PRESENTED TO

BY

ON THIS DATE

For God loved the world in this way:
He gave his one and only Son,
so that everyone who believes in him
will not perish but have eternal life.
JOHN 3:16

HOW CAN **THE BIBLE** HELP YOU?

Your Bible can help you in all life situations. Open it to find the verses below and read them. When you are angry, afraid, or sad, look to the Bible for help.

THE BIBLE CAN HELP YOU WHEN YOU ARE . . .

AFRAID—Isaiah 41:10; Hebrews 13:6

ANGRY—Proverbs 15:1; Matthew 5:21–26

DISCOURAGED—Romans 8:28

Feeling bad about **HURTING SOMEONE**—Luke 6:37

Feeling **GUILTY** about something you have done—1 John 1:9

Feeling **GREEDY**—Ecclesiastes 5:10; Hebrews 13:5

HAVING PROBLEMS with a friend—Luke 6:31; Ephesians 4:32; 1 John 4:7

Having problems with **YOUR PARENTS**—Ephesians 6:1–3

Needing to know **GOD'S WILL**—Proverbs 3:5–6

SAD—John 14:27

SICK—Jeremiah 17:14

TEMPTED—1 Corinthians 10:13

TEMPTED TO BE SELFISH—1 John 4:7–8

TEMPTED TO LIE—Colossians 3:8–9

Tempted to **GET BACK AT SOMEONE** who hurt you—Romans 12:17–21

WORRIED—Matthew 6:25–34; Philippians 4:6, 19

STUDYING
YOUR BIBLE

Bible study is exciting and can help you know what is true and what is not, how God wants you to live, and how to make good choices for the rest of your life. Read these Bible verses to discover why God wants you to study His Word: Psalm 119:105; Acts 17:11; 2 Timothy 2:15; 3:14–17; Hebrews 4:12.

Bible study is more than reading your Bible. If you are ready to begin an energizing discovery of truth, decide on what to study: a Bible book, a Bible person, or a Bible topic.

BIBLE BOOK Start with one of the Gospels such as Mark. Read a summary about the book. Read about 10 verses each day. If the verses talk about a place, look at one of the maps in this Bible to locate that place. Find a notebook and answer these questions: Who is the Bible writer talking to? What did God want the first readers or hearers to know or do? What does God want me to know or do?

PERSON Look at the "Kids in the Bible" article inserted at the beginning of the New Testament in this Bible. Read the Bible verses listed. In your notebook, answer as many of these questions as you can: Where did this person live? Whom did he know? What did he do? What can I learn from this person?

BIBLE TOPIC Find a topic such as "The Ten Plagues of Egypt" (see the article inserted among the pages of Exodus in this Bible). After reading the Bible verses, list in your notebook two or three things the Bible says about the topic. Then write what this means to you and what God wants you to do.

BIBLE SKILLS

Studying God's Word is important. You probably already have some Bible skills, and as you get older, you will learn more and more. Look at the checklist below and see how many skills you have already mastered. Check those off the list. Then ask your parents and Bible class teachers to help you learn new skills. The more you learn about the Word, the more you'll know about God and how to live your life for Him.

LEVEL 1 SKILLS

- ◆ I can locate the two main parts of the Bible—the Old Testament and the New Testament.
- ◆ I can pronounce the names of all the books of the Bible.
- ◆ I can find a book in the Bible by using the list of books in my Bible.
- ◆ I can read a Bible reference and locate the verse in my Bible.
- ◆ I can memorize a Bible verse. A verse I memorized is

_____

_____ .

- ◆ I know some of the books of the Bible in order.
- ◆ I am beginning to learn the five divisions of the Old Testament and the five divisions of the New Testament.
- ◆ I read my Bible every day.

LEVEL 2 SKILLS

◆ I can locate a verse in my Bible in a short time.

◆ I can find information about a person, place, or thing in the Bible by reading the verse.

◆ I can memorize Bible verses and short Bible passages. One passage I have memorized is

_____

_____ .

◆ I know all of the books of the Bible in order and can say them.

◆ I can identify which books of the Bible tell about Abraham, Moses, Daniel, and Jesus.

◆ I can identify some of the people whom God used to write the books of the Bible.

◆ I can name the ten divisions of the Old and New Testaments.

◆ I am beginning to use Bible study resources such as a Bible dictionary, a concordance, and an atlas.

◆ I read my Bible every day and find truths in it to apply to my life.

LEVEL 3 SKILLS

◆ I can locate any verse in my Bible in a short time.

◆ I can tell someone what verses and passages in the Bible mean to me.

◆ I can identify important Bible people by the books in which their stories are recorded.

◆ I can name the ten divisions of the Old and New Testaments in a short time.

◆ I can identify which Bible books belong in each division.

◆ I can easily use Bible study resources such as a Bible dictionary, a concordance, and an atlas.

◆ I can apply truths from the Bible to the personal and social issues I face each day.

TEST YOUR
BIBLE
KNOWLEDGE

Try to answer each question without using your Bible. Use your Bible to check your work.

QUESTIONS

1. What is the first color mentioned in the Bible? (Genesis 1:30)

2. Who beat his talking donkey three times? (Numbers 22:28)

3. Who was a left-handed judge who stabbed a fat king? (Judges 3:15–23)

4. What king had thousands of horses and chariots? (1 Kings 4:26)

5. Who made an iron ax head float? (2 Kings 6:1–6)

6. Which king of Judah became king when he was seven years old? (2 Kings 11:21–12:1)

7. What fruit was used to heal King Hezekiah's open sore? (2 Kings 20:7)

8. Who baked bread on a fire made from cow dung? (Ezekiel 1:3; 4:15)

9. Where did Peter find money to pay taxes? (Matthew 17:24–27)

10. What happened to the money the priests paid Judas? (Matthew 27:6–7)

11. Who ate locust and wild honey? (Mark 1:6)

12. Who fell out of a window while Paul was preaching? (Acts 20:9–10)

ANSWERS

A. Bought a graveyard

B. Elisha

C. Figs

D. Balaam

E. Solomon

F. In a fish's mouth

G. Eutychus

H. Green

I. John (the Baptist)

J. Joash

K. Ezekiel

L. Ehud

Answers: 1. h, 2. d, 3. l, 4. e, 5. b, 6. j, 7. c, 8. k, 9. f, 10. a, 11. i, 12. g.

FAVORITE **BIBLE** STORIES

The Bible is full of real stories about real people. When you read these stories, you learn about God and Jesus. You also discover how people reacted to different situations. As you read, ask yourself: What would I have done if I were in that story? How would I have treated the other people in the story? Would I have obeyed God? What are your favorite Bible stories? If they are not listed below, write the titles of the Bible stories you like to read and hear.

1. **CREATION** ◆ GENESIS 1–2

2. **ADAM AND EVE** ◆ GENESIS 1:26–31; 2:4–4:2

3. **NOAH** ◆ GENESIS 6:9–9:17

4. **MOSES** ◆ EXODUS 2:1–4:17

5. **DAVID & GOLIATH** ◆ 1 SAMUEL 17:1–50

6. **DANIEL & THE LIONS' DEN** ◆ DANIEL 6:1–23

7. **JONAH** ◆ JONAH

8. **JESUS' BIRTH** ◆ LUKE 2:1–20

9. **JESUS' CRUCIFIXION & DEATH** ◆ JOHN 19

10. **JESUS' RESURRECTION** ◆ JOHN 20:1–18

11. _____

12. _____

13. _____

14. _____

HOW DO I HAVE
QUIET TIME
WITH GOD?

Having quiet time with God is more than sitting still and being quiet. A quiet time is reading the Bible, praying, and listening to God in a quiet setting for at least five to ten minutes every day. If you miss some days, ask God to help you remember to have a quiet time more often. Here is how to get started:

◆ Decide the best time to have a quiet time, such as early in the morning or just before you go to bed at night.

◆ Find a private place where you will not be interrupted, such as your bedroom.

◆ Ask God to help you listen to Him as you read the Bible and pray.

◆ Read some Bible verses. A devotional magazine or book will suggest verses to read.

◆ In a journal or notebook, make a list of things and people to pray for.

◆ Pray:

> Praise and thank God.
> Ask God to forgive you.
> Pray for other people. Pray for yourself.
> Tell God you will do what He wants you to do.
> Ask God to bless you.
> Listen for God to speak to you.

◆ In one or two sentences, write in your journal what you think God wants you to remember from your quiet time today.

You have just had a quiet time! Thank God for the time you spent with Him and ask Him to help you do it again tomorrow.

THE
HOLY BIBLE

CHRISTIAN STANDARD BIBLE® | HOLMAN® BIBLES

HOLMAN BIBLE PUBLISHERS
NASHVILLE, TENNESSEE

The interior of the *CSB Kids Bible* was designed and typeset using Bible Serif created by 2K/DENMARK, Højbjerg, Denmark. Proofreading was provided by Peachtree Editorial Services, Peachtree City, Georgia.

Binding	ISBN
Hope LeatherTouch	978-1-4336-4896-0
Love LeatherTouch	978-1-4336-4897-7
Power LeatherTouch	978-1-4336-4898-4
Space LeatherTouch	978-1-4336-4899-1
Shiny Hearts LeatherTouch	978-1-4627-9282-5
Sports LeatherTouch	978-1-4627-9283-2

Printed in China
4 5 6 7 — 21 20 19
RRD

Books of the Bible / Contents

Introduction to the
Christian Standard Bible®

The Bible is God's revelation to humanity. It is our only source for completely reliable information about God, what happens when we die, and where history is headed. The Bible does these things because it is God's inspired Word, inerrant in the original manuscripts. Bible translation brings God's Word from the ancient languages (Hebrew, Greek, and Aramaic) into today's world. In dependence on God's Spirit to accomplish this sacred task, the Christian Standard Bible Translation Oversight Committee and Holman Bible Publishers present the CSB.

Textual Base of the CSB

The textual base for the New Testament (NT) is the Nestle-Aland *Novum Testamentum Graece*, 28th edition, and the United Bible Societies' *Greek New Testament*, 5th corrected edition. The text for the Old Testament (OT) is the *Biblia Hebraica Stuttgartensia*, 5th edition.

Where there are significant differences among Hebrew, Aramaic, or Greek manuscripts, the translators follow what they believe is the original reading and indicate the main alternative(s) in footnotes. The CSB uses the traditional verse divisions found in most Protestant Bibles.

Goals of This Translation

- Provide English-speaking people worldwide with an accurate translation in contemporary English.
- Provide an accurate translation for personal study, sermon preparation, private devotions, and memorization.
- Provide a text that is clear and understandable, suitable for public reading, and shareable so that all may access its life-giving message.
- Affirm the authority of Scripture and champion its absolute truth against skeptical viewpoints.

Translation Philosophy of the CSB

Most discussions of Bible translations speak of two opposite approaches: formal equivalence and dynamic equivalence. This terminology is meaningful, but Bible translations cannot be neatly sorted into these two categories. There is room for another category of translation philosophy that capitalizes on the strengths of the other two.

1. **Formal Equivalence:**
   Often called "word-for-word" (or "literal") translation, the principle of formal equivalence seeks as nearly as possible to preserve the structure of the original language. It seeks to represent each word of the original text with an exact equivalent word in the translation so that the reader

can see word for word what the original human author wrote. The merits of this approach include its consistency with the conviction that the Holy Spirit did inspire the very words of Scripture in the original manuscripts. It also provides the English Bible student some access to the structure of the text in the original language. Formal equivalence can achieve accuracy to the degree that English has an exact equivalent for each word and that the grammatical patterns of the original language can be reproduced in understandable English. However, it can sometimes result in awkward, if not incomprehensible, English or in a misunderstanding of the author's intent. The literal rendering of ancient idioms is especially difficult.

2. **Dynamic or Functional Equivalence:**
Often called "thought-for-thought" translation, the principle of dynamic equivalence rejects as misguided the attempt to preserve the structure of the original language. It proceeds by extracting the meaning of a text from its form and then translating that meaning so that it makes the same impact on modern readers that the ancient text made on its original readers. Strengths of this approach include a high degree of clarity and readability, especially in places where the original is difficult to render word for word. It also acknowledges that accurate and effective translation may require interpretation. However, the meaning of a text cannot always be neatly separated from its form, nor can it always be precisely determined. A biblical author may have intended multiple meanings, but these may be lost with the elimination of normal structures. In striving for readability, dynamic equivalence also sometimes overlooks and loses some of the less prominent elements of meaning. Furthermore, lack of formal correspondence to the original makes it difficult to verify accuracy and thus can affect the usefulness of the translation for in-depth Bible study.

3. **Optimal Equivalence:**
In practice, translations are seldom if ever purely formal or dynamic but favor one theory of Bible translation or the other to varying degrees. Optimal equivalence as a translation philosophy recognizes that form cannot always be neatly separated from meaning and should not be changed (for example, nouns to verbs or second person "you" to third person "they") unless comprehension demands it. The primary goal of translation is to convey the sense of the original with as much clarity as the original text and the translation language permit. Optimal equivalence appreciates the goals of formal equivalence but also recognizes its limitations. Optimal equivalence starts with an exhaustive analysis of

the text at every level (word, phrase, clause, sentence, discourse) in the original language to determine its original meaning and intention (or purpose). Then, relying on the latest and best language tools and experts, the nearest corresponding semantic and linguistic equivalents are used to convey as much of the information and intention of the original text with as much clarity and readability as possible. This process assures the maximum transfer of both the words and the thoughts contained in the original.

The CSB uses optimal equivalence as its translation philosophy. In the many places throughout the Bible where a word-for-word rendering is understandable, a literal translation is used. When a word-for-word rendering might obscure the meaning for a modern audience, a more dynamic translation is used. The CSB places equal value on fidelity to the original and readability for a modern audience, resulting in a translation that achieves both goals.

The Gender Language Usage in Bible Translation

The goal of the translators of the CSB has not been to promote a cultural ideology but to translate the Bible faithfully. Recognizing modern usage of English, the CSB regularly translates the plural of the Greek word ανθρωπος ("man") as "people" instead of "men," and occasionally the singular as "one," "someone," or "everyone," when the supporting pronouns in the original languages validate such a translation. While the CSB avoids using "he" or "him" unnecessarily, the translation does not restructure sentences to avoid them when they are in the text.

History of the CSB

After several years of preliminary development, Holman Bible Publishers, the oldest Bible publisher in North America, assembled an international, interdenominational team of 100 scholars, editors, stylists, and proofreaders, all of whom were committed to biblical inerrancy. Outside consultants and reviewers contributed valuable suggestions from their areas of expertise. Working with the original languages, an executive team of translators edited, polished, and reviewed the final manuscript that was first published as the Holman Christian Standard Bible (HCSB) in 2004.

A standing committee was also formed to maintain the HCSB translation and look for ways to improve readability without compromising accuracy. As with the original translation team, the committee that prepared this revision of the HCSB, renamed the CSB, is international and interdenominational, comprised of evangelical scholars who honor the inspiration and authority of God's written Word.

Traditional Features Found in the CSB

In keeping with a long line of Bible publications, the CSB has retained a number of features found in traditional Bibles:

1. Traditional theological vocabulary (for example, *justification, sanctification,*

redemption) has been retained since such terms have no other translation equivalent that adequately communicates their exact meaning.

2. Traditional spellings of names and places found in most Bibles have been used to make the CSB compatible with most Bible study tools.

3. Some editions of the CSB will print the words of Christ in red letters to help readers easily locate the spoken words of the Lord Jesus Christ.

4. Descriptive headings, printed above each section of Scripture, help readers quickly identify the contents of that section.

5. OT passages quoted in the NT are indicated. In the CSB, they are set in boldface type.

How the Names of God Are Translated

The CSB consistently translates the Hebrew names for God as follows:

Hebrew original:	CSB English:
Elohim	God
YHWH (*Yahweh*)	Lord
Adonai	Lord
Adonai Yahweh	Lord God
Yahweh Sabaoth	Lord of Armies
El Shaddai	God Almighty

Footnotes

Footnotes are used to show readers how the original biblical language has been understood in the CSB.

1. Old Testament (OT) Textual Footnotes

OT textual notes show important differences among Hebrew (Hb) manuscripts and ancient OT versions, such as the Septuagint and the Vulgate. See the list of abbreviations on page x for a list of other ancient versions used.

Some OT textual notes (like NT textual notes) give only an alternate textual reading. However, other OT textual notes also give the support for the reading chosen by the editors as well as for the alternate textual reading. For example, the CSB text of Psalm 12:7 reads,

> You, Lord, will guard us;
> you will protect us [G]
> from this generation
> forever.

The textual footnote for this verse reads,

[G] 12:7 Some Hb mss, LXX; other Hb mss read *him*

The textual note in this example means that there are two different readings found in the Hebrew manuscripts: some manuscripts read *us* and others read *him*. The CSB translators chose the reading *us*, which is also found in the Septuagint (LXX), and placed the other Hebrew reading *him* in the footnote.

Two other kinds OT textual notes are:

Alt Hb tradition reads ___ a variation given by scribes in the Hebrew manuscript tradition (known as *Kethiv/Qere* and *Tiqqune Sopherim* readings)

Hb uncertain
> when it is unclear what the original Hebrew text was

2. New Testament (NT) Textual Footnotes

NT textual notes indicate significant differences among Greek manuscripts (mss) and are normally indicated in one of three ways:

> Other mss read _____
> Other mss add _____
> Other mss omit _____

In the NT, some textual footnotes that use the word "add" or "omit" also have square brackets before and after the corresponding verses in the biblical text. Examples of this use of square brackets are Mark 16:9-20 and John 7:53–8:11.

3. Other Kinds of Footnotes

Lit ___
> a more literal rendering in English of the Hebrew, Aramaic, or Greek text

Or ___
> an alternate or less likely English translation of the same Hebrew, Aramaic, or Greek text

= an abbreviation for "it means" or "it is equivalent to"

Hb, Aramaic, Gk
> the actual Hebrew, Aramaic, or Greek word is given using equivalent English letters

Hb obscure
> the existing Hebrew text is especially difficult to translate

emend(ed) to ___
> the original Hebrew text is so difficult to translate that competent scholars have conjectured or inferred a restoration of the original text based on the context, probable root meanings of the words, and uses in comparative languages

In some editions of the CSB, additional footnotes clarify the meaning of certain biblical texts or explain biblical history, persons, customs, places, activities, and measurements. Cross references are given for parallel passages or passages with similar wording, and in the NT, for passages quoted from the OT.

Abbreviations in CSB Bibles

AD	In the year of our Lord
BC	before Christ
c.	century
ca	circa
chap(s).	chapter(s)
cp.	compare
DSS	Dead Sea Scrolls
e.g.	for example
Eng	English
etc.	et cetera
Gk	Greek
Hb	Hebrew
i.e.	that is
Lat	Latin
lit	literal(ly)
LXX	Septuagint—an ancient translation of the Old Testament into Greek
MT	Masoretic Text
NT	New Testament
ms(s)	manuscript(s)
OT	Old Testament
pl.	plural
Ps(s)	Psalm(s)
Sam	Samaritan Pentateuch
sg.	singular
Sym	Symmachus
Syr	Syriac
Tg	Targum
Theod	Theodotian
v./vv.	verse, verses
Vg	Vulgate—an ancient translation of the Bible into Latin
vol(s).	volume(s)

THE OLD TESTAMENT

THE OLD TESTAMENT

GENESIS

The Creation

1 In the beginning God created the heavens and the earth.[A] Jn 1:1-3 ² Now the earth was formless and empty, darkness covered the surface of the watery depths, and the Spirit of God was hovering over the surface of the waters. ³ Then God said, "Let there be light," and there was light. ⁴ God saw that the light was good, and God separated the light from the darkness. ⁵ God called the light "day," and the darkness he called "night." There was an evening, and there was a morning: one day. Jr 4:23; Jb 26:13; 33:4; Ps 33:6

⁶ Then God said, "Let there be an expanse between the waters, separating water from water." ⁷ So God made the expanse and separated the water under the expanse from the water above the expanse. And it was so. ⁸ God called the expanse "sky."[B] Evening came and then morning: the second day.

⁹ Then God said, "Let the water under the sky be gathered into one place, and let the dry land appear." And it was so. ¹⁰ God called the dry land "earth," and the gathering of the water he called "seas." And God saw that it was good. ¹¹ Then God said, "Let the earth produce vegetation: seed-bearing plants and fruit trees on the earth bearing fruit with seed in it according to their kinds." And it was so. ¹² The earth produced vegetation: seed-bearing plants according to their kinds and trees bearing fruit with seed in it according to their kinds. And God saw that it was good. ¹³ Evening came and then morning: the third day. Jb 38:8-11; Ps 33:7; 136:6; Jr 5:22

¹⁴ Then God said, "Let there be lights in the expanse of the sky to separate the day from the night. They will serve as signs for seasons[C] and for days and years. ¹⁵ They will be lights in the expanse of the sky to provide light on the earth." And it was so. ¹⁶ God made the two great lights — the greater light to rule over the day and the lesser light to rule over the night — as well as the stars. ¹⁷ God placed them in the expanse of the sky to provide light on the earth, ¹⁸ to rule the day and the night, and to separate light from darkness. And God saw that it was good. ¹⁹ Evening came and then morning: the fourth day.

²⁰ Then God said, "Let the water swarm with[D] living creatures, and let birds fly above the earth across the expanse of the sky." ²¹ So God created the large sea-creatures[E] and every living creature that moves and swarms in the water, according to their kinds. He also created every winged creature according to its kind. And God saw that it was good. ²² God blessed them: "Be fruitful, multiply, and fill the waters of the seas, and let the birds multiply on the earth." ²³ Evening came and then morning: the fifth day. Gn 8:17; 9:1; Ps 104:25-28

²⁴ Then God said, "Let the earth produce living creatures according

---

A 1:1 Or *created the universe* **B** 1:8 Or *"heavens."* **C** 1:14 Or *for the appointed times* **D** 1:20 Lit *with swarms of* **E** 1:21 Or *created sea monsters*

to their kinds: livestock, creatures that crawl, and the wildlife of the earth according to their kinds." And it was so. ²⁵ So God made the wildlife of the earth according to their kinds, the livestock according to their kinds, and all the creatures that crawl on the ground according to their kinds. And God saw that it was good.

²⁶ Then God said, "Let us make man ᴬ in ᴮ our image, according to our likeness. They will rule the fish of the sea, the birds of the sky, the livestock, the whole earth, ᶜ and the creatures that crawl ᴰ on the earth."
²⁷ So God created man
in his own image;
he created him in ᴱ the image of God;
he created them male and female.   Gn 5:2; Mt 19:4; Mk 10:6
²⁸ God blessed them, and God said to them, "Be fruitful, multiply, fill the earth, and subdue it. Rule the fish of the sea, the birds of the sky, and every creature that crawls ᶠ on the earth." ²⁹ God also said, "Look, I have given you every seed-bearing plant on the surface of the entire earth and every tree whose fruit contains seed. This will be food for you, ³⁰ for all the wildlife of the earth, for every bird of the sky, and for every creature that crawls on the earth — everything having the breath of life in it — I have given ᴳ every green plant for food." And it was so. ³¹ God saw all that he had made, and it was very good indeed. Evening came and then morning: the sixth day.   Gn 9:1,7; Gn 9:3; Ps 104:14-15

2 So the heavens and the earth and everything in them were completed. ² On the seventh ᴴ day God had completed his work that he had done, and he rested ᴵ on the seventh day from all his work that he had done. ³ God blessed the seventh day and declared it holy, for on it he rested from all his work of creation. ᴶ   Neh 9:6; Ps 33:6; Is 34:4; 45:12; 31:17

Man and Woman in the Garden

⁴ These are the records of the heavens and the earth, concerning their creation. At the time ᴷ that the Lᴏʀᴅ God made the earth and the heavens, ⁵ no shrub of the field had yet grown on the land, ᴸ and no plant of the field had yet sprouted, for the Lᴏʀᴅ God had not made it rain on the land, and there was no man to work the ground. ⁶ But mist would come up from the earth and water all the ground. ⁷ Then the Lᴏʀᴅ God formed the man out of the dust from the ground and breathed the breath of life into his nostrils, and the man became a living being.

⁸ The Lᴏʀᴅ God planted a garden in Eden, in the east, and there he placed the man he had formed. ⁹ The Lᴏʀᴅ God caused to grow out of the ground every tree pleasing in appearance and good for food, including the tree of life in the middle of the garden, as well as the tree of the knowledge of good and evil.

¹⁰ A river went ᴹ out from Eden to water the garden. From there it divided and became the source of four rivers. ᴺ ¹¹ The name of the first

ᴬ1:26 Or human beings; Hb 'adam, also in v. 27   ᴮ1:26 Or as   ᶜ1:26 Syr reads sky, and over every animal of the land   ᴰ1:26 Or scurry   ᴱ1:27 Or man as his own image; he created him as   ᶠ1:28 Or and all scurrying animals   ᴳ1:30 I have given added for clarity   ᴴ2:2 Sam, LXX, Syr read sixth   ᴵ2:2 Or ceased, also in v. 3   ᴶ2:3 Lit work that God created to make   ᴷ2:4 Lit creation on the day   ᴸ2:5 Or earth   ᴹ2:10 Or goes   ᴺ2:10 Lit became four heads is Pishon, which flows through the entire land of Havilah, ᴬ where there is gold. ¹² Gold from that land is pure; ᴮ bdellium ᶜ and onyx ᴰ are also there. ¹³ The name of the second river is Gihon, which flows through the entire land of Cush. ¹⁴ The name of the third river is Tigris, which runs east of Assyria. And the fourth river is the Euphrates.   Gn 10:7,29; 25:18; 1Sm 15:7; Dn 10:4

¹⁵ The LORD God took the man and placed him in the garden of Eden to work it and watch over it. ¹⁶ And the LORD God commanded the man, "You are free to eat from any tree of the garden, ¹⁷ but you must not eat from the tree of the knowledge of good and evil, for on the day you eat from it, you will certainly die." ¹⁸ Then the LORD God said, "It is not good for the man to be alone. I will make a helper corresponding to him." ¹⁹ The LORD God formed out of the ground every wild animal and every bird of the sky, and brought each to the man to see what he would call it. And whatever the man called a living creature, that was its name. ²⁰ The man gave names to all the livestock, to the birds of the sky, and to every wild animal; but for the man ᴱ no helper was found corresponding to him. ²¹ So the LORD God caused a deep sleep to come over the man, and he slept. God took one of his ribs and closed the flesh at that place. ²² Then the LORD God made the rib he had taken from the man into a woman and brought her to the man. ²³ And the man said: Gn 3:5; Dt 30:15,19-20

This one, at last, is bone
     of my bone
and flesh of my flesh;

this one will be
     called "woman,"
for she was taken from man.

²⁴ This is why a man leaves his father and mother and bonds with his wife, and they become one flesh. ²⁵ Both the man and his wife were naked, yet felt no shame.   Mal 2:15

The Temptation and the Fall

3 Now the serpent was the most cunning of all the wild animals that the LORD God had made. He said to the woman, "Did God really say, 'You can't eat from any tree in the garden'?"   Mt 10:16; 2Co 11:3; Rv 12:9
² The woman said to the serpent, "We may eat the fruit from the trees in the garden. ³ But about the fruit of the tree in the middle of the garden, God said, 'You must not eat it or touch it, or you will die.'"   Gn 2:17
⁴ "No! You will not die," the serpent said to the woman. ⁵ "In fact, God knows that when ᶠ you eat it your eyes will be opened and you will be like God, ᴳ knowing good and evil." ⁶ The woman saw that the tree was good for food and delightful to look at, and that it was desirable for obtaining wisdom. So she took some of its fruit and ate it; she also gave some to her husband, who was with her, and he ate it. ⁷ Then the eyes of both of them were opened, and they knew they were naked; so they sewed fig leaves together and made coverings for themselves.   Jn 8:44; 1Tm 2:14

Sin's Consequences

⁸ Then the man and his wife heard the sound of the LORD God walking in the garden at the time of

---

ᴬ**2:11** Or of the Havilah   ᴮ**2:12** Lit good   ᶜ**2:12** A yellowish, transparent gum resin   ᴰ**2:12** Identity of this precious stone uncertain   ᴱ**2:20** Or for Adam   ᶠ**3:5** Lit on the day   ᴳ**3:5** Or gods, or divine beings the evening breeze,^A and they hid from the LORD God among the trees of the garden. ⁹ So the LORD God called out to the man and said to him, "Where are you?"   Jb 34:22-23

¹⁰ And he said, "I heard you^B in the garden, and I was afraid because I was naked, so I hid."

¹¹ Then he asked, "Who told you that you were naked? Did you eat from the tree that I commanded you not to eat from?"

¹² The man replied, "The woman you gave to be with me — she gave me some fruit from the tree, and I ate."   Jb 31:33; Pr 28:13

¹³ So the LORD God asked the woman, "What is this you have done?" And the woman said, "The serpent deceived me, and I ate."   Rm 7:11

¹⁴ So the LORD God said to the serpent:

Because you have done this,
you are cursed more than
any livestock
and more than
any wild animal.
You will move on your belly
and eat dust all the days
of your life.   Is 65:25; Mc 7:17
¹⁵ I will put hostility between you
and the woman,
and between your offspring
and her offspring.
He will strike your head,
and you will strike your heel.

¹⁶ He said to the woman:
I will intensify
your labor pains;
you will bear children
with painful effort.   Jn 16:21
Your desire will be
for your husband,   Gn 4:7
yet he will rule over you.

¹⁷ And he said to the man, "Because you listened to your wife and ate from the tree about which I commanded you, 'Do not eat from it':

The ground is cursed
because of you.   Gn 5:29; Heb 6:8
You will eat from it
by means of painful labor^C
all the days of your life.
¹⁸ It will produce thorns
and thistles for you,
and you will eat the plants
of the field.   Gn 2:5
¹⁹ You will eat bread^D
by the sweat of your brow
until you return
to the ground,   Ps 90:3; 104:29
since you were taken from it.
For you are dust,
and you will return to dust."

²⁰ The man named his wife Eve^E because she was the mother of all the living. ²¹ The LORD God made clothing from skins for the man and his wife, and he clothed them. ²² The LORD God said, "Since the man has become like one of us, knowing good and evil, he must not reach out, take from the tree of life, eat, and live forever." ²³ So the LORD God sent him away from the garden of Eden to work the ground from which he was taken. ²⁴ He drove the man out and stationed the cherubim and the flaming, whirling sword east of the garden of Eden to guard the way to the tree of life.   Gn 2:9; Rv 2:7

Cain Murders Abel

4 The man was intimate with his wife Eve, and she conceived and gave birth to Cain. She said, "I have had a male child with the

---

^A**3:8** Lit *at the wind of the day*   ^B**3:10** Lit *the sound of you*   ^C**3:17** Lit *it through pain*   ^D**3:19** Or *food*
^E**3:20** Lit *Living,* or *Life*

Lord's help."ᴬ ² She also gave birth to his brother Abel. Now Abel became a shepherd of flocks, but Cain worked the ground. ³ In the course of time Cain presented some of the land's produce as an offering to the Lord. ⁴ And Abel also presented an offering — some of the firstborn of his flock and their fat portions. The Lord had regard for Abel and his offering, ⁵ but he did not have regard for Cain and his offering. Cain was furious, and he looked despondent. ᴮ Ex 23:19; 34:26; Neh 10:35; Pr 3:9

⁶ Then the Lord said to Cain, "Why are you furious? And why do you look despondent?ᶜ ⁷ If you do what is right, won't you be accepted? But if you do not do what is right, sin is crouching at the door. Its desire is for you, but you must rule over it." Gn 3:16; Jnh 4:4

⁸ Cain said to his brother Abel, "Let's go out to the field."ᴰ And while they were in the field, Cain attacked his brother Abel and killed him. Mt 23:35; Lk 11:51; 1Jn 3:12-15; Jd 11

⁹ Then the Lord said to Cain, "Where is your brother Abel?"

"I don't know," he replied. "Am I my brother's guardian?"

¹⁰ Then he said, "What have you done? Your brother's blood cries out to me from the ground! ¹¹ So now you are cursed, alienated from the ground that opened its mouth to receive your brother's blood you have shed.ᴱ ¹² If you work the ground, it will never again give you its yield. You will be a restless wanderer on the earth." Nm 35:33

¹³ But Cain answered the Lord, "My punishmentᶠ is too great to bear! ¹⁴ Since you are banishing me today from the face of the earth, and I must hide from your presence and become a restless wanderer on the earth, whoever finds me will kill me." Nm 35:26-27

¹⁵ Then the Lord replied to him, "In that case,ᴳ whoever kills Cain will suffer vengeance seven times over."ᴴ And he placed a mark on Cain so that whoever found him would not kill him. ¹⁶ Then Cain went out from the Lord's presence and lived in the land of Nod, east of Eden. Ex 9:4; Ezk 9:4,6; Rv 13:16-17

The Line of Cain

¹⁷ Cain was intimate with his wife, and she conceived and gave birth to Enoch. Then Cain became the builder of a city, and he named the city Enoch after his son. ¹⁸ Irad was born to Enoch, Irad fathered Mehujael, Mehujael fathered Methushael, and Methushael fathered Lamech. ¹⁹ Lamech took two wives for himself, one named Adah and the other named Zillah. ²⁰ Adah bore Jabal; he was the father of the nomadic herdsmen.ᴵ ²¹ His brother was named Jubal; he was the father of all who play the lyre and the flute. ²² Zillah bore Tubal-cain, who made all kinds of bronze and iron tools. Tubal-cain's sister was Naamah.

²³ Lamech said to his wives:
Adah and Zillah,
 hear my voice;
wives of Lamech,
 pay attention to my words.
For I killed a man
 for wounding me,
a young man for striking me.

ᴬ4:1 Lit the Lord ᴮ4:5 Lit and his face fell ᶜ4:6 Lit why has your face fallen ᴰ4:8 Sam, LXX, Syr, Vg; MT omits "Let's go out to the field." ᴱ4:11 Lit blood from your hand ᶠ4:13 Or sin ᴳ4:15 LXX, Syr, Vg read "Not so!" ᴴ4:15 Or suffer severely ᴵ4:20 Lit the dweller of tent and livestock

²⁴ If Cain is to be avenged
        seven times over,
    then for Lamech it will be
        seventy-seven times!

²⁵ Adam was intimate with his wife again, and she gave birth to a son and named him Seth, for she said, "God has given^A me another child^B in place of Abel, since Cain killed him." ²⁶ A son was born to Seth also, and he named him Enosh. At that time people began to call on the name of the LORD.   Gn 12:8; 26:25

The Line of Seth

5 This is the document containing the family^C records of Adam. ^D On the day that God created man, ^E he made him in the likeness of God; ² he created them male and female. When they were created, he blessed them and called them mankind. ^F   Gn 2:4; 26:25

³ Adam was 130 years old when he fathered a son in his likeness, according to his image, and named him Seth. ⁴ Adam lived 800 years after he fathered Seth, and he fathered other sons and daughters. ⁵ So Adam's life lasted 930 years; then he died.

⁶ Seth was 105 years old when he fathered Enosh. ⁷ Seth lived 807 years after he fathered Enosh, and he fathered other sons and daughters. ⁸ So Seth's life lasted 912 years; then he died.

⁹ Enosh was 90 years old when he fathered Kenan. ¹⁰ Enosh lived 815 years after he fathered Kenan, and he fathered other sons and daughters. ¹¹ So Enosh's life lasted 905 years; then he died.

¹² Kenan was 70 years old when he fathered Mahalalel. ¹³ Kenan lived 840 years after he fathered Mahalalel, and he fathered other sons and daughters. ¹⁴ So Kenan's life lasted 910 years; then he died.

¹⁵ Mahalalel was 65 years old when he fathered Jared. ¹⁶ Mahalalel lived 830 years after he fathered Jared, and he fathered other sons and daughters. ¹⁷ So Mahalalel's life lasted 895 years; then he died.

¹⁸ Jared was 162 years old when he fathered Enoch. ¹⁹ Jared lived 800 years after he fathered Enoch, and he fathered other sons and daughters. ²⁰ So Jared's life lasted 962 years; then he died.

²¹ Enoch was 65 years old when he fathered Methuselah. ²² And after he fathered Methuselah, Enoch walked with God 300 years and fathered other sons and daughters. ²³ So Enoch's life lasted 365 years. ²⁴ Enoch walked with God; then he was not there because God took him.   Gn 6:9; 17:1; 24:40; 48:15; 2Kg 2:11; Heb 11:5

²⁵ Methuselah was 187 years old when he fathered Lamech. ²⁶ Methuselah lived 782 years after he fathered Lamech, and he fathered other sons and daughters. ²⁷ So Methuselah's life lasted 969 years; then he died.

²⁸ Lamech was 182 years old when he fathered a son. ²⁹ And he named him Noah,^G saying, "This one will bring us relief from the agonizing labor of our hands, caused by the ground the LORD has cursed." ³⁰ Lamech lived 595 years after he fathered Noah, and he fathered other sons and daughters. ³¹ So Lamech's life lasted 777 years; then he died.

^A 4:25 The Hb word for *given* sounds like the name "Seth." ^B 4:25 Lit *seed* ^C 5:1 Lit *written family* ^D 5:1 Or *mankind* ^E 5:1 Or *Adam, human beings* ^F 5:2 Hb *'adam* ^G 5:29 In Hb, the name *Noah* sounds like "bring us relief."

³² Noah was 500 years old, and he fathered Shem, Ham, and Japheth.

Sons of God and Daughters of Mankind

6 When mankind began to multiply on the earth and daughters were born to them, ² the sons of God saw that the daughters of mankind were beautiful, and they took any they chose as wives ᴬ for themselves. ³ And the LORD said, "My Spirit will not remain ᴮ with ᶜ mankind forever, because they are corrupt. ᴰ Their days will be 120 years." ⁴ The Nephilim ᴱ were on the earth both in those days and afterward, when the sons of God came to the daughters of mankind, who bore children to them. They were the powerful men of old, the famous men. Jb 1:6; 2:1; 38:7; 1Pt 3:19-20; Jd 6

Judgment Decreed

⁵ When the LORD saw that human wickedness was widespread on the earth and that every inclination of the human mind was nothing but evil all the time, ⁶ the LORD regretted that he had made man on the earth, and he was deeply grieved. ᶠ ⁷ Then the LORD said, "I will wipe mankind, whom I created, off the face of the earth, together with the animals, creatures that crawl, and birds of the sky — for I regret that I made them." ⁸ Noah, however, found favor with the LORD. Gn 8:21

God Warns Noah

⁹ These are the family records of Noah. Noah was a righteous man, blameless among his contemporaries; Noah walked with God. ¹⁰ And Noah fathered three sons: Shem, Ham, and Japheth. Gn 2:4; 17:1; Jb 22:15; Ps 37:39; 2Pt 2:5

¹¹ Now the earth was corrupt in God's sight, and the earth was filled with wickedness. ᴳ ¹² God saw how corrupt the earth was, for every creature had corrupted its way on the earth. ¹³ Then God said to Noah, "I have decided to put an end to every creature, for the earth is filled with wickedness because of them; therefore I am going to destroy them along with the earth.

¹⁴ "Make yourself an ark of gopher ᴴ wood. Make rooms in the ark, and cover it with pitch inside and outside. ¹⁵ This is how you are to make it: The ark will be 450 feet long, 75 feet wide, and 45 feet high. ᴵ ¹⁶ You are to make a roof, ᴶ finishing the sides of the ark to within eighteen inches ᴷ of the roof. You are to put a door in the side of the ark. Make it with lower, middle, and upper decks.

¹⁷ "Understand that I am bringing a flood — floodwaters on the earth to destroy every creature under heaven with the breath of life in it. Everything on earth will perish. ¹⁸ But I will establish my covenant with you, and you will enter the ark with your sons, your wife, and your sons' wives. ¹⁹ You are also to bring into the ark two of all the living creatures, male and female, to keep them alive with you. ²⁰ Two of everything — from the birds according to their kinds, from the livestock according to their kinds, and from the animals that crawl on

---

ᴬ**6:2** Or women   ᴮ**6:3** Or strive   ᶜ**6:3** Or in   ᴰ**6:3** Lit flesh   ᴱ**6:4** Possibly means "fallen ones"; traditionally, "giants"; Nm 13:31-33   ᶠ**6:6** Lit was grieved to his heart   ᴳ**6:11** Or injustice, also in v. 13   ᴴ**6:14** Unknown species of tree; perhaps pine or cypress   ᴵ**6:15** Or 300 cubits long, 50 cubits wide, and 30 cubits high   ᴶ**6:16** Or window, or hatch; Hb uncertain   ᴷ**6:16** Lit to a cubit the ground according to their kinds — will come to you so that you can keep them alive. ²¹ Take with you every kind of food that is eaten; gather it as food for you and for them." ²² And Noah did this. He did everything that God had commanded him. _{Gn 7:4; 9:9-16; 17:7; 2Pt 2:5}

Entering the Ark

7 Then the LORD said to Noah, "Enter the ark, you and all your household, for I have seen that you alone are righteous before me in this generation. ² You are to take with you seven pairs, a male and its female, of all the clean animals, and two of the animals that are not clean, a male and its female, ³ and seven pairs, male and female, of the birds of the sky — in order to keep offspring alive throughout the earth. ⁴ Seven days from now I will make it rain on the earth forty days and forty nights, and every living thing I have made I will wipe off the face of the earth." ⁵ And Noah did everything that the LORD commanded him. _{Mt 24:38-39; Lk 17:26-27}

⁶ Noah was six hundred years old when the flood came and water covered the earth. ⁷ So Noah, his sons, his wife, and his sons' wives entered the ark because of the floodwaters. ⁸ From the clean animals, unclean animals, birds, and every creature that crawls on the ground, ⁹ two of each, male and female, came to Noah and entered the ark, just as God had commanded him. ¹⁰ Seven days later the floodwaters came on the earth.

The Flood

¹¹ In the six hundredth year of Noah's life, in the second month, on the seventeenth day of the month, on that day all the sources of the vast watery depths burst open, the floodgates of the sky were opened, ¹² and the rain fell on the earth forty days and forty nights. ¹³ On that same day Noah and his three sons, Shem, Ham, and Japheth, entered the ark, along with Noah's wife and his three sons' wives. ¹⁴ They entered it with all the wildlife according to their kinds, all livestock according to their kinds, all the creatures that crawl on the earth according to their kinds, every flying creature — all the birds and every winged creature — according to their kinds. ¹⁵ Two of every creature that has the breath of life in it came to Noah and entered the ark. ¹⁶ Those that entered, male and female of every creature, entered just as God had commanded him. Then the LORD shut him in. _{Gn 8:2}

¹⁷ The flood continued for forty days on the earth; the water increased and lifted up the ark so that it rose above the earth. ¹⁸ The water surged and increased greatly on the earth, and the ark floated on the surface of the water. ¹⁹ Then the water surged even higher on the earth, and all the high mountains under the whole sky were covered. ²⁰ The mountains were covered as the water surged above them more than twenty feet.ᴬ ²¹ Every creature perished — those that crawl on the earth, birds, livestock, wildlife, and those that swarmᴮ on the earth, as well as all mankind. ²² Everything with the breath of the spirit of life in its nostrils — everything on dry land died. ²³ He wiped out every living thing that was on the face of the earth, from mankind to

ᴬ**7:20** Lit *surged 15 cubits*   ᴮ**7:21** Lit *all the swarming swarms* livestock, to creatures that crawl, to the birds of the sky, and they were wiped off the earth. Only Noah was left, and those that were with him in the ark. ²⁴ And the water surged on the earth 150 days.　Gn 2:7; 1Pt 3:20

The Flood Recedes

8 God remembered Noah, as well as all the wildlife and all the livestock that were with him in the ark. God caused a windᴬ to pass over the earth, and the water began to subside. ² The sources of the watery depths and the floodgates of the sky were closed, and the rain from the sky stopped. ³ The water steadily receded from the earth, and by the end of 150 days the water had decreased significantly. ⁴ The ark came to rest in the seventh month, on the seventeenth day of the month, on the mountains of Ararat.　Gn 19:29; Ex 2:24; 1Sm 1:19; Ps 105:42

⁵ The water continued to recede until the tenth month; in the tenth month, on the first day of the month, the tops of the mountains were visible. ⁶ After forty days Noah opened the window of the ark that he had made, ⁷ and he sent out a raven. It went back and forth until the water had dried up from the earth. ⁸ Then he sent out a dove to see whether the water on the earth's surface had gone down, ⁹ but the dove found no resting place for its foot. It returned to him in the ark because water covered the surface of the whole earth. He reached out and brought it into the ark to himself. ¹⁰ So Noah waited seven more days and sent out the dove from the ark again. ¹¹ When the dove came to him at evening, there was a plucked olive leaf in its beak. So Noah knew that the water on the earth's surface had gone down. ¹² After he had waited another seven days, he sent out the dove, but it did not return to him again. ¹³ In the six hundred and first year,ᴮ in the first month, on the first day of the month, the water that had covered the earth was dried up. Then Noah removed the ark's cover and saw that the surface of the ground was drying. ¹⁴ By the twenty-seventh day of the second month, the earth was dry.

The Lᴏʀᴅ's Promise

¹⁵ Then God spoke to Noah, ¹⁶ "Come out of the ark, you, your wife, your sons, and your sons' wives with you. ¹⁷ Bring out all the living creaturesᶜ that are with you — birds, livestock, those that crawl on the earth — and they will spread over the earth and be fruitful and multiply on the earth." ¹⁸ So Noah, along with his sons, his wife, and his sons' wives, came out. ¹⁹ All the animals, all the creatures that crawl, and all the flying creatures — everything that moves on the earth — came out of the ark by their families.　9:1

²⁰ Then Noah built an altar to the Lᴏʀᴅ. He took some of every kind of clean animal and every kind of clean bird and offered burnt offerings on the altar. ²¹ When the Lᴏʀᴅ smelled the pleasing aroma, he said to himself, "I will never again curse the ground because of human beings, even though the inclination of the human heart is evil from youth onward. And I will never again strike down every living thing as I have done.　Ex 29:18; Lv 1:9
²² 　As long as the earth endures,
　　seedtime and harvest,
　　　cold and heat,

ᴬ **8:1** Or *spirit*; Gn 1:2　　ᴮ **8:13** = of Noah's life　　ᶜ **8:17** Lit *creatures of all flesh*

summer and winter,
and day and night
will not cease." *Jr 33:20,25*

God's Covenant with Noah

9 God blessed Noah and his sons and said to them, "Be fruitful and multiply and fill the earth. ² The fear and terror of you will be in every living creature on the earth, every bird of the sky, every creature that crawls on the ground, and all the fish of the sea. They are placed under your authority.ᴬ ³ Every creature that lives and moves will be food for you; as I gave the green plants, I have given you everything. ⁴ However, you must not eat meat with its lifeblood in it. ⁵ And I will require a penalty for your lifeblood;ᴮ I will require it from any animal and from any human; if someone murders a fellow human, I will require that person's life.ᶜ

⁶ Whoever sheds
human blood,
by humans his blood
will be shed, *Ex 21:12-14; Lv 24:17*
for God made humans in
his image. *Gn 1:26-27*

⁷ But you, be fruitful and multiply; spread out over the earth and multiply on it." *Gn 1:28*

⁸ Then God said to Noah and his sons with him, ⁹ "Understand that I am establishing my covenant with you and your descendants after you, ¹⁰ and with every living creature that is with you — birds, livestock, and all wildlife of the earth that are with you — all the animals of the earth that came out of the ark. ¹¹ I establish my covenant with you that never again will every creature be wiped out by floodwaters; there will never again be a flood to destroy the earth." *Gn 6:18; 8:22; 17:2*

¹² And God said, "This is the sign of the covenant I am making between me and you and every living creature with you, a covenant for all future generations: ¹³ I have placed my bow in the clouds, and it will be a sign of the covenant between me and the earth. ¹⁴ Whenever I form clouds over the earth and the bow appears in the clouds, ¹⁵ I will remember my covenant between me and you and all the living creatures:ᴰ water will never again become a flood to destroy every creature. ¹⁶ The bow will be in the clouds, and I will look at it and remember the permanent covenant between God and all the living creaturesᴱ on earth." ¹⁷ God said to Noah, "This is the sign of the covenant that I have established between me and every creature on earth." *Ez 1:28; Rv 4:3*

Prophecies About Noah's Family

¹⁸ Noah's sons who came out of the ark were Shem, Ham, and Japheth. Ham was the father of Canaan. ¹⁹ These three were Noah's sons, and from them the whole earth was populated. *Gn 9:1,7; 10:32*

²⁰ Noah, as a man of the soil, began by plantingᶠ a vineyard. ²¹ He drank some of the wine, became drunk, and uncovered himself inside his tent. ²² Ham, the father of Canaan, saw his father naked and told his two brothers outside. ²³ Then Shem and Japheth took a cloak and placed it over both their shoulders, and walking backward, they covered their father's

---

ᴬ**9:2** Lit *are given in your hand*   ᴮ**9:5** Lit *And your blood belonging to your life I will seek*   ᶜ**9:5** Lit *any human; from the hand of a man his brother I will seek the life of the human.*   ᴰ**9:15** Lit *and creatures of all flesh*   ᴱ**9:16** Lit *creatures of all flesh*   ᶠ**9:20** Or *Noah began to be a farmer and planted*

nakedness. Their faces were turned away, and they did not see their father naked. Lm 4:21; Hab 2:15
²⁴ When Noah awoke from his drinking and learned what his youngest son had done to him, ²⁵ he said:

Canaan is cursed.   Dt 27:16
He will be the lowest
  of slaves to his brothers.
²⁶ He also said:
Blessed be the LORD, the God
  of Shem;
Let Canaan be^A Shem's slave.
²⁷ Let God extend Japheth;^B
let Japheth dwell in the tents
  of Shem;
let Canaan be Shem's slave.

²⁸ Now Noah lived 350 years after the flood. ²⁹ So Noah's life lasted 950 years; then he died.

The Table of Nations

10 These are the family records of Noah's sons, Shem, Ham, and Japheth. They also had sons after the flood. Gn 2:4
² Japheth's sons: Gomer, Magog, Madai, Javan, Tubal, Meshech, and Tiras. ³ Gomer's sons: Ashkenaz, Riphath, and Togarmah. ⁴ And Javan's sons: Elishah, Tarshish, Kittim, and Dodanim.^C ⁵ From these descendants, the peoples of the coasts and islands spread out into their lands according to their clans in their nations, each with its own language.
⁶ Ham's sons: Cush, Mizraim, Put, and Canaan. ⁷ Cush's sons: Seba, Havilah, Sabtah, Raamah, and Sabteca. And Raamah's sons: Sheba and Dedan. 1Ch 1:8-10

⁸ Cush fathered Nimrod, who began to be powerful in the land. ⁹ He was a powerful hunter in the sight of the LORD. That is why it is said, "Like Nimrod, a powerful hunter in the sight of the LORD." ¹⁰ His kingdom started with Babylon, Erech,^D Accad,^E and Calneh,^F in the land of Shinar.^G ¹¹ From that land he went to Assyria and built Nineveh, Rehoboth-ir, Calah, ¹² and Resen, between Nineveh and the great city Calah. Gn 11:2,9; 14:1; Mc 5:6
¹³ Mizraim^H fathered the people of Lud, Anam, Lehab, Naphtuh, ¹⁴ Pathrus, Casluh (the Philistines came from them), and Caphtor.
¹⁵ Canaan fathered Sidon his firstborn and Heth, ¹⁶ as well as the Jebusites, the Amorites, the Girgashites, ¹⁷ the Hivites, the Arkites, the Sinites, ¹⁸ the Arvadites, the Zemarites, and the Hamathites. Afterward the Canaanite clans scattered. ¹⁹ The Canaanite border went from Sidon going toward Gerar as far as Gaza, and going toward Sodom, Gomorrah, Admah, and Zeboiim as far as Lasha. Gn 15:19-21
²⁰ These are Ham's sons by their clans, according to their languages, in their lands and their nations.
²¹ And Shem, Japheth's older brother, also had sons. Shem was the father of all the sons of Eber. ²² Shem's sons were Elam, Asshur, Arpachshad, Lud, and Aram.
²³ Aram's sons: Uz, Hul, Gether, and Mash.
²⁴ Arpachshad fathered^I Shelah, and Shelah fathered Eber. ²⁵ Eber had two sons. One was named

---

^A **9:26** As a wish or prayer; others interpret the verbs in vv. 26-27 as prophecy: *Canaan will be . . .*
^B **9:27** In Hb, the name *Japheth* sounds like the word "extend."   ^C **10:4** Some Hb mss, Sam, LXX read *Rodanim;* 1Ch 1:7   ^D **10:10** Or *Uruk*   ^E **10:10** Or *Akkad*   ^F **10:10** Or *and all of them*   ^G **10:10** Or *in Babylonia*
^H **10:13** = Egypt   ^I **10:24** LXX reads *fathered Cainan, and Cainan fathered*; Gn 11:12-13; Lk 3:35-36

Peleg,^A for during his days the earth was divided; his brother was named Joktan. ²⁶ And Joktan fathered Almodad, Sheleph, Hazarmaveth, Jerah, ²⁷ Hadoram, Uzal, Diklah, ²⁸ Obal, Abimael, Sheba, ²⁹ Ophir, Havilah, and Jobab. All these were Joktan's sons. ³⁰ Their settlements extended from Mesha to Sephar, the eastern hill country.

³¹ These are Shem's sons by their clans, according to their languages, in their lands and their nations.

³² These are the clans of Noah's sons, according to their family records, in their nations. The nations on earth spread out from these after the flood.   Gn 9:19

The Tower of Babylon

11 The whole earth had the same language and vocabulary.^B ² As people^C migrated from the east,^D they found a valley in the land of Shinar and settled there. ³ They said to each other, "Come, let us make oven-fired bricks." (They used brick for stone and asphalt for mortar.) ⁴ And they said, "Come, let us build ourselves a city and a tower with its top in the sky. Let us make a name for ourselves; otherwise, we will be scattered throughout the earth."   Gn 10:10; 14:1,10; Dn 1:2

⁵ Then the LORD came down to look over the city and the tower that the humans^E were building. ⁶ The LORD said, "If they have begun to do this as one people all having the same language, then nothing they plan to do will be impossible for them. ⁷ Come, let's go down there and confuse their language so that they will not understand one another's speech." ⁸ So from there the LORD scattered them throughout the earth, and they stopped building the city. ⁹ Therefore it is called Babylon,^F,G for there the LORD confused the language of the whole earth, and from there the LORD scattered them throughout the earth.

From Shem to Abram

¹⁰ These are the family records of Shem. Shem lived 100 years and fathered Arpachshad two years after the flood. ¹¹ After he fathered Arpachshad, Shem lived 500 years and fathered other sons and daughters. ¹² Arpachshad lived 35 years^H and fathered Shelah. ¹³ After he fathered Shelah, Arpachshad lived 403 years and fathered other sons and daughters. ¹⁴ Shelah lived 30 years and fathered Eber. ¹⁵ After he fathered Eber, Shelah lived 403 years and fathered other sons and daughters. ¹⁶ Eber lived 34 years and fathered Peleg. ¹⁷ After he fathered Peleg, Eber lived 430 years and fathered other sons and daughters. ¹⁸ Peleg lived 30 years and fathered Reu. ¹⁹ After he fathered Reu, Peleg lived 209 years and fathered other sons and daughters. ²⁰ Reu lived 32 years and fathered Serug. ²¹ After he fathered Serug, Reu lived 207 years and fathered other sons and daughters. ²² Serug lived 30 years and fathered Nahor. ²³ After he fathered Nahor, Serug lived 200 years and

---

^A 10:25 = Division   ^B 11:1 Lit one lip and the same words   ^C 11:2 Lit they   ^D 11:2 Or migrated eastward   ^E 11:5 Or the descendants of Adam   ^F 11:9 Hb Babel   ^G 11:9 In Hb, the name for "Babylon," babel sounds like the word for "confuse," balal.   ^H 11:12-13 LXX reads years and fathered Cainan. ¹³ After he fathered Cainan, Arpachshad lived 430 years and fathered other sons and daughters, and he died. Cainan lived 130 years and fathered Shelah. After he fathered Shelah, Cainan lived 330 years and fathered other sons and daughters, and he died; Gn 10:24; Lk 3:35-36 fathered other sons and daughters. [24] Nahor lived 29 years and fathered Terah. [25] After he fathered Terah, Nahor lived 119 years and fathered other sons and daughters. [26] Terah lived 70 years and fathered Abram, Nahor, and Haran. Gn 2:4; 11:27; Jos 24:2

[27] These are the family records of Terah. Terah fathered Abram, Nahor, and Haran, and Haran fathered Lot. [28] Haran died in his native land, in Ur of the Chaldeans, during his father Terah's lifetime. [29] Abram and Nahor took wives: Abram's wife was named Sarai, and Nahor's wife was named Milcah. She was the daughter of Haran, the father of both Milcah and Iscah. [30] Sarai was unable to conceive; she did not have a child. Gn 17:15; 20:12

[31] Terah took his son Abram, his grandson Lot (Haran's son), and his daughter-in-law Sarai, his son Abram's wife, and they set out together from Ur of the Chaldeans to go to the land of Canaan. But when they came to Haran, they settled there. [32] Terah lived 205 years and died in Haran. Gn 15:7; Neh 9:7; Ac 7:4

The Call of Abram

12 The LORD said to Abram:
Go out from your land,
your relatives,
and your father's house
to the land that I will show you.
[2] I will make you
    into a great nation, Gn 17:4-6
I will bless you, Gn 22:17
I will make your name great,
and you will be a blessing.
[3] I will bless those
    who bless you,
I will curse anyone
    who treats you
    with contempt, Gn 27:29

and all the peoples[A] on earth
will be blessed[B]
    through you.[C] Gn 18:18; 26:4; 28:14

[4] So Abram went, as the LORD had told him, and Lot went with him. Abram was seventy-five years old when he left Haran. [5] He took his wife Sarai, his nephew Lot, all the possessions they had accumulated, and the people they had acquired in Haran, and they set out for the land of Canaan. When they came to the land of Canaan, [6] Abram passed through the land to the site of Shechem, at the oak of Moreh. (At that time the Canaanites were in the land.) [7] The LORD appeared to Abram and said, "To your offspring I will give this land." So he built an altar there to the Lord who had appeared to him. [8] From there he moved on to the hill country east of Bethel and pitched his tent, with Bethel on the west and Ai on the east. He built an altar to the LORD there, and he called on the name of the LORD. [9] Then Abram journeyed by stages to the Negev. Gn 11:27, 31; 21:33

Abram in Egypt

[10] There was a famine in the land, so Abram went down to Egypt to stay there for a while because the famine in the land was severe. [11] When he was about to enter Egypt, he said to his wife Sarai, "Look, I know what a beautiful woman you are. [12] When the Egyptians see you, they will say, 'This is his wife.' They will kill me but let you live. [13] Please say you're my sister so it will go well for me because of you, and my life will be spared on your account." [14] When Abram entered Egypt, the Egyptians saw

---

[A] 12:3 Lit clans   [B] 12:3 Or will find blessing   [C] 12:3 Or will bless themselves by you that the woman was very beautiful. [15] Pharaoh's officials saw her and praised her to Pharaoh, so the woman was taken to Pharaoh's household. [16] He treated Abram well because of her, and Abram acquired flocks and herds, male and female donkeys, male and female slaves, and camels. Gn 26:1; 43:1 [17] But the LORD struck Pharaoh and his household with severe plagues because of Abram's wife Sarai. [18] So Pharaoh sent for Abram and said, "What have you done to me? Why didn't you tell me she was your wife? [19] Why did you say, 'She's my sister,' so that I took her as my wife? Now, here is your wife. Take her and go!" [20] Then Pharaoh gave his men orders about him, and they sent him away with his wife and all he had. Gn 20:18; 1Ch 16:21; Ps 105:14

Abram and Lot Separate

13 Abram went up from Egypt to the Negev — he, his wife, and all he had, and Lot with him. [2] Abram was very rich in livestock, silver, and gold. [3] He went by stages from the Negev to Bethel, to the place between Bethel and Ai where his tent had formerly been, [4] to the site where he had built the altar. And Abram called on the name of the LORD there. Gn 12:7-9

[5] Now Lot, who was traveling with Abram, also had flocks, herds, and tents. [6] But the land was unable to support them as long as they stayed together, for they had so many possessions that they could not stay together, [7] and there was quarreling between the herdsmen of Abram's livestock and the herdsmen of Lot's livestock. (At that time the Canaanites and the Perizzites were living in the land.) Gn 36:7

[8] So Abram said to Lot, "Please, let's not have quarreling between you and me, or between your herdsmen and my herdsmen, since we are relatives.[A] [9] Isn't the whole land before you? Separate from me: if you go to the left, I will go to the right; if you go to the right, I will go to the left."

[10] Lot looked out and saw that the entire plain[B] of the Jordan as far as[C] Zoar was well watered everywhere like the LORD's garden and the land of Egypt. (This was before the LORD destroyed Sodom and Gomorrah.) [11] So Lot chose the entire plain of the Jordan for himself. Then Lot journeyed eastward, and they separated from each other. [12] Abram lived in the land of Canaan, but Lot lived in the cities on the plain and set up his tent near Sodom. [13] (Now the men of Sodom were evil, sinning immensely[D] against the LORD.) Gn 19:17-29

[14] After Lot had separated from him, the LORD said to Abram, "Look from the place where you are. Look north and south, east and west, [15] for I will give you and your offspring forever all the land that you see. [16] I will make your offspring like the dust of the earth, so that if anyone could count the dust of the earth, then your offspring could be counted. [17] Get up and walk around the land, through its length and width, for I will give it to you." Gn 12:7; 15:18; 28:14

[18] So Abram moved his tent and went to live near the oaks of Mamre at Hebron, where he built an altar to the LORD. Gn 14:13; 18:1; 23:17-19

[A]**13:8** Lit *brothers*   [B]**13:10** Lit *circle* ; i.e., probably the large round plain where the Jordan River empties into the Dead Sea, also in v. 11   [C]**13:10** Lit *Jordan as you go to*   [D]**13:13** Lit *evil and sinful*

Abram Rescues Lot

14 In those days King Amraphel of Shinar, King Arioch of Ellasar, King Chedorlaomer of Elam, and King Tidal of Goiim[A] [2] waged war against King Bera of Sodom, King Birsha of Gomorrah, King Shinab of Admah, and King Shemeber of Zeboiim, as well as the king of Bela (that is, Zoar). [3] All of these came as allies to the Siddim Valley (that is, the Dead Sea). [4] They were subject to Chedorlaomer for twelve years, but in the thirteenth year they rebelled. [5] In the fourteenth year Chedorlaomer and the kings who were with him came and defeated the Rephaim in Ashteroth-karnaim, the Zuzim in Ham, the Emim in Shaveh-kiriathaim, [6] and the Horites in the mountains of Seir, as far as El-paran by the wilderness. [7] Then they came back to invade En-mishpat (that is, Kadesh), and they defeated the whole territory of the Amalekites, as well as the Amorites who lived in Hazazon-tamar. Gn 10:10; 11:2; Is 11:11

[8] Then the king of Sodom, the king of Gomorrah, the king of Admah, the king of Zeboiim, and the king of Bela (that is, Zoar) went out and lined up for battle in the Siddim Valley [9] against King Chedorlaomer of Elam, King Tidal of Goiim, King Amraphel of Shinar, and King Arioch of Ellasar — four kings against five. [10] Now the Siddim Valley contained many asphalt pits, and as the kings of Sodom and Gomorrah fled, some fell into them,[B] but the rest fled to the mountains. [11] The four kings took all the goods of Sodom and Gomorrah and all their food and went on. [12] They also took Abram's nephew Lot and his possessions, for he was living in Sodom, and they went on. Gn 13:12; 19:17

[13] One of the survivors came and told Abram the Hebrew, who lived near the oaks belonging to Mamre the Amorite, the brother of Eshcol and the brother of Aner. They were bound by a treaty with[C] Abram. [14] When Abram heard that his relative had been taken prisoner, he assembled[D] his 318 trained men, born in his household, and they went in pursuit as far as Dan. [15] And he and his servants deployed against them by night, defeated them, and pursued them as far as Hobah to the north of Damascus. [16] He brought back all the goods and also his relative Lot and his goods, as well as the women and the other people. Gn 39:14; 40:15

Melchizedek's Blessing

[17] After Abram returned from defeating Chedorlaomer and the kings who were with him, the king of Sodom went out to meet him in the Shaveh Valley (that is, the King's Valley). [18] Melchizedek, king of Salem,[E] brought out bread and wine; he was a priest to God Most High. [19] He blessed him and said: 2Sm 18:18

> Abram is blessed
> 　by God Most High,
> Creator[F] of heaven and earth,
> [20]　and blessed
> 　be God Most High
> who has handed over
> 　your enemies to you.

And Abram gave him a tenth of everything. Heb 7:4

[21] Then the king of Sodom said to Abram, "Give me the people, but take the possessions for yourself."

²² But Abram said to the king of Sodom, "I have raised my hand in an oath to the LORD, God Most High, Creator of heaven and earth, ²³ that I will not take a thread or sandal strap or anything that belongs to you, so you can never say, 'I made Abram rich.' ²⁴ I will take nothing^A except what the servants have eaten. But as for the share of the men who came with me — Aner, Eshcol, and Mamre — they can take their share."

The Abrahamic Covenant

15 After these events, the word of the LORD came to Abram in a vision: 1Sm 15:10; 2Sm 7:4; 1Kg 6:11; Is 38:4

Do not be afraid, Abram.
I am your shield;   Dt 33:29; Ps 3:3
your reward will be very great.

² But Abram said, "Lord GOD, what can you give me, since I am childless and the heir of my house is Eliezer of Damascus?"^B ³ Abram continued, "Look, you have given me no offspring, so a slave born in^C my house will be my heir."

⁴ Now the word of the LORD came to him: "This one will not be your heir; instead, one who comes from your own body^D will be your heir." ⁵ He took him outside and said, "Look at the sky and count the stars, if you are able to count them." Then he said to him, "Your offspring will be that numerous." Gn 22:17; 26:4; Dt 1:10

⁶ Abram believed the LORD, and he credited it to him as righteousness.   Rm 4:3,9,22; Gl 3:6; Jms 2:23

⁷ He also said to him, "I am the LORD who brought you from Ur of the Chaldeans to give you this land to possess." Gn 11:31; 12:1; Neh 9:7-8; Ac 7:2-4

⁸ But he said, "Lord GOD, how can I know that I will possess it?" Lk 1:18

⁹ He said to him, "Bring me a three-year-old cow, a three-year-old female goat, a three-year-old ram, a turtledove, and a young pigeon."

¹⁰ So he brought all these to him, cut them in half, and laid the pieces opposite each other, but he did not cut the birds in half. ¹¹ Birds of prey came down on the carcasses, but Abram drove them away. ¹² As the sun was setting, a deep sleep came over Abram, and suddenly great terror and darkness descended on him.   Gn 2:21; Lv 1:17

¹³ Then the LORD said to Abram, "Know this for certain: Your offspring will be resident aliens for four hundred years in a land that does not belong to them and will be enslaved and oppressed.^E ¹⁴ However, I will judge the nation they serve, and afterward they will go out with many possessions. ¹⁵ But you will go to your fathers in peace and be buried at a good old age. ¹⁶ In the fourth generation they will return here, for the iniquity of the Amorites has not yet reached its full measure."^F   Ac 7:6-7; Ex 22:21; 23:9

¹⁷ When the sun had set and it was dark, a smoking fire pot and a flaming torch appeared and passed between the divided animals. ¹⁸ On that day the LORD made a covenant with Abram, saying, "I give this land to your offspring, from the Brook of Egypt to the great river, the Euphrates River: ¹⁹ the land of the Kenites, Kenizzites, Kadmonites, ²⁰ Hethites, Perizzites, Rephaim, ²¹ Amorites, Canaanites, Girgashites, and Jebusites." Gn 12:7; 13:15; 17:8

---

^A **14:24** Lit nothing to me   ^B **15:2** Hb obscure   ^C **15:3** Lit a son of   ^D **15:4** Lit loins   ^E **15:13** Lit will serve them and they will oppress them   ^F **15:16** Lit Amorites is not yet complete

Hagar and Ishmael

16 Abram's wife Sarai had not borne any children for him, but she owned an Egyptian slave named Hagar. ² Sarai said to Abram, "Since the LORD has prevented me from bearing children, go to my slave; perhaps through her I can build a family." And Abram agreed to what Sarai said.^A ³ So Abram's wife Sarai took Hagar, her Egyptian slave, and gave her to her husband Abram as a wife for him. This happened after Abram had lived in the land of Canaan ten years. ⁴ He slept with ^B Hagar, and she became pregnant. When she saw that she was pregnant, her mistress became contemptible to her. ⁵ Then Sarai said to Abram, "You are responsible for my suffering!^C I put my slave in your arms, ^D and when she saw that she was pregnant, I became contemptible to her. May the LORD judge between me and you." Gn 31:49; Jos 22:25; 1Sm 24:12

⁶ Abram replied to Sarai, "Here, your slave is in your hands; do whatever you want with her." Then Sarai mistreated her so much that she ran away from her.

⁷ The angel of the LORD found her by a spring in the wilderness, the spring on the way to Shur. ⁸ He said, "Hagar, slave of Sarai, where have you come from and where are you going?" Gn 22:11; Ex 3:2; Nm 22:22; Jdg 2:1; Ps 34:7

She replied, "I'm running away from my mistress Sarai."

⁹ The angel of the LORD said to her, "Go back to your mistress and submit to her authority." ¹⁰ The angel of the LORD said to her, "I will greatly multiply your offspring, and they will be too many to count." Gn 15:5

¹¹ The angel of the LORD said to her, "You have conceived and will have a son. You will name him Ishmael, ^E for the LORD has heard your cry of affliction. ¹² This man will be like a wild donkey. His hand will be against everyone, and everyone's hand will be against him; he will settle near all his relatives." Gn 25:18

¹³ So she named the LORD who spoke to her: "You are El-roi,"^F for she said, "In this place, have I actually seen the one who sees me?"^G ¹⁴ That is why the well is called Beer-lahai-roi.^H It is between Kadesh and Bered. Gn 32:30; Ex 33:23; Ps 139:1-12

¹⁵ So Hagar gave birth to Abram's son, and Abram named his son (whom Hagar bore) Ishmael. ¹⁶ Abram was eighty-six years old when Hagar bore Ishmael to him.

Covenant Circumcision

17 When Abram was ninety-nine years old, the LORD appeared to him, saying, "I am God Almighty. Live^I in my presence and be blameless. ² I will set up my covenant between me and you, and I will multiply you greatly." Gn 28:3

³ Then Abram fell facedown and God spoke with him: ⁴ "As for me, here is my covenant with you: You will become the father of many nations. ⁵ Your name will no longer be Abram;^J your name will be Abraham,^K for I will make you the father of many nations. ⁶ I will make you extremely fruitful and will make nations and kings come from you. ⁷ I will confirm my covenant that

---

^A**16:2** Lit *Abram listened to the voice of Sarai*   ^B**16:4** Lit *He came to*   ^C**16:5** Or *"May my suffering be on you!*   ^D**16:5** Lit *bosom*   ^E**16:11** = God Hears   ^F**16:13** = God Sees Me   ^G**16:13** Hb obscure   ^H**16:14** = Well of the Living One Who Sees Me   ^I**17:1** Or *Walk*   ^J**17:5** = The Father Is Exalted   ^K**17:5** = Father of a Multitude is between me and you and your future offspring throughout their generations. It is a permanent covenant to be your God and the God of your offspring after you. ⁸ And to you and your future offspring I will give the land where you are residing — all the land of Canaan — as a permanent possession, and I will be their God." Gn 9:16; 35:11; 48:19

⁹ God also said to Abraham, "As for you, you and your offspring after you throughout their generations are to keep my covenant. ¹⁰ This is my covenant between me and you and your offspring after you, which you are to keep: Every one of your males must be circumcised. ¹¹ You must circumcise the flesh of your foreskin to serve as a sign of the covenant between me and you. ᴬ ¹² Throughout your generations, every male among you is to be circumcised at eight days old — every male born in your household or purchased from any foreigner and not your offspring. ¹³ Whether born in your household or purchased, he must be circumcised. My covenant will be marked in your flesh as a permanent covenant. ¹⁴ If any male is not circumcised in the flesh of his foreskin, that man will be cut off from his people; he has broken my covenant." Ex 12:48; Dt 10:16

¹⁵ God said to Abraham, "As for your wife Sarai, do not call her Sarai, for Sarah ᴮ will be her name. ¹⁶ I will bless her; indeed, I will give you a son by her. I will bless her, and she will produce nations; kings of peoples will come from her."

¹⁷ Abraham fell facedown. Then he laughed and said to himself, "Can a child be born to a hundred-year-old man? Can Sarah, a ninety-year-old woman, give birth?" ¹⁸ So Abraham said to God, "If only Ishmael were acceptable ᶜ to you!" Gn 21:6-7; Rm 4:19

¹⁹ But God said, "No. Your wife Sarah will bear you a son, and you will name him Isaac. ᴰ I will confirm my covenant with him as a permanent covenant for his future offspring. ²⁰ As for Ishmael, I have heard you. I will certainly bless him; I will make him fruitful and will multiply him greatly. He will father twelve tribal leaders, and I will make him into a great nation. ²¹ But I will confirm my covenant with Isaac, whom Sarah will bear to you at this time next year." ²² When he finished talking with him, God withdrew ᴱ from Abraham. Gn 18:10,14; 21:1; 25:13-16; 35:13

²³ So Abraham took his son Ishmael and those born in his household or purchased — every male among the members of Abraham's household — and he circumcised the flesh of their foreskin on that very day, just as God had said to him. ²⁴ Abraham was ninety-nine years old when the flesh of his foreskin was circumcised, ²⁵ and his son Ishmael was thirteen years old when the flesh of his foreskin was circumcised. ²⁶ On that same day Abraham and his son Ishmael were circumcised. ²⁷ And all the men of his household — whether born in his household or purchased from a foreigner — were circumcised with him.

Abraham's Three Visitors

18 The Lᴏʀᴅ appeared to Abraham at the oaks of Mamre while he was sitting at the entrance of his tent during the heat

ᴬ**17:11** *You* in v. 11 is pl.   ᴮ**17:15** = Princess   ᶜ**17:18** Lit *alive*   ᴰ**17:19** = He Laughs   ᴱ**17:22** Lit *went up*, or *ascended* of the day. [2] He looked up, and he saw three men standing near him. When he saw them, he ran from the entrance of the tent to meet them, bowed to the ground, [3] and said, "My lord, if I have found favor with you, please do not go on past your servant. [4] Let a little water be brought, that you may wash your feet and rest yourselves under the tree. [5] I will bring a bit of bread so that you may strengthen yourselves.[A] This is why you have passed your servant's way. Later, you can continue on."   Gn 13:18; 14:13

"Yes," they replied, "do as you have said."

[6] So Abraham hurried into the tent and said to Sarah, "Quick! Knead three measures[B] of fine flour and make bread."[C] [7] Abraham ran to the herd and got a tender, choice calf. He gave it to a young man, who hurried to prepare it. [8] Then Abraham took curds[D] and milk, as well as the calf that he had prepared, and set them before the men. He served[E] them as they ate under the tree.

Sarah Laughs

[9] "Where is your wife Sarah?" they asked him.

"There, in the tent," he answered.

[10] The LORD said, "I will certainly come back to you in about a year's time, and your wife Sarah will have a son!" Now Sarah was listening at the entrance of the tent behind him. [11] Abraham and Sarah were old and getting on in years.[F] Sarah had passed the age of childbearing.[G] [12] So she laughed to herself: "After

I am worn out and my lord is old, will I have delight?"   Gn 17:17; Rm 4:19

[13] But the LORD asked Abraham, "Why did Sarah laugh, saying, 'Can I really have a baby when I'm old?' [14] Is anything impossible for the LORD? At the appointed time I will come back to you, and in about a year she will have a son."   Jb 34:10

[15] Sarah denied it. "I did not laugh," she said, because she was afraid.

But he replied, "No, you did laugh."

Abraham's Plea for Sodom

[16] The men got up from there and looked out over Sodom, and Abraham was walking with them to see them off. [17] Then the LORD said, "Should I hide what I am about to do from Abraham? [18] Abraham is to become a great and powerful nation, and all the nations of the earth will be blessed through him. [19] For I have chosen[H] him so that he will command his children and his house after him to keep the way of the LORD by doing what is right and just. This is how the LORD will fulfill to Abraham what he promised him." [20] Then the LORD said, "The outcry against Sodom and Gomorrah is immense, and their sin is extremely serious. [21] I will go down to see if what they have done justifies the cry that has come up to me. If not, I will find out."   Gn 26:4; Am 3:7

[22] The men turned from there and went toward Sodom while Abraham remained standing before the LORD.[I] [23] Abraham stepped forward and said, "Will you really sweep away the righteous with the wicked? [24] What if there are fifty

---

[A]18:5 Lit *may sustain your heart*   [B]18:6 Lit *three seahs* ; about 21 quarts   [C]18:6 A round, thin, unleavened bread   [D]18:8 Or *butter*   [E]18:8 Lit *was standing by*   [F]18:11 Lit *days*   [G]18:11 Lit *The way of women had ceased for Sarah*   [H]18:19 Lit *known*   [I]18:22 Alt Hb tradition reads *while the LORD remained standing before Abraham* righteous people in the city? Will you really sweep it away instead of sparing the place for the sake of the fifty righteous people who are in it? ²⁵ You could not possibly do such a thing: to kill the righteous with the wicked, treating the righteous and the wicked alike. You could not possibly do that! Won't the Judge of the whole earth do what is just?"

²⁶ The LORD said, "If I find fifty righteous people in the city of Sodom, I will spare the whole place for their sake."   Jr 5:1

²⁷ Then Abraham answered, "Since I have ventured to speak to my lord — even though I am dust and ashes — ²⁸ suppose the fifty righteous lack five. Will you destroy the whole city for lack of five?"

He replied, "I will not destroy it if I find forty-five there."

²⁹ Then he spoke to him again, "Suppose forty are found there?"

He answered, "I will not do it on account of forty."

³⁰ Then he said, "Let my lord not be angry, and I will speak further. Suppose thirty are found there?"

He answered, "I will not do it if I find thirty there."

³¹ Then he said, "Since I have ventured to speak to my lord, suppose twenty are found there?"

He replied, "I will not destroy it on account of twenty."

³² Then he said, "Let my lord not be angry, and I will speak one more time. Suppose ten are found there?"   Jdg 6:39

He answered, "I will not destroy it on account of ten." ³³ When the LORD had finished speaking with Abraham, he departed, and Abraham returned to his place.

The Destruction of Sodom and Gomorrah

19 The two angels entered Sodom in the evening as Lot was sitting in Sodom's gateway. When Lot saw them, he got up to meet them. He bowed with his face to the ground ² and said, "My lords, turn aside to your servant's house, wash your feet, and spend the night. Then you can get up early and go on your way."   Gn 18:2,22

"No," they said. "We would rather spend the night in the square." ³ But he urged them so strongly that they followed him and went into his house. He prepared a feast and baked unleavened bread for them, and they ate.

⁴ Before they went to bed, the men of the city of Sodom, both young and old, the whole population, surrounded the house. ⁵ They called out to Lot and said, "Where are the men who came to you tonight? Send them out to us so we can have sex with them!"   Lv 18:22

⁶ Lot went out to them at the entrance and shut the door behind him. ⁷ He said, "Don't do this evil, my brothers. ⁸ Look, I've got two daughters who haven't been intimate with a man. I'll bring them out to you, and you can do whatever you want^A to them. However, don't do anything to these men, because they have come under the protection of my roof."   Jdg 19:24

⁹ "Get out of the way!" they said, adding, "This one came here as an alien, but he's acting like a judge! Now we'll do more harm to you than to them." They put pressure on Lot and came up to break down the door. ¹⁰ But the angels^B reached out, brought Lot into the

---

^A**19:8** Lit *do what is good in your eyes*   ^B**19:10** Lit *men,* also in v. 12

house with them, and shut the door. ¹¹ They struck the men who were at the entrance of the house, both young and old, with blindness ᴬ so that they were unable to find the entrance. Ex 2:14; Dt 28:28-29; 2Kg 6:18; Ac 13:11 ¹² Then the angels said to Lot, "Do you have anyone else here: a son-in-law, your sons and daughters, or anyone else in the city who belongs to you? Get them out of this place, ¹³ for we are about to destroy this place because the outcry against its people is so great before the LORD, that the LORD has sent us to destroy it." Gn 18:20-21; Ex 3:7; 22:23; 1Sm 9:16; Jb 27:9

¹⁴ So Lot went out and spoke to his sons-in-law, who were going to marry ᴮ his daughters. "Get up," he said. "Get out of this place, for the LORD is about to destroy the city!" But his sons-in-law thought he was joking. Nm 16:21,26,45; Jr 51:6; Rv 18:4

¹⁵ At daybreak the angels urged Lot on: "Get up! Take your wife and your two daughters who are here, or you will be swept away in the punishment ᶜ of the city." ¹⁶ But he hesitated. Because of the LORD's compassion for him, the men grabbed his hand, his wife's hand, and the hands of his two daughters. They brought him out and left him outside the city.

¹⁷ As soon as the angels got them outside, one of them ᴰ said, "Run for your lives! Don't look back and don't stop anywhere on the plain! Run to the mountains, or you will be swept away!"

¹⁸ But Lot said to them, "No, my lords ᴱ — please. ¹⁹ Your servant has indeed found favor with you, and you have shown me great kindness by saving my life. But I can't run to the mountains; the disaster will overtake me, and I will die. ²⁰ Look, this town is close enough for me to flee to. It is a small place. Please let me run to it — it's only a small place, isn't it? — so that I can survive."

²¹ And he said to him, "All right, ᶠ I'll grant your request ᴳ about this matter too and will not demolish the town you mentioned. ²² Hurry up! Run to it, for I cannot do anything until you get there." Therefore the name of the city is Zoar. ᴴ

²³ The sun had risen over the land when Lot reached Zoar. ²⁴ Then out of the sky the LORD rained on Sodom and Gomorrah burning sulfur from the LORD. ²⁵ He demolished these cities, the entire plain, all the inhabitants of the cities, and whatever grew on the ground. ²⁶ But Lot's wife looked back and became a pillar of salt. Dt 29:23; Ps 11:6

²⁷ Early in the morning Abraham went to the place where he had stood before the LORD. ²⁸ He looked down toward Sodom and Gomorrah and all the land of the plain, and he saw that smoke was going up from the land like the smoke of a furnace. ²⁹ So it was, when God destroyed the cities of the plain, he remembered Abraham and brought Lot out of the middle of the upheaval when he demolished the cities where Lot had lived. Gn 18:22

The Origin of Moab and Ammon

³⁰ Lot departed from Zoar and lived in the mountains along with his two daughters, because he was

---

ᴬ19:11 Or *a blinding light*   ᴮ19:14 Lit *take*   ᶜ19:15 Or *iniquity, or guilt*   ᴰ19:17 LXX, Syr, Vg read *outside, they*   ᴱ19:18 Or *my Lord*, or *my lord*   ᶠ19:21 Or *"Look!*   ᴳ19:21 Lit *I will lift up your face*   ᴴ19:22 In Hb, the name *Zoar* is related to "small" in v. 20; its previous name was "Bela"; Gn 14:2.

afraid to live in Zoar. Instead, he and his two daughters lived in a cave. ³¹ Then the firstborn said to the younger, "Our father is old, and there is no man in the land to sleep with us as is the custom of all the land. ³² Come, let's get our father to drink wine so that we can sleep with him and preserve our father's line." ³³ So they got their father to drink wine that night, and the first-born came and slept with her father; he did not know when she lay down or when she got up.

³⁴ The next day the firstborn said to the younger, "Look, I slept with my father last night. Let's get him to drink wine again tonight so you can go sleep with him and we can preserve our father's line." ³⁵ That night they again got their father to drink wine, and the younger went and slept with him; he did not know when she lay down or when she got up.

³⁶ So both of Lot's daughters became pregnant by their father. ³⁷ The firstborn gave birth to a son and named him Moab.ᴬ He is the father of the Moabites of today. ³⁸ The younger also gave birth to a son, and she named him Ben-ammi.ᴮ He is the father of the Ammonites of today.   Dt 2:9,19

Sarah Rescued from Abimelech

20 From there Abraham traveled to the region of the Negev and settled between Kadesh and Shur. While he was staying in Gerar, ² Abraham said about his wife Sarah, "She is my sister." So King Abimelech of Gerar had Sarah brought to him.   Gn 12:13; 26:7

³ But God came to Abimelech in a dream by night and said to him, "You are about to die because of the woman you have taken, for she is a married woman."ᶜ

⁴ Now Abimelech had not approached her, so he said, "Lord, would you destroy a nation even though it is innocent? ⁵ Didn't he himself say to me, 'She is my sister'? And she herself said, 'He is my brother.' I did this with a clear conscienceᴰ and cleanᴱ hands."

⁶ Then God said to him in the dream, "Yes, I know that you did this with a clear conscience.ᶠ I have also kept you from sinning against me. Therefore I have not let you touch her. ⁷ Now return the man's wife, for he is a prophet, and he will pray for you and you will live. But if you do not return her, know that you will certainly die, you and all who are yours."   1Sm 7:5; 2Kg 5:11

⁸ Early in the morning Abimelech got up, called all his servants together, and personallyᴳ told them all these things, and the men were terrified.

⁹ Then Abimelech called Abraham in and said to him, "What have you done to us? How did I sin against you that you have brought such enormous guilt on me and on my kingdom? You have done things to me that should never be done." ¹⁰ Abimelech also asked Abraham, "What made you do this?"   Gn 12:19

¹¹ Abraham replied, "I thought, 'There is absolutely no fear of God in this place. They will kill me because of my wife.' ¹² Besides, she really is my sister, the daughter of my father though not the daughter

---

ᴬ**19:37** = From My Father   ᴮ**19:38** = Son of My People   ᶜ**20:3** Lit *is possessed by a husband*   ᴰ**20:5** Lit *with integrity of my heart*   ᴱ**20:5** Lit *cleanness of my*   ᶠ**20:6** Lit *with integrity of your heart*   ᴳ**20:8** Lit *in their ears* of my mother, and she became my wife. ¹³ So when God had me wander from my father's house, I said to her: Show your loyalty to me wherever we go and say about me: 'He's my brother.'" Gn 12:1; 20:5; Neh 5:15; Pr 16:6

¹⁴ Then Abimelech took flocks and herds and male and female slaves, gave them to Abraham, and returned his wife Sarah to him. ¹⁵ Abimelech said, "Look, my land is before you. Settle wherever you want."ᴬ ¹⁶ And he said to Sarah, "Look, I am giving your brother one thousand pieces of silver. It is a verification of your honorᴮ to all who are with you. You are fully vindicated." Gn 13:9; 34:10; 47:6

¹⁷ Then Abraham prayed to God, and God healed Abimelech, his wife, and his female slaves so that they could bear children, ¹⁸ for the LORD had completely closed all the wombs in Abimelech's household on account of Sarah, Abraham's wife. Nm 12:13; 21:7; Jms 5:16

The Birth of Isaac

21 The LORD came to Sarah as he had said, and the LORD did for Sarah what he had promised. ² Sarah became pregnant and bore a son to Abraham in his old age, at the appointed time God had told him. ³ Abraham named his son who was born to him — the one Sarah bore to him — Isaac. ⁴ When his son Isaac was eight days old, Abraham circumcised him, as God had commanded him. ⁵ Abraham was a hundred years old when his son Isaac was born to him. Gn 17:16; 18:10

⁶ Sarah said, "God has made me laugh, and everyone who hears will laugh with me."ᶜ ⁷ She also said, "Who would have told Abraham that Sarah would nurse children? Yet I have borne a son for himᴰ in his old age." Gn 18:12-15

Hagar and Ishmael Sent Away

⁸ The child grew and was weaned, and Abraham held a great feast on the day Isaac was weaned. ⁹ But Sarah saw the son mocking — the one Hagar the Egyptian had borne to Abraham. ¹⁰ So she said to Abraham, "Drive out this slave with her son, for the son of this slave will not be a coheir with my son Isaac!"

¹¹ This was very distressing toᴱ Abraham because of his son. ¹² But God said to Abraham, "Do not be distressedᶠ about the boy and about your slave. Whatever Sarah says to you, listen to her, because your offspring will be traced through Isaac, ¹³ and I will also make a nation of the slave's son because he is your offspring." Gn 16:10; 21:18; Rm 9:7; Heb 11:18

¹⁴ Early in the morning Abraham got up, took bread and a waterskin, put them on Hagar's shoulders, and sent her and the boy away. She left and wandered in the Wilderness of Beer-sheba. ¹⁵ When the water in the skin was gone, she left the boy under one of the bushes ¹⁶ and went and sat at a distance, about a bowshot away, for she said, "I can't bear to watch the boy die!" While she sat at a distance, sheᴳ wept loudly.

¹⁷ God heard the boy crying, and theᴴ angel of God called to Hagar from heaven and said to her, "What's wrong, Hagar? Don't be afraid, for God has heard the boy crying from the place where he is. ¹⁸ Get up, help

---

ᴬ**20:15** Lit *Settle in the good in your eyes*   ᴮ**20:16** Lit *a covering of the eyes*   ᶜ**21:6** Isaac = He Laughs; Gn 17:19   ᴰ**21:7** Sam, Tg Jonathan; MT omits *him*   ᴱ**21:11** Lit *was very bad in the eyes of*   ᶠ**21:12** Lit *"Let it not be bad in your eyes*   ᴳ**21:16** LXX reads *the boy*   ᴴ**21:17** Or *an* the boy up, and grasp his hand, for I will make him a great nation." ¹⁹ Then God opened her eyes, and she saw a well. So she went and filled the waterskin and gave the boy a drink. ²⁰ God was with the boy, and he grew; he settled in the wilderness and became an archer. ²¹ He settled in the Wilderness of Paran, and his mother got a wife for him from the land of Egypt.   Nm 22:31

Abraham's Covenant with Abimelech

²² At that time Abimelech, accompanied by Phicol the commander of his army, said to Abraham, "God is with you in everything you do. ²³ Swear to me by God here and now, that you will not break an agreement with me or with my children and descendants. As I have been loyal to you, so you will be loyal to me and to the country where you are a resident alien."   Gn 20:2; 26:1,26

²⁴ And Abraham said, "I swear it." ²⁵ But Abraham complained to Abimelech because of the well that Abimelech's servants had seized. ²⁶ Abimelech replied, "I don't know who did this thing. You didn't report anything to me, so I hadn't heard about it until today."

²⁷ Abraham took flocks and herds and gave them to Abimelech, and the two of them made a covenant. ²⁸ Abraham separated seven ewe lambs from the flock. ²⁹ And Abimelech said to Abraham, "Why have you separated these seven ewe lambs?"   Gn 26:31

³⁰ He replied, "You are to accept the seven ewe lambs from me so that this act^A will serve as my witness that I dug this well." ³¹ Therefore that place was called Beer-sheba^B because it was there that the two of them swore an oath. ³² After they had made a covenant at Beer-sheba, Abimelech and Phicol, the commander of his army, left and returned to the land of the Philistines.   Gn 26:33

³³ Abraham planted a tamarisk tree in Beer-sheba, and there he called on the name of the LORD, the Everlasting God. ³⁴ And Abraham lived as an alien in the land of the Philistines for many days.   Ps 45:6

The Sacrifice of Isaac

22 After these things God tested Abraham and said to him, "Abraham!"   Dt 8:2,16; 1Co 10:13; Heb 11:17

"Here I am," he answered.

² "Take your son," he said, "your only son Isaac, whom you love, go to the land of Moriah, and offer him there as a burnt offering on one of the mountains I will tell you about."

³ So Abraham got up early in the morning, saddled his donkey, and took with him two of his young men and his son Isaac. He split wood for a burnt offering and set out to go to the place God had told him about. ⁴ On the third day Abraham looked up and saw the place in the distance. ⁵ Then Abraham said to his young men, "Stay here with the donkey. The boy and I will go over there to worship; then we'll come back to you." ⁶ Abraham took the wood for the burnt offering and laid it on his son Isaac. In his hand he took the fire and the knife, and the two of them walked on together.   Ex 19:11,16; Jos 3:1; 9:17; Jdg 20:30; 2Sm 1:2

⁷ Then Isaac spoke to his father Abraham and said, "My father."

And he replied, "Here I am, my son."

^A 21:30 Lit that it   ^B 21:31 = Well of the Oath, or Seven Wells

Isaac said, "The fire and the wood are here, but where is the lamb for the burnt offering?"

⁸ Abraham answered, "God himself will provide ᴬ the lamb for the burnt offering, my son." Then the two of them walked on together.

⁹ When they arrived at the place that God had told him about, Abraham built the altar there and arranged the wood. He bound his son Isaac ᴮ and placed him on the altar on top of the wood. ¹⁰ Then Abraham reached out and took the knife to slaughter his son.　Heb 11:17; Jms 2:21

¹¹ But the angel of the LORD called to him from heaven and said, "Abraham, Abraham!"

He replied, "Here I am."

¹² Then he said, "Do not lay a hand on the boy or do anything to him. For now I know that you fear God, since you have not withheld your only son from me." ¹³ Abraham looked up and saw a ram ᶜ caught in the thicket by its horns. So Abraham went and took the ram and offered it as a burnt offering in place of his son. ¹⁴ And Abraham named that place The LORD Will Provide, ᴰ so today it is said: "It will be provided ᴱ on the LORD's mountain."

¹⁵ Then the angel of the LORD called to Abraham a second time from heaven ¹⁶ and said, "By myself I have sworn," this is the LORD's declaration: "Because you have done this thing and have not withheld your only son, ¹⁷ I will indeed bless you and make your offspring as numerous as the stars of the sky and the sand on the seashore. Your offspring will possess the city gates of their enemies. ¹⁸ And all the nations of the earth will be blessed ᶠ by your offspring because you have obeyed my command."　Ps 105:9; Lk 1:73

¹⁹ Abraham went back to his young men, and they got up and went together to Beer-sheba. And Abraham settled in Beer-sheba.

Rebekah's Family

²⁰ Now after these things Abraham was told, "Milcah also has borne sons to your brother Nahor: ²¹ Uz his firstborn, his brother Buz, Kemuel the father of Aram, ²² Chesed, Hazo, Pildash, Jidlaph, and Bethuel." ²³ And Bethuel fathered Rebekah. Milcah bore these eight to Nahor, Abraham's brother. ²⁴ His concubine, whose name was Reumah, also bore Tebah, Gaham, Tahash, and Maacah.　Gn 11:29; 24:15

Sarah's Burial

23 Now Sarah lived 127 years; these were all the years of her life. ² Sarah died in Kiriath-arba (that is, Hebron) in the land of Canaan, and Abraham went to mourn for Sarah and to weep for her.

³ Then Abraham got up from beside his dead wife and spoke to the Hethites: ⁴ "I am an alien residing among you. Give me burial property among you so that I can bury my dead." ᴳ　Gn 17:8; Lv 25:23; 1Ch 29:15

⁵ The Hethites replied to Abraham, ᴴ ⁶ "Listen to us, my lord. You are a prince of God ᴵ among us. Bury your dead in our finest burial place. ᴶ None of us will withhold from you his burial place for burying your dead."

ᴬ22:8 Lit see　ᴮ22:9 Or Isaac hand and foot　ᶜ22:13 Some Hb mss, Sam, LXX, Syr, Tg; other Hb mss read saw behind him a ram　ᴰ22:14 = Yahweh-yireh　ᴱ22:14 Or "He will be seen　ᶠ22:18 Or will bless themselves, or will find blessing　ᴳ23:4 Lit dead from before me　ᴴ23:5 Lit Abraham, saying to him　ᴵ23:6 Or a mighty prince　ᴶ23:6 Or finest graves

⁷ Then Abraham rose and bowed down to the Hethites, the people of the land. ⁸ He said to them, "If you are willing for me to bury my dead, listen to me and ask Ephron son of Zohar on my behalf ⁹ to give me the cave of Machpelah that belongs to him; it is at the end of his field. Let him give it to me in your presence, for the full price, as burial property."

¹⁰ Ephron was sitting among the Hethites. So in the hearing[A] of all the Hethites who came to the gate of his city, Ephron the Hethite answered Abraham: ¹¹ "No, my lord. Listen to me. I give you the field, and I give you the cave that is in it. I give it to you in the sight[B] of my people. Bury your dead." Gn 34:20,24

¹² Abraham bowed down to the people of the land ¹³ and said to Ephron in the hearing of the people of the land, "Listen to me, if you please. Let me pay the price of the field. Accept it from me, and let me bury my dead there."

¹⁴ Ephron answered Abraham and said to him, ¹⁵ "My lord, listen to me. Land worth four hundred shekels of silver — what is that between you and me? Bury your dead." ¹⁶ Abraham agreed with Ephron, and Abraham weighed out to Ephron the silver that he had agreed to in the hearing of the Hethites: four hundred standard shekels[C] of silver. ¹⁷ So Ephron's field at Machpelah near Mamre — the field with its cave and all the trees anywhere within the boundaries of the field — became ¹⁸ Abraham's possession in the sight of all the Hethites who came to the gate of his city. ¹⁹ After this, Abraham buried his wife Sarah in the cave of the field at Machpelah near Mamre (that is, Hebron) in the land of Canaan. ²⁰ The field with its cave passed from the Hethites to Abraham as burial property. Ex 30:13; Jr 32:9

A Wife for Isaac

24 Abraham was now old, getting on in years,[D] and the LORD had blessed him in everything. ² Abraham said to his servant, the elder of his household who managed all he owned, "Place your hand under my thigh, ³ and I will have you swear by the LORD, God of heaven and God of earth, that you will not take a wife for my son from the daughters of the Canaanites among whom I live, ⁴ but will go to my land and my family to take a wife for my son Isaac." Gn 18:11; Jos 13:1; 23:1-2; 1Kg 1:1

⁵ The servant said to him, "Suppose the woman is unwilling to follow me to this land? Should I have your son go back to the land you came from?"

⁶ Abraham answered him, "Make sure that you don't take my son back there. ⁷ The LORD, the God of heaven, who took me from my father's house and from my native land, who spoke to me and swore to me, 'I will give this land to your offspring' — he will send his angel before you, and you can take a wife for my son from there. ⁸ If the woman is unwilling to follow you, then you are free from this oath to me, but don't let my son go back there." ⁹ So the servant placed his hand under his master Abraham's thigh and swore an oath to him concerning this matter. Gn 12:1; 13:15; 2Ch 36:23; Ezr 1:2

[A]23:10 Lit *ears*, also in vv. 13,16   [B]23:11 Lit *in the eyes of the sons*   [C]23:16 Lit *400 shekels passing to the merchant*   [D]24:1 Lit *days*

¹⁰ The servant took ten of his master's camels, and with all kinds of his master's goods in hand, he went to Aram-naharaim, to Nahor's town. ¹¹ At evening, the time when women went out to draw water, he made the camels kneel beside a well outside the town.

¹² "LORD, God of my master Abraham," he prayed, "make this happen for me today, and show kindness to my master Abraham. ¹³ I am standing here at the spring where the daughters of the men of the town are coming out to draw water. ¹⁴ Let the girl to whom I say, 'Please lower your water jug so that I may drink,' and who responds, 'Drink, and I'll water your camels also' — let her be the one you have appointed for your servant Isaac. By this I will know that you have shown kindness to my master."   Gn 24:43-44; 27:20

¹⁵ Before he had finished speaking, there was Rebekah — daughter of Bethuel son of Milcah, the wife of Abraham's brother Nahor — coming with a jug on her shoulder. ¹⁶ Now the girl was very beautiful, a virgin — no man had been intimate with her. She went down to the spring, filled her jug, and came up. ¹⁷ Then the servant ran to meet her and said, "Please let me have a little water from your jug."

¹⁸ She replied, "Drink, my lord." She quickly lowered her jug to her hand and gave him a drink. ¹⁹ When she had finished giving him a drink, she said, "I'll also draw water for your camels until they have had enough to drink."ᴬ ²⁰ She quickly emptied her jug into the trough and hurried to the well again to draw water. She drew water for all his camels ²¹ while the man silently watched her to see whether or not the LORD had made his journey a success.

²² As the camels finished drinking, the man took a gold ring weighing half a shekel, and for her wrists two bracelets weighing ten shekels of gold. ²³ "Whose daughter are you?" he asked. "Please tell me, is there room in your father's house for us to spend the night?"

²⁴ She answered him, "I am the daughter of Bethuel son of Milcah, whom she bore to Nahor." ²⁵ She also said to him, "We have plenty of straw and feed and a place to spend the night."

²⁶ Then the man knelt low, worshiped the LORD, ²⁷ and said, "Blessed be the LORD, the God of my master Abraham, who has not withheld his kindness and faithfulness from my master. As for me, the LORD has led me on the journey to the house of my master's relatives."   Ex 4:31; Ru 2:20; Ezr 9:9; Neh 9:17

²⁸ The girl ran and told her mother's household about these things. ²⁹ Now Rebekah had a brother named Laban, and Laban ran out to the man at the spring. ³⁰ As soon as he had seen the ring and the bracelets on his sister's wrists, and when he had heard his sister Rebekah's words — "The man said this to me!" — he went to the man. He was standing there by the camels at the spring.   Gn 25:20; 28:2; 29:5

³¹ Laban said, "Come, you who are blessed by the LORD. Why are you standing out here? I have prepared the house and a place for the camels." ³² So the man came to the house, and the camels were unloaded. Straw and feed were given to the camels, and water was

ᴬ24:19 Lit they are finished drinking

brought to wash his feet and the feet of the men with him. Gn 26:29

³³ A meal was set before him, but he said, "I will not eat until I have said what I have to say."

So Laban said, "Please speak."

³⁴ "I am Abraham's servant," he said. ³⁵ "The Lord has greatly blessed my master, and he has become rich. He has given him flocks and herds, silver and gold, male and female slaves, and camels and donkeys. ³⁶ Sarah, my master's wife, bore a son to my master in her^A old age, and he has given him everything he owns. ³⁷ My master put me under this oath: 'You will not take a wife for my son from the daughters of the Canaanites in whose land I live ³⁸ but will go to my father's family and to my clan to take a wife for my son.' ³⁹ But I said to my master, 'Suppose the woman will not come back with me?' ⁴⁰ He said to me, 'The Lord before whom I have walked will send his angel with you and make your journey a success, and you will take a wife for my son from my clan and from my father's family. ⁴¹ Then you will be free from my oath if you go to my family and they do not give her to you — you will be free from my oath.' Gn 17:1; 21:2; 25:5; 1Sm 2:30; 1Kg 2:4

⁴² "Today when I came to the spring, I prayed: Lord, God of my master Abraham, if only you will make my journey successful! ⁴³ I am standing here at a spring. Let the young woman^B who comes out to draw water, and I say to her, 'Please let me drink a little water from your jug,' ⁴⁴ and who responds to me, 'Drink, and I'll draw water for your camels also' — let her be the woman the Lord has appointed for my master's son.

⁴⁵ "Before I had finished praying silently, there was Rebekah coming with her jug on her shoulder, and she went down to the spring and drew water. So I said to her, 'Please let me have a drink.' ⁴⁶ She quickly lowered her jug from her shoulder and said, 'Drink, and I'll water your camels also.' So I drank, and she also watered the camels. ⁴⁷ Then I asked her, 'Whose daughter are you?' She responded, 'The daughter of Bethuel son of Nahor, whom Milcah bore to him.' So I put the ring on her nose and the bracelets on her wrists. ⁴⁸ Then I knelt low, worshiped the Lord, and blessed the Lord, the God of my master Abraham, who guided me on the right way to take the granddaughter of my master's brother for his son. ⁴⁹ Now, if you are going to show kindness and faithfulness to my master, tell me; if not, tell me, and I will go elsewhere."^C Gn 47:29; 1Sm 1:13

⁵⁰ Laban and Bethuel answered, "This is from the Lord; we have no choice in the matter.^D ⁵¹ Rebekah is here in front of you. Take her and go, and let her be a wife for your master's son, just as the Lord has spoken." Gn 31:24,29; 2Sm 13:22

⁵² When Abraham's servant heard their words, he bowed to the ground before the Lord. ⁵³ Then he brought out objects of silver and gold, and garments, and gave them to Rebekah. He also gave precious gifts to her brother and her mother. ⁵⁴ Then he and the men with him ate and drank and spent the night.

When they got up in the morning, he said, "Send me to my master."

^A 24:36 Sam, LXX read *his*   ^B 24:43 Or *the virgin*   ^C 24:49 Lit *go to the right or to the left*   ^D 24:50 Lit *we cannot say to you anything bad or good*

⁵⁵ But her brother and mother said, "Let the girl stay with us for about ten days.ᴬ Then sheᴮ can go."

⁵⁶ But he responded to them, "Do not delay me, since the Lᴏʀᴅ has made my journey a success. Send me away so that I may go to my master."

⁵⁷ So they said, "Let's call the girl and ask her opinion."ᶜ

⁵⁸ They called Rebekah and said to her, "Will you go with this man?"

She replied, "I will go." ⁵⁹ So they sent away their sister Rebekah with the one who had nursed and raised her,ᴰ and Abraham's servant and his men. Gn 35:8

⁶⁰ They blessed Rebekah, saying to her:

Our sister, may you become
thousands upon
ten thousands. Gn 17:16
May your offspring possess
the city gates
of theirᴱ enemies. Gn 22:17

⁶¹ Then Rebekah and her female servants got up, mounted the camels, and followed the man. So the servant took Rebekah and left.

⁶² Now Isaac was returning from Beer-lahai-roi,ᶠ for he was living in the Negev region. ⁶³ In the early evening Isaac went out to walkᴳ in the field, and looking up he saw camels coming. ⁶⁴ Rebekah looked up, and when she saw Isaac, she got down from her camel ⁶⁵ and asked the servant, "Who is that man in the field coming to meet us?" Gn 16:14; 25:11

The servant answered, "It is my master." So she took her veil and covered herself. ⁶⁶ Then the servant told Isaac everything he had done.

⁶⁷ And Isaac brought her into the tent of his mother Sarah and took Rebekah to be his wife. Isaac loved her, and he was comforted after his mother's death. Gn 23:1-2

Abraham's Other Wife and Sons

25 Abraham had takenᴴ another wife, whose name was Keturah, ² and she bore him Zimran, Jokshan, Medan, Midian, Ishbak, and Shuah. ³ Jokshan fathered Sheba and Dedan. Dedan's sons were the Asshurim, Letushim, and Leummim. ⁴ And Midian's sons were Ephah, Epher, Hanoch, Abida, and Eldaah. All these were sons of Keturah. ⁵ Abraham gave everything he owned to Isaac. ⁶ But Abraham gave gifts to the sons of his concubines, and while he was still alive he sent them eastward, away from his son Isaac, to the land of the East. Gn 24:35-36; 1Ch 1:32-33

Abraham's Death

⁷ This is the length of Abraham's life:ᴵ 175 years. ⁸ He took his last breath and died at a good old age, old and contented,ᴶ and he was gathered to his people. ⁹ His sons Isaac and Ishmael buried him in the cave of Machpelah near Mamre, in the field of Ephron son of Zohar the Hethite. ¹⁰ This was the field that Abraham bought from the Hethites. Abraham was buried there with his wife Sarah. ¹¹ After Abraham's death, God blessed his son Isaac, who lived near Beer-lahai-roi. Gn 15:15; 25:17; 35:29; 47:8-9; 50:13

ᴬ24:55 Lit *us days or tenth* ᴮ24:55 Or *you* ᶜ24:57 Lit *mouth* ᴰ24:59 Lit *with her wet nurse*; Gn 35:8 ᴱ24:60 Lit *his* ᶠ24:62 = A Well of the Living One Who Sees Me ᴳ24:63 Or *pray*, or *meditate*; Hb obscure ᴴ25:1 Or *Abraham took* ᴵ25:7 Lit *And these are the days of the years of the life of Abraham that he lived* ᴶ25:8 Sam, LXX, Syr read *full of days*

Ishmael's Family Records

¹² These are the family records of Abraham's son Ishmael, whom Hagar the Egyptian, Sarah's slave, bore to Abraham. ¹³ These are the names of Ishmael's sons; their names according to the family records are Nebaioth, Ishmael's firstborn, then Kedar, Adbeel, Mibsam, ¹⁴ Mishma, Dumah, Massa, ¹⁵ Hadad, Tema, Jetur, Naphish, and Kedemah. ¹⁶ These are Ishmael's sons, and these are their names by their settlements and encampments: twelve leaders ^A of their clans. ^B ¹⁷ This is the length ^C of Ishmael's life: 137 years. He took his last breath and died, and was gathered to his people. ¹⁸ And they ^D settled from Havilah to Shur, which is opposite Egypt as you go toward Asshur. ^E He ^F stayed near ^G all his relatives.   Gn 2:4; 17:20; 25:19; 1Ch 1:29-31

The Birth of Jacob and Esau

¹⁹ These are the family records of Isaac son of Abraham. Abraham fathered Isaac. ²⁰ Isaac was forty years old when he took as his wife Rebekah daughter of Bethuel the Aramean from Paddan-aram and sister of Laban the Aramean. ²¹ Isaac prayed to the LORD on behalf of his wife because she was childless. The LORD was receptive to his prayer, and his wife Rebekah conceived. ²² But the children inside her struggled with each other, and she said, "Why is this happening to me?" ^H So she went to inquire of the LORD. ²³ And the LORD said to her:

Two nations are
          in your womb;

two peoples will come
          from you and be separated.
One people will be stronger
          than the other,   2Sm 8:14; Ob 18-21
and the older will serve
          the younger.   Gn 27:29; Mal 1:2-3

²⁴ When her time came to give birth, there were indeed twins in her womb. ²⁵ The first one came out red-looking, ^I covered with hair ^J like a fur coat, and they named him Esau. ²⁶ After this, his brother came out grasping Esau's heel with his hand. So he was named Jacob. ^K Isaac was sixty years old when they were born.   Gn 27:11,16,23

Esau Sells His Birthright

²⁷ When the boys grew up, Esau became an expert hunter, an outdoorsman, ^L but Jacob was a quiet man who stayed at home. ^M ²⁸ Isaac loved Esau because he had a taste for wild game, but Rebekah loved Jacob.   Gn 27:4-9

²⁹ Once when Jacob was cooking a stew, Esau came in from the field exhausted. ³⁰ He said to Jacob, "Let me eat some of that red stuff, because I'm exhausted." That is why he was also named Edom. ^N ³¹ Jacob replied, "First sell me your birthright."

³² "Look," said Esau, "I'm about to die, so what good is a birthright to me?"

³³ Jacob said, "Swear to me first." So he swore to Jacob and sold his birthright to him. ³⁴ Then Jacob gave bread and lentil stew to Esau; he ate, drank, got up, and went

---

^A 25:16 Or chieftains   ^B 25:16 Or peoples   ^C 25:17 Lit And these are the years   ^D 25:18 LXX, Vg read he   ^E 25:18 Or Assyria   ^F 25:18 = Ishmael and his descendants   ^G 25:18 Or He settled down alongside of   ^H 25:22 Lit said, "If thus, why this I?"   ^I 25:25 In Hb, red-looking sounds like "Edom"; Gn 32:3.   ^J 25:25 In Hb, hair sounds like "Seir"; Gn 32:3.   ^K 25:26 = He Grasps the Heel   ^L 25:27 Lit a man of the field   ^M 25:27 Lit man living in tents   ^N 25:30 = Red away. So Esau despised his birthright.

Heb 12:16-17

The Promise Reaffirmed to Isaac

26 There was another famine in the land in addition to the one that had occurred in Abraham's time. And Isaac went to Abimelech, king of the Philistines, at Gerar. [2] The LORD appeared to him and said, "Do not go down to Egypt. Live in the land that I tell you about; [3] stay in this land as an alien, and I will be with you and bless you. For I will give all these lands to you and your offspring, and I will confirm the oath that I swore to your father Abraham. [4] I will make your offspring as numerous as the stars of the sky, I will give your offspring all these lands, and all the nations of the earth will be blessed[A] by your offspring, [5] because Abraham listened to me and kept my mandate, my commands, my statutes, and my instructions." [6] So Isaac settled in Gerar.   Gn 12:10

Isaac's Deception

[7] When the men of the place asked about his wife, he said, "She is my sister," for he was afraid to say "my wife," thinking, "The men of the place will kill me on account of Rebekah, for she is a beautiful woman." [8] When Isaac had been there for some time, Abimelech king of the Philistines looked down from the window and was surprised to see[B] Isaac caressing his wife Rebekah.   Gn 12:13; 20:5; 24:16; Pr 29:25

[9] Abimelech sent for Isaac and said, "So she is really your wife! How could you say, 'She is my sister'?"

Isaac answered him, "Because I thought I might die on account of her."

[10] Then Abimelech said, "What is this you've done to us? One of the people could easily have slept with your wife, and you would have brought guilt on us." [11] So Abimelech warned all the people, "Whoever harms this man or his wife will certainly be put to death."

Conflicts over Wells

[12] Isaac sowed seed in that land, and in that year he reaped[C] a hundred times what was sown. The LORD blessed him, [13] and the man became rich and kept getting richer until he was very wealthy. [14] He had flocks of sheep, herds of cattle, and many slaves, and the Philistines were envious of him. [15] Philistines stopped up all the wells that his father's servants had dug in the days of his father Abraham, filling them with dirt. [16] And Abimelech said to Isaac, "Leave us, for you are much too powerful for us."[D]   Gn 24:1,35

[17] So Isaac left there, camped in the Gerar Valley, and lived there. [18] Isaac reopened the wells that had been dug in the days of his father Abraham and that the Philistines had stopped up after Abraham died. He gave them the same names his father had given them. [19] Then Isaac's servants dug in the valley and found a well of spring[E] water there. [20] But the herdsmen of Gerar quarreled with Isaac's herdsmen and said, "The water is ours!" So he named the well Esek[F] because they argued with him. [21] Then they dug another well and quarreled over that one also, so he named it

---

[A]**26:4** Or *will bless themselves*   [B]**26:8** Or *and he looked and behold —*   [C]**26:12** Lit *found*   [D]**26:16** Or *are more numerous than we are*   [E]**26:19** Lit *living*   [F]**26:20** = Argument

Sitnah. [A] 22 He moved from there and dug another, and they did not quarrel over it. He named it Rehoboth [B] and said, "For now the Lord has made space for us, and we will be fruitful in the land."   Gn 21:25

The Lord Appears to Isaac

23 From there he went up to Beersheba, 24 and the Lord appeared to him that night and said, "I am the God of your father Abraham. Do not be afraid, for I am with you. I will bless you and multiply your offspring because of my servant Abraham."   Gn 17:7-8; 24:12; Ex 3:6; Ac 7:32

25 So he built an altar there, called on the name of the Lord, and pitched his tent there. Isaac's servants also dug a well there.   Gn 8:20; 12:7; 13:18; 35:7

Covenant with Abimelech

26 Now Abimelech came to him from Gerar with Ahuzzath his adviser and Phicol the commander of his army. 27 Isaac said to them, "Why have you come to me? You hated me and sent me away from you."

28 They replied, "We have clearly seen how the Lord has been with you. We think there should be an oath between two parties — between us and you. Let us make a covenant with you: 29 You will not harm us, just as we have not harmed you but have done only what was good to you, sending you away in peace. You are now blessed by the Lord."   Gn 24:31; Ps 115:15

30 So he prepared a banquet for them, and they ate and drank. 31 They got up early in the morning and swore an oath to each other. [C] Isaac sent them on their way, and they left him in peace. 32 On that same day Isaac's servants came to tell him about the well they had dug, saying to him, "We have found water!" 33 He called it Sheba. [D] Therefore the name of the city is still Beer-sheba [E] today.

Esau's Wives

34 When Esau was forty years old, he took as his wives Judith daughter of Beeri the Hethite, and Basemath daughter of Elon the Hethite. 35 They made life bitter [F] for Isaac and Rebekah.   Gn 27:46; 28:9; 36:2-3

The Stolen Blessing

27 When Isaac was old and his eyes were so weak that he could not see, he called his older son Esau and said to him, "My son."

And he answered, "Here I am."

2 He said, "Look, I am old and do not know the day of my death. 3 So now take your hunting gear, your quiver and bow, and go out in the field to hunt some game for me. 4 Then make me a delicious meal that I love and bring it to me to eat, so that I can bless you before I die."

5 Now Rebekah was listening to what Isaac said to his son Esau. So while Esau went to the field to hunt some game to bring in, 6 Rebekah said to her son Jacob, "Listen! I heard your father talking with your brother Esau. He said, 7 'Bring me game and make a delicious meal for me to eat so that I can bless you in the Lord's presence before I die.' 8 Now, my son, listen to me and do what I tell you. 9 Go to the flock and bring me two choice young goats, and I will make them into a delicious meal for your father — the kind he loves. 10 Then

---

[A] 26:21 = Hostility   [B] 26:22 = Open Spaces   [C] 26:31 Lit *swore, each man to his brother*   [D] 26:33 Or *Shibah*   [E] 26:33 = Well of the Oath   [F] 26:35 Lit *And they became bitterness of spirit* take it to your father to eat so that he may bless you before he dies."

¹¹ Jacob answered Rebekah his mother, "Look, my brother Esau is a hairy man, but I am a man with smooth skin. ¹² Suppose my father touches me. Then I will be revealed to him as a deceiver and bring a curse rather than a blessing on myself." Gn 25:25

¹³ His mother said to him, "Your curse be on me, my son. Just obey me and go get them for me."

¹⁴ So he went and got the goats and brought them to his mother, and his mother made the delicious food his father loved. ¹⁵ Then Rebekah took the best clothes of her older son Esau, which were in the house, and had her younger son Jacob wear them. ¹⁶ She put the skins of the young goats on his hands and the smooth part of his neck. ¹⁷ Then she handed the delicious food and the bread she had made to her son Jacob.

¹⁸ When he came to his father, he said, "My father."

And he answered, "Here I am. Who are you, my son?"

¹⁹ Jacob replied to his father, "I am Esau, your firstborn. I have done as you told me. Please sit up and eat some of my game so that you may bless me."

²⁰ But Isaac said to his son, "How did you ever find it so quickly, my son?"

He replied, "Because the LORD your God made it happen for me."

²¹ Then Isaac said to Jacob, "Please come closer so I can touch you, my son. Are you really my son Esau or not?"

²² So Jacob came closer to his father Isaac. When he touched him,

he said, "The voice is the voice of Jacob, but the hands are the hands of Esau." ²³ He did not recognize him, because his hands were hairy like those of his brother Esau; so he blessed him. ²⁴ Again he asked, "Are you really my son Esau?"

And he replied, "I am."

²⁵ Then he said, "Bring it closer to me, and let me eat some of my son's game so that I can bless you." Jacob brought it closer to him, and he ate; he brought him wine, and he drank.

²⁶ Then his father Isaac said to him, "Please come closer and kiss me, my son." ²⁷ So he came closer and kissed him. When Isaac smelled^A his clothes, he blessed him and said:

Ah, the smell of my son
is like the smell of a field
that the LORD has blessed.
²⁸ May God give to you —
from the dew of the sky　Dt 32:2
and from the richness
of the land —　Nm 18:12
an abundance of grain
and new wine.　Dt 7:13; Jl 2:19
²⁹ May peoples serve you　Gn 25:23
and nations bow in worship
to you.
Be master over your relatives;
may your mother's sons bow
in worship to you.
Those who curse you
will be cursed,
and those who bless you
will be blessed.　Gn 12:3; Nm 24:9

³⁰ As soon as Isaac had finished blessing Jacob and Jacob had left the presence of his father Isaac, his brother Esau arrived from his hunting. ³¹ He had also made some delicious food and brought it to his

---

^A27:27 Lit smelled the smell of

father. He said to his father, "Let my father get up and eat some of his son's game, so that you may bless me."

³² But his father Isaac said to him, "Who are you?"

He answered, "I am Esau your firstborn son."

³³ Isaac began to tremble uncontrollably. "Who was it then," he said, "who hunted game and brought it to me? I ate it all before you came in, and I blessed him. Indeed, he will be blessed!"

³⁴ When Esau heard his father's words, he cried out with a loud and bitter cry and said to his father, "Bless me too, my father!"

³⁵ But he replied, "Your brother came deceitfully and took your blessing."

³⁶ So he said, "Isn't he rightly named Jacob?ᴬ For he has cheated me twice now. He took my birthright, and look, now he has taken my blessing." Then he asked, "Haven't you saved a blessing for me?"

³⁷ But Isaac answered Esau, "Look, I have made him a master over you, have given him all of his relatives as his servants, and have sustained him with grain and new wine. What then can I do for you, my son?"

³⁸ Esau said to his father, "Do you have only one blessing, my father? Bless me too, my father!" And Esau wept loudly.ᴮ

³⁹ His father Isaac answered him,

Look, your dwelling place will be
away from the richness
of the land,
away from the dew
of the sky above.
⁴⁰ You will live by your sword,

and you will serve
your brother.
But when you rebel,ᶜ
you will break his yoke
from your neck.

Esau's Anger

⁴¹ Esau held a grudge against Jacob because of the blessing his father had given him. And Esau determined in his heart: "The days of mourning for my father are approaching; then I will kill my brother Jacob."

⁴² When the words of her older son Esau were reported to Rebekah, she summoned her younger son Jacob and said to him, "Listen, your brother Esau is consoling himself by planning to kill you. ⁴³ So now, my son, listen to me. Flee at once to my brother Laban in Haran, ⁴⁴ and stay with him for a few days until your brother's anger subsides — ⁴⁵ until your brother's rage turns away from you and he forgets what you have done to him. Then I will send for you and bring you back from there. Why should I lose you both in one day?"

⁴⁶ So Rebekah said to Isaac, "I'm sick of my life because of these Hethite girls. If Jacob marries someone from around here,ᴰ like these Hethite girls, what good is my life?"

Gn 24:3; 26:34-35; 28:8

Jacob's Departure

28 So Isaac summoned Jacob, blessed him, and commanded him, "Do not marry a Canaanite girl. ² Go at once to Paddan-aram, to the house of Bethuel, your mother's father. Marry one of the daughters of Laban, your mother's brother.

ᴬ27:36 = He Grasps the Heel ᴮ27:38 Lit *Esau lifted up his voice and wept* ᶜ27:40 Hb obscure
ᴰ27:46 Lit *someone like these daughters of the land*

³ May God Almighty bless you and make you fruitful and multiply you so that you become an assembly of peoples. ⁴ May God give you and your offspring the blessing of Abraham so that you may possess the land where you live as a foreigner, the land God gave to Abraham." ⁵ So Isaac sent Jacob to Paddan-aram, to Laban son of Bethuel the Aramean, the brother of Rebekah, the mother of Jacob and Esau. Gn 1:28

⁶ Esau noticed that Isaac blessed Jacob and sent him to Paddan-aram to get a wife there. When he blessed him, Isaac commanded Jacob, "Do not marry a Canaanite girl." ⁷ And Jacob listened to his father and mother and went to Paddan-aram. ⁸ Esau realized that his father Isaac disapproved of the Canaanite women, ⁹ so Esau went to Ishmael and married, in addition to his other wives, Mahalath daughter of Ishmael, Abraham's son. She was the sister of Nebaioth. Gn 24:3

Jacob at Bethel

¹⁰ Jacob left Beer-sheba and went toward Haran. ¹¹ He reached a certain place and spent the night there because the sun had set. He took one of the stones from the place, put it there at his head, and lay down in that place. ¹² And he dreamed: A stairway was set on the ground with its top reaching the sky, and God's angels were going up and down on it. ¹³ The LORD was standing there beside him,ᴬ saying, "I am the LORD, the God of your father Abraham and the God of Isaac. I will give you and your offspring the land on which you are lying. ¹⁴ Your offspring will be like the dust of the earth, and you will spread out toward the west, the east, the north, and the south. All the peoples on earth will be blessed through you and your offspring. ¹⁵ Look, I am with you and will watch over you wherever you go. I will bring you back to this land, for I will not leave you until I have done what I have promised you." Gn 41:1; Nm 12:6; Jb 33:15-16

¹⁶ When Jacob awoke from his sleep, he said, "Surely the LORD is in this place, and I did not know it." ¹⁷ He was afraid and said, "What an awesome place this is! This is none other than the house of God. This is the gate of heaven." Ex 3:4-6

¹⁸ Early in the morning Jacob took the stone that was near his head and set it up as a marker. He poured oil on top of it ¹⁹ and named the place Bethel,ᴮ though previously the city was named Luz. ²⁰ Then Jacob made a vow: "If God will be with me and watch over me during this journey I'm making, if he provides me with food to eat and clothing to wear, ²¹ and if I return safely to my father's family, then the LORD will be my God. ²² This stone that I have set up as a marker will be God's house, and I will give to you a tenth of all that you give me." Gn 31:13; 35:6; 48:3; Jdg 1:23,26

Jacob Meets Rachel

29 Jacob resumed his journeyᶜ and went to the eastern country.ᴰ ² He looked and saw a well in a field. Three flocks of sheep were lying there beside it because the sheep were watered from this well. But a large stone covered the opening of the well. ³ The shepherds would roll the stone from

---

ᴬ**28:13** Or there above it ᴮ**28:19** = House of God ᶜ**29:1** Lit Jacob picked up his feet ᴰ**29:1** Lit the land of the children of the east the opening of the well and water the sheep when all the flocks ᴬ were gathered there. Then they would return the stone to its place over the well's opening. Nm 23:7; Jdg 6:3

⁴ Jacob asked the men at the well, "My brothers! Where are you from?"

"We're from Haran," they answered.

⁵ "Do you know Laban grandson of Nahor?" Jacob asked them.

They answered, "We know him."

⁶ "Is he well?" Jacob asked.

"Yes," they said, "and here is his daughter Rachel, coming with his sheep."

⁷ Then Jacob said, "Look, it is still broad daylight. It's not time for the animals to be gathered. Water the flock, then go out and let them graze."

⁸ But they replied, "We can't until all the flocks have been gathered and the stone is rolled from the well's opening. Then we will water the sheep."

⁹ While he was still speaking with them, Rachel came with her father's sheep, for she was a shepherdess. ¹⁰ As soon as Jacob saw his uncle Laban's daughter Rachel with his sheep, ᴮ he went up and rolled the stone from the opening and watered his uncle Laban's sheep. ¹¹ Then Jacob kissed Rachel and wept loudly. ᶜ ¹² He told Rachel that he was her father's relative, Rebekah's son. She ran and told her father.

Jacob Deceived

¹³ When Laban heard the news about his sister's son Jacob, he ran to meet him, hugged him, and kissed him. Then he took him to his house, and Jacob told him all that had happened.

¹⁴ Laban said to him, "Yes, you are my own flesh and blood." ᴰ　Gn 2:23

After Jacob had stayed with him a month, ¹⁵ Laban said to him, "Just because you're my relative, should you work for me for nothing? Tell me what your wages should be."

¹⁶ Now Laban had two daughters: the older was named Leah, and the younger was named Rachel. ¹⁷ Leah had tender eyes, but Rachel was shapely and beautiful. ¹⁸ Jacob loved Rachel, so he answered Laban, "I'll work for you seven years for your younger daughter Rachel."

¹⁹ Laban replied, "Better that I give her to you than to some other man. Stay with me." ²⁰ So Jacob worked seven years for Rachel, and they seemed like only a few days to him because of his love for her.

²¹ Then Jacob said to Laban, "Since my time is complete, give me my wife, so I can sleep with ᴱ her." ²² So Laban invited all the men of the place and sponsored a feast. ²³ That evening, Laban took his daughter Leah and gave her to Jacob, and he slept with her. ²⁴ And Laban gave his slave Zilpah to his daughter Leah as her slave.

²⁵ When morning came, there was Leah! So he said to Laban, "What is this you have done to me? Wasn't it for Rachel that I worked for you? Why have you deceived me?"

²⁶ Laban answered, "It is not the custom in this place to give the younger daughter in marriage before the firstborn. ²⁷ Complete this week of wedding celebration, and we will also give you this younger

---

ᴬ29:3 Sam, some LXX mss read flocks and the shepherds　ᴮ29:10 Lit with the sheep of Laban his mother's brother　ᶜ29:11 Lit and he lifted his voice and wept　ᴰ29:14 Lit my bone and my flesh　ᴱ29:21 Lit can go to one in return for working yet another seven years for me."

²⁸ And Jacob did just that. He finished the week of celebration, and Laban gave him his daughter Rachel as his wife. ²⁹ And Laban gave his slave Bilhah to his daughter Rachel as her slave. ³⁰ Jacob slept with Rachel also, and indeed, he loved Rachel more than Leah. And he worked for Laban another seven years.

Jacob's Sons

³¹ When the LORD saw that Leah was unloved, he opened her womb; but Rachel was unable to conceive. ³² Leah conceived, gave birth to a son, and named him Reuben, ^A for she said, "The LORD has seen my affliction; surely my husband will love me now." Gn 25:28; Dt 21:15-16; 22:13

³³ She conceived again, gave birth to a son, and said, "The LORD heard that I am unloved and has given me this son also." So she named him Simeon. ^B

³⁴ She conceived again, gave birth to a son, and said, "At last, my husband will become attached to me because I have borne three sons for him." Therefore he was named Levi. ^C

³⁵ And she conceived again, gave birth to a son, and said, "This time I will praise the LORD." Therefore she named him Judah. ^D Then Leah stopped having children. Gn 49:8

30 When Rachel saw that she was not bearing Jacob any children, she envied her sister. "Give me sons, or I will die!" she said to Jacob. 1Sm 1:5-6

² Jacob became angry with Rachel and said, "Am I in God's place, who has withheld offspring ^E from you?"

³ Then she said, "Here is my maid Bilhah. Go sleep with her, and she'll bear children for me ^F so that through her I too can build a family." ⁴ So Rachel gave her slave Bilhah to Jacob as a wife, and he slept with her. ⁵ Bilhah conceived and bore Jacob a son. ⁶ Rachel said, "God has vindicated me; yes, he has heard me and given me a son," so she named him Dan. ^G   Gn 50:23

⁷ Rachel's slave Bilhah conceived again and bore Jacob a second son. ⁸ Rachel said, "In my wrestlings with God, ^H I have wrestled with my sister and won," and she named him Naphtali. ^I

⁹ When Leah saw that she had stopped having children, she took her slave Zilpah and gave her to Jacob as a wife. ¹⁰ Leah's slave Zilpah bore Jacob a son. ¹¹ Then Leah said, "What good fortune!" ^J and she named him Gad. ^K

¹² When Leah's slave Zilpah bore Jacob a second son, ¹³ Leah said, "I am happy that the women call me happy," so she named him Asher. ^L

¹⁴ Reuben went out during the wheat harvest and found some mandrakes in the field. When he brought them to his mother Leah, Rachel asked, "Please give me some of your son's mandrakes." Sg 7:13

¹⁵ But Leah replied to her, "Isn't it enough that you have taken my husband? Now you also want to take my son's mandrakes?"

^A 29:32 = See, a Son; in Hb, the name *Reuben* sounds like "has seen my affliction."   ^B 29:33 In Hb, the name *Simeon* sounds like "has heard."   ^C 29:34 In Hb, the name *Levi* sounds like "attached to."   ^D 29:35 In Hb, the name *Judah* sounds like "praise."   ^E 30:2 Lit *the fruit of the womb*   ^F 30:3 Lit *bear on my knees*   ^G 30:6 In Hb, the name *Dan* sounds like "has vindicated," or "has judged."   ^H 30:8 Or *"With mighty wrestlings"*   ^I 30:8 In Hb, the name *Naphtali* sounds like "my wrestling."   ^J 30:11 Alt Hb tradition, LXX, Vg read *"Good fortune has come!"*   ^K 30:11 = Good Fortune   ^L 30:13 = Happy

"Well then," Rachel said, "he can sleep with you tonight in exchange for your son's mandrakes."

¹⁶ When Jacob came in from the field that evening, Leah went out to meet him and said, "You must come with me, for I have hired you with my son's mandrakes." So Jacob slept with her that night.

¹⁷ God listened to Leah, and she conceived and bore Jacob a fifth son. ¹⁸ Leah said, "God has rewarded me for giving my slave to my husband," and she named him Issachar.ᴬ

¹⁹ Then Leah conceived again and bore Jacob a sixth son. ²⁰ "God has given me a good gift," Leah said. "This time my husband will honor me because I have borne six sons for him," and she named him Zebulun.ᴮ ²¹ Later, Leah bore a daughter and named her Dinah.

²² Then God remembered Rachel. He listened to her and opened her womb. ²³ She conceived and bore a son, and she said, "God has taken away my disgrace." ²⁴ She named him Josephᶜ and said, "May the LORD add another son to me." Is 4:1

Jacob's Flocks Multiply

²⁵ After Rachel gave birth to Joseph, Jacob said to Laban, "Send me on my way so that I can return to my homeland. ²⁶ Give me my wives and my children that I have worked for, and let me go. You know how hard I have worked for you." Gn 29:18,20,27

²⁷ But Laban said to him, "If I have found favor with you, stay. I have learned by divination that the LORD has blessed me because of you." ²⁸ Then Laban said, "Name your wages, and I will pay them." Gn 29:15; 31:7,41

²⁹ So Jacob said to him, "You know how I have served you and how your herds have fared with me. ³⁰ For you had very little before I came, but now your wealth has increased. The LORD has blessed you because of me. And now, when will I also do something for my own family?" Gn 31:6,38-40

³¹ Laban asked, "What should I give you?"

And Jacob said, "You don't need to give me anything. If you do this one thing for me, I will continue to shepherd and keep your flock. ³² Let me go through all your sheep today and remove every sheep that is speckled or spotted, every dark-colored sheep among the lambs, and the spotted and speckled among the female goats. Such will be my wages. ³³ In the future when you come to check on my wages, my honesty will testify for me. If I have any female goats that are not speckled or spotted, or any lambs that are not black, they will be considered stolen."

³⁴ "Good," said Laban. "Let it be as you have said."

³⁵ That day Laban removed the streaked and spotted male goats and all the speckled and spotted female goats — every one that had any white on it — and every dark-colored one among the lambs, and he placed his sons in charge of them. ³⁶ He put a three-day journey between himself and Jacob. Jacob, meanwhile, was shepherding the rest of Laban's flock.

³⁷ Jacob then took branches of fresh poplar, almond, and plane wood, and peeled the bark, exposing white stripes on the branches.

ᴬ**30:18** In Hb, the name *Issachar* sounds like "reward." "honored." ᶜ**30:24** = He Adds ᴮ**30:20** In Hb, the name *Zebulun* sounds like

³⁸ He set the peeled branches in the troughs in front of the sheep — in the water channels where the sheep came to drink. And the sheep bred when they came to drink. ³⁹ The flocks bred in front of the branches and bore streaked, speckled, and spotted young. ⁴⁰ Jacob separated the lambs and made the flocks face the streaked sheep and the completely dark sheep in Laban's flocks. Then he set his own stock apart and didn't put them with Laban's sheep. Gn 31:10-12

⁴¹ Whenever the stronger of the flock were breeding, Jacob placed the branches in the troughs, in full view of the flocks, and they would breed in front of the branches. ⁴² As for the weaklings of the flocks, he did not put out the branches. So it turned out that the weak sheep belonged to Laban and the stronger ones to Jacob. ⁴³ And the man became very rich.ᴬ He had many flocks, female and male slaves, and camels and donkeys. Gn 12:16;13:2;24:35

Jacob Separates from Laban

31 Now Jacob heard what Laban's sons were saying: "Jacob has taken all that was our father's and has built this wealth from what belonged to our father." ² And Jacob saw from Laban's face that his attitude toward him was not the same as before.

³ The LORD said to him, "Go back to the land of your fathers and to your family, and I will be with you."

⁴ Jacob had Rachel and Leah called to the field where his flocks were. ⁵ He said to them, "I can see from your father's face that his attitude toward me is not the same as before, but the God of my father has been with me. ⁶ You know that with all my strength I have served your father ⁷ and that he has cheated me and changed my wages ten times. But God has not let him harm me. ⁸ If he said, 'The spotted sheep will be your wages,' then all the sheep were born spotted. If he said, 'The streaked sheep will be your wages,' then all the sheep were born streaked. ⁹ God has taken away your father's herds and given them to me. Gn 30:29,32

¹⁰ "When the flocks were breeding, I saw in a dream that the streaked, spotted, and speckled males were mating with the females. ¹¹ In that dream the angel of God said to me, 'Jacob!' and I said, 'Here I am.' ¹² And he said, 'Look up and see: all the males that are mating with the flocks are streaked, spotted, and speckled, for I have seen all that Laban has been doing to you. ¹³ I am the God of Bethel, where you poured oil on the stone marker and made a solemn vow to me. Get up, leave this land, and return to your native land.'" Gn 30:37-40; Ex 3:7

¹⁴ Then Rachel and Leah answered him, "Do we have any portion or inheritance in our father's family? ¹⁵ Are we not regarded by him as outsiders? For he has sold us and has certainly spent our purchase price. ¹⁶ In fact, all the wealth that God has taken away from our father belongs to us and to our children. So do whatever God has said to you." Gn 29:19-30

¹⁷ So Jacob got up and put his children and wives on the camels. ¹⁸ He took all the livestock and possessions he had acquired in Paddan-aram, and he drove his herds to go to the land of Canaan, to his father

ᴬ**30:43** Lit *The man spread out very much, very much*

Isaac. ¹⁹ When Laban had gone to shear his sheep, Rachel stole her father's household idols. ²⁰ And Jacob deceived^A Laban the Aramean, not telling him that he was fleeing. ²¹ He fled with all his possessions, crossed the Euphrates, and headed for^B the hill country of Gilead.

Laban Overtakes Jacob

²² On the third day Laban was told that Jacob had fled. ²³ So he took his relatives with him, pursued Jacob for seven days, and overtook him in the hill country of Gilead. ²⁴ But God came to Laban the Aramean in a dream at night. "Watch yourself!" God warned him. "Don't say anything to Jacob, either good or bad."

²⁵ When Laban overtook Jacob, Jacob had pitched his tent in the hill country, and Laban and his relatives also pitched their tents in the hill country of Gilead. ²⁶ Laban said to Jacob, "What have you done? You have deceived me and taken my daughters away like prisoners of war! ²⁷ Why did you secretly flee from me, deceive me, and not tell me? I would have sent you away with joy and singing, with tambourines and lyres, ²⁸ but you didn't even let me kiss my grandchildren and my daughters. You have acted foolishly. ²⁹ I could do you great harm, but last night the God of your father said to me: 'Watch yourself! Don't say anything to Jacob, either good or bad.' ³⁰ Now you have gone off because you long for your father's family — but why have you stolen my gods?"   Gn 31:19; Jos 24:2

³¹ Jacob answered, "I was afraid, for I thought you would take your daughters from me by force. ³² If you find your gods with anyone here, he will not live! Before our relatives, point out anything that is yours and take it." Jacob did not know that Rachel had stolen the idols.   Gn 44:9

³³ So Laban went into Jacob's tent, Leah's tent, and the tents of the two concubines,^C but he found nothing. When he left Leah's tent, he went into Rachel's tent. ³⁴ Now Rachel had taken Laban's household idols, put them in the saddlebag of the camel, and sat on them. Laban searched the whole tent but found nothing.

³⁵ She said to her father, "Don't be angry, my lord, that I cannot stand up in your presence; I am having my period." So Laban searched, but could not find the household idols.

Jacob's Covenant with Laban

³⁶ Then Jacob became incensed and brought charges against Laban. "What is my crime?" he said to Laban. "What is my sin, that you have pursued me? ³⁷ You've searched all my possessions! Have you found anything of yours?^D Put it here before my relatives and yours, and let them decide between the two of us. ³⁸ I've been with you these twenty years. Your ewes and female goats have not miscarried, and I have not eaten the rams from your flock. ³⁹ I did not bring you any of the flock torn by wild beasts; I myself bore the loss. You demanded payment from me for what was stolen by day or by night. ⁴⁰ There I was — the heat consumed me by day and the frost by night, and sleep fled from my eyes. ⁴¹ For twenty years in your household I served you — fourteen

^A**31:20** Lit *And he stole the heart of*   ^B**31:21** Lit *and set his face to*   ^C**31:33** Lit *servants*   ^D**31:37** Lit *What have you found from all of the possessions of your house?*

years for your two daughters and six years for your flocks — and you have changed my wages ten times! ⁴² If the God of my father, the God of Abraham, the Fear of Isaac, had not been with me, certainly now you would have sent me off empty-handed. But God has seen my affliction and my hard work,^A and he issued his verdict last night."

⁴³ Then Laban answered Jacob, "The daughters are my daughters; the sons, my sons; and the flocks, my flocks! Everything you see is mine! But what can I do today for these daughters of mine or for the children they have borne? ⁴⁴ Come now, let's make a covenant, you and I. Let it be a witness between the two of us." Gn 21:27,32; 26:28

⁴⁵ So Jacob picked out a stone and set it up as a marker. ⁴⁶ Then Jacob said to his relatives, "Gather stones." And they took stones and made a mound, then ate there by the mound. ⁴⁷ Laban named the mound Jegar-sahadutha, but Jacob named it Galeed.^B Jos 24:26-27

⁴⁸ Then Laban said, "This mound is a witness between you and me today." Therefore the place was called Galeed ⁴⁹ and also Mizpah,^C for he said, "May the LORD watch between you and me when we are out of each other's sight. ⁵⁰ If you mistreat my daughters or take other wives, though no one is with us, understand that God will be a witness between you and me." ⁵¹ Laban also said to Jacob, "Look at this mound and the marker I have set up between you and me. ⁵² This mound is a witness and the marker is a witness that I will not

pass beyond this mound to you, and you will not pass beyond this mound and this marker to do me harm. ⁵³ The God of Abraham, and the gods of Nahor — the gods of their father^D — will judge between us." And Jacob swore by the Fear of his father Isaac. ⁵⁴ Then Jacob offered a sacrifice on the mountain and invited his relatives to eat a meal. So they ate a meal and spent the night on the mountain. ⁵⁵ Laban got up early in the morning, kissed his grandchildren and daughters, and blessed them. Then Laban left to return home. Jdg 11:29; 1Sm 7:5-6; Jb 16:19

Preparing to Meet Esau

32 Jacob went on his way, and God's angels met him. ² When he saw them, Jacob said, "This is God's camp." So he called that place Mahanaim.^E Ps 91:9-11

³ Jacob sent messengers ahead of him to his brother Esau in the land of Seir, the territory of Edom. ⁴ He commanded them, "You are to say to my lord Esau, 'This is what your servant Jacob says. I have been staying with Laban and have been delayed until now. ⁵ I have oxen, donkeys, flocks, and male and female slaves. I have sent this message to inform my lord, in order to seek your favor.' " Gn 33:8,15

⁶ When the messengers returned to Jacob, they said, "We went to your brother Esau; he is coming to meet you — and he has four hundred men with him." ⁷ Jacob was greatly afraid and distressed; he divided the people with him into two camps, along with the flocks, herds, and camels. ⁸ He thought,

---

^A31:42 Lit *and the work of my hands*   ^B31:47 *Jegar-sahadutha* is Aramaic, and *Galeed* is Hb; both names = Mound of Witness   ^C31:49 = Watchtower   ^D31:53 Two Hb mss, LXX omit *the gods of their father*   ^E32:2 = Two Camps

"If Esau comes to one camp and attacks it, the remaining one can escape." Gn 27:41; 33:1 ⁹ Then Jacob said, "God of my father Abraham and God of my father Isaac, the LORD who said to me, 'Go back to your land and to your family, and I will cause you to prosper,' ¹⁰ I am unworthy of all the kindness and faithfulness you have shown your servant. Indeed, I crossed over the Jordan with my staff, and now I have become two camps. ¹¹ Please rescue me from my brother Esau, for I am afraid of him; otherwise, he may come and attack me, the mothers, and their children. ¹² You have said, 'I will cause you to prosper, and I will make your offspring like the sand of the sea, too numerous to be counted.' " Gn 28:13; 31:42,53

¹³ He spent the night there and took part of what he had brought with him as a gift for his brother Esau: ¹⁴ two hundred female goats, twenty male goats, two hundred ewes, twenty rams, ¹⁵ thirty milk camels with their young, forty cows, ten bulls, twenty female donkeys, and ten male donkeys. ¹⁶ He entrusted them to his slaves as separate herds and said to them, "Go on ahead of me, and leave some distance between the herds."

¹⁷ And he told the first one: "When my brother Esau meets you and asks, 'Who do you belong to? Where are you going? And whose animals are these ahead of you?' ¹⁸ then tell him, 'They belong to your servant Jacob. They are a gift sent to my lord Esau. And look, he is behind us.' "

¹⁹ He also told the second one, the third, and everyone who was walking behind the animals, "Say the same thing to Esau when you find him. ²⁰ You are also to say, 'Look, your servant Jacob is right behind us.' " For he thought, "I want to appease Esau with the gift that is going ahead of me. After that, I can face him, and perhaps he will forgive me."

²¹ So the gift was sent on ahead of him while he remained in the camp that night. ²² During the night Jacob got up and took his two wives, his two slave women, and his eleven sons, and crossed the ford of Jabbok. ²³ He took them and sent them across the stream, along with all his possessions. Dt 2:37; 3:16; Jos 12:2

Jacob Wrestles with God

²⁴ Jacob was left alone, and a man wrestled with him until daybreak. ²⁵ When the man saw that he could not defeat him, he struck Jacob's hip socket as they wrestled and dislocated his hip. ²⁶ Then he said to Jacob, "Let me go, for it is daybreak."

But Jacob said, "I will not let you go unless you bless me."

²⁷ "What is your name?" the man asked.

"Jacob," he replied.

²⁸ "Your name will no longer be Jacob," he said. "It will be Israel^A because you have struggled with God and with men and have prevailed." Gn 35:10; 2Kg 17:34; Hs 12:3-4

²⁹ Then Jacob asked him, "Please tell me your name."

But he answered, "Why do you ask my name?" And he blessed him there. Jdg 13:18

³⁰ Jacob then named the place Peniel,^B "For I have seen God face to face," he said, "yet my life has been spared." ³¹ The sun shone on him as he passed by Penuel^C — limping

^A**32:28** In Hb, the name *Israel* sounds like "he struggled (with) God." ^B**32:30** = Face of God ^C**32:31** Variant of *Peniel* because of his hip. [32] That is why, still today, the Israelites don't eat the thigh muscle that is at the hip socket: because he struck Jacob's hip socket at the thigh muscle. [A]

Jacob Meets Esau

33 Now Jacob looked up and saw Esau coming toward him with four hundred men. So he divided the children among Leah, Rachel, and the two slave women. [2] He put the slaves and their children first, Leah and her children next, and Rachel and Joseph last. [3] He himself went on ahead and bowed to the ground seven times until he approached his brother.

[4] But Esau ran to meet him, hugged him, threw his arms around him, and kissed him. Then they wept. [5] When Esau looked up and saw the women and children, he asked, "Who are these with you?"

He answered, "The children God has graciously given your servant." [6] Then the slaves and their children approached him and bowed down. [7] Leah and her children also approached and bowed down, and then Joseph and Rachel approached and bowed down. Gn 48:9

[8] So Esau said, "What do you mean by this whole procession [B] I met?"

"To find favor with you, my lord," he answered. Gn 32:5

[9] "I have enough, my brother," Esau replied. "Keep what you have." [10] But Jacob said, "No, please! If I have found favor with you, take this gift from me. For indeed, I have seen your face, and it is like seeing God's face, since you have accepted me. [11] Please take my present that was brought to you, because God has been gracious to me and I have everything I need." So Jacob urged him until he accepted.

[12] Then Esau said, "Let's move on, and I'll go ahead of you."

[13] Jacob replied, "My lord knows that the children are weak, and I have nursing flocks and herds. If they are driven hard for one day, the whole herd will die. [14] Let my lord go ahead of his servant. I will continue on slowly, at a pace suited to the livestock and the children, until I come to my lord at Seir."

[15] Esau said, "Let me leave some of my people with you."

But he replied, "Why do that? Please indulge me, [C] my lord."

[16] That day Esau started on his way back to Seir, [17] but Jacob went to Succoth. He built a house for himself and shelters for his livestock; that is why the place was called Succoth. [D] Jos 13:27; Jdg 8:5; Ps 60:6

[18] After Jacob came from Paddan-aram, he arrived safely at Shechem in the land of Canaan and camped in front of the city. [19] He purchased a section of the field where he had pitched his tent from the sons of Hamor, Shechem's father, for a hundred pieces of silver. [E] [20] And he set up an altar there and called it God, the God of Israel. [F] Gn 28:21; Jos 24:1; Jdg 9:1

Dinah Defiled

34 Leah's daughter Dinah, whom Leah bore to Jacob, went out to see some of the young women of the area. [2] When Shechem — son of Hamor the Hivite, who was the region's chieftain — saw her, he took her and raped her. [3] He became infatuated with Jacob's daughter Dinah. He loved

---

[A]**32:32** Or *tendon*   [B]**33:8** Lit *camp*   [C]**33:15** Lit *May I find favor in your eyes*   [D]**33:17** = Stalls or Huts
[E]**33:19** Lit *100 qesitahs*; the value of this currency is unknown   [F]**33:20** = *El-Elohe-Israel*

the young girl and spoke tenderly to her. ^A^ ^4^ "Get me this girl as a wife," he told his father.   Gn 30:21; Jdg 14:2

^5^ Jacob heard that Shechem had defiled his daughter Dinah, but since his sons were with his livestock in the field, he remained silent until they returned. ^6^ Meanwhile, Shechem's father Hamor came to speak with Jacob. ^7^ Jacob's sons returned from the field when they heard about the incident and were deeply grieved and very angry. For Shechem had committed an outrage against Israel by raping Jacob's daughter, and such a thing should not be done. Dt 22:20-30; Jdg 20:6

^8^ Hamor said to Jacob's sons, "My son Shechem has his heart set on your^B^ daughter. Please give her to him as a wife. ^9^ Intermarry with us; give your daughters to us, and take our daughters for yourselves. ^10^ Live with us. The land is before you. Settle here, move about, and acquire property in it."

^11^ Then Shechem said to Dinah's father and brothers, "Grant me this favor,^C^ and I'll give you whatever you say. ^12^ Demand of me a high compensation^D^ and gift; I'll give you whatever you ask me. Just give the girl to be my wife!"

^13^ But Jacob's sons answered Shechem and his father Hamor deceitfully because he had defiled their sister Dinah. ^14^ "We cannot do this thing," they said to them. "Giving our sister to an uncircumcised man is a disgrace to us. ^15^ We will agree with you only on this condition: if all your males are circumcised as we are. ^16^ Then we will give you our daughters, take your daughters for ourselves, live with you,

and become one people. ^17^ But if you will not listen to us and be circumcised, then we will take our daughter and go."   Gn 17:23-27

^18^ Their words seemed good to Hamor and his son Shechem. ^19^ The young man did not delay doing this, because he was delighted with Jacob's daughter. Now he was the most important in all his father's family. ^20^ So Hamor and his son Shechem went to the gate of their city and spoke to the men of their city.

^21^ "These men are peaceful toward us," they said. "Let them live in our land and move about in it, for indeed, the region is large enough for them. Let us take their daughters as our wives and give our daughters to them. ^22^ But the men will agree to live with us and be one people only on this condition: if all our men are circumcised as they are. ^23^ Won't their livestock, their possessions, and all their animals become ours? Only let us agree with them, and they will live with us."

^24^ All the men who had come to the city gates listened to Hamor and his son Shechem, and all those men were circumcised. ^25^ On the third day, when they were still in pain, two of Jacob's sons, Simeon and Levi, Dinah's brothers, took their swords, went into the unsuspecting city, and killed every male. ^26^ They killed Hamor and his son Shechem with their swords, took Dinah from Shechem's house, and went away. ^27^ Jacob's sons came to the slaughter and plundered the city because their sister had been defiled. ^28^ They took their flocks, herds, donkeys, and whatever was

---

^A^ **34:3** Lit *spoke to her heart*   ^B^ **34:8** The Hb word for *your* is pl, showing that Hamor is speaking to Jacob and his sons.   ^C^ **34:11** Lit *"May I find favor in your eyes"*   ^D^ **34:12** Or *bride-price*, or *betrothal present* in the city and in the field. ²⁹ They captured all their possessions, dependents, and wives and plundered everything in the houses.   Gn 23:10

³⁰ Then Jacob said to Simeon and Levi, "You have brought trouble on me, making me odious to the inhabitants of the land, the Canaanites and the Perizzites. We are few in number; if they unite against me and attack me, I and my household will be destroyed."   Ex 5:21; 34:2; Jos 7:25

³¹ But they answered, "Should he treat our sister like a prostitute?"

Return to Bethel

35 God said to Jacob, "Get up! Go to Bethel and settle there. Build an altar there to the God who appeared to you when you fled from your brother Esau."   Gn 28:19

² So Jacob said to his family and all who were with him, "Get rid of the foreign gods that are among you. Purify yourselves and change your clothes. ³ We must get up and go to Bethel. I will build an altar there to the God who answered me in my day of distress. He has been with me everywhere I have gone."

⁴ Then they gave Jacob all their foreign gods and their earrings, and Jacob hid them under the oak near Shechem. ⁵ When they set out, a terror from God came over the cities around them, and they did not pursue Jacob's sons. ⁶ So Jacob and all who were with him came to Luz (that is, Bethel) in the land of Canaan. ⁷ Jacob built an altar there and called the place El-bethel ᴬ because it was there that God had revealed himself to him when he was fleeing from his brother.   Ex 23:27; 48:3

⁸ Deborah, the one who had nursed and raised Rebekah, ᴮ died and was buried under the oak south of Bethel. So Jacob named it Allon-bacuth. ᶜ   Gn 24:59

⁹ God appeared to Jacob again after he returned from Paddan-aram, and he blessed him. ¹⁰ God said to him, "Your name is Jacob; you will no longer be named Jacob, but your name will be Israel." So he named him Israel. ¹¹ God also said to him, "I am God Almighty. Be fruitful and multiply. A nation, indeed an assembly of nations, will come from you, and kings will descend from you. ᴰ ¹² I will give to you the land that I gave to Abraham and Isaac. And I will give the land to your future descendants." ¹³ Then God withdrew ᴱ from him at the place where he had spoken to him.   Gn 17:22; 18:33

¹⁴ Jacob set up a marker at the place where he had spoken to him — a stone marker. He poured a drink offering on it and anointed it with oil. ¹⁵ Jacob named the place where God had spoken with him Bethel.   Gn 28:18-19; 31:45

Rachel's Death

¹⁶ They set out from Bethel. When they were still some distance from Ephrath, Rachel began to give birth, and her labor was difficult. ¹⁷ During her difficult labor, the midwife said to her, "Don't be afraid, for you have another son." ¹⁸ With her last breath — for she was dying — she named him Ben-oni, ᶠ but his father called him Benjamin. ᴳ ¹⁹ So Rachel died and was buried on the way to Ephrath (that is, Bethlehem). ²⁰ Jacob set

---

ᴬ35:7 = God of Bethel   ᴮ35:8 Lit *Deborah, Rebekah's wet nurse* ; Gn 24:59   ᶜ35:8 = Oak of Weeping
ᴰ35:11 Lit *will come from your loins*   ᴱ35:13 Lit *went up*   ᶠ35:18 = Son of My Sorrow   ᴳ35:18 = Son of the Right Hand

up a marker on her grave; it is the marker at Rachel's grave still today.

Israel's Sons

²¹ Israel set out again and pitched his tent beyond the Tower of Eder. ᴬ ²² While Israel was living in that region, Reuben went in and slept with his father's concubine Bilhah, and Israel heard about it.   Gn 49:3-4

Jacob had twelve sons: 1Ch 2:1-2

²³ Leah's sons were Reuben (Jacob's firstborn), Simeon, Levi, Judah, Issachar, and Zebulun.

²⁴ Rachel's sons were Joseph and Benjamin.

²⁵ The sons of Rachel's slave Bilhah were Dan and Naphtali.

²⁶ The sons of Leah's slave Zilpah were Gad and Asher.

These are the sons of Jacob, who were born to him in Paddan-aram.

Isaac's Death

²⁷ Jacob came to his father Isaac at Mamre in Kiriath-arba (that is, Hebron), where Abraham and Isaac had stayed. ²⁸ Isaac lived 180 years. ²⁹ He took his last breath and died, and was gathered to his people, old and full of days. His sons Esau and Jacob buried him.   Gn 13:18; 18:1; 23:19

Esau's Family

36 These are the family records of Esau (that is, Edom). ² Esau took his wives from the Canaanite women: Adah daughter of Elon the Hethite, Oholibamah daughter of Anah and granddaughter ᴮ of Zibeon the Hivite, ³ and Basemath daughter of Ishmael and sister of Nebaioth. ⁴ Adah bore Eliphaz to Esau, Basemath bore Reuel, ⁵ and Oholibamah bore Jeush, Jalam, and Korah. These were Esau's sons, who were born to him in the land of Canaan.   Gn 2:4; 36:9

⁶ Esau took his wives, sons, daughters, and all the people of his household, as well as his herds, all his livestock, and all the property he had acquired in Canaan; he went to a land away from his brother Jacob. ⁷ For their possessions were too many for them to live together, and because of their herds, the land where they stayed could not support them. ⁸ So Esau (that is, Edom) lived in the mountains of Seir.   Gn 13:6

⁹ These are the family records of Esau, father of the Edomites in the mountains of Seir.

¹⁰ These are the names of Esau's sons: 1Ch 1:35-37
Eliphaz son of Esau's wife Adah,
and Reuel son of Esau's wife Basemath.

¹¹ The sons of Eliphaz were Teman, Omar, Zepho, Gatam, and Kenaz.

¹² Timna, a concubine of Esau's son Eliphaz, bore Amalek to Eliphaz. These are the sons of Esau's wife Adah.

¹³ These are Reuel's sons: Nahath, Zerah, Shammah, and Mizzah. These are the sons of Esau's wife Basemath.

¹⁴ These are the sons of Esau's wife Oholibamah daughter of Anah and granddaughter ᴮ of Zibeon: She bore Jeush, Jalam, and Korah to Edom.

ᴬ**35:21** Or *beyond Migdal-eder*   ᴮ**36:2,14** Sam, LXX read *Anah son*

¹⁵ These are the chiefs
among Esau's sons:
the sons of Eliphaz,
Esau's firstborn:
chief Teman, chief Omar,
chief Zepho, chief Kenaz,
¹⁶ chief Korah,^A chief Gatam,
and chief Amalek.
These are the chiefs
descended from Eliphaz
in the land of Edom.
These are the sons
of Adah.

¹⁷ These are the sons of Reuel,
Esau's son:
chief Nahath, chief Zerah,
chief Shammah, and chief
Mizzah.
These are the chiefs
descended from Reuel
in the land of Edom.
These are the sons
of Esau's wife Basemath.

¹⁸ These are the sons
of Esau's wife
Oholibamah:
chief Jeush, chief Jalam,
and chief Korah.
These are the
chiefs descended
from Esau's wife
Oholibamah
daughter of Anah.
¹⁹ These are the sons of Esau
(that is, Edom),
and these are their chiefs.

Seir's Family

²⁰ These are the sons of Seir
the Horite,   Gn 14:6; Dt 2:12,22
the inhabitants of the land:
Lotan, Shobal, Zibeon, Anah,
²¹ Dishon, Ezer, and Dishan.

These are the chiefs
among the Horites,
the sons of Seir, in the land
of Edom.
²² The sons of Lotan were Hori
and Heman.
Timna was Lotan's sister.
²³ These are Shobal's sons:
Alvan, Manahath, Ebal,
Shepho, and Onam.
²⁴ These are Zibeon's sons:
Aiah and Anah.
This was the Anah who
found the hot springs^B
in the wilderness
while he was pasturing
the donkeys of his father
Zibeon.
²⁵ These are the children
of Anah:
Dishon and Oholibamah
daughter of Anah.
²⁶ These are Dishon's sons:
Hemdan, Eshban, Ithran,
and Cheran.
²⁷ These are Ezer's sons:
Bilhan, Zaavan, and Akan.
²⁸ These are Dishan's sons:
Uz and Aran.
²⁹ These are the chiefs
among the Horites:
chief Lotan, chief Shobal,
chief Zibeon, chief Anah,
³⁰ chief Dishon, chief Ezer,
and chief Dishan.
These are the chiefs
among the Horites,
clan by clan,^C in the land
of Seir.

Rulers of Edom

³¹ These are the kings
who reigned in the land
of Edom   Gn 17:6,16; 35:11; 1Ch 1:43-54

---

^A **36:16** Sam omits *Korah*   ^B **36:24** Syr, Vg; Tg reads *the mules*; Hb obscure   ^C **36:30** Lit *Horites, for
their chiefs*

before any king reigned over the Israelites:

32 Bela son of Beor reigned in Edom;
the name of his city was Dinhabah.

33 When Bela died, Jobab son of Zerah from Bozrah reigned in his place.

34 When Jobab died, Husham from the land of the Temanites reigned in his place.

35 When Husham died, Hadad son of Bedad reigned in his place.
He defeated Midian in the field of Moab;
the name of his city was Avith.

36 When Hadad died, Samlah from Masrekah reigned in his place.

37 When Samlah died, Shaul from Rehoboth on the Euphrates River reigned in his place.

38 When Shaul died, Baal-hanan son of Achbor reigned in his place.

39 When Baal-hanan son of Achbor died, Hadar^A reigned in his place.
His city was Pau, and his wife's name was Mehetabel daughter of Matred daughter of Me-zahab.

40 These are the names of Esau's chiefs, according to their families and their localities, by their names:
chief Timna, chief Alvah, chief Jetheth,

41 chief Oholibamah, chief Elah, chief Pinon,

42 chief Kenaz, chief Teman, chief Mibzar,

43 chief Magdiel, and chief Iram.
These are Edom's chiefs, according to their settlements in the land they possessed.
Esau^B was father of the Edomites.

Joseph's Dreams

37 Jacob lived in the land where his father had stayed, the land of Canaan. ² These are the family records of Jacob.   Gn 26:3

At seventeen years of age, Joseph tended sheep with his brothers. The young man was working with the sons of Bilhah and Zilpah, his father's wives, and he brought a bad report about them to their father.   Gn 30:1-13; 1Sm 2:22-24

³ Now Israel loved Joseph more than his other sons because Joseph was a son born to him in his old age, and he made a robe of many colors^C for him. ⁴ When his brothers saw that their father loved him more than all his brothers, they hated him and could not bring themselves to speak peaceably to him.

⁵ Then Joseph had a dream. When he told it to his brothers, they hated him even more. ⁶ He said to them, "Listen to this dream I had: ⁷ There we were, binding sheaves of grain in the field. Suddenly my sheaf stood up, and your sheaves gathered around it and bowed down to my sheaf."   Gn 42:6,9; 43:26; 44:14

⁸ "Are you really going to reign over us?" his brothers asked him. "Are you really going to rule us?"

^A36:39 Many Hb mss, Sam, Syr read Hadad   ^B36:43 Lit He Esau   ^C37:3 Or robe with long sleeves; see 2Sm 13:18,19

So they hated him even more because of his dream and what he had said.

⁹ Then he had another dream and told it to his brothers. "Look," he said, "I had another dream, and this time the sun, moon, and eleven stars were bowing down to me."

¹⁰ He told his father and brothers, and his father rebuked him. "What kind of dream is this that you have had?" he said. "Am I and your mother and your brothers really going to come and bow down to the ground before you?" ¹¹ His brothers were jealous of him, but his father kept the matter in mind. Dn 7:28; Ac 7:9

Joseph Sold into Slavery

¹² His brothers had gone to pasture their father's flocks at Shechem. ¹³ Israel said to Joseph, "Your brothers, you know, are pasturing the flocks at Shechem. Get ready. I'm sending you to them."

"I'm ready," Joseph replied.

¹⁴ Then Israel said to him, "Go and see how your brothers and the flocks are doing, and bring word back to me." So he sent him from the Hebron Valley, and he went to Shechem. Gn 13:18; 35:27

¹⁵ A man found him there, wandering in the field, and asked him, "What are you looking for?"

¹⁶ "I'm looking for my brothers," Joseph said. "Can you tell me where they are pasturing their flocks?"

¹⁷ "They've moved on from here," the man said. "I heard them say, 'Let's go to Dothan.'" So Joseph set out after his brothers and found them at Dothan. 2Kg 6:13

¹⁸ They saw him in the distance, and before he had reached them, they plotted to kill him. ¹⁹ They said to one another, "Oh, look, here comes that dream expert!ᴬ ²⁰ So now, come on, let's kill him and throw him into one of the pits.ᴮ We can say that a vicious animal ate him. Then we'll see what becomes of his dreams!" Ps 31:13; 37:12,32

²¹ When Reuben heard this, he tried to save him from them.ᶜ He said, "Let's not take his life." ²² Reuben also said to them, "Don't shed blood. Throw him into this pit in the wilderness, but don't lay a hand on him" — intending to rescue him from them and return him to his father. Gn 42:22

²³ When Joseph came to his brothers, they stripped off Joseph's robe, the robe of many colors that he had on. ²⁴ Then they took him and threw him into the pit. The pit was empty, without water.

²⁵ They sat down to eat a meal, and when they looked up, there was a caravan of Ishmaelites coming from Gilead. Their camels were carrying aromatic gum, balsam, and resin, going down to Egypt. Gn 39:1; 42:21; 43:11; Jr 8:22; 46:11

²⁶ Judah said to his brothers, "What do we gain if we kill our brother and cover up his blood? ²⁷ Come on, let's sell him to the Ishmaelites and not lay a hand on him, for he is our brother, our own flesh," and his brothers agreed. ²⁸ When Midianite traders passed by, his brothers pulled Joseph out of the pit and sold him for twenty pieces of silver to the Ishmaelites, who took Joseph to Egypt. Dt 25:5,7

²⁹ When Reuben returned to the pit and saw that Joseph was not there, he tore his clothes. ³⁰ He went back to his brothers and said, "The boy is gone! What am I going

ᴬ**37:19** Lit comes the lord of the dreams   ᴮ**37:20** Or cisterns   ᶜ**37:21** Lit their hands to do?"^A ^31 So they took Joseph's robe, slaughtered a male goat, and dipped the robe in its blood. ^32 They sent the robe of many colors to their father and said, "We found this. Examine it. Is it your son's robe or not?" Gn 44:13; Nm 14:6; 2Sm 1:11; 3:31; Jb 1:20

^33 His father recognized it. "It is my son's robe," he said. "A vicious animal has devoured him. Joseph has been torn to pieces!" ^34 Then Jacob tore his clothes, put sackcloth around his waist, and mourned for his son many days. ^35 All his sons and daughters tried to comfort him, but he refused to be comforted. "No," he said. "I will go down to Sheol to my son, mourning." And his father wept for him. Gn 44:28

^36 Meanwhile, the Midianites sold Joseph in Egypt to Potiphar, an officer of Pharaoh and the captain of the guards.

Judah and Tamar

38 At that time Judah left his brothers and settled near an Adullamite named Hirah. ^2 There Judah saw the daughter of a Canaanite named Shua; he took her as a wife and slept with her. ^3 She conceived and gave birth to a son, and he named him Er. ^4 She conceived again, gave birth to a son, and named him Onan. ^5 She gave birth to another son and named him Shelah. It was at Chezib that^B,C she gave birth to him. Jos 15:35; 1Sm 22:1

^6 Judah got a wife for Er, his firstborn, and her name was Tamar. ^7 Now Er, Judah's firstborn, was evil in the LORD's sight, and the LORD put him to death. ^8 Then Judah said to Onan, "Sleep with your brother's wife. Perform your duty as her brother-in-law and produce offspring for your brother." ^9 But Onan knew that the offspring would not be his, so whenever he slept with his brother's wife, he released his semen on the ground so that he would not produce offspring for his brother. ^10 What he did was evil in the LORD's sight, so he put him to death also. Dt 25:5-10; 1Ch 2:3; Mt 22:24

^11 Then Judah said to his daughter-in-law Tamar, "Remain a widow in your father's house until my son Shelah grows up." For he thought, "He might die too, like his brothers." So Tamar went to live in her father's house. Ru 1:12-13

^12 After a long time^D Judah's wife, the daughter of Shua, died. When Judah had finished mourning, he and his friend Hirah the Adullamite went up to Timnah to his sheepshearers. ^13 Tamar was told, "Your father-in-law is going up to Timnah to shear his sheep." ^14 So she took off her widow's clothes, veiled her face, covered herself, and sat at the entrance to Enaim,^E which is on the way to Timnah. For she saw that, though Shelah had grown up, she had not been given to him as a wife. ^15 When Judah saw her, he thought she was a prostitute, for she had covered her face. Jos 15:10,57

^16 He went over to her and said, "Come, let me sleep with you," for he did not know that she was his daughter-in-law. Lv 18:15

She said, "What will you give me for sleeping with me?"

^17 "I will send you a young goat from my flock," he replied.

But she said, "Only if you leave something with me until you send it."

¹⁸ "What should I give you?" he asked.

She answered, "Your signet ring, your cord, and the staff in your hand." So he gave them to her and slept with her, and she became pregnant by him. ¹⁹ She got up and left, then removed her veil and put her widow's clothes back on.

²⁰ When Judah sent the young goat by his friend the Adullamite in order to get back the items he had left with the woman, he could not find her. ²¹ He asked the men of the place, "Where is the cult prostitute who was beside the road at Enaim?"

"There has been no cult prostitute here," they answered.

²² So the Adullamite returned to Judah, saying, "I couldn't find her, and besides, the men of the place said, 'There has been no cult prostitute here.' "

²³ Judah replied, "Let her keep the items for herself; otherwise we will become a laughingstock. After all, I did send this young goat, but you couldn't find her."

²⁴ About three months later Judah was told, "Your daughter-in-law, Tamar, has been acting like a prostitute, and now she is pregnant."

"Bring her out," Judah said, "and let her be burned to death!" Lv 20:14

²⁵ As she was being brought out, she sent her father-in-law this message: "I am pregnant by the man to whom these items belong." And she added, "Examine them. Whose signet ring, cord, and staff are these?"

²⁶ Judah recognized them and said, "She is more in the right ^A than I, since I did not give her to my son

Shelah." And he did not know her intimately again. 1Sm 24:17

²⁷ When the time came for her to give birth, there were twins in her womb. ²⁸ As she was giving birth, one of them put out his hand, and the midwife took it and tied a scarlet thread around it, announcing, "This one came out first." ²⁹ But then he pulled his hand back, out came his brother, and she said, "What a breakout you have made for yourself!" So he was named Perez. ^B ³⁰ Then his brother, who had the scarlet thread tied to his hand, came out, and was named Zerah. ^C

Joseph in Potiphar's House

39 Now Joseph had been taken to Egypt. An Egyptian named Potiphar, an officer of Pharaoh and the captain of the guards, bought him from the Ishmaelites who had brought him there. ² The LORD was with Joseph, and he became a successful man, serving ^D in the household of his Egyptian master. ³ When his master saw that the LORD was with him and that the LORD made everything he did successful, ⁴ Joseph found favor with his master and became his personal attendant. Potiphar also put him in charge of his household and placed all that he owned under his authority. ^E ⁵ From the time that he put him in charge of his household and of all that he owned, the LORD blessed the Egyptian's house because of Joseph. The LORD's blessing was on all that he owned, in his house and in his fields. ⁶ He left all that he owned under Joseph's authority; ^F he did not concern himself with anything except the food he ate.

^A**38:26** Or *more righteous* ^B**38:29** = Breaking Out ^C**38:30** = Brightness of Sunrise; perhaps related to the scarlet thread ^D**39:2** Lit *and he was* ^E**39:4** Lit *owned in his hand* ^F**39:6** Lit *owned in Joseph's hand*

Now Joseph was well-built and handsome. [7] After some time[A] his master's wife looked longingly at Joseph and said, "Sleep with me."

[8] But he refused. "Look," he said to his master's wife, "with me here my master does not concern himself with anything in his house, and he has put all that he owns under my authority.[B] [9] No one in this house is greater than I am. He has withheld nothing from me except you, because you are his wife. So how could I do this immense evil, and how could I sin against God?" Gn 20:6; 42:18; Ps 51:4

[10] Although she spoke to Joseph day after day, he refused to go to bed with her.[C] [11] Now one day he went into the house to do his work, and none of the household servants were there.[D] [12] She grabbed him by his garment and said, "Sleep with me!" But leaving his garment in her hand, he escaped and ran outside.

[13] When she saw that he had left his garment with her and had run outside, [14] she called her household servants. "Look," she said to them, "my husband brought a Hebrew man to make fools of us. He came to me so he could sleep with me, and I screamed as loud as I could. [15] When he heard me screaming for help,[E] he left his garment beside me and ran outside."

[16] She put Joseph's garment beside her until his master came home. [17] Then she told him the same story: "The Hebrew slave you brought to us came to make a fool of me, [18] but when I screamed for help,[F] he left his garment beside me and ran outside."

[19] When his master heard the story his wife told him — "These are the things your slave did to me" — he was furious [20] and had him thrown into prison, where the king's prisoners were confined. So Joseph was there in prison.

Joseph in Prison

[21] But the LORD was with Joseph and extended kindness to him. He granted him favor with the prison warden. [22] The warden put all the prisoners who were in the prison under Joseph's authority,[G] and he was responsible for everything that was done there. [23] The warden did not bother with anything under Joseph's authority,[H] because the LORD was with him, and the LORD made everything that he did successful.

Joseph Interprets Two Prisoners' Dreams

40 After this, the king of Egypt's cupbearer and baker offended their master, the king of Egypt. [2] Pharaoh was angry with his two officers, the chief cupbearer and the chief baker, [3] and put them in custody in the house of the captain of the guards in the prison where Joseph was confined. [4] The captain of the guards assigned Joseph to them as their personal attendant, and they were in custody for some time.[I] Neh 1:11

[5] The king of Egypt's cupbearer and baker, who were confined in the prison, each had a dream. Both had a dream on the same night, and each dream had its own meaning. [6] When Joseph came to them in the

---

[A]39:7 Lit And after these things   [B]39:8 Lit owns in my hand   [C]39:10 Lit he did not listen to her to lie beside her, to be with her   [D]39:11 Lit there in the house   [E]39:15 Lit he heard that I raised my voice and I screamed   [F]39:18 Lit I raised my voice and screamed   [G]39:22 Lit prison in the hand of Joseph   [H]39:23 Lit anything in his hand   [I]40:4 Lit custody days

THE BOOKS OF
LAW

The Bible is made up of sixty-six different books. The books are separated into ten divisions. The first five books of the Bible are in the division called the Pentateuch, or the books of Law. Although the focus is on the law, these books also deliver the plan of an even greater influence on God's people in the coming Messiah, Jesus Christ.

GENESIS is about the beginning of things, including how God created the world and everything in it, the great flood, the Tower of Babel, and the beginnings of the nation of Israel. Moses wrote this book. Even with the introduction of sin, God begins the plan of His redemption through His only Son, Jesus Christ.

EXODUS, also written by Moses, tells about the departure or exodus of the people of Israel from Egypt. Exodus also describes their wandering in the wilderness and how God gave His law to the people of Israel. Just as God used Moses to free His people from slavery in Egypt, God would one day free His people from slavery to sin through Jesus Christ.

LEVITICUS is a continuation of the history told in the book of Exodus. Moses wrote this book, and it contains the ceremonial and religious law. The Israelite tribe of Levi had the job of making sure the people followed that law. The laws recorded in this book would one day be completed with the perfect sacrifice of God's Son, Jesus Christ.

NUMBERS tells of the census or numbering of the people of Israel and the history of their journey after leaving Egypt. God shows His continual care and love by providing for His people, a care and love that would ultimately point to Christ and the cross. Moses wrote this book.

DEUTERONOMY was written mostly by Moses and consists of a second account of the giving of the Law. Moses shared the good news of another leader who would come after him, Jesus Christ. The book ends with Moses' death.

CREATION

One of the most important things God tells us about Himself in the Bible is that He created everything. There is no place you can go that God has not created and not a thing in the universe that He has not made.

Sometimes He makes things instantly, as He did with Adam and Eve. Sometimes He makes things by giving them a way to grow or change, like a seed that will become a tree or a caterpillar that will turn into a butterfly. And sometimes what He makes is used by people to build with and turn into other things such as houses or machines. But nobody can make something out of nothing—except for God. That's how powerful He is!

The book of Genesis tells us a lot about God's creation of the world, but it doesn't tell us all the things we sometimes wish we knew. For example, we know that some creatures lived a long time ago but don't exist anymore. Yes, it would be interesting to know how they fit into what the Bible says about the Creation. But the main thing the Bible tells us about Creation is not its date or how God did it; the most important thing is that God is the one who did it. Creation is not an accident. It did not happen by chance, and it did not always exist. God made the universe on purpose and for a reason.

When God was busy making the world, He wasn't just making all the things you can see and touch; He was also making things that are invisible. He made the gravity that holds you on the ground. He made the sounds you can hear plus lots of other sounds your ears don't even know are there. He made the numbers you use to count. He made the way you know about what's right and wrong. He even made time.

Think about that. Look around the room or out the window. Everything you see right now, everything you will ever see, touch, or hear was made by God on purpose. Every place you have ever been and every place you will ever go—even if it is all the way across the universe—was made by God. It all points to Him—including you! He made it all, and He rules it all, and those are just a few of the reasons He deserves our worship and praise.

FAMILY OF
ABRAHAM

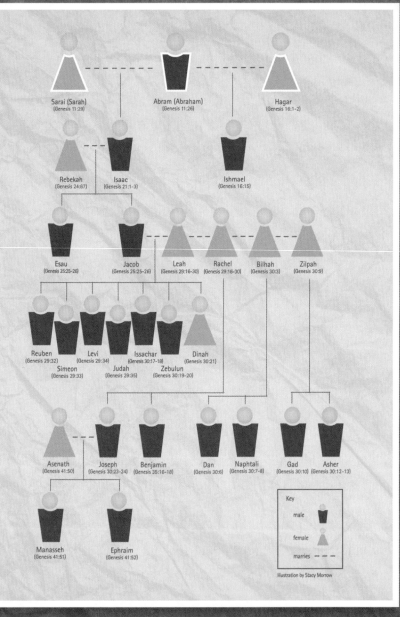

illustration by Stacy Morrow

THE NAMES OF
GOD

Bibles printed in English use several words for God's names. These names come from the Hebrew language. The Hebrew people described God by the actions He took toward His people or by the qualities of who He is. Think about all God's names, and praise Him for who He is.

HEBREW NAME	REFERENCE	MEANING	ENGLISH NAME
Elohim	Genesis 1:1	Powerful God	God
Adonai	Genesis 15:2	Lord	Lord GOD
El Elyon	Genesis 14:19–20	God Most High	God Most High
El Shaddai	Genesis 17:1	God Almighty	God Almighty
Jehovah Jireh	Genesis 22:14	The Lord Provides	The LORD Will Provide
Yahweh	Exodus 3:14	Israel's Covenantal God	I AM
Jehovah Rophe	Exodus 15:26	The Lord Heals	The LORD Who Heals You
Jehovah Nissi	Exodus 17:15–16	The Lord Is My Banner	The LORD Is My Banner
Jehovah Mekadesh	Leviticus 20:8	The Lord Who Sanctifies You	The LORD Who Sets You Apart
Jehovah Shalom	Judges 6:24	The Lord Is Peace	The LORD Is Peace
Jehovah Tsidkenu	Jeremiah 23:6	The Lord Is Our Righteousness	The LORD Is Our Righteousness
Jehovah Shammah	Ezekiel 48:35	The Lord Is There	The LORD Is There

Ken Hemphill, *The Names of God* (Nashville: Broadman & Holman, 2001) morning, he saw that they looked distraught. [7] So he asked Pharaoh's officers who were in custody with him in his master's house, "Why do you look so sad today?"   Neh 2:2

[8] "We had dreams," they said to him, "but there is no one to interpret them."

Then Joseph said to them, "Don't interpretations belong to God? Tell me your dreams."   Dn 2:11,20-24

[9] So the chief cupbearer told his dream to Joseph: "In my dream there was a vine in front of me. [10] On the vine were three branches. As soon as it budded, its blossoms came out and its clusters ripened into grapes. [11] Pharaoh's cup was in my hand, and I took the grapes, squeezed them into Pharaoh's cup, and placed the cup in Pharaoh's hand."

[12] "This is its interpretation," Joseph said to him. "The three branches are three days. [13] In just three days Pharaoh will lift up your head and restore you to your position. You will put Pharaoh's cup in his hand the way you used to when you were his cupbearer. [14] But when all goes well for you, remember that I was with you. Please show kindness to me by mentioning me to Pharaoh, and get me out of this prison. [15] For I was kidnapped from the land of the Hebrews, and even here I have done nothing that they should put me in the dungeon."[A]   Gn 41:12; Dn 2:36

[16] When the chief baker saw that the interpretation was positive, he said to Joseph, "I also had a dream. Three baskets of white bread were on my head. [17] In the top basket were all sorts of baked goods for Pharaoh, but the birds were eating them out of the basket on my head."

[18] "This is its interpretation," Joseph replied. "The three baskets are three days. [19] In just three days Pharaoh will lift up your head — from off you — and hang you on a tree.[B] Then the birds will eat the flesh from your body."[C]

[20] On the third day, which was Pharaoh's birthday, he gave a feast for all his servants. He elevated[D] the chief cupbearer and the chief baker among his servants. [21] Pharaoh restored the chief cupbearer to his position as cupbearer, and he placed the cup in Pharaoh's hand. [22] But Pharaoh hanged[E] the chief baker, just as Joseph had explained to them. [23] Yet the chief cupbearer did not remember Joseph; he forgot him.   2Kg 25:27; Ec 9:15-16; Jr 52:31; Mt 14:6

Joseph Interprets Pharaoh's Dreams

41 At the end of two years Pharaoh had a dream: He was standing beside the Nile, [2] when seven healthy-looking, well-fed cows came up from the Nile and began to graze among the reeds. [3] After them, seven other cows, sickly and thin, came up from the Nile and stood beside those cows along the bank of the Nile. [4] The sickly, thin cows ate the healthy, well-fed cows. Then Pharaoh woke up. [5] He fell asleep and dreamed a second time: Seven heads of grain, plump and good, came up on one stalk. [6] After them, seven heads of grain, thin and scorched by the east wind, sprouted up. [7] The thin heads of grain swallowed up the

---

[A]**40:15** Or *pit*, or *cistern*   [B]**40:19** Or *and impale you on a pole*   [C]**40:19** Lit *eat your flesh from upon you*   [D]**40:20** Lit *He lifted up the head of*   [E]**40:22** Or *impaled* seven plump, full ones. Then Pharaoh woke up, and it was only a dream. Gn 41:17-23

⁸ When morning came, he was troubled, so he summoned all the magicians of Egypt and all its wise men. Pharaoh told them his dreams, but no one could interpret them for him. Ex 7:11,22; Dn 1:20; 2:2; 2:1-3

⁹ Then the chief cupbearer said to Pharaoh, "Today I remember my faults. ¹⁰ Pharaoh was angry with his servants, and he put me and the chief baker in the custody of the captain of the guards. ¹¹ He and I had dreams on the same night; each dream had its own meaning. ¹² Now a young Hebrew, a slave of the captain of the guards, was with us there. We told him our dreams, he interpreted our dreams for us, and each had its own interpretation. ¹³ It turned out just the way he interpreted them to us: I was restored to my position, and the other man was hanged." Gn 40:1-22

¹⁴ Then Pharaoh sent for Joseph, and they quickly brought him from the dungeon.ᴬ He shaved, changed his clothes, and went to Pharaoh. ¹⁵ Pharaoh said to Joseph, "I have had a dream, and no one can interpret it. But I have heard it said about you that you can hear a dream and interpret it." Dn 5:16

¹⁶ "I am not able to," Joseph answered Pharaoh. "It is God who will give Pharaoh a favorable answer."ᴮ

¹⁷ So Pharaoh said to Joseph: "In my dream I was standing on the bank of the Nile, ¹⁸ when seven well-fed, healthy-looking cows came up from the Nile and grazed among the reeds. ¹⁹ After them, seven other cows — weak, very sickly, and thin — came up. I've never seen such sickly ones as these in all the land of Egypt. ²⁰ Then the thin, sickly cows ate the first seven well-fed cows. ²¹ When they had devoured them, you could not tell that they had devoured them; their appearance was as bad as it had been before. Then I woke up. ²² In my dream I also saw seven heads of grain, full and good, coming up on one stalk. ²³ After them, seven heads of grain — withered, thin, and scorched by the east wind — sprouted up. ²⁴ The thin heads of grain swallowed the seven good ones. I told this to the magicians, but no one can tell me what it means." Is 8:19; Dn 4:7

²⁵ Then Joseph said to Pharaoh, "Pharaoh's dreams mean the same thing. God has revealed to Pharaoh what he is about to do. ²⁶ The seven good cows are seven years, and the seven good heads are seven years. The dreams mean the same thing. ²⁷ The seven thin, sickly cows that came up after them are seven years, and the seven worthless, scorched heads of grain are seven years of famine. Dn 2:28-29,45; Rv 4:1

²⁸ "It is just as I told Pharaoh: God has shown Pharaoh what he is about to do. ²⁹ Seven years of great abundance are coming throughout the land of Egypt. ³⁰ After them, seven years of famine will take place, and all the abundance in the land of Egypt will be forgotten. The famine will devastate the land. ³¹ The abundance in the land will not be remembered because of the famine that follows it, for the famine will be very severe. ³² Since the dream was given twice to Pharaoh, it means that the matter has been determined by God, and he will carry it out soon. Gn 41:54,56; 47:13

ᴬ**41:14** Or *pit,* or *cistern*   ᴮ**41:16** Or *"God will answer Pharaoh with peace of mind."*

[33] "So now, let Pharaoh look for a discerning and wise man and set him over the land of Egypt. [34] Let Pharaoh do this: Let him appoint overseers over the land and take a fifth of the harvest of the land of Egypt during the seven years of abundance. [35] Let them gather all the excess food during these good years that are coming. Under Pharaoh's authority, store the grain in the cities, so they may preserve it as food. [36] The food will be a reserve for the land during the seven years of famine that will take place in the land of Egypt. Then the country will not be wiped out by the famine."

Joseph Exalted

[37] The proposal pleased Pharaoh and all his servants, [38] and he said to them, "Can we find anyone like this, a man who has God's spirit[A] in him?" [39] So Pharaoh said to Joseph, "Since God has made all this known to you, there is no one as discerning and wise as you are. [40] You will be over my house, and all my people will obey your commands.[B] Only I, as king, [C] will be greater than you." [41] Pharaoh also said to Joseph, "See, I am placing you over all the land of Egypt." [42] Pharaoh removed his signet ring from his hand and put it on Joseph's hand, clothed him with fine linen garments, and placed a gold chain around his neck. [43] He had Joseph ride in his second chariot, and servants called out before him, "Make way!"[D] So he placed him over all the land of Egypt. [44] Pharaoh said to Joseph, "I am Pharaoh and no one will be able to raise his hand or foot in all the land of Egypt without your permission." [45] Pharaoh gave Joseph the name Zaphenath-paneah and gave him a wife, Asenath daughter of Potiphera, priest at On.[E] And Joseph went throughout[F] the land of Egypt.

Joseph's Administration

[46] Joseph was thirty years old when he entered the service of Pharaoh king of Egypt. Joseph left Pharaoh's presence and traveled throughout the land of Egypt. [47] During the seven years of abundance the land produced outstanding harvests. [48] Joseph gathered all the excess food in the land of Egypt during the seven years and put it in the cities. He put the food in every city from the fields around it. [49] So Joseph stored up grain in such abundance — like the sand of the sea — that he stopped measuring it because it was beyond measure.

[50] Two sons were born to Joseph before the years of famine arrived. Asenath daughter of Potiphera, priest at On, bore them to him. [51] Joseph named the firstborn Manasseh[G] and said, "God has made me forget all my hardship and my whole family." [52] And the second son he named Ephraim[H] and said, "God has made me fruitful in the land of my affliction." Gn 46:20; 48:5

[53] Then the seven years of abundance in the land of Egypt came to an end, [54] and the seven years of famine began, just as Joseph had said. There was famine in every land, but in the whole land of Egypt there was food. [55] When the

---

whole land of Egypt was stricken with famine, the people cried out to Pharaoh for food. Pharaoh told all Egypt, "Go to Joseph and do whatever he tells you." ⁵⁶ Now the famine had spread across the whole region, so Joseph opened all the storehouses and sold grain to the Egyptians, for the famine was severe in the land of Egypt. ⁵⁷ Every land came to Joseph in Egypt to buy grain, for the famine was severe in every land.   Gn 12:10

Joseph's Brothers in Egypt

42 When Jacob learned that there was grain in Egypt, he said to his sons, "Why do you keep looking at each other? ² Listen," he went on, "I have heard there is grain in Egypt. Go down there and buy some for us so that we will live and not die." ³ So ten of Joseph's brothers went down to buy grain from Egypt. ⁴ But Jacob did not send Joseph's brother Benjamin with his brothers, for he thought, "Something might happen to him." Ac 7:12

⁵ The sons of Israel were among those who came to buy grain, for the famine was in the land of Canaan. ⁶ Joseph was in charge of the country; he sold grain to all its people. His brothers came and bowed down before him with their faces to the ground. ⁷ When Joseph saw his brothers, he recognized them, but he treated them like strangers and spoke harshly to them. Gn 37:7-10

"Where do you come from?" he asked.

"From the land of Canaan to buy food," they replied.

⁸ Although Joseph recognized his brothers, they did not recognize him. ⁹ Joseph remembered his dreams about them and said to them, "You are spies. You have come to see the weakness ᴬ of the land."

¹⁰ "No, my lord. Your servants have come to buy food," they said. ¹¹ "We are all sons of one man. We are honest; your servants are not spies."

¹² "No," he said to them. "You have come to see the weakness of the land."

¹³ But they replied, "We, your servants, were twelve brothers, the sons of one man in the land of Canaan. The youngest is now ᴮ with our father, and one is no longer living."

¹⁴ Then Joseph said to them, "I have spoken: ᶜ 'You are spies!' ¹⁵ This is how you will be tested: As surely as Pharaoh lives, you will not leave this place unless your youngest brother comes here. ¹⁶ Send one from among you to get your brother. The rest of you will be imprisoned so that your words can be tested to see if they are true. If they are not, then as surely as Pharaoh lives, you are spies!" ¹⁷ So Joseph imprisoned them together for three days.

¹⁸ On the third day Joseph said to them, "I fear God — do this and you will live. ¹⁹ If you are honest, let one of you ᴰ be confined to the guardhouse, while the rest of you go and take grain to relieve the hunger of your households. ²⁰ Bring your youngest brother to me so that your words can be confirmed; then you won't die." And they consented to this.   Gn 39:9; Lv 25:43; Neh 5:15

²¹ Then they said to each other, "Obviously, we are being punished

ᴬ42:9 Lit nakedness, also in v. 12   ᴮ42:13 Or today, also in v. 32   ᶜ42:14 Lit "That which I spoke to you saying: ᴰ42:19 Lit your brothers for what we did to our brother. We saw his deep distress when he pleaded with us, but we would not listen. That is why this trouble has come to us." Gn 37:26-28

²² But Reuben replied: "Didn't I tell you not to harm the boy? But you wouldn't listen. Now we must account for his blood!"ᴬ Gn 37:22

²³ They did not realize that Joseph understood them, since there was an interpreter between them. ²⁴ He turned away from them and wept. When he turned back and spoke to them, he took Simeon from them and had him bound before their eyes. ²⁵ Joseph then gave orders to fill their containers with grain, return each man's silver to his sack, and give them provisions for their journey. This order was carried out. ²⁶ They loaded the grain on their donkeys and left there.

The Brothers Return Home

²⁷ At the place where they lodged for the night, one of them opened his sack to get feed for his donkey, and he saw his silver there at the top of his bag. ²⁸ He said to his brothers, "My silver has been returned! It's here in my bag." Their hearts sank. Trembling, they turned to one another and said, "What is this that God has done to us?"

²⁹ When they reached their father Jacob in the land of Canaan, they told him all that had happened to them: ³⁰ "The man who is the lord of the country spoke harshly to us and accused us of spying on the country. ³¹ But we told him: We are honest and not spies. ³² We were twelve brothers, sons of the sameᴮ father. One is no longer living, and the youngest is now with our father

in the land of Canaan. ³³ The man who is the lord of the country said to us, 'This is how I will know if you are honest: Leave one brother with me, take food to relieve the hunger of your households, and go. ³⁴ Bring back your youngest brother to me, and I will know that you are not spies but honest men. I will then give your brother back to you, and you can trade in the country.'"

³⁵ As they began emptying their sacks, there in each man's sack was his bag of silver! When they and their father saw their bags of silver, they were afraid.

³⁶ Their father Jacob said to them, "It's me that you make childless. Joseph is gone, and Simeon is gone. Now you want to take Benjamin. Everything happens to me!"

³⁷ Then Reuben said to his father, "You can kill my two sons if I don't bring him back to you. Put him in my care,ᶜ and I will return him to you."

³⁸ But Jacob answered, "My son will not go down with you, for his brother is dead and he alone is left. If anything happens to him on your journey, you will bring my gray hairs down to Sheol in sorrow."

Decision to Return to Egypt

43 Now the famine in the land was severe. ² When they had used up the grain they had brought back from Egypt, their father said to them, "Go back and buy us a little food." Gn 12:10; 41:56-57; 47:20

³ But Judah said to him, "The man specifically warned us: 'You will not see me again unless your brother is with you.' ⁴ If you will send our brother with us, we will go down and buy food for you. ⁵ But if you

---

ᴬ**42:22** Lit *Even his blood is being sought!"*   ᴮ**42:32** Lit *of our*   ᶜ**42:37** Lit *hand* will not send him, we will not go, for the man said to us, 'You will not see me again unless your brother is with you.'" Gn 42:18-20; 44:23

⁶ "Why have you caused me so much trouble?" Israel asked. "Why did you tell the man that you had another brother?"

⁷ They answered, "The man kept asking about us and our family: 'Is your father still alive? Do you have another brother?' And we answered him accordingly. How could we know that he would say, 'Bring your brother here'?"

⁸ Then Judah said to his father Israel, "Send the boy with me. We will be on our way so that we may live and not die — neither we, nor you, nor our dependents. ⁹ I will be responsible for him. You can hold me personally accountable!ᴬ If I do not bring him back to you and set him before you, I will be guilty before you forever. ¹⁰ If we had not delayed, we could have come back twice by now." Gn 42:37; 44:32

¹¹ Then their father Israel said to them, "If it must be so, then do this: Put some of the best products of the land in your packs and take them down to the man as a gift — a little balsam and a little honey, aromatic gum and resin, pistachios and almonds. ¹² Take twice as much silver with you. Return the silver that was returned to you in the top of your bags. Perhaps it was a mistake. ¹³ Take your brother also, and go back at once to the man. ¹⁴ May God Almighty cause the man to be merciful to you so that he will release your other brother and Benjamin to you. As for me, if I am deprived of my sons, then I am deprived." Gn 37:25; Jr 8:22; Ezk 27:17

The Return to Egypt

¹⁵ The men took this gift, double the amount of silver, and Benjamin. They immediately went down to Egypt and stood before Joseph.

¹⁶ When Joseph saw Benjamin with them, he said to his steward, "Take the men to my house. Slaughter an animal and prepare it, for they will eat with me at noon." ¹⁷ The man did as Joseph had said and brought them to Joseph's house.

¹⁸ But the men were afraid because they were taken to Joseph's house. They said, "We have been brought here because of the silver that was returned in our bags the first time. They intend to overpower us, seize us, make us slaves, and take our donkeys." ¹⁹ So they approached Joseph's stewardᴮ and spoke to him at the doorway of the house.

²⁰ They said, "My lord, we really did come down here the first time only to buy food. ²¹ When we came to the place where we lodged for the night and opened our bags of grain, each one's silver was at the top of his bag! It was the full amount of our silver, and we have brought it back with us. ²² We have brought additional silver with us to buy food. We don't know who put our silver in the bags."

²³ Then the steward said, "May you be well. Don't be afraid. Your God and the God of your father must have put treasure in your bags. I received your silver." Then he brought Simeon out to them. ²⁴ The steward brought the men into Joseph's house, gave them water to wash their feet, and got feed for their donkeys. ²⁵ Since the men had heard that they were going to eat a meal there, they prepared their

---

ᴬ43:9 Lit can seek him from my hand   ᴮ43:19 Lit approached the one who was over the house

gift for Joseph's arrival at noon.
²⁶ When Joseph came home, they
brought him the gift they had carried into the house, and they bowed
to the ground before him. Gn 18:4; 19:2

²⁷ He asked if they were well, and
he said, "How is your elderly father that you told me about? Is he
still alive?"

²⁸ They answered, "Your servant
our father is well. He is still alive."
And they knelt low and paid homage to him.

²⁹ When he looked up and saw
his brother Benjamin, his mother's son, he asked, "Is this your
youngest brother that you told me
about?" Then he said, "May God be
gracious to you, my son." ³⁰ Joseph
hurried out because he was overcome with emotion for his brother, and he was about to weep. He
went into an inner room and wept
there. ³¹ Then he washed his face
and came out. Regaining his composure, he said, "Serve the meal."

³² They served him by himself, his
brothers by themselves, and the
Egyptians who were eating with
him by themselves, because Egyptians could not eat with Hebrews,
since that is detestable to them.
³³ They were seated before him in
order by age, from the firstborn
to the youngest. The men looked
at each other in astonishment.
³⁴ Portions were served to them
from Joseph's table, and Benjamin's
portion was five times larger than
any of theirs. They drank and became drunk with Joseph. Gn 46:34

Joseph's Final Test

44 Joseph commanded his
steward, "Fill the men's bags
with as much food as they can carry, and put each one's silver at the
top of his bag. ² Put my cup, the silver one, at the top of the youngest
one's bag, along with the silver for
his grain." So he did as Joseph told
him. Gn 42:25

³ At morning light, the men were
sent off with their donkeys. ⁴ They
had not gone very far from the city
when Joseph said to his steward,
"Get up. Pursue the men, and when
you overtake them, say to them,
'Why have you repaid evil for
good? ⁵ Isn't this the cup that my
master drinks from and uses for
divination? What you have done
is wrong!'" Gn 30:27; 44:15; Lv 19:26

⁶ When he overtook them, he
said these words to them. ⁷ They
said to him, "Why does my lord say
these things? Your servants could
not possibly do such a thing. ⁸ We
even brought back to you from the
land of Canaan the silver we found
at the top of our bags. How could
we steal silver or gold from your
master's house? ⁹ If it is found with
one of us, your servants, he must
die, and the rest of us will become
my lord's slaves." Gn 31:32

¹⁰ The steward replied, "What you
have said is right, but only the one
who is found to have it will be my
slave, and the rest of you will be
blameless."

¹¹ So each one quickly lowered his
sack to the ground and opened it.
¹² The steward searched, beginning
with the oldest and ending with the
youngest, and the cup was found in
Benjamin's sack. ¹³ Then they tore
their clothes, and each one loaded
his donkey and returned to the city.

¹⁴ When Judah and his brothers
reached Joseph's house, he was still
there. They fell to the ground before him. ¹⁵ "What is this you have
done?" Joseph said to them. "Didn't

you know that a man like me could uncover the truth by divination?"

¹⁶ "What can we say to my lord?" Judah replied. "How can we plead? How can we justify ourselves? God has exposed your servants' iniquity. We are now my lord's slaves — both we and the one in whose possession the cup was found."

¹⁷ Then Joseph said, "I swear that I will not do this. The man in whose possession the cup was found will be my slave. The rest of you can go in peace to your father."

Judah's Plea for Benjamin

¹⁸ But Judah approached him and said, "My lord, please let your servant speak personally to my lord.ᴬ Do not be angry with your servant, for you are like Pharaoh. ¹⁹ My lord asked his servants, 'Do you have a father or a brother?' ²⁰ and we answered my lord, 'We have an elderly father and a younger brother, the child of his old age. The boy's brother is dead. He is the only one of his mother's sons left, and his father loves him.' ²¹ Then you said to your servants, 'Bring him to me so that I can see him.' ²² But we said to my lord, 'The boy cannot leave his father. If he were to leave, his father would die.' ²³ Then you said to your servants, 'If your younger brother does not come down with you, you will not see me again.' Gn 37:3; 41:40-44

²⁴ "This is what happened when we went back to your servant my father: We reported to him the words of my lord. ²⁵ But our father said, 'Go again, and buy us a little food.' ²⁶ We told him, 'We cannot go down unless our younger brother goes with us. If our younger brother isn't with us, we cannot see the man.' ²⁷ Your servant my father said to us, 'You know that my wife bore me two sons. ²⁸ One is gone from me — I said he must have been torn to pieces — and I have never seen him again. ²⁹ If you also take this one from me and anything happens to him, you will bring my gray hairs down to Sheol in sorrow.'

³⁰ "So if I come to your servant my father and the boy is not with us — his life is wrapped up with the boy's life — ³¹ when he sees that the boy is not with us, he will die. Then your servants will have brought the gray hairs of your servant our father down to Sheol in sorrow. ³² Your servant became accountable to my father for the boy, saying, 'If I do not return him to you, I will always bear the guilt for sinning against you, my father.' ³³ Now please let your servant remain here as my lord's slave, in place of the boy. Let him go back with his brothers. ³⁴ For how can I go back to my father without the boy? I could not bear to see the grief that would overwhelm my father." Gn 43:9

Joseph Reveals his Identity

45 Joseph could no longer keep his composure in front of all his attendants,ᴮ so he called out, "Send everyone away from me!" No one was with him when he revealed his identity to his brothers. ² But he wept so loudly that the Egyptians heard it, and also Pharaoh's household heard it. ³ Joseph said to his brothers, "I am Joseph! Is my father still living?" But they could not answer him because they were terrified in his presence. Ac 7:13

ᴬ44:18 Lit *speak a word in my lord's ears*   ᴮ45:1 Lit *all those standing about him*

⁴ Then Joseph said to his brothers, "Please, come near me," and they came near. "I am Joseph, your brother," he said, "the one you sold into Egypt. ⁵ And now don't be grieved or angry with yourselves for selling me here, because God sent me ahead of you to preserve life. ⁶ For the famine has been in the land these two years, and there will be five more years without plowing or harvesting. ⁷ God sent me ahead of you to establish you as a remnant within the land and to keep you alive by a great deliverance.ᴬ ⁸ Therefore it was not you who sent me here, but God. He has made me a father to Pharaoh, lord of his entire household, and ruler over all the land of Egypt. Gn 37:18-36; 45:7-8

⁹ "Return quickly to my father and say to him, 'This is what your son Joseph says: "God has made me lord of all Egypt. Come down to me without delay.¹⁰ You can settle in the land of Goshen and be near me — you, your children, and your grandchildren, your flocks, your herds, and all you have.¹¹ There I will sustain you, for there will be five more years of famine. Otherwise, you, your household, and everything you have will become destitute."'¹² Look! Your eyes and the eyes of my brother Benjamin can see that I'mᴮ the one speaking to you. ¹³ Tell my father about all my glory in Egypt and about all you have seen. And bring my father here quickly."

¹⁴ Then Joseph threw his arms around his brother Benjamin and wept, and Benjamin wept on his shoulder. ¹⁵ Joseph kissed each of his brothers as he wept,ᶜ and afterward his brothers talked with him.

The Return for Jacob

¹⁶ When the news reached Pharaoh's palace, "Joseph's brothers have come," Pharaoh and his servants were pleased.¹⁷ Pharaoh said to Joseph, "Tell your brothers, 'Do this: Load your animals and go on back to the land of Canaan. ¹⁸ Get your father and your families, and come back to me. I will give you the best of the land of Egypt, and you can eat from the richness of the land.' ¹⁹ You are also commanded to tell them, 'Do this: Take wagons from the land of Egypt for your dependents and your wives and bring your father here. ²⁰ Do not be concerned about your belongings, for the best of all the land of Egypt is yours.'" Gn 46:5; Dt 32:9-14

²¹ The sons of Israel did this. Joseph gave them wagons as Pharaoh had commanded, and he gave them provisions for the journey. ²² He gave each of the brothers changes of clothes, but he gave Benjamin three hundred pieces of silver and five changes of clothes. ²³ He sent his father the following: ten donkeys carrying the best products of Egypt and ten female donkeys carrying grain, food, and provisions for his father on the journey. ²⁴ So Joseph sent his brothers on their way, and as they were leaving, he said to them, "Don't argueᴰ on the way."

²⁵ So they went up from Egypt and came to their father Jacob in the land of Canaan. ²⁶ They said, "Joseph is still alive, and he is ruler over all the land of Egypt!" Jacob was stunned,ᴱ for he did not believe them. ²⁷ But when they told Jacob all that Joseph had said to them, and when he saw the wagons

ᴬ45:7 Or keep alive for you many survivors ᴮ45:12 Lit that my mouth is ᶜ45:15 Lit brothers, and he wept over them ᴰ45:24 Or be anxious ᴱ45:26 Lit Jacob's heart was numb that Joseph had sent to transport him, the spirit of their father Jacob revived.

²⁸ Then Israel said, "Enough! My son Joseph is still alive. I will go to see him before I die."

Jacob Leaves for Egypt

46 Israel set out with all that he had and came to Beer-sheba, and he offered sacrifices to the God of his father Isaac. ² That night God spoke to Israel in a vision: "Jacob, Jacob!" he said.   Gn 21:14; 28:10

And Jacob replied, "Here I am."

³ God said, "I am God, the God of your father. Do not be afraid to go down to Egypt, for I will make you into a great nation there. ⁴ I will go down with you to Egypt, and I will also bring you back. Joseph will close your eyes when you die."ᴬ

⁵ Jacob left Beer-sheba. The sons of Israel took their father Jacob in the wagons Pharaoh had sent to carry him, along with their dependents and their wives. ⁶ They also took their cattle and possessions they had acquired in the land of Canaan. Then Jacob and all his offspring with him came to Egypt. ⁷ His sons and grandsons, his daughters and granddaughters, indeed all his offspring, he brought with him to Egypt.   Gn 45:19,21; Dt 26:5

Jacob's Family

⁸ These are the names of the sons of Israel who came to Egypt — Jacob and his sons: Ex 1:1-5; Nm 26:4-5

Jacob's firstborn: Reuben.
⁹ Reuben's sons: Hanoch, Pallu, Hezron, and Carmi.
¹⁰ Simeon's sons: Jemuel, Jamin, Ohad, Jachin, Zohar, and Shaul, the son of a Canaanite woman.
¹¹ Levi's sons: Gershon, Kohath, and Merari.   Ex 6:16; 1Ch 6:16
¹² Judah's sons: Er, Onan, Shelah, Perez, and Zerah; but Er and Onan died in the land of Canaan. The sons of Perez were Hezron and Hamul.   Gn 38:29
¹³ Issachar's sons: Tola, Puvah,ᴮ Jashub,ᶜ and Shimron.   1Ch 7:1
¹⁴ Zebulun's sons: Sered, Elon, and Jahleel.
¹⁵ These were Leah's sons born to Jacob in Paddan-aram, as well as his daughter Dinah. The total number of persons:ᴰ thirty-three.
¹⁶ Gad's sons: Ziphion, Haggi, Shuni, Ezbon, Eri, Arodi, and Areli.
¹⁷ Asher's sons: Imnah, Ishvah, Ishvi, Beriah, and their sister Serah. Beriah's sons were Heber and Malchiel.
¹⁸ These were the sons of Zilpah — whom Laban gave to his daughter Leah — that she bore to Jacob: sixteen persons.
¹⁹ The sons of Jacob's wife Rachel: Joseph and Benjamin.
²⁰ Manasseh and Ephraim were born to Joseph in the land of Egypt. They were born to him by Asenath daughter of Potiphera, a priest at On.ᴱ
²¹ Benjamin's sons: Bela, Becher, Ashbel, Gera, Naaman, Ehi, Rosh, Muppim, Huppim, and Ard.

ᴬ46:4 Lit will put his hand on your eyes   ᴮ46:13 Sam, Syr read *Puah*; 1Ch 7:1   ᶜ46:13 Sam, LXX; MT reads *Iob*   ᴰ46:15 Lit *All persons his sons and his daughters:*   ᴱ46:20 Or *Heliopolis*

22 These were Rachel's sons who were born to Jacob: fourteen persons.
23 Dan's son:[A] Hushim.
24 Naphtali's sons: Jahzeel, Guni, Jezer, and Shillem.
25 These were the sons of Bilhah, whom Laban gave to his daughter Rachel. She bore to Jacob: seven persons. Gn 29:29; 30:5-8
26 The total number of persons belonging to Jacob — his direct descendants,[B] not including the wives of Jacob's sons — who came to Egypt: sixty-six.
27 And Joseph's sons who were born to him in Egypt: two persons. All those of Jacob's household who came to Egypt: seventy[C] persons. Ex 1:5; Ac 7:14

Jacob Arrives in Egypt

28 Now Jacob had sent Judah ahead of him to Joseph to prepare for his arrival[D] at Goshen. When they came to the land of Goshen, 29 Joseph hitched the horses to his chariot and went up to Goshen to meet his father Israel. Joseph presented himself to him, threw his arms around him, and wept for a long time.
30 Then Israel said to Joseph, "I'm ready to die now because I have seen your face and you are still alive!"
31 Joseph said to his brothers and to his father's family, "I will go up and inform Pharaoh, telling him, 'My brothers and my father's family, who were in the land of Canaan, have come to me. 32 The men are shepherds; they also raise livestock. They have brought their flocks and herds and all that they have.' 33 When Pharaoh addresses you and asks, 'What is your occupation?' 34 you are to say, 'Your servants, both we and our fathers, have raised livestock[E] from our youth until now.' Then you will be allowed to settle in the land of Goshen, since all shepherds are detestable to Egyptians." Gn 47:1; Ex 8:26

Pharaoh Welcomes Jacob

47 So Joseph went and informed Pharaoh: "My father and my brothers, with their flocks and herds and all that they own, have come from the land of Canaan and are now in the land of Goshen." Gn 45:10; 46:28
2 He took five of his brothers and presented them to Pharaoh. 3 And Pharaoh asked his brothers, "What is your occupation?" Ac 7:13
They said to Pharaoh, "Your servants, both we and our fathers, are shepherds." 4 And they said to Pharaoh, "We have come to stay in the land for a while because there is no grazing land for your servants' sheep, since the famine in the land of Canaan has been severe. So now, please let your servants settle in the land of Goshen." Gn 46:32-34; Dt 26:5
5 Then Pharaoh said to Joseph, "Now that your father and brothers have come to you, 6 the land of Egypt is open before you; settle your father and brothers in the best part of the land. They can live in the land of Goshen. If you know of any capable men among them, put them in charge of my livestock."
7 Joseph then brought his father Jacob and presented him to

A46:23 Alt Hb tradition reads *sons;*   B46:26 Lit *Jacob who came out from his loins*   C46:27 LXX reads 75; Ac 7:14   D46:28 Lit *to give directions before him*   E46:34 Lit *fathers, are men of livestock*

Pharaoh, and Jacob blessed Pharaoh. [8] Pharaoh said to Jacob, "How many years have you lived?"

[9] Jacob said to Pharaoh, "My pilgrimage has lasted 130 years. My years have been few and hard, and they have not reached the years of my fathers during their pilgrimages." [10] So Jacob blessed Pharaoh and departed from Pharaoh's presence.   1Ch 29:15; Ps 39:12; 119:19,54; Heb 11:9,13

[11] Then Joseph settled his father and brothers in the land of Egypt and gave them property in the best part of the land, the land of Rameses, as Pharaoh had commanded. [12] And Joseph provided his father, his brothers, and all his father's family with food for their dependents.   Gn 45:10-11; 50:21; Ex 1:11; 12:37

The Land Becomes Pharaoh's

[13] But there was no food in the entire region, for the famine was very severe. The land of Egypt and the land of Canaan were exhausted by the famine. [14] Joseph collected all the silver to be found in the land of Egypt and the land of Canaan in exchange for the grain they were purchasing, and he brought the silver to Pharaoh's palace. [15] When the silver from the land of Egypt and the land of Canaan was gone, all the Egyptians came to Joseph and said, "Give us food. Why should we die here in front of you? The silver is gone!"   Gn 41:56

[16] But Joseph said, "Give me your livestock. Since the silver is gone, I will give you food in exchange for your livestock." [17] So they brought their livestock to Joseph, and he gave them food in exchange for the horses, the flocks of sheep, the herds of cattle, and the donkeys.

That year he provided them with food in exchange for all their livestock.

[18] When that year was over, they came the next year and said to him, "We cannot hide from our lord that the silver is gone and that all our livestock belongs to our lord. There is nothing left for our lord except our bodies and our land. [19] Why should we die here in front of you —both us and our land? Buy us and our land in exchange for food. Then we with our land will become Pharaoh's slaves. Give us seed so that we can live and not die, and so that the land won't become desolate."

[20] In this way, Joseph acquired all the land in Egypt for Pharaoh, because every Egyptian sold his field since the famine was so severe for them. The land became Pharaoh's, [21] and Joseph moved the people to the cities[A] from one end of Egypt to the other. [22] The only land he did not acquire belonged to the priests, for they had an allowance from Pharaoh. They ate from their allowance that Pharaoh gave them; therefore they did not sell their land.

[23] Joseph said to the people, "Understand today that I have acquired you and your land for Pharaoh. Here is seed for you. Sow it in the land. [24] At harvest, you are to give a fifth of it to Pharaoh, and four-fifths will be yours as seed for the field and as food for yourselves, your households, and your dependents."   Gn 41:34

[25] "You have saved our lives," they said. "We have found favor with our lord and will be Pharaoh's slaves." [26] So Joseph made it a law, still in effect today in the land of Egypt, that a fifth of the produce belongs

A**47:21** Sam, LXX, Vg read *and he made the people servants* to Pharaoh. Only the priests' land does not belong to Pharaoh.

Israel Settles in Goshen

²⁷ Israel settled in the land of Egypt, in the region of Goshen. They acquired property in it and became fruitful and very numerous. ²⁸ Now Jacob lived in the land of Egypt 17 years, and his life span was 147 years. ²⁹ When the time approached for him to die, he called his son Joseph and said to him, "If I have found favor with you, put your hand under my thigh and promise me that you will deal with me in kindness and faithfulness. Do not bury me in Egypt. ³⁰ When I rest with my fathers, carry me away from Egypt and bury me in their burial place." Gn 17:6; 26:4; 35:11; Ex 1:7

Joseph answered, "I will do what you have asked."

³¹ And Jacob said, "Swear to me." So Joseph swore to him. Then Israel bowed in thanks at the head of his bed.ᴬ   Gn 48:2; 1Kg 1:47; Heb 11:21

Jacob Blesses Ephraim and Manasseh

48 Some time after this, Joseph was told, "Your father is weaker." So he set out with his two sons, Manasseh and Ephraim. ² When Jacob was told, "Your son Joseph has come to you," Israel summoned his strength and sat up in bed.

³ Jacob said to Joseph, "God Almighty appeared to me at Luz in the land of Canaan and blessed me. ⁴ He said to me, 'I will make you fruitful and numerous; I will make many nations come from you, and I will give this land as a permanent possession to your future descendants.' ⁵ Your two sons born to you in the land of Egypt before I came to you in Egypt are now mine. Ephraim and Manasseh belong to me just as Reuben and Simeon do. ⁶ Children born to you after them will be yours and will be recorded under the names of their brothers with regard to their inheritance. ⁷ When I was returning from Paddan, to my sorrow Rachel died along the way, some distance from Ephrath in the land of Canaan. I buried her there along the way to Ephrath" (that is, Bethlehem). Gn 17:1

⁸ When Israel saw Joseph's sons, he said, "Who are these? "

⁹ And Joseph said to his father, "They are my sons God has given me here."

So Israel said, "Bring them to me and I will bless them." ¹⁰ Now his eyesight was poor because of old age; he could hardlyᴮ see. Joseph brought them to him, and he kissed and embraced them. ¹¹ Israel said to Joseph, "I never expected to see your face again, but now God has even let me see your offspring." ¹² Then Joseph took them from his father's knees and bowed with his face to the ground. Gn 27:4

Ephraim's Greater Blessing

¹³ Then Joseph took them both — with his right hand Ephraim toward Israel's left, and with his left hand Manasseh toward Israel's right — and brought them to Israel. ¹⁴ But Israel stretched out his right hand and put it on the head of Ephraim, the younger, and crossing his hands, put his left on Manasseh's head, although Manasseh was the firstborn. ¹⁵ Then he blessed Joseph and said: Gn 25:23; 27:18-30

ᴬ**47:31** Or *Israel worshiped while leaning on the top of his staff*   ᴮ**48:10** Lit *he was not able to*

The God before whom
my fathers Abraham
and Isaac walked, Gn 17:1; 24:40
the God who has been
my shepherd all my life
to this day, Gn 49:24; Ps 23:1; Jr 31:10
¹⁶ the angel who has redeemed
me from all harm —
may he bless these boys.
And may they be called
by my name
and the names of my fathers
Abraham and Isaac, Dt 28:10
and may they grow
to be numerous
within the land.

¹⁷ When Joseph saw that his father had placed his right hand on Ephraim's head, he thought it was a mistake[A] and took his father's hand to move it from Ephraim's head to Manasseh's. ¹⁸ Joseph said to his father, "Not that way, my father! This one is the firstborn. Put your right hand on his head."

¹⁹ But his father refused and said, "I know, my son, I know! He too will become a tribe,[B] and he too will be great; nevertheless, his younger brother will be greater than he, and his offspring will become a populous nation."[C] ²⁰ So he blessed them that day, putting Ephraim before Manasseh when he said, "The nation Israel will invoke blessings by you, saying, 'May God make you like Ephraim and Manasseh.'"

²¹ Israel said to Joseph, "Look, I am about to die, but God will be with you and will bring you back to the land of your fathers. ²² Over and above what I am giving your brothers, I am giving you the one

mountain slope[D] that I took from the Amorites with my sword and bow." Gn 34:25-29; 46:4; 50:24; Jos 24:32

Jacob's Last Words

49

Then Jacob called his sons and said, "Gather around, and I will tell you what will happen to you in the days to come.[E]

² Come together and listen,
sons of Jacob;
listen to your father Israel:
³ Reuben, you are my firstborn,
my strength
and the firstfruits
of my virility, Dt 21:17
excelling in prominence,
excelling in power.
⁴ Turbulent as water, you will
not excel,
because you got
into your father's bed
and you defiled it — he[F] got
into my bed.

⁵ Simeon and Levi are brothers;
their knives are
vicious weapons. Gn 34:25,30
⁶ May I never enter
their council;
may I never join
their assembly.
For in their anger
they kill men,
and on a whim
they hamstring oxen.
⁷ Their anger is cursed, for it
is strong,
and their fury, for it is cruel!
I will disperse them
throughout Jacob
and scatter them
throughout Israel. Ex 32:28

[A]48:17 Or he was displeased; lit head, it was bad in his eyes   [B]48:19 Lit people   [C]48:19 Or a multitude of nations; lit a fullness of nations   [D]48:22 Or Shechem, Joseph's burial place; lit one shoulder   [E]49:1 Or in the last days   [F]49:4 LXX, Syr, Tg read you

⁸ Judah, your brothers will
     praise you.   Gn 29:35
Your hand will
     be on the necks
     of your enemies;
your father's sons
     will bow down to you.   1Ch 5:2
⁹ Judah is a young lion —   Mc 5:8
my son, you return
     from the kill.
He crouches; he lies down
     like a lion
or a lioness — who dares
     to rouse him?
¹⁰ The scepter will not depart
     from Judah
or the staff from between
     his feet
until he whose right
     it is comes^A   Nm 2:9; 10:14; 24:17
and the obedience
     of the peoples belongs
     to him.   Ps 2:6-9; 72:8-11; Is 42:1,4; 49:6
¹¹ He ties his donkey to a vine,
and the colt of his donkey
     to the choice vine.
He washes his clothes in wine
and his robes in the blood
     of grapes.
¹² His eyes are darker than wine,
and his teeth are whiter
     than milk.

¹³ Zebulun will live
     by the seashore
and will be a harbor for ships,
and his territory will be
     next to Sidon.   Dt 33:19; Jos 19:10-16

¹⁴ Issachar is a strong donkey
lying down between
     the saddlebags.^B
¹⁵ He saw that his resting place
     was good

and that the land
     was pleasant,
so he leaned his shoulder
     to bear a load
and became a forced laborer.

¹⁶ Dan will judge his people
as one of the tribes of Israel.
¹⁷ Dan will be a snake
     by the road,
a viper beside the path,
that bites the horse's heels
so that its rider
     falls backward.

¹⁸ I wait for your salvation,
LORD.

¹⁹ Gad will be attacked
     by raiders,
but he will attack their heels.

²⁰ Asher's^C food will be rich,
and he will produce
     royal delicacies.   Dt 33:24-25

²¹ Naphtali is a doe set free
that bears beautiful fawns.

²² Joseph is a fruitful vine,
a fruitful vine beside a spring;
its branches^D climb
     over the wall.^E
²³ The archers attacked him,
shot at him, and were hostile
     toward him.
²⁴ Yet his bow remained steady,
and his strong arms
     were made agile
by the hands
     of the Mighty One of Jacob,
by the name
     of^F the Shepherd, the Rock
     of Israel,   Gn 48:15; Ps 23:1; Jr 31:10

---

^A49:10 Or *until tribute comes to him,* or *until Shiloh comes,* or *until he comes to Shiloh*   ^B49:14 Or
sheep pens   ^C49:19-20 LXX, Syr, Vg; MT reads *their heel.* ²⁰*From Asher*   ^D49:22 Lit *daughters*   ^E49:22
Hb obscure   ^F49:24 Syr, Tg; MT reads *Jacob, from there*

25 by the God of your father
who helps you,
and by the Almighty
who blesses you
with blessings
of the heavens above,
blessings of the deep
that lies below,
and blessings of the breasts
and the womb.
26 The blessings of your father
excel
the blessings
of my ancestors A
and B the bounty of
the ancient hills. C   Dt 33:15-16
May they rest on the head
of Joseph,
on the brow of the prince
of his brothers.

27 Benjamin is a wolf; he tears
his prey.
In the morning he devours
the prey,
and in the evening he divides
the plunder."   Jdg 5:14; 20:21

28 These are the tribes of Israel, twelve in all, and this is what their father said to them. He blessed them, and he blessed each one with a suitable blessing.

Jacob's Burial Instructions

29 Then he commanded them: "I am about to be gathered to my people. Bury me with my fathers in the cave in the field of Ephron the Hethite. 30 The cave is in the field of Machpelah near Mamre, in the land of Canaan. This is the field Abraham purchased from Ephron the Hethite as burial property. 31 Abraham and his wife Sarah are buried there, Isaac and his wife Rebekah

are buried there, and I buried Leah there. 32 The field and the cave in it were purchased from the Hethites." 33 When Jacob had finished giving charges to his sons, he drew his feet into the bed, took his last breath, and was gathered to his people.

Jacob's Burial

50 Then Joseph, leaning over his father's face, wept and kissed him. 2 He commanded his servants who were physicians to embalm his father. So they embalmed Israel. 3 They took forty days to complete this, for embalming takes that long, and the Egyptians mourned for him seventy days.   Gn 50:10; Nm 20:29; Dt 34:8

4 When the days of mourning were over, Joseph said to Pharaoh's household, "If I have found favor with you, please tell D Pharaoh that 5 my father made me take an oath, saying, 'I am about to die. You must bury me there in the tomb that I made for myself in the land of Canaan.' Now let me go and bury my father. Then I will return."   Gn 47:29-31

6 So Pharaoh said, "Go and bury your father in keeping with your oath."

7 Then Joseph went to bury his father, and all Pharaoh's servants, the elders of his household, and all the elders of the land of Egypt went with him, 8 along with all Joseph's family, his brothers, and his father's family. Only their dependents, their flocks, and their herds were left in the land of Goshen. 9 Horses and chariots went up with him; it was a very impressive procession. 10 When they reached the threshing floor of Atad, which is across the Jordan, they lamented and wept

A 49:26 Or *of the mountains*   B 49:26 Lit *to*   C 49:26 Hb obscure   D 50:4 Lit *please speak in the ears of* loudly, and Joseph mourned seven days for his father. [11] When the Canaanite inhabitants of the land saw the mourning at the threshing floor of Atad, they said, "This is a solemn mourning on the part of the Egyptians." Therefore the place is named Abel-mizraim. [A] It is across the Jordan.

[12] So Jacob's sons did for him what he had commanded them. [13] They carried him to the land of Canaan and buried him in the cave at Machpelah in the field near Mamre, which Abraham had purchased as burial property from Ephron the Hethite. [14] After Joseph buried his father, he returned to Egypt with his brothers and all who had gone with him to bury his father.

Joseph's Kindness

[15] When Joseph's brothers saw that their father was dead, they said to one another, "If Joseph is holding a grudge against us, he will certainly repay us for all the suffering we caused him." Gn 37:28; 42:21-22

[16] So they sent this message to Joseph, "Before he died your father gave a command: [17] 'Say this to Joseph: Please forgive your brothers' transgression and their sin — the suffering they caused you.' Therefore, please forgive the transgression of the servants of the God of your father." Joseph wept when their message came to him. [18] His brothers also came to him, bowed down before him, and said, "We are your slaves!" Gn 43:30; 46:29

[19] But Joseph said to them, "Don't be afraid. Am I in the place of God? [20] You planned evil against me; God planned it for good to bring about the present result — the survival of many people. [21] Therefore don't be afraid. I will take care of you and your children." And he comforted them and spoke kindly to them. [B]

Joseph's Death

[22] Joseph and his father's family remained in Egypt. Joseph lived 110 years. [23] He saw Ephraim's sons to the third generation; the sons of Manasseh's son Machir were recognized by [C,D] Joseph. Jb 42:16; Ps 128:6

[24] Joseph said to his brothers, "I am about to die, but God will certainly come to your aid and bring you up from this land to the land he swore to give to Abraham, Isaac, and Jacob." [25] So Joseph made the sons of Israel take an oath: "When God comes to your aid, you are to carry my bones up from here." Ex 35:19

[26] Joseph died at the age of 110. They embalmed him and placed him in a coffin in Egypt.

[A] 50:11 = Mourning of Egypt [B] 50:21 Lit spoke to their hearts [C] 50:23 Lit were born on the knees of
[D] 50:23 Referring to a ritual of adoption or of legitimation; Gn 30:3

EXODUS

Israel Oppressed in Egypt

1 These are the names of the sons of Israel who came to Egypt with Jacob; each came with his family:
² Reuben, Simeon, Levi, and Judah;
³ Issachar, Zebulun, and Benjamin;
⁴ Dan and Naphtali; Gad and Asher.
⁵ The total number of Jacob's descendants ^A was seventy; ^B Joseph was already in Egypt. Gn 46:26-27

⁶ Joseph and all his brothers and all that generation eventually died. ⁷ But the Israelites were fruitful, increased rapidly, multiplied, and became extremely numerous so that the land was filled with them.

⁸ A new king, who did not know about Joseph, came to power in Egypt. ⁹ He said to his people, "Look, the Israelite people are more numerous and powerful than we are. ¹⁰ Come, let's deal shrewdly with them; otherwise they will multiply further, and when war breaks out, they will join our enemies, fight against us, and leave the country." ¹¹ So the Egyptians assigned taskmasters over the Israelites to oppress them with forced labor. They built Pithom and Rameses as supply cities for Pharaoh. ¹² But the more they oppressed them, the more they multiplied and spread so that the Egyptians came to dread ^C the Israelites. ¹³ They worked the Israelites ruthlessly ¹⁴ and made their lives bitter with difficult labor in brick and mortar and in all kinds of fieldwork. They ruthlessly imposed all this work on them. Ac 7:19

¹⁵ The king of Egypt said to the Hebrew midwives — the first whose name was Shiphrah and the second whose name was Puah — ¹⁶ "When you help the Hebrew women give birth, observe them as they deliver. If the child is a son, kill him, but if it's a daughter, she may live." ¹⁷ The midwives, however, feared God and did not do as the king of Egypt had told them; they let the boys live. ¹⁸ So the king of Egypt summoned the midwives and asked them, "Why have you done this and let the boys live?" Ex 1:21

¹⁹ The midwives said to Pharaoh, "The Hebrew women are not like the Egyptian women, for they are vigorous and give birth before the midwife can get to them." Jos 2:4

²⁰ So God was good to the midwives, and the people multiplied and became very numerous. ²¹ Since the midwives feared God, he gave them families. ²² Pharaoh then commanded all his people: "You must throw every son born to the Hebrews into the Nile, but let every daughter live." Pr 11:18; Is 3:10

Moses's Birth and Adoption

2 Now a man from the family of Levi married a Levite woman. ² The woman became pregnant and gave birth to a son; when she saw that he was beautiful, ^D she hid him for three months. ³ But when

---

^A 1:5 Lit of people issuing from Jacob's loins   ^B 1:5 LXX, DSS read 75; Gn 46:27; Ac 7:14   ^C 1:12 Or Egyptians loathed   ^D 2:2 Or healthy she could no longer hide him, she got a papyrus basket for him and coated it with asphalt and pitch. She placed the child in it and set it among the reeds by the bank of the Nile. ⁴ Then his sister stood at a distance in order to see what would happen to him. Ex 6:20; Nm 26:59; 1Ch 23:14

⁵ Pharaoh's daughter went down to bathe at the Nile while her servant girls walked along the riverbank. She saw the basket among the reeds, sent her slave girl, took it, ⁶ opened it, and saw him, the child — and there he was, a little boy, crying. She felt sorry for him and said, "This is one of the Hebrew boys."

⁷ Then his sister said to Pharaoh's daughter, "Should I go and call a Hebrew woman who is nursing to nurse the boy for you?"

⁸ "Go," Pharaoh's daughter told her. So the girl went and called the boy's mother. ⁹ Then Pharaoh's daughter said to her, "Take this child and nurse him for me, and I will pay your wages." So the woman took the boy and nursed him. ¹⁰ When the child grew older, she brought him to Pharaoh's daughter, and he became her son. She named him Moses, ᴬ "Because," she said, "I drew him out of the water."

Moses in Midian

¹¹ Years later, ᴮ after Moses had grown up, he went out to his own people ᶜ and observed their forced labor. He saw an Egyptian striking a Hebrew, one of his people. ¹² Looking all around and seeing no one, he struck the Egyptian dead and hid him in the sand. ¹³ The next day

he went out and saw two Hebrews fighting. He asked the one in the wrong, "Why are you attacking your neighbor?" ᴰ   Ex 1:11; Ac 7:23

¹⁴ "Who made you a commander and judge over us?" the man replied. "Are you planning to kill me as you killed the Egyptian?"

Then Moses became afraid and thought, "What I did is certainly known."

¹⁵ When Pharaoh heard about this, he tried to kill Moses. But Moses fled from Pharaoh and went to live in the land of Midian, and sat down by a well. Gn 24:11; Ac 7:29; Heb 11:27

¹⁶ Now the priest of Midian had seven daughters. They came to draw water and filled the troughs to water their father's flock. ¹⁷ Then some shepherds arrived and drove them away, but Moses came to their rescue and watered their flock. ¹⁸ When they returned to their father Reuel, ᴱ he asked, "Why have you come back so quickly today?"

¹⁹ They answered, "An Egyptian rescued us from the shepherds. He even drew water for us and watered the flock."

²⁰ "So where is he?" he asked his daughters. "Why then did you leave the man behind? Invite him to eat dinner."

²¹ Moses agreed to stay with the man, and he gave his daughter Zipporah to Moses in marriage. ²² She gave birth to a son whom he named Gershom, ᶠ for he said, "I have been a resident alien in a foreign land."

²³ After a long time, the king of Egypt died. The Israelites groaned because of their difficult labor; and they cried out; and their cry for

help because of the difficult labor ascended to God. [24] And God heard their groaning; and God remembered his covenant with Abraham, with Isaac, and with Jacob; [25] and God saw the Israelites; and God knew.   Gn 9:15; Ex 3:7,9; 6:5; Dt 26:7; Jms 5:4

Moses and the Burning Bush

3 Meanwhile, Moses was shepherding the flock of his father-in-law Jethro, [A] the priest of Midian. He led the flock to the far side of the wilderness and came to Horeb, [B] the mountain of God. [2] Then the angel of the LORD appeared to him in a flame of fire within a bush. As Moses looked, he saw that the bush was on fire but was not consumed. [3] So Moses thought, "I must go over and look at this remarkable sight. Why isn't the bush burning up?"

[4] When the LORD saw that he had gone over to look, God called out to him from the bush, "Moses, Moses!"

"Here I am," he answered.

[5] "Do not come closer," he said. "Remove the sandals from your feet, for the place where you are standing is holy ground." [6] Then he continued, "I am the God of your father, [C] the God of Abraham, the God of Isaac, and the God of Jacob." Moses hid his face because he was afraid to look at God.   Jos 5:15; Ac 7:33

[7] Then the LORD said, "I have observed the misery of my people in Egypt, and have heard them crying out because of their oppressors. I know about their sufferings, [8] and I have come down to rescue them from the power of the Egyptians and to bring them from that land to a good and spacious land,

a land flowing with milk and honey — the territory of the Canaanites, Hethites, Amorites, Perizzites, Hivites, and Jebusites. [9] So because the Israelites' cry for help has come to me, and I have also seen the way the Egyptians are oppressing them, [10] therefore, go. I am sending you to Pharaoh so that you may lead my people, the Israelites, out of Egypt."

[11] But Moses asked God, "Who am I that I should go to Pharaoh and that I should bring the Israelites out of Egypt?"   Ex 6:12; 1Sm 18:18

[12] He answered, "I will certainly be with you, and this will be the sign to you that I am the one who sent you: when you bring the people out of Egypt, you will all worship [D] God at this mountain."   Gn 31:3

[13] Then Moses asked God, "If I go to the Israelites and say to them, 'The God of your fathers has sent me to you,' and they ask me, 'What is his name?' what should I tell them?"

[14] God replied to Moses, "I AM WHO I AM. [E] This is what you are to say to the Israelites: I AM has sent me to you." [15] God also said to Moses, "Say this to the Israelites: The LORD, the God of your fathers, the God of Abraham, the God of Isaac, and the God of Jacob, has sent me to you. This is my name forever; this is how I am to be remembered in every generation.   Ex 6:3; Ps 68:4; Jn 8:58

[16] "Go and assemble the elders of Israel and say to them: The LORD, the God of your fathers, the God of Abraham, Isaac, and Jacob, has appeared to me and said: I have paid close attention to you and to what has been done to you in

Egypt. ¹⁷ And I have promised you that I will bring you up from the misery of Egypt to the land of the Canaanites, Hethites, Amorites, Perizzites, Hivites, and Jebusites — a land flowing with milk and honey. ¹⁸ They will listen to what you say. Then you, along with the elders of Israel, must go to the king of Egypt and say to him: The LORD, the God of the Hebrews, has met with us. Now please let us go on a three-day trip into the wilderness so that we may sacrifice to the LORD our God. Gn 15:16; Ex 4:29; 5:1; Jos 24:11; Lk 1:68

¹⁹ "However, I know that the king of Egypt will not allow you to go, even under force from a strong hand. ²⁰ But when I stretch out my hand and strike Egypt with all my miracles that I will perform in it, after that, he will let you go. ²¹ And I will give these people such favor with the Egyptians that when you go, you will not go empty-handed. ²² Each woman will ask her neighbor and any woman staying in her house for silver and gold jewelry, and clothing, and you will put them on your sons and daughters. So you will plunder the Egyptians." Ex 5:2

Miraculous Signs for Moses

4 Moses answered, "What if they won't believe me and will not obey me but say, 'The LORD did not appear to you'?" Ex 3:18; 6:30

² The LORD asked him, "What is that in your hand?"

"A staff," he replied.

³ "Throw it on the ground," he said. So Moses threw it on the ground, it became a snake, and he ran from it. ⁴ The LORD told Moses, "Stretch out your hand and grab it

by the tail." So he stretched out his hand and caught it, and it became a staff in his hand. ⁵ "This will take place," he continued, "so that they will believe that the LORD, the God of their fathers, the God of Abraham, the God of Isaac, and the God of Jacob, has appeared to you."

⁶ In addition the LORD said to him, "Put your hand inside your cloak." So he put his hand inside his cloak, and when he took it out, his hand was diseased, resembling snow.ᴬ ⁷ "Put your hand back inside your cloak," he said. So he put his hand back inside his cloak, and when he took it out, it had again become like the rest of his skin. ⁸ "If they will not believe you and will not respond to the evidence of the first sign, they may believe the evidence of the second sign. ⁹ And if they don't believe even these two signs or listen to what you say, take some water from the Nile and pour it on the dry ground. The water you take from the Nile will become blood on the ground." Ex 7:19; Lv 13:3-4; Nm 12:10

¹⁰ But Moses replied to the LORD, "Please, Lord, I have never been eloquent — either in the past or recently or since you have been speaking to your servant — because my mouth and my tongue are sluggish."ᴮ Ex 6:12; Jr 1:6

¹¹ The LORD said to him, "Who placed a mouth on humans? Who makes a person mute or deaf, seeing or blind? Is it not I, the LORD? ¹² Now go! I will help you speakᶜ and I will teach you what to say."

¹³ Moses said, "Please, Lord, send someone else."ᴰ

¹⁴ Then the LORD's anger burned against Moses, and he said, "Isn't

ᴬ4:6 A reference to whiteness or flakiness of the skin   ᴮ4:10 Lit heavy of mouth and heavy of tongue
ᶜ4:12 Lit will be with your mouth   ᴰ4:13 Lit send by the hand of whom you will send

Aaron the Levite your brother? I know that he can speak well. And also, he is on his way now to meet you. He will rejoice when he sees you. [15] You will speak with him and tell him what to say. I will help both you and him to speak[A] and will teach you both what to do. [16] He will speak to the people for you. He will serve as a mouth for you, and you will serve as God to him. [17] And take this staff in your hand that you will perform the signs with."   Ex 4:2; 7:1-2; Nm 23:5,12,16

Moses's Return to Egypt

[18] Then Moses went back to his father-in-law Jethro and said to him, "Please let me return to my relatives in Egypt and see if they are still living."

Jethro said to Moses, "Go in peace."

[19] Now in Midian the LORD told Moses, "Return to Egypt, for all the men who wanted to kill you are dead." [20] So Moses took his wife and sons, put them on a donkey, and returned to the land of Egypt. And Moses took God's staff in his hand.

[21] The LORD instructed Moses, "When you go back to Egypt, make sure you do before Pharaoh all the wonders that I have put within your power. But I will harden his heart[B] so that he won't let the people go. [22] And you will say to Pharaoh: This is what the LORD says: Israel is my firstborn son. [23] I told you: Let my son go so that he may worship me, but you refused to let him go. Look, I am about to kill your firstborn son!"   Ex 7:13; 9:12,35; 14:8; Dt 2:30; Jos 11:20

[24] On the trip, at an overnight campsite, it happened that the LORD confronted him and intended

to put him to death. [25] So Zipporah took a flint, cut off her son's foreskin, threw it at Moses's feet, and said, "You are a bridegroom of blood to me!" [26] So he let him alone. At that time she said, "You are a bridegroom of blood," referring to the circumcision.   Gn 17:14

Reunion of Moses and Aaron

[27] Now the LORD had said to Aaron, "Go and meet Moses in the wilderness." So he went and met him at the mountain of God and kissed him. [28] Moses told Aaron everything the LORD had sent him to say, and about all the signs he had commanded him to do. [29] Then Moses and Aaron went and assembled all the elders of the Israelites. [30] Aaron repeated everything the LORD had said to Moses and performed the signs before the people. [31] The people believed, and when they heard that the LORD had paid attention to them and that he had seen their misery, they knelt low and worshiped.   Ex 2:25; 3:1,7,18; 4:14;

Moses Confronts Pharaoh

5 Later, Moses and Aaron went in and said to Pharaoh, "This is what the LORD, the God of Israel, says: Let my people go, so that they may hold a festival for me in the wilderness."   Ex 3:18; 10:9

[2] But Pharaoh responded, "Who is the LORD that I should obey him by letting Israel go? I don't know[C] the LORD, and besides, I will not let Israel go."   Ex 3:19; 1Sm 25:10; Pr 30:9; Jr 9:6

[3] They answered, "The God of the Hebrews has met with us. Please let us go on a three-day trip into the wilderness so that we may sacrifice

[A]4:15 Lit will be with your mouth and with his mouth   [B]4:21 Or will make him stubborn   [C]5:2 Or recognize to the LORD our God, or else he may strike us with plague or sword."

⁴ The king of Egypt said to them, "Moses and Aaron, why are you causing the people to neglect their work? Get to your labor!" ⁵ Pharaoh also said, "Look, the people of the land are so numerous, and you would stop them from their labor." Ex 1:7,9,11; 3:18

Further Oppression of Israel

⁶ That day Pharaoh commanded the overseers of the people as well as their foremen: ⁷ "Don't continue to supply the people with straw for making bricks, as before. They must go and gather straw for themselves. ⁸ But require the same quota of bricks from them as they were making before; do not reduce it. For they are slackers — that is why they are crying out, 'Let us go and sacrifice to our God.' ⁹ Impose heavier work on the men. Then they will be occupied with it and not pay attention to deceptive words." Ex 1:1; 2:23; 3:7; 5:15

¹⁰ So the overseers and foremen of the people went out and said to them, "This is what Pharaoh says: 'I am not giving you straw. ¹¹ Go get straw yourselves wherever you can find it, but there will be no reduction at all in your workload.'" ¹² So the people scattered throughout the land of Egypt to gather stubble for straw. ¹³ The overseers insisted, "Finish your assigned work each day, just as you did when straw was provided." ¹⁴ Then the Israelite foremen, whom Pharaoh's slave drivers had set over the people, were beaten and asked, "Why haven't you finished making your prescribed number of bricks yesterday or today, as you did before?" Ex 4:22; 5:1

¹⁵ So the Israelite foremen went in and cried for help to Pharaoh: "Why are you treating your servants this way? ¹⁶ No straw has been given to your servants, yet they say to us, 'Make bricks!' Look, your servants are being beaten, but it is your own people who are at fault."

¹⁷ But he said, "You are slackers. Slackers! That is why you are saying, 'Let us go sacrifice to the LORD.' ¹⁸ Now get to work. No straw will be given to you, but you must produce the same quantity of bricks."

¹⁹ The Israelite foremen saw that they were in trouble when they were told, "You cannot reduce your daily quota of bricks." ²⁰ When they left Pharaoh, they confronted Moses and Aaron, who stood waiting to meet them.

²¹ "May the LORD take note of you and judge," they said to them, "because you have made us reek to Pharaoh and his officials — putting a sword in their hand to kill us!" Gn 34:30; Ex 6:9; 14:11

²² So Moses went back to the LORD and asked, "Lord, why have you caused trouble for this people? And why did you ever send me? ²³ Ever since I went in to Pharaoh to speak in your name he has caused trouble for this people, and you haven't rescued your people at all." Nm 11:11; Jr 4:10

6 But the LORD replied to Moses, "Now you will see what I will do to Pharaoh: because of a strong hand he will let them go, and because of a strong hand he will drive them from his land." Ex 3:19; 12:31,33,39

God Promises Freedom

² Then God spoke to Moses, telling him, "I am the LORD. ³ I appeared

to Abraham, Isaac, and Jacob as God Almighty, but I was not known to them by my name 'the LORD.'[A] [4] I also established my covenant with them to give them the land of Canaan, the land they lived in as aliens. [5] Furthermore, I have heard the groaning of the Israelites, whom the Egyptians are forcing to work as slaves, and I have remembered my covenant. Gn 17:1

[6] "Therefore tell the Israelites: I am the LORD, and I will bring you out from the forced labor of the Egyptians and rescue you from slavery to them. I will redeem you with an outstretched arm and great acts of judgment. [7] I will take you as my people, and I will be your God. You will know that I am the LORD your God, who brought you out from the forced labor of the Egyptians. [8] I will bring you to the land that I swore[B] to give to Abraham, Isaac, and Jacob, and I will give it to you as a possession. I am the LORD." [9] Moses told this to the Israelites, but they did not listen to him because of their broken spirit and hard labor. Ex 3:17; Dt 7:8; 26:8; 1Ch 17:21

[10] Then the LORD spoke to Moses, [11] "Go and tell Pharaoh king of Egypt to let the Israelites go from his land."

[12] But Moses said in the LORD's presence: "If the Israelites will not listen to me, then how will Pharaoh listen to me, since I am such a poor speaker?"[C] [13] Then the LORD spoke to Moses and Aaron and gave them commands concerning both the Israelites and Pharaoh king of Egypt to bring the Israelites out of the land of Egypt. Ex 4:10; 6:30; Jr 1:6

Genealogy of Moses and Aaron

[14] These are the heads of their fathers' families:

The sons of Reuben,
　the firstborn of Israel: Gn 46:9
Hanoch and Pallu, Hezron
　and Carmi.
These are the clans of Reuben.

[15] The sons of Simeon: Gn 46:10
Jemuel, Jamin, Ohad, Jachin,
Zohar, and Shaul, the son
　of a Canaanite woman.
These are the clans of Simeon.

[16] These are the names
　of the sons of Levi
according to their family
　records;
Gershon, Kohath, and Merari.
Levi lived 137 years.

[17] The sons of Gershon:
Libni and Shimei,
　by their clans.

[18] The sons of Kohath:
Amram, Izhar, Hebron,
　and Uzziel.
Kohath lived 133 years.

[19] The sons of Merari:
Mahli and Mushi.
These are the clans
　of the Levites Nm 3:18-20; 23:21
according to their family
　records.

[20] Amram married
　his father's sister Jochebed,
and she bore him Aaron
　and Moses. Ex 2:1-2; Nm 26:59
Amram lived 137 years.

[21] The sons of Izhar: Nm 16:1
Korah, Nepheg, and Zichri.

[22] The sons of Uzziel:
Mishael, Elzaphan, and Sithri.

[A]6:3 LORD (in small capitals) stands for the personal name of God, which in Hb is *Yahweh*. There is a long tradition of substituting "LORD" for "Yahweh" out of reverence. [B]6:8 Lit *raised my hand* [C]6:12 Lit *I have uncircumcised lips*, also in v. 30

23 Aaron married Elisheba,
daughter of Amminadab
and sister of Nahshon. Mt 1:4
She bore him Nadab
and Abihu, Eleazar
and Ithamar. Lv 10:1; Nm 3:2; 26:60
24 The sons of Korah: Nm 26:11
Assir, Elkanah, and Abiasaph.
These are the clans
of the Korahites.
25 Aaron's son Eleazar married
one of the daughters of Putiel,
and she bore him Phinehas.
These are the heads
of the Levite families
by their clans.

26 It was this Aaron and Moses whom the LORD told, "Bring the Israelites out of the land of Egypt according to their military divisions." 27 Moses and Aaron were the ones who spoke to Pharaoh king of Egypt in order to bring the Israelites out of Egypt. Ex 7:4; 12:17, 51; Nm 33:1

Moses and Aaron Before Pharaoh

28 On the day the LORD spoke to Moses in the land of Egypt, 29 he said to him, "I am the LORD; tell Pharaoh king of Egypt everything I am telling you." Ex 6:11; 7:2
30 But Moses replied in the LORD's presence, "Since I am such a poor speaker, how will Pharaoh listen to me?" Ex 4:10; 6:12

7 The LORD answered Moses, "See, I have made you like God to Pharaoh, and Aaron your brother will be your prophet. 2 You must say whatever I command you; then Aaron your brother must declare it to Pharaoh so that he will let the Israelites go from his land. 3 But I will harden Pharaoh's heart and multiply my signs and wonders in

the land of Egypt. 4 Pharaoh will not listen to you, but I will put my hand into Egypt and bring the military divisions of my people the Israelites out of the land of Egypt by great acts of judgment. 5 The Egyptians will know that I am the LORD when I stretch out my hand against Egypt and bring out the Israelites from among them." Ex 4:21; 6:6; 7:17

6 So Moses and Aaron did this; they did just as the LORD commanded them. 7 Moses was eighty years old and Aaron eighty-three when they spoke to Pharaoh. Dt 29:5; 31:2

8 The LORD said to Moses and Aaron, 9 "When Pharaoh tells you, 'Perform a miracle,' tell Aaron, 'Take your staff and throw it down before Pharaoh. It will become a serpent.'" 10 So Moses and Aaron went in to Pharaoh and did just as the LORD had commanded. Aaron threw down his staff before Pharaoh and his officials, and it became a serpent. 11 But then Pharaoh called the wise men and sorcerers — the magicians of Egypt, and they also did the same thing by their occult practices. 12 Each one threw down his staff, and it became a serpent. But Aaron's staff swallowed their staffs. 13 However, Pharaoh's heart was hard, and he did not listen to them, as the LORD had said. Gn 41:8; Ex 4:2; Is 7:11; Jn 2:18; 6:30

The First Plague: Water Turned to Blood

14 Then the LORD said to Moses, "Pharaoh's heart is hard: He refuses to let the people go. 15 Go to Pharaoh in the morning. When you see him walking out to the water, stand ready to meet him by the bank of the Nile. Take in your hand the staff that turned into a snake.

¹⁶ Tell him: The Lᴏʀᴅ, the God of the Hebrews, has sent me to tell you: Let my people go, so that they may worship[A] me in the wilderness, but so far you have not listened. ¹⁷ This is what the Lᴏʀᴅ says: Here is how you will know that I am the Lᴏʀᴅ. Watch. I am about to strike the water in the Nile with the staff in my hand, and it will turn to blood. ¹⁸ The fish in the Nile will die, the river will stink, and the Egyptians will be unable to drink water from it."

¹⁹ So the Lᴏʀᴅ said to Moses, "Tell Aaron: Take your staff and stretch out your hand over the waters of Egypt — over their rivers, canals, ponds, and all their water reservoirs — and they will become blood. There will be blood throughout the land of Egypt, even in wooden and stone containers." Ex 9:22; 10:12,21

²⁰ Moses and Aaron did just as the Lᴏʀᴅ had commanded; in the sight of Pharaoh and his officials, he raised the staff and struck the water in the Nile, and all the water in the Nile was turned to blood. ²¹ The fish in the Nile died, and the river smelled so bad the Egyptians could not drink water from it. There was blood throughout the land of Egypt. Ex 17:5; Ps 78:44; 105:29

²² But the magicians of Egypt did the same thing by their occult practices. So Pharaoh's heart was hard, and he would not listen to them, as the Lᴏʀᴅ had said. ²³ Pharaoh turned around, went into his palace, and didn't take even this to heart. ²⁴ All the Egyptians dug around the Nile for water to drink because they could not drink the water from the river. ²⁵ Seven days passed after the Lᴏʀᴅ struck the Nile.

^A7:16 Or serve; Ex 4:23

The Second Plague: Frogs

8 Then the Lᴏʀᴅ said to Moses, "Go in to Pharaoh and tell him: This is what the Lᴏʀᴅ says: Let my people go, so that they may worship me. ² But if you refuse to let them go, then I will plague all your territory with frogs. ³ The Nile will swarm with frogs; they will come up and go into your palace, into your bedroom and on your bed, into the houses of your officials and your people, and into your ovens and kneading bowls. ⁴ The frogs will come up on you, your people, and all your officials." Ex 3:12,18; 4:23

⁵ The Lᴏʀᴅ then said to Moses, "Tell Aaron: Stretch out your hand with your staff over the rivers, canals, and ponds, and cause the frogs to come up onto the land of Egypt." ⁶ When Aaron stretched out his hand over the waters of Egypt, the frogs came up and covered the land of Egypt. ⁷ But the magicians did the same thing by their occult practices and brought frogs up onto the land of Egypt. Ex 7:19; 10:6

⁸ Pharaoh summoned Moses and Aaron and said, "Appeal to the Lᴏʀᴅ to remove the frogs from me and my people. Then I will let the people go and they can sacrifice to the Lᴏʀᴅ." Ex 8:28; 9:28; 10:17

⁹ Moses said to Pharaoh, "You may have the honor of choosing. When should I appeal on behalf of you, your officials, and your people, that the frogs be taken away from you and your houses, and remain only in the Nile?"

¹⁰ "Tomorrow," he answered.

Moses replied, "As you have said, so that you may know there is no one like the Lᴏʀᴅ our God, ¹¹ the frogs will go away from you, your houses, your officials, and your people. The frogs will remain only in the Nile." [12] After Moses and Aaron went out from Pharaoh, Moses cried out to the LORD for help concerning the frogs that he had brought against Pharaoh. [13] The LORD did as Moses had said: the frogs in the houses, courtyards, and fields died. [14] They piled them in countless heaps, and there was a terrible odor in the land. [15] But when Pharaoh saw there was relief, he hardened his heart and would not listen to them, as the LORD had said. Ex 9:14; Dt 33:26; 2Sm 7:22; 1Ch 17:20; Is 46:9

The Third Plague: Gnats

[16] Then the LORD said to Moses, "Tell Aaron: Stretch out your staff and strike the dust of the land, and it will become gnats[A] throughout the land of Egypt." [17] And they did this. Aaron stretched out his hand with his staff, and when he struck the dust of the land, gnats were on people and animals. All the dust of the land became gnats throughout the land of Egypt. [18] The magicians tried to produce gnats using their occult practices, but they could not. The gnats remained on people and animals. Ex 7:11; 9:11; Dn 5:8
[19] "This is the finger of God," the magicians said to Pharaoh. But Pharaoh's heart was hard, and he would not listen to them, as the LORD had said. Ps 8:3; Lk 11:20

The Fourth Plague: Swarms of Flies

[20] The LORD said to Moses, "Get up early in the morning and present yourself to Pharaoh when you see him going out to the water. Tell him: This is what the LORD says: Let my people go, so that they may worship[B] me. [21] But if you will not let my people go, then I will send swarms of flies[C] against you, your officials, your people, and your houses. The Egyptians' houses will swarm with flies, and so will the land where they live. [D] [22] But on that day I will give special treatment to the land of Goshen, where my people are living; no flies will be there. This way you will know that I, the LORD, am in the land. [23] I will make a distinction[E] between my people and your people. This sign will take place tomorrow." Ex 2:5; 7:15; 8:1; 9:4,6,13; 10:23
[24] And the LORD did this. Thick swarms of flies went into Pharaoh's palace and his officials' houses. Throughout Egypt the land was ruined because of the swarms of flies. [25] Then Pharaoh summoned Moses and Aaron and said, "Go sacrifice to your God within the country."
[26] But Moses said, "It would not be right[F] to do that, because what we will sacrifice to the LORD our God is detestable to the Egyptians. If we sacrifice what the Egyptians detest in front of them, won't they stone us? [27] We must go a distance of three days into the wilderness and sacrifice to the LORD our God as he instructs us." Gn 43:32; 46:34
[28] Pharaoh responded, "I will let you go and sacrifice to the LORD your God in the wilderness, but don't go very far. Make an appeal for me." Ex 8:8; 9:28; 1Kg 13:6
[29] "As soon as I leave you," Moses said, "I will appeal to the LORD, and tomorrow the swarms of flies will depart from Pharaoh, his officials, and his people. But Pharaoh

---

A8:16 Perhaps sand fleas or mosquitoes　B8:20 Or serve　C8:21 Or insects　D8:21 Lit are　E8:23 LXX, Syr, Vg; MT reads will place redemption　F8:26 Or allowable must not act deceptively again by refusing to let the people go and sacrifice to the LORD." ³⁰ Then Moses left Pharaoh's presence and appealed to the LORD. ³¹ The LORD did as Moses had said: He removed the swarms of flies from Pharaoh, his officials, and his people; not one was left. ³² But Pharaoh hardened his heart this time also and did not let the people go.

The Fifth Plague: Death of Livestock

9 Then the LORD said to Moses, "Go in to Pharaoh and say to him: This is what the LORD, the God of the Hebrews, says: Let my people go, so that they may worship me. ² But if you refuse to let them go and keep holding them, ³ then the LORD's hand will bring a severe plague against your livestock in the field — the horses, donkeys, camels, herds, and flocks. ⁴ But the LORD will make a distinction between the livestock of Israel and the livestock of Egypt, so that nothing of all that the Israelites own will die." ⁵ And the LORD set a time, saying, "Tomorrow the LORD will do this thing in the land." ⁶ The LORD did this the next day. All the Egyptian livestock died, but none among the Israelite livestock died. ⁷ Pharaoh sent messengers who saw that not a single one of the Israelite livestock was dead. But Pharaoh's heart was hard, and he did not let the people go.

The Sixth Plague: Boils

⁸ Then the LORD said to Moses and Aaron, "Take handfuls of furnace soot, and Moses is to throw it toward heaven in the sight of Pharaoh. ⁹ It will become fine dust over the entire land of Egypt. It will become festering boils on people and animals throughout the land of Egypt." ¹⁰ So they took furnace soot and stood before Pharaoh. Moses threw it toward heaven, and it became festering boils on people and animals. ¹¹ The magicians could not stand before Moses because of the boils, for the boils were on the magicians as well as on all the Egyptians. ¹² But the LORD hardened Pharaoh's heart and he did not listen to them, as the LORD had told Moses.

The Seventh Plague: Hail

¹³ Then the LORD said to Moses, "Get up early in the morning and present yourself to Pharaoh. Tell him: This is what the LORD, the God of the Hebrews says: Let my people go, so that they may worship me. ¹⁴ For this time I am about to send all my plagues against you,ᴬ your officials, and your people. Then you will know there is no one like me on the whole earth. ¹⁵ By now I could have stretched out my hand and struck you and your people with a plague, and you would have been obliterated from the earth. ¹⁶ However, I have let you live for this purpose: to show you my power and to make my name known on the whole earth. ¹⁷ You are still acting arrogantly againstᴮ my people by not letting them go. ¹⁸ Tomorrow at this time I will rain down the worst hail that has ever occurred in Egypt from the day it was founded until now. ¹⁹ Therefore give orders to bring your livestock and all that you have in the field into shelters. Every person and animal that is in the field and not brought inside will die when the hail falls on

ᴬ9:14 Lit *plagues to your heart*   ᴮ9:17 Or *still obstructing* them." ²⁰ Those among Pharaoh's officials who feared the word of the LORD made their servants and livestock flee to shelters, ²¹ but those who didn't take to heart the LORD's word left their servants and livestock in the field. Ex 3:20; 8:10,20; 14:17

²² Then the LORD said to Moses, "Stretch out your hand toward heaven and let there be hail throughout the land of Egypt — on people and animals and every plant of the field in the land of Egypt." ²³ So Moses stretched out his staff toward heaven, and the LORD sent thunder and hail. Lightning struck the land, and the LORD rained hail on the land of Egypt. ²⁴ The hail, with lightning flashing through it, was so severe that nothing like it had occurred in the land of Egypt since it had become a nation. ²⁵ Throughout the land of Egypt, the hail struck down everything in the field, both people and animals. The hail beat down every plant of the field and shattered every tree in the field. ²⁶ The only place it didn't hail was in the land of Goshen, where the Israelites were.

²⁷ Pharaoh sent for Moses and Aaron. "I have sinned this time," he said to them. "The LORD is the righteous one, and I and my people are the guilty ones. ²⁸ Make an appeal to the LORD. There has been enough of God's thunder and hail. I will let you go; you don't need to stay any longer." Ex 10:16; 2Ch 12:6; Ps 129:4

²⁹ Moses said to him, "When I have left the city, I will spread out my hands to the LORD. The thunder will cease, and there will be no more hail, so that you may know the earthᴬ belongs to the LORD.

³⁰ But as for you and your officials, I know that you still do not fear the LORD God." 1Kg 8:22,38; Ps 24:1; 143:6; Is 1:15

³¹ The flax and the barley were destroyed because the barley was ripeᴮ and the flax was budding, ³² but the wheat and the spelt were not destroyed since they are later crops.ᶜ Ru 1:22; 2:23

³³ Moses left Pharaoh and the city, and spread out his hands to the LORD. Then the thunder and hail ceased, and rain no longer poured down on the land. ³⁴ When Pharaoh saw that the rain, hail, and thunder had ceased, he sinned again and hardened his heart, he and his officials. ³⁵ So Pharaoh's heart was hard, and he did not let the Israelites go, as the LORD had said through Moses.

The Eighth Plague: Locusts

10 Then the LORD said to Moses, "Go to Pharaoh, for I have hardened his heart and the hearts of his officials so that I may do these miraculous signs of mine among them,ᴰ ² and so that you may tellᴱ your son and grandson how severely I dealt with the Egyptians and performed miraculous signs among them, and you will know that I am the LORD." Ex 4:21; 7:4,13; Dt 4:9

³ So Moses and Aaron went in to Pharaoh and told him, "This is what the LORD, the God of the Hebrews, says: How long will you refuse to humble yourself before me? Let my people go, that they may worship me. ⁴ But if you refuse to let my people go, then tomorrow I will bring locusts into your territory. ⁵ They will cover the surface of the land so that no one will be able to see the land.

ᴬ**9:29** Or land   ᴮ**9:31** Lit was ears of grain   ᶜ**9:32** Lit are late   ᴰ**10:1** Lit mine in his midst   ᴱ**10:2** Lit tell in the ears of

They will eat the remainder left to you that escaped the hail; they will eat every tree you have growing in the fields. [6] They will fill your houses, all your officials' houses, and the houses of all the Egyptians — something your fathers and grandfathers never saw since the time they occupied the land until today." Then he turned and left Pharaoh's presence.   Jms 4:10

[7] Pharaoh's officials asked him, "How long must this man be a snare to us? Let the men go, so that they may worship the LORD their God. Don't you realize yet that Egypt is devastated?"   Ex 23:33; Jos 23:13; 1Sm 18:21

[8] So Moses and Aaron were brought back to Pharaoh. "Go, worship the LORD your God," Pharaoh said. "But exactly who will be going?"

[9] Moses replied, "We will go with our young and with our old; we will go with our sons and with our daughters, with our flocks and with our herds because we must hold the LORD's festival."   Ex 5:1; 8:8

[10] He said to them, "The LORD would have to be with you if I would ever let you and your families go! Look out — you're heading for trouble. [11] No, go — just able-bodied men — worship the LORD, since that's what you want." And they were driven from Pharaoh's presence.

[12] The LORD then said to Moses, "Stretch out your hand over the land of Egypt, and the locusts will come up over it and eat every plant in the land, everything that the hail left." [13] So Moses stretched out his staff over the land of Egypt, and the LORD sent an east wind over the land all that day and through the night. By morning the east wind

had brought in the locusts. [14] The locusts went up over the entire land of Egypt and settled on the whole territory of Egypt. Never before had there been such a large number of locusts, and there never will be again. [15] They covered the surface of the whole land so that the land was black, and they consumed all the plants on the ground and all the fruit on the trees that the hail had left. Nothing green was left on the trees or the plants in the field throughout the land of Egypt.

[16] Pharaoh urgently sent for Moses and Aaron and said, "I have sinned against the LORD your God and against you. [17] Please forgive my sin once more and make an appeal to the LORD your God, so that he will just take this death away from me." [18] Moses left Pharaoh's presence and appealed to the LORD. [19] Then the LORD changed the wind to a strong west[A] wind, and it carried off the locusts and blew them into the Red Sea. Not a single locust was left in all the territory of Egypt. [20] But the LORD hardened Pharaoh's heart, and he did not let the Israelites go.   Ex 8:8,30; 9:27; 13:18; 15:4,22; 23:31

The Ninth Plague: Darkness

[21] Then the LORD said to Moses, "Stretch out your hand toward heaven, and there will be darkness over the land of Egypt, a darkness that can be felt." [22] So Moses stretched out his hand toward heaven, and there was thick darkness throughout the land of Egypt for three days. [23] One person could not see another, and for three days they did not move from where they were. Yet all the Israelites had light where they lived.   Ex 8:22; Ps 105:28

²⁴ Pharaoh summoned Moses and said, "Go, worship the LORD. Even your families may go with you; only your flocks and herds must stay behind."

²⁵ Moses responded, "You must also let us have^A sacrifices and burnt offerings to prepare for the LORD our God. ²⁶ Even our livestock must go with us; not a hoof will be left behind because we will take some of them to worship the LORD our God. We will not know what we will use to worship the LORD until we get there."

²⁷ But the LORD hardened Pharaoh's heart, and he was unwilling to let them go. ²⁸ Pharaoh said to him, "Leave me! Make sure you never see my face again, for on the day you see my face, you will die."

²⁹ "As you have said," Moses replied, "I will never see your face again."   Heb 11:27

The Tenth Plague: Death of the Firstborn

11 The LORD said^B to Moses, "I will bring one more plague on Pharaoh and on Egypt. After that, he will let you go from here. When he lets you go, ^C he will drive you out of here. ² Now announce to the people that both men and women should ask their neighbors for silver and gold items." ³ The LORD gave^D the people favor with the Egyptians. In addition, Moses himself was very highly regarded^E in the land of Egypt by^F Pharaoh's officials and the people.   Ex 3:21-22

⁴ So Moses said, "This is what the LORD says: About midnight I will go throughout Egypt, ⁵ and every firstborn male in the land of Egypt will die, from the firstborn of Pharaoh who sits on his throne to the firstborn of the servant girl who is at the grindstones, as well as every firstborn of the livestock. ⁶ Then there will be a great cry of anguish through all the land of Egypt such as never was before or ever will be again. ⁷ But against all the Israelites, whether people or animals, not even a dog will snarl, ^G so that you may know that the LORD makes a distinction between Egypt and Israel. ⁸ All these officials of yours will come down to me and bow before me, saying: Get out, you and all the people who follow you. ^H After that, I will get out." And he went out from Pharaoh's presence fiercely angry.   Ex 12:3; Am 5:17

⁹ The LORD said to Moses, "Pharaoh will not listen to you, so that my wonders may be multiplied in the land of Egypt." ¹⁰ Moses and Aaron did all these wonders before Pharaoh, but the LORD hardened Pharaoh's heart, and he would not let the Israelites go out of his land.

Instructions for the Passover

12 The LORD said to Moses and Aaron in the land of Egypt: ² "This month is to be the beginning of months for you; it is the first month of your year. ³ Tell the whole community of Israel that on the tenth day of this month they must each select an animal of the flock according to their fathers' families, one animal per family. ⁴ If the household is too small for a whole animal, that person and the neighbor nearest his house are to select one

---

^A10:25 Lit *also give in our hand*   ^B11:1 Or *had said*   ^C11:1 Or *go, it will be finished* —   ^D11:3 Or *had given*   ^E11:3 Lit *was very great*   ^F11:3 Or *in the eyes of*   ^G11:7 Lit *point its tongue*   ^H11:8 Lit *people at your feet* based on the combined number of people; you should apportion the animal according to what each will eat. ⁵ You must have an unblemished animal, a year-old male; you may take it from either the sheep or the goats. ⁶ You are to keep it until the fourteenth day of this month; then the whole assembly of the community of Israel will slaughter the animals at twilight. ⁷ They must take some of the blood and put it on the two doorposts and the lintel of the houses where they eat them. ⁸ They are to eat the meat that night; they should eat it, roasted over the fire along with unleavened bread and bitter herbs. ⁹ Do not eat any of it raw or cooked in boiling ᴬ water, but only roasted over fire — its head as well as its legs and inner organs. ¹⁰ You must not leave any of it until morning; any part of it left until morning you must burn. ¹¹ Here is how you must eat it: You must be dressed for travel, ᴮ your sandals on your feet, and your staff in your hand. You are to eat it in a hurry; it is the Lᴏʀᴅ's Passover. Ex 13:4; 23:15; 34:18; Lv 22:19-21; Dt 16:1

¹² "I will pass through the land of Egypt on that night and strike every firstborn male in the land of Egypt, both people and animals. I am the Lᴏʀᴅ; I will execute judgments against all the gods of Egypt. ¹³ The blood on the houses where you are staying will be a distinguishing mark for you; when I see the blood, I will pass over you. No plague will be among you to destroy you when I strike the land of Egypt. Ex 6:2; 11:4-5; Nm 33:4; Am 5:17

¹⁴ "This day is to be a memorial for you, and you must celebrate it as a festival to the Lᴏʀᴅ. You are to celebrate it throughout your generations as a permanent statute. ¹⁵ You must eat unleavened bread for seven days. On the first day you must remove yeast from your houses. Whoever eats what is leavened from the first day through the seventh day must be cut off from Israel. ¹⁶ You are to hold a sacred assembly on the first day and another sacred assembly on the seventh day. No work may be done on those days except for preparing what people need to eat — you may do only that. Ex 12:17,43; 13:9-10

¹⁷ "You are to observe the Festival of Unleavened Bread because on this very day I brought your military divisions out of the land of Egypt. You must observe this day throughout your generations as a permanent statute. ¹⁸ You are to eat unleavened bread in the first month, from the evening of the fourteenth day of the month until the evening of the twenty-first day. ¹⁹ Yeast must not be found in your houses for seven days. If anyone eats something leavened, that person, whether a resident alien or native of the land, must be cut off from the community of Israel. ²⁰ Do not eat anything leavened; eat unleavened bread in all your homes." ᶜ

²¹ Then Moses summoned all the elders of Israel and said to them, "Go, select an animal from the flock according to your families, and slaughter the Passover animal. ²² Take a cluster of hyssop, dip it in the blood that is in the basin, and brush the lintel and the two doorposts with some of the blood in the basin. None of you may go out the door of his house until morning. ²³ When the Lᴏʀᴅ passes through to strike Egypt and sees the blood

---

ᴬ**12:9** Or *or boiled at all in*   ᴮ**12:11** Lit *must have your waist girded*   ᶜ**12:20** Or *settlements* on the lintel and the two doorposts, he will pass over the door and not let the destroyer enter your houses to strike you. Ex 12:3,7; Mk 14:12-16

²⁴ "Keep this command permanently as a statute for you and your descendants. ²⁵ When you enter the land that the LORD will give you as he promised, you are to observe this ceremony. ²⁶ When your children ask you, 'What does this ceremony mean to you?' ²⁷ you are to reply, 'It is the Passover sacrifice to the LORD, for he passed over the houses of the Israelites in Egypt when he struck the Egyptians and spared our homes.'" So the people knelt low and worshiped. ²⁸ Then the Israelites went and did this; they did just as the LORD had commanded Moses and Aaron. Ex 10:2

The Exodus

²⁹ Now at midnight the LORD struck every firstborn male in the land of Egypt, from the firstborn of Pharaoh who sat on his throne to the firstborn of the prisoner who was in the dungeon, and every firstborn of the livestock. ³⁰ During the night Pharaoh got up, he along with all his officials and all the Egyptians, and there was a loud wailing throughout Egypt because there wasn't a house without someone dead. ³¹ He summoned Moses and Aaron during the night and said, "Get out immediately from among my people, both you and the Israelites, and go, worship the LORD as you have said. ³² Take even your flocks and your herds as you asked and leave, and also bless me." Ex 4:23

³³ Now the Egyptians pressured the people in order to send them quickly out of the country, for they said, "We're all going to die!" ³⁴ So the people took their dough before it was leavened, with their kneading bowls wrapped up in their clothes on their shoulders.

³⁵ The Israelites acted on Moses's word and asked the Egyptians for silver and gold items and for clothing. ³⁶ And the LORD gave the people such favor with the Egyptians that they gave them what they requested. In this way they plundered the Egyptians. Gn 15:14; Ex 3:21; Ps 105:37

³⁷ The Israelites traveled from Rameses to Succoth, about six hundred thousand able-bodied men on foot, besides their families. ³⁸ A mixed crowd also went up with them, along with a huge number of livestock, both flocks and herds. ³⁹ The people baked the dough they had brought out of Egypt into unleavened loaves, since it had no yeast; for when they were driven out of Egypt, they could not delay and had not prepared provisions for themselves. Gn 47:11; Nm 1:46; 33:3,5

⁴⁰ The time that the Israelites lived in Egypt ᴬ was 430 years. ⁴¹ At the end of 430 years, on that same day, all the LORD's military divisions went out from the land of Egypt. ⁴² It was a night of vigil in honor of the LORD, because he would bring them out of the land of Egypt. This same night is in honor of the LORD, a night vigil for all the Israelites throughout their generations.

Passover Instruction

⁴³ The LORD said to Moses and Aaron, "This is the statute of the Passover: no foreigner may eat it. ⁴⁴ But any slave a man has purchased may eat it, after you have circumcised him. ⁴⁵ A temporary resident

ᴬ**12:40** LXX, Sam add *and in Canaan*

or hired worker may not eat the Passover. ⁴⁶ It is to be eaten in one house. You may not take any of the meat outside the house, and you may not break any of its bones. ⁴⁷ The whole community of Israel must celebrate ᴬ it. ⁴⁸ If an alien resides among you and wants to observe the Lᴏʀᴅ's Passover, every male in his household must be circumcised, and then he may participate; ᴮ he will become like a native of the land. But no uncircumcised person may eat it. ⁴⁹ The same law will apply to both the native and the alien who resides among you."

⁵⁰ Then all the Israelites did this; they did just as the Lᴏʀᴅ had commanded Moses and Aaron. ⁵¹ On that same day the Lᴏʀᴅ brought the Israelites out of the land of Egypt according to their military divisions.   Ex 6:26; 12:41

13 The Lᴏʀᴅ spoke to Moses: ² "Consecrate every firstborn male to me, the firstborn from every womb among the Israelites, both man and domestic animal; it is mine."   Ex 13:12-13,15; 22:29-30; Nm 3:13

³ Then Moses said to the people, "Remember this day when you came out of Egypt, out of the place of slavery, for the Lᴏʀᴅ brought you out of here by the strength of his hand. Nothing leavened may be eaten. ⁴ Today, in the month of Abib, ᶜ you are going out. ⁵ When the Lᴏʀᴅ brings you into the land of the Canaanites, Hethites, Amorites, Hivites, and Jebusites, ᴰ which he swore to your fathers that he would give you, a land flowing with milk and honey, you must carry out this ceremony in this month. ⁶ For seven days you must eat unleavened bread, and on the seventh day there is to be a festival to the Lᴏʀᴅ. ⁷ Unleavened bread is to be eaten for those seven days. Nothing leavened may be found among you, and no yeast may be found among you in all your territory. ⁸ On that day explain to your son, 'This is because of what the Lᴏʀᴅ did for me when I came out of Egypt.' ⁹ Let it serve as a sign for you on your hand and as a reminder on your forehead, ᴱ so that the Lᴏʀᴅ's instruction may be in your mouth; for the Lᴏʀᴅ brought you out of Egypt with a strong hand. ¹⁰ Keep this statute at its appointed time from year to year.   Ex 6:1; 33:3

¹¹ "When the Lᴏʀᴅ brings you into the land of the Canaanites, as he swore to you and your fathers, and gives it to you, ¹² you are to present to the Lᴏʀᴅ every firstborn male of the womb. All firstborn offspring of the livestock you own that are males will be the Lᴏʀᴅ's. ¹³ You must redeem every firstborn of a donkey with a flock animal, but if you do not redeem it, break its neck. However, you must redeem every firstborn among your sons.   Ex 34:20

¹⁴ "In the future, when your son asks you, 'What does this mean?' say to him, 'By the strength of his hand the Lᴏʀᴅ brought us out of Egypt, out of the place of slavery. ¹⁵ When Pharaoh stubbornly refused to let us go, the Lᴏʀᴅ killed every firstborn male in the land of Egypt, both the firstborn of humans and the firstborn of livestock. That is why I sacrifice to the Lᴏʀᴅ all the firstborn of the

---

ᴬ 12:47 Lit *do*   ᴮ 12:48 Lit *may come near to do it*   ᶜ 13:4 March–April; called Nisan in the post-exilic period; Neh 2:1; Est 3:7   ᴰ 13:5 DSS, Sam, LXX, Syr add *Girgashites* and *Perizzites*; Jos 3:10   ᴱ 13:9 Lit *reminder between your eyes* womb that are males, but I redeem all the firstborn of my sons.' [16] So let it be a sign on your hand and a symbol[A] on your forehead, for the LORD brought us out of Egypt by the strength of his hand." Ex12:26-27

The Route of the Exodus

[17] When Pharaoh let the people go, God did not lead them along the road to the land of the Philistines, even though it was nearby; for God said, "The people will change their minds and return to Egypt if they face war." [18] So he led the people around toward the Red Sea along the road of the wilderness. And the Israelites left the land of Egypt in battle formation. Ex14:11; Nm 14:1-4

[19] Moses took the bones of Joseph with him, because Joseph had made the Israelites swear a solemn oath, saying, "God will certainly come to your aid; then you must take my bones with you from this place."

[20] They set out from Succoth and camped at Etham on the edge of the wilderness. [21] The LORD went ahead of them in a pillar of cloud to lead them on their way during the day and in a pillar of fire to give them light at night, so that they could travel day or night. [22] The pillar of cloud by day and the pillar of fire by night never left its place in front of the people. Ex14:19; Nm 9:15-16; Dt 1:33

14 Then the LORD spoke to Moses: [2] "Tell the Israelites to turn back and camp in front of Pi-hahiroth, between Migdol and the sea; you must camp in front of Baal-zephon, facing it by the sea. [3] Pharaoh will say of the Israelites: They are wandering around the land in confusion; the wilderness has boxed them in. [4] I will harden Pharaoh's heart so that he will pursue them. Then I will receive glory by means of Pharaoh and all his army, and the Egyptians will know that I am the LORD." So the Israelites did this. Ex 4:21; 13:18; Nm 33:7; Jr 44:1

The Egyptian Pursuit

[5] When the king of Egypt was told that the people had fled, Pharaoh and his officials changed their minds about the people and said: "What have we done? We have released Israel from serving us." [6] So he got his chariot ready and took his troops[B] with him; [7] he took six hundred of the best chariots and all the rest of the chariots of Egypt, with officers in each one. [8] The LORD hardened the heart of Pharaoh king of Egypt, and he pursued the Israelites, who were going out defiantly.[C] [9] The Egyptians — all Pharaoh's horses and chariots, his horsemen,[D] and his army — chased after them and caught up with them as they camped by the sea beside Pi-hahiroth, in front of Baal-zephon. Ex6:1

[10] As Pharaoh approached, the Israelites looked up and there were the Egyptians coming after them! The Israelites were terrified and cried out to the LORD for help. [11] They said to Moses: "Is it because there are no graves in Egypt that you have taken us away to die in the wilderness? What have you done to us by bringing us out of Egypt? [12] Isn't this what we told you in Egypt: Leave us alone so that we may serve the Egyptians? It would have been better for us to serve the Egyptians than to die in the wilderness."

[13] But Moses said to the people, "Don't be afraid. Stand firm and see the LORD's salvation that he

---

A **13:16** Or *phylactery*   B **14:6** Lit *people*   C **14:8** Lit *with a raised hand*   D **14:9** Or *chariot drivers* will accomplish for you today; for the Egyptians you see today, you will never see again. ¹⁴ The LORD will fight for you, and you must be quiet."

Escape Through the Red Sea

¹⁵ The LORD said to Moses, "Why are you crying out to me? Tell the Israelites to break camp. ¹⁶ As for you, lift up your staff, stretch out your hand over the sea, and divide it so that the Israelites can go through the sea on dry ground. ¹⁷ As for me, I am going to harden the hearts of the Egyptians so that they will go in after them, and I will receive glory by means of Pharaoh, all his army, and his chariots and horsemen. ¹⁸ The Egyptians will know that I am the LORD when I receive glory through Pharaoh, his chariots, and his horsemen." Ex 4:17; Nm 20:8-9; Is 10:26

¹⁹ Then the angel of God, who was going in front of the Israelite forces, moved and went behind them. The pillar of cloud moved from in front of them and stood behind them. ²⁰ It came between the Egyptian and Israelite forces. There was cloud and darkness, it lit up the night, and neither group came near the other all night long.

²¹ Then Moses stretched out his hand over the sea. The LORD drove the sea back with a powerful east wind all that night and turned the sea into dry land. So the waters were divided, ²² and the Israelites went through the sea on dry ground, with the waters like a wall to them on their right and their left.

²³ The Egyptians set out in pursuit — all Pharaoh's horses, his chariots, and his horsemen — and went into the sea after them.

²⁴ During the morning watch, the LORD looked down at the Egyptian forces from the pillar of fire and cloud, and threw the Egyptian forces into confusion. ²⁵ He caused their chariot wheels to swerve^A,B and made them drive^C with difficulty. "Let's get away from Israel," the Egyptians said, "because the LORD is fighting for them against Egypt!" Ex 13:21; Nm 14:14; Neh 9:12

²⁶ Then the LORD said to Moses, "Stretch out your hand over the sea so that the water may come back on the Egyptians, on their chariots and horsemen." ²⁷ So Moses stretched out his hand over the sea, and at daybreak the sea returned to its normal depth. While the Egyptians were trying to escape from it, the LORD threw them into the sea. ²⁸ The water came back and covered the chariots and horsemen, plus the entire army of Pharaoh that had gone after them into the sea. Not even one of them survived. ²⁹ But the Israelites had walked through the sea on dry ground, with the waters like a wall to them on their right and their left. ³⁰ That day the LORD saved Israel from the power of the Egyptians, and Israel saw the Egyptians dead on the seashore. ³¹ When Israel saw the great power that the LORD used against the Egyptians, the people feared the LORD and believed in him and in his servant Moses. Ps 106:12; Jn 2:11

Israel's Song

15 Then Moses and the Israelites sang this song to the LORD. They said:

> I will sing to the LORD,
>   for he is highly exalted;

---

^A14:25 Sam, LXX, Syr read *He bound their chariot wheels*   ^B14:25 Or *fall off*   ^C14:25 Or *and they drove them*

he has thrown the horse
and its rider into the sea.
2 The LORD is my strength
and my song;[A]
he has become my salvation.
This is my God,
and I will praise him,
my father's God,
and I will exalt him.   Gn 28:21
3 The LORD is a warrior;   Ps 24:8
the LORD is his name.   Ex 6:3

4 He threw Pharaoh's chariots
and his army into the sea;
the elite of his officers
were drowned in the Red Sea.
5 The floods covered them;
they sank to the depths
like a stone.   Ex 14:28; 15:10; Neh 9:11
6 LORD, your right hand
is glorious in power.
LORD, your right hand
shattered the enemy.
7 You overthrew
your adversaries
by your great majesty.
You unleashed
your burning wrath;
it consumed them
like stubble.   Dt 33:26; Is 5:24
8 The water heaped
up at the blast
from your nostrils;   Ex 14:21
the currents stood firm
like a dam.
The watery depths congealed
in the heart of the sea.
9 The enemy said:
"I will pursue, I will overtake,
I will divide the spoil.   Ex 14:9
My desire will be gratified
at their expense.
I will draw my sword;
my hand will destroy[B] them."
10 But you blew
with your breath,

and the sea covered them.
They sank like lead
in the mighty waters.
11 LORD, who is like you
among the gods?
Who is like you, glorious
in holiness,   Dt 3:24; 1Kg 8:23
revered with praises,
performing wonders?   Is 6:3
12 You stretched out
your right hand,
and the earth
swallowed them.
13 With your faithful love,
you will lead the people
you have redeemed;
you will guide them
to your holy dwelling
with your strength.   Ps 77:15,20

14 When the peoples hear,
they will shudder;
anguish will seize
the inhabitants of Philistia.
15 Then the chiefs of Edom
will be terrified;   Gn 36:15,40
trembling will seize
the leaders of Moab;
all the inhabitants of Canaan
will panic;
16 terror and dread will fall
on them.   Ex 23:27; Jos 2:9
They will be as still[C] as a stone
because of
your powerful arm
until your people pass by,
LORD,
until the people
whom you purchased[D]
pass by.   1Sm 25:37; Ps 74:2; 1Pt 2:9
17 You will bring them in
and plant them
on the mountain
of your possession;   Ps 44:2

A 15:2 Or might   B 15:9 Or conquer   C 15:16 Or silent   D 15:16 Or created

Lord, you have prepared
the place
for your dwelling;
Lord, [A] your hands
have established
the sanctuary.
18 The Lord will reign forever
and ever!   Ps 10:16; 29:10; Is 57:15

19 When Pharaoh's horses with his chariots and horsemen went into the sea, the Lord brought the water of the sea back over them. But the Israelites walked through the sea on dry ground. 20 Then the prophetess Miriam, Aaron's sister, took a tambourine in her hand, and all the women came out following her with tambourines and dancing. 21 Miriam sang to them: Nm 26:59

Sing to the Lord,
for he is highly exalted;
he has thrown the horse
and its rider into the sea.

Water Provided

22 Then Moses led Israel on from the Red Sea, and they went out to the Wilderness of Shur. They journeyed for three days in the wilderness without finding water. 23 They came to Marah, but they could not drink the water at Marah because it was bitter — that is why it was named Marah. [B] 24 The people grumbled to Moses, "What are we going to drink?" 25 So he cried out to the Lord, and the Lord showed him a tree. When he threw it into the water, the water became drinkable.

The Lord made a statute and ordinance for them at Marah, and he tested them there. 26 He said, "If you will carefully obey the Lord your God, do what is right in his sight, pay attention to his commands, and keep all his statutes, I will not inflict any illnesses on you that I inflicted on the Egyptians. For I am the Lord who heals you."   Ex 14:10

27 Then they came to Elim, where there were twelve springs and seventy date palms, and they camped there by the water.

Manna and Quail Provided

16 The entire Israelite community departed from Elim and came to the Wilderness of Sin, which is between Elim and Sinai, on the fifteenth day of the second month after they had left the land of Egypt. 2 The entire Israelite community grumbled against Moses and Aaron in the wilderness. 3 The Israelites said to them, "If only we had died by the Lord's hand in the land of Egypt, when we sat by pots of meat and ate all the bread we wanted. Instead, you brought us into this wilderness to make this whole assembly die of hunger!"

4 Then the Lord said to Moses, "I am going to rain bread from heaven for you. The people are to go out each day and gather enough for that day. This way I will test them to see whether or not they will follow my instructions. 5 On the sixth day, when they prepare what they bring in, it will be twice as much as they gather on other days." [C]   Dt 8:2

6 So Moses and Aaron said to all the Israelites: "This evening you will know that it was the Lord who brought you out of the land of Egypt, 7 and in the morning you will see the Lord's glory because he has heard your complaints about him. For who are we that you complain

A **15:17** Some Hb mss, DSS, Sam, Tg read LORD   B **15:23** = Bitter or Bitterness   C **16:5** Lit as gathering day to day about us?'" ⁸ Moses continued, "The LORD will give you meat to eat this evening and all the bread you want in the morning, for he has heard the complaints that you are raising against him. Who are we? Your complaints are not against us but against the LORD." Ex 6:7; Nm 16:28-30

⁹ Then Moses told Aaron, "Say to the entire Israelite community, 'Come before the LORD, for he has heard your complaints.'" ¹⁰ As Aaron was speaking to the entire Israelite community, they turned toward the wilderness, and there in a cloud the LORD's glory appeared.

¹¹ The LORD spoke to Moses, ¹² "I have heard the complaints of the Israelites. Tell them: At twilight you will eat meat, and in the morning you will eat bread until you are full. Then you will know that I am the LORD your God."

¹³ So at evening quail came and covered the camp. In the morning there was a layer of dew all around the camp. ¹⁴ When the layer of dew evaporated, there were fine flakes on the desert surface, as fine as frost on the ground. ¹⁵ When the Israelites saw it, they asked one another, "What is it?" because they didn't know what it was. Nm 11:9,31

Moses told them, "It is the bread the LORD has given you to eat. ¹⁶ This is what the LORD has commanded: 'Gather as much of it as each person needs to eat. You may take two quarts ᴬ per individual, according to the number of people each of you has in his tent.'" Ex 16:4; Jn 6:31

¹⁷ So the Israelites did this. Some gathered a lot, some a little. ¹⁸ When they measured it by quarts, ᴮ the person who gathered a lot had no surplus, and the person who gathered a little had no shortage. Each gathered as much as he needed to eat. ¹⁹ Moses said to them, "No one is to let any of it remain until morning." ²⁰ But they didn't listen to Moses; some people left part of it until morning, and it bred worms and stank. Therefore Moses was angry with them. 2Co 8:15

²¹ They gathered it every morning. Each gathered as much as he needed to eat, but when the sun grew hot, it melted. ²² On the sixth day they gathered twice as much food, four quarts ᶜ apiece, and all the leaders of the community came and reported this to Moses. ²³ He told them, "This is what the LORD has said: 'Tomorrow is a day of complete rest, a holy Sabbath to the LORD. Bake what you want to bake, and boil what you want to boil, and set aside everything left over to be kept until morning.'" Gn 2:3; Ex 20:8; 35:3

²⁴ So they set it aside until morning as Moses commanded, and it didn't stink or have maggots in it. ²⁵ "Eat it today," Moses said, "because today is a Sabbath to the LORD. Today you won't find any in the field. ²⁶ For six days you will gather it, but on the seventh day, the Sabbath, there will be none."

²⁷ Yet on the seventh day some of the people went out to gather, but they did not find any. ²⁸ Then the LORD said to Moses, "How long will you ᴰ refuse to keep my commands and instructions? ²⁹ Understand that the LORD has given you the Sabbath; therefore on the sixth day he will give you two days' worth of bread. Each of you stay where you are; no one is to leave his

ᴬ16:16 Lit an omer   ᴮ16:18 Lit by an omer   ᶜ16:22 Lit two omers   ᴰ16:28 The Hb word for you is pl, referring to the whole nation.

place on the seventh day." ³⁰ So the people rested on the seventh day.

³¹ The house of Israel named the substance manna.ᴬ It resembled coriander seed, was white, and tasted like wafers made with honey. ³² Moses said, "This is what the LORD has commanded: 'Two quartsᴮ of it are to be preserved throughout your generations, so that they may see the bread I fed you in the wilderness when I brought you out of the land of Egypt.'" Ex 16:14; Nm 11:7

³³ Moses told Aaron, "Take a container and put two quartsᶜ of manna in it. Then place it before the LORD to be preserved throughout your generations." ³⁴ As the LORD commanded Moses, Aaron placed it before the testimony to be preserved. Ex 25:16,21; 27:21; 40:20; Nm 17:10

³⁵ The Israelites ate manna for forty years, until they came to an inhabited land. They ate manna until they reached the border of the land of Canaan. ³⁶ (They used a measure called an omer, which held two quarts.ᴰ) Jos 5:12; Neh 9:20-21

Water from the Rock

17 The entire Israelite community left the Wilderness of Sin, moving from one place to the next according to the LORD's command. They camped at Rephidim, but there was no water for the people to drink. ² So the people complained to Moses, "Give us water to drink." Ex 16:1; Nm 33:12,14

"Why are you complaining to me?" Moses replied to them. "Why are you testing the LORD?" Nm 20:3

³ But the people thirsted there for water and grumbled against Moses.

They said, "Why did you ever bring us up from Egypt to kill us and our children and our livestock with thirst?" Ex 15:24; 16:2,7-8; Nm 14:2,27,29,36; 16:11

⁴ Then Moses cried out to the LORD, "What should I do with these people? In a little while they will stone me!" Nm 14:10; 1Sm 30:6; Jn 8:59; 10:31

⁵ The LORD answered Moses, "Go on ahead of the people and take some of the elders of Israel with you. Take the staff you struck the Nile with in your hand and go. ⁶ I am going to stand there in front of you on the rock at Horeb; when you hit the rock, water will come out of it and the people will drink." Moses did this in the sight of the elders of Israel. ⁷ He named the place Massahᴱ and Meribahᶠ because the Israelites complained, and because they tested the LORD, saying, "Is the LORD among us or not?" Ex 20:10-11

The Amalekites Attack

⁸ At Rephidim, Amalekᴳ came and fought against Israel. ⁹ Moses said to Joshua, "Select some men for us and go fight against Amalek. Tomorrow I will stand on the hilltop with God's staff in my hand." Gn 36:12

¹⁰ Joshua did as Moses had told him, and fought against Amalek, while Moses, Aaron, and Hur went up to the top of the hill. ¹¹ While Moses held up his hand,ᴴ Israel prevailed, but whenever he put his handᴴ down, Amalek prevailed. ¹² When Moses's hands grew heavy, they took a stone and put it under him, and he sat down on it. Then Aaron and Hur supported his hands, one on one side and one on the other so that his hands

---

ᴬ**16:31** = what?; Ex 16:15   ᴮ**16:32** Lit *A full omer*   ᶜ**16:33** Lit *a full omer*   ᴰ**16:36** Lit *(The omer is a tenth of an ephah.)*   ᴱ**17:7** = Testing   ᶠ**17:7** = Quarreling   ᴳ**17:8** A seminomadic people descended from *Amalek*, a grandson of Esau; Gn 36:12   ᴴ**17:11** Sam, LXX, Syr, Tg, Vg read *hands* remained steady until the sun went down. ¹³ So Joshua defeated Amalek and his army^A with the sword.

¹⁴ The LORD then said to Moses, "Write this down on a scroll as a reminder and recite it to Joshua: I will completely blot out the memory of Amalek under heaven."

¹⁵ And Moses built an altar and named it, "The LORD Is My Banner."^B ¹⁶ He said, "Indeed, my hand is lifted up toward^C the LORD's throne. The LORD will be at war with Amalek from generation to generation."

Jethro's Visit

18 Moses's father-in-law Jethro, the priest of Midian, heard about everything that God had done for Moses and for God's people Israel when the LORD brought Israel out of Egypt.   Ex 2:16,18; 3:1

² Now Jethro, Moses's father-in-law, had taken in Zipporah, Moses's wife, after he had sent her back, ³ along with her two sons, one of whom was named Gershom^D (because Moses had said, "I have been a resident alien in a foreign land") ⁴ and the other Eliezer (because he had said, "The God of my father was my helper and rescued me from Pharaoh's sword").^E   Ex 2:21,22; 4:25

⁵ Moses's father-in-law Jethro, along with Moses's wife and sons, came to him in the wilderness where he was camped at the mountain of God. ⁶ He sent word to Moses, "I, your father-in-law Jethro, am coming to you with your wife and her two sons."   Ex 3:1; 1Ch 23:15

⁷ So Moses went out to meet his father-in-law, bowed down, and then kissed him. They asked each other how they had been^F and went into the tent. ⁸ Moses recounted to his father-in-law all that the LORD had done to Pharaoh and the Egyptians for Israel's sake, all the hardships that confronted them on the way, and how the LORD rescued them.   Gn 29:13; Ex 15:6,16; 18:2; Ps 81:7

⁹ Jethro rejoiced over all the good things the LORD had done for Israel when he rescued them from the power of the Egyptians. ¹⁰ "Blessed be the LORD," Jethro exclaimed, "who rescued you from the power of Egypt and from the power of Pharaoh. He has rescued the people from under the power of Egypt! ¹¹ Now I know that the LORD is greater than all gods, because he did wonders when the Egyptians acted arrogantly against Israel."^G

¹² Then Jethro, Moses's father-in-law, brought a burnt offering and sacrifices to God, and Aaron came with all the elders of Israel to eat a meal with Moses's father-in-law in God's presence.

¹³ The next day Moses sat down to judge the people, and they stood around Moses from morning until evening. ¹⁴ When Moses's father-in-law saw everything he was doing for them he asked, "What is this thing you're doing for the people? Why are you alone sitting as judge, while all the people stand around you from morning until evening?"

¹⁵ Moses replied to his father-in-law, "Because the people come to me to inquire of God. ¹⁶ Whenever they have a dispute, it comes to me, and I make a decision between one man and another. I teach them God's statutes and laws."   Ex 24:14

---

^A**17:13** Or *people*   ^B**17:15** = *Yahweh-nissi*   ^C**17:16** Or *hand was on*, or *hand was against*; Hb obscure
^D**18:3** In Hb the name *Gershom* sounds like the phrase "a stranger there."   ^E**18:4** = My God Is Help
^F**18:7** Lit *other about well-being*   ^G**18:11** Hb obscure

¹⁷ "What you're doing is not good," Moses's father-in-law said to him. ¹⁸ "You will certainly wear out both yourself and these people who are with you, because the task is too heavy for you. You can't do it alone. ¹⁹ Now listen to me; I will give you some advice, and God be with you. You be the one to represent the people before God and bring their cases to him. ²⁰ Instruct them about the statutes and laws, and teach them the way to live and what they must do. ²¹ But you should select from all the people able men, God-fearing, trustworthy, and hating dishonest profit. Place them over the people as commanders of thousands, hundreds, fifties, and tens. ²² They should judge the people at all times. Then they can bring you every major case but judge every minor case themselves. In this way you will lighten your load,ᴬ and they will bear it with you. ²³ If you do this, and God so directs you, you will be able to endure, and also all these people will be able to go home satisfied."ᴮ

²⁴ Moses listened to his father-in-law and did everything he said. ²⁵ So Moses chose able men from all Israel and made them leaders over the people as commanders of thousands, hundreds, fifties, and tens. ²⁶ They judged the people at all times; they would bring the hard cases to Moses, but they would judge every minor case themselves.

²⁷ Moses let his father-in-law go, and he journeyed to his own land.

Israel at Sinai

19 In the third month from the very day the Israelites left the land of Egypt, they came to the Sinai Wilderness. ² They traveled from Rephidim, came to the Sinai Wilderness, and camped in the wilderness. Israel camped there in front of the mountain. Ex 3:1; 17:1,8

³ Moses went up the mountain to God, and the Lord called to him from the mountain: "This is what you must say to the house of Jacob and explain to the Israelites: ⁴ 'You have seen what I did to the Egyptians and how I carried you on eagles' wings and brought you to myself. ⁵ Now if you will carefully listen to me and keep my covenant, you will be my own possession out of all the peoples, although the whole earth is mine, ⁶ and you will be my kingdom of priests and my holy nation.' These are the words that you are to say to the Israelites."

⁷ After Moses came back, he summoned the elders of the people and set before them all these words that the Lord had commanded him. ⁸ Then all the people responded together, "We will do all that the Lord has spoken." So Moses brought the people's words back to the Lord.

⁹ The Lord said to Moses, "I am going to come to you in a dense cloud, so that the people will hear when I speak with you and will always believe you." Moses reported the people's words to the Lord, ¹⁰ and the Lord told Moses, "Go to the people and consecrate them today and tomorrow. They must wash their clothes ¹¹ and be prepared by the third day, for on the third day the Lord will come down on Mount Sinai in the sight of all the people. ¹² Put boundaries for the people all around the mountain and say: Be careful that you don't go up on the mountain or touch its base. Anyone who touches the mountain

ᴬ18:22 Lit *lighten from on you*　ᴮ18:23 Lit *go to their place in peace* must be put to death. ¹³ No hand may touch him;ᴬ instead he will be stoned or shot with arrows and not live, whether animal or human. When the ram's horn sounds a long blast, they may go up the mountain." Ex 24:15-16; Dt 4:12,36; Mt 17:5; Jn 12:29; 34:5

¹⁴ Then Moses came down from the mountain to the people and consecrated them, and they washed their clothes. ¹⁵ He said to the people, "Be prepared by the third day. Do not have sexual relations with women."

¹⁶ On the third day, when morning came, there was thunder and lightning, a thick cloud on the mountain, and a very loud trumpet sound, so that all the people in the camp shuddered. ¹⁷ Then Moses brought the people out of the camp to meet God, and they stood at the foot of the mountain. ¹⁸ Mount Sinai was completely enveloped in smoke because the Lord came down on it in fire. Its smoke went up like the smoke of a furnace, and the whole mountain shook violently. ¹⁹ As the sound of the trumpet grew louder and louder, Moses spoke and God answered him in the thunder. Ex 3:2; 24:17; Dt 4:11; 2Ch 7:1

²⁰ The Lord came down on Mount Sinai at the top of the mountain. Then the Lord summoned Moses to the top of the mountain, and he went up. ²¹ The Lord directed Moses, "Go down and warn the people not to break through to see the Lord; otherwise many of them will die. ²² Even the priests who come near the Lord must consecrate themselves, or the Lord will break out in anger against them." Ex 3:5

²³ Moses responded to the Lord, "The people cannot come up Mount Sinai, since you warned us: Put a boundary around the mountain and consecrate it." ²⁴ And the Lord replied to him, "Go down and come back with Aaron. But the priests and the people must not break through to come up to the Lord, or he will break out in anger against them." ²⁵ So Moses went down to the people and told them.

The Ten Commandments

20 Then God spoke all these words:

² I am the Lord your God, who brought you out of the land of Egypt, out of the place of slavery. Ex 13:3; Hs 13:4

³ Do not have other gods besides me. Dt 6:14; Jr 35:15

⁴ Do not make an idol for yourself, whether in the shape of anything in the heavens above or on the earth below or in the waters under the earth. ⁵ Do not bow in worship to them, and do not serve them; for I, the Lord your God, am a jealous God, punishing the children for the fathers' iniquity, to the third and fourth generations of those who hate me, ⁶ but showing faithful love to a thousand generations of those who love me and keep my commands.

⁷ Do not misuse the name of the Lord your God, because the Lord will not leave anyone unpunished who misuses his name. Lv 19:12; Mt 5:33

⁸ Remember the Sabbath day, to keep it holy: ⁹ You are to labor six days and do all your work, ¹⁰ but the seventh day is a Sabbath to the Lord your

ᴬ**19:13** Or *it*

God. You must not do any work — you, your son or daughter, your male or female servant, your livestock, or the resident alien who is within your city gates. ¹¹ For the LORD made the heavens and the earth, the sea, and everything in them in six days; then he rested on the seventh day. Therefore the LORD blessed the Sabbath day and declared it holy. Ex 31:13-16

¹² Honor your father and your mother so that you may have a long life in the land that the LORD your God is giving you.

¹³ Do not murder. Mt 5:21; Rm 13:9

¹⁴ Do not commit adultery. Dt 5:18

¹⁵ Do not steal. Lv 19:11; Mt 19:18

¹⁶ Do not give false testimony against your neighbor. Ex 23:1

¹⁷ Do not covet your neighbor's house. Do not covet your neighbor's wife, his male or female servant, his ox or donkey, or anything that belongs to your neighbor. Dt 5:21

The People's Reaction

¹⁸ All the people witnessed^A the thunder and lightning, the sound of the trumpet, and the mountain surrounded by smoke. When the people saw it^B they trembled and stood at a distance. ¹⁹ "You speak to us, and we will listen," they said to Moses, "but don't let God speak to us, or we will die." Ex 19:18; Heb 12:18

²⁰ Moses responded to the people, "Don't be afraid, for God has come to test you, so that you will fear him and will not^C sin." ²¹ And the people remained standing at a distance as Moses approached the total darkness where God was.

Moses Receives Additional Laws

²² Then the LORD told Moses, "This is what you are to say to the Israelites: You have seen that I have spoken to you from heaven. ²³ Do not make gods of silver to rival me; do not make gods of gold for yourselves.

²⁴ "Make an earthen altar for me, and sacrifice on it your burnt offerings and fellowship offerings, your flocks and herds. I will come to you and bless you in every place where I cause my name to be remembered. ²⁵ If you make a stone altar for me, do not build it out of cut stones. If you use your chisel on it, you will defile it. ²⁶ Do not go up to my altar on steps, so that your nakedness is not exposed on it.

21 "These are the ordinances that you are to set before them:

Laws About Slaves

² "When you buy a Hebrew slave, he is to serve for six years; then in the seventh he is to leave as a free man^D without paying anything. ³ If he arrives alone, he is to leave alone; if he arrives with^E a wife, his wife is to leave with him. ⁴ If his master gives him a wife and she bears him sons or daughters, the wife and her children belong to her master, and the man must leave alone. Dt 4:14; Jr 34:14

⁵ "But if the slave declares, 'I love my master, my wife, and my children; I do not want to leave as a free man,' ⁶ his master is to bring him to the judges^F and then bring him

---

^A 20:18 Lit saw ^B 20:18 Sam, LXX, Syr, Tg, Vg read smoke. The people (or they) were afraid, ^C 20:20 Lit that the fear of him may be in you, and you do not ^D 21:2 Lit to go forth ^E 21:3 Lit he is the husband of ^F 21:6 Or to God; that is, to his sanctuary or court to the door or doorpost. His master will pierce his ear with an awl, and he will serve his master for life.

[7] "When a man sells his daughter as a concubine,[A] she is not to leave as the male slaves do. [8] If she is displeasing to her master, who chose her for himself, then he must let her be redeemed. He has no right to sell her to foreigners because he has acted treacherously toward her. [9] Or if he chooses her for his son, he must deal with her according to the customary treatment of daughters. [10] If he takes an additional wife, he must not reduce the food, clothing, or marital rights of the first wife. [11] And if he does not do these three things for her, she may leave free of charge, without any payment.[B] Neh 5:5; 1Co 7:5

Laws About Personal Injury

[12] "Whoever strikes a person so that he dies must be put to death. [13] But if he did not intend any harm,[C] and yet God allowed it to happen, I will appoint a place for you where he may flee. [14] If a person schemes and willfully[D] acts against his neighbor to murder him, you must take him from my altar to be put to death.

[15] "Whoever strikes his father or his mother must be put to death.

[16] "Whoever kidnaps a person must be put to death, whether he sells him or the person is found in his possession. Gn 37:28; Ex 22:4; Dt 24:7

[17] "Whoever curses his father or his mother must be put to death.

[18] "When men quarrel and one strikes the other with a stone or his fist, and the injured man does not die but is confined to bed, [19] if he can later get up and walk around outside leaning on his staff, then the one who struck him will be exempt from punishment. Nevertheless, he must pay for his lost work time[E] and provide for his complete recovery.

[20] "When a man strikes his male or female slave with a rod, and the slave dies under his abuse,[F] the owner must be punished. [G] [21] However, if the slave can stand up after a day or two, the owner should not be punished[H] because he is his owner's property.[I] Lv 25:44-46

[22] "When men get in a fight and hit a pregnant woman so that her children are born prematurely but there is no injury, the one who hit her must be fined as the woman's husband demands from him, and he must pay according to judicial assessment. [23] If there is an injury, then you must give life for life, [24] eye for eye, tooth for tooth, hand for hand, foot for foot, [25] burn for burn, bruise for bruise, wound for wound. Ex 21:30; Lv 24:20; Dt 19:21; 22:18-19

[26] "When a man strikes the eye of his male or female slave and destroys it, he must let the slave go free in compensation for his eye. [27] If he knocks out the tooth of his male or female slave, he must let the slave go free in compensation for his tooth.

[28] "When an ox[J] gores a man or a woman to death, the ox must be stoned, and its meat may not be eaten, but the ox's owner is innocent. [29] However, if the ox was in the habit of goring, and its owner has been warned yet does not

---

[A]21:7 Or servant [B]21:11 She doesn't have to pay any redemption price. [C]21:13 Lit he was not lying in wait [D]21:14 Or maliciously [E]21:19 Lit his inactivity [F]21:20 Lit hand [G]21:20 Or must suffer vengeance [H]21:21 Or not suffer vengeance [I]21:21 Lit silver [J]21:28 Or a bull, or a steer restrain it, and it kills a man or a woman, the ox must be stoned, and its owner must also be put to death. ³⁰ If instead a ransom is demanded of him, he can pay a redemption price for his life in the full amount demanded from him. ³¹ If it gores a son or a daughter, he is to be dealt with according to this same law. ³² If the ox gores a male or female slave, he must give thirty shekels of silver^A to the slave's master, and the ox must be stoned. Gn 9:5; Nm 35:31

³³ "When a man uncovers a pit or digs a pit, and does not cover it, and an ox or a donkey falls into it, ³⁴ the owner of the pit must give compensation; he must pay to its owner, but the dead animal will become his.

³⁵ "When a man's ox injures his neighbor's ox and it dies, they must sell the live ox and divide its proceeds; they must also divide the dead animal. ³⁶ If, however, it is known that the ox was in the habit of goring, yet its owner has not restrained it, he must compensate fully, ox for ox; the dead animal will become his.

Laws About Theft

22 "When a man steals an ox or a sheep and butchers it or sells it, he must repay five cattle for the ox or four sheep for the sheep. ² If a thief is caught in the act of breaking in, and he is beaten to death, no one is guilty of bloodshed. ³ But if this happens after sunrise, the householder is guilty of bloodshed. A thief must make full restitution. If he is unable, he is to be sold because of his theft. ⁴ If what was stolen — whether ox, donkey, or sheep — is actually found alive in his possession, he must repay double.

Laws About Crop Protection

⁵ "When a man lets a field or vineyard be grazed in, and then allows his animals to go and graze in someone else's field, he must repay^B with the best of his own field or vineyard.

⁶ "When a fire gets out of control, spreads to thornbushes, and consumes stacks of cut grain, standing grain, or a field, the one who started the fire must make full restitution for what was burned.

Laws About Personal Property

⁷ "When a man gives his neighbor valuables^C or goods to keep, but they are stolen from that person's house, the thief, if caught, must repay double. ⁸ If the thief is not caught, the owner of the house must present himself to the judges^D to determine^E whether or not he has taken his neighbor's property. ⁹ In any case of wrongdoing involving an ox, a donkey, a sheep, a garment, or anything else lost, and someone claims, 'That's mine,'^F the case between the two parties is to come before the judges.^G The one the judges condemn^H must repay double to his neighbor. Dt 17:8-9

¹⁰ "When a man gives his neighbor a donkey, an ox, a sheep, or any other animal to care for, but it dies, is injured, or is stolen, while no one is watching, ¹¹ there must be an oath before the LORD between the two

---

^A21:32 About one pound of silver ^B22:5 LXX adds *from his field according to its produce. But if someone lets his animals graze an entire field, he must repay*; DSS, Sam also support this reading. ^C22:7 Lit *silver* ^D22:8 Or *to God* ^E22:8 LXX, Tg, Vg read *swear* ^F22:9 Lit *That is it* ^G22:9 Or *before God* ^H22:9 Or *one whom God condemns*

of them to determine whether or not he has taken his neighbor's property. Its owner must accept the oath, and the other man does not have to make restitution. ¹² But if, in fact, the animal was stolen from his custody, he must make restitution to its owner. ¹³ If it was actually torn apart by a wild animal, he is to bring it as evidence; he does not have to make restitution for the torn carcass.   Gn 31:39

¹⁴ "When a man borrows an animal from his neighbor, and it is injured or dies while its owner is not there with it, the man must make full restitution. ¹⁵ If its owner is there with it, the man does not have to make restitution. If it was rented, the loss is covered by ᴬ its rental price.

Laws About Seduction

¹⁶ "If a man seduces a virgin who is not engaged, and he sleeps with her, he must certainly pay the bridal price for her to be his wife. ¹⁷ If her father absolutely refuses to give her to him, he must pay an amount in silver equal to the bridal price for virgins.   Gn 34:12; Dt 22:28-29

Capital Offenses

¹⁸ "Do not allow a sorceress to live. ¹⁹ "Whoever has sexual intercourse with an animal must be put to death.   Lv 18:23; 20:15; Dt 27:21

²⁰ "Whoever sacrifices to any gods, except the LORD alone, is to be set apart for destruction.   Dt 17:2-5

Laws Protecting the Vulnerable

²¹ "You must not exploit a resident alien or oppress him, since you were resident aliens in the land of Egypt.   Lv 19:33; Dt 10:19

²² "You must not mistreat any widow or fatherless child. ²³ If you do mistreat them, they will no doubt cry to me, and I will certainly hear their cry. ²⁴ My anger will burn, and I will kill you with the sword; then your wives will be widows and your children fatherless.

²⁵ "If you lend silver to my people, to the poor person among you, you must not be like a creditor to him; you must not charge him interest. ²⁶ "If you ever take your neighbor's cloak as collateral, return it to him before sunset. ²⁷ For it is his only covering; it is the clothing for his body. ᴮ What will he sleep in? And if he cries out to me, I will listen because I am gracious.   Ex 34:6

Respect for God

²⁸ "You must not blaspheme God ᶜ or curse a leader among your people.

²⁹ "You must not hold back offerings from your harvest or your vats. Give me the firstborn of your sons. ³⁰ Do the same with your cattle and your flock. Let them stay with their mothers for seven days, but on the eighth day you are to give them to me.   Ex 13:2; 23:16; Lv 22:27

³¹ "Be my holy people. You must not eat the meat of a mauled animal found in the field; throw it to the dogs.   Ex 19:2; Ezk 4:14

Laws About Honesty and Justice

23 "You must not spread a false report. Do not join ᴰ the wicked to be a malicious witness. ² "You must not follow a crowd in wrongdoing. Do not testify in a lawsuit and go along with a crowd to pervert justice. ³ Do not show favoritism to a poor person in his lawsuit.   Dt 16:19; 24:17; 27:19

ᴬ**22:15** Lit *rented, it comes with*   ᴮ**22:27** Lit *skin*   ᶜ**22:28** Or *judges*   ᴰ**23:1** Lit *join hands with*

⁴ "If you come across your enemy's stray ox or donkey, you must return it to him.

⁵ "If you see the donkey of someone who hates you lying helpless under its load, and you want to refrain from helping it, you must help with it. ᴬ   Dt 22:1,4; Rm 12:20

⁶ "You must not deny justice to a poor person among you in his lawsuit. ⁷ Stay far away from a false accusation. Do not kill the innocent and the just, because I will not justify the guilty. ⁸ You must not take a bribe, for a bribe blinds the clear-sighted and corrupts the words ᴮ of the righteous. ⁹ You must not oppress a resident alien; you yourselves know how it feels to be a resident alien because you were resident aliens in the land of Egypt.   Dt 10:17; 16:19; Ec 5:8; Eph 4:25

Sabbaths and Festivals

¹⁰ "Sow your land for six years and gather its produce. ¹¹ But during the seventh year you are to let it rest and leave it uncultivated, so that the poor among your people may eat from it and the wild animals may consume what they leave. Do the same with your vineyard and your olive grove.   Lv 25:3-4

¹² "Do your work for six days but rest on the seventh day so that your ox and your donkey may rest, and the son of your female slave as well as the resident alien may be refreshed.   Ex 20:9

¹³ "Pay strict attention to everything I have said to you. You must not invoke the names of other gods;

they must not be heard on your lips. ᶜ   Dt 4:9; Jos 23:7; Hs 2:17; 1Tm 4:16

¹⁴ "Celebrate a festival in my honor three times a year. ¹⁵ Observe the Festival of Unleavened Bread. As I commanded you, you are to eat unleavened bread for seven days at the appointed time in the month of Abib, ᴰ because you came out of Egypt in that month. No one is to appear before me empty-handed. ¹⁶ Also observe the Festival of Harvest ᴱ with the firstfruits of your produce from what you sow in the field, and observe the Festival of Ingathering ᶠ at the end of the year, when you gather your produce ᴳ from the field. ¹⁷ Three times a year all your males are to appear before the Lord GOD.   Ex 12:15; 34:23; Dt 16:16

¹⁸ "You must not offer the blood of my sacrifices with anything leavened. The fat of my festival offering must not remain until morning.

¹⁹ "Bring the best of the firstfruits of your land to the house of the LORD your God.

"You must not boil a young goat in its mother's milk.   Ex 22:29; 26:2,10

Promises and Warnings

²⁰ "I am going to send an angel before you to protect you on the way and bring you to the place I have prepared. ²¹ Be attentive to him and listen to him. Do not defy him, because he will not forgive your acts of rebellion, for my name is in him. ²² But if you will carefully obey him and do everything I say, then I will be an enemy to your enemies and a foe to your foes. ²³ For my angel

---

ᴬ 23:5 Or *load, you must refrain from leaving it to him; you must set it free with him*   ᴮ 23:8 Or *and subverts the cause*   ᶜ 23:13 Lit *mouth*   ᴰ 23:15 March–April; called Nisan in the post-exilic period; Neh 2:1; Est 3:7   ᴱ 23:16 The *Festival of Harvest* is called Festival of Weeks elsewhere; Ex 34:22. In the NT it is called Pentecost; Ac 2:1.   ᶠ 23:16 The *Festival of Ingathering* is called Festival of Shelters elsewhere; Lv 23:34-36.   ᴳ 23:16 Lit *labors* will go before you and bring you to the land of the Amorites, Hethites, Perizzites, Canaanites, Hivites, and Jebusites, and I will wipe them out. 24 Do not bow in worship to their gods, and do not serve them. Do not imitate their practices. Instead, demolish them A and smash their sacred pillars to pieces. 25 Serve the LORD your God, and he B will bless your bread and your water. I will remove illnesses from you. 26 No woman will miscarry or be childless in your land. I will give you the full number of your days. Ex 7:15; 14:19

27 "I will cause the people ahead of you to feel terror C and will throw into confusion all the nations you come to. I will make all your enemies turn their backs to you in retreat. D 28 I will send hornets E in front of you, and they will drive the Hivites, Canaanites, and Hethites away from you. 29 I will not drive them out ahead of you in a single year; otherwise, the land would become desolate, and wild animals would multiply against you. 30 I will drive them out little by little ahead of you until you have become numerous F and take possession of the land. 31 I will set your borders from the Red Sea to the Mediterranean Sea, G and from the wilderness to the Euphrates River. H For I will place the inhabitants of the land under your control, and you will drive them out ahead of you. 32 You must not make a covenant with them or their gods. 33 They must not remain in your land, or else they will make you sin against me. If you serve their gods, it will be a snare for you." Dt 2:25; 7:20,23

The Covenant Ceremony

24 Then he said to Moses, "Go up to the LORD, you and Aaron, Nadab, and Abihu, and seventy of Israel's elders, and bow in worship at a distance. 2 Moses alone is to approach the LORD, but the others are not to approach, and the people are not to go up with him."

3 Moses came and told the people all the commands of the LORD and all the ordinances. Then all the people responded with a single voice, "We will do everything that the LORD has commanded." 4 And Moses wrote down all the words of the LORD. He rose early the next morning and set up an altar and twelve pillars for the twelve tribes of Israel at the base of the mountain. 5 Then he sent out young Israelite men, and they offered burnt offerings and sacrificed bulls as fellowship offerings to the LORD. 6 Moses took half the blood and set it in basins; the other half of the blood he splattered on the altar. 7 He then took the covenant scroll and read it aloud to the people. They responded, "We will do and obey all that the LORD has commanded." Ex 19:8; Dt 5:27; 31:9

8 Moses took the blood, splattered it on the people, and said, "This is the blood of the covenant that the LORD has made with you concerning all these words." Heb 9:18-20; 1Pt 1:2

9 Then Moses went up with Aaron, Nadab, and Abihu, and seventy of Israel's elders, 10 and they saw the God of Israel. Beneath his feet was something like a pavement made of lapis lazuli, as clear as the sky itself. 11 God did not harm I the

---

A **23:24** Probably the idols   B **23:25** LXX, Vg read I   C **23:27** Lit will send terror of me ahead of you
D **23:27** Or I will give your enemies to you by the neck   E **23:28** Or send panic   F **23:30** Lit fruitful
G **23:31** Lit the Sea of the Philistines   H **23:31** Lit the River   I **24:11** Lit not stretch out his hand against

Israelite nobles; they saw him, and they ate and drank. Jn1:18;1Jn4:12;Rv4:3

¹² The LORD said to Moses, "Come up to me on the mountain and stay there so that I may give you the stone tablets with the law and commandments I have written for their instruction." Ex32:15;Dt5:22

¹³ So Moses arose with his assistant Joshua and went up the mountain of God. ¹⁴ He told the elders, "Wait here for us until we return to you. Aaron and Hur are here with you. Whoever has a dispute should go to them." ¹⁵ When Moses went up the mountain, the cloud covered it. ¹⁶ The glory of the LORD settled on Mount Sinai, and the cloud covered it for six days. On the seventh day he called to Moses from the cloud. ¹⁷ The appearance of the LORD's glory to the Israelites was like a consuming fire on the mountaintop. ¹⁸ Moses entered the cloud as he went up the mountain, and he remained on the mountain forty days and forty nights. Ex3:1;17:9

Offerings to Build the Tabernacle

25 The LORD spoke to Moses: ² "Tell the Israelites to take an offering for me. You are to take my offering from everyone who is willing to give. ³ This is the offering you are to receive from them: gold, silver, and bronze; ⁴ blue, purple, and scarlet yarn; fine linen and goat hair; ⁵ ram skins dyed red and fine leather;ᴬ acacia wood; ⁶ oil for the light; spices for the anointing oil and for the fragrant incense; ⁷ and onyxᴮ along with other gemstones for mounting on the ephod and breastpiece.ᶜ Ex35:5,21;1Ch9:7;29:5

⁸ "They are to make a sanctuary for me so that I may dwell among them. ⁹ You must make it according to all that I show you — the pattern of the tabernacle as well as the pattern of all its furnishings. Ex36:1-5

The Ark

¹⁰ "They are to make an ark of acacia wood, forty-five inches long, twenty-seven inches wide, and twenty-seven inches high.ᴰ ¹¹ Overlay it with pure gold; overlay it both inside and out. Also make a gold molding all around it. ¹² Cast four gold rings for it and place them on its four feet, two rings on one side and two rings on the other side. ¹³ Make poles of acacia wood and overlay them with gold. ¹⁴ Insert the poles into the rings on the sides of the ark in order to carry the ark with them. ¹⁵ The poles are to remain in the rings of the ark; they must not be removed from it. ¹⁶ Put the tablets ofᴱ the testimony that I will give you into the ark. ¹⁷ Make a mercy seat of pure gold, forty-five inches long and twenty-seven inches wide.ᶠ ¹⁸ Make two cherubim of gold; make them of hammered work at the two ends of the mercy seat. ¹⁹ Make one cherub at one end and one cherub at the other end. At its two ends, make the cherubim of one piece with the mercy seat. ²⁰ The cherubim are to have wings spread out above, covering the mercy seat with their wings, and are to face one another. The faces of the cherubim should be toward the mercy seat. ²¹ Set the mercy seat on top of the ark and put the tablets of the testimony that

---

ᴬ**25:5** Hb obscure ᴮ**25:7** Or carnelian ᶜ**25:7** Traditionally, breastplate ᴰ**25:10** Lit two and a half cubits its length, one and a half cubits its width, and one and a half cubits its height ᴱ**25:16** the tablets of supplied for clarity, also in v. 21 ᶠ**25:17** Lit two and a half cubits its length, one and a half cubits its width

I will give you into the ark. ²² I will meet with you there above the mercy seat, between the two cherubim that are over the ark of the testimony; I will speak with you from there about all that I command you regarding the Israelites.   Ex 37:1,3-4

The Table

²³ "You are to construct a table of acacia wood, thirty-six inches long, eighteen inches wide, and twenty-seven inches high.ᴬ ²⁴ Overlay it with pure gold and make a gold molding all around it. ²⁵ Make a three-inchᴮ frame all around it and make a gold molding for it all around its frame. ²⁶ Make four gold rings for it, and attach the rings to the four corners at its four legs. ²⁷ The rings should be next to the frame as holders for the poles to carry the table. ²⁸ Make the poles of acacia wood and overlay them with gold, and the table can be carried by them. ²⁹ You are also to make its plates and cups, as well as its pitchers and bowls for pouring drink offerings. Make them out of pure gold. ³⁰ Put the Bread of the Presence on the table before me at all times.   Ex 37:10,16; 1Kg 7:48; 2Ch 4:8; Heb 9:2

The Lampstand

³¹ "You are to make a lampstand out of pure, hammered gold. It is to be made of one piece: its base and shaft, its ornamental cups, and its budsᶜ and petals. ³² Six branches are to extend from its sides, three branches of the lampstand from one side and three branches of the lampstand from the other side. ³³ There are to be three cups shaped like almond blossoms, each with a bud and petals, on one branch, and three cups shaped like almond blossoms, each with a bud and petals, on the next branch. It is to be this way for the six branches that extend from the lampstand. ³⁴ There are to be four cups shaped like almond blossoms on the lampstand shaft along with its buds and petals. ³⁵ For the six branches that extend from the lampstand, a bud must be under the first pair of branches from it, a bud under the second pair of branches from it, and a bud under the third pair of branches from it. ³⁶ Their buds and branches are to be of one piece.ᴰ All of it is to be a single hammered piece of pure gold.   Ex 37:17-24; 1Kg 7:49

³⁷ "Make its seven lamps, and set them up so that they illuminate the area in front of it. ³⁸ Its snuffers and firepans must be of pure gold. ³⁹ The lampstandᴱ with all these utensils is to be made from seventy-five poundsᶠ of pure gold. ⁴⁰ Be careful to make them according to the pattern you have been shown on the mountain.   Ex 27:21; 37:23; Lv 24:3-4

The Tabernacle

26 "You are to construct the tabernacle itself with ten curtains. You must make them of finely spun linen, and blue, purple, and scarlet yarn, with a design of cherubim worked into them. ² Each curtain should be forty-two feetᴳ long and six feetᴴ wide; all the curtains are to have the same measurements. ³ Five of the curtains should be joined together, and the other five curtains joined together.

ᴬ**25:23** Lit *two cubits its length, one cubit its width, and one and a half cubits its height*   ᴮ**25:25** Lit *Make it a handbreadth*   ᶜ**25:31** = the outer covering of a flower   ᴰ**25:36** Lit *piece with it*   ᴱ**25:39** Lit *It*   ᶠ**25:39** Lit *a talent*   ᴳ**26:2** Lit *28 cubits*   ᴴ**26:2** Lit *four cubits*, also in v. 8

⁴ Make loops of blue yarn on the edge of the last curtain in the first set, and do the same on the edge of the outermost curtain in the second set. ⁵ Make fifty loops on the one curtain and make fifty loops on the edge of the curtain in the second set, so that the loops line up together. ⁶ Also make fifty gold clasps and join the curtains together with the clasps, so that the tabernacle may be a single unit.

⁷ "You are to make curtains of goat hair for a tent over the tabernacle; make eleven of these curtains. ⁸ Each curtain should be forty-five feet[A] long and six feet wide. All eleven curtains are to have the same measurements. ⁹ Join five of the curtains by themselves, and the other six curtains by themselves. Then fold the sixth curtain double at the front of the tent. ¹⁰ Make fifty loops on the edge of one curtain, the outermost in the first set, and make fifty loops on the edge of the corresponding curtain of the second set. ¹¹ Make fifty bronze clasps; put the clasps through the loops and join the tent together so that it is a single unit. ¹² As for the flap that remains from the tent curtains, the leftover half curtain is to hang over the back of the tabernacle. ¹³ What remains along the length of the tent curtains — a half yard[B] on one side and a half yard on the other side — should hang over the sides of the tabernacle on either side to cover it. ¹⁴ Make a covering for the tent from ram skins dyed red and a covering of fine leather[C] on top of that.

¹⁵ "You are to make upright supports[D] of acacia wood for the tabernacle. ¹⁶ Each support is to be fifteen feet[E] long and twenty-seven[F] inches wide. ¹⁷ Each support will have two tenons for joining. Do the same for all the supports of the tabernacle. ¹⁸ Make the supports for the tabernacle as follows: twenty supports for the south side, ¹⁹ and make forty silver bases under the twenty supports, two bases under the first support for its two tenons, and two bases under the next support for its two tenons; ²⁰ twenty supports for the second side of the tabernacle, the north side, ²¹ along with their forty silver bases, two bases under the first support and two bases under each support; ²² and make six supports for the west side of the tabernacle. ²³ Make two additional supports for the two back corners of the tabernacle. ²⁴ They are to be paired at the bottom, and joined together[G] at the top in a single ring. So it should be for both of them; they will serve as the two corners. ²⁵ There are to be eight supports with their silver bases: sixteen bases; two bases under the first support and two bases under each support. Ex 25:28; 26:37; 38:6

²⁶ "You are to make five crossbars of acacia wood for the supports on one side of the tabernacle, ²⁷ five crossbars for the supports on the other side of the tabernacle, and five crossbars for the supports of the back side of the tabernacle on the west. ²⁸ The central crossbar is to run through the middle of the supports from one end to the other. ²⁹ Then overlay the supports with gold, and make their rings of gold as the holders for the crossbars. Also overlay the crossbars with

---

[A]26:8 Lit *30 cubits* [B]26:13 Lit *the cubit* [C]26:14 Hb obscure [D]26:15 Or *frames,* or *beams* [E]26:16 Lit *10 cubits* [F]26:16 Lit *a cubit and a half* [G]26:24 Lit *and together they are to be complete* gold. ³⁰ You are to set up the tabernacle according to the plan for it that you have been shown on the mountain.   Ex 25:9,40; Ac 7:44; Heb 8:5

³¹ "You are to make a curtain of blue, purple, and scarlet yarn, and finely spun linen with a design of cherubim worked into it. ³² Hang it on four gold-plated pillars of acacia wood that have gold hooks and that stand on four silver bases. ³³ Hang the curtain under the clasps ᴬ and bring the ark of the testimony there behind the curtain, so the curtain will make a separation for you between the holy place and the most holy place. ³⁴ Put the mercy seat on the ark of the testimony in the most holy place. ³⁵ Place the table outside the curtain and the lampstand on the south side of the tabernacle, opposite the table; put the table on the north side.   Ex 36:35; 2Ch 3:14; Mt 27:51

³⁶ "For the entrance to the tent you are to make a screen embroidered ᴮ with blue, purple, and scarlet yarn, and finely spun linen. ³⁷ Make five pillars of acacia wood for the screen and overlay them with gold; their hooks are to be gold, and you are to cast five bronze bases for them.

The Altar of Burnt Offering

27 "You are to construct the altar of acacia wood. The altar must be square, 7½ feet long, and 7½ feet wide; ᶜ it must be 4½ feet high. ᴰ ² Make horns for it on its four corners; the horns are to be of one piece. ᴱ Overlay it with bronze. ³ Make its pots for removing ashes, and its shovels, basins, meat forks, and firepans; make all its utensils of bronze. ⁴ Construct a grate for it of bronze mesh, and make four bronze rings on the mesh at its four corners. ⁵ Set it below, under the altar's ledge, ᶠ so that the mesh comes halfway up ᴳ the altar. ⁶ Then make poles for the altar, poles of acacia wood, and overlay them with bronze. ⁷ The poles are to be inserted into the rings so that the poles are on two sides of the altar when it is carried. ⁸ Construct the altar with boards so that it is hollow. They are to make it just as it was shown to you on the mountain.

The Courtyard

⁹ "You are to make the courtyard for the tabernacle. Make hangings for the south side of the courtyard out of finely spun linen, 150 feet ᴴ long on that side ¹⁰ including twenty posts and twenty bronze bases, with silver hooks and silver bands ᴵ for the posts. ¹¹ And so make hangings 150 feet long for the north side, including twenty posts and their twenty bronze bases, with silver hooks and silver bands for the posts. ¹² For the width of the courtyard, make hangings 75 feet ᴶ long for the west side, including their ten posts and their ten bases. ¹³ And for the width of the courtyard on the east side toward the sunrise, 75 feet, ¹⁴ make hangings 22½ feet ᴷ long for one side of the gate, including their three posts and their three bases. ¹⁵ And make hangings 22½ feet long for

---

ᴬ**26:33** The *clasps* that join the ten curtains of the tabernacle; Ex 26:6   ᴮ**26:36** Or *woven*   ᶜ**27:1** Lit *five cubits in length and five cubits in width*   ᴰ**27:1** Lit *wide; and its height three cubits*   ᴱ**27:2** Lit *piece with it*   ᶠ**27:5** Perhaps a *ledge* around the altar on which the priests could stand; Lv 9:22   ᴳ**27:5** Or *altar's rim, so that the grid comes halfway down*   ᴴ**27:9** Lit *100 cubits*, also in v. 11   ᴵ**27:10** Or *connecting rods*, also in v. 11   ᴶ**27:12** Lit *50 cubits*, also in v. 13   ᴷ**27:14** Lit *15 cubits*, also in v. 15

the other side, including their three posts and their three bases. ¹⁶ The gate of the courtyard is to have a 30-foot^A screen embroidered^B with blue, purple, and scarlet yarn, and finely spun linen. It is to have four posts and their four bases. Ex 38:9-20

¹⁷ "All the posts around the courtyard are to be banded with silver and have silver hooks and bronze bases. ¹⁸ The courtyard is to be 150 feet long, 75 feet wide at each end, and 7½ feet high, ^C all of it made of finely spun linen. The bases of the posts are to be bronze. ¹⁹ All the utensils of the tabernacle for every use and all its tent pegs as well as all the tent pegs of the courtyard are to be made of bronze.

The Lampstand Oil

²⁰ "You are to command the Israelites to bring you pure oil from crushed olives for the light, in order to keep the lamp burning regularly. ²¹ In the tent of meeting outside the curtain that is in front of the testimony, Aaron and his sons are to tend the lamp from evening until morning before the LORD. This is to be a permanent statute for the Israelites throughout their generations. Ex 26:31,33; 30:8; 1Sm 3:3; 2Ch 13:11

The Priestly Garments

28 "Have your brother Aaron, with his sons, come to you from the Israelites to serve me as priest — Aaron, his sons Nadab and Abihu, Eleazar and Ithamar. ² Make holy garments for your brother Aaron, for glory and beauty. ³ You are to instruct all the skilled artisans, ^D whom I have filled with a spirit of wisdom, to make Aaron's garments for consecrating him to serve me as priest. ⁴ These are the garments that they must make: a breastpiece, an ephod, a robe, a specially woven tunic, ^E a turban, and a sash. They are to make holy garments for your brother Aaron and his sons so that they may serve me as priests. ⁵ They should use ^F gold; blue, purple, and scarlet yarn; and fine linen. Ex 29:5,9; Nm 18:7; Ps 99:6; Heb 5:1

The Ephod

⁶ "They are to make the ephod of finely spun linen embroidered ^B with gold, and with blue, purple, and scarlet yarn. ⁷ It must have two shoulder pieces attached to its two edges so that it can be joined together. ⁸ The artistically woven waistband that is on the ephod ^G must be of one piece, ^H according to the same workmanship of gold, of blue, purple, and scarlet yarn, and of finely spun linen. Ex 39:2-7; Lv 8:7

⁹ "Take two onyx stones and engrave on them the names of Israel's sons: ¹⁰ six of their names on the first stone and the remaining six names on the second stone, in the order of their birth. ¹¹ Engrave the two stones with the names of Israel's sons as a gem cutter engraves a seal. Mount them, surrounded with gold filigree settings. ¹² Fasten both stones on the shoulder pieces of the ephod as memorial stones for the Israelites. Aaron will carry their names on his two shoulders before the LORD as a reminder. ¹³ Fashion gold filigree settings ¹⁴ and two chains of pure gold; you will make them of braided cord

---

^A 27:16 Lit 20-cubit   ^B 27:16; 28:6 Or woven   ^C 27:18 Lit be 100 by the cubit, and the width 50 by 50, and the height five cubits   ^D 28:3 Lit all wise of heart   ^E 28:4 Hb obscure   ^F 28:5 Lit receive   ^G 28:8 Lit waistband of its ephod, which is on it   ^H 28:8 Lit piece with the ephod work, and attach the cord chains to the settings. Ex 28:29; Jos 4:7; Zch 6:14

The Breastpiece

[15] "You are to make an embroidered breastpiece for making decisions.[A] Make it with the same workmanship as the ephod; make it of gold, of blue, purple, and scarlet yarn, and of finely spun linen. [16] It must be square and folded double, nine inches long and nine inches wide.[B] [17] Place a setting of gemstones[C] on it, four rows of stones: Ex 39:8-21

> The first row should be
> a row of carnelian, topaz,
> and emerald;[D]
[18]   the second row,
> a turquoise,[E] a lapis lazuli,
> and a diamond;[F]
[19]   the third row,
> a jacinth,[G] an agate,
> and an amethyst;
[20]   and the fourth row,
> a beryl, an onyx, and a jasper.

They should be adorned with gold filigree in their settings. [21] The twelve stones are to correspond to the names of Israel's sons. Each stone must be engraved like a seal, with one of the names of the twelve tribes.

[22] "You are to make braided chains[H] of pure gold cord work for the breastpiece. [23] Fashion two gold rings for the breastpiece and attach them to its two corners. [24] Then attach the two gold cords to the two gold rings at the corners of the breastpiece. [25] Attach the other ends of the two cords to the two filigree settings, and in this way attach them to the ephod's shoulder pieces in the front. [26] Make two other gold rings and put them at the two other corners of the breastpiece on the edge that is next to the inner border of the ephod. [27] Make two more gold rings and attach them to the bottom of the ephod's two shoulder pieces on its front, close to its seam,[I] and above the ephod's woven waistband. [28] The artisans are to tie the breastpiece from its rings to the rings of the ephod with a cord of blue yarn, so that the breastpiece is above the ephod's waistband and does not come loose from the ephod.

[29] "Whenever he enters the sanctuary, Aaron is to carry the names of Israel's sons over his heart on the breastpiece for decisions, as a continual reminder before the LORD. [30] Place the Urim and Thummim in the breastpiece for decisions, so that they will also be over Aaron's heart whenever he comes before the LORD. Aaron will continually carry the means of decisions for the Israelites over his heart before the LORD.   Lv 8:8; Nm 27:21; Dt 33:8; Ezr 2:63

The Robe

[31] "You are to make the robe of the ephod entirely of blue yarn. [32] There should be an opening at its top in the center of it. Around the opening, there should be a woven collar with an opening like that of body armor[G] so that it does not tear. [33] Make pomegranates of blue, purple, and scarlet yarn on its lower hem and all around it. Put gold bells between them all the way around, [34] so that gold bells and

---

[A] 28:15 Used for determining God's will; Nm 27:21   [B] 28:16 Lit *a span its length and a span its width*
[C] 28:17 Many of these stones cannot be identified with certainty.   [D] 28:17 Or *beryl*   [E] 28:18 Or *malachite*, or *garnet*   [F] 28:18 Hb obscure; LXX, Vg read *jasper*   [G] 28:19,32 Hb obscure   [H] 28:22 The same *chains* mentioned in v. 14   [I] 28:27 The place where the *shoulder pieces* join the front of the ephod

pomegranates alternate around the lower hem of the robe. [35] The robe will be worn by Aaron whenever he ministers, and its sound will be heard when he enters the sanctuary before the LORD and when he exits, so that he does not die. Ex 39:22-31

The Turban

[36] "You are to make a pure gold medallion and engrave it, like the engraving of a seal: HOLY TO THE LORD. [37] Fasten it to a cord of blue yarn so it can be placed on the turban; the medallion is to be on the front of the turban. [38] It will be on Aaron's forehead so that Aaron may bear the guilt connected with the holy offerings that the Israelites consecrate as all their holy gifts. It is always to be on his forehead, so that they may find acceptance with the LORD. Lv 8:9; 10:17; 22:16; Nm 18:1; Zch 14:20

Other Priestly Garments

[39] "You are to weave the tunic from fine linen, make a turban of fine linen, and make an embroidered sash. [40] Make tunics, sashes, and headbands for Aaron's sons to give them glory and beauty. [41] Put these on your brother Aaron and his sons; then anoint, ordain,[A] and consecrate them, so that they may serve me as priests. [42] Make them linen undergarments to cover their naked bodies; they must extend from the waist to the thighs. [43] These must be worn by Aaron and his sons whenever they enter the tent of meeting or approach the altar to minister in the sanctuary area, so that they do not incur guilt and die. This is to be a permanent

statute for Aaron and for his future descendants. Ex 39:41; Ezk 44:17-18

Instructions About Consecration

29 "This is what you are to do for them to consecrate them to serve me as priests. Take a young bull and two unblemished rams, [2] with unleavened bread, unleavened cakes mixed with oil, and unleavened wafers coated with oil. Make them out of fine wheat flour, [3] put them in a basket, and bring them in the basket, along with the bull and two rams. [4] Bring Aaron and his sons to the entrance to the tent of meeting and wash them with water. [5] Then take the garments and clothe Aaron with the tunic, the robe for the ephod, the ephod itself, and the breastpiece; fasten the ephod on him with its woven waistband. [6] Put the turban on his head and place the holy diadem on the turban. [7] Take the anointing oil, pour it on his head, and anoint him. [8] You must also bring his sons and clothe them with tunics. [9] Tie the sashes on Aaron and his sons and fasten headbands on them. The priesthood is to be theirs by a permanent statute. This is the way you will ordain Aaron and[B] his sons. Ex 40:12; Lv 2:4; 6:19-23; 8:6

[10] "You are to bring the bull to the front of the tent of meeting, and Aaron and his sons must lay their hands on the bull's head. [11] Slaughter the bull before the LORD at the entrance to the tent of meeting. [12] Take some of the bull's blood and apply it to the horns of the altar with your finger; then pour out all the rest of the blood at the base of the altar. [13] Take all the fat that covers the

---

A28:41 Lit anoint them, fill their hand　B29:9 Lit you will fill the hand of Aaron and the hand of; Ex 29:23-24 entrails, the fatty lobe of the liver, and the two kidneys with the fat on them, and burn them on the altar. ¹⁴ But burn the bull's flesh, its hide, and its waste outside the camp; it is a sin offering.   Ex 27:2; Lv 1:4; 8:14-15

¹⁵ "Take one ram, and Aaron and his sons are to lay their hands on the ram's head. ¹⁶ You are to slaughter the ram, take its blood, and splatter it on all sides of the altar. ¹⁷ Cut the ram into pieces. Wash its entrails and legs, and place them with its head and its pieces on the altar. ¹⁸ Then burn the whole ram on the altar; it is a burnt offering to the LORD. It is a pleasing aroma, a fire offering to the LORD. Lv 1:4; 8:18

¹⁹ "You are to take the second ram, and Aaron and his sons must lay their hands on the ram's head. ²⁰ Slaughter the ram, take some of its blood, and put it on Aaron's right earlobe, on his sons' right earlobes, on the thumbs of their right hands, and on the big toes of their right feet. Splatter the remaining blood on all sides of the altar. ²¹ Take some of the blood that is on the altar and some of the anointing oil, and sprinkle them on Aaron and his garments, as well as on his sons and their garments. So he and his garments will be holy, as well as his sons and their garments. Ex 29:3

²² "Take the fat from the ram, the fat tail, the fat covering the entrails, the fatty lobe of the liver, the two kidneys and the fat on them, and the right thigh (since this is a ram for ordinationᴬ); ²³ take one loaf of bread, one cake of bread made with oil, and one wafer from the basket of unleavened bread that is before

the LORD; ²⁴ and put all of them in the hands of Aaron and his ᴮ sons and present them as a presentation offering before the LORD. ²⁵ Take them from their hands and burn them on the altar on top of the burnt offering, as a pleasing aroma before the LORD; it is a fire offering to the LORD. Lv 7:30; 8:22

²⁶ "Take the breast from the ram of Aaron's ordination and present it as a presentation offering before the LORD; it is to be your portion. ²⁷ Consecrate for Aaron and his sons the breast of the presentation offering that is presented and the thigh of the contribution that is lifted up from the ram of ordination. ²⁸ This will belong to Aaron and his sons as a regular portion from the Israelites, for it is a contribution. It will be the Israelites' contribution from their fellowship sacrifices, their contribution to the LORD. Lv 8:29

²⁹ "The holy garments that belong to Aaron are to belong to his sons after him, so that they can be anointed and ordainedᶜ in them. ³⁰ Any priest who is one of his sons and who succeeds him and enters the tent of meeting to minister in the sanctuary must wear them for seven days. Lv 8:35; Nm 18:8; 20:26,28

³¹ "You are to take the ram of ordination and boil its flesh in a holy place. ³² Aaron and his sons are to eat the meat of the ram and the bread that is in the basket at the entrance to the tent of meeting. ³³ They must eat those things by which atonement was made at the time of their ordinationᴰ and consecration. An unauthorized person must not eat them, for these

---

ᴬ29:22 The priest would normally receive the right thigh to be eaten, but here it is burned; Lv 7:32-34.
ᴮ29:24 Lit in the hands of his   ᶜ29:29 Lit him for anointing in them and for filling their hand
ᴰ29:33 Lit made to fill their hand

things are holy. ³⁴ If any of the meat of ordination or any of the bread is left until morning, burn what is left over. It must not be eaten because it is holy.   Lv 8:31; Mt 12:4; 22:10

³⁵ "This is what you are to do for Aaron and his sons based on all I have commanded you. Take seven days to ordain them. ³⁶ Sacrifice a bull as a sin offering each day for atonement. Purify ^A the altar when you make atonement for it, and anoint it in order to consecrate it. ³⁷ For seven days you must make atonement for the altar and consecrate it. The altar will be especially holy. Whatever touches the altar will be consecrated.   Ex 40:10

³⁸ "This is what you are to offer regularly on the altar every day: two year-old lambs. ³⁹ In the morning offer one lamb, and at twilight offer the other lamb. ⁴⁰ With the first lamb offer two quarts ^B of fine flour mixed with one quart ^C of oil from crushed olives, and a drink offering of one quart of wine. ⁴¹ You are to offer the second lamb at twilight. Offer a grain offering and a drink offering with it, like the one in the morning, as a pleasing aroma, a fire offering to the Lord. ⁴² This will be a regular burnt offering throughout your generations at the entrance to the tent of meeting before the Lord, where I will meet you ^D to speak with you. ⁴³ I will also meet with the Israelites there, and that place will be consecrated by my glory. ⁴⁴ I will consecrate the tent of meeting and the altar; I will also consecrate Aaron and his sons to serve me as priests. ⁴⁵ I will dwell among the Israelites and be their God. ⁴⁶ And they will know that I am the Lord their God, who brought them out of the land of Egypt, so that I might dwell among them. I am the Lord their God.   Nm 28:3; Ezr 3:3

The Incense Altar

30 "You are to make an altar for the burning of incense; make it of acacia wood. ² It must be square, eighteen inches long and eighteen inches wide; ^E it must be thirty-six inches high. ^F Its horns must be of one piece with it. ³ Overlay its top, all around its sides, and its horns with pure gold; make a gold molding all around it. ⁴ Make two gold rings for it under the molding on two of its sides; put these on opposite sides of it to be holders for the poles to carry it with. ⁵ Make the poles of acacia wood and overlay them with gold.

⁶ "You are to place the altar in front of the curtain by the ark of the testimony — in front of the mercy seat that is over the testimony — where I will meet with you. ⁷ Aaron must burn fragrant incense on it; he must burn it every morning when he tends the lamps. ⁸ When Aaron sets up the lamps at twilight, he must burn incense. There is to be an incense offering before the Lord throughout your generations. ⁹ You must not offer unauthorized incense on it, or a burnt or grain offering; you are not to pour a drink offering on it.   Ex 27:21; 1Sm 2:28; 1Ch 23:13

¹⁰ "Once a year Aaron is to perform the atonement ceremony for the altar. Throughout your generations he is to perform the atonement ceremony for ^G it once a year,

---

^A **29:36** Or *Make a sin offering on*   ^B **29:40** Lit *offer a tenth*   ^C **29:40** Lit *a fourth of a hin*   ^D **29:42** = Moses
^E **30:2** Lit *one cubit its length and one cubit its width*   ^F **30:2** Lit *wide; and two cubits its height*
^G **30:10** Or *on*

with the blood of the sin offering for atonement on the horns. The altar is especially holy to the LORD."

The Atonement Money

[11] The LORD spoke to Moses: [12] "When you take a census of the Israelites to register them, each of the men must pay a ransom for his life to the LORD as they are registered. Then no plague will come on them as they are registered. [13] Everyone who is registered must pay half a shekel[A] according to the sanctuary shekel (twenty gerahs to the shekel). This half shekel is a contribution to the LORD. [14] Each man who is registered, twenty years old or more, must give this contribution to the LORD. [15] The wealthy may not give more and the poor may not give less than half a shekel when giving the contribution to the LORD to atone for[B] your lives. [16] Take the atonement price[C] from the Israelites and use it for the service of the tent of meeting. It will serve as a reminder for the Israelites before the LORD to atone for your lives."

The Bronze Basin

[17] The LORD spoke to Moses: [18] "Make a bronze basin for washing and a bronze stand for it. Set it between the tent of meeting and the altar, and put water in it. [19] Aaron and his sons must wash their hands and feet from the basin. [20] Whenever they enter the tent of meeting or approach the altar to minister by burning an offering to the LORD, they must wash with water so that they will not die. [21] They must wash their hands and feet so that they will not die; this is to be a permanent statute for them, for Aaron and his descendants throughout their generations."

The Anointing Oil

[22] The LORD spoke to Moses: [23] "Take for yourself the finest spices: 12½ pounds[D] of liquid myrrh, half as much (6¼ pounds[E]) of fragrant cinnamon, 6¼ pounds of fragrant cane, [24] 12½ pounds of cassia (by the sanctuary shekel), and a gallon[F] of olive oil. [25] Prepare from these a holy anointing oil, a scented blend, the work of a perfumer; it will be holy anointing oil.   Sg 4:14; Ezk 27:22

[26] "With it you are to anoint the tent of meeting, the ark of the testimony, [27] the table with all its utensils, the lampstand with its utensils, the altar of incense, [28] the altar of burnt offering with all its utensils, and the basin with its stand. [29] Consecrate them and they will be especially holy. Whatever touches them will be consecrated. [30] Anoint Aaron and his sons and consecrate them to serve me as priests.   Ex 40:9

[31] "Tell the Israelites: This will be my holy anointing oil throughout your generations. [32] It must not be used for ordinary anointing on a person's body, and you must not make anything like it using its formula. It is holy, and it must be holy to you. [33] Anyone who blends something like it or puts some of it on an unauthorized person must be cut off from his people."   Gn 17:14

The Sacred Incense

[34] The LORD said to Moses: "Take fragrant spices: stacte, onycha, and galbanum; the spices and pure frankincense are to be in

---

A **30:13** A shekel is about two-fifths of an ounce of silver   B **30:15** Or *to ransom*, also in v. 16   C **30:16** Lit *the silver of the atonement*   D **30:23** Lit *500* (shekels), also in v. 24   E **30:23** Lit *250* (shekels)   F **30:24** Lit *a hin* equal measures. ³⁵ Prepare expertly blended incense from these; it is to be seasoned with salt, pure and holy. ³⁶ Grind some of it into a fine powder and put some in front of the testimony in the tent of meeting, where I will meet with you. It must be especially holy to you. ³⁷ As for the incense you are making, you must not make any for yourselves using its formula. It is to be regarded by you as holy — belonging to the LORD. ³⁸ Anyone who makes something like it to smell its fragrance must be cut off from his people."   Ex 29:37; Lv 2:3

God's Provision of the Skilled Workers

31 The LORD also spoke to Moses: ² "Look, I have appointed by name Bezalel son of Uri, son of Hur, of the tribe of Judah. ³ I have filled him with God's Spirit, with wisdom, understanding, and ability in every craft ⁴ to design artistic works in gold, silver, and bronze, ⁵ to cut gemstones for mounting, and to carve wood for work in every craft. ⁶ I have also selected Oholiab ᴬ son of Ahisamach, of the tribe of Dan, to be with him. I have put wisdom in the heart of every skilled artisan ᴮ in order to make all that I have commanded you: ⁷ the tent of meeting, the ark of the testimony, the mercy seat that is on top of it, and all the other furnishings of the tent — ⁸ the table with its utensils, the pure gold lampstand with all its utensils, the altar of incense, ⁹ the altar of burnt offering with all its utensils, the basin with its stand — ¹⁰ the specially woven ᶜ garments, both the holy garments for the priest Aaron and

the garments for his sons to serve as priests, ¹¹ the anointing oil, and the fragrant incense for the sanctuary. They must make them according to all that I have commanded you."   Ex 35:30-31; 36:1; 1Ch 2:20; 1Kg 7:14

Observing the Sabbath

¹² The LORD said to Moses: ¹³ "Tell the Israelites: You must observe my Sabbaths, for it is a sign between me and you throughout your generations, so that you will know that I am the LORD who consecrates you. ¹⁴ Observe the Sabbath, for it is holy to you. Whoever profanes it must be put to death. If anyone does work on it, that person must be cut off from his people. ¹⁵ Work may be done for six days, but on the seventh day there must be a Sabbath of complete rest, holy to the LORD. Anyone who does work on the Sabbath day must be put to death. ¹⁶ The Israelites must observe the Sabbath, celebrating it throughout their generations as a permanent covenant. ¹⁷ It is a sign forever between me and the Israelites, for in six days the LORD made the heavens and the earth, but on the seventh day he rested and was refreshed."   Lv 19:3,30; Nm 15:35; Ezk 20:12,20

The Two Stone Tablets

¹⁸ When he finished speaking with Moses on Mount Sinai, he gave him the two tablets of the testimony, stone tablets inscribed by the finger of God.   Ex 24:12; 32:15-16; Dt 4:13; 5:22

The Gold Calf

32 When the people saw that Moses delayed in coming down from the mountain, they gathered around Aaron and said

ᴬ**31:6** LXX, Syr read *Eliab*   ᴮ**31:6** Lit *everyone wise of heart*   ᶜ**31:10** Hb obscure to him, "Come, make gods^A for us who will go before us because this Moses, the man who brought us up from the land of Egypt — we don't know what has happened to him!" Ex 13:21; 24:18; Dt 9:9; Ac 7:40

² Aaron replied to them, "Take off the gold rings that are on the ears of your wives, your sons, and your daughters and bring them to me." ³ So all the people took off the gold rings that were on their ears and brought them to Aaron. ⁴ He took the gold from them, fashioned it with an engraving tool, and made it into an image of a calf. Ex 35:22

Then they said, "Israel, these are your gods,^B who brought you up from the land of Egypt!" Dt 9:16

⁵ When Aaron saw this, he built an altar in front of it and made an announcement: "There will be a festival to the Lᴏʀᴅ tomorrow." ⁶ Early the next morning they arose, offered burnt offerings, and presented fellowship offerings. The people sat down to eat and drink, and got up to party. Lv 23:2,37; 2Kg 10:20

⁷ The Lᴏʀᴅ spoke to Moses: "Go down at once! For your people you brought up from the land of Egypt have acted corruptly. ⁸ They have quickly turned from the way I commanded them; they have made for themselves an image of a calf. They have bowed down to it, sacrificed to it, and said, 'Israel, these are your gods, who brought you up from the land of Egypt.'" ⁹ The Lᴏʀᴅ also said to Moses: "I have seen this people, and they are indeed a stiff-necked people. ¹⁰ Now leave me alone, so that my anger can burn against them and I can destroy them. Then I will make you into a great nation." Gn 6:11-12; Dt 9:12

¹¹ But Moses sought the favor of the Lᴏʀᴅ his God: "Lᴏʀᴅ, why does your anger burn against your people you brought out of the land of Egypt with great power and a strong hand? ¹² Why should the Egyptians say, 'He brought them out with an evil intent to kill them in the mountains and eliminate them from the face of the earth'? Turn from your fierce anger and relent concerning this disaster planned for your people. ¹³ Remember your servants Abraham, Isaac, and Israel — you swore to them by yourself and declared, 'I will make your offspring as numerous as the stars of the sky and will give your offspring all this land that I have promised, and they will inherit it forever.'" ¹⁴ So the Lᴏʀᴅ relented concerning the disaster he had said he would bring on his people. Gn 12:7

¹⁵ Then Moses turned and went down the mountain with the two tablets of the testimony in his hands. They were inscribed on both sides — inscribed front and back. ¹⁶ The tablets were the work of God, and the writing was God's writing, engraved on the tablets.

¹⁷ When Joshua heard the sound of the people as they shouted, he said to Moses, "There is a sound of war in the camp."

¹⁸ But Moses replied:

It's not the sound
of a victory cry
and not the sound of a cry
of defeat;
I hear the sound of singing!

¹⁹ As he approached the camp and saw the calf and the dancing, Moses became enraged and threw the tablets out of his hands, smashing them at the base of the mountain.

^A32:1 Or make a god, also in v. 23 ^B32:4 Or "Israel, this is your god or "Israel, this is your God, also in v. 8

²⁰ He took the calf they had made, burned it up, and ground it to powder. He scattered the powder over the surface of the water and forced the Israelites to drink the water.

²¹ Then Moses asked Aaron, "What did these people do to you that you have led them into such a grave sin?"

²² "Don't be enraged, my lord," Aaron replied. "You yourself know that the people are intent on evil. ²³ They said to me, 'Make gods for us who will go before us because this Moses, the man who brought us up from the land of Egypt — we don't know what has happened to him!' ²⁴ So I said to them, 'Whoever has gold, take it off,' and they gave it to me. When I threw it into the fire, out came this calf!" Gn 20:9; 26:10

²⁵ Moses saw that the people were out of control, for Aaron had let them get out of control, making them a laughingstock to their enemies. ᴬ ²⁶ And Moses stood at the camp's entrance and said, "Whoever is for the LORD, come to me." And all the Levites gathered around him. ²⁷ He told them, "This is what the LORD, the God of Israel, says, 'Every man fasten his sword to his side; go back and forth through the camp from entrance to entrance, and each of you kill his brother, his friend, and his neighbor.'" ²⁸ The Levites did as Moses commanded, and about three thousand men fell dead that day among the people. ²⁹ Afterward Moses said, "Today you have been dedicatedᴮ to the LORD, since each man went against his son and his brother. Therefore you have brought a blessing on yourselves today." Nm 25:5; Dt 33:9; Zch 13:3

³⁰ The following day Moses said to the people, "You have committed a grave sin. Now I will go up to the LORD; perhaps I will be able to atone for your sin." 1Sm 12:20; 2Sm 16:12

³¹ So Moses returned to the LORD and said, "Oh, these people have committed a grave sin; they have made a god of gold for themselves. ³² Now if you would only forgive their sin. But if not, please erase me from the book you have written." ³³ The LORD replied to Moses: "Whoever has sinned against me I will erase from my book. ³⁴ Now go, lead the people to the place I told you about; see, my angel will go before you. But on the day I settle accounts, I will hold them accountable for their sin." ³⁵ And the LORD inflicted a plague on the people for what they did with the calf Aaron had made. Dt 29:20; 32:35; Ps 9:5; Rm 2:5-6

The Tent Outside the Camp

33 The LORD spoke to Moses: "Go up from here, you and the people you brought up from the land of Egypt, to the land I promised to Abraham, Isaac, and Jacob, saying: I will give it to your offspring. ² I will send an angel ahead of you and will drive out the Canaanites, Amorites, Hethites, Perizzites, ᶜ Hivites, and Jebusites. ³ Go up to a land flowing with milk and honey. But I will not go up with you because you are a stiff-necked people; otherwise, I might destroy you on the way." ⁴ When the people heard this bad news, they mourned and didn't put on their jewelry. Gn 12:7; Ex 32:7, 34

⁵ For the LORD said to Moses: "Tell the Israelites: You are a stiff-necked

people. If I went up with you for a single moment, I would destroy you. Now take off your jewelry, and I will decide what to do with you." ⁶ So the Israelites remained stripped of their jewelry from Mount Horeb onward.

⁷ Now Moses took a tent and pitched it outside the camp, at a distance from the camp; he called it the tent of meeting. Anyone who wanted to consult the LORD would go to the tent of meeting that was outside the camp. ⁸ Whenever Moses went out to the tent, all the people would stand up, each one at the door of his tent, and they would watch Moses until he entered the tent. ⁹ When Moses entered the tent, the pillar of cloud would come down and remain at the entrance to the tent, and the LORD would speak with Moses. ¹⁰ As all the people saw the pillar of cloud remaining at the entrance to the tent, they would stand up, then bow in worship, each one at the door of his tent. ¹¹ The LORD would speak with Moses face to face, just as a man speaks with his friend, then Moses would return to the camp. His assistant, the young man Joshua son of Nun, would not leave the inside of the tent. Dt 4:29

The LORD's Glory

¹² Moses said to the LORD, "Look, you have told me, 'Lead this people up,' but you have not let me know whom you will send with me. You said, 'I know you by name, and you have also found favor with me.' ¹³ Now if I have indeed found favor with you, please teach me your ways, and I will know you, so that I may find favor with you. Now consider that this nation is your people." Ex 32:34; Jn 10:14-15; 2Tm 2:19

¹⁴ And he replied, "My presence will go with you, and I will give you rest." Jos 21:44; 22:4; Is 63:9

¹⁵ "If your presence does not go," Moses responded to him, "don't make us go up from here. ¹⁶ How will it be known that I and your people have found favor with you unless you go with us? I and your people will be distinguished by this from all the other people on the face of the earth." Ex 34:10; Nm 14:14

¹⁷ The LORD answered Moses, "I will do this very thing you have asked, for you have found favor with me, and I know you by name." ¹⁸ Then Moses said, "Please, let me see your glory." Ex 33:20; 1Tm 6:16

¹⁹ He said, "I will cause all my goodness to pass in front of you, and I will proclaim the name 'the LORD' before you. I will be gracious to whom I will be gracious, and I will have compassion on whom I will have compassion." ²⁰ But he added, "You cannot see my face, for humans cannot see me and live." ²¹ The LORD said, "Here is a place near me. You are to stand on the rock, ²² and when my glory passes by, I will put you in the crevice of the rock and cover you with my hand until I have passed by. ²³ Then I will take my hand away, and you will see my back, but my face will not be seen." Gn 32:30; Is 2:21; 6:5; Rm 9:15

New Stone Tablets

34 The LORD said to Moses, "Cut two stone tablets like the first ones, and I will write on them the words that were on the first tablets, which you broke. ² Be prepared by morning. Come up Mount Sinai in the morning and stand before me on the mountaintop. ³ No one may go up with you;

in fact, no one should be seen anywhere on the mountain. Even the flocks and herds are not to graze in front of that mountain." Ex 32:19

⁴ Moses cut two stone tablets like the first ones. He got up early in the morning, and taking the two stone tablets in his hand, he climbed Mount Sinai, just as the LORD had commanded him.

⁵ The LORD came down in a cloud, stood with him there, and proclaimed his name, "the LORD." ⁶ The LORD passed in front of him and proclaimed:

The LORD — the LORD is a compassionate and gracious God, slow to anger and abounding in faithful love and truth, ⁷ maintaining faithful love to a thousand generations, forgiving iniquity, rebellion, and sin. But he will not leave the guilty unpunished, bringing the fathers' iniquity on the children and grandchildren to the third and fourth generation. Nm 14:18

⁸ Moses immediately knelt low on the ground and worshiped. ⁹ Then he said, "My Lord, if I have indeed found favor with you, my Lord, please go with us (even though this is a stiff-necked people), forgive our iniquity and our sin, and accept us as your own possession."

Covenant Obligations

¹⁰ And the LORD responded: "Look, I am making a covenant. I will perform wonders in the presence of all your people that have never been doneᴬ in the whole earth or in any nation. All the people you live among will see the LORD's work, for what I am doing with you is awe-inspiring. ¹¹ Observe what I command you today. I am going to drive out before you the Amorites, Canaanites, Hethites, Perizzites, Hivites,ᴮ and Jebusites. ¹² Be careful not to make a treaty with the inhabitants of the land that you are going to enter; otherwise, they will become a snare among you. ¹³ Instead, you must tear down their altars, smash their sacred pillars, and chop down their Asherah poles. ¹⁴ Because the LORD is jealous for his reputation, you are never to bow down to another god.ᶜ He is a jealous God.

¹⁵ "Do not make a treaty with the inhabitants of the land, or else when they prostitute themselves with their gods and sacrifice to their gods, they will invite you, and you will eat their sacrifices. ¹⁶ Then you will take some of their daughters as brides for your sons. Their daughters will prostitute themselves with their gods and cause your sons to prostitute themselves with their gods. Nm 25:2

¹⁷ "Do not make cast images of gods for yourselves. Ex 32:8; Lv 19:14

¹⁸ "Observe the Festival of Unleavened Bread. You are to eat unleavened bread for seven days at the appointed time in the month of Abib,ᴰ as I commanded you, for you came out of Egypt in the month of Abib. Ex 12:15; 13:4

¹⁹ "The firstborn male from every womb belongs to me, including all your maleᴱ,ᶠ livestock, the firstborn of cattle or sheep. ²⁰ You may redeem the firstborn of a donkey with a sheep, but if you do not

---

ᴬ34:10 Lit created　ᴮ34:11 DSS, Sam, LXX add Girgashites　ᶜ34:14 Or the LORD — his name is Jealous or the LORD, being jealous by nature　ᴰ34:18 March–April; called Nisan in the post-exilic period; Neh 2:1; Est 3:7　ᴱ34:19 LXX, Theod, Vg, Tg read males　ᶠ34:19 Hb obscure

THE TEN
PLAGUES

When God wanted Pharaoh to free the Israelites who were slaves in Egypt, Pharaoh refused to let them go. Through Moses, God sent ten plagues on the country of Egypt.

1. ## WATER TURNED TO BLOOD • EXODUS 7:14–25
   The waters of the Nile turned to blood.

2. ## FROGS • EXODUS 8:1–15
   Frogs infested the land of Egypt.

3. ## GNATS • EXODUS 8:16–19
   Small stinging insects infested the land of Egypt.

4. ## SWARMS OF FLIES • EXODUS 8:20–32
   Swarms of flies infested the land of Egypt.

5. ## DEATH OF LIVESTOCK • EXODUS 9:1–7
   A serious disease infested the cattle belonging to Egyptians.

6. ## BOILS • EXODUS 9:8–12
   A skin disease infected the Egyptians.

7. ## HAIL • EXODUS 9:13–35
   A storm destroyed the grain fields of Egypt but spared the land of Goshen where the Israelites lived.

8. ## LOCUSTS • EXODUS 10:1–20
   An infestation of locusts stripped the land of Egypt of plant life.

9. ## DARKNESS • EXODUS 10:21–29
   A deep darkness covered the land of Egypt for three days.

10. ## DEATH OF THE FIRSTBORN • EXODUS 11:1–12:30
    The firstborn male of every Egyptian family died.

THE TEN
COMMMANDMENTS

God gave Moses the Ten Commandments on Mt. Sinai. The Commandments were written on tablets of stone by the finger of God. God wants people who believe in Him to obey these Commandments and live in ways that please Him. You can read the Ten Commandments in Exodus 20:1–17 and in Deuteronomy 5:6–21.

1. DO NOT HAVE OTHER GODS BESIDES ME.

2. DO NOT MAKE AN IDOL FOR YOURSELF.

3. DO NOT MISUSE THE NAME OF THE LORD YOUR GOD.

4. REMEMBER THE SABBATH DAY, TO KEEP IT HOLY.

5. HONOR YOUR FATHER AND YOUR MOTHER.

6. DO NOT MURDER.

7. DO NOT COMMIT ADULTERY.

8. DO NOT STEAL.

9. DO NOT GIVE DISHONEST TESTIMONY AGAINST YOUR NEIGHBOR.

10. DO NOT COVET.

redeem it, break its neck. You must redeem all the firstborn of your sons. No one is to appear before me empty-handed. Ex 13:2; 22:29; 23:15

²¹ "You are to labor six days but you must rest on the seventh day; you must even rest during plowing and harvesting times. Ex 20:9; Lk 13:14

²² "Observe the Festival of Weeks with the firstfruits of the wheat harvest, and the Festival of Ingathering ᴬ at the turn of the agricultural year. ²³ Three times a year all your males are to appear before the Lord GOD, the God of Israel. ²⁴ For I will drive out nations before you and enlarge your territory. No one will covet your land when you go up three times a year to appear before the LORD your God. Ex 19:8; 23:14

²⁵ "Do not present ᴮ the blood for my sacrifice with anything leavened. The sacrifice of the Passover Festival must not remain until morning. Ex 12:10; 23:18

²⁶ "Bring the best firstfruits of your land to the house of the LORD your God. Ex 23:19; Dt 26:2

"You must not boil a young goat in its mother's milk."

²⁷ The LORD also said to Moses, "Write down these words, for I have made a covenant with you and with Israel based on these words."

²⁸ Moses was there with the LORD forty days and forty nights; he did not eat food or drink water. He wrote the Ten Commandments, the words of the covenant, on the tablets. Ex 24:18; 31:18; Dt 4:13; 10:2,4

Moses's Radiant Face

²⁹ As Moses descended from Mount Sinai — with the two tablets of the testimony in his hands as he descended the mountain — he did not realize that the skin of his face shone as a result of his speaking with the LORD. ᶜ ³⁰ When Aaron and all the Israelites saw Moses, the skin of his face shone! They were afraid to come near him. ³¹ But Moses called out to them, so Aaron and all the leaders of the community returned to him, and Moses spoke to them. ³² Afterward all the Israelites came near, and he commanded them to do everything the LORD had told him on Mount Sinai. ³³ When Moses had finished speaking with them, he put a veil over his face. ³⁴ But whenever Moses went before the LORD to speak with him, he would remove the veil until he came out. After he came out, he would tell the Israelites what he had been commanded, ³⁵ and the Israelites would see that Moses's face ᴰ was radiant. Then Moses would put the veil over his face again until he went to speak with the LORD. Ex 32:15; Ps 34:5; Mt 17:2; 2Co 3:7,13

The Sabbath Command

35 Moses assembled the entire Israelite community and said to them, "These are the things that the LORD has commanded you to do: ² For six days work is to be done, but on the seventh day you are to have a holy day, a Sabbath of complete rest to the LORD. Anyone who does work on it must be executed. ³ Do not light a fire in any of your homes on the Sabbath day."

Building the Tabernacle

⁴ Then Moses said to the entire Israelite community, "This is what the LORD has commanded: ⁵ Take

---

ᴬ**34:22** The *Festival of Ingathering* is called Festival of Shelters elsewhere; Lv 23:34-36. ᴮ**34:25** Lit *slaughter* ᶜ**34:29** Lit *with him* ᴰ**34:35** Lit *see Moses's face, that the skin of his face* up an offering among you for the LORD. Let everyone whose heart is willing bring this as the LORD's offering: gold, silver, and bronze; [6] blue, purple, and scarlet yarn; fine linen and goat hair; [7] ram skins dyed red and fine leather;[A] acacia wood; [8] oil for the light; spices for the anointing oil and for the fragrant incense; [9] and onyx with gemstones to mount on the ephod and breastpiece.   Ex 25:2-7

[10] "Let all the skilled artisans[B] among you come and make everything that the LORD has commanded: [11] the tabernacle — its tent and covering, its clasps and supports, its crossbars, its pillars and bases; [12] the ark with its poles, the mercy seat, and the curtain for the screen; [13] the table with its poles, all its utensils, and the Bread of the Presence; [14] the lampstand for light with its utensils and lamps as well as the oil for the light; [15] the altar of incense with its poles; the anointing oil and the fragrant incense; the entryway screen for the entrance to the tabernacle; [16] the altar of burnt offering with its bronze grate, its poles, and all its utensils; the basin with its stand; [17] the hangings of the courtyard, its posts and bases, and the screen for the gate of the courtyard; [18] the tent pegs for the tabernacle and the tent pegs for the courtyard, along with their ropes; [19] and the specially woven[A] garments for ministering in the sanctuary — the holy garments for the priest Aaron and the garments for his sons to serve as priests."

[20] Then the entire Israelite community left Moses's presence. [21] Everyone whose heart was moved and whose spirit prompted him came and brought an offering to the LORD for the work on the tent of meeting, for all its services, and for the holy garments. [22] Both men and women came; all who had willing hearts brought brooches, earrings, rings, necklaces, and all kinds of gold jewelry — everyone who presented a presentation offering of gold to the LORD. [23] Everyone who possessed blue, purple, or scarlet yarn, fine linen or goat hair, ram skins dyed red or fine leather,[A] brought them. [24] Everyone making an offering of silver or bronze brought it as a contribution to the LORD. Everyone who possessed acacia wood useful for any task in the work brought it. [25] Every skilled[C] woman spun yarn with her hands and brought it: blue, purple, and scarlet yarn, and fine linen. [26] And all the women whose hearts were moved spun the goat hair by virtue of their skill. [27] The leaders brought onyx and gemstones to mount on the ephod and breastpiece, [28] as well as the spice and oil for the light, for the anointing oil, and for the fragrant incense. [29] So the Israelites brought a freewill offering to the LORD, all the men and women whose hearts prompted them to bring something for all the work that the LORD, through Moses, had commanded to be done.

Bezalel and Oholiab

[30] Moses then said to the Israelites: "Look, the LORD has appointed by name Bezalel son of Uri, son of Hur, of the tribe of Judah. [31] He has filled him with God's Spirit, with wisdom, understanding, and ability in every kind of craft [32] to design artistic

---

[A]35:7,19,23 Hb obscure   [B]35:10 Lit *the wise of heart*   [C]35:25 Lit *wise of heart* works in gold, silver, and bronze, [33] to cut gemstones for mounting, and to carve wood for work in every kind of artistic craft. [34] He has also given[A] both him and Oholiab son of Ahisamach, of the tribe of Dan, the ability to teach others. [35] He has filled them with skill[B] to do all the work of a gem cutter; a designer; an embroiderer[C] in blue, purple, and scarlet yarn and fine linen; and a weaver. They can do every kind of craft and design artistic designs.

36 [1] Bezalel, Oholiab, and all the skilled[D] people are to work based on everything the LORD has commanded. The LORD has given them wisdom and understanding to know how to do all the work of constructing the sanctuary."   Ex 25:8; 28:3; 31:1-6; 35:10,35

[2] So Moses summoned Bezalel, Oholiab, and every skilled person in whose heart the LORD had placed wisdom, all whose hearts moved them, to come to the work and do it. [3] They took from Moses's presence all the contributions that the Israelites had brought for the task of making the sanctuary. Meanwhile, the people continued to bring freewill offerings morning after morning.   Ex 25:2; 35:21,26; 1Ch 29:5

[4] Then all the artisans who were doing all the work for the sanctuary came one by one from the work they were doing [5] and said to Moses, "The people are bringing more than is needed for the construction of the work the LORD commanded to be done."   2Ch 31:10; 2Co 8:2-3

[6] After Moses gave an order, they sent a proclamation throughout the camp: "Let no man or woman make anything else as an offering for the sanctuary." So the people stopped. [7] The materials were sufficient for them to do all the work. There was more than enough.

Building the Tabernacle

[8] All the skilled artisans[E] among those doing the work made the tabernacle with ten curtains. Bezalel made them of finely spun linen, as well as blue, purple, and scarlet yarn, with a design of cherubim worked into them. [9] Each curtain was forty-two feet[F] long and six feet[G] wide; all the curtains had the same measurements. [10] He joined five of the curtains to each other, and the other five curtains he joined to each other. [11] He made loops of blue yarn on the edge of the last curtain in the first set and did the same on the edge of the outermost curtain in the second set. [12] He made fifty loops on the one curtain and fifty loops on the edge of the curtain in the second set, so that the loops lined up with each other. [13] He also made fifty gold clasps and joined the curtains to each other, so that the tabernacle became a single unit.   Ex 26:1-14

[14] He made curtains of goat hair for a tent over the tabernacle; he made eleven of them. [15] Each curtain was forty-five feet[H] long and six feet wide. All eleven curtains had the same measurements. [16] He joined five of the curtains together, and the other six together. [17] He made fifty loops on the edge of the outermost curtain in the first set and fifty loops on the edge of the corresponding curtain in the

---

A35:34 Lit *also put in his heart*   B35:35 Lit *with wisdom of heart*   C35:35 Or *weaver*   D36:1 Lit *wise of heart*, also in v. 2   E36:8 Lit *the wise of heart*   F36:9 Lit *28 cubits*   G36:9 Lit *four cubits*, also in v. 15   H36:15 Lit *30 cubits* second set. [18] He made fifty bronze clasps to join the tent together as a single unit. [19] He also made a covering for the tent from ram skins dyed red and a covering of fine leather[A] on top of it.

[20] He made upright supports[B] of acacia wood for the tabernacle. [21] Each support was fifteen feet[C] long and twenty-seven inches[D] wide. [22] Each support had two tenons for joining one to another. He did the same for all the supports of the tabernacle. [23] He made supports for the tabernacle as follows: twenty for the south side, [24] and he made forty silver bases to put under the twenty supports, two bases under the first support for its two tenons, and two bases under each of the following supports for their two tenons; [25] for the second side of the tabernacle, the north side, he made twenty supports, [26] with their forty silver bases, two bases under the first support and two bases under each of the following ones; [27] and for the back of the tabernacle, on the west side, he made six supports. [28] He also made two additional supports for the two back corners of the tabernacle. [29] They were paired at the bottom and joined together[E] at the[F] top in a single ring. This is what he did with both of them for the two corners. [30] So there were eight supports with their sixteen silver bases, two bases under each one. Ex 25:5; 26:15-29

[31] He made five crossbars of acacia wood for the supports on one side of the tabernacle, [32] five crossbars for the supports on the other side of the tabernacle, and five crossbars for those at the back of the tabernacle on the west. [33] He made the central crossbar run through the middle of the supports from one end to the other. [34] He overlaid them with gold and made their rings out of gold as holders for the crossbars. He also overlaid the crossbars with gold.

[35] Then he made the curtain with blue, purple, and scarlet yarn, and finely spun linen. He made it with a design of cherubim worked into it. [36] He made four pillars of acacia wood for it and overlaid them with gold; their hooks were of gold. And he cast four silver bases for the pillars. Ex 26:31-37

[37] He made a screen embroidered[G] with blue, purple, and scarlet yarn, and finely spun linen for the entrance to the tent, [38] together with its five pillars and their hooks. He overlaid the tops of the pillars and their bands with gold, but their five bases were bronze.

Making the Ark

37 Bezalel made the ark of acacia wood, forty-five inches long, twenty-seven inches wide, and twenty-seven inches high.[H] [2] He overlaid it with pure gold inside and out and made a gold molding all around it. [3] He cast four gold rings for it, for its four feet, two rings on one side and two rings on the other side. [4] He made poles of acacia wood and overlaid them with gold. [5] He inserted the poles into the rings on the sides of the ark for carrying the ark. Ex 25:10-20

[6] He made a mercy seat of pure gold, forty-five inches long and

---

[A]**36:19** Hb obscure   [B]**36:20** Or *made frames*   [C]**36:21** Lit *10 cubits*   [D]**36:21** Lit *a cubit and a half*
[E]**36:29** Lit *and together they are to be complete*   [F]**36:29** Lit *its*   [G]**36:37** Or *woven*   [H]**37:1** Lit *two and a half cubits its length, one and a half cubits its width, and one and a half cubits its height*

twenty-seven inches wide.^A ⁷He made two cherubim of gold; he made them of hammered work at the two ends of the mercy seat, ⁸one cherub at one end and one cherub at the other end. At each end, he made a cherub of one piece with the mercy seat. ⁹They had wings spread out. They faced each other and covered the mercy seat with their wings. The faces of the cherubim were looking toward the mercy seat.

Making the Table

¹⁰He constructed the table of acacia wood, thirty-six inches long, eighteen inches wide, and twenty-seven inches high. ^B ¹¹He overlaid it with pure gold and made a gold molding all around it. ¹²He made a three-inch^C frame all around it and made a gold molding all around its frame. ¹³He cast four gold rings for it and attached the rings to the four corners at its four legs. ¹⁴The rings were next to the frame as holders for the poles to carry the table. ¹⁵He made the poles for carrying the table from acacia wood and overlaid them with gold. ¹⁶He also made the utensils that would be on the table out of pure gold: its plates and cups, as well as its bowls and pitchers for pouring drink offerings. Ex 25:23-29

Making the Lampstand

¹⁷Then he made the lampstand out of pure hammered gold. He made it all of one piece: its base and shaft, its ornamental cups, and its buds and petals. ¹⁸Six branches extended from its sides, three branches of the lampstand from one side and three branches of the lampstand from the other side. ¹⁹There were three cups shaped like almond blossoms, each with a bud and petals, on one branch, and three cups shaped like almond blossoms, each with a bud and petals, on the next branch. It was this way for the six branches that extended from the lampstand. ²⁰There were four cups shaped like almond blossoms on the lampstand shaft along with its buds and petals. ²¹For the six branches that extended from it, a bud was under the first pair of branches from it, a bud under the second pair of branches from it, and a bud under the third pair of branches from it. ²²Their buds and branches were of one piece with it. All of it was a single hammered piece of pure gold. ²³He also made its seven lamps, snuffers, and firepans of pure gold. ²⁴He made it and all its utensils of seventy-five pounds^D of pure gold.

Making the Altar of Incense

²⁵He made the altar of incense out of acacia wood. It was square, eighteen inches long and eighteen inches wide; it was thirty-six inches high. ^E Its horns were of one piece with it. ²⁶He overlaid it, its top, all around its sides, and its horns with pure gold. Then he made a gold molding all around it. ²⁷He made two gold rings for it under the molding on two of its sides; he put these on opposite sides of it to be holders for the poles to carry it with. ²⁸He made the poles of acacia wood and overlaid them with gold.

²⁹He also made the holy anointing oil and the pure, fragrant, and expertly blended incense.

^A37:6 Lit two and a half cubits its length and one and a half cubits its width   ^B37:10 Lit two cubits its length, one cubit its width, and one and a half cubits its height   ^C37:12 Lit a handbreadth   ^D37:24 Lit a talent   ^E37:25 Lit a cubit its length, a cubit its width, and two cubits its height

Making the Altar of Burnt Offering

38 Bezalel constructed the altar of burnt offering from acacia wood. It was square, 7½ feet long and 7½ feet wide, ^A and was 4½ feet^B high. ² He made horns for it on its four corners; the horns were of one piece with it. Then he overlaid it with bronze.   Ex 27:1-8

³ He made all the altar's utensils: the pots, shovels, basins, meat forks, and firepans; he made all its utensils of bronze. ⁴ He constructed for the altar a grate of bronze mesh under its ledge, ^C halfway up from the bottom. ⁵ He cast four rings at the four corners of the bronze grate as holders for the poles. ⁶ He made the poles of acacia wood and overlaid them with bronze. ⁷ Then he inserted the poles into the rings on the sides of the altar in order to carry it with them. He constructed the altar with boards so that it was hollow.

Making the Bronze Basin

⁸ He made the bronze basin and its stand from the bronze mirrors of the women who served at the entrance to the tent of meeting.

Making the Courtyard

⁹ Then he made the courtyard. The hangings on the south side of the courtyard were of finely spun linen, 150 feet^D long, ¹⁰ including their twenty posts and their twenty bronze bases, with silver hooks and silver bands^E for the posts. ¹¹ The hangings on the north side were also 150 feet long, including their twenty posts and twenty bronze bases. The hooks and bands of the posts were silver. ¹² The hangings on the west side were 75 feet^F long, including their ten posts and their ten bases, with silver hooks and silver bands for the posts. ¹³ And for the east side toward the sunrise, 75 feet long, ¹⁴ the hangings on one side of the gate were 22½ feet, ^G including their three posts and their three bases. ¹⁵ It was the same for the other side of the courtyard gate. The hangings were 22½ feet, including their three posts and their three bases. ¹⁶ All the hangings around the courtyard were of finely spun linen. ¹⁷ The bases for the posts were bronze; the hooks and bands of the posts were silver; and the plating for the tops of the posts was silver. All the posts of the courtyard were banded with silver.   Ex 27:9-19

¹⁸ The screen for the gate of the courtyard was made of finely spun linen, expertly embroidered^H with blue, purple, and scarlet yarn. It was 30 feet^I long, and like the hangings of the courtyard, 7½ feet^J high.^K ¹⁹ It had four posts with their four bronze bases. Their hooks were silver, and their top plating and their bands were silver. ²⁰ All the tent pegs for the tabernacle and for the surrounding courtyard were bronze.

Inventory of Materials

²¹ This is the inventory for the tabernacle, the tabernacle of the testimony, that was recorded at Moses's command. It was the work of the

---

^A**38:1** Lit *five cubits its length and five cubits its width*   ^B**38:1** Lit *three cubits*   ^C**38:4** Or *rim*   ^D**38:9** Lit *100 cubits*, also in v.11   ^E**38:10** Or *connecting rods*, also in vv.11,17,19,28   ^F**38:12** Lit *50 cubits*, also in v.13   ^G**38:14** Lit *15 cubits*, also in v.15   ^H**38:18** Or *woven*   ^I**38:18** Lit *20 cubits*   ^J**38:18** Lit *five cubits*   ^K**38:18** Lit *high in width*

Levites under the direction of[A] Ithamar son of Aaron the priest. [22] Bezalel son of Uri, son of Hur, of the tribe of Judah, made everything that the LORD commanded Moses. [23] With him was Oholiab son of Ahisamach, of the tribe of Dan, a gem cutter, a designer, and an embroiderer with blue, purple, and scarlet yarn, and fine linen.

[24] All the gold of the presentation offering that was used for the project in all the work on the sanctuary, was 2,193 pounds, [B] according to the sanctuary shekel. [25] The silver from those of the community who were registered was 7,544 pounds, [C] according to the sanctuary shekel — [26] one-fifth of an ounce [D] per man, that is, half a shekel according to the sanctuary shekel, from everyone twenty years old or more who had crossed over to the registered group, 603,550 men. [27] There were 7,500 pounds[E] of silver used to cast the bases of the sanctuary and the bases of the curtain — one hundred bases from 7,500 pounds, 75 pounds[F] for each base. [28] With the remaining 44 pounds[G] he made the hooks for the posts, overlaid their tops, and supplied bands for them.

[29] The bronze of the presentation offering totaled 5,310 pounds.[H] [30] He made with it the bases for the entrance to the tent of meeting, the bronze altar and its bronze grate, all the utensils for the altar, [31] the bases for the surrounding courtyard, the bases for the gate of the courtyard, all the tent pegs for the tabernacle, and all the tent pegs for the surrounding courtyard.

Making the Priestly Garments

39 They made specially woven[I] garments for ministry in the sanctuary, and the holy garments for Aaron from the blue, purple, and scarlet yarn, just as the LORD had commanded Moses. Ex 28:2,4

Making the Ephod

[2] Bezalel made the ephod of gold, of blue, purple, and scarlet yarn, and of finely spun linen. [3] They hammered out thin sheets of gold, and he[J] cut threads from them to interweave with the blue, purple, and scarlet yarn, and the fine linen in a skillful design. [4] They made shoulder pieces for attaching it; it was joined together at its two edges. [5] The artistically woven waistband that was on the ephod was of one piece with the ephod, according to the same workmanship of gold, of blue, purple, and scarlet yarn, and of finely spun linen, just as the LORD had commanded Moses. Ex 28:6-12

[6] Then they mounted the onyx stones surrounded with gold filigree settings, engraved with the names of Israel's sons as a gem cutter engraves a seal. [7] He fastened them on the shoulder pieces of the ephod as memorial stones for the Israelites, just as the LORD had commanded Moses.

Making the Breastpiece

[8] He also made the embroidered[K] breastpiece with the same workmanship as the ephod of gold, of blue, purple, and scarlet yarn, and of finely spun linen. [9] They made the breastpiece square and folded

[A]38:21 Lit *Levites by the hand of*   [B]38:24 Lit *29 talents and 730 shekels*   [C]38:25 Lit *100 talents and 1,775 shekels*   [D]38:26 Lit *a beka*   [E]38:27 Lit *100 talents*   [F]38:27 Lit *one talent*   [G]38:28 Lit *1,775* (shekels)   [H]38:29 Lit *70 talents and 2,400 shekels*   [I]39:1 Hb obscure   [J]39:3 Sam, Syr, Tg read *they* [K]39:8 Or *woven* double, nine inches long and nine inches wide.[A] [10] They mounted four rows of gemstones[B] on it. Ex 28:15-28

The first row was
a row of carnelian, topaz, and emerald;[C]
[11] the second row,
a turquoise,[D] a lapis lazuli, and a diamond;[E]
[12] the third row,
a jacinth,[F] an agate, and an amethyst;
[13] and the fourth row,
a beryl, an onyx, and a jasper.
They were surrounded with gold filigree in their settings.

[14] The twelve stones corresponded to the names of Israel's sons. Each stone was engraved like a seal with one of the names of the twelve tribes.

[15] They made braided chains of pure gold cord for the breastpiece. [16] They also fashioned two gold filigree settings and two gold rings and attached the two rings to its two corners. [17] Then they attached the two gold cords to the two gold rings on the corners of the breastpiece. [18] They attached the other ends of the two cords to the two filigree settings, and in this way they attached them to the ephod's shoulder pieces in front. [19] They made two other gold rings and put them at the two other corners of the breastpiece on the edge that is next to the inner border of the ephod. [20] They made two more gold rings and attached them to the bottom of the ephod's two shoulder pieces on its front, close to its seam,[G] above the ephod's woven waistband. [21] Then they tied the breastpiece from its rings to the rings of the ephod with a cord of blue yarn, so that the breastpiece was above the ephod's waistband and did not come loose from the ephod. They did just as the LORD had commanded Moses.

Making the Robe

[22] They made the woven robe of the ephod entirely of blue yarn. [23] There was an opening in the center of the robe like that of body armor[F] with a collar around the opening so that it would not tear. [24] They made pomegranates of finely spun blue, purple, and scarlet yarn[H] on the lower hem of the robe. [25] They made bells of pure gold and attached the bells between the pomegranates, all around the hem of the robe between the pomegranates, [26] a bell and a pomegranate alternating all around the lower hem of the robe[I] to be worn for ministry. They made it just as the LORD had commanded Moses. Ex 28:31-34

The Other Priestly Garments

[27] They made the tunics of fine woven linen for Aaron and his sons. [28] They made the turban and the ornate headbands[J] of fine linen, the linen undergarments of finely spun linen, [29] and the sash of finely spun linen expertly embroidered with blue, purple, and scarlet yarn. They did just as the LORD had commanded Moses. Ex 28:39,42; Ezk 44:18

[A]39:9 Lit a span its length and a span its width   [B]39:10 Many of these stones cannot be identified with certainty.   [C]39:10 Or beryl   [D]39:11 Or malachite, or garnet   [E]39:11 Hb uncertain; LXX, Vg read jasper   [F]39:12,23 Hb obscure   [G]39:20 The place where the shoulder pieces join the front of the ephod   [H]39:24 Sam, LXX, Vg add and linen   [I]39:26 Lit bell and pomegranate, bell and pomegranate, on the hem of the robe around   [J]39:28 Lit and the headdresses of headbands

Making the Holy Diadem

[30] They made a medallion, the holy diadem, out of pure gold and wrote on it an inscription like the engraving on a seal: HOLY TO THE LORD. [31] They attached a cord of blue yarn to it in order to mount it on the turban, just as the LORD had commanded Moses. Ex 28:36-37; 29:6

Moses's Inspection of the Tabernacle

[32] So all the work for the tabernacle, the tent of meeting, was finished. The Israelites did everything just as the LORD had commanded Moses. [33] They brought the tabernacle to Moses: the tent with all its furnishings, its clasps, its supports, its crossbars, and its pillars and bases; [34] the covering of ram skins dyed red and the covering of fine leather;[A] the curtain for the screen; [35] the ark of the testimony with its poles and the mercy seat; [36] the table, all its utensils, and the Bread of the Presence; [37] the pure gold lampstand, with its lamps arranged and all its utensils, as well as the oil for the light; [38] the gold altar; the anointing oil; the fragrant incense; the screen for the entrance to the tent; [39] the bronze altar with its bronze grate, its poles, and all its utensils; the basin with its stand; [40] the hangings of the courtyard, its posts and bases, the screen for the gate of the courtyard, its ropes and tent pegs, and all the furnishings for the service of the tabernacle, the tent of meeting; [41] and the specially woven[A] garments for ministering in the sanctuary, the holy garments for the priest Aaron and the garments for his sons to serve as priests. [42] The Israelites had done all the work according to everything the LORD had commanded Moses. [43] Moses inspected all the work they had accomplished. They had done just as the LORD commanded. Then Moses blessed them. Ex 25:40; 30:3; 39:42-43

Setting up the Tabernacle

40 The LORD spoke to Moses: [2] "You are to set up the tabernacle, the tent of meeting, on the first day of the first month.[B] [3] Put the ark of the testimony there and screen off the ark with the curtain. [4] Then bring in the table and lay out its arrangement; also bring in the lampstand and set up its lamps. [5] Place the gold altar for incense in front of the ark of the testimony. Put up the screen for the entrance to the tabernacle. [6] Position the altar of burnt offering in front of the entrance to the tabernacle, the tent of meeting. [7] Place the basin between the tent of meeting and the altar, and put water in it. [8] Assemble the surrounding courtyard and hang the screen for the gate of the courtyard. Ex 12:12; 13:4

[9] "Take the anointing oil and anoint the tabernacle and everything in it; consecrate it along with all its furnishings so that it will be holy. [10] Anoint the altar of burnt offering and all its utensils; consecrate the altar so that it will be especially holy. [11] Anoint the basin and its stand and consecrate it.

[12] "Then bring Aaron and his sons to the entrance to the tent of meeting and wash them with water. [13] Clothe Aaron with the holy garments, anoint him, and consecrate him, so that he can serve me as a priest. [14] Have his sons come

---

[A] **39:34,41** Hb obscure   [B] **40:2** Lit *on the day of the first month, on the first of the month* forward and clothe them in tunics. [15] Anoint them just as you anointed their father, so that they may also serve me as priests. Their anointing will serve to inaugurate a permanent priesthood for them throughout their generations." Ex 28:41; Lv 8:1-3

[16] Moses did everything just as the LORD had commanded him. [17] The tabernacle was set up in the first month of the second year, on the first day of the month. [A] [18] Moses set up the tabernacle: He laid its bases, positioned its supports, inserted its crossbars, and set up its pillars. [19] Then he spread the tent over the tabernacle and put the covering of the tent on top of it, just as the LORD had commanded Moses.

[20] Moses took the testimony and placed it in the ark, and attached the poles to the ark. He set the mercy seat on top of the ark. [21] He brought the ark into the tabernacle, put up the curtain for the screen, and screened off the ark of the testimony, just as the LORD had commanded him. Ex 16:34; 25:16

[22] Moses placed the table in the tent of meeting on the north side of the tabernacle, outside the curtain. [23] He arranged the bread on it before the LORD, just as the LORD had commanded him. [24] He put the lampstand in the tent of meeting opposite the table on the south side of the tabernacle [25] and set up the lamps before the LORD, just as the LORD had commanded him.

[26] Moses installed the gold altar in the tent of meeting, in front of the curtain, [27] and burned fragrant incense on it, just as the LORD had commanded him. [28] He put up the screen at the entrance to the tabernacle. [29] He placed the altar of burnt offering at the entrance to the tabernacle, the tent of meeting, and offered the burnt offering and the grain offering on it, just as the LORD had commanded him.

[30] He set the basin between the tent of meeting and the altar and put water in it for washing. [31] Moses, Aaron, and his sons washed their hands and feet from it. [32] They washed whenever they came to the tent of meeting and approached the altar, just as the LORD had commanded Moses.

[33] Next Moses set up the surrounding courtyard for the tabernacle and the altar and hung a screen for the gate of the courtyard. So Moses finished the work. Ex 25:37

The LORD's Glory

[34] The cloud covered the tent of meeting, and the glory of the LORD filled the tabernacle. [35] Moses was unable to enter the tent of meeting because the cloud rested on it, and the glory of the LORD filled the tabernacle. Lv 16:2; Nm 9:15; 1Kg 8:10-11; 2Ch 5:13-14

[36] The Israelites set out whenever the cloud was taken up from the tabernacle throughout all the stages of their journey. [37] If the cloud was not taken up, they did not set out until the day it was taken up. [38] For the cloud of the LORD was over the tabernacle by day, and there was a fire inside the cloud by night, visible to the entire house of Israel throughout all the stages of their journey. Nm 9:17, 19-22; Neh 9:19

[A] 40:17 DSS, Sam, LXX add of their coming out of Egypt

LEVITICUS

The Burnt Offering

1 Then the LORD summoned Moses and spoke to him from the tent of meeting: ² "Speak to the Israelites and tell them: When any of you brings an offering to the LORD from the livestock, you may bring your offering from the herd or the flock. Ex 27:21; Ps 77:20; Mt 8:4; Heb 3:2

³ "If his offering is a burnt offering from the herd, he is to bring an unblemished male. He will bring it to the entrance to the tent of meeting so that he ᴬ may be accepted by the LORD. ⁴ He is to lay his hand on the head of the burnt offering so it can be accepted on his behalf to make atonement for him. ⁵ He is to slaughter the bull before the LORD; Aaron's sons the priests are to present the blood and splatter it on all sides of the altar that is at the entrance to the tent of meeting. ⁶ Then he is to skin the burnt offering and cut it into pieces. ᴮ ⁷ The sons of Aaron the priest will prepare a fire on the altar and arrange wood on the fire. ⁸ Aaron's sons the priests are to arrange the pieces, the head, and the fat on top of the burning wood on the altar. ⁹ The offerer is to wash its entrails and legs with water. Then the priest will burn all of it on the altar as a burnt offering, a fire offering of a pleasing aroma to the LORD. Gn 22:2; Ex 29:1; Lv 3:5; 19:5,7

¹⁰ "But if his offering for a burnt offering is from the flock, from sheep or goats, he is to present an unblemished male. ¹¹ He will slaughter it on the north side of the altar before the LORD. Aaron's sons the priests will splatter its blood against the altar on all sides. ¹² He will cut the animal into pieces with its head and its fat, and the priest will arrange them on top of the burning wood on the altar. ¹³ But he is to wash the entrails and legs with water. The priest will then present all of it and burn it on the altar; it is a burnt offering, a fire offering of a pleasing aroma to the LORD. Lv 4:23

¹⁴ "If his offering to the LORD is a burnt offering of birds, he is to present his offering from the turtledoves or young pigeons. ᶜ ¹⁵ Then the priest is to bring it to the altar, and will twist off its head and burn it on the altar; its blood should be drained at the side of the altar. ¹⁶ He will remove its digestive tract, ᴰ cutting off the tail feathers, and throw it on the east side of the altar at the place for ashes. ¹⁷ He will tear it open by its wings without dividing the bird. Then the priest is to burn it on the altar on top of the burning wood. It is a burnt offering, a fire offering of a pleasing aroma to the LORD. Gn 40:17; Lv 17:13; Nm 6:10; Ps 74:19

The Grain Offering

2 "When anyone presents a grain offering as an offering to the LORD, it is to consist of fine flour. He is to pour olive oil on it, put frankincense on it, ² and bring it to Aaron's sons the priests. The priest will take a handful of fine flour and oil from it, along with all its frankincense, and will burn this memorial

---

ᴬ**1:3** Or *it* ᴮ**1:6** Lit *its pieces,* also in v. 12 ᶜ**1:14** Or *or pigeons* ᴰ**1:16** Or *its crop,* or *its crissum* portion of it on the altar, a fire offering of a pleasing aroma to the LORD. [3] But the rest of the grain offering will belong to Aaron and his sons; it is the holiest part of the fire offerings to the LORD. Gn 18:6; Ex 40:29

[4] "When you present a grain offering baked in an oven, it is to be made of fine flour, either unleavened cakes mixed with oil or unleavened wafers coated with oil. [5] If your offering is a grain offering prepared on a griddle, it is to be unleavened bread made of fine flour mixed with oil. [6] Break it into pieces and pour oil on it; it is a grain offering. [7] If your offering is a grain offering prepared in a pan, it is to be made of fine flour with oil. [8] When you bring to the LORD the grain offering made in any of these ways, it is to be presented to the priest, and he will take it to the altar. [9] The priest will remove the memorial portion[A] from the grain offering and burn it on the altar, a fire offering of a pleasing aroma to the LORD. [10] But the rest of the grain offering will belong to Aaron and his sons; it is the holiest part of the fire offerings to the LORD. Ex 29:2,23; Lv 7:12; 8:26; Nm 6:15,19

[11] "No grain offering that you present to the LORD is to be made with yeast, for you are not to burn[B] any yeast or honey as a fire offering to the LORD. [12] You may present them to the LORD as an offering of firstfruits, but they are not to be offered on the altar as a pleasing aroma. [13] You are to season each of your grain offerings with salt; you must not omit from your grain offering the salt of the covenant with your God. You are to present salt with each of your offerings. Ex 12:14; Jdg 14:8

[14] "If you present a grain offering of firstfruits to the LORD, you are to present fresh heads of grain, crushed kernels, roasted on the fire, for your grain offering of firstfruits. [15] You are to put oil and frankincense on it; it is a grain offering. [16] The priest will then burn some of its crushed kernels and oil with all its frankincense as a fire offering to the LORD.

The Fellowship Offering

3 "If his offering is a fellowship sacrifice, and he is presenting an animal from the herd, whether male or female, he is to present one without blemish before the LORD. [2] He is to lay his hand on the head of his offering and slaughter it at the entrance to the tent of meeting. Then Aaron's sons the priests will splatter the blood on all sides of the altar. [3] He will present part of the fellowship sacrifice as a fire offering to the LORD: the fat surrounding the entrails, all the fat that is on the entrails, [4] and the two kidneys with the fat on them at the loins; he will also remove the fatty lobe of the liver with the kidneys. [5] Aaron's sons will burn it on the altar along with the burnt offering that is on the burning wood, a fire offering of a pleasing aroma to the LORD. Ex 23:18; 29:1,13,22; Lv 1:5; 7:11

[6] "If his offering as a fellowship sacrifice to the LORD is from the flock, he is to present a male or female without blemish. [7] If he is presenting a lamb for his offering, he is to present it before the LORD. [8] He must lay his hand on the head of his offering, then slaughter it before the tent of meeting. Aaron's sons will splatter its blood on all

A 2:9 Lit portion of it   B 2:11 Some Hb mss, Sam, LXX, Tg read present sides of the altar. [9] He will then present part of the fellowship sacrifice as a fire offering to the Lord consisting of its fat and the entire fat tail, which he is to remove close to the backbone. He will also remove the fat surrounding the entrails, all the fat on the entrails, [10] the two kidneys with the fat on them at the loins, and the fatty lobe of the liver above the kidneys. [11] Then the priest will burn the food on the altar, as a fire offering to the Lord.   Ex 29:22

[12] "If his offering is a goat, he is to present it before the Lord. [13] He must lay his hand on its head and slaughter it before the tent of meeting. Aaron's sons will splatter[A] its blood on all sides of the altar. [14] He will present part of his offering as a fire offering to the Lord: the fat surrounding the entrails, all the fat that is on the entrails, [15] and the two kidneys with the fat on them at the loins; he will also remove the fatty lobe of the liver with the kidneys. [16] Then the priest will burn the food on the altar, as a fire offering for a pleasing aroma. [B]   Lv 4:23

"All fat belongs to the Lord. [17] This is a permanent statute throughout your generations, wherever you live: you must not eat any fat or any blood."   Ex 28:43; Lv 7:26; 11:46; 17:10,14; 19:26

The Sin Offering

4 Then the Lord spoke to Moses: [2] "Tell the Israelites: When someone sins unintentionally against any of the Lord's commands and does anything prohibited by them —   Nm 15:22,24 [3] "If the anointed priest sins, bringing guilt on the people, he is to present to the Lord a young, unblemished bull as a sin[C] offering

for the sin he has committed. [4] He is to bring the bull to the entrance to the tent of meeting before the Lord, lay his hand on the bull's head, and slaughter it before the Lord. [5] The anointed priest will then take some of the bull's blood and bring it into the tent of meeting. [6] The priest is to dip his finger in the blood and sprinkle some of it seven times before the Lord in front of the curtain of the sanctuary. [7] The priest is to apply some of the blood to the horns of the altar of fragrant incense that is before the Lord in the tent of meeting. He must pour out the rest of the bull's blood at the base of the altar of burnt offering that is at the entrance to the tent of meeting. [8] He is to remove all the fat from the bull of the sin offering: the fat surrounding the entrails, all the fat that is on the entrails, [9] and the two kidneys with the fat on them at the loins. He will also remove the fatty lobe of the liver with the kidneys, [10] just as the fat is removed from the ox of the fellowship sacrifice. The priest is to burn them on the altar of burnt offering. [11] But the hide of the bull and all its flesh, with its head and legs, and its entrails and waste — [12] all the rest of the bull — he must bring to a ceremonially clean place outside the camp to the ash heap, and must burn it on a wood fire. It is to be burned at the ash heap.   Lv 4:16

[13] "Now if the whole community of Israel errs, and the matter escapes the notice of the assembly, so that they violate any of the Lord's commands and incur guilt by doing what is prohibited, [14] then the assembly must present a young bull as a sin offering. They are to

A [3:13] Or *dash*   B [3:16] Sam, LXX add *to the Lord*   C [4:3] Or *purification* bring it before the tent of meeting when the sin they have committed in regard to the command becomes known. ¹⁵ The elders of the community are to lay their hands on the bull's head before the LORD and it is to be slaughtered before the LORD. ¹⁶ The anointed priest will bring some of the bull's blood into the tent of meeting. ¹⁷ The priest is to dip his finger in the blood and sprinkle it seven times before the LORD in front of the curtain. ¹⁸ He is to apply some of the blood to the horns of the altar that is before the LORD in the tent of meeting. He will pour out the rest of the blood at the base of the altar of burnt offering that is at the entrance to the tent of meeting. ¹⁹ He is to remove all the fat from it and burn it on the altar. ²⁰ He is to offer this bull just as he did with the bull in the sin offering; he will offer it the same way. So the priest will make atonement on their behalf, and they will be forgiven. ²¹ Then he will bring the bull outside the camp and burn it just as he burned the first bull. It is the sin offering for the assembly. Ex 12:47

²² "When a leader^A sins and unintentionally violates any of the commands of the LORD his God by doing what is prohibited, and incurs guilt, ²³ or someone informs him about the sin he has committed, he is to bring an unblemished male goat as his offering. ²⁴ He is to lay his hand on the head of the goat and slaughter it at the place where the burnt offering is slaughtered before the LORD. It is a sin offering. ²⁵ Then the priest is to take some of the blood from the sin offering with his finger and apply it to the horns of the altar of burnt offering. The rest of its blood he is to pour out at the base of the altar of burnt offering. ²⁶ He must burn all its fat on the altar, like the fat of the fellowship sacrifice. In this way the priest will make atonement on his behalf for that person's sin, and he will be forgiven. Ex 34:31; Lv 9:3; 16:5

²⁷ "Now if any of the common people^B sins unintentionally by violating one of the LORD's commands, does what is prohibited, and incurs guilt, ²⁸ or if someone informs him about the sin he has committed, then he is to bring an unblemished female goat as his offering for the sin that he has committed. ²⁹ He is to lay his hand on the head of the sin offering and slaughter it at the place of the burnt offering. ³⁰ Then the priest is to take some of its blood with his finger and apply it to the horns of the altar of burnt offering. He is to pour out the rest of its blood at the base of the altar. ³¹ He is to remove all its fat just as the fat is removed from the fellowship sacrifice. The priest is to burn it on the altar as a pleasing aroma to the LORD. In this way the priest will make atonement on his behalf, and he will be forgiven.

³² "Or if the offering that he brings as a sin offering is a lamb, he is to bring an unblemished female. ³³ He is to lay his hand on the head of the sin offering and slaughter it as a sin offering at the place where the burnt offering is slaughtered. ³⁴ Then the priest is to take some of the blood of the sin offering with his finger and apply it to the horns of the altar of burnt offering. He is to pour out the rest of its blood at the base of the altar. ³⁵ He is to remove all its

---

^A 4:22 Or *ruler*   ^B 4:27 Lit *the people of the land*

fat just as the fat of the lamb is removed from the fellowship sacrifice. The priest will burn it on the altar along with the fire offerings to the LORD. In this way the priest will make atonement on his behalf for the sin he has committed, and he will be forgiven.   Lv 9:3

Cases Requiring Sin Offerings

5 "When someone sins in any of these ways:
If he has seen, heard, or known about something he has witnessed, and did not respond to a public call to testify, he will bear his iniquity.   Gn 4:13; Ex 20:5
² Or if someone touches anything unclean — a carcass of an unclean wild animal, or unclean livestock, or an unclean swarming creature — without being aware of it, he is unclean and incurs guilt.   Lv 11:4; Nm 19:13
³ Or if he touches human uncleanness — any uncleanness by which one can become defiled — without being aware of it, but later recognizes it, he incurs guilt.   Lv 11:24; 14:19
⁴ Or if someone swears rashly to do what is good or evil — concerning anything a person may speak rashly in an oath — without being aware of it, but later recognizes it, he incurs guilt in such an instance.   Ps 106:33
⁵ If someone incurs guilt in one of these cases, he is to confess he has committed that sin. ⁶ He must bring his penalty for guilt for the sin he has committed to the LORD: a female lamb or goat from the flock as a sin offering. In this way the priest will make atonement on his behalf for his sin.   Ex 30:15; Lv 14:12; 16:21

⁷ "But if he cannot afford an animal from the flock, then he may bring to the LORD two turtledoves or two young pigeons as penalty for guilt for his sin — one as a sin offering and the other as a burnt offering. ⁸ He is to bring them to the priest, who will first present the one for the sin offering. He is to twist its head at the back of the neck without severing it. ⁹ Then he will sprinkle some of the blood of the sin offering on the side of the altar, while the rest of the blood is to be drained out at the base of the altar; it is a sin offering. ¹⁰ He will prepare the second bird as a burnt offering according to the regulation. In this way the priest will make atonement on his behalf for the sin he has committed, and he will be forgiven.   Gn 15:10; Lv 1:14-15, 17

¹¹ "But if he cannot afford two turtledoves or two young pigeons, he may bring two quarts[A] of fine flour[B] as an offering for his sin. He must not put olive oil or frankincense on it, for it is a sin offering. ¹² He is to bring it to the priest, who will take a handful from it as its memorial portion and burn it on the altar along with the fire offerings to the LORD; it is a sin offering. ¹³ In this way the priest will make atonement on his behalf concerning the sin he has committed in any of these cases, and he will be forgiven. The rest will belong to the priest, like the grain offering."

The Guilt Offering

¹⁴ Then the LORD spoke to Moses: ¹⁵ "If someone offends by sinning unintentionally in regard to any of the LORD's holy things,[C] he must bring his penalty for guilt to the

---

A **5:11** Lit *one-tenth of an ephah*   B **5:11** Lit *flour as a sin offering*   C **5:15** Things dedicated to the LORD

Lord: an unblemished ram from the flock (based on your assessment of its value in silver shekels, according to the sanctuary shekel) as a guilt offering. ¹⁶ He is to make restitution for his sin regarding any holy thing, adding a fifth of its value to it, and give it to the priest. Then the priest will make atonement on his behalf with the ram of the guilt offering, and he will be forgiven. Lv 27:3; 24:18; Nm 15:24; Dt 32:51

¹⁷ "If someone sins and without knowing it violates any of the Lord's commands concerning anything prohibited, he is guilty, and he will bear his iniquity. ¹⁸ He must bring an unblemished ram from the flock according to your assessment of its value as a guilt offering to the priest. Then the priest will make atonement on his behalf for the error he has committed unintentionally, and he will be forgiven. ¹⁹ It is a guilt offering; he is indeed guilty before the Lord."

6 The Lord spoke to Moses: ² "When someone sins and offends the Lord by deceiving his neighbor in regard to a deposit, a security,^A or a robbery; or defrauds his neighbor; ³ or finds something lost and lies about it; or swears falsely about any of the sinful things a person may do — ⁴ once he has sinned and acknowledged his guilt — he must return what he stole or defrauded, or the deposit entrusted to him, or the lost item he found, ⁵ or anything else about which he swore falsely. He will make full restitution for it and add a fifth of its value to it. He is to pay it to its owner on the day he acknowledges his guilt. ⁶ Then he is to bring his guilt offering to the

Lord: an unblemished ram from the flock according to your assessment of its value as a guilt offering to the priest. ⁷ In this way the priest will make atonement on his behalf before the Lord, and he will be forgiven for anything he may have done to incur guilt." Lv 19:11

The Burnt Offering

⁸ The Lord spoke to Moses: ⁹ "Command Aaron and his sons: This is the law of the burnt offering; the burnt offering itself must remain on the altar's hearth all night until morning, while the fire of the altar is kept burning on it. ¹⁰ The priest is to put on his linen robe and linen undergarments. ^B He is to remove the ashes of the burnt offering fire has consumed on the altar, and place them beside the altar. ¹¹ Then he will take off his garments, put on other clothes, and bring the ashes outside the camp to a ceremonially clean place. ¹² The fire on the altar is to be kept burning; it must not go out. Every morning the priest will burn wood on the fire. He is to arrange the burnt offering on the fire and burn the fat portions from the fellowship offerings on it. ¹³ Fire must be kept burning on the altar continually; it must not go out. Ex 28:42-43; Lv 16:4; Ezk 44:17-19

The Grain Offering

¹⁴ "Now this is the law of the grain offering: Aaron's sons will present it before the Lord in front of the altar. ¹⁵ The priest is to remove a handful of fine flour and olive oil from the grain offering, with all the frankincense that is on the offering, and burn its memorial portion on the altar as a pleasing aroma to

^A6:2 Or an investment   ^B6:10 Lit undergarments on his flesh

the Lord.[16] Aaron and his sons may eat the rest of it. It is to be eaten in the form of unleavened bread in a holy place; they are to eat it in the courtyard of the tent of meeting. [17] It must not be baked with yeast; I have assigned it as their portion from my fire offerings. It is especially holy, like the sin offering and the guilt offering. [18] Any male among Aaron's descendants may eat it. It is a permanent portion[A] throughout your generations from the fire offerings to the Lord. Anything that touches the offerings will become holy."   Lv 2:1-16; 1Co 9:13

[19] The Lord spoke to Moses: [20] "This is the offering that Aaron and his sons are to present to the Lord on the day that he is anointed: two quarts[B] of fine flour as a regular grain offering, half of it in the morning and half in the evening. [21] It is to be prepared with oil on a griddle; you are to bring it well-kneaded. You are to present it as a grain offering of baked pieces,[C] a pleasing aroma to the Lord. [22] The priest, who is one of Aaron's sons and will be anointed to take his place, is to prepare it. It must be completely burned as a permanent portion for the Lord. [23] Every grain offering for a priest will be a whole burnt offering; it is not to be eaten."

The Sin Offering

[24] The Lord spoke to Moses: [25] "Tell Aaron and his sons: This is the law of the sin offering. The sin offering is most holy and must be slaughtered before the Lord at the place where the burnt offering is slaughtered. [26] The priest who offers it as a sin offering will eat it. It is

to be eaten in a holy place, in the courtyard of the tent of meeting. [27] Anything that touches its flesh will become holy, and if any of its blood spatters on a garment, then you must wash that garment[D] in a holy place. [28] A clay pot in which the sin offering is boiled is to be broken; if it is boiled in a bronze vessel, it is to be scoured and rinsed with water. [29] Any male among the priests may eat it; it is especially holy. [30] But no sin offering may be eaten if its blood has been brought into the tent of meeting to make atonement in the holy place; it must be burned.   Ex 29:14; Lv 16:24; 1Co 9:13

The Guilt Offering

7 "Now this is the law of the guilt[E] offering; it is especially holy. [2] The guilt offering is to be slaughtered at the place where the burnt offering is slaughtered, and the priest is to splatter its blood on all sides of the altar. [3] The offerer is to present all the fat from it: the fat tail, the fat surrounding the entrails,[F] [4] and the two kidneys with the fat on them at the loins; he will also remove the fatty lobe of the liver with the kidneys. [5] The priest will burn them on the altar as a fire offering to the Lord; it is a guilt offering. [6] Any male among the priests may eat it. It is to be eaten in a holy place; it is especially holy.

[7] "The guilt offering is like the sin offering; the law is the same for both. It belongs to the priest who makes atonement with it. [8] As for the priest who presents someone's burnt offering, the hide of the burnt offering he has presented belongs to him; it is the priest's. [9] Any grain

---

[A]6:18 Or statute   [B]6:20 Lit a tenth of an ephah   [C]6:21 Hb obscure   [D]6:27 Lit wash what it spattered on
[E]7:1 Or restitution   [F]7:3 LXX, Sam add and all the fat that is on the entrails; Lv 3:3,9,14; 4:8

offering that is baked in an oven or prepared in a pan or on a griddle belongs to the priest who presents it; it is his. ¹⁰ But any grain offering, whether dry or mixed with oil, belongs equally to all of Aaron's sons.

The Fellowship Sacrifice

¹¹ "Now this is the law of the fellowship sacrifice that someone may present to the Lord: ¹² If he presents it for thanksgiving, in addition to the thanksgiving sacrifice, he is to present unleavened cakes mixed with olive oil, unleavened wafers coated with oil, and well-kneaded cakes of fine flour mixed with oil. ¹³ He is to present as his offering cakes of leavened bread with his thanksgiving sacrifice of fellowship. ¹⁴ From the cakes he is to present one portion of each offering as a contribution to the Lord. It will belong to the priest who splatters the blood of the fellowship offering; it is his. ¹⁵ The meat of his thanksgiving sacrifice of fellowship must be eaten on the day he offers it; he may not leave any of it until morning.   Lv 3:1,3,6,9; 22:29

¹⁶ "If the sacrifice he offers is a vow or a freewill offering, it is to be eaten on the day he presents his sacrifice, and what is left over may be eaten on the next day. ¹⁷ But what remains of the sacrificial meat by the third day must be burned. ¹⁸ If any of the meat of his fellowship sacrifice is eaten on the third day, it will not be accepted. It will not be credited to the one who presents it; it is repulsive. The person who eats any of it will bear his iniquity.ᴬ

¹⁹ "Meat that touches anything unclean must not be eaten; it is to be burned. Everyone who is clean may eat any other meat. ²⁰ But the one who eats meat from the Lord's fellowship sacrifice while he is unclean, that person must be cut off from his people. ²¹ If someone touches anything unclean, whether human uncleanness, an unclean animal, or any unclean, abhorrentᴮ creature, and eats meat from the Lord's fellowship sacrifice, that person is to be cut off from his people."   Gn 17:14; Lv 7:27; 19:8; Nm 9:13; Is 66:17

Fat and Blood Prohibited

²² The Lord spoke to Moses: ²³ "Tell the Israelites: You are not to eat any fat of an ox, a sheep, or a goat. ²⁴ The fat of an animal that dies naturally or is mauled by wild beastsᶜ may be used for any other purpose, but you must not eat it. ²⁵ If anyone eats animal fat from a fire offering presented to the Lord, the person who eats it is to be cut off from his people. ²⁶ Wherever you live, you must not eat the blood of any bird or animal. ²⁷ Whoever eats any blood is to be cut off from his people."   Lv 17:15

The Portion for the Priests

²⁸ The Lord spoke to Moses: ²⁹ "Tell the Israelites: The one who presents a fellowship sacrifice to the Lord is to bring an offering to the Lord from his sacrifice. ³⁰ His own hands will bring the fire offerings to the Lord. He will bring the fat together with the breast. The breast is to be presented as a presentation offering before the Lord. ³¹ The priest is to burn the fat on the altar, but the breast belongs to Aaron and his sons. ³² You are to give the right thigh to the priest as a contribution

ᴬ7:18 Or will bear his guilt   ᴮ7:21 Some Hb mss, Sam, Syr, Tg read swarming   ᶜ7:24 Lit fat of a carcass or the fat of a mauled beast

from your fellowship sacrifices.
³³ The son of Aaron who presents the blood of the fellowship offering and the fat will have the right thigh as a portion. ³⁴ I have taken from the Israelites the breast of the presentation offering and the thigh of the contribution from their fellowship sacrifices, and have assigned them to the priest Aaron and to his sons as a permanent portion[A] from the Israelites." Ex 29:22,24; Lv 8:25-26; 9:21
³⁵ This is the portion from the fire offerings to the LORD for Aaron and his sons since the day they were presented to serve the LORD as priests. ³⁶ The LORD commanded this to be given to them by the Israelites on the day he anointed them. It is a permanent portion throughout their generations. 1Tm 5:17-18
³⁷ This is the law for the burnt offering, the grain offering, the sin offering, the guilt offering, the ordination offering, and the fellowship sacrifice, ³⁸ which the LORD commanded Moses on Mount Sinai on the day he[B] commanded the Israelites to present their offerings to the LORD in the Wilderness of Sinai.

Ordination of Aaron and His Sons

8 The LORD spoke to Moses:² "Take Aaron, his sons with him, the garments, the anointing oil, the bull of the sin[B] offering, the two rams, and the basket of unleavened bread, ³ and assemble the whole community at the entrance to the tent of meeting."⁴ So Moses did as the LORD commanded him, and the community assembled at the entrance to the tent of meeting. ⁵ Moses said to them, "This is what the LORD has commanded to be done." Ex 29:7

⁶ Then Moses presented Aaron and his sons and washed them with water. ⁷ He put the tunic on Aaron, wrapped the sash around him, clothed him with the robe, and put the ephod on him. He put the woven band of the ephod around him and fastened it to him. ⁸ Then he put the breastpiece on him and placed the Urim and Thummim into the breastpiece. ⁹ He also put the turban on his head and placed the gold medallion, the holy diadem, on the front of the turban, as the LORD had commanded Moses. Ex 28:4,30
¹⁰ Then Moses took the anointing oil and anointed the tabernacle and everything in it to consecrate them. ¹¹ He sprinkled some of the oil on the altar seven times, anointing the altar with all its utensils, and the basin with its stand, to consecrate them. ¹² He poured some of the anointing oil on Aaron's head and anointed and consecrated him. ¹³ Then Moses presented Aaron's sons, clothed them with tunics, wrapped sashes around them, and fastened headbands on them, as the LORD had commanded Moses. Ex 19:10,14,23
¹⁴ Then he brought the bull near for the sin offering, and Aaron and his sons laid their hands on the head of the bull for the sin offering. ¹⁵ Then Moses slaughtered it,[C] took the blood, and applied it with his finger to the horns of the altar on all sides, purifying the altar. He poured out the blood at the base of the altar and consecrated it so that atonement can be made on it.[D] ¹⁶ Moses took all the fat that was on the entrails, the fatty lobe of the liver, and the two kidneys with their fat, and he burned them on

---

[A]7:34 Or statute, also in v. 36   [B]8:2 Or purification   [C]8:14-15 Or offering, and he slaughtered it. ¹⁵Then Moses   [D]8:15 Or it by making atonement for it the altar. [17] He burned the bull with its hide, flesh, and waste outside the camp, as the LORD had commanded Moses. Ex 29:36; Lv 14:49,52; Ps 51:7

[18] Then he presented the ram for the burnt offering, and Aaron and his sons laid their hands on the head of the ram. [19] Moses slaughtered it and[A] splattered the blood on all sides of the altar. [20] Moses cut the ram into pieces and burned the head, the pieces, and the fat, [21] but he washed the entrails and legs with water. He then burned the entire ram on the altar. It was a burnt offering for a pleasing aroma, a fire offering to the LORD as he had commanded Moses. Lv 1:8

[22] Next he presented the second ram, the ram of ordination, and Aaron and his sons laid their hands on the head of the ram. [23] Moses slaughtered it,[B] took some of its blood, and put it on Aaron's right earlobe, on the thumb of his right hand, and on the big toe of his right foot. [24] Moses also presented Aaron's sons and put some of the blood on their right earlobes, on the thumbs of their right hands, and on the big toes of their right feet. Then Moses splattered the blood on all sides of the altar. [25] He took the fat — the fat tail, all the fat that was on the entrails, the fatty lobe of the liver, and the two kidneys with their fat — as well as the right thigh. [26] From the basket of unleavened bread that was before the LORD he took one cake of unleavened bread, one cake of bread made with oil, and one wafer, and placed them on the fat portions and the right thigh. [27] He put all these in the hands of Aaron and his sons and presented them before the LORD as a presentation offering. [28] Then Moses took them from their hands and burned them on the altar with the burnt offering. This was an ordination offering for a pleasing aroma, a fire offering to the LORD. [29] He also took the breast and presented it before the LORD as a presentation offering; it was Moses's portion of the ordination ram as the LORD had commanded him. Ex 29:22,26-34; Lv 7:37; 8:28-33

[30] Then Moses took some of the anointing oil and some of the blood that was on the altar and sprinkled them on Aaron and his garments, as well as on his sons and their garments. In this way he consecrated Aaron and his garments, as well as his sons and their garments. Ex 29:21

[31] Moses said to Aaron and his sons, "Boil the meat at the entrance to the tent of meeting and eat it there with the bread that is in the basket for the ordination offering as I commanded:[C] Aaron and his sons are to eat it. [32] Burn up what remains of the meat and bread. [33] Do not go outside the entrance to the tent of meeting for seven days, until the time your days of ordination are completed, because it will take seven days to ordain you.[D] [34] The LORD commanded what has been done today in order to make atonement for you. [35] You must remain at the entrance to the tent of meeting day and night for seven days and keep the LORD's charge so that you will not die, for this is what I was commanded." [36] So Aaron and his sons did everything the LORD had commanded through Moses. Lv 6:16,18

[A] 8:18-19 Or ram, [19] and he slaughtered it. Moses   [B] 8:22-23 Or ram, [23] and he slaughtered it. Moses
[C] 8:31 LXX, Syr, Tg read was commanded; Ex 29:31-32   [D] 8:33 Lit because he will fill your hands for seven days

The Priestly Ministry Inaugurated

9 On the eighth day Moses summoned Aaron, his sons, and the elders of Israel. [2] He said to Aaron, "Take a young bull for a sin[A] offering and a ram for a burnt offering, both without blemish, and present them before the LORD. [3] And tell the Israelites:[B] Take a male goat for a sin offering; a calf and a lamb, male yearlings without blemish, for a burnt offering; [4] an ox and a ram for a fellowship offering to sacrifice before the LORD; and a grain offering mixed with oil. For today the LORD is going to appear to you."

[5] They brought what Moses had commanded to the front of the tent of meeting, and the whole community came forward and stood before the LORD. [6] Moses said, "This is what the LORD commanded you to do, that the glory of the LORD may appear to you." [7] Then Moses said to Aaron, "Approach the altar and sacrifice your sin offering and your burnt offering; make atonement for yourself and the people.[C] Sacrifice the people's offering and make atonement for them, as the LORD commanded."   Ex 40:34; Lk 9:32; Heb 5:1-3

[8] So Aaron approached the altar and slaughtered the calf as a sin offering for himself. [9] Aaron's sons brought the blood to him, and he dipped his finger in the blood and applied it to the horns of the altar. He poured out the blood at the base of the altar. [10] He burned the fat, the kidneys, and the fatty lobe of the liver from the sin offering on the altar, as the LORD had commanded Moses. [11] He burned the flesh and the hide outside the camp.   Lv 7:8

[12] Then he slaughtered the burnt offering. Aaron's sons brought him the blood, and he splattered it on all sides of the altar. [13] They brought him the burnt offering piece by piece, along with the head, and he burned them on the altar. [14] He washed the entrails and the legs and burned them with the burnt offering on the altar.

[15] Aaron presented the people's offering. He took the male goat for the people's sin offering, slaughtered it, and made a sin offering with it as he did before. [16] He presented the burnt offering and sacrificed it according to the regulation. [17] Next he presented the grain offering, took a handful of it, and burned it on the altar in addition to the morning burnt offering.

[18] Finally, he slaughtered the ox and the ram as the people's fellowship sacrifice. Aaron's sons brought him the blood, and he splattered it on all sides of the altar. [19] They also brought the fat portions from the ox and the ram — the fat tail, the fat surrounding the entrails, the kidneys, and the fatty lobe of the liver — [20] and placed these on the breasts. Aaron burned the fat portions on the altar, [21] but he presented the breasts and the right thigh as a presentation offering before the LORD, as Moses had commanded.[D]   Ex 29:26-27; Lv 7:30-34; 8:26; 10:14-15

[22] Aaron lifted up his hands toward the people and blessed them. He came down after sacrificing the sin offering, the burnt offering, and the fellowship offering. [23] Moses and Aaron then entered the tent of meeting. When they came out, they blessed the people, and the glory of the LORD appeared to all

---

[A]9:2 Or *purification*   [B]9:3 Sam, LXX read *elders of Israel*   [C]9:7 LXX reads *and your household*
[D]9:21 Some Hb mss, LXX, Sam read *as the LORD commanded Moses*

the people. [24] Fire came from the LORD and consumed the burnt offering and the fat portions on the altar. And when all the people saw it, they shouted and fell facedown.

Nadab and Abihu

10 Aaron's sons Nadab and Abihu each took his own firepan, put fire in it, placed incense on it, and presented unauthorized fire before the LORD, which he had not commanded them to do. [2] Then fire came from the LORD and consumed them, and they died before the LORD. [3] Moses said to Aaron, "This is what the LORD has spoken:

I will demonstrate
  my holiness[A]   Nm 20:13; Ezk 20:41
to those who are near me,
and I will reveal my glory[B]
before all the people."

And Aaron remained silent.

[4] Moses summoned Mishael and Elzaphan, sons of Aaron's uncle Uzziel, and said to them, "Come here and carry your relatives away from the front of the sanctuary to a place outside the camp." [5] So they came forward and carried them in their tunics outside the camp, as Moses had said.   Ex 6:22; Lv 8:17; Nm 3:19; Heb 13:11-13

[6] Then Moses said to Aaron and his sons Eleazar and Ithamar, "Do not let your hair hang loose and do not tear your clothes, or else you will die, and the LORD will become angry with the whole community. However, your brothers, the whole house of Israel, may weep over the conflagration the LORD ignited. [7] You must not go outside the entrance to the tent of meeting or you will die, for the LORD's anointing oil is on you." So they did as Moses said.   Ex 6:23; Lv 13:45; 21:10

Regulations for Priests

[8] The LORD spoke to Aaron: [9] "You and your sons are not to drink wine or beer when you enter the tent of meeting, or else you will die; this is a permanent statute throughout your generations. [10] You must distinguish between the holy and the common, and the clean and the unclean, [11] and teach the Israelites all the statutes that the LORD has given to them through Moses."   Gn 9:21; Nm 6:3-4; Dt 7:13

[12] Moses spoke to Aaron and his remaining sons, Eleazar and Ithamar: "Take the grain offering that is left over from the fire offerings to the LORD, and eat it prepared without yeast beside the altar, because it is especially holy. [13] You must eat it in a holy place because it is your portion[C] and your sons' from the fire offerings to the LORD, for this is what I was commanded. [14] But you and your sons and your daughters may eat the breast of the presentation offering and the thigh of the contribution in any ceremonially clean place, because these portions have been assigned to you and your children from the Israelites' fellowship sacrifices. [15] They are to bring the thigh of the contribution and the breast of the presentation offering, together with the offerings of fat portions made by fire, to present as a presentation offering before the LORD. It will belong permanently to you and your children, as the LORD commanded."   Ex 29:28; 30:21; Lv 6:11,15; Dt 18:1

[16] Then Moses inquired carefully about the male goat of the sin offering, but it had already been burned up. He was angry with Eleazar and Ithamar, Aaron's surviving

A **10:3** Or *will be treated as holy*   B **10:3** Or *will be glorified*   C **10:13** Or *statute* sons, and asked, [17] "Why didn't you eat the sin offering in the sanctuary area? For it is especially holy, and he has assigned it to you to take away the guilt of the community and make atonement for them before the Lord. [18] Since its blood was not brought inside the sanctuary, you should have eaten it in the sanctuary area, as I commanded." Lv 6:26,29; Nm 5:31; Hs 14:2

[19] But Aaron replied to Moses, "See, today they presented their sin offering and their burnt offering before the Lord. Since these things have happened to me, if I had eaten the sin offering today, would it have been acceptable in the Lord's sight?" [20] When Moses heard this, it was acceptable to him.[A]

Clean and Unclean Land Animals

11 The Lord spoke to Moses and Aaron: [2] "Tell the Israelites: You may eat all these kinds of land animals. [3] You may eat any animal with divided hooves and that chews the cud. [4] But among the ones that chew the cud or have divided hooves you are not to eat these: Lv 11:1-23; Dt 14:3-21; Dn 1:3-16; Ac 10:9-16
camels, though they chew the cud, Gn 24:64; 31:34; Dt 14:7; Jr 2:23
do not have divided hooves — they are unclean for you;
[5] hyraxes, though they chew the cud, Dt 14:7; Ps 104:18; Pr 30:26
do not have hooves — they are unclean for you;
[6] hares, though they chew the cud,
do not have hooves — they are unclean for you;

[7] pigs, though they have divided hooves,
do not chew the cud — they are unclean for you.
[8] Do not eat any of their meat or touch their carcasses — they are unclean for you. Lv 7:21; 11:24-27; Is 52:11

Clean and Unclean Aquatic Animals

[9] "This is what you may eat from all that is in the water: You may eat everything in the water that has fins and scales, whether in the seas or streams. [10] But these are to be abhorrent to you: everything in the seas or streams that does not have fins and scales among all the swarming things and other living creatures in the water. [11] They are to remain abhorrent to you; you must not eat any of their meat, and you must abhor their carcasses. [12] Everything in the water that does not have fins and scales will be abhorrent to you.

Unclean Birds

[13] "You are to abhor these birds. They must not be eaten because they are abhorrent:
eagles, [B] bearded vultures,
Egyptian vultures, [C] [14] kites, [D]
any kind of falcon, [E] Dt 14:13
[15] every kind of raven,
[16] ostriches, [F]
short-eared owls, gulls, [G]
any kind of hawk, Dt 14:15; Jb 39:26
[17] little [H] owls, cormorants, [I]
long-eared owls, [J] Dt 14:16
[18] barn [K] owls, eagle owls, [L] Is 34:11
ospreys, [19] storks, [M]
any kind of heron, [N]
hoopoes, and bats.

[A]**10:20** Lit *acceptable in his sight*   [B]**11:13** Or *griffon-vultures*   [C]**11:13** Or *ospreys, or bearded vultures*
[D]**11:14** Or *hawks*   [E]**11:14** Or *buzzards, or hawks*   [F]**11:16** Or *eagle owls*   [G]**11:16** Or *long-eared owls*
[H]**11:17** Or *tawny*   [I]**11:17** Or *pelicans*   [J]**11:17** Or *ibis*   [K]**11:18** Or *little*   [L]**11:18** Or *pelicans, or horned owls*
[M]**11:19** Or *herons*   [N]**11:19** Or *cormorants, or hawks*

Clean and Unclean Flying Insects

20 "All winged insects that walk on all fours are to be abhorrent to you. 21 But you may eat these kinds of all the winged insects that walk on all fours: those that have jointed legs above their feet for hopping on the ground. 22 You may eat these:

any kind of locust, katydid, cricket, and grasshopper.

23 All other winged insects that have four feet are to be abhorrent to you.

Purification After Touching Dead Animals

24 "These will make you unclean. Whoever touches their carcasses will be unclean until evening, 25 and whoever carries any of their carcasses is to wash his clothes and will be unclean until evening. 26 All animals that have hooves but do not have a divided hoof and do not chew the cud are unclean for you. Whoever touches them becomes unclean. 27 All the four-footed animals that walk on their paws are unclean for you. Whoever touches their carcasses will be unclean until evening, 28 and anyone who carries their carcasses is to wash his clothes and will be unclean until evening. They are unclean for you.

29 "These creatures that swarm on the ground are unclean for you:

weasels,A mice,   1Sm 6:4-5,11,18

any kind of large lizard,B

30   geckos, monitor lizards,C common lizards,D skinks,E and chameleons.F

31 These are unclean for you among all the swarming creatures. Whoever touches them when they are dead will be unclean until evening.

32 When any one of them dies and falls on anything it becomes unclean — any item of wood, clothing, leather, sackcloth, or any implement used for work. It is to be rinsed with water and will remain unclean until evening; then it will be clean. 33 If any of them falls into any clay pot, everything in it will become unclean; you are to break it. 34 Any edible food coming into contact with that unclean water will become unclean, and any drinkable liquid in any container will become unclean. 35 Anything one of their carcasses falls on will become unclean. If it is an oven or stove, it is to be smashed; it is unclean and will remain unclean for you. 36 A spring or cistern containing water will remain clean, but someone who touches a carcass in it will become unclean. 37 If one of their carcasses falls on any seed that is to be sown, it is clean; 38 but if water has been put on the seed and one of their carcasses falls on it, it is unclean for you. Gn 37:34; Lv 26:5

39 "If one of the animals that you use for food dies, anyone who touches its carcass will be unclean until evening. 40 Anyone who eats some of its carcass is to wash his clothes and will be unclean until evening. Anyone who carries its carcass must wash his clothes and will be unclean until evening.

Unclean Swarming Creatures

41 "All the creatures that swarm on the earth are abhorrent; they must not be eaten. 42 Do not eat any of the creatures that swarm on the earth, anything that moves on its belly or

---

A11:29 Or mole rats, or rats   B11:29 Or of thorn-tailed, or dabb lizard, or of crocodile   C11:30 Or spotted lizards, or chameleons   D11:30 Or geckos, or newts, or salamanders   E11:30 Or sand lizards, or newts, or snails   F11:30 Or salamanders, or moles walks on all fours or on many feet,[A] for they are abhorrent. [43] Do not become contaminated by any creature that swarms; do not become unclean or defiled by them. [44] For I am the LORD your God, so you must consecrate yourselves and be holy because I am holy. Do not defile yourselves by any swarming creature that crawls on the ground. [45] For I am the LORD, who brought you up from the land of Egypt to be your God, so you must be holy because I am holy. Ex 19:22; 20:2; Nm 15:41

[46] "This is the law concerning animals, birds, all living creatures that move in the water, and all creatures that swarm on the ground, [47] in order to distinguish between the unclean and the clean, between the animals that may be eaten and those that may not be eaten." Lv 26:6

Purification After Childbirth

12 The LORD spoke to Moses: [2] "Tell the Israelites: When a woman becomes pregnant and gives birth to a male child, she will be unclean seven days, as she is during the days of her menstrual impurity. [3] The flesh of his foreskin must be circumcised on the eighth day. [4] She will continue in purification from her bleeding for thirty-three days. She must not touch any holy thing or go into the sanctuary until completing her days of purification. [5] But if she gives birth to a female child, she will be unclean for two weeks as she is during her menstrual impurity. She will continue in purification from her bleeding for sixty-six days.

[6] "When her days of purification are complete, whether for a son or daughter, she is to bring to the priest at the entrance to the tent of meeting a year-old male lamb for a burnt offering, and a young pigeon or a turtledove for a sin[B] offering. [7] He will present them before the LORD and make atonement on her behalf; she will be clean from her discharge of blood. This is the law for a woman giving birth, whether to a male or female. [8] But if she doesn't have sufficient means[C] for a sheep, she may take two turtledoves or two young pigeons, one for a burnt offering and the other for a sin offering. Then the priest will make atonement on her behalf, and she will be clean." Lv 14:21

Skin Diseases

13 The LORD spoke to Moses and Aaron: [2] "When a person has a swelling,[D] scab,[E] or spot on the skin of his body, and it may be a serious disease on the skin of his body, he is to be brought to the priest Aaron or to one of his sons, the priests. [3] The priest will examine the sore on the skin of his body. If the hair in the sore has turned white and the sore appears to be deeper than the skin of his body, it is in fact a serious skin disease. After the priest examines him, he must pronounce him unclean. [4] But if the spot on the skin of his body is white and does not appear to be deeper than the skin, and the hair in it has not turned white, the priest will quarantine the stricken person for seven days. [5] The priest will then reexamine him on the seventh day. If he sees that the sore remains unchanged and has not spread on the skin, the priest will

---

[A]**11:42** Lit *fours, to anything multiplying pairs of feet*   [B]**12:6** Or *purification*, also in v. 8   [C]**12:8** Lit *if her hand cannot obtain what is sufficient*   [D]**13:2** Or *discoloration*   [E]**13:2** Or *rash*, or *eruption* quarantine him for another seven days. [6] The priest will examine him again on the seventh day. If the sore has faded and has not spread on the skin, the priest is to pronounce him clean; it is a scab. The person is to wash his clothes and will become clean. [7] But if the scab spreads further on his skin after he has presented himself to the priest for his cleansing, he is to present himself again to the priest. [8] The priest will examine him, and if the scab has spread on the skin, then the priest must pronounce him unclean; he has a serious skin disease. Dt 24:8

[9] "When a case of serious skin disease may have developed on a person, he is to be brought to the priest. [10] The priest will examine him. If there is a white swelling on the skin that has turned the hair white, and there is a patch of raw flesh in the swelling, [11] it is a chronic serious disease on the skin of his body, and the priest must pronounce him unclean. He need not quarantine him, for he is unclean. [12] But if the skin disease breaks out all over the skin so that it covers all the skin of the stricken person from his head to his feet so far as the priest can see, [13] the priest will look, and if the skin disease has covered his entire body, he is to pronounce the stricken person clean. Since he has turned totally white, he is clean. [14] But whenever raw flesh appears on him, he will be unclean. [15] When the priest examines the raw flesh, he must pronounce him unclean. Raw flesh is unclean; this is a serious skin disease. [16] But if the raw flesh changes[A] and[B] turns white, he is to go to the priest. [17] The priest will examine him, and if the sore has turned white, the priest must pronounce the stricken person clean; he is clean. Lv 10:10; 11:4

[18] "When a boil appears on the skin of someone's body and it heals, [19] and a white swelling or a reddish-white spot develops where the boil was, the person is to present himself to the priest. [20] The priest will make an examination, and if the spot seems to be beneath the skin and the hair in it has turned white, the priest must pronounce him unclean; it is a case of serious skin disease that has broken out in the boil. [21] But when the priest examines it, if there is no white hair in it, and it is not beneath the skin but is faded, the priest will quarantine him seven days. [22] If it spreads further on the skin, the priest must pronounce him unclean; it is in fact a disease. [23] But if the spot remains where it is and does not spread, it is only the scar from the boil. The priest is to pronounce him clean.

[24] "When there is a burn on the skin of one's body produced by fire, and the patch made raw by the burn becomes reddish-white or white, [25] the priest is to examine it. If the hair in the spot has turned white and the spot appears to be deeper than the skin, it is a serious skin disease that has broken out in the burn. The priest must pronounce him unclean; it is a serious skin disease. [26] But when the priest examines it, if there is no white hair in the spot and it is not beneath the skin but is faded, the priest will quarantine him seven days. [27] The priest will reexamine him on the seventh day. If it has spread further on the skin, the priest must pronounce him

[A] 13:16 Or recedes [B] 13:16 Or flesh again

unclean; it is in fact a case of serious skin disease. ²⁸ But if the spot has remained where it was and has not spread on the skin but is faded, it is the swelling from the burn. The priest is to pronounce him clean, for it is only the scar from the burn.

²⁹ "When a man or woman has a condition on the head or chin, ³⁰ the priest is to examine the condition. If it appears to be deeper than the skin, and the hair in it is yellow and sparse, the priest must pronounce the person unclean. It is a scaly outbreak, a serious skin disease of the head or chin. ³¹ When the priest examines the scaly condition, if it does not appear to be deeper than the skin, and there is no black hair in it, the priest will quarantine the person with the scaly condition for seven days. ³² The priest will reexamine the condition on the seventh day. If the scaly outbreak has not spread and there is no yellow hair in it and it does not appear to be deeper than the skin, ³³ the person is to shave himself but not shave the scaly area. Then the priest will quarantine the person who has the scaly outbreak for another seven days. ³⁴ The priest will examine the scaly outbreak on the seventh day, and if it has not spread on the skin and does not appear to be deeper than the skin, the priest is to pronounce the person clean. He is to wash his clothes, and he will be clean. ³⁵ But if the scaly outbreak spreads further on the skin after his cleansing, ³⁶ the priest is to examine the person. If the scaly outbreak has spread on the skin, the priest does not need to look for yellow hair; the person is unclean. ³⁷ But if as far as he can see, the scaly outbreak remains unchanged and black hair has grown in it, then it has healed; he is clean. The priest is to pronounce the person clean.

³⁸ "When a man or a woman has white spots on the skin of the body, ³⁹ the priest is to make an examination. If the spots on the skin of the body are dull white, it is only a rash ᴬ that has broken out on the skin; the person is clean.

⁴⁰ "If a man loses the hair of his head, he is bald, but he is clean. ⁴¹ Or if he loses the hair at his hairline, he is bald on his forehead, but he is clean. ⁴² But if there is a reddish-white condition on the bald head or forehead, it is a serious skin disease breaking out on his head or forehead. ⁴³ The priest is to examine him, and if the swelling of the condition on his bald head or forehead is reddish-white, like the appearance of a serious skin disease on his body, ⁴⁴ the man is afflicted with a serious skin disease; he is unclean. The priest must pronounce him unclean; the infection is on his head.   Ex 4:6; 2Kg 2:23; 2Ch 26:19-20

⁴⁵ "The person who has a case of serious skin disease is to have his clothes torn and his hair hanging loose, and he must cover his mouth and cry out, 'Unclean, unclean!' ⁴⁶ He will remain unclean as long as he has the disease; he is unclean. He must live alone in a place outside the camp.   Lv 10:6; 21:10

Contaminated Fabrics

⁴⁷ "If a fabric is contaminated with mildew — in wool or linen fabric, ⁴⁸ in the warp or weft of linen or wool, or in leather or anything made of leather — ⁴⁹ and if the contamination is green or red in the

ᴬ13:39 Hb obscure

fabric, the leather, the warp, the weft, or any leather article, it is a mildew contamination and is to be shown to the priest. [50] The priest is to examine the contamination and quarantine the contaminated fabric for seven days. [51] The priest is to reexamine the contamination on the seventh day. If it has spread in the fabric, the warp, the weft, or the leather, regardless of how it is used, the contamination is harmful mildew; it is unclean. [52] He is to burn the fabric, the warp or weft in wool or linen, or any leather article, which is contaminated. Since it is harmful mildew it must be burned.

[53] "When the priest examines it, if the contamination has not spread in the fabric, the warp or weft, or any leather article, [54] the priest is to order whatever is contaminated to be washed and quarantined for another seven days. [55] After it has been washed, the priest is to reexamine the contamination. If the appearance of the contaminated article has not changed, it is unclean. Even though the contamination has not spread, you must burn the fabric. It is a fungus[A] on the front or back of the fabric.

[56] "If the priest examines it, and the contamination has faded after it has been washed, he is to cut the contaminated section out of the fabric, the leather, or the warp or weft. [57] But if it reappears in the fabric, the warp or weft, or any leather article, it has broken out again. You must burn whatever is contaminated. [58] But if the contamination disappears from the fabric, the warp or weft, or any leather article, which have been washed, it is to be washed again, and it will be clean.

[59] "This is the law concerning a mildew contamination in wool or linen fabric, warp or weft, or any leather article, in order to pronounce it clean or unclean."

Cleansing of Skin Diseases

14 The LORD spoke to Moses: [2] "This is the law concerning the person afflicted with a skin disease on the day of his cleansing. He is to be brought to the priest, [3] who will go outside the camp and examine him. If the skin disease has disappeared from the afflicted person,[B] [4] the priest will order that two live clean birds, cedar wood, scarlet yarn, and hyssop be brought for the one who is to be cleansed. [5] Then the priest will order that one of the birds be slaughtered over fresh water in a clay pot. [6] He is to take the live bird together with the cedar wood, scarlet yarn, and hyssop, and dip them all into the blood of the bird that was slaughtered over the fresh water. [7] He will then sprinkle the blood seven times on the one who is to be cleansed from the skin disease. He is to pronounce him clean and release the live bird over the open countryside. [8] The one who is to be cleansed must wash his clothes, shave off all his hair, and bathe with water; he is clean. Afterward he may enter the camp, but he must remain outside his tent for seven days. [9] He is to shave off all his hair again on the seventh day: his head, his beard, his eyebrows, and the rest of his hair. He is to wash his clothes and bathe himself with water; he is clean. _{Lv 11:46}

[10] "On the eighth day he must take two unblemished male lambs, an

unblemished year-old ewe lamb, a grain offering of six quarts[A] of fine flour mixed with olive oil, and one-third of a quart[B] of olive oil. ¹¹ The priest who performs the cleansing will place the person who is to be cleansed, together with these offerings, before the LORD at the entrance to the tent of meeting. ¹² The priest is to take one male lamb and present it as a guilt offering, along with the one-third quart of olive oil, and he will present them as a presentation offering before the LORD. ¹³ He is to slaughter the male lamb at the place in the sanctuary area where the sin offering and burnt offering are slaughtered, for like the sin offering, the guilt offering belongs to the priest; it is especially holy. ¹⁴ The priest is to take some of the blood from the guilt offering and put it on the lobe of the right ear of the one to be cleansed, on the thumb of his right hand, and on the big toe of his right foot. ¹⁵ Then the priest will take some of the one-third quart of olive oil and pour it into his left palm. ¹⁶ The priest will dip his right finger into the oil in his left palm and sprinkle some of the oil with his finger seven times before the LORD. ¹⁷ From the oil remaining in his palm the priest will put some on the lobe of the right ear of the one to be cleansed, on the thumb of his right hand, and on the big toe of his right foot, on top of the blood of the guilt offering. ¹⁸ What is left of the oil in the priest's palm he is to put on the head of the one to be cleansed. In this way the priest will make atonement for him before the LORD. ¹⁹ The priest is to sacrifice the sin offering and make atonement for the one to be cleansed from his uncleanness. Afterward he will slaughter the burnt offering. ²⁰ The priest is to offer the burnt offering and the grain offering on the altar. The priest will make atonement for him, and he will be clean.   Lv 3:5

²¹ "But if he is poor and cannot afford these, he is to take one male lamb for a guilt offering to be presented in order to make atonement for him, along with two quarts[C] of fine flour mixed with olive oil for a grain offering, one-third of a quart of olive oil, ²² and two turtledoves or two young pigeons, whatever he can afford, one to be a sin offering and the other a burnt offering. ²³ On the eighth day he is to bring these things for his cleansing to the priest at the entrance to the tent of meeting before the LORD. ²⁴ The priest will take the male lamb for the guilt offering and the one-third quart of olive oil, and present them as a presentation offering before the LORD. ²⁵ After he slaughters the male lamb for the guilt offering, the priest is to take some of the blood of the guilt offering and put it on the right earlobe of the one to be cleansed, on the thumb of his right hand, and on the big toe of his right foot. ²⁶ Then the priest will pour some of the oil into his left palm. ²⁷ With his right finger the priest will sprinkle some of the oil in his left palm seven times before the LORD. ²⁸ The priest will also put some of the oil in his palm on the right earlobe of the one to be cleansed, on the thumb of his right hand, and on the big toe of his right foot, on the same place as the blood of the guilt offering. ²⁹ What is left of the

---

A14:10 Lit three-tenths; probably three-tenths of an ephah   B14:10 Lit one log, also in vv. 12,15,21,24
C14:21 Lit him, and one-tenth; probably one-tenth of an ephah

oil in the priest's palm he is to put on the head of the one to be cleansed to make atonement for him before the LORD. ³⁰ He is to then sacrifice one type of what he can afford, either the turtledoves or young pigeons, ³¹ one as a sin offering and the other as a burnt offering, sacrificing what he can afford together with the grain offering. In this way the priest will make atonement before the LORD for the one to be cleansed. ³² This is the law for someone who has^A a skin disease and cannot afford the cost of his cleansing." Lv12:8

Cleansing of Contaminated Objects

³³ The LORD spoke to Moses and Aaron: ³⁴ "When you enter the land of Canaan that I am giving you as a possession, and I place a mildew contamination in a house in the land you possess,^B ³⁵ the owner of the house is to come and tell the priest: Something like mildew contamination has appeared^C in my house. ³⁶ The priest must order them to clear the house before he enters to examine the contamination, so that nothing in the house becomes unclean. Afterward the priest will come to examine the house. ³⁷ He will examine it, and if the contamination in the walls of the house consists of green or red indentations^D that appear to be beneath the surface of the wall, ³⁸ the priest is to go outside the house to its doorway and quarantine the house for seven days. ³⁹ The priest is to return on the seventh day and examine it. If the contamination has spread on the walls of the house, ⁴⁰ the priest must order that the stones with the contamination be pulled out and thrown into an unclean place outside the city. ⁴¹ He is to have the inside of the house completely scraped, and have the plaster^E that is scraped off dumped in an unclean place outside the city. ⁴² Then they are to take different stones to replace the former ones and take additional plaster to replaster the house. Gn 23:4; 37:1

⁴³ "If the contamination reappears in the house after the stones have been pulled out, and after the house has been scraped and replastered, ⁴⁴ the priest is to come and examine it. If the contamination has spread in the house, it is harmful mildew; the house is unclean. ⁴⁵ It must be torn down with its stones, its beams, and all its plaster, and taken outside the city to an unclean place. ⁴⁶ Whoever enters the house during any of the days the priest quarantines it will be unclean until evening. ⁴⁷ Whoever lies down in the house is to wash his clothes, and whoever eats in it is to wash his clothes.

⁴⁸ "But when the priest comes and examines it, if the contamination has not spread in the house after it was replastered, he is to pronounce the house clean because the contamination has disappeared.^F ⁴⁹ He is to take two birds, cedar wood, scarlet yarn, and hyssop to purify the house, ⁵⁰ and he is to slaughter one of the birds over a clay pot containing fresh water. ⁵¹ He will take the cedar wood, the hyssop, the scarlet yarn, and the live bird, dip them in the blood of the slaughtered bird and the fresh water, and sprinkle the house seven

^A14:32 Lit someone on whom there is   ^B14:34 Lit land of your possession   ^C14:35 Lit appeared to me
^D14:37 Or eruptions; Hb obscure   ^E14:41 Lit dust, also in v. 42   ^F14:48 Lit healed

times. [52] He will purify the house with the blood of the bird, the fresh water, the live bird, the cedar wood, the hyssop, and the scarlet yarn. [53] Then he is to release the live bird into the open countryside outside the city. In this way he will make atonement for the house, and it will be clean. Lv 14:7

[54] "This is the law for any skin disease or mildew, for a scaly outbreak, [55] for mildew in clothing or on a house, [56] and for a swelling, scab, or spot, [57] to determine when something is unclean or clean. This is the law regarding skin disease and mildew."

Bodily Discharges

15 The Lord spoke to Moses and Aaron: [2] "Speak to the Israelites and tell them: When any man has a discharge from his member, he is unclean. [3] This is uncleanness of his discharge: Whether his member secretes the discharge or retains it, he is unclean. All the days that his member secretes or retains anything because of his discharge,[A] he is unclean. [4] Any bed the man with the discharge lies on will be unclean, and any furniture he sits on will be unclean. [5] Anyone who touches his bed is to wash his clothes and bathe with water, and he will remain unclean until evening. [6] Whoever sits on furniture that the man with the discharge was sitting on is to wash his clothes and bathe with water, and he will remain unclean until evening. [7] Whoever touches the body[B] of the man with a discharge is to wash his clothes and bathe with water, and he will remain unclean until evening. [8] If

the man with the discharge spits on anyone who is clean, he is to wash his clothes and bathe with water, and he will remain unclean until evening. [9] Any saddle the man with the discharge rides on will be unclean. [10] Whoever touches anything that was under him will be unclean until evening, and whoever carries such things is to wash his clothes and bathe with water, and he will remain unclean until evening. [11] If the man with the discharge touches anyone without first rinsing his hands in water, the person who was touched is to wash his clothes and bathe with water, and he will remain unclean until evening. [12] Any clay pot that the man with the discharge touches must be broken, while any wooden utensil is to be rinsed with water. Lv 15:33; 22:4; Nm 5:2

[13] "When the man with the discharge has been cured of it, he is to count seven days for his cleansing, wash his clothes, and bathe his body in fresh water; he will be clean. [14] He must take two turtledoves or two young pigeons on the eighth day, come before the Lord at the entrance to the tent of meeting, and give them to the priest. [15] The priest is to sacrifice them, one as a sin offering and the other as a burnt offering. In this way the priest will make atonement for him before the Lord because of his discharge.

[16] "When a man has an emission of semen, he is to bathe himself completely with water, and he will remain unclean until evening. [17] Any clothing or leather on which there is an emission of semen is to be washed with water, and it will remain unclean until evening. [18] If a

---

A**15:3** DSS, Sam, LXX; MT omits *he is unclean. All the days that his member secretes or retains anything because of his discharge*   B**15:7** Or *member*, also in v. 13

man sleeps with a woman and has an emission of semen, both of them are to bathe with water, and they will remain unclean until evening.

¹⁹ "When a woman has a discharge, and it consists of blood from her body, she will be unclean because of her menstruation for seven days. Everyone who touches her will be unclean until evening. ²⁰ Anything she lies on during her menstruation will become unclean, and anything she sits on will become unclean. ²¹ Everyone who touches her bed is to wash his clothes and bathe with water, and he will remain unclean until evening. ²² Everyone who touches any furniture she was sitting on is to wash his clothes and bathe with water, and he will remain unclean until evening. ²³ If discharge is on the bed or the furniture she was sitting on, when he touches it he will be unclean until evening. ²⁴ If a man sleeps with her, and blood from her menstruation gets on him, he will be unclean for seven days, and every bed he lies on will become unclean.

²⁵ "When a woman has a discharge of her blood for many days, though it is not the time of her menstruation, or if she has a discharge beyond her period, she will be unclean all the days of her unclean discharge, as she is during the days of her menstruation. ²⁶ Any bed she lies on during the days of her discharge will be like her bed during menstrual impurity; any furniture she sits on will be unclean as in her menstrual period. ²⁷ Everyone who touches them will be unclean; he must wash his clothes and bathe with water, and he will remain unclean until evening. ²⁸ When she is cured of her discharge, she is to count seven days, and after that she will be clean. ²⁹ On the eighth day she must take two turtledoves or two young pigeons and bring them to the priest at the entrance to the tent of meeting. ³⁰ The priest is to sacrifice one as a sin offering and the other as a burnt offering. In this way the priest will make atonement for her before the LORD because of her unclean discharge.

³¹ "You must keep the Israelites from their uncleanness, so that they do not die by defiling my tabernacle that is among them. ³² This is the law for someone with a discharge: a man who has an emission of semen, becoming unclean by it; ³³ a woman who is in her menstrual period; anyone who has a discharge, whether male or female; and a man who sleeps with a woman who is unclean." Ex 25:9; Nm 5:2-3

The Day of Atonement

16 The LORD spoke to Moses after the death of two of Aaron's sons when they approached the presence of^A the LORD and died. ² The LORD said to Moses: "Tell your brother Aaron that he may not come whenever he wants into the holy place behind the curtain in front of the mercy seat on the ark or else he will die, because I appear in the cloud above the mercy seat.

³ "Aaron is to enter the most holy place in this way: with a young bull for a sin offering and a ram for a burnt offering. ⁴ He is to wear a holy linen tunic, and linen undergarments are to be on his body. He is to tie a linen sash around him and wrap his head with a linen turban. These are holy garments; he must

^A16:1 LXX, Tg, Syr, Vg read *they brought strange fire before* ; Nm 3:4

bathe his body with water before he wears them. ⁵ He is to take from the Israelite community two male goats for a sin offering and one ram for a burnt offering.   Gn 22:2; Lv 4:1-12

⁶ "Aaron will present the bull for his sin offering and make atonement for himself and his household. ⁷ Next he will take the two goats and place them before the LORD at the entrance to the tent of meeting. ⁸ After Aaron casts lots for the two goats, one lot for the LORD and the other for an uninhabitable place, A,B ⁹ he is to present the goat chosen by lot for the LORD and sacrifice it as a sin offering. ¹⁰ But the goat chosen by lot for an uninhabitable place is to be presented alive before the LORD to make atonement with it by sending it into the wilderness for an uninhabitable place.

¹¹ "When Aaron presents the bull for his sin offering and makes atonement for himself and his household, he will slaughter the bull for his sin offering. ¹² Then he is to take a firepan full of blazing coals from the altar before the LORD and two handfuls of finely ground fragrant incense, and bring them inside the curtain. ¹³ He is to put the incense on the fire before the LORD, so that the cloud of incense covers the mercy seat that is over the testimony, or else he will die. ¹⁴ He is to take some of the bull's blood and sprinkle it with his finger against the east side of the mercy seat; then he will sprinkle some of the blood with his finger before the mercy seat seven times.   Nm 7:14

¹⁵ "When he slaughters the male goat for the people's sin offering and brings its blood inside the curtain, he will do the same with its blood as he did with the bull's blood: He is to sprinkle it against the mercy seat and in front of it. ¹⁶ He will make atonement for the most holy place in this way for all their sins because of the Israelites' impurities and rebellious acts. He will do the same for the tent of meeting that remains among them, because it is surrounded by their impurities. ¹⁷ No one may be in the tent of meeting from the time he enters to make atonement in the most holy place until he leaves after he has made atonement for himself, his household, and the whole assembly of Israel. ¹⁸ Then he will go out to the altar that is before the LORD and make atonement for it. He is to take some of the bull's blood and some of the goat's blood and put it on the horns on all sides of the altar. ¹⁹ He is to sprinkle some of the blood on it with his finger seven times to cleanse and set it apart from the Israelites' impurities.

²⁰ "When he has finished making atonement for the most holy place, the tent of meeting, and the altar, he is to present the live male goat. ²¹ Aaron will lay both his hands on the head of the live goat and confess over it all the Israelites' iniquities and rebellious acts — all their sins. He is to put them on the goat's head and send it away into the wilderness by the man appointed for the task. C ²² The goat will carry all their iniquities into a desolate land, and the man will release it there.

²³ "Then Aaron is to enter the tent of meeting, take off the linen

---

A**16:8** Lit *for Azazel,* also in vv. 10 (2x),26   B**16:8** Perhaps a term that means "for the goat that departs," or "for removal," or "for a rough, difficult place," or "for a goat demon"; Hb obscure, also in vv. 10,26   C**16:21** Lit *wilderness in the hand of a ready man* garments he wore when he entered the most holy place, and leave them there. ²⁴ He will bathe his body with water in a holy place and put on his clothes. Then he must go out and sacrifice his burnt offering and the people's burnt offering; he will make atonement for himself and for the people. ²⁵ He is to burn the fat of the sin offering on the altar. ²⁶ The man who released the goat for an uninhabitable place is to wash his clothes and bathe his body with water; afterward he may reenter the camp. ²⁷ The bull for the sin offering and the goat for the sin offering, whose blood was brought into the most holy place to make atonement, must be brought outside the camp and their hide, flesh, and waste burned. ²⁸ The one who burns them is to wash his clothes and bathe himself with water; afterward he may reenter the camp.

²⁹ "This is to be a permanent statute for you: In the seventh month, on the tenth day of the month you are to practice self-denial and do no work, both the native and the alien who resides among you. ³⁰ Atonement will be made for you on this day to cleanse you, and you will be clean from all your sins before the LORD. ³¹ It is a Sabbath of complete rest for you, and you must practice self-denial; it is a permanent statute. ³² The priest who is anointed and ordained^A to serve as high priest in place of his father will make atonement. He will put on the linen garments, the holy garments, ³³ and make atonement for the most holy place. He will make atonement for the tent of meeting and the altar and will make

atonement for the priests and all the people of the assembly. ³⁴ This is to be a permanent statute for you, to make atonement for the Israelites once a year because of all their sins." And all this was done as the LORD commanded Moses.   Ex 28:43

Forbidden Sacrifices

17 The LORD spoke to Moses: ² "Speak to Aaron, his sons, and all the Israelites and tell them: This is what the LORD has commanded: ³ Anyone from the house of Israel who slaughters an ox, sheep, or goat in the camp, or slaughters it outside the camp, ⁴ instead of bringing it to the entrance to the tent of meeting to present it as an offering to the LORD before his tabernacle — that person will be considered guilty.^B He has shed blood and is to be cut off from his people. ⁵ This is so the Israelites will bring to the LORD the sacrifices they have been offering in the open country. They are to bring them to the priest at the entrance to the tent of meeting and offer them as fellowship sacrifices to the LORD. ⁶ The priest will then splatter the blood on the LORD's altar at the entrance to the tent of meeting and burn the fat as a pleasing aroma to the LORD. ⁷ They must no longer offer their sacrifices to the goat-demons that they have prostituted themselves with. This will be a permanent statute for them throughout their generations.

⁸ "Say to them: Anyone from the house of Israel or from the aliens who reside among them who offers a burnt offering or a sacrifice ⁹ but does not bring it to the entrance to the tent of meeting to sacrifice

---

^A 16:32 Lit *and will fill his hand*   ^B 17:4 Lit *tabernacle — blood will be charged against that person* it to the LORD, that person is to be cut off from his people. Gn19:9; Ex2:22

Eating Blood and Carcasses Prohibited

¹⁰ "Anyone from the house of Israel or from the aliens who reside among them who eats any blood, I will turn ᴬ against that person who eats blood and cut him off from his people. ¹¹ For the life of a creature is in the blood, and I have appointed it to you to make atonement on the altar for ᴮ your lives, since it is the lifeblood that makes atonement. ¹² Therefore I say to the Israelites: None of you and no alien who resides among you may eat blood.

¹³ "Any Israelite or alien residing among them, who hunts down a wild animal or bird that may be eaten must drain its blood and cover it with dirt. ¹⁴ Since the life of every creature is its blood, I have told the Israelites: You are not to eat the blood of any creature, because the life of every creature is its blood; whoever eats it must be cut off.

¹⁵ "Every person, whether the native or the resident alien, who eats an animal that died a natural death or was mauled by wild beasts is to wash his clothes and bathe with water, and he will remain unclean until evening; then he will be clean. ¹⁶ But if he does not wash his clothes and bathe himself, he will bear his iniquity." Ex 22:31; Lv 7:24; 16:29; 22:8; Dt 14:21

Prohibited Pagan Practices

18 The LORD spoke to Moses: ² "Speak to the Israelites and tell them: I am the LORD your God. ³ Do not follow the practices of the

land of Egypt, where you used to live, or follow the practices of the land of Canaan, where I am bringing you. You must not follow their customs. ⁴ You are to practice my ordinances and you are to keep my statutes by following them; I am the LORD your God. ⁵ Keep my statutes and ordinances; a person will live if he does them. I am the LORD.

⁶ "You are not to come near any close relative ᶜ for sexual intercourse; I am the LORD. ⁷ You are not to violate the intimacy that belongs to your father and mother. ᴰ She is your mother; you must not have sexual intercourse with her. ⁸ You are not to have sex with your father's wife; she is your father's family. ⁹ You are not to have sexual intercourse with your sister, either your father's daughter or your mother's, whether born at home or born elsewhere. You are not to have sex with her. ¹⁰ You are not to have sexual intercourse with your son's daughter or your daughter's daughter, for they are your family. ᴱ ¹¹ You are not to have sexual intercourse with your father's wife's daughter, who is adopted by ᶠ your father; she is your sister. ¹² You are not to have sexual intercourse with your father's sister; she is your father's close relative. ¹³ You are not to have sexual intercourse with your mother's sister, for she is your mother's close relative. ¹⁴ You are not to violate the intimacy that belongs to ᴳ your father's brother by approaching his wife to have sexual intercourse; she is your aunt. ¹⁵ You are not to have sexual intercourse with your

---

ᴬ**17:10** Lit will set my face   ᴮ**17:11** Or to ransom   ᶜ**18:6** Lit any flesh of his flesh   ᴰ**18:7** Lit Do not uncover your father's nakedness and your mother's nakedness   ᴱ**18:10** Lit because they are your nakedness   ᶠ**18:11** Lit daughter, a relative of   ᴳ**18:14** Lit Do not uncover the nakedness of daughter-in-law. She is your son's wife; you are not to have sex with her. [16] You are not to have sexual intercourse with your brother's wife; she is your brother's family. [17] You are not to have sexual intercourse with a woman and her daughter. You are not to marry her son's daughter or her daughter's daughter and have sex with her. They are close relatives; it is depraved. [18] You are not to marry a woman as a rival to her sister and have sexual intercourse with her during her sister's lifetime. Gn 20:4

[19] "You are not to approach a woman during her menstrual impurity to have sexual intercourse with her. [20] You are not to have sexual intercourse with [A] your neighbor's wife, defiling yourself with her. Gn 20:4; Ex 20:14; Lv 15:19-24; 20:18; Ezk 18:6

[21] "You are not to sacrifice any of your children in the fire [B] to Molech. Do not profane the name of your God; I am the LORD. [22] You are not to sleep with a man as with a woman; it is detestable. [23] You are not to have sexual intercourse with [C] any animal, defiling yourself with it; a woman is not to present herself to an animal to mate with it; it is a perversion. Lv 2:2-5; Dt 18:10; 1Kg 11:7

[24] "Do not defile yourselves by any of these practices, for the nations I am driving out before you have defiled themselves by all these things. [25] The land has become defiled, so I am punishing it for its iniquity, and the land will vomit out its inhabitants. [26] But you are to keep my statutes and ordinances. You must not commit any of these detestable acts — not the native or the alien who resides among you. [27] For the

people who were in the land prior to you have committed all these detestable acts, and the land has become defiled. [28] If you defile the land, it will vomit you out as it has vomited out the nations that were before you. [29] Any person who does any of these detestable practices is to be cut off from his people. [30] You must keep my instruction to not do any of the detestable customs that were practiced before you, so that you do not defile yourselves by them; I am the LORD your God."

Laws of Holiness

19 The LORD spoke to Moses: [2] "Speak to the entire Israelite community and tell them: Be holy because I, the LORD your God, am holy. Ex 19:5-6; Lv 11:44; 21:8

[3] "Each of you is to respect his mother and father. You are to keep my Sabbaths; I am the LORD your God. [4] Do not turn to idols or make cast images of gods for yourselves; I am the LORD your God. Ex 20:12; 21:15

[5] "When you offer a fellowship sacrifice to the LORD, sacrifice it so that you may be accepted. [6] It is to be eaten on the day you sacrifice it or on the next day, but what remains on the third day must be burned. [7] If any is eaten on the third day, it is a repulsive thing; it will not be accepted. [8] Anyone who eats it will bear his iniquity, for he has profaned what is holy to the LORD. That person is to be cut off from his people. Lv 1:4; 7:17-18,20

[9] "When you reap the harvest of your land, you are not to reap to the very edge of your field or gather the gleanings of your harvest. [10] Do not strip your vineyard bare or gather

---

[A] **18:20** Lit *to give your emission of semen to*   [B] **18:21** Lit *to make any of your children pass through the fire*   [C] **18:23** Lit *to give your emission to* its fallen grapes. Leave them for the poor and the resident alien; I am the LORD your God. Ex 2:22; Dt 24:20-21

¹¹ "Do not steal. Do not act deceptively or lie to one another. ¹² Do not swear falsely by my name, profaning the name of your God; I am the LORD. Ex 20:15; 22:1; Pr 30:9; 7:3; Rm 13:9; Eph 4:28

¹³ "Do not oppress your neighbor or rob him. The wages due a hired worker must not remain with you until morning. ¹⁴ Do not curse the deaf or put a stumbling block in front of the blind, but you are to fear your God; I am the LORD. Ex 12:45; 22:14

¹⁵ "Do not act unjustly when deciding a case. Do not be partial to the poor or give preference to the rich; judge your neighbor fairly. ¹⁶ Do not go about spreading slander among your people; do not jeopardize^A your neighbor's life; I am the LORD. Ex 23:2-3; Dt 1:17; 9:4; 25:16

¹⁷ "Do not harbor hatred against your brother.^B Rebuke your neighbor directly, and you will not incur guilt because of him. ¹⁸ Do not take revenge or bear a grudge against members of your community, but love your neighbor as yourself; I am the LORD. 2Th 3:15; 1Jn 2:9,11; 3:15; 4:20

¹⁹ "You are to keep my statutes. Do not crossbreed two different kinds of your livestock, sow your fields with two kinds of seed, or put on a garment made of two kinds of material. Dt 22:9-11

²⁰ "If a man has sexual intercourse with a woman who is a slave designated for another man, but she has not been redeemed or given her freedom, there must be punishment.^C They are not to be put to death, because she had not been

freed. ²¹ However, he must bring a ram as his guilt^D offering to the LORD at the entrance to the tent of meeting. ²² The priest will make atonement on his behalf before the LORD with the ram of the guilt offering for the sin he has committed, and he will be forgiven for the sin he committed. Ex 6:6; 21:7-11; Lv 27:29

²³ "When you come into the land and plant any kind of tree for food, you are to consider the fruit forbidden.^E It will be forbidden to you for three years; it is not to be eaten. ²⁴ In the fourth year all its fruit is to be consecrated as a praise offering to the LORD. ²⁵ But in the fifth year you may eat its fruit. In this way its yield will increase for you; I am the LORD your God. Lv 25:18-22; Jdg 9:27

²⁶ "You are not to eat anything with blood in it.^F You are not to practice divination or witchcraft. ²⁷ You are not to cut off the hair at the sides of your head or mar the edge of your beard. ²⁸ You are not to make gashes on your bodies for the dead or put tattoo marks on yourselves; I am the LORD. Gn 9:4; 41:5

²⁹ "Do not debase^G your daughter by making her a prostitute, or the land will be prostituted and filled with depravity. ³⁰ Keep my Sabbaths and revere my sanctuary; I am the LORD. Ex 34:31; Lv 20:3; 21:9,12; Dt 23:17-18

³¹ "Do not turn to mediums^H or consult spiritists,^I or you will be defiled by them; I am the LORD your God. Lv 20:6; Dt 18:11; Ac 16:16

³² "You are to rise in the presence of the elderly and honor the old. Fear your God; I am the LORD.

³³ "When an alien resides with you in your land, you must not

---

^A 19:16 Lit *not stand against*   ^B 19:17 Or *your fellow Israelite*   ^C 19:20 Or *compensation*   ^D 19:21 Or *restitution*   ^E 19:23 Lit *uncircumcised*   ^F 19:26 Or *anything over its blood*   ^G 19:29 Lit *profane*   ^H 19:31 Or *spirits of the dead*   ^I 19:31 Or *familiar spirits* oppress him. ³⁴ You will regard the alien who resides with you as the native-born among you. You are to love him as yourself, for you were aliens in the land of Egypt; I am the LORD your God.   Ex 23:9; Lv 19:18; Dt 23:16

³⁵ "Do not be unfair in measurements of length, weight, or volume. ³⁶ You are to have honest balances, honest weights, an honest dry measure, ᴬ and an honest liquid measure; ᴮ I am the LORD your God, who brought you out of the land of Egypt. ³⁷ Keep all my statutes and all my ordinances and do them; I am the LORD."   Dt 25:16; Hs 12:8; Am 8:5

Molech Worship and Spiritism

20 The LORD spoke to Moses: ² "Say to the Israelites: Any Israelite or alien residing in Israel who gives any of his children to Molech must be put to death; the people of the country are to stone him. ³ I will turn ᶜ against that man and cut him off from his people, because he gave his offspring to Molech, defiling my sanctuary and profaning my holy name. ⁴ But if the people of the country look the other way when that man ᴰ gives any of his children to Molech, and do not put him to death, ⁵ then I will turn against that man and his family, and cut off from their people both him and all who follow ᴱ him in prostituting themselves with Molech.   Lv 18:21; Dt 18:10; 2Kg 23:10; Ac 7:43

⁶ "Whoever turns to mediums ᶠ or spiritists ᴳ and prostitutes himself with them, I will turn against that person and cut him off from his people. ⁷ Consecrate yourselves and be holy, for I am the LORD your God. ⁸ Keep my statutes and do them; I am the LORD who sets you apart.

Family and Sexual Offenses

⁹ "If anyone curses his father or mother, he must be put to death. He has cursed his father or mother; his death is his own fault. ᴴ   Ex 21:17

¹⁰ "If a man commits adultery with a married woman — if he commits adultery with his neighbor's wife — both the adulterer and the adulteress must be put to death. ¹¹ If a man sleeps with his father's wife, he has violated the intimacy that belongs to his father. ᴵ Both of them must be put to death; their death is their own fault. ᴶ ¹² If a man sleeps with his daughter-in-law, both of them must be put to death. They have acted perversely; their death is their own fault. ¹³ If a man sleeps with a man as with a woman, they have both committed a detestable act. They must be put to death; their death is their own fault. ¹⁴ If a man marries ᴷ a woman and her mother, it is depraved. Both he and they must be burned, so that there will be no depravity among you. ¹⁵ If a man has sexual intercourse with ᴸ an animal, he must be put to death; you are also to kill the animal. ¹⁶ If a woman approaches any animal and mates with it, you are to kill the woman and the animal. They must be put to death; their death is their own fault. ¹⁷ If a man marries his sister, whether his father's daughter or

---

ᴬ**19:36** Lit honest ephah   ᴮ**19:36** Lit honest hin   ᶜ**20:3** Lit will set my face, also in vv. 5, 6   ᴰ**20:4** Lit country ever close their eyes from that man when he   ᴱ**20:5** Lit prostitute themselves with   ᶠ**20:6** Or spirits of the dead   ᴳ**20:6** Or familiar spirits   ᴴ**20:9** Lit his blood on him   ᴵ**20:11** Lit has uncovered his father's nakedness   ᴶ**20:11** Lit their blood on them, also in vv. 12,13,16,27   ᴷ**20:14** Lit takes, also in vv. 17,21   ᴸ**20:15** Lit man gives his emission to his mother's daughter, and they have sexual relations,[A] it is a disgrace. They are to be cut off publicly from their people. He has had sexual intercourse with his sister; he will bear his iniquity. [18] If a man sleeps with a menstruating woman and has sexual intercourse with her, he has exposed the source of her flow, and she has uncovered the source of her blood. Both of them are to be cut off from their people. [19] You must not have sexual intercourse with your mother's sister or your father's sister, for it is exposing one's own blood relative; both people will bear their iniquity. [20] If a man sleeps with his aunt, he has violated the intimacy that belongs to his uncle;[B] they will bear their guilt and die childless. [21] If a man marries his brother's wife, it is impurity. He has violated the intimacy that belongs to his brother;[C] they will be childless. Ex 20:14

Holiness in the Land

[22] "You are to keep all my statutes and all my ordinances, and do them, so that the land where I am bringing you to live will not vomit you out. [23] You must not follow the statutes of the nations I am driving out before you, for they did all these things, and I abhorred them. [24] And I promised you: You will inherit their land, since I will give it to you to possess, a land flowing with milk and honey. I am the LORD your God who set you apart from the peoples. [25] Therefore you are to distinguish the clean animal from the unclean one, and the unclean bird from the clean one. Do not

become contaminated by any land animal, bird, or whatever crawls on the ground; I have set these apart as unclean for you. [26] You are to be holy to me because I, the LORD, am holy, and I have set you apart from the nations to be mine. Lv 18:3,25

[27] "A man or a woman who is[D] a medium or a spiritist must be put to death. They are to be stoned; their death is their own fault."

The Holiness of the Priests

21 The LORD said to Moses: "Speak to Aaron's sons, the priests, and tell them: A priest is not to make himself ceremonially unclean for a dead person among his relatives, [2] except for his immediate family: his mother, father, son, daughter, or brother. [3] He may make himself unclean for his unmarried virgin sister in his immediate family. [4] He is not to make himself unclean for those related to him by marriage[E] and so defile himself. Nm 5:2-3; 6:6; 19:11-13; 31:19; Ezk 44:25

[5] "Priests may not make bald spots on their heads, shave the edge of their beards, or make gashes on their bodies. [6] They are to be holy to their God and not profane the name of their God. For they present the fire offerings to the LORD, the food of their God, and they must be holy. [7] They are not to marry a woman defiled by prostitution.[F] They are not to marry one divorced by her husband, for the priest is holy to his God. [8] You are to consider him holy since he presents the food of your God. He will be holy to you because I, the LORD who sets you apart, am holy. [9] If a priest's daughter defiles

---

[A]20:17 Lit and he sees her nakedness and she sees his nakedness [B]20:20 Lit has uncovered his uncle's nakedness [C]20:21 Lit has uncovered his brother's nakedness [D]20:27 Lit is in them [E]21:4 Lit unclean a husband among his people [F]21:7 Or a prostitute, or a defiled woman herself by promiscuity,^A she defiles her father; she must be burned to death. Ex 20:7; Lv 19:27-28; 20:3; Jn 10:25 ¹⁰ "The priest who is highest among his brothers, who has had the anointing oil poured on his head and has been ordained^B to wear the clothes, must not dishevel his hair^C or tear his clothes. ¹¹ He must not go near any dead person or make himself unclean even for his father or mother. ¹² He must not leave the sanctuary or he will desecrate the sanctuary of his God, for the consecration of the anointing oil of his God is on him; I am the LORD. Lv 10:6; Ezk 44:20,25; Mk 14:63

¹³ "He is to marry a woman who is a virgin. ¹⁴ He is not to marry a widow, a divorced woman, or one defiled by prostitution. He is to marry a virgin from his own people, ¹⁵ so that he does not corrupt his bloodline^D among his people, for I am the LORD who sets him apart." Ex 22:22

Physical Defects and Priests

¹⁶ The LORD spoke to Moses: ¹⁷ "Tell Aaron: None of your descendants throughout your generations who has a physical defect is to come near to present the food of his God. ¹⁸ No man who has any defect is to come near: no man who is blind, lame, facially disfigured, or deformed; ¹⁹ no man who has a broken foot or hand, ²⁰ or who is a hunchback or a dwarf,^E or who has an eye defect, a festering rash, scabs, or a crushed testicle. ²¹ No descendant of the priest Aaron who has a defect is to come near to present the fire offerings to the LORD. He has a defect and is not to come near to present the food of his God. ²² He

may eat the food of his God from what is especially holy as well as from what is holy. ²³ But because he has a defect, he must not go near the curtain or approach the altar. He is not to desecrate my holy places, for I am the LORD who sets them apart." ²⁴ Moses said this to Aaron and his sons and to all the Israelites.

Priests and Their Food

22 The LORD spoke to Moses: ² "Tell Aaron and his sons to deal respectfully with the holy offerings of the Israelites that they have consecrated to me, so they do not profane my holy name; I am the LORD. ³ Say to them: If any man from any of your descendants throughout your generations is in a state of uncleanness yet approaches the holy offerings that the Israelites consecrate to the LORD, that person will be cut off from my presence; I am the LORD. ⁴ No man of Aaron's descendants who has a skin disease^F or a discharge is to eat from the holy offerings until he is clean. Whoever touches anything made unclean by a dead person or by a man who has an emission of semen, ⁵ or whoever touches any swarming creature that makes him unclean or any person who makes him unclean — whatever his uncleanness — ⁶ the man who touches any of these will remain unclean until evening and is not to eat from the holy offerings unless he has bathed his body with water. ⁷ When the sun has set, he will become clean, and then he may eat from the holy offerings, for that is his food. ⁸ He must not eat an animal that died naturally or was mauled by wild beasts,^A making himself unclean by it; I am the LORD. ⁹ They must keep my instruction, or they will be guilty and die because they profane it; I am the LORD who sets them apart.   Ex 20:7

¹⁰ "No one outside a priest's family^B is to eat the holy offering. A foreigner staying with a priest or a hired worker is not to eat the holy offering. ¹¹ But if a priest purchases someone with his own silver, that person may eat it, and those born in his house may eat his food. ¹² If the priest's daughter is married to a man outside a priest's family,^C she is not to eat from the holy contributions.^D ¹³ But if the priest's daughter becomes widowed or divorced, has no children, and returns to her father's house as in her youth, she may share her father's food. But no outsider may share it. ¹⁴ If anyone eats a holy offering in error, he is to add a fifth to its value and give the holy offering to the priest. ¹⁵ The priests must not profane the holy offerings the Israelites give to the LORD ¹⁶ by letting the people eat their holy offerings and having them bear the penalty of restitution. For I am the LORD who sets them apart."   Ex 29:33; Nm 3:10

Acceptable Sacrifices

¹⁷ The LORD spoke to Moses: ¹⁸ "Speak to Aaron, his sons, and all the Israelites and tell them: Any man of the house of Israel or of the resident aliens in Israel who presents his offering — whether they present payment of vows or freewill gifts to the LORD as burnt offerings — ¹⁹ must offer an unblemished male from the cattle, sheep, or goats in order for you to be accepted. ²⁰ You are not to present anything that has a defect, because it will not be accepted on your behalf.   Ex 2:22; Lv 1:2

²¹ "When a man presents a fellowship sacrifice to the LORD to fulfill a vow or as a freewill offering from the herd or flock, it has to be unblemished to be acceptable; there must be no defect in it. ²² You are not to present any animal to the LORD that is blind, injured, maimed, or has a running sore, festering rash, or scabs; you may not put any of them on the altar as a fire offering to the LORD. ²³ You may sacrifice as a freewill offering any animal from the herd or flock that has an elongated or stunted limb, but it is not acceptable as a vow offering. ²⁴ You are not to present to the LORD anything that has bruised, crushed, torn, or severed testicles; you must not sacrifice them in your land. ²⁵ Neither you nor^E a foreigner are to present food to your God from any of these animals. They will not be accepted for you because they are deformed and have a defect."   Dt 28:27; 2Sm 23:38

²⁶ The LORD spoke to Moses: ²⁷ "When an ox, sheep, or goat is born, it is to remain with^F its mother for seven days; from the eighth day on, it will be acceptable as an offering, a fire offering to the LORD. ²⁸ But you are not to slaughter an animal from the herd or flock on the same day as its young. ²⁹ When you sacrifice a thank offering to the LORD, sacrifice it so that you may be accepted. ³⁰ It is to be eaten on the same day. Do not let any of it remain until morning; I am the LORD.   Ex 22:30; 23:19; Lv 7:12-15; Dt 22:6-7

^A **22:8** Lit *eat a carcass or a mauled beast*   ^B **22:10** Lit *"No stranger*   ^C **22:12** Lit *to a stranger*   ^D **22:12** Lit *the contribution of holy offerings*   ^E **22:25** Lit *nor from the hand of*   ^F **22:27** Lit *under*

³¹ "You are to keep my commands and do them; I am the LORD. ³² You must not profane my holy name; I must be treated as holy among the Israelites. I am the LORD who sets you apart, ³³ the one who brought you out of the land of Egypt to be your God; I am the LORD." Lv 19:12; 21:6-8,23

Holy Days

23 The LORD spoke to Moses: ² "Speak to the Israelites and tell them: These are my appointed times, the times of the LORD that you will proclaim as sacred assemblies. Lv 23:37,44; Nm 10:10; 2Ch 2:3; Ezr 3:5 ³ "Work may be done for six days, but on the seventh day there is to be a Sabbath of complete rest, a sacred assembly. You are not to do any work; it is a Sabbath to the LORD wherever you live. Ex 31:15; 35:2; Lv 16:31

⁴ "These are the LORD's appointed times, the sacred assemblies you are to proclaim at their appointed times. ⁵ The Passover to the LORD comes in the first month, at twilight on the fourteenth day of the month. ⁶ The Festival of Unleavened Bread to the LORD is on the fifteenth day of the same month. For seven days you must eat unleavened bread. ⁷ On the first day you are to hold a sacred assembly; you are not to do any daily work. ⁸ You are to present a fire offering to the LORD for seven days. On the seventh day there will be a sacred assembly; do not do any daily work." Ex 12:11,17

⁹ The LORD spoke to Moses: ¹⁰ "Speak to the Israelites and tell them: When you enter the land I am giving you and reap its harvest,ᴬ you are to bring the first sheaf of your harvest to the priest. ¹¹ He will present the sheaf before the LORD so that you may be accepted; the priest is to present it on the day after the Sabbath. ¹² On the day you present the sheaf, you are to offer a year-old male lambᴮ without blemish as a burnt offering to the LORD. ¹³ Its grain offering is to be four quartsᶜ of fine flour mixed with oil as a fire offering to the LORD, a pleasing aroma, and its drink offering will be one quartᴰ of wine. ¹⁴ You must not eat bread, roasted grain, or any new grainᴱ until this very day, and until you have brought the offering to your God. This is to be a permanent statute throughout your generations wherever you live. Ex 29:1

¹⁵ "You are to count sevenᶠ complete weeksᴳ starting from the day after the Sabbath, the day you brought the sheaf of the presentation offering. ¹⁶ You are to count fifty days until the day after the seventh Sabbath and then present an offering of new grain to the LORD. ¹⁷ Bring two loaves of bread from your settlements as a presentation offering, each of them made from four quarts of fine flour, baked with yeast, as firstfruits to the LORD. ¹⁸ You are to present with the bread seven unblemished male lambs a year old, one young bull, and two rams. They will be a burnt offering to the LORD, with their grain offerings and drink offerings, a fire offering of a pleasing aroma to the LORD. ¹⁹ You are also to prepare one male goat as a sin offering, and two male lambs a year old as a fellowship sacrifice. ²⁰ The priest will present the lambs with the bread of

---

ᴬ**23:10** = the barley harvest   ᴮ**23:12** Or *a male lamb in its first year*   ᶜ**23:13** Lit *two-tenths of an ephah*, also in v. 17   ᴰ**23:13** Lit *one-fourth of a hin*   ᴱ**23:14** Grain or bread from the new harvest   ᶠ**23:15** Lit *count; they will be seven*   ᴳ**23:15** Or *Sabbaths* firstfruits as a presentation offering before the LORD; the bread and the two lambs will be holy to the LORD for the priest. [21] On that same day you are to make a proclamation and hold a sacred assembly. You are not to do any daily work. This is to be a permanent statute wherever you live throughout your generations. [22] When you reap the harvest of your land, you are not to reap all the way to the edge of your field or gather the gleanings of your harvest. Leave them for the poor and the resident alien; I am the LORD your God." Ex 34:22; Nm 28:26

[23] The LORD spoke to Moses: [24] "Tell the Israelites: In the seventh month, on the first day of the month, you are to have a day of complete rest, commemoration, and trumpet blasts — a sacred assembly. [25] You must not do any daily work, but you must present a fire offering to the LORD." Lv 25:9; Nm 5:15

[26] The LORD again spoke to Moses: [27] "The tenth day of this seventh month is the Day of Atonement. You are to hold a sacred assembly and practice self-denial; you are to present a fire offering to the LORD. [28] On this particular day you are not to do any work, for it is a Day of Atonement to make atonement for yourselves before the LORD your God. [29] If any person does not practice self-denial on this particular day, he is to be cut off from his people. [30] I will destroy among his people anyone who does any work on this same day. [31] You are not to do any work. This is a permanent statute throughout your generations wherever you live. [32] It will be a Sabbath of complete rest for you, and you must practice self-denial. You are to observe your Sabbath from the evening of the ninth day of the month until the following evening."

[33] The LORD spoke to Moses: [34] "Tell the Israelites: The Festival of Shelters[A] to the LORD begins on the fifteenth day of this seventh month and continues for seven days. [35] There is to be a sacred assembly on the first day; you are not to do any daily work. [36] You are to present a fire offering to the LORD for seven days. On the eighth day you are to hold a sacred assembly and present a fire offering to the LORD. It is a solemn gathering; you are not to do any daily work. Ex 23:16

[37] "These are the LORD's appointed times that you are to proclaim as sacred assemblies for presenting fire offerings to the LORD, burnt offerings and grain offerings, sacrifices and drink offerings, each on its designated day. [38] These are in addition to the offerings for the LORD's Sabbaths, your gifts, all your vow offerings, and all your freewill offerings that you give to the LORD.

[39] "You are to celebrate the LORD's festival on the fifteenth day of the seventh month for seven days after you have gathered the produce of the land. There will be complete rest on the first day and complete rest on the eighth day. [40] On the first day you are to take the product of majestic trees — palm fronds, boughs of leafy trees, and willows of the brook — and rejoice before the LORD your God for seven days. [41] You are to celebrate it as a festival to the LORD seven days each year. This is a permanent statute for you throughout your generations; celebrate it in the seventh month. [42] You are to live in shelters

A 23:34 Or *Tabernacles,* or *Booths*

for seven days. All the native-born of Israel must live in shelters, ⁴³ so that your generations may know that I made the Israelites live in shelters when I brought them out of the land of Egypt; I am the LORD your God." ⁴⁴ So Moses declared the LORD's appointed times to the Israelites. Gn 1:11; Ex 15:27; Nm 33:9; Jdg 4:5; Jl 1:12

Tabernacle Oil and Bread

24 The LORD spoke to Moses: ² "Command the Israelites to bring you pure oil from crushed olives for the light, in order to keep the lamp burning regularly. ³ Aaron is to tend it continually from evening until morning before the LORD outside the curtain of the testimony in the tent of meeting. This is a permanent statute throughout your generations. ⁴ He must continually tend the lamps on the pure gold lampstand in the LORD's presence.

⁵ "Take fine flour and bake it into twelve loaves; each loaf is to be made with four quarts.^A ⁶ Arrange them in two rows, six to a row, on the pure gold table before the LORD. ⁷ Place pure frankincense near each row, so that it may serve as a memorial portion for the bread and a fire offering to the LORD. ⁸ The bread is to be set out before the LORD every Sabbath day as a permanent covenant obligation on the part of the Israelites. ⁹ It belongs to Aaron and his sons, who are to eat it in a holy place, for it is the holiest portion for him from the fire offerings to the LORD; this is a permanent rule." Ex 25:23,30

A Case of Blasphemy

¹⁰ Now the son of an Israelite mother and an Egyptian father was^B among the Israelites. A fight broke out in the camp between the Israelite woman's son and an Israelite man. ¹¹ Her son cursed and blasphemed the Name, and they brought him to Moses. (His mother's name was Shelomith, a daughter of Dibri of the tribe of Dan.) ¹² They put him in custody until the LORD's decision could be made clear to them. Ex 20:7

¹³ Then the LORD spoke to Moses: ¹⁴ "Bring the one who has cursed to the outside of the camp and have all who heard him lay their hands on his head; then have the whole community stone him. ¹⁵ And tell the Israelites: If anyone curses his God, he will bear the consequences of his sin. ¹⁶ Whoever blasphemes the name of the LORD must be put to death; the whole community is to stone him. If he blasphemes the Name, he is to be put to death, whether the resident alien or the native. Lv 19:7; 20:2,27; 24:16,23

¹⁷ "If a man kills anyone, he must be put to death. ¹⁸ Whoever kills an animal is to make restitution for it, life for life. ¹⁹ If any man inflicts a permanent injury on his neighbor, whatever he has done is to be done to him: ²⁰ fracture for fracture, eye for eye, tooth for tooth. Whatever injury he inflicted on the person, the same is to be inflicted on him. ²¹ Whoever kills an animal is to make restitution for it, but whoever kills a person is to be put to death. ²² You are to have the same law for the resident alien and the native, because I am the LORD your God."

²³ After Moses spoke to the Israelites, they brought the one who had cursed to the outside of the camp and stoned him. So the Israelites did as the LORD had commanded Moses.

^A**24:5** Lit two-tenths of an ephah   ^B**24:10** Lit went out

Sabbath Years and Jubilee

25 The LORD spoke to Moses on Mount Sinai: ² "Speak to the Israelites and tell them: When you enter the land I am giving you, the land will observe a Sabbath to the LORD. ³ You may sow your field for six years, and you may prune your vineyard and gather its produce for six years. ⁴ But there will be a Sabbath of complete rest for the land in the seventh year, a Sabbath to the LORD: you are not to sow your field or prune your vineyard. ⁵ You are not to reap what grows by itself from your crop, or harvest the grapes of your untended vines. It is to be a year of complete rest for the land. ⁶ Whatever the land produces during the Sabbath year can be food for you — for yourself, your male or female slave, and the hired worker or alien who resides with you. ⁷ All of its growth may serve as food for your livestock and the wild animals in your land. Lv 16:31

⁸ "You are to count seven sabbatical years, seven times seven years, so that the time period of the seven sabbatical years amounts to forty-nine. ⁹ Then you are to sound a trumpet loudly in the seventh month, on the tenth day of the month; you will sound it throughout your land on the Day of Atonement. ¹⁰ You are to consecrate the fiftieth year and proclaim freedom in the land for all its inhabitants. It will be your Jubilee, when each of you is to return to his property and each of you to his clan. ¹¹ The fiftieth year will be your Jubilee; you are not to sow, reap what grows by itself, or harvest its untended vines. ¹² It is to be holy to you because it is the Jubilee; you may only eat its produce directly from the field. Lv 23:27; 27:17-24; Nm 36:4; Dt 15:1

¹³ "In this Year of Jubilee, each of you will return to his property. ¹⁴ If you make a sale to your neighbor or a purchase from him, do not cheat one another. ¹⁵ You are to make the purchase from your neighbor based on the number of years since the last Jubilee. He is to sell to you based on the number of remaining harvest years. ¹⁶ You are to increase its price in proportion to a greater amount of years, and decrease its price in proportion to a lesser amount of years, because what he is selling to you is a number of harvests. ¹⁷ You are not to cheat one another, but fear your God, for I am the LORD your God.

¹⁸ "You are to keep my statutes and ordinances and carefully observe them, so that you may live securely in the land. ¹⁹ Then the land will yield its fruit, so that you can eat, be satisfied, and live securely in the land. ²⁰ If you wonder: 'What will we eat in the seventh year if we don't sow or gather our produce?' ²¹ I will appoint my blessing for you in the sixth year, so that it will produce a crop sufficient for three years. ²² When you sow in the eighth year, you will be eating from the previous harvest. You will be eating this until the ninth year when its harvest comes in. Lv 19:37

²³ "The land is not to be permanently sold because it is mine, and you are only aliens and temporary residents on my land.ᴬ ²⁴ You are to allow the redemption of any land you occupy. ²⁵ If your brother becomes destitute and sells part of his property, his nearest relative may come and redeem what his

ᴬ**25:23** Lit *residents with me*

brother has sold. [26] If a man has no family redeemer, but he prospers [A] and obtains enough to redeem his land, [27] he may calculate the years since its sale, repay the balance to the man he sold it to, and return to his property. [28] But if he cannot obtain enough to repay him, what he sold will remain in the possession of its purchaser until the Year of Jubilee. It is to be released at the Jubilee, so that he may return to his property.   1Ch 29:15; Heb 11:13

[29] "If a man sells a residence in a walled city, his right of redemption will last until a year has passed after its sale; his right of redemption will last a year. [30] If it is not redeemed by the end of a full year, then the house in the walled city is permanently transferred to its purchaser throughout his generations. It is not to be released on the Jubilee. [31] But houses in settlements that have no walls around them are to be classified as open fields. The right to redeem such houses stays in effect, and they are to be released at the Jubilee.

[32] "Concerning the Levitical cities, the Levites always have the right to redeem houses in the cities they possess. [33] Whatever property one of the Levites can redeem [B] — a house sold in a city they possess — is to be released at the Jubilee, because the houses in the Levitical cities are their possession among the Israelites. [34] The open pastureland around their cities may not be sold, for it is their permanent possession.   Nm 35:1-8; Dt 18:1-2; 19:2-9; Jos 21

[35] "If your brother becomes destitute and cannot sustain himself among [C] you, you are to support him as an alien or temporary resident, so that he can continue to live among you. [36] Do not profit or take interest from him, but fear your God and let your brother live among you. [37] You are not to lend him your silver with interest or sell him your food for profit. [38] I am the LORD your God, who brought you out of the land of Egypt to give you the land of Canaan and to be your God.   Ex 22:25; Dt 23:19-20; Ezk 22:12

[39] "If your brother among you becomes destitute and sells himself to you, you must not force him to do slave labor. [40] Let him stay with you as a hired worker or temporary resident; he may work for you until the Year of Jubilee. [41] Then he and his children are to be released from you, and he may return to his clan and his ancestral property. [42] They are not to be sold as slaves, [D] because they are my servants [E] that I brought out of the land of Egypt. [43] You are not to rule over them harshly but fear your God. [44] Your male and female slaves are to be from the nations around you; you may purchase male and female slaves. [45] You may also purchase them from the aliens residing with you, or from their families living among you — those born in your land. These may become your property. [46] You may leave them to your sons after you to inherit as property; you can make them slaves for life. But concerning your brothers, the Israelites, you must not rule over one another harshly.   2Kg 4:1

[47] "If an alien or temporary resident living among you prospers, but your brother living near him becomes destitute and sells himself

[A]25:26 Lit but his hand reaches   [B]25:33 Hb obscure   [C]25:35 Lit and his hand falters with   [D]25:42 Lit sold with a sale of a slave   [E]25:42 Or slaves to the alien living among you, or to a member of the resident alien's clan, ⁴⁸ he has the right of redemption after he has been sold. One of his brothers may redeem him. ⁴⁹ His uncle or cousin may redeem him, or any of his close relatives from his clan may redeem him. If he prospers, he may redeem himself. ⁵⁰ The one who purchased him is to calculate the time from the year he sold himself to him until the Year of Jubilee. The price of his sale will be determined by the number of years. It will be set for him like the daily wages of a hired worker. ⁵¹ If many years are still left, he must pay his redemption price in proportion to them based on his purchase price. ⁵² If only a few years remain until the Year of Jubilee, he will calculate and pay the price of his redemption in proportion to his remaining years. ⁵³ He will stay with him like a man hired year by year. A resident alien is not to rule over him harshly in your sight. ⁵⁴ If he is not redeemed in any of these ways, he and his children are to be released at the Year of Jubilee. ⁵⁵ For the Israelites are my servants. They are my servants that I brought out of the land of Egypt; I am the LORD your God.   Ex 4:10

Covenant Blessings and Discipline

26 "Do not make idols for yourselves, set up a carved image or sacred pillar for yourselves, or place a sculpted stone in your land to bow down to it, for I am the LORD your God. ² Keep my Sabbaths and revere my sanctuary; I am the LORD.

³ "If you follow my statutes and faithfully observe my commands,

⁴ I will give you rain at the right time, and the land will yield its produce, and the trees of the field will bear their fruit. ⁵ Your threshing will continue until grape harvest, and the grape harvest will continue until sowing time; you will have plenty of food to eat and live securely in your land. ⁶ I will give peace to the land, and you will lie down with nothing to frighten you. I will remove dangerous animals from the land, and no sword will pass through your land. ⁷ You will pursue your enemies, and they will fall before you by the sword. ⁸ Five of you will pursue a hundred, and a hundred of you will pursue ten thousand; your enemies will fall before you by the sword.   Lv 25:18-19; Dt 28:1-2,12; Is 30:21-23

⁹ "I will turn to you, make you fruitful and multiply you, and confirm my covenant with you. ¹⁰ You will eat the old grain of the previous year and will clear out the old to make room for the new. ¹¹ I will place my residenceᴬ among you, and I will not reject you. ¹² I will walk among you and be your God, and you will be my people. ¹³ I am the LORD your God, who brought you out of the land of Egypt, so that you would no longer be their slaves. I broke the bars of your yoke and enabled you to live in freedom. ᴮ

¹⁴ "But if you do not obey me and observe all these commands — ¹⁵ if you reject my statutes and despise my ordinances, and do not observe all my commands — and break my covenant, ¹⁶ then I will do this to you: I will bring terror on you — wasting disease and fever that will cause your eyes to fail and your life to ebb away. You will sow your seed

---

ᴬ**26:11** Or *tabernacle*   ᴮ**26:13** Lit *to walk uprightly* in vain because your enemies will eat it. [17] I will turn[A] against you, so that you will be defeated by your enemies. Those who hate you will rule over you, and you will flee even though no one is pursuing you.

[18] "But if after these things you will not obey me, I will proceed to discipline you seven times for your sins. [19] I will break down your strong pride. I will make your sky like iron and your land like bronze, [20] and your strength will be used up for nothing. Your land will not yield its produce, and the trees of the land will not bear their fruit.

[21] "If you act with hostility toward me and are unwilling to obey me, I will multiply your plagues seven times for your sins. [22] I will send wild animals against you that will deprive you of your children, ravage your livestock, and reduce your numbers until your roads are deserted.   Gn 4:15,24; Dt 32:24; Jdg 5:6; Is 33:8

[23] "If in spite of these things you do not accept my discipline, but act with hostility toward me, [24] then I will act with hostility toward you; I also will strike you seven times for your sins. [25] I will bring a sword against you to execute the vengeance of the covenant. Though you withdraw into your cities, I will send a pestilence among you, and you will be delivered into enemy hands. [26] When I cut off your supply of bread, ten women will bake your bread in a single oven and ration out your bread by weight, so that you will eat but not be satisfied.

[27] "And if in spite of this you do not obey me but act with hostility toward me, [28] I will act with furious hostility toward you; I will also discipline you seven times for

your sins. [29] You will eat the flesh of your sons; you will eat the flesh of your daughters. [30] I will destroy your high places, cut down your shrines,[B] and heap your lifeless bodies on the lifeless bodies of your idols; I will reject you. [31] I will reduce your cities to ruins and devastate your sanctuaries. I will not smell the pleasing aroma of your sacrifices. [32] I also will devastate the land, so that your enemies who come to live there will be appalled by it. [33] But I will scatter you among the nations, and I will draw a sword to chase after you. So your land will become desolate, and your cities will become ruins.   Dt 28:53-57; Jr 19:9

[34] "Then the land will make up for its Sabbath years during the time it lies desolate, while you are in the land of your enemies. At that time the land will rest and make up for its Sabbaths. [35] As long as it lies desolate, it will have the rest it did not have during your Sabbaths when you lived there.

[36] "I will put anxiety in the hearts of those of you who survive in the lands of their enemies. The sound of a wind-driven leaf will put them to flight, and they will flee as one flees from a sword, and fall though no one is pursuing them. [37] They will stumble over one another as if fleeing from a sword though no one is pursuing them. You will not be able to stand against your enemies. [38] You will perish among the nations; the land of your enemies will devour you. [39] Those[C] who survive in the lands of your enemies will waste away because of their iniquity; they will also waste away because of their fathers' iniquities along with theirs.

⁴⁰ "But when they confess their iniquity and the iniquity of their fathers — their unfaithfulness that they practiced against me, and how they acted with hostility toward me, ⁴¹ and I acted with hostility toward them and brought them into the land of their enemies — and when their uncircumcised hearts are humbled and they make amends for their iniquity, ⁴² then I will remember my covenant with Jacob. I will also remember my covenant with Isaac and my covenant with Abraham, and I will remember the land. ⁴³ For the land abandoned by them will make up for its Sabbaths by lying desolate without the people, while they make amends for their iniquity, because they rejected my ordinances and abhorred my statutes. ⁴⁴ Yet in spite of this, while they are in the land of their enemies, I will not reject or abhor them so as to destroy them and break my covenant with them, since I am the LORD their God. ⁴⁵ For their sake I will remember the covenant with their fathers, whom I brought out of the land of Egypt in the sight of the nations to be their God; I am the LORD." Dt 30:6; Jr 4:4; 9:25

⁴⁶ These are the statutes, ordinances, and laws the LORD established between himself and the Israelites through Moses on Mount Sinai.

Funding the Sanctuary

27 The LORD spoke to Moses: ² "Speak to the Israelites and tell them: When someone makes a special vow to the LORD that involves the assessment of people, ³ if the assessment concerns a male from twenty to sixty years old, your assessment is fifty silver shekels measured by the standard sanctuary shekel. ⁴ If the person is a female, your assessment is thirty shekels. ⁵ If the person is from five to twenty years old, your assessment for a male is twenty shekels and for a female ten shekels. ⁶ If the person is from one month to five years old, your assessment for a male is five silver shekels, and for a female your assessment is three shekels of silver. ⁷ If the person is sixty years or more, your assessment is fifteen shekels for a male and ten shekels for a female. ⁸ But if one is too poor to pay the assessment, he is to present the person before the priest and the priest will set a value for him. The priest will set a value for him according to what the one making the vow can afford. Ex 30:13; Lv 5:15; 27:8,25; 2Kg 15:20

⁹ "If the vow involves one of the animals that may be brought as an offering to the LORD, any of these he gives to the LORD will be holy. ¹⁰ He may not replace it or make a substitution for it, either good for bad, or bad for good. But if he does substitute one animal for another, both that animal and its substitute will be holy. Mal 1:8

¹¹ "If the vow involves any of the unclean animals that may not be brought as an offering to the LORD, the animal must be presented before the priest. ¹² The priest will set its value, whether high or low; the price will be set as the priest makes the assessment for you. ¹³ If the one who brought it decides to redeem it, he must add a fifth to the ᴬ assessed value. Gn 47:24; Lv 5:16; 6:5

¹⁴ "When a man consecrates his house as holy to the LORD, the priest

ᴬ27:13 Lit *your*, also in vv. 15,19,23

will assess its value, whether high or low. The price will stand just as the priest assesses it. [15] But if the one who consecrated his house redeems it, he must add a fifth to the assessed value, and it will be his.

[16] "If a man consecrates to the LORD any part of a field that he possesses, your assessment of value will be proportional to the seed needed to sow it, at the rate of fifty silver shekels for every five bushels[A] of barley seed.[B] [17] If he consecrates his field during the Year of Jubilee, the price will stand according to your assessment. [18] But if he consecrates his field after the Jubilee, the priest will calculate the price for him in proportion to the years left until the next Year of Jubilee, so that your assessment will be reduced. [19] If the one who consecrated the field decides to redeem it, he must add a fifth to the assessed value, and the field will transfer back to him. [20] But if he does not redeem the field or if he has sold it to another man, it is no longer redeemable. [21] When the field is released in the Jubilee, it will be holy to the LORD like a field permanently set apart; it becomes the priest's property.

[22] "If a person consecrates to the LORD a field he has purchased that is not part of his inherited landholding, [23] then the priest will calculate for him the amount of the assessment up to the Year of Jubilee, and the person will pay the assessed value on that day as a holy offering to the LORD. [24] In the Year of Jubilee the field will return to the one he bought it from, the original owner. [25] All your assessed values will be measured by the standard sanctuary shekel,[C] twenty gerahs to the shekel.   Ex 30:13; Lv 25:28; Nm 18:16

[26] "But no one can consecrate a firstborn of the livestock, whether an animal from the herd or flock, to the LORD, because a firstborn already belongs to the LORD. [27] If it is one of the unclean livestock, it can be ransomed according to your assessment by adding a fifth of its value to it. If it is not redeemed, it can be sold according to your assessment.   Ex 13:2,13,15; 34:19; Nm 18:15

[28] "Nothing that a man permanently sets apart to the LORD from all he owns, whether a person, an animal, or his inherited landholding, can be sold or redeemed; everything set apart is especially holy to the LORD. [29] No person who has been set apart for destruction is to be ransomed; he must be put to death.   Nm 21:1-3; 31:7,13-17; Jos 6:17; 1Sm 15:17-33

[30] "Every tenth of the land's produce, grain from the soil or fruit from the trees, belongs to the LORD; it is holy to the LORD. [31] If a man decides to redeem any part of this tenth, he must add a fifth to its value. [32] Every tenth animal from the herd or flock, which passes under the shepherd's rod, will be holy to the LORD. [33] He is not to inspect whether it is good or bad, and he is not to make a substitution for it. But if he does make a substitution, both the animal and its substitute will be holy; they cannot be redeemed."   Gn 28:22; Nm 18:21-32; Dt 14:22-29

[34] These are the commands the LORD gave Moses for the Israelites on Mount Sinai.   Nm 36:13

[A]27:16 Lit for a homer [B]27:16 Or grain [C]27:25 A shekel is about two-fifths of an ounce of silver

NUMBERS

The Census of Israel

1 The LORD spoke to Moses in the tent of meeting in the Wilderness of Sinai, on the first day of the second month of the second year after Israel's departure from the land of Egypt: ² "Take a census of the entire Israelite community by their clans and their fathers' families, ᴬ counting the names of every male one by one. ³ You and Aaron are to register those who are twenty years old or more by their military divisions — everyone who can serve in Israel's army.ᴮ ⁴ A man from each tribe is to be with you, each one the head of his ancestral family.ᶜ ⁵ These are the names of the men who are to assist you: Ex 19:1

Elizur son of Shedeur
from Reuben; Nm 2:3-30; 7:12-83
⁶ Shelumiel son of Zurishaddai
from Simeon;
⁷ Nahshon son of Amminadab
from Judah;
⁸ Nethanel son of Zuar
from Issachar;
⁹ Eliab son of Helon
from Zebulun;
¹⁰ from the sons of Joseph:
Elishama son of Ammihud
from Ephraim,
Gamaliel son of Pedahzur
from Manasseh;
¹¹ Abidan son of Gideoni
from Benjamin;
¹² Ahiezer son of Ammishaddai
from Dan;
¹³ Pagiel son of Ochran
from Asher;
¹⁴ Eliasaph son of Deuelᴰ
from Gad;
¹⁵ Ahira son of Enan
from Naphtali.

¹⁶ These are the men called from the community; they are leaders of their ancestral tribes, the heads of Israel's clans." Nm 1:47; 13:2; 26:55; 33:54

¹⁷ So Moses and Aaron took these men who had been designated by name, ¹⁸ and they assembled the whole community on the first day of the second month. They recorded their ancestry by their clans and their ancestral families, counting one by one the names of those twenty years old or more, ¹⁹ just as the LORD commanded Moses. He registered them in the Wilderness of Sinai:

²⁰ The descendants of Reuben, the firstborn of Israel: according to their family records by their clans and their ancestral families, counting one by one the names of every male twenty years old or more, everyone who could serve in the army, ²¹ those registered for the tribe of Reuben numbered 46,500.

²² The descendants of Simeon: according to their family records by their clans and their ancestral families, those registered counting one by one the names of every male twenty years old or more, everyone who could serve in the army, ²³ those registered for the tribe of Simeon numbered 59,300.

ᴬ**1:2** Lit *the house of their fathers*, also in vv. 18,20,22,24,26,28,30,32,34,36,38,40,42,45   ᴮ**1:3** Lit *everyone going out to war in Israel*   ᶜ**1:4** Lit *the house of his fathers*, also in v. 44   ᴰ**1:14** LXX, Syr read *Reuel*

²⁴ The descendants of Gad: according to their family records by their clans and their ancestral families, counting the names of those twenty years old or more, everyone who could serve in the army, ²⁵ those registered for the tribe of Gad numbered 45,650. Gn 30:11

²⁶ The descendants of Judah: according to their family records by their clans and their ancestral families, counting the names of those twenty years old or more, everyone who could serve in the army, ²⁷ those registered for the tribe of Judah numbered 74,600. Rv 5:5

²⁸ The descendants of Issachar: according to their family records by their clans and their ancestral families, counting the names of those twenty years old or more, everyone who could serve in the army, ²⁹ those registered for the tribe of Issachar numbered 54,400.

³⁰ The descendants of Zebulun: according to their family records by their clans and their ancestral families, counting the names of those twenty years old or more, everyone who could serve in the army, ³¹ those registered for the tribe of Zebulun numbered 57,400.

³² The descendants of Joseph:

The descendants of Ephraim: according to their family records by their clans and their ancestral families, counting the names of those twenty years old or more, everyone who could serve in the army, ³³ those registered for the tribe of Ephraim numbered 40,500.

³⁴ The descendants of Manasseh: according to their family records by their clans and their ancestral families, counting the names of those twenty years old or more, everyone who could serve in the army, ³⁵ those registered for the tribe of Manasseh numbered 32,200.

³⁶ The descendants of Benjamin: according to their family records by their clans and their ancestral families, counting the names of those twenty years old or more, everyone who could serve in the army, ³⁷ those registered for the tribe of Benjamin numbered 35,400.

³⁸ The descendants of Dan: according to their family records by their clans and their ancestral families, counting the names of those twenty years old or more, everyone who could serve in the army, ³⁹ those registered for the tribe of Dan numbered 62,700. Gn 30:6

⁴⁰ The descendants of Asher: according to their family records by their clans and their ancestral families, counting the names of those twenty years old or more, everyone who could serve in the army, ⁴¹ those registered for the tribe of Asher numbered 41,500. Gn 49:20

⁴² The descendants of Naphtali: according to their family

records by their clans and their ancestral families, counting the names of those twenty years old or more, everyone who could serve in the army, [43] those registered for the tribe of Naphtali numbered 53,400.

[44] These are the men Moses and Aaron registered, with the assistance of the twelve leaders of Israel; each represented his ancestral family. [45] So all the Israelites twenty years old or more, everyone who could serve in Israel's army, were registered by their ancestral families. [46] All those registered numbered 603,550. Ex 12:37; Nm 26:51

Duties of the Levites

[47] But the Levites were not registered with them by their ancestral tribe. [48] For the LORD had told Moses: [49] "Do not register or take a census of the tribe of Levi with the other Israelites. [50] Appoint the Levites over the tabernacle of the testimony, all its furnishings, and everything in it. They are to transport the tabernacle and all its articles, take care of it, and camp around it. [51] Whenever the tabernacle is to move, the Levites are to take it down, and whenever it is to stop at a campsite, the Levites are to set it up. Any unauthorized person who comes near it is to be put to death. Gn 34:25,30; 49:5-7; Ex 18:1; 32:26-29

[52] "The Israelites are to camp by their military divisions, each man with his encampment and under his banner. [53] The Levites are to camp around the tabernacle of the testimony and watch over it, so that no wrath will fall on the Israelite community." [54] The Israelites did everything just as the LORD had commanded Moses. Nm 3:7; 18:4-5; 36:10

Organization of the Camps

2 The LORD spoke to Moses and Aaron: [2] "The Israelites are to camp under their respective banners beside the flags of their ancestral families. [A] They are to camp around the tent of meeting at a distance from it:

[3] Judah's military divisions will camp on the east side toward the sunrise under their banner. The leader of the descendants of Judah is Nahshon son of Amminadab. [4] His military division numbers 74,600. [5] The tribe of Issachar will camp next to it. The leader of the Issacharites is Nethanel son of Zuar. [6] His military division numbers 54,400. [7] The tribe of Zebulun will be next. The leader of the Zebulunites is Eliab son of Helon. [8] His military division numbers 57,400. [9] The total number in their military divisions who belong to Judah's encampment is 186,400; they will move out first. Nm 1:3,52

[10] Reuben's military divisions will camp on the south side under their banner. The leader of the Reubenites is Elizur son of Shedeur. [11] His military division numbers 46,500. [12] The tribe of Simeon will camp next to it. The leader of the Simeonites is Shelumiel son of Zurishaddai. [13] His military division numbers 59,300. [14] The tribe of Gad will be next. The leader of the Gadites is Eliasaph son of Deuel. [B] [15] His military division numbers

A 2:2 Lit *the house of their fathers*, also in v. 32 B 2:14 Some Hb mss, Sam, Vg; other Hb mss read *Reuel*

45,650. [16] The total number in their military divisions who belong to Reuben's encampment is 151,450; they will move out second.

[17] The tent of meeting is to move out with the Levites' camp, which is in the middle of the camps. They are to move out just as they camp, each in his place, [A] with their banners.

[18] Ephraim's military divisions will camp on the west side under their banner. The leader of the Ephraimites is Elishama son of Ammihud. [19] His military division numbers 40,500. [20] The tribe of Manasseh will be next to it. The leader of the Manassites is Gamaliel son of Pedahzur. [21] His military division numbers 32,200. [22] The tribe of Benjamin will be next. The leader of the Benjaminites is Abidan son of Gideoni. [23] His military division numbers 35,400. [24] The total in their military divisions who belong to Ephraim's encampment number 108,100; they will move out third.

[25] Dan's military divisions will camp on the north side under their banner. The leader of the Danites is Ahiezer son of Ammishaddai. [26] His military division numbers 62,700. [27] The tribe of Asher will camp next to it. The leader of the Asherites is Pagiel son of Ochran. [28] His military division numbers 41,500. [29] The tribe of Naphtali will be next. The leader of the Naphtalites is Ahira

son of Enan. [30] His military division numbers 53,400. [31] The total number who belong to Dan's encampment is 157,600; they are to move out last, with their banners."

[32] These are the Israelites registered by their ancestral families. The total number in the camps by their military divisions is 603,550. [33] But the Levites were not registered among the Israelites, just as the LORD had commanded Moses. [34] The Israelites did everything the LORD commanded Moses; they camped by their banners in this way and moved out the same way, each man by his clan and by his ancestral family. [B]   Nm 10:10-28

Aaron's Sons and the Levites

3 These are the family records of Aaron and Moses at the time the LORD spoke with Moses on Mount Sinai. [2] These are the names of Aaron's sons: Nadab, the firstborn, and Abihu, Eleazar, and Ithamar. [3] These are the names of Aaron's sons, the anointed priests, who were ordained to serve as priests. [4] But Nadab and Abihu died in the LORD's presence when they presented unauthorized fire before the LORD in the Wilderness of Sinai, and they had no sons. So Eleazar and Ithamar served as priests under the direction of Aaron their father.   Ex 19:3; Lv 10:1-2,6; Nm 4:16,28,33

[5] The LORD spoke to Moses: [6] "Bring the tribe of Levi near and present them to the priest Aaron to assist him. [7] They are to perform duties for [C] him and the entire community before the tent of meeting

by attending to the service of the tabernacle. [8] They are to take care of all the furnishings of the tent of meeting and perform duties for the Israelites by attending to the service of the tabernacle. [9] Assign the Levites to Aaron and his sons; they have been assigned exclusively to him[A] from the Israelites. [10] You are to appoint Aaron and his sons to carry out their priestly responsibilities, but any unauthorized person who comes near the sanctuary is to be put to death." Nm 1:50-51,53; 8:16,19,22; 18:6

[11] The LORD spoke to Moses: [12] "See, I have taken the Levites from the Israelites in place of every firstborn Israelite from the womb. The Levites belong to me, [13] because every firstborn belongs to me. At the time I struck down every firstborn in the land of Egypt, I consecrated every firstborn in Israel to myself, both man and animal. They are mine; I am the LORD." Ex 8:16-18; 13:1-2; 32:26-29

The Levitical Census

[14] The LORD spoke to Moses in the Wilderness of Sinai: [15] "Register the Levites by their ancestral families[B] and their clans. You are to register every male one month old or more." [16] So Moses registered them in obedience to the LORD as he had been commanded:

[17] These were Levi's sons by name: Gershon, Kohath, and Merari. [18] These were the names of Gershon's sons by their clans: Libni and Shimei. [19] Kohath's sons by their clans were Amram, Izhar, Hebron, and Uzziel. [20] Merari's sons by their clans were Mahli and Mushi. These were the Levite clans by their ancestral families. Ex 6:17-19; 1Ch 6:1,16,20-29

[21] The Libnite clan and the Shimeite clan came from Gershon; these were the Gershonite clans. [22] Those registered, counting every male one month old or more, numbered 7,500. [23] The Gershonite clans camped behind the tabernacle on the west side, [24] and the leader of the Gershonite families[C] was Eliasaph son of Lael. [25] The Gershonites' duties at the tent of meeting involved the tabernacle, the tent, its covering, the screen for the entrance to the tent of meeting, [26] the hangings of the courtyard, the screen for the entrance to the courtyard that surrounds the tabernacle and the altar, and the tent ropes — all the work relating to these.

[27] The Amramite clan, the Izharite clan, the Hebronite clan, and the Uzzielite clan came from Kohath; these were the Kohathites. [28] Counting every male one month old or more, there were 8,600[D] responsible for the duties of[E] the sanctuary. [29] The clans of the Kohathites camped on the south side of the tabernacle, [30] and the leader of the families of the Kohathite clans was Elizaphan son of Uzziel. [31] Their duties involved the ark, the table, the lampstand, the altars, the sanctuary

A3:9 Some Hb mss, LXX, Sam read me ; Nm 8:16   B3:15 Lit the house of their fathers, also in v. 20
C3:24 Lit a father's house, also in vv. 30,35   D3:28 LXX reads 8,300   E3:28 Or for guarding, also in v. 32

utensils that were used with these, and the screen^A — and all the work relating to them. ³² The chief of the Levite leaders was Eleazar son of Aaron the priest; he had oversight of those responsible for the duties of the sanctuary.   Nm 2:10-16

³³ The Mahlite clan and the Mushite clan came from Merari; these were the Merarite clans. ³⁴ Those registered, counting every male one month old or more, numbered 6,200. ³⁵ The leader of the families of the Merarite clans was Zuriel son of Abihail; they camped on the north side of the tabernacle. ³⁶ The assigned duties of Merari's descendants involved the tabernacle's supports, crossbars, pillars, bases, all its equipment, and all the work related to these, ³⁷ in addition to the posts of the surrounding courtyard with their bases, tent pegs, and ropes.

³⁸ Moses, Aaron, and his sons, who performed the duties of^B the sanctuary as a service on behalf of the Israelites, camped in front of the tabernacle on the east, in front of the tent of meeting toward the sunrise. Any unauthorized person who came near it was to be put to death.   Nm 1:51; 2:3-9; 3:10; 8:19; 18:7

³⁹ The total number of all the Levite males one month old or more that Moses and Aaron^C registered by their clans at the LORD's command was 22,000.

Redemption of the Firstborn

⁴⁰ The LORD told Moses: "Register every firstborn male of the Israelites one month old or more, and list their names. ⁴¹ You are to take the Levites for me — I am the LORD — in place of every firstborn among the Israelites, and the Levites' cattle in place of every firstborn among the Israelites' cattle." ⁴² So Moses registered every firstborn among the Israelites, as the LORD commanded him. ⁴³ The total number of the firstborn males one month old or more listed by name was 22,273.   Ex 13:1-2; Nm 8:16-18

⁴⁴ The LORD spoke to Moses again: ⁴⁵ "Take the Levites in place of every firstborn among the Israelites, and the Levites' cattle in place of their cattle. The Levites belong to me; I am the LORD. ⁴⁶ As the redemption price for the 273 firstborn Israelites who outnumber the Levites, ⁴⁷ collect five shekels for each person, according to the standard sanctuary shekel — twenty gerahs to the shekel.^D ⁴⁸ Give the silver to Aaron and his sons as the redemption price for those who are in excess among the Israelites."   Nm 3:13,41; 10:10; 15:40-41

⁴⁹ So Moses collected the redemption amount from those in excess of the ones redeemed by the Levites. ⁵⁰ He collected the silver from the firstborn Israelites: 1,365 shekels^E measured by the standard sanctuary shekel. ⁵¹ He gave the redemption silver to Aaron and his sons in obedience to the LORD, just as the LORD commanded Moses.

---

^A 3:31 The screen between the most holy place and the holy place; Ex 35:12 ^B 3:38 Or who guarded
^C 3:39 Some Hb mss, Sam, Syr omit and Aaron   ^D 3:47 A shekel is about two-fifths of an ounce of silver
^E 3:50 Over 34 pounds of silver

Duties of the Kohathites

4 The LORD spoke to Moses and Aaron: [2] "Among the Levites, take a census of the Kohathites by their clans and their ancestral families, [A] [3] men from thirty years old to fifty years old — everyone who is qualified [B] to do work at the tent of meeting. Ex 6:16,18; Nm 3:27-31

[4] "The service of the Kohathites at the tent of meeting concerns the most holy objects. [5] Whenever the camp is about to move on, Aaron and his sons are to go in, take down the screening curtain, and cover the ark of the testimony with it. [6] They are to place over this a covering made of fine leather, [C] spread a solid blue cloth on top, and insert its poles. Ex 25:10-22; 26:14; Nm 3:30-31; 4:15-19

[7] "They are to spread a blue cloth over the table of the Presence and place the plates and cups on it, as well as the bowls and pitchers for the drink offering. The regular bread offering is to be on it. [8] They are to spread a scarlet cloth over them, cover them with a covering made of fine leather, and insert the poles in the table. Ex 25:30; Lv 24:5-9

[9] "They are to take a blue cloth and cover the lampstand used for light, with its lamps, snuffers, and firepans, as well as its jars of oil by which they service it. [10] Then they are to place it with all its utensils inside a covering made of fine leather and put them on the carrying frame.

[11] "They are to spread a blue cloth over the gold altar, cover it with a covering made of fine leather, and insert its poles. [12] They are to take all the serving utensils they use in the sanctuary, place them in a blue cloth, cover them with a covering made of fine leather, and put them on a carrying frame. Ex 30:1-3; 31:8; 39:38

[13] "They are to remove the ashes from the bronze altar, spread a purple cloth over it, [14] and place all the equipment on it that they use in serving: the firepans, meat forks, shovels, and basins — all the equipment of the altar. They are to spread a covering made of fine leather over it and insert its poles. [D]

[15] "Aaron and his sons are to finish covering the holy objects and all their equipment whenever the camp is to move on. The Kohathites will come and carry them, but they are not to touch the holy objects or they will die. These are the transportation duties of the Kohathites regarding the tent of meeting.

[16] "Eleazar, son of Aaron the priest, has oversight of the lamp oil, the fragrant incense, the daily grain offering, and the anointing oil. He has oversight of the entire tabernacle and everything in it, the holy objects and their utensils." [E]

[17] Then the LORD spoke to Moses and Aaron: [18] "Do not allow the Kohathite tribal clans to be wiped out from the Levites. [19] Do this for them so that they may live and not die when they come near the most holy objects: Aaron and his sons are to go in and assign each man his task and transportation duty. [20] The Kohathites are not to go in and look at the holy objects as they are covered [F] or they will die." Nm 3:31; 4:4

[A] **4:2** Lit *the house of their fathers*, also in vv. 22,29,34,38,40,42,46 [B] **4:3** Lit *everyone entering the service* [C] **4:6** Hb obscure, also in vv. 8,10,11,12,14,25 [D] **4:14** Sam, LXX add *They are to take a purple cloth and cover the wash basin and its base. They are to place them in a covering made of fine leather and put them on the carrying frame.* [E] **4:16** Or *the sanctuary and its furnishings* [F] **4:20** Or *objects, even long enough to swallow,*

Duties of the Gershonites

[21] The LORD spoke to Moses: [22] "Take a census of the Gershonites also, by their ancestral families and their clans. [23] Register men from thirty years old to fifty years old, everyone who is qualified to perform service, to do work at the tent of meeting. [24] This is the service of the Gershonite clans regarding work and transportation duties: [25] They are to transport the tabernacle curtains, the tent of meeting with its covering and the covering made of fine leather on top of it, the screen for the entrance to the tent of meeting, [26] the hangings of the courtyard, the screen for the entrance at the gate of the courtyard that surrounds the tabernacle and the altar, along with their ropes and all the equipment for their service. They will carry out everything that needs to be done with these items. Ex 26:1-13; Nm 3:17,21-26

[27] "All the service of the Gershonites, all their transportation duties and all their other work, is to be done at the command of Aaron and his sons; you are to assign to them all that they are responsible to carry. [28] This is the service of the Gershonite clans at the tent of meeting, and their duties will be under the direction of Ithamar son of Aaron the priest. Ex 6:23; 28:1; 38:21

Duties of the Merarites

[29] "As for the Merarites, you are to register them by their clans and their ancestral families. [30] Register men from thirty years old to fifty years old, everyone who is qualified to do the work of the tent of meeting. [31] This is what they are responsible to carry as the whole of their service at the tent of meeting: the supports of the tabernacle, with its crossbars, pillars, and bases, [32] the posts of the surrounding courtyard with their bases, tent pegs, and ropes, including all their equipment and all the work related to them. You are to assign by name the items that they are responsible to carry. [33] This is the service of the Merarite clans regarding all their work at the tent of meeting, under the direction of Ithamar son of Aaron the priest."

Census of the Levites

[34] So Moses, Aaron, and the leaders of the community registered the Kohathites by their clans and their ancestral families, [35] men from thirty years old to fifty years old, everyone who was qualified for work at the tent of meeting. [36] The men registered by their clans numbered 2,750. [37] These were the registered men of the Kohathite clans, everyone who could serve at the tent of meeting. Moses and Aaron registered them at the LORD's command through Moses.

[38] The Gershonites were registered by their clans and their ancestral families, [39] men from thirty years old to fifty years old, everyone who was qualified for work at the tent of meeting. [40] The men registered by their clans and their ancestral families numbered 2,630. [41] These were the registered men of the Gershonite clans. At the LORD's command Moses and Aaron registered everyone who could serve at the tent of meeting.

[42] The men of the Merarite clans were registered by their clans and their ancestral families, [43] those from thirty years old to fifty years old, everyone who was qualified for

work at the tent of meeting. ⁴⁴ The men registered by their clans numbered 3,200. ⁴⁵ These were the registered men of the Merarite clans; Moses and Aaron registered them at the LORD's command through Moses.

⁴⁶ Moses, Aaron, and the leaders of Israel registered all the Levites by their clans and their ancestral families, ⁴⁷ from thirty years old to fifty years old, everyone who was qualified to do the work of serving at the tent of meeting and transporting it. ⁴⁸ Their registered men numbered 8,580. ⁴⁹ At the LORD's command they were registered under the direction of Moses, each one according to his work and transportation duty, and his assignment was as the LORD commanded Moses.

Isolation of the Unclean

5 The LORD instructed Moses: ² "Command the Israelites to send away anyone from the camp who is afflicted with a skin disease, anyone who has a discharge, or anyone who is defiled because of a corpse. ³ Send away both male or female; send them outside the camp, so that they will not defile their camps where I dwell among them." ⁴ The Israelites did this, sending them outside the camp. The Israelites did as the LORD instructed Moses. Ex 4:6; Lv 13:42-44; Lv 15:2-33; Nm 12:10

Compensation for Wrongdoing

⁵ The LORD spoke to Moses: ⁶ "Tell the Israelites: When a man or woman commits any sin against another, that person acts unfaithfully toward the LORD and is guilty. ⁷ The person is to confess the sin he has committed. He is to pay full compensation, add a fifth of its value to it, and give it to the individual he has wronged. ⁸ But if that individual has no relative to receive compensation, the compensation goes to the LORD for the priest, along with the atonement ram by which the priest will make atonement for the guilty person. ⁹ Every holy contribution the Israelites present to the priest will be his. ¹⁰ Each one's holy contribution is his to give; what each one gives to the priest will be his." Lv 6:2,4

The Jealousy Ritual

¹¹ The LORD spoke to Moses: ¹² "Speak to the Israelites and tell them: If any man's wife goes astray, is unfaithful to him, ¹³ and sleeps with another, ᴬ but it is concealed from her husband, and she is undetected, even though she has defiled herself, since there is no witness against her, and she wasn't caught in the act; ¹⁴ and if a feeling of jealousy comes over the husband and he becomes jealous because of his wife who has defiled herself — or if a feeling of jealousy comes over him and he becomes jealous of her though she has not defiled herself — ¹⁵ then the man is to bring his wife to the priest. He is also to bring an offering for her of two quarts ᴮ of barley flour. He is not to pour oil over it or put frankincense on it because it is a grain offering of jealousy, a grain offering for remembrance to draw attention to guilt. Jb 5:2; Pr 6:34; 14:30; 27:4

¹⁶ "The priest is to bring her forward and have her stand before the LORD. ¹⁷ Then the priest is to take holy water in a clay bowl, take

ᴬ5:13 Lit and man lies with her and has an emission of semen   ᴮ5:15 Lit a tenth of an ephah some of the dust from the tabernacle floor, and put it in the water. ¹⁸ After the priest has the woman stand before the LORD, he is to let down her hair[A] and place in her hands the grain offering for remembrance, which is the grain offering of jealousy. The priest is to hold the bitter water that brings a curse. ¹⁹ The priest will require the woman to take an oath and will say to her, 'If no man has slept with you, if you have not gone astray and become defiled while under your husband's authority, be unaffected by this bitter water that brings a curse. ²⁰ But if you have gone astray while under your husband's authority, if you have defiled yourself and a man other than your husband has slept with you' — ²¹ at this point the priest will make the woman take the oath with the sworn curse, and he is to say to her — 'May the LORD make you into an object of your people's cursing and swearing when he makes your womb[B] shrivel and your belly swell. ²² May this water that brings a curse enter your stomach, causing your belly to swell and your womb to shrivel.'

"And the woman will reply, 'Amen, Amen.'

²³ "Then the priest is to write these curses on a scroll and wash them off into the bitter water. ²⁴ He will require the woman to drink the bitter water that brings a curse, and it will enter her to cause bitter suffering. ²⁵ The priest is to take the grain offering of jealousy from the woman, present the offering before the LORD, and bring it to the altar. ²⁶ The priest is to take a handful of the grain offering as a memorial

portion and burn it on the altar. Afterward, he will require the woman to drink the water. Lv 2:2,9,16; 5:12

²⁷ "When he makes her drink the water, if she has defiled herself and been unfaithful to her husband, the water that brings a curse will enter her to cause bitter suffering; her belly will swell, and her womb will shrivel. She will become a curse among her people. ²⁸ But if the woman has not defiled herself and is pure, she will be unaffected and will be able to conceive children.

²⁹ "This is the law regarding jealousy when a wife goes astray and defiles herself while under her husband's authority, ³⁰ or when a feeling of jealousy comes over a husband and he becomes jealous of his wife. He is to have the woman stand before the LORD, and the priest will carry out all these instructions for her. ³¹ The husband will be free of guilt, but that woman will bear her iniquity."

The Nazirite Vow

6 The LORD instructed Moses: ² "Speak to the Israelites and tell them: When a man or woman makes a special vow, a Nazirite vow, to consecrate himself to the LORD, ³ he is to abstain from wine and beer. He must not drink vinegar made from wine or from beer. He must not drink any grape juice or eat fresh grapes or raisins. ⁴ He is not to eat anything produced by the grapevine, from seeds to skin, during the period of his consecration.

⁵ "You must not cut his hair[C] throughout the time of his vow of consecration. He may be holy

---

^A**5:18** Or *to uncover her head*   ^B**5:21** Lit *thigh*, also in vv. 22,27   ^C**6:5** Lit *"A razor is not to pass over his head*

until the time is completed during which he consecrates himself to the LORD; he is to let the hair of his head grow long. [6] He must not go near a dead body during the time he consecrates himself to the LORD. [7] He is not to defile himself for his father or mother, or his brother or sister, when they die, while the mark of consecration to his God is on his head. [8] He is holy to the LORD during the time of consecration.

[9] "If someone suddenly dies near him, defiling his consecrated head, he must shave his head on the day of his purification; he is to shave it on the seventh day. [10] On the eighth day he is to bring two turtledoves or two young pigeons to the priest at the entrance to the tent of meeting. [11] The priest is to offer one as a sin offering and the other as a burnt offering to make atonement on behalf of the Nazirite, since he incurred guilt because of the corpse. On that day he is to consecrate his head again. [12] He is to rededicate his time of consecration to the LORD and to bring a year-old male lamb as a guilt offering. But do not count the initial period of consecration because it became defiled. Nm 19:11

[13] "This is the law of the Nazirite: On the day his time of consecration is completed, he is to be brought to the entrance to the tent of meeting. [14] He is to present an offering to the LORD of one unblemished year-old male lamb as a burnt offering, one unblemished year-old female lamb as a sin offering, one unblemished ram as a fellowship offering, [15] along with their grain offerings and drink offerings, and a basket of unleavened cakes made from fine flour mixed with oil, and unleavened wafers coated with oil.

[16] "The priest is to present these before the LORD and sacrifice the Nazirite's sin offering and burnt offering. [17] He will also offer the ram as a fellowship sacrifice to the LORD, together with the basket of unleavened bread. Then the priest will offer the accompanying grain offering and drink offering. [18] "The Nazirite is to shave his consecrated head at the entrance to the tent of meeting, take the hair from his head, and put it on the fire under the fellowship sacrifice. [19] The priest is to take the boiled shoulder from the ram, one unleavened cake from the basket, and one unleavened wafer, and put them into the hands of the Nazirite after he has shaved his consecrated head. [20] The priest is to present them as a presentation offering before the LORD. It is a holy portion for the priest, in addition to the breast of the presentation offering and the thigh of the contribution. After that, the Nazirite may drink wine. Ex 29:24-27; Lv 2:4-11

[21] "These are the instructions about the Nazirite who vows his offering to the LORD for his consecration, in addition to whatever else he can afford; he must fulfill whatever vow he makes in keeping with the instructions for his consecration." Ac 21:24

The Priestly Blessing

[22] The LORD spoke to Moses: [23] "Tell Aaron and his sons, 'This is how you are to bless the Israelites. You should say to them,

[24]   "May the LORD bless you
          and protect you; Ps 121:4,7; 128:5
[25]   may the LORD make his face
          shine on you
          and be gracious to you; Ps 67:1

²⁶ may the LORD look with favor
on you[A]
and give you peace."'   Ps 4:6
²⁷ In this way they will pronounce
my name over[B] the Israelites, and
I will bless them."

Offerings from the Leaders

7 On the day Moses finished
setting up the tabernacle, he
anointed and consecrated it and
all its furnishings, along with the
altar and all its utensils. After he
anointed and consecrated these
things, ² the leaders of Israel, the
heads of their ancestral families,[C]
presented an offering. They were
the tribal leaders who supervised
the registration. ³ They brought as
their offering before the LORD six
covered carts and twelve oxen, a
cart from every two leaders and
an ox from each one, and presented them in front of the tabernacle.
⁴ The LORD said to Moses, ⁵ "Accept these from them to be used
in the work of the tent of meeting,
and give this offering to the Levites,
to each division according to their
service."

⁶ So Moses took the carts and
oxen and gave them to the Levites.
⁷ He gave the Gershonites two carts
and four oxen corresponding to
their service, ⁸ and gave the Merarites four carts and eight oxen corresponding to their service, under
the direction of Ithamar son of Aaron the priest. ⁹ But he did not give
any to the Kohathites, since their
responsibility was service related
to the holy objects carried on their
shoulders.   Nm 3:36-37; 4:23-28,32; 4:30-33

¹⁰ The leaders also presented the
dedication gift for the altar when
it was anointed. The leaders presented their offerings in front of
the altar. ¹¹ The LORD told Moses,
"Each day have one leader present
his offering for the dedication of
the altar." Nm 7:11,84,88; 1Kg 8:62-64; 2Ch 7:4-9
¹² The one who presented his
offering on the first day was
Nahshon son of Amminadab
from the tribe of Judah. ¹³ His
offering was one silver dish
weighing 3 ¼ pounds[D] and
one silver basin weighing 1 ¾
pounds,[E] measured by the standard sanctuary shekel, both of
them full of fine flour mixed
with oil for a grain offering; ¹⁴ one gold bowl weighing
four ounces,[F] full of incense;
¹⁵ one young bull, one ram, and
one male lamb a year old, for
a burnt offering; ¹⁶ one male
goat for a sin offering; ¹⁷ and
two bulls, five rams, five male
goats, and five male lambs a
year old, for the fellowship sacrifice. This was the offering of
Nahshon son of Amminadab.

¹⁸ On the second day Nethanel
son of Zuar, leader of Issachar,
presented an offering. ¹⁹ As his
offering, he presented one silver dish weighing 3 ¼ pounds
and one silver basin weighing 1 ¾ pounds, measured by
the standard sanctuary shekel,
both of them full of fine flour
mixed with oil for a grain offering; ²⁰ one gold bowl weighing four ounces, full of incense;

[A]6:26 Lit *LORD lift his face to you*   [B]6:27 Or *put my name on*   [C]7:2 Lit *the house of their fathers*
[D]7:13 Lit *dish, 130 its shekel-weight*, also in vv. 19,25,31,37,43,49,55,61,67,73,79   [E]7:13 Lit *70 shekels*,
also in vv. 19,25,31,37,43,49,55,61,67,73,79   [F]7:14 Lit *10 (shekels)*, also in vv. 20,26,32,38,44,50,56,62,68,
74,80,86

²¹ one young bull, one ram, and one male lamb a year old, for a burnt offering; ²² one male goat for a sin offering; ²³ and two bulls, five rams, five male goats, and five male lambs a year old, for the fellowship sacrifice. This was the offering of Nethanel son of Zuar. Nm 1:8; 2:5; 10:15

²⁴ On the third day Eliab son of Helon, leader of the Zebulunites, presented an offering. ²⁵ His offering was one silver dish weighing 3 ¼ pounds and one silver basin weighing 1 ¾ pounds, measured by the standard sanctuary shekel, both of them full of fine flour mixed with oil for a grain offering; ²⁶ one gold bowl weighing four ounces, full of incense; ²⁷ one young bull, one ram, and one male lamb a year old, for a burnt offering; ²⁸ one male goat for a sin offering; ²⁹ and two bulls, five rams, five male goats, and five male lambs a year old, for the fellowship sacrifice. This was the offering of Eliab son of Helon. Nm 1:9; 2:7; 10:16

³⁰ On the fourth day Elizur son of Shedeur, leader of the Reubenites, presented an offering. ³¹ His offering was one silver dish weighing 3 ¼ pounds and one silver basin weighing 1 ¾ pounds, measured by the standard sanctuary shekel, both of them full of fine flour mixed with oil for a grain offering; ³² one gold bowl weighing four ounces, full of incense; ³³ one young bull, one ram, and one male lamb a year old, for a burnt offering; ³⁴ one male goat for a sin offering; ³⁵ and two bulls, five rams, five male goats, and five male lambs a year old, for the fellowship sacrifice. This was the offering of Elizur son of Shedeur. Nm 1:5; 2:10

³⁶ On the fifth day Shelumiel son of Zurishaddai, leader of the Simeonites, presented an offering. ³⁷ His offering was one silver dish weighing 3 ¼ pounds and one silver basin weighing 1 ¾ pounds, measured by the standard sanctuary shekel, both of them full of fine flour mixed with oil for a grain offering; ³⁸ one gold bowl weighing four ounces, full of incense; ³⁹ one young bull, one ram, and one male lamb a year old, for a burnt offering; ⁴⁰ one male goat for a sin offering; ⁴¹ and two bulls, five rams, five male goats, and five male lambs a year old, for the fellowship sacrifice. This was the offering of Shelumiel son of Zurishaddai. Nm 1:6; 2:12; 10:19

⁴² On the sixth day Eliasaph son of Deuel,ᴬ leader of the Gadites, presented an offering. ⁴³ His offering was one silver dish weighing 3 ¼ pounds and one silver basin weighing 1 ¾ pounds, measured by the standard sanctuary shekel, both of them full of fine flour mixed with oil for a grain offering; ⁴⁴ one gold bowl weighing four ounces full of incense; ⁴⁵ one young bull, one ram, and one male lamb a year old, for a burnt offering; ⁴⁶ one male

ᴬ **7:42** LXX, Syr read *Reuel*

goat for a sin offering; [47] and two bulls, five rams, five male goats, and five male lambs a year old, for the fellowship sacrifice. This was the offering of Eliasaph son of Deuel. [A]   Nm 1:14

[48] On the seventh day Elishama son of Ammihud, leader of the Ephraimites, presented an offering. [49] His offering was one silver dish weighing 3 1/4 pounds and one silver basin weighing 1 3/4 pounds, measured by the standard sanctuary shekel, both of them full of fine flour mixed with oil for a grain offering; [50] one gold bowl weighing four ounces, full of incense; [51] one young bull, one ram, and one male lamb a year old, for a burnt offering; [52] one male goat for a sin offering; [53] and two bulls, five rams, five male goats, and five male lambs a year old, for the fellowship sacrifice. This was the offering of Elishama son of Ammihud.   Nm 1:10; 2:18; 10:22

[54] On the eighth day Gamaliel son of Pedahzur, leader of the Manassites, presented an offering. [55] His offering was one silver dish weighing 3 1/4 pounds and one silver basin weighing 1 3/4 pounds, measured by the standard sanctuary shekel, both of them full of fine flour mixed with oil for a grain offering; [56] one gold bowl weighing four ounces, full of incense; [57] one young bull, one ram, and one male lamb a year old, for a burnt offering; [58] one male goat for a sin

offering; [59] and two bulls, five rams, five male goats, and five male lambs a year old, for the fellowship sacrifice. This was the offering of Gamaliel son of Pedahzur.   Nm 1:10; 2:20; 10:23

[60] On the ninth day Abidan son of Gideoni, leader of the Benjaminites, presented an offering. [61] His offering was one silver dish weighing 3 1/4 pounds and one silver basin weighing 1 3/4 pounds, measured by the standard sanctuary shekel, both of them full of fine flour mixed with oil for a grain offering; [62] one gold bowl weighing four ounces, full of incense; [63] one young bull, one ram, and one male lamb a year old, for a burnt offering; [64] one male goat for a sin offering; [65] and two bulls, five rams, five male goats, and five male lambs a year old, for the fellowship sacrifice. This was the offering of Abidan son of Gideoni.   Nm 1:11; 2:22; 10:24

[66] On the tenth day Ahiezer son of Ammishaddai, leader of the Danites, presented an offering. [67] His offering was one silver dish weighing 3 1/4 pounds and one silver basin weighing 1 3/4 pounds, measured by the standard sanctuary shekel, both of them full of fine flour mixed with oil for a grain offering; [68] one gold bowl weighing four ounces, full of incense; [69] one young bull, one ram, and one male lamb a year old, for a burnt offering; [70] one male goat for a sin offering; [71] and

[A] 7:47 LXX, Syr read *Reuel*

two bulls, five rams, five male goats, and five male lambs a year old, for the fellowship sacrifice. This was the offering of Ahiezer son of Ammishaddai.

⁷² On the eleventh day Pagiel son of Ochran, leader of the Asherites, presented an offering. ⁷³ His offering was one silver dish weighing 3¼ pounds and one silver basin weighing 1¾ pounds, measured by the standard sanctuary shekel, both of them full of fine flour mixed with oil for a grain offering; ⁷⁴ one gold bowl weighing four ounces, full of incense; ⁷⁵ one young bull, one ram, and one male lamb a year old, for a burnt offering; ⁷⁶ one male goat for a sin offering; ⁷⁷ and two bulls, five rams, five male goats, and five male lambs a year old, for the fellowship sacrifice. This was the offering of Pagiel son of Ochran. Nm 1:13; 2:27

⁷⁸ On the twelfth day Ahira son of Enan, leader of the Naphtalites, presented an offering. ⁷⁹ His offering was one silver dish weighing 3¼ pounds and one silver basin weighing 1¾ pounds, measured by the standard sanctuary shekel, both of them full of fine flour mixed with oil for a grain offering; ⁸⁰ one gold bowl weighing four ounces, full of incense; ⁸¹ one young bull, one ram, and one male lamb a year old, for a burnt offering; ⁸² one male goat for a sin offering; ⁸³ and two bulls, five rams, five male goats, and five male lambs a

year old, for the fellowship sacrifice. This was the offering of Ahira son of Enan. Nm 1:15; 2:29

⁸⁴ This was the dedication gift from the leaders of Israel for the altar when it was anointed: twelve silver dishes, twelve silver basins, and twelve gold bowls. ⁸⁵ Each silver dish weighed 3¼ pounds, ᴬ and each basin 1¾ pounds. ᴮ The total weight of the silver articles was 60 pounds ᶜ measured by the standard sanctuary shekel. ⁸⁶ The twelve gold bowls full of incense each weighed four ounces measured by the standard sanctuary shekel. The total weight of the gold bowls was 3 pounds. ᴰ ⁸⁷ All the livestock for the burnt offering totaled twelve bulls, twelve rams, and twelve male lambs a year old, with their grain offerings, and twelve male goats for the sin offering. ⁸⁸ All the livestock for the fellowship sacrifice totaled twenty-four bulls, sixty rams, sixty male goats, and sixty male lambs a year old. This was the dedication gift for the altar after it was anointed. Lv 1:1-13; 4:22-26; 6:8-13, 24-30; Nm 7:1,10

⁸⁹ When Moses entered the tent of meeting to speak with the LORD, he heard the voice speaking to him from above the mercy seat that was on the ark of the testimony, from between the two cherubim. He spoke to him that way. Nm 12:8; 37:1-9

The Lighting in the Tabernacle

8 The LORD spoke to Moses: ² "Speak to Aaron and tell him: When you set up the lamps, the seven lamps are to give light in front of the lampstand." ³ So Aaron did this; he set up its lamps to give light in front of the lampstand just as

ᴬ**7:85** Lit *130* (shekels) ᴮ**7:85** Lit *70* (shekels) ᶜ**7:85** Lit *2,400* (shekels) ᴰ**7:86** Lit *120* (shekels) the LORD had commanded Moses. [4] This is the way the lampstand was made: it was a hammered work of gold, hammered from its base to its flower petals. The lampstand was made according to the pattern the LORD had shown Moses.   Ex 25:31-40

Consecration of the Levites

[5] The LORD spoke to Moses: [6] "Take the Levites from among the Israelites and ceremonially cleanse them. [7] Do this to them for their purification: Sprinkle them with the purification water. Have them shave their entire bodies and wash their clothes, and so purify themselves.   Lv 14:51; Nm 19:7,13,17,20; Heb 9:13,23

[8] "They are to take a young bull and its grain offering of fine flour mixed with oil, and you are to take a second young bull for a sin offering. [9] Bring the Levites before the tent of meeting and assemble the entire Israelite community. [10] Then present the Levites before the LORD, and have the Israelites lay their hands on them. [11] Aaron is to present the Levites before the LORD as a presentation offering from the Israelites, so that they may perform the LORD's work. [12] Next the Levites are to lay their hands on the heads of the bulls. Sacrifice one as a sin offering and the other as a burnt offering to the LORD, to make atonement for the Levites.   Ex 29:4; Lv 8:1-6

[13] "You are to have the Levites stand before Aaron and his sons, and you are to present them before the LORD as a presentation offering. [14] In this way you are to separate the Levites from the rest of the Israelites so that the Levites will belong to me. [15] After that the Levites may come to serve at the tent of meeting, once you have ceremonially cleansed them and presented them as a presentation offering. [16] For they have been exclusively assigned to me from the Israelites. I have taken them for myself in place of all who come first from the womb, every Israelite firstborn. [17] For every firstborn among the Israelites is mine, both man and animal. I consecrated them to myself on the day I struck down every firstborn in the land of Egypt. [18] But I have taken the Levites in place of every firstborn among the Israelites. [19] From the Israelites, I have given the Levites exclusively to Aaron and his sons to perform the work for the Israelites at the tent of meeting and to make atonement on their behalf, so that no plague will come against the Israelites when they approach the sanctuary."   Ex 29:26-27; Lv 8:26-29

[20] Moses, Aaron, and the entire Israelite community did this to the Levites. The Israelites did everything to them the LORD commanded Moses regarding the Levites. [21] The Levites purified themselves and washed their clothes; then Aaron presented[A] them before the LORD as a presentation offering. Aaron also made atonement for them to cleanse them ceremonially. [22] After that, the Levites came to do their work at the tent of meeting in the presence of Aaron and his sons. So they did to them as the LORD had commanded Moses concerning the Levites.

[23] The LORD spoke to Moses: [24] "In regard to the Levites: From twenty-five years old or more, a man enters the service in the work at the tent of meeting. [25] But at fifty years

A 8:21 Lit waved

old he is to retire from his service in the work and no longer serve. [26] He may assist his brothers to fulfill responsibilities[A] at the tent of meeting, but he must not do the work. This is how you are to deal with the Levites regarding their duties." Nm 3:7-8; 4:3,23,30

The Second Passover

9 In the first month of the second year after their departure from the land of Egypt, the Lord told Moses in the Wilderness of Sinai: [2] "The Israelites are to observe the Passover at its appointed time. [3] You must observe it at its appointed time on the fourteenth day of this month at twilight; you are to observe it according to all its statutes and ordinances." [4] So Moses told the Israelites to observe the Passover, [5] and they observed it in the first month on the fourteenth day at twilight in the Wilderness of Sinai. The Israelites did everything as the Lord had commanded Moses. Ex 13:10; 19:1-2; Nm 1:1; 3:4,14

[6] But there were some men who were unclean because of a human corpse, so they could not observe the Passover on that day. These men came before Moses and Aaron the same day [7] and said to him, "We are unclean because of a human corpse. Why should we be excluded from presenting the Lord's offering at its appointed time with the other Israelites?" 2Ch 30:3

[8] Moses replied to them, "Wait here until I hear what the Lord commands for you."

[9] Then the Lord spoke to Moses: [10] "Tell the Israelites: When any one of you or your descendants is unclean because of a corpse or is on a distant journey, he may still observe the Passover to the Lord. [11] Such people are to observe it in the second month, on the fourteenth day at twilight. They are to eat the animal with unleavened bread and bitter herbs; [12] they may not leave any of it until morning or break any of its bones. They must observe the Passover according to all its statutes. Lv 21:1-3; Nm 5:2; 6:6-12

[13] "But the man who is ceremonially clean, is not on a journey, and yet fails to observe the Passover is to be cut off from his people, because he did not present the Lord's offering at its appointed time. That man will bear the consequences of his sin.

[14] "If an alien resides with you and wants to observe the Passover to the Lord, he is to do it according to the Passover statute and its ordinances. You are to apply the same statute to both the resident alien and the native of the land." Ex 12:48

Guidance by the Cloud

[15] On the day the tabernacle was set up, the cloud covered the tabernacle, the tent of the testimony, and it appeared like fire above the tabernacle from evening until morning. [16] It remained that way continuously: the cloud would cover it,[B] appearing like fire at night. [17] Whenever the cloud was lifted up above the tent, the Israelites would set out; at the place where the cloud stopped, there the Israelites camped. [18] At the Lord's command the Israelites set out, and at the Lord's command they camped. As long as the cloud stayed over the tabernacle, they camped. Ex 13:21-22; 40:17,34,38; Nm 7:1

[A]**8:26** Or to keep guard   [B]**9:16** LXX, Vg, Syr, Tg read it by day

¹⁹ Even when the cloud stayed over the tabernacle many days, the Israelites carried out the LORD's requirement and did not set out. ²⁰ Sometimes the cloud remained over the tabernacle for only a few days. They would camp at the LORD's command and set out at the LORD's command. ²¹ Sometimes the cloud remained only from evening until morning; when the cloud lifted in the morning, they set out. Or if it remained a day and a night, they moved out when the cloud lifted. ²² Whether it was two days, a month, or longer,^A the Israelites camped and did not set out as long as the cloud stayed over the tabernacle. But when it was lifted, they set out. ²³ They camped at the LORD's command, and they set out at the LORD's command. They carried out the LORD's requirement according to his command through Moses.

Two Silver Trumpets

10 The LORD spoke to Moses: ² "Make two trumpets of hammered silver to summon the community and have the camps set out. ³ When both are sounded in long blasts, the entire community is to gather before you at the entrance to the tent of meeting. ⁴ However, if one is sounded, only the leaders, the heads of Israel's clans, are to gather before you.

⁵ "When you sound short blasts, the camps pitched on the east are to set out. ⁶ When you sound short blasts a second time, the camps pitched on the south are to set out. Short blasts are to be sounded for them to set out. ⁷ When calling the assembly together, you are to sound long blasts, not short ones. ⁸ The sons of Aaron, the priests, are to sound the trumpets. Your use of these is a permanent statute throughout your generations.

⁹ "When you enter into battle in your land against an adversary who is attacking you, sound short blasts on the trumpets, and you will be remembered before the LORD your God and be saved from your enemies. ¹⁰ You are to sound the trumpets over your burnt offerings and your fellowship sacrifices and on your joyous occasions, your appointed festivals, and the beginning of each of your months. They will serve as a reminder for you before your God: I am the LORD your God." Ex 6:7; Dt 20:4; 2Ch 13:12; Ps 18:3

From Sinai to Paran

¹¹ During the second year, in the second month on the twentieth day of the month, the cloud was lifted up above the tabernacle of the testimony. ¹² The Israelites traveled on from the Wilderness of Sinai, moving from one place to the next until the cloud stopped in the Wilderness of Paran. ¹³ They set out for the first time according to the LORD's command through Moses.

¹⁴ The military divisions of the camp of Judah's descendants with their banner set out first, and Nahshon son of Amminadab was over their divisions. ¹⁵ Nethanel son of Zuar was over the division of the tribe of Issachar's descendants, ¹⁶ and Eliab son of Helon was over the division of the tribe of Zebulun's descendants. ¹⁷ The tabernacle was then taken down, and the Gershonites and the Merarites set out, transporting the tabernacle.

^A 9:22 Or *a year*

18 The military divisions of the camp of Reuben with their banner set out, and Elizur son of Shedeur was over their divisions. 19 Shelumiel son of Zurishaddai was over the division of the tribe of Simeon's descendants, 20 and Eliasaph son of Deuel A was over the division of the tribe of Gad's descendants. 21 The Kohathites then set out, transporting the holy objects; the tabernacle was to be set up before their arrival. Nm 1:6; 2:12; 3:27-31; 4:2-4,15,18-20; 7:36

22 Next the military divisions of the camp of Ephraim's descendants with their banner set out, and Elishama son of Ammihud was over their divisions. 23 Gamaliel son of Pedahzur was over the division of the tribe of Manasseh's descendants, 24 and Abidan son of Gideoni was over the division of the tribe of Benjamin's descendants.

25 The military divisions of the camp of Dan's descendants with their banner set out, serving as rear guard for all the camps, and Ahiezer son of Ammishaddai was over their divisions. 26 Pagiel son of Ochran was over the division of the tribe of Asher's descendants, 27 and Ahira son of Enan was over the division of the tribe of Naphtali's descendants. 28 This was the order of march for the Israelites by their military divisions as they set out.

29 Moses said to Hobab, descendant of Reuel the Midianite and Moses's relative by marriage: "We're setting out for the place the Lord promised: 'I will give it to you.' Come with us, and we will treat you well, for the Lord has promised good things to Israel." Gn 12:7; 15:7; Ex 2:16-18; 3:1; 4:18; Jdg 4:11

30 But he replied to him, "I don't want to go. Instead, I will go to my own land and my relatives."

31 "Please don't leave us," Moses said, "since you know where we should camp in the wilderness, and you can serve as our eyes. 32 If you come with us, whatever good the Lord does for us we will do for you." Jdg 1:16; 4:11

33 They set out from the mountain of the Lord on a three-day journey with the ark of the Lord's covenant traveling ahead of them for those three days to seek a resting place for them. 34 Meanwhile, the cloud of the Lord was over them by day when they set out from the camp.

35 Whenever the ark set out, Moses would say:

Arise, Lord!
Let your enemies
    be scattered,
and those who hate you flee
    from your presence. Ps 68:1

36 When it came to rest, he would say:

Return, Lord,
to the countless thousands
    of Israel. Gn 15:5; Dt 1:8,10

Complaints About Hardship

11 Now the people began complaining openly before B the Lord about hardship. When the Lord heard, his anger burned, and fire from the Lord blazed among them and consumed the outskirts of the camp. 2 Then the people cried out to Moses, and he prayed to the Lord, and the fire died down. 3 So that place was named Taberah, C because the Lord's fire had blazed among them. Ex 22:24; 32:10-11; Nm 11:1,33

A 10:20 LXX, Syr read Reuel   B 11:1 Lit in the ears of   C 11:3 = Blaze

Complaints About Food

[4] The riffraff[A] among them had a strong craving for other food. The Israelites wept again and said, "Who will feed us meat? [5] We remember the free fish we ate in Egypt, along with the cucumbers, melons, leeks, onions, and garlic. [6] But now our appetite is gone;[B] there's nothing to look at but this manna!"   Ex 12:38

[7] The manna resembled coriander seed, and its appearance was like that of bdellium.[C] [8] The people walked around and gathered it. They ground it on a pair of grinding stones or crushed it in a mortar, then boiled it in a cooking pot and shaped it into cakes. It tasted like a pastry cooked with the finest oil. [9] When the dew fell on the camp at night, the manna would fall with it.   Ex 16:4-35; Dt 8:3,16; Jos 5:12

[10] Moses heard the people, family after family, weeping at the entrance of their tents. The LORD was very angry; Moses was also provoked.[D] [11] So Moses asked the LORD, "Why have you brought such trouble on your servant? Why are you angry with me,[E] and why do you burden me with all these people? [12] Did I conceive all these people? Did I give them birth so you should tell me, 'Carry them at your breast, as a nanny carries a baby,' to the land that you swore to give their fathers? [13] Where can I get meat to give all these people? For they are weeping to me, 'Give us meat to eat!' [14] I can't carry all these people by myself. They are too much for me. [15] If you are going to treat me like this, please kill me right now if I have found favor with you, and don't let me see my misery[F] anymore."   Ex 22:24; 32:10-11; Nm 11:1,33; 32:13

Seventy Elders Anointed

[16] The LORD answered Moses, "Bring me seventy men from Israel known to you as elders and officers of the people. Take them to the tent of meeting and have them stand there with you. [17] Then I will come down and speak with you there. I will take some of the Spirit who is on you and put the Spirit on them. They will help you bear the burden of the people, so that you do not have to bear it by yourself.   2Kg 2:9,15

[18] "Tell the people: Consecrate yourselves in readiness for tomorrow, and you will eat meat because you wept in the LORD's hearing, 'Who will feed us meat? We were better off in Egypt.' The LORD will give you meat and you will eat. [19] You will eat, not for one day, or two days, or five days, or ten days, or twenty days, [20] but for a whole month — until it comes out of your nostrils and becomes nauseating to you — because you have rejected the LORD who is among you, and wept before him: 'Why did we ever leave Egypt?'"   Ex 17:3

[21] But Moses replied, "I'm in the middle of a people with six hundred thousand foot soldiers, yet you say, 'I will give them meat, and they will eat for a month.' [22] If flocks and herds were slaughtered for them, would they have enough? Or if all the fish in the sea were caught for them, would they have enough?"   Ex 12:37; Nm 1:45-46; 2:32

[A]11:4 Or *The mixed multitude*; Hb obscure [B]11:6 Or *our lives are wasting away*, or *our throat is dry*
[C]11:7 A yellowish, transparent gum resin [D]11:10 Lit *and it was evil in the eyes of Moses* [E]11:11 Lit *Why have I not found favor in your eyes* [F]11:15 Alt Hb tradition reads *your misery*

²³ The LORD answered Moses, "Is the LORD's arm weak?ᴬ Now you will see whether or not what I have promised will happen to you."

²⁴ Moses went out and told the people the words of the LORD. He brought seventy men from the elders of the people and had them stand around the tent. ²⁵ Then the LORD descended in the cloud and spoke to him. He took some of the Spirit that was on Moses and placed the Spirit on the seventy elders. As the Spirit rested on them, they prophesied, but they never did it again. ²⁶ Two men had remained in the camp, one named Eldad and the other Medad; the Spirit rested on them — they were among those listed, but had not gone out to the tent — and they prophesied in the camp. ²⁷ A young man ran and reported to Moses, "Eldad and Medad are prophesying in the camp."   Ex 19:9,20-24; 33:9-10

²⁸ Joshua son of Nun, assistant to Moses since his youth,ᴮ responded, "Moses, my lord, stop them!"

²⁹ But Moses asked him, "Are you jealous on my account? If only all the LORD's people were prophets and the LORD would place his Spirit on them!" ³⁰ Then Moses returned to the camp along with the elders of Israel.   Nm 12:2; 16:3

Quail in the Camp

³¹ A wind sent by the LORD came up and blew quail in from the sea; it dropped them all around the camp. They were flying three feetᶜ offᴰ the ground for about a day's journey in every direction. ³² The people were up all that day and night and all the next day gathering the quail — the one who took the least gathered fifty bushelsᴱ — and they spread them out all around the camp.ᶠ   Ex 14:21; 16:12-13; 2Sm 17:19; Ps 78:26-28

³³ While the meat was still between their teeth, before it was chewed, the LORD's anger burned against the people, and the LORD struck them with a very severe plague. ³⁴ So they named that place Kibroth-hattaavah,ᴳ because there they buried the people who had craved the meat.   Ex 22:24; 32:10-13

³⁵ From Kibroth-hattaavah the people moved on to Hazerothᴴ and remained there.   Nm 12:16; 33:16-17

Miriam and Aaron Rebel

12 Miriam and Aaron criticized Moses because of the Cushite woman he married (for he had married a Cushite woman). ² They said, "Does the LORD speak only through Moses? Does he not also speak through us?" And the LORD heard it. ³ Moses was a very humble man, more so than anyone on the face of the earth.   Ex 15:20-21; Nm 20:1

⁴ Suddenly the LORD said to Moses, Aaron, and Miriam, "You three come out to the tent of meeting." So the three of them went out. ⁵ Then the LORD descended in a pillar of cloud, stood at the entrance to the tent, and summoned Aaron and Miriam. When the two of them came forward, ⁶ he said: Dt 31:15

> "Listen to what I say:
> If there is a prophet
>   among you from the LORD,
> I make myself known to him
>   in a vision;   1Sm 3:15; Ezk 1:1
> I speak with him in a dream.

ᴬ**11:23** Lit *the LORD's arm too short*   ᴮ**11:28** Or *Moses, from his elite young men*   ᶜ**11:31** Lit *two cubits*
ᴰ**11:31** Or *They were three feet deep on*   ᴱ**11:32** Lit *10 homers*   ᶠ**11:32** To dry or cure the meat; 2Sm 17:19;
Ezk 26:5,14   ᴳ**11:34** = Graves of Craving   ᴴ**11:35** = Settlements; Nm 12:16; 33:16-17

7 Not so with my servant Moses;
he is faithful in[A] all
my household.   Heb 3:2,5
8 I speak with him directly,[B]
openly, and not in riddles;
he sees the form of the LORD.
So why were you not afraid to
speak against my servant Moses?"
9 The LORD's anger burned against
them, and he left.   Ex 22:24; 32:10-11,13

10 As the cloud moved away from
the tent, Miriam's skin suddenly became diseased, resembling snow.[C]
When Aaron turned toward her,
he saw that she was diseased 11 and
said to Moses, "My lord, please don't
hold against us this sin we have so
foolishly committed. 12 Please don't
let her be like a dead baby[D] whose
flesh is half eaten away when he
comes out of his mother's womb."

13 Then Moses cried out to the
LORD, "God, please heal her!"

14 The LORD answered Moses, "If
her father had merely spit in her
face, wouldn't she remain in disgrace for seven days? Let her be
confined outside the camp for
seven days; after that she may
be brought back in." 15 So Miriam
was confined outside the camp for
seven days, and the people did not
move on until Miriam was brought
back in. 16 After that, the people set
out from Hazeroth and camped in
the Wilderness of Paran.   Lv 13:46

Scouting out Canaan

13 The LORD spoke to Moses:
2 "Send men to scout out the
land of Canaan I am giving to the
Israelites. Send one man who is a
leader among them from each of
their ancestral tribes." 3 Moses sent

them from the Wilderness of Paran at the LORD's command. All the
men were leaders in Israel. 4 These
were their names: Ex 18:25-26; Dt 1:22-26
    Shammua son of Zaccur
        from the tribe of Reuben;
5   Shaphat son of Hori
        from the tribe of Simeon;
6   Caleb son of Jephunneh
        from the tribe of Judah;
7   Igal son of Joseph
        from the tribe of Issachar;
8   Hoshea son of Nun
        from the tribe of Ephraim;
9   Palti son of Raphu
        from the tribe of Benjamin;
10 Gaddiel son of Sodi
        from the tribe of Zebulun;
11 Gaddi son of Susi
        from the tribe of Manasseh
        (from the tribe of Joseph);
12 Ammiel son of Gemalli
        from the tribe of Dan;
13 Sethur son of Michael
        from the tribe of Asher;
14 Nahbi son of Vophsi
        from the tribe of Naphtali;
15 Geuel son of Machi
        from the tribe of Gad.
16 These were the names of the men
Moses sent to scout out the land,
and Moses renamed Hoshea son
of Nun, Joshua.

17 When Moses sent them to scout
out the land of Canaan, he told
them, "Go up this way to the Negev, then go up into the hill country. 18 See what the land is like, and
whether the people who live there
are strong or weak, few or many.
19 Is the land they live in good or
bad? Are the cities they live in encampments or fortifications? 20 Is
the land fertile or unproductive?

[A]12:7 Or is entrusted with   [B]12:8 Lit mouth to mouth   [C]12:10 A reference to whiteness or flakiness of
the skin   [D]12:12 Alt Hb tradition reads baby who comes out of our mother's womb and our flesh is half
eaten away.

Are there trees in it or not? Be courageous. Bring back some fruit from the land." It was the season for the first ripe grapes. Nm 14:7; Dt 3:5

²¹ So they went up and scouted out the land from the Wilderness of Zin ^A as far as Rehob near the entrance to Hamath. ^B ²² They went up through the Negev and came to Hebron, where Ahiman, Sheshai, and Talmai, the descendants of Anak, were living. Hebron was built seven years before Zoan in Egypt. ²³ When they came to the Valley of Eshcol, they cut down a branch with a single cluster of grapes, which was carried on a pole by two men. They also took some pomegranates and figs. ²⁴ That place was called the Valley of Eshcol ^C because of the cluster of grapes the Israelites cut there. ²⁵ At the end of forty days they returned from scouting out the land. Nm 13:28,33; Dt 1:28; 2:10-11,21; Is 19:11

Report About Canaan

²⁶ The men went back to Moses, Aaron, and the entire Israelite community in the Wilderness of Paran at Kadesh. They brought back a report for them and the whole community, and they showed them the fruit of the land. ²⁷ They reported to Moses: "We went into the land where you sent us. Indeed it is flowing with milk and honey, and here is some of its fruit. ²⁸ However, the people living in the land are strong, and the cities are large and fortified. We also saw the descendants of Anak there. ²⁹ The Amalekites are living in the land of the Negev; the Hethites, Jebusites, and Amorites live in the hill country; and the Canaanites live by the sea and along the Jordan." Nm 32:9; Dt 1:24-25; 3:5

³⁰ Then Caleb quieted the people in the presence of Moses and said, "Let's go up now and take possession of the land because we can certainly conquer it!" Nm 14:6,24,30,38

³¹ But the men who had gone up with him responded, "We can't attack the people because they are stronger than we are!" ³² So they gave a negative report to the Israelites about the land they had scouted: "The land we passed through to explore is one that devours its inhabitants, and all the people we saw in it are men of great size. ³³ We even saw the Nephilim there — the descendants of Anak come from the Nephilim! To ourselves we seemed like grasshoppers, and we must have seemed the same to them." Gn 6:4; Dt 2:10-11,20-21

Israel's Refusal to Enter Canaan

14 Then the whole community broke into loud cries, and the people wept that night. ² All the Israelites complained about Moses and Aaron, and the whole community told them, "If only we had died in the land of Egypt, or if only we had died in this wilderness! ³ Why is the LORD bringing us into this land to die by the sword? Our wives and children will become plunder. Wouldn't it be better for us to go back to Egypt?" ⁴ So they said to one another, "Let's appoint a leader and go back to Egypt." Ex 16:2,7-8

⁵ Then Moses and Aaron fell facedown in front of the whole assembly of the Israelite community. ⁶ Joshua son of Nun and Caleb son of Jephunneh, who were among those who scouted out the land, tore their clothes ⁷ and said to the entire Israelite community: "The land we

---

^A **13:21** Southern border of the promised land   ^B **13:21** Or *near Lebo-hamath*   ^C **13:24** = Cluster passed through and explored is an extremely good land. [8] If the LORD is pleased with us, he will bring us into this land, a land flowing with milk and honey, and give it to us. [9] Only don't rebel against the LORD, and don't be afraid of the people of the land, for we will devour them. Their protection has been removed from them, and the LORD is with us. Don't be afraid of them!" Ex 3:8; Dt 1:25

[10] While the whole community threatened to stone them, the glory of the LORD appeared to all the Israelites at the tent of meeting.

God's Judgment of Israel's Rebellion

[11] The LORD said to Moses, "How long will these people despise me? How long will they not trust in me despite all the signs I have performed among them? [12] I will strike them with a plague and destroy them. Then I will make you into a greater and mightier nation than they are." Ex 4:1–12:31; 14:11,21-22

[13] But Moses replied to the LORD, "The Egyptians will hear about it, for by your strength you brought up this people from them. [14] They will tell it to the inhabitants of this land. They have heard that you, LORD, are among these people, how you, LORD, are seen face to face, how your cloud stands over them, and how you go before them in a pillar of cloud by day and in a pillar of fire by night. [15] If you kill this people with a single blow,[A] the nations that have heard of your fame will declare, [16] 'Since the LORD wasn't able to bring this people into the land he swore to give them, he has slaughtered them in the wilderness.' Ex 13:21-22; 15:13-15; Dt 2:25

[17] "So now, may my Lord's power be magnified just as you have spoken: [18] The LORD is slow to anger and abounding in faithful love, forgiving iniquity and rebellion. But he will not leave the guilty unpunished, bringing the consequences of the fathers' iniquity on the children to the third and fourth generation. [19] Please pardon the iniquity of this people, in keeping with the greatness of your faithful love, just as you have forgiven them from Egypt until now." Neh 9:17; Ps 86:5,15; 103:8

[20] The LORD responded, "I have pardoned them as you requested. [21] Yet as surely as I live and as the whole earth is filled with the LORD's glory, [22] none of the men who have seen my glory and the signs I performed in Egypt and in the wilderness, and have tested me these ten times and did not obey me, [23] will ever see the land I swore to give their fathers. None of those who have despised me will see it. [24] But since my servant Caleb has a different spirit and has remained loyal to me, I will bring him into the land where he has gone, and his descendants will inherit it. [25] Since the Amalekites and Canaanites are living in the lowlands,[B] turn back tomorrow and head for the wilderness in the direction of the Red Sea." Gn 12:7; 13:14-17; 15:7; Ps 72:19; Hab 2:14

[26] Then the LORD spoke to Moses and Aaron: [27] "How long must I endure this evil community that keeps complaining about me? I have heard the Israelites' complaints that they make against me. [28] Tell them: As surely as I live — this is the LORD's declaration — I will do to you exactly as I heard you say. [29] Your corpses will fall in

[A]14:15 Lit people as one man   [B]14:25 Lit valley

this wilderness — all of you who were registered in the census, the entire number of you twenty years old or more — because you have complained about me. ³⁰ I swear that none of you will enter the land I promised ᴬ to settle you in, except Caleb son of Jephunneh and Joshua son of Nun. ³¹ I will bring your children whom you said would become plunder into the land you rejected, and they will enjoy it. ³² But as for you, your corpses will fall in this wilderness. ³³ Your children will be shepherds in the wilderness for forty years and bear the penalty for your acts of unfaithfulness until all your corpses lie scattered in the wilderness. ³⁴ You will bear the consequences of your iniquities forty years based on the number of the forty days that you scouted the land, a year for each day.ᴮ You will know my displeasure.ᶜ ³⁵ I, the Lord, have spoken. I swear that I will do this to the entire evil community that has conspired against me. They will come to an end in the wilderness, and there they will die."

³⁶ So the men Moses sent to scout out the land, and who returned and incited the entire community to complain about him by spreading a negative report about the land — ³⁷ those men who spread the negative report about the land were struck down by the Lord. ³⁸ Only Joshua son of Nun and Caleb son of Jephunneh remained alive of those men who went to scout out the land.

Israel Routed

³⁹ When Moses reported these words to all the Israelites, the people were overcome with grief. ⁴⁰ They got up early the next morning and went up the ridge of the hill country, saying, "Let's go to the place the Lord promised, for we were wrong."   Dt 1:41-44

⁴¹ But Moses responded, "Why are you going against the Lord's command? It won't succeed. ⁴² Don't go, because the Lord is not among you and you will be defeated by your enemies. ⁴³ The Amalekites and Canaanites are right in front of you, and you will fall by the sword. The Lord won't be with you, since you have turned from following him."

⁴⁴ But they dared to go up the ridge of the hill country, even though the ark of the Lord's covenant and Moses did not leave the camp. ⁴⁵ Then the Amalekites and Canaanites who lived in that part of the hill country came down, attacked them, and routed them as far as Hormah.   Nm 21:3; Jdg 1:17

Laws About Offerings

15 The Lord instructed Moses: ² "Speak to the Israelites and tell them: When you enter the land I am giving you to settle in, ³ and you make a fire offering to the Lord from the herd or flock — either a burnt offering or a sacrifice, to fulfill a vow, or as a freewill offering, or at your appointed festivals — to produce a pleasing aroma for the Lord, ⁴ the one presenting his offering to the Lord is also to present a grain offering of two quartsᴰ of fine flour mixed with a quartᴱ of oil. ⁵ Prepare a quart of wine as a drink offering with the burnt offering or sacrifice of each lamb.

ᴬ14:30 Lit *I raised my hand*   ᴮ14:34 Lit *a day for the year, a day for the year*   ᶜ14:34 Or *my opposition*
ᴰ15:4 Lit *a tenth* (of an ephah)   ᴱ15:4 Lit *a fourth hin*, also in v. 5

⁶ "If you prepare a grain offering with a ram, it is to be four quarts^A of fine flour mixed with a third of a gallon^B of oil. ⁷ Also present a third of a gallon of wine for a drink offering as a pleasing aroma to the LORD.

⁸ "If you prepare a young bull as a burnt offering or as a sacrifice, to fulfill a vow, or as a fellowship offering to the LORD, ⁹ a grain offering of six quarts^C of fine flour mixed with two quarts^D of oil is to be presented with the bull. ¹⁰ Also present two quarts of wine as a drink offering. It is a fire offering of pleasing aroma to the LORD. ¹¹ This is to be done for each ox, ram, lamb, or goat. ¹² This is how you are to prepare each of them, no matter how many. Nm 28:12

¹³ "Every Israelite is to prepare these things in this way when he presents a fire offering as a pleasing aroma to the LORD. ¹⁴ When an alien resides with you or someone else is among you and wants to prepare a fire offering as a pleasing aroma to the LORD, he is to do exactly as you do throughout your generations. ¹⁵ The assembly is to have the same statute for both you and the resident alien as a permanent statute throughout your generations. You and the alien will be alike before the LORD. ¹⁶ The same law and the same ordinance will apply to both you and the alien who resides with you." Ex 27:21; Lv 3:17; 7:36

¹⁷ The LORD instructed Moses: ¹⁸ "Speak to the Israelites and tell them: After you enter the land where I am bringing you, ¹⁹ you are to offer a contribution to the LORD when you eat from the food of the land. ²⁰ You are to offer a loaf from your first batch of dough as a contribution; offer it just like a contribution from the threshing floor. ²¹ Throughout your generations, you are to give the LORD a contribution from the first batch of your dough. Lv 2:14; Neh 10:37; Ezk 44:30

²² "When you sin unintentionally and do not obey all these commands that the LORD spoke to Moses — ²³ all that the LORD has commanded you through Moses, from the day the LORD issued the commands and onward throughout your generations — ²⁴ and if it was done unintentionally without the community's awareness, the entire community is to prepare one young bull for a burnt offering as a pleasing aroma to the LORD, with its grain offering and drink offering according to the regulation, and one male goat as a sin offering. ²⁵ The priest will then make atonement for the entire Israelite community so that they may be forgiven, for the sin was unintentional. They are to bring their offering, one made by fire to the LORD, and their sin offering before the LORD for their unintentional sin. ²⁶ The entire Israelite community and the alien who resides among them will be forgiven, since it happened to all the people unintentionally.

²⁷ "If one person sins unintentionally, he is to present a year-old female goat as a sin offering. ²⁸ The priest will then make atonement before the LORD on behalf of the person who acts in error sinning unintentionally, and when he makes atonement for him, he will be forgiven. ²⁹ You are to have the same law for the person who acts

^A 15:6 Lit two-tenths (of an ephah)   ^B 15:6 Lit a third hin, also in v. 7   ^C 15:9 Lit three-tenths (of an ephah)
^D 15:9 Lit a half hin, also in v. 10

in error, whether he is an Israelite or an alien who resides among you.

30 "But the person who acts defiantly,[A] whether native or resident alien, blasphemes the LORD. That person is to be cut off from his people. 31 He will certainly be cut off, because he has despised the LORD's word and broken his command; his guilt remains on him."   2Kg 19:6,22

Sabbath Violation

32 While the Israelites were in the wilderness, they found a man gathering wood on the Sabbath day. 33 Those who found him gathering wood brought him to Moses, Aaron, and the entire community. 34 They placed him in custody because it had not been decided what should be done to him. 35 Then the LORD told Moses, "The man is to be put to death. The entire community is to stone him outside the camp." 36 So the entire community brought him outside the camp and stoned him to death, as the LORD had commanded Moses.   Ex 35:2-3; Lv 20:27; Jos 7:25

Tassels for Remembrance

37 The LORD said to Moses, 38 "Speak to the Israelites and tell them that throughout their generations they are to make tassels for the corners of their garments, and put a blue cord on the tassel at each corner. 39 These will serve as tassels for you to look at, so that you may remember all the LORD's commands and obey them and not prostitute yourselves by following your own heart and your own eyes. 40 This way you will remember and obey all my commands and be holy to your God. 41 I am the LORD your God who brought you out of the land

A 15:30 Lit with a high hand

of Egypt to be your God; I am the LORD your God."   Dt 22:12; Mt 9:20; 14:36

Korah Incites Rebellion

16 Now Korah son of Izhar, son of Kohath, son of Levi, with Dathan and Abiram, sons of Eliab, and On son of Peleth, sons of Reuben, took 2 two hundred and fifty prominent Israelite men who were leaders of the community and representatives in the assembly, and they rebelled against Moses. 3 They came together against Moses and Aaron and told them, "You have gone too far! Everyone in the entire community is holy, and the LORD is among them. Why then do you exalt yourselves above the LORD's assembly?"   Ex 6:16-21; Nm 26:9; Dt 11:6

4 When Moses heard this, he fell facedown. 5 Then he said to Korah and all his followers, "Tomorrow morning the LORD will reveal who belongs to him, who is set apart, and the one he will let come near him. He will let the one he chooses come near him. 6 Korah, you and all your followers are to do this: take firepans, and tomorrow 7 place fire in them and put incense on them before the LORD. Then the man the LORD chooses will be the one who is set apart. It is you Levites who have gone too far!"   Ex 40:12-15; Nm 17:5

8 Moses also told Korah, "Now listen, Levites! 9 Isn't it enough for you that the God of Israel has separated you from the Israelite community to bring you near to himself, to perform the work at the LORD's tabernacle, and to stand before the community to minister to them? 10 He has brought you near, and all your fellow Levites who are with you, but you are pursuing the

priesthood as well. [11] Therefore, it is you and all your followers who have conspired against the LORD! As for Aaron, who is he[A] that you should complain about him?"

[12] Moses sent for Dathan and Abiram, the sons of Eliab, but they said, "We will not come! [13] Is it not enough that you brought us up from a land flowing with milk and honey to kill us in the wilderness? Do you also have to appoint yourself as ruler over us? [14] Furthermore, you didn't bring us to a land flowing with milk and honey or give us an inheritance of fields and vineyards. Will you gouge out the eyes of these men? We will not come!" Ex 3:8,17; 1Sm 11:2

[15] Then Moses became angry and said to the LORD, "Don't respect their offering. I have not taken one donkey from them or mistreated a single one of them." [16] So Moses told Korah, "You and all your followers are to appear before the LORD tomorrow — you, they, and Aaron. [17] Each of you is to take his firepan, place incense on it, and present his firepan before the LORD — 250 firepans. You and Aaron are each to present your firepan also."

[18] Each man took his firepan, placed fire in it, put incense on it, and stood at the entrance to the tent of meeting along with Moses and Aaron. [19] After Korah assembled the whole community against them at the entrance to the tent of meeting, the glory of the LORD appeared to the whole community. [20] The LORD spoke to Moses and Aaron, [21] "Separate yourselves from this community so I may consume them instantly." Ex 16:7,10; Nm 16:45; Jr 14:12

[22] But Moses and Aaron fell facedown and said, "God, God who gives breath to all,[B] when one man sins, will you vent your wrath on the whole community?" Gn 17:3

[23] The LORD replied to Moses, [24] "Tell the community: Get away from the dwellings of Korah, Dathan, and Abiram."

[25] Moses got up and went to Dathan and Abiram, and the elders of Israel followed him. [26] He warned the community, "Get away now from the tents of these wicked men. Don't touch anything that belongs to them, or you will be swept away because of all their sins." [27] So they got away from the dwellings of Korah, Dathan, and Abiram. Meanwhile, Dathan and Abiram came out and stood at the entrance of their tents with their wives, children, and infants. Gn 19:15,17; Is 52:11

[28] Then Moses said, "This is how you will know that the LORD sent me to do all these things and that it was not of my own will: [29] If these men die naturally as all people would, and suffer the fate of all, then the LORD has not sent me. [30] But if the LORD brings about something unprecedented, and the ground opens its mouth and swallows them along with all that belongs to them so that they go down alive into Sheol, then you will know that these men have despised the LORD." Ex 3:10-12; Zch 2:9,11

[31] Just as he finished speaking all these words, the ground beneath them split open. [32] The earth opened its mouth and swallowed them and their households, all Korah's people, and all their possessions. [33] They went down alive into Sheol with all that belonged to them. The earth closed over them, and they vanished from the assembly. [34] At their cries, all the people of

A[16:11] Or Aaron, what has he done   B[16:22] Or God of the spirits of all flesh

Israel who were around them fled because they thought, "The earth may swallow us too!" [35] Fire also came out from the LORD and consumed the 250 men who were presenting the incense. Ex 15:12; Nm 26:10

[36] Then the LORD spoke to Moses: [37] "Tell Eleazar son of Aaron the priest to remove the firepans from the burning debris, because they are holy, and scatter the fire far away. [38] As for the firepans of those who sinned at the cost of their own lives, make them into hammered sheets as plating for the altar, for they presented them before the LORD, and the firepans are holy. They will be a sign to the Israelites."

[39] So the priest Eleazar took the bronze firepans that those who were burned had presented, and they were hammered into plating for the altar, [40] just as the LORD commanded him through Moses. It was to be a reminder for the Israelites that no unauthorized person outside the lineage of Aaron should approach to offer incense before the LORD and become like Korah and his followers. Ex 28:1; Nm 3:10,38

[41] The next day the entire Israelite community complained about Moses and Aaron, saying, "You have killed the LORD's people!" [42] When the community assembled against them, Moses and Aaron turned toward the tent of meeting, and suddenly the cloud covered it, and the LORD's glory appeared. Ex 16:2,7-8; 17:3

[43] Moses and Aaron went to the front of the tent of meeting, [44] and the LORD said to Moses, [45] "Get away from this community so that I may consume them instantly." But they fell facedown. Nm 16:21

[46] Then Moses told Aaron, "Take your firepan, place fire from the altar in it, and add incense. Go quickly to the community and make atonement for them, because wrath has come from the LORD; the plague has begun." [47] So Aaron took his firepan as Moses had ordered, ran into the middle of the assembly, and saw that the plague had begun among the people. After he added incense, he made atonement for the people. [48] He stood between the dead and the living, and the plague was halted. [49] But those who died from the plague numbered 14,700, in addition to those who died because of the Korah incident. [50] Aaron then returned to Moses at the entrance to the tent of meeting, since the plague had been halted. Nm 25:1-9

Aaron's Staff Chosen

17 The LORD instructed Moses: [2] "Speak to the Israelites and take one staff from them for each ancestral tribe,[A] twelve staffs from all the leaders of their tribes.[B] Write each man's name on his staff. [3] Write Aaron's name on Levi's staff, because there is to be one staff for the head of each tribe. [4] Then place them in the tent of meeting in front of the testimony where I meet with you. [5] The staff of the man I choose will sprout, and I will rid myself of the Israelites' complaints that they have been making about you."

[6] So Moses spoke to the Israelites, and each of their leaders gave him a staff, one for each of the leaders of their tribes, twelve staffs in all. Aaron's staff was among them. [7] Moses placed the staffs before the LORD in the tent of the testimony.

[A]17:2 Lit father's house   [B]17:2 Lit the house of their fathers, also in vv. 3,6

⁸ The next day Moses entered the tent of the testimony and saw that Aaron's staff, representing the house of Levi, had sprouted, formed buds, blossomed, and produced almonds! ⁹ Moses then brought out all the staffs from the LORD's presence to all the Israelites. They saw them, and each man took his own staff. ¹⁰ The LORD told Moses, "Put Aaron's staff back in front of the testimony to be kept as a sign for the rebels, so that you may put an end to their complaints before me, or else they will die." ¹¹ So Moses did as the LORD commanded him.

¹² Then the Israelites declared to Moses, "Look, we're perishing! We're lost; we're all lost! ¹³ Anyone who comes near the LORD's tabernacle will die. Will we all perish?"

Provision for the Priesthood

18 The LORD said to Aaron, "You, your sons, and your ancestral family [A] will be responsible for iniquity against the sanctuary. You and your sons will be responsible for iniquity involving your priesthood. ² But also bring your relatives with you from the tribe of Levi, your ancestral tribe, so they may join you and assist you and your sons in front of the tent of the testimony. ³ They are to perform duties for you and for the whole tent. They must not come near the sanctuary equipment or the altar; otherwise, both they and you will die. ⁴ They are to join you and guard the tent of meeting, doing all the work at the tent, but no unauthorized person may come near you. Nm 8:5-26; 10:21

⁵ "You are to guard the sanctuary and the altar so that wrath may not fall on the Israelites again. ⁶ Look, I have selected your fellow Levites from the Israelites as a gift for you, assigned by the LORD to work at the tent of meeting. ⁷ But you and your sons will carry out your priestly responsibilities for everything concerning the altar and for what is inside the curtain, and you will do that work. I am giving you the work of the priesthood as a gift, ⁸ but an unauthorized person who comes near the sanctuary will be put to death." Nm 1:53; 16; 17:12-13; 1Ch 9:19; Ezk 44:11

Support for the Priests and Levites

⁸ Then the LORD spoke to Aaron, "Look, I have put you in charge of the contributions brought to me. As for all the holy offerings of the Israelites, I have given them to you and your sons as a portion and a permanent statute. ⁹ A portion of the holiest offerings kept from the fire will be yours; every one of their offerings that they give me, whether the grain offering, sin offering, or guilt offering will be most holy for you and your sons. ¹⁰ You are to eat it as a most holy offering. [C] Every male may eat it; it is to be holy to you. Ex 36:3; Lv 22:12; Nm 18:19; Dt 12:6,11,17

¹¹ "The contribution of their gifts also belongs to you. I have given all the Israelites' presentation offerings to you and to your sons and daughters as a permanent statute. Every ceremonially clean person in your house may eat it. ¹² I am giving you all the best of the fresh oil, new wine, and grain, which the Israelites give to the LORD as their firstfruits. ¹³ The firstfruits of all that is in their land, which they bring

[A] 18:1 Lit the house of your father   [B] 18:7 Or curtain. So you are to perform the service; a gift of your priesthood I grant   [C] 18:10 Or it in a most holy place to the LORD, belong to you. Every clean person in your house may eat them.   Ex 29:24-27; 35:22; 38:24,29; Lv 7:34-36

¹⁴ "Everything in Israel that is permanently dedicated to the LORD belongs to you. ¹⁵ The firstborn of every living thing, human or animal, presented to the LORD belongs to you. But you must certainly redeem a human firstborn, and redeem the firstborn of an unclean animal. ¹⁶ You will pay the redemption price for a month-old male according to your assessment: five shekels ᴬ of silver by the standard sanctuary shekel, which is twenty gerahs.   Ex 13:11-16; Lv 27:6,28; Nm 3:46-47

¹⁷ "However, you must not redeem the firstborn of an ox, a sheep, or a goat; they are holy. You are to splatter their blood on the altar and burn their fat as a fire offering for a pleasing aroma to the LORD. ¹⁸ But their meat belongs to you. It belongs to you like the breast of the presentation offering and the right thigh.

¹⁹ "I give to you and to your sons and daughters all the holy contributions that the Israelites present to the LORD as a permanent statute. It is a permanent covenant of salt before the LORD for you as well as your offspring."   Lv 2:13; 2Ch 13:5

²⁰ The LORD told Aaron, "You will not have an inheritance in their land; there will be no portion among them for you. I am your portion and your inheritance among the Israelites.   Dt 10:9; Jos 18:7; Ezk 44:28-30

²¹ "Look, I have given the Levites every tenth in Israel as an inheritance in return for the work they do, the work of the tent of meeting. ²² The Israelites must never again come near the tent of meeting, or

they will incur guilt and die. ²³ The Levites will do the work of the tent of meeting, and they will bear the consequences of their iniquity. The Levites will not receive an inheritance among the Israelites; this is a permanent statute throughout your generations. ²⁴ For I have given them the tenth that the Israelites present to the LORD as a contribution for their inheritance. That is why I told them that they would not receive an inheritance among the Israelites."   Dt 26:12; 2Ch 31:12; Neh 10:37-38

²⁵ The LORD instructed Moses, ²⁶ "Speak to the Levites and tell them: When you receive from the Israelites the tenth that I have given you as your inheritance, you are to present part of it as an offering to the LORD — a tenth of the tenth. ²⁷ Your offering will be credited to you as if it were your grain from the threshing floor or the full harvest from the winepress. ²⁸ You are to present an offering to the LORD from every tenth you receive from the Israelites. Give some of it to the priest Aaron as an offering to the LORD. ²⁹ You must present the entire offering due the LORD from all your gifts. The best part of the tenth is to be consecrated.   Nm 18:12

³⁰ "Tell them further: Once you have presented the best part of the tenth, and it is credited to you Levites as the produce of the threshing floor or the winepress, ³¹ then you and your household may eat it anywhere. It is your wage in return for your work at the tent of meeting. ³² You will not incur guilt because of it once you have presented the best part of it, but you must not defile the Israelites' holy offerings, so that you will not die."

ᴬ **18:16** A shekel is about two-fifths of an ounce

Purification Ritual

19 The Lord spoke to Moses and Aaron, ² "This is the legal statute that the Lord has commanded: Instruct the Israelites to bring you an unblemished red cow that has no defect and has never been yoked. ³ Give it to the priest Eleazar, and he will have it brought outside the camp and slaughtered in his presence. ⁴ The priest Eleazar is to take some of its blood with his finger and sprinkle it seven times toward the front of the tent of meeting. ⁵ The cow is to be burned in his sight. Its hide, flesh, and blood, are to be burned along with its waste. ⁶ The priest is to take cedar wood, hyssop, and crimson yarn, and throw them onto the fire where the cow is burning. ⁷ Then the priest must wash his clothes and bathe his body in water; after that he may enter the camp, but he will remain ceremonially unclean until evening. ⁸ The one who burned the cow must also wash his clothes and bathe his body in water, and he will remain unclean until evening. Dt 21:3; 1Sm 6:7; Heb 9:13; 28:1

⁹ "A man who is clean is to gather up the cow's ashes and deposit them outside the camp in a ceremonially clean place. The ashes will be kept by the Israelite community for preparing the water to remove impurity; it is a sin offering. ¹⁰ Then the one who gathers up the cow's ashes must wash his clothes, and he will remain unclean until evening. This is a permanent statute for the Israelites and for the alien who resides among them. Lv 4

¹¹ "The person who touches any human corpse will be unclean for seven days. ¹² He is to purify himself with the water^A on the third day and the seventh day; then he will be clean. But if he does not purify himself on the third and seventh days, he will not be clean. ¹³ Anyone who touches a body of a person who has died, and does not purify himself, defiles the tabernacle of the Lord. That person will be cut off from Israel. He remains unclean because the water for impurity has not been sprinkled on him, and his uncleanness is still on him. Nm 31:19

¹⁴ "This is the law when a person dies in a tent: everyone who enters the tent and everyone who is already in the tent will be unclean for seven days, ¹⁵ and any open container without a lid tied on it is unclean. ¹⁶ Anyone in the open field who touches a person who has been killed by the sword or has died, or who even touches a human bone, or a grave, will be unclean for seven days. ¹⁷ For the purification of the unclean person, they are to take some of the ashes of the burnt sin offering, put them in a jar, and add fresh water to them. ¹⁸ A person who is clean is to take hyssop, dip it in the water, and sprinkle the tent, all the furnishings, and the people who were there. He is also to sprinkle the one who touched a bone, a grave, a corpse, or a person who had been killed.

¹⁹ "The one who is clean is to sprinkle the unclean person on the third day and the seventh day. After he purifies the unclean person on the seventh day, the one being purified must wash his clothes and bathe in water, and he will be clean by evening. ²⁰ But a person who is unclean and does not purify himself, that person will be cut off

^A 19:12 Or *ashes*; lit *with it*

from the assembly because he has defiled the sanctuary of the LORD. The water for impurity has not been sprinkled on him; he is unclean. ²¹ This is a permanent statute for them. The person who sprinkles the water for impurity is to wash his clothes, and whoever touches the water for impurity will be unclean until evening. ²² Anything the unclean person touches will become unclean, and anyone who touches it will be unclean until evening."

Water from the Rock

20 The entire Israelite community entered the Wilderness of Zin in the first month, and they ^A settled in Kadesh. Miriam died and was buried there.   Nm 13:21; 27:14; 33:36

² There was no water for the community, so they assembled against Moses and Aaron. ³ The people quarreled with Moses and said, "If only we had perished when our brothers perished before the LORD. ⁴ Why have you brought the LORD's assembly into this wilderness for us and our livestock to die here? ⁵ Why have you led us up from Egypt to bring us to this evil place? It's not a place of grain, figs, vines, and pomegranates, and there is no water to drink!"   Ex 17:2

⁶ Then Moses and Aaron went from the presence of the assembly to the doorway of the tent of meeting. They fell facedown, and the glory of the LORD appeared to them. ⁷ The LORD spoke to Moses, ⁸ "Take the staff and assemble the community. You and your brother Aaron are to speak to the rock while they watch, and it will yield its water. You will bring out water for them from the rock and provide

drink for the community and their livestock."   Ex 4:2-5; 7:15,17,20; 17:4-9; Nm 17:8

⁹ So Moses took the staff from the LORD's presence just as he had commanded him. ¹⁰ Moses and Aaron summoned the assembly in front of the rock, and Moses said to them, "Listen, you rebels! Must we bring water out of this rock for you?" ¹¹ Then Moses raised his hand and struck the rock twice with his staff, so that abundant water gushed out, and the community and their livestock drank.   Nm 17:10

¹² But the LORD said to Moses and Aaron, "Because you did not trust me to demonstrate my holiness in the sight of the Israelites, you will not bring this assembly into the land I have given them." ¹³ These are the Waters of Meribah, ^B where the Israelites quarreled with the LORD, and he demonstrated his holiness to them.   Ex 17:7; Nm 27:12-14; Dt 1:37; 3:26; 32:51

Edom Denies Passage

¹⁴ Moses sent messengers from Kadesh to the king of Edom, "This is what your brother Israel says, 'You know all the hardships that have overtaken us. ¹⁵ Our fathers went down to Egypt, and we lived in Egypt many years, but the Egyptians treated us and our fathers badly. ¹⁶ When we cried out to the LORD, he heard our plea, ^C and sent an angel, ^D and brought us out of Egypt. Now look, we are in Kadesh, a city on the border of your territory. ¹⁷ Please let us travel through your land. We won't travel through any field or vineyard, or drink any well water. We will travel the King's Highway; we won't turn to the right or the left until we have traveled through your territory.' "   Gn 36:8

^A**20:1** Lit *the people*   ^B**20:13** = Quarreling   ^C**20:16** Lit *voice*   ^D**20:16** Or *a messenger*

[18] But Edom answered him, "You will not travel through our land, or we will come out and confront you with the sword."

[19] "We will go on the main road," the Israelites replied to them, "and if we or our herds drink your water, we will pay its price. There will be no problem; only let us travel through on foot."   Dt 2:1-7

[20] Yet Edom insisted, "You may not travel through." And they came out to confront them with a large force of heavily-armed people.[A] [21] Edom refused to allow Israel to travel through their territory, and Israel turned away from them.

Aaron's Death

[22] After they set out from Kadesh, the entire Israelite community came to Mount Hor. [23] The LORD said to Moses and Aaron at Mount Hor on the border of the land of Edom, [24] "Aaron will be gathered to his people; he will not enter the land I have given the Israelites, because you both rebelled against my command at the Waters of Meribah. [25] Take Aaron and his son Eleazar and bring them up Mount Hor. [26] Remove Aaron's garments and put them on his son Eleazar. Aaron will be gathered to his people and die there."   Nm 21:4; 33:37-41

[27] So Moses did as the LORD commanded, and they climbed Mount Hor in the sight of the whole community. [28] After Moses removed Aaron's garments and put them on his son Eleazar, Aaron died there on top of the mountain. Then Moses and Eleazar came down from the mountain. [29] When the whole community saw that Aaron had passed away, the entire house of Israel mourned for him thirty days.

Canaanite King Defeated

21 When the Canaanite king of Arad, who lived in the Negev, heard that Israel was coming on the Atharim road, he fought against Israel and captured some prisoners. [2] Then Israel made a vow to the LORD, "If you will hand this people over to us, we will completely destroy their cities." [3] The LORD listened to Israel's request and handed the Canaanites over to them, and Israel completely destroyed them and their cities. So they named the place Hormah.[B]   Dt 1:44; Nm 33:40; Jos 12:14; Jdg 1:16

The Bronze Snake

[4] Then they set out from Mount Hor by way of the Red Sea to bypass the land of Edom, but the people became impatient because of the journey. [5] The people spoke against God and Moses: "Why have you led us up from Egypt to die in the wilderness? There is no bread or water, and we detest this wretched food!" [6] Then the LORD sent poisonous[c] snakes among the people, and they bit them so that many Israelites died.   1Co 10:9

[7] The people then came to Moses and said, "We have sinned by speaking against the LORD and against you. Intercede with the LORD so that he will take the snakes away from us." And Moses interceded for the people.

[8] Then the LORD said to Moses, "Make a snake image and mount it on a pole. When anyone who is bitten looks at it, he will recover." [9] So Moses made a bronze snake

[A] 20:20 Lit *with numerous people and a strong hand*   [B] 21:3 = Destruction   [c] 21:6 Lit *Burning* and mounted it on a pole. Whenever someone was bitten, and he looked at the bronze snake, he recovered. 2Kg 18:4; Jn 3:14-15

Journey Around Moab

[10] The Israelites set out and camped at Oboth. [11] They set out from Oboth and camped at Iye-abarim in the wilderness that borders Moab on the east. [12] From there they went and camped at Zered Valley. [13] They set out from there and camped on the other side of the Arnon River, in the wilderness that extends from the Amorite border, because the Arnon was the Moabite border between Moab and the Amorites. [14] Therefore it is stated in the Book of the LORD's Wars: Nm 33:43-44

Waheb in Suphah
and the ravines of the Arnon,
[15] even the slopes of the ravines
that extend to the site of Ar
and lie along the border
of Moab.

[16] From there they went to Beer,[A] the well the LORD told Moses about, "Gather the people so I may give them water." [17] Then Israel sang this song:

Spring up, well — sing to it!
[18] The princes dug the well;
the nobles of the people
hollowed it out
with a scepter and with
their staffs.

They went from the wilderness to Mattanah, [19] from Mattanah to Nahaliel, from Nahaliel to Bamoth, [20] from Bamoth to the valley in the territory of Moab near the Pisgah highlands that overlook the wasteland.[B]

Amorite Kings Defeated

[21] Israel sent messengers to say to King Sihon of the Amorites: [22] "Let us travel through your land. We won't go into the fields or vineyards. We won't drink any well water. We will travel the King's Highway until we have traveled through your territory." [23] But Sihon would not let Israel travel through his territory. Instead, he gathered his whole army and went out to confront Israel in the wilderness. When he came to Jahaz, he fought against Israel. [24] Israel struck him with the sword and took possession of his land from the Arnon to the Jabbok, but only up to the Ammonite border, because it was fortified.[C] Nm 32:33; Dt 1:4; 2:24–4:46

[25] Israel took all the cities and lived in all these Amorite cities, including Heshbon and all its surrounding villages. [26] Heshbon was the city of King Sihon of the Amorites, who had fought against the former king of Moab and had taken control of all his land as far as the Arnon. [27] Therefore the poets[D] say:

Come to Heshbon,
let it be rebuilt;
let the city of Sihon
be restored.[E]
[28] For fire came out of Heshbon,
a flame from the city of Sihon.
It consumed Ar of Moab,
the citizens
of Arnon's heights.
[29] Woe to you, Moab!
You have been destroyed,
people of Chemosh! Jdg 11:24
He gave up his sons
as refugees,
and his daughters
into captivity

A 21:16 = Well   B 21:20 Or overlook Jeshimon   C 21:24 LXX reads because the Ammonite border was Jazer
D 21:27 Lit ones who speak proverbs   E 21:27 Or firmly founded

to Sihon the Amorite king.

30 We threw them down;
      Heshbon has been destroyed
         as far as Dibon.   Nm 32:34
      We caused desolation
         as far as Nophah,
      which reaches
         as far as Medeba.   Jos 13:9,16

31 So Israel lived in the Amorites' land. 32 After Moses sent spies to Jazer, Israel captured its surrounding villages and drove out the Amorites who were there.

33 Then they turned and went up the road to Bashan, and King Og of Bashan came out against them with his whole army to do battle at Edrei. 34 But the LORD said to Moses, "Do not fear him, for I have handed him over to you along with his whole army and his land. Do to him as you did to King Sihon of the Amorites, who lived in Heshbon." 35 So they struck him, his sons, and his whole army until no one was left, A and they took possession of his land.   Nm 32:33; Dt 3:1-13; 4:47

Balak Hires Balaam

22 The Israelites traveled on and camped in the plains of Moab near the Jordan across from Jericho. 2 Now Balak son of Zippor saw all that Israel had done to the Amorites. 3 Moab was terrified of the people because they were numerous, and Moab dreaded the Israelites. 4 So the Moabites said to the elders of Midian, "This horde will devour everything around us like an ox eats up the green plants in the field."   Jos 24:9-10; Jdg 11:25; Mc 6:5

Since Balak son of Zippor was Moab's king at that time, 5 he sent messengers to Balaam son of Beor at Pethor, which is by the Euphrates

in the land of his people. B,C Balak said to him: "Look, a people has come out of Egypt; they cover the surface of the land and are living right across from me. 6 Please come and put a curse on these people for me because they are more powerful than I am. I may be able to defeat them and drive them out of the land, for I know that those you bless are blessed and those you curse are cursed."   Dt 23:3-5; Jos 24:9-10; Mc 6:5; 2Pt 2:15-16

7 The elders of Moab and Midian departed with fees for divination in hand. They came to Balaam and reported Balak's words to him. 8 He said to them, "Spend the night here, and I will give you the answer the LORD tells me." So the officials of Moab stayed with Balaam.   Gn 30:27

9 Then God came to Balaam and asked, "Who are these men with you?"

10 Balaam replied to God, "Balak son of Zippor, king of Moab, sent this message to me: 11 'Look, a people has come out of Egypt, and they cover the surface of the land. Now come and put a curse on them for me. I may be able to fight against them and drive them away.'"

12 Then God said to Balaam, "You are not to go with them. You are not to curse this people, for they are blessed."

13 So Balaam got up the next morning and said to Balak's officials, "Go back to your land, because the LORD has refused to let me go with you."

14 The officials of Moab arose, returned to Balak, and reported, "Balaam refused to come with us."

15 Balak sent officials again who were more numerous and higher in rank than the others. 16 They came

A 21:35 Lit left to him   B 22:5 Sam, Vg, Syr read of the Ammonites   C 22:5 Or of the Amawites to Balaam and said to him, "This is what Balak son of Zippor says: 'Let nothing keep you from coming to me, ¹⁷ for I will greatly honor you and do whatever you ask me. So please come and put a curse on these people for me!'"

¹⁸ But Balaam responded to the servants of Balak, "If Balak were to give me his house full of silver and gold, I could not go against the command of the LORD my God to do anything small or great. ¹⁹ Please stay here overnight as the others did, so that I may find out what else the LORD has to tell me."

²⁰ God came to Balaam at night and said to him, "Since these men have come to summon you, get up and go with them, but you must only do what I tell you." ²¹ When he got up in the morning, Balaam saddled his donkey and went with the officials of Moab.

Balaam's Donkey and the Angel

²² But God was incensed that Balaam was going, and the angel of the LORD took his stand on the path to oppose him. Balaam was riding his donkey, and his two servants were with him. ²³ When the donkey saw the angel of the LORD standing on the path with a drawn sword in his hand, she turned off the path and went into the field. So Balaam hit her to return her to the path. ²⁴ Then the angel of the LORD stood in a narrow passage between the vineyards, with a stone wall on either side. ²⁵ The donkey saw the angel of the LORD and pressed herself against the wall, squeezing Balaam's foot against it. So he hit her once again. ²⁶ The angel of the LORD went ahead and stood in a narrow place where there was no room to turn to the right or the left. ²⁷ When the donkey saw the angel of the LORD, she crouched down under Balaam. So he became furious and beat the donkey with his stick.   Gn 16:7; 22:11; Ex 3:2; Jdg 2:1; 5:23; 6:1; 13:3

²⁸ Then the LORD opened the donkey's mouth, and she asked Balaam, "What have I done to you that you have beaten me these three times?"

²⁹ Balaam answered the donkey, "You made me look like a fool. If I had a sword in my hand, I'd kill you now!"

³⁰ But the donkey said, "Am I not the donkey you've ridden all your life until today? Have I ever treated you this way before?"

"No," he replied.

³¹ Then the LORD opened Balaam's eyes, and he saw the angel of the LORD standing in the path with a drawn sword in his hand. Balaam knelt low and bowed in worship on his face. ³² The angel of the LORD asked him, "Why have you beaten your donkey these three times? Look, I came out to oppose you, because I consider what you are doing to be evil.ᴬ ³³ The donkey saw me and turned away from me these three times. If she had not turned away from me, I would have killed you by now and let her live."

³⁴ Balaam said to the angel of the LORD, "I have sinned, for I did not know that you were standing in the path to confront me. And now, if it is evil in your sight, I will go back."

³⁵ Then the angel of the LORD said to Balaam, "Go with the men, but you are to say only what I tell you." So Balaam went with Balak's officials.

ᴬ22:32 Lit *because your way is perverse before me*

36 When Balak heard that Balaam was coming, he went out to meet him at the Moabite city[A] on the Arnon border at the edge of his territory. 37 Balak asked Balaam, "Did I not send you an urgent summons? Why didn't you come to me? Am I really not able to reward you?"

38 Balaam said to him, "Look, I have come to you, but can I say anything I want? I must speak only the message God puts in my mouth." 39 So Balaam went with Balak, and they came to Kiriath-huzoth.[B] 40 Balak sacrificed cattle, sheep, and goats and sent for Balaam and the officials who were with him.

41 In the morning, Balak took Balaam and brought him to Bamoth-baal.[C] From there he saw the outskirts of the people's camp.

Balaam's Oracles

23 Then Balaam said to Balak, "Build me seven altars here and prepare seven bulls and seven rams for me." 2 So Balak did as Balaam directed, and they offered a bull and a ram on each altar. 3 Balaam said to Balak, "Stay here by your burnt offering while I am gone. Maybe the LORD will meet with me. I will tell you whatever he reveals to me." So he went to a barren hill.   1Ch 15:26; 2Ch 29:21; Jb 42:8

4 God met with him and Balaam said to him, "I have arranged seven altars and offered a bull and a ram on each altar." 5 Then the LORD put a message in Balaam's mouth and said, "Return to Balak and say what I tell you."

6 So he returned to Balak, who was standing there by his burnt offering with all the officials of Moab.

Balaam's First Oracle

7 Balaam proclaimed his poem:

> Balak brought me
>   from Aram;   Dt 23:4
> the king of Moab,
>   from the eastern mountains:
> "Come, put a curse on Jacob
>   for me;
> come, denounce Israel!"
> 8 How can I curse someone
>   God has not cursed?
> How can I denounce
>   someone the LORD
>   has not denounced?
> 9 I see them from the top
>   of rocky cliffs,
> and I watch them
>   from the hills.
> There is a people living alone;
>   it does not consider itself
>   among the nations.
> 10 Who has counted the dust
>   of Jacob   Gn 13:16
> or numbered even
>   one-fourth of Israel?
> Let me die the death
>   of the upright;
> let the end of my life
>   be like theirs.

11 "What have you done to me?" Balak asked Balaam. "I brought you to curse my enemies, but look, you have only blessed them!"

12 He answered, "Shouldn't I say exactly what the LORD puts in my mouth?"   Nm 22:38

Balaam's Second Oracle

13 Then Balak said to him, "Please come with me to another place where you can see them. You will only see the outskirts of their camp; you won't see all of them. From there, put a curse on them for me." 14 So Balak took him to Lookout

A 22:36 Or at Ir-moab, or at Ar of Moab   B 22:39 = The City of Streets   C 22:41 = The High Places of Baal

Field^A on top of Pisgah, built seven altars, and offered a bull and a ram on each altar. _{Nm 21:20; 23:27}

^15 Balaam said to Balak, "Stay here by your burnt offering while I seek the Lord over there."

^16 The Lord met with Balaam and put a message in his mouth. Then he said, "Return to Balak and say what I tell you."

^17 So he returned to Balak, who was standing there by his burnt offering with the officials of Moab. Balak asked him, "What did the Lord say?"

^18 Balaam proclaimed his poem:

Balak, get up and listen;
son of Zippor, pay attention
to what I say!
^19 God is not a man, that he
might lie,
or a son of man, that he
might change his mind. _{Ti 1:2}
Does he speak and not act,
or promise and not fulfill?
^20 I have indeed received
a command to bless;
since he has blessed,^B
I cannot change it.
^21 He considers no disaster
for Jacob;
he sees no trouble for Israel.^C
The Lord their God is
with them, _{Gn 28:15; Nm 14:9; Dt 2:7}
and there is rejoicing
over the King among them.
^22 God brought them
out of Egypt;
he is like the horns
of a wild ox for them.^D
^23 There is no magic curse
against Jacob
and no divination
against Israel.

It will now be said
about Jacob and Israel,
"What great things
God has done!"
^24 A people rise up
like a lioness;
they rouse themselves
like a lion. _{Nm 24:9}
They will not lie down
until they devour the prey
and drink the blood
of the slain.

^25 Then Balak told Balaam, "Don't curse them and don't bless them!"

^26 But Balaam answered him, "Didn't I tell you: Whatever the Lord says, I must do?" _{Nm 22:38}

Balaam's Third Oracle

^27 Again Balak said to Balaam, "Please come. I will take you to another place. Maybe it will be agreeable to God that you can put a curse on them for me there." ^28 So Balak took Balaam to the top of Peor, which overlooks the wasteland.^E

^29 Balaam told Balak, "Build me seven altars here and prepare seven bulls and seven rams for me." ^30 So Balak did as Balaam said and offered a bull and a ram on each altar. _{Nm 23:1-2}

24 Since Balaam saw that it pleased the Lord to bless Israel, he did not go to seek omens as on previous occasions, but turned^F toward the wilderness. ^2 When Balaam looked up and saw Israel encamped tribe by tribe, the Spirit of God came on him, ^3 and he proclaimed his poem: _{Ex 35:31; 1Sm 10:10}

The oracle of Balaam
son of Beor,

---

^A23:14 Or *to the field of Zophim* ^B23:20 Sam, LXX read *since I will bless* ^C23:21 Or *He does not observe sin in Jacob; he does not see wrongdoing in Israel* ^D23:22 Or *Egypt; they have the horns of a wild ox* ^E23:28 Or *overlooks Jeshimon* ^F24:1 Lit *set his face*

the oracle of the man
  whose eyes are opened,
4 the oracle of one who hears
  the sayings of God,
who sees a vision
  from the Almighty,   Is 13:6,9
who falls into a trance
  with his eyes uncovered:
5 How beautiful are your tents,
  Jacob,
your dwellings, Israel.
6 They stretch out
  like river valleys, A
like gardens beside a stream,
like aloes the LORD
  has planted,
like cedars beside the water.
7 Water will flow
  from his buckets,
and his seed will be
  by abundant water.
His king will be greater
  than Agag,   Ex 17:14-16; 1Sm 15:8-33
and his kingdom
  will be exalted.
8 God brought him out of Egypt;
he is like B the horns
  of a wild ox for them.
He will feed
  on enemy nations
and gnaw their bones;
he will strike them
  with his arrows.
9 He crouches, he lies down
  like a lion
or a lioness — who dares
  to rouse him?   Gn 49:9; Nm 23:24
Those who bless you
  will be blessed,
and those who curse you
  will be cursed.   Gn 12:3; 27:29

10 Then Balak became furious with
Balaam, struck his hands together, and said to him, "I summoned
you to put a curse on my enemies,
but instead, you have blessed them
these three times. 11 Now go to your
home! I said I would reward you
richly, but look, the LORD has denied you a reward."   Nm 22:17

12 Balaam answered Balak, "Didn't
I previously tell the messengers you
sent me: 13 If Balak were to give me
his house full of silver and gold,
I could not go against the LORD's
command, to do anything good or
bad of my own will? I will say whatever the LORD says. 14 Now I am going back to my people, but first, let
me warn you what these people will
do to your people in the future."

Balaam's Fourth Oracle

15 Then he proclaimed his poem:
  The oracle of Balaam
    son of Beor,
  the oracle of the man
    whose eyes are opened;
16 the oracle of one who hears
    the sayings of God
  and has knowledge
    from the Most High,
  who sees a vision
    from the Almighty,
  who falls into a trance
    with his eyes uncovered:
17 I see him, but not now;
  I perceive him, but not near.
  A star will come from Jacob,
  and a scepter will arise
    from Israel.   Gn 49:10; Mt 2:2
  He will smash the forehead C
    of Moab
  and strike down D
    all the Shethites. E
18 Edom will become
    a possession;
  Seir will become
    a possession of its enemies,

A24:6 Or like date palms   B24:8 Or he has   C24:17 Or frontiers   D24:17 Sam reads and the skulls of;
Jr 48:45   E24:17 Or Sethites

but Israel will be triumphant.
19 One who comes from Jacob
    will rule;
    he will destroy
    the city's survivors.

20 Then Balaam saw Amalek and
proclaimed his poem:
    Amalek was first
        among the nations,   Ex 17:8-16
    but his future is destruction.

21 Next he saw the Kenites and
proclaimed his poem:
    Your dwelling place
        is enduring;
    your nest is set in the cliffs.
22 Kain will be destroyed
    when Asshur
        takes you captive.

23 Once more he proclaimed his
poem:
    Ah, who can live
        when God does this?
24 Ships will come
        from the coast of Kittim;
    they will carry out raids
        against Asshur and Eber,
    but they too will come
        to destruction.
25 Balaam then arose and went back
to his homeland, and Balak also
went his way.

Israel Worships Baal

25 While Israel was staying in
the Acacia Grove, [A] the people began to prostitute themselves
with the women of Moab. 2 The
women invited them to the sacrifices for their gods, and the people
ate and bowed in worship to their
gods. 3 So Israel aligned itself with
Baal of Peor, and the LORD's anger

burned against Israel. 4 The LORD
said to Moses, "Take all the leaders
of the people and execute [B] them in
broad daylight before the LORD so
that his burning anger may turn
away from Israel."   Nm 33:49; Jos 2:1; 3:1
5 So Moses told Israel's judges,
"Kill each of the men who aligned
themselves with Baal of Peor."

Phinehas Intervenes

6 An Israelite man came bringing a
Midianite woman to his relatives in
the sight of Moses and the whole
Israelite community while they
were weeping at the entrance to
the tent of meeting. 7 When Phinehas son of Eleazar, son of Aaron the
priest, saw this, he got up from the
assembly, took a spear in his hand,
8 followed the Israelite man into the
tent, [C] and drove it through both the
Israelite man and the woman —
through her belly. Then the plague
on the Israelites was stopped, 9 but
those who died in the plague numbered twenty-four thousand.
    10 The LORD spoke to Moses,
11 "Phinehas son of Eleazar, son of
Aaron the priest, has turned back
my wrath from the Israelites because he was zealous among them
with my zeal, [D] so that I did not destroy the Israelites in my zeal.
12 Therefore declare: I grant him
my covenant of peace. 13 It will be
a covenant of perpetual priesthood
for him and his future descendants,
because he was zealous for his God
and made atonement for the Isra-
elites."   Ex 34:14; Is 54:10; Ezk 34:25; 37:26; Zch 8:2
14 The name of the slain Israelite
man, who was struck dead with the
Midianite woman, was Zimri son
of Salu, the leader of a Simeonite

A 25:1 Or in Shittim   B 25:4 Or impale, or hang, or expose ; Hb obscure   C 25:8 Perhaps a tent shrine or
bridal tent   D 25:11 Or jealousy

family.[A] [15] The name of the slain Midianite woman was Cozbi, the daughter of Zur, a tribal head of a family in Midian.

Vengeance Against the Midianites

[16] The LORD told Moses: [17] "Attack the Midianites and strike them dead. [18] For they attacked you with the treachery that they used against you in the Peor incident. They did the same in the case involving their sister Cozbi, daughter of the Midianite leader who was killed the day the plague came at Peor."

The Second Census

26 After the plague, the LORD said to Moses and Eleazar son of Aaron the priest, [2] "Take a census of the entire Israelite community by their ancestral families[B] of those twenty years old or more who can serve in Israel's army."   Nm 1:2-3; 4:2,22; 2Sm 24:10; 2Kg 12:4

[3] So Moses and the priest Eleazar said to them in the plains of Moab by the Jordan across from Jericho, [4] "Take a census of those twenty years old or more, as the LORD had commanded Moses and the Israelites who came out of the land of Egypt."   Nm 22:1; 26:63; 31:12; 33:48-50; 35:1

[5] Reuben was the firstborn
    of Israel.   Gn 46:8-27; Ex 6:14-25
Reuben's descendants:
the Hanochite clan
    from Hanoch;
the Palluite clan from Pallu;
[6] the Hezronite clan
    from Hezron;
the Carmite clan from Carmi.
[7] These were
    the Reubenite clans,

and their registered men numbered 43,730.
[8] The son of Pallu was Eliab.
[9] The sons of Eliab
    were Nemuel, Dathan,
    and Abiram.
(It was Dathan and Abiram, chosen by the community, who fought against Moses and Aaron; they and Korah's followers fought against the LORD. [10] The earth opened its mouth and swallowed them with Korah, when his followers died and the fire consumed 250 men. They serve as a warning sign. [11] The sons of Korah, however, did not die.)   Nm 16:1-3,31-35

[12] Simeon's descendants
    by their clans:
the Nemuelite clan
    from Nemuel;   Gn 46:10; Ex 6:15
the Jaminite clan from Jamin;
the Jachinite clan
    from Jachin;
[13] the Zerahite clan from Zerah;
the Shaulite clan from Shaul.
[14] These were the
    Simeonite clans,
    numbering 22,200 men.

[15] Gad's descendants
    by their clans:
the Zephonite clan
    from Zephon;
the Haggite clan from Haggi;
the Shunite clan from Shuni;
[16] the Oznite clan from Ozni;
the Erite clan from Eri;
[17] the Arodite clan from Arod;
the Arelite clan from Areli.
[18] These were the Gadite
    clans numbered by their
    registered men: 40,500.

[A]**25:14** Lit *a father's house*, also in v. 15   [B]**26:2** Lit *the house of their fathers*

19 Judah's sons included Er and Onan, but they died in the land of Canaan. 20 Judah's descendants by their clans: the Shelanite clan from Shelah; the Perezite clan from Perez; the Zerahite clan from Zerah.

21 The descendants of Perez: the Hezronite clan from Hezron; the Hamulite clan from Hamul.

22 These were Judah's clans numbered by their registered men: 76,500.

23 Issachar's descendants by their clans: the Tolaite clan from Tola; the Punite clan from Puvah;^A

24 the Jashubite clan from Jashub; the Shimronite clan from Shimron.

25 These were Issachar's clans numbered by their registered men: 64,300.

26 Zebulun's descendants by their clans: the Seredite clan from Sered; the Elonite clan from Elon; the Jahleelite clan from Jahleel.

27 These were the Zebulunite clans numbered by their registered men: 60,500.

28 Joseph's descendants by their clans from Manasseh and Ephraim:

29 Manasseh's descendants: the Machirite clan from Machir.

Machir fathered Gilead; the Gileadite clan from Gilead.

30 These were Gilead's descendants: the Iezerite clan from Iezer; the Helekite clan from Helek;

31 the Asrielite clan from Asriel; the Shechemite clan from Shechem;

32 the Shemidaite clan from Shemida; the Hepherite clan from Hepher;

33 Zelophehad son of Hepher had no sons — only daughters. The names of Zelophehad's daughters were Mahlah, Noah, Hoglah, Milcah, and Tirzah.   Nm 27:1-11

34 These were Manasseh's clans, numbered by their registered men: 52,700.

35 These were Ephraim's descendants by their clans: the Shuthelahite clan from Shuthelah; the Becherite clan from Becher; the Tahanite clan from Tahan.

36 These were Shuthelah's descendants: the Eranite clan from Eran.

37 These were the Ephraimite clans numbered by their registered men: 32,500. These were Joseph's descendants by their clans.

38 Benjamin's descendants by their clans: the Belaite clan from Bela; the Ashbelite clan from Ashbel;

^A 26:23 Sam, LXX, Vg, Syr read *Puite clan from Puah*; 1Ch 7:1

the Ahiramite clan
from Ahiram;
³⁹ the Shuphamite clan
from Shupham;ᴬ
the Huphamite clan
from Hupham.
⁴⁰ Bela's descendants from Ard
and Naaman:
the Ardite clan from Ard;
the Naamite clan
from Naaman.
⁴¹ These were the Benjaminite
clans numbered by their
registered men: 45,600.

⁴² These were
Dan's descendants
by their clans:
the Shuhamite clan
from Shuham.
These were the clans of Dan
by their clans.
⁴³ All the Shuhamite clans
numbered by their
registered men: 64,400.

⁴⁴ Asher's descendants
by their clans:
the Imnite clan from Imnah;
the Ishvite clan from Ishvi;
the Beriite clan from Beriah.
⁴⁵ From Beriah's descendants:
the Heberite clan from Heber;
the Malchielite clan
from Malchiel.
⁴⁶ And the name
of Asher's daughter
was Serah.
⁴⁷ These were the Asherite
clans numbered by their
registered men: 53,400.

⁴⁸ Naphtali's descendants
by their clans:
the Jahzeelite clan
from Jahzeel;

the Gunite clan from Guni;
⁴⁹ the Jezerite clan from Jezer;
the Shillemite clan
from Shillem.
⁵⁰ These were the Naphtali
clans numbered by their
registered men: 45,400.

⁵¹ These registered
Israelite men
numbered 601,730.

⁵² The LORD spoke to Moses, ⁵³ "The
land is to be divided among them as
an inheritance based on the number of names. ⁵⁴ Increase the inheritance for a large tribe and decrease
it for a small one. Each is to be given
its inheritance according to those
who were registered in it. ⁵⁵ The
land is to be divided by lot; they will
receive an inheritance according to
the names of their ancestral tribes.
⁵⁶ Each inheritance will be divided
by lot among the larger and smaller tribes." Nm 33:53-54
⁵⁷ These were the Levites
registered by their clans:
the Gershonite clan
from Gershon;
the Kohathite clan
from Kohath;
the Merarite clan
from Merari.
⁵⁸ These were the Levite family
groups:
the Libnite clan,
the Hebronite clan,
the Mahlite clan,
the Mushite clan,
and the Korahite clan. Ex 6:21,24

Kohath was the ancestor of Amram. ⁵⁹ The name of Amram's wife
was Jochebed, a descendant of Levi,
born to Levi in Egypt. She bore to

Amram: Aaron, Moses, and their sister Miriam. ⁶⁰ Nadab, Abihu, Eleazar, and Ithamar were born to Aaron, ⁶¹ but Nadab and Abihu died when they presented unauthorized fire before the LORD. ⁶² Those registered were 23,000, every male one month old or more; they were not registered among the other Israelites, because no inheritance was given to them among the Israelites.

⁶³ These were the ones registered by Moses and the priest Eleazar when they registered the Israelites on the plains of Moab by the Jordan across from Jericho. ⁶⁴ But among them there was not one of those who had been registered by Moses and the priest Aaron when they registered the Israelites in the Wilderness of Sinai. ⁶⁵ For the LORD had said to them that they would all die in the wilderness. None of them was left except Caleb son of Jephunneh and Joshua son of Nun.

A Case of Daughters' Inheritance

27 The daughters of Zelophehad approached; Zelophehad was the son of Hepher, son of Gilead, son of Machir, son of Manasseh from the clans of Manasseh, the son of Joseph. These were the names of his daughters: Mahlah, Noah, Hoglah, Milcah, and Tirzah. ² They stood before Moses, the priest Eleazar, the leaders, and the entire community at the entrance to the tent of meeting and said, ³ "Our father died in the wilderness, but he was not among Korah's followers, who gathered together against the LORD. Instead, he died because of his own sin, and he had no sons. ⁴ Why should the name of

our father be taken away from his clan? Since he had no son, give us property among our father's brothers." Nm 16:1-3,11

⁵ Moses brought their case before the LORD, ⁶ and the LORD answered him, ⁷ "What Zelophehad's daughters say is correct. You are to give them hereditary property among their father's brothers and transfer their father's inheritance to them. ⁸ Tell the Israelites: When a man dies without having a son, transfer his inheritance to his daughter. ⁹ If he has no daughter, give his inheritance to his brothers. ¹⁰ If he has no brothers, give his inheritance to his father's brothers. ¹¹ If his father has no brothers, give his inheritance to the nearest relative of his clan, and he will take possession of it. This is to be a statutory ordinance for the Israelites as the LORD commanded Moses." Jos 17:4

Joshua Commissioned to Succeed Moses

¹² Then the LORD said to Moses, "Go up this mountain of the Abarim range^A and see the land that I have given the Israelites. ¹³ After you have seen it, you will also be gathered to your people, as Aaron your brother was. ¹⁴ When the community quarreled in the Wilderness of Zin, both of you rebelled against my command to demonstrate my holiness in their sight at the waters." Those were the Waters of Meribah-kadesh^B in the Wilderness of Zin. Nm 20:22-29; Dt 32:48-51

¹⁵ So Moses appealed to the LORD, ¹⁶ "May the LORD, the God who gives breath to all,^C appoint a man over the community ¹⁷ who

^A**27:12** = Mount Nebo; Nm 33:47-48; Dt 32:49; Jr 22:20   ^B**27:14** = Quarreling   ^C**27:16** Or *God of the spirits of all flesh*

will go out before them and come back in before them, and who will bring them out and bring them in, so that the LORD's community won't be like sheep without a shepherd." Jos 14:11

18 The LORD replied to Moses, "Take Joshua son of Nun, a man who has the Spirit in him, and lay your hands on him. 19 Have him stand before the priest Eleazar and the whole community, and commission him in their sight. 20 Confer some of your authority on him so that the entire Israelite community will obey him. 21 He will stand before the priest Eleazar who will consult the LORD for him with the decision of the Urim. He and all the Israelites with him, even the entire community, will go out and come back in at his command." Dt 34:9

22 Moses did as the LORD commanded him. He took Joshua, had him stand before the priest Eleazar and the entire community, 23 laid his hands on him, and commissioned him, as the LORD had spoken through Moses.

Prescribed Offerings

28 The LORD spoke to Moses, 2 "Command the Israelites and say to them: Be sure to present to me at its appointed time my offering and my food as my fire offering, a pleasing aroma to me. 3 And say to them: This is the fire offering you are to present to the LORD:

Daily Offerings

"Each day present two unblemished year-old male lambs as a regular burnt offering. 4 Offer one lamb in the morning and the other lamb at twilight, 5 along with two quarts A of fine flour for a grain offering mixed with a quart B of olive oil from crushed olives. 6 It is a regular burnt offering established at Mount Sinai for a pleasing aroma, a fire offering to the LORD. 7 The drink offering is to be a quart with each lamb. Pour out the offering of beer to the LORD in the sanctuary area. 8 Offer the second lamb at twilight, along with the same kind of grain offering and drink offering as in the morning. It is a fire offering, a pleasing aroma to the LORD. Ex 27:20; Lv 2:1; 24:2; Nm 15:4

Sabbath Offerings

9 "On the Sabbath day present two unblemished year-old male lambs, four quarts C of fine flour mixed with oil as a grain offering, and its drink offering. 10 It is the burnt offering for every Sabbath, in addition to the regular burnt offering and its drink offering. Ezk 46:4-5

Monthly Offerings

11 "At the beginning of each of your months present a burnt offering to the LORD: two young bulls, one ram, seven male lambs a year old — all unblemished — 12 with six quarts D of fine flour mixed with oil as a grain offering for each bull, four quarts of fine flour mixed with oil as a grain offering for the ram, 13 and two quarts E of fine flour mixed with oil as a grain offering for each lamb. It is a burnt offering, a pleasing aroma, a fire offering to the LORD. 14 Their

---

A 28:5 Lit *one-tenth of an ephah*   B 28:5 Lit *a fourth of a hin*, also in v. 7   C 28:9 Lit *two-tenths* (of an ephah), also in vv. 12,20,28   D 28:12 Lit *three-tenths* (of an ephah), also in vv. 20,28   E 28:13 Lit *one-tenth* (of an ephah), also in vv. 21,29 drink offerings are to be two quarts[A] of wine with each bull, one and a third quarts[B] with the ram, and one quart[C] with each male lamb. This is the monthly burnt offering for all the months of the year. [15] And one male goat is to be offered as a sin offering to the LORD, in addition to the regular burnt offering with its drink offering. 1Sm 20:5; 1Ch 23:31; 2Ch 2:4; Ezr 3:5

Offerings for Passover

[16] "The Passover to the LORD comes in the first month, on the fourteenth day of the month. [17] On the fifteenth day of this month there will be a festival; unleavened bread is to be eaten for seven days. [18] On the first day there is to be a sacred assembly; you are not to do any daily work. [19] Present a fire offering, a burnt offering to the LORD: two young bulls, one ram, and seven male lambs a year old. Your animals are to be unblemished. [20] The grain offering with them is to be of fine flour mixed with oil; offer six quarts with each bull and four quarts with the ram. [21] Offer two quarts with each of the seven lambs [22] and one male goat for a sin offering to make atonement for yourselves. [23] Offer these with the morning burnt offering that is part of the regular burnt offering. [24] You are to offer the same food each day for seven days as a fire offering, a pleasing aroma to the LORD. It is to be offered with its drink offering and the regular burnt offering. [25] On the seventh day you are to hold a sacred assembly; you are not to do any daily work. Ex 12:18; Lv 23:5-6; Ezk 45:21

Offerings for the Festival of Weeks

[26] "On the day of firstfruits, you are to hold a sacred assembly when you present an offering of new grain to the LORD at your Festival of Weeks; you are not to do any daily work. [27] Present a burnt offering for a pleasing aroma to the LORD: two young bulls, one ram, and seven male lambs a year old, [28] with their grain offering of fine flour mixed with oil, six quarts with each bull, four quarts with the ram, [29] and two quarts with each of the seven lambs, [30] and one male goat to make atonement for yourselves. [31] Offer them with their drink offerings in addition to the regular burnt offering and its grain offering. Your animals are to be unblemished. Ex 23:16; 34:22; Lv 23:10,15; Dt 16:9-10; Ac 2:1

Festival of Trumpets Offerings

29 "You are to hold a sacred assembly in the seventh month, on the first day of the month, and you are not to do any daily work. This will be a day of trumpet blasts for you. [2] Offer a burnt offering as a pleasing aroma to the LORD: one young bull, one ram, seven male lambs a year old — all unblemished — [3] with their grain offering of fine flour mixed with oil, six quarts[D] with the bull, four quarts[E] with the ram, [4] and two quarts[F] with each of the seven male lambs. [5] Also offer one male goat as a sin offering to make atonement

---

[A] 28:14 Lit a half hin   [B] 28:14 Lit bull, a third hin   [C] 28:14 Lit a fourth hin   [D] 29:3 Lit three-tenths (of an ephah), also in vv. 9,14   [E] 29:3 Lit two-tenths (of an ephah), also in vv. 9,14   [F] 29:4 Lit one-tenth (of an ephah), also in vv. 10,15 for yourselves. [6] These are in addition to the monthly and regular burnt offerings with their prescribed grain offerings and drink offerings. They are a pleasing aroma, a fire offering to the LORD.

Offerings for the Day of Atonement

[7] "You are to hold a sacred assembly on the tenth day of this seventh month and practice self-denial; do not do any work. [8] Present a burnt offering to the LORD, a pleasing aroma: one young bull, one ram, and seven male lambs a year old. All your animals are to be unblemished. [9] Their grain offering is to be of fine flour mixed with oil, six quarts with the bull, four quarts with the ram, [10] and two quarts with each of the seven lambs. [11] Offer one male goat for a sin offering. The regular burnt offering with its grain offering and drink offerings are in addition to the sin offering of atonement.   Lv 23:27-28

Offerings for the Festival of Shelters

[12] "You are to hold a sacred assembly on the fifteenth day of the seventh month; you do not do any daily work. You are to celebrate a seven-day festival for the LORD. [13] Present a burnt offering, a fire offering as a pleasing aroma to the LORD: thirteen young bulls, two rams, and fourteen male lambs a year old. They are to be unblemished. [14] Their grain offering is to be of fine flour mixed with oil, six quarts with each of the thirteen bulls, four quarts with each of the two rams, [15] and two quarts with each of the fourteen lambs. [16] Also offer one male goat as a sin offering.

These are in addition to the regular burnt offering with its grain and drink offerings.   Lv 23:34-35

[17] "On the second day present twelve young bulls, two rams, and fourteen male lambs a year old — all unblemished — [18] with their grain and drink offerings for the bulls, rams, and lambs, in proportion to their number. [19] Also offer one male goat as a sin offering. These are in addition to the regular burnt offering with its grain and drink and their drink offerings.

[20] "On the third day present eleven bulls, two rams, fourteen male lambs a year old — all unblemished — [21] with their grain and drink offerings for the bulls, rams, and lambs, in proportion to their number. [22] Also offer one male goat as a sin offering. These are in addition to the regular burnt offering with its grain and drink offerings.

[23] "On the fourth day present ten bulls, two rams, fourteen male lambs a year old — all unblemished — [24] with their grain and drink offerings for the bulls, rams, and lambs, in proportion to their number. [25] Also offer one male goat as a sin offering. These are in addition to the regular burnt offering with its grain and drink offerings.

[26] "On the fifth day present nine bulls, two rams, fourteen male lambs a year old — all unblemished — [27] with their grain and drink offerings for the bulls, rams, and lambs, in proportion to their number. [28] Also offer one male goat as a sin offering. These are in addition to the regular burnt offering with its grain and drink offerings.

[29] "On the sixth day present eight bulls, two rams, fourteen male lambs a year old — all

unblemished — [30] with their grain and drink offerings for the bulls, rams, and lambs, in proportion to their number. [31] Also offer one male goat as a sin offering. These are in addition to the regular burnt offering with its grain and drink offerings.

[32] "On the seventh day present seven bulls, two rams, and fourteen male lambs a year old — all unblemished — [33] with their grain and drink offerings for the bulls, rams, and lambs, in proportion to their number. [34] Also offer one male goat as a sin offering. These are in addition to the regular burnt offering with its grain and drink offerings.

[35] "On the eighth day you are to hold a solemn assembly; you are not to do any daily work. [36] Present a burnt offering, a fire offering as a pleasing aroma to the LORD: one bull, one ram, seven male lambs a year old — all unblemished — [37] with their grain and drink offerings for the bulls, rams, and lambs, in proportion to their number. [38] Also offer one male goat as a sin offering. These are in addition to the regular burnt offering with its grain and drink offerings.

[39] "Offer these to the LORD at your appointed times in addition to your vow and freewill offerings, whether burnt, grain, drink, or fellowship offerings." [40] So Moses told the Israelites everything the LORD had commanded him.

Regulations About Vows

30 Moses told the leaders of the Israelite tribes, "This is what the LORD has commanded: [2] When a man makes a vow to the LORD or swears an oath to put himself under an obligation, he must not break his word; he must do whatever he has promised. Dt 23:21; 1Kg 8:1

[3] "When a woman in her father's house during her youth makes a vow to the LORD or puts herself under an obligation, [4] and her father hears about her vow or the obligation she put herself under, and he says nothing to her, all her vows and every obligation she put herself under are binding. [5] But if her father prohibits her on the day he hears about it, none of her vows and none of the obligations she put herself under are binding. The LORD will release her because her father has prohibited her.

[6] "If a woman marries while her vows or the rash commitment she herself made are binding, [7] and her husband hears about it and says nothing to her when he finds out, her vows are binding, and the obligations she put herself under are binding. [8] But if her husband prohibits her when he hears about it, he will cancel her vow that is binding or the rash commitment she herself made, and the LORD will release her.

[9] "Every vow a widow or divorced woman puts herself under is binding on her.

[10] "If a woman in her husband's house has made a vow or put herself under an obligation with an oath, [11] and her husband hears about it, says nothing to her, and does not prohibit her, all her vows are binding, and every obligation she put herself under is binding. [12] But if her husband cancels them on the day he hears about it, nothing that came from her lips, whether her vows or her obligation, is binding. Her husband has canceled them, and the LORD will release her. [13] Her husband may confirm

or cancel any vow or any sworn obligation to deny herself. [14] If her husband says nothing at all to her from day to day, he confirms all her vows and obligations, which are binding. He has confirmed them because he said nothing to her when he heard about them. [15] But if he cancels them after he hears about them, he will be responsible for her commitment."[A]

[16] These are the statutes that the LORD commanded Moses concerning the relationship between a man and his wife, or between a father and his daughter in his house during her youth.

War with Midian

31 The LORD spoke to Moses, [2] "Execute vengeance for the Israelites against the Midianites. After that, you will be gathered to your people."   Nm 20:24-26; 27:13; Dt 32:50

[3] So Moses spoke to the people, "Equip some of your men for war. They will go against Midian to inflict the LORD's vengeance on them. [4] Send one thousand men to war from each Israelite tribe." [5] So one thousand were recruited from each Israelite tribe out of the thousands[B] in Israel — twelve thousand equipped for war. [6] Moses sent one thousand from each tribe to war. They went with Phinehas son of Eleazar the priest, in whose care were the holy objects and signal trumpets. Ps 18:47; 79:10; 94:1

[7] They waged war against Midian, as the LORD had commanded Moses, and killed every male. [8] Along with the others slain by them, they killed the Midianite kings — Evi, Rekem, Zur, Hur, and Reba, the five kings of Midian. They also killed Balaam son of Beor with the sword. [9] The Israelites took the Midianite women and their dependents captive, and they plundered all their cattle, flocks, and property. [10] Then they burned all the cities where the Midianites lived, as well as all their encampments, [11] and took away all the spoils of war and the captives, both people and animals. [12] They brought the prisoners, animals, and spoils of war to Moses, the priest Eleazar, and the Israelite community at the camp on the plains of Moab by the Jordan across from Jericho.   Gn 34:25

[13] Moses, the priest Eleazar, and all the leaders of the community went to meet them outside the camp. [14] But Moses became furious with the officers, the commanders of thousands and commanders of hundreds, who were returning from the military campaign. [15] "Have you let every female live?" he asked them. [16] "Yet they are the ones who, at Balaam's advice, incited the Israelites to unfaithfulness against the LORD in the Peor incident, so that the plague came against the LORD's community. [17] So now, kill every male among the dependents and kill every woman who has gone to bed with a man, [18] but keep alive for yourselves all the young females who have not gone to bed with a man.   Nm 25; 2Pt 2:15

[19] "You are to remain outside the camp for seven days. All of you and your prisoners who have killed a person or touched the dead are to purify yourselves on the third day and the seventh day. [20] Also purify everything: garments, leather goods, things made of goat hair, and every article of wood."   Lv 11:31

[A]30:15 Or *will bear her guilt*   [B]31:5 Or *clans*

²¹ Then the priest Eleazar said to the soldiers who had gone to battle, "This is the legal statute the LORD commanded Moses: ²² The gold, silver, bronze, iron, tin, and lead — ²³ everything that can withstand fire — you are to pass through fire, and it will be clean. It must still be purified with the purification water. Anything that cannot withstand fire, pass through the water. ²⁴ On the seventh day wash your clothes, and you will be clean. After that you may enter the camp." Ex 19:10; Nm 14:8; 19:1-9,17-20

²⁵ The LORD told Moses, ²⁶ "You, the priest Eleazar, and the family heads of the community are to take a count of what was captured, people and animals. ²⁷ Then divide the captives between the troops who went out to war and the entire community. ²⁸ Set aside a tribute for the LORD from what belongs to the fighting men who went out to war: one out of every five hundred people, cattle, donkeys, sheep, and goats. ²⁹ Take the tribute from their half and give it to the priest Eleazar as a contribution to the LORD. ³⁰ From the Israelites' half, take one out of every fifty from the people, cattle, donkeys, sheep, and goats, all the livestock, and give them to the Levites who perform the duties of ᴬ the LORD's tabernacle." 1Sm 30:24

³¹ So Moses and the priest Eleazar did as the LORD commanded Moses. ³² The captives remaining from the plunder the army had taken totaled:

    675,000 sheep and goats,
³³ 72,000 cattle,
³⁴ 61,000 donkeys,
³⁵ and 32,000 people,
    all the females

who had not gone to bed with a man.

³⁶ The half portion for those who went out to war numbered:

    337,500 sheep and goats,
³⁷ and the tribute to the LORD
    was 675
    from the sheep and goats;
³⁸ from the 36,000 cattle,
    the tribute to the LORD
    was 72;
³⁹ from the 30,500 donkeys,
    the tribute to the LORD
    was 61;
⁴⁰ and from the 16,000 people,
    the tribute to the LORD
    was 32 people.

⁴¹ Moses gave the tribute to the priest Eleazar as a contribution for the LORD, as the LORD had commanded Moses.

⁴² From the Israelites' half, which Moses separated from the men who fought, ⁴³ the community's half was:

    337,500 sheep and goats,
⁴⁴ 36,000 cattle,
⁴⁵ 30,500 donkeys,
⁴⁶ and 16,000 people.

⁴⁷ Moses took one out of every fifty, selected from the people and the livestock of the Israelites' half. He gave them to the Levites who perform the duties of the LORD's tabernacle, as the LORD had commanded him.

⁴⁸ The officers who were over the thousands of the army, the commanders of thousands and of hundreds, approached Moses ⁴⁹ and told him, "Your servants have taken a census of the fighting men under our command, and not one of us is missing. ⁵⁰ So we have presented to the LORD an offering of the gold

ᴬ **31:30** Or *who protect*

articles each man found — arm-
lets, bracelets, rings, earrings, and
necklaces — to make atonement
for ourselves before the LORD."

⁵¹ Moses and the priest Eleazar
received from them all the articles
made out of gold. ⁵² All the gold of
the contribution they offered to
the LORD, from the commanders
of thousands and of hundreds, was
420 pounds.ᴬ ⁵³ Each of the soldiers had taken plunder for himself. ⁵⁴ Moses and the priest Eleazar
received the gold from the commanders of thousands and of hundreds and brought it into the tent
of meeting as a memorial for the
Israelites before the LORD.   Dt 20:14

Transjordan Settlements

32 The Reubenites and Gadites had a very large number
of livestock. When they surveyed
the lands of Jazer and Gilead, they
saw that the region was a good
one for livestock. ² So the Gadites
and Reubenites came to Moses,
the priest Eleazar, and the leaders of the community and said:
³ "The territory of Ataroth, Dibon,
Jazer, Nimrah, Heshbon, Elealeh,
Sebam, ᴮ Nebo, and Beon, ⁴ which
the LORD struck down before the
community of Israel, is good land
for livestock, and your servants
own livestock." ⁵ They said, "If we
have found favor with you, let this
land be given to your servants as
a possession. Don't make us cross
the Jordan." Nm 21:32; Jos 13:25; 21:39; 33:47

⁶ But Moses asked the Gadites and
Reubenites, "Should your brothers go to war while you stay here?
⁷ Why are you discouraging the Israelites from crossing into the land
the LORD has given them? ⁸ That's

what your fathers did when I sent
them from Kadesh-barnea to see
the land. ⁹ After they went up as
far as Eshcol Valley and saw the
land, they discouraged the Israelites from entering the land the
LORD had given them. ¹⁰ So the
LORD's anger burned that day, and
he swore an oath: ¹¹ 'Because they
did not remain loyal to me, none of
the men twenty years old or more
who came up from Egypt will see
the land I swore to give Abraham,
Isaac, and Jacob — ¹² none except
Caleb son of Jephunneh the Kenizzite and Joshua son of Nun, because they did remain loyal to the
LORD.' ¹³ The LORD's anger burned
against Israel, and he made them
wander in the wilderness forty
years until the whole generation
that had done what was evil in the
LORD's sight was gone. ¹⁴ And here
you, a brood of sinners, stand in
your fathers' place adding even
more to the LORD's burning anger
against Israel. ¹⁵ If you turn back
from following him, he will once
again leave this people in the wilderness, and you will destroy all
of them." Nm 13:1-3, 32-33; Dt 1:22-28, 34-36

¹⁶ Then they approached him
and said, "We want to build sheep
pens here for our livestock and cities for our dependents. ¹⁷ But we
will arm ourselves and be ready
to go ahead of the Israelites until
we have brought them into their
place. Meanwhile, our dependents
will remain in the fortified cities
because of the inhabitants of the
land. ¹⁸ We will not return to our
homes until each of the Israelites
has taken possession of his inheritance. ¹⁹ Yet we will not have an
inheritance with them across the

ᴬ**31:52** Lit *16,750 shekels*   ᴮ**32:3** Sam, LXX read *Sibmah* (v. 38); Syr reads *Sebah*

Jordan and beyond, because our inheritance will be across the Jordan to the east." Dt 3:18; Jos 1:13-15; 4:12-13

²⁰ Moses replied to them, "If you do this — if you arm yourselves for battle before the LORD, ²¹ and every one of your armed men crosses the Jordan before the LORD until he has driven his enemies from his presence, ²² and the land is subdued before the LORD — afterward you may return and be free from obligation to the LORD and to Israel. And this land will belong to you as a possession before the LORD. ²³ But if you don't do this, you will certainly sin against the LORD; be sure your sin will catch up with you. ²⁴ Build cities for your dependents and pens for your flocks, but do what you have promised."

²⁵ The Gadites and Reubenites answered Moses, "Your servants will do just as my lord commands. ²⁶ Our dependents, wives, livestock, and all our animals will remain here in the cities of Gilead, ²⁷ but your servants are equipped for war before the LORD and will go across to the battle as my lord orders."

²⁸ So Moses gave orders about them to the priest Eleazar, Joshua son of Nun, and the family heads of the Israelite tribes. ²⁹ Moses told them, "If the Gadites and Reubenites cross the Jordan with you, every man in battle formation before the LORD, and the land is subdued before you, you are to give them the land of Gilead as a possession. ³⁰ But if they don't go across with you in battle formation, they must accept land in Canaan with you." Jos 22:9

³¹ The Gadites and Reubenites replied, "What the LORD has spoken to your servants is what we will do. ³² We will cross over in battle formation before the LORD into the land of Canaan, but we will keep our hereditary possession across the Jordan."

³³ So Moses gave them — the Gadites, Reubenites, and half the tribe of Manasseh son of Joseph — the kingdom of King Sihon of the Amorites and the kingdom of King Og of Bashan, the land including its cities with the territories surrounding them. ³⁴ The Gadites rebuilt Dibon, Ataroth, Aroer, ³⁵ Atroth-shophan, Jazer, Jogbehah, ³⁶ Beth-nimrah, and Beth-haran as fortified cities, and built sheep pens. ³⁷ The Reubenites rebuilt Heshbon, Elealeh, Kiriathaim, ³⁸ as well as Nebo and Baal-meon (whose names were changed), and Sibmah. They gave names to the cities they rebuilt. Dt 3:12-17; 29:8; Jos 12:6

³⁹ The descendants of Machir son of Manasseh went to Gilead, captured it, and drove out the Amorites who were there. ⁴⁰ So Moses gave Gilead to the clan of Machir son of Manasseh, and they settled in it. ⁴¹ Jair, a descendant of Manasseh, went and captured their villages, which he renamed Jair's Villages.ᴬ ⁴² Nobah went and captured Kenath with its surrounding villages and called it Nobah after his own name. Gn 50:23; Nm 26:29; Jos 17:1,3

Wilderness Travels Reviewed

33 These were the stages of the Israelites' journey when they went out of the land of Egypt by their military divisions under the leadership of Moses and Aaron. ² At the LORD's command, Moses wrote down the starting points for

ᴬ 32:41 Or *renamed Havvoth-jair*

the stages of their journey; these are the stages listed by their starting points:

³ They traveled from Rameses in the first month, on the fifteenth day of the month. On the day after the Passover the Israelites went out defiantly^A in the sight of all the Egyptians. ⁴ Meanwhile, the Egyptians were burying every firstborn male the LORD had struck down among them, for the LORD had executed judgment against their gods. ⁵ The Israelites traveled from Rameses and camped at Succoth.   Gn 47:11; Ex 1:1-48
⁶ They traveled from Succoth and camped at Etham, which is on the edge of the wilderness. ⁷ They traveled from Etham and turned back to Pi-hahiroth, which faces Baal-zephon, and they camped before Migdol. ⁸ They traveled from Pi-hahiroth^B and crossed through the middle of the sea into the wilderness. They took a three-day journey into the Wilderness of Etham and camped at Marah.   Ex 14:22-26
⁹ They traveled from Marah and came to Elim. There were twelve springs and seventy date palms at Elim, so they camped there.   Ex 15:27; 16:1
¹⁰ They traveled from Elim and camped by the Red Sea. ¹¹ They traveled from the Red Sea and camped in the Wilderness of Sin.   Ex 17:1
¹² They traveled from the Wilderness of Sin and camped in Dophkah.

¹³ They traveled from Dophkah and camped at Alush. ¹⁴ They traveled from Alush and camped at Rephidim, where there was no water for the people to drink.   Ex 17:1,1-8; 19:2
¹⁵ They traveled from Rephidim and camped in the Wilderness of Sinai.   Ex 19:1-2
¹⁶ They traveled from the Wilderness of Sinai and camped at Kibroth-hattaavah. ¹⁷ They traveled from Kibroth-hattaavah and camped at Hazeroth.   Nm 11:35; 12:16; Dt 1:1
¹⁸ They traveled from Hazeroth and camped at Rithmah. ¹⁹ They traveled from Rithmah and camped at Rimmon-perez. ²⁰ They traveled from Rimmon-perez and camped at Libnah. ²¹ They traveled from Libnah and camped at Rissah. ²² They traveled from Rissah and camped at Kehelathah. ²³ They traveled from Kehelathah and camped at Mount Shepher. ²⁴ They traveled from Mount Shepher and camped at Haradah. ²⁵ They traveled from Haradah and camped at Makheloth. ²⁶ They traveled from Makheloth and camped at Tahath. ²⁷ They traveled from Tahath and camped at Terah. ²⁸ They traveled from Terah and camped at Mithkah. ²⁹ They traveled from Mithkah and camped at Hashmonah. ³⁰ They traveled from Hashmonah and camped at Moseroth.

^A33:3 Lit *with a raised hand*; Ex 14:8   ^B33:8 Some Hb mss, Sam, Syr, Vg; other Hb mss read *from before Hahiroth*

³¹ They traveled from Moseroth and camped at Bene-jaakan. ³² They traveled from Bene-jaakan and camped at Hor-haggidgad. ³³ They traveled from Hor-haggidgad and camped at Jotbathah. ³⁴ They traveled from Jotbathah and camped at Abronah. ³⁵ They traveled from Abronah and camped at Ezion-geber. ³⁶ They traveled from Ezion-geber and camped in the Wilderness of Zin (that is, Kadesh).   Nm 10:12

³⁷ They traveled from Kadesh and camped at Mount Hor on the edge of the land of Edom. ³⁸ At the LORD's command, the priest Aaron climbed Mount Hor and died there on the first day of the fifth month in the fortieth year after the Israelites went out of the land of Egypt. ³⁹ Aaron was 123 years old when he died on Mount Hor. ⁴⁰ At that time the Canaanite king of Arad, who lived in the Negev in the land of Canaan, heard the Israelites were coming.   Nm 21:4; 33:37-41; Dt 32:50

⁴¹ They traveled from Mount Hor and camped at Zalmonah. ⁴² They traveled from Zalmonah and camped at Punon. ⁴³ They traveled from Punon and camped at Oboth.   Nm 21:10-11

⁴⁴ They traveled from Oboth and camped at Iye-abarim on the border of Moab.   Nm 21:11

⁴⁵ They traveled from Iyim ᴬ and camped at Dibon-gad. ⁴⁶ They traveled from Dibon-gad and camped at Almon-diblathaim.   Jr 48:22

⁴⁷ They traveled from Almon-diblathaim and camped in the Abarim range facing Nebo. ⁴⁸ They traveled from the Abarim range and camped on the plains of Moab by the Jordan across from Jericho. ⁴⁹ They camped by the Jordan from Beth-jeshimoth to the Acacia Meadow ᴮ on the plains of Moab.

Instructions for Occupying Canaan

⁵⁰ The LORD spoke to Moses in the plains of Moab by the Jordan across from Jericho, ⁵¹ "Tell the Israelites: When you cross the Jordan into the land of Canaan, ⁵² you must drive out all the inhabitants of the land before you, destroy all their stone images and cast images, and demolish all their high places. ⁵³ You are to take possession of the land and settle in it because I have given you the land to possess. ⁵⁴ You are to receive the land as an inheritance by lot according to your clans. Increase the inheritance for a large clan and decrease it for a small one. Whatever place the lot indicates for someone will be his. You will receive an inheritance according to your ancestral tribes. ⁵⁵ But if you don't drive out the inhabitants of the land before you, those you allow to remain will become barbs for your eyes and thorns for your sides; they will harass you in the land where you will live. ⁵⁶ And what I had planned to do to them, I will do to you."   Lv 26:1; 34:17

Boundaries of the Promised Land

34 The LORD spoke to Moses, ² "Command the Israelites and say to them: When you enter the land of Canaan, it will be

---

ᴬ **33:45** A shortened form of Iye-abarim   ᴮ **33:49** Or *to Abel-shittim* allotted to you as an inheritance[A] with these borders:

[3] Your southern side will be from the Wilderness of Zin along the boundary of Edom. Your southern border on the east will begin at the east end of the Dead Sea. [4] Your border will turn south of the Scorpions' Ascent,[B] proceed to Zin, and end south of Kadesh-barnea. It will go to Hazar-addar and proceed to Azmon. [5] The border will turn from Azmon to the Brook of Egypt, where it will end at the Mediterranean Sea. Jos 15:3

[6] Your western border will be the coastline of the Mediterranean Sea; this will be your western border.

[7] This will be your northern border: From the Mediterranean Sea draw a line to Mount Hor; [8] from Mount Hor draw a line to the entrance of Hamath,[C] and the border will reach Zedad. [9] Then the border will go to Ziphron and end at Hazar-enan. This will be your northern border. Nm 20:22-28; 2Ch 7:8

[10] For your eastern border, draw a line from Hazar-enan to Shepham. [11] The border will go down from Shepham to Riblah east of Ain. It will continue down and reach the eastern slope of the Sea of Chinnereth.[D] [12] Then the border will go down to the Jordan and end at the Dead Sea. This will be your land defined by its borders on all sides." Jos 12:3; 13:27; 15:32; Lk 5:1

[13] So Moses commanded the Israelites, "This is the land you are to receive by lot as an inheritance, which the LORD commanded to be given to the nine and a half tribes. [14] For the tribe of Reuben's descendants and the tribe of Gad's descendants have received their inheritance according to their ancestral families,[E] and half the tribe of Manasseh has received its inheritance. [15] The two and a half tribes have received their inheritance across the Jordan east of Jericho, toward the sunrise." Nm 32:33

Leaders for Distributing the Land

[16] The LORD spoke to Moses, [17] "These are the names of the men who are to distribute the land as an inheritance for you: the priest Eleazar and Joshua son of Nun. [18] Take one leader from each tribe to distribute the land. [19] These are the names of the men:

Caleb son of Jephunneh from the tribe of Judah; Nm 14:6,24,30,38 [20] Shemuel son of Ammihud from the tribe of Simeon's descendants; [21] Elidad son of Chislon from the tribe of Benjamin; [22] Bukki son of Jogli, a leader from the tribe of Dan's descendants; [23] from the sons of Joseph: Hanniel son of Ephod, a leader from the tribe of Manasseh's descendants, [24] Kemuel son of Shiphtan, a leader from the tribe of Ephraim's descendants; [25] Eli-zaphan son of Parnach, a leader from the tribe of Zebulun's descendants;

[A]34:2 Lit inheritance—the land of Canaan   [B]34:4 Lit of Scorpions; Jos 15:3; Jdg 1:36   [C]34:8 Or to Lebo-hamath   [D]34:11 = the Sea of Galilee; Jos 12:3; 13:27; Lk 5:1   [E]34:14 Lit the house of their fathers

²⁶ Paltiel son of Azzan, a leader from the tribe of Issachar's descendants;
²⁷ Ahihud son of Shelomi, a leader from the tribe of Asher's descendants;
²⁸ Pedahel son of Ammihud, a leader from the tribe of Naphtali's descendants."
²⁹ These are the ones the LORD commanded to distribute the inheritance to the Israelites in the land of Canaan.

Cities for the Levites

35 The LORD again spoke to Moses in the plains of Moab by the Jordan across from Jericho: ² "Command the Israelites to give cities out of their hereditary property for the Levites to live in and pastureland around the cities. ³ The cities will be for them to live in, and their pasturelands will be for their herds, flocks, and all their other animals. ⁴ The pasturelands of the cities you are to give the Levites will extend from the city wall five hundred yards[A] on every side. ⁵ Measure a thousand yards[B] outside the city for the east side, a thousand yards for the south side, a thousand yards for the west side, and a thousand yards for the north side, with the city in the center. This will belong to them as pasturelands for the cities. Nm 22:1
⁶ "The cities you give the Levites will include six cities of refuge, which you will provide so that the one who kills someone may flee there; in addition to these, give forty-two other cities. ⁷ The total number of cities you give the Levites will be forty-eight, along with their pasturelands. ⁸ Of the cities that you give from the Israelites' territory, you should take more from a larger tribe and less from a smaller one. Each tribe is to give some of its cities to the Levites in proportion to the inheritance it receives."

Cities of Refuge

⁹ The LORD said to Moses, ¹⁰ "Speak to the Israelites and tell them: When you cross the Jordan into the land of Canaan, ¹¹ designate cities to serve as cities of refuge for you, so that a person who kills someone unintentionally may flee there. ¹² You will have the cities as a refuge from the avenger, so that the one who kills someone will not die until he stands trial before the assembly. ¹³ The cities you select will be your six cities of refuge. ¹⁴ Select three cities across the Jordan and three cities in the land of Canaan to be cities of refuge. ¹⁵ These six cities will serve as a refuge for the Israelites and for the alien or temporary resident among them, so that anyone who kills a person unintentionally may flee there.

¹⁶ "If anyone strikes a person with an iron object and death results, he is a murderer; the murderer must be put to death. ¹⁷ If anyone has in his hand a stone capable of causing death and strikes another person and he dies, the murderer must be put to death. ¹⁸ If anyone has in his hand a wooden object capable of causing death and strikes another person and he dies, the murderer must be put to death. ¹⁹ The avenger of blood himself is to kill the murderer; when he finds him, he is to kill him. ²⁰ Likewise, if anyone in hatred pushes a person or throws an object at him with

A**35:4** Lit *1,000 cubits*   B**35:5** Lit *2,000 cubits*

malicious intent and he dies, [21] or if in hostility he strikes him with his hand and he dies, the one who struck him must be put to death; he is a murderer. The avenger of blood is to kill the murderer when he finds him. Ex 21:12-14; Lv 24:17; Dt 19:11-12

[22] "But if anyone suddenly pushes a person without hostility or throws any object at him without malicious intent [23] or without looking drops a stone that could kill a person and he dies, but he was not his enemy and didn't intend to harm him, [24] the assembly is to judge between the person who kills someone and the avenger of blood according to these ordinances. [25] The assembly is to protect the one who kills someone from the avenger of blood. Then the assembly will return him to the city of refuge he fled to, and he must live there until the death of the high priest who was anointed with the holy oil. Ex 21:13

[26] "If the one who kills someone ever goes outside the border of the city of refuge he fled to, [27] and the avenger of blood finds him outside the border of his city of refuge and kills him, the avenger will not be guilty of bloodshed, [28] for the one who killed a person was supposed to live in his city of refuge until the death of the high priest. Only after the death of the high priest may the one who has killed a person return to the land he possesses. [29] These instructions will be a statutory ordinance for you throughout your generations wherever you live.

[30] "If anyone kills a person, the murderer is to be put to death based on the word of witnesses. But no one is to be put to death based on the testimony of one witness. [31] You are not to accept a ransom for the life of someone who is guilty of murder; he must be put to death. [32] Neither should you accept a ransom for the person who flees to his city of refuge, allowing him to return and live in the land before the death of the high priest. Dt 17:6

[33] "Do not defile the land where you live, for bloodshed defiles the land, and there can be no atonement for the land because of the blood that is shed on it, except by the blood of the person who shed it. [34] Do not make the land unclean where you live and where I dwell; for I, the LORD, reside among the Israelites." Ps 106:38; Is 24:5; Jr 3:9

The Inheritance of Zelophehad's Daughters

36 The family heads from the clan of the descendants of Gilead — the son of Machir, son of Manasseh — who were from the clans of the sons of Joseph, approached and addressed Moses and the leaders who were heads of the Israelite families. [2] They said, "The LORD commanded my lord to give the land as an inheritance by lot to the Israelites. My lord was further commanded by the LORD to give our brother Zelophehad's inheritance to his daughters. [3] If they marry any of the men from the other Israelite tribes, their inheritance will be taken away from our fathers' inheritance and added to that of the tribe into which they marry. Therefore, part of our allotted inheritance would be taken away. [4] When the Jubilee comes for the Israelites, their inheritance will be added to that of the tribe into which they marry, and their inheritance will be taken away from the inheritance of our ancestral tribe." <small>Nm 26:29,33; 27:1-11</small>

⁵ So Moses commanded the Israelites at the word of the LORD, "What the tribe of Joseph's descendants says is right. ⁶ This is what the LORD has commanded concerning Zelophehad's daughters: They may marry anyone they like provided they marry within a clan of their ancestral tribe. ⁷ No inheritance belonging to the Israelites is to transfer from tribe to tribe, because each of the Israelites is to retain the inheritance of his ancestral tribe. ⁸ Any daughter who possesses an inheritance from an Israelite tribe must marry someone from the clan of her ancestral tribe, so that each of the Israelites

will possess the inheritance of his fathers. ⁹ No inheritance is to transfer from one tribe to another, because each of the Israelite tribes is to retain its inheritance." <small>Lv 25:23-24</small>

¹⁰ The daughters of Zelophehad did as the LORD commanded Moses. ¹¹ Mahlah, Tirzah, Hoglah, Milcah, and Noah, the daughters of Zelophehad, married cousins on their father's side. ¹² They married men from the clans of the descendants of Manasseh son of Joseph, and their inheritance remained within the tribe of their father's clan.

¹³ These are the commands and ordinances the LORD commanded the Israelites through Moses in the plains of Moab by the Jordan across from Jericho.

DEUTERONOMY

Introduction

1 These are the words Moses spoke to all Israel across the Jordan in the wilderness, in the Arabah opposite Suph,[A] between Paran and Tophel, Laban, Hazeroth, and Di-zahab. ² It is an eleven-day journey from Horeb to Kadesh-barnea by way of Mount Seir. ³ In the fortieth year, in the eleventh month, on the first of the month, Moses told the Israelites everything the LORD had commanded him to say to them. ⁴ This was after he had defeated King Sihon of the Amorites, who lived in Heshbon, and King Og of Bashan, who lived in Ashtaroth, at Edrei. ⁵ Across the Jordan in the land of Moab, Moses began to explain this law, saying: Gn 50:10-11; 11:30

Departure from Horeb

⁶ "The LORD our God spoke to us at Horeb: 'You have stayed at this mountain long enough. ⁷ Resume your journey and go to the hill country of the Amorites and their neighbors in the Arabah, the hill country, the Judean foothills,[B] the Negev and the sea coast — to the land of the Canaanites and to Lebanon as far as the great river, the Euphrates River. ⁸ See, I have set the land before you. Enter and take possession of the land the LORD swore to give to your fathers Abraham, Isaac, and Jacob and their future descendants.'

Leaders for the Tribes

⁹ "I said to you at that time: I can't bear the responsibility for you on my own. ¹⁰ The LORD your God has so multiplied you that today you are as numerous as the stars of the sky. ¹¹ May the LORD, the God of your fathers, increase you a thousand times more, and bless you as he promised you. ¹² But how can I bear your troubles, burdens, and disputes by myself? ¹³ Appoint for yourselves wise, understanding, and respected men from each of your tribes, and I will make them your leaders. Gn 22:17; 26:4; Ex 32:13

¹⁴ "You replied to me, 'What you propose to do is good.'

¹⁵ "So I took the leaders of your tribes, wise and respected men, and set them over you as leaders: commanders for thousands, hundreds, fifties, and tens, and officers for your tribes. ¹⁶ I commanded your judges at that time: Hear the cases between your brothers, and judge rightly between a man and his brother or his resident alien. ¹⁷ Do not show partiality when deciding a case; listen to small and great alike. Do not be intimidated by anyone, for judgment belongs to God. Bring me any case too difficult for you, and I will hear it. ¹⁸ At that time I commanded you about all the things you were to do. Lv 19:15

Israel's Disobedience at Kadesh-barnea

¹⁹ "We then set out from Horeb and went across all the great and terrible wilderness you saw on the way to the hill country of the Amorites, just as the LORD our God had

A1:1 LXX, Tg, Vg read *the Red Sea*   B1:7 Or *the Shephelah* commanded us. When we reached Kadesh-barnea, ²⁰ I said to you: You have reached the hill country of the Amorites, which the LORD our God is giving us. ²¹ See, the LORD your God has set the land before you. Go up and take possession of it as the LORD, the God of your fathers, has told you. Do not be afraid or discouraged.

²² "Then all of you approached me and said, 'Let's send men ahead of us, so that they may explore the land for us and bring us back a report about the route we should go up and the cities we will come to.' ²³ The plan seemed good to me, so I selected twelve men from among you, one man for each tribe. ²⁴ They left and went up into the hill country and came to the Valley of Eshcol, scouting the land. ²⁵ They took some of the fruit from the land in their hands, carried it down to us, and brought us back a report: 'The land the LORD our God is giving us is good.' Nm 13–14; Dt 8:7

²⁶ "But you were not willing to go up. You rebelled against the command of the LORD your God. ²⁷ You grumbled in your tents and said, 'The LORD brought us out of the land of Egypt to hand us over to the Amorites in order to destroy us, because he hates us. ²⁸ Where can we go? Our brothers have made us lose heart,^A saying: The people are larger and taller than we are; the cities are large, fortified to the heavens. We also saw the descendants of the Anakim there.' Ps 106:25

²⁹ "So I said to you: Don't be terrified or afraid of them! ³⁰ The LORD your God who goes before you will fight for you, just as you saw him do for you in Egypt. ³¹ And you saw in the wilderness how the LORD your God carried you as a man carries his son all along the way you traveled until you reached this place. ³² But in spite of this you did not trust the LORD your God, ³³ who went before you on the journey to seek out a place for you to camp. He went in the fire by night and in the cloud by day to guide you on the road you were to travel. Dt 31:6

³⁴ "When the LORD heard your^B words, he grew angry and swore an oath: ³⁵ 'None of these men in this evil generation will see the good land I swore to give your fathers, ³⁶ except Caleb the son of Jephunneh. He will see it, and I will give him and his descendants the land on which he has set foot, because he remained loyal to the LORD.' Dt 1:8; 6:18; 10:11; 11:21; 30:20; 31:7,20

³⁷ "The LORD was angry with me also because of you and said: 'You will not enter there either. ³⁸ Joshua son of Nun, who attends you, will enter it. Encourage him, for he will enable Israel to inherit it. ³⁹ Your children, whom you said would be plunder, your sons who^C don't yet know good from evil, will enter there. I will give them the land, and they will take possession of it. ⁴⁰ But you are to turn back and head for the wilderness by way of the Red Sea.' Nm 14:25; 20:12; 27:12-21

⁴¹ "You answered me, 'We have sinned against the LORD. We will go up and fight just as the LORD our God commanded us.' Then each of you put on his weapons of war and thought it would be easy to go up into the hill country.

⁴² "But the LORD said to me, 'Tell them: Don't go up and fight, for I am not with you to keep you from

^A1:28 Lit *have melted our hearts*   ^B1:34 Lit *the sound of your*   ^C1:39 Lit *who today*

being defeated by your enemies.' ⁴³ So I spoke to you, but you didn't listen. You rebelled against the LORD's command and defiantly went up into the hill country. ⁴⁴ Then the Amorites who lived there came out against you and chased you like a swarm of bees. They routed you from Seir as far as Hormah. ⁴⁵ When you returned, you wept before the LORD, but he didn't listen to your requests or pay attention to you. ⁴⁶ For this reason you stayed in Kadesh as long as you did. ᴬ

Nm 14:42,45

Journey past Seir

2 "Then we turned back and headed for the wilderness by way of the Red Sea, as the LORD had told me, and we traveled around the hill country of Seir for many days. ² The LORD then said to me, ³ 'You've been traveling around this hill country long enough; turn north. ⁴ Command the people: You are about to travel through the territory of your brothers, the descendants of Esau, who live in Seir. They will be afraid of you, so be very careful. ⁵ Don't provoke them, for I will not give you any of their land, not even a foot of it, ᴮ because I have given Esau the hill country of Seir as his possession. ⁶ You may purchase food from them, so that you may eat, and buy water from them to drink. ⁷ For the LORD your God has blessed you in all the work of your hands. He has watched over your journey through this immense wilderness. The LORD your God has been with you this past forty years, and you have lacked nothing.' Ex 10:19; 13:18

Journey past Moab

⁸ "So we bypassed our brothers, the descendants of Esau, who live in Seir. We turned away from the Arabah road and from Elath and Eziongeber. We traveled along the road to the Wilderness of Moab. ⁹ The LORD said to me, 'Show no hostility toward Moab, and do not provoke them to battle, for I will not give you any of their land as a possession, since I have given Ar as a possession to the descendants of Lot.' "

¹⁰ The Emim, a great and numerous people as tall as the Anakim, had previously lived there. ¹¹ They were also regarded as Rephaim, like the Anakim, though the Moabites called them Emim. ¹² The Horites had previously lived in Seir, but the descendants of Esau drove them out, destroying them completely ᶜ and settling in their place, just as Israel did in the land of its possession the LORD gave them.

¹³ "The LORD said, 'Now get up and cross the Zered Valley.' So we crossed the Zered Valley. ¹⁴ The time we spent traveling from Kadesh-barnea until we crossed the Zered Valley was thirty-eight years until the entire generation of fighting men had perished from the camp, as the LORD had sworn to them. ¹⁵ Indeed, the LORD's hand was against them, to eliminate them from the camp until they had all perished. Ex 14:24; 23:27; Nm 21:10-20; Dt 7:23

Journey past Ammon

¹⁶ "When all the fighting men had died among the people, ¹⁷ the LORD spoke to me, ¹⁸ 'Today you are going to cross the border of Moab at Ar. ¹⁹ When you get close to the

---

ᴬ**1:46** Lit *Kadesh for many days, according to the days you stayed*   ᴮ**2:5** Lit *land as far as the width of a sole of a foot*   ᶜ**2:12** Lit *them before them*

Ammonites, don't show any hostility to them or provoke them, for I will not give you any of the Ammonites' land as a possession; I have given it as a possession to the descendants of Lot.'" Gn 19:36,38

20 This too used to be regarded as the land of the Rephaim. The Rephaim lived there previously, though the Ammonites called them Zamzummim, 21 a great and numerous people, tall as the Anakim. The LORD destroyed the Rephaim at the advance of the Ammonites, so that they drove them out and settled in their place. 22 This was just as he had done for the descendants of Esau who lived in Seir, when he destroyed the Horites before them; they drove them out and have lived in their place until now. 23 The Caphtorim, who came from Caphtor, A destroyed the Avvites, who lived in villages as far as Gaza, and settled in their place. Gn 14:5

Defeat of Sihon the Amorite

24 "The LORD also said, 'Get up, move out, and cross the Arnon Valley. See, I have handed the Amorites' King Sihon of Heshbon and his land over to you. Begin to take possession of it; engage B him in battle. 25 Today I will begin to put the fear and dread of you on the peoples everywhere under heaven. They will hear the report about you, tremble, and be in anguish because of you.' Dt 1:27

26 "So I sent messengers with an offer of peace to King Sihon of Heshbon from the Wilderness of Kedemoth, saying, 27 'Let us travel through your land; we will keep strictly to the highway. We will not turn to the right or the left. 28 You can sell us food in exchange for silver so we may eat, and give us water for silver so we may drink. Only let us travel through on foot, 29 just as the descendants of Esau who live in Seir did for us, and the Moabites who live in Ar, until we cross the Jordan into the land the LORD our God is giving us.' 30 But King Sihon of Heshbon would not let us travel through his land, for the LORD your God had made his spirit stubborn and his heart obstinate in order to hand him over to you, as has now taken place.

31 "Then the LORD said to me, 'See, I have begun to give Sihon and his land to you. Begin to take possession of it.' 32 So Sihon and his whole army came out against us for battle at Jahaz. 33 The LORD our God handed him over to us, and we defeated him, his sons, and his whole army. 34 At that time we captured all his cities and completely destroyed the people of every city, including the women and children. We left no survivors. 35 We took only the livestock and the spoil from the cities we captured as plunder for ourselves. 36 There was no city that was inaccessible to C us, from Aroer on the rim of the Arnon Valley, along with the city in the valley, even as far as Gilead. The LORD our God gave everything to us. 37 But you did not go near the Ammonites' land, all along the bank of the Jabbok River, the cities of the hill country, or any place that the LORD our God had forbidden. Dt 7:2,23;20:13

Defeat of Og of Bashan

3 "Then we turned and went up the road to Bashan, and King Og of Bashan came out against us with his whole army to do battle at

A 2:23 Probably Crete B 2:24 Or provoke C 2:36 Or was too high for

Edrei. [2] But the LORD said to me, 'Do not fear him, for I have handed him over to you along with his whole army and his land. Do to him as you did to King Sihon of the Amorites, who lived in Heshbon.' [3] So the LORD our God also handed over King Og of Bashan and his whole army to us. We struck him until there was no survivor left. [4] We captured all his cities at that time. There wasn't a city that we didn't take from them: sixty cities, the entire region of Argob, the kingdom of Og in Bashan. [5] All these were fortified with high walls, gates, and bars, besides a large number of rural villages. [6] We completely destroyed them, as we had done to King Sihon of Heshbon, destroying the men, women, and children of every city. [7] But we took all the livestock and the spoil from the cities as plunder for ourselves.

The Land of the Transjordan Tribes

[8] "At that time we took the land from the two Amorite kings across the Jordan, from the Arnon Valley as far as Mount Hermon, [9] which the Sidonians call Sirion, but the Amorites call Senir, [10] all the cities of the plateau, Gilead, and Bashan as far as Salecah and Edrei, cities of Og's kingdom in Bashan. [11] (Only King Og of Bashan was left of the remnant of the Rephaim. His bed[A] was made of iron. Isn't it in Rabbah of the Ammonites? It is 13 ½ feet long and 6 feet wide by a standard measure.[B])   Gn 14:5; 50:10-11; Dt 1:1,5; Jos 1:14-15

[12] "At that time we took possession of this land. I gave to the Reubenites and Gadites the area extending from Aroer by the Arnon Valley, and half the hill country of Gilead along with its cities. [13] I gave to half the tribe of Manasseh the rest of Gilead and all Bashan, the kingdom of Og. The entire region of Argob, the whole territory of Bashan, used to be called the land of the Rephaim. [14] Jair, a descendant of Manasseh, took over the entire region of Argob as far as the border of the Geshurites and Maacathites. He called Bashan by his own name, Jair's Villages,[C] as it is today. [15] I gave Gilead to Machir, [16] and I gave to the Reubenites and Gadites the area extending from Gilead to the Arnon Valley (the middle of the valley was the border) and up to the Jabbok River, the border of the Ammonites. [17] The Arabah and Jordan are also borders from Chinnereth[D] as far as the Sea of the Arabah, the Dead Sea, under the slopes of Pisgah on the east. Gn 28:4

[18] "I commanded you at that time: The LORD your God has given you this land to possess. All your valiant men will cross over in battle formation ahead of your brothers the Israelites. [19] But your wives, dependents, and livestock — I know that you have a lot of livestock — will remain in the cities I have given you [20] until the LORD gives rest to your brothers as he has to you, and they also take possession of the land the LORD your God is giving them across the Jordan. Then each of you may return to his possession that I have given you.

The Transfer of Israel's Leadership

[21] "I commanded Joshua at that time: Your own eyes have seen

---

[A]3:11 Or *sarcophagus*   [B]3:11 Lit *nine cubits its length and four cubits its width, by a man's cubit*
[C]3:14 Or *Havvoth-jair*   [D]3:17 = the Sea of Galilee; Jos 12:3; 13:27; Lk 5:1

everything the LORD your God has done to these two kings. The LORD will do the same to all the kingdoms you are about to enter. ²² Don't be afraid of them, for the LORD your God fights for you.

²³ "At that time I begged the LORD: ²⁴ Lord GOD, you have begun to show your greatness and your strong hand to your servant, for what god is there in heaven or on earth who can perform deeds and mighty acts like yours? ²⁵ Please let me cross over and see the beautiful land on the other side of the Jordan, that good hill country and Lebanon.   Dt 8:7

²⁶ "But the LORD was angry with me because of you ᴬ and would not listen to me. The LORD said to me, 'That's enough! Do not speak to me again about this matter. ²⁷ Go to the top of Pisgah and look to the west, north, south, and east, and see it with your own eyes, for you will not cross the Jordan. ²⁸ But commission Joshua and encourage and strengthen him, for he will cross over ahead of the people and enable them to inherit this land that you will see.' ²⁹ So we stayed in the valley facing Beth-peor.   Nm 20:1-13

Call to Obedience

4 "Now, Israel, listen to the statutes and ordinances I am teaching you to follow, so that you may live, enter, and take possession of the land the LORD, the God of your fathers, is giving you. ² You must not add anything to what I command you or take anything away from it, so that you may keep the commands of the LORD your God I am giving you. ³ Your eyes have seen what the LORD did

at Baal-peor, for the LORD your God destroyed every one of you who followed Baal of Peor. ⁴ But you who have remained faithful ᴮ to the LORD your God are all alive today. ⁵ Look, I have taught you statutes and ordinances as the LORD my God has commanded me, so that you may follow them in the land you are entering to possess. ⁶ Carefully follow them, for this will show your wisdom and understanding in the eyes of the peoples. When they hear about all these statutes, they will say, 'This great nation is indeed a wise and understanding people.' ⁷ For what great nation is there that has a god near to it as the LORD our God is to us whenever we call to him? ⁸ And what great nation has righteous statutes and ordinances like this entire law I set before you today?   Ex 15:25; Lv 26:46; Dt 5:1; 11:32; 12:1; 1Kg 9:4

⁹ "Only be on your guard and diligently watch yourselves, so that you don't forget the things your eyes have seen and so that they don't slip from your mind ᶜ as long as you live. Teach them to your children and your grandchildren. ¹⁰ The day you stood before the LORD your God at Horeb, the LORD said to me, 'Assemble the people before me, and I will let them hear my words, so that they may learn to fear me all the days they live on the earth and may instruct their children.' ¹¹ You came near and stood at the base of the mountain, a mountain blazing with fire into the heavens and enveloped in a totally black cloud. ¹² Then the LORD spoke to you from the fire. You kept hearing the sound of the words, but didn't see a form; there was only a voice. ¹³ He declared his covenant

ᴬ**3:26** Or *me for your sake*   ᴮ**4:4** Lit *have held on*   ᶜ**4:9** Or *don't depart from your heart* to you. He commanded you to follow the Ten Commandments, which he wrote on two stone tablets. ¹⁴ At that time the LORD commanded me to teach you statutes and ordinances for you to follow in the land you are about to cross into and possess. Jos 22:5; Pr 13:3; 16:17; 4:5

Worshiping the True God

¹⁵ "Diligently watch yourselves — because you did not see any form on the day the LORD spoke to you out of the fire at Horeb — ¹⁶ so you don't act corruptly and make an idol for yourselves in the shape of any figure: a male or female form, ¹⁷ or the form of any animal on the earth, any winged creature that flies in the sky, ¹⁸ any creature that crawls on the ground, or any fish in the waters under the earth. ¹⁹ When you look to the heavens and see the sun, moon, and stars — all the stars in the sky — do not be led astray to bow in worship to them and serve them. The LORD your God has provided them for all people everywhere under heaven. ²⁰ But the LORD selected you and brought you out of Egypt's iron furnace to be a people for his inheritance, as you are today. Dt 17:3; Jr 11:4; Ezk 8:16; Zph 1:5

²¹ "The LORD was angry with me on your account. He swore that I would not cross the Jordan and enter the good land the LORD your God is giving you as an inheritance. ²² I won't be crossing the Jordan because I am going to die in this land. But you are about to cross over and take possession of this good land. ²³ Be careful not to forget the covenant of the LORD your God that he made with you, and make an idol for yourselves in the

shape of anything he has forbidden you. ²⁴ For the LORD your God is a consuming fire, a jealous God.

²⁵ "When you have children and grandchildren and have been in the land a long time, and if you act corruptly, make an idol in the form of anything, and do what is evil in the sight of the LORD your God, angering him, ²⁶ I call heaven and earth as witnesses against you today that you will quickly perish from the land you are about to cross the Jordan to possess. You will not live long there, but you will certainly be destroyed. ²⁷ The LORD will scatter you among the peoples, and you will be reduced to a few survivors ᴬ among the nations where the LORD your God will drive you. ²⁸ There you will worship man-made gods of wood and stone, which cannot see, hear, eat, or smell. ²⁹ But from there, you will search for the LORD your God, and you will find him when you seek him with all your heart and all your soul. ³⁰ When you are in distress and all these things have happened to you, in the future you will return to the LORD your God and obey him. ³¹ He will not leave you, destroy you, or forget the covenant with your fathers that he swore to them by oath, because the LORD your God is a compassionate God. Lv 26:33; Dt 8:19; 28:64

³² "Indeed, ask about the earlier days that preceded you, from the day God created mankind ᴮ on the earth and from one end of the heavens to the other: Has anything like this great event ever happened, or has anything like it been heard of? ³³ Has a people heard God's voice speaking from the fire as you have, and lived? ³⁴ Or has a god attempted

ᴬ4:27 Lit be left few in number   ᴮ4:32 Or Adam

to go and take a nation as his own out of another nation, by trials, signs, wonders, and war, by a strong hand and an outstretched arm, by great terrors, as the LORD your God did for you in Egypt before your eyes? ³⁵ You were shown these things so that you would know that the LORD is God; there is no other besides him. ³⁶ He let you hear his voice from heaven to instruct you. He showed you his great fire on earth, and you heard his words from the fire. ³⁷ Because he loved your fathers, he chose their descendants after them and brought you out of Egypt by his presence and great power, ³⁸ to drive out before you nations greater and stronger than you and to bring you in and give you their land as an inheritance, as is now taking place. ³⁹ Today, recognize and keep in mind that the LORD is God in heaven above and on earth below; there is no other. ⁴⁰ Keep his statutes and commands, which I am giving you today, so that you and your children after you may prosper and so that you may live long in the land the LORD your God is giving you for all time." 1Kg 8:60; Is 43:11

Cities of Refuge

⁴¹ Then Moses set apart three cities across the Jordan to the east. ⁴² Someone could flee there who committed manslaughter, killing his neighbor accidentally without previously hating him. He could flee to one of these cities and stay alive: ⁴³ Bezer in the wilderness on the plateau land, belonging to the Reubenites; Ramoth in Gilead, belonging to the Gadites; or Golan in Bashan, belonging to the Manassites. Nm 35:6-15; Dt 19:2-13; Jos 20:7-9

ᴬ **5:5** One Hb ms, DSS, Sam, LXX, Syr, Vg read *words*

Introduction to the Law

⁴⁴ This is the law Moses gave the Israelites. ⁴⁵ These are the decrees, statutes, and ordinances Moses proclaimed to them after they came out of Egypt, ⁴⁶ across the Jordan in the valley facing Beth-peor in the land of King Sihon of the Amorites. He lived in Heshbon, and Moses and the Israelites defeated him after they came out of Egypt. ⁴⁷ They took possession of his land and the land of Og king of Bashan, the two Amorite kings who were across the Jordan to the east, ⁴⁸ from Aroer on the rim of the Arnon Valley as far as Mount Sion (that is, Hermon) ⁴⁹ and all the Arabah on the east side of the Jordan as far as the Dead Sea below the slopes of Pisgah.

The Ten Commandments

5 Moses summoned all Israel and said to them, "Israel, listen to the statutes and ordinances I am proclaiming as you hear them today. Learn and follow them carefully. ² The LORD our God made a covenant with us at Horeb. ³ He did not make this covenant with our fathers, but with all of us who are alive here today. ⁴ The LORD spoke to you face to face from the fire on the mountain. ⁵ At that time I was standing between the LORD and you to report the word ᴬ of the LORD to you, because you were afraid of the fire and did not go up the mountain. And he said: Dt 4:31; 31:16

⁶ I am the LORD your God, who brought you out of the land of Egypt, out of the place of slavery. Ex 20:2-17; Lv 26:13; Dt 8:14

⁷ Do not have other gods besides me.

8 Do not make an idol for yourself in the shape of anything in the heavens above or on the earth below or in the waters under the earth. 9 Do not bow in worship to them, and do not serve them, because I, the LORD your God, am a jealous God, punishing the children for the fathers' iniquity to the third and fourth generations of those who hate me, 10 but showing faithful love to a thousand generations of those who love me and keep my commands. Ex 34:7; Nm 14:18

11 Do not misuse the name of the LORD your God, because the LORD will not leave anyone unpunished who misuses his name. Ex 3:13; 6:3; 33:19

12 Be careful to remember the Sabbath day, to keep it holy as the LORD your God has commanded you. 13 You are to labor six days and do all your work, 14 but the seventh day is a Sabbath to the LORD your God. Do not do any work — you, your son or daughter, your male or female slave, your ox or donkey, any of your livestock, or the resident alien who lives within your city gates, so that your male and female slaves may rest as you do.

15 Remember that you were a slave in the land of Egypt, and the LORD your God brought you out of there with a strong hand and an outstretched arm. That is why the LORD your God has commanded you to keep the Sabbath day.

16 Honor your father and your mother, as the LORD your God has commanded you, so that you may live long and so that you may prosper in the land the LORD your God is giving you. Mt 19:18-19; Mk 10:19

17 Do not murder. Mt 5:21; Jms 2:11

18 Do not commit adultery.

19 Do not steal.

20 Do not give dishonest testimony against your neighbor.

21 Do not covet your neighbor's wife or desire your neighbor's house, his field, his male or female slave, his ox or donkey, or anything that belongs to your neighbor.

The People's Response

22 "The LORD spoke these commands in a loud voice to your entire assembly from the fire, cloud, and total darkness on the mountain; he added nothing more. He wrote them on two stone tablets and gave them to me. 23 All of you approached me with your tribal leaders and elders when you heard the voice from the darkness and while the mountain was blazing with fire. 24 You said, 'Look, the LORD our God has shown us his glory and greatness, and we have heard his voice from the fire. Today we have seen that God speaks with a person, yet he still lives. 25 But now, why should we die? This great fire will consume us and we will die if we hear the voice of the LORD our God any longer. 26 For who out of all mankind has heard the voice of the living God speaking from the fire, as we have, and lived? 27 Go near and listen to everything the LORD our God says. Then you can tell us everything the LORD our God tells you; we will listen and obey.' Ex 20:18-21

²⁸ "The LORD heard your[A] words when you spoke to me. He said to me, 'I have heard the words that these people have spoken to you. Everything they have said is right. ²⁹ If only they had such a heart to fear me and keep all my commands always, so that they and their children would prosper forever. ³⁰ Go and tell them: Return to your tents. ³¹ But you stand here with me, and I will tell you every command — the statutes and ordinances — you are to teach them, so that they may follow them in the land I am giving them to possess.'

³² "Be careful to do as the LORD your God has commanded you; you are not to turn aside to the right or the left. ³³ Follow the whole instruction the LORD your God has commanded you, so that you may live, prosper, and have a long life in the land you will possess.

The Greatest Command

6 "This is the command — the statutes and ordinances — the LORD your God has commanded me to teach you, so that you may follow them in the land you are about to enter and possess. ² Do this so that you may fear the LORD your God all the days of your life by keeping all his statutes and commands I am giving you, your son, and your grandson, and so that you may have a long life. ³ Listen, Israel, and be careful to follow them, so that you may prosper and multiply greatly, because the LORD, the God of your fathers, has promised you a land flowing with milk and honey.   Dt 3:12; 6:24; 10:12; 14:23; 16:3

⁴ "Listen, Israel: The LORD our God, the LORD is one.[B] ⁵ Love the LORD your God with all your heart, with all your soul, and with all your strength. ⁶ These words that I am giving you today are to be in your heart. ⁷ Repeat them to your children. Talk about them when you sit in your house and when you walk along the road, when you lie down and when you get up. ⁸ Bind them as a sign on your hand and let them be a symbol[C] on your forehead.[D] ⁹ Write them on the doorposts of your house and on your city gates.

Remembering God Through Obedience

¹⁰ "When the LORD your God brings you into the land he swore to your fathers Abraham, Isaac, and Jacob that he would give you — a land with large and beautiful cities that you did not build, ¹¹ houses full of every good thing that you did not fill them with, cisterns that you did not dig, and vineyards and olive groves that you did not plant — and when you eat and are satisfied, ¹² be careful not to forget the LORD who brought you out of the land of Egypt, out of the place of slavery. ¹³ Fear the LORD your God, worship him, and take your oaths in his name. ¹⁴ Do not follow other gods, the gods of the peoples around you, ¹⁵ for the LORD your God, who is among you, is a jealous God. Otherwise, the LORD your God will become angry with you and obliterate you from the face of the earth. ¹⁶ Do not test the LORD your God as you tested him at Massah. ¹⁷ Carefully observe the commands

A5:28 Lit the sound of your   B6:4 Or the LORD is our God; the LORD is one, or The LORD is our God, the LORD alone, or The LORD our God is one LORD   C6:8 Or phylactery; Mt 23:5   D6:8 Lit symbol between your eyes of the LORD your God, the decrees and statutes he has commanded you. ¹⁸ Do what is right and good in the LORD's sight, so that you may prosper and so that you may enter and possess the good land the LORD your God swore to give your fathers, ¹⁹ by driving out all your enemies before you, as the LORD has said. Lv 26:13; Dt 8:10; Jos 24:13; Neh 9:25

²⁰ "When your son asks you in the future, 'What is the meaning of the decrees, statutes, and ordinances that the LORD our God has commanded you?' ²¹ tell him, 'We were slaves of Pharaoh in Egypt, but the LORD brought us out of Egypt with a strong hand. ²² Before our eyes the LORD inflicted great and devastating signs and wonders on Egypt, on Pharaoh, and on all his household, ²³ but he brought us from there in order to lead us in and give us the land that he swore to our fathers. ²⁴ The LORD commanded us to follow all these statutes and to fear the LORD our God for our prosperity always and for our preservation, as it is today. ²⁵ Righteousness will be ours if we are careful to follow every one of these commands before the LORD our God, as he has commanded us.' Ex 3:19; 6:1; 13:9; Jos 4:21

Israel to Destroy Idolatrous Nations

7 "When the LORD your God brings you into the land you are entering to possess, and he drives out many nations before you — the Hethites, Girgashites, Amorites, Canaanites, Perizzites, Hivites and Jebusites, seven nations more numerous and powerful than you — ² and when the LORD your God delivers them over to you and you defeat them, you must completely destroy them. Make no treaty with them and show them no mercy. ³ You must not intermarry with them, and you must not give your daughters to their sons or take their daughters for your sons, ⁴ because they will turn your sons away from me to worship other gods. Then the LORD's anger will burn against you, and he will swiftly destroy you. ⁵ Instead, this is what you are to do to them: tear down their altars, smash their sacred pillars, cut down their Asherah poles, and burn their carved images. ⁶ For you are a holy people belonging to the LORD your God. The LORD your God has chosen you to be his own possession out of all the peoples on the face of the earth. Ex 23:23-26; Dt 3:12

⁷ "The LORD had his heart set on you and chose you, not because you were more numerous than all peoples, for you were the fewest of all peoples. ⁸ But because the LORD loved you and kept the oath he swore to your fathers, he brought you out with a strong hand and redeemed you from the place of slavery, from the power of Pharaoh king of Egypt. ⁹ Know that the LORD your God is God, the faithful God who keeps his gracious covenant loyalty for a thousand generations with those who love him and keep his commands. ¹⁰ But he directly pays back ᴬ and destroys those who hate him. He will not hesitate to pay back directly ᴮ the one who hates him. ¹¹ So keep the command — the statutes and ordinances — that I am giving you to follow today. Dt 4:37; 9:26; 15:15; 24:18

¹² "If you listen to and are careful to keep these ordinances,

---

ᴬ7:10 Lit *He pays back to their faces*   ᴮ7:10 Lit *to pay back to their faces* the Lᴏʀᴅ your God will keep his covenant loyalty with you, as he swore to your fathers. ¹³ He will love you, bless you, and multiply you. He will bless your offspring,ᴬ and the produce of your land — your grain, new wine, and fresh oil — the young of your herds, and the newborn of your flocks, in the land he swore to your fathers that he would give you. ¹⁴ You will be blessed above all peoples; there will be no infertile male or female among you or your livestock. ¹⁵ The Lᴏʀᴅ will remove all sickness from you; he will not put on you all the terrible diseases of Egypt that you know about, but he will inflict them on all who hate you. ¹⁶ You must destroy all the peoples the Lᴏʀᴅ your God is delivering over to you and not look on them with pity. Do not worship their gods, for that will be a snare to you. Ex 15:26; 23:25; Dt 4:31; 28:4

¹⁷ "If you say to yourself, 'These nations are greater than I; how can I drive them out?' ¹⁸ do not be afraid of them. Be sure to remember what the Lᴏʀᴅ your God did to Pharaoh and all Egypt: ¹⁹ the great trials that you saw, the signs and wonders, the strong hand and outstretched arm, by which the Lᴏʀᴅ your God brought you out. The Lᴏʀᴅ your God will do the same to all the peoples you fear. ²⁰ The Lᴏʀᴅ your God will also send hornets against them until all the survivors and those hiding from you perish. ²¹ Don't be terrified of them, for the Lᴏʀᴅ your God, a great and awesome God, is among you. ²² The Lᴏʀᴅ your God will drive out these nations before you little by little. You will not be able to destroy them all at once; otherwise, the wild animals will

become too numerous for you. ²³ The Lᴏʀᴅ your God will give them over to you and throw them into great confusion until they are destroyed. ²⁴ He will hand their kings over to you, and you will wipe out their names under heaven. No one will be able to stand against you; you will annihilate them. ²⁵ Burn up the carved images of their gods. Don't covet the silver and gold on the images and take it for yourself, or else you will be ensnared by it, for it is detestable to the Lᴏʀᴅ your God. ²⁶ Do not bring any detestable thing into your house, or you will be set apart for destruction like it. You are to abhor and detest it utterly because it is set apart for destruction. Ex 23:28-30; Jos 24:12

Remember the Lᴏʀᴅ

8 "Carefully follow every command I am giving you today, so that you may live and increase, and may enter and take possession of the land the Lᴏʀᴅ swore to your fathers. ² Remember that the Lᴏʀᴅ your God led you on the entire journey these forty years in the wilderness, so that he might humble you and test you to know what was in your heart, whether or not you would keep his commands. ³ He humbled you by letting you go hungry; then he gave you manna to eat, which you and your fathers had not known, so that you might learn that man does not live on bread alone but on every word that comes from the mouth of the Lᴏʀᴅ. ⁴ Your clothing did not wear out, and your feet did not swell these forty years. ⁵ Keep in mind that the Lᴏʀᴅ your God has been disciplining you just as a man disciplines

ᴬ**7:13** Lit *bless the fruit of your womb*

his son. ⁶ So keep the commands of the LORD your God by walking in his ways and fearing him. ⁷ For the LORD your God is bringing you into a good land, a land with streams, springs, and deep water sources, flowing in both valleys and hills; ⁸ a land of wheat, barley, vines, figs, and pomegranates; a land of olive oil and honey; ⁹ a land where you will eat food without shortage, where you will lack nothing; a land whose rocks are iron and from whose hills you will mine copper. ¹⁰ When you eat and are full, you will bless the LORD your God for the good land he has given you. Dt 3:12; Mt 4:4; Lk 4:4; 3:25

¹¹ "Be careful that you don't forget the LORD your God by failing to keep his commands, ordinances, and statutes that I am giving you today. ¹² When you eat and are full, and build beautiful houses to live in, ¹³ and your herds and flocks grow large, and your silver and gold multiply, and everything else you have increases, ¹⁴ be careful that your heart doesn't become proud and you forget the LORD your God who brought you out of the land of Egypt, out of the place of slavery. ¹⁵ He led you through the great and terrible wilderness with its poisonousᴬ snakes and scorpions, a thirsty land where there was no water. He brought water out of the flint rock for you. ¹⁶ He fed you in the wilderness with manna, which your fathers had not known, in order to humble and test you, so that in the end he might cause you to prosper. ¹⁷ You may say to yourself, 'My power and my own ability have gained this wealth for me,' ¹⁸ but remember that the LORD your God gives you the power to gain wealth, in order

to confirm his covenant he swore to your fathers, as it is today. ¹⁹ If you ever forget the LORD your God and follow other gods to serve them and bow in worship to them, I testify against you today that you will perish. ²⁰ Like the nations the LORD is about to destroy before you, you will perish if you do not obey the LORD your God. Dt 6:12; 13:5,10; Jos 24:17

Warning Against Self-Righteousness

9 "Listen, Israel: Today you are about to cross the Jordan to enter and drive out nations greater and stronger than you, with large cities fortified to the heavens. ² The people are strong and tall, the descendants of the Anakim. You know about them and you have heard it said about them, 'Who can stand up to the sons of Anak?' ³ But understand that today the LORD your God will cross over ahead of you as a consuming fire; he will devastate and subdue them before you. You will drive them out and destroy them swiftly, as the LORD has told you. ⁴ When the LORD your God drives them out before you, do not say to yourself, 'The LORD brought me in to take possession of this land because of my righteousness.' Instead, the LORD will drive out these nations before you because of their wickedness. ⁵ You are not going to take possession of their land because of your righteousness or your integrity. Instead, the LORD your God will drive out these nations before you because of their wickedness, in order to fulfill the promise he swore to your fathers, Abraham, Isaac, and Jacob. ⁶ Understand that the

ᴬ8:15 Lit burning

LORD your God is not giving you this good land to possess because of your righteousness, for you are a stiff-necked people. Dt 4:38; 11:23; 21:11

Israel's Rebellion and Moses's Intercession

⁷ "Remember and do not forget how you provoked the LORD your God in the wilderness. You have been rebelling against the LORD from the day you left the land of Egypt until you reached this place. ⁸ You provoked the LORD at Horeb, and he was angry enough with you to destroy you. ⁹ When I went up the mountain to receive the stone tablets, the tablets of the covenant the LORD made with you, I stayed on the mountain forty days and forty nights. I did not eat food or drink water. ¹⁰ On the day of the assembly the LORD gave me the two stone tablets, inscribed by God's finger. The exact words were on them, which the LORD spoke to you from the fire on the mountain. ¹¹ The LORD gave me the two stone tablets, the tablets of the covenant, at the end of the forty days and forty nights.

¹² "The LORD said to me, 'Get up and go down immediately from here. For your people whom you brought out of Egypt have acted corruptly. They have quickly turned from the way that I commanded them; they have made a cast image for themselves.' ¹³ The LORD also said to me, 'I have seen this people, and indeed, they are a stiff-necked people. ¹⁴ Leave me alone, and I will destroy them and blot out their name under heaven. Then I will make you into a nation stronger and more numerous than they.' Ex 32:4,8; 34:17; Lv 19:4; Nm 33:52; Dt 27:15

¹⁵ "So I went back down the mountain, while it was blazing with fire, and the two tablets of the covenant were in my hands. ¹⁶ I saw how you had sinned against the LORD your God; you had made a calf image for yourselves. You had quickly turned from the way the LORD had commanded for you. ¹⁷ So I took hold of the two tablets and threw them from my hands, shattering them before your eyes. ¹⁸ I fell down like the first time in the presence of the LORD for forty days and forty nights; I did not eat food or drink water because of all the sin you committed, doing what was evil in the LORD's sight and angering him. ¹⁹ I was afraid of the fierce anger the LORD had directed against you, because he was about to destroy you. But again the LORD listened to me on that occasion. ²⁰ The LORD was angry enough with Aaron to destroy him. But I prayed for Aaron at that time also. ²¹ I took the sinful calf you had made and burned it. I crushed it, thoroughly grinding it to powder as fine as dust, and threw its dust into the stream that came down from the mountain. Ex 32:19

²² "You continued to provoke the LORD at Taberah, Massah, and Kibroth-hattaavah. ²³ When the LORD sent you from Kadesh-barnea, he said, 'Go up and possess the land I have given you'; you rebelled against the command of the LORD your God. You did not believe or obey him. ²⁴ You have been rebelling against the LORD ever since I have^A known you. Ex 17:1-7; Nm 11:1-35

²⁵ "I fell down in the presence of the LORD forty days and forty nights because the LORD had threatened to destroy you. ²⁶ I prayed to the LORD:

^A 9:24 Sam, LXX read *since he has*

Lord God, do not annihilate your people, your inheritance, whom you redeemed through your greatness and brought out of Egypt with a strong hand. [27] Remember your servants Abraham, Isaac, and Jacob. Disregard this people's stubbornness, and their wickedness and sin. [28] Otherwise, those in the land you brought us from will say, 'Because the Lord wasn't able to bring them into the land he had promised them, and because he hated them, he brought them out to kill them in the wilderness.' [29] But they are your people, your inheritance, whom you brought out by your great power and outstretched arm. Dt 7:8

The Covenant Renewed

10 "The Lord said to me at that time, 'Cut two stone tablets like the first ones and come to me on the mountain and make a wooden ark. [2] I will write on the tablets the words that were on the first tablets you broke, and you are to place them in the ark.' [3] So I made an ark of acacia wood, cut two stone tablets like the first ones, and climbed the mountain with the two tablets in my hand. [4] Then on the day of the assembly, the Lord wrote on the tablets what had been written previously, the Ten Commandments that he had spoken to you on the mountain from the fire. The Lord gave them to me, [5] and I went back down the mountain and placed the tablets in the ark I had made. And they have remained there, as the Lord commanded me." Ex 25:10,16; 37:1

[6] The Israelites traveled from Beeroth Bene-jaakan[A] to Moserah. Aaron died and was buried there, and Eleazar his son became priest in his place. [7] They traveled from there to Gudgodah, and from Gudgodah to Jotbathah, a land with flowing streams. Nm 20:22-29; 33:31-33

[8] "At that time the Lord set apart the tribe of Levi to carry the ark of the Lord's covenant, to stand before the Lord to serve him, and to pronounce blessings in his name, as it is today. [9] For this reason, Levi does not have a portion or inheritance like his brothers; the Lord is his inheritance, as the Lord your God told him. Ex 27:21-28:1; 32:26-29; 18:19

[10] "I stayed on the mountain forty days and forty nights like the first time. The Lord also listened to me on this occasion; he agreed not to annihilate you. [11] Then the Lord said to me, 'Get up. Continue your journey ahead of the people, so that they may enter and possess the land I swore to give their fathers.'

What God Requires

[12] "And now, Israel, what does the Lord your God ask of you except to fear the Lord your God by walking in all his ways, to love him, and to worship the Lord your God with all your heart and all your soul? [13] Keep the Lord's commands and statutes I am giving you today, for your own good. [14] The heavens, indeed the highest heavens, belong to the Lord your God, as does the earth and everything in it. [15] Yet the Lord had his heart set on your fathers and loved them. He chose their descendants after them — he chose you out of all the peoples, as it is today. [16] Therefore,

A **10:6** Or *from the wells of Bene-jaakan,* or *from the wells of the Jaakanites* circumcise your hearts and don't be stiff-necked any longer. [17] For the LORD your God is the God of gods and Lord of lords, the great, mighty, and awe-inspiring God, showing no partiality and taking no bribe. [18] He executes justice for the fatherless and the widow, and loves the resident alien, giving him food and clothing. [19] You are also to love the resident alien, since you were resident aliens in the land of Egypt. [20] You are to fear the LORD your God and worship him. Remain faithful[A] to him and take oaths in his name. [21] He is your praise and he is your God, who has done for you these great and awe-inspiring works your eyes have seen. [22] Your fathers went down to Egypt, seventy people in all, and now the LORD your God has made you numerous, like the stars of the sky.   Dt 6:5; 14:23

Remember and Obey

11 "Therefore, love the LORD your God and always keep his mandate and his statutes, ordinances, and commands. [2] Understand today that it is not your children who experienced or saw the discipline of the LORD your God:

His greatness, strong hand, and outstretched arm; [3] his signs and the works he did in Egypt to Pharaoh king of Egypt and all his land; [4] what he did to Egypt's army, its horses and chariots, when he made the water of the Red Sea flow over them as they pursued you, and he destroyed them completely;[B] [5] what he did to you in the wilderness until you reached this place; [6] and what he did to Dathan and Abiram, the sons of Eliab the Reubenite, when in the middle of the whole Israelite camp the earth opened its mouth and swallowed them, their households, their tents, and every living thing with them.   Ex 7–12; 14; 1Kg 8:42; 2Ch 6:32 [7] Your own eyes have seen every great work the LORD has done.

[8] "Keep every command I am giving you today, so that you may have the strength to cross into and possess the land you are to inherit, [9] and so that you may live long in the land the LORD swore to your fathers to give them and their descendants, a land flowing with milk and honey. [10] For the land you are entering to possess is not like the land of Egypt, from which you have come, where you sowed your seed and irrigated by hand[C] as in a vegetable garden. [11] But the land you are entering to possess is a land of mountains and valleys, watered by rain from the sky. [12] It is a land the LORD your God cares for. He is always watching over it from the beginning to the end of the year.

[13] "If you carefully obey my commands I am giving you today, to love the LORD your God and worship him with all your heart and all your soul, [14] I[D] will provide rain for your land in the proper time, the autumn and spring rains, and you will harvest your grain, new wine, and fresh oil. [15] I[E] will provide grass in your fields for your livestock. You will eat and be satisfied. [16] Be careful that you are not enticed to turn aside, serve, and bow in worship to other gods. [17] Then the LORD's anger will burn against

---

[A]**10:20** Lit *Hold on*   [B]**11:4** Lit *to this day*   [C]**11:10** Lit *foot*   [D]**11:14** DSS, Sam, LXX read *he*   [E]**11:15** DSS, Sam, LXX read *He* you. He will shut the sky, and there will be no rain; the land will not yield its produce, and you will perish quickly from the good land the LORD is giving you. Dt 7:13; Jr 5:24; Jms 5:7

[18] "Imprint these words of mine on your hearts and minds, bind them as a sign on your hands, and let them be a symbol[A] on your foreheads. [B] [19] Teach them to your children, talking about them when you sit in your house and when you walk along the road, when you lie down and when you get up. [20] Write them on the doorposts of your house and on your city gates, [21] so that as long as the heavens are above the earth, your days and those of your children may be many in the land the LORD swore to give your fathers. [22] For if you carefully observe every one of these commands I am giving you to follow — to love the LORD your God, walk in all his ways, and remain faithful[C] to him — [23] the LORD will drive out all these nations before you, and you will drive out nations greater and stronger than you are. [24] Every place the sole of your foot treads will be yours. Your territory will extend from the wilderness to Lebanon and from the Euphrates River[D] to the Mediterranean Sea. [25] No one will be able to stand against you; the LORD your God will put fear and dread of you in all the land where you set foot, as he has promised you. Dt 4:9-10; 9:1

A Blessing and a Curse

[26] "Look, today I set before you a blessing and a curse: [27] there will be a blessing, if you obey the commands of the LORD your God I am giving you today, [28] and a curse, if you do not obey the commands of the LORD your God and you turn aside from the path I command you today by following other gods you have not known. [29] When the LORD your God brings you into the land you are entering to possess, you are to proclaim the blessing at Mount Gerizim and the curse at Mount Ebal. [30] Aren't these mountains across the Jordan, beyond the western road in the land of the Canaanites, who live in the Arabah, opposite Gilgal, near the oaks[E] of Moreh? [31] For you are about to cross the Jordan to enter and take possession of the land the LORD your God is giving you. When you possess it and settle in it, [32] be careful to follow all the statutes and ordinances I set before you today. Jr 21:8

The Chosen Place of Worship

12 "Be careful to follow these statutes and ordinances in the land that the LORD, the God of your fathers, has given you to possess all the days you live on the earth. [2] Destroy completely all the places where the nations that you are driving out worship their gods — on the high mountains, on the hills, and under every green tree. [3] Tear down their altars, smash their sacred pillars, burn their Asherah poles, cut down the carved images of their gods, and wipe out their names from every[F] place. [4] Don't worship the LORD your God this way. [5] Instead, turn to the place the LORD your God chooses from all your tribes to put his name for his dwelling and go there. [6] You are to

[A]11:18 Or phylactery; Mt 23:5 [B]11:18 Lit symbol between your eyes; Ex 13:16; Dt 6:8 [C]11:22 Lit and hold on [D]11:24 Some Hb mss, LXX, Tg, Vg read the great river, the river Euphrates [E]11:30 Sam, LXX, Syr, Aq, Sym read oak; Gn 12:6 [F]12:3 Lit that bring there your burnt offerings and sacrifices, your tenths and personal contributions, [A] your vow offerings and freewill offerings, and the firstborn of your herds and flocks. [7] You will eat there in the presence of the LORD your God and rejoice with your household in everything you do, [B] because the LORD your God has blessed you. Dt 1:11,21

[8] "You are not to do as we are doing here today; everyone is doing whatever seems right in his own sight. [9] Indeed, you have not yet come into the resting place and the inheritance the LORD your God is giving you. [10] When you cross the Jordan and live in the land the LORD your God is giving you to inherit, and he gives you rest from all the enemies around you and you live in security, [11] then the LORD your God will choose the place to have his name dwell. Bring there everything I command you: your burnt offerings, sacrifices, offerings of the tenth, personal contributions, [C] and all your choice offerings you vow to the LORD. [12] You will rejoice before the LORD your God — you, your sons and daughters, your male and female slaves, and the Levite who is within your city gates, since he has no portion or inheritance among you. [13] Be careful not to offer your burnt offerings in all the sacred places you see. [14] You must offer your burnt offerings only in the place the LORD chooses in one of your tribes, and there you must do everything I command you.

Slaughtering Animals to Eat

[15] "But whenever you want, you may slaughter and eat meat within any of your city gates, according to the blessing the LORD your God has given you. Those who are clean or unclean may eat it, as they would a gazelle or deer, [16] but you must not eat the blood; pour it on the ground like water. [17] Within your city gates you may not eat the tenth of your grain, new wine, or fresh oil; the firstborn of your herd or flock; any of your vow offerings that you pledge; your freewill offerings; or your personal contributions. [D] [18] You are to eat them in the presence of the LORD your God at the place the LORD your God chooses — you, your son and daughter, your male and female slave, and the Levite who is within your city gates. Rejoice before the LORD your God in everything you do, [19] and be careful not to neglect the Levite, as long as you live in your land.

[20] "When the LORD your God enlarges your territory as he has promised you, and you say, 'I want to eat meat' because you have a strong desire to eat meat, you may eat it whenever you want. [21] If the place where the LORD your God chooses to put his name is too far from you, you may slaughter any of your herd or flock he has given you, as I have commanded you, and you may eat it within your city gates whenever you want. [22] Indeed, you may eat it as the gazelle and deer are eaten; both the clean and the unclean may eat it. [23] But don't eat the blood, since the blood is the life, and you must not eat the life with the meat. [24] Do not eat blood; pour it on the ground like water. [25] Do not eat it, so that you and your children after you will prosper, because you

---

[A] 12:6 Lit *and the contributions from your hands*   [B] 12:7 Lit *you put your hand to*, also in v. 18   [C] 12:11 Lit *tenth, the contributions from your hands*   [D] 12:17 Lit *or the contributions from your hands* will be doing what is right in the Lord's sight. Ex 34:24; Lv 3:17; 7:26; 17:11,14

26 "But you are to take the holy offerings you have and your vow offerings and go to the place the Lord chooses. 27 Present the meat and blood of your burnt offerings on the altar of the Lord your God. The blood of your other sacrifices is to be poured out beside the altar of the Lord your God, but you may eat the meat. 28 Be careful to obey all these things I command you, so that you and your children after you may prosper forever, because you will be doing what is good and right in the sight of the Lord your God.

29 "When the Lord your God annihilates the nations before you, which you are entering to take possession of, and you drive them out and live in their land, 30 be careful not to be ensnared by their ways after they have been destroyed before you. Do not inquire about their gods, asking, 'How did these nations worship their gods? I'll also do the same.' 31 You must not do the same to the Lord your God, because they practice every detestable act, which the Lord hates, for their gods. They even burn their sons and daughters in the fire to their gods. 32 Be careful to do everything I command you; do not add anything to it or take anything away from it. Ex 23:33; 34:12; Dt 3:12; 19:1

The False Prophet

13 "If a prophet or someone who has dreams arises among you and proclaims a sign or wonder to you, 2 and that sign or wonder he has promised you comes about, but he says, 'Let us follow other gods,' which you have not known, 'and let us worship them,' 3 do not listen to that prophet's words or to that dreamer. For the Lord your God is testing you to know whether you love the Lord your God with all your heart and all your soul. 4 You must follow the Lord your God and fear him. You must keep his commands and listen to him; you must worship him and remain faithfulA to him. 5 That prophet or dreamer must be put to death, because he has urged rebellion against the Lord your God who brought you out of the land of Egypt and redeemed you from the place of slavery, to turn you from the way the Lord your God has commanded you to walk. You must purge the evil from you.

Don't Tolerate Idolatry

6 "If your brother, the son of your mother,B or your son or daughter, or the wife you embrace, or your closest friend secretly entices you, saying, 'Let us go and worship other gods' — which neither you nor your fathers have known, 7 any of the gods of the peoples around you, near you or far from you, from one end of the earth to the other — 8 do not yield to him or listen to him. Show him no pity,C and do not spare him or shield him. 9 Instead, you must kill him. Your hand is to be the first against him to put him to death, and then the hands of all the people. 10 Stone him to death for trying to turn you away from the Lord your God who brought you out of the land of Egypt, out of the place of slavery. 11 All Israel

A13:4 Lit and hold on   B13:6 DSS, Sam, LXX read If the son of your father or the son of your mother
C13:8 Lit Your eye must not pity him

will hear and be afraid, and they will no longer do anything evil like this among you. Dt 7:16; 19:13,21; 25:12

¹² "If you hear it said about one of your cities the LORD your God is giving you to live in, ¹³ that wicked men have sprung up among you, led the inhabitants of their city astray, and said, 'Let us go and worship other gods,' which you have not known, ¹⁴ you are to inquire, investigate, and interrogate thoroughly. If the report turns out to be true that this detestable act has been done among you, ¹⁵ you must strike down the inhabitants of that city with the sword. Completely destroy everyone in it as well as its livestock with the sword. ¹⁶ You are to gather all its spoil in the middle of the city square and completely burn the city and all its spoil for the LORD your God. The city is to remain a mound of ruins forever; it is not to be rebuilt. ¹⁷ Nothing set apart for destruction is to remain in your hand, so that the LORD will turn from his burning anger and grant you mercy, show you compassion, and multiply you as he swore to your fathers. ¹⁸ This will occur if you obey the LORD your God, keeping all his commands I am giving you today, doing what is right in the sight of the LORD your God. Dt 17:2-5; Jr 25:9; 49:13; Mal 1:4

Forbidden Practices

14 "You are sons of the LORD your God; do not cut yourselves or make a bald spot on your head^A on behalf of the dead, ² for you are a holy people belonging to the LORD your God. The LORD has chosen you to be his own possession out of all the peoples on the face of the earth. Ex 4:22-23; Dt 7:6; 32:6

Clean and Unclean Foods

³ "You must not eat any detestable thing. ⁴ These are the animals you may eat:

    oxen, sheep, goats,
⁵   deer, gazelles, roe deer,
    wild goats, ibexes, antelopes,
    and mountain sheep.

⁶ You may eat any animal that has hooves divided in two and chews the cud. ^B ⁷ But among the ones that chew the cud or have divided hooves, you are not to eat these:

    camels, hares, and hyraxes,
    though they chew the cud,
      they do not have hooves —
    they are unclean for you;
⁸   and pigs, though they
      have hooves, they do not
      chew the cud —
    they are unclean for you.

Do not eat their meat or touch their carcasses. Lv 11:1-8

⁹ "You may eat everything from the water that has fins and scales, ¹⁰ but you may not eat anything that does not have fins and scales — it is unclean for you. Lv 11:9-12

¹¹ "You may eat every clean bird, ¹² but these are the ones you may not eat:

    eagles, bearded vultures,
    black vultures, ¹³ the kites,
    any kind of falcon, ^C
¹⁴   every kind of raven,
    ¹⁵ ostriches,
    short-eared owls, gulls,
    any kind of hawk,
¹⁶   little owls, long-eared owls,
    barn owls, ¹⁷ eagle owls,

---

^A **14:1** Or *forehead*   ^B **14:6** The Hb does not specify chewing the cud, but bringing up partially digested food and swallowing it again.   ^C **14:13** Some Hb mss, Sam, LXX; other Hb mss, Vg read *the falcon, the various kinds of kite* ospreys, cormorants, [18] storks, any kind of heron, hoopoes, and bats. [A]　Lv 11:13-19 [19] All winged insects are unclean for you; they may not be eaten. [20] But you may eat every clean flying creature.　Lv 11:20-23

[21] "You are not to eat any carcass; you may give it to a resident alien within your city gates, and he may eat it, or you may sell it to a foreigner. For you are a holy people belonging to the LORD your God. Do not boil a young goat in its mother's milk.

A Tenth for the LORD

[22] "Each year you are to set aside a tenth of all the produce grown in your fields. [23] You are to eat a tenth of your grain, new wine, and fresh oil, and the firstborn of your herd and flock, in the presence of the LORD your God at the place where he chooses to have his name dwell, so that you will always learn to fear the LORD your God. [24] But if the distance is too great for you to carry it, since the place where the LORD your God chooses to put his name is too far away from you and since the LORD your God has blessed you, [25] then exchange it for silver, take the silver in your hand, and go to the place the LORD your God chooses. [26] You may spend the silver on anything you want: cattle, sheep, goats, wine, beer, or anything you desire. You are to feast there in the presence of the LORD your God and rejoice with your family. [27] Do not neglect the Levite within your city gates, since he has no portion or inheritance among you.　Dt 12:11; 6:2

[28] "At the end of every three years, bring a tenth of all your produce for that year and store it within your city gates. [29] Then the Levite, who has no portion or inheritance among you, the resident alien, the fatherless, and the widow within your city gates may come, eat, and be satisfied. And the LORD your God will bless you in all the work of your hands that you do.　Dt 26:12; 30:9

Debts Canceled

15 "At the end of every seven years you must cancel debts. [2] This is how to cancel debt: Every creditor [B] is to cancel what he has lent his neighbor. He is not to collect anything from his neighbor or brother, because the LORD's release of debts has been proclaimed. [3] You may collect something from a foreigner, but you must forgive whatever your brother owes you.

[4] "There will be no poor among you, however, because the LORD is certain to bless you in the land the LORD your God is giving you to possess as an inheritance — [5] if only you obey the LORD your God and are careful to follow every one of these commands I am giving you today. [6] When the LORD your God blesses you as he has promised you, you will lend to many nations but not borrow; you will rule many nations, but they will not rule you.

Lending to the Poor

[7] "If there is a poor person among you, one of your brothers within any of your city gates in the land the LORD your God is giving you, do not be hardhearted or tightfisted toward your poor brother. [8] Instead, you are to open your hand to him and freely loan him enough for whatever need he has. [9] Be careful that there isn't this wicked thought

[A] 14:5-18 The identification of some of these animals is uncertain.　[B] 15:2 Lit *owner of a loan of his hand* in your heart, 'The seventh year, the year of canceling debts, is near,' and you are stingy toward your poor brother and give him nothing. He will cry out to the LORD against you, and you will be guilty. [10] Give to him, and don't have a stingy heart[A] when you give, and because of this the LORD your God will bless you in all your work and in everything you do. [B] [11] For there will never cease to be poor people in the land; that is why I am commanding you, 'Open your hand willingly to your poor and needy brother in your land.'

Release of Slaves

[12] "If your fellow Hebrew, a man or woman, is sold to you and serves you six years, you must set him free in the seventh year. [13] When you set him free, do not send him away empty-handed. [14] Give generously to him from your flock, your threshing floor, and your winepress. You are to give him whatever the LORD your God has blessed you with. [15] Remember that you were a slave in the land of Egypt and the LORD your God redeemed you; that is why I am giving you this command today. [16] But if your slave says to you, 'I don't want to leave you,' because he loves you and your family, and is well off with you, [17] take an awl and pierce through his ear into the door, and he will become your slave for life. Also treat your female slave the same way. [18] Do not regard it as a hardship[C] when you set him free, because he worked for you six years — worth twice the wages of a hired worker. Then the LORD your God will bless you in everything you do. Ex 15:13; Jr 34:14

Consecration of Firstborn Animals

[19] "Consecrate to the LORD your God every firstborn male produced by your herd and flock. You are not to put the firstborn of your oxen to work or shear the firstborn of your flock. [20] Each year you and your family are to eat it before the LORD your God in the place the LORD chooses. [21] But if there is a defect in the animal, if it is lame or blind or has any serious defect, you may not sacrifice it to the LORD your God. [22] Eat it within your city gates; both the unclean person and the clean may eat it, as though it were a gazelle or deer. [23] But you must not eat its blood; pour it on the ground like water. Lv 23:9-14; Dt 12:15-16,22-24

The Festival of Passover

16 "Set aside the month of Abib[D] and observe the Passover to the LORD your God, because the LORD your God brought you out of Egypt by night in the month of Abib. [2] Sacrifice to the LORD your God a Passover animal from the herd or flock in the place where the LORD chooses to have his name dwell. [3] Do not eat leavened bread with it. For seven days you are to eat unleavened bread with it, the bread of hardship — because you left the land of Egypt in a hurry — so that you may remember for the rest of your life the day you left the land of Egypt. [4] No yeast is to be found anywhere in your territory for seven days, and none of the meat you sacrifice in the evening of the first day is to remain until morning. [5] You are not to sacrifice the Passover animal in any of the

---

[A]**15:10** Lit and let not your heart be grudging [B]**15:10** Lit you put your hand to [C]**15:18** Lit Let it not be hard in your sight [D]**16:1** March–April; called Nisan in the post-exilic period; Neh 2:1; Est 3:7

towns the LORD your God is giving you. ⁶ Sacrifice the Passover animal only at the place where the LORD your God chooses to have his name dwell. Do this in the evening as the sun sets at the same time of day you departed from Egypt. ⁷ You are to cook and eat it in the place the LORD your God chooses, and you are to return to your tents in the morning. ⁸ Eat unleavened bread for six days. On the seventh day there is to be a solemn assembly to the LORD your God; do not do any work.

The Festival of Weeks

⁹ "You are to count seven weeks, counting the weeks from the time the sickle is first put to the standing grain. ¹⁰ You are to celebrate the Festival of Weeks to the LORD your God with a freewill offering that you give in proportion to how the LORD your God has blessed you. ¹¹ Rejoice before the LORD your God in the place where he chooses to have his name dwell — you, your son and daughter, your male and female slave, the Levite within your city gates, as well as the resident alien, the fatherless, and the widow among you. ¹² Remember that you were slaves in Egypt; carefully follow these statutes.   Lv 23:15-21

The Festival of Shelters

¹³ "You are to celebrate the Festival of Shelters for seven days when you have gathered in everything from your threshing floor and winepress. ¹⁴ Rejoice during your festival — you, your son and daughter, your male and female slave, as well as the Levite, the resident alien, the fatherless, and the widow within your city gates. ¹⁵ You are to hold a seven-day festival for the LORD your God in the place he chooses, because the LORD your God will bless you in all your produce and in all the work of your hands, and you will have abundant joy. Lv 23:34

¹⁶ "All your males are to appear three times a year before the LORD your God in the place he chooses: at the Festival of Unleavened Bread, the Festival of Weeks, and the Festival of Shelters. No one is to appear before the LORD empty-handed. ¹⁷ Everyone must appear with a gift suited to his means, according to the blessing the LORD your God has given you.   Ex 23:14,17; 34:23-24

Appointing Judges and Officials

¹⁸ "Appoint judges and officials for your tribes in all your towns the LORD your God is giving you. They are to judge the people with righteous judgment. ¹⁹ Do not deny justice or show partiality to anyone. Do not accept a bribe, for it blinds the eyes of the wise and twists the words of the righteous. ²⁰ Pursue justice and justice alone, so that you will live and possess the land the LORD your God is giving you.

Forbidden Worship

²¹ "Do not set up an Asherah of any kind of wood next to the altar you will build for the LORD your God, ²² and do not set up a sacred pillar; the LORD your God hates them. **17** "Do not sacrifice to the LORD your God an ox or sheep with a defect or any serious flaw, for that is detestable to the LORD your God.

The Judicial Procedure for Idolatry

² "If a man or woman among you in one of your towns that the LORD your God will give you is discovered

doing evil in the sight of the LORD your God and violating his covenant ³ and has gone to serve other gods by bowing in worship to the sun, moon, or all the stars in the sky — which I have forbidden — ⁴ and if you are told or hear about it, then investigate it thoroughly. If the report turns out to be true that this detestable act has been done in Israel, ⁵ you are to bring out to your city gates that man or woman who has done this evil thing and stone them to death. ⁶ The one condemned to die is to be executed on the testimony of two or three witnesses. No one is to be executed on the testimony of a single witness. ⁷ The witnesses' hands are to be the first in putting him to death, and after that, the hands of all the people. You must purge the evil from you. Dt 31:16; Jr 8:2

Difficult Cases

⁸ "If a case is too difficult for you — concerning bloodshed, lawsuits, or assaults — cases disputed at your city gates, then go up to the place the LORD your God chooses. ⁹ You are to go to the Levitical priests and to the judge who presides at that time. Ask, and they will give you a verdict in the case. ¹⁰ You must abide by the verdict they give you at the place the LORD chooses. Be careful to do exactly as they instruct you. ¹¹ You must abide by the instruction they give you and the verdict they announce to you. Do not turn to the right or the left from the decision they declare to you. ¹² The person who acts arrogantly, refusing to listen either to the priest who stands there serving the LORD your God or to the judge, must die. You must purge the evil

from Israel. ¹³ Then all the people will hear about it, be afraid, and no longer behave arrogantly.

Appointing a King

¹⁴ "When you enter the land the LORD your God is giving you, take possession of it, live in it, and say, 'I will set a king over me like all the nations around me,' ¹⁵ you are to appoint over you the king the LORD your God chooses. Appoint a king from your brothers. You are not to set a foreigner over you, or one who is not of your people. ¹⁶ However, he must not acquire many horses for himself or send the people back to Egypt to acquire many horses, for the LORD has told you, 'You are never to go back that way again.' ¹⁷ He must not acquire many wives for himself so that his heart won't go astray. He must not acquire very large amounts of silver and gold for himself. ¹⁸ When he is seated on his royal throne, he is to write a copy of this instruction for himself on a scroll in the presence of the Levitical priests. ¹⁹ It is to remain with him, and he is to read from it all the days of his life, so that he may learn to fear the LORD his God, to observe all the words of this instruction, and to do these statutes. ²⁰ Then his heart will not be exalted above his countrymen, he will not turn from this command to the right or the left, and he and his sons will continue reigning many years ᴬ in Israel. Gn 17:6,16; 35:11; Dt 26:1; 1Sm 8:4-22

Provisions for the Levites

18 "The Levitical priests, the whole tribe of Levi, will have no portion or inheritance with Israel. They will eat the LORD's fire

ᴬ17:20 Lit will lengthen days on his kingdom

offerings; that is their[A,B] inheritance. [2] Although Levi has no inheritance among his brothers, the LORD is his inheritance, as he promised him. [3] This is the priests' share from the people who offer a sacrifice, whether it is an ox, a sheep, or a goat; the priests are to be given the shoulder, jaws, and stomach. [4] You are to give him the firstfruits of your grain, new wine, and fresh oil, and the first sheared wool of your flock. [5] For the LORD your God has chosen him and his sons from all your tribes to stand and minister in his name from now on.[C] [6] When a Levite leaves one of your towns in Israel where he was staying and wants to go to the place the LORD chooses, [7] he may serve in the name of the LORD his God like all his fellow Levites who minister there in the presence of the LORD. [8] They will eat equal portions besides what he has received from the sale of the family estate.[D]   Nm 18:20; Dt 12:12; 14:27-29

Occult Practices Versus Prophetic Revelation

[9] "When you enter the land the LORD your God is giving you, do not imitate the detestable customs of those nations. [10] No one among you is to sacrifice his son or daughter in the fire,[E] practice divination, tell fortunes, interpret omens, practice sorcery, [11] cast spells, consult a medium or a spiritist, or inquire of the dead. [12] Everyone who does these acts is detestable to the LORD, and the LORD your God is driving out the nations before you because of these detestable acts. [13] You must be blameless before the LORD your God. [14] Though these nations you are about to drive out listen to fortune-tellers and diviners, the LORD your God has not permitted you to do this.   Ex 23:24; Dt 20:18; 1Kg 14:24; 2Kg 17:15

[15] "The LORD your God will raise up for you a prophet like me from among your own brothers. You must listen to him. [16] This is what you requested from the LORD your God at Horeb on the day of the assembly when you said, 'Let us not continue to hear the voice of the LORD our God or see this great fire any longer, so that we will not die!' [17] Then the LORD said to me, 'They have spoken well. [18] I will raise up for them a prophet like you from among their brothers. I will put my words in his mouth, and he will tell them everything I command him. [19] I will hold accountable whoever does not listen to my words that he speaks in my name. [20] But the prophet who presumes to speak a message in my name that I have not commanded him to speak, or who speaks in the name of other gods — that prophet must die.' [21] You may say to yourself, 'How can we recognize a message the LORD has not spoken?' [22] When a prophet speaks in the LORD's name, and the message does not come true or is not fulfilled, that is a message the LORD has not spoken. The prophet has spoken it presumptuously. Do not be afraid of him.   Mt 21:11; Lk 2:25-34; 7:16; 24:19; Jn 1:21,25

Cities of Refuge

19 "When the LORD your God annihilates the nations whose land he is giving you, so that you drive them out and live in their cities and houses, [2] you are to set apart three cities for yourselves within the land the Lord your God is giving you to possess. ³ You are to determine the distances ᴬ and divide the land the Lord your God is granting you as an inheritance into three regions, so that anyone who commits manslaughter can flee to these cities. ᴮ Nm 35:6-34; Dt 12:29

⁴ "Here is the law concerning a case of someone who kills a person and flees there to save his life, having killed his neighbor accidentally without previously hating him: ⁵ If, for example, he goes into the forest with his neighbor to cut timber, and his hand swings the ax to chop down a tree, but the blade flies off the handle and strikes his neighbor so that he dies, that person may flee to one of these cities and live. ⁶ Otherwise, the avenger of blood in the heat of his anger ᶜ might pursue the one who committed manslaughter, overtake him because the distance is great, and strike him dead. Yet he did not deserve to die, ᴰ since he did not previously hate his neighbor. ⁷ This is why I am commanding you to set apart three cities for yourselves. ⁸ If the Lord your God enlarges your territory as he swore to your fathers, and gives you all the land he promised to give them — ⁹ provided you keep every one of these commands I am giving you today and follow them, loving the Lord your God and walking in his ways at all times — you are to add three more cities to these three. ¹⁰ In this way, innocent blood will not be shed, and you will not become guilty of bloodshed in the land the Lord your God is giving you as an inheritance. ¹¹ But if someone hates his neighbor, lies in ambush for him, attacks him, and strikes him fatally, and flees to one of these cities, ¹² the elders of his city are to send for him, take him from there, and hand him over to the avenger of blood and he will die. ¹³ Do not look on him with pity but purge from Israel the guilt of shedding innocent blood, and you will prosper.   Dt 15:4

Boundary Markers

¹⁴ "Do not move your neighbor's boundary marker, established at the start in the inheritance you will receive in the land the Lord your God is giving you to possess.

Witnesses in Court

¹⁵ "One witness cannot establish any iniquity or sin against a person, whatever that person has done. A fact must be established by the testimony of two or three witnesses. Nm 35:30; Mt 18:16; Jn 8:17; 2Co 13:1

¹⁶ "If a malicious witness testifies against someone accusing him of a crime, ¹⁷ the two people in the dispute are to stand in the presence of the Lord before the priests and judges in authority at that time. ¹⁸ The judges are to make a careful investigation, and if the witness turns out to be a liar who has falsely accused his brother, ¹⁹ you must do to him as he intended to do to his brother. You must purge the evil from you. ²⁰ Then everyone else will hear and be afraid, and they will never again do anything evil like this among you. ²¹ Do not show pity: life for life, eye for eye, tooth for tooth, hand for hand, and foot for foot.   Ex 21:23-25; 23:1; Lv 24:19-20; Dt 13:11

ᴬ19:3 Or to prepare the roads   ᴮ19:3 Lit flee there   ᶜ19:6 Lit heart   ᴰ19:6 Lit did not have a judgment of death

Rules for War

20 "When you go out to war against your enemies and see horses, chariots, and an army larger than yours, do not be afraid of them, for the LORD your God, who brought you out of the land of Egypt, is with you. ² When you are about to engage in battle, the priest is to come forward and address the army. ³ He is to say to them: 'Listen, Israel: Today you are about to engage in battle with your enemies. Do not be cowardly. Do not be afraid, alarmed, or terrified because of them. ⁴ For the LORD your God is the one who goes with you to fight for you against your enemies to give you victory.' Jos 17:18

⁵ "The officers are to address the army, 'Has any man built a new house and not dedicated it? Let him leave and return home. Otherwise, he may die in battle and another man dedicate it. ⁶ Has any man planted a vineyard and not begun to enjoy its fruit?ᴬ Let him leave and return home. Otherwise he may die in battle and another man enjoy its fruit.ᴮ ⁷ Has any man become engaged to a woman and not married her? Let him leave and return home. Otherwise he may die in battle and another man marry her.' ⁸ The officers will continue to address the army and say, 'Is there any man who is afraid or cowardly? Let him leave and return home, so that his brothers won't lose heart as he did.'ᶜ ⁹ When the officers have finished addressing the army, they will appoint military commanders to lead it. Jdg 7:3

¹⁰ "When you approach a city to fight against it, make an offer of peace. ¹¹ If it accepts your offer of peace and opens its gates to you, all the people found in it will become forced laborers for you and serve you. ¹² However, if it does not make peace with you but wages war against you, lay siege to it. ¹³ When the LORD your God hands it over to you, strike down all its males with the sword. ¹⁴ But you may take the women, dependents, animals, and whatever else is in the city — all its spoil — as plunder. You may enjoy the spoil of your enemies that the LORD your God has given you. ¹⁵ This is how you are to treat all the cities that are far away from you and are not among the cities of these nations. ¹⁶ However, you must not let any living thing survive among the cities of these people the LORD your God is giving you as an inheritance. ¹⁷ You must completely destroy them — the Hethite, Amorite, Canaanite, Perizzite, Hivite, and Jebusite — as the LORD your God has commanded you, ¹⁸ so that they won't teach you to do all the detestable acts they do for their gods, and you sin against the LORD your God. Ex 1:11; Jos 16:10; 17:13; Jdg 1:28-35

¹⁹ "When you lay siege to a city for a long time, fighting against it in order to capture it, do not destroy its trees by putting an ax to them, because you can get food from them. Do not cut them down. Are trees of the field human, to come under siege by you? ²⁰ But you may destroy the trees that you know do not produce food. You may cut them down to build siege works against the city that is waging war against you, until it falls.

ᴬ20:6 Lit *not put it to use*   ᴮ20:6 Lit *man put it to use*   ᶜ20:8 Lit *brothers' hearts won't melt like his own*

Unsolved Murders

21

"If a murder victim is found lying in a field in the land the LORD your God is giving you to possess, and it is not known who killed him, [2] your elders and judges are to come out and measure the distance from the victim to the nearby cities. [3] The elders of the city nearest to the victim are to get a young cow that has not been yoked or used for work. [4] The elders of that city will bring the cow down to a continually flowing stream, to a place not tilled or sown, and they will break its neck there by the stream. [5] Then the priests, the sons of Levi, will come forward, for the LORD your God has chosen them to serve him and pronounce blessings in his name, and they are to give a ruling in[A] every dispute and case of assault. [6] All the elders of the city nearest to the victim will wash their hands by the stream over the young cow whose neck has been broken. [7] They will declare, 'Our hands did not shed this blood; our eyes did not see it. [8] LORD, wipe away the guilt of your people Israel whom you redeemed, and do not hold the shedding of innocent blood against them.' Then the responsibility for bloodshed will be wiped away from them. [9] You must purge from yourselves the guilt of shedding innocent blood, for you will be doing what is right in the LORD's sight.

Fair Treatment of Captured Women

[10] "When you go to war against your enemies and the LORD your God hands them over to you and you take some of them prisoner, and[11] if you see a beautiful woman among the captives, desire her, and want to take her as your wife, [12] you are to bring her into your house. She is to shave her head, trim her nails, [13] remove the clothes she was wearing when she was taken prisoner, live in your house, and mourn for her father and mother a full month. After that, you may have sexual relations with her and be her husband, and she will be your wife. [14] Then if you are not satisfied with her, you are to let her go where she wants, but you must not sell her or treat her as merchandise,[B] because you have humiliated her.

The Right of the Firstborn

[15] "If a man has two wives, one loved and the other unloved, and both the loved and the unloved bear him sons, and if the unloved wife has the firstborn son, [16] when that man gives what he has to his sons as an inheritance, he is not to show favoritism to the son of the loved wife as his firstborn over the firstborn of the unloved wife. [17] He must acknowledge the firstborn, the son of the unloved wife, by giving him two shares[C,D] of his estate, for he is the firstfruits of his virility; he has the rights of the firstborn.

A Rebellious Son

[18] "If a man has a stubborn and rebellious son who does not obey his father or mother and doesn't listen to them even after they discipline him, [19] his father and mother are to take hold of him and bring him to the elders of his city, to the gate of his hometown. [20] They will say to the elders of his city, 'This son of

---

[A] 21:5 Lit and according to their mouth will be   [B] 21:14 Hb obscure   [C] 21:17 Lit him mouth of two, or two mouthfuls   [D] 21:17 Or two-thirds ours is stubborn and rebellious; he doesn't obey us. He's a glutton and a drunkard.' ²¹ Then all the men of his city will stone him to death. You must purge the evil from you, and all Israel will hear and be afraid.

Display of Executed People

²² "If anyone is found guilty of an offense deserving the death penalty and is executed, and you hang his body on a tree, ²³ you are not to leave his corpse on the tree overnight but are to bury him that day, for anyone hung on a tree is under God's curse. You must not defile the land the LORD your God is giving you as an inheritance.   Gl 3:13

Caring for Your Brother's Property

22 "If you see your brother Israelite's ox or sheep straying, do not ignore it; make sure you return it to your brother. ² If your brother does not live near you or you don't know him, you are to bring the animal to your home to remain with you until your brother comes looking for it; then you can return it to him. ³ Do the same for his donkey, his garment, or anything your brother has lost and you have found. You must not ignore it. ⁴ If you see your brother's donkey or ox fallen down on the road, do not ignore it; help him lift it up.   Ex 23:4

Preserving Natural Distinctions

⁵ "A woman is not to wear male clothing, and a man is not to put on a woman's garment, for everyone who does these things is detestable to the LORD your God.

⁶ "If you come across a bird's nest with chicks or eggs, either in a tree or on the ground along the road, and the mother is sitting on the chicks or eggs, do not take the mother along with the young. ⁷ You may take the young for yourself, but be sure to let the mother go free, so that you may prosper and live long. ⁸ If you build a new house, make a railing around your roof, so that you don't bring bloodguilt on your house if someone falls from it. ⁹ Do not plant your vineyard with two types of seed; otherwise, the entire harvest, both the crop you plant and the produce of the vineyard, will be defiled. ¹⁰ Do not plow with an ox and a donkey together. ¹¹ Do not wear clothes made of both wool and linen. ¹² Make tassels on the four corners of the outer garment you wear.   Lv 19:19; Nm 15:38-39

Violations of Proper Sexual Conduct

¹³ "If a man marries a woman, has sexual relations with her, and comes to hate her, ¹⁴ and accuses her of shameful conduct, and gives her a bad name, saying, 'I married this woman and was intimate with her, but I didn't find any evidence of her virginity,' ¹⁵ the young woman's father and mother will take the evidence of her virginity and bring it to the city elders at the city gate. ¹⁶ The young woman's father will say to the elders, 'I gave my daughter to this man as a wife, but he hates her. ¹⁷ He has accused her of shameful conduct, saying: "I didn't find any evidence of your daughter's virginity," but here is the evidence of my daughter's virginity.' They will spread out the cloth before the city elders. ¹⁸ Then the elders of that city will take the man and punish him. ¹⁹ They will also

fine him a hundred silver shekels and give them to the young woman's father, because that man gave an Israelite virgin a bad name. She will remain his wife; he cannot divorce her as long as he lives. [20] But if this accusation is true and no evidence of the young woman's virginity is found, [21] they will bring the woman to the door of her father's house, and the men of her city will stone her to death. For she has committed an outrage in Israel by being promiscuous while living in her father's house. You must purge the evil from you. Dt 17:8; 21:19

[22] "If a man is discovered having sexual relations with another man's wife, both the man who had sex with the woman and the woman must die. You must purge the evil from Israel. [23] If there is a young woman who is a virgin engaged to a man, and another man encounters her in the city and sleeps with her, [24] take the two of them out to the gate of that city and stone them to death — the young woman because she did not cry out in the city and the man because he has violated his neighbor's fiancée. You must purge the evil from you. [25] But if the man encounters an engaged woman in the open country, and he seizes and rapes her, only the man who raped her must die. [26] Do nothing to the young woman, because she is not guilty of an offense deserving death. This case is just like one in which a man attacks his neighbor and murders him. [27] When he found her in the field, the engaged woman cried out, but there was no one to rescue her. [28] If a man encounters a young woman, a virgin who is not engaged, takes hold of her and rapes her, and they are discovered, [29] the man who raped her is to give the young woman's father fifty silver shekels, and she will become his wife because he violated her. He cannot divorce her as long as he lives. Ex 22:16-17

[30] "A man is not to marry his father's wife; he must not violate his father's marriage bed.[A] Lv 18:8; 20:10-11

Exclusion and Inclusion

23 "No man whose testicles have been crushed[B] or whose penis has been cut off may enter the LORD's assembly. [2] No one of illegitimate birth may enter the LORD's assembly; none of his descendants, even to the tenth generation, may enter the LORD's assembly. [3] No Ammonite or Moabite may enter the LORD's assembly; none of their descendants, even to the tenth generation, may ever enter the LORD's assembly. [4] This is because they did not meet you with food and water on the journey after you came out of Egypt, and because Balaam son of Beor from Pethor in Aram-naharaim was hired to curse you. [5] Yet the LORD your God would not listen to Balaam, but he turned the curse into a blessing for you because the LORD your God loves you. [6] Never pursue their welfare or prosperity as long as you live. [7] Do not despise an Edomite, because he is your brother. Do not despise an Egyptian, because you were a resident alien in his land. [8] The children born to them in the third generation may enter the LORD's assembly. Neh 13:1-2; Nm 22:5-6; Dt 4:37; 24:10

[A] **22:30** Lit *not uncover the edge of his father's garment*; Ru 3:9; Ezk 16:8　[B] **23:1** Lit *man bruised by crushing*

Cleanliness of the Camp

⁹ "When you are encamped against your enemies, be careful to avoid anything offensive. ¹⁰ If there is a man among you who is unclean because of a bodily emission during the night, he must go outside the camp; he may not come anywhere inside the camp. ¹¹ When evening approaches, he is to wash with water, and when the sun sets he may come inside the camp. ¹² You are to have a place outside the camp and go there to relieve yourself. ¹³ You are to have a digging tool in your equipment; when you relieve yourself, dig a hole with it and cover up your excrement. ¹⁴ For the LORD your God walks throughout your camp to protect you and deliver your enemies to you; so your encampments must be holy. He must not see anything indecent among you or he will turn away from you.

Fugitive Slaves

¹⁵ "Do not return a slave to his master when he has escaped from his master to you. ¹⁶ Let him live among you wherever he wants within your city gates. Do not mistreat him.

Cult Prostitution Forbidden

¹⁷ "No Israelite woman is to be a cult prostitute, and no Israelite man is to be a cult prostitute. ¹⁸ Do not bring a female prostitute's wages or a male prostitute's ᴬ earnings into the house of the LORD your God to fulfill any vow, because both are detestable to the LORD your God.

Interest on Loans

¹⁹ "Do not charge your brother interest on silver, food, or anything that can earn interest. ²⁰ You may charge a foreigner interest, but you must not charge your brother Israelite interest, so that the LORD your God may bless you in everything you do ᴮ in the land you are entering to possess.   Ex 22:25

Keeping Vows

²¹ "If you make a vow to the LORD your God, do not be slow to keep it, because he will require it of you, and it will be counted against you as sin. ²² But if you refrain from making a vow, it will not be counted against you as sin. ²³ Be careful to do whatever comes from your lips, because you have freely vowed what you promised ᶜ to the LORD your God.   Nm 30:2-15; Jb 22:27; Ps 50:14; 56:12

Neighbor's Crops

²⁴ "When you enter your neighbor's vineyard, you may eat as many grapes as you want until you are full, but do not put any in your container. ²⁵ When you enter your neighbor's standing grain, you may pluck heads of grain with your hand, but do not put a sickle to your neighbor's grain.

Marriage and Divorce Laws

24 "If a man marries a woman, but she becomes displeasing to him ᴰ because he finds something indecent about her, he may write her a divorce certificate, hand it to her, and send her away from his house. ² If after leaving his house she goes and becomes another man's wife, ³ and the second man hates her, writes her a divorce certificate, hands it to her, and sends her away from his

---

ᴬ**23:18** Lit *a dog's*   ᴮ**23:20** Lit *you put your hand to she does not find favor in his eyes*   ᶜ**23:23** Lit *promised with your mouth*   ᴰ**24:1** Lit house or if he dies, ⁴ the first husband who sent her away may not marry her again after she has been defiled, because that would be detestable to the LORD. You must not bring guilt on the land the LORD your God is giving you as an inheritance. Dt 15:4; Mt 5:31; 19:7; Mk 10:4

⁵ "When a man takes a bride, he must not go out with the army or be liable for any duty. He is free to stay at home for one year, so that he can bring joy to the wife he has married.

Safeguarding Life

⁶ "Do not take a pair of grindstones or even the upper millstone as security for a debt, because that is like taking a life as security.

⁷ "If a man is discovered kidnapping one of his Israelite brothers, whether he treats him as a slave or sells him, the kidnapper must die. You must purge the evil from you. Gn 40:15; Ex 21:16; 22:1; 1Sm 30:2-3,5

⁸ "Be careful with a person who has a case of serious skin disease, following carefully everything the Levitical priests instruct you to do. Be careful to do as I have commanded them. ⁹ Remember what the LORD your God did to Miriam on the journey after you left Egypt.

Consideration for People in Need

¹⁰ "When you make a loan of any kind to your neighbor, do not enter his house to collect what he offers as security. ¹¹ Stand outside while the man you are making the loan to brings the security out to you. ¹² If he is a poor man, do not sleep with the garment he has given as security. ¹³ Be sure to return it[A] to him at sunset. Then he will sleep in it and bless you, and this will be counted as righteousness to you before the LORD your God.

¹⁴ "Do not oppress a hired worker who is poor and needy, whether one of your Israelite brothers or one of the resident aliens in a town[B] in your land. ¹⁵ You are to pay him his wages each day before the sun sets, because he is poor and depends on them. Otherwise he will cry out to the LORD against you, and you will be held guilty. Lv 19:13

¹⁶ "Fathers are not to be put to death for their children, and children are not to be put to death for their fathers; each person will be put to death for his own sin. ¹⁷ Do not deny justice to a resident alien or fatherless child, and do not take a widow's garment as security. ¹⁸ Remember that you were a slave in Egypt, and the LORD your God redeemed you from there. Therefore I am commanding you to do this. 2Kg 14:6; 2Ch 25:4; Ezk 18:20; 33:10-20

¹⁹ "When you reap the harvest in your field, and you forget a sheaf in the field, do not go back to get it. It is to be left for the resident alien, the fatherless, and the widow, so that the LORD your God may bless you in all the work of your hands. ²⁰ When you knock down the fruit from your olive tree, do not go over the branches again. What remains will be for the resident alien, the fatherless, and the widow. ²¹ When you gather the grapes of your vineyard, do not glean what is left. What remains will be for the resident alien, the fatherless, and the widow. ²² Remember that you were a slave in the land of Egypt. Therefore I am commanding you to do this. Ex 22:26-27; 23:2-3,6-9; Dt 30:9

A24:13 Lit return what he has given as security   B24:14 Lit within the city gates

Fairness and Mercy

25
"If there is a dispute between men, they are to go to court, and the judges will hear their case. They will clear the innocent and condemn the guilty. ² If the guilty party deserves to be flogged, the judge will make him lie down and be flogged in his presence with the number of lashes appropriate for his crime. ³ He may be flogged with forty lashes, but no more. Otherwise, if he is flogged with more lashes than these, your brother will be degraded in your sight.

⁴ "Do not muzzle an ox while it treads out grain.   1Co 9:9; 1Tm 5:18

Preserving the Family Line

⁵ "When brothers live on the same property^A and one of them dies without a son, the wife of the dead man may not marry a stranger outside the family. Her brother-in-law is to take her as his wife, have sexual relations with her, and perform the duty of a brother-in-law for her. ⁶ The first son she bears will carry on the name of the dead brother, so his name will not be blotted out from Israel. ⁷ But if the man doesn't want to marry his sister-in-law, she is to go to the elders at the city gate and say, 'My brother-in-law refuses to preserve his brother's name in Israel. He isn't willing to perform the duty of a brother-in-law for me.' ⁸ The elders of his city will summon him and speak with him. If he persists and says, 'I don't want to marry her,' ⁹ then his sister-in-law will go up to him in the sight of the elders, remove his sandal from his foot, and spit in his face. Then she will declare, 'This is what is done to a man who will not build up his brother's house.' ¹⁰ And his family name in Israel will be 'The house of the man whose sandal was removed.'   Gn 38:8; Mt 22:24; Mk 12:19; Lk 20:28

¹¹ "If two men are fighting with each other, and the wife of one steps in to rescue her husband from the one striking him, and she puts out her hand and grabs his genitals, ¹² you are to cut off her hand. Do not show pity.

Honest Weights and Measures

¹³ "Do not have differing weights^B in your bag, one heavy and one light. ¹⁴ Do not have differing dry measures in your house, a larger and a smaller. ¹⁵ You must have a full and honest weight, a full and honest dry measure, so that you may live long in the land the LORD your God is giving you. ¹⁶ For everyone who does such things and acts unfairly is detestable to the LORD your God.

Revenge on the Amalekites

¹⁷ "Remember what the Amalekites did to you on the journey after you left Egypt. ¹⁸ They met you along the way and attacked all your stragglers from behind when you were tired and weary. They did not fear God. ¹⁹ When the LORD your God gives you rest from all the enemies around you in the land the LORD your God is giving you to possess as an inheritance, blot out the memory of Amalek under heaven. Do not forget.   Dt 3:20; 5:14; 12:9-11; 24:9; 30

Giving the Firstfruits

26
"When you enter the land the LORD your God is giving you as an inheritance, and you take possession of it and live in it, ² take some of the first of all the land's

^A 25:5 Lit *live together*   ^B 25:13 Lit *have a stone and a stone* produce that you harvest from the land the LORD your God is giving you and put it in a basket. Then go to the place where the LORD your God chooses to have his name dwell. [3] When you come before the priest who is serving at that time, say to him, 'Today I declare to the LORD your[A] God that I have entered the land the LORD swore to our fathers to give us.' Dt 12:11

[4] "Then the priest will take the basket from you and place it before the altar of the LORD your God. [5] You are to respond by saying in the presence of the LORD your God: My father was a wandering Aramean. He went down to Egypt with a few people and resided there as an alien. There he became a great, powerful, and populous nation. [6] But the Egyptians mistreated and oppressed us, and forced us to do hard labor. [7] So we called out to the LORD, the God of our fathers, and the LORD heard our cry and saw our misery, hardship, and oppression. [8] Then the LORD brought us out of Egypt with a strong hand and an outstretched arm, with terrifying power, and with signs and wonders. [9] He led us to this place and gave us this land, a land flowing with milk and honey. [10] I have now brought the first of the land's produce that you, LORD, have given me. You will then place the container before the LORD your God and bow down to him. [11] You, the Levites, and the resident aliens among you will rejoice in all the good things the LORD your God has given you and your household. Lv 23:40; Dt 12:12; 14:26

[A]26:3 LXX reads my

The Tenth in the Third Year

[12] "When you have finished paying all the tenth of your produce in the third year, the year of the tenth, you are to give it to the Levites, resident aliens, fatherless children and widows, so that they may eat in your towns and be satisfied. [13] Then you will say in the presence of the LORD your God: Dt 14:28-29

I have taken the consecrated portion out of my house; I have also given it to the Levites, resident aliens, fatherless children, and widows, according to all the commands you gave me. I have not violated or forgotten your commands. [14] I have not eaten any of it while in mourning, or removed any of it while unclean, or offered any of it for the dead. I have obeyed the LORD my God; I have done all you commanded me. [15] Look down from your holy dwelling, from heaven, and bless your people Israel and the land you have given us as you swore to our fathers, a land flowing with milk and honey. Jr 16:7; Hs 9:4

Covenant Summary

[16] "The LORD your God is commanding you this day to follow these statutes and ordinances. Follow them carefully with all your heart and all your soul. [17] Today you have affirmed that the LORD is your God and that you will walk in his ways, keep his statutes, commands, and ordinances, and obey him. [18] And today the LORD has affirmed that you are his own possession as he promised you, that you are to keep all his commands, [19] that he will elevate you to praise, fame, and glory

above all the nations he has made, and that you will be a holy people to the LORD your God as he promised."

The Law Written on Stones

27 Moses and the elders of Israel commanded the people, "Keep every command I am giving you today. ² When you cross the Jordan into the land the LORD your God is giving you, set up large stones and cover them with plaster. ³ Write all the words of this law on the stones after you cross to enter the land the LORD your God is giving you, a land flowing with milk and honey, as the LORD, the God of your fathers, has promised you. ⁴ When you have crossed the Jordan, you are to set up these stones on Mount Ebal, as I am commanding you today, and you are to cover them with plaster. ⁵ Build an altar of stones there to the LORD your God — do not use any iron tool on them. ⁶ Use uncut stones to build the altar of the LORD your God and offer burnt offerings to the LORD your God on it. ⁷ There you are to sacrifice fellowship offerings, eat, and rejoice in the presence of the LORD your God. ⁸ Write clearly all the words of this law on the plastered stones." Ex 20:25; Dt 11:9; Jos 8:30-32

The Covenant Curses

⁹ Moses and the Levitical priests spoke to all Israel, "Be silent, Israel, and listen! This day you have become the people of the LORD your God. ¹⁰ Obey the LORD your God and follow his commands and statutes I am giving you today."

¹¹ On that day Moses commanded the people, ¹² "When you have crossed the Jordan, these tribes will stand on Mount Gerizim to bless the people: Simeon, Levi, Judah, Issachar, Joseph, and Benjamin. ¹³ And these tribes will stand on Mount Ebal to deliver the curse: Reuben, Gad, Asher, Zebulun, Dan, and Naphtali. ¹⁴ The Levites will proclaim in a loud voice to every Israelite:

¹⁵ 'The person who makes a carved idol or cast image, which is detestable to the LORD, the work of a craftsman, and sets it up in secret is cursed.'
And all the people will reply, 'Amen!'

¹⁶ 'The one who dishonors his father or mother is cursed.'
And all the people will say, 'Amen!'

¹⁷ 'The one who moves his neighbor's boundary marker is cursed.'
And all the people will say, 'Amen!'

¹⁸ 'The one who leads a blind person astray on the road is cursed.'
And all the people will say, 'Amen!'

¹⁹ 'The one who denies justice to a resident alien, a fatherless child, or a widow is cursed.'
And all the people will say, 'Amen!'

²⁰ 'The one who sleeps with his father's wife is cursed, for he has violated his father's marriage bed.'ᴬ
And all the people will say, 'Amen!'

²¹ 'The one who has sexual intercourse with any animal is cursed.'
And all the people will say, 'Amen!'

ᴬ27:20 Lit *has uncovered the edge of his father's garment*; Ru 3:9; Ezk 16:8

²² 'The one who sleeps with his sister, whether his father's daughter or his mother's daughter is cursed.' And all the people will say, 'Amen!'

²³ 'The one who sleeps with his mother-in-law is cursed.' And all the people will say, 'Amen!'

²⁴ 'The one who secretly kills his neighbor is cursed.' And all the people will say, 'Amen!'

²⁵ 'The one who accepts a bribe to kill an innocent person is cursed.' And all the people will say, 'Amen!'

²⁶ 'Anyone who does not put the words of this law into practice is cursed.' And all the people will say, 'Amen!'

Blessings for Obedience

28 ¹ "Now if you faithfully obey the LORD your God and are careful to follow all his commands I am giving you today, the LORD your God will put you far above all the nations of the earth. ² All these blessings will come and overtake you, because you obey the LORD your God: Ex 15:5,26; 19:5; 23:22; Lv 26:3-13

³ You will be blessed
    in the city
    and blessed in the country.

⁴ Your offspring ^A
    will be blessed,
    and your land's produce,
    and the offspring
      of your livestock,
    including the young
      of your herds

and the newborn
    of your flocks.   Dt 7:13

⁵ Your basket
    and kneading bowl
    will be blessed.

⁶ You will be blessed
    when you come in
    and blessed when you go out.

⁷ "The LORD will cause the enemies who rise up against you to be defeated before you. They will march out against you from one direction but flee from you in seven directions. ⁸ The LORD will grant you a blessing on your barns and on everything you do; ^B he will bless you in the land the LORD your God is giving you. ⁹ The LORD will establish you as his holy people, as he swore to you, if you obey the commands of the LORD your God and walk in his ways. ¹⁰ Then all the peoples of the earth will see that you bear the LORD's name, and they will stand in awe of you. ¹¹ The LORD will make you prosper abundantly with offspring, ^C the offspring of your livestock, and your land's produce in the land the LORD swore to your fathers to give you. ¹² The LORD will open for you his abundant storehouse, the sky, to give your land rain in its season and to bless all the work of your hands. You will lend to many nations, but you will not borrow. ¹³ The LORD will make you the head and not the tail; you will only move upward and never downward if you listen to the LORD your God's commands I am giving you today and are careful to follow them. ¹⁴ Do not turn aside to the right or the left from all the things I am commanding you today, and

^A 28:4 Lit *The fruit of your womb,* also in v. 18   ^B 28:8 Lit *you put your hand to,* also in v. 20   ^C 28:11 Lit *abundantly in the fruit of your womb* do not follow other gods to worship them. Ex 22:31; Dt 7:6; 15:4; 30:16; Pr 3:10

Curses for Disobedience

15 "But if you do not obey the LORD your God by carefully following all his commands and statutes I am giving you today, all these curses will come and overtake you: Ps 7:5

16 You will be cursed in the city
and cursed in the country.
17 Your basket
and kneading bowl
will be cursed.
18 Your offspring will be cursed,
and your land's produce,
the young of your herds,
and the newborn
of your flocks.
19 You will be cursed
when you come in
and cursed when you go out.

20 The LORD will send against you curses, confusion, and rebuke in everything you do until you are destroyed and quickly perish, because of the wickedness of your actions in abandoning me. 21 The LORD will make pestilence cling to you until he has exterminated you from the land you are entering to possess. 22 The LORD will afflict you with wasting disease, fever, inflammation, burning heat, drought,A blight, and mildew; these will pursue you until you perish. 23 The sky above you will be bronze, and the earth beneath you iron. 24 The LORD will turn the rain of your land into fallingB dust; it will descend on you from the sky until you are destroyed. 25 The LORD will cause you to be defeated before your enemies. You will march out against them from one direction but flee from them in seven directions. You will be an object of horror to all the kingdoms of the earth. 26 Your corpses will be food for all the birds of the sky and the wild animals of the earth, with no one to scare them away. Dt 7:23,24; 28:45,48,51,61; Jos 23:15; Ezk 7:7

27 "The LORD will afflict you with the boils of Egypt, tumors, a festering rash, and scabies, from which you cannot be cured. 28 The LORD will afflict you with madness, blindness, and mental confusion, 29 so that at noon you will grope as a blind person gropes in the dark. You will not be successful in anything you do. You will only be oppressed and robbed continually, and no one will help you. 30 You will become engaged to a woman, but another man will rape her. You will build a house but not live in it. You will plant a vineyard but not enjoy its fruit. 31 Your ox will be slaughtered before your eyes, but you will not eat any of it. Your donkey will be taken away from you and not returned to you. Your flock will be given to your enemies, and no one will help you. 32 Your sons and daughters will be given to another people, while your eyes grow weary looking for them every day. But you will be powerless to do anything.C 33 A people you don't know will eat your land's produce and everything you have labored for. You will only be oppressed and crushed continually. 34 You will be driven mad by what you see. 35 The LORD will afflict you with painful and incurable boils on your knees and thighs — from the sole of your foot to the top of your head.

36 "The LORD will bring you and your king that you have appointed to a nation neither you nor your

A28:22 Or *sword*   B28:24 Lit *powder and*   C28:32 Lit *day, and not for power your hand* fathers have known, and there you will worship other gods, of wood and stone. ³⁷ You will become an object of horror, scorn, and ridicule among all the peoples where the LORD will drive you. Dt 4:28; 28:64

³⁸ "You will sow much seed in the field but harvest little, because locusts will devour it. ³⁹ You will plant and cultivate vineyards but not drink the wine or gather the grapes, because worms will eat them. ⁴⁰ You will have olive trees throughout your territory but not moisten your skin with oil, because your olives will drop off. ⁴¹ You will father sons and daughters, but they will not remain yours, because they will be taken prisoner. ⁴² Buzzing insects will take possession of all your trees and your land's produce. ⁴³ The resident alien among you will rise higher and higher above you, while you sink lower and lower. ⁴⁴ He will lend to you, but you won't lend to him. He will be the head, and you will be the tail.

⁴⁵ "All these curses will come, pursue, and overtake you until you are destroyed, since you did not obey the LORD your God and keep the commands and statutes he gave you. ⁴⁶ These curses will be a sign and a wonder against you and your descendants forever. ⁴⁷ Because you didn't serve the LORD your God with joy and a cheerful heart, even though you had an abundance of everything, ⁴⁸ you will serve your enemies the LORD will send against you, in famine, thirst, nakedness, and a lack of everything. He will place an iron yoke on your neck until he has destroyed you. ⁴⁹ The LORD will bring a nation from far away, from the ends of the earth, to swoop down on you like an eagle, a nation whose language you won't understand, ⁵⁰ a ruthless nation, ᴬ showing no respect for the old and not sparing the young. ⁵¹ They will eat the offspring of your livestock and your land's produce until you are destroyed. They will leave you no grain, new wine, fresh oil, young of your herds, or newborn of your flocks until they cause you to perish. ⁵² They will besiege you within all your city gates until your high and fortified walls, that you trust in, come down throughout your land. They will besiege you within all your city gates throughout the land the LORD your God has given you. Ex 7:3; Dt 4:34; 6:22; 7:19; 26:8; Is 8:18; Jr 32:20

⁵³ "You will eat your offspring, ᴮ the flesh of your sons and daughters the LORD your God has given you during the siege and hardship your enemy imposes on you. ⁵⁴ The most sensitive and refined man among you will look grudgingly ᶜ at his brother, the wife he embraces, ᴰ and the rest of his children, ⁵⁵ refusing to share with any of them his children's flesh that he will eat because he has nothing left during the siege and hardship your enemy imposes on you in all your towns. ⁵⁶ The most sensitive and refined woman among you, who would not venture to set the sole of her foot on the ground because of her refinement and sensitivity, will begrudge the husband she embraces, her son, and her daughter, ⁵⁷ the afterbirth that comes out from between her legs and the children she bears, because she will secretly eat them for lack of anything

ᴬ**28:50** Lit *a nation strong of face*   ᴮ**28:53** Lit *eat the fruit of your womb*   ᶜ**28:54** Lit *you his eye will be evil*   ᴰ**28:54** Lit *wife of his bosom* else during the siege and hardship your enemy imposes on you within your city gates. Lv 26:29; 2Kg 6:25-29

⁵⁸ "If you are not careful to obey all the words of this law, which are written in this scroll, by fearing this glorious and awe-inspiring name — the LORD, your God — ⁵⁹ he will bring wondrous plagues on you and your descendants, severe and lasting plagues, and terrible and chronic sicknesses. ⁶⁰ He will afflict you again with all the diseases of Egypt, which you dreaded, and they will cling to you. ⁶¹ The LORD will also afflict you with every sickness and plague not recorded in the book of this law, until you are destroyed. ⁶² Though you were as numerous as the stars of the sky, you will be left with only a few people, because you did not obey the LORD your God. ⁶³ Just as the LORD was glad to cause you to prosper and to multiply you, so he will also be glad to cause you to perish and to destroy you. You will be ripped out of the land you are entering to possess. ⁶⁴ Then the LORD will scatter you among all peoples from one end of the earth to the other, and there you will worship other gods, of wood and stone, which neither you nor your fathers have known. ⁶⁵ You will find no peace among those nations, and there will be no resting place for the sole of your foot. There the LORD will give you a trembling heart, failing eyes, and a despondent spirit. ⁶⁶ Your life will hang in doubt before you. You will be in dread night and day, never certain of survival. ⁶⁷ In the morning you will say, 'If only it were evening!' and in the evening you will say, 'If only it were morning!'

— because of the dread you will have in your heart and because of what you will see. ⁶⁸ The LORD will take you back in ships to Egypt by a route that I said you would never see again. There you will sell yourselves to your enemies as male and female slaves, but no one will buy you." Lv 26:33; Dt 4:27; 7:15; Neh 1:8; Ezk 22:15

Renewing the Covenant

29 These are the words of the covenant the LORD commanded Moses to make with the Israelites in the land of Moab, in addition to the covenant he had made with them at Horeb. ² Moses summoned all Israel and said to them, "You have seen with your own eyes everything the LORD did in Egypt to Pharaoh, to all his officials, and to his entire land. ³ You saw with your own eyes the great trials and those great signs and wonders. ⁴ Yet to this day the LORD has not given you a mind to understand, eyes to see, or ears to hear. ⁵ I led you forty years in the wilderness; your clothes and the sandals on your feet did not wear out; ⁶ you did not eat food or drink wine or beer — so that you might know that I am the LORD your God. ⁷ When you reached this place, King Sihon of Heshbon and King Og of Bashan came out against us in battle, but we defeated them. ⁸ We took their land and gave it as an inheritance to the Reubenites, the Gadites, and half the tribe of Manasseh. ⁹ Therefore, observe the words of this covenant and follow them, so that you will succeed in everything you do. Ex 3:1; 17:6; 33:6; Dt 1:2,6,19; 5:2; 31:16

¹⁰ "All of you are standing today before the LORD your God — your leaders, tribes, elders, officials, all

the men of Israel, [11] your dependents, your wives, and the resident aliens in your camps who cut your wood and draw your water — [12] so that you may enter into the covenant of the LORD your God, which he is making with you today, so that you may enter into his oath [13] and so that he may establish you today as his people and he may be your God as he promised you and as he swore to your fathers Abraham, Isaac, and Jacob. [14] I am making this covenant and this oath not only with you, [15] but also with those who are standing here with us today in the presence of the LORD our God and with those who are not here today. Dt 7:8,12-13; 8:18; 9:5

Abandoning the Covenant

[16] "Indeed, you know how we lived in the land of Egypt and passed through the nations where you traveled. [17] You saw their abhorrent images and idols made of wood, stone, silver, and gold, which were among them. [18] Be sure there is no man, woman, clan, or tribe among you today whose heart turns away from the LORD our God to go and worship the gods of those nations. Be sure there is no root among you bearing poisonous and bitter fruit. [19] When someone hears the words of this oath, he may consider himself exempt, [A] thinking, 'I will have peace even though I follow my own stubborn heart.' This will lead to the destruction of the well-watered land as well as the dry land. [20] The LORD will not be willing to forgive him. Instead, his anger and jealousy will burn against that person, and every curse written in this scroll will descend on him. The LORD will blot out his name under heaven, [21] and single him out for harm from all the tribes of Israel, according to all the curses of the covenant written in this book of the law. 2Ch 15:8; Jr 4:1; Ezk 16:36; Heb 12:15

[22] "Future generations of your children who follow you and the foreigner who comes from a distant country will see the plagues of that land and the sicknesses the LORD has inflicted on it. [23] All its soil will be a burning waste of sulfur and salt, unsown, producing nothing, with no plant growing on it, just like the fall of Sodom and Gomorrah, Admah and Zeboiim, which the LORD demolished in his fierce anger. [24] All the nations will ask, 'Why has the LORD done this to this land? Why this intense outburst of anger?' [25] Then people will answer, 'It is because they abandoned the covenant of the LORD, the God of their fathers, which he had made with them when he brought them out of the land of Egypt. [26] They began to serve other gods, bowing in worship to gods they had not known — gods that the LORD had not permitted them to worship. [27] Therefore the LORD's anger burned against this land, and he brought every curse written in this book on it. [28] The LORD uprooted them from their land in his anger, rage, and intense wrath, and threw them into another land where they are today.' [29] The hidden things belong to the LORD our God, but the revealed things belong to us and our children forever, so that we may follow all the words of this law. Gn 14:2,8; 19:23-29; Dt 4:19; 32:17

[A]29:19 Lit may bless himself in his heart

Returning to the LORD

30 "When all these things happen to you — the blessings and curses I have set before you — and you come to your senses while you are in all the nations where the LORD your God has driven you, ² and you and your children return to the LORD your God and obey him with all your heart and all your soul by doing ᴬ everything I am commanding you today, ³ then he will restore your fortunes, ᴮ have compassion on you, and gather you again from all the peoples where the LORD your God has scattered you. ⁴ Even if your exiles are at the farthest horizon, ᶜ he will gather you and bring you back from there. ⁵ The LORD your God will bring you into the land your fathers possessed, and you will take possession of it. He will cause you to prosper and multiply you more than he did your fathers. ⁶ The LORD your God will circumcise your heart and the hearts of your descendants, and you will love him with all your heart and all your soul so that you will live. ⁷ The LORD your God will put all these curses on your enemies who hate and persecute you. ⁸ Then you will again obey him and follow all his commands I am commanding you today. ⁹ The LORD your God will make you prosper abundantly in all the work of your hands, your offspring, ᴰ the offspring of your livestock, and the produce of your land. Indeed, the LORD will again delight in your prosperity, as he delighted in that of your fathers, ¹⁰ when you obey the LORD your God by keeping his commands and statutes that are written in this book of the law and return to him with all your heart and all your soul. Am 9:4

Choose Life

¹¹ "This command that I give you today is certainly not too difficult or beyond your reach. ¹² It is not in heaven so that you have to ask, 'Who will go up to heaven, get it for us, and proclaim it to us so that we may follow it?' ¹³ And it is not across the sea so that you have to ask, 'Who will cross the sea, get it for us, and proclaim it to us so that we may follow it?' ¹⁴ But the message is very near you, in your mouth and in your heart, so that you may follow it. ¹⁵ See, today I have set before you life and prosperity, death and adversity. ¹⁶ For ᴱ I am commanding you today to love the LORD your God, to walk in his ways, and to keep his commands, statutes, and ordinances, so that you may live ᶠ and multiply, and the LORD your God may bless you in the land you are entering to possess. ¹⁷ But if your heart turns away and you do not listen and you are led astray to bow in worship to other gods and serve them, ¹⁸ I tell you today that you will certainly perish and will not prolong your days in the land you are entering to possess across the Jordan. ¹⁹ I call heaven and earth as witnesses against you today that I have set before you life and death, blessing and curse. Choose life so that you and your descendants may live, ²⁰ love the LORD your God, obey him, and remain faithful ᴳ to him. For he is your life, and he will prolong your days as

---

ᴬ**30:2** Lit *soul according to*   ᴮ**30:3** Or *will end your captivity*   ᶜ**30:4** Lit *skies*   ᴰ**30:9** Lit *hands in the fruit of your womb*   ᴱ**30:16** LXX reads *If you obey the commands of the LORD your God that*   ᶠ**30:16** LXX reads *ordinances, then you will live*   ᴳ**30:20** Lit *and hold on* you live in the land the Lord swore to give to your fathers Abraham, Isaac, and Jacob." Dt 4:1; 11:26; Rm 10:6-8

Joshua Takes Moses's Place

31 Then Moses continued to speak these[A] words to all Israel, [2] saying, "I am now 120 years old; I can no longer act as your leader.[B] The Lord has told me, 'You will not cross the Jordan.' [3] The Lord your God is the one who will cross ahead of you. He will destroy these nations before you, and you will drive them out. Joshua is the one who will cross ahead of you, as the Lord has said. [4] The Lord will deal with them as he did Sihon and Og, the kings of the Amorites, and their land when he destroyed them. [5] The Lord will deliver them over to you, and you must do to them exactly as I have commanded you. [6] Be strong and courageous; don't be terrified or afraid of them. For the Lord your God is the one who will go with you; he will not leave you or abandon you." Dt 3:27; 9:3; Jos 14:10

[7] Moses then summoned Joshua and said to him in the sight of all Israel, "Be strong and courageous, for you will go with[C] this people into the land the Lord swore to give to their fathers. You will enable them to take possession of it. [8] The Lord is the one who will go before you. He will be with you; he will not leave you or abandon you. Do not be afraid or discouraged."

[9] Moses wrote down this law and gave it to the priests, the sons of Levi, who carried the ark of the Lord's covenant, and to all the elders of Israel. [10] Moses commanded them, "At the end of every seven years, at the appointed time in the year of debt cancellation, during the Festival of Shelters, [11] when all Israel assembles[D] in the presence of the Lord your God at the place he chooses, you are to read this law aloud before all Israel. [12] Gather the people — men, women, dependents, and the resident aliens within your city gates — so that they may listen and learn to fear the Lord your God and be careful to follow all the words of this law. [13] Then their children who do not know the law will listen and learn to fear the Lord your God as long as you live in the land you are crossing the Jordan to possess." Dt 15:1-2

[14] The Lord said to Moses, "The time of your death is now approaching. Call Joshua and present yourselves at the tent of meeting so that I may commission him." When Moses and Joshua went and presented themselves at the tent of meeting, [15] the Lord appeared at the tent in a pillar of cloud, and the cloud stood at the entrance to the tent. Ex 13:21-22; 33:9-10; Nm 12:5; Ps 99:7

[16] The Lord said to Moses, "You are about to rest with your fathers, and these people will soon prostitute themselves with the foreign gods of the land they are entering. They will abandon me and break the covenant I have made with them. [17] My anger will burn against them on that day; I will abandon them and hide my face from them so that they will become easy prey.[E] Many troubles and afflictions will come to them. On that day they will say, 'Haven't these troubles come to us because our God is no longer

---

A31:1 Some Hb mss, DSS, LXX, Syr, Vg read *all these*   B31:2 Lit *no longer go out or come in*   C31:7 Some Hb mss, Sam, Syr, Vg read *you will bring*   D31:11 Lit *comes to appear*   E31:17 Lit *will be for devouring* with us?' ¹⁸ I will certainly hide my face on that day because of all the evil they have done by turning to other gods. ¹⁹ Therefore write down this song for yourselves and teach it to the Israelites; have them sing it, ^A so that this song may be a witness for me against the Israelites. ²⁰ When I bring them into the land I swore to give their fathers, a land flowing with milk and honey, they will eat their fill and prosper.^B They will turn to other gods and worship them, despising me and breaking my covenant. ²¹ And when many troubles and afflictions come to them, this song will testify against them, because^C their descendants will not have forgotten it. For I know what they are prone to do,^D even before I bring them into the land I swore to give them." ²² So Moses wrote down this song on that day and taught it to the Israelites. Gn 47:30; 2Sm 7:12; 1Kg 2:10

²³ The LORD commissioned Joshua son of Nun, "Be strong and courageous, for you will bring the Israelites into the land I swore to them, and I will be with you."

Moses Warns the People

²⁴ When Moses had finished writing down on a scroll every single word^E of this law, ²⁵ he commanded the Levites who carried the ark of the LORD's covenant, ²⁶ "Take this book of the law and place it beside the ark of the covenant of the LORD your God so that it may remain there as a witness against you. ²⁷ For I know how rebellious and stiff-necked you are. If you are rebelling against the LORD now, while I am still alive, how much more will you rebel after I am dead! ²⁸ Assemble all your tribal elders and officers before me so that I may speak these words directly to them and call heaven and earth as witnesses against them. ²⁹ For I know that after my death you will become completely corrupt and turn from the path I have commanded you. Disaster will come to you in the future, because you will do what is evil in the LORD's sight, angering him with what your hands have made." ³⁰ Then Moses recited aloud every single word^F of this song to the entire assembly of Israel: Dt 4:25-26; 30:19; Jdg 2:6-13

Song of Moses

32 Pay attention, heavens,
  and I will speak;
listen, earth, to the words
  from my mouth.   Jdg 5:3; Pr 4:20

² Let my teaching fall like rain
and my word settle like dew,
like gentle rain on new grass
and showers
  on tender plants.

³ For I will proclaim the
  LORD's name.   Ex 33:19; Ps 22:22
Declare the greatness
  of our God!

⁴ The Rock — his work
  is perfect;   Gn 49:24; Dt 32:15,18,30-31
all his ways are just.   2Sm 22:31
A faithful God, without bias,
he is righteous and true.

⁵ His people have acted
  corruptly toward him;   Dt 9:12
this is their defect^G —
  they are not his children
but a devious
  and crooked generation.

⁶ Is this how you repay
    the Lᴏʀᴅ,
you foolish
    and senseless people?   Jr 4:22
Isn't he your Father
    and Creator?ᴬ   Mal 2:10
Didn't he make you
    and sustain you?
⁷ Remember the days of old;
consider the years of past
    generations.
Ask your father,
    and he will tell you,
your elders,
    and they will teach you.
⁸ When the Most High
    gave the nations
    their inheritanceᴮ
and divided the human race,
he set the boundaries
    of the peoples   Ac 17:26
according to the number
    of the people of Israel.ᶜ
⁹ But the Lᴏʀᴅ's portion is
    his people,
Jacob, his own inheritance.

¹⁰ He found him
    in a desolate land,
in a barren,
    howling wilderness;
he surrounded him,
    cared for him,   Ezk 16:6-14
and protected him
    as the pupil of his eye.   Pr 7:2
¹¹ He watches overᴰ his nest
    like an eagle
and hovers over his young;
he spreads his wings,
    catches him,
and carries him
    on his feathers.   Ex 19:4; Ps 91:4
¹² The Lᴏʀᴅ alone led him,

with no help from
    a foreign god.ᴱ
¹³ He made him ride
    on the heights of the land
and eat the produce
    of the field.
He nourished him
    with honey
    from the rock
and oil from flinty rock,
¹⁴ curds from the herd
    and milk from the flock,
with the fat of lambs,
rams from Bashan,
    and goats,   Ps 22:12; Ezk 39:18; Am 4:1
with the choicest grains
    of wheat;
you drank wine
    from the finest grapes.ᶠ
¹⁵ Thenᴳ Jeshurunᴴ became fat
    and rebelled —   Is 44:2
you became fat, bloated,
    and gorged.
He abandoned the God
    who made him
and scorned the Rock
    of his salvation.
¹⁶ They provoked his jealousy
    with different gods;
they enraged him
    with detestable practices.
¹⁷ They sacrificed to demons,
    not God,
to gods they had not known,
new gods that had
    just arrived,
which your fathers
    did not fear.   Ps 106:37; 1Co 10:19-20
¹⁸ You ignored the Rock
    who gave you birth;
you forgot the God
    who gave birth to you.

ᴬ**32:6** Or *Possessor*   ᴮ**32:8** Or *Most High divided the nations*   ᶜ**32:8** One DSS reads *number of the sons of God*; LXX reads *number of the angels of God*   ᴰ**32:11** Or *He stirs up*   ᴱ**32:12** Lit *him, and no foreign god with him*   ᶠ**32:14** Lit *drank the blood of grapes, fermenting wine*   ᴳ**32:15** DSS, Sam, LXX add *Jacob ate his fill;*   ᴴ**32:15** = Upright One, referring to Israel

¹⁹ When the LORD saw this,
he despised them,
angered by his sons
and daughters.
²⁰ He said: "I will hide my face
from them; Dt 31:17-18; Jb 13:24; 13:1
I will see what will become
of them,
for they are
a perverse generation —
unfaithful children.
²¹ They have provoked
my jealousy
with what is not a god;^A
they have enraged me
with their worthless idols.
So I will provoke
their jealousy
with what is not a people;^B
I will enrage them
with a foolish nation. Dt 32:6
²² For fire has been kindled
because of my anger
and burns to the depths
of Sheol; Ps 86:13; Pr 9:18; Is 7:11
it devours the land
and its produce,
and scorches the foundations
of the mountains.
²³ "I will pile disasters on them;
I will use up my arrows
against them.
²⁴ They will be weak
from hunger,
ravaged by pestilence
and bitter plague;
I will unleash on them
wild beasts with fangs,
as well as venomous snakes
that slither in the dust.
²⁵ Outside, the sword will take
their children,
and inside,
there will be terror;

the young man
and the young woman
will be killed,
the infant
and the gray-haired man.
²⁶ "I would have said:
I will cut them to pieces^C
and blot out the memory
of them from mankind,
²⁷ if I had not feared
provocation
from the enemy,
or feared that these foes
might misunderstand
and say: 'Our own hand
has prevailed;
it wasn't the LORD who did
all this.'"
²⁸ Israel is a nation
lacking sense
with no understanding
at all.^D Is 44:19; Jr 29:7
²⁹ If only they were wise,
they would
comprehend this;
they would understand
their fate.
³⁰ How could one pursue
a thousand,
or two put ten thousand
to flight, Lv 26:36
unless their Rock had sold
them,
unless the LORD had given
them up? Ps 127:1; Lm 3:37; Mk 13:20
³¹ But their "rock" is not
like our Rock,
as even our enemies concede.
³² For their vine is
from the vine of Sodom
and from the fields
of Gomorrah.
Their grapes are poisonous;

^A32:21 Lit with no gods ^B32:21 Lit with no people ^C32:26 LXX reads will scatter them ^D32:28 Lit understanding in them

their clusters are bitter.
³³ Their wine is
serpents' venom,
the deadly poison of cobras.

³⁴ "Is it not stored up with me,
sealed up in my vaults?
³⁵ Vengeance^A belongs to me;
I will repay.^B   1Sm 24:12; 2Sm 22:48
In time their foot will slip,
for their day of disaster
is near,
and their doom
is coming quickly."

³⁶ The LORD will indeed
vindicate his people
and have compassion
on his servants   Ps 135:14
when he sees that
their strength is gone
and no one is left —
slave or free.^C

³⁷ He will say:
"Where are their gods,
the 'rock'
they found refuge in?
³⁸ Who ate the fat
of their sacrifices
and drank the wine
of their drink offerings?
Let them rise up and help you;
let it^D be a shelter for you.
³⁹ See now that I alone am he;
there is no God but me.   Is 40:25
I bring death and I give life;
I wound and I heal.
No one can rescue anyone
from my power.   Dt 30:15,19; 4:8
⁴⁰ I raise my hand to heaven
and declare:

As surely as I live forever,
⁴¹ when I sharpen
my flashing sword,
and my hand takes hold
of judgment,
I will take vengeance
on my adversaries
and repay those
who hate me.
⁴² I will make my arrows drunk
with blood
while my sword devours
flesh —
the blood of the slain
and the captives,
the heads
of the enemy leaders."^E

⁴³ Rejoice, you nations,
concerning his people,^F
for he will avenge the blood
of his servants.^G
He will take vengeance
on his adversaries;^H   Ps 79:10
he will purify his land
and his people.^I

⁴⁴ Moses came with Joshua^J son of Nun and recited all the words of this song in the presence of the people. ⁴⁵ After Moses finished reciting all these words to all Israel, ⁴⁶ he said to them, "Take to heart all these words I am giving as a warning to you today, so that you may command your children to follow all the words of this law carefully. ⁴⁷ For they are not meaningless words to you but they are your life, and by them you will live long in

^A32:35 Sam, LXX read *On a day of vengeance*   ^B32:35 LXX, Tg, Vg read *me; and recompense I will recompense*   ^C32:36 Or *left—even the weak and impaired*; Hb obscure   ^D32:38 Sam, LXX, Tg, Vg read *them*   ^E32:42 Or *the long-haired heads of the enemy*   ^F32:43 LXX reads *Rejoice, you heavens, along with him, and let all the sons of God worship him; rejoice, you nations, with his people, and let all the angels of God strengthen themselves in him*; DSS read *Rejoice, you heavens, along with him, and let all the angels worship him*; Heb 1:6   ^G32:43 DSS, LXX read *sons*   ^H32:43 DSS, LXX add *and he will recompense those who hate him*; v. 41   ^I32:43 Syr, Tg; DSS, Sam, LXX, Vg read *his people's land*   ^J32:44 LXX, Syr, Vg; MT reads *Hoshea*; Nm 13:8,16

the land you are crossing the Jordan to possess." Dt 11:18; Ezk 3:10; Mal 2:2

Moses's Impending Death

⁴⁸ On that same day the LORD spoke to Moses, ⁴⁹ "Go up Mount Nebo in the Abarim range in the land of Moab, across from Jericho, and view the land of Canaan I am giving the Israelites as a possession. ⁵⁰ Then you will die on the mountain that you go up, and you will be gathered to your people, just as your brother Aaron died on Mount Hor and was gathered to his people. ⁵¹ For both of you broke faith with me among the Israelites at the Waters of Meribath-kadesh in the Wilderness of Zin by failing to treat me as holy in their presence. ⁵² Although from a distance you will view the land that I am giving the Israelites, you will not go there." Nm 27:12-14; Dt 34:1; Gn 25:8,17

Moses's Blessings

33 This is the blessing that Moses, the man of God, gave the Israelites before his death. ² He said:
The LORD came from Sinai
and appeared to them
    from Seir; Gn 14:6; 32:3; 36:8; Dt 1:2
he shone on them
    from Mount Paran Gn 21:21
and came with ten thousand
    holy ones, ᴬ
with lightning ᴮ
    from his right hand ᶜ
    for them. Jdg 5:4-5; Ps 68:7-8; Hab 3:3
³   Indeed he loves the people. ᴰ
All your ᴱ holy ones are
    in your hand,
and they assemble ᶠ
    at your feet.

Each receives your words.
⁴ Moses gave us instruction,
a possession for the assembly
    of Jacob.
⁵ So he became King
    in Jeshurun ᴳ Dt 32:15; 33:26
when the leaders
    of the people gathered
with the tribes of Israel.

⁶   Let Reuben live and not die
though his people
    become few. Gn 49:3-4; Jdg 5:15-16
⁷ He said this about Judah:
LORD, hear Judah's
    cry and bring him
    to his people.
He fights for his cause ᴴ
    with his own hands,
but may you be a help
    against his foes.
⁸ He said about Levi:
Your Thummim
    and Urim belong to
    your faithful one; ᴵ Ex 28:30
you tested him at Massah
and contended with him
    at the Waters of Meribah.
⁹   He said about his father
    and mother,
"I do not regard them."
He disregarded his brothers
and didn't acknowledge
    his sons,
for they kept your word
and maintained
    your covenant. Ex 32:25-29
¹⁰ They will teach
    your ordinances to Jacob
and your instruction
    to Israel; Dt 31:9-13
they will set incense
    before you

ᴬ**33:2** LXX reads *Mount Paran with ten thousands from Kadesh*   ᴮ**33:2** Or *fiery law*; Hb obscure
ᶜ**33:2** Or *ones, from his southland to the mountain slopes*   ᴰ**33:3** Or *peoples*   ᴱ**33:3** Lit *his*, or *its*
ᶠ**33:3** Hb obscure   ᴳ**33:5** = Upright One, referring to Israel, also in v. 26   ᴴ**33:7** Or *He contends for them*
ᴵ**33:8** DSS, LXX read *Give to Levi your Thummim, your Urim to your favored one*

and whole burnt offerings
    on your altar.
¹¹ LORD, bless his possessions, ᴬ
    and accept the work
        of his hands.
    Break the back ᴮ
        of his adversaries
        and enemies,
    so that they cannot rise again.
¹² He said about Benjamin:
    The LORD's beloved rests ᶜ
        securely on him.
    He ᴰ shields him all day long,
    and he rests on his shoulders. ᴱ
¹³ He said about Joseph:
    May his land be blessed
        by the LORD
    with the dew
        of heaven's bounty
    and the watery depths
        that lie beneath;   Pr 3:20
¹⁴ with the bountiful harvest
        from the sun
    and the abundant yield
        of the seasons;
¹⁵ with the best products
        of the ancient mountains
    and the bounty
        of the eternal hills;   Gn 49:26
¹⁶ with the choice gifts
        of the land
    and everything in it;
    and with the favor of him
    who appeared ᶠ
        in the burning bush.   Ex 3:2-4
    May these rest on the head
        of Joseph,
    on the brow of the prince
        of his brothers.   Gn 49:26
¹⁷ His firstborn bull
        has ᴳ splendor,
    and horns like ᴴ those
        of a wild ox;

he gores all the peoples
    with them
to the ends of the earth.
Such are the ten thousands
    of Ephraim,
and such are the thousands
    of Manasseh.
¹⁸ He said about Zebulun:
    Rejoice, Zebulun,
        in your journeys,
    and Issachar, in your tents.
¹⁹ They summon the peoples
        to a mountain;
    there they offer
        acceptable sacrifices.
    For they draw
        from the wealth of the seas
    and the hidden treasures
        of the sand.   Gn 49:13; Jdg 5:15,18
²⁰ He said about Gad:
    The one who enlarges
        Gad's territory
    will be blessed.
    He lies down like a lion
    and tears off an arm or even
        a head.   1Ch 12:8
²¹ He chose the best part
        for himself,
    because a ruler's portion
        was assigned there for him.
    He came with the leaders
        of the people;
    he carried out
        the LORD's justice
    and his ordinances for Israel.
²² He said about Dan:
    Dan is a young lion,
    leaping out of Bashan.   Jdg 5:17
²³ He said about Naphtali:
    Naphtali, enjoying approval,
    full of the LORD's blessing,
    take ᴵ possession to the west
        and the south.

ᴬ33:11 Or *abilities*   ᴮ33:11 Or *waist*   ᶜ33:12 Or *Let the LORD's beloved rest*   ᴰ33:12 LXX reads *The Most High*   ᴱ33:12 Or *and he dwells among his mountain slopes*   ᶠ33:16 Lit *dwelt*   ᴳ33:17 Some DSS, Sam, LXX, Syr, Vg read *A firstborn bull — he has*   ᴴ33:17 Lit *and his horns are*   ᴵ33:23 Sam, LXX, Syr, Vg, Tg read *he will take*

²⁴ He said about Asher:
　　May Asher^A be
　　　the most blessed of the sons;
　　may he be the most favored
　　　among his brothers
　　and dip his foot in olive oil.
²⁵　May the bolts of your gate
　　　be iron and bronze,
　　and your strength last
　　　as long as you live.

²⁶　There is none like the God
　　　of Jeshurun,
　　who rides the heavens
　　　to your aid,
　　the clouds in his majesty.
²⁷　The God of old is
　　　your dwelling place,　　Ps 91:9
　　and underneath are
　　　the everlasting arms.
　　He drives out the enemy
　　　before you
　　and commands, "Destroy!"
²⁸　So Israel dwells securely;
　　Jacob lives untroubled^B
　　in a land of grain
　　　and new wine;
　　even his skies drip with dew.
²⁹　How happy you are, Israel!
　　Who is like you,
　　a people saved by the LORD?
　　He is the shield
　　　that protects you,
　　the sword you boast in.
　　Your enemies will cringe
　　　before you,　　2Sm 22:44-46
　　and you will tread
　　　on their backs.^C　　Dt 32:13; Hab 3:19

Moses's Death

34 Then Moses went up from the plains of Moab to Mount Nebo, to the top of Pisgah, which faces Jericho, and the LORD showed him all the land: Gilead as far as Dan, ² all of Naphtali, the land of Ephraim and Manasseh, all the land of Judah as far as the Mediterranean^D Sea, ³ the Negev, and the plain in the Valley of Jericho, the City of Palms, as far as Zoar. ⁴ The LORD then said to him, "This is the land I promised Abraham, Isaac, and Jacob, 'I will give it to your descendants.' I have let you see it with your own eyes, but you will not cross into it." Dt 3:27; 32:48

⁵ So Moses the servant of the LORD died there in the land of Moab, according to the LORD's word. ⁶ He buried him^E in the valley in the land of Moab facing Beth-peor, and no one to this day knows where his grave is. ⁷ Moses was one hundred twenty years old when he died; his eyes were not weak, and his vitality had not left him. ⁸ The Israelites wept for Moses in the plains of Moab thirty days. Then the days of weeping and mourning for Moses came to an end. Jos 24:29; Jdg 2:8; 2Sm 3:18; 7:5,8; 14:8

⁹ Joshua son of Nun was filled with the spirit of wisdom because Moses had laid his hands on him. So the Israelites obeyed him and did as the LORD had commanded Moses. ¹⁰ No prophet has arisen again in Israel like Moses, whom the LORD knew face to face. ¹¹ He was unparalleled for all the signs and wonders the LORD sent him to do against the land of Egypt — to Pharaoh, to all his officials, and to all his land, ¹² and for all the mighty acts of power^F and terrifying deeds that Moses performed in the sight of all Israel. Ex 28:3; 31:3-6; 1Kg 4:29; 5:12; 7:14

---

^A33:24 = Happy or Blessed; Gn 30:13　　^B33:28 Text emended; MT reads *Jacob's fountain is alone*
^C33:29 Or *high places*　　^D34:2 Lit *Western*　　^E34:6 Or *he was buried*　　^F34:12 Lit *the strong hand*

JOSHUA

Encouragement of Joshua

1 After the death of Moses the LORD's servant, the LORD spoke to Joshua son of Nun, Moses's assistant: [2] "Moses my servant is dead. Now you and all the people prepare to cross over the Jordan to the land I am giving the Israelites. [3] I have given you every place where the sole of your foot treads, just as I promised Moses. [4] Your territory will be from the wilderness and Lebanon to the great river, the Euphrates River — all the land of the Hittites — and west to the Mediterranean Sea.[A] [5] No one will be able to stand against you as long as you live. I will be with you, just as I was with Moses. I will not leave you or abandon you. Ex 17:8-13; 33:11; Dt 34:5

[6] "Be strong and courageous, for you will distribute the land I swore to their fathers to give them as an inheritance. [7] Above all, be strong and very courageous to observe carefully the whole instruction my servant Moses commanded you. Do not turn from it to the right or the left, so that you will have success wherever you go. [8] This book of instruction must not depart from your mouth; you are to meditate on[B] it day and night so that you may carefully observe everything written in it. For then you will prosper and succeed in whatever you do. [9] Haven't I commanded you: be strong and courageous? Do not be afraid or discouraged, for the LORD your God is with you wherever you go." Jos 1:18; 10:25; 1Kg 2:2-3; 1Ch 22:13; 28:20; 31:24

Joshua Prepares the People

[10] Then Joshua commanded the officers of the people: [11] "Go through the camp and tell the people, 'Get provisions ready for yourselves, for within three days you will be crossing the Jordan to go in and take possession of the land the LORD your God is giving you to inherit.'" Jos 3:2

[12] Joshua said to the Reubenites, the Gadites, and half the tribe of Manasseh: [13] "Remember what Moses the LORD's servant commanded you when he said, 'The LORD your God will give you rest, and he will give you this land.' [14] Your wives, dependents, and livestock may remain in the land Moses gave you on this side of the Jordan. But your best soldiers must cross over in battle formation[C] ahead of your brothers and help them [15] until the LORD gives your brothers rest, as he has given you, and they too possess the land the LORD your God is giving them. You may then return to the land of your inheritance and take possession of what Moses the LORD's servant gave you on the east side of the Jordan." Nm 32:20-22; Jos 22:4

[16] They answered Joshua, "Everything you have commanded us we will do, and everywhere you send us we will go. [17] We will obey you, just as we obeyed Moses in everything. Certainly the LORD your God will be with you, as he was with Moses. [18] Anyone who rebels against your order and does not obey your words in all that you command

---

A[1:4] Lit *and to the Great Sea, the going down of the sun*   B[1:8] Or *to recite*   C[1:14] Or *over armed* him, will be put to death. Above all, be strong and courageous!"

Spies Sent to Jericho

2 Joshua son of Nun secretly sent two men as spies from the Acacia Grove,^A saying, "Go and scout the land, especially Jericho." So they left, and they came to the house of a prostitute named Rahab, and stayed there. Gn 42:9; Jos 7:2

² The king of Jericho was told, "Look, some of the Israelite men have come here tonight to investigate the land." ³ Then the king of Jericho sent word to Rahab and said, "Bring out the men who came to you and entered your house, for they came to investigate the entire land." Gn 19:5

⁴ But the woman had taken the two men and hidden them. So she said, "Yes, the men did come to me, but I didn't know where they were from. ⁵ At nightfall, when the city gate was about to close, the men went out, and I don't know where they were going. Chase after them quickly, and you can catch up with them!" ⁶ But she had taken them up to the roof and hidden them among the stalks of flax that she had arranged on the roof. ⁷ The men pursued them along the road to the fords of the Jordan, and as soon as they left to pursue them, the city gate was shut. 2Sm 17:19; Jms 2:25

The Promise to Rahab

⁸ Before the men fell asleep, she went up on the roof ⁹ and said to them, "I know that the LORD has given you this land and that the terror of you has fallen on us, and everyone who lives in the land is panicking because of you.^B ¹⁰ For we have heard how the LORD dried up the water of the Red Sea before you when you came out of Egypt, and what you did to Sihon and Og, the two Amorite kings you completely destroyed across the Jordan. ¹¹ When we heard this, we lost heart, and everyone's courage failed^C because of you, for the LORD your God is God in heaven above and on earth below. ¹² Now please swear to me by the LORD that you will also show kindness to my father's family,^D because I showed kindness to you. Give me a sure sign^E ¹³ that you will spare the lives of my father, mother, brothers, sisters, and all who belong to them, and save us from death." Nm 20:24; 7:5

¹⁴ The men answered her, "We will give our lives for yours. If you don't report our mission, we will show kindness and faithfulness to you when the LORD gives us the land."

¹⁵ Then she let them down by a rope through the window, since she lived in a house that was built into the wall of the city. ¹⁶ "Go to the hill country so that the men pursuing you won't find you," she said to them. "Hide there for three days until they return; afterward, go on your way."

¹⁷ The men said to her, "We will be free from this oath you made us swear, ¹⁸ unless, when we enter the land, you tie this scarlet cord to the window through which you let us down. Bring your father, mother, brothers, and all your father's family into your house. ¹⁹ If anyone goes out the doors of your house, his death will be his own fault,^F and we will be innocent. But

---

^A 2:1 Or from Shittim ^B 2:9 Or land panics at your approach ^C 2:11 Lit and spirit no longer remained in anyone ^D 2:12 Lit my father's house ^E 2:12 Or a sign of truth ^F 2:19 Lit his blood on his head if anyone with you in the house should be harmed,[A] his death will be our fault.[B] 20 And if you report our mission, we are free from the oath you made us swear." Mt 27:25

21 "Let it be as you say," she replied, and she sent them away. After they had gone, she tied the scarlet cord to the window.

22 So the two men went into the hill country and stayed there three days until the pursuers had returned. They searched all along the way, but did not find them. 23 Then the men returned, came down from the hill country, and crossed the Jordan. They went to Joshua son of Nun and reported everything that had happened to them. 24 They told Joshua, "The LORD has handed over the entire land to us. Everyone who lives in the land is also panicking because of us."[C]

Crossing the Jordan

3 Joshua started early the next morning and left the Acacia Grove[D] with all the Israelites. They went as far as the Jordan and stayed there before crossing. 2 After three days the officers went through the camp 3 and commanded the people: "When you see the ark of the covenant of the LORD your God carried by the Levitical priests, you are to break camp and follow it. 4 But keep a distance of about a thousand yards[E] between yourselves and the ark. Don't go near it, so that you can see the way to go, for you haven't traveled this way before."[F]

5 Joshua told the people, "Consecrate yourselves, because the LORD will do wonders among you

tomorrow." 6 Then he said to the priests, "Carry the ark of the covenant and go on ahead of the people." So they carried the ark of the covenant and went ahead of them.

7 The LORD spoke to Joshua: "Today I will begin to exalt you in the sight of all Israel, so they will know that I will be with you just as I was with Moses. 8 Command the priests carrying the ark of the covenant: When you reach the edge of the water,[G] stand in the Jordan." Jos 4:14

9 Then Joshua told the Israelites, "Come closer and listen to the words of the LORD your God." 10 He said: "You will know that the living God is among you and that he will certainly dispossess before you the Canaanites, Hethites, Hivites, Perizzites, Girgashites, Amorites, and Jebusites 11 when the ark of the covenant of the Lord of the whole earth goes ahead of you into the Jordan. 12 Now choose twelve men from the tribes of Israel, one man for each tribe. 13 When the feet[H] of the priests who carry the ark of the LORD, the Lord of the whole earth, come to rest in the Jordan's water, its water will be cut off. The water flowing downstream will stand up in a mass." Dt 5:26; Jr 10:10; Hs 1:10; 2Co 3:3

14 When the people broke camp to cross the Jordan, the priests carried the ark of the covenant ahead of the people. 15 Now the Jordan overflows its banks throughout the harvest season. But as soon as the priests carrying the ark reached the Jordan, their feet touched the water at its edge 16 and the water flowing downstream stood still, rising up in a mass that extended

---

A2:19 Lit *if a hand should be on him*　　B2:19 Lit *his blood on our heads*　　C2:24 Or *land also panics at our approach*　　D3:1 Or *left Shittim*　　E3:4 Lit *2,000 cubits*　　F3:4 Lit *yesterday and the day before*　　G3:8 Lit *waters of the Jordan*　　H3:13 Lit *soles of the feet* as far as^A Adam, a city next to Zarethan. The water flowing downstream into the Sea of the Arabah — the Dead Sea — was completely cut off, and the people crossed opposite Jericho. ¹⁷ The priests carrying the ark of the LORD's covenant stood firmly on dry ground in the middle of the Jordan, while all Israel crossed on dry ground until the entire nation had finished crossing the Jordan. 1Ch 12:15; Jr 12:5; Ac 7:44-45

The Memorial Stones

4 After the entire nation had finished crossing the Jordan, the LORD spoke to Joshua: ² "Choose twelve men from the people, one man for each tribe, ³ and command them: Take twelve stones from this place in the middle of the Jordan where the priests^B are standing, carry them with you, and set them down at the place where you spend the night." Ex 28:21; 39:14; Jos 3:12,17

⁴ So Joshua summoned the twelve men he had selected from the Israelites, one man for each tribe, ⁵ and said to them, "Go across to the ark of the LORD your God in the middle of the Jordan. Each of you lift a stone onto his shoulder, one for each^C of the Israelite tribes, ⁶ so that this will be a sign among you. In the future, when your children ask you, 'What do these stones mean to you?' ⁷ you should tell them, 'The water of the Jordan was cut off in front of the ark of the LORD's covenant. When it crossed the Jordan, the Jordan's water was cut off.' Therefore these stones will always be a memorial for the Israelites." Ex 12:26-27; 13:8-9,14

⁸ The Israelites did just as Joshua had commanded them. The twelve men took stones from the middle of the Jordan, one for each^D of the Israelite tribes, just as the LORD had told Joshua. They carried them to the camp and set them down there. ⁹ Joshua also set up twelve stones in the middle^E of the Jordan where the priests who carried the ark of the covenant were standing. The stones are still there today. Jos 6:25

¹⁰ The priests carrying the ark continued standing in the middle of the Jordan until everything was completed that the LORD had commanded Joshua to tell the people, in keeping with all that Moses had commanded Joshua. The people hurried across, ¹¹ and after everyone had finished crossing, the priests with the ark of the LORD crossed in the sight of the people. ¹² The Reubenites, Gadites, and half the tribe of Manasseh went in battle formation in front of the Israelites, as Moses had instructed them. ¹³ About forty thousand equipped for war crossed to the plains of Jericho in the LORD's presence. Nm 32:17

¹⁴ On that day the LORD exalted Joshua in the sight of all Israel, and they revered him throughout his life, as they had revered Moses. ¹⁵ The LORD told Joshua, ¹⁶ "Command the priests who carry the ark of the testimony to come up from the Jordan." Ex 25:16; Jos 3:7

¹⁷ So Joshua commanded the priests, "Come up from the Jordan." ¹⁸ When the priests carrying the ark of the LORD's covenant came up from the middle of the Jordan,

^A 3:16 Alt Hb tradition reads *mass at*   ^B 4:3 Lit *feet of the priests,* also in v. 9   ^C 4:5 Lit *shoulder according to the number*   ^D 4:8 Lit *Jordan according to the number*   ^E 4:9 Or *Now Joshua set up the twelve stones that had been in the middle* and their feet^A stepped out on solid ground, the water of the Jordan resumed its course, flowing over all the banks as before.

¹⁹ The people came up from the Jordan on the tenth day of the first month, and camped at Gilgal on the eastern limits of Jericho. ²⁰ Then Joshua set up in Gilgal the twelve stones they had taken from the Jordan, ²¹ and he said to the Israelites, "In the future, when your children ask their fathers, 'What is the meaning of these stones?' ²² you should tell your children, 'Israel crossed the Jordan on dry ground.' ²³ For the LORD your God dried up the water of the Jordan before you until you had crossed over, just as the LORD your God did to the Red Sea, which he dried up before us until we had crossed over. ²⁴ This is so that all the peoples of the earth may know that the LORD's hand is mighty, and so that you may always fear the LORD your God." Ex 12:3; 14:31

Circumcision of the Israelites

5 When all the Amorite kings across the Jordan to the west and all the Canaanite kings near the sea heard how the LORD had dried up the water of the Jordan before the Israelites until they had crossed over, they lost heart and their courage failed^B because of the Israelites. Nm 13:29; Dt 1:7; Jos 11:3 ² At that time the LORD said to Joshua, "Make flint knives and circumcise the Israelite men again." ³ So Joshua made flint knives and circumcised the Israelite men at Gibeath-haaraloth.^C ⁴ This is the reason Joshua circumcised them: All the people who came out of Egypt who were males — all the men of war — had died in the wilderness along the way after they had come out of Egypt. ⁵ Though all the people who came out were circumcised, none of the people born in the wilderness along the way were circumcised after they had come out of Egypt. ⁶ For the Israelites wandered in the wilderness forty years until all the nation's men of war who came out of Egypt had died off because they did not obey the LORD. So the LORD vowed never to let them see the land he had sworn to their fathers to give us, a land flowing with milk and honey. ⁷ He raised up their sons in their place; it was these Joshua circumcised. They were still uncircumcised, since they had not been circumcised along the way. ⁸ After the entire nation had been circumcised, they stayed where they were in the camp until they recovered. ⁹ The LORD then said to Joshua, "Today I have rolled away the disgrace of Egypt from you." Therefore, that place is still called Gilgal today. Gn 17:10-14; Ex 4:24-26; 12:44, 48

Food from the Land

¹⁰ While the Israelites camped at Gilgal on the plains of Jericho, they observed the Passover on the evening of the fourteenth day of the month. ¹¹ The day after Passover they ate unleavened bread and roasted grain from the produce of the land. ¹² And the day after they ate from the produce of the land, the manna ceased. Since there was no more manna for the Israelites, they ate from the crops of the land of Canaan that year. Ex 12:11, 18, 21; Lv 23:5

^A4:18 Lit and the soles of the feet of the priests ^B5:1 Lit and they did not have spirit in them any more
^C5:3 Or The Hill of Foreskins

Commander of the LORD's Army

¹³ When Joshua was near Jericho, he looked up and saw a man standing in front of him with a drawn sword in his hand. Joshua approached him and asked, "Are you for us or for our enemies?"   Gn 18:2; 32:24

¹⁴ "Neither," he replied. "I have now come as commander of the LORD's army."   Ex 7:4; 12:41; 1Sm 17:45

Then Joshua bowed with his face to the ground in worship and asked him, "What does my lord want to say to his servant?"   Gn 17:3

¹⁵ The commander of the LORD's army said to Joshua, "Remove the sandals from your feet, for the place where you are standing is holy." And Joshua did that.   Ex 3:5

The Conquest of Jericho

6 Now Jericho was strongly fortified because of the Israelites —no one leaving or entering. ² The LORD said to Joshua, "Look, I have handed Jericho, its king, and its best soldiers over to you. ³ March around the city with all the men of war, circling the city one time. Do this for six days. ⁴ Have seven priests carry seven ram's-horn trumpets in front of the ark. But on the seventh day, march around the city seven times, while the priests blow the trumpets. ⁵ When there is a prolonged blast of the horn and you hear its sound, have all the troops give a mighty shout. Then the city wall will collapse, and the troops will advance, each man straight ahead."   Dt 7:24; Jos 2:9,24

⁶ So Joshua son of Nun summoned the priests and said to them, "Take up the ark of the covenant and have seven priests carry seven trumpets in front of the ark of the LORD." ⁷ He said to the troops, "Move forward, march around the city, and have the armed men go ahead of the ark of the LORD."

⁸ After Joshua had spoken to the troops, seven priests carrying seven trumpets before the LORD moved forward and blew the trumpets; the ark of the LORD's covenant followed them. ⁹ While the trumpets were blowing, the armed men went in front of the priests who blew the trumpets, and the rear guard went behind the ark. ¹⁰ But Joshua had commanded the troops: "Do not shout or let your voice be heard. Don't let one word come out of your mouth until the time I say, 'Shout!' Then you are to shout." ¹¹ So the ark of the LORD was carried around the city, circling it once. They returned to the camp and spent the night there.ᴬ   Is 52:12

¹² Joshua got up early the next morning. The priests took the ark of the LORD, ¹³ and the seven priests carrying seven trumpets marched in front of the ark of the LORD. While the trumpets were blowing, the armed men went in front of them, and the rear guard went behind the ark of the LORD. ¹⁴ On the second day they marched around the city once and returned to the camp. They did this for six days.

¹⁵ Early on the seventh day, they started at dawn and marched around the city seven times in the same way. That was the only day they marched around the city seven times. ¹⁶ After the seventh time, the priests blew the trumpets, and Joshua said to the troops, "Shout! For the LORD has given you the city. ¹⁷ But the city and everything in it are set apart to the LORD for

ᴬ**6:11** Lit at the camp

destruction. Only Rahab the prostitute and everyone with her in the house will live, because she hid the messengers we sent. [18] But keep yourselves from the things set apart, or you will be set apart for destruction. If you[A] take any of those things, you will set apart the camp of Israel for destruction and make trouble for it. [19] For all the silver and gold, and the articles of bronze and iron, are dedicated to the LORD and must go into the LORD's treasury." Lv 27:29; Dt 7:26; 13:17

[20] So the troops shouted, and the trumpets sounded. When they heard the blast of the trumpet, the troops gave a great shout, and the wall collapsed. The troops advanced into the city, each man straight ahead, and they captured the city. [21] They completely destroyed everything in the city with the sword — every man and woman, both young and old, and every ox, sheep, and donkey. Jos 2:10

Rahab and Her Family Spared

[22] Joshua said to the two men who had scouted the land, "Go to the prostitute's house and bring the woman out of there, and all who are with her, just as you swore to her." [23] So the young men who had scouted went in and brought out Rahab and her father, mother, brothers, and all who belonged to her. They brought out her whole family and settled them outside the camp of Israel. Jos 2:14

[24] They burned the city and everything in it, but they put the silver and gold and the articles of bronze and iron into the treasury of the LORD's house. [25] However, Joshua spared Rahab the prostitute, her father's family, and all who belonged to her, because she hid the messengers Joshua had sent to spy on Jericho, and she still lives in Israel today. Ex 6:23; Ru 4:21-22; 1Ch 2:10-12; Mt 1:4-5; 5:9

[26] At that time Joshua imposed this curse:

The man who undertakes
  the rebuilding of this city,
    Jericho,
is cursed before the LORD.
He will lay its foundation
  at the cost of his firstborn;
he will finish its gates
  at the cost of his youngest.

[27] And the LORD was with Joshua, and his fame spread throughout the land. Gn 39:2,21; Jdg 1:19,22; 2:18; 1Sm 3:19

Defeat at Ai

7 The Israelites, however, were unfaithful regarding the things set apart for destruction. Achan son of Carmi, son of Zabdi, son of Zerah, of the tribe of Judah, took some of what was set apart, and the LORD's anger burned against the Israelites. Lv 6:2; Nm 5:27; 31:16; Dt 32:51

[2] Joshua sent men from Jericho to Ai, which is near Beth-aven, east of Bethel, and told them, "Go up and scout the land." So the men went up and scouted Ai. Jos 18:12; 1Sm 13:5

[3] After returning to Joshua they reported to him, "Don't send all the people, but send about two thousand or three thousand[B] men to attack Ai. Since the people of Ai are so few, don't wear out all our people there." [4] So about three thousand men[C] went up there, but they fled from the men of Ai. [5] The men of Ai struck down about thirty-six of

[A]**6:18** LXX reads *you covet and* ; Jos 7:21   [B]**7:3** Or *send two or three military units of*   [C]**7:4** Lit *men from the people* them and chased them from outside the city gate to the quarries,[A] striking them down on the descent. As a result, the people lost heart.[B]

⁶ Then Joshua tore his clothes and fell facedown to the ground before the ark of the LORD until evening, as did the elders of Israel; they all put dust on their heads. ⁷ "Oh, Lord GOD," Joshua said, "why did you ever bring these people across the Jordan to hand us over to the Amorites for our destruction? If only we had been content to remain on the other side of the Jordan! ⁸ What can I say, Lord, now that Israel has turned its back and run from its enemies? ⁹ When the Canaanites and all who live in the land hear about this, they will surround us and wipe out our name from the earth. Then what will you do about your great name?" Jb 1:20; Neh 9:1; Lm 2:10

¹⁰ The LORD then said to Joshua, "Stand up! Why have you fallen facedown? ¹¹ Israel has sinned. They have violated my covenant that I appointed for them. They have taken some of what was set apart. They have stolen, deceived, and put those things with their own belongings. ¹² This is why the Israelites cannot stand against their enemies. They will turn their backs and run from their enemies, because they have been set apart for destruction. I will no longer be with you unless you remove from among you what is set apart. Jos 6:18; Nm 14:45; Jdg 2:14

¹³ "Go and consecrate the people. Tell them to consecrate themselves for tomorrow, for this is what the LORD, the God of Israel, says: There are things that are set apart among you, Israel. You will not be able to stand against your enemies until you remove what is set apart. ¹⁴ In the morning, present yourselves tribe by tribe. The tribe the LORD selects is to come forward clan by clan. The clan the LORD selects is to come forward family by family. The family the LORD selects is to come forward man by man. ¹⁵ The one who is caught with the things set apart must be burned, along with everything he has, because he has violated the LORD's covenant and committed an outrage in Israel."

Achan Judged

¹⁶ Joshua got up early the next morning. He had Israel come forward tribe by tribe, and the tribe of Judah was selected. ¹⁷ He had the clans of Judah come forward, and the Zerahite clan was selected. He had the Zerahite clan come forward by heads of families,[C] and Zabdi was selected. ¹⁸ He then had Zabdi's family come forward man by man, and Achan son of Carmi, son of Zabdi, son of Zerah, of the tribe of Judah, was selected.

¹⁹ So Joshua said to Achan, "My son, give glory to the LORD, the God of Israel, and make a confession to him.[D] I urge you, tell me what you have done. Don't hide anything from me." 1Sm 6:5; 2Ch 30:22; Jr 13:16; Jn 9:24

²⁰ Achan replied to Joshua, "It is true. I have sinned against the LORD, the God of Israel. This is what I did: ²¹ When I saw among the spoils a beautiful cloak from Babylon,[E] five pounds[F] of silver, and a bar of gold weighing a pound and a quarter,[G] I coveted them and took them. You can see for yourself. They are concealed in the ground inside my tent,

with the silver under the cloak." ²² So Joshua sent messengers who ran to the tent, and there was the cloak, concealed in his tent, with the silver underneath. ²³ They took the things from inside the tent, brought them to Joshua and all the Israelites, and spread them out in the LORD's presence.   Gn 3:6; Jos 22:20

²⁴ Then Joshua and all Israel with him took Achan son of Zerah, the silver, the cloak, and the bar of gold, his sons and daughters, his ox, donkey, and sheep, his tent, and all that he had, and brought them up to the Valley of Achor. ²⁵ Joshua said, "Why have you brought us trouble? Today the LORD will bring you trouble!" So all Israel stoned them^A to death. They burned their bodies, threw stones on them, ²⁶ and raised over him a large pile of rocks that remains still today. Then the LORD turned from his burning anger. Therefore that place is called the Valley of Achor^B still today.

Conquest of Ai

8 The LORD said to Joshua, "Do not be afraid or discouraged. Take all the troops with you and go attack Ai. Look, I have handed over to you the king of Ai, his people, city, and land. ² Treat Ai and its king as you did Jericho and its king, except that you may plunder its spoil and livestock for yourselves. Set an ambush behind the city."   Dt 1:21; 7:18; 31:8

³ So Joshua and all the troops set out to attack Ai. Joshua selected thirty thousand of his best soldiers and sent them out at night. ⁴ He commanded them: "Pay attention. Lie in ambush behind the city, not too far from it, and all of you be ready. ⁵ Then I and all the people

who are with me will approach the city. When they come out against us as they did the first time, we will flee from them. ⁶ They will come after us until we have drawn them away from the city, for they will say, 'They are fleeing from us as before.' While we are fleeing from them, ⁷ you are to come out of your ambush and seize the city. The LORD your God will hand it over to you. ⁸ After taking the city, set it on fire. Follow the LORD's command — see that you do as I have ordered you." ⁹ So Joshua sent them out, and they went to the ambush site and waited between Bethel and Ai, to the west of Ai. But he spent that night with the troops.   Jdg 20:29

¹⁰ Joshua started early the next morning and mobilized them. Then he and the elders of Israel led the troops up to Ai. ¹¹ All those^C who were with him went up and approached the city, arriving opposite Ai, and camped to the north of it, with a valley between them and the city. ¹² Now Joshua had taken about five thousand men and set them in ambush between Bethel and Ai, to the west of the city. ¹³ The troops were stationed in this way: the main^D camp to the north of the city and its rear guard to the west of the city. And that night Joshua went into the valley.

¹⁴ When the king of Ai saw the Israelites, the men of the city hurried and went out early in the morning so that he and all his people could engage Israel in battle at a suitable place facing the Arabah. But he did not know there was an ambush waiting for him behind the city. ¹⁵ Joshua and all Israel pretended to be beaten back by them and

^A7:25 Lit him   ^B7:26 Or of Trouble   ^C8:11 Lit the people of war   ^D8:13 Lit way: all the fled toward the wilderness. ¹⁶ Then all the troops of Ai were summoned to pursue them, and they pursued Joshua and were drawn away from the city. ¹⁷ Not a man was left in Ai or Bethel who did not go out after Israel, leaving the city exposed while they pursued Israel. Jdg 20:36

¹⁸ Then the LORD said to Joshua, "Hold out the javelin in your hand toward Ai, for I will hand the city over to you." So Joshua held out his javelin toward it. ¹⁹ When he held out his hand, the men in ambush rose quickly from their position. They ran, entered the city, captured it, and immediately set it on fire.

²⁰ The men of Ai turned and looked back, and smoke from the city was rising to the sky! They could not escape in any direction, and the troops who had fled to the wilderness now became the pursuers. ²¹ When Joshua and all Israel saw that the men in ambush had captured the city and that smoke was rising from it, they turned back and struck down the men of Ai. ²² Then men in ambush came out of the city against them, and the men of Ai were trapped between the Israelite forces, some on one side and some on the other. They struck them down until no survivor or fugitive remained, ²³ but they captured the king of Ai alive and brought him to Joshua. Dt 7:2

²⁴ When Israel had finished killing everyone living in Ai who had pursued them into the open country, and when every last one of them had fallen by the sword, all Israel returned to Ai and struck it down with the sword. ²⁵ The total of those who fell that day, both men and women, was twelve thousand

— all the people of Ai. ²⁶ Joshua did not draw back his hand that was holding the javelin until all the inhabitants of Ai were completely destroyed. ²⁷ Israel plundered only the cattle and spoil of that city for themselves, according to the LORD's command that he had given Joshua. Nm 21:2-3; Dt 2:34; Jos 2:10; 6:21

²⁸ Joshua burned Ai and left it a permanent ruin, still desolate today. ²⁹ He hung ᴬ the body of the king of Ai on a tree ᴮ until evening, and at sunset Joshua commanded that they take his body down from the tree. They threw it down at the entrance of the city gate and put a large pile of rocks over it, which still remains today. Dt 13:16; Jos 6:25

Renewed Commitment to the Law

³⁰ At that time Joshua built an altar on Mount Ebal to the LORD, the God of Israel, ³¹ just as Moses the LORD's servant had commanded the Israelites. He built it according to what is written in the book of the law of Moses: an altar of uncut stones on which no iron tool has been used. Then they offered burnt offerings to the LORD and sacrificed fellowship offerings on it. ³² There on the stones, Joshua copied the law of Moses, which he had written in the presence of the Israelites. ³³ All Israel — resident alien and citizen alike — with their elders, officers, and judges, stood on either side of the ark of the LORD's covenant facing the Levitical priests who carried it. Half of them were in front of Mount Gerizim and half in front of Mount Ebal, as Moses the LORD's servant had commanded earlier concerning blessing the people of

ᴬ8:29 Or impaled   ᴮ8:29 Or wooden stake

Israel. ³⁴ Afterward, Joshua read aloud all the words of the law — the blessings as well as the curses — according to all that is written in the book of the law. ³⁵ There was not a word of all that Moses had commanded that Joshua did not read before the entire assembly of Israel, including the women, the dependents, and the resident aliens who lived ᴬ among them.   Dt 27:4-6

Deception by Gibeon

9 When all the kings heard about Jericho and Ai, those who were west of the Jordan in the hill country, in the Judean foothills, ᴮ and all along the coast of the Mediterranean Sea toward Lebanon — the Hethites, Amorites, Canaanites, Perizzites, Hivites, and Jebusites — ² they formed a unified alliance to fight against Joshua and Israel.

³ When the inhabitants of Gibeon heard what Joshua had done to Jericho and Ai, ⁴ they acted deceptively. They gathered provisions ᶜ and took worn-out sacks on their donkeys and old wineskins, cracked and mended. ⁵ They wore old, patched sandals on their feet and threadbare clothing on their bodies. Their entire provision of bread was dry and crumbly. ⁶ They went to Joshua in the camp at Gilgal and said to him and the men of Israel, "We have come from a distant land. Please make a treaty with us."   Jos 5:10; 10:2;

⁷ The men of Israel replied to the Hivites, "Perhaps you live among us. How can we make a treaty with you?"   Ex 23:32; Dt 7:2-5; 20:10-18

⁸ They said to Joshua, "We are your servants."   2Sm 15:15; 2Kg 10:5

Then Joshua asked them, "Who are you and where do you come from?"

⁹ They replied to him, "Your servants have come from a faraway land because of the reputation of the LORD your God. For we have heard of his fame, and all that he did in Egypt, ¹⁰ and all that he did to the two Amorite kings beyond the Jordan — King Sihon of Heshbon and King Og of Bashan, who was in Ashtaroth. ¹¹ So our elders and all the inhabitants of our land told us, 'Take provisions with you for the journey; go and meet them and say, "We are your servants. Please make a treaty with us." ' ¹² This bread of ours was warm when we took it from our houses as food on the day we left to come to you; but see, it is now dry and crumbly. ¹³ These wineskins were new when we filled them; but see, they are cracked. And these clothes and sandals of ours are worn out from the extremely long journey." ¹⁴ Then the men of Israel took some of their provisions, but did not seek the LORD's decision. ¹⁵ So Joshua established peace with them and made a treaty to let them live, and the leaders of the community swore an oath to them.   Ex 17:1; Lv 24:12; Nm 3:16; 9:18; 22:18

Gibeon's Deception Discovered

¹⁶ Three days after making the treaty with them, they heard that the Gibeonites were their neighbors, living among them. ¹⁷ So the Israelites set out and reached the Gibeonite cities on the third day. Now their cities were Gibeon, Chephirah, Beeroth, and Kiriath-jearim. ¹⁸ But the Israelites did not attack

ᴬ8:35 Lit *walked*   ᴮ9:1 Or *the Shephelah*   ᶜ9:4 Some Hb mss, LXX, Syr, Vg; other Hb mss read *They went disguised as ambassadors* them, because the leaders of the community had sworn an oath to them by the Lord, the God of Israel. Then the whole community grumbled against the leaders.

¹⁹ All the leaders answered them, "We have sworn an oath to them by the Lord, the God of Israel, and now we cannot touch them. ²⁰ This is how we will treat them: we will let them live, so that no wrath will fall on us because of the oath we swore to them." ²¹ They also said, "Let them live." So the Gibeonites became woodcutters and water carriers for the whole community, as the leaders had promised them.   Dt 29:11

²² Joshua summoned the Gibeonites and said to them, "Why did you deceive us by telling us you live far away from us, when in fact you live among us? ²³ Therefore you are cursed and will always be slaves — woodcutters and water carriers for the house of my God."

²⁴ The Gibeonites answered him, "It was clearly communicated to your servants that the Lord your God had commanded his servant Moses to give you all the land and to destroy all the inhabitants of the land before you. We greatly feared for our lives because of you, and that is why we did this. ²⁵ Now we are in your hands. Do to us whatever you think is right."ᴬ ²⁶ This is what Joshua did to them: he rescued them from the Israelites, and they did not kill them. ²⁷ On that day he made them woodcutters and water carriers — as they are today — for the community and for the Lord's altar at the place he would choose.   Gn 16:6; Dt 12:5; Jos 10:2; Jr 26:14; 38:5

The Day the Sun Stood Still

10 Now King Adoni-zedek of Jerusalem heard that Joshua had captured Ai and completely destroyed it, treating Ai and its king as he had Jericho and its king, and that the inhabitants of Gibeon had made peace with Israel and were living among them. ² So Adoni-zedek and his people wereᴮ greatly alarmed because Gibeon was a large city like one of the royal cities; it was larger than Ai, and all its men were warriors. ³ Therefore King Adoni-zedek of Jerusalem sent word to King Hoham of Hebron, King Piram of Jarmuth, King Japhia of Lachish, and King Debir of Eglon, saying, ⁴ "Come up and help me. We will attack Gibeon, because they have made peace with Joshua and the Israelites." ⁵ So the five Amorite kings — the kings of Jerusalem, Hebron, Jarmuth, Lachish, and Eglon — joined forces, advanced with all their armies, besieged Gibeon, and fought against it.

⁶ Then the men of Gibeon sent word to Joshua in the camp at Gilgal: "Don't give up onᶜ your servants. Come quickly and save us! Help us, for all the Amorite kings living in the hill country have joined forces against us." ⁷ So Joshua and all his troops, including all his best soldiers, came from Gilgal.

⁸ The Lord said to Joshua, "Do not be afraid of them, for I have handed them over to you. Not one of them will be able to stand against you."   Gn 14:20; Nm 21:34; Dt 2:30; 7:24; Jos 1:5

⁹ So Joshua caught them by surprise, after marching all night from Gilgal. ¹⁰ The Lord threw them into confusion before Israel. He

---

ᴬ**9:25** Lit *us as is good and as is right in your eyes do*   ᴮ**10:2** One Hb ms, Syr, Vg read *So he was*   ᶜ**10:6** Lit *Don't withdraw your hands from* defeated them in a great slaughter at Gibeon, chased them through the ascent of Beth-horon, and struck them down as far as Azekah and Makkedah. ¹¹ As they fled before Israel, the LORD threw large hailstones on them from the sky along the descent of Beth-horon all the way to Azekah, and they died. More of them died from the hail than the Israelites killed with the sword.

¹² On the day the LORD gave the Amorites over to the Israelites, Joshua spoke to the LORD in the presence of Israel:

"Sun, stand still over Gibeon,
    and moon, over the Valley
        of Aijalon."
¹³ And the sun stood still
    and the moon stopped
        until the nation
            took vengeance
                on its enemies.

Isn't this written in the Book of Jashar?ᴬ

So the sun stopped
    in the middle of the sky
    and delayed its setting
        almost a full day.

¹⁴ There has been no day like it before or since, when the LORD listened to a man, because the LORD fought for Israel. ¹⁵ Then Joshua and all Israel with him returned to the camp at Gilgal. Ex 14:14,25; Dt 1:30

Execution of the Five Kings

¹⁶ Now the five defeated kings had fled and hidden in the cave at Makkedah. ¹⁷ It was reported to Joshua: "The five kings have been found; they are hiding in the cave at Makkedah."

¹⁸ Joshua said, "Roll large stones against the mouth of the cave, and station men by it to guard the kings. ¹⁹ But as for the rest of you, don't stay there. Pursue your enemies and attack them from behind. Don't let them enter their cities, for the LORD your God has handed them over to you." ²⁰ So Joshua and the Israelites finished inflicting a terrible slaughter on them until they were destroyed, although a few survivors ran away to the fortified cities. ²¹ The people returned safely to Joshua in the camp at Makkedah. And no one dared to threatenᴮ the Israelites.

²² Then Joshua said, "Open the mouth of the cave, and bring those five kings to me out of there." ²³ That is what they did. They brought the five kings of Jerusalem, Hebron, Jarmuth, Lachish, and Eglon to Joshua out of the cave. ²⁴ When they had brought the kings to him, Joshua summoned all the men of Israel and said to the military commanders who had accompanied him, "Come here and put your feet on the necks of these kings." So the commanders came forward and put their feet on their necks. ²⁵ Joshua said to them, "Do not be afraid or discouraged. Be strong and courageous, for the LORD will do this to all the enemies you fight." Dt 31:7; Jos 1:6-7,9,18

²⁶ After this, Joshua struck them down and executed them. He hungᶜ their bodies on five treesᴰ and they were there until evening. ²⁷ At sunset Joshua commanded that they be taken down from the trees and thrown into the cave where they had hidden. Then large stones were placed against the mouth of the cave, and the stones are still there today. Dt 21:22-23; Jos 6:25; 8:29

ᴬ10:13 Or of the Upright   ᴮ10:21 Lit No one sharpened his tongue against   ᶜ10:26 Or impaled
ᴰ10:26 Or wooden stakes, also in v. 27

Conquest of Southern Cities

²⁸ On that day Joshua captured Makkedah and struck it down with the sword, including its king. He completely destroyed it ᴬ and everyone in it, leaving no survivors. So he treated the king of Makkedah as he had the king of Jericho.   Jos 6:21

²⁹ Joshua and all Israel with him crossed from Makkedah to Libnah and fought against Libnah. ³⁰ The Lᴏʀᴅ also handed it and its king over to Israel. He struck it down, putting everyone in it to the sword, and left no survivors in it. He treated Libnah's king as he had the king of Jericho.   Jos 7:24; 10:15,31,36; 21:13

³¹ From Libnah, Joshua and all Israel with him crossed to Lachish. They laid siege to it and attacked it. ³² The Lᴏʀᴅ handed Lachish over to Israel, and Joshua captured it on the second day. He struck it down, putting everyone in it to the sword, just as he had done to Libnah. ³³ At that time King Horam of Gezer went to help Lachish, but Joshua struck him down along with his people, leaving no survivors.   Jos 16:10; Jdg 1:29

³⁴ Then Joshua crossed from Lachish to Eglon and all Israel with him. They laid siege to it and attacked it. ³⁵ On that day they captured it and struck it down, putting everyone in it to the sword. He completely destroyed it that day, just as he had done to Lachish.

³⁶ Next, Joshua and all Israel with him went up from Eglon to Hebron and attacked it. ³⁷ They captured it and struck down its king, all its villages, and everyone in it with the sword. He left no survivors, just as he had done at Eglon. He completely destroyed Hebron and everyone in it.

³⁸ Finally, Joshua turned toward Debir and attacked it. And all Israel was with him. ³⁹ He captured it — its king and all its villages. They struck them down with the sword and completely destroyed everyone in it, leaving no survivors. He treated Debir and its king as he had treated Hebron and as he had treated Libnah and its king.   Jos 15:15; Jdg 1:11

⁴⁰ So Joshua conquered the whole region — the hill country, the Negev, the Judean foothills, ᴮ and the slopes — with all their kings, leaving no survivors. He completely destroyed every living being, as the Lᴏʀᴅ, the God of Israel, had commanded. ⁴¹ Joshua conquered everyone from Kadesh-barnea to Gaza, and all the land of Goshen as far as Gibeon. ⁴² Joshua captured all these kings and their land in one campaign, ᶜ because the Lᴏʀᴅ, the God of Israel, fought for Israel. ⁴³ Then Joshua returned with all Israel to the camp at Gilgal.   Dt 19:8

Conquest of Northern Cities

11 When King Jabin of Hazor heard this news, he sent a message to: King Jobab of Madon, the kings of Shimron and Achshaph, ² and the kings of the north in the hill country, the Arabah south of Chinnereth, the Judean foothills, ᴰ and the Slopes of Dor ᴱ to the west, ³ the Canaanites in the east and west, the Amorites, Hethites, Perizzites, and Jebusites in the hill country, and the Hivites at the foot of Hermon in the land of Mizpah. ⁴ They went out with all their armies — a multitude as numerous as the sand on the seashore — along with a vast number of horses and chariots. ⁵ All these

---

ᴬ**10:28** Some Hb mss read *them*   ᴮ**10:40** Or *the Shephelah*   ᶜ**10:42** Lit *land at one time*   ᴰ**11:2** Or *Shephelah*, also in v. 16   ᴱ**11:2** Or *and in Naphoth-dor* kings joined forces; they came and camped together at the Waters of Merom to attack Israel. Dt 3:17; Jos 12:3

⁶ The LORD said to Joshua, "Do not be afraid of them, for at this time tomorrow I will cause all of them to be killed before Israel. You are to hamstring their horses and burn their chariots." ⁷ So Joshua and all his troops surprised them at the Waters of Merom and attacked them. ⁸ The LORD handed them over to Israel, and they struck them down, pursuing them as far as greater Sidon and Misrephoth-maim, and to the east as far as the Valley of Mizpeh. They struck them down, leaving no survivors. ⁹ Joshua treated them as the LORD had told him; he hamstrung their horses and burned their chariots.

¹⁰ At that time Joshua turned back, captured Hazor, and struck down its king with the sword, because Hazor had formerly been the leader of all these kingdoms. ¹¹ They struck down everyone in it with the sword, completely destroying them; he left no one alive. Then he burned Hazor. Jos 10:1; 24:20; Jdg 1:17; 21:11

¹² Joshua captured all these kings and their cities and struck them down with the sword. He completely destroyed them, as Moses the LORD's servant had commanded. ¹³ However, Israel did not burn any of the cities that stood on their mounds except Hazor, which Joshua burned. ¹⁴ The Israelites plundered all the spoils and cattle of these cities for themselves. But they struck down every person with the sword until they had annihilated them, leaving no one alive. ¹⁵ Just as the LORD had commanded his servant Moses, Moses commanded Joshua. That is what Joshua did,

leaving nothing undone of all that the LORD had commanded Moses.

Summary of Conquests

¹⁶ So Joshua took all this land — the hill country, all the Negev, all the land of Goshen, the foothills, the Arabah, and the hill country of Israel with its foothills — ¹⁷ from Mount Halak, which ascends to Seir, as far as Baal-gad in the Valley of Lebanon at the foot of Mount Hermon. He captured all their kings and struck them down, putting them to death. ¹⁸ Joshua waged war with all these kings for a long time. ¹⁹ No city made peace with the Israelites except the Hivites who inhabited Gibeon; all of them were taken in battle. ²⁰ For it was the LORD's intention to harden their hearts, so that they would engage Israel in battle, be completely destroyed without mercy, and be annihilated, just as the LORD had commanded Moses. Jos 12:7; 15:51

²¹ At that time Joshua proceeded to exterminate the Anakim from the hill country — Hebron, Debir, Anab — all the hill country of Judah and of Israel. Joshua completely destroyed them with their cities. ²² No Anakim were left in the land of the Israelites, except for some remaining in Gaza, Gath, and Ashdod.

²³ So Joshua took the entire land, in keeping with all that the LORD had told Moses. Joshua then gave it as an inheritance to Israel according to their tribal allotments. After this, the land had rest from war.

Territory East of the Jordan

12 The Israelites struck down the following kings of the land and took possession of their land beyond the Jordan to the east and from the Arnon River to Mount

Hermon, including all the Arabah eastward: Dt 3:8-9

² King Sihon of the Amorites lived in Heshbon. He ruled from Aroer on the rim of the Arnon River, along the middle of the valley, and half of Gilead up to the Jabbok River (the border of the Ammonites), ³ the Arabah east of the Sea of Chinnereth to the Sea of Arabah (that is, the Dead Sea), eastward through Beth-jeshimoth and southwardᴬ below the slopes of Pisgah. Dt 2:36

⁴ King Ogᴮ of Bashan, of the remnant of the Rephaim, lived in Ashtaroth and Edrei. ⁵ He ruled over Mount Hermon, Salecah, all Bashan up to the Geshurite and Maacathite border, and half of Gilead to the border of King Sihon of Heshbon. ⁶ Moses the LORD's servant and the Israelites struck them down. And Moses the LORD's servant gave their land as an inheritance to the Reubenites, Gadites, and half the tribe of Manasseh. Nm 32:33; Dt 1:4; 3:10,14

Territory West of the Jordan

⁷ Joshua and the Israelites struck down the following kings of the land beyond the Jordan to the west, from Baal-gad in the Valley of Lebanon to Mount Halak, which ascends toward Seir (Joshua gave their land as an inheritance to the tribes of Israel according to their allotments: ⁸ the hill country, the Judean foothills,ᶜ the Arabah, the slopes, the wilderness, and the Negev — the lands of the Hethites, Amorites, Canaanites, Perizzites, Hivites, and Jebusites): Jos 11:16-17

⁹ the king of Jericho   one
   the king of Ai, which is
      next to Bethel   one
¹⁰ the king of Jerusalem   one
   the king of Hebron   one
¹¹ the king of Jarmuth   one
   the king of Lachish   one
¹² the king of Eglon   one
   the king of Gezer   one
¹³ the king of Debir   one
   the king of Geder   one
¹⁴ the king of Hormah   one
   the king of Arad   one
¹⁵ the king of Libnah   one
   the king of Adullam   one
¹⁶ the king of Makkedah   one
   the king of Bethel   one
¹⁷ the king of Tappuah   one
   the king of Hepher   one
¹⁸ the king of Aphek   one
   the king of Lasharon   one
¹⁹ the king of Madon   one
   the king of Hazor   one
²⁰ the king
      of Shimron-meron   one
   the king of Achshaph   one
²¹ the king of Taanach   one
   the king of Megiddo   one
²² the king of Kedesh   one
   the king of Jokneam
      in Carmel   one
²³ the king of Dor
      in Naphath-dorᴰ   one
   the king of Goiim
      in Gilgalᴱ   one
²⁴ the king of Tirzah   one
   the total number of
      all kings: thirty-one.

Unconquered Lands

13 Joshua was now old, advanced in age, and the LORD said to him, "You have become old, advanced in age, but a great deal of the land remains to be possessed. ² This is the land that remains:

All the districts of the Philistines and the Geshurites: ³ from

ᴬ**12:3** Or *and from Teman*   ᴮ**12:4** LXX; MT reads *The territory of Og*   ᶜ**12:8** Or *the Shephelah*
ᴰ**12:23** Or *in the Slopes of Dor*   ᴱ**12:23** LXX reads *Galilee*

the Shihor east of Egypt to the border of Ekron on the north (considered to be Canaanite territory) — the five Philistine rulers of Gaza, Ashdod, Ash-kelon, Gath, and Ekron, as well as the Avvites ⁴ in the south; all the land of the Canaanites, from Arah of the Sidonians to Aphek and as far as the bor-der of the Amorites; ⁵ the land of the Gebalites; and all Leba-non east from Baal-gad below Mount Hermon to the entrance of Hamath ᴬ — ⁶ all the inhab-itants of the hill country from Lebanon to Misrephoth-maim, all the Sidonians.   Jos 12:7; 1Kg 5:18
I will drive them out before the Is-raelites, only distribute the land as an inheritance for Israel, as I have commanded you. ⁷ Therefore, di-vide this land as an inheritance to the nine tribes and half the tribe of Manasseh."

The Inheritance East of the Jordan

⁸ With the other half of the tribe of Manasseh, the Reubenites and Gadites had received the inheri-tance Moses gave them beyond the Jordan to the east, just as Moses the LORD's servant had given them: ⁹ From Aroer on the rim of the Arnon Valley, along with the city in the middle of the val-ley, all the Medeba plateau as far as Dibon, ¹⁰ and all the cities of King Sihon of the Amorites, who reigned in Heshbon, to the border of the Ammonites; ¹¹ also Gilead and the territory of the Geshurites and Maaca-thites, all Mount Hermon, and all Bashan to Salecah — ¹² the whole kingdom of Og in Bashan, who reigned in Ashtaroth and Edrei; he was one of the remaining Rephaim. Moses struck them down and drove them out, ¹³ but the Israelites did not drive out the Geshurites and Maacathites. So Geshur and Maa-cath still live in Israel today.

¹⁴ He did not, however, give any inheritance to the tribe of Levi. This was their inheritance, just as he had promised: the offerings made by fire to the LORD, the God of Israel.

Reuben's Inheritance

¹⁵ To the tribe of Reuben's descen-dants by their clans, Moses gave ¹⁶ this as their territory:
From Aroer on the rim of the Arnon Valley, along with the city in the middle of the valley, the whole plateau as far as ᴮ Medeba, ¹⁷ with Heshbon and all its cities on the plateau — Dibon, Bamoth-baal, Beth-baal-meon, ¹⁸ Jahaz, Kede-moth, Mephaath, ¹⁹ Kiriathaim, Sibmah, Zereth-shahar on the hill in the valley, ²⁰ Beth-peor, the slopes of Pisgah, and Beth-jeshimoth — ²¹ all the cities of the plateau, and all the kingdom of King Sihon of the Amorites, who reigned in Heshbon. Moses had killed him and the chiefs of Midian — Evi, Rekem, Zur, Hur, and Reba — the princes of Sihon who lived in the land. ²² Along with those the Israelites put to death, they also killed the diviner, Balaam son of Beor, with the sword. ²³ The border of the Reubenites was the Jordan and its plain. This was the inheritance of the Reubenites

ᴬ13:5 Or to Lebo-hamath   ᴮ13:16 Some Hb mss read plateau near by their clans, with the cities and their settlements.

Gad's Inheritance

²⁴ To the tribe of the Gadites by their clans, Moses gave ²⁵ this as their territory:

Jazer and all the cities of Gilead, and half the land of the Ammonites to Aroer, near Rabbah; ²⁶ from Heshbon to Ramathmizpeh and Betonim, and from Mahanaim to the border of Debir;ᴬ ²⁷ in the valley: Bethharam, Beth-nimrah, Succoth, and Zaphon — the rest of the kingdom of King Sihon of Heshbon. Their land also included the Jordan and its territory as far as the edge of the Sea of Chinnereth on the east side of the Jordan.ᴮ

²⁸ This was the inheritance of the Gadites by their clans, with the cities and their settlements.

East Manasseh's Inheritance

²⁹ And to half the tribe of Manasseh (that is, to half the tribe of Manasseh's descendants by their clans) Moses gave ³⁰ this as their territory:

From Mahanaim through all Bashan — all the kingdom of King Og of Bashan, including all of Jair's Villagesᶜ that are in Bashan — sixty cities. ³¹ But half of Gilead, and Og's royal cities in Bashan — Ashtaroth and Edrei — are for the descendants of Machir son of Manasseh (that is, half the descendants of Machir by their clans). Nm 32:41

³² These were the portions Moses gave them on the plains of Moab beyond the Jordan east of Jericho. ³³ But Moses did not give a portion to the tribe of Levi. The LORD, the God of Israel, was their inheritance, just as he had promised them.

Israel's Inheritance in Canaan

14 The Israelites received these portions that the priest Eleazar, Joshua son of Nun, and the family heads of the Israelite tribes gave them in the land of Canaan. ² Their inheritance was by lot as the LORD commanded through Moses for the nine and a half tribes, ³ because Moses had given the inheritance to the two and a half tribes beyond the Jordan. But he gave no inheritance among them to the Levites. ⁴ The descendants of Joseph became two tribes, Manasseh and Ephraim. No portion of the land was given to the Levites except cities to live in, along with pasturelands for their cattle and livestock. ⁵ So the Israelites did as the LORD commanded Moses, and they divided the land. Nm 34:17-18; Jos 19:51

Caleb's Inheritance

⁶ The descendants of Judah approached Joshua at Gilgal, and Caleb son of Jephunneh the Kenizzite said to him, "You know what the LORD promised Moses the man of God at Kadesh-barnea about you and me. ⁷ I was forty years old when Moses the LORD's servant sent me from Kadesh-barnea to scout the land, and I brought back an honest report. ⁸ My brothers who went with me caused the people to lose heart,ᴰ but I followed the LORD my God completely. ⁹ On that day Moses swore to me: 'The land where

---

ᴬ13:26 Or *Lidbir*, or *Lo-debar*   ᴮ13:27 Lit *Chinnereth beyond the Jordan to the east*   ᶜ13:30 Or *all of Havvoth-jair*   ᴰ14:8 Lit *people's hearts to melt with fear* you have set foot will be an inheritance for you and your descendants forever, because you have followed the LORD my God completely.'

¹⁰ "As you see, the LORD has kept me alive these forty-five years as he promised, since the LORD spoke this word to Moses while Israel was journeying in the wilderness. Here I am today, eighty-five years old. ¹¹ I am still as strong today as I was the day Moses sent me out. My strength for battle and for daily tasks^A is now as it was then. ¹² Now give me this hill country the LORD promised me on that day, because you heard then that the Anakim are there, as well as large fortified cities. Perhaps the LORD will be with me and I will drive them out as the LORD promised."   Nm 14:30; 26:65; 32:12; Dt 1:28; 9:2; 34:7

¹³ Then Joshua blessed Caleb son of Jephunneh and gave him Hebron as an inheritance. ¹⁴ Therefore, Hebron still belongs to Caleb son of Jephunneh the Kenizzite as an inheritance today because he followed the LORD, the God of Israel, completely. ¹⁵ Hebron's name used to be Kiriath-arba; Arba was the greatest man among the Anakim. After this, the land had rest from war.   Nm 13:33; Jos 6:25; 15:13; Jdg 1:10,20

Judah's Inheritance

15 Now the allotment for the tribe of the descendants of Judah by their clans was in the southernmost region, south to the Wilderness of Zin and over to the border of Edom.   Nm 34:3

² Their southern border began at the tip of the Dead Sea on the south bay^B ³ and went south of the Scorpions' Ascent, ^C

proceeded to Zin, ascended to the south of Kadesh-barnea, passed Hezron, ascended to Addar, and turned to Karka. ⁴ It proceeded to Azmon and to the Brook of Egypt and so the border ended at the Mediterranean Sea. This is your^D southern border.   Jos 15:47; 1Kg 8:65; 2Kg 24:7

⁵ Now the eastern border was along the Dead Sea to the mouth of the Jordan.

The border on the north side was from the bay of the sea at the mouth of the Jordan. ⁶ It ascended to Beth-hoglah, proceeded north of Beth-arabah, and ascended to the Stone of Bohan son of Reuben. ⁷ Then the border ascended to Debir from the Valley of Achor, turning north to the Gilgal that is opposite the Ascent of Adummim, which is south of the ravine. The border proceeded to the Waters of En-shemesh and ended at En-rogel. ⁸ From there the border ascended Ben Hinnom Valley to the southern Jebusite slope (that is, Jerusalem) and ascended to the top of the hill that faces Hinnom Valley on the west, at the northern end of Rephaim Valley. ⁹ From the top of the hill the border curved to the spring of the Waters of Nephtoah, went to the cities of Mount Ephron, and then curved to Baalah (that is, Kiriath-jearim). ¹⁰ The border turned westward from Baalah to Mount Seir, went to the northern slope of Mount

---

^A14:11 Lit for going out and coming in   ^B15:2 Lit Sea at the tongue that turns southward   ^C15:3 Lit of scorpions   ^D15:4 LXX reads their

Jearim (that is, Chesalon), descended to Beth-shemesh, and proceeded to Timnah. ¹¹ Then the border reached to the slope north of Ekron, curved to Shikkeron, proceeded to Mount Baalah, went to Jabneel, and ended at the Mediterranean Sea.   Gn 38:13; Jdg 14:1; 1Ch 13:6

¹² Now the western border was the coastline of the Mediterranean Sea.

This was the boundary of the descendants of Judah around their clans.

Caleb and Othniel

¹³ He gave Caleb son of Jephunneh the following portion among the descendants of Judah based on the LORD's instruction to Joshua: Kiriath-arba (that is, Hebron; Arba was the father of Anak). ¹⁴ Caleb drove out from there the three sons of Anak: Sheshai, Ahiman, and Talmai, descendants of Anak. ¹⁵ From there he marched against the inhabitants of Debir, which used to be called Kiriath-sepher, ¹⁶ and Caleb said, "Whoever attacks and captures Kiriath-sepher, I will give my daughter Achsah to him as a wife." ¹⁷ So Othniel son of Caleb's brother, Kenaz, captured it, and Caleb gave his daughter Achsah to him as a wife. ¹⁸ When she arrived, she persuaded Othniel to ask her father for a field. As she got off her donkey, Caleb asked her, "What can I do for you?" ¹⁹ She replied, "Give me a blessing. Since you have given me land in the Negev, give me the springs also." So he gave her the upper and lower springs. Dt 9:2

Judah's Cities

²⁰ This was the inheritance of the tribe of the descendants of Judah by their clans.

²¹ These were the outermost cities of the tribe of the descendants of Judah toward the border of Edom in the Negev: Kabzeel, Eder, Jagur, ²² Kinah, Dimonah, Adadah, ²³ Kedesh, Hazor, Ithnan, ²⁴ Ziph, Telem, Bealoth, ²⁵ Hazor-hadattah, Kerioth-hezron (that is, Hazor), ²⁶ Amam, Shema, Moladah, ²⁷ Hazar-gaddah, Heshmon, Beth-pelet, ²⁸ Hazar-shual, Beer-sheba, Biziothiah, ²⁹ Baalah, Iim, Ezem, ³⁰ Eltolad, Chesil, Hormah, ³¹ Ziklag, Madmannah, Sansannah, ³² Lebaoth, Shilhim, Ain, and Rimmon — twenty-nine cities in all, with their settlements.

³³ In the Judean foothills:ᴬ Eshtaol, Zorah, Ashnah, ³⁴ Zanoah, En-gannim, Tappuah, ᴮ Enam, ³⁵ Jarmuth, Adullam, Socoh, ᶜ Azekah, ³⁶ Shaaraim, Adithaim, Gederah, and Gederothaim — fourteen cities, with their settlements; ³⁷ Zenan, Hadashah, Migdal-gad, ³⁸ Dilan, Mizpeh, Jokthe-el, ³⁹ Lachish, Bozkath, Eglon, ⁴⁰ Cabbon, Lahmam, Chitlish, ⁴¹ Gederoth, Beth-dagon, Naamah, and Makkedah — sixteen cities, with their settlements; ⁴² Libnah, Ether, Ashan, ⁴³ Iphtah, Ashnah, Nezib, ⁴⁴ Keilah, Achzib, and Mareshah — nine cities, with their settlements; ⁴⁵ Ekron, with its surrounding villages and settlements;

ᴬ15:33 Or the Shephelah   ᴮ15:34 Or En-gannim-tappuah   ᶜ15:35 Or Adullam-socoh

⁴⁶ from Ekron to the sea, all the cities near Ashdod, with their settlements; ⁴⁷ Ashdod, with its surrounding villages and settlements; Gaza, with its surrounding villages and settlements, to the Brook of Egypt and the coastline of the Mediterranean Sea.   1Sm 22:1

⁴⁸ In the hill country: Shamir, Jattir, Socoh, ⁴⁹ Dannah, Kiriath-sannah (that is, Debir), ⁵⁰ Anab, Eshtemoh, Anim, ⁵¹ Goshen, Holon, and Giloh — eleven cities, with their settlements; ⁵² Arab, Dumah, ᴬ Eshan, ⁵³ Janim, Beth-tappuah, Aphekah, ⁵⁴ Humtah, Kiriath-arba (that is, Hebron), and Zior — nine cities, with their settlements; ⁵⁵ Maon, Carmel, Ziph, Juttah, ⁵⁶ Jezreel, Jokdeam, Zanoah, ⁵⁷ Kain, Gibeah, and Timnah — ten cities, with their settlements; ⁵⁸ Halhul, Beth-zur, Gedor, ⁵⁹ Maarath, Beth-anoth, and Eltekon — six cities, with their settlements; ᴮ ⁶⁰ Kiriath-baal (that is, Kiriath-jearim), and Rabbah — two cities, with their settlements.

⁶¹ In the wilderness: Beth-arabah, Middin, Secacah, ⁶² Nibshan, the City of Salt, ᶜ and En-gedi — six cities, with their settlements.

⁶³ But the descendants of Judah could not drive out the Jebusites who lived in Jerusalem. So the Jebusites still live in Jerusalem among the descendants of Judah today.   Jos 6:25; 16:10; 22:17; Jdg 1:21; 2Sm 5:5-9

Joseph's Inheritance

16 The allotment for the descendants of Joseph went from the Jordan at Jericho to the Waters of Jericho on the east, through the wilderness ascending from Jericho into the hill country of Bethel. ² From Bethel it went to Luz and proceeded to the border of the Archites by Ataroth. ³ It then descended westward to the border of the Japhletites as far as the border of lower Beth-horon, then to Gezer, and ended at the Mediterranean Sea. ⁴ So Ephraim and Manasseh, the sons of Joseph, received their inheritance.   Jos 8:15; 18:12

Ephraim's Inheritance

⁵ This was the territory of the descendants of Ephraim by their clans:

The border of their inheritance went from Ataroth-addar on the east to Upper Beth-horon. ⁶ In the north the border went westward from Michmethath; it turned eastward from Taanath-shiloh and passed it east of Janoah. ⁷ From Janoah it descended to Ataroth and Naarah, and then reached Jericho and went to the Jordan. ⁸ From Tappuah the border went westward along the Brook of Kanah and ended at the Mediterranean Sea.   Jos 18:13

This was the inheritance of the tribe of the descendants of Ephraim by their clans, together with ⁹ the cities set apart for the

ᴬ**15:52** Some Hb mss read *Rumah*   ᴮ**15:59** LXX adds *Tekoa, Ephrathah (that is, Bethlehem), Peor, Etam, Culom, Tatam, Sores, Carem, Gallim, Baither, and Manach — eleven cities, with their settlements*
ᶜ**15:62** Or *Ir-hamelach*

descendants of Ephraim within the inheritance of the descendants of Manasseh — all these cities with their settlements. [10] However, they did not drive out the Canaanites who lived in Gezer. So the Canaanites still live in Ephraim today, but they are forced laborers.   Jdg 1:29

West Manasseh's Inheritance

17 This was the allotment for the tribe of Manasseh as Joseph's firstborn. Gilead and Bashan were given to Machir, the firstborn of Manasseh and the father of Gilead, because he was a man of war. [2] So the allotment was for the rest of Manasseh's descendants by their clans, for the sons of Abiezer, Helek, Asriel, Shechem, Hepher, and Shemida. These are the male descendants of Manasseh son of Joseph, by their clans. Gn 41:51; 46:20; 48:18

[3] Now Zelophehad son of Hepher, son of Gilead, son of Machir, son of Manasseh, had no sons, only daughters. These are the names of his daughters: Mahlah, Noah, Hoglah, Milcah, and Tirzah. [4] They came before the priest Eleazar, Joshua son of Nun, and the leaders, saying, "The LORD commanded Moses to give us an inheritance among our male relatives." So they gave them an inheritance among their father's brothers, in keeping with the LORD's instruction. [5] As a result, ten tracts fell to Manasseh, besides the land of Gilead and Bashan, which are beyond the Jordan, [A] [6] because Manasseh's daughters received an inheritance among his sons. The land of Gilead belonged to the rest of Manasseh's sons.   Nm 26:33; 27:1-11

[7] The border of Manasseh went from Asher to Michmethath near Shechem. It then went southward toward the inhabitants of En-tappuah. [8] The region of Tappuah belonged to Manasseh, but Tappuah itself on Manasseh's border belonged to the descendants of Ephraim. [9] From there the border descended to the Brook of Kanah; south of the brook, cities belonged to Ephraim among Manasseh's cities. Manasseh's border was on the north side of the brook and ended at the Mediterranean Sea. [10] Ephraim's territory was to the south and Manasseh's to the north, with the Sea as its border. They reached Asher on the north and Issachar on the east. [11] Within Issachar and Asher, Manasseh had Beth-shean, Ibleam, and the inhabitants of Dor with their surrounding villages; the inhabitants of En-dor, Taanach, and Megiddo — the three cities of [B] Naphath — with their surrounding villages.   Jos 16:8-9

[12] The descendants of Manasseh could not possess these cities, because the Canaanites were determined to stay in this land. [13] However, when the Israelites grew stronger, they imposed forced labor on the Canaanites but did not drive them out completely.

Joseph's Additional Inheritance

[14] Joseph's descendants said to Joshua, "Why did you give us only one tribal allotment [C] as an inheritance? We have many people, because the LORD has been blessing us greatly."

A **17:5** = east of the Jordan River B **17:11** LXX, Vg read *the third is* C **17:14** Lit *one lot and one territory*, also in v. 17

¹⁵ "If you have so many people," Joshua replied to them, "go to the forest and clear an area for yourselves there in the land of the Perizzites and the Rephaim, because Ephraim's hill country is too small for you."

¹⁶ But the descendants of Joseph said, "The hill country is not enough for us, and all the Canaanites who inhabit the valley area have iron chariots, both at Beth-shean with its surrounding villages and in the Jezreel Valley."

¹⁷ So Joshua replied to Joseph's family (that is, Ephraim and Manasseh), "You have many people and great strength. You will not have just one allotment, ¹⁸ because the hill country will be yours also. It is a forest; clear it and its outlying areas will be yours. You can also drive out the Canaanites, even though they have iron chariots and are strong."

Land Distribution at Shiloh

18 The entire Israelite community assembled at Shiloh and set up the tent of meeting there. The land had been subdued before them, ² but seven tribes among the Israelites were left who had not divided up their inheritance. ³ So Joshua asked the Israelites, "How long will you delay going out to take possession of the land that the LORD, the God of your fathers, gave you? ⁴ Appoint for yourselves three men from each tribe, and I will send them out. They are to go and survey the land, write a description of it for the purpose of their inheritance, and return to me. ⁵ Then they are to divide it into seven portions. Judah is to remain in its territory in the south and Joseph's family in their

territory in the north. ⁶ When you have written a description of the seven portions of land and brought it to me, I will cast lots for you here in the presence of the LORD our God. ⁷ But the Levites among you do not get a portion, because their inheritance is the priesthood of the LORD. Gad, Reuben, and half the tribe of Manasseh have taken their inheritance beyond the Jordan to the east, which Moses the LORD's servant gave them." Jos 19:51; Jdg 18:31; 1Sm 1:9; 3:3; 11:1

⁸ As the men prepared to go, Joshua commanded them^A to write down a description of the land, saying, "Go and survey the land, write a description of it, and return to me. I will then cast lots for you here in Shiloh in the presence of the LORD." ⁹ So the men left, went through the land, and described it by towns in a document of seven sections. They returned to Joshua at the camp in Shiloh. ¹⁰ Joshua cast lots for them at Shiloh in the presence of the LORD where he distributed the land to the Israelites according to their divisions.

Benjamin's Inheritance

¹¹ The lot came up for the tribe of Benjamin's descendants by their clans, and their allotted territory lay between Judah's descendants and Joseph's descendants.

¹² Their border on the north side began at the Jordan, ascended to the slope of Jericho on the north, through the hill country westward, and ended at the wilderness around Beth-aven. ¹³ From there the border went toward Luz, to the southern slope of Luz (that is, Bethel); it then went down by

^A 18:8 Lit *the ones going around*

Ataroth-addar, over the hill south of Lower Beth-horon.

¹⁴ On the west side, from the hill facing Beth-horon on the south, the border curved, turning southward, and ended at Kiriath-baal (that is, Kiriath-jearim), a city of the descendants of Judah. This was the west side of their border.

¹⁵ The south side began at the edge of Kiriath-jearim, and the border extended westward; it went to the spring at the Waters of Nephtoah. ¹⁶ The border descended to the foot of the hill that faces Ben Hinnom Valley at the northern end of Rephaim Valley. It ran down Hinnom Valley toward the south Jebusite slope and downward to En-rogel. ¹⁷ It curved northward and went to En-shemesh and on to Geliloth, which is opposite the Ascent of Adummim, and continued down to the Stone of Bohan son of Reuben. ¹⁸ Then it went north to the slope opposite the Arabah ^A and proceeded into the plains. ^B ¹⁹ The border continued to the north slope of Beth-hoglah and ended at the northern bay of the Dead Sea, at the southern end of the Jordan. This was the southern border. Jos 15:6

²⁰ The Jordan formed the border on the east side. This was the inheritance of Benjamin's descendants, by their clans, according to its surrounding borders.

Benjamin's Cities

²¹ These were the cities of the tribe of Benjamin's descendants by their clans:

Jericho, Beth-hoglah, Emek-keziz, ²² Beth-arabah, Zemaraim, Bethel, ²³ Avvim, Parah, Ophrah, ²⁴ Chephar-ammoni, Ophni, and Geba — twelve cities, with their settlements; ²⁵ Gibeon, Ramah, Beeroth, ²⁶ Mizpeh, Chephirah, Mozah, ²⁷ Rekem, Irpeel, Taralah, ²⁸ Zela, Haeleph, Jebus ^C (that is, Jerusalem), Gibeah, and Kiriath ^D — fourteen cities, with their settlements.

This was the inheritance for Benjamin's descendants by their clans.

Simeon's Inheritance

19 The second lot came out for Simeon, for the tribe of his descendants by their clans, but their inheritance was within the inheritance given to Judah's descendants. ² Their inheritance included Beer-sheba (or Sheba), Moladah, ³ Hazar-shual, Balah, Ezem, ⁴ Eltolad, Bethul, Hormah, ⁵ Ziklag, Beth-marcaboth, Hazar-susah, ⁶ Beth-lebaoth, and Sharuhen — thirteen cities, with their settlements; ⁷ Ain, Rimmon, Ether, and Ashan — four cities, with their settlements; ⁸ and all the settlements surrounding these cities as far as Baalath-beer (Ramah in the south ^E). 1Ch 4:28

This was the inheritance of the tribe of Simeon's descendants by their clans. ⁹ The inheritance of Simeon's descendants was within the territory of Judah's descendants,

^A **18:18** LXX reads *went northward to Beth-arabah*   ^B **18:18** Or *the Arabah*   ^C **18:28** Lit *Jebusite*
^D **18:28** LXX, Syr read *Kiriath-jearim*   ^E **19:8** Or *the Negev*

because the share for Judah's descendants was too large. So Simeon's descendants received an inheritance within Judah's portion.

Zebulun's Inheritance

¹⁰ The third lot came up for Zebulun's descendants by their clans. The territory of their inheritance stretched as far as Sarid; ¹¹ their border went up westward to Maralah, reached Dabbesheth, and met the brook east of Jokneam. ¹² From Sarid, it turned due east along the border of Chisloth-tabor, went to Daberath, and went up to Japhia. ¹³ From there, it went due east to Gath-hepher and to Eth-kazin; it extended to Rimmon, curving around to Neah. ¹⁴ The border then circled around Neah on the north to Hannathon and ended at Iphtah-el Valley, ¹⁵ along with Kattath, Nahalal, Shimron, Idalah, and Bethlehem — twelve cities, with their settlements. ¹⁶ This was the inheritance of Zebulun's descendants by their clans, these cities, with their settlements.

Issachar's Inheritance

¹⁷ The fourth lot came out for the tribe of Issachar's descendants by their clans. ¹⁸ Their territory went to Jezreel, and included Chesulloth, Shunem, ¹⁹ Hapharaim, Shion, Anaharath, ²⁰ Rabbith, Kishion, Ebez, ²¹ Remeth, En-gannim, En-haddah, and Beth-pazzez. ²² The border reached Tabor, Shahazumah, and Beth-shemesh, and ended at the Jordan — sixteen cities, with their settlements.

²³ This was the inheritance of the tribe of Issachar's descendants by their clans, the cities, with their settlements.

Asher's Inheritance

²⁴ The fifth lot came out for the tribe of Asher's descendants by their clans. ²⁵ Their boundary included Helkath, Hali, Beten, Achshaph, ²⁶ Allammelech, Amad, and Mishal and reached westward to Carmel and Shihor-libnath. ²⁷ It turned eastward to Beth-dagon, reached Zebulun and Iphtah-el Valley, north toward Beth-emek and Neiel, and went north to Cabul, ²⁸ Ebron, Rehob, Hammon, and Kanah, as far as greater Sidon. ²⁹ The boundary then turned to Ramah as far as the fortified city of Tyre; it turned back to Hosah and ended at the Mediterranean Sea, including Mahalab, Achzib, ^A ³⁰ Ummah, Aphek, and Rehob — twenty-two cities, with their settlements.   1Kg 9:13 ³¹ This was the inheritance of the tribe of Asher's descendants by their clans, these cities with their settlements.

Naphtali's Inheritance

³² The sixth lot came out for Naphtali's descendants by their clans. ³³ Their boundary went from Heleph and from the oak in Zaanannim, including Adaminekeb and Jabneel, as far as Lakkum, and ended at the Jordan. ³⁴ To the west, the boundary turned to Aznoth-tabor and went from there to Hukkok, reaching Zebulun on the

^A19:29 Or *Sea, in the region of Achzib*

south, Asher on the west, and Judah^A at the Jordan on the east. ³⁵ The fortified cities were Ziddim, Zer, Hammath, Rakkath, Chinnereth, ³⁶ Adamah, Ramah, Hazor, ³⁷ Kedesh, Edrei, En-hazor, ³⁸ Iron, Migdal-el, Horem, Beth-anath, and Beth-shemesh — nineteen cities, with their settlements.

³⁹ This was the inheritance of the tribe of Naphtali's descendants by their clans, the cities with their settlements.

Dan's Inheritance

⁴⁰ The seventh lot came out for the tribe of Dan's descendants by their clans.

⁴¹ The territory of their inheritance included Zorah, Eshtaol, Ir-shemesh, ⁴² Shaalabbin, Aijalon, Ithlah, ⁴³ Elon, Timnah, Ekron, ⁴⁴ Eltekeh, Gibbethon, Baalath, ⁴⁵ Jehud, Bene-berak, Gath-rimmon, ⁴⁶ Me-jarkon, and Rakkon, with the territory facing Joppa.   Jdg 1:35; 2Ch 2:16; Ezr 3:7

⁴⁷ When the territory of the descendants of Dan slipped out of their control, they went up and fought against Leshem, captured it, and struck it down with the sword. So they took possession of it, lived there, and renamed Leshem after their ancestor Dan. ⁴⁸ This was the inheritance of the tribe of Dan's descendants by their clans, these cities with their settlements. Jdg 18:1

Joshua's Inheritance

⁴⁹ When they had finished distributing the land into its territories, the Israelites gave Joshua son of Nun an inheritance among them. ⁵⁰ By the LORD's command, they gave him the city Timnath-serah in the hill country of Ephraim, which he requested. He rebuilt the city and lived in it.   Jos 24:30

⁵¹ These were the portions that the priest Eleazar, Joshua son of Nun, and the family heads distributed to the Israelite tribes by lot at Shiloh in the LORD's presence at the entrance to the tent of meeting. So they finished dividing up the land.   Jos 14:1

Cities of Refuge

20 Then the LORD spoke to Joshua, ² "Tell the Israelites: Select your cities of refuge, as I instructed you through Moses, ³ so that a person who kills someone unintentionally or accidentally may flee there. These will be your refuge from the avenger of blood. ⁴ When someone flees to one of these cities, stands at the entrance of the city gate, and states his case before^B the elders of that city, they are to bring him into the city and give him a place to live among them. ⁵ And if the avenger of blood pursues him, they must not hand the one who committed manslaughter over to him, for he killed his neighbor accidentally and did not hate him beforehand. ⁶ He is to stay in that city until he stands trial before the assembly and until the death of the high priest serving at that time. Then the one who committed manslaughter may return home to his own city from which he fled."   Nm 35:6-34; Dt 4:41-43; 19:1-13

⁷ So they designated Kedesh in the hill country of Naphtali in Galilee, Shechem in the hill country of Ephraim, and Kiriath-arba (that is, Hebron) in the hill country of

---

^A**19:34** LXX omits *Judah*　　^B**20:4** Lit *in the ears of*

Judah. **8** Across the Jordan east of Jericho, they selected Bezer on the wilderness plateau from Reuben's tribe, Ramoth in Gilead from Gad's tribe, and Golan in Bashan from Manasseh's tribe.   Jos 21:11; 1Ch 6:76

9 These are the cities appointed for all the Israelites and the aliens residing among them, so that anyone who kills a person unintentionally may flee there and not die at the hand of the avenger of blood until he stands before the assembly.   Nm 35:15

Cities of the Levites

21 The Levite family heads approached the priest Eleazar, Joshua son of Nun, and the family heads of the Israelite tribes. **2** At Shiloh, in the land of Canaan, they told them, "The LORD commanded through Moses that we be given cities to live in, with their pasturelands for our livestock." **3** So the Israelites, by the LORD'S command, gave the Levites these cities with their pasturelands from their inheritance.   Nm 35:4-5

4 The lot came out for the Kohathite clans: The Levites who were the descendants of the priest Aaron received thirteen cities by lot from the tribes of Judah, Simeon, and Benjamin. **5** The remaining descendants of Kohath received ten cities by lot from the clans of the tribes of Ephraim, Dan, and half the tribe of Manasseh.

6 Gershon's descendants received thirteen cities by lot from the clans of the tribes of Issachar, Asher, Naphtali, and half the tribe of Manasseh in Bashan.

7 Merari's descendants received twelve cities for their clans from the tribes of Reuben, Gad, and Zebulun.

8 The Israelites gave these cities with their pasturelands around them to the Levites by lot, as the LORD had commanded through Moses.

Cities of Aaron's Descendants

9 The Israelites gave these cities by name from the tribes of the descendants of Judah and Simeon **10** to the descendants of Aaron from the Kohathite clans of the Levites, because they received the first lot. **11** They gave them Kiriath-arba (that is, Hebron; Arba was the father of Anak) with its surrounding pasturelands in the hill country of Judah. **12** But they gave the fields and settlements of the city to Caleb son of Jephunneh as his possession.   1Ch 6:55

13 They gave to the descendants of the priest Aaron:

Hebron, the city of refuge for the one who commits manslaughter, with its pasturelands, Libnah with its pasturelands, **14** Jattir with its pasturelands, Eshtemoa with its pasturelands, **15** Holon with its pasturelands, Debir with its pasturelands, **16** Ain with its pasturelands, Juttah with its pasturelands, and Beth-shemesh with its pasturelands — nine cities from these two tribes.

17 From the tribe of Benjamin they gave:

Gibeon with its pasturelands, Geba with its pasturelands, **18** Anathoth with its pasturelands, and Almon with its pasturelands — four cities. **19** All thirteen cities with their pasturelands were for the priests, the descendants of Aaron.

Cities of Kohath's Other Descendants

²⁰ The allotted cities to the remaining clans of Kohath's descendants, who were Levites, came from the tribe of Ephraim. ²¹ The Israelites gave them:

Shechem, the city of refuge for the one who commits manslaughter, with its pasturelands in the hill country of Ephraim, Gezer with its pasturelands, ²² Kibzaim with its pasturelands, and Beth-horon with its pasturelands — four cities.

²³ From the tribe of Dan they gave: Elteke with its pasturelands, Gibbethon with its pasturelands, ²⁴ Aijalon with its pasturelands, and Gath-rimmon with its pasturelands — four cities.

²⁵ From half the tribe of Manasseh they gave:

Taanach with its pasturelands and Gath-rimmon^A with its pasturelands — two cities.

²⁶ All ten cities with their pasturelands were for the clans of Kohath's other descendants.

Cities of Gershon's Descendants

²⁷ From half the tribe of Manasseh, they gave to the descendants of Gershon, who were one of the Levite clans: 1Ch 6:71

Golan, the city of refuge for the one who commits manslaughter, with its pasturelands in Bashan, and Beeshterah with its pasturelands — two cities.

²⁸ From the tribe of Issachar they gave:

Kishion with its pasturelands, Daberath with its pasturelands, ²⁹ Jarmuth with its pasturelands, and En-gannim with its pasturelands — four cities.

³⁰ From the tribe of Asher they gave:

Mishal with its pasturelands, Abdon with its pasturelands, ³¹ Helkath with its pasturelands, and Rehob with its pasturelands — four cities.

³² From the tribe of Naphtali they gave:

Kedesh in Galilee, the city of refuge for the one who commits manslaughter, with its pasturelands, Hammoth-dor with its pasturelands, and Kartan with its pasturelands — three cities.

³³ All thirteen cities with their pasturelands were for the Gershonites by their clans.

Cities of Merari's Descendants

³⁴ From the tribe of Zebulun, they gave to the clans of the descendants of Merari, who were the remaining Levites: 1Ch 6:77

Jokneam with its pasturelands, Kartah with its pasturelands, ³⁵ Dimnah with its pasturelands, and Nahalal with its pasturelands — four cities.

³⁶ From the tribe of Reuben they gave:

Bezer with its pasturelands, Jahzah^B with its pasturelands, ³⁷ Kedemoth with its

A 21:25 Or Ibleam   B 21:36 Or Jahaz

pasturelands, and Mephaath with its pasturelands — four cities.[A]   Jos 20:8

38 From the tribe of Gad they gave: Ramoth in Gilead, the city of refuge for the one who commits manslaughter, with its pasturelands, Mahanaim with its pasturelands, **39** Heshbon with its pasturelands, and Jazer with its pasturelands — four cities in all. **40** All twelve cities were allotted to the clans of Merari's descendants, the remaining Levite clans.

41 Within the Israelite possession there were forty-eight cities in all with their pasturelands for the Levites. **42** Each of these cities had its own surrounding pasturelands; this was true for all the cities.

The Lord's Promises Fulfilled

43 So the Lord gave Israel all the land he had sworn to give their fathers, and they took possession of it and settled there. **44** The Lord gave them rest on every side according to all he had sworn to their fathers. None of their enemies were able to stand against them, for the Lord handed over all their enemies to them. **45** None of the good promises the Lord had made to the house of Israel failed. Everything was fulfilled.   Jos 23:14

Eastern Tribes Return Home

22 Joshua summoned the Reubenites, Gadites, and half the tribe of Manasseh **2** and told them, "You have done everything Moses the Lord's servant commanded you and have obeyed me

in everything I commanded you. **3** You have not deserted your brothers even once this whole time but have carried out the requirement of the command of the Lord your God. **4** Now that he has given your brothers rest, just as he promised them, return to your homes in your own land that Moses the Lord's servant gave you across the Jordan. **5** Only carefully obey the command and instruction that Moses the Lord's servant gave you: to love the Lord your God, walk in all his ways, keep his commands, be loyal to him, and serve him with all your heart and all your soul."   Dt 3:18-20

6 Joshua blessed them and sent them on their way, and they went to their homes. **7** Moses had given territory to half the tribe of Manasseh in Bashan, but Joshua had given territory to the other half,[B] with their brothers, on the west side of the Jordan. When Joshua sent them to their homes and blessed them, **8** he said, "Return to your homes with great wealth: a huge number of cattle, and silver, gold, bronze, iron, and a large quantity of clothing. Share the spoil of your enemies with your brothers."   Nm 32:33; Jos 14:13

Eastern Tribes Build an Altar

9 The Reubenites, Gadites, and half the tribe of Manasseh left the Israelites at Shiloh in the land of Canaan to return to their own land of Gilead, which they took possession of according to the Lord's command through Moses. **10** When they came to the region of [C] the Jordan in the land of Canaan, the Reubenites, Gadites, and half the tribe of Manasseh built a large, impressive altar there by the Jordan.

[A]21:36-37 Some Hb mss omit these vv.   [B]22:7 Lit *to his half*   [C]22:10 Or *to Geliloth by*

[11] Then the Israelites heard it said, "Look, the Reubenites, Gadites, and half the tribe of Manasseh have built an altar on the frontier of the land of Canaan at the region of [A] the Jordan, on the Israelite side." [12] When the Israelites heard this, the entire Israelite community assembled at Shiloh to go to war against them. Lv 17:8-9; Dt 13:12-15

Explanation of the Altar

[13] The Israelites sent Phinehas son of Eleazar the priest to the Reubenites, Gadites, and half the tribe of Manasseh, in the land of Gilead. [14] They sent ten leaders with him — one family leader for each tribe of Israel. All of them were heads of their ancestral families [B] among the clans of Israel. [15] They went to the Reubenites, Gadites, and half the tribe of Manasseh, in the land of Gilead, and told them, [16] "This is what the LORD's entire community says: 'What is this treachery you have committed today against the God of Israel by turning away from the LORD and building an altar for yourselves, so that you are in rebellion against the LORD today? [17] Wasn't the iniquity of Peor, which brought a plague on the LORD's community, enough for us? We have not cleansed ourselves from it even to this day, [18] and now would you turn away from the LORD? If you rebel against the LORD today, tomorrow he will be angry with the entire community of Israel. [19] But if the land you possess is defiled, cross over to the land the LORD possesses where the LORD's tabernacle stands, and take possession of it among us. But don't rebel against the LORD

or against us by building for yourselves an altar other than the altar of the LORD our God. [20] Wasn't Achan son of Zerah unfaithful regarding what was set apart for destruction, bringing wrath on the entire community of Israel? He was not the only one who perished because of his iniquity.'" Ex 6:25; Nm 25:7

[21] The Reubenites, Gadites, and half the tribe of Manasseh answered the heads of the Israelite clans, [22] "The Mighty One, God, the LORD! The Mighty One, God, the LORD! [C] He knows, and may Israel also know. Do not spare us today, if it was in rebellion or treachery against the LORD [23] that we have built for ourselves an altar to turn away from him. May the LORD himself hold us accountable if we intended to offer burnt offerings and grain offerings on it, or to sacrifice fellowship offerings on it. [24] We actually did this from a specific concern that in the future your descendants might say to our descendants, 'What relationship do you have with the LORD, the God of Israel? [25] For the LORD has made the Jordan a border between us and you descendants of Reuben and Gad. You have no share in the LORD!' So your descendants may cause our descendants to stop fearing the LORD. Dt 10:17; Ps 50:1; 136:2

[26] "Therefore we said: Let us take action and build an altar for ourselves, but not for burnt offering or sacrifice. [27] Instead, it is to be a witness between us and you, and between the generations after us, so that we may carry out the worship of the LORD in his presence with our burnt offerings, sacrifices, and

---

[A] 22:11 Or at Geliloth by   [B] 22:14 Lit the house of their fathers   [C] 22:22 Or The LORD is the God of gods! The LORD is the God of gods!

fellowship offerings. Then in the future, your descendants will not be able to say to our descendants, 'You have no share in the LORD!' [28] We thought that if they said this to us or to our generations in the future, we would reply: Look at the replica of the LORD's altar that our fathers made, not for burnt offering or sacrifice, but as a witness between us and you. [29] We would never ever rebel against the LORD or turn away from him today by building an altar for burnt offering, grain offering, or sacrifice, other than the altar of the LORD our God, which is in front of his tabernacle." Gn 31:48,52; Dt 31:19,26; Is 19:20

Conflict Resolved

[30] When the priest Phinehas and the community leaders, the heads of Israel's clans who were with him, heard what the descendants of Reuben, Gad, and Manasseh had to say, they were pleased. [31] Phinehas son of Eleazar the priest said to the descendants of Reuben, Gad, and Manasseh, "Today we know that the LORD is among us, because you have not committed this treachery against him. As a result, you have rescued the Israelites from the LORD's power." Lv 26:11-12

[32] Then the priest Phinehas son of Eleazar and the leaders returned from the Reubenites and Gadites in the land of Gilead to the Israelites in the land of Canaan and brought back a report to them. [33] The Israelites were pleased with the report, and they blessed God. They spoke no more about going to war against them to ravage the land where the Reubenites and Gadites lived. [34] So the Reubenites and Gadites named

the altar: It[A] is a witness between us that the LORD is God. 1Ch 29:20

Joshua's Farewell Address

23 A long time after the LORD had given Israel rest from all the enemies around them, Joshua was old, advanced in age. [2] So Joshua summoned all Israel, including its elders, leaders, judges, and officers, and said to them, "I am old, advanced in age, [3] and you have seen for yourselves everything the LORD your God did to all these nations on your account, because it was the LORD your God who was fighting for you. [4] See, I have allotted these remaining nations to you as an inheritance for your tribes, including all the nations I have destroyed, from the Jordan westward to the Mediterranean Sea. [5] The LORD your God will force them back on your account and drive them out before you so that you can take possession of their land, as the LORD your God promised you. Jos 13:1; 21:44

[6] "Be very strong and continue obeying all that is written in the book of the law of Moses, so that you do not turn from it to the right or left [7] and so that you do not associate with these nations remaining among you. Do not call on the names of their gods or make an oath to them; do not serve them or bow in worship to them. [8] Instead, be loyal to the LORD your God, as you have been to this day. Dt 5:32

[9] "The LORD has driven out great and powerful nations before you, and no one is able to stand against you to this day. [10] One of you routed a thousand because the LORD your God was fighting for you, as

A **22:34** Some Hb mss, Syr, Tg read *altar Witness because it* he promised.^A 11 So diligently watch yourselves! Love the LORD your God! 12 If you ever turn away and become loyal to the rest of these nations remaining among you, and if you intermarry or associate with them and they with you, 13 know for certain that the LORD your God will not continue to drive these nations out before you. They will become a snare and a trap for you, a sharp stick^B for your sides and thorns in your eyes, until you disappear from this good land the LORD your God has given you. Ex 23:30; Jos 1:5; Jdg 15:15-16

14 "I am now going the way of the whole earth, and you know with all your heart and all your soul that none of the good promises the LORD your God made to you has failed. Everything was fulfilled for you; not one promise has failed. 15 Since every good thing the LORD your God promised you has come about, so he will bring on you every bad thing until he has annihilated you from this good land the LORD your God has given you. 16 If you break the covenant of the LORD your God, which he commanded you, and go and serve other gods, and bow in worship to them, the LORD's anger will burn against you, and you will quickly disappear from this good land he has given you."

Review of Israel's History

24 Joshua assembled all the tribes of Israel at Shechem and summoned Israel's elders, leaders, judges, and officers, and they presented themselves before God. 2 Joshua said to all the people, "This is what the LORD, the God of Israel, says: 'Long ago your ancestors, including Terah,

the father of Abraham and Nahor, lived beyond the Euphrates River and worshiped other gods. 3 But I took your father Abraham from the region beyond the Euphrates River, led him throughout the land of Canaan, and multiplied his descendants. I gave him Isaac, 4 and to Isaac I gave Jacob and Esau. I gave the hill country of Seir to Esau as a possession. Gn 11:27-32; 12:1-7; Jos 23:2

" 'Jacob and his sons, however, went down to Egypt. 5 I sent Moses and Aaron, and I defeated Egypt by what I did within it, and afterward I brought you out. 6 When I brought your fathers out of Egypt and you reached the Red Sea, the Egyptians pursued your fathers with chariots and horsemen as far as the sea. 7 Your fathers cried out to the LORD, so he put darkness between you and the Egyptians, and brought the sea over them, engulfing them. Your own eyes saw what I did to Egypt. After that, you lived in the wilderness a long time.

8 " 'Later, I brought you to the land of the Amorites who lived beyond the Jordan. They fought against you, but I handed them over to you. You possessed their land, and I annihilated them before you. 9 Balak son of Zippor, king of Moab, set out to fight against Israel. He sent for Balaam son of Beor to curse you, 10 but I would not listen to Balaam. Instead, he repeatedly blessed you, and I rescued you from him.

11 " 'You then crossed the Jordan and came to Jericho. Jericho's citizens — as well as the Amorites, Perizzites, Canaanites, Hethites, Girgashites, Hivites, and Jebusites — fought against you, but I handed them over to you. 12 I sent hornets^C

^A **23:10** Lit *promised you*   ^B **23:13** Or *a whip*; Hb obscure   ^C **24:12** Or *sent terror* ahead of you, and they drove out the two Amorite kings before you. It was not by your sword or bow. [13] I gave you a land you did not labor for, and cities you did not build, though you live in them; you are eating from vineyards and olive groves you did not plant.' Jos 3:14,17

The Covenant Renewal

[14] "Therefore, fear the LORD and worship him in sincerity and truth. Get rid of the gods your fathers worshiped beyond the Euphrates River and in Egypt, and worship the LORD. [15] But if it doesn't please you to worship the LORD, choose for yourselves today: Which will you worship — the gods your fathers worshiped beyond the Euphrates River or the gods of the Amorites in whose land you are living? As for me and my family, we will worship the LORD." Gn 35:4; Dt 10:12; 1Sm 12:24

[16] The people replied, "We will certainly not abandon the LORD to worship other gods! [17] For the LORD our God brought us and our fathers out of the land of Egypt, out of the place of slavery, and performed these great signs before our eyes. He also protected us all along the way we went and among all the peoples whose lands we traveled through. [18] The LORD drove out before us all the peoples, including the Amorites who lived in the land. We too will worship the LORD, because he is our God." Lv 26:13; Dt 5:6; 6:12

[19] But Joshua told the people, "You will not be able to worship the LORD, because he is a holy God. He is a jealous God; he will not forgive your transgressions and sins. [20] If you abandon the LORD and worship foreign gods, he will turn against you, harm you, and completely destroy you, after he has been good to you." Ex 23:21; Lv 19:2

[21] "No!" the people answered Joshua. "We will worship the LORD."

[22] Joshua then told the people, "You are witnesses against yourselves that you yourselves have chosen to worship the LORD."

"We are witnesses," they said.

[23] "Then get rid of the foreign gods that are among you and turn your hearts to the LORD, the God of Israel."

[24] So the people said to Joshua, "We will worship the LORD our God and obey him."

[25] On that day Joshua made a covenant for the people at Shechem and established a statute and ordinance for them. [26] Joshua recorded these things in the book of the law of God; he also took a large stone and set it up there under the oak at the sanctuary of the LORD. [27] And Joshua said to all the people, "You see this stone — it will be a witness against us, for it has heard all the words the LORD said to us, and it will be a witness against you, so that you will not deny your God." [28] Then Joshua sent the people away, each to his own inheritance. Dt 31:24; Jos 22:27,34

Burial of Three Leaders

[29] After these things, the LORD's servant, Joshua son of Nun, died at the age of 110. [30] They buried him in his allotted territory at Timnath-serah, in the hill country of Ephraim north of Mount Gaash. [31] Israel worshiped the LORD throughout Joshua's lifetime and during the lifetimes of the elders who outlived Joshua and who had experienced all the works the LORD had done for Israel. Jos 19:49-50; Jdg 2:7

³² Joseph's bones, which the Israelites had brought up from Egypt, were buried at Shechem in the parcel of land Jacob had purchased from the sons of Hamor, Shechem's father, for a hundred pieces of silver.ᴬ It was an inheritance for Joseph's descendants. Gn 33:19; 50:25; Ex 13:19; Jb 42:11

³³ And Eleazar son of Aaron died, and they buried him at Gibeah,ᴮ which had been given to his son Phinehas in the hill country of Ephraim. Jos 22:13

THE BOOKS OF
OLD TESTAMENT HISTORY

The sixty-six books of the Bible are separated into ten divisions. Twelve books are in the division called Old Testament History. These history books share a view of the coming perfect prophet, judge, priest, and king in Jesus Christ.

JOSHUA tells how the Israelites entered the land God promised them and how God helped them become the new owners of the land. Joshua led God's people into this land just as Christ leads the way to an eternal promised land in heaven.

JUDGES explains about the different leaders God gave the Israelites after Joshua died and what those leaders did. God used these leaders to deliver His people from their enemies just as Christ provides an escape from eternal separation from God.

RUTH contains the story of God's care for Naomi and her daughter-in-law Ruth. The book also tells how Ruth met and married Boaz and had a son named Obed. Like Boaz redeemed and cared for Ruth, Christ redeems and cares for us. Ruth and Boaz are also part of Jesus' earthly lineage.

FIRST & SECOND SAMUEL are named for the prophet Samuel. The two books also include the selection and careers of the first two kings of Israel: Saul and David. These three great leaders represent Christ as priest, prophet, and king.

FIRST & SECOND KINGS continue the history of Israel from King Solomon's reign, through the division of Israel into two kingdoms, Israel and Judah, and into the exile of both kingdoms. These books cover a period of approximately 425 years. God provided prophets and kings to rule His people just as Jesus Christ rules over those who put their faith in Him.

FIRST & SECOND CHRONICLES are the records of the royal and religious history of the kingdoms of Israel and Judah. Regardless of whether God's people obeyed or disobeyed, God remained true to His promise to preserve a royal line that would eventually include Jesus Christ.

EZRA picks up the history of the Jews beginning with the return from the exile and covers a period of approximately eighty years, telling of the rebuilding of the Jerusalem temple and how the Jews decided to obey God again. Jesus Christ came to lead us back to a relationship with God just like Ezra led God's people back to their promised land.

NEHEMIAH continues the history of the Jews after their return from exile and tells how God used Nehemiah to rebuild Jerusalem's city wall. Nehemiah was determined to restore the city where God dwelt with His people just as Christ came to restore those who, by faith, dwell with God.

ESTHER tells how Esther became the beautiful Hebrew queen of King Ahasuerus and how she prevented Haman from carrying out his plan to slaughter the Jews. Just as Esther provided an escape from death for the Jews, Christ provides a way of escape from death for all Christians.

JUDGES

Judah's Leadership Against the Canaanites

1 After the death of Joshua, the Israelites inquired of the LORD, "Who will be the first to fight for us against the Canaanites?" Jos 1:1 ² The LORD answered, "Judah is to go. I have handed the land over to him." Gn 29:35; 35:12; 49:8-12; Jdg 20:18 ³ Judah said to his brother Simeon, "Come with me to my allotted territory, and let us fight against the Canaanites. I will also go with you to your allotted territory." So Simeon went with him.

⁴ When Judah attacked, the LORD handed the Canaanites and Perizzites over to them. They struck down ten thousand men in Bezek. ⁵ They found Adoni-bezek in Bezek, fought against him, and struck down the Canaanites and Perizzites. Gn 13:7; Dt 7:1; Jos 3:10; Ezr 9:1; 1Sm 11:8 ⁶ When Adoni-bezek fled, they pursued him, caught him, and cut off his thumbs and big toes. ⁷ Adoni-bezek said, "Seventy kings with their thumbs and big toes cut off used to pick up scraps ᴬ under my table. God has repaid me for what I have done." They brought him to Jerusalem, and he died there.

⁸ The men of Judah fought against Jerusalem, captured it, put it to the sword, and set the city on fire. ⁹ Afterward, the men of Judah marched down to fight against the Canaanites who were living in the hill country, the Negev, and the Judean foothills. ᴮ ¹⁰ Judah also marched against the Canaanites who were living in Hebron (Hebron was formerly named Kiriath-arba). They struck down Sheshai, Ahiman, and Talmai. ¹¹ From there they marched against the residents of Debir (Debir was formerly named Kiriath-sepher). Gn 13:18; 23:2; 35:27; Jos 14:15 ¹² Caleb said, "Whoever attacks and captures Kiriath-sepher, I will give my daughter Achsah to him as a wife." ¹³ So Othniel son of Kenaz, Caleb's youngest brother, captured it, and Caleb gave his daughter Achsah to him as his wife. Nm 13:6,13; 26:65

¹⁴ When she arrived, she persuaded Othniel to ask her father for a field. As she got off her donkey, Caleb asked her, "What do you want?" ¹⁵ She answered him, "Give me a blessing. Since you have given me land in the Negev, give me springs also." So Caleb gave her both the upper and lower springs. Gn 12:9

¹⁶ The descendants of the Kenite, Moses's father-in-law, had gone up with the men of Judah from the City of Palms ᶜ to the Wilderness of Judah, which was in the Negev of Arad. They went to live among the people. Ex 2:18; 3:1; 4:18; 18:1-12; Nm 10:29

¹⁷ Judah went with his brother Simeon, struck the Canaanites who were living in Zephath, and completely destroyed the town. So they named the town Hormah. ¹⁸ Judah captured Gaza and its territory, Ashkelon and its territory, and Ekron and its territory. ¹⁹ The LORD was with Judah and enabled them to take possession of the hill country, but they could not drive out the

---

ᴬ**1:7** Lit *toes cut off are gathering*   ᴮ**1:9** Or *the Shephelah*   ᶜ**1:16** = Jericho; Dt 34:3; Jdg 3:13; 2Ch 28:15

people who were living in the valley because those people had iron chariots. Gn 39:2,21; Nm 21:3; Dt 1:44; Jos 6:27

²⁰ Judah gave Hebron to Caleb, just as Moses had promised. Then Caleb drove out the three sons of Anak who lived there. Dt 1:36; Jos 14:9

Benjamin's Failure

²¹ At the same time the Benjaminites did not drive out the Jebusites who were living in Jerusalem. The Jebusites have lived among the Benjaminites in Jerusalem to this day. Jos 15:63

Success of the House of Joseph

²² The house of Joseph also attacked Bethel, and the LORD was with them. ²³ They sent spies to Bethel (the town was formerly named Luz). ²⁴ The spies saw a man coming out of the town and said to him, "Please show us how to get into town, and we will show you kindness." ²⁵ When he showed them the way into the town, they put the town to the sword but released the man and his entire family. ²⁶ Then the man went to the land of the Hittites, built a town, and named it Luz. That is its name still today.

Failure of the Other Tribes

²⁷ At that time Manasseh failed to take possession of Beth-shean and Taanach and their surrounding villages, or the residents of Dor, Ibleam, and Megiddo and their surrounding villages; the Canaanites were determined to stay in this land. ²⁸ When Israel became stronger, they made the Canaanites serve as forced labor but never drove them out completely.

²⁹ At that time Ephraim failed to drive out the Canaanites who were living in Gezer, so the Canaanites have lived among them in Gezer.

³⁰ Zebulun failed to drive out the residents of Kitron or the residents of Nahalol, so the Canaanites lived among them and served as forced labor. Jos 19:15; 21:35

³¹ Asher failed to drive out the residents of Acco or of Sidon, or Ahlab, Achzib, Helbah, Aphik, or Rehob. ³² The Asherites lived among the Canaanites who were living in the land, because they failed to drive them out.

³³ Naphtali did not drive out the residents of Beth-shemesh or the residents of Beth-anath. They lived among the Canaanites who were living in the land, but the residents of Beth-shemesh and Beth-anath served as their forced labor.

³⁴ The Amorites forced the Danites into the hill country and did not allow them to go down into the valley. ³⁵ The Amorites were determined to stay in ^A Har-heres, Aijalon, and Shaalbim. When the house of Joseph got the upper hand, ^B the Amorites ^C were made to serve as forced labor. ³⁶ The territory of the Amorites extended from the Scorpions' Ascent, that is from Sela upward. Ex 3:8; Nm 13:29; 21:31; Jos 2:10; 10:12

Pattern of Sin and Judgment

2 The angel of the LORD went up from Gilgal to Bochim and said, "I brought you out of Egypt and led you into the land I had promised to your fathers. I also said: I will never break my covenant with you. ² You are not to make a covenant with the inhabitants of this

---

^A 1:35 Or Amorites determined to live in   ^B 1:35 Lit When the hand of the house of Joseph was heavy
^C 1:35 LXX reads Joseph became strong on the Amorites, they

land. You are to tear down their altars. But you have not obeyed me. What is this you have done? ³ Therefore, I now say: I will not drive out these people before you. They will be thorns ᴬ,ᴮ in your sides, and their gods will be a trap for you." ⁴ When the angel of the LORD had spoken these words to all the Israelites, the people wept loudly. ⁵ So they named that place Bochim ᶜ and offered sacrifices there to the LORD. Gn 22:11; Ex 3:2; Ps 34:7

Joshua's Death

⁶ Previously, when Joshua had sent the people away, the Israelites had gone to take possession of the land, each to his own inheritance. ⁷ The people worshiped the LORD throughout Joshua's lifetime and during the lifetimes of the elders who outlived ᴰ Joshua. They had seen all the LORD's great works he had done for Israel. Dt 9:4; 11:31; 18:3

⁸ Joshua son of Nun, the servant of the LORD, died at the age of 110. ⁹ They buried him in the territory of his inheritance, in Timnath-heres, in the hill country of Ephraim, north of Mount Gaash. ¹⁰ That whole generation was also gathered to their ancestors. After them another generation rose up who did not know the LORD or the works he had done for Israel.

¹¹ The Israelites did what was evil in the LORD's sight. They worshiped the Baals ¹² and abandoned the LORD, the God of their fathers, who had brought them out of Egypt. They followed other gods from the surrounding peoples and bowed down to them. They angered the LORD, ¹³ for they abandoned him

and worshiped Baal and the Ashtoreths. Nm 32:12; Dt 4:25; 31:29; Jdg 3:7; 1Kg 11:6

¹⁴ The LORD's anger burned against Israel, and he handed them over to marauders who raided them. He sold them to ᴱ the enemies around them, and they could no longer resist their enemies. ¹⁵ Whenever the Israelites went out, the LORD ᶠ was against them and brought disaster on them, just as he had promised and sworn to them. So they suffered greatly.

¹⁶ The LORD raised up judges, who saved them from the power of their marauders, ¹⁷ but they did not listen to their judges. Instead, they prostituted themselves with other gods, bowing down to them. They quickly turned from the way of their fathers, who had walked in obedience to the LORD's commands. They did not do as their fathers did. ¹⁸ Whenever the LORD raised up a judge for the Israelites, the LORD was with him and saved the people from the power of their enemies while the judge was still alive. ᴳ The LORD was moved to pity whenever they groaned because of those who were oppressing and afflicting them. ¹⁹ Whenever the judge died, the Israelites would act even more corruptly than their fathers, following other gods to serve them and bow in worship to them. They did not turn from their evil practices or their obstinate ways.

²⁰ The LORD's anger burned against Israel, and he declared, "Because this nation has violated my covenant that I made with their fathers and disobeyed me, ²¹ I will no longer drive out before them any of the nations Joshua left when he

ᴬ 2:3 LXX reads affliction　ᴮ 2:3 Lit traps　ᶜ 2:5 Or Weeping　ᴰ 2:7 Lit extended their days after
ᴱ 2:14 Lit into the hand of　ᶠ 2:15 Lit the hand of the LORD　ᴳ 2:18 Lit enemies all the days of the judge

died. [22] I did this to test Israel and to see whether or not they would keep the LORD's way by walking in it, as their fathers had." [23] The LORD left these nations and did not drive them out immediately. He did not hand them over to Joshua. Jos 7:11,15

The LORD Tests Israel

3 These are the nations the LORD left in order to test all those in Israel who had experienced [A] none of the wars in Canaan. [2] This was to teach the future generations of the Israelites how to fight in battle, especially those who had not fought before. [B] [3] These nations included the five rulers of the Philistines and all of the Canaanites, the Sidonians, and the Hivites who lived in the Lebanese mountains from Mount Baal-hermon as far as the entrance to Hamath. [C] [4] The LORD left them to test Israel, to determine if they would keep the LORD's commands he had given their fathers through [D] Moses. [5] But they settled among the Canaanites, Hethites, Amorites, Perizzites, Hivites, and Jebusites. [6] The Israelites took their daughters as wives for themselves, gave their own daughters to their sons, and worshiped their gods.

Othniel, the First Judge

[7] The Israelites did what was evil in the LORD's sight; they forgot the LORD their God and worshiped the Baals and the Asherahs. [8] The LORD's anger burned against Israel, and he sold them to [E] King Cushan-rishathaim [F] of Aram-naharaim, [G] and the Israelites served him eight years. Gn 24:10; Dt 8:11,14,19; 1Sm 12:9; Jr 3:21

[9] The Israelites cried out to the LORD. So the LORD raised up Othniel son of Kenaz, Caleb's youngest brother, as a deliverer to save the Israelites. [10] The Spirit of the LORD came on him, and he judged Israel. Othniel went out to battle, and the LORD handed over King Cushan-rishathaim of Aram to him, so that Othniel overpowered him. [11] Then the land had peace for forty years, and Othniel son of Kenaz died.

Ehud

[12] The Israelites again did what was evil in the LORD's sight. He gave King Eglon of Moab power over Israel, because they had done what was evil in the LORD's sight. [13] After Eglon convinced the Ammonites and the Amalekites to join forces with him, he attacked and defeated Israel and took possession of the City of Palms. [H] [14] The Israelites served King Eglon of Moab eighteen years. Nm 22:3; Dt 2:8-9; 32:49; 34:3

[15] Then the Israelites cried out to the LORD, and he raised up Ehud son of Gera, a left-handed Benjaminite, [I] as a deliverer for them. The Israelites sent him with the tribute for King Eglon of Moab. Jdg 20:16

[16] Ehud made himself a double-edged sword eighteen inches long. [J] He strapped it to his right thigh under his clothes [17] and brought the tribute to King Eglon of Moab, who was an extremely fat man. [18] When Ehud had finished presenting the tribute, he dismissed the people who had carried it. [19] At the carved images near Gilgal he returned and said, "King Eglon, I have a secret message for you." The king said,

---

[A] 3:1 Lit *had known*   [B] 3:2 Lit *not known it*   [C] 3:3 Or *as Lebo-hamath*   [D] 3:4 Lit *by the hand of* [E] 3:8 Lit *into the hand of*   [F] 3:8 Lit *Doubly-Evil*   [G] 3:8 = Mesopotamia   [H] 3:13 = Jericho; Dt 34:3; Jdg 1:16; 2Ch 28:15   [I] 3:15 = son of the right hand   [J] 3:16 Lit *sword a gomed in length*

"Silence!" and all his attendants left him. [20] Then Ehud approached him while he was sitting alone in his upstairs room where it was cool. Ehud said, "I have a message from God for you," and the king stood up from his throne. [21] Ehud reached with his left hand, took the sword from his right thigh, and plunged it into Eglon's belly. [22] Even the handle went in after the blade, and Eglon's fat closed in over it, so that Ehud did not withdraw the sword from his belly. And the waste came out. [A] [23] Ehud escaped by way of the porch, closing and locking the doors of the upstairs room behind him.

[24] Ehud was gone when Eglon's servants came in. They looked and found the doors of the upstairs room locked and thought he was relieving himself [B] in the cool room. [25] The servants waited until they became embarrassed and saw that he had still not opened the doors of the upstairs room. So they took the key and opened the doors — and there was their lord lying dead on the floor!

[26] Ehud escaped while the servants waited. He passed the Jordan near the carved images and reached Seirah. [27] After he arrived, he sounded the ram's horn throughout the hill country of Ephraim. The Israelites came down with him from the hill country, and he became their leader. [28] He told them, "Follow me, because the LORD has handed over your enemies, the Moabites, to you." So they followed him, captured the fords of the Jordan leading to Moab, and did not allow anyone to cross over. [29] At that time they struck down about ten thousand Moabites, all stout and able-bodied men. Not one of them escaped. [30] Moab became subject to Israel that day, and the land had peace for eighty years.   Jdg 12:5-6

Shamgar

[31] After Ehud, Shamgar son of Anath became judge. He also delivered Israel, striking down six hundred Philistines with a cattle prod.

Deborah and Barak

4 The Israelites again did what was evil in the sight of the LORD after Ehud had died. [2] So the LORD sold them to King Jabin of Canaan, who reigned in Hazor. The commander of his army was Sisera who lived in Harosheth of the Nations. [C] [3] Then the Israelites cried out to the LORD, because Jabin had nine hundred iron chariots, and he harshly oppressed them twenty years.

[4] Deborah, a prophetess and the wife of Lappidoth, was judging Israel at that time. [5] She would sit under the palm tree of Deborah between Ramah and Bethel in the hill country of Ephraim, and the Israelites went up to her to settle disputes.   Ex 15:20; 2Kg 22:14; Neh 6:14; Is 8:3

[6] She summoned Barak son of Abinoam from Kedesh in Naphtali and said to him, "Hasn't the LORD, the God of Israel, commanded you: 'Go, deploy the troops on Mount Tabor, and take with you ten thousand men from the Naphtalites and Zebulunites? [7] Then I will lure Sisera commander of Jabin's army, his chariots, and his infantry at the Wadi Kishon to fight against you, and I will hand him over to you.'"

[A] 3:22 Or *And Eglon's bowels discharged*   [B] 3:24 Lit *was covering his feet*   [C] 4:2 Or *Harosheth-ha-goiim*, also in vv. 13, 16

⁸ Barak said to her, "If you will go with me, I will go. But if you will not go with me, I will not go."

⁹ "I will gladly go with you," she said, "but you will receive no honor on the road you are about to take, because the LORD will sell Sisera to a woman." So Deborah got up and went with Barak to Kedesh. ¹⁰ Barak summoned Zebulun and Naphtali to Kedesh; ten thousand men followed him, and Deborah also went with him.

¹¹ Now Heber the Kenite had moved away from the Kenites, the sons of Hobab, Moses's father-in-law, and pitched his tent beside the oak tree of Zaanannim, which was near Kedesh. Ex 3:1; 4:18; 18:1-27; Nm 10:29

¹² It was reported to Sisera that Barak son of Abinoam had gone up Mount Tabor. ¹³ Sisera summoned all his nine hundred iron chariots and all the troops who were with him from Harosheth of the Nations to the Wadi Kishon. ¹⁴ Then Deborah said to Barak, "Go! This is the day the LORD has handed Sisera over to you. Hasn't the LORD gone before you?" So Barak came down from Mount Tabor with ten thousand men following him.

¹⁵ The LORD threw Sisera, all his charioteers, and all his army into a panic before Barak's assault. Sisera left his chariot and fled on foot. ¹⁶ Barak pursued the chariots and the army as far as Harosheth of the Nations, and the whole army of Sisera fell by the sword; not a single man was left. Ex 14:24; 23:27; Jos 10:10; 144:6

¹⁷ Meanwhile, Sisera had fled on foot to the tent of Jael, the wife of Heber the Kenite, because there was peace between King Jabin of Hazor and the family of Heber the

Kenite. ¹⁸ Jael went out to greet Sisera and said to him, "Come in, my lord. Come in with me. Don't be afraid." So he went into her tent, and she covered him with a blanket. ¹⁹ He said to her, "Please give me a little water to drink for I am thirsty." She opened a container of milk, gave him a drink, and covered him again. ²⁰ Then he said to her, "Stand at the entrance to the tent. If a man comes and asks you, 'Is there a man here?' say, 'No.'"

²¹ While he was sleeping from exhaustion, Heber's wife Jael took a tent peg, grabbed a hammer, and went silently to Sisera. She hammered the peg into his temple and drove it into the ground, and he died.

²² When Barak arrived in pursuit of Sisera, Jael went out to greet him and said to him, "Come and I will show you the man you are looking for." So he went in with her, and there was Sisera lying dead with a tent peg through his temple!

²³ That day God subdued King Jabin of Canaan before the Israelites. ²⁴ The power of the Israelites continued to increase against King Jabin of Canaan until they destroyed him.

Deborah's Song

5 On that day Deborah and Barak son of Abinoam sang:

² When the leaders lead[A]
    in Israel,
  when the people volunteer,
    blessed be the LORD.
³ Listen, kings! Pay attention,
    princes!
  I will sing to the LORD;
  I will sing praise
    to the LORD God of Israel.

[A]**5:2** Or *the locks of hair are loose*

⁴ LORD, when you came
    from Seir,   Gn 14:6; 36:8-9; Dt 2:1
  when you marched
    from the fields of Edom,
  the earth trembled,   2Sm 22:8
  the skies poured rain,   Jb 29:22
  and the clouds poured water.
⁵ The mountains melted
    before the LORD,
  even Sinai,ᴬ before the LORD,
    the God of Israel.   Ex 5:1; Dt 6:4

⁶ In the days of Shamgar
    son of Anath,   Jdg 3:31
  in the days of Jael,   Jdg 4:17-22
  the main roads were deserted
  because travelers kept
    to the side roads.
⁷ Villages were deserted,ᴮ
  they were deserted in Israel,
  until I,ᶜ Deborah, arose,
  a mother in Israel.
⁸ Israel chose new gods,
  then there was war
    in the city gates.
  Not a shield or spear
    was seen
  among forty thousand
    in Israel.
⁹ My heart is with the leaders
    of Israel,
  with the volunteers
    of the people.
  Blessed be the LORD!
¹⁰ You who ride
    on whiteᴮ donkeys,
  who sit on saddle blankets,
  and who travel on the road,
    give praise!
¹¹ Let them tell
    the righteous acts
    of the LORD,   1Sm 12:7; Ps 103:6
  the righteous deeds
    of his warriors in Israel,

  with the voices of the singers
    at the watering places.ᴮ

  Then the LORD's people went
    down to the city gates.
¹² "Awake! Awake, Deborah!
  Awake! Awake, sing a song!
  Arise, Barak,
  and take your prisoners,
    son of Abinoam!"
¹³ Then the survivors came
    down to the nobles;   Nm 21:35
  the LORD's people came
    down to meᴰ
  with the warriors.
¹⁴ Those with their roots
    in Amalekᴱ came
    from Ephraim;
  Benjamin came with
    your people after you.
  The leaders came down
    from Machir,   Gn 50:23; Nm 26:29
  and those who carry
    a marshal's staff came
    from Zebulun.
¹⁵ The princes of Issachar were
    with Deborah;
  Issachar was with Barak;
  they were under his
    leadershipᶠ in the valley.
  There was great searchingᴳ
    of heart
  among the clans of Reuben.
¹⁶ Why did you sit
    among the sheep pensᴴ
  listening to the playing
    of pipes for the flocks?
  There was great searching
    of heart
  among the clans of Reuben.
¹⁷ Gilead remained
    beyond the Jordan.   Gn 31:25
  Dan, why did you linger
    at the ships?

ᴬ5:5 Or LORD, this one of Sinai   ᴮ5:7,10,11 Hb obscure   ᶜ5:7 Or you   ᴰ5:13 LXX reads down for him
ᴱ5:14 LXX reads in the valley   ᶠ5:15 Lit they set out as his feet   ᴳ5:15 Some Hb mss, Syr read There were
great resolves   ᴴ5:16 Or the campfires

Asher remained
at the seashore
and stayed in his harbors.
18 The people of Zebulun defied
death,
Naphtali also, on the heights
of the battlefield.

19 Kings came and fought.
Then the kings of Canaan
fought
at Taanach by the Waters
of Megiddo,
but they did not plunder the
silver.
20 The stars fought
from the heavens;
the stars fought with Sisera
from their paths.
21 The river Kishon swept them
away,   Jdg 4:15
the ancient river,
the river Kishon.
March on, my soul,
in strength!
22 The horses' hooves then
hammered —
the galloping, galloping
of his^A stallions.
23 "Curse Meroz," says the angel
of the LORD,
"Bitterly curse
her inhabitants,
for they did not come to help
the LORD,
to help the LORD with the
warriors."

24 Jael is most blessed
of women,
the wife of Heber the Kenite;
she is most blessed among
tent-dwelling women.
25 He asked for water; she gave
him milk.

She brought him cream
in a majestic bowl.   Gn 18:8; 29:6
26 She reached for a tent peg,
her right hand,
for a workman's hammer.
Then she hammered
Sisera —
she crushed his head;
she shattered and pierced
his temple.
27 He collapsed, he fell,
he lay down between
her feet;
he collapsed, he fell
between her feet;
where he collapsed,
there he fell — dead.

28 Sisera's mother looked
through the window;
she peered through
the lattice, crying out:
"Why is his chariot so long
in coming?
Why don't I hear
the hoofbeats
of his horses?"^B
29 Her wisest princesses
answer her;
she even answers herself:^C
30 "Are they not finding
and dividing the spoil —
a girl or two^D
for each warrior,
the spoil of colored garments
for Sisera,
the spoil of
an embroidered garment
or two for my neck?"^E

31 LORD, may all your enemies
perish as Sisera did.^F
But may those who love him
be like the rising of the sun
in its strength.

---

^A5:22 = Sisera's   ^B5:28 Lit Why have the hoofbeats of his chariots delayed   ^C5:29 Lit answers her
words   ^D5:30 Lit a womb or two wombs   ^E5:30 Hb obscure   ^F5:31 Lit perish in this way

And the land had peace for forty years.

Midian Oppresses Israel

6 The Israelites did what was evil in the sight of the LORD. So the LORD handed them over to Midian seven years, ² and they oppressed Israel. Because of Midian, the Israelites made hiding places for themselves in the mountains, caves, and strongholds. ³ Whenever the Israelites planted crops, the Midianites, Amalekites, and the Qedemites came and attacked them. ⁴ They encamped against them and destroyed the produce of the land, even as far as Gaza. They left nothing for Israel to eat, as well as no sheep, ox, or donkey. ⁵ For the Midianites came with their cattle and their tents like a great swarm of locusts. They and their camels were without number, and they entered the land to lay waste to it. ⁶ So Israel became poverty-stricken because of Midian, and the Israelites cried out to the LORD. Jdg 2:11; 3:7,12; 4:1; 10:6; 13:1

⁷ When the Israelites cried out to him because of Midian, ⁸ the LORD sent a prophet to them. He said to them, "This is what the LORD God of Israel says: 'I brought you out of Egypt and out of the place of slavery. ⁹ I rescued you from the power of Egypt and the power of all who oppressed you. I drove them out before you and gave you their land. ¹⁰ I said to you: I am the LORD your God. Do not fear the gods of the Amorites whose land you live in. But you did not obey me.'" Ex 7:1

The LORD Calls Gideon

¹¹ The angel of the LORD came, and he sat under the oak that was in Ophrah, which belonged to Joash, the Abiezrite. His son Gideon was threshing wheat in the winepress in order to hide it from the Midianites. ¹² Then the angel of the LORD appeared to him and said: "The LORD is with you, valiant warrior."

¹³ Gideon said to him, "Please, my lord, if the LORD is with us, why has all this happened? And where are all his wonders that our fathers told us about? They said, 'Hasn't the LORD brought us out of Egypt?' But now the LORD has abandoned us and handed us over to Midian."

¹⁴ The LORD turned to him and said, "Go in the strength you have and deliver Israel from the grasp of Midian. I am sending you!"

¹⁵ He said to him, "Please, Lord, how can I deliver Israel? Look, my family is the weakest in Manasseh, and I am the youngest in my father's family."

¹⁶ "But I will be with you," the LORD said to him. "You will strike Midian down as if it were one man."

¹⁷ Then he said to him, "If I have found favor with you, give me a sign that you are speaking with me. ¹⁸ Please do not leave this place until I return to you. Let me bring my gift and set it before you."

And he said, "I will stay until you return."

¹⁹ So Gideon went and prepared a young goat and unleavened bread from a half bushel^A of flour. He placed the meat in a basket and the broth in a pot. He brought them out and offered them to him under the oak.

²⁰ The angel of God said to him, "Take the meat with the unleavened bread, put it on this stone, and pour the broth on it." So he did that.

^A**6:19** Lit *an ephah*

21 The angel of the LORD extended the tip of the staff that was in his hand and touched the meat and the unleavened bread. Fire came up from the rock and consumed the meat and the unleavened bread. Then the angel of the LORD vanished from his sight.

22 When Gideon realized that he was the angel of the LORD, he said, "Oh no, Lord GOD! I have seen the angel of the LORD face to face!"

23 But the LORD said to him, "Peace to you. Don't be afraid, for you will not die." 24 So Gideon built an altar to the LORD there and called it The LORD Is Peace. A It is still in Ophrah of the Abiezrites today.

Gideon Tears Down a Baal Altar

25 On that very night the LORD said to him, "Take your father's young bull and a second bull seven years old. Then tear down the altar of Baal that belongs to your father and cut down the Asherah pole beside it. 26 Build a well-constructed altar to the LORD your God on the top of this mound. Take the second bull and offer it as a burnt offering with the wood of the Asherah pole you cut down." 27 So Gideon took ten of his male servants and did as the LORD had told him. But because he was too afraid of his father's family and the men of the city to do it in the daytime, he did it at night. Jdg 2:11,13

28 When the men of the city got up in the morning, they found Baal's altar torn down, the Asherah pole beside it cut down, and the second bull offered up on the altar that had been built. 29 They said to each other, "Who did this?" After they made a thorough investigation, they said, "Gideon son of Joash did it."

30 Then the men of the city said to Joash, "Bring out your son. He must die, because he tore down Baal's altar and cut down the Asherah pole beside it."

31 But Joash said to all who stood against him, "Would you plead Baal's case for him? Would you save him? Whoever pleads his case will be put to death by morning! If he is a god, let him plead his own case because someone tore down his altar." 32 That day he was called Jerubbaal, since Joash said, "Let Baal contend with him," because he tore down his altar.

The Sign of the Fleece

33 All the Midianites, Amalekites, and Qedemites gathered together, crossed over the Jordan, and camped in the Jezreel Valley. 34 The Spirit of the LORD enveloped B Gideon, and he blew the ram's horn and the Abiezrites rallied behind him. 35 He sent messengers throughout all of Manasseh, who rallied behind him. He also sent messengers throughout Asher, Zebulun, and Naphtali, who also came to meet him. Jdg 3:10; 11:29; 13:25

36 Then Gideon said to God, "If you will deliver Israel by my hand, as you said, 37 I will put a wool fleece here on the threshing floor. If dew is only on the fleece, and all the ground is dry, I will know that you will deliver Israel by my strength, as you said." 38 And that is what happened. When he got up early in the morning, he squeezed the fleece and wrung dew out of it, filling a bowl with water.

39 Gideon then said to God, "Don't be angry with me; let me speak one more time. Please allow me to make

---

A 6:24 = *Yahweh-shalom*   B 6:34 Lit *clothed*; 1Ch 12:18; 2Ch 24:20

one more test with the fleece. Let it remain dry, and the dew be all over the ground." ⁴⁰ That night God did as Gideon requested: only the fleece was dry, and dew was all over the ground.

God Selects Gideon's Army

7 Jerubbaal (that is, Gideon) and all the troops who were with him, got up early and camped beside the spring of Harod. The camp of Midian was north of them, below the hill of Moreh, in the valley. ² The LORD said to Gideon, "You have too many troops for me to hand the Midianites over to them, or else Israel might elevate themselves over me and say, ᴬ 'My own strength saved me.' ³ Now announce to the troops: 'Whoever is fearful and trembling may turn back and leave Mount Gilead.'" So twenty-two thousand of the troops turned back, but ten thousand remained.   Gn 31:21,23,25; Dt 3:12

⁴ Then the LORD said to Gideon, "There are still too many troops. Take them down to the water, and I will test them for you there. If I say to you, 'This one can go with you,' he can go. But if I say about anyone, 'This one cannot go with you,' he cannot go." ⁵ So he brought the troops down to the water, and the LORD said to Gideon, "Separate everyone who laps water with his tongue like a dog. Do the same with everyone who kneels to drink." ⁶ The number of those who lapped with their hands to their mouths was three hundred men, and all the rest of the troops knelt to drink water. ⁷ The LORD said to Gideon, "I will deliver you with the three hundred men who lapped and hand the Midianites over to you. But everyone else is to go home." ⁸ So Gideon sent all the Israelites to their tents but kept the three hundred troops, who took the provisions and their trumpets. The camp of Midian was below him in the valley.   Dt 20:4; Jr 42:11; Ezk 36:29; 37:23; Zch 8:13

Gideon Spies on the Midianite Camp

⁹ That night the LORD said to him, "Get up and attack the camp, for I have handed it over to you. ¹⁰ But if you are afraid to attack the camp, go down with Purah your servant. ¹¹ Listen to what they say, and then you will be encouraged ᴮ to attack the camp." So he went down with Purah his servant to the outpost of the troops ᶜ who were in the camp.   Dt 2:30; Jdg 4:7; 20:28; 2Sm 5:19; 1Kg 20:13

¹² Now the Midianites, Amalekites, and all the Qedemites had settled down in the valley like a swarm of locusts, and their camels were as innumerable as the sand on the seashore. ¹³ When Gideon arrived, there was a man telling his friend about a dream. He said, "Listen, I had a dream: a loaf of barley bread came tumbling into the Midianite camp, struck a tent, and it fell. The loaf turned the tent upside down so that it collapsed."   Gn 37:5-6,8-10; 41

¹⁴ His friend answered: "This is nothing less than the sword of Gideon son of Joash, the Israelite. God has handed the entire Midianite camp over to him."

Gideon Attacks the Midianites

¹⁵ When Gideon heard the account of the dream and its

ᴬ7:2 Lit brag against me   ᴮ7:11 Lit then your hands will be strengthened   ᶜ7:11 Lit of those who were arranged in companies of 50 interpretation, he bowed in worship. He returned to Israel's camp and said, "Get up, for the LORD has handed the Midianite camp over to you." ¹⁶ Then he divided the three hundred men into three companies and gave each of the men a trumpet in one hand and an empty pitcher with a torch inside it in the other hand.

¹⁷ "Watch me," he said to them, "and do what I do. When I come to the outpost of the camp, do as I do. ¹⁸ When I and everyone with me blow our trumpets, you are also to blow your trumpets all around the camp. Then you will say, 'For the LORD and for Gideon!'"

¹⁹ Gideon and the hundred men who were with him went to the outpost of the camp at the beginning of the middle watch after the sentries had been stationed. They blew their trumpets and broke the pitchers that were in their hands. ²⁰ The three companies blew their trumpets and shattered their pitchers. They held their torches in their left hands, their trumpets ᴬ in their right hands, and shouted, "A sword for the LORD and for Gideon!" ²¹ Each Israelite took his position around the camp, and the entire Midianite army began to run, and they cried out as they fled. ²² When Gideon's men blew their three hundred trumpets, the LORD caused the men in the whole army to turn on each other with their swords. They fled to Acacia House ᴮ in the direction of Zererah as far as the border of Abel-meholah near Tabbath. ²³ Then the men of Israel were called from Naphtali, Asher, and Manasseh, and they pursued the Midianites. 1Sm 14:20; 1Kg 4:12; 19:16

The Men of Ephraim Join the Battle

²⁴ Gideon sent messengers throughout the hill country of Ephraim with this message: "Come down to intercept the Midianites and take control of the watercourses ahead of them as far as Beth-barah and the Jordan." So all the men of Ephraim were called out, and they took control of the watercourses as far as Beth-barah and the Jordan. ²⁵ They captured Oreb and Zeeb, the two princes of Midian; they killed Oreb at the rock of Oreb and Zeeb at the winepress of Zeeb, while they were pursuing the Midianites. They brought the heads of Oreb and Zeeb to Gideon across the Jordan. Jdg 8:3; Ps 83:11; Is 10:26

8 The men of Ephraim said to him, "Why have you done this to us, not calling us when you went to fight against the Midianites?" And they argued with him violently.

² So he said to them, "What have I done now compared to you? Is not the gleaning of Ephraim better than the grape harvest of Abiezer? ³ God handed over to you Oreb and Zeeb, the two princes of Midian. What was I able to do compared to you?" When he said this, their anger against him subsided.

Gideon Pursues the Kings of Midian

⁴ Gideon and the three hundred men came to the Jordan and crossed it. They were exhausted but still in pursuit. ⁵ He said to the men of Succoth, "Please give some loaves of bread to the troops under my command, ᶜ because they are exhausted, for I am pursuing

ᴬ7:20 Lit trumpets to blow   ᴮ7:22 Or Beth-shittah   ᶜ8:5 Lit troops at my feet

Zebah and Zalmunna, the kings of Midian." Gn 33:17; Jos 13:27; 1Kg 7:46; 2Ch 4:17 ⁶ But the princes of Succoth asked, "AreᴬZebah and Zalmunna now in your hands that we should give bread to your army?"

⁷ Gideon replied, "Very well, when the LORD has handed Zebah and Zalmunna over to me, I will tearᴮ your flesh with thorns and briers from the wilderness!'" ⁸ He went from there to Penuel and asked the same thing from them. The men of Penuel answered just as the men of Succoth had answered. ⁹ He also told the men of Penuel, "When I return safely, I will tear down this tower!" Gn 32:31-32; 1Kg 12:25

¹⁰ Now Zebah and Zalmunna were in Karkor, and with them was their army of about fifteen thousand men, who were all those left of the entire army of the Qedemites. Those who had been killed were one hundred twenty thousand armed men.ᶜ ¹¹ Gideon traveled on the caravan routeᴰ east of Nobah and Jogbehah and attacked their army while the army felt secure. ¹² Zebah and Zalmunna fled, and he pursued them. He captured these two kings of Midian and routed the entire army. Nm 32:42

¹³ Gideon son of Joash returned from the battle by the Ascent of Heres. ¹⁴ He captured a youth from the men of Succoth and interrogated him. The youth wrote down for him the names of the seventy-seven leaders and elders of Succoth. ¹⁵ Then he went to the men of Succoth and said, "Here are Zebah and Zalmunna. You taunted me about them, saying, 'Are Zebah and Zalmunna now in your

power that we should give bread to your exhausted men?'" ¹⁶ So he took the elders of the city, and he took some thorns and briers from the wilderness, and he disciplined the men of Succoth with them. ¹⁷ He also tore down the tower of Penuel and killed the men of the city.

¹⁸ He asked Zebah and Zalmunna, "What kind of men did you kill at Tabor?"

"They were like you," they said. "Each resembled the son of a king."

¹⁹ So he said, "They were my brothers, the sons of my mother! As the LORD lives, if you had let them live, I would not kill you." ²⁰ Then he said to Jether, his firstborn, "Get up and kill them." The youth did not draw his sword, for he was afraid because he was still a youth.

²¹ Zebah and Zalmunna said, "Get up and strike us down yourself, for a man is judged by his strength." So Gideon got up, killed Zebah and Zalmunna, and took the crescent ornaments that were on the necks of their camels.

Gideon's Legacy

²² Then the Israelites said to Gideon, "Rule over us, you as well as your sons and your grandsons, for you delivered us from the power of Midian." Gn 3:16; 4:7; 37:8

²³ But Gideon said to them, "I will not rule over you, and my son will not rule over you; the LORD will rule over you." ²⁴ Then he said to them, "Let me make a request of you: Everyone give me an earring from his plunder." Now the enemy had gold earrings because they were Ishmaelites.

ᴬ8:6 Lit Are the hands of, also in v. 15   ᴮ8:7 Lit thresh   ᶜ8:10 Lit men who drew the sword   ᴰ8:11 Lit on the route of those who live in tents

²⁵ They said, "We agree to give them." So they spread out a cloak, and everyone threw an earring from his plunder on it. ²⁶ The weight of the gold earrings he requested was forty-three pounds ᴬ of gold, in addition to the crescent ornaments and ear pendants, the purple garments on the kings of Midian, and the chains on the necks of their camels. ²⁷ Gideon made an ephod from all this and put it in Ophrah, his hometown. Then all Israel prostituted themselves by worshiping it there, and it became a snare to Gideon and his household. Ex 25:7; 28:12; 39:12; 2Sm 6:14

²⁸ So Midian was subdued before the Israelites, and they were no longer a threat. ᴮ The land had peace for forty years during the days of Gideon. ²⁹ Jerubbaal (that is, Gideon) son of Joash went back to live at his house. Jdg 3:11; 5:31

³⁰ Gideon had seventy sons, his own offspring, since he had many wives. ³¹ His concubine who was in Shechem also bore him a son, and he named him Abimelech. ³² Then Gideon son of Joash died at a good old age and was buried in the tomb of his father Joash in Ophrah of the Abiezrites. Gn 12:6; 37:12-14; Jos 21:22; Ps 60:6

³³ When Gideon died, the Israelites turned and prostituted themselves by worshiping the Baals and made Baal-berith ᶜ their god. ³⁴ The Israelites did not remember the LORD their God who had rescued them from the hand of the enemies around them. ³⁵ They did not show kindness to the house of Jerubbaal (that is, Gideon) for all the good he had done for Israel. Ex 34:15-16; Dt 31:16; 2Ch 21:13

Abimelech Becomes King

9 Abimelech son of Jerubbaal went to Shechem and spoke to his uncles and to his mother's whole clan, saying, ² "Please speak in the hearing of all the citizens of Shechem, 'Is it better for you that seventy men, all the sons of Jerubbaal, rule over you or that one man rule over you?' Remember that I am your own flesh and blood." ᴰ

³ His mother's relatives spoke all these words about him in the hearing of all the citizens of Shechem, and they were favorable to Abimelech, for they said, "He is our brother." ⁴ So they gave him seventy pieces of silver from the temple of Baal-berith. ᶜ Abimelech used it to hire worthless and reckless men, and they followed him. ⁵ He went to his father's house in Ophrah and killed his seventy brothers, the sons of Jerubbaal, on top of a large stone. But Jotham, the youngest son of Jerubbaal, survived, because he hid. ⁶ Then all the citizens of Shechem and of Beth-millo gathered together and proceeded to make Abimelech king at the oak of the pillar in Shechem.

Jotham's Parable

⁷ When they told Jotham, he climbed to the top of Mount Gerizim, raised his voice, and called to them: Dt 11:29; 27:12; Jos 8:33

Listen to me,
　　citizens of Shechem,
　　and may God listen to you:

⁸ 　The trees decided
　　to anoint a king
　　over themselves.

ᴬ8:26 Lit 1,700 shekels　ᴮ8:28 Lit they no longer raised their head　ᶜ8:33; 9:4 Lit Baal of the Covenant, or Lord of the Covenant　ᴰ9:2 Lit your bone and your flesh

They said to the olive tree,
"Reign over us."
9 But the olive tree said to them,
"Should I stop giving my oil
that people use to honor
both God and men,
and rule^A over the trees?"

10 Then the trees said
to the fig tree,
"Come and reign over us."
11 But the fig tree said to them,
"Should I stop giving
my sweetness
and my good fruit,
and rule over trees?"

12 Later, the trees said
to the grapevine,
"Come and reign over us."
13 But the grapevine said
to them,
"Should I stop giving my wine
that cheers both God and man,
and rule over trees?"

14 Finally, all the trees said
to the bramble,
"Come and reign over us."
15 The bramble said to the trees,
"If you really are anointing me
as king over you,
come and find refuge
in my shade.
But if not,
may fire come out
from the bramble
and consume the cedars
of Lebanon."

16 "Now if you have acted faithfully and honestly in making Abimelech king, if you have done well by Jerubbaal and his family, and if you have rewarded him appropriately for what he did — 17 for my father fought for you, risked his life, and rescued you from Midian, 18 and now you have attacked my father's family today, killed his seventy sons on top of a large stone, and made Abimelech, the son of his slave woman, king over the citizens of Shechem 'because he is your brother' — 19 so if you have acted faithfully and honestly with Jerubbaal and his house this day, rejoice in Abimelech and may he also rejoice in you. 20 But if not, may fire come from Abimelech and consume the citizens of Shechem and Beth-millo, and may fire come from the citizens of Shechem and Beth-millo and consume Abimelech." 21 Then Jotham fled, escaping to Beer, and lived there because of his brother Abimelech.   1Sm 12:24

Abimelech's Punishment

22 When Abimelech had ruled over Israel three years, 23 God sent an evil spirit between Abimelech and the citizens of Shechem. They treated Abimelech deceitfully, 24 so that the crime against the seventy sons of Jerubbaal might come to justice and their blood would be avenged on their brother Abimelech, who killed them, and on the citizens of Shechem, who had helped him^B kill his brothers. 25 The citizens of Shechem rebelled against him by putting men in ambush on the tops of the mountains, and they robbed everyone who passed by them on the road. So this was reported to Abimelech.   Jos 8:2; 1Sm 16:14-23; 18:10-12; 19:9
26 Gaal son of Ebed came with his brothers and crossed into Shechem, and the citizens of Shechem trusted him. 27 So they went out to the countryside and harvested

A **9:9** Lit *and go to sway*, also in vv. 11,13   B **9:24** Lit *had strengthened his hands* grapes from their vineyards. They trampled the grapes and held a celebration. Then they went to the house of their god, and as they ate and drank, they cursed Abimelech. [28] Gaal son of Ebed said, "Who is Abimelech and who is Shechem that we should serve him? Isn't he the son of Jerubbaal, and isn't Zebul his officer? You are to serve the men of Hamor, the father of Shechem. Why should we serve Abimelech? [29] If only these people were in my power, I would remove Abimelech." So he said[A] to Abimelech, "Gather your army and come out."   Gn 33:19; 34:2-26; Lv 19:24; Jdg 21:20-21

[30] When Zebul, the ruler of the city, heard the words of Gaal son of Ebed, he was angry. [31] So he secretly sent messengers to Abimelech, saying, "Beware! Gaal son of Ebed, with his brothers, have come to Shechem and are turning the city against you.[B] [32] Now tonight, you and the troops with you, come and wait in ambush in the countryside. [33] Then get up early, and at sunrise attack the city. When he and the troops who are with him come out against you, do to him whatever you can." [34] So Abimelech and all the troops with him got up at night and waited in ambush for Shechem in four units.

[35] Gaal son of Ebed went out and stood at the entrance of the city gate. Then Abimelech and the troops who were with him got up from their ambush. [36] When Gaal saw the troops, he said to Zebul, "Look, troops are coming down from the mountaintops!" But Zebul said to him, "The shadows of the mountains look like men to you."

[37] Then Gaal spoke again, "Look, troops are coming down from the central part of the land, and one unit is coming from the direction of the Diviners' Oak." [38] Zebul replied, "What do you have to say now? You said, 'Who is Abimelech that we should serve him?' Aren't these the troops you despised? Now go and fight them!"   Ezk 38:12

[39] So Gaal went out leading the citizens of Shechem and fought against Abimelech, [40] but Abimelech pursued him, and Gaal fled before him. Numerous bodies were strewn as far as the entrance of the city gate. [41] Abimelech stayed in Arumah, and Zebul drove Gaal and his brothers from Shechem.   1Sm 17:52; 2Ch 13:17

[42] The next day when the people of Shechem[C] went into the countryside, this was reported to Abimelech. [43] He took the troops, divided them into three companies, and waited in ambush in the countryside. He looked, and the people were coming out of the city, so he arose against them and struck them down. [44] Then Abimelech and the units that were with him rushed forward and took their stand at the entrance of the city gate. The other two units rushed against all who were in the countryside and struck them down. [45] So Abimelech fought against the city that entire day, captured it, and killed the people who were in it. Then he tore down the city and sowed it with salt.   Dt 29:23

[46] When all the citizens of the Tower of Shechem heard, they entered the inner chamber[D] of the temple of El-berith.[E] [47] Then it was reported to Abimelech that all

A9:29 DSS read *They said*; LXX reads *I would say*   B9:31 Hb obscure   C9:42 *of Shechem* supplied for clarity   D9:46 Or *the crypt*, or *the vault*   E9:46 = God of the Covenant the citizens of the Tower of Shechem had gathered. ⁴⁸ So Abimelech and all the troops who were with him went up to Mount Zalmon. Abimelech took his ax in his hand and cut a branch from the trees. He picked up the branch, put it on his shoulder, and said to the troops who were with him, "Hurry and do what you have seen me do." ⁴⁹ Each of the troops also cut his own branch and followed Abimelech. They put the branches against the inner chamber and set it on fire; about a thousand men and women died, including all the men of the Tower of Shechem.

⁵⁰ Abimelech went to Thebez, camped against it, and captured it. ⁵¹ There was a strong tower inside the city, and all the men, women, and citizens of the city fled there. They locked themselves in and went up to the roof of the tower. ⁵² When Abimelech came to attack the tower, he approached its entrance to set it on fire. ⁵³ But a woman threw the upper portion of a millstone on Abimelech's head and fractured his skull. ⁵⁴ He quickly called his armor-bearer and said to him, "Draw your sword and kill me, or they'll say about me, 'A woman killed him.'" So his armor-bearer ran him through, and he died. ⁵⁵ When the Israelites saw that Abimelech was dead, they all went home.   2Sm 11:21; Ps 61:3; Pr 18:10

⁵⁶ In this way, God brought back Abimelech's evil—the evil that Abimelech had done to his father when he killed his seventy brothers. ⁵⁷ God also brought back to the men of Shechem all their evil. So the curse of Jotham son of Jerubbaal came upon them.   Jos 2:19; 8:32

Tola and Jair

10 After Abimelech, Tola son of Puah, son of Dodo became judge and began to deliver Israel. He was from Issachar and lived in Shamir in the hill country of Ephraim. ² Tola judged Israel twenty-three years and when he died, was buried in Shamir.

³ After him came Jair the Gileadite, who judged Israel twenty-two years. ⁴ He had thirty sons who rode on thirty donkeys. They had thirty towns ᴬ in Gilead, which are still called Jair's Villages ᴮ today. ⁵ When Jair died, he was buried in Kamon.   Nm 26:29-30; Jos 17:1,3; Jdg 11:1-2

Israel's Rebellion and Repentance

⁶ Then the Israelites again did what was evil in the sight of the LORD. They worshiped the Baals and the Ashtoreths, the gods of Aram, Sidon, and Moab, and the gods of the Ammonites and the Philistines. They abandoned the LORD and did not worship him. ⁷ So the LORD's anger burned against Israel, and he sold them to ᶜ the Philistines and the Ammonites. ⁸ They shattered and crushed the Israelites that year, and for eighteen years they did the same to all the Israelites who were on the other side of the Jordan in the land of the Amorites in Gilead. ⁹ The Ammonites also crossed the Jordan to fight against Judah, Benjamin, and the house of Ephraim. Israel was greatly oppressed, ¹⁰ so they cried out to the LORD, saying, "We have sinned against you. We have abandoned our God and worshiped the Baals."

¹¹ The LORD said to the Israelites, "When the Egyptians, Amorites,

ᴬ**10:4** LXX; MT reads *donkeys*   ᴮ**10:4** Or *called Havvoth-jair*   ᶜ**10:7** Lit *into the hand of*

Ammonites, Philistines, ¹² Sidonians, Amalekites, and Maonites^A oppressed you, and you cried out to me, did I not deliver you from them? ¹³ But you have abandoned me and worshiped other gods. Therefore, I will not deliver you again. ¹⁴ Go and cry out to the gods you have chosen. Let them deliver you whenever you are oppressed."

¹⁵ But the Israelites said, "We have sinned. Deal with us as you see fit;^B only rescue us today!" ¹⁶ So they got rid of the foreign gods among them and worshiped the LORD, and he became weary of Israel's misery.

¹⁷ The Ammonites were called together, and they camped in Gilead. So the Israelites assembled and camped at Mizpah. ¹⁸ The rulers^C of Gilead said to one another, "Which man will begin the fight against the Ammonites? He will be the leader of all the inhabitants of Gilead."

Jephthah Becomes Israel's Leader

11 Jephthah the Gileadite was a valiant warrior, but he was the son of a prostitute, and Gilead was his father. ² Gilead's wife bore him sons, and when they grew up, they drove Jephthah out and said to him, "You will have no inheritance in our father's family, because you are the son of another woman." ³ So Jephthah fled from his brothers and lived in the land of Tob. Then some worthless men joined Jephthah and went on raids with him.

⁴ Some time later, the Ammonites fought against Israel. ⁵ When the Ammonites made war with Israel, the elders of Gilead went to get Jephthah from the land of Tob. ⁶ They said to him, "Come, be our commander, and let's fight the Ammonites."

⁷ Jephthah replied to the elders of Gilead, "Didn't you hate me and drive me out of my father's family? Why then have you come to me now when you're in trouble?"

⁸ They answered Jephthah, "That's true. But now we turn to you. Come with us, fight the Ammonites, and you will become leader of all the inhabitants of Gilead."

⁹ So Jephthah said to them, "If you are bringing me back to fight the Ammonites and the LORD gives them to me, I will be your leader."

¹⁰ The elders of Gilead said to Jephthah, "The LORD is our witness if we don't do as you say." ¹¹ So Jephthah went with the elders of Gilead. The people made him their leader and commander, and Jephthah repeated all his terms in the presence of the LORD at Mizpah.

Jephthah Rejects Ammonite Claims

¹² Jephthah sent messengers to the king of the Ammonites, asking, "What do you have against me that you have come to fight me in my land?"

¹³ The king of the Ammonites said to Jephthah's messengers, "When Israel came from Egypt, they seized my land from the Arnon to the Jabbok and the Jordan. Now restore it peaceably." Nm 21:24; Dt 2:37; 3:16

¹⁴ Jephthah again sent messengers to the king of the Ammonites ¹⁵ to tell him, "This is what Jephthah says: Israel did not take away the land of Moab or the land of the Ammonites. ¹⁶ But when they came

^A**10:12** LXX reads *Midianites*   ^B**10:15** Lit *Do to us what is good in your eyes*   ^C**10:18** Lit *The people, rulers*

from Egypt, Israel traveled through the wilderness to the Red Sea and came to Kadesh. ¹⁷ Israel sent messengers to the king of Edom, saying, 'Please let us travel through your land,' but the king of Edom would not listen. They also sent messengers to the king of Moab, but he refused. So Israel stayed in Kadesh.

¹⁸ "Then they traveled through the wilderness and around the lands of Edom and Moab. They came to the east side of the land of Moab and camped on the other side of the Arnon but did not enter into the territory of Moab, for the Arnon was the boundary of Moab.

¹⁹ "Then Israel sent messengers to Sihon king of the Amorites, king of Heshbon. Israel said to him, 'Please let us travel through your land to our country,' ²⁰ but Sihon would not trust Israel to pass through his territory. Instead, Sihon gathered all his troops, camped at Jahaz, and fought with Israel. ²¹ Then the LORD God of Israel handed over Sihon and all his troops to Israel, and they defeated them. So Israel took possession of the entire land of the Amorites who lived in that country. ²² They took possession of all the territory of the Amorites from the Arnon to the Jabbok and from the wilderness to the Jordan.

²³ "The LORD God of Israel has now driven out the Amorites before his people Israel, and will you now force us out? ²⁴ Isn't it true that you can have whatever your god Chemosh conquers for you, and we can have whatever the LORD our God conquers for us? ²⁵ Now are you any better than Balak son of Zippor, king of Moab? Did he ever contend with Israel or fight against them? ²⁶ While Israel lived three hundred years in Heshbon and Aroer and their surrounding villages, and in all the cities that are on the banks of the Arnon, why didn't you take them back at that time? ²⁷ I have not sinned against you, but you are doing me wrong by fighting against me. Let the LORD who is the judge decide today between the Israelites and the Ammonites." ²⁸ But the king of the Ammonites would not listen to Jephthah's message that he sent him. Gn 18:25; Jb 9:15

Jephthah's Vow and Sacrifice

²⁹ The Spirit of the LORD came on Jephthah, who traveled through Gilead and Manasseh, and then through Mizpah of Gilead. He crossed over to the Ammonites from Mizpah of Gilead. ³⁰ Jephthah made this vow to the LORD: "If you in fact hand over the Ammonites to me, ³¹ whoever comes out the doors of my house to greet me when I return safely from the Ammonites will belong to the LORD, and I will offer that person as a burnt offering." Gn 28:20; Nm 30:2; 1Sm 1:11; Ps 66:13

³² Jephthah crossed over to the Ammonites to fight against them, and the LORD handed them over to him. ³³ He defeated twenty of their cities with a great slaughter from Aroer all the way to the entrance of Minnith and to Abel-keramim. So the Ammonites were subdued before the Israelites. Jdg 12:3; 1Sm 14:10

³⁴ When Jephthah went to his home in Mizpah, there was his daughter, coming out to meet him with tambourines and dancing! She was his only child; he had no other son or daughter besides her. ³⁵ When he saw her, he tore his clothes and said, "No! Not my daughter! You have devastated me!

You have brought great misery on me.[A] I have given my word to the LORD and cannot take it back."

³⁶ Then she said to him, "My father, you have given your word to the LORD. Do to me as you have said, for the LORD brought vengeance on your enemies, the Ammonites." ³⁷ She also said to her father, "Let me do this one thing: Let me wander two months through the mountains with my friends and mourn my virginity."

³⁸ "Go," he said. And he sent her away two months. So she left with her friends and mourned her virginity as she wandered through the mountains. ³⁹ At the end of two months, she returned to her father, and he kept the vow he had made about her. And she had never been intimate with a man. Now it became a custom in Israel ⁴⁰ that four days each year the young women of Israel would commemorate the daughter of Jephthah the Gileadite.

Conflict with Ephraim

12 The men of Ephraim were called together and crossed the Jordan to Zaphon. They said to Jephthah, "Why have you crossed over to fight against the Ammonites but didn't call us to go with you? We will burn your house with you in it!" Jos 13:27

² Then Jephthah said to them, "My people and I had a bitter conflict with the Ammonites. So I called for you, but you didn't deliver me from their power. ³ When I saw that you weren't going to deliver me, I took my life in my own hands and crossed over to the Ammonites, and the LORD handed them over

to me. Why then have you come today to fight against me?"

⁴ Then Jephthah gathered all of the men of Gilead. They fought and defeated Ephraim, because Ephraim had said, "You Gileadites are Ephraimite fugitives in the territories of Ephraim and Manasseh." ⁵ The Gileadites captured the fords of the Jordan leading to Ephraim. Whenever a fugitive from Ephraim said, "Let me cross over," the Gileadites asked him, "Are you an Ephraimite?" If he answered, "No," ⁶ they told him, "Please say Shibboleth." If he said, "Sibboleth," because he could not pronounce it correctly, they seized him and executed him at the fords of the Jordan. At that time forty-two thousand from Ephraim died.

⁷ Jephthah judged Israel six years, and when he died, he was buried in one of the cities of Gilead.[B]

Ibzan, Elon, and Abdon

⁸ Ibzan, who was from Bethlehem, judged Israel after Jephthah ⁹ and had thirty sons. He gave his thirty daughters in marriage to men outside the tribe and brought back thirty wives for his sons from outside the tribe. Ibzan judged Israel seven years, ¹⁰ and when he died, he was buried in Bethlehem. Ru 1:1-2

¹¹ Elon, who was from Zebulun, judged Israel after Ibzan. He judged Israel ten years, ¹² and when he died, he was buried in Aijalon in the land of Zebulun.

¹³ After Elon, Abdon son of Hillel, who was from Pirathon, judged Israel. ¹⁴ He had forty sons and thirty grandsons, who rode on seventy donkeys. Abdon judged Israel eight years, ¹⁵ and when he died, he was

---

A **11:35** Lit *have been among those who trouble me*   B **12:7** LXX reads *in his city in Gilead* buried in Pirathon in the land of Ephraim, in the hill country of the Amalekites. 2Sm 23:30; 1Ch 11:31; 27:14

Birth of Samson

13 The Israelites again did what was evil in the LORD's sight, so the LORD handed them over to the Philistines forty years. ² There was a certain man from Zorah, from the family of Dan, whose name was Manoah; his wife was unable to conceive and had no children. ³ The angel of the LORD appeared to the woman and said to her, "It is true that you are unable to conceive and have no children, but you will conceive and give birth to a son. ⁴ Now please be careful not to drink wine or beer, or to eat anything unclean; ⁵ for indeed, you will conceive and give birth to a son. You must never cut his hair,ᴬ because the boy will be a Nazirite to God from birth, and he will begin to save Israel from the power of the Philistines." Jdg 3:12; 4:1

⁶ Then the woman went and told her husband, "A man of God came to me. He looked like the awe-inspiring angel of God. I didn't ask him where he came from, and he didn't tell me his name. ⁷ He said to me, 'You will conceive and give birth to a son. Therefore, do not drink wine or beer, and do not eat anything unclean, because the boy will be a Nazirite to God from birth until the day of his death.'"

⁸ Manoah prayed to the LORD and said, "Please, Lord, let the man of God you sent come again to us and teach us what we should do for the boy who will be born." Gn 25:21; Ex 10:18

⁹ God listened toᴮ Manoah, and the angel of God came again to the woman. She was sitting in the field, and her husband Manoah was not with her. ¹⁰ The woman ran quickly to her husband and told him, "The man who came to me the other day has just come back!" Gn 16:11; Ex 16:8

¹¹ So Manoah got up and followed his wife. When he came to the man, he asked, "Are you the man who spoke to my wife?"

"I am," he said.

¹² Then Manoah asked, "When your words come true, what will be the boy's responsibilities and work?"

¹³ The angel of the LORD answered Manoah, "Your wife needs to do everything I told her. ¹⁴ She must not eat anything that comes from the grapevine or drink wine or beer. And she must not eat anything unclean. Your wife must do everything I have commanded her."

¹⁵ "Please stay here," Manoah told him, "and we will prepare a young goat for you." Gn 18:5

¹⁶ The angel of the LORD said to him, "If I stay, I won't eat your food. But if you want to prepare a burnt offering, offer it to the LORD." (Manoah did not know he was the angel of the LORD.)

¹⁷ Then Manoah said to him, "What is your name, so that we may honor you when your words come true?"

¹⁸ "Why do you ask my name," the angel of the LORD asked him, "since it is beyond understanding."

¹⁹ Manoah took a young goat and a grain offering and offered them on a rock to the LORD, who did something miraculousᶜ while Manoah and his wife were watching. ²⁰ When the flame went up from the altar to

---

ᴬ**13:5** Lit *And a razor is not to go up on his head*   ᴮ**13:9** Lit *to the voice of*   ᶜ**13:19** LXX reads *to the LORD, to the one who works wonders* the sky, the angel of the LORD went up in its flame. When Manoah and his wife saw this, they fell facedown on the ground. ²¹ The angel of the LORD did not appear again to Manoah and his wife. Then Manoah realized that it was the angel of the LORD.

²² "We're certainly going to die," he said to his wife, "because we have seen God!" Gn 33:10; Ex 24:10; 33:20

²³ But his wife said to him, "If the LORD had intended to kill us, he wouldn't have accepted the burnt offering and the grain offering from us, and he would not have shown us all these things or spoken to us like this."

²⁴ So the woman gave birth to a son and named him Samson. The boy grew, and the LORD blessed him. ²⁵ Then the Spirit of the LORD began to stir him in the Camp of Dan, ^A between Zorah and Eshtaol.

Samson's Riddle

14 Samson went down to Timnah and saw a young Philistine woman there. ² He went back and told his father and his mother: "I have seen a young Philistine woman in Timnah. Now get her for me as a wife." Jos 15:10; 19:43; 2Ch 28:18

³ But his father and mother said to him, "Can't you find a young woman among your relatives or among any of our people? Must you go to the uncircumcised Philistines for a wife?"

But Samson told his father, "Get her for me. She's the right one for me." ⁴ Now his father and mother did not know this was from the LORD, who wanted the Philistines to provide an opportunity for a confrontation. ^B At that time, the Philistines were ruling Israel.

⁵ Samson went down to Timnah with his father and mother and came to the vineyards of Timnah. Suddenly a young lion came roaring at him, ⁶ the Spirit of the LORD came powerfully on him, and he tore the lion apart with his bare hands as he might have torn a young goat. But he did not tell his father or mother what he had done. ⁷ Then he went and spoke to the woman, because she seemed right to Samson. Jdg 14:19; 15:14; 1Sm 10:6, 10

⁸ After some time, when he returned to marry her, he left the road to see the lion's carcass, and there was a swarm of bees with honey in the carcass. ⁹ He scooped some honey into his hands and ate it as he went along. When he came to his father and mother, he gave some to them and they ate it. But he did not tell them that he had scooped the honey from the lion's carcass. Lv 11:27

¹⁰ His father went to visit the woman, and Samson prepared a feast there, as young men were accustomed to do. ¹¹ When the Philistines saw him, they brought thirty men to accompany him.

¹² "Let me tell you a riddle," Samson said to them. "If you can explain it to me during the seven days of the feast and figure it out, I will give you thirty linen garments and thirty changes of clothes. ¹³ But if you can't explain it to me, you must give me thirty linen garments and thirty changes of clothes." Nm 12:8; Ps 49:4; Pr 1:6

"Tell us your riddle," they replied. ^C "Let's hear it."

¹⁴ So he said to them:

Out of the eater came
    something to eat,

---

^A 13:25 Or *in Mahaneh-dan*   ^B 14:4 *for a confrontation* supplied for clarity   ^C 14:13 Lit *replied to him* and out of the strong came something sweet.

After three days, they were unable to explain the riddle. [15] On the fourth[A] day they said to Samson's wife, "Persuade your husband to explain the riddle to us, or we will burn you and your father's family to death. Did you invite us here to rob us?"

[16] So Samson's wife came to him, weeping, and said, "You hate me and don't love me! You told my people the riddle, but haven't explained it to me."

"Look," he said, [B] "I haven't even explained it to my father or mother, so why should I explain it to you?"

[17] She wept the whole seven days of the feast, and at last, on the seventh day, he explained it to her, because she had nagged him so much. Then she explained it to her people. [18] On the seventh day, before sunset, the men of the city said to him:

What is sweeter than honey?
What is stronger than a lion?

So he said to them:
If you hadn't plowed with
     my young cow,
you wouldn't know
     my riddle now!

[19] The Spirit of the LORD came powerfully on him, and he went down to Ashkelon and killed thirty of their men. He stripped them and gave their clothes to those who had explained the riddle. In a rage, Samson returned to his father's house, [20] and his wife was given to one of the men who had accompanied him.

Samson's Revenge

15 Later on, during the wheat harvest, Samson took a young goat as a gift and visited his wife. "I want to go to my wife in her room," he said. But her father would not let him enter.

[2] "I was sure you hated her," her father said, "so I gave her to one of the men who accompanied you. Isn't her younger sister more beautiful than she is? Why not take her instead?"

[3] Samson said to them, "This time I will be blameless when I harm the Philistines." [4] So he went out and caught three hundred foxes. He took torches, turned the foxes tail-to-tail, and put a torch between each pair of tails. [5] Then he ignited the torches and released the foxes into the standing grain of the Philistines. He burned the piles of grain and the standing grain as well as the vineyards and olive groves. Nm 5:19,28,31; 1Sm 26:9; Jr 2:35

[6] Then the Philistines asked, "Who did this?"

They were told, "It was Samson, the Timnite's son-in-law, because he took Samson's wife and gave her to his companion." So the Philistines went to her and her father and burned them to death.

[7] Then Samson told them, "Because you did this, I swear that I won't rest until I have taken vengeance on you." [8] He tore them limb from limb[C] and then went down and stayed in the cave at the rock of Etam.

[9] The Philistines went up, camped in Judah, and raided Lehi. [10] So the men of Judah said, "Why have you attacked us?"

Jdg 16:15

They replied, "We have come to tie Samson up and pay him back for what he did to us."

[11] Then three thousand men of Judah went to the cave at the rock of Etam, and they asked Samson, "Don't you realize that the Philistines rule us? What have you done to us?" Lv 26:25; Dt 28:43; Jdg 13:1; 14:4

"I have done to them what they did to me," he answered. [A]

[12] They said to him, "We've come to tie you up and hand you over to the Philistines."

Then Samson told them, "Swear to me that you yourselves won't kill me."

[13] "No," they said, [B] "we won't kill you, but we will tie you up securely and hand you over to them." So they tied him up with two new ropes and led him away from the rock.

[14] When he came to Lehi, the Philistines came to meet him shouting. The Spirit of the LORD came powerfully on him, and the ropes that were on his arms and wrists became like burnt flax and fell off. [15] He found a fresh jawbone of a donkey, reached out his hand, took it, and killed a thousand men with it. [16] Then Samson said:

With the jawbone of a donkey
I have piled them in heaps.
With the jawbone
     of a donkey
I have killed a thousand men.

[17] When he finished speaking, he threw away the jawbone and named that place Ramath-lehi. [C] [18] He became very thirsty and called out to the LORD: "You have accomplished this great victory through your servant. Must I now die of thirst and fall into the hands of the uncircumcised?" [19] So God split a hollow place in the ground at Lehi, and water came out of it. After Samson drank, his strength returned, and he revived. That is why he named it En-hakkore, [D] which is still in Lehi today. [20] And he judged Israel twenty years in the days of the Philistines. Gn 45:27; 1Kg 17:22

Samson and Delilah

16 Samson went to Gaza, where he saw a prostitute and went to bed with her. [2] When the Gazites heard that Samson was there, they surrounded the place and waited in ambush for him all that night at the city gate. They kept quiet all night, saying, "Let's wait until dawn; then we will kill him." [3] But Samson stayed in bed only until midnight. Then he got up, took hold of the doors of the city gate along with the two gateposts, and pulled them out, bar and all. He put them on his shoulders and took them to the top of the mountain overlooking Hebron. Jos 15:47

[4] Some time later, he fell in love with a woman named Delilah, who lived in the Sorek Valley. [5] The Philistine leaders went to her and said, "Persuade him to tell you [E] where his great strength comes from, so we can overpower him, tie him up, and make him helpless. Each of us will then give you 1,100 pieces of silver." Jos 13:3

[6] So Delilah said to Samson, "Please tell me, where does your great strength come from? How could someone tie you up and make you helpless?"

[7] Samson told her, "If they tie me up with seven fresh bowstrings

---

[A]15:11 Lit *answered them*   [B]15:13 Lit *said to him of the One Who Cried Out*   [C]15:17 = High Place of the Jawbone   [D]15:19 = Spring   [E]16:5 Lit *him and see* that have not been dried, I will become weak and be like any other man."

⁸ The Philistine leaders brought her seven fresh bowstrings that had not been dried, and she tied him up with them. ⁹ While the men in ambush were waiting in her room, she called out to him, "Samson, the Philistines are here!"ᴬ But he snapped the bowstrings as a strand of yarn snaps when it touches fire. The secret of his strength remained unknown.

¹⁰ Then Delilah said to Samson, "You have mocked me and told me lies! Won't you please tell me how you can be tied up?"

¹¹ He told her, "If they tie me up with new ropes that have never been used, I will become weak and be like any other man." Jdg 15:13

¹² Delilah took new ropes, tied him up with them, and shouted, "Samson, the Philistines are here!" But while the men in ambush were waiting in her room, he snapped the ropes off his arms like a thread.

¹³ Then Delilah said to Samson, "You have mocked me all along and told me lies! Tell me how you can be tied up."

He told her, "If you weave the seven braids on my head into the fabric on a loom — "ᴮ

¹⁴ She fastened the braids with a pin and called to him, "Samson, the Philistines are here!" He awoke from his sleep and pulled out the pin, with the loom and the web.

¹⁵ "How can you say, 'I love you,'" she told him, "when your heart is not with me? This is the third time

you have mocked me and not told me what makes your strength so great!" Jdg 14:6

¹⁶ Because she nagged him day after day and pleaded with him until she wore him out,ᶜ ¹⁷ he told her the whole truth and said to her, "My hair has never been cut,ᴰ because I am a Nazirite to God from birth. If I am shaved, my strength will leave me, and I will become weak and be like any other man."

¹⁸ When Delilah realized that he had told her the whole truth, she sent this message to the Philistine leaders: "Come one more time, for he has told me the whole truth." The Philistine leaders came to her and brought the silver with them.

¹⁹ Then she let him fall asleep on her lap and called a man to shave off the seven braids on his head. In this way, she made him helpless, and his strength left him. ²⁰ Then she cried, "Samson, the Philistines are here!" When he awoke from his sleep, he said, "I will escape as I did before and shake myself free." But he did not know that the LORD had left him. Nm 14:9,42-43; Jos 7:12; 1Sm 16:14; 18:12

Samson's Defeat and Death

²¹ The Philistines seized him and gouged out his eyes. They brought him down to Gaza and bound him with bronze shackles, and he was forced to grind grain in the prison. ²² But his hair began to grow back after it had been shaved.

²³ Now the Philistine leaders gathered together to offer a great sacrifice to their god Dagon. They rejoiced and said: Jos 15:41; 19:27; 1Ch 10:10

ᴬ**16:9** Lit *are on you,* also in vv. 12,14,20　ᴮ**16:13-14** LXX reads *loom and fasten them with a pin into the wall and I will become weak and be like any other man."* ¹⁴*And while he was sleeping, Delilah wove the seven braids on his head into the loom.*　ᶜ**16:16** Lit *him and he became short to death*　ᴰ**16:17** Lit *A razor has not gone up on my head*

Our god has handed over
our enemy Samson to us.
²⁴ When the people saw him, they
praised their god and said: Dn 5:4
Our god has handed over
to us
our enemy who destroyed
our land
and who multiplied our dead.
²⁵ When they were in good spirits, ᴬ they said, "Bring Samson here
to entertain us." So they brought
Samson from prison, and he entertained them. They had him stand
between the pillars.

²⁶ Samson said to the young man
who was leading him by the hand,
"Lead me where I can feel the pillars supporting the temple, so I
can lean against them." ²⁷ The temple was full of men and women;
all the leaders of the Philistines
were there, and about three thousand men and women were on
the roof watching Samson entertain them. ²⁸ He called out to the
LORD: "Lord GOD, please remember me. Strengthen me, God, just
once more. With one act of vengeance, let me pay back the Philistines for my two eyes." ²⁹ Samson
took hold of the two middle pillars supporting the temple and
leaned against them, one on his
right hand and the other on his
left. ³⁰ Samson said, "Let me die
with the Philistines." He pushed
with all his might, and the temple fell on the leaders and all the
people in it. And those he killed at
his death were more than those he
had killed in his life.   Jr 15:15

³¹ Then his brothers and all his father's family came down, carried
him back, and buried him between
Zorah and Eshtaol in the tomb of

his father Manoah. So he judged
Israel twenty years.

Micah's Priest

17 There was a man from the hill
country of Ephraim named
Micah. ² He said to his mother, "The
1,100 pieces of silver taken from
you, and that I heard you place a
curse on — here's the silver. I took
it."

Then his mother said, "My son,
may you be blessed by the LORD!"

³ He returned the 1,100 pieces of
silver to his mother, and his mother
said, "I personally consecrate the
silver to the LORD for my son's benefit to make a carved image and a silver idol. ᴮ I will give it back to you."
⁴ So he returned the silver to his
mother, and she took five pounds
of silver and gave it to a silversmith.
He made it into a carved image and
a silver idol, and it was in Micah's
house.   Lv 22:2-3; 27:14-19; 1Ch 18:11; 26:26-28

⁵ This man Micah had a shrine,
and he made an ephod and household idols, and installed one of his
sons to be his priest. ⁶ In those days
there was no king in Israel; everyone did whatever seemed right to
him.   Gn 31:19, 34-35; Jdg 18:14; 1Sm 19:13; 2Kg 23:24

⁷ There was a young man, a Levite
from Bethlehem in Judah, who was
staying within the clan of Judah.
⁸ The man left the town of Bethlehem in Judah to stay wherever he
could find a place. On his way he
came to Micah's home in the hill
country of Ephraim.   Dt 18:6-7

⁹ "Where do you come from?" Micah asked him.

He answered him, "I am a Levite
from Bethlehem in Judah, and I'm
going to stay wherever I can find
a place."

ᴬ**16:25** Or *When they were feeling good*   ᴮ**17:3** Or *image and a cast image,* also in v. 4

¹⁰ Micah replied,^A "Stay with me and be my father and priest, and I will give you four ounces of silver a year, along with your clothing and provisions." So the Levite went in ¹¹ and agreed to stay with the man, and the young man became like one of his sons. ¹² Micah consecrated the Levite, and the young man became his priest and lived in Micah's house. ¹³ Then Micah said, "Now I know that the LORD will be good to me, because a Levite has become my priest." Gn 45:8; Jdg 18:19,30; Jr 3:19

Dan's Invasion and Idolatry

18 In those days, there was no king in Israel, and the Danite tribe was looking for territory to occupy. Up to that time no territory had been captured by them among the tribes of Israel. ² So the Danites sent out five brave men from all their clans, from Zorah and Eshtaol, to scout out the land and explore it. They told them, "Go and explore the land." Jdg 17:6; 19:1; 21:25 They came to the hill country of Ephraim as far as the home of Micah and spent the night there. ³ While they were near Micah's home, they recognized the accent of the young Levite. So they went over to him and asked, "Who brought you here? What are you doing in this place? What is keeping you here?" ⁴ He told them, "This is what Micah has done for me: He has hired me, and I became his priest." ⁵ Then they said to him, "Please inquire of God for us to determine if we will have a successful journey." ⁶ The priest told them, "Go in peace. The LORD is watching over the journey you are going on."

⁷ The five men left and came to Laish. They saw that the people who were there were living securely, in the same way as the Sidonians, quiet and unsuspecting. There was nothing lacking^B in the land and no oppressive ruler. They were far from the Sidonians, having no alliance with anyone.^C

⁸ When the men went back to their relatives at Zorah and Eshtaol, their relatives asked them, "What did you find out?" Jos 15:33 ⁹ They answered, "Come on, let's attack them, for we have seen the land, and it is very good. Why wait? Don't hesitate to go and invade and take possession of the land! ¹⁰ When you get there, you will come to an unsuspecting people and a spacious land, for God has handed it over to you. It is a place where nothing on earth is lacking." ¹¹ Six hundred Danites departed from Zorah and Eshtaol armed with weapons of war. ¹² They went up and camped at Kiriath-jearim in Judah. This is why the place is still called the Camp of Dan^D today; it is west of Kiriath-jearim. ¹³ From there they traveled to the hill country of Ephraim and arrived at Micah's house. Dt 8:9; Jos 9:17; 1Ch 13:5-6; 2Ch 1:4

¹⁴ The five men who had gone to scout out the land of Laish told their brothers, "Did you know that there are an ephod, household gods, and a carved image and a silver idol^E in these houses? Now think about what you should do." ¹⁵ So they detoured there and went to the house of the young Levite at the home of Micah and greeted him. ¹⁶ The six hundred Danite men were standing by the entrance of the city gate,

---

^A**17:10** Lit *replied to him*   ^B**18:7** Hb obscure   ^C**18:7** MT; some LXX mss, Sym, Old Lat, Syr read *Aram*
^D**18:12** Or *called Mahaneh-dan*   ^E**18:14** Or *image, the cast image*

armed with their weapons of war. [17] Then the five men who had gone to scout out the land went in and took the carved image, the ephod, the household idols, and the silver idol, [A] while the priest was standing by the entrance of the city gate with the six hundred men armed with weapons of war.

[18] When they entered Micah's house and took the carved image, the ephod, the household idols, and the silver idol, the priest said to them, "What are you doing?"

[19] They told him, "Be quiet. Keep your mouth shut. [B] Come with us and be a father and a priest to us. Is it better for you to be a priest for the house of one person or for you to be a priest for a tribe and family in Israel?" [20] So the priest was pleased and took his ephod, household idols, and carved image, and went with the people. [21] They prepared to leave, putting their dependents, livestock, and possessions in front of them. Jb 21:5; 29:9; 40:4; Mc 7:16

[22] After they were some distance from Micah's house, the men who were in the houses near it were mustered and caught up with the Danites. [23] They called to the Danites, who turned to face them, and said to Micah, "What's the matter with you that you mustered the men?"

[24] He said, "You took the gods I had made and the priest, and went away. What do I have left? How can you say to me, 'What's the matter with you?'"

[25] The Danites said to him, "Don't raise your voice against us, or angry men will attack you, and you and your family will lose your lives." [26] The Danites went on their way, and Micah turned to go back home, because he saw that they were stronger than he was.

[27] After they had taken the gods Micah had made and the priest that belonged to him, they went to Laish, to a quiet and unsuspecting people. They killed them with their swords and burned the city. [28] There was no one to rescue them because it was far from Sidon and they had no alliance with anyone. It was in a valley that belonged to Beth-rehob. They rebuilt the city and lived in it. [29] They named the city Dan, after the name of their ancestor Dan, who was born to Israel. The city was formerly named Laish.

[30] The Danites set up the carved image for themselves. Jonathan son of Gershom, son of Moses, [C] and his sons were priests for the Danite tribe until the time of the exile from the land. [31] So they set up for themselves Micah's carved image that he had made, and it was there as long as the house of God was in Shiloh. Jos 18:1; Jdg 21:12; 2Kg 15:29

Outrage in Benjamin

19 In those days, when there was no king in Israel, a Levite staying in a remote part of the hill country of Ephraim acquired a woman from Bethlehem in Judah as his concubine. [2] But she was unfaithful to [D] him and left him for her father's house in Bethlehem in Judah. She was there for four months. [3] Then her husband got up and followed her to speak kindly to her [E] and bring her back. He had his servant with him and a pair of donkeys. So she brought

[A]18:17 Or the cast image, also in v. 18   [B]18:19 Lit Put your hand on your mouth   [C]18:30 Some Hb mss, LXX, Vg; other Hb mss read Manasseh   [D]19:2 LXX reads was angry with   [E]19:3 Lit speak to her heart him to her father's house, and when the girl's father saw him, he gladly welcomed him. [4] His father-in-law, the girl's father, detained him, and he stayed with him for three days. They ate, drank, and spent the nights there.   Jdg 17:6; 18:1; 21:25

[5] On the fourth day, they got up early in the morning and prepared to go, but the girl's father said to his son-in-law, "Have something to eat to keep up your strength and then you can go." [6] So they sat down and the two of them ate and drank together. Then the girl's father said to the man, "Please agree to stay overnight and enjoy yourself." [7] The man got up to go, but his father-in-law persuaded him, so he stayed and spent the night there again. [8] He got up early in the morning of the fifth day to leave, but the girl's father said to him, "Please keep up your strength." So they waited until late afternoon and the two of them ate. [9] The man got up to go with his concubine and his servant, when his father-in-law, the girl's father, said to him, "Look, night is coming. Please spend the night. See, the day is almost over. Spend the night here, enjoy yourself, then you can get up early tomorrow for your journey and go home."   Gn 18:5; Jdg 16:25

[10] But the man was unwilling to spend the night. He got up, departed, and arrived opposite Jebus (that is, Jerusalem). The man had his two saddled donkeys and his concubine with him. [11] When they were near Jebus and the day was almost gone, the servant said to his master, "Please, why not let us stop at this Jebusite city and spend the night here?"   Jos 18:28; Jdg 19:9; 1Ch 11:4-5

[12] But his master replied to him, "We will not stop at a foreign city where there are no Israelites. Let's move on to Gibeah." [13] "Come on," he said, [A] "let's try to reach one of these places and spend the night in Gibeah or Ramah." [14] So they continued on their journey, and the sun set as they neared Gibeah in Benjamin. [15] They stopped [B] to go in and spend the night in Gibeah. The Levite went in and sat down in the city square, but no one took them into their home to spend the night.

[16] In the evening, an old man came in from his work in the field. He was from the hill country of Ephraim, but he was residing in Gibeah where the people were Benjaminites. [17] When he looked up and saw the traveler in the city square, the old man asked, "Where are you going, and where do you come from?"

[18] He answered him, "We're traveling from Bethlehem in Judah to the remote hill country of Ephraim, where I am from. I went to Bethlehem in Judah, and now I'm going to the house of the LORD. [C] No one has taken me into his home, [19] although there's straw and feed for the donkeys, and I have bread and wine for me, my concubine, and the servant [D] with us. There is nothing we lack."

[20] "Welcome!" said the old man. "I'll take care of everything you need. Only don't spend the night in the square." [21] So he brought him to his house and fed the donkeys. Then they washed their feet and ate and drank. [22] While they were enjoying themselves, all of a sudden, wicked men of the city surrounded the house and beat on the door.

They said to the old man who was the owner of the house, "Bring out the man who came to your house so we can have sex with him!"

²³ The owner of the house went out and said to them, "Please don't do this evil, my brothers. After all, this man has come into my house. Don't commit this horrible outrage. ²⁴ Here, let me bring out my virgin daughter and the man's concubine now. Abuse them and do whatever you want^A to them. But don't commit this outrageous thing against this man." Gn 34:7; Dt 22:21; Jdg 20:6; 2Sm 13:12

²⁵ But the men would not listen to him, so the man seized his concubine and took her outside to them. They raped^B her and abused her all night until morning. At daybreak they let her go. ²⁶ Early that morning, the woman made her way back, and as it was getting light, she collapsed at the doorway of the man's house where her master was.

²⁷ When her master got up in the morning, opened the doors of the house, and went out to leave on his journey, there was the woman, his concubine, collapsed near the doorway of the house with her hands on the threshold. ²⁸ "Get up," he told her. "Let's go." But there was no response. So the man put her on his donkey and set out for home.

²⁹ When he entered his house, he picked up a knife, took hold of his concubine, cut her into twelve pieces, limb by limb, and then sent her throughout the territory of Israel. ³⁰ Everyone who saw it said, "Nothing like this has ever happened or has been seen since the day the Israelites came out of the

land of Egypt until now.^C Think it over, discuss it, and speak up!"

War Against Benjamin

20 All the Israelites from Dan to Beer-sheba and from the land of Gilead came out, and the community assembled as one body before the LORD at Mizpah. ² The leaders of all the people and of all the tribes of Israel presented themselves in the assembly of God's people: four hundred thousand armed^D foot soldiers. ³ The Benjaminites heard that the Israelites had gone up to Mizpah. Gn 21:14; 22:19; 1Sm 3:20; 10:17

The Israelites asked, "Tell us, how did this evil act happen?"

⁴ The Levite, the husband of the murdered woman, answered: "I went to Gibeah in Benjamin with my concubine to spend the night. ⁵ Citizens of Gibeah came to attack me and surrounded the house at night. They intended to kill me, but they raped my concubine, and she died. ⁶ Then I took my concubine and cut her in pieces, and sent her throughout Israel's territory, because they have committed a wicked outrage in Israel. ⁷ Look, all of you are Israelites. Give your judgment and verdict here and now."

⁸ Then all the people stood united and said, "None of us will go to his tent or return to his house. ⁹ Now this is what we will do to Gibeah: we will attack it. By lot ¹⁰ we will take ten men out of every hundred from all the tribes of Israel, and one hundred out of every thousand, and one thousand out of every ten thousand to get provisions for the troops when they go to Gibeah in

---

^A**19:24** Lit *do what is good in your eyes*   ^B**19:25** Lit *knew*   ^C**19:30** LXX reads *until now." He commanded the men he sent out, saying, "You will say this to all the men of Israel: Has anything like this happened since the day the Israelites came out of Egypt until this day?*   ^D**20:2** Lit *drawing the sword*

Benjamin to punish them for all the outrage they committed in Israel." [11] So all the men of Israel gathered united against the city. [12] Then the tribes of Israel sent men throughout the tribe of Benjamin, saying, "What is this evil act that has happened among you? [13] Hand over the wicked men in Gibeah so we can put them to death and eradicate evil from Israel." But the Benjaminites would not listen to their fellow Israelites. [14] Instead, the Benjaminites gathered together from their cities to Gibeah to go out and fight against the Israelites. [15] On that day the Benjaminites mobilized twenty-six thousand armed men [A] from their cities, besides seven hundred fit young men rallied by the inhabitants of Gibeah. [16] There were seven hundred fit young men who were left-handed among all these troops; all could sling a stone at a hair and not miss. Dt 29:10; Jos 10:24; Jdg 20:33; 1Sm 11:15

[17] The Israelites, apart from Benjamin, mobilized four hundred thousand armed men, every one an experienced warrior. [18] They set out, went to Bethel, and inquired of God. The Israelites asked, "Who is to go first to fight for us against the Benjaminites?" Nm 27:21; Jdg 18:5

And the LORD answered, "Judah will be first."

[19] In the morning, the Israelites set out and camped near Gibeah. [20] The men of Israel went out to fight against Benjamin and took their battle positions against Gibeah. [21] The Benjaminites came out of Gibeah and slaughtered twenty-two thousand men of Israel on the field that day. [22] But the Israelite troops rallied and again took their battle positions in the same place where they positioned themselves on the first day. [23] They went up, wept before the LORD until evening, and inquired of him: "Should we again attack our brothers the Benjaminites?" Jos 7:6-7; 2Sm 1:12

And the LORD answered: "Fight against them."

[24] On the second day the Israelites advanced against the Benjaminites. [25] That same day the Benjaminites came out from Gibeah to meet them and slaughtered an additional eighteen thousand Israelites on the field; all were armed. [B]

[26] The whole Israelite army went to Bethel where they wept and sat before the LORD. They fasted that day until evening and offered burnt offerings and fellowship offerings to the LORD. [27] Then the Israelites inquired of the LORD. In those days, the ark of the covenant of God was there, [28] and Phinehas son of Eleazar, son of Aaron, was serving before it. The Israelites asked: "Should we again fight against our brothers the Benjaminites or should we stop?" Jdg 21:2; 1Sm 4:4; 2Sm 15:24; 1Ch 16:6

The LORD answered: "Fight, because I will hand them over to you tomorrow." [29] So Israel set up an ambush around Gibeah. [30] On the third day the Israelites fought against the Benjaminites and took their battle positions against Gibeah as before. [31] Then the Benjaminites came out against the troops and were drawn away from the city. They began to attack the troops as before, killing about thirty men of Israel on the highways, one of which goes up to Bethel and the other to Gibeah through the open country. [32] The Benjaminites said, "We are defeating them as before."

[A] 20:15 Lit *men drawing the sword*, also in vv. 17,46   [B] 20:25 Lit *were drawing the sword*, also in v. 35

But the Israelites said, "Let's flee and draw them away from the city to the highways." ³³ So all the men of Israel got up from their places and took their battle positions at Baal-tamar, while the Israelites in ambush charged out of their places west of ^A Geba. ³⁴ Then ten thousand fit young men from all Israel made a frontal assault against Gibeah, and the battle was fierce, but the Benjaminites did not know that disaster was about to strike them. ³⁵ The Lᴏʀᴅ defeated Benjamin in the presence of Israel, and on that day the Israelites slaughtered 25,100 men of Benjamin; all were armed. ³⁶ Then the Benjaminites realized they had been defeated.

The men of Israel had retreated before Benjamin, because they were confident in the ambush they had set against Gibeah. ³⁷ The men in ambush had rushed quickly against Gibeah; they advanced and put the whole city to the sword. ³⁸ The men of Israel had a prearranged signal with the men in ambush: when they sent up a great cloud of smoke from the city, ³⁹ the men of Israel would return to the battle. When Benjamin had begun to strike them down, killing about thirty men of Israel, they said, "They're defeated before us, just as they were in the first battle." ⁴⁰ But when the column of smoke began to go up from the city, Benjamin looked behind them, and the whole city was going up in smoke. ᴮ ⁴¹ Then the men of Israel returned, and the men of Benjamin were terrified when they realized that disaster had struck them. ⁴² They retreated before the men

of Israel toward the wilderness, but the battle overtook them, and those who came out of the cities ᶜ slaughtered those between them. ⁴³ They surrounded the Benjaminites, pursued them, and easily overtook them near Gibeah toward the east. ⁴⁴ There were eighteen thousand men who died from Benjamin; all were warriors. ⁴⁵ Then Benjamin turned and fled toward the wilderness to Rimmon Rock, and Israel killed five thousand men on the highways. They overtook them at Gidom and struck two thousand more dead. Dt 13:15; Jos 10:37,39; 11:12,14

⁴⁶ All the Benjaminites who died that day were twenty-five thousand armed men; all were warriors. ⁴⁷ But six hundred men escaped into the wilderness to Rimmon Rock and stayed there four months. ⁴⁸ The men of Israel turned back against the other Benjaminites and killed them with their swords — the entire city, the animals, and everything that remained. They also burned all the cities that remained.

Brides for Benjamin

21 The men of Israel had sworn an oath at Mizpah: "None of us will give his daughter to a Benjaminite in marriage." ² So the people went to Bethel and sat there before God until evening. They wept loudly and bitterly, ³ and cried out, "Why, Lᴏʀᴅ God of Israel, has it occurred ᴰ that one tribe is missing in Israel today?" ⁴ The next day the people got up early, built an altar there, and offered burnt offerings and fellowship offerings. ⁵ The Israelites asked, "Who of all the tribes of Israel didn't come to the Lᴏʀᴅ with

---

ᴬ20:33 LXX, Syr, Vg; MT reads *places in the plain of,* or *places in the cave of*   ᴮ20:40 Lit *up to the sky*
ᶜ20:42 LXX, Vg read *city*   ᴰ21:3 Lit *has this occurred in Israel*

the assembly?" For a great oath had been taken that anyone who had not come to the LORD at Mizpah would certainly be put to death.

⁶ But the Israelites had compassion on their brothers, the Benjaminites, and said, "Today a tribe has been cut off from Israel. ⁷ What should we do about wives for the survivors? We've sworn to the LORD not to give them any of our daughters as wives." ⁸ They asked, "Which city among the tribes of Israel didn't come to the LORD at Mizpah?" It turned out that no one from Jabesh-gilead had come to the camp and the assembly. ⁹ For when the roll was called, no men were there from the inhabitants of Jabesh-gilead.

¹⁰ The congregation sent twelve thousand brave warriors ᴬ there and commanded them: "Go and kill the inhabitants of Jabesh-gilead with the sword, including women and dependents. ¹¹ This is what you should do: Completely destroy every male, as well as every woman who has gone to bed with a man." ¹² They found among the inhabitants of Jabesh-gilead four hundred young virgins, who had not gone to bed with a man, and they brought them to the camp at Shiloh in the land of Canaan. Nm 31:17

¹³ The whole congregation sent a message of peace to the Benjaminites who were at Rimmon Rock. ¹⁴ Benjamin returned at that time, and Israel gave them the women they had kept alive from Jabesh-gilead. But there were not enough for them. Dt 20:10

¹⁵ The people had compassion on Benjamin, because the LORD had made this gap in the tribes of Israel. ¹⁶ The elders of the congregation said, "What should we do about wives for those who are left, since the women of Benjamin have been destroyed?" ¹⁷ They said, "There must be heirs for the survivors of Benjamin, so that a tribe of Israel will not be wiped out. ¹⁸ But we can't give them our daughters as wives." For the Israelites had sworn, "Anyone who gives a wife to a Benjaminite is cursed." ¹⁹ They also said, "Look, there's an annual festival to the LORD in Shiloh, which is north of Bethel, east of the highway that goes up from Bethel to Shechem, and south of Lebonah."

²⁰ Then they commanded the Benjaminites: "Go and hide in the vineyards. ²¹ Watch, and when you see the young women of Shiloh come out to perform the dances, each of you leave the vineyards and catch a wife for yourself from the young women of Shiloh, and go to the land of Benjamin. ²² When their fathers or brothers come to us and protest, we will tell them, 'Show favor to them, since we did not get enough wives for each of them in the battle. You didn't actually give the women to them, so ᴮ you are not guilty of breaking your oath.'" Ex 15:20

²³ The Benjaminites did this and took the number of women they needed from the dancers they caught. They went back to their own inheritance, rebuilt their cities, and lived in them. ²⁴ At that time, each of the Israelites returned from there to his own tribe and family. Each returned from there to his own inheritance. Jdg 20:48

²⁵ In those days there was no king in Israel; everyone did whatever seemed right to him. Jdg 17:6; 18:1; 19:1

ᴬ21:10 Lit *twelve thousand of their sons of valor*   ᴮ21:22 Lit *at this time*

RUTH

Naomi's Family in Moab

1 During the time[A] of the judges, there was a famine in the land. A man left Bethlehem[B] in Judah with his wife and two sons to stay in the territory of Moab for a while. [2] The man's name was Elimelech,[C] and his wife's name was Naomi.[D] The names of his two sons were Mahlon[E] and Chilion.[F] They were Ephrathites from Bethlehem in Judah. They entered the fields of Moab and settled there. [3] Naomi's husband Elimelech died, and she was left with her two sons. [4] Her sons took Moabite women as their wives: one was named Orpah and the second was named Ruth. After they lived in Moab about ten years, [5] both Mahlon and Chilion also died, and Naomi was left without her two children and without her husband. Gn 12:10; 26:1; 43:1; Jdg 2:16-18

Ruth's Loyalty to Naomi

[6] She and her daughters-in-law set out to return from the territory of Moab, because she had heard in Moab that the LORD had paid attention to his people's need by providing them food. [7] She left the place where she had been living, accompanied by her two daughters-in-law, and traveled along the road leading back to the land of Judah. [8] Naomi said to them, "Each of you go back to your mother's home. May the LORD show kindness to you as you have shown to the dead and to me. [9] May the LORD grant each of you rest in the house of a new husband." She kissed them, and they wept loudly. Gn 24:28; Ru 3:1

[10] They said to her, "We insist on returning with you to your people."

[11] But Naomi replied, "Return home, my daughters. Why do you want to go with me? Am I able to have any more sons who could become your husbands? [12] Return home, my daughters. Go on, for I am too old to have another husband. Even if I thought there was still hope for me to have a husband tonight and to bear sons, [13] would you be willing to wait for them to grow up? Would you restrain yourselves from remarrying?[G] No, my daughters, my life is much too bitter for you to share,[H] because the LORD's hand has turned against me." [14] Again they wept loudly, and Orpah kissed her mother-in-law, but Ruth clung to her. [15] Naomi said, "Look, your sister-in-law has gone back to her people and to her gods. Follow your sister-in-law." Gn 38:11

[16] But Ruth replied:

Don't plead with me
    to abandon you
or to return
    and not follow you.
For wherever you go, I will go,
and wherever you live,
    I will live;
your people will be
    my people,
and your God will be my God.

A1:1 Lit *In the days of the judging*   B1:1 = House of Bread   C1:2 = My God Is King   D1:2 = Pleasant
E1:2 = Sickly   F1:2 = Weak or Failing   G1:13 Lit *marrying a man*   H1:13 Lit *daughters, for more bitter to me than you*

¹⁷ Where you die, I will die,
and there I will be buried.
May the Lord punish me,^A
and do so severely,
if anything but death
separates you and me.

¹⁸ When Naomi saw that Ruth was determined to go with her, she stopped talking to her.

¹⁹ The two of them traveled until they came to Bethlehem. When they entered Bethlehem, the whole town was excited about their arrival^B and the local women exclaimed, "Can this be Naomi?"   Mt 21:10

²⁰ "Don't call me Naomi. Call me Mara,"^C she answered, "for the Almighty has made me very bitter. ²¹ I went away full, but the Lord has brought me back empty. Why do you call me Naomi, since the Lord has opposed^D me, and the Almighty has afflicted me?"   Gn 49:25; Ex 6:3; Jb 6:4

²² So Naomi came back from the territory of Moab with her daughter-in-law Ruth the Moabitess. They arrived in Bethlehem at the beginning of the barley harvest.

Ruth and Boaz Meet

2 Now Naomi had a relative on her husband's side. He was a prominent man of noble character from Elimelech's family. His name was Boaz.   Ru 1:2

² Ruth the Moabitess asked Naomi, "Will you let me go into the fields and gather fallen grain behind someone with whom I find favor?"   Lv 19:9-10; 23:22

Naomi answered her, "Go ahead, my daughter." ³ So Ruth left and entered the field to gather grain behind the harvesters. She happened to be in the portion of the field belonging to Boaz, who was from Elimelech's family.   Pr 16:33

⁴ Later, when Boaz arrived from Bethlehem, he said to the harvesters, "The Lord be with you."

"The Lord bless you," they replied.   Nm 6:24

⁵ Boaz asked his servant who was in charge of the harvesters, "Whose young woman is this?"

⁶ The servant answered, "She is the young Moabite woman who returned with Naomi from the territory of Moab. ⁷ She asked, 'Will you let me gather fallen grain among the bundles behind the harvesters?' She came and has been on her feet since early morning, except that she rested a little in the shelter."^E

⁸ Then Boaz said to Ruth, "Listen, my daughter.^F Don't go and gather grain in another field, and don't leave this one, but stay here close to my female servants. ⁹ See which field they are harvesting, and follow them. Haven't I ordered the young men not to touch you?^G When you are thirsty, go and drink from the jars the young men have filled."

¹⁰ She fell facedown, bowed to the ground, and said to him, "Why have I found favor with you, so that you notice me, although I am a foreigner?"

¹¹ Boaz answered her, "Everything you have done for your mother-in-law since your husband's death has been fully reported to me: how you left your father and mother and your native land, and how you came to a people you didn't

^A**1:17** A solemn oath formula; 1Sm 3:17; 2Sm 3:9,35; 1Kg 2:23; 2Kg 6:31   ^B**1:19** Lit *excited because of them*
^C**1:20** = Bitter   ^D**1:21** LXX, Syr, Vg read *has humiliated*   ^E**2:7** LXX reads *morning, and until evening she has not rested in the field a little*; Vg reads *morning until now and she did not return to the house*; Hb uncertain   ^F**2:8** Lit *"Haven't you heard, my daughter?*   ^G**2:9** Either sexual or physical harassment

previously know. [12] May the LORD reward you for what you have done, and may you receive a full reward from the LORD God of Israel, under whose wings you have come for refuge." 1Sm 24:19; Ru 1:16; Ps 17:8

[13] "My lord," she said, "I have found favor with you, for you have comforted and encouraged [A] your servant, although I am not like one of your female servants."

[14] At mealtime Boaz told her, "Come over here and have some bread and dip it in the vinegar sauce." So she sat beside the harvesters, and he offered her roasted grain. She ate and was satisfied and had some left over.

[15] When she got up to gather grain, Boaz ordered his young men, "Let her even gather grain among the bundles, and don't humiliate her. [16] Pull out some stalks from the bundles for her and leave them for her to gather. Don't rebuke her." [17] So Ruth gathered grain in the field until evening. She beat out what she had gathered, and it was about twenty-six quarts [B] of barley. [18] She picked up the grain and went into the town, where her mother-in-law saw what she had gleaned. She brought out what she had left over from her meal and gave it to her.

[19] Her mother-in-law said to her, "Where did you gather barley today, and where did you work? May the LORD bless the man who noticed you." Ps 41:1

Ruth told her mother-in-law whom she had worked with and said, "The name of the man I worked with today is Boaz."

[20] Then Naomi said to her daughter-in-law, "May the LORD bless him because he has not abandoned his kindness to the living or the dead." Naomi continued, "The man is a close relative. He is one of our family redeemers." Lv 25:25-26; 2Sm 2:5; Ru 1:8

[21] Ruth the Moabitess said, "He also told me, 'Stay with my young men until they have finished all of my harvest.'"

[22] So Naomi said to her daughter-in-law Ruth, "My daughter, it is good for you to work [C] with his female servants, so that nothing will happen to you in another field." [23] Ruth stayed close to Boaz's female servants and gathered grain until the barley and the wheat harvests were finished. And she lived with [D] her mother-in-law. Dt 16:9

Ruth's Appeal to Boaz

3 Ruth's mother-in-law Naomi said to her, "My daughter, shouldn't I find rest for you, so that you will be taken care of? [2] Now isn't Boaz our relative? Haven't you been working with his female servants? This evening he will be winnowing barley on the threshing floor. [3] Wash, put on perfumed oil, and wear your best clothes. Go down to the threshing floor, but don't let the man know you are there until he has finished eating and drinking. [4] When he lies down, notice the place where he's lying, go in and uncover his feet, and lie down. Then he will explain to you what you should do." Dt 25:5-10

[5] So Ruth said to her, "I will do everything you say." [E] [6] She went down to the threshing floor and did everything her mother-in-law had charged her to do. [7] After Boaz

[A]**2:13** Lit *and spoken to the heart of*   [B]**2:17** Lit *about an ephah*   [C]**2:22** Lit *go out*   [D]**2:23** Some Hb mss, Vg read *she returned to*   [E]**3:5** Alt Hb tradition reads *say to me* ate, drank, and was in good spirits, [A] he went to lie down at the end of the pile of barley, and she came secretly, uncovered his feet, and lay down.

[8] At midnight, Boaz was startled, turned over, and there lying at his feet was a woman! [9] So he asked, "Who are you?"

"I am Ruth, your servant," she replied. "Take me under your wing, [B] for you are a family redeemer."

[10] Then he said, "May the LORD bless you, my daughter. You have shown more kindness now than before, [C] because you have not pursued younger men, whether rich or poor. [11] Now don't be afraid, my daughter. I will do for you whatever you say, [D] since all the people in my town [E] know that you are a woman of noble character. [12] Yes, it is true that I am a family redeemer, but there is a redeemer closer than I am. [13] Stay here tonight, and in the morning, if he wants to redeem you, that's good. Let him redeem you. But if he doesn't want to redeem you, as the LORD lives, I will. Now lie down until morning."

[14] So she lay down at his feet until morning but got up while it was still dark. [F] Then Boaz said, "Don't let it be known that a [G] woman came to the threshing floor." [15] And he told Ruth, "Bring the shawl you're wearing and hold it out." When she held it out, he shoveled six measures of barley into her shawl, and she [H] went into the town.

[16] She went to her mother-in-law, Naomi, who asked her, "What happened, [I] my daughter?"

Then Ruth told her everything the man had done for her. [17] She said, "He gave me these six measures of barley, because he said, [J] 'Don't go back to your mother-in-law empty-handed.'"

[18] Naomi said, "My daughter, wait until you find out how things go, for he won't rest unless he resolves this today."

Ruth and Boaz Marry

4 Boaz went to the gate of the town and sat down there. Soon the family redeemer Boaz had spoken about came by. Boaz said, "Come over here [K] and sit down." So he went over and sat down. [2] Then Boaz took ten men of the town's elders and said, "Sit here." And they sat down. [3] He said to the redeemer, "Naomi, who has returned from the territory of Moab, is selling the portion of the field that belonged to our brother Elimelech. [4] I thought I should inform you: [L] Buy it back in the presence of those seated here and in the presence of the elders of my people. If you want to redeem it, do it. But if you do [M] not want to redeem it, tell me so that I will know, because there isn't anyone other than you to redeem it, and I am next after you." Ru 3:11-12; 2Sm 15:2; 18:4,24,33; 19:8

"I want to redeem it," he answered.

[5] Then Boaz said, "On the day you buy the field from Naomi, you will

---

[A]3:7 Lit *and his heart was glad*   [B]3:9 Or *"Spread the edge of your garment*; lit *"Spread the wing of your garment*; Ru 2:12   [C]3:10 Lit *kindness at the last than at the first*   [D]3:11 Some Hb mss, Orig, Syr, Tg, Vg read *say to me*   [E]3:11 Lit *all the gate of my people*   [F]3:14 Lit *up before a man could recognize his companion*   [G]3:14 LXX; MT reads *the*   [H]3:15 Some Hb mss, Aramaic, Syr, Vg; other Hb mss read *he*   [I]3:16 Lit *"Who are you*   [J]3:17 Alt Hb tradition, LXX, Syr, Tg read *said to me*   [K]4:1 Or *said, "Come here Mr. So-and-so*   [L]4:4 Lit *should uncover your ear, saying*   [M]4:4 Some Hb mss, LXX, Syr, Vg; other Hb mss read *if he does* acquire^A Ruth the Moabitess, the wife of the deceased man, to perpetuate the man's name on his property."^B Gn 38:6-11; Lv 25:23-34; Dt 25:5-10

⁶ The redeemer replied, "I can't redeem it myself, or I will ruin my own inheritance. Take my right of redemption, because I can't redeem it."

⁷ At an earlier period in Israel, a man removed his sandal and gave it to the other party in order to make any matter legally binding concerning the right of redemption or the exchange of property. This was the method of legally binding a transaction in Israel.   Dt 25:8-10

⁸ So the redeemer removed his sandal and said to Boaz, "Buy back the property yourself."

⁹ Boaz said to the elders and all the people, "You are witnesses today that I am buying from Naomi everything that belonged to Elimelech, Chilion, and Mahlon. ¹⁰ I have also acquired Ruth the Moabitess, Mahlon's widow, as my wife, to perpetuate the deceased man's name on his property, so that his name will not disappear among his relatives or from the gate of his hometown. You are witnesses today."

¹¹ All the people who were at the city gate, including the elders, said, "We are witnesses. May the LORD make the woman who is entering your house like Rachel and Leah, who together built the house of Israel. May you be powerful in Ephrathah and your name well known

in Bethlehem. ¹² May your house become like the house of Perez, the son Tamar bore to Judah, because of the offspring the LORD will give you by this young woman."

¹³ Boaz took Ruth and she became his wife. He slept with her, and the LORD granted conception to her, and she gave birth to a son. ¹⁴ The women said to Naomi, "Blessed be the LORD, who has not left you without a family redeemer today. May his name become well known in Israel. ¹⁵ He will renew your life and sustain you in your old age. Indeed, your daughter-in-law, who loves you and is better to you than seven sons, has given birth to him." ¹⁶ Naomi took the child, placed him on her lap, and became his nanny. ¹⁷ The neighbor women said, "A son has been born to Naomi," and they named him Obed.^C He was the father of Jesse, the father of David. Ru 1:16-17

David's Genealogy from Judah's Son

¹⁸ Now these are the family records of Perez:

Perez fathered Hezron,
¹⁹   Hezron fathered Ram,^D
     Ram fathered Amminadab,
²⁰   Amminadab
     fathered Nahshon,
     Nahshon fathered Salmon,
²¹   Salmon fathered Boaz,
     Boaz fathered Obed,
²²   Obed fathered Jesse,
     and Jesse fathered David.

---

^A4:5 Lit Naomi and from   ^B4:5 Alt Hb tradition reads Naomi, I will have already acquired from Ruth the Moabitess, the wife of the dead man, the privilege of raising up the name of the dead man on his property   ^C4:17 = Servant   ^D4:19 LXX reads Aram; Mt 1:3-4

1 SAMUEL

Hannah's Vow

1 There was a man from Ramathaim-zophim in^A the hill country of Ephraim. His name was Elkanah son of Jeroham, son of Elihu, son of Tohu, son of Zuph, an Ephraimite. ² He had two wives, the first named Hannah and the second Peninnah. Peninnah had children, but Hannah was childless. ³ This man would go up from his town every year to worship and to sacrifice to the Lord of Armies at Shiloh, where Eli's two sons, Hophni and Phinehas, were the Lord's priests. Dt 21:15-17; Jos 17:14-18; Jdg 17:1; 1Sm 1:19

⁴ Whenever Elkanah offered a sacrifice, he always gave portions of the meat to his wife Peninnah and to each of her sons and daughters. ⁵ But he gave a double^B portion to Hannah, for he loved her even though the Lord had kept her from conceiving. ⁶ Her rival would taunt her severely just to provoke her, because the Lord had kept Hannah from conceiving. ⁷ Year after year, when she went up to the Lord's house, her rival taunted her in this way. Hannah would weep and would not eat. ⁸ "Hannah, why are you crying?" her husband Elkanah would ask. "Why won't you eat? Why are you troubled? Am I not better to you than ten sons?"

⁹ On one occasion, Hannah got up after they ate and drank at Shiloh.^C The priest Eli was sitting on a chair by the doorpost of the Lord's temple. ¹⁰ Deeply hurt, Hannah prayed to the Lord and wept with many tears. ¹¹ Making a vow, she pleaded, "Lord of Armies, if you will take notice of your servant's affliction, remember and not forget me, and give your servant a son,^D I will give him to the Lord all the days of his life, and his hair will never be cut."^E Nm 6:5; 1Sm 3:3

¹² While she continued praying in the Lord's presence, Eli watched her mouth. ¹³ Hannah was praying silently,^F and though her lips were moving, her voice could not be heard. Eli thought she was drunk ¹⁴ and said to her, "How long are you going to be drunk? Get rid of your wine!" Gn 24:42-45; Ac 2:4,13

¹⁵ "No, my lord," Hannah replied. "I am a woman with a broken heart. I haven't had any wine or beer; I've been pouring out my heart before the Lord. ¹⁶ Don't think of me as a wicked woman; I've been praying from the depth of my anguish and resentment." 1Sm 2:12; Ps 62:8; Lk 6:45

¹⁷ Eli responded, "Go in peace, and may the God of Israel grant the request you've made of him."

¹⁸ "May your servant find favor with you," she replied. Then Hannah went on her way; she ate and no longer looked despondent.^G

Samuel's Birth and Dedication

¹⁹ The next morning Elkanah and Hannah got up early to worship before the Lord. Afterward, they

---

^A**1:1** Or *from Ramathaim, a Zuphite from* ^B**1:5** Or *gave only one* ; Hb obscure ^C**1:9** LXX adds *and presented herself before the Lord* ^D**1:11** Lit *a seed of men* ^E**1:11** Lit *and no razor will go up on his head* ^F**1:13** Lit *praying to her heart* ^G**1:18** Lit *and her face was not to her again* returned home to Ramah. Then Elkanah was intimate with his wife Hannah, and the LORD remembered her. ²⁰ After some time, ^A Hannah conceived and gave birth to a son. She named him Samuel, ^B because she said, "I requested him from the LORD."   Gn 8:1; 30:22; 1Sm 1:1,11; 2:11;

²¹ When Elkanah and all his household went up to make the annual sacrifice and his vow offering to the LORD, ²² Hannah did not go and explained to her husband, "After the child is weaned, I'll take him to appear in the LORD's presence and to stay there permanently."   Dt 12:11; 1Sm 1:3,11,28; Lk 2:22

²³ Her husband Elkanah replied, "Do what you think is best, ^C and stay here until you've weaned him. May the LORD confirm your ^D word." So Hannah stayed there and nursed her son until she weaned him. ²⁴ When she had weaned him, she took him with her to Shiloh, as well as a three-year-old bull, ^E half a bushel ^F of flour, and a clay jar of wine. Though the boy was still young, ^G she took him to the LORD's house at Shiloh. ²⁵ Then they slaughtered the bull and brought the boy to Eli.   Nm 30:10-11,13; Jos 18:1

²⁶ "Please, my lord," she said, "as surely as you live, my lord, I am the woman who stood here beside you praying to the LORD. ²⁷ I prayed for this boy, and since the LORD gave me what I asked him for, ²⁸ I now give the boy to the LORD. For as long as he lives, he is given to the LORD." Then he ^H worshiped the LORD there. ^I   1Sm 1:11-13; 2Kg 2:2,4,6

Hannah's Triumphant Prayer

2 Hannah prayed: Ps 72:20; Hab 3:1

My heart rejoices
   in the LORD;   Ps 75:4-5,10; 92:10
my horn is lifted up
   by the LORD.
My mouth boasts
   over my enemies,
because I rejoice
   in your salvation.   Is 12:2-3

² There is no one holy
   like the LORD.   Ex 15:11
There is no one besides you!
And there is no rock
   like our God.   2Sm 7:22; Ps 18:31

³ Do not boast so proudly,
   or let arrogant words come
      out of your mouth,
for the LORD is a God
   of knowledge,
and actions are weighed
   by him.   Pr 16:2; 24:12

⁴ The bows of the warriors
   are broken,   Ps 37:15; 46:9
but the feeble are clothed
   with strength.   Ps 18:39

⁵ Those who are full hire
   themselves out for food,
but those who are starving
   hunger no more.
The woman who is childless
   gives birth to seven,   Ru 4:15
but the woman
   with many sons pines away.

⁶ The LORD brings death
   and gives life;   Dt 32:39
he sends some down
   to Sheol, and he raises
      others up.   Is 26:19

⁷ The LORD brings poverty
   and gives wealth;   Dt 8:17-18
he humbles and he exalts.

---

^A**1:20** Lit *In the turning of the days* ^B**1:20** In Hb, the name *Samuel* sounds like the phrase "requested from God." ^C**1:23** Lit *what is good in your eyes* ^D**1:23** DSS, LXX, Syr; MT reads *his* ^E**1:24** DSS, LXX, Syr; MT reads *Shiloh with three bulls* ^F**1:24** Lit *bull and an ephah* ^G**1:24** Lit *And the youth was a young* ^H**1:28** DSS read *she*; some Hb mss, Syr, Vg read *they* ^I**1:28** LXX reads *Then she left him there before the LORD*

8 He raises the poor
from the dust   Jb 42:10-12; Ps 75:7
and lifts the needy
from the trash heap.   2Sm 7:8
He seats them with noblemen
and gives them a throne
of honor.[A]
For the foundations
of the earth are the LORD's;
he has set the world on them.
9 He guards the steps[B]
of his faithful ones,   Ps 91:11-12
but the wicked perish
in darkness,   Mt 8:12
for a person does not prevail
by his own strength.
10 Those who oppose the LORD
will be shattered;[C]   Ps 2:9
he will thunder
in the heavens against them.
The LORD will judge the ends
of the earth.   Ps 96:13; 98:9
He will give power to his king;
he will lift up the horn
of his anointed.[D]   1Sm 2:35; 12:3

11 Elkanah went home to Ramah, but the boy served the LORD in the presence of the priest Eli.   1Sm 1:1,19

Eli's Family Judged

12 Eli's sons were wicked men; they did not respect the LORD 13 or the priests' share of the sacrifices from the people. When anyone offered a sacrifice, the priest's servant would come with a three-pronged meat fork while the meat was boiling 14 and plunge it into the container, kettle, cauldron, or cooking pot. The priest would claim for himself whatever the meat fork brought up. This is the way they treated all the Israelites who came there to Shiloh. 15 Even before the fat was burned, the priest's servant would come and say to the one who was sacrificing, "Give the priest some meat to roast, because he won't accept boiled meat from you — only raw." 16 If that person said to him, "The fat must be burned first; then you can take whatever you want for yourself," the servant would reply, "No, I insist that you hand it over right now. If you don't, I'll take it by force!" 17 So the servants' sin was very severe in the presence of the LORD, because the men treated the LORD's offering with contempt.

18 Samuel served in the LORD's presence — this mere boy was dressed in the linen ephod. 19 Each year his mother made him a little robe and took it to him when she went with her husband to offer the annual sacrifice. 20 Eli would bless Elkanah and his wife: "May the LORD give you children by this woman in place of the one she[E] has given to the LORD." Then they would go home.   1Sm 2:11,28; 3:1

21 The LORD paid attention to Hannah's need, and she conceived and gave birth to three sons and two daughters. Meanwhile, the boy Samuel grew up in the presence of the LORD.   Gn 21:1; 1Sm 2:26; 3:19-21; Lk 2:40

22 Now Eli was very old. He heard about everything his sons were doing to all Israel and how they were sleeping with the women who served at the entrance to the tent of meeting. 23 He said to them, "Why are you doing these things? I have heard about your evil actions from all these people. 24 No, my sons, the news I hear the LORD's people

[A]2:8 DSS, LXX add *He gives the vow of the one who makes a vow and he blesses the years of the just.*
[B]2:9 Lit *feet*   [C]2:10 DSS, LXX read *The LORD shatters those who dispute with him*   [D]2:10 Or *Messiah*
[E]2:20 DSS; MT reads *he*

spreading is not good. [25] If one person sins against another, God can intercede for him, but if a person sins against the LORD, who can intercede for him?" But they would not listen to their father, since the LORD intended to kill them. [26] By contrast, the boy Samuel grew in stature and in favor with the LORD and with people. Ex 5:2; 38:8; 1Sm 2:13-17

[27] A man of God came to Eli and said to him, "This is what the LORD says: 'Didn't I reveal myself to your forefather's family [A] when they were in Egypt and belonged to Pharaoh's palace? [28] Out of all the tribes of Israel, I chose your house [B] to be my priests, to offer sacrifices on my altar, to burn incense, and to wear an ephod in my presence. I also gave your forefather's family all the Israelite fire offerings. [29] Why, then, do all of you despise my sacrifices and offerings that I require at the place of worship? You have honored your sons more than me, by making yourselves fat with the best part of all of the offerings of my people Israel.' Dt 33:1

[30] "Therefore, this is the declaration of the LORD, the God of Israel: 'I did say that your family and your forefather's family would walk before me forever. But now,' this is the LORD's declaration, 'no longer! For those who honor me I will honor, but those who despise me will be disgraced. [31] Look, the days are coming when I will cut off your strength and the strength of your forefather's house, so that none in your family will reach old age. [32] You will see distress in the place of worship, in spite of all that is good in Israel, and no one in your family will ever again reach old age. [33] Any man from your family I do not cut off from my altar will bring grief [C] and sadness to you. All your descendants will die violently. [D, E] [34] This will be the sign that will come to you concerning your two sons Hophni and Phinehas: both of them will die on the same day.

[35] "Then I will raise up a faithful priest for myself. He will do whatever is in my heart and mind. I will establish a lasting dynasty for him, and he will walk before my anointed one for all time. [36] Anyone who is left in your family will come and bow down to him for a piece of silver or a loaf of bread. He will say: Please appoint me to some priestly office so I can have a piece of bread to eat.' " 1Sm 3:20; 8:3-5; 1Kg 11:38; 12:3; 16:13

Samuel's Call

3 The boy Samuel served the LORD in Eli's presence. In those days the word of the LORD was rare and prophetic visions were not widespread. 1Sm 2:11,18; Ps 74:9; Ezk 7:26; Am 8:11-12

[2] One day Eli, whose eyesight was failing, was lying in his usual place. [3] Before the lamp of God had gone out, Samuel was lying down in the temple of the LORD, where the ark of God was located. Ex 27:20-21; 1Sm 4:15

[4] Then the LORD called Samuel, [F] and he answered, "Here I am." [5] He ran to Eli and said, "Here I am; you called me."

"I didn't call," Eli replied. "Go back and lie down." So he went and lay down.

[6] Once again the LORD called, "Samuel!"

Samuel got up, went to Eli, and said, "Here I am; you called me."

"I didn't call, my son," he replied. "Go back and lie down."

⁷ Now Samuel did not yet know the LORD, because the word of the LORD had not yet been revealed to him. ⁸ Once again, for the third time, the LORD called Samuel. He got up, went to Eli, and said, "Here I am; you called me."

Then Eli understood that the LORD was calling the boy. ⁹ He told Samuel, "Go and lie down. If he calls you, say, 'Speak, LORD, for your servant is listening.'" So Samuel went and lay down in his place.

¹⁰ The LORD came, stood there, and called as before, "Samuel, Samuel!"

Samuel responded, "Speak, for your servant is listening."

¹¹ The LORD said to Samuel, "I am about to do something in Israel that everyone who hears about it will shudder.ᴬ ¹² On that day I will carry out against Eli everything I said about his family, from beginning to end. ¹³ I told him that I am going to judge his family forever because of the iniquity he knows about: his sons are cursing God,ᴮ and he has not stopped them. ¹⁴ Therefore, I have sworn to Eli's family: The iniquity of Eli's family will never be wiped out by either sacrifice or offering." Dt 17:12; 1Sm 2:27-36; 2Kg 21:12; Jr 19:3;

¹⁵ Samuel lay down until the morning; then he opened the doors of the LORD's house. He was afraid to tell Eli the vision, ¹⁶ but Eli called him and said, "Samuel, my son."

"Here I am," answered Samuel.

¹⁷ "What was the message he gave you?" Eli asked. "Don't hide it from me. May God punish you and do so severely if you hide anything from me that he told you." ¹⁸ So Samuel told him everything and did not hide anything from him. Eli responded, "He is the LORD. Let him do what he thinks is good."ᶜ Lv 10:3

¹⁹ Samuel grew, and the LORD was with him, and he fulfilled everything Samuel prophesied.ᴰ ²⁰ All Israel from Dan to Beer-sheba knew that Samuel was a confirmed prophet of the LORD. ²¹ The LORD continued to appear in Shiloh, because there he revealed himself to

4 Samuel by his word. ¹ And Samuel's words came to all Israel.

The Ark Captured by the Philistines

Israel went out to meet the Philistines in battle andᴱ camped at Ebenezer while the Philistines camped at Aphek. ² The Philistines lined up in battle formation against Israel, and as the battle intensified, Israel was defeated by the Philistines, who struck down about four thousand men on the battlefield.

³ When the troops returned to the camp, the elders of Israel asked, "Why did the LORD defeat us today before the Philistines? Let's bring the ark of the LORD's covenant from Shiloh. Then itᶠ will go with us and save us from our enemies." ⁴ So the people sent men to Shiloh to bring back the ark of the covenant of the LORD of Armies, who is enthroned between the cherubim. Eli's two sons, Hophni and Phinehas, were there with the ark of the covenant of God. ⁵ When the ark of the covenant of the LORD entered

---

ᴬ**3:11** Lit about it, his two ears will tingle; Hb obscure   ᴮ**3:13** LXX, Old Lat; MT reads them   ᶜ**3:18** Lit what is good in his eyes   ᴰ**3:19** Lit he let none of his words fall to the ground   ᴱ**4:1** LXX reads In those days the Philistines gathered together to fight against Israel, and Israel went out to engage them in battle. They   ᶠ**4:3** or he the camp, all the Israelites raised such a loud shout that the ground shook. Ex 25:22; Nm 10:35; Jos 6:6; 7:7-8 ⁶ The Philistines heard the sound of the war cry and asked, "What's this loud shout in the Hebrews' camp?" When the Philistines discovered that the ark of the LORD had entered the camp, ⁷ they panicked. "A god has entered their camp!" they said. "Woe to us, nothing like this has happened before.ᴬ ⁸ Woe to us, who will rescue us from these magnificent gods? These are the gods that slaughtered the Egyptians with all kinds of plagues in the wilderness. ⁹ Show some courage and be men, Philistines! Otherwise, you'll serve the Hebrews just as they served you. Now be men and fight!" Jdg 13:1; 1Sm 14:21; 1Co 16:13 ¹⁰ So the Philistines fought, and Israel was defeated, and each man fled to his tent. The slaughter was severe — thirty thousand of the Israelite foot soldiers fell. ¹¹ The ark of God was captured, and Eli's two sons, Hophni and Phinehas, died. Dt 28:15,25; 1Sm 4:2; 2Sm 18:17; 2Kg 14:12

Eli's Death and Ichabod's Birth

¹² That same day, a Benjaminite man ran from the battle and came to Shiloh. His clothes were torn, and there was dirt on his head. ¹³ When he arrived, there was Eli sitting on his chair beside the road watching, because he was anxious about the ark of God. When the man entered the city to give a report, the entire city cried out. Jos 7:6,22; 1Sm 8:11 ¹⁴ Eli heard the outcry and asked, "Why this commotion?" The man quickly came and reported to Eli. ¹⁵ At that time Eli was ninety-eight

years old, and his eyes didn't moveᴮ because he couldn't see. 1Kg 14:4 ¹⁶ The man said to Eli, "I'm the one who came from the battle.ᶜ I fled from there today."

"What happened, my son?" Eli asked. 2Sm 1:4 ¹⁷ The messenger answered, "Israel has fled from the Philistines, and also there was a great slaughter among the people. Your two sons, Hophni and Phinehas, are both dead, and the ark of God has been captured." ¹⁸ When he mentioned the ark of God, Eli fell backward off the chair by the city gate, and since he was old and heavy, his neck broke and he died. Eli had judged Israel forty years. 1Sm 4:13 ¹⁹ Eli's daughter-in-law, the wife of Phinehas, was pregnant and about to give birth. When she heard the news about the capture of God's ark and the deaths of her father-in-law and her husband, she collapsed and gave birth because her labor pains came on her. ²⁰ As she was dying,ᴰ the women taking care of her said, "Don't be afraid. You've given birth to a son!" But she did not respond or pay attention. ²¹ She named the boy Ichabod,ᴱ saying, "The glory has departed from Israel," referring to the capture of the ark of God and to the deaths of her father-in-law and her husband. ²² "The glory has departed from Israel," she said, "because the ark of God has been captured." Gn 35:16-19

The Ark in Philistine Hands

5 After the Philistines had captured the ark of God, they took it from Ebenezer to Ashdod, ² brought it into the temple

---

ᴬ4:7 Lit yesterday or the day before   ᴮ4:15 Lit his eyes stood; 1Kg 14:4   ᶜ4:16 LXX reads camp
ᴰ4:20 LXX reads And in her time of delivery, she was about to die   ᴱ4:21 = Where Is Glory?

of Dagon[A] and placed it next to his statue.[B] ³ When the people of Ashdod got up early the next morning, there was Dagon, fallen with his face to the ground before the ark of the LORD. So they took Dagon and returned him to his place. ⁴ But when they got up early the next morning, there was Dagon, fallen with his face to the ground before the ark of the LORD. This time, Dagon's head and both of his hands were broken off and lying on the threshold. Only Dagon's torso remained.[C] ⁵ That is why, still today, the priests of Dagon and everyone who enters the temple of Dagon in Ashdod do not step on Dagon's threshold. _{Jos 13:3; Jdg 16:23-24; 1Sm 4:1; 7:12}

⁶ The LORD's hand was heavy on the people of Ashdod. He terrified the people of Ashdod and its territory and afflicted them with tumors.[D,E] ⁷ When the people of Ashdod saw what was happening, they said, "The ark of Israel's God must not stay here with us, because his hand is strongly against us and our god Dagon." ⁸ So they called all the Philistine rulers together and asked, "What should we do with the ark of Israel's God?" _{Ex 9:3; 1Sm 6:5}

"The ark of Israel's God should be moved to Gath," they replied. So they moved the ark of Israel's God. ⁹ After they had moved it, the LORD's hand was against the city of Gath, causing a great panic. He afflicted the people of the city, from the youngest to the oldest, with an outbreak of tumors. _{1Sm 5:11; 7:13}

¹⁰ The people of Gath then sent the ark of God to Ekron, but when it got there, the Ekronites cried out, "They've moved the ark of Israel's God to us to kill us and our people!"[F]

¹¹ The Ekronites called all the Philistine rulers together. They said, "Send the ark of Israel's God away. Let it return to its place so it won't kill us and our people!"[G] For the fear of death pervaded the city; God's hand was oppressing them. ¹² Those who did not die were afflicted with tumors, and the outcry of the city went up to heaven.

The Return of the Ark

6 When the ark of the LORD had been in Philistine territory for seven months, ² the Philistines summoned the priests and the diviners and pleaded, "What should we do with the ark of the LORD? Tell us how we can send it back to its place." _{Gn 41:8; Ex 7:11; Is 2:6}

³ They replied, "If you send the ark of Israel's God away, do not send it without an offering. Send back a guilt offering to him, and you will be healed. Then the reason his hand hasn't been removed from you will be revealed."[H] _{Lv 5:15-16; Dt 16:16}

⁴ They asked, "What guilt offering should we send back to him?"

And they answered, "Five gold tumors and five gold mice corresponding to the number of Philistine rulers, since there was one plague for both you[I] and your rulers. ⁵ Make images of your tumors

---

[A]5:2 A Philistine god of the sea, grain, or storm [B]5:2 Lit *to Dagon* [C]5:4 LXX; Hb reads *Only Dagon remained on it* [D]5:6 LXX adds *He brought up mice against them, and they swarmed in their ships. Then mice went up into the land and there was a mortal panic in the city*. [E]5:6 Perhaps bubonic plague [F]5:10 DSS, LXX read *"Why have you moved . . . people?"* [G]5:11 DSS, LXX read *"Why don't you return it to . . . people?"* [H]6:3 DSS, LXX read *healed, and an atonement shall be made for you. Shouldn't his hand be removed from you?"* [I]6:4 Some Hb mss, LXX; other Hb mss read *them* and of your mice that are destroying the land. Give glory to Israel's God, and perhaps he will stop oppressing you, [A] your gods, and your land. [6] Why harden your hearts as the Egyptians and Pharaoh hardened theirs? When he afflicted them, didn't they send Israel away, and Israel left?   Jos 13:3; 1Sm 5:6,9,12; 6:17

[7] "Now then, prepare one new cart and two milk cows that have never been yoked. Hitch the cows to the cart, but take their calves away and pen them up. [8] Take the ark of the LORD, place it on the cart, and put the gold objects that you're sending him as a guilt offering in a box beside the ark. Send it off and let it go its way. [9] Then watch: If it goes up the road to its homeland toward Beth-shemesh, it is the LORD who has made this terrible trouble for us. However, if it doesn't, we will know that it was not his hand that punished us — it was just something that happened to us by chance."   Nm 19:2; 1Sm 6:4-5

[10] The men did this: They took two milk cows, hitched them to the cart, and confined their calves in the pen. [11] Then they put the ark of the LORD on the cart, along with the box containing the gold mice and the images of their tumors. [12] The cows went straight up the road to Beth-shemesh. They stayed on that one highway, lowing as they went; they never strayed to the right or to the left. The Philistine rulers were walking behind them to the territory of Beth-shemesh.   1Sm 6:9

[13] The people of Beth-shemesh were harvesting wheat in the valley, and when they looked up and saw the ark, they were overjoyed to see it. [14] The cart came to the field of Joshua of Beth-shemesh and stopped there near a large rock. The people of the city chopped up the cart and offered the cows as a burnt offering to the LORD. [15] The Levites removed the ark of the LORD, along with the box containing the gold objects, and placed them on the large rock. That day the people of Beth-shemesh offered burnt offerings and made sacrifices to the LORD. [16] When the five Philistine rulers observed this, they returned to Ekron that same day.   Nm 4:1-33; Jos 13:3; 1Kg 19:21

[17] As a guilt offering to the LORD, the Philistines had sent back one gold tumor for each city: Ashdod, Gaza, Ashkelon, Gath, and Ekron. [18] The number of gold mice also corresponded to the number of Philistine cities of the five rulers, the fortified cities and the outlying villages. The large rock [B] on which the ark of the LORD was placed is still in the field of Joshua of Beth-shemesh today.   Dt 3:5; 1Sm 6:4,14-15

[19] God struck down the people of Beth-shemesh because they looked inside the ark of the LORD. [C] He struck down seventy persons. [D] The people mourned because the LORD struck them with a great slaughter. [20] The people of Beth-shemesh asked, "Who is able to stand in the presence of the LORD this holy God? To whom should the ark go from here?"   Nm 4:15-20; 17:13; 2Sm 6:7; Ps 76:7

[21] They sent messengers to the residents of Kiriath-jearim, saying,

---

[A] 6:5 Lit will lighten the heaviness of his hand from you   [B] 6:18 Some Hb mss, DSS, LXX, Tg; other Hb mss read meadow   [C] 6:19 LXX reads But the sons of Jeconiah did not rejoice with the men of Beth-shemesh when they saw the ark of the LORD.   [D] 6:19 Some Hb mss, Josephus; other Hb mss read 70 men, 50,000 men

"The Philistines have returned the ark of the LORD. Come down and get it."[A] Jos 9:17; 15:9,60

7 So the people of Kiriath-jearim came for the ark of the LORD and took it to Abinadab's house on the hill. They consecrated his son Eleazar to take care of it. 2Sm 6:3-4

Victory at Mizpah

[2] Time went by until twenty years had passed since the ark had been taken to Kiriath-jearim. Then the whole house of Israel longed for the LORD. [3] Samuel told them, "If you are returning to the LORD with all your heart, get rid of the foreign gods and the Ashtoreths that are among you, dedicate yourselves to[B] the LORD, and worship only him. Then he will rescue you from the Philistines." [4] So the Israelites removed the Baals and the Ashtoreths and only worshiped the LORD.

[5] Samuel said, "Gather all Israel at Mizpah, and I will pray to the LORD on your behalf." [6] When they gathered at Mizpah, they drew water and poured it out in the LORD's presence. They fasted that day, and there they confessed, "We have sinned against the LORD." And Samuel judged the Israelites at Mizpah.

[7] When the Philistines heard that the Israelites had gathered at Mizpah, their rulers marched up toward Israel. When the Israelites heard about it, they were afraid because of the Philistines. [8] The Israelites said to Samuel, "Don't stop crying out to the LORD our God for us, so that he will save us from the Philistines."

[9] Then Samuel took a young lamb and offered it as a whole burnt offering to the LORD. He cried out to the LORD on behalf of Israel, and the LORD answered him. [10] Samuel was offering the burnt offering as the Philistines approached to fight against Israel. The LORD thundered loudly against the Philistines that day and threw them into such confusion that they were defeated by Israel. [11] Then the men of Israel charged out of Mizpah and pursued the Philistines striking them down all the way to a place below Beth-car. Lv 22:27; 1Sm 2:10; Ps 99:6; Jr 15:1

[12] Afterward, Samuel took a stone and set it upright between Mizpah and Shen. He named it Ebenezer,[C] explaining, "The LORD has helped us to this point." [13] So the Philistines were subdued and[D] did not invade Israel's territory again. The LORD's hand was against the Philistines all of Samuel's life. [14] The cities from Ekron to Gath, which they had taken from Israel, were restored; Israel even rescued their surrounding territories from Philistine control. There was also peace between Israel and the Amorites. Jos 4:9; 1Sm 13:5

[15] Samuel judged Israel throughout his life. [16] Every year he would go on a circuit to Bethel, Gilgal, and Mizpah and would judge Israel at all these locations. [17] Then he would return to Ramah because his home was there, he judged Israel there, and he built an altar to the LORD there. 1Sm 1:1,19; 2:11; 7:6; 12:11

Israel's Demand for a King

8 When Samuel grew old, he appointed his sons as judges over Israel. [2] His firstborn son's name was Joel and his second was Abijah. They were judges in Beer-sheba.

[A]6:21 Lit and bring it up to you   [B]7:3 Lit you and set your hearts on   [C]7:12 = Stone of Help   [D]7:13 LXX reads The LORD humbled the Philistines and they

³ However, his sons did not walk in his ways — they turned toward dishonest profit, took bribes, and perverted justice. Gn 22:19; Dt 16:18-19

⁴ So all the elders of Israel gathered together and went to Samuel at Ramah. ⁵ They said to him, "Look, you are old, and your sons do not walk in your ways. Therefore, appoint a king to judge us the same as all the other nations have."

⁶ When they said, "Give us a king to judge us," Samuel considered their demand wrong, so he prayed to the LORD. ⁷ But the LORD told him, "Listen to the people and everything they say to you. They have not rejected you; they have rejected me as their king. ⁸ They are doing the same thing to you that they have done to me,ᴬ since the day I brought them out of Egypt until this day, abandoning me and worshiping other gods. ⁹ Listen to them, but solemnly warn them and tell them about the customary rights of the king who will reign over them."

¹⁰ Samuel told all the LORD's words to the people who were asking him for a king. ¹¹ He said, "These are the rights of the king who will reign over you: He will take your sons and put them to his use in his chariots, on his horses, or running in front of his chariots. ¹² He can appoint them for his use as commanders of thousands or commanders of fifties, to plow his ground and reap his harvest, or to make his weapons of war and the equipment for his chariots. ¹³ He can take your daughters to become perfumers, cooks, and bakers. ¹⁴ He can take your best fields, vineyards, and olive orchards and give them to his servants. ¹⁵ He can take a tenth of your grain and your vineyards and give them to his officials and servants. ¹⁶ He can take your male servants, your female servants, your best young men,ᴮ and your donkeys and use them for his work. ¹⁷ He can take a tenth of your flocks, and you yourselves can become his servants. ¹⁸ When that day comes, you will cry out because of the king you've chosen for yourselves, but the LORD won't answer you on that day." Nm 31:14

¹⁹ The people refused to listen to Samuel. "No!" they said. "We must have a king over us. ²⁰ Then we'll be like all the other nations: our king will judge us, go out before us, and fight our battles." Nm 27:17; 1Sm 18:13

²¹ Samuel listened to all the people's words and then repeated them to the LORD.ᶜ ²² "Listen to them," the LORD told Samuel. "Appoint a king for them." 1Sm 8:7

Then Samuel told the men of Israel, "Each of you, go back to your city."

Saul Anointed King

9 There was a prominent man of Benjamin named Kish son of Abiel, son of Zeror, son of Becorath, son of Aphiah, son of a Benjaminite. ² He had a son named Saul, an impressive young man. There was no one more impressive among the Israelites than he. He stood a head taller than anyone else.ᴰ 1Sm 14:51

³ One day the donkeys of Saul's father Kish wandered off. Kish said to his son Saul, "Take one of the servants with you and go look for the donkeys." ⁴ Saul and his servant went through the hill country of Ephraim and then through the

---

ᴬ8:8 LXX; MT omits *to me*   ᴮ8:16 LXX reads *best cattle*   ᶜ8:21 Lit *them in the LORD's ears*   ᴰ9:2 Lit *From his shoulder and up higher than any of the people*

region of Shalishah, but they didn't find them. They went through the region of Shaalim — nothing. Then they went through the Benjaminite region but still didn't find them.

⁵ When they came to the land of Zuph, Saul said to the servant who was with him, "Come on, let's go back, or my father will stop worrying about the donkeys and start worrying about us."   1Sm 1:1; 10:2

⁶ "Look," the servant said, "there's a man of God in this city who is highly respected; everything he says is sure to come true. Let's go there now. Maybe he'll tell us which way we should go."   Dt 33:1; 2Kg 5:8

⁷ "Suppose we do go," Saul said to his servant, "what do we take the man? The food from our packs is gone, and there's no gift to take to the man of God. What do we have?"

⁸ The servant answered Saul: "Here, I have a littleᴬ silver. I'll give it to the man of God, and he will tell us which way we should go."

⁹ Formerly in Israel, a man who was going to inquire of God would say, "Come, let's go to the seer," for the prophet of today was formerly called the seer.   2Sm 24:11; 1Ch 9:22; 26:28

¹⁰ "Good," Saul replied to his servant. "Come on, let's go." So they went to the city where the man of God was. ¹¹ As they were climbing the hill to the city, they found some young women coming out to draw water and asked, "Is the seer here?"

¹² The women answered, "Yes, he is ahead of you. Hurry, he just now entered the city, because there's a sacrifice for the people at the high place today. ¹³ As soon as you enter the city, you will find him before he goes to the high place to eat. The people won't eat until he comes because he must bless the sacrifice; after that, the guests can eat. Go up immediately — you can find him now." ¹⁴ So they went up toward the city.   Nm 28:11-15; 1Sm 7:17; 10:5

Saul and his servant were entering the city when they saw Samuel coming toward them on his way to the high place. ¹⁵ Now the day before Saul's arrival, the LORD had informed Samuel, ᴮ ¹⁶ "At this time tomorrow I will send you a man from the land of Benjamin. Anoint him ruler over my people Israel. He will save them from the Philistines because I have seen the affliction of my people, for their cry has come to me." ¹⁷ When Samuel saw Saul, the LORD told him, "Here is the man I told you about; he will govern my people."   Ex 3:7,9; 1Sm 10:1; 15:1; Ac 13:21

¹⁸ Saul approached Samuel in the city gate and asked, "Would you please tell me where the seer's house is?"

¹⁹ "I am the seer," Samuel answered. ꟲ "Go up ahead of me to the high place and eat with me today. When I send you off in the morning, I'll tell you everything that's in your heart. ²⁰ As for the donkeys that wandered away from you three days ago, don't worry about them because they've been found. And who does all Israel desire but you and all your father's family?"   1Sm 8:5; 9:3; 12:13

²¹ Saul responded, "Am I not a Benjaminite from the smallest of Israel's tribes and isn't my clan the least important of all the clans of the Benjaminite tribe? So why have you said something like this to me?"   Jdg 20:46-48; 1Sm 15:17

ᴬ9:8 Lit a quarter of a shekel (about a tenth of an ounce)   ᴮ9:15 Lit had uncovered Samuel's ear, saying
ꟲ9:19 Lit answered Saul

²² Samuel took Saul and his servant, brought them to the banquet hall, and gave them a place at the head of the thirty ^A or so men who had been invited. ²³ Then Samuel said to the cook, "Get the portion of meat that I gave you and told you to set aside."

²⁴ The cook picked up the thigh and what was attached to it and set it before Saul. Then Samuel said, "Notice that the reserved piece is set before you. Eat it because it was saved for you for this solemn event at the time I said, 'I've invited the people.'" So Saul ate with Samuel that day. ²⁵ Afterward, they went down from the high place to the city, and Samuel spoke with Saul on the roof. ^B Ex 29:22,27; Lv 7:32-33; Nm 18:18

²⁶ They got up early, and just before dawn, Samuel called to Saul on the roof, "Get up, and I'll send you on your way!" Saul got up, and both he and Samuel went outside. ²⁷ As they were going down to the edge of the city, Samuel said to Saul, "Tell the servant to go on ahead of us, but you stay for a while, and I'll reveal the word of God to you." So the servant went on.

10 Samuel took the flask of oil, poured it out on Saul's head, kissed him, and said, "Hasn't the LORD anointed you ruler over his inheritance? ^C ² Today when you leave me, you'll find two men at Rachel's Grave at Zelzah in the territory of Benjamin. They will say to you, 'The donkeys you went looking for have been found, and now your father has stopped being concerned about the donkeys and is worried about you, asking: What should I do about my son?' Ex 30:23-33; 1Sm 16:13

³ "You will proceed from there until you come to the oak of Tabor. Three men going up to God at Bethel will meet you there, one bringing three goats, one bringing three loaves of bread, and one bringing a clay jar of wine. ⁴ They will ask how you are and give you two loaves ^D of bread, which you will accept from them. Gn 28:19; 35:8

⁵ "After that you will come to Gibeah of God where there are Philistine garrisons. ^E When you arrive at the city, you will meet a group of prophets coming down from the high place prophesying. They will be preceded by harps, tambourines, flutes, and lyres. ⁶ The Spirit of the LORD will come powerfully on you, you will prophesy with them, and you will be transformed. ⁷ When these signs have happened to you, do whatever your circumstances require ^F because God is with you. ⁸ Afterward, go ahead of me to Gilgal. I will come to you to offer burnt offerings and to sacrifice fellowship offerings. Wait seven days until I come to you and show you what to do." 1Sm 13:2-3; Ec 9:10

⁹ When Saul turned around ^G to leave Samuel, God changed his heart, ^H and all the signs came about that day. ¹⁰ When Saul and his servant arrived at Gibeah, a group of prophets met him. Then the Spirit of God came powerfully on him, and he prophesied along with them.

---

^A **9:22** LXX reads *70*   ^B **9:25** LXX reads *city. They prepared a bed for Saul on the roof, and he slept.*
^C **10:1** LXX adds *And you will reign over the LORD's people, and you will save them from the hand of their enemies all around. And this is the sign to you that the LORD has anointed you ruler over his inheritance.*
^D **10:4** DSS, LXX read *wave offerings*   ^E **10:5** Or *governors*   ^F **10:7** Lit *do for yourself whatever your hand finds*   ^G **10:9** Lit *turned his shoulder*   ^H **10:9** Lit *God turned to him another heart*

¹¹ Everyone who knew him previously and saw him prophesy with the prophets asked each other, "What has happened to the son of Kish? Is Saul also among the prophets?" 1Sm 19:24; Am 7:14-15; Mt 13:54-57

¹² Then a man who was from there asked, "And who is their father?"

As a result, "Is Saul also among the prophets?" became a popular saying. ¹³ Then Saul finished prophesying and went to the high place.

¹⁴ Saul's uncle asked him and his servant, "Where did you go?"

"To look for the donkeys," Saul answered. "When we saw they weren't there, we went to Samuel."

¹⁵ "Tell me," Saul's uncle asked, "what did Samuel say to you?"

¹⁶ Saul told him, "He assured us the donkeys had been found." However, Saul did not tell him what Samuel had said about the matter of kingship.

Saul Received as King

¹⁷ Samuel summoned the people to the LORD at Mizpah ¹⁸ and said to the Israelites, "This is what the LORD, the God of Israel, says: 'I brought Israel out of Egypt, and I rescued you from the power of the Egyptians and all the kingdoms that were oppressing you.' ¹⁹ But today you have rejected your God, who saves you from all your troubles and afflictions. You said to him, 'You ᴬ must set a king over us.' Now therefore present yourselves before the LORD by your tribes and clans." Jdg 6:8-9; 1Sm 7:5; 8:6-7,19

²⁰ Samuel had all the tribes of Israel come forward, and the tribe of Benjamin was selected. ²¹ Then he had the tribe of Benjamin come forward by its clans, and the Matrite clan was selected. ᴮ Finally, Saul son of Kish was selected. But when they searched for him, they could not find him. ²² They again inquired of the LORD, "Has the man come here yet?" Ex 28:30; Nm 27:21; Jos 7:16-18

The LORD replied, "There he is, hidden among the supplies."

²³ They ran and got him from there. When he stood among the people, he stood a head taller than anyone else. ᶜ ²⁴ Samuel said to all the people, "Do you see the one the LORD has chosen? There is no one like him among the entire population." Dt 17:15; 1Sm 9:2; 2Sm 21:6

And all the people shouted, ᴰ "Long live the king!" 1Kg 1:25,34,39

²⁵ Samuel proclaimed to the people the rights of kingship. He wrote them on a scroll, which he placed in the presence of the LORD. Then Samuel sent all the people home. Dt 17:18-20; 1Sm 8:11-17

²⁶ Saul also went to his home in Gibeah, and brave men whose hearts God had touched went with him. ²⁷ But some wicked men said, "How can this guy save us?" They despised him and did not bring him a gift, but Saul said nothing. ᴱ,ᶠ

ᴬ10:19 Some Hb mss, LXX, Syr, Vg read You said, 'No, you ᴮ10:21 LXX adds And he had the Matrite clan come forward, man by man. ᶜ10:23 Lit people, and he was higher than any of the people from his shoulder and up ᴰ10:24 LXX reads acknowledged and said ᴱ10:27 DSS add Nahash king of the Ammonites had been severely oppressing the Gadites and Reubenites. He gouged out the right eye of each of them and brought fear and trembling on Israel. Of the Israelites beyond the Jordan none remained whose right eye Nahash, king of the Ammonites, had not gouged out. But there were seven thousand men who had escaped from the Ammonites and entered Jabesh-gilead. ᶠ10:27 Lit gift, and he was like a mute person

Saul's Deliverance of Jabesh-gilead

11 Nahash[A] the Ammonite came up and laid siege to Jabesh-gilead. All the men of Jabesh said to him, "Make a treaty with us, and we will serve you." 1Sm 12:12

² Nahash the Ammonite replied, "I'll make one with you on this condition: that I gouge out everyone's right eye and humiliate all Israel."

³ "Don't do anything to us for seven days," the elders of Jabesh said to him, "and let us send messengers throughout the territory of Israel. If no one saves us, we will surrender to you."

⁴ When the messengers came to Gibeah, Saul's hometown, and told the terms to[B] the people, all wept aloud. ⁵ Just then Saul was coming in from the field behind his oxen. "What's the matter with the people? Why are they weeping?" Saul inquired, and they repeated to him the words of the men from Jabesh.

⁶ When Saul heard these words, the Spirit of God suddenly came powerfully on him, and his anger burned furiously. ⁷ He took a team of oxen, cut them in pieces, and sent them throughout the territory of Israel by messengers who said, "This is what will be done to the ox of anyone who doesn't march behind Saul and Samuel." As a result, the terror of the LORD fell on the people, and they went out united.

⁸ Saul counted them at Bezek. There were three hundred thousand[C] Israelites and thirty thousand[D] men from Judah. ⁹ He told the messengers who had come, "Tell this to the men of Jabesh-gilead: 'Deliverance will be yours tomorrow by the time the sun is hot.'" So the messengers told the men of Jabesh, and they rejoiced. Jdg 1:5

¹⁰ Then the men of Jabesh said to Nahash, "Tomorrow we will come out, and you can do whatever you want[E] to us."

¹¹ The next day Saul organized the troops into three divisions. During the morning watch, they invaded the Ammonite camp and slaughtered them until the heat of the day. There were survivors, but they were so scattered that no two of them were left together.

Saul's Confirmation as King

¹² Afterward, the people said to Samuel, "Who said that Saul should not[F] reign over us? Give us those men so we can kill them!" 1Sm 10:27

¹³ But Saul ordered, "No one will be executed this day, for today the LORD has provided deliverance in Israel." Ex 14:13; 1Sm 19:5

¹⁴ Then Samuel said to the people, "Come, let's go to Gilgal, so we can renew the kingship there." ¹⁵ So all the people went to Gilgal, and there in the LORD's presence they made Saul king. There they sacrificed fellowship offerings in the LORD's presence, and Saul and all the men of Israel rejoiced greatly.

Samuel's Final Public Speech

12 Then Samuel said to all Israel, "I have carefully listened to everything you said to me and placed a king over you. ² Now you can see that the king is leading you. As for me, I'm old and gray, and my sons are here with you. I

[A]**11:1** DSS, LXX read *About a month later, Nahash*   [B]**11:4** Lit *in the ears of*   [C]**11:8** LXX reads *600,000*
[D]**11:8** DSS, LXX read *70,000*   [E]**11:10** Lit *do what is good in your eyes*   [F]**11:12** Some Hb mss, LXX; other Hb mss omit *not*

have led you from my youth until now. ³ Here I am. Bring charges against me before the LORD and his anointed: Whose ox or donkey have I taken? Whom have I wronged or mistreated? From whom have I accepted a bribe to overlook something?^(A,B) I will return it to you."

⁴ "You haven't wronged us, you haven't mistreated us, and you haven't taken anything from anyone," they responded.

⁵ He said to them, "The LORD is a witness against you, and his anointed is a witness today that you haven't found anything in my hand."   Ex 22:4; Ac 23:9; 24:20

"He is a witness," they said.

⁶ Then Samuel said to the people, "The LORD, who appointed Moses and Aaron and who brought your ancestors up from the land of Egypt, is a witness.^C ⁷ Now present yourselves, so I may confront you before the LORD about all the righteous acts he has done for you and your ancestors.   Ex 6:26

⁸ "When Jacob went to Egypt,^D your ancestors cried out to the LORD, and he sent them Moses and Aaron, who led your ancestors out of Egypt and settled them in this place. ⁹ But they forgot the LORD their God, so he handed them over to Sisera commander of the army of Hazor, to the Philistines, and to the king of Moab. These enemies fought against them. ¹⁰ Then they cried out to the LORD and said, 'We have sinned, for we abandoned the LORD and worshiped the Baals and the Ashtoreths. Now rescue us from the power of our enemies, and we

will serve you.' ¹¹ So the LORD sent Jerubbaal, Barak,^E Jephthah, and Samuel. He rescued you from the power of the enemies around you, and you lived securely. ¹² But when you saw that Nahash king of the Ammonites was coming against you, you said to me, 'No, we must have a king reign over us' — even though the LORD your God is your king.   Ex 2:23-25; 3:1-10; Jdg 4:1-2; 11:1

¹³ "Now here is the king you've chosen, the one you requested. Look, this is the king the LORD has placed over you. ¹⁴ If you fear the LORD, worship and obey him, and if you don't rebel against the LORD's command, then both you and the king who reigns over you will follow the LORD your God. ¹⁵ However, if you disobey the LORD and rebel against his command, the LORD's hand will be against you as it was against your ancestors.^F   1Sm 10:24

¹⁶ "Now, therefore, present yourselves and see this great thing that the LORD will do before your eyes. ¹⁷ Isn't the wheat harvest today? I will call on the LORD, and he will send thunder and rain so that you will recognize^G what an immense evil you committed in the LORD's sight by requesting a king for yourselves." ¹⁸ Samuel called on the LORD, and on that day the LORD sent thunder and rain. As a result, all the people greatly feared the LORD and Samuel.   Ex 14:13; Pr 26:1

¹⁹ They pleaded with Samuel, "Pray to the LORD your God for your servants so we won't die! For we have added to all our sins the evil of requesting a king for ourselves."

---

^A 12:3 LXX reads bribe or a pair of shoes? Testify against me.   ^B 12:3 Lit bribe and will hide my eyes with it?   ^C 12:6 LXX; MT omits is a witness   ^D 12:8 LXX reads "When Jacob and his sons went to Egypt and Egypt humbled them   ^E 12:11 LXX, Syr; MT reads Bedan; Jdg 4:6; Heb 11:32   ^F 12:15 LXX against you and against your king   ^G 12:17 Lit know and see

²⁰ Samuel replied, "Don't be afraid. Even though you have committed all this evil, don't turn away from following the LORD. Instead, worship the LORD with all your heart. ²¹ Don't turn away to follow worthless ^A things that can't profit or rescue you; they are worthless. ²² The LORD will not abandon his people, because of his great name and because he has determined to make you his own people.   Dt 11:16; Is 44:9-20

²³ "As for me, I vow that I will not sin against the LORD by ceasing to pray for you. I will teach you the good and right way. ²⁴ Above all, fear the LORD and worship him faithfully with all your heart; consider the great things he has done for you. ²⁵ However, if you continue to do what is evil, both you and your king will be swept away."

Saul's Failure

13 Saul was thirty years ^B old when he became king, and he reigned forty-two years ^C over Israel. ^D ² He chose three thousand men from Israel for himself: two thousand were with Saul at Michmash and in Bethel's hill country, and one thousand were with Jonathan in Gibeah of Benjamin. He sent the rest of the troops away, each to his own tent.   1Sm 14:31

³ Jonathan attacked the Philistine garrison ^E that was in Geba, and the Philistines heard about it. So Saul blew the ram's horn throughout the land saying, "Let the Hebrews hear!" ^F ⁴ And all Israel heard the news, "Saul has attacked the Philistine garrison, and Israel is now repulsive to the Philistines." Then the troops were summoned to join Saul at Gilgal.   1Sm 10:5; 13:16; 14:5

⁵ The Philistines also gathered to fight against Israel: three thousand ^G chariots, six thousand horsemen, and troops as numerous as the sand on the seashore. They went up and camped at Michmash, east of Beth-aven. ^H   Jos 11:4; 1Sm 14:23

⁶ The men of Israel saw that they were in trouble because the troops were in a difficult situation. They hid in caves, in thickets, among rocks, and in holes and cisterns. ⁷ Some Hebrews even crossed the Jordan to the land of Gad and Gilead.   Jdg 6:2

Saul, however, was still at Gilgal, and all his troops were gripped with fear. ⁸ He waited seven days for the appointed time that Samuel had set, but Samuel didn't come to Gilgal, and the troops were deserting him. ⁹ So Saul said, "Bring me the burnt offering and the fellowship offerings." Then he offered burnt offering.   1Sm 10:8

¹⁰ Just as he finished offering the burnt offering, Samuel arrived. So Saul went out to greet him, ¹¹ and Samuel asked, "What have you done?"

Saul answered, "When I saw that the troops were deserting me and you didn't come within the appointed days and the Philistines were gathering at Michmash, ¹² I thought, 'The Philistines will now descend on me at Gilgal, and I haven't sought the LORD's favor.' So I forced myself to offer the burnt offering."

---

^A 12:21 LXX reads *away after empty*   ^B 13:1 Some LXX mss; MT reads *was one year*   ^C 13:1 Text emended; MT reads *two years*   ^D 13:1 Some LXX mss omit v. 1   ^E 13:3 Or *governor*, also in v. 4   ^F 13:3 LXX reads *"The slaves have revolted"*   ^G 13:5 One LXX ms, Syr; MT reads *30,000*   ^H 13:5 LXX reads *Michmash, opposite Beth-horon to the south*

¹³ Samuel said to Saul, "You have been foolish. You have not kept the command the LORD your God gave you. It was at this time that the LORD would have permanently established your reign over Israel, ¹⁴ but now your reign will not endure. The LORD has found a man after his own heart, ^A and the LORD has appointed him as ruler over his people, because you have not done what the LORD commanded." ¹⁵ Then Samuel went ^B from Gilgal to Gibeah in Benjamin. Saul registered the troops who were with him, about six hundred men.

¹⁶ Saul, his son Jonathan, and the troops who were with them were staying in Geba of Benjamin, and the Philistines were camped at Michmash. ¹⁷ Raiding parties went out from the Philistine camp in three divisions. One division headed toward the Ophrah road leading to the land of Shual. ¹⁸ The next division headed toward the Bethhoron road, and the last division headed down the border road that looks out over the Zeboim Valley toward the wilderness. 1Sm 13:2-3; 14:15

¹⁹ No blacksmith could be found in all the land of Israel because the Philistines had said, "Otherwise, the Hebrews will make swords or spears." ²⁰ So all the Israelites went to the Philistines to sharpen their plows, mattocks, axes, and sickles. ^C ²¹ The price was two-thirds of a shekel ^D for plows and mattocks, and one-third of a shekel for pitchforks and axes, and for putting a point on a cattle prod. ²² So on the day of battle not a sword or spear could be found in the hand of any of the troops who were with Saul and Jonathan; only Saul and his son Jonathan had weapons. Jdg 5:8

Jonathan's Victory over the Philistines

²³ Now a Philistine garrison took control of the pass at Michmash.

14 ¹ That same day Saul's son Jonathan said to the attendant who carried his weapons, "Come on, let's cross over to the Philistine garrison on the other side." However, he did not tell his father.

² Saul was staying under the pomegranate tree in Migron on the outskirts of Gibeah. ^E The troops with him numbered about six hundred. ³ Ahijah, who was wearing an ephod, was also there. He was the son of Ahitub, the brother of Ichabod son of Phinehas, son of Eli the LORD's priest at Shiloh. But the troops did not know that Jonathan had left. 1Sm 1:3; 13:15-16; Is 10:28

⁴ There were sharp columns ^F of rock on both sides of the pass that Jonathan intended to cross to reach the Philistine garrison. One was named Bozez and the other Seneh; ⁵ one stood to the north in front of Michmash and the other to the south in front of Geba. ⁶ Jonathan said to the attendant who carried his weapons, "Come on, let's cross over to the garrison of these uncircumcised men. Perhaps the LORD will help us. Nothing can keep the LORD from saving, whether by many or by few." 1Sm 13:23; 17:26,36

⁷ His armor-bearer responded, "Do what is in your heart. You

choose. I'm right here with you whatever you decide."

8 "All right," Jonathan replied, "we'll cross over to the men and then let them see us. 9 If they say, 'Wait until we reach you,' then we will stay where we are and not go up to them. 10 But if they say, 'Come on up,' then we'll go up, because the LORD has handed them over to us — that will be our sign."

11 They let themselves be seen by the Philistine garrison, and the Philistines said, "Look, the Hebrews are coming out of the holes where they've been hiding!" 12 The men of the garrison called to Jonathan and his armor-bearer. "Come on up, and we'll teach you a lesson!" they said.

"Follow me," Jonathan told his armor-bearer, "for the LORD has handed them over to Israel." 13 Jonathan climbed up using his hands and feet, with his armor-bearer behind him. Jonathan cut them down, and his armor-bearer followed and finished them off. 14 In that first assault Jonathan and his armor-bearer struck down about twenty men in a half-acre field.   2Sm 5:24

A Defeat for the Philistines

15 Terror spread through the Philistine camp and the open fields to all the troops. Even the garrison and the raiding parties were terrified. The earth shook, and terror spread from God. A 16 When Saul's watchmen in Gibeah of Benjamin looked, they saw the panicking troops scattering in every direction. 17 So Saul said to the troops with him, "Call the roll and determine who has left us." They called the roll and saw that Jonathan and his armor-bearer were gone.   1Sm 7:10; 13:17-18; 2Kg 7:6

18 Saul told Ahijah, "Bring the ark of God," for it was with the Israelites B at that time. 19 While Saul spoke to the priest, the panic in the Philistine camp increased in intensity. So Saul said to the priest, "Stop what you're doing." C   Nm 27:21

20 Saul and all the troops with him assembled and marched to the battle, and there the Philistines were, fighting against each other in great confusion! 21 There were Hebrews from the area who had gone earlier into the camp to join the Philistines, but even they joined the Israelites who were with Saul and Jonathan. 22 When all the Israelite men who had been hiding in the hill country of Ephraim heard that the Philistines were fleeing, they also joined Saul and Jonathan in the battle. 23 So the LORD saved Israel that day.

Saul's Rash Oath

The battle extended beyond Bethaven, 24 and the men of Israel were worn out that day, for Saul had D placed the troops under an oath: "The man who eats food before evening, before I have taken vengeance on my enemies is cursed." So none of the troops tasted any food.

25 Everyone E went into the forest, and there was honey on the ground. 26 When the troops entered the forest, they saw the flow of honey, but none of them ate any of it F because they feared the oath. 27 However, Jonathan had not heard his father make the troops swear the oath. He reached out with the

end of the staff he was carrying and dipped it into the honeycomb. When he ate the honey,[A] he had renewed energy.[B] 28 Then one of the troops said, "Your father made the troops solemnly swear, 'The man who eats food today is cursed,' and the troops are exhausted." 1Sm 14:43

29 Jonathan replied, "My father has brought trouble to the land. Just look at how I have renewed energy[C] because I tasted a little of this honey. 30 How much better if the troops had eaten freely today from the plunder they took from their enemies! Then the slaughter of the Philistines would have been much greater." 1Kg 18:17-18

31 The Israelites struck down the Philistines that day from Michmash all the way to Aijalon. Since the Israelites were completely exhausted, 32 they rushed to the plunder, took sheep, goats, cattle, and calves, slaughtered them on the ground, and ate meat with the blood still in it. 33 Some reported to Saul: "Look, the troops are sinning against the LORD by eating meat with the blood still in it." Gn 9:4; Jos 10:12; 1Sm 14:5; 15:19

Saul said, "You have been unfaithful. Roll a large stone over here at once." 34 He then said, "Go among the troops and say to them, 'Let each man bring me his ox or his sheep. Do the slaughtering here and then you can eat. Don't sin against the LORD by eating meat with the blood in it.'" So everyone of the troops brought his ox that night and slaughtered it there. 35 Then Saul built an altar to the LORD; it was the first time he had built an altar to the LORD. 1Sm 7:12,17

36 Saul said, "Let's go down after the Philistines tonight and plunder them until morning. Don't let even one remain!"

"Do whatever you want,"[D] the troops replied.

But the priest said, "Let's approach God here." Jdg 18:5-6; 1Sm 14:3,18-19

37 So Saul inquired of God, "Should I go after the Philistines? Will you hand them over to Israel?" But God did not answer him that day. 1Sm 10:22; 28:6

38 Saul said, "All you leaders of the troops, come here. Let us investigate[E] how this sin has occurred today. 39 As surely as the LORD lives who saves Israel, even if it is because of my son Jonathan, he must die!" Not one of the troops answered him.

40 So he said to all Israel, "You will be on one side, and I and my son Jonathan will be on the other side."

And the troops replied, "Do whatever you want."

41 So Saul said to the LORD, "God of Israel, why have you not answered your servant today? If the unrighteousness is in me or in my son Jonathan, LORD God of Israel, give Urim; but if the fault is in your people Israel, give Thummim."[F] Jonathan and Saul were selected, and the troops were cleared of the charge. Ac 1:24

42 Then Saul said, "Cast the lot between me and my son Jonathan," and Jonathan was selected. 43 Saul commanded him, "Tell me what you did." Jos 7:19

Jonathan told him, "I tasted a little honey with the end of the staff I was carrying. I am ready to die!"

A 14:27 Lit he returned his hand to his mouth   B 14:27 Lit his eyes became bright   C 14:29 Lit how my eyes became bright   D 14:36 Lit Do what is good in your eyes, also in v. 40   E 14:38 Lit know and see
F 14:41 LXX; MT reads said to the LORD, "God of Israel, give us the right decision."

⁴⁴ Saul declared to him, "May God punish me and do so severely if you do not die, Jonathan!" 1Sm 25:22

⁴⁵ But the people said to Saul, "Must Jonathan die, who accomplished such a great deliverance for Israel? No, as the LORD lives, not a hair of his head will fall to the ground, for he worked with God's help today." So the people redeemed Jonathan, and he did not die. ⁴⁶ Then Saul gave up the pursuit of the Philistines, and the Philistines returned to their own territory. 2Sm 14:11; 1Kg 1:52

Summary of Saul's Kingship

⁴⁷ When Saul assumed the kingship over Israel, he fought against all his enemies in every direction: against Moab, the Ammonites, Edom, the kings of Zobah, and the Philistines. Wherever he turned, he caused havoc.ᴬ ⁴⁸ He fought bravely, defeated the Amalekites, and rescued Israel from those who plundered them. 1Sm 11:1-13; 15:3,7; 2Sm 8:3-10

⁴⁹ Saul's sons were Jonathan, Ishvi, and Malchishua. The names of his two daughters were Merab, his firstborn, and Michal, the younger. ⁵⁰ The name of Saul's wife was Ahinoam daughter of Ahimaaz. The name of the commander of his army was Abner son of Saul's uncle Ner. ⁵¹ Saul's father was Kish. Abner's father was Ner son of Abiel.

⁵² The conflict with the Philistines was fierce all of Saul's days, so whenever Saul noticed any strong or valiant man, he enlisted him.

Saul Rejected as King

15 Samuel told Saul, "The LORD sent me to anoint you as king over his people Israel. Now, listen to the words of the LORD. ² This is

what the LORD of Armies says: 'I witnessedᴮ what the Amalekites did to the Israelites when they opposed them along the way as they were coming out of Egypt. ³ Now go and attack the Amalekites and completely destroy everything they have. Do not spare them. Kill men and women, infants and nursing babies, oxen and sheep, camels and donkeys.'" Ex 17:8-16; 1Sm 9:16

⁴ Then Saul summoned the troops and counted them at Telaim: two hundred thousand foot soldiers and ten thousand men from Judah. ⁵ Saul came to the city of Amalek and set up an ambush in the wadi. ⁶ He warned the Kenites, "Since you showed kindness to all the Israelites when they came out of Egypt, go on and leave! Get away from the Amalekites, or I'll sweep you away with them." So the Kenites withdrew from the Amalekites. Ex 18:9-10; Nm 10:29-32; Jdg 1:16; 4:11

⁷ Then Saul struck down the Amalekites from Havilah all the way to Shur, which is next to Egypt. ⁸ He captured King Agag of Amalek alive, but he completely destroyed all the rest of the people with the sword. ⁹ Saul and the troops spared Agag, and the best of the sheep, goats, cattle, and choice animals,ᶜ as well as the young rams and the best of everything else. They were not willing to destroy them, but they did destroy all the worthless and unwanted things. 1Sm 14:48; Est 3:1

¹⁰ Then the word of the LORD came to Samuel, ¹¹ "I regret that I made Saul king, for he has turned away from following me and has not carried out my instructions." So Samuel became angry and cried out to the LORD all night. Gn 6:6-7; Ex 32:14

ᴬ14:47 LXX reads *he was victorious*   ᴮ15:2 LXX reads *I will avenge*   ᶜ15:9 Lit *and the second ones*

¹² Early in the morning Samuel got up to confront Saul, but it was reported to Samuel, "Saul went to Carmel where he set up a monument for himself. Then he turned around and went down to Gilgal." ¹³ When Samuel came to him, Saul said, "May the LORD bless you. I have carried out the LORD's instructions." Jos 15:55; 1Sm 13:13-14; 25:2

¹⁴ Samuel replied, "Then what is this sound of sheep, goats,ᴬ and cattle I hear?"

¹⁵ Saul answered, "The troops brought them from the Amalekites and spared the best sheep, goats, and cattle in order to offer a sacrifice to the LORD your God, but the rest we destroyed." Gn 3:12-13

¹⁶ "Stop!" exclaimed Samuel. "Let me tell you what the LORD said to me last night."

"Tell me," he replied.

¹⁷ Samuel continued, "Although you once considered yourself unimportant, have you not become the leader of the tribes of Israel? The LORD anointed you king over Israel ¹⁸ and then sent you on a mission and said: 'Go and completely destroy the sinful Amalekites. Fight against them until you have annihilated them.' ¹⁹ So why didn't you obey the LORD? Why did you rush on the plunder and do what was evil in the LORD's sight?" 1Sm 9:21

²⁰ "But I did obey the LORD!" Saul answered.ᴮ "I went on the mission the LORD gave me: I brought back King Agag of Amalek, and I completely destroyed the Amalekites. ²¹ The troops took sheep, goats, and cattle from the plunder — the best of what was set apart for destruction — to sacrifice to the LORD your God at Gilgal." Ex 32:22-23

²² Then Samuel said:

Does the LORD take pleasure
    in burnt offerings
    and sacrifices   Ps 40:6-8; 51:16-17
as much as in obeying
    the LORD?

Look: to obey is better
    than sacrifice,
to pay attention is better
    than the fat of rams.   Heb 10:5-7
²³ For rebellion is like the sin
    of divination,   Dt 18:10
and defiance is
    like wickedness
    and idolatry.   Gn 31:19,34
Because you have rejected
    the word of the LORD,
he has rejected you as king.

²⁴ Saul answered Samuel, "I have sinned. I have transgressed the LORD's command and your words. Because I was afraid of the people, I obeyed them. ²⁵ Now therefore, please forgive my sin and return with me so I can worship the LORD."

²⁶ Samuel replied to Saul, "I will not return with you. Because you rejected the word of the LORD, the LORD has rejected you from being king over Israel." ²⁷ When Samuel turned to go, Saul grabbed the corner of his robe, and it tore. ²⁸ Samuel said to him, "The LORD has torn the kingship of Israel away from you today and has given it to your neighbor who is better than you. ²⁹ Furthermore, the Eternal One of Israel does not lie or change his mind, for he is not man who changes his mind." 1Sm 13:14; 16:1; 28:17-18

³⁰ Saul said, "I have sinned. Please honor me now before the elders of my people and before Israel. Come back with me so I can bow

ᴬ15:14 Lit sheep in my ears   ᴮ15:20 Lit answered Samuel

in worship to the LORD your God." ³¹ Then Samuel went back, following Saul, and Saul bowed down to the LORD.   Is 29:13; Jn 12:43

³² Samuel said, "Bring me King Agag of Amalek."

Agag came to him trembling,ᴬ for he thought, "Certainly the bitterness of death has come."ᴮ˒ᶜ

³³ Samuel declared:

As your sword has made
    women childless,
so your mother will be
    childless among women.

Then he hacked Agag to pieces before the LORD at Gilgal.

³⁴ Samuel went to Ramah, and Saul went up to his home in Gibeah of Saul. ³⁵ Even to the day of his death, Samuel never saw Saul again. Samuel mourned for Saul, and the LORD regretted he had made Saul king over Israel. 1Sm 7:17

Samuel Anoints David

16 The LORD said to Samuel, "How long are you going to mourn for Saul, since I have rejected him as king over Israel? Fill your horn with oil and go. I am sending you to Jesse of Bethlehem because I have selected a king from his sons."

² Samuel asked, "How can I go? Saul will hear about it and kill me!"

The LORD answered, "Take a young cow with you and say, 'I have come to sacrifice to the LORD.' ³ Then invite Jesse to the sacrifice, and I will let you know what you are to do. You are to anoint for me the one I indicate to you." 1Sm 20:29

⁴ Samuel did what the LORD directed and went to Bethlehem. When the elders of the town met him, they trembledᴰ and asked, "Doᴱ you come in peace?" Gn 48:7

⁵ "In peace," he replied. "I've come to sacrifice to the LORD. Consecrate yourselves and come with me to the sacrifice."ᶠ Then he consecrated Jesse and his sons and invited them to the sacrifice. ⁶ When they arrived, Samuel saw Eliab and said, "Certainly the LORD's anointed one is here before him." Gn 35:2; Ex 19:10

⁷ But the LORD said to Samuel, "Do not look at his appearance or his stature because I have rejected him. Humans do not see what the LORD sees,ᴳ for humans see what is visible,ᴴ but the LORD sees the heart."

⁸ Jesse called Abinadab and presented him to Samuel. "The LORD hasn't chosen this one either," Samuel said. ⁹ Then Jesse presented Shammah, but Samuel said, "The LORD hasn't chosen this one either." ¹⁰ After Jesse presented seven of his sons to him, Samuel told Jesse, "The LORD hasn't chosen any of these." ¹¹ Samuel asked him, "Are these all the sons you have?" 1Sm 17:13

"There is still the youngest," he answered, "but right now he's tending the sheep." Samuel told Jesse, "Send for him. We won't sit down to eat until he gets here." ¹² So Jesse sent for him. He had beautiful eyes and a healthy,ᴵ handsome appearance. 1Sm 17:12,42; 2Sm 13:3

Then the LORD said, "Anoint him, for he is the one." ¹³ So Samuel took the horn of oil and anointed him in the presence of his brothers, and the Spirit of the LORD came powerfully on David from that day

---

ᴬ15:32 Hb obscure   ᴮ15:32 LXX reads "Is death bitter in this way?"   ᶜ15:32 Lit turned   ᴰ16:4 LXX reads were astonished   ᴱ16:4 DSS, LXX read "Seer, do   ᶠ16:5 LXX reads and rejoice with me today   ᴳ16:7 LXX reads God does not see as a man sees   ᴴ16:7 Lit for the man sees according to the eyes   ᴵ16:12 Or ruddy forward. Then Samuel set out and went to Ramah.   1Sm 9:17; 10:1; Ezk 36:27

David in Saul's Court

¹⁴ Now the Spirit of the LORD had left Saul, and an evil spirit sent from the LORD began to torment him, ¹⁵ so Saul's servants said to him, "You see that an evil spirit from God is tormenting you. ¹⁶ Let our lord command your servants here in your presence to look for someone who knows how to play the lyre. Whenever the evil spirit from God comes on you, that person can play the lyre, and you will feel better."   1Sm 11:6; 18:10,12; 19:9; 28:15; 2Kg 3:15

¹⁷ Then Saul commanded his servants, "Find me someone who plays well and bring him to me."

¹⁸ One of the young men answered, "I have seen a son of Jesse of Bethlehem who knows how to play the lyre. He is also a valiant man, a warrior, eloquent, handsome, and the LORD is with him."

¹⁹ Then Saul dispatched messengers to Jesse and said, "Send me your son David, who is with the sheep." ²⁰ So Jesse took a donkey loaded with bread, a wineskin, and one young goat and sent them by his son David to Saul. ²¹ When David came to Saul and entered his service, Saul loved him very much, and David became his armor-bearer. ²² Then Saul sent word to Jesse: "Let David remain in my service, for he has found favor with me." ²³ Whenever the spirit from God came on Saul, David would pick up his lyre and play, and Saul would then be relieved, feel better, and the evil spirit would leave him.   1Sm 10:4,27; Pr 18:16

David versus Goliath

17 The Philistines gathered their forces for war at Socoh in Judah and camped between Socoh and Azekah in Ephes-dammim. ² Saul and the men of Israel gathered and camped in the Valley of Elah; then they lined up in battle formation to face the Philistines.   Jos 10:10; 1Sm 13:5; 1Ch 11:13; 2Ch 28:18

³ The Philistines were standing on one hill, and the Israelites were standing on another hill with a ravine between them. ⁴ Then a champion named Goliath, from Gath, came out from the Philistine camp. He was nine feet, nine inches ᴬ,ᴮ tall ⁵ and wore a bronze helmet ᶜ and bronze scale armor that weighed one hundred twenty-five pounds. ᴰ ⁶ There was bronze armor on his shins, and a bronze javelin was slung between his shoulders. ⁷ His spear shaft was like a weaver's beam, and the iron point of his spear weighed fifteen pounds. ᴱ In addition, a shield-bearer was walking in front of him.   2Sm 21:18-22; 1Ch 11:23

⁸ He stood and shouted to the Israelite battle formations: "Why do you come out to line up in battle formation?" He asked them, "Am I not a Philistine and are you not servants of Saul? Choose one of your men and have him come down against me. ⁹ If he wins in a fight against me and kills me, we will be your servants. But if I win against him and kill him, then you will be our servants and serve us." ¹⁰ Then the Philistine said, "I defy the ranks of Israel today. Send me a man so we can fight each other!" ¹¹ When Saul and all Israel heard these words from the Philistine,

---

ᴬ **17:4** DSS, LXX read *four cubits and a span*   ᴮ **17:4** Lit *was six cubits and a span*   ᶜ **17:5** Lit *helmet on his head*   ᴰ **17:5** Lit *5,000 shekels*   ᴱ **17:7** Lit *600 shekels* they lost their courage and were terrified. 1Sm 8:17; 17:26,36,45; 2Sm 2:12-16

[12] Now David was the son of the Ephrathite from Bethlehem of Judah named Jesse. Jesse had eight sons and during Saul's reign was already an old man. [13] Jesse's three oldest sons had followed Saul to the war, and their names were Eliab, the firstborn, Abinadab, the next, and Shammah, the third, [14] and David was the youngest. The three oldest had followed Saul, [15] but David kept going back and forth from Saul to tend his father's flock in Bethlehem. Gn 35:19; 1Sm 16:10-11; 1Ch 2:13-15

[16] Every morning and evening for forty days the Philistine came forward and took his stand. [17] One day Jesse had told his son David: "Take this half-bushel[A] of roasted grain along with these ten loaves of bread for your brothers and hurry to their camp. [18] Also take these ten portions of cheese to the field commander.[B] Check on the well-being of your brothers and bring a confirmation from them. [19] They are with Saul and all the men of Israel in the Valley of Elah fighting with the Philistines." 1Sm 25:18

[20] So David got up early in the morning, left the flock with someone to keep it, loaded up, and set out as Jesse had charged him.

He arrived at the perimeter of the camp as the army was marching out to its battle formation shouting their battle cry. [21] Israel and the Philistines lined up in battle formation facing each other. [22] David left his supplies in the care of the quartermaster and ran to the battle line. When he arrived, he asked his brothers how they were. [23] While he was speaking with them, suddenly the champion named Goliath, the Philistine from Gath, came forward from the Philistine battle line and shouted his usual words, which David heard. [24] When all the Israelite men saw Goliath, they retreated from him terrified. Jdg 18:21; 1Sm 26:5,7

[25] Previously, an Israelite man had declared: "Do you see this man who keeps coming out? He comes to defy Israel. The king will make the man who kills him very rich and will give him his daughter. The king will also make the family of that man's father exempt from paying taxes in Israel." Jos 15:16; 1Sm 8:11

[26] David spoke to the men who were standing with him: "What will be done for the man who kills that Philistine and removes this disgrace from Israel? Just who is this uncircumcised Philistine that he should defy the armies of the living God?" Dt 5:26; 1Sm 11:2; 14:6; 17:36

[27] The troops told him about the offer, concluding, "That is what will be done for the man who kills him."

[28] David's oldest brother Eliab listened as he spoke to the men, and he became angry with him. "Why did you come down here?" he asked. "Who did you leave those few sheep with in the wilderness? I know your arrogance and your evil heart — you came down to see the battle!" Gn 37:4,8-36

[29] "What have I done now?" protested David. "It was just a question." [30] Then he turned from those beside him to others in front of him and asked about the offer. The people gave him the same answer as before. 1Sm 17:26-27

[31] What David said was overheard and reported to Saul, so he had David brought to him. [32] David said to

[A]17:17 Lit this ephah   [B]17:18 Lit the leader of 1,000

Saul, "Don't let anyone be discouraged by ^A him; your servant will go and fight this Philistine!" Dt 20:1-4

³³ But Saul replied, "You can't go fight this Philistine. You're just a youth, and he's been a warrior since he was young."

³⁴ David answered Saul: "Your servant has been tending his father's sheep. Whenever a lion or a bear came and carried off a lamb from the flock, ³⁵ I went after it, struck it down, and rescued the lamb from its mouth. If it reared up against me, I would grab it by its fur, ^B strike it down, and kill it. ³⁶ Your servant has killed lions and bears; this uncircumcised Philistine will be like one of them, for he has defied the armies of the living God." ³⁷ Then David said, "The LORD who rescued me from the paw of the lion and the paw of the bear will rescue me from the hand of this Philistine."

Saul said to David, "Go, and may the LORD be with you." 1Sm 20:13

³⁸ Then Saul had his own military clothes put on David. He put a bronze helmet on David's head and had him put on armor. ³⁹ David strapped his sword on over the military clothes and tried to walk, but he was not used to them. "I can't walk in these," David said to Saul, "I'm not used to them." So David took them off. ⁴⁰ Instead, he took his staff in his hand and chose five smooth stones from the wadi and put them in the pouch, in his shepherd's bag. Then, with his sling in his hand, he approached the Philistine. Jdg 20:16

⁴¹ The Philistine came closer and closer to David, with the shield-bearer in front of him. ⁴² When the Philistine looked and saw David, he despised him because he was just a youth, healthy ^C and handsome. ⁴³ He said to David, "Am I a dog that you come against me with sticks?" ^D Then he cursed David by his gods. ⁴⁴ "Come here," the Philistine called to David, "and I'll give your flesh to the birds of the sky and the wild beasts!"

⁴⁵ David said to the Philistine: "You come against me with a sword, spear, and javelin, but I come against you in the name of the LORD of Armies, the God of the ranks of Israel — you have defied him. ⁴⁶ Today, the LORD will hand you over to me. Today, I'll strike you down, remove your head, and give the corpses ^E of the Philistine camp to the birds of the sky and the wild creatures of the earth. Then all the world will know that Israel has a God, ⁴⁷ and this whole assembly will know that it is not by sword or by spear that the LORD saves, for the battle is the LORD's. He will hand you over to us." 2Ch 32:7-8; Ps 124:8; Is 37:20

⁴⁸ When the Philistine started forward to attack him, David ran quickly to the battle line to meet the Philistine. ⁴⁹ David put his hand in the bag, took out a stone, slung it, and hit the Philistine on his forehead. The stone sank into his forehead, and he fell facedown to the ground. ⁵⁰ David defeated the Philistine with a sling and a stone. David overpowered the Philistine and killed him without having a sword. ⁵¹ David ran and stood over him. He grabbed the Philistine's sword, pulled it from

---

^A 17:32 Lit let a man's heart fall over   ^B 17:35 LXX reads throat; lit beard   ^C 17:42 Or ruddy   ^D 17:43 Some LXX mss add and stones?" And David said, "No! Worse than a dog!"   ^E 17:46 LXX reads give your limbs and the limbs its sheath, and used it to kill him. Then he cut off his head. When the Philistines saw that their hero was dead, they fled. ⁵² The men of Israel and Judah rallied, shouting their battle cry, and chased the Philistines to the entrance of the valley and to the gates of Ekron. ᴬ Philistine bodies were strewn all along the Shaaraim road to Gath and Ekron.   1Sm 21:9; Ps 27:3; Heb 11:34

⁵³ When the Israelites returned from the pursuit of the Philistines, they plundered their camps. ⁵⁴ David took Goliath's ᴮ head and brought it to Jerusalem, but he put Goliath's weapons in his own tent.

⁵⁵ ᶜ When Saul had seen David going out to confront the Philistine, he asked Abner the commander of the army, "Whose son is this youth, Abner?"   1Sm 16:17-22; 17:25

"Your Majesty, as surely as you live, I don't know," Abner replied. ⁵⁶ The king said, "Find out whose son this young man is!"

⁵⁷ When David returned from killing the Philistine, Abner took him and brought him before Saul with the Philistine's head still in his hand. ⁵⁸ Saul said to him, "Whose son are you, young man?"   1Sm 17:54

"The son of your servant Jesse of Bethlehem," David answered.

David's Success

18 When David had finished speaking with Saul, Jonathan was bound to David in close friendship, ᴰ and loved him as much as he loved himself. ² Saul kept David with him from that day on and did not let him return to his father's house.   1Sm 20:17; 2Sm 1:26

³ Jonathan made a covenant with David because he loved him as much as himself. ⁴ Then Jonathan removed the robe he was wearing and gave it to David, along with his military tunic, his sword, his bow, and his belt.   Gn 41:42; 1Sm 20:8,16; 23:18

⁵ David marched out with the army and was successful in everything Saul sent him to do. Saul put him in command of the fighting men, which pleased all the people and Saul's servants as well.

⁶ As the troops were coming back, when David was returning from killing the Philistine, the women came out from all the cities of Israel to meet King Saul, singing and dancing with tambourines, with shouts of joy, and with three-stringed instruments. ⁷ As they danced, the women sang:

Saul has killed his thousands,
  but David his tens
    of thousands.   1Sm 21:11; 29:5

⁸ Saul was furious and resented this song. ᴱ "They credited tens of thousands to David," he complained, "but they only credited me with thousands. What more can he have but the kingdom?" ⁹ So Saul watched David jealously from that day forward.   1Sm 15:28; 24:20

Saul Attempts to Kill David

¹⁰ The next day an evil spirit sent from God came powerfully on Saul, and he began to rave ᶠ inside the palace. David was playing the lyre as usual, but Saul was holding a spear, ¹¹ and he threw it, thinking, "I'll pin David to the wall." But David got away from him twice.

ᴬ**17:52** LXX reads *Ashkelon*   ᴮ**17:54** Lit *the Philistine's*   ᶜ**17:55** LXX omits 1Sm 17:55–18:5   ᴰ**18:1** Lit *the life of Jonathan was bound to the life of David*   ᴱ**18:8** Lit *furious; this saying was evil in his eyes*   ᶠ**18:10** Or *prophesy*

¹² Saul was afraid of David, because the LORD was with David but had left Saul. ¹³ Therefore, Saul sent David away from him and made him commander over a thousand men. David led the troops ¹⁴ and continued to be successful in all his activities because the LORD was with him. ¹⁵ When Saul observed that David was very successful, he dreaded him. ¹⁶ But all Israel and Judah loved David because he was leading their troops. ¹⁷ Saul told David, "Here is my oldest daughter Merab. I'll give her to you as a wife, if you will be a warrior for me and fight the LORD's battles." But Saul was thinking, "I don't need to raise a hand against him; let the hand of the Philistines be against him." 1Sm 16:13,18; 18:15,29

¹⁸ Then David responded, "Who am I, and what is my family or my father's clan in Israel that I should become the king's son-in-law?" ¹⁹ When it was time to give Saul's daughter Merab to David, she was given to Adriel the Meholathite as a wife. Jdg 7:22; 1Sm 9:21; 18:23; 2Sm 7:18

David's Marriage to Michal

²⁰ Now Saul's daughter Michal loved David, and when it was reported to Saul, it pleased him. ᴬ ²¹ "I'll give her to him," Saul thought. "She'll be a trap for him, and the hand of the Philistines will be against him." So Saul said to David a second time, "You can now be my son-in-law." 1Sm 18:17,28

²² Saul then ordered his servants, "Speak to David in private and tell him, 'Look, the king is pleased with you, and all his servants love you.

Therefore, you should become the king's son-in-law.'"

²³ Saul's servants reported these words directly to David, ᴮ but he replied, "Is it trivial in your sight to become the king's son-in-law? I am a poor commoner." Gn 29:20; 34:12

²⁴ The servants reported back to Saul, "These are the words David spoke."

²⁵ Then Saul replied, "Say this to David: 'The king desires no other bride-price except a hundred Philistine foreskins, to take revenge on his enemies.'" Actually, Saul intended to cause David's death at the hands of the Philistines. Ex 22:17

²⁶ When the servants reported these terms to David, he was pleased ᶜ to become the king's son-in-law. Before the wedding day arrived, ᴰ ²⁷ David and his men went out and killed two hundred ᴱ Philistines. He brought their foreskins and presented them as full payment to the king to become his son-in-law. Then Saul gave his daughter Michal to David as his wife. ²⁸ Saul realized ᶠ that the LORD was with David and that his daughter Michal loved him, ²⁹ and he became even more afraid of David. As a result, Saul was David's enemy from then on. 2Sm 3:14

³⁰ Every time the Philistine commanders came out to fight, David was more successful than all of Saul's officers. So his name became well known. 1Sm 18:5; 2Sm 11:1

David Delivered from Saul

19 Saul ordered his son Jonathan and all his servants to kill David. But Saul's son Jonathan liked David very much, ² so he told him:

ᴬ **18:20** Lit *Saul, the thing was right in his eyes*   ᴮ **18:23** Lit *words in David's ears*   ᶜ **18:26** Lit *David, it was right in David's eyes*   ᴰ **18:26** Lit *And the days were not full*   ᴱ **18:27** LXX reads *100*   ᶠ **18:28** Lit *saw and knew*

"My father Saul intends to kill you. Be on your guard in the morning and hide in a secret place and stay there. ³ I'll go out and stand beside my father in the field where you are and talk to him about you. When I see what he says, I'll tell you."

⁴ Jonathan spoke well of David to his father Saul. He said to him: "The king should not sin against his servant David. He hasn't sinned against you; in fact, his actions have been a great advantage to you. ⁵ He took his life in his hands when he struck down the Philistine, and the LORD brought about a great victory for all Israel. You saw it and rejoiced, so why would you sin against innocent blood by killing David for no reason?" Gn 44:22; Pr 17:13

⁶ Saul listened to Jonathan's advice and swore an oath: "As surely as the LORD lives, David will not be killed." ⁷ So Jonathan summoned David and told him all these words. Then Jonathan brought David to Saul, and he served him as he did before. 1Sm 16:21; 18:2,10,13

⁸ When war broke out again, David went out and fought against the Philistines. He defeated them with such great force that they fled from him.

⁹ Now an evil spirit sent from the LORD came on Saul as he was sitting in his palace holding a spear. David was playing the lyre, ¹⁰ and Saul tried to pin David to the wall with the spear. As the spear struck the wall, David eluded Saul, ran away, and escaped that night. ¹¹ Saul sent agents to David's house to watch for him and kill him in the morning. But his wife Michal warned David, "If you don't escape tonight, you will be dead tomorrow!" ¹² So she lowered David from the window, and he fled and escaped. ¹³ Then Michal took the household idol and put it on the bed, placed some goat hair on its head, and covered it with a garment. ¹⁴ When Saul sent agents to seize David, Michal said, "He's sick." 1Sm 16:14-16; 18:10-11

¹⁵ Saul sent the agents back to see David and said, "Bring him on his bed so I can kill him." ¹⁶ When the agents arrived, to their surprise, the household idol was on the bed with some goat hair on its head.

¹⁷ Saul asked Michal, "Why did you deceive me like this? You sent my enemy away, and he has escaped!"

She answered him, "He said to me, 'Let me go! Why should I kill you?'"

¹⁸ So David fled and escaped and went to Samuel at Ramah and told him everything Saul had done to him. Then he and Samuel left and stayed at Naioth. 1Sm 7:17; 2Kg 6:1-2

¹⁹ When it was reported to Saul that David was at Naioth in Ramah, ²⁰ he sent agents to seize David. However, when they saw the group of prophets prophesying with Samuel leading them, the Spirit of God came on Saul's agents, and they also started prophesying. ²¹ When they reported to Saul, he sent other agents, and they also began prophesying. So Saul tried again and sent a third group of agents, and even they began prophesying. ²² Then Saul himself went to Ramah. He came to the large cistern at Secu and asked, "Where are Samuel and David?" 1Sm 19:11; Jn 7:32

"At Naioth in Ramah," someone said.

²³ So he went to Naioth in Ramah. The Spirit of God also came on him, and as he walked along, he prophesied until he entered Naioth in

Ramah. ²⁴ Saul then removed his clothes and also prophesied before Samuel; he collapsed and lay naked all that day and all that night. That is why they say, "Is Saul also among the prophets?"   1Sm 10:10

Jonathan Protects David

20 David fled from Naioth in Ramah and came to Jonathan and asked, "What have I done? What did I do wrong? How have I sinned against your father so that he wants to take my life?"   1Sm 24:9

² Jonathan said to him, "No, you won't die. Listen, my father doesn't do anything, great or small, without telling me.ᴬ So why would he hide this matter from me? This can't be true."

³ But David said, "Your father certainly knows that I have found favor with you. He has said, 'Jonathan must not know of this, or else he will be grieved.'" David also swore, "As surely as the LORD lives and as you yourself live, there is but a step between me and death."   1Sm 25:26

⁴ Jonathan said to David, "Whatever you say, I will do for you."

⁵ So David told him, "Look, tomorrow is the New Moon, and I'm supposed to sit down and eat with the king. Instead, let me go, and I'll hide in the countryside for the next two nights.ᴮ ⁶ If your father misses me at all, say, 'David urgently requested my permission to go quickly to his hometown Bethlehem for an annual sacrifice there involving the whole clan.'⁷ If he says, 'Good,' then your servant is safe, but if he becomes angry, you will know he

has evil intentions. ⁸ Deal kindly withᶜ your servant, for you have brought me into a covenant with you before the LORD. If I have done anything wrong, then kill me yourself; why take me to your father?"

⁹ "No!" Jonathan responded. "If I ever find out my father has evil intentions against you, wouldn't I tell you about it?"

¹⁰ So David asked Jonathan, "Who will tell me if your father answers you harshly?"

¹¹ He answered David, "Come on, let's go out to the countryside." So both of them went out to the countryside. ¹² "By the LORD, the God of Israel, I will sound out my father by this time tomorrow or the next day. If I find out that he is favorable toward you, will I not send for you and tell you?ᴰ ¹³ If my father intends to bring evil on you, may the LORD punish Jonathan and do so severely if I do not tell youᴱ and send you away so you may leave safely. May the LORD be with you, just as he was with my father. ¹⁴ If I continue to live, show me kindnessᶠ from the LORD, but if I die, ¹⁵ don't ever withdraw your kindness from my household — not even when the LORD cuts off every one of David's enemies from the face of the earth." ¹⁶ Then Jonathan made a covenant with the house of David, saying, "May the LORD hold David's enemies accountable."ᴳ ¹⁷ Jonathan once again swore to Davidᴴ in his love for him, because he loved him as he loved himself.   Ru 1:17; 1Sm 3:17

¹⁸ Then Jonathan said to him, "Tomorrow is the New Moon; you'll be

---

ᴬ20:2 Lit without uncovering my ear   ᴮ20:5 Lit countryside until the third night   ᶜ20:8 Or Show loyalty to   ᴰ20:12 Lit and uncover your ear   ᴱ20:13 Lit severely — I will uncover your ear   ᶠ20:14 Or loyalty, also in v. 15   ᴳ20:16 Lit LORD require it from the hand of David's enemies   ᴴ20:17 LXX; MT reads Jonathan once again made David swear missed because your seat will be empty. ¹⁹ The following day hurry down and go to the place where you hid on the day this incident began and stay beside the rock Ezel. ²⁰ I will shoot three arrows beside it as if I'm aiming at a target. ²¹ Then I will send a servant and say, 'Go and find the arrows!' Now, if I expressly say to the servant, 'Look, the arrows are on this side of you — get them,' then come, because as the LORD lives, it is safe for you and there is no problem. ²² But if I say this to the youth, 'Look, the arrows are beyond you!' then go, for the LORD is sending you away. ²³ As for the matter you and I have spoken about, the LORD will be a witness^A between you and me forever."

²⁴ So David hid in the countryside.

At the New Moon, the king sat down to eat the meal. ²⁵ He sat at his usual place on the seat by the wall. Jonathan sat facing him^B and Abner took his place beside Saul, but David's place was empty. ²⁶ Saul did not say anything that day because he thought, "Something unexpected has happened; he must be ceremonially unclean — yes, that's it, he is unclean." Lv 7:20-21; 1Sm 20:18

²⁷ However, the day after the New Moon, the second day, David's place was still empty, and Saul asked his son Jonathan, "Why didn't Jesse's son come to the meal either yesterday or today?"

²⁸ Jonathan answered, "David asked for my permission to go to Bethlehem. ²⁹ He said, 'Please let me go because our clan is holding a sacrifice in the town, and my brother has told me to be there. So now, if I have found favor with you, let me go so I can see my brothers.' That's why he didn't come to the king's table." 1Sm 20:6

³⁰ Then Saul became angry with Jonathan and shouted, "You son of a perverse and rebellious woman! Don't I know that you are siding with Jesse's son to your own shame and to the disgrace of your mother?^C ³¹ Every day Jesse's son lives on earth you and your kingship are not secure. Now send for him and bring him to me — he must die!" 2Sm 12:5

³² Jonathan answered his father back: "Why is he to be killed? What has he done?" 1Sm 19:5

³³ Then Saul threw his spear at Jonathan to kill him, so he knew that his father was determined to kill David. ³⁴ He got up from the table fiercely angry and did not eat any food that second day of the New Moon, for he was grieved because of his father's shameful behavior toward David. 1Sm 18:11; 19:10

³⁵ In the morning Jonathan went out to the countryside for the appointed meeting with David. A young servant was with him. ³⁶ He said to the servant, "Run and find the arrows I'm shooting." As the servant ran, Jonathan shot an arrow beyond him. ³⁷ He came to the location of the arrow that Jonathan had shot, but Jonathan called to him and said, "The arrow is beyond you, isn't it?" ³⁸ Then Jonathan called to him, "Hurry up and don't stop!" Jonathan's servant picked up the arrow and returned to his master. ³⁹ He did not know anything; only Jonathan and David knew the arrangement. ⁴⁰ Then Jonathan gave his equipment to the servant who

---

^A20:23 LXX; MT omits *a witness*   ^B20:25 Text emended; MT reads *Jonathan got up*   ^C20:30 Lit *your mother's nakedness* was with him and said, "Go, take it back to the city." 1Sm 20:20-22

⁴¹ When the servant had gone, David got up from the south side of the stone Ezel, fell facedown to the ground, and paid homage three times. Then he and Jonathan kissed each other and wept with each other, though David wept more.

⁴² Jonathan then said to David, "Go in the assurance the two of us pledged in the name of the LORD when we said: The LORD will be a witness between you and me and between my offspring and your offspring forever." Then David left, and Jonathan went into the city. 1Sm 20:15-23

David Flees to Nob

21 David went to the priest Ahimelech at Nob. Ahimelech was afraid to meet David, so he said to him, "Why are you alone and no one is with you?" 1Sm 14:3

² David answered the priest Ahimelech, "The king gave me a mission, but he told me, 'Don't let anyone know anything about the mission I'm sending you on or what I have ordered you to do.' I have stationed my young men at a certain place. ³ Now what do you have on hand? Give me five loaves of bread or whatever can be found."

⁴ The priest told him, "There is no ordinary bread on hand. However, there is consecrated bread, but the young men may eat it ᴬ only if they have kept themselves from women." Ex 19:15; 25:30; Lv 24:5-9; Mt 12:3-4

⁵ David answered him, "I swear that women are being kept from us, as always when I go out to battle. The young men's bodies ᴮ are

consecrated even on an ordinary mission, so of course their bodies are consecrated today." ⁶ So the priest gave him the consecrated bread, for there was no bread there except the Bread of the Presence that had been removed from the presence of the LORD. When the bread was removed, it had been replaced with warm bread. 2Sm 11:11

⁷ One of Saul's servants, detained before the LORD, was there that day. His name was Doeg the Edomite, chief of Saul's shepherds. 1Sm 22:9

⁸ David said to Ahimelech, "Do you have a spear or sword on hand? I didn't even bring my sword or my weapons since the king's mission was urgent."

⁹ The priest replied, "The sword of Goliath the Philistine, whom you killed in the Valley of Elah, is here, wrapped in a cloth behind the ephod. If you want to take it for yourself, then take it, for there isn't another one here." 1Sm 17:51

"There's none like it!" David said. "Give it to me."

David Flees to Gath

¹⁰ David fled that day from Saul's presence and went to King Achish of Gath. ¹¹ But Achish's servants said to him, "Isn't this David, the king of the land? Don't they sing about him during their dances:

Saul has killed his thousands,
    but David his tens
        of thousands?" 1Sm 18:7; 29:5

¹² David took this to heart ᶜ and became very afraid of King Achish of Gath, ¹³ so he pretended to be insane in their presence. He acted like a madman around them, ᴰ

ᴬ21:4 DSS; MT omits *may eat it*   ᴮ21:5 Lit *vessels*   ᶜ21:12 Lit *David placed these words in his heart*
ᴰ21:13 Lit *madman in their hand*

scribbling^A on the doors of the city gate and letting saliva run down his beard. ^Ps 34 title

^14 "Look! You can see the man is crazy," Achish said to his servants. "Why did you bring him to me? ^15 Do I have such a shortage of crazy people that you brought this one to act crazy around me? Is this one going to come into my house?" ^Ps 34 title

Saul's Increasing Paranoia

22 So David left Gath and took refuge in the cave of Adullam. When David's brothers and his father's whole family heard, they went down and joined him there. ^2 In addition, every man who was desperate, in debt, or discontented rallied around him, and he became their leader. About four hundred men were with him. ^Pss 57; 142 titles

^3 From there David went to Mizpeh of Moab where he said to the king of Moab, "Please let my father and mother stay with you until I know what God will do for me." ^4 So he left them in the care of the king of Moab, and they stayed with him the whole time David was in the stronghold.

^5 Then the prophet Gad said to David, "Don't stay in the stronghold. Leave and return to the land of Judah." So David left and went to the forest of Hereth. ^1Ch 21:9; 29:29

^6 Saul heard that David and his men had been discovered. At that time Saul was in Gibeah, sitting under the tamarisk tree at the high place. His spear was in his hand, and all his servants were standing around him. ^7 Saul said to his servants, "Listen, men of Benjamin: Is Jesse's son going to give all of you fields and vineyards? Do you think he'll make all of you commanders of thousands and commanders of hundreds? ^8 That's why all of you have conspired against me! Nobody tells me^B when my own son makes a covenant with Jesse's son. None of you cares about me or tells me^C that my son has stirred up my own servant to wait in ambush for me, as is the case today." ^Jdg 4:5; 1Sm 14:2

^9 Then Doeg the Edomite, who was in charge of Saul's servants, answered: "I saw Jesse's son come to Ahimelech son of Ahitub at Nob. ^10 Ahimelech inquired of the LORD for him and gave him provisions. He also gave him the sword of Goliath the Philistine." ^1Sm 21:1; Ps 52 title

Slaughter of the Priests

^11 The king sent messengers to summon the priest Ahimelech son of Ahitub, and his father's whole family, who were priests in Nob. All of them came to the king. ^12 Then Saul said, "Listen, son of Ahitub!"

"I'm at your service, my lord," he said. ^1Sm 3:4-6; 2Sm 1:7

^13 Saul asked him, "Why did you and Jesse's son conspire against me? You gave him bread and a sword and inquired of God for him, so he could rise up against me and wait in ambush, as is the case today." ^1Sm 22:8

^14 Ahimelech replied to the king: "Who among all your servants is as faithful as David? He is the king's son-in-law, captain of your bodyguard, and honored in your house. ^15 Was today the first time I inquired of God for him? Of course not! Please don't let the king make an accusation against your servant or any of my father's family,

^A 21:13 LXX reads *drumming*   ^B 22:8 Lit *No one uncovers my ear*   ^C 22:8 Lit *or uncovers my ear* for your servant didn't have any idea^A about all this." 1Sm 19:4-5

¹⁶ But the king said, "You will die, Ahimelech — you and your father's whole family!"

¹⁷ Then the king ordered the guards standing by him, "Turn and kill the priests of the LORD because they sided with David. For they knew he was fleeing, but they didn't tell me."^B But the king's servants would not lift a hand to execute the priests of the LORD.

¹⁸ So the king said to Doeg, "Go and execute the priests!" So Doeg the Edomite went and executed the priests himself. On that day, he killed eighty-five men who wore linen ephods. ¹⁹ He also struck down Nob, the city of the priests, with the sword — both men and women, infants and nursing babies, oxen, donkeys, and sheep.

²⁰ However, one of the sons of Ahimelech son of Ahitub escaped. His name was Abiathar, and he fled to David. ²¹ Abiathar told David that Saul had killed the priests of the LORD. ²² Then David said to Abiathar, "I knew that Doeg the Edomite was there that day and that he was sure to report to Saul. I myself am responsible for^C the lives of everyone in your father's family. ²³ Stay with me. Don't be afraid, for the one who wants to take my life wants to take your life. You will be safe with me." 1Sm 23:9; 30:7; 2Sm 2:1; 1Kg 2:26-27

Deliverance at Keilah

23 It was reported to David: "Look, the Philistines are fighting against Keilah and raiding the threshing floors." Jos 15:44

² So David inquired of the LORD: "Should I launch an attack against these Philistines?" 1Sm 23:4,6,9-12

The LORD answered David, "Launch an attack against the Philistines and rescue Keilah."

³ But David's men said to him, "Look, we're afraid here in Judah; how much more if we go to Keilah against the Philistine forces!"

⁴ Once again, David inquired of the LORD, and the LORD answered him: "Go at once to Keilah, for I will hand the Philistines over to you."

⁵ Then David and his men went to Keilah, fought against the Philistines, drove their livestock away, and inflicted heavy losses on them. So David rescued the inhabitants of Keilah. ⁶ Abiathar son of Ahimelech fled to David at Keilah, and he brought an ephod with him.

⁷ When it was reported to Saul that David had gone to Keilah, he said, "God has handed him over to me, for he has trapped himself by entering a town with barred gates." ⁸ Then Saul summoned all the troops to go to war at Keilah and besiege David and his men.

⁹ When David learned that Saul was plotting evil against him, he said to the priest Abiathar, "Bring the ephod." 1Sm 22:20; 23:6; 30:7

¹⁰ Then David said, "LORD God of Israel, your servant has reliable information that Saul intends to come to Keilah and destroy the town because of me. ¹¹ Will the citizens of Keilah hand me over to him? Will Saul come down as your servant has heard? LORD God of Israel, please tell your servant."

The LORD answered, "He will come down."

---

^A 22:15 Lit didn't know a thing, small or large   ^B 22:17 Lit didn't uncover my ear   ^C 22:22 LXX, Syr, Vg; MT reads I myself turn in

¹² Then David asked, "Will the citizens of Keilah hand me and my men over to Saul?"

"They will," the LORD responded. ¹³ So David and his men, numbering about six hundred, left Keilah at once and moved from place to place. When it was reported to Saul that David had escaped from Keilah, he called off the expedition. ¹⁴ David then stayed in the wilderness strongholds and in the hill country of the Wilderness of Ziph. Saul searched for him every day, but God did not hand David over to him.   Jos 15:55; 1Sm 22:2; 25:13; 2Sm 15:20

A Renewed Covenant

¹⁵ David was in the Wilderness of Ziph in Horesh when he saw that Saul had come out to take his life. ¹⁶ Then Saul's son Jonathan came to David in Horesh and encouraged him in his faith^A in God, ¹⁷ saying, "Don't be afraid, for my father Saul will never lay a hand on you. You yourself will be king over Israel, and I'll be your second-in-command. Even my father Saul knows it is true." ¹⁸ Then the two of them made a covenant in the LORD's presence. Afterward, David remained in Horesh, while Jonathan went home.   1Sm 16:1-13; 20:31; 24:20-22; 30:6

David's Narrow Escape

¹⁹ Some Ziphites came up to Saul at Gibeah and said, "David is^B hiding among us in the strongholds in Horesh on the hill of Hachilah south of Jeshimon. ²⁰ Now, whenever the king wants to come down, let him come down. Our part will be to hand him over to the king."   1Sm 23:12; 26:1; Ps 54 title

²¹ "May you be blessed by the LORD," replied Saul, "for you have shown concern for me. ²² Go and check again. Investigate^C where he goes^D and who has seen him there; they tell me he is extremely cunning. ²³ Investigate^E all the places where he hides. Then come back to me with accurate information, and I'll go with you. If it turns out he really is in the region, I'll search for him among all the clans^F of Judah." ²⁴ So they went to Ziph ahead of Saul.   1Sm 22:8

Now David and his men were in the wilderness near Maon in the Arabah south of Jeshimon, ²⁵ and Saul and his men went to look for him. When David was told about it, he went down to the rock and stayed in the Wilderness of Maon. Saul heard of this and pursued David there.   Jos 15:55; 1Sm 25:2

²⁶ Saul went along one side of the mountain and David and his men went along the other side. Even though David was hurrying to get away from Saul, Saul and his men were closing in on David and his men to capture them. ²⁷ Then a messenger came to Saul saying, "Come quickly, because the Philistines have raided the land!" ²⁸ So Saul broke off his pursuit of David and went to engage the Philistines. Therefore, that place was named the Rock of Separation. ²⁹ From there David went up and stayed in the strongholds of En-gedi.

David Spares Saul

24 When Saul returned from pursuing the Philistines, he was told, "David is in the wilderness near En-gedi." ² So Saul took

^A **23:16** Lit *and strengthened his hand*   ^B **23:19** Lit *"Is David not . . . Jeshimon?*   ^C **23:22** Lit *Know and see*
^D **23:22** Lit *watch his place where his foot will be*   ^E **23:23** Lit *See and know*   ^F **23:23** Or *thousands*

three thousand of Israel's fit young men and went to look for David and his men in front of the Rocks of the Wild Goats. [3] When Saul came to the sheep pens along the road, a cave was there, and he went in to relieve himself.[A] David and his men were staying in the recesses of the cave, [4] so they said to him, "Look, this is the day the LORD told you about: 'I will hand your enemy over to you so you can do to him whatever you desire.'" Then David got up and secretly cut off the corner of Saul's robe.   1Sm 23:19,28-29

[5] Afterward, David's conscience bothered[B] him because he had cut off the corner of Saul's robe.[C] [6] He said to his men, "I swear before the LORD: I would never do such a thing to my lord, the LORD's anointed. I will never lift my hand against him, since he is the LORD's anointed." [7] With these words David persuaded[D] his men, and he did not let them rise up against Saul.   1Sm 10:1; 2Sm 24:10

Then Saul left the cave and went on his way. [8] After that, David got up, went out of the cave, and called to Saul, "My lord the king!" When Saul looked behind him, David knelt low with his face to the ground and paid homage. [9] David said to Saul, "Why do you listen to the words of people who say, 'Look, David intends to harm you'? [10] You can see with your own eyes that the LORD handed you over to me today in the cave. Someone advised me to kill you, but I[E,F] took pity on you and said: I won't lift my hand against my lord, since he is the LORD's anointed. [11] Look, my father! Look at the corner of your robe in my hand,

for I cut it off, but I didn't kill you. Recognize[G] that I've committed no crime or rebellion. I haven't sinned against you even though you are hunting me down to take my life.

[12] "May the LORD judge between me and you, and may the LORD take vengeance on you for me, but my hand will never be against you. [13] As the old proverb says, 'Wickedness comes from wicked people.' My hand will never be against you. [14] Who has the king of Israel come after? What are you chasing after? A dead dog? A single flea? [15] May the LORD be judge and decide between you and me. May he take notice and plead my case and deliver[H] me from you."   1Sm 26:10-11,23

[16] When David finished saying these things to him, Saul replied, "Is that your voice, David my son?" Then Saul wept aloud [17] and said to David, "You are more righteous than I, for you have done what is good to me though I have done what is evil to you. [18] You yourself have told me today what good you did for me: when the LORD handed me over to you, you didn't kill me. [19] When a man finds his enemy, does he let him go unharmed?[I] May the LORD repay you with good for what you've done for me today. [20] "Now I know for certain you will be king, and the kingdom of Israel will be established[J] in your hand. [21] Therefore swear to me by the LORD that you will not cut off my descendants or wipe out my name from my father's family." [22] So David swore to Saul. Then Saul went back home, and David and his men went up to the stronghold.   1Sm 13:14

[A]24:3 Lit *to cover his feet*   [B]24:5 Lit *David's heart struck*   [C]24:5 Some Hb mss, LXX, Syr, Vg; other Hb mss omit *robe*   [D]24:7 Or *restrained*   [E]24:10 LXX, Syr, Tg; MT reads *she* or *it*   [F]24:10 Or *my eye*   [G]24:11 Lit *Know and see*   [H]24:15 Lit *render a verdict for*   [I]24:19 Lit *go on a good way*   [J]24:20 Or *will flourish*

David, Nabal, and Abigail

25 Samuel died, and all Israel assembled to mourn for him, and they buried him by his home in Ramah. David then went down to the Wilderness of Paran.[A] Dt 34:8

2 A man in Maon had a business in Carmel; he was a very rich man with three thousand sheep and one thousand goats and was shearing his sheep in Carmel. 3 The man's name was Nabal, and his wife's name, Abigail. The woman was intelligent and beautiful, but the man, a Calebite, was harsh and evil in his dealings. Jos 15:13,55; 1Sm 23:24

4 While David was in the wilderness, he heard that Nabal was shearing sheep, 5 so David sent ten young men instructing them, "Go up to Carmel, and when you come to Nabal, greet him[B] in my name. 6 Then say this: 'Long life to you,[C] and peace to you, peace to your family, and peace to all that is yours. 7 I hear that you are shearing.[D] When your shepherds were with us, we did not harass them, and nothing of theirs was missing the whole time they were in Carmel. 8 Ask your young men, and they will tell you. So let my young men find favor with you, for we have come on a feast[E] day. Please give whatever you have on hand to your servants and to your son David.'" 1Sm 23:24-25; 25:15-16; 1Ch 12:18

9 David's young men went and said all these things to Nabal on David's behalf,[F] and they waited.[G] 10 Nabal asked them, "Who is David? Who is Jesse's son? Many slaves these days are running away from their masters. 11 Am I supposed to take my bread, my water, and my meat that I butchered for my shearers and give them to these men? I don't know where they are from." Jdg 9:28

12 David's young men retraced their steps. When they returned to him, they reported all these words. 13 He said to his men, "All of you, put on your swords!" So each man put on his sword, and David also put on his sword. About four hundred men followed David while two hundred stayed with the supplies. 1Sm 23:13; 30:9-10

14 One of Nabal's young men informed Abigail, Nabal's wife: "Look, David sent messengers from the wilderness to greet our master, but he screamed at them. 15 The men treated us very well. When we were in the field, we weren't harassed and nothing of ours was missing the whole time we were living among them. 16 They were a wall around us, both day and night, the entire time we were with them herding the sheep. 17 Now consider carefully[H] what you should do, because there is certain to be trouble for our master and his entire family. He is such a worthless fool nobody can talk to him!" 1Sm 13:10; 15:13

18 Abigail hurried, taking two hundred loaves of bread, two clay jars of wine, five butchered sheep, a bushel[I] of roasted grain, one hundred clusters of raisins, and two hundred cakes of pressed figs, and loaded them on donkeys. 19 Then she said to her male servants, "Go ahead of me. I will be right behind you." But she did not tell her husband Nabal. Gn 32:16,20; 2Sm 16:1; 1Ch 12:40

A 25:1 LXX reads to Maon   B 25:5 Or Nabal, ask him for peace   C 25:6 Lit 'To life   D 25:7 Lit you have shearers   E 25:8 Lit good   F 25:9 Lit name   G 25:9 LXX reads and he became arrogant   H 25:17 Lit Now know and see   I 25:18 Lit sheep, five seahs

²⁰ As she rode the donkey down a mountain pass hidden from view, she saw David and his men coming toward her and met them. ²¹ David had just said, "I guarded everything that belonged to this man in the wilderness for nothing. He was not missing anything, yet he paid me back evil for good. ²² May God punish me ᴬ and do so severely if I let any of his males ᴮ survive until morning." 1Sm 3:17; 20:13; 1Kg 14:10

²³ When Abigail saw David, she quickly got off the donkey and knelt down with her face to the ground and paid homage to David. ²⁴ She knelt at his feet and said, "The guilt is mine, my lord, but please let your servant speak to you directly. Listen to the words of your servant. ²⁵ My lord should pay no attention to this worthless fool Nabal, for he lives up to his name: ᶜ His name means 'stupid,' and stupidity is all he knows. ᴰ I, your servant, didn't see my lord's young men whom you sent. ²⁶ Now my lord, as surely as the LORD lives and as you yourself live— it is the LORD who kept you from participating in bloodshed and avenging yourself by your own hand—may your enemies and those who intend to harm my lord be like Nabal. ²⁷ Let this gift your servant has brought to my lord be given to the young men who follow my lord. ²⁸ Please forgive your servant's offense, for the LORD is certain to make a lasting dynasty for my lord because he fights the LORD's battles. Throughout your life, may evil ᴱ not be found in you. 1Sm 20:41; 2Sm 18:32; 22:14; Heb 10:30

²⁹ "Someone is pursuing you and intends to take your life. My lord's life is tucked safely in the place ᶠ where the LORD your God protects the living, but he is flinging away your enemies' lives like stones from a sling. ³⁰ When the LORD does for my lord all the good he promised you and appoints you ruler over Israel, ³¹ there will not be remorse or a troubled conscience for my lord because of needless bloodshed or my lord's revenge. And when the LORD does good things for my lord, may you remember me your servant." Gn 40:14; 1Sm 13:14; 25:30; Jr 10:18

³² Then David said to Abigail, "Blessed be the LORD God of Israel, who sent you to meet me today! ³³ May your discernment be blessed, and may you be blessed. Today you kept me from participating in bloodshed and avenging myself by my own hand. ³⁴ Otherwise, as surely as the LORD God of Israel lives, who prevented me from harming you, if you had not come quickly to meet me, Nabal wouldn't have had any males ᴳ left by morning light." ³⁵ Then David accepted what she had brought him and said, "Go home in peace. See, I have heard what you said and have granted your request." 2Kg 5:19

³⁶ Then Abigail went to Nabal, and there he was in his house, holding a feast fit for a king. Nabal's heart was cheerful, ᴴ and he was very drunk, so she didn't say anything ᴵ to him until morning light. ³⁷ In the morning when Nabal sobered up, ᴶ his wife told him about

---

ᴬ25:22 LXX; MT reads *David's enemies*   ᴮ25:22 Lit *of those of his who are urinating against the wall*
ᶜ25:25 Lit *for as is his name is, so he is*   ᴰ25:25 Lit *and foolishness is with him*   ᴱ25:28 Or *trouble*
ᶠ25:29 Lit *bundle*   ᴳ25:34 Lit *had anyone urinating against a wall*   ᴴ25:36 Lit *Nabal's heart was good*
on him   ᴵ25:36 Lit *anything at all*   ᴶ25:37 Lit *when the wine had gone out of Nabal*

these events. His heart died^A and he became a stone. ³⁸ About ten days later, the LORD struck Nabal dead.

³⁹ When David heard that Nabal was dead, he said, "Blessed be the LORD who championed my cause against Nabal's insults and restrained his servant from doing evil. The LORD brought Nabal's evil deeds back on his own head."

Then David sent messengers to speak to Abigail about marrying him. ⁴⁰ When David's servants came to Abigail at Carmel, they said to her, "David sent us to bring you to him as a wife."

⁴¹ She stood up, paid homage with her face to the ground, and said, "Here I am, your servant, a slave to wash the feet of my lord's servants." ⁴² Then Abigail got up quickly, and with her five female servants accompanying her, rode on the donkey following David's messengers. And so she became his wife.

⁴³ David also married Ahinoam of Jezreel, and the two of them became his wives. ⁴⁴ But Saul gave his daughter Michal, David's wife, to Palti son of Laish, who was from Gallim. Jos 15:56; 1Sm 18:27; 2Sm 3:14-15; Is 10:30

David Again Spares Saul

26 Then the Ziphites came to Saul at Gibeah saying, "David is hiding on the hill of Hachilah opposite Jeshimon." ² So Saul, accompanied by three thousand of the fit young men of Israel, went immediately to the Wilderness of Ziph to search for David there. ³ Saul camped beside the road at the hill of Hachilah opposite Jeshimon. David was living in the wilderness and discovered Saul had come there after him. ⁴ So David sent out spies and knew for certain that Saul had come. ⁵ Immediately, David went to the place where Saul had camped. He saw the place where Saul and Abner son of Ner, the commander of his army, were lying down. Saul was lying inside the inner circle of the camp with the troops camped around him. ⁶ Then David asked Ahimelech the Hethite and Joab's brother Abishai son of Zeruiah, "Who will go with me into the camp to Saul?" 1Sm 23:19

"I'll go with you," answered Abishai.

⁷ That night, David and Abishai came to the troops, and Saul was lying there asleep in the inner circle of the camp with his spear stuck in the ground by his head. Abner and the troops were lying around him. ⁸ Then Abishai said to David, "Today God has delivered your enemy to you. Let me thrust the spear through him into the ground just once. I won't have to strike him twice!"

⁹ But David said to Abishai, "Don't destroy him, for who can lift a hand against the LORD's anointed and be innocent?" ¹⁰ David added, "As the LORD lives, the LORD will certainly strike him down: either his day will come and he will die, or he will go into battle and perish. ¹¹ However, because of the LORD, I will never lift my hand against the LORD's anointed. Instead, take the spear and the water jug by his head, and let's go." Dt 32:35; 1Sm 10:1; 24:6-7; 2Sm 1:14,16

¹² So David took the spear and the water jug by Saul's head, and they went their way. No one saw them, no one knew, and no one woke up; they all remained asleep because a deep sleep from the LORD came

^**25:37** Lit *Then his heart died within him*

over them. ¹³ David crossed to the other side and stood on top of the mountain at a distance; there was a considerable space between them. ¹⁴ Then David shouted to the troops and to Abner son of Ner: "Aren't you going to answer, Abner?"   Gn 2:21

"Who are you who calls to the king?" Abner asked.

¹⁵ David called to Abner, "You're a man, aren't you? Who in Israel is your equal? So why didn't you protect your lord the king when one of the people came to destroy him? ¹⁶ What you have done is not good. As the LORD lives, all of you deserve to die^A since you didn't protect your lord, the LORD's anointed. Now look around; where are the king's spear and water jug that were by his head?"   1Sm 20:31

¹⁷ Saul recognized David's voice and asked, "Is that your voice, my son David?"   1Sm 24:16; 26:21,25

"It is my voice, my lord and king," David said. ¹⁸ Then he continued, "Why is my lord pursuing his servant? What have I done? What crime have I committed? ¹⁹ Now, may my lord the king please hear the words of his servant: If it is the LORD who has incited you against me, then may he accept an offering. But if it is people, may they be cursed in the presence of the LORD, for today they have banished me from sharing in the inheritance of the LORD saying, 'Go and worship other gods.' ²⁰ So don't let my blood fall to the ground far from the LORD's presence, for the king of Israel has come out to search for a single flea, like one who pursues a partridge in the mountains."

²¹ Saul responded, "I have sinned. Come back, my son David, I will never harm you again because today you considered my life precious. I have been a fool! I've committed a grave error."   1Sm 15:24,30; 24:17

²² David answered, "Here is the king's spear; have one of the young men come over and get it. ²³ The LORD will repay every man for his righteousness and his loyalty. I wasn't willing to lift my hand against the LORD's anointed, even though the LORD handed you over to me today. ²⁴ Just as I considered your life valuable today, so may the LORD consider my life valuable and rescue me from all trouble."

²⁵ Saul said to him, "You are blessed, my son David. You will certainly do great things and will also prevail." Then David went on his way, and Saul returned home.

David Flees to Ziklag

27 David said to himself, "One of these days I'll be swept away by Saul. There is nothing better for me than to escape immediately to the land of the Philistines. Then Saul will give up searching for me everywhere in Israel, and I'll escape from him." ² So David set out with his six hundred men and went over to Achish son of Maoch, the king of Gath. ³ David and his men stayed with Achish in Gath. Each man had his family with him, and David had his two wives: Ahinoam of Jezreel and Abigail of Carmel, Nabal's widow. ⁴ When it was reported to Saul that David had fled to Gath, he no longer searched for him.

⁵ Now David said to Achish, "If I have found favor with you, let me be given a place in one of the outlying towns, so I can live there. Why should your servant live in the royal

^A**26:16** Lit *you are sons of death*

city with you?" ⁶ That day Achish gave Ziklag to him, and it still belongs to the kings of Judah today. ⁷ The length of time that David stayed in Philistine territory amounted to a year and four months. Jos 15:31; 19:5

⁸ David and his men went up and raided the Geshurites, the Girzites,ᴬ and the Amalekites. From ancient times they had been the inhabitants of the region through Shur as far as the land of Egypt. ⁹ Whenever David attacked the land, he did not leave a single person alive, either man or woman, but he took flocks, herds, donkeys, camels, and clothing. Then he came back to Achish, ¹⁰ who inquired, "Where did you raid today?"ᴮ Ex 17:8; Jos 13:2,13; 1Sm 15:7-8

David replied, "The south country of Judah," "The south country of the Jerahmeelites," or "The south country of the Kenites." 1Sm 30:29

¹¹ David did not let a man or woman live to be brought to Gath, for he said, "Or they will inform on us and say, 'This is what David did.'" This was David's custom during the whole time he stayed in the Philistine territory. ¹² So Achish trusted David, thinking, "Since he has made himself repulsive to his people Israel, he will be my servant forever."

Saul and the Medium

28 At that time, the Philistines gathered their military units into one army to fight against Israel. So Achish said to David, "You know, of course, that you and your men must march out in the armyᶜ with me." 1Sm 29:1

² David replied to Achish, "Good, you will find out what your servant can do."

So Achish said to David, "Very well, I will appoint you as my permanent bodyguard." 1Sm 1:22,28

³ By this time Samuel had died, all Israel had mourned for him and buried him in Ramah, his city, and Saul had removed the mediums and spiritists from the land. ⁴ The Philistines gathered and camped at Shunem. So Saul gathered all Israel, and they camped at Gilboa. ⁵ When Saul saw the Philistine camp, he was afraid and his heart pounded. ⁶ He inquired of the LORD, but the LORD did not answer him in dreams or by the Urim or by the prophets. ⁷ Saul then said to his servants, "Find me a woman who is a medium, so I can go and consult her." 1Sm 25:1

His servants replied, "There is a woman at En-dor who is a medium." Jos 17:1; Ps 83:10; Ac 16:16

⁸ Saul disguised himself by putting on different clothes and set out with two of his men. They came to the woman at night, and Saul said, "Consult a spirit for me. Bring up for me the one I tell you." 2Ch 18:29

⁹ But the woman said to him, "You surely know what Saul has done, how he has cut off the mediums and spiritists from the land. Why are you setting a trap for me to get me killed?" 1Sm 28:3

¹⁰ Then Saul swore to her by the LORD: "As surely as the LORD lives, no punishment will come to youᴰ from this."

¹¹ "Who is it that you want me to bring up for you?" the woman asked.

"Bring up Samuel for me," he answered.

¹² When the woman saw Samuel, she screamed, and then she asked

Saul, "Why did you deceive me? You are Saul!"

¹³ But the king said to her, "Don't be afraid. What do you see?"

"I see a spirit form ^A coming up out of the earth," the woman answered.

¹⁴ Then Saul asked her, "What does he look like?"

"An old man is coming up," she replied. "He's wearing a robe." Then Saul knew that it was Samuel, and he knelt low with his face to the ground and paid homage. 1Sm 15:27

¹⁵ "Why have you disturbed me by bringing me up?" Samuel asked Saul.

"I'm in serious trouble," replied Saul. "The Philistines are fighting against me and God has turned away from me. He doesn't answer me anymore, either through the prophets or in dreams. So I've called on you to tell me what I should do." 1Sm 16:13-14; 18:12; 28:6

¹⁶ Samuel answered, "Since the LORD has turned away from you and has become your enemy, why are you asking me? ¹⁷ The LORD has done ^B exactly what he said through me: The LORD has torn the kingship out of your hand and given it to your neighbor David. ¹⁸ You did not obey the LORD and did not carry out his burning anger against Amalek; therefore the LORD has done this to you today. ¹⁹ The LORD will also hand Israel over to the Philistines along with you. Tomorrow you and your sons will be with me, ^C and the LORD will hand Israel's army over to the Philistines." 1Sm 15:1-9,28

²⁰ Immediately, Saul fell flat on the ground. He was terrified by Samuel's words and was also weak because he had not eaten anything all day and all night. ²¹ The woman came over to Saul, and she saw that he was terrified and said to him, "Look, your servant has obeyed you. I took my life in my hands and did what you told me to do. ²² Now please listen to your servant. Let me set some food in front of you. Eat and it will give you strength so you can go on your way." 1Sm 19:5

²³ He refused, saying, "I won't eat," but when his servants and the woman urged him, he listened to them. He got up off the ground and sat on the bed. 2Kg 5:13; Est 1:6; Ezk 23:41

²⁴ The woman had a fattened calf at her house, and she quickly slaughtered it. She also took flour, kneaded it, and baked unleavened bread. ²⁵ She served it to Saul and his servants, and they ate. Afterward, they got up and left that night. Gn 18:6-7

Philistines Reject David

29 The Philistines brought all their military units together at Aphek while Israel was camped by the spring in Jezreel. ² As the Philistine leaders were passing in review with their units of hundreds and thousands, David and his men were passing in review behind them with Achish. ³ Then the Philistine commanders asked, "What are these Hebrews doing here?" Jos 12:18; 1Sm 4:1; 28:1-2; 1Kg 18:19

Achish answered the Philistine commanders, "That is David, servant of King Saul of Israel. He has been with me a considerable period of time. ^D From the day he defected until today, I've found no fault with him." 1Sm 27:4-12

^A **28:13** Or *a god*, or *a divine being*　^B **28:17** Some Hb, some LXX mss, Vg read *done to you*　^C **28:19** LXX reads *sons will fall*　^D **29:3** Hb obscure

⁴ The Philistine commanders, however, were enraged with Achish and told him, "Send that man back and let him return to the place you assigned him. He must not go down with us into battle only to become our adversary during the battle. What better way could he ingratiate himself with his master than with the heads of our men? ⁵ Isn't this the David they sing about during their dances: 1Sm 14:21; 27:6

Saul has killed his thousands,
    but David his tens
    of thousands?"   1Sm 18:7; 21:11

⁶ So Achish summoned David and told him, "As the LORD lives, you are an honorable man. I think it is good^A to have you fighting^B in this unit with me, because I have found no fault in you from the day you came to me until today. But the leaders don't think you are reliable. ⁷ Now go back quietly and you won't be doing anything the Philistine leaders think is wrong."

⁸ "But what have I done?" David replied to Achish. "From the first day I entered your service until today, what have you found against your servant to keep me from going to fight against the enemies of my lord the king?"   1Sm 27:10-12

⁹ Achish answered David, "I'm convinced that you are as reliable as an angel of God. But the Philistine commanders have said, 'He must not go into battle with us.' ¹⁰ So get up early in the morning, you and your masters' servants who came with you.^C When you've all gotten up early, go as soon as it's light." ¹¹ So David and his men got up early in the morning to return to the land of the Philistines. And the Philistines went up to Jezreel.   1Sm 29:4; 2Sm 14:17,20; 19:27; 1Ch 12:19,22

David's Defeat of the Amalekites

30 David and his men arrived in Ziklag on the third day. The Amalekites had raided the Negev and attacked and burned Ziklag. ² They also had kidnapped the women and everyone^D in it from youngest to oldest. They had killed no one but had carried them off as they went on their way.   Gn 14:1-16

³ When David and his men arrived at the town, they found it burned. Their wives, sons, and daughters had been kidnapped. ⁴ David and the troops with him wept loudly until they had no strength left to weep. ⁵ David's two wives, Ahinoam the Jezreelite and Abigail the widow of Nabal the Carmelite, had also been kidnapped. ⁶ David was in an extremely difficult position because the troops talked about stoning him, for they were all very bitter over the loss of their sons and daughters. But David found strength in the LORD his God.

⁷ David said to the priest Abiathar son of Ahimelech, "Bring me the ephod." So Abiathar brought it to him, ⁸ and David asked the LORD: "Should I pursue these raiders? Will I overtake them?"   1Sm 23:2,4,6-9

The LORD replied to him, "Pursue them, for you will certainly overtake them and rescue the people."

⁹ So David and the six hundred men with him went. They came to the Wadi Besor, where some stayed behind. ¹⁰ David and four hundred

---

^A29:6 Lit It was good in my eyes   ^B29:6 Lit you going out and coming in   ^C29:10 LXX adds and go to the place I appointed you to. Don't take this evil matter to heart, for you are good before me.   ^D30:2 LXX; MT omits and everyone of the men continued the pursuit, while two hundred stopped because they were too exhausted to cross the Wadi Besor. 1Sm 27:2

¹¹ David's men found an Egyptian in the open country and brought him to David. They gave him some bread to eat and water to drink. ¹² Then they gave him some pressed figs and two clusters of raisins. After he ate he revived, for he hadn't eaten food or drunk water for three days and three nights. Jdg 15:19

¹³ Then David said to him, "Who do you belong to? Where are you from?"

"I'm an Egyptian, the slave of an Amalekite man," he said. "My master abandoned me when I got sick three days ago. ¹⁴ We raided the south country of the Cherethites, the territory of Judah, and the south country of Caleb, and we burned Ziklag." Jos 14:13; 1Sm 30:16; 2Sm 8:18

¹⁵ David then asked him, "Will you lead me to these raiders?"

He said, "Swear to me by God that you won't kill me or turn me over to my master, and I will lead you to them."

¹⁶ So he led him, and there were the Amalekites, spread out over the entire area, eating, drinking, and celebrating because of the great amount of plunder they had taken from the land of the Philistines and the land of Judah. ¹⁷ David slaughtered them from twilight until the evening of the next day. None of them escaped, except four hundred young men who got on camels and fled. Jdg 7:12; 1Sm 11:11; 15:3; 30:14

¹⁸ David recovered everything the Amalekites had taken; he also rescued his two wives. ¹⁹ Nothing of theirs was missing from the youngest to the oldest, including the sons and daughters, and all the plunder the Amalekites had taken. David got everything back. ²⁰ He took all the flocks and herds, which were driven ahead of the other livestock, and the people shouted, "This is David's plunder!" 1Sm 30:8

²¹ When David came to the two hundred men who had been too exhausted to go with him and had been left at the Wadi Besor, they came out to meet him and to meet the troops with him. When David approached the men, he greeted them, ²² but all the corrupt and worthless men among those who had gone with David argued, "Because they didn't go with us, we will not give any of the plunder we recovered to them except for each man's wife and children. They may take them and go." 1Sm 30:9-10

²³ But David said, "My brothers, you must not do this with what the LORD has given us. He protected us and handed over to us the raiders who came against us. ²⁴ Who can agree to your proposal? The share of the one who goes into battle is to be the same as the share of the one who remains with the supplies. They will share equally." ²⁵ And it has been so from that day forward. David established this policy^A as a law and an ordinance for Israel and it still continues today. Nm 31:25-27; Jos 22:8

²⁶ When David came to Ziklag, he sent some of the plunder to his friends, the elders of Judah, saying, "Here is a gift for you from the plunder of the LORD's enemies." ²⁷ He sent gifts^B to those in Bethel, in Ramoth of the Negev, and in Jattir; ²⁸ to those in Aroer, in

^A 30:25 *this policy* supplied for clarity   ^B 30:27 *He sent gifts* supplied for clarity

Siphmoth, and in Eshtemoa; ²⁹ to those in Racal, in the towns of the Jerahmeelites, and in the towns of the Kenites; ³⁰ to those in Hormah, in Bor-ashan, and in Athach; ³¹ to those in Hebron, and to those in all the places where David and his men had roamed.   1Sm 25:27-28

The Death of Saul and his Sons

31 The Philistines fought against Israel, and Israel's men fled from them and were killed on Mount Gilboa. ² The Philistines pursued Saul and his sons and killed his sons, Jonathan, Abinadab, and Malchishua. ³ When the battle intensified against Saul, the archers found him and severely wounded him.ᴬ ⁴ Then Saul said to his armorbearer, "Draw your sword and run me through with it, or these uncircumcised men will come and run me through and torture me!" But his armor-bearer would not do it because he was terrified. Then Saul took his sword and fell on it. ⁵ When his armor-bearer saw that Saul was dead, he also fell on his own sword and died with him. ⁶ So on that day, Saul died together with his three sons, his armor-bearer, and all his men.   1Sm 28:4; 2Sm 1:6,12; 1Ch 10:1-12

⁷ When the men of Israel on the other side of the valley and on the other side of the Jordan saw that Israel's men had fled and that Saul and his sons were dead, they abandoned the cities and fled. So the Philistines came and settled in them.

⁸ The next day when the Philistines came to strip the slain, they found Saul and his three sons dead on Mount Gilboa. ⁹ They cut off Saul's head, stripped off his armor, and sent messengers throughout the land of the Philistines to spread the good news in the temples of their idols and among the people. ¹⁰ Then they put his armor in the temple of the Ashtoreths and hung his body on the wall of Beth-shan.   2Sm 1:20; Jdg 16:23-24

¹¹ When the residents of Jabeshgilead heard what the Philistines had done to Saul, ¹² all their brave men set out, journeyed all night, and retrieved the body of Saul and the bodies of his sons from the wall of Beth-shan. When they arrived at Jabesh, they burned the bodies there. ¹³ Afterward, they took their bones and buried them under the tamarisk tree in Jabesh and fasted seven days.   1Sm 11:1-13; 2Sm 2:4-7

ᴬ31:3 LXX reads *and he was wounded under the ribs*

2 SAMUEL

Responses to Saul's Death

1 After the death of Saul, David returned from defeating the Amalekites and stayed at Ziklag two days. ² On the third day a man with torn clothes and dust on his head came from Saul's camp. When he came to David, he fell to the ground and paid homage. ³ David asked him, "Where have you come from?"

He replied to him, "I've escaped from the Israelite camp."

⁴ "What was the outcome? Tell me," David asked him.

"The troops fled from the battle," he answered. "Many of the troops have fallen and are dead. Also, Saul and his son Jonathan are dead."

⁵ David asked the young man who had brought him the report, "How do you know Saul and his son Jonathan are dead?"

⁶ "I happened to be on Mount Gilboa," he replied, "and there was Saul, leaning on his spear. At that very moment the chariots and the cavalry were closing in on him. ⁷ When he turned around and saw me, he called out to me, so I answered: I'm at your service. ⁸ He asked me, 'Who are you?' I told him: I'm an Amalekite. ⁹ Then he begged me, 'Stand over me and kill me, for I'm mortally wounded,ᴬ but my life still lingers.' ¹⁰ So I stood over him and killed him because I knew that after he had fallen he couldn't survive. I took the crown that was on his head and the armband that was on his arm, and I've brought them here to my lord." 1Sm 31:1-5; 1Ch 10:1-6

¹¹ Then David took hold of his clothes and tore them, and all the men with him did the same. ¹² They mourned, wept, and fasted until the evening for those who died by the sword — for Saul, his son Jonathan, the LORD's people, and the house of Israel. Jos 7:6; 2Sm 3:31; 13:31

¹³ David inquired of the young man who had brought him the report, "Where are you from?"

"I'm the son of a resident alien," he said. "I'm an Amalekite."

¹⁴ David questioned him, "How is it that you were not afraid to lift your hand to destroy the LORD's anointed?" ¹⁵ Then David summoned one of his servants and said, "Come here and kill him!" The servant struck him, and he died. ¹⁶ For David had said to the Amalekite, "Your blood is on your own head because your own mouth testified against you by saying, 'I killed the LORD's anointed.'"

¹⁷ David sang the following lament for Saul and his son Jonathan, ¹⁸ and he ordered that the Judahites be taught The Song of the Bow. It is written in the Book of Jashar:ᴮ

¹⁹ The splendor of Israel
 lies slain on your heights.
 How the mighty have fallen!
²⁰ Do not tell it in Gath,
 don't announce it
  in the marketplaces
  of Ashkelon,
 or the daughters
  of the Philistines will rejoice,
 and the daughters
  of the uncircumcised
  will celebrate.

ᴬ1:9 LXX reads *for terrible darkness has taken hold of me* ᴮ1:18 Or *of the Upright*

²¹ Mountains of Gilboa,
    let no dew or rain be on you,
    or fields of offerings, ^A
for there the shield
    of the mighty
    was defiled —   1Sm 31:4
the shield of Saul, no longer
    anointed with oil.   1Sm 10:1
²² Jonathan's bow
    never retreated,
Saul's sword never returned
    unstained, ^B
from the blood of the slain,
from the flesh ^C of the mighty.
²³ Saul and Jonathan,
    loved and delightful,
they were not parted in life
    or in death.
They were swifter than eagles,
    stronger than lions.
²⁴ Daughters of Israel,
    weep for Saul,
who clothed you in scarlet,
    with luxurious things,
who decked your garments
    with gold ornaments.
²⁵ How the mighty have fallen
    in the thick of battle!
Jonathan lies slain
    on your heights.
²⁶ I grieve for you, Jonathan,
    my brother.
You were such a friend to me.
Your love for me was
    more wondrous
than the love of women.
²⁷ How the mighty have fallen
    and the weapons of war
    have perished!

David, King of Judah

2 Some time later, David inquired
    of the LORD: "Should I go to one
of the towns of Judah?"   1Sm 23:1-12
    The LORD answered him, "Go."

Then David asked, "Where should
I go?"
    "To Hebron," the LORD replied.
² So David went there with his
two wives, Ahinoam the Jezreelite and Abigail, the widow of Nabal the Carmelite. ³ In addition,
David brought the men who were
with him, each one with his family,
and they settled in the towns near
Hebron. ⁴ Then the men of Judah
came, and there they anointed David king over the house of Judah.
They told David: "It was the men
of Jabesh-gilead who buried Saul."
⁵ David sent messengers to the
men of Jabesh-gilead and said to
them, "The LORD bless you, because
you have shown this kindness to
Saul your lord when you buried
him. ⁶ Now, may the LORD show
kindness and faithfulness to you,
and I will also show the same goodness to you because you have done
this deed. ⁷ Therefore, be strong ^D
and valiant, for though Saul your
lord is dead, the house of Judah has
anointed me king over them."

⁸ Abner son of Ner, commander
of Saul's army, took Saul's son Ish-
bosheth ^E,F and moved him to Mahanaim. ⁹ He made him king over
Gilead, Asher, Jezreel, Ephraim,
Benjamin — over all Israel. ¹⁰ Saul's
son Ish-bosheth was forty years
old when he became king over Israel; he reigned for two years. The
house of Judah, however, followed
David. ¹¹ The length of time that David was king in Hebron over the
house of Judah was seven years
and six months.   1Sm 14:50; 2Sm 5:5; 1Kg 2:11
¹² Abner son of Ner and soldiers
of Ish-bosheth son of Saul marched
out from Mahanaim to Gibeon. ¹³ So

---

^A 1:21 LXX reads *firstfruits*   ^B 1:22 Lit *empty*   ^C 1:22 Lit *fat*   ^D 2:7 Lit *Therefore, strengthen your hands*
^E 2:8 Some LXX mss read *Ishbaal*; 1Ch 8:33; 9:39   ^F 2:8 = Man of Shame

Joab son of Zeruiah and David's soldiers marched out and met them by the pool of Gibeon. The two groups took up positions on opposite sides of the pool.   Jr 41:11-12

¹⁴ Then Abner said to Joab, "Let's have the young men get up and compete in front of us."

"Let them get up," Joab replied.

¹⁵ So they got up and were counted off — twelve for Benjamin and Ish-bosheth son of Saul, and twelve from David's soldiers. ¹⁶ Then each man grabbed his opponent by the head and thrust his sword into his opponent's side so that they all died together. So this place, which is in Gibeon, is named Field of Blades.^A

¹⁷ The battle that day was extremely fierce, and Abner and the men of Israel were defeated by David's soldiers. ¹⁸ The three sons of Zeruiah were there: Joab, Abishai, and Asahel. Asahel was a fast runner, like one of the wild gazelles. ¹⁹ He chased Abner and did not turn to the right or the left in his pursuit of him. ²⁰ Abner glanced back and said, "Is that you, Asahel?"   1Ch 2:16

"Yes it is," Asahel replied.

²¹ Abner said to him, "Turn to your right or left, seize one of the young soldiers, and take whatever you can get from him." But Asahel would not stop chasing him. ²² Once again, Abner warned Asahel, "Stop chasing me. Why should I strike you to the ground? How could I ever look your brother Joab in the face?"

²³ But Asahel refused to turn away, so Abner hit him in the stomach with the butt of his spear. The spear went through his body, and he fell and died right there. As they all came to the place where Asahel had fallen and died, they stopped,

²⁴ but Joab and Abishai pursued Abner. By sunset, they had gone as far as the hill of Ammah, which is opposite Giah on the way to the wilderness of Gibeon.

²⁵ The Benjaminites rallied to Abner; they formed a unit and took their stand on top of a hill. ²⁶ Then Abner called out to Joab: "Must the sword devour forever? Don't you realize this will only end in bitterness? How long before you tell the troops to stop pursuing their brothers?"

²⁷ "As God lives," Joab replied, "if you had not spoken up, the troops wouldn't have stopped pursuing their brothers until morning." ²⁸ Then Joab blew the ram's horn, and all the troops stopped; they no longer pursued Israel or continued to fight. ²⁹ So Abner and his men marched through the Arabah all that night. They crossed the Jordan, marched all morning,^B and arrived at Mahanaim.   2Sm 2:8,14

³⁰ When Joab had turned back from pursuing Abner, he gathered all the troops. In addition to Asahel, nineteen of David's soldiers were missing, ³¹ but they had killed 360 of the Benjaminites and Abner's men. ³² Afterward, they carried Asahel to his father's tomb in Bethlehem and buried him. Then Joab and his men marched all night and reached Hebron at dawn.

Civil War

3 During the long war between the house of Saul and the house of David, David was growing stronger and the house of Saul was becoming weaker.   1Sm 20:16; 1Kg 12:19

² Sons were born to David in Hebron:

^A 2:16 Or Helkath-hazzurim   ^B 2:29 Or marched through the Bithron

His firstborn was Amnon,
by Ahinoam the Jezreelite;
³ his second was Chileab,
by Abigail, the widow
of Nabal the Carmelite;
the third was Absalom,
son of Maacah the daughter
of King Talmai of Geshur;
⁴ the fourth was Adonijah,
son of Haggith;
the fifth was Shephatiah,
son of Abital;
⁵ the sixth was Ithream,
by David's wife Eglah.
These were born to David in Hebron.   1Ch 3:1-5

⁶ During the war between the house of Saul and the house of David, Abner kept acquiring more power in the house of Saul. ⁷ Now Saul had a concubine whose name was Rizpah daughter of Aiah, and Ish-bosheth questioned Abner, "Why did you sleep with my father's concubine?"   2Sm 2:8-9; 21:8-10

⁸ Abner was very angry about Ish-bosheth's accusation. "Am I a dog's head^A who belongs to Judah?" he asked. "All this time I've been loyal to the family of your father Saul, to his brothers, and to his friends and haven't betrayed you to David, but now you accuse me of wrongdoing with this woman! ⁹ May God punish Abner and do so severely if I don't do for David what the LORD swore to him: ¹⁰ to transfer the kingdom from the house of Saul and establish the throne of David over Israel and Judah from Dan to Beer-sheba." ¹¹ Ish-bosheth did not dare respond to Abner because he was afraid of him.   Ex 22:31; 1Sm 17:43; 24:14; 2Sm 9:8; 16:9

¹² Abner sent messengers as his representatives to say to David,

"Whose land is it? Make your covenant with me, and you can be certain I am on your side to turn all Israel over to you."

¹³ David replied, "Good, I will make a covenant with you. However, there's one thing I require of you: You will not see my face unless you first bring Saul's daughter Michal when you come to see me."   1Sm 14:49

¹⁴ Then David sent messengers to say to Ish-bosheth son of Saul, "Give me back my wife, Michal. I was engaged to her for the price of a hundred Philistine foreskins."

¹⁵ So Ish-bosheth sent someone to take her away from her husband, Paltiel son of Laish. ¹⁶ Her husband followed her, weeping all the way to Bahurim. Abner said to him, "Go back." So he went back.   1Sm 25:44

The Assassination of Abner

¹⁷ Abner conferred with the elders of Israel: "In the past you wanted David to be king over you. ¹⁸ Now take action, because the LORD has spoken concerning David: 'Through my servant David I will save my people Israel from the power of the Philistines and the power of all Israel's enemies.'"

¹⁹ Abner also informed the Benjaminites and went to Hebron to inform David about all that was agreed on by Israel and the whole house of Benjamin. ²⁰ When Abner and twenty men came to David at Hebron, David held a banquet for him and his men.   1Ch 12:29

²¹ Abner said to David, "Let me now go and I will gather all Israel to my lord the king. They will make a covenant with you, and you will reign over all you desire." So David

^A 3:8 = a despised person

dismissed Abner, and he went in peace. 2Sm 3:12

²² Just then David's soldiers and Joab returned from a raid and brought a large amount of plundered goods with them. Abner was not with David in Hebron because David had dismissed him, and he had gone in peace. ²³ When Joab and his whole army arrived, Joab was informed, "Abner son of Ner came to see the king, the king dismissed him, and he went in peace."

²⁴ Joab went to the king and said, "What have you done? Look here, Abner came to you. Why did you dismiss him? Now he's getting away. ²⁵ You know that Abner son of Ner came to deceive you and to find out about your military activities ᴬ and everything you're doing." ²⁶ Then Joab left David and sent messengers after Abner. They brought him back from the well ᴮ of Sirah, but David was unaware of it. ²⁷ When Abner returned to Hebron, Joab pulled him aside to the middle of the city gate, as if to speak to him privately, and there Joab stabbed him in the stomach. So Abner died in revenge for the death of Asahel, ᶜ Joab's brother. 2Sm 2:23; 1Kg 2:5,32

²⁸ David heard about it later and said: "I and my kingdom are forever innocent before the Lᴏʀᴅ concerning the blood of Abner son of Ner. ²⁹ May it hang over Joab's head and his father's whole family, and may the house of Joab never be without someone who has a discharge or a skin disease, or a man who can only work a spindle, ᴰ or someone who falls by the sword or starves." ³⁰ Joab and his

brother Abishai killed Abner because he had put their brother Asahel to death in the battle at Gibeon. Lv 14:2-8; 2Sm 2:23

³¹ David then ordered Joab and all the people who were with him, "Tear your clothes, put on sackcloth, and mourn over Abner." And King David walked behind the coffin. ᴱ Gn 37:34; Jos 7:6

³² When they buried Abner in Hebron, the king wept aloud at Abner's tomb. All the people wept, ³³ and the king sang a lament for Abner: 2Sm 1:17; 2Ch 35:25

Should Abner die as a fool
    dies?
³⁴   Your hands were not bound,
    your feet not placed
        in bronze shackles.
    You fell like one who falls
        victim to criminals.
And all the people wept over him even more.

³⁵ Then they came to urge David to eat food while it was still day, but David took an oath: "May God punish me and do so severely if I taste bread or anything else before sunset!" ³⁶ All the people took note of this, and it pleased them. In fact, everything the king did pleased them. ³⁷ On that day all the troops and all Israel were convinced that the king had no part in the killing of Abner son of Ner. 2Sm 12:17

³⁸ Then the king said to his soldiers, "You must know that a great leader has fallen in Israel today. ³⁹ As for me, even though I am the anointed king, I have little power today. These men, the sons of Zeruiah, are too fierce for me. May the Lᴏʀᴅ repay the evildoer according to his evil!" 2Sm 16:10; 19:22; Ps 28:4; 2Tm 4:14

ᴬ3:25 Lit your going out and your coming in   ᴮ3:26 Or cistern   ᶜ3:27 Lit And he died for the blood of Asahel   ᴰ3:29 LXX reads who uses a crutch   ᴱ3:31 Or the bier; lit the bed

The Assassination of Ish-bosheth

4 When Saul's son Ish-bosheth heard that Abner had died in Hebron, he gave up, [A] and all Israel was dismayed. ² Saul's son had two men who were leaders of raiding parties: one named Baanah and the other Rechab, sons of Rimmon the Beerothite of the Benjaminites. Beeroth is also considered part of Benjamin, ³ and the Beerothites fled to Gittaim and still reside there as aliens today.

⁴ Saul's son Jonathan had a son whose feet were crippled. He was five years old when the report about Saul and Jonathan came from Jezreel. His nanny [B] picked him up and fled, but as she was hurrying to flee, he fell and became lame. His name was Mephibosheth.

⁵ Rechab and Baanah, the sons of Rimmon the Beerothite, set out and arrived at Ish-bosheth's house during the heat of the day while the king was taking his midday nap. ⁶ They entered the interior of the house as if to get wheat and stabbed him in the stomach. Then Rechab and his brother Baanah escaped. ⁷ They had entered the house while Ish-bosheth was lying on his bed in his bedroom and stabbed and killed him. They removed his head, took it, and traveled by way of the Arabah all night. ⁸ They brought Ish-bosheth's head to David at Hebron and said to the king, "Here's the head of Ish-bosheth son of Saul, your enemy who intended to take your life. Today the LORD has granted vengeance to my lord the king against Saul and his offspring."

⁹ But David answered Rechab and his brother Baanah, sons of Rimmon the Beerothite, "As the LORD lives, the one who has redeemed my life from every distress, ¹⁰ when the person told me, 'Look, Saul is dead,' he thought he was a bearer of good news, but I seized him and put him to death at Ziklag. That was my reward to him for his news! ¹¹ How much more when wicked men kill a righteous man in his own house on his own bed! So now, should I not require his blood from you and purge you from the earth?" 1Kg1:29

¹² So David gave orders to the young men, and they killed Rechab and Baanah. They cut off their hands and feet and hung their bodies by the pool in Hebron, but they took Ish-bosheth's head and buried it in Abner's tomb in Hebron.

David, King of Israel

5 All the tribes of Israel came to David at Hebron and said, "Here we are, your own flesh and blood. [C] ² Even while Saul was king over us, you were the one who led us out to battle and brought us back. The LORD also said to you, 'You will shepherd my people Israel, and you will be ruler over Israel.'" 1Ch 11:1-3

³ So all the elders of Israel came to the king at Hebron. King David made a covenant with them at Hebron in the LORD's presence, and they anointed David king over Israel. 2Sm 3:12-13,21

⁴ David was thirty years old when he began his reign; he reigned forty years. ⁵ In Hebron he reigned over Judah seven years and six months, and in Jerusalem he reigned thirty-three years over all Israel and Judah. 1Kg 2:11; 1Ch 29:26-27

⁶ The king and his men marched to Jerusalem against the Jebusites who inhabited the land. The

---

^A **4:1** Lit *his hands dropped*   ^B **4:4** Lit *His nurse*   ^C **5:1** Lit *your bone and your flesh*

Jebusites had said to David: "You will never get in here. Even the blind and lame can repel you" thinking, "David can't get in here." ⁷ Yet David did capture the stronghold of Zion, that is, the city of David. ⁸ He said that day, "Whoever attacks the Jebusites must go through the water shaft to reach the lame and the blind who are despised by David." ᴬ For this reason it is said, "The blind and the lame will never enter the house." ᴮ Lk 2:4

⁹ David took up residence in the stronghold, which he named the city of David. He built it up all the way around from the supporting terraces inward. ¹⁰ David became more and more powerful, and the Lᴏʀᴅ God of Armies was with him. ¹¹ King Hiram of Tyre sent envoys to David; he also sent cedar logs, carpenters, and stonemasons, and they built a palace for David. ¹² Then David knew that the Lᴏʀᴅ had established him as king over Israel and had exalted his kingdom for the sake of his people Israel. 2Sm 3:1

¹³ After he arrived from Hebron, David took more concubines and wives from Jerusalem, and more sons and daughters were born to him. ¹⁴ These are the names of those born to him in Jerusalem: Shammua, Shobab, Nathan, Solomon, ¹⁵ Ibhar, Elishua, Nepheg, Japhia, ¹⁶ Elishama, Eliada, and Eliphelet. 1Ch 3:5-8; 14:1-7; Lk 3:31

¹⁷ When the Philistines heard that David had been anointed king over Israel, they all went in search of David, but he heard about it and went down to the stronghold. ¹⁸ So the Philistines came and spread out in the Valley of Rephaim. 1Ch 14:8-17

¹⁹ Then David inquired of the Lᴏʀᴅ: "Should I attack the Philistines? Will you hand them over to me?" 2Sm 2:1

The Lᴏʀᴅ replied to David, "Attack, for I will certainly hand the Philistines over to you."

²⁰ So David went to Baal-perazim and defeated them there and said, "Like a bursting flood, the Lᴏʀᴅ has burst out against my enemies before me." Therefore, he named that place The Lord Bursts Out. ᶜ ²¹ The Philistines abandoned their idols there, and David and his men carried them off. Is 28:21

²² The Philistines came up again and spread out in the Valley of Rephaim. ²³ So David inquired of the Lᴏʀᴅ, and he answered, "Do not attack directly, but circle around behind them and come at them opposite the balsam trees. ²⁴ When you hear the sound of marching in the tops of the balsam trees, act decisively, for then the Lᴏʀᴅ will have gone out ahead of you to strike down the army of the Philistines." ²⁵ So David did exactly as the Lᴏʀᴅ commanded him, and he struck down the Philistines all the way from Geba to Gezer. 2Kg 7:6

David Moves the Ark

6 David again assembled all the fit young men in Israel: thirty thousand. ² He and all his troops set out to bring the ark of God from Baale-judah. ᴰ The ark bears the Name, the name of the Lᴏʀᴅ of Armies who is enthroned between the cherubim. ³ They set the ark of God on a new cart and transported it from Abinadab's house, which was on the hill. Uzzah and Ahio, ᴱ

ᴬ**5:8** Alt Hb tradition, LXX, Tg, Syr read *who despise David*   ᴮ**5:8** Or *temple*, or *palace*   ᶜ**5:20** Or *Baal-perazim* ; 2Sm 6:8; 1Ch 13:11   ᴰ**6:2** = Kiriath-jearim in 1Sm 7:1; 1Ch 13:6; 2Ch 1:4   ᴱ**6:3** Or *And his brothers* sons of Abinadab, were guiding the cart [4] and brought it with the ark of God from Abinadab's house on the hill. Ahio walked in front of the ark. [5] David and the whole house of Israel were dancing before the LORD with all kinds of fir wood instruments, [A] lyres, harps, tambourines, sistrums, [B] and cymbals.

[6] When they came to Nacon's threshing floor, Uzzah reached out to the ark of God and took hold of it because the oxen had stumbled. [7] Then the LORD's anger burned against Uzzah, and God struck him dead on the spot for his irreverence, and he died there next to the ark of God. [8] David was angry because of the LORD's outburst against Uzzah, so he named that place Outburst Against Uzzah, [C] as it is today. [9] David feared the LORD that day and said, "How can the ark of the LORD ever come to me?" [10] So he was not willing to bring the ark of the LORD to the city of David; instead, he diverted it to the house of Obed-edom of Gath. [11] The ark of the LORD remained in his house three months, and the LORD blessed Obed-edom and his whole family.

[12] It was reported to King David: "The LORD has blessed Obed-edom's family and all that belongs to him because of the ark of God." So David went and had the ark of God brought up from Obed-edom's house to the city of David with rejoicing. [13] When those carrying the ark of the LORD advanced six steps, he sacrificed an ox and a fattened calf. [14] David was dancing [D] with all his might before the LORD wearing a linen ephod. [15] He and the whole house of Israel were bringing up the ark of the LORD with shouts and the sound of the ram's horn. [16] As the ark of the LORD was entering the city of David, Saul's daughter Michal looked down from the window and saw King David leaping and dancing before the LORD, and she despised him in her heart.

[17] They brought the ark of the LORD and set it in its place inside the tent David had pitched for it. Then David offered burnt offerings and fellowship offerings in the LORD's presence. [18] When David had finished offering the burnt offering and the fellowship offerings, he blessed the people in the name of the LORD of Armies. [19] Then he distributed a loaf of bread, a date cake, and a raisin cake to each one in the entire Israelite community, both men and women. Then all the people went home. _{1Ch 15:1; 2Ch 1:4}

[20] When David returned home to bless his household, Saul's daughter Michal came out to meet him. "How the king of Israel honored himself today!" she said. "He exposed himself today in the sight of the slave girls of his subjects like a vulgar person would expose himself." _{1Ch 16:43}

[21] David replied to Michal, "It was before the LORD who chose me over your father and his whole family to appoint me ruler over the LORD's people Israel. I will dance before the LORD, [22] and I will dishonor myself and humble myself even more. [E,F] However, by the slave girls you spoke about, I will be honored." [23] And Saul's daughter Michal had no child to the day of her death.

The LORD's Covenant with David

7 When the king had settled into his palace and the LORD had given him rest on every side from all his enemies, [2] the king said to the prophet Nathan, "Look, I am living in a cedar house while the ark of God sits inside tent curtains."

[3] So Nathan told the king, "Go and do all that is on your mind, for the LORD is with you."

[4] But that night the word of the LORD came to Nathan: [5] "Go to my servant David and say, 'This is what the LORD says: Are you to build me a house to dwell in? [6] From the time I brought the Israelites out of Egypt until today I have not dwelt in a house; instead, I have been moving around with a tent as my dwelling. [7] In all my journeys with all the Israelites, have I ever spoken a word to one of the tribes of Israel, whom I commanded to shepherd my people Israel, asking: Why haven't you built me a house of cedar?'   1Kg 5:3

[8] "So now this is what you are to say to my servant David: 'This is what the LORD of Armies says: I took you from the pasture, from tending the flock, to be ruler over my people Israel. [9] I have been with you wherever you have gone, and I have destroyed all your enemies before you. I will make a great name for you like that of the greatest on the earth. [10] I will designate a place for my people Israel and plant them, so that they may live there and not be disturbed again. Evildoers will not continue to oppress them as they have done [11] ever since the day I ordered judges to be over my people Israel. I will give you rest from all your enemies.   Gn 11:4; 12:2; 1Sm 16:11-13; 2Sm 7:23

" 'The LORD declares to you: The LORD himself will make a house for you. [12] When your time comes and you rest with your fathers, I will raise up after you your descendant, who will come from your body, and I will establish his kingdom. [13] He is the one who will build a house for my name, and I will establish the throne of his kingdom forever. [14] I will be his father, and he will be my son. When he does wrong, I will discipline him with a rod of men and blows from mortals. [15] But my faithful love will never leave him as it did when I removed it from Saul, whom I removed from before you. [16] Your house and kingdom will endure before me[A] forever, and your throne will be established forever.' "   1Kg 5:2-5; 6:12; 8:18-19; Ac 13:23

[17] Nathan reported all these words and this entire vision to David.

David's Prayer of Thanksgiving

[18] Then King David went in, sat in the LORD's presence, and said,

Who am I, Lord GOD, and what is my house that you have brought me this far? [19] What you have done so far[B] was a little thing to you, Lord GOD, for you have also spoken about your servant's house in the distant future. And this is a revelation[C] for mankind, Lord GOD. [20] What more can David say to you? You know your servant, Lord GOD. [21] Because of your word and according to your will, you have revealed all these great things to your servant.

[22] This is why you are great, Lord GOD. There is no one like you, and there is no God besides

you, as all we have heard confirms. [23] And who is like your people Israel? God came to one nation on earth in order to redeem a people for himself, to make a name for himself, and to perform for them[A] great and awesome acts,[B] driving out nations and their gods before your people you redeemed for yourself from Egypt. [24] You established your people Israel to be your own people forever, and you, LORD, have become their God.

[25] Now, LORD God, fulfill the promise forever that you have made to your servant and his house. Do as you have promised, [26] so that your name will be exalted forever, when it is said, "The LORD of Armies is God over Israel." The house of your servant David will be established before you [27] since you, LORD of Armies, God of Israel, have revealed this to your servant when you said, "I will build a house for you." Therefore, your servant has found the courage to pray this prayer to you. [28] Lord GOD, you are God; your words are true, and you have promised this good thing to your servant. [29] Now, please bless your servant's house so that it will continue before you forever. For you, Lord GOD, have spoken, and with your blessing your servant's house will be blessed forever.

2Sm 22:51; Ps 89:28-29; Lk 1:69

David's Victories

8 After this, David defeated the Philistines, subdued them, and took Metheg-ammah[C] from Philistine control.[D] [2] He also defeated the Moabites, and after making them lie down on the ground, he measured them off with a cord. He measured every two cord lengths of those to be put to death and one full length of those to be kept alive. So the Moabites became David's subjects and brought tribute.

[3] David also defeated Hadadezer son of Rehob, king of Zobah, when he went to restore his control at the Euphrates River. [4] David captured seventeen hundred horsemen[E] and twenty thousand foot soldiers from him, and he hamstrung all the horses and kept a hundred chariots.[F]

[5] When the Arameans of Damascus came to assist King Hadadezer of Zobah, David struck down twenty-two thousand Aramean men. [6] Then he placed garrisons in Aram of Damascus, and the Arameans became David's subjects and brought tribute. The LORD made David victorious wherever he went. Gn 14:15

[7] David took the gold shields of Hadadezer's officers and brought them to Jerusalem. [8] King David also took huge quantities of bronze from Betah[G] and Berothai, Hadadezer's cities. 2Kg 11:10; 2Ch 23:9

[9] When King Toi of Hamath heard that David had defeated the entire army of Hadadezer, [10] he sent his son Joram to King David to greet him and to congratulate him because David had fought against Hadadezer and defeated him, for

---

[A]7:23 Some Hb mss, Tg, Vg, Syr; other Hb mss read you   [B]7:23 LXX; MT reads acts for your land
[C]8:1 Or took control of the mother city; Hb obscure   [D]8:1 LXX reads them, and David took tribute out of the hand of the Philistines   [E]8:4 LXX, DSS read 1,000 chariots and 7,000 horsemen   [F]8:4 Or chariot horses   [G]8:8 Some LXX mss, Syr read Tebah

Toi and Hadadezer had fought many wars. Joram had items of silver, gold, and bronze with him. ¹¹ King David also dedicated these to the LORD, along with the silver and gold he had dedicated from all the nations he had subdued — ¹² from Edom, ᴬ Moab, the Ammonites, the Philistines, the Amalekites, and the spoil of Hadadezer son of Rehob, king of Zobah.   Gn 10:15-18; Ezk 47:16-17

¹³ David made a reputation for himself when he returned from striking down eighteen thousand Edomites ᴮ in Salt Valley. ᶜ ¹⁴ He placed garrisons throughout Edom, and all the Edomites were subject to David. The LORD made David victorious wherever he went.   Gn 25:23; 27:29-40; 2Sm 7:9; 2Kg 14:7

¹⁵ So David reigned over all Israel, administering justice and righteousness for all his people.   1Kg 10:9

¹⁶   Joab son of Zeruiah was
          over the army;
       Jehoshaphat son of Ahilud
          was court historian;
¹⁷   Zadok son of Ahitub and
          Ahimelech son of Abiathar
          were priests;
       Seraiah was court secretary;
¹⁸   Benaiah son of Jehoiada
          was over the Cherethites
          and the Pelethites;
       and David's sons were
          chief officials. ᴰ

David's Kindness to Mephibosheth

9 David asked, "Is there anyone remaining from the family of Saul I can show kindness to for Jonathan's sake?" ² There was a servant of Saul's family named Ziba. They summoned him to David,

and the king said to him, "Are you Ziba?"   Gn 19:19; 24:12; 40:14; 47:29; Jos 2:12

"I am your servant," he replied.

³ So the king asked, "Is there anyone left of Saul's family that I can show the kindness of God to?"

Ziba said to the king, "There is still Jonathan's son who was injured in both feet."   2Sm 4:4

⁴ The king asked him, "Where is he?"

Ziba answered the king, "You'll find him in Lo-debar at the house of Machir son of Ammiel." ⁵ So King David had him brought from the house of Machir son of Ammiel in Lo-debar.

⁶ Mephibosheth son of Jonathan son of Saul came to David, fell facedown, and paid homage. David said, "Mephibosheth!"

"I am your servant," he replied.

⁷ "Don't be afraid," David said to him, "since I intend to show you kindness for the sake of your father Jonathan. I will restore to you all your grandfather Saul's fields, and you will always eat meals at my table."   1Kg 2:7

⁸ Mephibosheth paid homage and said, "What is your servant that you take an interest in a dead dog like me?"   1Sm 24:14; 2Sm 16:9

⁹ Then the king summoned Saul's attendant Ziba and said to him, "I have given to your master's grandson all that belonged to Saul and his family. ¹⁰ You, your sons, and your servants are to work the ground for him, and you are to bring in the crops so your master's grandson will have food to eat. But Mephibosheth, your master's grandson, is always to eat at my table." Now Ziba had fifteen sons and twenty servants.

ᴬ**8:12** Some Hb mss, LXX, Syr; other Hb mss read *Aram* ; 1Ch 18:11   ᴮ**8:13** Some Hb mss, LXX, Syr; other Hb mss read *Arameans* ; 1Ch 18:12   ᶜ**8:13** = the Dead Sea region   ᴰ**8:18** LXX; MT reads *were priests* ; 1Ch 18:17

¹¹ Ziba said to the king, "Your servant will do all my lord the king commands."

So Mephibosheth ate at David's ^A table just like one of the king's sons. ¹² Mephibosheth had a young son whose name was Mica. All those living in Ziba's house were Mephibosheth's servants. ¹³ However, Mephibosheth lived in Jerusalem because he always ate at the king's table. His feet had been injured.

War with the Ammonites

10 Some time later, the king of the Ammonites died, and his son Hanun became king in his place. ² Then David said, "I'll show kindness to Hanun son of Nahash, just as his father showed kindness to me." 1Ch 19:1-19

So David sent his emissaries to console Hanun concerning his father. However, when they arrived in the land of the Ammonites, ³ the Ammonite leaders said to Hanun their lord, "Just because David has sent men with condolences for you, do you really believe he's showing respect for your father? Instead, hasn't David sent his emissaries in order to scout out the city, spy on it, and demolish it?" ⁴ So Hanun took David's emissaries, shaved off half their beards, cut their clothes in half at the hips, and sent them away.

⁵ When this was reported to David, he sent someone to meet them, since they were deeply humiliated. The king said, "Stay in Jericho until your beards grow back; then return."

⁶ When the Ammonites realized they had become repulsive to David, they hired twenty thousand foot soldiers from the Arameans of Beth-rehob and Zobah, one thousand men from the king of Maacah, and twelve thousand men from Tob.

⁷ David heard about it and sent Joab and all the elite troops. ⁸ The Ammonites marched out and lined up in battle formation at the entrance to the city gate while the Arameans of Zobah and Rehob and the men of Tob and Maacah were in the field by themselves. ⁹ When Joab saw that there was a battle line in front of him and another behind him, he chose some of Israel's finest young men and lined up in formation to engage the Arameans. ¹⁰ He placed the rest of the forces under the command of his brother Abishai. They lined up in formation to engage the Ammonites.

¹¹ "If the Arameans are too strong for me," Joab said, "then you will be my help. However, if the Ammonites are too strong for you, I'll come to help you. ¹² Be strong! Let's prove ourselves strong for our people and for the cities of our God. May the LORD's will be done." ^B Dt 31:6; Jos 1:6

¹³ Joab and his troops advanced to fight against the Arameans, and they fled before him. ¹⁴ When the Ammonites saw that the Arameans had fled, they too fled before Abishai and entered the city. So Joab withdrew from the attack against the Ammonites and went to Jerusalem.

¹⁵ When the Arameans saw that they had been defeated by Israel, they regrouped. ¹⁶ Hadadezer sent messengers to bring the Arameans who were beyond the Euphrates River, and they came to Helam with

---

^A 9:11 LXX; Syr reads *the king's*; Vg reads *your*; MT reads *my*   ^B 10:12 Lit the LORD do what is good in his eyes

Shobach, commander of Hadadezer's army, leading them.

¹⁷ When this was reported to David, he gathered all Israel, crossed the Jordan, and went to Helam. Then the Arameans lined up to engage David in battle and fought against him. ¹⁸ But the Arameans fled before Israel, and David killed seven hundred of their charioteers and forty thousand foot soldiers. ᴬ He also struck down Shobach commander of their army, who died there. ¹⁹ When all the kings who were Hadadezer's subjects saw that they had been defeated by Israel, they made peace with Israel and became their subjects. After this, the Arameans were afraid to ever help the Ammonites again.

David's Adultery with Bathsheba

11 In the spring when kings march out to war, David sent Joab with his officers and all Israel. They destroyed the Ammonites and besieged Rabbah, but David remained in Jerusalem. 2Sm 12:26-29

² One evening David got up from his bed and strolled around on the roof of the palace. From the roof he saw a woman bathing — a very beautiful woman. ³ So David sent someone to inquire about her, and he said, "Isn't this Bathsheba, daughter of Eliam and wife of Uriah the Hethite?" ᴮ 2Sm 12:24; Ps 51; Mt 1:6

⁴ David sent messengers to get her, and when she came to him, he slept with her. Now she had just been purifying herself from her uncleanness. Afterward, she returned home. ⁵ The woman conceived and sent word to inform David: "I am pregnant." Lv 15:18-30; 18:19

⁶ David sent orders to Joab: "Send me Uriah the Hethite." So Joab sent Uriah to David. ⁷ When Uriah came to him, David asked how Joab and the troops were doing and how the war was going. ⁸ Then he said to Uriah, "Go down to your house and wash your feet." So Uriah left the palace, and a gift from the king followed him. ⁹ But Uriah slept at the door of the palace with all his master's servants; he did not go down to his house.

¹⁰ When it was reported to David, "Uriah didn't go home," David questioned Uriah, "Haven't you just come from a journey? Why didn't you go home?"

¹¹ Uriah answered David, "The ark, Israel, and Judah are dwelling in tents, and my master Joab and his soldiers ᶜ are camping in the open field. How can I enter my house to eat and drink and sleep with my wife? As surely as you live and by your life, I will not do this!" 1Sm 21:5

¹² "Stay here today also," David said to Uriah, "and tomorrow I will send you back." So Uriah stayed in Jerusalem that day and the next. ¹³ Then David invited Uriah to eat and drink with him, and David got him drunk. He went out in the evening to lie down on his cot with his master's servants, but he did not go home.

Uriah's Death Arranged

¹⁴ The next morning David wrote a letter to Joab and sent it with Uriah. ¹⁵ In the letter he wrote:

Put Uriah at the front of the fiercest fighting, then withdraw from him so that he is struck down and dies. Mt 1:6

ᴬ**10:18** Some LXX mss; MT reads *horsemen* ; 1Ch 19:18 *servants*   ᴮ**11:3** DSS add *Joab's armor-bearer*   ᶜ**11:11** Lit

16 When Joab was besieging the city, he put Uriah in the place where he knew the best enemy soldiers were. 17 Then the men of the city came out and attacked Joab, and some of the men from David's soldiers fell in battle; Uriah the Hethite also died.

18 Joab sent someone to report to David all the details of the battle, 19 He commanded the messenger, "When you've finished telling the king all the details of the battle — 20 if the king's anger gets stirred up and he asks you, 'Why did you get so close to the city to fight? Didn't you realize they would shoot from the top of the wall? 21 At Thebez, who struck Abimelech son of Jerubbesheth?A,B Didn't a woman drop an upper millstone on him from the top of the wall so that he died? Why did you get so close to the wall?' — then say, 'Your servant Uriah the Hethite is dead also.'" 22 Then the messenger left. Jdg 9:50-54

When he arrived, he reported to David all that Joab had sent him to tell. 23 The messenger reported to David, "The men gained the advantage over us and came out against us in the field, but we counterattacked right up to the entrance of the city gate. 24 However, the archers shot down on your servants from the top of the wall, and some of the king's servants died. Your servant Uriah the Hethite is also dead."

25 David told the messenger, "Say this to Joab: 'Don't let this matter upset you because the sword devours all alike. Intensify your fight against the city and demolish it.' Encourage him."

26 When Uriah's wife heard that her husband Uriah had died, she mourned for him. C 27 When the time of mourning ended, David had her brought to his house. She became his wife and bore him a son. However, the LORD considered what David had done to be evil. Mt1:6;2Sm12:9

Nathan's Parable and David's Repentance

12 So the LORD sent Nathan to David. When he arrived, he said to him: Ps 51 title

There were two men in a certain city, one rich and the other poor. 2 The rich man had very large flocks and herds, 3 but the poor man had nothing except one small ewe lamb that he had bought. He raised her, and she grew up with him and with his children. From his meager food she would eat, from his cup she would drink, and in his arms she would sleep. She was like a daughter to him. 4 Now a traveler came to the rich man, but the rich man could not bring himself to take one of his own sheep or cattle to prepare for the traveler who had come to him. Instead, he took the poor man's lamb and prepared it for his guest. D

5 David was infuriated with the man and said to Nathan: "As the LORD lives, the man who did this deserves to die! 6 Because he has done this thing and shown no pity, he must pay four lambs for that lamb." Ex 22:1; Lk 19:8

7 Nathan replied to David, "You are the man! This is what the LORD

A11:21 LXX reads Jerubbaal   B11:21 = Gideon   C11:26 Lit her husband   D12:4 Lit for the man who had come to him

God of Israel says: 'I anointed you king over Israel, and I rescued you from Saul. [8] I gave your master's house to you and your master's wives into your arms, [A] and I gave you the house of Israel and Judah, and if that was not enough, I would have given you even more. [9] Why then have you despised the LORD's command by doing what I consider[B] evil? You struck down Uriah the Hethite with the sword and took his wife as your own wife — you murdered him with the Ammonite's sword. [10] Now therefore, the sword will never leave your house because you despised me and took the wife of Uriah the Hethite to be your own wife.' Nm 15:30-31; 1Sm 16:13

[11] "This is what the LORD says, 'I am going to bring disaster on you from your own family: I will take your wives and give them to another[C] before your very eyes, and he will sleep with them in broad daylight. [D] [12] You acted in secret, but I will do this before all Israel and in broad daylight.' "[E]   2Sm 16:21-22

[13] David responded to Nathan, "I have sinned against the LORD."

Then Nathan replied to David, "And the LORD has taken away your sin; you will not die. [14] However, because you treated[F] the LORD with such contempt in this matter, the son born to you will die." [15] Then Nathan went home.   Lv 20:10; 24:17

The Death of Bathsheba's Son

The LORD struck the baby that Uriah's wife had borne to David, and he became deathly ill. [16] David pleaded with God for the boy. He fasted, went home, and spent the night lying on the ground. [17] The elders of his house stood beside him to get him up from the ground, but he was unwilling and would not eat anything with them. Jb 1:20; Mt 1:6

[18] On the seventh day the baby died. But David's servants were afraid to tell him the baby was dead. They said, "Look, while the baby was alive, we spoke to him, and he wouldn't listen to us. So how can we tell him the baby is dead? He may do something desperate."

[19] When David saw that his servants were whispering to each other, he guessed that the baby was dead. So he asked his servants, "Is the baby dead?"

"He is dead," they replied.

[20] Then David got up from the ground. He washed, anointed himself, changed his clothes, went to the LORD's house, and worshiped. Then he went home and requested something to eat. So they served him food, and he ate.

[21] His servants asked him, "Why have you done this? While the baby was alive, you fasted and wept, but when he died, you got up and ate food."

[22] He answered, "While the baby was alive, I fasted and wept because I thought, 'Who knows? The LORD may be gracious to me and let him live.' [23] But now that he is dead, why should I fast? Can I bring him back again? I'll go to him, but he will never return to me."   Jb 7:8-10

The Birth of Solomon

[24] Then David comforted his wife Bathsheba; he went to her and slept with her. She gave birth to a son and

---

named^A him Solomon. ^B The LORD loved him, ²⁵ and he sent a message through the prophet Nathan, who named^C him Jedidiah, ^D because of the LORD. Gn 37:35; Ps 23:4; 119:76,82; 1Ch 22:9

Capture of the City of Rabbah

²⁶ Joab fought against Rabbah of the Ammonites and captured the royal fortress. ²⁷ Then Joab sent messengers to David to say, "I have fought against Rabbah and have also captured its water supply. ²⁸ Now therefore, assemble the rest of the troops, lay siege to the city, and capture it. Otherwise I will be the one to capture the city, and it will be named after me." ²⁹ So David assembled all the troops and went to Rabbah; he fought against it and captured it. ³⁰ He took the crown from the head of their king, ^E and it was placed on David's head. The crown weighed seventy-five pounds^F of gold, and it had a precious stone in it. In addition, David took away a large quantity of plunder from the city. ³¹ He removed the people who were in the city and put them to work with saws, iron picks, and iron axes, and to labor at brickmaking. He did the same to all the Ammonite cities. Then he and all his troops returned to Jerusalem. Ex 1:13-14; 1Ch 20:1-3

Amnon Rapes Tamar

13 Some time passed. David's son Absalom had a beautiful sister named Tamar, and David's son Amnon was infatuated with her. ² Amnon was frustrated to the point of making himself sick over his sister Tamar because she was a virgin, but it seemed impossible to do anything to her. ³ Amnon had a friend named Jonadab, a son of David's brother Shimeah. Jonadab was a very shrewd man, ⁴ and he asked Amnon, "Why are you, the king's son, so miserable every morning? Won't you tell me?"

Amnon replied, "I'm in love with Tamar, my brother Absalom's sister."

⁵ Jonadab said to him, "Lie down on your bed and pretend you're sick. When your father comes to see you, say to him, 'Please let my sister Tamar come and give me something to eat. Let her prepare a meal in my presence so I can watch and eat from her hand.'" Jr 7:18

⁶ So Amnon lay down and pretended to be sick. When the king came to see him, Amnon said to him, "Please let my sister Tamar come and make a couple of cakes in my presence so I can eat from her hand."

⁷ David sent word to Tamar at the palace: "Please go to your brother Amnon's house and prepare a meal for him."

⁸ Then Tamar went to his house while Amnon was lying down. She took dough, kneaded it, made cakes in his presence, and baked them. ⁹ She brought the pan and set it down in front of him, but he refused to eat. Amnon said, "Everyone leave me!" And everyone left him. ¹⁰ "Bring the meal to the bedroom," Amnon told Tamar, "so I can eat from your hand." Tamar took the cakes she had made and went to her brother Amnon's bedroom. ¹¹ When she brought them to him

^A12:24 Alt Hb tradition reads *he named*   ^B12:24 In Hb, the name *Solomon* sounds like "peace."   ^C12:25 Or *prophet to name*   ^D12:25 = Beloved of the LORD   ^E12:30 LXX reads *of Milcom*; some emend to *Molech*; 1Kg 11:5,33   ^F12:30 Lit *a talent* to eat, he grabbed her and said,[A] "Come sleep with me, my sister!"

[12] "Don't, my brother!" she cried. "Don't disgrace me, for such a thing should never be done in Israel. Don't commit this outrage! [13] Where could I ever go with my humiliation? And you — you would be like one of the outrageous fools in Israel! Please, speak to the king, for he won't keep me from you." [14] But he refused to listen to her, and because he was stronger than she was, he disgraced her by raping her. Dt 21:14; Ru 2:15; 2Sm 19:3; Jb 19:3

[15] So Amnon hated Tamar with such intensity that the hatred he hated her with was greater than the love he had loved her with. "Get out of here!" he said.

[16] "No," she cried,[B] "sending me away is much worse than the great wrong you've already done to me!"

But he refused to listen to her. [17] Instead, he called to the servant who waited on him: "Get this away from me, throw her out, and bolt the door behind her!" [18] Amnon's servant threw her out and bolted the door behind her. Now Tamar was wearing a long-sleeved[C] garment, because this is what the king's virgin daughters wore. [19] Tamar put ashes on her head and tore the long-sleeved garment she was wearing. She put her hand on her head and went away crying out.

[20] Her brother Absalom said to her: "Has your brother Amnon been with you? Be quiet for now, my sister. He is your brother. Don't take this thing to heart." So Tamar lived as a desolate woman in the house of her brother Absalom. Is 54:1; 62:4

Absalom Murders Amnon

[21] When King David heard about all these things, he was furious.[D] [22] Absalom didn't say anything to Amnon, either good or bad, because he hated Amnon since he disgraced his sister Tamar.

[23] Two years later, Absalom's sheepshearers were at Baal-hazor near Ephraim, and Absalom invited all the king's sons. [24] Then he went to the king and said, "Your servant has just hired sheepshearers. Will the king and his servants please come with your servant?"

[25] The king replied to Absalom, "No, my son, we should not all go, or we would be a burden to you." Although Absalom urged him, he wasn't willing to go, though he did bless him.

[26] "If not," Absalom said, "please let my brother Amnon go with us."

The king asked him, "Why should he go with you?" [27] But Absalom urged him, so he sent Amnon and all the king's sons.[E]

[28] Now Absalom commanded his young men, "Watch Amnon until he is in a good mood from the wine. When I order you to strike Amnon, then kill him. Don't be afraid. Am I not the one who has commanded you? Be strong and valiant!" [29] So Absalom's young men did to Amnon just as Absalom had commanded. Then all the rest of the king's sons got up, and each fled on his mule. Jos 1:9

[30] While they were on the way, a report reached David: "Absalom struck down all the king's sons; not even one of them survived!" [31] In response the king stood up, tore

his clothes, and lay down on the ground, and all his servants stood by with their clothes torn.   2Sm 1:11

³² But Jonadab, son of David's brother Shimeah, spoke up: "My lord must not think they have killed all the young men, the king's sons, because only Amnon is dead. In fact, Absalom has planned this ᴬ ever since the day Amnon disgraced his sister Tamar. ³³ So now, my lord the king, don't take seriously the report that says all the king's sons are dead. Only Amnon is dead."   2Sm 13:3-5

³⁴ Meanwhile, Absalom had fled. When the young man who was standing watch looked up, there were many people coming from the road west of him from the side of the mountain. ᴮ ³⁵ Jonadab said to the king, "Look, the king's sons have come! It's exactly like your servant said." ³⁶ Just as he finished speaking, the king's sons entered and wept loudly. Then the king and all his servants also wept very bitterly. ³⁷ But Absalom fled and went to Talmai son of Ammihud, king of Geshur. And David mourned for his son ᶜ every day.   2Sm 3:3; 1Ch 3:2

³⁸ After Absalom had fled to Geshur and had been there three years, ³⁹ King David ᴰ longed to go to Absalom, for David had finished grieving over Amnon's death.

Absalom Restored to David

14 Joab son of Zeruiah realized that the king's mind was on Absalom. ² So Joab sent someone to Tekoa to bring a wise woman from there. He told her, "Pretend to be in mourning: dress in mourning clothes and don't put on any oil. Act like a woman who has been mourning for the dead for a long time. ³ Go to the king and speak these words to him." Then Joab told her exactly what to say. ᴱ   2Sm 13:3; 14:20; 2Ch 20:20; Am 1:1

⁴ When the woman from Tekoa came ᶠ to the king, she fell facedown to the ground, paid homage, and said, "Help me, Your Majesty!"

⁵ "What's the matter?" the king asked her.

"Sadly, I am a widow; my husband died," she said. ⁶ "Your servant had two sons. They were fighting in the field with no one to separate them, and one struck the other and killed him. ⁷ Now the whole clan has risen up against your servant and said, 'Hand over the one who killed his brother so we may put him to death for the life of the brother he murdered. We will eliminate the heir!' They would extinguish my one remaining ember by not preserving my husband's name or posterity on earth."   2Sm 12:1; Nah 1:14

⁸ The king told the woman, "Go home. I will issue a command on your behalf."

⁹ Then the woman of Tekoa said to the king, "My lord the king, may any blame be on me and my father's family, and may the king and his throne be innocent."   1Sm 25:24

¹⁰ "Whoever speaks to you," the king said, "bring him to me. He will not trouble you again!"

¹¹ She replied, "Please, may the king invoke the LORD your God, so that the avenger of blood will not increase the loss, and they will not eliminate my son!"   Nm 35:19-21

ᴬ**13:32** Lit *In fact, it was established on the mouth of Absalom*   ᴮ**13:34** LXX adds *And the watchman came and reported to the king saying, "I see men on the Horonaim road on the side of the mountain."*
ᶜ**13:37** Probably Amnon   ᴰ**13:39** DSS, LXX, Tg read *David's spirit*   ᴱ**14:3** Lit *Joab put the words into her mouth*   ᶠ**14:4** Some Hb mss, LXX, Syr, Tg, Vg; other Hb mss read *spoke*

"As the LORD lives," he vowed, "not a hair of your son will fall to the ground." 1Sm 14:45; Dn 3:27; Lk 21:18; Ac 27:34

¹² Then the woman said, "Please, may your servant speak a word to my lord the king?"

"Speak," he replied.

¹³ The woman asked, "Why have you devised something similar against the people of God? When the king spoke as he did about this matter, he has pronounced his own guilt. The king has not brought back his own banished one. ¹⁴ We will certainly die and be like water poured out on the ground, which can't be recovered. But God would not take away a life; he would devise plans so that the one banished from him does not remain banished. Jn 8:51

¹⁵ "Now therefore, I've come to present this matter to my lord the king because the people have made me afraid. Your servant thought: I must speak to the king. Perhaps the king will grant his servant's request. ¹⁶ The king will surely listen in order to keep his servant from the grasp of this man who would eliminate both me and my son from God's inheritance. ¹⁷ Your servant thought: May the word of my lord the king bring relief, for my lord the king is able to discern the good and the bad like the angel of God. May the LORD your God be with you."

¹⁸ Then the king answered the woman, "I'm going to ask you something; don't conceal it from me!"

"Let my lord the king speak," the woman replied.

¹⁹ The king asked, "Did Joab put you up to^A all this?"

The woman answered. "As you live, my lord the king, no one can turn to the right or left from all my lord the king says. Yes, your servant Joab is the one who gave orders to me; he told your servant exactly what to say.^B ²⁰ Joab your servant has done this to address the issue indirectly,^C but my lord has wisdom like the wisdom of the angel of God, knowing everything on earth."

²¹ Then the king said to Joab, "I hereby grant this request. Go, bring back the young man Absalom."

²² Joab fell with his face to the ground in homage and blessed the king. "Today," Joab said, "your servant knows I have found favor with you, my lord the king, because the king has granted the request of your servant."

²³ So Joab got up, went to Geshur, and brought Absalom to Jerusalem. ²⁴ However, the king added, "He may return to his house, but he may not see my face." So Absalom returned to his house, but he did not see the king.^D 2Sm 13:38

²⁵ No man in all Israel was as handsome and highly praised as Absalom. From the sole of his foot to the top of his head, he did not have a single flaw. ²⁶ When he shaved his head — he shaved it at the end of every year because his hair got so heavy for him that he had to shave it off — he would weigh the hair from his head and it would be five pounds^E according to the royal standard. Gn 39:6

²⁷ Three sons were born to Absalom, and a daughter named Tamar, who was a beautiful woman. ²⁸ Absalom resided in Jerusalem

^A 14:19 Lit "Is the hand of Joab in   ^B 14:19 Lit he put all these words into the mouth of your servant   ^C 14:20 Lit to go around the face of the matter   ^D 14:24 Lit king's face   ^E 14:26 Lit 200 shekels two years but never saw the king. ²⁹ Then Absalom sent for Joab in order to send him to the king, but Joab was unwilling to come to him. So he sent again, a second time, but he still would not come. ³⁰ Then Absalom said to his servants, "See, Joab has a field right next to mine, and he has barley there. Go and set fire to it!" So Absalom's servants set the field on fire.ᴬ

³¹ Then Joab came to Absalom's house and demanded, "Why did your servants set my field on fire?"

³² "Look," Absalom explained to Joab, "I sent for you and said, 'Come here. I want to send you to the king to ask: Why have I come back from Geshur? I'd be better off if I were still there.' So now, let me see the king. If I am guilty, let him kill me."

³³ Joab went to the king and told him. So David summoned Absalom, who came to the king and paid homage with his face to the ground before him. Then the king kissed Absalom.

Absalom's Revolt

15 After this, Absalom got himself a chariot, horses, and fifty men to run before him. ² He would get up early and stand beside the road leading to the city gate. Whenever anyone had a grievance to bring before the king for settlement, Absalom called out to him and asked, "What city are you from?" If he replied, "Your servant is from one of the tribes of Israel," ³ Absalom said to him, "Look, your claims are good and right, but the king does not have anyone to listen to you." ⁴ He added, "If only someone would appoint me judge in the land. Then anyone who had a grievance or dispute could come to me, and I would make sure he received justice." ⁵ When a person approached to pay homage to him, Absalom reached out his hand, took hold of him, and kissed him. ⁶ Absalom did this to all the Israelites who came to the king for a settlement. So Absalom stole the hearts of the men of Israel. 1Sm 8:11

⁷ When fourᴮ years had passed, Absalom said to the king, "Please let me go to Hebron to fulfill a vow I made to the LORD. ⁸ For your servant made a vow when I lived in Geshur of Aram, saying: If the LORD really brings me back to Jerusalem, I will worship the LORD in Hebron."ᶜ Gn 28:20-21; 1Sm 1:11; 2Sm 13:37-38

⁹ "Go in peace," the king said to him. So he went to Hebron. Ex 4:18

¹⁰ Then Absalom sent agents throughout the tribes of Israel with this message: "When you hear the sound of the ram's horn, you are to say, 'Absalom has become king in Hebron!'" 2Sm 6:15; 1Kg 1:41; Jr 4:19,21

¹¹ Two hundred men from Jerusalem went with Absalom. They had been invited and were going innocently, for they did not know the whole situation. ¹² While he was offering the sacrifices, Absalom sent for David's adviser Ahithophel the Gilonite, from his city of Giloh. So the conspiracy grew strong, and the people supporting Absalom continued to increase. 1Ch 27:33; Ps 41:9

¹³ Then an informer came to David and reported, "The hearts of the men of Israel are with Absalom."

¹⁴ David said to all the servants with him in Jerusalem, "Get up. We have to flee, or we will not escape from Absalom! Leave quickly, or he will overtake us quickly, heap disaster on us, and strike the city with the edge of the sword." Ps 3 title

¹⁵ The king's servants said to the king, "Whatever my lord the king decides, we are your servants." ¹⁶ Then the king set out, and his entire household followed him. But he left behind ten concubines to take care of the palace. ¹⁷ So the king set out, and all the people followed him. They stopped at the last house ¹⁸ while all his servants marched past him. Then all the Cherethites, the Pelethites, and the people of Gath— six hundred men who came with him from there — marched past the king. 1Sm 27:2-7

¹⁹ The king said to Ittai of Gath, "Why are you also going with us? Go back and stay with the new king since you're both a foreigner and an exile from your homeland. ²⁰ Besides, you only arrived yesterday; should I make you wander around with us today while I go wherever I can? Go back and take your brothers with you. May the LORD show you ᴬ kindness and faithfulness."

²¹ But in response, Ittai vowed to the king, "As the LORD lives and as my lord the king lives, wherever my lord the king is, whether it means life or death, your servant will be there!" Ru 1:16

²² "March on," David replied to Ittai. So Ittai of Gath marched past with all his men and the dependents who were with him. ²³ Everyone in the countryside was weeping loudly while all the people were marching out of the city. As the king was crossing the Kidron Valley, all the people were marching past on the road that leads to the wilderness.

²⁴ Zadok was also there, and all the Levites with him were carrying the ark of the covenant of God. They set the ark of God down, and Abiathar offered sacrifices ᴮ until the people had finished marching past. ²⁵ Then the king instructed Zadok, "Return the ark of God to the city. If I find favor with the LORD, he will bring me back and allow me to see both it and its ᶜ dwelling place. ²⁶ However, if he should say, 'I do not delight in you,' then here I am — he can do with me whatever pleases him." ᴰ 1Sm 4:3; 2Sm 8:17; 20:25

²⁷ The king also said to the priest Zadok, "Look, ᴱ return to the city in peace and your two sons with you: your son Ahimaaz and Abiathar's son Jonathan. ²⁸ Remember, I'll wait at the fords ᶠ of the wilderness until word comes from you to inform me." ²⁹ So Zadok and Abiathar returned the ark of God to Jerusalem and stayed there. 2Sm 8:17

³⁰ David was climbing the slope of the Mount of Olives, weeping as he ascended. His head was covered, and he was walking barefoot. All of the people with him covered their heads and went up, weeping as they ascended. Zch 14:4; Mt 21:1; 24:3

³¹ Then someone reported to David: "Ahithophel is among the conspirators with Absalom."

"LORD," David pleaded, "please turn the counsel of Ahithophel into foolishness!" 2Sm 16:21; 17:14,23

ᴬ15:20 LXX; MT omits Lit *May the LORD show you*   ᴮ15:24 Or *Abiathar went up*   ᶜ15:25 Or *his*   ᴰ15:26 Lit *me what is good in his eyes*   ᴱ15:27 LXX; MT reads *"Are you a seer?*   ᶠ15:28 Alt Hb tradition reads *plains*

³² When David came to the summit where he used to worship God, Hushai the Archite was there to meet him with his robe torn and dust on his head. ³³ David said to him, "If you go away with me, you'll be a burden to me, ³⁴ but if you return to the city and tell Absalom, 'I will be your servant, Your Majesty! Previously, I was your father's servant, but now I will be your servant,' then you can counteract Ahithophel's counsel for me. ³⁵ Won't the priests Zadok and Abiathar be there with you? Report everything you hear from the palace to the priests Zadok and Abiathar. ³⁶ Take note: their two sons are there with them—Zadok's son Ahimaaz and Abiathar's son Jonathan. Send them to tell me everything you hear." ³⁷ So Hushai, David's personal adviser, entered Jerusalem just as Absalom was entering the city. Jos 16:2; 1Ch 27:33

Ziba Helps David

16 When David had gone a little beyond the summit, ᴬ Ziba, Mephibosheth's servant, was right there to meet him. He had a pair of saddled donkeys loaded with two hundred loaves of bread, one hundred clusters of raisins, one hundred bunches of summer fruit, and a clay jar of wine. ² The king said to Ziba, "Why do you have these?"

Ziba answered, "The donkeys are for the king's household to ride, the bread and summer fruit are for the young men to eat, and the wine is for those to drink who become exhausted in the wilderness."

³ "Where is your master's grandson?" the king asked.

"Why, he's staying in Jerusalem," Ziba replied to the king, "for he said, 'Today, the house of Israel will restore my grandfather's kingdom to me.'" 2Sm 19:26-27

⁴ The king said to Ziba, "All that belongs to Mephibosheth is now yours!" 2Sm 9:3-11

"I bow before you," Ziba said. "May I find favor with you, my lord the king!"

Shimei Curses David

⁵ When King David got to Bahurim, a man belonging to the family of the house of Saul was just coming out. His name was Shimei son of Gera, and he was yelling curses as he approached. ⁶ He threw stones at David and at all the royal ᴮ servants, the people and the warriors on David's right and left. ⁷ Shimei said as he cursed: "Get out, get out, you man of bloodshed, you wicked man! ⁸ The LORD has paid you back for all the blood of the house of Saul in whose place you became king, and the LORD has handed the kingdom over to your son Absalom. Look, you are in trouble because you're a man of bloodshed!"

⁹ Then Abishai son of Zeruiah said to the king, "Why should this dead dog curse my lord the king? Let me go over and remove his head!"

¹⁰ The king replied, "Sons of Zeruiah, do we agree on anything? He curses me this way because the LORD ᶜ told him, 'Curse David!' Therefore, who can say, 'Why did you do that?'" ¹¹ Then David said to Abishai and all his servants, "Look, my own son, my own flesh and blood, ᴰ intends to take my life — how much more now this

---

ᴬ16:1 = Mount of Olives   ᴮ16:6 Lit *all King David's* LORD   ᶜ16:10 Alt Hb tradition reads *If he curses, and if the* LORD   ᴰ16:11 Lit *son who came from my belly*

Benjaminite! Leave him alone and let him curse me; the LORD has told him to. ¹² Perhaps the LORD will see my affliction ᴬ and restore goodness to me instead of Shimei's curses today." ¹³ So David and his men proceeded along the road as Shimei was going along the ridge of the hill opposite him. As Shimei went, he cursed David, threw stones at him, and kicked up dust. ¹⁴ Finally, the king and all the people with him arrived ᴮ exhausted, so they rested there.   1Sm 17:43; 2Sm 3:39; 19:22

Absalom's Advisers

¹⁵ Now Absalom and all the Israelites came to Jerusalem. Ahithophel was also with him. ¹⁶ When David's friend Hushai the Archite came to Absalom, Hushai said to Absalom, "Long live the king! Long live the king!"   1Sm 10:24; 1Kg 1:25; 2Kg 11:12

¹⁷ "Is this your loyalty to your friend?" Absalom asked Hushai. "Why didn't you go with your friend?"

¹⁸ "Not at all," Hushai answered Absalom. "I am on the side of the one that the LORD, this people, and all the men of Israel have chosen. I will stay with him. ¹⁹ Furthermore, whom will I serve if not his son? As I served in your father's presence, I will also serve in yours."   2Sm 15:34

²⁰ Then Absalom said to Ahithophel, "Give me your advice. What should we do?"

²¹ Ahithophel replied to Absalom, "Sleep with your father's concubines whom he left to take care of the palace. When all Israel hears that you have become repulsive to your father, everyone with you will be encouraged." ᶜ

²² So they pitched a tent for Absalom on the roof, and he slept with his father's concubines in the sight of all Israel.   2Sm 12:11-12; 15:16; 20:3

²³ Now the advice Ahithophel gave in those days was like someone asking about a word from God — such was the regard that both David and Absalom had for Ahithophel's advice. ¹ Ahithophel said to Absalom, "Let me choose twelve thousand men, and I will set out in pursuit of David tonight. ² I will attack him while he is weary and discouraged, ᴰ throw him into a panic, and all the people with him will scatter. I will strike down only the king ³ and bring all the people back to you. When everyone returns except the man you're looking for, all ᴱ the people will be at peace." ⁴ This proposal seemed right to Absalom and all the elders of Israel.   1Kg 22:31

⁵ Then Absalom said, "Summon Hushai the Archite also. Let's hear what he has to say as well."

⁶ So Hushai came to Absalom, and Absalom told him: "Ahithophel offered this proposal. Should we carry out his proposal? If not, what do you say?"

⁷ Hushai replied to Absalom, "The advice Ahithophel has given this time is not good." ⁸ Hushai continued, "You know your father and his men. They are warriors and are desperate like a wild bear robbed of her cubs. Your father is an experienced soldier who won't spend the night with the people. ⁹ He's

---

ᴬ**16:12** Some Hb mss, LXX, Syr, Vg; one Hb tradition reads *iniquity*; alt Hb tradition reads *eyes*; another Hb tradition reads *will look with his eye*   ᴮ**16:14** LXX adds *at the Jordan*   ᶜ**16:21** Lit *father, the hands of everyone with you will be strong*   ᴰ**17:2** Lit *and weak of hands*   ᴱ**17:3** LXX reads *to you as a bride returns to her husband. You seek the life of only one man, and all* probably already hiding in one of the caves[A] or some other place. If some of our troops fall[B] first, someone is sure to hear and say, 'There's been a slaughter among the people who follow Absalom.' [10] Then, even a brave man with the heart of a lion will lose heart[C] because all Israel knows that your father and the valiant men with him are warriors. [11] Instead, I advise that all Israel from Dan to Beer-sheba — as numerous as the sand by the sea — be gathered to you and that you personally go into battle. [12] Then we will attack David wherever we find him, and we will descend on him like dew on the ground. Not even one will be left—neither he nor any of the men with him. [13] If he retreats to some city, all Israel will bring ropes to that city, and we will drag its stones[D] into the valley until not even a pebble can be found there." [14] Since the LORD had decreed that Ahithophel's good advice be undermined in order to bring about Absalom's ruin, Absalom and all the men of Israel said, "The advice of Hushai the Archite is better than Ahithophel's advice."   Pr 17:12; Hs 13:8

David Informed of Absalom's Plans

[15] Hushai then told the priests Zadok and Abiathar, "This is what[E] Ahithophel advised Absalom and the elders of Israel, and this is what[F] I advised. [16] Now send someone quickly and tell David, 'Don't spend the night at the wilderness ford,[G] but be sure to cross over the Jordan,[H] or the king and all the people with him will be devoured.' "

[17] Jonathan and Ahimaaz were staying at En-rogel, where a servant girl would come and pass along information to them. They in turn would go and inform King David, because they dared not be seen entering the city. [18] However, a young man did see them and informed Absalom. So the two left quickly and came to the house of a man in Bahurim. He had a well in his courtyard, and they climbed down into it. [19] Then his wife took the cover, placed it over the mouth of the well, and scattered grain on it so nobody would know anything.

[20] Absalom's servants came to the woman at the house and asked, "Where are Ahimaaz and Jonathan?"

"They passed by toward the water,"[I] the woman replied to them. The men searched but did not find them, so they returned to Jerusalem.

[21] After they had gone, Ahimaaz and Jonathan climbed out of the well and went and informed King David. They told him, "Get up and immediately ford the river, for Ahithophel has given this advice against you." [22] So David and all the people with him got up and crossed the Jordan. By daybreak, there was no one who had not crossed the Jordan. [23] When Ahithophel realized that his advice had not been followed, he saddled his donkey and set out for his house in his hometown. He set his house in order and hanged himself. So he died and was buried in his father's tomb.

[24] David had arrived at Mahanaim by the time Absalom crossed

the Jordan with all the men of Israel. ²⁵ Now Absalom had appointed Amasa over the army in Joab's place. Amasa was the son of a man named Ithra ᴬ the Israelite; ᴮ Ithra had married Abigail daughter of Nahash. ᶜ Abigail was a sister to Zeruiah, Joab's mother. ²⁶ And Israel and Absalom camped in the land of Gilead. ²⁷ When David came to Mahanaim, Shobi son of Nahash from Rabbah of the Ammonites, Machir son of Ammiel from Lo-debar, and Barzillai the Gileadite from Rogelim ²⁸ brought beds, basins, ᴰ and pottery items. They also brought wheat, barley, flour, roasted grain, beans, lentils, ᴱ ²⁹ honey, curds, sheep, goats, and cheese ᶠ from the herd for David and the people with him to eat. They had reasoned, "The people must be hungry, exhausted, and thirsty in the wilderness."   2Sm 9:4; 19:13; 20:9-12

Absalom's Defeat

18 David reviewed his troops and appointed commanders of thousands and of hundreds over them. ² He then sent out the troops, a third under Joab, a third under Joab's brother Abishai son of Zeruiah, and a third under Ittai of Gath. The king said to the troops, "I must also march out with you."

³ "You must not go!" the people pleaded. "If we have to flee, they will not pay any attention to us. Even if half of us die, they will not pay any attention to us because you are worth ᴳ ten thousand of us. Therefore, it is better if you support us from the city."   2Sm 21:17

⁴ "I will do whatever you think is best," the king replied to them. So he stood beside the city gate while all the troops marched out by hundreds and thousands. ⁵ The king commanded Joab, Abishai, and Ittai, "Treat the young man Absalom gently for my sake." All the people heard the king's orders to all the commanders about Absalom.

⁶ Then David's forces marched into the field to engage Israel in battle, which took place in the forest of Ephraim. ⁷ Israel's army was defeated by David's soldiers, and the slaughter there was vast that day — twenty thousand dead. ⁸ The battle spread over the entire area, and that day the forest claimed more people than the sword.

Absalom's Death

⁹ Absalom was riding on his mule when he happened to meet David's soldiers. When the mule went under the tangled branches of a large oak tree, Absalom's head was caught fast in the tree. The mule under him kept going, so he was suspended in midair. ᴴ ¹⁰ One of the men saw him and informed Joab. He said, "I just saw Absalom hanging in an oak tree!"

¹¹ "You just saw him!" Joab exclaimed. ᴵ "Why didn't you strike him to the ground right there? I would have given you ten silver pieces ᴶ and a belt!"

¹² The man replied to Joab, "Even if I had the weight of a thousand pieces of silver ᴷ in my hand, I would not raise my hand against the

---

ᴬ17:25 Or *Jether*   ᴮ17:25 Some LXX mss read *Ishmaelite*   ᶜ17:25 Some LXX mss read *Jesse*   ᴰ17:28 LXX reads *brought 10 embroidered beds with double coverings, 10 vessels*   ᴱ17:28 LXX, Syr; MT adds *roasted grain*   ᶠ 17:29 Hb obscure   ᴳ18:3 Some Hb mss, LXX, Vg; other Hb mss read *because there would now be about*   ᴴ18:9 Lit *was between heaven and earth*   ᴵ18:11 Lit *Joab said to the man who told him*   ᴶ18:11 About four ounces of silver   ᴷ18:12 About 25 pounds of silver king's son. For we heard the king command you, Abishai, and Ittai, 'Protect the young man Absalom for me.'[A] [13] If I had jeopardized my own[B] life — and nothing is hidden from the king — you would have abandoned me."   2Sm 18:5

[14] Joab said, "I'm not going to waste time with you!" He then took three spears in his hand and thrust them into Absalom's chest. While Absalom was still alive in the oak tree, [15] ten young men who were Joab's armor-bearers surrounded Absalom, struck him, and killed him. [16] Joab blew the ram's horn, and the troops broke off their pursuit of Israel because Joab restrained them. [17] They took Absalom, threw him into a large pit in the forest, and raised up a huge mound of stones over him. And all Israel fled, each to his tent.

[18] When he was alive, Absalom had taken a pillar and raised it up for himself in the King's Valley, since he thought, "I have no son to preserve the memory of my name." So he named the pillar after himself. It is still called Absalom's Monument today.   Gn 28:18; Dt 16:22

[19] Ahimaaz son of Zadok said, "Please let me run and tell the king the good news that the LORD has vindicated him by freeing him from his enemies."   2Sm 15:36

[20] Joab replied to him, "You are not the man to take good news today. You may do it another day, but today you aren't taking good news, because the king's son is dead." [21] Joab then said to a Cushite, "Go tell the king what you have seen." The Cushite bowed to Joab and took off running.

[22] However, Ahimaaz son of Zadok persisted and said to Joab, "No matter what, please let me also run behind the Cushite!"

Joab replied, "My son, why do you want to run since you won't get a reward?"[C]

[23] "No matter what, I want to run!"

"Then run!" Joab said to him. So Ahimaaz ran by way of the plain and outran the Cushite.

[24] David was sitting between the city gates when the watchman went up to the roof of the city gate and over to the wall. The watchman looked out and saw a man running alone. [25] He called out and told the king.   2Sm 13:34; 19:8; 2Kg 9:17

The king said, "If he's alone, he bears good news."

As the first runner came closer, [26] the watchman saw another man running. He called out to the gatekeeper, "Look! Another man is running alone!"

"This one is also bringing good news," said the king.

[27] The watchman said, "The way the first man runs looks to me like the way Ahimaaz son of Zadok runs."   2Kg 9:20

"This is a good man; he comes with good news," the king commented.   1Kg 1:42

[28] Ahimaaz called out to the king, "All is well," and paid homage to the king with his face to the ground. He continued, "Blessed be the LORD your God! He delivered up the men who rebelled against my lord the king."

[29] The king asked, "Is the young man Absalom all right?"

Ahimaaz replied, "When Joab sent the king's servant and your

A18:12 Some Hb mss, LXX, Tg, Vg; other Hb mss read 'Protect, whoever, the young man Absalom'; Hb obscure   B18:13 Alt Hb tradition reads jeopardized his   C18:22 Or you have no good news?

servant, I saw a big disturbance, but I don't know what it was."

³⁰ The king said, "Move aside and stand here." So he stood to one side.

³¹ Just then the Cushite came and said, "May my lord the king hear the good news: The LORD has vindicated you today by freeing you from all who rise against you!"

³² The king asked the Cushite, "Is the young man Absalom all right?"

The Cushite replied, "I wish that the enemies of my lord the king, along with all who rise up against you with evil intent, would become like that young man." 1Sm 25:26

³³ The king was deeply moved and went up to the chamber above the city gate and wept. As he walked, he cried, "My son Absalom! My son, my son Absalom! If only I had died instead of you, Absalom, my son, my son!" 2Sm 19:4

David's Kingdom Restored

19 It was reported to Joab, "The king is weeping. He's mourning over Absalom." ² That day's victory was turned into mourning for all the troops because on that day the troops heard, "The king is grieving over his son." ³ So they returned to the city quietly that day like troops come in when they are humiliated after fleeing in battle. ⁴ But the king covered his face and cried loudly, "My son Absalom! Absalom, my son, my son!" 2Sm 15:30

⁵ Then Joab went into the house to the king and said, "Today you have shamed all your soldiers — those who saved your life as well as your sons, your wives, and your concubines — ⁶ by loving your enemies and hating those who love you! Today you have made it clear that the commanders and soldiers mean nothing to you. In fact, today I know that if Absalom were alive and all of us were dead, it would be fine with you!ᴬ

⁷ "Now get up! Go out and encourageᴮ your soldiers, for I swear by the LORD that if you don't go out, not a man will remain with you tonight. This will be worse for you than all the trouble that has come to you from your youth until now!"

⁸ So the king got up and sat in the city gate, and all the people were told: "Look, the king is sitting in the city gate." Then they all came into the king's presence. 2Sm 18:4,24,33

Meanwhile, each Israelite had fled to his tent. ⁹ People throughout all the tribes of Israel were arguing among themselves, saying, "The king rescued us from the grasp of our enemies, and he saved us from the grasp of the Philistines, but now he has fled from the land because of Absalom. ¹⁰ But Absalom, the man we anointed over us, has died in battle. So why do you say nothing about restoring the king?" 2Sm 5:20; 8:1-14; 8:1; 18:17

¹¹ King David sent word to the priests Zadok and Abiathar: "Say to the elders of Judah, 'Why should you be the last to restore the king to his palace? The talk of all Israel has reached the king at his house. ¹² You are my brothers, my flesh and blood.ᶜ So why should you be the last to restore the king?' ¹³ And tell Amasa, 'Aren't you my flesh and blood?ᴰ May God punish me and do so severely if you don't become commander of my army from now on instead of Joab!'" Gn 29:14; 2Sm 15:29

ᴬ**19:6** Lit *be right in your eyes*   ᴮ**19:7** Lit *speak to the heart of*   ᶜ**19:12** Lit *my bone and my flesh*
ᴰ**19:13** Lit *my bone and my flesh?*

¹⁴ So he won over^A all the men of Judah, and they unanimously sent word to the king: "Come back, you and all your servants." ¹⁵ Then the king returned. When he arrived at the Jordan, Judah came to Gilgal to meet the king and escort him across the Jordan.

¹⁶ Shimei son of Gera, the Benjaminite from Bahurim, hurried down with the men of Judah to meet King David. ¹⁷ There were a thousand men from Benjamin with him. Ziba, an attendant from the house of Saul, with his fifteen sons and twenty servants also rushed down to the Jordan ahead of the king. ¹⁸ They forded the Jordan to bring the king's household across and do whatever the king desired.^B   2Sm 16:1-5; 1Kg 2:8

When Shimei son of Gera crossed the Jordan, he fell facedown before the king ¹⁹ and said to him, "My lord, don't hold me guilty, and don't remember your servant's wrongdoing on the day my lord the king left Jerusalem. May the king not take it to heart. ²⁰ For your servant knows that I have sinned. But look! Today I am the first one of the entire house of Joseph to come down to meet my lord the king."   2Sm 16:5-13

²¹ Abishai son of Zeruiah asked, "Shouldn't Shimei be put to death for this, because he cursed the LORD's anointed?"   Ex 22:28

²² David answered, "Sons of Zeruiah, do we agree on anything? Have you become my adversary today? Should any man be killed in Israel today? Am I not aware that today I'm king over Israel?" ²³ So the king said to Shimei, "You will not die." Then the king gave him his oath.

²⁴ Mephibosheth, Saul's grandson, also went down to meet the king. He had not taken care of his feet, trimmed his mustache, or washed his clothes from the day the king left until the day he returned safely. ²⁵ When he came from Jerusalem to meet the king, the king asked him, "Mephibosheth, why didn't you come with me?"   2Sm 9:6

²⁶ "My lord the king," he replied, "my servant Ziba betrayed me. Actually your servant said: 'I'll saddle the donkey for myself^C so that I may ride it and go with the king' — for your servant is lame. ²⁷ Ziba slandered your servant to my lord the king. But my lord the king is like the angel of God, so do whatever you think best.^D ²⁸ For my grandfather's entire family deserves death from my lord the king, but you set your servant among those who eat at your table. So what further right do I have to keep on making appeals to the king?"   2Sm 4:4; 9:3; 14:17,20; 16:1-4

²⁹ The king said to him, "Why keep on speaking about these matters of yours? I hereby declare: you and Ziba are to divide the land."   2Sm 9:9

³⁰ Mephibosheth said to the king, "Instead, since my lord the king has come to his palace safely, let Ziba take it all!"

³¹ Barzillai the Gileadite had come down from Rogelim and accompanied the king to the Jordan River to see him off at the Jordan. ³² Barzillai was a very old man — eighty years old — and since he was a very wealthy man, he had provided for the needs of the king while he stayed in Mahanaim.

^A19:14 Lit he turned the heart of ^B19:18 Lit do what is good in his eyes ^C19:26 LXX, Syr, Vg read said to him, 'Saddle the donkey for me ^D19:27 Lit do what is good in your eyes

³³ The king said to Barzillai, "Cross over with me, and I'll provide for you ᴬ at my side in Jerusalem."

³⁴ Barzillai replied to the king, "How many years of my life are left that I should go up to Jerusalem with the king? ³⁵ I'm now eighty years old. Can I discern what is pleasant and what is not? Can your servant taste what he eats or drinks? Can I still hear the voice of male and female singers? Why should your servant be an added burden to my lord the king? ³⁶ Since your servant is only going with the king a little way across the Jordan, why should the king repay me with such a reward? ³⁷ Please let your servant return so that I may die in my own city near the tomb of my father and mother. But here is your servant Chimham: let him cross over with my lord the king. Do for him what seems good to you." ᴮ   2Sm 15:33; 1Kg 2:7; Ps 90:10; Jr 41:17

³⁸ The king replied, "Chimham will cross over with me, and I will do for him what seems good to you, and whatever you desire from me I will do for you." ³⁹ So all the people crossed the Jordan, and then the king crossed. The king kissed Barzillai and blessed him, and Barzillai returned to his home.

⁴⁰ The king went on to Gilgal, and Chimham went with him. All the troops of Judah and half of Israel's escorted the king. ⁴¹ Suddenly, all the men of Israel came to the king. They asked him, "Why did our brothers, the men of Judah, take you away secretly and transport the king and his household across the Jordan, along with all of David's men?"

⁴² All the men of Judah responded to the men of Israel, "Because the king is our relative. Why does this make you angry? Have we ever eaten anything of the king's or been honored at all?" ᶜ

⁴³ The men of Israel answered the men of Judah: "We have ten shares in the king, so we have a greater claim to David than you. Why then do you despise us? Weren't we the first to speak of restoring our king?" But the words of the men of Judah were harsher than those of the men of Israel.   1Kg 11:31

Sheba's Revolt

20 Now a wicked man, a Benjaminite named Sheba son of Bichri, happened to be there. He blew the ram's horn and shouted:

We have no portion in David,
no inheritance in Jesse's son.
Each man to his tent, ᴰ Israel!

² So all the men of Israel deserted David and followed Sheba son of Bichri, but the men of Judah from the Jordan all the way to Jerusalem remained loyal to their king.

³ When David came to his palace in Jerusalem, he took the ten concubines he had left to take care of the palace and placed them under guard. He provided for them, but he was not intimate with them. They were confined until the day of their death, living as widows.   2Sm 15:16

⁴ The king said to Amasa, "Summon the men of Judah to me within three days and be here yourself." ⁵ Amasa went to summon Judah, but he took longer than the time allotted him. ⁶ So David said to Abishai, "Sheba son of Bichri will do more harm to us than Absalom.

ᴬ19:33 LXX reads *for your old age*; Ru 4:15   ᴮ19:37 Lit *what is good in your eyes*, also in v. 38   ᶜ19:42 LXX reads *king's or has he given us a gift or granted us a portion*   ᴰ20:1 Alt Hb tradition reads *gods*

Take your lord's soldiers and pursue him, or he will find fortified cities and elude us."^A

⁷ So Joab's men, the Cherethites, the Pelethites, and all the warriors marched out under Abishai's command;^B they left Jerusalem to pursue Sheba son of Bichri. ⁸ They were at the great stone in Gibeon when Amasa joined them. Joab was wearing his uniform and over it was a belt around his waist with a sword in its sheath. As he approached, the sword fell out. ⁹ Joab asked Amasa, "Are you well, my brother?" Then with his right hand Joab grabbed Amasa by the beard to kiss him. ¹⁰ Amasa was not on guard against the sword in Joab's hand, and Joab stabbed him in the stomach with it and spilled his intestines out on the ground. Joab did not stab him again, and Amasa died.   Mt 26:49; Mk 14:45; Lk 22:47

Joab and his brother Abishai pursued Sheba son of Bichri. ¹¹ One of Joab's young men had stood over Amasa saying, "Whoever favors Joab and whoever is for David, follow Joab!" ¹² Now Amasa had been writhing in his blood in the middle of the highway, and the man had seen that all the troops stopped. So he moved Amasa from the highway to the field and threw a garment over him because he realized that all those who encountered Amasa were stopping. ¹³ When he was removed from the highway, all the men passed by and followed Joab to pursue Sheba son of Bichri.

¹⁴ Sheba passed through all the tribes of Israel to Abel of Beth-maacah. All the Berites^C came together and followed him. ¹⁵ Joab's troops came and besieged Sheba in Abel of Beth-maacah. They built a siege ramp against the outer wall of the city. While all the troops with Joab were battering the wall to make it collapse, ¹⁶ a wise woman called out from the city, "Listen! Listen! Please tell Joab to come here and let me speak with him."   2Kg 19:32; 26:8

¹⁷ When he had come near her, the woman asked, "Are you Joab?"

"I am," he replied.

"Listen to the words of your servant," she said to him.

He answered, "I'm listening."

¹⁸ She said, "In the past they used to say, 'Seek counsel in Abel,' and that's how they settled disputes. ¹⁹ I am one of the peaceful and faithful in Israel, but you're trying to destroy a city that is like a mother in Israel. Why would you devour the LORD's inheritance?"

²⁰ Joab protested: "Never! I would never devour or demolish! ²¹ That is not the case. There is a man named Sheba son of Bichri, from the hill country of Ephraim, who has rebelled against King David. Deliver this one man, and I will withdraw from the city."

The woman replied to Joab, "Watch! His head will be thrown over the wall to you." ²² The woman went to all the people with her wise counsel, and they cut off the head of Sheba son of Bichri and threw it to Joab. So he blew the ram's horn, and they dispersed from the city, each to his own tent. Joab returned to the king in Jerusalem.   Ec 9:14-15

²³ Joab commanded the whole army of Israel;   2Sm 8:16-18
Benaiah son of Jehoiada was over the Cherethites and Pelethites;

---

^A20:6 Lit and snatch away our eyes   ^B20:7 Lit out following him   ^C20:14 LXX, Vg read Bichrites

24 Adoram[A] was over forced labor;   1Kg 12:18
Jehoshaphat son of Ahilud was court historian;
25 Sheva was court secretary; Zadok and Abiathar were priests;
26 and in addition, Ira the Jairite was David's priest.

Justice for the Gibeonites

21 During David's reign there was a famine for three successive years, so David inquired[B] of the LORD. The LORD answered, "It is due to Saul and to his bloody family, because he killed the Gibeonites."

² The Gibeonites were not Israelites but rather a remnant of the Amorites. The Israelites had taken an oath concerning them, but Saul had tried to kill them in his zeal for the Israelites and Judah. So David summoned the Gibeonites and spoke to them. ³ He asked the Gibeonites, "What should I do for you? How can I make atonement so that you will bring a blessing on[C] the LORD's inheritance?"

⁴ The Gibeonites said to him, "We are not asking for silver and gold from Saul or his family, and we cannot put anyone to death in Israel."

"Whatever you say, I will do for you," he said.

⁵ They replied to the king, "As for the man who annihilated us and plotted to destroy us so we would not exist within the whole territory of Israel, ⁶ let seven of his male descendants be handed over to us so we may hang[D] them in the presence of the LORD at Gibeah of Saul, the LORD's chosen."   Nm 25:4; 1Sm 15:34

The king answered, "I will hand them over."

⁷ David spared Mephibosheth, the son of Saul's son Jonathan, because of the oath of the LORD that was between David and Jonathan, Saul's son. ⁸ But the king took Armoni and Mephibosheth, who were the two sons whom Rizpah daughter of Aiah had borne to Saul, and the five sons whom Merab[E] daughter of Saul had borne to Adriel son of Barzillai the Meholathite ⁹ and handed them over to the Gibeonites. They hanged[F] them on the hill in the presence of the LORD; the seven of them died together. They were executed in the first days of the harvest at the beginning of the barley harvest.[G]   1Sm 18:3; 20:12-17; 23:18; 2Sm 3:7

The Burial of Saul's Family

¹⁰ Rizpah, Aiah's daughter, took sackcloth and spread it out for herself on the rock from the beginning of the harvest[H] until the rain poured down from heaven on the bodies. She kept the birds of the sky from them by day and the wild animals by night.

¹¹ When it was reported to David what Saul's concubine Rizpah daughter of Aiah had done, ¹² he went and got the bones of Saul and his son Jonathan from the citizens of Jabesh-gilead. They had stolen them from the public square of Beth-shan where the Philistines had hung the bodies the day the Philistines killed Saul at Gilboa. ¹³ David had the bones brought from there. They gathered up the bones of Saul's family who had been hanged ¹⁴ and buried the

---

[A]**20:24** Some Hb mss, LXX, Syr read *Adoniram* ; 1Kg 4:6; 5:14   [B]**21:1** Lit *sought the face of*   [C]**21:3** Lit *will bless*   [D]**21:6** Or *impale*, or *expose*   [E]**21:8** Some Hb mss, LXX, Syr, Tg; other Hb mss read *Michal*   [F]**21:9** Or *impaled*, or *exposed*, also in v. 13   [G]**21:9** = March–April   [H]**21:10** = April to October bones of Saul and his son Jonathan at Zela in the land of Benjamin in the tomb of Saul's father Kish. They did everything the king commanded. After this, God was receptive to prayer for the land. 1Sm 31:11-13

The Philistine Giants

¹⁵ The Philistines again waged war against Israel. David went down with his soldiers, and they fought the Philistines, but David became exhausted. ¹⁶ Then Ishbi-benob, one of the descendants of the giant,^A whose bronze spear weighed about eight pounds^B and who wore new armor, intended to kill David. ¹⁷ But Abishai son of Zeruiah came to his aid, struck the Philistine, and killed him. Then David's men swore to him: "You must never again go out with us to battle. You must not extinguish the lamp of Israel."

¹⁸ After this, there was another battle with the Philistines at Gob. At that time Sibbecai the Hushathite killed Saph, who was one of the descendants of the giant. 1Ch 20:4-8

¹⁹ Once again there was a battle with the Philistines at Gob, and Elhanan son of Jaare-oregim the Bethlehemite killed^C Goliath of Gath. The shaft of his spear was like a weaver's beam. 1Sm 17:7

²⁰ At Gath there was still another battle. A huge man was there with six fingers on each hand and six toes on each foot — twenty-four in all. He, too, was descended from the giant. ²¹ When he taunted Israel, Jonathan, son of David's brother Shimei, killed him.

²² These four were descended from the giant in Gath and were killed by David and his soldiers.

David's Song of Thanksgiving

22 David spoke the words of this song to the Lord on the day the Lord rescued him from the grasp of all his enemies and from the grasp of Saul. ² He said:

The Lord is my rock,
  my fortress,
  and my deliverer, Ps 31:3; 71:3
³ my God,^D my rock where
  I seek refuge.
My shield, the horn
  of my salvation,
  my stronghold, my refuge,
and my Savior, you save me
  from violence.
⁴ I called to the Lord,
  who is worthy of praise,
  and I was saved
  from my enemies.
⁵ For the waves of death
  engulfed me; Ps 42:7; Jnh 2:3
  the torrents of destruction
  terrified me.
⁶ The ropes of Sheol
  entangled me;
  the snares of death
  confronted me. Ps 116:3

⁷ I called to the Lord
  in my distress;
I called to my God. Ps 116:4; 120:1
From his temple he heard
  my voice,
and my cry for help reached
  his ears.
⁸ Then the earth shook
  and quaked;
  the foundations
  of the heavens^E trembled;
they shook because
  he burned with anger.
⁹ Smoke rose from his nostrils,
  and consuming fire came
  from his mouth;

---

^A21:16 Or *Raphah*, also in vv. 18, 20, 22 ^B21:16 Lit *300* (shekels) ^C21:19 1Ch 20:5 adds *the brother of*
^D22:3 LXX, Ps 18:2 read *my God*; MT reads *God of* ^E22:8 Some Hb mss, Syr, Vg read *mountains*; Ps 18:7

coals were set ablaze by it. ᴬ

10 He bent the heavens
   and came down,   Ps 144:5; Is 64:1
   total darkness
   beneath his feet.
11 He rode on a cherub and flew,
   soaring ᴮ on the wings
   of the wind.
12 He made darkness a canopy
   around him,
   a gathering ᶜ of water
   and thick clouds.   Ps 97:2
13 From the radiance
   of his presence,
   blazing coals were ignited.
14 The LORD thundered
   from heaven;
   the Most High made his voice
   heard.   Jb 37:4
15 He shot arrows
   and scattered them;   Dt 32:23
   he hurled lightning bolts
   and routed them.   Ps 144:6
16 The depths of the sea
   became visible,
   the foundations of the world
   were exposed
   at the rebuke of the LORD,
   at the blast of the breath
   of his nostrils.   Jb 4:9; Is 30:33

17 He reached down from on
   high
   and took hold of me;
   he pulled me
   out of deep water.   Ps 144:7
18 He rescued me
   from my powerful enemy
   and from those
   who hated me,
   for they were too strong
   for me.
19 They confronted me
   in the day of my calamity,
   but the LORD was my support.
20 He brought me out
   to a spacious place;   Ps 31:8
   he rescued me because
   he delighted in me.
21 The LORD rewarded me
   according to
   my righteousness;   1Sm 26:23
   he repaid me
   according to the cleanness
   of my hands.   Ps 24:3-4
22 For I have kept the ways
   of the LORD   Pr 8:32
   and have not turned
   from my God
   to wickedness.
23 Indeed, I let
   all his ordinances
   guide me ᴰ   Ps 119:30,102
   and have not disregarded
   his statutes.
24 I was blameless before him
   and kept myself from my
   iniquity.
25 So the LORD repaid me
   according to
   my righteousness,
   according to my cleanness ᴱ
   in his sight.
26 With the faithful
   you prove yourself faithful,
   with the blameless
   you prove
   yourself blameless,
27 with the pure
   you prove yourself pure;
   but with the crooked
   you prove yourself shrewd.
28 You rescue
   an oppressed people,
   but your eyes are set
   against the proud —

ᴬ22:9 Or *him*   ᴮ22:11 Some Hb mss; other Hb mss, Syr, Tg read *he was seen*   ᶜ22:12 Or *sieve*, or *mass*; Hb obscure   ᴰ22:23 Lit *Indeed, all his ordinances have been in front of me*   ᴱ22:25 LXX, Syr, Vg read *to the cleanness of my hands*; Ps 18:24

you humble them.   Is 2:11-12,17

²⁹ LORD, you are my lamp;
the LORD illuminates
    my darkness.   Jb 29:3; Ps 27:1

³⁰ With you I can attack
    a barricade,ᴬ
and with my God I can leap
    over a wall.   2Sm 5:6-9

³¹ God — his way is perfect;
the word of the LORD is pure.
He is a shield to all
    who take refuge in him.

³² For who is God
    besides the LORD?
And who is a rock?
    Only our God.

³³ God is my strong refuge;ᴮ
he makes my way perfect.ᶜ

³⁴ He makes my feet like
    the feet of a deer
and sets me securely
    on theᴰ heights.ᴱ

³⁵ He trains my hands for war;
my arms can bend a bow
    of bronze.

³⁶ You have given me the shield
    of your salvation;   Eph 6:16-17
your helpᶠ exalts me.

³⁷ You make a spacious place
    beneath me for my steps,
and my ankles do not
    give way.

³⁸ I pursue my enemies
    and destroy them;
I do not turn back
    until they are wiped out.

³⁹ I wipe them out
    and crush them,
and they do not rise;
they fall beneath my feet.

⁴⁰ You have clothed me
    with strength for battle;

you subdue my adversaries
    beneath me.   Ps 44:5

⁴¹ You have made my enemies
    retreat before me;ᴳ
I annihilate those
    who hate me.

⁴² They look, but there is no one
    to save them —
they look to the LORD,
    but he does not
    answer them.   1Sm 28:6; Pr 1:28

⁴³ I pulverize them like dust
    of the earth;
I crush them
    and trample them like mud
    in the streets.   Is 10:6; Mc 7:10

⁴⁴ You have freed me
    from the feuds
    among my people;   2Sm 2:8-10
you have preserved me
    as head of nations;
a people I had not known
    serve me.   2Sm 8:1-14; Is 55:5

⁴⁵ Foreigners submit to me
    cringing;
as soon as they hear,
    they obey me.

⁴⁶ Foreigners lose heart
and come trembling
    from their fortifications.

⁴⁷ The LORD lives —
    blessed be my rock!
God, the rock of my salvation,
    is exalted.   Ps 89:26; 95:1

⁴⁸ God — he grants
    me vengeance
and casts down peoples
    under me.   Ps 144:2

⁴⁹ He frees me from my enemies.
You exalt me
    above my adversaries;

ᴬ **22:30** Or *a ridge*, or *raiders*   ᴮ**22:33** DSS, some LXX mss, Syr, Vg read *God clothes me with strength*; Ps 18:32   ᶜ**22:33** Some LXX mss, Syr; MT reads *he sets free the blameless his way*; Hb obscure   ᴰ**22:34** LXX; some Hb mss read *my*; other Hb mss read *his*   ᴱ**22:34** Or *on my high places*   ᶠ**22:36** LXX reads *humility*; Ps 18:35   ᴳ**22:41** Lit *you gave me the neck of my enemies*

you rescue me
from violent men. Ps 140:1

50 Therefore I will give
thanks to you among
the nations, Lord;
I will sing praises
about your name. Rm 15:9
51 He is a tower of salvation
for^A his king;
he shows loyalty
to his anointed,
to David and his descendants
forever. 2Sm 7:12-16; Lk 1:55

David's Last Words

23 These are the last words of
David:
The declaration of David
son of Jesse, Lk 3:32
the declaration of the man
raised on high, ^B
the one anointed by the God
of Jacob. 1Sm 16:12-13; Ps 89:20
This is the most delightful
of Israel's songs.
2 The Spirit of the Lord spoke
through me,
his word was on my tongue.
3 The God of Israel spoke;
the Rock of Israel said to me,
"The one who rules
the people with justice,
who rules in the fear of God,
4 is like the morning light
when the sun rises
on a cloudless morning,
the glisten of rain
on sprouting grass."

5 Is it not true my house is
with God?
For he has established
a permanent covenant
with me, Gn 9:16; 17:7,19; 1Ch 16:17

ordered and secured
in every detail. 2Sm 7:12-16
Will he not bring about
my whole salvation
and my every desire?
6 But all the wicked are
like thorns raked aside;
they can never be picked up
by hand.
7 The man who touches them
must be armed with iron
and the shaft of a spear.
They will be completely
burned up on the spot.

Exploits of David's Warriors

8 These are the names of David's
warriors: 1Ch 11:11-47
Josheb-basshebeth the Tahche-
monite was chief of the officers. ^C
He wielded his spear^D against eight
hundred men that he killed at one
time.
9 After him, Eleazar son of Dodo
son of an Ahohite was among the
three warriors with David when
they defied the Philistines. The men
of Israel retreated in the place they
had gathered for battle, 10 but Eleazar stood his ground and attacked
the Philistines until his hand was
tired and stuck to his sword. The
Lord brought about a great victory
that day. Then the troops came back
to him, but only to plunder the dead.
11 After him was Shammah son of
Agee the Hararite. The Philistines
had assembled in formation where
there was a field full of lentils. The
troops fled from the Philistines,
12 but Shammah took his stand in
the middle of the field, defended
it, and struck down the Philistines.
So the Lord brought about a great
victory.

^A 22:51 DSS read *he gives great victory to*   ^B 23:1 Or *raised up by the high God*   ^C 23:8 Some Hb mss,
LXX read *Three*   ^D 23:8 Some Hb mss; other Hb mss, LXX read *He was Adino the Eznite*

¹³ Three of the thirty leading warriors went down at harvest time and came to David at the cave of Adullam, while a company of Philistines was camping in the Valley of Rephaim. ¹⁴ At that time David was in the stronghold, and a Philistine garrison was at Bethlehem. ¹⁵ David was extremely thirsty ᴬ and said, "If only someone would bring me water to drink from the well at the city gate of Bethlehem!" ¹⁶ So three of the warriors broke through the Philistine camp and drew water from the well at the gate of Bethlehem. They brought it back to David, but he refused to drink it. Instead, he poured it out to the LORD. ¹⁷ David said, "LORD, I would never do such a thing! Is this not the blood of men who risked their lives?" So he refused to drink it. Such were the exploits of the three warriors.   1Sm 22:1

¹⁸ Abishai, Joab's brother and son of Zeruiah, was leader of the Three. ᴮ He wielded his spear against three hundred men and killed them, gaining a reputation among the Three. ¹⁹ Was he not more honored than the Three? He became their commander even though he did not become one of the Three.   1Sm 26:3-6; 1Ch 11:21

²⁰ Benaiah son of Jehoiada was the son of a brave man from Kabzeel, a man of many exploits. Benaiah killed two sons ᶜ of Ariel ᴰ of Moab, and he went down into a pit on a snowy day and killed a lion. ²¹ He also killed an Egyptian, an impressive man. Even though the Egyptian had a spear in his hand, Benaiah went down to him with a club, snatched the spear out of the Egyptian's hand, and then killed him with his own spear. ²² These were the exploits of Benaiah son of Jehoiada, who had a reputation among the three warriors. ²³ He was the most honored of the Thirty, but he did not become one of the Three. David put him in charge of his bodyguard.   2Sm 8:18; 20:23

²⁴ Among the Thirty were
Joab's brother Asahel,   1Ch 27:7
Elhanan son of Dodo
      of Bethlehem,
²⁵   Shammah the Harodite,
      Elika the Harodite,
²⁶   Helez the Paltite,
      Ira son of Ikkesh the Tekoite,
²⁷   Abiezer the Anathothite,
      Mebunnai the Hushathite,
²⁸   Zalmon the Ahohite,
      Maharai the Netophathite,
²⁹   Heleb son of Baanah
      the Netophahite,
      Ittai son of Ribai from Gibeah
      of the Benjaminites,
³⁰   Benaiah the Pirathonite,
      Hiddai from the wadis
      of Gaash, ᴱ
³¹   Abi-albon the Arbathite,
      Azmaveth the Barhumite,
³²   Eliahba the Shaalbonite,
      the sons of Jashen,
      Jonathan son of ᶠ ³³ Shammah
      the Hararite,
      Ahiam son of Sharar
      the Hararite,
³⁴   Eliphelet son of Ahasbai
      son of the Maacathite,
      Eliam son of Ahithophel
      the Gilonite,   2Sm 15:12
³⁵   Hezro the Carmelite,
      Paarai the Arbite,
³⁶   Igal son of Nathan from Zobah,

ᴬ23:15 Lit And David craved   ᴮ23:18 Some Hb mss, Syr read the Thirty   ᶜ23:20 LXX; MT omits sons
ᴰ23:20 Or two warriors   ᴱ23:30 Or from Nahale-gaash   ᶠ23:32 Some LXX mss; MT omits son of;
1Ch 11:34

Bani the Gadite,
37 Zelek the Ammonite,
Naharai the Beerothite,
the armor-bearer for Joab
son of Zeruiah,
38 Ira the Ithrite,
Gareb the Ithrite,
39 and Uriah the Hethite.　Mt 1:6
There were thirty-seven in all.

David's Military Census

24 The LORD's anger burned against Israel again, and he stirred up David against them to say: "Go, count the people of Israel and Judah." 1Ch 21:1-28

2 So the king said to Joab, the commander of his army, "Go through all the tribes of Israel from Dan to Beer-sheba and register the troops so I can know their number."

3 Joab replied to the king, "May the LORD your God multiply the troops a hundred times more than they are — while my lord the king looks on! But why does my lord the king want to do this?" Dt 1:11

4 Yet the king's order prevailed over Joab and the commanders of the army. So Joab and the commanders of the army left the king's presence to register the troops of Israel.

5 They crossed the Jordan and camped in Aroer, south of the town in the middle of the valley, and then proceeded toward Gad and Jazer. 6 They went to Gilead and to the land of the Hittites^A and continued on to Dan-jaan and around to Sidon. 7 They went to the fortress of Tyre and all the cities of the Hivites and Canaanites. Afterward, they went to the Negev of Judah at Beer-sheba. Dt 2:36; Jos 13:16,19

8 When they had gone through the whole land, they returned to Jerusalem at the end of nine months and twenty days. 9 Joab gave the king the total of the registration of the troops. There were eight hundred thousand valiant armed men^B from Israel and five hundred thousand men from Judah. Nm 1:45-46

10 David's conscience troubled him after he had taken a census of the troops. He said to the LORD, "I have sinned greatly in what I've done. Now, LORD, because I've been very foolish, please take away your servant's guilt." Nm 12:9-12; 1Sm 24:5

David's Punishment

11 When David got up in the morning, the word of the LORD had come to the prophet Gad, David's seer: 12 "Go and say to David, 'This is what the LORD says: I am offering you three choices. Choose one of them, and I will do it to you.'" 1Sm 22:5

13 So Gad went to David, told him the choices, and asked him, "Do you want three^C years of famine to come on your land, to flee from your foes three months while they pursue you, or to have a plague in your land three days? Now, consider carefully^D what answer I should take back to the one who sent me."

14 David answered Gad, "I have great anxiety. Please, let us fall into the LORD's hands because his mercies are great, but don't let me fall into human hands." Ps 103:8-18; 119:156

15 So the LORD sent a plague on Israel from that morning until the appointed time, and from Dan to Beer-sheba seventy thousand men died. 16 Then the angel extended his hand toward Jerusalem to destroy

^A 24:6 LXX; MT reads *of Tahtim-hodshi*; Hb obscure　^B 24:9 Lit *men of valor drawing the sword*
^C 24:13 LXX; MT reads *seven*; 1Ch 21:12　^D 24:13 Lit *Now, know and see*

it, but the LORD relented concerning the destruction and said to the angel who was destroying the people, "Enough, withdraw your hand now! " The angel of the LORD was then at the threshing floor of Araunah [A] the Jebusite.   Ex 32:14; 2Kg 19:35

[17] When David saw the angel striking the people, he said to the LORD, "Look, I am the one who has sinned; I am the one [B] who has done wrong. But these sheep, what have they done? Please, let your hand be against me and my father's family."

David's Altar

[18] Gad came to David that day and said to him, "Go up and set up an altar to the LORD on the threshing floor of Araunah the Jebusite." [19] David went up in obedience to Gad's command, just as the LORD had commanded. [20] Araunah looked down and saw the king and his servants coming toward him, so he went out and paid homage to the king with his face to the ground.

[21] Araunah said, "Why has my lord the king come to his servant? "

David replied, "To buy the threshing floor from you in order to build an altar to the LORD, so the plague on the people may be halted."

[22] Araunah said to David, "My lord the king may take whatever he wants [C] and offer it. Here are the oxen for a burnt offering and the threshing sledges and ox yokes for the wood. [23] Your Majesty, Araunah gives everything here to the king." Then he said to the king, "May the LORD your God accept you."

[24] The king answered Araunah, "No, I insist on buying it from you for a price, for I will not offer to the LORD my God burnt offerings that cost me nothing." David bought the threshing floor and the oxen for twenty ounces [D] of silver. [25] He built an altar to the LORD there and offered burnt offerings and fellowship offerings. Then the LORD was receptive to prayer for the land, and the plague on Israel ended.

[A] 24:16 = Ornan in 1Ch 21:15-28; 2Ch 3:1   [B] 24:17 LXX reads shepherd   [C] 24:22 Lit take what is good in his eyes   [D] 24:24 Lit 50 shekels

1 KINGS

David's Last Days

1 Now King David was old and advanced in age. Although they covered him with bedclothes, he could not get warm. ² So his servants said to him: "Let us^A search for a young virgin for my lord the king. She is to attend the king and be his caregiver. She is to lie by your side so that my lord the king will get warm." ³ They searched for a beautiful girl throughout the territory of Israel; they found Abishag the Shunammite^B and brought her to the king. ⁴ The girl was of unsurpassed beauty, and she became the king's caregiver. She attended to him, but he was not intimate with^C her. 2Sm 5:4; 1Kg 2:10-11; 1Ch 23:1; Est 2:2; Ec 4:11

Adonijah's Bid for Power

⁵ Adonijah son of Haggith kept exalting himself, saying, "I will be king!" He prepared chariots, cavalry, and fifty men to run ahead of him.^D ⁶ But his father had never once infuriated him by asking, "Why did you do that?" In addition, he was quite handsome and was born after Absalom. ⁷ He conspired^E with Joab son of Zeruiah and with the priest Abiathar. They supported Adonijah, ⁸ but the priest Zadok, Benaiah son of Jehoiada, prophet Nathan, Shimei, ... d's royal guard^F did ... nijah. 2Sm 2:1-25; 3:4 ... ed sheep, ... cattle

near the stone of Zoheleth, which is next to En-rogel. He invited all his royal brothers and all the men of Judah, the servants of the king, ¹⁰ but he did not invite the prophet Nathan, Benaiah, the royal guard, or his brother Solomon. Jos 15:7; 18:16

Nathan's and Bathsheba's Appeals

¹¹ Then Nathan said to Bathsheba, Solomon's mother, "Have you not heard that Adonijah son of Haggith has become king and our lord David does not know it? ¹² Now please come and let me advise you. Save your life and the life of your son Solomon. ¹³ Go, approach King David and say to him, 'My lord the king, did you not swear to your servant: Your son Solomon is to become king after me, and he is the one who is to sit on my throne? So why has Adonijah become king?' ¹⁴ At that moment, while you are still there speaking with the king, I'll come in after you and confirm your words." 2Sm 12:1,25; 1Kg 1:8,10,25

¹⁵ So Bathsheba went to the king in his bedroom. Since the king was very old, Abishag the Shunammite was attending to him. ¹⁶ Bathsheba knelt low and paid homage to the king, and he asked, "What do you want?" 1Kg 1:1-4

¹⁷ She replied, "My lord, you swore to your servant by the LORD your God, 'Your son Solomon is to become king after me, and he is

country of Issachar at the foot of Mt. Moreh; Jos 19:17–18. ... procession ^E1:7 Lit *His words were* ^F1:8 Lit

... miss; LXX, alt Hb tradition ... 9:8; Jr 28:6

the one who is to sit on my throne.' [18] Now look, Adonijah has become king. And, [A] my lord the king, you didn't know it. [19] He has lavishly sacrificed oxen, fattened cattle, and sheep. He invited all the king's sons, the priest Abiathar, and Joab the commander of the army, but he did not invite your servant Solomon. [20] Now, my lord the king, the eyes of all Israel are on you to tell them who will sit on the throne of my lord the king after him. [21] Otherwise, when my lord the king rests with his fathers, I and my son Solomon will be regarded as criminals."   Dt 31:16; 2Sm 7:12; 1Kg 1:12; 2:10

[22] At that moment, while she was still speaking with the king, the prophet Nathan arrived, [23] and it was announced to the king, "The prophet Nathan is here." He came into the king's presence and paid homage to him with his face to the ground.   1Kg 1:14

[24] "My lord the king," Nathan said, "did you say, 'Adonijah is to become king after me, and he is the one who is to sit on my throne'? [25] For today he went down and lavishly sacrificed oxen, fattened cattle, and sheep. He invited all the sons of the king, the commanders of the army, and the priest Abiathar. And look! They're eating and drinking in his presence, and they're saying, 'Long live King Adonijah!' [26] But he did not invite me — me, your servant — or the priest Zadok or Benaiah son of Jehoiada or your servant Solomon. [27] I'm certain my lord the king would not have let this happen without letting your servant [B] know who will sit on my lord the king's throne after him."

Solomon Confirmed King

[28] King David responded by saying, "Call in Bathsheba for me." So she came into the king's presence and stood before him. [29] The king swore an oath and said, "As the LORD lives, who has redeemed my life from every difficulty, [30] just as I swore to you by the LORD God of Israel: Your son Solomon is to become king after me, and he is the one who is to sit on my throne in my place, that is exactly what I will do this very day."   2Sm 4:9; 1Kg 1:13,33-35

[31] Bathsheba knelt low with her face to the ground, paying homage to the king, and said, "May my lord King David live forever!"   1Kg 1:16

[32] King David then said, "Call in the priest Zadok, the prophet Nathan, and Benaiah son of Jehoiada for me." So they came into the king's presence. [33] The king said to them, "Take my servants with you, have my son Solomon ride on my own mule, and take him down to Gihon. [34] There, the priest Zadok and the prophet Nathan are to anoint him as king over Israel. You are to blow the ram's horn and say, 'Long live King Solomon!' [35] You are to come up after him, and he is to come in and sit on my throne. He is the one who is to become king in my place; he is the one I have commanded to be ruler over Israel and Judah."   2Sm 18:9; 20:6; 1Kg 1:8,10,26; Est 6:8

[36] "Amen," Benaiah son of Jehoiada replied to the king. "May the LORD, the God of my lord the king, so affirm it. [37] Just as the LORD was with my lord the king, so may he [C] be with Solomon and make his throne greater than the throne of my lord King David."   1Sm 20:1

³⁸ Then the priest Zadok, the prophet Nathan, Benaiah son of Jehoiada, the Cherethites, and the Pelethites went down, had Solomon ride on King David's mule, and took him to Gihon. ³⁹ The priest Zadok took the horn of oil from the tabernacle and anointed Solomon. Then they blew the ram's horn, and all the people proclaimed, "Long live King Solomon!" ⁴⁰ All the people went up after him, playing flutes and rejoicing with such a great joy that the earth split open from the sound.ᴬ   2Sm 8:18; 1Ch 29:22

Adonijah Hears of Solomon's Coronation

⁴¹ Adonijah and all the invited guests who were with him heard the noise as they finished eating. Joab heard the sound of the ram's horn and said, "Why is the town in such an uproar?" ⁴² He was still speaking when Jonathan son of Abiathar the priest, suddenly arrived. Adonijah said, "Come in, for you are an important man, and you must be bringing good news."

⁴³ "Unfortunately not," Jonathan answered him. "Our lord King David has made Solomon king. ⁴⁴ And with Solomon, the king has sent the priest Zadok, the prophet Nathan, Benaiah son of Jehoiada, the Cherethites, and the Pelethites, and they have had him ride on the king's mule. ⁴⁵ The priest Zadok and the prophet Nathan have anointed him king in Gihon. They have gone up from there rejoicing. The town has been in an uproar; that's the noise you heard. ⁴⁶ Solomon has even taken his seat on the royal throne.   1Kg 1:33-35; 1Ch 29:23

⁴⁷ "The king's servants have also gone to congratulate our lord King David, saying, 'May your God make the name of Solomon more well known than your name, and may he make his throne greater than your throne.' Then the king bowed in worship on his bed. ⁴⁸ And the king went on to say this: 'Blessed be the LORD God of Israel! Today he has provided one to sit on my throne, and I am a witness.'"ᴮ

⁴⁹ Then all of Adonijah's guests got up trembling and went their separate ways. ⁵⁰ Adonijah was afraid of Solomon, so he got up and went to take hold of the horns of the altar.   Ex 21:12-14; 1Kg 2:28

⁵¹ It was reported to Solomon: "Look, Adonijah fears King Solomon, and he has taken hold of the horns of the altar, saying, 'Let King Solomon firstᶜ swear to me that he will not kill his servant with the sword.'"

⁵² Then Solomon said, "If he is a man of character, not a single hair of his will fall to the ground, but if evil is found in him, he dies." ⁵³ So King Solomon sent for him, and they took him down from the altar. He came and paid homage to King Solomon, and Solomon said to him, "Go to your home."   1Sm 14:45

David's Dying Instructions to Solomon

2 As the time approached for David to die, he ordered his son Solomon, ² "As for me, I am going the way of all of the earth. Be strong and be a man, ³ and keep your obligation to the LORD your God to walk in his ways and to keep his statutes, commands,

ᴬ1:40 LXX reads *the land resounded with their noise* mss, LXX, Syr, Vg read *today*   ᴮ1:48 Lit *and my eyes are seeing*   ᶜ1:51 Some Hb ordinances, and decrees. This is written in the law of Moses, so that you will have success in everything you do and wherever you turn, [4] and so that the LORD will fulfill his promise that he made to me: 'If your sons guard their way to walk faithfully before me with all their heart and all their soul, you will never fail to have a man on the throne of Israel.'   Gn 47:29

[5] "You also know what Joab son of Zeruiah did to me and what he did to the two commanders of Israel's army, Abner son of Ner and Amasa son of Jether. He murdered them in a time of peace to avenge blood shed in war. He spilled that blood on his own waistband and on the sandals of his feet.[A] [6] Act according to your wisdom, and do not let his gray head descend to Sheol in peace.   2Sm 3:27; 18:5,12,14; 20:10

[7] "Show kindness to the sons of Barzillai the Gileadite and let them be among those who eat at your table because they supported me when I fled from your brother Absalom.   2Sm 9:7; 19:28,31-39

[8] "Keep an eye on Shimei son of Gera, the Benjaminite from Bahurim who is with you. He uttered malicious curses against me the day I went to Mahanaim. But he came down to meet me at the Jordan River, and I swore to him by the LORD: 'I will never kill you with the sword.' [9] So don't let him go unpunished, for you are a wise man. You know how to deal with him to bring his gray head down to Sheol with blood."   2Sm 16:5-13; 19:16-23

[10] Then David rested with his fathers and was buried in the city of David. [11] The length of time David reigned over Israel was forty years: he reigned seven years in Hebron and thirty-three years in Jerusalem. [12] Solomon sat on the throne of his father David, and his kingship was firmly established.   Ac 2:29

Adonijah's Foolish Request

[13] Now Adonijah son of Haggith came to Bathsheba, Solomon's mother. She asked, "Do you come peacefully?"   1Kg 1:5,51-53

"Peacefully," he replied, [14] and then asked, "May I talk with you?"[B]

"Go ahead," she answered.

[15] "You know the kingship was mine," he said. "All Israel expected me to be king, but then the kingship was turned over to my brother, for the LORD gave it to him. [16] So now I have just one request of you; don't turn me down."[C]   1Kg 1:11,38-46; 1Ch 28:5,7

She said to him, "Go on."

[17] He replied, "Please speak to King Solomon since he won't turn you down. Let him give me Abishag the Shunammite as a wife."

[18] "Very well," Bathsheba replied. "I will speak to the king for you."

[19] So Bathsheba went to King Solomon to speak to him about Adonijah. The king stood up to greet her, bowed to her, sat down on his throne, and had a throne placed for the king's mother. So she sat down at his right hand.   2Sm 15:16

[20] Then she said, "I have just one small request of you. Don't turn me down."

"Go ahead and ask, mother," the king replied, "for I won't turn you down."

[21] So she said, "Let Abishag the Shunammite be given to your brother Adonijah as a wife."

[A]2:5 LXX, Old Lat read *on my waistband and . . . my feet*; v. 31   [B]2:14 Lit *then said, "I have a word for you."*
[C]2:16 Lit *don't make me turn my face*

²² King Solomon answered his mother, "Why are you requesting Abishag the Shunammite for Adonijah? Since he is my elder brother, you might as well ask the kingship for him, for the priest Abiathar, and for Joab son of Zeruiah." ᴬ ²³ Then King Solomon took an oath by the LORD: "May God punish me and do so severely if Adonijah has not made this request at the cost of his life. ²⁴ And now, as the LORD lives — the one who established me, seated me on the throne of my father David, and made me a dynasty as he promised — I swear Adonijah will be put to death today!" ²⁵ Then King Solomon dispatched Benaiah son of Jehoiada, who struck down Adonijah, and he died.   2Sm 16:20-22; 1Kg 1:6-7; 1Ch 3:2,5

Abiathar's Banishment

²⁶ The king said to the priest Abiathar, "Go to your fields in Anathoth. Even though you deserve to die, I will not put you to death today, since you carried the ark of the Lord GOD in the presence of my father David and you suffered through all that my father suffered." ²⁷ So Solomon banished Abiathar from being the LORD's priest, and it fulfilled the LORD's prophecy he had spoken at Shiloh against Eli's family.   Jos 21:18; 1Kg 1:7,19

Joab's Execution

²⁸ The news reached Joab. Since he had supported Adonijah but not Absalom, Joab fled to the LORD's tabernacle and took hold of the horns of the altar.   2Sm 18:1-5; 1Kg 1:7

²⁹ It was reported to King Solomon: "Joab has fled to the LORD's tabernacle and is now beside the altar." Then Solomon sent ᴮ Benaiah son of Jehoiada and told him, "Go and strike him down!"   1Kg 1:8
³⁰ So Benaiah went to the tabernacle and said to Joab, "This is what the king says: 'Come out!'"   Ex 21:14
But Joab said, "No, for I will die here."
So Benaiah took a message back to the king, "This is what Joab said, and this is how he answered me."
³¹ The king said to him, "Do just as he says. Strike him down and bury him in order to remove from me and from my father's family the blood that Joab shed without just cause. ³² The LORD will bring back his own blood on his head because he struck down two men more righteous and better than he, without my father David's knowledge. With his sword, Joab murdered Abner son of Ner, commander of Israel's army, and Amasa son of Jether, commander of Judah's army. ³³ The responsibility for their deaths will come back to Joab and to his descendants ᶜ forever, but for David, his descendants, his dynasty, and his throne, there will be peace from the LORD forever."   Nm 35:33; Dt 21:8-9; 2Sm 3:26-27; 20:8-10
³⁴ Benaiah son of Jehoiada went up, struck down Joab, and put him to death. He was buried at his house in the wilderness. ³⁵ Then the king appointed Benaiah son of Jehoiada in Joab's place over the army, and he appointed the priest Zadok in Abiathar's place.   2Sm 2:32; 1Kg 4:4; 2Kg 2:25

ᴬ2:22 LXX, Vg, Syr read kingship for him, and on his side are Abiathar the priest and Joab son of Zeruiah ᴮ2:29 LXX adds Joab a message: "What is the matter with you, that you have fled to the altar?" And Joab replied, "Because I feared you, I have fled to the Lord." And Solomon the king sent ᶜ2:33 Lit Their blood will return on the head of Joab and on the head of his seed

Shimei's Banishment and Execution

36 Then the king summoned Shimei and said to him, "Build a house for yourself in Jerusalem and live there, but don't leave there and go anywhere else. **37** On the day you do leave and cross the Kidron Valley, know for sure that you will certainly die. Your blood will be on your own head." 2Sm 16:5-13; 1Kg 2:8-9; Jn 18:1

38 Shimei said to the king, "The sentence is fair; your servant will do as my lord the king has spoken." And Shimei lived in Jerusalem for a long time.

39 But then, at the end of three years, two of Shimei's slaves ran away to Achish son of Maacah, king of Gath. Shimei was informed, "Look, your slaves are in Gath." **40** So Shimei saddled his donkey and set out to Achish at Gath to search for his slaves. He went and brought them back from Gath. Jos 13:3; 1Sm 27:2

41 It was reported to Solomon that Shimei had gone from Jerusalem to Gath and had returned. **42** So the king summoned Shimei and said to him, "Didn't I make you swear by the LORD and warn you, saying, 'On the day you leave and go anywhere else, know for sure that you will certainly die'? And you said to me, 'The sentence is fair; I will obey.' **43** So why have you not kept the LORD's oath and the command that I gave you?" **44** The king also said, "You yourself know all the evil that you did to my father David. Therefore, the LORD has brought back your evil on your head, **45** but King Solomon will be blessed, and David's throne will remain established before the LORD forever."

46 Then the king commanded Benaiah son of Jehoiada, and he went out and struck Shimei down, and he died. So the kingdom was established in Solomon's hand.

The LORD Appears to Solomon

3 Solomon made an alliance[A] with Pharaoh king of Egypt by marrying Pharaoh's daughter. Solomon brought her to the city of David until he finished building his palace, the LORD's temple, and the wall surrounding Jerusalem. **2** However, the people were sacrificing on the high places, because until that time a temple for the LORD's name had not been built. **3** Solomon loved the LORD by walking in the statutes of his father David, but he also sacrificed and burned incense on the high places. Dt 7:3; 1Kg 7:8; 9:24

4 The king went to Gibeon to sacrifice there because it was the most famous high place. He offered a thousand burnt offerings on that altar. **5** At Gibeon the LORD appeared to Solomon in a dream at night. God said, "Ask. What should I give you?" Nm 12:6; Jos 9:3-27; 21:17; 2Ch 1:3,6

6 And Solomon replied, "You have shown great and faithful love to your servant, my father David, because he walked before you in faithfulness, righteousness, and integrity.[B] You have continued this great and faithful love for him by giving him a son to sit on his throne, as it is today. 1Kg 1:48; 2:4; 9:4; 2Ch 1:8

7 "LORD my God, you have now made your servant king in my father David's place. Yet I am just a youth with no experience in leadership.[C] **8** Your servant is among your people you have chosen, a people

---

A 3:1 Lit Solomon made himself a son-in-law   **B** 3:6 Lit and uprightness of heart with you   **C** 3:7 Lit am a little youth and do not know to go out or come in too many to be numbered or counted. ⁹ So give your servant a receptive heart to judge your people and to discern between good and evil. For who is able to judge this great people of yours?" Dt 7:6; 1Ch 29:1; 2Ch 1:8

¹⁰ Now it pleased the Lord that Solomon had requested this. ¹¹ So God said to him, "Because you have requested this and did not ask for long life^A or riches for yourself, or the death^B of your enemies, but you asked discernment for yourself to administer justice, ¹² I will therefore do what you have asked. I will give you a wise and understanding heart, so that there has never been anyone like you before and never will be again. ¹³ In addition, I will give you what you did not ask for: both riches and honor, so that no king will be your equal during your entire life. ¹⁴ If you walk in my ways and keep my statutes and commands just as your father David did, I will give you a long life." 1Ch 22:12; Jms 4:3; 1Jn 5:14-15

¹⁵ Then Solomon woke up and realized it had been a dream. He went to Jerusalem, stood before the ark of the Lord's covenant, and offered burnt offerings and fellowship offerings. Then he held a feast for all his servants. Gn 41:7; 2Sm 6:12; Dn 2:3; 4:5

Solomon's Wisdom

¹⁶ Then two women who were prostitutes came to the king and stood before him. ¹⁷ One woman said, "Please, my lord, this woman and I live in the same house, and I had a baby while she was in the house. ¹⁸ On the third day after I gave birth, she also had a baby and we were alone. No one else^C

was with us in the house; just the two of us were there. ¹⁹ During the night this woman's son died because she lay on him. ²⁰ She got up in the middle of the night and took my son from my side while your servant was asleep. She laid him in her arms, and she put her dead son in my arms. ²¹ When I got up in the morning to nurse my son, I discovered he was dead. That morning, when I looked closely at him I realized that he was not the son I gave birth to." Dt 16:18-19; 2Sm 15:2-4

²² "No," the other woman said. "My son is the living one; your son is the dead one."

The first woman said, "No, your son is the dead one; my son is the living one." So they argued before the king.

²³ The king replied, "This woman says, 'This is my son who is alive, and your son is dead,' but that woman says, 'No, your son is dead, and my son is alive.'" ²⁴ The king continued, "Bring me a sword." So they brought the sword to the king. ²⁵ And the king said, "Cut the living boy in two and give half to one and half to the other."

²⁶ The woman whose son was alive spoke to the king because she felt great compassion^D for her son. "My lord, give her the living baby," she said, "but please don't have him killed!" Gn 43:30; Jr 31:20; Hs 11:8

But the other one said, "He will not be mine or yours. Cut him in two!"

²⁷ The king responded, "Give the living baby to the first woman, and don't kill him. She is his mother." ²⁸ All Israel heard about the judgment the king had given, and they

^A 3:11 Lit for many days   ^B 3:11 Lit life   ^C 3:18 Lit No stranger   ^D 3:26 Lit because her compassion grew hot stood in awe of the king because they saw that God's wisdom was in him to carry out justice. 2Sm 14:20

Solomon's Officials

4 King Solomon reigned over all Israel, ² and these were his officials: 2Sm 5:5; 8:15; 1Kg 12:6
Azariah son of Zadok, priest;
³ Elihoreph and Ahijah the sons of Shisha, secretaries;
Jehoshaphat son of Ahilud, court historian;
⁴ Benaiah son of Jehoiada, in charge of the army;
Zadok and Abiathar, priests;
⁵ Azariah son of Nathan, in charge of the deputies;
Zabud son of Nathan, a priest and adviser to the king;
⁶ Ahishar, in charge of the palace;
and Adoniram son of Abda, in charge of forced labor.

⁷ Solomon had twelve deputies for all Israel. They provided food for the king and his household; each one made provision for one month out of the year. ⁸ These were their names: 1Kg 4:27
Ben-hur, in the hill country of Ephraim;
⁹ Ben-deker, in Makaz, Shaalbim, Beth-shemesh, and Elon-beth-hanan;
¹⁰ Ben-hesed, in Arubboth (he had Socoh and the whole land of Hepher);
¹¹ Ben-abinadab, in all Naphath-dor (Taphath daughter of Solomon was his wife);
¹² Baana son of Ahilud, in Taanach, Megiddo, and all Beth-shean which is beside Zarethan below Jezreel, from Beth-shean to Abel-meholah, as far as the other side of Jokmeam;
¹³ Ben-geber, in Ramoth-gilead (he had the villages of Jair son of Manasseh, which are in Gilead, and he had the region of Argob, which is in Bashan, sixty great cities with walls and bronze bars);
¹⁴ Ahinadab son of Iddo, in Mahanaim;
¹⁵ Ahimaaz, in Naphtali (he also had married a daughter of Solomon — Basemath);
¹⁶ Baana son of Hushai, in Asher and Bealoth;
¹⁷ Jehoshaphat son of Paruah, in Issachar;
¹⁸ Shimei son of Ela, in Benjamin;
¹⁹ Geber son of Uri, in the land of Gilead, the country of King Sihon of the Amorites and of King Og of Bashan.
There was one deputy in the land of Judah. ᴬ

Solomon's Provisions

²⁰ Judah and Israel were as numerous as the sand by the sea; they were eating, drinking, and rejoicing. ²¹ Solomon ruled all the kingdoms from the Euphrates River to the land of the Philistines and as far as the border of Egypt. They offered tribute and served Solomon all the days of his life. Gn 22:17; 1Kg 3:8
²² Solomon's provisions for one day were 150 bushels ᴮ of fine flour and 300 bushels ᶜ of meal, ²³ ten fattened cattle, twenty range cattle, and a hundred sheep and goats, besides deer, gazelles, roebucks, and pen-fed poultry, ᴰ ²⁴ for he had dominion over everything west

ᴬ4:19 LXX; MT omits *of Judah*   ᴮ4:22 Lit *30 cors*   ᶜ4:22 Lit *60 cors*   ᴰ4:23 Hb obscure of the Euphrates from Tiphsah to Gaza and over all the kings west of the Euphrates. He had peace on all his surrounding borders. ²⁵ Throughout Solomon's reign, Judah and Israel lived in safety from Dan to Beer-sheba, each person under his own vine and his own fig tree. ²⁶ Solomon had forty thousand^A stalls of horses for his chariots, and twelve thousand horsemen. ²⁷ Each of those deputies for a month in turn provided food for King Solomon and for everyone who came to King Solomon's table. They neglected nothing. ²⁸ Each man brought the barley and the straw for the chariot teams and the other horses to the required place according to his assignment.^B Jdg 20:1; 1Kg 10:5; Neh 5:18

Solomon's Wisdom and Literary Gifts

²⁹ God gave Solomon wisdom, very great insight, and understanding as vast as the sand on the seashore. ³⁰ Solomon's wisdom was greater than the wisdom of all the people of the East, greater than all the wisdom of Egypt. ³¹ He was wiser than anyone — wiser than Ethan the Ezrahite, and Heman, Calcol, and Darda, sons of Mahol. His reputation extended to all the surrounding nations. Gn 29:1; 1Kg 3:12; Is 19:11; Ac 7:22

³² Solomon spoke 3,000 proverbs, and his songs numbered 1,005. ³³ He spoke about trees, from the cedar in Lebanon to the hyssop growing out of the wall. He also spoke about animals, birds, reptiles, and fish. ³⁴ Emissaries of all peoples, sent by every king on earth who had heard of his wisdom, came to listen to Solomon's wisdom. Pr 1:1; Sg 1:1

Hiram's Building Materials

5 King Hiram of Tyre sent his emissaries to Solomon when he heard that he had been anointed king in his father's place, for Hiram had always been friends with David. 2Sm 5:11; 1Kg 1:34,39; 1Ch 14:1; 2Ch 2:3

² Solomon sent this message to Hiram: ³ "You know my father David was not able to build a temple for the name of the LORD his God. This was because of the warfare all around him until the LORD put his enemies under his feet. ⁴ The LORD my God has now given me rest on every side; there is no enemy or crisis. ⁵ So I plan to build a temple for the name of the LORD my God, according to what the LORD promised my father David: 'I will put your son on your throne in your place, and he will build the temple for my name.' 1Kg 4:24-25; 1Ch 28:2-3; 2Ch 2:4

⁶ "Therefore, command that cedars from Lebanon be cut down for me. My servants will be with your servants, and I will pay your servants' wages according to whatever you say, for you know that not a man among us knows how to cut timber like the Sidonians." 2Ch 2:8

⁷ When Hiram heard Solomon's words, he rejoiced greatly and said, "Blessed be the LORD today! He has given David a wise son to be over this great people!" ⁸ Then Hiram sent a reply to Solomon, saying, "I have heard your message; I will do everything you want regarding the cedar and cypress timber. ⁹ My servants will bring the logs down from Lebanon to the sea, and I will make them into rafts to go by sea to the place you indicate. I will break them apart there, and you can take them away. You then can

^A**4:26** 2Ch 9:25 reads *4,000 stalls* ^B**4:28** Lit *judgment*

meet my needs by providing my household with food." 1Kg 10:9; Ezr 3:7

¹⁰ So Hiram provided Solomon with all the cedar and cypress timber he wanted, ¹¹ and Solomon provided Hiram with one hundred thousand bushels^A of wheat as food for his household and one hundred ten thousand gallons^B of oil from crushed olives. Solomon did this for Hiram year after year. 2Ch 2:10

¹² The LORD gave Solomon wisdom, as he had promised him. There was peace between Hiram and Solomon, and the two of them made a treaty. 1Kg 3:12; 15:19

Solomon's Workforce

¹³ Then King Solomon drafted forced laborers from all Israel; the labor force numbered thirty thousand men. ¹⁴ He sent ten thousand to Lebanon each month in shifts; one month they were in Lebanon, two months they were at home. Adoniram was in charge of the forced labor. ¹⁵ Solomon had seventy thousand porters and eighty thousand stonecutters in the mountains, ¹⁶ not including his thirty-three hundred^C deputies in charge of the work. They supervised the people doing the work. ¹⁷ The king commanded them to quarry large, costly stones to lay the foundation of the temple with dressed stones. ¹⁸ So Solomon's builders and Hiram's builders, along with the Gebalites, quarried the stone and prepared the timber and stone for the temple's construction. 1Kg 4:6; 9:15; 2Ch 2:17-18

Building the Temple

6 Solomon began to build the temple for the LORD in the four hundred eightieth year after the Israelites came out of the land of Egypt, in the fourth year of his reign over Israel, in the month of Ziv, which is the second month.^D ² The temple that King Solomon built for the LORD was ninety feet^E long, thirty feet^F wide, and forty-five feet^G high. ³ The portico in front of the temple sanctuary was thirty feet long extending across the temple's width, and fifteen feet deep^H in front of the temple. ⁴ He also made windows with beveled frames^I for the temple.

⁵ He then built a chambered structure^J along the temple wall, encircling the walls of the temple, that is, the sanctuary and the inner sanctuary. And he made side chambers^K all around. ⁶ The lowest chamber was 7½ feet^L wide, the middle was 9 feet^M wide, and the third was 10½ feet^N wide. He also provided offset ledges for the temple all around the outside so that nothing would be inserted into the temple walls. ⁷ The temple's construction used finished stones cut at the quarry so that no hammer, chisel, or any iron tool was heard in the temple while it was being built.

⁸ The door for the lowest^O side chamber was on the right side of the temple. They^P went up a stairway¹ to the middle chamber, and from the middle to the third. ⁹ When he finished building the temple, he paneled it with boards and planks of cedar. ¹⁰ He built the chambers

^A5:11 Lit 20,000 cors   ^B5:11 LXX reads 20,000 baths; MT reads 20 cors   ^C5:16 Some LXX mss read 3,600; 2Ch 2:2,18   ^D6:1 April–May   ^E6:2 Lit 60 cubits   ^F6:2 Lit 20 cubits, also in vv. 3,16,20
^G6:2 Lit 30 cubits   ^H6:3 Lit 10 cubits wide   ^I6:4,8 Hb obscure   ^J6:5 Lit built the temple of chamber
^K6:5 Lit made ribs or sides   ^L6:6 Lit five cubits, also in vv. 10,24   ^M6:6 Lit six cubits   ^N6:6 Lit seven cubits   ^O6:8 LXX, Tg; MT reads middle   ^P6:8 = People

along the entire temple, joined to the temple with cedar beams; each story was 7 ½ feet high. 1Kg 6:1,14,38

¹¹ The word of the LORD came to Solomon: ¹² "As for this temple you are building — if you walk in my statutes, observe my ordinances, and keep all my commands by walking in them, I will fulfill my promise to you, which I made to your father David. ¹³ I will dwell among the Israelites and not abandon my people Israel." 1Kg 3:5,11-15; 9:2

¹⁴ When Solomon finished building the temple, ᴬ ¹⁵ he paneled the interior temple walls with cedar boards; from the temple floor to the surface of the ceiling he overlaid the interior with wood. He also overlaid the floor with cypress boards. ¹⁶ Then he lined thirty feet of the rear of the temple with cedar boards from the floor to the surface of the ceiling, ᴮ and he built the interior as an inner sanctuary, the most holy place. ¹⁷ The temple, that is, the sanctuary in front of the most holy place, ᶜ was sixty feet ᴰ long. ¹⁸ The cedar paneling inside the temple was carved with ornamental gourds and flower blossoms. Everything was cedar; not a stone could be seen. 1Kg 6:1,38; 7:7

¹⁹ He prepared the inner sanctuary inside the temple to put the ark of the LORD's covenant there. ²⁰ The interior of the sanctuary was thirty feet long, thirty feet wide, and thirty feet high; he overlaid it with pure gold. He also overlaid the cedar altar. ²¹ Next, Solomon overlaid the interior of the temple with pure gold, and he hung ᴱ gold chains across the front of the inner sanctuary

and overlaid it with gold. ²² So he added the gold overlay to the entire temple until everything was completely finished, including the entire altar that belongs to the inner sanctuary. Ezk 41:3-4; Dt 10:16; Jos 3:11

²³ In the inner sanctuary he made two cherubim 15 feet ᶠ high out of olive wood. ²⁴ One wing of the first cherub was 7 ½ feet long, and the other wing was 7 ½ feet long. The wingspan was 15 feet from tip to tip. ²⁵ The second cherub also was 15 feet; both cherubim had the same size and shape. ²⁶ The first cherub's height was 15 feet and so was the second cherub's. ²⁷ Then he put the cherubim inside the inner temple. Since their wings were spread out, the first one's wing touched one wall while the second cherub's wing touched the other ᴳ wall, and in the middle of the temple their wings were touching wing to wing. ²⁸ He also overlaid the cherubim with gold. Ex 25:18-22; 2Ch 3:10-13; 5:8

²⁹ He carved all the surrounding temple walls with carved engravings — cherubim, palm trees, and flower blossoms — in the inner and outer sanctuaries. ³⁰ He overlaid the temple floor with gold in both the inner and the outer sanctuaries.

³¹ For the entrance of the inner sanctuary, he made olive wood doors. The pillars of the doorposts were five-sided. ᴴ ³² The two doors were made of olive wood. He carved cherubim, palm trees, and flower blossoms on them and overlaid them with gold, hammering gold over the cherubim and palm trees. ³³ In the same way, he made four-sided ᴴ olive wood doorposts

ᴬ 6:11-14 LXX omits these vv. ᴮ 6:16 LXX; MT omits *of the ceiling* ; 1Kg 6:15 ᶜ 6:17 Lit *front of me* ; Hb obscure ᴰ 6:17 Lit *40 cubits* ᴱ 6:21 Lit *he caused to pass across* ᶠ 6:23 Lit *10 cubits*, also in vv. 24,25,26 ᴳ 6:27 Lit *the second* ᴴ 6:31,33 Hb obscure for the sanctuary entrance. ³⁴ The two doors were made of cypress wood; the first door had two folding sides, and the second door had two folding panels. ³⁵ He carved cherubim, palm trees, and flower blossoms on them and overlaid them with gold applied evenly over the carving. ³⁶ He built the inner courtyard with three rows of dressed stone and a row of trimmed cedar beams.   Ezk 41:23

³⁷ The foundation of the LORD's temple was laid in Solomon's fourth year in the month of Ziv. ³⁸ In his eleventh year in the month of Bul, which is the eighth month,ᴬ the temple was completed in every detail and according to every specification. So he built it in seven years.   1Kg 6:1,14; 7:1

Solomon's Palace Complex

7 Solomon completed his entire palace complex after thirteen years of construction. ² He built the House of the Forest of Lebanon. It was one hundred fifty feetᴮ long, seventy-five feetᶜ wide, and forty-five feetᴰ high on four rows of cedar pillars, with cedar beams on top of the pillars. ³ It was paneled above with cedar at the top of the chambers that rested on forty-five pillars, fifteen per row. ⁴ There were three rows of window frames, facing each otherᴱ in three tiers.ᶠ ⁵ All the doors and doorposts had rectangular frames, the openings facing each otherᴳ in three tiers. ⁶ He made the hall of pillars seventy-five feet long and forty-five

feet wide. A portico was in front of the pillars, and a canopy with pillarsᴴ was in front of them. ⁷ He made the Hall of the Throne where he would judge — the Hall of Judgment. It was paneled with cedar from the floor to the rafters.ᴵ ⁸ Solomon's own palace where he would live, in the other courtyard behind the hall, was of similar construction. And he made a house like this hall for Pharaoh's daughter, his wife.ᴶ   1Kg 3:16-28; 9:10; 10:16-17,21; 2Ch 8:1

⁹ All of these buildings were of costly stones, cut to size and sawed with saws on the inner and outer surfaces, from foundation to coping and from the outside to the great courtyard. ¹⁰ The foundation was made of large, costly stones twelve and fifteen feetᴷ long. ¹¹ Above were also costly stones, cut to size, as well as cedar wood. ¹² Around the great courtyard, as well as the inner courtyard of the LORD's temple and the portico of the temple, were three rows of dressed stone and a row of trimmed cedar beams.   1Kg 6:36

¹³ King Solomon had Hiramᴸ brought from Tyre. ¹⁴ He was a widow's son from the tribe of Naphtali, and his father was a man of Tyre, a bronze craftsman. Hiram had great skill, understanding, and knowledge to do every kind of bronze work. So he came to King Solomon and carried out all his work.

The Bronze Pillars

¹⁵ He cast two bronze pillars, each 27 feetᴹ high and 18 feetᴺ in

---

ᴬ6:38 = October–November   ᴮ7:2 Lit *100 cubits*   ᶜ7:2 Lit *50 cubits*, also in v. 6   ᴰ7:2 Lit *30 cubits*, also in vv. 6,23   ᴱ7:4 Lit *frames, window to window*   ᶠ7:4 Lit *three times* ; = at 3 different places, also in v. 5   ᴳ7:5 Lit *frames, opposing window to window*   ᴴ7:6 Hb obscure   ᴵ7:7 Syr, Vg; MT reads *floor*   ᴶ7:8 Lit *daughter he had taken*   ᴷ7:10 Lit *ten cubits and eight cubits*   ᴸ7:13 = Huram in 2Ch 4:11   ᴹ7:15 Lit *18 cubits*   ᴺ7:15 Lit *12 cubits* circumference.[A] [16] He also made two capitals of cast bronze to set on top of the pillars; 7½ feet[B] was the height of the first capital, and 7½ feet was also the height of the second capital. [17] The capitals on top of the pillars had gratings of latticework, wreaths[C] made of chainwork — seven for the first capital and seven for the second.   2Ch 3:15

[18] He made the pillars with two encircling rows of pomegranates on the one grating to cover the capital on top; he did the same for the second capital. [19] And the capitals on top of the pillars in the portico were shaped like lilies, six feet[D] high. [20] The capitals on the two pillars were also immediately above the rounded surface next to the grating, and two hundred pomegranates were in rows encircling each[E] capital. [21] He set up the pillars at the portico of the sanctuary: he set up the right pillar and named it Jachin;[F] then he set up the left pillar and named it Boaz.[G] [22] The tops of the pillars were shaped like lilies. Then the work of the pillars was completed.   1Kg 6:3; 2Ch 3:16-17; 4:13

The Basin

[23] He made the cast metal basin,[H] 15 feet[I] from brim to brim, perfectly round. It was 7½ feet high and 45 feet in circumference. [24] Ornamental gourds encircled it below the brim, ten every half yard,[J] completely encircling the basin. The gourds were cast in two rows when the basin was cast. [25] It stood on twelve oxen, three facing north, three facing west, three facing south, and three facing east. The basin was on top of them and all their hindquarters were toward the center. [26] The basin was three inches[K] thick, and its rim was fashioned like the brim of a cup or of a lily blossom. It held eleven thousand gallons.[L]   2Kg 25:13

The Bronze Water Carts

[27] Then he made ten bronze water carts.[M] Each water cart was 6 feet long, 6 feet wide, and 4½ feet[N] high. [28] This was the design of the carts: They had frames; the frames were between the cross-pieces, [29] and on the frames between the cross-pieces were lions, oxen, and cherubim. On the cross-pieces there was a pedestal above, and below the lions and oxen were wreaths of hanging[O] work. [30] Each cart had four bronze wheels with bronze axles. Underneath the four corners of the basin were cast supports, each next to a wreath. [31] And the water cart's opening inside the crown on top was eighteen inches[P] wide. The opening was round, made as a pedestal twenty-seven inches[Q] wide. On it were carvings, but their frames were square, not round. [32] There were four wheels under the frames, and the wheel axles were part of the water cart; each wheel was twenty-seven inches[R] tall. [33] The wheels' design was similar to that of chariot wheels: their axles, rims, spokes, and hubs were all of cast metal.

[A]7:15 LXX adds *and the thickness of the pillar was four fingers hollowed and similarly the second pillar*   [B]7:16 Lit *five cubits,* also in v. 23   [C]7:17 Lit *tassels*   [D]7:19 Lit *four cubits,* also in vv. 27, 38   [E]7:20 Lit *encircling the second*   [F]7:21 = He Will Establish   [G]7:21 = In Him Is Strength   [H]7:23 Lit *sea*   [I]7:23 Lit *10 cubits*   [J]7:24 Lit *10 per cubit*   [K]7:26 Lit *a handbreadth*   [L]7:26 Lit *2,000 baths*   [M]7:27 Lit *bronze stands*   [N]7:27 Lit *three cubits*   [O]7:29 Or *hammered-down*   [P]7:31 Lit *a cubit*   [Q]7:31 Lit *one and a half cubits*   [R]7:32 Lit *was one and a half cubits*

³⁴ Four supports were at the four corners of each water cart; each support was one piece with the water cart. ³⁵ At the top of the cart was a band nine inches ᴬ high encircling it; also, at the top of the cart, its braces and its frames were one piece with it. ³⁶ He engraved cherubim, lions, and palm trees on the plates of its braces and on its frames, wherever each had space, with encircling wreaths. ³⁷ In this way he made the ten water carts using the same casting, dimensions, and shape for all of them.

Bronze Basins and Other Utensils

³⁸ Then he made ten bronze basins — each basin held 220 gallons ᴮ and each was six feet wide — one basin for each of the ten water carts. ³⁹ He set five water carts on the right side of the temple and five on the left side. He put the basin near the right side of the temple toward the southeast. ⁴⁰ Then Hiram made the basins, the shovels, and the sprinkling basins.   Ex 30:18

Completion of the Bronze Works

So Hiram finished all the work that he was doing for King Solomon on the LORD's temple: ⁴¹ two pillars; bowls for the capitals that were on top of the two pillars; the two gratings for covering both bowls of the capitals that were on top of the pillars; ⁴² the four hundred pomegranates for the two gratings (two rows of pomegranates for each grating covering both capitals' bowls on top of the pillars); ⁴³ the ten water carts; the ten basins on the water carts; ⁴⁴ the basin; the twelve oxen underneath the basin; ⁴⁵ and the pots, shovels, and sprinkling basins. All the utensils that Hiram made for King Solomon at the LORD's temple were made of burnished bronze. ⁴⁶ The king had them cast in clay molds in the Jordan Valley between Succoth and Zarethan. ⁴⁷ Solomon left all the utensils unweighed because there were so many; the weight of the bronze was not determined.

Completion of the Gold Furnishings

⁴⁸ Solomon also made all the equipment in the LORD's temple: the gold altar; the gold table that the Bread of the Presence was placed on; ⁴⁹ the pure gold lampstands in front of the inner sanctuary, five on the right and five on the left; the gold flowers, lamps, and tongs; ⁵⁰ the pure gold ceremonial bowls, wick trimmers, sprinkling basins, ladles, ᶜ and firepans; and the gold hinges for the doors of the inner temple (that is, the most holy place) and for the doors of the temple sanctuary.   Ex 25:30; 30:1-3; 2Ch 29:18

⁵¹ So all the work King Solomon did in the LORD's temple was completed. Then Solomon brought in the consecrated things of his father David — the silver, the gold, and the utensils — and put them in the treasuries of the LORD's temple.

Solomon's Dedication of the Temple

8 At that time Solomon assembled the elders of Israel, all the tribal heads and the ancestral leaders of the Israelites before him at Jerusalem in order to bring the ark of the LORD's covenant from the city of David, that is Zion. ² So all the men of Israel were assembled in the presence of King Solomon in the month of Ethanim, which is the seventh month, [A] at the festival.

³ All the elders of Israel came, and the priests picked up the ark. ⁴ The priests and the Levites brought the ark of the LORD, the tent of meeting, and the holy utensils that were in the tent. ⁵ King Solomon and the entire congregation of Israel, who had gathered around him and were with him in front of the ark, were sacrificing sheep, goats, and cattle that could not be counted or numbered, because there were so many. ⁶ The priests brought the ark of the LORD's covenant to its place, into the inner sanctuary of the temple, to the most holy place beneath the wings of the cherubim. ⁷ For the cherubim were spreading their wings over [B] the place of the ark, so that the cherubim covered the ark and its poles from above. ⁸ The poles were so long that their ends were seen from the holy place in front of the inner sanctuary, but they were not seen from outside the sanctuary; they are still there today. ⁹ Nothing was in the ark except the two stone tablets that Moses had put there at Horeb, [C] where the LORD made a covenant with the Israelites when they came out of the land of Egypt. Nm 11:16; Dt 31:9; 2Ch 1:3

¹⁰ When the priests came out of the holy place, the cloud filled the LORD's temple, ¹¹ and because of the cloud, the priests were not able to continue ministering, for the glory of the LORD filled the temple. 2Ch 7:1

¹² Then Solomon said:
The LORD said that
he would dwell
in total darkness. Ex 20:21

¹³ I have indeed built
an exalted temple for you,
a place
for your dwelling forever.

¹⁴ The king turned around and blessed the entire congregation of Israel while they were standing. ¹⁵ He said: Ex 39:43; 2Sm 6:18; 1Kg 8:55

Blessed be the LORD God
of Israel!
He spoke directly
to my father David,
and he has fulfilled
the promise by his power.
He said,

¹⁶ "Since the day I brought
my people Israel
out of Egypt, 2Sm 7:6; 1Ch 17:5
I have not chosen a city
to build a temple in
among any of the tribes
of Israel,
so that my name
would be there. Dt 12:5,11
But I have chosen David
to rule my people Israel."

¹⁷ My father David had his
heart set
on building a temple
for the name of the LORD,
the God of Israel. 2Sm 7:2-3

¹⁸ But the LORD said
to my father David,
"Since your heart was set
on building a temple
for my name,
you have done well to have
this desire. [D] 2Ch 6:8

¹⁹ Yet you are not the one
to build it;
instead, your son,
your own offspring,
will build it for my name."

²⁰ The LORD has fulfilled
what he promised.

ᴬ8:2 = September–October ᴮ8:7 LXX; MT reads *toward* ᶜ8:9 = Sinai ᴰ8:18 Lit *well because it was with your heart*

I have taken the place
  of my father David,   2Sm 7:12
and I sit on the throne of Israel,
  as the LORD promised.
I have built the temple
  for the name of the LORD,
  the God of Israel.
21 I have provided a place there
  for the ark,
where the LORD's covenant is
that he made
  with our ancestors
when he brought them out
  of the land of Egypt.   Dt 31:26

Solomon's Prayer

22 Then Solomon stood before the altar of the LORD in front of the entire congregation of Israel and spread out his hands toward heaven. 23 He said: 2Ch 6:12-42; 1Kg 8:54; 2Ch 6:12
LORD God of Israel,
  there is no God like you
in heaven above or on earth
  below,   1Sm 2:2; 2Sm 7:22
who keeps
  the gracious covenant
with your servants who walk
  before you
with all their heart.   Dt 7:16; Dn 9:4
24 You have kept
  what you promised
to your servant,
  my father David.
You spoke directly to him
and you fulfilled your promise
  by your power
as it is today.   2Sm 7:15-16
25 Therefore, LORD God of Israel,
keep what you promised
to your servant,
  my father David:
You will never fail to have
  a man
to sit before me on the throne
  of Israel,   1Kg 2:4; 9:5

if only your sons take care
  to walk before me
as you have walked
  before me.   1Kg 9:4-9; 2Ch 7:17-22
26 Now LORD^A God of Israel,
please confirm
  what you promised
to your servant,
  my father David.   2Sm 7:25
27 But will God indeed live
  on earth?
Even heaven,
  the highest heaven,
  cannot contain you,
much less this temple
  I have built.   2Ch 2:6; Ac 7:47; 17:24
28 Listen^B to your servant's
  prayer and his petition,
LORD my God,
so that you may hear the cry
  and the prayer
that your servant prays
  before you today,
29 so that your eyes
  may watch over this temple
  night and day,   2Ch 7:15; Neh 1:6
toward the place
  where you said,
"My name will be there,"
and so that you may hear
  the prayer
that your servant prays
  toward this place.
30 Hear the petition
  of your servant   Neh 1:6; Dn 9:4
and your people Israel,
which they pray
  toward this place.   Dn 6:10
May you hear
  in your dwelling place
  in heaven.
May you hear and forgive.
31 When a man sins
  against his neighbor

^A 8:26 Some Hb mss, LXX, Syr, Tg, Vg, 2Ch 6:16; other Hb mss omit LORD   ^B 8:28 Lit Turn

and is forced to take an oath,^A
and he comes to take an oath
before your altar
  in this temple,
32 may you hear in heaven
  and act.
May you judge your servants,
condemning the wicked man
  by bringing
what he has done
  on his own head
and providing justice
  for the righteous
by rewarding him
  according to
  his righteousness.   Dt 25:1

33 When your people
  Israel are defeated
  before an enemy,
because they have sinned
  against you,   Lv 26:17,25,39
and they return to you
  and praise your name,
and they pray and plead
  with you
for mercy in this temple,
34 may you hear in heaven
  and forgive the sin
  of your people Israel.
May you restore them
  to the land
you gave their ancestors.

35 When the skies are shut
  and there is no rain,
because they have sinned
  against you,   Dt 28:23-24
and they pray
  toward this place
and praise your name,
and they turn from their sins
because you
  are afflicting them,   Dt 30:1-3
36 may you hear in heaven

and forgive the sin
  of your servants
and your people Israel,
so that you may teach them
  the good way
they should walk in.   1Sm 12:23
May you send rain
  on your land
that you gave your people
  for an inheritance.   Dt 11:14

37 When there is famine
  in the land,
when there is pestilence,
when there is blight or mildew,
  locust or grasshopper,
when their enemy
  besieges them
in the land and its cities,^B
when there is any plague
  or illness,
38 every prayer or petition
that any person or that
  all your people Israel
  may have —
they each know
  their own affliction ^C —
as they spread out their hands
  toward this temple,   Ex 9:29
39 may you hear in heaven,
  your dwelling place,
and may you forgive, act,
  and give to everyone
according to all their ways,
  since you know each heart,
for you alone know
  every human heart,   1Sm 16:7
40 so that they may fear you
all the days they live
  on the land   Dt 12:1
you gave our ancestors.

41 Even for the foreigner
  who is not
  of your people Israel

---

^A **8:31** Lit *and he lifts a curse against him to curse him*   ^B **8:37** Lit *land of its gates*   ^C **8:38** Lit *know in his heart of a plague*

but has come
　from a distant land　Lv 24:22
because of your name —
42 for they will hear
　of your great name,
strong hand,
　and outstretched arm,　Dt 3:24
and will come and pray
　toward this temple —　1Kg 10:1
43 may you hear in heaven,
　your dwelling place,
and do according to all
　the foreigner asks.
Then all peoples of earth
　will know your name,　Jos 4:24
to fear you
　as your people Israel do
and to know that this temple
　I have built
bears your name.

44 When your people
　go out to fight
　against their enemies,[A]
wherever you send them,
and they pray to the LORD
in the direction of the city
　you have chosen　Dt 12:11
and the temple I have built
　for your name,
45 may you hear their prayer
　and petition in heaven
and uphold their cause.　Ps 9:4

46 When they sin against you —
for there is no one
　who does not sin —
and you are angry with them
and hand them over
　to the enemy,
and their captors deport them
　to the enemy's country —
　whether distant or nearby —
47 and when they come
　to their senses[B]

in the land where
　they were deported
and repent and petition you
　in their captors' land:
"We have sinned
　and done wrong;
we have been wicked,"　Neh 1:6
48 and when they return to you
　with all their heart and
　all their soul
in the land of their enemies
　who took them captive,
and when they pray
　to you in the direction
　of their land
that you gave their ancestors,
the city you have chosen,
and the temple I have built
　for your name,
49 may you hear in heaven,
　your dwelling place,
their prayer and petition
　and uphold their cause.
50 May you forgive
　your people
who sinned against you
and all their rebellions[C]
　against you,
and may you grant
　them compassion
before their captors,
so that they may treat them
　compassionately.　2Kg 25:28
51 For they are your people
　and your inheritance;　Ex 32:11
you brought them
　out of Egypt,
out of the middle
　of an iron furnace.　Dt 4:20
52 May your eyes be open
　to your servant's petition
and to the petition
　of your people Israel,
listening to them whenever
　they call to you.

[A] 8:44 Some Hb mss, some ancient versions, 2Ch 6:34; other Hb mss read *enemy*　[B] 8:47 Lit *they return to their heart*　[C] 8:50 Lit *rebellions that they have rebelled*

53 For you, Lord GOD,
    have set them apart
    as your inheritance
    from all peoples of the earth,
    as you spoke
    through your servant Moses
    when you brought
    our ancestors
    out of Egypt. Ex 19:5-6; Dt 9:26-29

Solomon's Blessing

54 When Solomon finished praying this entire prayer and petition to the LORD, he got up from kneeling before the altar of the LORD, with his hands spread out toward heaven, 55 and he stood and blessed the whole congregation of Israel with a loud voice: 56 "Blessed be the LORD! He has given rest to his people Israel according to all he has said. Not one of all the good promises he made through his servant Moses has failed. 57 May the LORD our God be with us as he was with our ancestors. May he not abandon us or leave us 58 so that he causes us to be devotedᴬ to him, to walk in all his ways, and to keep his commands, statutes, and ordinances, which he commanded our ancestors. 59 May my words with which I have made my petition before the LORD be near the LORD our God day and night. May he uphold his servant's cause and the cause of his people Israel, as each day requires. 60 May all the peoples of the earth know that the LORD is God. There is no other! 61 Be wholeheartedly devoted to the LORD our God to walk in his statutes and to keep his commands, as it is today." 2Ch 6:12-13

62 The king and all Israel with him were offering sacrifices in the LORD's presence. 63 Solomon offered a sacrifice of fellowship offerings to the LORD: twenty-two thousand cattle and one hundred twenty thousand sheep and goats. In this manner the king and all the Israelites dedicated the LORD's temple. Dt 20:5; 1Ch 29:21; 2Ch 7:4-5; Ezr 6:16-17

64 On the same day, the king consecrated the middle of the courtyard that was in front of the LORD's temple because that was where he offered the burnt offering, the grain offering, and the fat of the fellowship offerings since the bronze altar before the LORD was too small to accommodate the burnt offerings, the grain offerings, and the fat of the fellowship offerings.

65 Solomon and all Israel with him — a great assembly, from the entrance of Hamathᴮ to the Brook of Egypt — observed the festival at that time in the presence of the LORD our God, seven days, and seven more days — fourteen days.ᶜ 66 On the fifteenth dayᴰ he sent the people away. So they blessed the king and went to their homesᴱ rejoicing and with happy hearts for all the goodness that the LORD had done for his servant David and for his people Israel. Gn 15:18; Nm 13:21; 34:8

The LORD's Response

9 When Solomon finished building the temple of the LORD, the royal palace, and all that Solomon desired to do, 2 the LORD appeared to Solomon a second time just as he had appeared to him at Gibeon. 3 The LORD said to him: 2Ch 7:11-22
    I have heard your prayer and
    petition you have made before
    me. I have consecrated this

ᴬ8:58 Lit causes our hearts to be inclined ᴮ8:65 Or from Lebo-hamath ᶜ8:65 Temple dedication lasted seven days, and the Festival of Shelters lasted seven days. ᴰ8:66 Lit the eighth day ᴱ8:66 Lit tents temple you have built, to put [A] my name there forever; my eyes and my heart will be there at all times.   1Kg 8:29; 2Ch 6:40

[4] As for you, if you walk before me as your father David walked, with a heart of integrity and in what is right, doing everything I have commanded you, and if you keep my statutes and ordinances, [5] I will establish your royal throne over Israel forever, as I promised your father David: You will never fail to have a man on the throne of Israel.   1Kg 3:6,14; 11:4,6

[6] If you or your sons turn away from following me and do not keep my commands — my statutes that I have set before you — and if you go and serve other gods and bow in worship to them, [7] I will cut off Israel from the land I gave them, and I will reject [B] the temple I have sanctified for my name. Israel will become an object of scorn and ridicule among all the peoples. [8] Though this temple is now exalted, [C] everyone who passes by will be appalled and will scoff. [D] They will say: Why did the LORD do this to this land and this temple? [9] Then they will say: Because they abandoned the LORD their God who brought their ancestors out of the land of Egypt. They held on to other gods and bowed in worship to them and served them. Because of this, the LORD brought all this ruin on them.

King Hiram's Twenty Towns

[10] At the end of twenty years during which Solomon had built the two houses, the LORD's temple and the royal palace — [11] King Hiram of Tyre having supplied him with cedar and cypress logs and gold for his every wish — King Solomon gave Hiram twenty towns in the land of Galilee. [12] So Hiram went out from Tyre to look over the towns that Solomon had given him, but was not pleased with them. [13] So he said, "What are these towns you've given me, my brother?" So he called them the Land of Cabul, [E] as they are still called today. [14] Now Hiram had sent the king nine thousand pounds [F] of gold.   1Kg 6:38; 7:1; 2Ch 8:1

Solomon's Forced Labor

[15] This is the account of the forced labor that King Solomon had imposed to build the LORD's temple, his own palace, the supporting terraces, the wall of Jerusalem, and Hazor, Megiddo, and Gezer. [16] Pharaoh king of Egypt had attacked and captured Gezer. He then burned it, killed the Canaanites who lived in the city, and gave it as a dowry to his daughter, Solomon's wife. [17] Then Solomon rebuilt Gezer, Lower Beth-horon, [18] Baalath, Tamar [G,H] in the Wilderness of Judah, [19] all the storage cities that belonged to Solomon, the chariot cities, the cavalry cities, and whatever Solomon desired to build in Jerusalem, Lebanon, or anywhere else in the land of his dominion.

[20] As for all the peoples who remained of the Amorites, Hethites, Perizzites, Hivites, and Jebusites,

---

[A] 9:3 Or by putting   [B] 9:7 Lit send from my presence   [C] 9:8 Some ancient versions read temple will become a ruin   [D] 9:8 Lit hiss   [E] 9:13 = Like Nothing   [F] 9:14 Lit 120 talents   [G] 9:18 Alt Hb traditions, LXX, Syr, Tg, Vg read Tadmor; 2Ch 8:4   [H] 9:18 Tamar was a city in southern Judah; Ezk 47:19; 48:28.

who were not Israelites — [21] their descendants who remained in the land after them, those whom the Israelites were unable to destroy completely — Solomon imposed forced labor on them; it is still this way today. [22] But Solomon did not consign the Israelites to slavery; they were soldiers, his servants, his commanders, his captains, and commanders of his chariots and his cavalry. [23] These were the deputies who were over Solomon's work: 550 who supervised the people doing the work. Jdg 1:21-36; 3:1

Solomon's Other Activities

[24] Pharaoh's daughter moved from the city of David to the house that Solomon had built for her; he then built the terraces. 2Sm 5:7; 1Kg 7:8; 2Ch 8:11

[25] Three times a year Solomon offered burnt offerings and fellowship offerings on the altar he had built for the LORD, and he burned incense with them in the LORD's presence. So he completed the temple. Dt 16:16; 2Ch 8:16

[26] King Solomon put together a fleet of ships at Ezion-geber, which is near Eloth on the shore of the Red Sea in the land of Edom. [27] With the fleet, Hiram sent his servants, experienced seamen, along with Solomon's servants. [28] They went to Ophir and acquired gold there — sixteen tons [A] — and delivered it to Solomon. Nm 33:48; 1Kg 10:11; 22:48

The Queen of Sheba

10 The queen of Sheba heard about Solomon's fame connected with the name of the LORD and came to test him with riddles. [2] She came to Jerusalem with a very large entourage, with camels bearing spices, gold in great abundance, and precious stones. She came to Solomon and spoke to him about everything that was on her mind. [3] So Solomon answered all her questions; nothing was too difficult for the king to explain to her. [4] When the queen of Sheba observed all of Solomon's wisdom, the palace he had built, [5] the food at his table, his servants' residence, his attendants' service and their attire, his cupbearers, and the burnt offerings he offered at the LORD's temple, it took her breath away.

[6] She said to the king, "The report I heard in my own country about your words and about your wisdom is true. [7] But I didn't believe the reports until I came and saw with my own eyes. Indeed, I was not even told half. Your wisdom and prosperity far exceed the report I heard. [8] How happy are your men. [B] How happy are these servants of yours, who always stand in your presence hearing your wisdom. [9] Blessed be the LORD your God! He delighted in you and put you on the throne of Israel, because of the LORD's eternal love for Israel. He has made you king to carry out justice and righteousness."

[10] Then she gave the king four and a half tons [C] of gold, a great quantity of spices, and precious stones. Never again did such a quantity of spices arrive as those the queen of Sheba gave to King Solomon.

[11] In addition, Hiram's fleet that carried gold from Ophir brought from Ophir a large quantity of almug [D] wood and precious stones. [12] The king made the almug wood

into steps for the LORD's temple and the king's palace and into lyres and harps for the singers. Never before did such almug wood arrive, and the like has not been seen again. 1Kg 9:27-28

¹³ King Solomon gave the queen of Sheba her every desire — whatever she asked — besides what he had given her out of his royal bounty. Then she, along with her servants, returned to her own country.

Solomon's Wealth

¹⁴ The weight of gold that came to Solomon annually was twenty-five tons, ᴬ ¹⁵ besides what came from merchants, traders' merchandise, and all the Arabian kings and governors of the land. 2Ch 1:16; 9:13-24

¹⁶ King Solomon made two hundred large shields of hammered gold; fifteen pounds ᴮ of gold went into each shield. ¹⁷ He made three hundred small shields of hammered gold; nearly four pounds ᶜ of gold went into each shield. The king put them in the House of the Forest of Lebanon. 1Kg 7:2-5

¹⁸ The king also made a large ivory throne and overlaid it with fine gold. ¹⁹ The throne had six steps; there was a rounded top at the back of the throne, armrests on either side of the seat, and two lions standing beside the armrests. ²⁰ Twelve lions were standing there on the six steps, one at each end. Nothing like it had ever been made in any other kingdom.

²¹ All of King Solomon's drinking cups were gold, and all the utensils of the House of the Forest of Lebanon were pure gold. There was no silver, since it was considered as nothing in Solomon's time, ²² for the king had ships of Tarshish at sea with Hiram's fleet, and once every three years the ships of Tarshish would arrive bearing gold, silver, ivory, apes, and peacocks. ᴰ

²³ King Solomon surpassed all the kings of the world in riches and in wisdom. ²⁴ The whole world wanted an audience with Solomon to hear the wisdom that God had put in his heart. ²⁵ Every man would bring his annual tribute: items ᴱ of silver and gold, clothing, weapons, ᶠ spices, and horses and mules.

²⁶ Solomon accumulated 1,400 chariots and 12,000 horsemen and stationed them in the chariot cities and with the king in Jerusalem. ²⁷ The king made silver as common in Jerusalem as stones, and he made cedar as abundant as sycamore in the Judean foothills. ²⁸ Solomon's horses were imported from Egypt and Kue. ᴳ The king's traders bought them from Kue at the going price. ²⁹ A chariot was imported from Egypt for fifteen pounds ᴴ of silver, and a horse for nearly four pounds. ᴵ In the same way, they exported them to all the kings of the Hittites and to the kings of Aram through their agents. 1Kg 4:26; 9:19

Solomon's Unfaithfulness to God

11 King Solomon loved many foreign women in addition to Pharaoh's daughter: Moabite, Ammonite, Edomite, Sidonian, and Hittite women ² from the nations about which the LORD had told the Israelites, "You must not intermarry with them, and they must not

ᴬ**10:14** Lit *666 talents*   ᴮ**10:16** Lit *600* (shekels)   ᶜ**10:17** Lit *three minas*   ᴰ**10:22** Or *baboons*
ᴱ**10:25** Or *vessels*, or *weapons*   ᶠ**10:25** Or *fragrant balsam*   ᴳ**10:28** = Cilicia   ᴴ**10:29** Lit *600 shekels*
ᴵ**10:29** Lit *150 shekels*

intermarry with you, because they will turn your heart away to follow their gods." To these women Solomon was deeply attached[A] in love. [3] He had seven hundred wives who were princesses and three hundred who were concubines, and they turned his heart away. 1Kg 3:1; 7:8

[4] When Solomon was old, his wives turned his heart away to follow other gods. He was not wholeheartedly devoted to the LORD his God, as his father David had been. [5] Solomon followed Ashtoreth, the goddess of the Sidonians, and Milcom, the abhorrent idol of the Ammonites. [6] Solomon did what was evil in the LORD's sight, and unlike his father David, he did not remain loyal to the LORD. 1Kg 8:61; 9:4; 15:3,14

[7] At that time, Solomon built a high place for Chemosh, the abhorrent idol of Moab, and for Milcom,[B] the abhorrent idol of the Ammonites, on the hill across from Jerusalem. [8] He did the same for all his foreign wives, who were burning incense and offering sacrifices to their gods. Nm 21:29; 33:52; 1Kg 3:2-3

[9] The LORD was angry with Solomon, because his heart had turned away from the LORD, the God of Israel, who had appeared to him twice. [10] He had commanded him about this, so that he would not follow other gods, but Solomon did not do what the LORD had commanded. 1Kg 3:5; 6:12; 9:2,6-7

[11] Then the LORD said to Solomon, "Since you have done this[C] and did not keep my covenant and my statutes, which I commanded you, I will tear the kingdom away from you and give it to your servant. [12] However, I will not do it during your lifetime for the sake of your father David; I will tear it out of your son's hand. [13] Yet I will not tear the entire kingdom away from him. I will give one tribe to your son for the sake of my servant David and for the sake of Jerusalem that I chose."

Solomon's Enemies

[14] So the LORD raised up Hadad the Edomite as an enemy against Solomon. He was of the royal family in Edom. [15] Earlier, when David was in Edom, Joab, the commander of the army, had gone to bury the dead and had struck down every male in Edom. [16] For Joab and all Israel had remained there six months, until he had killed every male in Edom. [17] Hadad fled to Egypt, along with some Edomites from his father's servants. At the time Hadad was a small boy. [18] Hadad and his men set out from Midian and went to Paran. They took men with them from Paran and went to Egypt, to Pharaoh king of Egypt, who gave Hadad a house, ordered that he be given food, and gave him land. [19] Pharaoh liked Hadad so much[D] that he gave him a wife, the sister of his own wife, Queen Tahpenes. [20] Tahpenes's sister gave birth to Hadad's son Genubath. Tahpenes herself weaned him in Pharaoh's palace, and Genubath lived there along with Pharaoh's sons. 1Kg 5:4

[21] When Hadad heard in Egypt that David rested with his fathers and that Joab, the commander of the army, was dead, Hadad said to Pharaoh, "Let me leave, so I may go to my own country."

[22] But Pharaoh asked him, "What do you lack here with me for you

A 11:2 Lit *Solomon clung*   B 11:7 Lit *Molech*   C 11:11 Lit *"Since this was with you*   D 11:19 Lit *Hadad found much favor in Pharaoh's eyes* to want to go back to your own country?"

"Nothing," he replied, "but please let me leave."

²³ God raised up Rezon son of Eliada as an enemy against Solomon. Rezon had fled from his master King Hadadezer of Zobah ²⁴ and gathered men to himself. He became leader of a raiding party when David killed the Zobaites. He^A went to Damascus, lived there, and became king in Damascus. ²⁵ Rezon was Israel's enemy throughout Solomon's reign, adding to the trouble Hadad had caused. He reigned over Aram^B and loathed Israel.

²⁶ Now Solomon's servant, Jeroboam son of Nebat, was an Ephraimite from Zeredah. His widowed mother's name was Zeruah. Jeroboam rebelled against Solomon, ²⁷ and this is the reason he rebelled against the king: Solomon had built the supporting terraces and repaired the opening in the wall of the city of his father David. ²⁸ Now the man Jeroboam was capable, and Solomon noticed the young man because he was getting things done. So he appointed him over the entire labor force of the house of Joseph. 1Kg 9:15,24; 11:11,40; 2Ch 13:6

²⁹ During that time, the prophet Ahijah the Shilonite met Jeroboam on the road as Jeroboam came out of Jerusalem. Now Ahijah had wrapped himself with a new cloak, and the two of them were alone in the open field. ³⁰ Then Ahijah took hold of the new cloak he had on, tore it into twelve pieces, ³¹ and said to Jeroboam, "Take ten pieces for yourself, for this is what the LORD God of Israel says: 'I am about to tear the kingdom out of Solomon's hand. I will give you ten tribes, ³² but one tribe will remain his for the sake of my servant David and for the sake of Jerusalem, the city I chose out of all the tribes of Israel. ³³ For they have abandoned me; they have bowed down to Ashtoreth, the goddess of the Sidonians, to Chemosh, the god of Moab, and to Milcom, the god of the Ammonites. They have not walked in my ways to do what is right in my sight and to carry out my statutes and my judgments as his father David did. 1Sm 15:27-28; 1Kg 11:11-13; 12:15; 14:2

³⁴ "'However, I will not take the whole kingdom from him but will let him be ruler all the days of his life for the sake of my servant David, whom I chose and who kept my commands and my statutes. ³⁵ I will take ten tribes of the kingdom from his son and give them to you. ³⁶ I will give one tribe to his son, so that my servant David will always have a lamp before me in Jerusalem, the city I chose for myself to put my name there. ³⁷ I will appoint you, and you will reign as king over all you want, and you will be king over Israel. 1Kg 3:14; 12:16-17; Am 11:12-13

³⁸ "'After that, if you obey all I command you, walk in my ways, and do what is right in my sight in order to keep my statutes and my commands as my servant David did, I will be with you. I will build you a lasting dynasty just as I built for David, and I will give you Israel. ³⁹ I will humble David's descendants, because of their unfaithfulness, but not forever.'" ^C 1Kg 11:11

⁴⁰ Therefore, Solomon tried to kill Jeroboam, but he fled to Egypt, to

^A11:24 LXX; Hb reads *They*   ^B11:25 Some Hb mss, LXX, Syr read *Edom*   ^C11:38-39 LXX omits *and I will give . . . but not forever*

King Shishak of Egypt, where he remained until Solomon's death.

Solomon's Death

⁴¹ The rest of the events of Solomon's reign, along with all his accomplishments and his wisdom, are written in the Book of Solomon's Events. ⁴² The length of Solomon's reign in Jerusalem over all Israel totaled forty years. ⁴³ Solomon rested with his fathers and was buried in the city of his father David. His son Rehoboam became king in his place.   1Kg 15:7,23; 2Ch 9:29

The Kingdom Divided

12 Then Rehoboam went to Shechem, for all Israel had gone to Shechem to make him king. ² When Jeroboam son of Nebat heard about it, he stayed in Egypt, where he had fled from King Solomon's presence. Jeroboam stayed in Egypt. [A] ³ But they summoned him, and Jeroboam and the whole assembly of Israel came and spoke to Rehoboam: ⁴ "Your father made our yoke harsh. You, therefore, lighten your father's harsh service and the heavy yoke he put on us, and we will serve you."

⁵ Rehoboam replied, "Go away for three days and then return to me." So the people left. ⁶ Then King Rehoboam consulted with the elders who had served his father Solomon when he was alive, asking, "How do you advise me to respond to this people?"   1Kg 4:2-19

⁷ They replied, "Today if you will be a servant to this people and serve them, and if you respond to them by speaking kind words to them, they will be your servants forever."   2Ch 10:7; Pr 15:1

⁸ But he rejected the advice of the elders who had advised him and consulted with the young men who had grown up with him and attended him. ⁹ He asked them, "What message do you advise that we send back to this people who said to me, 'Lighten the yoke your father put on us'?"   Lv 19:32

¹⁰ Then the young men who had grown up with him told him, "This is what you should say to this people who said to you, 'Your father made our yoke heavy, but you, make it lighter on us!' This is what you should tell them: 'My little finger is thicker than my father's waist! ¹¹ Although my father burdened you with a heavy yoke, I will add to your yoke; my father disciplined you with whips, but I will discipline you with barbed whips.'" [B]   Ex 1:13-14

¹² So Jeroboam and all the people came to Rehoboam on the third day, as the king had ordered: "Return to me on the third day." ¹³ Then the king answered the people harshly. He rejected the advice the elders had given him ¹⁴ and spoke to them according to the young men's advice: "My father made your yoke heavy, but I will add to your yoke; my father disciplined you with whips, but I will discipline you with barbed whips."

¹⁵ The king did not listen to the people, because this turn of events came from the LORD to carry out his word, which the LORD had spoken through Ahijah the Shilonite to Jeroboam son of Nebat. ¹⁶ When all Israel saw that the king had not listened to them, the people answered him: Dt 2:30; 1Kg 11:29-39; 12:24

> What portion do we have
> in David?

[A] **12:2** LXX, Vg read *Jeroboam returned from Egypt* ; 2Ch 10:2   [B] **12:11** Lit *with scorpions*, also in v. 14

We have no inheritance
in the son of Jesse.   2Sm 5:3,5
Israel, return to your tents;
David, now look
after your own house!
So Israel went to their tents, [17] but Rehoboam reigned over the Israelites living in the cities of Judah.

[18] Then King Rehoboam sent Adoram, [A] who was in charge of forced labor, but all Israel stoned him to death. King Rehoboam managed to get into the chariot and flee to Jerusalem. [19] Israel is still in rebellion against the house of David today.   2Sm 20:24; 1Kg 4:6; 5:14

Rehoboam in Jerusalem

[20] When all Israel heard that Jeroboam had come back, they summoned him to the assembly and made him king over all Israel. No one followed the house of David except the tribe of Judah alone. [21] When Rehoboam arrived in Jerusalem, he mobilized one hundred eighty thousand fit young soldiers from the entire house of Judah and the tribe of Benjamin to fight against the house of Israel to restore the kingdom to Rehoboam son of Solomon. [22] But the word of God came to Shemaiah, the man of God: [23] "Say to Rehoboam son of Solomon, king of Judah, to the whole house of Judah and Benjamin, and to the rest of the people, [24] 'This is what the LORD says: You are not to march up and fight against your brothers, the Israelites. Each of you return home, for this situation is from me.'"   1Kg 11:11,13,36; 12:3;

So they listened to the word of the LORD and went back according to the word of the LORD.

Jeroboam's Idolatry

[25] Jeroboam built Shechem in the hill country of Ephraim and lived there. From there he went out and built Penuel. [26] Jeroboam said to himself, "The kingdom might now return to the house of David. [27] If these people regularly go to offer sacrifices in the LORD's temple in Jerusalem, the heart of these people will return to their lord, King Rehoboam of Judah. They will kill me and go back to the king of Judah." [28] So the king sought advice.   Gn 12:6; Jdg 9:6; 1Kg 12:1

Then he made two golden calves, and he said to the people, "Going to Jerusalem is too difficult for you. Israel, here are your gods [B] who brought you up from the land of Egypt." [29] He set up one in Bethel, and put the other in Dan. [30] This led to sin; the people walked in procession before one of the calves all the way to Dan. [C]   Gn 12:8; Ex 32:4,8

[31] Jeroboam also made shrines [D] on the high places and made priests from the ranks of the people who were not Levites. [32] Jeroboam made a festival in the eighth month on the fifteenth day of the month, like the festival in Judah. He offered sacrifices on the altar; he made this offering in Bethel to sacrifice to the calves he had made. He also stationed the priests in Bethel for the high places he had made. [33] He offered sacrifices on [E] the altar he had set up in Bethel on the fifteenth day of the eighth month. He chose this month on his own. He made a festival for the Israelites, offered sacrifices on the altar, and burned incense.   Lv 23:33-34; 1Kg 3:3; 11:7; 2Kg 17:32

[A]12:18 LXX reads *Adoniram*; 1Kg 4:6; 5:14   [B]12:28 Or *here is your God*, or *here is your god*   [C]12:30 Some LXX mss read *calves to Bethel and the other to Dan*   [D]12:31 Lit *a house*   [E]12:33 Or *He went up to*

Judgment on Jeroboam

13 A man of God came, however, from Judah to Bethel by the word of the LORD while Jeroboam was standing beside the altar to burn incense. ² The man of God cried out against the altar by the word of the LORD: "Altar, altar, this is what the LORD says, 'A son will be born to the house of David, named Josiah, and he will sacrifice on you the priests of the high places who are burning incense on you. Human bones will be burned on you.'" ³ He gave a sign that day. He said, "This is the sign that the LORD has spoken: 'The altar will now be ripped apart, and the ashes that are on it will be poured out.'" 1Kg 12:22; 2Kg 23:17

⁴ When the king heard the message that the man of God had cried out against the altar at Bethel, Jeroboam stretched out his hand from the altar and said, "Arrest him!" But the hand he stretched out against him withered, and he could not pull it back to himself. ⁵ The altar was ripped apart, and the ashes poured from the altar, according to the sign that the man of God had given by the word of the LORD.

⁶ Then the king responded to the man of God, "Plead for the favor of the LORD your God and pray for me so that my hand may be restored to me." So the man of God pleaded for the favor of the LORD, and the king's hand was restored to him and became as it had been at first. ⁷ Then the king declared to the man of God, "Come home with me, refresh yourself, and I'll give you a reward." 1Sm 9:7; 2Kg 5:15

⁸ But the man of God replied, "If you were to give me half your house, I still wouldn't go with you, and I wouldn't eat food or drink water in this place, ⁹ for this is what I was commanded by the word of the LORD: 'You must not eat food or drink water or go back the way you came.'" ¹⁰ So he went another way; he did not go back by the way he had come to Bethel. Nm 22:18; Est 5:3

The Old Prophet and the Man of God

¹¹ Now a certain old prophet was living in Bethel. His son^A came and told him all the deeds that the man of God had done that day in Bethel. His sons also told their father the words that he had spoken to the king. ¹² Then their father asked them, "Which way did he go?" His sons had seen^B the way taken by the man of God who had come from Judah. ¹³ Then he said to his sons, "Saddle the donkey for me." So they saddled the donkey for him, and he got on it. ¹⁴ He followed the man of God and found him sitting under an oak tree. He asked him, "Are you the man of God who came from Judah?"

"I am," he said. 1Kg 12:32; 13:1-6

¹⁵ Then he said to him, "Come home with me and eat some food."

¹⁶ But he answered, "I cannot go back with you or accompany you; I will not eat food or drink water with you in this place. ¹⁷ For a message came to me by the word of the LORD: 'You must not eat food or drink water there or go back by the way you came.'" 1Kg 13:8-9

¹⁸ He said to him, "I am also a prophet like you. An angel spoke to me by the word of the LORD: 'Bring him back with you to your house so that he may eat food and drink water.'" The old prophet deceived him,

^A**13:11** Some Hb mss, LXX, Syr, Vg read *sons*   ^B**13:12** LXX, Syr, Tg, Vg read *sons showed him*

¹⁹ and the man of God went back with him, ate food in his house, and drank water. Dt 13:1-3; 1Jn 4:1

²⁰ While they were sitting at the table, the word of the LORD came to the prophet who had brought him back, ²¹ and the prophet cried out to the man of God who had come from Judah, "This is what the LORD says: 'Because you rebelled against the LORD's command and did not keep the command that the LORD your God commanded you — ²² but you went back and ate food and drank water in the place that he said to you, "Do not eat food and do not drink water" — your corpse will never reach the grave of your fathers.'" 1Kg 13:8-9,30

²³ So after he had eaten food and after he had drunk, the old prophet saddled the donkey for the prophet he had brought back. ²⁴ When he left,ᴬ a lion attackedᴮ him along the way and killed him. His corpse was thrown on the road, and the donkey was standing beside it; the lion was standing beside the corpse too.

²⁵ There were men passing by who saw the corpse thrown on the road and the lion standing beside it, and they went and spoke about it in the city where the old prophet lived. ²⁶ When the prophet who had brought him back from his way heard about it, he said, "He is the man of God who disobeyed the LORD's command. The LORD has given him to the lion, and it has mauled and killed him, according to the word of the LORD that he spoke to him."

²⁷ Then the old prophet instructed his sons, "Saddle the donkey for me." They saddled it, ²⁸ and he went and found the corpse thrown on the road with the donkey and the lion standing beside the corpse. The lion had not eaten the corpse or mauled the donkey. ²⁹ So the prophet lifted the corpse of the man of God and laid it on the donkey and brought it back. The old prophet came into the city to mourn and to bury him. ³⁰ Then he laid the corpse in his own grave, and they mourned over him: "Oh, my brother!"

³¹ After he had buried him, he said to his sons, "When I die, bury me in the grave where the man of God is buried; lay my bones beside his bones, ³² for the message that he cried out by the word of the LORD against the altar in Bethel and against all the shrines of the high places in the cities of Samaria is certain to happen." 1Kg 13:1-3; 2Kg 17:29

³³ Even after this, Jeroboam did not repent of his evil way but again made priests for the high places from the ranks of the people. He ordained whoever so desired it, and they became priests of the high places. ³⁴ This was the sin that caused the house of Jeroboam to be cut off and obliterated from the face of the earth. Jdg 17:5; 1Kg 13:1-6,24

Disaster on the House of Jeroboam

14 At that time Abijah son of Jeroboam became sick. ² Jeroboam said to his wife, "Go disguise yourself, so they won't know that you're Jeroboam's wife, and go to Shiloh. The prophet Ahijah is there; it was he who told about me becoming king over this people. ³ Take with you ten loaves of bread, some cakes, and a jar of honey, and go to him. He will tell you what will happen to the boy." 1Kg 14:12,17-18

ᴬ13:23-24 LXX reads *donkey, and he turned* ²⁴*and left, and*   ᴮ13:24 Lit *met*

⁴ Jeroboam's wife did that: she went to Shiloh and arrived at Ahijah's house. Ahijah could not see; he was blind ᴬ due to his age. ⁵ But the Lᴏʀᴅ had said to Ahijah, "Jeroboam's wife is coming soon to ask you about her son, for he is sick. You are to say such and such to her. When she arrives, she will be disguised."   1Sm 3:2; 4:15; 2Sm 14:1-2

⁶ When Ahijah heard the sound of her feet entering the door, he said, "Come in, wife of Jeroboam! Why are you disguised? I have bad news for you. ⁷ Go tell Jeroboam, 'This is what the Lᴏʀᴅ God of Israel says: I raised you up from among the people, appointed you ruler over my people Israel, ⁸ tore the kingdom away from the house of David, and gave it to you. But you were not like my servant David, who kept my commands and followed me with all his heart, doing only what is right in my sight. ⁹ You behaved more wickedly than all who were before you. In order to anger me, you have proceeded to make for yourself other gods and cast images, but you have flung me behind your back. ¹⁰ Because of all this, I am about to bring disaster on the house of Jeroboam: 1Sm 28:12

I will wipe out all of
   Jeroboam's males, ᴮ
   both slave and free, ᶜ in Israel;
I will sweep away the house
   of Jeroboam
as one sweeps away dung
   until it is all gone!   1Kg 15:29
¹¹   Anyone who belongs
   to Jeroboam and dies
   in the city,
   the dogs will eat,
and anyone who dies
   in the field,
the birds ᴰ will eat,   1Kg 16:4; 21:24
for the Lᴏʀᴅ has spoken!'

¹² "As for you, get up and go to your house. When your feet enter the city, the boy will die. ¹³ All Israel will mourn for him and bury him. He alone out of Jeroboam's house will be given a proper burial because out of the house of Jeroboam something favorable to the Lᴏʀᴅ God of Israel was found in him. ¹⁴ The Lᴏʀᴅ will raise up for himself a king over Israel, who will wipe out the house of Jeroboam. This is the day, yes, ᴱ even today! ¹⁵ For the Lᴏʀᴅ will strike Israel so that they will ᶠ shake as a reed shakes in water. He will uproot Israel from this good soil that he gave to their ancestors. He will scatter them beyond the Euphrates because they made their Asherah poles, angering the Lᴏʀᴅ. ¹⁶ He will give up Israel because of Jeroboam's sins that he committed and caused Israel to commit."   1Kg 14:17

¹⁷ Then Jeroboam's wife got up and left and went to Tirzah. As she was crossing the threshold of the house, the boy died. ¹⁸ He was buried, and all Israel mourned for him, according to the word of the Lᴏʀᴅ he had spoken through his servant the prophet Ahijah.   1Kg 15:33; Sg 6:4

¹⁹ As for the rest of the events of Jeroboam's reign, how he waged war and how he reigned, note that they are written in the Historical Record of Israel's Kings. ²⁰ The length of Jeroboam's reign was twenty-two years. He rested with

---

ᴬ14:4 Lit *see, for his eyes stood*; 1Sm 4:15   ᴮ14:10 Lit *eliminate Jeroboam's one who urinates against the wall*   ᶜ14:10 Or *males, even the weak and impaired*; Hb obscure   ᴰ14:11 Lit *birds of the sky*   ᴱ14:14 Hb obscure   ᶠ14:15 *so that they will* supplied for clarity his fathers, and his son Nadab became king in his place.　1Kg 14:30

Judah's King Rehoboam

[21] Now Rehoboam, Solomon's son, reigned in Judah. Rehoboam was forty-one years old when he became king; he reigned seventeen years in Jerusalem, the city where the LORD had chosen from all the tribes of Israel to put his name. Rehoboam's mother's name was Naamah the Ammonite. Dt 12:5; 1Kg 12:1-24 [22] Judah did what was evil in the LORD's sight. They provoked him to jealous anger more than all that their ancestors had done with the sins they committed. [23] They also built for themselves high places, sacred pillars, and Asherah poles on every high hill and under every green tree; [24] there were even male cult prostitutes in the land. They imitated all the detestable practices of the nations the LORD had dispossessed before the Israelites. [25] In the fifth year of King Rehoboam, King Shishak of Egypt went to war against Jerusalem. [26] He seized the treasuries of the LORD's temple and the treasuries of the royal palace. He took everything. He took all the gold shields that Solomon had made. [27] King Rehoboam made bronze shields to replace them and committed them into the care of the captains of the guards [A] who protected the entrance to the king's palace. [28] Whenever the king entered the LORD's temple, the guards would carry the shields, then they would take them back to the armory. [B]　1Kg 10:16-17; 11:40; 2Ch 12:2-11 [29] The rest of the events of Rehoboam's reign, along with all

his accomplishments, are written about in the Historical Record of Judah's Kings. [30] There was war between Rehoboam and Jeroboam throughout their reigns. [31] Rehoboam rested with his fathers and was buried with his fathers in the city of David. His mother's name was Naamah the Ammonite. His son Abijam [C] became king in his place.

Judah's King Abijam

15 In the eighteenth year of Israel's King Jeroboam son of Nebat, Abijam became king over Judah, [2] and he reigned three years in Jerusalem. His mother's name was Maacah daughter [D] of Abishalom.

[3] Abijam walked in all the sins his father before him had committed, and he was not wholeheartedly devoted to the LORD his God as his ancestor David had been. [4] But for the sake of David, the LORD his God gave him a lamp in Jerusalem by raising up his son after him and by preserving Jerusalem. [5] For David did what was right in the LORD's sight, and he did not turn aside from anything he had commanded him all the days of his life, except in the matter of Uriah the Hethite.　2Sm 21:17; 1Kg 9:4; 11:4; 14:21-22

[6] There had been war between Rehoboam and Jeroboam all the days of Rehoboam's life. [7] The rest of the events of Abijam's reign, along with all his accomplishments, are written in the Historical Record of Judah's Kings. There was also war between Abijam and Jeroboam. [8] Abijam rested with his fathers and was buried in the city of David. His son Asa became king in his place.　1Kg 14:29-30; 2Ch 12:15

[A]14:27 Lit the runners　[B]14:28 Lit the chamber of the runners　[C]14:31 = Abijah in 2Ch 13
[D]15:2 Possibly granddaughter, also in v. 10; 2Ch 13:2

Judah's King Asa

[9] In the twentieth year of Israel's King Jeroboam, Asa became king of Judah, [10] and he reigned forty-one years in Jerusalem. His grandmother's[A] name was Maacah daughter of Abishalom.   1Kg 15:1-2

[11] Asa did what was right in the LORD's sight, as his ancestor David had done. [12] He banished the male cult prostitutes from the land and removed all of the idols that his fathers had made. [13] He also removed his grandmother[B] Maacah from being queen mother because she had made an obscene image of Asherah. Asa chopped down her obscene image and burned it in the Kidron Valley. [14] The high places were not taken away, but Asa was wholeheartedly devoted to the LORD his entire life. [15] He brought his father's consecrated gifts and his own consecrated gifts into the LORD's temple: silver, gold, and utensils. Dt 23:17; 1Kg 9:4-5; 15:3; 2Ch 14:2

[16] There was war between Asa and King Baasha of Israel throughout their reigns. [17] Israel's King Baasha went to war against Judah. He built Ramah in order to keep anyone from leaving or coming to King Asa of Judah. [18] So Asa withdrew all the silver and gold that remained in the treasuries of the LORD's temple and the treasuries of the royal palace and gave it to his servants. Then King Asa sent them to Ben-hadad son of Tabrimmon son of Hezion king of Aram who lived in Damascus, saying, [19] "There is a treaty between me and you, between my father and your father. Look, I have sent you a gift of silver and gold. Go and break your treaty with King Baasha of Israel so that he will withdraw from me."

[20] Ben-hadad listened to King Asa and sent the commanders of his armies against the cities of Israel. He attacked Ijon, Dan, Abel-beth-maacah, all Chinnereth, and the whole land of Naphtali. [21] When Baasha heard about it, he quit building Ramah and stayed in Tirzah. [22] Then King Asa gave a command to everyone without exception in Judah, and they carried away the stones of Ramah and the timbers Baasha had built it with. Then King Asa built Geba of Benjamin and Mizpah with them. Jdg 18:29; 2Kg 15:29

[23] The rest of all the events of Asa's reign, along with all his might, all his accomplishments, and the cities he built, are written in the Historical Record of Judah's Kings. But in his old age he developed a disease in his feet. [24] Then Asa rested with his fathers and was buried in the city of his ancestor David. His son Jehoshaphat became king in his place.   2Ch 16:11-14

Israel's King Nadab

[25] Nadab son of Jeroboam became king over Israel in the second year of Judah's King Asa; he reigned over Israel two years. [26] Nadab did what was evil in the LORD's sight and walked in the ways of his father and the sin he had caused Israel to commit.   1Kg 14:16,20

[27] Then Baasha son of Ahijah of the house of Issachar conspired against Nadab, and Baasha struck him down at Gibbethon of the Philistines while Nadab and all Israel were besieging Gibbethon. [28] In the third year of Judah's King Asa,

---

A 15:10 Lit mother's   B 15:13 Lit mother

Baasha killed Nadab and reigned in his place.   Jos 19:44; 1Kg 14:14; 15:16

²⁹ When Baasha became king, he struck down the entire house of Jeroboam. He did not leave Jeroboam any survivors but ᴬ destroyed his family according to the word of the Lᴏʀᴅ he had spoken through his servant Ahijah the Shilonite. ³⁰ This was because Jeroboam had angered ᴮ the Lᴏʀᴅ God of Israel by the sins he had committed and had caused Israel to commit.   1Kg 13:34; 14:7-9,10

³¹ The rest of the events of Nadab's reign, along with all his accomplishments, are written in the Historical Record of Israel's Kings. ³² There was war between Asa and King Baasha of Israel throughout their reigns.   1Kg 14:19; 15:16; 16:5

Israel's King Baasha

³³ In the third year of Judah's King Asa, Baasha son of Ahijah became king over all Israel, and he reigned in Tirzah twenty-four years. ³⁴ He did what was evil in the Lᴏʀᴅ's sight and walked in the ways of Jeroboam and the sin he had caused Israel to commit.   1Kg 14:16; 15:21

16 Now the word of the Lᴏʀᴅ came to Jehu son of Hanani against Baasha: ² "Because I raised you up from the dust and made you ruler over my people Israel, but you have walked in the ways of Jeroboam and have caused my people Israel to sin, angering me with their sins, ³ take note: I will eradicate Baasha and his house, and I will make your house like the house of Jeroboam son of Nebat:

⁴   Anyone who belongs
        to Baasha and dies in the city,

the dogs will eat,
    and anyone who is his
        and dies in the field,
    the birds ᶜ will eat."   1Kg 14:11; 21:24

⁵ The rest of the events of Baasha's reign, along with all his accomplishments and might, are written in the Historical Record of Israel's Kings. ⁶ Baasha rested with his fathers and was buried in Tirzah. His son Elah became king in his place. ⁷ But through the prophet Jehu son of Hanani the word of the Lᴏʀᴅ also had come against Baasha and against his house because of all the evil he had done in the Lᴏʀᴅ's sight. His actions angered the Lᴏʀᴅ, and Baasha's house became like the house of Jeroboam, because he had struck it down.   1Kg 14:19; 15:31

Israel's King Elah

⁸ In the twenty-sixth year of Judah's King Asa, Elah son of Baasha became king over Israel, and he reigned in Tirzah two years.

⁹ His servant Zimri, commander of half his chariots, conspired against him while Elah was in Tirzah getting drunk in the house of Arza, who was in charge of the household at Tirzah. ¹⁰ In the twenty-seventh year of Judah's King Asa, Zimri went in, struck Elah down, killing him. Then Zimri became king in his place.   2Kg 9:30-33

¹¹ When he became king, as soon as he was seated on his throne, Zimri struck down the entire house of Baasha. He did not leave a single male, ᴰ including his kinsmen and his friends. ¹² So Zimri destroyed the entire house of Baasha, according

---

ᴬ**15:29** Lit *Jeroboam anyone breathing until he*   ᴮ**15:30** Lit *provoked in the provocation of*   ᶜ**16:4** Lit *birds of the sky*   ᴰ**16:11** Lit *leave him one who urinates against the wall* to the word of the LORD he had spoken against Baasha through the prophet Jehu. [13] This happened because of all the sins of Baasha and those of his son Elah, which they committed and caused Israel to commit, angering the LORD God of Israel with their worthless idols.

[14] The rest of the events of Elah's reign, along with all his accomplishments, are written in the Historical Record of Israel's Kings.

Israel's King Zimri

[15] In the twenty-seventh year of Judah's King Asa, Zimri became king for seven days in Tirzah. Now the troops were encamped against Gibbethon of the Philistines. [16] When these troops heard that Zimri had not only conspired but had also struck down the king, then all Israel made Omri, the army commander, king over Israel that very day in the camp. [17] Omri along with all Israel marched up from Gibbethon and besieged Tirzah. [18] When Zimri saw that the city was captured, he entered the citadel of the royal palace and burned it down over himself. He died [19] because of the sin he committed by doing what was evil in the LORD's sight and by walking in the ways of Jeroboam and the sin he caused Israel to commit.

[20] The rest of the events of Zimri's reign, along with the conspiracy that he instigated, are written in the Historical Record of Israel's Kings. [21] At that time the people of Israel were divided: half the people followed Tibni son of Ginath, to make him king, and half followed Omri. [22] However, the people who followed Omri proved stronger than those who followed Tibni son

of Ginath. So Tibni died and Omri became king.

Israel's King Omri

[23] In the thirty-first year of Judah's King Asa, Omri became king over Israel, and he reigned twelve years. He reigned six years in Tirzah, [24] then he bought the hill of Samaria from Shemer for 150 pounds[A] of silver, and he built up the hill. He named the city he built Samaria[B] based on the name Shemer, the owner of the hill.   1Kg 13:32; 15:21

[25] Omri did what was evil in the LORD's sight; he did more evil than all who were before him. [26] He walked in all the ways of Jeroboam son of Nebat in every respect and continued in his sins that he caused Israel to commit, angering the LORD God of Israel with their worthless idols. [27] The rest of the events of Omri's reign, along with his accomplishments and the might he exercised, are written in the Historical Record of Israel's Kings. [28] Omri rested with his fathers and was buried in Samaria. His son Ahab became king in his place.   1Kg 14:9; 16:13,19,30

Israel's King Ahab

[29] Ahab son of Omri became king over Israel in the thirty-eighth year of Judah's King Asa; Ahab son of Omri reigned over Israel in Samaria twenty-two years. [30] But Ahab son of Omri did what was evil in the LORD's sight more than all who were before him. [31] Then, as if following the sin of Jeroboam son of Nebat were not enough, he married Jezebel, the daughter of Ethbaal king of the Sidonians, and then proceeded to serve Baal and bow

[A]16:24 Lit for two talents   [B]16:24 = Belonging to Shemer's Clan in worship to him. ³² He set up an altar for Baal in the temple of Baal that he had built in Samaria. ³³ Ahab also made an Asherah pole. Ahab did more to anger the LORD God of Israel than all the kings of Israel who were before him. 1Kg 14:9

³⁴ During his reign, Hiel the Bethelite built Jericho. At the cost of Abiram his firstborn, he laid its foundation, and at the cost of Segub his youngest, he finished its gates, according to the word of the LORD he had spoken through Joshua son of Nun. Jos 6:26

Elijah Announces Famine

17 Now Elijah the Tishbite, from the Gilead settlers, ᴬ said to Ahab, "As the LORD God of Israel lives, in whose presence I stand, there will be no dew or rain during these years except by my command!" 1Kg 17–19; 2Kg 1–2; Mal 4:5; Mt 11:14

² Then the word of the LORD came to him: ³ "Leave here, turn eastward, and hide at the Wadi Cherith where it enters the Jordan. ⁴ You are to drink from the wadi. I have commanded the ravens to provide for you there." 1Kg 17:9; 18:4; Jb 38:41; Lk 12:24

⁵ So he proceeded to do what the LORD commanded. Elijah left and lived at the Wadi Cherith where it enters the Jordan. ⁶ The ravens kept bringing him bread and meat in the morning and in the evening, and he would drink from the wadi. ⁷ After a while, the wadi dried up because there had been no rain in the land. Ex 16:8

Elijah and the Widow

⁸ Then the word of the LORD came to him: ⁹ "Get up, go to Zarephath that belongs to Sidon and stay there.

Look, I have commanded a woman who is a widow to provide for you there." ¹⁰ So Elijah got up and went to Zarephath. When he arrived at the city gate, there was a widow gathering wood. Elijah called to her and said, "Please bring me a little water in a cup and let me drink." ¹¹ As she went to get it, he called to her and said, "Please bring me a piece of bread in your hand." Ob 20; Lk 4:26

¹² But she said, "As the LORD your God lives, I don't have anything baked — only a handful of flour in the jar and a bit of oil in the jug. Just now, I am gathering a couple of sticks in order to go prepare it for myself and my son so we can eat it and die." 1Kg 17:1; 2Kg 4:2-7

¹³ Then Elijah said to her, "Don't be afraid; go and do as you have said. But first make me a small loaf from it and bring it out to me. Afterward, you may make some for yourself and your son, ¹⁴ for this is what the LORD God of Israel says, 'The flour jar will not become empty and the oil jug will not run dry until the day the LORD sends rain on the surface of the land.'" 1Kg 17:1

¹⁵ So she proceeded to do according to the word of Elijah. Then the woman, Elijah, and her household ate for many days. ¹⁶ The flour jar did not become empty, and the oil jug did not run dry, according to the word of the LORD he had spoken through ᴮ Elijah. Mt 6:11

The Widow's Son Raised

¹⁷ After this, the son of the woman who owned the house became ill. His illness got worse until he stopped breathing. ¹⁸ She said to Elijah, "Man of God, why are you here? Have you come to call attention to

ᴬ **17:1** LXX reads *from Tishbe of Gilead*　ᴮ **17:16** Lit *by the hand of* my iniquity so that my son is put to death?"   1Kg 12:22; Lk 5:8; Ac 9:37

¹⁹ But Elijah said to her, "Give me your son." So he took him from her arms, brought him up to the upstairs room where he was staying, and laid him on his own bed. ²⁰ Then he cried out to the LORD and said, "LORD my God, have you also brought tragedy on the widow I am staying with by killing her son?" ²¹ Then he stretched himself out over the boy three times. He cried out to the LORD and said, "LORD my God, please let this boy's life come into him again!"   Ac 9:37,39

²² So the LORD listened to Elijah, and the boy's life came into him again, and he lived. ²³ Then Elijah took the boy, brought him down from the upstairs room into the house, and gave him to his mother. Elijah said, "Look, your son is alive."   Lk 7:14-15; Heb 11:35

²⁴ Then the woman said to Elijah, "Now I know you are a man of God and the LORD's word from your mouth is true."   1Kg 22:16; Jn 3:2

Elijah's Message to Ahab

18 After a long time, the word of the LORD came to Elijah in the third year: "Go and present yourself to Ahab. I will send rain on the surface of the land." ² So Elijah went to present himself to Ahab.

The famine was severe in Samaria. ³ Ahab called for Obadiah, who was in charge of the palace. Obadiah was a man who greatly feared the LORD ⁴ and took a hundred prophets and hid them, fifty men to a cave, and provided them with food and water when Jezebel slaughtered the LORD's prophets. ⁵ Ahab said to Obadiah, "Go

throughout the land to every spring and to every wadi. Perhaps we'll find grass so we can keep the horses and mules alive and not have to destroy any cattle." ⁶ They divided the land between them in order to cover it. Ahab went one way by himself, and Obadiah went the other way by himself.   1Kg 16:24,29

⁷ While Obadiah was walking along the road, Elijah suddenly met him. When Obadiah recognized him, he fell facedown and said, "Is it you, my lord Elijah?"

⁸ "It is I," he replied. "Go tell your lord, 'Elijah is here!' " ᴬ

⁹ But Obadiah said, "What sin have I committed, that you are handing your servant over to Ahab to put me to death? ¹⁰ As the LORD your God lives, there is no nation or kingdom where my lord has not sent someone to search for you. When they said, 'He is not here,' he made that kingdom or nation swear they had not found you.   1Kg 17:18

¹¹ "Now you say, 'Go tell your lord, "Elijah is here!" ' ¹² But when I leave you, the Spirit of the LORD may carry you off to some place I don't know. Then when I go report to Ahab and he doesn't find you, he will kill me. But I, your servant, have feared the LORD from my youth. ¹³ Wasn't it reported to my lord what I did when Jezebel slaughtered the LORD's prophets? I hid a hundred of the prophets of the LORD, fifty men to a cave, and I provided them with food and water. ¹⁴ Now you say, 'Go tell your lord, "Elijah is here!" ' He will kill me!"

¹⁵ Then Elijah said, "As the LORD of Armies lives, in whose presence

---

ᴬ**18:8** The Hb words translated 'Elijah is here' also mean 'Look, my God is the LORD'

I stand, today I will present myself to Ahab." _{1Kg 17:1}

¹⁶ Obadiah went to meet Ahab and told him. Then Ahab went to meet Elijah. ¹⁷ When Ahab saw Elijah, Ahab said to him, "Is that you, the one ruining Israel?" _{Jos 7:25}

¹⁸ He replied, "I have not ruined Israel, but you and your father's family have, because you have abandoned the LORD's commands and followed the Baals. ¹⁹ Now summon all Israel to meet me at Mount Carmel, along with the 450 prophets of Baal and the 400 prophets of Asherah who eat at Jezebel's table."

Elijah at Mount Carmel

²⁰ So Ahab summoned all the Israelites and gathered the prophets at Mount Carmel. ²¹ Then Elijah approached all the people and said, "How long will you waver between two opinions?ᴬ If the LORD is God, follow him. But if Baal, follow him." But the people didn't answer him a word. _{Jos 24:15; 2Kg 17:41; Mt 6:24}

²² Then Elijah said to the people, "I am the only remaining prophet of the LORD, but Baal's prophets are 450 men. ²³ Let two bulls be given to us. They are to choose one bull for themselves, cut it in pieces, and place it on the wood but not light the fire. I will prepare the other bull and place it on the wood but not light the fire. ²⁴ Then you call on the name of your god, and I will call on the name of the LORD. The God who answers with fire, he is God."

All the people answered, "That's fine."

²⁵ Then Elijah said to the prophets of Baal, "Since you are so numerous, choose for yourselves one bull and prepare it first. Then call on the name of your god but don't light the fire."

²⁶ So they took the bull that he gave them, prepared it, and called on the name of Baal from morning until noon, saying, "Baal, answer us!" But there was no sound; no one answered. Then they dancedᴮ around the altar they had made.

²⁷ At noon Elijah mocked them. He said, "Shout loudly, for he's a god! Maybe he's thinking it over; maybe he has wandered away;ᶜ or maybe he's on the road. Perhaps he's sleeping and will wake up!" ²⁸ They shouted loudly, and cut themselves with knives and spears, according to their custom, until blood gushed over them. ²⁹ All afternoon they kept on raving until the offering of the evening sacrifice, but there was no sound; no one answered, no one paid attention.

³⁰ Then Elijah said to all the people, "Come near me." So all the people approached him. Then he repaired the LORD's altar that had been torn down: ³¹ Elijah took twelve stones — according to the number of the tribes of the sons of Jacob, to whom the word of the LORD had come, saying, "Israel will be your name" — ³² and he built an altar with the stones in the name of the LORD. Then he made a trench around the altar large enough to hold about four gallons.ᴰ,ᴱ ³³ Next, he arranged the wood, cut up the bull, and placed it on the wood. He said, "Fill four water pots with water and pour it on the offering to be burned and on the wood." ³⁴ Then

---

ᴬ**18:21** Lit *you hobble on two crutches?*   ᴮ**18:26** Or *hobbled*   ᶜ**18:27** Or *has turned aside*; possibly to relieve himself   ᴰ**18:32** LXX reads *trench containing two measures of seed*   ᴱ**18:32** Lit *altar corresponding to a house of two seahs of seed* he said, "A second time!" and they did it a second time. And then he said, "A third time!" and they did it a third time. ³⁵ So the water ran all around the altar; he even filled the trench with water.   1Kg 19:10

³⁶ At the time for offering the evening sacrifice, the prophet Elijah approached the altar and said, "LORD, the God of Abraham, Isaac, and Israel, today let it be known that you are God in Israel and I am your servant, and that at your word I have done all these things. ³⁷ Answer me, LORD! Answer me so that this people will know that you, the LORD, are God and that you have turned their hearts back."   1Kg 18:29

³⁸ Then the LORD's fire fell and consumed the burnt offering, the wood, the stones, and the dust, and it licked up the water that was in the trench. ³⁹ When all the people saw it, they fell facedown and said, "The LORD, he is God! The LORD, he is God!"   Lv 9:24; 1Kg 18:21,24; Mt 17:6

⁴⁰ Then Elijah ordered them, "Seize the prophets of Baal! Do not let even one of them escape." So they seized them, and Elijah brought them down to the Wadi Kishon and slaughtered them there. ⁴¹ Elijah said to Ahab, "Go up, eat and drink, for there is the sound of a rainstorm."   Jdg 4:7; 5:21

⁴² So Ahab went to eat and drink, but Elijah went up to the summit of Carmel. He bent down on the ground and put his face between his knees. ⁴³ Then he said to his servant, "Go up and look toward the sea."   1Sm 12:17; 1Kg 18:19; Jms 5:18

So he went up, looked, and said, "There's nothing."

Seven times Elijah said, "Go back." ⁴⁴ On the seventh time, he reported, "There's a cloud as small as a man's hand coming up from the sea."   Jos 6:15; Lk 12:54

Then Elijah said, "Go and tell Ahab, 'Get your chariot ready and go down so the rain doesn't stop you.'"

⁴⁵ In a little while, the sky grew dark with clouds and wind, and there was a downpour. So Ahab got in his chariot and went to Jezreel. ⁴⁶ The power of the LORD was on Elijah, and he tucked his mantle under his belt and ran ahead of Ahab to the entrance of Jezreel.

Elijah's Journey to Horeb

19 Ahab told Jezebel everything that Elijah had done and how he had killed all the prophets with the sword. ² So Jezebel sent a messenger to Elijah, saying, "May the gods punish me and do so severely if I don't make your life like the life of one of them by this time tomorrow!"   1Kg 16:31; 18:4,14,30-38

³ Then Elijah became afraid ᴬ and immediately ran for his life. When he came to Beer-sheba that belonged to Judah, he left his servant there, ⁴ but he went on a day's journey into the wilderness. He sat down under a broom tree and prayed that he might die. He said, "I have had enough! LORD, take my life, for I'm no better than my fathers." ⁵ Then he lay down and slept under the broom tree.   Gn 31:21; Pr 29:25

Suddenly, an angel touched him. The angel told him, "Get up and eat." ⁶ Then he looked, and there at his head was a loaf of bread baked over hot stones, and a jug of water. So he ate and drank and lay down again. ⁷ Then the angel of the LORD returned for a second time and touched him. He said, "Get up and

ᴬ19:3 Some Hb mss, LXX, Syr, Vg; other Hb mss read *He saw*

eat, or the journey will be too much for you." ⁸ So he got up, ate, and drank. Then on the strength from that food, he walked forty days and forty nights to Horeb, the mountain of God. ⁹ He entered a cave there and spent the night.   Ex 4:27

Elijah's Encounter with the LORD

Suddenly, the word of the LORD came to him, and he said to him, "What are you doing here, Elijah?"

¹⁰ He replied, "I have been very zealous for the LORD God of Armies, but the Israelites have abandoned your covenant, torn down your altars, and killed your prophets with the sword. I alone am left, and they are looking for me to take my life."

¹¹ Then he said, "Go out and stand on the mountain in the LORD's presence."   Ex 19:20

At that moment, the LORD passed by. A great and mighty wind was tearing at the mountains and was shattering cliffs before the LORD, but the LORD was not in the wind. After the wind there was an earthquake, but the LORD was not in the earthquake. ¹² After the earthquake there was a fire, but the LORD was not in the fire. And after the fire there was a voice, a soft whisper. ¹³ When Elijah heard it, he wrapped his face in his mantle and went out and stood at the entrance of the cave.   Ex 33:21-22; Ezk 1:4; Am 1:1; Ac 2:2; Rv 6:12

Suddenly, a voice came to him and said, "What are you doing here, Elijah?"

¹⁴ "I have been very zealous for the LORD God of Armies," he replied, "but the Israelites have abandoned your covenant, torn down your altars, and killed your prophets with the sword. I alone am left,

and they're looking for me to take my life."   1Kg 19:10; Rm 11:3

¹⁵ Then the LORD said to him, "Go and return by the way you came to the Wilderness of Damascus. When you arrive, you are to anoint Hazael as king over Aram. ¹⁶ You are to anoint Jehu son of Nimshi as king over Israel and Elisha son of Shaphat from Abel-meholah as prophet in your place. ¹⁷ Then Jehu will put to death whoever escapes the sword of Hazael, and Elisha will put to death whoever escapes the sword of Jehu. ¹⁸ But I will leave seven thousand in Israel — every knee that has not bowed to Baal and every mouth that has not kissed him."   2Kg 8:8-15; 19:1-10

Elisha's Appointment as Elijah's Successor

¹⁹ Elijah left there and found Elisha son of Shaphat as he was plowing. Twelve teams of oxen were in front of him, and he was with the twelfth team. Elijah walked by him and threw his mantle over him. ²⁰ Elisha left the oxen, ran to follow Elijah, and said, "Please let me kiss my father and mother, and then I will follow you."   1Kg 19:16-17; 2Kg 2:8,13-14

"Go on back," he replied, "for what have I done to you?"

²¹ So he turned back from following him, took the team of oxen, and slaughtered ᴬ them. With the oxen's wooden yoke and plow, he cooked the meat and gave it to the people, and they ate. Then he left, followed Elijah, and served him.   1Sm 6:14

Victory over Ben-hadad

20 Now King Ben-hadad of Aram assembled his entire army. Thirty-two kings, along with

ᴬ**19:21** Or *sacrificed*

horses and chariots, were with him. He marched up, besieged Samaria, and fought against it. ² He sent messengers into the city to King Ahab of Israel and said to him, "This is what Ben-hadad says: ³ 'Your silver and your gold are mine! And your best wives and children are mine as well!' " 1Kg 15:18,20; 16:24,29; 22:31

⁴ Then the king of Israel answered, "Just as you say, my lord the king: I am yours, along with all that I have."

⁵ The messengers then returned and said, "This is what Ben-hadad says: 'I have sent messengers to you, saying: You are to give me your silver, your gold, your wives, and your children. ⁶ But at this time tomorrow I will send my servants to you, ^A and they will search your palace and your servants' houses. They will lay their hands on and take away whatever is precious to you.' " Lm 2:4; Ezk 24:16,21,25

⁷ Then the king of Israel called for all the elders of the land and said, "Recognize ^B that this one is only looking for trouble, for he demanded my wives, my children, my silver, and my gold, and I didn't turn him down." 2Kg 5:7

⁸ All the elders and all the people said to him, "Don't listen or agree."

⁹ So he said to Ben-hadad's messengers, "Say to my lord the king, 'Everything you demanded of your servant the first time, I will do, but this thing I cannot do.' " So the messengers left and took word back to him.

¹⁰ Then Ben-hadad sent messengers to him and said, "May the gods punish me and do so severely if Samaria's dust amounts to a handful for each of the people who follow me." 2Sm 22:43; 1Kg 19:2; 2Kg 6:31

¹¹ The king of Israel answered, "Say this: 'Don't let the one who puts on his armor boast like the one who takes it off.' " Pr 27:1

¹² When Ben-hadad heard this response, while he and the kings were drinking in their quarters, ^C he said to his servants, "Take your positions." So they took their positions against the city. 1Kg 16:9

¹³ A prophet approached King Ahab of Israel and said, "This is what the LORD says: 'Do you see this whole huge army? Watch, I am handing it over to you today so that you may know that I am the LORD.' " 1Kg 20:28

¹⁴ Ahab asked, "By whom?"

And the prophet said, "This is what the LORD says: 'By the young men of the provincial leaders.' "

Then he asked, "Who is to start the battle?" Jdg 1:1; 20:18

He said, "You."

¹⁵ So Ahab mobilized the young men of the provincial leaders, and there were 232. After them he mobilized all the Israelite troops: 7,000. ¹⁶ They marched out at noon while Ben-hadad and the thirty-two kings who were helping him were getting drunk in their quarters. ¹⁷ The young men of the provincial leaders marched out first. Then Ben-hadad sent out scouts, and they reported to him, saying, "Men are marching out of Samaria." Jdg 7:2; 1Kg 16:24; 20:1

¹⁸ So he said, "If they have marched out in peace, take them alive, and if they have marched out for battle, take them alive." 2Kg 14:8

¹⁹ The young men of the provincial leaders and the army behind them marched out from the city, ²⁰ and each one struck down his opponent. So the Arameans fled

---

^A **20:6** Lit *take all the delight of your eyes*　　^B **20:7** Lit *"Know and see*　　^C **20:12** Lit *booths*, also in v. 16

and Israel pursued them, but King Ben-hadad of Aram escaped on a horse with the cavalry. ²¹ Then the king of Israel marched out and attacked the cavalry and the chariots. He inflicted a severe slaughter on Aram.   1Sm 14:13-14,22; 2Sm 2:15-16

²² The prophet approached the king of Israel and said to him, "Go and strengthen yourself, then consider carefully ᴬ what you should do, for in the spring the king of Aram will attack you."   2Sm 11:1

²³ Now the king of Aram's servants said to him, "Their gods are gods of the hill country. That's why they were stronger than we were. Instead, we should fight with them on the plain; then we will certainly be stronger than they are. ²⁴ Also do this: remove each king from his position and appoint captains in their place. ²⁵ Raise another army for yourself like the army you lost — horse for horse, chariot for chariot — and let's fight with them on the plain; and we will certainly be stronger than they are." The king listened to them and did it.   1Kg 14:23

²⁶ In the spring, Ben-hadad mobilized the Arameans and went up to Aphek to battle Israel. ²⁷ The Israelites mobilized, gathered supplies, and went to fight them. The Israelites camped in front of them like two little flocks of goats, while the Arameans filled the landscape.

²⁸ Then the man of God approached and said to the king of Israel, "This is what the LORD says: 'Because the Arameans have said: The LORD is a god of the mountains and not a god of the valleys, I will hand over all this whole huge army

to you. Then you will know that I am the LORD.'"   1Kg 17:18; 20:23

²⁹ They camped opposite each other for seven days. On the seventh day, the battle took place, and the Israelites struck down the Arameans — one hundred thousand foot soldiers in one day. ³⁰ The ones who remained fled into the city of Aphek, and the wall fell on those twenty-seven thousand remaining men.   Jos 6:15

Ben-hadad also fled and went into an inner room in the city. ³¹ His servants said to him, "Consider this: we have heard that the kings of the house of Israel are merciful kings. So let's put sackcloth around our waists and ropes around our heads, and let's go out to the king of Israel. Perhaps he will spare your life."   Gn 37:34; 1Kg 22:25

³² So they dressed with sackcloth around their waists and ropes around their heads, went to the king of Israel, and said, "Your servant Ben-hadad says, 'Please spare my life.'"

So he said, "Is he still alive? He is my brother."

³³ Now the men were looking for a sign of hope, so they quickly picked up on this ᴮ and responded, "Yes, it is your brother Ben-hadad."

Then he said, "Go and bring him."

So Ben-hadad came out to him, and Ahab had him come up into the chariot. ³⁴ Then Ben-hadad said to him, "I restore to you the cities that my father took from your father, and you may set up marketplaces for yourself in Damascus, like my father set up in Samaria."   1Kg 15:20

Ahab responded, "On the basis of this treaty, I release you." So he

ᴬ20:22 Lit then know and see   ᴮ20:33 Some Hb mss, alt Hb tradition, LXX; other Hb mss read they hastened and caught hold; "Is this it?"

made a treaty with him and released him.

Ahab Rebuked by the LORD

³⁵ One of the sons of the prophets said to his fellow prophet by the word of the LORD, "Strike me!" But the man refused to strike him. ³⁶ He told him, "Because you did not listen to the LORD, mark my words: When you leave me, a lion will kill you." When he left him, a lion attacked and killed him.

³⁷ The prophet found another man and said to him, "Strike me!" So the man struck him, inflicting a wound. ³⁸ Then the prophet went and waited for the king on the road. He disguised himself with a bandage over his eyes. ³⁹ As the king was passing by, he cried out to the king and said, "Your servant marched out into the middle of the battle. Suddenly, a man turned aside and brought someone to me and said, 'Guard this man! If he is ever missing, it will be your life in place of his life, or you will weigh out seventy-five pounds ᴬ of silver.' ⁴⁰ But while your servant was busy here and there, he disappeared." 1Kg 14:2

The king of Israel said to him, "That will be your sentence; you yourself have decided it." 2Sm 12:5

⁴¹ He quickly removed the bandage from his eyes. The king of Israel recognized that he was one of the prophets. ⁴² The prophet said to him, "This is what the LORD says: 'Because you released from your hand the man I had set apart for destruction, it will be your life in place of his life and your people in place of his people.'" ⁴³ The king of Israel left for home resentful and angry, and he entered Samaria.

ᴬ**20:39** Lit *a talent*

Ahab and Naboth's Vineyard

21 Some time passed after these events. Naboth the Jezreelite had a vineyard; it was in Jezreel next to the palace of King Ahab of Samaria. ² So Ahab spoke to Naboth, saying, "Give me your vineyard so I can have it for a vegetable garden, since it is right next to my palace. I will give you a better vineyard in its place, or if you prefer, I will give you its value in silver."

³ But Naboth said to Ahab, "I will never give you my fathers' inheritance to you." Lv 25:23; Nm 36:7

⁴ So Ahab went to his palace resentful and angry because of what Naboth the Jezreelite had told him. He had said, "I will not give you my fathers' inheritance." He lay down on his bed, turned his face away, and didn't eat any food. 1Kg 20:43

⁵ Then his wife Jezebel came to him and said to him, "Why are you so upset that you refuse to eat?"

⁶ "Because I spoke to Naboth the Jezreelite," he replied. "I told him: Give me your vineyard for silver, or if you wish, I will give you a vineyard in its place. But he said, 'I won't give you my vineyard!'"

⁷ Then his wife Jezebel said to him, "Now, exercise your royal power over Israel. Get up, eat some food, and be happy. For I will give you the vineyard of Naboth the Jezreelite." ⁸ So she wrote letters in Ahab's name and sealed them with his seal. She sent the letters to the elders and nobles who lived with Naboth in his city. ⁹ In the letters, she wrote: 1Sm 8:14; 2Sm 11:14; Est 3:12; 8:8,10

Proclaim a fast and seat Naboth at the head of the people. ¹⁰ Then seat two wicked men opposite him and have them testify against him, saying, "You have cursed God and the king!" Then take him out and stone him to death. Ex 23:1; 1Sm 7:5-6

¹¹ The men of his city, the elders and nobles who lived in his city, did as Jezebel had sent word to them, just as it was written in the letters she had sent them. ¹² They proclaimed a fast and seated Naboth at the head of the people. ¹³ The two wicked men came in and sat opposite him. Then the wicked men testified against Naboth in the presence of the people, saying, "Naboth has cursed God and the king!" So they took him outside the city and stoned him to death with stones. ¹⁴ Then they sent word to Jezebel: "Naboth has been stoned to death." Lv 24:16

¹⁵ When Jezebel heard that Naboth had been stoned to death, she said to Ahab, "Get up and take possession of the vineyard of Naboth the Jezreelite who refused to give it to you for silver, since Naboth isn't alive, but dead." ¹⁶ When Ahab heard that Naboth was dead, he got up to go down to the vineyard of Naboth the Jezreelite to take possession of it. 1Kg 21:2-3

The Lord's Judgment on Ahab

¹⁷ Then the word of the Lord came to Elijah the Tishbite: ¹⁸ "Get up and go to meet King Ahab of Israel, who is in Samaria. He's in Naboth's vineyard, where he has gone to take possession of it. ¹⁹ Tell him, 'This is what the Lord says: Have you murdered and also taken possession?' Then tell him, 'This is what the Lord

says: In the place where the dogs licked up Naboth's blood, the dogs will also lick up your blood!'"

²⁰ Ahab said to Elijah, "So, my enemy, you've found me, have you?"

He replied, "I have found you because you devoted yourself to do what is evil in the Lord's sight. ²¹ This is what the Lord says:ᴬ 'I am about to bring disaster on you and will eradicate your descendants:

I will wipe out all of
　　Ahab's males,ᴮ
　　both slave and free,ᶜ in Israel;
²² I will make your house like the house of Jeroboam son of Nebat and like the house of Baasha son of Ahijah, because you have angered me and caused Israel to sin.' ²³ The Lord also speaks of Jezebel: 'The dogs will eat Jezebel in the plot of landᴰ at Jezreel: 1Kg 14:10-11; 16:3-4
²⁴ Anyone who belongs
　　to Ahab and dies in the city,
　　the dogs will eat,
　　and anyone who dies
　　in the field, the birdsᴱ
　　will eat.'" 1Kg 14:11; 16:4

²⁵ Still, there was no one like Ahab, who devoted himself to do what was evil in the Lord's sight, because his wife Jezebel incited him. ²⁶ He committed the most detestable acts by following idols as the Amorites had, whom the Lord had dispossessed before the Israelites. Gn 15:16; 1Kg 16:30-33; 2Kg 17:12; 21:11

²⁷ When Ahab heard these words, he tore his clothes, put sackcloth over his body, and fasted. He lay down in sackcloth and walked around subdued. ²⁸ Then the word of the Lord came to

---

ᴬ**21:21** LXX; MT omits *This is what the Lord says* 　ᴮ**21:21** Lit *eliminate Ahab's one who urinates against the wall* 　ᶜ**21:21** Or *males, even the weak and impaired*; Hb obscure 　ᴰ**21:23** Some Hb mss, Syr, Tg, Vg, 2Kg 9:36; other Hb mss, LXX read *the rampart* 　ᴱ**21:24** Lit *birds of the sky*

Elijah the Tishbite: [29] "Have you seen how Ahab has humbled himself before me? I will not bring the disaster during his lifetime, because he has humbled himself before me. I will bring the disaster on his house during his son's lifetime."   Gn 37:34; 2Sm 3:31

Jehoshaphat's Alliance with Ahab

22 There was a lull of three years without war between Aram and Israel. [2] However, in the third year, King Jehoshaphat of Judah went to visit the king of Israel. [3] The king of Israel had said to his servants, "Don't you know that Ramoth-gilead is ours, but we're doing nothing to take it from the king of Aram?" [4] So he asked Jehoshaphat, "Will you go with me to fight Ramoth-gilead?"   2Ch 18:1-8

Jehoshaphat replied to the king of Israel, "I am as you are, my people as your people, my horses as your horses." [5] But Jehoshaphat said to the king of Israel, "First, please ask what the Lord's will is."   2Kg 3:7

[6] So the king of Israel gathered the prophets, about four hundred men, and asked them, "Should I go against Ramoth-gilead for war or should I refrain?"   1Kg 18:19

They replied, "March up, and the Lord will hand it over to the king."

[7] But Jehoshaphat asked, "Isn't there a prophet of the Lord here anymore? Let's ask him."   2Kg 1:3; 3:11

[8] The king of Israel said to Jehoshaphat, "There is still one man who can inquire of the Lord, but I hate him because he never prophesies good about me, but only disaster. He is Micaiah son of Imlah."

"The king shouldn't say that!" Jehoshaphat replied.

[9] So the king of Israel called an officer and said, "Hurry and get Micaiah son of Imlah!"

[10] Now the king of Israel and King Jehoshaphat of Judah, clothed in royal attire, were each sitting on his own throne. They were on the threshing floor at the entrance to the gate of Samaria, and all the prophets were prophesying in front of them. [11] Then Zedekiah son of Chenaanah made iron horns and said, "This is what the Lord says: 'You will gore the Arameans with these until they are finished off.'" [12] And all the prophets were prophesying the same: "March up to Ramoth-gilead and succeed, for the Lord will hand it over to the king."   Dt 33:17; Jdg 6:37; 1Kg 22:24; 2Ch 18:9-11

Micaiah's Message of Defeat

[13] The messenger who went to call Micaiah instructed him, "Look, the words of the prophets are unanimously favorable for the king. So let your words be like theirs, and speak favorably."   2Ch 18:12-27

[14] But Micaiah said, "As the Lord lives, I will say whatever the Lord says to me."   Nm 22:28; 24:13; 1Kg 18:10,15

[15] So he went to the king, and the king asked him, "Micaiah, should we go to Ramoth-gilead for war, or should we refrain?"

Micaiah told him, "March up and succeed. The Lord will hand it over to the king."

[16] But the king said to him, "How many times must I make you swear not to tell me anything but the truth in the name of the Lord?"

[17] So Micaiah said:

I saw all Israel scattered
    on the hills
like sheep
    without a shepherd.   Mt 9:36

And the LORD said,
"They have no master;
  let everyone return home
    in peace."   1Kg 22:35-36

 18 So the king of Israel said to Jehoshaphat, "Didn't I tell you he never prophesies good about me, but only disaster?"

19 Then Micaiah said, "Therefore, hear the word of the LORD: I saw the LORD sitting on his throne, and the whole heavenly army was standing by him at his right hand and at his left hand. **20** And the LORD said, 'Who will entice Ahab to march up and fall at Ramoth-gilead?' So one was saying this and another was saying that.   Jb 1:6; Is 6:1; Dn 7:9-10

21 "Then a spirit came forward, stood in the LORD's presence, and said, 'I will entice him.'

22 "The LORD asked him, 'How?'

"He said, 'I will go and become a lying spirit in the mouth of all his prophets.'   Jdg 9:23; 1Sm 16:14; Jr 20:7; Ezk 14:9

"Then he said, 'You will certainly entice him and prevail. Go and do that.'   2Th 2:11

23 "You see, the LORD has put a lying spirit into the mouth of all these prophets of yours, and the LORD has pronounced disaster against you."

24 Then Zedekiah son of Chenaanah came up, hit Micaiah on the cheek, and demanded, "Did^A the Spirit of the LORD leave me to speak to you?"   1Kg 22:11; 2Ch 18:23

25 Micaiah replied, "You will soon see when you go to hide in an inner chamber on that day."   1Kg 20:30

26 Then the king of Israel ordered, "Take Micaiah and return him to Amon, the governor of the city, and to Joash, the king's son, **27** and say, 'This is what the king says: Put this guy in prison and feed him only a little bread and water^B until I come back safely.'"   1Kg 22:40; 2Ch 16:10; Heb 11:36

28 But Micaiah said, "If you ever return safely, the LORD has not spoken through me." Then he said, "Listen, all you people!"^C   Dt 18:22

Ahab's Death

29 Then the king of Israel and Judah's King Jehoshaphat went up to Ramoth-gilead. **30** But the king of Israel said to Jehoshaphat, "I will disguise myself and go into battle, but you wear your royal attire." So the king of Israel disguised himself and went into battle.   2Ch 18:28-32

31 Now the king of Aram had ordered his thirty-two chariot commanders, "Do not fight with anyone at all^D except the king of Israel."

32 When the chariot commanders saw Jehoshaphat, they shouted, "He must be the king of Israel!" So they turned to fight against him, but Jehoshaphat cried out. **33** When the chariot commanders saw that he was not the king of Israel, they turned back from pursuing him.

34 But a man drew his bow without taking special aim and struck the king of Israel through the joints of his armor. So he said to his charioteer, "Turn around and take me out of the battle,^E for I am badly wounded!" **35** The battle raged throughout that day, and the king was propped up in his chariot facing the Arameans. He died that evening, and blood from his wound flowed into the bottom of

---

^A 22:24 Lit "Which way did"   ^B 22:27 Lit him on bread of oppression and water of oppression
^C 22:28 LXX omits Then he said, "Listen, all you people!"   ^D 22:31 Lit with small or with great
^E 22:34 LXX; MT reads camp

the chariot. ³⁶ Then the cry rang out in the army as the sun set, declaring:

> Each man to his own city,
> and each man
>   to his own land!   2Sm 20:1

³⁷ So the king died and was brought to Samaria. They buried the king in Samaria. ³⁸ Then someone washed the chariot at the pool of Samaria. The dogs licked up his blood, and the prostitutes bathed in it, according to the word of the LORD that he had spoken.   1Kg 16:28

³⁹ The rest of the events of Ahab's reign, along with all his accomplishments, including the ivory palace he built, and all the cities he built, are written in the Historical Record of Israel's Kings. ⁴⁰ Ahab rested with his fathers, and his son Ahaziah became king in his place.

Judah's King Jehoshaphat

⁴¹ Jehoshaphat son of Asa became king over Judah in the fourth year of Israel's King Ahab. ⁴² Jehoshaphat was thirty-five years old when he became king; he reigned twenty-five years in Jerusalem. His mother's name was Azubah daughter of Shilhi. ⁴³ He walked in all the ways of his father Asa; he did not turn away from them but did what was right in the LORD's sight. However, the high places were not taken away;ᴬ the people still sacrificed and burned incense on the high places. ⁴⁴ Jehoshaphat also made peace with the king of Israel.   1Kg 15:11; 2Ch 20:3

⁴⁵ The rest of the events of Jehoshaphat's reign, along with the might he exercised and how he waged war, are written in the Historical Record of Judah's Kings. ⁴⁶ He eradicated from the land the rest of the male cult prostitutes who were left from the days of his father Asa. ⁴⁷ There was no king in Edom; a deputy served as king. ⁴⁸ Jehoshaphat made ships of Tarshish to go to Ophir for gold, but they did not go because the ships were wrecked at Ezion-geber. ⁴⁹ At that time, Ahaziah son of Ahab said to Jehoshaphat, "Let my servants go with your servants in the ships," but Jehoshaphat was not willing. ⁵⁰ Jehoshaphat rested with his fathers and was buried with them in the city of his ancestor David. His son Jehoram became king in his place.   1Kg 15:12,23; 2Ch 20:34

Israel's King Ahaziah

⁵¹ Ahaziah son of Ahab became king over Israel in Samaria in the seventeenth year of Judah's King Jehoshaphat, and he reigned over Israel two years. ⁵² He did what was evil in the LORD's sight. He walked in the ways of his father, in the ways of his mother, and in the ways of Jeroboam son of Nebat, who had caused Israel to sin. ⁵³ He served Baal and bowed in worship to him. He angered the LORD God of Israel just as his father had done.   1Kg 22:40

ᴬ22:43 LXX, Syr, Vg read *he did not remove the high places*

2 KINGS

Ahaziah's Sickness and Death

1 After Ahab's death, Moab rebelled against Israel. ² Ahaziah had fallen through the latticed window of his upstairs room in Samaria and was injured. So he sent messengers, instructing them, "Go inquire of Baal-zebub,^A the god of Ekron, whether I will recover from this injury." Gn 19:37; 2Sm 8:2; 2Kg 3:5

³ But the angel of the LORD said to Elijah the Tishbite, "Go and meet the messengers of the king of Samaria and say to them, 'Is it because there is no God in Israel that you are going to inquire of Baal-zebub, the god of Ekron? ⁴ Therefore, this is what the LORD says: You will not get up from your sickbed; you will certainly die.'" Then Elijah left.

⁵ The messengers returned to the king, who asked them, "Why have you come back?"

⁶ They replied, "A man came to meet us and said, 'Go back to the king who sent you and declare to him: This is what the LORD says: Is it because there is no God in Israel that you're sending these men to inquire of Baal-zebub, the god of Ekron? Therefore, you will not get up from your sickbed; you will certainly die.'"

⁷ The king asked them, "What sort of man came up to meet you and spoke those words to you?"

⁸ They replied, "A hairy man with a leather belt around his waist."

He said, "It's Elijah the Tishbite."

⁹ So King Ahaziah sent a captain with his fifty men to Elijah. When the captain went up to him, he was sitting on top of the hill. He announced, "Man of God, the king declares, 'Come down!'" 2Kg 6:13-14

¹⁰ Elijah responded to the captain, "If I am a man of God, may fire come down from heaven and consume you and your fifty men." Then fire came down from heaven and consumed him and his fifty men.

¹¹ So the king sent another captain with his fifty men to Elijah. He took in the situation^B and announced, "Man of God, this is what the king says: 'Come down immediately!'"

¹² Elijah responded, "If I am a man of God, may fire come down from heaven and consume you and your fifty men." So a divine fire^C came down from heaven and consumed him and his fifty men.

¹³ Then the king sent a third captain with his fifty men. The third captain went up and fell on his knees in front of Elijah and begged him, "Man of God, please let my life and the lives of these fifty servants of yours be precious to you. ¹⁴ Already fire has come down from heaven and consumed the first two captains with their companies, but this time let my life be precious to you." 1Sm 26:21; 1Kg 13:1; Ps 72:14

¹⁵ The angel of the LORD said to Elijah, "Go down with him. Don't be afraid of him." So he got up and went down with him to the king.

¹⁶ Then Elijah said to King Ahaziah, "This is what the LORD says: 'Because you have sent messengers to inquire of Baal-zebub, the god

^A1:2 = Lord of the Flies   ^B1:11 Lit *He answered*   ^C1:12 Lit *a fire of God* of Ekron — is it because there is no God in Israel for you to inquire of his will? — you will not get up from your sickbed; you will certainly die.'"

[17] Ahaziah died according to the word of the LORD that Elijah had spoken. Since he had no son, Joram[A] became king in his place. This happened in the second year of Judah's King Jehoram son of Jehoshaphat. [B] [18] The rest of the events of Ahaziah's reign, along with his accomplishments, are written in the Historical Record of Israel's Kings. [C]

Elijah in the Whirlwind

2 The time had come for the LORD to take Elijah up to heaven in a whirlwind. Elijah and Elisha were traveling from Gilgal, [2] and Elijah said to Elisha, "Stay here; the LORD is sending me on to Bethel." Gn 5:24

But Elisha replied, "As the LORD lives and as you yourself live, I will not leave you." So they went down to Bethel. 1Sm 1:26; 2Kg 4:30

[3] Then the sons of the prophets who were at Bethel came out to Elisha and said, "Do you know that the LORD will take your master away from you today?" 1Sm 10:5; 1Kg 20:35

He said, "Yes, I know. Be quiet."

[4] Elijah said to him, "Elisha, stay here; the LORD is sending me to Jericho." Jos 6:16; 1Kg 16:34

But Elisha said, "As the LORD lives and as you yourself live, I will not leave you." So they went to Jericho.

[5] Then the sons of the prophets who were in Jericho came up to Elisha and said, "Do you know that the LORD will take your master away from you today?"

He said, "Yes, I know. Be quiet."

[6] Elijah said to him, "Stay here; the LORD is sending me to the Jordan."

But Elisha said, "As the LORD lives and as you yourself live, I will not leave you." So the two of them went on.

[7] Fifty men from the sons of the prophets came and stood observing them at a distance while the two of them stood by the Jordan. [8] Elijah took his mantle, rolled it up, and struck the water, which parted to the right and left. Then the two of them crossed over on dry ground. [9] When they had crossed over, Elijah said to Elisha, "Tell me what I can do for you before I am taken from you." Ex 14:21-22; 1Kg 19:13,19

So Elisha answered, "Please, let me inherit two shares of your spirit." Nm 11:16-25; Dt 21:15-17

[10] Elijah replied, "You have asked for something difficult. If you see me being taken from you, you will have it. If not, you won't." Ac 1:9-11

[11] As they continued walking and talking, a chariot of fire with horses of fire suddenly appeared and separated the two of them. Then Elijah went up into heaven in the whirlwind. [12] As Elisha watched, he kept crying out, "My father, my father, the chariots and horsemen of Israel!" 2Kg 2:1; 6:17; 13:14

Elisha Succeeds Elijah

When he could see him no longer, he took hold of his own clothes, tore them in two, [13] picked up the mantle that had fallen off Elijah, and went back and stood on the bank of the Jordan. [14] He took the mantle Elijah had dropped, and he struck the water. "Where is the LORD God of Elijah?" he asked.

A[1:17] Lit *Jehoram*; 2Kg 8:16   B[1:17] LXX omits *in the second year . . . Jehoshaphat*   C[1:18] LXX adds 4 more vv. here similar to 2Kg 3:1-3.

He struck the water himself, and it parted to the right and the left, and Elisha crossed over. Gn 37:29,34

¹⁵ When the sons of the prophets from Jericho who were observing saw him, they said, "The spirit of Elijah rests on Elisha." They came to meet him and bowed down to the ground in front of him.

¹⁶ Then the sons of the prophets said to Elisha, "Since there are fifty strong men here with your servants, please let them go and search for your master. Maybe the Spirit of the LORD has carried him away and put him on one of the mountains or into one of the valleys."

He answered, "Don't send them."

¹⁷ However, they urged him to the point of embarrassment, so he said, "Send them." They sent fifty men, who looked for three days but did not find him. ¹⁸ When they returned to him in Jericho where he was staying, he said to them, "Didn't I tell you not to go?" Jdg 3:25

¹⁹ The men of the city said to Elisha, "My lord can see that even though the city's location is good, the water is bad and the land unfruitful." Dt 28:15-18; Jos 6:26; 1Kg 16:34

²⁰ He replied, "Bring me a new bowl and put salt in it." Lv 2:13; Nm 18:19

After they had brought him one, ²¹ Elisha went out to the spring, threw salt in it, and said, "This is what the LORD says: 'I have healed this water. No longer will death or unfruitfulness result from it.'" ²² Therefore, the water still remains healthy today according to the word that Elisha spoke. Ex 15:25-26

²³ From there Elisha went up to Bethel. As he was walking up the path, some small boys came out of the city and jeered at him, chanting, "Go up, baldy! Go up, baldy!"

²⁴ He turned around, looked at them, and cursed them in the name of the LORD. Then two female bears came out of the woods and mauled forty-two of the children. ²⁵ From there Elisha went to Mount Carmel, and then he returned to Samaria.

Israel's King Joram

3 Joram son of Ahab became king over Israel in Samaria during the eighteenth year of Judah's King Jehoshaphat, and he reigned twelve years. ² He did what was evil in the LORD's sight, but not like his father and mother, for he removed the sacred pillar of Baal his father had made. ³ Nevertheless, Joram clung to the sins that Jeroboam son of Nebat had caused Israel to commit. He did not turn away from them.

Moab's Rebellion Against Israel

⁴ King Mesha of Moab was a sheep breeder. He used to pay the king of Israel one hundred thousand lambs and the wool of one hundred thousand rams, ⁵ but when Ahab died, the king of Moab rebelled against the king of Israel. ⁶ So King Joram marched out from Samaria at that time and mobilized all Israel. ⁷ Then he sent a message to King Jehoshaphat of Judah: "The king of Moab has rebelled against me. Will you go with me to fight against Moab?"

Jehoshaphat said, "I will go. I am as you are, my people as your people, my horses as your horses."

⁸ He asked, "Which route should we take?"

He replied, "The route of the Wilderness of Edom."

⁹ So the king of Israel, the king of Judah, and the king of Edom set out. After they had traveled their indirect route for seven days, they

had no water for the army or the animals with them. 1Kg 22:47; 2Kg 8:20

¹⁰ Then the king of Israel said, "Oh no, the LORD has summoned these three kings, only to hand them over to Moab."

¹¹ But Jehoshaphat said, "Isn't there a prophet of the LORD here? Let's inquire of the LORD through him." 1Kg 22:7

One of the servants of the king of Israel answered, "Elisha son of Shaphat, who used to pour water on Elijah's hands, is here." 2Kg 2:9

¹² Jehoshaphat affirmed, "The word of the LORD is with him." So the king of Israel and Jehoshaphat and the king of Edom went to him.

¹³ However, Elisha said to King Joram of Israel, "What do we have in common? Go to the prophets of your father and your mother!"

But the king of Israel replied, "No, because it is the LORD who has summoned these three kings to hand them over to Moab."

¹⁴ Elisha responded, "By the life of the LORD of Armies, before whom I stand: If I did not have respect for King Jehoshaphat of Judah, I wouldn't look at you; I would not take notice of you. ¹⁵ Now, bring me a musician." 1Kg 17:1; 22:41-50; 2Kg 5:16

While the musician played, the LORD's hand came on Elisha. ¹⁶ Then he said, "This is what the LORD says: 'Dig ditch after ditch in this wadi.' ¹⁷ For the LORD says, 'You will not see wind or rain, but the wadi will be filled with water, and you will drink — you and your cattle and your animals.' ¹⁸ This is easy in the LORD's sight. He will also hand Moab over to you. ¹⁹ Then you will attack every fortified city and every choice city. You will cut down every good tree and stop up every spring. You will ruin every good piece of land with stones." 1Sm 16:23; Ps 107:35; Ezk 3:14

²⁰ About the time for the grain offering the next morning, water suddenly came from the direction of Edom and filled the land.

²¹ All Moab had heard that the kings had come up to fight against them. So all who could bear arms, from the youngest to the oldest, were summoned and took their stand at the border. ²² When they got up early in the morning, the sun was shining on the water, and the Moabites saw that the water across from them was red like blood. ²³ "This is blood!" they exclaimed. "The kings have crossed swordsᴬ and their men have killed one another. So, to the spoil, Moab!" Ex 7:17,20; 2Kg 3:9

²⁴ However, when the Moabites came to Israel's camp, the Israelites attacked them, and they fled from them. So Israel went into the land attacking the Moabites. ²⁵ They would destroy the cities, and each of them would throw a stone to cover every good piece of land. They would stop up every spring and cut down every good tree. This went on until only the buildings of Kirhareseth were left. Then men with slings surrounded the city and attacked it. Jr 48:31,36

²⁶ When the king of Moab saw that the battle was too fierce for him, he took seven hundred swordsmen with him to try to break through to the king of Edom, but they could not do it. ²⁷ So he took his firstborn son, who was to become king in his place, and offered him as a burnt offering on the city wall. Great wrath was on the Israelites, and

ᴬ3:23 Or have been laid waste

they withdrew from him and returned to their land. Dt 12:31; 2Kg 3:9

The Widow's Oil Multiplied

4 One of the wives of the sons of the prophets cried out to Elisha, "Your servant, my husband, has died. You know that your servant feared the LORD. Now the creditor is coming to take my two children as his slaves." 2Kg 2:3,15; Pr 1:7

² Elisha asked her, "What can I do for you? Tell me, what do you have in the house?"

She said, "Your servant has nothing in the house except a jar of oil."

³ Then he said, "Go out and borrow empty containers from all your neighbors. Do not get just a few. ⁴ Then go in and shut the door behind you and your sons, and pour oil into all these containers. Set the full ones to one side." ⁵ So she left.

After she had shut the door behind her and her sons, they kept bringing her containers, and she kept pouring. ⁶ When they were full, she said to her son, "Bring me another container." Mt 14:17-21

But he replied, "There aren't any more." Then the oil stopped.

⁷ She went and told the man of God, and he said, "Go sell the oil and pay your debt; you and your sons can live on the rest." 1Kg 12:22

The Shunammite Woman's Hospitality

⁸ One day Elisha went to Shunem. A prominent woman who lived there persuaded him to eat some food. So whenever he passed by, he stopped there to eat. ⁹ Then she said to her husband, "I know that the one who often passes by here is a holy man of God, ¹⁰ so let's make a small, walled-in upper room and

put a bed, a table, a chair, and a lamp there for him. Whenever he comes, he can stay there." Jos 19:18; Mt 10:40-42

The Shunammite Woman's Son

¹¹ One day he came there and stopped at the upstairs room to lie down. ¹² He ordered his attendant Gehazi, "Call this Shunammite woman." So he called her and she stood before him. 2Kg 4:29-31; 5:20-27

¹³ Then he said to Gehazi, "Say to her, 'Look, you've gone to all this trouble for us. What can we do for you? Can we speak on your behalf to the king or to the commander of the army?'" 2Kg 4:2

She answered, "I am living among my own people."

¹⁴ So he asked, "Then what should be done for her?"

Gehazi answered, "Well, she has no son, and her husband is old."

¹⁵ "Call her," Elisha said. So Gehazi called her, and she stood in the doorway. ¹⁶ Elisha said, "At this time next year you will have a son in your arms." Gn 18:9-14; Lk 1:7-13

Then she said, "No, my lord. Man of God, do not lie to your servant."

¹⁷ The woman conceived and gave birth to a son at the same time the following year, as Elisha had promised her.

The Shunammite's Son Raised

¹⁸ The child grew and one day went out to his father and the harvesters. ¹⁹ Suddenly he complained to his father, "My head! My head!"

His father told his servant, "Carry him to his mother." ²⁰ So he picked him up and took him to his mother. The child sat on her lap until noon and then died. ²¹ She went up and laid him on the bed of the man of God, shut him in, and left.

²² She summoned her husband and said, "Please send me one of the servants and one of the donkeys, so I can hurry to the man of God and come back again."

²³ But he said, "Why go to him today? It's not a New Moon or a Sabbath." Nm 10:10; 28:11

She replied, "Everything is all right." 2Sm 18:28; 2Kg 4:26

²⁴ Then she saddled the donkey and said to her servant, "Go fast; don't slow the pace for me unless I tell you." ²⁵ So she came to the man of God at Mount Carmel. 1Kg 18:19-20

When the man of God saw her at a distance, he said to his attendant Gehazi, "Look, there's the Shunammite woman. ²⁶ Run out to meet her and ask, 'Are you all right? Is your husband all right? Is your son all right?'" 2Kg 4:8,12

And she answered, "Everything's all right."

²⁷ When she came up to the man of God at the mountain, she clung to his feet. Gehazi came to push her away, but the man of God said, "Leave her alone — she is in severe anguish, and the LORD has hidden it from me. He hasn't told me." Ru 1:19-21; 1Sm 1:15; Zch 12:10; Mt 28:9

²⁸ Then she said, "Did I ask my lord for a son? Didn't I say, 'Do not lie to me?'" 2Kg 4:16

²⁹ So Elisha said to Gehazi, "Tuck your mantle under your belt, take my staff with you, and go. If you meet anyone, don't stop to greet him, and if a man greets you, don't answer him. Then place my staff on the boy's face." 1Kg 18:46; 2Kg 9:1

³⁰ The boy's mother said to Elisha, "As the LORD lives and as you yourself live, I will not leave you." So he got up and followed her.

³¹ Gehazi went ahead of them and placed the staff on the boy's face, but there was no sound or sign of life, so he went back to meet Elisha and told him, "The boy didn't wake up." Jn 11:11

³² When Elisha got to the house, he discovered the boy lying dead on his bed. ³³ So he went in, closed the door behind the two of them, and prayed to the LORD. ³⁴ Then he went up and lay on the boy: he put mouth to mouth, eye to eye, hand to hand. While he bent down over him, the boy's flesh became warm. ³⁵ Elisha got up, went into the house, and paced back and forth. Then he went up and bent down over him again. The boy sneezed seven times and opened his eyes. 2Kg 4:21; Mt 6:6; Ac 20:10

³⁶ Elisha called Gehazi and said, "Call the Shunammite woman." He called her and she came. Then Elisha said, "Pick up your son." ³⁷ She came, fell at his feet, and bowed to the ground; she picked up her son and left. Heb 11:35

The Deadly Stew

³⁸ When Elisha returned to Gilgal, there was a famine in the land. The sons of the prophets were sitting before him. He said to his attendant, "Put on the large pot and make stew for the sons of the prophets."

³⁹ One went out to the field to gather herbs and found a wild vine from which he gathered as many wild gourds as his garment would hold. Then he came back and cut them up into the pot of stew, but they were unaware of what they were. ᴬ

⁴⁰ They served some for the men to eat, but when they ate the stew they cried out, "There's death in the

ᴬ4:39 *of what they were* added for clarity

pot, man of God!" And they were unable to eat it.   Ex 10:17

⁴¹ Then Elisha said, "Get some flour." He threw it into the pot and said, "Serve it for the people to eat." And there was nothing bad in the pot.   Ex 15:25; 2Kg 2:21

The Multiplied Bread

⁴² A man from Baal-shalishah came to the man of God with his sack full of ᴬ twenty loaves of barley bread from the first bread of the harvest. Elisha said, "Give it to the people to eat."   1Sm 9:4; Mt 14:17

⁴³ But Elisha's attendant asked, "What? Am I to set this before a hundred men?"   Lk 9:13; Jn 6:9

"Give it to the people to eat," Elisha said, "for this is what the LORD says: 'They will eat, and they will have some left over.'" ⁴⁴ So he set it before them, and as the LORD had promised, they ate and had some left over.   Mt 14:20

Naaman's Disease Healed

5 Naaman, commander of the army for the king of Aram, was a man important to his master and highly regarded because through him, the LORD had given victory to Aram. The man was a valiant warrior, but he had a skin disease.

² Aram had gone on raids and brought back from the land of Israel a young girl who served Naaman's wife. ³ She said to her mistress, "If only my master were with the prophet who is in Samaria, he would cure him of his skin disease."   2Kg 6:23; 13:20

⁴ So Naaman went and told his master what the girl from the land of Israel had said. ⁵ Therefore, the king of Aram said, "Go, and I will send a letter with you to the king of Israel."

So he went and took with him 750 pounds ᴮ of silver, 150 pounds ᶜ of gold, and ten sets of clothing. ⁶ He brought the letter to the king of Israel, and it read: Jdg 14:12; 2Kg 5:22

When this letter comes to you, note that I have sent you my servant Naaman for you to cure him of his skin disease.

⁷ When the king of Israel read the letter, he tore his clothes and asked, "Am I God, killing and giving life that this man expects me to cure a man of his skin disease? Recognize ᴰ that he is only picking a fight with me."   Gn 37:29; 2Kg 11:14

⁸ When Elisha the man of God heard that the king of Israel had torn his clothes, he sent a message to the king, "Why have you torn your clothes? Have him come to me, and he will know there is a prophet in Israel." ⁹ So Naaman came with his horses and chariots and stood at the door of Elisha's house.

¹⁰ Then Elisha sent him a messenger, who said, "Go wash seven times in the Jordan and your skin will be restored and you will be clean."   Lv 14:7; Nm 5:1-4; Jn 9:7

¹¹ But Naaman got angry and left, saying, "I was telling myself: He will surely come out, stand and call on the name of the LORD his God, and wave his hand over the place and cure the skin disease. ¹² Aren't Abana and Pharpar, the rivers of Damascus, better than all the waters of Israel? Couldn't I wash in them and be clean?" So he turned and left in a rage.   Ex 7:19; Pr 14:17; 19:11; Is 8:6

ᴬ**4:42** Or *with some heads of fresh grain and Know and see*   ᴮ**5:5** Lit *10 talents*   ᶜ**5:5** Lit *6,000 shekels*   ᴰ**5:7** Lit

¹³ But his servants approached and said to him, "My father, if the prophet had told you to do some great thing, would you not have done it? How much more should you do it when he only tells you, 'Wash and be clean'?" ¹⁴ So Naaman went down and dipped himself in the Jordan seven times, according to the command of the man of God. Then his skin was restored and became like the skin of a small boy, and he was clean.   2Kg 2:12; 6:21; 13:14

¹⁵ Then Naaman and his whole company went back to the man of God, stood before him, and declared, "I know there's no God in the whole world except in Israel. Therefore, please accept a gift from your servant."   Gn 33:11; Jos 2:11; 1Sm 17:46-47

¹⁶ But Elisha said, "As the LORD lives, in whose presence I stand, I will not accept it." Naaman urged him to accept it, but he refused.

¹⁷ Naaman responded, "If not, please let your servant be given as much soil as a pair of mules can carry, for your servant will no longer offer a burnt offering or a sacrifice to any other god but the LORD. ¹⁸ However, in a particular matter may the LORD pardon your servant: When my master, the king of Aram, goes into the temple of Rimmon to bow in worship while he is leaning on my arm,ᴬ and I have to bow in the temple of Rimmon — when I bowᴮ in the temple of Rimmon, may the LORD pardon your servant in this matter."   Ex 20:24; Dt 6:4; 2Kg 7:2

¹⁹ So he said to him, "Go in peace."

Gehazi's Greed Punished

After Naaman had traveled a short distance from Elisha, ²⁰ Gehazi, the attendant of Elisha the man of God, thought, "My master has let this Aramean Naaman off lightly by not accepting from him what he brought. As the LORD lives, I will run after him and get something from him."   Ex 20:7; 2Kg 4:12,31

²¹ So Gehazi pursued Naaman. When Naaman saw someone running after him, he got down from the chariot to meet him and asked, "Is everything all right?"

²² Gehazi said, "It's all right. My master has sent me to say, 'I have just now discovered that two young men from the sons of the prophets have come to me from the hill country of Ephraim. Please give them seventy-five poundsᶜ of silver and two sets of clothing.'"

²³ But Naaman insisted, "Please, accept one hundred fifty pounds."ᴰ He urged Gehazi and then packed one hundred fifty pounds of silver in two bags with two sets of clothing. Naaman gave them to two of his attendants who carried them ahead of Gehazi. ²⁴ When Gehazi came to the hill,ᴱ he took the gifts from them and deposited them in the house. Then he dismissed the men, and they left.   2Kg 1:9

²⁵ Gehazi came and stood by his master. "Where did you go, Gehazi?" Elisha asked him.

He replied, "Your servant didn't go anywhere."

²⁶ "And my heart didn't goᶠ when the man got down from his chariot to meet you," Elisha said. "Is this a time to accept silver and clothing, olive orchards and vineyards, flocks and herds, and male and female slaves? ²⁷ Therefore, Naaman's skin disease will cling to you and

---

ᴬ5:18 Lit worship, and he leans on my hand   ᴮ5:18 LXX, Vg read when he bows himself   ᶜ5:22 Lit a talent   ᴰ5:23 Lit two talents   ᴱ5:24 Or citadel   ᶠ5:26 Or "Did not my heart go your descendants forever." So Gehazi went out from his presence diseased, resembling snow.ᴬ   Ex 4:6

The Floating Ax Head

6 The sons of the prophets said to Elisha, "Please notice that the place where we live under your supervisionᴮ is too small for us. ² Please let us go to the Jordan where we can each get a log and can build ourselves a place to live there."   1Sm 10:5; 2Kg 2:3,5,7; 4:38

"Go," he said.

³ Then one said, "Please come with your servants."

"I'll come," he answered.

⁴ So he went with them, and when they came to the Jordan, they cut down trees. ⁵ As one of them was cutting down a tree, the iron ax head fell into the water, and he cried out, "Oh, my master, it was borrowed!"   Ex 22:14

⁶ Then the man of God asked, "Where did it fall?"   2Kg 4:8-9

When he showed him the place, the man of God cut a piece of wood, threw it there, and made the iron float. ⁷ Then he said, "Pick it up." So he reached out and took it.   Ex 15:25

The Aramean War

⁸ When the king of Aram was waging war against Israel, he conferred with his servants, "My camp will be at such and such a place."

⁹ But the man of God sent word to the king of Israel: "Be careful passing by this place, for the Arameans are going down there." ¹⁰ Consequently, the king of Israel sent word to the place the man of God had told him about. The man of God repeatedlyᶜ warned the king, so the king would be on his guard.   2Kg 4:8-9

¹¹ The king of Aram was enraged because of this matter, and he called his servants and demanded of them, "Tell me, which one of us is for the king of Israel?"

¹² One of his servants said, "No one, my lord the king. Elisha, the prophet in Israel, tells the king of Israel even the words you speak in your bedroom."

¹³ So the king said, "Go and see where he is, so I can send men to capture him."

When he was told, "Elisha is in Dothan," ¹⁴ he sent horses, chariots, and a massive army there. They went by night and surrounded the city.   Gn 37:17

¹⁵ When the servant of the man of God got up early and went out, he discovered an army with horses and chariots surrounding the city. So he asked Elisha, "Oh, my master, what are we to do?"

¹⁶ Elisha said, "Don't be afraid, for those who are with us outnumber those who are with them."   Ex 14:13

¹⁷ Then Elisha prayed, "LORD, please open his eyes and let him see." So the LORD opened the servant's eyes, and he saw that the mountain was covered with horses and chariots of fire all around Elisha.   2Kg 2:11; Ps 34:7

¹⁸ When the Arameans came against him, Elisha prayed to the LORD, "Please strike this nation with blindness."ᴰ So he struck them with blindness, according to Elisha's word. ¹⁹ Then Elisha said to them, "This is not the way, and this is not the city. Follow me, and I will take you to the man you're looking

for." And he led them to Samaria. ²⁰ When they entered Samaria, Elisha said, "LORD, open these men's eyes and let them see." So the LORD opened their eyes, and they saw that they were in the middle of Samaria.

²¹ When the king of Israel saw them, he said to Elisha, "Should I kill them, should I kill them, my father?"   2Kg 2:12; 5:13

²² Elisha replied, "Don't kill them. Do you kill those you have captured with your sword or your bow? Set food and water in front of them so they can eat and drink and go to their master."   2Ch 28:8-15; Rm 12:20

²³ So he prepared a big feast for them. When they had eaten and drunk, he sent them away, and they went to their master. The Aramean raiders did not come into Israel's land again.   2Kg 5:2; 24:2

The Siege of Samaria

²⁴ Some time later, King Ben-hadad of Aram brought all his military units together and marched up and laid siege to Samaria. ²⁵ So there was a severe famine in Samaria, and they continued the siege against it until a donkey's head sold for thirty-four ounces ᴬ of silver, and a cup ᴮ of dove's dung ᶜ sold for two ounces ᴰ of silver.   1Kg 20:1; 2Kg 4:38

²⁶ As the king of Israel was passing by on the wall, a woman cried out to him, "My lord the king, help!"

²⁷ He answered, "If the LORD doesn't help you, where can I get help for you? From the threshing floor or the winepress?" ²⁸ Then the king asked her, "What's the matter?"   2Sm 14:4-5; Hs 9:2

She said, "This woman said to me, 'Give up your son, and we will eat him today. Then we will eat my son tomorrow.' ²⁹ So we boiled my son and ate him, and I said to her the next day, 'Give up your son, and we will eat him,' but she has hidden her son."   Lv 26:29; Dt 28:53,57

³⁰ When the king heard the woman's words, he tore his clothes. Then, as he was passing by on the wall, the people saw that there was sackcloth under his clothes next to his skin. ³¹ He announced, "May God punish me and do so severely if the head of Elisha son of Shaphat remains on his shoulders today."

³² Elisha was sitting in his house, and the elders were sitting with him. The king sent a man ahead of him, but before the messenger got to him, Elisha said to the elders, "Do you see how this murderer has sent someone to remove my head? Look, when the messenger comes, shut the door to keep him out. Isn't the sound of his master's feet behind him?"   Ezk 8:1; 14:1; Lk 12:31-32

³³ While Elisha was still speaking with them, the messenger ᴱ came down to him. Then he said, "This disaster is from the LORD. Why should I wait for the LORD any longer?"

7 Elisha replied, "Hear the word of the LORD! This is what the LORD says: 'About this time tomorrow at Samaria's gate, six quarts ᶠ of fine flour will sell for a half ounce of silver ᴳ and twelve quarts ᴴ of barley will sell for a half ounce of silver.'"

² Then the captain, the king's right-hand man, ᴵ responded to the man of God, "Look, even if the LORD

ᴬ6:25 Lit for 80; "shekels" is assumed   ᴮ6:25 Lit a fourth of a kab   ᶜ6:25 Or seedpods, or wild onions   ᴰ6:25 Lit for five; "shekels" is assumed   ᴱ6:33 Some emend to king   ᶠ7:1 Lit a seah, also in vv. 16,18   ᴳ7:1 Lit for a shekel, also in vv. 16,18   ᴴ7:1 Lit two seahs, also in vv. 16,18   ᴵ7:2 Lit captain, upon whose hand the king leaned, also in v. 17

were to make windows in heaven, could this really happen?" 2Kg 5:18

Elisha announced, "You will in fact see it with your own eyes, but you won't eat any of it." 2Kg 7:17

³ Now four men with a skin disease were at the entrance to the city gate. They said to each other, "Why just sit here until we die? ⁴ If we say, 'Let's go into the city,' we will die there because the famine is in the city, but if we sit here, we will also die. So now, come on. Let's surrender to the Arameans' camp. If they let us live, we will live; if they kill us, we will die." Nm 5:2-4; 2Kg 5:1

⁵ So the diseased men got up at twilight to go to the Arameans' camp. When they came to the camp's edge, they discovered that no one was there, ⁶ for the Lord^A had caused the Aramean camp to hear the sound of chariots, horses, and a large army. The Arameans had said to each other, "The king of Israel must have hired the kings of the Hittites and the kings of Egypt to attack us." ⁷ So they had gotten up and fled at twilight, abandoning their tents, horses, and donkeys. The camp was intact, and they had fled for their lives. 2Sm 5:24; 2Kg 5:16-17

⁸ When these diseased men came to the edge of the camp, they went into a tent to eat and drink. Then they picked up the silver, gold, and clothing and went off and hid them. They came back and entered another tent, picked things up, and hid them. ⁹ Then they said to each other, "We're not doing what is right. Today is a day of good news. If we are silent and wait until morning light, our punishment will catch up with us. So let's go tell the king's household." Jos 7:21; Pr 15:27; 21:17-18

¹⁰ The diseased men came and called to the city's gatekeepers and told them, "We went to the Aramean camp and no one was there — no human sounds. There was nothing but tethered horses and donkeys, and the tents were intact." ¹¹ The gatekeepers called out, and the news was reported to the king's household.

¹² So the king got up in the night and said to his servants, "Let me tell you what the Arameans have done to us. They know we are starving, so they have left the camp to hide in the open country, thinking, 'When they come out of the city, we will take them alive and go into the city.'" Jos 8:4-12; 2Kg 6:25

¹³ But one of his servants responded, "Please, let messengers take five of the horses that are left in the city. Their fate is like the entire Israelite community who will die, ᴮ so let's send them and see."

¹⁴ The messengers took two chariots with horses, and the king sent them after the Aramean army, saying, "Go and see." ¹⁵ So they followed them as far as the Jordan. They saw that the whole way was littered with clothes and equipment the Arameans had thrown off in their haste. The messengers returned and told the king.

¹⁶ Then the people went out and plundered the Aramean camp. It was then that six quarts of fine flour sold for a half ounce of silver and twelve quarts of barley sold for a half ounce of silver, according to the word of the Lᴏʀᴅ. ¹⁷ The

^A 7:6 Some Hb mss read Lᴏʀᴅ ᴮ 7:13 Some Hb mss, LXX, Syr, Vg; other Hb mss read *left in it. Indeed, they are like the whole multitude of Israel that are left in it; indeed, they are like the whole multitude of Israel who will die.*

king had appointed the captain, his right-hand man, to be in charge of the city gate, but the people trampled him in the gate. He died, just as the man of God had predicted when the king had come to him. [18] When the man of God had said to the king, "About this time tomorrow twelve quarts of barley will sell for a half ounce of silver and six quarts of fine flour will sell for a half ounce of silver at Samaria's gate," [19] this captain had answered the man of God, "Look, even if the LORD were to make windows in heaven, could this really happen?" Elisha had said, "You will in fact see it with your own eyes, but you won't eat any of it." [20] This is what happened to him: the people trampled him in the city gate, and he died.   2Kg 7:8

The Shunammite's Land Restored

8 Elisha said to the woman whose son he had restored to life, "Get ready, you and your household, and go live as a resident alien wherever you can. For the LORD has announced a seven-year famine, and it has already come to the land."   Gn 41:27,54; 2Kg 4:8-37

[2] So the woman got ready and did what the man of God said. She and her household lived as resident aliens in the land of the Philistines for seven years. [3] When the woman returned from the land of the Philistines at the end of seven years, she went to appeal to the king for her house and field.

[4] The king had been speaking to Gehazi, the attendant of the man of God, saying, "Tell me all the great things Elisha has done."   2Kg 4:12

[5] While he was telling the king how Elisha restored the dead son

to life, the woman whose son he had restored to life came to appeal to the king for her house and field. So Gehazi said, "My lord the king, this is the woman and this is the son Elisha restored to life."   2Kg 4:35

[6] When the king asked the woman, she told him the story. So the king appointed a court official for her, saying, "Restore all that was hers, along with all the income from the field from the day she left the country until now."

Aram's King Hazael

[7] Elisha came to Damascus while King Ben-hadad of Aram was sick, and the king was told, "The man of God has come here." [8] So the king said to Hazael, "Take a gift with you and go meet the man of God. Inquire of the LORD through him, 'Will I recover from this sickness?'"

[9] Hazael went to meet Elisha, taking with him a gift: forty camel-loads of all the finest products of Damascus. When he came and stood before him, he said, "Your son, King Ben-hadad of Aram, has sent me to ask you, 'Will I recover from this sickness?'"   2Kg 5:13

[10] Elisha told him, "Go say to him, 'You are sure to [A] recover.' But the LORD has shown me that he is sure to die." [11] Then he stared steadily at him until he was ashamed.   Jdg 3:25

The man of God wept, [12] and Hazael asked, "Why is my lord weeping?"   Lk 19:41

He replied, "Because I know the evil you will do to the people of Israel. You will set their fortresses on fire. You will kill their young men with the sword. You will dash their children to pieces. You will rip open their pregnant women."   1Kg 19:17

A 8:10 Alt Hb tradition reads *You will not*

¹³ Hazael said, "How could your servant, a mere dog, do such a mighty deed?" 2Sm 9:8

Elisha answered, "The LORD has shown me that you will be king over Aram." 1Kg 19:15

¹⁴ Hazael left Elisha and went to his master, who asked him, "What did Elisha say to you?"

He responded, "He told me you are sure to recover." ¹⁵ The next day Hazael took a heavy cloth, dipped it in water, and spread it over the king's face. Ben-hadad died, and Hazael reigned in his place.

Judah's King Jehoram

¹⁶ In the fifth year of Israel's King Joram son of Ahab, Jehoram ᴬ son of Jehoshaphat became king of Judah, replacing his father. ᴮ ¹⁷ He was thirty-two years old when he became king, and he reigned eight years in Jerusalem. ¹⁸ He walked in the ways of the kings of Israel, as the house of Ahab had done, for Ahab's daughter was his wife. He did what was evil in the LORD's sight. ¹⁹ For the sake of his servant David, the LORD was unwilling to destroy Judah, since he had promised to give a lamp to David and his sons forever. 2Kg 1:17; 3:1; 2Ch 21:5-20

²⁰ During Jehoram's reign, Edom rebelled against Judah's control and appointed their own king. ²¹ So Jehoram crossed over to Zair with all his chariots. Then at night he set out to attack the Edomites who had surrounded him and the chariot commanders, but his troops fled to their tents. ²² So Edom is still in rebellion against Judah's control today. Libnah also rebelled at that time. Jos 21:13; 2Sm 18:17; 19:8; 1Kg 22:47; 2Kg 3:9

²³ The rest of the events of Jehoram's reign, along with all his accomplishments, are written in the Historical Record of Judah's Kings. ²⁴ Jehoram rested with his fathers and was buried with his fathers in the city of David, and his son Ahaziah became king in his place.

Judah's King Ahaziah

²⁵ In the twelfth year of Israel's King Joram son of Ahab, Ahaziah son of Jehoram became king of Judah. ²⁶ Ahaziah was twenty-two years old when he became king, and he reigned one year in Jerusalem. His mother's name was Athaliah, granddaughter of Israel's King Omri. ²⁷ He walked in the ways of the house of Ahab and did what was evil in the LORD's sight like the house of Ahab, for his father had married into ᶜ the house of Ahab.

²⁸ Ahaziah went with Joram son of Ahab to fight against King Hazael of Aram in Ramoth-gilead, and the Arameans wounded Joram. ²⁹ So King Joram returned to Jezreel to recover from the wounds that the Arameans had inflicted on him in Ramoth-gilead ᴰ when he fought against Aram's King Hazael. Then Judah's King Ahaziah son of Jehoram went down to Jezreel to visit Joram son of Ahab since Joram was ill. 1Kg 19:15; 21:1; 22:3,29; 2Kg 9:15

Jehu Anointed as Israel's King

9 The prophet Elisha called one of the sons of the prophets and said, "Tuck your mantle under your belt, take this flask of oil with you, and go to Ramoth-gilead. ² When you get there, look for Jehu son of Jehoshaphat, son of Nimshi. Go in,

ᴬ8:16 = The LORD is Exalted ᴮ8:16 Lit Judah; Jehoshaphat had been king of Judah ᶜ8:27 Lit for he was related by marriage to ᴰ8:29 Lit Ramah get him away from his colleagues, and take him to an inner room. ³ Then take the flask of oil, pour it on his head, and say, 'This is what the LORD says: "I anoint you king over Israel."' Open the door and escape. Don't wait." ⁴ So the young prophet ᴬ went to Ramoth-gilead.

⁵ When he arrived, the army commanders were sitting there, so he said, "I have a message for you, commander."

Jehu asked, "For which one of us?"

He answered, "For you, commander."

⁶ So Jehu got up and went into the house. The young prophet poured the oil on his head and said, "This is what the LORD God of Israel says: 'I anoint you king over the LORD's people, Israel. ⁷ You are to strike down the house of your master Ahab so that I may avenge the blood shed by the hand of Jezebel — the blood of my servants the prophets and of all the servants of the LORD. ⁸ The whole house of Ahab will perish, and I will wipe out all of Ahab's males, ᴮ both slave and free, ᶜ in Israel. ⁹ I will make the house of Ahab like the house of Jeroboam son of Nebat and like the house of Baasha son of Ahijah. ¹⁰ The dogs will eat Jezebel in the plot of land at Jezreel — no one will bury her.'" Then the young prophet opened the door and escaped. 1Kg 18:4; 21:15

¹¹ When Jehu came out to his master's servants, they asked, "Is everything all right? Why did this crazy person come to you?" 1Sm 10:11; Mk 3:21

Then he said to them, "You know the sort and their ranting."

¹² But they replied, "That's a lie! Tell us!"

So Jehu said, "He talked to me about this and that and said, 'This is what the LORD says: I anoint you king over Israel.'"

¹³ Each man quickly took his garment and put it under Jehu on the bare steps. ᴰ They blew the ram's horn and proclaimed, "Jehu is king!" 2Sm 15:10; 1Kg 1:39; Mt 21:8

¹⁴ Then Jehu son of Jehoshaphat, son of Nimshi, conspired against Joram. Joram and all Israel had been at Ramoth-gilead on guard against King Hazael of Aram. ¹⁵ But King Joram had returned to Jezreel to recover from the wounds that the Arameans had inflicted on him when he fought against Aram's King Hazael. Jehu said, "If you commanders wish to make me king, ᴱ then don't let anyone escape from the city to go tell about it in Jezreel."

Jehu Kills Joram and Ahaziah

¹⁶ Jehu got into his chariot and went to Jezreel since Joram was laid up there and King Ahaziah of Judah had gone down to visit Joram. ¹⁷ Now the watchman was standing on the tower in Jezreel. He saw Jehu's mob approaching and shouted, "I see a mob!" 1Sm 14:16

Joram responded, "Choose a rider and send him to meet them and have him ask, 'Do you come in peace?'" 1Sm 16:4

¹⁸ So a horseman went to meet Jehu and said, "This is what the king asks: 'Do you come in peace?'"

Jehu replied, "What do you have to do with peace? ᶠ Fall in behind me."

ᴬ9:4 Or the young man, the attendant of the prophet   ᴮ9:8 Lit wipe out Ahab's one who urinates against a wall   ᶜ9:8 Or males, even the weak and impaired; Hb obscure   ᴰ9:13 Lit on the bones of the steps   ᴱ9:15 Lit "If your desire exists   ᶠ9:18 Lit What to you and to peace, also in v. 19

The watchman reported, "The messenger reached them but hasn't started back."

¹⁹ So he sent out a second horseman, who went to them and said, "This is what the king asks: 'Do you come in peace?'"

Jehu answered, "What do you have to do with peace? Fall in behind me."

²⁰ Again the watchman reported, "He reached them but hasn't started back. Also, the driving is like that of Jehu son of Nimshi — he drives like a madman." 1Kg 19:17

²¹ "Get the chariot ready!" Joram shouted, and they got it ready. Then King Joram of Israel and King Ahaziah of Judah set out, each in his own chariot, and met Jehu at the plot of land of Naboth the Jezreelite. ²² When Joram saw Jehu he asked, "Do you come in peace, Jehu?"

He answered, "What peace can there be as long as there is so much prostitution and sorcery from your mother Jezebel?" 1Kg 16:30-33; 2Ch 21:13

²³ Joram turned around and fled, shouting to Ahaziah, "It's treachery, Ahaziah!" 2Kg 11:14

²⁴ Then Jehu drew his bow and shot Joram between the shoulders. The arrow went through his heart, and he slumped down in his chariot. ²⁵ Jehu said to Bidkar his aide, "Pick him up and throw him on the plot of ground belonging to Naboth the Jezreelite. For remember when you and I were riding side by side behind his father Ahab, and the LORD uttered this pronouncement against him: ²⁶ 'As surely as I saw the blood of Naboth and the blood of his sons yesterday' — this is the LORD's declaration — 'so will I repay you on this plot of land' — this

is the LORD's declaration. So now, according to the word of the LORD, pick him up and throw him on the plot of land." 1Kg 21:1; 22:34-35

²⁷ When King Ahaziah of Judah saw what was happening, he fled up the road toward Beth-haggan. Jehu pursued him, shouting, "Shoot him too!" So they shot him in his chariotᴬ at Gur Pass near Ibleam, but he fled to Megiddo and died there. ²⁸ Then his servants carried him to Jerusalem in a chariot and buried him in his fathers' tomb in the city of David. ²⁹ It was in the eleventh year of Joram son of Ahab that Ahaziah had become king over Judah. Jos 17:11; Jdg 1:27; 2Kg 23:29; 2Ch 22:7,9

Jehu Kills Jezebel

³⁰ When Jehu came to Jezreel, Jezebel heard about it, so she painted her eyes, fixed her hair,ᴮ and looked down from the window. ³¹ As Jehu entered the city gate, she said, "Do you come in peace, Zimri, killer of your master?" Jr 4:30; Ezk 23:40

³² He looked up toward the window and said, "Who is on my side? Who?" Two or three eunuchs looked down at him, ³³ and he said, "Throw her down!" So they threw her down, and some of her blood splattered on the wall and on the horses, and Jehu rode over her. Est 2:14

³⁴ Then he went in, ate and drank, and said, "Take care of this cursed woman and bury her, since she's a king's daughter." ³⁵ But when they went out to bury her, they did not find anything but the skull, the feet, and the hands. ³⁶ So they went back and told him, and he said, "This fulfills the LORD's word that he spoke through his servant Elijah the Tishbite: 'In the plot of land at Jezreel, the

ᴬ9:27 LXX, Syr, Vg; MT omits *So they shot him*　　ᴮ9:30 Lit *made her head pleasing* dogs will eat Jezebel's flesh. ³⁷ Jezebel's corpse will be like manure on the surface of the ground in the plot of land at Jezreel so that no one will be able to say: This is Jezebel.'"

Jehu Kills the House of Ahab

10 Since Ahab had seventy sons in Samaria, Jehu wrote letters and sent them to Samaria to the rulers of Jezreel, to the elders, and to the guardians of Ahab's sons,ᴬ saying: 1Kg 16:24,29; 21:1; 2Kg 9:30
² Your master's sons are with you, and you have chariots, horses, a fortified city, and weaponry, so when this letter arrives ³ select the most qualifiedᴮ of your master's sons, set him on his father's throne, and fight for your master's house.

⁴ However, they were terrified and reasoned, "Look, two kings couldn't stand against him; how can we?"   2Kg 9:24,27
⁵ So the overseer of the palace, the overseer of the city, the elders, and the guardians sent a message to Jehu: "We are your servants, and we will do whatever you tell us. We will not make anyone king. Do whatever you think is right."ᶜ   Jos 9:8,11
⁶ Then Jehu wrote them a second letter, saying:

If you are on my side, and if you will obey me, bring me the heads of your master's sonsᴰ at this time tomorrow at Jezreel.

All seventy of the king's sons were being cared for by the city's prominent men. ⁷ When the letter came to them, they took the king's sons and slaughtered all seventy, put their heads in baskets, and sent them to Jehu at Jezreel. ⁸ When the messenger came and told him, "They have brought the heads of the king's sons," the king said, "Pile them in two heaps at the entrance of the city gate until morning."

⁹ The next morning when he went out and stood at the gate, he said to all the people, "You are innocent. It was I who conspired against my master and killed him. But who struck down all these? ¹⁰ Know, then, that not a word the LORD spoke against the house of Ahab will fail, for the LORD has done what he promised through his servant Elijah." ¹¹ So Jehu killed all who remained of the house of Ahab in Jezreel — all his great men, close friends, and priests — leaving him no survivors.   2Kg 9:14-24
¹² Then he set out and went to Samaria. On the way, while he was at Beth-eked of the Shepherds, ¹³ Jehu met the relatives of King Ahaziah of Judah and asked, "Who are you?"

They answered, "We're Ahaziah's relatives. We've come down to greet the king's sons and the queen mother's sons."   2Kg 9:27-29
¹⁴ Then Jehu ordered, "Take them alive." So they took them alive and then slaughtered them at the pit of Beth-eked — forty-two men. He didn't spare any of them.   2Ch 22:8
¹⁵ When he left there, he found Jehonadab son of Rechab coming to meet him. He greeted him and then asked, "Is your heart one with mine?"ᴱ   Jr 35:6-19

"It is," Jehonadab replied.

Jehu said, "If it is,ᶠ give me your hand."   Ezr 10:19

ᴬ**10:1** LXX; MT reads *of Ahab*   ᴮ**10:3** Lit *the good and the upright*   ᶜ**10:5** Lit *Do what is good in your eyes*   ᴰ**10:6** Lit *heads of the men of the sons of your master*   ᴱ**10:15** Lit *heart upright like my heart is with your heart*   ᶠ**10:15** LXX, Syr, Vg; MT reads *mine?" Jehonadab said, "It is and it is*

So he gave him his hand, and Jehu pulled him up into the chariot with him. ¹⁶ Then he said, "Come with me and see my zeal for the LORD!" So he let him ride with him in his chariot. ¹⁷ When Jehu came to Samaria, he struck down all who remained from the house of Ahab in Samaria until he had annihilated his house, according to the word of the LORD spoken to Elijah.

Jehu Kills the Baal Worshipers

¹⁸ Then Jehu brought all the people together and said to them, "Ahab served Baal a little, but Jehu will serve him a lot. ¹⁹ Now, therefore, summon to me all the prophets of Baal, all his servants, and all his priests. None must be missing, for I have a great sacrifice for Baal. Whoever is missing will not live." However, Jehu was acting deceptively in order to destroy the servants of Baal. ²⁰ Jehu commanded, "Consecrate a solemn assembly for Baal." So they called one.   1Kg 16:31-32

²¹ Then Jehu sent messengers throughout all Israel, and all the servants of Baal ᴬ came; no one failed to come. They entered the temple of Baal, and it was filled from one end to the other. ²² Then he said to the custodian of the wardrobe, "Bring out the garments for all the servants of Baal." So he brought out their garments.

²³ Then Jehu and Jehonadab son of Rechab entered the temple of Baal, and Jehu said to the servants of Baal, "Look carefully to see that there are no servants of the LORD here among you — only servants of Baal." ²⁴ Then they went in to offer sacrifices and burnt offerings.

Now Jehu had stationed eighty men outside, and he warned them, "Whoever allows any of the men I am placing in your hands to escape will forfeit his life for theirs." ²⁵ When he finished offering the burnt offering, Jehu said to the guards and officers, "Go in and kill them. Don't let anyone out." So they struck them down with the sword. Then the guards and officers threw the bodies out and went into the inner room of the temple of Baal. ²⁶ They brought out the pillar of the temple of Baal and burned it, ²⁷ and they tore down the pillar of Baal. Then they tore down the temple of Baal and made it a latrine — which it still is today.   1Kg 14:23; 18:40; 20:39

Evaluation of Jehu's Reign

²⁸ Jehu eliminated Baal worship from Israel, ²⁹ but he did not turn away from the sins that Jeroboam son of Nebat had caused Israel to commit — worshiping the gold calves that were in Bethel and Dan. ³⁰ Nevertheless, the LORD said to Jehu, "Because you have done well in carrying out what is right in my sight and have done to the house of Ahab all that was in my heart, four generations of your sons will sit on the throne of Israel."   2Kg 15:12

³¹ Yet Jehu was not careful to follow the instruction of the LORD God of Israel with all his heart. He did not turn from the sins that Jeroboam had caused Israel to commit.

³² In those days the LORD began to reduce the size of Israel. Hazael defeated the Israelites throughout their territory ³³ from the Jordan eastward: the whole land of Gilead — the Gadites, the Reubenites,

ᴬ 10:21 LXX adds — all his priests and all his prophets —

and the Manassites — from Aroer which is by the Arnon Valley through Gilead to Bashan.[A]

³⁴ The rest of the events of Jehu's reign, along with all his accomplishments and all his might, are written in the Historical Record of Israel's Kings. ³⁵ Jehu rested with his fathers and was buried in Samaria. His son Jehoahaz became king in his place. ³⁶ The length of Jehu's reign over Israel in Samaria was twenty-eight years. 2Kg 1:18

Athaliah Usurps the Throne

11 When Athaliah, Ahaziah's mother, saw that her son was dead, she proceeded to annihilate all the royal heirs. ² Jehosheba, who was King Jehoram's daughter and Ahaziah's sister, secretly rescued Joash son of Ahaziah from among the king's sons who were being killed and put him and the one who nursed him in a bedroom. So he was hidden from Athaliah and was not killed. ³ Joash was in hiding with her in the LORD's temple six years while Athaliah reigned over the land. 2Kg 8:26; 9:27; 2Ch 22:10

Athaliah Overthrown

⁴ In the seventh year, Jehoiada sent for the commanders of hundreds, the Carites, and the guards. He had them come to him in the LORD's temple, where he made a covenant with them and put them under oath. He showed them the king's son ⁵ and commanded them, "This is what you are to do: A third of you who come on duty on the Sabbath are to provide protection for the king's palace. ⁶ A third are to be at the Foundation[B] Gate and a third at the gate behind the guards. You are to take turns providing protection for the palace.[C] 2Ch 23:1-15

⁷ "Your two divisions that go off duty on the Sabbath are to provide the king protection at the LORD's temple. ⁸ Completely surround the king with weapons in hand. Anyone who approaches the ranks is to be put to death. Be with the king in all his daily tasks."[D] Nm 27:16-17

⁹ So the commanders of hundreds did everything the priest Jehoiada commanded. They each brought their men — those coming on duty on the Sabbath and those going off duty — and came to the priest Jehoiada. ¹⁰ The priest gave to the commanders of hundreds King David's spears and shields that were in the LORD's temple. ¹¹ Then the guards stood with their weapons in hand surrounding the king — from the right side of the temple to the left side, by the altar and by the temple. 2Sm 8:7; 1Ch 18:72; Ch 23:8

¹² Jehoiada brought out the king's son, put the crown on him, gave him the testimony,[E] and made him king. They anointed him and clapped their hands and cried, "Long live the king!" Ex 31:18; 2Sm 1:10

¹³ When Athaliah heard the noise from the guard and the crowd, she went out to the people at the LORD's temple. ¹⁴ She looked, and there was the king standing by the pillar according to the custom. The commanders and the trumpeters were by the king, and all the people of the land were rejoicing and blowing trumpets. Athaliah tore her clothes and screamed "Treason! Treason!"

[A]**10:33** Lit *Arnon Valley and Gilead and Bashan*　[B]**11:6** See 2Ch 23:5; MT here reads *Sur*　[C]**11:6** Hb obscure　[D]**11:8** Lit *king when he goes out and when he comes in*　[E]**11:12** Or *him the copy of the covenant*, or *him a diadem*, or *him jewels*

¹⁵ Then the priest Jehoiada ordered the commanders of hundreds in charge of the army, "Take her out between the ranks, and put to death by the sword anyone who follows her," for the priest had said, "She is not to be put to death in the LORD's temple." ¹⁶ So they arrested her, and she went through the horse entrance to the king's palace, where she was put to death.

Jehoiada's Reforms

¹⁷ Then Jehoiada made a covenant between the LORD, the king, and the people that they would be the LORD's people and another covenant between the king and the people.ᴬ ¹⁸ So all the people of the land went to the temple of Baal and tore it down. They smashed its altars and images to pieces, and they killed Mattan, the priest of Baal, at the altars.   Jos 24:25; 2Ch 23:16-21; 34:31

Then Jehoiada the priest appointed guards for the LORD's temple. ¹⁹ He took the commanders of hundreds, the Carites, the guards, and all the people of the land, and they brought the king from the LORD's temple. They entered the king's palace by way of the guards' gate. Then Joash sat on the throne of the kings. ²⁰ All the people of the land rejoiced, and the city was quiet, for they had put Athaliah to death by the sword in the king's palace.

Judah's King Joash

²¹ Joashᴮ was seven years old when

12 he became king. ¹ In the seventh year of Jehu, Joash became king, and he reigned forty years in Jerusalem. His mother's name was Zibiah; she was from Beer-sheba. ² Throughout the time the priest Jehoiada instructed him, Joash did what was right in the LORD's sight. ³ Yet the high places were not taken away; the people continued sacrificing and burning incense on the high places.   1Kg 3:3; 2Kg 11:2,21

Repairing the Temple

⁴ Then Joash said to the priests, "All the dedicated silver brought to the LORD's temple, census silver, silver from vows, and all silver voluntarily given for the LORD's temple — ⁵ each priest is to take it from his assessorᶜ and repair whatever damage is found in the temple."ᴰ

⁶ But by the twenty-third year of the reign of King Joash, the priests had not repaired the damageᴱ to the temple. ⁷ So King Joash called the priest Jehoiada and the other priests and asked, "Why haven't you repaired the temple's damage? Since you haven't, don't take any silver from your assessors; instead, hand it over for the repair of the temple." ⁸ So the priests agreed that they would receive no silver from the people and would not be the ones to repair the temple's damage.   2Kg 11:4-6,21; 2Ch 24:5

⁹ Then the priest Jehoiada took a chest, bored a hole in its lid, and set it beside the altar on the right side as one enters the LORD's temple; the priests who guarded the threshold put into the chest all the silver that was brought to the LORD's temple. ¹⁰ Whenever they saw there was a large amount of silver in the chest, the king's secretary and the high priest would

ᴬ **11:17** Some Gk versions, 2Ch 23:16 omit *and another covenant between the king and the people*
ᴮ **11:21** = The LORD Has Bestowed   ᶜ **12:5** Hb obscure   ᴰ **12:5** Lit *repair the breach of the temple wherever there is found a breach*   ᴱ **12:6** Lit *breach* in 2Kg 12:5-12

go bag up and tally the silver found in the LORD's temple. ¹¹ Then they would give the weighed silver to those doing the work — those who oversaw the LORD's temple. They in turn would pay it out to those working on the LORD's temple — the carpenters, the builders, ¹² the masons, and the stonecutters — and would use it to buy timber and quarried stone to repair the damage to the LORD's temple and for all expenses for temple repairs.

¹³ However, no silver bowls, wick trimmers, sprinkling basins, trumpets, or any articles of gold or silver were made for the LORD's temple from the contributions ᴬ brought to the LORD's temple. ¹⁴ Instead, it was given to those doing the work, and they repaired the LORD's temple with it. ¹⁵ No accounting was required from the men who received the silver to pay those doing the work, since they worked with integrity. ¹⁶ The silver from the guilt offering and the sin offering was not brought to the LORD's temple since it belonged to the priests.

Aramean Invasion of Judah

¹⁷ At that time King Hazael of Aram marched up and fought against Gath and captured it. Then he planned to attack Jerusalem. ¹⁸ So King Joash of Judah took all the items consecrated by himself and by his ancestors — Judah's kings Jehoshaphat, Jehoram, and Ahaziah — as well as all the gold found in the treasuries of the LORD's temple and in the king's palace, and he sent them to King Hazael of Aram. Then Hazael withdrew from Jerusalem.   1Kg 19:17; 2Kg 8:12; 10:32; 2Ch 24:23-27

Joash Assassinated

¹⁹ The rest of the events of Joash's reign, along with all his accomplishments, are written in the Historical Record of Judah's Kings. ²⁰ Joash's servants conspired against him and attacked him at Beth-millo on the road that goes down to Silla. ²¹ It was his servants Jozabad ᴮ son of Shimeath and Jehozabad son of Shomer who attacked him. He died and they buried him with his fathers in the city of David, and his son Amaziah became king in his place.   1Kg 22:45

Israel's King Jehoahaz

13 In the twenty-third year of Judah's King Joash son of Ahaziah, Jehoahaz son of Jehu became king over Israel in Samaria, and he reigned seventeen years. ² He did what was evil in the LORD's sight and followed the sins that Jeroboam son of Nebat had caused Israel to commit; he did not turn away from them. ³ So the LORD's anger burned against Israel, and he handed them over to King Hazael of Aram and to his son Ben-hadad during their reigns.   2Kg 12:1,17

⁴ Then Jehoahaz sought the LORD's favor, and the LORD heard him, for he saw the oppression the king of Aram inflicted on Israel. ⁵ Therefore, the LORD gave Israel a deliverer, and they escaped from the power of the Arameans. Then the people of Israel returned to their former way of life, ᶜ ⁶ but they didn't turn away from the sins that the house of Jeroboam had caused Israel to commit. Jehoahaz continued them, and the Asherah pole also remained standing in Samaria. ⁷ Jehoahaz did not

---

have an army left, except for fifty horsemen, ten chariots, and ten thousand foot soldiers, because the king of Aram had destroyed them, making them like dust at threshing. Ex 3:7-9; Nm 21:7-9; Jdg 2:18; 2Kg 14:26; Am 1:3

8 The rest of the events of Jehoahaz's reign, along with all his accomplishments and his might, are written in the Historical Record of Israel's Kings. 9 Jehoahaz rested with his fathers, and he was buried in Samaria. His son Jehoash^A became king in his place. 2Kg 1:17-18

Israel's King Jehoash

10 In the thirty-seventh year of Judah's King Joash, Jehoash son of Jehoahaz became king over Israel in Samaria, and he reigned sixteen years. 11 He did what was evil in the LORD's sight. He did not turn away from all the sins that Jeroboam son of Nebat had caused Israel to commit, but he continued them. 12 The rest of the events of Jehoash's reign, along with all his accomplishments and the power he had to wage war against Judah's King Amaziah, are written in the Historical Record of Israel's Kings. 13 Jehoash rested with his fathers, and Jeroboam sat on his throne. Jehoash was buried in Samaria with the kings of Israel. 2Kg 14:15-16,23

Elisha's Death

14 When Elisha became sick with the illness from which he died, King Jehoash of Israel went down and wept over him and said, "My father, my father, the chariots and horsemen of Israel!" 2Kg 2:12

15 Elisha responded, "Get a bow and arrows." So he got a bow and arrows. 16 Then Elisha said to the king of Israel, "Grasp the bow." So the king grasped it, and Elisha put his hands on the king's hands. 17 Elisha said, "Open the east window." So he opened it. Elisha said, "Shoot!" So he shot. Then Elisha said, "The LORD's arrow of victory, yes, the arrow of victory over Aram. You are to strike down the Arameans in Aphek until you have put an end to them." Jos 8:18; 1Sm 20:20

18 Then Elisha said, "Take the arrows!" So he took them. Then Elisha said to the king of Israel, "Strike the ground!" So he struck the ground three times and stopped. 19 The man of God was angry with him and said, "You should have struck the ground five or six times. Then you would have struck down Aram until you had put an end to them, but now you will strike down Aram only three times." 20 Then Elisha died and was buried. 2Kg 2:1,11; 5:20

Now Moabite raiders used to come into the land in the spring of the year. 21 Once, as the Israelites were burying a man, suddenly they saw a raiding party, so they threw the man into Elisha's tomb. When he touched Elisha's bones, the man revived and stood up! 2Kg 24:2

God's Mercy on Israel

22 King Hazael of Aram oppressed Israel throughout the reign of Jehoahaz, 23 but the LORD was gracious to them, had compassion on them, and turned toward them because of his covenant with Abraham, Isaac, and Jacob. He was not willing to destroy them. Even now he has not banished them from his presence. 1Kg 8:28; 19:17; 2Kg 8:12-13

24 King Hazael of Aram died, and his son Ben-hadad became king in

^A 13:9 Lit Joash

his place. ²⁵ Then Jehoash son of Jehoahaz took back from Ben-hadad
son of Hazael the cities that Hazael had taken in war from Jehoash's
father Jehoahaz. Jehoash defeated
Ben-hadad three times and recov-
ered the cities of Israel.   2Kg 13:3

Judah's King Amaziah

14 In the second year of Israel's
King Jehoash ᴬ son of Jehoahaz, ᴮ Amaziah son of Joash became
king of Judah. ² He was twenty-five
years old when he became king,
and he reigned twenty-nine years
in Jerusalem. His mother's name
was Jehoaddin; ᶜ she was from Jerusalem. ³ He did what was right
in the LORD's sight, but not like his
ancestor David. He did everything
his father Joash had done. ⁴ Yet the
high places were not taken away,
and the people continued sacrificing and burning incense on the
high places.   2Kg 13:10; 2Ch 25:1-24

⁵ As soon as the kingdom was
firmly in his grasp, Amaziah killed
his servants who had killed his father the king. ⁶ However, he did
not put the children of the killers
to death, as it is written in the book
of the law of Moses where the LORD
commanded, "Fathers are not to be
put to death because of children,
and children are not to be put to
death because of fathers; instead,
each one will be put to death for his
own sin." Dt 24:16; 2Kg 12:20; Jr 31:30; Ezk 18:4,20

⁷ Amaziah killed ten thousand
Edomites in Salt Valley. He took
Sela in battle and called it Jokthe-
el, which is still its name today.
⁸ Amaziah then sent messengers
to Jehoash son of Jehoahaz, son of
Jehu, king of Israel, and challenged
him: "Come, let's meet face to face."

⁹ King Jehoash of Israel sent word
to King Amaziah of Judah, saying,
"The thistle in Lebanon once sent a
message to the cedar in Lebanon,
saying, 'Give your daughter to my
son as a wife.' Then a wild animal
in Lebanon passed by and trampled
the thistle. ¹⁰ You have indeed defeated Edom, and you have become
overconfident. ᴰ Enjoy your glory
and stay at home. Why should you
stir up such trouble that you fall —
you and Judah with you?" 1Kg 4:33

¹¹ But Amaziah would not listen,
so King Jehoash of Israel advanced.
He and King Amaziah of Judah met
face to face at Beth-shemesh that
belonged to Judah. ¹² Judah was
routed before Israel, and each man
fled to his own tent. ¹³ King Jehoash of Israel captured Judah's King
Amaziah son of Joash, ᴱ son of Ahaziah, at Beth-shemesh. Then Jehoash went to Jerusalem and broke
down two hundred yardsᶠ of Jerusalem's wall from the Ephraim
Gate to the Corner Gate. ¹⁴ He took
all the gold and silver, all the articles found in the LORD's temple
and in the treasuries of the king's
palace, and some hostages. Then
he returned to Samaria. Jos 19:38; 21:16

Jehoash's Death

¹⁵ The rest of the events of Jehoash's reign, along with his accomplishments, his might, and how he
waged war against King Amaziah
of Judah, are written in the Historical Record of Israel's Kings. ¹⁶ Jehoash rested with his fathers, and
he was buried in Samaria with the

ᴬ**14:1** Lit *Joash*, also in vv. 23,27   ᴮ**14:1** Lit *Joahaz*   ᶜ**14:2** Alt Hb tradition, some Hb mss, Syr, Tg, Vg,
2Ch 25:1; other Hb mss, LXX read *Jehoaddin*   ᴰ**14:10** Lit *and your heart has lifted you*   ᴱ**14:13** Lit *Jehoash*
ᶠ**14:13** Lit *400 cubits*

kings of Israel. His son Jeroboam became king in his place. 2Kg13:12-13

Amaziah's Death

¹⁷ Judah's King Amaziah son of Joash lived fifteen years after the death of Israel's King Jehoash son of Jehoahaz. ¹⁸ The rest of the events of Amaziah's reign are written in the Historical Record of Judah's Kings. ¹⁹ A conspiracy was formed against him in Jerusalem, and he fled to Lachish. However, men were sent after him to Lachish, and they put him to death there. ²⁰ They carried him back on horses, and he was buried in Jerusalem with his fathers in the city of David.

²¹ Then all the people of Judah took Azariah, ᴬ who was sixteen years old, and made him king in place of his father Amaziah. ²² After Amaziah the king rested with his fathers, Azariah rebuilt Elath ᴮ and restored it to Judah.   2Kg15:13

Israel's King Jeroboam

²³ In the fifteenth year of Judah's King Amaziah son of Joash, Jeroboam son of Jehoash became king of Israel in Samaria, and he reigned forty-one years. ²⁴ He did what was evil in the LORD's sight. He did not turn away from all the sins Jeroboam son of Nebat had caused Israel to commit.   1Kg12:30; 15:30; 2Kg13:13

²⁵ He restored Israel's border from Lebo-hamath as far as the Sea of the Arabah, according to the word the LORD, the God of Israel, had spoken through his servant, the prophet Jonah son of Amittai from Gath-hepher. ²⁶ For the LORD saw that the affliction of Israel was very bitter for both slaves and free people. ᶜ There was no one to help Israel. ²⁷ The LORD had not said he would blot out the name of Israel under heaven, so he delivered them by the hand of Jeroboam son of Jehoash.   Nm 34:3-9; 1Kg 8:65; 2Kg 13:25

²⁸ The rest of the events of Jeroboam's reign — along with all his accomplishments, the power he had to wage war, and how he recovered for Israel Damascus and Hamath, which had belonged to Judah ᴰ — are written in the Historical Record of Israel's Kings. ²⁹ Jeroboam rested with his fathers, the kings of Israel. His son Zechariah became king in his place.

Judah's King Azariah

15 In the twenty-seventh year of Israel's King Jeroboam, Azariah ᴱ son of Amaziah became king of Judah. ² He was sixteen years old when he became king, and he reigned fifty-two years in Jerusalem. His mother's name was Jecoliah; she was from Jerusalem. ³ Azariah did what was right in the LORD's sight just as his father Amaziah had done. ⁴ Yet the high places were not taken away; the people continued sacrificing and burning incense on the high places.

⁵ The LORD afflicted the king, and he had a serious skin disease until the day of his death. He lived in quarantine, ᶠ while Jotham, the king's son, was over the household governing the people of the land.

⁶ The rest of the events of Azariah's reign, along with all his accomplishments, are written in the Historical Record of Judah's Kings.

ᴬ14:21 = Uzziah in 2Ch 26:1   ᴮ14:22 = Eloth in 2Ch 26:2   ᶜ14:26 Hb obscure   ᴰ14:28 Lit recovered Damascus and for Judah in Israel; Hb obscure   ᴱ15:1 = Uzziah in 2Ch 26:3   ᶠ15:5 Lit in a house of exemption from duty

⁷ Azariah rested with his fathers and was buried with his fathers in the city of David. His son Jotham became king in his place. 2Kg 14:18

Israel's King Zechariah

⁸ In the thirty-eighth year of Judah's King Azariah, Zechariah son of Jeroboam reigned over Israel in Samaria for six months. ⁹ He did what was evil in the LORD's sight as his fathers had done. He did not turn away from the sins Jeroboam son of Nebat had caused Israel to commit. 1Kg 12:28-33; 13:33-34; 2Kg 14:24,29

¹⁰ Shallum son of Jabesh conspired against Zechariah. He struck him down publicly,ᴬ killed him, and became king in his place. ¹¹ As for the rest of the events of Zechariah's reign, they are written in the Historical Record of Israel's Kings. ¹² The word of the LORD that he spoke to Jehu was, "Four generations of your sons will sit on the throne of Israel," and it was so.

Israel's King Shallum

¹³ In the thirty-ninth year of Judah's King Uzziah,ᴮ Shallum son of Jabesh became king; he reigned in Samaria a full month. ¹⁴ Then Menahem son of Gadi came up from Tirzah to Samaria and struck down Shallum son of Jabesh there. He killed him and became king in his place. ¹⁵ As for the rest of the events of Shallum's reign, along with the conspiracy that he formed, they are written in the Historical Record of Israel's Kings. 1Kg 14:17; 16:24

Israel's King Menahem

¹⁶ At that time, starting from Tirzah, Menahem attacked Tiphsah, all who were in it, and its territory because they wouldn't surrender. He ripped open all the pregnant women. Dt 20:11; 1Kg 4:24; 2Kg 8:12; Hs 13:16

¹⁷ In the thirty-ninth year of Judah's King Azariah, Menahem son of Gadi became king over Israel, and he reigned ten years in Samaria. ¹⁸ He did what was evil in the LORD's sight. Throughout his reign, he did not turn away from the sins Jeroboam son of Nebat had caused Israel to commit. 1Kg 12:28-33

¹⁹ King Pulᶜ of Assyria invaded the land, so Menahem gave Pul seventy-five thousand poundsᴰ of silver so that Pul would support him to strengthen his grasp on the kingdom. ²⁰ Then Menahem exacted twenty ouncesᴱ of silver from each of the prominent men of Israel to give to the king of Assyria. So the king of Assyria withdrew and did not stay there in the land.

²¹ The rest of the events of Menahem's reign, along with all his accomplishments, are written in the Historical Record of Israel's Kings. ²² Menahem rested with his fathers, and his son Pekahiah became king in his place. 2Kg 14:29

Israel's King Pekahiah

²³ In the fiftieth year of Judah's King Azariah, Pekahiah son of Menahem became king over Israel in Samaria, and he reigned two years. ²⁴ He did what was evil in the LORD's sight and did not turn away from the sins Jeroboam son of Nebat had caused Israel to commit. 1Kg 12:28-33

²⁵ Then his officer, Pekah son of Remaliah, conspired against him and struck him down in Samaria at the citadel of the king's palace

ᴬ15:10 Some LXX mss read *down at Ibleam*; Hb uncertain　ᴮ15:13 = Azariah, also in vv. 30,32,34
ᶜ15:19 = Tiglath-pileser　ᴰ15:19 Lit *1,000 talents*　ᴱ15:20 Lit *50 shekels*

— with Argob and Arieh.[A] There were fifty Gileadite men with Pekah. He killed Pekahiah and became king in his place. 2Ch 28:6

²⁶ As for the rest of the events of Pekahiah's reign, along with all his accomplishments, they are written in the Historical Record of Israel's Kings.

Israel's King Pekah

²⁷ In the fifty-second year of Judah's King Azariah, Pekah son of Remaliah became king over Israel in Samaria, and he reigned twenty years. ²⁸ He did what was evil in the LORD's sight. He did not turn away from the sins Jeroboam son of Nebat had caused Israel to commit.

²⁹ In the days of King Pekah of Israel, King Tiglath-pileser of Assyria came and captured Ijon, Abel-beth-maacah, Janoah, Kedesh, Hazor, Gilead, and Galilee — all the land of Naphtali — and deported the people to Assyria. 1Kg 15:29; 1Ch 5:6,26

³⁰ Then Hoshea son of Elah organized a conspiracy against Pekah son of Remaliah. He attacked him, killed him, and became king in his place in the twentieth year of Jotham son of Uzziah. 2Kg 17:1

³¹ As for the rest of the events of Pekah's reign, along with all his accomplishments, they are written in the Historical Record of Israel's Kings.

Judah's King Jotham

³² In the second year of Israel's King Pekah son of Remaliah, Jotham son of Uzziah became king of Judah. ³³ He was twenty-five years old when he became king, and he reigned sixteen years in Jerusalem. His mother's name was Jerusha daughter of Zadok. ³⁴ He did what was right in the LORD's sight just as his father Uzziah had done. ³⁵ Yet the high places were not taken away; the people continued sacrificing and burning incense on the high places. 2Kg 15:5,7

Jotham built the Upper Gate of the LORD's temple. ³⁶ The rest of the events of Jotham's reign, along with all his accomplishments, are written in the Historical Record of Judah's Kings. ³⁷ In those days the LORD began sending Aram's King Rezin and Pekah son of Remaliah against Judah. ³⁸ Jotham rested with his fathers and was buried with his fathers in the city of his ancestor David. His son Ahaz became king in his place. 2Ch 27:3; Is 7:1

Judah's King Ahaz

16 In the seventeenth year of Pekah son of Remaliah, Ahaz son of Jotham became king of Judah. ² Ahaz was twenty years old when he became king, and he reigned sixteen years in Jerusalem. He did not do what was right in the sight of the LORD his God like his ancestor David ³ but walked in the ways of the kings of Israel. He even sacrificed his son in the fire,[B] imitating the detestable practices of the nations the LORD had dispossessed before the Israelites. ⁴ He sacrificed and burned incense on the high places, on the hills, and under every green tree. 2Ch 28:1-4; Is 1:1

⁵ Then Aram's King Rezin and Israel's King Pekah son of Remaliah came to wage war against Jerusalem. They besieged Ahaz but were not able to conquer him. ⁶ At that time Aram's King Rezin recovered Elath for Aram and expelled

---

[A]15:25 Hb obscure   [B]16:3 Lit even made his son pass through the fire

¹⁷ Then the king of Assyria sent the field marshal, the chief of staff, and his royal spokesman, along with a massive army, from Lachish to King Hezekiah at Jerusalem. They advanced and came to Jerusalem, and ᴬ they took their position by the aqueduct of the upper pool, by the road to the Launderer's Field. ¹⁸ They called for the king, but Eliakim son of Hilkiah, who was in charge of the palace, Shebnah the court secretary, and Joah son of Asaph, the court historian, came out to them. Is 7:3; 20:1

The Royal Spokesman's Speech

¹⁹ Then the royal spokesman said to them, "Tell Hezekiah this is what the great king, the king of Assyria, says: 'What are you relying on?ᴮ ²⁰ You think mere words are strategy and strength for war. Who are you now relying on so that you have rebelled against me? ²¹ Now look, you are relying on Egypt, that splintered reed of a staff that will pierce the hand of anyone who grabs it and leans on it. This is what Pharaoh king of Egypt is to all who rely on him. ²² Suppose you say to me, "We rely on the LORD our God." Isn't he the one whose high places and altars Hezekiah has removed, saying to Judah and to Jerusalem, "You must worship at this altar in Jerusalem"?' 2Kg 18:5; 2Ch 32:10; Is 36:4-22

²³ "So now, make a bargain with my master the king of Assyria. I'll give you two thousand horses if you're able to supply riders for them! ²⁴ How then can you drive back a single officer among the least of my master's servants? How can you rely on Egypt for chariots and for horsemen? ²⁵ Now, have I attacked this place to destroy it without the LORD's approval? The LORD said to me, 'Attack this land and destroy it.' " 2Kg 19:6,22; 24:3; 2Ch 35:21; Is 10:8

²⁶ Then Eliakim son of Hilkiah, Shebnah, and Joah said to the royal spokesman, "Please speak to your servants in Aramaic, since we understand it. Don't speak with us in Hebrewᶜ within earshot of the people on the wall." Ezr 4:7; Dn 2:4

²⁷ But the royal spokesman said to them, "Has my master sent me to speak these words only to your master and to you? Hasn't he also sent me to the men who sit on the wall, destined with you to eat their own excrement and drink their own urine?" Is 36:11-12

²⁸ The royal spokesman stood and called out loudly in Hebrew: "Hear the word of the great king, the king of Assyria. ²⁹ This is what the king says: 'Don't let Hezekiah deceive you; he can't rescue you from my power. ³⁰ Don't let Hezekiah persuade you to rely on the LORD by saying, "Certainly the LORD will rescue us! This city will not be handed over to the king of Assyria." '

³¹ "Don't listen to Hezekiah, for this is what the king of Assyria says: 'Make peaceᴰ with me and surrender to me. Then each of you may eat from his own vine and his own fig tree, and each may drink water from his own cistern ³² until I come and take you away to a land like your own land — a land of grain and new wine, a land of bread and vineyards, a land of olive trees and honey — so that you may live and not die. But don't listen to Hezekiah when he misleads you, saying,

ᴬ18:17 LXX, Syr, Vg; MT reads and came and ᴮ18:19 Lit 'What is this trust which you trust ᶜ18:26 Lit Judahite, also in v. 28 ᴰ18:31 Lit a blessing

"The LORD will rescue us." ³³ Has any of the gods of the nations ever rescued his land from the power of the king of Assyria? ³⁴ Where are the gods of Hamath and Arpad? Where are the gods of Sepharvaim, Hena, and Ivvah?ᴬ Have they rescued Samaria from my power? ³⁵ Who among all the gods of the lands has rescued his land from my power? So will the LORD rescue Jerusalem from my power?'"

³⁶ But the people kept silent; they did not answer him at all, for the king's command was, "Don't answer him." ³⁷ Then Eliakim son of Hilkiah, who was in charge of the palace, Shebna the court secretary, and Joah son of Asaph, the court historian, came to Hezekiah with their clothes torn and reported to him the words of the royal spokesman. 2Kg 6:30; 18:26; 19:2; Is 33:7

Hezekiah Seeks Isaiah's Counsel

19 When King Hezekiah heard their report, he tore his clothes, covered himself with sackcloth, and went into the LORD's temple. ² He sent Eliakim, who was in charge of the palace, Shebna the court secretary, and the leading priests, who were wearing sackcloth, to the prophet Isaiah son of Amoz. ³ They said to him, "This is what Hezekiah says: 'Today is a day of distress, rebuke, and disgrace, for children have come to the point of birth, but there is no strength to deliver them. ⁴ Perhaps the LORD your God will hear all the words of the royal spokesman, whom his master the king of Assyria sent to mock the living God, and will rebuke him for the words that the

LORD your God has heard. Therefore, offer a prayer for the surviving remnant.'" 1Kg 21:27; 2Kg 18:37; Ps 69:11

⁵ So the servants of King Hezekiah went to Isaiah, ⁶ who said to them, "Tell your master, 'The LORD says this: Don't be afraid because of the words you have heard, with which the king of Assyria's attendants have blasphemed me. ⁷ I am about to put a spirit in him, and he will hear a rumor and return to his own land, where I will cause him to fall by the sword.'" 2Kg 18:17; Is 37:6

Sennacherib's Departing Threat

⁸ When the royal spokesman heard that the king of Assyria had pulled out of Lachish, he left and found him fighting against Libnah. ⁹ The king had heard concerning King Tirhakah of Cush, "Look, he has set out to fight against you." So he again sent messengers to Hezekiah, saying, ¹⁰ "Say this to King Hezekiah of Judah: 'Don't let your God, on whom you rely, deceive you by promising that Jerusalem will not be handed over to the king of Assyria. ¹¹ Look, you have heard what the kings of Assyria have done to all the countries: They completely destroyed them. Will you be rescued? ¹² Did the gods of the nations that my predecessors destroyed rescue them — nations such as Gozan, Haran, Rezeph, and the Edenites in Telassar? ¹³ Where is the king of Hamath, the king of Arpad, the king of the city ofᴮ Sepharvaim, Hena, or Ivvah?'" 2Kg 18:5; Is 37:8-13

Hezekiah's Prayer

¹⁴ Hezekiah took the letter from the messengers' hands, read it,

then went up to the LORD's temple, and spread it out before the LORD. **15** Then Hezekiah prayed before the LORD: 2Kg 5:7; Is 37:14-20

LORD God of Israel, enthroned between the cherubim, you are God — you alone — of all the kingdoms of the earth. You made the heavens and the earth. **16** Listen closely, LORD, and hear; open your eyes, LORD, and see. Hear the words that Sennacherib has sent to mock the living God. **17** LORD, it is true that the kings of Assyria have devastated the nations and their lands. **18** They have thrown their gods into the fire, for they were not gods but made by human hands — wood and stone. So they have destroyed them. **19** Now, LORD our God, please save us from his power so that all the kingdoms of the earth may know that you, LORD, are God — you alone. Gn 1:1; Ex 25:22

God's Answer Through Isaiah

20 Then Isaiah son of Amoz sent a message to Hezekiah: "The LORD, the God of Israel says, 'I have heard your prayer to me about King Sennacherib of Assyria.' **21** This is the word the LORD has spoken against him: 2Kg 20:5; Is 37:21-35

Virgin Daughter Zion Jr 14:17
despises you and scorns you;
Daughter Jerusalem
shakes her head
behind your back. Ps 22:7-8
22 Who is it you mocked
and blasphemed? 2Kg 19:4,6
Against whom
have you raised your voice
and lifted your eyes in pride?

Against the Holy One of Israel!
23 You have mocked the Lord A
through B your messengers.
You have said, 'With my
many chariots Ps 20:7; Jr 50:37
I have gone up to the heights
of the mountains,
to the far recesses
of Lebanon.
I cut down its tallest cedars,
its choice cypress trees.
I came to its farthest outpost,
its densest forest.
24 I dug wells
and drank water
in foreign lands.
I dried up all the streams
of Egypt Is 19:6
with the soles of my feet.'

25 Have you not heard? Is 40:21; 45:7
I designed it long ago;
I planned it in days gone by.
I have now brought it to pass,
and you have crushed
fortified cities
into piles of rubble.
26 Their inhabitants have
become powerless,
dismayed, and ashamed.
They are plants of the field,
tender grass,
grass on the rooftops, Ps 129:6
blasted by the east wind. C
27 But I know your sitting down,
your going out
and your coming in,
and your raging against me.
28 Because your raging
against me
and your arrogance
have reached my ears,
I will put my hook
in your nose Ezk 19:9; 29:4; 38:4

A**19:23** Many mss read LORD　B**19:23** Lit by the hand of　C**19:26** DSS; MT reads blasted before standing grain; Is 37:27

and my bit in your mouth;
I will make you go back
the way you came.

²⁹ "This will be the sign for you: This year you will eat what grows on its own, and in the second year what grows from that. But in the third year sow and reap, plant vineyards and eat their fruit. ³⁰ The surviving remnant of the house of Judah will again take root downward and bear fruit upward. ³¹ For a remnant will go out from Jerusalem, and survivors, from Mount Zion. The zeal of the LORD of Armies will accomplish this. Ex 3:14; 2Kg 20:8-9

³² Therefore, this is
   what the LORD says
   about the king of Assyria:
He will not enter this city,
   shoot an arrow here,
come before it with a shield,
   or build up a siege ramp
   against it. Is 8:7-10
³³ He will go back
   the way he came,
   and he will not enter this city.
   This is the LORD's declaration.
³⁴ I will defend this city
   and rescue it
for my sake and for the sake
   of my servant David." Is 31:5

Defeat and Death of Sennacherib

³⁵ That night the angel of the LORD went out and struck down one hundred eighty-five thousand in the camp of the Assyrians. When the people got up the next morning — there were all the dead bodies! ³⁶ So King Sennacherib of Assyria broke camp and left. He returned home and lived in Nineveh. 2Ch 32:21; Is 37:36

ᴬ20:3 Lit *what is good in your eyes*

³⁷ One day, while he was worshiping in the temple of his god Nisroch, his sons Adrammelech and Sharezer struck him down with the sword and escaped to the land of Ararat. Then his son Esar-haddon became king in his place. 2Kg 17:31

Hezekiah's Illness and Recovery

20 In those days Hezekiah became terminally ill. The prophet Isaiah son of Amoz came and said to him, "This is what the LORD says: 'Set your house in order, for you are about to die; you will not recover.'" 2Ch 32:24; Is 1:1; 2:1; 38:1-8

² Then Hezekiah turned his face to the wall and prayed to the LORD, ³ "Please, LORD, remember how I have walked before you faithfully and wholeheartedly and have done what pleases you."ᴬ And Hezekiah wept bitterly. 1Kg 21:4; Neh 5:19; 13:14,22,31

⁴ Isaiah had not yet gone out of the inner courtyard when the word of the LORD came to him: ⁵ "Go back and tell Hezekiah, the leader of my people, 'This is what the LORD God of your ancestor David says: I have heard your prayer; I have seen your tears. Look, I will heal you. On the third day from now you will go up to the LORD's temple. ⁶ I will add fifteen years to your life. I will rescue you and this city from the grasp of the king of Assyria. I will defend this city for my sake and for the sake of my servant David.'" 1Sm 9:16

⁷ Then Isaiah said, "Bring a lump of pressed figs." So they brought it and applied it to his infected skin, and he recovered. Is 38:21

⁸ Hezekiah had asked Isaiah, "What is the sign that the LORD will heal me and that I will go up to the LORD's temple on the third day?"

⁹ Isaiah said, "This is the sign to you from the LORD that he will do what he has promised: Should the shadow go ahead ten steps or go back ten steps?"   Is 38:7

¹⁰ Then Hezekiah answered, "It's easy for the shadow to lengthen ten steps. No, let the shadow go back ten steps." ¹¹ So the prophet Isaiah called out to the LORD, and he brought the shadow ᴬ back the ten steps it had descended on the stairway of Ahaz. ᴮ   Jos 10:12-14; Is 38:8

Hezekiah's Folly

¹² At that time Merodach-baladan ᶜ son of Baladan, king of Babylon, sent letters and a gift to Hezekiah since he heard that he had been sick. ¹³ Hezekiah listened to the letters and showed the envoys his whole treasure house — the silver, the gold, the spices, and the precious oil — and his armory, and everything that was found in his treasuries. There was nothing in his palace and in all his realm that Hezekiah did not show them.

¹⁴ Then the prophet Isaiah came to King Hezekiah and asked him, "Where did these men come from and what did they say to you?"

Hezekiah replied, "They came from a distant country, from Babylon."

¹⁵ Isaiah asked, "What have they seen in your palace?"

Hezekiah answered, "They have seen everything in my palace. There isn't anything in my treasuries that I didn't show them."

¹⁶ Then Isaiah said to Hezekiah, "Hear the word of the LORD: ¹⁷ 'Look, the days are coming when everything in your palace and all that your fathers have stored up until today will be carried off to Babylon; nothing will be left,' says the LORD. ¹⁸ 'Some of your descendants — who come from you, whom you father — will be taken away, and they will become eunuchs ᴰ in the palace of the king of Babylon.'"

¹⁹ Then Hezekiah said to Isaiah, "The word of the LORD that you have spoken is good," for he thought: Why not, if there will be peace and security during my lifetime?

Hezekiah's Death

²⁰ The rest of the events of Hezekiah's reign, along with all his might and how he made the pool and the tunnel and brought water into the city, are written in the Historical Record of Judah's Kings. ²¹ Hezekiah rested with his fathers, and his son Manasseh became king in his place.   2Ch 32:30; 2Kg 16:19; Neh 3:16; Is 7:3

Judah's King Manasseh

21 Manasseh was twelve years old when he became king, and he reigned fifty-five years in Jerusalem. His mother's name was Hephzibah. ² He did what was evil in the LORD's sight, imitating the detestable practices of the nations that the LORD had dispossessed before the Israelites. ³ He rebuilt the high places that his father Hezekiah had destroyed and reestablished the altars for Baal. He made an Asherah, as King Ahab of Israel had done; he also bowed in worship to all the stars in the sky and served them. ⁴ He built altars in the

---

ᴬ 20:11 Lit *shadow on the steps*   ᴮ 20:11 Tg, Vg; DSS read *on the steps of Ahaz's roof chamber*; Is 38:8   ᶜ 20:12 Some Hb mss, LXX, Syr, Tg, some Vg mss, Is 39:1; other Hb mss read *Berodach-baladan*   ᴰ 20:18 Or *court officials*

LORD's temple, where the LORD had said, "Jerusalem is where I will put my name." ⁵ He built altars to all the stars in the sky in both courtyards of the LORD's temple. ⁶ He sacrificed his son in the fire, ᴬ practiced witchcraft and divination, and consulted mediums and spiritists. He did a huge amount of evil in the LORD's sight, angering him.

⁷ Manasseh set up the carved image of Asherah, which he made, in the temple that the LORD had spoken about to David and his son Solomon: "I will establish my name forever in this temple and in Jerusalem, which I have chosen out of all the tribes of Israel. ⁸ I will never again cause the feet of the Israelites to wander from the land I gave to their ancestors if only they will be careful to do all I have commanded them — the whole law that my servant Moses commanded them." ⁹ But they did not listen; Manasseh caused them to stray so that they did worse evil than the nations the LORD had destroyed before the Israelites. Dt 12:5; 2Sm 7:10; 1Kg 9:1-9; 11:32

¹⁰ The LORD said through his servants the prophets, ¹¹ "Since King Manasseh of Judah has committed all these detestable acts — worse evil than the Amorites who preceded him had done — and by means of his idols has also caused Judah to sin, ¹² this is what the LORD God of Israel says: 'I am about to bring such disaster on Jerusalem and Judah that everyone who hears about it will shudder. ᴮ ¹³ I will stretch over Jerusalem the measuring line used on Samaria and the mason's level used on the house of Ahab, and I will wipe Jerusalem clean as one wipes a bowl — wiping it and turning it upside down. ¹⁴ I will abandon the remnant of my inheritance and hand them over to their enemies. They will become plunder and spoil to all their enemies, ¹⁵ because they have done what is evil in my sight and have angered me from the day their ancestors came out of Egypt until today.' " Gn 15:16; 1Sm 3:11; 1Kg 21:16; 2Kg 21:2; 24:3-4

¹⁶ Manasseh also shed so much innocent blood that he filled Jerusalem with it from one end to another. This was in addition to his sin that he caused Judah to commit, so that they did what was evil in the LORD's sight. 2Kg 24:4

Manasseh's Death

¹⁷ The rest of the events of Manasseh's reign, along with all his accomplishments and the sin that he committed, are written in the Historical Record of Judah's Kings. ¹⁸ Manasseh rested with his fathers and was buried in the garden of his own house, the garden of Uzza. His son Amon became king in his place. 2Kg 20:20; 2Ch 33:18-20

Judah's King Amon

¹⁹ Amon was twenty-two years old when he became king, and he reigned two years in Jerusalem. His mother's name was Meshullemeth daughter of Haruz; she was from Jotbah. ²⁰ He did what was evil in the LORD's sight, just as his father Manasseh had done. ²¹ He walked in all the ways his father had walked; he served the idols his father had served, and he bowed in worship to them. ²² He abandoned the LORD God of his ancestors and did not walk in the ways of the LORD.

ᴬ **21:6** Lit *He made his son pass through the fire*   ᴮ **21:12** Lit *about it, his two ears will tingle*; Hb obscure

²³ Amon's servants conspired against him and put the king to death in his own house. ²⁴ The common people[A] killed all who had conspired against King Amon, and they made his son Josiah king in his place.   2Kg 12:20; 14:5,19; 22:1

²⁵ The rest of the events of Amon's reign, along with his accomplishments, are written in the Historical Record of Judah's Kings. ²⁶ He was buried in his tomb in the garden of Uzza, and his son Josiah became king in his place.

Judah's King Josiah

22 Josiah was eight years old when he became king, and he reigned thirty-one years in Jerusalem. His mother's name was Jedidah the daughter of Adaiah; she was from Bozkath. ² He did what was right in the LORD's sight and walked in all the ways of his ancestor David; he did not turn to the right or the left.   Jos 1:7; 15:39; 2Ch 34:1-2

Josiah Repairs the Temple

³ In the eighteenth year of King Josiah, the king sent the court secretary Shaphan son of Azaliah, son of Meshullam, to the LORD's temple, saying, ⁴ "Go up to the high priest Hilkiah so that he may total up the silver brought into the LORD's temple — the silver the doorkeepers have collected from the people. ⁵ It is to be given to those doing the work — those who oversee the LORD's temple. They in turn are to give it to the workmen in the LORD's temple to repair the damage. ⁶ They are to give it to the carpenters, builders, and masons to buy timber and quarried stone to repair the temple. ⁷ But no accounting is to

be required from them for the silver given to them since they work with integrity."   2Kg 12:4,9-10; 2Ch 34:8

The Book of the Law Found

⁸ The high priest Hilkiah told the court secretary Shaphan, "I have found the book of the law in the LORD's temple," and he gave the book to Shaphan, who read it. ⁹ Then the court secretary Shaphan went to the king and reported,[B] "Your servants have emptied out the silver that was found in the temple and have given it to those doing the work — those who oversee the LORD's temple." ¹⁰ Then the court secretary Shaphan told the king, "The priest Hilkiah has given me a book," and Shaphan read it in the presence of the king.   Dt 17:18-20

¹¹ When the king heard the words of the book of the law, he tore his clothes. ¹² Then he commanded the priest Hilkiah, Ahikam son of Shaphan, Achbor son of Micaiah, the court secretary Shaphan, and the king's servant Asaiah: ¹³ "Go and inquire of the LORD for me, the people, and all Judah about the words in this book that has been found. For great is the LORD's wrath that is kindled against us because our ancestors have not obeyed the words of this book in order to do everything written about us."   Gn 37:34; Jos 7:6; 2Kg 25:22; Jr 26:24

Huldah's Prophecy of Judgment

¹⁴ So the priest Hilkiah, Ahikam, Achbor, Shaphan, and Asaiah went to the prophetess Huldah, wife of Shallum son of Tikvah, son of Harhas, keeper of the wardrobe. She lived in Jerusalem in the Second District. They spoke with her.

[A]21:24 Lit The people of the land [B]22:9 Lit and returned a word to the king and said

¹⁵ She said to them, "This is what the LORD God of Israel says: Say to the man who sent you to me, ¹⁶ 'This is what the LORD says: I am about to bring disaster on this place and on its inhabitants, fulfilling ᴬ all the words of the book that the king of Judah has read, ¹⁷ because they have abandoned me and burned incense to other gods in order to anger me with all the work of their hands. My wrath will be kindled against this place, and it will not be quenched.' ¹⁸ Say this to the king of Judah who sent you to inquire of the LORD: 'This is what the LORD God of Israel says: As for the words that you heard, ¹⁹ because your heart was tender and you humbled yourself before the LORD when you heard what I spoke against this place and against its inhabitants, that they would become a desolation and a curse, and because you have torn your clothes and wept before me, I myself have heard' — this is the LORD's declaration. ²⁰ 'Therefore, I will indeed gather you to your fathers, and you will be gathered to your grave in peace. Your eyes will not see all the disaster that I am bringing on this place.'"

Then they reported ᴮ to the king.

Covenant Renewal

23 So the king sent messengers, and they gathered all the elders of Judah and Jerusalem to him. ² Then the king went to the LORD's temple with all the men of Judah and all the inhabitants of Jerusalem, as well as the priests and the prophets — all the people from the youngest to the oldest. He read in their hearing all the words of the book of the covenant that had been found in the LORD's temple. ³ Next, the king stood by the pillar ᶜ and made a covenant in the LORD's presence to follow the LORD and to keep his commands, his decrees, and his statutes with all his heart and with all his soul in order to carry out the words of this covenant that were written in this book; all the people agreed to ᴰ the covenant. Dt 31:10-13; 2Kg 10:1; 2Ch 34:29-32

Josiah's Reforms

⁴ Then the king commanded the high priest Hilkiah and the priests of the second rank and the doorkeepers to bring out of the LORD's sanctuary all the articles made for Baal, Asherah, and all the stars in the sky. He burned them outside Jerusalem in the fields of the Kidron and carried their ashes to Bethel. ⁵ Then he did away with the idolatrous priests the kings of Judah had appointed to burn incense at the high places in the cities of Judah and in the areas surrounding Jerusalem. They had burned incense to Baal, and to the sun, moon, constellations, and all the stars in the sky. ⁶ He brought out the Asherah pole from the LORD's temple to the Kidron Valley outside Jerusalem. He burned it at the Kidron Valley, beat it to dust, and threw its dust on the graves of the common people. ᴱ ⁷ He also tore down the houses of the male cult prostitutes that were in the LORD's temple, in which the women were weaving tapestries ᶠ for Asherah. 2Kg 22:8,14; 25:18; Jr 35:4

⁸ Then Josiah brought all the priests from the cities of Judah,

---

ᴬ**22:16** *fulfilling* supplied for clarity   ᴮ**22:20** Lit *returned a word*   ᶜ**23:3** 2Ch 34:31 reads *platform*
ᴰ**23:3** Lit *people took a stand in*   ᴱ**23:6** Lit *the sons of the people*   ᶠ**23:7** Or *clothing*

and he defiled the high places from Geba to Beer-sheba, where the priests had burned incense. He tore down the high places of the city gates at the entrance of the gate of Joshua the governor of the city (on the left at the city gate). ⁹ The priests of the high places, however, did not come up to the altar of the LORD in Jerusalem; instead, they ate unleavened bread with their fellow priests. Jos 21:17; 1Kg 15:22; 2Kg 18:4

¹⁰ He defiled Topheth, which is in Ben Hinnom Valley, so that no one could sacrifice his son or daughter in the fire ᴬ to Molech. ¹¹ He did away with the horses that the kings of Judah had dedicated to the sun. They had been at the entrance of the LORD's temple in the precincts by the chamber of Nathan-melech, the eunuch. He also burned the chariots of the sun. Is 30:33; Jr 7:31-32

¹² The king tore down the altars that the kings of Judah had made on the roof of Ahaz's upper chamber. He also tore down the altars that Manasseh had made in the two courtyards of the LORD's temple. Then he smashed them ᴮ there and threw their dust into the Kidron Valley. ¹³ The king also defiled the high places that were across from Jerusalem, to the south of the Mount of Destruction, which King Solomon of Israel had built for Ashtoreth, the abhorrent idol of the Sidonians; for Chemosh, the abhorrent idol of Moab; and for Milcom, the detestable idol of the Ammonites. ¹⁴ He broke the sacred pillars into pieces, cut down the Asherah poles, then filled their places with human bones. 2Kg 20:11; Jr 19:13; Zph 1:4-5

¹⁵ He even tore down the altar at Bethel and the high place that had been made by Jeroboam son of Nebat, who caused Israel to sin. He burned the high place, crushed it to dust, and burned the Asherah. ¹⁶ As Josiah turned, he saw the tombs there on the mountain. He sent someone to take the bones out of the tombs, and he burned them on the altar. He defiled it according to the word of the LORD proclaimed by the man of God ᶜ who proclaimed these things. ¹⁷ Then he said, "What is this monument I see?" 1Kg 12:28-33; 13:1-3; 2Kg 23:6

The men of the city told him, "It is the tomb of the man of God who came from Judah and proclaimed these things that you have done to the altar at Bethel." 1Kg 13:1,31-32

¹⁸ So he said, "Let him rest. Don't let anyone disturb his bones." So they left his bones undisturbed with the bones of the prophet who came from Samaria. 1Kg 13:29-31

¹⁹ Josiah also removed all the shrines of the high places that were in the cities of Samaria, which the kings of Israel had made to anger the LORD. Josiah did the same things to them that he had done at Bethel. ²⁰ He slaughtered on the altars all the priests of those high places, and he burned human bones on the altars. Then he returned to Jerusalem. 1Kg 13:2; 2Ch 34:6-7

Passover Observed

²¹ The king commanded all the people, "Observe the Passover of the LORD your God as written in the book of the covenant." ²² No such Passover had ever been observed

---

ᴬ **23:10** Lit *could make his son or daughter pass through the fire*   ᴮ**23:12** Text emended; MT reads *he ran from*   ᶜ**23:16** LXX adds *when Jeroboam stood by the altar of the feast. And he turned and raised his eyes to the tomb of the man of God* from the time of the judges who judged Israel through the entire time of the kings of Israel and Judah. ²³ But in the eighteenth year of King Josiah, the LORD's Passover was observed in Jerusalem.

Further Zeal for the LORD

²⁴ In addition, Josiah eradicated the mediums, the spiritists, household idols, images, and all the abhorrent things that were seen in the land of Judah and in Jerusalem. He did this in order to carry out the words of the law that were written in the book that the priest Hilkiah found in the LORD's temple. ²⁵ Before him there was no king like him who turned to the LORD with all his heart and with all his soul and with all his strength according to all the law of Moses, and no one like him arose after him. Gn 31:19; Lv 19:31; Dt 7:26; 2Kg 16:3; 21:6

²⁶ In spite of all that, the LORD did not turn from the fury of his intense burning anger, which burned against Judah because of all the affronts with which Manasseh had angered him. ²⁷ For the LORD had said, "I will also remove Judah from my presence just as I have removed Israel. I will reject this city Jerusalem, that I have chosen, and the temple about which I said, 'My name will be there.'" 2Kg 21:11-13; Jr 15:4

Josiah's Death

²⁸ The rest of the events of Josiah's reign, along with all his accomplishments, are written in the Historical Record of Judah's Kings. ²⁹ During his reign, Pharaoh Neco king of Egypt marched up to help the king of Assyria at the Euphrates River. King Josiah went to confront him, and at Megiddo when Neco saw him he killed him. ³⁰ From Megiddo his servants carried his dead body in a chariot, brought him into Jerusalem, and buried him in his own tomb. Then the common people^A took Jehoahaz son of Josiah, anointed him, and made him king in place of his father. 2Ch 35:20-27

Judah's King Jehoahaz

³¹ Jehoahaz was twenty-three years old when he became king, and he reigned three months in Jerusalem. His mother's name was Hamutal daughter of Jeremiah; she was from Libnah. ³² He did what was evil in the LORD's sight just as his ancestors had done. ³³ Pharaoh Neco imprisoned him at Riblah in the land of Hamath to keep him from reigning in Jerusalem, and he imposed on the land a fine of seventy-five hundred pounds^B of silver and seventy-five pounds^C of gold. 2Kg 24:18; 1Ch 3:15; 2Ch 36:2-3; Jr 22:11

Judah's King Jehoiakim

³⁴ Then Pharaoh Neco made Eliakim son of Josiah king in place of his father Josiah and changed Eliakim's name to Jehoiakim. But Neco took Jehoahaz and went to Egypt, and he died there. ³⁵ So Jehoiakim gave the silver and the gold to Pharaoh, but at Pharaoh's command he taxed the land to give it. He exacted the silver and the gold from the common people, each according to his assessment, to give it to Pharaoh Neco. 1Ch 3:15; 2Ch 36:4-5

³⁶ Jehoiakim was twenty-five years old when he became king, and he reigned eleven years in Jerusalem. His mother's name was Zebidah daughter of Pedaiah; she

^A23:30 Lit the people of the land, also in v. 35　^B23:33 Lit 100 talents　^C23:33 Lit one talent

was from Rumah. ³⁷ He did what was evil in the LORD's sight just as his ancestors had done.   Jr 22:13-19

Jehoiakim's Rebellion and Death

24 During Jehoiakim's reign, King Nebuchadnezzar of Babylon attacked. Jehoiakim became his vassal for three years, and then he turned and rebelled against him. ² The LORD sent Chaldean, Aramean, Moabite, and Ammonite raiders against Jehoiakim. He sent them against Judah to destroy it, according to the word of the LORD he had spoken through his servants the prophets. ³ Indeed, this happened to Judah at the LORD's command to remove them from his presence. It was because of the sins of Manasseh, according to all he had done, ⁴ and also because of all the innocent blood he had shed. He had filled Jerusalem with innocent blood, and the LORD was not willing to forgive. 2Kg 24:10-11; 2Ch 36:6-8

⁵ The rest of the events of Jehoiakim's reign, along with all his accomplishments, are written in the Historical Record of Judah's Kings. ⁶ Jehoiakim rested with his fathers, and his son Jehoiachin became king in his place.   2Kg 23:28

⁷ Now the king of Egypt did not march out of his land again, for the king of Babylon took everything that had belonged to the king of Egypt, from the Brook of Egypt to the Euphrates River.   Jr 37:5-7; 46:2

Judah's King Jehoiachin

⁸ Jehoiachin was eighteen years old when he became king, and he reigned three months in Jerusalem. His mother's name was Nehushta daughter of Elnathan; she was from Jerusalem. ⁹ He did what was evil in the LORD's sight just as his father had done. 2Ch 36:9; Jr 22:24-30

Deportations to Babylon

¹⁰ At that time the servants of King Nebuchadnezzar of Babylon marched up to Jerusalem, and the city came under siege. ¹¹ King Nebuchadnezzar of Babylon came to the city while his servants were besieging it. ¹² King Jehoiachin of Judah, along with his mother, his servants, his commanders, and his officials, ᴬ surrendered to the king of Babylon.   2Kg 24:1; 2Ch 36:10; Dn 1:1

So the king of Babylon took him captive in the eighth year of his reign. ¹³ He also carried off from there all the treasures of the LORD's temple and the treasures of the king's palace, and he cut into pieces all the gold articles that King Solomon of Israel had made for the LORD's sanctuary, just as the LORD had predicted. ¹⁴ He deported all Jerusalem and all the commanders and all the best soldiers — ten thousand captives including all the craftsmen and metalsmiths. Except for the poorest people of the land, no one remained. 1Kg 7:48-50; 2Kg 20:16-18

¹⁵ Nebuchadnezzar deported Jehoiachin to Babylon. He took the king's mother, the king's wives, his officials, and the leading men of the land into exile from Jerusalem to Babylon. ¹⁶ The king of Babylon brought captive into Babylon all seven thousand of the best soldiers and one thousand craftsmen and metalsmiths — all strong and fit for war. ¹⁷ And the king of Babylon made Mattaniah, Jehoiachin's ᴮ uncle, king in his place and changed his name to Zedekiah. 2Ch 36:10; Jr 1:3

ᴬ**24:12** Or *eunuchs*   ᴮ**24:17** Lit *his*

Judah's King Zedekiah

[18] Zedekiah was twenty-one years old when he became king, and he reigned eleven years in Jerusalem. His mother's name was Hamutal daughter of Jeremiah; she was from Libnah. [19] Zedekiah did what was evil in the LORD's sight just as Jehoiakim had done. [20] Because of the LORD's anger, it came to the point in Jerusalem and Judah that he finally banished them from his presence. Then Zedekiah rebelled against the king of Babylon.

Nebuchadnezzar's Siege of Jerusalem

25 In the ninth year of Zedekiah's reign, on the tenth day of the tenth month, King Nebuchadnezzar of Babylon advanced against Jerusalem with his entire army. They laid siege to the city and built a siege wall against it all around. [2] The city was under siege until King Zedekiah's eleventh year.

[3] By the ninth day of the fourth month the famine was so severe in the city that the common people had no food. [4] Then the city was broken into, and all the warriors fled at night by way of the city gate between the two walls near the king's garden, even though the Chaldeans surrounded the city. As the king made his way along the route to the Arabah, [5] the Chaldean army pursued him and overtook him in the plains of Jericho. Zedekiah's entire army left him and scattered. [6] The Chaldeans seized the king and brought him up to the king of Babylon at Riblah, and they passed sentence on him. [7] They slaughtered Zedekiah's sons before his eyes. Finally, the king of Babylon blinded Zedekiah, bound him in bronze chains, and took him to Babylon.   2Kg 6:24-25; Lm 4:9-10; Jr 39:2

Jerusalem Destroyed

[8] On the seventh day of the fifth month — which was the nineteenth year of King Nebuchadnezzar of Babylon — Nebuzaradan, the captain of the guards, a servant of the king of Babylon, entered Jerusalem. [9] He burned the LORD's temple, the king's palace, and all the houses of Jerusalem; he burned down all the great houses. [10] The whole Chaldean army with the captain of the guards tore down the walls surrounding Jerusalem. [11] Nebuzaradan, the captain of the guards, deported the rest of the people who remained in the city, the deserters who had defected to the king of Babylon, and the rest of the population. [12] But the captain of the guards left some of the poorest of the land to be vinedressers and farmers.   Jr 40:7

[13] Now the Chaldeans broke into pieces the bronze pillars of the LORD's temple, the water carts, and the bronze basin,[A] which were in the LORD's temple, and carried the bronze to Babylon. [14] They also took the pots, shovels, wick trimmers, dishes, and all the bronze articles used in the priests' service. [15] The captain of the guards took away the firepans and sprinkling basins — whatever was gold or silver.   Jr 20:5

[16] As for the two pillars, the one basin, and the water carts that Solomon had made for the LORD's temple, the weight of the bronze of all these articles was beyond measure. [17] One pillar was twenty-seven feet[B] tall and had a bronze capital on top of it. The capital, encircled

A 25:13 Lit sea   B 25:17 Lit 18 cubits

by a grating and pomegranates of bronze, stood five feet[A] high. The second pillar was the same, with its own grating. 1Kg 7:15-22,47

[18] The captain of the guards also took away Seraiah the chief priest, Zephaniah the priest of the second rank, and the three doorkeepers. [19] From the city he took a court official[B] who had been appointed over the warriors; five trusted royal aides[C] found in the city; the secretary of the commander of the army, who enlisted the people of the land for military duty; and sixty men from the common people[D] who were found within the city. [20] Nebuzaradan, the captain of the guards, took them and brought them to the king of Babylon at Riblah. [21] The king of Babylon put them to death at Riblah in the land of Hamath. So Judah went into exile from its land. Jr 21:1; 39:9-13

Gedaliah Made Governor

[22] King Nebuchadnezzar of Babylon appointed Gedaliah son of Ahikam, son of Shaphan, over the rest of the people he left in the land of Judah. [23] When all the commanders of the armies — they and their men — heard that the king of Babylon had appointed Gedaliah, they came to Gedaliah at Mizpah. The commanders included Ishmael son of Nethaniah, Johanan son of Kareah, Seraiah son of Tanhumeth the Netophathite, and Jaazaniah son of the Maacathite — they and their men. [24] Gedaliah swore an oath to them and their men, assuring them, "Don't be afraid of the servants of the Chaldeans. Live in the land and serve the king of Babylon, and it will go well for you." Is 1:9; Jr 39:14; 40:7-9

[25] In the seventh month, however, Ishmael son of Nethaniah, son of Elishama, of the royal family, came with ten men and struck down Gedaliah, and he died. Also, they killed the Judeans and the Chaldeans who were with him at Mizpah. [26] Then all the people, from the youngest to the oldest, and the commanders of the army, left and went to Egypt, for they were afraid of the Chaldeans. Is 30:2; Jr 41:1-2; 43:4-7

Jehoiachin Pardoned

[27] On the twenty-seventh day of the twelfth month of the thirty-seventh year of the exile of Judah's King Jehoiachin, in the year Evil-merodach became king of Babylon, he pardoned King Jehoiachin of Judah and released him[E] from prison. [28] He spoke kindly to him and set his throne over the thrones of the kings who were with him in Babylon. [29] So Jehoiachin changed his prison clothes, and he dined regularly in the presence of the king of Babylon for the rest of his life. [30] As for his allowance, a regular allowance was given to him by the king, a portion for each day, for the rest of his life. Gn 40:13,20; 2Kg 24:12; Jr 52:31-34

[A]25:17 Lit three cubits   [B]25:19 Or eunuch   [C]25:19 Lit five men who look on the king's face   [D]25:19 Lit the people of the land   [E]25:27 and released him supplied for clarity

1 CHRONICLES

From Adam to Abraham

1 Adam, Seth, Enosh, Gn 4:25–5:32
² Kenan, Mahalalel, Jared,
³ Enoch, Methuselah, Lamech,
⁴ Noah, Noah's sons:ᴬ
Shem, Ham, and Japheth.

⁵ Japheth's sons: Gomer,
Magog, Madai, Javan, Tubal,
Meshech, and Tiras. Gn 10:2-4
⁶ Gomer's sons: Ashkenaz,
Riphath,ᴮ and Togarmah.
⁷ Javan's sons: Elishah,
Tarshish, Kittim, and
Rodanim.ᶜ

⁸ Ham's sons: Cush, Mizraim,ᴰ
Put, and Canaan.
⁹ Cush's sons: Seba, Havilah,
Sabta, Raama, and Sabteca.
Raama's sons: Sheba and
Dedan.
¹⁰ Cush fathered Nimrod, who
was the first to become a great
warrior on earth.
¹¹ Mizraim fathered the
people of Lud, Anam, Lehab,
Naphtuh, ¹² Pathrus, Casluh (the
Philistines came from them),
and Caphtor. Gn 10:13-18; Dt 2:23; Am 9:7
¹³ Canaan fathered Sidon as his
firstborn and Heth, ¹⁴ as well
as the Jebusites, Amorites,
Girgashites, ¹⁵ Hivites, Arkites,
Sinites, ¹⁶ Arvadites, Zemarites,
and Hamathites.

¹⁷ Shem's sons: Elam, Asshur,
Arpachshad, Lud, Aram, Uz,
Hul, Gether, and Meshech.

¹⁸ Arpachshad fathered
Shelah, and Shelah fathered
Eber. ¹⁹ Two sons were born
to Eber. One of them was
named Pelegᴱ because the
earth was divided during
his lifetime, and the name
of his brother was Joktan.
²⁰ Joktan fathered Almodad,
Sheleph, Hazarmaveth, Jerah,
²¹ Hadoram, Uzal, Diklah,
²² Ebal, Abimael, Sheba,
²³ Ophir, Havilah, and Jobab.
All of these were Joktan's
sons.

²⁴ Shem, Arpachshad, Shelah,
²⁵ Eber, Peleg, Reu,
²⁶ Serug, Nahor, Terah,
²⁷ and Abram (that is,
Abraham).

Abraham's Descendants

²⁸ Abraham's sons: Isaac
and Ishmael.

²⁹ These are their family
records: Nebaioth, Ishmael's
firstborn, Kedar, Adbeel,
Mibsam, ³⁰ Mishma, Dumah,
Massa, Hadad, Tema, ³¹ Jetur,
Naphish, and Kedemah.
These were Ishmael's sons.

³² The sons born to Keturah,
Abraham's concubine: Zimran,
Jokshan, Medan, Midian,
Ishbak, and Shuah. Gn 25:1-4
Jokshan's sons: Sheba and
Dedan.

ᴬ **1:4** LXX; MT omits *Noah's sons* ᴮ **1:6** Some Hb mss, LXX, Vg; other Hb mss read *Diphath* ; Gn 10:3
ᶜ **1:7** Some Hb mss, Syr read *Dodanim* ; Gn 10:4 ᴰ **1:8** = Egypt ᴱ **1:19** = Division

³³ Midian's sons: Ephah, Epher, Hanoch, Abida, and Eldaah. All of these were Keturah's descendants.

³⁴ Abraham fathered Isaac. Isaac's sons: Esau and Israel. ³⁵ Esau's sons: Eliphaz, Reuel, Jeush, Jalam, and Korah. ³⁶ Eliphaz's sons: Teman, Omar, Zephi, Gatam, and Kenaz; and by Timna, Amalek. ᴬ ³⁷ Reuel's sons: Nahath, Zerah, Shammah, and Mizzah.

The Edomites

³⁸ Seir's sons: Lotan, Shobal, Zibeon, Anah, Dishon, Ezer, and Dishan. Gn 36:20-30 ³⁹ Lotan's sons: Hori and Homam. Timna was Lotan's sister. ⁴⁰ Shobal's sons: Alian, Manahath, Ebal, Shephi, and Onam. Zibeon's sons: Aiah and Anah. ⁴¹ Anah's son: Dishon. Dishon's sons: Hamran, Eshban, Ithran, and Cheran. ⁴² Ezer's sons: Bilhan, Zaavan, and Jaakan. Dishan's sons: Uz and Aran.

⁴³ These were the kings who reigned in the land of Edom Gn 36:31-39 before any king reigned over the Israelites: Bela son of Beor. Bela's town was named Dinhabah. ⁴⁴ When Bela died, Jobab son of Zerah from Bozrah reigned in his place. Is 34:6 ⁴⁵ When Jobab died, Husham from the land of the Temanites reigned in his place. Jb 2:11 ⁴⁶ When Husham died, Hadad son of Bedad, who defeated Midian in the territory of Moab, reigned in his place. Hadad's town was named Avith. ⁴⁷ When Hadad died, Samlah from Masrekah reigned in his place. ⁴⁸ When Samlah died, Shaul from Rehoboth on the Euphrates River reigned in his place. ⁴⁹ When Shaul died, Baal-hanan son of Achbor reigned in his place. ⁵⁰ When Baal-hanan died, Hadad reigned in his place. Hadad's city was named Pai, and his wife's name was Mehetabel daughter of Matred, daughter of Me-zahab. ⁵¹ Then Hadad died.

Edom's chiefs: Timna, Alvah, ᴮ Jetheth, ⁵² Oholibamah, Elah, Pinon, ⁵³ Kenaz, Teman, Mibzar, ⁵⁴ Magdiel, and Iram. Gn 36:40-43 These were Edom's chiefs.

Israel's Sons

2 These were Israel's sons: Reuben, Simeon, Levi, Judah, Issachar, Zebulun, ² Dan, Joseph, Benjamin, Naphtali, Gad, and Asher.

Judah's Descendants

³ Judah's sons: Er, Onan, and Shelah. These three were born to him by Bath-shua the Canaanite woman. Er, Judah's

ᴬ**1:36** LXX; MT reads *and Timna and Amalek* ; Gn 36:12　ᴮ**1:51** Alt Hb tradition reads *Aliah* firstborn, was evil in the LORD's sight, so he put him to death. ⁴ Judah's daughter-in-law Tamar bore Perez and Zerah to him. Judah had five sons in all. Gn 46:12

⁵ Perez's sons: Hezron and Hamul.
⁶ Zerah's sons: Zimri, Ethan, Heman, Calcol, and Dara ᴬ — five in all. 1Kg 4:31
⁷ Carmi's son: Achar, ᴮ who brought trouble on Israel when he was unfaithful by taking the things set apart for destruction. Jos 7:1,16-26
⁸ Ethan's son: Azariah.
⁹ Hezron's sons, who were born to him: Jerahmeel, Ram, and Chelubai. ᶜ

¹⁰ Ram fathered Amminadab, and Amminadab fathered Nahshon, a leader of Judah's descendants. ¹¹ Nahshon fathered Salma, and Salma fathered Boaz. ¹² Boaz fathered Obed, and Obed fathered Jesse. ¹³ Jesse fathered Eliab, his firstborn; Abinadab was born second, Shimea third, ¹⁴ Nethanel fourth, Raddai fifth, ¹⁵ Ozem sixth, and David seventh. ¹⁶ Their sisters were Zeruiah and Abigail. Zeruiah's three sons: Abishai, Joab, and Asahel. ¹⁷ Amasa's mother was Abigail, and his father was Jether the Ishmaelite.

¹⁸ Caleb son of Hezron had children by his wife Azubah and by Jerioth. These were Azubah's sons: Jesher, Shobab, and Ardon. ¹⁹ When Azubah died, Caleb married Ephrath, and she bore Hur to him. ²⁰ Hur fathered Uri, and Uri fathered Bezalel. ²¹ After this, Hezron slept with the daughter of Machir the father of Gilead. Hezron had married her when he was sixty years old, and she bore Segub to him. ²² Segub fathered Jair, who possessed twenty-three towns in the land of Gilead. ²³ But Geshur and Aram captured ᴰ Jair's Villages ᴱ along with Kenath and its surrounding villages — sixty towns. All these were the descendants of Machir father of Gilead. ²⁴ After Hezron's death in Caleb-ephrathah, his wife Abijah bore ᶠ Ashhur to him. He was the father of Tekoa. Nm 26:29

²⁵ The sons of Jerahmeel, Hezron's firstborn: Ram, his firstborn, Bunah, Oren, Ozem, and Ahijah. ²⁶ Jerahmeel had another wife named Atarah, who was the mother of Onam. ²⁷ The sons of Ram, Jerahmeel's firstborn: Maaz, Jamin, and Eker. ²⁸ Onam's sons: Shammai and Jada.
Shammai's sons: Nadab and Abishur. ²⁹ Abishur's wife was named Abihail, who bore Ahban and Molid to him. ³⁰ Nadab's sons: Seled and Appaim. Seled died without children. ³¹ Appaim's son: Ishi.
Ishi's son: Sheshan.
Sheshan's descendant: Ahlai.

ᴬ **2:6** Some Hb mss, LXX, Syr, Tg, Vg read *Darda* ; 1Kg 4:31   ᴮ **2:7** = Trouble; Achan in Jos 7:1,16-26
ᶜ **2:9** = Caleb   ᴰ **2:23** Lit *took from them*   ᴱ **2:23** Or *captured Havvoth-jair*   ᶠ **2:24** LXX, Vg read *death,*
Caleb slept with Ephrath (Hezron's wife was Abijah) and she bore

³² The sons of Jada, brother of Shammai: Jether and Jonathan. Jether died without children. ³³ Jonathan's sons: Peleth and Zaza. These were the descendants of Jerahmeel.
³⁴ Sheshan had no sons, only daughters, but he did have an Egyptian servant whose name was Jarha. ³⁵ Sheshan gave his daughter in marriage to his servant Jarha, and she bore Attai to him.

³⁶ Attai fathered Nathan, and Nathan fathered Zabad. ³⁷ Zabad fathered Ephlal, and Ephlal fathered Obed. ³⁸ Obed fathered Jehu, and Jehu fathered Azariah. ³⁹ Azariah fathered Helez, and Helez fathered Elasah. ⁴⁰ Elasah fathered Sismai, and Sismai fathered Shallum. ⁴¹ Shallum fathered Jekamiah, and Jekamiah fathered Elishama.

⁴² The sons of Caleb brother of Jerahmeel: Mesha, his firstborn, fathered Ziph, and Mareshah, his second son, ᴬ fathered Hebron. ⁴³ Hebron's sons: Korah, Tappuah, Rekem, and Shema. ⁴⁴ Shema fathered Raham, who fathered Jorkeam, and Rekem fathered Shammai. ⁴⁵ Shammai's son was Maon, and Maon fathered Beth-zur. ⁴⁶ Caleb's concubine Ephah was the mother of Haran, Moza, and Gazez. Haran fathered Gazez. ⁴⁷ Jahdai's sons: Regem, Jotham, Geshan, Pelet, Ephah, and Shaaph.

⁴⁸ Caleb's concubine Maacah was the mother of Sheber and Tirhanah. ⁴⁹ She was also the mother of Shaaph, Madmannah's father, and of Sheva, the father of Machbenah and Gibea. Caleb's daughter was Achsah. ⁵⁰ These were Caleb's descendants.

The sons of Hur, Ephrathah's firstborn:
Shobal fathered Kiriath-jearim;
⁵¹ Salma fathered Bethlehem, and Hareph fathered Beth-gader.

⁵² These were the descendants of Shobal the father of Kiriath-jearim: Haroeh, half of the Manahathites, ᴮ ⁵³ and the families of Kiriath-jearim — the Ithrites, Puthites, Shumathites, and Mishraites. The Zorathites and Eshtaolites descended from these.

⁵⁴ Salma's descendants: Bethlehem, the Netophathites, Atroth-beth-joab, and half of the Manahathites, the Zorites, ⁵⁵ and the families of scribes who lived in Jabez — the Tirathites, Shimeathites, and Sucathites. These are the Kenites who came from Hammath, the father of Rechab's family.

David's Descendants

3 These were David's sons who were born to him in Hebron:
Amnon was the firstborn, by Ahinoam of Jezreel;
Daniel was born second, by Abigail of Carmel;

ᴬ 2:42 Lit *and the sons of Mareshah*   ᴮ 2:52 Lit *Manuhoth*

² Absalom son of Maacah, daughter of King Talmai of Geshur, was third; Adonijah son of Haggith was fourth; ³ Shephatiah, by Abital, was fifth; and Ithream, by David's wife Eglah, was sixth. ⁴ Six sons were born to David in Hebron, where he reigned seven years and six months, and he reigned in Jerusalem thirty-three years.   2Sm 2:11; 5:4-5

⁵ These sons were born to him in Jerusalem: 2Sm 5:14-16; 1Ch 14:4-7 Shimea, Shobab, Nathan, and Solomon. These four were born to him by Bath-shua daughter of Ammiel.   2Sm 12:24-25 ⁶ David's other sons: Ibhar, Elishua,ᴬ Eliphelet, ⁷ Nogah, Nepheg, Japhia, ⁸ Elishama, Eliada, and Eliphelet — nine sons.   2Sm 5:15; 1Ch 14:5 ⁹ These were all David's sons, with their sister Tamar, in addition to the sons by his concubines.   2Sm 13:1

Judah's Kings

¹⁰ Solomon's son was Rehoboam; his son was Abijah, his son Asa, his son Jehoshaphat, ¹¹ his son Jehoram,ᴮ,ᶜ his son Ahaziah, his son Joash, ¹² his son Amaziah, his son Azariah, his son Jotham, ¹³ his son Ahaz, his son Hezekiah, his son Manasseh, ¹⁴ his son Amon, and his son Josiah.

¹⁵ Josiah's sons: Johanan was the firstborn, Jehoiakim second, Zedekiah third, and Shallum fourth. ¹⁶ Jehoiakim's sons: his sons Jeconiah and Zedekiah.

David's Line after the Exile

¹⁷ The sons of Jeconiah the captive: his sons Shealtiel, ¹⁸ Malchiram, Pedaiah, Shenazzar, Jekamiah, Hoshama, and Nedabiah. ¹⁹ Pedaiah's sons: Zerubbabel and Shimei. Zerubbabel's sons: Meshullam and Hananiah, with their sister Shelomith; ²⁰ and five others — Hashubah, Ohel, Berechiah, Hasadiah, and Jushab-hesed. ²¹ Hananiah's descendants: Pelatiah, Jeshaiah, and the sons of Rephaiah, Arnan, Obadiah, and Shecaniah.ᴰ ²² The sonᴱ of Shecaniah: Shemaiah. Shemaiah's sons: Hattush, Igal, Bariah, Neariah, and Shaphat — six. ²³ Neariah's sons: Elioenai, Hizkiah, and Azrikam — three. ²⁴ Elioenai's sons: Hodaviah, Eliashib, Pelaiah, Akkub, Johanan, Delaiah, and Anani — seven.

Judah's Descendants

4 Judah's sons: Perez, Hezron, Carmi, Hur, and Shobal. ² Reaiah son of Shobal fathered Jahath, and Jahath fathered Ahumai and Lahad.

ᴬ3:6 Lit Elishama ; 2Sm 5:15; 1Ch 14:5   ᴮ3:11 Lit Joram   ᶜ3:11 = The Lᴏʀᴅ is Exalted   ᴰ3:21 LXX reads Jeshaiah, his son Rephaiah, his son Arnan, his son Obadiah, and his son Shecaniah   ᴱ3:22 LXX; MT reads sons

These were the families of the Zorathites.

³ These were Etam's sons:[A] Jezreel, Ishma, and Idbash, and their sister was named Hazzelelponi.

⁴ Penuel fathered Gedor, and Ezer fathered Hushah.

These were the sons of Hur, Ephrathah's firstborn and the father of Bethlehem:

⁵ Ashhur fathered Tekoa and had two wives, Helah and Naarah.

⁶ Naarah bore Ahuzzam, Hepher, Temeni, and Haahashtari to him. These were Naarah's sons.

⁷ Helah's sons: Zereth, Zohar,[B] and Ethnan. ⁸ Koz fathered Anub, Zobebah,[C] and the families of Aharhel son of Harum.

⁹ Jabez[D] was more honored than his brothers. His mother named him Jabez and said, "I gave birth to him in pain."

¹⁰ Jabez called out to the God of Israel: "If only you would bless me, extend my border, let your hand be with me, and keep me from harm, so that I will not experience pain."[E] And God granted his request.

¹¹ Chelub brother of Shuhah fathered Mehir, who was the father of Eshton. ¹² Eshton fathered Beth-rapha, Paseah, and Tehinnah the father of Irnahash. These were the men of Recah.

¹³ Kenaz's sons: Othniel and Seraiah.

Othniel's sons: Hathath and Meonothai.[F]

¹⁴ Meonothai fathered Ophrah, and Seraiah fathered Joab, the ancestor of those in the Craftsmen's Valley,[G] for they were craftsmen.

¹⁵ The sons of Caleb son of Jephunneh: Iru, Elah, and Naam.

Elah's son: Kenaz.

¹⁶ Jehallelel's sons: Ziph, Ziphah, Tiria, and Asarel.

¹⁷ Ezrah's sons: Jether, Mered, Epher, and Jalon. Mered's wife Bithiah gave birth to Miriam, Shammai, and Ishbah the father of Eshtemoa. ¹⁸ These were the sons of Pharaoh's daughter Bithiah; Mered had married her. His Judean wife gave birth to Jered the father of Gedor, Heber the father of Soco, and Jekuthiel the father of Zanoah. ¹⁹ The sons of Hodiah's wife, the sister of Naham: the father of Keilah the Garmite and the father of Eshtemoa the Maacathite.

²⁰ Shimon's sons: Amnon, Rinnah, Ben-hanan, and Tilon. Ishi's sons: Zoheth and Ben-zoheth.

²¹ The sons of Shelah son of Judah: Er the father of Lecah, Laadah the father of Mareshah, the families of the guild[H] of linen workers at Beth-ashbea, ²² Jokim, the men of Cozeba; and Joash and Saraph, who married Moabites[I] and returned to Lehem.[J] These names

---

are from ancient records. ²³ They were the potters and residents of Netaim and Gederah. They lived there in the service of the king.

Simeon's Descendants

²⁴ Simeon's sons: Nemuel, Jamin, Jarib, Zerah, and Shaul; ²⁵ Shaul's sons: his son Shallum, his son Mibsam, and his son Mishma.
²⁶ Mishma's sons: his son Hammuel, his son Zaccur, and his son Shimei.

²⁷ Shimei had sixteen sons and six daughters, but his brothers did not have many children, so their whole family did not become as numerous as the Judeans. ²⁸ They lived in Beer-sheba, Moladah, Hazarshual, ²⁹ Bilhah, Ezem, Tolad, ³⁰ Bethuel, Hormah, Ziklag, ³¹ Beth-marcaboth, Hazarsusim, Beth-biri, and Shaaraim. These were their cities until David became king. ³² Their villages were Etam, Ain, Rimmon, Tochen, and Ashan — five cities, ³³ and all their surrounding villages as far as Baal. These were their settlements, and they kept a genealogical record for themselves.

³⁴ Meshobab, Jamlech, Joshah son of Amaziah, ³⁵ Joel, Jehu son of Joshibiah, son of Seraiah, son of Asiel, ³⁶ Elioenai, Jaakobah, Jeshohaiah, Asaiah, Adiel, Jesimiel, Benaiah, ³⁷ and Ziza son of Shiphi, son of Allon, son of Jedaiah, son of Shimri, son of Shemaiah —

³⁸ these mentioned by name were leaders in their families. Their ancestral houses increased greatly. ³⁹ They went to the entrance of Gedor, to the east side of the valley to seek pasture for their flocks. ⁴⁰ They found rich, good pasture, and the land was broad, peaceful, and quiet, for some Hamites had lived there previously.

⁴¹ These who were recorded by name came in the days of King Hezekiah of Judah, attacked the Hamites' tents and the Meunites who were found there, and set them apart for destruction, as they are today. Then they settled in their place because there was pasture for their flocks. ⁴² Now five hundred men from these sons of Simeon went with Pelatiah, Neariah, Rephaiah, and Uzziel, the descendants of Ishi, as their leaders to Mount Seir. ⁴³ They struck down the remnant of the Amalekites who had escaped, and they still live there today. 1Ch 4:33-38; Nm 21:3; 7:2

Reuben's Descendants

5 These were the sons of Reuben the firstborn of Israel. He was the firstborn, but his birthright was given to the sons of Joseph son of Israel, because Reuben defiled his father's bed. He is not listed in the genealogy according to birthright. ² Although Judah became strong among his brothers and a ruler came from him, the birthright was given to Joseph. Gn 29:32; 35:22; 1Ch 2:1
³ The sons of Reuben, Israel's firstborn: Gn 46:9; Nm 26:5-9
Hanoch, Pallu, Hezron, and Carmi.
⁴ Joel's sons: his son Shemaiah,

his son Gog, his son Shimei,
⁵ his son Micah, his son
    Reaiah,
his son Baal, ⁶ and his son
    Beerah.

Beerah was a leader of the Reubenites, and King Tiglath-pileser^A of Assyria took him into exile. ⁷ His relatives by their families as they are recorded in their family records: 1Ch 5:17

Jeiel the chief, Zechariah,
⁸ and Bela son of Azaz,
son of Shema, son of Joel.
They settled in Aroer as far as Nebo and Baal-meon. ⁹ They also settled in the east as far as the edge of the desert that extends to the Euphrates River, because their herds had increased in the land of Gilead. ¹⁰ During Saul's reign they waged war against the Hagrites, who were defeated by their power. And they lived in their tents throughout the region east of Gilead.   Nm 32:34; Jos 12:2; 22:8-9; 1Ch 5:19-21

Gad's Descendants

¹¹ The sons of Gad lived next to them in the land of Bashan as far as Salecah: Gn 46:16; Nm 26:15-18
¹² Joel the chief, Shapham the second in command, Janai, and Shaphat in Bashan.
¹³ Their relatives according to their ancestral houses:
Michael, Meshullam, Sheba, Jorai, Jacan, Zia, and Eber — seven.
¹⁴ These were the sons of Abihail son of Huri,
son of Jaroah, son of Gilead,
son of Michael, son of Jeshishai,
son of Jahdo, son of Buz.

¹⁵ Ahi son of Abdiel, son of Guni, was head of their ancestral family.^B ¹⁶ They lived in Gilead, in Bashan and its surrounding villages, and throughout the pasturelands of Sharon. ¹⁷ All of them were registered in the genealogies during the reigns of Judah's King Jotham and Israel's King Jeroboam.   2Kg 15:5,32; 1Ch 27:29

¹⁸ The descendants of Reuben and Gad and half the tribe of Manasseh had 44,760 warriors who could serve in the army — men who carried shield and sword, drew the bow, and were trained for war. ¹⁹ They waged war against the Hagrites, Jetur, Naphish, and Nodab. ²⁰ They received help against these enemies because they cried out to God in battle, and the Hagrites and all their allies were handed over to them. He was receptive to their prayer because they trusted in him. ²¹ They captured the Hagrites' livestock — fifty thousand of their camels, two hundred fifty thousand sheep, and two thousand donkeys — as well as one hundred thousand people. ²² Many of the Hagrites were killed because it was God's battle. And they lived there in the Hagrites' place until the exile.   Nm 1:3; 1Ch 1:31; 5:10; 2Ch 14:11-13

Half the Tribe of Manasseh

²³ The descendants of half the tribe of Manasseh settled in the land from Bashan to Baal-hermon (that is, Senir or Mount Hermon); they were numerous. ²⁴ These were the heads of their ancestral families: Epher, Ishi, Eliel, Azriel, Jeremiah, Hodaviah, and Jahdiel. They were

---

^A5:6 LXX; MT reads *Tilgath-pilneser*   ^B5:15 Lit *the house of their fathers,* also in v. 24

valiant warriors, famous men, and heads of their ancestral houses. ²⁵ But they were unfaithful to the God of their ancestors. They prostituted themselves with the gods of the nations[A] God had destroyed before them. ²⁶ So the God of Israel roused the spirit of King Pul (that is, Tiglath-pileser[B]) of Assyria, and he took the Reubenites, Gadites, and half the tribe of Manasseh into exile. He took them to Halah, Habor, Hara, and Gozan's river, where they are until today. Ex 34:15; Dt 3:9; 2Kg 17:7-8

The Levites

6 Levi's sons: Gershom,[C] Kohath, and Merari. Gn 46:11

² Kohath's sons: Amram, Izhar, Hebron, and Uzziel.

³ Amram's children: Aaron, Moses, and Miriam.
Aaron's sons: Nadab, Abihu, Eleazar, and Ithamar.

⁴ Eleazar fathered Phinehas; Phinehas fathered Abishua;

⁵ Abishua fathered Bukki; Bukki fathered Uzzi;

⁶ Uzzi fathered Zerahiah; Zerahiah fathered Meraioth;

⁷ Meraioth fathered Amariah; Amariah fathered Ahitub;

⁸ Ahitub fathered Zadok; Zadok fathered Ahimaaz;

⁹ Ahimaaz fathered Azariah; Azariah fathered Johanan;

¹⁰ Johanan fathered Azariah, who served as priest in the temple that Solomon built in Jerusalem;

¹¹ Azariah fathered Amariah; Amariah fathered Ahitub;

¹² Ahitub fathered Zadok; Zadok fathered Shallum;

¹³ Shallum fathered Hilkiah;

Hilkiah fathered Azariah;

¹⁴ Azariah fathered Seraiah; and Seraiah fathered Jehozadak.

¹⁵ Jehozadak went into exile when the LORD sent Judah and Jerusalem into exile at the hands of Nebuchadnezzar. 2 Kg 25:1,8

¹⁶ Levi's sons: Gershom, Kohath, and Merari. Ex 6:16-19

¹⁷ These are the names of Gershom's sons: Libni and Shimei.

¹⁸ Kohath's sons: Amram, Izhar, Hebron and Uzziel.

¹⁹ Merari's sons: Mahli and Mushi.
These are the Levites' families according to their fathers:

²⁰ Of Gershom: his son Libni, his son Jahath, his son Zimmah,

²¹ his son Joah, his son Iddo, his son Zerah, and his son Jeatherai.

²² Kohath's sons: his son Amminadab, his son Korah, his son Assir,

²³ his son Elkanah, his son Ebiasaph, his son Assir, ²⁴ his son Tahath, his son Uriel, his son Uzziah, and his son Shaul.

²⁵ Elkanah's sons: Amasai and Ahimoth,

²⁶ his son Elkanah, his son Zophai, his son Nahath, ²⁷ his son Eliab, his son Jeroham, and his son Elkanah.

[A]**5:25** Lit *the peoples of the land*   [B]**5:26** LXX; MT reads *Tilgath-pilneser*   [C]**6:1** In Hb Levi's son's name is spelled "Gershon" here and many other places

²⁸ Samuel's sons: his firstborn
Joel,^A   1Sm 8:2
and his second son Abijah.
²⁹ Merari's sons: Mahli, his son
Libni,
his son Shimei, his son Uzzah,
³⁰ his son Shimea, his son
Haggiah,
and his son Asaiah.

The Musicians

³¹ These are the men David put in charge of the music in the LORD's temple after the ark came to rest there. ³² They ministered with song in front of the tabernacle, the tent of meeting, until Solomon built the LORD's temple in Jerusalem, and they performed their task according to the regulations given to them. ³³ These are the men who served with their sons.   1Ch 15:16-22

From the Kohathites:
Heman the singer,
son of Joel, son of Samuel,
³⁴ son of Elkanah,
son of Jeroham,
son of Eliel, son of Toah,
³⁵ son of Zuph, son of Elkanah,
son of Mahath,
son of Amasai,
³⁶ son of Elkanah, son of Joel,
son of Azariah,
son of Zephaniah,
³⁷ son of Tahath, son of Assir,
son of Ebiasaph,
son of Korah,
³⁸ son of Izhar, son of Kohath,
son of Levi, son of Israel.

³⁹ Heman's relative was Asaph,
who stood at his right hand:
Asaph son of Berechiah,
son of Shimea,
⁴⁰ son of Michael,
son of Baaseiah,

son of Malchijah,
⁴¹ son of Ethni,
son of Zerah, son of Adaiah,
⁴² son of Ethan,
son of Zimmah,
son of Shimei,
⁴³ son of Jahath,
son of Gershom, son of Levi.

⁴⁴ On the left, their relatives
were Merari's sons:
Ethan son of Kishi,
son of Abdi,
son of Malluch,
⁴⁵ son of Hashabiah,
son of Amaziah,
son of Hilkiah,
⁴⁶ son of Amzi, son of Bani,
son of Shemer,
⁴⁷ son of Mahli,
son of Mushi, son of Merari,
son of Levi.

Aaron's Descendants

⁴⁸ Their relatives, the Levites, were assigned to all the service of the tabernacle, God's temple. ⁴⁹ But Aaron and his sons did all the work of the most holy place. They presented the offerings on the altar of burnt offerings and on the altar of incense to make atonement for Israel according to all that Moses the servant of God had commanded.   Ex 27:1-8; 30:1-7,10-16
⁵⁰ These are Aaron's sons:
his son Eleazar,   1Ch 6:4-8
his son Phinehas, his son
Abishua,
⁵¹ his son Bukki, his son Uzzi,
his son Zerahiah, ⁵² his son
Meraioth,
his son Amariah, his son
Ahitub,
⁵³ his son Zadok, and his son
Ahimaaz.

^A**6:28** Some LXX mss, Syr, Arabic; other Hb mss omit *Joel*; 1Sm 8:2

The Settlements of the Levites

54 These were the places assigned to Aaron's descendants from the Kohathite family for their settlements in their territory, because the first lot was for them. **55** They were given Hebron in the land of Judah and its surrounding pasturelands, **56** but the fields and settlements around the city were given to Caleb son of Jephunneh. **57** Aaron's descendants were given: Jos 14:13; 15:13; 21:4,10,13,19

Hebron (a city of refuge), Libnah and its pasturelands, Jattir, Eshtemoa and its pasturelands, **58** Hilen[A] and its pasturelands, Debir and its pasturelands, **59** Ashan and its pasturelands, and Beth-shemesh and its pasturelands. **60** From the tribe of Benjamin they were given Geba and its pasturelands, Alemeth and its pasturelands, and Anathoth and its pasturelands. They had thirteen towns in all among their families.

61 To the rest of the Kohathites, ten towns from half the tribe of Manasseh were assigned by lot.

62 The Gershomites were assigned thirteen towns from the tribes of Issachar, Asher, Naphtali, and Manasseh in Bashan according to their families.

63 The Merarites were assigned by lot twelve towns from the tribes of Reuben, Gad, and Zebulun according to their families. **64** So the Israelites gave these towns and their pasturelands to the Levites. **65** They assigned by lot the towns named above from the tribes of the descendants of Judah, Simeon, and Benjamin.   Jos 21:3,7,41-42; 1Ch 6:77-81

66 Some of the families of the Kohathites were given towns from the tribe of Ephraim for their territory: Jos 21:20-40
67 Shechem (a city of refuge) with its pasturelands in the hill country of Ephraim, Gezer and its pasturelands, **68** Jokmeam and its pasturelands, Beth-horon and its pasturelands, **69** Aijalon and its pasturelands, and Gath-rimmon and its pasturelands. **70** From half the tribe of Manasseh, Aner and its pasturelands, and Bileam and its pasturelands were given to the rest of the families of the Kohathites.

71 The Gershomites received: Golan in Bashan and its pasturelands, and Ashtaroth and its pasturelands from the families of half the tribe of Manasseh. **72** From the tribe of Issachar they received Kedesh and its pasturelands, Daberath and its pasturelands, **73** Ramoth and its pasturelands, and Anem and its pasturelands. **74** From the tribe of Asher they received Mashal and its pasturelands, Abdon and its pasturelands, **75** Hukok and its pasturelands, and Rehob and its pasturelands. **76** From the tribe of Naphtali they received Kedesh in Galilee and its pasturelands, Hammon and its pasturelands, and Kiriathaim and its pasturelands.

77 The rest of the Merarites received:
From the tribe of Zebulun they received Rimmono and its

<hr>

A**6:58** Some Hb mss, LXX; other Hb mss read *Hilez*

pasturelands and Tabor and its pasturelands. ⁷⁸ From the tribe of Reuben across the Jordan at Jericho, to the east of the Jordan, they received Bezer in the desert and its pasturelands, Jahzah and its pasturelands, ⁷⁹ Kedemoth and its pasturelands, and Mephaath and its pasturelands. ⁸⁰ From the tribe of Gad they received Ramoth in Gilead and its pasturelands, Mahanaim and its pasturelands, ⁸¹ Heshbon and its pasturelands, and Jazer and its pasturelands.

Issachar's Descendants

7 Issachar's sons: Tola, Puah, Jashub, and Shimron — four. ² Tola's sons: Uzzi, Rephaiah, Jeriel, Jahmai, Ibsam, and Shemuel, the heads of their ancestral families. ^A During David's reign, 22,600 descendants of Tola were recorded as valiant warriors in their family records.   2Sm 24:1-9 ³ Uzzi's son: Izrahiah. Izrahiah's sons: Michael, Obadiah, Joel, Isshiah. All five of them were chiefs. ⁴ Along with them, they had 36,000 troops for battle according to the family records of their ancestral families, for they had many wives and children. ⁵ Their tribesmen who were valiant warriors belonging to all the families of Issachar totaled 87,000 in their genealogies.

Benjamin's Descendants

⁶ Three of Benjamin's sons: Bela, Becher, and Jediael. Gn 46:21

⁷ Bela's sons: Ezbon, Uzzi, Uzziel, Jerimoth, and Iri — five. They were valiant warriors and heads of their ancestral families; 22,034 were listed in their genealogies. ⁸ Becher's sons: Zemirah, Joash, Eliezer, Elioenai, Omri, Jeremoth, Abijah, Anathoth, and Alemeth; all these were Becher's sons. ⁹ Their family records were recorded according to the heads of their ancestral families — 20,200 valiant warriors. ¹⁰ Jediael's son: Bilhan. Bilhan's sons: Jeush, Benjamin, Ehud, Chenaanah, Zethan, Tarshish, and Ahishahar. ¹¹ All these sons of Jediael listed by family heads were valiant warriors; there were 17,200 who could serve in the army. ¹² Shuppim and Huppim were sons of Ir, and the Hushim were the sons of Aher.

Naphtali's Descendants

¹³ Naphtali's sons: Jahziel, Guni, Jezer, and Shallum — Bilhah's sons. Gn 46:24-25

Manasseh's Descendants

¹⁴ Manasseh's sons through his Aramean concubine: Asriel and Machir the father of Gilead. ¹⁵ Machir took wives from Huppim and Shuppim. The name of his sister was Maacah. Another descendant was named Zelophehad, but he had only daughters. Nm 26:29-34 ¹⁶ Machir's wife Maacah gave birth to a son, and she named him Peresh. His brother was named Sheresh, and his sons were Ulam and Rekem.

^A**7:2** Lit *the house of their fathers,* also in vv. 4,7,9,40

¹⁷ Ulam's son: Bedan. These were the sons of Gilead son of Machir, son of Manasseh. ¹⁸ His sister Hammolecheth gave birth to Ishhod, Abiezer, and Mahlah. ¹⁹ Shemida's sons: Ahian, Shechem, Likhi, and Aniam.

Ephraim's Descendants

²⁰ Ephraim's sons: Shuthelah,
and his son Bered,   Nm 26:35-36
his son Tahath,
his son Eleadah,
his son Tahath,
²¹ his son Zabad,
his son Shuthelah, also Ezer,
and Elead.

The men of Gath, born in the land, killed them because they went down to raid their cattle. ²² Their father Ephraim mourned a long time, and his relatives^A came to comfort him. ²³ He slept with his wife, and she conceived and gave birth to a son. So he named him Beriah, because there had been misfortune in his home.^B ²⁴ His daughter was Sheerah, who built Lower and Upper Beth-horon and Uzzen-sheerah,

²⁵ his son Rephah,^C
his son Resheph,
his son Telah, his son Tahan,
²⁶ his son Ladan,
his son Ammihud,
his son Elishama,
²⁷ his son Nun,
and his son Joshua.   Ex 17:9-14

²⁸ Their holdings and settlements were Bethel and its surrounding villages; Naaran to the east, Gezer and its villages to the west, and Shechem and its villages as far as Ayyah and its villages, ²⁹ and along the borders of the descendants of Manasseh, Beth-shean, Taanach, Megiddo, and Dor with their surrounding villages. The sons of Joseph son of Israel lived in these towns.   Jos 16:2

Asher's Descendants

³⁰ Asher's sons: Imnah, Ishvah, Ishvi, and Beriah, with their sister Serah.   Gn 46:17; Nm 26:44-46
³¹ Beriah's sons: Heber, and Malchiel, who fathered Birzaith.
³² Heber fathered Japhlet, Shomer, and Hotham, with their sister Shua.
³³ Japhlet's sons: Pasach, Bimhal, and Ashvath. These were Japhlet's sons.
³⁴ Shemer's sons: Ahi, Rohgah, Hubbah, and Aram.
³⁵ His brother Helem's sons: Zophah, Imna, Shelesh, and Amal.
³⁶ Zophah's sons: Suah, Harnepher, Shual, Beri, Imrah, ³⁷ Bezer, Hod, Shamma, Shilshah, Ithran, and Beera.
³⁸ Jether's sons: Jephunneh, Pispa, and Ara.
³⁹ Ulla's sons: Arah, Hanniel, and Rizia.
⁴⁰ All these were Asher's descendants. They were the heads of their ancestral families, chosen men, valiant warriors, and chiefs among the leaders. The number of men listed in their genealogies for military service was 26,000.

^A 7:22 Or his brothers   ^B 7:23 In Hb, the name Beriah sounds like "in misfortune."   ^C 7:25 Probably Ephraim's son

Benjamin's Descendants

8 Benjamin fathered Bela, his firstborn; Ashbel was born second, Aharah third, ² Nohah fourth, and Rapha fifth. Gn 46:21

³ Bela's sons: Addar, Gera, Abihud,^A ⁴ Abishua, Naaman, Ahoah, ⁵ Gera, Shephuphan, and Huram.

⁶ These were Ehud's sons, who were the heads of the families living in Geba and who were deported to Manahath: ⁷ Naaman, Ahijah, and Gera. Gera deported them and was the father of Uzza and Ahihud.

⁸ Shaharaim had sons in the territory of Moab after he had divorced his wives Hushim and Baara. ⁹ His sons by his wife Hodesh: Jobab, Zibia, Mesha, Malcam, ¹⁰ Jeuz, Sachia, and Mirmah. These were his sons, family heads. ¹¹ He also had sons by Hushim: Abitub and Elpaal.

¹² Elpaal's sons: Eber, Misham, and Shemed who built Ono and Lod and its surrounding villages, ¹³ Beriah and Shema, who were the family heads of Aijalon's residents and who drove out the residents of Gath, ¹⁴ Ahio,^B Shashak, and Jeremoth.

¹⁵ Zebadiah, Arad, Eder, ¹⁶ Michael, Ishpah, and Joha were Beriah's sons.

¹⁷ Zebadiah, Meshullam, Hizki, Heber, ¹⁸ Ishmerai, Izliah, and Jobab were Elpaal's sons.

¹⁹ Jakim, Zichri, Zabdi, ²⁰ Elienai, Zillethai, Eliel, ²¹ Adaiah, Beraiah, and Shimrath were Shimei's sons.

²² Ishpan, Eber, Eliel, ²³ Abdon, Zichri, Hanan, ²⁴ Hananiah, Elam, Anthothijah, ²⁵ Iphdeiah, and Penuel were Shashak's sons.

²⁶ Shamsherai, Shehariah, Athaliah, ²⁷ Jaareshiah, Elijah, and Zichri were Jeroham's sons.

²⁸ These were family heads, chiefs according to their family records; they lived in Jerusalem. 1Ch 9:34-44

²⁹ Jeiel^C fathered Gibeon and lived in Gibeon. His wife's name was Maacah. ³⁰ Abdon was his firstborn son, then Zur, Kish, Baal, Nadab, ³¹ Gedor, Ahio, Zecher, ³² and Mikloth who fathered Shimeah. These also lived opposite their relatives in Jerusalem, with their other relatives. 1Ch 9:35

³³ Ner fathered Kish, Kish fathered Saul, and Saul fathered Jonathan, Malchishua, Abinadab, and Esh-baal.^D

³⁴ Jonathan's son was Merib-baal,^E and Merib-baal fathered Micah.

³⁵ Micah's sons: Pithon, Melech, Tarea, and Ahaz.

³⁶ Ahaz fathered Jehoaddah, Jehoaddah fathered Alemeth, Azmaveth, and Zimri, and Zimri fathered Moza.

³⁷ Moza fathered Binea. His son was Raphah, his son Elasah, and his son Azel.

³⁸ Azel had six sons, and these were their names: Azrikam, Bocheru, Ishmael, Sheariah, Obadiah, and Hanan. All these were Azel's sons.

^A 8:3 Or *Gera father of Ehud*; Jdg 3:15   ^B 8:13-14 LXX reads *Gath* ¹⁴*and their brother*   ^C 8:29 LXX; MT omits *Jeiel*; 1Ch 9:35   ^D 8:33 = Man of Baal   ^E 8:34 = Baal Contends

[39] His brother Eshek's sons: Ulam was his firstborn, Jeush second, and Eliphelet third. [40] Ulam's sons were valiant warriors and archers. [A] They had many sons and grandsons — 150 of them.

All these were among Benjamin's sons.

After the Exile

9 All Israel was registered in the genealogies that are written in the Book of the Kings of Israel. But Judah was exiled to Babylon because of their unfaithfulness. [2] The first to live in their towns on their own property again were Israelites, priests, Levites, and temple servants. 1Ch 6:15; Ezr 2:43,58; 8:20; Neh 11:3-9

[3] These people from the descendants of Judah, Benjamin, Ephraim, and Manasseh settled in Jerusalem: [4] Uthai son of Ammihud, son of Omri, son of Imri, son of Bani, a descendant [B] of Perez son of Judah; [5] from the Shilonites: Asaiah the firstborn and his sons; [6] and from the descendants of Zerah: Jeuel and their relatives — 690 in all.

[7] The Benjaminites: Sallu son of Meshullam, son of Hodaviah, son of Hassenuah; [8] Ibneiah son of Jeroham; Elah son of Uzzi, son of Michri; Meshullam son of Shephatiah, son of Reuel, son of Ibnijah; [9] and their relatives according to their family records — 956

in all. All these men were heads of their ancestral families. [C]

[10] The priests: Jedaiah; Jehoiarib; Jachin;   Neh 11:10-18
[11] Azariah son of Hilkiah, son of Meshullam, son of Zadok, son of Meraioth, son of Ahitub, the chief official of God's temple; [12] Adaiah son of Jeroham, son of Pashhur, son of Malchijah; Maasai son of Adiel, son of Jahzerah, son of Meshullam, son of Meshillemith, son of Immer; [13] and their relatives, the heads of their ancestral families — 1,760 in all. They were capable men employed in the ministry of God's temple.

[14] The Levites: Shemaiah son of Hasshub, son of Azrikam, son of Hashabiah of the Merarites; [15] Bakbakkar, Heresh, Galal, and Mattaniah, son of Mica, son of Zichri, son of Asaph; [16] Obadiah son of Shemaiah, son of Galal, son of Jeduthun; and Berechiah son of Asa, son of Elkanah who lived in the settlements of the Netophathites.

[17] The gatekeepers: Shallum, Akkub, Talmon, Ahiman, and their relatives.   1Ch 26:1-19; Ezr 2:42
Shallum was their chief; [18] he was previously stationed at the King's Gate on the east side. These were the gatekeepers from the camp of the Levites. [19] Shallum son of Kore, son of Ebiasaph, son of Korah and his relatives from his

A 8:40 Lit *valiant ones who string the bow*   B 9:4 Lit *Bani, from the sons*   C 9:9 Lit *the house of their fathers*, also in v. 13

father's family,^A the Korahites, were assigned to guard the thresholds of the tent.^B Their ancestors had been assigned to the LORD's camp as guardians of the entrance. ²⁰ In earlier times Phinehas son of Eleazar had been their leader, and the LORD was with him. ²¹ Zechariah son of Meshelemiah was the gatekeeper at the entrance to the tent of meeting.   Nm 4:1-20; 26:11

²² The total number of those chosen to be gatekeepers at the thresholds was 212. They were registered by genealogy in their settlements. David and the seer Samuel had appointed them to their trusted positions. ²³ So they and their sons were assigned as guards to the gates of the LORD's temple, which had been the tent-temple. ²⁴ The gatekeepers were on the four sides: east, west, north, and south. ²⁵ Their relatives came from their settlements at fixed times to be with them seven days, ²⁶ but the four chief gatekeepers, who were Levites, were entrusted with the rooms and the treasuries of God's temple. ²⁷ They spent the night in the vicinity of God's temple, because they had guard duty and were in charge of opening it every morning.   1Ch 26:1

²⁸ Some of them were in charge of the utensils used in worship. They would count them when they brought them in and when they took them out. ²⁹ Others were put in charge of the furnishings and all the utensils of the sanctuary, as well as the fine flour, wine, oil, incense, and spices. ³⁰ Some of the priests' sons mixed the spices. ³¹ A Levite called Mattithiah, the firstborn of Shallum the Korahite, was entrusted with baking the bread.^C ³² Some of the Kohathites' relatives were responsible for preparing the rows of the Bread of the Presence every Sabbath.   Lv 24:5-9; Nm 3:31; 1Ch 23:29

³³ The singers, the heads of the Levite families, stayed in the temple chambers and were exempt from other tasks because they were on duty day and night. ³⁴ These were the heads of the Levite families, chiefs according to their family records; they lived in Jerusalem.

Saul's Family

³⁵ Jeiel fathered Gibeon and lived in Gibeon. His wife's name was Maacah. ³⁶ Abdon was his firstborn son, then Zur, Kish, Baal, Ner, Nadab, ³⁷ Gedor, Ahio, Zechariah, and Mikloth. ³⁸ Mikloth fathered Shimeam. These also lived opposite their relatives in Jerusalem with their other relatives. ³⁹ Ner fathered Kish, Kish fathered Saul, and Saul fathered Jonathan, Malchishua, Abinadab, and Esh-baal. ⁴⁰ Jonathan's son was Merib-baal, and Merib-baal fathered Micah. ⁴¹ Micah's sons: Pithon, Melech, Tahrea, and Ahaz.^D ⁴² Ahaz fathered Jarah; Jarah fathered Alemeth, Azmaveth, and Zimri; Zimri fathered Moza. ⁴³ Moza fathered Binea. His son was Rephaiah, his son Elasah, and his son Azel.

^A 9:19 Lit the house of his father   ^B 9:19 = the temple   ^C 9:31 Lit with things prepared in pans
^D 9:41 LXX, Syr, Tg, Vg, Arabic; MT omits and Ahaz; 1Ch 8:35

⁴⁴ Azel had six sons, and these were their names: Azrikam, Bocheru, Ishmael, Sheariah, Obadiah, and Hanan. These were Azel's sons.

The Death of Saul and His Sons

10 The Philistines fought against Israel, and Israel's men fled from them. Many were killed on Mount Gilboa. ² The Philistines pursued Saul and his sons and killed his sons Jonathan, Abinadab, and Malchishua. ³ When the battle intensified against Saul, the archers spotted him and severely wounded him. ⁴ Then Saul said to his armorbearer, "Draw your sword and run me through with it, or these uncircumcised men will come and torture me." But his armor-bearer would not do it because he was terrified. Then Saul took his sword and fell on it. ⁵ When his armor-bearer saw that Saul was dead, he also fell on his own sword and died. ⁶ So Saul and his three sons died — his whole house died together.

⁷ When all the men of Israel in the valley saw that the army had fled and that Saul and his sons were dead, they abandoned their cities and fled. So the Philistines came and settled in them.

⁸ The next day when the Philistines came to strip the slain, they found Saul and his sons dead on Mount Gilboa. ⁹ They stripped Saul, cut off his head, took his armor, and sent messengers throughout the land of the Philistines to spread the good news to their idols and the people. ¹⁰ Then they put his armor in the temple of their gods and hung his skull in the temple of Dagon.   1Sm 5:1-4; 17:54

¹¹ When all Jabesh-gilead heard of everything the Philistines had done to Saul, ¹² all their brave men set out and retrieved the body of Saul and the bodies of his sons and brought them to Jabesh. They buried their bones under the oak^A in Jabesh and fasted seven days.

¹³ Saul died for his unfaithfulness to the Lord because he did not keep the Lord's word. He even consulted a medium for guidance, ¹⁴ but he did not inquire of the Lord. So the Lord put him to death and turned the kingdom over to David son of Jesse.   1Sm 13:13-14; 15:23,28; 28:7

David's Anointing as King

11 All Israel came together to David at Hebron and said, "Here we are, your own flesh and blood.^B ² Even previously when Saul was king, you were leading Israel out to battle and bringing us back. The Lord your God also said to you, 'You will shepherd my people Israel, and you will be ruler over my people Israel.' "   2Sm 5:1-3

³ So all the elders of Israel came to the king at Hebron. David made a covenant with them at Hebron in the Lord's presence, and they anointed David king over Israel, in keeping with the Lord's word through Samuel.   1Sm 16:1-13

David's Capture of Jerusalem

⁴ David and all Israel marched to Jerusalem (that is, Jebus); the Jebusites who inhabited the land were there. ⁵ The inhabitants of Jebus said to David, "You will never get in here." Yet David did capture the stronghold of Zion, that is, the city of David.

⁶ David said, "Whoever is the first to kill a Jebusite will become chief

^A10:12 Or terebinth, or large tree   ^B11:1 Lit your bone and your flesh commander." Joab son of Zeruiah went up first, so he became the chief. 2Sm 8:16; 1Ch 18:15

⁷ Then David took up residence in the stronghold; therefore, it was called the city of David. ⁸ He built up the city all the way around, from the supporting terraces to the surrounding parts, and Joab restored the rest of the city. ⁹ David steadily grew more powerful, and the LORD of Armies was with him. 2Sm 3:1

Exploits of David's Warriors

¹⁰ The following were the chiefs of David's warriors who, together with all Israel, strongly supported him in his reign to make him king according to the LORD's word about Israel. ¹¹ This is the list of David's warriors: 2Sm 23:8-23; 1Ch 11:3

Jashobeam son of Hachmoni was chief of the Thirty;^A he wielded his spear against three hundred and killed them at one time. 1Ch 12:18

¹² After him, Eleazar son of Dodo the Ahohite was one of the three warriors. ¹³ He was with David at Pas-dammim when the Philistines had gathered there for battle. There was a portion of a field full of barley, where the troops had fled from the Philistines. ¹⁴ But Eleazar and David^B took their stand in the middle of the field and defended it. They killed the Philistines, and the LORD gave them a great victory.

¹⁵ Three of the thirty chief men went down to David, to the rock at the cave of Adullam, while the Philistine army was encamped in the Valley of Rephaim. ¹⁶ At that time David was in the stronghold, and a Philistine garrison was at Bethlehem. ¹⁷ David was extremely thirsty^C and said, "If only someone would bring me water to drink from the well at the city gate of Bethlehem!" ¹⁸ So the Three broke through the Philistine camp and drew water from the well at the gate of Bethlehem. They brought it back to David, but he refused to drink it. Instead, he poured it out to the LORD. ¹⁹ David said, "I would never do such a thing in the presence of my God! How can I drink the blood of these men who risked their lives?" For they brought it at the risk of their lives. So he would not drink it. Such were the exploits of the three warriors. 1Sm 22:1; 1Ch 14:9

²⁰ Abishai, Joab's brother, was the leader of the Three.^D He raised his spear against three hundred men and killed them, gaining a reputation among the Three. ²¹ He was more honored than the Three and became their commander even though he did not become one of the Three. 1Sm 26:6; 2Sm 18:2

²² Benaiah son of Jehoiada was the son of a brave man^E from Kabzeel, a man of many exploits. Benaiah killed two sons of Ariel of Moab,^F and he went down into a pit on a snowy day and killed a lion. ²³ He also killed an Egyptian who was seven and a half feet tall.^G Even though the Egyptian had a spear in his hand like a weaver's beam, Benaiah went down to him with a club, snatched the spear out of the Egyptian's hand, and then killed him with his own spear. ²⁴ These were the exploits of Benaiah son of Jehoiada, who had a reputation among the three warriors. ²⁵ He

---

^A **11:11** Alt Hb tradition reads *Three*   ^B **11:14** Lit *But they*   ^C **11:17** Lit *And David craved*   ^D **11:20** Syr reads *Thirty*   ^E **11:22** Or *was a valiant man*   ^F **11:22** Or *He killed two Moabite warriors*   ^G **11:23** Lit *who measured five cubits* was the most honored of the Thirty, but he did not become one of the Three. David put him in charge of his bodyguard.   2Sm 8:18; 20:23; 23:20-23

26 The best soldiers were
     Joab's brother Asahel,
     Elhanan son of Dodo
        of Bethlehem,
27 Shammoth the Harorite,
     Helez the Pelonite,
28 Ira son of Ikkesh the Tekoite,
     Abiezer the Anathothite,
29 Sibbecai the Hushathite,
     Ilai the Ahohite,
30 Maharai the Netophathite,
     Heled son of Baanah
        the Netophathite,
31 Ithai son of Ribai from Gibeah
        of the Benjaminites,
     Benaiah the Pirathonite,
32 Hurai from the wadis
        of Gaash,
     Abiel the Arbathite,
33 Azmaveth the Baharumite,
     Eliahba the Shaalbonite,
34 the sons of A Hashem
        the Gizonite,   2Sm 23:32
     Jonathan son of Shagee
        the Hararite,
35 Ahiam son of Sachar
        the Hararite,
     Eliphal son of Ur,
36 Hepher the Mecherathite,
     Ahijah the Pelonite,
37 Hezro the Carmelite,
     Naarai son of Ezbai,
38 Joel the brother of Nathan,
     Mibhar son of Hagri,
39 Zelek the Ammonite,
     Naharai the Beerothite,
        the armor-bearer for Joab
        son of Zeruiah,
40 Ira the Ithrite,
     Gareb the Ithrite,
41 Uriah the Hethite,
     Zabad son of Ahlai,

A11:34 LXX omits *the sons of*; 2Sm 23:32

42 Adina son of Shiza
     the Reubenite, chief
     of the Reubenites,
     and thirty with him,
43 Hanan son of Maacah,
     Joshaphat the Mithnite,
44 Uzzia the Ashterathite,
     Shama and Jeiel the sons
        of Hotham the Aroerite,
45 Jediael son of Shimri
     and his brother Joha
        the Tizite,
46 Eliel the Mahavite,
     Jeribai and Joshaviah,
        the sons of Elnaam,
     Ithmah the Moabite,
47 Eliel, Obed, and Jaasiel
        the Mezobaite.

David's First Supporters

12 The following were the men who came to David at Ziklag while he was still banned from the presence of Saul son of Kish. They were among the warriors who helped him in battle. 2 They were archers who could use either the right or left hand, both to sling stones and shoot arrows from a bow. They were Saul's relatives from Benjamin: Jdg 3:15; 20:16; 1Sm 27:1-7
3 Their chief was Ahiezer son of Shemaah the Gibeathite. Then there was his brother Joash; Jeziel and Pelet sons of Azmaveth; Beracah, Jehu the Anathothite; 4 Ishmaiah the Gibeonite, a warrior among the Thirty and a leader over the Thirty; Jeremiah, Jahaziel, Johanan, Jozabad the Gederathite; 5 Eluzai, Jerimoth, Bealiah, Shemariah, Shephatiah the Haruphite;

⁶ Elkanah, Isshiah, Azarel, Joezer, and Jashobeam, the Korahites; ⁷ and Joelah and Zebadiah, the sons of Jeroham from Gedor.

⁸ Some Gadites defected to David at his stronghold in the desert. They were valiant warriors, trained for battle, expert with shield and spear. Their faces were like the faces of lions, and they were as swift as gazelles on the mountains.   2Sm 2:18

⁹ Ezer was the chief,
  Obadiah second,
  Eliab third,
¹⁰ Mishmannah fourth,
  Jeremiah fifth,
¹¹ Attai sixth, Eliel seventh,
¹² Johanan eighth,
  Elzabad ninth,
¹³ Jeremiah tenth, and
  Machbannai eleventh.

¹⁴ These Gadites were army commanders; the least of them was a match for a hundred, and the greatest of them for a thousand. ¹⁵ These are the men who crossed the Jordan in the first month^A when it was overflowing all its banks, and put to flight all those in the valleys to the east and to the west.   Lv 26:8

¹⁶ Other Benjaminites and men from Judah also went to David at the stronghold. ¹⁷ David went out to meet them and said to them, "If you have come in peace to help me, my heart will be united with you, but if you have come to betray me to my enemies even though my hands have done no wrong, may the God of our ancestors look on it and judge."   1Sm 22:1-2

¹⁸ Then the Spirit enveloped^B Amasai, chief of the Thirty, and he said: Jdg 6:34; 1Ch 2:17; 2Ch 24:20

We are yours, David,
we are with you, son of Jesse!
Peace, peace to you,
and peace to him
  who helps you,   1Sm 25:5-6
for your God helps you.

So David received them and made them leaders of his troops.

¹⁹ Some Manassites defected to David when he went with the Philistines to fight against Saul. However, they did not help the Philistines because the Philistine rulers sent David away after a discussion. They said, "It will be our heads if he defects to his master Saul." ²⁰ When David went to Ziklag, some men from Manasseh defected to him: Adnah, Jozabad, Jediael, Michael, Jozabad, Elihu, and Zillethai, chiefs of thousands in Manasseh. ²¹ They helped David against the raiders, for they were all valiant warriors and commanders in the army. ²² At that time, men came day after day to help David until there was a great army, like an army of God.^C   Gn 32:1-2; 1Sm 29:1-11; 30:1-20

David's Soldiers in Hebron

²³ The numbers of the armed troops who came to David at Hebron to turn Saul's kingdom over to him, according to the LORD's word, were as follows: 1Sm 15:28; 1Ch 10:14; 11:10

²⁴ From the Judahites: 6,800
  armed troops bearing
  shields and spears.
²⁵ From the Simeonites:
  7,100 valiant warriors
  ready for war.
²⁶ From the Levites: 4,600 ²⁷ in
  addition to Jehoiada, leader
  of the house of Aaron, with
  3,700 men; ²⁸ and Zadok,
  a young valiant warrior,

^A **12:15** = Nisan (March–April)   ^B **12:18** Lit *clothed* ; Jdg 6:34; 2Ch 24:20   ^C **12:22** Or *like the ultimate army* with 22 commanders from his father's family. [A]   2Sm 8:17

29 From the Benjaminites, the relatives of Saul: 3,000 (up to that time the majority of the Benjaminites maintained their allegiance to the house of Saul).   1Ch 12:2

30 From the Ephraimites: 20,800 valiant warriors who were famous men in their ancestral families. [B]

31 From half the tribe of Manasseh: 18,000 designated by name to come and make David king.

32 From the Issacharites, who understood the times and knew what Israel should do: 200 chiefs with all their relatives under their command.

33 From Zebulun: 50,000 who could serve in the army, trained for battle with all kinds of weapons of war, with one purpose to help David. [C]   Ps 12:2

34 From Naphtali: 1,000 commanders accompanied by 37,000 men with shield and spear.

35 From the Danites: 28,600 trained for battle.

36 From Asher: 40,000 who could serve in the army, trained for battle.

37 From across the Jordan — from the Reubenites, Gadites, and half the tribe of Manasseh: 120,000 men equipped with all the military weapons of war.

38 All these warriors, lined up in battle formation, came to Hebron wholeheartedly determined to make David king over all Israel. All the rest of Israel was also of one mind to make David king. 39 They spent three days there eating and drinking with David, for their relatives had provided for them. 40 In addition, their neighbors from as far away as Issachar, Zebulun, and Naphtali came and brought food on donkeys, camels, mules, and oxen — abundant provisions of flour, fig cakes, raisins, wine and oil, herds, and flocks. Indeed, there was joy in Israel.   1Sm 25:18; 2Sm 5:1-3

David and the Ark

13 David consulted with all his leaders, the commanders of hundreds and of thousands. 2 Then he said to the whole assembly of Israel, "If it seems good to you, and if this is from the LORD our God, let us spread out and send the message to the rest of our relatives in all the districts of Israel, including the priests and Levites in their cities with pasturelands, that they should gather together with us. 3 Then let us bring back the ark of our God, for we did not inquire of him [D] in Saul's days." 4 Since the proposal seemed right to all the people, the whole assembly agreed to do it.

5 So David assembled all Israel, from the Shihor of Egypt to the entrance of Hamath, [E] to bring the ark of God from Kiriath-jearim. 6 David and all Israel went to Baalah (that is, Kiriath-jearim that belongs to Judah) to take from there the ark of God, which bears the name of the LORD who is enthroned between

[A]12:28 Lit the house of his father   [B]12:30 Lit the house of their fathers   [C]12:33 LXX; MT omits David   [D]13:3 Or did not seek it   [E]13:5 Or to Lebo-hamath the cherubim. [7] At Abinadab's house they set the ark of God on a new cart. Uzzah and Ahio[A] were guiding the cart. 2Sm 6:1; 1Ch 15:3; 1Kg 8:65

[8] David and all Israel were dancing with all their might before God with songs and with lyres, harps, tambourines, cymbals, and trumpets. [9] When they came to Chidon's threshing floor, Uzzah reached out to hold the ark because the oxen had stumbled. [10] Then the LORD's anger burned against Uzzah, and he struck him dead because he had reached out to the ark. So he died there in the presence of God.

[11] David was angry because of the LORD's outburst against Uzzah, so he named that place Outburst Against Uzzah,[B] as it is still named today. [12] David feared God that day and said, "How can I ever bring the ark of God to me?" [13] So David did not bring the ark of God home[C] to the city of David; instead, he diverted it to the house of Obed-edom of Gath. [14] The ark of God remained with Obed-edom's family in his house for three months, and the LORD blessed his family and all that he had. 1Ch 26:4-5; 2Ch 25:23-24

God's Blessing on David

14 King Hiram of Tyre sent envoys to David, along with cedar logs, stonemasons, and carpenters to build a palace for him. [2] Then David knew that the LORD had established him as king over Israel and that his kingdom had been exalted for the sake of his people Israel. 2Sm 5:11-25

[3] David took more wives in Jerusalem, and he became the father of more sons and daughters. [4] These are the names of the children born to him in Jerusalem: Shammua, Shobab, Nathan, Solomon, [5] Ibhar, Elishua, Elpelet, [6] Nogah, Nepheg, Japhia, [7] Elishama, Beeliada, and Eliphelet. 1Ch 3:5-8

[8] When the Philistines heard that David had been anointed king over all Israel, they all went in search of David; when David heard of this, he went out to face them. [9] Now the Philistines had come and raided in the Valley of Rephaim, [10] so David inquired of God, "Should I attack the Philistines? Will you hand them over to me?" 1Ch 11:15; 14:13

The LORD replied, "Attack, and I will hand them over to you."

[11] So the Israelites went up to Baal-perazim, and David defeated the Philistines there. Then David said, "Like a bursting flood, God has used me to burst out against my enemies." Therefore, they named that place The Lord Bursts Out.[D] [12] The Philistines abandoned their idols there, and David ordered that they be burned in the fire.

[13] Once again the Philistines raided in the valley. [14] So David again inquired of God, and God answered him, "Do not pursue them directly. Circle around them and attack them opposite the balsam trees. [15] When you hear the sound of marching in the tops of the balsam trees, then go out to battle, for God will have gone out ahead of you to strike down the army of the Philistines." [16] So David did as God commanded him, and they struck down the Philistine army from Gibeon to Gezer. [17] Then David's fame spread throughout the lands, and the LORD caused all the nations to be terrified of him. Ex 15:14-16; Dt 2:25

A**13:7** Or And his brothers   B**13:11** Or Perez-uzzah   C**13:13** Lit to himself   D**14:11** Or Baal-perazim

The Ark Comes to Jerusalem

15 David built houses for himself in the city of David, and he prepared a place for the ark of God and pitched a tent for it. ² Then David said, "No one but the Levites may carry the ark of God, because the LORD has chosen them to carry the ark of the LORD and to minister before him forever." 1Ch 16:1; 17:1-5

³ David assembled all Israel at Jerusalem to bring the ark of the LORD to the place he had prepared for it. ⁴ Then he gathered together the descendants of Aaron and the Levites: 2Sm 6:12,17; 1Ch 13:5; 15:12

⁵ From the Kohathites, Uriel the leader and 120 of his relatives; ⁶ from the Merarites, Asaiah the leader and 220 of his relatives; ⁷ from the Gershomites, ᴬ Joel the leader and 130 of his relatives; ⁸ from the Elizaphanites, Shemaiah the leader and 200 of his relatives; ⁹ from the Hebronites, Eliel the leader and 80 of his relatives; ¹⁰ from the Uzzielites, Amminadab the leader and 112 of his relatives.

¹¹ David summoned the priests Zadok and Abiathar and the Levites Uriel, Asaiah, Joel, Shemaiah, Eliel, and Amminadab. ¹² He said to them, "You are the heads of the Levite families. You and your relatives must consecrate yourselves so that you may bring the ark of the LORD God of Israel to the place I have prepared for it. ¹³ For the LORD our God burst out in anger against us because you Levites were not with us the first time, for we didn't inquire of him about the proper procedures." ¹⁴ So the priests and the Levites consecrated themselves to bring up the ark of the LORD God of Israel. ¹⁵ Then the Levites carried the ark of God the way Moses had commanded according to the word of the LORD: on their shoulders with the poles. 1Ch 12:28; 18:16

¹⁶ Then David told the leaders of the Levites to appoint their relatives as singers and to have them raise their voices with joy accompanied by musical instruments — harps, lyres, and cymbals. ¹⁷ So the Levites appointed Heman son of Joel; from his relatives, Asaph son of Berechiah; and from their relatives the Merarites, Ethan son of Kushaiah. ¹⁸ With them were their relatives second in rank: Zechariah, Jaaziel, ᴮ Shemiramoth, Jehiel, Unni, Eliab, Benaiah, Maaseiah, Mattithiah, Eliphelehu, Mikneiah, and the gatekeepers Obed-edom and Jeiel. ¹⁹ The singers Heman, Asaph, and Ethan were to sound the bronze cymbals; ²⁰ Zechariah, Aziel, Shemiramoth, Jehiel, Unni, Eliab, Maaseiah, and Benaiah were to play harps according to *Alamoth* ᶜ ²¹ and Mattithiah, Eliphelehu, Mikneiah, Obed-edom, Jeiel, and Azaziah were to lead the music with lyres according to the *Sheminith.* ²² Chenaniah, the leader of the Levites in music, was to direct the music because he was skillful. ²³ Berechiah and Elkanah were to be gatekeepers for the ark. ²⁴ The priests, Shebaniah, Joshaphat, Nethanel, Amasai, Zechariah, Benaiah, and Eliezer, were to blow trumpets before the ark of God. Obed-edom and Jehiah were also to be gatekeepers for the ark. 1Ch 13:8; 16:6; 25:1

ᴬ15:7 = Gershonites　ᴮ15:18 Some Hb mss, LXX; other Hb mss read *Zechariah son and Jaaziel*
ᶜ15:20 This may refer to a high pitch, perhaps a tune sung by soprano voices; the Hb word means "young women"; Ps 46 title

²⁵ David, the elders of Israel, and the commanders of thousands went with rejoicing to bring the ark of the covenant of the LORD from the house of Obed-edom. ²⁶ Because God helped the Levites who were carrying the ark of the covenant of the LORD, with God's help, they sacrificed seven bulls and seven rams. 2Sm 6:12-16; 1Ch 13:13

²⁷ Now David was dressed in a robe of fine linen, as were all the Levites who were carrying the ark, as well as the singers and Chenaniah, the music leader of the singers. David also wore a linen ephod. ²⁸ So all Israel brought up the ark of the covenant of the LORD with shouts, the sound of the ram's horn, trumpets, and cymbals, and the playing of harps and lyres. ²⁹ As the ark of the covenant of the LORD was entering the city of David, Saul's daughter Michal looked down from the window and saw King David leaping ᴬ and dancing, and she despised him in her heart.

16 They brought the ark of God and placed it inside the tent David had pitched for it. Then they offered burnt offerings and fellowship offerings in God's presence. ² When David had finished offering the burnt offerings and the fellowship offerings, he blessed the people in the name of the LORD. ³ Then he distributed to each and every Israelite, both men and women, a loaf of bread, a date cake, and a raisin cake. 2Sm 6:17-19; 1Ch 15:1

⁴ David appointed some of the Levites to be ministers before the ark of the LORD, to celebrate the LORD God of Israel, and to give thanks and praise to him. ⁵ Asaph was the chief and Zechariah was second to him. Jeiel, Shemiramoth, Jehiel, Mattithiah, Eliab, Benaiah, Obed-edom, and Jeiel played the harps and lyres, while Asaph sounded the cymbals ⁶ and the priests Benaiah and Jahaziel blew the trumpets regularly before the ark of the covenant of God.

David's Psalm of Thanksgiving

⁷ On that day David decreed for the first time that thanks be given to the LORD by Asaph and his relatives:

⁸ Give thanks to the LORD;
  call on his name; Ps 105:1-15
  proclaim his deeds among
    the peoples. 1Kg 8:43; 2Kg 19:19
⁹ Sing to him; sing praise
    to him;
  tell about all
    his wondrous works!
¹⁰ Honor his holy name;
  let the hearts of those
    who seek the LORD rejoice.
¹¹ Seek the LORD
    and his strength;
  seek his face always. Ps 24:6
¹² Remember
    the wondrous works
    he has done, Ps 103:2
  his wonders,
    and the judgments
    he has pronounced, ᴮ
¹³ you offspring of Israel
    his servant,
  Jacob's descendants —
    his chosen ones.

¹⁴ He is the LORD our God;
  his judgments govern
    the whole earth. Ps 48:10
¹⁵ Remember his covenant
    forever —
  the promise he ordained
    for a thousand generations,

ᴬ**15:29** Or *whirling*   ᴮ**16:12** Lit *judgments of his mouth*

¹⁶ the covenant he made
  with Abraham,
swore^A to Isaac,   Gn 17:2; 22:16-18
¹⁷ and confirmed to Jacob
  as a decree,
and to Israel
  as a permanent covenant:
¹⁸ "I will give the land
  of Canaan to you
as your inherited portion."

¹⁹ When they^B were few
  in number,
very few indeed,
  and resident aliens
  in Canaan   Gn 34:30; Dt 7:7
²⁰ wandering from nation
  to nation
and from one kingdom
  to another,
²¹ he allowed no one to oppress
  them;
he rebuked kings
  on their behalf: Gn 12:17; 20:3
²² "Do not touch
  my anointed ones
or harm my prophets."   Gn 20:7

²³ Let the whole earth sing to
  the LORD.   Ps 96
Proclaim his salvation
  from day to day.
²⁴ Declare his glory
  among the nations,
his wondrous works
  among all peoples.

²⁵ For the LORD is great
  and highly praised;   Ps 144:3-6
he is feared above all gods.
²⁶ For all the gods
  of the peoples are idols,
but the LORD made
  the heavens.   Ps 102:25
²⁷ Splendor and majesty are
  before him;

strength and joy are
  in his place.
²⁸ Ascribe to the LORD, families
  of the peoples,
ascribe to the LORD glory
  and strength.
²⁹ Ascribe to the LORD the glory
  of his name;
bring an offering and come
  before him.
Worship the LORD
  in the splendor
  of his holiness;   Ps 29:2
³⁰ let the whole earth tremble
  before him.   Ps 93:1

The world is
  firmly established;
it cannot be shaken.
³¹ Let the heavens be glad
  and the earth rejoice,   Is 44:23
and let them say
  among the nations,
"The LORD reigns!"
³² Let the sea and all that fills it
  resound;
let the fields and everything
  in them exult.   Ps 98:7
³³ Then the trees of the forest
  will shout for joy
  before the LORD,
for he is coming to judge
  the earth.

³⁴ Give thanks to the LORD,
  for he is good;
his faithful love
  endures forever.   Ps 106:1; 136:1
³⁵ And say: "Save us,
  God of our salvation;
gather us and rescue us from
  the nations
so that we may
  give thanks to
  your holy name
and rejoice in your praise.

^A**16:16** Lit *and his oath*   ^B**16:19** One Hb ms, LXX, Vg; other Hb mss read *you*

³⁶ Blessed be the LORD God
of Israel   1Kg 8:15,56; Ps 72:18
from everlasting
to everlasting."
Then all the people said, "Amen"
and "Praise the LORD."

³⁷ So David left Asaph and his relatives there before the ark of the LORD's covenant to minister regularly before the ark according to the daily requirements. ³⁸ He assigned Obed-edom and his ᴬ sixty-eight relatives. Obed-edom son of Jeduthun and Hosah were to be gatekeepers. ³⁹ David left the priest Zadok and his fellow priests before the tabernacle of the LORD at the high place in Gibeon ⁴⁰ to offer burnt offerings regularly, morning and evening, to the LORD on the altar of burnt offerings and to do everything that was written in the law of the LORD, which he had commanded Israel to keep. ⁴¹ With them were Heman, Jeduthun, and the rest who were chosen and designated by name to give thanks to the LORD — for his faithful love endures forever. ⁴² Heman and Jeduthun had with them trumpets and cymbals to play and musical instruments of God. Jeduthun's sons were at the city gate.   1Ch 16:4-5; 2Ch 8:14

⁴³ Then all the people went home, and David returned home to bless his household.   2Sm 6:19-20

The LORD's Covenant with David

17 When David had settled into his palace, he said to the prophet Nathan, "Look! I am living in a cedar house while the ark of the LORD's covenant is under tent curtains."   2Sm 7:1-3; Hg 1:4

² So Nathan told David, "Do all that is on your mind, for God is with you."

³ But that night the word of God came to Nathan: ⁴ "Go to David my servant and say, 'This is what the LORD says: You are not the one to build me a house to dwell in. ⁵ From the time I brought Israel out of Egypt until today I have not dwelt in a house; instead, I have moved from one tent site to another, and from one tabernacle location to another.ᴮ ⁶ In all my journeys throughout Israel, have I ever spoken a word to even one of the judges of Israel, whom I commanded to shepherd my people, asking: Why haven't you built me a house of cedar?'

⁷ "So now this is what you are to say to my servant David: 'This is what the LORD of Armies says: I took you from the pasture, from tending the flock, to be ruler over my people Israel. ⁸ I have been with you wherever you have gone, and I have destroyed all your enemies before you. I will make a name for you like that of the greatest on the earth. ⁹ I will designate a place for my people Israel and plant them, so that they may live there and not be disturbed again. Evildoers will not continue to oppress them as they have done ¹⁰ ever since the day I ordered judges to be over my people Israel. I will also subdue all your enemies.   Ex 15:17; 1Sm 16:11-13

" 'Furthermore, I declare to you that the LORD himself will build a house for you. ¹¹ When your time comes to be with your fathers, I will raise up after you your descendant, who is one of your own sons, and I will establish his kingdom. ¹² He is the one who will build a house for me, and I will establish his throne forever. ¹³ I will be his father, and he will be my son. I will not remove

---

ᴬ**16:38** LXX, Syr, Vg; Hb reads their   ᴮ**17:5** Lit I was from tent to tent and from tabernacle my faithful love from him as I removed it from the one who was before you. ¹⁴ I will appoint him over my house and my kingdom forever, and his throne will be established forever.'" 1Kg 5:2-5; 6:14,38; 8:17-20; 2Ch 6:2

¹⁵ Nathan reported all these words and this entire vision to David.

David's Prayer of Thanksgiving

¹⁶ Then King David went in, sat in the LORD's presence, and said,

Who am I, LORD God, and what is my house that you have brought me this far? ¹⁷ This was a little thing to you,ᴬ God, for you have spoken about your servant's house in the distant future. You regard me as a man of distinction,ᴮ LORD God. ¹⁸ What more can David say to you for honoring your servant? You know your servant. ¹⁹ LORD, you have done this whole great thing, making known all these great promises for the sake of your servant and according to your will. ²⁰ LORD, there is no one like you, and there is no God besides you, as all we have heard confirms. ²¹ And who is like your people Israel? God, you came to one nation on earth to redeem a people for yourself, to make a name for yourself through great and awesome works by driving out nations before your people you redeemed from Egypt. ²² You made your people Israel your own people forever, and you, LORD, have become their God.

²³ Now, LORD, let the word that you have spoken concerning your servant and his house be confirmed forever, and do as you have promised. ²⁴ Let your name be confirmed and magnified forever in the saying, "The LORD of Armies, the God of Israel, is God over Israel." May the house of your servant David be established before you. ²⁵ Since you, my God, have revealed toᶜ your servant that you will build him a house, your servant has found courage to pray in your presence. ²⁶ LORD, you indeed are God, and you have promised this good thing to your servant. ²⁷ So now, you have been pleased to bless your servant's house that it may continue before you forever. For you, LORD, have blessed it, and it is blessed forever. Ex 6:7; 19:5-6

David's Military Campaigns

18 After this, David defeated the Philistines, subdued them, and took Gath and its surrounding villages from Philistine control. ² He also defeated the Moabites, and they became David's subjects and brought tribute. 2Sm 8:1-14

³ David also defeated King Hadadezer of Zobah at Hamath when he went to establish his control at the Euphrates River. ⁴ David captured one thousand chariots, seven thousand horsemen, and twenty thousand foot soldiers from him, hamstrung all the horses, and kept a hundred chariots.ᴰ

⁵ When the Arameans of Damascus came to assist King Hadadezer of Zobah, David struck down twenty-two thousand Aramean

ᴬ**17:17** Lit thing in your eyes   ᴮ**17:17** Hb obscure   ᶜ**17:25** Lit have uncovered the ear of   ᴰ**18:4** Or chariot horses men. ⁶ Then he placed garrisons ᴬ in Aram of Damascus, and the Arameans became David's subjects and brought tribute. The LORD made David victorious wherever he went. 2Sm 8:6; 1Ch 18:9; 19:6

⁷ David took the gold shields carried by Hadadezer's officers and brought them to Jerusalem. ⁸ From Tibhath and Cun, Hadadezer's cities, David also took huge quantities of bronze, from which Solomon made the bronze basin, ᴮ the pillars, and the bronze articles. 1Kg 7:15-47

⁹ When King Tou of Hamath heard that David had defeated the entire army of King Hadadezer of Zobah, ¹⁰ he sent his son Hadoram to King David to greet him and to congratulate him because David had fought against Hadadezer and defeated him, for Tou and Hadadezer had fought many wars. Hadoram brought all kinds of gold, silver, and bronze items. ¹¹ King David also dedicated these to the LORD, along with the silver and gold he had carried off from all the nations — from Edom, Moab, the Ammonites, the Philistines, and the Amalekites.

¹² Abishai son of Zeruiah struck down eighteen thousand Edomites in the Salt Valley. ¹³ He put garrisons in Edom, and all the Edomites were subject to David. The LORD made David victorious wherever he went.

¹⁴ So David reigned over all Israel, administering justice and righteousness for all his people.

¹⁵ Joab son of Zeruiah was over the army; 1Ch 11:6
Jehoshaphat son of Ahilud was court historian;
¹⁶ Zadok son of Ahitub and Ahimelech ᶜ

son of Abiathar were priests; 2Sm 8:17; 1Ch 24:6,31
Shavsha was court secretary;
¹⁷ Benaiah son of Jehoiada was over the Cherethites and the Pelethites;
and David's sons were the chief officials at the king's side.

War with the Ammonites

19 Some time later, King Nahash of the Ammonites died, and his son became king in his place. ² Then David said, "I'll show kindness to Hanun son of Nahash, because his father showed kindness to me." 2Sm 10:1-5

So David sent messengers to console him concerning his father. However, when David's emissaries arrived in the land of the Ammonites to console him, ³ the Ammonite leaders said to Hanun, "Just because David has sent men with condolences for you, do you really believe he's showing respect for your father? Instead, haven't his emissaries come in order to scout out, overthrow, and spy on the land?" ⁴ So Hanun took David's emissaries, shaved them, cut their clothes in half at the hips, and sent them away. Is 7:20; 20:4

⁵ It was reported to David about his men, so he sent messengers to meet them, since the men were deeply humiliated. The king said, "Stay in Jericho until your beards grow back; then return."

⁶ When the Ammonites realized they had made themselves repulsive to David, Hanun and the Ammonites sent thirty-eight tons ᴰ of silver to hire chariots and

ᴬ**18:6** Some Hb mss, LXX, Vg; other Hb mss omit *garrisons*; 2Sm 8:6　ᴮ**18:8** Lit *sea*　ᶜ**18:16** Some Hb mss, LXX, Syr, Vg; other Hb mss read *Abimelech*; 2Sm 8:17　ᴰ**19:6** Lit *1,000 talents* horsemen from Aram-naharaim, Aram-maacah, and Zobah. [7] They hired thirty-two thousand chariots and the king of Maacah with his army, who came and camped near Medeba. The Ammonites also came together from their cities for the battle. Nm 21:30; 2Sm 10:6-19; 1Ch 18:5,9

[8] David heard about this and sent Joab and all the elite troops. [9] The Ammonites marched out and lined up in battle formation at the entrance of the city while the kings who had come were in the field by themselves. [10] When Joab saw that there was a battle line in front of him and another behind him, he chose some of Israel's finest young men [A] and lined up in formation to engage the Arameans. [11] He placed the rest of the forces under the command of his brother Abishai. They lined up in formation to engage the Ammonites. 2Sm 6:1

[12] "If the Arameans are too strong for me," Joab said, "then you'll be my help. However, if the Ammonites are too strong for you, I'll help you. [13] Be strong! Let's prove ourselves strong for our people and for the cities of our God. May the LORD's will be done." [B] Jos 1:6

[14] Joab and the people with him approached the Arameans for battle, and they fled before him. [15] When the Ammonites saw that the Arameans had fled, they likewise fled before Joab's brother Abishai and entered the city. Then Joab went to Jerusalem.

[16] When the Arameans realized that they had been defeated by Israel, they sent messengers to summon the Arameans who were beyond the Euphrates River. They were led by Shophach, the commander of Hadadezer's army.

[17] When this was reported to David, he gathered all Israel and crossed the Jordan. He came up to the Arameans and lined up against them. When David lined up to engage them, they fought against him. [18] But the Arameans fled before Israel, and David killed seven thousand of their charioteers and forty thousand foot soldiers. He also killed Shophach, commander of the army. [19] When Hadadezer's subjects saw that they had been defeated by Israel, they made peace with David and became his subjects. After this, the Arameans were never willing to help the Ammonites again.

Capture of the City of Rabbah

20 In the spring [C] when kings march out to war, Joab led the army and destroyed the Ammonites' land. He came to Rabbah and besieged it, but David remained in Jerusalem. Joab attacked Rabbah and demolished it. [2] Then David took the crown from the head of their king, [D,E] and it was placed on David's head. He found that the crown weighed seventy-five pounds [F] of gold, and there was a precious stone in it. In addition, David took away a large quantity of plunder from the city. [3] He brought out the people who were in it and put them to work with saws, [G] iron picks, and axes. [H] David did the same to all the Ammonite

---

cities. Then he and all his troops returned to Jerusalem. 2Sm 12:26-31

The Philistine Giants

⁴ After this, a war broke out with the Philistines at Gezer. At that time Sibbecai the Hushathite killed Sippai, a descendant of the Rephaim, ^A^ and the Philistines were subdued.

⁵ Once again there was a battle with the Philistines, and Elhanan son of Jair killed Lahmi the brother of Goliath of Gath. The shaft of his spear was like a weaver's beam.

⁶ There was still another battle at Gath where there was a man of extraordinary stature with six fingers on each hand and six toes on each foot — twenty-four in all. He, too, was descended from the giant. ^B^ ⁷ When he taunted Israel, Jonathan son of David's brother Shimei killed him.

⁸ These were the descendants of the giant in Gath killed by David and his soldiers.

David's Military Census

21 Satan^C^ rose up against Israel and incited David to count the people of Israel. ² So David said to Joab and the commanders of the troops, "Go and count Israel from Beer-sheba to Dan and bring a report to me so I can know their number." 2Sm 24:1-10; 1Ch 27:23-24; Jb 1:6; Zch 3:1-2

³ Joab replied, "May the LORD multiply the number of his people a hundred times over! My lord the king, aren't they all my lord's servants? Why does my lord want to do this? Why should he bring guilt on Israel?" Dt 1:11

⁴ Yet the king's order prevailed over Joab. So Joab left and traveled throughout Israel and then returned to Jerusalem. ⁵ Joab gave the total troop registration to David. In all Israel there were one million one hundred thousand armed men ^D^ and in Judah itself four hundred seventy thousand armed men. ⁶ But he did not include Levi and Benjamin in the count because the king's command was detestable to him. ⁷ This command was also evil in God's sight, so he afflicted Israel.

⁸ David said to God, "I have sinned greatly because I have done this thing. Now, please take away your servant's guilt, for I've been very foolish." 2Sm 12:13

David's Punishment

⁹ Then the LORD instructed Gad, David's seer, ¹⁰ "Go and say to David, 'This is what the LORD says: I am offering you three choices. Choose one of them for yourself, and I will do it to you.'" 1Sm 9:9; 2Sm 24:11-17; 1Ch 29:29

¹¹ So Gad went to David and said to him, "This is what the LORD says: 'Take your choice: ¹² three years of famine, or three months of devastation by your foes with the sword of your enemy overtaking you, or three days of the sword of the LORD — a plague on the land, the angel of the LORD bringing destruction to the whole territory of Israel.' Now decide what answer I should take back to the one who sent me."

¹³ David answered Gad, "I'm in anguish. Please, let me fall into the LORD's hands because his mercies are very great, but don't let me fall into human hands." Ps 51:1; 130:4,7

¹⁴ So the LORD sent a plague on Israel, and seventy thousand Israelite men died. ¹⁵ Then God sent

---

^A^**20:4** Or *the Rephaites* ^B^**20:6** Or *Raphah,* also in v. 8 ^C^**21:1** Or *An adversary* ; Jb 1:6; Zch 3:1-2 ^D^**21:5** Lit *men drawing the sword* an angel to Jerusalem to destroy it, but when the angel was about to destroy the city,[A] the LORD looked, relented concerning the destruction, and said to the angel who was destroying the people, "Enough, withdraw your hand now!" The angel of the LORD was then standing at the threshing floor of Ornan[B] the Jebusite. Ex 32:14; 1Sm 15:11; 2Sm 24:16

[16] When David looked up and saw the angel of the LORD standing between earth and heaven, with his drawn sword in his hand stretched out over Jerusalem, David and the elders, clothed in sackcloth, fell facedown. [17] David said to God, "Wasn't I the one who gave the order to count the people? I am the one who has sinned and acted very wickedly. But these sheep, what have they done? LORD my God, please let your hand be against me and against my father's family, but don't let the plague be against your people." 1Kg 21:27

David's Altar

[18] So the angel of the LORD ordered Gad to tell David to go and set up an altar to the LORD on the threshing floor of Ornan the Jebusite. [19] David went up at Gad's command spoken in the name of the LORD. 2Sm 24:18-25 [20] Ornan was threshing wheat when he turned and saw the angel. His four sons, who were with him, hid. [21] David came to Ornan, and when Ornan looked and saw David, he left the threshing floor and bowed to David with his face to the ground. [22] Then David said to Ornan, "Give me this threshing-floor plot so that I may build an altar to the LORD on

it. Give it to me for the full price, so the plague on the people may be stopped."

[23] Ornan said to David, "Take it! My lord the king may do whatever he wants.[C] See, I give the oxen for the burnt offerings, the threshing sledges for the wood, and the wheat for the grain offering — I give it all." [24] King David answered Ornan, "No, I insist on paying the full price, for I will not take for the LORD what belongs to you or offer burnt offerings that cost me nothing."

[25] So David gave Ornan fifteen pounds of gold[D] for the plot. [26] He built an altar to the LORD there and offered burnt offerings and fellowship offerings. He called on the LORD, and he answered him with fire from heaven on the altar of burnt offering. Lv 9:24; Jdg 6:21

[27] Then the LORD spoke to the angel, and he put his sword back into its sheath. [28] At that time, David offered sacrifices there when he saw that the LORD answered him at the threshing floor of Ornan the Jebusite. [29] The tabernacle of the LORD, which Moses made in the wilderness, and the altar of burnt offering were at the high place in Gibeon, [30] but David could not go before it to inquire of God, because he was terrified of the sword of the LORD's angel. **22** [1] Then David said, "This is the house of the LORD God, and this is the altar of burnt offering for Israel." 1Ch 21:18-28; 2Ch 3:1

David's Preparations for the Temple

[2] So David gave orders to gather the resident aliens that were in the land of Israel, and he appointed

A **21:15** Lit *but as he was destroying*   B **21:15-28** = Araunah in 2Sm 24:16-24   C **21:23** Lit *do what is good in his eyes*   D **21:25** Lit *600 shekels of gold by weight* stonecutters to cut finished stones for building God's house. ³ David supplied a great deal of iron to make the nails for the doors of the gates and for the fittings, together with an immeasurable quantity of bronze, ⁴ and innumerable cedar logs because the Sidonians and Tyrians had brought a large quantity of cedar logs to David. ⁵ David said, "My son Solomon is young and inexperienced, and the house that is to be built for the LORD must be exceedingly great and famous and glorious in all the lands. Therefore, I will make provision for it." So David made lavish preparations for it before his death. 1Kg 9:20-21; 2Ch 2:17

⁶ Then he summoned his son Solomon and charged him to build a house for the LORD God of Israel. ⁷ "My son," David said to Solomon, "It was in my heart to build a house for the name of the LORD my God, ⁸ but the word of the LORD came to me: 'You have shed much blood and waged great wars. You are not to build a house for my name because you have shed so much blood on the ground before me. ⁹ But a son will be born to you; he will be a man of rest. I will give him rest from all his surrounding enemies, for his name will be Solomon,ᴬ and I will give peace and quiet to Israel during his reign. ¹⁰ He is the one who will build a house for my name. He will be my son, and I will be his father. I will establish the throne of his kingdom over Israel forever.'

¹¹ "Now, my son, may the LORD be with you, and may you succeed in building the house of the LORD your God, as he said about you. ¹² Above all, may the LORD give you insight and understanding when he puts you in charge of Israel so that you may keep the law of the LORD your God. ¹³ Then you will succeed if you carefully follow the statutes and ordinances the LORD commanded Moses for Israel. Be strong and courageous. Don't be afraid or discouraged. 1Kg 3:9-12; 1Ch 22:16; 2Ch 1:10-12

¹⁴ "Notice I have taken great pains to provide for the house of the LORD — 3,775 tons of gold, 37,750 tons of silver,ᴮ and bronze and iron that can't be weighed because there is so much of it. I have also provided timber and stone, but you will need to add more to them. ¹⁵ You also have many workers: stonecutters, masons, carpenters, and people skilled in every kind of work¹⁶ in gold, silver, bronze, and iron — beyond number. Now begin the work, and may the LORD be with you."

¹⁷ Then David ordered all the leaders of Israel to help his son Solomon: ¹⁸ "The LORD your God is with you, isn't he? And hasn't he given you rest on every side? For he has handed the land's inhabitants over to me, and the land has been subdued before the LORD and his people. ¹⁹ Now determine in your mind and heart to seek the LORD your God. Get started building the LORD God's sanctuary so that you may bring the ark of the LORD's covenant and the holy articles of God to the temple that is to be built for the name of the LORD." 1Ch 22:9; 23:25

The Divisions of the Levites

23 When David was old and full of days, he installed his son Solomon as king over Israel. ² Then he gathered all the leaders of Israel,

---

ᴬ**22:9** In Hb, the name *Solomon* sounds like "peace." ᴮ**22:14** Lit *100,000 talents of gold and 1,000,000 talents of silver* the priests, and the Levites. ³ The Levites thirty years old or more were counted; the total number of men was thirty-eight thousand by headcount. ⁴ "Of these," David said, "twenty-four thousand are to be in charge of the work on the LORD's temple, six thousand are to be officers and judges, ⁵ four thousand are to be gatekeepers, and four thousand are to praise the LORD with the instruments that I have made for worship." 1Ch 29:28

⁶ Then David divided them into divisions according to Levi's sons: Gershom,ᴬ Kohath, and Merari. ⁷ The Gershonites: Ladan and Shimei. ⁸ Ladan's sons: Jehiel was the first, then Zetham, and Joel — three. ⁹ Shimei's sons: Shelomoth, Haziel, and Haran — three. Those were the heads of the families of Ladan. ¹⁰ Shimei's sons: Jahath, Zizah,ᴮ Jeush, and Beriah. Those were Shimei's sons — four. ¹¹ Jahath was the first and Zizah was the second; however, Jeush and Beriah did not have many sons, so they became one familyᶜ and received a single assignment. ¹² Kohath's sons: Amram, Izhar, Hebron, and Uzziel — four. ¹³ Amram's sons: Aaron and Moses. Ex 6:20

Aaron, along with his descendants, was set apart forever to consecrate the most holy things, to burn incense in the presence of the LORD, to minister to him, and to pronounce blessings in his name forever. ¹⁴ As for Moses the man of God, his sons were named among the tribe of Levi. Ex 28:1; 30:6-10; Dt 33:1

¹⁵ Moses's sons: Gershom and Eliezer. ¹⁶ Gershom's sons: Shebuel was first. ¹⁷ Eliezer's sons were Rehabiah, first; Eliezer did not have any other sons, but Rehabiah's sons were very numerous. ¹⁸ Izhar's sons: Shelomith was first. ¹⁹ Hebron's sons: Jeriah was first, Amariah second, Jahaziel third, and Jekameam fourth. ²⁰ Uzziel's sons: Micah was first, and Isshiah second. ²¹ Merari's sons: Mahli and Mushi.

Mahli's sons: Eleazar and Kish. ²² Eleazar died having no sons, only daughters. Their cousins, the sons of Kish, married them. ²³ Mushi's sons: Mahli, Eder, and Jeremoth — three.

²⁴ These were the descendants of Levi by their ancestral familiesᴰ — the family heads, according to their registration by name in the headcount — twenty years old or more, who worked in the service of the LORD's temple. ²⁵ For David said, "The LORD God of Israel has given rest to his people, and he has come to stay in Jerusalem forever. ²⁶ Also, the Levites no longer need to carry the tabernacle or any of the equipment for its service" — ²⁷ for according to the last words of David, the Levites twenty years old or more were to be counted — ²⁸ "but their duty will be to assist the descendants of Aaron with the service of the LORD's temple, being

ᴬ23:6 Lit Gershon   ᴮ23:10 LXX, Vg; MT reads Zina   ᶜ23:11 Lit a father's house   ᴰ23:24 Lit the house of their fathers responsible for the courts and the chambers, the purification of all the holy things, and the work of the service of God's temple — ²⁹ as well as the rows of the Bread of the Presence, the fine flour for the grain offering, the wafers of unleavened bread, the baking, ᴬ the mixing, and all measurements of volume and length. ³⁰ They are also to stand every morning to give thanks and praise to the LORD, and likewise in the evening. ³¹ Whenever burnt offerings are offered to the LORD on the Sabbaths, New Moons, and appointed festivals, they are to offer them regularly in the LORD's presence according to the number prescribed for them. ³² They are to carry out their responsibilities for the tent of meeting, for the holy place, and for their relatives, the descendants of Aaron, in the service of the LORD's temple." Nm 4:5,15

The Divisions of the Priests

24 The divisions of the descendants of Aaron were as follows: Aaron's sons were Nadab, Abihu, Eleazar, and Ithamar. ² But Nadab and Abihu died before their father, and they had no sons, so Eleazar and Ithamar served as priests. ³ Together with Zadok from the descendants of Eleazar and Ahimelech from the descendants of Ithamar, David divided them according to the assigned duties of their service. ⁴ Since more leaders were found among Eleazar's descendants than Ithamar's, they were divided accordingly: sixteen heads of ancestral families ᴮ were from Eleazar's descendants, and eight heads of ancestral families were from Ithamar's. ⁵ They were assigned by lot, for there were officers of the sanctuary and officers of God among both Eleazar's and Ithamar's descendants. Ex 6:23; 24:6,31

⁶ The secretary, Shemaiah son of Nethanel, a Levite, recorded them in the presence of the king and the officers, the priest Zadok, Ahimelech son of Abiathar, and the heads of families of the priests and the Levites. One ancestral family ᶜ was taken for Eleazar, and then one for Ithamar. 2Sm 8:17; 1Ch 18:16; 24:31

⁷ The first lot fell to Jehoiarib,
    the second to Jedaiah,
⁸ the third to Harim, the fourth
    to Seorim,
⁹ the fifth to Malchijah,
    the sixth to Mijamin,
¹⁰ the seventh to Hakkoz,
    the eighth to Abijah, Neh 12:4
¹¹ the ninth to Jeshua, the tenth
    to Shecaniah,
¹² the eleventh to Eliashib,
    the twelfth to Jakim,
¹³ the thirteenth to Huppah,
    the fourteenth
    to Jeshebeab,
¹⁴ the fifteenth to Bilgah,
    the sixteenth to Immer,
¹⁵ the seventeenth to Hezir,
    the eighteenth
    to Happizzez,
¹⁶ the nineteenth to Pethahiah,
    the twentieth to Jehezkel,
¹⁷ the twenty-first to Jachin,
    the twenty-second
    to Gamul,
¹⁸ the twenty-third to Delaiah,
    and the twenty-fourth
    to Maaziah.

¹⁹ These had their assigned duties for service when they entered the LORD's temple, according to their regulations, which they received

---

ᴬ23:29 Lit *the griddle*   ᴮ24:4 Lit *house of fathers*   ᶜ24:6 Lit *father's house* from their ancestor Aaron, as the LORD God of Israel had commanded him.

The Rest of the Levites

²⁰ As for the rest of Levi's sons: from Amram's sons: Shubael; from Shubael's sons: Jehdeiah. ²¹ From Rehabiah: from Rehabiah's sons: Isshiah was the first. ²² From the Izharites: Shelomoth; from Shelomoth's sons: Jahath. ²³ Hebron's ᴬ sons: 1Ch 23:19
Jeriah the first, Amariah the second,
Jahaziel the third, and Jekameam the fourth. ²⁴ From Uzziel's sons: Micah; from Micah's sons: Shamir. ²⁵ Micah's brother: Isshiah; from Isshiah's sons: Zechariah. ²⁶ Merari's sons: Mahli and Mushi,
and from his sons, Jaaziah his son. ᴮ ²⁷ Merari's sons, by his son Jaaziah: ᶜ
Shoham, Zaccur, and Ibri. ²⁸ From Mahli: Eleazar, who had no sons. ²⁹ From Kish, from Kish's sons: Jerahmeel. ³⁰ Mushi's sons: Mahli, Eder, and Jerimoth.

Those were the descendants of the Levites according to their ancestral families. ᴰ ³¹ They also cast lots the same way as their relatives the descendants of Aaron did in the presence of King David, Zadok, Ahimelech, and the heads of the families of the priests and Levites — the family heads and their younger brothers alike.   1Ch 24:5-6

The Levitical Musicians

25 David and the officers of the army also set apart some of the sons of Asaph, Heman, and Jeduthun, who were to prophesy accompanied by lyres, harps, and cymbals. This is the list of the men who performed their service: ² From Asaph's sons: Zaccur, Joseph, Nethaniah, and Asarelah, sons of Asaph, under Asaph's authority, who prophesied under the authority of the king. ³ From Jeduthun: Jeduthun's sons: 1Ch 16:41-42
Gedaliah, Zeri, Jeshaiah, Shimei, ᴱ Hashabiah, and Mattithiah — six — under the authority of their father Jeduthun, prophesying to the accompaniment of lyres, giving thanks and praise to the LORD. ⁴ From Heman: Heman's sons: Bukkiah, Mattaniah, Uzziel, Shebuel, Jerimoth, Hananiah, Hanani, Eliathah, Giddalti, Romamti-ezer, Joshbekashah, Mallothi, Hothir, and Mahazioth. ⁵ All these sons of Heman, the king's seer, were given by the promises of God to exalt him, ꟻ for God had given Heman fourteen sons and three daughters.   1Sm 9:9

⁶ All these men were under their own fathers' authority for the music in the LORD's temple, with cymbals, harps, and lyres for the service of God's temple. Asaph,

---

Jeduthun, and Heman were under the king's authority. ⁷ They numbered 288 together with their relatives who were all trained and skillful in music for the LORD. ⁸ They cast lots for their duties, young and old alike, teacher as well as pupil.   1Ch 26:13

9   The first lot for Asaph
      fell to Joseph, his sons,
      and his relatives —   12 ᴬ
         to Gedaliah the second:
      him, his relatives,
      and his sons —   12
10   the third to Zaccur, his sons,
      and his relatives —   12
11   the fourth to Izri, ᴮ his sons,
      and his relatives —   12
12   the fifth to Nethaniah,
      his sons,
      and his relatives —   12
13   the sixth to Bukkiah, his sons,
      and his relatives —   12
14   the seventh
      to Jesarelah, his sons,
      and his relatives —   12
15   the eighth to Jeshaiah,
      his sons,
      and his relatives —   12
16   the ninth to Mattaniah,
      his sons,
      and his relatives —   12
17   the tenth to Shimei, his sons,
      and his relatives —   12
18   the eleventh
      to Azarel, ᶜ his sons,
      and his relatives —   12
19   the twelfth
      to Hashabiah, his sons,
      and his relatives —   12
20   the thirteenth
      to Shubael, his sons,
      and his relatives —   12
21   the fourteenth
      to Mattithiah, his sons,
      and his relatives —   12

22   the fifteenth
      to Jeremoth, his sons,
      and his relatives —   12
23   the sixteenth
      to Hananiah, his sons,
      and his relatives —   12
24   the seventeenth
      to Joshbekashah, his sons,
      and his relatives —   12
25   the eighteenth
      to Hanani, his sons,
      and his relatives —   12
26   the nineteenth
      to Mallothi, his sons,
      and his relatives —   12
27   the twentieth
      to Eliathah, his sons,
      and his relatives —   12
28   the twenty-first
      to Hothir, his sons,
      and his relatives —   12
29   the twenty-second
      to Giddalti, his sons,
      and his relatives —   12
30   the twenty-third
      to Mahazioth, his sons,
      and his relatives —   12
31   and the twenty-fourth
      to Romamti-ezer, his sons,
      and his relatives —   12.

The Levitical Gatekeepers

26 The following were the divisions of the gatekeepers:
From the Korahites:
Meshelemiah son of Kore, one of the sons of Asaph. ² Meshelemiah had sons:
Zechariah the firstborn, Jediael the second,
Zebadiah the third, Jathniel the fourth,
³ Elam the fifth, Jehohanan the sixth,
and Eliehoenai the seventh. ⁴ Obed-edom also had sons:

ᴬ25:9 LXX; MT lacks *his sons, and his relatives* —12   ᴮ25:11 Variant of Zeri   ᶜ25:18 Variant of Uzziel

Shemaiah the firstborn,
Jehozabad the second,
Joah the third, Sachar the fourth,
Nethanel the fifth, ⁵ Ammiel
the sixth,
Issachar the seventh, and
Peullethai the eighth,
for God blessed him.

⁶ Also, to his son Shemaiah were born sons who ruled their ancestral families ᴬ because they were strong, capable men. ⁷ Shemaiah's sons: Othni, Rephael, Obed, and Elzabad; his relatives Elihu and Semachiah were also capable men. ⁸ All of these were among the sons of Obed-edom with their sons and relatives; they were capable men with strength for the work — sixty-two from Obed-edom.

⁹ Meshelemiah also had sons and relatives who were capable men — eighteen.

¹⁰ Hosah, from the Merarites, also had sons: Shimri the first (although he was not the firstborn, his father had appointed him as the first), ¹¹ Hilkiah the second, Tebaliah the third, and Zechariah the fourth. The sons and relatives of Hosah were thirteen in all.

¹² These divisions of the gatekeepers, under their leading men, had duties for ministering in the LORD's temple, just as their relatives did. ¹³ They cast lots for each temple gate according to their ancestral families, young and old alike. 1Ch 24:5,31

¹⁴ The lot for the east gate fell to Shelemiah.ᴮ They also cast lots for his son Zechariah, an insightful counselor, and his lot came out for the north gate. ¹⁵ Obed-edom's was the south gate, and his sons' lot was for the storehouses; ¹⁶ it was the west gate and the gate of Shallecheth on the ascending highway for Shuppim and Hosah.

There were guards stationed at every watch. ¹⁷ There were six Levites each dayᶜ on the east, four each day on the north, four each day on the south, and two pair at the storehouses. ¹⁸ As for the court on the west, there were four at the highway and two at the court. ¹⁹ Those were the divisions of the gatekeepers from the descendants of the Korahites and Merarites.

The Levitical Treasurers and Other Officials

²⁰ From the Levites, Ahijah was in charge of the treasuries of God's temple and the treasuries of what had been dedicated. ²¹ From the sons of Ladan, who were the descendants of the Gershonites through Ladan and were the family heads belonging to Ladan the Gershonite: Jehieli. ²² The sons of Jehieli, Zetham and his brother Joel, were in charge of the treasuries of the LORD's temple. 1Ch 26:24,26; 28:12

²³ From the Amramites, the Izharites, the Hebronites, and the Uzzielites: ²⁴ Shebuel, a descendant of Moses's son Gershom, was the officer in charge of the treasuries. ²⁵ His relatives through Eliezer: his son Rehabiah, his son Jeshaiah, his son Joram, his son Zichri, and his son Shelomith.ᴰ ²⁶ This Shelomith and his relatives were in charge of all the treasuries of what had been dedicated by King David,

---

by the family heads who were the commanders of thousands and of hundreds, and by the army commanders. ²⁷ They dedicated part of the plunder from their battles for the repair of the LORD's temple. ²⁸ All that the seer Samuel, Saul son of Kish, Abner son of Ner, and Joab son of Zeruiah had dedicated, along with everything else that had been dedicated, were in the care of Shelomith and his relatives. 2Sm 8:11

²⁹ From the Izrahites: Chenaniah and his sons had duties outside the temple ᴬ as officers and judges over Israel. ³⁰ From the Hebronites: Hashabiah and his relatives, 1,700 capable men, had assigned duties in Israel west of the Jordan for all the work of the LORD and for the service of the king. ³¹ From the Hebronites: Jerijah was the head of the Hebronites, according to the family records of his ancestors. A search was made in the fortieth year of David's reign and strong, capable men were found among them at Jazer in Gilead. ³² There were among Jerijah's relatives 2,700 capable men who were family heads. King David appointed them over the Reubenites, the Gadites, and half the tribe of Manasseh as overseers in every matter relating to God and the king. Neh 11:16; 1Ch 23:4; 27:17

David's Secular Officials

27 This is the list of the Israelites, the family heads, the commanders of thousands and the commanders of hundreds, and their officers who served the king in every matter to do with the divisions that were on rotated military duty each month throughout ᴮ the year. There were 24,000 in each division:

² Jashobeam son of Zabdiel was in charge of the first division, for the first month; 24,000 were in his division. ³ He was a descendant of Perez and chief of all the army commanders for the first month. 2Sm 23:8-30

⁴ Dodai the Ahohite was in charge of the division for the second month, and Mikloth was the leader; 24,000 were in his division.

⁵ The third army commander, as chief for the third month, was Benaiah son of the priest Jehoiada; 24,000 were in his division. ⁶ This Benaiah was a mighty man among the Thirty and over the Thirty, and his son Ammizabad was in charge ᶜ of his division.

⁷ The fourth commander, for the fourth month, was Joab's brother Asahel, and his son Zebadiah was commander after him; 24,000 were in his division.

⁸ The fifth, for the fifth month, was the commander Shamhuth the Izrahite; 24,000 were in his division.

⁹ The sixth, for the sixth month, was Ira son of Ikkesh the Tekoite; 24,000 were in his division.

¹⁰ The seventh, for the seventh month, was Helez the Pelonite from the descendants of Ephraim; 24,000 were in his division.

¹¹ The eighth, for the eighth month, was Sibbecai the

ᴬ26:29 the temple added for clarity　ᴮ27:1 Lit that came in and went out month by month for all months of　ᶜ27:6 LXX; MT omits in charge

Hushathite, a Zerahite; 24,000 were in his division.

¹² The ninth, for the ninth month, was Abiezer the Anathothite, a Benjaminite; 24,000 were in his division. ¹³ The tenth, for the tenth month, was Maharai the Netophathite, a Zerahite; 24,000 were in his division. ¹⁴ The eleventh, for the eleventh month, was Benaiah the Pirathonite from the descendants of Ephraim; 24,000 were in his division. ¹⁵ The twelfth, for the twelfth month, was Heldai the Netophathite, of Othniel's family;ᴬ 24,000 were in his division.

¹⁶ The following were in charge of the tribes of Israel:
For the Reubenites, Eliezer son of Zichri was the chief official; for the Simeonites, Shephatiah son of Maacah; ¹⁷ for the Levites, Hashabiah son of Kemuel; for Aaron, Zadok; ¹⁸ for Judah, Elihu, one of David's brothers; for Issachar, Omri son of Michael; ¹⁹ for Zebulun, Ishmaiah son of Obadiah;
for Naphtali, Jerimoth son of Azriel; ²⁰ for the Ephraimites, Hoshea son of Azaziah;
for half the tribe of Manasseh, Joel son of Pedaiah; ²¹ for half the tribe of Manasseh in Gilead, Iddo son of Zechariah;
for Benjamin, Jaasiel son of Abner;

²² for Dan, Azarel son of Jeroham.
Those were the leaders of the tribes of Israel. 1Ch 28:1

²³ David didn't count the men aged twenty or under, for the LORD had said he would make Israel as numerous as the stars of the sky. ²⁴ Joab son of Zeruiah began to count them, but he didn't complete it. There was wrath against Israel because of this census, and the number was not entered in the Historical Recordᴮ of King David. Gn 15:5; 2Sm 24:1-15; 1Ch 21:1-7

²⁵ Azmaveth son of Adiel was in charge of the king's storehouses.
Jonathan son of Uzziah was in charge of the storehouses in the country, in the cities, in the villages, and in the fortresses. ²⁶ Ezri son of Chelub was in charge of those who worked in the fields tilling the soil. ²⁷ Shimei the Ramathite was in charge of the vineyards.
Zabdi the Shiphmite was in charge of the produce of the vineyards for the wine cellars. ²⁸ Baal-hanan the Gederite was in charge of the olive and sycamore trees in the Judean foothills.ᶜ 1Kg 10:27; 2Ch 1:15
Joash was in charge of the stores of olive oil.
²⁹ Shitrai the Sharonite was in charge of the herds that grazed in Sharon, while Shaphat son of Adlai was in charge of the herds in the valleys. 1Ch 5:16
³⁰ Obil the Ishmaelite was in charge of the camels.
Jehdeiah the Meronothite was in charge of the donkeys.

ᴬ**27:15** Lit *belonging to Othniel*   ᴮ**27:24** LXX; MT reads *the number of the Historical Record*   ᶜ**27:28** Or *the Shephelah*

³¹ Jaziz the Hagrite was in charge of the flocks. 1Ch 5:10,18-21 All these were officials in charge of King David's property.

³² David's uncle Jonathan was a counselor; he was a man of understanding and a scribe. Jehiel son of Hachmoni attended^A the king's sons. ³³ Ahithophel was the king's counselor. Hushai the Archite was the king's friend. ³⁴ After Ahithophel came Jehoiada son of Benaiah, then Abiathar. Joab was the commander of the king's army. 2Sm 15:12

David Commissions Solomon to Build the Temple

28 David assembled all the leaders of Israel in Jerusalem: the leaders of the tribes, the leaders of the divisions in the king's service, the commanders of thousands and the commanders of hundreds, and the officials in charge of all the property and cattle of the king and his sons, along with the court officials, the fighting men, and all the best soldiers. ² Then King David rose to his feet and said, "Listen to me, my brothers and my people. It was in my heart to build a house as a resting place for the ark of the LORD's covenant and as a footstool for our God. I had made preparations to build, ³ but God said to me, 'You are not to build a house for my name because you are a man of war and have shed blood.'

⁴ "Yet the LORD God of Israel chose me out of all my father's family to be king over Israel forever. For he chose Judah as leader, and from the house of Judah, my father's family, and from my father's sons, he was pleased to make me king over all Israel. ⁵ And out of all my sons — for the LORD has given me many sons — he has chosen my son Solomon to sit on the throne of the LORD's kingdom over Israel. ⁶ He said to me, 'Your son Solomon is the one who is to build my house and my courts, for I have chosen him to be my son, and I will be his father. ⁷ I will establish his kingdom forever if he perseveres in keeping my commands and my ordinances as he is doing today.' 1Sm 16:6-13; 1Ch 17:23,27

⁸ "So now in the sight of all Israel, the assembly of the LORD, and in the hearing of our God, observe and follow all the commands of the LORD your God so that you may possess this good land and leave it as an inheritance to your descendants forever.

⁹ "As for you, Solomon my son, know the God of your father, and serve him wholeheartedly and with a willing mind, for the LORD searches every heart and understands the intention of every thought. If you seek him, he will be found by you, but if you abandon him, he will reject you forever. ¹⁰ Realize now that the LORD has chosen you to build a house for the sanctuary. Be strong, and do it." Gn 6:5; 1Kg 8:61; 1Ch 29:17-19; Ps 139

¹¹ Then David gave his son Solomon the plans for the portico of the temple and its buildings, treasuries, upstairs rooms, inner rooms, and a room for the mercy seat. ¹² The plans contained everything he had in mind^B for the courts of the LORD's house, all the surrounding chambers, the treasuries of God's house, and the treasuries for what is dedicated. ¹³ Also included were plans for the divisions of the priests

^A 27:32 Lit was with   ^B 28:12 Or he received from the Spirit and the Levites; all the work of service in the LORD's house; all the articles of service of the LORD's house; ¹⁴ the weight of gold for all the articles for every kind of service; the weight of all the silver articles for every kind of service; ¹⁵ the weight of the gold lampstands and their gold lamps, including the weight of each lampstand and its lamps; the weight of each silver lampstand and its lamps, according to the service of each lampstand; ¹⁶ the weight of gold for each table for the rows of the Bread of the Presence and the silver for the silver tables; ¹⁷ the pure gold for the forks, sprinkling basins, and pitchers; the weight of each gold dish; the weight of each silver bowl; ¹⁸ the weight of refined gold for the altar of incense; and the plans for the chariot of ᴬ the gold cherubim that spread out their wings and cover the ark of the LORD's covenant.

¹⁹ David concluded, "By the LORD's hand on me, he enabled me to understand everything in writing, all the details of the plan."ᴮ

²⁰ Then David said to his son Solomon, "Be strong and courageous, and do the work. Don't be afraid or discouraged, for the LORD God, my God, is with you. He won't leave you or abandon you until all the work for the service of the LORD's house is finished. ²¹ Here are the divisions of the priests and the Levites for all the service of God's house. Every willing person of any skill will be at your disposal for the work, and the leaders and all the people are at your every command." Jos 1:6-7

Contributions for Building the Temple

29 Then King David said to all the assembly, "My son Solomon — God has chosen him alone — is young and inexperienced. The task is great because the building will not be built for a human but for the LORD God. ² So to the best of my ability I've made provision for the house of my God: gold for the gold articles, silver for the silver, bronze for the bronze, iron for the iron, and wood for the wood, as well as onyx, stones for mounting, ᶜ antimony, ᴰ stones of various colors, all kinds of precious stones, and a great quantity of marble. ³ Moreover, because of my delight in the house of my God, I now give my personal treasures of gold and silver for the house of my God over and above all that I've provided for the holy house: ⁴ 100 tons ᴱ of gold (gold of Ophir) and 250 tons ᶠ of refined silver for overlaying the walls of the buildings, ⁵ the gold for the gold work and the silver for the silver, for all the work to be done by the craftsmen. Now who will volunteer to consecrate himself to the LORD today?" 1Ch 22:3-5; 29:19

⁶ Then the leaders of the households, the leaders of the tribes of Israel, the commanders of thousands and of hundreds, and the officials in charge of the king's work gave willingly. ⁷ For the service of God's house they gave 185 tons ᴳ of gold and 10,000 gold coins, ᴴ 375 tons ᴵ of silver, 675 tons ᴶ of bronze, and 4,000 tons ᴷ of iron. ⁸ Whoever had precious stones gave them

---

ᴬ**28:18** Or *chariot, that is*; Ps 18:10; Ezk 1:5,15   ᴮ**28:19** Hb obscure   ᶜ**29:2** Or *mosaic*   ᴰ**29:2** In Hb, the word *antimony* is similar to "turquoise"; Ex 28:18.   ᴱ**29:4** Lit *3,000 talents*   ᶠ**29:4** Lit *7,000 talents*   ᴳ**29:7** Lit *5,000 talents*   ᴴ**29:7** Or *drachmas*, or *darics*   ᴵ**29:7** Lit *10,000 talents*   ᴶ**29:7** Lit *18,000 talents*   ᴷ**29:7** Lit *100,000 talents* to the treasury of the LORD's house under the care of Jehiel the Gershonite. [9] Then the people rejoiced because of their leaders' willingness to give, for they had given to the LORD wholeheartedly. King David also rejoiced greatly. 1Ch 27:1; 28:1

David's Prayer

[10] Then David blessed the LORD in the sight of all the assembly. David said,

May you be blessed, LORD God of our father Israel, from eternity to eternity. [11] Yours, LORD, is the greatness and the power and the glory and the splendor and the majesty, for everything in the heavens and on earth belongs to you. Yours, LORD, is the kingdom, and you are exalted as head over all. [12] Riches and honor come from you, and you are the ruler of everything. Power and might are in your hand, and it is in your hand to make great and to give strength to all. [13] Now therefore, our God, we give you thanks and praise your glorious name. 2Ch 1:12; Mt 6:13; Rv 5:13

[14] But who am I, and who are my people, that we should be able to give as generously as this? For everything comes from you, and we have given you only what comes from your own hand. [A] [15] For we are aliens and temporary residents in your presence as were all our ancestors. Our days on earth are like a shadow, without hope. [16] LORD our God, all this wealth that we've provided

for building you a house for your holy name comes from your hand; everything belongs to you. [17] I know, my God, that you test the heart and that you are pleased with what is right. I have willingly given all these things with an upright heart, and now I have seen your people who are present [B] here giving joyfully and [C] willingly to you. [18] LORD God of Abraham, Isaac, and Israel, our ancestors, keep this desire forever in the thoughts of the hearts of your people, and confirm their hearts toward you. [19] Give my son Solomon an undivided heart to keep and to carry out all your commands, your decrees, and your statutes, and to build the building for which I have made provision. Lv 25:23

[20] Then David said to the whole assembly, "Blessed be the LORD your God." So the whole assembly praised the LORD God of their ancestors. They knelt low and paid homage to the LORD and the king. [21] The following day they offered sacrifices to the LORD and burnt offerings to the LORD: a thousand bulls, a thousand rams, and a thousand lambs, along with their drink offerings, and sacrifices in abundance for all Israel. [22] They ate and drank with great joy in the LORD's presence that day. 1Kg 8:62-63

The Enthronement of Solomon

Then, for a second time, they made David's son Solomon king; they anointed him [D] as the LORD's ruler, and Zadok as the priest. [23] Solomon

---

[A] 29:14 Lit and from your hand we have given to you [B] 29:17 Lit found [C] 29:17 Or now with joy I've seen your people who are present here giving [D] 29:22 LXX, Tg, Vg; MT omits him sat on the LORD's throne as king in place of his father David. He prospered, and all Israel obeyed him. [24] All the leaders and the mighty men, and all of King David's sons as well, pledged their allegiance to King Solomon. [25] The LORD highly exalted Solomon in the sight of all Israel and bestowed on him such royal majesty as had not been bestowed on any king over Israel before him.   1Kg 1:33-39; 2:12; 1Ch 23:1; 2Ch 1:1

A Summary of David's Life

[26] David son of Jesse was king over all Israel. [27] The length of his reign over Israel was forty years; he reigned in Hebron for seven years and in Jerusalem for thirty-three. [28] He died at a good old age, full of days, riches, and honor, and his son Solomon became king in his place. [29] As for the events of King David's reign, from beginning to end, note that they are written in the Events of the Seer Samuel, the Events of the Prophet Nathan, and the Events of the Seer Gad, [30] along with all his reign, his might, and the incidents that affected him and Israel and all the kingdoms of the surrounding lands.   Gn 15:15; 2Sm 5:4-5; 1Kg 2:11; 1Ch 18:14

2 CHRONICLES

Solomon's Request for Wisdom

1 Solomon son of David strengthened his hold on his kingdom. The LORD his God was with him and highly exalted him. ² Then Solomon spoke to all Israel, to the commanders of thousands and of hundreds, to the judges, and to every leader in all Israel — the family heads. ³ Solomon and the whole assembly with him went to the high place that was in Gibeon because God's tent of meeting, which the LORD's servant Moses had made in the wilderness, was there. ⁴ Now David had brought the ark of God from Kiriath-jearim to the place^A he had set up for it, because he had pitched a tent for it in Jerusalem, ⁵ but he put^B the bronze altar, which Bezalel son of Uri, son of Hur, had made, in front of the LORD's tabernacle. Solomon and the assembly inquired of him^C there. ⁶ Solomon offered sacrifices there in the LORD's presence on the bronze altar at the tent of meeting; he offered a thousand burnt offerings on it. 1Kg 2:12,46; 1Ch 28:1; 29:25

⁷ That night God appeared to Solomon and said to him: "Ask. What should I give you?" 1Kg 3:5-15

⁸ And Solomon said to God: "You have shown great and faithful love to my father David, and you have made me king in his place. ⁹ LORD God, let your promise to my father David now come true. For you have made me king over a people as numerous as the dust of the earth. ¹⁰ Now grant me wisdom and knowledge so that I may lead these people, for who can judge this great people of yours?" 2Sm 7:12-16; 1Ch 28:5

¹¹ God said to Solomon, "Since this was in your heart, and you have not requested riches, wealth, or glory, or for the life of those who hate you, and you have not even requested long life, but you have requested for yourself wisdom and knowledge that you may judge my people over whom I have made you king, ¹² wisdom and knowledge are given to you. I will also give you riches, wealth, and glory, unlike what was given to the kings who were before you, or will be given to those after you." ¹³ So Solomon went to Jerusalem from^D the high place that was in Gibeon in front of the tent of meeting, and he reigned over Israel. 1Ch 29:25; 2Ch 9:22

Solomon's Horses and Wealth

¹⁴ Solomon accumulated 1,400 chariots and 12,000 horsemen, which he stationed in the chariot cities and with the king in Jerusalem. ¹⁵ The king made silver and gold as common in Jerusalem as stones, and he made cedar as abundant as sycamore in the Judean foothills. ¹⁶ Solomon's horses came from Egypt and Kue.^E The king's traders would get them from Kue at the going price. ¹⁷ A chariot could be imported from Egypt for fifteen pounds^F of silver and a horse for nearly four pounds.^G In the same way, they exported them to all the kings of the

<hr>

^A1:4 Vg; MT omits *the place*   ^B1:5 Some Hb mss, Tg, Syr; other Hb mss, LXX, Vg read *but there was*
^C1:5 Or *it*   ^D1:13 LXX, Vg; MT reads *to*   ^E1:16 = Cilicia   ^F1:17 Lit *600 shekels*   ^G1:17 Lit *150 shekels*

Hittites and to the kings of Aram through their agents. 1Kg 10:26-29

Solomon's Letter to Hiram

2 Solomon decided to build a temple for the name of the LORD and a royal palace for himself, ² so he assigned 70,000 men as porters, 80,000 men as stonecutters in the mountains, and 3,600 as supervisors over them. 1Kg 5:5; 2Ch 2:12; 9:23; 8:10 ³ Then Solomon sent word to King Hiram ᴬ of Tyre: 2Sm 5:11; 1Kg 5:1-2

Do for me what you did for my father David. You sent him cedars to build him a house to live in. ⁴ Now I am building a temple for the name of the LORD my God in order to dedicate it to him for burning fragrant incense before him, for displaying the rows of the Bread of the Presence continuously, and for sacrificing burnt offerings for the morning and the evening, the Sabbaths and the New Moons, and the appointed festivals of the LORD our God. This is ordained for Israel permanently. ⁵ The temple that I am building will be great, for our God is greater than any of the gods. ⁶ But who is able to build a temple for him, since even heaven and the highest heaven cannot contain him? Who am I then that I should build a temple for him except as a place to burn incense before him? ⁷ Therefore, send me an artisan who is skilled in engraving to work with gold, silver, bronze, and iron, and with purple, crimson,

and blue yarn. He will work with the artisans who are with me in Judah and Jerusalem, appointed by my father David. ⁸ Also, send me cedar, cypress, and algum ᴮ logs from Lebanon, for I know that your servants know how to cut the trees of Lebanon. Note that my servants will be with your servants ⁹ to prepare logs for me in abundance because the temple I am building will be great and wondrous. ¹⁰ I will give your servants, the woodcutters who cut the trees, one hundred thousand bushels ᶜ of wheat flour, one hundred thousand bushels of barley, one hundred ten thousand gallons ᴰ of wine, and one hundred ten thousand gallons of oil. Ex 25:30; 30:7; 1Ch 14:1

Hiram's Reply

¹¹ Then King Hiram of Tyre wrote a letter ᴱ and sent it to Solomon:

Because the LORD loves his people, he set you over them as king. 1Kg 10:9; 2Ch 9:8

¹² Hiram also said:

Blessed be the LORD God of Israel, who made the heavens and the earth! He gave King David a wise son with insight and understanding, who will build a temple for the LORD and a royal palace for himself. ¹³ I have now sent Huram-abi, ᶠ a skillful man who has understanding. ¹⁴ He is the son of a woman from the daughters of Dan. His father is a man of Tyre. He knows how to work with gold, silver, bronze, iron,

---

ᴬ2:3 Some Hb mss, LXX, Syr, Vg; other Hb mss read *Huram*; 2Sm 5:11; 1Kg 5:1-2   ᴮ2:8 = almug in 1Kg 10:11-12   ᶜ2:10 Lit *20,000 cors*   ᴰ2:10 Lit *20,000 baths*   ᴱ2:11 Lit *Tyre said in writing*   ᶠ2:13 Lit *Huram my father* stone, and wood, with purple, blue, crimson yarn, and fine linen. He knows how to do all kinds of engraving and to execute any design that may be given him. I have sent him to be with your artisans and the artisans of my lord, your father David. [15] Now, let my lord send the wheat, barley, oil, and wine to his servants as promised. [16] We will cut logs from Lebanon, as many as you need, and bring them to you as rafts by sea to Joppa. You can then take them up to Jerusalem. **Ps 33:6; 102:25**

Solomon's Workforce

[17] Solomon took a census of all the resident alien men in the land of Israel, after the census that his father David had conducted, and the total was 153,600. [18] Solomon made 70,000 of them porters, 80,000 stonecutters in the mountains, and 3,600 supervisors to make the people work. **2Sm 24:1-9; 1Ch 21:1-5**

Building the Temple

3 Then Solomon began to build the LORD's temple in Jerusalem on Mount Moriah where the LORD[A] had appeared to his father David, at the site David had prepared on the threshing floor of Ornan[B] the Jebusite. [2] He began to build on the second day of the second month in the fourth year of his reign. [3] These are Solomon's foundations[C] for building God's temple: the length[D] was ninety feet,[E] and the width thirty feet.[F] [4] The portico, which was across the front extending across the width of the temple, was thirty feet wide; its height was thirty feet;[G] he overlaid its inner surface with pure gold. [5] The larger room[H] he paneled with cypress wood, overlaid with fine gold, and decorated with palm trees and chains. [6] He adorned the temple with precious stones for beauty, and the gold was the gold of Parvaim. [7] He overlaid the temple — the beams, the thresholds, its walls and doors — with gold, and he carved cherubim on the walls. **Gn 22:2; 1Kg 6:1-3**

The Most Holy Place

[8] Then he made the most holy place; its length corresponded to the width of the temple, 30 feet, and its width was 30 feet. He overlaid it with forty-five thousand pounds[I] of fine gold. [9] The weight of the nails was twenty ounces[J] of gold, and he overlaid the ceiling with gold. **1Kg 6:16**

[10] He made two cherubim of sculptured work, for the most holy place, and he overlaid them with gold. [11] The overall length of the wings of the cherubim was 30 feet: the wing of one was 7 1/2 feet,[K] touching the wall of the room; its other wing was 7 1/2 feet, touching the wing of the other cherub. [12] The wing of the other[L] cherub was 7 1/2 feet, touching the wall of the room; its other wing was 7 1/2 feet, reaching the wing of the other cherub. [13] The wingspan of these cherubim was 30 feet. They stood on their feet and faced the larger room.[M]

[A]**3:1** LXX; Tg reads *the angel of the LORD*; MT reads *he*　　[B]**3:1** = Araunah in 2Sm 24:16-24　　[C]**3:3** Tg reads *The measurements which Solomon decreed*　　[D]**3:3** Lit *length — cubits in the former measure —*　　[E]**3:3** Lit *60 cubits*　　[F]**3:3** Lit *20 cubits*, also in vv. 4,8,11,13　　[G]**3:4** LXX, Syr; MT reads *120 cubits*　　[H]**3:5** Lit *The house*　　[I]**3:8** Lit *600 talents*　　[J]**3:9** Lit *50 shekels*　　[K]**3:11** Lit *five cubits*, also in vv. 12,15　　[L]**3:12** Syr, Vg; MT reads *the one*　　[M]**3:13** Lit *the house*

¹⁴ He made the curtain of blue, purple, and crimson yarn and fine linen, and he wove cherubim into it.

The Bronze Pillars

¹⁵ In front of the temple he made two pillars, each 27 feet^A high. The capital on top of each was 7 ½ feet high. ¹⁶ He had made chainwork in the inner sanctuary and also put it on top of the pillars. He made a hundred pomegranates and fastened them into the chainwork. ¹⁷ Then he set up the pillars in front of the sanctuary, one on the right and one on the left. He named the one on the right Jachin^B and the one on the left Boaz.^C 1Kg 7:15-22; 7:17

The Altar, Reservoir, and Basins

4 He made a bronze altar 30 feet^D long, 30 feet wide, and 15 feet^E high. Ex 27:1-2; 2Kg 16:14

² Then he made the cast metal basin,^F 15 feet from brim to brim, perfectly round. It was 7 ½ feet^G high and 45 feet^H in circumference. ³ The likeness of oxen^I was below it, completely encircling it, ten every half yard,^J completely surrounding the basin. The oxen were cast in two rows when the basin was cast. ⁴ It stood on twelve oxen, three facing north, three facing west, three facing south, and three facing east. The basin was on top of them and all their hindquarters were toward the center. ⁵ The basin was three inches^K thick, and its rim was fashioned like the brim of a cup or a lily blossom. It could hold eleven thousand gallons.^L 1Kg 7:23-26; Rv 22:1

⁶ He made ten basins for washing and he put five on the right and five on the left. The parts of the burnt offering were rinsed in them, but the basin was used by the priests for washing. 1Kg 7:38-39; Ezk 40:38

The Lampstands, Tables, and Courts

⁷ He made the ten gold lampstands according to their specifications and put them in the sanctuary, five on the right and five on the left. ⁸ He made ten tables and placed them in the sanctuary, five on the right and five on the left. He also made a hundred gold bowls. Ex 37:17-24

⁹ He made the courtyard of the priests and the large court, and doors for the court. He overlaid the doors with bronze. ¹⁰ He put the basin on the right side, toward the southeast. ¹¹ Then Huram^M made the pots, the shovels, and the bowls.

Completion of the Bronze Furnishings

So Huram finished doing the work that he was doing for King Solomon in God's temple: ¹² two pillars; the bowls and the capitals on top of the two pillars; the two gratings for covering both bowls of the capitals that were on top of the pillars; ¹³ the four hundred pomegranates for the two gratings (two rows of pomegranates for each grating covering both capitals' bowls on top of the pillars). ¹⁴ He also made the water carts^N and the basins on the water carts. ¹⁵ The one basin and the twelve oxen underneath it, ¹⁶ the pots, the shovels, the forks, and

---

^A3:15 Syr reads *18 cubits* (27 feet); Hb reads *35 cubits* (52 1/2 feet) ^B3:17 = He Will Establish
^C3:17 = Strength Is in Him ^D4:1 Lit *20 cubits* ^E4:1 Lit *10 cubits*, also in v. 2 ^F4:2 Lit *sea* ^G4:2 Lit *five cubits*
^H4:2 Lit *30 cubits* ^I4:3 = gourds in 1Kg 7:24 ^J4:3 Lit *10 per cubit* ^K4:5 Lit *a handbreadth* ^L4:5 Text
emended; MT reads *3,000 baths* in 1Kg 7:26 ^M4:11 = Hiram in 1Kg 7:13,40,45 ^N4:14 Lit *the stands*

all their utensils — Huram-abi[A] made them for King Solomon for the LORD's temple. All these were made of polished bronze. [17] The king had them cast in clay molds in the Jordan Valley between Succoth and Zeredah. [18] Solomon made all these utensils in such great abundance that the weight of the bronze was not determined. 1Kg 7:20,27-37

Completion of the Gold Furnishings

[19] Solomon also made all the equipment in God's temple: the gold altar; the tables on which to put the Bread of the Presence; [20] the lampstands and their lamps of pure gold to burn in front of the inner sanctuary according to specifications; [21] the flowers, lamps, and gold tongs — of purest gold; [22] the wick trimmers, sprinkling basins, ladles, [B] and firepans — of purest gold; and the entryway to the temple, its inner doors to the most holy place, and the doors of the temple sanctuary — of gold. Ex 25:31-40; Lv 24:5-9

5 So all the work Solomon did for the LORD's temple was completed. Then Solomon brought the consecrated things of his father David — the silver, the gold, and all the utensils — and put them in the treasuries of God's temple.

Preparations for the Temple Dedication

[2] At that time Solomon assembled at Jerusalem the elders of Israel — all the tribal heads, the ancestral chiefs of the Israelites — in order to bring the ark of the covenant of the LORD up from the city of David, that is, Zion. [3] So all the men of Israel were assembled in the king's presence at the festival; this was in the seventh month. [C] 1Kg 8:1-11; 2Ch 1:4

[4] All the elders of Israel came, and the Levites picked up the ark. [5] They brought up the ark, the tent of meeting, and the holy utensils that were in the tent. The priests and the Levites brought them up. [6] King Solomon and the entire congregation of Israel who had gathered around him were in front of the ark sacrificing sheep, goats, and cattle that could not be counted or numbered because there were so many. [7] The priests brought the ark of the LORD's covenant to its place, into the inner sanctuary of the temple, to the most holy place, beneath the wings of the cherubim. [8] And the cherubim spread their wings over the place of the ark so that the cherubim formed a cover above the ark and its poles. [9] The poles were so long that their ends were seen from the holy place [D] in front of the inner sanctuary, but they were not seen from outside; they are still there today. [10] Nothing was in the ark except the two tablets that Moses had put in it at Horeb, [E] where the LORD had made a covenant with the Israelites when they came out of Egypt. 2Ch 3:10

[11] Now all the priests who were present had consecrated themselves regardless of their divisions. When the priests came out of the holy place, [12] the Levitical singers dressed in fine linen and carrying cymbals, harps, and lyres were standing east of the altar, and with them were 120 priests blowing trumpets. The Levitical singers were descendants of Asaph,

---

[A]4:16 Lit Huram my father [B]4:22 Or dishes, or spoons; lit palms [C]5:3 = Tishri (September–October)
[D]5:9 Some Hb mss, LXX; other Hb mss read the ark; 1Kg 8:8 [E]5:10 = Sinai

Heman, and Jeduthun and their sons and relatives. ¹³ The trumpeters and singers joined together to praise and thank the LORD with one voice. They raised their voices, accompanied by trumpets, cymbals, and musical instruments, in praise to the LORD: 1Ch 13:8

For he is good;
his faithful love
endures forever.   1Ch 16:34

The temple, the LORD's temple, was filled with a cloud. ¹⁴ And because of the cloud, the priests were not able to continue ministering, for the glory of the LORD filled God's temple.   Ex 40:34-35; Lv 16:2; Nm 9:15-16; Dt 4:11

Solomon's Dedication of the Temple

6 Then Solomon said: 1Kg 8:12-53
The LORD said he would dwell
in total darkness,   Ex 20:21; 5:22
² but I have built
an exalted temple for you,
a place
for your residence forever.

³ Then the king turned and blessed the entire congregation of Israel while they were standing. ⁴ He said:

Blessed be the LORD God
of Israel!
He spoke directly
to my father David,
and he has fulfilled
the promise
by his power.
He said,
⁵ "Since the day I brought
my people Israel
out of the land of Egypt,
I have not chosen a city
to build a temple in
among any of the tribes
of Israel,

so that my name
would be there,
and I have not chosen a man
to be ruler
over my people Israel.
⁶ But I have chosen Jerusalem
so that my name will be there,
and I have chosen David
to be over my people Israel."

⁷ My father David had his
heart set
on building a temple
for the name of the LORD,
the God of Israel.   2Sm 7:2-3
⁸ However, the LORD said
to my father David,
"Since it was your desire
to build a temple
for my name,
you have done well to have
this desire.
⁹ Yet, you are not the one
to build the temple,
but your son,
your own offspring,
will build the temple
for my name."
¹⁰ So the LORD has fulfilled
what he promised.
I have taken the place
of my father David
and I sit on the throne
of Israel, as the
LORD promised.
I have built the temple
for the name of the LORD,
the God of Israel.
¹¹ I have put the ark there,
where the LORD's covenant is
that he made
with the Israelites.   2Ch 5:7,10

Solomon's Prayer

¹² Then Solomon stood before the altar of the LORD in front of the entire congregation of Israel and

spread out his hands. ¹³ For Solomon had made a bronze platform 7½ feet ᴬ long, 7½ feet wide, and 4½ feet ᴮ high and put it in the court. He stood on it, knelt down in front of the entire congregation of Israel, and spread out his hands toward heaven. ¹⁴ He said: Ex 9:29,33; Ezr 9:5

LORD God of Israel,
  there is no God like you
  in heaven or on earth,   Ex 15:11
who keeps
  his gracious covenant
with your servants who walk
  before you
with all their heart.   Dt 7:9
¹⁵ You have kept
  what you promised
to your servant,
  my father David.
You spoke directly to him,
and you fulfilled
  your promise
  by your power,
as it is today.   1Ch 22:9-10
¹⁶ Therefore, LORD God
  of Israel,
keep what you promised
to your servant,
  my father David:
"You will never fail to have
  a man
to sit before me on the throne
  of Israel,   1Kg 2:4; 2Ch 7:18
if only your sons guard
  their way to walk in my Law
as you have walked
  before me."
¹⁷ Now, LORD God of Israel,
  please confirm
what you promised
  to your servant David.

¹⁸ But will God indeed live
  on earth with humans?

Even heaven,
  the highest heaven,
  cannot contain you,   2Ch 2:6
much less this temple
  I have built.
¹⁹ Listen ᶜ to your servant's
  prayer and his petition,
LORD my God,
so that you may hear the cry
  and the prayer
that your servant prays
  before you,
²⁰ so that your eyes watch over
  this temple
day and night,
toward the place
  where you said
you would put your name;
and so that you may hear
  the prayer
your servant prays
  toward this place.
²¹ Hear the petitions
  of your servant
and your people Israel,
  which they pray
  toward this place.
May you hear
  in your dwelling place
  in heaven.
May you hear and forgive.

²² If a man sins
  against his neighbor
and is forced to take an oath ᴰ
and he comes to take an oath
before your altar
  in this temple,
²³ may you hear in heaven
  and act.
May you judge your servants,
condemning the wicked man
  by bringing
what he has done
  on his own head

ᴬ6:13 Lit *five cubits*   ᴮ6:13 Lit *three cubits*   ᶜ6:19 Lit *Turn*   ᴰ6:22 Lit *and he lifts a curse against him to curse him*

and providing justice
    for the righteous
by rewarding him
    according to
    his righteousness.

24 If your people Israel
    are defeated
    before an enemy,
because they have sinned
    against you,
and they return to you
    and praise your name,
and they pray and plead
    for mercy
before you in this temple,
25 may you hear in heaven
and forgive the sin
    of your people Israel.
May you restore them
    to the land
you gave them
    and their ancestors.

26 When the skies are shut
    and there is no rain
because they have sinned
    against you,
and they pray
    toward this place
and praise your name,
and they turn
    from their sins
because you are
    afflicting[A] them, 1Kg 8:35
27 may you hear in heaven
and forgive the sin
    of your servants
and your people Israel,
so that you may teach them
    the good way
they should walk in.
May you send rain
    on your land

that you gave your people
    for an inheritance.
28 When there is famine
    in the land,
when there is pestilence,
when there is blight
    or mildew, locust
    or grasshopper,
when their enemies
    besiege them
in the land and its cities,[B,C]
when there is any plague
    or illness,
29 every prayer or petition
that any person or that
    all your people Israel
    may have —
they each know
    their own affliction[D]
    and suffering —
as they spread out their hands
    toward this temple,
30 may you hear in heaven,
    your dwelling place,
and may you forgive
    and give to everyone[E]
according to all their ways,
    since you know each heart,
for you alone know
    the human heart, 1Sm 16:7
31 so that they may fear you
and walk in your ways
all the days they live
    on the land
you gave our ancestors.

32 Even for the foreigner who is
    not of your people Israel
but has come from
    a distant land
because of your great name
and your strong hand
    and outstretched arm:

[A]6:26 LXX, Vg; MT reads *answering*; 1Kg 8:35   [B]6:28 Lit *land of its gates*   [C]6:28 Lit *if his* (Israel's) *enemies besiege him in the land of his gates*; Jos 2:7; Jdg 16:2-3   [D]6:29 Lit *plague*   [E]6:30 Lit *give for the man*

when he comes and prays
   toward this temple,
33 may you hear in heaven
   in your dwelling place,
and do all the foreigner
   asks you.
Then all the peoples
   of the earth will know
   your name,
to fear you as your people
   Israel do
and know that this temple
   I have built
bears your name.   2Ch 7:14

34 When your people go
   out to fight against
   their enemies,
wherever you send them,
and they pray to you
in the direction of this city
   you have chosen   Dt 12:11
and the temple that
   I have built for your name,
35 may you hear their prayer
   and petition in heaven
   and uphold their cause.

36 When they sin against you —
   for there is no one
   who does not sin —   Jb 15:14-16
and you are angry with them
and hand them over
   to the enemy,
and their captors
   deport them
to a distant
   or nearby country,
37 and when they come
   to their senses
in the land where they
   were deported
and repent and petition you
   in their captors' land,
saying: "We have sinned
   and done wrong;

we have been wicked,"
38 and when they return to you
   with all their mind and all
   their heart
in the land of their captivity
   where they were
   taken captive,
and when they pray
   in the direction
   of their land
that you gave their ancestors,
and the city you have chosen,
and toward the temple
   I have built for your name,
39 may you hear their prayer
   and petitions in heaven,
your dwelling place,
and uphold their cause. A
May you forgive your people
   who sinned against you.
40 Now, my God,
please let your eyes be open
and your ears attentive
to the prayer of this place.
41 Now therefore: Ps 132:8-10

Arise, Lᴏʀᴅ God, come
   to your resting place,
you and your powerful ark.
May your priests, Lᴏʀᴅ God,
   be clothed with salvation,
and may your faithful people
   rejoice in goodness.
42 Lᴏʀᴅ God, do not reject
   your anointed one; B
remember the promises
   to your servant David.   Is 55:3

The Dedication Ceremonies

7 When Solomon finished praying, fire descended from heaven and consumed the burnt offering and the sacrifices, and the glory of the Lᴏʀᴅ filled the temple. 2 The priests were not able to enter the

---

A 6:39 Lit and do their judgment, or justice   B 6:42 Some Hb mss, LXX; other Hb mss read ones; Ps 132:10

LORD's temple because the glory of the LORD filled the temple of the LORD. ³ All the Israelites were watching when the fire descended and the glory of the LORD came on the temple. They bowed down on the pavement with their faces to the ground. They worshiped and praised the LORD: Gn 15:7-17; 1Kg 8:54

> For he is good,
> for his faithful love
> endures forever.   1Ch 16:41

⁴ The king and all the people were offering sacrifices in the LORD's presence. ⁵ King Solomon offered a sacrifice of twenty-two thousand cattle and one hundred twenty thousand sheep and goats. In this manner the king and all the people dedicated God's temple. ⁶ The priests and the Levites were standing at their stations. The Levites had the musical instruments of the LORD, which King David had made to give thanks to the LORD — "for his faithful love endures forever" — when he offered praise with them. Across from the Levites, the priests were blowing trumpets, and all the people were standing. ⁷ Since the bronze altar that Solomon had made could not accommodate the burnt offering, the grain offering, and the fat of the fellowship offerings, Solomon first consecrated the middle of the courtyard that was in front of the LORD's temple and then offered the burnt offerings and the fat of the fellowship offerings there. 1Kg 8:62-63; 1Ch 15:16-21; 16:42; 23:5

⁸ So Solomon and all Israel with him — a very great assembly, from the entrance to Hamath^A to the Brook of Egypt — observed the festival at that time for seven days. ⁹ On the eighth day^B they held a sacred assembly, for the dedication of the altar lasted seven days and the festival seven days. ¹⁰ On the twenty-third day of the seventh month he sent the people home,^C rejoicing and with happy hearts for the goodness the LORD had done for David, for Solomon, and for his people Israel. ¹¹ So Solomon finished the LORD's temple and the royal palace. Everything that had entered Solomon's heart to do for the LORD's temple and for his own palace succeeded.

The LORD's Response

¹² Then the LORD appeared to Solomon at night and said to him:

> I have heard your prayer and have chosen this place for myself as a temple of sacrifice. ¹³ If I shut the sky so there is no rain, or if I command the grasshopper to consume the land, or if I send pestilence on my people, ¹⁴ and my people, who bear my name, humble themselves, pray and seek my face, and turn from their evil ways, then I will hear from heaven, forgive their sin, and heal their land. ¹⁵ My eyes will now be open and my ears attentive to prayer from this place. ¹⁶ And I have now chosen and consecrated this temple so that my name may be there forever; my eyes and my heart will be there at all times.   Dt 12:5,11; 2Ch 6:26-28

¹⁷ As for you, if you walk before me as your father David walked, doing everything I have commanded you, and if you

---

^A 7:8 Or from Lebo-hamath   ^B 7:9 = the day after the festival, or the 15th day   ^C 7:10 Lit people to their tents keep my statutes and ordinances, ¹⁸ I will establish your royal throne, as I promised your father David: You will never fail to have a man ruling in Israel.

¹⁹ However, if you turn away and abandon my statutes and my commands that I have set before you and if you go and serve other gods and bow in worship to them, ²⁰ then I will uproot Israel from the soil that I gave them, and this temple that I have sanctified for my name I will banish from my presence; I will make it an object of scorn and ridicule among all the peoples. ²¹ As for this temple, which was exalted, everyone who passes by will be appalled and will say: Why did the Lord do this to this land and this temple? ²² Then they will say: Because they abandoned the Lord God of their ancestors who brought them out of the land of Egypt. They clung to other gods and bowed in worship to them and served them. Because of this, he brought all this ruin on them.

Solomon's Later Building Projects

8 At the end of twenty years during which Solomon had built the Lord's temple and his own palace — ² Solomon had rebuilt the cities Hiram ᴬ gave him and settled Israelites there — ³ Solomon went to Hamath-zobah and seized it. ⁴ He built Tadmor in the wilderness along with all the storage cities that he built in Hamath. ⁵ He built Upper Beth-horon and Lower

Beth-horon — fortified cities with walls, gates, and bars — ⁶ Baalath, all the storage cities that belonged to Solomon, all the chariot cities, the cavalry cities, and everything Solomon desired to build in Jerusalem, Lebanon, or anywhere else in the land of his dominion. 1Ch 7:24
⁷ As for all the peoples who remained of the Hethites, Amorites, Perizzites, Hivites, and Jebusites, who were not from Israel — ⁸ their descendants who remained in the land after them, those the Israelites had not completely destroyed — Solomon imposed forced labor on them; it is this way today. ⁹ But Solomon did not consign the Israelites to be slaves for his work; they were soldiers, commanders of his captains, and commanders of his chariots and his cavalry. ¹⁰ These were King Solomon's deputies: 250 who supervised the people. 1Kg 4:6

¹¹ Solomon brought the daughter of Pharaoh from the city of David to the house he had built for her, for he said, "My wife must not live in the house ᴮ of King David of Israel because the places the ark of the Lord has come into are holy."

Public Worship Established at the Temple

¹² At that time Solomon offered burnt offerings to the Lord on the Lord's altar he had made in front of the portico. ¹³ He followed the daily requirement for offerings according to the commandment of Moses for Sabbaths, New Moons, and the three annual appointed festivals: the Festival of Unleavened Bread, the Festival of Weeks, and the Festival of Shelters. ¹⁴ According to the ordinances of his father

ᴬ8:2 = the king of Tyre   ᴮ8:11 LXX reads *city*

David, he appointed the divisions of the priests over their service, of the Levites over their responsibilities to offer praise and to minister before the priests following the daily requirement, and of the gatekeepers by their divisions with respect to each temple gate, for this had been the command of David, the man of God. **15** They did not turn aside from the king's command regarding the priests and the Levites concerning any matter or concerning the treasuries. **16** All of Solomon's work was carried out from the day the foundation was laid for the LORD's temple until it was finished. So the LORD's temple was completed. 1Kg9:25; 2Ch4:1

Solomon's Fleet

17 At that time Solomon went to Ezion-geber and to Eloth on the seashore in the land of Edom. **18** So Hiram[A] sent ships to him by his servants along with crews of experienced seamen. They went with Solomon's servants to Ophir, took from there seventeen tons[B] of gold, and delivered it to King Solomon.

The Queen of Sheba

9 The queen of Sheba heard of Solomon's fame, so she came to test Solomon with difficult questions at Jerusalem with a very large entourage, with camels bearing spices, gold in abundance, and precious stones. She came to Solomon and spoke with him about everything that was on her mind. **2** So Solomon answered all her questions; nothing was too difficult for Solomon to explain to her. **3** When the queen of Sheba observed Solomon's wisdom, the palace he had built,

4 the food at his table, his servants' residence, his attendants' service and their attire, his cupbearers and their attire, and the burnt offerings he offered at the LORD's temple, it took her breath away. 1Kg10:1-13

5 She said to the king, "The report I heard in my own country about your words and about your wisdom is true. **6** But I didn't believe their reports until I came and saw with my own eyes. Indeed, I was not even told half of your great wisdom! You far exceed the report I heard. **7** How happy are your men.[C] How happy are these servants of yours, who always stand in your presence hearing your wisdom. **8** Blessed be the LORD your God! He delighted in you and put you on his throne as king for the LORD your God. Because your God loved Israel enough to establish them forever, he has set you over them as king to carry out justice and righteousness." Dt7:8; 1Kg10:8; 1Ch28:5; 29:23; 2Ch2:11

9 Then she gave the king four and a half tons[D] of gold, a great quantity of spices, and precious stones. There never were such spices as those the queen of Sheba gave to King Solomon. **10** In addition, Hiram's servants and Solomon's servants who brought gold from Ophir also brought algum wood and precious stones. **11** The king made the algum wood into walkways for the LORD's temple and for the king's palace and into lyres and harps for the singers. Never before had anything like them been seen in the land of Judah. 2Ch8:18

12 King Solomon gave the queen of Sheba her every desire, whatever she asked — far more than she had brought the king. Then she, along

A**8:18** Lit *Huram*   B**8:18** Lit *450 talents*   C**9:7** LXX, Old Lat read *wives*; 1Kg10:8   D**9:9** Lit *120 talents* with her servants, returned to her own country.

Solomon's Wealth

[13] The weight of gold that came to Solomon annually was twenty-five tons,[A][14] besides what was brought by the merchants and traders. All the Arabian kings and governors of the land also brought gold and silver to Solomon.   1Kg 10:14-25

[15] King Solomon made two hundred large shields of hammered gold; 15 pounds[B] of hammered gold went into each shield. [16] He made three hundred small shields of hammered gold; 7 ½ pounds[C] of gold went into each shield. The king put them in the House of the Forest of Lebanon.   1Kg 7:2-5

[17] The king also made a large ivory throne and overlaid it with pure gold. [18] The throne had six steps; there was a footstool covered in gold for the throne, armrests on either side of the seat, and two lions standing beside the armrests. [19] Twelve lions were standing there on the six steps, one at each end. Nothing like it had ever been made in any other kingdom.

[20] All of King Solomon's drinking cups were gold, and all the utensils of the House of the Forest of Lebanon were pure gold. There was no silver, since it was considered as nothing in Solomon's time, [21] for the king's ships kept going to Tarshish with Hiram's servants, and once every three years the ships of Tarshish would arrive bearing gold, silver, ivory, apes, and peacocks.[D]

[22] King Solomon surpassed all the kings of the world in riches and wisdom. [23] All the kings of the world wanted an audience with Solomon to hear the wisdom God had put in his heart. [24] Each of them would bring his own gift — items[E] of silver and gold, clothing, weapons,[F,G] spices, and horses and mules — as an annual tribute.   1Kg 3:13

[25] Solomon had four thousand stalls for horses and chariots, and twelve thousand horsemen. He stationed them in the chariot cities and with the king in Jerusalem. [26] He ruled over all the kings from the Euphrates River to the land of the Philistines and as far as the border of Egypt. [27] The king made silver as common in Jerusalem as stones, and he made cedar as abundant as sycamore in the Judean foothills. [28] They were bringing horses for Solomon from Egypt and from all the countries.   Dt 17:16; 1Kg 4:26; 10:26-29

Solomon's Death

[29] The remaining events of Solomon's reign, from beginning to end, are written in the Events of the Prophet Nathan, the Prophecy of Ahijah the Shilonite, and the Visions of the Seer Iddo concerning Jeroboam son of Nebat. [30] Solomon reigned in Jerusalem over all Israel for forty years. [31] Solomon rested with his fathers and was buried in the city of his father David. His son Rehoboam became king in his place.   1Kg 11:41-43; 1Ch 29:29; 2Ch 12:15; 13:22

The Kingdom Divided

10 Then Rehoboam went to Shechem, for all Israel had gone to Shechem to make him king. [2] When Jeroboam son of Nebat heard about it — for he was in Egypt where he had fled from

---

[A]**9:13** Lit *666 talents*   [B]**9:15** Lit *600* (shekels)   [C]**9:16** Lit *300* (shekels)   [D]**9:21** Or *baboons*   [E]**9:24** Or *vessels,* or *weapons*   [F]**9:24** LXX reads *resin*   [G]**9:24** Or *fragrant balsam*

King Solomon's presence — Jeroboam returned from Egypt. ³ So they summoned him. Then Jeroboam and all Israel came and spoke to Rehoboam: ⁴ "Your father made our yoke harsh. Therefore, lighten your father's harsh service and the heavy yoke he put on us, and we will serve you." 1Kg 11:40; 12:1-20

⁵ Rehoboam replied, "Return to me in three days." So the people left.

⁶ Then King Rehoboam consulted with the elders who had attended his father Solomon when he was alive, asking, "How do you advise me to respond to this people?"

⁷ They replied, "If you will be kind to this people and please them by speaking kind words to them, they will be your servants forever."

⁸ But he rejected the advice of the elders who had advised him, and he consulted with the young men who had grown up with him, the ones attending him. ⁹ He asked them, "What message do you advise we send back to this people who said to me, 'Lighten the yoke your father put on us'?"

¹⁰ Then the young men who had grown up with him told him, "This is what you should say to the people who said to you, 'Your father made our yoke heavy, but you, make it lighter on us!' This is what you should say to them: 'My little finger is thicker than my father's waist! ¹¹ Now therefore, my father burdened you with a heavy yoke, but I will add to your yoke; my father disciplined you with whips, but I, with barbed whips.' "ᴬ

¹² So Jeroboam and all the people came to Rehoboam on the third day, just as the king had ordered, saying, "Return to me on the third day." ¹³ Then the king answered them harshly. King Rehoboam rejected the elders' advice ¹⁴ and spoke to them according to the young men's advice, saying, "My father made your yoke heavy,ᴮ but I will add to it; my father disciplined you with whips, but I, with barbed whips."

¹⁵ The king did not listen to the people because the turn of events came from God, in order that the LORD might carry out his word that he had spoken through Ahijah the Shilonite to Jeroboam son of Nebat.

¹⁶ When all Israel sawᶜ that the king had not listened to them, the people answered the king: 1Kg 12:16

What portion do we have
  in David?
We have no inheritance
  in the son of Jesse.
Israel, each to your tent;
David, look after
  your own house now!

So all Israel went to their tents. ¹⁷ But as for the Israelites living in the cities of Judah, Rehoboam reigned over them.

¹⁸ Then King Rehoboam sent Hadoram,ᴰ who was in charge of the forced labor, but the Israelites stoned him to death. However, King Rehoboam managed to get into his chariot to flee to Jerusalem. ¹⁹ Israel is in rebellion against the house of David until today. 1Kg 4:6; 5:14; 12:18

Rehoboam in Jerusalem

11 When Rehoboam arrived in Jerusalem, he mobilized the house of Judah and Benjamin — one hundred eighty thousand fit

---

ᴬ**10:11** Lit *with scorpions*, also in v. 14   ᴮ**10:14** Some Hb mss, LXX; other Hb mss read *I will make your yoke heavy*; 1Kg 12:14   ᶜ**10:16** Some Hb mss, LXX; other Hb mss omit *saw*; 1Kg 12:16   ᴰ**10:18** = Adoram in 1Kg 12:18

young soldiers — to fight against Israel to restore the reign to Rehoboam. ² But the word of the LORD came to Shemaiah, the man of God: ³ "Say to Rehoboam son of Solomon, king of Judah, to all Israel in Judah and Benjamin, and to the rest of the people: ⁴ 'This is what the LORD says: You are not to march up and fight against your brothers. Each of you return home, for this incident has come from me.'" 2Ch 28:8-11

So they listened to what the LORD said and turned back from going against Jeroboam.

Judah's King Rehoboam

⁵ Rehoboam stayed in Jerusalem, and he fortified cities[A] in Judah. ⁶ He built up Bethlehem, Etam, Tekoa, ⁷ Beth-zur, Soco, Adullam, ⁸ Gath, Mareshah, Ziph, ⁹ Adoraim, Lachish, Azekah, ¹⁰ Zorah, Aijalon, and Hebron, which are fortified cities in Judah and in Benjamin. ¹¹ He strengthened their fortifications and put leaders in them with supplies of food, oil, and wine. ¹² He also put large shields and spears in each and every city to make them very strong. So Judah and Benjamin were his. 2Ch 8:2-6; 11:23

¹³ The priests and Levites from all their regions throughout Israel took their stand with Rehoboam, ¹⁴ for the Levites left their pasturelands and their possessions and went to Judah and Jerusalem, because Jeroboam and his sons refused to let them serve as priests of the LORD. ¹⁵ Jeroboam appointed his own priests for the high places, the goat-demons, and the golden calves he had made. ¹⁶ Those from every tribe of Israel who had determined in their hearts to seek the LORD their God followed the Levites to Jerusalem to sacrifice to the LORD, the God of their ancestors. ¹⁷ So they strengthened the kingdom of Judah and supported Rehoboam son of Solomon for three years, because they walked in the ways of David and Solomon for three years. Lv 17:7; Nm 35:2-5; 2Ch 13:9

¹⁸ Rehoboam married Mahalath, daughter of David's son Jerimoth and of Abihail daughter of Jesse's son Eliab. ¹⁹ She bore sons to him: Jeush, Shemariah, and Zaham. ²⁰ After her, he married Maacah daughter[B] of Absalom. She bore Abijah, Attai, Ziza, and Shelomith to him. ²¹ Rehoboam loved Maacah daughter of Absalom more than all his wives and concubines. He acquired eighteen wives and sixty concubines and was the father of twenty-eight sons and sixty daughters. Dt 17:17; 1Sm 16:6; 2Ch 13:2

²² Rehoboam appointed Abijah son of Maacah as chief, leader among his brothers, intending to make him king. ²³ Rehoboam also showed discernment by dispersing some of his sons to all the regions of Judah and Benjamin and to all the fortified cities. He gave them plenty of provisions and sought many wives for them. Dt 21:15-17

Shishak's Invasion

12 When Rehoboam had established his sovereignty and royal power, he abandoned the law of the LORD — he and all Israel with him. ² Because they were unfaithful to the LORD, in the fifth year of King Rehoboam, King Shishak of Egypt went to war against Jerusalem ³ with 1,200 chariots, 60,000 cavalrymen, and countless people

A11:5 Lit he built cities for a fortress　B11:20 Possibly granddaughter, also in v. 21; 2Ch 13:2

who came with him from Egypt — Libyans, Sukkiim, and Cushites. ⁴ He captured the fortified cities of Judah and came as far as Jerusalem.

⁵ Then the prophet Shemaiah went to Rehoboam and the leaders of Judah who were gathered at Jerusalem because of Shishak. He said to them: "This is what the LORD says: 'You have abandoned me; therefore, I have abandoned you to Shishak.'"   Dt 28:15,25; 2Ch 11:2

⁶ So the leaders of Israel and the king humbled themselves and said, "The LORD is righteous."   Dn 9:14

⁷ When the LORD saw that they had humbled themselves, the LORD's message came to Shemaiah: "They have humbled themselves; I will not destroy them but will grant them a little deliverance. My wrath will not be poured out on Jerusalem through Shishak. ⁸ However, they will become his servants so that they may recognize the difference between serving me and serving the kingdoms of other lands."

⁹ So King Shishak of Egypt went to war against Jerusalem. He seized the treasuries of the LORD's temple and the treasuries of the royal palace. He took everything. He took the gold shields that Solomon had made. ¹⁰ King Rehoboam made bronze shields to replace them and committed them into the care of the captains of the guards^A who protected the entrance to the king's palace. ¹¹ Whenever the king entered the LORD's temple, the guards would carry the shields and take them back to the armory.^B ¹² When Rehoboam humbled himself, the LORD's anger turned away from him, and he did not destroy him

completely. Besides that, conditions were good in Judah.   1Kg 14:25-28

Rehoboam's Last Days

¹³ King Rehoboam established his royal power in Jerusalem. Rehoboam was forty-one years old when he became king, and he reigned seventeen years in Jerusalem, the city the LORD had chosen from all the tribes of Israel to put his name. Rehoboam's mother's name was Naamah the Ammonite. ¹⁴ Rehoboam did what was evil, because he did not determine in his heart to seek the LORD.   Dt 12:5; 1Kg 14:21-22

¹⁵ The events of Rehoboam's reign, from beginning to end, are written in the Events of the Prophet Shemaiah and of the Seer Iddo concerning genealogies. There was war between Rehoboam and Jeroboam throughout their reigns. ¹⁶ Rehoboam rested with his fathers and was buried in the city of David. His son Abijah^C became king in his place.   1Kg 14:29-31; 2Ch 9:29; 12:5

Judah's King Abijah

13 In the eighteenth year of Israel's King Jeroboam, Abijah^C became king over Judah, ² and he reigned three years in Jerusalem. His mother's name was Micaiah^D daughter of Uriel; she was from Gibeah.   1Kg 15:1-2, 7; 2Ch 11:20,22

There was war between Abijah and Jeroboam. ³ Abijah set his army of warriors in order with four hundred thousand fit young men. Jeroboam arranged his mighty army of eight hundred thousand fit young men in battle formation against him. ⁴ Then Abijah stood on Mount Zemaraim, which is in

---

^A **12:10** Lit *the runners*   ^B **12:11** Lit *the chamber of the runners*   ^C **12:16; 13:1** = Abijam in 1Kg 14:31–15:8
^D **13:2** LXX, Syr, Arabic read *Maacah*; 1Kg 15:2; 2Ch 11:22

the hill country of Ephraim, and said, "Jeroboam and all Israel, hear me. [5] Don't you know that the LORD God of Israel gave the kingship over Israel to David and his descendants forever by a covenant of salt? [6] But Jeroboam son of Nebat, a servant of Solomon son of David, rose up and rebelled against his lord. [7] Then worthless and wicked men gathered around him to resist Rehoboam son of Solomon when Rehoboam was young, inexperienced, and unable to assert himself against them. Jos 18:22; 2Sm 7:12-16

[8] "And now you are saying you can assert yourselves against the LORD's kingdom, which is in the hand of one of David's sons. You are a vast number and have with you the golden calves that Jeroboam made for you as gods.[A] [9] Didn't you banish the priests of the LORD, the descendants of Aaron and the Levites, and make your own priests like the peoples of other lands do? Whoever comes to ordain himself with a young bull and seven rams may become a priest of what are not gods. Ex 29:29-33; 1Kg 12:28; 2Ch 11:14

[10] "But as for us, the LORD is our God. We have not abandoned him; the priests ministering to the LORD are descendants of Aaron, and the Levites serve at their tasks. [11] They offer a burnt offering and fragrant incense to the LORD every morning and every evening, and they set the rows of the Bread of the Presence on the ceremonially clean table. They light the lamps of the gold lampstand every evening. We are carrying out the requirements of the LORD our God, while you have abandoned him. [12] Look, God and

his priests are with us at our head. The trumpets are ready to sound the charge against you. Israelites, don't fight against the LORD God of your ancestors, for you will not succeed." Ex 25:30; 29:38; Lv 24:5-9; 2Ch 2:4

[13] Now Jeroboam had sent an ambush around to advance from behind them. So they were in front of Judah, and the ambush was behind them. [14] Judah turned and discovered that the battle was in front of them and behind them, so they cried out to the LORD. Then the priests blew the trumpets, [15] and the men of Judah raised the battle cry. When the men of Judah raised the battle cry, God routed Jeroboam and all Israel before Abijah and Judah. [16] So the Israelites fled before Judah, and God handed them over to them. [17] Then Abijah and his people struck them with a mighty blow, and five hundred thousand fit young men of Israel were killed. [18] The Israelites were subdued at that time. The Judahites succeeded because they depended on the LORD, the God of their ancestors. Jos 8:4-9; 2Ch 14:11-12; 16:8

[19] Abijah pursued Jeroboam and captured some cities from him: Bethel, Jeshanah, and Ephron,[B] along with their surrounding villages. [20] Jeroboam no longer retained his power[C] during Abijah's reign; ultimately, the LORD struck him and he died. 1Sm 25:38; 1Kg 14:20

[21] However, Abijah grew strong, acquired fourteen wives, and fathered twenty-two sons and sixteen daughters. [22] The rest of the events of Abijah's reign, along with his ways and his sayings, are written in the Writing of the Prophet

[A]13:8 Or God; 1Kg 12:28 [B]13:19 Alt Hb tradition reads Ephrain [C]13:20 Lit He did not restrain the power of Jeroboam

14

Iddo. [1] Abijah rested with his fathers and was buried in the city of David. His son Asa became king in his place. During his reign the land experienced peace for ten years.

1Kg 15:7-8; 2Ch 9:29; 12:15

Judah's King Asa

[2] Asa did what was good and right in the sight of the LORD his God. [3] He removed the pagan altars and the high places. He shattered their sacred pillars and chopped down their Asherah poles. [4] He told the people of Judah to seek the LORD God of their ancestors and to carry out the instruction and the commands. [5] He also removed the high places and the shrines[A] from all the cities of Judah, and the kingdom experienced peace under him.

[6] Because the land experienced peace, Asa built fortified cities in Judah. No one made war with him in those days because the LORD gave him rest. [7] So he said to the people of Judah, "Let's build these cities and surround them with walls and towers, with doors and bars. The land is still ours because we sought the LORD our God. We sought him and he gave us rest on every side." So they built and succeeded.

The Cushite Invasion

[8] Asa had an army of three hundred thousand from Judah bearing large shields and spears, and two hundred eighty thousand from Benjamin bearing regular shields and drawing the bow. All these were valiant warriors. [9] Then Zerah the Cushite came against them with an army of one million men and three hundred[B] chariots. They came as far as Mareshah. [10] So Asa marched out against him and lined up in battle formation in Zephathah Valley at Mareshah.

2Ch 11:8; 13:3

[11] Then Asa cried out to the LORD his God: "LORD, there is no one besides you to help the mighty and those without strength. Help us, LORD our God, for we depend on you, and in your name we have come against this large army. LORD, you are our God. Do not let a mere mortal hinder you."

2Ch 13:14,18

[12] So the LORD routed the Cushites before Asa and before Judah, and the Cushites fled. [13] Then Asa and the people who were with him pursued them as far as Gerar. The Cushites fell until they had no survivors, for they were crushed before the LORD and his army. So the people of Judah carried off a great supply of loot. [14] Then they attacked all the cities around Gerar because the terror of the LORD was on them. They also plundered all the cities, since there was a great deal of plunder in them. [15] They also attacked the tents of the herdsmen and captured many sheep and camels. Then they returned to Jerusalem.

Revival under Asa

15

The Spirit of God came on Azariah son of Oded. [2] So he went out to meet Asa and said to him, "Asa and all Judah and Benjamin, hear me. The LORD is with you when you are with him. If you seek him, he will be found by you, but if you abandon him, he will abandon you. [3] For many years Israel has been without the true God, without a teaching priest, and without instruction, [4] but when they turned to the LORD God of Israel in their distress and sought him, he was

A 14:5 Or *incense altars*   B 14:9 Syr, Arabic read *30,000* found by them. ⁵ In those times there was no peace for those who went about their daily activities because the residents of the lands had many conflicts. ⁶ Nation was crushed by nation and city by city, for God troubled them with every possible distress. ⁷ But as for you, be strong; don't give up, ᴬ for your work has a reward."   2Ch 20:14; 24:20

⁸ When Asa heard these words and the prophecy of Azariah son of Oded the prophet, he took courage and removed the abhorrent idols from the whole land of Judah and Benjamin and from the cities he had captured in the hill country of Ephraim. He renovated the altar of the Lᴏʀᴅ that was in front of the portico of the Lᴏʀᴅ's temple. ⁹ Then he gathered all Judah and Benjamin, as well as those from the tribes of Ephraim, Manasseh, and Simeon who were residing among them, for they had defected to him from Israel in great numbers when they saw that the Lᴏʀᴅ his God was with him.

¹⁰ They were gathered in Jerusalem in the third month of the fifteenth year of Asa's reign. ¹¹ At that time they sacrificed to the Lᴏʀᴅ seven hundred cattle and seven thousand sheep and goats from all the plunder they had brought. ¹² Then they entered into a covenant to seek the Lᴏʀᴅ God of their ancestors with all their heart and all their soul. ¹³ Whoever would not seek the Lᴏʀᴅ God of Israel would be put to death, young or old, ᴮ man or woman. ¹⁴ They took an oath to the Lᴏʀᴅ in a loud voice, with shouting, with trumpets, and with rams' horns. ¹⁵ All Judah rejoiced over the oath,

for they had sworn it with all their mind. They had sought him with all their heart, and he was found by them. So the Lᴏʀᴅ gave them rest on every side.   Dt 17:2-7; 2Ch 14:13-15; 23:16

¹⁶ King Asa also removed Maacah, his grandmother, ᶜ from being queen mother because she had made an obscene image of Asherah. Asa chopped down her obscene image, then crushed it and burned it in the Kidron Valley. ¹⁷ The high places were not taken away from Israel; nevertheless, Asa was wholeheartedly devoted his entire life. ᴰ ¹⁸ He brought his father's consecrated gifts and his own consecrated gifts into God's temple: silver, gold, and utensils.

¹⁹ There was no war until the thirty-fifth year of Asa's reign.

Asa's Treaty with Aram

16 In the thirty-sixth year of Asa, Israel's King Baasha went to war against Judah. He built Ramah in order to keep anyone from leaving or coming to King Asa of Judah. ² So Asa brought out the silver and gold from the treasuries of the Lᴏʀᴅ's temple and the royal palace and sent it to Aram's King Ben-hadad, who lived in Damascus, saying, ³ "There's a treaty between me and you, between my father and your father. Look, I have sent you silver and gold. Go break your treaty with Israel's King Baasha so that he will withdraw from me."   1Kg 15:17-22

⁴ Ben-hadad listened to King Asa and sent the commanders of his armies to the cities of Israel. They attacked Ijon, Dan, Abel-maim, ᴱ and all the storage cities ᶠ

ᴬ15:7 Lit don't let your hands drop   ᴮ15:13 Or insignificant or great   ᶜ15:16 Lit mother; 1Kg 15:2; 2Ch 11:22   ᴰ15:17 Lit wholehearted all his days   ᴱ16:4 Abel-beth-maacah in 1Kg 15:20   ᶠ16:4 = all Chinnereth in 1Kg 15:20

of Naphtali. ⁵ When Baasha heard about it, he quit building Ramah and stopped his work. ⁶ Then King Asa brought all Judah, and they carried away the stones of Ramah and the timbers Baasha had built it with. Then he built Geba and Mizpah with them.

Hanani's Rebuke of Asa

⁷ At that time, the seer Hanani came to King Asa of Judah and said to him, "Because you depended on the king of Aram and have not depended on the LORD your God, the army of the king of Aram has escaped from you. ⁸ Were not the Cushites and Libyans a vast army with many chariots and horsemen? When you depended on the LORD, he handed them over to you. ⁹ For the eyes of the LORD roam throughout the earth to show himself strong for those who are wholeheartedly devoted to him. You have been foolish in this matter. Therefore, you will have wars from now on." ¹⁰ Asa was enraged with the seer and put him in prison^A because of his anger over this. And Asa mistreated some of the people at that time.   Pr 15:3

Asa's Death

¹¹ Note that the events of Asa's reign, from beginning to end, are written in the Book of the Kings of Judah and Israel. ¹² In the thirty-ninth year of his reign, Asa developed a disease in his feet, and his disease became increasingly severe. Yet even in his disease he didn't seek the LORD but only the physicians. ¹³ Asa rested with his fathers; he died in the forty-first year of his reign. ¹⁴ He was buried in his own tomb that he had made for himself in the city of David. They laid him out in a coffin that was full of spices and various mixtures of prepared ointments; then they made a great fire in his honor.

Judah's King Jehoshaphat

17 His son Jehoshaphat became king in his place and strengthened himself against Israel. ² He stationed troops in every fortified city of Judah and set garrisons in the land of Judah and in the cities of Ephraim that his father Asa had captured.   1Kg 15:24

³ Now the LORD was with Jehoshaphat because he walked in the former ways of his father David.^B He did not seek the Baals ⁴ but sought the God of his father and walked by his commands, not according to the practices of Israel. ⁵ So the LORD established the kingdom in his hand. Then all Judah brought him tribute, and he had riches and honor in abundance. ⁶ His mind rejoiced in the LORD's ways, and he again removed the high places and Asherah poles from Judah. 1Kg 12:28

Jehoshaphat's Educational Plan

⁷ In the third year of his reign, Jehoshaphat sent his officials — Ben-hail,^C Obadiah, Zechariah, Nethanel, and Micaiah — to teach in the cities of Judah. ⁸ The Levites with them were Shemaiah, Nethaniah, Zebadiah,^D Asahel, Shemiramoth, Jehonathan, Adonijah, Tobijah, and Tob-adonijah; the priests, Elishama and Jehoram, were with these Levites. ⁹ They taught throughout Judah, having the book of the LORD's instruction with them. They went

---

^A 16:10 Lit the house of stocks   ^B 17:3 Some Hb mss, LXX omit David   ^C 17:7 = Son of Power   ^D 17:8 Some Hb mss, Syr, Tg, Arabic read Zechariah throughout the towns of Judah and taught the people. Dt 6:4-9; 2Ch 15:3; 35:3

¹⁰ The terror of the LORD was on all the kingdoms of the lands that surrounded Judah, so they didn't fight against Jehoshaphat. ¹¹ Some of the Philistines also brought gifts and silver as tribute to Jehoshaphat, and the Arabs brought him flocks: 7,700 rams and 7,700 male goats.

Jehoshaphat's Military Might

¹² Jehoshaphat grew stronger and stronger. He built fortresses and storage cities in Judah ¹³ and carried out great works in the towns of Judah. He had fighting men, valiant warriors, in Jerusalem. ¹⁴ These are their numbers according to their ancestral families.ᴬ For Judah, the commanders of thousands: 2Ch27:4

Adnah the commander and
      three hundred thousand
      valiant warriors with him;
¹⁵   next to him, Jehohanan
      the commander and two
      hundred eighty thousand
      with him;
¹⁶   next to him, Amasiah son
      of Zichri, the volunteer of
      the LORD, and two hundred
      thousand valiant warriors
      with him;   Jdg 5:2,9; 1Ch 29:9
¹⁷   from Benjamin, Eliada, a
      valiant warrior, and two
      hundred thousand with
      him armed with bow and
      shield;
¹⁸   next to him, Jehozabad
      and one hundred eighty
      thousand with him
      equipped for war.

¹⁹ These were the ones who served the king, besides those he stationed in the fortified cities throughout all Judah.   2Ch 17:2

Jehoshaphat's Alliance with Ahab

18 Now Jehoshaphat had riches and honor in abundance, and he made an alliance with Ahab through marriage.ᴮ ² Then after some years, he went down to visit Ahab in Samaria. Ahab sacrificed many sheep, goats, and cattle for him and for the people who were with him. Then he persuaded him to attack Ramoth-gilead, ³ for Israel's King Ahab asked Judah's King Jehoshaphat, "Will you go with me to Ramoth-gilead?" 1Kg 22:1-35; 2Ch 17:5

He replied to him, "I am as you are, my people as your people; we will be with you in the battle." ⁴ But Jehoshaphat said to the king of Israel, "First, please ask what the LORD's will is."

⁵ So the king of Israel gathered the prophets, four hundred men, and asked them, "Should we go to Ramoth-gilead for war or should I refrain?"

They replied, "March up, and God will hand it over to the king."

⁶ But Jehoshaphat asked, "Isn't there a prophet of the LORD here anymore? Let's ask him." 2Kg 3:11

⁷ The king of Israel said to Jehoshaphat, "There is still one man who can inquire of the LORD, but I hate him because he never prophesies good about me, but only disaster. He is Micaiah son of Imlah."

"The king shouldn't say that," Jehoshaphat replied.

⁸ So the king of Israel called an officer and said, "Hurry and get Micaiah son of Imlah!"

⁹ Now the king of Israel and King Jehoshaphat of Judah, clothed in royal attire, were each sitting on his own throne. They were sitting

ᴬ17:14 Lit the house of their fathers   ᴮ18:1 Lit made himself a son-in-law to Ahab ; 1Kg 3:1; Ezr 9:14

on the threshing floor at the entrance to Samaria's gate, and all the prophets were prophesying in front of them. [10] Then Zedekiah son of Chenaanah made iron horns and said, "This is what the LORD says: 'You will gore the Arameans with these until they are finished off.'" [11] And all the prophets were prophesying the same, saying, "March up to Ramoth-gilead and succeed, for the LORD will hand it over to the king."   Ru 4:1

Micaiah's Message of Defeat

[12] The messenger who went to call Micaiah instructed him, "Look, the words of the prophets are unanimously favorable for the king. So let your words be like theirs, and speak favorably."

[13] But Micaiah said, "As the LORD lives, I will say whatever my God says."[A]   Nm 22:35,38; 24:13

[14] So he went to the king, and the king asked him, "Micaiah, should we go to Ramoth-gilead for war, or should I[B] refrain?"

Micaiah said, "March up and succeed, for they will be handed over to you."

[15] But the king said to him, "How many times must I make you swear not to tell me anything but the truth in the name of the LORD?"

[16] So Micaiah said:

I saw all Israel scattered
    on the hills
like sheep without a shepherd.
And the LORD said,
"They have no master;
    let each return home in peace."

[17] So the king of Israel said to Jehoshaphat, "Didn't I tell you he never prophesies good about me, but only disaster?"

[18] Then Micaiah said, "Therefore, hear the word of the LORD. I saw the LORD sitting on his throne, and the whole heavenly army was standing at his right hand and at his left hand. [19] And the LORD said, 'Who will entice King Ahab of Israel to march up and fall at Ramoth-gilead?' So one was saying this and another was saying that.   Is 6:1-5

[20] "Then a spirit came forward, stood before the LORD, and said, 'I will entice him.'   Dt 13:1-5; 1Sm 16:14

"The LORD asked him, 'How?'

[21] "So he said, 'I will go and become a lying spirit in the mouth of all his prophets.'

"Then he said, 'You will entice him and also prevail. Go and do that.'

[22] "Now, you see, the LORD has put a lying spirit into the mouth of[C] these prophets of yours, and the LORD has pronounced disaster against you."

[23] Then Zedekiah son of Chenaanah came up, hit Micaiah on the cheek, and demanded, "Which way did the spirit from the LORD leave me to speak to you?"

[24] Micaiah replied, "You will soon see when you go to hide in an inner chamber on that day."   1Kg 20:30

[25] Then the king of Israel ordered, "Take Micaiah and return him to Amon, the governor of the city, and to Joash, the king's son, [26] and say, 'This is what the king says: Put this guy in prison and feed him only a little bread and water[D] until I come back safely.'"   2Ch 16:10; 18:8; 34:8

[27] But Micaiah said, "If you ever return safely, the LORD has not

A18:13 LXX, Vg add to me; 1Kg 22:14   B18:14 LXX reads we; 1Kg 22:15   C18:22 Some Hb mss, LXX, Syr, Vg add all; 1Kg 22:23   D18:26 Lit him on bread of oppression and water of oppression spoken through me." Then he said, "Listen, all you people!" Mc 1:2

Ahab's Death

²⁸ Then the king of Israel and Judah's King Jehoshaphat went up to Ramoth-gilead. ²⁹ But the king of Israel said to Jehoshaphat, "I will disguise myself and go into battle, but you wear your royal attire." So the king of Israel disguised himself, and they went into battle. 2Ch 35:22

³⁰ Now the king of Aram had ordered his chariot commanders, "Do not fight with anyone at all ᴬ except the king of Israel."

³¹ When the chariot commanders saw Jehoshaphat, they shouted, "He must be the king of Israel!" So they turned to attack him, but Jehoshaphat cried out and the LORD helped him. God drew them away from him. ³² When the chariot commanders saw that he was not the king of Israel, they turned back from pursuing him. 2Ch 13:14-15

³³ But a man drew his bow without taking special aim and struck the king of Israel through the joints of his armor. So he said to the charioteer, "Turn around and take me out of the battle, ᴮ for I am badly wounded!" ³⁴ The battle raged throughout that day, and the king of Israel propped himself up in his chariot facing the Arameans until evening. Then he died at sunset.

Jehu's Rebuke of Jehoshaphat

19 King Jehoshaphat of Judah returned to his home in Jerusalem in peace. ² Then Jehu son of the seer Hanani went out to confront him ᶜ and said to King Jehoshaphat, "Do you help the wicked and love those who hate the LORD? Because of this, the LORD's wrath is on you. ³ However, some good is found in you, for you have eradicated the Asherah poles from the land and have decided to seek God." 1Kg 16:1

Jehoshaphat's Reforms

⁴ Jehoshaphat lived in Jerusalem, and once again he went out among the people from Beer-sheba to the hill country of Ephraim and brought them back to the LORD, the God of their ancestors. ⁵ He appointed judges in all the fortified cities of the land of Judah, city by city. ⁶ Then he said to the judges, "Consider what you are doing, for you do not judge for a mere mortal, but for the LORD, who is with you in the matter of judgment. ⁷ And now, may the terror of the LORD be on you. Watch what you do, for there is no injustice or partiality or taking bribes with the LORD our God." Lv 19:15; Dt 1:17; 16:18-20; 2Ch 15:8-13

⁸ Jehoshaphat also appointed in Jerusalem some of the Levites and priests and some of the Israelite family heads for deciding the LORD's will and for settling disputes of the residents of ᴰ Jerusalem. ⁹ He commanded them, saying, "In the fear of the LORD, with integrity, and wholeheartedly, you are to do the following: ¹⁰ For every dispute that comes to you from your brothers who dwell in their cities — whether it regards differences of bloodguilt, law, commandment, statutes, or judgments — you are to warn them, so they will not incur guilt before the LORD and wrath will not come on you and your brothers. Do this, and you will not incur guilt.

ᴬ18:30 Lit with small or with great   ᴮ18:33 LXX, Vg; MT reads camp   ᶜ19:2 Lit to his face   ᴰ19:8 LXX, Vg; MT reads disputes and they returned to

11 "Note that Amariah, the chief priest, is over you in all matters related to the LORD, and Zebadiah son of Ishmael, the ruler of the house of Judah, in all matters related to the king, and the Levites are officers in your presence. Be strong; may the LORD be with those who do what is good."   1Ch 28:20

War against Eastern Enemies

20 After this, the Moabites and Ammonites, together with some of the Meunites,ᴬ came to fight against Jehoshaphat. 2 People came and told Jehoshaphat, "A vast number from beyond the Dead Sea and from Edomᴮ has come to fight against you; they are already in Hazazon-tamar" (that is, En-gedi). 3 Jehoshaphat was afraid, and he resolved to seek the LORD. Then he proclaimed a fast for all Judah, 4 who gathered to seek the LORD. They even came from all the cities of Judah to seek him.   2Ch 26:7

Jehoshaphat's Prayer

5 Then Jehoshaphat stood in the assembly of Judah and Jerusalem in the LORD's temple before the new courtyard. 6 He said:

LORD, God of our ancestors, are you not the God who is in heaven, and do you not rule over all the kingdoms of the nations? Power and might are in your hand, and no one can stand against you. 7 Are you not our God who drove out the inhabitants of this land before your people Israel and who gave it forever to the descendants of Abraham your friend? 8 They have lived in the land and have built you a sanctuary in it for your name and have said, 9 "If disaster comes on us — sword or judgment, pestilence or famine — we will stand before this temple and before you, for your name is in this temple. We will cry out to you because of our distress, and you will hear and deliver."   Dt 4:39; 1Ch 29:11; Is 41:8

10 Now here are the Ammonites, Moabites, and the inhabitants of Mount Seir. You did not let Israel invade them when Israel came out of the land of Egypt, but Israel turned away from them and did not destroy them. 11 Look how they repay us by coming to drive us out of your possession that you gave us as an inheritance. 12 Our God, will you not judge them? For we are powerless before this vast number that comes to fight against us. We do not know what to do, but we look to you.ᶜ

God's Answer

13 All Judah was standing before the LORD with their dependents, their wives, and their children. 14 In the middle of the congregation, the Spirit of the LORD came on Jahaziel (son of Zechariah, son of Benaiah, son of Jeiel, son of Mattaniah, a Levite from Asaph's descendants), 15 and he said, "Listen carefully, all Judah and you inhabitants of Jerusalem, and King Jehoshaphat. This is what the LORD says: 'Do not be afraid or discouraged because of this vast number, for the battle is not yours, but God's. 16 Tomorrow, go down against them. You

ᴬ20:1 LXX; MT reads *Ammonites* ; 2Ch 26:7   ᴮ20:2 Some Hb mss, Old Lat; other Hb mss read *Aram*
ᶜ20:12 Lit *but on you our eyes*

will see them coming up the Ascent of Ziz, and you will find them at the end of the valley facing the Wilderness of Jeruel. [17] You do not have to fight this battle. Position yourselves, stand still, and see the salvation of the LORD. He is with you, Judah and Jerusalem. Do not be afraid or discouraged. Tomorrow, go out to face them, for the LORD is with you.' "   2Ch 14:12; 15:1; 24:20

[18] Then Jehoshaphat knelt low with his face to the ground, and all Judah and the inhabitants of Jerusalem fell down before the LORD to worship him. [19] Then the Levites from the sons of the Kohathites and the Korahites stood up to praise the LORD God of Israel shouting loudly.

Victory and Plunder

[20] In the morning they got up early and went out to the wilderness of Tekoa. As they were about to go out, Jehoshaphat stood and said, "Hear me, Judah and you inhabitants of Jerusalem. Believe in the LORD your God, and you will be established; believe in his prophets, and you will succeed." [21] Then he consulted with the people and appointed some to sing for the LORD and some to praise the splendor of his holiness. When they went out in front of the armed forces, they kept singing: [A]   1Ch 16:29; Ps 29:2; Is 7:9

Give thanks to the LORD,
    for his faithful love
      endures forever.   1Ch 16:34; 2Ch 7:3

[22] The moment they began their shouts and praises, the LORD set an ambush against the Ammonites, Moabites, and the inhabitants of Mount Seir who came to fight against Judah, and they were defeated. [23] The Ammonites and Moabites turned against the inhabitants of Mount Seir and completely annihilated them. When they had finished with the inhabitants of Seir, they helped destroy each other.   Jdg 7:22; 2Ch 13:13; Ezk 38:21; Hg 2:22; Zch 14:13

[24] When Judah came to a place overlooking the wilderness, they looked for the large army, but there were only corpses lying on the ground; nobody had escaped. [25] Then Jehoshaphat and his people went to gather the plunder. They found among them [B] an abundance of goods on the bodies [C] and valuable items. So they stripped them until nobody could carry any more. They were gathering the plunder for three days because there was so much. [26] They assembled in the Valley of Beracah [D] on the fourth day, for there they blessed the LORD. Therefore, that place is still called the Valley of Beracah today.

[27] Then all the men of Judah and Jerusalem turned back with Jehoshaphat their leader, returning joyfully to Jerusalem, for the LORD enabled them to rejoice over their enemies. [28] So they came into Jerusalem to the LORD's temple with harps, lyres, and trumpets.

[29] The terror of God was on all the kingdoms of the lands when they heard that the LORD had fought against the enemies of Israel. [30] Then Jehoshaphat's kingdom was quiet, for his God gave him rest on every side.   2Ch 14:14; 17:10

Summary of Jehoshaphat's Reign

[31] Jehoshaphat became king over Judah. He was thirty-five years

[A]20:21 Lit saying   [B]20:25 LXX reads found cattle   [C]20:25 Some Hb mss, Old Lat, Vg read goods, garments   [D]20:26 = Blessing old when he became king, and he reigned twenty-five years in Jerusalem. His mother's name was Azubah daughter of Shilhi. ³² He walked in the ways of Asa his father; he did not turn away from it but did what was right in the LORD's sight. ³³ However, the high places were not taken away; the people had not yet set their hearts on the God of their ancestors. 1Kg 22:41-45

³⁴ The rest of the events of Jehoshaphat's reign from beginning to end are written in the Events of Jehu son of Hanani, which is recorded in the Book of Israel's Kings.

Jehoshaphat's Fleet of Ships

³⁵ After this, Judah's King Jehoshaphat made an alliance with Israel's King Ahaziah, who was guilty of wrongdoing. ³⁶ Jehoshaphat formed an alliance with him to make ships to go to Tarshish, and they made the ships in Ezion-geber. ³⁷ Then Eliezer son of Dodavahu of Mareshah prophesied against Jehoshaphat, saying, "Because you formed an alliance with Ahaziah, the LORD has broken up what you have made." So the ships were wrecked and were not able to go to Tarshish. 1Kg 22:48-49; 2Ch 9:21

Jehoram Becomes King over Judah

21 Jehoshaphat rested with his fathers and was buried with his fathers in the city of David. His son Jehoram ᴬ became king in his place. ² He had brothers, sons of Jehoshaphat: Azariah, Jehiel, Zechariah, Azariah, Michael, and Shephatiah; all these were the sons of King Jehoshaphat of Judah. ᴮ ³ Their father had given them many gifts of silver, gold, and valuable things, along with fortified cities in Judah, but he gave the kingdom to Jehoram because he was the firstborn. ⁴ When Jehoram had established himself over his father's kingdom, he strengthened his position by killing with the sword all his brothers as well as some of the princes of Israel.

Judah's King Jehoram

⁵ Jehoram was thirty-two years old when he became king, and he reigned eight years in Jerusalem. ⁶ He walked in the ways of the kings of Israel, as the house of Ahab had done, for Ahab's daughter was his wife. He did what was evil in the LORD's sight, ⁷ but for the sake of the covenant the LORD had made with David, he was unwilling to destroy the house of David since the LORD had promised to give a lamp to David and to his sons forever.

⁸ During Jehoram's reign, Edom rebelled against Judah's control and appointed their own king. ⁹ So Jehoram crossed into Edom with his commanders and all his chariots. Then at night he set out to attack the Edomites who had surrounded him and the chariot commanders. ¹⁰ And now Edom is still in rebellion against Judah's control today. Libnah also rebelled at that time against his control because he had abandoned the LORD, the God of his ancestors. ¹¹ Jehoram also built high places in the hills ᶜ of Judah, and he caused the inhabitants of Jerusalem to prostitute themselves, and he led Judah astray. Lv 20:5; 1Kg 11:7

ᴬ 21:1 = Joram   ᴮ 21:2 Some Hb mss, LXX, Syr, Vg, Arabic; other Hb mss read *Israel*   ᶜ 21:11 Some Hb mss, LXX, Vg read *cities*

Elijah's Letter to Jehoram

[12] Then a letter came to Jehoram from the prophet Elijah, saying: This is what the LORD, the God of your ancestor David says: "Because you have not walked in the ways of your father Jehoshaphat or in the ways of King Asa of Judah [13] but have walked in the ways of the kings of Israel, have caused Judah and the inhabitants of Jerusalem to prostitute themselves like the house of Ahab prostituted itself, and also have killed your brothers, your father's family, who were better than you, [14] the LORD is now about to strike your people, your sons, your wives, and all your possessions with a horrible affliction. [15] You yourself will be struck with many illnesses, including a disease of the intestines, until your intestines come out day after day because of the disease." 2Ch 17:3-4

Jehoram's Last Days

[16] The LORD roused the spirit of the Philistines and the Arabs who lived near the Cushites to attack Jehoram. [17] So they went to war against Judah and invaded it. They carried off all the possessions found in the king's palace and also his sons and wives; not a son was left to him except Jehoahaz, [A] his youngest son. [18] After all these things, the LORD afflicted him in his intestines with an incurable disease. [19] This continued day after day until two full years passed. Then his intestines came out because of his disease,

and he died from severe [B] illnesses. But his people did not hold a fire in his honor like the fire in honor of his fathers. 2Ch 16:14

[20] Jehoram was thirty-two years old when he became king; he reigned eight years in Jerusalem. He died to no one's regret [C] and was buried in the city of David but not in the tombs of the kings. 2Kg 8:17,24

Judah's King Ahaziah

22 Then the inhabitants of Jerusalem made Ahaziah, his youngest son, king in his place, because the troops that had come with the Arabs to the camp had killed all the older sons. [D] So Ahaziah son of Jehoram became king of Judah. [2] Ahaziah was twenty-two [E] years old when he became king, and he reigned one year in Jerusalem. His mother's name was Athaliah, granddaughter [F] of Omri.

[3] He walked in the ways of the house of Ahab, for his mother gave him evil advice. [4] So he did what was evil in the LORD's sight like the house of Ahab, for they were his advisers after the death of his father, to his destruction. [5] He also followed their advice and went with Joram [G] son of Israel's King Ahab to fight against King Hazael of Aram, in Ramoth-gilead. The Arameans [H] wounded Joram, [6] so he returned to Jezreel to recover from the wounds they inflicted on him in Ramoth-gilead [I] when he fought against King Hazael of Aram. Then Judah's King Ahaziah [J] son of Jehoram went down to Jezreel to visit Joram son of Ahab since Joram was ill.

[A] 21:17 LXX, Syr, Tg read *Ahaziah*   [B] 21:19 Lit *evil*   [C] 21:20 Lit *He walked in no desirability*   [D] 22:1 Lit *the former ones*   [E] 22:2 Some LXX mss, Syr; MT reads *42*; 2Kg 8:26   [F] 22:2 Lit *daughter*   [G] 22:5 = Jehoram   [H] 22:5 Lit *Rammites*   [I] 22:6 Lit *in Ramah*   [J] 22:6 Some Hb mss, LXX, Syr, Vg; other Hb mss read *Azariah*

⁷ Ahaziah's downfall came from God when he went to Joram. When Ahaziah arrived, he went out with Joram to meet Jehu son of Nimshi, whom the LORD had anointed to destroy the house of Ahab. ⁸ So when Jehu executed judgment on the house of Ahab, he found the rulers of Judah and the sons of Ahaziah's brothers who were serving Ahaziah, and he killed them. ⁹ Then Jehu looked for Ahaziah, and Jehu's soldiers captured him (he was hiding in Samaria). So they brought Ahaziah to Jehu, and they killed him. The soldiers buried him, for they said, "He is the grandson of Jehoshaphat who sought the LORD with all his heart." So no one from the house of Ahaziah had the strength to rule the kingdom. 2Kg 9:21; 2Ch 10:15

Athaliah Usurps the Throne

¹⁰ When Athaliah, Ahaziah's mother, saw that her son was dead, she proceeded to annihilate all the royal heirs ᴬ of the house of Judah. ¹¹ Jehoshabeath, ᴮ the king's daughter, rescued Joash son of Ahaziah from the king's sons who were being killed and put him and the one who nursed him in a bedroom. Now Jehoshabeath was the daughter of King Jehoram and the wife of the priest Jehoiada. Since she was Ahaziah's sister, she hid Joash from Athaliah so that she did not kill him. ¹² While Athaliah reigned over the land, he was hiding with them in God's temple six years. 2Kg 11:1-3

Athaliah Overthrown

23 Then, in the seventh year, Jehoiada summoned his courage and took the commanders of hundreds into a covenant with him: Azariah son of Jeroham, Ishmael son of Jehohanan, Azariah son of Obed, Maaseiah son of Adaiah, and Elishaphat son of Zichri. ² They made a circuit throughout Judah. They gathered the Levites from all the cities of Judah and the family heads of Israel, and they came to Jerusalem. 2Kg 11:4-20

³ Then the whole assembly made a covenant with the king in God's temple. Jehoiada said to them, "Here is the king's son! He will reign, just as the LORD promised concerning David's sons. ⁴ This is what you are to do: a third of you, priests and Levites who are coming on duty on the Sabbath, are to be gatekeepers. ⁵ A third are to be at the king's palace, and a third are to be at the Foundation Gate, and all the troops will be in the courtyards of the LORD's temple. ⁶ No one is to enter the LORD's temple but the priests and those Levites who serve; they may enter because they are holy, but all the people are to obey the requirement of the LORD. ⁷ Completely surround the king with weapons in hand. Anyone who enters the temple is to be put to death. Be with the king in all his daily tasks." ᶜ 1Ch 9:25; 2Ch 21:7

⁸ So the commanders of hundreds did everything the priest Jehoiada commanded. They each brought their men — those coming on duty on the Sabbath and those going off duty on the Sabbath — for the priest Jehoiada did not release the divisions. ⁹ The priest Jehoiada gave to the commanders of hundreds King David's spears, shields, and quivers ᴰ that were in

---

ᴬ22:10 Lit seed   ᴮ22:11 = Jehosheba; 2Kg 11:2   ᶜ23:7 Lit king when he comes in and when he goes out
ᴰ23:9 Or spears and large and small shields

God's temple. ¹⁰ Then he stationed all the troops with their weapons in hand surrounding the king — from the right side of the temple to the left side, by the altar and by the temple.   1Ch 24:1

¹¹ They brought out the king's son, put the crown on him, gave him the testimony, and made him king. Jehoiada and his sons anointed him and cried, "Long live the king!"

¹² When Athaliah heard the noise from the troops, the guards, and those praising the king, she went to the troops in the LORD's temple. ¹³ As she looked, there was the king standing by his pillar^A at the entrance. The commanders and the trumpeters were by the king, and all the people of the land were rejoicing and blowing trumpets while the singers with musical instruments were leading the praise. Athaliah tore her clothes and screamed, "Treason! Treason!"   Nm 10:7-10

¹⁴ Then the priest Jehoiada sent out the commanders of hundreds, those in charge of the army, saying, "Take her out between the ranks, and put anyone who follows her to death by the sword," for the priest had said, "Don't put her to death in the LORD's temple." ¹⁵ So they arrested her, and she went by the entrance of the Horse Gate to the king's palace, where they put her to death.   Neh 3:28; Jr 31:40

Jehoiada's Reforms

¹⁶ Then Jehoiada made a covenant between himself, the king, and the people that they would be the LORD's people. ¹⁷ So all the people went to the temple of Baal and tore it down. They smashed its altars and images and killed Mattan, the priest of Baal, at the altars.   Dt 13:6-9

¹⁸ Then Jehoiada put the oversight of the LORD's temple into the hands of the Levitical priests, whom David had appointed over the LORD's temple, to offer burnt offerings to the LORD as it is written in the law of Moses, with rejoicing and song ordained by^B David. ¹⁹ He stationed gatekeepers at the gates of the LORD's temple so that nothing unclean could enter for any reason. ²⁰ Then he took with him the commanders of hundreds, the nobles, the governors of the people, and all the people of the land and brought the king down from the LORD's temple. They entered the king's palace through the Upper Gate and seated the king on the throne of the kingdom. ²¹ All the people of the land rejoiced, and the city was quiet, for they had put Athaliah to death by the sword.   2Kg 14:6; 1Ch 23:6,25-31; 2Ch 5:5

Judah's King Joash

24 Joash was seven years old when he became king, and he reigned forty years in Jerusalem. His mother's name was Zibiah; she was from Beer-sheba. ² Throughout the time of the priest Jehoiada, Joash did what was right in the LORD's sight. ³ Jehoiada acquired two wives for him, and he was the father of sons and daughters.   2Kg 11:21; 12:1-2; 2Ch 26:4-5

Repairing the Temple

⁴ Afterward, Joash took it to heart to renovate the LORD's temple. ⁵ So he gathered the priests and Levites and said, "Go out to the cities of Judah and collect silver from all Israel to repair the temple of your God

---

^A**23:13** LXX reads *post*   ^B**23:18** Lit *song on the hands of* as needed year by year, and do it quickly." Ex 30:12-16; 2Kg 12:4-12; 2Ch 24:7

However, the Levites did not hurry. [6] So the king called Jehoiada the high priest and said, "Why haven't you required the Levites to bring from Judah and Jerusalem the tax imposed by the LORD's servant Moses and the assembly of Israel for the tent of the testimony? [7] For the sons of that wicked Athaliah broke into the LORD's temple and even used the sacred things of the LORD's temple for the Baals." Nm 1:50

[8] At the king's command a chest was made and placed outside the gate of the LORD's temple. [9] Then a proclamation was issued in Judah and Jerusalem that the tax God's servant Moses imposed on Israel in the wilderness be brought to the LORD. [10] All the leaders and all the people rejoiced, brought the tax, and put it in the chest until it was full. [11] Whenever the chest was brought by the Levites to the king's overseers, and when they saw that there was a large amount of silver, the king's secretary and the high priest's deputy came and emptied the chest, picked it up, and returned it to its place. They did this daily and gathered the silver in abundance. [12] Then the king and Jehoiada gave it to those in charge of the labor on the LORD's temple, who were hiring stonecutters and carpenters to renovate the LORD's temple, also blacksmiths and coppersmiths to repair the LORD's temple. 2Ch 36:22

[13] The workmen did their work, and through them the repairs progressed. They restored God's temple to its specifications and reinforced it. [14] When they finished, they presented the rest of the silver to the king and Jehoiada, who made articles for the LORD's temple with it — articles for ministry and for making burnt offerings, and ladles [A] and articles of gold and silver. They regularly offered burnt offerings in the LORD's temple throughout Jehoiada's life.

Joash's Apostasy

[15] Jehoiada died when he was old and full of days; he was 130 years old at his death. [16] He was buried in the city of David with the kings because he had done what was good in Israel with respect to God and his temple. 2Ch 21:20; 24:25

[17] However, after Jehoiada died, the rulers of Judah came and paid homage to the king. Then the king listened to them, [18] and they abandoned the temple of the LORD, the God of their ancestors, and served the Asherah poles and the idols. So there was wrath against Judah and Jerusalem for this guilt of theirs. [19] Nevertheless, he sent them prophets to bring them back to the LORD; they admonished them, but the people would not listen. Jr 7:25

[20] The Spirit of God enveloped [B] Zechariah son of Jehoiada the priest. He stood above the people and said to them, "This is what God says, 'Why are you transgressing the LORD's commands so that you do not prosper? Because you have abandoned the LORD, he has abandoned you.'" [21] But they conspired against him and stoned him at the king's command in the courtyard of the LORD's temple. [22] King Joash didn't remember the kindness that Zechariah's father Jehoiada had extended to him, but killed his son. While he was dying, he said, "May

A 24:14 Or dishes, or spoons; lit palms   B 24:20 Lit clothed the LORD see and demand an account."   Nm 14:41; Jdg 6:34; 1Ch 12:18; 2Ch 15:2

Aramean Invasion of Judah

²³ At the turn of the year, an Aramean army attacked Joash. They entered Judah and Jerusalem and destroyed all the leaders of the people among them and sent all the plunder to the king of Damascus. ²⁴ Although the Aramean army came with only a few men, the LORD handed over a vast army to them because the people of Judah had abandoned the LORD, the God of their ancestors. So they executed judgment on Joash.

Joash Assassinated

²⁵ When the Arameans saw that Joash had many wounds, they left him. His servants conspired against him, and killed him on his bed, because he had shed the blood of the sons of the priest Jehoiada. So he died, and they buried him in the city of David, but they did not bury him in the tombs of the kings. ²⁶ Those who conspired against him were Zabad, son of the Ammonite woman Shimeath, and Jehozabad, son of the Moabite woman Shimrith. ^A ²⁷ The accounts concerning his sons, the many divine pronouncements about him, and the restoration of God's temple are recorded in the Writing of the Book of the Kings. His son Amaziah became king in his place.

Judah's King Amaziah

25 Amaziah became king when he was twenty-five years old, and he reigned twenty-nine years in Jerusalem. His mother's name was Jehoaddan; she was from Jerusalem. ² He did what was right in the LORD's sight but not wholeheartedly.   2Kg 14:2-6; 25:14

³ As soon as the kingdom was firmly in his grasp, ^B he executed his servants who had killed his father the king. ⁴ However, he did not put their children to death, because — as it is written in the Law, in the book of Moses, where the LORD commanded — "Fathers are not to die because of children, and children are not to die because of fathers, but each one will die for his own sin."   Dt 24:16; 2Ch 17:9; 23:18; Jr 31:30

Amaziah's Campaign Against Edom

⁵ Then Amaziah gathered Judah and assembled them according to ancestral families, ^C according to commanders of thousands, and according to commanders of hundreds. He numbered those twenty years old or more for all Judah and Benjamin. He found there to be three hundred thousand fit young men who could serve in the army, bearing spear and shield. ⁶ Then for 7,500 pounds ^D of silver he hired one hundred thousand valiant warriors from Israel.   Nm 1:3; 2Ch 26:13

⁷ However, a man of God came to him and said, "King, do not let Israel's army go with you, for the LORD is not with Israel — all the Ephraimites. ⁸ But if you go with them, do it! Be strong for battle! But God will make you stumble before the enemy, for God has the power to help or to make one stumble."

⁹ Then Amaziah said to the man of God, "What should I do about the 7,500 pounds of silver I gave to Israel's division?"

---

^A 24:26 = Shomer in 2Kg 12:21   ^B 25:3 LXX, Syr; MT reads *was strong on him*; 1Kg 14:4   ^C 25:5 Lit *house of fathers*   ^D 25:6 Lit *100 talents*, also in v. 9

The man of God replied, "The LORD is able to give you much more than this."

¹⁰ So Amaziah released the division that came to him from Ephraim to go home. But they got very angry with Judah and returned home in a fierce rage.

¹¹ Amaziah strengthened his position and led his people to the Salt Valley. He struck down ten thousand Seirites, ^A ¹² and the Judahites captured ten thousand alive. They took them to the top of a cliff where they threw them off, and all of them were dashed to pieces.

¹³ As for the men of the division that Amaziah sent back so they would not go with him into battle, they raided the cities of Judah from Samaria to Beth-horon, struck down three thousand of their people, and took a great deal of plunder.

¹⁴ After Amaziah came from the attack on the Edomites, he brought the gods of the Seirites and set them up as his gods. He worshiped before them and burned incense to them. ¹⁵ So the LORD's anger was against Amaziah, and he sent a prophet to him, who said, "Why have you sought a people's gods that could not rescue their own people from you?"   2Ch 25:11-12; 28:23

¹⁶ While he was still speaking to him, the king asked, "Have we made you the king's counselor? Stop, why should you lose your life?"

So the prophet stopped, but he said, "I know that God intends to destroy you, because you have done this and have not listened to my advice."

Amaziah's War with Israel's King Jehoash

¹⁷ King Amaziah of Judah took counsel and sent word to Jehoash ^B son of Jehoahaz, son of Jehu, king of Israel, and challenged him: "Come, let's meet face to face."   2Kg 14:8-14

¹⁸ King Jehoash of Israel sent word to King Amaziah of Judah, saying, "The thistle in Lebanon sent a message to the cedar in Lebanon, saying, 'Give your daughter to my son as a wife.' Then a wild animal in Lebanon passed by and trampled the thistle. ¹⁹ You have said, 'Look, I ^C have defeated Edom,' and you have become overconfident ^D that you will get glory. Now stay at home. Why stir up such trouble so that you fall and Judah with you?"   Jdg 9:8-15; 2Ch 26:16

²⁰ But Amaziah would not listen, for this turn of events was from God in order to hand them over to their enemies because they went after the gods of Edom. ²¹ So King Jehoash of Israel advanced. He and King Amaziah of Judah met face to face at Beth-shemesh that belonged to Judah. ²² Judah was routed before Israel, and each man fled to his own tent. ²³ King Jehoash of Israel captured Judah's King Amaziah son of Joash, son of Jehoahaz, ^E at Beth-shemesh. Then Jehoash took him to Jerusalem and broke down two hundred yards ^F of Jerusalem's wall from the Ephraim Gate to the Corner Gate. ^G ²⁴ He took all the gold, silver, all the utensils that were found with Obed-edom in God's temple, the treasures of the king's palace, and the hostages. Then he returned to Samaria.   2Kg 14:13; 1Ch 26:15; 2Ch 21:17; 22:1

^A 25:11 = Edomites, also in v. 14   ^B 25:17 Lit *Joash*   ^C 25:19 Some LXX mss, Old Lat, Tg, Vg; MT reads *you*
^D 25:19 Lit *and your heart has lifted you*   ^E 25:23 = Ahaziah in 2Kg 14:13   ^F 25:23 Lit *400 cubits*
^G 25:23 Some Hb mss; other Hb mss read *to Happoneh*

Amaziah's Death

²⁵ Judah's King Amaziah son of Joash lived fifteen years after the death of Israel's King Jehoash son of Jehoahaz. ²⁶ The rest of the events of Amaziah's reign, from beginning to end, are written in the Book of the Kings of Judah and Israel. 2Kg 14:17-20

²⁷ From the time Amaziah turned from following the LORD, a conspiracy was formed against him in Jerusalem, and he fled to Lachish. However, men were sent after him to Lachish, and they put him to death there. ²⁸ They carried him back on horses and buried him with his fathers in the city of Judah.ᴬ 2Kg 14:20

Judah's King Uzziah

26 All the people of Judah took Uzziah,ᴮ who was sixteen years old, and made him king in place of his father Amaziah. ² After Amaziah the king rested with his fathers, Uzziah rebuilt Elothᶜ and restored it to Judah. 2Kg 14:21-22

³ Uzziah was sixteen years old when he became king, and he reigned fifty-two years in Jerusalem. His mother's name was Jecoliah; she was from Jerusalem. ⁴ He did what was right in the LORD's sight just as his father Amaziah had done. ⁵ He sought God throughout the lifetime of Zechariah, the teacher of the fearᴰ of God. During the time that he sought the LORD, God gave him success. 2Kg 15:2-3; 2Ch 24:2

Uzziah's Exploits

⁶ Uzziah went out to wage war against the Philistines, and he tore down the wall of Gath, the wall of Jabneh, and the wall of Ashdod. Then he built cities in the vicinity of Ashdod and among the Philistines. ⁷ God helped him against the Philistines, the Arabs that live in Gur-baal, and the Meunites. ⁸ The Ammonitesᴱ paid tribute to Uzziah, and his fame spread as far as the entrance of Egypt, for God made him very powerful. ⁹ Uzziah built towers in Jerusalem at the Corner Gate, the Valley Gate, and the corner buttress, and he fortified them. ¹⁰ Since he had many cattle both in the Judean foothillsᶠ and the plain, he built towers in the desert and dug many wells. And since he was a lover of the soil, he had farmers and vinedressers in the hills and in the fertile lands.ᴳ 2Ch 17:11; Is 14:29

¹¹ Uzziah had an army equipped for combat that went out to war by division according to their assignments, as recorded by Jeiel the court secretary and Maaseiah the officer under the authority of Hananiah, one of the king's commanders. ¹² The total number of family heads was 2,600 valiant warriors. ¹³ Under their authority was an army of 307,500 equipped for combat, a powerful force to help the king against the enemy. ¹⁴ Uzziah provided the entire army with shields, spears, helmets, armor, bows, and slingstones. ¹⁵ He made skillfully designed devices in Jerusalem to shoot arrows and catapult large stones for use on the towers and on the corners. So his fame spread even to distant places, for he was wondrously helped until he became strong. 2Ch 25:5

ᴬ25:28 Some Hb mss read city of David ᴮ26:1 = Azariah in 2Kg 14:21 ᶜ26:2 LXX, Syr, Vg read Elath ᴰ26:5 Some Hb mss, LXX, Syr, Tg, Arabic; other Hb mss, Vg read visions ᴱ26:8 LXX reads Meunites ᶠ26:10 Or the Shephelah ᴳ26:10 Or in Carmel

Uzziah's Disease

¹⁶ But when he became strong, he grew arrogant, and it led to his own destruction. He acted unfaithfully against the LORD his God by going into the LORD's sanctuary to burn incense on the incense altar. ¹⁷ The priest Azariah, along with eighty brave priests of the LORD, went in after him. ¹⁸ They took their stand against King Uzziah and said, "Uzziah, you have no right to offer incense to the LORD — only the consecrated priests, the descendants of Aaron, have the right to offer incense. Leave the sanctuary, for you have acted unfaithfully! You will not receive honor from the LORD God." Dt 32:15; 1Kg 13:1-4; 2Ch 25:19

¹⁹ Uzziah, with a firepan in his hand to offer incense, was enraged. But when he became enraged with the priests, in the presence of the priests in the LORD's temple beside the altar of incense, a skin disease broke out on his forehead. ²⁰ Then Azariah the chief priest and all the priests turned to him and saw that he was diseased on his forehead. They rushed him out of there. He himself also hurried to get out because the LORD had afflicted him. ²¹ So King Uzziah was diseased to the time of his death. He lived in quarantine^A with a serious skin disease and was excluded from access to the LORD's temple, while his son Jotham was over the king's household governing the people of the land. Lv 13:46; 2Kg 5:25-27; 15:5-7

²² Now the prophet Isaiah son of Amoz wrote about the rest of the events of Uzziah's reign, from beginning to end. ²³ Uzziah rested with his fathers, and he was buried with his fathers in the burial ground of the kings' cemetery, for they said, "He has a skin disease." His son Jotham became king in his place. 2Ch 21:20; Is 1:1

Judah's King Jotham

27 Jotham was twenty-five years old when he became king, and he reigned sixteen years in Jerusalem. His mother's name was Jerushah daughter of Zadok. ² He did what was right in the LORD's sight just as his father Uzziah had done. In addition, he didn't enter the LORD's sanctuary, but the people still behaved corruptly. 2Kg 15:33-35; 2Ch 26:16-18; 27:8

³ Jotham built the Upper Gate of the LORD's temple, and he built extensively on the wall of Ophel. ⁴ He also built cities in the hill country of Judah and fortresses and towers in the forests. ⁵ He waged war against the king of the Ammonites. He overpowered the Ammonites, and that year they gave him 7,500 pounds^B of silver, 50,000 bushels^C of wheat, and 50,000 bushels of barley. They paid him the same in the second and third years. ⁶ So Jotham strengthened his position because he did not waver in obeying^D the LORD his God. 2Ch 33:14

⁷ As for the rest of the events of Jotham's reign, along with all his wars and his ways, note that they are written in the Book of the Kings of Israel and Judah. ⁸ He was twenty-five years old when he became king, and he reigned sixteen years in Jerusalem. ⁹ Jotham rested with his fathers and was buried in the city of David. His son Ahaz became king in his place. 2Kg 15:36-38

^A26:21 Lit *in a house of exemption from duty*   ^B27:5 Lit *100 talents*   ^C27:5 Lit *10,000 cors*   ^D27:6 Lit *he established his ways before*

Judah's King Ahaz

28 Ahaz was twenty years old when he became king, and he reigned sixteen years in Jerusalem. He did not do what was right in the LORD's sight like his ancestor David, ² for he walked in the ways of the kings of Israel and made cast images of the Baals. ³ He burned incense in Ben Hinnom Valley and burned his children in ᴬ the fire, imitating the detestable practices of the nations the LORD had dispossessed before the Israelites. ⁴ He sacrificed and burned incense on the high places, on the hills, and under every green tree.   2Kg 16:2-4; 18:16

⁵ So the LORD his God handed Ahaz over to the king of Aram. He attacked him and took many captives to Damascus.   2Ch 24:24

Ahaz was also handed over to the king of Israel, who struck him with great force: ⁶ Pekah son of Remaliah killed one hundred twenty thousand in Judah in one day — all brave men — because they had abandoned the LORD God of their ancestors. ⁷ An Ephraimite warrior named Zichri killed the king's son Maaseiah, Azrikam governor of the palace, and Elkanah who was second to the king. ⁸ Then the Israelites took two hundred thousand captives from their brothers — women, sons, and daughters. They also took a great deal of plunder from them and brought it to Samaria.   2Ch 11:4

⁹ A prophet of the LORD named Oded was there. He went out to meet the army that came to Samaria and said to them, "Look, the LORD God of your ancestors handed them over to you because of his wrath against Judah, but you slaughtered them in a rage that has reached heaven. ¹⁰ Now you plan to reduce the people of Judah and Jerusalem, male and female, to slavery. Are you not also guilty before the LORD your God? ¹¹ Listen to me and return the captives you took from your brothers, for the LORD's burning anger is on you."   Is 47:6

¹² So some men who were leaders of the Ephraimites — Azariah son of Jehohanan, Berechiah son of Meshillemoth, Jehizkiah son of Shallum, and Amasa son of Hadlai — stood in opposition to those coming from the war. ¹³ They said to them, "You must not bring the captives here, for you plan to bring guilt on us from the LORD to add to our sins and our guilt. For we have much guilt, and burning anger is on Israel."

¹⁴ The army left the captives and the plunder in the presence of the officers and the congregation. ¹⁵ Then the men who were designated by name took charge of the captives and provided clothes for their naked ones from the plunder. They clothed them, gave them sandals, food and drink, dressed their wounds, and provided donkeys for all the feeble. The Israelites brought them to Jericho, the City of Palms, among their brothers. Then they returned to Samaria.   2Kg 6:22; 2Ch 28:12

¹⁶ At that time King Ahaz asked the king of Assyria for help. ¹⁷ The Edomites came again, attacked Judah, and took captives. ¹⁸ The Philistines also raided the cities of the Judean foothills ᴮ and the Negev of Judah. They captured and occupied Beth-shemesh, Aijalon, and Gederoth, as well as Soco, Timnah,

ᴬ**28:3** LXX, Syr, Tg read *and passed his children through*   ᴮ**28:18** Or *the Shephelah* and Gimzo with their surrounding villages. ¹⁹ For the LORD humbled Judah because of King Ahaz of Judah, ^A who threw off restraint in Judah and was unfaithful to the LORD. ²⁰ Then King Tiglath-pileser ^B of Assyria came against Ahaz; he oppressed him and did not give him support. ²¹ Although Ahaz plundered the LORD's temple and the palace of the king and of the rulers and gave the plunder to the king of Assyria, it did not help him.   2Kg 16:7; Ezk 16:57; Ob 10-14

²² At the time of his distress, King Ahaz himself became more unfaithful to the LORD. ²³ He sacrificed to the gods of Damascus which had defeated him; he said, "Since the gods of the kings of Aram are helping them, I will sacrifice to them so that they will help me." But they were the downfall of him and of all Israel.   Jr 44:17-18

²⁴ Then Ahaz gathered up the utensils of God's temple, cut them into pieces, shut the doors of the LORD's temple, and made himself altars on every street corner in Jerusalem. ²⁵ He made high places in every city of Judah to offer incense to other gods, and he angered the LORD, the God of his ancestors.

Ahaz's Death

²⁶ As for the rest of his deeds and all his ways, from beginning to end, they are written in the Book of the Kings of Judah and Israel. ²⁷ Ahaz rested with his fathers and was buried in the city, in Jerusalem, but they did not bring him into the tombs of the kings of Israel. His son Hezekiah became king in his place.   2Kg 16:19-20

Judah's King Hezekiah

29 Hezekiah was twenty-five years old when he became king, and he reigned twenty-nine years in Jerusalem. His mother's name was Abijah ^C daughter of Zechariah. ² He did what was right in the LORD's sight just as his ancestor David had done.   2Kg 18:2-3

³ In the first year of his reign, in the first month, he opened the doors of the LORD's temple and repaired them. ⁴ Then he brought in the priests and Levites and gathered them in the eastern public square. ⁵ He said to them, "Hear me, Levites. Consecrate yourselves now and consecrate the temple of the LORD, the God of your ancestors. Remove everything impure from the holy place. ⁶ For our fathers were unfaithful and did what is evil in the sight of the LORD our God. They abandoned him, turned their faces away from the LORD's dwelling place, and turned their backs on him. ^D ⁷ They also closed the doors of the portico, extinguished the lamps, did not burn incense, and did not offer burnt offerings in the holy place of the God of Israel. ⁸ Therefore, the wrath of the LORD was on Judah and Jerusalem, and he made them an object of terror, horror, and mockery, ^E as you see with your own eyes. ⁹ Our fathers fell by the sword, and our sons, our daughters, and our wives are in captivity because of this. ¹⁰ It is in my heart now to make a covenant with the LORD, the God of Israel so that his burning anger may turn away from us. ¹¹ My sons, don't be negligent now, for the LORD has chosen you to stand in his presence,

^A **28:19** Some Hb mss; other Hb mss read *Israel*   ^B **28:20** Text emended; MT reads *Tilgath-pilneser*;
1Ch 5:6,26   ^C **29:1** = Abi in 2Kg 18:2   ^D **29:6** Lit *and they gave the back of the neck*   ^E **29:8** Lit *hissing*

to serve him, and to be his ministers and burners of incense."

Cleansing the Temple

¹² Then the Levites stood up:

Mahath son of Amasai and Joel son of Azariah from the Kohathites; 2Ch 31:13

Kish son of Abdi and Azariah son of Jehallelel from the Merarites; Nm 3:19-20

Joah son of Zimmah and Eden son of Joah from the Gershonites;

¹³ Shimri and Jeuel from the Elizaphanites;

Zechariah and Mattaniah from the Asaphites;

¹⁴ Jehiel^A and Shimei from the Hemanites;

Shemaiah and Uzziel from the Jeduthunites.

¹⁵ They gathered their brothers together, consecrated themselves, and went according to the king's command by the words of the LORD to cleanse the LORD's temple.

¹⁶ The priests went to the entrance of the LORD's temple to cleanse it. They took all the unclean things they found in the LORD's sanctuary to the courtyard of the LORD's temple. Then the Levites received them and took them outside to the Kidron Valley. ¹⁷ They began the consecration on the first day of the first month, and on the eighth day of the month they came to the portico of the LORD's temple. They consecrated the LORD's temple for eight days, and on the sixteenth day of the first month they finished.

¹⁸ Then they went inside to King Hezekiah and said, "We have cleansed the whole temple of the LORD, the altar of burnt offering and all its utensils, and the table for the rows of the Bread of the Presence and all its utensils. ¹⁹ We have set up and consecrated all the utensils that King Ahaz rejected during his reign when he became unfaithful. They are in front of the altar of the LORD." 2Ch 28:24

Renewal of Temple Worship

²⁰ King Hezekiah got up early, gathered the city officials, and went to the LORD's temple. ²¹ They brought seven bulls, seven rams, seven lambs, and seven male goats as a sin offering for the kingdom, for the sanctuary, and for Judah. Then he told the descendants of Aaron, the priests, to offer them on the altar of the LORD. ²² So they slaughtered the bulls, and the priests received the blood and splattered it on the altar. They slaughtered the rams and splattered the blood on the altar. They slaughtered the lambs and splattered the blood on the altar. ²³ Then they brought the goats for the sin offering right into the presence of the king and the congregation, who laid their hands on them. ²⁴ The priests slaughtered the goats and put their blood on the altar for a sin offering, to make atonement for all Israel, for the king said that the burnt offering and sin offering were for all Israel. Lv 4:15,18,26

²⁵ Hezekiah stationed the Levites in the LORD's temple with cymbals, harps, and lyres according to the command of David, Gad the king's seer, and the prophet Nathan. For the command was from the LORD through his prophets. ²⁶ The Levites stood with the instruments of David, and the priests with the trumpets. 2Sm 7:2; 24:11; 1Ch 15:16; 25:6; 2Ch 8:14

^A 29:14 Alt Hb tradition reads *Jehuel*

²⁷ Then Hezekiah ordered that the burnt offering be offered on the altar. When the burnt offerings began, the song of the Lord and the trumpets began, accompanied by the instruments of King David of Israel. ²⁸ The whole assembly was worshiping, singing the song, and blowing the trumpets — all this continued until the burnt offering was completed. ²⁹ When the burnt offerings were completed, the king and all those present with him bowed down and worshiped. ³⁰ Then King Hezekiah and the officials told the Levites to sing praise to the Lord in the words of David and of the seer Asaph. So they sang praises with rejoicing and knelt low and worshiped.   2Ch 20:18

³¹ Hezekiah concluded, "Now you are consecrated^A to the Lord. Come near and bring sacrifices and thank offerings to the Lord's temple." So the congregation brought sacrifices and thank offerings, and all those with willing hearts brought burnt offerings. ³² The number of burnt offerings the congregation brought was seventy bulls, one hundred rams, and two hundred lambs; all these were for a burnt offering to the Lord. ³³ Six hundred bulls and three thousand sheep and goats were consecrated.   Ex 35:5,22

³⁴ However, since there were not enough priests, they weren't able to skin all the burnt offerings, so their Levite brothers helped them until the work was finished and until the priests consecrated themselves. For the Levites were more conscientious^B to consecrate themselves than the priests were. ³⁵ Furthermore, the burnt offerings were abundant, along with the fat of the fellowship offerings and with the drink offerings for the burnt offering.   Lv 3:16; 2Ch 30:3; 35:11; Ps 32:11; 64:10

So the service of the Lord's temple was established. ³⁶ Then Hezekiah and all the people rejoiced over how God had prepared the people, for it had come about suddenly.

Celebration of the Passover

30 Then Hezekiah sent word throughout all Israel and Judah, and he also wrote letters to Ephraim and Manasseh to come to the Lord's temple in Jerusalem to observe the Passover of the Lord, the God of Israel. ² For the king and his officials and the entire congregation in Jerusalem decided to observe the Passover of the Lord in the second month, ³ because they were not able to observe it at the appropriate time. Not enough of the priests had consecrated themselves, and the people hadn't been gathered together in Jerusalem. ⁴ The proposal pleased the king and the congregation, ⁵ so they affirmed the proposal and spread the message throughout all Israel, from Beer-sheba to Dan, to come to observe the Passover of the Lord, the God of Israel in Jerusalem, for they hadn't observed it often, ^C as prescribed.^D   Ex 12:1-28; 13:1-10; Nm 9:6-14

⁶ So the couriers went throughout Israel and Judah with letters from the hand of the king and his officials, and according to the king's command, saying, "Israelites, return to the Lord, the God of Abraham, Isaac, and Israel so that he may return to those of you who remain, who have escaped

^A 29:31 Lit Now you have filled your hands   ^B 29:34 Lit upright of heart; Ps 32:11; 64:10   ^C 30:5 Or in great numbers   ^D 30:5 Lit often, according to what is written the grasp of the kings of Assyria. ⁷ Don't be like your fathers and your brothers who were unfaithful to the LORD, the God of their ancestors so that he made them an object of horror as you yourselves see. ⁸ Don't become obstinate ᴬ now like your fathers did. Give your allegiance ᴮ to the LORD, and come to his sanctuary that he has consecrated forever. Serve the LORD your God so that he may turn his burning anger away from you, ⁹ for when you return to the LORD, your brothers and your sons will receive mercy in the presence of their captors and will return to this land. For the LORD your God is gracious and merciful; he will not turn his face away from you if you return to him." 2Ch 28:20; Est 8:14; Jb 9:25; Jr 51:31

¹⁰ The couriers traveled from city to city in the land of Ephraim and Manasseh as far as Zebulun, but the inhabitants ᶜ laughed at them and mocked them. ¹¹ But some from Asher, Manasseh, and Zebulun humbled themselves and came to Jerusalem. ¹² Also, the power of God was at work in Judah to unite them ᴰ to carry out the command of the king and his officials by the word of the LORD. 2Ch 36:16

¹³ A very large assembly of people was gathered in Jerusalem to observe the Festival of Unleavened Bread in the second month. ¹⁴ They proceeded to take away the altars that were in Jerusalem, and they took away the incense altars and threw them into the Kidron Valley. ¹⁵ They slaughtered the Passover lamb on the fourteenth day of the second month. The priests and Levites were ashamed, and

they consecrated themselves and brought burnt offerings to the LORD's temple. ¹⁶ They stood at their prescribed posts, according to the law of Moses, the man of God. The priests splattered the blood received from the Levites, ¹⁷ for there were many in the assembly who had not consecrated themselves, and so the Levites were in charge of slaughtering the Passover lambs for every unclean person to consecrate the lambs to the LORD. ¹⁸ A large number of the people — many from Ephraim, Manasseh, Issachar, and Zebulun — were ritually unclean, yet they had eaten the Passover contrary to what was written. But Hezekiah had interceded for them, saying, "May the good LORD provide atonement on behalf of ¹⁹ whoever sets his whole heart on seeking God, the LORD, the God of his ancestors, even though not according to the purification rules of the sanctuary." ²⁰ So the LORD heard Hezekiah and healed the people. ²¹ The Israelites who were present in Jerusalem observed the Festival of Unleavened Bread seven days with great joy, and the Levites and the priests praised the LORD day after day with loud instruments. ²² Then Hezekiah encouraged ᴱ all the Levites who performed skillfully before the LORD. They ate at the appointed festival for seven days, sacrificing fellowship offerings and giving thanks to the LORD, the God of their ancestors. 2Ch 28:24

²³ The whole congregation decided to observe seven more days, so they observed seven days with joy, ²⁴ for King Hezekiah of Judah

ᴬ 30:8 Lit Don't stiffen your neck   ᴮ 30:8 Lit hand   ᶜ 30:10 Lit but they   ᴰ 30:12 Lit to give them one heart   ᴱ 30:22 Lit spoke to the heart of contributed one thousand bulls and seven thousand sheep for the congregation. Also, the officials contributed one thousand bulls and ten thousand sheep for the congregation, and many priests consecrated themselves. ²⁵ Then the whole assembly of Judah with the priests and Levites, the whole assembly that came from Israel, the resident aliens who came from the land of Israel, and those who were living in Judah, rejoiced. ²⁶ There was great rejoicing in Jerusalem, for nothing like this was known since the days of Solomon son of David, the king of Israel. 1Kg 8:65; 2Ch 29:34; 30:3; 35:7-8

²⁷ Then the priests and the Levites stood to bless the people, and God heard them, and their prayer came into his holy dwelling place in heaven. Nm 6:23-27; Dt 26:15; 2Ch 23:18

Removal of Idolatry

31 When all this was completed, all Israel who had attended went out to the cities of Judah and broke up the sacred pillars, chopped down the Asherah poles, and tore down the high places and altars throughout Judah and Benjamin, as well as in Ephraim and Manasseh, to the last one.^A Then all the Israelites returned to their cities, each to his own possession.

Offerings for Levites

² Hezekiah reestablished the divisions of the priests and Levites for the burnt offerings and fellowship offerings, for ministry, for giving thanks, and for praise in the gates of the camp of the LORD, each division corresponding to his service among the priests and Levites. ³ The king contributed^B from his own possessions for the regular morning and evening burnt offerings, the burnt offerings of the Sabbaths, of the New Moons, and of the appointed feasts, as written in the law of the LORD. ⁴ He told the people who lived in Jerusalem to give a contribution for the priests and Levites so that they could devote their energy to the law of the LORD. ⁵ When the word spread, the Israelites gave liberally of the best of the grain, new wine, fresh oil, honey, and of all the produce of the field, and they brought in an abundance, a tenth of everything. ⁶ As for the Israelites and Judahites who lived in the cities of Judah, they also brought a tenth of the herds and flocks, and a tenth of the dedicated things that were consecrated to the LORD their God. They gathered them into large piles. ⁷ In the third month they began building up the piles, and they finished in the seventh month. ⁸ When Hezekiah and his officials came and viewed the piles, they blessed the LORD and his people Israel. 1Ch 23:6-23; 24:1-19; 2Ch 35:7

⁹ Hezekiah asked the priests and Levites about the piles. ¹⁰ The chief priest Azariah, of the household of Zadok, answered him, "Since they began bringing the offering to the LORD's temple, we eat and are satisfied and there is plenty left over because the LORD has blessed his people; this abundance is what is left over." 1Ch 6:8-9; Mal 3:10

¹¹ Hezekiah told them to prepare chambers in the LORD's temple, and they prepared them. ¹² The offering, the tenth, and the dedicated things were brought faithfully. Conaniah the Levite was the officer in charge of them, and his

^A31:1 Lit Manasseh, until finishing   ^B31:3 Lit The king's portion

brother Shimei was second. ¹³ Jehiel, Azaziah, Nahath, Asahel, Jerimoth, Jozabad, Eliel, Ismachiah, Mahath, and Benaiah were deputies under the authority of Cozaniah and his brother Shimei by appointment of King Hezekiah and of Azariah the chief official of God's temple.   1Kg 6:5; 2Ch 35:9

¹⁴ Kore son of Imnah the Levite, the keeper of the East Gate, was over the freewill offerings to God to distribute the contribution to the LORD and the consecrated things. ¹⁵ Eden, Miniamin, Jeshua, Shemaiah, Amariah, and Shecaniah in the cities of the priests were to distribute it faithfully under his authority to their brothers by divisions, whether large or small. ¹⁶ In addition, they distributed it to males registered by genealogy three^A years old and above; to all who would enter the LORD's temple for their daily duty, for their service in their responsibilities according to their divisions. ¹⁷ They distributed also to those recorded by genealogy of the priests by their ancestral families and the Levites twenty years old and above, by their responsibilities in their divisions; ¹⁸ to those registered by genealogy — with all their dependents, wives, sons, and daughters — of the whole assembly (for they had faithfully consecrated themselves as holy); ¹⁹ and to the descendants of Aaron, the priests, in the common fields of their cities, in each and every city. There were men who were registered by name to distribute a portion to every male among the priests and to every Levite recorded by genealogy.   1Ch 26:26-28; 2Ch 29:12

²⁰ Hezekiah did this throughout all Judah. He did what was good and upright and true before the LORD his God. ²¹ He was diligent in every deed that he began in the service of God's temple, in the instruction and the commands, in order to seek his God, and he prospered.   2Kg 20:3

Sennacherib's Invasion

32 After these faithful deeds, King Sennacherib of Assyria came and entered Judah. He laid siege to the fortified cities and intended^B to break into them. ² Hezekiah saw that Sennacherib had come and that he planned^C war on Jerusalem, ³ so he consulted with his officials and his warriors about stopping up the water of the springs that were outside the city, and they helped him. ⁴ Many people gathered and stopped up all the springs and the stream that flowed through the land; they said, "Why should the kings of Assyria come and find abundant water?" ⁵ Then Hezekiah strengthened his position by rebuilding the entire broken-down wall and heightening the towers and the other outside wall. He repaired the supporting terraces of the city of David, and made an abundance of weapons and shields.   2Kg 18:13; 20:20; Is 36:1

⁶ He set military commanders over the people and gathered the people in the square of the city gate. Then he encouraged them,^D saying, ⁷ "Be strong and courageous! Don't be afraid or discouraged before the king of Assyria or before the large army that is with him, for there are more with us than with him. ⁸ He has only human strength,^E but we

---

^A**31:16** Or *30*; 1Ch 23:3   ^B**32:1** Lit *said to himself*   ^C**32:2** Lit *that his face was for*   ^D**32:6** Lit *he spoke to their hearts*   ^E**32:8** Lit *With him an arm of flesh* have the LORD our God to help us and to fight our battles." So the people relied on the words of King Hezekiah of Judah. Dt 31:6; Jos 1:6-9; 2Ch 30:22

Sennacherib's Servant's Speech

9 After this, while King Sennacherib of Assyria with all his armed forces besieged^A Lachish, he sent his servants to Jerusalem against King Hezekiah of Judah and against all those of Judah who were in Jerusalem, saying, 10 "This is what King Sennacherib of Assyria says: 'What are you relying on that you remain in Jerusalem under siege? 11 Isn't Hezekiah misleading you to give you over to death by famine and thirst when he says, "The LORD our God will keep us from the grasp of the king of Assyria"? 12 Didn't Hezekiah himself remove his high places and his altars and say to Judah and Jerusalem, "You must worship before one altar, and you must burn incense on it"? 2Kg 18:17-22; 2Ch 31:1; Is 36:2-7

13 " 'Don't you know what I and my fathers have done to all the peoples of the lands? Have any of the national gods of the lands been able to rescue their land from my power? 14 Who among all the gods of these nations that my predecessors completely destroyed was able to rescue his people from my power, that your God should be able to deliver you from my power? 15 So now, don't let Hezekiah deceive you, and don't let him mislead you like this. Don't believe him, for no god of any nation or kingdom has been able to rescue his people from my power or the power of my fathers. How much less will your God rescue you from my power!'" 2Kg 18:33-35; Is 36:18-20

16 His servants said more against the LORD God and against his servant Hezekiah. 17 He also wrote letters to mock the LORD, the God of Israel, saying against him:

Just like the national gods of the lands that did not rescue their people from my power, so Hezekiah's God will not rescue his people from my power.

18 Then they called out loudly in Hebrew^B to the people of Jerusalem, who were on the wall, to frighten and discourage them in order that he might capture the city. 19 They spoke against the God of Jerusalem like they had spoken against the gods of the peoples of the earth, which were made by human hands.

Deliverance from Sennacherib

20 King Hezekiah and the prophet Isaiah son of Amoz prayed about this and cried out to heaven, 21 and the LORD sent an angel who annihilated every valiant warrior, leader, and commander in the camp of the king of Assyria. So the king of Assyria returned in disgrace to his land. He went to the temple of his god, and there some of his own children struck him down with the sword. 2Kg 19:15,35-37; Is 37:15-16

22 So the LORD saved Hezekiah and the inhabitants of Jerusalem from the power of King Sennacherib of Assyria and from the power of all others. He gave them rest^C on every side. 23 Many were bringing an offering to the LORD to Jerusalem and valuable gifts to King Hezekiah of Judah, and he was exalted in the eyes of all the nations after that. 2Sm 8:10; 2Ch 9:23-24; Ps 23:2

^A32:9 Lit with his dominion was against　^B32:18 Lit Judahite　^C32:22 Lit He led them; Ps 23:2

Hezekiah's Illness and Pride

24 In those days Hezekiah became sick to the point of death, so he prayed to the LORD, and he spoke to him and gave him a miraculous sign. 25 However, because his heart was proud, Hezekiah didn't respond according to the benefit that had come to him. So there was wrath on him, Judah, and Jerusalem. 26 Then Hezekiah humbled himself for the pride of his heart — he and the inhabitants of Jerusalem — so the LORD's wrath didn't come on them during Hezekiah's lifetime. 2Kg 20:1-3,8-11; 2Ch 26:16; Is 38:1-3,7-8

Hezekiah's Wealth and Works

27 Hezekiah had abundant riches and glory, and he made himself treasuries for silver, gold, precious stones, spices, shields, and every desirable item. 28 He made warehouses for the harvest of grain, new wine, and fresh oil, and stalls for all kinds of cattle, and pens for flocks. 29 He made cities for himself, and he acquired vast numbers of flocks and herds, for God gave him abundant possessions.

30 This same Hezekiah blocked the outlet of the water of the Upper Gihon and channeled it smoothly downward and westward to the city of David. Hezekiah succeeded in everything he did. 31 When the ambassadors of Babylon's rulers were sent^A to him to inquire about the miraculous sign that happened in the land, God left him to test him and discover what was in his heart.

Hezekiah's Death

32 As for the rest of the events of Hezekiah's reign and his deeds of faithful love, note that they are written in the Visions of the Prophet Isaiah son of Amoz, and in the Book of the Kings of Judah and Israel. 33 Hezekiah rested with his fathers and was buried on the ascent to the tombs of David's descendants. All Judah and the inhabitants of Jerusalem paid him honor at his death. His son Manasseh became king in his place.

Judah's King Manasseh

33 Manasseh was twelve years old when he became king, and he reigned fifty-five years in Jerusalem. 2 He did what was evil in the LORD's sight, imitating the detestable practices of the nations that the LORD had dispossessed before the Israelites. 3 He rebuilt the high places that his father Hezekiah had torn down and reestablished the altars for the Baals. He made Asherah poles, and he bowed in worship to all the stars in the sky and served them. 4 He built altars in the LORD's temple, where the LORD had said, "Jerusalem is where my name will remain forever." 5 He built altars to all the stars in the sky in both courtyards of the LORD's temple. 6 He passed his sons through the fire in Ben Hinnom Valley. He practiced witchcraft, divination, and sorcery, and consulted mediums and spiritists. He did a huge amount of evil in the LORD's sight, angering him.

7 Manasseh set up a carved image of the idol, which he had made, in God's temple that God had spoken about to David and his son Solomon: "I will establish my name forever^B in this temple and in Jerusalem, which I have chosen out of all the tribes of Israel. 8 I will never

A 32:31 LXX, Tg, Vg; MT reads *of Babylon sent*   B 33:7 LXX, Syr, Tg, Vg; 2Kg 21:7; MT reads *name for Elom* again remove the feet of the Israelites from the land where I stationed your[A] ancestors, if only they will be careful to do all I have commanded them through Moses — all the law, statutes, and judgments." [9] So Manasseh caused Judah and the inhabitants of Jerusalem to stray so that they did worse evil than the nations the LORD had destroyed before the Israelites.   Dt 16:21; 1Kg 9:1-9

Manasseh's Repentance

[10] The LORD spoke to Manasseh and his people, but they didn't listen. [11] So he brought against them the military commanders of the king of Assyria. They captured Manasseh with hooks, bound him with bronze shackles, and took him to Babylon. [12] When he was in distress, he sought the favor of the LORD his God and earnestly humbled himself before the God of his ancestors. [13] He prayed to him, and the LORD was receptive to his prayer. He granted his request and brought him back to Jerusalem, to his kingdom. So Manasseh came to know that the LORD is God.   2Kg 21:10-16

[14] After this, he built the outer wall of the city of David from west of Gihon in the valley to the entrance of the Fish Gate; he brought it around the Ophel, and he heightened it considerably. He also placed military commanders in all the fortified cities of Judah.   1Kg 1:33; 2Ch 32:30

[15] He removed the foreign gods and the idol from the LORD's temple, along with all the altars that he had built on the mountain of the LORD's temple and in Jerusalem, and he threw them outside the city. [16] He built[B] the altar of the LORD and offered fellowship and thank offerings on it. Then he told Judah to serve the LORD, the God of Israel. [17] However, the people still sacrificed at the high places, but only to the LORD their God.   2Ch 32:12

Manasseh's Death

[18] The rest of the events of Manasseh's reign, along with his prayer to his God and the words of the seers who spoke to him in the name of the LORD, the God of Israel, are written in the Events of Israel's Kings. [19] His prayer and how God was receptive to his prayer, and all his sin and unfaithfulness and the sites where he built high places and set up Asherah poles and carved images before he humbled himself, they are written in the Events of Hozai. [20] Manasseh rested with his fathers, and he was buried in his own house. His son Amon became king in his place.   2Kg 21:17-24; 2Ch 33:12-13

Judah's King Amon

[21] Amon was twenty-two years old when he became king, and he reigned two years in Jerusalem. [22] He did what was evil in the LORD's sight, just as his father Manasseh had done. Amon sacrificed to all the carved images that his father Manasseh had made, and he served them. [23] But he did not humble himself before the LORD like his father Manasseh humbled himself; instead, Amon increased his guilt.

[24] So his servants conspired against him and put him to death in his own house. [25] The common people[C] killed all who had conspired against King Amon, and they made his son Josiah king in his place.

[A]33:8 LXX, Syr, Vg read *land I gave to their*; 2Kg 21:8 LXX, Vg read *restored*   [B]33:16 Some Hb mss, Syr, Tg, Arabic; other Hb mss, LXX, Vg read *restored*   [C]33:25 Lit *The people of the land*

Judah's King Josiah

34 Josiah was eight years old when he became king, and he reigned thirty-one years in Jerusalem. ² He did what was right in the LORD's sight and walked in the ways of his ancestor David; he did not turn aside to the right or the left. 2Kg 22:1-2; 2Ch 29:2

Josiah's Reform

³ In the eighth year of his reign, while he was still a youth, Josiah began to seek the God of his ancestor David, and in the twelfth year he began to cleanse Judah and Jerusalem of the high places, the Asherah poles, the carved images, and the cast images. ⁴ Then in his presence the altars of the Baals were torn down, and he chopped down the shrines ᴬ that were above them. He shattered the Asherah poles, the carved images, and the cast images, crushed them to dust, and scattered them over the graves of those who had sacrificed to them. ⁵ He burned the bones of the priests on their altars. So he cleansed Judah and Jerusalem. ⁶ He did the same in the cities of Manasseh, Ephraim, and Simeon, and as far as Naphtali and on their surrounding mountain shrines. ᴮ ⁷ He tore down the altars, and he smashed the Asherah poles and the carved images to powder. He chopped down all the shrines throughout the land of Israel and returned to Jerusalem.

Josiah's Repair of the Temple

⁸ In the eighteenth year of his reign, in order to cleanse the land and the temple, Josiah sent Shaphan son of Azaliah, along with Maaseiah the governor of the city and the court historian Joah son of Joahaz, to repair the temple of the LORD his God.

⁹ So they went to the high priest Hilkiah and gave him the silver brought into God's temple. The Levites and the doorkeepers had collected it from Manasseh, Ephraim, and from the entire remnant of Israel, and from all Judah, Benjamin, and the inhabitants of Jerusalem. ¹⁰ They gave it to those doing the work — those who oversaw the LORD's temple. They gave it to the workmen who were working in the LORD's temple, to repair and restore the temple; ¹¹ they gave it to the carpenters and builders and also used it to buy quarried stone and timbers — for joining and making beams — for the buildings that Judah's kings had destroyed. 2Ch 34:14; 35:8

¹² The men were doing the work with integrity. Their overseers were Jahath and Obadiah, Levites from the Merarites, and Zechariah and Meshullam from the Kohathites as supervisors. The Levites were all skilled with musical instruments. ¹³ They were also over the porters and were supervising all those doing the work task by task. Some of the Levites were secretaries, officers, and gatekeepers.

The Recovery of the Book of the Law

¹⁴ When they brought out the silver that had been deposited in the LORD's temple, the priest Hilkiah found the book of the law of the LORD written by the hand of Moses. ¹⁵ Consequently, Hilkiah told the court secretary Shaphan, "I

ᴬ34:4 Lit *incense altars*, also in v. 7 ᴮ34:6 One Hb tradition reads *Naphtali with their swords*; alt Hb tradition, Syr, Vg read *Naphtali, the ruins all around*; Hb obscure have found the book of the law in the LORD's temple," and he gave the book to Shaphan.   Dt 31:24-26

¹⁶ Shaphan took the book to the king, and also reported, "Your servants are doing all that was placed in their hands. ¹⁷ They have emptied out the silver that was found in the LORD's temple and have given it to the overseers and to those doing the work." ¹⁸ Then the court secretary Shaphan told the king, "The priest Hilkiah gave me a book," and Shaphan read from it in the presence of the king.   Dt 17:18-20

¹⁹ When the king heard the words of the law, he tore his clothes. ²⁰ Then he commanded Hilkiah, Ahikam son of Shaphan, Abdon son of Micah, the court secretary Shaphan, and the king's servant Asaiah, ²¹ "Go and inquire of the LORD for me and for those remaining in Israel and Judah, concerning the words of the book that was found. For great is the LORD's wrath that is poured out on us because our ancestors have not kept the word of the LORD in order to do everything written in this book."   Jos 7:6

Huldah's Prophecy of Judgment

²² So Hilkiah and those the king had designated^A went to the prophetess Huldah, the wife of Shallum son of Tokhath, son of Hasrah, keeper of the wardrobe. She lived in Jerusalem in the Second District. They spoke with her about this.

²³ She said to them, "This is what the LORD God of Israel says: Say to the man who sent you to me, ²⁴ 'This is what the LORD says: I am about to bring disaster on this place and on its inhabitants, fulfilling^B all the curses written in the book that they

read in the presence of the king of Judah, ²⁵ because they have abandoned me and burned incense to other gods so as to anger me with all the works of their hands. My wrath will be poured out on this place, and it will not be quenched.' ²⁶ Say this to the king of Judah who sent you to inquire of the LORD: 'This is what the LORD God of Israel says: As for the words that you heard, ²⁷ because your heart was tender and you humbled yourself before God when you heard his words against this place and against its inhabitants, and because you humbled yourself before me, and you tore your clothes and wept before me, I myself have heard' — this is the LORD's declaration. ²⁸ 'I will indeed gather you to your fathers, and you will be gathered to your grave in peace. Your eyes will not see all the disaster that I am bringing on this place and on its inhabitants.'"

Then they reported to the king.

Affirmation of the Covenant by Josiah and the People

²⁹ So the king sent messengers and gathered all the elders of Judah and Jerusalem. ³⁰ The king went up to the LORD's temple with all the men of Judah and the inhabitants of Jerusalem, as well as the priests and the Levites — all the people from the oldest to the youngest. He read in their hearing all the words of the book of the covenant that had been found in the LORD's temple. ³¹ Then the king stood at his post and made a covenant in the LORD's presence to follow the LORD and to keep his commands, his decrees, and his statutes with all his heart and with all his soul in order to

---

^A 34:22 LXX; MT omits *designated*   ^B 34:24 *fulfilling* supplied for clarity carry out the words of the covenant written in this book. 2Kg 11:14; Neh 8:1-3

³² He had all those present in Jerusalem and Benjamin agree[A] to it. So all the inhabitants of Jerusalem carried out the covenant of God, the God of their ancestors.

³³ So Josiah removed everything that was detestable from all the lands belonging to the Israelites, and he required all who were present in Israel to serve the LORD their God. Throughout his reign they did not turn aside from following the LORD, the God of their ancestors.

Josiah's Passover Observance

35 Josiah observed the LORD's Passover and slaughtered the Passover lambs on the fourteenth day of the first month. ² He appointed the priests to their responsibilities and encouraged them to serve in the LORD's temple. ³ He said to the Levites who taught all Israel the holy things of the LORD, "Put the holy ark in the temple built by Solomon son of David king of Israel. Since you do not have to carry it on your shoulders, now serve the LORD your God and his people Israel. Ex 12:6; Nm 9:3; 2Kg 23:21

⁴ "Organize your ancestral families[B] by your divisions according to the written instruction of King David of Israel and that of his son Solomon. ⁵ Serve in the holy place by the groupings of the ancestral families[C] for your brothers, the lay people,[D] and according to the division of the Levites by family. ⁶ Slaughter the Passover lambs, consecrate yourselves, and make preparations for your brothers

to carry out the word of the LORD through Moses." 1Ch 9:10-13; 2Ch 8:14

⁷ Then Josiah donated thirty thousand sheep, lambs, and young goats, plus three thousand cattle from his own possessions, for the Passover sacrifices for all the lay people who were present.

⁸ His officials also donated willingly for the people, the priests, and the Levites. Hilkiah, Zechariah, and Jehiel, chief officials of God's temple, gave twenty-six hundred Passover sacrifices and three hundred cattle for the priests. ⁹ Conaniah and his brothers Shemaiah and Nethanel, and Hashabiah, Jeiel, and Jozabad, officers of the Levites, donated five thousand Passover sacrifices for the Levites, plus five hundred cattle. 2Ch 31:12-13

¹⁰ So the service was established; the priests stood at their posts and the Levites in their divisions according to the king's command. ¹¹ Then they slaughtered the Passover lambs, and while the Levites were skinning the animals, the priests splattered the blood[E] they had been given.[F] ¹² They removed the burnt offerings so that they might be given to the groupings of the ancestral families[G] of the lay people to offer to the LORD, according to what is written in the book of Moses; they did the same with the cattle. ¹³ They roasted the Passover lambs with fire according to regulation. They boiled the holy sacrifices in pots, kettles, and bowls; and they quickly brought them to the lay people. ¹⁴ Afterward, they made preparations for themselves and for the priests, since the priests,

[A]34:32 Lit take a stand.   [B]35:4 Lit the house of your fathers   [C]35:5 Lit the house of the fathers
[D]35:5 Lit the sons of the people, also in vv. 7,12,13   [E]35:11 LXX, Vg, Tg; MT omits blood   [F]35:11 Lit
splattered from their hand   [G]35:12 Lit house of fathers

the descendants of Aaron, were busy offering up burnt offerings and fat until night. So the Levites made preparations for themselves and for the priests, the descendants of Aaron. Ex 12:8-9; 2Ch 29:34; 35:5

¹⁵ The singers, the descendants of Asaph, were at their stations according to the command of David, Asaph, Heman, and Jeduthun the king's seer. Also, the gatekeepers were at each temple gate. None of them left their tasks because their Levite brothers had made preparations for them. 1Ch 25:1; 26:12-19

¹⁶ So all the service of the LORD was established that day for observing the Passover and for offering burnt offerings on the altar of the LORD, according to the command of King Josiah. ¹⁷ The Israelites who were present in Judah also observed the Passover at that time and the Festival of Unleavened Bread for seven days. ¹⁸ No Passover had been observed like it in Israel since the days of the prophet Samuel. None of the kings of Israel ever observed a Passover like the one that Josiah observed with the priests, the Levites, all Judah, the Israelites who were present in Judah, and the inhabitants of Jerusalem. ¹⁹ In the eighteenth year of Josiah's reign, this Passover was observed. 2Ch 30:21

Josiah's Last Deeds and Death

²⁰ After all this that Josiah had prepared for the temple, King Neco of Egypt marched up to fight at Carchemish by the Euphrates, and Josiah went out to confront him. ²¹ But Neco sent messengers to him, saying, "What is the issue between you and me, king of Judah? I have not come against you today ᴬ but I am fighting another dynasty. ᴮ God told me to hurry. Stop opposing God who is with me; don't make him destroy you! " 2Kg 23:29-30a; Is 10:9; Jr 46:2

²² But Josiah did not turn away from him; instead, in order to fight with him he disguised himself. ᶜ He did not listen to Neco's words from the mouth of God, but went to the Valley of Megiddo to fight. ²³ The archers shot King Josiah, and he said to his servants, "Take me away, for I am severely wounded! " ²⁴ So his servants took him out of the war chariot, carried him in his second chariot, and brought him to Jerusalem. Then he died, and they buried him in the tomb of his fathers. All Judah and Jerusalem mourned for Josiah. ²⁵ Jeremiah chanted a dirge over Josiah, and all the male and female singers still speak of Josiah in their dirges today. They established them as a statute for Israel, and indeed they are written in the Dirges. Jdg 5:19; 2Ch 18:29,33; Zch 12:11

²⁶ The rest of the events of Josiah's reign, along with his deeds of faithful love according to what is written in the law of the LORD, ²⁷ and his words, from beginning to end, are written in the Book of the Kings of Israel and Judah.

Judah's King Jehoahaz

36 Then the common people ᴰ took Jehoahaz son of Josiah and made him king in Jerusalem in place of his father. 2Kg 23:30b-34

² Jehoahaz ᴱ was twenty-three years old when he became king, and he reigned three months in

Jerusalem. ³ The king of Egypt deposed him in Jerusalem and fined the land seventy-five hundred pounds ^A of silver and seventy-five pounds ^B of gold.

Judah's King Jehoiakim

⁴ Then King Neco of Egypt made Jehoahaz's brother Eliakim king over Judah and Jerusalem and changed Eliakim's name to Jehoiakim. But Neco took his brother Jehoahaz and brought him to Egypt. Jr 22:10-12

⁵ Jehoiakim was twenty-five years old when he became king, and he reigned eleven years in Jerusalem. He did what was evil in the sight of the LORD his God. ⁶ Now King Nebuchadnezzar of Babylon attacked him and bound him in bronze shackles to take him to Babylon. ⁷ Also Nebuchadnezzar took some of the articles of the LORD's temple to Babylon and put them in his temple in Babylon. 2Kg 23:36-37

⁸ The rest of the deeds of Jehoiakim, the detestable actions he committed, and what was found against him, are written in the Book of Israel's Kings. His son Jehoiachin became king in his place. 2Kg 24:5-6

Judah's King Jehoiachin

⁹ Jehoiachin was eighteen ^C years old when he became king, and he reigned three months and ten days in Jerusalem. He did what was evil in the LORD's sight. ¹⁰ In the spring ^D Nebuchadnezzar sent for him and brought him to Babylon along with the valuable articles of the LORD's temple. Then he made Jehoiachin's brother Zedekiah king over Judah and Jerusalem. 2Sm 11:1; 2Kg 24:8-17; Jr 37:1

Judah's King Zedekiah

¹¹ Zedekiah was twenty-one years old when he became king, and he reigned eleven years in Jerusalem. ¹² He did what was evil in the sight of the LORD his God and did not humble himself before the prophet Jeremiah at the LORD's command. ¹³ He also rebelled against King Nebuchadnezzar who had made him swear allegiance by God. He became obstinate ^E and hardened his heart against returning to the LORD, the God of Israel. ¹⁴ All the leaders of the priests and the people multiplied their unfaithful deeds, imitating all the detestable practices of the nations, and they defiled the LORD's temple that he had consecrated in Jerusalem. 2Kg 24:18-20; 2Ch 33:23; Jr 52:1-3

The Destruction of Jerusalem

¹⁵ But the LORD, the God of their ancestors sent word against them by the hand of his messengers, sending them time and time again, for he had compassion on his people and on his dwelling place. ¹⁶ But they kept ridiculing God's messengers, despising his words, and scoffing at his prophets, until the LORD's wrath was so stirred up against his people that there was no remedy. ¹⁷ So he brought up against them the king of the Chaldeans, who killed their fit young men with the sword in the house of their sanctuary. He had no pity on young men or young women, elderly or aged; he handed them all over to him. ¹⁸ He took everything to Babylon — all the articles of God's temple, large and small,

^A 36:3 Lit 100 talents ^B 36:3 Lit one talent ^C 36:9 Some Hb mss, LXX; 2Kg 24:8; other Hb mss read eight ^D 36:10 Lit At the return of the year ^E 36:13 Lit He stiffened his neck the treasures of the LORD's temple, and the treasures of the king and his officials. [19] Then the Chaldeans burned God's temple. They tore down Jerusalem's wall, burned all its palaces, and destroyed all its valuable articles. Jr 7:13; 25:3,11-12

[20] He deported those who escaped from the sword to Babylon, and they became servants to him and his sons until the rise of the Persian[A] kingdom. [21] This fulfilled the word of the LORD through Jeremiah, and the land enjoyed its Sabbath rest all the days of the desolation until seventy years were fulfilled. Lv 25:4; 26:33; Jr 25:11-12; 27:7; 29:10

The Decree of Cyrus

[22] In the first year of King Cyrus of Persia, in order to fulfill the word of the LORD spoken through[B] Jeremiah, the LORD roused the spirit of King Cyrus of Persia to issue a proclamation throughout his entire kingdom and also to put it in writing:

[23] This is what King Cyrus of Persia says: The LORD, the God of the heavens, has given me all the kingdoms of the earth and has appointed me to build him a temple at Jerusalem in Judah. Any of his people among you may go up, and may the LORD his God be with him.

A 36:20 LXX reads Median   B 36:22 Lit LORD by the mouth of

EZRA

The Decree of Cyrus

1 In the first year of King Cyrus of Persia, in order to fulfill the word of the LORD spoken through Jeremiah, the LORD roused the spirit of King Cyrus to issue a proclamation throughout his entire kingdom and to put it in writing:

² This is what King Cyrus of Persia says: "The LORD, the God of the heavens, has given me all the kingdoms of the earth and has appointed me to build him a house at Jerusalem in Judah. ³ Any of his people among you, may his God be with him, and may he go to Jerusalem in Judah and build the house of the LORD, the God of Israel, the God who is in Jerusalem. ⁴ Let every survivor, wherever he resides, be assisted by the men of that region with silver, gold, goods, and livestock, along with a freewill offering for the house of God in Jerusalem."

Return from Exile

⁵ So the family heads of Judah and Benjamin, along with the priests and Levites — everyone whose spirit God had roused — prepared to go up and rebuild the LORD's house in Jerusalem. ⁶ All their neighbors supported them[A] with silver articles, gold, goods, livestock, and valuables, in addition to all that was given as a freewill offering. ⁷ King Cyrus also brought out the articles of the LORD's house that Nebuchadnezzar had taken from Jerusalem and had placed in the house of his gods. ⁸ King Cyrus of Persia had them brought out under the supervision of Mithredath the treasurer, who counted them out to Sheshbazzar the prince of Judah. ⁹ This was the inventory:

30 gold basins,
1,000 silver basins,
29 silver knives,
¹⁰ 30 gold bowls,
410 various[B] silver bowls,
and 1,000 other articles.

¹¹ The gold and silver articles totaled 5,400. Sheshbazzar brought all of them when the exiles went up from Babylon to Jerusalem.

The Exiles Who Returned

2 These now are the people of the province who came from those captive exiles King Nebuchadnezzar of Babylon[C] had deported to Babylon. They returned to Jerusalem and Judah, each to his own town. ² They came with Zerubbabel, Jeshua, Nehemiah, Seraiah, Reelaiah, Mordecai, Bilshan, Mispar, Bigvai, Rehum, and Baanah. 1Ch3:19

The number of the Israelite men included[D]

³	Parosh's descendants	2,172
⁴	Shephatiah's descendants	372
⁵	Arah's descendants	775
⁶	Pahath-moab's descendants: Jeshua's and Joab's descendants	2,812
⁷	Elam's descendants	1,254
⁸	Zattu's descendants	945

A1:6 Lit strengthened their hands   B1:10 Or similar   C2:1 Nebuchadnezzar reigned 605–562 BC
D2:2 Lit the men of the people of Israel

⁹ Zaccai's descendants   760
¹⁰ Bani's descendants   642
¹¹ Bebai's descendants   623
¹² Azgad's descendants   1,222
¹³ Adonikam's descendants 666
¹⁴ Bigvai's descendants   2,056
¹⁵ Adin's descendants   454
¹⁶ Ater's descendants:
   of Hezekiah   98
¹⁷ Bezai's descendants   323
¹⁸ Jorah's descendants   112
¹⁹ Hashum's descendants   223
²⁰ Gibbar's descendants   95
²¹ Bethlehem's people   123
²² Netophah's men   56
²³ Anathoth's men   128
²⁴ Azmaveth's people   42
²⁵ Kiriatharim's, Chephirah's,
   and Beeroth's people   743
²⁶ Ramah's
   and Geba's people   621
²⁷ Michmas's men   122
²⁸ Bethel's and Ai's men   223
²⁹ Nebo's people   52
³⁰ Magbish's people   156
³¹ the other Elam's people   1,254
³² Harim's people   320
³³ Lod's, Hadid's, and Ono's
   people   725
³⁴ Jericho's people   345
³⁵ Senaah's people   3,630

³⁶ The priests included
   Jedaiah's descendants of
     the house of Jeshua   973
³⁷ Immer's descendants   1,052
³⁸ Pashhur's descendants   1,247
³⁹ and Harim's descendants
                    1,017

⁴⁰ The Levites included
   Jeshua's and Kadmiel's
     descendants
   from Hodaviah's
     descendants   74

⁴¹ The singers included
   Asaph's descendants   128

⁴² The gatekeepers' descendants
included   1Ch 9:17-32; Neh 12:25-26
   Shallum's descendants,
   Ater's descendants,
   Talmon's descendants,
   Akkub's descendants,
   Hatita's descendants,
   Shobai's descendants,
   in all   139

⁴³ The temple servants included
   Ziha's descendants,
   Hasupha's descendants,
   Tabbaoth's descendants,
⁴⁴ Keros's descendants,
   Siaha's descendants,
   Padon's descendants,
⁴⁵ Lebanah's descendants,
   Hagabah's descendants,
   Akkub's descendants,
⁴⁶ Hagab's descendants,
   Shalmai's ^A descendants,
   Hanan's descendants,
⁴⁷ Giddel's descendants,
   Gahar's descendants,
   Reaiah's descendants,
⁴⁸ Rezin's descendants,
   Nekoda's descendants,
   Gazzam's descendants,
⁴⁹ Uzza's descendants,
   Paseah's descendants,
   Besai's descendants,
⁵⁰ Asnah's descendants,
   Meunim's ^B descendants,
   Nephusim's ^C
     descendants,
⁵¹ Bakbuk's descendants,
   Hakupha's descendants,
   Harhur's descendants,
⁵² Bazluth's descendants,
   Mehida's descendants,
   Harsha's descendants,

^A **2:46** Alt Hb tradition reads *Shamlai's* ^B **2:50** Alt Hb tradition reads *Meinim's* ^C **2:50** Alt Hb tradition reads *Nephisim's*

⁵³ Barkos's descendants,
   Sisera's descendants,
   Temah's descendants,
     ⁵⁴ Neziah's descendants,
   and Hatipha's descendants.

⁵⁵ The descendants of Solomon's
servants included   Neh 11:3
   Sotai's descendants,
   Hassophereth's descendants,
   Peruda's descendants,
     ⁵⁶ Jaalah's descendants,
   Darkon's descendants,
   Giddel's descendants,
⁵⁷ Shephatiah's descendants,
   Hattil's descendants,
   Pochereth-hazzebaim's
     descendants,
   and Ami's descendants.
⁵⁸ All the temple servants
   and the descendants
   of Solomon's servants 392.

⁵⁹ The following are those who
came from Tel-melah, Tel-harsha,
Cherub, Addan, and Immer but
were unable to prove that their ancestral families ᴬ and their lineage
were Israelite:
⁶⁰ Delaiah's descendants,
   Tobiah's descendants,
   Nekoda's descendants 652
⁶¹ and from the descendants of the
priests: the descendants of Hobaiah, the descendants of Hakkoz, the descendants of Barzillai
— who had taken a wife from the
daughters of Barzillai the Gileadite and who bore their name.
⁶² These searched for their entries in the genealogical records,
but they could not be found, so
they were disqualified from the
priesthood. ⁶³ The governor ordered them not to eat the most
holy things until there was a priest
who could consult the Urim and
Thummim. Ex 28:30; Ezr 6:7; Neh 5:14; Hg 1:1
⁶⁴ The whole combined
   assembly numbered 42,360
⁶⁵ not including their 7,337 male
   and female servants,
   and their 200 male
   and female singers.   2Ch 35:25
⁶⁶ They had 736 horses,
   245 mules,
⁶⁷ 435 camels,
   and 6,720 donkeys.

Gifts for the Work

⁶⁸ After they arrived at the LORD's
house in Jerusalem, some of the
family heads gave freewill offerings for the house of God in order
to have it rebuilt on its original site.
⁶⁹ Based on what they could give,
they gave 61,000 gold coins, ᴮ 6,250
pounds ᶜ of silver, and 100 priestly
garments to the treasury for the
project. ⁷⁰ The priests, Levites, singers, gatekeepers, temple servants,
and some of the people settled in
their towns, and the rest of Israel
settled in their towns.   Nm 15:3; Ezr 1:4

Sacrifice Restored

3 When the seventh month arrived, and the Israelites were
in their towns, the people gathered
as one in Jerusalem. ² Jeshua son
of Jozadak and his brothers the
priests along with Zerubbabel son
of Shealtiel and his brothers began
to build the altar of Israel's God in
order to offer burnt offerings on it,
as it is written in the law of Moses,
the man of God. ³ They set up the
altar on its foundation and offered
burnt offerings for the morning
and evening on it to the LORD even
though they feared the surrounding peoples. ⁴ They celebrated the

ᴬ 2:59 Lit that the house of their fathers   ᴮ 2:69 Or drachmas, or darics   ᶜ 2:69 Lit 5,000 minas

Festival of Shelters as prescribed, and offered burnt offerings each day, based on the number specified by ordinance for each festival day. ⁵ After that, they offered the regular burnt offering and the offerings for the beginning of each month ᴬ and for all the LORD's appointed holy occasions, as well as the freewill offerings brought to ᴮ the LORD. Lv 23:23-43; Nm 29:1-38; Neh 7:73-8:1

⁶ On the first day of the seventh month they began to offer burnt offerings to the LORD, even though the foundation of the LORD's temple had not yet been laid. ⁷ They gave money to the stonecutters and artisans, and gave food, drink, and oil to the people of Sidon and Tyre, so they would bring cedar wood from Lebanon to Joppa by sea, according to the authorization given them by King Cyrus of Persia. Lv 23:23-25; Ezr 1:2

Rebuilding the Temple

⁸ In the second month of the second year after they arrived at God's house in Jerusalem, Zerubbabel son of Shealtiel, Jeshua son of Jozadak, and the rest of their brothers, including the priests, the Levites, and all who had returned to Jerusalem from the captivity, began to build. They appointed the Levites who were twenty years old or more to supervise the work on the LORD's house. ⁹ Jeshua with his sons and brothers, Kadmiel with his sons, and the sons of Judah ᶜ and of Henadad, with their sons and brothers, the Levites, joined together to supervise those working on the house of God. Ezr 2:40; 4:3; 5:2; Hg 1:1

Temple Foundation Completed

¹⁰ When the builders had laid the foundation of the LORD's temple, the priests, dressed in their robes and holding trumpets, and the Levites descended from Asaph, holding cymbals, took their positions to praise the LORD, as King David of Israel had instructed. ¹¹ They sang with praise and thanksgiving to the LORD: "For he is good; his faithful love to Israel endures forever." Then all the people gave a great shout of praise to the LORD because the foundation of the LORD's house had been laid. 1Ch 6:31; Ezr 2:41

¹² But many of the older priests, Levites, and family heads, who had seen the first temple, wept loudly when they saw the foundation of this temple, but many others shouted joyfully. ¹³ The people could not distinguish the sound of the joyful shouting from that of the ᴰ weeping, because the people were shouting so loudly. And the sound was heard far away. Ps 126:5-6; Hg 2:3

Opposition to Rebuilding the Temple

4 When the enemies of Judah and Benjamin heard that the returned exiles ᴱ were building a temple for the LORD, the God of Israel, ² they approached Zerubbabel and the family heads and said to them, "Let us build with you, for we also worship your God and have been sacrificing to him ᶠ since the time King Esar-haddon of Assyria brought us here." Ezr 1:11; 2:1; Neh 2:19-20

³ But Zerubbabel, Jeshua, and the other heads of Israel's families answered them, "You may have no

---

ᴬ3:5 Lit for the new moons   ᴮ3:5 Lit well as those of everyone making a freewill offering to
ᶜ3:9 Or Hodaviah; Neh 7:43; 1 Esdras 5:58   ᴰ3:13 Lit the people   ᴱ4:1 Lit the sons of the exile   ᶠ4:2 Alt
Hb tradition reads have not been sacrificing

part with us in building a house for our God, since we alone will build it for the LORD, the God of Israel, as King Cyrus, the king of Persia has commanded us." ⁴ Then the people who were already in the land^A discouraged^B the people of Judah and made them afraid to build. ⁵ They also bribed officials to act against them to frustrate their plans throughout the reign of King Cyrus of Persia and until the reign of King Darius of Persia.

Opposition to Rebuilding the City

⁶ At the beginning of the reign of Ahasuerus, the people who were already in the land wrote an accusation against the residents of Judah and Jerusalem. ⁷ During the time of King Artaxerxes of Persia, Bishlam, Mithredath, Tabeel and the rest of his colleagues wrote to King Artaxerxes. The letter was written in Aramaic and translated.^C

⁸ Rehum the chief deputy and Shimshai the scribe wrote a letter to King Artaxerxes concerning Jerusalem as follows: Ezr 4:17,23-24

⁹ From Rehum^D the chief deputy, Shimshai the scribe, and the rest of their colleagues — the judges and magistrates^E from Tripolis, Persia, Erech, Babylon, Susa (that is, the people of Elam),^F ¹⁰ and the rest of the peoples whom the great and illustrious Ashurbanipal^G deported and settled in the cities of Samaria and the region west of the Euphrates River. Neh 1:1

¹¹ This is the text of the letter they sent to him:

To King Artaxerxes from your servants, the men from the region west of the Euphrates River:

¹² Let it be known to the king that the Jews who came from you have returned to us at Jerusalem. They are rebuilding that rebellious and evil city, finishing its walls, and repairing its foundations. ¹³ Let it now be known to the king that if that city is rebuilt and its walls are finished, they will not pay tribute, duty, or land tax, and the royal revenue^F will suffer. ¹⁴ Since we have taken an oath of loyalty to the king,^H and it is not right for us to witness his dishonor, we have sent to inform the king ¹⁵ that a search should be made in your fathers' record books. In these record books you will discover and verify that the city is a rebellious city, harmful to kings and provinces. There have been revolts in it since ancient times. That is why this city was destroyed. ¹⁶ We advise the king that if this city is rebuilt and its walls are finished, you will not have any possession west of the Euphrates. Ezr 4:16,21; Neh 1:3; 7:24

Artaxerxes's Reply

¹⁷ The king sent a reply to his chief deputy Rehum, Shimshai the scribe, and the rest of their colleagues living in Samaria and elsewhere in the region west of the Euphrates River: Greetings.

¹⁸ The letter you sent us has been translated and read^I in my

---

^A4:4 Lit *people of the land,* also in v. 6 ^B4:4 Lit *weakened the hands of* ^C4:7 Ezr 4:8–6:18 is written in Aramaic. ^D4:9 Lit *Then Rehum* ^E4:9 Or *ambassadors* ^F4:9,13 Aramaic obscure ^G4:10 Lit *Osnappar*
^H4:14 Lit *have eaten the salt of the palace* ^I4:18 Or *been read clearly*

presence. [19] I issued a decree and a search was conducted. It was discovered that this city has had uprisings against kings since ancient times, and there have been rebellions and revolts in it. [20] Powerful kings have also ruled over Jerusalem and exercised authority over the whole region west of the Euphrates River, and tribute, duty, and land tax were paid to them. [21] Therefore, issue an order for these men to stop, so that this city will not be rebuilt until a further decree has been pronounced by me. [22] See that you not neglect this matter. Otherwise, the damage will increase and the royal interests[A] will suffer.   Neh 8:8

[23] As soon as the text of King Artaxerxes's letter was read to Rehum, Shimshai the scribe, and their colleagues, they immediately went to the Jews in Jerusalem and forcibly stopped them.   Ezr 4:8-10,17

Rebuilding of the Temple Resumed

[24] Now the construction of God's house in Jerusalem had stopped and remained at a standstill until the second year of the reign of King Darius of Persia. **5** [1] But when the prophets Haggai and Zechariah son of Iddo prophesied to the Jews who were in Judah and Jerusalem, in the name of the God of Israel who was over them, [2] Zerubbabel son of Shealtiel and Jeshua son of Jozadak began to rebuild God's house in Jerusalem. The prophets of God were with them, helping them.

[3] At that time Tattenai the governor of the region west of the Euphrates River, Shethar-bozenai, and their colleagues came to the Jews and asked, "Who gave you the order to rebuild this temple and finish this structure?"[B] [4] They also asked them, "What are the names of the workers[C] who are constructing this building?" [5] But God was watching[D] over the Jewish elders. These men wouldn't stop them until a report was sent to Darius, so that they could receive written instructions about this matter.   Ezr 1:1-4; 5:9,13; 6:6,13

The Letter to Darius

[6] This is the text of the letter that Tattenai the governor of the region west of the Euphrates River, Shethar-bozenai, and their colleagues, the officials in the region, sent to King Darius. [7] They sent him a report, written as follows:

To King Darius:

All greetings.

[8] Let it be known to the king that we went to the house of the great God in the province of Judah. It is being built with cut[E] stones, and its beams are being set in the walls. This work is being done diligently and succeeding through the people's efforts. [9] So we questioned the elders and asked, "Who gave you the order to rebuild this temple and finish this structure?" [10] We also asked them for their names, so that we could write down the names of their leaders for your information.

[A]4:22 Lit the kings   [B]5:3 Or finish its furnishings, also in v. 9   [C]5:4 One Aramaic ms, LXX, Syr; MT reads Then we told them exactly what the names of the men were   [D]5:5 Lit But the eye of their God was   [E]5:8 Or huge

¹¹ This is the reply they gave us:

We are the servants of the God of the heavens and earth, and we are rebuilding the temple that was built many years ago, which a great king of Israel built and finished. ¹² But since our fathers angered the God of the heavens, he handed them over to King Nebuchadnezzar of Babylon, the Chaldean, who destroyed this temple and deported the people to Babylon. ¹³ However, in the first year of King Cyrus of Babylon, he issued a decree to rebuild the house of God. ¹⁴ He also took from the temple in Babylon the gold and silver articles of God's house that Nebuchadnezzar had taken from the temple in Jerusalem and carried them to the temple in Babylon. He released them from the temple in Babylon to a man named Sheshbazzar, the governor by the appointment of King Cyrus. ¹⁵ Cyrus told him, "Take these articles, put them in the temple in Jerusalem, and let the house of God be rebuilt on its original site." ¹⁶ Then this same Sheshbazzar came and laid the foundation of God's house in Jerusalem. It has been under construction from that time until now, but it has not been completed.   1Kg 6:1,37-38; 2Ch 36:19-20

¹⁷ So if it pleases the king, let a search of the royal archives ᴬ in Babylon be conducted to see if it is true that a decree was issued by King Cyrus to rebuild the house of God in Jerusalem. Let the king's decision regarding this matter be sent to us.

Darius's Search

6 King Darius gave the order, and they searched in the library of Babylon in the archives. ᴮ ² But it was in the fortress of Ecbatana in the province of Media that a scroll was found with this record written on it: Ezr 4:15; 5:17; Dn 9:1; Ac 2:9
³ In the first year of King Cyrus, he issued a decree concerning the house of God in Jerusalem:

Let the house be rebuilt as a place for offering sacrifices, and let its original foundations be retained. ᶜ Its height is to be ninety feet ᴰ and its width ninety feet, ⁴ with three layers of cut ᴱ stones and one of timber. The cost is to be paid from the royal treasury. ᶠ ⁵ The gold and silver articles of God's house that Nebuchadnezzar took from the temple in Jerusalem and carried to Babylon must also be returned. They are to be brought to the temple in Jerusalem where they belong ᴳ and put into the house of God.   1Kg 6:2

Darius's Decree

⁶ Therefore, you must stay away from that place, Tattenai governor of the region west of the Euphrates River, Shethar-bozenai, and your ᴴ colleagues, the officials in the region. ⁷ Leave the construction of the house of God alone. Let the

---

ᴬ **5:17** Lit *treasure house*   ᴮ **6:1** Lit *Babylon where the treasures were stored*   ᶜ **6:3** Lit *be brought forth*
ᴰ **6:3** Lit *60 cubits*   ᴱ **6:4** Or *huge*   ᶠ **6:4** Lit *the king's house*   ᴳ **6:5** Lit *Jerusalem, to its place,*   ᴴ **6:6** Lit *their*

governor and elders of the Jews rebuild this house of God on its original site. Ezr 5:3,6; 6:13

⁸ I hereby issue a decree concerning what you are to do, so that the elders of the Jews can rebuild the house of God:

The cost is to be paid in full to these men out of the royal revenues from the taxes of the region west of the Euphrates River, so that the work will not stop. ⁹ Whatever is needed — young bulls, rams, and lambs for burnt offerings to the God of the heavens, or wheat, salt, wine, and oil, as requested by the priests in Jerusalem — let it be given to them every day without fail, ¹⁰ so that they can offer sacrifices of pleasing aroma to the God of the heavens and pray for the life of the king and his sons. Ezr 7:17,20-22

¹¹ I also issue a decree concerning any man who interferes with this directive:

Let a beam be torn from his house and raised up; he will be impaled on it, and his house will be made into a garbage dump because of this offense. ¹² May the God who caused his name to dwell there overthrow any king or people who dares ᴬ to harm or interfere with this house of God in Jerusalem. I, Darius, have issued the decree. Let it be carried out diligently.

¹³ Then Tattenai governor of the region west of the Euphrates River, Shethar-bozenai, and their colleagues diligently carried out what King Darius had decreed. ¹⁴ So the Jewish elders continued successfully with the building under the prophesying of Haggai the prophet and Zechariah son of Iddo. They finished the building according to the command of the God of Israel and the decrees of Cyrus, Darius, and King Artaxerxes of Persia. ¹⁵ This house was completed on the third day of the month of Adar in the sixth year of the reign of King Darius. Ezr 5:1-3,6; 6:3-6; Hg 1:1; Zch 1:1

Temple Dedication and the Passover

¹⁶ Then the Israelites, including the priests, the Levites, and the rest of the exiles, celebrated the dedication of the house of God with joy. ¹⁷ For the dedication of God's house they offered one hundred bulls, two hundred rams, and four hundred lambs, as well as twelve male goats as a sin offering for all Israel — one for each Israelite tribe. ¹⁸ They also appointed the priests by their divisions and the Levites by their groups to the service of God in Jerusalem, according to what is written in the book of Moses. 2Ch 7:4-5

¹⁹ The exiles observed the Passover on the fourteenth day of the first month. ²⁰ All of the priests and Levites were ceremonially clean, because they had purified themselves. They killed the Passover lamb for themselves, their priestly brothers, and all the exiles. ²¹ The Israelites who had returned from exile ate it, together with all who had separated themselves from the uncleanness of the Gentiles of the land ᴮ in order to worship the LORD,

ᴬ6:12 Lit who stretches out its hand   ᴮ6:21 Lit land to them the God of Israel. ²² They observed the Festival of Unleavened Bread for seven days with joy, because the LORD had made them joyful, having changed the Assyrian king's attitude toward them, so that he supported them^A in the work on the house of the God of Israel.

Ezra's Arrival

7 After these events, during the reign of King Artaxerxes of Persia, Ezra — Ezr 4:7; 6:14; Neh 2:1
Seraiah's son, Azariah's son, Hilkiah's son, ² Shallum's son, Zadok's son, Ahitub's son,
³ Amariah's son, Azariah's son, Meraioth's son,
⁴ Zerahiah's son, Uzzi's son, Bukki's son,
⁵ Abishua's son, Phinehas's son, Eleazar's son, the chief priest Aaron's son 1Ch 6:3-15
⁶ — came up from Babylon. He was a scribe skilled in the law of Moses, which the LORD, the God of Israel, had given. The king had granted him everything he requested because the hand of the LORD his God was on him. ⁷ Some of the Israelites, priests, Levites, singers, gatekeepers, and temple servants accompanied him to Jerusalem in the seventh year of King Artaxerxes.

⁸ Ezra^B came to Jerusalem in the fifth month, during the seventh year of the king. ⁹ He began the journey from Babylon on the first day of the first month and arrived in Jerusalem on the first day of the fifth month since the gracious hand of his God was on him. ¹⁰ Now Ezra had determined in his heart to study the law of the LORD, obey it, and teach its statutes and ordinances in Israel. Ezr 8:15,21,31

Letter from Artaxerxes

¹¹ This is the text of the letter King Artaxerxes gave to Ezra the priest and scribe, an expert in matters of the LORD's commands and statutes for Israel:^C

¹² Artaxerxes, king of kings, to Ezra the priest, an expert in the law of the God of the heavens:

Greetings.

¹³ I issue a decree that any of the Israelites in my kingdom, including their priests and Levites, who want to go to Jerusalem, may go with you. ¹⁴ You are sent by the king and his seven counselors to evaluate Judah and Jerusalem according to the law of your God, which is in your possession. ¹⁵ You are also to bring the silver and gold the king and his counselors have willingly given to the God of Israel, whose dwelling is in Jerusalem, ¹⁶ and all the silver and gold you receive throughout the province of Babylon, together with the freewill offerings given by the people and the priests to the house of their God in Jerusalem. ¹⁷ Then you are to be diligent to buy with this money bulls, rams, and lambs, along with their grain and drink offerings, and offer them on the altar at the house of your God in Jerusalem. ¹⁸ You may do whatever seems best to you and your brothers with the rest of the silver and gold, according to the will of your God. ¹⁹ Deliver to the God of Jerusalem all the articles given to you

---

^A 6:22 Lit strengthened their hands   ^B 7:8 LXX, Syr, Vg read They   ^C 7:11 Ezr 7:12-26 is written in Aramaic.

for the service of the house of your God. 20 You may use the royal treasury A to pay for anything else needed for the house of your God.   Ezr 1:3,6; Est 1:14; Hg 2:8

21 I, King Artaxerxes, issue a decree to all the treasurers in the region west of the Euphrates River: Ezr 4:10; 7:25

Whatever Ezra the priest, an expert in the law of the God of the heavens, asks of you must be provided in full, 22 up to 7,500 pounds B of silver, 500 bushels C of wheat, 550 gallons D of wine, 550 gallons of oil, and salt without limit. E 23 Whatever is commanded by the God of heaven must be done diligently for the house of the God of the heavens, so that wrath will not fall on the realm of the king and his sons. 24 Be advised that you do not have authority to impose tribute, duty, and land tax on any priests, Levites, singers, doorkeepers, temple servants, or other servants of this house of God.   Ezr 6:8,10

25 And you, Ezra, according to F God's wisdom that you possess, appoint magistrates and judges to judge all the people in the region west of the Euphrates who know the laws of your God and to teach anyone who does not know them. 26 Anyone who does not keep the law of your God and the law of the king, let the appropriate judgment be executed against him, whether death, banishment, confiscation of property, or imprisonment.

27 Blessed be the LORD, the God of our fathers, who has put it into the king's mind to glorify the house of the LORD in Jerusalem, 28 and who has shown favor to me before the king, his counselors, and all his powerful officers. So I took courage because I was strengthened by the hand of the LORD my God, G and I gathered Israelite leaders to return with me.   Ezr 6:22; 9:9; Is 60:7,13

Those Returning with Ezra

8 These are the family heads and the genealogical records of those who returned with me from Babylon during the reign of King Artaxerxes: Ezr 7:7
2   Gershom, from Phinehas's
        descendants;
    Daniel, from Ithamar's
        descendants;
    Hattush, from
        David's descendants,
3   who was of Shecaniah's
        descendants;   1Ch 3:22
    Zechariah, from Parosh's
        descendants,   Ezr 2:3; 10:25
    and 150 men H with him
        who were registered
        by genealogy;
4   Eliehoenai son of Zerahiah
        from Pahath-moab's
        descendants,   Ezr 2:6
    and 200 men with him;
5   Shecaniah I son of Jahaziel
        from Zattu's descendants,
        and 300 men with him;
6   Ebed son of Jonathan
        from Adin's descendants,

and 50 men with him;
7 Jeshaiah son of Athaliah from Elam's descendants, and 70 men with him;
8 Zebadiah son of Michael from Shephatiah's descendants, and 80 men with him;
9 Obadiah son of Jehiel from Joab's descendants, and 218 men with him;
10 Shelomith^A son of Josiphiah from Bani's descendants, and 160 men with him;
11 Zechariah son of Bebai from Bebai's descendants, and 28 men with him;
12 Johanan son of Hakkatan from Azgad's descendants, and 110 men with him;
13 these are the last ones, from Adonikam's descendants, and their names are Eliphelet, Jeuel, and Shemaiah, and 60 men with them;
14 Uthai and Zaccur^B from Bigvai's descendants, and 70 men with them.

15 I gathered them at the river^C that flows to Ahava, and we camped there for three days. I searched among the people and priests, but found no Levites there. 16 Then I summoned the leaders: Eliezer, Ariel, Shemaiah, Elnathan, Jarib, Elnathan, Nathan, Zechariah, and Meshullam, as well as the teachers Joiarib and Elnathan. 17 I sent them to Iddo, the leader at Casiphia, with a message for^D him and his brothers, the temple servants at Casiphia, that they should bring us ministers for the house of our God. 18 Since the gracious hand of our God was on us, they brought us Sherebiah — a man of insight from the descendants of Mahli, a descendant of Levi son of Israel — along with his sons and brothers, 18 men, 19 plus Hashabiah, along with Jeshaiah, from the descendants of Merari, and his brothers and their sons, 20 men. 20 There were also 220 of the temple servants, who had been appointed by David and the leaders for the work of the Levites. All were identified by name.

Preparing to Return

21 I proclaimed a fast by the Ahava River,^E so that we might humble ourselves before our God and ask him for a safe journey for us, our dependents, and all our possessions. 22 I did this because I was ashamed to ask the king for infantry and cavalry to protect us from enemies during the journey, since we had told him, "The hand of our God is gracious to all who seek him, but his fierce anger is against all who abandon him." 23 So we fasted and pleaded with our God about this, and he was receptive to our prayer.   Dt 31:6,17; Is 58:3-8

24 I selected twelve of the leading priests, along with Sherebiah, Hashabiah, and ten of their brothers. 25 I weighed out to them the silver, the gold, and the articles — the contribution for the house of our God that the king, his counselors, his leaders, and all the Israelites who were present had offered. 26 I weighed out to them 24 tons^F of silver, silver articles weighing

---

^A 8:10 Some LXX mss, 1 Esdras 8:36; MT reads the descendants of Shelomith   ^B 8:14 Alt Hb tradition, some LXX mss read Zabud   ^C 8:15 Or canal   ^D 8:17 Lit Casiphia, and I put in their mouth the words to speak to
^E 8:21 Or Canal, also in v. 31   ^F 8:26 Lit 650 talents

7,500 pounds,[A] 7,500 pounds of gold, [27] twenty gold bowls worth a thousand gold coins,[B] and two articles of fine gleaming bronze, as valuable as gold. [28] Then I said to them, "You are holy to the Lord, and the articles are holy. The silver and gold are a freewill offering to the Lord God of your fathers. [29] Guard them carefully until you weigh them out in the chambers of the Lord's house before the leading priests, Levites, and heads of the Israelite families in Jerusalem." [30] So the priests and Levites took charge of the silver, the gold, and the articles that had been weighed out, to bring them to the house of our God in Jerusalem. Ezr 7:15-20; Neh 10:9,11

Arrival in Jerusalem

[31] We set out from the Ahava River on the twelfth day of the first month to go to Jerusalem. We were strengthened by our God,[C] and he kept us from the grasp of the enemy and from ambush along the way. [32] So we arrived at Jerusalem and rested there for three days. [33] On the fourth day the silver, the gold, and the articles were weighed out in the house of our God into the care of the priest Meremoth son of Uriah. Eleazar son of Phinehas was with him. The Levites Jozabad son of Jeshua and Noadiah son of Binnui were also with them. [34] Everything was verified by number and weight, and the total weight was recorded at that time. Ezr 7:9

[35] The exiles who had returned from the captivity offered burnt offerings to the God of Israel: twelve bulls for all Israel, ninety-six rams, and seventy-seven lambs, along with twelve male goats as a sin offering. All this was a burnt offering for the Lord. [36] They also delivered the king's edicts to the royal satraps and governors of the region west of the Euphrates, so that they would support the people and the house of God. Lv 1:3-15; 2 Ch 29:24,27,31-35; Ezr 2:1; 6:16

Israel's Intermarriage

9 After these things had been done, the leaders approached me and said: "The people of Israel, the priests, and the Levites have not separated themselves from the surrounding peoples whose detestable practices are like those of the Canaanites, Hethites, Perizzites, Jebusites, Ammonites, Moabites, Egyptians, and Amorites. [2] Indeed, the Israelite men[D] have taken some of their daughters as wives for themselves and their sons, so that the holy seed has become mixed with the surrounding peoples. The leaders[E] and officials have taken the lead in this unfaithfulness!" [3] When I heard this report, I tore my tunic and robe, pulled out some of the hair from my head and beard, and sat down devastated. Dt 7:1; 12:29-31; Ezk 5:10-12

Ezra's Confession

[4] Everyone who trembled at the words of the God of Israel gathered around me, because of the unfaithfulness of the exiles, while I sat devastated until the evening offering. [5] At the evening offering, I got up from my time of humiliation, with my tunic and robe torn. Then I fell on my knees and spread out my hands to the Lord my God. [6] And I said: Ezr 2:1; 6:16; 10:3; Is 66:2,5

[A]8:26 Lit *100 talents* [B]8:27 Or *1,000 drachmas*, or *1,000 darics* [C]8:31 Lit *The hand of our God was on us* [D]9:2 Lit *they* [E]9:2 Lit *hand of the leaders*

My God, I am ashamed and embarrassed to lift my face toward you, my God, because our iniquities are higher than our heads and our guilt is as high as the heavens. ⁷ Our guilt has been terrible from the days of our fathers until the present. Because of our iniquities we have been handed over, along with our kings and priests, to the surrounding kings, and to the sword, captivity, plundering, and open shame, as it is today. ⁸ But now, for a brief moment, grace has come from the Lord our God to preserve a remnant for us and give us a stake in his holy place. Even in our slavery, God has given us a little relief and light to our eyes. ⁹ Though we are slaves, our God has not abandoned us in our slavery. He has extended grace to us in the presence of the Persian kings, giving us relief, so that we can rebuild the house of our God and repair its ruins, to give us a wall in Judah and Jerusalem. Jr 51:9; Dn 9:7; Rv 18:5

¹⁰ Now, our God, what can we say in light of ᴬ this? For we have abandoned the commands ¹¹ you gave through your servants the prophets, saying: "The land you are entering to possess is an impure land. The surrounding peoples have filled it from end to end with their uncleanness by their impurity and detestable practices. ¹² So do not give your daughters to their sons in marriage or take their daughters for your sons. Never pursue

their welfare or prosperity, so that you will be strong, eat the good things of the land, and leave it as an inheritance to your sons forever." ¹³ After all that has happened to us because of our evil deeds and terrible guilt — though you, our God, have punished us less than our iniquities deserve and have allowed us to survive ᴮ — ¹⁴ should we break your commands again and intermarry with the peoples who commit these detestable practices? Wouldn't you become so angry with us that you would destroy us, leaving neither remnant nor survivor? ¹⁵ Lord God of Israel, you are righteous, for we survive as a remnant today. Here we are before you with our guilt, though no one can stand in your presence because of this. Dt 7:1-4; 12:29-31; Ezr 9:1

Sending Away Foreign Wives

10 While Ezra prayed and confessed, weeping and falling facedown before the house of God, an extremely large assembly of Israelite men, women, and children gathered around him. The people also wept bitterly. ² Then Shecaniah son of Jehiel, an Elamite, responded to Ezra: "We have been unfaithful to our God by marrying foreign women from the surrounding peoples, but there is still hope for Israel in spite of this. ³ Let us therefore make a covenant before our God to send away all the foreign wives and their children, according to the counsel of my lord and of those who tremble at the command of our God. Let it be done according

ᴬ**9:10** Lit say after   ᴮ**9:13** Lit and gave us a remnant like this to the law. ⁴ Get up, for this matter is your responsibility, and we support you. Be strong and take action!" Ezr 9:3,5; 10:26; Neh 1:4; Dn 9:3-4,20

⁵ Then Ezra got up and made the leading priests, Levites, and all Israel take an oath to do what had been said; so they took the oath. ⁶ Ezra then went from the house of God and walked to the chamber of Jehohanan son of Eliashib, where he spent the night. ᴬ He did not eat food or drink water, because he was mourning over the unfaithfulness of the exiles. Dt 9:18-19; Neh 10:29-30; 13:25

⁷ They circulated a proclamation throughout Judah and Jerusalem that all the exiles should gather at Jerusalem. ⁸ Whoever did not come within three days would forfeit all his possessions, ᴮ according to the decision of the leaders and elders, and would be excluded from the assembly of the exiles. Ezr 7:26

⁹ So all the men of Judah and Benjamin gathered in Jerusalem within the three days. On the twentieth day of the ninth month, all the people sat in the square at the house of God, trembling because of this matter and because of the heavy rain. ¹⁰ Then the priest Ezra stood up and said to them, "You have been unfaithful by marrying foreign women, adding to Israel's guilt. ¹¹ Therefore, make a confession to the LORD, the God of your fathers, and do his will. Separate yourselves from the surrounding peoples and your foreign wives." Ezr 9:1-2; Neh 8:1; 13:23-27

¹² Then all the assembly responded loudly: "Yes, we will do as you say! ¹³ But there are many people, and it is the rainy season. We don't have the stamina to stay out in the open. This isn't something that can be done in a day or two, for we have rebelled terribly in this matter. ¹⁴ Let our leaders represent the entire assembly. Then let all those in our towns who have married foreign women come at appointed times, together with the elders and judges of each town, in order to avert the fierce anger of our God concerning ᶜ this matter." ¹⁵ Only Jonathan son of Asahel and Jahzeiah son of Tikvah opposed this, with Meshullam and Shabbethai the Levite supporting them. 2Ch 29:10

¹⁶ The exiles did what had been proposed. The priest Ezra selected men ᴰ who were family heads, all identified by name, to represent ᴱ their ancestral families. ᶠ They convened on the first day of the tenth month to investigate the matter, ¹⁷ and by the first day of the first month they had dealt with all the men who had married foreign women.

Those Married to Foreign Wives

¹⁸ The following were found to have married foreign women from the descendants of the priests:

from the descendants of Jeshua son of Jozadak and his brothers: Maaseiah, Eliezer, Jarib, and Gedaliah. ¹⁹ They pledged ᴳ to send their wives away, and being guilty, they offered a ram from the flock for their guilt; Lv 5:14–6:7

ᴬ10:6 1 Esdras 9:2, Syr; MT, Vg read he went   ᴮ10:8 Lit would set apart all his possessions for destruction   ᶜ10:14 Some Hb mss, LXX, Vg; other Hb mss read until   ᴰ10:16 1 Esdras 9:16, Syr; MT, Vg read priest and men were selected   ᴱ10:16 Lit name, for   ᶠ10:16 Lit the house of their fathers   ᴳ10:19 Lit gave their hand

20 Hanani and Zebadiah from Immer's descendants;
21 Maaseiah, Elijah, Shemaiah, Jehiel, and Uzziah from Harim's descendants;
22 Elioenai, Maaseiah, Ishmael, Nethanel, Jozabad, and Elasah from Pashhur's descendants.
23 The Levites: Ezr 2:40
Jozabad, Shimei, Kelaiah (that is Kelita), Pethahiah, Judah, and Eliezer.
24 The singers: Ezr 2:41
Eliashib.
The gatekeepers: Ezr 2:42
Shallum, Telem, and Uri.
25 The Israelites: Ezr 2:3-35; Neh 7:8-38
Parosh's descendants:
Ramiah, Izziah, Malchijah, Mijamin, Eleazar, Malchijah,ᴬ and Benaiah;
26 Elam's descendants:
Mattaniah, Zechariah, Jehiel, Abdi, Jeremoth, and Elijah; Ezr 2:7; 10:2
27 Zattu's descendants:
Elioenai, Eliashib, Mattaniah, Jeremoth, Zabad, and Aziza; Ezr 2:8
28 Bebai's descendants:
Jehohanan, Hananiah, Zabbai, and Athlai; Ezr 2:11
29 Bani's descendants:
Meshullam, Malluch, Adaiah, Jashub, Sheal, and Jeremoth; Ezr 2:10
30 Pahath-moab's descendants:
Adna, Chelal, Benaiah, Maaseiah, Mattaniah, Bezalel, Binnui, and Manasseh; Ezr 2:6
31 Harim's descendants:
Eliezer, Isshijah, Malchijah, Shemaiah, Shimeon,
32 Benjamin, Malluch, and Shemariah; Ezr 2:32
33 Hashum's descendants:
Mattenai, Mattattah, Zabad, Eliphelet, Jeremai, Manasseh, and Shimei;
34 Bani's descendants: Maadai, Amram, Uel, 35 Benaiah, Bedeiah, Cheluhi, 36 Vaniah, Meremoth, Eliashib, 37 Mattaniah, Mattenai, Jaasu, 38 Bani, Binnui, Shimei, 39 Shelemiah, Nathan, Adaiah, 40 Machnadebai, Shashai, Sharai, 41 Azarel, Shelemiah, Shemariah, 42 Shallum, Amariah, and Joseph; Ezr 2:10
43 Nebo's descendants: Jeiel, Mattithiah, Zabad, Zebina, Jaddai, Joel, and Benaiah.
44 All of these had married foreign women, and some of the wives had given birth to children. Ezr 10:18-43

ᴬ10:25 Some LXX mss, 1 Esdras 9:26 read *Hashabiah*

NEHEMIAH

1 The words of Nehemiah son of Hacaliah:
Neh 10:1

News from Jerusalem

During the month of Chislev in the twentieth year, when I was in the fortress city of Susa, ² Hanani, one of my brothers, arrived with men from Judah, and I questioned them about Jerusalem and the Jewish remnant that had survived the exile. ³ They said to me, "The remnant in the province, who survived the exile, are in great trouble and disgrace. Jerusalem's wall has been broken down, and its gates have been burned." Ezr 7:1,8; Neh 2:1; Zch 7:1

Nehemiah's Prayer

⁴ When I heard these words, I sat down and wept. I mourned for a number of days, fasting and praying before the God of the heavens. ⁵ I said, Ezr 9:3; 10:1; Ps 35:13; Dn 9:3; Lk 2:37

Lord, the God of the heavens, the great and awe-inspiring God who keeps his gracious covenant with those who love him and keep his commands, ⁶ let your eyes be open and your ears be attentive to hear your servant's prayer that I now pray to you day and night for your servants, the Israelites. I confess the sins ᴬ we have committed against you. Both I and my father's family have sinned. ⁷ We have acted corruptly toward you and have not kept the commands, statutes, and ordinances you gave your servant Moses. ⁸ Please remember what you commanded your servant Moses: "If you are unfaithful, I will scatter you among the peoples. ⁹ But if you return to me and carefully observe my commands, even though your exiles were banished to the farthest horizon, ᴮ I will gather them from there and bring them to the place where I chose to have my name dwell." ¹⁰ They are your servants and your people. You redeemed them by your great power and strong hand. ¹¹ Please, Lord, let your ear be attentive to the prayer of your servant and to that of your servants who delight to revere your name. Give your servant success today, and grant him compassion in the presence of this man. ᶜ Dt 6:5; 7:9-11; 9:4; Rm 8:28

At the time, I was the king's cupbearer. Gn 40:20

Nehemiah Sent to Jerusalem

2 During the month of Nisan in the twentieth year of King Artaxerxes, when wine was set before him, I took the wine and gave it to the king. I had never been sad in his presence, ² so the king said to me, "Why are you ᴰ sad, when you aren't sick? This is nothing but sadness of heart." Ezr 7:1,8; Neh 1:1; Pr 15:13

I was overwhelmed with fear ³ and replied to the king, "May the

---

ᴬ1:6 Lit sins of the Israelites   ᴮ1:9 Lit skies   ᶜ1:11 = the king   ᴰ2:2 Lit "Why is your face king live forever! Why should I[A] not be sad when the city where my ancestors are buried lies in ruins and its gates have been destroyed by fire?" Ezr 4:12,21; Neh 1:3

⁴ Then the king asked me, "What is your request?"

So I prayed to the God of the heavens ⁵ and answered the king, "If it pleases the king, and if your servant has found favor with you, send me to Judah and to the city where my ancestors are buried, [B] so that I may rebuild it." Ezr 4:21; Neh 1:3-4

⁶ The king, with the queen seated beside him, asked me, "How long will your journey take, and when will you return?" So I gave him a definite time, and it pleased the king to send me. Neh 13:6

⁷ I also said to the king: "If it pleases the king, let me have letters written to the governors of the region west of the Euphrates River, so that they will grant me safe passage until I reach Judah. ⁸ And let me have a letter written to Asaph, keeper of the king's forest, so that he will give me timber to rebuild the gates of the temple's fortress, the city wall, and the home where I will live."[C] The king granted my requests, for the gracious hand of my God was on me. Ezr 3:7; 4:8-9; 8:22,36; Neh 7:2

⁹ I went to the governors of the region west of the Euphrates and gave them the king's letters. The king had also sent officers of the infantry and cavalry with me. ¹⁰ When Sanballat the Horonite and Tobiah the Ammonite official heard that someone had come to pursue the prosperity of the Israelites, they were greatly displeased. Ezr 8:36

Preparing to Rebuild the Walls

¹¹ After I arrived in Jerusalem and had been there three days, ¹² I got up at night and took a few men with me. I didn't tell anyone what my God had laid on my heart to do for Jerusalem. The only animal I took[D] was the one I was riding. ¹³ I went out at night through the Valley Gate toward the Serpent's[E] Well and the Dung Gate, and I inspected the walls of Jerusalem that had been broken down and its gates that had been destroyed by fire. ¹⁴ I went on to the Fountain Gate and the King's Pool, but farther down it became too narrow for my animal to go through. ¹⁵ So I went up at night by way of the valley and inspected the wall. Then heading back, I entered through the Valley Gate and returned. ¹⁶ The officials did not know where I had gone or what I was doing, for I had not yet told the Jews, priests, nobles, officials, or the rest of those who would be doing the work. ¹⁷ So I said to them, "You see the trouble we are in. Jerusalem lies in ruins and its gates have been burned. Come, let's rebuild Jerusalem's wall, so that we will no longer be a disgrace." ¹⁸ I told them how the gracious hand of my God had been on me, and what the king had said to me. Ezr 4:12; 8:32; Neh 1:3; 3:13,15

They said, "Let's start rebuilding," and their hands were strengthened[F] to do this good work.

¹⁹ When Sanballat the Horonite, Tobiah the Ammonite official, and Geshem the Arab heard about this, they mocked and despised us, and said, "What is this you're doing? Are you rebelling against the king?"

[A]2:3 Lit my face   [B]2:5 Lit city, the house of the graves of my fathers,   [C]2:8 Lit enter   [D]2:12 Lit animal with me   [E]2:13 Or Dragon's   [F]2:18 Lit they put their hands

²⁰ I gave them this reply, "The God of the heavens is the one who will grant us success. We, his servants, will start building, but you have no share, right, or historic claim in Jerusalem." Ezr 4:3-4

Rebuilding the Walls

3 The high priest Eliashib and his fellow priests began rebuilding the Sheep Gate. They dedicated it and installed its doors. After building the wall to the Tower of the Hundred and the Tower of Hananel, they dedicated it. ² The men of Jericho built next to Eliashib, and next to them Zaccur son of Imri built.

Fish Gate

³ The sons of Hassenaah built the Fish Gate. They built it with beams and installed its doors, bolts, and bars. ⁴ Next to them Meremoth son of Uriah, son of Hakkoz, made repairs. Beside them Meshullam son of Berechiah, son of Meshezabel, made repairs. Next to them Zadok son of Baana made repairs. ⁵ Beside them the Tekoites made repairs, but their nobles did not lift a finger to help ᴬ their supervisors.

Old Gate, Broad Wall, and Tower of the Ovens

⁶ Joiada son of Paseah and Meshullam son of Besodeiah repaired the Old ᴮ Gate. They built it with beams and installed its doors, bolts, and bars. ⁷ Next to them the repairs were done by Melatiah the Gibeonite, Jadon the Meronothite, and the men of Gibeon and Mizpah, who were under the authority ᶜ of the governor of the region west of the Euphrates River. ⁸ After him

Uzziel son of Harhaiah, the goldsmith, made repairs, and next to him Hananiah son of the perfumer made repairs. They restored Jerusalem as far as the Broad Wall. ⁹ Next to them Rephaiah son of Hur, ruler of half the district of Jerusalem, made repairs. ¹⁰ After them Jedaiah son of Harumaph made repairs across from his house. Next to him Hattush the son of Hashabneiah made repairs. ¹¹ Malchijah son of Harim and Hasshub son of Pahath-moab made repairs to another section, as well as to the Tower of the Ovens. ¹² Beside him Shallum son of Hallohesh, ruler of half the district of Jerusalem, made repairs — he and his daughters.

Valley Gate, Dung Gate, and Fountain Gate

¹³ Hanun and the inhabitants of Zanoah repaired the Valley Gate. They rebuilt it and installed its doors, bolts, and bars, and repaired five hundred yards ᴰ of the wall to the Dung Gate. ¹⁴ Malchijah son of Rechab, ruler of the district of Bethhaccherem, repaired the Dung Gate. He rebuilt it and installed its doors, bolts, and bars. Neh 2:13 ¹⁵ Shallun ᴱ son of Col-hozeh, ruler of the district of Mizpah, repaired the Fountain Gate. He rebuilt it and roofed it. Then he installed its doors, bolts, and bars. He also made repairs to the wall of the Pool of Shelah near the king's garden, as far as the stairs that descend from the city of David. Neh 2:14; 12:37; Is 8:6 ¹⁶ After him Nehemiah son of Azbuk, ruler of half the district of Beth-zur, made repairs up to a point opposite the tombs of David,

ᴬ3:5 Lit not bring their neck to the work of   ᴮ3:6 Or Jeshanah   ᶜ3:7 Or Mizpah, the seat   ᴰ3:13 Lit 1,000 cubits   ᴱ3:15 Some Hb mss, Syr read Shallum as far as the artificial pool and the House of the Warriors. ¹⁷ Next to him the Levites made repairs under Rehum son of Bani. Beside him Hashabiah, ruler of half the district of Keilah, made repairs for his district. ¹⁸ After him their fellow Levites made repairs under Binnui^A son of Henadad, ruler of half the district of Keilah. ¹⁹ Next to him Ezer son of Jeshua, ruler of Mizpah, made repairs to another section opposite the ascent to the armory at the Angle. Jos 15:58; 1Ch 2:45

The Angle, Water Gate, and Tower on the Ophel

²⁰ After him Baruch son of Zabbai^B diligently repaired another section, from the Angle to the door of the house of the high priest Eliashib. ²¹ Beside him Meremoth son of Uriah, son of Hakkoz, made repairs to another section, from the door of Eliashib's house to the end of his house. ²² And next to him the priests from the surrounding area made repairs. Ezr 8:33; Neh 3:1; 12:10

²³ After them Benjamin and Hasshub made repairs opposite their house. Beside them Azariah son of Maaseiah, son of Ananiah, made repairs beside his house. ²⁴ After him Binnui son of Henadad made repairs to another section, from the house of Azariah to the Angle and the corner. ²⁵ Palal son of Uzai made repairs opposite the Angle and tower that juts out from the king's upper palace, ^C by the courtyard of the guard. Beside him Pedaiah son of Parosh ²⁶ and the temple servants living on Ophel made repairs opposite the Water Gate toward the east and the tower that juts out. ²⁷ Next to him the Tekoites made repairs to another section from a point opposite the great tower that juts out, as far as the wall of Ophel. Ezr 8:33; Neh 12:37

Horse Gate, Inspection Gate, and Sheep Gate

²⁸ Each of the priests made repairs above the Horse Gate, each opposite his own house. ²⁹ After them Zadok son of Immer made repairs opposite his house. And beside him Shemaiah son of Shecaniah, guard of the East Gate, made repairs. ³⁰ Next to him Hananiah son of Shelemiah and Hanun the sixth son of Zalaph made repairs to another section. 2Ch 23:15

After them Meshullam son of Berechiah made repairs opposite his room. ³¹ Next to him Malchijah, one of the goldsmiths, made repairs to the house of the temple servants and the merchants, opposite the Inspection^D Gate, and as far as the upstairs room on the corner. ³² The goldsmiths and merchants made repairs between the upstairs room on the corner and the Sheep Gate. Neh 3:8; 7:46-56; Jn 5:2

Progress in Spite of Opposition

4 When Sanballat heard that we were rebuilding the wall, he became furious. He mocked the Jews ² before his colleagues and the powerful men^E of Samaria, and said, "What are these pathetic Jews doing? Can they restore it by themselves? Will they offer sacrifices? Will they ever finish it? Can they bring these burnt stones back to

^A3:18 Some Hb mss, Syr, LXX; Neh 3:24; other Hb mss, Vg read *Bavvai*   ^B3:20 Alt Hb tradition, Vg read *Zaccai*; Ezr 2:9   ^C3:25 Or *and the upper tower that juts out from the palace*   ^D3:31 Or *Muster*   ^E4:2 Or *the army*

life from the mounds of rubble?" ³ Then Tobiah the Ammonite, who was beside him, said, "Indeed, even if a fox climbed up what they are building, he would break down their stone wall!" Neh 2:10,19; 4:7

⁴ Listen, our God, for we are despised. Make their insults return on their own heads and let them be taken as plunder to a land of captivity. ⁵ Do not cover their guilt or let their sin be erased from your sight, because they have angeredᴬ the builders. Neh 6:14; Jr 18:23

⁶ So we rebuilt the wall until the entire wall was joined together up to half its height, for the people had the will to keep working. Neh 2:20

⁷ When Sanballat, Tobiah, and the Arabs, Ammonites, and Ashdodites heard that the repair to the walls of Jerusalem was progressing and that the gaps were being closed, they became furious. ⁸ They all plotted together to come and fight against Jerusalem and throw it into confusion. ⁹ So we prayed to our God and stationed a guard because of them day and night.

¹⁰ In Judah, it was said:ᴮ

The strength of the laborer fails,
  since there is so much rubble.
We will never be able
  to rebuild the wall.

¹¹ And our enemies said, "They won't realize itᶜ until we're among them and can kill them and stop the work." ¹² When the Jews who lived nearby arrived, they said to us time and again,ᴰ "Everywhere you turn, they attackᴱ us." ¹³ So I stationed people behind the lowest sections of the wall, at the vulnerable areas.

I stationed them by families with their swords, spears, and bows. ¹⁴ After I made an inspection, I stood up and said to the nobles, the officials, and the rest of the people, "Don't be afraid of them. Remember the great and awe-inspiring Lord, and fight for your countrymen, your sons and daughters, your wives and homes." Neh 2:16

Sword and Trowel

¹⁵ When our enemies heard that we knew their scheme and that God had frustrated it, every one of us returned to his own work on the wall. ¹⁶ From that day on, half of my men did the work while the other half held spears, shields, bows, and armor. The officers supported all the people of Judah, ¹⁷ who were rebuilding the wall. The laborers who carried the loads worked with one hand and held a weapon with the other. ¹⁸ Each of the builders had his sword strapped around his waist while he was building, and the trumpeter was beside me. ¹⁹ Then I said to the nobles, the officials, and the rest of the people: "The work is enormous and spread out, and we are separated far from one another along the wall. ²⁰ Wherever you hear the trumpet sound, rally to us there. Our God will fight for us!" ²¹ So we continued the work, while half of the men were holding spears from daybreak until the stars came out. ²² At that time, I also said to the people, "Let everyone and his servant spend the night inside Jerusalem, so that they can stand guard by night and work by day." ²³ And I, my brothers, my servants, and the

ᴬ4:5 Or provoked you in front of   ᴮ4:10 Lit Judah said   ᶜ4:11 Lit won't know or see   ᴰ4:12 Lit us 10 times   ᴱ4:12 Or again from every place, "You must return to men of the guard with me never took off our clothes. Each carried his weapon, even when washing. [A]

Social Injustice

5 There was a widespread outcry from the people and their wives against their Jewish countrymen. [2] Some were saying, "We, our sons, and our daughters are numerous. Let us get grain so that we can eat and live." [3] Others were saying, "We are mortgaging our fields, vineyards, and homes to get grain during the famine." [4] Still others were saying, "We have borrowed money to pay the king's tax on our fields and vineyards. [5] We and our children are just like our countrymen and their children, yet we are subjecting our sons and daughters to slavery. Some of our daughters are already enslaved, but we are powerless [B] because our fields and vineyards belong to others." Hg 1:5-11

[6] I became extremely angry when I heard their outcry and these complaints. [7] After seriously considering the matter, I accused the nobles and officials, saying to them, "Each of you is charging his countrymen interest." So I called a large assembly against them [8] and said, "We have done our best to buy back our Jewish countrymen who were sold to foreigners, but now you sell your own countrymen, and we have to buy them back." They remained silent and could not say a word. [9] Then I said, "What you are doing isn't right. Shouldn't you walk in the fear of our God and not invite the reproach of our foreign enemies? [10] Even I, as well as my brothers and my servants, have been lending them money and grain. Please, let us stop charging this interest. [C] [11] Return their fields, vineyards, olive groves, and houses to them immediately, along with the percentage [D] of the money, grain, new wine, and fresh oil that you have been assessing them." Ex 11:8

[12] They responded: "We will return these things and require nothing more from them. We will do as you say." Neh 10:31

So I summoned the priests and made everyone take an oath to do this. [13] I also shook the folds of my robe and said, "May God likewise shake from his house and property everyone who doesn't keep this promise. May he be shaken out and have nothing!" Ezr 10:5; Ac 18:6

The whole assembly said, "Amen," and they praised the LORD. Then the people did as they had promised.

Good and Bad Governors

[14] Furthermore, from the day King Artaxerxes appointed me to be their governor in the land of Judah — from the twentieth year until his thirty-second year, twelve years — I and my associates never ate from the food allotted to the governor. [15] The governors who preceded me had heavily burdened the people, taking from them food and wine as well as a pound [E] of silver. Their subordinates also oppressed the people, but because of the fear of God, I didn't do this. [16] Instead, I devoted myself to the construction of this wall, and all my subordinates were gathered there for the work. We didn't buy any land. Ezr 4:7; 7:1

[17] There were 150 Jews and officials, as well as guests from the

---

[A] **4:23** Lit *Each his weapon the water*   [B] **5:5** Lit *but there is not the power in our hand*   [C] **5:10** Or *us forgive these debts*   [D] **5:11** Lit *hundred*   [E] **5:15** Lit *40 shekels* surrounding nations at my table. ¹⁸ Each ᴬ day, one ox, six choice sheep, and some fowl were prepared for me. An abundance of all kinds of wine was provided every ten days. But I didn't demand the food allotted to the governor, because the burden on the people was so heavy.   1Kg 4:22-23,27;18:19

¹⁹ Remember me favorably, my God, for all that I have done for this people.   Neh 13:14,22,31

Attempts to Discourage the Builders

6 When Sanballat, Tobiah, Geshem the Arab, and the rest of our enemies heard that I had rebuilt the wall and that no gap was left in it — though at that time I had not installed the doors in the city gates — ² Sanballat and Geshem sent me a message: "Come, let's meet together in the villages of ᴮ the Ono Valley." They were planning to harm me.   Neh 2:10,19; 4:6-7

³ So I sent messengers to them, saying, "I am doing important work and cannot come down. Why should the work cease while I leave it and go down to you?" ⁴ Four times they sent me the same proposal, and I gave them the same reply.

⁵ Sanballat sent me this same message a fifth time by his aide, who had an open letter in his hand. ⁶ In it was written: Neh 2:10

It is reported among the nations — and Geshem ᶜ agrees — that you and the Jews plan to rebel. This is the reason you are building the wall. According to these reports, you are to become their king ⁷ and have even set up the prophets

in Jerusalem to proclaim on your behalf: "There is a king in Judah." These rumors will be heard by the king. So come, let's confer together.   Neh 2:19

⁸ Then I replied to him, "There is nothing to these rumors you are spreading; you are inventing them in your own mind." ⁹ For they were all trying to intimidate us, saying, "They will drop their hands from ᴰ the work, and it will never be finished."   Ezr 3:3; 4:4; Jb 13:4; Ps 52:2

But now, my God, strengthen my hands.   Neh 5:19; 13:22; Ps 138:3

Attempts to Intimidate Nehemiah

¹⁰ I went to the house of Shemaiah son of Delaiah, son of Mehetabel, who was restricted to his house. He said:

Let's meet at the house
    of God,
inside the temple.
Let's shut the temple doors
    because they're coming
    to kill you.
They're coming to kill you
    tonight! ᴱ

¹¹ But I said, "Should a man like me run away? How can someone like me enter the temple and live? I will not go." ¹² I realized that God had not sent him, because of the prophecy he spoke against me. Tobiah and Sanballat had hired him. ¹³ He was hired, so that I would be intimidated, do as he suggested, sin, and get a bad reputation, in order that they could discredit me.   Nm 18:7; Neh 2:10; 6:1

¹⁴ My God, remember Tobiah and Sanballat for what they have done, and also the prophetess Noadiah

ᴬ5:18 Lit *And that which was prepared each*   ᴮ6:2 Or *together at Kephirim in*   ᶜ6:6 Lit *Gashmu*
ᴰ6:9 Or *will give up on*   ᴱ6:10 Or *by night*

and the other prophets who wanted to intimidate me. Neh 13:29; Rv 2:20

The Wall Completed

15 The wall was completed in fifty-two days, on the twenty-fifth day of the month Elul. 16 When all our enemies heard this, all the surrounding nations were intimidated and lost their confidence,^A for they realized that this task had been accomplished by our God. Neh 4:1,7; 6:1

17 During those days, the nobles of Judah sent many letters to Tobiah, and Tobiah's letters came to them. 18 For many in Judah were bound by oath to him, since he was a son-in-law of Shecaniah son of Arah, and his son Jehohanan had married the daughter of Meshullam son of Berechiah. 19 These nobles kept mentioning Tobiah's good deeds to me, and they reported my words to him. And Tobiah sent letters to intimidate me. Neh 6:1; 13:4-5,7-8

The Exiles Return

7 When the wall had been rebuilt and I had the doors installed, the gatekeepers, singers, and Levites were appointed. 2 Then I put my brother Hanani in charge of Jerusalem, along with Hananiah, commander of the fortress, because he was a faithful man who feared God more than most. 3 I said to them, "Do not open the gates of Jerusalem until the sun is hot, and let the doors be shut and securely fastened while the guards are on duty. Station the citizens of Jerusalem as guards, some at their posts and some at their homes." Neh 6:1

4 The city was large and spacious, but there were few people in it, and no houses had been built yet. 5 Then my God put it into my mind to assemble the nobles, the officials, and the people to be registered by genealogy. I found the genealogical record of those who came back first, and I found the following written in it: Ezr 2:1-70; Neh 11:1; Pr 2:6

6 These are the people of the province who went up among the captive exiles deported by King Nebuchadnezzar of Babylon. Each of them returned to Jerusalem and Judah, to his own town. 7 They came with Zerubbabel, Jeshua, Nehemiah, Azariah, Raamiah, Nahamani, Mordecai, Bilshan, Mispereth, Bigvai, Nehum, and Baanah. 2Ch 36:20

The number of the Israelite men included^B

8	Parosh's descendants	2,172
9	Shephatiah's descendants	372
10	Arah's descendants	652
11	Pahath-moab's descendants: Jeshua's and Joab's descendants	2,818
12	Elam's descendants	1,254
13	Zattu's descendants	845
14	Zaccai's descendants	760
15	Binnui's descendants	648
16	Bebai's descendants	628
17	Azgad's descendants	2,322
18	Adonikam's descendants	667
19	Bigvai's descendants	2,067
20	Adin's descendants	655
21	Ater's descendants: of Hezekiah	98
22	Hashum's descendants	328
23	Bezai's descendants	324
24	Hariph's descendants	112
25	Gibeon's^C descendants	95
26	Bethlehem's and Netophah's men	188

^A 6:16 Lit and fell greatly in their eyes   ^B 7:7 Lit the men of the people of Israel   ^C 7:25 = Gibbar's in Ezr 2:20

27 Anathoth's men   128
28 Beth-azmaveth's men   42
29 Kiriath-jearim's,
   Chephirah's,
   and Beeroth's men   743
30 Ramah's and Geba's men   621
31 Michmas's men   122
32 Bethel's and Ai's men   123
33 the other Nebo's men   52
34 the other Elam's
   people   1,254
35 Harim's people   320
36 Jericho's people   345
37 Lod's, Hadid's,
   and Ono's people   721
38 Senaah's people   3,930.

39 The priests included
   Jedaiah's descendants
   of the house
   of Jeshua   973
40 Immer's descendants   1,052
41 Pashhur's descendants   1,247.
42 Harim's descendants   1,017

43 The Levites included   Ezr 2:40; 7:7
   Jeshua's descendants:
   of Kadmiel   .
   Hodevah's descendants   74

44 The singers included   1Ch 15:16.
   Asaph's descendants   148

45 The gatekeepers included
   Shallum's descendants,
   Ater's descendants,
   Talmon's descendants,
   Akkub's descendants,
   Hatita's descendants,   .
   Shobai's descendants   138

46 The temple servants included
   Ziha's descendants,
   Hasupha's descendants,
   Tabbaoth's descendants,
47 Keros's descendants,

Sia's descendants,
Padon's descendants,
48 Lebanah's descendants,
   Hagabah's descendants,
   Shalmai's descendants,
49 Hanan's descendants,
   Giddel's descendants,
   Gahar's descendants,
50 Reaiah's descendants,
   Rezin's descendants,
   Nekoda's descendants,
51 Gazzam's descendants,
   Uzza's descendants,
   Paseah's descendants,
52 Besai's descendants,
   Meunim's descendants,
   Nephishesim's [A] descendants,
53 Bakbuk's descendants,
   Hakupha's descendants,
   Harhur's descendants,
54 Bazlith's descendants,
   Mehida's descendants,
   Harsha's descendants,
55 Barkos's descendants,
   Sisera's descendants,
   Temah's descendants,
56 Neziah's descendants,
   Hatipha's descendants.

57 The descendants of Solomon's
servants included   1Kg 9:21; Ezr 2:55
   Sotai's descendants,
   Sophereth's descendants,
   Perida's descendants,
58 Jaala's descendants,
   Darkon's descendants,
   Giddel's descendants,
59 Shephatiah's descendants,
   Hattil's descendants,
   Pochereth-hazzebaim's
   descendants,
   Amon's descendants.

60 All the temple servants
   and the descendants of
   Solomon's servants   392.

A 7:52 Alt Hb tradition reads *Nephushesim's*

⁶¹ The following are those who came from Tel-melah, Tel-harsha, Cherub, Addon, and Immer, but were unable to prove that their ancestral families[A] and their lineage were Israelite: Ezr 2:59-60

⁶² Delaiah's descendants,
Tobiah's descendants,
and Nekoda's
descendants   642

⁶³ and from the priests: the descendants of Hobaiah, the descendants of Hakkoz, and the descendants of Barzillai — who had taken a wife from the daughters of Barzillai the Gileadite and who bore their name. ⁶⁴ These searched for their entries in the genealogical records, but they could not be found, so they were disqualified from the priesthood. ⁶⁵ The governor ordered them not to eat the most holy things until there was a priest who could consult the Urim and Thummim. Ex 28:30; Lv 8:8; Ezr 2:63

⁶⁶ The whole combined
assembly numbered 42,360
⁶⁷ not including
their 7,337 male
and female servants,
as well as their 245 male
and female singers.
⁶⁸ They had 736 horses,
245 mules,[B]
⁶⁹ 435 camels,
and 6,720 donkeys.

⁷⁰ Some of the family heads contributed to the project. The governor gave 1,000 gold coins,[C] 50 bowls, and 530 priestly garments to the treasury. ⁷¹ Some of the family heads gave 20,000 gold coins and 2,200 silver minas to the treasury for the project. ⁷² The rest of the people gave 20,000 gold coins, 2,000 silver minas, and 67 priestly garments. ⁷³ The priests, Levites, gatekeepers, temple singers, some of the people, temple servants, and all Israel settled in their towns.

Public Reading of the Law

When the seventh month came and the Israelites had settled in their towns, ¹ all the people gathered together at the square in front of the Water Gate. They asked the scribe Ezra to bring the book of the law of Moses that the LORD had given Israel. ² On the first day of the seventh month, the priest Ezra brought the law before the assembly of men, women, and all who could listen with understanding. ³ While he was facing the square in front of the Water Gate, he read out of it from daybreak until noon before the men, the women, and those who could understand. All the people listened attentively[D] to the book of the law. ⁴ The scribe Ezra stood on a high wooden platform made for this purpose. Mattithiah, Shema, Anaiah, Uriah, Hilkiah, and Maaseiah stood beside him on his right; to his left were Pedaiah, Mishael, Malchijah, Hashum, Hash-baddanah, Zechariah, and Meshullam. ⁵ Ezra opened the book in full view of all the people, since he was elevated above everyone. As he opened it, all the people stood up. ⁶ Ezra blessed the LORD, the great God, and with their hands uplifted all the people said, "Amen, Amen!" Then they knelt low and worshiped the LORD with their faces to the ground. Ezr 3:1; Neh 3:26; 8:16

⁷ Jeshua, Bani, Sherebiah, Jamin, Akkub, Shabbethai, Hodiah,

Maaseiah, Kelita, Azariah, Jozabad, Hanan, and Pelaiah, who were Levites, [A] explained the law to the people as they stood in their places. [8] They read out of the book of the law of God, translating and giving the meaning so that the people could understand what was read. [9] Nehemiah the governor, Ezra the priest and scribe, and the Levites who were instructing the people said to all of them, "This day is holy to the LORD your God. Do not mourn or weep." For all the people were weeping as they heard the words of the law. [10] Then he said to them, "Go and eat what is rich, drink what is sweet, and send portions to those who have nothing prepared, since today is holy to our Lord. Do not grieve, because the joy of the LORD is your strength." [B] [11] And the Levites quieted all the people, saying, "Be still, since today is holy. Don't grieve." [12] Then all the people began to eat and drink, send portions, and have a great celebration, because they had understood the words that were explained to them.

Festival of Shelters Observed

[13] On the second day, the family heads of all the people, along with the priests and Levites, assembled before the scribe Ezra to study the words of the law. [14] They found written in the law how the LORD had commanded through Moses that the Israelites should dwell in shelters during the festival of the seventh month. [15] So they proclaimed and spread this news throughout their towns and in Jerusalem, saying, "Go out to the hill country and bring back branches of olive, wild olive, myrtle, palm, and other leafy trees to make shelters, just as it is written." [16] The people went out, brought back branches, and made shelters for themselves on each of their rooftops and courtyards, the court of the house of God, the square by the Water Gate, and the square by the Ephraim Gate. [17] The whole community that had returned from exile made shelters and lived in them. The Israelites had not celebrated like this from the days of Joshua son of Nun until that day. And there was tremendous joy. [18] Ezra [C] read out of the book of the law of God every day, from the first day to the last. The Israelites celebrated the festival for seven days, and on the eighth day there was an assembly, according to the ordinance. Ezr 7:6; 8:1; Neh 10:28-29

National Confession of Sin

9 On the twenty-fourth day of this month the Israelites assembled; they were fasting, wearing sackcloth, and had put dust on their heads. [2] Those of Israelite descent separated themselves from all foreigners, and they stood and confessed their sins and the iniquities of their fathers. [3] While they stood in their places, they read from the book of the law of the LORD their God for a fourth of the day and spent another fourth of the day in confession and worship of the LORD their God. [4] Jeshua, Bani, Kadmiel, Shebaniah, Bunni, Sherebiah, Bani, and Chenani stood on the raised platform built for the Levites and cried out loudly to the LORD their God. [5] Then the Levites — Jeshua, Kadmiel, Bani, Hashabneiah, Sherebiah,

[A] 8:7 Vg, 1 Esdras 9:48; MT reads *Pelaiah and the Levites*   [B] 8:10 Or *stronghold*   [C] 8:18 Some Hb mss, Syr read *They*

Hodiah, Shebaniah, and Pethahiah
— said, "Stand up. Blessed be the
Lord your God from everlasting
to everlasting."

Blessed be
your glorious name,
and may it be exalted above
all blessing and praise.

6 You, [A] Lord, are the only
God. [B]   Dt 6:4
You created the heavens,
the highest heavens with all
their stars,
the earth and all that is on it,
the seas and all that is in
them.
You give life to all of them,
and all the stars
of heaven worship you.

7 You, the Lord,
are the God who chose
Abram
and brought him out of Ur
of the Chaldeans,   Gn 11:28,31
and changed his name
to Abraham.   Gn 17:5

8 You found his heart faithful
in your sight,   Gn 15:6; 22:15-18
and made a covenant
with him
to give the land
of the Canaanites,
Hethites, Amorites, Perizzites,
Jebusites, and Girgashites —
to give it to his descendants.
You have fulfilled
your promise,
for you are righteous.

9 You saw the oppression
of our ancestors in Egypt
and heard their cry
at the Red Sea.

10 You performed
signs and wonders
against Pharaoh,

all his officials, and all
the people of his land,   Ex 3:20
for you knew how arrogantly
they treated our ancestors.
You made a name
for yourself
that endures to this day.

11 You divided the sea
before them,
and they crossed through it
on dry ground.   Ex 14:21-22
You hurled their pursuers
into the depths
like a stone into raging water.

12 You led them with a pillar
of cloud by day,
and with a pillar of fire
by night,
to illuminate the way
they should go.   Dt 1:32-33

13 You came down
on Mount Sinai,   Ex 19:20
and spoke to them
from heaven.
You gave them
impartial ordinances,
reliable instructions,
and good statutes
and commands.

14 You revealed
your holy Sabbath to them,
and gave them commands,
statutes, and instruction
through your servant Moses.

15 You provided bread
from heaven
for their hunger;   Ex 16:4
you brought them
water from the rock
for their thirst.   Ex 17:6
You told them to go in
and possess the land
you had sworn [C] to give them.

16 But our ancestors
acted arrogantly;

A 9:6 LXX reads *And Ezra said: You*   B 9:6 Lit *are alone*   C 9:15 Lit *lifted your hand*

they became stiff-necked
and did not listen
to your commands.
17 They refused to listen
and did not remember
your wonders
you performed among them.
They became stiff-necked
and appointed a leader
to return to their slavery
in Egypt.ᴬ
But you are a forgiving God,
gracious and compassionate,
slow to anger
and abounding
in faithful love,   Ex 34:6; Ps 86:15
and you did not abandon
them.
18 Even after they had cast
an image of a calf
for themselves and said,
"This is your god
who brought you
out of Egypt,"   Ex 32:4
and they had committed
terrible blasphemies,
19 you did not abandon them
in the wilderness
because of
your great compassion.
During the day the pillar
of cloud
never turned away
from them,
guiding them
on their journey.
And during the night
the pillar of fire
illuminated the way
they should go.   Ex 16:4; 17:6
20 You sent your good Spirit
to instruct them.   Nm 11:17
You did not withhold
your manna
from their mouths,   Ex 16:14-15

and you gave them water
for their thirst.   Ex 17:6
21 You provided for them
in the wilderness
forty years,   Dt 2:7; 29:5
and they lacked nothing.
Their clothes did not
wear out,
and their feet did not swell.

22 You gave them kingdoms
and peoples
and established boundaries
for them.
They took possession
of the land of King Sihonᴮ
of Heshbon
and of the land of King Og
of Bashan.   Nm 21:21-35
23 You multiplied
their descendants
like the stars of the sky   Gn 15:5
and brought them
to the land
you told their ancestors
to go in and possess.
24 So their descendants went in
and possessed the land:
You subdued the Canaanites
who inhabited the land
before them
and handed their kings
and the surrounding
peoples over to them,
to do as they pleased
with them.
25 They captured fortified cities
and fertile land
and took possession of
well-supplied houses,
cisterns cut out of rock,
vineyards,
olive groves, and fruit trees
in abundance.   Dt 6:11; 11:11-12
They ate, were filled,

ᴬ9:17 Some Hb mss, LXX; other Hb mss read *in their rebellion*   ᴮ9:22 One Hb ms, LXX; other Hb mss, Vg
read *of Sihon, even the land of the king*

became prosperous,
and delighted
in your great goodness.

26 But they were disobedient
and rebelled against you.
They flung your law
behind their backs   1Kg 14:9
and killed your prophets
who warned them
in order to turn them back
to you.
They committed
terrible blasphemies.

27 So you handed them over
to their enemies,
who oppressed them.
In their time of distress,
they cried out to you,
and you heard from heaven.
In your abundant
compassion
you gave them deliverers,
who rescued them
from the power
of their enemies.

28 But as soon as they had relief,
they again did what was evil
in your sight.
So you abandoned
them to the power
of their enemies,
who dominated them.
When they cried out to you
again,
you heard from heaven
and rescued them
many times
in your compassion.

29 You warned them
to turn back to your law,
but they acted arrogantly
and would not obey your
commands.
They sinned against
your ordinances,

which a person will live by
if he does them.   Lv 18:5; Dt 30:16
They stubbornly resisted, [A]
stiffened their necks,
and would not obey.

30 You were patient with them
for many years,
and your Spirit warned them
through your prophets,
but they would not listen.
Therefore,
you handed them over
to the surrounding peoples.

31 However, in your
abundant compassion,
you did not destroy them
or abandon them,   Jr 4:27
for you are a gracious
and compassionate God.

32 So now, our God — the great,
mighty,
and awe-inspiring
God who keeps
his gracious covenant —
do not view lightly
all the hardships
that have afflicted us,
our kings and leaders,
our priests and prophets,
our ancestors and all
your people,
from the days
of the Assyrian kings
until today.   2Kg 15:19; 17:3-6

33 You are righteous concerning
all that has happened to us,
because you have acted
faithfully,
while we have acted
wickedly.

34 Our kings, leaders, priests,
and ancestors
did not obey your law
or listen to your commands
and warnings you gave them.

A 9:29 Lit *They gave a stubborn shoulder*

35 When they were
in their kingdom,
with your abundant goodness
that you gave them,
and in the spacious
and fertile land you set
before them,   Neh 9:25
they would not
serve you or turn
from their wicked ways.

36 Here we are today,
slaves in the land you gave
our ancestors
so that they could enjoy
its fruit and its goodness.
Here we are — slaves in it!
37 Its abundant harvest goes
to the kings
you have set over us,
because of our sins.
They rule over our bodies
and our livestock
as they please.   Dt 28:33,51
We are in great distress.

Israel's Vow of Faithfulness

38 In view of all this, we are making a binding agreement in writing on a sealed document containing the names of our leaders, Levites, and priests.   2Ch 23:16; Neh 10:1-39

10 Those whose seals were on the document were
the governor Nehemiah
son of Hacaliah,
and Zedekiah,   Neh 5:14; 8:9; 12:26
2 Seraiah, Azariah, Jeremiah,
3 Pashhur, Amariah, Malchijah,
4 Hattush, Shebaniah, Malluch,
5 Harim, Meremoth, Obadiah,
6 Daniel, Ginnethon, Baruch,
7 Meshullam, Abijah, Mijamin,
8 Maaziah, Bilgai, and
Shemaiah.
These were the priests.

9 The Levites were   Neh 8:7; 9:4-5
Jeshua son of Azaniah,
Binnui of the sons
of Henadad, Kadmiel,
10 and their brothers
Shebaniah, Hodiah, Kelita,
Pelaiah, Hanan,
11 Mica, Rehob, Hashabiah,
12 Zaccur, Sherebiah,
Shebaniah,
13 Hodiah, Bani, and Beninu.

14 The heads of the people were
Parosh, Pahath-moab, Elam,
Zattu, Bani,
15 Bunni, Azgad, Bebai,
16 Adonijah, Bigvai, Adin,   Ezr 8:6
17 Ater, Hezekiah, Azzur,
18 Hodiah, Hashum, Bezai,
19 Hariph, Anathoth, Nebai,
20 Magpiash, Meshullam,
Hezir,
21 Meshezabel, Zadok, Jaddua,
22 Pelatiah, Hanan, Anaiah,
23 Hoshea, Hananiah, Hasshub,
24 Hallohesh, Pilha, Shobek,
25 Rehum, Hashabnah,
Maaseiah,
26 Ahijah, Hanan, Anan,
27 Malluch, Harim, Baanah.

28 The rest of the people — the priests, Levites, gatekeepers, singers, and temple servants, along with their wives, sons, and daughters, everyone who is able to understand and who has separated themselves from the surrounding peoples to obey the law of God — 29 join with their noble brothers and commit themselves with a sworn oath [A] to follow the law of God given through God's servant Moses and to obey carefully all the commands, ordinances, and statutes of the LORD our Lord.   Neh 8:2-3

[A]**10:29** Lit and enter in a curse and in an oath

Details of the Vow

[30] We will not give our daughters in marriage to the surrounding peoples and will not take their daughters as wives for our sons. Ex 34:16; Neh 13:23

[31] When the surrounding peoples bring merchandise or any kind of grain to sell on the Sabbath day, we will not buy from them on the Sabbath or a holy day. We will also leave the land uncultivated in the seventh year and will cancel every debt. Ex 23:10-11; Lv 25:1-7; Dt 15:1-3; Neh 13:16

[32] We will impose the following commands on ourselves:

To give an eighth of an ounce of silver[A] yearly for the service of the house of our God: [33] the bread displayed before the LORD,[B] the daily grain offering, the regular burnt offering, the Sabbath and New Moon offerings, the appointed festivals, the holy things, the sin offerings to atone for Israel, and for all the work of the house of our God. Ex 30:11-16; Lv 24:5-9; Nm 10:10; Mt 17:24

[34] We have cast lots among the priests, Levites, and people for the donation of wood by our ancestral families[C] at the appointed times each year. They are to bring the wood to our God's house to burn on the altar of the LORD our God, as it is written in the law. Lv 16:8; Neh 11:1

[35] We will bring the firstfruits of our land and of every fruit tree to the LORD's house year by year. [36] We will also bring the firstborn of our sons and our livestock, as prescribed by the law, and will bring the firstborn of our herds and flocks to the house of our God, to the priests who serve in our God's house. [37] We will bring a loaf from our first batch of dough to the priests at the storerooms of the house of our God. We will also bring the firstfruits of our grain offerings, of every fruit tree, and of the new wine and fresh oil. A tenth of our land's produce belongs to the Levites, for the Levites are to collect the one-tenth offering in all our agricultural towns. [38] A priest from Aaron's descendants is to accompany the Levites when they collect the tenth, and the Levites are to take a tenth of this offering to the storerooms of the treasury in the house of our God. [39] For the Israelites and the Levites are to bring the contributions of grain, new wine, and fresh oil to the storerooms where the articles of the sanctuary are kept and where the priests who minister are, along with the gatekeepers and singers. We will not neglect the house of our God. Lv 26:1-10; Nm 18:12-13

Resettling Jerusalem

11 Now the leaders of the people stayed in Jerusalem, and the rest of the people cast lots for one out of ten to come and live in Jerusalem, the holy city, while the other nine-tenths remained in their towns. [2] The people blessed all

A 10:32 Lit give one-third of a shekel   B 10:33 Lit rows of bread   C 10:34 Lit the house of our fathers the men who volunteered to live in Jerusalem. Neh 7:4; 10:34; 11:18; Is 48:2 ³ These are the heads of the province who stayed in Jerusalem (but in the villages of Judah each lived on his own property in their towns — the Israelites, priests, Levites, temple servants, and descendants of Solomon's servants — ⁴ while some of the descendants of Judah and Benjamin settled in Jerusalem): 1Ch 9:2-34; Neh 7:73; 11:20

Judah's descendants: 1Ch 9:3-21

Athaiah son of Uzziah, son of Zechariah, son of Amariah, son of Shephatiah, son of Mahalalel, of Perez's descendants; ⁵ and Maaseiah son of Baruch, son of Col-hozeh, son of Hazaiah, son of Adaiah, son of Joiarib, son of Zechariah, a descendant of the Shilonite. ⁶ The total number of Perez's descendants, who settled in Jerusalem, was 468 capable men.

⁷ These were Benjamin's descendants:

Sallu son of Meshullam, son of Joed, son of Pedaiah, son of Kolaiah, son of Maaseiah, son of Ithiel, son of Jeshaiah, ⁸ and after him Gabbai and Sallai: 928. ⁹ Joel son of Zichri was the officer over them, and Judah son of Hassenuah was second in command over the city.

¹⁰ The priests:

Jedaiah son of Joiarib, Jachin, and ¹¹ Seraiah son of Hilkiah, son of Meshullam, son of Zadok, son of Meraioth, son

of Ahitub, the chief official of God's temple, ¹² and their relatives who did the work at the temple: 822. Adaiah son of Jeroham, son of Pelaliah, son of Amzi, son of Zechariah, son of Pashhur, son of Malchijah ¹³ and his relatives, the heads of families: 242. Amashsai son of Azarel, son of Ahzai, son of Meshillemoth, son of Immer, ¹⁴ and their relatives, capable men: 128. Zabdiel son of Haggedolim, was their chief.

¹⁵ The Levites:

Shemaiah son of Hasshub, son of Azrikam, son of Hashabiah, son of Bunni; ¹⁶ and Shabbethai and Jozabad, from the heads of the Levites, who supervised the work outside the house of God; ¹⁷ Mattaniah son of Mica, son of Zabdi, son of Asaph, the one ᴬ who began the thanksgiving in prayer; Bakbukiah, second among his relatives; and Abda son of Shammua, son of Galal, son of Jeduthun. ¹⁸ All the Levites in the holy city: 284.

¹⁹ The gatekeepers:

Akkub, Talmon, and their relatives, who guarded the city gates: 172.

²⁰ The rest of Israel, the priests, and the Levites were in all the villages of Judah, each on his own inherited property. ²¹ The temple servants lived on Ophel; Ziha and Gishpa supervised the temple servants. Nm 36:3; Neh 3:26; 11:3

ᴬ11:17 Lit the head

The Levites and Priests

²² The leader of the Levites in Jerusalem was Uzzi son of Bani, son of Hashabiah, son of Mattaniah, son of Mica, of the descendants of Asaph, who were singers for the service of God's house. ²³ There was, in fact, a command of the king regarding them, and an ordinance regulating the singers' daily tasks. ²⁴ Pethahiah son of Meshezabel, of the descendants of Zerah son of Judah, was the king's agent ᴬ in every matter concerning the people.   1Ch 15:16; Neh 2:1; 7:44

²⁵ As for the farming settlements with their fields:

Some of Judah's descendants
lived in Kiriath-arba   Jos 14:15
and Dibon and their
surrounding villages,
and Jekabzeel and
its settlements;   Jos 3:9,17
²⁶ in Jeshua, Moladah,
Beth-pelet,   Jos 15:26-28
²⁷ Hazar-shual, and Beer-sheba
and its surrounding
villages;   2Sm 17:11
²⁸ in Ziklag and Meconah
and its surrounding
villages;   1Sm 27:6
²⁹ in En-rimmon, Zorah,
Jarmuth, and   Jos 10:5; 15:33
³⁰ Zanoah and Adullam
with their settlements;
in Lachish with its
fields and Azekah
and its surrounding villages.
So they settled
from Beer-sheba
to Hinnom Valley.   Jos 15:27

³¹ Benjamin's descendants:
from Geba, ᴮ Michmash, Aija,
and Bethel
and its surrounding villages,
³² Anathoth, Nob, Ananiah,   Jr 1:1
³³ Hazor, Ramah, Gittaim,   Jos 11:1
³⁴ Hadid, Zeboim, Neballat,
³⁵ Lod, and Ono,
in Craftsmen's Valley.   1Ch 8:12
³⁶ Some of the Judean
divisions of Levites were
in Benjamin.

12 These are the priests and Levites who went up with Zerubbabel son of Shealtiel and with Jeshua: Ezr 2:1-2; 3:2; 7:7; Neh 12:12-21

Seraiah, Jeremiah, Ezra,
² Amariah, Malluch, Hattush,
³ Shecaniah, Rehum,
Meremoth,
⁴ Iddo, Ginnethoi, Abijah,   Zch 1:1
⁵ Mijamin, Maadiah, Bilgah,
⁶ Shemaiah, Joiarib, Jedaiah,
⁷ Sallu, Amok, Hilkiah, Jedaiah.
These were the heads of the priests and their relatives in the days of Jeshua.   Ezr 2:2; 3:2

⁸ The Levites:
Jeshua, Binnui, Kadmiel,
Sherebiah, Judah,
and Mattaniah —   Neh 11:17
he and his relatives
were in charge
of the songs of praise.
⁹ Bakbukiah, Unni, ᶜ
and their relatives
stood opposite them
in the services.
¹⁰ Jeshua fathered Joiakim,
Joiakim fathered Eliashib,
Eliashib fathered Joiada,
¹¹ Joiada fathered Jonathan,
and Jonathan fathered
Jaddua. ᴰ

ᴬ11:24 Lit was at the king's hand   ᴮ11:31 Or descendants from Geba lived in   ᶜ12:9 Alt Hb tradition reads Unno   ᴰ12:10-11 These men were high priests.

¹² In the days of Joiakim, the heads of the priestly families were

Meraiah	of Seraiah,
Hananiah	of Jeremiah,
¹³ Meshullam	of Ezra,
Jehohanan	of Amariah,
¹⁴ Jonathan	of Malluchi,
Joseph	of Shebaniah,
¹⁵ Adna	of Harim,
Helkai	of Meraioth,
¹⁶ Zechariah	of Iddo,
Meshullam	of Ginnethon,
¹⁷ Zichri	of Abijah,
Piltai	of Moadiah,
	of Miniamin,
¹⁸ Shammua	of Bilgah,
Jehonathan	of Shemaiah,
¹⁹ Mattenai	of Joiarib,
Uzzi	of Jedaiah,
²⁰ Kallai	of Sallai,
Eber	of Amok,
²¹ Hashabiah	of Hilkiah,
and Nethanel	of Jedaiah.

²² In the days of Eliashib, Joiada, Johanan, and Jaddua, the heads of the families of the Levites and priests were recorded while Darius the Persian ruled. ²³ Levi's descendants, the family heads, were recorded in the Book of the Historical Events during the days of Johanan son of Eliashib. ²⁴ The heads of the Levites — Hashabiah, Sherebiah, and Jeshua son of Kadmiel, along with their relatives opposite them — gave praise and thanks, division by division, as David the man of God had prescribed. ²⁵ This included Mattaniah, Bakbukiah, and Obadiah. Meshullam, Talmon, and Akkub were gatekeepers who guarded the storerooms at the city gates. ²⁶ These served in the days of Joiakim son of Jeshua, son of Jozadak, and in the days of Nehemiah the governor and Ezra the priest and scribe.   1Ch 9:14-22; 16:4; 23:30

Dedication of the Wall

²⁷ At the dedication of the wall of Jerusalem, they sent for the Levites wherever they lived and brought them to Jerusalem to celebrate the joyous dedication with thanksgiving and singing accompanied by cymbals, harps, and lyres. ²⁸ The singers gathered from the region around Jerusalem, from the settlements of the Netophathites, ²⁹ from Beth-gilgal, and from the fields of Geba and Azmaveth, for they had built settlements for themselves around Jerusalem. ³⁰ After the priests and Levites had purified themselves, they purified the people, the city gates, and the wall.   1Ch 15:16; Ezr 6:16

³¹ Then I brought the leaders of Judah up on top of the wall, and I appointed two large processions that gave thanks. One went to the right on the wall, toward the Dung Gate. ³² Hoshaiah and half the leaders of Judah followed, ³³ along with Azariah, Ezra, Meshullam, ³⁴ Judah, Benjamin, Shemaiah, Jeremiah, ³⁵ and some of the priests' sons with trumpets, and Zechariah son of Jonathan, son of Shemaiah, son of Mattaniah, son of Micaiah, son of Zaccur, son of Asaph followed ³⁶ as well as his relatives — Shemaiah, Azarel, Milalai, Gilalai, Maai, Nethanel, Judah, and Hanani, with the musical instruments of David, the man of God. Ezra the scribe went in front of them. ³⁷ At the Fountain Gate they climbed the steps of the city of David on the ascent of the wall and went above the house of David to the Water Gate on the east.

³⁸ The second thanksgiving procession went to the left, and I followed it with half the people along the top of the wall, past the Tower of the Ovens to the Broad Wall, ³⁹ above the Ephraim Gate, and by the Old Gate, the Fish Gate, the Tower of Hananel, and the Tower of the Hundred, to the Sheep Gate. They stopped at the Gate of the Guard. ⁴⁰ The two thanksgiving processions stood in the house of God. So did I and half of the officials accompanying me, ⁴¹ as well as the priests:

Eliakim, Maaseiah,
   Miniamin,
Micaiah, Elioenai, Zechariah,
   and Hananiah,
   with trumpets;
⁴²   and Maaseiah, Shemaiah,
   Eleazar,
   Uzzi, Jehohanan, Malchijah,
   Elam, and Ezer.

Then the singers sang, with Jezrahiah as the leader. ⁴³ On that day they offered great sacrifices and rejoiced because God had given them great joy. The women and children also celebrated, and Jerusalem's rejoicing was heard far away.

Support of the Levites' Ministry

⁴⁴ On that same day men were placed in charge of the rooms that housed the supplies, contributions, firstfruits, and tenths. The legally required portions for the priests and Levites were gathered from the village fields, because Judah was grateful to the priests and Levites who were serving. ⁴⁵ They performed the service of their God and the service of purification, along with the singers and gatekeepers, as David and his son Solomon had prescribed. ⁴⁶ For long ago, in the days of David and Asaph, there were heads ᴬ of the singers and songs of praise and thanksgiving to God. ⁴⁷ So in the days of Zerubbabel and Nehemiah, all Israel contributed the daily portions for the singers and gatekeepers. They also set aside daily portions for the Levites, and the Levites set aside daily portions for Aaron's descendants.   Dt 18:8; Neh 10:37-39; 13:4,13

Nehemiah's Further Reforms

13 At that time the book of Moses was read publicly to ᴮ the people. The command was found written in it that no Ammonite or Moabite should ever enter the assembly of God, ² because they did not meet the Israelites with food and water. Instead, they hired Balaam against them to curse them, but our God turned the curse into a blessing. ³ When they heard the law, they separated all those of mixed descent from Israel.   Dt 28:61; Neh 12:27

⁴ Now before this, the priest Eliashib had been put in charge of the storerooms of the house of our God. He was a relative ᶜ of Tobiah ⁵ and had prepared a large room for him where they had previously stored the grain offerings, the frankincense, the articles, and the tenths of grain, new wine, and fresh oil prescribed for the Levites, singers, and gatekeepers, along with the contributions for the priests.

⁶ While all this was happening, I was not in Jerusalem, because I had returned to King Artaxerxes of Babylon in the thirty-second year of his reign. It was only later that I asked the king for a leave of absence ⁷ so I could return to Jerusalem. Then I discovered the

---

ᴬ12:46 Alt Hb tradition reads *there was a head*   ᴮ13:1 Lit *read in the ears of*   ᶜ13:4 Or *an associate* evil that Eliashib had done on behalf of Tobiah by providing him a room in the courts of God's house. ⁸ I was greatly displeased and threw all of Tobiah's household possessions out of the room. ⁹ I ordered that the rooms be purified, and I had the articles of the house of God restored there, along with the grain offering and frankincense. ¹⁰ I also found out that because the portions for the Levites had not been given, each of the Levites and the singers performing the service had gone back to his own field. ¹¹ Therefore, I rebuked the officials, asking, "Why has the house of God been neglected?" I gathered the Levites and singers together and stationed them at their posts. ¹² Then all Judah brought a tenth of the grain, new wine, and fresh oil into the storehouses. ¹³ I appointed as treasurers over the storehouses the priest Shelemiah, the scribe Zadok, and Pedaiah of the Levites, with Hanan son of Zaccur, son of Mattaniah to assist them, because they were considered trustworthy. They were responsible for the distribution to their colleagues.   Ezr 5:13; Neh 2:1-8

¹⁴ Remember me for this, my God, and don't erase the deeds of faithful love I have done for the house of my God and for its services.

¹⁵ At that time I saw people in Judah treading winepresses on the Sabbath. They were also bringing in stores of grain and loading them on donkeys, along with wine, grapes, and figs. All kinds of goods were being brought to Jerusalem on the Sabbath day. So I warned them against selling food on that day. ¹⁶ The Tyrians living there were importing fish and all kinds of merchandise and selling them on the Sabbath to the people of Judah in Jerusalem.   Ex 20:8-11; Dt 5:12-15; Neh 10:31

¹⁷ I rebuked the nobles of Judah and said to them: "What is this evil you are doing — profaning the Sabbath day? ¹⁸ Didn't your ancestors do the same, so that our God brought all this disaster on us and on this city? And now you are rekindling his anger against Israel by profaning the Sabbath!"

¹⁹ When shadows began to fall on the city gates of Jerusalem just before the Sabbath, I gave orders that the city gates be closed and not opened until after the Sabbath. I posted some of my men at the gates, so that no goods could enter during the Sabbath day. ²⁰ Once or twice the merchants and those who sell all kinds of goods camped outside Jerusalem, ²¹ but I warned them, "Why are you camping in front of the wall? If you do it again, I'll use force^A against you." After that they did not come again on the Sabbath. ²² Then I instructed the Levites to purify themselves and guard the city gates in order to keep the Sabbath day holy.   Lv 23:32; Neh 7:1,3; Jr 17:21-22

Remember me for this also, my God, and look on me with compassion according to the abundance of your faithful love.   Neh 5:19; 13:14,31

²³ In those days I also saw Jews who had married women from Ashdod, Ammon, and Moab. ²⁴ Half of their children spoke the language of Ashdod or the language of one of the other peoples but could not speak Hebrew. ^B ²⁵ I rebuked them, cursed them, beat some of their men, and pulled out their hair. I forced them to take

---

^A 13:21 Lit *again, I will send a hand*   ^B 13:24 Lit *Judahite* an oath before God and said, "You must not give your daughters in marriage to their sons or take their daughters as wives for your sons or yourselves! ²⁶ Didn't King Solomon of Israel sin in matters like this? There was not a king like him among many nations. He was loved by his God, and God made him king over all Israel, yet foreign women drew him into sin. ²⁷ Why then should we hear about you doing all this terrible evil and acting unfaithfully against our God by marrying foreign women?" ²⁸ Even one of the sons of Jehoiada, son of the high priest Eliashib, had become a son-in-law to Sanballat the Horonite. So I drove him away from me.   Ezr 9:1-2; Neh 10:30

²⁹ Remember them, my God, for defiling the priesthood as well as the covenant of the priesthood and the Levites.   Neh 6:14; Mal 2:4-8

³⁰ So I purified them from everything foreign and assigned specific duties to each of the priests and Levites. ³¹ I also arranged for the donation of wood at the appointed times and for the firstfruits.

Remember me, my God, with favor.   Neh 5:19; 13:14,22

ESTHER

Vashti Angers the King

1 These events took place during the days of Ahasuerus, who ruled 127 provinces from India to Cush. ² In those days King Ahasuerus reigned from his royal throne in the fortress at Susa. ³ He held a feast in the third year of his reign for all his officials and staff, the army of Persia and Media, the nobles, and the officials from the provinces. ⁴ He displayed the glorious wealth of his kingdom and the magnificent splendor of his greatness for a total of 180 days. Ezr 4:6

⁵ At the end of this time, the king held a week-long banquet in the garden courtyard of the royal palace for all the people, from the greatest to the least, who were present in the fortress of Susa. ⁶ White and violet linen hangings were fastened with fine white and purple linen cords to silver rods on marble^A columns. Gold and silver couches were arranged on a mosaic pavement of red feldspar,^B marble, mother-of-pearl, and precious stones. 2Kg 21:18

⁷ Drinks were served in an array of gold goblets, each with a different design. Royal wine flowed freely, according to the king's bounty. ⁸ The drinking was according to royal decree: "There are no restrictions." The king had ordered every wine steward in his household to serve whatever each person wanted. ⁹ Queen Vashti also gave a feast for the women of King Ahasuerus's palace.

¹⁰ On the seventh day, when the king was feeling good from the wine, Ahasuerus commanded Mehuman, Biztha, Harbona, Bigtha, Abagtha, Zethar, and Carkas — the seven eunuchs who personally served him — ¹¹ to bring Queen Vashti before him with her royal crown. He wanted to show off her beauty to the people and the officials, because she was very beautiful. ¹² But Queen Vashti refused to come at the king's command that was delivered by his eunuchs. The king became furious and his anger burned within him. 2Sm 13:28; Est 7:9

The King's Decree

¹³ The king consulted the wise men who understood the times,^C for it was his normal procedure to confer with experts in law and justice. ¹⁴ The most trusted ones^D were Carshena, Shethar, Admatha, Tarshish, Meres, Marsena, and Memucan. They were the seven officials of Persia and Media who had personal access to the king and occupied the highest positions in the kingdom. ¹⁵ The king asked, "According to the law, what should be done with Queen Vashti, since she refused to obey King Ahasuerus's command that was delivered by the eunuchs?" 1Ch 12:32; Jr 10:7; Dn 2:2,12; Mt 2:1

¹⁶ Memucan said in the presence of the king and his officials, "Queen Vashti has wronged not only the king, but all the officials and the peoples who are in every one of King Ahasuerus's provinces. ¹⁷ For the queen's action will become public knowledge to all the women

^A 1:6 Or *alabaster*   ^B 1:6 Or *of porphyry*   ^C 1:13 Or *understood propitious times*   ^D 1:14 Lit *Those near him* and cause them to despise their husbands and say, 'King Ahasuerus ordered Queen Vashti brought before him, but she did not come.' ¹⁸ Before this day is over, the noble women of Persia and Media who hear about the queen's act will say the same thing to all the king's officials, resulting in more contempt and fury. Est 1:1,3,5; 9:30

¹⁹ "If it meets the king's approval, he should personally issue a royal decree. Let it be recorded in the laws of Persia and Media, so that it cannot be revoked: Vashti is not to enter King Ahasuerus's presence, and her royal position is to be given to another woman who is more worthy than she. ²⁰ The decree the king issues will be heard throughout his vast kingdom, so all women will honor their husbands, from the greatest to the least." Est 1:1; 8:8

²¹ The king and his counselors approved the proposal, and he followed Memucan's advice. ²² He sent letters to all the royal provinces, to each province in its own script and to each ethnic group in its own language, that every man should be master of his own house and speak in the language of his own people.

The Search for a New Queen

2 Some time later, when King Ahasuerus's rage had cooled down, he remembered Vashti, what she had done, and what was decided against her. ² The king's personal attendants suggested, "Let a search be made for beautiful young virgins for the king. ³ Let the king appoint commissioners in each province of his kingdom, so that they may gather all the beautiful young virgins to the harem at the fortress of Susa.

Put them under the supervision of Hegai, the king's eunuch, keeper of the women, and give them the required beauty treatments. ⁴ Then the young woman who pleases the king will become queen instead of Vashti." This suggestion pleased the king, and he did accordingly.

⁵ In the fortress of Susa, there was a Jewish man named Mordecai son of Jair, son of Shimei, son of Kish, a Benjaminite. ⁶ He had been taken into exile from Jerusalem with the other captives when King Nebuchadnezzar of Babylon took King Jeconiah of Judah into exile. ⁷ Mordecai was the legal guardian of his cousin ^A Hadassah (that is, Esther), because she had no father or mother. The young woman had a beautiful figure and was extremely good-looking. When her father and mother died, Mordecai had adopted her as his own daughter. Ezr 2:2

⁸ When the king's command and edict became public knowledge and when many young women were gathered at the fortress of Susa under Hegai's supervision, Esther was taken to the palace, into the supervision of Hegai, keeper of the women. ⁹ The young woman pleased him and gained his favor so that he accelerated the process of the beauty treatments and the special diet that she received. He assigned seven hand-picked female servants to her from the palace and transferred her and her servants to the harem's best quarters.

¹⁰ Esther did not reveal her ethnicity or her family background, because Mordecai had ordered her not to make them known. ¹¹ Every day Mordecai took a walk in front of the harem's courtyard to learn

^A**2:7** Lit *uncle's daughter*

how Esther was doing and to see what was happening to her.

¹² During the year before each young woman's turn to go to King Ahasuerus, the harem regulation required her to receive beauty treatments with oil of myrrh for six months and then with perfumes and cosmetics for another six months. ¹³ When the young woman would go to the king, she was given whatever she requested to take with her from the harem to the palace. ¹⁴ She would go in the evening, and in the morning she would return to a second harem under the supervision of the king's eunuch Shaashgaz, keeper of the concubines. She never went to the king again, unless he desired her and summoned her by name.   1Kg 11:3; Est 4:11; Dn 5:2

Esther Becomes Queen

¹⁵ Esther was the daughter of Abihail, the uncle of Mordecai who had adopted her as his own daughter. When her turn came to go to the king, she did not ask for anything except what Hegai, the king's eunuch, keeper of the women, suggested. Esther gained favor in the eyes of everyone who saw her.

¹⁶ She was taken to King Ahasuerus in the palace in the tenth month, the month Tebeth, in the seventh year of his reign. ¹⁷ The king loved Esther more than all the other women. She won more favor and approval from him than did any of the other virgins. He placed the royal crown on her head and made her queen in place of Vashti. ¹⁸ The king held a great banquet for all his officials and staff. It was Esther's banquet. He freed his provinces from tax payments and gave gifts worthy of the king's bounty.   Est 1:2-3,7,10-11; 2:4

Mordecai Saves the King

¹⁹ When the virgins were gathered a second time, Mordecai was sitting at the King's Gate. ²⁰ (Esther had not revealed her family background or her ethnicity, as Mordecai had directed. She obeyed Mordecai's orders, as she always had while he raised her.)   Est 2:12-14; 5:13

²¹ During those days while Mordecai was sitting at the King's Gate, Bigthan and Teresh, two of the king's eunuchs who guarded the entrance, became infuriated and planned to assassinate ᴬ King Ahasuerus. ²² When Mordecai learned of the plot, he reported it to Queen Esther, and she told the king on Mordecai's behalf. ²³ When the report was investigated and verified, both men were hanged on the gallows. This event was recorded in the Historical Record in the king's presence.   Gn 40:19,22; Est 1:10,12; 2:3,14; 6:2-3

Haman's Plan to Kill the Jews

3 After all this took place, King Ahasuerus honored Haman, son of Hammedatha the Agagite. He promoted him in rank and gave him a higher position than all the other officials. ² The entire royal staff at the King's Gate bowed down and paid homage to Haman, because the king had commanded this to be done for him. But Mordecai would not bow down or pay homage. ³ The members of the royal staff at the King's Gate asked Mordecai, "Why are you disobeying the king's command?" ⁴ When they had warned him day after day and he

ᴬ2:21 Lit and they sought to stretch out a hand against

still would not listen to them, they told Haman in order to see if Mordecai's actions would be tolerated, since he had told them he was a Jew. ⁵ When Haman saw that Mordecai was not bowing down or paying him homage, he was filled with rage. ⁶ And when he learned of Mordecai's ethnic identity, it seemed repugnant to Haman to do away with ᴬ Mordecai alone. He planned to destroy all of Mordecai's people, the Jews, throughout Ahasuerus's kingdom.

⁷ In the first month, the month of Nisan, in King Ahasuerus's twelfth year, the Pur — that is, the lot — was cast before Haman for each day in each month, and it fell on the twelfth month, the month Adar. ⁸ Then Haman informed King Ahasuerus, "There is one ethnic group, scattered throughout the peoples in every province of your kingdom, keeping themselves separate. Their laws are different from everyone else's and they do not obey the king's laws. It is not in the king's best interest to tolerate them. ⁹ If the king approves, let an order be drawn up authorizing their destruction, and I will pay 375 tons of silver to ᴮ the officials for deposit in the royal treasury." Est 1:1-2; 2:16

¹⁰ The king removed his signet ring from his finger and gave it to Haman son of Hammedatha the Agagite, the enemy of the Jewish people. ¹¹ Then the king told Haman, "The money and people are given to you to do with as you see fit."

¹² The royal scribes were summoned on the thirteenth day of the first month, and the order was written exactly as Haman commanded. It was intended for the royal satraps, the governors of each of the provinces, and the officials of each ethnic group and written for each province in its own script and to each ethnic group in its own language. It was written in the name of King Ahasuerus and sealed with the royal signet ring. ¹³ Letters were sent by couriers to each of the royal provinces telling the officials to destroy, kill, and annihilate all the Jewish people — young and old, women and children — and plunder their possessions on a single day, the thirteenth day of Adar, the twelfth month. ᶜ Ezr 8:36; Est 1:22; 8:9

¹⁴ A copy of the text, issued as law throughout every province, was distributed to all the peoples so that they might get ready for that day. ¹⁵ The couriers left, spurred on by royal command, and the law was issued in the fortress of Susa. The king and Haman sat down to drink, while the city of Susa was in confusion. Est 7:1; 8:13-15

Mordecai Appeals to Esther

4 When Mordecai learned all that had occurred, he tore his clothes, put on sackcloth and ashes, went into the middle of the city, and cried loudly and bitterly. ² He went only as far as the King's Gate, since the law prohibited anyone wearing sackcloth from entering the King's Gate. ³ There was great mourning among the Jewish people in every province where the king's command and edict came. They fasted, wept, and lamented, and many lay in sackcloth and ashes.

⁴ Esther's female servants and her eunuchs came and reported

ᴬ3:6 Lit *to stretch out a hand against*   ᴮ3:9 Lit *will weigh 10,000 silver talents on the hands of*
ᶜ3:13 LXX adds the text of Ahasuerus's letter here.

the news to her, and the queen was overcome with fear. She sent clothes for Mordecai to wear so that he would take off his sackcloth, but he did not accept them. [5] Esther summoned Hathach, one of the king's eunuchs who attended her, and dispatched him to Mordecai to learn what he was doing and why. [A] [6] So Hathach went out to Mordecai in the city square in front of the King's Gate. [7] Mordecai told him everything that had happened as well as the exact amount of money Haman had promised to pay the royal treasury for the slaughter of the Jews. Est 3:9-15; 7:6

[8] Mordecai also gave him a copy of the written decree issued in Susa ordering their destruction, so that Hathach might show it to Esther, explain it to her, and command her to approach the king, implore his favor, and plead with him personally for her people. [9] Hathach came and repeated Mordecai's response to Esther. Est 7:3-4

[10] Esther spoke to Hathach and commanded him to tell Mordecai, [11] "All the royal officials and the people of the royal provinces know that one law applies to every man or woman who approaches the king in the inner courtyard and who has not been summoned — the death penalty — unless the king extends the gold scepter, allowing that person to live. I have not been summoned to appear before the king for the last [B] thirty days." [12] Esther's response was reported to Mordecai. Est 5:1; Dn 2:9,12-13

[13] Mordecai told the messenger to reply to Esther, "Don't think that you will escape the fate of all the Jews because you are in the king's palace. [14] If you keep silent at this time, relief and deliverance will come to the Jewish people from another place, but you and your father's family will be destroyed. Who knows, perhaps you have come to your royal position for such a time as this." Gn 45:5-7; 50:20

[15] Esther sent this reply to Mordecai: [16] "Go and assemble all the Jews who can be found in Susa and fast for me. Don't eat or drink for three days, night or day. I and my female servants will also fast in the same way. After that, I will go to the king even if it is against the law. If I perish, I perish." [17] So Mordecai went and did everything Esther had commanded him. Est 5:1

Esther Approaches the King

5 On the third day, Esther dressed in her royal clothing and stood in the inner courtyard of the palace facing it. The king was sitting on his royal throne in the royal courtroom, [C] facing its entrance. [2] As soon as the king saw Queen Esther standing in the courtyard, she gained favor in his eyes. The king extended the gold scepter in his hand toward Esther, and she approached and touched the tip of the scepter. Est 8:4

[3] "What is it, Queen Esther?" the king asked her. "Whatever you want, even to half the kingdom, will be given to you." Est 7:2; Mk 6:23

[4] "If it pleases the king," Esther replied, "may the king and Haman come today to the banquet I have prepared for them." Est 1:3,5; 2:18

[5] The king said, "Hurry, and get Haman so we can do as Esther has requested." So the king and Haman went to the banquet Esther had prepared.

[A] **4:5** Lit *what is this and why is this*   [B] **4:11** Lit *king these*   [C] **5:1** Lit *house*

⁶ While drinking the ᴬ wine, the king asked Esther, "Whatever you ask will be given to you. Whatever you want, even to half the kingdom, will be done." Est 1:7-8,10; 7:1-2

⁷ Esther answered, "This is my petition and my request: ⁸ If I have found favor in the eyes of the king, and if it pleases the king to grant my petition and perform my request, may the king and Haman come to the banquet I will prepare for them. Tomorrow I will do what the king has asked." Est 6:14; 7:3; 8:5

⁹ That day Haman left full of joy and in good spirits. ᴮ But when Haman saw Mordecai at the King's Gate, and Mordecai didn't rise or tremble in fear at his presence, Haman was filled with rage toward Mordecai. ¹⁰ Yet Haman controlled himself and went home. He sent for his friends and his wife Zeresh to join him. ¹¹ Then Haman described for them his glorious wealth and his many sons. He told them all how the king had honored him and promoted him in rank over the other officials and the royal staff. ¹² "What's more," Haman added, "Queen Esther invited no one but me to join the king at the banquet she had prepared. I am invited again tomorrow to join her with the king. ¹³ Still, none of this satisfies me since I see Mordecai the Jew sitting at the King's Gate all the time." 1Kg 8:66; 2Ch 7:10; Pr 15:15

¹⁴ His wife Zeresh and all his friends told him, "Have them build a gallows seventy-five feet ᶜ tall. Ask the king in the morning to hang Mordecai on it. Then go to the banquet with the king and enjoy yourself." The advice pleased Haman, so he had the gallows constructed.

Mordecai Honored by the King

6 That night sleep escaped the king, so he ordered the book recording daily events to be brought and read to the king. ² They found the written report of how Mordecai had informed on Bigthana and Teresh, two of the king's eunuchs who guarded the entrance, when they planned to assassinate King Ahasuerus. ³ The king inquired, "What honor and special recognition have been given to Mordecai for this act?" Est 2:21-23; Dn 6:18

The king's personal attendants replied, "Nothing has been done for him."

⁴ The king asked, "Who is in the court?" Now Haman was just entering the outer court of the palace to ask the king to hang Mordecai on the gallows he had prepared for him. Est 5:14

⁵ The king's attendants answered him, "Haman is there, standing in the court."

"Have him enter," the king ordered. ⁶ Haman entered, and the king asked him, "What should be done for the man the king wants to honor?" Est 3:8-9

Haman thought to himself, "Who is it the king would want to honor more than me?" ⁷ Haman told the king, "For the man the king wants to honor: ⁸ Have them bring a royal garment that the king himself has worn and a horse the king himself has ridden, which has a royal crown on its head. ⁹ Put the garment and the horse under the charge of one of the king's most noble officials. Have them clothe the man the king wants to honor, parade him on the horse through the city square, and proclaim before

---

ᴬ **5:6** Lit *During the banquet of*   ᴮ **5:9** Lit *left rejoicing and good of heart*   ᶜ **5:14** Lit *50 cubits* him, 'This is what is done for the man the king wants to honor.'"

¹⁰ The king told Haman, "Hurry, and do just as you proposed. Take a garment and a horse for Mordecai the Jew, who is sitting at the King's Gate. Do not leave out anything you have suggested."   Est 3:6

¹¹ So Haman took the garment and the horse. He clothed Mordecai and paraded him through the city square, crying out before him, "This is what is done for the man the king wants to honor."

¹² Then Mordecai returned to the King's Gate, but Haman hurried off for home, mournful and with his head covered. ¹³ Haman told his wife Zeresh and all his friends everything that had happened. His advisers and his wife Zeresh said to him, "Since Mordecai is Jewish, and you have begun to fall before him, you won't overcome him, because your downfall is certain." ¹⁴ While they were still speaking with him, the king's eunuchs arrived and rushed Haman to the banquet Esther had prepared.   2Sm 15:30; Est 5:9,13

Haman Is Executed

7 The king and Haman came to feast ᴬ with Esther the queen. ² Once again, on the second day while drinking wine, the king asked Esther, "Queen Esther, whatever you ask will be given to you. Whatever you seek, even to half the kingdom, will be done."

³ Queen Esther answered, "If I have found favor in your eyes, Your Majesty, and if the king is pleased, spare my life; this is my request. And spare my people; this is my desire. ⁴ For my people and I have been sold to destruction, death, and extermination. If we had merely been sold as male and female slaves, I would have kept silent. Indeed, the trouble wouldn't be worth burdening the king."

⁵ King Ahasuerus spoke up and asked Queen Esther, "Who is this, and where is the one who would devise such a scheme? " ᴮ   Est 3:5-6,8-9

⁶ Esther answered, "The adversary and enemy is this evil Haman."

Haman stood terrified before the king and queen. ⁷ The king arose in anger and went from where they were drinking wine to the palace garden. ᶜ Haman remained to beg Queen Esther for his life because he realized the king was planning something terrible for him. ⁸ Just as the king returned from the palace garden to the banquet hall, ᴰ Haman was falling on the couch where Esther was reclining. The king exclaimed, "Would he actually violate the queen while I am in the house?" As soon as the statement left the king's mouth, they covered Haman's face.   Est 1:6,12; 4:4; Pr 20:2

⁹ Harbona, one of the king's eunuchs, said: "There is a gallows seventy-five feet ᴱ tall at Haman's house that he made for Mordecai, who gave the report that saved ᶠ the king."   Est 1:12; 2:21-23; 5:14; 6:1-2

The king said, "Hang him on it."

¹⁰ They hanged Haman on the gallows he had prepared for Mordecai. Then the king's anger subsided.

Esther Intervenes for the Jews

8 That same day King Ahasuerus awarded Queen Esther the estate of Haman, the enemy of the Jews. Mordecai entered the king's

---

ᴬ **7:1** Lit *drink*   ᴮ **7:5** Lit *who would fill his heart to do this*   ᶜ **7:7** Lit *the garden of the house,* also in v. 8
ᴰ **7:8** Or *the house of wine*   ᴱ **7:9** Lit *50 cubits*   ᶠ **7:9** Lit *who spoke good for*

presence because Esther had revealed her relationship to Mordecai. ² The king removed his signet ring he had recovered from Haman and gave it to Mordecai, and Esther put him in charge of Haman's estate. Est 2:7,10; 3:9-10,12; 5:11; 7:6

³ Then Esther addressed the king again. She fell at his feet, wept, and begged him to revoke the evil of Haman the Agagite and his plot he had devised against the Jews. ⁴ The king extended the gold scepter toward Esther, so she got up and stood before the king. Est 7:3-4,6

⁵ She said, "If it pleases the king and I have found favor before him, if the matter seems right to the king and I am pleasing in his eyes, let a royal edict be written. Let it revoke the documents the scheming Haman son of Hammedatha the Agagite wrote to destroy the Jews who are in all the king's provinces. ⁶ For how could I bear to see the disaster that would come on my people? How could I bear to see the destruction of my relatives?"

⁷ King Ahasuerus said to Esther the queen and to Mordecai the Jew, "Look, I have given Haman's estate to Esther, and he was hanged on the gallows because he attacked^A the Jews. ⁸ Write in the king's name whatever pleases you concerning the Jews, and seal it with the royal signet ring. A document written in the king's name and sealed with the royal signet ring cannot be revoked." Est 3:9,11; 5:11; 8:1; Pr 13:22

⁹ On the twenty-third day of the third month — that is, the month Sivan — the royal scribes were summoned. Everything was written exactly as Mordecai commanded for the Jews, to the satraps, the governors, and the officials of the 127 provinces from India to Cush. The edict was written for each province in its own script, for each ethnic group in its own language, and to the Jews in their own script and language. Ezr 8:36; Est 3:7,12

¹⁰ Mordecai wrote in King Ahasuerus's name and sealed the edicts with the royal signet ring. He sent the documents by mounted couriers, who rode fast horses bred in the royal stables. 1Kg 4:26,28; Est 3:12-13

¹¹ The king's edict gave the Jews in each and every city the right to assemble and defend themselves, to destroy, kill, and annihilate every ethnic and provincial army hostile to them, including women and children, and to take their possessions as spoils of war. ¹² This would take place on a single day throughout all the provinces of King Ahasuerus, on the thirteenth day of the twelfth month, the month Adar.

¹³ A copy of the text, issued as law throughout every province, was distributed to all the peoples so the Jews could be ready to avenge themselves against their enemies on that day. ¹⁴ The couriers rode out in haste on their royal horses at the king's urgent command. The law was also issued in the fortress of Susa. Est 3:14-15

¹⁵ Mordecai went from the king's presence clothed in royal purple and white, with a great gold crown and a purple robe of fine linen. The city of Susa shouted and rejoiced, ¹⁶ and the Jews celebrated^B with gladness, joy, and honor. ¹⁷ In every province and every city, wherever the king's command and his law reached, joy and rejoicing took place among the Jews. There was

^A 8:7 Lit *stretched out his hand against*   ^B 8:16 Lit *had light* a celebration and a holiday.^A And many of the ethnic groups of the land professed themselves to be Jews because fear of the Jews had overcome them. Gn 41:42; Est 5:11; Dn 5:29

Victories of the Jews

9 The king's command and law went into effect on the thirteenth day of the twelfth month, the month Adar. On the day when the Jews' enemies had hoped to overpower them, just the opposite happened. The Jews overpowered those who hated them. ² In each of King Ahasuerus's provinces the Jews assembled in their cities to attack those who intended to harm them.^B Not a single person could withstand them; fear of them fell on every nationality.   Est 3:7; 8:7-8,10

³ All the officials of the provinces, the satraps, the governors, and the royal civil administrators^C aided the Jews because they feared Mordecai. ⁴ For Mordecai exercised great power in the palace, and his fame spread throughout the provinces as he became more and more powerful.   Est 3:12; 8:9,17; 10:2-3

⁵ The Jews put all their enemies to the sword, killing and destroying them. They did what they pleased to those who hated them. ⁶ In the fortress of Susa the Jews killed and destroyed five hundred men, ⁷ including Parshandatha, Dalphon, Aspatha, ⁸ Poratha, Adalia, Aridatha, ⁹ Parmashta, Arisai, Aridai, and Vaizatha. ¹⁰ They killed these ten sons of Haman son of Hammedatha, the enemy of the Jews. However, they did not seize^D any plunder.   Est 1:2; 3:13,15; 5:11; 7:6; 8:14

¹¹ On that day the number of people killed in the fortress of Susa was reported to the king. ¹² The king said to Queen Esther, "In the fortress of Susa the Jews have killed and destroyed five hundred men, including Haman's ten sons. What have they done in the rest of the royal provinces? Whatever you ask will be given to you. Whatever you seek will also be done."   Est 5:6; 7:2; 8:8

¹³ Esther answered, "If it pleases the king, may the Jews who are in Susa also have tomorrow to carry out today's law, and may the bodies of Haman's ten sons be hung on the gallows." ¹⁴ The king gave the orders for this to be done, so a law was announced in Susa, and they hung the bodies of Haman's ten sons. ¹⁵ The Jews in Susa assembled again on the fourteenth day of the month of Adar and killed three hundred men in Susa, but they did not seize any plunder.   Est 8:12; 9:1

¹⁶ The rest of the Jews in the royal provinces assembled, defended themselves, and gained relief from their enemies. They killed seventy-five thousand^E of those who hated them, but they did not seize any plunder. ¹⁷ They fought on the thirteenth day of the month of Adar and rested on the fourteenth, and it became a day of feasting and rejoicing.   Lv 26:7-8; Est 9:5

¹⁸ But the Jews in Susa had assembled on the thirteenth and the fourteenth days of the month. They rested on the fifteenth day of the month, and it became a day of feasting and rejoicing. ¹⁹ This explains why the rural Jews who live in villages observe the fourteenth day

---

^A **8:17** Lit good day   ^B **9:2** Lit cities to send out a hand against the seekers of their evil   ^C **9:3** Lit and those who do the king's work ; Est 3:9   ^D **9:10** Lit not put their hands on, also in vv. 15,16   ^E **9:16** Some LXX mss read 10,107 ; other LXX mss read 15,000 of the month of Adar as a time of rejoicing and feasting. It is a holiday when they send gifts to one another. Est 8:16-17; 9:22; Neh 8:10,12

20 Mordecai recorded these events and sent letters to all the Jews in all of King Ahasuerus's provinces, both near and far. 21 He ordered them to celebrate the fourteenth and fifteenth days of the month of Adar every year 22 because during those days the Jews gained relief from their enemies. That was the month when their sorrow was turned into rejoicing and their mourning into a holiday. They were to be days of feasting, rejoicing, and of sending gifts to one another and to the poor. 23 So the Jews agreed to continue the practice they had begun, as Mordecai had written them to do. 24 For Haman son of Hammedatha the Agagite, the enemy of all the Jews, had plotted against the Jews to destroy them. He cast the Pur — that is, the lot — to crush and destroy them. 25 But when the matter was brought before the king, he commanded by letter that the evil plan Haman had devised against the Jews return on his own head and that he should be hanged with his sons on the gallows. 26 For this reason these days are called Purim, from the word Pur. Because of all the instructions in this letter as well as what they had witnessed and what had happened to them, 27 the Jews bound themselves, their descendants, and all who joined with them to a commitment that they would not fail to celebrate these two days each and every year according to the written instructions and according to the time appointed. 28 These days are remembered and celebrated by every generation, family, province, and city, so that these days of Purim will not lose their significance in Jewish life A and their memory will not fade from their descendants.

29 Queen Esther, daughter of Abihail, along with Mordecai the Jew, wrote this second letter with full authority to confirm the letter about Purim. 30 He sent letters with assurances of peace and security B to all the Jews who were in the 127 provinces of the kingdom of Ahasuerus, 31 in order to confirm these days of Purim at their proper time just as Mordecai the Jew and Esther the queen had established them and just as they had committed themselves and their descendants to the practices of fasting and lamentation. 32 So Esther's command confirmed these customs of Purim, which were then written into the record. Est 2:7,15; 5:13

Mordecai's Fame

10 King Ahasuerus imposed a tax throughout the land even to the farthest shores. C 2 All of his powerful and magnificent accomplishments and the detailed account of Mordecai's great rank with which the king had honored him, have they not been written in the Book of the Historical Events of the Kings of Media and Persia? 3 Mordecai the Jew was second only to King Ahasuerus. He was famous among the Jews and highly esteemed by many of his relatives. He continued to pursue prosperity for his people and to speak for the well-being of all his descendants.

A 9:28 LXX reads *will be celebrated into all times*   B 9:30 Or *of peace and faithfulness*   C 10:1 Or *imposed forced labor on the land and the coasts of the sea*

JOB

Job and His Family

1 There was a man in the country of Uz named Job. He was a man of complete integrity, who feared God and turned away from evil. ² He had seven sons and three daughters. ³ His estate included seven thousand sheep and goats, three thousand camels, five hundred yoke of oxen, five hundred female donkeys, and a very large number of servants. Job was the greatest man among all the people of the east. Jr 25:20; Lm 4:21; Ezk 14:14,20

⁴ His sons used to take turns having banquets at their homes. They would send an invitation to their three sisters to eat and drink with them. ⁵ Whenever a round of banqueting was over, Job would send for his children and purify them, rising early in the morning to offer burnt offerings forᴬ all of them. For Job thought, "Perhaps my children have sinned, having cursed God in their hearts." This was Job's regular practice. Jb 42:8

Satan's First Test of Job

⁶ One day the sons of God came to present themselves before the LORD, and Satanᴮ also came with them. ⁷ The LORD asked Satan, "Where have you come from?"

"From roaming through the earth," Satan answered him, "and walking around on it." 1Pt 5:8

⁸ Then the LORD said to Satan, "Have you considered my servant Job? No one else on earth is like him, a man of perfect integrity,

who fears God and turns away from evil." Jb 28:28; Ps 25:21; Pr 3:7; 29:10

⁹ Satan answered the LORD, "Does Job fear God for nothing? ¹⁰ Haven't you placed a hedge around him, his household, and everything he owns? You have blessed the work of his hands, and his possessions have increased in the land. ¹¹ But stretch out your hand and strike everything he owns, and he will surely curse you to your face." Jb 2:5; 4:5; 5:19; Ps 34:7

¹² "Very well," the LORD told Satan, "everything he owns is in your power. However, do not lay a hand on Job himself." So Satan left the LORD's presence.

¹³ One day when Job's sons and daughters were eating and drinking wine in their oldest brother's house, ¹⁴ a messenger came to Job and reported: "While the oxen were plowing and the donkeys grazing nearby, ¹⁵ the Sabeans swooped down and took them away. They struck down the servants with the sword, and I alone have escaped to tell you!" Gn 10:7; Jb 6:19; Is 45:14

¹⁶ He was still speaking when another messenger came and reported: "God's fire fell from heaven. It burned the sheep and the servants and devoured them, and I alone have escaped to tell you!" Gn 19:24

¹⁷ That messenger was still speaking when yet another came and reported: "The Chaldeans formed three bands, made a raid on the camels, and took them away. They struck down the servants with the

ᴬ**1:5** Lit *for the number of* ᴮ**1:6** Or *the adversary* sword, and I alone have escaped to tell you!"

¹⁸ He was still speaking when another messenger came and reported: "Your sons and daughters were eating and drinking wine in their oldest brother's house. ¹⁹ Suddenly a powerful wind swept in from the desert and struck the four corners of the house. It collapsed on the young people so that they died, and I alone have escaped to tell you!"

²⁰ Then Job stood up, tore his robe, and shaved his head. He fell to the ground and worshiped, ²¹ saying: Gn 37:29,34; Jos 7:6; Jb 2:12; Jr 7:29; Ezk 7:18

> Naked I came
>   from my mother's womb,
>   and naked I will leave
>   this life.ᴬ Ps 139:13,15
> The LORD gives, and the LORD
>   takes away.
> Blessed be the name of the
>   LORD. Jb 38:1; Ps 113:2; 118:26

²² Throughout all this Job did not sin or blame God for anything.ᴮ

Satan's Second Test of Job

2 One day the sons of God came again to present themselves before the LORD, and Satan also came with them to present himself before the LORD. ² The LORD asked Satan, "Where have you come from?"

"From roaming through the earth," Satan answered him, "and walking around on it."

³ Then the LORD said to Satan, "Have you considered my servant Job? No one else on earth is like him, a man of perfect integrity, who fears God and turns away from evil. He still retains his integrity, even though you incited

me against him, to destroy him for no good reason." Jb 1:1,8; 6:29; 28:28; Pr 3:7

⁴ "Skin for skin!" Satan answered the LORD. "A man will give up everything he owns in exchange for his life. ⁵ But stretch out your hand and strike his flesh and bones, and he will surely curse you to your face." Jb 1:11; 4:5; 19:21

⁶ "Very well," the LORD told Satan, "he is in your power; only spare his life." ⁷ So Satan left the LORD's presence and infected Job with terrible boils from the soles of his feet to the top of his head. ⁸ Then Job took a piece of broken pottery to scrape himself while he sat among the ashes. Dt 28:27,35; 2Sm 13:19; Jb 42:6

⁹ His wife said to him, "Are you still holding on to your integrity? Curse God and die!"

¹⁰ "You speak as a foolish woman speaks," he told her. "Should we accept only good from God and not adversity?" Throughout all this Job did not sin in what he said.ᶜ

Job's Three Friends

¹¹ Now when Job's three friends — Eliphaz the Temanite, Bildad the Shuhite, and Zophar the Naamathite — heard about all this adversity that had happened to him, each of them came from his home. They met together to go and sympathize with him and comfort him. ¹² When they looked from a distance, they could barely recognize him. They wept aloud, and each man tore his robe and threw dust into the air and on his head. ¹³ Then they sat on the ground with him seven days and nights, but no one spoke a word to him because they saw that his suffering was very intense. Gn 36:34; 1Ch 1:45; Jb 8:1; 42:9

ᴬ**1:21** Lit will return there; Ps 139:13,15　ᴮ**1:22** Lit or ascribe blame to God　ᶜ**2:10** Lit sin with his lips

Job's Opening Speech

3 After this, Job began to speak
and cursed the day he was born.
² He said:

³ May the day
    I was born perish,
  and the night that said,
  "A boy is conceived."   Jb 5:7; Is 7:14
⁴ If only that day had turned
    to darkness!
  May God above not care
    about it,
  or light shine on it.
⁵ May darkness and gloom
    reclaim it,   Jb 10:21-22; 12:22; 28:3
  and a cloud settle over it.
  May what darkens the day
    terrify it.
⁶ If only darkness had taken
    that night away!
  May it not appearᴬ
    among the days of the year
  or be listed in the calendar.ᴮ
⁷ Yes, may that night be barren;
  may no joyful shout be heard
    in it.   Jb 20:5; Ps 63:5
⁸ Let those who curse days
    condemn it,   Nm 22:11,17; Jb 5:3
  those who are ready
    to rouse Leviathan.   Jb 41
⁹ May its morning stars
    grow dark.
  May it wait for daylight
    but have none;
  may it not see the breakingᶜ
    of dawn.
¹⁰ For that night did not shut
    the doors
    of my mother's womb,
  and hide sorrow
    from my eyes.

¹¹ Why was I not stillborn;
  why didn't I die as I came
    from the womb?   Jb 1:21; 10:17-18
¹² Why did the knees receive me,

and why were there breasts
  for me to nurse?   Sg 8:1; Is 66:12
¹³ Now I would certainly
    be lying down in peace;
  I would be asleep.   Ps 13:3; Mt 8:24
  Then I would be at rest   Jb 17:16
¹⁴ with the kings
    and counselors
    of the earth,   Is 14:9; Jr 51:57
  who rebuilt ruined cities
    for themselves,
¹⁵ or with princes
    who had gold,
  who filled their houses
    with silver.   Jb 17:13; 30:23; Ec 12:5
¹⁶ Or why was I not hidden
    like a miscarried child,   Ec 6:3
  like infants who never
    see daylight?
¹⁷ There the wicked cease
    to make trouble,   Jb 9:22; 11:20
  and there the weary
    find rest.
¹⁸ The captives are completely
    at rest;   Pr 1:33; Jr 30:10; 46:27
  they do not hear
    a taskmaster's voice.   Ex 3:7
¹⁹ Both small and
    great are there,
  and the slave is set free
    from his master.   Jb 9:22; Ec 9:2-3

²⁰ Why is light given
    to one burdened with grief,
  and life to those
    whose existence is bitter,
²¹ who wait for death,
    but it does not come,   1Kg 19:4
  and search for it more than
    for hidden treasure,
²² who are filled with much joy
  and are glad when they reach
    the grave?   Jb 5:26; 10:19; 17:1
²³ Why is life given to a man
    whose path is hidden,   Jb 19:8
  whom God has hedged in?

ᴬ**3:6** LXX, Syr, Tg, Vg; MT reads *rejoice*   ᴮ**3:6** Lit *or enter the number of months*   ᶜ**3:9** Lit *the eyelids*

²⁴ I sigh when food is put
    before me,ᴬ Jb 6:7; 33:20; Ps 102:4
and my groans pour out
    like water. Ps 6:6; 22:1,14; 32:3
²⁵ For the thing I feared
    has overtaken me,
and what I dreaded
    has happened to me. Jb 9:28
²⁶ I cannot relax or be calm;
I have no rest,
    for turmoil has come. Jb 30:17

FIRST SERIES OF SPEECHES

Eliphaz Speaks

4 Then Eliphaz the Temanite replied:
² Should anyone try to speak
    with you
when you are exhausted?
Yet who can keep
    from speaking?
³ Indeed, you have
    instructed many
and have strengthened
    weak hands. Jb 26:2; Is 35:3
⁴ Your words have steadied
    the one who was stumbling
and braced the knees
    that were buckling. Dt 3:28
⁵ But now that this
    has happened to you,
you have become exhausted.
It strikes you, and you
    are dismayed. Jb 5:19; 6:7; 19:21
⁶ Isn't your piety
    your confidence,
and the integrity of your lifeᴮ
    your hope? Jb 11:18; Ps 119:116
⁷ Consider: Who has perished
    when he was innocent?
Where have the honestᶜ
    been destroyed? Jb 8:20; Ps 37:25
⁸ In my experience,
    those who plow injustice

and those who sow trouble
    reap the same. Jb 5:7; 15:35; Is 59:4
⁹ They perish at a single blast
    from God 2Sm 22:26; Jb 37:10
and come to an end
    by the breath of his nostrils.
¹⁰ The lion may roar and
    the fierce lion growl, Ps 10:9
but the teeth of young lions
    are broken. Jb 29:17; Ps 3:7; 58:6
¹¹ The strong lion dies
    if it catches no prey,
and the cubs of the lioness
    are scattered. Ps 59:11; Pr 20:8,20
¹² A word was brought to me
    in secret;
my ears caught a whisper of it.
¹³ Among unsettling thoughts
    from visions in the night,
when deep sleep comes
    over men, Gn 2:21; 15:12; Jb 33:15
¹⁴ fear and trembling came
    over me Jb 21:6; Ps 55:5; 119:120
and made all my bones shake.
¹⁵ I felt a draftᴰ on my face,
and the hair on my body
    stood up.
¹⁶ A figure stood there,
but I could not recognize
    its appearance;
a form loomed
    before my eyes.
I heard a whispering voice:
¹⁷ "Can a mortal be righteous
    before God?
Can a man be more pure
    than his Maker?" Jb 15:14; 25:4
¹⁸ If God puts no trust
    in his servants
and he charges his angels
    with foolishness,ᴱ Jb 15:15; 21:22
¹⁹ how much more
    those who dwell
    in clay houses, Jb 10:9; 33:6; Is 64:8

ᴬ3:24 Or *My sighing serves as my food*　ᴮ4:6 Lit *ways*　ᶜ4:7 Or *the upright*, or *those with integrity*
ᴰ4:15 Or *a spirit*　ᴱ4:18 Or *error*; Hb obscure

whose foundation is
  in the dust,
who are crushed like a moth!

20 They are smashed to pieces
  from dawn to dusk;
they perish forever
  while no one notices. Jb 14:2

21 Are their tent cords not
  pulled up?
They die without wisdom.

5 Call out! Will anyone
  answer you?
Which of the holy ones
  will you turn to? Jb 15:15; Dn 4:17

2 For anger kills a fool,
and jealousy slays
  the gullible. Pr 12:16; 14:18; 19:19

3 I have seen a fool taking root,
but I immediately
  pronounced a curse
  on his home.

4 His children are far
  from safety.
They are crushed
  at the city gate, Jb 31:21; Pr 22:22
with no one to rescue them.

5 The hungry consume
  his harvest,
even taking it
  out of the thorns. A
The thirsty B pant
  for his children's wealth.

6 For distress does not grow
  out of the soil,
and trouble does not sprout
  from the ground.

7 But humans are born
  for trouble Jb 4:8; 15:35; Is 59:4
as surely as sparks fly upward.

8 However, if I were you,
I would appeal to God
and would present my case
  to him. Jb 13:18; 23:4; Lm 3:59

9 He does great
  and unsearchable things,
wonders without number.

10 He gives rain to the earth
and sends water to the fields.

11 He sets the lowly on high,
and mourners are lifted
  to safety. 1Sm 2:7; Ps 113:6-7; Mt 5:4

12 He frustrates the schemes
  of the crafty
so that they C achieve
  no success.

13 He traps the wise
  in their craftiness
so that the plans
  of the deceptive
are quickly brought
  to an end. Ps 9:15-16; Is 29:14

14 They encounter darkness
  by day,
and they grope at noon
  as if it were night. Dt 28:29; Is 59:10

15 He saves the needy
  from their sharp words D
and from the clutches
  of the powerful.

16 So the poor have hope,
and injustice shuts its mouth.

17 See how happy is
  the person whom
  God corrects;
so do not reject the discipline
  of the Almighty.

18 For he wounds but he also
  bandages;
he strikes, but his hands
  also heal. Dt 32:39; 1Sm 2:6; Hs 6:1

19 He will rescue you
  from six calamities;
no harm will touch you
  in seven.

20 In famine he will redeem you
  from death,
and in battle, from the power
  of the sword. Ps 33:19; 37:19; 144:10

A5:5 Hb obscure B5:5 Aq, Sym, Syr, Vg; MT reads *snares* C5:12 Lit *their hands* D5:15 Lit *from the sword of their mouth*; Ps 55:21; 59:7

²¹ You will be safe from slander^A
   and not fear destruction
      when it comes.   Ps 27:5; 31:20; 91:5
²² You will laugh at destruction
   and hunger
   and not fear the land's wild
      creatures.
²³ For you will have a covenant
   with the stones of the field,
   and the wild animals will be
      at peace with you.   Ps 91:12
²⁴ You will know that your tent
      is secure,   Jb 8:6; 12:6; 21:9
   and nothing will be missing
      when you inspect
      your home.
²⁵ You will also know
      that your offspring
      will be many
   and your descendants
      like the grass of the earth.
²⁶ You will approach the grave
      in full vigor,   Jb 3:22; 10:19; 17:1; 25:8
   as a stack of sheaves
      is gathered in its season.

²⁷ We have investigated this,
      and it is true!
   Hear it and understand it
      for yourself.

Job's Reply to Eliphaz

6 Then Job answered:
² If only my grief
      could be weighed
   and my devastation placed
      with it on the scales.   Jb 30:13
³ For then it would outweigh
      the sand of the seas!
   That is why my words
      are rash.
⁴ Surely the arrows
      of the Almighty
   have pierced^B me;
   my spirit drinks their poison.

God's terrors are arrayed
   against me.   Jb 30:15; Ps 38:2; 88:16
⁵ Does a wild donkey bray
      over fresh grass
   or an ox low over its fodder?
⁶ Is bland food eaten
      without salt?
   Is there flavor
      in an egg white?^C
⁷ I refuse to touch them;
   they are like
      contaminated food.   Jb 3:24

⁸ If only my request
      would be granted
   and God would provide what
      I hope for:
⁹ that he would decide
      to crush me,
   to unleash his power
      and cut me off!
¹⁰ It would still bring me
      comfort,
   and I would leap for joy
      in unrelenting pain
   that I have not denied^D
      the words of the Holy One.

¹¹ What strength do I have,
      that I should continue
      to hope?
   What is my future,
      that I should be patient?
¹² Is my strength that of stone,
   or my flesh made of bronze?
¹³ Since I cannot help myself,
   the hope for success
      has been banished
      from me.

¹⁴ A despairing man
      should receive loyalty
      from his friends,^E   Jb 19:21
   even if he abandons the fear
      of the Almighty.

---

^A**5:21** Lit *be hidden from the whip of the tongue*   ^B**6:4** Lit *Almighty are in*   ^C**6:6** Hb obscure   ^D**6:10** Lit *hidden*   ^E**6:14** Lit *To the despairing his friend loyalty*

¹⁵ My brothers are
   as treacherous as a wadi,
as seasonal streams
   that overflow
¹⁶ and become darkened^A
   because of ice,
and the snow melts into them.
¹⁷ The wadis evaporate
   in warm weather;
they disappear
   from their channels
   in hot weather.
¹⁸ Caravans turn away
   from their routes,
go up into the desert,
   and perish.
¹⁹ The caravans of Tema look
   for these streams.
The traveling merchants
   of Sheba hope for them.
²⁰ They are ashamed because
   they had been confident
   of finding water.
When they arrive there,
   they are disappointed. **Jr 14:3**
²¹ So this is what you have
   now become to me.^B
When you see something
   dreadful, you are afraid.
²² Have I ever said:
   "Give me something"
or "Pay a bribe for me
   from your wealth"
²³ or "Deliver me
   from the enemy's hand"
or "Redeem me from the hand
   of the ruthless"?
²⁴ Teach me, and I will be silent.
Help me understand
   what I did wrong.
²⁵ How painful honest words
   can be!
But what does your rebuke
   prove?

²⁶ Do you think that you
   can disprove my words
or that a despairing
   man's words are
   mere wind? **Jb 8:2; 15:2; 16:3**
²⁷ No doubt you would cast lots
   for a fatherless child
and negotiate a price to sell
   your friend. **Jl 3:3; Nah 3:10; 2Pt 2:3**
²⁸ But now, please look at me;
I will not lie to your face.
²⁹ Reconsider; don't be unjust.
Reconsider;
   my righteousness is still
   the issue. **Jb 2:3**
³⁰ Is there injustice on my tongue
or can my palate
   not taste disaster? **Jb 12:11; 27:4**

7

Isn't each person consigned
   to forced labor on earth?
Are not his days like those
   of a hired worker?
² Like a slave he longs
   for shade;
like a hired worker he waits
   for his pay.
³ So I have been made
   to inherit months of futility,
and troubled nights
   have been assigned to me.
⁴ When I lie down I think,
   "When will I get up?"
But the evening drags
   on endlessly,
and I toss and turn until dawn.
⁵ My flesh is clothed
   with maggots
   and encrusted with dirt.^C
My skin forms scabs^D
   and then oozes. **Dt 28:35; Ps 38:5**
⁶ My days pass more swiftly
   than a weaver's shuttle;

^A**6:16** Or *turbid*   ^B**6:21** Alt Hb tradition reads *So you have now become nothing*   ^C**7:5** Or *and dirty scabs*
^D**7:5** Lit *skin hardens*

they come to an end
  without hope.   Jb 14:19; 17:15; 19:10
7 Remember that my life is
     but a breath.
   My eye will never again see
     anything good.   Jb 9:25; Ps 78:39
8 The eye of anyone who looks
     on me
   will no longer see me.
   Your eyes will look for me,
     but I will be gone.   Jb 7:21; 20:9
9 As a cloud fades away
     and vanishes,
   so the one who goes down
     to Sheol will never
     rise again.   Jb 11:8; 14:13; 17:13,16
10 He will never return
     to his house;
   his hometown will no longer
     remember[A] him.   Jb 8:18; 20:9

11 Therefore I will not restrain
     my mouth.
   I will speak in the anguish
     of my spirit;
   I will complain
     in the bitterness of my soul.
12 Am I the sea[B]
     or a sea monster,   Jb 26:12; Is 27:1
   that you keep me
     under guard?
13 When I say, "My bed
     will comfort me,
   and my couch will ease
     my complaint,"
14 then you frighten me
     with dreams,
   and terrify me with visions,
15 so that I prefer strangling[C]—
   death rather than life
     in this body.[D]   1Kg 19:4; Jb 3:21
16 I give up! I will not
     live forever.
   Leave me alone, for my days
     are a breath.[E]   Jb 7:19; 10:20

17 What is a mere human,
     that you think so highly
     of him
   and pay so much attention
     to him?   Ps 8:4; 144:3; Heb 2:6
18 You inspect him
     every morning,
   and put him to the test
     every moment.   Ps 17:3; 73:14
19 Will you ever look away
     from me,
   or leave me alone
     long enough to swallow?[F]
20 If I have sinned, what have
     I done to you,
   Watcher of humanity?
   Why have you made me
     your target,   Jb 16:12; Lm 3:12
   so that I have become
     a burden to you?[G]
21 Why not forgive my sin
   and pardon my iniquity?
   For soon I will lie down
     in the grave.   Jb 17:16; 20:11; Is 26:19
   You will eagerly seek me,
     but I will be gone.   Jb 3:13; 7:8

Bildad Speaks

8 Then Bildad the Shuhite replied:
   2 How long will you
     go on saying these things?
   Your words are a blast
     of wind.   Jb 6:26; 11:2; Pr 10:19; Ec 5:3
3 Does God pervert justice?
   Does the Almighty pervert
     what is right?   Gn 18:25; Jb 34:17
4 Since your children sinned
     against him,
   he gave them over
     to their rebellion.
5 But if you earnestly
     seek God
   and ask the Almighty
     for mercy,   Jb 9:15; 33:24; Ps 30:8
6 if you are pure and upright,

[A]7:10 Lit know   [B]7:12 Or the sea god   [C]7:15 Or suffocation   [D]7:15 Lit than my bones   [E]7:16 Or are
futile   [F]7:19 Lit swallow my saliva?   [G]7:20 Alt Hb tradition, LXX; MT, Vg read myself

then he will move even now
  on your behalf
and restore the home where
  your righteousness dwells.
⁷ Then, even if your beginnings
  were modest,
your final days will be
  full of prosperity.   Jb 36:11

⁸ For ask the previous
  generation,
and pay attention to what
  their fathers discovered,
⁹ since we were born only
  yesterday and know
  nothing.
Our days on earth are
  but a shadow.   Ps 102:11; 144:4
¹⁰ Will they not teach you
  and tell you
and speak from
  their understanding?
¹¹ Does papyrus grow where
  there is no marsh?
Do reeds flourish
  without water?
¹² While still uncut shoots,
they would dry up quicker
  than any other plant.
¹³ Such is the destiny ᴬ of all
  who forget God;
the hope of the godless
  will perish.   Jb 13:16; 15:34; 27:8
¹⁴ His source of confidence
  is fragile; ᴮ
what he trusts in is
  a spider's web.   Jb 27:18; Is 59:5
¹⁵ He leans on his web,
  but it doesn't stand firm.
He grabs it, but it does not
  hold up.
¹⁶ He is a well-watered plant
  in the sunshine;
his shoots spread out
  over his garden.

¹⁷ His roots are intertwined
  around a pile of rocks.
He looks for a home
  among the stones.
¹⁸ If he is uprooted ᶜ
  from his place,
it will deny knowing him,
  saying, "I never saw you."
¹⁹ Surely this is the joy
  of his way of life;
yet others will sprout
  from the dust.
²⁰ Look, God does not reject
  a person of integrity,
and he will not support ᴰ
  evildoers.   Gn 18:25; Jb 36:6; 2Pt 2:9
²¹ He will yet fill your mouth
  with laughter
and your lips with a shout
  of joy.   Jb 33:26; Ps 27:6; 47:5
²² Your enemies will be clothed
  with shame;   Ps 35:26; 109:29
the tent of the wicked
  will no longer exist.   Jb 18:6,14

Job's Reply to Bildad

9 Then Job answered:
² Yes, I know what you've said
  is true,
but how can a person
  be justified before God?
³ If one wanted to take him
  to court,   Jb 13:19; 33:13; 40:2
he could not answer God ᴱ
  once in a thousand times.
⁴ God is wise and all-powerful.
Who has opposed him
  and come out unharmed?
⁵ He removes mountains
  without their knowledge,
overturning them
  in his anger.   Jdg 5:5; Ps 18:7; Mc 1:4
⁶ He shakes the earth
  from its place
so that its pillars tremble.

ᴬ8:13 Lit *Such are the ways*   ᴮ8:14 Or *cut off*; Hb obscure   ᶜ8:18 Or *destroyed*   ᴰ8:20 Lit *grasp the hand of*   ᴱ9:3 Or *court, God would not answer him*

7 He commands the sun
    not to shine
 and seals off the stars. Is 13:10
8 He alone stretches out
    the heavens   Ps 104:2-3; Is 40:22
 and treads on the waves
    of the sea. A
9 He makes the stars: the Bear, B
    Orion,
 the Pleiades,
    and the constellations C
    of the southern sky. Jb 38:31-32
10 He does great
    and unsearchable things,
    wonders without number.
11 If he passed by me,
    I wouldn't see him;   Jb 23:8-9
 if he went by,
    I wouldn't recognize him.
12 If he snatches something,
    who can stop D him?
 Who can ask him, "What are
    you doing?"   Jb 11:10; Is 45:9
13 God does not hold back
    his anger;
 Rahab's assistants cringe
    in fear beneath him!   Jb 26:12

14 How then can I answer him
 or choose my arguments
    against him?
15 Even if I were in the right,
    I could not answer.
 I could only beg my Judge
    for mercy.   Jb 8:5; 10:15
16 If I summoned him
    and he answered me,
 I do not believe he would
    pay attention to
    what I said.
17 He batters me
    with a whirlwind   Jb 30:22
 and multiplies my wounds
    without cause.

18 He doesn't let me catch
    my breath
 but fills me
    with bitter experiences.
19 If it is a matter
    of strength, look, he is
    the powerful one!   Jb 9:4; Is 28:2
 If it is a matter of justice,
    who can summon him? E
20 Even if I were in the right,
    my own mouth would
    condemn me;   Jb 9:28; 40:8; Is 50:9
 if I were blameless,
    my mouth would
    declare me guilty.

21 Though I am blameless,
 I no longer care
    about myself;
 I renounce my life.   Jb 7:16; 10:1
22 It is all the same. Therefore
    I say,
 "He destroys both
    the blameless
    and the wicked."   Jb 3:19; Ec 9:2-3
23 When catastrophe F brings
    sudden death,
 he mocks the despair
    of the innocent.
24 The earth G is handed over
    to the wicked;
 he blindfolds H its judges.
 If it isn't he, then who is it?

25 My days fly by faster
    than a runner; I   2Sm 18:19-33
 they flee without seeing
    any good.   Jb 7:7; Ps 78:39; Jms 4:14
26 They sweep by like boats
    made of papyrus,
 like an eagle swooping down
    on its prey.   Jb 39:29; Is 18:2; Hab 1:8
27 If I said, "I will forget
    my complaint,

A9:8 Or and walks on the back of the sea god   B9:9 Or Aldebaran   C9:9 Or chambers   D9:12 Or
dissuade   E9:19 LXX; MT reads me   F9:23 Or whip; Hb obscure   G9:24 Or land   H9:24 Lit covers the
faces of   I9:25 = a royal messenger

change my expression,
and smile,"

28 I would still live in terror
of all my pains.   Jb 3:25; 13:11
I know you will not
acquit me.   Jb 10:14; Jl 3:21; Nah 1:3

29 Since I will be found guilty,
why should I struggle in vain?

30 If I wash myself with snow,
and cleanse my hands
with lye,

31 then you dip me in a pit
of mud,
and my own clothes
despise me!

32 For he is not a man like me,
that I can answer him,   Ec 6:10
that we can take each other
to court.

33 There is
no mediator between us,
to lay his hand on both of us.

34 Let him take his rod away
from me
so his terror will no longer
frighten me.   Jb 6:4; 13:21; Ps 39:10

35 Then I would speak and not
fear him.
But that is not the case; I am
on my own.

10 I am disgusted with my life.
I will give vent to
my complaint
and speak in the bitterness
of my soul.

2 I will say to God,
"Do not declare me guilty!
Let me know why
you prosecute me.

3 Is it good for you to oppress,
to reject the work
of your hands,   Ps 128:2
and favor^A the plans
of the wicked?   Jb 21:16; Ps 1:1

4 Do you have eyes of flesh,
or do you see
as a human sees?

5 Are your days like those
of a human,
or your years like those
of a man,   Jb 36:26; Ps 90:4; 2Pt 3:8

6 that you look for my iniquity
and search for my sin,

7 even though you know that
I am not wicked
and that there is no one
who can rescue
from your power?   Dt 32:39

8 "Your hands shaped me
and formed me.   Gn 2:7,8,19
Will you now
turn and destroy me?

9 Please remember that you
formed me like clay.
Will you now return me
to dust?   Gn 2:7; Jb 4:19; 34:15

10 Did you not pour me out
like milk
and curdle me like cheese?

11 You clothed me with skin
and flesh,
and wove me together
with bones and tendons.

12 You gave me life
and faithful love,
and your care has guarded
my life.

13 "Yet you concealed
these thoughts
in your heart;
I know that this was
your hidden plan:^B

14 if I sin, you would notice,^C
and would not acquit me
of my iniquity.   Ex 34:7; Jb 7:21

15 If I am wicked, woe to me!
And even if I am righteous,
I cannot lift up my head.

^A 10:3 Lit shine on   ^B 10:13 Lit was with you   ^C 10:14 Lit notice me

I am filled with shame   Hab 2:16
and have drunk deeply of^A
   my affliction.   Jb 9:15; Ps 25:18
¹⁶ If I am proud,^B you hunt me
   like a lion
and again display
   your miraculous power
   against me.   Jb 5:9; Is 38:13; Lm 3:10
¹⁷ You produce new witnesses^C
   against me
and multiply your anger
   toward me.
Hardships assault me,
   wave after wave.^D

¹⁸ "Why did you bring me out of
   the womb?   Jb 1:21; 10:18-19
I should have died and never
   been seen.
¹⁹ I wish^E I had never existed
but had been carried
   from the womb
   to the grave.   Jb 3:22; 5:26; 17:1
²⁰ Are my days not few? Stop it!^F
Leave me alone, so that
   I can smile a little
²¹ before I go to a land
   of darkness and gloom,
never to return.
²² It is a land of blackness
   like the deepest darkness,
gloomy and chaotic,
   where even the light is
   like^G the darkness."

Zophar Speaks

11 Then Zophar the Naamathite
   replied:
² Should this abundance
   of words go unanswered
   and such a talker^H
   be acquitted?
³ Should your babbling
   put others to silence,

so that you can keep on
   ridiculing
with no one to humiliate you?
⁴ You have said, "My teaching
   is sound,   Dt 32:2; Pr 4:2; Is 29:24
and I am pure in your sight."
⁵ But if only God would speak
and open his lips against you!
⁶ He would show you
   the secrets of wisdom,
for true wisdom has
   two sides.
Know then that God
   has chosen to overlook
   some of your iniquity.   Ezr 9:13

⁷ Can you fathom the depths
   of God
or discover the limits
   of the Almighty?   Ec 3:11; 8:17
⁸ They are higher
   than the heavens —
   what can you do?
They are deeper than Sheol
   — what can you know?
⁹ Their measure is longer
   than the earth
and wider than the sea.

¹⁰ If he passes by and throws
   someone in prison
or convenes a court, who can
   stop him?   Jb 9:12; 23:13; Rv 3:7
¹¹ Surely he knows
   which people are worthless.
If he sees iniquity, will he not
   take note of it?   Jb 34:25; Ps 10:14
¹² But a stupid person
   will gain understanding
as soon as a wild donkey
   is born a human!

¹³ As for you, if you redirect
   your heart

---

^A10:15 Or *and look at*   ^B10:16 Lit *If he lifts up*   ^C10:17 Or *You bring fresh troops*   ^D10:17 Lit *Changes and a host are with me*   ^E10:19 Lit *As if*   ^F10:20 Alt Hb tradition reads *Will he not leave my few days alone?*   ^G10:22 Lit *chaotic, and shines as*   ^H11:2 Lit *a man of lips*

and spread out your hands
to him in prayer —
14 if there is iniquity
in your hand, remove it,
and don't allow injustice
to dwell in your tents —
15 then you will hold
your head high,
free from fault.
You will be firmly established
and unafraid.   Jb 22:26; Ps 119:6
16 For you will forget
your suffering,
recalling it only as water
that has flowed by.
17 Your life will be brighter
than noonday;
its darkness^A will be
like the morning.   Jb 17:12
18 You will be confident,
because there is hope.   Jb 4:6
You will look carefully about
and lie down in safety.   Ps 4:8
19 You will lie down with no one
to frighten you,
and many will seek
your favor.   Ps 45:12; Pr 19:6; 29:26
20 But the sight of the wicked
will fail.   Jb 3:17; 9:22; 18:5
Their way of escape will be
cut off,
and their only hope
is their last breath.   Jb 8:13; 11:7

Job's Reply to Zophar

12 Then Job answered:
2 No doubt you are
the people,
and wisdom will die
with you!
3 But I also have a mind like you;
I am not inferior to you.
Who doesn't know the things
you are talking about?^B

4 I am a laughingstock
to my^C friends,
by calling on God,
who answers me.^D
The righteous
and upright man is
a laughingstock.   Jb 30:1,9; Jr 20:7
5 The one who is at ease
holds calamity in contempt
and thinks it is prepared
for those whose feet
are slipping.
6 The tents of robbers are safe,
and those who trouble God
are secure;
God holds them in his
hands.^E   Ps 73:11; Jr 12:1; Mt 5:45
7 But ask the animals,
and they will instruct you;
ask the birds of the sky,
and they will tell you.   Jb 35:11
8 Or speak to the earth,
and it will instruct you;
let the fish of the sea
inform you.
9 Which of all these
does not know
that the hand of the LORD
has done this?   Ru 1:13; Jb 19:21
10 The life of every living thing
is in his hand,
as well as the breath
of all mankind.   Gn 2:7; Jb 27:3
11 Doesn't the ear test words
as the palate tastes food?
12 Wisdom is found
with the elderly,
and understanding comes
with long life.   Jb 12:20; 32:7,9
13 Wisdom and strength belong
to God;
counsel and understanding
are his.   Jb 9:4; 36:5; 38:36

^A 11:17 Text emended; MT reads *noonday; you are dark, you*   ^B 12:3 Lit *With whom are not such things as these?*   ^C 12:4 Lit *his*   ^D 12:4 Lit *him*   ^E 12:6 Or *secure; to those who bring their god in their hands*

¹⁴ Whatever he tears down
      cannot be rebuilt;
   whoever he imprisons
      cannot be released.   Jb 11:10
¹⁵ When he withholds water,
      everything dries up,
   and when he releases it,
      it destroys the land.   Is 41:18
¹⁶ True wisdom and power
      belong to him.
   The deceived
      and the deceiver are his.
¹⁷ He leads counselors away
      barefoot
   and makes judges
      go mad.   Jb 9:24; Is 29:14; 44:25
¹⁸ He releases the bonds ^A
      put on by kings   Jb 12:21; Is 45:1
   and fastens a belt
      around their waists.
¹⁹ He leads priests away
      barefoot
   and overthrows
      established leaders.   Is 40:23
²⁰ He deprives trusted advisers
      of speech
   and takes away the elders'
      good judgment.
²¹ He pours out contempt
      on nobles
   and disarms ^B the strong.
²² He reveals mysteries
      from the darkness
   and brings
      the deepest darkness
      into the light.   Ps 90:8; Dn 2:22
²³ He makes nations great,
      then destroys them;
   he enlarges nations,
      then leads them away.   Is 9:3
²⁴ He deprives
      the world's leaders
      of reason,
   and makes them wander
      in a trackless wasteland.

²⁵ They grope around
      in darkness without light;
   he makes them stagger like a
      drunkard.   Dt 28:29; Jb 5:14; Is 59:10

13

Look, my eyes have seen
      all this;
   my ears have heard
      and understood it.   Jb 4:12; 33:16
² Everything you know,
      I also know;
   I am not inferior to you.   Jb 12:3
³ Yet I prefer to speak
      to the Almighty
   and argue my case before God.
⁴ You use lies like plaster;
   you are all worthless healers.
⁵ If only you would shut up
   and let that be your wisdom!

⁶ Hear now my argument,
   and listen to my defense. ^C
⁷ Would you testify unjustly
      on God's behalf
   or speak deceitfully for him?
⁸ Would you show partiality
      to him   Dt 10:17; Jb 32:21; 34:19
   or argue the case
      in his defense?
⁹ Would it go well
      if he examined you?
   Could you deceive him
      as you would deceive
      a man?   Ps 44:21; Pr 18:17; Jr 17:10
¹⁰ Surely he would rebuke you
   if you secretly
      showed partiality.
¹¹ Would God's majesty
      not terrify you?   Ex 15:16; Jb 31:23
   Would his dread not fall
      on you?
¹² Your memorable sayings
      are proverbs of ash;   1Sm 24:13
   your defenses are made
      of clay.

^A12:18 Text emended; MT reads *discipline*   ^B12:21 Lit *and loosens the belt of*   ^C13:6 Lit *to the claims of my lips*

¹³ Be quiet, ᴬ and I will speak.
   Let whatever comes happen
     to me.
¹⁴ I will put ᴮ myself at risk ᶜ
   and take my life
     in my own hands.
¹⁵ Even if he kills me, I will hope
     in him. ᴰ
   I will still defend my ways
     before him.   Jb 13:3; 15:3; 23:7
¹⁶ Yes, this will result
     in my deliverance,
   for no godless person
     can appear before him.
¹⁷ Pay close attention
     to my words;
   let my declaration ring
     in your ears.
¹⁸ Now then, I have prepared
     my case;   Jb 5:8; 23:4; Lm 3:59
   I know that I am right.
¹⁹ Can anyone indict me?
   If so, I will be silent and die.

²⁰ Only grant these two things
     to me, God,
   so that I will not have to hide
     from your presence:
²¹ remove your hand from me,
   and do not let your terror
     frighten me.   Jb 6:4; 9:34; Ps 39:10
²² Then call, and I will answer,
   or I will speak, and you
     can respond to me.
²³ How many
     iniquities and sins
   have I committed? ᴱ   Jb 7:21
   Reveal to me
     my transgression and sin.
²⁴ Why do you hide your face
   and consider me
     your enemy?   Jb 19:11; 33:10; Lm 2:5
²⁵ Will you frighten
   a wind-driven leaf?

Will you chase after
     dry straw?
²⁶ For you record
     bitter accusations
   against me
   and make me inherit
     the iniquities of my youth.
²⁷ You put my feet in the stocks
   and stand watch over all
     my paths,
   setting a limit for the soles ᶠ
     of my feet.
²⁸ A person wears out
     like something rotten,
   like a moth-eaten garment.

14 Anyone born of woman
   is short of days and full
     of trouble.   Jb 5:7; 15:35; Is 59:4
² He blossoms like a flower,
     then withers;   Ps 103:15-16
   he flees like a shadow
     and does not last.
³ Do you really take notice
     of one like this?
   Will you bring me
     into judgment
   against you? ᴳ   Jb 22:4; Ps 143:2
⁴ Who can produce
     something pure from what
     is impure?
   No one!
⁵ Since a person's days
     are determined
   and the number
     of his months depends
     on you,
   and since you have
     set ᴴ limits he cannot pass,
⁶ look away from him
     and let him rest
   so that he can enjoy his day
     like a hired worker.   Jb 7:16

ᴬ**13:13** Lit quiet before me   ᴮ**13:14** LXX; MT reads Why do I put   ᶜ**13:14** Lit I take my flesh in my teeth
ᴰ**13:15** Some Hb mss read I will be without hope   ᴱ**13:23** Lit sins are to me   ᶠ**13:27** Lit paths. You mark
a line around the roots   ᴳ**14:3** LXX, Syr, Vg read him   ᴴ**14:5** Lit set his

7 There is hope for a tree:
   If it is cut down, it will
      sprout again,
   and its shoots will not die.
8 If its roots grow old
      in the ground
   and its stump starts to die
      in the soil,
9 the scent of water
      makes it thrive
   and produce twigs
      like a sapling.   Jb 29:19; Ps 1:3
10 But a person dies
      and fades away;
   he breathes his last —
      where is he?
11 As water disappears
      from a lake
   and a river becomes parched
      and dry,
12 so people lie down never
      to rise again.
   They will not wake up
      until the heavens are
      no more;   Is 51:6; Rv 20:11; 21:1
   they will not stir
      from their sleep.

13 If only you would hide me
      in Sheol   Jb 11:8; 17:16; Am 9:2
   and conceal me
      until your anger passes.
   If only you would appoint
      a time for me
   and then remember me.
14 When a person dies, will he
      come back to life?
   If so, I would wait all the days
      of my struggle   Jb 6:8; 13:13; 35:14
   until my relief comes.
15 You would call, and I would
      answer you.
   You would long for the work
      of your hands.   Jb 9:16; 10:3; 13:22
16 For then you would count
      my steps   Jb 10:6; 31:4; 34:21

but would not take note of
   my sin.   Jb 10:14; 33:11; Ps 130:3
17 My rebellion would be
      sealed up in a bag,
   and you would cover over
      my iniquity.

18 But as a mountain collapses
      and crumbles
   and a rock is dislodged
      from its place,
19 as water wears away stones
   and torrents wash away
      the soil from the land,
   so you destroy a man's hope.
20 You completely overpower
      him, and he passes on;
   you change his appearance
      and send him away.
21 If his sons receive honor,
      he does not know it;
   if they become insignificant,
      he is unaware of it.   Jb 21:21
22 He feels only the pain
      of his own body
   and mourns only for himself.

SECOND SERIES OF SPEECHES

Eliphaz Speaks

15 Then Eliphaz the Temanite
   replied:
2 Does a wise man answer
      with empty[A] counsel   Jb 2:10
   or fill himself[B]
      with the hot east wind?
3 Should he argue
      with useless talk   Jb 13:3,15; 23:7
   or with words that serve
      no good purpose?
4 But you even undermine
      the fear of God
   and hinder meditation
      before him.
5 Your iniquity teaches you
      what to say,   Jb 13:23,26; 14:17; 22:5

[A]**15:2** Lit *windy*; Jb 16:3   [B]**15:2** Lit *his belly*

and you choose
the language of the crafty.

6 Your own mouth
condemns you, not I;
your own lips testify
against you.   2Sm 1:16; Jb 9:20

7 Were you the first human
ever born,
or were you brought forth
before the hills?   Jb 38:21; Ps 90:2

8 Do you listen in
on the council of God,
or have a monopoly
on wisdom?   Jr 23:18; Rm 11:34

9 What do you know that
we don't?
What do you understand that
is not clear to us?

10 Both the gray-haired
and the elderly are
with us—
older than your father.

11 Are God's consolations
not enough for you,
even the words
that deal gently with you?

12 Why has your heart
misled you,
and why do your eyes flash

13 as you turn your anger A
against God
and allow such words
to leave your mouth?

14 What is a mere human,
that he should be pure,
or one born
of a woman, that he
should be righteous?

15 If God puts no trust
in his holy ones   Jb 5:1; Ps 89:5-7
and the heavens are not pure
in his sight,   Jb 4:18; 21:22; 25:5

16 how much less one
who is revolting and corrupt,
who drinks injustice
like water?   Jb 34:7; Ps 14:3

17 Listen to me and I will
inform you.
I will describe what
I have seen,

18 what the wise have declared
and not concealed,
that came from
their ancestors,   Dt 4:32; 32:7

19 to whom alone the land
was given
when no foreigner passed
among them.

20 A wicked person writhes
in pain all his days,
throughout the number
of years reserved
for the ruthless.

21 Dreadful sounds fill his ears;
when he is at peace, a robber
attacks him.

22 He doesn't believe
he will return
from darkness;
he is destined for the sword.

23 He wanders about for food,
asking, "Where is it?"
He knows the day
of darkness is at hand.

24 Trouble and distress
terrify him,   1Sm 22:2; Jb 36:19
overwhelming him
like a king prepared
for battle.

25 For he has stretched out
his hand against God   Is 5:25
and has arrogantly opposed
the Almighty.

26 He rushes headlong at him
with his thick, studded shields.

27 Though his face is covered
with fat B
and his waistline bulges
with it,

A 15:13 Or spirit   B 15:27 Lit with his fat

28 he will dwell in ruined cities,
in abandoned houses
destined to become piles
of rubble.   Jb 3:14; Ps 109:10; Is 5:9

29 He will no longer be rich;
his wealth will not endure.
His possessions [A]
will not increase
in the land.

30 He will not escape
from the darkness;
flames will wither his shoots,
and by the breath
of God's mouth,
he will depart.   Jb 4:9; 22:20

31 Let him not put trust
in worthless things, being
led astray,
for what he gets in exchange
will prove worthless.

32 It will be accomplished
before his time,
and his branch
will not flourish.

33 He will be like a vine
that drops its unripe grapes
and like an olive tree
that sheds its blossoms.

34 For the company
of the godless will have
no children,   Jb 8:13; 13:16; 27:8
and fire will consume
the tents of those
who offer bribes.

35 They conceive trouble
and give birth to evil;   Jb 4:8
their womb
prepares deception.   Jb 32:19

Job's Reply to Eliphaz

16 Then Job answered:
2 I have heard many things
like these.
You are all
miserable comforters.   Jb 13:4

3 Is there no end
to your empty [B] words?
What provokes you that you
continue testifying?

4 If you were in my place
I could also talk like you.
I could string words together
against you
and shake my head at you.

5 Instead, I would encourage
you with my mouth,
and the consolation
from my lips
would bring relief.   Dt 3:28

6 If I speak, my suffering
is not relieved,
and if I hold back, does any of
it leave me?

7 Surely he [C] has now
exhausted me.
You have devastated
my entire family.

8 You have shriveled me up [D] —
it has become a witness;
my frailty rises up against me
and testifies to my face.

9 His anger tears at me,
and he harasses me.   Gn 49:23
He gnashes his teeth at me.
My enemy pierces me
with his eyes.

10 They open their mouths
against me
and strike my cheeks
with contempt;   1Kg 22:24; Mc 5:1
they join themselves
together against me.

11 God hands me over to the
unjust; [E]
he throws me to the wicked.

12 I was at ease,
but he shattered me;
he seized me by the scruff
of the neck

A15:29 Text emended; MT reads *Their gain*   B16:3 Lit *windy*; Jb 15:2   C16:7 Or *it*   D16:8 Or *have seized me*; Hb obscure   E16:11 LXX, Vg; MT reads *to a boy*

and smashed me to pieces.
He set me up as his target;
13   his archers^A surround me.
He pierces my kidneys
      without mercy
and pours my bile
      on the ground.
14   He breaks through
      my defenses again
      and again;^B
he charges at me
      like a warrior.   Jb 30:14; Jl 2:7

15   I have sewn sackcloth
      over my skin;
I have buried my strength^C
      in the dust.   Jb 30:19; Ps 7:5; 75:10
16   My face has grown red
      with weeping,
and darkness covers my eyes,
17   although my hands are free
      from violence   Is 53:9; 59:6; Jnh 3:8
and my prayer is pure.

18   Earth, do not cover my blood;
may my cry for help find
      no resting place.   Gn 4:10; Is 26:21
19   Even now my witness is
      in heaven,
and my advocate is
      in the heights!   Jb 22:12; Rm 1:9
20   My friends scoff at me
      as I weep before God.
21   I wish that someone might
      argue for a man with God
just as anyone^D would
      for a friend.
22   For only a few years will pass
before I go the way
      of no return.

17 My spirit is broken.
My days are extinguished.
A graveyard awaits me.   Jb 3:22

2   Surely mockers
      surround^E me,
and my eyes must gaze
      at their rebellion.   Ps 22:7; 119:51

3   Accept my pledge! Put up
      security for me.   Gn 43:9; Pr 6:1
Who else will be my sponsor?^F
4   You have closed their minds
      to understanding,
therefore you will not
      honor them.
5   If a man
      denounces his friends
      for a price,
the eyes of his children
      will fail.

6   He has made me an object
      of scorn to the people;
I have become a man people
      spit at.^G   Nm 12:14; Is 50:6; Mt 27:30
7   My eyes have grown dim
      from grief,
and my whole body
      has become but a shadow.
8   The upright are appalled
      at this,   Jb 18:20; 21:5; Dn 4:19
and the innocent are roused
      against the godless.
9   Yet the righteous person
      will hold to his way,
and the one
      whose hands are clean
      will grow stronger.   2Sm 22:21
10   But come back and try again,
      all of you.^H
I will not find a wise man
      among you.

11   My days have slipped by;
my plans have been ruined,
even the things dear
      to my heart.

^A16:13 Or arrows   ^B16:14 Lit through me, breach on breach   ^C16:15 Lit horn   ^D16:21 Lit a son of man
^E17:2 Lit are with   ^F17:3 Or Who is there that will shake hands with me?   ^G17:6 Lit become a spitting
to the faces   ^H17:10 Some Hb mss, LXX, Vg; other Hb mss read them

12 They turned night into day
　　and made light seem near
　　　in the face of darkness.
13 If I await Sheol as my home,
　　spread out my bed
　　　in darkness,
14 and say to corruption,
　　　"You are my father,"
　　and to the maggot,
　　　"My mother"
　　　or "My sister,"　　　Jb 3:15; 30:23
15 where then is my hope?　　Jb 7:6
　　Who can see any hope
　　　for me?
16 Will it go down to the gates
　　　of Sheol,　　Jb 7:9; 11:8; 14:13
　　or will we descend together
　　　to the dust?

Bildad Speaks

18 Then Bildad the Shuhite re-
　　plied:　　　Jb 2:11; 8:1; 25:1
2 How long until you
　　stop talking?
　　Show some sense, and then
　　　we can talk.
3 Why are we regarded
　　　as cattle,
　　as stupid in your sight?
4 You who tear yourself
　　　in anger[A] —
　　should the earth
　　　be abandoned
　　　on your account,
　　or a rock be removed
　　　from its place?

5 Yes, the light of the wicked
　　is extinguished;　　Jb 21:17; Pr 13:9
　　the flame of his fire does
　　　not glow.
6 The light in his tent
　　grows dark,　　Jb 8:22; 18:14; Ps 52:5
　　and the lamp beside him
　　　is put out.

7 His powerful stride
　　is shortened,
　　and his own schemes
　　　trip him up.　　Jb 5:13; Pr 4:12
8 For his own feet lead him
　　　into a net,
　　and he strays into its mesh.
9 A trap catches him
　　　by the heel;
　　a noose seizes him.
10 A rope lies hidden for him
　　　on the ground,
　　and a snare waits for him
　　　along the path.
11 Terrors frighten him
　　on every side　　Jb 20:25; 27:20
　　and harass him at every step.
12 His strength is depleted;
　　disaster lies ready for him
　　　to stumble.[B]
13 Parts of his skin
　　are eaten away;
　　death's firstborn consumes
　　　his limbs.
14 He is ripped
　　from the security of his tent
　　and marched away
　　　to the king of terrors.
15 Nothing he owned remains
　　　in his tent.
　　Burning sulfur is scattered
　　　over his home.　　Gn 19:24; Ps 11:6
16 His roots below dry up,
　　and his branches above
　　　wither away.　　Is 5:24; Hs 9:16; Am 2:9
17 All memory of him perishes
　　　from the earth;　　Ps 34:16; 109:13,15
　　he has no name anywhere.[C]
18 He is driven from light
　　　to darkness
　　and chased
　　　from the inhabited world.
19 He has no children
　　　or descendants
　　　among his people,

[A]**18:4** Lit *He who tears himself in his anger*　[B]**18:12** Or *disaster hungers for him*　[C]**18:17** Or *name in the streets*

no survivor where he
used to live. Gn 21:23; Is 14:22

20 Those in the west
are appalled at his fate, 32:10
while those in the east
tremble in horror.

21 Indeed, such is the dwelling
of the unjust man,
and this is the place of the one
who does not know God.

Job's Reply to Bildad

19 Then Job answered:
² How long will you
torment me
and crush me with words?

3 You have humiliated me
ten times now,
and you mistreat^A me
without shame. Gn 31:7; Nm 14:22

4 Even if it is true that
I have sinned,
my mistake concerns
only^B me.

5 If you really want to appear
superior to me Ps 35:26; 38:16
and would use my disgrace
as evidence against me,

6 then understand
that it is God
who has wronged me
and caught me in his net.

7 I cry out: "Violence!"
but get no response; Jb 30:20
I call for help, but there is
no justice.

8 He has blocked my way
so that I cannot
pass through; Jb 3:23; Lm 3:9
he has veiled my paths
with darkness. Jb 29:3; 30:26

9 He has stripped me
of my honor

and removed the crown
from my head.

10 He tears me down
on every side so that
I am ruined.^C
He uproots my hope
like a tree. Dt 28:63; Jb 24:20; Ps 52:5

11 His anger burns against me,
and he regards me as one of
his enemies. Jb 13:24; 33:10; Lm 2:5

12 His troops advance together;
they construct a ramp^D
against me
and camp around my tent.

13 He has removed my brothers
from me;
my acquaintances
have abandoned me. Ps 31:11

14 My relatives stop coming by,
and my close friends
have forgotten me.

15 My house guests^E
and female servants
regard me as a stranger;
I am a foreigner
in their sight. Gn 31:15; Ps 69:8

16 I call for my servant, but he
does not answer,
even if I beg him
with my own mouth.

17 My breath is offensive
to my wife,
and my own family^F
finds me repulsive.

18 Even young boys scorn me.
When I stand up,
they mock me. 2Kg 2:23; Jb 29:8

19 All of my best friends^G
despise me, Jb 30:10; Ps 89:38
and those I love have turned
against me. Ps 41:9; 55:11-12; Jn 13:18

20 My skin and my flesh cling
to my bones;

---

^A 19:3 Hb obscure   ^B 19:4 Lit *mistake lives with*   ^C 19:10 Lit *gone*   ^D 19:12 Lit *they raise up their way*
^E 19:15 Or *The resident aliens in my household*   ^F 19:17 Lit *and the sons of my belly*   ^G 19:19 Lit *of the men of my council*

I have escaped with only
   the skin of my teeth.

21 Have mercy on me,
   my friends, have mercy,
for God's hand
   has struck me. Ru 1:13; Jb 2:5; 12:9
22 Why do you persecute me
   as God does?
Will you never get enough
   of my flesh?

23 I wish that my words
   were written down,
that they were recorded
   on a scroll
24 or were inscribed
   in stone forever
by an iron stylus and lead!
25 But I know that my Redeemer
   lives, A Jb 16:19; Pr 23:11; Jr 50:34
and at the end he will stand
   on the dust. Is 44:6; 48:12; Rv 1:17-18
26 Even after my skin
   has been destroyed, B
yet I will see God
   in C my flesh. Ps 17:15; Is 6:1
27 I will see him myself;
my eyes will look at him,
   and not as a stranger. D
My heart longs E within me.

28 If you say, "How will
   we pursue him,
since the root
   of the problem lies
   with him?" F
29 then be afraid of the sword,
because wrath
   brings punishment
   by the sword, Jb 15:22; Is 66:16
so that you may know
   there is a judgment.

Zophar Speaks

20 Then Zophar the Naamathite
replied: Jb 2:11; 11:1; 42:9
2 This is why
   my unsettling thoughts
   compel me to answer,
because I am upset! G
3 I have heard a rebuke
   that insults me,
and my understanding H
   makes me reply. Jb 19:3; 32:18

4 Don't you know that
   ever since antiquity,
from the time a human
   was placed on earth,
5 the joy of the wicked
   has been brief
and the happiness
   of the godless has lasted
   only a moment? Jb 8:12-13; Ps 92:7
6 Though his arrogance
   reaches heaven,
and his head touches
   the clouds, Gn 11:4; Is 14:13-14
7 he will vanish forever
   like his own dung.
Those who know I him
   will ask, "Where is he?"
8 He will fly away like a dream
   and never be found;
he will be chased away
   like a vision in the night.
9 The eye that saw him
   will see him no more, Jb 7:8,21
and his household
   will no longer see him. Jb 8:18
10 His children will beg
   from J the poor,
for his own hands
   must give back his wealth.
11 His frame may be full of
   youthful vigor,

A19:25 Or know my living Redeemer B19:26 Lit skin which they destroyed, or skin they destroyed in this way C19:26 Or apart from D19:27 Or not a stranger E19:27 Lit My kidneys grow faint F19:28 Some Hb mss, LXX, Vg; other Hb mss read me G20:2 Lit because of my feeling within me H20:3 Lit and a spirit from my understanding I20:7 Lit have seen J20:10 Or children must compensate

but it will lie down with him
in dust. Jb 7:21; 17:16; Ps 7:5

12 Though evil tastes sweet
in his mouth
and he conceals it
under his tongue,
13 though he cherishes it
and will not let it go
but keeps it in his mouth,
14 yet the food in his stomach
turns
into cobras' venom
inside him.
15 He swallows wealth but must
vomit it up;
God will force it
from his stomach.
16 He will suck the poison
of cobras;
a viper's fangs^A will kill him.
17 He will not enjoy the streams,
the rivers flowing
with honey and curds. Jb 29:6
18 He must return
the fruit of his labor
without consuming it;
he doesn't enjoy the profits
from his trading.
19 For he oppressed
and abandoned the poor;
he seized a house
he did not build. Dt 28:30; Is 5:8

20 Because his appetite
is never satisfied,^B
he does not let anything
he desires escape.
21 Nothing is left for him
to consume; Jb 15:29; Pr 17:1; Ec 5:13
therefore, his prosperity
will not last.
22 At the height of his success^C
distress will come to him;

the full weight of misery^D
will crush him.
23 When he fills his stomach,
God will send
his burning anger
against him,
raining it down on him
while he is eating.^E Gn 19:24
24 If he flees
from an iron weapon,
an arrow from a bronze bow
will pierce him.
25 He pulls it out of his back,
the flashing tip out of
his liver.^F
Terrors come over him. Jb 18:11
26 Total darkness is reserved
for his treasures.
A fire unfanned
by human hands
will consume him; Jb 15:34
it will feed on what is left
in his tent.
27 The heavens will expose
his iniquity, Jb 13:23,26; 15:5; 22:5
and the earth will rise up
against him. Dt 4:26; Jb 16:18-19
28 The possessions in his house
will be removed,
flowing away on the day
of God's anger.
29 This is
the wicked person's lot
from God, Jb 27:13; 31:2; Ps 17:14
the inheritance God ordained
for him.

Job's Reply to Zophar

21 Then Job answered:
2 Pay close attention
to my words;
let this be the consolation
you offer.
3 Bear with me while I speak;

---

^A 20:16 Lit tongue   ^B 20:20 Lit Because he does not know ease in his stomach   ^C 20:22 Lit In the
fullness of his excess   ^D 20:22 Some Hb mss, LXX, Vg; other Hb mss read the hand of everyone in misery
^E 20:23 Text emended; MT reads him, against his flesh   ^F 20:25 Or gallbladder

then after I have spoken,
  you may continue mocking.

4 As for me, is my complaint
    against a human being?
  Then why shouldn't I
    be impatient?
5 Look at me and shudder;
  put your hand
    over your mouth.   Jdg 18:19; 40:4
6 When I think about it,
    I am terrified
  and my body trembles
    in horror.   Jb 4:14; Ps 55:5; 119:120
7 Why do the wicked continue
    to live,
  growing old and becoming
    powerful?
8 Their children are
    established while they are
    still alive, ^A
  and their descendants,
    before their eyes.
9 Their homes are secure
    and free of fear;   Jb 5:24; 8:6; 12:6
  no rod from God strikes
    them.   Jb 9:34; Ps 73:5
10 Their bulls breed
    without fail;
  their cows calve
    and do not miscarry.
11 They let their little ones run
    around like lambs;
  their children skip about,
12 singing to the tambourine
    and lyre
  and rejoicing at the sound
    of the flute.   Jb 30:31; Ps 81:2; 150:4
13 They spend ^B their days
    in prosperity   Jb 36:11; Ps 37:7
  and go down to Sheol
    in peace.
14 Yet they say to God,
    "Leave us alone!

We don't want to know
  your ways.   Jb 22:17; Ps 95:10; Pr 1:29
15 Who is the Almighty, that we
    should serve him,
  and what will we gain
    by pleading with him?"
16 But their prosperity is not
    of their own doing.
  The counsel of the wicked is
    far from me!   Jb 22:18; Ps 1:1; Pr 1:10
17 How often is the lamp
    of the wicked put out?   Jb 18:5
  Does disaster ^C come on them?
  Does he apportion
    destruction in his anger?
18 Are they like straw
    before the wind,
  like chaff a storm
    sweeps away?   Ps 1:4; 35:5; Is 17:13
19 God reserves
    a person's punishment
    for his children.   Ex 20:5; Jr 31:29
  Let God repay
    the person himself, so that
    he may know it.
20 Let his own eyes see
    his demise;
  let him drink from
    the Almighty's wrath!   Ps 75:8
21 For what does he care
    about his family once
    he is dead,   Jb 14:21; Ec 9:5; Is 63:16
  when the number
    of his months has run out?

22 Can anyone teach God
    knowledge,   Is 40:13-14; Rm 11:34
  since he judges
    the exalted ones? ^D
23 One person dies
    in excellent health, ^E
  completely secure ^F
    and at ease.

24 His body is^A well fed,^B
   and his bones are full
      of marrow.^C
25 Yet another person dies
   with a bitter soul,   1Sm 1:10
   having never
      tasted prosperity.
26 But they both lie in the dust,
   and worms cover them. Jb 20:11

27 I know your thoughts
   very well,
   the schemes by which
      you would wrong me.
28 For you say, "Where now is
   the nobleman's house?"
   and "Where are the tents
      the wicked lived in?" Ps 55:15
29 Have you never consulted
   those who travel
      the roads?
   Don't you accept
      their reports?^D
30 Indeed, the evil person
   is spared from the day
      of disaster,
   rescued from the day
      of wrath.
31 Who would denounce
   his behavior to his face?
   Who would repay him
      for what he has done? Dt 7:10
32 He is carried to the grave,
   and someone
      keeps watch over his tomb.
33 The dirt on his grave
   is^E sweet to him.
   Everyone follows
      behind him,
   and those who go before him
      are without number.

34 So how can you offer me
   such futile comfort?
   Your answers are deceptive.

THIRD SERIES OF SPEECHES

Eliphaz Speaks

22 Then Eliphaz the Temanite
      replied:
2 Can a man be of any use
   to God?
   Can even a wise man be
      of use to him?
3 Does it delight the Almighty
   if you are righteous?
   Does he profit if you perfect
      your behavior? Jb 35:7; Ps 16:2

4 Does he correct you
   and take you to court
   because of your piety? Jb 14:3
5 Isn't your wickedness
      abundant
   and aren't your iniquities
      endless?
6 For you took collateral
   from your brothers
      without cause, Ex 22:26; Dt 24:6,17
   stripping off their clothes
      and leaving them naked.
7 You gave no water
   to the thirsty
   and withheld food
      from the famished, Jb 31:17
8 while the land belonged
   to a powerful man
   and an influential man lived
      on it.
9 You sent widows away
      empty-handed,
   and the strength
      of the fatherless
      was^F crushed. Jb 24:3; Is 10:2
10 Therefore snares
      surround you,
   and sudden dread
      terrifies you, Jb 3:25; 23:15; 31:23
11 or darkness,
   so you cannot see,

---

^A21:24 Or *His sides are*; Hb obscure   ^B21:24 Lit *is full of milk*   ^C21:24 Lit *and the marrow of his bones is watered*   ^D21:29 Lit *signs*   ^E21:33 Lit *The clods of the wadi are*   ^F22:9 LXX, Syr, Vg, Tg read *you have*

and a flood of water
   covers you.   Jb 38:34; Ps 69:1-2

¹² Isn't God as high
   as the heavens?
And look at the highest stars
   — how lofty they are!
¹³ Yet you say, "What does
   God know?
Can he judge
   through total darkness?
¹⁴ Clouds veil him so that
   he cannot see,   2Sm 22:12; Jb 26:8
as he walks on the circle
   of the sky."
¹⁵ Will you continue
   on the ancient path
that wicked men have
   walked?
¹⁶ They were snatched away
   before their time,
and their foundations
   were washed away
   by a river.   Jb 4:19; Lm 4:11; Ezk 30:4
¹⁷ They were the ones
   who said to God,
"Leave us alone!"
and "What can the Almighty
   do to us?" ᴬ   Jb 21:14; Ps 95:10; 107:42
¹⁸ But it was he who filled
   their houses
   with good things.
The counsel of the wicked is
   far from me!
¹⁹ The righteous see this
   and rejoice;
the innocent mock them,
   saying,   Ps 52:6; 58:10; Pr 1:26-27
²⁰ "Surely our opponents
   are destroyed,
and fire has consumed
   what they left behind."   Jb 1:16

²¹ Come to terms with God
   and be at peace;   Ps 119:165; Pr 3:2

in this way ᴮ good will come
   to you.
²² Receive instruction
   from his mouth,   Dt 8:3; Pr 2:6
and place his sayings
   in your heart.   Jb 6:10; 23:12
²³ If you return to the Almighty,
   you will be renewed.   Is 31:6
If you banish injustice
   from your tent
²⁴ and consign your gold
   to the dust,
the gold of Ophir
   to the stones in the wadis,
²⁵ the Almighty will be
   your gold
and your finest silver.
²⁶ Then you will delight in
   the Almighty   Jb 27:10; Ps 37:4
and lift up your face to God.
²⁷ You will pray to him,
   and he will hear you,   Jb 33:26
and you will fulfill your vows.
²⁸ When you make a decision,
   it will be carried out, ᶜ
and light will shine
   on your ways.   Pr 4:18; Is 60:3
²⁹ When others are humiliated
   and you say, "Lift them up,"
God will save the humble. ᴰ
³⁰ He will even rescue
   the guilty one,
who will be rescued
   by the purity of your hands.

Job's Reply to Eliphaz

23 Then Job answered:
   ² Today also my complaint
   is bitter. ᴱ   Jb 7:11; 10:1; 21:4
His ᶠ hand is heavy
   despite my groaning.
³ If only I knew how to find him,
so that I could go to his throne.
⁴ I would plead my case
   before him   Jb 5:8; 13:18; 35:14

ᴬ22:17 LXX, Syr; MT reads *them*   ᴮ22:21 Lit *peace; by them*   ᶜ22:28 Lit *out for you*   ᴰ22:29 Lit *bowed of eyes*   ᴱ23:2 Syr, Tg, Vg; MT reads *rebellion*   ᶠ23:2 LXX, Syr; MT reads *My*

and fill my mouth
   with arguments.
5 I would learn how[A] he would
   answer me;
and understand what
   he would say to me.
6 Would he prosecute
   me forcefully?   Jb 13:19; 33:13
No, he would certainly
   pay attention to me.
7 Then an upright man
   could reason with him,
and I would escape
   from my Judge[B] forever.

8 If I go east, he is not there,
and if I go west, I cannot
   perceive him.   Jb 9:11; 35:14
9 When he is at work
   to the north, I cannot
   see him;
when he turns south,
   I cannot find him.
10 Yet he knows the way
   I have taken;[C]
when he has tested me,
   I will emerge as pure gold.
11 My feet have followed
   in his tracks;
I have kept to his way
   and not turned aside.   Jb 17:9
12 I have not departed
   from the commands
   from his lips;
I have treasured[D] the words
   from his mouth   Jb 6:10; 22:22
more than my daily food.

13 But he is unchangeable;
   who can oppose him?
He does what he desires.
14 He will certainly accomplish
   what he has decreed for me,
and he has many more things
   like these in mind.[E]

15 Therefore I am terrified
   in his presence;   Jb 4:14; 22:10
when I consider this,
   I am afraid of him.
16 God has made my heart faint;
   the Almighty
   has terrified me.
17 Yet I am not destroyed[F]
   by the darkness,   Jb 19:8; 29:3
by the thick darkness
   that covers my face.

24

Why does the Almighty
not reserve times
for judgment?   Ec 9:12; Is 2:12
Why do those who know him
   never see his days?
2 The wicked displace
   boundary markers.
They steal a flock
   and provide pasture for it.
3 They drive away the donkeys
   owned by the fatherless
and take the widow's ox
   as collateral.
4 They push the needy off
   the road;
the poor of the land
   are forced into hiding.   Jdg 5:6
5 Like wild donkeys
   in the wilderness,
the poor go out to their task
   of foraging for food;
the desert provides
   nourishment
   for their children.
6 They gather their fodder
   in the field
and glean the vineyards
   of the wicked.
7 Without clothing, they spend
   the night naked,
having no covering
   against the cold.   Ex 22:26-27
8 Drenched by mountain rains,

A23:5 Lit the words   B23:7 Or judgment   C23:10 Lit way with me   D23:12 LXX, Vg read treasured in
my bosom   E23:14 Lit these with him   F23:17 Or silenced

they huddle against^A the rocks,
    shelterless.

9 The fatherless infant
    is snatched from the breast;
the nursing child of the poor
    is seized as collateral.^B

10 Without clothing,
    they wander about naked.
They carry sheaves
    but go hungry.   Dt 24:19; 2Tm 2:6

11 They crush olives
    in their presses;^C
they tread the winepresses,
    but go thirsty.

12 From the city, men^D groan;
the mortally wounded cry
    for help,
yet God pays no attention
    to this crime.   Jb 1:22; Ps 69:26

13 The wicked are those
    who rebel against the light.
They do not recognize
    its ways
or stay on its paths.

14 The murderer rises at dawn
    to kill the poor and needy,
and by night he becomes
    a thief.

15 The adulterer's eye watches
    for twilight,
thinking, "No eye
    will see me,"
and he covers his face.

16 In the dark they break^E
    into houses;
by day they lock
    themselves in,^F
never experiencing the light.

17 For the morning is
    like darkness to them.
Surely they are familiar
    with the terrors of darkness!

18 They float^G on the surface
    of the water.
Their section of the land
    is cursed,
so that they never go
    to their vineyards.

19 As dry ground
    and heat snatch away
    the melted snow,
so Sheol steals those
    who have sinned.   Jb 7:9; Ps 9:17

20 The womb forgets them;
worms feed on them;
they are remembered
    no more.   Jb 18:17; Pr 10:7; Jr 11:19
So injustice is broken
    like a tree.

21 They prey on^H
    the childless woman
    who is unable to conceive,
and do not deal kindly
    with the widow.

22 Yet God drags away^I
    the mighty by his power;
when he rises up, they have
    no assurance of life.

23 He gives them a sense
    of security, so they can rely
    on it,   Jb 11:18; Ps 4:8; Pr 3:24
but his eyes watch
    over their ways.   Ps 11:4; Pr 15:3

24 They are exalted
    for a moment, then gone;
they are brought
    low and shrivel up
    like everything else.^J
They wither like heads
    of grain.   Jb 14:21; Ps 37:10; 106:43

25 If this is not true, then who
    can prove me a liar   Jb 6:28
and show that my speech
    is worthless?

Bildad Speaks

25 Then Bildad the Shuhite replied:

2 Dominion and dread belong
　　to him,　　2Ch 20:29; Jb 13:11; Ps 36:1
　the one who establishes
　　harmony in his heights.
3 Can his troops be numbered?
　Does his light not shine
　　on everyone?
4 How can a human
　　be justified before God?
　How can one born of woman
　　be pure?　　Jb 4:17; 15:14; Pr 20:9
5 If even the moon
　　does not shine
　and the stars are not pure
　　in his sight,　　Jb 4:18; 15:15; 21:22
6 how much less a human,
　　who is a maggot,
　a son of man,^A who is a worm!

Job's Reply to Bildad

26 Then Job answered:
2 How you have helped
　　the powerless　　Jb 4:3; Is 35:3
　and delivered the arm
　　that is weak!
3 How you have counseled
　　the unwise　　Jb 11:6; Ps 73:24; Jms 1:5
　and abundantly
　　provided insight!
4 With whom did you speak
　　these words?
　Whose breath came out of
　　your mouth?

5 The departed spirits tremble
　beneath the waters and all
　　that inhabit them.　　Ps 88:10
6 Sheol is naked before God,
　and Abaddon has
　　no covering.　　Jb 28:22; Pr 27:20
7 He stretches
　　the northern skies
　　over empty space;

　he hangs the earth
　　on nothing.
8 He wraps up the water
　　in his clouds,
　yet the clouds do not burst
　　beneath its weight.　　Jb 37:11
9 He obscures the view
　　of his throne,
　spreading his cloud over it.
10 He laid out the horizon
　　on the surface of the waters
　at the boundary
　　between light and darkness.
11 The pillars that hold up
　　the sky tremble,
　astounded at his rebuke.　Ps 104:7
12 By his power he stirred
　　the sea,　　Is 51:15; Jr 31:35
　and by his understanding
　　he crushed Rahab.　　Jb 9:13
13 By his breath
　　the heavens gained
　　their beauty;
　his hand pierced
　　the fleeing serpent.^B　　Jb 41
14 These are but the fringes
　　of his ways;
　how faint is the word
　　we hear of him!
　Who can understand
　　his mighty thunder?

27 Job continued his discourse,
　　saying:
2 As God lives, who has
　　deprived me of justice,
　and the Almighty who has
　　made me bitter,　　Ex 1:14; Ru 1:20
3 as long as my breath is still
　　in me
　and the breath from God
　　remains in my nostrils,
4 my lips will not
　　speak unjustly,
　and my tongue will not
　　utter deceit.

^A 25:6 Or *a mere mortal*　　^B 26:13 = Leviathan

⁵ I will never affirm that you
    are right.
I will maintain my integrity ᴬ
    until I die.   Jb 2:3,9; 31:6; Pr 11:3
⁶ I will cling to
    my righteousness
    and never let it go.
My conscience will not
    accuse me as long as I live!

⁷ May my enemy be
    like the wicked
and my opponent
    like the unjust.
⁸ For what hope does
    the godless person have
    when he is cut off,   Jb 17:8; 20:5
when God takes away his life?
⁹ Will God hear his cry
when distress comes on him?
¹⁰ Will he delight
    in the Almighty?   Jb 22:26; Ps 37:4
Will he call on God
    at all times?
¹¹ I will teach you
    about God's power.
I will not conceal
    what the Almighty
    has planned. ᴮ
¹² All of you have seen this
    for yourselves,
why do you keep up
    this empty talk?   Jb 2:10; 15:2

¹³ This is a wicked man's lot
    from God,   Jb 20:29; 31:2; Ps 17:14
the inheritance the ruthless
    receive from the Almighty.
¹⁴ Even if his children
    increase, they are destined
    for the sword;
his descendants will never
    have enough food.
¹⁵ Those who survive
    him will be buried
    by the plague,

yet their widows
    will not weep for them.
¹⁶ Though he piles up silver
    like dust
and heaps up fine clothing
    like clay —
¹⁷ he may heap it up,
    but the righteous
    will wear it,
and the innocent
    will divide up his silver.
¹⁸ The house he built is
    like a moth's cocoon
or a shelter set up
    by a watchman.   Jb 4:19; Is 1:8
¹⁹ He lies down wealthy,
    but will do so no more;
when he opens his eyes,
    it is gone.
²⁰ Terrors overtake him
    like a flood;   Jb 18:11; 20:25; Jr 6:25
a storm wind sweeps him
    away at night.   Jb 21:18; Ps 83:15
²¹ An east wind picks him up,
    and he is gone;
it carries him away
    from his place.
²² It blasts at him
    without mercy,
while he flees desperately
    from its force.
²³ It claps its hands at him   Lm 2:15
and scoffs at him
    from its place.

A Hymn to Wisdom

28 Surely there is a mine
    for silver
and a place where gold
    is refined.
² Iron is taken
    from the ground,
and copper is smelted
    from ore.
³ A miner puts an end
    to the darkness;

ᴬ**27:5** Lit *will not remove my integrity from me*   ᴮ**27:11** Lit *what is with the Almighty*

he probes[A]
  the deepest recesses
for ore in the gloomy darkness.

4 He cuts a shaft far
    from human habitation,
  in places unknown to those
    who walk above ground.
  Suspended far away
    from people,
  the miners swing back
    and forth.
5 Food may come
    from the earth,
  but below the surface
    the earth is transformed
    as by fire.
6 Its rocks are a source
    of lapis lazuli,   Ex 24:10; Ezk 1:26
  containing flecks of gold.
7 No bird of prey knows
    that path;
  no falcon's eye has seen it.
8 Proud beasts
    have never walked on it;
  no lion has ever prowled
    over it.
9 The miner uses a flint tool
  and turns up ore
    from the root
    of the mountains.
10 He cuts out channels
    in the rocks,
  and his eyes spot
    every treasure.
11 He dams up the streams
    from flowing[B]
  so that he may bring to light
    what is hidden.

12 But where can wisdom
    be found,   Jb 28:20; Pr 16:16; Ec 7:23,25
  and where is understanding
    located?
13 No one can know its value,[C]
  since it cannot be found
    in the land of the living.

14 The ocean depths say,
    "It's not in me,"
  while the sea declares,
    "I don't have it."   Dt 30:11-13
15 Gold cannot be exchanged
    for it,
  and silver
    cannot be weighed out
    for its price.
16 Wisdom cannot be valued
    in the gold of Ophir,   1Kg 9:28
  in precious onyx or lapis
    lazuli.   Pr 3:14-16; 8:10-11; 16:16
17 Gold and glass
    do not compare with it,
  and articles of fine gold
    cannot be exchanged for it.
18 Coral and quartz are not
    worth mentioning.
  The price of wisdom
    is beyond pearls.
19 Topaz from Cush
    cannot compare with it,
  and it cannot be valued
    in pure gold.
20 Where then does wisdom
    come from,
  and where is understanding
    located?
21 It is hidden from the eyes
    of every living thing
  and concealed from the birds
    of the sky.
22 Abaddon and Death say,   Jb 25:6
    "We have heard news of it
    with our ears."
23 But God understands the way
    to wisdom,
  and he knows its location.
24 For he looks to the ends
    of the earth
  and sees everything
    under the heavens.
25 When God fixed the weight
    of the wind

A **28:3** Lit probes all   B **28:11** LXX, Vg read He explores the sources of the streams   C **28:13** LXX reads way

and distributed the water
  by measure,   Ps 135:7; Pr 30:4
26 when he established a limit ᴬ
  for the rain   Jb 5:10; 37:6; 38:25
  and a path for the lightning,
27 he considered wisdom
  and evaluated it;
  he established it
  and examined it.
28 He said to mankind,
  "The fear of the Lord—
  that is wisdom.
  And to turn from evil
  is understanding."   Dt 4:6; Pr 1:7

Job's Final Claim of Innocence

29 Job continued his discourse,
      saying:
2 If only I could be
  as in months gone by,
  in the days when God
  watched over me,
3 when his lamp shone
  above my head,
  and I walked through darkness
  by his light!   Jb 11:17; Ps 18:28
4 I would be as I was
  in the days of my youth
  when God's friendship
  rested on my tent,   Ps 25:14
5 when the Almighty was still
  with me
  and my children were
  around me,
6 when my feet were bathed
  in curds
  and the rock poured out
  streams of oil for me!   Dt 32:13

7 When I went out
  to the city gate   Dt 25:7; 2Sm 15:2
  and took my seat
  in the town square,
8 the young men saw me
  and withdrew,

while older men stood
  to their feet.
9 City officials stopped talking
  and covered their mouths
  with their hands.   Jdg 18:19
10 The noblemen's voices
  were hushed,
  and their tongues stuck
  to the roof of their mouths.
11 When they heard me,
  they blessed me,
  and when they saw me,
  they spoke well of me. ᴮ
12 For I rescued
  the poor who cried out
  for help,
  and the fatherless
  child who had no one
  to support him.   Ex 22:22; Dt 24:17
13 The dying blessed me,
  and I made the widow's heart
  rejoice.
14 I clothed myself
  in righteousness,   Ps 132:9
  and it enveloped me;
  my just decisions were
  like a robe and a turban.
15 I was eyes to the blind
  and feet to the lame.   Is 35:6
16 I was a father to the needy,
  and I examined the case
  of the stranger.
17 I shattered the fangs
  of the unjust   Jb 4:10; Ps 3:7; 58:6
  and snatched the prey
  from his teeth.
18 So I thought, "I will die
  in my own nest
  and multiply my days
  as the sand. ᶜ
19 My roots will have access
  to water,   Jb 14:9; Ps 1:3; Ezk 31:7
  and the dew will rest
  on my branches all night.

ᴬ**28:26** Or *decree*   ᴮ**29:11** Lit *When an ear heard, it called me blessed, and when an eye saw, it testified for me*   ᶜ**29:18** Or *as the phoenix*

20 My whole being
 will be refreshed within me,
and my bow will be renewed
 in my hand." Gn 49:24; Is 40:31; 41:1

21 Men listened to me
 with expectation,
waiting silently
 for my advice.

22 After a word from me
 they did not speak again;
my speech settled on them
 like dew. Dt 32:2

23 They waited for me as for
 the rain
and opened their mouths
 as for spring showers.

24 If I smiled at them,
 they couldn't believe it;
they were thrilled
 at^A the light
 of my countenance.

25 I directed their course
 and presided as chief.
I lived as a king
 among his troops,
like one who comforts
 those who mourn.

30
But now they mock me,
men younger than I am,
whose fathers I would have
 refused to put
with my sheep dogs.

2 What use to me was
 the strength
 of their hands?
Their vigor had left them.

3 Emaciated from poverty
 and hunger,
they gnawed the dry land,
the desolate wasteland
 by night.

4 They plucked mallow^B
 among the shrubs, Jb 12:4

and the roots
 of the broom tree were
 their food.

5 They were banished
 from human society;
people shouted at them
 as if they were thieves.

6 They are living on the slopes
 of the wadis,
among the rocks and in holes
 in the ground.

7 They bray
 among the shrubs;
they huddle
 beneath the thistles.

8 Foolish men,
 without even a name. Ec 7:5
They were forced to leave
 the land.

9 Now I am mocked
 by their songs; Jb 12:4; 30:1
I have become an object
 of scorn to them.

10 They despise me and keep
 their distance from me;
they do not hesitate to spit
 in my face. Nm 12:14; Is 50:6

11 Because God has loosened
 my^C bowstring
 and oppressed me,
they have cast off restraint
 in my presence. Jb 12:18; 29:20

12 The rabble^D rise up
 at my right;
they trap^E my feet
and construct
 their siege ramp^F
 against me. Jb 16:10; 19:12

13 They tear up my path;
they contribute
 to my destruction, Jb 6:2; Ps 57:1
without anyone to help them.

14 They advance as through
 a gaping breach;

---

^A 29:24 Lit they did not cast down   ^B 30:4 Or saltwort   ^C 30:11 Alt Hb tradition, LXX, Vg read his
^D 30:12 Hb obscure   ^E 30:12 Lit stretch out   ^F 30:12 Lit and raise up their destructive paths

they keep rolling in through
   the ruins.   *Jb 16:14; Jl 2:7*

15 Terrors are turned loose
   against me;   *Jb 18:11; 27:20; Ps 73:19*
they chase my dignity away
   like the wind,
and my prosperity
   has passed by like a cloud.

16 Now my life is poured out
   before me,
and days of suffering
   have seized me.   *Jb 10:15; 30:27*
17 Night pierces my bones,
but my gnawing pains
   never rest.   *Jb 33:19; Ps 6:2; 38:3*
18 My clothing is distorted
   with great force;
he chokes me by the neck
   of my garment.ᴬ
19 He throws me into the mud,
and I have become like dust
   and ashes.   *Jb 16:15; Ps 7:5; 75:10*

20 I cry out to you for help,
   but you do not answer me;
when I stand up,
   you merely look at me.
21 You have turned against me
   with cruelty;
you harass me
   with your strong hand.
22 You lift me up on the wind
   and make me ride it;
you scatter me in the storm.
23 Yes, I know that
   you will lead me to death —
the place appointed for all
   who live.   *Jb 3:15; 17:13; Ec 12:5*

24 Yet no one would stretch out
   his hand
against a ruined personᴮ
when he cries out to him
   for help

because of his distress.   *Jb 12:5*
25 Have I not wept for those
   who have fallen
   on hard times?
Has my soul not grieved
   for the needy?   *Jb 5:15; 24:4,14*
26 But when I hoped for good,
   evil came;
when I looked for light,
   darkness came.   *Jb 19:8; Is 59:9*
27 I am churning withinᶜ
   and cannot rest;
days of suffering
   confront me.
28 I walk about blackened,
   but not by the sun.ᴰ
I stood in the assembly
   and cried out for help.
29 I have become a brother
   to jackals
and a companion
   of ostriches.
30 My skin blackens
   and flakes off,ᴱ
and my bones burn
   with fever.   *Ps 102:3; Lm 4:8; 5:10*
31 My lyre is used for mourning
and my flute for the sound
   of weeping.   *Is 24:8; Ezk 26:13*

31 I have made a covenant
   with my eyes.   *Pr 4:25; Is 33:15*
How then could I look
   at a young woman?ᶠ   *Ex 22:6*
2 For what portion
   would I have
   from God above,   *Jb 20:29; 27:13*
or what inheritance
   from the Almighty
   on high?
3 Doesn't disaster come
   to the unjust
and misfortune to evildoers?
4 Does he not see my ways
   and number all my steps?

ᴬ**30:18** Hb obscure   ᴮ**30:24** Lit *a heap of ruins*   ᶜ**30:27** Lit *My bowels boil*   ᴰ**30:28** Or *walk in sunless gloom*   ᴱ**30:30** Lit *blackens away from me*   ᶠ**31:1** Or *a virgin*

5 If I have walked in falsehood
  or my foot has rushed
    to deceit,
6 let God weigh me on
    accurate scales,   Jb 6:2; Dn 5:27
  and he will recognize
    my integrity.   Jb 2:3,9; 27:5; Pr 11:3

7 If my step has turned
    from the way,
  my heart has followed
    my eyes,
  or impurity has stained
    my hands,   Nm 15:39; Jb 23:11; Ps 7:3
8 let someone else eat
    what I have sown,
  and let my crops
    be uprooted.   Lv 26:16; Dt 28:30

9 If my heart has gone
    astray over a woman
  or I have lurked at my
    neighbor's door,
10 let my own wife grind grain
    for another man,
  and let other men
    sleep with^A her.
11 For that would be a disgrace;
  it would be an iniquity
    deserving punishment.
12 For it is a fire that consumes
    down to Abaddon;
  it would destroy
    my entire harvest.   Jb 26:6; 28:22

13 If I have dismissed
    the case of my male
    or female servants
  when they made a complaint
    against me,
14 what could I do when God
    stands up to judge?
  How should I answer
    him when he calls me
    to account?

15 Did not the one
    who made me in the womb
    also make them?
  Did not the same God
    form us both in the womb?
16 If I have refused the wishes
    of the poor
  or let the widow's eyes
    go blind,   Jb 22:9; 24:3,21; 29:13
17 if I have eaten
    my few crumbs alone
  without letting the fatherless
    eat any of it —
18 for from my youth,
    I raised him as his father,
  and since the day I was born^B
    I guided the widow —
19 if I have seen anyone dying
    for lack of clothing
  or a needy person
    without a cloak,   Ex 22:26; Jb 22:6
20 if he^C did not bless me
  while warming himself
    with the fleece
    from my sheep,
21 if I ever cast my vote^D
    against a fatherless child
  when I saw that
    I had support
    in the city gate,   Jb 5:4; Pr 22:22
22 then let my shoulder blade
    fall from my back,
  and my arm be pulled
    from its socket.
23 For disaster from God
    terrifies me,
  and because of his majesty
    I could not do these things.
24 If I placed my confidence
    in gold
  or called fine gold my trust,
25 if I have rejoiced because
    my wealth is great

^A**31:10** Lit *men kneel down over*   ^B**31:18** Lit *and from my mother's womb*   ^C**31:20** Lit *his loins*
^D**31:21** Lit *I raise my hand*

or because my own hand
   has acquired so much,
26 if I have gazed at the sun
   when it was shining
or at the moon moving
   in splendor,   Dt 4:19; 17:3; Ezk 8:16
27 so that my heart
   was secretly enticed
and I threw them a kiss, A
28 this would also be an iniquity
   deserving punishment,
for I would have denied God
   above.

29 Have I rejoiced over
   my enemy's distress,
or become excited
   when trouble came his way?
30 I have not allowed my mouth
   to sin
by asking for his life
   with a curse.
31 Haven't the members
   of my household said,
"Who is there who has not
   had enough to eat
   at Job's table?"
32 No stranger had to spend
   the night on the street,
for I opened my door
   to the traveler.
33 Have I covered
   my transgressions
   as others do B   Jb 7:21; 22:5; 33:9
by hiding my iniquity
   in my heart   Ps 32:3-5; Pr 28:13
34 because I greatly feared
   the crowds
and because the contempt
   of the clans terrified me,
so I grew silent
   and would not go outside?

35 If only I had someone to hear
   my case!   Jb 16:21; Ec 6:10; Is 45:9

Here is my signature;
   let the Almighty answer me.
Let my Opponent compose
   his indictment.
36 I would surely carry it
   on my shoulder
and wear it like a crown.   Pr 4:9
37 I would give him an account
   of all my steps;
I would approach him
   like a prince.

38 If my land cries out
   against me
and its furrows join
   in weeping,
39 if I have consumed
   its produce
   without payment
or shown contempt
   for its tenants, C
40 then let thorns grow
   instead of wheat   Gn 3:18; Is 34:13
and stinkweed
   instead of barley.   Pr 24:31; Is 5:2

The words of Job are concluded.

Elihu's Angry Response

32 So these three men quit answering Job, because he was righteous in his own eyes. 2 Then Elihu son of Barachel the Buzite from the family of Ram became angry. He was angry at Job because he had justified himself rather than God. 3 He was also angry at Job's three friends because they had failed to refute him and yet had condemned him. D   Jb 10:7; 33:9; 34:5-6

4 Now Elihu had waited to speak to Job because they were all older than he. 5 But when he saw that the three men could not answer Job, he became angry.

A **31:27** Lit *and my hand kissed my mouth*   B **31:33** Or *as Adam*   C **31:39** Lit *or caused the breath of its tenants to breathe out*   D **32:3** Alt Hb tradition reads *condemned God*

⁶ So Elihu son of Barachel the Buzite replied:

I am young in years,
while you are old;
therefore I was timid
and afraid
to tell you what I know.   Jb 15:17
⁷ I thought that age
should speak
and maturity should teach
wisdom.
⁸ But it is the spirit
in a person—
the breath
from the Almighty—   Gn 2:7
that gives anyone
understanding.
⁹ It is not only the old
who are wise
or the elderly
who understand
how to judge.
¹⁰ Therefore I say, "Listen to me.
I too will declare what I know."
¹¹ Look, I waited
for your conclusions;
I listened to your insights
as you sought for words.
¹² I paid close attention to you.
Yet no one proved Job wrong;
not one of you refuted
his arguments.
¹³ So do not claim,
"We have found wisdom;
let God deal with him,
not man."
¹⁴ But Job has not directed
his argument to me,
and I will not respond to him
with your arguments.

¹⁵ Job's friends are dismayed
and can no longer answer;
words have left them.
¹⁶ Should I continue to wait
now that they are silent,
now that they stand there
and no longer answer?
¹⁷ I too will answer;ᴬ
yes, I will tell what I know.
¹⁸ For I am full of words,
and my spiritᴮ compels me
to speak.   Jb 19:3; 32:18; Ac 4:20
¹⁹ My heartᶜ is
like unvented wine;
it is about to burst
like new wineskins.   Jb 15:35
²⁰ I must speak so that
I can find relief;
I must open my lips
and respond.
²¹ I will be partial to no one,
and I will not give anyone
an undeserved title.
²² For I do not know how to give
such titles;
otherwise, my Maker
would remove me
in an instant.

Elihu Confronts Job

33 But now, Job, pay attention
to my speech,
and listen to all my words.
² I am going to open
my mouth;
my tongue will form words
on my palate.
³ My words come from
my upright heart,   1Kg 9:4
and my lips speak
with sincerity
what they know.
⁴ The Spirit of God has made me,
and the breath of the Almighty
gives me life.   Jb 27:2; 32:8; 35:13
⁵ Refute me if you can.
Prepare your case
against me; take your stand.
⁶ I am just like you before God;
I was also pinched off
from a piece of clay.   Jb 4:19

ᴬ32:17 Lit *answer my part*   ᴮ32:18 Lit *and the spirit of my belly*   ᶜ32:19 Lit *belly*

THE BOOKS OF
POETRY

One of the ten divisions of the Bible is called Poetry. Five books containing poetry and wisdom are located in the middle of your Bible. Glory, wisdom, and love are unveiled as perfect attributes in Jesus Christ.

JOB is the story of a man named Job whom God tested. The book explores questions concerning the sovereignty of God and the problem of suffering. In the middle of his suffering, Job cried out for a redeemer. We now worship the great Redeemer, Jesus Christ.

PSALMS is a collection of 150 "songs" written by different authors over a long period of time. King David wrote many of the psalms. Every form of sorrow, joy, repentance, ambition, prayer, or hope is found in this book. In the middle of these psalms is the great promise of a Messiah whom we now know as Jesus Christ.

PROVERBS contains godly wisdom, most of which was recorded by King Solomon. The book calls people to live in ways that please God, gives practical advice, and makes wise observations. The wisdom mentioned in this book is seen in all its fullness in Jesus Christ.

ECCLESIASTES is another book of wisdom written by Solomon. The title means "the teacher" or "the preacher" and tells of the meaninglessness of life apart from God. Christ is the answer to the meaningless life as He came to give abundant life.

THE SONG OF SOLOMON is a remarkable love poem that King Solomon wrote. This love between husband and wife is like the love expressed between Christ and His Church.

PSALMS
FOR ALL TIMES

The book of Psalms has been called the songbook of the Bible. Each psalm is a poem or song to God. You can read a psalm as a prayer, sing it as a song, or say it as a confession to God. Look at the list. Use your Bible to find a psalm that fits a need in your life.

PSALM 8 & PSALM 19 can help you praise God for His creation.

PSALM 15 can help you know how to live in ways that please God.

PSALM 18:1–3 can help you know God cares for you.

PSALM 23 can help you find comfort in God.

PSALM 25:4–7 can help you pray for God's guidance.

PSALM 32 & PSALM 51 can help you ask God for forgiveness.

PSALM 36:5–7 & PSALM 136 can help you thank God for His love for you.

PSALM 37:3–8 can help you trust in God.

PSALM 46 can help you know God's power.

PSALM 62 can help you find hope in God.

PSALM 92:1–5; PSALM 95:1–7; PSALM 96; & PSALM 98 can help you praise God.

PSALM 100 can help you worship God.

PSALM 119 can help you know about God's Word.

PSALM 121 can help you know about God's protection.

PSALM 139 can help you know that God is all-seeing, all-knowing, and all-powerful.

PSALM 148, PSALM 149, & PSALM 150 can help you praise God.

⁷ Fear of me should not
      terrify you;   Jb 20:25; Ps 55:4; 88:15
   no pressure from me
      should weigh you down.

⁸ Surely you have spoken
      in my hearing,
   and I have heard
      these very ᴬ words:
⁹ "I am pure,
      without transgression;
   I am clean and have
      no iniquity.   Jb 9:21; 11:4; 34:6
¹⁰ But he finds reasons
      to oppose me;
   he regards me as his enemy.
¹¹ He puts my feet in the stocks;
   he stands watch over
      all my paths."   Jb 10:14; 14:16

¹² But I tell you that you
      are wrong in this matter,
   since God is greater
      than man.   Jb 4:17; 9:2; 15:14
¹³ Why do you take him to court
   for not answering anything
      a person asks? ᴮ
¹⁴ For God speaks time
      and again,
   but a person may not notice it.
¹⁵ In a dream, a vision
      in the night,   Jb 4:13; 7:14; 20:8
   when deep sleep comes
      over people   Gn 2:21; 15:12; Jb 4:13
   as they slumber on their beds,
¹⁶ he uncovers their ears   Jb 4:12
   and terrifies them ᶜ
      with warnings,
¹⁷ in order to turn a person
      from his actions
   and suppress the pride
      of a person.
¹⁸ God spares his soul
      from the Pit,   Jb 33:28,30; 36:16

his life from crossing
      the river of death. ᴰ
¹⁹ A person may be disciplined
      on his bed with pain   Jb 7:13
   and constant distress
      in his bones,   Jb 30:17; Ps 6:2; 38:3
²⁰ so that he detests bread,
   and his soul despises his
      favorite food.   Jb 3:24; 6:7; Ps 102:4
²¹ His flesh wastes away
      to nothing, ᴱ
   and his unseen bones
      stick out.
²² He draws near to the Pit,
   and his life
      to the executioners.
²³ If there is an angel
      on his side,   Ex 23:20,23; Ps 34:7
   one mediator out of
      a thousand,
   to tell a person what is right
      for him ᶠ
²⁴ and to be gracious to him
      and say,
   "Spare him from going down
      to the Pit;
   I have found a ransom,"   Ps 49:7
²⁵ then his flesh
      will be healthier ᴳ than
      in his youth,
   and he will return
      to the days
      of his youthful vigor.   Dt 34:7
²⁶ He will pray to God, and God
      will delight in him.
   That person will see his face
      with a shout of joy,   Gn 33:10
   and God will restore
      his righteousness to him.
²⁷ He will look at men and say,
   "I have sinned and perverted
      what was right;
   yet I did not get
      what I deserved. ᴴ

ᴬ 33:8 Lit heard a sound of   ᴮ 33:13 Lit court, for he does not answer all his words   ᶜ 33:16 LXX; MT
reads and seals   ᴰ 33:18 Or from perishing by the sword   ᴱ 33:21 Lit away from sight   ᶠ 33:23 Or to
vouch for a person's uprightness   ᴳ 33:25 Hb obscure   ᴴ 33:27 Lit and the same was not to me

²⁸ He redeemed my soul
    from going down to the Pit,
and I will continue to see
    the light."
²⁹ God certainly does all
    these things
    two or three times
    to a person
³⁰ in order to turn him back
    from the Pit,
so he may shine
    with the light of life.   Ps 56:13
³¹ Pay attention, Job, and listen
    to me.
Be quiet, and I will speak.
³² But if you have something
    to say,^A answer me;
speak, for I would like
    to justify you.
³³ If not, then listen to me;
be quiet, and I will teach
    you wisdom.

34 Then Elihu continued,^B saying:

² Hear my words,
    you wise ones,
and listen to me,
    you knowledgeable ones.
³ Doesn't the ear test words
    as the palate tastes food?
⁴ Let us judge for ourselves
    what is right;
let us decide together
    what is good.
⁵ For Job has declared,
    "I am righteous,
yet God has deprived me
    of justice.   Jb 10:7; 27:2; 33:9
⁶ Would I lie about my case?
My wound^C is incurable,
    though I am
    without transgression."
⁷ What man is like Job?
He drinks derision like water.

⁸ He keeps company
    with evildoers
and walks with wicked men.
⁹ For he has said,
    "A man gains nothing
when he becomes
    God's friend."   Ex 5:2; Jb 21:15
¹⁰ Therefore listen to me,
    you men of understanding.
It is impossible for God
    to do wrong,
and for the Almighty
    to act unjustly.   Dt 32:4; Ps 92:15
¹¹ For he repays a person
    according to his deeds,
and he gives him what his
    conduct deserves.^D
¹² Indeed, it is true that God
    does not act wickedly
and the Almighty does not
    pervert justice.   2Ch 19:6; Jb 8:3
¹³ Who gave him authority
    over the earth?
Who put him in charge of
    the entire world?   Jb 38:4
¹⁴ If he put his mind to it
and withdrew the spirit
    and breath he gave,   Ps 104:29
¹⁵ every living thing
    would perish together
and mankind would return
    to the dust.   Gn 2:7; Jb 4:19; 10:9

¹⁶ If you have understanding,
    hear this;
listen to what I have to say.
¹⁷ Could one who hates justice
    govern the world?
Will you condemn the mighty
    Righteous One,   Gn 18:25; 2Sm 23:3
¹⁸ who says to a king,
    "Worthless man!"
and to nobles,
    "Wicked men!"?   Ex 22:28; Jb 12:21

^A33:32 Lit If there are words   ^B34:1 Lit answered   ^C34:6 Lit arrow   ^D34:11 Lit and like a path of a man, he causes him to find

¹⁹ God is not partial to princes
and does not favor the rich
over the poor,
for they are all the work
of his hands.
²⁰ They die suddenly
in the middle of the night;
people shudder,
then pass away.
Even the mighty are removed
without effort.

²¹ For his eyes watch over
a man's ways,
and he observes all his steps.
²² There is no darkness,
no deep darkness,
where evildoers can hide.
²³ God does not need to examine
a person further,
that one should^A
approach him in court.
²⁴ He shatters the mighty
without an investigation
and sets others in their place.
²⁵ Therefore, he recognizes
their deeds   Jb 11:11; Ps 10:14
and overthrows them
by night, and they
are crushed.
²⁶ In full view of the public,^B
he strikes them
for their wickedness,
²⁷ because they turned aside
from following him
and did not understand any
of his ways
²⁸ but caused the poor
to cry out to him,
and he heard the outcry
of the needy.   Ex 3:7; 22:23; Jms 5:4
²⁹ But when God is silent,
who can declare him guilty?
When he hides his face,
who can see him?

Yet he watches over both
individuals and nations,
³⁰ so that godless men
should not rule
or ensnare the people.

³¹ Suppose someone says
to God,
"I have endured
my punishment;
I will no longer act wickedly.
³² Teach me what I cannot see;
if I have done wrong, I won't
do it again."
³³ Should God repay you
on your terms
when you have rejected his?
You must choose, not I!
So declare what you know.
³⁴ Reasonable men will say
to me,
along with the wise men
who hear me,
³⁵ "Job speaks
without knowledge;   Jb 35:16
his words are
without insight."
³⁶ If only Job were tested
to the limit,
because his answers are
like those of wicked men.
³⁷ For he adds rebellion
to his sin;
he scornfully claps
in our presence,   Nm 24:10
while multiplying his words
against God.   Jb 16:4; 35:16; Ezk 35:13

35

Then Elihu continued, saying:
² Do you think it is just
when you say,
"I am righteous before God"?
³ For you ask, "What does
it profit you,^C

^A**34:23** Some emend to *God has not appointed a time for man to*   ^B**34:26** Lit *In a place of spectators*
^C**35:3** Some emend to *me*

and what benefit comes
   to me, if I do not sin?"   Jb 9:29

4 I will answer you
   and your friends with you.
5 Look at the heavens and see;
   gaze at the clouds high
      above you.
6 If you sin, how does it
      affect God?
   If you multiply
      your transgressions,
   what does it do to him?
7 If you are righteous,
      what do you give him,
   or what does he receive
      from your hand?   Jb 22:3; 41:11
8 Your wickedness affects
      a person like yourself,
   and your righteousness, a
      son of man.ᴬ
9 People cry out because of
      severe oppression;
   they shout for help
      because of the power
      of the mighty.   Ex 2:23; Jb 24:12
10 But no one asks,
   "Where is God my Maker,
   who provides us with songs
      in the night,   Ps 42:8; 77:6; Ac 16:25
11 who gives us
      more understanding
   than the animals of the earth
   and makes us wiser
      than the birds of the sky?"
12 There they cry out,
      but he does not answer,
   because of the pride
      of evil people.   Pr 1:28; Is 1:15
13 Indeed, God does not listen
      to empty cries,
   and the Almighty does not
      take note of it —
14 how much less
      whenᴮ you complainᶜ
   that you do not see him,

that your case is before him
   and you are waiting for him.
15 But now, because God's anger
      does not punish
   and he does not pay attention
      to transgression,ᴰ
16 Job opens his mouth in vain
   and multiplies words
      without knowledge.   Jb 15:2

36 Then Elihu continued, say-
      ing:
2 Be patient with me
      a little longer, and I will
      inform you,
   for there is still more
      to be said on God's behalf.
3 I will get my knowledge from
      a distant place
   and ascribe justice
      to my Maker.
4 Indeed, my words are
      not false;
   one who has complete
      knowledge is with you.

5 Yes, God is mighty,
      but he despises no one;
   he understands all things.ᴱ
6 He does not keep
      the wicked alive,   Gn 18:25
   but he gives justice
      to the oppressed.
7 He does not withdraw
      his gaze from the righteous,
   but he seats them forever
      with enthroned kings,
   and they are exalted.

8 If people are bound
      with chains
   and trapped by the cords
      of affliction,
9 God tells them
      what they have done

ᴬ35:8 Or a mere mortal   ᴮ35:14 Or how then can   ᶜ35:14 Lit say   ᴰ35:15 LXX, Vg; MT reads folly, or arrogance; Hb obscure   ᴱ36:5 Lit he is mighty in strength of heart

and how arrogantly
   they have transgressed.
¹⁰ He opens their ears
   to correction   Jb 4:12; 13:1; 33:16
and tells them to repent
   from iniquity.
¹¹ If they listen and serve him,
they will end their days
   in prosperity
and their years in happiness.
¹² But if they do not listen,
they will cross the river
   of death^A
and die without knowledge.

¹³ Those who have
   a godless heart
   harbor anger;
even when God binds them,
   they do not cry for help.
¹⁴ They die in their youth;
their life ends among
   male cult prostitutes. Dt 23:17
¹⁵ God rescues the afflicted by
   their affliction;
he instructs them
   by their torment.

¹⁶ Indeed, he lured you
   from the jaws^B of distress
to a spacious
   and unconfined place.
Your table was spread
   with choice food.
¹⁷ Yet now you are obsessed
   with the judgment due
   the wicked;
judgment and justice
   have seized you.
¹⁸ Be careful that
   no one lures you
   with riches;^C
do not let a large ransom^D
   lead you astray. 1Sm 12:3; Ps 26:10

¹⁹ Can your wealth^E or all
   your physical exertion
keep you from distress?
²⁰ Do not long for the night
when nations will disappear
   from their places.
²¹ Be careful that
   you do not turn to iniquity,
for that is why you
   have been tested
   by^F affliction.

²² Look, God shows himself
   exalted by his power.
Who is a teacher like him?
²³ Who has appointed his way
   for him,
and who has declared,
   "You have done wrong"?
²⁴ Remember that you
   should praise his work,
which people
   have sung about. Ps 92:5; 104:33
²⁵ All mankind has seen it;
people have looked at it
   from a distance. Ps 19:3; Heb 11:13
²⁶ Yes, God is exalted
   beyond our knowledge;
the number of his years
   cannot be counted.   Ps 90:2
²⁷ For he makes waterdrops
   evaporate;^G
they distill the rain
   into its^H mist,   Gn 2:6; Jb 38:28
²⁸ which the clouds pour out
   and shower abundantly
   on mankind.
²⁹ Can anyone understand
   how the clouds
   spread out
or how the thunder roars
   from God's pavilion?   Jb 26:14
³⁰ See how he spreads
   his lightning around him

^A**36:12** Or *will perish by the sword*   ^B**36:16** Lit *from a mouth of narrowness*   ^C**36:18** Or *you into mockery*   ^D**36:18** Or *bribe*   ^E**36:19** Or *cry for help*   ^F**36:21** Or *for you have preferred this to*   ^G**36:27** Lit *he draws in waterdrops*   ^H**36:27** Or *his*

and covers the depths
of the sea.
31 For he judges the nations
with these;
he gives food
in abundance. Jb 37:13; Ps 136:25
32 He covers his hands
with lightning
and commands it to hit
its mark.
33 The^A thunder declares
his presence;^B
the cattle also,
the approaching storm.

37 My heart pounds at this
and leaps from my chest.^C
2 Just listen to
his thunderous voice
and the rumbling that comes
from his mouth.
3 He lets it loose beneath
the entire sky;
his lightning to the ends
of the earth. Jb 38:13; Is 11:12; Ezk 7:2

4 Then there comes
a roaring sound;
God thunders
with his majestic voice.
He does not restrain
the lightning
when his rumbling voice
is heard.
5 God thunders wondrously
with his voice;
he does great things that
we cannot comprehend.
6 For he says to the snow,
"Fall to the earth," Jb 6:16; 24:19
and the torrential rains,
his mighty torrential rains,
7 serve as his sign
to all mankind,
so that all men may know
his work.

8 The wild animals enter
their lairs
and stay in their dens. Jb 38:40
9 The windstorm comes
from its chamber,
and the cold from the
driving north winds.
10 Ice is formed by the breath
of God, 2Sm 22:21; Jb 4:9; Is 30:33
and watery expanses
are frozen.
11 He saturates clouds
with moisture; Jb 26:8; 36:29; 38:9
he scatters his lightning
through them.
12 They swirl about,
turning round and round
at his direction,
accomplishing everything
he commands them
over the surface
of the inhabited world.
13 He causes this to happen
for punishment,
for his land,
or for his faithful love.

14 Listen to this, Job.
Stop and consider
God's wonders.
15 Do you know
how God directs his clouds
or makes their lightning
flash?
16 Do you understand
how the clouds float,
those wonderful works
of him who has
perfect knowledge?
17 You whose clothes get hot
when the south wind
brings calm to the land,
18 can you help God spread out
the skies
as hard as
a cast metal mirror?

^A**36:33** Lit *His*, or *Its*   ^B**36:33** Lit *thunder announces concerning him* or *it*   ^C**37:1** Lit *from its place*

¹⁹ Teach us what we should say
        to him;   Jb 9:3,14; 40:2; Jms 1:5
    we cannot prepare our case
        because of our darkness.
²⁰ Should he be told that I want
        to speak?
    Can a man speak
        when he is confused?
²¹ Now no one can even look
        at the sun
    when it is in the skies,
    after a wind
        has swept through and
        cleared the clouds away. ^A
²² Yet out of the north he comes,
        shrouded in a golden glow;
    awesome majesty
        surrounds him.   Ex 15:11; Dt 7:21
²³ The Almighty — we cannot
        reach him —
    he is exalted in power!
    He will not violate justice and
        abundant righteousness,
²⁴ therefore, men fear him.
    He does not look favorably
        on any who are wise
        in heart.   Pr 3:7; 26:5,12,16; 28:11

The Lord Speaks

38 Then the Lord answered Job
        from the whirlwind. He said:
² Who is this who obscures
        my counsel
    with ignorant words?   Jb 34:35
³ Get ready to answer me
        like a man;
    when I question you,
        you will inform me.   2Sm 11:7
⁴ Where were you
        when I established
        the earth?   Ps 89:11; 102:25; 104:5
    Tell me, if you have ^B
        understanding.
⁵ Who fixed its dimensions?
        Certainly you know!

Who stretched
        a measuring line across it?
⁶ What supports
        its foundations?
    Or who laid its cornerstone
⁷ while the morning stars
        sang together
    and all the sons of God
        shouted for joy?   Gn 6:2,4; Jb 1:6

⁸ Who enclosed the sea
        behind doors
    when it burst from the womb,
⁹ when I made the clouds
        its garment
    and total darkness
        its blanket, ^C   2Sm 22:10; Jb 22:13
¹⁰ when I determined
        its boundaries ^D
    and put its bars and doors
        in place,
¹¹ when I declared:
    "You may come this far,
        but no farther;
    your proud waves stop here"?

¹² Have you ever in your life
        commanded the morning
    or assigned the dawn
        its place,
¹³ so it may seize the edges
        of the earth
    and shake the wicked
        out of it?
¹⁴ The earth is changed as clay
        is by a seal;
    its hills stand out
        like the folds of a garment.
¹⁵ Light ^E is withheld
        from the wicked,
    and the arm raised
        in violence is broken.

¹⁶ Have you traveled
        to the sources of the sea

---

^A**37:21** Lit and cleaned them   ^B**38:4** Lit know   ^C**38:9** Lit swaddling clothes   ^D**38:10** Lit I broke my statute on it   ^E**38:15** Lit Their light

or walked in the depths
of the oceans?

¹⁷ Have the gates of death
been revealed to you?   Ps 9:13
Have you seen the gates
of deep darkness?

¹⁸ Have you comprehended
the extent of the earth?
Tell me, if you know all this.

¹⁹ Where is the road
to the home of light?
Do you know
where darkness lives,

²⁰ so you can lead it back
to its border?
Are you familiar
with the paths to its home?

²¹ Don't you know? You were
already born;   Jb 15:7; Ps 90:2
you have lived so long!ᴬ

²² Have you entered the place
where the snow is stored?
Or have you seen
the storehouses of hail,

²³ which I hold in reserve
for times of trouble,
for the day of warfare
and battle?   Jos 10:11; Is 30:30

²⁴ What road leads to the place
where light is dispersed?ᴮ
Where is the source of
the east wind that spreads
across the earth?

²⁵ Who cuts a channel
for the flooding rain
or clears the way for lightning,

²⁶ to bring rain
on an uninhabited land,
on a desert
with no human life,ᶜ

²⁷ to satisfy
the parched wasteland

and cause the grass
to sprout?   Gn 1:11; 2Sm 23:4

²⁸ Does the rain have a father?
Who fathered the drops
of dew?   Jb 5:10; Ps 147:8; Jr 14:22

²⁹ Whose womb did the ice
come from?
Who gave birth to the frost
of heaven

³⁰ when water becomes as hard
as stone,ᴰ
and the surface
of the watery depths
is frozen?   Jb 37:10; Ps 147:16-17

³¹ Can you fasten the chains
of the Pleiades
or loosen the belt of Orion?

³² Can you bring out
the constellationsᴱ
in their season
and lead the Bearᶠ
and her cubs?   Jb 9:9; Is 40:26

³³ Do you know the laws
of heaven?   Jr 31:35; 33:25
Can you impose
itsᴳ authority on earth?

³⁴ Can you commandᴴ
the clouds
so that a flood of water
covers you?   Jb 22:11; Ps 69:1-2

³⁵ Can you send out
lightning bolts,
and they go?   Ex 19:16; Ps 18:14; 97:4
Do they report to you:
"Here we are"?

³⁶ Who put wisdom in the heartᴵ
or gave
the mind understanding?

³⁷ Who has the wisdom
to number the clouds?
Or who can tilt the water jars
of heaven

38 when the dust hardens
     like cast metal
and the clods of dirt
     stick together?

39 Can you hunt prey
     for a lioness
or satisfy the appetite
     of young lions   Ps 104:21; 145:15-16
40 when they crouch
     in their dens
and lie in wait
     within their lairs?
41 Who provides
     the raven's food   1Kg 17:4,6
when its young cry out to God
and wander about for lack
     of food?

39 Do you know when
     mountain goats give birth?
Have you watched the deer
     in labor?
2 Can you count the months
     they are pregnant[A]
so you can know the time
     they give birth?
3 They crouch down
     to give birth to their young;
they deliver their newborn.[B]
4 Their offspring
     are healthy and grow up
     in the open field.
They leave
     and do not return.[C]

5 Who set the wild donkey free?
Who released
     the swift donkey
     from its harness?
6 I made the desert its home,
and the salty wasteland
     its dwelling.   Dt 29:23; Ps 107:34
7 It scoffs at the noise
     of the village

and never hears the shouts
     of a driver.   Ex 3:7; 5:10,13-14; Jb 3:18
8 It roams the mountains
     for its pastureland,
searching
     for anything green.
9 Would the wild ox be willing
     to serve you?
Would it spend the night
     by your feeding trough?
10 Can you hold the wild ox
     to a furrow by its harness?
Will it plow the valleys
     behind you?
11 Can you depend on it
     because its strength
     is great?
Would you leave it to do
     your hard work?
12 Can you trust the wild ox
     to harvest your grain
and bring it
     to your threshing floor?

13 The wings of the ostrich
     flap joyfully,
but are her feathers
     and plumage
     like the stork's?[D]   Ps 104:17; Jr 8:7
14 She abandons her eggs
     on the ground
and lets them be warmed
     in the sand.
15 She forgets that a foot
     may crush them
or that some wild animal
     may trample them.
16 She treats her young harshly,
     as if they were not her own,
with no fear that her labor
     may have been in vain.
17 For God has deprived her
     of wisdom;
he has not endowed her
     with understanding.   Jb 35:11

A 39:2 Lit *months they fulfill*   B 39:3 Or *they send away their labor pains*   C 39:4 Lit *return to them*
D 39:13 Hb obscure

¹⁸ When she proudly^A spreads
    her wings,
  she laughs at the horse
    and its rider.

¹⁹ Do you give strength
    to the horse?
  Do you adorn his neck
    with a mane?^A
²⁰ Do you make him leap
    like a locust?
  His proud snorting
    fills one with terror.
²¹ He paws^B in the valley
    and rejoices in his strength;
  he charges into battle.^C
²² He laughs at fear,
    since he is afraid of nothing;
  he does not run
    from the sword.
²³ A quiver rattles at his side,
  along with a flashing spear
    and a javelin.
²⁴ He charges ahead^D
    with trembling rage;
  he cannot stand still
    at the trumpet's sound.
²⁵ When the trumpet blasts,
    he snorts defiantly.^E
  He smells the battle
    from a distance;
  he hears the officers' shouts
    and the battle cry.

²⁶ Does the hawk take flight
    by your understanding
  and spread its wings
    to the south?
²⁷ Does the eagle soar
    at your command
  and make its nest on high?
²⁸ It lives on a cliff
    where it spends the night;
  its stronghold is
    on a rocky crag.

²⁹ From there it searches
    for prey;   Jb 9:26; Hab 1:8
  its eyes penetrate
    the distance.
³⁰ Its brood gulps down blood,
  and where the slain are,
    it is there.   Ezk 39:17; Mt 24:28

40

The LORD answered Job:
² Will the one
who contends
with the Almighty
correct him?
Let him who argues with God
give an answer.^F

³ Then Job answered the LORD:
⁴ I am so insignificant.
  How can I answer you?
  I place my hand
    over my mouth.
⁵ I have spoken once,
    and I will not reply;
  twice, but now
    I can add nothing.   Jb 9:3,15

⁶ Then the LORD answered Job
from the whirlwind: Jb 38:1; Jr 30:23
⁷ Get ready to answer me
    like a man;
  When I question you,
    you will inform me.   2Sm 11:7
⁸ Would you really challenge
    my justice?
  Would you declare me guilty
    to justify yourself?   Jb 9:20,28
⁹ Do you have an arm
    like God's?
  Can you thunder with a voice
    like his?

¹⁰ Adorn yourself with majesty
    and splendor,   Ps 93:1; 96:6; 104:1
  and clothe yourself
    with honor and glory.

---

^A**39:18,19** Hb obscure   ^B**39:21** LXX, Syr; MT reads *They dig*   ^C**39:21** Lit *he goes out to meet the weaponry*   ^D**39:24** Lit *He swallows the ground*   ^E**39:25** Lit *he says, "Aha!"*   ^F**40:2** Lit *God respond to it*

11 Pour out your raging anger;
  look on every proud person
    and humiliate him. Is 2:11
12 Look on every proud person
    and humble him; Ps 18:27; 63:3
  trample the wicked
    where they stand. A
13 Hide them together
    in the dust;
  imprison them in the grave. B
14 Then I will confess to you
    that your own right hand
      can deliver you. Ps 17:7; 20:6; 49:7

15 Look at Behemoth,
  which I made along with you.
  He eats grass like cattle.
16 Look at the strength
    of his back C
  and the power in the muscles
    of his belly.
17 He stiffens his tail
    like a cedar tree;
  the tendons of his thighs
    are woven firmly together.
18 His bones are bronze tubes;
  his limbs are like iron rods.
19 He is the foremost
    of God's works; Jb 26:14; Pr 8:22
  only his Maker can draw
    the sword against him.
20 The hills yield food for him,
  while all sorts of
    wild animals play there.
21 He lies
    under the lotus plants,
  hiding in the protection D
    of marshy reeds.
22 Lotus plants cover him
    with their shade;
  the willows by the brook
    surround him.
23 Though the river rages,
    Behemoth is unafraid;

he remains confident, even if
    the Jordan surges up
      to his mouth.
24 Can anyone capture him
    while he looks on, E
  or pierce his nose
    with snares?

41 Can you pull in Leviathan
      with a hook Jb 3:8; Ps 104:26
  or tie his tongue down
    with a rope?
2 Can you put a cord F
    through his nose
  or pierce his jaw
    with a hook? 2Kg 19:28; Jb 40:24
3 Will he beg you for mercy
  or speak softly to you?
4 Will he make a covenant
    with you
  so that you can take him
    as a slave forever? Ex 21:6
5 Can you play with him
    like a bird
  or put him on a leash G
    for your girls?
6 Will traders bargain for him
  or divide him
    among the merchants?
7 Can you fill his hide
    with harpoons
  or his head
    with fishing spears?
8 Lay a H hand on him.
  You will remember the battle
  and never repeat it!
9 Any hope of capturing him
    proves false.
  Does a person not collapse
    at the very sight of him?
10 No one is ferocious enough
    to rouse Leviathan; Jb 3:8
  who then can stand
    against me?

A 40:12 Lit wicked in their place   B 40:13 Lit together; bind their faces in the hidden place   C 40:16 Or
waist   D 40:21 Lit plants, in the hiding place   E 40:24 Lit capture it in its eyes   F 41:2 Lit reed   G 41:5 Lit
or bind him   H 41:8 Lit your

¹¹ Who confronted me, that I
  should repay him?
Everything under heaven
  belongs to me.   Ps 24:1; Rm 11:35

¹² I cannot be silent
  about his limbs,
his power,
  and his graceful proportions.

¹³ Who can strip off
  his outer covering?
Who can penetrate
  his double layer
  of armor?^A   Jr 46:4; 51:3

¹⁴ Who can open his jaws,^B
surrounded by
  those terrifying teeth?

¹⁵ His pride is in his rows
  of scales,
closely sealed together.

¹⁶ One scale is so close
  to another^C
that no air can pass
  between them.

¹⁷ They are joined
  to one another,
so closely connected^D
  they cannot be separated.

¹⁸ His snorting^E flashes
  with light,
while his eyes are
  like the rays^F of dawn.

¹⁹ Flaming torches shoot
  from his mouth;
fiery sparks fly out!

²⁰ Smoke billows
  from his nostrils   2Sm 22:9
as from a boiling pot
  or burning reeds.

²¹ His breath sets coals ablaze,
  and flames pour out
  of his mouth.

²² Strength resides in his neck,

and dismay dances
  before him.

²³ The folds of his flesh
  are joined together,
solid as metal^G
  and immovable.

²⁴ His heart is as hard as a rock,
  as hard as a lower millstone!

²⁵ When Leviathan rises,
  the mighty^H are terrified;
they withdraw because of
  his thrashing.

²⁶ The sword that reaches him
  will have no effect,
nor will a spear, dart,
  or arrow.

²⁷ He regards iron as straw,
and bronze as rotten wood.

²⁸ No arrow can make
  him flee;
slingstones become
  like stubble to him.

²⁹ A club is regarded as stubble,
and he laughs at the sound
  of a javelin.   2Ch 30:10; Jb 39:7,18

³⁰ His undersides are
  jagged potsherds,
spreading the mud
  like a threshing sledge.

³¹ He makes the depths seethe
  like a cauldron;
he makes the sea
  like an ointment jar.

³² He leaves a shining wake
  behind him;^I
one would think the deep
  had gray hair!

³³ He has no equal on earth —
  a creature devoid of fear!

³⁴ He surveys everything
  that is haughty;
he is king over all
  the proud beasts.^J

^A**41:13** LXX; MT reads *double bridle*   ^B**41:14** Lit *open the doors of his face*   ^C**41:16** Lit *One by one they
approach*   ^D**41:17** Lit *another; they cling together and*   ^E**41:18** Or *sneezing*   ^F**41:18** Lit *eyelids*
^G**41:23** Lit *together, hard on him*   ^H**41:25** Or *the divine beings*   ^I**41:32** Lit *a path*   ^J**41:34** Lit *the
children of pride*

Job Replies to the LORD

42 Then Job replied to the LORD: ² I^A know that you can do anything
and no plan of yours
   can be thwarted.   Gn 18:14

³ You asked, "Who is this
   who conceals my counsel
   with ignorance?"   Jb 34:35; 35:16
Surely I spoke about things
   I did not understand,
things too wondrous for me
   to^B know.   Ps 40:5; 131:1; 139:6

⁴ You said, "Listen now,
   and I will speak.
When I question you,
   you will inform me."   Jb 38:3

⁵ I had heard reports
   about you,
but now my eyes
   have seen you.   Jb 19:27; Ps 123:1-2

⁶ Therefore, I reject my words
   and am sorry for them;
I am dust and ashes. ^C,D

⁷ After the LORD had finished speaking^E to Job, he said to Eliphaz the Temanite: "I am angry with you and your two friends, for you have not spoken the truth about me, as my servant Job has. ⁸ Now take seven bulls and seven rams, go to my servant Job, and offer a burnt offering for yourselves. Then my servant Job will pray for you. I will surely accept his prayer and not deal with you as your folly deserves. For you have not spoken the truth about me, as my servant Job has." ⁹ Then Eliphaz the Temanite, Bildad the Shuhite, and Zophar the Naamathite went and did as the LORD had told them, and the LORD accepted Job's prayer.   Gn 20:17; Nm 23:1; 1Jn 5:16

God Restores Job

¹⁰ After Job had prayed for his friends, the LORD restored his fortunes and doubled his previous possessions. ¹¹ All his brothers, sisters, and former acquaintances came to him and dined with him in his house. They sympathized with him and comforted him concerning all the adversity the LORD had brought on him. Each one gave him a piece of silver^F and a gold earring.   Jb 2:11; 19:13; Ps 14:7; Is 40:2; Mt 5:44

¹² So the LORD blessed the last part of Job's life more than the first. He owned fourteen thousand sheep and goats, six thousand camels, one thousand yoke of oxen, and one thousand female donkeys. ¹³ He also had seven sons and three daughters. ¹⁴ He named his first daughter Jemimah, his second Keziah, and his third Keren-happuch. ¹⁵ No women as beautiful as Job's daughters could be found in all the land, and their father granted them an inheritance with their brothers.

¹⁶ Job lived 140 years after this and saw his children and their children to the fourth generation. ¹⁷ Then Job died, old and full of days.   Gn 25:8

---

^A 42:2 Alt Hb tradition reads *You*   ^B 42:3 Lit *me, and I did not*   ^C 42:6 LXX reads *I despise myself and melt; I consider myself dust and ashes*   ^D 42:6 Lit *I reject and I relent, concerning dust and ashes*
^E 42:7 Lit *speaking these words*   ^F 42:11 Lit *a qesitah*; the value of this currency is unknown

PSALMS

BOOK I (Psalms 1–41)

The Two Ways

1 How happy is the one who
does not
walk in the advice
of the wicked
or stand in the pathway
with sinners
or sit in the company
of mockers!   Ps 26:4-5; Pr 4:14-15

2 Instead, his delight is in the
LORD's instruction,
and he meditates on it day
and night.   Jos 1:8; Ps 40:8; 119:14-16

3 He is like a tree planted
beside flowing streams[A]
that bears its fruit
in its season   Rv 22:2
and whose leaf
does not wither.   Ps 92:12-14
Whatever he does prospers.

4 The wicked are not like this;
instead, they are like chaff
that the wind blows away.

5 Therefore the wicked
will not stand up in
the judgment,   Ps 5:5; 9:16; 76:7
nor sinners in the assembly
of the righteous.

6 For the LORD watches over
the way of the righteous,
but the way of the wicked
leads to ruin.   Pr 21:12; Jn 3:16

Coronation of the Son

2 Why do the nations rage
and the peoples plot
in vain?   Ps 83:2-3

2 The kings of the earth take
their stand,   Jr 49:19; 50:44
and the rulers conspire
together
against the LORD
and his Anointed One:[B]

3 "Let's tear off their chains
and throw their ropes
off of us."   Is 58:6; Jr 5:5; Nah 1:13

4 The one enthroned[C]
in heaven laughs;
the Lord ridicules them.   Ps 59:8

5 Then he speaks to them
in his anger
and terrifies them
in his wrath: Ps 90:7

6 "I have installed my king
on Zion, my holy mountain."

7 I will declare the
LORD's decree.
He said to me, "You are
my Son;[D]
today I have become
your Father.   Mt 3:17; Lk 3:22; Heb 1:5

8 Ask of me,
and I will make the nations
your inheritance
and the ends of the earth
your possession.   Jos 23:4

9 You will break them
with an iron scepter;
you will shatter them
like pottery."   Ps 89:23; Rv 2:26-27

10 So now, kings, be wise;
receive instruction,
you judges of the earth.

11 Serve the LORD
with reverential awe

[A]1:3 Or *beside irrigation channels*   [B]2:2 Or *anointed one*   [C]2:4 Lit *who sits*   [D]2:7 Or *son*, also in v. 12

and rejoice with trembling.
¹² Pay homage to ^A the Son or he
will be angry
and you will perish
in your rebellion, ^B   Jn 3:18
for his anger may ignite
at any moment.   2Th 1:7-8
All who take refuge in him
are happy.   Ps 5:11; 34:8,22

Confidence in Troubled Times

3 *A psalm of David when he fled from
his son Absalom.*   2Sm 15:13-17

¹ LORD, how my foes increase!
There are many
who attack me.   2Sm 15:12; Ps 69:4
² Many say about me,
"There is no help for him
in God."   *Selah*

³ But you, LORD, are a shield
around me,   Gn 15:1; Dt 33:29; Ps 5:12
my glory, and the one
who lifts up my head.   Ps 62:7
⁴ I cry aloud to the LORD,
and he answers me
from his holy mountain.
          Selah

⁵ I lie down and sleep;
I wake again because
the LORD sustains me.   Lv 26:6
⁶ I will not be afraid
of thousands of people
who have taken their stand
against me on every side.

⁷ Rise up, LORD!   Ps 7:6
Save me, my God!
You strike all my enemies
on the cheek;   Jb 16:10; Mc 5:1
you break the teeth
of the wicked.   Ps 58:6
⁸ Salvation belongs
to the LORD;   Jnh 2:9; Rv 7:10; 19:1

may your blessing be
on your people.   *Selah*

A Night Prayer

4 *For the choir director: with stringed
instruments. A psalm of David.*

¹ Answer me when I call,
God, who vindicates me. ^C
You freed me from affliction;
be gracious to me and hear
my prayer.

² How long, exalted ones, ^D
will my honor be insulted?
How long will you love
what is worthless   Ps 12:2
and pursue a lie?   *Selah*
³ Know that the LORD
has set apart
the faithful for himself;
the LORD will hear when I call
to him.
⁴ Be angry ^E and do not sin;
on your bed, reflect
in your heart and be still.
          Selah
⁵ Offer sacrifices
in righteousness ^F   Dt 33:19
and trust in the LORD.   Ps 37:3,5

⁶ Many are asking,
"Who can show us
anything good?"
Let the light of your face
shine on us, LORD.   Nm 6:25

⁷ You have put more joy
in my heart
than they have
when their grain
and new wine abound.   Is 9:3
⁸ I will both lie down and sleep
in peace,   Ps 3:5
for you alone, LORD, make me
live in safety.   Lv 25:18; Dt 12:10

^A**2:12** Lit *Kiss*   ^B**2:12** Lit *perish in the way*   ^C**4:1** Or *God of my righteousness*   ^D**4:2** Lit *long, sons of a man*
^E**4:4** Or *Tremble*   ^F**4:5** Or *Offer right sacrifices*

The Refuge of the Righteous

5 *For the choir director: with the flutes. A psalm of David.*

1 Listen to my words, LORD;
consider my sighing. Ps 38:9
2 Pay attention to the sound
of my cry, Ps 28:2
my King and my God, Ps 84:3
for I pray to you.

3 In the morning, LORD,
you hear my voice; Ps 88:13
in the morning I plead
my case to you and watch
expectantly. Jb 13:18; 23:4; Ps 50:21

4 For you are not
a God who delights
in wickedness;
evil cannot dwell with you.
5 The boastful cannot stand
in your sight; Ps 1:5; 73:3; 75:4
you hate all evildoers. Jb 8:20
6 You destroy those
who tell lies; Rv 21:8
the LORD abhors
violent and treacherous
people. Ps 55:23

7 But I enter your house
by the abundance
of your faithful love; Ps 69:13
I bow down toward
your holy temple
in reverential awe of you.
8 LORD, lead me
in your righteousness
because of my adversaries;
make your way straight
before me. Pr 4:11

9 For there is nothing reliable
in what they say; Ps 52:2
destruction is within them;
their throat
is an open grave;

they flatter
with their tongues. Ps 12:3
10 Punish them, God;
let them fall
by their own schemes. Ps 9:16
Drive them out because of
their many crimes, Mt 13:41-42
for they rebel against you.

11 But let all who take refuge
in you rejoice; Ps 2:12; 64:10
let them shout for joy forever.
May you shelter them, Ps 31:20
and may those who love
your name boast about you.
12 For you, LORD, bless
the righteous one;
you surround him with favor
like a shield. Gn 15:1; Dt 33:29

A Prayer for Mercy

6 *For the choir director: with stringed instruments, according to Sheminith. A psalm of David.* 1Ch 15:21

1 LORD, do not rebuke me
in your anger;
do not discipline me
in your wrath. Ps 38:1; Jr 10:24
2 Be gracious to me, LORD,
for I am weak;[A] Ps 142:6
heal me, LORD, for my bones
are shaking; Jb 4:14; Ps 41:4; Jr 17:14
3 my whole being is shaken
with terror. Jb 9:28; Jn 12:27
And you, LORD — how long?

4 Turn, LORD! Rescue me;
save me because of
your faithful love. Ps 31:16
5 For there is no remembrance
of you in death;
who can thank you in Sheol?

6 I am weary from my groaning;
with my tears I dampen
my bed

A **6:2** Or *sick*

and drench my couch
   every night.   Ps 42:3; 102:9
⁷ My eyes are swollen
   from grief;   Jb 17:7; Ps 31:9; 88:9
they grow old because of all
   my enemies.

⁸ Depart from me, all evildoers,
for the Lord has heard
   the sound of my weeping.
⁹ The Lord has heard my plea
   for help;   Ps 28:6
the Lord accepts my prayer.
¹⁰ All my enemies will be
   ashamed and shake
   with terror;
they will turn back
   and suddenly be disgraced.

Prayer for Justice

7 A Shiggaion *of David, which he sang
to the Lord concerning the words of
Cush, a Benjaminite.*

¹ Lord my God, I seek refuge
   in you;   Ps 11:1; 31:1; 71:1
save me from all my pursuers
   and rescue me   Ps 31:15
² or they ᴬ will tear me
   like a lion,
ripping me apart with no one
   to rescue me.   Ps 57:4; Is 5:29

³ Lord my God,
   if I have done this,
if there is injustice
   on my hands,   1Sm 24:11
⁴ if I have done harm to one
   at peace with me   Ps 55:20
or have plundered ᴮ
   my adversary
   without cause,   1Sm 24:11; 26:18
⁵ may an enemy pursue
   and overtake me;
may he trample me
   to the ground   Am 2:7

and leave my honor
   in the dust.   *Selah*

⁶ Rise up, Lord, in your anger;
lift yourself up
   against the fury
   of my adversaries;   Ps 3:7; 17:13
awake for me; ᶜ   Ps 59:4
you have ordained
   a judgment.   Jr 15:3
⁷ Let the assembly of peoples
   gather around you;   Ps 22:27
take your seat on high over it.
⁸ The Lord judges the peoples;
vindicate me, Lord,
according to
   my righteousness
   and my integrity.   Ps 26:1; 35:24

⁹ Let the evil of the wicked
   come to an end,   Ps 94:23
but establish the righteous.
The one who examines
   the thoughts
   and emotions ᴰ
is a righteous God.   Heb 4:12
¹⁰ My shield is with God, 2Sm 22:3
who saves the upright
   in heart.   Ps 36:10
¹¹ God is a righteous judge
and a God who shows his
   wrath every day.   Ps 9:4; Is 11:4

¹² If anyone does not repent,
he will sharpen his sword;
he has strung his bow
   and made it ready.   Ps 37:14
¹³ He has prepared
   his deadly weapons;
he tips his arrows with fire.

¹⁴ See, the wicked one is
   pregnant with evil,
conceives trouble,
   and gives birth to deceit.

ᴬ**7:2** Lit *he*   ᴮ**7:4** Or *me and have spared*   ᶜ**7:6** LXX reads *awake, Lord my God*   ᴰ**7:9** Lit *examines hearts and kidneys*

15 He dug a pit and
    hollowed it out
  but fell into the hole
    he had made. Ps 9:15; 57:6; Pr 26:27
16 His trouble comes back
    on his own head;
  his own violence comes
    down on top of his head.

17 I will thank the LORD
    for his righteousness;
  I will sing about the name
    of the LORD Most High. Ps 9:2

God's Glory, Human Dignity

8 *For the choir director: on the* Gittith.
A psalm of David.   Pss 81; 84 titles

1 LORD, our Lord,
    how magnificent
    is your name
    throughout the earth! Is 12:4

  You have covered the heavens
    with your majesty.[A]   Ps 113:4
2 From the mouths of infants
    and nursing babies, Mt 21:16
  you have established
    a stronghold[B]
  on account of your
    adversaries
  in order to silence the enemy
    and the avenger.

3 When I observe your heavens,
  the work of your fingers,
  the moon and the stars,
  which you set in place, Ps 33:6
4 what is a human being
    that you remember him,
  a son of man[C] that you look
    after him?   Jb 7:17-18; Ps 144:3
5 You made him little less
    than God[D,E]
  and crowned him with glory
    and honor.

6 You made him ruler
    over the works
    of your hands;
  you put everything
    under his feet: 1Co 15:27; Eph 1:22
7 all the sheep and oxen,
    as well as the animals
    in the wild,
8 the birds of the sky,
  and the fish of the sea
    that pass through
    the currents of the seas.

9 LORD, our Lord,
  how magnificent is your name
    throughout the earth!

Celebration of God's Justice

9 *For the choir director: according to*
Muth-labben. *A psalm of David.*

1 I will thank the LORD with all
    my heart;
  I will declare all
    your wondrous works. Ps 96:3
2 I will rejoice and boast
    about you;   Ps 5:11
  I will sing about your name,
    Most High.   Ps 7:17; 92:1

3 When my enemies retreat,
  they stumble and perish
    before you.   Lv 26:37; Ps 27:2; 92:9
4 For you have upheld
    my just cause;   1Kg 8:45,49,59
  you are seated
    on your throne
  as a righteous judge.   Ps 7:11
5 You have rebuked
    the nations: Is 17:3
  You have destroyed
    the wicked;   Ps 68:2
  you have erased their name
    forever and ever.   Zch 13:2
6 The enemy has come
    to eternal ruin.

A **8:1** Lit *earth, which has set your splendor upon the heavens*   B **8:2** LXX reads *established praise*
C **8:4** Or *a mere mortal*   D **8:5** LXX reads *angels*   E **8:5** Or *heavenly beings;* Hb *Elohim*

You have uprooted the cities,
and the very memory
of them has perished. Ps 34:16

7 But the LORD sits enthroned
forever; Ps 29:10; 102:12; Lm 5:19
he has established his throne
for judgment. Ps 89:14
8 And he judges the world
with righteousness;
he executes judgment
on the nations
with fairness. Ps 96:13; 98:9
9 The LORD is a refuge
for the persecuted,
a refuge in times of trouble.
10 Those who know your name
trust in you
because you have not
abandoned
those who seek you, LORD.

11 Sing to the LORD, who dwells
in Zion; Ps 76:2
proclaim his deeds
among the nations. 1Ch 16:8
12 For the one who seeks
an accounting
for bloodshed
remembers them; Gn 9:5
he does not forget the cry
of the oppressed. Ps 12:5

13 Be gracious to me, LORD;
consider my affliction
at the hands of those
who hate me. Ps 69:14
Lift me up from the gates
of death, Ps 30:3; 86:13
14 so that I may declare
all your praises.
I will rejoice
in your salvation 1Sm 2:1
within the gates
of Daughter Zion.

15 The nations have fallen
into the pit they made;
their foot is caught in the net
they have concealed. Ps 7:15
16 The LORD has made himself
known;
he has executed justice, Is 56:1
snaring the wicked
by the work of their hands.
Higgaion. Selah

17 The wicked will return
to Sheol — Ps 31:17; 49:14; 55:15
all the nations that forget God.
18 For the needy will not always
be forgotten;
the hope of the oppressed[A]
will not perish forever. Ps 72:4

19 Rise up, LORD! Do not let
mere humans prevail;
let the nations be judged
in your presence. Ps 82:8; 110:6
20 Put terror in them, LORD;
let the nations know they are
only humans. *Selah*

Need for God's Justice

10 LORD, [B,C] why do you stand
so far away? Ps 22:1; 35:22; 38:21
Why do you hide in times
of trouble? Jb 13:24; Ps 44:24; 88:14
2 In arrogance the wicked
relentlessly pursue
their victims;
let them be caught
in the schemes
they have devised. Ps 7:15-16
3 For the wicked one boasts
about his own cravings;
the one who is greedy
curses[D] and despises
the LORD. 2Pt 2:3
4 In all his scheming,

A9:18 Alt Hb tradition reads *humble*   B10:1 Some Hb mss, LXX connect Pss 9–10.   C10:1 Together Pss 9–10
form a partial acrostic.   D10:3 Or *he blesses the greedy*

the wicked person
  arrogantly thinks,[A]
"There's no accountability,
  since there's no God."   Ps 14:1
5 His ways are always secure;[B]
your lofty judgments have
  no effect on him;[C]
he scoffs at
  all his adversaries.   Ps 52:7
6 He says to himself, "I will
  never be moved —
from generation
  to generation
  without calamity."   Ps 49:11
7 Cursing, deceit, and violence
  fill his mouth;
trouble and malice are
  under his tongue.   Ps 73:8; 140:3
8 He waits in ambush
  near settlements;   Ps 59:3
he kills the innocent
  in secret places.
His eyes are on the lookout
  for the helpless;   Ps 64:4; 94:6
9 he lurks in secret like a lion
  in a thicket.
He lurks in order to seize
  a victim;
he seizes a victim
  and drags him in his net.
10 So he is oppressed
  and beaten down;
helpless people fall
  because of the wicked
  one's strength.   Ps 17:11-12
11 He says to himself,
  "God has forgotten;
he hides his face and will
  never see."   Jb 22:13; Ps 59:3
12 Rise up, Lord God! Lift up
  your hand.   Mc 5:9
Do not forget the oppressed.
13 Why has the wicked person
  despised God?

He says to himself,
  "You will not demand
  an account."   Ps 73:11
14 But you yourself have seen
  trouble and grief,
observing it in order to take
  the matter
  into your hands.   Ps 33:13-15
The helpless one entrusts
  himself to you;
you are a helper
  of the fatherless.   Ps 68:5; 146:9
15 Break the arm of the wicked,
  evil person,   Ps 37:17
until you look for his
  wickedness,
but it can't be found.   Ps 89:32
16 The Lord is King forever
  and ever;   Ex 15:18; Ps 29:10; Rv 11:15
the nations will perish
  from his land.   Dt 8:20
17 Lord, you have heard
  the desire of the humble;
you will strengthen
  their hearts.
You will listen carefully,
18 doing justice
  for the fatherless
  and the oppressed
so that mere humans
  from the earth
  may terrify them no more.

Refuge in the Lord

11 *For the choir director. Of David.*
I have taken refuge
  in the Lord.   Ps 7:1; 31:1; 71:1
How can you say to me,
  "Escape to the mountains[D]
  like a bird!   Ps 121:1
2 For look, the wicked
  string bows;
they put their arrows
  on bowstrings

[A]10:4 Lit *wicked according to the height of his nose away from in front of him*   [B]10:5 Or *prosperous*   [C]10:5 Lit *judgments are*   [D]11:1 Lit *your mountain*

to shoot from the shadows
  at the upright in heart.   Ps 64:4
³ When the foundations
  are destroyed,
what can the righteous do? "

⁴ The LORD is in
  his holy temple;   Ps 27:4; Hab 2:20
the LORD—his throne is
  in heaven.   Ps 103:19; Is 66:1; Ac 7:49
His eyes watch;
his gaze^A
  examines everyone.^B
⁵ The LORD examines
  the righteous,
but he hates the wicked
and^C those who
  love violence.   Ps 33:13-15
⁶ Let him rain burning coals^D
  and sulfur on the wicked;
let a scorching wind be
  the portion in their cup.
⁷ For the LORD is righteous;
  he loves righteous deeds.
The upright will see his face.

Oppression by the Wicked

12 For the choir director: according to Sheminith. A psalm of David.

¹ Help, LORD, for no
  faithful one remains;
the loyal have disappeared
  from the human race.^E
² They lie to one another;
they speak with
  flattering lips
  and deceptive hearts.   Ps 41:6
³ May the LORD cut off
  all flattering lips
and the tongue
  that speaks boastfully.   Ps 5:9
⁴ They say, "Through
  our tongues we have power;

our lips are our own —
  who can be our master? "

⁵ "Because of the devastation
  of the needy
and the groaning of the poor,
I will now rise up,"
  says the LORD.
"I will provide safety for the
  one who longs for it."   Ps 9:18

⁶ The words of the LORD
  are pure words,
like silver refined
  in an earthen furnace,
purified seven times.   Ps 18:30
⁷ You, LORD, will guard us;^F
you will protect us^G
  from this generation
  forever.   Ps 37:28; 97:10
⁸ The wicked prowl^H
  all around,
and what is
  worthless is exalted
  by the human race.   Ps 4:2

A Plea for Deliverance

13 For the choir director. A psalm of David.

¹ How long, LORD? Will you
  forget me forever?
How long will you hide
  your face from me?   Jb 13:24
² How long will I store up
  anxious concerns^I
  within me,
agony in my mind every day?
How long will my enemy
  dominate me?   Ps 6:3; 38:6; 42:9

³ Consider me and answer,
  LORD my God.

---

^A11:4 Lit *eyelids*   ^B11:4 Or *examines the descendants of Adam*   ^C11:5 Or *righteous and the wicked, and he hates*   ^D11:6 Sym; MT reads *rain snares, fire*   ^E12:1 Or *the descendants of Adam*, also in v. 8   ^F12:7 Some Hb mss, LXX, Jer; other Hb mss read *them*   ^G12:7 Some Hb mss, LXX; other Hb mss read *him*   ^H12:8 Lit *walk about*   ^I13:2 Or *up counsels*

Restore brightness to my eyes;
otherwise, I will sleep in death.

4 My enemy will say,
"I have triumphed over him,"
and my foes will rejoice
because I am shaken. Ps 89:42

5 But I have trusted in
your faithful love; Ps 52:8
my heart will rejoice in
your deliverance. Ps 9:14

6 I will sing to the LORD
because he has treated
me generously. Ps 119:17; 142:7

A Portrait of Sinners

14 *For the choir director. Of David.*
The fool says in his heart,
"There's no God." Ps 10:4; 53:1
They are corrupt; they do
vile deeds.
There is no one
who does good.

2 The LORD looks
down from heaven
on the human race[A]
to see if there is one
who is wise,
one who seeks God.

3 All have turned away;
all alike have become corrupt.
There is no
one who does good,
not even one. Ps 12:1; 53:1-3; Mc 7:2

4 Will evildoers never
understand?
They consume my people
as they consume bread;
they do not call on the LORD.

5 Then[B] they will be filled
with dread,
for God is with those
who are[C] righteous. Ps 53:5

6 You sinners frustrate
the plans of the oppressed,
but the LORD is his refuge.

7 Oh, that Israel's deliverance
would come from Zion!
When the LORD restores the
fortunes of his people,[D]
let Jacob rejoice, let
Israel be glad. Ps 53:6

A Description of the Godly

15 *A psalm of David.*
LORD, who can dwell
in your tent? Ps 61:4
Who can live on
your holy mountain? Ps 43:3

2 The one who lives
blamelessly,
practices righteousness,
and acknowledges the truth
in his heart — Ps 24:3-5

3 who does not slander
with his tongue, Pr 10:18
who does not harm his friend
or discredit his neighbor,

4 who despises the one
rejected by the LORD[E]
but honors those who fear
the LORD, Gn 14:17-24; Ps 119:63
who keeps his word
whatever the cost, Lv 5:4

5 who does not lend his silver
at interest Lv 25:35-38; Dt 33:19
or take a bribe
against the innocent —
the one who does
these things will never
be shaken. Ps 16:8; 112:6

Confidence in the LORD

16 *A Miktam of David.* Pss 56–60 titles
Protect me, God, for I take
refuge in you. Ps 94:22

[A]14:2 Or *the descendants of Adam*   [B]14:5 Or *There*   [C]14:5 Lit *with the generation of the*   [D]14:7 Or *restores his captive people*   [E]15:4 Lit *in his eyes the rejected is despised*

2 I[A] said to the LORD, "You are
   my Lord;
   I have nothing good besides
   you."[B]   Ps 73:25
3 As for the holy people
   who are in the land,   Dt 7:6; 14:2
   they are the noble ones.
   All my delight is in them.
4 The sorrows of those who
   take another god
   for themselves will multiply;
   I will not pour out
   their drink offerings
   of blood,
   and I will not speak
   their names with my lips.

5 LORD, you are my portion[C]
   and my cup of blessing;
   you hold my future.   Nm 18:20
6 The boundary lines
   have fallen for me
   in pleasant places;
   indeed, I have
   a beautiful inheritance.

7 I will bless the LORD
   who counsels me —   Ps 73:24
   even at night when my
   thoughts trouble me.[D]   Ps 77:6
8 I always let the LORD
   guide me.[E]
   Because he is at my right hand,
   I will not be shaken.   Ps 15:5; 112:6
9 Therefore my heart is glad
   and my whole being rejoices;
   my body also rests securely.
10 For you will not abandon me
   to Sheol;   Ps 49:10; 86:13
   you will not allow
   your faithful one
   to see decay.   Jb 33:18,28; Ps 30:3

11 You reveal the path of life
   to me;
   in your presence is
   abundant joy;   Ps 21:6
   at your right hand are
   eternal pleasures.   Ac 2:25-28

A Prayer for Protection

17 *A prayer of David.*

   LORD, hear a just cause;   Ps 9:4
   pay attention to my cry;
   listen to my prayer —
   from lips free of deceit.   Jb 27:4
2 Let my vindication come
   from you,
   for you see what is right.
3 You have tested my heart;
   you have examined me
   at night.
   You have tried me and found
   nothing evil;   Jb 23:10; Ps 26:2
   I have determined that
   my mouth will not sin.[F]
4 Concerning what people do:
   by the words from your lips
   I have avoided the ways
   of the violent.   Pr 4:14-15
5 My steps are on your paths;
   my feet have not slipped.
6 I call on you, God,
   because you will answer me;
   listen closely to me;
   hear what I say.
7 Display the wonders
   of your faithful love,   Ps 85:7
   Savior of all who seek refuge
   from those who rebel
   against your right hand.[G]
8 Protect me as the pupil
   of your eye;   Pr 7:2
   hide me in the shadow
   of your wings   Ps 36:7; 57:1; 63:7

[A]16:2 Some Hb mss, LXX, Syr, Jer; other Hb mss read *You you."* [B]16:2 Or *"Lord, my good; there is none besides you."* [C]16:5 Or *allotted portion* [D]16:7 Or *at night my heart instructs me* [E]16:8 Lit *I place the LORD in front of me always* [F]17:3 Or *evil; my mouth will not sin* [G]17:7 Or *love, you who save with your right hand those seeking refuge from adversaries*

9 from^A the wicked
  who treat me violently,^B
my deadly enemies
  who surround me.   Ps 18:48

10 They are uncaring;^C   Ps 119:70
   their mouths speak
   arrogantly.

11 They advance against me;^D
   now they surround me.
They are determined^E
to throw me to the ground.

12 They are^F like a lion
   eager to tear,
like a young lion lurking
   in ambush.   Ps 7:2; 10:9

13 Rise up, Lord!
Confront him;
   bring him down.   Ps 55:23
With your sword, save me
   from the wicked.   Ps 7:12

14 With your hand, Lord,
   save me from men,
from men of the world
whose portion is in this life:
You fill their bellies
   with what you have in store;
their sons are satisfied,
and they leave their surplus
   to their children.   Ps 73:3-7

15 But I will see your face
   in righteousness;   Ps 11:7; Rv 22:4
when I awake, I will be satisfied
   with your presence.^G   Ps 16:11

Praise for Deliverance

18 For the choir director. Of the
     servant of the Lord, David, who
spoke the words of this song to the
Lord on the day the Lord rescued him
from the grasp of all his enemies and
from the power of Saul. He said: 2Sm 22

1 I love you, Lord, my strength.
2 The Lord is my rock,
  my fortress, and my deliverer,
my God, my rock
  where I seek refuge,
my shield and the horn
  of my salvation,   Gn 15:1; Dt 33:29
my stronghold.
3 I called to the Lord, who is
  worthy of praise,   Ps 48:1; 96:4
and I was saved
  from my enemies.   Ps 138:7

4 The ropes of death
  were wrapped around me;
the torrents of destruction
  terrified me.   Ps 124:4
5 The ropes of Sheol
  entangled me;
the snares of death
  confronted me.   Ps 116:3
6 I called to the Lord
  in my distress,
and I cried to my God for help.
From his temple he heard
  my voice,   Ps 3:4
and my cry to him
  reached his ears.   Ps 34:15

7 Then the earth shook
  and quaked;
the foundations
  of the mountains trembled;
they shook
  because he burned
  with anger.
8 Smoke rose from his nostrils,
  and consuming fire came
  from his mouth;
coals were set ablaze by it.^H
9 He bent the heavens
  and came down,   Ps 144:5; Is 64:1
total darkness
  beneath his feet.

^A 17:9 Lit from the presence of   ^B 17:9 Or who plunder me   ^C 17:10 Lit have closed up their fat
^D 17:11 Vg; MT reads Our steps   ^E 17:11 Lit They set their eyes   ^F 17:12 Lit He is   ^G 17:15 Lit form
^H 18:8 Or him

¹⁰ He rode on a cherub and flew,
    soaring on the wings
        of the wind.   Ps 104:3
¹¹ He made darkness
    his hiding place,
    dark storm clouds his canopy
        around him.   Ps 97:2
¹² From the radiance
    of his presence,   Ps 50:2; Is 60:3
    his clouds swept onward
    with hail and blazing coals.
¹³ The LORD thundered
    from ᴬ heaven;
    the Most High made
    his voice heard. ᴮ   Ps 29:3; 104:7
¹⁴ He shot his arrows
    and scattered them;
    he hurled ᶜ lightning bolts
    and routed them.   Ps 144:6
¹⁵ The depths of the sea
    became visible,
    the foundations of the world
        were exposed,
    at your rebuke, LORD,
    at the blast of the breath
        of your nostrils.   Ex 15:8; Ps 106:9

¹⁶ He reached down
    from on high
    and took hold of me;
    he pulled me out of
        deep water.   Ps 144:7
¹⁷ He rescued me
    from my powerful enemy
    and from those who hated me,
    for they were too strong
        for me.   Ps 35:10; 59:1; 142:6
¹⁸ They confronted me
    in the day of my calamity,
    but the LORD was my support.
¹⁹ He brought me out
    to a spacious place;   Ps 31:8
    he rescued me
    because he delighted in me.

²⁰ The LORD rewarded me
    according to
        my righteousness;   Ps 7:8
    he repaid me
    according to the cleanness
        of my hands.   Ps 24:4
²¹ For I have kept the ways
    of the LORD
    and have not turned
        from my God
    to wickedness.   Jb 23:11; Ps 119:101
²² Indeed, I let all
    his ordinances guide me ᴰ
    and have not disregarded
    his statutes.   Lv 18:4-5
²³ I was blameless
    toward him
    and kept myself from
        my iniquity.
²⁴ So the LORD repaid me
    according to
        my righteousness,   2Ch 6:23
    according to
    the cleanness of my hands
        in his sight.

²⁵ With the faithful
    you prove yourself faithful,
    with the blameless
    you prove yourself
        blameless,
²⁶ with the pure
    you prove yourself pure;
    but with the crooked
    you prove yourself shrewd.
²⁷ For you rescue
    an oppressed people,   Ps 72:12
    but you humble those
    with haughty eyes.   Ps 138:6
²⁸ LORD, you light my lamp;
    my God illuminates
        my darkness.   Ps 112:4; Is 42:16
²⁹ With you I can attack
    a barricade, ᴱ

ᴬ**18:13** Some Hb mss, LXX, Tg, Jer; other Hb mss read *in*   ᴮ**18:13** Some Hb mss read *voice, with hail and blazing coals*   ᶜ**18:14** Or *multiplied*   ᴰ**18:22** Lit *Indeed, all his ordinances have been in front of me*   ᴱ**18:29** Or *a ridge*, or *raiders*

and with my God
  I can leap over a wall. Php 4:13

30 God — his way is perfect;
  the word of the LORD is pure.
He is a shield to all
  who take refuge in him.
31 For who is God
  besides the LORD? Dt 32:39
And who is a rock?
  Only our God. Ps 62:2
32 God — he clothes me
  with strength Is 45:5
and makes my way perfect.
33 He makes my feet
  like the feet of a deer Hab 3:19
and sets me securely
  on the heights. A Dt 32:13; Is 58:14
34 He trains my hands for war;
my arms can bend a bow
  of bronze. Jb 29:20
35 You have given me the shield
  of your salvation;
your right hand upholds me,
and your humility exalts me.
36 You make a spacious place
  beneath me for my steps,
and my ankles do not
  give way. Ps 66:9; Pr 4:12
37 I pursue my enemies
  and overtake them;
I do not turn back
  until they are wiped out.
38 I crush them,
  and they cannot get up;
they fall beneath my feet.
39 You have clothed me
  with strength for battle;
you subdue my adversaries
  beneath me. 1Ch 17:10; Ps 81:14
40 You have made my enemies
  retreat before me; B Ex 23:27
I annihilate those
  who hate me. Dt 7:10

41 They cry for help, but there is
  no one to save them —
they cry to the LORD,
  but he does not
  answer them. Mc 3:4
42 I pulverize them like dust
  before the wind; 2Kg 13:7
I trample them C like mud
  in the streets. Is 10:6; Mc 7:10
43 You have freed me
  from the feuds
  among the people;
you have appointed me
  the head of nations; 2Sm 8:1-14
a people I had not known
  serve me. Is 55:5
44 Foreigners submit to me
  cringing;
as soon as they hear
  they obey me. Dt 33:29; Ps 66:3
45 Foreigners lose heart
and come trembling
  from their fortifications.
46 The LORD lives — blessed be
  my rock!
The God of my salvation
  is exalted. Ps 62:2,6
47 God — he grants
  me vengeance 2Sm 4:8; Ps 94:1
and subdues peoples
  under me. Ps 47:3; 144:2
48 He frees me from my enemies.
You exalt me
  above my adversaries;
you rescue me
  from violent men. Ps 59:1; 140:1
49 Therefore I will give
  thanks to you among
  the nations, LORD;
I will sing praises about
  your name. Rm 15:9
50 He gives great victories
  to his king; Ps 144:10

A 18:33 Or on my high places B 18:40 Or You gave me the necks of my enemies C 18:42 Some Hb mss,
LXX, Syr, Tg; other Hb mss read I poured them out

he shows loyalty
   to his anointed,
to David
   and his descendants forever.

The Witness of Creation and Scripture

19 *For the choir director.*
A psalm of David.

1 The heavens declare
   the glory of God,
and the expanse proclaims
   the work of his hands. Gn 1:6
2 Day after day
   they pour out speech;
night after night
   they communicate
   knowledge.[A]
3 There is no speech; there are
   no words;
their voice is not heard.
4 Their message[B] has gone out
   to the whole earth,
and their words to the ends
   of the world. Rm 10:18

In the heavens he has pitched
   a tent for the sun. Is 40:22
5 It is like a bridegroom
   coming from his home;
it rejoices like an athlete
   running a course.
6 It rises from one end
   of the heavens
and circles to their other end;
nothing is hidden
   from its heat.

7 The instruction of the LORD
   is perfect,
renewing one's life; Ps 111:7
the testimony of the LORD
   is trustworthy,
making the inexperienced
   wise. Ps 93:5; 119:130

8 The precepts of the LORD
   are right,
making the heart glad; Ps 119:14
the command of the LORD
   is radiant,
making the eyes light up.
9 The fear of the LORD is pure,
   enduring forever; Ps 111:10
the ordinances of the LORD
   are reliable
and altogether righteous.
10 They are more desirable
   than gold —
than an abundance
   of pure gold; Ps 119:72,127
and sweeter than honey
   dripping from a honeycomb.
11 In addition, your servant
   is warned by them,
and in keeping them there is
   an abundant reward. Pr 29:18

12 Who perceives
   his unintentional sins?
Cleanse me
   from my hidden faults.
13 Moreover, keep your servant
   from willful sins; Nm 15:30
do not let them rule me. Gn 4:7
Then I will be blameless
and cleansed
   from blatant rebellion.
14 May the words
   of my mouth
and the meditation
   of my heart
be acceptable to you, Ps 104:34
LORD, my rock
   and my Redeemer. Ps 78:35

Deliverance in Battle

20 *For the choir director.*
A psalm of David.

1 May the LORD answer you
   in a day of trouble; Ps 50:15

A **19:2** Or *Day to day pours out speech, and night to night communicates knowledge*   B **19:4** LXX, Sym, Syr, Vg; MT reads *line*

may the name of Jacob's God
protect you.   Ps 46:7,11

2 May he send you help
from the sanctuary
and sustain you from Zion.

3 May he remember
all your offerings
and accept
your burnt offering.   *Selah*

4 May he give you what
your heart desires   Ps 21:2
and fulfill your whole purpose.

5 Let us shout for joy
at your victory   Ps 21:1
and lift the banner
in the name of our God.
May the LORD fulfill
all your requests.   Ps 21:2

6 Now I know that
the LORD gives victory
to his anointed;   Ps 18:50
he will answer him
from his holy heaven
with mighty victories
from his right hand.   Ps 44:3

7 Some take pride in chariots,
and others in horses,
but we take pride
in the name of the LORD
our God.   Ps 33:17; Is 31:1

8 They collapse and fall,
but we rise and stand firm.

9 LORD, give victory to the king!
May he[A] answer us
on the day that we call.

The King's Victory

21 *For the choir director.*
A psalm of David.

1 LORD, the king finds joy
in your strength.
How greatly he rejoices
in your victory!   Ps 28:7-8

2 You have given him
his heart's desire   Ps 20:4; 145:19
and have not denied
the request
of his lips.   *Selah*

3 For you meet him
with rich blessings;
you place a crown
of pure gold on his head.

4 He asked you for life,
and you gave it to him —
length of days forever
and ever.   Ps 61:6; 91:16

5 His glory is great
through your victory;
you confer majesty
and splendor on him.   Ps 8:5

6 You give him blessings
forever;   1Ch 17:27
you cheer him with joy
in your presence.   Ps 16:11

7 For the king relies
on the LORD;
through the faithful love
of the Most High
he is not shaken.   Ps 10:6; 16:8

8 Your hand will capture
all your enemies;
your right hand will seize
those who hate you.   Ex 15:6

9 You will make them burn
like a fiery furnace
when you appear;
the LORD will engulf them
in his wrath,
and fire will devour them.

10 You will wipe their progeny
from the earth
and their offspring
from the human race.[B]

11 Though they intend
to harm[C] you
and devise a wicked plan,
they will not prevail.   Ps 2:1-3

[A]**20:9** Or LORD, *save. May the king*   [B]**21:10** Or *the descendants of Adam*   [C]**21:11** Lit *they stretch out harm against*

¹² Instead, you will put them
    to flight
when you ready
    your bowstrings to shoot
    at them.   Ps 7:12

¹³ Be exalted, LORD,
    in your strength;
we will sing and praise
    your might.   Ps 59:16; 81:1

From Suffering to Praise

22 For the choir director: according
to "The Deer of the Dawn."
A psalm of David.

¹ My God, my God,
    why have you
    abandoned me?   Mt 27:46
Why are you so far
    from my deliverance   Ps 10:1
and from my words
    of groaning?   Ps 32:3; 38:8
² My God, I cry by day, but you
    do not answer,
by night, yet I have no rest.
³ But you are holy,
    enthroned on the praises
    of Israel.   Ps 99:3
⁴ Our fathers trusted in you;
    they trusted,
    and you rescued them.
⁵ They cried to you and were
    set free;
they trusted in you
    and were not disgraced.

⁶ But I am a worm and not
    a man,   Jb 25:6
scorned by mankind
    and despised by people.
⁷ Everyone who sees me
    mocks me;
they sneerᴬ and shake
    their heads: Mt 27:39; Mk 15:29
⁸ "He relies onᴮ the LORD;

let him save him;
let the LORDᶜ rescue him,
since he takes pleasure
    in him."   Mt 27:43

⁹ It was you who brought me
    out of the womb,
making me secure
    at my mother's breast.   Ps 71:6
¹⁰ I was given over to you
    at birth;ᴰ
you have been my God
    from my mother's womb.

¹¹ Don't be far from me,
    because distress is near
and there's no one to help.

¹² Many bulls surround me;
strong ones of Bashan
    encircle me.   Ps 68:30; Am 4:1
¹³ They open their mouths
    against me —
lions, mauling and roaring.
¹⁴ I am poured out like water,
and all my bones
    are disjointed;   Jb 4:14; Ps 6:2; 32:3
my heart is like wax,
    melting within me.   Nah 2:10
¹⁵ My strength is dried up
    like baked clay;   Ps 38:10
my tongue sticks to the roof
    of my mouth.   Lm 4:4
You put me into the dust
    of death.   Ps 104:29
¹⁶ For dogs have
    surrounded me;   Ps 59:6,14
a gang of evildoers
    has closed in on me;
they piercedᴱ my hands
    and my feet.   Jn 20:25
¹⁷ I can count all my bones;
people ꜰ look and stare at me.
¹⁸ They divided my garments
    among themselves,

ᴬ**22:7** Lit *separate with the lip* ᴮ**22:8** Or *Rely on* ᶜ**22:8** Lit *let him* ᴰ**22:10** Lit *was cast on you from
the womb* ᴱ**22:16** Some Hb mss, LXX, Syr; other Hb mss read *me; like a lion* ꜰ**22:17** Lit *they*

and they cast lots
  for my clothing.   Mt 27:35

19 But you, LORD, don't be
  far away.   Ps 10:1
My strength, come quickly
  to help me.   Ps 70:5
20 Rescue my life
  from the sword,   Jr 39:18
my only life^A from the power
  of these dogs.
21 Save me
  from the lion's mouth,
from the horns of wild oxen.

You answered me!^B

22 I will proclaim your name
  to my brothers and sisters;
I will praise you
  in the assembly.   Ps 40:10; Heb 2:12
23 You who fear the LORD,
  praise him!   Rv 19:5
All you descendants of Jacob,
  honor him!
All you descendants of Israel,
  revere him!   Ps 135:20
24 For he has not despised
  or abhorred
the torment
  of the oppressed.   Ps 69:33
He did not hide his face
  from him   Ezk 39:29
but listened when he cried
  to him for help.   Ps 28:2

25 I will give praise
  in the great assembly
because of you;   Ps 35:18; 40:9-10
I will fulfill my vows
  before those who fear you.^C
26 The humble will eat
  and be satisfied;   Ps 107:9
those who seek the LORD
  will praise him.
May your hearts live forever!

27 All the ends of the earth
  will remember
and turn to the LORD.
All the families
  of the nations
will bow down before you,
28 for kingship
  belongs to the LORD;
he rules the nations.   1Ch 16:31
29 All who prosper on earth
  will eat and bow down;
all those who go down
  to the dust
will kneel before him —
even the one who cannot
  preserve his life.   Is 45:23
30 Their descendants
  will serve him;
the next generation
  will be told
about the Lord.   Ps 102:18,28
31 They will come and declare
  his righteousness;
to a people yet to be born
they will declare
  what he has done.   Ps 71:18; 78:6

The Good Shepherd

23 *A psalm of David.*
  The LORD is my shepherd;
I have what I need.   Ps 34:9-10
2 He lets me lie down
  in green pastures;   Ps 65:11-13
he leads me beside
  quiet waters.   Ps 36:8
3 He renews my life;
he leads me
  along the right paths^D
for his name's sake.   Ps 5:8; Pr 4:11
4 Even when I go
  through the darkest valley,^E
I fear no danger,
for you are with me;   Is 43:2
your rod and your staff —
  they comfort me.   Mc 7:14

^A22:20 Lit my only one   ^B22:21 Or oxen you rescued me   ^C22:25 Lit him   ^D23:3 Or me in paths of
righteousness   ^E23:4 Or the valley of the shadow of death

5 You prepare a table before me
in the presence of my enemies;
you anoint my head with oil;
my cup overflows.   Ps 16:5
6 Only goodness
and faithful love
will pursue me
all the days of my life,   Ps 25:7
and I will dwell in^A the house
of the LORD
as long as I live.^B   Ps 27:4-6

The King of Glory

24 *A psalm of David.*
The earth and everything
in it,
the world and its inhabitants,
belong to the LORD;   Dt 10:14
2 for he laid its foundation
on the seas
and established it
on the rivers.   Ps 104:5; Pr 8:29

3 Who may ascend
the mountain of the LORD?
Who may stand
in his holy place?   Ps 15:1
4 The one who has clean hands
and a pure heart,   Jb 22:30
who has not appealed
to^C what is false,   Ps 31:6; 119:37
and who has not
sworn deceitfully.
5 He will receive blessing
from the LORD,   Ps 115:13
and righteousness^D
from the God
of his salvation.   Ps 65:5
6 Such is the
generation of those
who inquire of him,
who seek the face of the God
of Jacob.^E   *Selah*

7 Lift up your heads, you gates!
Rise up, ancient doors!
Then the King of glory
will come in.   Ps 118:19-20; Is 26:2
8 Who is this King of glory?
The LORD, strong and mighty,
the LORD, mighty in battle.
9 Lift up your heads, you gates!
Rise up, ancient doors!
Then the King of glory
will come in.
10 Who is he, this King of glory?
The LORD of Armies,
he is the King of glory.   *Selah*

Dependence on the LORD

25 *Of David.*
LORD, I appeal to you.^F
2 My God, I trust in you.
Do not let me be disgraced;
do not let my enemies gloat
over me.   Ps 13:4; 41:11
3 No one who waits for you
will be disgraced;   Is 49:23
those who act treacherously
without cause
will be disgraced.   Pr 2:22; Is 21:2
4 Make your ways known
to me, LORD;
teach me your paths.   Ex 33:13
5 Guide me in your truth
and teach me,   Jn 16:13
for you are the God
of my salvation;   Ex 15:2
I wait for you all day long.
6 Remember, LORD,
your compassion
and your faithful love,
for they have existed
from antiquity.^G   Ps 98:3; 103:17
7 Do not remember the sins
of my youth   Jb 13:26

---

^A**23:6** LXX, Sym, Syr, Tg, Vg, Jer; MT reads *will return to*   ^B**23:6** Lit *LORD for length of days* ; traditionally *LORD forever*   ^C**24:4** Lit *not lifted up his soul to*   ^D**24:5** Or *vindication*   ^E**24:6** LXX; some Hb mss, Syr read *seek your face, God of Jacob* ; some Hb mss read *seek your face, Jacob*   ^F**25:1** Or *To you, LORD, I lift up my soul*   ^G**25:6** Or *everlasting*

or my acts of rebellion;　Ps 51:1
in keeping with
　your faithful love,
　remember me
because of your goodness,
LORD.　Neh 13:22

8 The LORD is good
　and upright;　Ps 100:5; Nah 1:7
therefore he shows sinners
　the way.　Ps 32:8
9 He leads the humble in what
　is right　Ps 23:3
and teaches them his way.
10 All the LORD's ways show
　faithful love and truth
to those who keep
　his covenant and decrees.
11 LORD, for the sake of
　your name,
forgive my iniquity, for
　it is immense.　Jb 7:21; Ps 103:3

12 Who is this person
　who fears the LORD?　Ps 31:19
He will show him the way
　he should choose.　Ps 37:23
13 He will live a good life,
and his descendants
　will inherit the land.ᴬ　Ps 37:11
14 The secret counsel
　of the LORD
is for those who fear him,
and he reveals his covenant
　to them.　Jn 7:17; 1Co 2:9
15 My eyes are always
　on the LORD,
for he will pull my feet
　out of the net.　Ps 31:4; 124:7
16 Turn to me and be gracious
　to me,
for I am alone and afflicted.
17 The distresses of my heart
　increase;ᴮ　Lm 1:20
bring me out of my sufferings.

18 Consider my affliction
　and trouble,　Ps 31:7
and forgive all my sins.　Rm 11:27
19 Consider my enemies;
　they are numerous,　Ps 3:1
and they hate me violently.
20 Guard me and rescue me;
do not let me be put
　to shame,
for I take refuge in you.　Ps 86:2
21 May integrity
　and what is right
watch over me,
for I wait for you.　Ps 41:12

22 God, redeem Israel, from all
　its distresses.　Ps 34:22; 130:8

Prayer for Vindication

26 *Of David.*
Vindicate me, LORD,
because I have lived
　with integrity
and have trusted in the LORD
　without wavering.　2Kg 20:3
2 Test me, LORD, and try me;
examine my heart and mind.
3 For your faithful love
　guides me,ᶜ
and I live by your truth.　Ps 40:10

4 I do not sit
　with the worthless
or associate
　with hypocrites.
5 I hate a crowd of evildoers,
and I do not sit
　with the wicked.　Ps 1:1; Pr 4:14-15
6 I wash my hands
　in innocence　Ps 73:13
and go around your altar,
LORD,　Ps 43:4
7 raising my voice
　in thanksgiving　Jnh 2:9
and telling about
　your wondrous works.　Ps 9:1

ᴬ25:13 Or *earth*　ᴮ25:17 Or *Relieve the distresses of my heart*　ᶜ26:3 Lit *love is in front of my eyes*

8 LORD, I love the house
  where you dwell,
the place where
  your glory resides.   Ps 27:4

9 Do not destroy me
  along with sinners,
or my life along with men
  of bloodshed   Ps 28:3

10 in whose hands are
  evil schemes
and whose right hands
  are filled with bribes.   Ex 23:8

11 But I live with integrity;
  redeem me and be gracious
  to me.   Jb 31:6; Ps 7:8

12 My foot stands
  on level ground;   Ps 27:11
I will bless the LORD
  in the assemblies.   Ps 35:18

My Stronghold

27 *Of David.*
The LORD is my light
  and my salvation —
whom should I fear?   Is 60:20
The LORD is the stronghold
  of my life —
  whom should I dread?   Ps 28:8

2 When evildoers came
  against me to devour
  my flesh,   Ps 14:4
my foes and my enemies
  stumbled and fell.   Ps 9:3

3 Though an army deploys
  against me,
my heart will not be afraid;
though a war breaks out
  against me,
I will still be confident.   Ps 3:6

4 I have asked one thing
  from the LORD;
it is what I desire:
to dwell in the house
  of the LORD

all the days of my life,   Ps 23:6
gazing on the beauty
  of the LORD   Ps 93:5
and seeking him
  in his temple.   Mal 3:1

5 For he will conceal me
  in his shelter
in the day of adversity;
he will hide me
  under the cover of his tent;
he will set me high on a rock.

6 Then my head will be high
above my enemies
  around me;   Ps 3:3
I will offer sacrifices
  in his tent with shouts of joy.
I will sing and make music
  to the LORD.   Eph 5:19

7 LORD, hear my voice
  when I call;
be gracious to me
  and answer me.   Ps 4:3; 30:10

8 My heart says this about you:
"Seek[A] his face."
LORD, I will seek your face.

9 Do not hide your face
  from me;   Ps 69:17; 102:2; 143:7
do not turn your servant
  away in anger.   Ps 6:1
You have been my helper;
do not leave me
  or abandon me,
God of my salvation.

10 Even if my father and mother
  abandon me,
the LORD cares for me.   Ps 37:28

11 Because of my adversaries,
show me your way, LORD,
and lead me on a level path.

12 Do not give me over
  to the will of my foes,
for false witnesses rise up
  against me,
breathing violence.   Ps 35:11; 41:2

A 27:8 The command is pl in Hb

13 I am certain that I will see the
    LORD's goodness
    in the land of the living. Ps 116:9
14 Wait for the LORD;
    be strong, and let your heart
        be courageous. Jos 1:6
    Wait for the LORD. Ps 37:34; 130:5

My Strength

28
Of David.
LORD, I call to you;
my rock, do not be deaf to me.
If you remain silent to me,
I will be like
    those going down to the Pit.
2 Listen to the sound
    of my pleading
when I cry to you for help,
when I lift up my hands
toward your holy sanctuary.

3 Do not drag me away
    with the wicked,
with the evildoers,
who speak in friendly ways
    with their neighbors
while malice is
    in their hearts. Ps 26:9-10
4 Repay them according to
    what they have done —
according to the evil
    of their deeds.
Repay them according to
    the work of their hands;
give them back
    what they deserve. Jr 50:29
5 Because they do not consider
what the LORD has done
or the work of his hands,
he will tear them down
    and not rebuild them. Is 5:12

6 Blessed be the LORD,
for he has heard the sound
    of my pleading. Ps 31:22

7 The LORD is my strength
    and my shield;
my heart trusts in him,
    and I am helped. Gn 15:1; Dt 33:29
Therefore my heart
    celebrates,
and I give thanks to him
    with my song. Ps 59:17; 69:30

8 The LORD is the strength
    of his people;[A]
he is a stronghold of salvation
    for his anointed. Ps 20:6; 27:1
9 Save your people,
    bless your possession,
shepherd them, and carry
    them forever. Ps 33:12; Is 40:11

The Voice of the LORD

29
A psalm of David.
Ascribe to the LORD,
    you heavenly beings,[B]
ascribe to the LORD glory
    and strength.
2 Ascribe to the LORD the glory
    due his name;
worship the LORD
    in the splendor of his
        holiness.[C] 1Ch 16:28-29; Ps 96:7-9

3 The voice of the LORD is
    above the waters.
The God of glory thunders —
the LORD, above the
    vast water, Jb 37:4-5; Ps 18:13; 104:7
4 the voice of the LORD
    in power,
the voice of the LORD
    in splendor. Ps 68:33
5 The voice of the LORD
    breaks the cedars;
the LORD shatters the cedars
    of Lebanon. Ps 104:16
6 He makes Lebanon skip
    like a calf, Ps 114:4,6

A28:8 Some Hb mss, LXX, Syr; other Hb mss read *strength for them*   B29:1 Or *you sons of gods,* or *you sons of mighty ones*   C29:2 Or *in holy attire,* or *in holy appearance*

and Sirion,
   like a young wild ox.   Dt 3:8-9
7 The voice of the LORD flashes
   flames of fire.   Dt 4:12,33
8 The voice of the LORD shakes
   the wilderness;
the LORD shakes
   the wilderness of Kadesh.
9 The voice of the LORD
   makes the deer give birth^A
and strips the woodlands
   bare.   Is 24:1,3

In his temple all cry, "Glory!"

10 The LORD sits enthroned
   over the flood;
the LORD sits enthroned,
   King forever.   Ps 9:7; 10:17
11 The LORD gives
   his people strength;   Ps 28:8
the LORD blesses his people
   with peace.   Php 4:7

Joy in the Morning

30 *A psalm; a dedication song for the house. Of David.*

1 I will exalt you, LORD,
   because you have lifted
   me up   Ps 3:3
and have not allowed
   my enemies
to triumph over me.   Ps 25:2; 35:19
2 LORD my God,
I cried to you for help,
   and you healed me.   Ps 88:13
3 LORD, you brought me up
   from Sheol;   Ps 86:13
you spared me
   from among those
going down^B to the Pit.   Ps 28:1

4 Sing to the LORD,
   you his faithful ones,
and praise his holy name.

5 For his anger lasts
   only a moment,
but his favor, a lifetime.
Weeping may stay overnight,
but there is joy
   in the morning.   Ps 103:9; Is 54:7-8

6 When I was secure, I said,
   "I will never be shaken."   Ps 10:6
7 LORD, when you showed
   your favor,
you made me stand
   like a strong mountain;
when you hid your face,
   I was terrified.   Ps 104:29
8 LORD, I called to you;
I sought favor from my Lord:
9 "What gain is there
   in my death,
if I go down to the Pit?
Will the dust praise you?
Will it proclaim your truth?
10 LORD, listen and be gracious
   to me;
LORD, be my helper."   Ps 4:1; 27:7

11 You turned my lament
   into dancing;
you removed my sackcloth
   and clothed me
   with gladness,   Ec 3:4; Is 61:10
12 so that I can sing to you
   and not be silent.
LORD my God, I will praise
   you forever.   Ps 44:8; 108:1

A Plea for Protection

31 *For the choir director. A psalm of David.*

1 LORD, I seek refuge in you;
let me never be disgraced.
Save me
   by your righteousness.
2 Listen closely to me;
   rescue me quickly.

^A29:9 Or *the oaks shake*   ^B30:3 Some Hb mss, LXX, Theod, Orig, Syr; other Hb mss, Aq, Sym, Tg, Jer read *from going down*

Be a rock of refuge for me,
a mountain fortress
to save me.   Ps 71:1-2

3 For you are my rock
and my fortress;   Ps 18:2; 71:3
you lead and guide me
for your name's sake.   Ps 23:3

4 You will free me from the net
that is secretly set for me,
for you are my refuge.   Ps 25:15

5 Into your hand I entrust
my spirit;   Lk 23:46
you have redeemed me, A
LORD, God of truth.   Ps 25:5

6 I B hate those
who are devoted
to worthless idols,
but I trust in the LORD.   Ps 26:5

7 I will rejoice and be glad
in your faithful love
because you have seen
my affliction.
You know the troubles
of my soul   Ps 10:14

8 and have not handed me over
to the enemy.   Dt 32:30
You have set my feet
in a spacious place.   Jb 36:16

9 Be gracious to me, LORD,
because I am in distress;
my eyes are worn out
from frustration —
my whole being C as well. Ps 6:7

10 Indeed, my life is consumed
with grief
and my years with groaning;
my strength has failed
because of my iniquity, D
and my bones waste away.

11 I am ridiculed by all
my adversaries
and even by my neighbors.

I am dreaded by
my acquaintances;
those who see me
in the street run from me.

12 I am forgotten:
gone from memory
like a dead person —
like broken pottery.   Ps 88:5

13 I have heard the gossip
of many;
terror is on every side.   Jr 20:10
When they conspired
against me,
they plotted to take my life.

14 But I trust in you, LORD;
I say, "You are my God."   Ps 140:6

15 The course of my life is
in your power;   Jb 14:5; 24:1
rescue me from the power
of my enemies
and from my persecutors.

16 Make your face shine on
your servant;   Nm 6:25
save me by your faithful love.

17 LORD, do not let me
be disgraced when I call
on you.   Ps 25:2-3,20
Let the wicked
be disgraced;
let them be quiet E,F in Sheol.

18 Let lying lips   Ps 120:2
that arrogantly speak
against the righteous
in proud contempt
be silenced.   1Sm 2:3; Ps 94:4

19 How great is your goodness
that you have stored up
for those who fear you
and accomplished
in the sight of everyone G
for those who take refuge
in you.   Ps 5:11; 23:5

A31:5 Or spirit. Redeem me   B31:6 One Hb ms, LXX, Syr, Vg, Jer read You   C31:9 Lit my soul and my belly
D31:10 LXX, Syr, Sym read affliction   E31:17 LXX reads brought down   F31:17 Or them wail   G31:19 Or
of the descendants of Adam

20 You hide them
  in the protection
  of your presence;
you conceal them in a shelter
from human schemes,
from quarrelsome tongues.
21 Blessed be the LORD,
for he has wondrously shown
  his faithful love to me
in a city under siege. Ps 28:6
22 In my alarm I said,
"I am cut off from your sight."
But you heard the sound
  of my pleading
when I cried to you for help.

23 Love the LORD,
  all his faithful ones. Ps 30:4
The LORD protects the loyal,
but fully repays
  the arrogant. Ps 94:2
24 Be strong, and let your heart
  be courageous,
all you who put your hope
  in the LORD. Ps 27:14

The Joy of Forgiveness

32 *Of David. A* Maskil.
  How joyful is the one
whose transgression
  is forgiven,
whose sin is covered! Ps 85:2
2 How joyful is a person whom
the LORD does not charge
  with iniquity Rm 4:7-8
and in whose spirit is
  no deceit! Jn 1:47

3 When I kept silent, my bones
  became brittle
from my groaning
  all day long. Ps 31:10; 38:8
4 For day and night your hand
  was heavy on me; Jb 23:2
my strength was drained A
as in the summer's heat. *Selah*

5 Then I acknowledged my sin
  to you
and did not conceal
  my iniquity.
I said, "I will confess
  my transgressions
  to the LORD,"
and you forgave the guilt
  of my sin. *Selah*

6 Therefore let everyone
  who is faithful pray to you
  immediately. B Is 55:6
When great
  floodwaters come,
they will not reach him. Is 43:2
7 You are my hiding place; Ps 91:1
you protect me
  from trouble.
You surround me
  with joyful shouts
  of deliverance. *Selah*

8 I will instruct you
  and show you the way to go;
with my eye on you,
  I will give counsel. Ps 33:18
9 Do not be like a horse
  or mule,
without understanding,
that must be controlled
  with bit and bridle
or else it will not come
  near you. Pr 26:3; Jms 3:3

10 Many pains come
  to the wicked, Pr 13:21; Rm 2:9
but the one who trusts
  in the LORD
will have faithful love
  surrounding him. Ps 5:12
11 Be glad in the LORD
  and rejoice,
you righteous ones;
shout for joy,
all you upright in heart. Ps 68:3

A**32:4** Hb obscure B**32:6** Lit *you at a time of finding*

Praise to the Creator

33 Rejoice in the LORD,
　　you righteous ones;
praise from the upright
　　is beautiful.   Ps 32:11; 147:1; Php 4:4

2 Praise the LORD
　　with the lyre;
make music to him
　　with a ten-stringed harp.

3 Sing a new song to him;   Ps 40:3
play skillfully on the strings,
　　with a joyful shout.   Ps 150:4

4 For the word of the LORD
　　is right,
and all his work
　　is trustworthy.   Ps 19:8

5 He loves righteousness
　　and justice;   Ps 11:7; 37:28
the earth is full of the LORD's
　　unfailing love.   Ps 119:64

6 The heavens were made
　　by the word of the LORD,
and all the stars,
　　by the breath of his mouth.

7 He gathers the water
　　of the sea into a heap;^A
he puts the depths
　　into storehouses.   Ex 15:8

8 Let the whole earth
　　fear the LORD;
let all the inhabitants
　　of the world stand in awe
　　of him.   Ps 67:7; 96:9

9 For he spoke, and it came
　　into being;
he commanded, and it came
　　into existence.   Gn 1:3; Ps 147:15,18

10 The LORD frustrates
　　the counsel of the nations;
he thwarts the plans
　　of the peoples.   Ps 2:1-3; Is 8:10

11 The counsel of the LORD
　　stands forever,

the plans of his heart
　　from generation
　　to generation.   Ps 139:17; Pr 19:21

12 Happy is the nation
　　whose God is the LORD —
the people he has chosen
　　to be his own possession!

13 The LORD looks down
　　from heaven;
he observes everyone.   Jb 28:24

14 He gazes on all
　　the inhabitants
　　of the earth
from his dwelling place.

15 He forms the hearts
　　of them all;
he considers all
　　their works.   Jb 34:21

16 A king is not saved by
　　a large army;
a warrior will not be rescued
　　by great strength.   Ps 44:6; 60:11

17 The horse is a false hope
　　for safety;
it provides no escape by
　　its great power.   Ps 20:7; 147:10

18 But look, the LORD
　　keeps his eye on those
　　who fear him —
those who depend on
　　his faithful love   Jb 36:7; Ps 34:15

19 to rescue them from death
and to keep them alive
　　in famine.   Jb 5:20; Ps 37:19; 56:13

20 We wait for the LORD;   Ps 130:6
he is our help and shield.   Ps 3:3

21 For our hearts rejoice
　　in him   Ps 13:5; 28:7; Jn 16:22
because we trust in
　　his holy name.   Zph 3:12

22 May your faithful love rest
　　on us, LORD,
for we put our hope in you.

^A33:7 LXX, Tg, Syr, Vg, Jer read *sea as in a bottle*

The LORD Delivers the Righteous

34 *Concerning David, when he pretended to be insane in the presence of Abimelech, who drove him out, and he departed.*   1Sm 21:10-15

¹ I will bless the LORD
    at all times;
his praise will always be
    on my lips.   Ps 71:6; Eph 5:20
² I will boast in the LORD;   Ps 44:8
    the humble will hear
    and be glad.   Ps 69:32
³ Proclaim the
    LORD's greatness with me;
    let us exalt his name together.

⁴ I sought the LORD,
    and he answered me
    and rescued me from all
    my fears.   Ps 34:6,17,19
⁵ Those who look to him
    are[A] radiant with joy;   Is 60:5
    their faces will never
    be ashamed.   Ps 25:3
⁶ This poor man cried,
    and the LORD heard him
    and saved him from all
    his troubles.   Ps 34:4
⁷ The angel of the LORD
    encamps
    around those who fear him,
    and rescues them.   Ps 91:11

⁸ Taste and see that the LORD
    is good.   1Pt 2:3
    How happy is the person
    who takes refuge in him!
⁹ You who are his holy ones,
    fear the LORD,
    for those who fear him
    lack nothing.   Ps 23:1
¹⁰ Young lions[B] lack food
    and go hungry,   Jb 4:10-11
    but those who seek the LORD
    will not lack any good thing.

¹¹ Come, children, listen to me;
    I will teach you the fear
    of the LORD.   Ps 66:16; 111:10
¹² Who is someone
    who desires life,
    loving a long life to enjoy
    what is good?   Ec 3:13; 6:6
¹³ Keep your tongue from evil
    and your lips
    from deceitful speech.   Ps 39:1
¹⁴ Turn away from evil and do
    what is good;   Ps 37:27; Is 1:16-17
    seek peace and pursue it.

¹⁵ The eyes of the LORD are
    on the righteous,
    and his ears are open
    to their cry for help.   Jb 36:7
¹⁶ The face of the LORD is set
    against those who do
    what is evil,   1Pt 3:10-12
    to remove[C] all memory
    of them from the earth.
¹⁷ The righteous[D] cry out,
    and the LORD hears,
    and rescues them from all
    their troubles.   Ps 145:19
¹⁸ The LORD is near
    the brokenhearted;
    he saves those crushed
    in spirit.   Ps 51:17; 147:3; Is 61:1

¹⁹ One who is righteous has
    many adversities,
    but the LORD rescues him
    from them all.   Ps 71:20
²⁰ He protects all his bones;
    not one of them is broken.
²¹ Evil brings death
    to the wicked,
    and those who hate
    the righteous
    will be punished.   Ps 94:23; 140:11
²² The LORD redeems the life
    of his servants,

[A]**34:5** Some Hb mss, LXX, Aq, Syr, Jer read *Look to him and be*   [B]**34:10** LXX, Syr, Vg read *The rich*
[C]**34:16** Or *cut off*   [D]**34:17** Lit *They*

and all who take
refuge in him will not
be punished. Ps 37:40; Rm 8:33-34

Prayer for Victory

35 *Of David.*
Oppose my opponents,
Lord;
fight those who fight me.
2 Take your shields —
large and small —
and come to my aid. Ps 5:12; 91:4
3 Draw the spear and javelin
against my pursuers,
and assure me: "I am
your deliverance." Ps 13:5; 40:17

4 Let those who intend to take
my life
be disgraced and humiliated;
let those who plan
to harm me
be turned back and ashamed.
5 Let them be like chaff
in the wind,
with the angel of the Lord
driving them away. Jb 21:18
6 Let their way be dark
and slippery,
with the angel of the Lord
pursuing them. Ps 73:18; Jr 23:12
7 They hid their net for me
without cause;
they dug a pit for me
without cause. Ps 140:5
8 Let ruin come
on him unexpectedly,
and let the net that he hid
ensnare him;
let him fall into it —
to his ruin. Jb 18:8; Ps 7:15

9 Then I will rejoice in the Lord;
I will delight
in his deliverance. Ps 9:14; 13:5
10 All my bones will say,

"Lord, who is like you, Ex 15:11
rescuing the poor from one
too strong for him,
the poor or the needy
from one who robs him?"

11 Malicious witnesses
come forward;
they question me
about things I do not know.
12 They repay me evil for good,
making me desolate. Ps 38:20
13 Yet when they were sick,
my clothing was sackcloth;
I humbled myself with fasting,
and my prayer was genuine. A
14 I went about mourning as if
for my friend or brother;
I was bowed down with grief,
like one mourning for
a mother. Ps 38:6
15 But when I stumbled,
they gathered in glee;
they gathered against me.
Assailants I did not know
tore at me and did not stop.
16 With godless mockery B
they gnashed their teeth
at me. Jb 16:9; Ps 37:12; Lm 2:16

17 Lord, how long will you
look on? Ps 13:1; Hab 1:13
Rescue me
from their ravages;
rescue my precious life
from the young lions.
18 I will praise you
in the great assembly;
I will exalt you
among many people. Ps 40:9-10
19 Do not let
my deceitful enemies
rejoice over me;
do not let those who hate me
without cause Ps 38:19; Jn 15:25
wink at me maliciously. Ps 13:4

A 35:13 Lit *prayer returned to my chest*   B 35:16 Hb obscure

20 For they do not speak
    in friendly ways,
but contrive
    fraudulent schemes[A]
against those who live
    peacefully in the land.   Jr 9:8

21 They open their mouths wide
    against me and say,
"Aha, aha! We saw it!"[B]   Jb 16:10

22 You saw it, LORD; do not
    be silent.
Lord, do not be far from me.

23 Wake up and rise
    to my defense,
to my cause, my God
    and my Lord!   Ps 7:6; 44:23; 59:4

24 Vindicate me, LORD my God,
in keeping with
    your righteousness,
and do not let them rejoice
    over me.   Ps 26:1; 43:1

25 Do not let them say
    in their hearts,
"Aha! Just what we wanted."
Do not let them say,
"We have swallowed him up!"

26 Let those who rejoice
    at my misfortune
be disgraced and humiliated;
let those who exalt
    themselves over me
be clothed with shame
    and reproach.   Jb 8:22; Ps 40:14

27 Let those who want
    my vindication
shout for joy and be glad;
let them continually say,
"The LORD be exalted.
He takes pleasure in
    his servant's well-being."

28 And my tongue will proclaim
    your righteousness,
your praise all day long.

Human Wickedness and God's Love

36 *For the choir director. Of David, the LORD's servant.*

1 An oracle within my heart
    concerning the transgression
    of the wicked person:
Dread of God has no effect
    on him.[C]   Rm 3:18

2 For with his flattering
    opinion of himself,
he does not discover
    and hate his iniquity.   Dt 29:19

3 The words from his mouth
    are malicious
    and deceptive;   Ps 10:7
he has stopped acting wisely
    and doing good.   Jr 4:22

4 Even on his bed he makes
    malicious plans.   Pr 4:16
He sets himself on a path
    that is not good,
and he does not reject evil.

5 LORD, your faithful love
    reaches to heaven,
your faithfulness
    to the clouds.   Ps 57:10; 103:11; 108:4

6 Your righteousness is
    like the highest mountains,
your judgments
    like the deepest sea.   Ps 71:19
LORD, you preserve people
    and animals.   Ps 104:14-15

7 How priceless your
    faithful love is, God!
People take refuge
    in the shadow of your wings.

8 They are filled
    from the abundance
    of your house.
You let them drink from
    your refreshing stream.

9 For the wellspring of life is
    with you.   Jn 4:10,14

[A]35:20 Lit *but devise fraudulent words* [B]35:21 Lit *Our eyes saw!* [C]36:1 Lit *There is no dread of God in front of his eyes*

By means of your light
    we see light.   Jn 1:9; Ac 26:18

10 Spread your faithful love
    over those who know you,
and your righteousness
    over the upright in heart.
11 Do not let the foot of
    the arrogant come near me
or the hand of the wicked
    drive me away.   Ps 38:16; 119:122
12 There! The evildoers have
    fallen.
They have been thrown
    down and cannot rise.   Ps 1:5

Instruction in Wisdom

37 *Of David.*
    Do not be agitated
    by evildoers;
do not envy those
    who do wrong.   Ps 73:3; Pr 3:31
2 For they wither quickly
    like grass
and wilt like tender
    green plants.   Ps 92:7; 129:6; Jms 1:11

3 Trust in the Lord and do
    what is good;   Ps 62:8
dwell in the land
    and live securely. A   Pr 2:21
4 Take delight in the Lord,
and he will give you
    your heart's desires.   Ps 21:2

5 Commit your way
    to the Lord;
trust in him, and he will act,
6 making your righteousness
    shine like the dawn,
your justice like the noonday.

7 Be silent before the Lord
    and wait expectantly for him;
do not be agitated by one
    who prospers in his way,

by the person
    who carries out evil plans.

8 Refrain from anger
    and give up your rage;
do not be agitated —
    it can only bring harm.
9 For evildoers
    will be destroyed,
but those who put their hope
    in the Lord
will inherit the land.   Pr 2:21; 60:21

10 A little while, and
    the wicked person will be
    no more;
though you look for him,
    he will not be there.   Jb 7:10
11 But the humble will inherit
    the land   Mt 5:5
and will enjoy
    abundant prosperity.   Ps 72:7

12 The wicked person schemes
    against the righteous
and gnashes his teeth
    at him.
13 The Lord laughs at him   Ps 2:4
because he sees that his day
    is coming.   1Sm 26:10

14 The wicked have drawn
    the sword and strung
    the B bow
to bring down the poor
    and needy
and to slaughter those
    whose way is upright.   Ps 11:2
15 Their swords will enter
    their own hearts,
and their bows
    will be broken.   1Sm 2:4; Ps 46:9
16 The little that
    the righteous person has
    is better

A **37:3** Or *and cultivate faithfulness,* or *and befriend faithfulness*   B **37:14** Lit *their*

than the abundance
　　of many wicked people.
17 For the arms of the wicked
　　　will be broken, Ps 10:15
but the LORD supports
　　the righteous. Ps 145:14

18 The LORD watches over
　　the blameless all their days,
and their inheritance
　　will last forever. Ps 1:6
19 They will not be disgraced
　　in times of adversity;
they will be satisfied in days
　　of hunger. Jb 5:20; Ps 33:19

20 But the wicked will perish;
the LORD's enemies,
　　like the glory of the pastures,
will fade away —
they will fade away like smoke.

21 The wicked person borrows
　　and does not repay,
but the righteous one
　　is gracious and giving.
22 Those who are blessed
　　by the LORD will inherit
　　the land,
but those cursed by him
　　will be destroyed. Pr 3:33

23 A person's steps
　　are established by the LORD,
and he takes pleasure
　　in his way. 1Sm 2:9; Ps 66:9
24 Though he falls, he will not
　　be overwhelmed,
because the LORD supports
　　him with his hand. Ps 145:14

25 I have been young and now
　　I am old,
yet I have not seen
　　the righteous abandoned
or his children begging
　　for bread. Is 41:17

26 He is always generous,
　　always lending,
and his children are
　　a blessing. Dt 15:8; Ps 112:5,9; Mt 5:42

27 Turn away from evil, do
　　what is good,
and settle permanently. Ps 34:14
28 For the LORD loves justice
and will not abandon
　　his faithful ones. Dt 31:6
They are kept safe forever,
but the children
　　of the wicked
　　will be destroyed. Ps 21:10
29 The righteous will inherit
　　the land
and dwell in it permanently.

30 The mouth of the righteous
　　utters wisdom;
his tongue speaks
　　what is just. Ps 49:3; 119:13; Pr 10:13
31 The instruction of his God is
　　in his heart;
his steps do not falter. Dt 6:6

32 The wicked one lies in wait
　　for the righteous
and intends to kill him; Ps 10:8
33 the LORD will not leave him
in the power of
　　the wicked one
or allow him
　　to be condemned
　　when he is judged. Ps 34:22

34 Wait for the LORD and keep
　　his way,
and he will exalt you
　　to inherit the land.
You will watch
　　when the wicked
　　are destroyed. Ps 27:14; 52:5-6

35 I have seen
　　a wicked, violent person

well-rooted,^A like
a flourishing native tree.

36 Then I^B passed by
and noticed he was gone;
I searched for him,
but he could not be found.

37 Watch the blameless
and observe the upright,
for the person of peace
will have a future.^C   Is 57:1-2

38 But transgressors will all
be eliminated;
the future of the wicked
will be destroyed.   Ps 1:4-6

39 The salvation of the
righteous is from the LORD,
their refuge in a time
of distress.   Ps 3:8; 9:9; 62:1

40 The LORD helps
and delivers them;
he will deliver them
from the wicked
and will save them
because they take refuge
in him.   Ps 22:4; 34:22; 54:4

Prayer of a Suffering Sinner

38 *A psalm of David for
remembrance.*   Ps 70 title

1 LORD, do not punish me
in your anger
or discipline me
in your wrath.   Ps 6:1

2 For your arrows have sunk
into me,
and your hand has
pressed down on me.   Jb 6:4

3 There is no soundness
in my body
because of your indignation;
there is no health^D in my bones
because of my sin.   Jb 33:19; 102:10

4 For my iniquities
have flooded over my head;
they are a burden too heavy
for me to bear.   Ezr 9:6; Ps 40:12

5 My wounds are foul
and festering
because of my foolishness.

6 I am bent over
and brought very low;
all day long I go around
in mourning.   Ps 35:14

7 For my insides are full of
burning pain,
and there is no soundness
in my body.   Ps 38:3; Lm 1:13

8 I am faint and severely
crushed;
I groan because of
the anguish of my heart.

9 Lord, my every desire is
in front of you;
my sighing is not hidden
from you.   Ps 10:17

10 My heart races, my strength
leaves me,
and even the light of my eyes
has faded.^E   Ps 6:7; 69:3; 88:9

11 My loved ones
and friends stand back
from my affliction,
and my relatives stand
at a distance.   Jb 19:13-20; Ps 31:11

12 Those who intend to kill me
set traps,
and those who want
to harm me threaten
to destroy me;
they plot treachery
all day long.   Ps 35:4,20; 54:3; 140:5

13 I am like a deaf person;
I do not hear.
I am like a speechless person
who does not open his mouth.

^A37:35 Hb obscure   ^B37:36 LXX, Syr, Vg, Jer; MT reads *he*   ^C37:37 Or *posterity*, also in v. 38   ^D38:3 Hb
shalom   ^E38:10 Or *and the light of my eyes —even that is not with me*

14 I am like a man
    who does not hear
and has no arguments
    in his mouth.   Jb 23:4
15 For I put my hope in you,
    LORD;
you will answer me, my Lord,
    my God.   Ps 17:6; 39:7
16 For I said,
    "Don't let them rejoice
        over me —
those who are
    arrogant toward me
    when I stumble."   Ps 13:4; 35:26
17 For I am about to fall,
and my pain is constantly
    with me.   Ps 13:2; 35:15
18 So I confess my iniquity;
I am anxious because of
    my sin.   Ps 32:5; 2Co 7:9-10
19 But my enemies are vigorous
    and powerful; A
many hate me for no reason.
20 Those who repay evil
    for good
attack me for pursuing good.

21 LORD, do not abandon me;
my God, do not be far
    from me.   Ps 22:19; 35:22
22 Hurry to help me,
my Lord, my salvation.

The Fleeting Nature of Life

39 For the choir director, for
Jeduthun. A psalm of David.

1 I said, "I will guard my ways
so that I may not sin
    with my tongue;
I will guard my mouth
    with a muzzle
as long as the wicked are
    in my presence."   Ps 34:13
2 I was speechless and quiet;
I kept silent, even from
    speaking good,

and my pain intensified.
3 My heart grew hot
    within me;
as I mused, a fire burned.
I spoke with my tongue:
4 "LORD, make me
    aware of my end
and the number of my days
so that I will know how
    short-lived I am.   Ps 78:39; 90:12
5 In fact, you have made
    my days just inches long,
and my life span is as nothing
    to you.
Yes, every human being
    stands as only a vapor.
                                Selah
6 Yes, a person goes about
    like a mere shadow.
Indeed, they rush around
    in vain,
gathering possessions
without knowing
    who will get them.   Ps 49:10
7 "Now, Lord, what do I wait for?
My hope is in you.   Ps 38:15
8 Rescue me from all
    my transgressions;
do not make me the taunt
    of fools.   Ps 44:13; 79:4; 119:22
9 I am speechless; I do not
    open my mouth
because of what
    you have done.   Ps 39:2
10 Remove your torment
    from me.
Because of the force
    of your hand I am finished.
11 You discipline a person
    with punishment
    for iniquity,
consuming like a moth
    what is precious to him;
yes, every human being is
    only a vapor.   Selah

A 38:19 Or numerous

¹² "Hear my prayer, LORD,
and listen to my cry for help;
do not be silent at my tears.
For I am here with you
  as an alien,
a temporary resident like all
  my ancestors. 1Ch 29:15; Heb 11:13
¹³ Turn your angry gaze from me
so that I may be cheered up
before I die and am gone."

Thanksgiving and a Cry for Help

40 *For the choir director.*
A psalm of David.

¹ I waited patiently for the LORD,
and he turned to me
and heard my cry for help.
² He brought me up
  from a desolate ᴬ pit,
out of the muddy clay, Ps 69:2,14
and set my feet on a rock,
making my steps secure.
³ He put a new song
  in my mouth,
a hymn of praise to our God.
Many will see and fear,
and they will trust in the LORD.

⁴ How happy is anyone
who has put his trust
  in the LORD
and has not turned
  to the proud
or to those who run after lies!
⁵ LORD my God, you have done
  many things —
your wondrous works
  and your plans for us;
none can compare with you.
If I were to report and speak
  of them,
they are more than can be told.

⁶ You do not delight
  in sacrifice and offering;

you open my ears to listen. ᴮ
You do not ask for
  a whole burnt offering
or a sin offering. 1Sm 15:22
⁷ Then I said, "See, I have come;
in the scroll it is written
  about me. Lk 24:44
⁸ I delight to do your will,
  my God, Ps 119:16,24; Jn 4:34
and your instruction is deep
  within me." Ps 119:11; Heb 10:5-9

⁹ I proclaim righteousness
  in the great assembly;
see, I do not keep
  my mouth closed ᶜ —
as you know, LORD. Ps 22:22,25
¹⁰ I did not hide
  your righteousness
  in my heart;
I spoke about
  your faithfulness
  and salvation;
I did not conceal
  your constant love and truth
from the great assembly.

¹¹ LORD, you do not ᴰ withhold
  your compassion from me.
Your constant love and truth
  will always guard me. Ps 36:5
¹² For troubles without number
  have surrounded me;
my iniquities have overtaken
  me; I am unable to see.
They are more than the hairs
  of my head,
and my courage leaves me.
¹³ LORD, be pleased
  to rescue me;
hurry to help me, LORD. Ps 70:1

¹⁴ Let those who intend to take
  my life
be disgraced and confounded.

ᴬ**40:2** Or *watery* ᴮ**40:6** Lit *you hollow out ears for me* ᶜ**40:9** Lit *not restrain my lips* ᴰ**40:11** Or
LORD, *do not*

Let those who wish me harm
be turned back
and humiliated.   Ps 35:4,26; 63:9
15 Let those who say to me,
"Aha, aha!"
be appalled because of
their shame.   Ps 35:21,25; 70:3

16 Let all who seek you rejoice
and be glad in you;
let those who love
your salvation
continually say,
"The LORD is great!"   Ps 35:27; 70:4
17 I am oppressed and needy;
may the Lord think of me.
You are my helper
and my deliverer;
my God, do not delay.   Ps 86:1

Victory in Spite of Betrayal

41 For the choir director.
A psalm of David.

1 Happy is one who is
considerate of the poor;
the LORD will save him
in a day of adversity.   Ps 82:3-4
2 The LORD will keep him
and preserve him;
he will be blessed in the land.
You will not give him over
to the desire of his enemies.
3 The LORD will sustain him
on his sickbed;
you will heal him on the bed
where he lies.   Jr 17:14

4 I said, "LORD, be gracious
to me;
heal me, for I have sinned
against you."   Ps 6:2; 51:4
5 My enemies
speak maliciously
about me:
"When will he die
and be forgotten?"   Ps 38:12

6 When one of them
comes to visit,
he speaks deceitfully;
he stores up evil in his heart;
he goes out and talks.   Ps 12:2
7 All who hate me
whisper together about me;
they plan to harm me.   Ps 56:5
8 "Something awful has
overwhelmed him,^A
and he won't rise again
from where he lies!"
9 Even my friend^B in whom
I trusted,
one who ate my bread,
has raised his heel
against me.   Jb 19:19; Ps 55:12-13
10 But you, LORD, be gracious
to me and raise me up;
then I will repay them.   Ps 9:13
11 By this I know
that you delight in me:
my enemy does not shout
in triumph over me.   Ps 25:2
12 You supported me because of
my integrity   Ps 37:17
and set me
in your presence forever.

13 Blessed be the LORD God
of Israel,
from everlasting
to everlasting.
Amen and amen.   Ps 72:18-19; 89:52

BOOK II (Psalms 42–72)

Longing for God

42 For the choir director.
A Maskil of the sons of Korah.

1 As a deer longs for
flowing streams,
so I long for you, God.   Ps 84:2
2 I thirst for God,
the living God.

---

^A **41:8** Lit *"A thing of worthlessness has been poured into him*   ^B **41:9** Lit *Even a man of my peace*

When can I come and appear
  before God? Ps 63:1
3 My tears have been my food
  day and night,
while all day long people say
  to me,
"Where is your God?" Ps 79:10
4 I remember this as I pour out
  my heart: Ps 62:8
how I walked with many,
leading
  the festive procession
  to the house of God,
with joyful
  and thankful shouts. Ps 55:14

5 Why, my soul, are you
  so dejected?
Why are you in
  such turmoil?
Put your hope in God,
  for I will still praise him,
my Savior and my God. Ps 38:6
6 I A am deeply depressed;
therefore I remember you
  from the land of Jordan
and the peaks of Hermon,
  from Mount Mizar. Ps 61:2
7 Deep calls to deep in the roar
  of your waterfalls;
all your breakers
  and your billows
  have swept over me. Ps 69:1-2
8 The Lord will send
  his faithful love by day;
his song will be with me
  in the night —
a prayer to the God of my life.

9 I will say to God, my rock,
"Why have you forgotten me?
Why must I go about
  in sorrow
because of
  the enemy's oppression?"

10 My adversaries taunt me,
as if crushing my bones,
while all day long they say
  to me,
"Where is your God?" Jl 2:17
11 Why, my soul, are you
  so dejected?
Why are you in
  such turmoil?
Put your hope in God,
  for I will still praise him,
my Savior and my God. Ps 43:5

43 B Vindicate me, God,
  and champion my cause
against an unfaithful nation;
rescue me from the deceitful
  and unjust person. Ps 5:6; 26:1
2 For you are the God
  of my refuge.
Why have you rejected me?
Why must I go about
  in sorrow
because of
  the enemy's oppression?

3 Send your light
  and your truth; let them
  lead me. Ps 36:9
Let them bring me
  to your holy mountain,
to your dwelling place. Ps 2:6
4 Then I will come to the altar
  of God,
to God, my greatest joy. Ps 26:6
I will praise you with the lyre,
God, my God. Ps 33:2; 57:8

5 Why, my soul, are you
  so dejected?
Why are you in
  such turmoil?
Put your hope in God,
  for I will still praise him,
my Savior and my God.

A 42:5-6 Some Hb mss, LXX, Syr; other Hb mss read *him, the salvation of his presence.* 6 *My God, I*
B Ps 43 Many Hb mss connect Pss 42 and 43

Israel's Complaint

44 *For the choir director.*
A Maskil of the sons of Korah.

1 God, we have heard
   with our ears —
   our ancestors have told us —
   the work you accomplished
   in their days,
   in days long ago: Dt 32:7; Ps 78:3

2 In order to plant them,
   you displaced the nations
   by your hand;
   in order to settle them,
   you brought disaster on
   the peoples.   2Sm 7:10; Ps 78:55; 80:8

3 For they did not take
   the land by their sword —
   their arm did not
   bring them victory —
   but by your right hand,
   your arm,
   and the light of your face,
   because you were favorable
   toward them.   Dt 7:7-8; Ps 77:15

4 You are my King, my God,
   who ordains[A] victories
   for Jacob.   Ps 42:8; 74:12

5 Through you we drive back
   our foes;
   through your name
   we trample our enemies.

6 For I do not trust in my bow,
   and my sword does not
   bring me victory.   1Sm 17:47

7 But you give us victory
   over our foes
   and let those who hate us
   be disgraced.   Ps 35:4; 53:5

8 We boast in God
   all day long;
   we will praise
   your name forever.   *Selah*

9 But you have rejected
   and humiliated us;

10 you do not march out
   with our armies.   Ps 60:1,10; 74:1

10 You make us retreat
   from the foe,
   and those who hate us
   have taken plunder
   for themselves.   Lv 26:17; Dt 28:25

11 You hand us over to be eaten
   like sheep
   and scatter us
   among the nations.   Lv 26:33

12 You sell your people
   for nothing;
   you make no profit
   from selling them.   Dt 32:30

13 You make us an object
   of reproach
   to our neighbors,
   a source of mockery
   and ridicule to those
   around us.   Dt 28:37; Ps 79:4

14 You make us a joke
   among the nations,
   a laughingstock[B]
   among the peoples.   Jb 17:6

15 My disgrace is before me
   all day long,
   and shame has covered
   my face,   2Ch 32:21; Ps 69:7

16 because of the taunts[C]
   of the scorner and reviler,
   because of the enemy
   and avenger.   Ps 8:2; 74:10

17 All this has happened to us,
   but we have not
   forgotten you
   or betrayed your covenant.

18 Our hearts have not
   turned back;
   our steps have not strayed
   from your path.   Jb 23:11; Ps 37:31

19 But you have crushed us
   in a haunt of jackals
   and have covered us
   with deepest darkness.

A 44:4 LXX, Syr, Aq; MT reads *King, God; ordain*   B 44:14 Lit *shaking of the head*   C 44:16 Lit *voice*

20 If we had forgotten the name
   of our God
   and spread out our hands
   to a foreign god,   Dt 6:14; Jb 11:13
21 wouldn't God have found
   this out,
   since he knows the secrets
   of the heart?   Ps 139:1-2; Jr 17:10
22 Because of you we are being
   put to death all day long;
   we are counted as sheep
   to be slaughtered. Is 53:7; Jr 12:3

23 Wake up, LORD!
   Why are you sleeping?
   Get up!
   Don't reject us forever! Ps 7:6
24 Why do you hide
   and forget our affliction
   and oppression?   Jb 13:24
25 For we have sunk down
   to the dust;
   our bodies cling to the ground.
26 Rise up! Help us!
   Redeem us because of
   your faithful love.   Ps 25:22

A Royal Wedding Song

45 For the choir director: according
to "The Lilies." A Maskil of the
sons of Korah. A love song.   Pss 60; 69

1 My heart is moved
   by a noble theme
   as I recite my verses
   to the king;
   my tongue is the pen
   of a skillful writer.   Ezr 7:6
2 You are the most handsome
   of men;[A]
   grace flows from your lips.
   Therefore God
   has blessed you forever.

3 Mighty warrior,
   strap your sword
   at your side.

In your majesty
   and splendor —   Is 49:2; Rv 1:16
4 in your splendor
   ride triumphantly
   in the cause of truth,
   humility, and justice.
   May your right hand show
   your awe-inspiring acts.
5 Your sharpened arrows
   pierce the hearts
   of the king's enemies;
   the peoples fall under you.

6 Your throne, God, is[B] forever
   and ever;   Heb 1:8-9
   the scepter of your kingdom
   is a scepter of justice.   Ps 93:2
7 You love righteousness
   and hate wickedness;   Ps 33:5
   therefore God, your God,
   has anointed you
   with the oil of joy
   more than your companions.
8 Myrrh, aloes, and cassia
   perfume all your garments;
   from ivory palaces harps
   bring you joy.   Sg 4:14; Jn 19:39
9 Kings' daughters are among
   your honored women;   Sg 6:8
   the queen, adorned with gold
   from Ophir,
   stands at your right hand.

10 Listen, daughter,
   pay attention
   and consider:
   forget your people
   and your father's house,
11 and the king will desire
   your beauty.
   Bow down to him,
   for he is your lord.   Eph 5:33
12 The daughter of Tyre,
   the wealthy people,
   will seek your favor
   with gifts. Ps 68:29; 72:10-11; Is 49:23

A45:2 Or of the descendants of Adam   B45:6 Or Your divine throne is, or Your throne is God's

¹³ In her chamber,
  the royal daughter
  is all glorious,
  her clothing embroidered
  with gold.   Ex 39:2-3; Rv 19:7-8
¹⁴ In colorful garments
  she is led to the king;
  after her, the virgins,
  her companions,
  are brought to you.   Ezk 16:18
¹⁵ They are led in with gladness
  and rejoicing;
  they enter the king's palace.

¹⁶ Your sons will succeed
  your ancestors;
  you will make them princes
  throughout the land.   1Pt 2:9
¹⁷ I will cause your name
  to be remembered
  for all generations;
  therefore the peoples
  will praise you forever
  and ever.   Mal 1:11

God Our Refuge

46
*For the choir director.
A song of the sons of Korah.*
According to Alamoth.   1Ch 15:20

¹ God is our refuge and strength,
  a helper who is always found
  in times of trouble.   Ps 9:9; 62:7-8
² Therefore we
  will not be afraid,
  though the earth trembles
  and the mountains topple
  into the depths of the seas,
³ though its water roars
  and foams
  and the mountains quake
  with its turmoil.   *Selah*

⁴ There is a river —
  its streams delight the city
  of God,
  the holy dwelling place
  of the Most High.   Ps 43:3

⁵ God is within her;
  she will not be toppled.
  God will help her
  when the morning dawns.
⁶ Nations rage,
  kingdoms topple;
  the earth melts when he lifts
  his voice.   Ps 2:1; Jr 25:30
⁷ The Lᴏʀᴅ of Armies is
  with us;
  the God of Jacob is
  our stronghold.   *Selah*

⁸ Come, see the works
  of the Lᴏʀᴅ,
  who brings devastation
  on the earth.   Ps 66:5
⁹ He makes wars cease
  throughout the earth.
  He shatters bows
  and cuts spears to pieces;
  he sets wagons ablaze.   Ps 76:3
¹⁰ "Stop your fighting,
  and know that I am God,
  exalted among the nations,
  exalted on the earth."   Ps 100:3
¹¹ The Lᴏʀᴅ of Armies is with us;
  the God of Jacob is
  our stronghold.   *Selah*

God Our King

47
*For the choir director.
A psalm of the sons of Korah.*

¹ Clap your hands,
  all you peoples;   Is 55:12
  shout to God
  with a jubilant cry.   Ps 95:1
² For the Lᴏʀᴅ, the Most High,
  is awe-inspiring,
  a great King over
  the whole earth.   Dt 7:21; Neh 1:5
³ He subdues peoples under us
  and nations under our feet.
⁴ He chooses for us
  our inheritance —
  the pride of Jacob,
  whom he loves.   *Selah*

5 God ascends among
   shouts of joy,
 the LORD, with the sound
   of trumpets.   2Sm 6:15; Ps 68:18
6 Sing praise to God, sing praise;
 sing praise to our King,
   sing praise!   Ps 68:4; 89:18
7 Sing a song of wisdom,[A]
 for God is King of
   the whole earth.   Zch 14:9

8 God reigns over the nations;
 God is seated
   on his holy throne.   1Ch 16:31
9 The nobles of the peoples
   have assembled
 with the people of the God
   of Abraham.   Ps 102:22
 For the leaders[B] of the earth
   belong to God;
 he is greatly exalted.   Ps 72:11

Zion Exalted

48 A song. A psalm of the sons
of Korah.

1 The LORD is great and
   highly praised
 in the city of our God.   Ps 2:6
 His holy mountain,
   2 rising splendidly,
 is the joy of the whole earth.
 Mount Zion — the summit
   of Zaphon —
 is the city of the great King.
3 God is known as a stronghold
 in its citadels.   Ps 46:7; 50:2

4 Look! The kings assembled;
 they advanced together.
5 They looked and froze
   with fear;
 they fled in terror.   Ex 15:15
6 Trembling seized them there,
 agony like that of a woman
   in labor,   Is 13:8; Hs 13:13

7 as you wrecked the ships
   of Tarshish
 with the east wind.   1Kg 22:48
8 Just as we heard,
   so we have seen
 in the city of the LORD
   of Armies,
 in the city of our God;
 God will establish
   it forever.   *Selah*

9 God, within your temple,
 we contemplate
   your faithful love.   Ps 26:3; 40:10
10 Like your name, God,
   so your praise
 reaches to the ends
   of the earth;   Ps 113:3; Mal 1:11
 your right hand is filled
   with justice.   Ps 45:4
11 Mount Zion is glad.
 Judah's villages[C] rejoice
 because of your judgments.

12 Go around Zion,
   encircle it;
 count its towers,
13 note its ramparts;
   tour its citadels
 so that you can tell
 a future generation: Ps 78:5-7
14 "This God, our God
   forever and ever —
 he will always lead us."[D]

Misplaced Trust in Wealth

49 For the choir director.
A psalm of the sons of Korah.

1 Hear this, all you peoples;
 listen, all who inhabit
   the world,   Ps 78:1; Mc 1:2
2 both low and high,
 rich and poor together.   Ps 62:9
3 My mouth speaks wisdom;

[A] 47:7 Or *Sing* a maskil   [B] 47:9 Lit *shields*   [C] 48:11 Lit *daughters*   [D] 48:14 Some Hb mss, LXX; other Hb mss read *over death*

my heart's meditation
brings understanding.
4 I turn my ear to a proverb;
I explain my riddle with a lyre.

5 Why should I fear in times
of trouble?
The iniquity of my foes
surrounds me.   Ps 23:4; 27:1
6 They trust in their wealth
and boast of
their abundant riches.   Ps 52:7
7 Yet these cannot redeem
a person[A]
or pay his ransom to God —
8 since the price
of redeeming him is
too costly,
one should forever
stop trying[B] —   Mt 16:26
9 so that he may live forever
and not see the Pit.   Jb 33:28

10 For one can see that the
wise die;
the foolish and stupid also
pass away.   Ec 2:16
Then they leave their wealth
to others.   Ps 39:6; Ec 2:18-19; Lk 12:20
11 Their graves are
their permanent homes,[C]
their dwellings
from generation
to generation,
though they have named
estates after themselves.
12 But despite his assets,[D]
mankind will not last;
he is like the animals
that perish.   Ec 3:19

13 This is the way of those
who are arrogant,

and of their followers,
who approve of
their words.[E]   Selah
14 Like sheep they are headed
for Sheol;
Death will shepherd them.
The upright
will rule over them
in the morning,   Rv 2:26
and their form
will waste away in Sheol,[F]
far from their lofty abode.
15 But God will redeem me
from the power of Sheol,
for he will take me.   Selah

16 Do not be afraid
when a person gets rich,
when the wealth[G]
of his house increases.
17 For when he dies, he will take
nothing at all;
his wealth will not follow
him down.   Jb 27:19; Ps 17:14; 1Tm 6:7
18 Though he blesses himself
during his lifetime —
and you are acclaimed
when you do well
for yourself —   Dt 29:19; Ps 10:3,6
19 he will go to the generation
of his fathers;
they will never see
the light.   Gn 15:15; Jb 33:30; Ps 56:13
20 Mankind, with his assets
but without understanding,
is like the animals
that perish.   Ec 3:19

God as Judge

50 A psalm of Asaph.   1Ch 16:5,7
The Mighty One, God,[H]
the Lord, speaks;
he summons the earth

[A]**49:7** Or *Certainly he cannot redeem himself,* or *Yet he cannot redeem a brother*   [B]**49:8** Or *costly, it will cease forever*   [C]**49:11** LXX, Syr, Tg; MT reads *Their inner thought is that their houses are eternal*   [D]**49:12** Or *honor*   [E]**49:13** Lit *and after them with their mouth they were pleased*   [F]**49:14** Hb obscure   [G]**49:16** Or *glory,* also in v. 17   [H]**50:1** Or *The God of gods*

from the rising of the sun
  to its setting.   Jos 22:22; Ps 113:3
2 From Zion, the perfection
    of beauty,
  God appears in radiance.[A]
3 Our God is coming;
    he will not be silent!
  Devouring fire precedes him,
  and a storm rages
    around him.   Ps 18:12-13; 97:3
4 On high, he summons heaven
    and earth
  in order to judge his people:
5 "Gather my faithful ones
    to me,
  those who made a covenant
    with me by sacrifice."   2Ch 6:11
6 The heavens proclaim
    his righteousness,   Ps 89:5; 97:6
  for God is the Judge.   *Selah*

7 "Listen, my people,
    and I will speak;
  I will testify
    against you, Israel.
  I am God, your God.   Dt 31:21
8 I do not rebuke you
    for your sacrifices
  or for your burnt offerings,
  which are continually
    before me.   1Sm 15:22; Ps 40:6; 51:16
9 I will not take a bull
    from your household
  or male goats
    from your pens,   Ps 69:31
10 for every animal of the forest
    is mine,
  the cattle on a thousand hills.
11 I know every bird
    of the mountains,
  and the creatures of the field
    are mine.   Ex 19:5; Ps 104:24
12 If I were hungry, I would not
    tell you,
  for the world and everything
    in it is mine.   Dt 10:14; Ps 24:1

13 Do I eat the flesh of bulls
  or drink the blood of goats?
14 Sacrifice a thank offering
    to God,   Lv 7:12; Ps 107:22; 116:17
  and pay your vows
    to the Most High.   Dt 23:21
15 Call on me in a day of trouble;
  I will rescue you,
    and you will honor me."

16 But God says to the wicked:
  "What right do you have
    to recite my statutes
  and to take my covenant
    on your lips?   Is 29:13
17 You hate instruction
  and fling my words
    behind you.   Pr 5:12; 12:1
18 When you see a thief,
  you make friends with him,
  and you associate
    with adulterers.   Rm 1:32
19 You unleash your mouth
    for evil
  and harness your tongue
    for deceit.   Ps 10:7; 36:3; 52:2
20 You sit,
    maligning your brother,
  slandering
    your mother's son.   Jb 19:18
21 You have done these things,
    and I kept silent;
  you thought I was just
    like you.   Is 42:14; 57:11
  But I will rebuke you
  and lay out the case
    before you.[B]   Ps 90:8

22 "Understand this,
    you who forget God,
  or I will tear you apart,
  and there will be no one to
    rescue you.   Jb 8:13; Ps 9:17
23 Whoever sacrifices
    a thank offering
  honors me,

[A]50:2 Or *God shines forth*   [B]50:21 Lit *lay it out before your eyes*

and whoever orders
  his conduct,
I will show him the salvation
  of God."   Ps 85:13; 91:16; Gl 6:16

A Prayer for Restoration

51 *For the choir director.
A psalm of David, when the
prophet Nathan came to him after he
had gone to Bathsheba.*   2Sm 12:1

¹ Be gracious to me, God,
  according to your faithful love;
  according to your abundant
    compassion,
  blot out my rebellion.   Is 43:25
² Completely wash away
    my guilt
  and cleanse me from my sin.
³ For I am conscious
    of my rebellion,
  and my sin is always
    before me.   Ps 32:5; Pr 28:13; Is 59:12
⁴ Against you — you alone —
    I have sinned
  and done this evil
    in your sight.   Ps 41:4
  So you are right
    when you pass sentence;
  you are blameless
    when you judge.   Rm 3:4
⁵ Indeed, I was guilty
    when I was born;
  I was sinful when my mother
    conceived me.   Jb 15:14; Ps 58:3
⁶ Surely you desire integrity
    in the inner self,
  and you teach me wisdom
    deep within.   Jb 38:36; Pr 2:6; Ec 2:26
⁷ Purify me with hyssop,
    and I will be clean;
  wash me, and I will be
    whiter than snow.   Lv 14:4,49
⁸ Let me hear joy and gladness;
  let the bones
    you have crushed rejoice.

⁹ Turn your face away^A
    from my sins
  and blot out all my guilt.
¹⁰ God, create a clean heart
    for me
  and renew a steadfast^B spirit
    within me.   Ps 24:4; Mt 5:8; Jms 4:8
¹¹ Do not banish me
    from your presence
  or take your Holy Spirit
    from me.   2Kg 13:23; Is 63:10-11; Jr 7:15
¹² Restore the joy
    of your salvation to me,
  and sustain me by giving me
    a willing spirit.   Ps 13:5
¹³ Then I will teach
    the rebellious your ways,
  and sinners will return
    to you.   Ex 33:13; Ps 25:4; Jr 2:33
¹⁴ Save me from the guilt
    of bloodshed, God —   Ps 26:9
  God of my salvation —
  and my tongue will sing
    of your righteousness.
¹⁵ Lord, open my lips,
  and my mouth will declare
    your praise.   Ex 4:15; Ps 9:14
¹⁶ You do not want a sacrifice,
    or I would give it;
  you are not pleased
    with a burnt offering.   Ps 40:6
¹⁷ The sacrifice pleasing to God
    is^C a broken spirit.
  You will not despise a broken
    and humbled heart, God.
¹⁸ In your good pleasure,
    cause Zion to prosper;
  build the walls of Jerusalem.
¹⁹ Then you will delight
    in righteous sacrifices,
  whole burnt offerings;
  then bulls will be offered
    on your altar.   Ps 4:5; 66:13,15

^A**51:9** Lit *Hide your face*   ^B**51:10** Or *right*   ^C**51:17** Lit *The sacrifices of God are*

God Judges the Proud

52 *For the choir director. A* Maskil *of David. When Doeg the Edomite went and reported to Saul, telling him, "David went to Ahimelech's house."*

1 Why boast about evil,
   you hero!   Ps 94:4
   God's faithful love
   is constant.   Ps 40:10-11; 138:2
2 Like a sharpened razor,
   your tongue
   devises destruction,
   working treachery. Ps 5:9; 50:19
3 You love evil instead of good,
   lying instead of
   speaking truthfully.   *Selah*
4 You love any words
   that destroy,
   you treacherous tongue!

5 This is why God will bring
   you down forever.
   He will take you, ripping you
   out of your tent;
   he will uproot you
   from the land of the living.
                          Selah
6 The righteous will see
   and fear,
   and they will derisively say
   about that hero,[A]   Jb 22:19-20
7 "Here is the man
   who would not make God
   his refuge,
   but trusted in the abundance
   of his riches,
   taking refuge
   in his destructive behavior."

8 But I am like
   a flourishing olive tree
   in the house of God;   Ps 1:3; 128:3
   I trust in God's faithful love
   forever and ever.   Ps 143:8
9 I will praise you forever
   for what you have done.

In the presence
   of your faithful people,
I will put my hope
   in your name, for it is good.

A Portrait of Sinners

53 *For the choir director: on* Mahalath. *A* Maskil *of David.*

1 The fool says in his heart,
   "There's no God."
   They are corrupt, and they do
   vile deeds.
   There is no one
   who does good.   Ps 10:4; 14:1
2 God looks down from heaven
   on the human race[B]
   to see if there is one
   who is wise,
   one who seeks God.   Ps 33:13-15
3 All have turned away;
   all alike have
   become corrupt.
   There is no one
   who does good,
   not even one.   Rm 3:10-12
4 Will evildoers
   never understand?
   They consume my people
   as they consume bread;
   they do not call on God. Is 64:7
5 Then they will be filled
   with dread —
   dread like no other — Lv 26:36
   because God will scatter
   the bones of those
   who besiege you.   Jr 8:1-2
   You will put them to shame,
   for God has rejected them.
6 Oh, that Israel's deliverance
   would come from Zion!
   When God restores the
   fortunes of his people,[C]
   let Jacob rejoice, let
   Israel be glad.   Ps 14:7; Is 52:7-9

[A]**52:6** Lit *about him* [B]**53:2** Or *the descendants of Adam* [C]**53:6** Or *restores his captive people*

Prayer for Deliverance

54 *For the choir director: with stringed instruments. A* Maskil *of David. When the Ziphites went and said to Saul, "Is David not hiding among us?"*

1 God, save me by your name,
   and vindicate me
   by your might! Ps 6:1; 7:8; 35:24

2 God, hear my prayer;
   listen to the words
   from my mouth. Ps 5:1; 17:6; 55:1

3 For strangers rise up
   against me,
   and violent men intend to
   kill me.
   They do not let God
   guide them. [A]   *Selah*

4 God is my helper;
   the Lord is the sustainer
   of my life. [B] Ps 118:7; Is 41:10

5 He will repay my adversaries
   for their evil.
   Because of your faithfulness,
   annihilate them. Ps 94:23; 143:12

6 I will sacrifice
   a freewill offering to you.
   I will praise your name, LORD,
   because it is good. Ps 52:9

7 For he has rescued me
   from every trouble,
   and my eye
   has looked down on
   my enemies. Ps 59:10; 92:11

Betrayal by a Friend

55 *For the choir director: with stringed instruments. A* Maskil *of David.*

1 God, listen to my prayer
   and do not hide from my plea
   for help. Lm 3:56

2 Pay attention to me
   and answer me. Ps 4:1; 5:1-2; 54:2

I am restless and in turmoil
   with my complaint, Ps 64:1

3 because of
   the enemy's words, [C]
   because of the pressure [D]
   of the wicked.
   For they bring down disaster
   on me
   and harass me in anger. Ps 71:11

4 My heart shudders
   within me; Ps 38:8
   terrors of death sweep
   over me.

5 Fear and trembling grip me;
   horror has overwhelmed me.

6 I said, "If only I had wings
   like a dove!
   I would fly away and find rest.

7 How far away I would flee;
   I would stay
   in the wilderness. *Selah*

8 I would hurry to my shelter
   from the raging wind
   and the storm." Is 4:6; 25:4

9 Lord, confuse [E] and confound
   their speech, [F] Gn 10:25; 11:7
   for I see violence and strife
   in the city;

10 day and night they make
   the rounds on its walls.
   Crime and trouble are
   within it; Jr 6:7; Hab 1:3

11 destruction is inside it;
   oppression and deceit
   never leave its marketplace.

12 Now it is not an enemy
   who insults me —
   otherwise I could bear it;
   it is not a foe who rises up
   against me —
   otherwise I could hide
   from him.

[A] **54:3** Lit *They do not set God in front of them*   [B] **54:4** Or *is with those who sustain my life*   [C] **55:3** Lit *voice*   [D] **55:3** Or *threat,* or *oppression*   [E] **55:9** Or *destroy*   [F] **55:9** Lit *and divide their tongue*

¹³ But it is you, a man who is
        my peer,
    my companion
        and good friend! Jb 19:13,19
¹⁴ We used to have
        close fellowship;
    we walked with the crowd
        into the house of God. Ps 42:4

¹⁵ Let death take them
        by surprise; Pr 6:15; Is 47:11; 1Th 5:3
    let them go down
        to Sheol alive,
    because evil is in their homes
        and within them. Nm 16:30,33
¹⁶ But I call to God,
    and the LORD will save me.
¹⁷ I complain and groan
        morning, noon, and night,
    and he hears my voice. Ps 64:1
¹⁸ Though many are against me,
    he will redeem me
        from my battle unharmed.
¹⁹ God, the one enthroned
        from long ago, Ps 93:2
    will hear and
    will humiliate them *Selah*
    because they do not change
    and do not fear God. Dt 33:27

²⁰ My friend acts violently
    against those at peace
        with him; Ps 7:4
    he violates his covenant.
²¹ His buttery words
        are smooth,
    but war is in his heart.
    His words are softer than oil,
    but they are drawn swords.

²² Cast your burden
        on the LORD,
    and he will sustain you; 1Pt 5:7
    he will never allow
        the righteous to be shaken.

²³ God, you will
        bring them down
    to the Pit of destruction;
    men of bloodshed
        and treachery
    will not live out half their days.
    But I will trust in you. Ps 56:3

A Call for God's Protection

56 *For the choir director: according
to "A Silent Dove Far Away."*
A Miktam *of David. When the Philistines
seized him in Gath.* 1Sm 21:10-11; 22:1

¹ Be gracious to me, God,
        for a man is trampling me;
    he fights and oppresses me
        all day long.
² My adversaries trample me
        all day,
    for many arrogantly fight
        against me. ^A Ps 35:1; 57:3

³ When I am afraid,
    I will trust in you. Ps 112:7; Pr 29:25
⁴ In God, whose word I praise,
    in God I trust; I will not
        be afraid.
    What can mere mortals do
        to me? Ps 27:1; 118:6; Heb 13:6

⁵ They twist my words
        all day long;
    all their thoughts against me
        are evil. Ps 41:7; 2Pt 3:16
⁶ They stir up strife, ^B they lurk;
    they watch my steps
    while they wait to take my life.
⁷ Will they escape in spite of
        such sin?
    God, bring down the nations
        in wrath. Ezk 17:15; Rm 2:3

⁸ You yourself have recorded
        my wanderings. ^C
    Put my tears in your bottle.

^A**56:2** Or *many fight against me, O exalted one,* or *many fight against me from the heights*   ^B**56:6** Or
They attack   ^C**56:8** Or *misery*

Are they not in your book?
9 Then my enemies will retreat
  on the day when I call.   Ps 9:3
This I know: God is for me.

10 In God, whose word I praise,
  in the LORD,
    whose word I praise,
11 in God I trust; I will not
  be afraid.
What can mere humans do
  to me?   Ps 112:7; Pr 29:25; Is 12:2

12 I am obligated by vows A
  to you, God;
I will make
  my thank offerings to you.
13 For you rescued me
  from death,
even my feet from stumbling,
to walk before God
  in the light of life.   Jb 33:30

Praise for God's Protection

57 For the choir director: "Do Not
Destroy." A Miktam of David.
When he fled before Saul into the cave.

1 Be gracious to me, God,
  be gracious to me,
for I take refuge in you.
I will seek refuge
  in the shadow of your wings
until danger passes.   Ru 2:12
2 I call to God Most High,
to God who fulfills
  his purpose for me. B   Ps 138:8
3 He reaches down
  from heaven and saves me,
challenging the one
  who tramples me.   Selah
God sends his faithful love
  and truth.   Ps 25:10; 40:11
4 I am surrounded by lions;
I lie down
  among devouring lions —

people whose teeth
  are spears and arrows,
whose tongues
  are sharp swords.   Ps 58:6; 64:3
5 God, be exalted
  above the heavens;
let your glory be over
  the whole earth.   Ps 108:5; 113:4
6 They prepared a net
  for my steps;
I was despondent.
They dug a pit ahead of me,
but they fell into it!   Selah

7 My heart is confident, God,
  my heart is confident.
I will sing; I will sing praises.
8 Wake up, my soul!
Wake up, harp and lyre!
I will wake up the dawn.
9 I will praise you, Lord,
  among the peoples;
I will sing praises to you
  among the nations.   2Sm 22:50
10 For your faithful love is
  as high as the heavens;
your faithfulness reaches
  the clouds.   Ps 36:5; 103:11
11 God, be exalted
  above the heavens;   Ps 113:4
let your glory be
  over the whole earth.

A Cry Against Injustice

58 For the choir director: "Do Not
Destroy." A Miktam of David.

1 Do you really
  speak righteously,
    you mighty ones? C
Do you judge people fairly?
2 No, you practice injustice
  in your hearts;
with your hands
  you weigh out violence
    in the land.   Ps 94:20; Is 10:1; Mal 3:15

A 56:12 Lit On me the vows   B 57:2 Or who avenges me   C 58:1 Or Can you really speak righteousness
in silence?

3 The wicked go astray
     from the womb;
  liars wander about
     from birth.   Ps 51:5; Is 48:8
4 They have venom
     like the venom
     of a snake,
  like the deaf cobra
     that stops up its ears,   Dt 32:33
5 that does not listen
     to the sound
     of the charmers
  who skillfully weave spells.

6 God, knock the teeth
     out of their mouths;
  LORD, tear out
     the young lions' fangs.   Jb 4:10
7 May they vanish like water
     that flows by;
  may they aim
     their blunted arrows. A   Jos 7:5
8 Like a slug that moves along
     in slime,
  like a woman's miscarried
     child,
  may they not see the sun.

9 Before your pots can feel
     the heat of the thorns —
  whether green
     or burning —
  he will sweep them away. B
10 The righteous one
     will rejoice
  when he sees
     the retribution;   Jb 22:19
  he will wash his feet
     in the blood
     of the wicked.   Ps 68:23; Jr 11:20
11 Then people will say,
  "Yes, there is a reward
     for the righteous!
  There is a God who judges
     on earth! "   Ps 9:8; 67:4; 75:7

God Our Stronghold

59 *For the choir director: "Do Not Destroy." A Miktam of David. When Saul sent agents to watch the house and kill him.*   1Sm 19:11

1 Rescue me from my enemies,
     my God;   Ps 143:9
  protect me from those
     who rise up against me.
2 Rescue me from those
     who practice sin,
  and save me from men
     of bloodshed.   Ps 5:6; 17:7
3 Because look, LORD, they set
     an ambush for me.   Pr 1:11,18
  Powerful men attack me,
  but not because of any sin
     or rebellion of mine.   1Sm 20:1
4 For no fault of mine,
  they run and take up
     a position.
  Awake to help me,
     and take notice.   Ps 7:3-4; 69:4
5 LORD God of Armies, you are
     the God of Israel.
  Rise up to punish
     all the nations;
  do not show favor
     to any wicked traitors. *Selah*

6 They return at evening,
     snarling like dogs
  and prowling
     around the city.
7 Look, they spew
     from their mouths —
  sharp words from C their lips.
  "For who," they say,
     "will hear? "   Ps 73:11
8 But you laugh at them, LORD;
  you ridicule all the nations.
9 I will keep watch for you,
     my D strength,
  because God is
     my stronghold.   Ps 28:8; Jr 16:19

A58:7 Hb obscure   B58:9 Or *thorns, he will sweep it away, whether raw or cooking*   C59:7 Lit *swords are on*   D59:9 Some Hb mss, LXX, Vg, Tg; other Hb mss read *his*

10 My faithful God^A will come
  to meet me;
  God will let me look down on
  my adversaries.   Ps 54:7

11 Do not kill them; otherwise,
  my people will forget.
  By your power, make them
    homeless wanderers   Hs 9:17
  and bring them down,
  Lord, our shield.   Gn 15:1; Dt 33:29

12 For the sin of their mouths
    and the words of their lips,
  let them be caught
    in their pride.
  They utter curses and lies.

13 Consume them in rage;
  consume them until
    they are gone.   Ps 104:35
  Then people will know
    throughout^B the earth
  that God rules over Jacob.
                              Selah

14 And they return at evening,
    snarling like dogs
  and prowling around the city.

15 They scavenge for food;
  they growl if they are not
    satisfied.   Jb 15:23; Ps 109:10

16 But I will sing
    of your strength
  and will joyfully proclaim
  your faithful love
    in the morning.   Ps 5:3; 88:13; 92:2
  For you have been
    a stronghold for me,
  a refuge in my day of trouble.

17 To you, my strength,
    I sing praises,
  because God is
    my stronghold —
    my faithful God.   Ps 28:8; Jr 16:19

Prayer in Difficult Times

60 *For the choir director: according
to "The Lily of Testimony."*
A Miktam *of David for teaching. When
he fought with Aram-naharaim and
Aram-zobah, and Joab returned and
struck Edom in Salt Valley, killing twelve
thousand.*   1Ch 18:3,12; Pss 45; 69; 80 titles

1 God, you have rejected us;
  you have broken us down;
  you have been angry.
    Restore us!^C   Ps 44:9,23; 79:5

2 You have shaken the land
    and split it open.
  Heal its fissures,
    for it shudders.   Ps 18:7

3 You have made your people
    suffer hardship;
  you have given us wine
    to drink
  that made us stagger.   Is 51:17-23

4 You have given a signal flag
    to those who fear you,
  so that they can flee
    before the archers.^D   *Selah*

5 Save with your right hand,
    and answer me,
  so that those you love
    may be rescued.   Ps 17:7; 20:6

6 God has spoken
    in his sanctuary:^E
  "I will celebrate!
  I will divide up Shechem.
  I will apportion the Valley
    of Succoth.   Gn 33:17

7 Gilead is mine,
    Manasseh is mine,
  and Ephraim is my helmet;
  Judah is my scepter.   Gn 49:10

8 Moab is my washbasin.   2Sm 8:2
  I throw my sandal on Edom;
  I shout in triumph
    over Philistia."   2Sm 8:1

^A**59:10** Alt Hb tradition reads *My God in his faithful love*   ^B**59:13** Lit *know to the ends of*   ^C**60:1** Or
Turn back to us   ^D**60:4** Or *can rally before the archers,* or *can rally because of the truth*   ^E**60:6** Or *has
promised by his holy nature*

9 Who will bring me
    to the fortified city?
  Who will lead me to Edom?
10 God, haven't you rejected us?
   God, you do not march out
     with our armies.   Ps 44:9
11 Give us aid against the foe,
   for human help is worthless.
12 With God
     we will perform valiantly;
   he will trample our foes.

Security in God

61 *For the choir director: on stringed
    instruments. Of David.*

1 God, hear my cry;
    pay attention to my prayer.
2 I call to you from the ends
    of the earth
  when my heart is
    without strength.   Ps 88:4
  Lead me to a rock that is
    high above me,   Ps 27:5
3 for you have been a refuge
    for me,
  a strong tower in the face
    of the enemy.   Pr 18:10
4 I will dwell in your tent forever
  and take refuge
    under the shelter
    of your wings.   *Selah*

5 God, you have heard
    my vows;   Jb 22:27; Ps 56:12
  you have given a heritage
  to those who fear your name.
6 Add days to the king's life;
  may his years span
    many generations.   Ps 21:4
7 May he sit enthroned
    before God forever.   Ps 41:12
  Appoint faithful love
    and truth to guard him.
8 Then I will continually sing
    of your name,   Ps 7:17; 9:2; 18:49
  fulfilling my vows day by day.

Trust in God Alone

62 *For the choir director: according
    to Jeduthun. A psalm of David.*

1 I am at rest in God alone;
  my salvation comes
    from him.   Ps 33:20; 37:39
2 He alone is my rock
    and my salvation,   Dt 32:15
  my stronghold;
    I will never be shaken.

3 How long will you
    threaten a man?
  Will all of you attack^A
  as if he were a leaning wall
  or a tottering fence?   Is 30:13
4 They only plan to bring him
    down
  from his high position.
  They take pleasure in lying;
  they bless with their mouths,
  but they curse inwardly. *Selah*

5 Rest in God alone, my soul,
  for my hope comes from him.
6 He alone is my rock
    and my salvation,   Ps 89:26; 95:1
  my stronghold; I will not
    be shaken.   Ps 16:8; 21:7
7 My salvation and glory
    depend on God,
    my strong rock.
  My refuge is in God.   Ps 18:2
8 Trust in him at all times,
    you people;
  pour out your hearts
    before him.
  God is our refuge.   *Selah*

9 Common people are only
    a vapor;
  important people, an illusion.
  Together on a scale,
  they weigh less than^B a vapor.
10 Place no trust in oppression,
   or false hope in robbery.

^A62:3 Some Hb mss read *you be struck down*   ^B62:9 Lit *they go up more than*

If wealth increases,
don't set your heart on it.

11 God has spoken once;
I have heard this twice:
strength belongs to God,
12 and faithful love belongs
to you, Lord.
For you repay each
according to his works.

Praise God Who Satisfies

63 *A psalm of David. When he was in the Wilderness of Judah.*

1 God, you are my God;
I eagerly seek you.
I thirst for you;
my body faints for you
in a land that is dry, desolate,
and without water.   Ps 42:2
2 So I gaze on you
in the sanctuary
to see your strength
and your glory.   Jb 19:26-27; 27:4

3 My lips will glorify you
because your faithful love
is better than life.   Ps 69:16
4 So I will bless you as long as
I live;
at your name, I will lift up
my hands.   Ps 28:2; 143:6; Lm 3:41
5 You satisfy me as with
rich food; A   Ps 36:8
my mouth will praise you
with joyful lips.   Ps 71:23

6 When I think of you as I lie
on my bed,
I meditate on you
during the night watches
7 because you are
my helper;   Ps 27:9; 40:17
I will rejoice in the shadow
of your wings.   Ps 17:8; 36:7; 57:1
8 I follow close to you;

your right hand holds on
to me.   Ps 18:35

9 But those who intend
to destroy my life
will go into the depths
of the earth.   Ps 55:15; Ezk 26:20
10 They will be given over
to the power of the sword;
they will become a meal
for jackals.
11 But the king will rejoice
in God;   Ps 21:1
all who swear by him
will boast,
for the mouths of liars
will be shut.   Ps 107:42; Rm 3:19

Protection from Evildoers

64 *For the choir director. A psalm of David.*

1 God, hear my voice
when I am in anguish.   Ps 55:2
Protect my life from the terror
of the enemy.   Ps 140:1
2 Hide me from the scheming
of wicked people,   Ps 35:20; 37:12
from the mob of evildoers,
3 who sharpen their tongues
like swords
and aim bitter words
like arrows,   Ps 52:2; 57:4; Pr 25:18
4 shooting
from concealed places
at the blameless.
They shoot at him suddenly
and are not afraid.   Ps 10:8; 11:2
5 They adopt B an evil plan;
they talk about hiding traps
and say,
"Who will see them?" C   Ps 35:7
6 They devise crimes and say,
"We have perfected
a secret plan."   Ps 21:11; 83:3
The inner man and the heart
are mysterious.

A **63:5** Lit *with fat and fatness*   B **64:5** Or *They strengthen themselves with*   C **64:5** Or *it*

⁷ But God will shoot them
    with arrows;
  suddenly, they will be
    wounded.   Ps 7:13; 45:5; 144:6
⁸ They will be made
    to stumble;
  their own tongues work
    against them.
  All who see them will shake
    their heads.   Jr 18:16; 48:27; Lm 2:15
⁹ Then everyone will fear
  and will tell
    about God's work,
  for they will understand
    what he has done.   Ps 40:3

¹⁰ The righteous one rejoices
    in the LORD
  and takes refuge in him;
  all those who are upright
    in heart
  will offer praise.   Ps 32:11; 68:3

God's Care for the Earth

65 For the choir director.
      A psalm of David. A song.

¹ Praise is rightfully yours, ᴬ
  God, in Zion;
  vows to you will be fulfilled.
² All humanity will come to you,
  the one who hears prayer.
³ Iniquities overwhelm me;
  only you can atone for
    our rebellions.   Ps 38:14; 40:12
⁴ How happy is the one
    you choose
  and bring near to live
    in your courts!
  We will be satisfied
    with the goodness
    of your house,
  the holiness of your temple. ᴮ

⁵ You answer us
    in righteousness,

with awe-inspiring works,
  God of our salvation,
  the hope of all the ends
    of the earth
  and of the distant seas.   Dt 10:21
⁶ You establish the mountains
    by your power;
  you are robed with strength.
⁷ You silence the roar
    of the seas,
  the roar of their waves,
  and the tumult
    of the nations.   Ps 107:29; Is 17:13
⁸ Those who live far away
    are awed by your signs;
  you make east and west
    shout for joy.   Ps 2:8; 139:9; Is 24:16

⁹ You visit the earth
    and water it abundantly,
  enriching it greatly.
  God's stream is filled
    with water,
  for you prepare the earth
    in this way,
  providing people
    with grain.   Ps 104:13; 147:8; Is 45:8
¹⁰ You soften it with showers
    and bless its growth,
  soaking its furrows
    and leveling its ridges.
¹¹ You crown the year
    with your goodness;
  your carts overflow
    with plenty. ᶜ   Ps 104:28; 147:14
¹² The wilderness pastures
    overflow,
  and the hills are robed
    with joy.   Jb 38:26-27; Is 55:12; Jl 2:22
¹³ The pastures are clothed
    with flocks
  and the valleys covered
    with grain.   Ps 72:16; 144:13; Is 30:23
  They shout in triumph;
    indeed, they sing.   Is 44:23

ᴬ**65:1** Or *Praise is silence to you,* or *Praise awaits you*   ᴮ**65:4** Or *house, your holy temple*   ᶜ**65:11** Lit
your paths drip with fat

Praise for God's Mighty Acts

66 *For the choir director. A song.*
A psalm.

¹ Let the whole earth shout
  joyfully to God! *Ps 98:4; 100:1*
² Sing about the glory
  of his name;
  make his praise glorious.
³ Say to God,
  "How awe-inspiring
  are your works!
  Your enemies will cringe
  before you
  because of your great
  strength. *Ps 18:44; 47:2; 145:6*
⁴ The whole earth will worship
  you
  and sing praise to you.
  They will sing praise
  to your name." *Selah*

⁵ Come and see the wonders
  of God; *Ps 46:8*
  his acts for humanity^A
  are awe-inspiring.
⁶ He turned the sea
  into dry land,
  and they crossed the river
  on foot. *Ex 14:21; Ps 106:9*
  There we rejoiced in him.
⁷ He rules forever by his might;
  he keeps his eye
  on the nations. *Ps 14:2; 33:13-14*
  The rebellious should not
  exalt themselves. *Selah*
⁸ Bless our God, you peoples;
  let the sound of his praise
  be heard. *Ps 98:4*
⁹ He keeps us alive^B
  and does not allow our feet
  to slip. *Ps 94:18; 121:3*

¹⁰ For you, God, tested us;
  you refined us as silver
  is refined. *Jb 23:10; Ps 17:3; Is 48:10*

¹¹ You lured us into a trap;
  you placed burdens
  on our backs. *Lm 1:13; Ezk 12:13*
¹² You let men ride
  over our heads;
  we went through fire
  and water,
  but you brought us out
  to abundance.^C *Ps 18:19; Is 43:2*

¹³ I will enter your house
  with burnt offerings;
  I will pay you my vows *Ps 22:25*
¹⁴ that my lips promised
  and my mouth spoke
  during my distress. *Ps 18:6*
¹⁵ I will offer you
  fattened sheep
  as burnt offerings,
  with the fragrant smoke
  of rams;
  I will sacrifice bulls
  with goats. *Selah*

¹⁶ Come and listen,
  all who fear God,
  and I will tell what
  he has done for me. *Ps 9:1; 34:11*
¹⁷ I cried out to him
  with my mouth,
  and praise was
  on my tongue. *Ps 35:28*
¹⁸ If I had been aware of malice
  in my heart,
  the Lord would not
  have listened. *Jb 36:21; Jn 9:31*
¹⁹ However, God has listened;
  he has paid attention
  to the sound
  of my prayer. *Ps 116:1-2*
²⁰ Blessed be God!
  He has not turned away
  my prayer
  or turned his faithful love
  from me. *Ps 22:24; 68:35*

^A **66:5** Or *for the descendants of Adam*　^B **66:9** Lit *He sets our soul in life*　^C **66:12** Or *a place of satisfaction*

All Will Praise God

67 *For the choir director: with stringed instruments. A psalm. A song.*

1 May God be gracious to us
   and bless us;
may he make his face shine
   upon us   *Selah*
2 so that your way
   may be known on earth,
your salvation
   among all nations.   Ps 98:2

3 Let the peoples praise you,
   God;
let all the peoples praise you.
4 Let the nations rejoice
   and shout for joy,
for you judge the peoples
   with fairness
and lead the nations
   on earth.   *Selah*
5 Let the peoples praise
   you, God,
let all the peoples praise you.

6 The earth has produced
   its harvest;
God, our God, blesses us.
7 God will bless us,
and all the ends of the earth
   will fear him.   1Kg 8:43; 2Ch 6:33

God's Majestic Power

68 *For the choir director. A psalm of David. A song.*

1 God arises.
   His enemies scatter,
and those who hate him flee
   from his presence.   Nm 10:35
2 As smoke is blown away,
so you blow them away.
As wax melts before the fire,
so the wicked are destroyed
   before God.   Ps 37:20; Hs 13:3

3 But the righteous are glad;
they rejoice before God
   and celebrate with joy.

4 Sing to God! Sing praises
   to his name.
Exalt him who rides
   on the clouds [A] —
his name is the LORD [B] —
   and celebrate before him.
5 God in his holy dwelling is
a father of the fatherless
and a champion of widows.
6 God provides homes
   for those who are deserted.
He leads out the prisoners
   to prosperity, [C]
but the rebellious live
   in a scorched land.   Ps 107:14

7 God, when you went out
   before your people,
when you marched
   through the desert,   *Selah*
8 the earth trembled
   and the skies poured rain
before God, the God of Sinai, [D]
before God, the God of Israel.
9 You, God, showered
   abundant rain;
you revived your inheritance
   when it languished.   Lv 26:4
10 Your people settled in it;
God, you provided for
   the poor by your goodness.

11 The Lord gave the command;
a great company of women
   brought the good news:
12 "The kings of the armies flee
   — they flee!"
She who stays at home
   divides the spoil.   Jos 10:16
13 While [E] you lie among
   the sheep pens, [F]

[A] **68:4** Or *rides through the desert*   [B] **68:4** Hb *Yah*   [C] **68:6** Or *prisoners with joyous music*; Hb uncertain
[D] **68:8** Or *God, this one of Sinai*   [E] **68:13** Or *If*   [F] **68:13** Or *the campfires*, or *the saddlebags*; Hb obscure

the wings of a dove
    are covered with silver,
and its feathers
    with glistening gold.   Gn 49:14

14 When the Almighty scattered
    kings in the land,
it snowed on Zalmon.^A   Jos 10:10

15 Mount Bashan is
    God's towering mountain;
Mount Bashan is a mountain
    of many peaks.   Ps 36:6
16 Why gaze with envy,
    you mountain peaks,
at the mountain God desired
    for his abode?
The LORD will
    dwell there forever!   Ps 48:1-2
17 God's chariots are tens
    of thousands,
thousands and thousands;
the Lord is among them
    in the sanctuary^B
as he was at Sinai.   Dt 33:2
18 You ascended to the heights,
    taking away captives;
you received gifts
    from^C people,
even from the rebellious,
so that the LORD God
    might dwell there.^D   Dt 21:10

19 Blessed be the Lord!
Day after day he bears
    our burdens;
God is our salvation.   *Selah*
20 Our God is a God of salvation,
    and escape from death
    belongs to the LORD my
    Lord.   Dt 32:39; Ps 49:15; 56:13
21 Surely God crushes the heads
    of his enemies,
the hairy brow of
    one who goes on
    in his guilty acts.   Ps 110:6

22 The Lord said,
    "I will bring them back
    from Bashan;
I will bring them back
    from the depths of the sea
23 so that your foot may wade^E
    in blood
and your dogs' tongues
    may have their share
from the enemies."   1Kg 21:19
24 People have seen
    your procession, God,
the procession of my God,
    my King, in the sanctuary.
25 Singers lead the way,
    with musicians following;
among them are
    young women
    playing tambourines.   Ex 15:20
26 Bless God in the assemblies;
bless the LORD
    from the fountain
    of Israel.
27 There is Benjamin,
    the youngest,
    leading them,
the rulers of Judah
    in their assembly,^F
the rulers of Zebulun,
    the rulers of Naphtali.

28 Your God has decreed
    your strength.
Show your strength, God,
you who have acted
    on our behalf.   Ps 44:4; Is 26:12
29 Because of your temple
    at Jerusalem,
kings will bring tribute
    to you.   Ps 72:10; Is 18:7; Hg 2:7
30 Rebuke the beast
    in the reeds,
the herd of bulls
    with the calves
    of the peoples.   Ps 22:12

^A68:14 Or *Black Mountain*   ^B68:17 Or *in holiness*, also in v. 24   ^C68:18 Lit *among*   ^D68:18 Or *even those rebelling against the LORD God's living there*; Hb obscure   ^E68:23 LXX, Syr read *dip*   ^F68:27 Hb obscure

Trample underfoot those
    with bars of silver. [A]
Scatter the peoples
    who take pleasure in war.
31 Ambassadors will come [B]
    from Egypt;
Cush will stretch out
    its hands to God.   Is 45:14

32 Sing to God, you kingdoms
    of the earth;
sing praise to the Lord,   *Selah*
33 to him who rides
    in the ancient,
    highest heavens.   Dt 33:26
Look, he thunders
    with his powerful voice!
34 Ascribe power to God.
His majesty is over Israel,
    his power is among the clouds.
35 God, you are awe-inspiring
    in your sanctuaries.
The God of Israel gives power
    and strength to his people.
Blessed be God!   Dt 10:21; Ps 29:11

A Plea for Rescue

69 For the choir director: according
to "The Lilies." Of David.   Pss 45; 60

1 Save me, God,
for the water has risen
    to my neck.   Jb 22:11; Ps 32:6; Jnh 2:5
2 I have sunk in deep mud,
    and there is no footing;
I have come into deep water,
and a flood sweeps over me.
3 I am weary from my crying;
my throat is parched.
My eyes fail,
    looking for my God.   Ps 6:6
4 Those who hate me
    without cause
are more numerous
    than the hairs of my head;

my deceitful enemies,
    who would destroy me,
are powerful.   Ps 38:19
Though I did not steal,
    I must repay.   Lv 6:2-5; Ps 35:19

5 God, you know
    my foolishness,
and my guilty acts are
    not hidden from you.   Ps 38:5
6 Do not let those who put
    their hope in you
be disgraced because of me,
Lord GOD of Armies;
do not let those
    who seek you
be humiliated because of me,
God of Israel.   Ps 25:2-3
7 For I have endured insults
    because of you,
and shame has covered
    my face.   Ps 44:15; Is 50:6; Jr 51:51
8 I have become a stranger
    to my brothers
and a foreigner
    to my mother's sons   Ps 31:11
9 because zeal for your house
    has consumed me,   Jn 2:17
and the insults of those
    who insult you
have fallen on me.   Ps 89:50
10 I mourned and fasted,
but it brought me insults.
11 I wore sackcloth
    as my clothing,
and I was a joke to them.
12 Those who sit at the city gate
    talk about me,
and drunkards
    make up songs about me.

13 But as for me, LORD,
my prayer to you is for a time
    of favor.

[A]68:30 Or *peoples, trampling on those who take pleasure in silver,* or *peoples, trampling on the bars of silver,* or *peoples, who trample each other for bars of silver*   [B]68:31 Or *They bring red cloth,* or *They bring bronze*

In your abundant,
  faithful love, God,
answer me with
  your sure salvation.   Ps 109:4

14 Rescue me
  from the miry mud;
  don't let me sink.
Let me be rescued from those
  who hate me
and from the deep water.

15 Don't let the floodwaters
  sweep over me
or the deep swallow me up;
don't let the Pit close
  its mouth over me.   Nm 16:33

16 Answer me, LORD,
  for your faithful love is good.
In keeping with
  your abundant compassion,
turn to me.   Ps 25:16; 109:21

17 Don't hide your face
  from your servant,
for I am in distress.
Answer me quickly!   Ps 27:9; 102:2

18 Come near to me
  and redeem me;
ransom me because of
  my enemies.   Ps 119:134

19 You know the insults
  I endure —
my shame and disgrace.
You are aware of
  all my adversaries.   Jr 15:15

20 Insults have broken my heart,
and I am in despair.
I waited for sympathy,
but there was none;
for comforters, but found
  no one.   Ps 142:4; Is 63:5

21 Instead, they gave me gall
  for my food,
and for my thirst
they gave me vinegar to drink.

22 Let their table set
  before them be a snare,

and let it be a trap
  for their allies.   Ps 35:4-8; 1Th 5:3

23 Let their eyes grow too dim
  to see,
and let their hips
  continually quake.   Is 6:10

24 Pour out your rage on them,
and let your burning anger
  overtake them.   Ps 79:6; Ezk 21:31

25 Make their fortification
  desolate;
may no one live in their tents.

26 For they persecute the one
  you struck
and talk about the pain
  of those you wounded.

27 Charge them with crime
  on top of crime;
do not let them share
  in your righteousness.

28 Let them be erased
  from the book of life
and not be recorded
  with the righteous.   Ex 32:32

29 But as for me —
  poor and in pain —
let your salvation
  protect me, God.   Ps 20:1; 70:5

30 I will praise God's name
  with song
and exalt him
  with thanksgiving.   Ps 100:4

31 That will please the LORD
  more than an ox,
more than a bull with horns
  and hooves.   Ps 50:13-14; 51:16

32 The humble will see it
  and rejoice.
You who seek God, take heart!

33 For the LORD listens
  to the needy
and does not despise
his own who are prisoners.

34 Let heaven and earth
  praise him,

the seas and everything
that moves in them,   Ps 96:11
35 for God will save Zion
and build up^A the cities
of Judah.
They will live there
and possess it.   Ps 147:2; Is 44:26
36 The descendants
of his servants
will inherit it,
and those who love his name
will live in it.   Ps 102:28; Is 65:9

A Call for Deliverance

70 *For the choir director. Of David.
To bring remembrance.*   Ps 38 title

1 God, hurry to rescue me.
LORD, hurry to help me!

2 Let those who seek to kill me
be disgraced
and confounded;
let those who wish me harm
be turned back
and humiliated.
3 Let those who say, "Aha, aha!"
retreat because of
their shame.   Ps 35:25; 40:14-15

4 Let all who seek you rejoice
and be glad in you;
let those who love
your salvation
continually say,
"God is great!"   Ps 35:27; 77:13
5 I am oppressed and needy;
hurry to me, God.
You are my help
and my deliverer;
LORD, do not delay.   Ps 40:17; 141:1

God's Help in Old Age

71 LORD, I seek refuge in you;
let me never be disgraced.
2 In your justice, rescue
and deliver me;

^A **69:35** Or *and rebuild*

listen closely to me
and save me.   Ps 17:6
3 Be a rock of refuge for me,
where I can always go.
Give the command
to save me,
for you are my rock
and fortress.   Ps 31:1-3
4 Deliver me, my God, from
the power of the wicked,
from the grasp of the unjust
and oppressive.   Ps 140:1,4
5 For you are my hope, Lord
GOD,
my confidence
from my youth.   Ps 39:7; Jr 17:13
6 I have leaned on you
from birth;
you took me from
my mother's womb.   Ps 22:9-10
My praise is always about you.
7 I am like a miraculous sign
to many,
and you are my strong refuge.
8 My mouth is full of praise
and honor to you all day long.

9 Don't discard me in my
old age.
As my strength fails,
do not abandon me.   Ps 27:9
10 For my enemies talk
about me,
and those who spy on me
plot together,   Ps 31:13; 56:6; 83:3
11 saying, "God
has abandoned him;
chase him and catch him,
for there is no one
to rescue him."   Ps 3:2
12 God, do not be far from me;
my God, hurry to help me.
13 May my adversaries
be disgraced and destroyed;
may those who intend
to harm me

be covered with disgrace
and humiliation. Ps 71:24

¹⁴ But I will hope continually
and will praise you more
and more. Ps 84:4; 130:7; 147:11

¹⁵ My mouth will tell
about your righteousness
and your salvation
all day long,
though I cannot sum them up.

¹⁶ I come because of
the mighty acts
of the Lord God;
I will proclaim
your righteousness,
yours alone. Ps 51:14; 106:2

¹⁷ God, you have taught me
from my youth,
and I still proclaim your
wondrous works. Dt 4:5; 6:7

¹⁸ Even while I am old and gray,
God, do not abandon me,
while I proclaim your power
to another generation,
your strength to all who are
to come. Ps 22:30-31; 78:4,6

¹⁹ Your righteousness reaches
the heights, God,
you who have done
great things;
God, who is like you? Ex 15:11

²⁰ You caused me to experience
many troubles
and misfortunes, Ps 60:3
but you will revive me again.
You will bring me up again,
even from the depths
of the earth. Hs 6:1-2

²¹ You will increase my honor
and comfort me once again.

²² Therefore, I will praise you
with a harp
for your faithfulness, my God;
I will sing to you with a lyre,

Holy One of Israel. Ps 33:2; 81:2

²³ My lips will shout for joy
when I sing praise to you
because you have
redeemed me. Ps 34:22; 55:18

²⁴ Therefore, my tongue
will proclaim
your righteousness
all day long,
for those who intend
to harm me
will be disgraced
and confounded. Ps 35:28; 71:13

A Prayer for the King

72 *Of Solomon.* Ps 127 title
God, give your justice
to the king
and your righteousness
to the king's son. 1Kg 3:9; Ps 24:5

² He will judge your people
with righteousness
and your afflicted ones
with justice. Is 9:7; 11:2-5; 32:1

³ May the mountains
bring well-being ᴬ
to the people
and the hills, righteousness.

⁴ May he vindicate the afflicted
among the people,
help the poor,
and crush the oppressor. Is 11:4

⁵ May they fear you ᴮ while the
sun endures
and as long as the moon,
throughout all generations.

⁶ May the king be like rain
that falls on the cut grass,
like spring showers
that water the earth. Dt 32:2

⁷ May the righteous ᶜ flourish
in his days
and well-being abound
until the moon is no more.

ᴬ72:3 Or *peace*, also in v. 7　ᴮ72:5 LXX reads *May he continue*　ᶜ72:7 Some Hb mss, LXX, Syr, Jer read *May righteousness*

8 May he rule from sea to sea
and from the Euphrates
to the ends of the earth.
9 May desert tribes kneel
before him
and his enemies lick the dust.
10 May the kings of Tarshish
and the coasts and islands
bring tribute,
the kings of Sheba and Seba
offer gifts.   1Kg 10:22; 2Ch 9:21
11 Let all kings bow in homage
to him,
all nations serve him.   Ps 86:9

12 For he will rescue the poor
who cry out
and the afflicted who have
no helper.   Jb 29:12-17
13 He will have pity on the poor
and helpless
and save the lives of the poor.
14 He will redeem them
from oppression
and violence,
for their lives are[A] precious[B]
in his sight.   Ps 69:18; 116:15

15 May he live long!
May gold from Sheba
be given to him.
May prayer be offered
for him continually,
and may he be blessed
all day long.   Is 60:6
16 May there be plenty of grain
in the land;
may it wave on the tops
of the mountains.
May its crops be like Lebanon.
May people flourish
in the cities
like the grass of the field.
17 May his name
endure forever;

as long as the sun shines,
may his fame increase.
May all nations be blessed
by him
and call him blessed.   Gn 12:2-3

18 Blessed be the LORD God,
the God of Israel,
who alone does wonders.
19 Blessed be his glorious name
forever;
the whole earth is filled
with his glory.   Nm 14:21; Is 6:3
Amen and amen.
20 The prayers of David
son of Jesse are concluded.

BOOK III (Psalms 73–89)

God's Ways Vindicated

73 *A psalm of Asaph.*   1Ch 16:5,7
God is indeed good
to Israel,
to the pure in heart.   Ps 24:4; 51:10
2 But as for me, my feet
almost slipped;
my steps nearly went astray.
3 For I envied the arrogant;
I saw the prosperity
of the wicked.   Ps 37:1; Pr 23:17

4 They have an easy time
until they die,[C]
and their bodies
are well fed.[D]   Jb 21:23-24
5 They are not in trouble
like others;
they are not afflicted
like most people.   Jb 21:4
6 Therefore, pride is
their necklace,
and violence covers them
like a garment.   Ps 37:35; Pr 16:29
7 Their eyes bulge out
from fatness;

[A]72:14 Lit their blood is   [B]72:14 Or valuable   [C]73:4 Lit For there are no pangs to their death
[D]73:4 Lit fat

the imaginations
of their hearts run wild.
8 They mock,
and they speak maliciously;
they arrogantly
threaten oppression. Ps 17:10
9 They set their mouths
against heaven,
and their tongues strut
across the earth. Rv 13:6
10 Therefore his people turn
to them^A
and drink in their
overflowing words.^B Jb 15:16
11 The wicked say,
"How can God know?
Does the Most High
know everything?" Jb 22:13
12 Look at them — the wicked!
They are always at ease,
and they increase their wealth.
13 Did I purify my heart
and wash my hands
in innocence for nothing?
14 For I am afflicted all day long
and punished every morning.
15 If I had decided to say
these things aloud,
I would have betrayed
your people.^C Ps 44:17; 89:33
16 When I tried to understand
all this,
it seemed hopeless^D Ec 8:17
17 until I entered God's sanctuary.
Then I understood
their destiny. Jb 8:13; Ps 37:38
18 Indeed, you put them
in slippery places;
you make them fall into ruin.
19 How suddenly they become
a desolation!
They come to an end,
swept away by terrors.

20 Like one waking
from a dream,
Lord, when arising,
you will despise their image.
21 When I became embittered
and my innermost being^E
was wounded, Ps 109:22
22 I was stupid
and didn't understand;
I was an unthinking animal
toward you. Jb 11:12; Ps 92:6
23 Yet I am always with you;
you hold my right hand. Ps 63:8
24 You guide me
with your counsel,
and afterward you will
take me up in glory.^F Ps 49:15
25 Who do I have in heaven
but you?
And I desire nothing on earth
but you. Ps 16:2; Php 3:8
26 My flesh and my heart
may fail,
but God is the strength^G
of my heart,
my portion forever. Ps 16:5; 38:10
27 Those far from you
will certainly perish;
you destroy all who are
unfaithful to you. 1Ch 5:25
28 But as for me, God's presence
is my good.
I have made the Lord God
my refuge,
so I can tell about all you do.

Prayer for Israel

74 A Maskil of Asaph. 1Ch 16:5,7
Why have you
rejected us forever, God?
Why does your anger burn
against the sheep
of your pasture? Ex 32:11; Ps 108:11

---

^A**73:10** Lit turn here   ^B**73:10** Lit and waters of fullness are drained by them   ^C**73:15** Lit betrayed the generation of your sons   ^D**73:16** Lit it was trouble in my eyes   ^E**73:21** Lit my kidneys   ^F**73:24** Or will receive me with honor   ^G**73:26** Lit rock

2 Remember
   your congregation,
which you purchased
   long ago
and redeemed as the tribe
   for your own possession.
Remember Mount Zion
   where you dwell.   Is 8:18
3 Make your way ^A
   to the perpetual ruins,
to all that the enemy
   has destroyed
   in the sanctuary.   Ps 79:1; Is 61:4
4 Your adversaries roared
   in the meeting place
where you met with us. ^B
They set up their emblems
   as signs.   Nm 2:2; Lm 2:6-7
5 It was like men in a thicket
   of trees,
wielding axes,   Jr 46:22
6 then smashing
   all the carvings
with hatchets and picks.   Lm 2:2
7 They set your sanctuary
   on fire;
they utterly ^C desecrated
the dwelling place
   of your name.   2Kg 25:9; Ps 79:1
8 They said in their hearts,
   "Let us
   oppress them relentlessly."
They burned every place
   throughout the land
where God met with us. ^D
9 There are no signs for us
   to see.
There is no longer a prophet.
And none of us knows
   how long this will last.   Lm 2:9
10 God, how long will the
   enemy mock?
Will the foe insult
   your name forever?   Ps 79:12

11 Why do you hold back
   your hand?
Stretch out ^E your right hand
   and destroy them!   Ps 59:13
12 God my King is
   from ancient times,
performing saving acts
   on the earth.   Ps 47:6-8; 95:3
13 You divided the sea
   with your strength;
you smashed the heads
   of the sea monsters
   in the water;   Ex 14:21; Is 51:9
14 you crushed the heads
   of Leviathan;
you fed him to the creatures
   of the desert.   Jb 41:1; Ps 104:26
15 You opened up springs
   and streams;   Ps 104:10-11
you dried up
   ever-flowing rivers.   Is 42:15
16 The day is yours,
   also the night;
you established the moon
   and the sun.   Gn 1:14-18; Ps 104:19
17 You set all the boundaries
   of the earth;
you made summer
   and winter.   Gn 8:22; Jb 38:10-11

18 Remember this: the enemy
   has mocked the LORD,
and a foolish people
   has insulted your name.
19 Do not give to beasts the life
   of your dove; ^F
do not forget the lives
   of your poor people
   forever.   Ps 9:18; 68:10
20 Consider the covenant,   Dt 4:31
for the dark places
   of the land
   are full of violence.   Ezk 7:23

^A74:3 Lit Lift up your steps   ^B74:4 Lit in your meeting place   ^C74:7 Lit they to the ground   ^D74:8 Lit every meeting place of God in the land   ^E74:11 Lit From your bosom   ^F74:19 One Hb ms, LXX, Syr read life that praises you

21 Do not let the oppressed
　　turn away in shame;
　let the poor and needy
　　praise your name.　Ps 9:9; 103:6
22 Rise up, God,
　　champion your cause!　Ps 9:19
　Remember the insults
　that fools bring against you
　　all day long.　Ps 79:12
23 Do not forget the clamor
　　of your adversaries,
　the tumult of your opponents
　that goes up constantly.

God Judges the Wicked

75 For the choir director: "Do Not
Destroy." A psalm of Asaph.
A song.　　　　　　　1Ch 16:5,7

1 We give thanks to you, God;
　we give thanks to you,
　　for your name is near.
　People tell about
　　your wondrous works.　Dt 4:7

2 "When I choose a time,
　I will judge fairly.　Ps 9:8; 96:10
3 When the earth and all
　　its inhabitants shake,
　I am the one who steadies
　　its pillars.　　　　　Selah
4 I say to the boastful,
　'Do not boast,'
　and to the wicked, 'Do not
　　lift up your horn.　Pr 27:1; Jr 9:23
5 Do not lift up your horn
　　against heaven[A]
　or speak arrogantly.' "　1Sm 2:3

6 Exaltation does not come
　from the east, the west,
　　or the desert,
7 for God is the Judge:
　He brings down one
　　and exalts another.　1Sm 2:7-8
8 For there is a cup
　　in the LORD's hand,

full of wine blended
　with spices, and he pours
　　from it.
All the wicked of the earth
　　will drink,
draining it to the dregs.

9 As for me, I will tell
　　about him forever;
　I will sing praise to the God
　　of Jacob.　Ps 9:2; 18:49; 81:1

10 "I will cut off all the horns
　　of the wicked,　Jr 48:25
　but the horns
　of the righteous will be
　　lifted up."　Ps 89:17; 92:10; 148:14

God, the Powerful Judge

76 For the choir director:
with stringed instruments.
A psalm of Asaph. A song.　1Ch 16:5,7

1 God is known in Judah;
　his name is great in Israel.
2 His tent is in Salem,
　his dwelling place in Zion.
3 There he shatters the bow's
　　flaming arrows,
　the shield, the sword,
　　and the weapons
　of war.　　　　　　Selah

4 You are resplendent
　　and majestic
　coming down
　　from the mountains
　of prey.　Is 14:25; Nah 2:13
5 The brave-hearted
　　have been plundered;
　they have slipped
　　into their final sleep.
None of the warriors
　　was able to lift a hand.
6 At your rebuke, God of Jacob,
　both chariot and horse
　　lay still.　Ex 13:1,21

[A]75:5 Lit horn to the height

⁷ And you — you are
  to be feared.ᴬ
When you are angry,
who can stand before you?
⁸ From heaven
  you pronounced judgment.
The earth feared
  and grew quiet   2Ch 20:29-30
⁹ when God rose up to judge
  and to save all the lowly
    of the earth.   *Selah*
¹⁰ Even human wrath
  will praise you;
you will clothe yourself
with the wrath that remains.ᴮ

¹¹ Make and keep your vows
  to the LORD your God;   Ps 50:14
let all who are around him
    bring tribute
to the awe-inspiring one.ᶜ
¹² He humbles the spirit
    of leaders;
he is feared by the kings
    of the earth.   Dn 4:37

Confidence in a Time of Crisis

77 *For the choir director: according
to Jeduthun. Of Asaph. A psalm.*

¹ I cry aloud to God,
  aloud to God, and he
    will hear me.   Ps 3:4; 142:1
² I sought the Lord in my day
    of trouble.
My hands were continually
    lifted up
all night long;
I refused to be comforted.
³ I think of God; I groan;
I meditate; my spirit
    becomes weak.   *Selah*

⁴ You have kept me
  from closing my eyes;
I am troubled
  and cannot speak.   Ps 39:9

⁵ I consider days of old,
  years long past.   Dt 32:7; Ps 143:5
⁶ At night I remember
    my music;
I meditate in my heart,
  and my spirit ponders.   Ps 4:4

⁷ "Will the Lord reject forever
and never again
  show favor?   Ps 44:9,23; 74:1; Lm 2:7
⁸ Has his faithful love
  ceased forever?
Is his promise at an end
  for all generations?   Ps 33:11
⁹ Has God forgotten
  to be gracious?
Has he in anger withheld
  his compassion?"   *Selah*

¹⁰ So I say, "I am grieved
that the right hand
  of the Most High
  has changed."ᴮ   Ps 31:22; 73:14
¹¹ I will remember
  the LORD's works;
yes, I will remember
  your ancient wonders.
¹² I will reflect on
  all you have done
and meditate on your actions.

¹³ God, your way is holy.
What god is great like God?
¹⁴ You are the God
  who works wonders;
you revealed your strength
  among the peoples.   Ps 72:18
¹⁵ With power you redeemed
    your people,
the descendants of Jacob
  and Joseph.   *Selah*

¹⁶ The water saw you, God.
The water saw you;
  it trembled.
Even the depths shook.   Ps 114:3

ᴬ**76:7** Or *are awe-inspiring*   ᴮ**76:10; 77:10** Hb obscure   ᶜ**76:11** Or *tribute with awe*

¹⁷ The clouds poured
    down water.
The storm clouds thundered;
your arrows flashed
    back and forth.   Ps 18:14; Hab 3:11
¹⁸ The sound of your thunder
    was in the whirlwind;
lightning lit up the world.
The earth shook and quaked.
¹⁹ Your way went through
    the sea
and your path through
    the vast water,
but your footprints
    were unseen.   Is 43:16
²⁰ You led your people like a flock
by the hand of Moses
    and Aaron.   Ps 105:26; Is 63:11-13

Lessons from Israel's Past

78   *A* Maskil *of Asaph.*   1Ch 16:5,7
My people,
    hear my instruction;
listen to the words
    from my mouth.   Pr 5:7; 7:24
² I will declare wise sayings;
I will speak mysteries
    from the past —   Ps 49:4; Pr 1:6
³ things we have heard
    and known
and that our fathers
    have passed down to us.
⁴ We will not hide them
    from their children,
but will tell
    a future generation
the praiseworthy acts
    of the LORD,
his might,
    and the wondrous works
he has performed.   Dt 6:7; 11:19
⁵ He established a testimony
    in Jacob
and set up a law in Israel,
which he commanded
    our fathers
to teach to their children

⁶ so that a future generation —
children yet to be born —
    might know.
They were to rise and tell
    their children   Dt 11:19; Ps 22:31
⁷ so that they might
    put their confidence in God
and not forget God's works,
but keep his commands.   Dt 6:12
⁸ Then they would not be
    like their fathers,
a stubborn and rebellious
    generation,
a generation whose heart
    was not loyal
and whose spirit
    was not faithful to God.

⁹ The Ephraimite archers
    turned back
on the day of battle.   Ps 44:10
¹⁰ They did not keep
    God's covenant
and refused to live
    by his law.   1Kg 11:11; 2Kg 17:15
¹¹ They forgot what
    he had done,
the wondrous works
    he had shown them.   Ps 106:13
¹² He worked wonders in
    the sight of their fathers
in the land of Egypt,
    the territory of Zoan.   Ex 7–12
¹³ He split the sea
    and brought them across;
the water stood firm
    like a wall.   Ex 14:21; 15:8; Ps 136:13
¹⁴ He led them with a cloud
    by day
and with a fiery light
    throughout the night.   Ex 13:21
¹⁵ He split rocks
    in the wilderness
and gave them drink
    as abundant as the depths.
¹⁶ He brought streams out of
    the stone

and made water flow down
   like rivers.   Ps 105:41; 114:8

17 But they continued to sin
   against him,
rebelling in the desert
   against the Most High.
18 They deliberately^A tested God,
demanding the food
   they craved.   Ex 17:2,7; Ps 106:14
19 They spoke
   against God, saying,
"Is God able to provide food
   in the wilderness?
20 Look! He struck the rock
   and water gushed out;
torrents overflowed.   Nm 20:11
But can he also provide bread
or furnish meat
   for his people?"   Ex 16:3; Nm 11:4
21 Therefore, the LORD heard
   and became furious;
then fire broke out
   against Jacob,
and anger flared up
   against Israel   Nm 11:1
22 because they did not
   believe God
or rely on his salvation.   Dt 1:23
23 He gave a command
   to the clouds above
and opened the doors
   of heaven.   Gn 7:11; Mal 3:10
24 He rained manna for them
   to eat;
he gave them grain
   from heaven.   Ex 16:4,31; Jn 6:31
25 People^B ate the bread
   of angels.^C
He sent them
   an abundant supply
   of food.   Ex 16:3
26 He made the east wind blow
   in the skies
and drove the south wind
   by his might.   Nm 11:31

27 He rained meat on them
   like dust,
and winged birds
   like the sand of the seas.
28 He made them fall
   in the camp,
all around the tents.   Ex 16:13
29 The people ate and were
   completely satisfied,
for he gave them
   what they craved.   Nm 11:4,34
30 Before they had turned from
   what they craved,
while the food was still
   in their mouths,
31 God's anger flared up
   against them,
and he killed
   some of their best men.
He struck down Israel's fit
   young men.   Nm 11:33-34; Jb 20:23

32 Despite all this,
   they kept sinning
and did not believe
   his wondrous works.
33 He made their days end
   in futility,
their years
   in sudden disaster.   Nm 14:29,35
34 When he killed some of them,
the rest began to seek him;
they repented
   and searched for God.   Ps 63:1
35 They remembered that God
   was their rock,
the Most High God,
   their Redeemer.   Is 44:6,8
36 But they deceived him
   with their mouths,
they lied to him
   with their tongues,   Is 29:13
37 their hearts were insincere
   toward him,
and they were unfaithful
   to his covenant.   Ps 51:10; 78:8

^A78:18 Lit *in their heart*   ^B78:25 Lit *Man*   ^C78:25 Lit *mighty ones*

38 Yet he was compassionate;
    he atoned for their iniquity
  and did not destroy them.
  He often turned
    his anger aside
  and did not unleash[A]
    all his wrath.   Nm 14:18-20; Dt 4:31
39 He remembered that
    they were only flesh,
  a wind that passes
    and does not return.   Dt 31:27

40 How often they rebelled
    against him
  in the wilderness
  and grieved him in the desert.
41 They constantly tested God
  and provoked the Holy One
    of Israel.   Dt 9:7-8,22; Ps 106:29
42 They did not remember
    his power shown
  on the day he redeemed them
    from the foe,   Jdg 8:34; Ps 44:3
43 when he performed
    his miraculous signs
    in Egypt
  and his wonders in
    the territory of Zoan.   Ex 4:21
44 He turned their rivers
    into blood,
  and they could not drink
    from their streams.   Ex 7:14-25
45 He sent among them swarms
    of flies,   Ex 8:17; Ps 105:31
  which fed on them,
  and frogs,
    which devastated them.
46 He gave their crops
    to the caterpillar
  and the fruit of their labor
    to the locust.   Ex 10:14-15; Ps 105:34
47 He killed their vines with hail
  and their sycamore fig trees
    with a flood.
48 He handed over
    their livestock to hail

and their cattle
    to lightning bolts.   Ex 9:23-24
49 He sent his burning anger
    against them:
  fury, indignation,
    and calamity —
  a band
    of deadly messengers.[B]
50 He cleared a path
    for his anger.
  He did not spare them
    from death
  but delivered their lives
    to the plague.   Ex 12:29-30
51 He struck all the firstborn
    in Egypt,   Ex 13:15; Ps 105:36
  the first progeny of the tents
    of Ham.   Ps 105:23,27
52 He led his people out
    like sheep
  and guided them like a flock
    in the wilderness.   Ex 15:22
53 He led them safely,
    and they were not afraid;
  but the sea covered
    their enemies.   Ex 14; 15:19; Jos 24:7
54 He brought them
    to his holy territory,
  to the mountain
    his right hand acquired.
55 He drove out nations
    before them.   Jos 11:16-23; Ps 44:2
  He apportioned
    their inheritance by lot
  and settled the tribes
    of Israel in their tents.
56 But they rebelliously tested
    the Most High God,
  for they did not keep
    his decrees.   Jdg 2:11-13
57 They treacherously
    turned away
    like their fathers;
  they became warped
    like a faulty bow.   Ezk 20:27-28

A78:38 Or stir up   B78:49 Or angels

58 They enraged him
    with their high places
and provoked his jealousy
    with their carved images.
59 God heard
    and became furious;
he completely rejected Israel.
60 He abandoned the tabernacle
    at Shiloh,
the tent where he resided
    among mankind.   Jr 7:12,14; 26:6
61 He gave up his strength
    to captivity
and his splendor to the hand
    of a foe.   1Sm 4:17
62 He surrendered his people
    to the sword
because he was enraged
    with his heritage.   Jdg 20:21
63 Fire consumed
    his chosen young men,
and his young women
    had no wedding songs.ᴬ
64 His priests fell by the sword,
    and the widows
        could not lament.   Jb 27:15

65 The Lord awoke as if
    from sleep,
like a warrior
    from the effects of wine.
66 He beat back his foes;
    he gave them lasting disgrace.
67 He rejected the tent of Joseph
    and did not choose the tribe
        of Ephraim.
68 He chose instead the tribe
    of Judah,
Mount Zion, which he loved.
69 He built his sanctuary
    like the heights,
like the earth that
    he established forever.   1Kg 6
70 He chose David his servant
    and took him from
        the sheep pens;   1Sm 16:11-13

ᴬ**78:63** Lit *virgins were not praised*

71 he brought him
    from tending ewes
to be shepherd
    over his people Jacob —
over Israel, his inheritance.
72 He shepherded them
    with a pure heart
and guided them
    with his skillful hands.

Faith amid Confusion

79 *A psalm of Asaph.*   1Ch 16:5,7
    God, the nations
    have invaded
    your inheritance,
desecrated your holy temple,
and turned Jerusalem
    into ruins.   Jr 26:18; Lm 1:10; Mc 3:12
2 They gave the corpses
    of your servants
to the birds of the sky for food,
the flesh of your faithful ones
    to the beasts of the earth.
3 They poured out their blood
    like water
    all around Jerusalem,
and there was no one
    to bury them.   Jr 14:16; 16:4; 22:19
4 We have become an object
    of reproach
    to our neighbors,
a source of mockery
    and ridicule
to those around us.   Ps 44:13-14

5 How long, LORD? Will you
    be angry forever?
Will your jealousy
    keep burning like fire?
6 Pour out your wrath
    on the nations
that don't acknowledge you,
on the kingdoms that don't
    call on your name,   Ps 14:4
7 for they have devoured Jacob
    and devastated his homeland.

8 Do not hold past iniquities[A]
  against us;
let your compassion come
  to us quickly,
for we have
  become very weak.   Ps 142:6

9 God of our salvation,
  help us —   1Ch 16:35; Ps 85:4
for the glory of your name.
Rescue us and atone for
  our sins,
for your name's sake.   Ps 25:11
10 Why should the nations ask,
"Where is their God?"   Ps 42:3,10
Before our eyes,
let vengeance
  for the shed blood
  of your servants
be known among the nations.
11 Let the groans
  of the prisoners reach you;
according to your great power,
preserve those condemned
  to die.   Ps 102:20

12 Pay back sevenfold
  to our neighbors   Lv 26:21,28
the reproach they have hurled
  at you, Lord.   Ps 74:10,18,22
13 Then we, your people,
  the sheep of your pasture,
will thank you forever;
we will declare your praise
to generation after generation.

A Prayer for Restoration

80 *For the choir director: according
to "The Lilies." A testimony of
Asaph. A psalm.*   1Ch 16:5,7; Pss 45; 60; 69 titles

1 Listen, Shepherd of Israel,
who leads Joseph like a flock;
you who sit enthroned
  between the cherubim,
shine ² on Ephraim,   Dt 33:2

Benjamin, and Manasseh.
Rally your power and come
  to save us.   Ps 35:23; 106:47; 118:25
3 Restore us, God;
make your face shine on us,
so that we may be saved.

4 Lord God of Armies,
how long will you be angry
with your people's prayers?
5 You fed them the bread
  of tears
and gave them a full measure[B]
of tears to drink.   Ps 102:9; Is 30:20
6 You put us at odds
  with our neighbors;
our enemies mock us.   Ps 44:13
7 Restore us, God of Armies;
make your face shine on us,
  so that we may be saved.

8 You dug up a vine
  from Egypt;
you drove out the nations
  and planted it.   Jr 2:21; 32:41
9 You cleared a place for it;
it took root and filled the land.
10 The mountains were covered
  by its shade,
and the mighty cedars[C]
  with its branches.   Ezk 17:22-24
11 It sent out sprouts
  toward the Sea[D]
and shoots toward the River.[E]

12 Why have you broken down
  its walls
so that all who pass by
  pick its fruit?   Ps 89:40; Is 5:5
13 Boars from the forest tear at it
and creatures of the field
  feed on it.   Jr 5:6
14 Return, God of Armies.   Ps 6:4
Look down from heaven
  and see;

A 79:8 Or *hold the sins of past generations*   B 80:5 Lit *a one-third measure*   C 80:10 Lit *the cedars of
God*   D 80:11 = the Mediterranean   E 80:11 = the Euphrates

take care of this vine,
¹⁵ the root^A
your right hand planted,
the son^B that you made strong
for yourself. Is 63:15
¹⁶ It was cut down and burned;
they^C perish at the rebuke
of your countenance. Ps 39:11
¹⁷ Let your hand be
with the man
at your right hand,
with the son of man
you have made strong
for yourself. Ps 89:21
¹⁸ Then we will not turn away
from you;
revive us, and we will call
on your name. Ps 71:20; 85:6
¹⁹ Restore us, LORD,
God of Armies; Ps 60:1; 85:4
make your face shine on us,
so that we may be saved.

A Call to Obedience

81 For the choir director:
on the Gittith. Of Asaph. 1Ch 16:5,7

¹ Sing for joy to God
our strength;
shout in triumph to the God
of Jacob. Ps 59:16; 95:1-2; 98:4
² Lift up a song —
play the tambourine,
the melodious lyre,
and the harp. Ps 33:2; 71:22; 92:3
³ Blow the horn on the day of
our feasts^D
during the new moon Lv 23:24
and during the full moon.
⁴ For this is a statute for Israel,
an ordinance of the God
of Jacob. 1Ch 16:17; Ps 105:10
⁵ He set it up as a decree
for Joseph
when he went throughout^E
the land of Egypt. Ps 78:5; 122:4

I heard
an unfamiliar language:
⁶ "I relieved his shoulder
from the burden;
his hands were freed
from carrying the basket.
⁷ You called out in distress,
and I rescued you;
I answered you
from the thundercloud.
I tested you at the Waters
of Meribah. *Selah*
⁸ Listen, my people, and I will
admonish you.
Israel, if you
would only listen to me!
⁹ There must not be
a strange god among you;
you must not bow down
to a foreign god. Ex 20:3-5; 22:20
¹⁰ I am the LORD your God,
who brought you up
from the land of Egypt. Dt 5:6
Open your mouth wide,
and I will fill it. Ps 78:25; 107:9

¹¹ "But my people did not listen
to my voice;
Israel did not obey me. Jr 7:24
¹² So I gave them over
to their stubborn hearts
to follow their own plans.
¹³ If only my people
would listen to me
and Israel would follow
my ways, Dt 5:29; Is 48:18
¹⁴ I would quickly subdue
their enemies
and turn my hand
against their foes." Ps 18:47
¹⁵ Those who hate the LORD
would cower to him; Ps 18:44
their doom would last forever.
¹⁶ But he would feed Israel^F
with the best wheat.

^A**80:15** Hb obscure ^B**80:15** Or *shoot* ^C**80:16** Or *may they* ^D**81:3** Lit *feast* ^E**81:5** Or *went out against*
^F**81:16** Lit *him*

"I would satisfy you
with honey from the rock."

A Plea for Righteous Judgment

82 *A psalm of Asaph.* 1Ch 16:5,7
God stands
in the divine assembly;
he pronounces judgment
among the gods:[A] Jb 21:22

2 "How long will you
judge unjustly
and show partiality
to the wicked? *Selah*

3 Provide justice for the needy
and the fatherless;
uphold the rights
of the oppressed
and the destitute. Dt 24:17; Is 11:4

4 Rescue the poor and needy;
save them from the power
of the wicked." Jb 29:12; Pr 24:11

5 They do not know
or understand;
they wander in darkness.
All the foundations
of the earth are shaken.

6 I said, "You are gods; Jn 10:34
you are all sons
of the Most High. Ps 82:1; Lk 6:35

7 However, you will die
like humans
and fall like any other ruler."

8 Rise up, God,
judge the earth,
for all the nations
belong to you. Ps 58:11; 96:13

Prayer Against Enemies

83 *A song. A psalm of Asaph.*
God, do not keep silent.
Do not be deaf, God; do not
be quiet. Ps 28:1; 39:12; Is 62:1

2 See how your enemies
make an uproar;
those who hate you
have acted arrogantly.[B] Ps 2:1

3 They devise clever schemes
against your people;
they conspire against
your treasured ones. Ps 37:12

4 They say, "Come, let us
wipe them out as a nation
so that Israel's name
will no longer
be remembered." Ps 41:5; Jr 11:19

5 For they have conspired
with one mind;
they form an alliance[C]
against you — Ps 2:2

6 the tents of Edom
and the Ishmaelites, Ps 137:7
Moab and the Hagrites, 1Ch 5:10

7 Gebal, Ammon, and Amalek,
Philistia with the inhabitants
of Tyre. 1Sm 4:1; Ezk 27:3

8 Even Assyria has joined them;
they lend support[D]
to the sons of Lot.[E] *Selah*

9 Deal with them as you did
with Midian, Nm 31:7; Jdg 7:1-24
as you did with Sisera
and Jabin at the Kishon River.

10 They were destroyed
at En-dor;
they became manure
for the ground. Jr 9:22; 16:4; 25:33

11 Make their nobles like Oreb
and Zeeb, Jdg 7:25; 8:3
and all their tribal leaders
like Zebah and Zalmunna,

12 who said, "Let us
seize God's pastures
for ourselves." 2Ch 20:11

13 Make them like tumbleweed,
my God,

A82:1 Or *the heavenly beings*, or *the earthly rulers*; Hb *elohim* B83:2 Lit *have lifted their head*
C83:5 Lit *they cut a covenant* D83:8 Lit *they are an arm* E83:8 = Moab and Ammon

like straw before the wind.
14 As fire burns a forest,
as a flame blazes
through mountains,   Is 9:18
15 so pursue them
with your tempest
and terrify them
with your storm.   Jb 9:17; Ps 58:9
16 Cover their faces with shame
so that they will seek
your name, LORD.   Ps 35:26; 132:18
17 Let them be put to shame
and terrified forever;
let them perish in disgrace.
18 May they know
that you alone —
whose name is the LORD —
are the Most High
over the whole earth.   Ps 97:9

Longing for God's House

84 For the choir director: on the Gittith. A psalm of the sons of Korah.   Pss 8; 81 titles

1 How lovely is
your dwelling place,
LORD of Armies.   Ps 43:3; 132:5
2 I long and yearn
for the courts of the LORD;
my heart and flesh cry out
for[A] the living God.   Ps 42:1-2

3 Even a sparrow finds a home,
and a swallow, a nest
for herself
where she places her young —
near your altars,
LORD of Armies,
my King and my God.   Ps 5:2; 43:4
4 How happy are those
who reside in your house,
who praise you
continually.   *Selah*

5 Happy are the people
whose strength is in you,

whose hearts are set
on pilgrimage.   Ps 119:2; 122:1
6 As they pass
through the Valley of Baca,[B]
they make it a source
of spring water;
even the autumn
rain will cover it
with blessings.[C]   Ezk 34:26; Jl 2:23
7 They go from strength
to strength;
each appears before God
in Zion.   Pr 4:18; Is 40:31

8 LORD God of Armies,
hear my prayer;
listen, God of Jacob.   *Selah*
9 Consider our shield,[D] God;
look on the face
of your anointed one.

10 Better a day in your courts
than a thousand
anywhere else.
I would rather stand
at the threshold
of the house of my God
than live in the tents
of wicked people.   Ps 27:4
11 For the LORD God is a sun
and shield.   Ps 3:3; 5:12; 18:2; 28:7
The LORD grants favor
and honor;
he does not withhold
the good
from those who live
with integrity.   Pr 2:7
12 Happy is the person
who trusts in you,
LORD of Armies!   Ps 40:4

Restoration of Favor

85 For the choir director. A psalm of the sons of Korah.

1 LORD, you showed favor
to your land;   Ps 106:4

A 84:2 Or *flesh shout for joy to*   B 84:6 Or *Valley of Tears*   C 84:6 Or *pools*   D 84:9 = the king

you restored the fortunes
   of Jacob.^A   Dt 30:3; Ps 14:7; Jr 29:14

2 You forgave
   your people's guilt;
you covered all their sin.
                   Selah

3 You withdrew all your fury;
you turned from
   your burning anger.   Ps 78:38

4 Return to us,
   God of our salvation,
and abandon
   your displeasure with us.

5 Will you be angry
   with us forever?
Will you prolong your anger
   for all generations?   Ps 74:1

6 Will you not revive us again
so that your people
   may rejoice in you?   Ps 71:20

7 Show us
   your faithful love, LORD,
and give us your salvation.

8 I will listen to what
   God will say;
surely the LORD will declare
   peace
to his people,
   his faithful ones,
and not let them go back
   to foolish ways.   Hg 2:9; Zch 9:10

9 His salvation is very near
   those who fear him,
so that glory may dwell
   in our land.   Is 46:13; Zch 2:5; Jn 1:14

10 Faithful love and truth
   will join together;
righteousness and peace
   will embrace.   Ps 72:3; 89:14

11 Truth will spring up
   from the earth,
and righteousness will look
   down from heaven.   Is 45:8

12 Also, the LORD will provide
   what is good,
and our land will yield
   its crops.   Ps 65:12-13; 67:6; Ezk 34:27

13 Righteousness will go
   before him
to prepare the way
   for his steps.   Ps 89:14; Is 40:3,10

Lament and Petition

86 *A prayer of David.*
Listen, LORD,
   and answer me,
for I am poor and needy.   Ps 17:6

2 Protect my life,
   for I am faithful.   1Sm 2:9
You are my God;
   save your servant
   who trusts in you.   Ps 109:26

3 Be gracious to me, Lord,
for I call to you all day long.

4 Bring joy
   to your servant's life,
because I appeal to you, Lord.

5 For you, Lord, are kind
   and ready to forgive,   Ps 130:4
abounding in faithful love
   to all who call on you.   Ps 145:8

6 LORD, hear my prayer;
listen to my plea for mercy.

7 I call on you in the day
   of my distress,
for you will answer me.   Gn 35:3

8 Lord, there is no one like you
   among the gods,
and there are no works
   like yours.   Ex 15:11; Dt 3:24; Ps 89:6

9 All the nations you have made
will come and bow down
   before you, Lord,
and will honor your name.

10 For you are great
   and perform wonders;
you alone are God.   2Kg 19:15

11 Teach me your way, LORD,
  and I will live by your truth.
  Give me an undivided mind
    to fear your name.   Ps 25:4-5
12 I will praise you
  with all my heart,
  Lord my God,
  and will honor
    your name forever.   Ps 111:1
13 For your faithful love for me
    is great,
  and you rescue my life
    from the depths of Sheol.
14 God, arrogant people
    have attacked me;
  a gang of ruthless men
    intends to kill me.
  They do not let you
    guide them.^A   Ps 54:3
15 But you, Lord, are
    a compassionate
    and gracious God,
  slow to anger
    and abounding
    in faithful love and truth.
16 Turn to me and be gracious
    to me.
  Give your strength
    to your servant;
  save the son
    of your female servant.
17 Show me a sign
    of your goodness;
  my enemies will see
    and be put to shame
  because you, LORD,
    have helped
    and comforted me.   Ps 112:10

Zion, the City of God

87 A psalm of the sons of Korah.
  A song.
1 The city he founded^B is
  on the holy mountains.

2 The LORD loves Zion's
    city gates
  more than all the dwellings
    of Jacob.   Ps 78:67-68
3 Glorious things are said
    about you,
  city of God.   *Selah*
4 "I will make a record of those
    who know me:
  Rahab, Babylon, Philistia,
    Tyre, and Cush —
  each one was born there."
5 And it will be said of Zion,
  "This one and that one
    were born in her."
  The Most High himself
    will establish her.   Ps 48:8; Is 2:2
6 When he registers
    the peoples,
  the LORD will record,
  "This one
    was born there."   *Selah*
7 Singers and dancers^C alike
    will say,^D
  "My whole source of joy is^E
    in you."   Ps 46:4; 68:25

A Cry of Desperation

88 A song. A psalm of the sons
  of Korah. For the choir director:
according to Mahalath Leannoth.
A Maskil *of Heman the Ezrahite.* 1Kg 4:31
1 LORD, God of my salvation,
  I cry out before you
    day and night.   Ps 22:2; 86:3
2 May my prayer reach
    your presence;
  listen to my cry.   Ps 18:6; 31:2; 86:1

3 For I have had enough
    troubles,
  and my life is near Sheol.
4 I am counted among those
    going down to the Pit.   Ps 28:1

^A86:14 Lit *They do not set you in front of them*   ^B87:1 Lit *His foundation*   ^C87:7 Or *musicians*
^D87:7 Or *As they dance they will sing*   ^E87:7 Lit *"All my springs, are*

I am like a man
　　without strength,　　Ps 61:2
5 abandoned^A among the dead.
I am like the slain lying
　　in the grave,　　Ps 31:12
whom you
　　no longer remember,
and who are cut off
　　from your care.^B　Ps 31:22; Is 53:8

6 You have put me
　　in the lowest part of the Pit,
in the darkest places,
　　in the depths.　　Ps 69:15; 86:13
7 Your wrath weighs heavily
　　on me;　　Ps 32:4; 39:10
you have overwhelmed me
　　with all your waves.　　*Selah*
8 You have distanced
　　my friends from me;
you have made me repulsive
　　to them.　　Jb 19:13-22; Ps 31:11
I am shut in and cannot go out.
9 My eyes are worn out
　　from crying.　　Ps 6:7; 31:9
LORD, I cry out to you
　　all day long;　　Ps 86:3
I spread out my hands to you.

10 Do you work wonders
　　for the dead?
Do departed spirits rise up
　　to praise you?　　*Selah*
11 Will your faithful love
　　be declared in the grave,
your faithfulness
　　in Abaddon?　　Jb 26:6; Pr 15:11; 27:20
12 Will your wonders be known
　　in the darkness
or your righteousness
　　in the land of oblivion?　　Ec 9:5

13 But I call to you for help, LORD;
in the morning my prayer
　　meets you.　　Ps 5:3; 119:147
14 LORD, why do you reject me?

Why do you hide your face
　　from me?　　Jb 13:24; Ps 10:1; 13:1
15 From my youth,
I have been suffering
　　and near death.
I suffer your horrors;
　　I am desperate.　　Jb 31:23
16 Your wrath sweeps
　　over me;
your terrors destroy me.　　Jb 6:4
17 They surround me
　　like water all day long;
they close in on me
　　from every side.　　Ps 22:12,16
18 You have distanced loved one
　　and neighbor from me;
darkness is my only friend.^C

Perplexity About God's Promises

89 A Maskil *of Ethan the Ezrahite.*
I will sing about the LORD's
　　faithful love forever;　　Ps 101:1
I will proclaim
　　your faithfulness to all
　　generations
with my mouth.　　Ps 92:2; 119:90
2 For I will declare,
　　"Faithful love
　　is built up forever;
you establish
　　your faithfulness
　　in the heavens."　　Ps 36:5

3 The LORD said,
　　"I have made a covenant
　　with my chosen one;
I have sworn an oath
　　to David my servant:
4 'I will establish
　　your offspring forever
and build up your throne
　　for all generations.'"　　*Selah*

5 LORD, the heavens praise
　　your wonders —　　Ps 19:1; 97:6
your faithfulness also —

^A**88:5** Or *set free*　^B**88:5** Or *hand*　^C**88:18** Or *from me, my friends. Oh darkness!*

in the assembly
of the holy ones.   Ps 149:1
⁶ For who in the skies
can compare with the LORD?
Who among
the heavenly beings ᴬ is
like the LORD?   Ps 86:8; 113:5
⁷ God is greatly feared
in the council
of the holy ones,
more awe-inspiring than ᴮ
all who surround him.
⁸ LORD God of Armies,
who is strong like you, LORD?
Your faithfulness
surrounds you.
⁹ You rule the raging sea;
when its waves surge,
you still them.   Jb 38:11; Ps 104:9
¹⁰ You crushed Rahab like one
who is slain;   Is 30:7; 51:9-10
you scattered your enemies
with your powerful arm.
¹¹ The heavens are yours;
the earth also is yours.
The world and everything
in it — you founded them.
¹² North and south —
you created them.   Jb 26:7
Tabor and Hermon shout
for joy at your name.   Ps 133:3
¹³ You have a mighty arm;
your hand is powerful;
your right hand is lifted high.
¹⁴ Righteousness and justice
are the foundation
of your throne;   Ps 97:2
faithful love and truth
go before you.   Ps 85:13
¹⁵ Happy are the people
who know the joyful shout;
LORD, they walk in the light
from your face.   Nm 6:25; Ps 56:13
¹⁶ They rejoice in your name
all day long,

and they are exalted
by your righteousness.
¹⁷ For you are their
magnificent strength;   Ps 28:8
by your favor our horn
is exalted.   Ps 148:14
¹⁸ Surely our shield ᶜ
belongs to the LORD,
our king to the Holy One
of Israel.   Ps 84:9
¹⁹ You once spoke in a vision
to your faithful ones
and said: "I have granted help
to a warrior;
I have exalted one chosen ᴰ
from the people.   2Sm 17:10
²⁰ I have found David
my servant;
I have anointed him
with my sacred oil.   1Sm 16:13
²¹ My hand will always be
with him,
and my arm will
strengthen him.   Ps 18:35; 80:17
²² The enemy will not
oppress ᴱ him;
the wicked will not
afflict him.   2Sm 7:10
²³ I will crush his foes
before him
and strike those
who hate him.   2Sm 7:9; Ps 2:9
²⁴ My faithfulness and love
will be with him,
and through my name
his horn will be exalted.   Ps 21:7
²⁵ I will extend his power
to the sea
and his right hand
to the rivers.   Ps 72:8
²⁶ He will call to me, 'You are
my Father,   2Sm 7:14; 1Ch 22:10
my God, the rock
of my salvation.'   2Sm 22:47

ᴬ**89:6** Or *the angels,* or *the sons of the mighty*   ᴮ**89:7** Or *ones, revered by*   ᶜ**89:18** = the king
ᴰ**89:19** Or *exalted a young man*   ᴱ**89:22** Or *not exact tribute from*

27 I will also make him
my firstborn,
greatest of the kings
of the earth. Ex 4:22; Jr 31:9; Col 1:15

28 I will always preserve
my faithful love for him,
and my covenant with him
will endure. 2Ch 13:5; Ps 105:8

29 I will establish
his line forever,
his throne as long as
heaven lasts. A Is 9:7; Jr 33:17

30 If his sons abandon
my instruction
and do not live
by my ordinances, 2Sm 7:14

31 if they dishonor my statutes
and do not keep
my commands, 1Sm 12:15

32 then I will call their rebellion
to account with the rod,
their iniquity with blows.

33 But I will not withdraw
my faithful love from him
or betray my faithfulness.

34 I will not violate
my covenant
or change what my lips
have said. Lv 26:44; Jdg 2:1

35 Once and for all
I have sworn an oath
by my holiness;
I will not lie to David. Am 4:2

36 His offspring
will continue forever,
his throne like the sun
before me, Ps 72:5,17

37 like the moon,
established forever,
a faithful witness
in the sky." Selah

38 But you have spurned
and rejected him;
you have become enraged
with your anointed. 1Ch 28:9

39 You have repudiated
the covenant
with your servant;
you have completely
dishonored his crown. B

40 You have broken down
all his walls;
you have reduced
his fortified cities to ruins.

41 All who pass by plunder him;
he has become an object of
ridicule
to his neighbors. Ps 44:13; 79:4

42 You have lifted high
the right hand of his foes;
you have made all
his enemies rejoice. Ps 13:4

43 You have also turned back
his sharp sword
and have not let him stand
in battle. Ps 44:10

44 You have made
his splendor C cease
and have overturned
his throne. Ezk 28:7

45 You have shortened the days
of his youth;
you have covered him
with shame. Selah

46 How long, LORD?
Will you hide forever?
Will your anger keep burning
like fire? Ps 6:3; 13:1; 35:17; 79:5

47 Remember how short
my life is.
Have you created everyone
for nothing? Ps 39:6-7; 90:5-6,9-10

48 What courageous person can
live and never see death?
Who can save himself
from the power of Sheol?
Selah

49 Lord, where are
the former acts
of your faithful love

A 89:29 Lit as days of heaven B 89:39 Lit have dishonored his crown to the ground C 89:44 Hb obscure

that you swore to David
in your faithfulness? 2Sm 7:15

50 Remember, Lord, the ridicule
against your servants —
in my heart I carry abuse
from all the peoples —

51 how your enemies
have ridiculed, Lord,
how they have
ridiculed every step
of your anointed. Ps 69:9

52 Blessed be the Lord forever.
Amen and amen. Ps 41:13; 72:19-20

BOOK IV (Psalms 90–106)

Eternal God and Mortal Man

90
A prayer of Moses,
the man of God.

1 Lord, you have been
our refuge ᴬ
in every generation. Ps 71:3

2 Before the mountains
were born,
before you gave birth
to the earth and the world,
from eternity to eternity,
you are God. Jb 36:26; Ps 102:27

3 You return mankind
to the dust,
saying, "Return,
descendants of Adam."

4 For in your sight
a thousand years
are like yesterday that
passes by,
like a few hours of the night.

5 You end their lives; ᴮ they sleep.
They are like grass that grows
in the morning —

6 in the morning it sprouts
and grows;

by evening it withers
and dries up. Jb 14:1-2; Ps 37:2

7 For we are consumed
by your anger;
we are terrified
by your wrath. Ps 39:11

8 You have set our iniquities
before you,
our secret sins in the light
of your presence. Ps 19:12

9 For all our days ebb away
under your wrath;
we end our years like a sigh.

10 Our lives last ᶜ seventy years
or, if we are strong,
eighty years.
Even the best of them
are ᴰ struggle and sorrow;
indeed, they pass quickly
and we fly away. Jb 20:8; Ps 78:39

11 Who understands the power
of your anger?
Your wrath matches the fear
that is due you. Ps 76:7

12 Teach us to number
our days carefully
so that we may
develop wisdom
in our hearts. ᴱ Dt 32:29; Ps 39:4

13 Lord — how long?
Turn and have compassion
on your servants. Dt 32:36

14 Satisfy us in the morning
with your faithful love
so that we may shout
with joy and be glad
all our days. Ps 36:8; 65:4; 103:5

15 Make us rejoice
for as many days
as you have humbled us,
for as many years as
we have seen adversity.

ᴬ90:1 Some Hb mss, LXX; other Hb mss read *dwelling place* ᴮ90:5 Or *You overwhelm them* ; Hb obscure
ᶜ90:10 Lit *The days of our years in them* ᴰ90:10 LXX, Tg, Syr, Vg read *Even their span is* ; Hb obscure
ᴱ90:12 Or *develop a heart of wisdom*

16 Let your work be seen
　　by your servants,
　　and your splendor
　　by their children. Ps 96:6; Is 35:2
17 Let the favor of the Lord
　　our God be on us;
　　establish for us the work
　　of our hands —
　　establish the work
　　of our hands! Ps 27:4; Is 26:12

The Protection of the Most High

91
The one who lives
　　under the protection
of the Most High
dwells in the shadow
　　of the Almighty. Ps 27:5; 32:7

2 I will say[A]
　　concerning the LORD,
　　who is my refuge
　　and my fortress,
　　my God in whom I trust: Ps 18:2
3 He himself will rescue you
　　from the bird trap, Ps 124:7
　　from the destructive
　　plague.
4 He will cover you
　　with his feathers;
　　you will take refuge
　　under his wings. Ps 57:1; 63:7
　　His faithfulness will be
　　a protective shield. Ps 5:12
5 You will not fear the terror
　　of the night,
　　the arrow that flies by day,
6 the plague that stalks
　　in darkness,
　　or the pestilence
　　that ravages at noon.
7 Though a thousand fall
　　at your side
　　and ten thousand
　　at your right hand,
　　the pestilence will not
　　reach you. 2Ch 20:9

8 You will only see it
　　with your eyes
　　and witness the punishment
　　of the wicked. Ps 37:34; 58:10

9 Because you have made
　　the LORD — my refuge,
　　the Most High —
　　your dwelling place, Ps 121:5
10 no harm will come to you;
　　no plague will come near
　　your tent. Pr 12:21
11 For he will give his angels
　　orders concerning you,
　　to protect you in all
　　your ways. Ps 34:7
12 They will support you
　　with their hands
　　so that you will not strike
　　your foot against a stone.
13 You will tread on the lion
　　and the cobra;
　　you will trample
　　the young lion
　　and the serpent. Lk 10:19

14 Because he has his heart
　　set on me,
　　I will deliver him;
　　I will protect him
　　because he knows
　　my name. Ps 9:10; 37:40; 107:41
15 When he calls out to me,
　　I will answer him;
　　I will be with him in trouble.
　　I will rescue him
　　and give him honor. 2Sm 22:20
16 I will satisfy him
　　with a long life Dt 4:40; Ps 21:4
　　and show him my salvation.

God's Love and Faithfulness

92
*A psalm. A song for the
Sabbath day.*
1 It is good to give thanks
　　to the LORD,

[A]**91:1-2** LXX, Syr, Jer read ²*Almighty, saying,* or ²*Almighty, he will say*

to sing praise to your name,
Most High,   Ps 135:3; 147:1
2 to declare your faithful love
in the morning
and your faithfulness
at night,   Ps 59:16; 89:1; Lm 3:22-23
3 with a ten-stringed harp[A]
and the music of a lyre.   Ps 33:2

4 For you have made me
rejoice, LORD,
by what you have done;
I will shout for joy
because of the works
of your hands.   Ps 40:5; 143:5
5 How magnificent are
your works, LORD,
how profound your thoughts!
6 A stupid person
does not know,
a fool does not
understand this: Ps 73:22
7 though the wicked sprout
like grass
and all evildoers flourish,
they will be
eternally destroyed.   Ps 90:5-6
8 But you, LORD,
are exalted forever.   Ps 93:4
9 For indeed, LORD,
your enemies —
indeed, your enemies
will perish;
all evildoers will be scattered.
10 You have lifted up my horn
like that of a wild ox;
I have been anointed[B] with
the finest oil.   Ps 45:7
11 My eyes look at my enemies;
when evildoers rise
against me,
my ears hear them.   Ps 37:34; 54:7

12 The righteous thrive
like a palm tree
and grow like a cedar tree
in Lebanon.   Ps 1:3; Is 61:3; Jr 17:8
13 Planted in the house
of the LORD,
they thrive in the courts of
our God.   Is 60:21
14 They will still bear fruit
in old age,
healthy and green,   Is 37:31; 46:4
15 to declare:
"The LORD is just;
he is my rock,
and there is
no unrighteousness
in him."   Dt 32:4; Ps 18:2; 94:22

God's Eternal Reign

93 The LORD reigns!
He is robed in majesty;
the LORD is robed,
enveloped in strength.
The world is
firmly established;
it cannot be shaken.   1Ch 16:30-31
2 Your throne
has been established
from the beginning;[C]
you are from eternity.   Ps 9:7
3 The floods have
lifted up, LORD,
the floods have lifted up
their voice;
the floods lift up
their pounding waves.
4 Greater than the roar of a
huge torrent —
the mighty breakers
of the sea —
the LORD on high
is majestic.   Ps 65:7; 89:9; Ezk 43:2

5 LORD, your testimonies
are completely reliable;
holiness adorns your house
for all the days to come.   Ps 29:2

[A]**92:3** Or *ten-stringed instrument and a harp*   [B]**92:10** Syr reads *you have anointed me*   [C]**93:2** Lit *from then*

The Just Judge

94

LORD, God of vengeance —
God of vengeance, shine!

2 Rise up, Judge of the earth;
repay the proud
what they deserve.   Ps 7:6; 28:4

3 LORD, how long will
the wicked —
how long will
the wicked celebrate?   Rv 6:10

4 They pour out arrogant
words;
all the evildoers boast.   1Sm 2:3

5 LORD, they crush your people;
they oppress your heritage.

6 They kill the widow and
the resident alien
and murder the fatherless.

7 They say, "The LORD
doesn't see it.
The God of Jacob
doesn't pay attention."

8 Pay attention,
you stupid people!
Fools, when will you be wise?

9 Can the one who shaped
the ear not hear,
the one who formed the eye
not see?   Ex 4:11; Pr 20:12

10 The one who instructs nations,
the one who teaches
mankind knowledge —
does he not discipline?   Jb 35:11

11 The LORD knows the
thoughts of mankind;
they are futile.   Ps 139:2; Is 66:18

12 LORD, how happy is anyone
you discipline
and teach from your law

13 to give him relief
from troubled times
until a pit is dug
for the wicked.   Ps 7:15; 9:15

14 The LORD will not leave
his people
or abandon his heritage,

15 for the administration
of justice will again
be righteous,
and all the upright in heart
will follow[A] it.   Ps 36:10; 64:10

16 Who stands up for me
against the wicked?
Who takes a stand for me
against evildoers?   Ps 59:2

17 If the LORD had not been
my helper,
I would soon rest
in the silence of death.

18 If I say, "My foot is slipping,"
your faithful love
will support me, LORD.   Ps 66:9

19 When I am filled with cares,
your comfort brings me joy.

20 Can a corrupt throne
be your ally,
a throne that makes
evil laws?   Ps 50:16; 58:2

21 They band together
against the life
of the righteous
and condemn the innocent
to death.   2Kg 21:16; Ps 106:38; Jr 26:15

22 But the LORD is my refuge;
my God is the rock
of my protection.   2Sm 22:3

23 He will pay them back
for their sins
and destroy them for their evil.
The LORD our God
will destroy them.   Ps 73:27

Worship and Warning

95

Come, let us shout joyfully
to the LORD,
shout triumphantly
to the rock of our salvation!

A94:15 Or heart will support; lit heart after

² Let us enter his presence
    with thanksgiving;
let us shout triumphantly
    to him in song.   Ps 100:4; Jnh 2:9

³ For the LORD is a great God,
a great King above all gods.
⁴ The depths of the earth are
    in his hand,
and the mountain peaks
    are his.   Ps 135:6
⁵ The sea is his; he made it.
His hands formed the dry land.

⁶ Come, let us worship
    and bow down;
let us kneel before the LORD
    our Maker.   Ps 96:9; 100:3; Is 17:7
⁷ For he is our God,
and we are the people
    of his pasture,
the sheep under his care.^A

Today, if you hear his voice:
⁸ Do not harden your hearts
    as at Meribah,
as on that day at Massah
    in the wilderness   Ex 17:7; Dt 6:16
⁹ where your fathers
    tested me;
they tried me, though
    they had seen what I did.
¹⁰ For forty years
    I was disgusted
    with that generation;
I said, "They are a people
    whose hearts go astray;
they do not know my ways."
¹¹ So I swore in my anger,
"They will not enter my rest."

King of the Earth

96 Sing a new song
    to the LORD;
let the whole earth sing
    to the LORD.   1Ch 16:23; Ps 98:1

^A**95:7** Lit *sheep of his hand*

² Sing to the LORD,
    bless his name;
proclaim his salvation
    from day to day.   Is 25:9; 52:7
³ Declare his glory
    among the nations,
his wondrous works
    among all peoples.   1Ch 16:9,24

⁴ For the LORD is great and is
    highly praised;
he is feared above all gods.
⁵ For all the gods
    of the peoples are idols,
but the LORD made
    the heavens.   1Ch 16:27; Jr 10:11
⁶ Splendor and majesty are
    before him;
strength and beauty are
    in his sanctuary.   Ps 104:1

⁷ Ascribe to the LORD, you
    families of the peoples,
ascribe to the LORD glory
    and strength.   1Ch 16:28-29; Ps 29:1
⁸ Ascribe to the LORD the glory
    of his name;   Ps 79:9
bring an offering and enter
    his courts.   Ps 100:4
⁹ Worship the LORD
    in the splendor
    of his holiness;   Ps 29:2
let the whole earth tremble
    before him.   Ps 33:8; 114:7

¹⁰ Say among the nations:
    "The LORD reigns.   Ps 93:1; 97:1
The world is firmly
    established; it cannot
    be shaken.   1Ch 16:30
He judges
    the peoples fairly."   Ps 9:8; 67:4
¹¹ Let the heavens be glad
    and the earth rejoice;
let the sea and all
    that fills it resound.   Ps 69:34

12 Let the fields and everything
   in them celebrate.
Then all the trees of the forest
   will shout for joy Is 35:1; 55:12-13
13 before the LORD,
   for he is coming —
for he is coming to judge
   the earth.
He will judge the world
   with righteousness
and the peoples
   with his faithfulness. Ps 98:9

The Majestic King

97 The LORD reigns! Let
   the earth rejoice;
let the many coasts and
   islands be glad. Ps 93:1; 96:10

2 Clouds and total darkness
   surround him;
righteousness and justice
   are the foundation
   of his throne. Dt 4:11; 5:20; Ps 18:11
3 Fire goes before him
and burns up his foes
   on every side. Ps 18:8; 50:3
4 His lightning lights up
   the world;
the earth sees and trembles.
5 The mountains melt like wax
at the presence
   of the LORD —
at the presence of the Lord
   of the whole earth. Neh 1:5

6 The heavens proclaim
   his righteousness; Ps 50:6
all the peoples see his glory.

7 All who serve carved images,
those who boast in idols,
   will be put to shame. Is 44:9,11
All the gods[A]
   must worship him. Heb 1:6

8 Zion hears and is glad,
Judah's villages[B] rejoice
because of
   your judgments, LORD.
9 For you, LORD,
are the Most High over
   the whole earth;
you are exalted above all
   the gods. 1Ch 16:25; Ps 95:3; 96:4

10 You who love the LORD,
   hate evil! Am 5:15
He protects the lives
   of his faithful ones; Ps 145:20
he rescues them
   from the power of
   the wicked. Ps 37:40
11 Light dawns[C,D]
   for the righteous,
gladness for the upright
   in heart. Ps 112:4; Pr 4:18
12 Be glad in the LORD,
   you righteous ones,
and give thanks to
   his holy name.[E] Ps 30:4; 32:11

Praise the King

98 A psalm.
   Sing a new song
   to the LORD, Ps 33:3
for he has
   performed wonders;
his right hand
   and holy arm
have won him victory. Ex 15:6
2 The LORD has made
   his victory known;
he has revealed
   his righteousness
in the sight of the nations.
3 He has remembered his love
and faithfulness
   to the house of Israel;
all the ends of the earth
have seen our God's victory.

---

4 Let the whole earth shout
    to the LORD;
be jubilant, shout for joy,
    and sing.   Ps 66:1; 100:1; Is 44:23
5 Sing to the LORD with the lyre,
with the lyre
    and melodious song.   Ps 51:3
6 With trumpets and the blast
    of the ram's horn
shout triumphantly
in the presence of the LORD,
    our King.   Nm 10:10; 2Ch 15:14
7 Let the sea and all that fills it,
the world and those who live
    in it, resound.   1Ch 16:31-32; Ps 93:1
8 Let the rivers clap
    their hands;
let the mountains
    shout together for joy   Is 55:12
9 before the LORD,
for he is coming to judge
    the earth.
He will judge
    the world righteously
and the peoples fairly.   Ps 9:8

The King Is Holy

99 The LORD reigns! Let
        the peoples tremble.
He is enthroned
    between the cherubim.
Let the earth quake.   Ps 33:8
2 The LORD is great in Zion;
he is exalted above
    all the peoples.   Ps 48:1; 113:4
3 Let them praise your great
and awe-inspiring name.
He is holy.   Is 6:3

4 The mighty King loves justice.
You have established
    fairness;
you have
    administered justice
and righteousness in Jacob.

5 Exalt the LORD our God;
bow in worship
    at his footstool.   Ps 132:7
He is holy.   Is 6:3
6 Moses and Aaron were
    among his priests;   Ex 24:6-8
Samuel also was among
    those calling on his name.
They called to the LORD
    and he answered them.
7 He spoke to them in a pillar
    of cloud;   Nm 12:5; 14:14; Dt 31:15-18
they kept his decrees
    and the statutes
    he gave them.
8 LORD our God,
    you answered them.
You were a forgiving God
    to them,   Ps 78:38
but an avenger of their
    sinful actions.   Jr 46:28

9 Exalt the LORD our God;
bow in worship
    at his holy mountain,
for the LORD our God is holy.

Be Thankful

100 *A psalm of thanksgiving.*
        Let the whole earth
        shout triumphantly
        to the LORD!   Ps 66:1; 98:4
2 Serve the LORD
    with gladness;
come before him
    with joyful songs.   Ps 95:1-2
3 Acknowledge that the LORD
    is God.
He made us,
    and we are his[A]—   Dt 32:6
his people, the sheep
    of his pasture.   Ps 79:13; 95:7
4 Enter his gates
    with thanksgiving   Ps 119:90
and his courts with praise.

A 100:3 Alt Hb tradition, some Hb mss, LXX, Syr, Vg read *and not we ourselves*

Give thanks to him and bless
his name.   Ps 75:1; 116:17
5 For the LORD is good,
and his faithful love
endures forever;
his faithfulness,
through all generations.

A Vow of Integrity

101 *A psalm of David.*
I will sing of faithful love
and justice;
I will sing praise
to you, LORD.   Ps 89:1; 145:7
2 I will pay attention to the way
of integrity.
When will you come to me?
I will live with a heart
of integrity in my house.
3 I will not let
anything worthless
guide me. ^A
I hate the practice
of transgression;
it will not cling to me.   Dt 15:9
4 A devious heart will be far
from me;
I will not be involved
with ^B evil.   Pr 3:32; 14:2

5 I will destroy anyone
who secretly slanders
his neighbor;   Ps 50:20
I cannot tolerate anyone
with haughty eyes
or an arrogant heart.   Ps 18:27
6 My eyes favor the faithful
of the land
so that they may sit down
with me.
The one who follows the way
of integrity
may serve me.   Ps 119:1; Pr 11:20
7 No one who acts deceitfully
will live in my palace;

the one who tells lies
will not be retained here
to guide me. ^C   Ps 31:18; 52:3; 63:11
8 Every morning I will destroy
all the wicked of the land,
wiping out all evildoers
from the LORD's city.   Ps 119:119

Affliction in Light of Eternity

102 *A prayer of a suffering person
who is weak and pours out his
lament before the LORD.*   Ps 142:2

1 LORD, hear my prayer;
let my cry for help come
before you.   Ps 18:6; 39:12; 61:1
2 Do not hide your face
from me in my day
of trouble.
Listen closely to me;
answer me quickly
when I call.   Ps 27:9; 31:2; 69:17

3 For my days vanish
like smoke,
and my bones burn
like a furnace.   Jb 30:30; Ps 31:10
4 My heart is suffering,
withered like grass;   Ps 37:2
I even forget to eat my food.
5 Because of the sound
of my groaning,
my flesh sticks to my bones.
6 I am like an eagle owl,
like a little owl
among the ruins.   Is 34:11
7 I stay awake;   Ps 77:4
I am like a solitary bird
on a roof.
8 My enemies taunt me
all day long;
they ridicule and use
my name as a curse.   Ps 31:11
9 I eat ashes like bread
and mingle my drinks
with tears   Ps 42:3; 80:5

^A 101:3 Lit *I will not put a worthless thing in front of my eyes*   ^B 101:4 Lit *not know*   ^C 101:7 Lit *be
established in front of my eyes*

10 because of your indignation
  and wrath;
 for you have picked me up
  and thrown me aside. Jb 30:22
11 My days are like
  a lengthening shadow,
 and I wither away like grass.

12 But you, LORD,
  are enthroned forever; Ps 9:7
 your fame endures
  to all generations. Ps 135:13
13 You will rise up
  and have compassion
  on Zion,
 for it is time to show favor
  to her —
 the appointed time has come.
14 For your servants
  take delight in its stones
 and favor its dust. Neh 4:2; Lm 4:1

15 Then the nations will fear
  the name of the LORD,
 and all the kings of the earth
  your glory, Ps 138:4; Is 60:3
16 for the LORD will rebuild Zion;
 he will appear in his glory.
17 He will pay attention
  to the prayer of the destitute
 and will not despise
  their prayer. Ps 22:24

18 This will be written
  for a later generation,
 and a people who have
  not yet been created
 will praise the LORD: Dt 31:19
19 He looked down from
  his holy heights —
 the LORD gazed out
  from heaven to earth —
20 to hear a prisoner's groaning,
 to set free those condemned
  to die, A Ps 79:11
21 so that they might declare

the name of the LORD in Zion
 and his praise in Jerusalem,
22 when peoples and kingdoms
  are assembled
 to serve the LORD. Ps 22:27; 86:9

23 He has broken my B strength
  in midcourse;
 he has shortened my days.
24 I say: "My God, do not
  take me
 in the middle of my life! C
 Your years continue
  through all generations.
25 Long ago you established
  the earth,
 and the heavens are the work
  of your hands. Neh 9:6; Ps 96:5
26 They will perish, but you
  will endure;
 all of them will wear out
  like clothing.
 You will change them
  like a garment,
 and they will pass away. Is 34:4
27 But you are the same,
 and your years
  will never end. Mal 3:6; Jms 1:17
28 Your servants' children
  will dwell securely,
 and their offspring will be
  established before you."

The Forgiving God

103 Of David.

My soul, bless the LORD,
 and all that is within me,
  bless his holy name. Ps 30:4
2 My soul, bless the LORD,
 and do not forget
  all his benefits. Dt 6:12; 8:11

3 He forgives all your iniquity;
 he heals all your diseases.
4 He redeems your life
  from the Pit; Ps 49:15

A 102:20 Lit free sons of death   B 102:23 Some Hb mss, LXX read his   C 102:24 Lit my days

he crowns you
  with faithful love
  and compassion.   Ps 5:12

5 He satisfies you^A with
  good things;   Ps 107:9
your youth is renewed
  like the eagle.   Is 40:31

6 The LORD executes acts
  of righteousness
and justice for all
  the oppressed.   Ps 147:7

7 He revealed his ways
  to Moses,   Ex 33:13
his deeds to the people
  of Israel.   Ps 78:11; 99:7

8 The LORD is compassionate
  and gracious,
slow to anger and abounding
  in faithful love.   Ex 34:6; Nm 14:18

9 He will not always accuse us
  or be angry forever.   Is 57:16

10 He has not dealt with us as
  our sins deserve
or repaid us according to
  our iniquities.   Ezr 9:13; Lm 3:22

11 For as high as the heavens
  are above the earth,
so great is his faithful love
  toward those who fear him.

12 As far as the east is
  from the west,
so far has he removed
  our transgressions from us.

13 As a father has compassion
  on his children,
so the LORD has compassion
  on those who fear him.

14 For he knows what we are
  made of,
remembering
  that we are dust.   Gn 3:19

15 As for man, his days are
  like grass —

he blooms like a flower
  of the field;   Jb 14:2; 1Pt 1:24

16 when the wind passes over it,
  it vanishes,
and its place is no longer
  known.^B   Is 40:6-7

17 But from eternity to eternity
the LORD's faithful love is
  toward those who fear him,
and his righteousness
  toward the grandchildren

18 of those who keep
  his covenant,
who remember to observe
  his precepts.   Dt 7:9; Ps 25:10

19 The LORD has established
  his throne in heaven,
and his kingdom rules
  over all.   Ps 11:4; 47:2

20 Bless the LORD,
all his angels
  of great strength,
who do his word,
obedient to his command.

21 Bless the LORD, all his armies,
his servants who do his will.

22 Bless the LORD, all his works
in all the places
  where he rules.   Ps 145:10
My soul, bless the LORD!

God the Creator

104
My soul, bless the LORD!
LORD my God, you are
  very great;
you are clothed with majesty
  and splendor.   Ps 93:1; 103:22

2 He wraps himself in light
  as if it were a robe,
spreading out the sky
  like a canopy,   Jb 9:8; Is 40:22

3 laying the beams of his palace
on the waters above,   Am 9:6
making the clouds
  his chariot,   Is 19:1

^A 103:5 Lit satisfies your ornament; Hb obscure   ^B 103:16 Lit place no longer knows it

walking on the wings
   of the wind,   Ps 18:10
4 and making the winds
   his messengers, ^A
flames of fire his servants.

5 He established the earth
   on its foundations;
it will never be shaken.   Jb 38:4
6 You covered it with the deep
as if it were a garment;
the water stood
   above the mountains.   Gn 7:19
7 At your rebuke
   the water fled;
at the sound of your thunder
   they hurried away —   Ps 18:15
8 mountains rose
   and valleys sank ^B —
to the place you established
   for them.   Ps 65:6; Am 4:13
9 You set a boundary
   they cannot cross;
they will never cover
   the earth again. Jb 26:10; 38:10-11

10 He causes the springs to gush
   into the valleys;
they flow
   between the mountains.
11 They supply water
   for every wild beast;
the wild donkeys quench
   their thirst.   Jb 39:5
12 The birds of the sky live
   beside the springs;
they make their voices heard
   among the foliage.   Mt 8:20
13 He waters the mountains
   from his palace;
the earth is satisfied
   by the fruit of your labor.

14 He causes grass to grow
   for the livestock

and provides crops for man
   to cultivate,
producing food
   from the earth,   Jb 28:5; Ps 147:8
15 wine that makes
   human hearts glad —
making his face shine
   with oil —
and bread that sustains
   human hearts.   Gn 18:5; Ps 141:5
16 The trees of the LORD
   flourish, ^C
the cedars of Lebanon
   that he planted.   Nm 24:6
17 There the birds make
   their nests;
storks make their homes
   in the pine trees.   Lv 11:19
18 The high mountains are
   for the wild goats;
the cliffs are a refuge
   for hyraxes.   Lv 11:5; Pr 30:26

19 He made the moon to mark
   the ^D festivals; ^E
the sun knows when to set.
20 You bring darkness,
   and it becomes night,
when all
   the forest animals stir.
21 The young lions roar
   for their prey
and seek their food
   from God.   Jb 38:39
22 The sun rises; they go back
and lie down in their dens.
23 Man goes out to his work
and to his labor
   until evening.   Gn 3:19

24 How countless are
   your works, LORD!
In wisdom
   you have made them all;

the earth is full of
your creatures. [A]   Pr 3:19; Jr 10:12
25 Here is the sea, vast and wide,
teeming with creatures
beyond number —
living things both large
and small.   Gn 1:21; Ps 69:34
26 There the ships move about,
and Leviathan,
which you formed
to play there.   Jb 41:1; Ps 74:14

27 All of them wait for you
to give them their food
at the right time.   Ps 136:25; 147:9
28 When you give it to them,
they gather it;
when you open your hand,
they are satisfied
with good things.   Ps 145:16
29 When you hide your face,
they are terrified;
when you take away
their breath,
they die and return
to the dust.   Jb 10:9; Ps 90:3
30 When you send your breath, [B]
they are created,
and you renew the surface
of the ground.   Jb 33:4

31 May the glory of the LORD
endure forever;
may the LORD rejoice
in his works.   Ps 72:17
32 He looks at the earth,
and it trembles;
he touches the mountains,
and they pour out smoke.
33 I will sing to the LORD
all my life;
I will sing praise to my God
while I live.   Ps 63:4; 146:2
34 May my meditation
be pleasing to him;
I will rejoice in the LORD.

35 May sinners vanish
from the earth
and wicked people be
no more.   Ps 37:10; 59:13
My soul, bless the LORD!
Hallelujah!

God's Faithfulness to His People

105 Give thanks to the LORD,
call on his name;
proclaim his deeds
among the peoples.   Ps 9:11
2 Sing to him, sing praise
to him;
tell about all
his wondrous works!   Ps 96:3
3 Honor his holy name;
let the hearts of those
who seek the LORD rejoice.
4 Seek the LORD
and his strength;
seek his face always.   Ps 27:8; 63:2
5 Remember
the wondrous works
he has done,
his wonders,
and the judgments
he has pronounced, [C]   Ps 77:11
6 you offspring of Abraham
his servant,
Jacob's descendants —
his chosen ones.   Ps 135:4

7 He is the LORD our God;
his judgments govern
the whole earth.   Is 26:9
8 He remembers his covenant
forever,
the promise he ordained
for a thousand
generations —   Dt 7:9; Ps 106:45
9 the covenant he made
with Abraham,
swore [D] to Isaac,   Gn 12:7; 22:16-18
10 and confirmed to Jacob
as a decree

[A] **104:24** Lit *possessions*   [B] **104:30** Or *Spirit*   [C] **105:5** Lit *judgments of his mouth*   [D] **105:9** Lit *and his oath*

and to Israel
as a permanent covenant:
11 "I will give the land
of Canaan to you
as your inherited portion."

12 When they were few
in number,
very few indeed,
and resident aliens
in Canaan,   Gn 34:30; Dt 7:7
13 wandering from nation
to nation
and from one kingdom
to another,   Dt 26:5
14 he allowed no one
to oppress them;
he rebuked kings
on their behalf: Gn 12:17; 20:3,7
15 "Do not touch
my anointed ones,   Gn 20:6-7
or harm my prophets."

16 He called down famine
against the land
and destroyed
the entire food supply.
17 He had sent a man ahead
of them —
Joseph, who was sold
as a slave.   Gn 37:28-36; 45:5; Ac 7:9
18 They hurt his feet
with shackles;
his neck was put in
an iron collar.   Gn 39:20
19 Until the time
his prediction
came true,
the word of the LORD
tested him.   Gn 40:20-21
20 The king sent for him
and released him;
the ruler of peoples set
him free.   Gn 41:14
21 He made him master
of his household,

ruler over all
his possessions —   Gn 41:40-43
22 binding A his officials at will
and instructing his elders.

23 Then Israel went to Egypt;
Jacob lived as an alien
in the land of Ham. B   Gn 46:6
24 The LORD C made his people
very fruitful;
he made them
more numerous
than their foes,   Ex 1:7,9; Dt 26:5
25 whose hearts he turned
to hate his people
and to deal deceptively
with his servants.   Ex 1:8-14
26 He sent Moses his servant,
and Aaron,
whom he had chosen.   Ex 3:10
27 They performed
his miraculous signs
among them,
and wonders in the land
of Ham.   Ex 7:3; 11:9-10; Ps 78:43-51
28 He sent darkness,
and it became dark —
for did they not defy
his commands?   Ex 10:21-23
29 He turned their water
into blood
and caused their fish to die.
30 Their land was overrun
with frogs,
even in their royal chambers.
31 He spoke,
and insects came —   Ex 8:21
gnats
throughout their country.
32 He gave them hail for rain,
and lightning throughout
their land.   Ex 9:23-25
33 He struck their vines
and fig trees
and shattered the trees
of their territory.   Ps 78:47

A 105:22 LXX, Syr, Vg read *teaching*   B 105:23 = Egypt, also in v. 27   C 105:24 Lit *He*

³⁴ He spoke,
and locusts came —
young locusts
without number.
³⁵ They devoured
all the vegetation
in their land
and consumed the produce
of their land.　Ex 10:12-15
³⁶ He struck all the firstborn
in their land,
all their first progeny.　Ex 12:29

³⁷ Then he brought Israel out
with silver and gold,
and no one among
his tribes stumbled.
³⁸ Egypt was glad
when they left,
for the dread of Israel^A
had fallen on them.　Ex 12:33
³⁹ He spread a cloud
as a covering
and gave a fire to light up
the night.　Ex 13:21; Neh 9:12; Ps 78:14
⁴⁰ They asked,
and he brought quail
and satisfied them
with bread
from heaven.　Ex 16:15; Ps 78:24
⁴¹ He opened a rock,
and water gushed out;
it flowed like a stream
in the desert.　Ex 17:6; Nm 20:11
⁴² For he remembered
his holy promise
to Abraham his servant.
⁴³ He brought his people out
with rejoicing,
his chosen ones with shouts
of joy.　Ex 15:1; Ps 106:12
⁴⁴ He gave them the lands
of the nations,
and they inherited
what other peoples
had worked for.　Jos 24:13

^A 105:38 Lit them

⁴⁵ All this happened
so that they might keep
his statutes
and obey his instructions.
Hallelujah!

Israel's Unfaithfulness to God

106 Hallelujah!
Give thanks to the LORD,
for he is good;
his faithful love
endures forever.　1Ch 16:34,41
² Who can declare
the LORD's mighty acts
or proclaim all the praise
due him?　Ps 145:4,12; 150:2
³ How happy are those
who uphold justice,
who practice righteousness
at all times.　Ps 15:2
⁴ Remember me, LORD,
when you show favor
to your people.　Ps 119:132
Come to me
with your salvation
⁵ so that I may enjoy
the prosperity
of your chosen ones,
rejoice in the joy
of your nation,
and boast
about your heritage.　Dt 32:9
⁶ Both we and our fathers
have sinned;
we have done wrong
and have acted wickedly.
⁷ Our fathers in Egypt did not
grasp
the significance of
your wondrous works
or remember your many acts
of faithful love;
instead, they rebelled
by the sea — the Red Sea.

⁸ Yet he saved them for
   his name's sake,
   to make his power known.
⁹ He rebuked the Red Sea,
   and it dried up;
   he led them through
   the depths as through
   a desert.   Ps 18:15; 104:7; Is 63:11-13
¹⁰ He saved them
   from the power
   of the adversary;
   he redeemed them
   from the power
   of the enemy.   Ex 14:30; Ps 107:2
¹¹ Water covered their foes;
   not one of them remained.
¹² Then they believed
   his promises
   and sang his praise.   Ex 14:31

¹³ They soon forgot his works
   and would not wait
   for his counsel.   Ex 15:24; Ps 78:11
¹⁴ They were seized
   with craving
   in the wilderness
   and tested God in the desert.
¹⁵ He gave them what
   they asked for,
   but sent a wasting disease
   among them.   Nm 11:31; Ps 78:29

¹⁶ In the camp
   they were envious
   of Moses
   and of Aaron,
   the LORD's holy one.   Nm 16:1-3
¹⁷ The earth opened up
   and swallowed Dathan;
   it covered the assembly
   of Abiram.   Nm 16:31-32; Dt 11:6
¹⁸ Fire blazed throughout
   their assembly;
   flames consumed
   the wicked.   Nm 16:35

¹⁹ At Horeb they made a calf
   and worshiped
   the cast metal image.   Ex 32:4
²⁰ They exchanged
   their glory A,B
   for the image
   of a grass-eating ox.   Jr 2:11
²¹ They forgot God their Savior,
   who did great things
   in Egypt,   Dt 10:21; Ps 78:11
²² wondrous works in the land
   of Ham, C
   awe-inspiring acts
   at the Red Sea.   Ps 105:27
²³ So he said he would have
   destroyed them —
   if Moses his chosen one
   had not stood before him
   in the breach
   to turn his wrath away
   from destroying them.

²⁴ They despised
   the pleasant land
   and did not believe
   his promise.   Nm 14:31; Dt 9:23
²⁵ They grumbled
   in their tents
   and did not listen
   to the LORD.   Nm 14:2; Dt 1:27
²⁶ So he raised his hand
   against them
   with an oath
   that he would make them
   fall in the desert   Nm 14:28-35
²⁷ and would disperse
   their descendants D
   among the nations,
   scattering them
   throughout the lands.   Dt 4:27

²⁸ They aligned themselves
   with Baal of Peor
   and ate sacrifices offered
   to lifeless gods. E   Nm 25:3; Dt 4:3

A **106:20** Alt Hb tradition reads *his glory*, or *my glory*   B **106:20** = God   C **106:22** = Egypt   D **106:27** Syr;
MT reads *would make their descendants fall*   E **106:28** Lit *sacrifices for dead ones*

²⁹ They angered the Lᴏʀᴅ
with their deeds,
and a plague broke out
against them.   Nm 25:4

³⁰ But Phinehas stood up
and intervened,
and the plague was stopped.

³¹ It was credited to him
as righteousness
throughout all generations
to come.   Gn 15:6; Nm 25:10-13

³² They angered the Lᴏʀᴅ
at the Waters of Meribah,
and Moses suffered ᴬ
because of them;   Nm 20:2-13

³³ for they embittered
his spirit, ᴮ
and he spoke rashly
with his lips.   Ps 78:40; Is 63:10

³⁴ They did not destroy
the peoples
as the Lᴏʀᴅ
had commanded them

³⁵ but mingled
with the nations
and adopted their ways.

³⁶ They served their idols,
which became a snare
to them.   Dt 7:16; Jdg 2:12

³⁷ They sacrificed their sons
and daughters
to demons.   Lv 17:7; Dt 32:17

³⁸ They shed innocent blood —
the blood of their sons
and daughters
whom they sacrificed
to the idols of Canaan;
so the land became polluted
with blood.   Nm 35:33; Is 24:5

³⁹ They defiled themselves
by their actions
and prostituted themselves
by their deeds.   Lv 18:24

⁴⁰ Therefore the Lᴏʀᴅ's anger
burned against his people,
and he abhorred
his own inheritance.   Dt 32:19

⁴¹ He handed them over
to the nations;
those who hated them
ruled over them.   Jdg 2:14

⁴² Their enemies
oppressed them,
and they were subdued
under their power.   Jdg 4:3

⁴³ He rescued them
many times,
but they continued
to rebel deliberately
and were beaten down
by their iniquity.   Jdg 2:16-18

⁴⁴ When he heard their cry,
he took note of
their distress,   Jdg 3:3; 6:7; 10:10

⁴⁵ remembered his covenant
with them,
and relented according to
the abundance
of his faithful love.   Lv 26:42

⁴⁶ He caused them
to be pitied
before all their captors.   Ezr 9:9

⁴⁷ Save us, Lᴏʀᴅ our God,
and gather us
from the nations,
so that we may give thanks
to your holy name
and rejoice in your praise.

⁴⁸ Blessed be the Lᴏʀᴅ God
of Israel,
from everlasting
to everlasting.   Ps 41:13; 72:18
Let all the people
say, "Amen!"
Hallelujah!   1Ch 16:35-36

ᴬ**106:32** Lit *and it was evil for Moses*   ᴮ**106:33** Some Hb mss, LXX, Syr, Jer; other Hb mss read *they rebelled against his Spirit*

BOOK V (Psalms 107–150)

Thanksgiving for God's Deliverance

107 Give thanks to the LORD,
for he is good;
his faithful love
endures forever. 1Ch 16:34

2 Let the redeemed
of the LORD proclaim
that he has redeemed them
from the power of the foe

3 and has gathered them
from the lands —
from the east and the west,
from the north and the south.

4 Some[A] wandered
in the desolate wilderness,
finding no way to a city
where they could live.

5 They were hungry and thirsty;
their spirits failed[B]
within them. Ps 77:3

6 Then they cried out
to the LORD in their trouble;
he rescued them
from their distress. Ps 106:44

7 He led them by the right path
to go to a city where
they could live. Jr 31:9

8 Let them give thanks
to the LORD
for his faithful love
and his wondrous works for
all humanity. Ps 75:1

9 For he has satisfied the thirsty
and filled the hungry
with good things. Ps 22:26; 34:10

10 Others sat in darkness
and gloom[C] —
prisoners in cruel chains —

11 because they rebelled
against God's commands
and despised the counsel
of the Most High. 2Ch 36:16

12 He broke their spirits[D]
with hard labor;
they stumbled, and there was
no one to help. Ex 6:9; Dt 26:6

13 Then they cried out
to the LORD in their trouble;
he saved them
from their distress. Ex 2:23-25

14 He brought them
out of darkness and gloom
and broke
their chains apart. Jr 2:20

15 Let them give thanks
to the LORD
for his faithful love
and his wondrous works for
all humanity. Ps 75:1

16 For he has broken down
the bronze gates
and cut through
the iron bars. Is 45:1-2

17 Fools suffered affliction
because of
their rebellious ways
and their iniquities. Jr 30:14-15

18 They loathed all food
and came near the gates
of death. Jb 33:20

19 Then they cried out
to the LORD in their trouble;
he saved them
from their distress. Nm 21:7-9

20 He sent his word
and healed them;
he rescued them from the Pit.

21 Let them give thanks
to the LORD
for his faithful love
and his wondrous works for
all humanity. Ps 75:1

22 Let them offer sacrifices
of thanksgiving

A**107:4** Lit *They*, also in vv. 10, 23   B**107:5** Lit *their soul fainted*   C**107:10** Or *the shadow of death*, also in v. 14   D**107:12** Lit *hearts*

and announce his works
  with shouts of joy. Ps 9:11; 116:17

23 Others went to sea in ships,
  conducting trade
    on the vast water. Is 42:10
24 They saw the LORD's works,
  his wondrous works
    in the deep. Is 33:21
25 He spoke and raised
    a stormy wind
  that stirred up the waves
    of the sea.^A Ps 93:3-4; Ezk 26:19
26 Rising up to the sky,
  sinking down to the depths,
  their courage^B melting away
    in anguish, Ps 22:14; 119:28
27 they reeled and staggered
    like a drunkard,
  and all their skill was useless.
28 Then they cried out
    to the LORD in their trouble,
  and he brought them
    out of their distress. Jnh 1:14
29 He stilled the storm
    to a whisper,
  and the waves of the sea^C
    were hushed. Ps 89:9; Mt 8:26
30 They rejoiced
    when the waves^D grew quiet.
  Then he guided
    them to the harbor
    they longed for. Ex 15:13; Ps 78:72
31 Let them give thanks
    to the LORD
  for his faithful love
  and his wondrous works for
    all humanity. Ps 75:1
32 Let them exalt him
    in the assembly of the people
  and praise him in the council
    of the elders. Ps 22:22,25

33 He turns rivers into desert,
  springs into thirsty ground,
34 and fruitful land
  into salty wasteland,
  because of the wickedness
    of its inhabitants. Gn 19:24-28
35 He turns a desert into a pool,
  dry land into springs. Is 35:6-7
36 He causes the hungry
    to settle there,
  and they establish a city
    where they can live. Ps 60:9
37 They sow fields
    and plant vineyards
  that yield a fruitful harvest.
38 He blesses them,
    and they multiply greatly;
  he does not let
    their livestock decrease.
39 When they are diminished
    and are humbled
  by cruel oppression
    and sorrow, Ps 44:25
40 he pours contempt on nobles
  and makes them wander
    in a trackless wasteland.
41 But he lifts the needy out of
    their suffering 1Sm 2:8; Ps 113:7-8
  and makes their families
    multiply like flocks. Jb 21:11
42 The upright see it and rejoice,
  and all injustice shuts
    its mouth. Jb 5:16

43 Let whoever is wise
    pay attention
  to these things
  and consider the LORD's acts
    of faithful love. Ps 64:9; Hs 14:9

A Plea for Victory

108 *A song. A psalm of David.*
My heart
  is confident, God;
I will sing; I will sing praises
  with the whole of my being.^E

A **107:25** Lit *of it* B **107:26** Lit *souls* C **107:29** Lit *of them* D **107:30** Lit *when they* E **108:1** Lit *praises, even my glory*

2 Wake up, harp and lyre!
  I will wake up the dawn.   Ps 81:2
3 I will praise you, LORD,
    among the peoples;
  I will sing praises to you
    among the nations.   2Sm 22:50
4 For your faithful love
    is higher than the heavens,
  and your faithfulness
    reaches to the clouds.   Ps 36:5
5 God, be exalted above
    the heavens,   Ps 113:4
  and let your glory be over
    the whole earth.   Ps 57:7-11
6 Save with your right hand
    and answer me
  so that those you love
    may be rescued.   Ps 17:7; 20:6

7 God has spoken
    in his sanctuary:^A
  "I will celebrate!
  I will divide up Shechem.
  I will apportion the Valley
    of Succoth.   Gn 33:17
8 Gilead is mine, Manasseh is
    mine,
  and Ephraim is my helmet;
  Judah is my scepter.   Gn 49:10
9 Moab is my washbasin;   2Sm 8:2
  I throw my sandal on Edom.
  I shout in triumph
    over Philistia."   2Sm 8:1

10 Who will bring me
     to the fortified city?
   Who will lead me to Edom?
11 God, haven't you rejected us?
   God, you do not march out
     with our armies.   Ps 44:9
12 Give us aid against the foe,
   for human help is worthless.
13 With God we will
     perform valiantly;   Nm 24:18
   he will trample our foes.

Prayer Against an Enemy

109

*For the choir director.
A psalm of David.*

1 God of my praise,
    do not be silent.   Ps 28:1; 83:1
2 For wicked
    and deceitful mouths open
    against me;
  they speak against me
    with lying tongues.   Ps 10:7
3 They surround me
    with hateful words
  and attack me without cause.
4 In return for my love
    they accuse me,
  but I continue to pray.^B   Ps 69:13
5 They repay me evil for good,
    and hatred for my love.   Ps 35:12

6 Set a wicked person
    over him;
  let an accuser^C stand
    at his right hand.   Zch 3:1
7 When he is judged, let him
    be found guilty,
  and let his prayer be counted
    as sin.   Ps 1:5; Pr 28:9
8 Let his days be few;
  let another take over
    his position.   Ps 55:23; Ac 1:20
9 Let his children be fatherless
  and his wife a widow.   Ex 22:24
10 Let his children wander
     as beggars,
   searching for food
     far^D from their
     demolished homes.   Jb 30:5-8
11 Let a creditor seize all he has;
   let strangers plunder
     what he has worked for.
12 Let no one show him
     kindness,
   and let no one be gracious
     to his fatherless children.

---

^A **108:7** Or *has promised by his holy nature*   ^B **109:4** Lit *but I, prayer*   ^C **109:6** Or *adversary*
^D **109:10** LXX reads *beggars, driven far*

¹³ Let the line
      of his descendants
      be cut off;
   let their name be blotted out
      in the next generation. Ps 9:5
¹⁴ Let the iniquity of his fathers
   be remembered
      before the LORD,   Ex 20:5
   and do not let
      his mother's sin
      be blotted out. Neh 4:5; Jr 18:23
¹⁵ Let their sins^A always remain
      before the LORD,
   and let him remove^B
      all memory of them
      from the earth. Ps 34:16; 90:8

¹⁶ For he did not think
      to show kindness,
   but pursued the suffering,
      needy, and brokenhearted
   in order to put them to death.
¹⁷ He loved cursing — let it fall
      on him;
   he took no delight in blessing
      — let it be far from him.
¹⁸ He wore cursing
      like his coat —
   let it enter his body like water
   and go into his bones like oil.
¹⁹ Let it be like a robe he wraps
      around himself,
   like a belt he always wears.
²⁰ Let this be the LORD's
      payment to my accusers,
   to those who speak evil
      against me. Ps 54:5; 94:23; Is 3:11

²¹ But you, LORD, my Lord,
   deal kindly with me
      for your name's sake; Ps 79:9
   because your faithful love is
      good, rescue me. Ps 69:16
²² For I am suffering and needy;
   my heart is wounded
      within me. Ps 143:4

²³ I fade away like a
      lengthening shadow; Ps 102:11
   I am shaken off like a locust.
²⁴ My knees are weak
      from fasting,
   and my body is emaciated.^C
²⁵ I have become an object
      of ridicule to my accusers;^D
   when they see me, they shake
      their heads in scorn. Ps 22:6-7

²⁶ Help me, LORD my God;
   save me according to
      your faithful love Ps 119:86
²⁷ so they may know that this is
      your hand
   and that you, LORD,
      have done it. Jb 37:7
²⁸ Though they curse,
      you will bless.
   When they rise up,
      they will be put to shame,
   but your servant will rejoice.
²⁹ My accusers will be clothed
      with disgrace;
   they will wear their shame
      like a cloak. Jb 8:22; Ps 35:26; 132:18
³⁰ I will fervently thank the LORD
      with my mouth;
   I will praise him
      in the presence of many.
³¹ For he stands
      at the right hand of
      the needy
   to save him from
      those who would
      condemn him. Ps 16:8; 110:5; 121:5

The Priestly King

110 *A psalm of David.*
This is the declaration
   of the LORD
to my Lord:
"Sit at my right hand
until I make your enemies
   your footstool." Mt 22:44

---

^A**109:15** Lit *Let them*   ^B**109:15** Or *cut off*   ^C**109:24** Lit *denied from fat*   ^D**109:25** Lit *to them*

² The LORD will extend
  your mighty scepter
  from Zion.
Rule^A over your
  surrounding^B enemies.
³ Your people will volunteer
  on your day of battle.^C   Jdg 5:2
In holy splendor,
  from the womb of the dawn,
the dew of your youth
  belongs to you.^D   1Ch 16:29
⁴ The LORD has sworn an oath
  and will not take it back:
"You are a priest forever
according to the pattern
  of Melchizedek."   Gn 14:18

⁵ The Lord is
  at your right hand;
he will crush kings
  on the day of his anger.   68:14
⁶ He will judge the nations,
  heaping up corpses;   Is 66:24
he will crush leaders
  over the entire world.
⁷ He will drink from the brook
  by the road;   Jdg 7:5-6
therefore, he will lift up
  his head.   Ps 27:6

Praise for the LORD's Works

111 Hallelujah!^E
      I will praise the LORD
  with all my heart
in the assembly
  of the upright
  and in the congregation.

² The LORD's works are great,
  studied by all who delight
  in them.   Ps 92:5; 143:5
³ All that he does is splendid
  and majestic;   Ps 145:5
his righteousness
  endures forever.   Ps 112:3,9

⁴ He has caused
  his wondrous works
  to be remembered.   Ps 78:4
The LORD is gracious
  and compassionate.   Ps 103:8
⁵ He has provided food
  for those who fear him;
he remembers
  his covenant forever.   Ps 105:8
⁶ He has shown his people
  the power of his works
by giving them
  the inheritance
  of the nations.   Dt 4:38; 32:8
⁷ The works of his hands
  are truth and justice;
all his instructions
  are trustworthy.   Ps 19:7; 93:5
⁸ They are established forever
  and ever,
enacted in truth
  and in uprightness.   Ps 119:160
⁹ He has sent redemption
  to his people.   Lk 1:68
He has ordained
  his covenant forever.
His name is holy
  and awe-inspiring.   Ps 99:3

¹⁰ The fear of the LORD is
  the beginning of wisdom;
all who follow his
  instructions^F have
  good insight.   Ps 119:98
His praise endures forever.

The Traits of the Righteous

112 Hallelujah!^E
      Happy is the person
  who fears the LORD,
taking great delight
  in his commands.   Ps 1:2; 119:16

² His descendants will be
  powerful in the land;

^A**110:2** One Hb ms, LXX, Tg read *You will rule*   ^B**110:2** Lit *Rule in the midst of your*   ^C**110:3** Lit *power*
^D**110:3** Hb obscure   ^E**111:1; 112:1** The lines of this poem form an acrostic.   ^F**111:10** Lit *follow them*

the generation of the upright
will be blessed. Ps 102:28

3 Wealth and riches are
in his house, Pr 3:16; 8:18
and his righteousness
endures forever. Ps 111:3

4 Light shines in the darkness
for the upright. Ps 97:11
He is gracious,
compassionate,
and righteous. Ex 34:6; Neh 9:17

5 Good will come to the one
who lends generously
and conducts
his business fairly. Ps 15:5; 37:26

6 He will never be shaken.
The righteous one will be
remembered forever. Pr 10:7

7 He will not fear bad news;
his heart is confident,
trusting in the LORD. Ps 56:4

8 His heart is assured;
he will not fear. Ps 27:1; 56:11
In the end he will look
in triumph on his foes.

9 He distributes freely
to the poor;
his righteousness
endures forever. 2Co 9:9
His horn will be exalted
in honor. Ps 75:10; 89:17

10 The wicked one will see it
and be angry;
he will gnash his teeth
in despair. Jb 16:9; Ps 35:16
The desire of the wicked
leads to ruin. Pr 10:28; 11:7

Praise to the Merciful God

113 Hallelujah!
Give praise, servants
of the LORD;
praise the name of the LORD.

2 Let the name of the LORD
be blessed
both now and forever. Ps 115:18

3 From the rising of the sun
to its setting,
let the name of the LORD
be praised. Mal 1:11

4 The LORD is exalted above
all the nations, Ps 99:2
his glory above the heavens.

5 Who is like the LORD
our God —
the one enthroned on high,

6 who stoops down to look
on the heavens and the earth?

7 He raises the poor
from the dust
and lifts the needy
from the trash heap 1Sm 2:8

8 in order to seat them
with nobles —
with the nobles of his people.

9 He gives the childless woman
a household,
making her the joyful mother
of children. 1Sm 2:5; Ps 68:6
Hallelujah!

God's Deliverance of Israel

114 When Israel came
out of Egypt —
the house of Jacob
from a people
who spoke
a foreign language — Ex 13:3

2 Judah became his sanctuary,
Israel, his dominion. Ex 15:17

3 The sea looked and fled;
the Jordan turned back.

4 The mountains skipped
like rams,
the hills, like lambs. Ex 19:18

5 Why was it, sea,
that you fled?
Jordan, that you turned back?

6 Mountains, that you skipped
like rams?
Hills, like lambs? Hab 3:10

⁷ Tremble, earth,
 at the presence of the Lord,
 at the presence of the God
 of Jacob,   Ps 96:9
⁸ who turned the rock
 into a pool,
 the flint into a spring.   Ex 17:6

Glory to God Alone

115 Not to us, Lord, not to us,
 but to your name give
 glory
because of your faithful love,
 because of your truth.
² Why should the nations say,
 "Where is their God?"   Ps 42:3,10
³ Our God is in heaven
and does whatever
 he pleases.   Ps 135:6; Dn 4:35
⁴ Their idols are silver
 and gold,
made by human hands.   Is 37:19
⁵ They have mouths
 but cannot speak,
eyes, but cannot see.
⁶ They have ears
 but cannot hear,
noses, but cannot smell.   Is 46:7
⁷ They have hands
 but cannot feel,
feet, but cannot walk.   Jr 10:5
They cannot make a sound
 with their throats.   Hab 2:18
⁸ Those who make them are[A]
 just like them,
as are all who trust in them.

⁹ Israel,[B] trust in the Lord!
He is their help and shield.
¹⁰ House of Aaron,
 trust in the Lord!   Ps 118:3; 135:19
He is their help and shield.
¹¹ You who fear the Lord,
 trust in the Lord!   Ps 22:23; 118:4

He is their help and shield.
¹² The Lord remembers us
 and will bless us.
He will bless the house
 of Israel;
he will bless the house
 of Aaron;   Ps 98:3
¹³ he will bless those who fear
 the Lord —
small and great alike.   Rv 11:18

¹⁴ May the Lord add to
 your numbers,
both yours
 and your children's.   Dt 1:11
¹⁵ May you be blessed
 by the Lord,
the Maker of heaven
 and earth.   Ps 121:2; 124:8; 134:3
¹⁶ The heavens are the Lord's,[C]
but the earth he has given
 to the human race.   Ps 89:11
¹⁷ It is not the dead who praise
 the Lord,
nor any of those descending
 into the silence of death.
¹⁸ But we will bless the Lord,
both now and forever.   Ps 113:2
Hallelujah!

Thanks to God for Deliverance

116 I love the Lord
 because he has heard
my appeal for mercy.   Ps 18:1
² Because he has turned
 his ear to me,
I will call out to him
 as long as I live.   Ps 17:6; 40:1

³ The ropes of death
 were wrapped around me,
and the torments of Sheol
 overcame me;
I encountered trouble
 and sorrow.   Ps 18:4-5

[A]**115:8** Or *May those who make them become*   [B]**115:9** Some Hb mss, LXX, Syr read *House of Israel*
[C]**115:16** Lit *the Lord's heavens*

4 Then I called on the name
    of the LORD:
  "LORD, save me!"   Ps 18:6; 118:5

5 The LORD is gracious
    and righteous;
  our God is compassionate.
6 The LORD guards
    the inexperienced;
  I was helpless,
    and he saved me.   Ps 19:7; 79:8
7 Return to your rest,
    my soul,
  for the LORD has been good
    to you.   Ps 13:6; Jr 6:16
8 For you, LORD, rescued me
    from death,
  my eyes from tears,
  my feet from stumbling.
9 I will walk before the LORD
  in the land of the living. Ps 27:13
10 I believed, even when I said,
  "I am severely oppressed."
11 In my alarm I said,
  "Everyone is a liar."   Ps 31:22; 62:9

12 How can I repay the LORD
  for all the good he has done
    for me?   2Ch 32:25; 1Th 3:9
13 I will take the cup
    of salvation
  and call on the name of the
    LORD.   Ps 16:5; 105:1
14 I will fulfill my vows
    to the LORD
  in the presence of all
    his people.   Ps 22:25; 50:14

15 The death of his faithful ones
  is valuable
    in the LORD's sight.   Ps 72:14
16 LORD, I am indeed
    your servant;
  I am your servant, the son
    of your female servant.
  You have loosened my bonds.

17 I will offer you a sacrifice
    of thanksgiving
  and call on the name
    of the LORD.   Lv 7:12; Ps 50:14
18 I will fulfill my vows
    to the LORD
  in the presence of all
    his people,   Ps 22:25; 50:14
19 in the courts
    of the LORD's house —
  within you, Jerusalem.   Ps 96:8
  Hallelujah!

Universal Call to Praise

117 Praise the LORD,
          all nations!
  Glorify him, all peoples!
2 For his faithful love to
    us is great;
  the LORD's faithfulness
    endures forever.   Ps 100:5; 103:11
  Hallelujah!

Thanksgiving for Victory

118 Give thanks to the LORD,
          for he is good;
  his faithful love
    endures forever.   2Ch 5:13
2 Let Israel say,
  "His faithful love
    endures forever."   Ps 115:9
3 Let the house of Aaron say,
  "His faithful love
    endures forever."   Ps 115:10
4 Let those who fear the LORD
    say,
  "His faithful love
    endures forever."   Ps 22:23; 115:11

5 I called to the LORD
    in distress;   Ps 18:6; 120:1
  the LORD answered me
  and put me in a spacious
    place. A   Ps 18:19
6 The LORD is for me;
    I will not be afraid.

A 118:5 Or *answered me with freedom*

What can a mere mortal do
  to me? Ps 56:4,11; Heb 13:6
7 The LORD is my helper,
Therefore, I will look
  in triumph on those
  who hate me. Ps 54:4,7; 59:10

8 It is better to take refuge
  in the LORD
than to trust in humanity.
9 It is better to take refuge
  in the LORD
than to trust in nobles. Ps 146:3

10 All the nations
  surrounded me;
in the name of the LORD
  I destroyed them. Ps 3:6; 88:17
11 They surrounded me, yes,
  they surrounded me;
in the name of the LORD
  I destroyed them. Ps 18:40
12 They surrounded me
  like bees; Dt 1:44
they were extinguished
  like a fire among thorns;
in the name of the LORD
  I destroyed them. Ps 58:9
13 They^A pushed me hard
  to make me fall,
but the LORD helped me.
14 The LORD is my strength
  and my song;
he has become my salvation.

15 There are shouts of joy
  and victory
in the tents
  of the righteous:
"The LORD's right hand
  performs valiantly! Ex 15:6
16 The LORD's right hand
  is raised.
The LORD's right hand
  performs valiantly!" Ps 89:13
17 I will not die, but I will live

^A 118:13 Lit You

and proclaim what the LORD
  has done. Ps 73:28; Hab 1:12
18 The LORD disciplined me
  severely
but did not give me over
  to death. Ps 86:13; Jr 30:11; 2Co 6:9

19 Open the gates
  of righteousness for me;
I will enter through them
and give thanks to the LORD.
20 This is the LORD's gate;
the righteous will enter
  through it. Ps 24:3-6; Rv 22:14
21 I will give thanks to you
because you have
  answered me
and have become
  my salvation. Ps 116:1
22 The stone that
  the builders rejected
has become the cornerstone.
23 This came from the LORD;
it is wondrous in our sight.
24 This is the day the LORD
  has made;
let us rejoice and be glad in it.
25 LORD, save us!
LORD, please grant us
  success! Neh 2:20; Ps 122:6-7
26 He who comes in the name
of the LORD is blessed. Mt 21:9
From the house of the LORD
  we bless you. Ps 129:8
27 The LORD is God
  and has given us light.
Bind the festival sacrifice
  with cords
to the horns of the altar. Ex 27:2
28 You are my God,
  and I will give you thanks.
You are my God;
  I will exalt you. Is 25:1
29 Give thanks to the LORD,
  for he is good;

his faithful love
endures forever.   2Ch 5:13

Delight in God's Word

א Aleph

119 How[A] happy are those
whose way is blameless,
who walk according
to the LORD's instruction!

2 Happy are those who keep
his decrees   Ps 25:10; 119:10,22,168
and seek him with all
their heart.   Dt 4:29; 10:12; 11:13; 13:3

3 They do nothing wrong;   1Jn 3:9
they walk in his ways.

4 You have commanded
that your precepts   Dt 4:13
be diligently kept.

5 If only my ways
were committed
to keeping your statutes!

6 Then I would not be ashamed
when I think about
all your commands.

7 I will praise you
with an upright heart
when I learn
your righteous judgments.

8 I will keep your statutes;
never abandon me.   Ps 38:21

ב Beth

9 How can a young man keep
his way pure?
By keeping your[B] word.   Ps 12:6

10 I have sought you
with all my heart;   Ps 119:2
don't let me wander
from your commands.

11 I have treasured your word
in my heart   Ps 37:31; 40:8; Lk 2:19,51
so that I may not sin
against you.

12 LORD, may you be blessed;
teach me your statutes.

13 With my lips I proclaim

all the judgments
from your mouth.   Ps 40:9

14 I rejoice in the way
revealed by your decrees
as much as in all riches.

15 I will meditate on
your precepts   Ps 1:2
and think about your ways.

16 I will delight in your statutes;
I will not forget your word.

ג Gimel

17 Deal generously
with your servant   Ps 13:6
so that I might live;
then I will keep your word.

18 Open my eyes so that
I may contemplate
wondrous things
from your instruction.

19 I am a resident alien on earth;
do not hide your commands
from me.

20 I am continually overcome
with longing for
your judgments.   Ps 42:1-2; 63:1

21 You rebuke the arrogant,
the ones under a curse,   Dt 27:26
who wander
from your commands.

22 Take insult and contempt
away from me,   Ps 39:8; 119:39
for I have kept your decrees.

23 Though princes sit together
speaking against me,
your servant will think
about your statutes;

24 your decrees are my delight
and my counselors.   Ps 119:16

ד Daleth

25 My life is down in the dust;
give me life through
your word.

26 I told you about my life,
and you answered me;

A 119:1 The stanzas of this poem form an acrostic.   B 119:9 Or keeping it according to your teach me your statutes.   Ps 25:4

²⁷ Help me understand
the meaning of your precepts
so that I can meditate on
your wonders.   Ps 105:2; 145:5

²⁸ I am weary^A from grief;
strengthen me through
your word.   1Pt 5:10

²⁹ Keep me from the way
of deceit
and graciously give me
your instruction.

³⁰ I have chosen the way
of truth;
I have set your ordinances
before me.   Ps 16:8

³¹ I cling to your decrees;
LORD, do not put me to shame.

³² I pursue the way of
your commands,
for you broaden
my understanding.^B   1Kg 4:29

ה He

³³ Teach me, LORD,
the meaning^C
of your statutes,
and I will always keep them.^D

³⁴ Help me understand
your instruction,
and I will obey it
and follow it with all
my heart.   1Ch 22:12; Ps 119:2,69

³⁵ Help me stay on the path
of your commands,   Ps 25:4
for I take pleasure in it.   Ps 119:16

³⁶ Turn my heart
to your decrees   1Kg 8:58
and not to dishonest profit.

³⁷ Turn my eyes
from looking at
what is worthless;   Is 33:15
give me life in your ways.^E

³⁸ Confirm what you said
to your servant,   2Sm 7:25

for it produces reverence
for you.

³⁹ Turn away the disgrace
I dread;   Ps 119:22
indeed, your judgments
are good.

⁴⁰ How I long for your precepts!
Give me life through
your righteousness.

ו Waw

⁴¹ Let your faithful love
come to me, LORD,   Ps 119:77
your salvation,
as you promised.

⁴² Then I can answer the one
who taunts me,   Ps 102:8; Pr 27:11
for I trust in your word.

⁴³ Never take the word of truth
from my mouth,
for I hope in
your judgments.

⁴⁴ I will always obey
your instruction,
forever and ever.   Ps 119:33

⁴⁵ I will walk freely
in an open place   Pr 4:12
because I study
your precepts.   Ps 119:94,155

⁴⁶ I will speak of your decrees
before kings
and not be ashamed.   Mt 10:18

⁴⁷ I delight in your commands,
which I love.   Ps 119:16,97,127,159

⁴⁸ I will lift up my hands
to your commands,   Ps 63:4
which I love,
and will meditate
on your statutes.   Ps 119:15

ז Zayin

⁴⁹ Remember your word
to your servant;
you have given me hope
through it.

^A119:28 Or *I weep*   ^B119:32 Lit *you enlarge my heart*   ^C119:33 Lit *way*   ^D119:33 Or *will keep it as my reward*   ^E119:37 Some Hb mss, Tg read *word*

⁵⁰ This is my comfort
   in my affliction: Rm 15:4
   Your promise has given
   me life.
⁵¹ The arrogant constantly
   ridicule me,
   but I do not turn away
   from your instruction.
⁵² LORD, I remember
   your judgments
   from long ago
   and find comfort.
⁵³ Rage seizes me because of
   the wicked   Ezr 9:3; Neh 13:25
   who reject your instruction.
⁵⁴ Your statutes are
   the theme of my song
   during my earthly life. ᴬ
⁵⁵ LORD, I remember your name
   in the night,   Ps 42:8; 63:6; 92:2
   and I obey your instruction.
⁵⁶ This is my practice:
   I obey your precepts.

ה Cheth

⁵⁷ The LORD is my portion; ᴮ
   I have promised to keep
   your words.
⁵⁸ I have sought your favor
   with all my heart;   1Kg 13:6
   be gracious to me
   according to your promise.
⁵⁹ I thought about my ways
   and turned my steps back
   to your decrees.
⁶⁰ I hurried, not hesitating
   to keep your commands.
⁶¹ Though the ropes
   of the wicked   Jb 36:8; Ps 140:5
   were wrapped around me,
   I did not forget
   your instruction.
⁶² I rise at midnight
   to thank you   Ps 119:55
   for your righteous
   judgments.   Ps 119:7

⁶³ I am a friend to all
   who fear you,   Ps 101:6
   to those who keep
   your precepts.
⁶⁴ LORD, the earth is filled with
   your faithful love;   Ps 33:5
   teach me your statutes.

ט Teth

⁶⁵ LORD, you have treated
   your servant well,
   just as you promised.
⁶⁶ Teach me good judgment
   and discernment,   Php 1:9-10
   for I rely on your commands.
⁶⁷ Before I was afflicted
   I went astray,   Ps 119:71,75
   but now I keep your word.
⁶⁸ You are good, and you do
   what is good;   Ps 100:5; 106:1; 107:1
   teach me your statutes.
⁶⁹ The arrogant
   have smeared me with lies,
   but I obey your precepts
   with all my heart.   Ps 119:56
⁷⁰ Their hearts are hard
   and insensitive,   Ps 17:10
   but I delight in
   your instruction.   Ps 119:16
⁷¹ It was good for me
   to be afflicted   Ps 119:67,75
   so that I could learn
   your statutes.
⁷² Instruction from your lips
   is better for me   Ps 19:10; 119:127
   than thousands of gold
   and silver pieces.

י Yod

⁷³ Your hands made me
   and formed me;   Jb 10:8; 31:15
   give me understanding
   so that I can learn
   your commands.   Ps 119:34
⁷⁴ Those who fear you
   will see me and rejoice,

ᴬ**119:54** Lit *song in the house of my sojourning*   ᴮ**119:57** Lit *You are my portion, LORD*

for I put my hope
in your word.   Ps 119:43
75 I know, Lord,
that your judgments are just
and that you have afflicted
me fairly.   Ps 119:138; Heb 12:10
76 May your faithful love
comfort me
as you promised
your servant.
77 May your compassion
come to me   Ps 119:41
so that I may live,
for your instruction is
my delight.   Ps 119:16
78 Let the arrogant be
put to shame   Jr 50:32
for slandering me with lies;
I will meditate on
your precepts.
79 Let those who fear you,
those who know
your decrees, turn to me.
80 May my heart be blameless
regarding your statutes
so that I will not be put
to shame.

כ **Kaph**

81 I long for your salvation;
I put my hope in your word.
82 My eyes grow weary
looking for what
you have promised;   Ps 69:3
I ask, "When will you
comfort me?"
83 Though I have become
like a wineskin dried
by smoke,
I do not forget your statutes.
84 How many days must
your servant wait?
When will you
execute judgment
on my persecutors?   Rv 6:10
85 The arrogant have dug pits
for me;   Ps 35:7; 57:6; Jr 18:22

they violate your instruction.
86 All your commands are true;
people persecute me
with lies — help me!   Ps 35:19
87 They almost ended my life
on earth,
but I did not abandon
your precepts.
88 Give me life in accordance
with your faithful love,
and I will obey the decree
you have spoken.

ל **Lamed**

89 Lord, your word is forever;
it is firmly fixed in heaven.
90 Your faithfulness is
for all generations;   Ps 89:1-2
you established the earth,
and it stands firm.   Ps 148:6
91 Your judgments stand firm
today,   Jr 31:35
for all things are
your servants.   Ps 104:2-4
92 If your instruction
had not been my delight,
I would have died
in my affliction.   Ps 119:16,50
93 I will never forget
your precepts,
for you have given me life
through them.   Ps 119:16,25
94 I am yours; save me,   Ps 119:146
for I have studied
your precepts.   Ps 119:45
95 The wicked hope to destroy
me,   Ps 40:14
but I contemplate
your decrees.
96 I have seen a limit
to all perfection,
but your command is
without limit.

מ **Mem**

97 How I love your instruction!
It is my meditation all day long.

⁹⁸ Your commands make me
    wiser than my enemies,
for they are always with me.
⁹⁹ I have more insight than
    all my teachers
because your decrees are
    my meditation.   Ps 119:15
¹⁰⁰ I understand more
    than the elders   Jb 32:7-9
because I obey your precepts.
¹⁰¹ I have kept my feet
    from every evil path   Pr 1:15
to follow your word.
¹⁰² I have not turned from
    your judgments,   Dt 17:20
for you yourself have
    instructed me.
¹⁰³ How sweet your word is
    to my taste —   Ps 19:10; Pr 8:11
sweeter than honey in
    my mouth.
¹⁰⁴ I gain understanding
    from your precepts;   Ps 119:130
therefore I hate
    every false way.   Ps 119:128

ב Nun

¹⁰⁵ Your word is a lamp
    for my feet   Pr 6:23
and a light on my path.
¹⁰⁶ I have solemnly sworn
    to keep
    your righteous judgments.
¹⁰⁷ I am severely afflicted;
Lord, give me life according
    to your word.   Ps 119:25,50
¹⁰⁸ Lord, please accept
    my freewill offerings
    of praise,   Hs 14:2; Heb 13:15
and teach me
    your judgments.   Ps 119:12
¹⁰⁹ My life is constantly
    in danger,ᴬ
yet I do not forget
    your instruction.   Ps 119:16

¹¹⁰ The wicked have set a trap
    for me,   Ps 140:5; 141:9
but I have not wandered
    from your precepts.   Ps 119:10
¹¹¹ I have your decrees
    as a heritage forever;
indeed, they are the joy
    of my heart.   Ps 119:14,162
¹¹² I am resolved to obey
    your statutes
to the very end.ᴮ   Ps 119:33,36

ס Samek

¹¹³ I hate those who are
    double-minded,   1Kg 18:21; Jms 1:8
but I love your instruction.
¹¹⁴ You are my shelter
    and my shield;   Gn 15:1; Dt 33:29
I put my hope in your word.
¹¹⁵ Depart from me,
    you evil ones,   Ps 6:8; 139:19; Mt 4:10
so that I may obey
    my God's commands.
¹¹⁶ Sustain me as you promised,
    and I will live;   Ps 54:4
do not let me be ashamed
    of my hope.   Ps 25:20; 31:1; Rm 9:33
¹¹⁷ Sustain me so that I can
    be safe   Pr 29:25
and always be concerned
    about your statutes.   Ps 119:15
¹¹⁸ You reject all who stray
    from your statutes,   Ps 119:10,21
for their deceit is a lie.
¹¹⁹ You remove all the wicked
    on earth
as if they wereᶜ dross
    from metal;   Is 1:25; Ezk 22:18-19
therefore, I love your decrees.
¹²⁰ I trembleᴰ in awe of you;
I fear your judgments.

ע Ayin

¹²¹ I have done what is just
    and right;   Jb 29:14

ᴬ**119:109** Lit *in my hand*   ᴮ**119:112** Or *statutes; the reward is eternal*   ᶜ**119:119** Some Hb mss, DSS, LXX,
Aq, Sym, Jer read *All the wicked of the earth you count as*   ᴰ**119:120** Lit *My flesh shudders*

do not leave me to
 my oppressors.

122 Guarantee your servant's
  well-being;   Ps 119:134
do not let the arrogant
 oppress me.

123 My eyes grow weary
  looking for your salvation
and for your righteous
 promise.

124 Deal with your servant
  based on
  your faithful love;   Ps 51:1
teach me your statutes.

125 I am your servant;
  give me understanding
so that I may know
 your decrees.

126 It is time for the LORD to act,
 for they have violated
 your instruction.

127 Since I love your commands
  more than gold,
  even the purest gold,

128 I carefully follow all
  your precepts   Ps 19:8
and hate every false way.

פ *Pe*

129 Your decrees are wondrous;
  therefore I obey them.   Ps 119:22

130 The revelation of your words
  brings light   Pr 6:23
and gives understanding
 to the inexperienced.   Ps 19:7

131 I open my mouth and pant
 because I long
 for your commands.

132 Turn to me and be gracious
  to me,   Ps 25:16
as is your practice
 toward those who love
 your name.

133 Make my steps steady
 through your promise;
don't let any sin
 dominate me.   Ps 19:13; Rm 6:12

134 Redeem me
 from human oppression,
and I will keep your precepts.

135 Make your face shine on
  your servant,   Nm 6:25; Ps 31:16
and teach me your statutes.

136 My eyes pour out streams
  of tears   Jr 9:1; 14:17; Lm 3:48
because people do not follow
 your instruction.

צ *Tsade*

137 You are righteous, LORD,   145:17
and your judgments are just.

138 The decrees you issue
  are righteous
and altogether trustworthy.

139 My anger overwhelms me
 because my foes forget
  your words.   Ps 69:9; Jn 2:17

140 Your word is completely pure,
and your servant loves it.

141 I am insignificant
  and despised,   Ps 22:6
but I do not forget
  your precepts.   Ps 119:61

142 Your righteousness
  is an everlasting
  righteousness,
and your instruction is true.

143 Trouble and distress
  have overtaken me,
but your commands are
  my delight.   Ps 119:24

144 Your decrees are
  righteous forever.   Ps 19:9
Give me understanding,
 and I will live.

ק *Qoph*

145 I call with all my heart;
  answer me, LORD.
I will obey your statutes.

146 I call to you; save me,
and I will keep your decrees.

147 I rise before dawn
  and cry out for help;   Ps 5:3

I put my hope in your word.

148 I am awake through
each watch of the night
to meditate on your promise.

149 In keeping with
your faithful love,
hear my voice.
LORD, give me life
in keeping with
your justice.   Ps 119:25,124

150 Those who pursue evil plans ^A
come near;   Pr 6:17,18
they are far from
your instruction.

151 You are near, LORD,   Ps 34:18; 145:18
and all your commands
are true.   Ps 119:142

152 Long ago I learned from
your decrees
that you have established
them forever.   Ps 119:89; Lk 21:33

ר Resh

153 Consider my affliction
and rescue me,   Ps 119:50; Lm 5:1
for I have not forgotten
your instruction.   Ps 119:16

154 Champion my cause
and redeem me;   1Sm 24:15
give me life as you promised.

155 Salvation is far
from the wicked
because they do not study
your statutes.   Ps 119:45,94

156 Your compassions are
many, LORD;   2Sm 24:14
give me life according to
your judgments.

157 My persecutors and foes
are many.   Ps 7:1
I have not turned
from your decrees.   Ps 119:51

158 I have seen the disloyal
and feel disgust Ps 139:21; Pr 14:14
because they do not keep
your word.

159 Consider how I love
your precepts;
LORD, give me life according to
your faithful love.   Ps 119:25,47

160 The entirety of your word
is truth,
each of your righteous
judgments endures forever.

ש Sin / ש Shin

161 Princes have persecuted me
without cause,
but my heart fears only
your word.   Ps 119:23,120

162 I rejoice over your promise
like one who finds
vast treasure.

163 I hate and abhor falsehood,
but I love your instruction.

164 I praise you seven times
a day
for your righteous judgments.

165 Abundant peace belongs
to those   Pr 3:1-2; Is 26:3; 32:17
who love your instruction;
nothing makes them
stumble.   Pr 3:23; Is 63:13

166 LORD, I hope for
your salvation   Gn 49:18
and carry out your commands.

167 I obey your decrees
and love them greatly.

168 I obey your precepts
and decrees,
for all my ways are before you.

ת Taw

169 Let my cry reach you, LORD;
give me understanding
according to your word.

170 Let my plea reach you;   Ps 28:2
rescue me according to
your promise.   Ps 22:20; 59:1

171 My lips pour out praise,   Ps 51:15
for you teach me
your statutes.   Ps 119:12

^A 119:150 Some Hb mss, LXX, Sym, Jer read *who maliciously persecute me*

172 My tongue sings
    about your promise,   Ps 51:14
for all your commands
    are righteous.   Ps 119:138
173 May your hand be ready
    to help me,   Ps 37:24; 73:23
for I have chosen
    your precepts.   Jos 24:22
174 I long for your salvation,
    LORD,
and your instruction is
    my delight.   Ps 119:16,24,166
175 Let me live, and I will
    praise you;   Ps 119:25
may your judgments
    help me.
176 I wander like a lost sheep;
seek your servant,   Mt 18:12; Lk 15:4
for I do not forget
    your commands.   Ps 119:16

A Cry for Truth and Peace

120 *A song of ascents.*
In my distress I called
to the LORD,
and he answered me.   Ps 18:6
2 "LORD, rescue me
    from lying lips
and a deceitful tongue."   Pr 12:22

3 What will he give you,
and what will he do to you,
you deceitful tongue?   Zph 3:13
4 A warrior's sharp arrows
with burning charcoal!ᴬ

5 What misery that I have
    stayed in Meshech,ᴮ   Ezk 27:13
that I have lived among
    the tents of Kedar!ᶜ   Sg 1:5
6 I have dwelt too long
with those who hate peace.
7 I am for peace;
    but when I speak,
they are for war.   Ps 109:4

The LORD Our Protector

121 *A song of ascents.*
I lift my eyes
toward the mountains.
Where will my help
    come from?   Ps 87:1; 123:1
2 My help comes
    from the LORD,
the Maker of heaven
    and earth.   Ps 115:15; 124:8

3 He will not allow your foot
    to slip;
your Protector will not
    slumber.   Ps 41:2; 66:9; 127:1
4 Indeed, the Protector
    of Israel
does not slumber or sleep.

5 The LORD protects you;
the LORD is a shelter right
    by your side.ᴰ   Ps 16:8; 91:1,4
6 The sun will not strike you
    by day
or the moon by night.   Is 49:10

7 The LORD will protect you
    from all harm;
he will protect your life.   Ps 41:2
8 The LORD will protect
    your coming and going
both now and forever.   Dt 28:6

A Prayer for Jerusalem

122 *A song of ascents. Of David.*
I rejoiced with those
    who said to me,
"Let us go to the house
    of the LORD."   Is 2:3; Mc 4:2; Zch 8:21
2 Our feet were standing
within your gates,
    Jerusalem —   Ps 9:14; Jr 7:2

3 Jerusalem, built as a city
    should be,

ᴬ120:4 Lit *with coals of the broom bush*   ᴮ120:5 = a people far to the north of Palestine
ᶜ120:5 = a nomadic people of the desert to the southeast   ᴰ121:5 Lit *is your shelter at your right hand*

solidly united,   Neh 4:6; Ps 147:2
4 where the tribes, the LORD's
tribes, go up
to give thanks to the name
of the LORD.   Is 2:3; Mc 4:2
(This is an ordinance
for Israel.)   1Ch 22:13
5 There, thrones for judgment
are placed,
thrones of the house
of David.   Dt 17:8; 2Ch 19:8

6 Pray for the well-being[A]
of Jerusalem:
"May those who love you
be secure;   Ps 51:18; Jr 29:7
7 may there be peace
within your walls,
security
within your fortresses."
8 Because of my brothers
and friends,
I will say, "May peace be
in you."[B]   1Sm 25:6; Ps 85:8
9 Because of the house
of the LORD our God,
I will pursue your prosperity.

Looking for God's Favor

123 *A song of ascents.*
I lift my eyes to you,
the one enthroned in heaven.
2 Like a servant's eyes
on his master's hand,
like a servant girl's eyes
on her mistress's hand,
so our eyes are on the LORD
our God
until he shows us favor.   Ps 25:15

3 Show us favor, LORD,
show us favor,
for we've had more than
enough contempt.   Neh 4:4
4 We've had more than enough
scorn from the arrogant

and contempt
from the proud.   Is 32:9,11; Am 6:1

The LORD Is on Our Side

124 *A song of ascents. Of David.*
If the LORD had not been
on our side —
let Israel say —
2 If the LORD had not been
on our side   Ps 94:17
when people attacked us,
3 then they would have
swallowed us alive
in their burning anger
against us.   Ps 35:25; 56:1; Pr 1:12
4 Then the water would have
engulfed us;
the torrent would have swept
over us;
5 the raging water would have
swept over us.   Jb 22:11; Ps 32:6

6 Blessed be the LORD,
who has not let us be
ripped apart by their teeth.
7 We have escaped like a bird
from the hunter's net;
the net is torn,
and we have escaped.   Ps 91:3
8 Our help is in the name
of the LORD,
the Maker of heaven
and earth.   Ps 115:15; 121:2

Israel's Stability

125 *A song of ascents.*
Those who trust
in the LORD are
like Mount Zion.
It cannot be shaken;
it remains forever.   Ps 46:5
2 The mountains surround
Jerusalem
and the LORD surrounds
his people,
both now and forever.   Zch 2:5

[A]122:6 Or *peace*   [B]122:8 = Jerusalem

3 The scepter of the wicked
    will not remain
over the land allotted
    to the righteous,
so that the righteous
    will not apply their hands
    to injustice.   Ps 89:22; Is 14:5
4 Do what is good, Lord,
    to the good,
to those whose hearts
    are upright.   Ps 7:10; 119:68
5 But as for those
    who turn aside
    to crooked ways,
the Lord will banish them
    with the evildoers.   Ps 92:7,9

Peace be with Israel.   Ps 128:5-6

Zion's Restoration

126 *A song of ascents.*
    When the Lord restored
    the fortunes of Zion, [A]
we were like those
    who dream.   Ps 85:1; Jr 29:14
2 Our mouths were filled
    with laughter then,   Jb 8:21
and our tongues with shouts
    of joy.   Ps 51:14
Then they said
    among the nations,
"The Lord has done
    great things for them."
3 The Lord had done
    great things for us;
we were joyful.   Is 25:9

4 Restore our fortunes, [B] Lord,
    like watercourses
    in the Negev.   Is 35:6; 43:19
5 Those who sow in tears
    will reap with shouts of joy.
6 Though one goes along
    weeping,
    carrying the bag of seed,

he will surely come back
    with shouts of joy,
    carrying his sheaves.   Is 35:10

The Blessing of the Lord

127 *A song of ascents.*
    Of Solomon.
1 Unless the Lord builds
    a house,
its builders labor over it
    in vain;   Ps 78:69
unless the Lord watches over
    a city,
the watchman stays alert
    in vain.   Ps 121:4
2 In vain you get up early
    and stay up late,
working hard to have
    enough food —
yes, he gives sleep to the one
    he loves. [C]   Ps 3:5; 4:8; Pr 3:24

3 Sons are indeed a heritage
    from the Lord,
offspring, a reward.   Dt 7:13
4 Like arrows in the hand
    of a warrior
are the sons born in
    one's youth.   Ps 120:4
5 Happy is the man who
    has filled his quiver
    with them.   Ps 128:2-3
They will never be put
    to shame
when they speak
    with their enemies
    at the city gate.   Jl 2:26-27

Blessings for Those Who Fear God

128 *A song of ascents.*
    How happy is everyone
    who fears the Lord,
    who walks in his ways!   Ps 112:1
2 You will surely eat

[A]126:1 Or *Lord returned those of Zion who had been captives*   [B]126:4 Or *Return our captives*
[C]127:2 Or *yes, he gives such things to his loved ones while they sleep*

what your hands
 have worked for.   Is 3:10
You will be happy,
 and it will go well for you.
3 Your wife will be
  like a fruitful vine
 within your house,
 your children,
  like young olive trees
 around your table.   Ps 52:8
4 In this very way
 the man who fears the LORD
 will be blessed.   Ps 115:13

5 May the LORD bless you
  from Zion,
 so that you will see
  the prosperity
  of Jerusalem
 all the days of your life   Ps 20:2
6 and will see your children's
  children!

 Peace be with Israel.   Ps 125:5

Protection of the Oppressed

129 *A song of ascents.*
 Since my youth they
  have often attacked me —
 let Israel say —
2 Since my youth they have
  often attacked me,
 but they have not prevailed
  against me.   Jr 1:19; 20:11
3 Plowmen plowed
  over my back;
 they made
  their furrows long.   Mc 3:12
4 The LORD is righteous;
 he has cut the ropes
  of the wicked.   Ps 2:3

5 Let all who hate Zion
 be driven back in disgrace.
6 Let them be like grass
  on the rooftops,

which withers before
 it grows up[A]   2Kg 19:26; Is 37:27
7 and can't even fill the hands
  of the reaper
 or the arms of the one
  who binds sheaves.   Ps 79:12
8 Then none who pass by
  will say,
 "May the LORD's blessing be
  on you.
 We bless you in the name
  of the LORD."   Ru 2:4; Ps 118:26

Awaiting Redemption

130 *A song of ascents.*
 Out of the depths
  I call to you, LORD!   Ps 69:2
2 Lord, listen to my voice;
 let your ears be attentive
  to my cry for help.   2Ch 6:40; Ps 140:6

3 LORD, if you kept an account
  of iniquities,
 Lord, who could stand?   Ps 76:7
4 But with you there is
  forgiveness,
 so that you may
  be revered.   1Kg 8:39-40; Ps 86:5

5 I wait for the LORD; I wait
 and put my hope
  in his word.   Ps 33:20; 119:74,81
6 I wait for the Lord
 more than watchmen
  for the morning —
 more than watchmen
  for the morning.   Ps 63:6; 119:147

7 Israel, put your hope
  in the LORD.   Ps 131:3
For there is faithful love
  with the LORD,
 and with him is redemption
  in abundance.   Ps 111:9
8 And he will redeem Israel
 from all its iniquities.   Lk 1:68

A 129:6 Or *it can be pulled out*

A Childlike Spirit

131

A song of ascents. Of David.

LORD, my heart is not proud;
my eyes are not haughty.
I do not get involved
   with things
too great or too wondrous
   for me.   Jb 42:3; Ps 139:6

2 Instead, I have calmed
   and quieted my soul
like a weaned child
   with its mother;
my soul is like a
   weaned child.   Mt 18:3; 1Co 14:20

3 Israel, put your hope
   in the LORD,
both now and forever.   Ps 130:7

David and Zion Chosen

132

A song of ascents.

LORD, remember David
and all the hardships
   he endured,   2Sm 16:12

2 and how he swore an oath
   to the LORD,
making a vow
   to the Mighty One of Jacob:

3 "I will not enter my house
or get into my bed,

4 I will not allow my eyes
   to sleep
or my eyelids to slumber   Pr 6:4

5 until I find a place
   for the LORD,
a dwelling
   for the Mighty One
   of Jacob."   1Ch 22:7; Ac 7:46

6 We heard of the ark
   in Ephrathah;[A]   Gn 35:19; Ru 4:11
we found it in the fields
   of Jaar.[B]   1Sm 7:1

7 Let us go
   to his dwelling place;

let us worship
   at his footstool.   1Ch 28:2; Ps 99:5

8 Rise up, LORD, come to
   your resting place,
you and your powerful ark.

9 May your priests be clothed
   with righteousness,
and may your faithful people
   shout for joy.   Jb 29:14; Ps 149:5

10 For the sake of
   your servant David,
do not reject
   your anointed one.[C]   2Ch 6:42

11 The LORD swore an oath
   to David,
a promise he will not
   abandon:
"I will set
   one of your offspring[D]
on your throne.   2Sm 7:12-16; Ps 89:3

12 If your sons keep
   my covenant
and my decrees
   that I will teach them,
their sons will also sit on
   your throne forever."   1Kg 8:25

13 For the LORD has chosen
   Zion;
he has desired it
   for his home: Ps 68:16; 78:68

14 "This is my resting
   place forever;
I will make my home here
   because I have desired it.

15 I will abundantly bless
   its food;
I will satisfy its needy
   with bread.   Ps 107:9; 147:14

16 I will clothe its priests
   with salvation,
and its faithful people
   will shout for joy.   2Ch 6:41

17 There I will make
   a horn grow for David;

A132:6 = Bethlehem   B132:6 = Kiriath-jearim   C132:10 = the king   D132:11 Lit *set the fruit of your belly*

I have prepared a lamp for
my anointed one.   1Kg 11:36
18 I will clothe his enemies
with shame,   Jb 8:22
but the crown he wears^A
will be glorious."   Ps 21:3

Living in Harmony

133 *A song of ascents. Of David.*
How good and pleasant
it is
when brothers live together
in harmony!   Gn 13:8; Heb 13:1
2 It is like fine oil on the head,
running down on the beard,
running down Aaron's beard
onto his robes.   Ex 30:25,30; Lv 8:12
3 It is like the dew of Hermon^B
falling on the mountains
of Zion.   Ps 48:1-2; Mc 5:7
For there the Lord
has appointed
the blessing —
life forevermore.   Ps 21:4

Call to Evening Worship

134 *A song of ascents.*
Now bless the Lord,
all you servants of the Lord
who stand
in the Lord's house at night!
2 Lift up your hands in the
holy place
and bless the Lord!   Ps 28:2; 63:2

3 May the Lord,
Maker of heaven and earth,
bless you from Zion.   Ps 115:15

The Lord Is Great

135 Hallelujah!
Praise the name
of the Lord.
Give praise, you servants
of the Lord   Ps 113:1; 134:1

2 who stand in the house
of the Lord,
in the courts of the house
of our God.   Ps 92:13; 116:19
3 Praise the Lord, for the Lord
is good;
sing praise to his name,
for it is delightful.   Ps 100:5; 147:1
4 For the Lord has chosen Jacob
for himself,
Israel as his treasured
possession.   Ex 19:5; Dt 7:6-7; 10:15
5 For I know that the Lord
is great;
our Lord is greater
than all gods.   Ps 95:3; 97:9
6 The Lord does
whatever he pleases
in heaven and on earth,
in the seas and all the depths.
7 He causes the clouds to rise
from the ends of the earth.
He makes lightning
for the rain
and brings the wind
from his storehouses.   Jr 10:13

8 He struck down the firstborn
of Egypt,
both people and animals.
9 He sent signs and wonders
against you, Egypt,
against Pharaoh and all
his officials.   Dt 6:22; Ps 78:43
10 He struck down many nations
and slaughtered
mighty kings: Ps 44:2; 136:17-22
11 Sihon king of the Amorites,
Og king of Bashan,
and all the kings of Canaan.
12 He gave their land
as an inheritance,
an inheritance to his people
Israel.   Dt 29:8; Ps 78:55

---

^A**132:18** Lit *but on him his crown*   ^B**133:3** The tallest mountain in the region, noted for its abundant precipitation

¹³ Lord, your name
   endures forever,
your reputation, Lord,
through all generations. Ex 3:15

¹⁴ For the Lord will vindicate
   his people
and have compassion
   on his servants. Dt 32:36; Ps 90:13

¹⁵ The idols of the nations are
   of silver and gold,
made by human hands. Is 37:19

¹⁶ They have mouths
   but cannot speak,   Hab 2:18
eyes, but cannot see.

¹⁷ They have ears
   but cannot hear;
indeed, there is no breath
   in their mouths.   Is 46:7

¹⁸ Those who make them
   are just like them,
as are all who trust in them.

¹⁹ House of Israel,
   bless the Lord!   Ps 115:9; 118:2
House of Aaron,
   bless the Lord!   Ps 115:10; 118:3

²⁰ House of Levi, bless the Lord!
You who revere the Lord,
   bless the Lord!   Ps 22:23; 115:11

²¹ Blessed be the Lord from Zion;
he dwells in Jerusalem.
Hallelujah!

God's Love Is Eternal

136
 Give thanks to the Lord,
   for he is good. Ps 106:1; 107:1
   His faithful love
   endures forever.

² Give thanks to the God
   of gods.
   His faithful love
   endures forever.

³ Give thanks to the Lord
   of lords.   Dt 10:17
   His faithful love
   endures forever.

⁴ He alone does great wonders.
   His faithful love
   endures forever.

⁵ He made the heavens skillfully.
   His faithful love
   endures forever.

⁶ He spread the land
   on the waters.   Ps 24:2
   His faithful love
   endures forever.

⁷ He made the great lights:
   His faithful love
   endures forever.

⁸ the sun to rule by day,
   His faithful love
   endures forever.

⁹ the moon and stars to rule
   by night.   Gn 1:16
   His faithful love
   endures forever.

¹⁰ He struck the firstborn
   of the Egyptians   Ex 12:29
   His faithful love
   endures forever.

¹¹ and brought Israel out
   from among them
   His faithful love
   endures forever.

¹² with a strong hand
   and outstretched arm. Ex 6:1
   His faithful love
   endures forever.

¹³ He divided the Red Sea   Ex 14:21
   His faithful love
   endures forever.

¹⁴ and led Israel through,   Ps 106:9
   His faithful love
   endures forever.

¹⁵ but hurled Pharaoh
   and his army
   into the Red Sea.   Ex 14:27; 106:11
   His faithful love
   endures forever.

¹⁶ He led his people
   in the wilderness.   Dt 8:15
   His faithful love
   endures forever.

17 He struck down great kings
   His faithful love
   endures forever.
18 and slaughtered
   famous kings —
   His faithful love
   endures forever.
19 Sihon king of the Amorites
   His faithful love
   endures forever.
20 and Og king of Bashan —
   His faithful love
   endures forever.
21 and gave their land as
   an inheritance,
   His faithful love
   endures forever.
22 an inheritance to Israel
   his servant.   Nm 21:21-35
   His faithful love
   endures forever.
23 He remembered us
   in our humiliation   Ps 106:45
   His faithful love
   endures forever.
24 and rescued us
   from our foes.
   His faithful love
   endures forever.
25 He gives food
   to every creature.   Ps 104:27
   His faithful love
   endures forever.
26 Give thanks to the God
   of heaven!   Neh 1:5
   His faithful love
   endures forever.

Lament of the Exiles

137 By the rivers
      of Babylon —
   there we sat down and wept
   when we remembered Zion.
2 There we hung up our lyres
   on the poplar trees,   Jb 30:31

3 for our captors there asked
   us for songs,
   and our tormentors,
   for rejoicing:
   "Sing us one of the songs
   of Zion."   Ps 80:6
4 How can we sing
   the LORD's song
   on foreign soil?   Neh 12:46
5 If I forget you, Jerusalem,
   may my right hand forget
   its skill.   Is 65:11
6 May my tongue stick
   to the roof of my mouth
   if I do not remember you,
   if I do not exalt Jerusalem
   as my greatest joy!   Jb 29:10
7 Remember, LORD,
   what the Edomites said
   that day A at Jerusalem:
   "Destroy it! Destroy it
   down to its foundations!"
8 Daughter Babylon,
   doomed to destruction,
   happy is the one
   who pays you back
   what you have done to us.
9 Happy is he who takes
   your little ones
   and dashes them
   against the rocks.   2Kg 8:12

A Thankful Heart

138 *Of David.*
   I will give you thanks
   with all my heart;   Ps 111:1
   I will sing your praise before
   the heavenly beings. B Ps 95:3
2 I will bow down
   toward your holy temple
   and give thanks to your name
   for your constant love
   and truth.

A **137:7** The day Jerusalem fell to the Babylonians in 586 BC   B **138:1** Or *before the gods*, or *before judges*,
or *before kings* ; Hb *elohim*

You have exalted your name
and your promise above
everything else.[A]   1Kg 8:29; Ps 5:7

³ On the day I called,
you answered me;
you increased strength
within me.[B]   Ps 28:7; 46:1

⁴ All the kings on earth
will give you thanks, LORD,
when they hear what you
have promised.[C]   Ps 72:11; 102:15

⁵ They will sing of
the LORD's ways,
for the LORD's glory is great.

⁶ Though the LORD is exalted,
he takes note of the humble;
but he knows the haughty
from a distance.   Ps 113:4-7

⁷ If I walk into the thick
of danger,
you will preserve my life
from the anger
of my enemies.   Ps 23:4
You will extend your hand;
your right hand will save me.

⁸ The LORD will fulfill
his purpose for me.   Ps 57:2
LORD, your faithful love
endures forever;
do not abandon the work
of your hands.   Jb 10:3; Ps 100:3

The All-Knowing, Ever-Present God

139
*For the choir director.
A psalm of David.*

¹ LORD, you have searched me
and known me.   Ps 17:3; 44:21

² You know when I sit down
and when I stand up;
you understand my thoughts
from far away.   2Kg 19:27; Is 66:18

³ You observe my travels
and my rest;
you are aware of all
my ways.   Jb 14:16; 31:4

⁴ Before a word is
on my tongue,
you know all about it, LORD.

⁵ You have encircled me;
you have placed your hand
on me.   Jb 9:33; Ps 125:2

⁶ This wondrous knowledge is
beyond me.
It is lofty; I am unable
to reach it.   Jb 42:3; Rm 11:33

⁷ Where can I go to escape
your Spirit?
Where can I flee
from your presence?   Jr 23:24

⁸ If I go up to heaven,
you are there;   Am 9:2-4
if I make my bed in Sheol,
you are there.   Jb 26:6; Is 14:11

⁹ If I live at the eastern horizon
or settle
at the western limits,[D]

¹⁰ even there your hand
will lead me;
your right hand will hold on
to me.   Ps 23:2-3

¹¹ If I say, "Surely the darkness
will hide me,
and the light around me
will be night" —   Jb 22:13-14

¹² even the darkness is not dark
to you.
The night shines like the day;
darkness and light are alike
to you.   Jb 34:22; Dn 2:22

¹³ For it was you who created
my inward parts;[E]
you knit me together
in my mother's womb.

[A]138:2 Or *You have exalted your promise above all your name*   [B]138:3 Hb obscure   [C]138:4 Lit *hear the words of your mouth*   [D]139:9 Lit *I take up the wings of the dawn; I dwell at the end of the sea*   [E]139:13 Lit *my kidneys*

¹⁴ I will praise you
because I have
   been remarkably
   and wondrously made. [A,B]
Your works are wondrous,
and I know this very well.
¹⁵ My bones were not hidden
   from you
when I was made in secret,
when I was formed
   in the depths
   of the earth.
¹⁶ Your eyes saw me when
   I was formless;
all my days were written
   in your book and planned
before a single one of them
   began.   Jb 14:5

¹⁷ God, how precious [C]
   your thoughts are
   to me;
how vast their sum is!
¹⁸ If I counted them,
they would outnumber
   the grains of sand;   Ps 40:5; 92:5
when I wake up, [D]
   I am still with you.   Ps 3:5

¹⁹ God, if only you would kill
   the wicked —
you bloodthirsty men,
   stay away from me —   Ps 5:6
²⁰ who invoke you deceitfully.
Your enemies swear
   by you falsely.   Ex 20:7; Jd 15
²¹ Lord, don't I hate those
   who hate you,
and detest those who rebel
   against you?
²² I hate them
   with extreme hatred;
I consider them
   my enemies.

²³ Search me, God, and know
   my heart;
test me and know
   my concerns.   Jb 31:6; Ps 26:2
²⁴ See if there is any
   offensive [E] way in me;
lead me in the
   everlasting way.   Ps 16:11

Prayer for Rescue

140 *For the choir director.
A psalm of David.*

¹ Rescue me, Lord,
   from evil men.
Keep me safe
   from violent men   Ps 18:48; 71:4
² who plan evil in their hearts.
They stir up wars all day
   long.   Ps 36:4; 56:6; Pr 6:14
³ They make their tongues
as sharp as a snake's bite;
viper's venom is under
   their lips.   *Selah*

⁴ Protect me, Lord,
from the power of the wicked.
Keep me safe
   from violent men
who plan
   to make me stumble. [F] Ps 36:11
⁵ The proud hide a trap
   with ropes for me;
they spread a net along
   the path
and set snares for me.   *Selah*

⁶ I say to the Lord,
   "You are my God."
Listen, Lord, to my cry
   for help.   Ps 31:14; 130:2
⁷ Lord, my Lord,
   my strong Savior,
you shield my head
   on the day of battle.   Ps 28:8

[A] **139:14** DSS, some LXX mss, Syr, Jer read *because you are remarkable and wonderful*   [B] **139:14** Hb obscure   [C] **139:17** Or *difficult*   [D] **139:18** Some Hb mss read *I come to an end*   [E] **139:24** Or *idolatrous*   [F] **140:4** Lit *to trip up my steps*

⁸ LORD, do not grant
    the desires of the wicked;
do not let them achieve
    their goals.
Otherwise, they will become
    proud.   *Selah*

⁹ When those
    who surround me
    rise up, ^A
may the trouble their lips
    cause overwhelm them.

¹⁰ Let hot coals fall on them.
Let them be thrown
    into the fire,
into the abyss, never again
    to rise.   Ps 11:6; 36:12

¹¹ Do not let a slanderer stay
    in the land.
Let evil relentlessly ^B
    hunt down a violent man.

¹² I ^C know that the LORD
    upholds
the just cause of the poor,
    justice for the needy.   1Kg 8:45,49

¹³ Surely the righteous
    will praise your name;
the upright will live in
    your presence.   Ps 11:7; 64:10

Protection from Sin and Sinners

141
A psalm of David.
    LORD, I call on you; hurry
to help me.
Listen to my voice when I call
    on you.   Ps 22:19; 38:22; 70:5

² May my prayer be set
    before you as incense,   Ex 30:8
the raising of my hands
    as the evening offering.

³ LORD, set up a guard
    for my mouth;

keep watch at the door
    of my lips.   Ps 34:13; 39:1; Pr 13:3

⁴ Do not let my heart turn
    to any evil thing
or perform wicked acts
with men who commit sin.
Do not let me feast
    on their delicacies.   Ps 119:36

⁵ Let the righteous one
    strike me —
it is an act of
    faithful love;
let him rebuke me —
it is oil for my head;
let me ^D not refuse it.   Ec 7:5; Gl 6:1
Even now my prayer
    is against
the evil acts
    of the wicked. ^E   Ps 109:4

⁶ When their rulers ^F
    will be thrown off
the sides of a cliff,
the people ^G will listen
    to my words,
for they are pleasing.   2Ch 25:12

⁷ As when one plows and
    breaks up the soil,
turning up rocks,
so our ^H bones
    have been scattered
at the mouth of Sheol.   Ps 53:5

⁸ But my eyes look to you,
    LORD, my Lord.
I seek refuge in you; do not
    let me die. ^I   Ps 7:1; 57:1; 144:2

⁹ Protect me from the trap
    they have set for me,
and from the snares
    of evildoers.   Ps 38:12; 140:5

¹⁰ Let the wicked fall
    into their own nets,
while I pass by safely.   Ps 7:15

---

^A **140:9** Lit *Head of those who surround me*   ^B **140:11** Hb obscure   ^C **140:12** Alt Hb tradition reads *You*
^D **141:5** Lit *my head*   ^E **141:5** Lit *of them*   ^F **141:6** Or *judges*   ^G **141:6** Lit *cliff, and they*   ^H **141:7** DSS reads
my; some LXX mss, Syr read *their*   ^I **141:8** Or *not pour out my life*

A Cry of Distress

142

A Maskil of David. When he was in the cave. A prayer.

1 I cry aloud to the LORD;   Ps 3:4
I plead aloud to the LORD
    for mercy.   Ps 30:8

2 I pour out my complaint
    before him;
I reveal my trouble to him.

3 Although my spirit is weak
    within me,
you know my way.   Ps 77:3; 143:4

Along this path I travel
they have hidden a trap
    for me.   Ps 140:5

4 Look to the right and see:[A]
no one stands up for me;
there is no refuge for me;
no one cares about me.   Ps 69:20

5 I cry to you, LORD;
I say, "You are my shelter,
my portion in the land
    of the living."   Ps 16:5; 27:13

6 Listen to my cry,
for I am very weak.   Ps 79:8; 116:6
Rescue me from those
    who pursue me,
for they are too strong for me.

7 Free me from prison
so that I can praise
    your name.
The righteous will gather
    around me
because you deal generously
    with me.   Ps 13:6; 143:11

A Cry for Help

143

A psalm of David.

LORD, hear my prayer.
In your faithfulness
    listen to my plea,
and in your righteousness
    answer me.   Ps 71:2; 140:6

2 Do not bring your servant
    into judgment,   Jb 14:3
for no one alive is righteous
    in your sight.   Jb 15:14; Ps 130:3

3 For the enemy
    has pursued me,
crushing me to the ground,
making me live in darkness
like those long dead.   Ps 88:3-6

4 My spirit is weak
    within me;
my heart is overcome
    with dismay.   Ps 77:3; 142:3

5 I remember the days of old;
I meditate on
    all you have done;
I reflect on the work
    of your hands.   Ps 77:5,10-12

6 I spread out my hands to you;
I am like parched land
    before you.   *Selah*

7 Answer me quickly, LORD;
my spirit fails.   Ps 69:17; 102:2
Don't hide your face
    from me,
or I will be like those
going down to the Pit.   Ps 28:1

8 Let me experience
your faithful love
    in the morning,
for I trust in you.   Ps 90:14
Reveal to me the way
    I should go
because I appeal to you.

9 Rescue me from my enemies,
    LORD;
I come to you for
    protection.[B]   Ps 31:15; 59:1; 142:6

10 Teach me to do your will,
for you are my God.   Ps 25:4-5; 63:1
May your gracious Spirit
lead me on level ground.

[A]**142:4** DSS, LXX, Syr, Vg, Tg read *I look to the right and I see*   [B]**143:9** One Hb ms, LXX; some Hb mss read *I cover myself to you*

11 For your name's
   sake, Lord,
let me live.
In your righteousness
   deliver me from trouble,
12 and in your faithful love
   destroy my enemies.
Wipe out all those
   who attack me,
for I am your servant.   Ps 54:5

A King's Prayer

144 *Of David.*
   Blessed be the Lord,
   my rock   1Sm 2:2; Ps 18:2; 19:14; 92:15
who trains my hands
   for battle
and my fingers for warfare.
2 He is my faithful love
   and my fortress,
my stronghold
   and my deliverer.
He is my shield, and I take
   refuge in him;   Dt 33:29; Ps 3:3; 91:4
he subdues my people^A
   under me.   Ps 18:39,47

3 Lord, what is a human
   that you care for him,
a son of man^B that you think
   of him?   Jb 7:17; Ps 8:4; Heb 2:6
4 A human is like a breath;
his days are like
   a passing shadow.   Ps 102:11

5 Lord, part your heavens
   and come down.   2Sm 22:10
Touch the mountains,
   and they will smoke.   Ps 104:32
6 Flash your lightning
   and scatter the foe;^C
shoot your arrows and rout
   them.   Ps 18:14; Hab 3:11; Zch 9:14
7 Reach down^D from on high;

rescue me from deep water,
   and set me free
from the grasp of foreigners
8 whose mouths speak lies,
whose right hands
   are deceptive.   Ps 12:2; 41:6; 106:26

9 God, I will sing a new song
   to you;
I will play on a ten-stringed
   harp for you —   Ps 33:2-3; 40:3
10 the one who gives victory
   to kings,
who frees his servant David
   from the deadly sword.   Ps 18:50
11 Set me free and rescue me
   from foreigners   Ps 69:14
whose mouths speak lies,
whose right hands
   are deceptive.   Ps 12:2; 41:6; 106:26

12 Then our sons will be
   like plants
nurtured in their youth,
our daughters,
   like corner pillars
that are carved
   in the palace style.   Ps 92:12-14
13 Our storehouses will be full,
supplying all kinds of produce;
our flocks will increase
   by thousands
and tens of thousands in
   our open fields.   Pr 3:9-10
14 Our cattle will be well fed.^E
There will be no breach
   in the walls,
no going into captivity,^F
and no cry of lament in
   our public squares.   Is 24:11
15 Happy are the people with
   such blessings.
Happy are the people
   whose God is the Lord.

^A**144:2** Some Hb mss, DSS, Aq, Syr, Tg, Jer read *subdues peoples*; 2Sm 22:48; Ps 18:47   ^B**144:3** Or *a mere mortal*   ^C**144:6** Lit *scatter them*   ^D**144:7** Lit *down your hands*   ^E**144:14** Or *will bear heavy loads*, or *will be pregnant*   ^F**144:14** Or *be no plague, no miscarriage*

Praising God's Greatness

145 *A hymn of David.*
I[A] exalt you, my God
the King,
and bless your name
forever and ever.   Ps 30:1; 34:1

2 I will bless you every day;
I will praise your name
forever and ever.   Ps 146:2

3 The LORD is great
and is highly praised;   Ps 48:1
his greatness is
unsearchable.   Jb 5:9; 9:10; Is 40:28

4 One generation will declare
your works to the next
and will proclaim
your mighty acts.   Ps 22:30-31

5 I[B] will speak of your splendor
and glorious majesty
and[C] your wondrous works.

6 They will proclaim the power
of your awe-inspiring acts,
and I will declare
your greatness.[D]   Dt 10:21

7 They will give a testimony
of your great goodness
and will joyfully sing
of your righteousness.   Is 63:7

8 The LORD is gracious
and compassionate,
slow to anger and great
in faithful love.   Ex 34:6; Ps 86:5,15

9 The LORD is good
to everyone;   Ac 14:17
his compassion rests
on all he has made.   Ps 100:5

10 All you have made
will thank you, LORD;
the[E] faithful will bless you.

11 They will speak of the glory
of your kingdom

and will declare
your might,   Jr 14:21

12 informing all people
of your mighty acts
and of the glorious splendor
of your[F] kingdom.   Ps 105:1

13 Your kingdom is
an everlasting kingdom;
your rule is for all
generations.   Ps 10:16; 2Pt 1:11
The LORD is faithful in all
his words
and gracious in all
his actions.[G]   Ps 103:8

14 The LORD helps all who fall;
he raises up all
who are oppressed.[H]   Ps 37:24

15 All eyes look to you,
and you give them their food
at the proper time.   Ps 104:27

16 You open your hand
and satisfy the desire
of every living thing.   Ps 104:28

17 The LORD is righteous
in all his ways
and faithful in all his acts.

18 The LORD is near all
who call out to him,
all who call out to him
with integrity.   Dt 4:7; Ps 34:18

19 He fulfills the desires
of those who fear him;
he hears their cry for help
and saves them.   Ps 10:17; 21:2

20 The LORD guards all those
who love him,
but he destroys
all the wicked.   Ps 31:23; 97:10

21 My mouth will declare
the LORD's praise;
let every living thing

[A]145:1 The lines of this poem form an acrostic.   [B]145:5 LXX, Syr read *They*   [C]145:5 LXX, Syr read *and they will tell of*   [D]145:6 Alt Hb tradition, Jer read *great deeds*   [E]145:10 Lit *your*   [F]145:12 LXX, Syr, Jer; MT reads *his*   [G]145:13 One Hb ms, DSS, LXX, Syr; some Hb mss omit *The LORD is faithful in all his words and gracious in all his actions.*   [H]145:14 Lit *bowed down*

bless his holy name forever
and ever.   Ps 65:2; 150:6

The God of Compassion

146
Hallelujah!
My soul,
praise the LORD.   Ps 103:1

2 I will praise the LORD
all my life;
I will sing to my God
as long as I live.   Ps 63:4; 104:33

3 Do not trust in nobles,
in a son of man,[A]
who cannot save.   Ps 60:11; 108:12

4 When his breath[B]
leaves him,
he returns to the ground;
on that day his plans die.

5 Happy is the one whose help
is the God of Jacob,
whose hope is in the LORD
his God,   Ps 144:15; Jr 17:7

6 the Maker of heaven
and earth,
the sea and everything
in them.   Ps 115:15; Ac 14:15
He remains faithful forever,

7 executing justice
for the exploited
and giving food
to the hungry.   Ps 103:6; 107:9
The LORD frees prisoners.

8 The LORD opens the eyes of
the blind.   Mt 9:27-30; Jn 9:7
The LORD raises up those
who are oppressed.[C]   Ps 145:15
The LORD loves the righteous.

9 The LORD protects
resident aliens
and helps the fatherless
and the widow,   Ex 22:22-23
but he frustrates the ways
of the wicked.   Ps 147:6

10 The LORD reigns forever;
Zion, your God reigns
for all generations.   Ex 15:18
Hallelujah!

God Restores Jerusalem

147
Hallelujah!
How good it is to sing
to our God,
for praise is pleasant
and lovely.   Ps 33:1; 135:3

2 The LORD rebuilds Jerusalem;
he gathers Israel's
exiled people.   Dt 30:3; Ezk 39:28

3 He heals the brokenhearted
and bandages their wounds.

4 He counts the number
of the stars;
he gives names to all of them.

5 Our Lord is great,
vast in power;
his understanding is infinite.[D]

6 The LORD helps
the oppressed
but brings the wicked
to the ground.   Ps 146:8-9

7 Sing to the LORD
with thanksgiving;
play the lyre to our God,   Ps 33:2

8 who covers the sky
with clouds,
prepares rain for the earth,
and causes grass to grow
on the hills.   Jb 5:10; 38:27; Ps 104:14

9 He provides the animals
with their food,
and the young ravens,
what they cry for.   Jb 38:41

10 He is not impressed
by the strength of a horse;
he does not value the power
of a warrior.[E]   Ps 33:17

[A]146:3 Or a mere mortal   [B]146:4 Or spirit   [C]146:8 Lit bowed down   [D]147:5 Lit understanding has no number   [E]147:10 Lit the legs of the man

11 The LORD values
  those who fear him,
  those who put their hope
  in his faithful love.   Ps 33:18

12 Exalt the LORD, Jerusalem;
  praise your God, Zion!   Ps 99:5,9

13 For he strengthens the bars
  of your city gates
  and blesses your children
  within you.   Neh 7:3

14 He endows your territory
  with prosperity;ᴬ   Is 54:13
  he satisfies you
  with the finest wheat.   Ps 81:16

15 He sends his command
  throughout the earth;
  his word runs swiftly.   Ps 104:4

16 He spreads snow like wool;
  he scatters frost
  like ashes;   Jb 37:6; 38:29

17 he throws his hailstones
  like crumbs.
  Who can withstand
  his cold?   Jb 37:9-10

18 He sends his word
  and melts them;
  he unleashes his winds,ᴮ
  and the water flows.   Ps 33:9

19 He declares his word
  to Jacob,
  his statutes and judgments
  to Israel.   Dt 33:2-4; Mal 4:4

20 He has not done this
  for every nation;
  they do not know
  his judgments.   Dt 4:7,32-34
  Hallelujah!

Creation's Praise of the LORD

148
Hallelujah!
Praise the LORD
from the heavens;
praise him in the heights.

2 Praise him, all his angels;
  praise him, all
  his heavenly armies.

3 Praise him, sun and moon;
  praise him, all
  you shining stars.   1Co 15:41

4 Praise him,
  highest heavens,
  and you waters above
  the heavens.   Gn 1:7; Dt 10:14

5 Let them praise the name
  of the LORD,
  for he commanded,
  and they were created.

6 He set them in position
  forever and ever;
  he gave an order
  that will never pass away.

7 Praise the LORD
  from the earth,
  all sea monsters
  and ocean depths,   Gn 1:2,21

8 lightningᶜ and hail,
  snow and cloud,
  stormy wind that executes
  his command,   Ps 18:12; 103:20

9 mountains and all hills,
  fruit trees and all cedars,

10 wild animals and all cattle,
  creatures that crawl
  and flying birds,   Is 43:20; Hs 2:18

11 kings of the earth
  and all peoples,
  princes and all judges
  of the earth,   Ps 102:15

12 young men as well as
  young women,
  old and young together.   Rv 7:9

13 Let them praise the name
  of the LORD,
  for his name alone is exalted.
  His majesty covers
  heaven and earth.   Ps 8:1; 113:4

14 He has raised up a horn
  for his people,

ᴬ147:14 Or peace   ᴮ147:18 Or breath   ᶜ148:8 Or fire

resulting in praise to all
    his faithful ones,
to the Israelites, the people
    close to him.   Dt 10:21; Jr 17:14
Hallelujah!

Praise for God's Triumph

149 Hallelujah!
    Sing to the LORD
    a new song,   Ps 33:3
his praise in the assembly
    of the faithful.   Ps 35:18; 89:5
² Let Israel celebrate its Maker;
    let the children of Zion
    rejoice in their King.   Ps 95:6
³ Let them praise his name
    with dancing
and make music to him
    with tambourine and lyre.
⁴ For the LORD takes pleasure
    in his people;   Ps 147:11; Rm 8:8
he adorns the humble
    with salvation.   Ps 35:27; Is 61:3
⁵ Let the faithful celebrate
    in triumphal glory;
let them shout for joy
    on their beds.   Jb 35:10; Ps 132:16

⁶ Let the exaltation of God be
    in their mouths ᴬ
and a double-edged sword
    in their hands,   Ps 66:17; Heb 4:12
⁷ inflicting vengeance
    on the nations
and punishment
    on the peoples,   Ezk 25:16-17

⁸ binding their kings
    with chains
and their dignitaries
    with iron shackles,   Jb 36:8
⁹ carrying out the judgment
    decreed against them.
This honor is for
    all his faithful people.
Hallelujah!

Praise the LORD

150 Hallelujah!
    Praise God
    in his sanctuary.
Praise him
    in his mighty expanse.   Gn 1:6
² Praise him for his
    powerful acts;   Ps 145:12
praise him for his abundant
    greatness.   Dt 3:24

³ Praise him with trumpet blast;
praise him with harp
    and lyre.   Ps 33:2
⁴ Praise him with tambourine
    and dance;   Ps 149:3
praise him with strings
    and flute.   Jb 21:12; Ps 45:8
⁵ Praise him
    with resounding cymbals;
praise him
    with clashing cymbals.

⁶ Let everything that breathes
    praise the LORD.   Ps 145:21
Hallelujah!

ᴬ**149:6** Lit *throat*

PROVERBS

The Purpose of Proverbs

1 The proverbs of Solomon
son of David, king of Israel:
² For learning wisdom
and discipline;
for understanding
insightful sayings;
³ for receiving
prudent instruction
in righteousness, justice,
and integrity;   Pr 2:9
⁴ for teaching shrewdness
to the inexperienced, ᴬ   Pr 8:5
knowledge and discretion
to a young man —   Pr 2:11; 3:21
⁵ let a wise person listen
and increase learning,   Pr 9:9
and let a discerning person
obtain guidance —
⁶ for understanding a proverb
or a parable, ᴮ
the words of the wise,
and their riddles.   Nm 12:8

⁷ The fear of the LORD
is the beginning
of knowledge;   Jb 28:28; Ps 111:10
fools despise wisdom
and discipline.   Eph 5:17

Avoid the Path of the Violent

⁸ Listen, my son,
to your father's instruction,
and don't reject
your mother's teaching,
⁹ for they will be a garland
of favor on your head   Pr 4:9
and pendants ᶜ
around your neck.   Gn 41:42

¹⁰ My son, if sinners entice you,
don't be persuaded.   Ps 141:4
¹¹ If they say — "Come with us!
Let's set an ambush
and kill someone. ᴰ   Pr 12:6
Let's attack
some innocent person
just for fun! ᴱ   Ps 10:8
¹² Let's swallow them alive,
like Sheol,   Ps 124:3
whole, like those
who go down to the Pit.
¹³ We'll find all kinds
of valuable property
and fill our houses
with plunder.   Pr 24:4
¹⁴ Throw in your lot with us,
and we'll all share
the loot" ᶠ —
¹⁵ my son, don't travel that road
with them   Ps 1:1; Pr 4:14
or set foot on their path,
¹⁶ because their feet run
toward evil
and they hurry to shed blood.
¹⁷ It is useless to spread a net
where any bird can see it,
¹⁸ but they set an ambush
to kill themselves; ᴳ
they attack their own lives.
¹⁹ Such are the paths
of all who make
profit dishonestly;   Pr 15:27
it takes the lives of those
who receive it. ᴴ

Wisdom's Plea

²⁰ Wisdom calls out
in the street;

ᴬ**1:4** Or *simple,* or *gullible*   ᴮ**1:6** Or *an enigma*   ᶜ**1:9** Lit *chains*   ᴰ**1:11** Lit *Let's ambush for blood*
ᴱ**1:11** Lit *person for no reason*   ᶠ**1:14** Lit *us; one bag will be for all of us*   ᴳ**1:18** Lit *they ambush for their blood*   ᴴ**1:19** Lit *takes the life of its masters*

she makes her voice heard
in the public squares. Pr 8:1-3

21 She cries out above[A]
the commotion;
she speaks at the entrance
of the city gates:

22 "How long,
inexperienced ones,
will you love ignorance?
How long will you mockers
enjoy mocking Ps 1:1
and you fools
hate knowledge? Jb 21:14; Pr 1:29

23 If you respond to
my warning,[B] Pr 3:11; 15:5, 31-32
then I will pour out my spirit
on you Jl 2:28
and teach you my words.

24 Since I called out
and you refused, Is 65:12; 66:4
extended my hand
and no one paid attention,

25 since you neglected all
my counsel Ps 107:11; Lk 7:30
and did not accept
my correction,

26 I, in turn, will laugh at
your calamity. Ps 2:4
I will mock when terror
strikes you,

27 when terror strikes you
like a storm
and your calamity comes
like a whirlwind,
when trouble and stress
overcome you.

28 Then they will call me,
but I won't answer;
they will search for me,
but won't find me. 1Sm 8:18

29 Because
they hated knowledge,
didn't choose to fear the LORD,

30 were not interested
in my counsel,

and rejected
all my correction, Pr 5:12; 15:5

31 they will eat the fruit
of their way Jr 6:19
and be glutted with
their own schemes. Pr 14:14

32 For the apostasy
of the inexperienced
will kill them, Jr 2:19
and the complacency of fools
will destroy them.

33 But whoever listens to me
will live securely
and be undisturbed
by the dread of danger."

Wisdom's Worth

2 My son, if you accept
my words Pr 4:10
and store up my commands
within you,

2 listening closely[C] to wisdom
and directing your heart
to understanding;

3 furthermore, if you call out
to insight
and lift your voice
to understanding,

4 if you seek it like silver
and search for it
like hidden treasure, Jb 3:21

5 then you will understand
the fear of the LORD
and discover the knowledge
of God.

6 For the LORD gives wisdom;
from his mouth
come knowledge
and understanding. Jb 32:8

7 He stores up success[D]
for the upright;
He is a shield for those
who live with integrity

8 so that he may guard
the paths of justice

[A]1:21 Lit at the head of   [B]1:23 Lit you turn back to my reprimand   [C]2:2 Lit you, stretching out your ear
[D]2:7 Or resourcefulness

and protect the way
of his faithful followers.

9 Then you will understand
righteousness, justice,
and integrity —
every good path.

10 For wisdom will enter
your heart,
and knowledge
will delight you.

11 Discretion will watch
over you,
and understanding
will guard you.   Pr 4:6; 6:22

12 It will rescue you
from the way of evil —
from anyone who says
perverse things,

13 from those who abandon
the right paths
to walk in ways of darkness,

14 from those who enjoy
doing evil   Pr 10:23
and celebrate perversion,

15 whose paths are crooked,
and whose ways are devious.

16 It will rescue you
from a forbidden woman,
from a wayward woman
with her flattering talk,

17 who abandons
the companion of her youth
and forgets the covenant
of her God;

18 for her house sinks down
to death
and her ways to the land
of the departed spirits.

19 None return who go to her;
none reach the paths of life.

20 So follow the way
of the good,   Heb 6:12
and keep to the paths
of the righteous.

21 For the upright will inhabit
the land,

and those of integrity
will remain in it;   Pr 10:30

22 but the wicked will be cut off
from the land,   Ps 37:38
and the treacherous ripped
out of it.   Dt 28:63; Ps 52:5

Trust the LORD

3 My son, don't forget
my teaching,
but let your heart keep
my commands;   Dt 30:16

2 for they will bring you
many days, a full life, [A]
and well-being.   Ps 91:16; Pr 3:16

3 Never let loyalty
and faithfulness
leave you.
Tie them around your neck;
write them on the tablet
of your heart.   Pr 1:9; 6:21; 7:3

4 Then you will find favor
and high regard
with God and people.   Dt 4:6

5 Trust in the LORD with all
your heart,   Ps 37:3,5
and do not rely on
your own understanding;

6 in all your ways know him,
and he will make your
paths straight.   Pr 11:5

7 Don't be wise in your
own eyes;   Pr 26:5,12; 28:11,26
fear the LORD and turn away
from evil.   Jb 1:1; 28:28; Ps 37:27

8 This will be healing
for your body [B]   Pr 4:22
and strengthening
for your bones.   Jb 21:24

9 Honor the LORD
with your possessions
and with the first produce
of your entire harvest;

10 then your barns will be
completely filled,

A3:2 Lit *days, years of life*   B3:8 Lit *navel*

and your vats will overflow
with new wine. Dt 28:8; Mal 3:10

11 Do not despise
the LORD's instruction,
my son,
and do not loathe
his discipline; Pr 5:11-13; 15:5,31-33

12 for the LORD disciplines
the one he loves,
just as a father disciplines
the son in whom
he delights. Dt 8:5; Jb 5:17-18

Wisdom Brings Happiness

13 Happy is a man
who finds wisdom Pr 8:32,34
and who acquires
understanding,

14 for she is more profitable
than silver,
and her revenue is better
than gold. Jb 28:15-19; Pr 8:10,19; 22:1

15 She is more precious
than jewels; Jb 28:18
nothing you desire can
equal her. Pr 8:11; 20:15

16 Long life^A is
in her right hand;
in her left, riches and honor.

17 Her ways are pleasant, Mt 11:19
and all her paths, peaceful.

18 She is a tree of life to those
who embrace her, Gn 2:9; 13:12
and those who hold on to her
are happy.

19 The LORD founded the earth
by wisdom Ps 104:24; Pr 8:27
and established the heavens
by understanding.

20 By his knowledge
the watery depths
broke open, Gn 7:11
and the clouds dripped
with dew. Dt 33:28; Jb 36:28

21 Maintain sound wisdom
and discretion.
My son, don't lose sight
of them. Pr 4:21

22 They will be life for you^B
and adornment^C
for your neck.

23 Then you will go safely
on your way;
your foot will not stumble.

24 When you lie^D down,
you will not be afraid; Jb 11:19
you will lie down,
and your sleep
will be pleasant.

25 Don't fear sudden danger
or the ruin of the wicked
when it comes, Jb 5:21; Ps 91:5

26 for the LORD will be
your confidence^E
and will keep your foot
from a snare. 1Sm 2:9

Treat Others Fairly

27 When it is in your power,^F
don't withhold good
from the one to whom
it belongs. Gl 6:10

28 Don't say to your neighbor,
"Go away!
Come back later.
I'll give it tomorrow" —
when it is there with you.

29 Don't plan any harm
against your neighbor,
for he trusts you and lives
near you.

30 Don't accuse anyone
without cause, Pr 24:28; Rm 12:18
when he has done you
no harm.

31 Don't envy a violent man
or choose any of his ways;

32 for the devious are detestable
to the LORD,

---

^A3:16 Lit *Length of days*   ^B3:22 Or *be your throat*   ^C3:22 Or *grace*   ^D3:24 LXX reads *sit*   ^E3:26 Or *be*
at your side   ^F3:27 Lit *in the power of your hands*

but he is a friend[A]
to the upright.   Ps 25:14; Pr 11:20

33 The LORD's curse is
on the household
of the wicked,   Zch 5:3-4; Mal 2:2
but he blesses the home
of the righteous;

34 He mocks those who mock,
but gives grace
to the humble.   Jms 4:6; 1Pt 5:5

35 The wise will inherit honor,
but he holds up fools
to dishonor.[B]

A Father's Example

4 Listen, sons,
to a father's discipline,   Pr 1:8
and pay attention so that
you may gain understanding,

2 for I am giving you
good instruction.   Jb 11:4
Don't abandon my teaching.

3 When I was a son
with my father,
tender and precious
to my mother,

4 he taught me and said:
"Your heart must hold on
to my words.
Keep my commands and live.

5 Get wisdom,
get understanding;   Pr 16:16
don't forget or turn away
from the words
from my mouth.

6 Don't abandon
wisdom, and she will
watch over you;
love her, and she will
guard you.   2Th 2:10

7 Wisdom is supreme —
so get wisdom.
And whatever else you get,
get understanding.   Pr 16:16

8 Cherish her, and she will
exalt you;

if you embrace her, she will
honor you.   1Sm 2:30

9 She will place a garland
of favor on your head;
she will give you a crown
of beauty."   Pr 1:9; 16:31

Two Ways of Life

10 Listen, my son.
Accept my words,   Pr 2:1
and you will live many years.

11 I am teaching you the way
of wisdom;
I am guiding you
on straight paths.   1Sm 12:23

12 When you walk, your steps
will not be hindered;   Jb 18:7
when you run,
you will not stumble.   Pr 3:23

13 Hold on to instruction;
don't let go.   Pr 3:18
Guard it, for it is your life.

14 Keep off the path
of the wicked;   Ps 1:1; Pr 1:15
don't proceed on the way
of evil ones.

15 Avoid it; don't travel on it.
Turn away from it,
and pass it by.

16 For they can't sleep
unless they have done
what is evil;
they are robbed of sleep
unless they make
someone stumble.   Ps 36:4

17 They eat the bread
of wickedness
and drink the wine of violence.

18 The path of the righteous is
like the light of dawn,
shining brighter and brighter
until midday.

19 But the way of the wicked is
like the darkest gloom;
they don't know what makes
them stumble.   Pr 24:16; Jn 11:10

[A]**3:32** Or *confidential counsel*   [B]**3:35** Or *but haughty fools dishonor*, or *but fools exalt dishonor*

The Straight Path

20 My son, pay attention
    to my words;
  listen closely to my sayings.
21 Don't lose sight of them;   Pr 3:21
  keep them within your heart.
22 For they are life to those
    who find them,
  and health to
    one's whole body.
23 Guard your heart
    above all else,[A]
  for it is the source of life.
24 Don't let your mouth
    speak dishonestly,   Pr 6:12
  and don't let your lips
    talk deviously.
25 Let your eyes look forward;
  fix your gaze[B] straight ahead.
26 Carefully consider the path[C]
    for your feet,   Pr 5:6,21; Heb 12:13
  and all your ways
    will be established.
27 Don't turn to the right
    or to the left;   Dt 5:32-33; 28:13-14
  keep your feet away from evil.

Avoid Seduction

5 My son, pay attention
    to my wisdom;
  listen closely[D]
    to my understanding   Pr 4:20
2 so that you may maintain
    discretion
  and your lips safeguard
    knowledge.   Mal 2:7
3 Though the lips
    of the forbidden woman
    drip honey
  and her words are[E]
    smoother than oil,
4 in the end she's as bitter
    as wormwood   Pr 5:8-11; 6:32-33
  and as sharp as
    a double-edged sword.

5 Her feet go down to death;
  her steps head straight
    for Sheol.   Pr 7:27; 9:18
6 She doesn't consider the path
    of life;
  she doesn't know
    that her ways are unstable.
7 So now, sons, listen to me,
  and don't turn away
    from the words
    from my mouth.   Pr 7:24
8 Keep your way far from her.
  Don't go near the door
    of her house.   Pr 2:18; 7:8; 9:14
9 Otherwise, you will give up
    your vitality to others
  and your years
    to someone cruel;
10 strangers will drain
    your resources,
  and your hard-earned
    pay will end up
    in a foreigner's house.
11 At the end of your life,
    you will lament
  when your physical body
    has been consumed,
12 and you will say,
  "How I hated discipline,
  and how my heart
    despised correction.   Ps 107:11
13 I didn't obey my teachers
  or listen closely[F]
    to my instructors.
14 I am on the verge
    of complete ruin
  before the entire
    community."

Enjoy Marriage

15 Drink water
    from your own cistern,
  water flowing
    from your own well.   Sg 4:12,15

[A]4:23 Or heart with all diligence   [B]4:25 Lit eyelids   [C]4:26 Or Clear a path   [D]5:1 Lit wisdom; stretch out your ear   [E]5:3 Lit her palate is   [F]5:13 Lit or turn my ear

¹⁶ Should your springs flow
   in the streets,
streams
   in the public squares?   Pr 7:12
¹⁷ They should be for you alone
   and not for you to share
   with strangers.
¹⁸ Let your fountain be blessed,
   and take pleasure in the wife
   of your youth.   Ec 9:9; Mal 2:14
¹⁹ A loving deer,
   a graceful doe ᴬ —
let her breasts
   always satisfy you;   Sg 4:5
be lost in her love forever.
²⁰ Why, my son, would you
   lose yourself
with a forbidden woman
or embrace
   a wayward woman?   Pr 2:16
²¹ For a man's ways are before
   the LORD's eyes,   Jb 14:16; Hs 7:2
and he considers
   all his paths.   Pr 4:25-26
²² A wicked man's iniquities
   will trap him;   Nm 32:23; Ps 7:15-16
he will become tangled
   in the ropes of his own sin.
²³ He will die because there is
   no discipline,   Jb 4:21
and be lost because of
   his great stupidity.

Financial Entanglements

6 My son, if you have
   put up security
   for your neighbor ᴮ
or entered into an agreement
   with ᶜ a stranger,   Pr 11:15; 17:18
² you have been snared
   by the words
   of your mouth
trapped by the words
   from your mouth.
³ Do this, then, my son,
   and free yourself,

for you have put yourself
   in your neighbor's power:
Go, humble yourself,
   and plead
   with your neighbor.
⁴ Don't give sleep to your eyes
   or slumber to your eyelids.
⁵ Escape like a gazelle
   from a hunter, ᴰ
like a bird from
   a hunter's trap. ᴰ   Ps 91:3; 124:7

Laziness

⁶ Go to the ant, you slacker!
Observe its ways
   and become wise.
⁷ Without leader,
   administrator, or ruler,
⁸ it prepares its provisions
   in summer;
it gathers its food
   during harvest.   Pr 10:5; 30:25
⁹ How long will you stay
   in bed, you slacker?
When will you get up
   from your sleep?
¹⁰ A little sleep, a little slumber,
a little folding of the arms
   to rest,
¹¹ and your poverty will come
   like a robber,
your need, like a bandit.

The Malicious Man

¹² A worthless person,
   a wicked man   1Sm 25:25; Pr 16:27
goes around
   speaking dishonestly,   Pr 4:24
¹³ winking his eyes, signaling
   with his feet,   Ps 35:19; Pr 10:10
and gesturing
   with his fingers.
¹⁴ He always plots evil
   with perversity
   in his heart;   Pr 3:29; Mc 2:1
he stirs up trouble.   Pr 6:19; 28:25

ᴬ**5:19** Or *graceful mountain goat*   ᴮ**6:1** Or *friend*   ᶜ**6:1** Lit *or slapped hands for*   ᴰ**6:5** Lit *hand*

¹⁵ Therefore calamity
　　will strike him suddenly;
　he will be shattered instantly,
　　beyond recovery.　2Ch 36:16

What the LORD Hates

¹⁶ The LORD hates six things;
　in fact, seven are detestable
　　to him:
¹⁷ arrogant eyes,
　　a lying tongue,　Ps 18:27; Pr 21:4
　hands that shed
　　innocent blood,　Dt 19:10; Pr 1:16
¹⁸ a heart that plots
　　wicked schemes,　Gn 6:5
　feet eager to run to evil,　Pr 1:16
¹⁹ a lying witness who gives
　　false testimony,　Ex 20:16; Ps 27:12
　and one who stirs up trouble
　　among brothers.　Pr 6:14; 28:25

Warning Against Adultery

²⁰ My son, keep
　　your father's command,
　and don't reject
　　your mother's teaching.
²¹ Always bind them
　　to your heart;
　tie them around your neck.
²² When you walk here
　　and there, they will
　　guide you;
　when you lie down, they will
　　watch over you;
　when you wake up, they will
　　talk to you.
²³ For a command is a lamp,
　　teaching is a light,　Ps 119:105
　and corrective discipline is
　　the way to life.　Pr 3:1-2; 4:4; 7:2
²⁴ They will protect you
　　from an evil woman,ᴬ
　from the flatteringᴮ tongue
　　of a wayward woman.　Pr 7:5

²⁵ Don't lust in your heart
　　for her beauty　Mt 5:28
　or let her captivate you
　　with her eyelashes.　Sg 4:9
²⁶ For a prostitute's fee is
　　only a loaf of bread,ᶜ
　but the wife of another manᴰ
　　goes after a precious life.
²⁷ Can a man embrace fire
　and his clothes not
　　be burned?
²⁸ Can a man walk
　　on burning coals
　without scorching his feet?
²⁹ So it is with the one
　　who sleeps with
　another man's wife;
　no one who touches her
　　will go unpunished.　Pr 16:5
³⁰ People don't despise the thief
　if he steals
　to satisfy himself
　　when he is hungry.　Jr 49:9; Ob 5
³¹ Still, if caught, he must pay
　　seven times as much;　Ps 79:12
　he must give up all the wealth
　　in his house.
³² The one who
　　commits adulteryᴱ
　　lacks sense;
　whoever does so
　　destroys himself.　Pr 7:22-23
³³ He will get a beatingᶠ
　　and dishonor,
　and his disgrace will
　　never be removed.
³⁴ For jealousy enrages
　　a husband,　Pr 27:4; Sg 8:6
　and he will show no mercy
　　when he takes revenge.
³⁵ He will not be appeased
　　by anything
　or be persuaded
　　by lavish bribes.

7

My son, obey my words,
and treasure my commands.
2 Keep my commands and live,
and guard my instructions
as you would the pupil
of your eye. Dt 32:10; Ps 17:8; Zch 2:8
3 Tie them to your fingers;
write them on the tablet
of your heart. Dt 11:18; Pr 3:3; 6:21
4 Say to wisdom, "You are
my sister," Sg 4:9
and call understanding
your relative.
5 She will keep you
from a forbidden woman,
a wayward woman with
her flattering talk. Pr 5:3,20

A Story of Seduction

6 At the window of my house
I looked through my lattice.
7 I saw among
the inexperienced,[A]
I noticed among the youths,
a young man lacking sense.
8 Crossing the street
near her corner,
he strolled down the road
to her house
9 at twilight, in the evening,
in the dark of the night. Jb 24:15
10 A woman came to meet him
dressed like a prostitute,
having a hidden agenda.[B]
11 She is loud and defiant; Pr 9:13
her feet do not stay at home.
12 Now in the street,
now in the squares, Pr 5:16; 9:14
she lurks at every corner.
13 She grabs him
and kisses him;
she brazenly says[C] to him,
14 "I've made
fellowship offerings;

today I've fulfilled my vows.
15 So I came out to meet you,
to search for you,
and I've found you.
16 I've spread coverings
on my bed — Pr 31:22
richly colored linen
from Egypt. Ezk 27:7
17 I've perfumed my bed
with myrrh, aloes,
and cinnamon. Ex 30:23; Ps 45:8
18 Come, let's drink
deeply of lovemaking
until morning. Sg 5:1
Let's feast on
each other's love!
19 My husband isn't home;
he went on a long journey.
20 He took a bag of silver
with him
and will come home
at the time of the full moon."
21 She seduces him
with her persistent pleading;
she lures
with her flattering[D] talk.
22 He follows her impulsively
like an ox going
to the slaughter,
like a deer bounding
toward a trap[E]
23 until an arrow pierces
its[F] liver, Pr 2:16-19; 5:3-6; 23:27-28
like a bird darting
into a snare — Ec 9:12
he doesn't know
it will cost him his life.
24 Now, sons, listen to me,
and pay attention
to the words
from my mouth.
25 Don't let your heart
turn aside to her ways;

A**7:7** Or simple, or gullible, or naive   B**7:10** Or prostitute with a guarded heart   C**7:13** Lit she makes her
face strong and says   D**7:21** Lit smooth   E**7:22** Text emended; MT reads like a shackle to the discipline
of a fool; Hb obscure   F**7:23** Or his

don't stray onto her paths.

26 For she has brought many
   down to death;
   her victims are countless. ᴬ

27 Her house is the road
   to Sheol,
   descending to the chambers
   of death.   Pr 2:18; 5:5; 9:18; 1Co 6:9

Wisdom's Appeal

8 Doesn't wisdom call out?
   Doesn't understanding make
   her voice heard?

2 At the heights overlooking
   the road,
   at the crossroads, she takes
   her stand.

3 Beside the gates leading
   into the city,   Jb 29:7
   at the main entrance,
   she cries out:

4 "People, I call out to you;
   my cry is to the children of
   Adam.

5 Learn to be shrewd,
   you who are inexperienced;
   develop common sense,
   you who are foolish.

6 Listen, for I speak
   of noble things,
   and what my lips say
   is right.

7 For my mouth tells the truth,
   and wickedness is detestable
   to my lips.

8 All the words from my mouth
   are righteous;
   none of them are deceptive
   or perverse.   Dt 32:5; Pr 2:15

9 All of them are clear
   to the perceptive,   Pr 14:6
   and right to those
   who discover knowledge.

10 Accept my instruction
   instead of silver,

and knowledge rather
   than pure gold.   Pr 3:14-15; 8:19

11 For wisdom is better
   than jewels,   Jb 28:12-19
   and nothing desirable
   can equal it.   Pr 3:15; 20:15

12 I, wisdom, share a home
   with shrewdness
   and have knowledge
   and discretion.   Pr 1:4

13 To fear the LORD is
   to hate evil.   Pr 16:6
   I hate arrogant pride,
   evil conduct,
   and perverse speech.

14 I possess good advice
   and sound wisdom; ᴮ
   I have understanding
   and strength.   Ec 7:19

15 It is by me that kings reign
   and rulers enact just law;

16 by me, princes lead,
   as do nobles
   and all righteous judges. ᶜ

17 I love those who love me,
   and those who search for me
   find me.   Pr 1:28; 2:4-5; Jms 1:5

18 With me are riches and honor,
   lasting wealth
   and righteousness.   Ps 112:3

19 My fruit is better
   than solid gold,
   and my harvest
   than pure silver.   Jb 28:15; Pr 3:14

20 I walk in the ways
   of righteousness,
   along the paths of justice,

21 giving wealth
   as an inheritance to those
   who love me,
   and filling their treasuries.

22 "The LORD acquiredᴰ me
   at the beginning
   of his creation, ᴱ

ᴬ**7:26** Or *and powerful men are all her victims*   ᴮ**8:14** Or *resourcefulness*   ᶜ**8:16** Some Hb mss, LXX read *nobles who judge the earth*   ᴰ**8:22** Or *possessed*, or *made*   ᴱ**8:22** Lit *way* before his works of long ago.

23 I was formed[A]
before ancient times,
from the beginning,
before the earth began.

24 I was born
when there were
no watery depths   Gn 1:2; Pr 3:20
and no springs filled
with water.

25 Before the mountains
were established,
prior to the hills, I was
given birth —   Ps 90:2

26 before he made the land,
the fields,
or the first soil on earth.

27 I was there
when he established
the heavens,   Pr 3:19
when he laid out the horizon
on the surface of the ocean,

28 when he placed
the skies above,
when the fountains
of the ocean gushed out,

29 when he set a limit
for the sea
so that the waters
would not violate
his command,   Jb 38:8-11; Ps 104:9
when he laid out
the foundations of the earth.

30 I was a skilled craftsman[B]
beside him.   Jb 28:20-27; 38–39
I was his[C] delight every day,
always rejoicing before him.

31 I was rejoicing in
his inhabited world,   Jb 38:4-7
delighting in
the children of Adam.

32 "And now, sons, listen to me;
those who keep my ways
are happy.   Ps 119:1-2; 128:1; Lk 11:28

33 Listen to instruction
and be wise;   Pr 4:1
don't ignore it.

34 Anyone who listens to me
is happy,   Pr 3:13
watching at my doors
every day,
waiting by the posts
of my doorway.

35 For the one who finds me
finds life   Pr 4:4,22; 7:2; 9:11; 12:28
and obtains favor
from the LORD,   Pr 3:4; 12:2; 13:13

36 but the one who misses me[D]
harms himself;   Pr 15:32
all who hate me love death."

Wisdom Versus Foolishness

9 Wisdom has built her house;
she has carved out
her seven pillars.

2 She has prepared her meat;
she has mixed her wine;
she has also set her table.

3 She has sent out
her female servants;   Ps 68:11
she calls out from
the highest points
of the city: Pr 8:2-3; 9:14-15; Mt 10:27

4 "Whoever is inexperienced,
enter here!"
To the one who lacks sense,
she says,   Pr 6:32

5 "Come, eat my bread,   Is 55:1
and drink the wine
I have mixed.

6 Leave inexperience behind,
and you will live;
pursue the way
of understanding.

7 The one who corrects
a mocker
will bring abuse on himself;
the one who rebukes
the wicked will get hurt.[E]

A 8:23 Or consecrated   B 8:30 Or a confidant, or a child, or was constantly   C 8:30 LXX; MT omits his
D 8:36 Or who sins against me   E 9:7 Lit man: his blemish

8 Don't rebuke a mocker,
    or he will hate you; Pr 15:12
  rebuke the wise, and he will
    love you. Ps 141:5
9 Instruct the wise, and he will
    be wiser still;
  teach the righteous,
    and he will learn more. Pr 1:5

10 "The fear of the LORD is
    the beginning of wisdom,
  and the knowledge
    of the Holy One
    is understanding. Pr 30:3; Rv 16:5
11 For by me your days
    will be many,
  and years will be added
    to your life.
12 If you are wise, you are wise
    for your own benefit; Jb 22:2
  if you mock, you
    alone will bear
    the consequences."

13 Folly is a rowdy woman; Pr 7:11
  she is gullible
    and knows nothing. Pr 5:6
14 She sits by the doorway
    of her house,
  on a seat at the highest point
    of the city,
15 calling to those
    who pass by,
  who go straight ahead
    on their paths: Pr 7:11-12; 9:3-4
16 "Whoever is inexperienced,
    enter here!"
  To the one who lacks sense,
    she says,
17 "Stolen water is sweet,
    and bread eaten secretly
    is tasty!" Pr 20:17
18 But he doesn't know
    that the departed spirits
    are there, Pr 2:18; 21:16
  that her guests are
    in the depths of Sheol. Pr 5:5

A Collection of Solomon's Proverbs

10 Solomon's proverbs: Pr 1:1
  A wise son brings joy
    to his father,
  but a foolish son, heartache
    to his mother. Pr 15:20; 17:25

2 Ill-gotten gains do not
    profit anyone,
  but righteousness rescues
    from death. Pr 11:4,18; 12:28; 21:6

3 The LORD will not let
    the righteous go hungry,
  but he denies the wicked
    what they crave. Ps 112:10

4 Idle hands make one poor,
  but diligent hands
    bring riches. Pr 12:24,27; 13:4,11

5 The son who gathers
    during summer is prudent;
  the son who sleeps
    during harvest
    is disgraceful. Pr 6:6-11; 30:25

6 Blessings are on the head
    of the righteous,
  but the mouth of the wicked
    conceals violence. Pr 10:11

7 The remembrance
    of the righteous is
    a blessing,
  but the name of the wicked
    will rot. Ps 9:5-6; 112:6

8 A wise heart
    accepts commands, Mt 7:24
  but foolish lips
    will be destroyed.

9 The one who lives
    with integrity
    lives securely, Ps 23:4; Pr 2:7; 3:23

but whoever perverts
  his ways will be found out.

10 A sly wink of the eye
    causes grief, Ps 35:19; Pr 6:13; 16:30
  and foolish lips
    will be destroyed.

11 The mouth of the righteous is
    a fountain of life, Ps 37:30; 14:27
  but the mouth of the wicked
    conceals violence. Pr 10:6

12 Hatred stirs up conflicts,
  but love covers all offenses.

13 Wisdom is found on the lips
    of the discerning,
  but a rod is for the back
    of the one who lacks sense.

14 The wise
    store up knowledge,
  but the mouth of the fool
    hastens destruction. Pr 10:8

15 The wealth of the rich is
    his fortified city; Ps 52:7; Pr 18:11
  the poverty of the poor is
    their destruction.

16 The reward of the righteous
    is life;
  the wages of the wicked
    is punishment. Pr 11:19

17 The one who follows
    instruction is on the path
    to life,
  but the one who rejects
    correction goes astray.

18 The one who conceals hatred
    has lying lips,
  and whoever spreads slander
    is a fool. Pr 11:13

19 When there are many words,
    sin is unavoidable,
  but the one who controls
    his lips is prudent. Pr 17:27-28

20 The tongue of the righteous
    is pure silver;
  the heart of the wicked is
    of little value. Pr 8:19; 10:32

21 The lips of the righteous
    feed many,
  but fools die for lack of sense.

22 The LORD's blessing enriches,
  and he adds no painful
    effort to it. ᴬ Mt 6:31-32

23 As shameful conduct is
    pleasure for a fool, Pr 2:14; 15:21
  so wisdom is for a person
    of understanding.

24 What the wicked dreads
    will come to him, Pr 1:26-27
  but what the righteous desire
    will be given to them. Ps 37:4

25 When the whirlwind passes,
    the wicked are no more,
  but the righteous
    are secure forever. Ps 15:5

26 Like vinegar to the teeth
    and smoke to the eyes,
  so the slacker is to the one
    who sends him
    on an errand.

27 The fear of the LORD
    prolongs life, ᴮ Pr 3:2
  but the years of the wicked
    are cut short. Jb 15:32-33

28 The hope of the righteous
    is joy, Pr 11:23; 23:18; Jr 29:11

ᴬ10:22 Or and painful effort adds nothing to it   ᴮ10:27 Lit LORD adds to days

but the expectation
of the wicked will perish.

29 The way of the LORD
is a stronghold
for the honorable,
but destruction awaits
the malicious.   Pr 13:6; 21:15

30 The righteous will never
be shaken,
but the wicked
will not remain
on the earth.   Ps 21:7; 37:29; 125:1

31 The mouth of the righteous
produces wisdom,   Ps 37:30
but a perverse tongue will be
cut out.   Ps 37:38; 120:2-4

32 The lips of the righteous
know what is appropriate,
but the mouth
of the wicked,
only what is perverse.   Pr 2:12

11 Dishonest scales
are detestable to the LORD,
but an accurate weight is
his delight.   Lv 19:36; Pr 16:11

2 When arrogance comes,
disgrace follows,
but with humility
comes wisdom.   Pr 15:33; 18:12

3 The integrity of the upright
guides them,   Pr 13:6
but the perversity
of the treacherous
destroys them.   Pr 11:17-19; 19:3

4 Wealth is not profitable
on a day of wrath,
but righteousness rescues
from death.   Gn 7:1; Pr 10:2; 11:28

5 The righteousness
of the blameless
clears his path,
but the wicked person
will fall because of
his wickedness.

6 The righteousness
of the upright rescues them,
but the treacherous
are trapped
by their own desires.   Pr 5:22

7 When the wicked person dies,
his expectation
comes to nothing,
and hope placed in wealth^A,B
vanishes.   Jb 8:13; Pr 10:28; 24:14

8 The righteous one is rescued
from trouble;
in his place, the wicked one
goes in.   Pr 21:18

9 With his mouth the ungodly
destroys his neighbor,
but through knowledge
the righteous are rescued.

10 When the righteous thrive,
a city rejoices;   Pr 28:12
when the wicked die, there is
joyful shouting.

11 A city is built up
by the blessing
of the upright,   Pr 14:34
but it is torn down
by the mouth of the wicked.

12 Whoever shows contempt
for his neighbor
lacks sense,
but a person
with understanding
keeps silent.   Pr 14:21

^A 11:7 LXX reads *hope of the ungodly*   ^B 11:7 Or *strength*

13 A gossip goes around
     revealing a secret,
    but a trustworthy person
     keeps a confidence.   Lv 19:16

14 Without guidance, a people
     will fall,
    but with many counselors
     there is deliverance.   Pr 15:22

15 If someone puts up security
     for a stranger,
    he will suffer for it,   Pr 6:1-2; 17:18
    but the one who hates
     such agreements
     is protected.

16 A gracious woman
     gains honor,
    but violent[A] people gain
     only riches.

17 A kind man benefits himself,
    but a cruel person
     brings ruin on himself.

18 The wicked person earns
     an empty wage,
    but the one
     who sows righteousness,
     a true reward.   Pr 10:2-3; Hs 10:12

19 Genuine righteousness leads
     to life,
        Pr 10:16-17; 19:23
    but pursuing evil leads
     to death.   Rm 6:23; Jms 1:15

20 Those with twisted minds
     are detestable
     to the LORD,
    but those with blameless
     conduct are his delight.

21 Be assured[B] that
     a wicked person
     will not go unpunished,   Pr 16:5

    but the offspring
     of the righteous
     will escape.

22 A beautiful woman
     who rejects good sense
    is like a gold ring
     in a pig's snout.   Gn 24:47

23 The desire of the righteous
     turns out well,   Ps 37:4-5; Pr 10:24
    but the hope of the wicked
     leads to wrath.   Pr 10:28; 11:7

24 One person gives freely,
     yet gains more;   Ps 112:9; Pr 11:25
    another withholds
     what is right,
    only to become poor.   Pr 13:7

25 A generous person
     will be enriched,   Pr 3:9-10
    and the one who gives
     a drink of water
    will receive water.   Mt 5:7; 10:42

26 People will curse anyone
     who hoards grain,   Pr 24:24
    but a blessing will come
     to the one who sells it.

27 The one who searches
     for what is good
     seeks favor,   Php 4:8
    but if someone looks for
     trouble, it will come to him.

28 Anyone trusting in his riches
     will fall,   Ps 49:6
    but the righteous
     will flourish like foliage.

29 The one who brings ruin
     on his household   Pr 15:27
    will inherit the wind,   Ec 5:16
    and a fool will be a slave

A 11:16 Or ruthless   B 11:21 Lit Hand to hand

to someone whose heart
  is wise.

30 The fruit of the righteous is
    a tree of life,   Pr 3:18
and a wise person
    captivates people.

31 If the righteous will be repaid
    on earth,
how much more the wicked
    and sinful.   Dt 32:25; Pr 13:21; 1Pt 4:18

12 Whoever loves discipline
    loves knowledge,
but one who hates correction
    is stupid.   Pr 3:11; 5:11-13; 15:5, 31-32

2 One who is good obtains
    favor from the LORD,   Pr 8:35
but he condemns a person
    who schemes.   Pr 14:17; 24:8

3 No one can be made secure
    by wickedness,
but the root of the righteous
    is immovable.   Ps 16:8; 21:7

4 A wife of noble character[A] is
    her husband's crown,   Pr 18:22
but a wife who causes shame
is like rottenness
    in his bones.   Pr 14:30

5 The thoughts of the righteous
    are just,
but guidance from the wicked
    is deceitful.

6 The words of the wicked are
    a deadly ambush,   Pr 1:11
but the speech of the upright
    rescues them.   Pr 14:2

7 The wicked are overthrown
    and perish,   Jb 34:25

but the house
    of the righteous will stand.

8 A man is praised
    for his insight,
but a twisted mind is despised.

9 Better to be disregarded,
    yet have a servant,
than to act important
    but have no food.   Pr 11:24; 13:7

10 The righteous cares about
    his animal's health,   Dt 25:4
but even the merciful acts
    of the wicked are cruel.

11 The one who works his land
    will have plenty of food,
but whoever chases fantasies
    lacks sense.   Pr 28:19

12 The wicked desire what
    evil people have caught,[B]
but the root of the righteous
    is productive.

13 By rebellious speech an evil
    person is trapped,   Pr 10:14; 13:3
but a righteous person
    escapes from trouble.   Pr 21:23

14 A person will be satisfied
    with good
by the fruit of his mouth,
and the work of
    a person's hands
    will reward him.   Pr 1:31; 28:19

15 A fool's way is right
    in his own eyes,   Pr 16:2; 21:2
but whoever listens
    to counsel is wise.

16 A fool's displeasure is known
    at once,

[A]12:4 Or A wife of quality, or A wife of good character   [B]12:12 Or desire a stronghold of evil

but whoever ignores
an insult is sensible.   Pr 11:13

17 Whoever speaks the truth
declares what is right,
but a false witness speaks
deceit.   Pr 6:19; 14:5,25

18 There is one
who speaks rashly,
like a piercing sword;   Ps 57:4
but the tongue of the wise
brings healing.   Pr 4:22; 15:4

19 Truthful lips endure forever,
but a lying tongue,
only a moment.   Ps 52:4-5; Pr 19:9

20 Deceit is in the hearts
of those who plot evil,
but those who promote
peace have joy.   Pr 14:22

21 No disaster overcomes
the righteous,   Ps 91:10; 1Pt 3:13
but the wicked are full
of misery.

22 Lying lips are detestable
to the LORD,   Rv 22:15
but faithful people
are his delight.   Pr 3:32; 11:20

23 A shrewd person
conceals knowledge,
but a foolish heart
publicizes stupidity.   Pr 11:13

24 The diligent hand will rule,
but laziness will lead to
forced labor.   Pr 10:4; 13:4; 19:15

25 Anxiety in a person's heart
weighs it down,
but a good word cheers it up.

26 A righteous person is
careful in dealing
with his neighbor, A
but the ways of the wicked
lead them astray.   Pr 14:22

27 A lazy hunter doesn't roast
his game,   Pr 19:15,24; 26:15
but to a diligent person,
his wealth is precious.   Pr 10:4

28 There is life in the path
of righteousness,
and in its path there is
no death. B   Pr 10:2; 13:14; 14:27

13 A wise son responds to his
father's discipline,
but a mocker doesn't listen
to rebuke.

2 From the fruit of his mouth,
a person will enjoy
good things,   Pr 12:14
but treacherous people have
an appetite for violence.

3 The one who guards
his mouth protects his life;
the one who opens his lips
invites his own ruin.   Pr 10:14

4 The slacker craves,
yet has nothing,
but the diligent is
fully satisfied.   Pr 10:4; 12:24,27

5 The righteous hate lying,
but the wicked bring
disgust and shame.

6 Righteousness guards people
of integrity, C
but wickedness undermines
the sinner.   Pr 10:29; 11:3

A 12:26 Or person guides his neighbor   B 12:28 Or righteousness, but the crooked way leads to death
C 13:6 Lit guards integrity of way

7 One person pretends
   to be rich
   but has nothing;   Pr 11:24
another pretends to be poor
   but has abundant wealth.

8 Riches are a ransom
   for a person's life,   Jb 2:4; Pr 10:15
but a poor person
   hears no threat.

9 The light of the righteous
   shines brightly,   Pr 4:18
but the lamp of the wicked
   is put out.   Jb 18:5-6; Pr 20:20; 24:20

10 Arrogance leads to nothing
    but strife,   Pr 17:19
but wisdom is gained
   by those who take advice.

11 Wealth obtained by fraud
    will dwindle,   Pr 10:2; 20:21; 23:5
but whoever earns
   it through labor^A
   will multiply it.   Pr 10:4; 21:5-6

12 Hope delayed makes
    the heart sick,
but desire fulfilled is a tree
   of life.   Pr 11:30; 15:4

13 The one who has contempt
    for instruction will pay
    the penalty,   Nm 15:31; 2Ch 36:16
but the one who
   respects a command
   will be rewarded.   Pr 3:1-2; 4:4

14 A wise person's instruction is
    a fountain of life,   Pr 10:11; 14:27
turning people away
   from the snares of death.

15 Good sense wins favor,   Pr 3:4

but the way of the treacherous
   never changes.^B

16 Every sensible person
    acts knowledgeably,
but a fool displays
   his stupidity.   Pr 12:23; 15:2; Ec 10:3

17 A wicked envoy falls
    into trouble,
but a trustworthy courier
   brings healing.   Pr 25:13

18 Poverty and disgrace
    come to those
    who ignore discipline,
but the one who accepts
   correction will be honored.

19 Desire fulfilled is sweet
    to the taste,
but to turn from evil is
   detestable to fools.   Pr 16:22

20 The one who walks
    with the wise
    will become wise,
but a companion of fools
   will suffer harm.

21 Disaster pursues sinners,
but good rewards
   the righteous.   Ps 32:10; Pr 11:31

22 A good man leaves
    an inheritance
    to his^C grandchildren,
but the sinner's
   wealth is stored up
   for the righteous.   Jb 27:13-17

23 The uncultivated field of the
    poor yields abundant food,
but without justice, it is
   swept away.

^A 13:11 Lit *whoever gathers upon his hand*   ^B 13:15 LXX, Syr, Tg read *treacherous will perish*   ^C 13:22 Or
inheritance: his

24 The one who will not use
    the rod hates his son,   Pr 19:18
but the one who loves him
    disciplines him diligently.

25 A righteous person eats
    until he is satisfied,
but the stomach
    of the wicked is empty.

14 Every wise woman builds
    her house,   Ru 4:11; Pr 9:1; 24:3
but a foolish one tears it
    down with her own hands.

2 Whoever lives with integrity
    fears the LORD,   Pr 19:1; 28:6
but the one who is devious
    in his ways despises him.

3 The proud speech of a fool
    brings a rod of discipline, A
but the lips of the wise
    protect them.   Pr 12:6

4 Where there are no oxen, the
    feeding trough is empty, B
but an abundant harvest
    comes through
    the strength of an ox.

5 An honest witness
    does not deceive,
but a dishonest witness
    utters lies.   Ex 20:16; 23:1; Pr 6:19

6 A mocker seeks wisdom
    and doesn't find it,
but knowledge comes easily
    to the perceptive.

7 Stay away
    from a foolish person;
you will gain no knowledge
    from his speech.   Pr 20:15

8 The sensible person's
    wisdom is to consider
    his way,
but the stupidity of fools
    deceives them.

9 Fools mock at making
    reparation, C
but there is goodwill
    among the upright.

10 The heart knows
    its own bitterness,
and no outsider shares
    in its joy.

11 The house of the wicked
    will be destroyed,
but the tent of the upright
    will flourish.   Pr 10:25; 11:28; 12:7

12 There is a way
    that seems right
    to a person,   Pr 12:15; 16:25
but its end is the way
    to death.   Pr 5:4; Rm 6:21

13 Even in laughter a heart
    may be sad,
and joy may end in grief.

14 The disloyal one will get
    what his conduct deserves,
and a good one,
    what his deeds deserve.

15 The inexperienced one
    believes anything,   Eph 4:14
but the sensible one
    watches D his steps.

16 A wise person is cautious
    and turns from evil,   Jb 28:28
but a fool is easily angered
    and is careless. E

A 14:3 Some emend to In the mouth of a fool is a rod for his back   B 14:4 Or clean   C 14:9 Or at guilt
offerings   D 14:15 Lit the prudent understands   E 14:16 Or and falls

¹⁷ A quick-tempered person
    acts foolishly,
and one who schemes
    is hated.   Pr 12:2; 24:8

¹⁸ The inexperienced inherit
    foolishness,
but the sensible are crowned
    with knowledge.

¹⁹ The evil bow before those
    who are good,
and the wicked, at the gates
    of the righteous.

²⁰ A poor person is hated even
    by his neighbor,   Pr 19:7
but there are many who love
    the rich.   Pr 19:4

²¹ The one who despises
    his neighbor sins,   Pr 11:12
but whoever shows
    kindness to the poor
    will be happy.   Ps 41:1

²² Don't those who plan evil
    go astray?   Pr 6:14-15; 12:26
But those who plan
    good find loyalty
    and faithfulness.   Pr 12:20

²³ There is profit in all
    hard work,
but endless talk^A leads only
    to poverty.   Pr 21:5

²⁴ The crown of the wise is
    their wealth,
but the foolishness of fools
    produces foolishness.

²⁵ A truthful witness
    rescues lives,
but one who utters lies
    is deceitful.   Pr 6:19; 12:17; 14:5

²⁶ In the fear of the LORD
    one has strong confidence
and his children have
    a refuge.   Pr 29:25

²⁷ The fear of the LORD is
    a fountain of life,
turning people away
    from the snares of death.

²⁸ A large population is
    a king's splendor,
but a shortage of people is
    a ruler's devastation.

²⁹ A patient person shows great
    understanding,   Pr 16:32; 19:11
but a quick-tempered one
    promotes foolishness.

³⁰ A tranquil heart is life
    to the body,   Pr 3:8; 4:22; 16:24
but jealousy is rottenness
    to the bones.   Pr 12:4; 27:4; Jms 3:16

³¹ The one who oppresses
    the poor person insults
    his Maker,   Pr 17:5; 21:13; Mt 25:40
but one who is kind
    to the needy honors him.

³² The wicked one is thrown
    down by his own sin,   Ps 17:15
but the righteous one has
    a refuge in his death. Pr 10:25

³³ Wisdom resides
    in the heart
    of the discerning;   Pr 15:14; 18:15
she is known^B even
    among fools.

³⁴ Righteousness exalts
    a nation,
but sin is a disgrace
    to any people.   Pr 11:11

^A**14:23** Lit *but word of lips*   ^B**14:33** LXX reads *unknown*

35 A king favors
 a prudent servant,   Pr 22:29
but his anger falls on
 a disgraceful one.

15
A gentle answer
 turns away anger,   Jdg 8:1-3
but a harsh word
 stirs up wrath.   1Sm 25:10-13

2 The tongue of the wise
 makes knowledge attractive,
but the mouth of fools
 blurts out foolishness.

3 The eyes of the LORD
 are everywhere,
observing the wicked
 and the good.   2Ch 16:9; Jb 31:4

4 The tongue that heals is
 a tree of life,   Pr 11:30; 13:12
but a devious tongue^A
 breaks the spirit.

5 A fool despises
 his father's discipline,
but a person who
 accepts correction
 is sensible.   Pr 3:11; 12:1; 15:31-33

6 The house of the righteous
 has great wealth,
but trouble accompanies
 the income
 of the wicked.

7 The lips of the wise
 broadcast knowledge,
but not so the heart
 of fools.

8 The sacrifice of the wicked
 is detestable to the LORD,
but the prayer of the upright
 is his delight.   Pr 15:29

9 The LORD detests the way
 of the wicked,
but he loves the one
 who pursues righteousness.

10 Discipline is harsh
 for the one who leaves
 the path;
the one who hates correction
 will die.

11 Sheol and Abaddon lie open
 before the LORD —   Jb 26:6
how much more,
 human hearts.   1Sm 16:7; 2Ch 6:30

12 A mocker doesn't love one
 who corrects him;   Pr 9:8
he will not consult the wise.

13 A joyful heart makes
 a face cheerful,
but a sad heart produces
 a broken spirit.   Pr 12:25; 14:30

14 A discerning mind
 seeks knowledge,   Pr 14:33; 18:15
but the mouth
 of fools feeds
 on foolishness.   Mt 12:34

15 All the days
 of the oppressed
 are miserable,
but a cheerful heart has
 a continual feast.

16 Better a little with the fear
 of the LORD
than great treasure
 with turmoil.   Ps 37:16; Pr 16:8

17 Better a meal of vegetables
 where there is love
than a fattened ox
 with hatred.   Mt 22:4; Lk 15:23

^A 15:4 Lit but crookedness in it

18 A hot-tempered person
      stirs up conflict,   Pr 16:28; 26:21
   but one slow to anger
      calms strife.   Pr 14:29

19 A slacker's way is like
      a thorny hedge,
   but the path of the upright is
      a highway.   Pr 16:17,31; 22:5-6

20 A wise son brings joy
      to his father,
   but a foolish man despises
      his mother.   Pr 10:1; 23:24-25; 29:3,15

21 Foolishness brings joy
      to one without sense,
   but a person with
      understanding walks
      a straight path.   Pr 4:11,25; 10:23

22 Plans fail when there is
      no counsel,
   but with many advisers
      they succeed.   Pr 8:14-16; 11:14; 24:6

23 A person takes joy in giving
      an answer;^A
   and a timely word —
      how good that is!   Pr 25:11; Is 50:4

24 For the prudent the path
      of life leads upward,
   so that he may avoid
      going down to Sheol.

25 The LORD tears apart
      the house of the proud,
   but he protects
      the widow's territory.   Ps 68:5

26 The LORD detests the plans
      of the one who is evil,
   but pleasant words
      are pure.   Pr 11:20; 15:8-9; 16:24

27 The one who profits
      dishonestly troubles
      his household,   Pr 1:19; Jr 17:11
   but the one who hates bribes
      will live.   Ex 23:8; Dt 16:19; Ps 15:5

28 The mind
      of the righteous person
      thinks before answering,
   but the mouth of the wicked
      blurts out evil things.   Pr 15:2

29 The LORD is far
      from the wicked,   Ps 18:41
   but he hears the prayer
      of the righteous.   Ps 145:18-19

30 Bright eyes cheer the heart;
   good news strengthens^B
      the bones.   Pr 14:30; 15:13; 17:22

31 One who^C listens
      to life-giving rebukes   Pr 3:11
   will be at home
      among the wise.

32 Anyone who ignores
      discipline despises himself,
   but whoever listens
      to correction acquires
      good sense.^D   Pr 3:11; 5:12-14

33 The fear of the LORD is what
      wisdom teaches,
   and humility comes
      before honor.   Pr 18:12; 22:4; 29:23

16 The reflections of the heart
      belong to mankind,
   but the answer of the tongue
      is from the LORD.   Pr 16:9; 19:21

2 All a person's ways
      seem right to him,
   but the LORD weighs motives.^E

^A**15:23** Lit *in an answer of his mouth*   ^B**15:30** Lit *makes fat*   ^C**15:31** Lit *An ear that*   ^D**15:32** Lit
acquires a heart   ^E**16:2** Lit *spirits*

³ Commit your activities
   to the LORD,
and your plans
   will be established.   Ps 37:4-5

⁴ The LORD has
   prepared everything
   for his purpose —
even the wicked for the day
   of disaster.   Ex 9:16; Rm 9:21-22

⁵ Everyone with a proud heart
   is detestable to the LORD;
be assured,ᴬ he will not
   go unpunished.   Ps 101:5; Pr 11:21

⁶ Iniquity is atoned for
   by loyalty and faithfulness,
and one turns from evil
   by the fear of the LORD.   Pr 3:7

⁷ When a person's ways please
   the LORD,
he makes even his enemies
   to be at peace with him.

⁸ Better a little
   with righteousness
than great income
   with injustice.   Ps 37:16; Pr 15:16-17

⁹ A person's heart plans
   his way,
but the LORD determines
   his steps.   Ps 37:23; Pr 16:1; 19:21

¹⁰ God's verdict is on the lips
   of a king;ᴮ   2Sm 14:17,20; 1Kg 3:28
his mouth should not give
   an unfair judgment.   Pr 18:14-15

¹¹ Honest balances and scales
   are the LORD's;
all the weights in the bag are
   his concern.   Lv 19:36; Pr 11:1; Mc 6:11

¹² Wicked behavior
   is detestable to kings,
since a throne is established
   through righteousness.

¹³ Righteous lips are
   a king's delight,
and he loves one
   who speaks honestly.

¹⁴ A king's fury is a messenger
   of death,
but a wise person
   appeases it.   Ec 10:4

¹⁵ When a king's face lights up,
   there is life;
his favor is like a cloud
   with spring rain.

¹⁶ Get wisdom —
how much better it is
   than gold!
And get understanding —
it is preferable to silver.   Pr 3:14

¹⁷ The highway of the upright
   avoids evil;   Is 35:8
the one who guards his way
   protects his life.   Pr 2:11-13; 15:19

¹⁸ Pride comes before
   destruction,
and an arrogant spirit
   before a fall.   Pr 11:2; 16:5; 18:12

¹⁹ Better to be lowly of spirit
   with the humbleᶜ   Pr 29:23
than to divide plunder
   with the proud.   Ex 15:9; Ps 37:16

²⁰ The one who understands
   a matter finds success,   Pr 19:8
and the one who trusts
   in the LORD will be happy.

ᴬ**16:5** Lit *hand to hand*   ᴮ**16:10** Or *A divination is on the lips of a king*   ᶜ**16:19** Alt Hb tradition reads *afflicted*

21 Anyone with a wise heart
 is called discerning,
and pleasant speech[A]
 increases learning. Pr 1:5; 9:9

22 Insight is a fountain of life
 for its possessor, Pr 10:11; 13:14
but the discipline of fools
 is folly.

23 The heart of a wise person
 instructs his mouth;
it adds learning to his speech.[B]

24 Pleasant words are
 a honeycomb: Ps 19:10; Pr 15:26
sweet to the taste[C] and health
 to the body.[D] Pr 4:22; 15:30; 25:13

25 There is a way that seems
 right to a person,
but its end is the way to death.

26 A worker's appetite works
 for him
because his hunger[E]
 urges him on.

27 A worthless person
 digs up evil,
and his speech is like
 a scorching fire. Pr 6:12; 19:28

28 A contrary person
 spreads conflict,
and a gossip separates
 close friends. Pr 6:14,19; 17:9; 28:25

29 A violent person lures
 his neighbor, Pr 1:10
leading him on a path that is
 not good. 1Sm 12:23; Ps 36:4; Pr 28:10

30 The one who narrows his eyes
 is planning deceptions;

the one who compresses
 his lips brings about evil.

31 Gray hair is a glorious crown;
 it is found in the ways
 of righteousness. Pr 3:1-2

32 Patience is better than power,
 and controlling one's
 emotions,[F] than capturing
 a city. Pr 25:15,28; 29:11

33 The lot is cast into the lap,
 but its every decision is
 from the LORD. Pr 16:1; 19:21; 21:31

17 Better a dry crust with peace
 than a house full of feasting
 with strife. Pr 15:17; 21:9,19; 25:24

2 A prudent servant will
 rule over a disgraceful son
 and share an inheritance
 among brothers.

3 A crucible for silver, and
 a smelter for gold, Pr 27:21
and the LORD is the tester
 of hearts. 1Ch 29:17; Ps 26:2; Pr 16:2

4 A wicked person listens to
 malicious talk;[G]
a liar pays attention to
 a destructive tongue.

5 The one who mocks the poor
 insults his Maker, Pr 14:31; 21:13
and one who rejoices over
 calamity
will not go unpunished.

6 Grandchildren are the crown
 of the elderly,
and the pride of children is
 their fathers.

A**16:21** Lit and sweetness of lips B**16:23** Lit learning upon his lips C**16:24** Lit throat D**16:24** Lit bones
E**16:26** Lit mouth F**16:32** Lit and ruling over one's spirit G**17:4** Lit to lips of iniquity

⁷ Eloquent words are
   not appropriate
   on a fool's lips;
how much worse are lies
   for a ruler.

⁸ A bribe seems like
   a magic stone to its owner;
wherever he turns,
   he succeeds.   Pr 18:16; 19:6; 21:14

⁹ Whoever conceals an offense
   promotes love,   Pr 10:12; Jms 5:20
but whoever gossips about it
   separates friends.   Lv 19:16

¹⁰ A rebuke cuts into
   a perceptive person
more than a hundred lashes
   into a fool.

¹¹ An evil person desires
   only rebellion;
a cruel messenger^A
   will be sent against him.

¹² Better for a person to meet
   a bear robbed of her cubs
than a fool
   in his foolishness.

¹³ If anyone returns evil
   for good,   Ps 35:12; 109:5
evil will never depart
   from his house.   2Sm 12:10

¹⁴ To start a conflict is
   to release a flood;
stop the dispute before
   it breaks out.   Pr 20:3; 25:8

¹⁵ Acquitting the guilty
   and condemning
   the just —   Ex 23:7; Pr 17:26; 18:5
both are detestable
   to the LORD.

¹⁶ Why does a fool have money
   in his hand
with no intention
   of buying wisdom?   Pr 4:5,7

¹⁷ A friend loves at all times,
and a brother is born for
   a difficult time.

¹⁸ One without sense enters
   an agreement^B
and puts up security
   for his friend.   Pr 6:1-5; 11:15; 22:26

¹⁹ One who loves to offend
   loves strife;   Pr 29:22
one who builds
   a high threshold
   invites injury.

²⁰ One with a twisted mind
   will not succeed,
and one with deceitful
   speech will fall into ruin.

²¹ A man fathers a fool
   to his own sorrow;
the father of a fool has no joy.

²² A joyful heart is
   good medicine,
but a broken spirit dries up
   the bones.   Ps 22:15; Pr 14:30; 15:13

²³ A wicked person secretly
   takes a bribe   Pr 17:8
to subvert the course
   of justice.   Dt 16:19; Ps 15:5; Pr 18:5

²⁴ Wisdom is the focus
   of the perceptive,
but a fool's eyes roam
   to the ends of the earth.

²⁵ A foolish son is grief
   to his father

^A 17:11 Or *a merciless angel*   ^B 17:18 Lit *sense slaps hands*

and bitterness to the one
who bore him.   Pr 10:1; 17:21; 19:13

26 It is certainly not good to fine
an innocent person
or to beat a noble
for his honesty. ^A   Pr 17:15; 18:5

27 The one who has knowledge
restrains his words,   Pr 10:19
and one who keeps
a cool head ^B
is a person of understanding.

28 Even a fool is considered wise
when he keeps silent —
discerning, when he seals
his lips.   Jb 13:5; Pr 10:19

18

One who isolates himself
pursues selfish desires;
he rebels against
all sound wisdom.

2 A fool does not delight
in understanding,
but only wants to show off
his opinions. ^C   Pr 12:23; 13:16

3 When a wicked
person comes,
contempt also comes,
and along with dishonor,
derision.

4 The words
of a person's mouth
are deep waters,   Pr 20:5
a flowing river, a fountain
of wisdom. ^D

5 It is not good
to show partiality
to the guilty,   Lv 19:15; Dt 1:17; 24:17

denying an innocent person
justice.   Pr 17:15

6 A fool's lips lead to strife,
and his mouth provokes
a beating.   Pr 19:29

7 A fool's mouth is
his devastation,
and his lips are a trap
for his life.   Ps 64:8; 140:9; Pr 10:14

8 A gossip's words are
like choice food
that goes down to one's
innermost being. ^E   Pr 26:22

9 The one who is lazy
in his work
is brother to a vandal. ^F   Pr 28:24

10 The name of the LORD is
a strong tower;   Ps 18:2; 61:3; 91:2
the righteous run to it
and are protected. ^G   Pr 29:25

11 The wealth of the rich is
his fortified city;
in his imagination it is
like a high wall.   Pr 10:15

12 Before his downfall
a person's heart is proud,
but humility comes
before honor.   Pr 11:2; 15:33; 29:23

13 The one who gives
an answer
before he listens —
this is foolishness
and disgrace for him.   Pr 15:28

14 A person's spirit can
endure sickness,

^A 17:26 Or noble unfairly   ^B 17:27 Lit spirit   ^C 18:2 Lit to uncover his heart   ^D 18:4 Or waters; a fountain
of wisdom is a flowing river   ^E 18:8 Lit to the chambers of the belly   ^F 18:9 Lit master of destruction
^G 18:10 Lit raised high

but who can survive
a broken spirit? Pr 15:13; 17:22

15 The mind of the discerning
acquires knowledge,
and the ear of the wise
seeks it. Pr 14:33; 15:14

16 A person's gift opens doors [A]
for him
and brings him
before the great. Gn 32:20

17 The first to state his case
seems right
until another comes
and cross-examines him.

18 Casting the lot
ends quarrels Pr 16:33
and separates
powerful opponents.

19 An offended brother is
harder to reach [B]
than a fortified city,
and quarrels are
like the bars of a fortress.

20 From the fruit of a
person's mouth
his stomach is satisfied;
he is filled with the product
of his lips. Pr 1:31; 12:14; 14:14

21 Death and life are
in the power
of the tongue,
and those who love it will eat
its fruit. Pr 13:2; Mt 12:37; 15:11,18-20

22 A man who finds a wife finds
a good thing Pr 12:4; 19:14; 31:10-31
and obtains favor
from the LORD. Pr 8:35

23 The poor person pleads, Pr 19:7
but the rich one
answers roughly. Jms 2:6

24 One with many friends
may be harmed, [C]
but there is a friend
who stays closer
than a brother. Pr 17:17; 27:10

19 Better a poor person
who lives with integrity
than someone who has
deceitful lips and is a fool.

2 Even zeal is not good
without knowledge, Rm 10:2
and the one who acts
hastily [D] sins. Pr 21:5; 28:20; 29:20

3 A person's own
foolishness leads
him astray,
yet his heart rages
against the LORD. Is 8:21

4 Wealth attracts
many friends, Pr 14:20; 19:6
but a poor person
is separated
from his friend.

5 A false witness will not
go unpunished, Dt 19:16-19
and one who utters lies
will not escape. Pr 6:19

6 Many seek a ruler's favor,
and everyone is a friend
of one who gives gifts.

7 All the brothers
of a poor person hate him;
how much more do
his friends

[A] **18:16** Lit *gift makes room* [B] **18:19** LXX, Syr, Tg, Vg read *is stronger* [C] **18:24** Some LXX mss, Syr, Tg, Vg
read *friends must be friendly* [D] **19:2** Lit *who is hasty with feet*

keep their distance from him!
He may pursue them
  with words,   Pr 18:23
but they are not there. ᴬ

8 The one who acquires
     good sense ᴮ loves himself;
   one who safeguards
     understanding
     finds success.   Pr 16:20

9 A false witness will not
     go unpunished,
   and one who utters
     lies perishes.   Pr 19:5; 21:28

10 Luxury is not appropriate
      for a fool —   Pr 17:7; 26:1
    how much less for a slave
      to rule over princes!   Pr 30:22

11 A person's insight gives
      him patience,   Pr 14:29
    and his virtue is to overlook
      an offense.   Pr 11:13; 17:9

12 A king's rage is like the
      roaring of a lion,   Pr 16:14
    but his favor is like dew
      on the grass.   Ps 133:3; Pr 20:2; 28:15

13 A foolish son is
      his father's ruin,   Pr 10:1; 17:25
    and a wife's nagging is
      an endless dripping.   Pr 21:9,19

14 A house and wealth
      are inherited from fathers,
    but a prudent wife is
      from the LORD.

15 Laziness induces deep sleep,
    and a lazy person
      will go hungry.   Pr 6:9-11; 10:4; 13:4

16 The one who keeps commands
      preserves himself;   Lk 10:28
    one who disregards ᶜ
      his ways will die.   Pr 3:1-2; 4:4

17 Kindness to the poor is a loan
      to the LORD,   Dt 15:7-10; Pr 14:31
    and he will give a reward
      to the lender. ᴰ   Lk 6:38

18 Discipline your son
      while there is hope;
    don't set your heart on being
      the cause of his death. ᴱ

19 A person with intense anger
      bears the penalty;
    if you rescue him, you'll have
      to do it again.   Pr 22:24-25; 29:22

20 Listen to counsel
      and receive instruction
    so that you may be wise
      later in life. ᶠ   Pr 12:1; 15:5, 31-32

21 Many plans are
      in a person's heart,
    but the LORD's decree
      will prevail.   Ps 33:10-11; Pr 16:1,9,33

22 What is desirable in a person
      is his fidelity;
    better to be a poor person
      than a liar.   Pr 19:1; 28:6

23 The fear of the LORD leads
      to life;
    one will sleep at night ᴳ
      without danger.   Pr 14:26-27

24 The slacker buries his hand
      in the bowl;
    he doesn't even bring it back
      to his mouth!   Pr 12:27; 20:4

ᴬ**19:7** Hb uncertain   ᴮ**19:8** Lit *acquires a heart*   ᶜ**19:16** Or *despises,* or *treats lightly*   ᴰ**19:17** Lit *to him*
ᴱ**19:18** Lit *don't lift up your soul to his death*   ᶠ**19:20** Lit *in your end*   ᴳ**19:23** Lit *will spend the night satisfied*

25 Strike a mocker,
and the inexperienced
learn a lesson; Pr 21:11
rebuke the discerning,
and he gains knowledge.

26 The one who plunders
his father and evicts
his mother
is a disgraceful
and shameful son.

27 If you stop listening
to correction, my son,
you will stray from the words
of knowledge.

28 A worthless witness
mocks justice,
and a wicked mouth
swallows iniquity. Jb 15:16; 34:7

29 Judgments are prepared
for mockers,
and beatings for the backs
of fools. Pr 10:13; 18:6; 26:3

20 Wine is a mocker, beer is
a brawler; Gn 9:21; Pr 23:29-30
whoever goes astray A
because of them
is not wise.

2 A king's terrible wrath is
like the roaring of a lion;
anyone who provokes him
endangers himself. Nm 16:38

3 Honor belongs to the person
who ends a dispute, Pr 17:14
but any fool can get himself
into a quarrel. Pr 15:18; 18:6; 22:10

4 The slacker does not plow
during planting season; B
at harvest time he looks, C
and there is nothing.

5 Counsel in a person's heart is
deep water; Pr 18:4
but a person of understanding
draws it out.

6 Many a person proclaims
his own loyalty,
but who can find
a trustworthy person? Lk 18:8

7 A righteous person acts
with integrity; Pr 2:7,20-21; 10:9
his children who come
after him will be happy.

8 A king sitting on a throne
to judge
separates out all evil
with his eyes. Pr 20:26; 25:5

9 Who can say, "I have kept
my heart pure;
I am cleansed from my sin"?

10 Differing weights
and varying measures D —
both are detestable
to the LORD. Dt 25:14-15; Pr 11:1

11 Even a young man is known
by his actions —
by whether his behavior
is pure and upright. Pr 21:8

12 The hearing ear
and the seeing eye —
the LORD made them both.

13 Don't love sleep, or you will
become poor;
open your eyes, and you'll have
enough to eat. Pr 6:10-11; 19:15

A **20:1** Or whoever staggers   B **20:4** Lit plow in winter   C **20:4** Lit inquires   D **20:10** Lit Stone and stone, measure and measure

14 "It's worthless,
  it's worthless!"
  the buyer says,
but after he is on his way,
  he gloats.

15 There is gold and a multitude
  of jewels,
but knowledgeable lips are
  a rare treasure. Pr 3:15; 8:11

16 Take his garment,
  for he has put up security
  for a stranger;
get collateral if it is
  for foreigners. Dt 24:12-13; Pr 6:1-5

17 Food gained by fraud
  is sweet to a person, Pr 9:17
but afterward his mouth
  is full of gravel.

18 Finalize plans with counsel,
and wage war with
  sound guidance. Pr 24:6; Lk 14:31

19 The one who reveals secrets
  is a constant gossip; Lv 19:16
avoid someone
  with a big mouth. Pr 13:3

20 Whoever curses his father
  or mother — Ex 21:17; Pr 24:20
his lamp will go out
  in deep darkness. Jb 18:5

21 An inheritance gained
  prematurely
will not be blessed
  ultimately. Pr 21:5; 23:5; 28:22

22 Don't say, "I will avenge
  this evil!" Pr 24:29; Mt 5:39; 1Th 5:15
Wait on the LORD, and he will
  rescue you. Ps 27:14; 37:7-9

23 Differing weights[A]
  are detestable to the LORD,
and dishonest scales
  are unfair. Pr 11:1

24 Even a courageous person's
  steps are determined
  by the LORD, Pr 16:9, 33; 19:21
so how can anyone
  understand his own way?

25 It is a trap for anyone
  to dedicate something rashly
and later to reconsider
  his vows. Nm 30:2; Dt 23:21; Ec 5:4-6

26 A wise king separates out
  the wicked Pr 20:8
and drives
  the threshing wheel
  over them. Is 28:27

27 The LORD's lamp sheds light on
  a person's life,[B]
searching
  the innermost parts.[C] Pr 20:30

28 Loyalty and faithfulness
  guard a king;
through loyalty he maintains
  his throne.

29 The glory of young men is
  their strength,
and the splendor of old men
  is gray hair. Lv 19:32; Pr 16:31

30 Lashes and wounds
  purge away evil, Is 53:5
and beatings cleanse
  the innermost parts.[D]

21 A king's heart is like
  channeled water
  in the LORD's hand:

A20:23 Lit *A stone and a stone* B20:27 Lit *breath* C20:27 Lit *the chambers of the belly* D20:30 Lit *beatings the chambers of the belly*

He directs it wherever
   he chooses.   Ezr 6:22

2 All a person's ways
   seem right to him,
but the LORD weighs hearts.

3 Doing what is righteous
   and just
is more acceptable
   to the LORD than sacrifice.

4 The lamp that guides
   the wicked —
haughty eyes
   and an arrogant heart —
is sin.   Ps 101:5; Pr 6:16-17; 30:13

5 The plans of the diligent
   certainly lead to profit,
but anyone who is reckless
   certainly becomes poor.

6 Making a fortune
   through a lying tongue
is a vanishing mist,[A]
   a pursuit of death.[B,C]   Pr 8:36

7 The violence of the wicked
   sweeps them away
because they refuse
   to act justly.

8 A guilty one's conduct
   is crooked,   Pr 2:15
but the behavior
   of the innocent is upright.

9 Better to live on the corner
   of a roof
than to share a house
   with a nagging wife.

10 A wicked person
   desires evil;

he has no consideration[D]
   for his neighbor.   Pr 14:21

11 When a mocker
   is punished,
the inexperienced
   become wiser;
when one teaches
   a wise man,
he acquires knowledge.   Pr 19:25

12 The Righteous One[E]
   considers the house
   of the wicked;
he brings the wicked to ruin.

13 The one who shuts his ears
   to the cry of the poor
will himself also call out
   and not be answered.   Pr 14:31

14 A secret gift soothes anger,
and a covert bribe,
   fierce rage.   Pr 17:8; 18:16; 19:6

15 Justice executed is a joy
   to the righteous
but a terror to those
   who practice iniquity.

16 The person who strays
   from the way of prudence
will come to rest in
   the assembly of
   the departed spirits.   Ps 49:14

17 The one who loves pleasure
   will become poor;
whoever loves wine and oil
   will not get rich.   Ec 2:1-3,10-11

18 The wicked are a ransom
   for the righteous,
and the treacherous,
   for[F] the upright.   Pr 11:8; Is 43:3

[A] 21:6 Or *a breath blown away*   [B] 21:6 Some Hb mss, LXX, Vg read *a snare of death*   [C] 21:6 Lit *is vanity, ones seeking death*   [D] 21:10 Or *favor*   [E] 21:12 Or *righteous one*   [F] 21:18 Or *in place of*

¹⁹ Better to live in a wilderness
    than with a nagging
       and hot-tempered wife.

²⁰ Precious treasure and oil
    are in the dwelling of
       a wise person,
    but a fool consumes them. ^A

²¹ The one who pursues
    righteousness
       and faithful love
    will find life, righteousness,
       and honor.   Pr 3:16; 8:18; 15:9; Mt 5:6

²² A wise person
    went up against a city
       of warriors
    and brought down
       its secure fortress.   2Sm 5:6-9

²³ The one who guards
    his mouth and tongue
    keeps himself out of trouble.

²⁴ The arrogant
    and proud person,
       named "Mocker,"
    acts with excessive
       arrogance.   Ps 1:1; Pr 1:22; 21:11

²⁵ A slacker's craving
    will kill him
    because his hands refuse
       to work.   Pr 10:4; 12:24; 13:4; 19:15,24
²⁶ He is filled with craving ^B
    all day long,
    but the righteous give
       and don't hold back.   Ps 37:26

²⁷ The sacrifice
    of a wicked person
       is detestable —
    how much more so
    when he brings it
       with ulterior motives!   Pr 15:8

²⁸ A lying witness will perish,
    but the one who listens
       will speak successfully.

²⁹ A wicked person puts on
    a bold face,   Pr 7:13
    but the upright one
       considers his way.

³⁰ No wisdom,
    no understanding,
       and no counsel
    will prevail against the LORD.

³¹ A horse is prepared
    for the day of battle,   Ps 20:7
    but victory comes
       from the LORD.   Jr 3:23; 1Co 15:57

22 A good name is to be chosen
    over great wealth;
    favor is better than silver
       and gold.   Pr 10:7; 8:10; Ec 7:1

² Rich and poor have this
    in common: ^C
    the LORD makes them all.

³ A sensible person sees
    danger and takes cover,
    but the inexperienced
       keep going
       and are punished.   Pr 14:16; 27:12

⁴ Humility, the fear of the LORD,
    results in wealth, honor,
       and life.   Pr 15:33; 21:21; 29:23

⁵ There are thorns and snares
    on the way of the crooked;
    the one who guards himself
       stays far from them.

⁶ Start a youth out on his way;
    even when he grows old
       he will not depart from it.

^A**21:20** Lit *it*   ^B**21:26** Lit *He craves a craving*   ^C**22:2** Lit *poor meet*

⁷ The rich rule over the poor,
  and the borrower is a slave
    to the lender.   Dt 28:12-13

⁸ The one who sows injustice
    will reap disaster,   Jb 4:8
  and the rod of his fury
    will be destroyed.

⁹ A generous person^A
    will be blessed,   Pr 19:17; 2Co 9:6
  for he shares his food
    with the poor.   Lk 14:13-14

¹⁰ Drive out a mocker,
    and conflict goes too;
  then quarreling
    and dishonor will cease.

¹¹ The one who loves a pure heart
  and gracious lips —
    the king is his friend.   Pr 16:13

¹² The Lord's eyes keep watch
    over knowledge,
  but he overthrows the words
    of the treacherous.

¹³ The slacker says,
    "There's a lion outside!
  I'll be killed
    in the public square!"   Pr 26:13

¹⁴ The mouth
    of the forbidden woman
  is a deep pit;
  a man cursed by the Lord
    will fall into it.   Pr 2:16-19; 23:27-28

¹⁵ Foolishness is bound
    to the heart of a youth;
  a rod of discipline
    will separate it from him.

¹⁶ Oppressing the poor
    to enrich oneself,
  and giving to the rich —
    both lead only to poverty.

Words of the Wise

¹⁷ Listen closely,^B pay attention
    to the words of the wise,
  and apply your mind
    to my knowledge.

¹⁸ For it is pleasing
    if you keep them
    within you
  and if they are^C constantly
    on your lips.

¹⁹ I have instructed you today
    — even you —
  so that your confidence
    may be in the Lord.

²⁰ Haven't I written for you
    thirty sayings^D
  about counsel
    and knowledge,

²¹ in order to teach you true
    and reliable words,
  so that you may give
    a dependable report^E   Lk 1:3-4
  to those who sent you?   Pr 10:26

²² Don't rob a poor person
    because he is poor,
  and don't crush
    the oppressed at
    the city gate,   Ex 23:6; Jb 31:16

²³ for the Lord will
    champion their cause   Ps 12:5
  and will plunder those
    who plunder them.

²⁴ Don't make friends
    with an angry person,^F
  and don't be a companion
    of a hot-tempered one,

---

^A 22:9 Lit *Good of eye*   ^B 22:17 Lit *Stretch out your ear*   ^C 22:18 Or *you; let them be*, or *you, so that they are*   ^D 22:20 Text emended; one Hb tradition reads *you previously*; alt Hb tradition reads *you excellent things*; LXX, Syr, Vg read *you three times*   ^E 22:21 Lit *give dependable words*   ^F 22:24 Lit *with a master of anger*

²⁵ or you will learn his ways
and entangle yourself
in a snare.

²⁶ Don't be one of those
who enter agreements, ^A
who put up security
for loans. Pr 6:1-5; 11:15; 17:18

²⁷ If you have nothing with
which to pay,
even your bed will be taken
from under you. Ex 22:26

²⁸ Don't move
an ancient boundary marker
that your fathers set up.

²⁹ Do you see a person skilled
in his work?
He will stand in the presence
of kings.
He will not stand
in the presence
of the unknown. Gn 41:46

23
When you sit down
to dine with a ruler,
consider carefully what ^B is
before you,

² and put a knife
to your throat
if you have a big ^C appetite;

³ don't desire his choice food,
for that food is deceptive.

⁴ Don't wear yourself out
to get rich; Pr 15:27; 28:20; Mt 6:19
because you know better,
stop!

⁵ As soon as your eyes fly to it,
it disappears, Pr 27:24
for it makes wings for itself
and flies like an eagle
to the sky.

⁶ Don't eat
a stingy person's bread, ^D
and don't desire
his choice food, Pr 23:3

⁷ for it's like someone
calculating inwardly. ^E Mt 6:21
"Eat and drink,"
he says to you,
but his heart is not with you.

⁸ You will vomit the little
you've eaten
and waste
your pleasant words.

⁹ Don't speak to ^F a fool,
for he will despise the insight
of your words. Mt 7:6

¹⁰ Don't move an ancient
boundary marker, Pr 22:28
and don't encroach
on the fields
of the fatherless,

¹¹ for their Redeemer is strong,
and he will champion
their cause against you.

¹² Apply yourself to discipline
and listen to words
of knowledge.

¹³ Don't withhold discipline
from a youth;
if you punish him with a rod,
he will not die. Pr 13:24; 19:18

¹⁴ Punish him with a rod,
and you will rescue his life
from Sheol. 1Co 5:5

¹⁵ My son, if your heart
is wise,
my heart will indeed rejoice.

¹⁶ My innermost being
will celebrate

^A**22:26** Lit *Don't be among hand slappers* ^B**23:1** Or *who* ^C**23:2** Lit *you are the master of an*
^D**23:6** Lit *eat bread of an evil eye* ^E**23:7** LXX reads *it is like someone swallowing a hair in the throat*
^F**23:9** Lit *in the ears of*

when your lips say
   what is right.   Pr 8:6

¹⁷ Don't let your heart
   envy sinners;   Ps 37:1; Pr 24:1,19
instead, always fear the LORD.

¹⁸ For then you will have
   a future,
and your hope will not
   be dashed.   Ps 9:18; Pr 10:28; 24:14

¹⁹ Listen, my son, and be wise;
keep your mind
   on the right course.

²⁰ Don't associate with those
   who drink too much wine
or with those
   who gorge themselves
   on meat.   Pr 28:7

²¹ For the drunkard
   and the glutton
   will become poor,
and grogginess
   will clothe them in rags.

²² Listen to your father
   who gave you life,
and don't despise your mother
   when^A she is old.   Pr 1:8; 15:20

²³ Buy — and do not sell — truth,
wisdom, instruction,
   and understanding.   Pr 4:5,7

²⁴ The father of a righteous son
   will rejoice greatly,
and one who fathers
   a wise son will delight
   in him.   Pr 10:1; 23:15; 29:3

²⁵ Let your father and mother
   have joy,   Pr 27:11
and let her who gave birth
   to you rejoice.

²⁶ My son, give me your heart,
and let your eyes observe
   my ways.

²⁷ For a prostitute is a deep pit,
and a wayward woman is
   a narrow well;

²⁸ indeed, she sets an ambush
   like a robber   Pr 6:26; 7:12,22-23
and increases the number
   of unfaithful people.

²⁹ Who has woe?
   Who has sorrow?
Who has conflicts?
   Who has complaints?
Who has wounds
   for no reason?   Pr 23:35
Who has red eyes?

³⁰ Those who linger over wine;
those who go looking
   for mixed wine.   Is 5:11,22

³¹ Don't gaze at wine
   because it is red,   Eph 5:18
because it gleams in the cup
and goes down smoothly.

³² In the end it bites
   like a snake
and stings like a viper.

³³ Your eyes will see
   strange things,
and you will say
   absurd things.^B   Is 28:7

³⁴ You'll be like someone
   sleeping out at sea
or lying down on the top
   of a ship's mast.

³⁵ "They struck me, but^C I feel
   no pain!
They beat me, but I didn't
   know it!   Pr 23:29; Jr 5:3
When will I wake up?
I'll look for another drink."

24 Don't envy the evil   Ps 37:1
   or desire to be with them,
² for their hearts plan violence,
and their words
   stir up trouble.   Ps 10:7

^A**23:22** Or *because* ^B**23:33** Or *will speak perversities*, or *inverted things* ^C**23:35** LXX, Syr, Tg, Vg read *me," you will say, "but*

3 A house is built
     by wisdom,   Pr 14:1
  and it is established
     by understanding;
4 by knowledge the rooms
     are filled
  with every precious
     and beautiful treasure.

5 A wise warrior is better
     than a strong one, ᴬ
  and a man of knowledge
     than one of strength; ᴮ
6 for you should wage war
     with sound guidance —
  victory comes
     with many counselors.

7 Wisdom is inaccessible
     to ᶜ a fool;   Pr 14:6; 17:16,24
  he does not open his mouth
     at the city gate.   Jb 5:4; Ps 127:5

8 The one who plots evil   Rm 1:30
     will be called a schemer.
9 A foolish scheme is sin,
  and a mocker is detestable
     to people.

10 If you do nothing
     in a difficult time,
   your strength is limited.
11 Rescue those being taken off
     to death,
   and save those stumbling
     toward slaughter.   Ps 82:4
12 If you say,
     "But we didn't know
     about this,"
   won't he who weighs hearts
     consider it?   1Sm 16:7; Ps 44:21
   Won't he who protects
     your life know?   Ps 121:3-8
   Won't he repay a person
     according to his work?

13 Eat honey, my son,
     for it is good,   Pr 25:16
   and the honeycomb is sweet
     to your palate;   Sg 5:1
14 realize that wisdom is
     the same for you.   Ps 19:10
   If you find it, you will have
     a future,
   and your hope will never fade.

15 Don't set an ambush, you
     wicked one,
   at the camp
     of the righteous man;
   don't destroy his dwelling.
16 Though a righteous person
     falls seven times,
   he will get up,   Jb 5:19; Ps 37:24
   but the wicked will stumble
     into ruin.   Pr 14:32; 29:16

17 Don't gloat when your enemy
     falls,
   and don't let your heart
     rejoice when he stumbles,
18 or the LORD will see,
     be displeased,
   and turn his wrath away
     from him.

19 Don't be agitated
     by evildoers,
   and don't envy the wicked.
20 For the evil have no future;
   the lamp of the wicked
     will be put out.   Jb 18:5; 21:17

21 My son, fear the LORD,
     as well as the king,   Mt 22:21
   and don't associate
     with rebels, ᴰ
22 for destruction will come
     suddenly from them;
   who knows what distress
     these two can bring?

ᴬ**24:5** LXX, Syr; MT reads *is in strength*   ᴮ**24:5** LXX, Syr, Tg; MT reads *knowledge exerts strength*
ᶜ**24:7** Lit *is too high for*   ᴰ**24:21** Or *those given to change*

23 These sayings also
belong to the wise: Pr 1:6; 22:17

It is not good
to show partiality
in judgment. Dt 1:17; 16:19; Pr 18:5
24 Whoever says to the guilty,
"You are innocent" — Pr 17:15
peoples will curse
him, and nations
will denounce him; Pr 11:26
25 but it will go well with those
who convict the guilty,
and a generous blessing
will come to them.

26 He who gives
an honest answer
gives a kiss on the lips.

27 Complete your outdoor
work, and prepare
your field; Pr 20:4
afterward, build your house.

28 Don't testify against
your neighbor
without cause. Ex 20:16; Pr 25:18
Don't deceive with your lips.
29 Don't say, "I'll do to him
what he did to me;
I'll repay the man for what
he has done." Dt 32:35; Pr 20:22

30 I went by the field
of a slacker
and by the vineyard of one
lacking sense.
31 Thistles had come up
everywhere,
weeds covered the ground,
and the stone wall was ruined.
32 I saw, and took it to heart;
I looked,
and received instruction:

33 a little sleep, a little slumber,
a little folding of the arms
to rest,
34 and your poverty will come
like a robber,
and your need, like a bandit.

Hezekiah's Collection

25 These too are proverbs
of Solomon, Pr 1:1
which the men
of King Hezekiah of Judah
copied. 2Kg 18–20

2 It is the glory of God
to conceal a matter Dt 29:29
and the glory of kings
to investigate a matter.
3 As the heavens are high
and the earth is deep,
so the hearts of kings cannot
be investigated.

4 Remove impurities
from silver, Ezk 22:18; Mal 3:2-3
and material
will be produced[A]
for a silversmith.[B] 2Tm 2:21
5 Remove the wicked
from the king's presence,
and his throne
will be established
in righteousness. Pr 16:12

6 Don't boast about yourself
before the king,
and don't stand in the place
of the great;
7 for it is better for him to say
to you, "Come up here!"
than to demote you
in plain view of a noble.[C]

8 Don't take a matter
to court hastily. Pr 17:14; Mt 5:25

Otherwise, what will
you do afterward
if your opponent[A]
humiliates you?

9 Make your case
with your opponent
without revealing
another's secret; Pr17:9; Mt18:15

10 otherwise, the one who hears
will disgrace you,
and you'll never live it down.[B]

11 A word spoken
at the right time
is like gold apples
in silver settings. Pr8:10; 15:23

12 A wise correction
to a receptive ear Pr15:31
is like a gold ring
or an ornament of gold.

13 To those who send him,
a trustworthy envoy
is like the coolness of snow
on a harvest day;
he refreshes the life
of his masters. Pr13:17; 16:24

14 The one who boasts
about a gift
that does not exist
is like clouds and wind
without rain. Jd12

15 A ruler can be persuaded
through patience,
and a gentle tongue
can break a bone. Pr15:1; Ec10:4

16 If you find honey, eat only
what you need; Jdg14:8; 1Sm14:25
otherwise, you'll get sick
from it and vomit. Pr25:27

17 Seldom set foot
in your neighbor's house;
otherwise, he'll get sick
of you and hate you.

18 A person giving
false testimony
against his neighbor Ex20:16
is like a club, a sword,
or a sharp arrow. Ps57:4

19 Trusting an unreliable
person in a difficult time
is like a rotten tooth
or a faltering foot. 2Kg18:21

20 Singing songs
to a troubled heart
is like taking off clothing
on a cold day
or like pouring vinegar
on soda.[C] Rm12:15

21 If your enemy is hungry,
give him food to eat,
and if he is thirsty, give him
water to drink; Ex23:4-5; 2Kg6:22

22 for you will heap burning
coals on his head,
and the LORD will reward you.

23 The north wind produces rain,
and a backbiting tongue,
angry looks.

24 Better to live on the corner
of a roof
than to share a house
with a nagging wife. Pr15:17

25 Good news
from a distant land
is like cold water
to a parched throat.[D] Pr15:30

26 A righteous person
who yields to the wicked
is like a muddied spring
or a polluted well. Ezk32:2

27 It is not good to eat
too much honey Pr25:16
or to seek glory after glory.[E]

28 A person who does not
control his temper Pr16:32

is like a city whose wall
  is broken down.   Neh 1:3

26 Like snow in summer
  and rain at harvest,
honor is inappropriate
  for a fool.   Pr 17:7; 19:10
2 Like a flitting sparrow
  or a fluttering swallow,
an undeserved curse
  goes nowhere.   Nm 23:8; Dt 23:5
3 A whip for the horse, a bridle
  for the donkey,   Ps 32:9
and a rod for the backs
  of fools.   Pr 10:13; 19:29
4 Don't answer a fool
  according to his foolishness
or you'll be like him yourself.
5 Answer a fool according to
  his foolishness   Mt 16:1-4; 21:24-27
or he'll become wise
  in his own eyes.   Pr 26:12; 28:11
6 The one who sends
  a message by a fool's hand
cuts off his own feet
  and drinks violence.   Pr 13:2
7 A proverb in the mouth
  of a fool
is like lame legs that hang limp.
8 Giving honor to a fool
is like binding a stone
  in a sling.
9 A proverb in the mouth
  of a fool
is like a stick with thorns,
brandished by[A] the hand
  of a drunkard.
10 The one who hires
  a fool or who hires
  those passing by
is like an archer
  who wounds everyone.
11 As a dog returns to its vomit,
so also a fool repeats
  his foolishness.   2Pt 2:22

12 Do you see a person
  who is wise in his own eyes?
There is more hope for a fool
  than for him.   Pr 29:20
13 The slacker says,
  "There's a lion in the road —
a lion in the public square!"
14 A door turns on its hinges,
and a slacker, on his bed.
15 The slacker buries his hand
  in the bowl;
he is too weary to bring it
  to his mouth!   Pr 12:27; 19:24
16 In his own eyes, a slacker
  is wiser   Pr 26:5,12; 28:11
than seven
  who can answer sensibly.

17 A person who is passing by
  and meddles in a quarrel
  that's not his
is like one who grabs a dog
  by the ears.
18 Like a madman who throws
  flaming darts
  and deadly arrows,   Is 50:11
19 so is the person who deceives
  his neighbor
and says, "I was only joking!"

20 Without wood, fire goes out;
without a gossip,
  conflict dies down.   Pr 16:28
21 As charcoal for embers
  and wood for fire,
so is a quarrelsome person
  for kindling strife.   Pr 15:18
22 A gossip's words are
  like choice food
that goes down to
  one's innermost being.[B]

23 Smooth[C] lips
  with an evil heart

A26:9 Lit *thorn that goes up into* B26:22 Lit *to the chambers of the belly* C26:23 LXX; MT reads *Burning*

are like glaze
     on an earthen vessel. Mt 23:27
24 A hateful person
     disguises himself
     with his speech
and harbors deceit within.
25 When he speaks graciously,
     don't believe him,
for there are
     seven detestable things
     in his heart. Ps 28:3
26 Though his hatred
     is concealed by deception,
his evil will be revealed
     in the assembly.
27 The one who digs a pit
     will fall into it,
and whoever rolls a stone —
     it will come back on him. Jb 4:8
28 A lying tongue hates
     those it crushes,
and a flattering mouth
     causes ruin.

27 Don't boast
     about tomorrow,
for you don't know what
     a day might bring. Lk 12:19-20

2 Let another praise you,
     and not your own mouth —
a stranger, and not
     your own lips. Pr 25:27

3 A stone is heavy and sand,
     a burden,
but aggravation from a fool
     outweighs them both.

4 Fury is cruel, and anger
     a flood,
but who can withstand
     jealousy? Pr 6:34

5 Better an open reprimand
     than concealed love. Pr 28:23

6 The wounds of a friend
     are trustworthy, Ps 141:5
but the kisses of an enemy
     are excessive. Lk 22:48

7 A person who is full tramples
     on a honeycomb, Pr 25:16
but to a hungry person,
     any bitter thing is sweet.

8 Anyone wandering
     from his home
is like a bird wandering
     from its nest. Pr 26:2

9 Oil and incense bring joy
     to the heart, Ps 23:5
and the sweetness of a friend
     is better than self-counsel. A

10 Don't abandon your friend
     or your father's friend,
and don't go
     to your brother's house
in your time of calamity;
better a neighbor nearby
     than a brother far away.

11 Be wise, my son, and bring
     my heart joy, Pr 10:1; 23:24-25; 29:3
so that I can answer anyone
     who taunts me. Ps 119:42; 127:5

12 A sensible person
     sees danger
     and takes cover;
the inexperienced keep going
     and are punished. Pr 22:3

13 Take his garment,
for he has put up security
     for a stranger;
get collateral if it is
     for foreigners. B Pr 6:1-5; 11:15

14 If one blesses his neighbor

A **27:9** LXX reads *heart, but the soul is torn up by affliction*   B **27:13** Lit *a foreign woman*

with a loud voice early
in the morning,
it will be counted as a curse
to him.

15 An endless dripping
on a rainy day
and a nagging wife are alike;
16 the one who controls her
controls the wind
and grasps oil
with his right hand.

17 Iron sharpens iron,
and one person
sharpens another.[A]

18 Whoever tends a fig tree
will eat its fruit,   Am 7:14; Sg 8:12
and whoever looks after
his master will be honored.

19 As water reflects the face,
so the heart reflects
the person.

20 Sheol and Abaddon are
never satisfied,   Jb 26:6; Pr 15:11
and people's eyes are
never satisfied.   Ec 1:8; 4:8

21 A crucible refines silver,
a smelter refines gold,
and a person
refines his praise.   Pr 16:2; 17:3

22 Though you grind a fool
in a mortar with a pestle
along with grain,
you will not separate
his foolishness from him.

23 Know well the condition
of your flock,   Ezk 34:12; Jn 10:3,14
and pay attention
to your herds,

24 for wealth is not forever;
not even a crown lasts
for all time.
25 When hay is removed
and new growth appears
and the grain from the hills
is gathered in,
26 lambs will provide
your clothing,
and goats, the price of a field;
27 there will be enough
goat's milk for your food —
food for your household
and nourishment for your
female servants.   Pr 31:15

28 The wicked flee
when no one
is pursuing them,   Lv 26:17
but the righteous are as bold
as a lion.   Eph 6:19-20

2 When a land is in rebellion,
it has many rulers,   1Kg 16:8-28
but with a discerning
and knowledgeable person,
it endures.

3 A destitute leader[B]
who oppresses the poor
is like a driving rain
that leaves no food.   Ex 9:25

4 Those who reject the law
praise the wicked,   Rm 1:32
but those who keep
the law pit themselves
against them.   1Kg 18:18; Mt 3:7

5 The evil do not
understand justice,   Ps 92:6
but those who seek the LORD
understand everything.

6 Better the poor person
who lives with integrity

A 27:17 Lit and a man sharpens his friend's face   B 28:3 LXX reads A wicked man

than the rich one who
distorts right and wrong. [A]

7 A discerning son keeps
the law,
but a companion of gluttons
humiliates his father.   Dt 21:20

8 Whoever increases
his wealth through
excessive interest   Ex 22:25
collects it for one who is kind
to the poor.   Jb 27:17; Pr 13:22

9 Anyone who turns his ear
away from hearing
the law —
even his prayer is detestable.

10 The one who leads
the upright into an evil way
will fall into his own pit,   Ps 7:15
but the blameless will inherit
what is good.   Mt 5:6

11 A rich person is wise in
his own eyes,
but a poor one
who has discernment
sees through him.

12 When the righteous triumph,
there is great rejoicing, [B]
but when the wicked come
to power,
people hide.   Pr 11:10; 28:28; 29:2

13 The one who conceals his sins
will not prosper,   Jb 31:33; Ps 32:3
but whoever confesses
and renounces them
will find mercy.   Ps 32:5; Jms 5:16

14 Happy is the one who is
always reverent,   2Ch 19:7

but one who hardens
his heart falls into trouble.

15 A wicked ruler over
a helpless people   Ex 1:14; Pr 29:2
is like a roaring lion
or a charging bear.   Pr 19:12

16 A leader who lacks
understanding
is very oppressive,
but one who hates dishonest
profit
prolongs his life.   1Kg 12:1-19; Ps 15:5

17 Someone burdened
by bloodguilt [C]
will be a fugitive until death.
Let no one help him.   Nm 35:31

18 The one who lives
with integrity
will be helped,
but one who distorts right
and wrong [D]
will suddenly fall.   Pr 2:7; 10:9; 20:7

19 The one who works his land
will have plenty of food,
but whoever chases fantasies
will have his fill of poverty.

20 A faithful person will have
many blessings,   Pr 10:6; Mt 25:21
but one in a hurry to get rich
will not go unpunished.

21 It is not good
to show partiality —   Pr 18:5
yet even a courageous
person may sin for a piece
of bread.   Ezk 13:19

22 A greedy one [E] is in a hurry
for wealth;

[A]28:6 Lit who twists two ways   [B]28:12 Lit glory   [C]28:17 Lit the blood of a person   [D]28:18 Lit who is twisted regarding two ways   [E]28:22 Lit A man with an evil eye

he doesn't know
that poverty will come
to him. Pr 13:11; 20:21; 21:5; 22:16

23 One who rebukes a person
will later find more favor
than one who flatters[A]
with his tongue. Pr 26:28; 29:5

24 The one who robs his father
or mother Pr 19:26
and says, "That's no sin,"
is a companion to a person
who destroys. Pr 18:9

25 A greedy person stirs
up conflict, Pr 15:18
but whoever trusts
in the LORD will prosper.

26 The one who trusts
in himself[B] is a fool,
but one who walks
in wisdom will be safe.

27 The one who gives
to the poor
will not be in need,
but one who turns
his eyes away[C]
will receive many curses.

28 When the wicked come
to power,
people hide,
but when they
are destroyed,
the righteous flourish. Pr 28:12

29

One who becomes
stiff-necked,
after many reprimands
will be shattered instantly —
beyond recovery. Pr 1:24-31; 6:14-15

2 When the righteous flourish,
the people rejoice,
but when the wicked rule,
people groan. Ex 2:23; Est 8:15

3 A man who loves wisdom
brings joy to his father,
but one who consorts
with prostitutes
destroys his wealth. Pr 5:9-10

4 By justice a king brings
stability to a land,
but a person who demands
"contributions"[D]
demolishes it. Pr 17:23

5 A person who flatters[E]
his neighbor
spreads a net for his feet.

6 An evil person is caught
by sin, Pr 12:13; 18:7; Ec 9:12
but the righteous one sings
and rejoices. Ex 15:1

7 The righteous person knows
the rights[F] of the poor, Ps 41:1
but the wicked one does not
understand these concerns.

8 Mockers inflame a city, Pr 11:11
but the wise turn away anger.

9 If a wise person goes to court
with a fool,
there will be ranting
and raving
but no resolution.[G] Pr 26:4

10 Bloodthirsty men hate
an honest person, Gn 4:5-8
but the upright care
about him.[H]

[A] 28:23 Lit *is smooth*　[B] 28:26 Lit *his heart*　[C] 28:27 Lit *who shuts his eyes*　[D] 29:4 The Hb word for *contributions* usually refers to offerings in worship.　[E] 29:5 Lit *is smooth on*　[F] 29:7 Lit *justice*　[G] 29:9 Lit *rest*　[H] 29:10 Or *person, and seek the life of the upright*

11 A fool gives full vent
     to his anger,[A]   Pr 12:16
   but a wise person holds it
     in check.   Pr 16:32; 25:28

12 If a ruler listens to lies,
   all his officials
     will be wicked.

13 The poor and the oppressor
     have this in common:[B]
   the LORD gives light
     to the eyes of both.   Pr 22:2

14 A king who judges the poor
     with fairness —
   his throne will be
     established forever.   Ps 72:4

15 A rod of correction
     imparts wisdom,   Pr 13:24; 22:15
   but a youth left
     to himself[C]
   is a disgrace to his mother.

16 When the wicked increase,
     rebellion increases,
   but the righteous will see
     their downfall.   Ps 37:34,36; 58:10

17 Discipline your child,
     and it will bring you
     peace of mind   Pr 13:24
   and give you delight.

18 Without revelation[D] people
     run wild,   1Sm 3:1; Ps 74:9; Am 8:11-12
   but one who follows
     divine instruction
     will be happy.   Ps 119:2; Pr 8:32

19 A servant cannot be
     disciplined by words;
   though he understands,
     he doesn't respond.   Mt 18:17

20 Do you see someone
     who speaks too soon?   Lv 5:4
   There is more hope for a fool
     than for him.   Pr 26:12

21 A servant pampered
     from his youth
   will become arrogant[E]
     later on.

22 An angry person
     stirs up conflict,
   and a hot-tempered one[F]
     increases rebellion.   Pr 15:18

23 A person's pride
     will humble him,   2Sm 22:28
   but a humble spirit
     will gain honor.   Pr 11:2; 15:33

24 To be a thief's partner is
     to hate oneself;
   he hears the curse but
     will not testify.   Lv 5:1

25 The fear of mankind is
     a snare,   Gn 12:12; 20:2; 1Sm 13:11
   but the one who trusts
     in the LORD is protected.[G]

26 Many desire a ruler's favor,
   but a person receives justice
     from the LORD.   Is 49:4; 1Co 4:4-5

27 An unjust person
     is detestable
     to the righteous,
   and one whose way
     is upright
   is detestable to the wicked.

The Words of Agur

30 The words of Agur
     son of Jakeh.
   The pronouncement.[H]

A 29:11 Lit *spirit*   B 29:13 Lit *oppressor meet*   C 29:15 Lit *youth sent away*   D 29:18 Lit *vision*   E 29:21 Hb obscure   F 29:22 Lit *a master of rage*   G 29:25 Lit *raised high*   H 30:1 Or *son of Jakeh from Massa*; Pr 31:1

The man's oration to Ithiel,
 to Ithiel and Ucal:[A]

2 I am more stupid than
 any other person,[B]
and I lack a human's ability
 to understand.   1Kg 3:7
3 I have not gained wisdom,
and I have no knowledge
 of the Holy One.   Pr 9:10
4 Who has gone up to heaven
 and come down?   Jn 3:13
Who has gathered the wind
 in his hands?
Who has bound up
 the waters in a cloak?   Jb 26:8
Who has established
 all the ends of the earth?
What is his name,
and what is the name
 of his son —
if you know?   Mt 11:27; Rv 19:12-13
5 Every word of God is pure;[C]
he is a shield to those
 who take refuge in him.
6 Don't add to his words,   Dt 4:2
or he will rebuke you,
 and you will be proved a liar.

7 Two things I ask of you;
don't deny them to me
 before I die:
8 Keep falsehood
 and deceitful words
 far from me.
Give me neither poverty
 nor wealth;
feed me with the food I need.
9 Otherwise, I might have
 too much   Dt 6:10-12; 8:11-14
and deny you, saying,
 "Who is the LORD?"   Jos 24:27

or I might have nothing
 and steal,   Ex 20:5; Eph 4:28
profaning[D] the name
 of my God.   Lv 19:11-12

10 Don't slander a servant
 to his master
or he will curse you,
 and you will become guilty.

11 There is a generation
 that curses its father
and does not bless
 its mother.   Ex 21:17; Pr 20:20
12 There is a generation
 that is pure in its own eyes,
yet is not washed
 from its filth.
13 There is a generation —
 how haughty its eyes
and pretentious its looks.[E]
14 There is a generation
 whose teeth are swords,
whose fangs are knives,
devouring the oppressed
 from the land   Ps 14:4
and the needy from among
 mankind.

15 The leech has two daughters:
 "Give, Give!"
Three things are
 never satisfied;   Pr 6:16
four never say, "Enough!":
16 Sheol; a childless womb;
earth, which is
 never satisfied with water;
and fire, which never says,
 "Enough!"

17 As for the eye that ridicules
 a father   Gn 9:22

[A]30:1 Hb uncertain. Sometimes read with different word division as *oration: I am weary, God, I am weary, God, and I am exhausted,* or *oration: I am not God, I am not God, that I should prevail.* LXX reads *My son, fear my words and when you have received them repent. The man says these things to the believers in God, and I pause.* [B]30:2 Lit *I am more stupid than a man* [C]30:5 Lit *refined* [D]30:9 Lit *grabbing* [E]30:13 Lit *and its eyelids lifted up*

and despises obedience
to a mother,
may ravens of the valley
pluck it out
and young vultures eat it.

18 Three things are too
wondrous for me;
four I can't understand:
19 the way of an eagle in the sky,
the way of a snake on a rock,
the way of a ship at sea,
and the way of a man
with a young woman.

20 This is the way
of an adulteress:
she eats and wipes her mouth
and says, "I've done
nothing wrong."   Pr 28:24; 1Jn 1:8

21 The earth trembles
under three things;
it cannot bear up under four:
22 a servant
when he becomes king,
a fool when he is stuffed
with food,
23 an unloved woman
when she marries,   Gn 29:30-31
and a servant girl
when she ousts her queen.

24 Four things on earth are small,
yet they are extremely wise:
25 ants are not a strong people,
yet they store up their food
in the summer;   Pr 6:6-8
26 hyraxes are not
a mighty people,
yet they make their homes
in the cliffs;   Lv 11:5; Ps 104:18
27 locusts have no king,
yet all of them march
in ranks;   Jl 2:7-8

28 a lizard[A] can be caught
in your hands,
yet it lives in kings' palaces.

29 Three things are stately
in their stride;
four are stately in their walk:
30 a lion, which is mightiest
among beasts
and doesn't retreat
before anything;
31 a strutting rooster;[B] a goat;
and a king at the head
of his army.[C]

32 If you have been foolish
by exalting yourself
or if you've been scheming,
put your hand
over your mouth.   Jb 21:5
33 For the churning of milk
produces butter,
and twisting a nose
draws blood,
and stirring up anger
produces strife.   Pr 10:12; 29:22

The Words of Lemuel

31 The words of King Lemuel,
a pronouncement[D] that
his mother taught him:

2 What should I say, my son?
What, son of my womb?   Is 49:15
What, son of my vows?
3 Don't spend your energy
on women   Pr 5:9
or your efforts on those
who destroy kings.   Dt 17:17
4 It is not for kings, Lemuel,
it is not for kings
to drink wine   1Kg 16:9; 20:16
or for rulers to desire beer.
5 Otherwise, he will drink,
forget what is decreed,   Hs 4:11

A 30:28 Or *spider*   B 30:31 Or *a greyhound*   C 30:31 LXX reads *king addressing his people*   D 31:1 Or *of Lemuel, king of Massa,* or *of King Lemuel, a burden*

and pervert justice for all
the oppressed.[A] Ps 72:1-2; Is 28:7

6 Give beer to one who is dying
and wine to one whose life
is bitter. Jb 3:20

7 Let him drink so that
he can forget his poverty
and remember his trouble
no more. Ps 104:15

8 Speak up[B] for those
who have no voice,[C]
for the justice of all
who are dispossessed.[D]

9 Speak up, judge righteously,
and defend the cause of
the oppressed and needy.

In Praise of a Wife of Noble Character

10 Who can find a wife
of noble character?[E] Ru 3:11
She is far more precious
than jewels.[F]

11 The heart of her husband
trusts in her,
and he will not lack
anything good.

12 She rewards him with good,
not evil,
all the days of her life.

13 She selects wool and flax
and works
with willing hands.

14 She is like
the merchant ships,
bringing her food
from far away. 1Kg 10:22

15 She rises while it is still night
and provides food
for her household
and portions[G] for
her female servants. Pr 27:27

16 She evaluates a field
and buys it;
she plants a vineyard
with her earnings.[H] Mt 21:33

17 She draws
on her strength[I]
and reveals that her arms
are strong. Pr 31:25

18 She sees that her profits
are good,
and her lamp never goes out
at night. Mt 25:8

19 She extends her hands
to the spinning staff,
and her hands hold
the spindle. Pr 31:13

20 Her hands reach[J] out
to the poor,
and she extends her hands
to the needy. Dt 15:11; Pr 22:9; 31:9

21 She is not afraid
for her household
when it snows,
for all in her household
are doubly clothed.[K]

22 She makes
her own bed coverings;
her clothing is fine linen
and purple. Gn 41:42; Rv 19:8,14

23 Her husband is known
at the city gates,
where he sits among
the elders
of the land. Ru 4:1-2

24 She makes and sells
linen garments;
she delivers belts[L]
to the merchants.

25 Strength and honor are
her clothing, Pr 31:17; 1Tm 2:9-10
and she can laugh
at the time to come. Pr 31:21

[A]**31:5** Lit *sons of affliction*   [B]**31:8** Lit *Open your mouth*, also in v. 9   [C]**31:8** Lit *who are mute*
[D]**31:8** Lit *all the sons of passing away*   [E]**31:10** Or *a wife of quality*, or *a capable wife*   [F]**31:10** Vv. 10-31
form an acrostic.   [G]**31:15** Or *tasks*   [H]**31:16** Or *vineyard by her own labors*   [I]**31:17** Lit *She wraps strength
around her like a belt*   [J]**31:20** Lit *Her hand reaches*   [K]**31:21** LXX, Vg; MT reads *are dressed in scarlet*
[L]**31:24** Or *sashes*

²⁶ Her mouth speaks wisdom,
  and loving instruction^A is
    on her tongue.
²⁷ She watches over
    the activities
    of her household   Pr 31:15
  and is never idle.^B
²⁸ Her children rise up
    and call her blessed;
  her husband also
    praises her:

²⁹ "Many women^C have done
    noble deeds,
  but you surpass them all!"
³⁰ Charm is deceptive
    and beauty is fleeting,
  but a woman who fears
    the Lord will be praised.
³¹ Give her the reward
    of her labor,^D
  and let her works praise her
    at the city gates.

---

^A**31:26** Or *and the teaching of kindness*   ^B**31:27** Lit *and does not eat the bread of idleness*   ^C**31:29** Lit *daughters*   ^D**31:31** Lit *the fruit of her hands*

ECCLESIASTES

Everything Is Futile

1 The words of the Teacher,[A] son of David, king in Jerusalem.
² "Absolute futility,"
    says the Teacher.
"Absolute futility. Everything
    is futile." Ps 39:5-6; 62:9; 144:4; Ec 12:8
³ What does a person gain
    for all his efforts
    that he labors at
    under the sun? Ec 2:11,22; 3:9; 5:16
⁴ A generation goes
    and a generation comes,
    but the earth remains
        forever. Ps 104:5; 119:90; 1Jn 2:17
⁵ The sun rises and the sun sets;
    panting, it returns to the place
    where it rises.
⁶ Gusting to the south,
    turning to the north,
    turning, turning,
        goes the wind, Ec 11:5; Jn 3:8
    and the wind returns
    in its cycles.
⁷ All the streams flow to the sea,
    yet the sea is never full;
    to the place where the
        streams flow,
    there they flow again.
⁸ All things[B] are wearisome,
    more than anyone can say.
    The eye is not satisfied
        by seeing Pr 27:20; Ec 4:8
    or the ear filled with hearing.
⁹ What has been is what will be,
    and what has been done is
        what will be done;
    there is nothing new
        under the sun.

¹⁰ Can one say about anything,
    "Look, this is new"?
    It has already existed
        in the ages before us.
¹¹ There is no remembrance
    of those who[C] came before;
    and of those
        who will come after
    there will also be
        no remembrance
    by those who follow them.

The Limitations of Wisdom

¹² I, the Teacher, have been[D] king over Israel in Jerusalem. ¹³ I applied my mind to examine and explore through wisdom all that is done under heaven. God has given people[E] this miserable task to keep them occupied. ¹⁴ I have seen all the things that are done under the sun and have found everything to be futile, a pursuit of the wind.[F]
¹⁵ What is crooked cannot
        be straightened; Ec 7:13
    what is lacking cannot
        be counted.

¹⁶ I said to myself, "See, I have amassed wisdom far beyond all those who were over Jerusalem before me, and my mind has thoroughly grasped[G] wisdom and knowledge." ¹⁷ I applied my mind to know wisdom and knowledge, madness and folly; I learned that this too is a pursuit of the wind.
¹⁸ For with much wisdom is
        much sorrow; Ec 2:23; 12:12

A**1:1** Or of Qoheleth, or of the Leader of the Assembly   B**1:8** Or words   C**1:11** Or of the things that
D**1:12** Or Teacher, was   E**1:13** Or given the descendants of Adam   F**1:14** Or a feeding on wind, or an affliction of spirit; also in v. 17   G**1:16** Or discerned

as knowledge increases,
  grief increases.

The Emptiness of Pleasure

2 I said to myself, "Go ahead, I will test you with pleasure; enjoy what is good." But it turned out to be futile. ² I said about laughter, "It is madness," and about pleasure, "What does this accomplish?" ³ I explored with my mind the pull of wine on my body — my mind still guiding me with wisdom — and how to grasp folly, until I could see what is good for people to do under heaven^A during the few days of their lives.   Pr 14:13; Ec 7:4; 8:15; Lk 12:19

The Emptiness of Possessions

⁴ I increased my achievements. I built houses and planted vineyards for myself. ⁵ I made gardens and parks for myself and planted every kind of fruit tree in them. ⁶ I constructed reservoirs for myself from which to irrigate a grove of flourishing trees. ⁷ I acquired male and female servants and had slaves who were born in my house. I also owned livestock — large herds and flocks — more than all who were before me in Jerusalem. ⁸ I also amassed silver and gold for myself, and the treasure of kings and provinces. I gathered male and female singers for myself, and many concubines, the delights of men.^B,C ⁹ So I became great and surpassed all who were before me in Jerusalem; my wisdom also remained with me. ¹⁰ All that my eyes desired, I did not deny them. I did not refuse myself any pleasure, for I took pleasure in all my struggles. This was my reward for all my struggles. ¹¹ When I considered all that I had accomplished^D and what I had labored to achieve, I found everything to be futile and a pursuit of the wind.^E There was nothing to be gained under the sun.   1Kg 7:1-12

The Relative Value of Wisdom

¹² Then I turned to consider wisdom, madness, and folly, for what will the king's successor^F be like? He^G will do what has already been done. ¹³ And I realized that there is an advantage to wisdom over folly, like the advantage of light over darkness.   Ec 1:9-10,17; 3:15; 7:11-12,19

¹⁴   The wise person has eyes
        in his head,
      but the fool walks
        in darkness.   Pr 2:10-13; 1Jn 2:11
Yet I also knew that one fate comes to them both. ¹⁵ So I said to myself, "What happens to the fool will also happen to me. Why then have I been overly wise?" And I said to myself that this is also futile. ¹⁶ For, just like the fool, there is no lasting remembrance of the wise, since in the days to come both will be forgotten. How is it that the wise person dies just like the fool? ¹⁷ Therefore, I hated life because the work that was done under the sun was distressing to me. For everything is futile and a pursuit of the wind.   Ps 49:10; Ec 3:19; 6:6

The Emptiness of Work

¹⁸ I hated all my work that I labored at under the sun because I must leave it to the one who comes after me. ¹⁹ And who knows whether he

---

^A**2:3** Two Hb mss, LXX, Syr read *the sun*   ^B**2:8** LXX, Theod, Syr read *and male cupbearers and female cupbearers*; Aq, Tg, Vg read *a cup and cups*; Hb obscure   ^C**2:8** Or *many treasures that people delight in*   ^D**2:11** Lit *all my works that my hands had done*   ^E**2:11** Or *a feeding on wind*, or *an affliction of spirit*; also in vv. 17,26   ^F**2:12** Lit *the man who comes after the king*   ^G**2:12** Some Hb mss read *They* will be wise or a fool? Yet he will take over all my work that I labored at skillfully under the sun. This too is futile. [20] So I began to give myself over[A] to despair concerning all my work that I had labored at under the sun. [21] When there is a person whose work was done with wisdom, knowledge, and skill, and he must give his portion to a person who has not worked for it, this too is futile and a great wrong. [22] For what does a person get with all his work and all his efforts that he labors at under the sun? [23] For all his days are filled with grief, and his occupation is sorrowful; even at night, his mind does not rest. This too is futile. Ps 39:6; 49:10; Pr 13:22; Ec 1:3; 2:11

[24] There is nothing better for a person than to eat, drink, and enjoy[B,C] his work. I have seen that even this is from God's hand, [25] because who can eat and who can enjoy life[D] apart from him?[E] [26] For to the person who is pleasing in his sight, he gives wisdom, knowledge, and joy; but to the sinner he gives the task of gathering and accumulating in order to give to the one who is pleasing in God's sight. This too is futile and a pursuit of the wind. Ec 2:3; 3:12-13,22; 5:18; 6:12; 8:15

The Mystery of Time

3 There is an occasion
for everything,
and a time for every activity
under heaven: Ec 3:17; 8:6
[2] a time to give birth
and a time to die;   Jb 14:5
a time to plant and a time
to uproot;[F]

[3] a time to kill and a time
to heal;
a time to tear down
and a time to build;
[4] a time to weep and a time
to laugh;   Rm 12:15
a time to mourn and a time
to dance;   Ex 15:20
[5] a time to throw stones
and a time to gather stones;
a time to embrace and a time
to avoid embracing;   1Co 7:5
[6] a time to search and a time
to count as lost;
a time to keep and a time
to throw away;
[7] a time to tear and a time
to sew;
a time to be silent and a time
to speak;   Am 5:13; 1Co 14:26-32
[8] a time to love and a time
to hate;
a time for war and a time
for peace.   Mt 5:9; 10:34

[9] What does the worker gain from his struggles? [10] I have seen the task that God has given the children of Adam to keep them occupied. [11] He has made everything appropriate[G] in its time. He has also put eternity in their hearts,[H] but no one can discover the work God has done from beginning to end. [12] I know that there is nothing better for them than to rejoice and enjoy the[I] good life. [13] It is also the gift of God whenever anyone eats, drinks, and enjoys all his efforts. [14] I know that everything God does will last forever; there is no adding to it or taking from it. God works so that people will be in awe of him. [15] Whatever

---

is, has already been, and whatever will be, already is. However, God seeks justice for the persecuted. [A]

The Mystery of Injustice and Death

[16] I also observed under the sun: there is wickedness at the place of judgment and there is wickedness at the place of righteousness. [17] I said to myself, "God will judge the righteous and the wicked, since there is a time for every activity and every work." [18] I said to myself, "This happens so that God may test the children of Adam and they may see for themselves that they are like animals." [19] For the fate of the children of Adam and the fate of animals is the same. As one dies, so dies the other; they all have the same breath. People have no advantage over animals since everything is futile. [20] All are going to the same place; all come from dust, and all return to dust. [21] Who knows if the spirits of the children of Adam go upward and the spirits of animals go downward to the earth? [22] I have seen that there is nothing better than for a person to enjoy his activities because that is his reward. For who can enable him to see what will happen after he dies? [B]

4 Again, I observed all the acts of oppression being done under the sun. Look at the tears of those who are oppressed; they have no one to comfort them. Power is with those who oppress them; they have no one to comfort them. [2] So I commended the dead, who have already died, more than the living, who are still alive. [3] But better than either of them is the one who has

not yet existed, who has not seen the evil activity that is done under the sun.   Jb 3:11-26; 35:9; Ec 3:16; 5:8; 6:3

The Loneliness of Wealth

[4] I saw that all labor and all skillful work is due to one person's jealousy of another. This too is futile and a pursuit of the wind. [C]   1Sm 18:9; Ec 2:21

[5]   The fool folds his arms   Pr 6:10
        and consumes his own flesh.
[6]   Better one handful with rest
        than two handfuls
        with effort and a pursuit
        of the wind.   Pr 15:16-17

[7] Again, I saw futility under the sun: [8] There is a person without a companion, [D] without even a son or brother, and though there is no end to all his struggles, his eyes are still not content with riches. "Who am I struggling for," he asks, "and depriving myself of good things?" This too is futile and a miserable task.   Pr 27:20; Ec 1:8; 5:10

[9] Two are better than one because they have a good reward for their efforts. [10] For if either falls, his companion can lift him up; but pity the one who falls without another to lift him up. [11] Also, if two lie down together, they can keep warm; but how can one person alone keep warm? [12] And if someone overpowers one person, two can resist him. A cord of three strands is not easily broken.   1Kg 1:1-4

[13] Better is a poor but wise youth than an old but foolish king who no longer pays attention to warnings. [14] For he came from prison to be king, even though he was born poor in his kingdom. [15] I saw all the living, who move about under the

sun, follow[A] a second youth who succeeds him. [16] There is no limit to all the people who were before them, yet those who come later will not rejoice in him. This too is futile and a pursuit of the wind.   Ec 9:15

Caution in God's Presence

5 Guard your steps when you go to the house of God. Better to approach in obedience than to offer the sacrifice as fools do, for they ignorantly do wrong. [2] Do not be hasty to speak, and do not be impulsive to make a speech before God. God is in heaven and you are on earth, so let your words be few. [3] Just as dreams accompany much labor, so also a fool's voice comes with many words. [4] When you make a vow to God, don't delay fulfilling it, because he does not delight in fools. Fulfill what you vow. [5] Better that you do not vow than that you vow and not fulfill it. [6] Do not let your mouth bring guilt on you, and do not say in the presence of the messenger that it was a mistake. Why should God be angry with your words and destroy the work of your hands? [7] For many dreams bring futility, so do many words. Therefore, fear God.   Pr 10:19

The Realities of Wealth

[8] If you see oppression of the poor and perversion of justice and righteousness in the province, don't be astonished at the situation, because one official protects another official, and higher officials protect them. [9] The profit from the land is taken by all; the king is served by the field. [B]   Pr 27:23-27; Ec 4:1; 1Pt 4:12

[10] The one who loves silver is never satisfied with silver, and whoever loves wealth is never satisfied with income. This too is futile. [11] When good things increase, the ones who consume them multiply; what, then, is the profit to the owner, except to gaze at them with his eyes? [12] The sleep of the worker is sweet, whether he eats little or much, but the abundance of the rich permits him no sleep.

[13] There is a sickening tragedy I have seen under the sun: wealth kept by its owner to his harm. [14] That wealth was lost in a bad venture, so when he fathered a son, he was empty-handed. [15] As he came from his mother's womb, so he will go again, naked as he came; he will take nothing for his efforts that he can carry in his hands. [16] This too is a sickening tragedy: exactly as he comes, so he will go. What does the one gain who struggles for the wind? [17] What is more, he eats in darkness all his days, with much frustration, sickness, and anger.

[18] Here is what I have seen to be good: It is appropriate to eat, drink, and experience good in all the labor one does under the sun during the few days of his life God has given him, because that is his reward. [19] Furthermore, everyone to whom God has given riches and wealth, he has also allowed him to enjoy them, take his reward, and rejoice in his labor. This is a gift of God, [20] for he does not often consider the days of his life because God keeps him occupied with the joy of his heart.   2Ch 1:12; Ec 2:10,24; 3:13; 6:2

6 Here is a tragedy I have observed under the sun, and it weighs heavily on humanity: [C] [2] God gives a person riches, wealth, and honor so that he lacks nothing of

[A]**4:15** Lit *with*   [B]**5:9** Hb obscure   [C]**6:1** Or *it is common among men* all he desires for himself, but God does not allow him to enjoy them. Instead, a stranger will enjoy them. This is futile and a sickening tragedy. [3] A man may father a hundred children and live many years. No matter how long he lives, [A] if he is not satisfied by good things and does not even have a proper burial, I say that a stillborn child is better off than he. [4] For he comes in futility and he goes in darkness, and his name is shrouded in darkness. [5] Though a stillborn child does not see the sun and is not conscious, it has more rest than he. [6] And if a person lives a thousand years twice, but does not experience happiness, do not both go to the same place?   1Kg 3:13; Ps 17:14; 73:7; Ec 5:13

[7]   All of a person's labor is
     for his stomach, [B]   Pr 16:26
     yet the appetite is
     never satisfied.

[8] What advantage then does the wise person have over the fool? What advantage is there for the poor person who knows how to conduct himself before others? [9] Better what the eyes see than wandering desire. This too is futile and a pursuit of the wind. [C]

[10] Whatever exists was given its name long ago, [D] and it is known what mankind is. But he is not able to contend with the one stronger than he. [11] For when there are many words, they increase futility. What is the advantage for mankind? [12] For who knows what is good for anyone in life, in the few days of his futile life that he spends like a shadow? Who can tell anyone what will happen after him under the sun?

Wise Sayings

7   A good name is better than
     fine perfume,   Pr 22:1; Ezk 36:21
and the day of one's death
     is better than the day
     of one's birth.   Ec 4:2

[2]   It is better to go to a house
     of mourning
than to go to a house
     of feasting,
since that is the end
     of all mankind,
and the living should take it
     to heart.   Ps 90:12

[3]   Grief is better than laughter,
for when a face is sad, a heart
     may be glad.   Pr 14:13

[4]   The heart of the wise is
     in a house of mourning,
but the heart of fools is
     in a house of pleasure.

[5]   It is better to listen to rebuke
     from a wise person
than to listen to the song
     of fools,   Pr 13:1

[6]   for like the crackling
     of burning thorns
     under the pot,   Ps 58:9; 118:12
so is the laughter of the fool.
This too is futile.

[7]   Surely, the practice
     of extortion turns
     a wise person into a fool,
and a bribe corrupts the mind.

[8]   The end of a matter is better
     than its beginning;
a patient spirit is better
     than a proud spirit.   Pr 14:29

[9]   Don't let your spirit rush
     to be angry,
for anger abides in the heart
     of fools.   Pr 14:17; Jms 1:19

[10]   Don't say, "Why were
     the former days better
     than these?"   Jdg 6:13

[A] 6:3 Lit *how many years*   [B] 6:7 Lit *mouth*   [C] 6:9 Or *a feeding on wind,* or *an affliction of spirit*
[D] 6:10 Lit *name already*

since it is not wise of you
   to ask this.
11 Wisdom is as good
   as an inheritance
and an advantage to those
   who see the sun,
12 because wisdom
   is protection as silver
   is protection;
but the advantage
   of knowledge
is that wisdom preserves
   the life of its owner.   Pr 3:18
13 Consider the work of God,
   for who can straighten out
what he has made crooked?

14 In the day of prosperity be joyful, but in the day of adversity, consider: God has made the one as well as the other, so that no one can discover anything that will come after him.   Ec 3:22; Lm 3:38

Avoiding Extremes

15 In my futile life[A] I have seen everything: someone righteous perishes in spite of his righteousness, and someone wicked lives long in spite of his evil. 16 Don't be excessively righteous, and don't be overly wise. Why should you destroy yourself? 17 Don't be excessively wicked, and don't be foolish. Why should you die before your time? 18 It is good that you grasp the one and do not let the other slip from your hand. For the one who fears God will end up with both of them.
19 Wisdom makes
   the wise person stronger
   than ten rulers of a city.
20 There is certainly no one
   righteous on the earth
   who does good and never sins.

21 Don't pay attention[B] to everything people say, or you may hear your servant cursing you, 22 for in your heart you know that many times you yourself have cursed others.   Pr 30:10

What the Teacher Found

23 I have tested all this by wisdom. I resolved, "I will be wise," but it was beyond me. 24 What exists is beyond reach and very deep. Who can discover it? 25 I turned my thoughts to know, explore, and examine wisdom and an explanation for things, and to know that wickedness is stupidity and folly is madness. 26 And I find more bitter than death the woman who is a trap: her heart a net and her hands chains. The one who pleases God will escape her, but the sinner will be captured by her. 27 "Look," says the Teacher, "I have discovered this by adding one thing to another to find out the explanation, 28 which my soul continually searches for but does not find: I found one person in a thousand, but none of those was a woman. 29 Only see this: I have discovered that God made people upright, but they pursued many schemes."   Pr 5:4; 6:25; Ec 1:15,17; Rm 11:33

Wisdom, Authorities, and Inequities

8 Who is like the wise person, and who knows the interpretation of a matter? A person's wisdom brightens his face, and the sternness of his face is changed.   Dt 28:50
2 Keep[C] the king's command because of your oath made before God. 3 Do not be in a hurry; leave his presence, and don't persist in a

A7:15 Lit days   B7:21 Lit Don't give your heart   C8:2 Some Hb mss, LXX, Vg, Tg, Syr; other Hb mss read I, keep bad cause, since he will do whatever he wants. ⁴ For the king's word is authoritative, and who can say to him, "What are you doing?" ⁵ The one who keeps a command will not experience anything harmful, and a wise heart knows the right time and procedure. ⁶ For every activity there is a right time and procedure, even though a person's troubles are heavy on him. ⁷ Yet no one knows what will happen because who can tell him what will happen? ⁸ No one has authority over the wind ᴬ to restrain it, and there is no authority over the day of death; no one is discharged during battle, and wickedness will not allow those who practice it to escape. ⁹ All this I have seen, applying my mind to all the work that is done under the sun, at a time when one person has authority over another to his harm.

¹⁰ In such circumstances, I saw the wicked buried. They came and went from the holy place, and they were praised ᴮ in the city where they did those things. This too is futile. ¹¹ Because the sentence against an evil act is not carried out quickly, the heart of people is filled with the desire to commit evil. ¹² Although a sinner does evil a hundred times and prolongs his life, I also know that it will go well with God-fearing people, for they are reverent before him. ¹³ However, it will not go well with the wicked, and they will not lengthen their days like a shadow, for they are not reverent before God. Ec 7:15; 9:5; Rm 2:4; 2Pt 3:9

¹⁴ There is a futility that is done on the earth: there are righteous people who get what the actions of the wicked deserve, and there are wicked people who get what the actions of the righteous deserve. I say that this too is futile. ¹⁵ So I commended enjoyment because there is nothing better for a person under the sun than to eat, drink, and enjoy himself, for this will accompany him in his labor during the days of his life that God gives him under the sun. Jb 21:7; Ps 73:3; Ec 7:15; Jr 12:1

¹⁶ When I applied my mind to know wisdom and to observe the activity that is done on the earth (even though one's eyes do not close in sleep day or night), ¹⁷ I observed all the work of God and concluded that a person is unable to discover the work that is done under the sun. Even though a person labors hard to explore it, he cannot find it; even if a wise person claims to know it, he is unable to discover it. Ec 1:13-14; 3:11; 7:25-29; 11:5

Enjoy Life Despite Death

9 Indeed, I took all this to heart and explained it all: The righteous, the wise, and their works are in God's hands. People don't know whether to expect love or hate. Everything lies ahead of them. ² Everything is the same for everyone: There is one fate for the righteous and the wicked, for the good and the bad, ᶜ for the clean and the unclean, for the one who sacrifices and the one who does not sacrifice. As it is for the good, so also it is for the sinner; as it is for the one who takes an oath, so also for the one who fears an oath. ³ This is an evil in all that is done under the sun: there is one fate for everyone. In addition, the hearts of people are full of evil, and madness is in their

ᴬ8:8 Or life-breath ᴮ8:10 Some Hb mss, LXX, Aq, Theod, Sym; other Hb mss read forgotten ᶜ9:2 LXX, Aq, Syr, Vg; MT omits and the bad hearts while they live; after that they go to the dead. ⁴ But there is hope for whoever is joinedᴬ with all the living, since a live dog is better than a dead lion. ⁵ For the living know that they will die, but the dead don't know anything. There is no longer a reward for them because the memory of them is forgotten. ⁶ Their love, their hate, and their envy have already disappeared, and there is no longer a portion for them in all that is done under the sun.   Dt 33:3; Jb 9:22; Ec 1:17; 2:14

⁷ Go, eat your bread with pleasure, and drink your wine with a cheerful heart, for God has already accepted your works. ⁸ Let your clothes be white all the time, and never let oil be lacking on your head. ⁹ Enjoy life with the wife you love all the days of your fleetingᴮ life, which has been given to you under the sun, all your fleeting days. For that is your portion in life and in your struggle under the sun. ¹⁰ Whatever your hands find to do, do with all your strength, because there is no work, planning, knowledge, or wisdom in Sheol where you are going. Ps 23:5; Ec 2:24; 3:13; 5:18; 8:15

The Limitations of Wisdom

¹¹ Again I saw under the sun that the race is not to the swift, or the battle to the strong, or bread to the wise, or riches to the discerning, or favor to the skillful; rather, time and chance happen to all of them. ¹² For certainly no one knows his time: like fish caught in a cruel net or like birds caught in a trap, so people are trapped in an evil time as it suddenly falls on them. Am 2:14-15

¹³ I have observed that this also is wisdom under the sun, and it is significant to me: ¹⁴ There was a small city with few men in it. A great king came against it, surrounded it, and built large siege works against it. ¹⁵ Now a poor wise man was found in the city, and he delivered the city by his wisdom. Yet no one remembered that poor man. ¹⁶ And I said, "Wisdom is better than strength, but the wisdom of the poor man is despised, and his words are not heeded." Ec 4:13

¹⁷ The calm words of the wise
   are heeded
more than the shouts
   of a ruler over fools.
¹⁸ Wisdom is better
   than weapons of war,
but one sinner can destroy
   much good.   Jos 7:1

The Burden of Folly

10 Dead flies make
   a perfumer's oil ferment
   and stink;   Ex 30:25
so a little folly outweighs
   wisdom and honor.
² A wise person's heart goes
   to theᶜ right,
but a fool's heart to the left.
³ Even when the fool walks
   along the road, his heart
   lacks sense,
and he shows everyone he is
   a fool.   Pr 13:16; 18:2
⁴ If the ruler's anger rises
   against you, don't leave
   your post,   Ec 8:3
for calmness puts
   great offenses to rest.   Pr 25:15

⁵ There is an evil I have seen under the sun, an error proceeding from the presence of the ruler:
⁶ The fool is appointed
   to great heights,   Est 3:1; Pr 28:12

ᴬ9:4 Alt Hb tradition reads *chosen*   ᴮ9:9 Or *futile*   ᶜ10:2 Lit *his*

but the rich remain
in lowly positions.
7 I have seen slaves on horses,
but princes walking
on the ground like slaves.

8 The one who digs a pit
may fall into it,   Ps 7:15
and the one who breaks
through a wall
may be bitten by a snake.
9 The one who quarries stones
may be hurt by them;
the one who splits logs
may be endangered
by them.
10 If the ax is dull, and one
does not sharpen its edge,
then one must exert
more strength;
however, the advantage
of wisdom is that
it brings success.
11 If the snake bites before
it is charmed,   Jr 8:17
then there is no advantage
for the charmer.ᴬ
12 The words from the mouth
of a wise person
are gracious,   Pr 10:32; 22:11; Lk 4:22
but the lips of a fool
consume him.   Pr 18:7
13 The beginning of the words
from his mouth is folly,
but the end of his speaking
is evil madness;
14 yet the fool multiplies words.
No one knows
what will happen,
and who can tell anyone
what will happen
after him?   Ec 8:7,17
15 The struggles of fools
weary them,
for they don't know how
to go to the city.

16 Woe to you, land,
when your king is a youth
and your princes feast
in the morning.
17 Blessed are you, land,
when your king is a son
of nobles
and your princes feast
at the proper time —
for strength and not
for drunkenness.   Pr 31:4; Is 5:11
18 Because of laziness the roof
caves in,
and because of
negligent hands
the house leaks.
19 A feast is prepared
for laughter,
and wine makes life happy,
and moneyᴮ is the answer
for everything.   Ec 7:12
20 Do not curse the king
even in your thoughts,
and do not curse
a rich person
even in your bedroom,
for a bird of the sky
may carry the message,
and a winged creature
may report the matter.

Invest in Life

11 Send your bread
on the surface of the water,
for after many days
you may find it.
2 Give a portion to seven
or even to eight,   Ps 112:9; Mt 5:42
for you don't know
what disaster may happen
on earth.
3 If the clouds are full,
they will pour out rain
on the earth;
whether a tree falls
to the south or the north,

ᴬ10:11 Lit master of the tongue   ᴮ10:19 Lit silver

the place where the tree falls,
　　there it will lie.
4 One who watches the wind
　　will not sow,
and the one who looks
　　at the clouds will not reap.
5 Just as you don't know
　　the path of the wind,
or how bones develop
　　in[A] the womb
　　of a pregnant woman,
so also you don't know
　　the work of God
　　who makes everything.
6 In the morning sow your seed,
and at evening do not let
　　your hand rest,
because you don't know
　　which will succeed,
whether one or the other,
or if both of them will be
　　equally good.
7 Light is sweet,
and it is pleasing for the eyes
　　to see the sun.　　Ec 6:5; 7:11
8 Indeed, if someone lives
　　many years,
let him rejoice in them all,
and let him remember
　　the days of darkness,
　　since they will be many.
All that comes is futile.
9 Rejoice, young person,
　　while you are young,
and let your heart be glad
　　in the days of your youth.
And walk in the ways
　　of your heart
and in the desire of your eyes;
but know that for all
　　of these things
　　God will bring you
　　to judgment.
10 Remove sorrow
　　from your heart,

and put away pain
　　from your flesh,　　2Co 7:1
because youth and the prime
　　of life are fleeting.

The Twilight of Life

12 So remember your Creator in
　　the days of your youth:
Before the days of adversity
　　come,
and the years approach
　　when you will say,　　Ec 11:8
"I have no delight in them";
2 before the sun and the light
　　are darkened,　　Is 5:30; Ezk 32:7-8
and the moon and the stars,
and the clouds return
　　after[B] the rain;
3 on the day
　　when the guardians
　　of the house tremble,
and the strong men stoop,
the women who grind grain
　　cease because they are few,
and the ones who watch
　　through the windows
　　see dimly,　　Gn 27:1; 48:10; 1Sm 3:2
4 the doors at the street
　　are shut
while the sound of the mill
　　fades;　　Jr 25:10; Rv 18:22
when one rises at the sound
　　of a bird,
and all the daughters of song
　　grow faint.
5 Also, they are afraid
　　of heights and dangers
　　on the road;
the almond tree blossoms,
the grasshopper loses
　　its spring,[C]
and the caper berry has
　　no effect;
for the mere mortal is
　　headed to his eternal home,

[A]11:5 Or *know how the life-breath comes to the bones in* [B]12:2 Or *with* [C]12:5 Or *grasshopper is weighed down,* or *grasshopper drags itself along*

and mourners will walk
around in the street;   Jr 9:17

6 before the silver cord
is snapped,[A]
and the gold bowl is broken,
and the jar is shattered
at the spring,
and the wheel is broken
into the well;

7 and the dust returns
to the earth as it once was,
and the spirit returns to God
who gave it.   Gn 2:7; 3:19; Ec 3:21

8 "Absolute futility," says the Teacher. "Everything is futile."   Ec 1:2

The Teacher's Objectives and Conclusion

9 In addition to the Teacher being a wise man, he constantly taught the people knowledge; he weighed, explored, and arranged many proverbs. 10 The Teacher sought to find delightful sayings and write words of truth accurately. 11 The sayings of the wise are like cattle prods, and those from masters of collections are like firmly embedded nails. The sayings are given by one Shepherd.[B]   1Kg 4:32; Ezr 9:8; Pr 1:1,6; 22:17

12 But beyond these, my son, be warned: there is no end to the making of many books, and much study wearies the body. 13 When all has been heard, the conclusion of the matter is this: fear God and keep his commands, because this is for all[C] humanity. 14 For God will bring every act to judgment, including every hidden thing, whether good or evil.   1Kg 4:32-33; Pr 1:7; Ec 1:18; 3:14; Jn 21:25

A 12:6 Alt Hb tradition reads *removed*   B 12:11 Or *by a shepherd*   C 12:13 Or *is the whole duty of*

SONG OF SONGS

1 The Song of Songs, which is
Solomon's.   1Kg 4:32

Woman
2   Oh, that he would kiss
    me with the kisses
    of his mouth!
    For your caresses^A are
    more delightful than wine.
3   The fragrance
    of your perfume
    is intoxicating;   Jn 12:3
    your name is perfume
    poured out.   Ec 7:1
    No wonder young women^B
    adore you.
4   Take me with you —
    let's hurry.   Hs 11:4
    Oh, that the king
    would bring^C me
    to his chambers.

Young Women
    We will rejoice and be glad
    in you;
    we will celebrate your caresses
    more than wine.

Woman
    It is only right that
    they adore you.

5   Daughters of Jerusalem,   Sg 2:7
    I am dark like the tents
    of Kedar,   Ps 120:5; Is 60:7
    yet lovely like the curtains
    of Solomon.   Sg 2:14; 4:3; 6:4
6   Do not stare at me because
    I am dark,

    for the sun has gazed on me.
    My mother's sons
    were angry with me;   Ps 69:8
    they made me take care
    of the vineyards.   Sg 8:11
    I have not taken care of
    my own vineyard.

7   Tell me, you whom I love:
    Where do you pasture
    your sheep?   Sg 2:16; 6:3
    Where do you let them rest
    at noon?   Is 13:20; Jr 33:12
    Why should I be like one
    who veils herself^D
    beside the flocks
    of your companions?   Sg 8:13

Man^E
8   If you do not know,
    most beautiful of women,
    follow^F the tracks of the flock,
    and pasture
    your young goats
    near the shepherds' tents.

9   I compare you, my darling,
    to a^G mare
    among Pharaoh's chariots.
10 Your cheeks are beautiful
    with jewelry,   Sg 5:13
    your neck with its necklace.
11 We will make gold jewelry
    for you,
    accented with silver.

Woman
12 While the king is
    on his couch,^H

---

^A1:2 Or *acts of love*   ^B1:3 Or *wonder virgins*   ^C1:4 Or *The king has brought*   ^D1:7 Or *who wanders*
^E1:8 Some understand the young women to be the speakers in this verse.   ^F1:8 Lit *go out for yourself into*
^G1:9 Lit *my*   ^H1:12 Or *is at his table*

my perfume^A releases
its fragrance.   Sg 4:14; Mk 14:3

13 The one I love is a sachet
   of myrrh to me,   Ps 45:8; Jn 19:39
spending the night
   between my breasts.

14 The one I love is a cluster
   of henna blossoms to me,
in the vineyards of En-gedi.

Man

15 How beautiful you are,
   my darling.
How very beautiful!
Your eyes are doves.   Sg 4:1

Woman

16 How handsome you are,
   my love.   Sg 2:3
How delightful!
Our bed is verdant;

17 the beams of our house
   are cedars,
and our rafters
   are cypresses.^B

2 I am a wildflower^C of Sharon,
a lily^D of the valleys.   Sg 5:13

Man

2 Like a lily among thorns,
so is my darling
   among the young women.

Woman

3 Like an apricot^E tree
   among the trees
   of the forest,
so is my love
   among the young men.
I delight to sit in his shade,
and his fruit is sweet
   to my taste.

4 He brought me
   to the banquet hall,^F   Sg 1:4

and he looked on me
   with love.^G   Ps 20:5

5 Sustain me with raisins;
refresh me with apricots,^H
for I am lovesick.   Sg 5:8

6 May his left hand be
   under my head,
and his right arm
   embrace me.   Sg 8:3

7 Young women of Jerusalem,
   I charge you
by the gazelles
   and the wild does
   of the field,
do not stir up or awaken love
until the appropriate time.^I

8 Listen! My love
   is approaching.
Look! Here he comes,
leaping over the mountains,
bounding over the hills.

9 My love is like a gazelle
or a young stag.   Sg 2:17; 8:14
See, he is standing
   behind our wall,
gazing through the windows,
peering through the lattice.

10 My love calls to me:

Man

Arise, my darling.   Sg 2:13
Come away,
   my beautiful one.

11 For now the winter is past;
the rain has ended
   and gone away.

12 The blossoms appear
   in the countryside.
The time of singing^J
   has come,
and the turtledove's cooing
   is heard in our land.   Jr 8:7

13 The fig tree ripens its figs;

---

^A1:12 Lit *nard*   ^B1:17 Or *firs*, or *pines*   ^C2:1 Traditionally *rose*   ^D2:1 Or *lotus*   ^E2:3 Or *apple*   ^F2:4 Lit
the house of wine   ^G2:4 Or *and his banner over me is love*   ^H2:5 Or *apples*   ^I2:7 Lit *until it pleases*
^J2:12 Or *pruning*

the blossoming vines give off
  their fragrance.　　　Sg 7:12
Arise, my darling.
Come away, my beautiful one.

¹⁴ My dove, in the clefts
  of the rock,　　　Sg 5:2; 6:9; Jr 48:28
in the crevices of the cliff,
let me see your face, ᴬ
let me hear your voice;　　Sg 8:13
for your voice is sweet,
and your face is lovely.　　Sg 1:5

Woman ᴮ
¹⁵ Catch the foxes for us —
the little foxes that ruin
  the vineyards —
for our vineyards are in bloom.

Woman
¹⁶ My love is mine and I am his;
he feeds among the lilies.
¹⁷ Until the day breaks ᶜ
and the shadows flee,
turn around, my love, and be
  like a gazelle
or a young stag
  on the divided mountains. ᴰ

3 In my bed at night ᴱ
I sought the one I love;　　Sg 1:7
I sought him, but did not
  find him. ᶠ　　　Sg 5:6
² I will arise now and go
  about the city,
through the streets
  and the plazas.　　Jr 5:1
I will seek the one I love.
I sought him, but did not
  find him.
³ The guards who go
  about the city found me.
I asked them, "Have you seen
  the one I love?"

⁴ I had just passed them
when I found the one I love.
I held on to him
  and would not let him go
until I brought him
  to my mother's house —
to the chamber of the one
  who conceived me.
⁵ Young women of Jerusalem,
  I charge you
by the gazelles
  and the wild does
  of the field,
do not stir up
  or awaken love
until the appropriate time. ᴳ

Narrator
⁶ Who is this coming up
  from the wilderness　　Sg 6:10
like columns of smoke,
scented with myrrh
  and frankincense　　Sg 4:6,14
from every fragrant powder
  of the merchant?

⁷ Look! Solomon's bed
surrounded by sixty warriors
from the mighty men
  of Israel.
⁸ All of them are skilled
  with swords
and trained in warfare.
Each has his sword
  at his side　　　Ps 45:3
to guard against the terror
  of the night.　　　Ps 91:5

⁹ King Solomon made
  a carriage for himself
with wood from Lebanon.
¹⁰ He made its posts of silver,
its back ᴴ of gold,
and its seat of purple.

ᴬ2:14 Or *form*　　ᴮ2:15 The speaker could be the woman, the man, or both.　　ᶜ2:17 Lit *breathes*　　ᴰ2:17 Or
the Bether mountains, or *the mountains of spices* ; Hb obscure　　ᴱ3:1 Or *bed night after night*　　ᶠ3:1 LXX
adds *I called him, but he did not answer me*　　ᴳ3:5 Lit *until it pleases*　　ᴴ3:10 Or *base*, or *canopy*

Its interior is inlaid with love[A]
by the young women
  of Jerusalem.   Sg 1:5

11 Go out, young women of Zion,
and gaze at King Solomon,
wearing the crown
  his mother placed on him
on the day of his wedding —
the day of his
  heart's rejoicing.

Man

4 How beautiful you are,
  my darling.
How very beautiful!
Behind your veil,
your eyes are doves.   Sg 1:15; 5:12
Your hair is like a flock
  of goats
streaming down
  Mount Gilead.   Sg 6:5

2 Your teeth are like a flock
  of newly shorn sheep
coming up from washing,
each one bearing twins,
and none has lost its young.[B]

3 Your lips are
  like a scarlet cord,   Jos 2:18
and your mouth[C] is lovely.
Behind your veil,
your brow[D] is like a slice
  of pomegranate.   Sg 6:7

4 Your neck is like the tower
  of David,   Sg 7:4
constructed in layers.
A thousand shields are hung
  on it —
all of them shields
  of warriors.

5 Your breasts are
  like two fawns,
twins of a gazelle, that feed
  among the lilies.   Sg 7:3

6 Until the day breaks[E]

and the shadows flee,   Sg 2:17
I will make my way
  to the mountain of myrrh
and the hill of frankincense.

7 You are absolutely beautiful,
  my darling;   Sg 1:15; Eph 5:27
there is no imperfection
  in you.

8 Come with me
  from Lebanon,[F] my bride;
come with me from Lebanon!
Descend from the peak
  of Amana,
from the summit of Senir
  and Hermon,   Dt 3:9; 1Ch 5:23
from the dens of the lions,
from the mountains
  of the leopards.

9 You have captured my heart,
  my sister, my bride.   Sg 6:5; 7:5
You have captured
  my heart with one glance
  of your eyes,
with one jewel
  of your necklace.

10 How delightful
  your caresses are,
  my sister, my bride.
Your caresses are much
  better than wine,   Sg 1:2,4
and the fragrance
  of your perfume
  than any balsam.

11 Your lips drip sweetness like
  the honeycomb, my bride.
Honey and milk are
  under your tongue.   Ex 3:8,17
The fragrance
  of your garments is like
  the fragrance of Lebanon.

12 My sister, my bride, you are
  a locked garden —

[A]3:10 Or *leather* [B]4:2 Lit *and no one bereaved among them* [C]4:3 Or *speech* [D]4:3 Or *temple*, or *cheek*, or *lips* [E]4:6 Lit *breathes* [F]4:8 In Hb, the word for *Lebanon* is similar to "frankincense" in Sg 4:6,14,15.

a locked garden^A
and a sealed spring.   1Kg 21:8

¹³ Your branches
are a paradise^B
of pomegranates
with choicest fruits;   Sg 7:13
henna with nard,

¹⁴ nard and saffron, calamus
and cinnamon,   Ex 30:23
with all the trees
of frankincense,   Sg 4:6
myrrh and aloes,   Sg 3:6; Jn 19:39
with all the best spices.

¹⁵ You are a garden spring,
a well of flowing water   Gn 26:19
streaming from Lebanon.

Woman

¹⁶ Awaken, north wind;   Sg 2:7; 3:5
come, south wind.
Blow on my garden,
and spread the fragrance
of its spices.
Let my love come
to his garden
and eat its choicest fruits.

Man

5 I have come to my garden —
my sister, my bride.
I gather^C my myrrh
with my spices.
I eat my honeycomb
with my honey.
I drink my wine
with my milk.

Narrator

Eat, friends!
Drink, be intoxicated
with caresses!^D   Pr 5:19

Woman

² I was sleeping, but my heart
was awake.

A sound! My love
was knocking!   Sg 2:8

Man

Open to me, my sister,
my darling,
my dove, my perfect one.
For my head is drenched
with dew,
my hair with droplets
of the night.

Woman

³ I have taken off my clothing.
How can I put it back on?
I have washed my feet.
How can I get them dirty?

⁴ My love thrust his hand
through the opening,
and my feelings were stirred
for him.

⁵ I rose to open for my love.
My hands dripped with myrrh,
my fingers
with flowing myrrh
on the handles of the bolt.

⁶ I opened to my love,
but my love had turned
and gone away.
My heart sank^E because
he had left.^F
I sought him, but did not
find him.   Sg 3:1-2
I called him, but he
did not answer.

⁷ The guards who go
about the city found me.
They beat and wounded me;
they took my cloak^G
from me —
the guardians of the walls.

⁸ Young women of Jerusalem,
I charge you,   Sg 2:7; 3:5; 8:4
if you find my love,
tell him that I am lovesick.

^A**4:12** Some Hb mss read *locked fountain*   ^B**4:13** Or *park*, or *orchard*   ^C**5:1** Lit *pluck*   ^D**5:1** Or *Drink your fill, lovers*   ^E**5:6** Lit *My soul went out*   ^F**5:6** Or *spoken*   ^G**5:7** Or *veil*, or *shawl*

Young Women

9 What makes the one you love
   better than another,
most beautiful of women?
What makes him better
   than another,
that you would give us
   this charge?

Woman

10 My love is fit and strong,^A
notable among ten thousand.
11 His head is purest gold.
His hair is wavy^B   Sg 5:2
and black as a raven.
12 His eyes are like doves   Sg 1:15
beside flowing streams,
washed in milk
and set like jewels.^C
13 His cheeks are like beds
   of spice,   Sg 1:10
mounds of^D perfume.
His lips are lilies,
dripping with flowing myrrh.
14 His arms^E are rods of gold
set^F with beryl.   Ex 28:20; 39:13
His body^G is an ivory panel
covered with lapis lazuli.
15 His legs are alabaster pillars
set on pedestals of pure gold.
His presence is like Lebanon,
as majestic as the cedars.
16 His mouth is sweetness.
He is absolutely desirable.
This is my love, and this is
   my friend,
young women of Jerusalem.

Young Women

6 Where has your love gone,
most beautiful of women?
Which way has he^H turned?
We will seek him with you.

Woman

2 My love has gone down
   to his garden,   Sg 4:16; 5:1
to beds of spice,   Sg 5:13
to feed in the gardens   Sg 1:7
and gather lilies.   Sg 2:1
3 I am my love's and my love
   is mine;   Sg 2:16; 7:10; 8:6
he feeds among the lilies.

Man

4 You are as beautiful
   as Tirzah, my darling,
lovely as Jerusalem,
awe-inspiring as an army
   with banners.   Nm 2:2-3; Sg 6:10
5 Turn your eyes away from me,
for they captivate me.   Sg 4:9
Your hair is like a flock
   of goats
streaming down from Gilead.
6 Your teeth are like a flock
   of ewes
coming up from washing,
each one having a twin,
and not one missing.^I   Sg 4:2
7 Behind your veil,   Sg 4:3
your brow^J is like a slice
   of pomegranate.
8 There are sixty queens
and eighty concubines   1Kg 11:3
and young women^K
   without number.
9 But my dove,
   my virtuous one, is unique;
she is the favorite
   of her mother,
perfect to the one who gave
   her birth.
Women see her and declare
   her fortunate;   Gn 30:13
queens and concubines also,
   and they sing her praises:

---

^A5:10 Or *is radiant and ruddy*   ^B5:11 Or *is like palm leaves*; Hb obscure   ^C5:12 Lit *milk sitting in fullness*
^D5:13 LXX, Vg read *spice, yielding*   ^E5:14 Lit *hands*   ^F5:14 Lit *filled*; Sg 5:2,12   ^G5:14 Lit *abdomen*
^H6:1 Lit *your love*   ^I6:6 Lit *and no one bereaved among them*   ^J6:7 Or *temple*, or *cheek*, or *lips*
^K6:8 Or *and virgins*; Sg 1:3

¹⁰ Who is this who shines
     like the dawn,   Sg 3:6; 8:5
as beautiful as the moon,
bright as the sun,
awe-inspiring as an army
     with banners?   Sg 6:4

Woman
¹¹ I came down
     to the walnut grove
to see the blossoms
     of the valley,
to see if the vines
     were budding   Sg 7:12
and the
     pomegranates blooming.
¹² I didn't know what was
     happening to me.
I felt like I was
in a chariot with a
     nobleman.^A

Young Women
¹³ Come back, come back,
     Shulammite!^B
Come back, come back, that
     we may look at you!

Man
How you gaze
     at the Shulammite,
as you look at the dance
     of the two camps!^C   Jdg 21:21

7 How beautiful are
     your sandaled feet,
     princess!^D   Ps 45:13
The curves of your thighs
     are like jewelry,
the handiwork of a master.
² Your navel is a rounded bowl;
it never lacks mixed wine.
Your belly is a mound of wheat
surrounded by lilies.

³ Your breasts are
     like two fawns,
twins of a gazelle.   Sg 4:5
⁴ Your neck is like a tower
     of ivory,   Sg 4:4
your eyes like pools
     in Heshbon
by Bath-rabbim's gate.
Your nose is like the tower
     of Lebanon
looking toward Damascus.
⁵ Your head crowns you^E
     like Mount Carmel,
the hair of your head
     like purple cloth —
a king could be held captive
     in your tresses.   Sg 4:9
⁶ How beautiful you are
     and how pleasant,   Sg 1:15-16
my love, with such delights!
⁷ Your stature is
     like a palm tree;
your breasts are clusters
     of fruit.
⁸ I said, "I will climb
     the palm tree
and take hold of its fruit."
May your breasts be
     like clusters of grapes,
and the fragrance
     of your breath like apricots.
⁹ Your mouth^F is
     like fine wine —   Sg 5:16

Woman
flowing smoothly
     for my love,
gliding past my lips
     and teeth!^G
¹⁰ I am my love's,
and his desire is for me.   Gn 3:16

¹¹ Come, my love,
     let's go to the field;

---

^A**6:12** Hb obscure   ^B**6:13** Or *the perfect one*, or *the peaceable one*   ^C**6:13** Or *dance of Mahanaim*
^D**7:1** Lit *daughter of a nobleman*, or *prince*   ^E**7:5** Lit *head upon you is*   ^F**7:9** Lit *palate*   ^G**7:9** LXX, Syr, Vg;
MT reads *past lips of sleepers*

let's spend the night
among the henna blossoms.[A]

12 Let's go early to the vineyards;
let's see if the vine has budded,
if the blossom has opened,
if the pomegranates are
in bloom.   Sg 6:11
There I will give you
my caresses.

13 The mandrakes give off
a fragrance,   Gn 30:14-16
and at our doors is
every delicacy,
both new and old.
I have treasured them up
for you, my love.

8 If only I could treat you
like my brother,[B]
one who nursed
at my mother's breasts,
I would find you in public
and kiss you,
and no one would scorn me.

2 I would lead you,
I would take you,
to the house of my mother
who taught me.[C]   Sg 3:4
I would give you spiced wine
to drink
from the juice of my
pomegranate.

3 May his left hand be
under my head,
and his right arm embrace me.

4 Young women of Jerusalem,
I charge you,
do not stir up or awaken love
until the appropriate time.

Young Women

5 Who is this coming up
from the wilderness,   Sg 3:6
leaning on the one she loves?

Woman

I awakened you under
the apricot tree.   Sg 2:3
There your mother
conceived you;
there she conceived and gave
you birth.

6 Set me as a seal
on your heart,
as a seal on your arm.   Sg 2:16; 6:3
For love is as strong as death;
jealousy is as unrelenting
as Sheol.
Love's flames are
fiery flames —   Dt 32:21-22
an almighty flame![D]

7 A huge torrent cannot
extinguish love;
rivers cannot sweep it away.
If a man were to give all
his wealth[E] for love,   Pr 6:35
it would be utterly scorned.

Brothers

8 Our sister is young;
she has no breasts.   Ezk 16:7
What will we do for our sister
on the day she is spoken for?

9 If she is a wall,
we will build
a silver barricade on her.
If she is a door,
we will enclose her
with cedar planks.   1Kg 6:15

Woman

10 I am[F] a wall
and my breasts like towers.
So in his eyes I have become
like one who finds[G] peace.[H]

11 Solomon owned a vineyard
in Baal-hamon.   Ec 2:4

[A]7:11 Or *the villages*   [B]8:1 Lit *Would that you were like a brother to me*   [C]8:2 LXX adds *and into the chamber of the one who bore me*   [D]8:6 Or *the blaze of the Lord*   [E]8:7 Lit *all the wealth of his house*   [F]8:10 Or *was*   [G]8:10 Or *brings*   [H]8:10 In Hb, the word for *peace* sounds similar to Solomon and Shulammite.

He leased the vineyard
    to tenants.   Mt 21:33
Each was to bring
    for his fruit
one thousand pieces
    of silver.   Is 7:23
12 I have my own vineyard. A
The one thousand are
    for you, Solomon,
but two hundred for those
    who take care of its fruits.

Man

13 You B who dwell in the gardens,
companions are listening
    for your voice;   Sg 1:7
let me hear you!   Sg 2:14

Woman

14 Run away with me, C my love,
and be like a gazelle
or a young stag
on the mountains of spices.

A 8:12 Lit *My vineyard, which is mine, is before me* ; Sg 1:6   B 8:13 In Hb, the word for *You* is feminine.
C 8:14 Lit *Flee*

ISAIAH

1 The vision concerning Judah and Jerusalem that Isaiah son of Amoz saw during the reigns^A,B of Kings Uzziah, Jotham, Ahaz, and Hezekiah of Judah. Pr 29:18; Dn 8:1; Ob 1

Judah on Trial

² Listen, heavens,
and pay attention, earth,
for the LORD has spoken:
"I have raised children^C
and brought them up,
but they have rebelled
against me. Is 30:1
³ The ox knows its owner,
and the donkey its master's
feeding trough,
but Israel does not know;
my people do not understand."

⁴ Oh sinful nation,
people weighed down
with iniquity, Is 13:11
brood of evildoers, Is 14:20; Mt 3:7
depraved children!
They have abandoned
the LORD; Dt 4:31
they have despised
the Holy One of Israel; Pr 5:12
they have turned their backs
on him.

⁵ Why do you want
more beatings?
Why do you
keep on rebelling?
The whole head is hurt,
and the whole heart is sick.
⁶ From the sole of the foot
even to the head, Jb 2:7
no spot is uninjured — Ps 38:3
wounds, welts,
and festering sores
not cleansed, bandaged,
or soothed with oil.

⁷ Your land is desolate,
your cities burned down;
foreigners devour your fields
right in front of you —
a desolation, like a place
demolished by foreigners.
⁸ Daughter Zion is abandoned
like a shelter in a vineyard,
like a shack
in a cucumber field,
like a besieged city.
⁹ If the LORD of Armies 1Sm 17:45
had not left us
a few survivors, Is 10:21-22
we would be like Sodom,
we would
resemble Gomorrah. Is 3:9

¹⁰ Hear the word of the LORD,
you rulers of Sodom!
Listen to the instruction
of our God,
you people of Gomorrah! Is 3:9
¹¹ "What are all your sacrifices
to me?"
asks the LORD.
"I have had enough
of burnt offerings and rams
and the fat of well-fed cattle;
I have no desire for the blood
of bulls,
lambs, or male goats. 1Sm 15:22
¹² When you come to appear
before me,
who requires this from you —
this trampling of my courts?

---

^A **1:1** Lit *saw in the days* ^B **1:1** ca 792–686 BC ^C **1:2** Or *sons*, also in v. 4

¹³ Stop bringing
useless offerings. Mal 1:10
Your incense is detestable
to me.
New Moons and Sabbaths,
and the calling
of solemn assemblies —
I cannot stand iniquity
with a festival. Is 13:11
¹⁴ I hate your New Moons
and prescribed festivals.
They have become a burden
to me;
I am tired of putting up
with them.
¹⁵ When you spread out
your hands in prayer, 1Kg 8:22
I will refuse to look at you;
even if you offer
countless prayers,
I will not listen. Is 59:2; Jr 7:16
Your hands are covered
with blood. Pr 1:28; Is 59:1-3; Mc 3:4

Purification of Jerusalem

¹⁶ "Wash yourselves.
Cleanse yourselves. Ps 26:6
Remove your evil deeds
from my sight.
Stop doing evil. Jr 25:5
¹⁷ Learn to do what is good.
Pursue justice. Dt 16:20; 1Kg 3:11; 11:4
Correct the oppressor.^A
Defend the rights
of the fatherless.
Plead the widow's cause.
¹⁸ "Come, let us settle this,"
says the LORD.
"Though your sins are scarlet,
they will be as white as snow;
though they are crimson red,
they will be like wool.
¹⁹ If you are willing
and obedient,

you will eat the good things
of the land. Dt 30:15-20
²⁰ But if you refuse and rebel,
you will be devoured
by the sword." Jr 12:12
For the mouth of the LORD
has spoken. Is 24:3; 40:5; 58:14

²¹ The faithful town —
what an adulteress^B
she has become!
She was once full of justice.
Righteousness once dwelt
in her,
but now, murderers!
²² Your silver has become dross
to be discarded,
your beer^C is diluted
with water.
²³ Your rulers are rebels,
friends of thieves. Hs 5:10
They all love graft
and chase after bribes. Ex 23:8
They do not defend the rights
of the fatherless,
and the widow's case
never comes
before them. Ex 22:22; Dt 24:17

²⁴ Therefore the Lord GOD
of Armies,
the Mighty One
of Israel, declares:
"Ah, I will get even with
my foes;
I will take revenge
against my enemies. Is 35:4
²⁵ I will turn my hand
against you Ps 81:14; Is 5:25; Am 1:8
and will burn away
your dross completely;^D
I will remove
all your impurities. Ezk 22:20
²⁶ I will restore my judges
to what they were at first,^E

^A1:17 Or Aid the oppressed ^B1:21 Or prostitute ^C1:22 Or wine ^D1:25 Lit dross as with lye
^E1:26 Lit judges as at the first

and your advisers to what
   they were at the start. [A]
Afterward you will be called
   the Righteous City,   Is 33:5; 60:14
a Faithful Town."

27 Zion will be redeemed
   by justice,
those who repent,
   by righteousness.   Rm 3:26
28 At the same time both rebels
   and sinners
   will be broken,
and those who abandon
   the LORD will perish.
29 Indeed, they [B]
   will be ashamed
   of the sacred trees
you desired,   Is 2:8; 57:5; Hs 4:13
and you
   will be embarrassed
   because of the garden
   shrines
you have chosen.   Is 65:3; 66:17
30 For you will become
   like an oak
whose leaves are withered,
and like a garden
   without water.   Ps 1:3; Is 64:6
31 The strong one
   will become tinder,
and his work a spark;
both will burn together,   Is 5:24
with no one to extinguish
   the flames.   Is 66:24; Mt 3:12; Mk 9:43

The City of Peace

2 The vision that Isaiah son of
Amoz saw concerning Judah
and Jerusalem: 2Kg 19:2; 20:1; 2Ch 26:22; 13:1
2 In the last days   Mc 4:1-4; Rm 2:20
   the mountain
   of the LORD's house
   will be established   2Ch 33:15
at the top of the mountains

and will be raised
   above the hills.
All nations will stream to it,
3 and many peoples will come
   and say,
"Come, let us go up
   to the mountain
   of the LORD,
to the house of the God
   of Jacob.   Is 29:23; 45:23; 60:13; 66:18
He will teach us
   about his ways
so that we may walk
   in his paths."
For instruction will go
   out of Zion
and the word of the LORD
   from Jerusalem.
4 He will settle disputes
   among the nations
and provide arbitration
   for many peoples.
They will beat their swords
   into plows
and their spears
   into pruning knives.   Is 11:6-9
Nation will not take up
   the sword against nation,
and they will
   never again train for war.

The Day of the LORD

5 House of Jacob,
   come and let us walk
   in the LORD's light.   Ps 27:1; 43:3
6 For you have abandoned
   your people,   Dt 31:17; Ps 94:14; Is 1:4
the house of Jacob,
because they are
   full of divination
   from the East
and of fortune-tellers
   like the Philistines.   Lv 19:26
They are in league [C]
   with foreigners.

[A]**1:26** Lit *advisers as at the beginning*   [B]**1:29** Some Hb mss; other Hb mss, Tg read *you*   [C]**2:6** Or *They teem*, or *They partner*; Hb obscure

7 Their^(A,B) land is full of silver
  and gold,
and there is no limit
  to their treasures;
their land is full of horses,
and there is no limit
  to their chariots.   Dt 17:17
8 Their land is full of idols;
they worship the work
  of their hands,
what their fingers
  have made.   Is 41:21-29; 44:9-17
9 So humanity is brought low,
and each person is humbled.
Do not forgive them!   Ex 34:7
10 Go into the rocks   Rv 6:15
  and hide in the dust
from the terror of the LORD
and from
  his majestic splendor.   2Th 1:9
11 The pride of mankind^C
  will be humbled,   Ps 18:27; Is 2:17
and human loftiness
  will be brought low;
the LORD alone
  will be exalted on that day.

12 For a day belonging to
  the LORD of Armies
  is coming
against all that is proud
  and lofty,   Mal 4:1
against all that is lifted up —
  it will be humbled —
13 against all the cedars
  of Lebanon,   Ps 29:5; Is 14:8; Hs 14:5
lofty and lifted up,
against all the oaks
  of Bashan,   Ezk 27:6; Zch 11:2
14 against all
  the high mountains,   Is 40:4
against all the lofty hills,
15 against every high tower,
against every fortified wall,
16 against every ship
  of Tarshish,   1Kg 10:22; Is 23:1,14

and against every splendid
  sea vessel.
17 The pride of mankind will be
  brought low,
and human loftiness
  will be humbled;
the LORD alone
  will be exalted on that day.
18 The idols
  will vanish completely.
19 People will go into caves
  in the rocks   Is 2:10
and holes in the ground,
away from the terror
  of the LORD
and
  from his majestic splendor,
when he rises to terrify
  the earth.   Ps 18:7; Is 13:13; 24:1,19-20
20 On that day people will throw
their silver and gold idols,
which they made to worship,
to the moles and the bats.
21 They will go into the caves
  of the rocks
and the crevices in the cliffs,
away from the terror
  of the LORD
and from
  his majestic splendor,   Is 2:10
when he rises to terrify
  the earth.
22 Put no more trust in a mere
  human,
who has only the breath
  in his nostrils.   Ps 39:11; 144:4
What is he really worth?

Judah's Leaders Judged

3 Note this: The Lord GOD
  of Armies
is about to remove
  from Jerusalem
  and from Judah
every kind of security:

^A 2:7 Lit Its   ^B 2:7 = the house of Jacob   ^C 2:11 Lit Mankind's proud eyes

the entire supply of bread
and water,

2 heroes and warriors,　2Kg 24:14
judges and prophets,
fortune-tellers and elders,

3 commanders of fifty
and dignitaries,
counselors,
cunning magicians, A
and necromancers. B

4 "I will make youths
their leaders,　Ec 10:16
and unstable rulers C
will govern them."

5 The people will oppress
one another,　Mc 7:3-6
man against man, neighbor
against neighbor;
the young will act arrogantly
toward the old,
and the worthless
toward the honorable.

6 A man will even seize
his brother
in his father's house, saying:
"You have a cloak — you be
our leader!
This heap of rubble will be
under your control."

7 On that day
he will cry out, saying:
"I'm not a healer.
I don't even have food
or clothing in my house.
Don't make me the leader
of the people!"

8 For Jerusalem has stumbled
and Judah has fallen
because they have spoken
and acted against the LORD,
defying
his glorious presence.　Is 43:7

9 The look on their faces
testifies against them,
and like Sodom, they flaunt
their sin;　Is 1:9-10; 13:19

they do not conceal it.
Woe to them,
for they have brought
disaster on themselves.

10 Tell the righteous that
it will go well for them,
for they will eat the fruit
of their labor.

11 Woe to the wicked —
it will go badly for them,
for what they have done
will be done to them.

12 Youths oppress my people,
and women rule over them.
My people, your leaders
mislead you;
they confuse the direction
of your paths.　Is 28:14-22

13 The LORD rises to argue
the case
and stands to judge the people.

14 The LORD brings this charge
against the elders
and leaders of his people:
"You have devastated
the vineyard.
The plunder from the poor is
in your houses.　Ezk 18:10-18; 33:15

15 Why do you crush my people
and grind the faces
of the poor?"
This is the declaration
of the Lord GOD of Armies.

Jerusalem's Women Judged

16 The LORD also says:
Because the daughters
of Zion are haughty,　Is 32:9-15
walking with heads
held high
and seductive eyes,
prancing along,
jingling their ankle bracelets,

17 the Lord will put scabs
on the heads

A3:3 Or *skilled craftsmen*　B3:3 Or *mediums*　C3:4 Or *mischief-makers*

of the daughters of Zion,
and the Lord will shave
their foreheads bare.

¹⁸ On that day the Lord will strip their finery: ankle bracelets, headbands, crescents, ¹⁹ pendants, bracelets, veils, ²⁰ headdresses, ankle jewelry, sashes, perfume bottles, amulets, ²¹ signet rings, nose rings, ²² festive robes, capes, cloaks, purses, ²³ garments, linen clothes, turbans, and shawls. Jdg 8:21,26; Is 27:12

²⁴ Instead of perfume
there will be a stench;
instead of a belt, a rope;
instead of beautifully
styled hair, baldness; 1Pt 3:3
instead of
fine clothes, sackcloth; Is 15:3
instead of beauty, branding. ᴬ
²⁵ Your men will fall
by the sword,
your warriors in battle.
²⁶ Then her gates will lament
and mourn; Jr 14:2; Lm 1:4
deserted, she will sit
on the ground. Jb 2:13; Is 47:1

4 On that day seven women will seize one man, saying, "We will eat our own bread and provide
our own clothing.
Just let us bear your name.
Take away our disgrace."

Zion's Future Glory

² On that day the Branch ᴮ of the Lord will be beautiful and glorious, and the fruit of the land will be the pride and glory of Israel's survivors. ³ Whoever remains in Zion and whoever is left in Jerusalem will be called holy — all in Jerusalem written in the book of life ᶜ — ⁴ when the Lord has washed away the filth of the daughters of Zion and cleansed the bloodguilt from the heart of Jerusalem by a spirit of judgment and a spirit of burning. ⁵ Then the Lord will create a cloud of smoke by day and a glowing flame of fire by night over the entire site of Mount Zion and over its assemblies. For there will be a canopy over all the glory, ᴰ ⁶ and there will be a shelter for shade from heat by day, and a refuge and shelter from storm and rain.

Song of the Vineyard

5 I will sing about the one
I love,
a song about
my loved one's vineyard:
The one I love had a vineyard
on a very fertile hill.
² He broke up the soil,
cleared it of stones,
and planted it
with the finest vines. Jr 2:21
He built a tower in the middle
of it
and even dug out
a winepress there.
He expected it to yield
good grapes, Is 40:31
but it yielded
worthless grapes. Mt 21:19

³ So now,
residents of Jerusalem
and men of Judah,
please judge between me
and my vineyard.
⁴ What more could I have done
for my vineyard
than I did? Mc 6:3-4; Mt 23:37
Why, when I expected a yield
of good grapes,

ᴬ3:24 DSS read shame ᴮ4:2 Or plant ᶜ4:3 Lit Jerusalem recorded for life ᴰ4:5 Or For glory will be a canopy over all did it yield worthless grapes?

5 Now I will tell you
what I am about to do
to my vineyard:
I will remove its hedge,   Ps 89:40
and it will be consumed;
I will tear down its wall,
and it will be trampled.
6 I will make it a wasteland.
It will not be pruned
or weeded;
thorns and briers
will grow up.   Gn 3:18; Is 7:23-25
I will also give orders
to the clouds
that rain should not fall on it.
7 For the vineyard of the LORD
of Armies
is the house of Israel,   Ps 80:8-11
and the men[A] of Judah,
the plant he delighted in.
He expected justice
but saw injustice;
he expected righteousness,
but heard cries of despair.

Judah's Sins Denounced

8 Woe to those who add house
to house   Jr 22:13-17; Mc 2:2
and join field to field
until there is no more room
and you alone are left
in the land.

9 I heard the LORD of Armies say:
Indeed, many houses
will become desolate,
grand and lovely ones
without inhabitants.
10 For a ten-acre[B] vineyard
will yield
only six gallons of wine,[C]
and ten bushels[D] of seed
will yield
only one bushel of grain.[E]

11 Woe to those who rise early
in the morning
in pursuit of beer,   Lv 10:9; Nm 6:3
who linger into the evening,
inflamed by wine.
12 At their feasts they have
lyre, harp,
tambourine, flute, and wine.
They do not perceive
the LORD's actions,   Dt 32:4; 44:1
and they do not see the work
of his hands.   Ex 32:16; 34:10

13 Therefore my people will go
into exile
because they
lack knowledge;   Is 1:3; 27:11
her[F] dignitaries are starving,
and her masses are parched
with thirst.
14 Therefore Sheol enlarges
its throat
and opens wide
its enormous jaws,   Pr 30:16
and down go Zion's
dignitaries, her masses,
her crowds, and those
who celebrate in her!
15 Humanity is brought low,
each person is humbled,
and haughty eyes
are humbled.   Is 2:9,11,17; 10:33
16 But the LORD of Armies
is exalted by his justice,
and the holy God shows that
he is holy through
his righteousness.   Is 6:3; 8:13
17 Lambs will graze
as if in[G] their own pastures,
and resident aliens[H] will eat
among the ruins of the rich.

18 Woe to those
who drag iniquity
with cords of deceit   Pr 5:22

[A]5:7 Lit *man*   [B]5:10 Lit *ten-yoke*   [C]5:10 Lit *one bath*   [D]5:10 Lit *one homer*   [E]5:10 Lit *yield an ephah*
[F]5:13 Lit *its*   [G]5:17 Syr reads *graze in*   [H]5:17 LXX reads *sheep*

and pull sin along
　with cart ropes,
19 to those who say:
"Let him hurry up and do
　his work quickly
so that we can see it!
Let the plan of the Holy One
　of Israel take place　Jb 38:2; 42:3
so that we can know it!"
20 Woe to those who call
　evil good
and good evil,　　　Pr 17:15; Am 5:7
who substitute darkness
　for light
and light for darkness,
who substitute bitter
　for sweet
and sweet for bitter.
21 Woe to those
　who consider themselves
　wise
and judge themselves
　clever.ᴬ　　　Pr 3:7; Rm 12:16; 1Co 3:18
22 Woe to those who are heroes
　at drinking wine,
who are champions at
　pouring beer,　　　Is 5:11
23 who acquit the guilty
　for a bribe　　Ex 23:8; Pr 17:15; Is 1:23
and deprive the innocent
　of justice.

24 Therefore, as a tongue of fire
　consumes straw
and as dry grass shrivels
　in the flame,
so their roots will become
　like something rotten
and their blossoms
　will blow away like dust,
for they have rejected　　Is 8:6
the instruction of the LORD
　of Armies,
and they have despised
the word of the Holy One
　of Israel.　　　Is 5:19; Jr 51:5

25 Therefore the LORD's anger
　burned against his people.
He raised his hand
　against them
　and struck them;
the mountains quaked,　　Am 1:1
and their corpses were
　like garbage in the streets.
In all this, his anger has
　not turned away,
and his hand is still raised
　to strike.　　Is 9:12,17,21; 10:4; 14:27

26 He raises a signal flag
　for the distant nations　Is 10:5
and whistles for them
　from the ends
　of the earth.　　Is 7:18; Zch 10:8
Look — how quickly
　and swiftly they come!
27 None of them grows weary
　or stumbles;　　　1Jn 2:10
no one slumbers or sleeps.
No belt is loose
and no sandal strap broken.
28 Their arrows are sharpened,
and all their bows strung.
Their horses' hooves are
　like flint;
their chariot wheels are
　like a whirlwind.
29 Their roaring is
　like a lion's;　　Jdg 14:5; Hs 13:8; Jl 1:6
they roar like young lions;
they growl and seize
　their prey
and carry it off,
and no one can rescue it.
30 On that day they will roar
　over it,
like the roaring of the sea.
When one looks at the land,
there will be darkness
　and distress;
light will be obscured
　by clouds.ᴮ

ᴬ5:21 Lit and clever before their face　　ᴮ5:30 Lit its clouds

Isaiah's Call and Mission

6 In the year that King Uzziah died, I saw the Lord seated on a high and lofty throne, and the hem of his robe filled the temple. ² Seraphim ᴬ were standing above him; they each had six wings: with two they covered their faces, with two they covered their feet, and with two they flew. ³ And one called to another: Gn 32:30; 2Kg 15:1-7; Is 1:1; 14:28

Holy, holy, holy is the LORD
    of Armies;
his glory fills
    the whole earth. Ex 16:10; Is 35:2
⁴ The foundations of the doorways shook at the sound of their voices, and the temple was filled with smoke. Ex 19:8; Hab 3:3-10; Rv 15:8
⁵ Then I said:
Woe is me for I am ruined ᴮ
because I am a man
    of unclean lips
and live among a people
    of unclean lips, Ex 6:12,30
and because my eyes
    have seen the King,
the LORD of Armies.

⁶ Then one of the seraphim flew to me, and in his hand was a glowing coal that he had taken from the altar with tongs. ⁷ He touched my mouth with it and said: Lv 6:12-13
Now that this has touched
    your lips,
your iniquity is removed
and your sin is atoned for.

⁸ Then I heard the voice of the Lord asking:
Who should I send?
Who will go for us?

I said:
Here I am. Send me.

⁹ And he replied:
Go! Say to these people:
Keep listening,
    but do not understand;
keep looking,
    but do not perceive.
¹⁰ Make the minds ꟲ of these
    people dull;
deafen their ears and blind
    their eyes;
otherwise they might see
    with their eyes
and hear with their ears,
understand
    with their minds,
turn back, and be healed.

¹¹ Then I said, "Until when, Lord?"
And he replied: Ps 79:5; 89:46
Until cities lie in ruins
    without inhabitants, Is 1:7
houses are without people,
the land is ruined
    and desolate,
¹² and the LORD drives
    the people far away,
leaving great emptiness
    in the land.
¹³ Though a tenth will remain
    in the land,
it will be burned again.
Like the terebinth or the oak
that leaves a stump
    when felled,
the holy seed is the stump.

The Message to Ahaz

7 This took place during the reign of Ahaz, son of Jotham, son of Uzziah king of Judah: Aram's King Rezin and Israel's King Pekah son of Remaliah went to fight against Jerusalem, but they were not able to conquer it. 2Kg 15:25,37; 16:5; Is 1:1
² When it became known to the house of David that Aram had

ᴬ **6:2** = heavenly beings   ᴮ **6:5** Or *I must be silent*   ꟲ **6:10** Lit *heart* occupied Ephraim, the heart of Ahaz^A and the hearts of his people trembled like trees of a forest shaking in the wind. Is 7:13; 9:7; 16:5; 29:1

³ The LORD said to Isaiah, "Go out with your son Shear-jashub^B to meet Ahaz at the end of the conduit of the upper pool, by the road to the Launderer's Field. ⁴ Say to him: Calm down and be quiet. Don't be afraid or cowardly because of these two smoldering sticks, the fierce anger of Rezin and Aram, and the son of Remaliah. ⁵ For Aram, along with Ephraim and the son of Remaliah, has plotted harm against you. They say, ⁶ 'Let us go up against Judah, terrorize it, and conquer it for ourselves. Then we can install Tabeel's son as king in it.' " Gn 15:1; Ex 14:13; 2Kg 18:17; Is 8:3,18; 36:2

⁷ This is what the Lord GOD says:

It will not happen;
it will not occur. Is 8:10
⁸ The^C chief city of Aram
is Damascus,
the chief of Damascus
is Rezin
(within sixty-five years
Ephraim will be
too shattered to be
a people),
⁹ the chief city of Ephraim
is Samaria,
and the chief of Samaria
is the son of Remaliah.
If you do not stand firm
in your faith,
then you will not stand at all.

The Immanuel Prophecy

¹⁰ Then the LORD spoke again to Ahaz: ¹¹ "Ask for a sign from the LORD your God — it can be as deep as Sheol or as high as heaven."

¹² But Ahaz replied, "I will not ask. I will not test the LORD."

¹³ Isaiah said, "Listen, house of David! Is it not enough for you to try the patience of men? Will you also try the patience of my God? ¹⁴ Therefore, the Lord himself will give you^D a sign: See, the virgin will conceive,^E have a son, and name him Immanuel.^F ¹⁵ By the time he learns to reject what is bad and choose what is good, he will be eating curds^G and honey. ¹⁶ For before the boy knows to reject what is bad and choose what is good, the land of the two kings you dread will be abandoned. ¹⁷ The LORD will bring on you, your people, and your father's house such a time as has never been since Ephraim separated from Judah: He will bring the king of Assyria." Is 1:14; 43:24; Mt 3:3; 12:17

¹⁸   On that day   Is 27:12
the LORD will whistle to flies
at the farthest streams
of the Nile
and to bees in the land
of Assyria.
¹⁹   All of them will come
and settle
in the steep ravines,
in the clefts of the rocks,
in all the thornbushes, and in
all the water holes.

²⁰ On that day the Lord will use a razor hired from beyond the Euphrates River — the king of Assyria — to shave the hair on your heads, the hair on your legs, and even your beards. 2Kg 18:13-16; Is 8:7; 11:15; 24:1; Ezk 5:1-4

²¹   On that day
a man will raise a young cow
and two sheep,

^A7:2 Lit Aram has rested upon Ephraim, his heart   ^B7:3 = A Remnant Will Return   ^C7:8 Lit For the
^D7:14 In Hb, the word you is pl   ^E7:14 Or virgin is pregnant, will   ^F7:14 = God With Us   ^G7:15 Or sour milk

22 and from the abundant milk
   they give
he will eat curds,
for every survivor in the land
   will eat curds and honey.

23 And on that day
every place where there were
   a thousand vines,
worth a thousand pieces
   of silver,
will become thorns
   and briers.   Is 5:6
24 A man will go there with bow
   and arrows
because the whole land
   will be thorns and briers.
25 You will not go to all the hills
that were once tilled
   with a hoe,
for fear of the thorns
   and briers.
Those hills will be places
   for oxen to graze
and for sheep to trample.

The Coming Assyrian Invasion

8 Then the Lord said to me, "Take a large piece of parchment[A] and write on it with an ordinary pen:[B] Maher-shalal-hash-baz.[C] 2 I have appointed[D] trustworthy witnesses — the priest Uriah and Zechariah son of Jeberechiah."

3 I was then intimate with the prophetess, and she conceived and gave birth to a son. The Lord said to me, "Name him Maher-shalal-hash-baz, 4 for before the boy knows how to call 'Father,' or 'Mother,' the wealth of Damascus and the spoils of Samaria will be carried off to the king of Assyria."

5 The Lord spoke to me again:
6 Because these
   people rejected
the slowly flowing water
   of Shiloah
and rejoiced with[E] Rezin
and the son of Remaliah,   Is 7:1
7 the Lord will certainly bring
   against them
the mighty rushing water
   of the Euphrates River —
the king of Assyria
   and all his glory.
It will overflow its channels
and spill over all its banks.
8 It will pour into Judah,
flood over it,
and sweep through,
reaching up to the neck;
and its flooded banks[F]
will fill your entire land,
   Immanuel!   Is 7:14; 8:10

9 Band together,[G] peoples,
   and be broken;
pay attention,
   all you distant lands;
prepare for war,
   and be broken;
prepare for war,
   and be broken.
10 Devise a plan; it will fail.
Make a prediction;
   it will not happen.
For God is with us.[H]   Is 8:8

The Lord of Armies, the Only Refuge

11 For this is what the Lord said to me with great power, to keep[I] me from going the way of this people:
12 Do not call everything
   a conspiracy

A 8:1 Hb obscure   B 8:1 Lit *with the pen of a man*   C 8:1 = Speeding to the Plunder, Hurrying to the Spoil
D 8:2 Vg; MT, one DSS ms read *I will appoint*; one DSS ms, LXX, Syr, Tg read *Appoint*   E 8:6 Or *and rejoiced over*   F 8:8 Lit *its outspread wings*   G 8:9 Or *Raise the war cry*, or *Be shattered*   H 8:10 Hb *Immanuel*
I 8:11 DSS; MT reads *instruct*

these people say is
  a conspiracy.   Is 7:2; 30:1
Do not fear what they fear;
do not be terrified.
13 You are to regard
     only the LORD of Armies
     as holy.   Nm 20:12
Only he should be feared;
only he should be held
  in awe.
14 He will be a sanctuary;   Is 4:6
but for the two houses
  of Israel,
he will be a stone
  to stumble over   Ps 91:12; Is 26:4
and a rock to trip over,   Lk 2:34
and a trap and a snare
  to the inhabitants
  of Jerusalem.
15 Many will stumble
     over these;   Is 28:13; 59:10; Lk 20:18
they will fall and be broken;
they will be snared
  and captured.

16 Bind up the testimony.   Is 8:1-2
Seal up the instruction
  among my disciples.   Dn 12:4
17 I will wait for the LORD,   Ps 27:14
who is hiding his face
  from the house of Jacob.
I will wait for him.

18 Here I am with the children the
LORD has given me to be signs and
wonders in Israel from the LORD of
Armies who dwells on Mount Zion.
19 When they say to you, "Inquire of
the mediums and the spiritists who
chirp and mutter," shouldn't a people inquire of their God? A Should
they inquire of the dead on behalf
of the living? 20 Go to God's instruction and testimony! If they do not
speak according to this word, there
will be no dawn for them.   Heb 2:13

21 They will wander through the
land, dejected and hungry. When
they are famished, they will become enraged, and, looking upward, will curse their king and
their God. 22 They will look toward the earth and see only distress, darkness, and the gloom of
affliction, and they will be driven
into thick darkness. Is 5:30; 59:9; Jr 13:16

Birth of the Prince of Peace

9 Nevertheless, the gloom of the
  distressed land will not be like
that of the former times when he
humbled the land of Zebulun and
the land of Naphtali. But in the future he will bring honor to the way
of the sea, to the land east of the
Jordan, and to Galilee of the na-
tions.   Mt 4:15
2 The people walking
     in darkness
   have seen a great light;   Mt 4:16
   a light has dawned
   on those living in the land
     of darkness.   Lk 1:79
3 You have enlarged the nation
   and increased its joy. B   Is 26:15
   The people have rejoiced
     before you
   as they rejoice
     at harvest time
   and as they rejoice
     when dividing spoils.
4 For you have shattered
     their oppressive yoke   Is 10:27
   and the rod
     on their shoulders,
   the staff of their oppressor,
   just as you did on the day
     of Midian.   Jdg 7:25; Is 10:26
5 For every trampling boot
     of battle
   and the bloodied garments
     of war

A 8:19 Or gods   B 9:3 Alt Hb tradition reads *have not increased joy*

will be burned as fuel
    for the fire.
6 For a child will be born
    for us,
a son will be given to us,   Is 7:14
and the government will be
    on his shoulders.   Is 22:22
He will be named
Wonderful Counselor,
    Mighty God,   Dt 10:17; Is 28:29
Eternal Father,
    Prince of Peace.   Is 63:16; 64:8
7 The dominion will be vast,
and its prosperity will
    never end.   Ps 89:4; Dn 2:44
He will reign on the throne
    of David
and over his kingdom,
to establish and sustain it
with justice and
    righteousness from now on
    and forever.
The zeal of the
    LORD of Armies
    will accomplish this.   Is 37:32

The Hand Raised Against Israel

8 The Lord sent a message
    against Jacob;
it came against Israel.
9 All the people —
Ephraim and the inhabitants
    of Samaria — will know it.
They will say with pride
    and arrogance:
10 "The bricks have fallen,
but we will rebuild
    with cut stones;
the sycamores have been
    cut down,
but we will replace them
    with cedars."
11 The LORD has raised up
    Rezin's adversaries
    against him
and stirred up his enemies.

12 Aram from the east
    and Philistia from the west
have consumed Israel
    with open mouths.
In all this, his anger
    has not turned away,
and his hand is still raised
    to strike.   Is 5:25
13 The people did not turn
    to him who struck them;
they did not seek the LORD
    of Armies.
14 So the LORD cut off
    Israel's head and tail,   Is 19:15
palm branch and reed
    in a single day.
15 The head is the elder,
    the honored one;   Is 3:2-3
the tail is the prophet,
    the one teaching lies.   Is 28:15
16 The leaders of the people
    mislead them,
and those they mislead
    are swallowed up. A
17 Therefore the Lord does not
    rejoice
over B Israel's young men
and has no compassion
on its fatherless and widows,
for everyone is
    a godless evildoer,   Is 1:4; 10:6
and every mouth speaks folly.
In all this, his anger
    has not turned away,
and his hand is still raised
    to strike.
18 For wickedness burns
    like a fire   Ps 83:14; Is 1:7; Nah 1:10
that consumes thorns
    and briers
and kindles
    the forest thickets
so that they go up
    in a column of smoke.

A 9:16 Or are confused   B 9:17 DSS read not spare

^19 The land is scorched
by the wrath of the Lord
of Armies,
and the people are like fuel
for the fire.   Is 1:31; 24:6
No one has compassion
on his brother.   Mc 7:2,6
^20 They carve meat on the right,
but they are still hungry;
they have eaten on the left,
but they are still not satisfied.
Each one eats the flesh
of his own arm.   Dt 28:53-57
^21 Manasseh is with Ephraim,
and Ephraim with Manasseh;
together, both are
against Judah.   2Ch 28:6,8; Is 11:13
In all this, his anger has
not turned away,
and his hand is still raised
to strike.   Is 5:25

10 Woe to those enacting
crooked statutes   Is 5:8; 28:1
and writing oppressive laws
^2 to keep the poor from getting
a fair trial
and to deprive the needy
among my people of justice,
so that widows can be
their spoil
and they can plunder
the fatherless.   Ex 22:22; Dt 24:17
^3 What will you do on the day
of punishment
when devastation comes
from far away?
Who will you run to for help?
Where will you leave
your wealth?
^4 There will be nothing to do
except crouch
among the prisoners
or fall among the slain.
In all this, his anger
has not turned away,

and his hand is still raised
to strike.   Is 5:25; 9:12,17,21

Assyria, the Instrument of Wrath

^5 Woe to Assyria, the rod
of my anger —
the staff in their hands is
my wrath.
^6 I will send him against
a godless nation;
I will command him to go
against a people destined
for my rage,
to take spoils, to plunder,
and to trample them down
like clay in the streets.
^7 But this is not
what he intends;
this is not what he plans.
It is his intent to destroy
and to cut off many nations.
^8 For he says,
"Aren't all
my commanders kings?
^9 Isn't Calno like Carchemish?
Isn't Hamath like Arpad?
Isn't Samaria
like Damascus? ^A   Ac 1:8
^10 As my hand seized
the idolatrous kingdoms,
whose idols exceeded
those of Jerusalem
and Samaria,
^11 and as I did to Samaria
and its worthless images
will I not also do to Jerusalem
and its idols? "   2Kg 21:11; 23:24

Judgment on Assyria

^12 But when the Lord finishes all his
work against Mount Zion and Jerusalem, he will say, "I ^B will punish
the king of Assyria for his arrogant
acts and the proud look in his eyes."
^13 For he said: Jr 50:31

^A **10:9** Cities conquered by Assyria   ^B **10:12** LXX reads *Jerusalem, he*

I have done this
  by my own strength
and wisdom, for I am clever.
I abolished the borders
  of nations
and plundered
  their treasures; Jr 15:13; 17:3; 20:5
like a mighty warrior,
  I subjugated
  the inhabitants. ᴬ   2Sm 22:48

¹⁴ My hand has reached out,
  as if into a nest,
to seize the wealth
  of the nations.
Like one gathering
  abandoned eggs,
I gathered the whole earth.
No wing fluttered;
  no beak opened or chirped.

¹⁵ Does an ax exalt itself
above the one who chops
  with it?
Does a saw magnify itself
above the one who saws
  with it?
It would be like a rod waving
  the one who lifts ᴮ it!
It would be like a staff
  lifting the one
  who isn't wood!

¹⁶ Therefore the Lord GOD
  of Armies
will inflict
  an emaciating disease
on the well-fed of Assyria,
and he will kindle
  a burning fire
under its glory.

¹⁷ Israel's Light will become
  a fire,
and its Holy One, a flame. Is 4:5
In one day it will
  burn and consume
  Assyria's thorns
  and thistles. Gn 3:18; Is 5:6; 7:23-25

¹⁸ He will completely destroy
the glory of its forests
  and orchards
as a sickness consumes
  a person.

¹⁹ The remaining trees
  of its forest
will be so few in number
that a child could count them.

The Remnant Will Return

²⁰ On that day the remnant of Israel and the survivors of the house of Jacob will no longer depend on the one who struck them, but they will faithfully depend on the LORD, the Holy One of Israel. Is 1:4

²¹ The remnant will return,
  the remnant of Jacob,
  to the Mighty God.

²² Israel, even if your people
  were as numerous
  as the sand of the sea,
  only a remnant of them
  will return. 2Kg 19:30,31; Ezr 9:8,15
Destruction has been
  decreed;
justice overflows.

²³ For throughout the land
  the Lord GOD of Armies
  is carrying out a destruction
  that was decreed.

²⁴ Therefore, the Lord GOD of Armies says this: "My people who dwell in Zion, do not fear Assyria, though they strike you with a rod and raise their staff over you as the Egyptians did. ²⁵ In just a little while my wrath will be spent and my anger will turn to their destruction." ²⁶ And the LORD of Armies will brandish a whip against him as he did when he struck Midian at the rock of Oreb; and he will raise his staff over the sea as he did in Egypt.

ᴬ10:13 Or I brought down their kings   ᴮ10:15 Some Hb mss, Syr, Vg read wave he who lifts

God Will Judge Assyria

27 On that day
his burden will fall
    from your shoulders,
and his yoke
    from your neck.
The yoke will be broken
    because your neck will be
    too large. A   Gn 27:40; Dt 28:48; 30:8
28 Assyria has come to Aiath
and has gone
    through Migron,
storing their equipment
    at Michmash.
29 They crossed over
    at the ford, saying,
"We will spend the night
    at Geba."
The people of Ramah
    are trembling;
those at Gibeah of Saul
    have fled.
30 Cry aloud, daughter
    of Gallim!
Listen, Laishah!
Anathoth is miserable.
31 Madmenah has fled.
The inhabitants of Gebim
    have sought refuge.
32 Today the Assyrians will
    stand at Nob,
shaking their fists
    at the mountain
    of Daughter Zion,
the hill of Jerusalem.
33 Look, the Lord GOD
    of Armies
will chop off the branches
    with terrifying power,
and the tall trees will be
    cut down,
the high trees felled.
34 He is clearing the thickets
    of the forest with an ax,
and Lebanon with its majesty
    will fall.

Reign of the Davidic King

11 Then a shoot will grow
    from the stump of Jesse,
and a branch from his roots
    will bear fruit.   Is 14:19; 60:21
2 The Spirit of the LORD
    will rest on him — Is 42:1; 48:16
a Spirit of wisdom
    and understanding,
a Spirit of counsel
    and strength,
a Spirit of knowledge
    and of the fear of the LORD.
3 His delight will be in the fear
    of the LORD.
He will not judge
by what he sees with his eyes,
he will not execute justice
by what he hears with his ears,
4 but he will judge
    the poor righteously   Is 3:14
and execute justice
    for the oppressed
    of the land.
He will strike the land
with a scepter B
    from his mouth,   Ps 2:9; Is 49:2
and he will kill the wicked
with a command C
    from his lips.   Jb 4:9; Is 30:28,33
5 Righteousness will be a belt
    around his hips;   Eph 6:14
faithfulness will be a belt
    around his waist.   Eph 6:14
6 The wolf will dwell
    with the lamb,   Is 65:25; Jr 5:6
and the leopard will lie down
    with the goat.
The calf, the young lion,
    and the fattened calf
    will be together,
and a child will lead them.
7 The cow and the bear
    will graze,
their young ones
    will lie down together,

A 10:27 Lit *because of fatness*; Hb obscure   B 11:4 Lit *the rod*   C 11:4 Lit *with the breath*

and the lion will eat straw
    like cattle.
8   An infant will play
        beside the cobra's pit,
    and a toddler will put
        his hand into a snake's den.
9   They will not harm or
        destroy each other
    on my entire holy mountain,
    for the land will be as full
    of the knowledge of the LORD
    as the sea is filled with water.

Israel Regathered

10 On that day the root of Jesse
    will stand as a banner
        for the peoples.   Is 49:22; 62:10
    The nations will look to him
        for guidance,   Rm 15:12; Rv 5:5
    and his resting place
        will be glorious.   Is 14:3; 28:12

11 On that day the Lord will extend
his hand a second time to recover
the remnant of his people who survive — from Assyria, Egypt, Pathros, Cush, Elam, Shinar, Hamath,
and the coasts and islands of the
west.   Is 10:20-22; 27:12; 37:4,31-32; 46:3
12 He will lift up a banner
        for the nations
    and gather the dispersed
        of Israel;   Is 56:8; Zph 3:10; Zch 10:6
    he will collect the scattered
        of Judah
    from the four corners
        of the earth.   Rv 7:1; 20:8
13 Ephraim's envy will cease;
    Judah's harassing will end.
    Ephraim will no longer
        be envious of Judah,
    and Judah will not harass
        Ephraim.
14 But they will swoop down
        on the Philistine flank
        to the west.

Together they will plunder
    the people of the east.   Jr 49:28
They will extend their power
    over Edom and Moab,
and the Ammonites will be
    their subjects.   Ps 60:8; 83:6
15 The LORD will divide^A,B
        the Gulf of Suez.^C
He will wave his hand
    over the Euphrates
with his mighty wind   Is 7:20; 8:7
and will split it
    into seven streams,
letting people walk through
    on foot.
16 There will be a highway
        for the remnant
        of his people
    who will survive
        from Assyria,   Is 19:23; 35:8; 40:3
    as there was for Israel
    when they came up
        from the land of Egypt.

A Song of Praise

12 On that day you will say:
"I will give thanks to you,
    LORD,
although you were angry
    with me.
Your anger has turned away,
    and you have comforted me.
2   Indeed, God is my salvation;
    I will trust him and not
        be afraid,
    for the LORD,
        the LORD himself,
    is my strength and my song.
    He has become my salvation."
3   You will joyfully draw water
    from the springs of salvation,
4   and on that day you will say:
    "Give thanks to the LORD;
        proclaim his name!
    Make his works known
        among the peoples.   1Ch 16:8

^A 11:15 Text emended; MT reads *destroy*   ^B 11:15 Or *dry up*   ^C 11:15 Lit *the Sea of Egypt*

Declare that his name
   is exalted.
5 Sing to the LORD,
   for he has done
   glorious things.   Ex 15:1; Ps 98:1
Let this be known
   throughout the earth.
6 Cry out and sing,
   citizen of Zion,
for the Holy One of Israel is
   among you   Is 1:4
in his greatness."

A Pronouncement
Against Babylon

13 A pronouncement concerning Babylon that Isaiah son
of Amoz saw: Is 14:28; 15:1; 17:1; 19:1; 22:1
2 Lift up a banner
   on a barren mountain.   Is 5:26
Call out to them.
Signal with your hand,
   and they will go
through the gates
   of the nobles.
3 I have commanded
   my consecrated ones;
yes, I have called
   my warriors,
who celebrate my triumph,
to execute my wrath.   Ps 78:21,50
4 Listen, a commotion
   on the mountains,
like that of a mighty people!
Listen, an uproar
   among the kingdoms,
like nations being
   gathered together!
The LORD of Armies
   is mobilizing an army
   for war.
5 They are coming
   from a distant land,
from the farthest horizon —
   the LORD and the weapons
   of his wrath —

to destroy
   the whole country.^A
6 Wail! For the day of the LORD
   is near.   Is 2:12; 10:3; 13:9; 34:2,8; 61:2
It will come as destruction
   from the Almighty.   Is 10:25
7 Therefore everyone's hands
   will become weak,
and every man will lose
   heart.^B
8 They will be horrified;
pain and agony
   will seize them;
they will be in anguish
   like a woman in labor.   Is 26:17
They will look at each other,
their faces flushed with fear.
9 Look, the day of the LORD
   is coming —   Mt 25:13
cruel, with rage
   and burning anger —
to make the earth a desolation
and to destroy its sinners.
10 Indeed, the stars of the sky
   and its constellations^C
will not give their light.
The sun will be dark
   when it rises,
and the moon will not shine.
11 I will punish the world
   for its evil,   Jr 23:2; 36:31; 44:29
and wicked people
   for their iniquities.
I will put an end to the pride
   of the arrogant   Is 2:11; 23:9
and humiliate the insolence
   of tyrants.
12 I will make a human more
   scarce than fine gold,
and mankind more rare
   than the gold of Ophir.
13 Therefore I will make
   the heavens tremble,
and the earth will shake
   from its foundations   Ps 18:7

^A**13:5** Or earth   ^B**13:7** Lit every man's heart will melt   ^C**13:10** Or Orions

at the wrath of the LORD
of Armies,
on the day
of his burning anger.
14 Like wandering gazelles
and like sheep
without a shepherd,   1Kg 22:17
each one will turn
to his own people,
each one will flee
to his own land.
15 Whoever is found
will be stabbed,
and whoever is caught
will die by the sword.
16 Their children will be
dashed to pieces
before their eyes;   Ps 137:8-9
their houses will be looted,
and their wives raped.
17 Look! I am stirring up
the Medes against them,
who cannot be bought off
with^A silver
and who have no desire
for gold.
18 Their bows will cut
young men to pieces.
They will have
no compassion
on offspring;
they will not look with pity
on children.

19 And Babylon, the jewel
of the kingdoms,
the glory of the pride
of the Chaldeans,
will be like Sodom
and Gomorrah
when God overthrew them.
20 It will never be inhabited
or lived in from generation
to generation;   Is 14:23; 34:10-15
a nomad will not pitch
his tent there,

and shepherds will not let
their flocks rest there.
21 But desert creatures
will lie down there,
and owls will fill the houses.
Ostriches will dwell there,
and wild goats
will leap about.   Is 34:11-15; Rv 18:2
22 Hyenas will howl
in the fortresses,
and jackals,
in the luxurious palaces.
Babylon's time is almost up;
her days are almost over.

Israel's Return

14 For the LORD will have compassion on Jacob and will
choose Israel again. He will settle
them on their own land. The resident alien will join them and be
united with the house of Jacob.
2 The nations will escort Israel and
bring it to its homeland. Then the
house of Israel will possess them
as male and female slaves in the
LORD's land. They will make captives of their captors and will rule
over their oppressors.   Dt 7:7; 1Kg 3:26

Downfall of the King of Babylon

3 When the LORD gives you rest
from your pain, torment, and the
hard labor you were forced to do,
4 you will sing this song of contempt about the king of Babylon
and say: Gn 3:16; Ex 1:14; Is 14:3; Jr 44:19; Mc 2:4
How the oppressor
has quieted down,
and how the raging^B
has become quiet!
5 The LORD has broken
the staff of the wicked,
the scepter of the rulers.
6 It struck the peoples in anger
with unceasing blows.

^A 13:17 Lit who have no regard for   ^B 14:4 DSS; Hb uncertain

It subdued the nations
in rage
with relentless persecution.
⁷ The whole earth is calm
and at rest;
people shout
with a ringing cry.
⁸ Even the cypresses
and the cedars of Lebanon
rejoice over you: Ps 104:16; Is 55:12
"Since you have been
laid low,
no lumberjack has come
against us."

⁹ Sheol below is eager to greet
your coming,
stirring up the spirits
of the departed for you —
all the rulers ᴬ of the earth —
making all the kings
of the nations
rise from their thrones.
¹⁰ They all respond
to you, saying,
"You too have become
as weak as we are;
you have become like us!
¹¹ Your splendor has been
brought down to Sheol,
along with the music
of your harps.
Maggots are spread out
under you,
and worms cover you."

¹² Shining morning star, ᴮ 2Pt 1:19
how you have fallen
from the heavens! Is 34:4
You destroyer of nations,
you have been cut down
to the ground.
¹³ You said to yourself,
"I will ascend to the heavens;
I will set up my throne
above the stars of God.

I will sit on the mount
of the gods' assembly,
in the remotest parts
of the North. ᶜ Ps 48:2
¹⁴ I will ascend above
the highest clouds;
I will make myself
like the Most High."
¹⁵ But you will be brought down
to Sheol
into the deepest regions
of the Pit. Ps 28:1; Is 38:18; Ezk 28:8

¹⁶ Those who see you will stare
at you;
they will look closely at you:
"Is this the man who caused
the earth to tremble,
who shook the kingdoms,
¹⁷ who turned the world
into a wilderness, Jl 1:19-20; 3:19
who destroyed its cities
and would not release
the prisoners
to return home?"
¹⁸ All the kings of the nations
lie in splendor,
each in his own tomb.
¹⁹ But you are thrown out
without a grave,
like a worthless branch,
covered by those slain
with the sword
and dumped into a rocky pit
like a trampled corpse.
²⁰ You will not join them
in burial,
because you destroyed
your land
and slaughtered
your own people.
The offspring of evildoers
will never be mentioned
again. Jb 18:16,19; Ps 21:10; 37:28; Is 1:4
²¹ Prepare a place of slaughter
for his sons,

ᴬ14:9 Lit rams ᴮ14:12 Or Day Star, son of the dawn ᶜ14:13 Or of Zaphon

because of the iniquity
of their fathers.   Is 13:11
They will never rise up
to possess a land
or fill the surface of the earth
with cities.

²² "I will rise up against them" —
this is the declaration of the Lᴏʀᴅ
of Armies — "and I will cut off from
Babylon her reputation, remnant,
offspring, and posterity" — this is
the Lᴏʀᴅ's declaration. ²³ "I will make
her a swampland and a region for
herons, ᴬ and I will sweep her away
with the broom of destruction."
This is the declaration of
the Lᴏʀᴅ of Armies.

Assyria Will Be Destroyed

²⁴ The Lᴏʀᴅ of Armies has sworn:
As I have purposed,
so it will be;
as I have planned it,
so it will happen.   Pr 16:4; Is 46:11
²⁵ I will break Assyria
in my land;   Is 8:7; 10:5-15,27
I will tread him down
on my mountain.
Then his yoke will be taken
from them,
and his burden
will be removed
from their shoulders.
²⁶ This is the plan prepared
for the whole earth,
and this is the hand
stretched out
against all the nations.
²⁷ The Lᴏʀᴅ of Armies himself
has planned it;
therefore, who can stand
in its way?
It is his hand
that is outstretched,
so who can turn it back?

A Pronouncement Against Philistia

²⁸ In the year that King Ahaz died,
this pronouncement came:
²⁹ Don't rejoice, all of you
in Philistia,
because the rod of the one
who struck you is broken.
For a viper will come
from the root ᴮ of a snake,
and from its egg comes
a flying serpent.   Ex 4:2-3; 7:10-12
³⁰ Then the firstborn
of the poor will be well fed,
and the impoverished
will lie down in safety,
but I will kill your root
with hunger,
and your remnant
will be slain.
³¹ Wail, you gates! Cry out, city!
Tremble with fear,
all Philistia!   Jos 2:9,24
For a cloud of dust is coming
from the north,   Is 41:25; Jr 1:13-14
and there is no one missing
from the invader's ranks.
³² What answer will be
given to the messengers
from that nation?
The Lᴏʀᴅ has founded Zion,
and his oppressed people
find refuge in her.

A Pronouncement Against Moab

15 A pronouncement concerning Moab: Gn 19:31-37; Is 11:14; 25:10
Ar in Moab is devastated,
destroyed in a night.
Kir in Moab is devastated,
destroyed in a night.
² Dibon went up to its temple
to weep at its high places.
Moab wails on Nebo
and at ᶜ Medeba.
Every head is shaved;

ᴬ14:23 Or hedgehogs; Hb obscure ᴮ14:29 Or stock ᶜ15:2 Or wails over Nebo and over

every beard is chopped short.
3 In its streets
    they wear sackcloth;
on its rooftops
    and in its public squares
    everyone wails,
falling down and weeping.
4 Heshbon and Elealeh cry out;
their voices are heard
    as far away as Jahaz. Nm 21:28
Therefore the soldiers
    of Moab cry out,
and they tremble.A
5 My heart cries out
    over Moab,
whose fugitives flee
    as far as Zoar,   Gn 19:21-22
to Eglath-shelishiyah;
they go up the Ascent
    of Luhith weeping;
they raise a cry
    of destruction
on the road to Horonaim.
6 The Waters of Nimrim
    are desolate; Nm 32:3,36; Jos 13:27
the grass is withered,
    the foliage is gone,
and the vegetation
    has vanished.
7 So they carry their wealth
    and belongings
over the Wadi of the Willows.
8 For their cry echoes
throughout the territory
    of Moab.
Their wailing
    reaches Eglaim;
their wailing
    reaches Beer-elim.
9 The Waters of DibonB are full
    of blood,   2Kg 3:22-23
but I will bring on DibonB
    even more than this —
a lion for those who escape
    from Moab,

and for the survivors
    in the land. 2Sm 23:20; 1Ch 11:22

16 Send lambs to the ruler
    of the land,   2Kg 3:4
from Sela in the desert 2Kg 14:7
to the mountain
    of Daughter Zion.
2 Like a bird fleeing,
forced from the nest,
the daughters of Moab
will be at the fords
    of the Arnon.

3 Give us counsel and make
    a decision.
Shelter us at noonday
with shade that is as dark
    as night.
Hide the refugees;   1Kg 18:4
do not betray the one
    who flees.
4 Let my refugees stay
    with you;
be a refuge for MoabC
    from the aggressor.

When the oppressor
    has gone,
destruction has ended,
and marauders
    have vanished
    from the land,
5 a throne will be established
    in love,   Is 9:6-7; 32:1; 55:4; Dn 7:14
and one will sit on it
    faithfullyD
in the tent of David,
judging and pursuing what is
    right,
quick to execute justice.

6 We have heard
    of Moab's pride —   Jr 48:29
how very proud he is —

A 15:4 Lit out, he trembles within himself B 15:9 DSS, some LXX mss, Vg; MT reads Dimon C 16:4 Or you;
Moab — be a refuge for him D 16:5 Or continually

his haughtiness, his pride,
   his arrogance,
and his empty boasting.
⁷ Therefore let Moab wail;
let every one of them wail
   for Moab.
You who are
   completely devastated,
   mourn
for the raisin cakes
   of Kir-hareseth.   2Sm 6:19; Sg 2:5
⁸ For Heshbon's terraced
   vineyards
and the grapevines
   of Sibmah have withered.
The rulers of the nations
have trampled
   its choice vines
that reached as far as Jazer
and spread to the desert.
Their shoots spread out
and reached the sea.   Jr 48:32
⁹ So I join with Jazer
to weep for the vines
   of Sibmah;
I drench Heshbon
   and Elealeh
   with my tears.
Triumphant shouts
   have fallen silent ᴬ
over your summer fruit
   and your harvest.
¹⁰ Joy and rejoicing
   have been removed
   from the orchard;   Is 24:8
no one is singing or shouting
   for joy in the vineyards.
No one tramples grapes ᴮ
   in the winepresses.
I have put an end
   to the shouting.
¹¹ Therefore I moan like
   the sound of a lyre
   for Moab,   Is 15:5; 63:15; Jr 48:36
as does my innermost being
   for Kir-heres.

¹² When Moab appears
and tires himself out on
   the high place   1Kg 18:29
and comes to his sanctuary
   to pray,
it will do him no good.   Is 15:2

¹³ This is the message that the
LORD previously announced about
Moab. ¹⁴ And now the LORD says,
"In three years, as a hired worker
counts years, Moab's splendor will
become an object of contempt, in
spite of a very large population.
And those who are left will be few
and weak."   Jb 7:1; 14:6; Is 21:16

A Pronouncement Against Damascus

17 A pronouncement concerning Damascus: Gn 14:15; 15:2; Is 13:1
Look, Damascus is no longer
   a city.
It has become a ruined heap.
² The cities of Aroer
   are abandoned;
they will be places
   for flocks.
They will lie down
   without fear.
³ The fortress disappears
   from Ephraim,   Is 7:8,16; 8:4
and a kingdom
   from Damascus.
The remnant of Aram will be
like the splendor
   of the Israelites.
This is the declaration
   of the LORD of Armies.

Judgment Against Israel

⁴ On that day
the splendor of Jacob
   will fade,
and his healthy body ᶜ
   will become emaciated.

ᴬ**16:9** Or *Battle cries have fallen*   ᴮ**16:10** Lit *wine*   ᶜ**17:4** Lit *and the fat of his flesh*

⁵ It will be as if a reaper
　had gathered
　standing grain —
　his arm harvesting the heads
　of grain —
　and as if one had gleaned
　heads of grain
in the Valley of Rephaim.
⁶ Only gleanings will be left
　in Israel,　Dt 4:27; Is 24:13; 27:12; Ob 5
as if an olive tree
　had been beaten —
two or three olives
　at the very top of the tree,
four or five
　on its fruitful branches.
　This is the declaration
　of the Lord,
　the God of Israel.

⁷ On that day people will look to
their Maker and will turn their eyes
to the Holy One of Israel. ⁸ They will
not look to the altars they made
with their hands or to the Asherahs and shrines ᴬ they made with
their fingers.　Ex 34:13; 2Ch 34:7; Is 1:4; 27:9
⁹ On that day their strong cities
　will be
　like the abandoned woods
　　and mountaintops
　that were abandoned
　　because of the Israelites;
　there will be desolation.
¹⁰ For you have forgotten
　　the God of your salvation,
　and you have failed
　　to remember
　the rock of your strength;
　therefore you will plant
　　beautiful plants
　and set out cuttings
　　from exotic vines.
¹¹ On the day that you plant,
　you will help them to grow,
　and in the morning

you will help your seed
　to sprout,
but the harvest will vanish
on the day of disease
　and incurable pain.

Judgment Against the Nations

¹² Ah! The roar
　of many peoples —
they roar like the roaring
　of the seas.
The raging of the nations —
they rage
　like the rumble
　of rushing water.　Ps 93:1-5
¹³ The nations rage
　like the rumble of a
　huge torrent.　Is 33:3
He rebukes them,
　and they flee far away,　Ps 9:5
driven before the wind
　like chaff on the hills　Jb 21:18
and like tumbleweeds
　before a gale.
¹⁴ In the evening —
　sudden terror!
Before morning —
　it is gone!
This is the fate of those
　who plunder us
and the lot of those
　who ravage us.

The Lord's Message to Cush

18 Woe to the land
　　of buzzing insect wings ᴮ
beyond the rivers of Cush,
² which sends envoys by sea,
in reed vessels
　over the water.

Go, swift messengers,
to a nation tall
　and smooth-skinned,
to a people feared
　far and near,

ᴬ17:8 Or incense altars　ᴮ18:1 Or of sailing ships

a powerful nation
  with a strange language, [A]
whose land is divided
  by rivers.
³ All you inhabitants
    of the world
and you who live on the earth,
when a banner is raised
  on the mountains, look!
When a trumpet sounds,
  listen!

⁴ For the Lord said to me:
I will quietly look out
  from my place,
like shimmering heat
  in sunshine,
like a rain cloud
  in harvest heat.
⁵ For before the harvest,
  when the blossoming is over
and the blossom becomes
  a ripening grape,
he will cut off the shoots
  with a pruning knife,
and tear away and remove
  the branches.
⁶ They will all be left
  for the birds of prey
  on the hills
and for the wild animals
  of the land.
The birds of prey will spend
  the summer feeding
  on them,
and all the wild animals
  the winter.

⁷ At that time a gift will be brought to the Lord of Armies from [B] a people tall and smooth-skinned, a people feared far and near, a powerful nation with a strange language, whose land is divided by rivers — to Mount Zion, the place of the name of the Lord of Armies.

A Pronouncement Against Egypt

19 A pronouncement concerning Egypt: Is 13:1; Jr 46:13-26; Jl 3:19
Look, the Lord rides
  on a swift cloud Ps 18:9-10; 104:3
and is coming to Egypt.
Egypt's idols will tremble
  before him, Ex 12:12; Jr 43:12; 44:8
and Egypt will lose heart. [C]
² I will provoke Egyptians
    against Egyptians;
each will fight
    against his brother Mk 13:12
and each against his friend,
city against city,
    kingdom against kingdom.
³ Egypt's spirit will be
    disturbed within it,
and I will frustrate its plans.
Then they will inquire of
    idols, ghosts,
and spiritists. 1Ch 10:13; Is 8:19; Dn 2:2
⁴ I will hand over Egypt
    to harsh masters, Is 20:4
and a strong king
    will rule it.
This is the declaration
  of the Lord God of Armies.

⁵ The water of the sea
    will dry up,
and the river will be parched
    and dry.
⁶ The channels will stink;
they will dwindle,
    and Egypt's canals
    will be parched.
Reed and rush will wilt.
⁷ The reeds by the Nile,
    by the mouth of the river,
and all the cultivated areas
    of the Nile
will wither, blow away,
    and vanish.
⁸ Then the fishermen
    will mourn.

[A] 18:2 Hb obscure [B] 18:7 DSS, LXX, Vg; MT omits *from* [C] 19:1 Lit *Egypt's heart will melt within it*

All those who cast hooks
    into the Nile will lament,
and those who spread nets
    on the water will give up.
9 Those who work with flax
    will be dismayed;   Pr 7:16
those combing it
    and weaving linen
    will turn pale.A
10 Egypt's weaversB
    will be dejected;
all her wage earners
    will be demoralized.

11 The princes of Zoan
    are complete fools;   Nm 13:22
Pharaoh's wisest advisers
    give stupid advice!
How can you say
    to Pharaoh,
"I am oneC of the wise,
a studentD of eastern kings"?
12 Where then are
    your wise men?
Let them tell you and reveal
what the LORD of Armies
    has planned against Egypt.
13 The princes of Zoan
    have been fools;
the princes of Memphis
    are deceived.   Jr 2:16; 46:14,19
Her tribal chieftains have led
    Egypt astray.
14 The LORD has mixed
    within her a spirit
    of confusion.
The leaders have made Egypt
    stagger in all she does,
as a drunkard staggers
    in his vomit.
15 No head or tail,
    palm or reed,   Is 9:14-16
will be able to do anything
    for Egypt.

Egypt Will Know the LORD

16 On that day Egypt will be like women and will tremble with fear because of the threatening hand of the LORD of Armies when he raises it against them. 17 The land of Judah will terrify Egypt; whenever Judah is mentioned, Egypt will tremble because of what the LORD of Armies has planned against it.   Is 5:19

18 On that day five cities in the land of Egypt will speak the language of Canaan and swear loyalty to the LORD of Armies. One of the cities will be called the City of the Sun.E,F

19 On that day there will be an altar to the LORD in the center of the land of Egypt and a pillar to the LORD near her border. 20 It will be a sign and witness to the LORD of Armies in the land of Egypt. When they cry out to the LORD because of their oppressors, he will send them a savior and leader, and he will rescue them. 21 The LORD will make himself known to Egypt, and Egypt will know the LORD on that day. They will offer sacrifices and offerings; they will make vows to the LORD and fulfill them. 22 The LORD will strike Egypt, striking and healing. Then they will turn to the LORD and he will be receptive to their prayers and heal them.   Gn 28:18; Ex 24:4; Jdg 3:9,15

23 On that day there will be a highway from Egypt to Assyria. Assyria will go to Egypt, Egypt to Assyria, and Egypt will worship with Assyria.   Is 11:16; 35:8; 49:11; 62:10

24 On that day Israel will form a triple alliance with Egypt and Assyria — a blessing within the land. 25 The LORD of Armies will bless

---

A19:9 DSS, Tg; MT reads *weavers of white cloth*   B19:10 Or *foundations*   C19:11 Lit *a son*   D19:11 Lit *a son of ancient*   E19:18 Some Hb mss, DSS, Sym, Tg, Vg, Arabic; other Hb mss read *of Destruction*; LXX reads *of Righteousness*   F19:18 = the ancient Egyptian city Heliopolis them, saying, "Egypt my people, Assyria my handiwork, and Israel my inheritance are blessed."

No Help from Cush or Egypt

20 In the year that the chief commander, sent by King Sargon of Assyria, came to Ashdod and attacked and captured it — ² during that time the LORD had spoken through Isaiah son of Amoz, saying, "Go, take off your sackcloth ᴬ and remove the sandals from your feet," and he did that, going stripped and barefoot — ³ the LORD said, "As my servant Isaiah has gone stripped and barefoot three years as a sign and omen against Egypt and Cush, ⁴ so the king of Assyria will lead the captives of Egypt and the exiles of Cush, young and old alike, stripped and barefoot, with bared buttocks — to Egypt's shame. ⁵ Those who made Cush their hope and Egypt their boast will be dismayed and ashamed. ⁶ And the inhabitants of this coastland will say on that day, 'Look, this is what has happened to those we relied on and fled to for help to rescue us from the king of Assyria! Now, how will we escape?'"

A Judgment on Babylon

21 A pronouncement concerning the desert by the sea:
Like storms that pass
  over the Negev,
it comes from the desert,
  from the land of terror.
² A troubling vision is declared
  to me:
"The treacherous one
  acts treacherously,   Is 24:16; 33:1
and the destroyer destroys.

Advance, Elam! Lay siege,
  you Medes!
I will put an end to all
  the groaning."
³ Therefore I am ᴮ filled
  with anguish.
Pain grips me, like the pain
  of a woman in labor.   Ps 48:6
I am too perplexed to hear,
too dismayed to see.
⁴ My heart staggers;
  horror terrifies me.
He has turned
  my last glimmer of hope ᶜ
into sheer terror.   Dt 28:67
⁵ Prepare a table,
  and spread out a carpet!
Eat and drink!
Rise up, you princes, and oil
  the shields!

⁶ For the Lord has said to me,
"Go, post a lookout;
let him report what he sees.
⁷ When he sees riders —
pairs of horsemen,
riders on donkeys,
riders on camels —
he must pay close attention."
⁸ Then the lookout ᴰ reported,
"Lord, I stand
  on the watchtower all day,
and I stay at my post all night.
⁹ Look, riders come —
horsemen in pairs."
And he answered, saying,
"Babylon has fallen,
  has fallen.   2Sm 1:19; Is 3:8; 14:12
All the images of her gods
have been shattered
  on the ground."   Is 46:1; Jr 50:2

¹⁰ My people who have
  been crushed

ᴬ20:2 Lit *off the sackcloth from your waist*   ᴮ21:3 Lit *my waist is,* or *my insides are*   ᶜ21:4 Lit *my twilight*   ᴰ21:8 DSS, Syr; MT reads *Then a lion*

on the threshing floor,   Jr 51:33
I have declared to you
what I have heard
   from the LORD of Armies,
the God of Israel.

A Pronouncement Against Dumah

¹¹ A pronouncement concerning
Dumah: ᴬ   Gn 25:14; Is 21:1
   One calls to me from Seir,
   "Watchman, what is left
      of the night?
   Watchman, what is left
      of the night?"
¹² The watchman said,
   "Morning has come,
      and also night.
   If you want to ask, ask!
   Come back again."

A Pronouncement Against Arabia

¹³ A pronouncement concerning
Arabia: Jr 25:23-24; 49:28
   In the desert ᴮ brush
   you will camp for the night,
   you caravans of Dedanites.
¹⁴ Bring water for the thirsty.
   The inhabitants of the land
      of Tema   Gn 25:15; Jb 6:19
   meet ᶜ the refugees with food.
¹⁵ For they have fled
      from swords,
   from the drawn sword,
   from the bow that is strung,
   and from the stress of battle.

¹⁶ For the Lord said this to me:
"Within one year, as a hired worker
counts years, all the glory of Kedar
will be gone. ¹⁷ The remaining Ke-
darite archers will be few in number." For the LORD, the God of Israel,
has spoken.   Ps 120:5; Sg 1:5; Is 16:14; 42:11

A Pronouncement Against Jerusalem

22 A pronouncement concerning the Valley of Vision:
What's the matter with you?
Why have all of you gone up
   to the rooftops?   Is 15:3
² The noisy city,
   the jubilant town,   Is 23:7; 32:13
is filled with celebration.
Your dead did not die
   by the sword;
they were not killed
   in battle.
³ All your rulers
   have fled together,
captured without a bow.
All your fugitives
   were captured together;
they had fled far away.
⁴ Therefore I said,
"Look away from me!
   Let me weep bitterly!   Is 15:3
Do not try to comfort me
about the destruction
   of my dear ᴰ people."
⁵ For the Lord GOD of Armies
had a day of tumult,
   trampling, and confusion
in the Valley of Vision —
   people shouting ᴱ and crying
   to the mountains;
⁶ Elam took up a quiver
with chariots
   and horsemen, ᶠ
and Kir uncovered
   the shield.   2Kg 16:9; Am 1:5; 9:7
⁷ Your best valleys were full
   of chariots,
and horsemen
   were positioned at the city
   gates.
⁸ He removed the defenses
   of Judah.

On that day you looked to the weapons in the House of the Forest. ⁹ You saw that there were many breaches in the walls of the city of David. You collected water from the lower pool. ¹⁰ You counted the houses of Jerusalem so that you could tear them down to fortify the wall. ¹¹ You made a reservoir between the walls for the water of the ancient pool, but you did not look to the one who made it, or consider the one who created it long ago. 1Kg 7:2; 10:17; 2Kg 20:20; Neh 3:16; Lk 2:4

¹² On that day the Lord GOD
of Armies
called for weeping,
for wailing,
for shaven heads,   Is 32:11; Jl 1:13
and for the wearing
of sackcloth.

¹³ But look: joy and gladness,
butchering of cattle,
slaughtering of sheep and
goats,
eating of meat, and drinking
of wine —
"Let us eat and drink,
for tomorrow we die!"

¹⁴ The LORD of Armies has
directly revealed to me:
"This iniquity will not be
wiped out for you people as
long as you live."ᴬ   1Sm 3:14
The Lord GOD of Armies
has spoken.

A Pronouncement
Against Shebna

¹⁵ The Lord GOD of Armies said: "Go to Shebna, that steward who is in charge of the palace, and say to him: ¹⁶ What are you doing here? Who authorized you to carve out a tomb for yourself here, carving your tomb on the height and cutting a resting place for yourself out of rock? ¹⁷ Look, you strong man! The LORD is about to shake you violently. He will take hold of you, ¹⁸ wind you up into a ball, and sling you into a wide land.ᴮ There you will die, and there your glorious chariots will be — a disgrace to the house of your lord. ¹⁹ I will remove you from your office; you will be ousted from your position. 2Kg 18:18,26,37

²⁰ "On that day I will call for my servant, Eliakim son of Hilkiah. ²¹ I will clothe him with your robe and tie your sash around him. I will hand your authority over to him, and he will be like a father to the inhabitants of Jerusalem and to the house of Judah. ²² I will place the key of the house of David on his shoulder; what he opens, no one can close; what he closes, no one can open. ²³ I will drive him, like a peg, into a firm place. He will be a throne of honor for his father's family. ²⁴ They will hang on him all the glory of his father's family: the descendants and the offshoots — all the small vessels, from bowls to every kind of jar. ²⁵ On that day" — the declaration of the LORD of Armies — "the peg that was driven into a firm place will give way, be cut off, and fall, and the load on it will be destroyed." Indeed, the LORD has spoken. 2Kg 18:18; Is 36:3,22; 37:2

A Pronouncement Against Tyre

23 A pronouncement concerning Tyre: Jos 19:29; 1Kg 5:1; 47:4; Is 13:1
Wail, ships of Tarshish,   Gn 10:4
for your haven
has been destroyed.
Word has reached them
from the land of Cyprus.ᶜ

ᴬ22:14 Lit for you until you die   ᴮ22:17-18 Hb obscure   ᶜ23:1 Hb Kittim

² Mourn, inhabitants
    of the coastland,
you merchants of Sidon;
your agents have crossed
    the sea ᴬ
³ over deep water.
Tyre's revenue was the grain
    from Shihor —
the harvest of the Nile.
She was the merchant
    among the nations. Ezk 27:3-23
⁴ Be ashamed, Sidon,
    the stronghold of the sea,
for the sea has spoken:
"I have not been in labor
    or given birth.
I have not raised young men
or brought up
    young women."
⁵ When the news reaches
    Egypt,
they will be in anguish
    over the news about Tyre.
⁶ Cross over to Tarshish;
wail, inhabitants
    of the coastland!
⁷ Is this your jubilant city,
whose origin was
    in ancient times,
whose feet have taken her
to reside far away?
⁸ Who planned this
    against Tyre,
the bestower of crowns,
whose traders are princes,
whose merchants are
    the honored ones
    of the earth?
⁹ The Lᴏʀᴅ of Armies
    planned it,
to desecrate all
    its glorious beauty,
to disgrace all
    the honored ones
    of the earth.

¹⁰ Overflow ᴮ your
    land like the Nile,
    daughter of Tarshish;
there is no longer anything
    to restrain you. ᶜ
¹¹ He stretched out his hand
    over the sea; Ex 14:21; Is 14:26
he made kingdoms tremble.
The Lᴏʀᴅ has commanded
that the Canaanite fortresses
    be destroyed.
¹² He said,
"You will not celebrate
    anymore,
ravished young woman,
    daughter of Sidon.
Get up and cross over
    to Cyprus — Is 23:1; Jr 2:10; Ezk 27:6
even there you will have
    no rest! "
¹³ Look at the land
    of the Chaldeans —
a people who no longer exist.
Assyria destined it
    for desert creatures.
They set up their siege towers
and stripped its palaces.
They made it a ruin.
¹⁴ Wail, ships of Tarshish,
because your fortress
    is destroyed!

¹⁵ On that day Tyre will be forgotten for seventy years — the
life span of one king. At the end of
seventy years, what the song says
about the prostitute will happen
to Tyre:
¹⁶ Pick up your lyre,
    stroll through the city,
    you forgotten prostitute.
Play skillfully,
    sing many a song
so that you will be
    remembered.

ᴬ23:2 DSS; MT reads *Sidon, whom the seafarers have filled*   ᴮ23:10 DSS, LXX read *Work*   ᶜ23:10 Or
longer any harbor

¹⁷ And at the end of the seventy years, the LORD will restore Tyre and she will go back into business, prostituting herself with all the kingdoms of the world throughout the earth. ¹⁸ But her profits and wages will be dedicated to the LORD. They will not be stored or saved, for her profit will go to those who live in the LORD's presence, to provide them with ample food and sacred clothing. Jr 25:11,22

The Earth Judged

24 Look, the LORD is stripping the earth bare
and making it desolate.
He will twist its surface
and scatter its inhabitants:
² people and priest alike,
servant and master,
female servant and mistress,
buyer and seller,
lender and borrower,
creditor and debtor.
³ The earth will be stripped
completely bare
and will be totally plundered,
for the LORD has spoken
this message. Is 1:20; 6:11

⁴ The earth mourns
and withers;
the world wastes away
and withers;
the exalted people
of the earth waste away.
⁵ The earth is polluted
by its inhabitants, Gn 3:17
for they have transgressed
teachings,
overstepped decrees,
and broken
the permanent covenant.
⁶ Therefore a curse
has consumed the earth,

and its inhabitants
have become guilty;
the earth's inhabitants
have been burned,
and only a few survive.
⁷ The new wine mourns; Is 16:10
the vine withers.
All the carousers now groan.
⁸ The joyful tambourines
have ceased. Ex 15:20; Jdg 11:34
The noise of the jubilant
has stopped.
The joyful lyre has ceased.
⁹ They no longer sing
and drink wine;
beer is bitter to those
who drink it.
¹⁰ The city of chaos is shattered;
every house is closed
to entry. Is 23:1
¹¹ In the streets they cryᴬ
for wine.
All joy grows dark;
earth's rejoicing goes
into exile.
¹² Only desolation remains
in the city;
its gate has collapsed
in ruins.
¹³ For this is how it will be
on earth
among the nations:
like a harvested olive tree,
like a gleaning after
a grape harvest. Is 17:6

¹⁴ They raise their voices,
they sing out;
they proclaim in the west
the majesty of the LORD.
¹⁵ Therefore, in the east
honor the LORD!
In the coasts and islands
of the west
honor the name of the LORD,
the God of Israel.

ᴬ24:11 Lit streets she cries

¹⁶ From the ends of the earth
    we hear songs:
The Splendor
    of the Righteous One.   Ex 9:27

But I said, "I waste away!
    I waste away!^A
Woe is me."
The treacherous
    act treacherously;
the treacherous deal
    very treacherously.   Is 21:2; 33:1

¹⁷ Panic, pit, and trap await you
    who dwell on the earth.
¹⁸ Whoever flees at the sound
    of panic
will fall into a pit,
and whoever escapes
    from the pit
will be caught in a trap.
For the windows on high
    are opened,   Gn 7:11
and the foundations
    of the earth are shaken.
¹⁹ The earth is
    completely devastated;
the earth is split open;
the earth is violently shaken.
²⁰ The earth staggers
    like a drunkard   Is 19:14
and sways like a hut.
Earth's rebellion
    weighs it down,
and it falls,
    never to rise again.

²¹ On that day the LORD
    will punish   Is 27:12
the army of the heights in the
    heights
and the kings of the ground
    on the ground.
²² They will be
    gathered together
like prisoners in a pit.   Rv 20:1-3

^A**24:16** Hb obscure

They will be confined
    to a dungeon;   Rv 20:2
after many days
    they will be punished.
²³ The moon will be
    put to shame
and the sun disgraced,
because the LORD of Armies
    will reign as king
on Mount Zion in Jerusalem,
and he will display his glory
    in the presence
    of his elders.   Is 2:2-4; 1Co 15:54

Salvation and Judgment on That Day

25 LORD, you are my God;
    I will exalt you.
I will praise your name,
for you have accomplished
    wonders,
plans formed long ago,
    with perfect faithfulness.
² For you have turned the city
    into a pile of rocks,   Is 17:1; 26:5
a fortified city, into ruins;
the fortress of barbarians is
    no longer a city;   Col 3:11
it will never be rebuilt.
³ Therefore, a strong people
    will honor you.
The cities of violent nations
    will fear you.
⁴ For you have been
    a stronghold for the poor
    person,
a stronghold for the needy
    in his distress,   Mt 11:29
a refuge from storms and
    a shade from heat.   Is 4:6; 32:2
When the breath
    of the violent
is like a storm against a wall,
⁵ like heat in a dry land,
you will subdue the uproar
    of barbarians.

As the shade of a cloud cools
　　the heat of the day,
so he will silence the song
　　of the violent.

6 On this mountain, [A]   Is 2:2-4
　　the LORD of Armies
　　will prepare for all the
　　peoples a feast of choice
　　meat,   Is 24:23; Rv 19:9
a feast with aged wine,
　　prime cuts of choice meat, [B]
　　fine vintage wine.
7 On this mountain
he will destroy
　　the burial shroud,
the shroud over
　　all the peoples,
the sheet covering
　　all the nations;   2Co 3:15-16
8 he will destroy death forever.
The Lord GOD will wipe away
　　the tears
from every face   Is 30:19; 35:10; 51:11
and remove
　　his people's disgrace   Is 51:7
from the whole earth,
for the LORD has spoken.

9 On that day it will be said,
"Look, this is our God;
we have waited for him,
　　and he has saved us.
This is the LORD;
　　we have waited for him.
Let us rejoice and be glad
　　in his salvation."   Is 35:1-2,10
10 For the LORD's power
　　will rest on this mountain.

But Moab will be trampled
　　in his place [C]   Nm 24:17; Is 15:1
as straw is trampled
　　in a dung pile.
11 He will spread out his arms
　　in the middle of it,

as a swimmer spreads out
　　his arms to swim.
His pride will be
　　brought low,
along with the trickery
　　of his hands.   Is 2:10-12,15-17
12 The high-walled fortress
　　will be brought down,
thrown to the ground,
　　to the dust.   Is 26:5-6

The Song of Judah

26 On that day this song will be
　　sung in the land of Judah:
We have a strong city.
Salvation is established
　　as walls and ramparts.
2 Open the gates
so a righteous nation
　　can come in —
one that remains faithful.
3 You will keep the mind that is
　　dependent on you
in perfect peace,   Is 26:12; 27:5; 57:19
for it is trusting in you.
4 Trust in the LORD forever,
because in the LORD,
　　the LORD himself, is
　　an everlasting rock!   Ps 73:26
5 For he has humbled
　　those who live
　　in lofty places —
an inaccessible city.   Is 25:10-12
He brings it down;
　　he brings it down
　　to the ground;
he throws it to the dust.
6 Feet trample it,
the feet of the humble,
　　the steps of the poor.

God's People Vindicated

7 The path of the righteous
　　is level;   Ps 27:11
you clear a straight path
　　for the righteous.

[A]**25:6** = Mount Zion　　[B]**25:6** Lit *wine, fat full of marrow*　　[C]**25:10** Or *trampled under him*

⁸ Yes, LORD, we wait for you
  in the path
    of your judgments.
Our desire is for your name
  and renown.   Ex 3:15
⁹ I long for you in the night;
yes, my spirit within me
  diligently seeks you,
for when your judgments are
  in the land,
the inhabitants of the world
  will learn righteousness.
¹⁰ But if the wicked man is
  shown favor,
he does not
  learn righteousness.
In a righteous land
  he acts unjustly
and does not see the majesty
  of the LORD.

¹¹ LORD, your hand is lifted up
  to take action,
but they do not see it.
Let them see your zeal
  for your people
and be put to shame.
Let fire consume your
  adversaries.
¹² LORD, you will establish
  peace for us,
for you have also done
  all our work for us.
¹³ LORD our God, lords other
  than you have owned ᴬ us,
but we remember
  your name alone.   Jn 10:25
¹⁴ The dead do not live;
departed spirits do not
  rise up.
Indeed, you have punished
  and destroyed them;
you have wiped out
  all memory of them.   Jb 18:17

¹⁵ You have added
  to the nation, LORD.   Is 9:3
You have added to the nation;
  you are honored.
You have expanded
  all the borders of the land.
¹⁶ LORD, they went to you
  in their distress;   Is 37:3; Hs 5:15
they poured out
  whispered prayers
because your discipline fell
  on them. ᴮ
¹⁷ As a pregnant woman
  about to give birth
writhes and cries out
  in her pains,   Is 13:8
so we were before you, LORD.
¹⁸ We became pregnant,
  we writhed in pain;
we gave birth to wind.
We have won no victories
  on earth,
and the earth's inhabitants
  have not fallen.
¹⁹ Your dead will live;
  their bodies ᶜ will rise.   Is 25:8
Awake and sing, you who
  dwell in the dust!
For you will be covered
  with the morning dew, ᴰ
and the earth will bring out
  the departed spirits.

²⁰ Go, my people,
  enter your rooms
and close your doors
  behind you.
Hide for a little while
  until the wrath has passed.
²¹ For look, the LORD is coming
  from his place   Mc 1:3
to punish the inhabitants
  of the earth
  for their iniquity.   Is 13:11

ᴬ**26:13** Or *married*   ᴮ**26:16** Hb obscure   ᶜ**26:19** Lit *live; my body they*   ᴰ**26:19** Lit *For your dew is a dew of lights*

The earth will reveal
the blood shed on it
and will no longer conceal
her slain.

Leviathan Slain

27 On that day the LORD with
his relentless, large, strong
sword will bring judgment on Leviathan, the fleeing serpent — Leviathan, the twisting serpent. He will
slay the monster that is in the sea.

The LORD's Vineyard

2 On that day
sing about
a desirable vineyard: Ps 80:8
3 I am the LORD, who
watches over it
to water it regularly.
So that no one disturbs it,
I watch over it night and day.
4 I am not angry.
If only there were thorns
and briers for me to battle,
I would trample them
and burn them to the ground.
5 Or let it take hold
of my strength;
let it make peace with me —
make peace with me.
6 In days to come,
Jacob will take root.   Is 37:31
Israel will blossom
and bloom   Is 35:1-2; Hs 14:5-6
and fill the whole world
with fruit.

7 Did the LORD strike Israel
as he struck the one
who struck Israel?   Is 10:12,17
Was Israel killed like those
killed by the LORD?
8 You disputed with Israel
by banishing and driving her
away. A

A 27:8 Hb obscure

He removed her
with his severe storm
on the day of the east wind.
9 Therefore Jacob's iniquity
will be atoned for
in this way,   Is 13:11
and the result of the removal
of his sin will be this: Rm 11:27
when he makes all
the altar stones
like crushed bits of chalk,
no Asherah poles
or incense altars
will remain standing.
10 For the fortified city
will be desolate,
pastures deserted
and abandoned
like a wilderness.
Calves will graze there,
and there they will spread
out and strip its branches.
11 When its branches dry out,
they will be broken off.
Women will come
and make fires with them,
for they are not a people
with understanding.   Ps 32:9
Therefore their Maker
will not have compassion
on them,   Jb 4:17; Ps 95:6; Pr 14:31
and their Creator will not
be gracious to them.

12 On that day   Is 3:18; 7:18,20; 11:11; 24:21
the LORD will thresh grain
from the Euphrates River
as far as the Wadi of Egypt,
and you Israelites
will be gathered
one by one.
13 On that day
a great trumpet
will be blown,   Lv 25:9; 1Ch 15:24
and those lost in the land
of Assyria will come,

as well as those dispersed
  in the land of Egypt;
and they will worship
  the LORD
at Jerusalem
  on the holy mountain.

Woe to Samaria

28 Woe to the majestic crown
  of Ephraim's drunkards,
and to the fading flower
  of its beautiful splendor,
which is on the summit
  above the rich valley.
Woe to those overcome
  with wine.

² Look, the Lord has a strong
  and mighty one —   Is 8:7; 40:10
like a devastating hail storm,
like a storm with strong
  flooding water.
He will bring it
  across the land
  with his hand.

³ The majestic crown
  of Ephraim's drunkards
will be trampled underfoot.

⁴ The fading flower
  of his beautiful splendor,
which is on the summit
  above the rich valley,
will be like a ripe fig
  before the summer harvest.
Whoever sees it
  will swallow it
while it is still in his hand.

⁵ On that day
  the LORD of Armies
  will become a crown
  of beauty
and a diadem of splendor
to the remnant of his people,

⁶ a spirit of justice
to the one who sits
  in judgment,   1Kg 3:28; Is 11:2
and strength

to those who repel attacks
  at the city gate.

⁷ Even these stagger
  because of wine
and stumble
  under the influence
  of beer:
priest and prophet stagger
  because of beer,
they are confused by wine.
They stumble
  because of beer,
they are muddled
  in their visions,
they stumble
  in their judgments.

⁸ Indeed, all their tables
  are covered with vomit;
there is no place
  without a stench.

⁹ Who is he trying to teach?
Who is he trying to instruct?
Infants ᴬ just weaned
  from milk?
Babies ᴬ removed
  from the breast?

¹⁰ "Law after law,
  law after law,
line after line, line after line,
a little here, a little there." ᴮ

¹¹ For he will speak
  to this people
with stammering speech
and in a foreign language.

¹² He had said to them:
"This is the place of rest;
let the weary rest;   Is 11:10; 30:15
this is the place of repose."
But they would not listen.

¹³ The word of the LORD will
  come to them:
"Law after law, law after law,
line after line, line after line,
a little here, a little there,"

ᴬ**28:9** Lit *Those*   ᴮ**28:10** Hb obscure, also in v. 13

so they go
   stumbling backward,
to be broken, trapped,
   and captured.   Is 8:15; Mt 21:44

A Deal with Death

14 Therefore hear the word
   of the LORD, you scoffers
who rule this people
   in Jerusalem.
15 For you said, "We have made
   a covenant with Death,
and we have an agreement
   with Sheol;
when the overwhelming
   catastrophe[A]
   passes through,   Is 8:7-8
it will not touch us,
because we have
   made falsehood our refuge
and have hidden
   behind treachery."
16 Therefore the Lord GOD said:
"Look, I have laid a stone
   in Zion,   Is 8:14; 26:4
a tested stone,
a precious cornerstone,
   a sure foundation;   Mt 21:42
the one who believes
   will be unshakable.[B]   Rm 9:33
17 And I will make justice
   the measuring line
and righteousness
   the mason's level."   2Kg 21:13
Hail will sweep away
   the false refuge,
and water will flood
   your hiding place.
18 Your covenant with Death
   will be dissolved,
and your agreement
   with Sheol will not last.
When the overwhelming
   catastrophe
   passes through,

you will be trampled.
19 Every time it passes through,
   it will carry you away;
it will pass through
   every morning —
every day and every night.
Only terror will cause you
   to understand the message.[C]
20 Indeed, the bed is too short
   to stretch out on,
and its cover too small
   to wrap up in.
21 For the LORD will rise up
   as he did at Mount Perazim.
He will rise in wrath,
   as at the Valley of Gibeon,
to do his work,
   his unexpected work,
and to perform his task,
   his unfamiliar task.
22 So now, do not scoff,
or your shackles
   will become stronger.
Indeed, I have heard
   from the Lord GOD
   of Armies
a decree of destruction
   for the whole land.   Is 10:22-23

God's Wonderful Advice

23 Listen and hear my voice.
Pay attention and hear
   what I say.
24 Does the plowman plow
   every day to plant seed?
Does he continuously
   break up and cultivate
   the soil?
25 When he has leveled
   its surface,
does he not then
   scatter black cumin
   and sow cumin?
He plants wheat in rows
   and barley in plots,

A 28:15 Or *whip*; Hb obscure, also in v. 18   B 28:16 Lit *will not hurry*   C 28:19 Or *The understanding of the message will cause sheer terror*

with spelt as their border.
26 His God teaches him order;
he instructs him.
27 Certainly black cumin
is not threshed
with a threshing board,
and a cart wheel is not rolled
over the cumin.
But black cumin is beaten out
with a stick,
and cumin with a rod.
28 Bread grain is crushed,
but is not
threshed endlessly.
Though the wheel
of the farmer's cart rumbles,
his horses do not crush it.
29 This also comes
from the LORD of Armies.
He gives wondrous advice;
he gives great wisdom.   Is 9:6

Woe to Jerusalem

29 Woe to Ariel,[A] Ariel,
the city where David
camped!   2Sm 5:9
Continue year after year;
let the festivals recur.
2 I will oppress Ariel,
and there will be mourning
and crying,
and she will be to me
like an Ariel.
3 I will camp in a circle
around you;
I will besiege you
with earth ramps,
and I will set up
my siege towers
against you.
4 You will be brought down;
you will speak
from the ground,
and your words will come
from low in the dust.

Your voice will be like that
of a spirit
from the ground;   Is 8:19
your speech will whisper
from the dust.
5 Your many foes[B] will be
like fine dust,   Is 17:13; 41:15-16
and many of the ruthless,
like blowing chaff.
Then suddenly, in an instant,
6 you will be punished
by the LORD of Armies
with thunder, earthquake,
and loud noise,
storm, tempest, and a flame
of consuming fire.   Ex 9:23
7 All the many nations   Mc 4:11-12
going out to battle
against Ariel —
all the attackers, the siege
works against her,
and those
who oppress her —
will then be like a dream,
a vision in the night.   Jb 20:8
8 It will be like a hungry one
who dreams he is eating,
then wakes and is
still hungry;
and like a thirsty one
who dreams
he is drinking,
then wakes and is still thirsty,
longing for water.
So it will be for all the
many nations
who go to battle
against Mount Zion.
9 Stop and be astonished;
blind yourselves
and be blind!
They are drunk,[C] but not
with wine;

A **29:1** Or *Altar Hearth*, or *Lion of God*; Hb obscure, also in v. 2   B **29:5** Lit *foreigners*   C **29:9** LXX, Tg, Vg read *Be drunk*

they stagger,^A but not
with beer. Lk 1:15

10 For the LORD has poured out
on you
an overwhelming urge
to^B sleep; Ps 69:23; Is 6:9-10; Mc 3:6
he has shut your eyes
(the prophets)
and covered your heads
(the seers). Rm 11:8

11 For you the entire vision will be like the words of a sealed document. If it is given to one who can read and he is asked to read it,^C he will say, "I can't read it, because it is sealed." 12 And if the document is given to one who cannot read and he is asked to read it,^D he will say, "I can't read." Is 8:16; Dn 12:4,9; Mt 13:11

13 The Lord said:
These people approach me
with their speeches Ezk 33:31
to honor me
with lip-service^E —
yet their hearts are far
from me,
and human rules direct their
worship of me.^F

14 Therefore, I will again
confound these people
with wonder after wonder.
The wisdom of their wise
will vanish, Is 44:25; Jr 8:9; 49:7
and the perception
of their perceptive
will be hidden.

15 Woe to those who go
to great lengths
to hide their plans
from the LORD. Ps 10:11,13; Is 28:15
They do their works in the
dark,

and say, "Who sees us?
Who knows us?" Jb 22:13

16 You have turned things
around,
as if the potter were the same
as the clay.
How can what is made say
about its maker,
"He didn't make me"? Rm 9:20
How can what is formed
say about the one
who formed it,
"He doesn't understand
what he's doing"?

17 Isn't it true that in just
a little while
Lebanon will become
an orchard,
and the orchard will seem
like a forest? Ps 84:6; 107:33,35

18 On that day the deaf
will hear Is 35:5; 42:18-19; 43:8
the words of a document,
and out of a deep darkness
the eyes of the blind will see.

19 The humble will have joy
after joy in the LORD,
and the poor people
will rejoice Ps 69:32; Is 49:13
in the Holy One of Israel. Is 1:4

20 For the ruthless one
will vanish,
the scorner will disappear,
and all those who lie in wait
with evil intent
will be killed —

21 those who, with their speech,
accuse a person
of wrongdoing,
who set a trap for the
one mediating at the city
gate

---

^A 29:9 Tg, Vg read *wine;* stagger   ^B 29:10 Lit *you a spirit of*   ^C 29:11 Lit *If one gives it to one who knows the document, saying, "Read this, please"*   ^D 29:12 Lit *who does not know the document, saying, "Read this, please"*   ^E 29:13 Lit *their mouth and honor me with its lips*   ^F 29:13 Lit *their fearing of me is a taught command of men*

and without cause deprive
the righteous of justice.

²² Therefore, the LORD who redeemed Abraham says this about
the house of Jacob: Is 41:8; 51:2; 63:16
Jacob will no longer
be ashamed,
and his face will no longer
be pale.
²³ For when he sees
his children,
the work of my hands
within his nation,
they will honor my name,
they will honor the Holy One
of Jacob   2Sm 23:1; Ps 24:6; 76:6; 114:7
and stand in awe of the God
of Israel.   Is 5:16; 8:13
²⁴ Those who are confused
will gain understanding,
and those who grumble
will accept instruction.

Condemnation of the Egyptian Alliance

30 Woe to the rebellious
children!   Dt 21:18-21; Is 1:2,23; 30:9
This is
the LORD's declaration.
They carry out a plan,
but not mine;   Is 29:15
they make an alliance,
but against my will,
piling sin on top of sin.
² Without asking my advice
they set out to go down
to Egypt   Is 31:1; Jr 43:7
in order to seek shelter
under Pharaoh's protection
and take refuge
in Egypt's shadow.   Is 36:9
³ But Pharaoh's protection
will become your shame,
and refuge in Egypt's shadow
your humiliation.   Is 20:5-6; 36:6

⁴ For though his ᴬ princes are
at Zoan   Is 19:11
and his messengers reach
as far as Hanes,
⁵ everyone will be ashamed
because of a people
who can't help.
They are of no benefit,
they are no help;
they are good for nothing
but shame and disgrace.

⁶ A pronouncement concerning
the animals of the Negev: ᴮ   Is 13:1
Through a land of trouble
and distress,
of lioness and lion,
of viper and flying serpent,
they carry their wealth
on the backs of donkeys
and their treasures
on the humps of camels,
to a people who will not
help them.
⁷ Egypt's help is
completely worthless;
therefore, I call her:
Rahab Who Just Sits.   Ps 87:4

⁸ Go now, write it on a tablet
in their presence
and inscribe it on a scroll;
it will be for the future,
forever and ever.
⁹ They are a rebellious people,
deceptive children,   Is 30:1
children who do not
want to listen to
the LORD's instruction.
¹⁰ They say to the seers,
"Do not see,"
and to the prophets,
"Do not prophesy the truth
to us.
Tell us flattering things.   Jr 6:14
Prophesy illusions.

ᴬ**30:4** Or *Judah's*   ᴮ**30:6** Or *Southland*

11 Get out of the way!
Leave the pathway.
Rid us of the Holy One
of Israel." Is 1:4; 41:14-20; 43:14; 45:11
12 Therefore the Holy One
of Israel says:
"Because you have rejected
this message
and have trusted
in oppression and deceit,
and have depended on them,
13 this iniquity of yours will be
like a crumbling gap,
a bulge in a high wall
whose collapse will come
in an instant — suddenly!
14 Its collapse will be
like the shattering
of a potter's jar,
crushed to pieces, Ps 2:9
so that not even a fragment
of pottery
will be found among
its shattered remains —
no fragment large enough
to take fire from a hearth
or scoop water
from a cistern."
15 For the Lord GOD, the Holy One
of Israel, has said:
"You will be delivered
by returning and resting;
your strength will lie
in quiet confidence.
But you are not willing."
16 You say, "No!
We will escape on horses" —
therefore you will escape! —
and, "We will ride
on fast horses" —
but those who pursue you
will be faster. Is 31:1,3
17 One thousand will flee
at the threat of one, Lv 26:36
at the threat of five
you will flee,

until you remain
like a solitary pole
on a mountaintop
or a banner on a hill.

The LORD's Mercy to Israel

18 Therefore the LORD is waiting
to show you mercy,
and is rising up
to show you compassion,
for the LORD is a just God.
All who wait patiently
for him are happy.

19 For people will live on Zion in Jerusalem. You will never weep again; he will show favor to you at the sound of your outcry; as soon as he hears, he will answer you. 20 The Lord will give you meager bread and water during oppression, but your Teacher[A] will not hide any longer. Your eyes will see your Teacher, 21 and whenever you turn to the right or to the left, your ears will hear this command behind you: "This is the way. Walk in it." 22 Then you will defile your silver-plated idols and your gold-plated images. You will throw them away like menstrual cloths, and call them filth. 1Kg 22:27; Ps 80:5; Is 35:8-9

23 Then he will send rain for your seed that you have sown in the ground, and the food, the produce of the ground, will be rich and plentiful. On that day your cattle will graze in open pastures. 24 The oxen and donkeys that work the ground will eat salted fodder scattered with winnowing shovel and fork. 25 Streams flowing with water will be on every high mountain and every raised hill on the day of great slaughter when the towers fall. 26 The moonlight will

A **30:20** Or *teachers*

be as bright as the sunlight, and the sunlight will be seven times brighter — like the light of seven days — on the day that the LORD bandages his people's injuries and heals the wounds he inflicted.   Ps 144:13; Is 32:20

Annihilation of the Assyrians

27 Look there! The LORD^A is
     coming from far away,
   his anger burning and heavy
     with smoke.^B
   His lips are full of fury,
   and his tongue is
     like a consuming fire.
28 His breath is like
     an overflowing torrent
   that rises to the neck.   Is 8:8
   He comes to sift the nations
     in a sieve of destruction
   and to put a bridle
     on the jaws of the peoples
   to lead them astray.   2Kg 19:28
29 Your singing will be like that
   on the night
     of a holy festival,
   and your heart will rejoice
   like one who walks
     to the music of a flute,
   going up to the mountain
     of the LORD,
   to the Rock of Israel.   Is 8:14; 26:4
30 And the LORD will
     make the splendor
     of his voice heard
   and reveal his arm striking in
     angry wrath   Ex 6:6; Dt 4:34; Jb 40:9
   and a flame
     of consuming fire,
   in driving rain, a torrent,
     and hailstones.
31 Assyria will be shattered
     by the voice of the LORD.
   He will strike with a rod.
32 And every stroke
     of the appointed^C staff

that the LORD brings down
     on him
   will be to the sound
     of tambourines and lyres;
   he will fight against him
     with brandished weapons.
33 Indeed! Topheth
     has been ready   2Kg 23:10; Jr 7:31
   for the king for a long time.
   Its funeral pyre is deep
     and wide,
   with plenty of fire
     and wood.
   The breath of the
     LORD, like a torrent
     of burning sulfur,   Is 40:7
   kindles it.

The LORD, the Only Help

31 Woe to those who go down
     to Egypt for help   Is 30:2,7
   and who depend on horses!
   They trust in the abundance
     of chariots
   and in the large number
     of horsemen.   Dt 17:16; Ps 20:7
   They do not look
     to the Holy One of Israel
   and they do not seek
     the LORD.
2 But he also is wise
     and brings disaster.   Is 45:7
   He does not go back on what
     he says;   Nm 23:19; Is 22:14; Jr 44:29
   he will rise up
     against the house
     of the wicked
   and against the allies
     of evildoers.
3 Egyptians are men,
     not God;
   their horses are flesh,
     not spirit.
   When the LORD
     raises his hand to strike,
   the helper will stumble

^A30:27 Or Look, the name of the LORD   ^B30:27 Hb obscure   ^C30:32 Some Hb mss read punishing

and the one who is helped
    will fall;
both will perish together.

⁴ For this is what the LORD said
to me:
    As a lion or young lion
        growls over its prey   Nm 24:9
    when a band of shepherds
        is called out against it,
    and is not terrified
        by their shouting
    or subdued by their noise,
    so the LORD of Armies
        will come down
    to fight on Mount Zion
        and on its hill.   Is 42:13; Zch 12:8

⁵ Like hovering birds,
    so the LORD of Armies
        will protect Jerusalem —
    by protecting it,
        he will rescue it,
    by sparing it,
        he will deliver it.

⁶ Return to the one the Israelites have greatly rebelled against.
⁷ For on that day, every one of you
will reject the silver and gold idols
that your own hands have sinfully
made.   Is 1:5; 2:20; 30:22; 59:13
⁸ Then Assyria will fall,
    but not by human sword;
    a sword will devour him,
    but not one made by man.
    He will flee from the sword;
    his young men will be put
        to forced labor.   Gn 49:15; Is 14:2
⁹ His rockᴬ will pass away
    because of fear,   Dt 32:31,37
    and his officers will be afraid
        because of the signal flag.
This is the LORD's declaration —
whose fire is in Zion and whose
furnace is in Jerusalem.   Lv 10:2; Is 10:17
ᴬ 31:9 Perhaps the Assyrian king

The Righteous Kingdom Announced

32 Indeed, a king
    will reign righteously,
and rulers will rule justly.
² Each will be like a shelter
        from the wind,
    a refuge from the rain,   Is 4:6
    like flowing streams
        in a dry land   Is 30:25
    and the shade
        of a massive rock
        in an arid land.
³ Then the eyes of those
        who see will not be closed,
    and the ears of those
        who hear will listen.   Is 29:18
⁴ The reckless mind
        will gain knowledge,
    and the stammering
        tongue will speak clearly
        and fluently.   Is 33:19
⁵ A fool will no longer be called
        a noble,   Ps 107:40; 118:9; 146:3
    nor a scoundrel said
        to be important.
⁶ For a fool speaks foolishness
    and his mind plots iniquity.
    He lives in a godless way
    and speaks falsely
        about the LORD.
    He leaves the hungry empty
    and deprives the thirsty
        of drink.   Is 3:15; 10:2
⁷ The scoundrel's weapons
        are destructive;
    he hatches plots to destroy
        the needy with lies,
    even when the poor person
        says what is right.
⁸ But a noble person plans
        noble things;
    he stands up for noble causes.
⁹ Stand up,
    you complacent women;

listen to me.
Pay attention to what I say,
you overconfident daughters.
¹⁰ In a little more than a year
you overconfident ones
will shudder,
for the grapes will fail
and the harvest
will not come.
¹¹ Shudder, you complacent ones;
tremble,
you overconfident ones!
Strip yourselves bare   Is 47:2-3
and put sackcloth
around your waists.
¹² Beat your breasts
in mourning   Nah 2:7
for the delightful fields
and the fruitful vines,
¹³ for the ground of my people
growing thorns and briers,
indeed, for every joyous
house in the jubilant city.
¹⁴ For the palace
will be deserted,
the busy city abandoned.
The hill and the watchtower
will become
barren places forever,
the joy of wild donkeys,
and a pasture for flocks,
¹⁵ until the Spirit ᴬ from on high
is poured out on us.   Is 11:2; 44:3
Then the desert will become
an orchard,
and the orchard will seem
like a forest.   Is 29:17; 35:1-2
¹⁶ Then justice will inhabit
the wilderness,
and righteousness will dwell
in the orchard.
¹⁷ The result of righteousness
will be peace;   Ps 72:2-3; 85:8; Is 2:4
the effect of righteousness
will be quiet
confidence forever.

¹⁸ Then my people will dwell
in a peaceful place,
in safe and secure dwellings.
¹⁹ But hail will level the forest, ᴮ
and the city will sink
into the depths.   Is 24:10,12; 26:5
²⁰ You will be happy as you
sow seed
beside abundant water,   Nm 24:7
and as you let oxen
and donkeys range freely.

The Lᴏʀᴅ Rises Up

33 Woe, you destroyer
never destroyed,
you traitor never betrayed!
When you have
finished destroying,
you will be destroyed.
When you have
finished betraying,
they will betray you.   2Kg 18:14-36

² Lᴏʀᴅ, be gracious to us!
We wait for you.   Is 25:9; 26:8
Be our strength
every morning
and our salvation in time
of trouble.   Ex 15:2; Ps 28:8; Is 12:2
³ The peoples flee
at the thunderous noise;
the nations scatter
when you rise
in your majesty.
⁴ Your spoil will be gathered
as locusts are gathered;
people will swarm over it
like an infestation of locusts.
⁵ The Lᴏʀᴅ is exalted,
for he dwells on high;
he has filled Zion with justice
and righteousness.
⁶ There will be times
of security for you —
a storehouse of salvation,
wisdom, and knowledge.

ᴬ**32:15** Or *a wind*   ᴮ**32:19** Hb obscure

The fear of the LORD is
   Zion's treasure.   Is 11:2-3; Ac 9:31

7 Listen! Their warriors
   cry loudly in the streets;
the messengers of peace
   weep bitterly.   2Kg 18:18,37

8 The highways are deserted;
travel has ceased.
An agreement has been
   broken,   2Kg 18:14-17; Is 24:5
cities A despised,
and human life disregarded.

9 The land mourns
   and withers;   Is 3:26; 24:4; 29:2
Lebanon is ashamed
   and wilted.
Sharon is like a desert;
Bashan and Carmel shake off
   their leaves.

10 "Now I will rise up,"
   says the LORD.   Ps 12:5; Is 2:19,21
"Now I will lift myself up.
Now I will be exalted.

11 You will conceive chaff;   Ps 7:14
you will give birth to stubble.
Your breath is fire that will
   consume you.

12 The peoples will be burned
   to ashes,
like thorns cut down
   and burned in a fire.

13 You who are far off,
   hear what I have done;
you who are near,
   know my strength."   Is 18:2

14 The sinners in Zion
   are afraid;
trembling seizes the ungodly:
"Who among us can dwell
   with a consuming fire?
Who among us can dwell
   with ever-burning flames?"

15 The one who
   lives righteously

and speaks rightly,   Ps 15:2; 24:4
who refuses profit
   from extortion,
whose hand never
   takes a bribe,
who stops his ears
   from listening
   to murderous plots
and shuts his eyes against
   evil schemes —   Ps 119:37

16 he will dwell on the heights;
his refuge will be
   the rocky fortresses,
his food provided,
   his water assured.

17 Your eyes will see the King
   in his beauty;   Is 6:5; 24:23; Zch 9:9
you will see a vast land.

18 Your mind will meditate
   on the past terror:
"Where is the accountant? B
Where is
   the tribute collector? C
Where is the one
   who spied out
   our defenses?" D

19 You will no longer see
   the barbarians,
a people whose
   speech is difficult
   to comprehend —
who stammer in a language
   that is not understood.   Jr 5:15

20 Look at Zion, the city
   of our festival times.
Your eyes will
   see Jerusalem,
a peaceful pasture, a tent
   that does not wander;   Ps 46:5
its tent pegs will not
   be pulled up
nor will any of its cords
   be loosened.   Is 54:2

21 For the majestic one,
   our LORD, will be there,

a place of rivers
  and broad streams
where ships that are rowed
  will not go,
and majestic vessels
  will not pass. Is 41:18; 43:19-20
22 For the LORD is our Judge,
  the LORD is our Lawgiver,
  the LORD is our King.
He will save us. 2Sm 22:3; 23:5
23 Your ropes are slack;
they cannot hold the base
  of the mast
or spread out the flag.
Then abundant spoil
  will be divided,
the lame will plunder it,
24 and none there will say,
  "I am sick."
The people who dwell there
will be forgiven
  their iniquity. Is 13:11; 40:2; 44:22

The Judgment of the Nations

34 You nations, come here
  and listen;
you peoples, pay attention!
Let the earth and all
  that fills it hear,
the world and all that comes
  from it. Ps 24:1; Is 6:3; 42:5
2 The LORD is angry with all
  the nations,
furious with all
  their armies. Is 13:5; Jr 10:10; 50:13
He will set them apart
  for destruction, Jos 6:21; 1Sm 15:3
giving them over
  to slaughter.
3 Their slain will be
  thrown out,
and the stench
  of their corpses will rise;
the mountains will flow A
  with their blood. Ps 46:2-3

4 All B the stars in the sky
  will dissolve. 2Kg 17:16; 21:3,5
The sky will roll up
  like a scroll, Rv 6:12-14
and its stars will all wither
as leaves wither on the vine,
and foliage on the fig tree.

The Judgment of Edom

5 When my sword has drunk
  its fill C in the heavens,
it will then come down
  on Edom Nm 20:14-21; Is 63:1
and on the people I have
  set apart for destruction.
6 The LORD'S sword is covered
  with blood.
It drips with fat,
with the blood of lambs
  and goats,
with the fat of the kidneys
  of rams. Is 25:6; 30:32; Jr 46:10; 51:40
For the LORD has a sacrifice
  in Bozrah, Gn 36:33; Is 63:1
a great slaughter in the land
  of Edom.
7 The wild oxen
  will be struck D down
  with them,
and young bulls
  with the mighty bulls.
Their land will be soaked
  with E blood,
and their soil
  will be saturated with fat.
8 For the LORD has a day
  of vengeance, Is 13:6; 35:4; 47:3
a time of paying back Edom
for its hostility against Zion.
9 Edom's streams
  will be turned into pitch,
her soil into sulfur; Gn 19:24
her land will become
  burning pitch.

A34:3 Or melt, or dissolve   B34:4 DSS read And the valleys will be split, and all   C34:5 DSS read sword
will appear   D34:7 Or will go   E34:7 Or will drink its fill of

¹⁰ It will never go out —
　　 day or night.
Its smoke will go up forever.
It will be desolate,
　　 from generation
　　 to generation;
no one will pass
　　 through it forever and ever.
¹¹ Eagle owls^A and herons^B
　　 will possess it,
and long-eared owls
　　 and ravens will dwell there.
The LORD will stretch out
　　 a measuring line
and a plumb line over her
for her destruction
　　 and chaos.　2Kg 21:13; Is 24:10; Lm 2:8
¹² No nobles will be left
　　 to proclaim a king,
and all her princes will come
　　 to nothing.
¹³ Her palaces
　　 will be overgrown
　　 with thorns;
her fortified cities,
　　 with thistles and briers.
She will become a dwelling
　　 for jackals,
an abode^C for ostriches.　Is 13:22
¹⁴ The desert creatures
　　 will meet hyenas,
and one wild goat will call
　　 to another.
Indeed, the night birds
　　 will stay there
and will find a resting place.
¹⁵ Sand partridges^D will make
　　 their nests there;
they will lay and hatch
　　 their eggs
and will gather their broods
　　 under their shadows.
Indeed, the birds of prey
　　 will gather there,

each with its mate.　Dt 14:13
¹⁶ Search and read the scroll
　　 of the LORD:　Ps 40:7; 139:16; Is 8:16
Not one of them
　　 will be missing,
none will be lacking its mate,
because he has ordered it
　　 by my^E mouth,
and he will gather them
　　 by his Spirit.
¹⁷ He has cast the lot for them;
his hand allotted
　　 their portion
　　 with a measuring line.
They will possess it forever;
they will dwell in it
　　 from generation
　　 to generation.

The Ransomed Return to Zion

35 The wilderness
　　 and the dry land
　　 will be glad;
the desert will rejoice
　　 and blossom
　　 like a wildflower.^F　Ps 65:12
² It will blossom abundantly
and will also rejoice with joy
　　 and singing.
The glory of Lebanon
　　 will be given to it,
the splendor of Carmel
　　 and Sharon.　Sg 2:1; 5:15; 7:5; Is 33:9
They will see the glory
　　 of the LORD,　Ex 16:7,10; Lv 9:6,23
the splendor of our God.
³ Strengthen the weak hands,
steady the shaking knees!
⁴ Say to the cowardly:
"Be strong; do not fear!
Here is your God;
　　 vengeance is coming.　Is 1:24
God's retribution is coming;
　　 he will save you."　Is 33:22

^A**34:11** Or *Pelicans*　^B**34:11** Or *hedgehogs*　^C**34:13** DSS, LXX, Syr, Tg; MT reads *jackals, grass*
^D**34:15** Or *Arrow snakes*, or *Owls*　^E**34:16** Some Hb mss, other Hb mss, DSS, Syr, Tg read *his*　^F**35:1** Or
meadow saffron ; traditionally *rose*

5 Then the eyes of the blind
   will be opened,
   and the ears
   of the deaf unstopped.
6 Then the lame will leap
   like a deer, Zph 3:19; Mt 11:5; 15:30-31
   and the tongue of the mute
   will sing for joy, Ex 4:11; Mk 7:32
   for water will gush
   in the wilderness,
   and streams in the desert;
7 the parched ground
   will become a pool,
   and the thirsty land springs.
   In the haunt of jackals,
   in their lairs, Is 13:22; 34:13
   there will be grass, reeds,
   and papyrus.
8 A road will be there
   and a way; Is 40:3; 42:16; 43:16,19
   it will be called the Holy Way.
   The unclean will not travel
   on it, Is 52:1; Rv 21:27
   but it will be for the one
   who walks the path. Ps 139:24
   Fools will not wander on it.
9 There will be no lion there,
   and no vicious beast
   will go up on it;
   they will not be found there.
   But the redeemed will walk
   on it,
10 and the redeemed
   of the LORD will return
   and come to Zion with singing,
   crowned with unending joy.
   Joy and gladness
   will overtake them,
   and sorrow and sighing
   will flee. Is 65:19; Rm 9:2; Rv 21:4

Sennacherib's Invasion

36 In the fourteenth year of
King Hezekiah, King Sen-
nacherib of Assyria attacked all
the fortified cities of Judah and

captured them. 2 Then the king of
Assyria sent his royal spokesman,
along with a massive army, from
Lachish to King Hezekiah at Jerusalem. The Assyrian stood near the
conduit of the upper pool, by the
road to the Launderer's Field. 3 Eliakim son of Hilkiah, who was in
charge of the palace, Shebna the
court secretary, and Joah son of
Asaph, the court historian, came
out to him. 2Kg 18:13,17-37; 2Ch 32:1-16,18

4 The royal spokesman said to
them, "Tell Hezekiah:
The great king, the king of
Assyria, says this: What are
you relying on?A 5 YouB think
mere words are strategy and
strength for war. Who are you
now relying on that you have
rebelled against me? 6 Look,
you are relying on Egypt, that
splintered reed of a staff that
will pierce the hand of anyone who grabs it and leans on
it. This is how Pharaoh king
of Egypt is to all who rely on
him. 7 Suppose you say to me,
'We rely on the LORD our God.'
Isn't he the one whose high
places and altars Hezekiah has
removed, saying to Judah and
Jerusalem, 'You are to worship
at this altar'? 2Kg 18:7; Ezk 29:6-7

8 "Now make a deal with my
master, the king of Assyria. I'll
give you two thousand horses if you're able to supply riders for them! 9 How then can
you drive back a single officer
among the least of my master's
servants? How can you rely on
Egypt for chariots and horsemen? 10 Have I attacked this
land to destroy it without the

A36:4 Lit *What is this trust that you trust*   B36:5 Many Hb mss, DSS, 2Kg 18:20; MT reads *I*

LORD's approval? The LORD said to me, 'Attack this land and destroy it.'"   Is 20:5; 30:2-5,7; 31:3

[11] Then Eliakim, Shebna, and Joah said to the royal spokesman, "Please speak to your servants in Aramaic, since we understand it. Don't speak to us in Hebrew[A] within earshot of the people who are on the wall."   Ezr 4:7; Dn 2:4

[12] But the royal spokesman replied, "Has my master sent me to speak these words to your master and to you, and not to the men who are sitting on the wall, who are destined with you to eat their own excrement and drink their own urine?"

[13] Then the royal spokesman stood and called out loudly in Hebrew:

Listen to the words of the great king, the king of Assyria! [14] This is what the king says: "Don't let Hezekiah deceive you, for he cannot rescue you. [15] Don't let Hezekiah persuade you to rely on the LORD, saying, 'The LORD will certainly rescue us! This city will not be handed over to the king of Assyria.'"   Is 37:10

[16] Don't listen to Hezekiah, for this is what the king of Assyria says: "Make peace[B] with me and surrender to me. Then every one of you may eat from his own vine and his own fig tree and drink water from his own cistern [17] until I come and take you away to a land like your own land — a land of grain and new wine, a land of bread and vineyards. [18] Beware that Hezekiah does not mislead you by

saying, 'The LORD will rescue us.' Has any one of the gods of the nations rescued his land from the power of the king of Assyria? [19] Where are the gods of Hamath and Arpad? Where are the gods of Sepharvaim? Have they rescued Samaria from my power? [20] Who among all the gods of these lands ever rescued his land from my power? So will the LORD rescue Jerusalem from my power?"   Mc 4:4

[21] But they kept silent; they didn't say anything, for the king's command was, "Don't answer him." [22] Then Eliakim son of Hilkiah, who was in charge of the palace, Shebna the court secretary, and Joah son of Asaph, the court historian, came to Hezekiah with their clothes torn and reported to him the words of the royal spokesman.   Pr 26:4

Hezekiah Seeks Isaiah's Counsel

37 When King Hezekiah heard their report, he tore his clothes, put on sackcloth, and went to the LORD's temple. [2] He sent Eliakim, who was in charge of the palace, Shebna the court secretary, and the leading priests, who were wearing sackcloth, to the prophet Isaiah son of Amoz. [3] They said to him, "This is what Hezekiah says: 'Today is a day of distress, rebuke, and disgrace. It is as if children have come to the point of birth, and there is no strength to deliver them. [4] Perhaps the LORD your God will hear all the words of the royal spokesman, whom his master the king of Assyria sent to mock the living God, and will rebuke him for the words that the LORD your God has

A **36:11** Lit *Judahite*, also in v. 13   B **36:16** Lit *a blessing*

THE BOOKS OF THE
MAJOR PROPHETS

Prophets (men who spoke for God) wrote seventeen Old Testament books. Five of these books are in the division of the Bible called the Major Prophets. The other twelve books are called the Minor Prophets because these books are shorter than the books of the Major Prophets. These prophets called God's people to faithfulness and holiness while preparing them for the coming Christ.

ISAIAH, like the other books by prophets, takes its name from its author. The book includes prophecy about the coming of the Messiah. Isaiah is filled with references to Christ and His expected birth and suffering for the sins of the world.

JEREMIAH calls the people of Judah to turn away from their idol worship and other sins. Just like Jeremiah, Christ loves people and mourns their sin.

LAMENTATIONS is a lament, or a song of mourning, over the sins of Judah and the destruction of Jerusalem by the Babylonians. Jeremiah wrote this book. It is a great example of the need for salvation that can only come from Jesus Christ.

EZEKIEL was the prophet to the Jewish exiles in Babylon. He spoke of God's judgment on Israel and other nations but also predicted the future blessings of God and salvation of His people. God refers to Ezekiel as "Son of man," a reference that would later identify Jesus Christ as not just a human being, like Ezekiel, but also as God the Son.

DANIEL was a Jew in exile in Babylon who was blessed by God for his faithfulness. The book also speaks of the power of God over people of all nations. Half of the book is history and half is prophecy. The prophecy includes Christ's first and second coming and His eternal Kingdom.

THE BOOKS OF THE
MINOR PROPHETS

Twelve of the seventeen Old Testament books written by prophets are called the Minor Prophets. The minor prophets were messengers destined to keep God's people united physically and spiritually as they awaited the arrival of Jesus Christ.

HOSEA expresses God's love for His sinful people, Israel. Similarly, Christ expresses God's love as a sacrifice for all sinful people.

JOEL is written to the people of Judah, calling the people to repent and warning them about God's judgment. Joel also foretold the coming of the Holy Spirit on all believers. His message was much like Christ's message to repent.

AMOS calls on the people of Israel to stop worshiping idols and to quit being mean to the poor. Amos preached on issues dealing with righteousness. His words would often be echoed by the righteous one, Jesus Christ.

OBADIAH teaches that God will punish those who trouble His people. The prophet also promised a future kingdom and judgment, the same message later proclaimed by Christ Himself.

JONAH tells the story of the prophet who did not want to tell Israel's enemies about God's love. He was caught in a violent storm at sea, swallowed by a great fish, and rescued by God. Just as Jonah was confined inside the big fish for three days, Christ endured burial in a grave for three days before His resurrection.

MICAH warns the people of Israel and Judah of coming judgment and offers pardon for those who repent. The prophet also foretold Jesus' birth in Bethlehem.

NAHUM speaks of God's judgment of Nineveh in order to offer comfort to Judah. This book magnifies the destruction that sin causes, but Jesus Christ gives us hope through faith and repentance.

HABAKKUK speaks of God's power over the nations. That same power and authority came to earth in Jesus Christ.

ZEPHANIAH foretells the day of wrath and the reward of the good. Zephaniah also recognizes that the king of Israel, a title later given to Jesus Christ, was in the midst of God's people.

HAGGAI calls those who returned to Jerusalem from exile to complete the rebuilding of the temple. Haggai realized the importance of the temple, where Jesus Christ would one day be dedicated and teach.

ZECHARIAH contains many references to the coming of the Messiah. This gave hope to the Jews who had returned to Jerusalem from exile.

MALACHI was the last book written in the Old Testament. The book contains prophecies about the Messiah and calls the Jews in Jerusalem to turn from their sins and renew their relationship with God.

heard. Therefore offer a prayer for the surviving remnant.'" 2Kg 19:1-34

⁵ So the servants of King Hezekiah went to Isaiah, ⁶ who said to them, "Tell your master, 'The LORD says this: Don't be afraid because of the words you have heard, with which the king of Assyria's attendants have blasphemed me. ⁷ I am about to put a spirit in him and he will hear a rumor and return to his own land, where I will cause him to fall by the sword.'" Is 7:4; 35:4; 52:5

Sennacherib's Letter

⁸ When the royal spokesman heard that the king of Assyria had pulled out of Lachish, he left and found him fighting against Libnah. ⁹ The king had heard concerning King Tirhakah of Cush, "He has set out to fight against you." So when he heard this, he sent messengers to Hezekiah, saying, ¹⁰ "Say this to King Hezekiah of Judah: 'Don't let your God, on whom you rely, deceive you by promising that Jerusalem won't be handed over to the king of Assyria. ¹¹ Look, you have heard what the kings of Assyria have done to all the countries: they completely destroyed them. Will you be rescued? ¹² Did the gods of the nations that my predecessors destroyed rescue them — Gozan, Haran, Rezeph, and the Edenites in Telassar? ¹³ Where is the king of Hamath, the king of Arpad, the king of the city of ᴬ Sepharvaim, Hena, or Ivvah?'" Nm 33:20; Jos 10:31-32

Hezekiah's Prayer

¹⁴ Hezekiah took the letter from the messengers' hands, read it, then went up to the LORD's temple and spread it out before the LORD. ¹⁵ Then Hezekiah prayed to the LORD: Dt 22:17; 1Kg 8:22; 2Ch 32:20; Ezk 2:10 ¹⁶ LORD of Armies, God of Israel, enthroned between the cherubim, you are God — you alone — of all the kingdoms of the earth. You made the heavens and the earth. ¹⁷ Listen closely, LORD, and hear; open your eyes, LORD, and see. Hear all the words that Sennacherib has sent to mock the living God. ¹⁸ LORD, it is true that the kings of Assyria have devastated all these countries and their lands. ¹⁹ They have thrown their gods into the fire, for they were not gods but made from wood and stone by human hands. So they have destroyed them. ²⁰ Now, LORD our God, save us from his power so that all the kingdoms of the earth may know that you, LORD, are God ᴮ — you alone. Ex 25:22; Nm 7:89

God's Answer Through Isaiah

²¹ Then Isaiah son of Amoz sent a message to Hezekiah: "The LORD, the God of Israel, says, 'Because you prayed to me about King Sennacherib of Assyria, ²² this is the word the LORD has spoken against him:

Virgin Daughter Zion Lm 2:13; 4:4
despises you and scorns you;
Daughter Jerusalem
shakes her head Jb 16:4; Ps 22:7
behind your back.
²³ Who is it you have mocked
and blasphemed? Ps 74:10,18
Against whom have you
raised your voice
and lifted your eyes in pride?
Against the Holy One of Israel!
²⁴ You have mocked the Lord
through ᶜ your servants.

ᴬ37:13 Or king of Lair,   ᴮ37:20 are God supplied for clarity; see v. 16   ᶜ37:24 Lit by the hand of

You have said, "With my
  many chariots Ex 14:26-28; 15:4,19
I have gone up to the heights
  of the mountains,
to the far recesses
  of Lebanon.
I cut down its tallest cedars,
  its choice cypress trees.
I came to its distant heights,
  its densest forest.
²⁵ I dug wells and drank water
  in foreign lands. ᴬ
I dried up all the streams
  of Egypt
with the soles of my feet."

²⁶ Have you not heard? Is 40:21,28
  I designed it long ago;
I planned it in days gone by.
I have now brought it to pass,
  and you have crushed
    fortified cities Is 34:13
into piles of rubble.
²⁷ Their inhabitants have
  become powerless,
dismayed, and ashamed.
They are plants of the field,
  tender grass,
grass on the rooftops,
  blasted by the east wind. ᴮ

²⁸ But I know
  your sitting down,
your going out
  and your coming in, Ps 139:1
and your raging against me.
²⁹ Because your raging
  against me
and your arrogance
  have reached my ears, Is 10:12
I will put my hook
  in your nose Ezk 19:9; 29:4; 38:4
and my bit in your mouth;
I will make you go back
  the way you came.

³⁰ " 'This will be the sign for you:
This year you will eat what grows
on its own, and in the second year
what grows from that. But in the
third year sow and reap, plant vineyards and eat their fruit. ³¹ The surviving remnant of the house of
Judah will again take root downward and bear fruit upward. ³² For
a remnant will go out from Jerusalem, and survivors from Mount
Zion. The zeal of the Lᴏʀᴅ of Armies
will accomplish this.' Ex 3:12; 1Sm 2:34
³³ "Therefore, this is what the
Lᴏʀᴅ says about the king of Assyria:
  He will not enter this city,
  shoot an arrow here,
  come before it with a shield,
  or build up a siege ramp
    against it.
³⁴ He will go back
  the way he came,
  and he will not enter this city.
  This is
    the Lᴏʀᴅ's declaration.
³⁵ I will defend this city
  and rescue it
  for my sake Is 43:25; 48:9,11
  and for the sake of
    my servant David." 2Kg 20:6

Defeat and Death of Sennacherib

³⁶ Then the angel of the Lᴏʀᴅ went
out and struck down one hundred
eighty-five thousand in the camp
of the Assyrians. When the people
got up the next morning — there
were all the dead bodies! ³⁷ So King
Sennacherib of Assyria broke camp
and left. He returned home and
lived in Nineveh. 2Kg 19:35-37; 2Ch 32:21
³⁸ One day, while he was worshiping in the temple of his god Nisroch, his sons Adrammelech and

---

ᴬ37:25 DSS, 2Kg 19:24; MT omits *in foreign lands* ᴮ37:27 DSS; MT reads *rooftops, field before standing
grain*

Sharezer struck him down with the sword and escaped to the land of Ararat. Then his son Esar-haddon became king in his place.   Gn 8:4

Hezekiah's Illness and Recovery

38 In those days Hezekiah became terminally ill. The prophet Isaiah son of Amoz came and said to him, "This is what the LORD says: 'Set your house in order, for you are about to die; you will not recover.' "[A]   2Kg 20:1-6,9-11
[2] Then Hezekiah turned his face to the wall and prayed to the LORD. [3] He said, "Please, LORD, remember how I have walked before you faithfully and wholeheartedly, and have done what pleases you."[B] And Hezekiah wept bitterly.   Gn 17:1; 1Kg 2:4; 3:6
[4] Then the word of the LORD came to Isaiah: [5] "Go and tell Hezekiah, 'This is what the LORD God of your ancestor David says: I have heard your prayer; I have seen your tears. Look, I am going to add fifteen years to your life.[C] [6] And I will rescue you and this city from the grasp of the king of Assyria; I will defend this city. [7] This is the sign to you from the LORD that he will do what[D] he has promised:[E] [8] I am going to make the sun's shadow that goes down on the stairway of Ahaz go back by ten steps.'" So the sun's shadow[F] went back the ten steps it had descended.   2Kg 18:2,13
[9] A poem by King Hezekiah of Judah after he had been sick and had recovered from his illness:

[10] I said: In the prime[G] of my life
   I must go to the gates of Sheol;
   I am deprived of the rest
   of my years.

[11] I said: I will never see
   the LORD,
   the LORD in the land
   of the living;   Ps 27:13; 116:9
   I will not look on humanity
   any longer
   with the inhabitants of what
   is passing away.[H]

[12] My dwelling is plucked up
   and removed from me
   like a shepherd's tent.   2Co 5:1,4
   I have rolled up my life
   like a weaver;   Jb 7:6; Heb 1:12
   he cuts me off
   from the loom.   Jb 6:9
   By nightfall[I] you make an
   end of me.   Jb 4:20; Ps 73:14

[13] I thought until the morning:
   He will break all my bones
   like a lion.
   By nightfall you make an end
   of me.

[14] I chirp like a swallow
   or a crane;
   I moan like a dove.   Is 59:11; Ezk 7:16
   My eyes grow weak
   looking upward.
   Lord, I am oppressed;
   support me.   Jb 17:3; Ps 119:122

[15] What can I say?
   He has spoken to me,
   and he himself has done it.
   I walk along slowly
   all my years   1Kg 21:27
   because of the bitterness
   of my soul.   1Sm 1:10; Ezk 27:31; 7:11

[16] Lord, by such things
   people live,   Ps 119:71,75
   and in every one of them my
   spirit finds life;
   you have restored me
   to health   Ps 39:13
   and let me live.   Ps 119:25

[A]**38:1** Lit *live*   [B]**38:3** Lit *what is good in your eyes*   [C]**38:5** Lit *days*, also in v. 10   [D]**38:7** Lit *this thing*
[E]**38:7** Lit *said*   [F]**38:8** Lit *And the sun*   [G]**38:10** Lit *quiet*   [H]**38:11** Some Hb mss, Tg read *of the world*
[I]**38:12** Lit *From day until night*, also in v. 13

¹⁷ Indeed, it was for
     my own well-being
that I had
     such intense bitterness;
but your love
     has delivered me
from the Pit of destruction,
for you have
     thrown all my sins
     behind your back.   Is 43:25
¹⁸ For Sheol cannot thank you;
Death cannot praise you.   Ps 6:5
Those who go down to the Pit
cannot hope
     for your faithfulness.
¹⁹ The living, only the living
     can thank you,
as I do today;
a father will make
     your faithfulness known
     to children.   Dt 6:7; 11:19; Ps 78:5-7
²⁰ The LORD is ready to save me;
we will play
     stringed instruments
all the days of our lives
at the house of the LORD.

²¹ Now Isaiah had said, "Let them take a lump of pressed figs and apply it to his infected skin, so that he may recover." ²² And Hezekiah had asked, "What is the sign that I will go up to the LORD's temple?"

Hezekiah's Folly

39 At that time Merodach-baladan son of Baladan, king of Babylon, sent letters and a gift to Hezekiah since he heard that he had been sick and had recovered. ² Hezekiah was pleased with the letters, and he showed the envoys his treasure house — the silver, the gold, the spices, and the precious oil — and all his armory, and everything that was found in his treasuries. There was nothing in his palace and in all his realm that Hezekiah did not show them.   2Kg 20:12-19; 2Ch 32:31

³ Then the prophet Isaiah came to King Hezekiah and asked him, "What did these men say, and where did they come to you from?"

Hezekiah replied, "They came to me from a distant country, from Babylon."

⁴ Isaiah asked, "What have they seen in your palace?"

Hezekiah answered, "They have seen everything in my palace. There isn't anything in my treasuries that I didn't show them."

⁵ Then Isaiah said to Hezekiah, "Hear the word of the LORD of Armies: ⁶ 'Look, the days are coming when everything in your palace and all that your fathers have stored up until today will be carried off to Babylon; nothing will be left,' says the LORD. ⁷ 'Some of your descendants — who come from you, whom you father — will be taken away, and they will become eunuchs in the palace of the king of Babylon.'"   Is 28:14; Zch 7:4; 8:1,18

⁸ Then Hezekiah said to Isaiah, "The word of the LORD that you have spoken is good," for he thought: There will be peace and security during my lifetime.   2Ch 32:26

God's People Comforted

40 "Comfort, comfort
     my people,"   Is 12:1; 49:13
says your God.
² "Speak tenderly to^A Jerusalem,
and announce to her
     that her time of forced labor
     is over,
her iniquity has been
     pardoned,   Lv 26:41,43; Is 13:11; 27:9

^A**40:2** Lit *Speak to the heart of*

and she has received
  from the LORD's hand
double for all her sins." Jr 16:18

³ A voice of one crying out:
  Prepare the way of the LORD
    in the wilderness;   Mal 3:1; 4:5-6
  make a straight highway
    for our God in the desert.
⁴ Every valley will be lifted up,
  and every mountain and hill
    will be leveled;
  the uneven ground
    will become smooth
  and the rough places, a plain.
⁵ And the glory of the LORD
    will appear,   Is 35:2
  and all humanity^A together
    will see it,   Is 52:10; Jl 2:28
  for the mouth of the LORD
    has spoken.   Is 1:20; 34:16; 58:14

⁶ A voice was saying, "Cry out!"
  Another said,^B
    "What should I cry out?"
  "All humanity is grass,
  and all its goodness is
    like the flower of the field.
⁷ The grass withers,
    the flowers fade
  when the breath^C of the LORD
    blows on them;^D
  indeed, the people are grass.
⁸ The grass withers,
    the flowers fade,   Jms 1:11
  but the word of our God
    remains forever."   Is 55:11; 59:21

⁹ Zion, herald of good news,
  go up on a high mountain.
  Jerusalem, herald
    of good news,   Is 61:1
  raise your voice loudly.
  Raise it, do not be afraid!
  Say to the cities of Judah,

"Here is your God!"   Is 25:9; 35:2
¹⁰ See, the Lord GOD comes
    with strength,
  and his power establishes
    his rule.   Is 59:16-18
  His wages are with him,   Is 62:11
  and his reward
    accompanies him.
¹¹ He protects his flock
    like a shepherd;   Jr 31:10; Mc 5:4
  he gathers the lambs
    in his arms
  and carries them in the fold
    of his garment.
  He gently leads those
    that are nursing.

¹² Who has measured
    the waters in the hollow
    of his hand
  or marked off the heavens
    with the span of his hand?
  Who has gathered the dust
    of the earth in a measure
  or weighed the mountains
    on a balance
  and the hills on the scales?
¹³ Who has directed^E the Spirit
    of the LORD,
  or who gave him counsel?
¹⁴ Who did he consult?
  Who gave him
    understanding   Jb 21:22; Col 2:3
  and taught him the paths
    of justice?
  Who taught him knowledge
  and showed him the way
    of understanding?
¹⁵ Look, the nations are
    like a drop in a bucket;
  they are considered
    as a speck of dust on
    the scales;
  he lifts up the islands
    like fine dust.

^A**40:5** Lit *flesh*   ^B**40:6** DSS, LXX, Vg read *I said*   ^C**40:7** Or *wind*, or *Spirit*   ^D**40:7** Lit *it*   ^E**40:13** Or
measured, or *comprehended*

16 Lebanon's cedars are not
   enough for fuel,
or its animals enough
   for a burnt offering.   Ps 50:9-11

17 All the nations are as nothing
   before him;
they are considered by him
   as empty nothingness.   Is 29:7

18 With whom will you
   compare God?
What likeness will you set up
   for comparison with him?

19 An idol? — something that
   a smelter casts
and a metalworker plates
   with gold
and makes silver chains for?

20 A poor person contributes
   wood for a pedestal
that will not rot.[A]
He looks for
   a skilled craftsman
to set up an idol that will not
   fall over.   1Sm 5:3; Is 44:9-15; 46:6-7

21 Do you not know?   Ps 19:1; 50:6
Have you not heard?
Has it not been declared
   to you
from the beginning?
Have you not considered
the foundations of the earth?

22 God is enthroned above
   the circle of the earth;
its inhabitants are
   like grasshoppers.   Nm 13:33
He stretches out the heavens
   like thin cloth   Jb 9:8; Is 37:16; 42:5
and spreads them out
   like a tent to live in.   Jb 36:29

23 He reduces princes
   to nothing   Jb 12:21; Ps 107:40
and makes judges of the earth
   like a wasteland.

24 They are barely planted,
   barely sown,
their stem hardly takes root
   in the ground
when he blows on them
   and they wither,
and a whirlwind carries
   them away like stubble.

25 "To whom will you
   compare me,   Is 46:5; Ac 17:29
or who is my equal?"
   asks the Holy One.

26 Look up[B] and see!
Who created these?   Is 42:5
He brings out the stars
   by number;
he calls all of them by name.
Because of his great power
   and strength,
not one of them is missing.

27 Jacob, why do you say,
and, Israel, why do you assert:
"My way is hidden
   from the LORD,
and my claim is ignored
   by my God"?   Is 7:13; 49:4,14

28 Do you not know?
Have you not heard?
The LORD is
   the everlasting God,   Gn 21:33
the Creator
   of the whole earth.
He never becomes faint
   or weary;
there is no limit
   to his understanding.   Ps 147:5

29 He gives strength to the faint
and strengthens
   the powerless.

30 Youths may become faint
   and weary,
and young men stumble
   and fall,

[A]40:20 Or who is too poor for such an offering, or who chooses mulberry wood as a votive gift; Hb obscure   [B]40:26 Lit Lift up your eyes on high

31 but those who trust
    in the LORD
will renew their strength;
they will soar on wings
    like eagles;   Ex 19:4; Dt 32:11; Lk 18:1
they will run and not
    become weary,
they will walk and not faint.

The LORD Versus the Nations' Gods

41 "Be silent before me,
    coasts and islands!   Is 11:11
And let peoples renew
    their strength.
Let them approach;
    let them testify;
let's come together
    for the trial.
2 Who has stirred up someone
    from the east?   Is 41:25; 45:1-3
In righteousness he calls him
    to serve.[A,B]   Is 42:6
The LORD hands nations over
    to him,   2Ch 36:23; Ezr 1:2
and he subdues kings.
He makes them like dust
    with his sword,
like wind-driven stubble
    with his bow.
3 He pursues them,
    going on safely,
hardly touching the path
    with his feet.
4 Who has performed
    and done this,
calling the generations
    from the beginning?
I am the LORD, the first
and with the last — I am he."

5 The coasts and islands see
    and are afraid,
the whole earth trembles.
They approach and arrive.
6 Each one helps the other,

and says to another,
    "Take courage!"
7 The craftsman encourages
    the metalworker;   Is 40:19
the one who flattens
    with the hammer
encourages the one
    who strikes the anvil,
saying of the soldering,
    "It is good."
He fastens it with nails
    so that it will not fall over.

8 But you, Israel, my servant,
Jacob, whom I have chosen,
descendant of Abraham,
    my friend —   2Ch 20:7; Jms 2:23
9 I brought[C] you from the ends
    of the earth
and called you
    from its farthest corners.
I said to you: You are
    my servant;
I have chosen you; I haven't
    rejected you.   Is 43:5-7
10 Do not fear, for I am with you;
do not be afraid, for I am
    your God.   Ezk 34:31
I will strengthen you; I will
    help you;
I will hold on to you
    with my righteous
    right hand.   Ex 15:6,12; Ps 18:35; 63:8

11 Be sure that all
    who are enraged
    against you
will be ashamed
    and disgraced;   Is 45:24
those who contend with you
will become as nothing
    and will perish.
12 You will look for those
    who contend with you,
but you will not find them.
Those who war against you

A 41:2 Or *Righteousness calls him to serve*   B 41:2 Lit *to his foot*   C 41:9 Or *seized*

will become
absolutely nothing.
13 For I am the LORD your God,
who holds your right hand,
who says to you, 'Do not fear,
I will help you.
14 Do not fear, you worm Jacob,
you men^A of Israel.
I will help you' —
this is
the LORD's declaration.
Your Redeemer is
the Holy One of Israel.   Is 43:14
15 See, I will make you
into a sharp threshing board,
new, with many teeth.
You will thresh mountains
and pulverize them
and make hills into chaff.
16 You will winnow them   Jr 51:2
and a wind
will carry them away,
a whirlwind will scatter
them.
But you will rejoice
in the LORD;
you will boast in the Holy One
of Israel.

17 The poor and the
needy seek water,
but there is none;
their tongues are parched
with thirst.
I will answer them.   Is 43:20; 44:3
I am the LORD, the God
of Israel. I will not
abandon them.
18 I will open rivers
on the barren heights,
and springs in the middle
of the plains.
I will turn the desert
into a pool
and dry land into springs.

19 I will plant cedars,
acacias, myrtles,
and olive trees
in the wilderness.   Is 35:1; 55:13
I will put juniper trees,
elms,
and cypress trees together
in the desert,
20 so that all may see and know,
consider and understand,
that the hand of the LORD
has done this,   Jb 12:9; Is 66:14
the Holy One of Israel
has created it.   Is 4:5

21 "Submit your case,"
says the LORD.
"Present your arguments,"
says Jacob's King.
22 "Let them come and tell us
what will happen.   Is 44:7-8; 45:21
Tell us the past events,
so that we may reflect
on them
and know the outcome,
or tell us the future.
23 Tell us the coming events,
then we will know
that you are gods.
Indeed, do something good
or bad,
then we will be in awe^B when
we see it.
24 Look, you are nothing   Ps 115:8
and your work is worthless.
Anyone who chooses you
is detestable.

25 "I have stirred up one
from the north,
and he has come,   Jr 50:3
one from the east
who invokes my^C name.
He will march over rulers
as if they were mud,

^A 41:14 LXX reads *small number*; DSS read *dead ones*   ^B 41:23 DSS read *we may hear*   ^C 41:25 DSS read *his*

like a potter who treads
  the clay.

26 Who told about this
  from the beginning,
so that we might know,
and from times past,
so that we might say,
  'He is right'?
No one announced it,
no one told it,
no one heard your words.

27 I was the first to say to Zion, [A]
'Look! Here they are!'
And I gave Jerusalem a
  herald with good news.

28 When I look, there is no one;
there is no counselor
  among them;
when I ask them, they have
  nothing to say.   Is 46:7

29 Look, all of them are
  a delusion; [B]
their works are nonexistent;
their images are wind
  and emptiness.

The Servant's Mission

42 "This is my servant;
    I strengthen him, Mt 12:18-21
this is my chosen one;
  I delight in him.   Is 41:8-9; Lk 9:35
I have put my Spirit on him;
he will bring justice [C]
  to the nations.   Is 2:4; 51:4-5

2 He will not cry out or shout
or make his voice heard
  in the streets.

3 He will not break
  a bruised reed,
and he will not put out
  a smoldering wick;
he will faithfully
  bring justice.

4 He will not grow weak
  or be discouraged

until he has established
  justice on earth.
The coasts and islands will
  wait for his instruction."

5 This is what God, the
  LORD, says —
who created the heavens
  and stretched them out,
who spread out the earth
  and what comes from it,
who gives breath
  to the people on it
and spirit to those who walk
  on it —   Jb 12:10; 33:4; Is 57:16; Dn 5:23

6 "I am the LORD. I
  have called you
for a righteous purpose, [D]
and I will hold you
  by your hand.   Is 41:10,13
I will watch over you, and I
  will appoint you
to be a covenant
  for the people   Is 49:8
and a light to the nations,

7 in order to open blind eyes,
to bring out prisoners
  from the dungeon, Is 35:5; 49:9
and those sitting in darkness
  from the prison house.

8 I am the LORD. That is
  my name,
and I will not give my glory
  to another   Ex 20:3-5; Is 48:11
or my praise to idols.

9 The past events
  have indeed happened.
Now I declare new events;
I announce them to you
  before they occur."

A Song of Praise

10 Sing a new song to the LORD;
sing his praise from the ends
  of the earth,

you who go down to the sea
with all that fills it,   Ps 96:11
you coasts and islands
with your[A] inhabitants.
11 Let the desert
and its cities shout,
the settlements
where Kedar dwells
cry aloud.   Is 21:16; 60:7
Let the inhabitants of Sela
sing for joy;   Is 16:1
let them cry out
from the mountaintops.
12 Let them give glory
to the LORD
and declare his praise
in the coasts and islands.
13 The LORD advances
like a warrior;
he stirs up his zeal
like a soldier.   Is 9:7; 26:11; 37:32
He shouts, he roars aloud,
he prevails over his enemies.

14 "I have kept silent
from ages past;
I have been quiet
and restrained myself.
But now, I will groan
like a woman in labor,   Is 13:8
gasping breathlessly.
15 I will lay waste mountains
and hills
and dry up all their vegetation.
I will turn rivers into islands
and dry up marshes.   Is 44:27
16 I will lead the blind by a way
they did not know;   Is 29:18; 32:3
I will guide them on paths
they have not known.
I will turn darkness to light
in front of them   Eph 5:8
and rough places
into level ground.   Is 40:4; Lk 3:5
This is what I will do for them,
and I will not abandon them.
17 They will be turned back
and utterly ashamed —
those who trust in an idol
and say to a cast image,
'You are our gods!'   Ps 97:7; Is 1:29

Israel's Blindness and Deafness

18 "Listen, you deaf!
Look, you blind, so that
you may see.   Is 35:5
19 Who is blind but my servant,
or deaf like my messenger
I am sending?
Who is blind
like my dedicated one,[B]
or blind like the servant
of the LORD?
20 Though seeing many things,[C]
you pay no attention.
Though his ears are open,
he does not listen."   Rm 2:21-23

21 Because of his righteousness,
the LORD was pleased
to magnify his instruction
and make it glorious.
22 But this is a people plundered
and looted,
all of them trapped in holes
or imprisoned in dungeons.
They have become plunder
with no one to rescue them
and loot, with no one saying,
"Give it back!"
23 Who among you
will hear this?
Let him listen and obey
in the future.
24 Who gave Jacob
to the robber,[D]
and Israel to the plunderers?
Was it not the LORD?
Have we not sinned
against him?

[A]42:10 Lit their   [B]42:19 Hb obscure   [C]42:20 Alt Hb tradition reads You see many things;   [D]42:24 Lit
to loot

They were not willing
  to walk in his ways,
and they would not listen
  to his instruction.
²⁵ So he poured out
  his furious anger
and the power of war on Jacob.
It surrounded him with fire,
  but he did not know it;
it burned him, but he didn't
  take it to heart. Is 29:13; 47:7; 57:1

Restoration of Israel

43
Now this is what the
  LORD says —
the one who created
  you, Jacob,
and the one who formed
  you, Israel — Is 43:7,15,21
"Do not fear, for I have
  redeemed you; Is 44:22-23; 48:20
I have called you by your
  name; you are mine. Gn 32:28
² I will be with you Dt 31:6,8,23
when you pass
  through the waters, Ps 66:12
and when you pass
  through the rivers,
they will not overwhelm you.
You will not be scorched
when you walk
  through the fire, Is 29:6; 30:27-29
and the flame will not
  burn you.
³ For I am the LORD your God,
the Holy One of Israel,
  and your Savior. Is 19:20; 43:11
I have given Egypt
  as a ransom for you,
Cush and Seba in your place.
⁴ Because you are precious
  in my sight 2Kg 1:13-14; Ps 36:7
and honored, and I love you,
I will give people
  in exchange for you
and nations instead of
  your life.

⁵ Do not fear, for I am with you;
I will bring your descendants
  from the east, Is 41:8; 61:9
and gather you from the west.
⁶ I will say to the north,
  'Give them up!'
and to the south,
  'Do not hold them back!'
Bring my sons from far away,
and my daughters
  from the ends
  of the earth — Is 45:22
⁷ everyone who bears
  my name
and is created for my glory.
I have formed them;
  indeed, I have made them."

⁸ Bring out a people
  who are blind, yet have eyes,
and are deaf, yet have ears.
⁹ All the nations
  are gathered together,
and the peoples
  are assembled. Is 34:1; 41:1
Who among them
  can declare this, Is 41:22-23,26
and tell us the former things?
Let them present
  their witnesses
to vindicate themselves,
so that people may hear
  and say, "It is true."
¹⁰ "You are my witnesses" —
  this is
  the LORD's declaration —
"and my servant
  whom I have chosen, Is 41:8
so that you may know
  and believe me
and understand that I am he.
No god was formed
  before me,
and there will be none
  after me. Is 44:6,8; 45:5-6
¹¹ I — I am the LORD.
Besides me, there is no Savior.

12 I alone declared, saved,
   and proclaimed —
and not some foreign god [A]
   among you.
So you are my witnesses" —
   this is
   the LORD's declaration —
"and [B] I am God.   Ps 46:10; 50:7
13 Also, from today on
   I am he alone,
and none can rescue
   from my power.   Dt 32:39
I act, and who can
   reverse it?"   Jb 9:12; Is 14:27

God's Deliverance of Rebellious Israel

14 This is what the LORD, your Redeemer, the Holy One of Israel says:
   Because of you, I will send an
      army [C] to Babylon
   and bring all of them
      as fugitives, [D]
   even the Chaldeans
      in the ships in which
      they rejoice. [E]   Is 23:13
15 I am the LORD, your Holy One,
   the Creator of Israel,
      your King.

16 This is what the LORD says —
who makes a way in the sea,
and a path
   through raging water,   Is 11:15
17 who brings out the chariot
      and horse,   Ex 15:19
   the army
      and the mighty one together
   (they lie down, they do not
      rise again;
   they are extinguished, put
      out like a wick) —   Ps 118:12
18 "Do not remember
      the past events,

pay no attention to things
   of old.   Is 65:17; Jr 23:7
19 Look, I am about to do
   something new;   Is 42:9; 48:6
even now it is coming.
   Do you not see it?
Indeed, I will make a way
   in the wilderness,   Ex 17:6
rivers [F] in the desert.
20 Wild animals —
   jackals and ostriches — will
      honor me,
because I provide water
   in the wilderness,
and rivers in the desert,
to give drink
   to my chosen people.
21 The people I formed
   for myself
will declare my praise.   Ps 102:18

22 "But, Jacob, you have not
   called on me,
because, Israel, you have
   become weary of me.   Mc 6:3
23 You have not brought
   me your sheep
   for burnt offerings
or honored me
   with your sacrifices.   Zch 7:5-6
I have not burdened you
   with offerings
or wearied you with incense. [G]
24 You have not bought me
   aromatic cane with silver,
or satisfied me with the fat
   of your sacrifices.
But you have burdened me
   with your sins;
you have wearied me
   with your iniquities.   Ps 95:10
25 "I — I sweep away
   your transgressions   Is 44:22

[A]43:12 Lit not a foreigner   [B]43:12 Or that   [C]43:14 an army supplied for clarity   [D]43:14 Or will break down all their bars   [E]43:14 Hb obscure   [F]43:19 DSS read paths   [G]43:23 I.e., with demands for offerings and incense

for my own sake   Is 37:35; 48:9,11
and remember your sins
   no more.   Is 38:17; Jr 31:34; Mk 2:7
²⁶ Remind me. Let's argue
   the case together.   Is 1:18; 41:1
Recount the facts, so that
   you may be vindicated.
²⁷ Your first father sinned,   Is 51:2
and your mediators
   have rebelled against me.
²⁸ So I defiled the officers
   of the sanctuary,
and set Jacob apart
   for destruction   Is 24:6; 34:5
and Israel for scorn.

Spiritual Blessing

44 "And now listen,
        Jacob my servant,
Israel whom I have chosen.
² This is the word of the LORD
your Maker, the one
   who formed you
   from the womb:
He will help you.
Do not fear, Jacob my servant,
Jeshurun^A whom I have
   chosen.   Dt 32:15; 33:5,26
³ For I will pour water on
   the thirsty land
and streams
   on the dry ground;
I will pour out my Spirit
   on your descendants   Is 32:15
and my blessing
   on your offspring.
⁴ They will sprout
   among^B the grass
like poplars by
   flowing streams.
⁵ This one will say, 'I am
   the LORD's';
another will use the name
   of Jacob;
still another will write
   on his hand, 'The LORD's,'

and take on the name
   of Israel."

No God Other Than the LORD

⁶ This is what the LORD, the King of
Israel and its Redeemer, the LORD
of Armies, says: Is 41:14; 43:14
I am the first and I am
   the last.   Is 41:4; 43:10; 48:12; Rv 1:8,17
There is no God but me.   Is 43:11
⁷ Who, like me, can announce
   the future?
Let him say so and make
   a case before me,   Is 41:22,26
since I have established
   an ancient people.
Let these gods declare^C
   the coming things,
and what will take place.
⁸ Do not be startled or afraid.
Have I not told you
   and declared it long ago?
You are my witnesses!   Is 43:10
Is there any God but me?   Jl 2:27
There is no other Rock;
   I do not know any.   Is 17:10; 26:4

⁹ All who make idols
   are nothing,
and what they treasure
   benefits no one.
Their witnesses do not see
   or know anything,
so they will be put
   to shame.   Ps 97:7; Is 42:17; 44:11
¹⁰ Who makes a god or casts
   a metal image
that benefits no one?   Is 41:29
¹¹ Look, all its worshipers
   will be put to shame,
and the craftsmen
   are humans.
They all will assemble
   and stand;
they all will be startled
   and put to shame.

^A44:2 = Upright One   ^B44:4 Some Hb mss, DSS, LXX read as among   ^C44:7 Lit declare them —

12 The ironworker labors
over the coals,
shapes the idol
with hammers,
and works it
with his strong arm.
Also he grows hungry
and his strength fails;
he doesn't drink water
and is faint.

13 The woodworker
stretches out
a measuring line,
he outlines it with a stylus;
he shapes it with chisels
and outlines it with a compass.
He makes it according to
a human form,   Ps 115:5-7
like a beautiful person,
to dwell in a temple.

14 He cuts down^A cedars
for his use,
or he takes a cypress or an oak.
He lets it grow strong
among the trees
of the forest.
He plants a laurel,
and the rain makes it grow.

15 A person can use it for fuel.
He takes some of it
and warms himself;
also he kindles a fire
and bakes bread;
he even makes it into a god
and worships it;
he makes an idol from it
and bows down to it.

16 He burns half of it in a fire,
and he roasts meat
on that half.
He eats the roast
and is satisfied.
He warms himself
and says, "Ah!
I am warm, I see the blaze."

17 He makes a god or his idol
with the rest of it.
He bows down to it
and worships;
he prays to it, "Save me, for
you are my god."   1Kg 18:26,28

18 Such people^B
do not comprehend
and cannot understand,
for he has shut their eyes^C
so they cannot see,
and their minds
so they cannot understand.

19 No one comes to his senses;^D
no one has the perception
or insight to say,
"I burned half of it in the fire,
I also baked bread on its coals,
I roasted meat and ate.
Should I make
something detestable
with the rest of it?   Dt 27:15
Should I bow down to a block
of wood?"

20 He feeds on^E ashes.
His deceived mind
has led him astray,
and he cannot rescue himself,
or say, "Isn't there a lie
in my right hand?"   Is 57:11

21 Remember these things,
Jacob,
and Israel, for you are
my servant;
I formed you, you are
my servant;
Israel, you will never
be forgotten by me.^F   Is 49:15

22 I have swept away
your transgressions
like a cloud,   Ps 51:1,9; Is 43:25
and your sins like a mist.
Return to me,   Is 31:6; 55:7
for I have redeemed you.

---

^A 44:14 Lit To cut down for himself   ^B 44:18 Lit They   ^C 44:18 Or for their eyes are shut   ^D 44:19 Lit No one returns to his heart   ^E 44:20 Or He shepherds   ^F 44:21 DSS, LXX, Tg read Israel, do not forget me

23 Rejoice, heavens,
　for the LORD has acted;
shout, depths of the earth.
Break out
　into singing, mountains,
forest, and every tree in it.
For the LORD
　has redeemed Jacob,
and glorifies himself
　through Israel.　　Is 49:3; 61:3

Restoration of Israel Through Cyrus

24 This is what the LORD, your Redeemer who formed you from the womb, says:　　Is 41:14; 43:14; 44:2
I am the LORD,
　who made everything;
who stretched out
　the heavens by myself;
who alone spread out
　the earth;
25 who destroys the omens
　of the false prophets
and makes fools of diviners;
who confounds the wise
and makes
　their knowledge foolishness;
26 who confirms the message
　of his servant
and fulfills the counsel
　of his messengers;
who says to Jerusalem,
　"She will be inhabited,"
and to the cities of Judah,
　"They will be rebuilt,"
and I will restore her ruins;
27 who says to the depths
　of the sea, "Be dry,"
and I will dry up your rivers;
28 who says to Cyrus,
　"My shepherd,　　Is 45:1
he will fulfill
　all my pleasure"　　Eph 1:9
and says to Jerusalem,
　"She will be rebuilt,"　　Ezr 1:1

and of the temple,
　"Its foundation will be laid."

45 The LORD says this
　to Cyrus, his anointed,
whose right hand
　I have grasped　　Ps 73:23; Is 41:13
to subdue nations
　before him
and disarm^A kings,　　Jb 12:21; Is 45:5
to open doors before him,
and even city gates will not
　be shut:
2 "I will go before you
and level the uneven places;^B
I will shatter
　the bronze doors
and cut the iron bars in two.
3 I will give you the treasures
　of darkness
and riches
　from secret places,　　Jr 41:8
so that you may know that I
　am the LORD.
I am the God of Israel, who
　calls you by your name.
4 I call you by your name,
for the sake of my servant Jacob
and Israel my chosen one.
I give a name to you,
though you do not know me.
5 I am the LORD, and there is
　no other;　　Is 45:6,14,18,21; 46:9
there is no God but me.　　Is 44:6,8
I will strengthen^C you,
though you do not know me,
6 so that all may know
　from the rising of the sun
　to its setting
that there is no one but me.
I am the LORD, and there is
　no other.
7 I form light
　and create darkness,　　Ps 104:20
I make success
　and create disaster;　　Gn 50:20

^A45:1 Lit *unloosen the waist of*　^B45:2 DSS, LXX read *the mountains*　^C45:5 Lit *gird*

I am the LORD, who
    does all these things.

8 "Heavens, sprinkle
        from above,
    and let the skies
        shower righteousness.
    Let the earth open up
    so that salvation will sprout
    and righteousness will
        spring up with it.   Ps 85:11
    I, the LORD, have created it.

9 "Woe to the one who argues
        with his Maker —
    one clay pot among many. A
    Does clay say to the one
        forming it,
    'What are you making?' Is 29:16
    Or does your work say,
    'He has no hands'? B

10 Woe to the one who says
        to his father,
    'What are you fathering?'
    or to his mother, C
    'What are you
        giving birth to?'"

11 This is what the LORD,
    the Holy One of Israel
        and its Maker, says: Is 1:4
    "Ask me what is to happen
        to D my sons,   Jr 31:9
    and instruct me
        about the work
        of my hands.   Is 19:25; 29:23; 60:21

12 I made the earth,
    and created humans on it.
    It was my hands
        that stretched out
        the heavens,   Ps 104:2; Is 42:5; 44:24
    and I commanded
        everything in them.

13 I have stirred him up
        in righteousness,   Is 41:2
    and will level all roads for him.

He will rebuild my city,   Is 44:28
    and set my exiles free,   Is 52:3
    not for a price or a bribe,"
    says the LORD of Armies.

God Alone Is the Savior

14 This is what the LORD says:
    "The products of Egypt
        and the merchandise
        of Cush
    and the Sabeans,
        men of stature,   Is 18:1; 43:3
    will come over to you   Is 14:1-2
    and will be yours;
    they will follow you,
    they will come over in chains
    and bow down to you.
    They will confess E to you,
    'God is indeed with you,
        and there is no other;
    there is no other God.'"

15 Yes, you are a God who hides,
    God of Israel, Savior.   Is 43:3

16 All of them are put to shame,
        even humiliated;   Is 42:17; 44:9
    the makers of idols
        go in humiliation together.

17 Israel will be saved
        by the LORD
    with an everlasting salvation;
    you will not be put to shame
        or humiliated
    for all eternity.   Is 49:23; 50:7; 54:4

18 For this is
        what the LORD says —
    the Creator of the heavens,
    the God who formed the
        earth and made it,
    the one who established it
    (he did not create it to be
        a wasteland,
    but formed it
        to be inhabited) —   Gn 1:26

A 45:9 Lit a clay pot with clay pots of the ground   B 45:9 Or making? Your work has no hands.
C 45:10 Lit to a woman   D 45:11 Or me the coming things about   E 45:14 Lit pray

he says, "I am the LORD,
and there is no other.
¹⁹ I have not spoken in secret,
somewhere in a land
of darkness.
I did not say
to the descendants of Jacob:
Seek me in a wasteland.
I am the LORD, who
speaks righteously,   Ps 19:8; 63:1
who declares what is right.

²⁰ "Come, gather together,
and approach, you fugitives
of the nations.
Those who carry
their wooden idols
and pray to a god
who cannot save   Is 44:17; 46:1,7
have no knowledge.   Is 44:18-19
²¹ Speak up and present
your case ᴬ —   Is 41:21-23; 43:9
yes, let them
consult each other.
Who predicted this long ago?
Who announced it
from ancient times?
Was it not I, the LORD?
There is no other God but me,
a righteous God and Savior;
there is no one except me.
²² Turn to me and be saved,
all the ends of the earth.
For I am God,
and there is no other.
²³ By myself I have sworn;   Is 62:8
truth has gone
from my mouth,   Is 55:11
a word that will not
be revoked:
Every knee will bow to me,
every tongue will
swear allegiance.
²⁴ It will be said about
me, 'Righteousness
and strength

are found only in the LORD.'"
All who are enraged
against him
will come to him and be
put to shame.   Is 41:11
²⁵ All the descendants of Israel
will be justified and find glory
through the LORD.

There Is No One like God

46 Bel crouches;
Nebo cowers.   Jr 50:2-4; 51:44
Idols depicting them are
consigned to beasts
and cattle.
The images you carry
are loaded,
as a burden
for the weary animal.
² The gods cower;
they crouch together;
they are not able to rescue
the burden,
but they themselves go
into captivity.   Jdg 18:17-18,24

³ "Listen to me, house of Jacob,
all the remnant of the house
of Israel,
who have been sustained
from the womb,
carried along since birth.
⁴ I will be the same
until your old age,   Ps 71:18
and I will bear you up
when you turn gray.
I have made you,
and I will carry you;
I will bear and rescue you.

⁵ "Who will you compare me
or make me equal to?
Who will you
measure me with,
so that we should be
like each other?   Is 40:18,25

ᴬ**45:21** Lit and approach

6 Those who pour out
  their bags of gold
and weigh out silver
  on scales —
they hire a goldsmith
  and he makes it into a god.
Then they kneel
  and bow down to it.   Is 40:19
7 They lift it to their shoulder
  and bear it along;   Is 45:20; 46:1
they set it in its place,
  and there it stands;
it does not budge
  from its place.   Is 40:20; 41:7
They cry out to it
  but it doesn't answer;
it saves no one
  from his trouble.

8 "Remember this
  and be brave;ᴬ
take it to heart,
  you transgressors!
9 Remember what happened
  long ago,   Dt 32:7; Is 42:9; 65:17
for I am God, and there is
  no other;
I am God, and no one is
  like me.
10 I declare the end
  from the beginning,
and from long ago what is
  not yet done,
saying: my plan
  will take place,
and I will do all my will.   Ps 33:11
11 I call a bird of preyᴮ
  from the east,   Is 44:28–45:1
a man for my purpose
  from a far country.
Yes, I have spoken;
  so I will also bring it about.
I have planned it;
  I will also do it.
12 Listen to me,
  you hardhearted,

far removed from justice:
13 I am bringing
  my justice near;   Is 51:5; 61:11
it is not far away,
and my salvation
  will not delay.
I will put salvation in Zion,
my splendor in Israel.

The Fall of Babylon

47 "Go down and sit
  in the dust,   Is 3:26; Jr 48:18
Virgin Daughter Babylon.
Sit on the ground
  without a throne,
Daughter Chaldea!
For you will no longer
  be called pampered
  and spoiled.
2 Take millstones
  and grind flour;   Ex 11:5; Jb 31:10
remove your veil,
strip off your skirt,
  bare your thigh,
wade through the streams.
3 Your nakedness
  will be uncovered,
and your disgrace
  will be exposed.   Jr 13:26; Lm 1:8
I will take vengeance;
I will spare no one."ᴬ
4 The Holy One of Israel is
  our Redeemer;   Is 41:14; 43:14
The LORD of Armies is
  his name.

5 "Daughter Chaldea,
sit in silence and go
  into darkness.   Is 23:2; Jr 8:14
For you will no longer
  be called mistress
  of kingdoms.
6 I was angry with my people;
I profaned my possession,
and I handed them over
  to you.

ᴬ46:8; 47:3 Hb obscure   ᴮ46:11 = Cyrus

You showed them no mercy;
you made your yoke
    very heavy on the elderly.
7 You said, 'I will be
    the queen forever.'
You did not take these things
    to heart
or think about their outcome.

8 "So now hear this,
    lover of luxury,
who sits securely,   Zph 2:15
who says to herself,
'I am, and there is
    no one else.
I will never be a widow
or know the loss of children.'
9 These two things will happen
    to you
suddenly, in one day:
loss of children
    and widowhood.
They will happen to you
    in their entirety,
in spite of
    your many sorceries   Is 47:13
and the potency
    of your spells.
10 You were secure
    in your wickedness;
you said, 'No one sees me.'
Your wisdom and knowledge
led you astray.
You said to yourself,
'I am, and there is
    no one else.'
11 But disaster will happen
    to you;
you will not know how
    to avert it.
And it will fall on you,
but you will be unable
    to ward it off.ᴬ
Devastation will happen
    to you suddenly
and unexpectedly.   Is 13:6; Jr 51:8,43

12 So take your stand
    with your spells
and your many sorceries,
which you have
    wearied yourself with
    from your youth.
Perhaps you will be able
    to succeed;
perhaps you will
    inspire terror!
13 You are worn out
    with your many
    consultations.
So let the astrologers stand
    and save you —
those who observe the stars,
those who predict monthly
what will happen to you.
14 Look, they are like stubble;
fire burns them.   Is 10:17
They cannot
    rescue themselves
from the powerᴮ
    of the flame.
This is not a coal
    for warming themselves,
or a fire to sit beside!
15 This is what they are
    to you —
those who have wearied you
and have traded with you
    from your youth —
each wanders
    on his own way;
no one can save you.

Israel Must Leave Babylon

48 "Listen to this,
    house of Jacob —
those who are called
    by the name Israel
and have descended
    fromᶜ Judah,   Nm 24:7; Dt 33:28
who swear by the name
    of the LORD   Dt 6:13; Is 45:23; 65:16
and declare the God of Israel,

ᴬ47:11 Or to atone for it   ᴮ47:14 Lit hand   ᶜ48:1 Lit have come from the waters of

but not in truth
or righteousness.
² For they are named
after the Holy City,
and lean on the God of Israel;
his name is the LORD
of Armies.
³ I declared the past events
long ago;
they came out of my mouth;
I proclaimed them.
Suddenly I acted,
and they occurred.
⁴ Because I know
that you are stubborn,
and your neck is iron^A
and your forehead bronze,
⁵ therefore I declared to you
long ago.
I announced it to you
before it occurred,
so you could not claim,
'My idol caused them;
my carved image
and cast idol control them.'
⁶ You have heard it.
Observe it all.
Will you not acknowledge it?
From now on
I will announce new things
to you,
hidden things that
you have not known.   Is 42:9
⁷ They have been created now,
and not long ago;
you have not heard of them
before today,
so you could not claim,
'I already knew them!'
⁸ You have never heard;
you have never known;
for a long time your ears
have not been open.
For I knew that you
were very treacherous,

and were known as a rebel
from birth.   Dt 9:7,24; Ps 58:3; Is 46:8
⁹ I will delay my anger
for the sake of my name,
and I will restrain
myself for your benefit
and for my praise,
so that you will not be
destroyed.
¹⁰ Look, I have refined you,
but not as silver;   Dt 4:20; 1Kg 8:51
I have tested^B you
in the furnace
of affliction.
¹¹ I will act for my own sake,
indeed, my own,   Is 43:25
for how can I^C be defiled?
I will not give my glory
to another.   Is 42:8

¹² "Listen to me, Jacob,
and Israel, the one called
by me:
I am he; I am the first,
I am also the last.   Is 41:4; 43:10-13
¹³ My own hand founded
the earth,
and my right hand spread out
the heavens;   Heb 1:10-12
when I summoned them,
they stood up together.
¹⁴ All of you, assemble
and listen!
Who among the idols^D
has declared these things?
The LORD loves him;^E
he will accomplish his will
against Babylon,   Is 13:4-5,17-19
and his arm will be against
the Chaldeans.
¹⁵ I — I have spoken;
yes, I have called him;   Is 41:2
I have brought him,
and he will succeed
in his mission.   Is 53:10

^A 48:4 Lit *is an iron sinew*   ^B 48:10 DSS; MT reads *chosen*   ^C 48:11 DSS, Syr; MT reads *it*   ^D 48:14 Lit *among them*   ^E 48:14 = Cyrus

16 Approach me and listen
   to this.
From the beginning
   I have not spoken in secret;
from the time anything
   existed, I was there."
And now the Lord GOD
has sent me and his Spirit.

17 This is what the LORD, your
Redeemer, the Holy One of Israel
says: Is 1:4; 41:14; 43:14
   I am the LORD your God,
   who teaches you
     for your benefit,
   who leads you in the way
     you should go.
18 If only you had paid attention
   to my commands.
Then your peace
   would have been
   like a river,   Is 32:16-18; 66:12
and your righteousness
   like the waves of the sea.
19 Your descendants
   would have been
   as countless as the sand,
and the offspring
   of your body like its grains;
their name would not
   be cut off
or eliminated
   from my presence.

20 Leave Babylon,
   flee from the Chaldeans!
Declare with a shout of joy,
   proclaim this,
let it go out to the end
   of the earth;
announce,
"The LORD has redeemed
   his servant Jacob!"   Is 41:8-9
21 They did not thirst
when he led them
   through the deserts;

he made water flow
   from the rock for them;
he split the rock, and water
   gushed out.
22 "There is no peace
   for the wicked,"
   says the LORD.   Is 57:21

The Servant Brings Salvation

49
Coasts and islands, [A]
   listen to me;
distant peoples,
   pay attention.
The LORD called me
   before I was born.   Is 44:2,24
He named me while I was
   in my mother's womb.   Lk 1:15
2 He made my words
   like a sharp sword;   Is 11:4
he hid me in the shadow
   of his hand.   Is 51:16
He made me
   like a sharpened arrow;
he hid me in his quiver.
3 He said to me, "You are
   my servant,   Is 41:8-9; 42:1; 49:5-7
Israel, in whom I will
   be glorified."
4 But I myself said:
   I have labored in vain,
I have spent my strength
   for nothing and futility;
yet my vindication is
   with the LORD,
and my reward is
   with my God.
5 And now, says the LORD,
who formed me
   from the womb to be
   his servant,
to bring Jacob back to him
so that Israel
   might be gathered to him;
for I am honored in the sight
   of the LORD,
and my God is my strength —

A 49:1 Or *Islands*

6 he says,
"It is not enough for you to be
my servant
raising up the tribes of Jacob
and restoring
the protected ones of Israel.
I will also make you a light
for the nations, Is 42:6; 51:4
to be my salvation to the ends
of the earth." Ac 13:47

7 This is what the LORD,
the Redeemer of Israel,
his Holy One, says Is 41:14; 43:14
to one who is despised,
to one abhorred by people, A
to a servant of rulers:
"Kings will see, princes will
stand up,
and they B will all bow down
because of the LORD,
who is faithful,
the Holy One of Israel —
and he has chosen you."

8 This is what the LORD says:
I will answer you in a time
of favor,
and I will help you in the day
of salvation. Ps 69:13; 2Co 6:2
I will keep you,
and I will appoint you
to be a covenant
for the people, Is 42:6
to restore the land,
to make them possess
the desolate inheritances,
9 saying to the prisoners:
Come out, Is 42:7; 61:1; Lk 4:18
and to those who
are in darkness:
Show yourselves.
They will feed
along the pathways,
and their pastures will be
on all the barren heights.

10 They will not hunger
or thirst,
the scorching heat or sun
will not strike them;
for their compassionate one
will guide them,
and lead them to springs.
11 I will make all my mountains
into a road,
and my highways will be
raised up. Is 40:4
12 See, these will come
from far away,
from the north
and from the west, C Is 43:5-6
and from the land of Sinim. D, E

13 Shout for joy, you heavens!
Earth, rejoice!
Mountains break
into joyful shouts!
For the LORD has comforted
his people, Is 40:1
and will have compassion
on his afflicted ones. Is 54:7-10

Zion Remembered

14 Zion says, "The LORD
has abandoned me;
the Lord has forgotten me!"
15 "Can a woman forget
her nursing child,
or lack compassion
for the child of her womb?
Even if these forget,
yet I will not forget you.
16 Look, I have inscribed you
on the palms of my hands;
your walls are continually
before me.
17 Your builders F hurry;
those who destroy
and devastate you
will leave you.
18 Look up, and look around.

A 49:7 Or by the nation   B 49:7 Lit princes and they   C 49:12 Lit sea   D 49:12 DSS read of the Syenites
E 49:12 Perhaps modern Aswan in southern Egypt   F 49:17 DSS, Aq, Theod, Vg; MT, Syr, Sym read sons

They all gather together;
   they come to you.   Is 60:4
As I live" —
   this is
   the Lord's declaration —
"you will wear
   all your children^A as jewelry,
and put them on
   as a bride does.
19 For your waste
   and desolate places
and your land marked
   by ruins —
will now be indeed too small
   for the inhabitants,   Is 54:1-2
and those who swallowed
   you up will be far away.
20 Yet as you listen, the children
   that you have been
     deprived of will say,
   'This place is too small
     for me;
make room for me so that
   I may settle.'   Is 54:1-3
21 Then you will say
   within yourself,
'Who fathered these for me?
I was deprived of my children
   and unable to conceive,
exiled and wandering —
but who brought them up?
See, I was left by myself —
but these, where did they
   come from?' "^B

22 This is what the Lord God says:
Look, I will lift up my hand
   to the nations,
and raise my banner
   to the peoples.   Is 11:10-12; 18:3
They will bring your sons
   in their arms,
and your daughters
   will be carried
   on their shoulders.   Is 14:2; 43:6

23 Kings will be your guardians
and their queens^C
   your nursing mothers.
They will bow down to you
   with their faces
     to the ground
and lick the dust at your feet.
Then you will know that I am
   the Lord;   Is 41:20; 43:10; 60:16
those who put their hope
   in me
will not be put to shame.   Jl 2:27

24 Can the prey be taken from
   a mighty man,
or the captives of a tyrant^D
   be delivered?
25 For this is what
   the Lord says:
"Even the captives
   of a mighty man
     will be taken,
and the prey of a tyrant
   will be delivered;
I will contend with the one
   who contends with you,
and I will save
   your children.
26 I will make your oppressors
   eat their own flesh,   Is 9:20
and they will be drunk
   with their own blood
   as with sweet wine.
Then all people will know
that I, the Lord,
   am your Savior,   Is 43:3
and your Redeemer,
   the Mighty One of Jacob."

50 This is what the Lord says:
   Where is your mother's
     divorce certificate
that I used to send her away?
Or to which of my creditors
   did I sell you?   Dt 32:30; 2Kg 4:1

---

^A49:18 Lit *all of them*   ^B49:21 Lit *where are they*   ^C49:23 Lit *princesses*   ^D49:24 DSS, Syr, Vg; MT reads *a righteous man*

Look, you were sold
for your iniquities,   Is 13:11
and your mother was
sent away
because of
your transgressions.
² Why was no one there
when I came?
Why was there no one
to answer when I called?
Is my arm too weak
to redeem?   Gn 18:14; Nm 11:23
Or do I have no power
to rescue?
Look, I dry up the sea
by my rebuke;   Ex 14:21; Is 43:16
I turn the rivers
into a wilderness;
their fish rot because of lack
of water
and die of thirst.
³ I dress the heavens in black
and make sackcloth
their clothing.   Rv 6:12

The Obedient Servant

⁴ The Lord GOD has given me
the tongue of those
who are instructed   Is 8:16
to know how to sustain
the weary with a word.
He awakens me
each morning;
he awakens my ear to listen
like those being instructed.
⁵ The Lord GOD has opened
my ear,
and I was not rebellious;
I did not turn back.   Jn 8:29; 14:31
⁶ I gave my back to those
who beat me,
and my cheeks to those
who tore out my beard.
I did not hide my face
from scorn and spitting.
⁷ The Lord GOD will help me;

therefore I have not
been humiliated;
therefore I have set my face
like flint,   Ezk 3:8-9
and I know I will not
be put to shame.
⁸ The one who vindicates me
is near;   Is 45:25
who will contend with me?
Let us confront each other. ᴬ
Who has a case against me? ᴮ
Let him come near me!
⁹ In truth, the Lord GOD
will help me;
who will condemn me?
Indeed, all of them
will wear out
like a garment;
a moth will devour them.
¹⁰ Who among you fears
the LORD
and listens to his servant?
Who among you walks
in darkness,
and has no light?
Let him trust in the name
of the LORD;
let him lean on his God.
¹¹ Look, all you who kindle
a fire,
who encircle yourselves
with ᶜ torches;
walk in the light of your fire
and of the torches
you have lit!
This is what you'll get
from my hand:
you will lie down in a place
of torment.

Salvation for Zion

51 Listen to me, you
who pursue righteousness,
you who seek the LORD:
Look to the rock from which
you were cut,

ᴬ**50:8** Lit *us stand*   ᴮ**50:8** Lit *Who is lord of my judgment*   ᶜ**50:11** Syr reads *who set ablaze*

and to the quarry
  from which you were dug.
2 Look to Abraham your father,
  and to Sarah who gave birth
    to you.
When I called him, he was
  only one;
I blessed him
  and made him many.   Gn 12:1
3 For the LORD
  will comfort Zion;   Is 40:1
he will comfort
  all her waste places,
and he will make
  her wilderness like Eden,
and her desert
  like the garden of the LORD.
Joy and gladness
  will be found in her,
thanksgiving
  and melodious song.

4 Pay attention to me,
  my people,
and listen to me, my nation;
for instruction will come
  from me,
and my justice for a light
  to the nations.   Is 42:6; 49:6
I will bring it about quickly.
5 My righteousness is near,
my salvation appears,
and my arms
  will bring justice
  to the nations.   Is 40:10
The coasts and islands
  will put their hope in me,
and they will look
  to my strength. A
6 Look up to the heavens,
  and look
    at the earth beneath;
for the heavens will vanish
  like smoke,
the earth will wear out
  like a garment,

and its inhabitants will die
  like gnats. B   Ps 102:25-26; Is 34:4
But my salvation
  will last forever,   Is 45:17; Heb 5:9
and my righteousness
  will never be shattered.

7 Listen to me, you who
  know righteousness,
the people in whose heart is
  my instruction: Ps 37:31
do not fear disgrace by men,
and do not be shattered
  by their taunts.
8 For moths will devour them
  like a garment,   Is 50:9
and worms will eat them
  like wool.   Is 14:11
But my righteousness
  will last forever,
and my salvation
  for all generations.

9 Wake up, wake up!
Arm of the LORD, clothe
  yourself with strength.
Wake up as in days past,
as in generations long ago.
Wasn't it you
  who hacked Rahab
    to pieces,   Jb 26:12; Ps 89:10; Is 30:7
who pierced the sea monster?
10 Wasn't it you who dried up
  the sea,   Is 11:15-16; 50:2; 63:11-12
the waters of the great deep,
who made the sea-bed
  into a road
for the redeemed
  to pass over?   Ex 15:13
11 And the redeemed
  of the LORD will return
and come to Zion
  with singing,
crowned with unending joy.
Joy and gladness
  will overtake them,

A 51:5 Lit *arm*   B 51:6 Or *die in like manner*

and sorrow and sighing
will flee.

12 I — I am the one
who comforts you.
Who are you that you should
fear humans who die, Ps 118:6
or a son of man who
is given up like grass? 1Pt 1:24
13 But you have forgotten
the LORD, your Maker,
who stretched out
the heavens
and laid the foundations
of the earth. Is 44:24; 45:12; Am 9:6
You are in constant dread
all day long
because of the fury
of the oppressor,
who has set himself
to destroy.
But where is the fury
of the oppressor? Is 49:26
14 The prisoner[A] is soon to be
set free;
he will not die and go
to the Pit,
and his food will not
be lacking.
15 For I am the LORD your God
who stirs up the sea so that
its waves roar — Ps 107:25
his name is the LORD
of Armies.
16 I have put my words
in your mouth, Is 59:21
and covered you
in the shadow of my hand,
in order to plant[B]
the heavens,
to found the earth,
and to say to Zion, "You are
my people."

17 Wake yourself,
wake yourself up!

Stand up, Jerusalem,
you who have drunk the cup
of his fury Jb 21:20; Is 63:6; Jr 25:15
from the LORD's hand;
you who have drunk
the goblet to the dregs —
the cup that causes people
to stagger.
18 There is no one to guide her
among all the children
she has raised;
there is no one to take hold
of her hand
among all the offspring
she has brought up.
19 These two things
have happened to you: Is 47:9
devastation and destruction,
famine and sword.
Who will grieve for you?
How can I[C] comfort you?
20 Your children have fainted;
they lie at the head
of every street
like an antelope in a net.
They are full
of the LORD's fury,
the rebuke of your God.
21 So listen to this, suffering
and drunken one — but not
with wine. Is 29:9
22 This is what
your Lord says —
the LORD, even your God,
who defends his people —
"Look, I have removed
from your hand
the cup that causes
staggering;
that goblet, the cup
of my fury.
You will never drink it again.
23 I will put it into the hands
of your tormentors,
who said to you: Is 49:26; Zch 12:2

A 51:14 Hb obscure   B 51:16 Syr reads to stretch out   C 51:19 DSS, LXX, Syr, Vg read you? Who can

Lie down, so we can walk
     over you.
You made your back
     like the ground,
and like a street for those
     who walk on it.

52

"Wake up, wake up;
     put on your strength, Zion!
Put on
     your beautiful garments,
Jerusalem, the Holy City!
For the uncircumcised
     and the unclean
will no longer enter you.   Is 35:8
2 Stand up, shake the dust
     off yourself!
Take your seat, Jerusalem.
Remove the bonds[A]
     from your neck,
captive Daughter Zion."
3 For this is what
     the LORD says:
"You were sold for nothing,
and you will be redeemed
     without silver."   Is 45:13; 1Pt 1:18
4 For this is what the Lord
     GOD says:
"At first my people
     went down to Egypt
     to reside there,   Gn 46:6
then Assyria oppressed them
     without cause.[B]
5 So now what have I here" —
     this is
     the LORD's declaration —
"that my people
     are taken away
     for nothing?
Its rulers wail" —
     this is
     the LORD's declaration —
"and my name is continually
     blasphemed all day long.
6 Therefore my people
     will know my name;   Is 49:23

therefore they will know
     on that day
that I am he who says:
Here I am."

7 How beautiful
     on the mountains
are the feet of the herald,
who proclaims peace,
who brings news
     of good things,   Nah 1:15; Rm 10:15
who proclaims salvation,
who says to Zion,
     "Your God reigns!"   Ps 93:1
8 The voices
     of your watchmen —   Is 62:6
they lift up their voices,
shouting for joy together;
for every eye will see
when the LORD returns
     to Zion.
9 Be joyful, rejoice together,
you ruins of Jerusalem!   Is 44:26
For the LORD has comforted
     his people;   Is 40:1
he has redeemed Jerusalem.
10 The LORD has displayed
     his holy arm
in the sight of
     all the nations;   Ps 98:1-3; Is 51:9
all the ends of the earth
     will see
the salvation of our God.   Is 40:5

11 Leave, leave, go out
     from there!   Is 48:20; Jr 50:8
Do not touch
     anything unclean;
go out from her,
     purify yourselves,   2Co 6:17
you who carry the vessels
     of the LORD.
12 For you will not leave
     in a hurry,   Ex 12:11,33; Dt 16:3
and you will not have
     to take flight;

because the Lord is going
before you,   Ex 23:23; Dt 1:30; 31:8
and the God of Israel is
your rear guard.   Jos 6:9,13

The Servant's Suffering and Exaltation

13 See, my servant[A]
will be successful;[B]   Is 42:1; 50:10
he will be raised
and lifted up
and greatly exalted.   Php 2:9-11
14 Just as many were appalled
at you[C] —
his appearance
was so disfigured
that he did not look
like a man,
and his form
did not resemble
a human being —
15 so he will sprinkle
many nations.[D]   Nm 19:18-21
Kings will shut their mouths
because of him,
for they will see
what had not been told them,
and they will understand
what they had not heard.

53
Who has believed
what we have heard?[E]
And to whom has the arm
of the Lord been revealed?
2 He grew up before him
like a young plant   Is 11:1
and like a root out of
dry ground.
He didn't have an
impressive form
or majesty that we
should look at him,
no appearance
that we should desire him.

3 He was despised and rejected
by men,   Ps 22:6; Is 49:7; Lk 18:31-33
a man of suffering who knew
what sickness was.   Mk 8:31
He was like someone
people turned away from;[F]
he was despised,
and we didn't value him.
4 Yet he himself bore
our sicknesses,
and he carried our pains;
but we in turn
regarded him stricken,
struck down by God,
and afflicted.   Ps 69:26
5 But he was pierced
because of our rebellion,
crushed because of
our iniquities;   Is 1:4
punishment for our peace
was on him,   Jr 2:30; Zph 3:2; Heb 5:8
and we are healed
by his wounds.   1Pt 2:24-25
6 We all went astray
like sheep;   Mt 18:12
we all have turned
to our own way;
and the Lord
has punished him
for[G] the iniquity of us all.
7 He was oppressed
and afflicted,
yet he did not open
his mouth.
Like a lamb led
to the slaughter
and like a sheep silent
before her shearers,
he did not open his mouth.
8 He was taken away
because of oppression
and judgment;

[A]52:13 Tg adds *the Messiah*   [B]52:13 Or *will act wisely*   [C]52:14 Some Hb mss, Syr, Tg read *him*
[D]52:15 LXX reads *so many nations will marvel at him*   [E]53:1 Or *believed our report*   [F]53:3 Lit *And like a hiding of faces from him*   [G]53:6 Or *has placed on him*; lit *with*

and who considered
  his fate?[A]
For he was cut off
  from the land
  of the living;
he was struck because of
  my people's rebellion.

9 He was assigned a grave
  with the wicked,
but he was with a rich man
  at his death,   Mt 27:57-60
because he had done
  no violence
and had not
  spoken deceitfully.   Heb 4:15

10 Yet the LORD was pleased
  to crush him severely.[B]
When[C] you make him
  a guilt offering,   Lv 5:1-19
he will see his seed,
  he will prolong his days,
and by his hand, the
  LORD's pleasure
  will be accomplished.   Is 46:10

11 After his anguish,
he will see light[D] and be
  satisfied.
By his knowledge,
my righteous servant
  will justify many,   Is 42:1; 1Jn 2:1
and he will carry
  their iniquities.

12 Therefore I will give him[E]
  the many as a portion,
and he will receive[F]
  the mighty as spoil,
because he willingly
  submitted to death,   Mt 26:42
and was counted
  among the rebels;   Lk 22:37
yet he bore the sin
  of many   Heb 9:28
and interceded
  for the rebels.   Lk 23:34; Rm 8:34

Future Glory for Israel

54 "Rejoice, childless one,
  who did not give birth;
burst into song and shout,
you who have not been
  in labor!   Gl 4:27
For the children
  of the desolate one
  will be more
than the children
  of the married woman,"
says the LORD.

2 "Enlarge the site of your tent,
and let your tent curtains
  be stretched out;   Is 49:19-20
do not hold back;
lengthen your ropes,
and drive your pegs deep.

3 For you will spread out
  to the right and to the left,
and your descendants
  will dispossess nations
and inhabit
  the desolate cities.

4 "Do not be afraid,
  for you will not
  be put to shame;   Is 45:17
don't be humiliated,
  for you will not
  be disgraced.
For you will forget the shame
  of your youth,
and you will
  no longer remember
the disgrace
  of your widowhood.   Is 4:1; 51:7

5 Indeed, your husband is
  your Maker —   Jr 3:14; Hs 2:19
his name is the
  LORD of Armies —
and the Holy One of Israel is
  your Redeemer;   Is 1:4; 41:14
he is called the God of the
  whole earth.

[A]53:8 Or *and as for his generation, who considered him?*   [B]53:10 Or *him; he made him sick.*
[C]53:10 Or *If*   [D]53:11 DSS, LXX; MT omits *light*   [E]53:12 Or *him with*   [F]53:12 Or *receive with*

⁶ For the LORD has called you,
like a wife deserted
and wounded in spirit,
a wife of one's youth
when she is rejected," Mal 2:14
says your God.

⁷ "I deserted you
for a brief moment, Is 26:20
but I will take you back
with abundant compassion.

⁸ In a surge of anger
I hid my face from you
for a moment, Dt 31:17-18; Is 8:17
but I will have compassion
on you
with everlasting love," Ps 100:5
says the LORD
your Redeemer.

⁹ "For this is like the days ᴬ
of Noah to me:
when I swore that the water
of Noah
would never flood
the earth again, Gn 9:11
so I have sworn that I will not
be angry with you
or rebuke you. Ezk 39:29

¹⁰ Though the mountains move
and the hills shake,
my love will not be removed
from you
and my covenant of peace
will not be shaken," Nm 25:12
says your compassionate
LORD.

¹¹ "Poor Jerusalem, storm-tossed,
and not comforted,
I will set your stones
in black mortar,ᴮ
and lay your foundations
in lapis lazuli. Rv 21:19

¹² I will make
your fortifications ᶜ
out of rubies,
your gates out of
sparkling stones,
and all your walls out of
precious stones.

¹³ Then all your children
will be taught
by the LORD, Jn 6:45
their prosperity
will be great,

¹⁴ and you will be established
on a foundation of
righteousness.
You will be far
from oppression,
you will certainly not
be afraid;
you will be far from terror,
it will certainly not
come near you.

¹⁵ If anyone attacks you,
it is not from me;
whoever attacks you
will fall before you.

¹⁶ Look, I have created
the craftsman
who blows on
the charcoal fire
and produces
a weapon suitable
for its task;
and I have created
the destroyer
to cause havoc.

¹⁷ No weapon formed
against you will succeed,
and you will refute
any accusation ᴰ
raised against you
in court.
This is the heritage
of the LORD's servants, Lk 1:54
and their vindication is
from me." Is 45:24; 46:13
This is
the LORD's declaration.

Come to the LORD

55 "Come, everyone
who is thirsty,   Ps 42:1-2; 63:1
come to the water;
and you without silver,
come, buy, and eat!
Come, buy wine and milk
without silver
and without cost!
2 Why do you spend silver
on what is not food,
and your wages on what
does not satisfy?
Listen carefully to me,
and eat what is good,
and you will enjoy
the choicest of foods. ^A
3 Pay attention and come
to me;
listen, so that you will live.
I will make
a permanent covenant
with you   Gn 9:16; 17:7; 2Sm 23:5
on the basis of the faithful
kindnesses of David. ^B
4 Since I have made him
a witness to the peoples,
a leader and commander
for the peoples,   Ezk 34:24; Dn 9:25
5 so you will summon a nation
you do not know,   Is 45:14,22-24
and nations who do not
know you will run to you.
For the LORD your God,
even the Holy One
of Israel,   Is 1:4
has glorified you."   Is 60:9

6 Seek the LORD
while he may be found;
call to him while he is near.
7 Let the wicked one abandon
his way
and the sinful one
his thoughts;   Ps 33:10; Is 32:7; 59:7
let him return to the LORD,

so he may have compassion
on him,
and to our God, for he will
freely forgive.   Is 1:18; 43:25; 44:22

8 "For my thoughts are not
your thoughts,
and your ways are not
my ways."
This is
the LORD's declaration.
9 "For as heaven is higher
than earth,   Ps 103:11
so my ways are higher
than your ways,
and my thoughts
than your thoughts.
10 For just as rain and snow fall
from heaven
and do not return there
without saturating
the earth
and making it germinate
and sprout,
and providing seed to sow
and food to eat,   2Co 9:10
11 so my word that comes
from my mouth
will not return to me empty,
but it will accomplish
what I please
and will prosper
in what I send it to do."

12 You will indeed go out
with joy
and be peacefully guided;
the mountains and the hills
will break into singing
before you,
and all the trees of the field
will clap their hands.   Ps 98:8
13 Instead of the thornbush,
a cypress will come up,
and instead of the brier,
a myrtle will come up;

^A55:2 Lit enjoy fatness   ^B55:3 Or with you, the faithful acts of kindness shown to David

this will stand as a
monument for the LORD,
an everlasting sign
that will not be destroyed.

A House of Prayer for All

56 This is what the LORD says:
Preserve justice and do
what is right,   Gn 18:19; Ps 106:3
for my salvation
is coming soon,
and my righteousness
will be revealed.   Ps 98:2; Is 46:13

2 Happy is the person
who does this,
the son of man who
holds it fast,
who keeps the Sabbath
without desecrating it,
and keeps his hand
from doing any evil.   Is 58:13

3 No foreigner who has
joined himself to the LORD
should say,
"The LORD will exclude me
from his people,"   Is 14:1; 56:6
and the eunuch should not say,
"Look, I am a dried-up tree."

4 For the LORD says this:
"For the eunuchs who keep
my Sabbaths,
and choose what pleases me,
and hold firmly
to my covenant,

5 I will give them, in my house
and within my walls,
a memorial and a name
better than sons
and daughters.
I will give each of them
an everlasting name
that will never be cut off.

6 As for the foreigners
who join themselves
to the LORD

to minister to him, to
love the name of the LORD,
and to become his servants —
all who keep the Sabbath
without desecrating it
and who hold firmly
to my covenant —

7 I will bring them
to my holy mountain   Is 2:2-3
and let them rejoice
in my house of prayer.
Their burnt offerings
and sacrifices
will be acceptable
on my altar,   Mal 1:11
for my house will be called
a house of prayer
for all nations."   Jr 7:11; Mt 21:13

8 This is the declaration
of the Lord GOD,
who gathers the dispersed
of Israel:
"I will gather to them
still others
besides those
already gathered."   Is 11:12

Unrighteous Leaders Condemned

9 All you animals of the field
and forest,
come and eat!

10 Israel's^A watchmen are blind,
all of them,
they know nothing;
all of them are mute dogs,
they cannot bark;
they dream, lie down,
and love to sleep.

11 These dogs have
fierce appetites;
they never have enough.
And they are shepherds
who have no discernment;
all of them turn
to their own way,

^A 56:10 Or *His*, or *Its*

every last one
for his own profit. Jr 10:21; 23:1

12 "Come, let me get some wine,
let's guzzle some beer;
and tomorrow will be
like today,
only far better!" Lk 12:19; 1Co 15:32

57

The righteous
person perishes,
and no one takes it to heart;
the faithful are taken away,
with no one realizing
that the righteous person
is taken away
because of [A] evil.

2 He will enter into peace —
they will rest
on their beds [B] —
everyone who lives uprightly.

Pagan Religion Denounced

3 But come here,
you witch's sons,
offspring of an adulterer
and a prostitute! [C]

4 Who are you mocking?
Who are you opening
your mouth
and sticking out
your tongue at?
Isn't it you,
you rebellious children,
you offspring of liars,

5 who burn with lust
among the oaks,
under every green tree, Jr 2:20
who slaughter children
in the wadis
below the clefts of the rocks?

6 Your portion is
among the smooth stones
of the wadi;
indeed, they are your lot.

You have even poured out
a drink offering to them;
you have offered
a grain offering;
should I be satisfied
with these?

7 You have placed your bed
on a high and lofty mountain;
you also went up there
to offer sacrifice.

8 You have set up
your memorial
behind the door
and doorpost.
For away from me,
you stripped,
went up, and made
your bed wide, Ezk 23:17-18
and you have made
a bargain [D] for yourself
with them.
You have loved their bed;
you have gazed on
their genitals. [E,F]

9 You went to the king with oil
and multiplied
your perfumes;
you sent your envoys
far away Ezk 16:26-29
and sent them down
even to Sheol.

10 You became weary
on your many journeys,
but you did not say,
"It's hopeless!" Jr 2:25; 18:12
You found a renewal
of your strength; [G]
therefore you did not
grow weak.

11 Who was it you dreaded
and feared,
so that you lied and didn't
remember me
or take it to heart?

[A]57:1 Or taken away from the presence of [B]57:2 Either their deathbeds or their graves [C]57:3 Lit and
she acted as a prostitute [D]57:8 Lit you cut [E]57:8 Lit hand [F]57:8 In Hb, the word "hand" is probably a
euphemism for genitals. [G]57:10 Lit found life of your hand

I have kept silent
  for a long time, haven't I? [A]
So you do not fear me.
12 I will announce
  your righteousness,
and your works —
  they will not profit you.
13 When you cry out,
  let your collection of idols
    rescue you!
The wind will carry
  all of them off,
a breath will take them away.
But whoever takes refuge
  in me
will inherit the land   Ps 37:3,9
and possess
  my holy mountain.   Is 65:9

Healing and Peace

14 He said,
"Build it up, build it up,
  prepare the way,
remove every obstacle
  from my people's way." [A]
15 For the High and Exalted One,
who lives forever,
  whose name is holy,
  says this: Lk 1:49
"I live in a high and holy place,
and with the oppressed
  and lowly of spirit,   Ps 34:18
to revive the spirit
  of the lowly
and revive the heart
  of the oppressed.   Ps 147:3
16 For I will not
  accuse you forever,
and I will not always
  be angry;   Gn 6:3; Ps 103:9; Jr 3:12
for then the spirit
  would grow weak
  before me,
even the breath,
  which I have made.

17 Because of his sinful greed
  I was angry,   Is 2:7; 56:11; Jr 6:13
so I struck him; I was angry
  and hid;
but he went on turning back
  to the desires of his heart.
18 I have seen his ways,
  but I will heal him;
I will lead him and
  restore comfort
to him and his mourners,
19 creating words of praise." [B]
The LORD says,
"Peace, peace to the one
  who is far or near,   Ac 2:39
and I will heal him.
20 But the wicked are
  like the storm-tossed sea,
for it cannot be still,
and its water churns up mire
  and muck.
21 There is no peace
  for the wicked,"
says my God.   Is 48:22; 59:8

True Fasting

58 "Cry out loudly, [C]
  don't hold back!
Raise your voice
  like a trumpet.
Tell my people
  their transgression
and the house of Jacob
  their sins.
2 They seek me day after day
and delight to know
  my ways,
like a nation that does
  what is right
and does not abandon
  the justice of their God.
They ask me
  for righteous judgments;
they delight in the nearness
  of God."   Ps 119:151; Is 29:13; 57:3

[A] **57:11** LXX reads *And I, when I see you, I pass by*   [B] **57:19** Lit *creating fruit of the lips*   [C] **58:1** Lit *with throat*

3 "Why have we fasted,
   but you have not seen?
We have denied ourselves,
   but you haven't noticed!" ᴬ
"Look, you do as you please
   on the day of your fast,
and oppress
   all your workers.   Is 22:12-13
4 You fast with contention
   and strife
to strike viciously
   with your fist.
You cannot fast
   as you do today,
hoping to make your voice
   heard on high.
5 Will the fast I choose
   be like this:
A day for a person
   to deny himself,
to bow his head like a reed,
and to spread out sackcloth
   and ashes?   Est 4:3; Dn 9:3
Will you call this a fast
and a day acceptable
   to the LORD?
6 Isn't this the fast I choose:
To break the chains
   of wickedness,   Jb 36:8; Ps 107:10
to untie the ropes of the yoke,
to set the oppressed free,
and to tear off every yoke?
7 Is it not to share your bread
   with the hungry,   Jb 31:19-20
to bring the poor
   and homeless
   into your house,
to clothe the naked
   when you see him,   Mt 25:35-36
and not to ignore
   your own flesh and blood? ᴮ
8 Then your light will appear
   like the dawn,
and your recovery
   will come quickly.   Is 30:26

Your righteousness will go
   before you,   Ps 85:13; Is 62:1
and the LORD's glory will be
   your rear guard.   Ex 14:19; Is 52:12
9 At that time, when you call,
   the LORD will answer;   Ps 50:15
when you cry out, he will say,
   'Here I am.'
If you get rid of the yoke
   among you,
the finger-pointing
   and malicious speaking,
10 and if you offer yourself ᶜ
   to the hungry,
and satisfy the afflicted one,
then your light will shine
   in the darkness,   Jb 11:17; Ps 37:6
and your night will be
   like noonday.
11 The LORD will always
   lead you,
satisfy you in a parched land,
and strengthen your bones.
You will be
   like a watered garden   Sg 4:15
and like a spring
   whose water
   never runs dry.   Jn 4:14; 7:38
12 Some of you will rebuild
   the ancient ruins;   Ezr 6:14
you will restore
   the foundations laid
   long ago;   1Kg 6:37; Ezr 3:10-12
you will be called
   the repairer
   of broken walls,
the restorer of streets
   where people live.
13 "If you keep from desecrating ᴰ
   the Sabbath,   Ex 31:16-17; 35:2-3
from doing whatever
   you want on my holy day;
if you call the Sabbath
   a delight,

ᴬ**58:3** These are Israel's words to God. ᴮ**58:7** Lit *not hide yourself from your flesh* ᶜ**58:10** Some Hb mss,
LXX, Syr read *offer your bread* ᴰ**58:13** Lit *keep your foot from*

and the holy day
   of the LORD honorable;
if you honor it, not going
   your own ways,   Is 55:8
seeking your own pleasure,
   or talking business;[A,B]
14 then you will delight
   in the LORD,   Jb 22:26; Ps 37:4
and I will make you ride
   over the heights of the land,
and let you enjoy the heritage
   of your father Jacob."
For the mouth of the LORD
   has spoken.   Is 1:20; 40:5

Sin and Redemption

59 Indeed, the LORD's arm
   is not too weak to save,
and his ear is not too deaf
   to hear.
2 But your iniquities
   are separating you   Is 13:11
from your God,
and your sins
   have hidden his face
   from you   Dt 31:17-18; 32:20; Is 50:6
so that he does not listen.
3 For your hands are defiled
   with blood
and your fingers,
   with iniquity;
your lips have spoken lies,
and your tongues
   mutter injustice.
4 No one makes claims justly;
no one pleads honestly.
They trust in empty
   and worthless words;
they conceive trouble
   and give birth to iniquity.
5 They hatch viper's eggs
   and weave spider's webs.
Whoever eats their eggs
   will die;
crack one open, and a viper
   is hatched.

6 Their webs cannot
   become clothing,
and they cannot
   cover themselves
   with their works.
Their works are
   sinful works,
and violent acts are
   in their hands.
7 Their feet run after evil,
and they rush to shed
   innocent blood.   Pr 1:16; 6:17
Their thoughts are
   sinful thoughts;   Mk 7:21-22
ruin and wretchedness are
   in their paths.
8 They have not known
   the path of peace,   Lk 1:79
and there is no justice
   in their ways.
They have made
   their roads crooked;
no one who walks on them
   will know peace.   Is 57:20-21

9 Therefore justice is far
   from us,
and righteousness does not
   reach us.
We hope for light,
   but there is darkness;
for brightness, but we live
   in the night.
10 We grope along a wall
   like the blind;
we grope like those
   without eyes.   Dt 28:29; Jb 5:14
We stumble at noon
   as though it were twilight;
we are like the dead
   among those
   who are healthy.
11 We all growl like bears
   and moan like doves.   Is 38:14
We hope for justice,
   but there is none;

A **58:13** Or *idly*   B **58:13** Lit *or speak a word*

for salvation, but it is
  far from us.
¹² For our transgressions
  have multiplied before you,
and our sins testify
  against us.   Is 3:9; Jr 14:7; Hs 5:5
For our transgressions are
  with us,
and we know our iniquities:
¹³ transgression and deception
  against the LORD,
turning away from following
  our God,
speaking oppression
  and revolt,
conceiving and uttering
  lying words
  from the heart.
¹⁴ Justice is turned back,
and righteousness stands
  far off.
For truth has stumbled
  in the public square,
and honesty cannot enter.
¹⁵ Truth is missing,
and whoever turns from evil
  is plundered.

The LORD saw that there was
  no justice,
and he was offended.
¹⁶ He saw that there was
  no man —
he was amazed
  that there was
  no one interceding;   Is 41:28
so his own arm
  brought salvation,
and his own righteousness
  supported him.
¹⁷ He put on righteousness
  as body armor,
and a helmet of salvation
  on his head;   Eph 6:14,17; 1Th 5:8
he put on garments
  of vengeance for clothing,

and he wrapped himself
  in zeal as in a cloak.   Is 9:7
¹⁸ So he will repay according to
  their deeds: Jr 25:14; Rv 22:12
fury to his enemies,
retribution to his foes,
and he will repay the coasts
  and islands.
¹⁹ They will fear the name
  of the LORD in the west
and his glory in the east;ᴬ
for he will come
  like a rushing stream   Is 30:28
driven by the wind of the LORD.
²⁰ "The Redeemer will come
  to Zion,   Is 41:14; 43:14
and to those
  in Jacob who turn
  from transgression."
This is
  the LORD's declaration.

²¹ "As for me, this is my covenant
with them," says the LORD: "My
Spirit who is on you, and my words
that I have put in your mouth, will
not depart from your mouth, or
from the mouths of your children,
or from the mouths of your children's children, from now on and
forever," says the LORD.   Jr 31:31-34

The LORD's Glory in Zion

60 Arise, shine, for your light
  has come,   Is 9:2; 26:19; 30:26; 52:2
and the glory
  of the LORD shines
  over you.ᴮ   Is 40:5; 58:8; Mal 4:2
² For look, darkness will
  cover the earth,
and total darkness
  the peoples;
but the LORD will shine
  over you,
and his glory will appear
  over you.

ᴬ**59:19** Lit *sunrise*   ᴮ**60:1** = Jerusalem

³ Nations will come
    to your light,
and kings
    to your shining brightness.
⁴ Raise your eyes
    and look around:
they all gather and come
    to you;
your sons will come
    from far away,
and your daughters
    on the hips of nannies.
⁵ Then you will see
    and be radiant,   Ps 34:5
and your heart will tremble
    and rejoice,ᴬ
because the riches of the sea
    will become yours
and the wealth of the nations
    will come to you.   Is 61:6
⁶ Caravans of camels
    will cover your landᴮ —
young camels of Midian
    and Ephah —
all of them will come
    from Sheba.   Gn 25:3; Ps 72:10
They will carry gold
    and frankincense   Mt 2:11
and proclaim the praises
    of the LORD.
⁷ All the flocks of Kedar
    will be gathered to you;
the rams of Nebaioth
    will serve you   Gn 25:13
and go up on my altar
    as an acceptable sacrifice.
I will glorify
    my beautiful house.   Is 60:13
⁸ Who are these who fly
    like a cloud,
like doves to their shelters?
⁹ Yes, the coasts and islands
    will wait for me   Is 51:5
with the ships of Tarshish
    in the lead,   Ps 48:7; Is 2:16

to bring your children
    from far away,   Is 14:2; 43:6; 49:22
their silver and gold
    with them,
for the honor of the LORD
    your God,
the Holy One of Israel,   Is 1:4
who has glorified you.   Is 55:5
¹⁰ Foreigners will
    rebuild your walls,   Is 14:1-2
and their kings will
    serve you.   Is 49:7,23; Rv 21:24
Although I struck you
    in my wrath,
yet I will show mercy to you
    with my favor.   Hab 3:2
¹¹ Your city gates will always
    be open;
they will never be shut
    day or night
so that the wealth
    of the nations
may be brought into you,
with their kings being led
    in procession.
¹² For the nation
    and the kingdom
that will not serve
    you will perish;
those nations
    will be annihilated.
¹³ The glory of Lebanon
    will come to you —   Is 35:2
its pine, elm,
    and cypress together —
to beautify the place
    of my sanctuary,
and I will glorify
    my dwelling place.ᶜ
¹⁴ The sons of your oppressors
will come and bow down
    to you;   Is 14:1-2; Zch 8:23
all who reviled you
will fall facedown at your feet.
They will call you the City
    of the LORD,

ᴬ60:5 Lit expand   ᴮ60:6 Lit cover you   ᶜ60:13 Lit glorify the place of my feet

Zion of the Holy One of Israel.
¹⁵ Instead of your
    being deserted and hated,
with no one
    passing through,   Is 34:10
I will make you an object
    of eternal pride,   Is 65:18
a joy from age to age.
¹⁶ You will nurse on the milk
    of nations,
and nurse at the breast
    of kings;   Is 49:23; 66:11-12
you will know that I, the
    LORD, am your Savior   Is 43:3
and Redeemer,
    the Mighty One of Jacob.

¹⁷ I will bring gold
    instead of bronze;
I will bring silver
    instead of iron,
bronze instead of wood,
and iron instead of stones.
I will appoint peace
    as your government
and righteousness
    as your overseers.
¹⁸ Violence will never again
    be heard of in your land;
devastation and destruction
will be gone
    from your borders.
You will call your
    walls Salvation   Is 26:1
and your city gates Praise.
¹⁹ The sun will no longer be
    your light by day,
and the brightness
    of the moon will not shine
    on you.
The LORD will be
    your everlasting light,
and your God will be
    your splendor.
²⁰ Your sun will no longer set,
    and your moon will not fade;

for the LORD will be
    your everlasting light,
and the days of your sorrow
    will be over.   Is 35:10; 65:19; Rv 21:4
²¹ All your people
    will be righteous;   Is 52:1
they will possess
    the land forever;   Ps 37:9
they are the branch I planted,
the work of my^A hands,
so that I may be glorified.
²² The least will become
    a thousand,
the smallest a mighty nation.
I am the LORD;
I will accomplish it quickly
    in its time.

Messiah's Jubilee

61 The Spirit of the Lord GOD
    is on me,   Is 11:2; 42:1; 48:16
because the LORD
    has anointed me
to bring good news
    to the poor.   Lk 7:22
He has sent me to heal^B
    the brokenhearted,
to proclaim liberty
    to the captives
and freedom
    to the prisoners;   Is 42:7; 49:9
² to proclaim the year
    of the LORD's favor,   Is 49:8
and the day
    of our God's vengeance;
to comfort all who mourn,
³ to provide for those
    who mourn in Zion;
to give them a crown
    of beauty instead of ashes,
festive oil
    instead of mourning,   Ps 45:7
and splendid clothes
    instead of despair.^C
And they will be called
    righteous trees,

^A**60:21** LXX, DSS read *his*   ^B**61:1** Lit *bind up*   ^C**61:3** Lit *a dim spirit*

planted by the LORD
to glorify him. Is 60:21; Jr 17:7-8

4 They will rebuild
the ancient ruins; Is 49:8; 58:12
they will restore
the former devastations;
they will renew
the ruined cities,
the devastations
of many generations.
5 Strangers will stand and feed
your flocks,
and foreigners will
be your plowmen
and vinedressers. Is 14:2; 60:10
6 But you will be called
the LORD's priests; Ex 19:6
they will speak of you
as ministers of our God;
you will eat the wealth
of the nations,
and you will boast
in their riches.
7 In place of your shame, you
will have a double portion;
in place of disgrace, they will
rejoice over their share.
So they will possess double
in their land, Is 40:2; Zch 9:12
and eternal joy will be theirs.

8 For I the LORD love justice;
I hate robbery and injustice;^A
I will faithfully reward my
people
and make
a permanent covenant
with them. Is 24:5; 55:3
9 Their descendants
will be known
among the nations,
and their posterity
among the peoples.
All who see them
will recognize

that they are a people
the LORD has blessed.

10 I rejoice greatly in the LORD,
I exult in my God;
for he has clothed me
with the garments
of salvation
and wrapped me in a robe
of righteousness, Is 49:18; 52:1
as a groom wears a turban
and as a bride adorns herself
with her jewels. Rv 21:2
11 For as the earth produces
its growth,
and as a garden enables
what is sown to spring up,
so the Lord GOD
will cause righteousness
and praise
to spring up
before all the nations.

Zion's Restoration

62 I will not keep silent
because of Zion,
and I will not keep still
because of Jerusalem, Ps 83:1
until her righteousness
shines like a bright light
and her salvation,
like a flaming torch.
2 Nations will see
your righteousness Is 60:3
and all kings, your glory.
You will be given
a new name
that the LORD's mouth
will announce. Is 60:14; Rv 2:17
3 You will be a glorious crown
in the LORD's hand,
and a royal diadem
in the palm of your God's
hand. Is 28:5; Zch 9:16; 1Th 2:19
4 You will no longer
be called Deserted, Is 54:6-7

^A 61:8 Some Hb mss, DSS, LXX, Syr, Tg, Vg; other Hb mss read *robbery with a burnt offering*

and your land will not
  be called Desolate;
instead, you will be called
  My Delight Is in Her, [A]
and your land Married; [B]
for the LORD delights in you,
and your land
  will be married.

5 For as a young man marries
    a young woman,
  so your sons
    will marry you;
  and as a groom rejoices
    over his bride,
  so your God will rejoice
    over you.   Is 65:19

6 Jerusalem,
  I have appointed watchmen
    on your walls;   Is 52:8; Jr 6:17
  they will never be silent,
    day or night.
  There is no rest for you,
  who remind the LORD.

7 Do not give him rest
  until he establishes
    and makes Jerusalem
  the praise of the earth.   Is 60:18

8 The LORD has sworn
    with his right hand
  and his strong arm:
  I will no longer give
    your grain
  to your enemies for food,   Is 1:7
  and foreigners will not drink
    the new wine
  for which you have labored.

9 For those who gather grain
    will eat it
  and praise the LORD,
  and those who harvest
    the grapes will drink
    the wine
  in my holy courts.

10 Go out, go out
     through the city gates;
   prepare a way
     for the people!
   Build it up, build up
     the highway;   Is 11:16; 19:23; 35:8
   clear away the stones!
   Raise a banner
     for the peoples.   Is 11:10,12; 49:22

11 Look, the LORD
     has proclaimed
   to the ends of the earth,
   "Say to Daughter Zion: Zch 9:9
   Look, your salvation
     is coming,
   his wages are with him,   Is 40:10
   and his reward
     accompanies him."

12 And they will be called [C]
     the Holy People,   Dt 7:6; Is 4:3
   the LORD's Redeemed;
   and you will be called
     Cared For,
   A City Not Deserted.

The LORD's Day of Vengeance

63

Who is this coming
  from Edom   Ps 137:7; Is 34:5-6
in crimson-stained garments
  from Bozrah —
this one who is splendid
  in his apparel,
striding in his formidable [D]
  might?

It is I,
  proclaiming vindication, [E]
powerful to save.

2 Why are your clothes red,
  and your garments like one
    who treads a winepress?

3 I trampled
    the winepress alone,

A 62:4 Or *Hephzibah*   B 62:4 Or *Beulah*   C 62:12 Lit *will call them*   D 63:1 Syr, Vg read *apparel, striding forward in*   E 63:1 Or *righteousness*

and no one from the nations
    was with me.
I trampled them in my anger
and ground them underfoot
    in my fury;
their blood spattered
    my garments,
and all my clothes
    were stained.
⁴ For I planned the day
    of vengeance,   Is 34:8; 61:2; Jr 46:10
and the year
    of my redemption ᴬ came.
⁵ I looked, but there was
    no one to help,   Is 59:16
and I was amazed
    that no one assisted;
so my arm accomplished
    victory for me,
and my wrath assisted me.
⁶ I crushed nations
    in my anger;
I made them drunk
    with my wrath   Is 29:9; 51:17
and poured out their blood
    on the ground.   Rv 14:20

Remembrance of Grace

⁷ I will make known
    the LORD's faithful love
and the LORD's
    praiseworthy acts,
because of all the LORD
    has done for us —
even the many good things
he has done for the house
    of Israel,
which he did for them
    based on his compassion
and the abundance of
    his faithful love.
⁸ He said, "They are indeed
    my people,
children who will not
    be disloyal,"

and he became their Savior.
⁹ In all their suffering,
    he suffered, ᴮ   Jdg 10:16
and the angel of his presence
    saved them.
He redeemed them
because of his love
    and compassion;   Dt 7:7-8
he lifted them up
    and carried them
all the days of the past.   Dt 1:31
¹⁰ But they rebelled
and grieved his Holy Spirit.
So he became their enemy
and fought against them.
¹¹ Then he ᶜ remembered
    the days of the past,
the days of Moses
    and his people.
Where is he who
    brought them out of the sea
with the shepherds ᴰ
    of his flock?
Where is he who
    put his Holy Spirit
    among the flock?
¹² He made
    his glorious strength
available at the right hand of
    Moses,
divided the water
    before them   Ex 14:21; Ps 74:13
to make an eternal name
    for himself,
¹³ and led them
    through the depths
like a horse in the wilderness,
so that they did not stumble.
¹⁴ Like cattle that go down
    into the valley,
the Spirit of the LORD
    gave them ᴱ rest.
You led your people this way
to make a glorious name
    for yourself.

ᴬ63:4 Or blood retribution   ᴮ63:9 Alt Hb tradition reads did not suffer   ᶜ63:11 Or they   ᴰ63:11 LXX, Tg,
Syr read shepherd   ᴱ63:14 Lit him

Israel's Prayer

15 Look down from heaven
and see   Dt 26:15; Ps 80:14
from your lofty home —
holy and beautiful.
Where is your zeal
and your might?
Your yearning[A]
and your compassion
are withheld from me.

16 Yet you are our Father,
even though Abraham
does not know us
and Israel doesn't
recognize us.
You, Lord, are our Father;
your name is
Our Redeemer   Is 41:14; 43:14
from Ancient Times.

17 Why, Lord, do you
make us stray
from your ways?
You harden our hearts
so we do not fear[B] you.   Is 6:10
Return, because of
your servants,
the tribes of your heritage.

18 Your holy people
had a possession[C]
for a little while,
but our enemies
have trampled down
your sanctuary.   Ps 74:3-7; Is 64:11

19 We have become like those
you never ruled,
like those who did not bear
your name.   Dt 28:10; Is 43:7; 65:1

64

If only you would tear
the heavens open
and come down,   Ex 19:18; Ps 18:9
so that mountains
would quake
at your presence —   Jdg 5:5

2 just as fire kindles
brushwood,
and fire boils water —
to make your name known
to your enemies,
so that nations will tremble
at your presence!

3 When you did
awesome works   Dt 10:21; Ps 65:5
that we did not expect,
you came down,   Mc 1:3-4
and the mountains quaked
at your presence.

4 From ancient times no one
has heard,
no one has listened to,
no eye has seen any God
except you
who acts on behalf
of the one who waits
for him.   1Co 2:9

5 You welcome the one
who joyfully does
what is right;
they remember you
in your ways.
But we have sinned, and you
were angry.
How can we be saved if we
remain in our sins?[D]

6 All of us have become
like something unclean,
and all our righteous acts are
like a polluted[E] garment;
all of us wither like a leaf,
and our iniquities carry us
away like the wind.   Is 13:11

7 No one calls on your name,
striving to take hold of you.
For you have hidden
your face from us   Is 54:8
and made us melt
because of[F,G] our iniquity.

[A]63:15 Lit *The agitation of your inward parts*   [B]63:17 Lit *our heart from fearing*   [C]63:18 Or *Your people possessed your holy place*   [D]64:5 Lit *angry; in them continually and we will be saved*; Hb obscure   [E]64:6 Lit *menstrual*   [F]64:7 LXX, Syr, Vg, Tg read *and delivered us into the hand of*   [G]64:7 Lit *melt by the hand of*

⁸ Yet L<small>ORD</small>, you are our Father;
we are the clay, and you are
    our potter;
we all are the work
    of your hands.   Is 29:16; 45:9

⁹ L<small>ORD</small>, do not be terribly angry
or remember
    our iniquity forever.   Is 43:25
Please look — all of us are
    your people!

¹⁰ Your holy cities have become
    a wilderness;
Zion has become
    a wilderness,
Jerusalem a desolation.   Is 62:4

¹¹ Our holy
    and beautiful^A temple,
where our fathers
    praised you,
has been burned down,
and all that was dear to us
    lies in ruins.   2Kg 25:9; Ps 74:5-7

¹² L<small>ORD</small>, after all this, will you
    restrain yourself?
Will you keep silent
    and afflict us severely?

The L<small>ORD</small>'s Response

65 "I was sought by those
    who did not ask;
I was found by those
    who did not seek me.
I said, 'Here I am, here I am,'
to a nation that did not call
    on^B my name.   Is 63:19; Hs 1:10

² I spread out my hands
    all day long
to a rebellious people   Rm 10:21
who walk in the path that is
    not good,
following
    their own thoughts.

³ These people
    continually anger me
to my face,
sacrificing in gardens,   Is 1:29
burning incense on bricks,

⁴ sitting among the graves,
spending nights
    in secret places,
eating the meat of pigs,   Lv 11:7
and putting polluted broth
    in their bowls.^C

⁵ They say, 'Keep to yourself,
don't come near me, for I am
    too holy for you!'
These practices are smoke
    in my nostrils,
a fire that burns all day long.

⁶ Look, it is written in front of
    me:
I will not keep silent,
    but I will repay;   Ps 50:3,21; 64:12
I will repay them fully^D

⁷ for your iniquities
    and the iniquities   Is 13:11
of your^E fathers together,"
says the L<small>ORD</small>.
"Because they burned
    incense on the mountains
and reproached me
    on the hills,   Ezk 20:27-28; Hs 9:10
I will reward them fully^F
for their former deeds."

⁸ The L<small>ORD</small> says this:
"As the new wine is found
    in a bunch of grapes,
and one says,
    'Don't destroy it,
for there's some good^G in it,'
so I will act because of
    my servants
and not destroy them all.

⁹ I will produce descendants
    from Jacob,   Jr 31:36-37
and heirs to my mountains
    from Judah;

---

^A**64:11** Or *glorious*; Is 60:7   ^B**65:1** Or *that was not called by*   ^C**65:3-4** These vv. describe pagan worship.
^D**65:6** Lit *repay into their lap*   ^E**65:7** LXX, Syr read *for their iniquities and the iniquities of their*
^F**65:7** Lit *reward into their lap*   ^G**65:8** Or *there's a blessing*

my chosen ones
　　will possess it,　　　　　Is 41:8
and my servants
　　will dwell there.　　Is 49:8; 60:21

10 Sharon will be a pasture
　　for flocks,　　　　Is 33:9; 35:2
and the Valley of Achor
　　a place for herds to lie down,
for my people
　　who have sought me.　Is 51:1

11 But you who abandon
　　the Lord,
who forget my holy mountain,
who prepare a table
　　for Fortune
and fill bowls of mixed wine
　　for Destiny, A

12 I will destine you
　　for the sword,
and all of you will kneel down
　　to be slaughtered,
because I called
　　and you did not answer,
I spoke and you did not hear;
you did what was evil
　　in my sight
and chose what I did not
　　delight in."　2Ch 36:15-16; Pr 1:24

13 Therefore, this is what the Lord
God says:
"My servants will eat,
but you will be hungry;
my servants will drink,
but you will be thirsty;
my servants will rejoice,
but you will be put to shame.

14 My servants will shout
　　for joy from a glad heart,
but you will cry out
　　from an anguished heart,
and you will lament out of
　　a broken spirit.

15 You will leave
　　your name behind

as a curse
　　for my chosen ones,　　Jr 24:9
and the Lord God will kill you;
but he will give his servants
　　another name.　　　Is 62:2

16 Whoever asks for a blessing
　　in the land
will ask for a blessing
　　by the God of truth,　　Ps 31:5
and whoever swears
　　in the land
will swear by the God
　　of truth.
For the former troubles
　　will be forgotten
and hidden from my sight.

A New Creation

17 "For I will create a new heaven
　　and a new earth;　Is 66:22; Rv 21:1
the past events will not
　　be remembered or come
　　to mind.

18 Then be glad
　　and rejoice forever
in what I am creating;
for I will create Jerusalem
　　to be a joy
and its people to be a delight.

19 I will rejoice in Jerusalem
and be glad in my people.
The sound of weeping
　　and crying
will no longer be heard in her.

20 In her, a nursing infant
　　will no longer live
only a few days, B
or an old man not live out
　　his days.
Indeed, the one who dies
　　at a hundred years old
will be mourned as
　　a young man, C
and the one who misses
　　a hundred years

A65:11 Pagan gods　B65:20 Lit her, no longer infant of days　C65:20 Lit the youth of a hundred years
will die

will be considered cursed.
²¹ People will build houses
and live in them;
they will plant vineyards
and eat their fruit.   Jos 24:13
²² They will not build
and others live in them;
they will not plant
and others eat.
For my people's lives
will be
like the lifetime of a tree.
My chosen ones
will fully enjoy
the work of their hands.
²³ They will not labor
without success   Dt 28:3-12
or bear children destined
for disaster,
for they will be a people
blessed by the LORD
along with their
descendants.   Is 61:9
²⁴ Even before they call,
I will answer;   Ps 91:15; Is 55:6; 58:9
while they are still speaking,
I will hear.
²⁵ The wolf and the lamb
will feed together,ᴬ
and the lion will eat straw
like cattle,   Is 11:6-9
but the serpent's food
will be dust!   Gn 3:14; Mc 7:17
They will not do what is evil
or destroy
on my entire holy mountain,"
says the LORD.

Final Judgment and Joyous Restoration

66 This is what the LORD says:
Heaven is my throne,   Ps 11:4
and earth is my footstool.
Where could you
possibly build a house
for me?

And where would my resting
place be?   2Sm 7:5; 1Kg 8:27; Jr 23:24
² My hand made
all these things,
and so they all came
into being.
This is
the LORD's declaration.
I will look favorably
on this kind of person:
one who is humble,
submissiveᴮ in spirit,   Ps 86:1
and trembles at my word.
³ One person slaughters an ox,
another kills a person;
one person sacrifices
a lamb, another breaks
a dog's neck;
one person offers
a grain offering,
another offers pig's blood;
one person offers incense,
another praises an idol —
all these have chosen
their ways
and delight in their
abhorrent practices.
⁴ So I will choose
their punishment,
and I will bring on them
what they dread
because I called
and no one answered;
I spoke and they did not
listen;
they did what was evil
in my sight
and chose what I did
not delight in.   2Kg 21:2,6; Is 59:7
⁵ You who tremble at his word,
hear the word of the LORD:
"Your brothers who hate
and exclude you
for my name's sake have said,
'Let the LORD be glorified

ᴬ**65:25** Lit *as one*   ᴮ**66:2** Lit *broken*

so that we can see your joy!'
But they will be put to shame."

6 A sound of uproar
    from the city!
A voice from the temple —
    the voice of the LORD,
paying back his enemies
    what they deserve!   Is 59:18

7 Before Zion was in labor,
    she gave birth;
before she was in pain,
    she delivered a boy.
8 Who has heard of
    such a thing?
Who has seen such things?
Can a land be born in one day
or a nation be delivered
    in an instant?
Yet as soon as Zion was
    in labor,
she gave birth to her sons.
9 "Will I bring a baby
    to the point of birth
and not deliver it?"
says the LORD;
"or will I who deliver,
    close the womb?"
says your God.
10 Be glad for Jerusalem
    and rejoice over her,
all who love her.   Ps 122:6; 137:6
Rejoice greatly with her,
all who mourn over her —
11 so that you may nurse
    and be satisfied
from her comforting breast
and drink deeply
    and delight yourselves
from her glorious breasts.

12 For this is what the LORD says:
I will make peace flow to her
    like a river,   Ps 72:3,7; Is 48:18

and the wealth^A of nations
    like a flood;   Is 61:6
you will nurse and be carried
    on her hip   Is 60:4-5
and bounced on her lap.
13 As a mother comforts
    her son,
so I will comfort you,   Ps 86:17
and you will be comforted
    in Jerusalem.

14 You will see, you will rejoice,
and you^B will flourish
    like grass;   Ps 72:16; Pr 11:28; Is 58:11
then the LORD's power
    will be revealed
to his servants,
but he will show his wrath
    against his enemies.
15 Look, the LORD will come
    with fire —   Is 33:14; Mal 3:1-2
his chariots are
    like the whirlwind —   Ps 68:17
to execute his anger
    with fury
and his rebuke with flames
    of fire.
16 For the LORD
    will execute judgment
on all people
    with his fiery sword,   Gn 6:12
and many will be slain
    by the LORD.

17 "Those who dedicate and purify themselves to enter the groves
following their leader,^C eating meat
from pigs, vermin,^D and rats, will
perish together."   Is 65:3-5
    This is
    the LORD's declaration.
18 "Knowing^E their works and
their thoughts, I have come to gather all nations and languages; they
will come and see my glory. 19 I will

^A66:12 Or *glory*   ^B66:14 Lit *your bones*   ^C66:17 Hb obscure   ^D66:17 Lit *abhorrent things*   ^E66:18 LXX,
Syr; MT omits *Knowing*

establish a sign among them, and I will send survivors from them to the nations — to Tarshish, Put,[A] Lud (who are archers), Tubal, Javan, and the coasts and islands far away — who have not heard about me or seen my glory. And they will proclaim my glory among the nations. ²⁰ They will bring all your brothers from all the nations as a gift to the LORD on horses and chariots, in litters, and on mules and camels, to my holy mountain Jerusalem," says the LORD, "just as the Israelites bring an offering in a clean vessel to the house of the LORD. ²¹ I will also take some of them as priests and Levites," says the LORD.   Jr 3:17

²² "For just as the new heavens and the new earth,   Is 65:17
which I will make,
will remain before me" —
    this is
    the LORD's declaration —
"so your offspring
    and your name will remain.
²³ All mankind will come
    to worship me
from one New Moon
    to another
and from one Sabbath
    to another,"
says the LORD.

²⁴ "As they leave, they will see the dead bodies of those who have rebelled against me; for their worm will never die, their fire will never go out, and they will be a horror to all mankind."   Jb 7:5; Is 1:2; 5:25; 14:11; 34:3

JEREMIAH

1 The words of Jeremiah, the son of Hilkiah, one of the priests living in Anathoth in the territory of Benjamin. ² The word of the LORD came to him in the thirteenth year of the reign of Josiah son of Amon, king of Judah. ³ It also came throughout the days of Jehoiakim son of Josiah, king of Judah, until the fifth month of the eleventh year of Zedekiah son of Josiah, king of Judah, when the people of Jerusalem went into exile.   2Ch 35:25; 36:12

The Call of Jeremiah

⁴ The word of the LORD came to me:
⁵   I chose you
      before I formed you
      in the womb;
    I set you apart
      before you were born.   Is 44:2
    I appointed you a prophet
      to the nations.   Jr 25:15-26

⁶ But I protested, "Oh no, Lord GOD! Look, I don't know how to speak since I am only a youth."
⁷ Then the LORD said to me:
    Do not say, "I am only a youth,"
    for you will go to everyone
      I send you to
    and speak whatever I tell you.
⁸   Do not be afraid of anyone,
      for I will be with you
        to rescue you.   Gn 26:3; 31:3; Ex 3:12
    This is
      the LORD's declaration.

⁹ Then the LORD reached out his hand, touched my mouth, and told me: Is 6:7

    I have now filled
      your mouth
      with my words.   Is 51:16
¹⁰   See, I have
      appointed you today
    over nations and kingdoms
    to uproot and tear down,
    to destroy and demolish,
    to build and plant.   Jr 12:14-17; 19:7

Two Visions

¹¹ Then the word of the LORD came to me, asking, "What do you see, Jeremiah?"   Jr 24:3; Am 8:2; Zch 4:2
    I replied, "I see a branch of an almond tree."
¹² The LORD said to me, "You have seen correctly, for I watch over^A my word to accomplish it." ¹³ Again the word of the LORD came to me asking, "What do you see?"   Jr 31:28; Php 1:6
    And I replied, "I see a boiling pot, its lip tilted from the north to the south."   Ezk 24:3
¹⁴ Then the LORD said to me, "Disaster will be poured out^B from the north on all who live in the land. ¹⁵ Indeed, I am about to summon all the clans and kingdoms of the north."   Jr 4:1,6,20; 15:12; 47:2; 50:3,9,41; 51:48
    This is
      the LORD's declaration.
    They will come,
      and each king will set up
      his throne
    at the entrance
      to Jerusalem's gates.
    They will attack
      all her surrounding walls
    and all the other cities
      of Judah.

^A **1:12** In Hb, the word for *almond tree* sounds like the word for *watch over*   ^B **1:14** LXX reads *will boil*

¹⁶ "I will pronounce my judgments against them for all the evil they did when they abandoned me to burn incense to other gods and to worship the works of their own hands.   Ex 20:3; Is 37:19; 44:15; Ac 7:41

¹⁷ "Now, get ready. Stand up and tell them everything that I command you. Do not be intimidated by them or I will cause you to cower before them. ¹⁸ Today, I am the one who has made you a fortified city, an iron pillar, and bronze walls against the whole land — against the kings of Judah, its officials, its priests, and the population. ¹⁹ They will fight against you but never prevail over you, since I am with you to rescue you."   Jr 15:20; Ezk 2:6-7; 1Th 2:2

This is
the LORD's declaration.

Israel Accused of Apostasy

2 The word of the LORD came to me: ² "Go and announce directly to Jerusalem that this is what the LORD says:

I remember the loyalty
of your youth,   Ezk 16:8, 60; Rv 2:4
your love as a bride —
how you followed me
in the wilderness,
in a land not sown.
³ Israel was holy to the LORD,
the firstfruits of his harvest.
All who ate of it found
themselves guilty;   Gn 12:3
disaster came on them."
This is
the LORD's declaration.

⁴ Hear the word of the LORD,
house of Jacob
and all families of the house
of Israel.
⁵ This is what the LORD says:

What fault did your fathers
find in me   Is 5:4; Mc 6:3
that they went so far
from me,
followed worthless idols,
and became worthless
themselves?   Ps 115:8; Hs 9:10
⁶ They stopped asking,
"Where is the LORD   Jdg 6:13
who brought us
from the land of Egypt,
who led us
through the wilderness,
through a land of deserts
and ravines,
through a land of drought
and darkness, ᴬ
a land no one
traveled through
and where no one lived?"
⁷ I brought you to
a fertile land   Ex 3:8; Dt 8:7-10
to eat its fruit and bounty,
but after you entered,
you defiled my land;   Nm 35:33
you made
my inheritance detestable.
⁸ The priests quit asking,
"Where is the LORD?"
The experts in the law
no longer knew me,   Hs 4:6
and the rulers rebelled
against me.   Jr 23:1-4; Ezk 34
The prophets prophesied
by ᴮ Baal   Jr 2:23; 9:14
and followed useless idols.
⁹ Therefore, I will bring a case
against you again.
This is
the LORD's declaration.
I will bring a case against
your children's children.
¹⁰ Cross over
to the coasts of Cyprus ᶜ
and take a look.   Gn 10:4; Nm 24:24

ᴬ2:6 Or shadow of death   ᴮ2:8 = in the name of   ᶜ2:10 Lit to the islands of Kittim

Send someone to Kedar
and consider carefully;
see if there has ever been
anything like this:
¹¹ Has a nation ever exchanged
its gods?   Mc 4:5
(But they were not gods!)   Gl 4:8
Yet my people
have exchanged
their^A Glory
for useless idols.   Ps 106:20; Hs 4:7
¹² Be appalled at this, heavens;
be shocked
and utterly desolated!
This is
the LORD's declaration.

¹³ For my people
have committed
a double evil:
They have abandoned me,
the fountain of living water,
and dug cisterns
for themselves —
cracked cisterns that cannot
hold water.   Is 55:2; Gl 1:6-7

Consequences of Apostasy

¹⁴ Is Israel a slave?
Was he born into slavery?^B
Why else has he become
a prey?
¹⁵ The young lions have roared
at him;   Is 5:29
they have roared loudly.
They have laid waste his land.
His cities are in ruins,
without inhabitants.
¹⁶ The men of Memphis
and Tahpanhes   Jr 44:1; 46:14,19
have also broken your skull.
¹⁷ Have you not brought this
on yourself   Jr 4:18
by abandoning the LORD
your God

while he was leading you
along the way?
¹⁸ Now what will you gain
by traveling along the way
to Egypt   Is 30:1-2; 31:1
to drink the water of the Nile?^C
What will you gain
by traveling along the way
to Assyria   Hs 7:11
to drink the water
of the Euphrates?   Is 8:7
¹⁹ Your own evil
will discipline you;   Is 3:9; Hs 5:5
your own apostasies
will reprimand you.
Recognize^D how evil
and bitter it is   Jr 4:18
for you to abandon the LORD
your God
and to have no fear of me.
This is the declaration
of the Lord GOD of Armies.

²⁰ For long ago I^E broke
your yoke;   Lv 26:13; Is 10:27; Nah 1:13
I^E tore off your chains.
You insisted,
"I will not serve!"
On every high hill
and under every green tree
you lay down
like a prostitute.   Ezk 16:28; Hs 2:5
²¹ I planted you, a choice vine
from the very best seed.
How then could you turn into
a degenerate, foreign vine?
²² Even if you wash with lye
and use a great amount
of bleach,^F   Ps 51:2,7; Mal 3:2
the stain of your iniquity
is still in front of me.   Ps 90:8
This is
the Lord GOD's declaration.

^A2:11 Alt Hb tradition reads *my*   ^B2:14 Lit *born of a house*   ^C2:18 Lit *of Shihor*   ^D2:19 Lit *Know and see*
^E2:20 LXX reads *you*   ^F2:22 Lit *cleansing agent*

23 How can you protest, "I am
     not defiled;
   I have not followed
     the Baals"?   Jr 2:8; 9:14
   Look at your behavior
     in the valley;
   acknowledge
     what you have done.   Gn 3:13
   You are a swift young camel
   twisting and turning
     on her way,
24 a wild donkey at home[A]
     in the wilderness.   Jb 39:5; Hs 8:9
   She sniffs the wind
     in the heat of her desire.
   Who can control
     her passion?
   All who look for her will not
     become weary;
   they will find her
     in her mating season.[B]
25 Keep your feet
     from going bare
   and your throat from thirst.
   But you say, "It's hopeless;
   I love strangers,   Dt 32:16; Jr 3:13
   and I will continue
     to follow them."

26 Like the shame of a thief
     when he is caught,
   so the house of Israel
     has been put to shame.
   They, their kings,
     their officials,
   their priests,
     and their prophets   Ezr 9:7
27 say to a tree, "You are
     my father,"
   and to a stone,
     "You gave birth to me."
   For they have
     turned their back to me
   and not their face,   2Ch 29:6; 32:33
   yet in their time of disaster
     they beg,   Jdg 10:9-10; Is 26:16

   "Rise up and save us!"
28 But where are your gods
     you made for yourself?
   Let them rise up and save you
   in your time of disaster
     if they can,
   for your gods are
     as numerous
   as your cities, Judah.

Judgment Deserved

29 Why do you bring a case
     against me?   Jr 2:9
   All of you have rebelled
     against me.
   This is
     the LORD's declaration.
30 I have struck down
     your children in vain;
   they would not
     accept discipline.   Pr 3:11; Is 1:5
   Your own sword
     has devoured
     your prophets   Mt 23:34
   like a ravaging lion.
31 Evil generation,
   pay attention to the word
     of the LORD!
   Have I been a wilderness
     to Israel
   or a land of dense darkness?
   Why do my people claim,
   "We will go where we want;[C]
   we will no longer come
     to you"?
32 Can a young woman forget
     her jewelry   Is 61:10
   or a bride
     her wedding sash?
   Yet my people
     have forgotten me   Ps 106:21
   for countless days.
33 How skillfully
     you pursue love;
   you also teach evil women
     your ways.

A2:24 Lit donkey taught   B2:24 Lit her month   C2:31 Or "We have taken control, or "We can roam

³⁴ Moreover, your skirts
    are stained
with the blood
    of the innocent poor.
You did not catch them
    breaking and entering.
But in spite of
    all these things
³⁵ you claim, "I am innocent.
His anger is sure
    to turn away from me."
But I will certainly judge you
    because you have said,
    "I have not sinned." Pr 28:13
³⁶ How unstable you are, Jms 1:8
    constantly changing
        your ways!
You will be put to shame
    by Egypt Is 30:3
just as you were put to shame
    by Assyria.
³⁷ Moreover, you will be led out
    from here
with your hands
    on your head 2Sm 13:19
since the LORD has rejected
    those you trust; 1Sm 15:23,26
you will not succeed
    even with their help. ᴬ

Wages of Apostasy

3 If ᴮ a man divorces his wife
    and she leaves him
        to marry another,
can he ever return to her?
Wouldn't such a land ᶜ
    become totally defiled?
But you!
You have prostituted yourself
    with many partners —
can you return to me? Hs 2:7
    This is
    the LORD's declaration.
²   Look to the barren heights
    and see. Dt 12:2; Ezk 16:52

Where have you not
    been immoral?
You sat waiting for them
    beside the highways Gn 38:14
like a nomad in the desert.
You have defiled the land
    with your prostitution
    and wickedness. Nm 14:33
³ This is why the showers
    haven't come — Zch 14:7
why there has been
    no spring rain.
You have the brazen look
    of a prostitute ᴰ Ezk 3:7-8
and refuse to be ashamed.
⁴ Haven't you recently
    called to me, "My Father.
You were my friend
    in my youth. Ps 71:17; Hs 2:15
⁵ Will he bear
    a grudge forever? Lv 19:18
Will he be
    endlessly infuriated?"
This is what you have said,
but you have done
    the evil things
    you are capable of.

Unfaithful Israel, Treacherous Judah

⁶ In the days of King Josiah the LORD asked me, "Have you seen what unfaithful Israel has done? She has ascended every high hill and gone under every green tree to prostitute herself there. ⁷ I thought, 'After she has done all these things, she will return to me.' But she didn't return, and her treacherous sister Judah saw it. ⁸ I ᴱ observed that it was because unfaithful Israel had committed adultery that I had sent her away and had given her a certificate of divorce. Nevertheless, her treacherous sister Judah was

---

ᴬ2:37 Lit *with them*   ᴮ3:1 One Hb ms, LXX, Syr; other Hb mss read *Saying: If*   ᶜ3:1 LXX reads *woman*
ᴰ3:3 Lit *have a prostitute's forehead*   ᴱ3:8 One Hb ms, Syr read *She*

not afraid but also went and prostituted herself. ⁹ Indifferent to ᴬ her prostitution, she defiled the land and committed adultery with stones and trees. ¹⁰ Yet in spite of all this, her treacherous sister Judah didn't return to me with all her heart — only in pretense."   Jr 2:20

This is
the LORD's declaration.

¹¹ The LORD announced to me, "Unfaithful Israel has shown herself more righteous than treacherous Judah. ¹² Go, proclaim these words to the north, and say,

'Return, unfaithful Israel.
This is
the LORD's declaration.
I will not look on you
    with anger, ᴮ
for I am unfailing in my love.
This is
the LORD's declaration.
I will not be angry forever.
¹³ Only acknowledge
    your guilt —   Lv 26:40; 1Jn 1:9
you have rebelled
    against the LORD
    your God.
You have scattered
    your favors to strangers
under every green tree   Dt 12:2
and have not obeyed me.
This is
the LORD's declaration.
¹⁴ " 'Return, you faithless children
— this is the LORD's declaration
— for I am your master, ᶜ and I will take you, one from a city and two from a family, and I will bring you to Zion. ¹⁵ I will give you shepherds who are loyal to me, ᴰ and they will shepherd you with knowledge and skill. ¹⁶ When you multiply and increase in the land, in those days

— this is the LORD's declaration
— no one will say again, "The ark of the LORD's covenant." It will never come to mind, and no one will remember or miss it. Another one will not be made. ᴱ ¹⁷ At that time Jerusalem will be called The LORD's Throne, and all the nations will be gathered to it, to the name of the LORD in Jerusalem. They will cease to follow the stubbornness of their evil hearts. ¹⁸ In those days the house of Judah will join with the house of Israel, and they will come together from the land of the north to the land I have given your ancestors to inherit.' "   Hs 2:16-17; 14:1

True Repentance

¹⁹ I thought, "How I long
    to make you my sons
    and give you a desirable land,
    the most beautiful
        inheritance of all
    the nations."   Dt 32:8-9; Ps 16:6
I thought, "You will call me
    'My Father'
    and never turn away
        from me."
²⁰ However, as a woman
    may betray her lover, ᶠ
so you have betrayed me,
    house of Israel.   Ex 21:8-9; Is 48:8
This is
    the LORD's declaration.

²¹ A sound is heard
    on the barren heights:
    the children of Israel
    weeping and begging
        for mercy,
    for they have perverted
        their way;
    they have forgotten the LORD
        their God.   Is 17:10

ᴬ3:9 Lit From the lightness of   ᴮ3:12 Lit not cause my face to fall on you   ᶜ3:14 Or husband
ᴰ3:15 Lit shepherds according to my heart   ᴱ3:16 Or It will no longer be done   ᶠ3:20 Lit friend

²² Return,
   you faithless children.
I will heal
   your unfaithfulness.   Is 57:18
"Here we are, coming to you,
for you are the Lord our God.
²³ Surely, falsehood comes
   from the hills,
commotion
   from the mountains,   Ps 121:1-2
but the salvation of Israel
is only in the Lord our God.
²⁴ From the time of our youth
the shameful one^A
   has consumed
what our fathers
   have worked for —
their flocks and their herds,
their sons
   and their daughters.
²⁵ Let us lie down
   in our shame;
let our disgrace cover us.
We have sinned
   against the Lord our God,
both we and our fathers,
from the time of our youth
   even to this day.   Ezr 9:7; Ezk 2:3
We have not obeyed the Lord
our God."

Blessing or Curse

4 If you return,^B Israel —
   this is
   the Lord's declaration —
you will return to me,   Zch 1:3
if you remove
   your abhorrent idols   Jr 7:30
from my presence
and do not waver,
² then you can swear,
   "As the Lord lives,"   Dt 6:13; Jr 5:2
in truth, in justice,
   and in righteousness,   Is 65:16
then the nations
   will be blessed^C by him

and will pride themselves
   in him.   Gn 12:1-3; 18:18; 22:18; 1Co 1:31

³ For this is what the Lord says to
the men of Judah and Jerusalem:
   Break up
   the unplowed ground;
do not sow among the thorns.
⁴ Circumcise yourselves
   to the Lord;
remove the foreskin
   of your hearts,   Gn 17:14; Dt 10:16
men of Judah and residents
   of Jerusalem.
Otherwise, my wrath
   will break out like fire
and burn with no one
   to extinguish it   Is 1:31; Jr 21:12
because of your evil deeds.

Judgment from the North

⁵ Declare in Judah, proclaim in Jerusalem, and say:
   Blow the ram's horn
      throughout the land.   Jr 6:1
   Cry out loudly and say:
   Assemble yourselves,
   and let's flee
   to the fortified cities.
⁶ Lift up a signal flag
   toward Zion.   Is 62:10
Run for cover!
   Don't stand still!
For I am bringing disaster
   from the north —
a crushing blow.   Is 14:31; 41:25
⁷ A lion has gone up
   from his thicket;   Ps 10:9; 17:12
a destroyer of nations
   has set out.
He has left his lair
to make your land a waste.
Your cities will be reduced
   to uninhabited ruins.   Is 1:7
⁸ Because of this,
   put on sackcloth;

^A3:24 = Baal   ^B4:1 Or *Repent*   ^C4:2 Or *will bless themselves*

mourn and wail,   Jl 1:13
for the LORD's burning anger
has not turned away from us.

⁹ "On that day" — this is the
LORD's declaration — "the king
and the officials will lose their
courage. The priests will tremble
in fear, and the prophets will be
scared speechless."

¹⁰ I said, "Oh no, Lord GOD, you
have certainly deceived this people and Jerusalem, by announcing, 'You will have peace,' while a
sword is at ᴬ our throats."   1Kg 22:22

¹¹ "At that time it will be said to this
people and to Jerusalem, 'A sear-
ing wind blows from the barren
heights in the wilderness on the
way to my dear ᴮ people. It comes
not to winnow or to sift; ¹² a wind
too strong for this comes at my
call. ᶜ Now I will also pronounce
judgments against them.' "   Ezk 17:10

¹³ Look, he advances
        like clouds;   Rv 1:7
    his chariots are like a storm.
    His horses are
        swifter than eagles.   2Sm 1:23
    Woe to us, for we are ruined!
¹⁴ Wash the evil from
        your heart, Jerusalem,   Is 1:16
    so that you will be delivered.
    How long will you harbor
        malicious thoughts?   Ps 119:113
¹⁵ For a voice announces
        from Dan,
    proclaiming malice
        from Mount Ephraim.
¹⁶ Warn the nations: Look!
    Proclaim to Jerusalem:
    Those who besiege
        are coming
    from a distant land;   Is 39:3
    they raise their voices

against the cities of Judah.
¹⁷ They have her surrounded
    like those who guard a field,
    because she has rebelled
        against me.   Is 1:20
    This is
        the LORD's declaration.
¹⁸ Your way and your actions
    have brought this on you.
    This is your punishment. It is
        very bitter,
    because it has reached
        your heart!

Jeremiah's Lament

¹⁹ My anguish, my anguish! ᴰ
        I writhe in agony!
    Oh, the pain in ᴱ my heart!
    My heart pounds;
    I cannot be silent.
    For you, my soul,
    have heard the sound
        of the ram's horn —
    the shout of battle.
²⁰ Disaster after disaster
        is reported   Ezk 7:26
    because the whole land
        is destroyed.
    Suddenly my tents
        are destroyed,
    my tent curtains,
        in a moment.
²¹ How long must I see
        the signal flag
    and hear the sound
        of the ram's horn?

²² "For my people are fools;
    they do not know me.
    They are foolish children,
    without understanding.   Ps 82:5
    They are skilled in doing
        what is evil,
    but they do not know how
        to do what is good."   Rm 16:19

ᴬ 4:10 Lit sword touches   ᴮ 4:11 Lit to the daughter of my   ᶜ 4:12 Lit comes for me   ᴰ 4:19 Lit My inner
parts, my inner parts   ᴱ 4:19 Lit the walls of

²³ I looked at the earth,
and it was formless
and empty.   Gn 1:2; Jb 26:7; Is 45:18
I looked to the heavens,
and their light was gone.
²⁴ I looked at the mountains,
and they were quaking;   Jdg 5:5
all the hills shook.
²⁵ I looked, and there was no
human being,   Gn 2:5
and all the birds of the sky
had fled.   Zph 1:3
²⁶ I looked, and the fertile field
was a wilderness.   Jr 2:7
All its cities were torn down
because of the LORD
and his burning anger.   Ps 76:7

²⁷ For this is what the LORD says:
The whole land will be
a desolation,   Is 6:11
but I will not finish it off.
²⁸ Because of this, the earth
will mourn;   Jr 8:13; 14:2; Hs 4:3
the skies above
will grow dark.   Ps 105:28; Is 13:10
I have spoken;
I have planned,
and I will not relent
or turn back from it.   Nm 23:19

²⁹ Every city flees   2Kg 25:4
at the sound of the horseman
and the archer.
They enter the thickets
and climb among the rocks.
Every city is abandoned;
no inhabitant is left.
³⁰ And you, devastated one,
what are you doing   Is 10:3
that you dress yourself
in scarlet,
that you adorn yourself
with gold jewelry,
that you enhance your eyes
with makeup?   2Kg 9:30

You beautify yourself
for nothing.
Your lovers reject you;   Jr 30:14
they intend to take your life.
³¹ I hear a cry like a woman
in labor,   Ps 48:6; Is 13:8; 21:3; 42:14
a cry of anguish
like one bearing
her first child.
The cry of Daughter Zion
gasping for breath,
stretching out her hands:
"Woe is me, for my life
is weary
because of the murderers!"

The Depravity of Jerusalem

5 Roam through the streets
of Jerusalem.   2Ch 16:9
Investigate;ᴬ
search in her squares.
If you find one person,   Ps 14:1-3
any who acts justly,
who pursues faithfulness,
then I will forgive her.
² When they say,
"As the LORD lives,"   Jr 4:2
they are swearing falsely.   Jr 7:9
³ LORD, don't your eyes
look for faithfulness?   Ps 51:6
You have struck them,
but they felt no pain.   Pr 23:35
You finished them off,
but they refused
to accept discipline.   Pr 27:22
They made their faces harder
than rock,   Ezk 3:7-9
and they refused to return.

⁴ Then I thought:
They are just the poor;
they have been foolish.
For they don't understand
the way of the LORD,   Gn 18:19
the justice of their God.   Mc 3:1
⁵ I will go to the powerful

ᴬ**5:1** Lit *See and know*

and speak to them.
Surely they know the way
 of the LORD,
the justice of their God.   Ps 103:7
However, these also
 had broken the yoke
and torn off the chains.   Ps 2:3

6 Therefore, a lion
 from the forest
 will strike them down.   Jr 4:7
A wolf from arid plains
 will ravage them.
A leopard stalks their cities.
Anyone who leaves them
 will be torn to pieces
because their rebellious acts
 are many,   Is 59:12
their unfaithful deeds
 numerous.   Jr 3:6,8,11-12,22; 14:7

7 Why should I forgive you?
Your children
 have abandoned me
and sworn by those who are
 not gods.   Dt 32:21; Jos 23:7; Gl 4:8
I satisfied their needs, yet they
 committed adultery;   Hs 4:10
they gashed themselves
 at theᴬ prostitute's house.

8 They are well-fed,ᴮ
 eagerᶜ stallions,   Ezk 23:20
each neighing after
 someone else's wife.   Jr 13:27

9 Should I not punish them
 for these things?   Jr 5:29; 8:10; 9:9
This is
 the LORD's declaration.
Should I not avenge myself
 on such a nation as this?

10 Go up among
 her vineyard terraces
 and destroy them,   2Kg 24:2
but do not finish them off.
Prune away her shoots,

for they do not belong
 to the LORD.   Hs 1:9
11 They, the house of Israel
 and the house of Judah,
have dealt very treacherously
 with me.   Is 21:2; 24:16; 48:8; Hs 6:7
This is
 the LORD's declaration.
12 They have contradicted
 the LORD
and insisted,
 "It won't happen.ᴰ   Is 28:15
Harm won't come to us;
we won't see sword
 or famine."
13 The prophets become
 only wind,
for the LORD's word is not
 in them.
This will in fact happen
 to them.

Coming Judgment

14 Therefore, this is what the Lord
GOD of Armies says:
Because you have spoken
 this word,
I am going to make my words
become fire in your mouth.
These people are the wood,
and the fire
 will consume them.   Zch 12:6
15 I am about to bring a nation
from far away against you,
house of Israel.
This is
 the LORD's declaration.
It is an established nation,
an ancient nation,
a nation whose language
 you do not know
and whose speech
 you do not understand.
16 Their quiver is
 like an open grave;   Ps 5:9

ᴬ5:7 Or adultery and trooped to the, or adultery and lodged at the ; Hb obscure   ᴮ5:8 Lit well-equipped ;
Hb obscure   ᶜ5:8 Lit early-rising ; Hb obscure   ᴰ5:12 Lit "He does not exist

they are all warriors.
17 They will consume
  your harvest and your food.
They will consume your sons
  and your daughters.
They will consume
  your flocks and your herds.
They will consume your vines
  and your fig trees.
With the sword they will
    destroy
  your fortified cities in which
    you trust.   Hs 8:14

18 "But even in those days" — this is the LORD's declaration — "I will not finish you off. 19 When people ask, 'For what offense has the LORD our God done all these things to us?' You will respond to them, 'Just as you abandoned me and served foreign gods in your land, so will you serve strangers in a land that is not yours.'   2Ch 12:12; Jr 4:27; 5:10; 30:11

20 "Declare this in the house of Jacob; proclaim it in Judah, saying:
21   Hear this,
  you foolish
    and senseless[A] people.
They have eyes,
  but they don't see.
They have ears,
  but they don't hear.   Ps 115:5-6
22 Do you not fear me?
  This is
    the LORD's declaration.
Do you not tremble
  before me,
the one who set the sand
  as the boundary of the sea,
an enduring barrier that
  it cannot cross?   Jb 26:10; 38:10-11
The waves surge, but they
  cannot prevail.
They roar but cannot
  pass over it.

23 But these people
  have stubborn
    and rebellious hearts.   Ps 78:8
They have turned aside
  and have gone away.
24 They have not said
  to themselves,
'Let's fear the LORD our God,
who gives the seasonal rains,
  both autumn and spring,
who guarantees to
  us the fixed weeks
  of the harvest.'
25 Your guilty acts
  have diverted these things
    from you.
Your sins have withheld
  my bounty from you,   Is 59:2
26 for wicked men live
  among my people.
They watch like hunters[B]
  lying in wait.[C]   Pr 1:11
They set a trap;   Ps 10:9
  they catch men.
27 Like a cage full of birds,
so their houses are full
    of deceit.   Ps 10:7; 50:19; Is 3:14; 5:18
Therefore they have
  grown powerful and rich.
28 They have become fat
  and sleek.   Dt 32:15
They have also excelled
  in evil matters.
They have not
  taken up cases,
such as the case
  of the fatherless,
  so they might prosper,
and they have not defended
  the rights of the needy.
29 Should I not punish them
  for these things?
  This is
    the LORD's declaration.
Should I not avenge myself
  on such a nation as this?

A 5:21 Lit without heart   B 5:26 Lit hunters of birds   C 5:26 Hb obscure

30 An appalling, horrible thing
   has taken place in the land.
31 The prophets
      prophesy falsely,   Jr 6:13; 8:10
   and the priests rule
   by their own authority.
   My people love it like this.
   But what will you do
      at the end of it?   Dt 32:29; Is 10:3

Threatened Siege of Jerusalem

6 "Run for cover   Ex 9:19; Is 10:31; Jr 4:6
   out of Jerusalem,
      Benjaminites.
   Sound the ram's horn
      in Tekoa;   2Ch 11:6; Jr 4:5; 51:27; Am 3:6
   raise a smoke signal
      over Beth-haccherem, ^A
   for disaster threatens
      from the north,   Jr 1:13; 4:6, 20
   even a crushing blow.
2 Though she is beautiful
      and delicate,
   I will destroy ^B Daughter Zion.
3 Shepherds and their flocks
      will come against her;
   they will pitch their tents
      all around her.   Jr 4:17
   Each will pasture
      his own portion.
4 Set them apart for war
      against her;   Jr 51:27; Mc 3:5
   rise up, let's attack at noon.
   Woe to us, for the day
      is passing;
   the evening shadows
      grow long.
5 Rise up, let's attack by night.
   Let us destroy her fortresses."

6 For this is what the LORD of Armies says:
   Cut down the trees;   Dt 20:19-20
   raise a siege ramp
      against Jerusalem.

This city must be punished.
There is nothing
   but oppression within her.
7 As a well gushes out
      its water,
   so she pours out her evil. ^C
   Violence and destruction
      resound in her.   Jr 20:8; Am 3:10
   Sickness and wounds
      keep coming
      to my attention.
8 Be warned, Jerusalem,
   or I will turn away from you;
   I will make you a desolation,
   a land without inhabitants.

Wrath on Israel

9 This is what the LORD of Armies
says:
   Glean the remnant of Israel
      as thoroughly as a vine.
   Pass your hand once more
      like a grape gatherer
      over the branches.
10 Who can I speak to and give
      such a warning ^D
   that they will listen?
   Look, their ear
      is uncircumcised, ^E   Lv 26:41
   so they cannot pay attention.
   See, the word of the LORD
      has become contemptible
      to them —
   they find no pleasure in it.
11 But I am full
      of the LORD's wrath;
   I am tired of holding it back.
   Pour it out on the children
      in the street,   Jr 9:21
   on the gathering
      of young men as well.
   For both husband and wife
      will be captured,
   the old with the very old. ^F

^A 6:1 = House of the Vineyard   ^B 6:2 Or *silence*   ^C 6:7 Or *well keeps its water fresh, so she keeps her evil fresh*   ^D 6:10 Or *and bear witness*   ^E 6:10 They are unresponsive to God.   ^F 6:11 Lit *with fullness of days*

12 Their houses will be
    turned over to others,
their fields and wives
    as well,
for I will stretch out my hand
against the inhabitants
    of the land.
    This is
    the LORD's declaration.

13 For from the least
    to the greatest of them,
everyone is making
    profit dishonestly.   Pr 1:19; 15:27
From prophet to priest,
everyone deals falsely.   Jr 5:31

14 They have treated
    my people's brokenness
    superficially,
claiming, "Peace, peace,"
when there is no peace.

15 Were they ashamed
    when they acted
    so detestably?
They weren't at all ashamed.
They can no longer
    feel humiliation.   Jr 3:3; 8:12
Therefore, they will fall
    among the fallen.
When I punish them,
    they will collapse,   Jr 8:10-12
says the LORD.

Disaster Because of Disobedience

16 This is what the LORD says:
    Stand by the roadways
    and look.
    Ask about the ancient paths,
    "Which is the way to what
    is good?"
    Then take it
    and find rest for yourselves.
    But they protested,
    "We won't!"

17 I appointed watchmen
    over you   Is 21:11; 58:1; Hs 9:8
and said, "Listen for the sound
    of the ram's horn."
But they protested,
    "We won't listen!"

18 Therefore listen, you nations
    and you witnesses,
learn what the charge is
    against them.

19 Listen, earth!
I am about to bring disaster
    on these people,
the fruit
    of their own plotting,   Pr 1:31
for they have paid
    no attention to my words.
They have rejected
    my instruction.   Is 5:24; Jr 23:17

20 What use to me is
    frankincense from Sheba
or sweet cane
    from a distant land?   Ex 30:23
Your burnt offerings
    are not acceptable;
your sacrifices do not
    please me.   Ps 40:6; Is 1:11; 43:23; 66:3

21 Therefore, this is what
    the LORD says:
I am going to place
    stumbling blocks
    before these people;
fathers and sons together
    will stumble over them;
friends and neighbors
    will also perish.

A Cruel Nation from the North

22 This is what the LORD says:
    Look, an army is coming
    from a northern land;
a great nation will be
    stirred up
from the remote regions
    of the earth.   Jr 25:32; 31:8

23 They grasp bow and javelin.
They are cruel and show
    no mercy.   Is 13:18; Jr 50:42; Hab 1:6-17

Their voice roars like the sea,
and they ride on horses,
lined up like men
    in battle formation
against you, Daughter Zion.

24 We have heard about it,
    and our hands have become
        weak.
    Distress has seized us —
    pain, like a woman in labor.
25 Don't go out to the fields;
    don't walk on the road.
    For the enemy has a sword;
    terror is on every side.   Ps 31:13

26 My dear[A] people,
        dress yourselves
        in sackcloth
    and roll in the dust.   Jr 25:34
    Mourn as you would for
        an only son,   Am 8:10
    a bitter lament,
    for suddenly the destroyer
        will come on us.   Ex 12:23; Is 21:2

Jeremiah Appointed as an Examiner

27 I have appointed you
        to be an assayer
        among my people —
    a refiner[B] —
    so you may know and assay
        their way of life.   1Ch 29:17; Ps 7:9
28 All are stubborn rebels
    spreading slander.   Lv 19:16; Pr 11:13
    They are bronze and iron;
    all of them are corrupt.   Is 1:4
29 The bellows blow,
    blasting the lead with fire.
    The refining is completely
        in vain;
    the evil ones are not
        separated out.
30 They are called rejected silver,

for the LORD
    has rejected them.   1Sm 15:23,26

False Trust in the Temple

7 This is the word that came to Jeremiah from the LORD: [2] "Stand in the gate of the house of the LORD and there call out this word: 'Hear the word of the LORD, all you people of Judah who enter through these gates to worship the LORD.   Jr 26:2

[3] "This is what the LORD of Armies, the God of Israel, says: Correct your ways and your actions, and I will allow you to live in this place. [4] Do not trust deceitful words, chanting, "This is the temple of the LORD, the temple of the LORD, the temple of the LORD." [5] Instead, if you really correct your ways and your actions, if you act justly toward one another,[C] [6] if you no longer oppress the resident alien, the fatherless, and the widow and no longer shed innocent blood in this place or follow other gods, bringing harm on yourselves, [7] I will allow you to live in this place, the land I gave to your ancestors long ago and forever. [8] But look, you keep trusting in deceitful words that cannot help.   Dt 19:10,13; Jr 4:18; 18:11; 22:3; 26:13

[9] "Do you steal, murder, commit adultery, swear falsely, burn incense to Baal, and follow other gods that you have not known? [10] Then do you come and stand before me in this house that bears my name and say, "We are rescued, so we can continue doing all these detestable acts"? [11] Has this house, which bears my name, become a den of robbers in your view? Yes, I too have seen it.   Ex 20:3-17; Lv 19:11-12

This is
    the LORD's declaration.

Shiloh as a Warning

¹² " 'But return to my place that was at Shiloh, where I made my name dwell at first. See what I did to it because of the evil of my people Israel. ¹³ Now, because you have done all these things — this is the Lᴏʀᴅ's declaration — and because I have spoken to you time and time again ᴬ but you wouldn't listen, and I have called to you, but you wouldn't answer, ¹⁴ what I did to Shiloh I will do to the house that bears my name — the house in which you trust — the place that I gave you and your ancestors. ¹⁵ I will banish you from my presence, just as I banished all of your brothers, all the descendants of Ephraim.' Dt 12:11; 14:23; 16:6,11

Do Not Pray for Judah

¹⁶ "As for you, do not pray for these people. Do not offer a cry or a prayer on their behalf, and do not beg me, for I will not listen to you. ¹⁷ Don't you see how they behave in the cities of Judah and in the streets of Jerusalem? ¹⁸ The sons gather wood, the fathers light the fire, and the women knead dough to make cakes for the queen of heaven, ᴮ and they pour out drink offerings to other gods so that they provoke me to anger. ¹⁹ But are they really provoking me? " This is the Lᴏʀᴅ's declaration. "Isn't it they themselves being provoked to disgrace? "

²⁰ Therefore, this is what the Lord Gᴏᴅ says: "Look, my anger — my burning wrath — is about to be poured out on this place, on people and animals, on the tree of the field, and on the produce of the land. My wrath will burn and not be quenched." Jr 42:18; Lm 4:11; Nah 1:6

Obedience over Sacrifice

²¹ This is what the Lᴏʀᴅ of Armies, the God of Israel, says: "Add your burnt offerings to your other sacrifices, and eat the meat yourselves, ²² for when I brought your ancestors out of the land of Egypt, I did not speak with them or command them concerning burnt offering and sacrifice. ²³ However, I did give them this command: 'Obey me, and then I will be your God, and you will be my people. Follow every way I command you so that it may go well with you.' ²⁴ Yet they didn't listen or pay attention but followed their own advice and their own stubborn, evil heart. They went backward and not forward. ²⁵ Since the day your ancestors came out of the land of Egypt until today, I have sent all my servants the prophets to you time and time again. ᶜ ²⁶ However, my people wouldn't listen to me or pay attention but became obstinate; ᴰ they did more evil than their ancestors. Dt 12:4-28; Ps 50:13; Hs 8:13

A Lament for Disobedient Judah

²⁷ "When you speak all these things to them, they will not listen to you. When you call to them, they will not answer you. ²⁸ Therefore, declare to them, 'This is the nation that would not listen to the Lᴏʀᴅ their God and would not accept discipline. Truth ᴱ has perished — it has disappeared from their mouths. ²⁹ Cut off the hair of your sacred vow ᶠ and throw it away. Raise up a dirge on the barren heights, for the Lᴏʀᴅ has rejected and abandoned the generation under his wrath.'

³⁰ "For the Judeans have done what is evil in my sight." This is the

LORD's declaration. "They have set up their abhorrent things in the house that bears my name in order to defile it. ³¹ They have built the high places of Topheth ᴬ in Ben Hinnom Valley ᴮ in order to burn their sons and daughters in the fire, a thing I did not command; I never entertained the thought. ᶜ   Jr 4:1; 16:18

³² "Therefore, look, the days are coming" — the LORD's declaration — "when this place will no longer be called Topheth and Ben Hinnom Valley, but the Valley of Slaughter. Topheth will become a cemetery, ᴰ because there will be no other burial place. ³³ The corpses of these people will become food for the birds of the sky and for the wild animals of the land, with no one to scare them away. ³⁴ I will remove from the cities of Judah and the streets of Jerusalem the sound of joy and gladness and the voices of the groom and the bride, for the land will become a desolate waste.   Jr 16:14; 19:6-7; 23:5; 48:12; 49:2

Death over Life

8 "At that time" — this is the LORD's declaration — "the bones of the kings of Judah, the bones of her officials, the bones of the priests, the bones of the prophets, and the bones of the residents of Jerusalem will be brought out of their graves. ² They will be exposed to the sun, the moon, and all the stars in the sky, which they have loved, served, followed, consulted, and worshiped. Their bones will not be collected and buried but will become like manure on the soil's surface. ³ Death will be chosen over life by all the survivors of this evil

family, those who remain wherever I have banished them." This is the declaration of the LORD of Armies.   2Sm 21:12-14; 2Kg 9:37; 23:16; Am 2:1

⁴ "You are to say to them: This is what the LORD says:

Do people fall and not
     get up again?   Is 24:20; Jr 25:27
If they turn away, do they
     not return?
⁵ Why have these people
     turned away?
Why is Jerusalem always
     turning away?
They take hold of deceit;
     they refuse to return.   Jr 5:3
⁶ I have paid careful attention.
They do not speak
     what is right.
No one regrets his evil,
     asking, 'What have I done?'
Everyone has stayed
     his course
like a horse rushing into battle.
⁷ Even storks in the sky
know their seasons.
Turtledoves, swallows,
     and cranes ᴱ
are aware of their migration,
but my people do not know
the requirements
     of the LORD.   2Kg 17:26; Ps 95:10

Punishment for Judah's Leaders

⁸ "How can you claim,
     'We are wise;
the law of the LORD is with us'?
In fact, the lying pen
     of scribes   Jb 19:24; Ps 45:1; Jr 17:1
has produced falsehood.
⁹ The wise will be put to shame;
they will be dismayed
     and snared.
They have rejected the word
     of the LORD,   1Sm 15:23,26

ᴬ**7:31** Lit *of the fireplace*   ᴮ**7:31** A valley south of Jerusalem   ᶜ**7:31** Lit *command, and it did not arise on my heart*   ᴰ**7:32** Lit *They will bury in Topheth*   ᴱ**8:7** Hb obscure

so what wisdom do they
   really have?
10 Therefore, I will give
   their wives to other men,
   their fields to new occupants,
   for from the least
     to the greatest,   Est 1:20; Jr 6:13
   everyone is making
    profit dishonestly.
   From prophet to priest,
   everyone deals falsely.
11 They have treated
    the brokenness
  of my dear[A] people
    superficially,
  claiming, 'Peace, peace,'
  when there is no peace.
12 Were they ashamed
   when they acted
   so detestably?
  They weren't at all ashamed.
  They can no longer
   feel humiliation.
  Therefore, they will fall
   among the fallen.
  When I punish them,
   they will collapse," Jr 10:15; 49:8
  says the LORD.

13 I will gather them
   and bring them to an end.[B]
   This is
   the LORD's declaration.
  There will be no grapes
   on the vine,
  no figs on the fig tree,
  and even the leaf will wither.
  Whatever I have given them
   will be lost to them.

God's People Unrepentant

14 Why are we just sitting here?
  Gather together; let us enter
   the fortified cities
  and perish there,[C]

for the LORD our God
  has destroyed[D] us.
He has given us
  poisoned water to drink,
because we have sinned
  against the LORD. Is 64:5; Jr 3:25
15 We hoped for peace,
  but there was
  nothing good;
for a time of healing,
  but there was only terror.

16 From Dan, the snorting
  of horses is heard.
At the sound of the neighing
  of mighty steeds, Jdg 5:22
the whole land quakes.
They come to devour the land
  and everything in it,
the city and all its residents.
17 Indeed, I am about to send
  snakes among you,
poisonous vipers that cannot
  be charmed. Nm 21:6-9; Dt 32:24
They will bite you.
  This is
  the LORD's declaration.

Lament over Judah

18 My joy has flown away;
  grief has settled on me.
My heart is sick. Lm 5:17
19 Listen — the cry
  of my dear people
from a faraway land,
"Is the LORD no longer
  in Zion, Ps 99:2; 102:21; Jr 14:9; Mc 3:11
her King not within her?"
Why have they angered me
with their carved images,
with their worthless
  foreign idols? Dt 32:21; Jr 2:5
20 Harvest has passed,
  summer has ended,
but we have not been saved.

[A]**8:11** Lit *of the daughter of my,* also in vv. 19,21,22 [B]**8:13** Lit *Gathering I will end them* [C]**8:14** Or *there be silenced* [D]**8:14** Or *silenced*

21 I am broken
  by the brokenness
  of my dear people.   Jr 6:14; 8:11
I mourn; horror has
  taken hold of me.

22 Is there no balm in Gilead?
  Is there no physician there?
  So why has the healing
  of my dear people
  not come about?

9 If my head were a flowing
  spring,
  my eyes a fountain of tears,
  I would weep day and night
  over the slain
  of my dear[A] people.

2 If only I had a traveler's
  lodging place
  in the wilderness,   1Kg 19:9-10
  I would abandon my people
  and depart from them,
  for they are all adulterers,
  a solemn assembly
  of treacherous people.

3 They bent their tongues
  like their bows;
  lies and not faithfulness
  prevail in the land,
  for they proceed
  from one evil to another,
  and they do not take me
  into account.   Jr 4:22
  This is
  the LORD's declaration.

Imminent Ruin and Exile

4 Everyone has to be on guard
  against his friend.
  Don't trust any brother,
  for every brother will
  certainly deceive,   Gn 27:36
  and every friend
  spread slander.   Jr 6:28

5 Each one betrays his friend;
  no one tells the truth.
  They have taught
  their tongues to speak lies;
  they wear themselves out
  doing wrong.

6 You live in a world
  of deception.[B]   Gn 27:35-36; 34:13
  In their deception
  they refuse to know me.
  This is
  the LORD's declaration.

7 Therefore, this is what the LORD
of Armies says:
  I am about to refine them
  and test them,   Is 1:25; Jr 6:27
  for what else can I do
  because of
  my dear[C] people?[D]

8 Their tongues are
  deadly arrows —
  they speak deception.   Ps 28:3
  With his mouth
  one speaks peaceably
  with his friend,
  but inwardly he sets up
  an ambush.

9 Should I not punish them
  for these things?
  This is
  the LORD's declaration.
  Should I not avenge myself
  on such a nation as this?

10 I will raise weeping
  and a lament
  over the mountains,
  a dirge over the wilderness
  grazing land,
  for they have been
  so scorched
  that no one passes through.
  The sound of cattle is
  no longer heard.

[A]9:1 Lit slain among the daughter of my   [B]9:6 LXX reads Oppression on oppression, deceit on deceit
[C]9:7 Lit of the daughter of my   [D]9:7 LXX, Tg read because of their evils

From the birds of the sky
  to the animals,   Jr 4:25; 12:4
everything has fled —
  they have gone away.
11 I will make Jerusalem a heap
  of rubble,   2Kg 19:25; Is 25:2
a jackals' den.   Jr 10:22; 49:33; 51:37
I will make the cities of Judah
  a desolation,
an uninhabited place.

12 Who is the person wise enough to understand this? Who has the LORD spoken to, that he may explain it? Why is the land destroyed and scorched like a wilderness, so no one can pass through? Ps 107:43; Ec 8:1

13 The LORD said, "It is because they abandoned my instruction, which I set before them, and did not obey my voice or walk according to it. 14 Instead, they followed the stubbornness of their hearts and followed the Baals as their fathers taught them." 15 Therefore, this is what the LORD of Armies, the God of Israel, says: "I am about to feed this people wormwood and give them poisonous water to drink. 16 I will scatter them among the nations that they and their fathers have not known. I will send a sword after them until I have finished them off."

Mourning over Judah

17 This is what the LORD of Armies says:

Consider, and summon
  the women who mourn;
send for the skillful women.
18 Let them come quickly
  to raise a lament over us
so that our eyes
  may overflow with tears,
our eyelids be soaked
  with weeping.

19 For a sound of lamentation
  is heard from Zion:
How devastated we are.
We are greatly ashamed,   Jr 2:26
for we have abandoned
  the land;
our dwellings have been
  torn down.

20 Now hear the word
  of the LORD, you women.
Pay attention to A the words
  from his mouth.
Teach your daughters
  a lament
and one another a dirge,
21 for Death has climbed
  through our windows;
it has entered our fortresses,
cutting off children
  from the streets,
young men
  from the squares.

22 "Speak as follows: 'This is what the LORD declares: Human corpses will fall like manure on the surface of the field, like newly cut grain after the reaper with no one to gather it.   2Kg 9:30,32,37; Am 2:13; Mc 4:12; Zch 12:6

Boast in the LORD

23 " 'This is what the LORD says:
The wise person
  should not boast
  in his wisdom;
the strong should not boast
  in his strength;
the wealthy should not boast
  in his wealth.
24 But the one who boasts
  should boast in this:
that he understands
  and knows me —   Ps 34:2; 64:10
that I am the LORD,
  showing faithful love,

A9:20 Lit Your ears must receive

justice, and righteousness
　　on the earth,
for I delight in these things.
　　This is
　　the LORD's declaration.

²⁵ " 'Look, the days are coming — this is the LORD's declaration — when I will punish all the
circumcised yet uncircumcised:
²⁶ Egypt, Judah, Edom, the Ammonites, Moab, and all the inhabitants
of the desert who clip the hair on
their temples. ᴬ All these nations
are uncircumcised, and the whole
house of Israel is uncircumcised in
heart.' "   Lv 19:27; Jr 4:4; 25:23; Rm 2:28-29

False Gods Contrasted
with the Creator

10 Hear the word that the LORD
　　has spoken to ᴮ you, house of
Israel. ² This is what the LORD says:
　　Do not learn the way
　　　of the nations   Jr 2:23,36
　　or be terrified by signs
　　　in the heavens,
　　although the nations
　　　are terrified by them,
³ for the customs
　　　of the peoples
　　are worthless.
　　Someone cuts down a tree
　　　from the forest;
　　it is worked by the hands
　　　of a craftsman
　　　with a chisel.
⁴ He decorates it with silver
　　　and gold.   Is 40:19
　　It is fastened with hammer
　　　and nails,   Is 41:7
　　so it won't totter.
⁵ Like scarecrows
　　　in a cucumber patch,
　　their idols cannot speak.

They must be carried
　　because they cannot walk.
Do not fear them for they
　　can do no harm —   Is 41:23-24
and they cannot do any good.

⁶ LORD, there is no one
　　like you.   Ex 15:11; 2Sm 7:22; 1Kg 8:23
You are great;
　　your name is great in power.
⁷ Who should not fear you,
　　King of the nations?   Ps 22:28
It is what you deserve.
For among all the wise people
　　of the nations
and among
　　all their kingdoms,
there is no one like you.
⁸ They are both stupid
　　and foolish,
instructed by worthless idols
made of wood!
⁹ Beaten silver is brought
　　from Tarshish   Ezk 27:12,25; 38:13
and gold from Uphaz. ᶜ   Dn 10:5
The work of a craftsman
and of a goldsmith's hands
is clothed in blue and purple,
all the work
　　of skilled artisans.
¹⁰ But the LORD is the true God;
　　he is the living God
　　and eternal King.   Dt 5:26
The earth quakes at his wrath,
　　and the nations
　　cannot endure his rage.
¹¹ You are to say this to them: "The
gods that did not make the heavens
and the earth will perish from the
earth and from under these heavens." ᴰ   Ps 96:5; Is 2:18
¹² He made the earth
　　by his power,
established the world
　　by his wisdom,   Jb 38:4; Ps 93:1

ᴬ9:26 Or *who live in distant places*　ᴮ10:1 Or *against*　ᶜ10:9 Or *Ophir*　ᴰ10:11 This is the only Aramaic
v. in Jr.

and spread out the heavens
   by his understanding.   Jb 9:8
13 When he thunders, ^A
   the waters in the heavens
      are in turmoil,   Jr 5:22; 31:35
   and he causes the clouds
      to rise
   from the ends of the earth.
   He makes lightning
      for the rain
   and brings the wind
      from his storehouses.

14 Everyone is stupid
      and ignorant.
   Every goldsmith
      is put to shame
   by his carved image,   Is 40:18-31
   for his cast images are a lie;
      there is no breath in them.
15 They are worthless, a work
      to be mocked.
   At the time
      of their punishment
   they will be destroyed.   Jr 8:12
16 Jacob's Portion ^B is not
      like these
   because he is the one
      who formed all things.
   Israel is the tribe
      of his inheritance;   Dt 4:20
   the LORD of Armies is
      his name.   Jr 51:15-19

Exile After the Siege

17 Gather up your belongings ^C
      from the ground,   Ezk 12:3
   you who live under siege.

18 For this is what the LORD says:
   Look, I am flinging away
   the land's residents
      at this time
   and bringing them
      such distress
   that they will feel it.

Jeremiah Grieves

19 Woe to me because of
      my brokenness —
   I am severely wounded!   Jr 14:17
   I exclaimed, "This is
      my intense suffering,
   but I must bear it."
20 My tent is destroyed;   Jr 4:20
   all my tent cords
      are snapped.
   My sons have departed
      from me and are no more.
   I have no one to pitch
      my tent again
   or to hang up my curtains.
21 For the shepherds are stupid:
   They don't seek the LORD.
   Therefore they have not
      prospered,
   and their whole flock
      is scattered.
22 Listen! A noise —
      it is coming —
   a great commotion
      from the land to the north.
   The cities of Judah will be
      made desolate,
   a jackals' den.   Jr 9:11

23 I know, LORD,
   that a person's way of life
      is not his own;
   no one who walks
      determines his own steps.
24 Discipline me, LORD,
      but with justice —
   not in your anger,   Ps 6:1; 38:1
   or you will reduce me
      to nothing.
25 Pour out your wrath
      on the nations
   that don't recognize you
   and on the families
   that don't call on your name,
   for they have consumed
      Jacob;

---

^A 10:13 Lit *At his giving of the voice*   ^B 10:16 = the LORD   ^C 10:17 Lit *bundle*

they have consumed him
  and finished him off
and made his homeland
  desolate.   Ps 79:6-7

Reminder of the Covenant

11 This is the word that came to Jeremiah from the LORD: ² "Listen to the words of this covenant and tell them to the men of Judah and the residents of Jerusalem. ³ Tell them, 'This is what the LORD, the God of Israel, says: "Let a curse be on the man who does not obey the words of this covenant, ⁴ which I commanded your ancestors when I brought them out of the land of Egypt, out of the iron furnace." I declared, "Obey me, and do everything that I command you, and you will be my people, and I will be your God," ⁵ in order to establish the oath I swore to your ancestors, to give them a land flowing with milk and honey, as it is today.'"

I answered, "Amen, LORD."

⁶ The LORD said to me, "Proclaim all these words in the cities of Judah and in the streets of Jerusalem: 'Obey the words of this covenant and carry them out.' ⁷ For I strongly warned your ancestors when I brought them out of the land of Egypt until today, warning them time and time again,^A 'Obey me.' ⁸ Yet they would not obey or pay attention; each one followed the stubbornness of his evil heart. So I brought on them all the curses of this covenant, because they had not done what I commanded them to do." 2Ch 36:15; Jr 7:13,25; 25:3; 26:5; 29:19; 32:33

⁹ The LORD said to me, "A conspiracy has been discovered among the men of Judah and the residents of Jerusalem. ¹⁰ They have returned to the iniquities of their fathers who refused to obey my words and have followed other gods to worship them. The house of Israel and the house of Judah broke my covenant I made with their ancestors.

¹¹ "Therefore, this is what the LORD says: I am about to bring on them disaster that they cannot escape. They will cry out to me, but I will not hear them. ¹² Then the cities of Judah and the residents of Jerusalem will go and cry out to the gods they have been burning incense to, but they certainly will not save them in their time of disaster. ¹³ Your gods are indeed as numerous as your cities, Judah, and the altars you have set up to Shame^B — altars to burn incense to Baal — as numerous as the streets of Jerusalem.

¹⁴ "As for you, do not pray for these people. Do not raise up a cry or a prayer on their behalf, for I will not be listening when they call out to me at the time of their disaster.   Jr 7:16; 14:11

¹⁵   What right does
      my beloved have
    to be in my house,   Jr 7:1-15
    having carried out so many
      evil schemes?
    Can holy meat^C prevent
      your disaster^D   Hg 2:12
    so you can celebrate?
¹⁶   The LORD named you
    a flourishing olive tree,   Ps 52:8
    beautiful with
      well-formed fruit.
    He has set fire to it,
    and its branches
      are consumed^E   Ezk 31:12
    with the sound of a mighty
      tumult.   Ezk 1:24

^A**11:7** Lit *today, rising early and warning*   ^B**11:13** = Baal   ^C**11:15** = sacrificial meat   ^D**11:15** LXX; MT reads *meat pass from you*   ^E**11:16** Vg; MT reads *broken*

17 "The LORD of Armies who planted you has decreed disaster against you, because of the disaster[A] the house of Israel and the house of Judah brought on themselves when they angered me by burning incense to Baal."   Is 5:2,7; Jr 2:21

18   The LORD informed me,
         so I knew.
      Then you helped me to see
         their deeds,
19   for I was like a docile[B] lamb
         led to slaughter.   Ps 44:11,22
      I didn't know that they had
         devised plots against me:
      "Let's destroy the tree
         with its fruit;[C]
      let's cut him off from the land
         of the living   Ps 27:13; Is 53:8
      so that his name will
         no longer be remembered."
20   But, LORD of Armies,
         who judges righteously,
      who tests heart[D]
         and mind,   Jr 9:7; 12:3; Ps 7:9; 17:3
      let me see your vengeance
         on them,
      for I have presented my case
         to you.   Jr 20:12

21 Therefore, here is what the LORD says concerning the people of Anathoth who intend to take your life. They warn, "Do not prophesy in the name of the LORD, or you will certainly die at our hand." 22 Therefore, this is what the LORD of Armies says: "I am about to punish them. The young men will die by the sword; their sons and daughters will die by famine. 23 They will have no remnant, for I will bring disaster on the people of Anathoth in the year of their punishment."   Jr 1:1; 23:12; 32:7-9; Am 7:13

Jeremiah's Complaint

12 You will be righteous, LORD,
         even if I bring a case
         against you.
      Yet, I wish to contend with you:
      Why does the way
         of the wicked prosper?   Ps 73
      Why do all the treacherous
         live at ease?
2   You planted them, and they
         have taken root.   Ps 1:3; Jr 17:7-8
      They have grown
         and produced fruit.
      You are ever on their lips,[E]
      but far from
         their conscience.[D]   Ps 28:3
3   As for you, LORD,
         you know me; you see me.
      You test whether my heart is
         with you.   Ps 7:9; Jr 11:20
      Drag the wicked away
         like sheep to slaughter
      and set them apart
         for the day of killing.
4   How long will the land mourn
         and the grass of every field
         wither?
      Because of the evil
         of its residents,
      animals and birds have been
         swept away,   Zph 1:3
      for the people have said,
      "He cannot see what our end
         will be."[F]   Dt 32:20; Jb 22:13; Jr 29:11

The LORD's Response

5   If you have raced
         with runners
      and they have worn you out,
      how can you compete
         with horses?
      If you stumble[G]
         in a peaceful land,
      what will you do
         in the thickets of the Jordan?

[A]11:17 Or evil   [B]11:19 Or pet   [C]11:19 Lit bread   [D]11:20; 12:2 Lit kidneys   [E]12:2 Lit are near in their mouth   [F]12:4 LXX reads see our ways   [G]12:5 Or you are secure

⁶ Even your brothers —
    your own father's family —
even they were treacherous
    to you;   Jn 1:11
even they have
    cried out loudly after you.
Do not have confidence
    in them,
though they speak well
    of you.

⁷ I have abandoned my house;
I have deserted
    my inheritance.
I have handed the love
    of my life
over to her enemies.

⁸ My inheritance has behaved
    toward me
like a lion in the forest.
She has roared against me.
Therefore, I hate her.   Hs 9:15

⁹ Is my inheritance
    like a hyenaᴬ to me?
Are birds of prey
    circling her?
Go, gather all
    the wild animals;   Is 56:9; Jr 7:33
bring them to devour her.

¹⁰ Many shepherds
    have destroyed
    my vineyard;
they have trampled my plot
    of land.   Is 63:18
They have turned
    my desirable plot
into a desolate wasteland.

¹¹ They have made it
    a desolation.
It mourns, desolate,
    before me.
All the land is desolate,
but no one takes it to heart.

¹² Over all the barren heights
    in the wilderness
the destroyers have come,

for the Lᴏʀᴅ has a sword
    that devours
from one end of the earth
    to the other.
No one has peace.   2Ch 15:5; Is 48:22

¹³ They have sown wheat
    but harvested thorns.   Lv 26:16
They have exhausted
    themselves but have
    no profit.   Is 55:2
Be put to shame
    by your harvests
because of the Lᴏʀᴅ's
    burning anger.   Jr 4:26; 25:37-38

¹⁴ This is what the Lᴏʀᴅ says: "Concerning all my evil neighbors who attack the inheritance that I bequeathed to my people, Israel, I am about to uproot them from their land, and I will uproot the house of Judah from them. ¹⁵ After I have uprooted them, I will once again have compassion on them and return each one to his inheritance and to his land. ¹⁶ If they will diligently learn the ways of my people — to swear by my name, 'As the Lᴏʀᴅ lives,' just as they taught my people to swear by Baal — they will be built up among my people. ¹⁷ However, if they will not obey, then I will uproot and destroy that nation."   Jr 1:10; 18:7-8; 30:18; 31:20; 33:26; 42:12
    This is
    the Lᴏʀᴅ's declaration.

Linen Underwear

13 This is what the Lᴏʀᴅ said to me: "Go and buy yourself a linen undergarment and put it on.ᴮ But do not put it in water." ² So I bought underwear as the Lᴏʀᴅ instructed me and put it on.   Lv 16:4 ³ Then the word of the Lᴏʀᴅ came to me a second time: ⁴ "Take the

ᴬ**12:9** Hb obscure   ᴮ**13:1** Lit *around your waist*

underwear that you bought and are wearing, [A] and go at once to the Euphrates [B] and hide it in a rocky crevice." [5] So I went and hid it by the Euphrates, as the LORD commanded me.   Jr 51:63

[6] A long time later the LORD said to me, "Go at once to the Euphrates and get the underwear that I commanded you to hide there." [7] So I went to the Euphrates and dug up the underwear and got it from the place where I had hidden it, but it was ruined — of no use at all.

[8] Then the word of the LORD came to me: [9] "This is what the LORD says: Just like this I will ruin the great pride of both Judah and Jerusalem. [10] These evil people, who refuse to listen to me, who follow the stubbornness of their own hearts, and who have followed other gods to serve and bow in worship — they will be like this underwear, of no use at all. [11] Just as underwear clings to one's waist, so I fastened the whole house of Israel and of Judah to me" — this is the LORD's declaration — "so that they might be my people for my fame, praise, and glory, but they would not obey.

The Wine Jars

[12] "Say this to them: 'This is what the LORD, the God of Israel, says: Every jar should be filled with wine.' Then they will respond to you, 'Don't we know that every jar should be filled with wine?' [13] And you will say to them, 'This is what the LORD says: I am about to fill all who live in this land — the kings who reign for David on his throne, the priests, the prophets, and all the residents of Jerusalem — with drunkenness. [14] I will smash them against each other, fathers and sons alike — this is the LORD's declaration. I will allow no mercy, pity, or compassion to keep me from destroying them.'"   Lm 2:2,17,21

The LORD's Warning

[15] Listen and pay attention.
    Do not be proud,
for the LORD has spoken.
[16] Give glory to the LORD
    your God   Jos 7:19; 1Sm 6:5; Ps 29:1-2
before he brings darkness,
before your feet stumble
on the mountains at dusk.
You wait for light,
but he brings darkest gloom [C]
and makes total darkness.
[17] But if you will not listen,
my innermost being
    will weep in secret
because of your pride.
My eyes will overflow
    with tears,
for the LORD's flock has been
    taken captive.   Ps 80:1; 95:7

[18] Say to the king
    and the queen mother:
Take a humble seat,
for your glorious crowns
have fallen from your heads.
[19] The cities of the Negev are
    under siege;
no one can help them.
All of Judah has been taken
    into exile,
taken completely into exile.
[20] Look up and see
those coming from the north.
Where is the flock entrusted
    to you,
the sheep that were
    your pride?

[A]13:4 Lit wearing around your waist   [B]13:4-7 Perhaps a place near Anathoth with the same spelling as the river   [C]13:16 Or brings a shadow of death

The Destiny of Jerusalem

21 What will you say
   when he appoints
close friends as leaders
   over you,
ones you yourself trained?
Won't labor pains seize you,
   as they do a woman in labor?
22 And when you ask yourself,
   "Why have these things
      happened to me?"
it is because of
   your great guilt   Jr 5:6; 30:15
that your skirts have been
      stripped off,   Ezk 16:37-39; Hs 2:3,10
your body exposed. A
23 Can the Cushite change
      his skin,
or a leopard his spots?
If so, you might be able to do
      what is good,   Ec 5:1; Jr 4:22; Hs 5:4
you who are instructed in evil.
24 I will scatter you B
      like drifting chaff   Jb 13:25
before the desert wind.
25 This is your lot,
what I have decreed
      for you —
      this is
      the LORD's declaration —
because you have
      forgotten me   Ps 106:21; Jr 2:32
and trusted in lies.   Jr 3:23
26 I will pull your skirts up
      over your face
so that your shame
      might be seen.   Is 47:2-3; Jr 49:10
27 Your adulteries and
      your lustful neighing,
your depraved prostitution
   on the hills, in the fields —
I have seen
      your abhorrent acts.
Woe to you, Jerusalem!
You are unclean —
for how long yet?   Hs 8:5

The Drought

14 This is the word of the LORD
      that came to Jeremiah con-
cerning the drought: Jr 17:8
2 Judah mourns;
   her city gates languish.   Is 3:26
Her people are on the ground
   in mourning;
Jerusalem's cry rises up.
3 Their nobles send
      their servants C for water.
They go to the cisterns;
they find no water;
their containers return empty.
They are ashamed
   and humiliated;
they cover their heads.   Est 6:12
4 The ground is cracked
since no rain has fallen
   on the land.
The farmers are ashamed;
they cover their heads.
5 Even the doe in the field
gives birth and abandons
      her fawn
since there is no grass.
6 Wild donkeys stand
   on the barren heights   Jr 2:24
panting for air like jackals.
Their eyes fail
because there are
   no green plants.

7 Though our iniquities testify
      against us,
LORD, act for
   your name's sake.
Indeed, our rebellions
   are many;   Jr 2:19; 3:6,22; 5:6
we have sinned against you.
8 Hope of Israel,   Jr 17:13; 50:7
its Savior in time of distress,
why are you like a resident
   alien in the land,
like a traveler stopping only
      for the night?

A 13:22 Lit *your heels have suffered violence*   B 13:24 Lit *them*   C 14:3 Lit *little ones*

⁹ Why are you
   like a helpless man,
   like a warrior unable to save?
   Yet you are among us, LORD,
   and we bear your name.
   Don't leave us!

¹⁰ This is what the LORD says concerning these people:
   Truly they love to wander;
   they never rest their feet.
   So the LORD does not
   accept them.
   Now he will remember
   their iniquity
   and punish their sins.   Hs 8:13

False Prophets to Be Punished

¹¹ Then the LORD said to me, "Do not
pray for the well-being of these
people. ¹² If they fast, I will not hear
their cry of despair. If they offer
burnt offering and grain offering, I
will not accept them. Rather, I will
finish them off by sword, famine,
and plague."   Jr 5:12; 7:16; 11:14; 15:1

¹³ And I replied, "Oh no, Lord GOD!
The prophets are telling them, 'You
won't see sword or suffer famine. I
will certainly give you lasting peace
in this place.'"   Jr 4:10; 6:13-14; 8:10-12

¹⁴ But the LORD said to me, "These
prophets are prophesying a lie in
my name. I did not send them, nor
did I command them or speak to
them. They are prophesying to you
a false vision, worthless divination,
the deceit of their own minds.

¹⁵ "Therefore, this is what the
LORD says concerning the prophets
who prophesy in my name, though
I did not send them, and who say,
'There will never be sword or famine in this land.' By sword and famine these prophets will meet their
end. ¹⁶ The people they are prophesying to will be thrown into the

streets of Jerusalem because of the
famine and the sword. There will be
no one to bury them — they, their
wives, their sons, and their daughters. I will pour out their own evil
on them."   Jr 7:33; 9:22

Jeremiah's Request

¹⁷ You are to speak this word
   to them:
   Let my eyes overflow
   with tears;
   day and night may they
   not stop,   Jr 9:1,10; 13:17
   for the virgin daughter
   of my people
   has been destroyed
   by a crushing blow,   Jr 4:6; 6:1
   an extremely severe wound.

¹⁸ If I go out to the field,
   look — those slain
   by the sword!
   If I enter the city,
   look — those ill from famine!
   For both prophet and priest
   travel to a land
   they do not know.

¹⁹ Have you completely
   rejected Judah?
   Do you detest Zion?
   Why do you strike us
   with no hope of healing
   for us?
   We hoped for peace,
   but there was nothing good;
   for a time of healing,
   but there was only terror.

²⁰ We acknowledge
   our wickedness, LORD,
   the iniquity of our fathers;
   indeed, we have sinned
   against you.

²¹ For your name's sake,
   don't despise us.
   Don't disdain
   your glorious throne.   Dt 32:19

Remember your covenant
with us; Lv 26:44; Jdg 2:1; Is 33:8
do not break it.
22 Can any of the worthless idols
of the nations bring rain?
Or can the skies alone
give showers?
Are you not the LORD our God?
We therefore put our hope
in you, Is 8:17; 25:9
for you have done
all these things.

The LORD's Negative Response

15 Then the LORD said to me:
"Even if Moses and Samuel
should stand before me, my compassions would not reach out to
these people. Send them from my
presence, and let them go. 2 If they
ask you, 'Where will we go?' tell
them: This is what the LORD says:

Those destined for death,
to death; Jr 14:12; 43:11; Ezk 5:12
those destined for the sword,
to the sword.
Those destined for famine,
to famine;
those destined for captivity,
to captivity.

3 "I will ordain four kindsᴬ of
judgment for them" — this is the
LORD's declaration — "the sword
to kill, the dogs to drag away, and
the birds of the sky and the wild
animals of the land to devour and
destroy. 4 I will make them a horror to all the kingdoms of the earth
because of Manasseh son of Hezekiah, the king of Judah, for what
he did in Jerusalem. Jr 22:19; 49:20–50:45
5 Who will have pity on you,
Jerusalem? Lm 1:1-2; Am 5:2
Who will show sympathy
toward you? Is 51:19; Nah 3:7

ᴬ15:3 Lit families

Who will turn aside
to ask about your well-being?
6 You have left me." Dt 32:15
This is
the LORD's declaration.
"You have turned your back,
so I have stretched out
my hand against you
and destroyed you.
I am tired of
showing compassion. Is 1:14
7 I scattered them
with a winnowing fork
at the city gates of the land.
I made them childless;
I destroyed my people.
They would not turn
from their ways. Jdg 2:19; 2Ch 7:14
8 I made their widows
more numerous
than the sand of the seas.
I brought a destroyer
at noon
against the mother
of young men.
I suddenly released on her
agitation and terrors.
9 The mother of seven
grew faint; Ru 4:15; 1Sm 2:5; Jb 42:13
she breathed her last breath.
Her sun set while it was
still day;
she was ashamed
and humiliated.
The rest of them I will
give over to the sword
in the presence
of their enemies."
This is
the LORD's declaration.

Jeremiah's Complaint

10 Woe is me, my mother,
that you gave birth to me,
a man who incites dispute
and conflict

in all the land.
I did not lend or borrow,
yet everyone curses me.   Is 53:3

The LORD's Response

¹¹ The LORD said:
Haven't I set you loose for
your good?
Haven't I punished you
in a time of trouble,
in a time of distress
with the enemy?ᴬ
¹² Can anyone smash iron,
iron from the north,
or bronze?
¹³ I will give up your wealth
and your treasures
as plunder,
without cost, for all
your sins   Ps 44:12; Is 52:3
in all your borders.
¹⁴ Then I will make you serve
your enemiesᴮ
in a land you do not know,
for my anger will kindle
a fire
that will burn against you.

Jeremiah's Prayer for Vengeance

¹⁵ You know, LORD;   Jr 12:3
remember me and take note
of me.   Jdg 16:28; Neh 5:19; 13:14,22,31
Avenge me
against my persecutors.
In your patience, ᶜ
don't take me away.
Know that I suffer disgrace
for your honor.   Ps 69:7-9
¹⁶ Your words were found,
and I ate them.   Ezk 3:3
Your words became a delight
to me
and the joy of my heart,
for I bear your name,   Jr 14:9
LORD God of Armies.

¹⁷ I never sat with the band
of revelers,
and I did not celebrate
with them.
Because your hand was
on me, I sat alone,   2Kg 3:15
for you filled me
with indignation.
¹⁸ Why has my pain
become unending,
my wound incurable,   Jr 19:8
refusing to be healed?
You truly have become
like a mirage to me —
water that is not reliable.

Jeremiah Told to Repent

¹⁹ Therefore, this is what the LORD
says:
If you return, I will take you
back;
you will stand
in my presence.
And if you speak
noble words,
rather than worthless ones,
you will be my spokesman.
It is they who must return
to you;
you must not return to them.
²⁰ Then I will make you
a fortified wall of bronze
to this people.
They will fight against you
but will not overcome you,
for I am with you
to save you and rescue you.
This is
the LORD's declaration.
²¹ I will rescue you
from the power
of evil people
and redeem you
from the grasp
of the ruthless.

ᴬ15:11 Hb obscure   ᴮ15:14 Some Hb mss, LXX, Syr, Tg; other Hb mss read *you pass through*   ᶜ15:15 Lit *In the slowness of your anger*

No Marriage for Jeremiah

16 The word of the LORD came to me: ² "Do not marry or have sons or daughters in this place. ³ For this is what the LORD says concerning sons and daughters born in this place as well as concerning the mothers who bear them and the fathers who father them in this land: ⁴ They will die from deadly diseases. They will not be mourned or buried but will be like manure on the soil's surface. They will be finished off by sword and famine. Their corpses will become food for the birds of the sky and for the wild animals of the land. Dt 28:26; Is 18:6; Jr 8:2; 9:22; 25:33

⁵ "For this is what the LORD says: Don't enter a house where a mourning feast is taking place. ^A Don't go to lament or sympathize with them, for I have removed my peace from these people as well as my faithful love and compassion." This is the LORD's declaration. ⁶ "Both great and small will die in this land without burial. No lament will be made for them, nor will anyone cut himself or shave his head for them. ^B ⁷ Food won't be provided for the mourner to comfort him because of the dead. A consoling drink won't be given him for the loss of his father or mother. ⁸ Do not enter the house where feasting is taking place to sit with them to eat and drink. ⁹ For this is what the LORD of Armies, the God of Israel, says: I am about to eliminate from this place, before your very eyes and in your time, the sound of joy and gladness, the voice of the groom and the bride. Dt 14:1; Ps 25:6; 40:11; 69:16; Hs 9:4

Abandoning the LORD and His Law

¹⁰ "When you tell these people all these things, they will say to you, 'Why has the LORD declared all this terrible disaster against us? What is our iniquity? What is our sin that we have committed against the LORD our God?' ¹¹ Then you will answer them, 'Because your fathers abandoned me — this is the LORD's declaration — and followed other gods, served them, and bowed in worship to them. Indeed, they abandoned me and did not keep my instruction. ¹² You did more evil than your fathers. Look, each one of you was following the stubbornness of his evil heart, not obeying me. ¹³ So I will hurl you from this land into a land that you and your fathers are not familiar with. There you will worship other gods both day and night, for I will not grant you grace.' ^C Dt 29:25; Jr 1:16; 2:13,17,19; 5:19

¹⁴ "However, look, the days are coming" — the LORD's declaration — "when it will no longer be said, 'As the LORD lives who brought the Israelites from the land of Egypt,' ¹⁵ but rather, 'As the LORD lives who brought the Israelites from the land of the north and from all the other lands where he had banished them.' For I will return them to their land that I gave to their ancestors. Jr 7:32; 19:6; 23:5; 48:12; 49:2; 51:47,52

Punishment of Exile

¹⁶ "I am about to send for many fishermen" — this is the LORD's declaration — "and they will fish for them. Then I will send for many hunters, and they will hunt them down on every mountain and hill

---

^A 16:5 Lit *house of mourning*   ^B 16:6 This custom demonstrated pagan mourning rituals.   ^C 16:13 Or *compassion*

and out of the clefts of the rocks,
[17] for my gaze takes in all their ways.
They are not concealed from me,
and their iniquity is not hidden
from my sight. [18] I will first repay
them double for their iniquity and
sin because they have polluted my
land. They have filled my inheritance with the carcasses of their
abhorrent and detestable idols."

[19] LORD, my strength
    and my stronghold,
  my refuge in a time
    of distress,   Ps 37:39; Nah 1:7
  the nations will come to you
    from the ends of the earth,
    and they will say,
  "Our fathers inherited
    only lies,
  worthless idols of no benefit
    at all."   Jr 8:19; 10:8,15; 14:22
[20] Can one make gods
    for himself?
  But they are not gods.   Gn 1:26
[21] "Therefore, I am about
    to inform them,
  and this time I will
    make them know
  my power and my might;
  then they will know
    that my name is the LORD."

The Persistent Sin of Judah

17 The sin of Judah
    is inscribed
  with an iron stylus.   Jb 19:24
  With a diamond point
  it is engraved on the tablet
    of their hearts   Pr 3:3; 7:3
  and on the horns
    of their[A] altars,
[2] while their children
    remember their altars
  and their Asherah poles,
    by the green trees
  on the high hills —   Dt 16:21

[3] my mountains
    in the countryside.
  I will give up your wealth
  and all your treasures
    as plunder   Ps 44:10; Is 10:6; 42:22-24
  because of the sin
    of your high places[B]
  in all your borders.   Jr 15:13
[4] You will, on your own,
    relinquish your inheritance
  that I gave you.
  I will make you serve
    your enemies
  in a land you do not know,
  for you have set my anger
    on fire;   Dt 32:22; Jr 15:14
  it will burn forever.

Curse and Blessing

[5] This is what the LORD says:
  Cursed is the person
    who trusts in mankind.
  He makes human flesh
    his strength,   2Ch 32:8
  and his heart turns
    from the LORD.
[6] He will be like a juniper
    in the Arabah;   Jr 48:6
  he cannot see
    when good comes
  but dwells
    in the parched places
    in the wilderness,
  in a salt land
    where no one lives.   Gn 19:24-26
[7] The person who trusts
    in the LORD,
  whose confidence indeed is
    the LORD, is blessed.   Ps 40:4
[8] He will be like a tree planted
    by water: Ps 1:3; Ezk 17:5-8
  it sends its roots out
    toward a stream,
  it doesn't fear
    when heat comes,
  and its foliage remains green.

[A]17:1 Some Hb mss, Syr, Vg; other Hb mss read *your*   [B]17:3 Lit *plunder, your high places because of sin*

It will not worry in a year
　　of drought
or cease producing fruit.

The Deceitful Heart

⁹ The heart is more deceitful
　　than anything else,　　Gn 6:5
and incurable —
　　who can understand it?
¹⁰ I, the LORD,
　　examine the mind,
I test the heart ᴬ　　Dt 8:2; Ps 17:3; 26:2
to give to each according to
　　his way,
according to what
　　his actions deserve.　　Jr 4:18
¹¹ He who makes
　　a fortune unjustly
is like a partridge
　　that hatches eggs
　　it didn't lay.
In the middle of his life
　　his riches will abandon him,
so in the end he will be a fool.

¹² A glorious throne　　Is 6:1-3; Jr 14:21
　　on high from the beginning
　　is the place of our sanctuary.
¹³ LORD, the hope of Israel,　　Jr 14:8
all who abandon you
will be put to shame.
All who turn away from me
will be written in the dirt,
for they have abandoned
　　the LORD, the fountain
　　of living water.　　Jr 2:13

Jeremiah's Plea

¹⁴ Heal me, LORD,
　　and I will be healed;
save me, and I will be saved,
for you are my praise.　　Ps 22:25
¹⁵ Hear how they keep
　　challenging me,　　Is 5:19; 2Pt 3:4
"Where is the word
　　of the LORD?

Let it come!"
¹⁶ But I have not run away
　　from being your shepherd,
and I have not longed for
　　the fatal day.　　Am 5:18
You know my words
　　were spoken
　　in your presence.
¹⁷ Don't become a terror to me.
You are my refuge in the day
　　of disaster.　　Ps 46:1; 61:3; 62:7-8
¹⁸ Let my persecutors be
　　put to shame,　　Ps 35:4
but don't let me be
　　put to shame.
Let them be terrified,
　　but don't let me
　　be terrified.
Bring on them the day
　　of disaster;　　Ps 35:8
shatter them
　　with total ᴮ destruction.

Observing the Sabbath

¹⁹ This is what the LORD said to me, "Go and stand at the People's Gate, through which the kings of Judah enter and leave, as well as at all the gates of Jerusalem. ²⁰ Announce to them, 'Hear the word of the LORD, kings of Judah, all Judah, and all the residents of Jerusalem who enter through these gates. ²¹ This is what the LORD says: Watch yourselves; do not pick up a load and bring it in through Jerusalem's gates on the Sabbath day. ²² Do not carry a load out of your houses on the Sabbath day or do any work, but keep the Sabbath day holy, just as I commanded your ancestors. ²³ They wouldn't listen or pay attention but became obstinate, not listening or accepting discipline. Jn 5:9-12

²⁴ "'However, if you listen to me — this is the LORD's declaration

ᴬ 17:10 Lit kidneys　　ᴮ 17:18 Lit double

— and do not bring loads through the gates of this city on the Sabbath day, but keep the Sabbath day holy and do no work on it, ²⁵ kings and princes will enter through the gates of this city. They will sit on the throne of David; they will ride in chariots and on horses with their officials, the men of Judah, and the residents of Jerusalem. This city will be inhabited forever. ²⁶ Then people will come from the cities of Judah and from the area around Jerusalem, from the land of Benjamin and from the Judean foothills, from the hill country and from the Negev bringing burnt offerings and sacrifices, grain offerings and frankincense, and thank offerings to the house of the LORD. ²⁷ But if you do not listen to me to keep the Sabbath day holy by not carrying a load while entering the gates of Jerusalem on the Sabbath day, I will set fire to its gates, and it will consume the citadels of Jerusalem and not be extinguished.'"   Jr 22:2,30; 29:16; 36:30

Parable of the Potter

18 This is the word that came to Jeremiah from the LORD: ² "Go down at once to the potter's house; there I will reveal my words to you." ³ So I went down to the potter's house, and there he was, working away at the wheel.ᴬ ⁴ But the jar that he was making from the clay became flawed in the potter's hand, so he made it into another jar, as it seemed right for him to do.   Is 29:16

⁵ The word of the LORD came to me: ⁶ "House of Israel, can I not treat you as this potter treats his clay?" — this is the LORD's declaration. "Just like clay in the potter's

hand, so are you in my hand, house of Israel. ⁷ At one moment I might announce concerning a nation or a kingdom that I will uproot, tear down, and destroy it. ⁸ However, if that nation about which I have made the announcement turns from its evil, I will relent concerning the disaster I had planned to do to it. ⁹ At another time I might announce concerning a nation or a kingdom that I will build and plant it. ¹⁰ However, if it does what is evil in my sight by not listening to me, I will relent concerning the good I had said I would do to it. ¹¹ So now, say to the men of Judah and to the residents of Jerusalem, 'This is what the LORD says: Look, I am about to bring harm to you and make plans against you. Turn now, each from your evil way, and correct your ways and your deeds.' ¹² But they will say, 'It's hopeless. We will continue to follow our plans, and each of us will continue to act according to the stubbornness of his evil heart.'"   Gn 2:7-8; Is 43:1; 64:8; Jr 1:10

Deluded Israel

¹³ Therefore, this is what the LORD says:

> Ask among the nations,
> who has heard things
> like these?
> Virgin Israel has done
> a most horrible thing.   Jr 5:30
> ¹⁴ Does the snow
> of Lebanon ever leave
> the highland crags?
> Or does cold water flowing
> from a distance ever fail?
> ¹⁵ Yet my people
> have forgotten me.   Jr 2:32; 3:21
> They burn incense
> to worthless idols

ᴬ**18:3** Lit *pair of stones*

that make them stumble
in their ways   Ezk 14:3,4,7; 44:12
on the ancient roads,   Jr 6:16
and make them walk on new
    paths, not the highway.
¹⁶ They have made their land
    a horror,   Dt 28:37; 2Ch 29:8; 30:7
    a perpetual object of scorn; ^A
    all who pass by it
    will be appalled   Jr 19:8; 49:17
    and shake their heads.   Jb 2:11
¹⁷ I will scatter them
    before the enemy
    like the east wind.   Ex 10:13
    I will show them ^B my back
    and not my face   2Ch 29:6; Jr 2:27
    on the day of their calamity.

Plot Against Jeremiah

¹⁸ Then certain ones said, "Come,
let's make plans against Jeremiah,
for instruction will never be lost
from the priest, or counsel from
the wise, or a word from the prophet. Come, let's denounce him ^c and
pay no attention to all his words."
¹⁹ Pay attention to me, LORD.
    Hear what my opponents
        are saying!   Ps 55:2-3; 142:6
²⁰ Should good be repaid
        with evil?
    Yet they have dug a pit for me.
    Remember how I stood
        before you
    to speak good on their behalf,
    to turn your anger
        from them.
²¹ Therefore, hand their children
        over to famine,   Ps 109:9-20
    and give them over to the
        power of the sword.
    Let their wives
        become childless
    and widowed,

their husbands slain
    by deadly disease, ^D
their young men
    struck down by the sword
    in battle.
²² Let a cry be heard
    from their houses
when you suddenly
    bring raiders against them,
for they have dug a pit
    to capture me
and have hidden snares
    for my feet.   Ps 140:5; 142:3
²³ But you, LORD, know
    all their deadly plots
        against me.
Do not wipe out their iniquity;
do not blot out their sin
    before you.
Let them be forced
    to stumble before you;
deal with them in the time
    of your anger.

The Clay Jar

19 This is what the LORD says: "Go,
buy a potter's clay jar. Take ^E
some of the elders of the people and
some of the leading priests ² and
go out to Ben Hinnom Valley near
the entrance of the Potsherd Gate.
Proclaim there the words I speak
to you. ³ Say, 'Hear the word of the
LORD, kings of Judah and residents
of Jerusalem. This is what the LORD
of Armies, the God of Israel, says: I
am going to bring such disaster on
this place that everyone who hears
about it will shudder ^{F 4} because they
have abandoned me and made this
a foreign place. They have burned
incense in it to other gods that they,
their fathers, and the kings of Judah
have never known. They have filled

^A**18:16** Lit *hissing*   ^B**18:17** LXX, Lat, Syr, Tg; MT reads *will look at them*   ^C**18:18** Lit *let's strike him with the tongue*   ^D**18:21** Lit *by death*   ^E**19:1** Syr, Tg; MT omits *Take*   ^F**19:3** Lit *about it, his ears will tingle*; Hb obscure

this place with the blood of the innocent. ⁵ They have built high places to Baal on which to burn their children in the fire as burnt offerings to Baal, something I have never commanded or mentioned; I never entertained the thought. ᴬ

⁶ " 'Therefore, look, the days are coming — this is the LORD's declaration — when this place will no longer be called Topheth and Ben Hinnom Valley, but Slaughter Valley. ⁷ I will spoil the plans of Judah and Jerusalem in this place. I will make them fall by the sword before their enemies, by the hand of those who intend to take their life. I will provide their corpses as food for the birds of the sky and for the wild animals of the land. ⁸ I will make this city desolate, an object of scorn. Everyone who passes by it will be appalled and scoff because of all its wounds. ⁹ I will make them eat the flesh of their sons and their daughters, and they will eat each other's flesh in the distressing siege inflicted on them by their enemies who intend to take their life.'

¹⁰ "Then you are to shatter the jar in the presence of the people going with you, ¹¹ and you are to proclaim to them, 'This is what the LORD of Armies says: I will shatter these people and this city, like one shatters a potter's jar that can never again be mended. They will bury the dead in Topheth because there is no other place for burials. ¹² That is what I will do to this place — this is the declaration of the LORD — and to its residents, making this city like Topheth. ¹³ The houses of Jerusalem and the houses of the kings of Judah will become impure like that place Topheth — all the houses on

whose rooftops they have burned incense to all the stars in the sky and poured out drink offerings to other gods.' " Dt 4:19; 2Kg 17:16; 23:4-5; Jr 7:32

¹⁴ Jeremiah returned from Topheth, where the LORD had sent him to prophesy, stood in the courtyard of the LORD's temple, and proclaimed to all the people, ¹⁵ "This is what the LORD of Armies, the God of Israel, says: 'I am about to bring on this city — and on all its cities — every disaster that I spoke against it, for they have become obstinate, not obeying my words.' " 2Ch 20:5

Jeremiah Beaten by Pashhur

20 Pashhur the priest, the son of Immer and chief official in the temple of the LORD, heard Jeremiah prophesying these things. ² So Pashhur had the prophet Jeremiah beaten and put him in the stocks at the Upper Benjamin Gate in the LORD's temple. ³ The next day, when Pashhur released Jeremiah from the stocks, Jeremiah said to him, "The LORD does not call you Pashhur, but Terror Is on Every Side, ᴮ ⁴ for this is what the LORD says, 'I am about to make you a terror to both yourself and those you love. They will fall by the sword of their enemies before your very eyes. I will hand Judah over to the king of Babylon, and he will deport them to Babylon and put them to the sword. ⁵ I will give away all the wealth of this city, all its products and valuables. Indeed, I will hand all the treasures of the kings of Judah over to their enemies. They will plunder them, seize them, and carry them off to Babylon. ⁶ As for you, Pashhur, and all who live in your house, you will go into captivity. You will

ᴬ**19:5** Lit mentioned, and it did not arise on my heart　　ᴮ**20:3** = Magor-missabib go to Babylon. There you will die, and there you will be buried, you and all your friends to whom you prophesied lies.'" 1Ch 9:12; Jr 21:1; 38:1

Jeremiah Compelled to Preach

7 You deceived me, LORD,
　　and I was deceived. 2Ch 18:20
You seized me and prevailed.
I am a laughingstock
　　all the time; Gn 38:23; Jb 12:4
everyone ridicules me.
8 For whenever I speak,
　　I cry out,
I proclaim, "Violence
　　and destruction!" Jr 6:7
so the word of the LORD
　　has become my
constant disgrace
　　and derision.
9 I say, "I won't mention him
or speak any longer
　　in his name." Ex 5:23; Dt 18:20
But his message becomes
　　a fire burning in my heart,
shut up in my bones.
I become tired of holding it in,
and I cannot prevail.
10 For I have heard the gossip
　　of many people,
"Terror is on every side! Jr 6:25
Report him; let's report him!"
Everyone I trusted^A watches
　　for my fall. Ps 35:15; 41:9; 56:6
"Perhaps he will be deceived
so that we might prevail
　　against him
and take our vengeance
　　on him."
11 But the LORD is with me
　　like a violent warrior. Ex 15:3
Therefore, my persecutors
　　will stumble
　　and not prevail.
Since they have not succeeded,
　　they will be utterly shamed,

an everlasting
　　humiliation that will
　　never be forgotten. Mc 3:7
12 LORD of Armies, testing
　　the righteous
and seeing the heart^B
　　and mind,
let me see your vengeance
　　on them,
for I have presented my case
　　to you. Jr 11:20
13 Sing to the LORD!
Praise the LORD,
for he rescues the life
　　of the needy
from evil people.

Jeremiah's Lament

14 May the day I was born
be cursed. Jb 3:3
May the day my mother
　　bore me
　　never be blessed.
15 May the man be cursed
who brought the news
　　to my father, saying,
"A male child is born to you,"
bringing him great joy.
16 Let that man be
　　like the cities
the LORD demolished
　　without compassion. Gn 19:25
Let him hear an outcry
　　in the morning Jr 18:22
and a war cry at noontime
17 because he didn't kill me
　　in the womb Jb 3:10-11
so that my mother
　　might have been my grave,
her womb
　　eternally pregnant.
18 Why did I come out
　　of the womb
to see only struggle
　　and sorrow, Jb 3:20; Lm 3:1
to end my life in shame?

^A20:10 Lit *Every man of my peace*　^B20:12 Lit *kidneys*

Zedekiah's Request Denied

21 This is the word that came to Jeremiah from the LORD when King Zedekiah sent Pashhur son of Malchijah and the priest Zephaniah son of Maaseiah to Jeremiah, asking, [2] "Inquire of the LORD on our behalf, since King Nebuchadnezzar[A] of Babylon is making war against us. Perhaps the LORD will perform for us something like all his past wondrous works so that Nebuchadnezzar will withdraw from us." 1Ch 9:12; Jr 38:1

[3] But Jeremiah answered, "This is what you are to say to Zedekiah: [4] 'This is what the LORD, the God of Israel, says: I am about to repel the weapons of war in your hands, those you are using to fight the king of Babylon and the Chaldeans[B] who are besieging you outside the wall, and I will bring them into the center of this city. [5] I myself will fight against you with an outstretched hand and a strong arm, with anger, rage, and intense wrath. [6] I will strike the residents of this city, both people and animals. They will die in a severe plague. [7] Afterward — this is the LORD's declaration — King Zedekiah of Judah, his officers, and the people — those in this city who survive the plague, the sword, and the famine — I will hand over to King Nebuchadnezzar of Babylon, to their enemies, yes, to those who intend to take their lives. He will put them to the sword; he won't spare them or show pity or compassion.'

A Warning for the People

[8] "But tell this people, 'This is what the LORD says: Look, I am setting before you the way of life and the way of death. [9] Whoever stays in this city will die by the sword, famine, and plague, but whoever goes out and surrenders to the Chaldeans who are besieging you will live and will retain his life like the spoils of war. [10] For I have set my face against this city to bring disaster and not good — this is the LORD's declaration. It will be handed over to the king of Babylon, who will burn it.'

[11] "And to the house of the king of Judah say this: 'Hear the word of the LORD! [12] House of David, this is what the LORD says:

Administer justice
   every morning,
and rescue the victim
   of robbery
from his oppressor,   Dt 28:29
or my anger will flare up
   like fire
and burn unquenchably
because of your evil deeds.
[13] Beware! I am against you,
   you who sit above the valley,
   you atop the rocky plateau —
   this is
      the LORD's declaration —
   you who say, "Who can
      come down against us?
Who can enter our
   hiding places?"
[14] I will punish you according to
      what you have done —
   this is
      the LORD's declaration.
I will kindle a fire
   in your forest   Ezk 20:47
that will consume everything
   around it.'"   Jr 50:32

Judgment Against Sinful Kings

22 This is what the LORD says: "Go down to the palace of the king of Judah and announce this word there. [2] You are to say,

---

'Hear the word of the LORD, king of Judah, you who sit on the throne of David — you, your officers, and your people who enter these gates. ³ This is what the LORD says: Administer justice and righteousness. Rescue the victim of robbery from his oppressor. Don't exploit or brutalize the resident alien, the fatherless, or the widow. Don't shed innocent blood in this place. ⁴ For if you conscientiously carry out this word, then kings sitting on David's throne will enter through the gates of this palace riding on chariots and horses — they, their officers, and their people. ⁵ But if you do not obey these words, then I swear by myself — this is the LORD's declaration — that this house will become a ruin.' " 2Sm 3:10; 1Kg 2:12,24,45; Is 9:7; Jr 17:25

⁶ For this is what the LORD says concerning the house of the king of Judah:

"You are like Gilead to me,
   or the summit of Lebanon,
but I will certainly turn you
   into a wilderness,
   uninhabited cities.
⁷ I will set apart destroyers
   against you,   Ex 12:23; 2Sm 24:16
each with his weapons.
   They will cut down
   the choicest of your cedars
   and throw them
   into the fire.

⁸ "Many nations will pass by this city and ask one another, 'Why did the LORD do such a thing to this great city?' ⁹ They will answer, 'Because they abandoned the covenant of the LORD their God and bowed in worship to other gods and served them.' " Dt 29:24-25; 30:17

ᴬ22:14 Lit *my windows*

A Message concerning Shallum

¹⁰ Do not weep for the dead;
   do not mourn for him.
Weep bitterly for the one
   who has gone away,
   for he will never return again
   and see his native land.

¹¹ For this is what the LORD says concerning Shallum son of Josiah, king of Judah, who became king in place of his father Josiah, and who has left this place: "He will never return here again, ¹² but he will die in the place where they deported him, never seeing this land again."

A Message Concerning Jehoiakim

¹³ Woe for the one who builds
   his palace
   through unrighteousness,
   his upstairs rooms
   through injustice,
   who makes his neighbor
   serve without pay
   and will not give him
   his wages,   Lv 19:13; Jms 5:4
¹⁴ who says, "I will build myself
   a massive palace,
   with spacious
   upstairs rooms."
He will cut windowsᴬ in it,
   and it will be paneled
   with cedar   1Kg 6:9,15,18; 7:3,7
   and painted bright red.
¹⁵ Are you a king
   because you excel in cedar?
Didn't your father
   eat and drink
   and administer justice
   and righteousness?   Jr 22:3
Then it went well with him.
¹⁶ He took up the case
   of the poor and needy;
   then it went well.

Is this not what it means
  to know me?
This is
  the LORD's declaration.
¹⁷ But you have eyes and a heart
  for nothing
except your own
  dishonest profit,
shedding innocent blood
and committing extortion
  and oppression.   Is 30:12; 59:9-15

¹⁸ Therefore, this is what the LORD
says concerning Jehoiakim son of
Josiah, king of Judah: 2Kg 23:34–24:6
They will not mourn
  for him, saying,
"Woe, my brother!" or "Woe,
  my sister!"
They will not mourn
  for him, saying,
"Woe, lord! Woe,
  his majesty!"
¹⁹ He will be buried
  like a donkey,   Jr 36:30
dragged off and thrown
  outside Jerusalem's gates.
²⁰ Go up to Lebanon and cry out;
raise your voice in Bashan;
cry out from Abarim,   Nm 27:12
for all your lovers ᴬ
  have been crushed.   Jr 3:1
²¹ I spoke to you when
  you were secure.
You said, "I will not listen."
This has been your way
  since youth;   Jr 3:25
indeed, you have
  never listened to me.
²² The wind will take charge
  of ᴮ all your shepherds,
and your lovers will go
  into captivity.
Then you will be ashamed
  and humiliated   Is 41:11

because of all your evil.
²³ You residents of Lebanon,
  nestled among the cedars,
how you will groan ᶜ
  when pains come on you,
agony like a woman in labor.

A Message Concerning Coniah

²⁴ "As I live" — this is the LORD's
declaration — "though you, Coniah ᴰ son of Jehoiakim, the king
of Judah, were a signet ring on my
right hand, I would tear you from
it. ²⁵ In fact, I will hand you over
to those you dread, who intend
to take your life, to Nebuchadnezzar king of Babylon and the
Chaldeans. ²⁶ I will hurl you and
the mother who gave birth to you
into another land, where neither
of you were born, and there you
will both die. ²⁷ They will never
return to the land they long to re-
turn to."   Gn 38:18; 2Kg 24:6-17; Jr 37:1; 52:31
²⁸ Is this man Coniah
  a despised, shattered pot,
  a jar no one wants?
Why are he
  and his descendants
    hurled out
and cast into a land
  they have not known?
²⁹ Earth, earth, earth,
hear the word of the LORD!

³⁰ This is what the LORD says:
Record this man as childless,
a man who will
  not be successful
  in his lifetime.
None of his descendants
  will succeed
in sitting on the throne
  of David   Jr 36:30
or ruling again in Judah.

ᴬ22:20 Or *friends*, or *allies*, also in v. 22   ᴮ22:22 Lit *will shepherd*   ᶜ22:23 LXX, Syr, Vg; MT reads *will be
pitied*   ᴰ22:24 = Jehoiachin

The LORD and His Sheep

23 "Woe to the shepherds who destroy and scatter the sheep of my pasture!" This is the LORD's declaration. ² "Therefore, this is what the LORD, the God of Israel, says about the shepherds who tend my people: You have scattered my flock, banished them, and have not attended to them. I am about to attend to you because of your evil acts" — this is the LORD's declaration. ³ "I will gather the remnant of my flock from all the lands where I have banished them, and I will return them to their grazing land. They will become fruitful and numerous. ⁴ I will raise up shepherds over them who will tend them. They will no longer be afraid or discouraged, nor will any be missing." This is the LORD's declaration. Ps 100:3; Ezk 34:2,31; Zch 11:5-7,15-17

The Righteous Branch of David

5   "Look, the days are
        coming" — this is
        the LORD's declaration —
    "when I will raise
        up a Righteous
        Branch for David.   1Kg 12:16
    He will reign wisely as king
    and administer justice and
        righteousness in the land.
6   In his days Judah will
        be saved,
    and Israel will dwell securely.
    This is the name he will
        be called:
    The LORD
        Is Our Righteousness.ᴬ   Ps 4:1

    ⁷ "Look, the days are coming" —
the LORD's declaration — "when it
will no longer be said, 'As the LORD
lives who brought the Israelites
from the land of Egypt,' ⁸ but, 'As
the LORD lives, who brought and led
the descendants of the house of Israel from the land of the north and
from all the other countries where
Iᴮ had banished them.' They will
dwell once more in their own land."

False Prophets Condemned

⁹ Concerning the prophets:
    My heart is broken
        within me,   Hab 3:16
    and all my bones tremble.
    I have become
        like a drunkard,
    like a man overcome by wine,
    because of the LORD,
    because of his holy words.
10   For the land is full
        of adulterers;   Jr 9:2; Hs 7:4; Mal 3:5
    the land mourns because
        of the curse,   Jr 12:4; Am 1:2; Rm 8:22
    and the grazing lands
        in the wilderness
        have dried up.
    Their way of lifeᶜ
        has become evil,
    and their power is not
        rightly used
11   because both prophet
        and priest are ungodly,   Jr 6:13
    even in my house
    I have found their evil.
    This is
        the LORD's declaration.
12   Therefore, their way
        will seem
    like slippery paths
        in the gloom.   Ps 35:6; 73:18
    They will be driven away
        and fall down there,
    for I will bring disaster
        on them,
    the year of their punishment.
    This is
        the LORD's declaration.

ᴬ**23:6** = *Yahweh-zidkenu*   ᴮ**23:8** LXX reads *he*   ᶜ**23:10** Lit *Their manner of running*

¹³ Among the prophets
of Samaria
I saw something disgusting:
They prophesied by Baal
and led
my people Israel astray.
¹⁴ Among the prophets
of Jerusalem also
I saw a horrible thing: Jr 5:30
They commit adultery
and walk in lies.
They strengthen the hands
of evildoers,
and none turns his back
on evil.
They are all like Sodom
to me;   Gn 13:10-13; 18:16–19:28
Jerusalem's residents are
like Gomorrah.

¹⁵ Therefore, this is what the
LORD of Armies says concerning
the prophets:
I am about
to feed them wormwood
and give them
poisoned water to drink,
for from the prophets
of Jerusalem
ungodliness^A has spread
throughout the land.

¹⁶ This is what the LORD of Armies
says: "Do not listen to the words of
the prophets who prophesy to you.
They are deluding you. They speak
visions from their own minds, not
from the LORD's mouth. ¹⁷ They keep
on saying to those who despise me,
'The LORD has spoken: You will have
peace.' They have said to everyone
who follows the stubbornness of
his heart, 'No harm will come to
you.'"   Jr 14:14; Lm 2:9; Ezk 7:26; 12:24; 13:16; Mc 3:6
¹⁸ For who has stood
in the council of the LORD

to see and hear his word?
Who has paid attention
to his word and obeyed?
¹⁹ Look, a storm from the LORD!
Wrath has gone out,
a whirling storm.
It will whirl about the heads
of the wicked.
²⁰ The LORD's anger will not
turn away   Gn 27:45; Is 5:25; 10:4
until he has completely
fulfilled the purposes
of his heart.
In time to come you will
understand it clearly.
²¹ I did not send out
these prophets,   Jr 14:14
yet they ran.   Jos 7:22; 2Sm 18:21
I did not speak to them,
yet they prophesied.
²² If they had really stood
in my council,
they would have enabled
my people to hear
my words
and would have turned them
from their evil ways
and their evil deeds.   Jr 4:18

²³ "Am I a God who is only near" —
this is the LORD's declaration — "and
not a God who is far away? ²⁴ Can a
person hide in secret places where
I cannot see him?" — the LORD's
declaration. "Do I not fill the heavens and the earth?" — the LORD's
declaration.   Gn 3:8; 4:14; Ps 139:1-10; Am 9:2-3
²⁵ "I have heard what the prophets
who prophesy a lie in my name have
said: 'I had a dream! I had a dream!'
²⁶ How long will this continue in
the minds of the prophets prophesying lies, prophets of the deceit
of their own minds? ²⁷ Through
their dreams that they tell one

another, they plan to cause my people to forget my name as their fathers forgot my name through Baal worship. ²⁸ The prophet who has only a dream should recount the dream, but the one who has my word should speak my word truthfully, for what is straw compared to grain?" — this is the LORD's declaration. ²⁹ "Is not my word like fire" — this is the LORD's declaration — "and like a hammer that pulverizes rock? ³⁰ Therefore, take note! I am against the prophets" — the LORD's declaration — "who steal my words from each other. ³¹ I am against the prophets" — the LORD's declaration — "who use their own tongues to make a declaration. ³² I am against those who prophesy false dreams" — the LORD's declaration — "telling them and leading my people astray with their reckless lies. It was not I who sent or commanded them, and they are of no benefit at all to these people" — this is the LORD's declaration.

The Burden of the LORD

³³ "Now when these people or a prophet or a priest asks you, 'What is the burden ᴬ of the LORD?' you will respond to them, 'What is the burden? I will throw you away! This is the LORD's declaration.' ³⁴ As for the prophet, priest, or people who say, 'The burden of the LORD,' I will punish that man and his household. ³⁵ This is what each man is to say to his friend and to his brother: 'What has the LORD answered?' or 'What has the LORD spoken?' ³⁶ But no longer refer to ᴮ the burden of the LORD, for each man's word becomes his burden and you pervert the words of the living God, the LORD of Armies, our God. ³⁷ Say to the prophet, 'What has the LORD answered you?' or 'What has the LORD spoken?' ³⁸ But if you say, 'The burden of the LORD,' then this is what the LORD says: Because you have said, 'The burden of the LORD,' and I specifically told you not to say, 'The burden of the LORD,' ³⁹ I will surely forget you. ᶜ I will throw you away from my presence — both you and the city that I gave you and your fathers. ⁴⁰ I will bring on you everlasting disgrace and humiliation that will never be forgotten." Ps 78:66

The Good and the Bad Figs

24 After King Nebuchadnezzar of Babylon had deported Jeconiah ᴰ son of Jehoiakim king of Judah, the officials of Judah, and the craftsmen and metalsmiths from Jerusalem and had brought them to Babylon, the LORD showed me two baskets of figs placed in front of the temple of the LORD. ² One basket contained very good figs, like early figs, but the other basket contained very bad figs, so bad they were inedible. ³ The LORD said to me, "What do you see, Jeremiah?"

I said, "Figs! The good figs are very good, but the bad figs are extremely bad, so bad they are inedible."

⁴ The word of the LORD came to me: ⁵ "This is what the LORD, the God of Israel, says: Like these good figs, so I regard as good the exiles from Judah I sent away from this place to the land of the Chaldeans. ⁶ I will keep my eyes on them for

---

ᴬ**23:33** The Hb word for *burden* (Ex 23:5; 2Sm 15:33) can also mean "oracle" (Is 13:1; Nah 1:10).
ᴮ**23:36** Or *longer remember*   ᶜ**23:39** Some Hb mss; other Hb mss, LXX, Syr, Vg read *surely lift you up*
ᴰ**24:1** = Jehoiachin

their good and will return them to this land. I will build them up and not demolish them; I will plant them and not uproot them. ⁷ I will give them a heart to know me, that I am the LORD. They will be my people, and I will be their God because they will return to me with all their heart. Dt 30:6; Jr 1:10; 31:33; 32:40; Am 9:4

⁸ "But as for the bad figs, so bad they are inedible, this is what the LORD says: In this way I will deal with King Zedekiah of Judah, his officials, and the remnant of Jerusalem — those remaining in this land or living in the land of Egypt. ⁹ I will make them an object of horror and a disaster to all the kingdoms of the earth, an example for disgrace, scorn, ridicule, and cursing, wherever I have banished them. ¹⁰ I will send the sword, famine, and plague against them until they have perished from the land I gave to them and their ancestors." Jr 29:17; 44:1

The Seventy-Year Exile

25 This is the word that came to Jeremiah concerning all the people of Judah in the fourth year of Jehoiakim son of Josiah, king of Judah (which was the first year of King Nebuchadnezzar of Babylon). ² The prophet Jeremiah spoke concerning all the people of Judah and all the residents of Jerusalem as follows: ³ "From the thirteenth year of Josiah son of Amon, king of Judah, until this very day — twenty-three years — the word of the LORD has come to me, and I have spoken to you time and time again, ᴬ but you have not obeyed. ⁴ The LORD sent all his servants the prophets to you time and time again, ᴮ but

you have not obeyed or even paid attention. ᶜ ⁵ He announced, 'Turn, each of you, from your evil way of life and from your evil deeds. Live in the land the LORD gave to you and your ancestors long ago and forever. ⁶ Do not follow other gods to serve them and to bow in worship to them, and do not anger me by the work of your hands. Then I will do you no harm. 2Kg 23:34–24:6

⁷ " 'But you have not obeyed me' — this is the LORD's declaration — 'with the result that you have angered me by the work of your hands and brought disaster on yourselves.'

⁸ "Therefore, this is what the LORD of Armies says: 'Because you have not obeyed my words, ⁹ I am going to send for all the families of the north' — this is the LORD's declaration — 'and send for my servant Nebuchadnezzar king of Babylon, and I will bring them against this land, against its residents, and against all these surrounding nations, and I will completely destroy them and make them an example of horror and scorn, and ruins forever. ¹⁰ I will eliminate the sound of joy and gladness from them — the voice of the groom and the bride, the sound of the millstones and the light of the lamp. ¹¹ This whole land will become a desolate ruin, and these nations will serve the king of Babylon for seventy years. ¹² When the seventy years are completed, I will punish the king of Babylon and that nation' — this is the LORD's declaration — 'the land of the Chaldeans, for their iniquity, and I will make it a ruin forever. ¹³ I will bring on that land all my words

ᴬ**25:3** Lit *you; rising early and speaking*   ᴮ**25:4** Lit *to you, rising early and sending*   ᶜ**25:4** Lit *even inclined your ear to hear*

I have spoken against it, all that is written in this book that Jeremiah prophesied against all the nations. ¹⁴ For many nations and great kings will enslave them, and I will repay them according to their deeds and the work of their hands.' " Jr 1:13

The Cup of God's Wrath

¹⁵ This is what the LORD, the God of Israel, said to me: "Take this cup of the wine of wrath from my hand and make all the nations to whom I am sending you drink from it. ¹⁶ They will drink, stagger, ᴬ and go out of their minds because of the sword I am sending among them."

¹⁷ So I took the cup from the LORD's hand and made all the nations to whom the LORD sent me drink from it.

¹⁸ Jerusalem and the other cities of Judah, its kings and its officials, to make them a desolate ruin, an example for scorn and cursing — as it is today;
¹⁹ Pharaoh king of Egypt, his officers, his leaders, all his people,
²⁰ and all the mixed peoples; all the kings of the land of Uz; all the kings of the land of the Philistines — Ashkelon, Gaza, Ekron, and the remnant of Ashdod;
²¹ Edom, Moab, and the Ammonites;
²² all the kings of Tyre, all the kings of Sidon, and the kings of the coasts and islands;
²³ Dedan, Tema, Buz, and all those who clip the hair on their temples; ᴮ Lv 19:27; Jr 9:26; 49:32
²⁴ all the kings of Arabia,

and all the kings of the mixed peoples who have settled in the desert;
²⁵ all the kings of Zimri, all the kings of Elam, and all the kings of Media;
²⁶ all the kings of the north, both near and far from one another; that is, all the kingdoms of the world throughout the earth. Finally, the king of Sheshach ᶜ will drink after them. Jr 51:41

²⁷ "Then you are to say to them, 'This is what the LORD of Armies, the God of Israel, says: Drink, get drunk, and vomit. Fall down and never get up again, as a result of the sword I am sending among you.' ²⁸ If ᴰ they refuse to accept the cup from your hand and drink, you are to say to them, 'This is what the LORD of Armies says: You must drink! ²⁹ For I am already bringing disaster on the city that bears my name, so how could you possibly go unpunished? You will not go unpunished, for I am summoning a sword against all the inhabitants of the earth. This is the declaration of the LORD of Armies.' Jr 25:16; Hab 2:16

Judgment on the Whole World

³⁰ "As for you, you are to prophesy all these things to them, and say to them:

The LORD roars from on high;
  he makes his voice heard
    from his holy dwelling. Jl 3:16
He roars loudly
  over his grazing land;
he calls out with a shout,
  like those
  who tread grapes,
against all the inhabitants
  of the earth.

ᴬ25:16 Or vomit ᴮ25:23 Or who live in distant places ᶜ25:26 = Babylon ᴰ25:28 Or When

³¹ The tumult reaches
    to the ends of the earth
because the LORD brings
    a case against the nations.
He enters into judgment
    with all people.   Is 66:16
As for the wicked,
    he hands them over
    to the sword —
this is
    the LORD's declaration.

³² "This is what the LORD of Armies says:
    Pay attention!
      Disaster spreads
from nation to nation.
A huge storm is stirred up
from the ends of the earth."

³³ Those slain by the LORD on that day will be scattered from one end of the earth to the other. They will not be mourned, gathered, or buried. They will be like manure on the soil's surface.   Is 66:16; Jr 16:4

³⁴ Wail, you shepherds,
    and cry out.
Roll in the dust, you leaders
    of the flock.   Jb 2:8,12; Jr 6:26
Because the days
    of your slaughter
    have come,   Jr 7:32; 19:6
you will fall
    and become shattered
    like a precious vase.
³⁵ Flight will be impossible
    for the shepherds,
and escape, for the leaders
    of the flock.
³⁶ Hear the sound
    of the shepherds' cry,
the wail of the leaders
    of the flock,
for the LORD is destroying
    their pasture.

³⁷ Peaceful grazing land
    will become lifeless
because of
    the LORD's burning anger.
³⁸ He has left his den like a lion,
for their land has become
    a desolation
because of the sword^A
    of the oppressor,   Jr 46:16
because of his burning anger.

Jeremiah's Speech in the Temple

26 At the beginning of the reign of Jehoiakim son of Josiah, king of Judah, this word came from the LORD: ² "This is what the LORD says: Stand in the courtyard of the LORD's temple and speak all the words I have commanded you to speak to all Judah's cities that are coming to worship there. Do not hold back a word. ³ Perhaps they will listen and turn — each from his evil way of life — so that I might relent concerning the disaster that I plan to do to them because of the evil of their deeds. ⁴ You are to say to them, 'This is what the LORD says: If you do not listen to me by living according to my instruction that I set before you ⁵ and by listening to the words of my servants the prophets — whom I have been sending to you time and time again, ^B though you did not listen — ⁶ I will make this temple like Shiloh. I will make this city an example for cursing for all the nations of the earth.' "   Dt 4:2

Jeremiah Seized

⁷ The priests, the prophets, and all the people heard Jeremiah speaking these words in the temple of the LORD. ⁸ When he finished the address the LORD had commanded him to deliver to all the people,

^A**25:38** Some Hb mss, LXX, Tg; other Hb mss read *burning*   ^B**26:5** Lit *you, rising early and sending*

immediately the priests, the prophets, and all the people took hold of him, yelling, "You must surely die! ⁹ How dare you prophesy in the name of the LORD, 'This temple will become like Shiloh and this city will become an uninhabited ruin'!" Then all the people crowded around Jeremiah at the LORD's temple.

¹⁰ When the officials of Judah heard about these things, they went from the king's palace to the LORD's temple and sat at the entrance of the New Gate of the LORD's temple. ᴬ ¹¹ Then the priests and prophets said to the officials and all the people, "This man deserves the death sentence because he has prophesied against this city, as you have heard with your own ears." Jr 36:10; Ezk 46:1,3

Jeremiah's Defense

¹² Then Jeremiah said to all the officials and all the people, "The LORD sent me to prophesy all the words that you have heard against this temple and city. ¹³ So now, correct your ways and deeds, and obey the LORD your God so that he might relent concerning the disaster he had pronounced against you. ¹⁴ As for me, here I am in your hands; do to me what you think is good and right. ¹⁵ But know for certain that if you put me to death, you will bring innocent blood on yourselves, on this city, and on its residents, for it is certain the LORD has sent me to speak all these things directly to you." Dt 19:10,13; 21:8-9; Jr 4:18; 7:3-5; 18:11

Jeremiah Released

¹⁶ Then the officials and all the people told the priests and prophets,

"This man doesn't deserve the death sentence, for he has spoken to us in the name of the LORD our God!"

¹⁷ Some of the elders of the land stood up and said to all the assembled people, ¹⁸ "Micah the Moreshite prophesied in the days of King Hezekiah of Judah and said to all the people of Judah, 'This is what the LORD of Armies says:

Zion will be plowed
   like a field,
Jerusalem will become ruins,
  and the temple's mountain
    will be a high thicket.' Mc 3:12

¹⁹ Did King Hezekiah of Judah and all the people of Judah put him to death? Did not the king fear the LORD and plead for the LORD's favor, ᴮ and did not the LORD relent concerning the disaster he had pronounced against them? We are about to bring a terrible disaster on ourselves!" Ex 32:14; 2Sm 24:16; 2Ch 32:26

The Prophet Uriah

²⁰ Another man was also prophesying in the name of the LORD —Uriah son of Shemaiah from Kiriath-jearim. He prophesied against this city and against this land in words like all those of Jeremiah. ²¹ King Jehoiakim, all his warriors, and all the officials heard his words, and the king tried to put him to death. When Uriah heard, he fled in fear and went to Egypt. ²² But King Jehoiakim sent men to Egypt: Elnathan son of Achbor and certain other men with him went to Egypt. ²³ They brought Uriah out of Egypt and took him to King Jehoiakim, who executed him with the sword and threw his corpse

---

ᴬ26:10 Many Hb mss, Syr, Tg, Vg; other Hb mss read *the New Gate of the LORD*   ᴮ26:19 Or *and appease the LORD* into the burial place of the common people.[A] Jos 9:17; 1Sm 6:21; 7:2; Jr 36:12 [24] But Ahikam son of Shaphan supported Jeremiah, so he was not handed over to the people to be put to death. 2Kg 22:12,14; Jr 39:14; 40:5–43:6

The Yoke of Babylon

27 At the beginning of the reign of Zedekiah[B] son of Josiah, king of Judah, this word came to Jeremiah from the LORD:[C] [2] This is what the LORD said to me: "Make chains and yoke bars for yourself and put them on your neck. [3] Send word to the king of Edom, the king of Moab, the king of the Ammonites, the king of Tyre, and the king of Sidon through messengers who are coming to King Zedekiah of Judah in Jerusalem. [4] Command them to go to their masters, saying, 'This is what the LORD of Armies, the God of Israel, says: Tell this to your masters: [5] "By my great strength and outstretched arm, I made the earth, and the people, and animals on the face of the earth. I give it to anyone I please.[D] [6] So now I have placed all these lands under the authority of my servant Nebuchadnezzar, king of Babylon. I have even given him the wild animals to serve him. [7] All nations will serve him, his son, and his grandson until the time for his own land comes, and then many nations and great kings will enslave him. 2Kg 24:17; Jr 1:3; 2:20; 5:5; 21:1; 28:10-13

[8] " ' "As for the nation or kingdom that does not serve King Nebuchadnezzar of Babylon and does not place its neck under the yoke of the king of Babylon, that nation I will punish by sword, famine, and plague — this is the LORD's

declaration — until through him I have destroyed it. [9] So you should not listen to your prophets, diviners, dreamers, fortune-tellers, or sorcerers who say to you, 'Don't serve the king of Babylon!' [10] They are prophesying a lie to you so that you will be removed from your land. I will banish you, and you will perish. [11] But as for the nation that will put its neck under the yoke of the king of Babylon and serve him, I will leave it in its own land, and that nation will cultivate[E] it and reside in it. This is the LORD's declaration." ' " Lv 19:26; Dt 18:10,14; Jr 14:14; 29:8

Warning to Zedekiah

[12] I spoke to King Zedekiah of Judah in the same way: "Put your necks under the yoke of the king of Babylon, serve him and his people, and live! [13] Why should you and your people die by the sword, famine, and plague as the LORD has threatened against any nation that does not serve the king of Babylon? [14] Do not listen to the words of the prophets who are telling you, 'Don't serve the king of Babylon,' for they are prophesying a lie to you. [15] 'I have not sent them' — this is the LORD's declaration — 'and they are prophesying falsely in my name; therefore, I will banish you, and you will perish — you and the prophets who are prophesying to you.' "

[16] Then I spoke to the priests and all these people, saying, "This is what the LORD says: 'Do not listen to the words of your prophets. They are prophesying to you, claiming, "Look, very soon now the articles of the LORD's temple will be brought back from Babylon." They

---

[A]26:23 Lit *the sons of the people*　[B]27:1 Some Hb mss, Syr, Arabic; other Hb mss, DSS read *Jehoiakim*　[C]27:1 LXX omits this v.　[D]27:5 Lit *to whomever is upright in my eyes*　[E]27:11 Lit *work* are prophesying a lie to you. [17] Do not listen to them. Serve the king of Babylon and live! Why should this city become a ruin? [18] If they are indeed prophets and if the word of the LORD is with them, let them intercede with the LORD of Armies not to let the articles that remain in the LORD's temple, in the palace of the king of Judah, and in Jerusalem go to Babylon.' [19] For this is what the LORD of Armies says about the pillars, the basin, [A] the water carts, and the rest of the articles that still remain in this city, [20] those King Nebuchadnezzar of Babylon did not take when he deported Jeconiah [B] son of Jehoiakim, king of Judah, from Jerusalem to Babylon along with all the nobles of Judah and Jerusalem. [21] Yes, this is what the LORD of Armies, the God of Israel, says about the articles that remain in the temple of the LORD, in the palace of the king of Judah, and in Jerusalem: [22] 'They will be taken to Babylon and will remain there until I attend to them again.' This is the LORD's declaration. 'Then I will bring them up and restore them to this place.'"   2Kg 24:13; Jr 28:3

Hananiah's False Prophecy

28 In that same year, at the beginning of the reign of King Zedekiah of Judah, in the fifth month of the fourth year, the prophet Hananiah son of Azzur from Gibeon said to me in the temple of the LORD in the presence of the priests and all the people, [2] "This is what the LORD of Armies, the God of Israel, says: 'I have broken the yoke of the king of Babylon. [3] Within two years I will restore to this place all the articles of the LORD's temple that King Nebuchadnezzar of Babylon took from here and transported to Babylon. [4] And I will restore to this place Jeconiah [B] son of Jehoiakim, king of Judah, and all the exiles from Judah who went to Babylon' — this is the LORD's declaration — 'for I will break the yoke of the king of Babylon.'"   Jr 27:12

Jeremiah's Response to Hananiah

[5] The prophet Jeremiah replied to the prophet Hananiah in the presence of the priests and all the people who were standing in the temple of the LORD. [6] The prophet Jeremiah said, "Amen! May the LORD do that. May the LORD make the words you have prophesied come true and may he restore the articles of the LORD's temple and all the exiles from Babylon to this place! [7] Only listen to this message I am speaking in your hearing and in the hearing of all the people. [8] The prophets who preceded you and me from ancient times prophesied war, disaster, [C] and plague against many lands and great kingdoms. [9] As for the prophet who prophesies peace — only when the word of the prophet comes true will the prophet be recognized as one the LORD has truly sent."   1Kg 1:36

Hananiah Breaks Jeremiah's Yoke

[10] The prophet Hananiah then took the yoke bar from the neck of the prophet Jeremiah and broke it. [11] In the presence of all the people Hananiah proclaimed, "This is what the LORD says: 'In this way, within two years I will break the yoke of King Nebuchadnezzar of Babylon from the neck of all the nations.'" The

[A] 27:19 Lit *sea*   [B] 27:20; 28:4 = Jehoiachin   [C] 28:8 Some Hb mss, Vg read *famine* prophet Jeremiah then went on his way. Jr 27:2

The Lord's Word Against Hananiah

¹² After the prophet Hananiah had broken the yoke bar from the neck of the prophet Jeremiah, the word of the Lord came to Jeremiah: ¹³ "Go say to Hananiah, 'This is what the Lord says: You broke a wooden yoke bar, but in its place you will make an iron yoke bar. ¹⁴ For this is what the Lord of Armies, the God of Israel, says: I have put an iron yoke on the neck of all these nations that they might serve King Nebuchadnezzar of Babylon, and they will serve him. I have even put the wild animals under him.'"

¹⁵ The prophet Jeremiah said to the prophet Hananiah, "Listen, Hananiah! The Lord did not send you, but you have led these people to trust in a lie. ¹⁶ Therefore, this is what the Lord says: 'I am about to send you off the face of the earth. You will die this year because you have preached rebellion against the Lord.'" ¹⁷ And the prophet Hananiah died that year in the seventh month. Dt 13:5; Is 59:13; Jr 29:31-32; Ezk 13:22

Jeremiah's Letter to the Exiles

29 This is the text of the letter that the prophet Jeremiah sent from Jerusalem to the remaining exiled elders, the priests, the prophets, and all the people Nebuchadnezzar had deported from Jerusalem to Babylon. ² This was after King Jeconiah,ᴬ the queen mother, the court officials, the officials of Judah and Jerusalem, the craftsmen, and the metalsmiths had left Jerusalem. ³ He sent the letter with Elasah son of Shaphan and Gemariah son of Hilkiah, whom Zedekiah king of Judah sent to Babylon to King Nebuchadnezzar of Babylon. The letter stated: 2Sm 11:14-15; 1Kg 21:8-11

⁴ This is what the Lord of Armies, the God of Israel, says to all the exiles I deported from Jerusalem to Babylon: ⁵ "Build houses and live in them. Plant gardens and eat their produce. ⁶ Find wives for yourselves, and have sons and daughters. Find wives for your sons and give your daughters to men in marriage so that they may bear sons and daughters. Multiply there; do not decrease. ⁷ Pursue the well-beingᴮ of the city I have deported you to. Pray to the Lord on its behalf, for when it thrives, you will thrive." Gn 17:5-6; 35:10-11; Ezr 6:10; Jr 29:28

⁸ For this is what the Lord of Armies, the God of Israel, says: "Don't let your prophets who are among you and your diviners deceive you, and don't listen to the dreams you elicit from them, ⁹ for they are prophesying falsely to you in my name. I have not sent them." This is the Lord's declaration. Jr 5:31; 14:14; 20:6; 27:9,15

¹⁰ For this is what the Lord says: "When seventy years for Babylon are complete, I will attend to you and will confirm my promise concerning you to restore you to this place. ¹¹ For I know the plans I have for you" — this is the Lord's declaration — "plans for your well-being, not for disaster, to give

ᴬ **29:2** = Jehoiachin　ᴮ **29:7** Or *peace*

you a future and a hope. ¹² You will call to me and come and pray to me, and I will listen to you. ¹³ You will seek me and find me when you search for me with all your heart. ¹⁴ I will be found by you" — this is the LORD's declaration — "and I will restore your fortunes ᴬ and gather you from all the nations and places where I banished you" — this is the LORD's declaration. "I will restore you to the place from which I deported you." Ps 33:10; Jr 25:12; 26:3; Dn 9:2

¹⁵ You have said, "The LORD has raised up prophets for us in Babylon!" ¹⁶ But this is what the LORD says concerning the king sitting on David's throne and concerning all the people living in this city — that is, concerning your brothers who did not go with you into exile. ¹⁷ This is what the LORD of Armies says: "I am about to send sword, famine, and plague against them, and I will make them like rotten figs that are inedible because they are so bad. ¹⁸ I will pursue them with sword, famine, and plague. I will make them a horror to all the kingdoms of the earth — a curse and a desolation, an object of scorn and a disgrace among all the nations where I have banished them. ¹⁹ I will do this because they have not listened to my words" — this is the LORD's declaration — "the words that I sent to them with my servants the prophets time and time again. ᴮ

And you too have not listened." This is the LORD's declaration.

²⁰ Hear the word of the LORD, all you exiles I have sent from Jerusalem to Babylon. ²¹ This is what the LORD of Armies, the God of Israel, says about Ahab son of Kolaiah and concerning Zedekiah son of Maaseiah, the ones prophesying a lie to you in my name: "I am about to hand them over to King Nebuchadnezzar of Babylon, and he will kill them before your very eyes. ²² Based on what happens to them, all the exiles of Judah who are in Babylon will create a curse that says, 'May the LORD make you like Zedekiah and Ahab, whom the king of Babylon roasted in the fire!' ²³ because they have committed an outrage in Israel by committing adultery with their neighbors' wives and have spoken in my name a lie, which I did not command them. I am he who knows, and I am a witness." This is the LORD's declaration. Is 65:15; Jr 14:14; 24:5; 29:9; Dn 3:6

²⁴ To Shemaiah the Nehelamite you are to say, ²⁵ "This is what the LORD of Armies, the God of Israel, says: You ᶜ in your own name have sent out letters to all the people of Jerusalem, to the priest Zephaniah son of Maaseiah, and to all the priests, saying, ²⁶ 'The LORD has appointed you priest in place of the priest Jehoiada to be the chief officer in the temple of the LORD, responsible for

ᴬ29:14 Or will end your captivity ᴮ29:19 Lit prophets, rising up early and sending ᶜ29:25 Lit Because you every madman who acts like a prophet. You must confine him in the stocks and an iron collar. [27] So now, why have you not rebuked Jeremiah of Anathoth who has been acting like a prophet among you? [28] For he has sent word to us in Babylon, claiming, "The exile will be long. Build houses and settle down. Plant gardens and eat their produce." ' " Jr 21:1; 37:3; 52:24-27 [29] The priest Zephaniah read this letter in the hearing of the prophet Jeremiah.

A Message About Shemaiah

[30] Then the word of the LORD came to Jeremiah: [31] "Send a message to all the exiles, saying, 'This is what the LORD says concerning Shemaiah the Nehelamite. Because Shemaiah prophesied to you, though I did not send him, and made you trust a lie, [32] this is what the LORD says: I am about to punish Shemaiah the Nehelamite and his descendants. There will not be even one of his descendants living among these people, nor will any ever see the good that I will bring to my people — this is the LORD's declaration — for he has preached rebellion against the LORD.' " Jr 27:10,14-16; 28:15

Restoration from Captivity

30 This is the word that came to Jeremiah from the LORD. [2] "This is what the LORD, the God of Israel, says: Write on a scroll all the words that I have spoken to you, [3] for look, the days are coming" — this is the LORD's declaration — "when I will restore the fortunes[A] of my people Israel and Judah," says the LORD. "I will restore

[A] **30:3** Or *will end the captivity*

them to the land I gave to their ancestors and they will possess it."

[4] These are the words the LORD spoke to Israel and Judah. [5] This is what the LORD says:

> We have heard a cry of terror,
>   of dread — there is no peace.
> [6] Ask and see
>   whether a male can give birth.
> Why then do I see every man
>   with his hands
>   on his stomach
>   like a woman in labor
>   and every face turned pale?
> [7] How awful that day will be!
>   There will be no other like it!
> It will be a time of trouble
>   for Jacob,
> but he will be saved out of it.

> [8] On that day —
>   this is the declaration
>   of the LORD of Armies —
> I will break his yoke from
>   your neck   Gn 27:40; Jr 2:20; 28:4,11
> and tear off your chains,   Jr 27:2
> and strangers will never
>   again enslave him.   Ezk 34:27
> [9] They will serve the LORD
>   their God
> and David their king,
>   whom I will raise up for
>   them.   Is 55:3-5; Ezk 34:23-24; 37:24-25

> [10] As for you, my servant Jacob,
>   do not be afraid —
>   this is
>   the LORD's declaration —
> and do not
>   be discouraged, Israel,
> for without fail I will
>   save you out of a distant
>   place,
> your descendants,
>   from the land
>   of their captivity!

Jacob will return
and have calm and quiet
with no one
to frighten him. Lv 26:6; Jr 46:27
11 For I will be with you —
this is
the Lord's declaration —
to save you! 2Kg 19:34; Is 37:35; Jr 15:20
I will bring destruction
on all the nations
where I have scattered you;
however, I will not
bring destruction on you.
I will discipline you justly,
and I will by no means
leave you unpunished.

Healing Zion's Wounds

12 For this is what the Lord says:
Your injury is incurable;
your wound most severe.
13 You have no defender for
your case. Hs 5:13
There is no remedy for your
sores,
and no healing for you. A
14 All your lovers
have forgotten you; Jr 4:30
they no longer look
for you,
for I have struck
you as an enemy would,
with the discipline
of someone cruel, Jr 2:30; 5:3
because of
your enormous guilt
and your innumerable sins.
15 Why do you cry out
about your injury?
Your pain has no cure!
I have done these things
to you
because of
your enormous guilt
and your innumerable sins.

16 Nevertheless, all
who devoured you
will be devoured, Jr 10:25
and all your adversaries —
all of them —
will go off into exile.
Those who plunder you
will be plundered,
and all who raid you
will be raided. Ezk 39:10; Hab 2:8
17 But I will bring you health
and will heal you
of your wounds —
this is
the Lord's declaration —
for they call you Outcast,
Zion whom no one
cares about.

Restoration of the Land

18 This is what the Lord says:
I will certainly restore
the fortunes B
of Jacob's tents Jr 30:3
and show compassion
on his dwellings. Jr 12:15; 31:20
Every city will be rebuilt
on its mound;
every citadel will stand
on its proper site.
19 Thanksgiving will come
out of them,
a sound of rejoicing.
I will multiply them,
and they will not decrease;
I will honor them,
and they will not
be insignificant.
20 His children will be
as in past days;
his congregation
will be established
in my presence.
I will punish
all his oppressors. Jdg 10:12

A 30:13 Or No one pleads that your sores should be healed. There is no remedy for you. B 30:18 Or
certainly end the captivity

21 Jacob's leader will be
    one of them;
  his ruler will issue from him.
  I will invite him to me,
    and he will approach me,
  for who would
    otherwise risk his life
    to approach me?
  This is
    the Lord's declaration.
22 You will be my people,
  and I will be your God.   Jr 11:4

The Wrath of God

23 Look, a storm from the Lord!
  Wrath has gone out,
  a churning storm.
  It will whirl about the heads
    of the wicked.
24 The Lord's burning anger
    will not turn back
  until he has
    completely fulfilled
    the purposes of his heart.
  In time to come you will
    understand it.   Jr 23:19-20

God's Relationship
with His People

31 "At that time" — this is the
   Lord's declaration — "I will
be the God of all the families of Israel, and they will be my people."
  2 This is what the Lord says:
  The people who survived
    the sword
  found favor
    in the wilderness.   Ex 33:12-17
  When Israel went to find rest,
3   the Lord appeared to him A
    from far away.
  I have loved you
    with an everlasting love;
  therefore, I have continued
    to extend faithful love
    to you.   Ps 36:10; 109:12

4 Again I will build you so that
    you will be rebuilt,
  Virgin Israel.   Jr 18:13; 31:21; Am 5:2
  You will take up
    your tambourines again
  and go out in joyful dancing.
5 You will plant
    vineyards again   Am 5:11
  on the mountains of Samaria;
  the planters will plant
    and will enjoy the fruit.
6 For there will be a day
    when watchmen
    will call out
  in the hill country
    of Ephraim,
  "Come, let's go up to Zion,
  to the Lord our God!"

God's People Brought Home

7 For this is what the Lord says:
  Sing with joy for Jacob;
  shout for the foremost
    of the nations!
  Proclaim, praise, and say,
  "Lord, save your people,
  the remnant of Israel!"   Is 10:20
8 Watch! I am going
    to bring them
    from the northern land.
  I will gather them
    from remote regions
    of the earth —   Neh 1:9; Is 43:6
  the blind and the lame will be
    with them,   Lv 21:18; Mt 11:5; Lk 14:13
  along with those
    who are pregnant
    and those
    about to give birth.
  They will return here
    as a great assembly!   Ezk 38:15
9 They will come weeping,
  but I will bring them back
    with consolation. B   Jb 15:11
  I will lead them to wadis
    filled with water,

A31:3 LXX; MT reads me   B31:9 LXX; MT reads supplications

by a smooth way where
   they will not stumble,   Pr 4:12
for I am Israel's Father,
and Ephraim is my firstborn.

10 Nations, hear the word
   of the LORD,
and tell it among the
   far off coasts, and islands!
Say, "The one who scattered
   Israel will gather him.   Dt 30:3
He will watch over
   him as a shepherd
   guards his flock,

11 for the LORD has ransomed
   Jacob
and redeemed him
   from the power of one
   stronger than he."   Is 41:14; 43:1

12 They will come and shout
   for joy on the heights of Zion;
they will be radiant with joy
because of
   the LORD's goodness,
because of the grain,
   the new wine, the fresh oil,
and because of the young
   of the flocks and herds.
Their life will be
   like an irrigated garden,
and they will no longer
   grow weak from hunger.

13 Then the young women will
   rejoice with dancing,
while young and old men
   rejoice together.
I will turn their mourning
   into joy,   Ps 105:43; Is 35:10; 51:3,11
give them consolation,
and bring happiness
   out of grief.

14 I will refresh the priests
   with an abundance,A   Dt 31:20
and my people will be satisfied
   with my goodness.
This is
   the LORD's declaration.

A 31:14 Lit *fatness*

Lament Turned to Joy

15 This is what the LORD says:
   A voice was heard in Ramah,
   a lament
     with bitter weeping —
Rachel weeping
   for her children,
refusing to be comforted
   for her children
because they are no more.

16 This is what the LORD says:
Keep your voice from weeping
and your eyes from tears,
for the reward for your work
   will come —
   this is
   the LORD's declaration —
and your children will return
   from the enemy's land.

17 There is hope
   for your future —   Jr 5:31; 23:20
   this is
   the LORD's declaration —
and your children will return
   to their own territory.

18 I have surely heard
   Ephraim moaning,
"You disciplined me,
   and I have been disciplined
like an untrained calf.   Hs 4:16
Take me back, so
   that I can return,
for you, LORD, are my God.

19 After my return, I felt regret;
After I was instructed,
   I struck my thigh in grief.
I was ashamed
   and humiliated   Ps 35:4; Ezr 9:6
because I bore the disgrace
   of my youth."

20 Isn't Ephraim a precious son
   to me,
   a delightful child?   Is 5:7; Hs 11:1
Whenever I speak
   against him,

I certainly still think
   about him.
Therefore, my inner being
   yearns for him;
I will truly have compassion
   on him.   Jr 12:15; 30:18; 33:26; 42:12
This is
   the LORD's declaration.

Repentance and Restoration

²¹ Set up road markers
   for yourself;   2Kg 23:17; Ezk 39:15
establish signposts!
Keep the highway in mind,
the way you have traveled.
Return, Virgin Israel!
Return to these cities
   of yours.
²² How long will you turn
   here and there,
faithless daughter?   Jr 3:14,22; 49:4
For the LORD creates
   something new
   in the land ᴬ —
a female ᴮ will shelter ᶜ a man.

²³ This is what the LORD of Armies,
the God of Israel, says: "When I restore their fortunes, ᴰ they will once
again speak this word in the land
of Judah and in its cities: 'May the
LORD bless you, righteous settlement, holy mountain.' ²⁴ Judah and
all its cities will live in it together — also farmers and those who
move ᴱ with the flocks — ²⁵ for I satisfy the thirsty person and feed all
those who are weak."   Jb 8:6; Jr 50:7
²⁶ At this I awoke and looked
around. My sleep had been most
pleasant to me.
²⁷ "Look, the days are coming" —
this is the LORD's declaration —
"when I will sow the house of Israel
and the house of Judah with the

seed of people and the seed of animals. ²⁸ Just as I watched over them
to uproot and to tear them down,
to demolish and to destroy, and to
cause disaster, so will I watch over
them to build and to plant them"
— this is the LORD's declaration.
²⁹ "In those days, it will never again
be said,   Jr 21:10; 39:16; 44:27; Ezk 36:9,11; Hs 2:23
'The fathers have eaten
   sour grapes,
and the children's teeth
   are set on edge.'   Ezk 18:2
³⁰ Rather, each will die for his own
iniquity. Anyone who eats sour
grapes — his own teeth will be
set on edge.   Dt 24:6; Ezk 18:20

The New Covenant

³¹ "Look, the days are coming" —
this is the LORD's declaration —
"when I will make a new covenant
with the house of Israel and with
the house of Judah. ³² This one will
not be like the covenant I made
with their ancestors on the day
I took them by the hand to lead
them out of the land of Egypt —
my covenant that they broke even
though I am their master" ᶠ — the
LORD's declaration. ³³ "Instead, this
is the covenant I will make with the
house of Israel after those days" —
the LORD's declaration. "I will put
my teaching within them and write
it on their hearts. I will be their God,
and they will be my people. ³⁴ No
longer will one teach his neighbor or his brother, saying, 'Know
the LORD,' for they will all know
me, from the least to the greatest
of them" — this is the LORD's declaration. "For I will forgive their iniquity and never again remember
their sin.   Ezk 37:26; Hs 2:18; Heb 8:8-12; 10:16-17

ᴬ31:22 Or new on earth   ᴮ31:22 Or woman   ᶜ31:22 Or female surrounds, or female courts; Hb obscure
ᴰ31:23 Or I end their captivity   ᴱ31:24 Tg, Vg, Aq, Sym; MT reads and they will move   ᶠ31:32 Or husband

35 "This is what the LORD says:
  The one who gives the sun
    for light by day,
  the fixed order of moon
    and stars for light
    by night,
  who stirs up the sea
    and makes
    its waves roar — Ps 46:3; Is 51:15
  the LORD of Armies is
    his name:
36 If this fixed order departs
    from before me —
  this is
    the LORD's declaration —
  only then will
  Israel's descendants cease
    to be a nation
    before me forever. Jr 33:18

37 "This is what the LORD says:
  Only if the heavens above
    can be measured
  and the foundations
    of the earth below explored,
  will I reject all of
  Israel's descendants
    because of
  all they have done —
  this is
    the LORD's declaration.

38 "Look, the days are coming" —
the LORD's declaration — "when
the city^A from the Tower of Hananel
to the Corner Gate will be rebuilt
for the LORD. 39 A measuring line
will once again stretch out straight
to the hill of Gareb and then turn
toward Goah. 40 The whole valley
— the corpses, the ashes, and all
the fields as far as the Kidron Valley
to the corner of the Horse Gate to
the east — will be holy to the LORD.
It will never be uprooted or demolished again." Neh 3:1; 12:39; 2Kg 14:13; Zch 2:1

Jeremiah's Land Purchase

32 This is the word that came
to Jeremiah from the LORD
in the tenth year of King Zedekiah of Judah, which was the eighteenth year of Nebuchadnezzar.
2 At that time, the army of the king
of Babylon was besieging Jerusalem, and the prophet Jeremiah was
imprisoned in the guard's courtyard in the palace of the king of Judah. 3 King Zedekiah of Judah had
imprisoned him, saying, "Why are
you prophesying as you do? You
say, 'This is what the LORD says:
Look, I am about to hand this city
over to Babylon's king, and he will
capture it. 4 King Zedekiah of Judah
will not escape from the Chaldeans; indeed, he will certainly be
handed over to Babylon's king.
They will speak face to face^B and
meet eye to eye. 5 He will take Zedekiah to Babylon, where he will
stay until I attend to him — this
is the LORD's declaration. For you
will fight the Chaldeans, but you
will not succeed.' " 2Kg 24:17-20; Jr 29:1
6 Jeremiah replied, "The word of
the LORD came to me: 7 Watch! Hanamel, the son of your uncle Shallum, is coming to you to say, 'Buy
my field in Anathoth for yourself,
for you own the right of redemption to buy it.' 1Kg 2:26; Jr 1:1; 11:21,23
8 "Then, as the LORD had said,
my cousin Hanamel came to the
guard's courtyard and urged me,
'Please buy my field in Anathoth
in the land of Benjamin, for you
own the right of inheritance and
redemption. Buy it for yourself.'
Then I knew that this was the word
of the LORD. 9 So I bought the field
in Anathoth from my cousin Hanamel, and I weighed out the silver

^A31:38 = Jerusalem   ^B32:4 Lit *His mouth will speak with his mouth* to him — seventeen shekels A of silver. ¹⁰ I recorded it on a scroll, sealed it, called in witnesses, and weighed out the silver on the scales. ¹¹ I took the purchase agreement — the sealed copy with its terms and conditions and the open copy — ¹² and gave the purchase agreement to Baruch son of Neriah, son of Mahseiah. I did this in the sight of my cousin B Hanamel, the witnesses who had signed the purchase agreement, and all the Judeans sitting in the guard's courtyard.

¹³ "I charged Baruch in their sight, ¹⁴ 'This is what the Lord of Armies, the God of Israel, says: Take these scrolls — this purchase agreement with the sealed copy and this open copy — and put them in an earthen storage jar so they will last a long time. ¹⁵ For this is what the Lord of Armies, the God of Israel, says: Houses, fields, and vineyards will again be bought in this land.'   Jr 32:43

¹⁶ "After I had given the purchase agreement to Baruch, son of Neriah, I prayed to the Lord: ¹⁷ Oh, Lord God! You yourself made the heavens and earth by your great power and with your outstretched arm. Nothing is too difficult for you! ¹⁸ You show faithful love to thousands but lay the fathers' iniquity on their sons' laps after them, great and mighty God whose name is the Lord of Armies, ¹⁹ the one great in counsel and powerful in action. Your eyes are on all the ways of the children of men C in order to reward each person according to his ways and as the result of his actions. ²⁰ You performed signs and wonders in the land of Egypt and still do today, both in Israel and among all mankind. You made a name for yourself, as is the case today. ²¹ You brought your people Israel out of Egypt with signs and wonders, with a strong hand and an outstretched arm, and with great terror. ²² You gave them this land you swore to give to their ancestors, a land flowing with milk and honey. ²³ They entered and possessed it, but they did not obey you or live according to your instructions. They failed to perform all you commanded them to do, and so you have brought all this disaster on them. ²⁴ Look! Siege ramps have come against the city to capture it, and the city, as a result of the sword, famine, and plague, has been handed over to the Chaldeans who are fighting against it. What you have spoken has happened. Look, you can see it! ²⁵ Yet you, Lord God, have said to me, 'Purchase the field and call in witnesses' — even though the city has been handed over to the Chaldeans!"   Is 37:16; Jr 42:4

²⁶ The word of the Lord came to Jeremiah: ²⁷ "Look, I am the Lord, the God over every creature. Is anything too difficult for me? ²⁸ Therefore, this is what the Lord says: I am about to hand this city over to the Chaldeans, to Babylon's king Nebuchadnezzar, and he will capture it. ²⁹ The Chaldeans who are fighting against this city will come and set this city on fire. They will burn it, including the houses where incense has been burned to Baal on their rooftops and where drink offerings have been poured out to other gods to anger me. ³⁰ From their youth, the Israelites and Judeans have done nothing but what is evil in my sight! They have done

A 32:9 About seven ounces   B 32:12 Some Hb mss, LXX, Syr; other Hb mss read *uncle*   C 32:19 Or *Adam* nothing but anger me by the work of their hands" — this is the LORD's declaration — ³¹"for this city has caused my wrath and fury from the day it was built until now. I will therefore remove it from my presence ³² because of all the evil the Israelites and Judeans have done to anger me — they, their kings, their officials, their priests, and their prophets, the men of Judah, and the residents of Jerusalem. ³³ They have turned their backs to me and not their faces. Though I taught them time and time again, ᴬ they do not listen and receive discipline. ³⁴ They have placed their abhorrent things in the house that bears my name and have defiled it. ³⁵ They have built the high places of Baal in Ben Hinnom Valley to sacrifice their sons and daughters in the fireᴮ to Molech — something I had not commanded them. I had never entertained the thoughtᶜ that they do this detestable act causing Judah to sin!   Gn 18:4; Nm 16:22; Jr 32:3

³⁶ "Now therefore, this is what the LORD, the God of Israel, says to this city about which you said, 'It has been handed over to Babylon's king through sword, famine, and plague': ³⁷ I will certainly gather them from all the lands where I have banished them in my anger, rage and intense wrath, and I will return them to this place and make them live in safety. ³⁸ They will be my people, and I will be their God. ³⁹ I will give them integrity of heart and actionᴰ so that they will fear me always, for their good and for the good of their descendants after them.   Dt 12:10; Is 11:12; Jr 23:3; 29:14; 30:10

⁴⁰ "I will make a permanent covenant with them: I will never turn away from doing good to them, and I will put fear of me in their hearts so they will never again turn away from me. ⁴¹ I will take delight in them to do what is good for them, and with all my heart and mind I will faithfully plant them in this land.   Gn 17:7,13,19; Is 55:3; 61:8; Jr 50:5; Ezk 16:60

⁴² "For this is what the LORD says: Just as I have brought all this terrible disaster on these people, so am I about to bring on them all the good I am promising them. ⁴³ Fields will be bought in this land about which you are saying, 'It's a desolation without people or animals; it has been handed over to the Chaldeans!' ⁴⁴ Fields will be purchased, the transaction written on a scroll and sealed, and witnesses will be called on in the land of Benjamin, in the areas surrounding Jerusalem, and in Judah's cities — the cities of the hill country, the cities of the Judean foothills, and the cities of the Negev — because I will restore their fortunes."ᴱ   Jr 32:15; 31:28

This is

the LORD's declaration.

Israel's Restoration

33 While he was still confined in the guard's courtyard, the word of the LORD came to Jeremiah a second time: ² "The LORD who made the earth,ᶠ the LORD who forms it to establish it, the LORD is his name, says this: ³ Call to me and I will answer you and tell you great and incomprehensible things you do not know. ⁴ For this is what the LORD, the God of

---

ᴬ**32:33** Lit them, rising up early and teaching   ᴮ**32:35** Lit to make their sons and daughters pass through the fire   ᶜ**32:35** Lit them, and it did not arise on my heart   ᴰ**32:39** Lit give them one heart and one way   ᴱ**32:44** Or will end their captivity   ᶠ**33:2** LXX; MT reads made it

Israel, says concerning the houses of this city and the palaces of Judah's kings, the ones torn down for defense against the assault ramps and the sword: ⁵ The people coming to fight the Chaldeans will fill the houses with the corpses of their own men that I strike down in my wrath and rage. I have hidden my face from this city because of all their evil. ⁶ Yet I will certainly bring health and healing to it and will indeed heal them. I will let them experience the abundance ᴬ of true peace. ⁷ I will restore the fortunes ᴮ of Judah and of Israel and will rebuild them as in former times. ⁸ I will purify them from all the iniquity they have committed against me, and I will forgive all the iniquities they have committed against me, rebelling against me. ⁹ This city will bear on my behalf a name of joy, praise, and glory before all the nations of the earth, who will hear of all the prosperity I will give them. They will tremble with awe because of all the good and all the peace I will bring about for them. Gn 2:18-19; Ex 6:3; Ps 91:15; Jr 32:2

¹⁰ "This is what the LORD says: In this place, which you say is a ruin, without people or animals — that is, in Judah's cities and Jerusalem's streets that are a desolation without people, without inhabitants, and without animals — there will be heard again ¹¹ a sound of joy and gladness, the voice of the groom and the bride, and the voice of those saying, Jr 7:34; 16:9; 25:10; 32:43

Give thanks to the LORD
    of Armies,
for the LORD is good;
    his faithful love
    endures forever

as they bring thank offerings to the temple of the LORD. For I will restore the fortunes of the land as in former times, says the LORD.

¹² "This is what the LORD of Armies says: In this desolate place — without people or animals — and in all its cities there will once more be a grazing land where shepherds may rest flocks. ¹³ The flocks will again pass under the hands of the one who counts them in the cities of the hill country, the cities of the Judean foothills, the cities of the Negev, the land of Benjamin — the areas around Jerusalem and in Judah's cities, says the LORD. Lv 27:32; Is 65:10; Ezk 34:12-15

God's Covenant with David

¹⁴ "Look, the days
        are coming" —
    this is
        the LORD's declaration —
    "when I will fulfill
        the good promise
    that I have spoken
    concerning the
        house of Israel
    and the house of Judah.
¹⁵ In those days and
        at that time
    I will cause
        a Righteous Branch   Is 4:2
    to sprout up for David,
    and he will administer justice
    and righteousness
        in the land.
¹⁶ In those days Judah
        will be saved,
    and Jerusalem
        will dwell securely,   Dt 33:12
    and this is what she
        will be named:
    The LORD
        Is Our Righteousness. ᶜ

ᴬ33:6 Or fragrance; Hb obscure   ᴮ33:7 Or will end the captivity, also in v. 11   ᶜ33:16 = Yahweh-zidkenu

17 "For this is what the LORD says: David will never fail to have a man sitting on the throne of the house of Israel. 18 The Levitical priests will never fail to have a man always before me to offer burnt offerings, to burn grain offerings, and to make sacrifices." 1Kg 2:4; 8:25; 9:5; Jr 31:36; 35:19

19 The word of the LORD came to Jeremiah: 20 "This is what the LORD says: If you can break my covenant with the day and my covenant with the night so that day and night cease to come at their regular time, 21 then also my covenant with my servant David may be broken. If that could happen, then he would not have a son reigning on his throne and the Levitical priests would not be my ministers. 22 Even as the stars of heaven cannot be counted, and the sand of the sea cannot be measured, so too I will make innumerable the descendants of my servant David and the Levites who minister to me."

23 The word of the LORD came to Jeremiah: 24 "Have you not noticed what these people have said? They say, 'The LORD has rejected the two families he had chosen.' My people are treated with contempt and no longer regarded as a nation among them. 25 This is what the LORD says: If I do not keep my covenant with the day and with the night, and if I fail to establish the fixed order of heaven and earth, 26 then I might also reject the descendants of Jacob and of my servant David. That is, I would not take rulers from his descendants to rule over the descendants of Abraham, Isaac, and Jacob. But in fact, I will restore their fortunes A and have compassion on them." Dt 7:6; 14:2; Ps 74:16-17; Jr 12:15; 30:18; 33:7

Jeremiah's Word to King Zedekiah

34 This is the word that came to Jeremiah from the LORD when King Nebuchadnezzar of Babylon, his whole army, all the kingdoms of the lands under his control, and all other peoples were fighting against Jerusalem and all its surrounding cities: 2 "This is what the LORD, the God of Israel, says: Go, speak to King Zedekiah of Judah, and tell him, 'This is what the LORD says: I am about to hand this city over to the king of Babylon, and he will burn it. 3 As for you, you will not escape from him but are certain to be captured and handed over to him. You will meet the king of Babylon eye to eye and speak face to face; B you will go to Babylon.

4 " 'Yet hear the LORD's word, King Zedekiah of Judah. This is what the LORD says concerning you: You will not die by the sword; 5 you will die peacefully. There will be a burning ceremony for you just like the burning ceremonies for your ancestors, the kings of old who came before you. "Oh, master!" will be the lament for you, for I have spoken this word. This is the LORD's declaration.' " 2Ch 16:14; 21:19

6 So the prophet Jeremiah related all these words to King Zedekiah of Judah in Jerusalem 7 while the king of Babylon's army was attacking Jerusalem and all of Judah's remaining cities — that is, Lachish and Azekah, for they were the only ones left of Judah's fortified cities.

The People and Their Slaves

8 This is the word that came to Jeremiah from the LORD after King Zedekiah made a covenant with all the

A **33:26** Or I will end their captivity   B **34:3** Lit and his mouth will speak to your mouth people who were in Jerusalem to proclaim freedom to them. ⁹ As a result, each was to let his male and female Hebrew slaves go free, and no one was to enslave his fellow Judean. ¹⁰ All the officials and people who entered into covenant to let their male and female slaves go free — in order not to enslave them any longer — obeyed and let them go free. ¹¹ Afterward, however, they changed their minds and took back their male and female slaves they had let go free and forced them to become slaves again. Lv 25:10; Is 61:1

¹² Then the word of the LORD came to Jeremiah from the LORD: ¹³ "This is what the LORD, the God of Israel, says: I made a covenant with your ancestors when I brought them out of the land of Egypt, out of the place of slavery, saying, ¹⁴ 'At the end of seven years, each of you must let his fellow Hebrew who sold himself^A to you go. He may serve you six years, but then you must let him go free from your service.' But your ancestors did not obey me or pay any attention. ¹⁵ Today you repented and did what pleased me, each of you proclaiming freedom for his neighbor. You made a covenant before me at the house that bears my name. ¹⁶ But you have changed your minds and profaned my name. Each has taken back his male and female slaves who had been let go free to go wherever they wanted, and you have again forced them to be your slaves. Jr 31:32

¹⁷ "Therefore, this is what the LORD says: You have not obeyed me by proclaiming freedom, each for his fellow Hebrew and for his neighbor. I hereby proclaim freedom for you — this is

the LORD's declaration — to the sword, to plague, and to famine! I will make you a horror to all the earth's kingdoms. ¹⁸ As for those who disobeyed my covenant, not keeping the terms of the covenant they made before me, I will treat them like the calf they cut in two in order to pass between its pieces. ¹⁹ The officials of Judah and Jerusalem, the court officials, the priests, and all the people of the land who passed between the pieces of the calf — ²⁰ all these I will hand over to their enemies, to those who intend to take their life. Their corpses will become food for the birds of the sky and for the wild animals of the land. ²¹ I will hand King Zedekiah of Judah and his officials over to their enemies, to those who intend to take their lives, to the king of Babylon's army that is withdrawing. ²² I am about to give the command — this is the LORD's declaration — and I will bring them back to this city. They will fight against it, capture it, and burn it. I will make Judah's cities a desolation, without inhabitant." Is 9:19

The Rechabites' Example

35 This is the word that came to Jeremiah from the LORD in the days of Jehoiakim son of Josiah, king of Judah: ² "Go to the house of the Rechabites, speak to them, and bring them to one of the chambers of the temple of the LORD to offer them a drink of wine." 2Kg 23:34–24:19

³ So I took Jaazaniah son of Jeremiah, son of Habazziniah, and his brothers and all his sons — the entire house of the Rechabites — ⁴ and I brought them into the temple of the LORD to a chamber

^A**34:14** Or who was sold

occupied by the sons of Hanan son of Igdaliah, a man of God, who had a chamber near the officials' chamber, which was above the chamber of Maaseiah son of Shallum the doorkeeper. ⁵ I set jars filled with wine and some cups before the sons of the house of the Rechabites and said to them, "Drink wine!"

⁶ But they replied, "We do not drink wine, for Jonadab, son of our ancestor Rechab, commanded: 'You and your descendants must never drink wine. ⁷ You must not build a house or sow seed or plant a vineyard. Those things are not for you. Rather, you must live in tents your whole life, so you may live a long time on the soil where you stay as a resident alien.' ⁸ We have obeyed Jonadab, son of our ancestor Rechab, in all he commanded us. So we haven't drunk wine our whole life — we, our wives, our sons, and our daughters. ⁹ We also have not built houses to live in and do not have vineyard, field, or seed. ¹⁰ But we have lived in tents and have obeyed and done everything our ancestor Jonadab commanded us. ¹¹ However, when King Nebuchadnezzar of Babylon marched into the land, we said, 'Come, let's go into Jerusalem to get away from the Chaldean and Aramean armies.' So we have been living in Jerusalem." Ex 20:12; 2Kg 10:15,23

¹² Then the word of the LORD came to Jeremiah: ¹³ "This is what the LORD of Armies, the God of Israel, says: Go, say to the men of Judah and the residents of Jerusalem, 'Will you not accept discipline by listening to my words? — this is the LORD's declaration. ¹⁴ The words of Jonadab, son of Rechab, have been carried out. He commanded

his descendants not to drink wine, and they have not drunk to this day because they have obeyed their ancestor's command. But I have spoken to you time and time again,^A and you have not obeyed me! ¹⁵ Time and time again^B I have sent you all my servants the prophets, proclaiming, "Turn, each one from his evil way, and correct your actions. Stop following other gods to serve them. Live in the land that I gave you and your ancestors." But you did not pay attention or obey me. ¹⁶ Yes, the sons of Jonadab son of Rechab carried out their ancestor's command he gave them, but these people have not obeyed me. ¹⁷ Therefore, this is what the LORD, the God of Armies, the God of Israel, says: I will certainly bring on Judah and on all the residents of Jerusalem all the disaster I have pronounced against them because I have spoken to them, but they have not obeyed, and I have called to them, but they did not answer.'"

¹⁸ But to the house of the Rechabites Jeremiah said, "This is what the LORD of Armies, the God of Israel, says: 'Because you have obeyed the command of your ancestor Jonadab and have kept all his commands and have done everything he commanded you, ¹⁹ this is what the LORD of Armies, the God of Israel, says: Jonadab son of Rechab will never fail to have a man to stand before me always.'" Jr 31:36; 33:18

Jeremiah Dictates a Scroll

36 In the fourth year of Jehoiakim son of Josiah, king of Judah, this word came to Jeremiah from the LORD: ² "Take a scroll, and write on it all the words I have

^A 35:14 Lit *you, rising up early and speaking*   ^B 35:15 Lit *Rising up early and sending* spoken to you concerning Israel, Judah, and all the nations from the time I first spoke to you during Josiah's reign until today. [3] Perhaps when the house of Judah hears about all the disaster I am planning to bring on them, each one of them will turn from his evil way. Then I will forgive their iniquity and their sin." Jr 25:1; 45:1; 46:2; Ps 40:7

[4] So Jeremiah summoned Baruch son of Neriah. At Jeremiah's dictation, [A] Baruch wrote on a scroll all the words the LORD had spoken to Jeremiah. [5] Then Jeremiah commanded Baruch, "I am restricted; I cannot enter the temple of the LORD, [6] so you must go and read from the scroll — which you wrote at my dictation [B] — the words of the LORD in the hearing of the people at the temple of the LORD on a day of fasting. Read his words in the hearing of all the Judeans who are coming from their cities. [7] Perhaps their petition will come before the LORD, and each one will turn from his evil way, for the anger and fury that the LORD has pronounced against this people are intense." [8] So Baruch son of Neriah did everything the prophet Jeremiah had commanded him. At the LORD's temple he read the LORD's words from the scroll. Jr 32:12-16; 45:1-2

Baruch Reads the Scroll

[9] In the fifth year of Jehoiakim son of Josiah, king of Judah, in the ninth month, all the people of Jerusalem and all those coming in from Judah's cities into Jerusalem proclaimed a fast before the LORD. [10] Then at the LORD's temple, in the chamber of Gemariah son of Shaphan the scribe, in the upper courtyard at the opening of the New Gate of the LORD's temple, in the hearing of all the people, Baruch read Jeremiah's words from the scroll. 2Kg 22:3-14; 2Ch 20:3; Jr 29:3; 36:22

[11] When Micaiah son of Gemariah, son of Shaphan, heard all the words of the LORD from the scroll, [12] he went down to the scribe's chamber in the king's palace. All the officials were sitting there — Elishama the scribe, Delaiah son of Shemaiah, Elnathan son of Achbor, Gemariah son of Shaphan, Zedekiah son of Hananiah, and all the other officials. [13] Micaiah reported to them all the words he had heard when Baruch read from the scroll in the hearing of the people. [14] Then all the officials sent word to Baruch through Jehudi son of Nethaniah, son of Shelemiah, son of Cushi, saying, "Bring the scroll that you read in the hearing of the people, and come." So Baruch son of Neriah took the scroll and went to them. [15] They said to him, "Sit down and read it in our hearing." So Baruch read it in their hearing. Jr 26:22

[16] When they had heard all the words, they turned to each other in fear and said to Baruch, "We must surely tell the king all these things." [17] Then they asked Baruch, "Tell us, how did you write all these words? At his dictation?" [C]

[18] Baruch said to them, "At his dictation. He recited all these words to me while I was writing on the scroll in ink."

Jehoiakim Burns the Scroll

[19] The officials said to Baruch, "You and Jeremiah must hide and tell no one where you are." [20] Then, after depositing the scroll in the

A **36:4** Lit *From Jeremiah's mouth*   B **36:6** Lit *wrote from my mouth*   C **36:17** Lit *From his mouth*, also in v. 18

chamber of Elishama the scribe, the officials came to the king at the courtyard and reported everything in the hearing of the king. ²¹ The king sent Jehudi to get the scroll, and he took it from the chamber of Elishama the scribe. Jehudi then read it in the hearing of the king and all the officials who were standing by the king. ²² Since it was the ninth month, the king was sitting in his winter quarters with a fire burning in front of him. ²³ As soon as Jehudi would read three or four columns, Jehoiakim would cut the scroll^A with a scribe's knife and throw the columns into the fire in the hearth until the entire scroll was consumed by the fire in the hearth. ²⁴ As they heard all these words, the king and all of his servants did not become terrified or tear their clothes. ²⁵ Even though Elnathan, Delaiah, and Gemariah had urged the king not to burn the scroll, he did not listen to them. ²⁶ Then the king commanded Jerahmeel the king's son, Seraiah son of Azriel, and Shelemiah son of Abdeel to seize the scribe Baruch and the prophet Jeremiah, but the LORD hid them. Jr 36:16; Am 3:15

Jeremiah Dictates Another Scroll

²⁷ After the king had burned the scroll and the words Baruch had written at Jeremiah's dictation,^B the word of the LORD came to Jeremiah: ²⁸ "Take another scroll, and once again write on it the original words that were on the original scroll that King Jehoiakim of Judah burned. ²⁹ You are to proclaim concerning King Jehoiakim of Judah, 'This is what the LORD says:

You have burned the scroll, asking, "Why have you written on it that the king of Babylon will certainly come and destroy this land and cause it to be without people or animals?" ³⁰ Therefore, this is what the LORD says concerning King Jehoiakim of Judah: He will have no one to sit on David's throne, and his corpse will be thrown out to be exposed to the heat of day and the frost of night. ³¹ I will punish him, his descendants, and his officers for their iniquity. I will bring on them, on the residents of Jerusalem, and on the people of Judah all the disaster, which I warned them about but they did not listen.' "

³² Then Jeremiah took another scroll and gave it to Baruch son of Neriah, the scribe, and he wrote on it at Jeremiah's dictation^C all the words of the scroll that Jehoiakim, Judah's king, had burned in the fire. And many other words like them were added. Jr 36:4,18

Jerusalem's Last Days

37 Zedekiah son of Josiah reigned as king in the land of Judah in place of Coniah^D son of Jehoiakim, for King Nebuchadnezzar of Babylon made him king. ² He and his officers and the people of the land did not obey the words of the LORD that he spoke through the prophet Jeremiah. 2Kg 24:17; Jr 22:24

³ Nevertheless, King Zedekiah sent Jehucal son of Shelemiah and Zephaniah son of Maaseiah, the priest, to the prophet Jeremiah, requesting, "Please pray to the LORD our God for us!" ⁴ Jeremiah was going about his daily tasks^E among the people, for he had not

---

^A**36:23** Lit *columns, he would tear it* ^B**36:27** Lit *written from Jeremiah's mouth* ^C**36:32** Lit *it from Jeremiah's mouth* ^D**37:1** = Jehoiachin ^E**37:4** Lit *was coming in and going out*

yet been put into the prison. ⁵ Pharaoh's army had left Egypt, and when the Chaldeans, who were besieging Jerusalem, heard the report, they withdrew from Jerusalem. 2Kg 25:18-21; Jr 21:1; 29:24-29; 38:1

⁶ The word of the LORD came to the prophet Jeremiah: ⁷ "This is what the LORD, the God of Israel, says: This is what you will say to Judah's king, who is sending you to inquire of me: 'Watch: Pharaoh's army, which has come out to help you, is going to return to its own land of Egypt. ⁸ The Chaldeans will then return and fight against this city. They will capture it and burn it. ⁹ This is what the LORD says: Don't deceive yourselves by saying, "The Chaldeans will leave us for good," for they will not leave. ¹⁰ Indeed, if you were to strike down the entire Chaldean army that is fighting with you, and there remained among them only the badly wounded ^A men, each in his tent, they would get up and burn this city.' " Jr 21:1-2

Jeremiah's Imprisonment

¹¹ When the Chaldean army withdrew from Jerusalem because of Pharaoh's army, ¹² Jeremiah started to leave Jerusalem to go to the land of Benjamin to claim his portion there among the people. ¹³ But when he was at the Benjamin Gate, an officer of the guard was there, whose name was Irijah son of Shelemiah, son of Hananiah, and he apprehended the prophet Jeremiah, saying, "You are defecting to the Chaldeans." Jr 32:1-15; 38:7; Zch 14:10

¹⁴ "That's a lie," Jeremiah replied. "I am not defecting to the Chaldeans!" Irijah would not listen to him but apprehended Jeremiah and

took him to the officials. ¹⁵ The officials were angry at Jeremiah and beat him and placed him in jail in the house of Jonathan the scribe, for it had been made into a prison. ¹⁶ So Jeremiah went into a cell in the dungeon and stayed there many days. Gn 40:15; Is 24:22; Jr 38:26; Zch 9:11

Jeremiah Summoned by Zedekiah

¹⁷ King Zedekiah later sent for him and received him, and in his house privately asked him, "Is there a word from the LORD?" Jr 38:14-16

"There is," Jeremiah responded. He continued, "You will be handed over to the king of Babylon." ¹⁸ Then Jeremiah said to King Zedekiah, "How have I sinned against you or your servants or these people that you have put me in prison? ¹⁹ Where are your prophets who prophesied to you, claiming, 'The king of Babylon will not come against you and this land'? ²⁰ So now please listen, my lord the king. May my petition come before you. Don't send me back to the house of Jonathan the scribe, or I will die there." Jr 21:7

²¹ So King Zedekiah gave orders, and Jeremiah was placed in the guard's courtyard. He was given a loaf of bread each day from the bakers' street until all the bread was gone from the city. So Jeremiah remained in the guard's courtyard.

Jeremiah Thrown into a Cistern

38 Now Shephatiah son of Mattan, Gedaliah son of Pashhur, Jucal ^B son of Shelemiah, and Pashhur son of Malchijah heard the words Jeremiah was speaking to all the people: ² "This is what the LORD says: 'Whoever stays in this

^A 37:10 Lit the pierced　^B 38:1 = Jehucal in Jr 37:3

city will die by the sword, famine, and plague, but whoever surrenders to the Chaldeans will live. He will retain his life like the spoils of war and will live.' ³ This is what the LORD says: 'This city will most certainly be handed over to the king of Babylon's army, and he will capture it.'" Jr 14:12; 21:9; 24:10; 27:8; 29:17-18; 37:3

⁴ The officials then said to the king, "This man ought to die, because he is weakening the morale ᴬ of the warriors who remain in this city and of all the people by speaking to them in this way. This man is not pursuing the welfare of this people, but their harm." Jr 29:11

⁵ King Zedekiah said, "Here he is; he's in your hands since the king can't do anything against you." ⁶ So they took Jeremiah and dropped him into the cistern of Malchiah the king's son, which was in the guard's courtyard, lowering Jeremiah with ropes. There was no water in the cistern, only mud, and Jeremiah sank in the mud.

⁷ But Ebed-melech, a Cushite court official in the king's palace, heard Jeremiah had been put into the cistern. While the king was sitting at the Benjamin Gate, ⁸ Ebed-melech went from the king's palace and spoke to the king: ⁹ "My lord the king, these men have been evil in all they have done to the prophet Jeremiah. They have dropped him into the cistern where he will die from hunger, because there is no more bread in the city." Jr 20:2; 37:21

¹⁰ So the king commanded Ebed-melech, the Cushite, "Take from here thirty men under your authority ᴮ and pull the prophet Jeremiah up from the cistern before he dies."

¹¹ So Ebed-melech took the men under his authority ᶜ and went to the king's palace to a place below the storehouse. ᴰ From there he took old rags and worn-out clothes and lowered them by ropes to Jeremiah in the cistern. ¹² Ebed-melech the Cushite called down to Jeremiah, "Place these old rags and clothes between your armpits and the ropes." Jeremiah did this. ¹³ They pulled him up with the ropes and lifted him out of the cistern, but he remained in the guard's courtyard.

Zedekiah's Final Meeting with Jeremiah

¹⁴ King Zedekiah sent for the prophet Jeremiah and received him at the third entrance of the LORD's temple. The king said to Jeremiah, "I am going to ask you something; don't hide anything from me."

¹⁵ Jeremiah replied to Zedekiah, "If I tell you, you will kill me, won't you? Besides, if I give you advice, you won't listen to me anyway."

¹⁶ King Zedekiah swore to Jeremiah in private, "As the LORD lives, who has given us this life, I will not kill you or hand you over to these men who intend to take your life."

¹⁷ Jeremiah therefore said to Zedekiah, "This is what the LORD, the God of Armies, the God of Israel, says: 'If indeed you surrender to the officials of the king of Babylon, then you will live, this city will not be burned, and you and your household will survive. ¹⁸ But if you do not surrender to the officials of the king of Babylon, then this city will be handed over to the Chaldeans. They will burn it, and you yourself will not escape from them.'" 2Kg 24:12; Jr 22:25; 27:12; 38:2; 39:3

ᴬ38:4 Lit hands   ᴮ38:10 Lit men in your hand   ᶜ38:11 Lit men in his hand   ᴰ38:11 Or treasury

¹⁹ But King Zedekiah said to Jeremiah, "I am worried about the Judeans who have defected to the Chaldeans. They may hand me over to the Judeans to abuse me."

²⁰ "They will not hand you over," Jeremiah replied. "Obey the LORD in what I am telling you, so it may go well for you and you can live. ²¹ But if you refuse to surrender, this is the verdict ᴬ that the LORD has shown me: ²² 'All the women ᴮ who remain in the palace of Judah's king will be brought out to the officials of the king of Babylon and will say to you, ᶜ

"Your trusted friends ᴰ
    misled ᴱ you
and overcame you.
Your feet sank into the mire,
    and they deserted you."

²³ All your wives and children will be brought out to the Chaldeans. You yourself will not escape from them, for you will be seized by the king of Babylon and this city will burn.'" Jr 39:6; 41:10

²⁴ Then Zedekiah warned Jeremiah, "Don't let anyone know about this conversation ᶠ or you will die. ²⁵ The officials may hear that I have spoken with you and come and demand of you, 'Tell us what you said to the king; don't hide anything from us and we won't kill you. Also, what did the king say to you?' ²⁶ If they do, tell them, 'I was bringing before the king my petition that he not return me to the house of Jonathan to die there.'" ²⁷ All the officials did come to Jeremiah, and they questioned him. He reported the exact words to them the king had commanded, and they quit speaking with him because the conversation ᴳ had not been overheard. ²⁸ Jeremiah remained in the guard's courtyard until the day Jerusalem was captured, and he was there when it happened. ᴴ Jr 38:4-6

The Fall of Jerusalem to Babylon

39 In the ninth year of King Zedekiah of Judah, in the tenth month, King Nebuchadnezzar of Babylon advanced against Jerusalem with his entire army and laid siege to it. ² In the fourth month of Zedekiah's eleventh year, on the ninth day of the month, the city was broken into. ³ All the officials of the king of Babylon entered and sat at the Middle Gate: Nergal-sharezer, Samgar, Nebusarsechim ᴵ the chief of staff, Nergal-sharezer the chief soothsayer, and all the rest of the officials of Babylon's king.

⁴ When King Zedekiah of Judah and all the fighting men saw them, they fled. They left the city at night by way of the king's garden through the city gate between the two walls. They left along the route to the Arabah. ⁵ However, the Chaldean army pursued them and overtook Zedekiah in the plains of Jericho. They arrested him and brought him up to Nebuchadnezzar, Babylon's king, at Riblah in the land of Hamath. The king passed sentence on him there. Dt 2:8; Neh 3:15

⁶ At Riblah the king of Babylon slaughtered Zedekiah's sons before his eyes, and he also slaughtered all Judah's nobles. ⁷ Then he blinded Zedekiah and put him in bronze chains to take him to Babylon. ⁸ The Chaldeans next burned down the

ᴬ38:21 Or *promise*; lit *word*   ᴮ38:22 Or *wives*   ᶜ38:22 *to you* supplied for clarity   ᴰ38:22 Lit *"The men of your peace*   ᴱ38:22 Or *incited*   ᶠ38:24 Lit *about these words*   ᴳ38:27 Lit *word*   ᴴ38:28 Or *captured. This is what happened when Jerusalem was captured:*   ᴵ39:3 LXX; MT reads *Samgar-nebu, Sarsechim* king's palace and the people's houses and tore down the walls of Jerusalem. ⁹ Nebuzaradan, the captain of the guards, deported the rest of the people to Babylon — those who had remained in the city and those deserters who had defected to him along with the rest of the people who remained. ¹⁰ However, Nebuzaradan, the captain of the guards, left in the land of Judah some of the poor people who owned nothing, and he gave them vineyards and fields at that time.

Jeremiah Freed by Nebuchadnezzar

¹¹ Speaking through Nebuzaradan, captain of the guards, King Nebuchadnezzar of Babylon gave orders concerning Jeremiah: ¹² "Take him and look after him. Don't do him any harm, but do for him whatever he says." ¹³ Nebuzaradan, captain of the guards, Nebushazban the chief of staff, Nergal-sharezer the chief soothsayer, and all the captains of Babylon's king ¹⁴ had Jeremiah brought from the guard's courtyard and turned him over to Gedaliah son of Ahikam, son of Shaphan, to take him home. So he settled among his own people.

¹⁵ Now the word of the LORD had come to Jeremiah when he was confined in the guard's courtyard: ¹⁶ "Go tell Ebed-melech the Cushite, 'This is what the LORD of Armies, the God of Israel, says: I am about to fulfill my words for disaster and not for good against this city. They will take place before your eyes on that day. ¹⁷ But I will rescue you on that day — this is the LORD's declaration — and you will

not be handed over to the men you dread. ¹⁸ Indeed, I will certainly deliver you so that you do not fall by the sword. Because you have trusted in me, you will retain your life like the spoils of war. This is the LORD's declaration.'"   Jr 33:1; 38:1-13

Jeremiah Stays in Judah

40 This is the word that came to Jeremiah from the LORD after Nebuzaradan, captain of the guards, released him at Ramah. When he found him, he was bound in chains with all the exiles of Jerusalem and Judah who were being exiled to Babylon. ² The captain of the guards took Jeremiah and said to him, "The LORD your God decreed this disaster on this place, ³ and the LORD has fulfilled it. He has done just what he decreed. Because you people have sinned against the LORD and have not obeyed him, this thing has happened. ⁴ Now pay attention: Today I am setting you free from the chains that were on your hands. If it pleases you to come with me to Babylon, come, and I will take care of you. But if it seems wrong to you to come with me to Babylon, go no farther. ᴬ Look — the whole land is in front of you. Wherever it seems good and right for you to go, go there." ⁵ When Jeremiah had not yet turned to go, Nebuzaradan said to him, ᴮ "Return ᶜ to Gedaliah son of Ahikam, son of Shaphan, whom the king of Babylon has appointed over the cities of Judah, and stay with him among the people or go wherever it seems right for you to go." So the captain of the guards gave him a ration and a gift and

---

ᴬ40:4 Lit Babylon, stop   ᴮ40:5 Nebuzaradan said to him supplied for clarity   ᶜ40:5 LXX reads "But if not, run, return; Hb obscure released him. ⁶ Jeremiah therefore went to Gedaliah son of Ahikam at Mizpah, and he stayed with him among the people who remained in the land. 1Kg 15:17-22; 2Ch 16:1-6; Dn 9:10-12

Gedaliah Advises Peace

⁷ All the commanders of the armies that were in the countryside — they and their men — heard that the king of Babylon had appointed Gedaliah son of Ahikam over the land. He had been put in charge of the men, women, and children from among the poorest of the land, who had not been deported to Babylon. ⁸ So they came to Gedaliah at Mizpah. The commanders included Ishmael son of Nethaniah, Johanan and Jonathan the sons of Kareah, Seraiah son of Tanhumeth, the sons of Ephai the Netophathite, and Jezaniah son of the Maacathite — they and their men.

⁹ Gedaliah son of Ahikam, son of Shaphan, swore an oath to them and their men, assuring them, "Don't be afraid to serve the Chaldeans. Live in the land and serve the king of Babylon, and it will go well for you. ¹⁰ As for me, I am going to live in Mizpah to represent youᴬ before the Chaldeans who come to us. As for you, gather wine, summer fruit, and oil, place them in your storage jars, and live in the cities you have captured." Dt 1:38

¹¹ When all the Judeans in Moab and among the Ammonites and in Edom and in all the other lands also heard that the king of Babylon had left a remnant in Judah and had appointed Gedaliah son of Ahikam, son of Shaphan, over them, ¹² they all returned from all the places where they had been banished and came to the land of Judah, to Gedaliah at Mizpah, and harvested a great amount of wine and summer fruit. Nm 22:1; 1Sm 11:1; 12:12

¹³ Meanwhile, Johanan son of Kareah and all the commanders of the armies in the countryside came to Gedaliah at Mizpah ¹⁴ and warned him, "Don't you realize that Baalis, king of the Ammonites, has sent Ishmael son of Nethaniah to kill you?" But Gedaliah son of Ahikam would not believe them. ¹⁵ Then Johanan son of Kareah suggested to Gedaliah in private at Mizpah, "Let me go kill Ishmael son of Nethaniah. No one will know it. Why should he kill you and allow all of Judah that has gathered around you to scatter and the remnant of Judah to perish?" Jr 40:13-16; 41:10; 42:2

¹⁶ But Gedaliah son of Ahikam responded to Johanan son of Kareah, "Don't do that! What you're saying about Ishmael is a lie."

Gedaliah Assassinated by Ishmael

41 In the seventh month, Ishmael son of Nethaniah, son of Elishama, of the royal family and one of the king's chief officers, came with ten men to Gedaliah son of Ahikam at Mizpah. They ate a meal together there in Mizpah, ² but then Ishmael son of Nethaniah and the ten men who were with him got up and struck down Gedaliah son of Ahikam, son of Shaphan, with the sword; he killed the one the king of Babylon had appointed in the land. ³ Ishmael also struck down all the Judeans who were with Gedaliah at Mizpah, as well as the Chaldean soldiers who were there. 2Kg 25:25; Jr 52:30

ᴬ**40:10** Lit *to stand*

⁴ On the day after he had killed Gedaliah, when no one knew yet, ⁵ eighty men came from Shechem, Shiloh, and Samaria who had shaved their beards, torn their clothes, and gashed themselves, and who were carrying grain and incense offerings to bring to the temple of the LORD. ⁶ Ishmael son of Nethaniah came out of Mizpah to meet them, weeping as he came. When he encountered them, he said, "Come to Gedaliah son of Ahikam!" ⁷ But when they came into the city, Ishmael son of Nethaniah and the men with him slaughtered them and threw them into^A a cistern.

⁸ However, there were ten men among them who said to Ishmael, "Don't kill us, for we have hidden treasure in the field — wheat, barley, oil, and honey!" So he stopped and did not kill them along with their companions. ⁹ Now the cistern where Ishmael had thrown all the corpses of the men he had struck down was a large one^B that King Asa had made in the encounter with King Baasha of Israel. Ishmael son of Nethaniah filled it with the slain.   1Kg 15:16-22

¹⁰ Then Ishmael took captive all the rest of the people of Mizpah including the daughters of the king — all those who remained in Mizpah over whom Nebuzaradan, captain of the guards, had appointed Gedaliah son of Ahikam. Ishmael son of Nethaniah took them captive and set off to cross over to the Ammonites.   Jr 40:14

The Captives Rescued by Johanan

¹¹ When Johanan son of Kareah and all the commanders of the armies with him heard of all the evil that Ishmael son of Nethaniah had done, ¹² they took all their men and went to fight with Ishmael son of Nethaniah. They found him by the great pool in Gibeon. ¹³ When all the people held by Ishmael saw Johanan son of Kareah and all the commanders of the army with him, they rejoiced. ¹⁴ All the people whom Ishmael had taken captive from Mizpah turned around and rejoined Johanan son of Kareah. ¹⁵ But Ishmael son of Nethaniah escaped from Johanan with eight men and went to the Ammonites. ¹⁶ Johanan son of Kareah and all the commanders of the armies with him then took from Mizpah all the remnant of the people whom he had recovered from Ishmael son of Nethaniah after Ishmael had killed Gedaliah son of Ahikam — men, soldiers, women, children, and court officials whom he brought back from Gibeon. ¹⁷ They left, stopping in Geruth Chimham, which is near Bethlehem, in order to make their way into Egypt, ¹⁸ away from the Chaldeans. For they feared them because Ishmael son of Nethaniah had struck down Gedaliah son of Ahikam, whom the king of Babylon had appointed over the land.

The People Seek Jeremiah's Counsel

42 Then all the commanders of the armies, along with Johanan son of Kareah, Jezaniah son of Hoshaiah, and all the people from the least to the greatest, approached ² the prophet Jeremiah and said, "May our petition come before you; pray to the LORD

^A **41:7** Syr; MT reads *slaughtered them in*   ^B **41:9** LXX; MT reads *down by the hand of Gedaliah* your God on our behalf, on behalf of this entire remnant (for few of us remain out of the many, as you can see with your own eyes), ³ that the LORD your God may tell us the way we should go and the thing we should do." Est 1:20; Jr 6:13; 40:13; 41:11

⁴ So the prophet Jeremiah said to them, "I have heard. I will now pray to the LORD your God according to your words, and I will tell you every word that the LORD answers you; I won't withhold a word from you."

⁵ And they said to Jeremiah, "May the LORD be a true and faithful witness against us if we don't act according to every word the LORD your God sends you to tell us. ⁶ Whether it is pleasant or unpleasant, we will obey the LORD our God to whom we are sending you so that it may go well with us. We will certainly obey the LORD our God!"

Jeremiah's Advice to Stay

⁷ At the end of ten days, the word of the LORD came to Jeremiah, ⁸ and he summoned Johanan son of Kareah, all the commanders of the armies who were with him, and all the people from the least to the greatest. ⁹ He said to them, "This is what the LORD says, the God of Israel to whom you sent me to bring your petition before him: ¹⁰ 'If you will indeed stay in this land, then I will rebuild and not demolish you, and I will plant and not uproot you, because I relent concerning the disaster that I have brought on you. ¹¹ Don't be afraid of the king of Babylon whom you now fear; don't be afraid of him' — this is the LORD's declaration — 'because I am with you to save you and rescue you

from him. ¹² I will grant you compassion, and heᴬ will have compassion on you and allow you to return to your own soil.' Jr 18:8; 24:6

¹³ "But if you say, 'We will not stay in this land,' in order to disobey the LORD your God, ¹⁴ and if you say, 'No, instead we'll go to the land of Egypt where we will not see war or hear the sound of the ram's horn or hunger for food, and we'll live there,' ¹⁵ then hear the word of the LORD, remnant of Judah! This is what the LORD of Armies, the God of Israel, says: 'If you are firmly resolved to go to Egypt and stay there for a while, ¹⁶ then the sword you fear will overtake you there in the land of Egypt, and the famine you are worried about will follow on your heelsᴮ there to Egypt, and you will die there. ¹⁷ All who resolve to go to Egypt to stay there for a while will die by the sword, famine, and plague. They will have no survivor or fugitive from the disaster I will bring on them.' Jr 4:19,21; 41:17; 44:16-17

¹⁸ "For this is what the LORD of Armies, the God of Israel, says: 'Just as my anger and fury were poured out on Jerusalem's residents, so will my fury pour out on you if you go to Egypt. You will become an example for cursing, scorn, execration, and disgrace, and you will never see this place again.' ¹⁹ The LORD has spoken concerning you, remnant of Judah: 'Don't go to Egypt.' Know for certain that I have warned you today! ²⁰ You have gone astray at the cost of your livesᶜ because you are the ones who sent me to the LORD your God, saying, 'Pray to the LORD our God on our behalf, and as for all that the LORD our God says, tell it to us, and we'll act

ᴬ**42:12** LXX reads *I*   ᴮ**42:16** Lit *will cling after you*   ᶜ**42:20** Or *You have led your own selves astray* accordingly.' ²¹ For I have told you today, but you have not obeyed the LORD your God in everything he has sent me to tell you. ²² Now therefore, know for certain that by the sword, famine, and plague you will die in the place where you desired to go to stay for a while."   Jr 7:20

Jeremiah's Counsel Rejected

43 When Jeremiah had finished speaking to all the people all the words of the LORD their God — all these words the LORD their God had sent him to give them — ² then Azariah^A son of Hoshaiah, Johanan son of Kareah, and all the other arrogant men responded to Jeremiah, "You are speaking a lie! The LORD our God has not sent you to say, 'You must not go to Egypt to stay there for a while!' ³ Rather, Baruch son of Neriah is inciting you against us to hand us over to the Chaldeans to put us to death or to deport us to Babylon!"   Jr 42:1

⁴ So Johanan son of Kareah, all the commanders of the armies, and all the people failed to obey the LORD's command to stay in the land of Judah. ⁵ Instead, Johanan son of Kareah and all the commanders of the armies led away the whole remnant of Judah, those who had returned to stay in the land of Judah from all the nations where they had been banished. ⁶ They led away the men, women, children, king's daughters, and everyone whom Nebuzaradan, captain of the guards, had allowed to remain with Gedaliah son of Ahikam son of Shaphan. They also led the prophet Jeremiah and Baruch son of Neriah away. ⁷ They went to the land of Egypt because they did not obey the LORD. They went as far as Tahpanhes.   Jr 39:10; 40:7,11-12; 44:1

God's Sign to the People in Egypt

⁸ Then the word of the LORD came to Jeremiah at Tahpanhes: ⁹ "Pick up some large stones and set them in the mortar of the brick pavement that is at the opening of Pharaoh's palace at Tahpanhes. Do this in the sight of the Judean men ¹⁰ and tell them, 'This is what the LORD of Armies, the God of Israel, says: I will send for my servant Nebuchadnezzar king of Babylon, and I will place his throne on these stones that I have embedded, and he will pitch his pavilion over them. ¹¹ He will come and strike down the land of Egypt — those destined for death, to death; those destined for captivity, to captivity; and those destined for the sword, to the sword. ¹² I^B will kindle a fire in the temples of Egypt's gods, and he will burn them and take them captive. He will clean the land of Egypt as a shepherd picks lice off^C his clothes, and he will leave there unscathed. ¹³ He will smash the sacred pillars of the sun temple^D,E in the land of Egypt and burn the temples of the Egyptian gods.'"   Jr 15:2; 44:13; 46:13-26

God's Judgment Against His People in Egypt

44 This is the word that came to Jeremiah for all the Jews living in the land of Egypt — at Migdol, Tahpanhes, Memphis, and in the land of Pathros: ² "This is what the LORD of Armies, the God of Israel, says: You have seen all the disaster I brought against Jerusalem and all Judah's cities. Look, they are

---

^A43:2 = Jezaniah   ^B43:12 LXX, Syr, Vg read *He*   ^C43:12 Or *will wrap himself in the land of Egypt as a shepherd wraps himself in*   ^D43:13 Or *Beth-shemesh*   ^E43:13 = of Heliopolis a ruin today without an inhabitant in them. ³ because of the evil they committed to anger me, by going and burning incense to serve other gods that they, you, and your fathers did not know. ⁴ So I sent you all my servants the prophets time and time again, ᴬ saying, 'Don't commit this detestable action that I hate.' ⁵ But they did not listen or pay attention; they did not turn from their evil or stop burning incense to other gods. ⁶ So my fierce wrath poured out and burned in Judah's cities and Jerusalem's streets so that they became the desolate ruin they are today. Ex 14:2; Nm 33:7; Jr 46:14

⁷ "So now, this is what the LORD, the God of Armies, the God of Israel, says: Why are you doing such terrible harm to yourselves? You are cutting off man and woman, infant and nursing baby from Judah, leaving yourselves without a remnant. ⁸ You are angering me by the work of your hands. You are burning incense to other gods in the land of Egypt where you have gone to stay for a while. As a result, you will be cut off and become an example for cursing and insult among all the nations of earth. ⁹ Have you forgotten the evils of your fathers, the evils of Judah's kings, the evils of their wives, your own evils, and the evils of your wives that were committed in the land of Judah and in the streets of Jerusalem? ¹⁰ They have not become humble to this day, and they have not feared or followed my instruction or my statutes that I set before you and your ancestors. 1Sm 15:3; 22:19; Jr 11:23; 40:15; 44:15

¹¹ "Therefore, this is what the LORD of Armies, the God of Israel, says: I am about to set my face against you to bring disaster, to cut off all Judah. ¹² And I will take away the remnant of Judah, those who have set their face to go to the land of Egypt to stay there. All of them will meet their end in the land of Egypt. They will fall by the sword; they will meet their end by famine. From the least to the greatest, they will die by the sword and by famine. Then they will become an example for cursing, scorn, execration, and disgrace. ¹³ I will punish those living in the land of Egypt just as I punished Jerusalem by sword, famine, and plague. ¹⁴ Then the remnant of Judah — those going to live for a while there in the land of Egypt — will have no fugitive or survivor to return to the land of Judah where they are longing ᴮ to return to stay, for they will not return except for a few fugitives." 1Sm 20:15; Is 10:7; Jr 21:10

The People's Stubborn Response

¹⁵ However, all the men who knew that their wives were burning incense to other gods, all the women standing by — a great assembly — and all the people who were living in the land of Egypt at Pathros answered Jeremiah, ¹⁶ "As for the word you spoke to us in the name of the LORD, we are not going to listen to you! ¹⁷ Instead, we will do everything we promised: ᶜ we will burn incense to the queen of heaven ᴰ and offer drink offerings to her just as we, our fathers, our kings, and our officials did in Judah's cities and in Jerusalem's streets. Then we had enough food, we were well off, and we saw no disaster, ¹⁸ but from the time we ceased to burn incense

ᴬ44:4 Lit prophets, rising up early and sending   ᴮ44:14 Lit lifting up their soul   ᶜ44:17 Lit do every word that came from our mouth   ᴰ44:17 = Ashtoreth, or Astarte to the queen of heaven and to offer her drink offerings, we have lacked everything, and through sword and famine we have met our end."

¹⁹ And the women said,^A "When we burned incense to the queen of heaven and poured out drink offerings to her, was it apart from our husbands' knowledge that we made sacrificial cakes in her image and poured out drink offerings to her?"   Nm 30:6-7

²⁰ But Jeremiah responded to all the people — the men, women, and all the people who were answering him: ²¹ "As for the incense you burned in Judah's cities and in Jerusalem's streets — you, your fathers, your kings, your officials, and the people of the land — did the Lord not remember them? He brought this to mind. ²² The Lord can no longer bear your evil deeds and the detestable acts you have committed, so your land has become a waste, a desolation, and an example for cursing, without inhabitant, as you see today. ²³ Because you burned incense and sinned against the Lord and didn't obey the Lord and didn't follow his instruction, his statutes, and his testimonies, this disaster has come to you, as you see today."

²⁴ Then Jeremiah said to all the people, including all the women, "Hear the word of the Lord, all you people of Judah who are in the land of Egypt. ²⁵ This is what the Lord of Armies, the God of Israel, says: 'As for you and your wives, you women have spoken with your mouths, and you men fulfilled it by your deeds, saying, "We will keep our vows that we have made to burn incense to the queen of heaven and

to pour out drink offerings for her." Go ahead, confirm your vows! Keep your vows!'   Jr 43:7

²⁶ "Therefore, hear the word of the Lord, all you Judeans who live in the land of Egypt: 'I have sworn by my great name, says the Lord, that my name will never again be invoked by anyone of Judah in all the land of Egypt, saying, "As the Lord God lives." ²⁷ I am watching over them for disaster and not for good, and everyone from Judah who is in the land of Egypt will meet his end by sword or famine until they are finished off. ²⁸ Those who escape the sword will return from the land of Egypt to the land of Judah only few in number, and the whole remnant of Judah, the ones going to the land of Egypt to stay there for a while, will know whose word stands, mine or theirs! ²⁹ This will be a sign to you' — this is the Lord's declaration — 'that I will punish you in this place, so you may know that my words of disaster concerning you will certainly come to pass. ³⁰ This is what the Lord says: I am about to hand over Pharaoh Hophra, Egypt's king, to his enemies, to those who intend to take his life, just as I handed over Judah's King Zedekiah to Babylon's King Nebuchadnezzar, who was his enemy, the one who intended to take his life.'"   Gn 22:16

The Lord's Message to Baruch

45 This is the word that the prophet Jeremiah spoke to Baruch son of Neriah when he wrote these words on a scroll at Jeremiah's dictation^B in the fourth year of Jehoiakim son of Josiah, king of Judah: ² "This is what the

---

^A 44:19 LXX, Syr; MT omits *And the women said*   ^B 45:1 Lit *scroll from Jeremiah's mouth*

LORD, the God of Israel, says to you, Baruch: ³ 'You have said, "Woe is me, because the LORD has added misery to my pain! I am worn out with ^A groaning and have found no rest."'

⁴ "This is what you are to say to him: 'This is what the LORD says: "What I have built I am about to demolish, and what I have planted I am about to uproot — the whole land! ⁵ But as for you, do you pursue great things for yourself? Stop pursuing! For I am about to bring disaster on everyone" — this is the LORD's declaration — "but I will grant you your life like the spoils of war wherever you go."'"   Jr 24:6

PROPHECIES AGAINST THE NATIONS

46 This is the word of the LORD that came to the prophet Jeremiah about the nations:

Prophecies Against Egypt

² About Egypt and the army of Pharaoh Neco, Egypt's king, which was defeated at Carchemish on the Euphrates River by King Nebuchadnezzar of Babylon in the fourth year of Judah's King Jehoiakim son of Josiah: 2Kg 23:29; 2Ch 35:20; Jr 45:1

³ Deploy small shields
   and large;   Jr 49:14; Ob 1
approach for battle!
⁴ Harness the horses;
  mount the steeds; ^B
take your positions
  with helmets on!
Polish the lances;
  put on armor!   Jb 41:13; Jr 51:3
⁵ Why have I seen this?
They are terrified,
they are retreating,
  their warriors are crushed,

they flee headlong,
they never look back,
  terror is on every side!   Jr 6:25
This is
  the LORD's declaration.
⁶ The swift cannot flee,
and the warrior
  cannot escape!   Am 2:14
In the north by the bank
  of the Euphrates River,
they stumble and fall.   Dn 11:19
⁷ Who is this,
  rising like the Nile,   Jr 47:2
with waters
  that churn like rivers?
⁸ Egypt rises like the Nile,   Am 8:8
and its waters churn
  like rivers.
He boasts, "I will go up,
I will cover the earth;
I will destroy cities
  with their residents."
⁹ Rise up, you cavalry!
Race furiously, you chariots!
Let the warriors march out —
Cush and Put,   Gn 10:6; Ezk 30:5
who are able
  to handle shields,
and the men of Lud,   Gn 10:13
who are able to handle
  and string the bow.   Is 66:19
¹⁰ That day belongs to the Lord,
  the GOD of Armies,
a day of vengeance
to avenge himself
against his adversaries.
The sword will devour
  and be satisfied;
it will drink its fill
  of their blood,
because it will be a sacrifice
to the Lord, the GOD
  of Armies,   Is 34:5-8; Ezk 39:17-20
in the northern land
  by the Euphrates River.

---

^A **45:3** Lit *I labored in my*   ^B **46:4** Or *mount up, riders*

¹¹ Go up to Gilead
     and get balm,   Gn 37:25; Jr 8:22
Virgin Daughter Egypt!
You have multiplied
     remedies in vain;
there is no healing for you.
¹² The nations have heard
     of your dishonor,   Jr 13:26; Hs 4:7
and your cries fill the earth,
because warrior stumbles
     against warrior
and together both of them
     have fallen.

¹³ This is the word the LORD spoke
to the prophet Jeremiah about the
coming of King Nebuchadnezzar of
Babylon to defeat the land of Egypt:
¹⁴ Announce it in Egypt,
     and proclaim it
     in Migdol!   Jr 2:16; 43:7-9; 44:1
Proclaim it in Memphis
     and in Tahpanhes!
Say, "Take positions!
     Prepare yourself,
for the sword devours
     all around you."   Jr 46:10
¹⁵ Why have your strong ones
     been swept away?
Each has not stood,
for the LORD
     has thrust him down.
¹⁶ He continues to stumble.
Indeed, each falls
     over the other.
They say, "Get up! Let's return
     to our people
and to our native land,
away from the oppressor's
     sword."   Jr 50:16
¹⁷ There they will cry out,
     "Pharaoh king of Egypt
     was all noise;
he let the
     opportune moment pass."

¹⁸ As I live —
     this is
     the King's declaration;
     the LORD of Armies is
     his name —   Jr 48:15; 51:57
the king of Babylon ^A
     will come like Tabor
     among the mountains
and like Carmel by the sea.
¹⁹ Get your bags ready for exile,
inhabitant of Daughter Egypt!
For Memphis will become
     a desolation,
uninhabited ruins.

²⁰ Egypt is
     a beautiful young cow,
but a horsefly from the north
     is coming against her. ^B
²¹ Even her mercenaries
     among her
are like stall-fed calves.
They too will turn back;
together they will flee;
they will not take their stand,
for the day of their calamity
     is coming on them,
the time of their punishment.
²² Egypt will hiss
     like a slithering snake, ^C
for the enemy will come
     with an army;
with axes they will come
     against her
like those who cut trees.
²³ They will cut down
     her forest —
     this is
     the LORD's declaration —
though it is dense,
for they are more numerous
     than locusts;
they cannot be counted.   Jdg 6:5
²⁴ Daughter Egypt will be
     put to shame,

^A**46:18** Lit *He*   ^B**46:20** Some Hb mss, LXX, Syr; other Hb mss read *is coming, coming*   ^C**46:22** Lit *Her sound is like a snake as it goes*

handed over
　　to a northern people.　Jr 1:15

25 The LORD of Armies, the God of Israel, says, "I am about to punish Amon, god of Thebes, along with Pharaoh, Egypt, her gods, and her kings — Pharaoh and those trusting in him. **26** I will hand them over to those who intend to take their lives — to King Nebuchadnezzar of Babylon and his officers. But after this, Egypt^A will be inhabited again as in ancient times." Jr 44:30; Ezk 30:14-16
　　This is
　　the LORD's declaration.

Reassurance for Israel

27 But you, my servant Jacob,
　　do not be afraid,　Is 41:8; 44:2
and do not
　　be discouraged, Israel,
for without fail
　　I will save you
　　from far away,
and your descendants
　　from the land
　　of their captivity!
Jacob will return
　　and have calm and quiet
with no one
　　to frighten him.
28 And you, my servant Jacob,
　　do not be afraid —
　　this is
　　the LORD's declaration —
for I will be with you.　Jr 1:8,19
I will bring destruction
　　on all the nations
where I have banished you,
but I will not
　　bring destruction on you.
I will discipline you
　　with justice,
and I will by no means
　　leave you unpunished.

Prophecies Against the Philistines

47 This is the word of the LORD that came to the prophet Jeremiah about the Philistines before Pharaoh defeated Gaza. **2** This is what the LORD says:　Jr 25:20; Am 1:6-7
　　Look, water is rising
　　　from the north　Jr 1:13; 4:6,20; 6:1
and becoming
　　an overflowing wadi.
It will overflow the land
　　and everything in it,　Is 8:7-8
the cities
　　and their inhabitants.
The people will cry out,
　　and every inhabitant
　　of the land will wail.
3 At the sound
　　of the stomping hooves
　　of his stallions,　Jdg 5:22; Jr 8:16
the rumbling of his chariots,
　　and the clatter
　　of their wheels,　Nah 3:2-3
fathers will not turn back
　　for their sons.
They will be utterly helpless^B
4 on account of the day
　　that is coming
to destroy all the Philistines,
to cut off from Tyre and Sidon
every remaining ally.　Jr 25:22
Indeed, the LORD is
　　about to destroy
　　the Philistines,
the remnant of the coastland
　　of Caphtor.^C　Gn 10:14; Am 9:7
5 Baldness is coming to Gaza;
Ashkelon will become silent.
Remnant of their valley,
　　how long will you
　　gash yourself?

6 Oh, sword of the LORD!
How long will you
　　be restless?

---

^A 46:26 Lit it　　^B 47:3 Lit Because of weakened hands　　^C 47:4 Probably Crete

Go back to your sheath;
be still; be silent!

7 How can it[A] rest
when the LORD has given it
a command?   Ezk 14:17
He has assigned it   Mc 6:9
against Ashkelon
and the shore of the sea.

Prophecies Against Moab

48 About Moab, this is what the
LORD of Armies, the God of
Israel, says: Gn 19:37; Nm 22:1; 24:17; 25:1

Woe to Nebo, because it is
about to be destroyed;
Kiriathaim will be
put to shame; it will be
taken captive.   Nm 32:37; Jr 48:23
The fortress will
be put to shame
and dismayed!

2 There is no longer praise
for Moab;
they plan harm against her
in Heshbon: Jr 48:34,45; 49:3
Come, let's cut her off
from nationhood.
Also, Madmen, you will
be silenced;
the sword will follow you.

3 A voice cries out
from Horonaim,   Is 15:5; Jr 48:34
"devastation
and a crushing blow!"

4 Moab will be shattered;
her little ones will cry out.

5 For on the Ascent to Luhith
they will be
weeping continually,[B]
and on the descent
to Horonaim
will be heard cries of distress
over the destruction: Is 15:5

6 Flee! Save your lives!   Jr 51:6,45

Be like a juniper bush[C]
in the wilderness.   Is 41:19; Jr 17:6

7 Because you trust
in your works
and treasures,
you will be captured also.
Chemosh will go into exile
with his priests and officials.

8 The destroyer will move
against every town;   Jr 6:26
not one town will escape.
The valley will perish,
and the plain
will be annihilated,
as the LORD has said.

9 Make Moab a salt marsh,[D]
for she will run away;[E]
her towns will become
a desolation,
without inhabitant.   Jos 8:26; Is 5:9

10 The one who does
the LORD's business
deceitfully[F] is cursed,
and the one who withholds
his sword from bloodshed
is cursed.

11 Moab has been left quiet
since his youth,
settled like wine
on its dregs.   Ps 75:8; Zph 1:12
He hasn't been poured
from one container
to another
or gone into exile.
So his taste has remained
the same,
and his aroma
hasn't changed.

12 Therefore look, the days
are coming —   Jr 7:32; 16:14; 19:6
this is
the LORD's declaration —

A47:7 LXX, Vg; MT reads *you*   B48:5 Lit *Luhith, weeping goes up with weeping*   C48:6 Or *like Aroer*;
Is 17:2; Jr 48:19   D48:9 LXX reads *a sign*; Vg reads *a flower*; Syr, Tg read *a crown*   E48:9 Hb obscure
F48:10 Or *negligently*

when I will send
pourers to him,
who will pour him out.
They will empty
his containers
and smash his jars.

13 Moab will be put to shame
because of Chemosh,
just as the house of Israel
was put to shame
because of Bethel
that they trusted in.

14 How can you say,
"We are warriors —
valiant men for battle"?

15 The destroyer of Moab
and its towns
has come up, [A]
and the best of its young men
have gone down to slaughter.
This is
the King's declaration;
the LORD of Armies is
his name.   Jr 46:18; 51:57

16 Moab's calamity is near
at hand;
his disaster is rushing swiftly.

17 Mourn for him,
all you surrounding nations,
everyone who knows
his name.
Say, "How the mighty scepter
is shattered,   Ps 110:2; Ezk 19:11-12,14
the glorious staff!"

18 Come down from glory;
sit on parched ground,
resident of the daughter
of Dibon,   Jos 13:8-9; Jr 46:19
for the destroyer of Moab
has come against you;
he has destroyed
your fortresses.

19 Stand by the highway
and watch,

resident of Aroer!   Dt 2:36
Ask him who is fleeing or her
who is escaping,   1Sm 4:13,16
"What happened?"

20 Moab is put to shame,
indeed dismayed.
Wail and cry out!   Is 14:31; Jr 25:34
Declare by the Arnon
that Moab is destroyed.

21 "Judgment has come to the land
of the plateau — to Holon, Jahzah,
Mephaath, 22 Dibon, Nebo, Beth-
diblathaim, 23 Kiriathaim, Beth-
gamul, Beth-meon, 24 Kerioth,
Bozrah, and all the towns of the
land of Moab, those far and near.
25 Moab's horn is chopped off; his
arm is shattered."   Jos 13:17-19
This is
the LORD's declaration.

26 "Make him drunk, because he
has exalted himself against the
LORD. Moab will wallow in his own
vomit, and he will also become a
laughingstock. 27 Wasn't Israel a
laughingstock to you? Was he ever
found among thieves? For whenever you speak of him you shake
your head."   Gn 38:23; Jb 12:4; Jr 20:7; 48:42

28 Abandon the towns!
Live in the cliffs,
residents of Moab!
Be like a dove
that nests inside the mouth
of a cave.   Is 2:19-21

29 We have heard
of Moab's pride,
great pride, indeed —
his insolence, arrogance,
pride,
and haughty heart.

30 I know his outburst.
This is
the LORD's declaration.

It is empty.
His boast is empty.
³¹ Therefore, I will wail
     over Moab.
I will cry out for Moab,
     all of it;
he will moan for the men
     of Kir-heres.
³² I will weep for you,
     vine of Sibmah,
with more than the weeping
     for Jazer.
Your tendrils have extended
     to the sea;
they have reached to the sea
     and to Jazer.^A
The destroyer has fallen
     on your summer fruit
     and grape harvest.
³³ Gladness and
     celebration are taken
     from the fertile field
and from the land of Moab.
I have stopped
     the flow of wine
     from the winepresses;
no one will tread with shouts
     of joy.
The shouting is not a shout
     of joy.   Is 16:7-10

³⁴ "There is a cry from Heshbon to Elealeh; they make their voices heard as far as Jahaz — from Zoar to Horonaim and Eglath-shelishiyah — because even the Waters of Nimrim have become desolate. ³⁵ In Moab, I will stop" — this is the LORD's declaration — "the one who offers sacrifices on the high place and burns incense to his gods. ³⁶ Therefore, my heart moans like flutes for Moab, and my heart moans like flutes for the people of Kir-heres. And therefore, the wealth he has

gained has perished. ³⁷ Indeed, every head is bald and every beard is chopped short. On every hand is a gash and sackcloth around the waist. ³⁸ On all the rooftops of Moab and in her public squares, everyone is mourning because I have shattered Moab like a jar no one wants." This is the LORD's declaration. ³⁹ "How broken it is! They wail! How Moab has turned his back! He is ashamed. Moab will become a laughingstock and a shock to all those around him."

⁴⁰ For this is what the LORD says:
Look! He will swoop down
     like an eagle
and spread his wings
     against Moab.   Dt 28:49; Jr 49:22
⁴¹ The towns
     have^B been captured,
and the strongholds seized.
In that day the heart
     of Moab's warriors
will be like the heart
     of a woman
     with contractions.   Is 13:8
⁴² Moab will be destroyed
     as a people
because he has
     exalted himself
     against the LORD.   Jr 48:26
⁴³ Panic, pit, and trap   Jr 30:5; 49:5
     await you, resident of Moab.
     This is
     the LORD's declaration.
⁴⁴ He who flees from the panic
     will fall in the pit,
and he who climbs
     from the pit
will be captured in the trap,
for I will bring against Moab
     the year
     of their punishment.
     This is
     the LORD's declaration.

^A48:32 Some Hb mss read *reached as far as Jazer*   ^B48:41 Or *Kerioth has*

⁴⁵ Those who flee
     will stand exhausted
     in Heshbon's shadow
 because fire has come out
     from Heshbon
 and a flame
     from within Sihon.
 It will devour
     Moab's forehead
 and the skull
     of the noisemakers.
⁴⁶ Woe to you, Moab!
 The people of Chemosh
     have perished
 because your sons have been
     taken captive
 and your daughters have
     gone into captivity.
⁴⁷ Yet, I will restore
     the fortunes ᴬ of Moab
     in the last days.   Jr 49:6,39
 This is
     the Lᴏʀᴅ's declaration.
 The judgment on Moab
     ends here.

Prophecies Against Ammon

49 About the Ammonites, this
     is what the Lᴏʀᴅ says: Dt 2:19
 Does Israel have no sons?
 Is he without an heir?
 Why then has Milcom ᴮ˙ᶜ
     dispossessed Gad 1Kg 11:5,7,33
 and his people settled
     in their cities?
 ² Therefore look, the days
     are coming — Jr 7:32; 16:14; 19:6
 this is
     the Lᴏʀᴅ's declaration —
 when I will make the shout
     of battle heard Jr 4:19
 against Rabbah
     of the Ammonites. Dt 3:11
 It will become
     a desolate mound,

and its surrounding villages
     will be set on fire.
 Israel will dispossess
     their dispossessors,
 says the Lᴏʀᴅ.
 ³ Wail, Heshbon, for Ai
     is devastated; Nm 21:21-25,34
 cry out, daughters of Rabbah!
 Clothe yourselves
     with sackcloth, and lament;
 run back and forth
     within your walls, ᴰ
 because Milcom will go
     into exile
 together with his priests
     and officials. Jr 48:7
 ⁴ Why do you boast
     about your valleys,
 your flowing valley, ᴱ
 you faithless daughter —
 you who trust
     in your treasures
 and say,
     "Who can attack me?"
 ⁵ Look, I am about
     to bring terror on you —
     this is the declaration
     of the Lord Gᴏᴅ
     of Armies —
 from all those around you.
 You will be banished,
     each person headlong,
 with no one to gather up
     the fugitives.
 ⁶ But after that, I will restore
     the fortunes ᶠ
     of the Ammonites. Jr 48:47
 This is
     the Lᴏʀᴅ's declaration.

Prophecies Against Edom

⁷ About Edom, this is what the Lᴏʀᴅ
 of Armies says: Gn 25:30; 32:3; 36:1
 Is there no longer wisdom
     in Teman? Gn 36:15; Ezk 25:13

ᴬ**48:47** Or *will end the captivity*   ᴮ**49:1** LXX, Syr, Vg; MT reads *Malkam*   ᶜ**49:1** = Molech   ᴰ**49:3** Or *sheep pens*   ᴱ**49:4** Or *about your strength, your ebbing strength*   ᶠ**49:6** Or *will end the captivity*, also in v. 39

Has counsel perished
from the prudent?
Has their wisdom
rotted away? Ob 8-9
8 Run! Turn back! Lie low,
residents of Dedan, Gn 25:1-3
for I will bring
Esau's calamity on him
at the time I punish him. Jr 6:15
9 If grape harvesters
came to you,
wouldn't they leave
some gleanings? Dt 24:21
Were thieves to come
in the night,
they would destroy only
what they wanted. Ob 5
10 But I will strip Esau bare;
I will uncover his secret places.
He will try to hide,
but he will be unable. Ob 3
His descendants
will be destroyed
along with his relatives
and neighbors.
He will exist no longer. Mal 1:3-4
11 Abandon your fatherless;
I will preserve them;
let your widows trust in me.

12 For this is what the LORD says:
"If those who do not deserve to
drink the cup must drink it, can
you possibly remain unpunished?
You will not remain unpunished,
for you must drink it too. 13 For by
myself I have sworn" — this is the
LORD's declaration — "Bozrah^A will
become a desolation, a disgrace, a
ruin, and an example for cursing,
and all its surrounding cities will
become ruins forever." Gn 22:16
14 I have heard an envoy
from the LORD;
a messenger has been sent
among the nations:

Assemble yourselves to come
against her.
Rise up for war!
15 I will certainly make you
insignificant
among the nations,
despised among humanity.
16 As to the terror you cause,^B
your arrogant heart
has deceived you.
You who live in the clefts
of the rock,^C
you who occupy
the mountain summit,
though you elevate your nest
like the eagles,
even from there I will bring
you down.
This is
the LORD's declaration.

17 "Edom will become a desolation.
Everyone who passes by her will
be appalled and scoff because of
all her wounds. 18 As when Sodom
and Gomorrah were overthrown
along with their neighbors," says
the LORD, "no one will live there;
no human being will stay in it even
temporarily. Dt 28:37; 2Ch 29:8
19 "Look, it will be like a lion coming from the thickets^D of the Jordan to the watered grazing land.
I will chase Edom away from her
land in a flash. I will appoint whoever is chosen for her. For who is
like me? Who will issue me a summons? Who is the shepherd who
can stand against me?" Jb 9:19; Jr 50:44
20 Therefore, hear the plans that
the LORD has drawn up against
Edom and the strategies he has
devised against the people of Teman: The flock's little lambs will
certainly be dragged away, and

^A49:13 = Edom's capital ^B49:16 Lit Your horror ^C49:16 = Petra ^D49:19 Lit pride their grazing land will be made desolate because of them. ²¹ At the sound of their fall the earth will quake; the sound of her cry will be heard at the Red Sea. ²² Look! It will be like an eagle soaring upward, then swooping down and spreading its wings over Bozrah. In that day the hearts of Edom's warriors will be like the heart of a woman with contractions.

Prophecies Against Damascus

²³ About Damascus: Is 17:1; Am 1:3
    Hamath and Arpad are
        put to shame,   2Kg 18:34
    for they have heard
        a bad report
        and are agitated,
    likeᴬ the anxious sea
        that cannot be calmed.
²⁴ Damascus has become weak;
    she has turned to run;
    panic has gripped her.
    Distress and labor pains
        have seized her
    like a woman in labor.   Is 13:8
²⁵ How can the city of praise
        not be abandoned,   Jr 33:9
    the town that brings me joy?
²⁶ Therefore, her
        young men will fall
        in her public squares;
    all the warriors will perish
        in that day.
    This is the declaration
        of the Lord of Armies.
²⁷ I will set fire to the wall
        of Damascus;
    it will consume
        Ben-hadad's citadels.   Am 1:4

Prophecies Against Kedar and Hazor

²⁸ About Kedar and the kingdoms of Hazor, which King Nebuchadnezzar

of Babylon defeated, this is what the Lord says: Gn 25:13; Ps 120:5; Is 21:16-17
    Rise up, attack Kedar,
    and destroy the people
        of the east!
²⁹ They will take their tents
        and their flocks
    along with
        their tent curtains
        and all their equipment.
    They will take their camels
        for themselves.
    They will call out to them,
    "Terror is on every side!"
³⁰ Run! Escape quickly! Lie low,
    residents of Hazor —
        this is
        the Lord's declaration —
    for King Nebuchadnezzar
        of Babylon
    has drawn up a plan
        against you;
    he has devised a strategy
        against you.
³¹ Rise up, attack a nation
        at ease,
    one living in security.
        This is
        the Lord's declaration.
    They have no doors, not even
        a gate bar;
    they live alone.   Jdg 18:7-10; Ps 73:12
³² Their camels will
        become plunder,
    and their massive herds
        of cattle will become spoil.
    I will scatter them
        to the wind
        in every direction,
    those who clip the hair on
        their temples;
    I will bring calamity on them
        across all their borders.
        This is
        the Lord's declaration.

ᴬ49:23 Lit in

33 Hazor will become
   a jackals' den, *Jr 9:11; 10:22; 51:37*
   a desolation forever.
   No one will live there;
   no human being
   will stay in it even
   temporarily. *Jr 49:18; 50:40*

Prophecies Against Elam

34 This is the word of the LORD
that came to the prophet Jeremiah about Elam[A] at the beginning
of the reign of King Zedekiah of
Judah. 35 This is what the LORD of
Armies says: *Jr 27:12; 28:1; 29:3*
   I am about to shatter
   Elam's bow, *Is 22:6*
   the source[B] of their might.
36 I will bring the four winds
   against Elam
   from the four corners
   of the heavens,
   and I will scatter them
   to all these winds.
   There will not be a nation
   to which
   Elam's banished ones
   will not go.
37 I will devastate Elam
   before their enemies,
   before those who intend
   to take their lives.
   I will bring disaster
   on them,
   my burning anger.
   This is
   the LORD's declaration.
   I will send the sword
   after them *Jr 9:16*
   until I finish them off.
38 I will set my throne in Elam,
   and I will destroy the king
   and officials from there.
   This is
   the LORD's declaration.

39 Yet, in the last days,
   I will restore the fortunes
   of Elam. *Jr 48:47; 49:6*
   This is
   the LORD's declaration.

Prophecies Against Babylon

50 This is the word the LORD
spoke about Babylon, the
land of the Chaldeans, through
the prophet Jeremiah: *Is 13:1*
2 Announce to the nations;
   proclaim and raise up
   a signal flag; *Ps 60:4; Is 5:26; 18:3*
   proclaim, and hide nothing.
   Say, "Babylon is captured;
   Bel is put to shame; *Is 46:1; Jr 51:44*
   Marduk is terrified."
   Her idols are put to shame;
   her false gods, devastated.
3 For a nation from the north
   will attack her; *Is 41:25; Jr 1:13-15*
   it will make
   her land desolate.
   No one will be living in it —
   both people and animals
   will escape.[C] *Ps 135:8; Jr 7:20; 21:6*
4 In those days
   and at that time —
   this is
   the LORD's declaration —
   the Israelites and Judeans
   will come together, *Is 11:12-13*
   weeping as they come,
   and will seek the LORD
   their God. *2Ch 11:16; 15:4; Hs 3:5*
5 They will ask about Zion,
   turning their faces
   to this road.
   They will come
   and join themselves[D]
   to the LORD
   in a permanent covenant
   that will never
   be forgotten.

A49:34 = modern Iran B49:35 Lit *first* C50:3 Lit *escape; they will walk* D50:5 LXX; MT reads *Come and join yourselves*

⁶ My people were lost sheep;
  their shepherds
      led them astray,   Jr 23:2,13
  guiding them the wrong way
      in the mountains.   Ezk 34:6
  They wandered
      from mountain to hill;
  they forgot their resting place.
⁷ Whoever found them
      devoured them.
  Their adversaries said,
      "We're not guilty;
  instead, they have sinned
      against the LORD,
  their righteous grazing land,
  the hope of their ancestors,
      the LORD."   Jr 14:8; 17:13

⁸ Escape from Babylon;   Jr 51:6
  depart from
      the Chaldeans' land.
  Be like the rams that lead
      the flock.
⁹ For I will soon stir up
      and bring against Babylon
  an assembly of great nations
      from the north country.
  They will line up
      in battle formation
      against her;   Jr 6:23; 50:14,42; 51:27
  from there she
      will be captured.
  Their arrows will be
      like a skilled ᴬ warrior
  who does not
      return empty-handed.
¹⁰ The Chaldeans will
      become plunder;
  all Babylon's plunderers
      will be fully satisfied.
      This is
      the LORD's declaration.
¹¹ Because you rejoice,
  because you celebrate —
  you who plundered
      my inheritance —

because you frolic
    like a young cow
    treading grain
and neigh like stallions,   Jr 8:16
¹² your mother will be
    utterly humiliated;   Jr 2:31; 51:47
  she who bore you will be
    put to shame.
  Look! She will lag behind
    all ᴮ the nations —
  an arid wilderness, a desert.
¹³ Because of the LORD's wrath,
  she will not be inhabited;
  she will become
    a desolation, every bit
    of her.
  Everyone who passes
    through Babylon
  will be appalled
  and scoff because of
    all her wounds.   Dt 28:37; 2Ch 29:8
¹⁴ Line up in battle formation
    around Babylon,
  all you archers!
  Shoot at her! Do not spare
    an arrow,
  for she has sinned
    against the LORD.
¹⁵ Raise a war cry against her
    on every side!
  She has thrown up her hands
    in surrender;
  her defense towers
    have fallen;
  her walls are demolished.
  Since this is
    the LORD's vengeance,   Jr 46:10
  take your vengeance on her;
  as she has done, do the same
    to her.
¹⁶ Cut off the sower
    from Babylon
  as well as him who wields
    the sickle at harvest time.
  Because of
    the oppressor's sword,

ᴬ**50:9** Some Hb mss, LXX, Syr; other Hb mss read *bereaving*   ᴮ**50:12** Lit *Look! The last of*

each will turn
to his own people,   Is 13:14
each will flee to his own land.

The Return of God's People

17 Israel is a stray lamb,
chased by lions.   Jr 2:15; 4:7
The first who devoured him
was the king of Assyria;
the last who crushed
his bones
was King Nebuchadnezzar
of Babylon.   2Kg 24:10-12; 25:1-7

18 Therefore, this is what the LORD
of Armies, the God of Israel, says:
I am about to punish the king of
Babylon and his land just as I punished the king of Assyria.   Is 10:12
19 I will return Israel
to his grazing land,   Jr 22:6; 23:3
and he will feed on Carmel
and Bashan;
he will be satisfied
in the hill country
of Ephraim and of Gilead.
20 In those days
and at that time —
this is
the LORD's declaration —
one will search
for Israel's iniquity,
but there will be none,
and for Judah's sins,
but they will not be found,
for I will forgive those I leave
as a remnant.   Nm 14:20; Jr 31:34

The Invasion of Babylon

21 Attack the land
of Merathaim,
and those living in Pekod.
Put them to the sword;
completely destroy them —
this is
the LORD's declaration —

do everything I have
commanded you.   1Kg 9:4
22 The sound of war is
in the land —   Jr 51:54-56
a crushing blow!
23 How the hammer
of the whole earth
is cut down and smashed!
What a horror Babylon
has become
among the nations!   Jr 51:41
24 Babylon, I laid a trap for you,
and you were caught,   Jr 51:31
but you did not even know it.
You were found and captured
because you pitted yourself
against the LORD.
25 The LORD opened his armory
and brought out his weapons
of wrath,   Is 13:5
because it is a task
of the Lord GOD of Armies
in the land of the Chaldeans.
26 Come against her from
the most distant places. A
Open her granaries;
pile her up like mounds
of grain
and completely destroy her.
Leave her no survivors.
27 Put all her young bulls
to the sword;
let them go down
to the slaughter.
Woe to them
because their day has come,
the time of their punishment.

The Humiliation of Babylon

28 There is a voice of fugitives
and refugees
from the land of Babylon.
The voice announces in Zion
the vengeance of the LORD
our God,
the vengeance for his temple.

A 50:26 Lit from the end

29 Summon the archers
     to Babylon,
all who string the bow;
camp all around her;
     let none escape.
Repay her according to
     her deeds;   Ps 28:4; Pr 24:12,29
just as she has done,
     do the same to her,
for she has acted arrogantly
     against the Lord,
against the Holy One
     of Israel.
30 Therefore, her young men
     will fall
in her public squares;
all the warriors will perish
     in that day.
     This is
     the Lord's declaration.
31 Look, I am against you,
     you arrogant one —
     this is the declaration of
     the Lord God of Armies —
for your day has come,
the time when I will
     punish you.
32 The arrogant will stumble
     and fall   Ps 27:2; Pr 24:16-17; Is 3:8; 8:15
with no one to pick him up.
I will set fire to his cities,
and it will
     consume everything
     around him.   Jr 21:14

The Desolation of Babylon

33 This is what the Lord of Armies
says:
     Israelites and Judeans alike
          have been oppressed.
     All their captors
          hold them fast;   2Ch 28:11; 30:9
     they refuse to release them.
34 Their Redeemer is strong;
     the Lord of Armies
          is his name.

He will fervently
     champion their cause   Pr 23:11
so that he might bring rest
     to the earth
but turmoil to those who live
     in Babylon.   Mc 4:10
35 A sword is
     over the Chaldeans —
     this is
     the Lord's declaration —
against those who live
     in Babylon,
against her officials,
     and against her sages.
36 A sword is
     against the diviners,
and they will act foolishly.
A sword is
     against her heroic warriors,
and they will be terrified.
37 A sword is
     against his horses
     and chariots
and against
     all the foreigners
          among them,   Ex 12:38; Neh 13:1-3
and they will be like women.
A sword is
     against her treasuries,
and they will be plundered.
38 A drought will come
     on her waters,
and they will be dried up.
For it is a land
     of carved images,
and they go mad because of
     terrifying things. A   Ex 15:16

39 Therefore, desert creatures B
     will live with hyenas,
and ostriches will also live
     in her.
It will never again
     be inhabited
or lived in
     through all generations.

A 50:38 Or of dreaded gods   B 50:39 Or desert demons

40 Just as God
demolished Sodom
and Gomorrah
and their neighboring
towns —   Gn 19:24-25
this is
the LORD's declaration —
so no one will live there;
no human being
will stay in it even
temporarily
as a temporary resident.

The Conquest of Babylon

41 Look! A people comes
from the north.   Jr 6:22-24; 49:24
A great nation
and many kings will be
stirred up
from the remote regions
of the earth.   Jr 6:22; 25:32; 31:8
42 They grasp bow and javelin.
They are cruel and show
no mercy.
Their voice roars like the sea,
and they ride on horses,
lined up like men
in battle formation
against you, Daughter
Babylon.
43 The king of Babylon
has heard about them;
his hands have become weak.
Distress has seized him —
pain, like a woman in labor.

44 "Look, it will be like a lion coming from the thickets^A of the Jordan to the watered grazing land. I
will chase Babylon^B away from her
land in a flash. I will appoint whoever is chosen for her. For who is
like me? Who will issue me a summons? Who is the shepherd who
can stand against me?"   Ps 10:9; 17:12

45 Therefore, hear the plans that
the LORD has drawn up against
Babylon and the strategies he
has devised against the land of
the Chaldeans: Certainly the
flock's little lambs will be dragged
away; certainly the grazing land
will be made desolate because of
them. 46 At the sound of Babylon's
conquest the earth will quake;
a cry will be heard among the
nations.   Jr 49:19-21; 51:29

God's Judgment on Babylon

51 This is what the LORD says:
I am about to rouse the
spirit of a destroyer^C
against Babylon   Jr 4:11-12; 50:9
and against the population
of Leb-qamai.^D,E
2 I will send strangers
to Babylon
who will scatter her and strip
her land bare,   Jr 15:7; Mt 3:12
for they will come
against her
from every side in the day
of disaster.
3 Don't let the archer string
his bow;
don't let him put on^F
his armor.   Jb 41:13; Jr 46:4
Don't spare her young men;
completely destroy
her entire army!
4 Those who were slain
will fall in the land
of the Chaldeans,
those who were
pierced through,
in her streets.   Jr 51:47,52
5 For Israel and Judah are not
left widowed
by their God, the LORD
of Armies,

^A 50:44 Lit pride   ^B 50:44 Lit them   ^C 51:1 Or to stir up a destructive wind   ^D 51:1 Lit heart of my
adversaries   ^E 51:1 = Chaldeans   ^F 51:3 Hb obscure

though their land is
  full of guilt
against the Holy One of Israel.

6 Leave Babylon;   Jr 50:8; Rv 18:4
save your lives, each of you!
Don't perish because of
  her guilt.
For this is the time
  of the LORD's vengeance —
he will pay her
  what she deserves.   Ps 28:4
7 Babylon was a gold cup
  in the LORD's hand,   Rv 17:4
making the whole earth
  drunk.
The nations drank her wine;
therefore, the nations
  go mad.
8 Suddenly Babylon fell
  and was shattered.
Wail for her;
get balm for her wound —
perhaps she can be healed.

9 We tried to heal Babylon,
but she could not be healed.
Abandon her!
Let each of us go
  to his own land,   Is 13:14
for her judgment extends
  to the sky
and reaches as far
  as the clouds.   Rv 18:5

10 The LORD has brought about
  our vindication;   Ps 37:6
come, let's tell in Zion
what the LORD our God
  has accomplished.   Jr 50:28

11 Sharpen the arrows!   Is 5:28
Fill the quivers!A
The LORD has roused the
  spirit
of the kings of the Medes

because his plan is aimed
  at Babylon
to destroy her,
for it is
  the LORD's vengeance,
vengeance for his temple.
12 Raise up a signal flag   Ps 60:4
against the walls of Babylon;
fortify the watch post;
set the watchmen in place;
prepare the ambush.
For the LORD
  has both planned
  and accomplished
what he has threatened
against those who live
  in Babylon.   Is 14:26; 19:12,17; 23:8
13 You who reside
  by abundant water,   Rv 17:1
rich in treasures,
your end has come,
your life thread is cut.

14 The LORD of Armies has sworn
by himself:
  I will fill you up with men
    as with locusts,
  and they will sing
    the victory song over you.

15 He made the earth
  by his power,
established the world
  by his wisdom,   Jb 38:4; Ps 93:1
and spread out the heavens
  by his understanding.   Jb 9:8
16 When he thunders,B
the waters in the heavens are
  tumultuous,   Jr 5:22; 31:35
and he causes the clouds
to rise from the ends
  of the earth.
He makes lightning
  for the rain
and brings the wind
  from his storehouses.

A 51:11 Or Grasp the shields!   B 51:16 Lit At his giving of the voice

¹⁷ Everyone is stupid
and ignorant.
Every goldsmith
is put to shame
by his carved image,
for his cast images
are a lie;   Is 41:29
there is no breath in them.
¹⁸ They are worthless, a work
to be mocked.   Jr 10:3,8
At the time
of their punishment
they will be destroyed.   Jr 6:15
¹⁹ Jacob's Portion^A is not
like these
because he is the one
who formed all things.   Is 43:1
Israel is the tribe
of his inheritance;   Dt 4:20
the LORD of Armies is
his name.   Jr 10:12-16

²⁰ You are my war club,
my weapons of war.
With you I will smash
nations;
with you I will bring
kingdoms to ruin.
²¹ With you I will smash
the horse and its rider;
with you I will smash
the chariot and its rider.
²² With you I will smash man
and woman;   2Ch 36:17; Is 13:15-18
with you I will smash
the old man and the youth;
with you I will smash
the young man
and the young woman.
²³ With you I will smash
the shepherd and his flock;
with you I will
smash the farmer
and his ox-team.^B
With you I will smash
governors and officials.

²⁴ "Before your very eyes, I will repay Babylon and all the residents
of Chaldea for all their evil they
have done in Zion." 2Sm 12:11; Is 1:7; Jr 16:9
This is
the LORD's declaration.
²⁵ Look, I am against you,
devastating mountain.
This is
the LORD's declaration.
You devastate
the whole earth.
I will stretch out my hand
against you,   Jr 15:6; Ezk 6:14; 25:7
roll you down
from the cliffs,
and turn you into
a charred mountain.
²⁶ No one will be able
to retrieve a cornerstone
or a foundation stone
from you,
because you will become
desolate forever.
This is
the LORD's declaration.

²⁷ Raise a signal flag
in the land;   Ps 60:4; Is 5:26; 18:3
blow a ram's horn
among the nations;   Jr 4:5; 6:1
set apart the nations
against her.   Jr 6:4; 22:7; 50:9
Summon kingdoms
against her —
Ararat, Minni, and Ashkenaz.
Appoint a marshal
against her;
bring up horses
like a swarm^C of locusts.
²⁸ Set apart the nations
for battle against her —
the kings of Media,
her governors
and all her officials,
and all the lands they rule.

^A 51:19 = The LORD   ^B 51:23 Lit yoke   ^C 51:27 Hb obscure

²⁹ The earth quakes
and trembles   Ps 18:7; Is 13:13
because the LORD's intentions
against Babylon stand:
to make the land of Babylon
a desolation, without
inhabitant.
³⁰ Babylon's warriors have
stopped fighting;   Jr 50:37
they sit in their strongholds.
Their might is exhausted;
they have become
like women.
Babylon's homes have been
set ablaze,
her gate bars are shattered.
³¹ Messenger races
to meet messenger,   2Ch 30:6
and herald to meet herald,
to announce to the king
of Babylon
that his city has been captured
from end to end.   Jr 50:24
³² The fords have been seized,
the marshes set on fire,
and the fighting men
are terrified.

³³ For this is what the LORD of Armies, the God of Israel, says:
Daughter Babylon is
like a threshing floor
at the time it is trampled.
In just a little while
her harvest time will come.

³⁴ "King Nebuchadnezzar
of Babylon
has devoured me;
he has crushed me.
He has set me aside
like an empty dish;
he has swallowed me
like a sea monster;   Ps 74:13
he filled his belly
with my delicacies;

he has vomited me out.^A
³⁵ Let the violence done to me
and my family be done
to Babylon,"
says the inhabitant of Zion.
"Let my blood be
on the inhabitants
of Chaldea,"
says Jerusalem.

³⁶ Therefore, this is what the LORD says:
I am about to champion
your cause   1Sm 24:15; Pr 23:11
and take vengeance
on your behalf;
I will dry up her sea
and make her fountain
run dry.
³⁷ Babylon will become a heap
of rubble,
a jackals' den,
a desolation and an object
of scorn,   2Ch 29:8; Jr 18:16; 19:8
without inhabitant.   Jr 4:7; 9:11
³⁸ They will roar together
like young lions;
they will growl
like lion cubs.
³⁹ While they are flushed
with heat, I will serve them
a feast,
and I will make them drunk
so that they celebrate.^B
Then they will fall
asleep forever
and never wake up.
This is
the LORD's declaration.
⁴⁰ I will bring them down
like lambs to the slaughter,
like rams together
with male goats.   Is 34:6

⁴¹ How Sheshach^C
has been captured,   Jr 25:26

^A**51:34** Lit *has rinsed me off*   ^B**51:39** LXX reads *pass out*   ^C**51:41** = Babylon

the praise
of the whole earth seized.
What a horror Babylon
has become
among the nations! Jr 50:23
42 The sea has risen
over Babylon; Is 8:7-8
she is covered
with its tumultuous waves.
43 Her cities have become
a desolation, Jr 50:12
an arid desert,
a land where no one lives,
where no human being even
passes through.
44 I will punish Bel in Babylon.
I will make him vomit
what he swallowed. Jb 20:15
The nations will
no longer stream to him;
even Babylon's wall will fall.

45 Come out from among her,
my people! Jr 51:6
Save your lives, each of you,
from the LORD's burning anger.
46 May you not become cowardly
and fearful
when the report
is proclaimed in the land,
for the report will come
one year,
and then another
the next year.
There will be violence
in the land
with ruler against ruler.
47 Therefore, look, the days
are coming Jr 7:32; 16:14; 19:6; 23:7
when I will punish
Babylon's carved images.
Her entire land
will suffer shame,
and all her slain will lie fallen
within her. Jr 50:12
48 Heaven and earth
and everything in them

will shout for joy
over Babylon Is 44:23; 49:13
because the destroyers
from the north Is 41:25; Jr 4:6,20
will come against her.
This is
the LORD's declaration.

49 Babylon must fall because of
the slain of Israel,
even as the slain of the
whole earth fell
because of Babylon.
50 You who have escaped
the sword, Jr 44:28
go and do not stand still!
Remember the LORD
from far away,
and let Jerusalem come
to your mind.

51 We are ashamed
because we have
heard insults. Ps 44:15
Humiliation covers
our faces
because foreigners
have entered
the holy places
of the LORD's temple. Lm 1:10

52 Therefore, look, the days
are coming —
this is
the LORD's declaration —
when I will punish
her carved images,
and the wounded will groan
throughout her land.
53 Even if Babylon
should ascend
to the heavens Gn 11:4; Is 14:12-14
and fortify her tall fortresses,
destroyers will come
against her from me.
This is
the LORD's declaration.

⁵⁴ The sound of a cry
	from Babylon! 			Jr 50:22
The sound
	of terrible destruction 	Jr 4:6
from the land
	of the Chaldeans!
⁵⁵ For the Lord is going
	to devastate Babylon;
he will silence
	her mighty voice.
Their waves roar like a
	huge torrent;
the tumult
	of their voice resounds,
⁵⁶ for a destroyer is coming
	against her,
against Babylon.
Her warriors will be captured,
	their bows shattered,
for the Lord is a God
	of retribution;
he will certainly repay.
⁵⁷ I will make her princes
	and sages drunk,
along with her governors,
	officials, and warriors.
Then they will fall
	asleep forever
and never wake up. 		Jr 51:39
	This is
	the King's declaration;
	the Lord of Armies is
	his name. 		Jr 46:18; 48:15

⁵⁸ This is what the Lord of Armies
says:
Babylon's thick walls will be
	totally demolished, 		Jr 50:15
and her high gates set ablaze.
The peoples will have
	labored for nothing; 	Hab 2:13
the nations will
	weary themselves
	only to feed the fire.

⁵⁹ This is what the prophet Jeremiah commanded Seraiah son of Neriah son of Mahseiah, the quartermaster, when he went to Babylon with King Zedekiah of Judah in the fourth year of Zedekiah's reign. ⁶⁰ Jeremiah wrote on one scroll about all the disaster that would come to Babylon; all these words were written against Babylon. 		Jr 32:12; 36:2

⁶¹ Jeremiah told Seraiah, "When you get to Babylon, see that you read all these words aloud. ⁶² Say, 'Lord, you have threatened to cut off this place so that no one will live in it — people or animals. Indeed, it will remain desolate forever.' ⁶³ When you have finished reading this scroll, tie a stone to it and throw it into the middle of the Euphrates River. ⁶⁴ Then say, 'In the same way, Babylon will sink and never rise again because of the disaster I am bringing on her. They will grow weary.'" 		1Sm 20:15; Ps 109:13

The words of Jeremiah end here.

The Fall of Jerusalem

52 Zedekiah was twenty-one years old when he became king, and he reigned eleven years in Jerusalem. His mother's name was Hamutal daughter of Jeremiah; she was from Libnah. ² Zedekiah did what was evil in the Lord's sight just as Jehoiakim had done. ³ Because of the Lord's anger, it came to the point in Jerusalem and Judah that he finally banished them from his presence. Then Zedekiah rebelled against the king of Babylon. 		2Kg 23:34–24:6; 2Ch 36:4-8

⁴ In the ninth year of Zedekiah's reign, on the tenth day of the tenth month, King Nebuchadnezzar of Babylon advanced against Jerusalem with his entire army. They laid siege to the city and built a siege

wall against it all around. 5 The city was under siege until King Zedekiah's eleventh year.

6 By the ninth day of the fourth month the famine was so severe in the city that the common people had no food. 7 Then the city was broken into, and all the warriors fled. They left the city at night by way of the city gate between the two walls near the king's garden, though the Chaldeans surrounded the city. They made their way along the route to the Arabah. 8 The Chaldean army pursued the king and overtook Zedekiah in the plains of Jericho. Zedekiah's entire army left him and scattered. 9 The Chaldeans seized the king and brought him to the king of Babylon at Riblah in the land of Hamath, and he passed sentence on him.   Dt 2:8

10 At Riblah the king of Babylon slaughtered Zedekiah's sons before his eyes, and he also slaughtered the Judean commanders. 11 Then he blinded Zedekiah and bound him with bronze chains. The king of Babylon brought Zedekiah to Babylon, where he kept him in custodyA until his dying day.   2Kg 25:1-7

12 On the tenth day of the fifth month — which was the nineteenth year of King Nebuchadnezzar, king of Babylon — Nebuzaradan, the captain of the guards, entered Jerusalem as the representative ofB the king of Babylon. 13 He burned the LORD's temple, the king's palace, all the houses of Jerusalem; he burned down all the great houses. 14 The whole Chaldean army with the captain of the guards tore down all the walls surrounding Jerusalem. 15 Nebuzaradan, the captain of the guards, deported some of the poorest of the people, as well as the rest of the people who remained in the city, the deserters who had defected to the king of Babylon, and the rest of the craftsmen. 16 But Nebuzaradan, the captain of the guards, left some of the poorest of the land to be vinedressers and farmers.   2Kg 25:8-12; 2Ch 36:19

17 Now the Chaldeans broke into pieces the bronze pillars for the LORD's temple and the water carts and the bronze basinC that were in the LORD's temple, and they carried all the bronze to Babylon. 18 They also took the pots, shovels, wick trimmers, sprinkling basins, dishes, and all the bronze articles used in the temple service. 19 The captain of the guards took away the bowls, firepans, sprinkling basins, pots, lampstands, pans, and drink offering bowls — whatever was gold or silver.   Ex 25:29; 37:16; 1Kg 7:23,27

20 As for the two pillars, the one basin, with the twelve bronze oxen under it, and the water cartsD that King Solomon had made for the LORD's temple, the weight of the bronze of all these articles was beyond measure. 21 One pillar was 27 feetE tall, had a circumference of 18 feet,F was hollow — four fingers thick — 22 and had a bronze capital on top of it. One capital, encircled by bronze grating and pomegranates, stood 7 1/2 feetG high. The second pillar was the same, with pomegranates. 23 Each capital had ninety-six pomegranates

---

A52:11 Lit in a house of guards   B52:12 Lit Jerusalem; he stood before   C52:17 Lit sea   D52:20 LXX, Syr; MT reads oxen under the water carts   E52:21 Lit 18 cubits   F52:21 Lit 12 cubits   G52:22 Lit five cubits all around it. All the pomegranates around the grating numbered one hundred. 1Kg 7:16-20,41-42; 2Ch 4:12-13

²⁴ The captain of the guards also took away Seraiah the chief priest, Zephaniah the priest of the second rank, and the three doorkeepers. ²⁵ From the city he took a court official[A] who had been appointed over the warriors; seven trusted royal aides[B] found in the city; the secretary of the commander of the army, who enlisted the people of the land for military duty; and sixty men from the common people[C] who were found within the city. ²⁶ Nebuzaradan, the captain of the guards, took them and brought them to the king of Babylon at Riblah. ²⁷ The king of Babylon put them to death at Riblah in the land of Hamath. So Judah went into exile from its land. 2Kg 25:13-21

²⁸ These are the people Nebuchadnezzar deported: in the seventh year, 3,023 Jews; ²⁹ in his eighteenth year,[D] 832 people from Jerusalem; ³⁰ in Nebuchadnezzar's twenty-third year, Nebuzaradan, the captain of the guards, deported 745 Jews. Altogether, 4,600 people were deported. 2Kg 24:12-16

Jehoiachin Pardoned

³¹ On the twenty-fifth day of the twelfth month of the thirty-seventh year of the exile of Judah's King Jehoiachin, King Evil-merodach of Babylon, in the first year of his reign, pardoned King Jehoiachin of Judah and released him from prison. ³² He spoke kindly to him and set his throne above the thrones of the kings who were with him in Babylon. ³³ So Jehoiachin changed his prison clothes, and he dined regularly in the presence of the king of Babylon for the rest of his life. ³⁴ As for his allowance, a regular allowance was given to him by the king of Babylon, a portion for each day until the day of his death, for the rest of his life. 2Kg 25:27-30

A 52:25 Or a eunuch   B 52:25 Lit seven men who look on the king's face   C 52:25 Lit the people of the land   D 52:29 Some Hb mss, Syr add he deported

LAMENTATIONS

Lament over Jerusalem

א Aleph

1 How[A] she sits alone,　Lm 3:28
the city once crowded
　with people!　Lm 1:17
She who was great
　among the nations
has become like a widow.
The princess
　among the provinces
has been put to forced labor.

ב Beth

2 She weeps bitterly
　during the night,　Ps 6:6
with tears on her cheeks.
There is no one to offer
　her comfort,
not one from
　all her lovers.[B]　Jr 3:1; 22:20-22
All her friends
　have betrayed her;
they have become
　her enemies.

ג Gimel

3 Judah has gone into exile
　following[C] affliction
　and harsh slavery;
she lives among the nations
but finds no place to rest.
All her pursuers
　have overtaken her
in narrow places.

ד Daleth

4 The roads to Zion mourn,
　for no one comes
　　to the appointed festivals.
All her gates are deserted;
　her priests groan,

her young women grieve,
and she herself is bitter.

ה He

5 Her adversaries have become
　her masters;　Dt 28:13,44
her enemies are at ease,　Jb 3:26
for the LORD has made
　her suffer
because of her
　many transgressions.
Her children have gone away
as captives
　before the adversary.

ו Waw

6 All the splendor
　has vanished　Ezk 27:10
from Daughter Zion.　Lm 2:1,4,8
Her leaders are like stags
　that find no pasture;
they stumble away exhausted
before the hunter.　Jr 39:4-7

ז Zayin

7 During the days
　of her affliction
　and homelessness　Is 58:7
Jerusalem remembers all
　her precious belongings
that were hers in days of old.
When her people fell
　into the adversary's hand,
she had no one to help.
The adversaries looked
　at her,
laughing over her downfall.

ח Cheth

8 Jerusalem has
　sinned grievously;

A **1:1** The stanzas in Lm 1–4 form an acrostic.　B **1:2** = Jerusalem's political allies　C **1:3** Or *because of*

therefore, she has become
   an object of scorn. [A]
All who honored her
   now despise her,
for they have seen
   her nakedness.
She herself groans
   and turns away.

ט Teth

9   Her uncleanness stains
     her skirts.   Jr 13:22,26; Nah 3:5
She never considered
   her end.
Her downfall
   was astonishing;   Dt 28:43
there was no one
   to comfort her.
LORD, look on my affliction,
   for the enemy boasts.

י Yod

10   The adversary has seized
     all her precious belongings.
She has even seen the nations
enter her sanctuary —
those you had forbidden
to enter your assembly.   Dt 23:3

כ Kaph

11   All her people groan
     while they search for bread.
They have traded
   their precious belongings
   for food
in order to stay alive.   Lm 1:19; 4:10
LORD, look and see
how I have become despised.

ל Lamed

12   Is this nothing to you, all you
     who pass by?   Ps 89:41; Jr 22:8
Look and see!
Is there any pain like mine,

which was dealt out to me,
which the LORD
   made me suffer
on the day of his
   burning anger?   Am 5:18

מ Mem

13   He sent fire from on high
     into my bones;   Gn 19:24; Hs 8:14
he made it descend. [B]   1Kg 18:38
He spread a net for my feet
and turned me back.
He made me desolate,
sick all day long.

נ Nun

14   My transgressions
     have been formed
     into a yoke, [C,D]   Gn 27:40; Lv 26:13
fastened together
   by his hand;
they have been placed
   on my neck,
and the Lord has broken
   my strength.
He has handed me over
to those I cannot withstand.

ס Samek

15   The Lord has rejected   Ps 119:118
all the mighty men
   within me.
He has summoned an army [E]
   against me
to crush my young warriors.
The Lord has trampled
   Virgin Daughter Judah
like grapes in a winepress.

ע Ayin

16   I weep because of these things;
my eyes flow [F] with tears.
For there is no one nearby
   to comfort me,   Is 40:1

[A]1:8 Or *become impure*   [B]1:13 DSS, LXX; MT reads *bones, and it prevailed against them*   [C]1:14 Some Hb mss, LXX read *He kept watch over my transgressions*   [D]1:14 Or *The yoke of my transgressions is bound*; Hb obscure   [E]1:15 Or *has announced an appointed time*   [F]1:16 Lit *my eye, my eye flows*

no one to keep me alive.
My children are desolate
because the enemy
has prevailed.

פ Pe

17 Zion stretches out
her hands;
there is no one
to comfort her.
The LORD has issued a decree
against Jacob
that his neighbors should be
his adversaries.
Jerusalem has become
something impure
among them.   Lv 15:19-20

צ Tsade

18 The LORD is just,
for I have rebelled
against his command.
Listen, all you people;
look at my pain.
My young women
and young men
have gone into captivity.   Ezr 9:7

ק Qoph

19 I called to my lovers,   Lm 1:2
but they betrayed me.
My priests and elders
perished in the city
while searching for food
to keep themselves alive.

ר Resh

20 LORD, see how I am
in distress.
I am churning within;   Jb 30:27
my heart is broken,^A
for I have been
very rebellious.
Outside, the sword takes
the children;
inside, there is death.   Dt 32:25

^A **1:20** Lit *is turned within me*

ש Shin

21 People have heard
me groaning,   Lm 1:4,8
but there is no one
to comfort me.
All my enemies have heard
of my misfortune;
they are glad that
you have caused it.   Lm 2:15-17
Bring on the day
you have announced,
so that they may become
like me.   Is 62:8–63:6; Ezk 38–39

ת Taw

22 Let all their wickedness come
before you,
and deal with them
as you have dealt with me
because of all
my transgressions.   Lm 4:21-22
For my groans are many,
and I am sick at heart.

Judgment on Jerusalem

א Aleph

2 How the Lord
has overshadowed
Daughter Zion
with his anger!
He has thrown down
Israel's glory
from heaven to earth.
He did not acknowledge
his footstool   1Ch 28:2; Ps 99:5
in the day of his anger.   Jb 20:28

ב Beth

2 Without compassion
the Lord
has swallowed up   Jb 16:13
all the dwellings of Jacob.
In his wrath
he has demolished
the fortified cities
of Daughter Judah.   Is 2:12,15

He brought them
  to the ground
and defiled the kingdom
  and its leaders.   Ps 89:39; Is 43:28

ℷ Gimel
3 He has cut off every horn
    of Israel   Ps 75:5,10; Jr 48:25
  in his burning anger
  and withdrawn
    his right hand   Ex 6:6; Dt 4:34
  in the presence of the enemy.
  He has blazed against Jacob
    like a flaming fire
  that consumes everything.

ℸ Daleth
4 He has strung his bow
    like an enemy;   Ps 7:12; Lm 3:12
  his right hand is positioned
    like an adversary.
  He has killed everyone
    who was the delight to the
    eye,   1Kg 20:6; Ezk 24:16,21,25
  pouring out his wrath
    like fire
  on the tent of Daughter Zion.

ה He
5 The Lord is like an enemy;
  he has swallowed up Israel.
  He swallowed up
    all its palaces
  and destroyed
    its fortified cities.
  He has multiplied mourning
    and lamentation
  within Daughter Judah.   Is 29:2

ו Waw
6 He has wrecked his temple^A
  as if it were merely a shack in
    a field,^B
  destroying his place
    of meeting.   Ps 74:4
  The LORD has abolished

appointed festivals
  and Sabbaths in Zion.
He has despised king
  and priest
in his fierce anger.

ז Zayin
7 The Lord has rejected
    his altar,
  repudiated his sanctuary;
  he has handed the walls
    of her palaces
  over to the enemy.
  They have raised a shout
    in the house of the LORD
  as on the day
    of an appointed festival.

ח Cheth
8 The LORD determined
    to destroy
  the wall of Daughter Zion.
  He stretched out
    a measuring line   2Kg 21:13
  and did not restrain himself
    from destroying.
  He made the ramparts
    and walls grieve;
  together they waste away.

ט Teth
9 Zion's gates have fallen
    to the ground;   Neh 1:3; Jr 14:2
  he has destroyed
    and shattered the bars
    on her gates.
  Her king and her leaders live
    among the nations,
  instruction^C is no more,
  and even her
    prophets receive
  no vision from the LORD.

י Yod
10 The elders of Daughter Zion
  sit on the ground in silence.

^A**2:6** Lit *booth*   ^B**2:6** Lit *it were a garden*   ^C**2:9** Or *the law*

They have thrown dust
   on their heads   Gn 37:34; Jos 7:6
and put on sackcloth.
The young women
   of Jerusalem
have bowed their heads
   to the ground.   Jb 10:15; Is 58:5

 כ **Kaph**

¹¹ My eyes are worn out
   from weeping;   Ps 69:3; Jr 9:1; 14:17
I am churning within.
My heart is poured out
   in grief^A   Ps 22:14; Jr 4:19
because of the destruction
   of my dear people,   Lm 3:48
because infants and nursing
   babies faint
in the streets of the city.   Jr 44:7

ל **Lamed**

¹² They cry out
   to their mothers,
"Where is the grain
   and wine?"   Dt 28:51; Hs 2:8-9; 7:14
as they faint
   like the wounded
in the streets of the city,
as their life pours out
in the arms of their mothers.

מ **Mem**

¹³ What can I say
   on your behalf?
What can I compare you to,
   Daughter Jerusalem?
What can I liken you to,
so that I may console you,
   Virgin Daughter Zion?
For your ruin is as vast
   as the sea.
Who can heal you?   Nah 3:19

נ **Nun**

¹⁴ Your prophets saw visions
   for you

that were empty
   and deceptive;^B   Jr 5:12-13; 23:9-40
they did not reveal
   your iniquity
and so restore your fortunes.
They saw pronouncements
   for you
that were empty
   and misleading.

ס **Samek**

¹⁵ All who pass by
   scornfully clap their hands
     at you.   Nm 24:10; Ezk 25:6
They hiss and shake
   their heads   1Kg 9:8; Ps 22:7; Jr 19:8
at Daughter Jerusalem:
Is this the city that was called
the perfection of beauty,
the joy of the whole earth?

פ **Pe**

¹⁶ All your enemies
open their mouths
   against you.   Dt 28:37; Jb 16:10
They hiss and gnash
   their teeth,   Jb 16:9; Ps 35:16; 37:12
saying, "We have swallowed
   her up.   Lm 2:2,5,8
This is the day
   we have waited for!
We have lived to see it."

ע **Ayin**

¹⁷ The LORD has done
   what he planned;
he has accomplished
   his decree,
which he ordained in days
   of old.
He has demolished
   without compassion,   Lm 3:43
letting the enemy gloat
   over you
and exalting the horn
   of your adversaries.

^A**2:11** Lit *My liver is poured out on the ground*   ^B**2:14** Or *insipid*

צ Tsade

18 The hearts of the people
  cry out to the Lord.
Wall of Daughter Zion,   Lm 2:8
let your tears run down
  like a river
day and night.   Jr 4:31; 14:17
Give yourself no relief
and your^A eyes no rest.

ק Qoph

19 Arise, cry out in the night
  from the first watch
  of the night.
Pour out your heart
  like water
before the Lord's presence.
Lift up your hands to him
for the lives of your children
who are fainting
  from hunger
at the head of every street.

ר Resh

20 Lord, look and consider
  to whom you have done this.
Should women eat
  their own children,   Lv 26:27-29
the infants they
  have nurtured?^B
Should priests and prophets
  be killed
  in the Lord's sanctuary?

ש Shin

21 Both young and old
  are lying on the ground
  in the streets.
My young women and young
  men
have fallen by the sword.
You have killed them
  in the day of your anger,
slaughtering
  without compassion.   Lm 3:43

ת Taw

22 You summon those who
  terrorize me^C on every side,
as if for an appointed
  festival day;
on the day
  of the Lord's anger
no one escaped or survived.
My enemy has destroyed
  those I nurtured^D and reared.

Hope Through God's Mercy

א Aleph

3 I am the man
  who has seen affliction
  under the rod of God's wrath.
2 He has driven me away
  and forced me to walk
  in darkness instead of light.
3 Yes, he repeatedly
  turns his hand
  against me all day long.

ב Beth

4 He has worn away my flesh
  and skin;   Jb 13:28; Ps 32:3; 38:3; 49:14
he has broken my bones.
5 He has laid siege against me,
  encircling me with bitterness
  and hardship.   Lm 3:19
6 He has made me dwell
  in darkness
like those who
  have been dead for ages.

ג Gimel

7 He has walled me in
  so I cannot get out;   Jb 19:8
he has weighed me down
  with chains.
8 Even when I cry out
  and plead for help,
he blocks out my prayer.   Is 59:2
9 He has walled in my ways
  with blocks of stone;   Jb 13:27

^A2:18 Lit *and the daughter of your*   ^B2:20 Or *infants in a healthy condition*; Hb obscure   ^C2:22 Or *terrors*   ^D2:22 Or *I bore healthy*; Hb obscure

he has made
    my paths crooked.   Jb 19:8

ד Daleth

¹⁰ He is^A a bear waiting
    in ambush,
    a lion in hiding.   Hs 13:7-8
¹¹ He forced me off my way
    and tore me to pieces;
he left me desolate.
¹² He strung his bow   Ps 7:12; Lm 2:4
and set me as the target
    for his arrow.

ה He

¹³ He pierced my kidneys
    with shafts from his quiver.
¹⁴ I am a laughingstock
    to all my people,^B   Jb 12:4; Jr 20:7
mocked by their songs
    all day long.   Jb 30:9; Ps 69:12
¹⁵ He filled me with bitterness,
satiated me with wormwood.

ו Waw

¹⁶ He ground my teeth
    with gravel   Ps 3:7; 58:6; Pr 20:17
and made me cower^C
    in the dust.
¹⁷ I have been deprived^D
    of peace;   Ps 88:15; Lm 3:31
I have forgotten
    what prosperity is.
¹⁸ Then I thought, "My future^E
    is lost,
as well as my hope
    from the Lᴏʀᴅ."

ז Zayin

¹⁹ Remember^F my affliction
    and my homelessness,   Is 58:7
the wormwood
    and the poison.   Dt 29:18; Jr 9:15

²⁰ I continually remember them
    and have become
        depressed.^G   Ps 42:5-6,11; 43:5; 44:25
²¹ Yet I call this to mind,
    and therefore I have hope:

ח Cheth

²² Because of the Lᴏʀᴅ's
    faithful love   Ps 89:1; 103:17; Is 63:7
we do not perish,^H
for his mercies never end.
²³ They are new every morning;
    great is your faithfulness!
²⁴ I say, "The Lᴏʀᴅ is my portion,
    therefore I will put my hope
    in him."

ט Teth

²⁵ The Lᴏʀᴅ is good to those
    who wait for him,   Ps 25:3; 49:23
to the person who seeks him.
²⁶ It is good to wait quietly   Ps 37:7
    for salvation from the Lᴏʀᴅ.
²⁷ It is good for a man to bear
    the yoke   Jr 27:11; Lm 1:14
while he is still young.

י Yod

²⁸ Let him sit alone
    and be silent,   Jr 15:17
for God has disciplined^I him.
²⁹ Let him put his mouth
    in the dust —   Nm 22:31; Jos 7:6
perhaps there is still hope.
³⁰ Let him offer his cheek
    to the one
    who would strike him;   Is 50:6
let him be filled
    with disgrace.

כ Kaph

³¹ For the Lord
    will not reject us forever.

---

^A**3:10** Lit *is to me*   ^B**3:14** Some Hb mss, LXX, Vg; other Hb mss, Syr read *all peoples*   ^C**3:16** Or *and trampled me*   ^D**3:17** Syr, Vg; MT reads *You deprived my soul*   ^E**3:18** Or *splendor*   ^F**3:19** Or *I remember*   ^G**3:20** Alt Hb tradition reads *and you cause me to collapse*   ^H**3:22** One Hb mss, Syr, Tg read *The Lᴏʀᴅ's faithful love, indeed, does not perish*   ^I**3:28** Lit *has laid a burden on*

32 Even if he causes suffering,
   he will show compassion
   according to the abundance
   of his faithful love. Ps 106:43-45
33 For he does not enjoy
   bringing affliction Heb 12:10-11
   or suffering on mankind.

ל Lamed

34 Crushing all the prisoners
   of the land^A
   beneath one's feet,
35 denying justice to a man
   in the presence
   of the Most High,
36 or subverting a person in his
   lawsuit — Ex 23:2-3
   the Lord does not approve
   of these things.

מ Mem

37 Who is there who speaks
   and it happens,
   unless the Lord
   has ordained it? Ps 33:9-11
38 Do not both adversity
   and good
   come from the mouth
   of the Most High? Gn 50:20
39 Why should any living
   person complain,
   any man, because
   of the punishment
   for his sins?

נ Nun

40 Let us examine and probe
   our ways,
   and turn back to the LORD.
41 Let us lift up our hearts
   and our hands Ps 25:1
   to God in heaven:
42 "We have sinned
   and rebelled;
   you have not forgiven. Dt 29:20

ס Samek

43 "You have covered yourself
   in anger and pursued us;
   you have killed
   without compassion. Ezk 8:18
44 You have covered yourself
   with a cloud
   so that no prayer
   can get through. Lm 3:8
45 You have made
   us disgusting filth
   among the peoples. 1Co 4:13

פ Pe

46 "All our enemies
   open their mouths
   against us. Lm 2:16
47 We have experienced panic
   and pitfall, Is 24:17; Jr 48:43
   devastation and destruction."
48 My eyes flow with streams
   of tears
   because of the destruction
   of my dear people.

ע Ayin

49 My eyes
   overflow unceasingly,
   without end, Jr 9:1,18; Lm 1:16; 2:11
50 until the LORD looks down
   from heaven and sees. Ps 14:2
51 My eyes bring me grief
   because of the fate of
   all the women in my city.

צ Tsade

52 For no reason, my enemies^B
   hunted me like a bird. Ps 35:7
53 They smothered my life
   in^C a pit Gn 37:20-29; Jr 38:6-13
   and threw stones on me.
54 Water flooded
   over my head, Ps 42:7; 69:1-2
   and I thought, "I'm going
   to die!" Ezk 37:11

---

^A 3:34 Or earth   ^B 3:52 Or Those who were my enemies for no reason   ^C 3:53 Or They ended my life in ;
Hb obscure

ק **Qoph**

55 I called on your name, LORD,
      from the depths of the pit.
56 You heard my plea:
      Do not ignore my cry
        for relief.
57 You came near
      whenever I called you;
    you said, "Do not be afraid."

ר **Resh**

58 You championed
      my cause, Lord;   Ps 43:1; Pr 23:11
    you redeemed my life.   Ps 103:4
59 LORD, you saw the wrong
      done to me;
    judge my case.
60 You saw all
      their vengefulness,
    all their plots against me.

ש **Sin / ש Shin**

61 LORD, you heard
      their insults,   Lm 5:1
    all their plots against me.
62 The slander[A]
      and murmuring
      of my opponents
    attack me all day long.
63 When they sit and when
      they rise, look,
    I am mocked by their songs.

ת **Taw**

64 You will pay them back
      what they deserve, LORD,
    according to the work
      of their hands.   Ps 28:4; Rm 2:6
65 You will give them a heart
      filled with anguish.[B]   Is 6:10
    May your curse be on them!
66 You will pursue them
      in anger
      and destroy them
    under your heavens.[C]   Ps 8:3

Terrors of the Besieged City

א **Aleph**

4 How the gold
      has become tarnished,
    the fine gold become dull!
    The stones of the temple[D]
      lie scattered
    at the head of every street.

ב **Beth**

2 Zion's precious children —
      once worth their weight
        in pure gold —   Is 62:3; Zch 9:16
    how they are regarded
      as clay jars,
    the work of a potter's hands!

ג **Gimel**

3 Even jackals
      offer their breasts
    to nurse their young,
    but my dear people
      have become cruel
    like ostriches
      in the wilderness.   Jb 39:13-18

ד **Daleth**

4 The nursing baby's tongue
      clings to the roof
      of his mouth from thirst.
    Infants beg for food,
    but no one gives them any.

ה **He**

5 Those who used
      to eat delicacies
    are destitute in the streets;
    those who were reared
      in purple garments   Jdg 8:26
    huddle in trash heaps.

ו **Waw**

6 The punishment
      of my dear people
    is greater than that of Sodom,

A 3:62 Lit *lips*   B 3:65 Or *them an obstinate heart*; Hb obscure   C 3:66 Lit *under the LORD's heavens*
D 4:1 Or *The sacred gems*

which was overthrown
  in an instant
without a hand laid on it.

ז Zayin
7 Her dignitaries were brighter
    than snow,
  whiter than milk;
  their bodies^A were
    more ruddy than coral,
  their appearance
    like lapis lazuli.

ח Cheth
8 Now they appear darker
    than soot;   Jb 30:30; Lm 5:10
  they are not recognized
    in the streets.
  Their skin has shriveled
    on their bones;
  it has become dry like wood.

ט Teth
9 Those slain by the sword are
    better off
  than those slain by hunger,
  who waste away,
    pierced with pain
  because the fields
    lack produce.

י Yod
10 The hands
    of compassionate women
  have cooked
    their own children;   Dt 28:53
  they became their food
  during the destruction
    of my dear people.   Jr 8:11,21

כ Kaph
11 The LORD has exhausted
    his wrath,
  poured out
    his burning anger;
  he has ignited a fire in Zion,

and it has consumed
  her foundations.   Lm 2:3-4

ל Lamed
12 The kings of the earth
  and all
    the world's inhabitants
    did not believe
  that an enemy or adversary
  could enter Jerusalem's
    gates.   2Sm 5:6-8; Ps 48:1-5

מ Mem
13 Yet it happened because of
    the sins of her prophets
  and the iniquities
    of her priests,
  who shed the blood
    of the righteous within her.

נ Nun
14 Blind, they stumbled
    in the streets,   Dt 28:29; Is 59:10
  defiled by this blood,   Lv 21:11
  so that no one dared
  to touch their garments.

ס Samek
15 "Stay away! Unclean!"
    people shouted at them.
  "Away, away!
    Don't touch us!"   Lv 13:45-46
  So they wandered aimlessly.
  It was said
    among the nations,
  "They can stay here
    no longer."

פ Pe
16 The LORD himself
    has scattered them;
  he no longer watches over
    them.
  The priests
    are not respected;
  the elders find no favor.

^A 4:7 Lit bones

ע Ayin

17 All the while our eyes
         were failing
     as we looked in vain for help;
     we watched
         from our towers
     for a nation that would not
         save us.

צ Tsade

18 Our steps
         were closely followed
     so that we could not walk
         in our streets.
     Our end approached;
         our time ran out.   Ezk 7:2-12
     Our end had come!

ק Qoph

19 Those who chased us
         were swifter
     than eagles in the sky;   Jr 4:13
     they relentlessly pursued us
         over the mountains
     and ambushed us
         in the wilderness.

ר Resh

20 The Lᴏʀᴅ's anointed,
         the breath of our life, ᴬ   Gn 2:7
     was captured in their traps.
     We had said about him,
     "We will live
         under his protection
         among the nations."

שׁ Sin

21 So rejoice and be glad,
         Daughter Edom,   Ezk 35:15; Ob 12
     you resident of the land
         of Uz!   Jr 25:20
     Yet the cup will pass to you
         as well;   Is 51:17; Jr 25:15-16; Hab 2:16
     you will get drunk
         and expose yourself.

ת Taw

22 Daughter Zion,
         your punishment
         is complete;
     he will not lengthen
         your exile. ᴮ
     But he will punish
         your iniquity,
         Daughter Edom,
     and will expose your sins.

Prayer for Restoration

5 Lᴏʀᴅ, remember
         what has happened to us.
     Look, and see our disgrace!
2 Our inheritance
         has been turned over
         to strangers,
     our houses to foreigners.
3 We have become
         orphans, fatherless;
     our mothers are widows.
4 We must pay for the water
         we drink;
     our wood comes at a price.
5 We are closely pursued;
     we are tired, and no one
         offers us rest.
6 We made a treaty with ᶜ Egypt
         and with Assyria,
     to get enough food.   Hs 12:1
7 Our fathers sinned;
         they no longer exist,
     but we bear
         their punishment.
8 Slaves rule over us;   Pr 30:21-23
     no one rescues us from them.
9 We secure our food
         at the risk of our lives
     because of the sword
         in the wilderness.
10 Our skin is as hot ᴰ as an oven
     from the ravages of hunger.
11 Women have been raped
         in Zion,

A **4:20** Lit *nostrils*   B **4:22** Or *not deport you again*   C **5:6** Lit *We gave the hand to*   D **5:10** Or *black*; Hb obscure virgins in the cities of Judah.

¹² Princes have been hung up
by their hands;
elders are shown no respect.

¹³ Young men labor
at millstones; Ex 11:5; Jdg 16:21
boys stumble
under loads of wood.

¹⁴ The elders have left
the city gate,
the young men, their music.

¹⁵ Joy has left our hearts; Am 8:10
our dancing has turned
to mourning.

¹⁶ The crown has fallen
from our head. Jb 19:9; Is 28:3
Woe to us,
for we have sinned. Jr 8:14

¹⁷ Because of this, our heart
is sick;
because of these, our eyes
grow dim: Ps 69:23; Ec 12:3

¹⁸ because of Mount Zion,
which lies desolate
and has jackals
prowling in it. Is 13:19-22; 34:11-15

¹⁹ You, LORD,
are enthroned forever;
your throne endures
from generation
to generation. Ps 9:7; 45:6; 102:12

²⁰ Why do you continually
forget us, Ps 13:1
abandon us
for our entire lives?

²¹ LORD, bring us back
to yourself, so we
may return; Jr 15:19; 31:18
renew our days
as in former times,

²² unless you have completely
rejected us
and are intensely angry
with us.

EZEKIEL

1 In the thirtieth year, in the fourth month, on the fifth day of the month, while I was among the exiles by the Chebar Canal, the heavens were opened and I saw visions of God. ² On the fifth day of the month — it was the fifth year of King Jehoiachin's exile — ³ the word of the LORD came directly to the priest Ezekiel son of Buzi, in the land of the Chaldeans by the Chebar Canal. The LORD's hand was on him there.   Ezk 3:15,23; 10:15,20,22; Mt 3:16

Vision of the LORD's Glory

⁴ I looked, and there was a whirlwind coming from the north, a huge cloud with fire flashing back and forth and brilliant light all around it. In the center of the fire, there was a gleam like amber. ⁵ The likeness of four living creatures came from it, and this was their appearance: They looked something like a human, ⁶ but each of them had four faces and four wings. ⁷ Their legs were straight, and the soles of their feet were like the hooves of a calf, sparkling like the gleam of polished bronze. ⁸ They had human hands under their wings on their four sides. All four of them had faces and wings. ⁹ Their wings were touching. The creatures did not turn as they moved; each one went straight ahead. ¹⁰ Their faces looked something like the face of a human, and each of the four had the face of a lion on the right, the face of an ox on the left, and the face of an eagle.

¹¹ That is what their faces were like. Their wings were spread upward; each had two wings touching that of another and two wings covering its body. ¹² Each creature went straight ahead. Wherever the Spiritᴬ wanted to go, they went without turning as they moved.   2Kg 2:1

¹³ The likeness of the living creatures was like the appearance of blazing coals of fire or like torches. Fire was moving back and forth between the living creatures; it was bright, with lightning coming out of it. ¹⁴ The creatures were darting back and forth like flashes of lightning.   Ps 104:4; Zch 4:10; Mt 24:27; Lk 17:24; Rv 4:5

¹⁵ When I looked at the living creatures, there was one wheel on the ground beside each of the four-faced creatures. ¹⁶ The appearance of the wheels and their craftsmanship was like the gleam of beryl, and all four had the same likeness. Their appearance and craftsmanship was like a wheel within a wheel. ¹⁷ When they moved, they went in any of the four directions, without turning as they moved. ¹⁸ Their rims were tall and awe-inspiring. Each of their four rims were full of eyes all around. ¹⁹ When the living creatures moved, the wheels moved beside them, and when the creatures rose from the earth, the wheels also rose. ²⁰ Wherever the Spirit wanted to go, the creatures went in the direction the Spirit was moving. The wheels rose alongside them, for the spirit of

ᴬ**1:12** Or *spirit,* also in v. 20

the living creatures was in the wheels. ²¹ When the creatures moved, the wheels moved; when the creatures stopped, the wheels stopped; and when the creatures rose from the earth, the wheels rose alongside them, for the spirit of the living creatures was in the wheels. Ezk 10:9-12; Dn 10:6; Rv 4:6,8

²² Over the heads of the living creatures the likeness of an expanse was spread out. It gleamed like awe-inspiring crystal, ²³ and under the expanse their wings extended one toward another. They each also had two wings covering their bodies. ²⁴ When they moved, I heard the sound of their wings like the roar of a huge torrent, like the voice of the Almighty, and a sound of tumult like the noise of an army. When they stopped, they lowered their wings. Gn 1:6-8; Ezk 10:1; 43:2; Rv 4:6

²⁵ A voice came from above the expanse over their heads; when they stopped, they lowered their wings. ²⁶ Something like a throne with the appearance of lapis lazuli was above the expanse over their heads. On the throne, high above, was someone who looked like a human. ²⁷ From what seemed to be his waist up, I saw a gleam like amber, with what looked like fire enclosing it all around. From what seemed to be his waist down, I also saw what looked like fire. There was a brilliant light all around him. ²⁸ The appearance of the brilliant light all around was like that of a rainbow in a cloud on a rainy day. This was the appearance of the likeness of the LORD's glory. When I saw it, I fell face-down and heard a voice speaking. Ezk 10:1; 24:10; Is 6:1

Mission to Rebellious Israel

2 He said to me, "Son of man, stand up on your feet and I will speak with you." ² As he spoke to me, the Spirit entered me and set me on my feet, and I listened to the one who was speaking to me. ³ He said to me, "Son of man, I am sending you to the Israelites, to ^A the rebellious pagans who have rebelled against me. The Israelites and their ancestors have transgressed against me to this day. ⁴ The descendants are obstinate ^B and hardhearted. I am sending you to them, and you must say to them, 'This is what the Lord GOD says.' ⁵ Whether they listen or refuse to listen — for they are a rebellious house — they will know that a prophet has been among them.

⁶ "But you, son of man, do not be afraid of them and do not be afraid of their words, even though briers and thorns are beside you and you live among scorpions. Don't be afraid of their words or discouraged by the look on their faces, for they are a rebellious house. ⁷ Speak my words to them whether they listen or refuse to listen, for they are rebellious. 2Sm 23:6; Jr 1:8,17; Ezk 3:9

⁸ "And you, son of man, listen to what I tell you: Do not be rebellious like that rebellious house. Open your mouth and eat what I am giving you." ⁹ So I looked and saw a hand reaching out to me, and there was a written scroll in it. ¹⁰ When he unrolled it before me, it was written on the front and back; words of lamentation, mourning, and woe were written on it. Jr 15:16

3 He said to me: "Son of man, eat what you find here. Eat this scroll, then go and speak to the house of Israel." ² So I opened my

^A**2:3** Or *Israelites and to*   ^B**2:4** Lit *hard of face*

mouth, and he fed me the scroll. ³ "Son of man," he said to me, "feed your stomach and fill your belly with this scroll I am giving you." So I ate it, and it was as sweet as honey in my mouth.   Jr 15:16; Ezk 2:8-9

⁴ Then he said to me: "Son of man, go to the house of Israel and speak my words to them. ⁵ For you are not being sent to a people of unintelligible speech or a difficult language but to the house of Israel — ⁶ not to the many peoples of unintelligible speech or a difficult language, whose words you cannot understand. No doubt, if I sent you to them, they would listen to you. ⁷ But the house of Israel will not want to listen to you because they do not want to listen to me. For the whole house of Israel is hardheaded and hardhearted. ⁸ Look, I have made your face as hard as their faces and your forehead as hard as their foreheads. ⁹ I have made your forehead like a diamond, harder than flint. Don't be afraid of them or discouraged by the look on their faces, though they are a rebellious house."   Jn 15:20

¹⁰ Next he said to me: "Son of man, listen carefully to all my words that I speak to you and take them to heart. ¹¹ Go to your people, the exiles, and speak to them. Tell them, 'This is what the Lord GOD says,' whether they listen or refuse to listen."   Ezk 2:5,7

¹² The Spirit then lifted me up, and I heard a loud rumbling sound behind me — bless the glory of the LORD in his place! — ¹³ with the^A sound of the living creatures' wings brushing against each other and the sound of the wheels beside them, a loud rumbling sound.

¹⁴ The Spirit lifted me up and took me away. I left in bitterness and in an angry spirit, and the LORD's hand was on me powerfully. ¹⁵ I came to the exiles at Tel-abib, who were living by the Chebar Canal, and I sat there among them stunned for seven days.   Jb 2:13; Ezk 1:15,24; 8:3; Ac 8:39

Ezekiel as a Watchman

¹⁶ Now at the end of seven days the word of the LORD came to me: ¹⁷ "Son of man, I have made you a watchman over the house of Israel. When you hear a word from my mouth, give them a warning from me. ¹⁸ If I say to the wicked person, 'You will surely die,' but you do not warn him — you don't speak out to warn him about his wicked way in order to save his life — that wicked person will die for his iniquity. Yet I will hold you responsible for his blood. ¹⁹ But if you warn a wicked person and he does not turn from his wickedness or his wicked way, he will die for his iniquity, but you will have rescued yourself. ²⁰ Now if a righteous person turns from his righteousness and acts unjustly, and I put a stumbling block in front of him, he will die. If you did not warn him, he will die because of his sin, and the righteous acts he did will not be remembered. Yet I will hold you responsible for his blood. ²¹ But if you warn the righteous person that he should not sin, and he does not sin, he will indeed live because he listened to your warning, and you will have rescued yourself."   Is 52:8; 56:10; Jr 42:7

²² The hand of the LORD was on me there, and he said to me, "Get up, go out to the plain, and I will speak with you there." ²³ So I got up and

went out to the plain. The Lord's glory was present there, like the glory I had seen by the Chebar Canal, and I fell facedown. ²⁴ The Spirit entered me and set me on my feet. He spoke with me and said: "Go, shut yourself inside your house. ²⁵ As for you, son of man, they will put ropes on you and bind you with them so you cannot go out among them. ²⁶ I will make your tongue stick to the roof of your mouth, and you will be mute and unable to be a mediator for ᴬ them, for they are a rebellious house. ²⁷ But when I speak with you, I will open your mouth, and you will say to them, 'This is what the Lord God says.' Let the one who listens, listen, and let the one who refuses, refuse — for they are a rebellious house.

Jerusalem's Siege Dramatized

4 "Now you, son of man, take a brick, set it in front of you, and draw the city of Jerusalem on it. ² Then lay siege against it: Construct a siege wall, build a ramp, pitch military camps, and place battering rams against it on all sides. ³ Take an iron plate and set it up as an iron wall between yourself and the city. Face it so that it is under siege, and besiege it. This will be a sign for the house of Israel.   Jr 6:6

⁴ "Then lie down on your left side and place the iniquity ᴮ of the house of Israel on it. You will bear their iniquity for the number of days you lie on your side. ⁵ For I have assigned you the years of their iniquity according to the number of days you lie down, 390 days; so you will bear the iniquity of the house of Israel. ⁶ When you have completed

these days, lie down again, but on your right side, and bear the iniquity of the house of Judah. I have assigned you forty days, a day for each year. ⁷ Face the siege of Jerusalem with your arm bared, and prophesy against it. ⁸ Be aware that I will put cords on you so you cannot turn from side to side until you have finished the days of your siege.   Nm 14:34; Ezk 3:25

⁹ "Also take wheat, barley, beans, lentils, millet, and spelt. Put them in a single container and make them into bread for yourself. You are to eat it during the number of days you lie on your side, 390 days. ¹⁰ The food you eat each day will weigh eight ounces; ᶜ you will eat it at set times. ᴰ ¹¹ You will also drink a ration of water, a sixth of a gallon, ᴱ which you will drink at set times. ¹² You will eat it as you would a barley cake and bake it over dried human excrement in their sight." ¹³ The Lord said, "This is how the Israelites will eat their bread — ceremonially unclean — among the nations where I will banish them."

¹⁴ But I said, "Oh, Lord God, I have never been defiled. From my youth until now I have not eaten anything that died naturally or was mauled by wild beasts. And impure meat has never entered my mouth."   228

¹⁵ He replied to me, "Look, I will let you use cow dung instead of human excrement, and you can make your bread over that." ¹⁶ He said to me, "Son of man, I am going to cut off the supply of bread in Jerusalem. They will anxiously eat food they have weighed out and in dread drink rationed water ¹⁷ for lack of bread and water. Everyone

---

ᴬ**3:26** Or *to rebuke*   ᴮ**4:4** Or *punishment*   ᶜ**4:10** Lit *20 shekels*   ᴰ**4:10** Lit *from time to time,* also in v. 11
ᴱ**4:11** Lit *hin*

will be devastated and waste away because of their iniquity.   Lv 26:26

Ezekiel Dramatizes Jerusalem's Fall

5 "Now you, son of man, take a sharp sword, use it as you would a barber's razor, and shave your head and beard. Then take a set of scales and divide the hair. ² You are to burn a third of it in the city when the days of the siege have ended; you are to take a third and slash it with the sword all around the city; and you are to scatter a third to the wind, for I will draw a sword to chase after them. ³ But you are to take a few strands from the hair and secure them in the folds of your robe. ⁴ Take some more of them, throw them into the fire, and burn them in it. A fire will spread from it to the whole house of Israel.

⁵ "This is what the Lord GOD says: I have set this Jerusalem in the center of the nations, with countries all around her. ⁶ She has rebelled against my ordinances with more wickedness than the nations, and against my statutes more than the countries that surround her. For her people have rejected my ordinances and have not walked in my statutes.

⁷ "Therefore, this is what the Lord GOD says: Because you have been more insubordinate than the nations around you — you have not walked in my statutes or kept my ordinances; you have not even kept the ordinances of the nations around you — ⁸ therefore, this is what the Lord GOD says: See, I myself am against you, Jerusalem, and I will execute judgments within you in the sight of the nations. ⁹ Because of all your detestable practices, I will do to you what I have never done before and what I will never do again. ¹⁰ As a result, fathers will eat their sons within Jerusalem, ᴬ and sons will eat their fathers. I will execute judgments against you and scatter all your survivors to every direction of the wind.   Jr 2:10-11; Dn 9:12

¹¹ "Therefore, as I live" — this is the declaration of the Lord GOD — "I will withdraw and show you no pity, because you have defiled my sanctuary with all your abhorrent acts and detestable practices. Yes, I will not spare you. ¹² A third of your people will die by plague and be consumed by famine within you; a third will fall by the sword all around you; and I will scatter a third to every direction of the wind, and I will draw a sword to chase after them. ¹³ When my anger is spent and I have vented my wrath on them, I will be appeased. Then after I have spent my wrath on them, they will know that I, the LORD, have spoken in my jealousy.

¹⁴ "I will make you a ruin and a disgrace among the nations around you, in the sight of everyone who passes by. ¹⁵ So you ᴮ will be a disgrace and a taunt, a warning and a horror, to the nations around you when I execute judgments against you in anger, wrath, and furious rebukes. I, the LORD, have spoken. ¹⁶ When I shoot deadly arrows of famine at them, arrows for destruction that I will send to destroy you, inhabitants of Jerusalem, I will intensify the famine against you and cut off your supply of bread. ¹⁷ I will send famine and dangerous animals against you. They will leave you childless. Plague and

ᴬ**5:10** Lit *you*   ᴮ**5:15** DSS, LXX, Syr, Tg, Vg; MT reads *she* bloodshed will sweep through you, and I will bring a sword against you. I, the Lord, have spoken."

Prophecy Against Israel's Idolatry

6 The word of the Lord came to me: [2] "Son of man, face the mountains of Israel and prophesy against them. [3] You are to say: Mountains of Israel, hear the word of the Lord God! This is what the Lord God says to the mountains and the hills, to the ravines and the valleys: I am about to bring a sword against you, and I will destroy your high places. [4] Your altars will be desolated and your shrines[A] smashed. I will throw down your slain in front of your idols. [5] I will lay the corpses of the Israelites in front of their idols and scatter your bones around your altars. [6] Wherever you live the cities will be in ruins and the high places will be desolate, so that your altars will lie in ruins and be desecrated,[B] your idols smashed and obliterated, your shrines cut down, and what you have made wiped out. [7] The slain will fall among you, and you will know that I am the Lord.

[8] "Yet I will leave a remnant when you are scattered among the nations, for throughout the countries there will be some of you who will escape the sword. [9] Then your survivors will remember me among the nations where they are taken captive, how I was crushed by their promiscuous hearts that turned away from me and by their eyes that lusted after their idols. They will loathe themselves because of the evil things they did, their detestable actions of every kind. [10] And they will know that I am the Lord; I did not threaten to bring this disaster on them without a reason.   Dt 4:29; Ps 78:40; Jr 44:14,28; Ezk 7:16; 20:43

Lament over the Fall of Jerusalem

[11] "This is what the Lord God says: Clap your hands, stamp your feet, and cry out over all the evil and detestable practices of the house of Israel, who will fall by the sword, famine, and plague. [12] The one who is far off will die by plague; the one who is near will fall by the sword; and the one who remains and is spared[C] will die of famine. In this way I will exhaust my wrath on them. [13] You will all know that I am the Lord when their slain lie among their idols around their altars, on every high hill, on all the mountaintops, and under every green tree and every leafy oak — the places where they offered pleasing aromas to all their idols. [14] I will stretch out my hand against them, and wherever they live I will make the land a desolate waste, from the wilderness to Diblah.[D] Then they will know that I am the Lord."   Ezk 5:12-13; 21:14,17; 25:6

Announcement of the End

7 The word of the Lord came to me: [2] "Son of man, this is what the Lord God says to the land of Israel:

An end! The end has come
on the four corners
of the earth.   Am 8:2,10
[3] The end is now upon you;
I will send my anger
against you

A **6:4** Or *incense altars*, also in v. 6   B **6:6** Hb obscure   C **6:12** Or *besieged*   D **6:14** Some Hb mss, some LXX mss read *Riblah*; 2Kg 23:33; Jr 39:5

and judge you according to
    your ways.
I will punish you for all
    your detestable practices.
4   I will not look on you
        with pity or spare you,
    but I will punish you
        for your ways   Ezk 11:21
    and for your
        detestable practices
        within you.
    Then you will know that I am
        the LORD."   Ezk 6:7,14

5 This is what the Lord GOD says:
    Look, one disaster
        after another is coming!
6   An end has come; the end
        has come!
    It has awakened against you.
    Look, it is coming!
7   Doom[A] has come on you,
        inhabitants of the land.
    The time has come; the day
        is near.
    There will be panic
        on the mountains
    and not celebration.   Jl 2:1-2

8   I will pour out my wrath
        on you very soon;   Ezk 20:8,21
    I will exhaust my anger
        against you
    and judge you
        according to your ways.
    I will punish you for all your
        detestable practices.
9   I will not look on you
        with pity or spare you.
    I will punish you
        for your ways
    and for your
        detestable practices
        within you.
    Then you will know

that it is I, the LORD,
    who strikes.
10 Here is the day! Here it
        comes!
    Doom is on its way.   Ezk 7:7
    The rod has blossomed;   Nm 17:8
    arrogance has bloomed.   Is 10:5
11 Violence has grown
        into a rod of wickedness.
    None of them will remain:
    none of that crowd,
    none of their wealth,
    and none of the eminent[B]
        among them.

12 The time has come; the day
        has arrived.
    Let the buyer not rejoice
    and the seller not mourn,
    for wrath is on
        her whole crowd.   Is 24:2
13 The seller will certainly
        not return
    to what was sold
    as long as he and the buyer
        remain alive.[C]
    For the vision concerning
        her whole crowd
    will not be revoked,
    and because of the iniquity
        of each one,
    none will preserve his life.

14 They have blown
        the trumpet   Nm 10:9
    and prepared everything,
    but no one goes to war,
    for my wrath is on
        her whole crowd.
15 The sword is on the outside;
    plague and famine are
        on the inside.
    Whoever is in the field
        will die by the sword,

A7:7 Or A leash; Hb obscure, also in v. 10   B7:11 Some Hb mss, Syr, Vg read and no rest   C7:13 Lit sold,
while still in life is their life

and famine and plague
will devour
whoever is in the city.

16 The survivors among them
will escape   Ezk 6:8; 14:22
and live on the mountains.
Like doves of the valley,
all of them will moan,
each over his own iniquity.

17 All their hands
will become weak,   Is 13:7
and all their knees will run
with urine. [A]

18 They will put on sackcloth,
and horror will
overwhelm them.
Shame will cover all
their faces,
and all their heads
will be bald.   Is 15:2-3; Am 8:10

19 They will throw their silver
into the streets,
and their gold will seem like
something filthy.   Is 2:20; 30:22
Their silver and gold
will be unable to save them
in the day
of the LORD's wrath.   Pr 11:4
They will not satisfy
their appetites
or fill their stomachs,
for these were
the stumbling blocks   Ezk 14:3
that brought
about their iniquity.

20 He appointed
his beautiful ornaments
for majesty,
but [B] they made
their detestable images
from them,
their abhorrent things.   Jr 7:30
Therefore, I have made these

into something filthy
to them.

21 I will hand these things over
to foreigners as plunder
and to the wicked
of the earth as spoil,
and they will profane them.

22 I will turn my face from them
as they profane
my treasured place.
Violent men will enter it
and profane it.

23 Forge the chain,   Jr 27:2
for the land is filled
with crimes of bloodshed,
and the city is filled
with violence.   Ezk 8:17; 9:9

24 So I will bring the most evil
of nations   Ezk 21:31; 28:7
to take possession
of their houses.
I will put an end to the pride
of the strong,
and their sacred places
will be profaned.   2Ch 7:20

25 Anguish is coming!
They will look for peace,
but there will be none.

26 Disaster after disaster
will come,   Is 47:11; Jr 4:20
and there will be rumor
after rumor.   Ezk 21:7
Then they will look for
a vision from a prophet,
but instruction will perish
from the priests
and counsel from the elders.

27 The king will mourn;
the prince will be clothed
in grief;
and the hands of the people
of the land will tremble.
I will deal with
them according to
their own conduct,

[A]7:17 Lit knees will go water   [B]7:20 Or They turned their beautiful ornaments into objects of pride, and

and I will judge them
   by their own standards.
Then they will know that
   I am the LORD.

Visionary Journey to Jerusalem

8 In the sixth year, in the sixth month, on the fifth day of the month, I was sitting in my house and the elders of Judah were sitting in front of me, and there the hand of the Lord GOD came down on me. ² I looked, and there was someone who looked like a man.ᴬ From what seemed to be his waist down was fire, and from his waist up was something that looked bright, like the gleam of amber. ³ He stretched out what appeared to be a hand and took me by the hair of my head. Then the Spirit lifted me up between earth and heaven and carried me in visions of God to Jerusalem, to the entrance of the inner gate that faces north, where the offensive statue that provokes jealousy was located. ⁴ I saw the glory of the God of Israel there, like the vision I had seen in the plain.

Pagan Practices in the Temple

⁵ The LORD said to me, "Son of man, look toward the north." I looked to the north, and there was this offensive statue north of the Altar Gate, at the entrance. ⁶ He said to me, "Son of man, do you see what they are doing here — more detestable acts that the house of Israel is committing — so that I must depart from my sanctuary? You will see even more detestable acts."   Ezk 5:11; 8:9,17

⁷ Then he brought me to the entrance of the court, and when I looked there was a hole in the wall. ⁸ He said to me, "Son of man, dig

through the wall." So I dug through the wall and discovered a doorway. ⁹ He said to me, "Go in and see the detestable, wicked acts they are committing here."

¹⁰ I went in and looked, and there engraved all around the wall was every kind of abhorrent thing — crawling creatures and beasts — as well as all the idols of the house of Israel. ¹¹ Seventy elders from the house of Israel were standing before them, with Jaazaniah son of Shaphan standing among them. Each had a firepan in his hand, and a fragrant cloud of incense was rising up. ¹² He said to me, "Son of man, do you see what the elders of the house of Israel are doing in the darkness, each at the shrine of his idol? For they are saying, 'The LORD does not see us. The LORD has abandoned the land.'" ¹³ Again he said to me, "You will see even more detestable acts that they are committing."   Ex 20:4; Nm 11:16,25; Dt 4:16-18; Rm 1:23

¹⁴ Then he brought me to the entrance of the north gate of the LORD's house, and I saw women sitting there weeping for Tammuz. ¹⁵ And he said to me, "Do you see this, son of man? You will see even more detestable acts than these."

¹⁶ So he brought me to the inner court of the LORD's house, and there were about twenty-five men at the entrance of the LORD's temple, between the portico and the altar, with their backs to the LORD's temple and their faces turned to the east. They were bowing to the east in worship of the sun. ¹⁷ And he said to me, "Do you see this, son of man? Is it not enough for the house of Judah to commit the detestable acts they are doing here, that they must

ᴬ**8:2** LXX; MT, Vg read *like fire*

also fill the land with violence and repeatedly anger me, even putting the branch to their nose?[A] [18] Therefore I will respond with wrath. I will not show pity or spare them. Though they call loudly in my hearing, I will not listen to them." Jl 2:17

Vision of Slaughter in Jerusalem

9 Then he called loudly in my hearing, "Come near, executioners of the city, each of you with a destructive weapon in his hand." [2] And I saw six men coming from the direction of the Upper Gate, which faces north, each with a war club in his hand. There was another man among them, clothed in linen, carrying writing equipment. They came and stood beside the bronze altar. Lv 16:4; 2Kg 15:35; Jr 20:2

[3] Then the glory of the God of Israel rose from above the cherub where it had been, to the threshold of the temple. He called to the man clothed in linen and carrying writing equipment. [4] "Pass throughout the city of Jerusalem," the LORD said to him, "and put a mark on the foreheads of the men who sigh and groan over all the detestable practices committed in it." Ezk 10:4

[5] He spoke to the others in my hearing: "Pass through the city after him and start killing; do not show pity or spare them! [6] Slaughter the old men, the young men and women, as well as the children and older women, but do not come near anyone who has the mark. Begin at my sanctuary." So they began with the elders who were in front of the temple. [7] Then he said to them, "Defile the temple and fill the courts with the slain. Go!" So they went out killing people in the city. Ezk 5:11

[8] While they were killing, I was left alone. And I fell facedown and cried out, "Oh, Lord GOD! Are you going to destroy the entire remnant of Israel when you pour out your wrath on Jerusalem?" Ezk 11:13

[9] He answered me, "The iniquity of the house of Israel and Judah is extremely great; the land is full of bloodshed, and the city full of perversity. For they say, 'The LORD has abandoned the land; he does not see.' [10] But as for me, I will not show pity or spare them. I will bring their conduct down on their own heads."

[11] Then the man clothed in linen and carrying writing equipment reported back, "I have done all that you commanded me."

God's Glory Leaves the Temple

10 Then I looked, and there above the expanse over the heads of the cherubim was something like a throne with the appearance of lapis lazuli. [2] The LORD spoke to the man clothed in linen and said, "Go inside the wheelwork beneath the cherubim. Fill your hands with blazing coals from among the cherubim and scatter them over the city." So he went in as I watched. Ezk 1:13,22,26; Rv 8:5

[3] Now the cherubim were standing to the south of the temple when the man went in, and the cloud filled the inner court. [4] Then the glory of the LORD rose from above the cherub to the threshold of the temple. The temple was filled with the cloud, and the court was filled with the brightness of the LORD's glory. [5] The sound of the cherubim's wings could be heard as far as the outer court; it was like the voice of God Almighty when he speaks.

[A]**8:17** Alt Hb tradition reads *my nose*

⁶ After the LORD commanded the man clothed in linen, saying, "Take fire from inside the wheelwork, from among the cherubim," the man went in and stood beside a wheel. ⁷ Then the cherub reached out his hand to the fire that was among them. He took some and put it into the hands of the man clothed in linen, who took it and went out. ⁸ The cherubim appeared to have the form of human hands under their wings. Ezk 1:8

⁹ I looked, and there were four wheels beside the cherubim, one wheel beside each cherub. The luster of the wheels was like the gleam of beryl. ¹⁰ In appearance, all four looked alike, like a wheel within a wheel. ¹¹ When they moved, they would go in any of the four directions, without pivoting as they moved. But wherever the head faced, they would go in that direction, without pivoting as they went. ¹² Their entire bodies, including their backs, hands, wings, and the wheels that the four of them had, were full of eyes all around. ¹³ As I listened the wheels were called "the wheelwork." ¹⁴ Each one had four faces: one was the face of a cherub, the second the face of a man, the third the face of a lion, and the fourth the face of an eagle.

¹⁵ The cherubim ascended; these were the living creatures I had seen by the Chebar Canal. ¹⁶ When the cherubim moved, the wheels moved beside them, and when they lifted their wings to rise from the earth, even then the wheels did not veer away from them. ¹⁷ When the cherubim stopped, the wheels stood still, and when they ascended, the wheels ascended with them,

for the spirit of the living creatures was in them. Ezk 1:3,5,21

¹⁸ Then the glory of the LORD moved away from the threshold of the temple and stopped above the cherubim. ¹⁹ The cherubim lifted their wings and ascended from the earth right before my eyes; the wheels were beside them as they went. The glory of the God of Israel was above them, and it stopped at the entrance to the eastern gate of the LORD's house. Ps 18:10; Ezk 10:4

²⁰ These were the living creatures I had seen beneath the God of Israel by the Chebar Canal, and I recognized that they were cherubim. ²¹ Each had four faces and each had four wings, with what looked something like human hands under their wings. ²² Their faces looked like the same faces I had seen by the Chebar Canal. Each creature went straight ahead.

Vision of Israel's Corrupt Leaders

11 The Spirit then lifted me up and brought me to the eastern gate of the LORD's house, which faces east, and at the gate's entrance were twenty-five men. Among them I saw Jaazaniah son of Azzur, and Pelatiah son of Benaiah, leaders of the people. ² The LORDᴬ said to me, "Son of man, these are the men who plot evil and give wicked advice in this city. ³ They are saying, 'Isn't the time near to build houses?ᴮ The city is the pot, and we are the meat.' ⁴ Therefore, prophesy against them. Prophesy, son of man!" Gn 6:5; Ps 36:4; Ezk 3:12,14; 8:3

⁵ Then the Spirit of the LORD came on me, and he told me, "You are to say, 'This is what the LORD says: That is what you are thinking, house of

ᴬ**11:2** Lit *He*   ᴮ**11:3** Or *"The time is not near to build houses.*

Israel; and I know the thoughts that arise in your mind. ⁶ You have multiplied your slain in this city, filling its streets with them. Jr 17:10; Ezk 2:2

⁷ " 'Therefore, this is what the Lord GOD says: The slain you have put within it are the meat, and the city is the pot, but I ᴬ will take you out of it. ⁸ You fear the sword, so I will bring the sword against you. This is the declaration of the Lord GOD. ⁹ I will take you out of the city and hand you over to foreigners; I will execute judgments against you. ¹⁰ You will fall by the sword, and I will judge you at the border of Israel. Then you will know that I am the LORD. ¹¹ The city will not be a pot for you, and you will not be the meat within it. I will judge you at the border of Israel, ¹² so you will know that I am the LORD, whose statutes you have not followed and whose ordinances you have not practiced. Instead, you have acted according to the ordinances of the nations around you.' " Ezk 24:3-13

¹³ Now while I was prophesying, Pelatiah son of Benaiah died. Then I fell facedown and cried out loudly, "Oh, Lord GOD! You are bringing the remnant of Israel to an end!"

Promise of Israel's Restoration

¹⁴ The word of the LORD came to me again: ¹⁵ "Son of man, your own relatives, those who have the right to redeem your property, ᴮ,ᶜ along with the entire house of Israel — all of them — are those to whom the residents of Jerusalem have said, 'You are far from the LORD; this land has been given to us as a possession.'

¹⁶ "Therefore say, 'This is what the Lord GOD says: Though I sent them far away among the nations and scattered them among the countries, yet for a little while I have been a sanctuary for them in the countries where they have gone.'

¹⁷ "Therefore say, 'This is what the Lord GOD says: I will gather you from the peoples and assemble you from the countries where you have been scattered, and I will give you the land of Israel.'

¹⁸ "When they arrive there, they will remove all its abhorrent acts and detestable practices from it. ¹⁹ I will give them integrity of ᴰ heart and put a new spirit within them; I will remove their heart of stone from their bodies ᴱ and give them a heart of flesh, ²⁰ so that they will follow my statutes, keep my ordinances, and practice them. They will be my people, and I will be their God. ²¹ But as for those whose hearts pursue their desire for abhorrent acts and detestable practices, I will bring their conduct down on their own heads." This is the declaration of the Lord GOD. Ps 51:10; Jr 32:39; Ezk 5:11; 37:23; Zch 7:12

God's Glory Leaves Jerusalem

²² Then the cherubim, with the wheels beside them, lifted their wings, and the glory of the God of Israel was above them. ²³ The glory of the LORD rose up from within the city and stopped on the mountain east of the city. ᶠ ²⁴ The Spirit lifted me up and brought me to Chaldea and to the exiles in a vision from the Spirit of God. After the vision I had seen left me, ²⁵ I spoke to the

---

ᴬ11:7 Some Hb mss, LXX, Syr, Tg, Vg; other Hb mss read *he*   ᴮ11:15 LXX, Syr read *your relatives, your fellow exiles*   ᶜ11:15 Or *own brothers, your relatives*   ᴰ11:19 Lit *give them one*   ᴱ11:19 Lit *flesh*   ᶠ11:23 = the Mount of Olives exiles about all the things the LORD had shown me.   Ezk 8:4; 10:19; Zch 14:4

Ezekiel Dramatizes the Exile

12 The word of the LORD came to me: ² "Son of man, you are living among a rebellious house. They have eyes to see but do not see, and ears to hear but do not hear, for they are a rebellious house.

³ "Now you, son of man, get your bags ready for exile and go into exile in their sight during the day. You will go into exile from your place to another place while they watch; perhaps they will understand, though they are a rebellious house. ⁴ During the day, bring out your bags like an exile's bags while they look on. Then in the evening go out in their sight like those going into exile. ⁵ As they watch, dig through the wall and take the bags out through it. ⁶ And while they look on, lift the bags to your shoulder and take them out in the dark; cover your face so that you cannot see the land. For I have made you a sign to the house of Israel."   Ezk 4:3

⁷ So I did just as I was commanded. In the daytime I brought out my bags like an exile's bags. In the evening I dug through the wall by hand; I took them out in the dark, carrying them on my shoulder in their sight.

⁸ In the morning the word of the LORD came to me: ⁹ "Son of man, hasn't the house of Israel, that rebellious house, asked you, 'What are you doing?' ¹⁰ Say to them, 'This is what the Lord GOD says: This pronouncement concerns the prince^A in Jerusalem and the whole house of Israel living there.'^B ¹¹ You are to say, 'I am a sign for you. Just as I have done, it will be done to them; they will go into exile, into captivity.' ¹² The prince who is among them will lift his bags to his shoulder in the dark and go out. They^C will dig through the wall to bring him out through it. He will cover his face so he cannot see the land with his eyes. ¹³ But I will spread my net over him, and he will be caught in my snare. I will bring him to Babylon, the land of the Chaldeans, yet he will not see it, and he will die there. ¹⁴ I will also scatter all the attendants who surround him and all his troops to every direction of the wind, and I will draw a sword to chase after them. ¹⁵ They will know that I am the LORD when I disperse them among the nations and scatter them among the countries. ¹⁶ But I will spare a few of them from the sword, famine, and plague, so that among the nations where they go they can tell about all their detestable practices. Then they will know that I am the LORD."   Ezk 2:5-8; 17:12; 20:49; 24:19

Ezekiel Dramatizes Israel's Anxiety

¹⁷ The word of the LORD came to me: ¹⁸ "Son of man, eat your bread with trembling and drink your water with anxious shaking. ¹⁹ Then say to the people of the land, 'This is what the Lord GOD says about the residents of Jerusalem in the land of Israel: They will eat their bread with anxiety and drink their water in dread, for their^{D,E} land will be stripped of everything in it because of the violence of all who live there. ²⁰ The inhabited cities will

^A**12:10** = King Zedekiah   ^B**12:10** Lit *Israel among them*   ^C**12:12** LXX, Syr read *He*   ^D**12:19** Lit *its*
^E**12:19** = Jerusalem's

be destroyed, and the land will become dreadful. Then you will know that I am the Lord.'" Ezk 4:16; Zch 7:14

A Deceptive Proverb Stopped

21 Again the word of the Lord came to me: 22 "Son of man, what is this proverb you people have about the land of Israel, which goes, 'The days keep passing by, and every vision fails'? 23 Therefore say to them, 'This is what the Lord God says: I will put a stop to this proverb, and they will not use it again in Israel.' But say to them, 'The days have arrived, as well as the fulfillment of every vision. 24 For there will no longer be any false vision or flattering divination within the house of Israel. 25 But I, the Lord, will speak whatever message I will speak, and it will be done. It will no longer be delayed. For in your days, rebellious house, I will speak a message and bring it to pass. This is the declaration of the Lord God.'" Ezk 16:44

26 The word of the Lord came to me: 27 "Son of man, notice that the house of Israel is saying, 'The vision that he sees concerns many years from now; he prophesies about distant times.' 28 Therefore say to them, 'This is what the Lord God says: None of my words will be delayed any longer. The message I speak will be fulfilled. This is the declaration of the Lord God.'"

Israel's False Prophets Condemned

13 The word of the Lord came to me: 2 "Son of man, prophesy against the prophets of Israel who are prophesying. Say to those who prophesy out of their own imagination, 'Hear the word of the Lord!

3 This is what the Lord God says: Woe to the foolish prophets who follow their own spirit and have seen nothing. 4 Your prophets, Israel, are like jackals among ruins. 5 You did not go up to the gaps or restore the wall around the house of Israel so that it might stand in battle on the day of the Lord. 6 They saw false visions and their divinations were a lie. They claimed, "This is the Lord's declaration," when the Lord did not send them, yet they wait for the fulfillment of their message. 7 Didn't you see a false vision and speak a lying divination when you proclaimed, "This is the Lord's declaration," even though I had not spoken? Jr 23:16,26; Ezk 22:25,28

8 " 'Therefore, this is what the Lord God says: You have spoken falsely and had lying visions; that's why you discover that I am against you. This is the declaration of the Lord God. 9 My hand will be against the prophets who see false visions and speak lying divinations. They will not be present in the council of my people or be recorded in the register of the house of Israel, and they will not enter the land of Israel. Then you will know that I am the Lord God. Jr 20:3-6; 28:15-17

10 " 'Since they have led my people astray by saying, "Peace," when there is no peace, and since when a flimsy wall is being built, they plaster it with whitewash, 11 therefore, tell those plastering it with whitewash that it will fall. Torrential rain will come, and I will send hailstones plunging[A] down, and a whirlwind will be released. 12 When the wall has fallen, will you not be asked, "Where's the whitewash you plastered on it?" Jr 6:14; 8:11; 14:13; Mc 3:5

A13:11 One Hb ms, LXX, Vg; other Hb mss read *and you, hailstones, will plunge*

13 " 'So this is what the Lord God says: I will release a whirlwind in my wrath. Torrential rain will come in my anger, and hailstones will fall in destructive fury. 14 I will demolish the wall you plastered with whitewash and knock it to the ground so that its foundation is exposed. The city will fall, and you will be destroyed within it. Then you will know that I am the Lord. 15 After I exhaust my wrath against the wall and against those who plaster it with whitewash, I will say to you, "The wall is no more and neither are those who plastered it — 16 those prophets of Israel who prophesied to Jerusalem and saw a vision of peace for her when there was no peace." This is the declaration of the Lord God.'

17 "Now you, son of man, face^A the women among your people who prophesy out of their own imagination, and prophesy against them. 18 Say, 'This is what the Lord God says: Woe to the women who sew magic bands on the wrist of every hand and who make veils for the heads of people of every size in order to ensnare lives. Will you ensnare the lives of my people but preserve your own? 19 You profane me among my people for handfuls of barley and scraps of bread; you put those to death who should not die and spare those who should not live, when you lie to my people, who listen to lies. Jdg 4:4; 2Kg 22:14 20 " 'Therefore, this is what the Lord God says: I am against your magic bands with which you ensnare people like birds, and I will tear them from your arms. I will free the people you have ensnared like birds. 21 I will also tear off your veils and rescue my people from your hands, so that they will no longer be prey in your hands. Then you will know that I am the Lord. 22 Because you have disheartened the righteous person with lies (when I intended no distress), and because you have supported^B the wicked person so that he does not turn from his evil way to save his life, 23 therefore you will no longer see false visions or practice divination. I will rescue my people from your hands. Then you will know that I am the Lord.' " Ps 91:3; 124:7; Jr 23:14; 28:15

Idolatrous Elders Punished

14 Some of the elders of Israel came to me and sat down in front of me. 2 Then the word of the Lord came to me: 3 "Son of man, these men have set up idols in their hearts and have put their sinful stumbling blocks in front of themselves. Should I actually let them inquire of me? Ezk 7:19; 8:1; 20:1

4 "Therefore, speak to them and tell them, 'This is what the Lord God says: When anyone from the house of Israel sets up idols in his heart and puts his sinful stumbling block in front of himself, and then comes to the prophet, I, the Lord, will answer him appropriately.^C I will answer him according to his many idols, 5 so that I may take hold of the house of Israel by their hearts. They are all estranged from me because of their idols.'

6 "Therefore, say to the house of Israel, 'This is what the Lord God says: Repent and turn away from your idols; turn your faces away from all your detestable things.

---

^A 13:17 Lit set your face   ^B 13:22 Lit strengthened the hand of   ^C 14:4 Alt Hb tradition reads him who comes

⁷ For when anyone from the house of Israel or from the aliens who reside in Israel separates himself from me, setting up idols in his heart and putting his sinful stumbling block in front of himself, and then comes to the prophet to inquire of me, I, the Lord, will answer him myself. ⁸ I will turn against that one and make him a sign and a proverb; I will cut him off from among my people. Then you will know that I am the Lord. 1Sm 7:3;15:7

⁹ "'But if the prophet is deceived and speaks a message, it was I, the Lord, who deceived that prophet. I will stretch out my hand against him and destroy him from among my people Israel. ¹⁰ They will bear their punishment — the punishment of the one who inquires will be the same as that of the prophet — ¹¹ in order that the house of Israel may no longer stray from following me and no longer defile themselves with all their transgressions. Then they will be my people and I will be their God. This is the declaration of the Lord God.'"

Four Devastating Judgments

¹² The word of the Lord came to me: ¹³ "Son of man, suppose a land sins against me by acting faithlessly, and I stretch out my hand against it to cut off its supply of bread, to send famine through it, and to wipe out both man and animal from it. ¹⁴ Even if these three men — Noah, Daniel, and Job — were in it, they would rescue only themselves by their righteousness." This is the declaration of the Lord God.

¹⁵ "Suppose I allow dangerous animals to pass through the land and depopulate it so that it becomes desolate, with no one passing through it for fear of the animals. ¹⁶ Even if these three men were in it, as I live" — the declaration of the Lord God — "they could not rescue their sons or daughters. They alone would be rescued, but the land would be desolate. Lv 26:22

¹⁷ "Or suppose I bring a sword against that land and say, 'Let a sword pass through it,' so that I wipe out both man and animal from it. ¹⁸ Even if these three men were in it, as I live" — the declaration of the Lord God — "they could not rescue their sons or daughters, but they alone would be rescued.

¹⁹ "Or suppose I send a plague into that land and pour out my wrath on it with bloodshed to wipe out both man and animal from it. ²⁰ Even if Noah, Daniel, and Job were in it, as I live" — the declaration of the Lord God — "they could not rescue their son or daughter. They would rescue only themselves by their righteousness. 2Sm 24:15; Ezk 38:22

²¹ "For this is what the Lord God says: How much worse will it be when I send my four devastating judgments against Jerusalem — sword, famine, dangerous animals, and plague — in order to wipe out both man and animal from it! ²² Even so, there will be survivors left in it, sons and daughters who will be brought out. Indeed, they will come out to you, and you will observe their conduct and actions. Then you will be consoled about the devastation I have brought on Jerusalem, about all I have brought on it. ²³ They will bring you consolation when you see their conduct and actions, and you will know that it was not without cause that I have done what I did to it." This is the declaration of the Lord God.

Parable of the Useless Vine

15 Then the word of the LORD came to me: ² "Son of man, how does the wood of the vine, that branch among the trees of the forest, compare to any other wood? ³ Can wood be taken from it to make something useful? Or can anyone make a peg from it to hang things on? ⁴ In fact, it is put into the fire as fuel. The fire devours both of its ends, and the middle is charred. Can it be useful for anything? ⁵ Even when it was whole it could not be made into a useful object. How much less can it ever be made into anything useful when the fire has devoured it and it is charred!" Ps 80:8-16; Is 5:1-7; Hs 10:1; Jn 15:6

⁶ Therefore, this is what the Lord GOD says, "Like the wood of the vine among the trees of the forest, which I have given to the fire as fuel, so I will give up the residents of Jerusalem. ⁷ I will turn against them. They may have escaped from the fire, but it will still consume them. And you will know that I am the LORD when I turn against them. ⁸ I will make the land desolate because they have acted unfaithfully." This is the declaration of the Lord GOD. Ezk 14:8

Parable of God's Adulterous Wife

16 The word of the LORD came to me again: ² "Son of man, confront Jerusalem with her detestable practices. ³ You are to say, 'This is what the Lord GOD says to Jerusalem: Your origin and your birth were in the land of the Canaanites. Your father was an Amorite and your mother a Hethite. ⁴ As for your birth, your umbilical cord wasn't cut on the day you were born, and you weren't washed clean ᴬ with water. You were not rubbed with salt or wrapped in cloths. ⁵ No one cared enough about you to do even one of these things out of compassion for you. But you were thrown out into the open field because you were despised on the day you were born. Dt 7:1; Jdg 3:5; Is 58:1; Ezk 16:45; 20:4; 22:2

⁶ " 'I passed by you and saw you thrashing around in your blood, and I said to you as you lay in your blood, "Live!" Yes, I said to you as you lay in your blood, "Live!" ᴮ ⁷ I made you thrive ᶜ like plants of the field. You grew up and matured and became very beautiful. ᴰ Your breasts were formed and your hair grew, but you were stark naked. Ex 1:7

⁸ " 'Then I passed by you and saw you, and you were indeed at the age for love. So I spread the edge of my garment over you and covered your nakedness. I pledged myself to you, entered into a covenant with you — this is the declaration of the Lord GOD — and you became mine. ⁹ I washed you with water, rinsed off your blood, and anointed you with oil. ¹⁰ I clothed you in embroidered cloth and provided you with fine leather ᴬ sandals. I also wrapped you in fine linen and covered you with silk. ¹¹ I adorned you with jewelry, putting bracelets on your wrists and a necklace around your neck. ¹² I put a ring in your nose, earrings on your ears, and a beautiful crown on your head. ¹³ So you were adorned with gold and silver, and your clothing was made of fine linen, silk, and embroidered cloth. You ate fine

ᴬ**16:4,10** Hb obscure   ᴮ**16:6** Some Hb mss, LXX, Syr omit *Yes, I said to you as you lay in your blood, "Live!"*   ᶜ**16:7** LXX reads *Thrive; I made you*   ᴰ**16:7** Or *matured and developed the loveliest of ornaments* flour, honey, and oil. You became extremely beautiful and attained royalty. [14] Your fame spread among the nations because of your beauty, for it was perfect through my splendor, which I had bestowed on you. This is the declaration of the Lord God.　　Gn 22:16-18; Ru 3:9; Jr 2:2

[15] " 'But you trusted in your beauty and acted like a prostitute because of your fame. You lavished your sexual favors on everyone who passed by. Your beauty became his. [A] [16] You took some of your clothing and made colorful high places for yourself, and you engaged in prostitution on them. These places should not have been built, and this should never have happened! [A] [17] You also took your beautiful jewelry made from the gold and silver I had given you, and you made male images so that you could engage in prostitution with them. [18] Then you took your embroidered clothing to cover them and set my oil and incense before them. [19] The food that I gave you — the fine flour, oil, and honey that I fed you — you set it before them as a pleasing aroma. That is what happened. This is the declaration of the Lord God.　　Pr 7:8-13; Is 57:8; Jr 2:20

[20] " 'You even took your sons and daughters you bore to me and sacrificed them to these images as food. Wasn't your prostitution enough? [21] You slaughtered my children and gave them up when you passed them through the fire to the images. [22] In all your detestable practices and acts of prostitution, you did not remember the days of your youth when you were stark naked and thrashing around in your blood.　　Lv 18:21; Jr 7:31; 19:5; Ezk 23:37

[23] " 'Then after all your evil — Woe, woe to you! — the declaration of the Lord God — [24] you built yourself a mound and made yourself an elevated place in every square. [25] You built your elevated place at the head of every street and turned your beauty into a detestable thing. You spread your legs to everyone who passed by and increased your prostitution. [26] You engaged in promiscuous acts with Egyptian men, your well-endowed neighbors, and increased your prostitution to anger me.　　Pr 9:14; Jr 11:13; Ezk 23:19-20

[27] " 'Therefore, I stretched out my hand against you and reduced your provisions. I gave you over to the desire of those who hate you, the Philistine women, who were embarrassed by your indecent conduct. [28] Then you engaged in prostitution with the Assyrian men because you were not satisfied. Even though you did this with them, you were still not satisfied. [29] So you extended your prostitution to Chaldea, the land of merchants, but you were not even satisfied with this!　　Jr 2:18,36; Ezk 16:57

[30] " 'How your heart was inflamed with lust [B] — the declaration of the Lord God — when you did all these things, the acts of a brazen prostitute, [31] building your mound at the head of every street and making your elevated place in every square. But you were unlike a prostitute because you scorned payment. [32] You adulterous wife, who receives strangers instead of her husband! [33] Men give gifts to all prostitutes, but you gave gifts to all your lovers. You bribed them to come to you from all around for your sexual favors. [34] So you were

the opposite of other women in your acts of prostitution; no one solicited you. When you paid a fee instead of one being paid to you, you were the opposite.   Is 52:3

35 " 'Therefore, you prostitute, hear the word of the LORD! 36 This is what the Lord GOD says: Because your lust was poured out and your nakedness exposed by your acts of prostitution with your lovers, and because of all your detestable idols and the blood of your children that you gave to them, 37 I am therefore going to gather all the lovers you pleased — all those you loved as well as all those you hated. I will gather them against you from all around and expose your nakedness to them so they see you completely naked. 38 I will judge you the way adulteresses and those who shed blood are judged. Then I will bring about the shedding of your blood in jealous wrath. 39 I will hand you over to them, and they will demolish your mounds and tear down your elevated places. They will strip off your clothes, take your beautiful jewelry, and leave you stark naked. 40 They will bring a mob against you to stone you and to cut you to pieces with their swords. 41 They will burn your houses and execute judgments against you in the sight of many women. I will stop you from being a prostitute, and you will never again pay fees for lovers. 42 So I will satisfy my wrath against you, and my jealousy will turn away from you. Then I will be calm and no longer angry. 43 Because you did not remember the days of your youth but enraged me with all these things, I will also

bring your conduct down on your own head. This is the declaration of the Lord GOD. Haven't you committed depravity in addition to all your detestable practices?

44 " 'Look, everyone who uses proverbs will quote this proverb about you: "Like mother, like daughter." 45 You are the daughter of your mother, who despised her husband and children. You are the sister of your sisters, who despised their husbands and children. Your mother was a Hethite and your father an Amorite. 46 Your older sister was Samaria, who lived with her daughters to the north of you, and your younger sister was Sodom, who lived with her daughters to the south of you. 47 Didn't you walk in their ways and do their detestable practices? It was only a short time before all your ways were more corrupt than theirs.   Ezk 16:31; 23:2

48 " 'As I live — the declaration of the Lord GOD — your sister Sodom and her daughters have not behaved as you and your daughters have. 49 Now this was the iniquity of your sister Sodom: She and her daughters had pride, plenty of food, and comfortable security, but didn't support A the poor and needy. 50 They were haughty and did detestable acts before me, so I removed them when I saw this. B 51 But Samaria did not commit even half your sins. You have multiplied your detestable practices beyond theirs and made your sisters appear righteous by all the detestable acts you have committed. 52 You must also bear your disgrace, since you have helped your sisters out. C For they appear

A 16:49 Lit strengthen the hand of   B 16:50 Or them as you have seen   C 16:52 Lit you have been the advocate for your sisters more righteous than you because of your sins, which you committed more detestably than they did. So you also, be ashamed and bear your disgrace, since you have made your sisters appear righteous. Gn 13:10; 18:20-21; Mt 10:15; 11:23-24

53 " 'I will restore their fortunes, the fortunes of Sodom and her daughters and those of Samaria and her daughters. I will also restore^A your fortunes among them, 54 so you will bear your disgrace and be ashamed of all you did when you comforted them. 55 As for your sisters, Sodom and her daughters and Samaria and her daughters will return to their former state. You and your daughters will also return to your former state. 56 Didn't you treat your sister Sodom as an object of scorn when you were proud, 57 before your wickedness was exposed? It was like the time you were scorned by the daughters of Aram^B and all those around her, and by the daughters of the Philistines — those who treated you with contempt from every side. 58 You yourself must bear the consequences of your depravity and detestable practices — this is the LORD's declaration. Is 1:9; Jr 20:16

59 " 'For this is what the Lord GOD says: I will deal with you according to what you have done, since you have despised the oath by breaking the covenant. 60 But I will remember the covenant I made with you in the days of your youth, and I will establish a permanent covenant with you. 61 Then you will remember your ways and be ashamed when you^C receive your older and younger

sisters. I will give them to you as daughters, but not because of your covenant. 62 I will establish my covenant with you, and you will know that I am the LORD, 63 so that when I make atonement for all you have done, you will remember and be ashamed, and never open your mouth again because of your disgrace. This is the declaration of the Lord GOD.' " Is 55:3; Jr 32:38-41; Ezk 17:19

Parable of the Eagles

17 The word of the LORD came to me: 2 "Son of man, pose a riddle and speak a parable to the house of Israel. 3 You are to say, 'This is what the Lord GOD says: A huge eagle with powerful wings, long feathers, and full plumage of many colors came to Lebanon and took the top of the cedar. 4 He plucked off its topmost shoot, brought it to the land of merchants, and set it in a city of traders. 5 Then he took some of the land's seed and put it in a fertile field; he set it like a willow, a plant^D by abundant water. 6 It sprouted and became a spreading vine, low in height with its branches turned toward him, yet its roots stayed under it. So it became a vine, produced branches, and sent out shoots. Is 44:4; Jr 48:40; Ezk 17:12; 20:49; 24:3

7 " 'But there was another huge eagle with powerful wings and thick plumage. And this vine bent its roots toward him! It stretched out its branches to him from the plot where it was planted, so that he might water it. 8 It had been planted in a good field by abundant water in order to produce branches, bear fruit, and become a splendid vine.' Ezk 31:4

^A16:53 LXX, Vg; MT reads *Samaria and her daughters and the fortunes of*   ^B16:57 Some Hb mss, Syr read *Edom*   ^C16:61 Some LXX mss, Syr read *I*   ^D17:5 Hb obscure

⁹ "You are to say, 'This is what the Lord God says: Will it flourish? Will he not tear out its roots and strip off its fruit so that it shrivels? All its fresh leaves will wither! Great strength and many people will not be needed to pull it from its roots. ¹⁰ Even though it is planted, will it flourish? Won't it wither completely when the east wind strikes it? It will wither on the plot where it sprouted.'" Gn 41:6; 2Kg 19:26; 25:7

¹¹ The word of the Lord came to me: ¹² "Now say to that rebellious house, 'Don't you know what these things mean?' Tell them, 'The king of Babylon came to Jerusalem, took its king and officials, and brought them back with him to Babylon. ¹³ He took one of the royal family and made a covenant with him, putting him under oath. Then he took away the leading men of the land, ¹⁴ so that the kingdom would be humble and not exalt itself but would keep his covenant in order to endure. ¹⁵ However, this king revolted against him by sending his ambassadors to Egypt so they might give him horses and a large army. Will he flourish? Will the one who does such things escape? Can he break a covenant and still escape? 2Kg 24:11-15,17; Ezk 2:3-5; 12:9-11

¹⁶ "'As I live — this is the declaration of the Lord God — he will die in Babylon, in the land of the king who put him on the throne, whose oath he despised and whose covenant he broke. ¹⁷ Pharaoh with his mighty army and vast company will not help him in battle, when ramps are built and siege walls constructed to destroy many lives. ¹⁸ He despised the oath by breaking the covenant. He did all these things

even though he gave his hand in pledge. He will not escape! Ezk 12:13

¹⁹ "'Therefore, this is what the Lord God says: As I live, I will bring down on his head my oath that he despised and my covenant that he broke. ²⁰ I will spread my net over him, and he will be caught in my snare. I will bring him to Babylon and execute judgment on him there for the treachery he committed against me. ²¹ All the fugitives[A] among his troops will fall by the sword, and those who survive will be scattered to every direction of the wind. Then you will know that I, the Lord, have spoken. Jr 39:5

²² "'This is what the Lord God says:

I will take a sprig
from the lofty top
    of the cedar and plant it.
I will pluck a tender sprig
from its topmost shoots,
and I will plant it
on a high towering mountain.
²³ I will plant it on Israel's
    high mountain Ezk 20:40
so that it may bear branches,
    produce fruit,
and become a majestic cedar.
Birds of every kind will nest
    under it, Dn 4:12
taking shelter in the shade
    of its branches.
²⁴ Then all the trees of the field
    will know
    that I am the Lord.
I bring down the tall tree,
    and make the low tree tall.
I cause the green tree
    to wither
and make
    the withered tree thrive.
I, the Lord, have spoken
and I will do it.'" Nm 14:35; Ps 33:9

A17:21 Some Hb mss, LXX, Syr, Tg read *choice men*

Personal Responsibility for Sin

18 The word of the LORD came to me: ² "What do you mean by using this proverb concerning the land of Israel:

'The fathers eat sour grapes,
and the children's teeth
are set on edge'?   Jr 31:29

³ As I live" — this is the declaration of the Lord GOD — "you will no longer use this proverb in Israel. ⁴ Look, every life belongs to me. The life of the father is like the life of the son — both belong to me. The person who sins is the one who will die.   Nm 16:22; 27:16; Dt 24:16; Ezk 12:23; 18:20

⁵ "Suppose a man is righteous and does what is just and right: ⁶ He does not eat at the mountain shrines^A or look to the idols of the house of Israel. He does not defile his neighbor's wife or approach a woman during her menstrual impurity. ⁷ He doesn't oppress anyone but returns his collateral to the debtor. He does not commit robbery, but gives his bread to the hungry and covers the naked with clothing. ⁸ He doesn't lend at interest or for profit but keeps his hand from injustice and carries out true justice between men. ⁹ He follows my statutes and keeps my ordinances, acting faithfully. Such a person is righteous; he will certainly live." This is the declaration of the Lord GOD.   Ex 20:17-18; 22:9

¹⁰ "But suppose the man has a violent son, who sheds blood and does any of these things, ¹¹ though the father has done none of them. Indeed, when the son eats at the mountain shrines and defiles his neighbor's wife, ¹² and when he oppresses the poor and needy, commits robbery, and does not return

collateral, and when he looks to the idols, commits detestable acts, ¹³ and lends at interest or for profit, will he live? He will not live! Since he has committed all these detestable acts, he will certainly die. His death will be his own fault. ^B

¹⁴ "Now suppose he has a son who sees all the sins his father has committed, and though he sees them, he does not do likewise. ¹⁵ He does not eat at the mountain shrines or look to the idols of the house of Israel. He does not defile his neighbor's wife. ¹⁶ He doesn't oppress anyone, hold collateral, or commit robbery. He gives his bread to the hungry and covers the naked with clothing. ¹⁷ He keeps his hand from harming the poor, not taking interest or profit on a loan. He practices my ordinances and follows my statutes. Such a person will not die for his father's iniquity. He will certainly live.

¹⁸ "As for his father, he will die for his own iniquity because he practiced fraud, robbed his brother, and did among his people what was not good. ¹⁹ But you may ask, 'Why doesn't the son suffer punishment for the father's iniquity?' Since the son has done what is just and right, carefully observing all my statutes, he will certainly live. ²⁰ The person who sins is the one who will die. A son won't suffer punishment for the father's iniquity, and a father won't suffer punishment for the son's iniquity. The righteousness of the righteous person will be on him, and the wickedness of the wicked person will be on him.   Ex 20:5; Dt 24:16; Ezk 3:18; 18:4

²¹ "But if the wicked person turns from all the sins he has committed,

---

^A **18:6** Lit *the mountains*, also in vv. 11,15   ^B **18:13** Lit *His blood will be on him* keeps all my statutes, and does what is just and right, he will certainly live; he will not die. ²² None of the transgressions he has committed will be held against him. He will live because of the righteousness he has practiced. ²³ Do I take any pleasure in the death of the wicked?" This is the declaration of the Lord God. "Instead, don't I take pleasure when he turns from his ways and lives? ²⁴ But when a righteous person turns from his righteousness and acts unjustly, committing the same detestable acts that the wicked do, will he live? None of the righteous acts he did will be remembered. He will die because of the treachery he has engaged in and the sin he has committed. Ps 18:20-24; Ezk 33:12,16,19

²⁵ "But you say, 'The Lord's way isn't fair.' Now listen, house of Israel: Is it my way that is unfair? Instead, isn't it your ways that are unfair? ²⁶ When a righteous person turns from his righteousness and acts unjustly, he will die for this. He will die because of the injustice he has committed. ²⁷ But if a wicked person turns from the wickedness he has committed and does what is just and right, he will preserve his life. ²⁸ He will certainly live because he thought it over and turned from all the transgressions he had committed; he will not die. ²⁹ But the house of Israel says, 'The Lord's way isn't fair.' Is it my ways that are unfair, house of Israel? Instead, isn't it your ways that are unfair? Ezk 18:29; 33:17,20

³⁰ "Therefore, house of Israel, I will judge each one of you according to his ways." This is the declaration of the Lord God.

ᴬ19:7 Tg, Aq; MT reads *knew their widows*

"Repent and turn from all your rebellious acts, so they will not become a sinful stumbling block to you. ³¹ Throw off all the transgressions you have committed, and get yourselves a new heart and a new spirit. Why should you die, house of Israel? ³² For I take no pleasure in anyone's death." This is the declaration of the Lord God. "So repent and live! Jr 32:39; Ezk 7:3,8; 33:20

A Lament for Israel's Princes

19 "As for you, take up a lament for the princes of Israel, ² and say: Ezk 26:17; 27:2

What was your mother?
   A lioness!
She lay down
   among the lions;
she reared her cubs
   among the young lions.
³ She brought up one
   of her cubs,
and he became a young lion.
After he learned to tear prey,
   he devoured people.
⁴ When the nations
   heard about him,
he was caught in their pit.
Then they led him away
   with hooks
to the land of Egypt. 2Kg 23:34

⁵ When she saw that she
   waited in vain,
that her hope was lost,
she took another of her cubs
and made him a young lion.
⁶ He prowled among the lions,
and he became a young lion.
After he learned to tear prey,
   he devoured people.
⁷ He devastated
   their strongholdsᴬ
and destroyed their cities.

The land and everything
in it shuddered
at the sound of his roaring.
8 Then the nations from
the surrounding provinces
set out against him. 2Kg 24:2,11
They spread their net
over him;
he was caught in their pit.
9 They put a wooden yoke
on him A with hooks 2Ch 36:6
and led him away to the king
of Babylon.
They brought him into the
fortresses
so his roar could no longer
be heard
on the mountains of Israel.

10 Your mother was like a vine
in your vineyard, B Ps 80:8-11
planted by the water;
it was fruitful and full
of branches Dt 8:7-9
because of abundant water.
11 It had strong branches, fit for
the scepters of rulers;
its height towered
among the clouds. C
So it was conspicuous
for its height
as well as its many branches.
12 But it was uprooted in fury,
thrown to the ground,
and the east wind dried up
its fruit.
Its strong branches were
torn off and dried up; Hs 13:15
fire consumed them.
13 Now it is planted
in the wilderness, 2Kg 24:12-16
in a dry and thirsty land.
14 Fire has gone out from its
main branch D

and has devoured its fruit,
so that it no longer has
a strong branch,
a scepter for ruling. Lm 2:5
This is a lament and should be used
as a lament."

Israel's Rebellion

20 In the seventh year, in the
fifth month, on the tenth day
of the month, some of Israel's elders came to inquire of the LORD,
and they sat down in front of me.
2 Then the word of the LORD came
to me: 3 "Son of man, speak with the
elders of Israel and tell them, 'This
is what the Lord GOD says: Are you
coming to inquire of me? As I live, I
will not let you inquire of me. This
is the declaration of the Lord GOD.'

4 "Will you pass judgment against
them, will you pass judgment, son
of man? Explain the detestable
practices of their fathers to them.
5 Say to them, 'This is what the Lord
GOD says: On the day I chose Israel, I swore an oath E to the descendants of Jacob's house and made
myself known to them in the land of
Egypt. I swore to them, saying, "I am
the LORD your God." 6 On that day I
swore F to them that I would bring
them out of the land of Egypt into
a land I had searched out for them,
a land flowing with milk and honey, the most beautiful of all lands.
7 I also said to them, "Throw away,
each of you, the abhorrent things
that you prize, G and do not defile
yourselves with the idols of Egypt.
I am the LORD your God." Ezk 16:2; 22:2

8 " 'But they rebelled against me
and were unwilling to listen to
me. None of them threw away the

A 19:9 Or put him in a cage B 19:10 Some Hb mss; other Hb mss read blood C 19:11 Or thick foliage
D 19:14 Lit from the branch of its parts E 20:5 Lit I lifted my hand F 20:6 Lit lifted my hand, also in
vv. 15,23,28,42 G 20:7 Lit things of your eyes

abhorrent things that they prized, [A] and they did not abandon the idols of Egypt. So I considered pouring out my wrath on them, exhausting my anger against them within the land of Egypt. [9] But I acted for the sake of my name, so that it would not be profaned in the eyes of the nations they were living among, in whose sight I had made myself known to Israel by bringing them out of Egypt.   Ezk 5:13; 7:8; 36:21-22

[10] " 'So I brought them out of the land of Egypt and led them into the wilderness. [11] Then I gave them my statutes and explained my ordinances to them — the person who does them will live by them. [12] I also gave them my Sabbaths to serve as a sign between me and them, so that they would know that I am the LORD who consecrates them.

[13] " 'But the house of Israel rebelled against me in the wilderness. They did not follow my statutes and they rejected my ordinances — the person who does them will live by them. They also completely profaned my Sabbaths. So I considered pouring out my wrath on them in the wilderness to put an end to them. [14] But I acted for the sake of my name, so that it would not be profaned in the eyes of the nations in whose sight I had brought them out. [15] However, I swore to them in the wilderness that I would not bring them into the land I had given them — the most beautiful of all lands, flowing with milk and honey — [16] because they rejected my ordinances, profaned my Sabbaths, and did not follow my statutes. For their hearts went after their idols. [17] Yet I spared them from destruction and did not bring them to an end in the wilderness.   Lv 18:5; Nm 14:11-12,22; Ezk 22:8; 23:38

[18] " 'Then I said to their children in the wilderness, "Don't follow the statutes of your fathers, defile yourselves with their idols, or keep their ordinances. [19] I am the LORD your God. Follow my statutes, keep my ordinances, and practice them. [20] Keep my Sabbaths holy, and they will be a sign between me and you, so you may know that I am the LORD your God."   Dt 5:32-33; Jr 17:22; Mt 15:1-3

[21] " 'But the children rebelled against me. They did not follow my statutes or carefully keep my ordinances — the person who does them will live by them. They also profaned my Sabbaths. So I considered pouring out my wrath on them and exhausting my anger against them in the wilderness. [22] But I withheld my hand and acted for the sake of my name, so that it would not be profaned in the eyes of the nations in whose sight I brought them out. [23] However, I swore to them in the wilderness that I would disperse them among the nations and scatter them among the countries. [24] For they did not practice my ordinances but rejected my statutes and profaned my Sabbaths, and their eyes were fixed on their fathers' idols. [25] I also gave them statutes that were not good and ordinances they could not live by. [26] When they sacrificed every firstborn in the fire, [B] I defiled them through their gifts in order to devastate them so they would know that I am the LORD.'   Nm 21:5; 25:1-3

[27] "Therefore, son of man, speak to the house of Israel, and tell them, 'This is what the Lord GOD says: In this way also your fathers

---

[A] 20:8 Lit *things of their eyes*   [B] 20:26 Lit *they made every firstborn pass through the fire* blasphemed me by committing treachery against me: ²⁸ When I brought them into the land that I swore to give them and they saw any high hill or leafy tree, they offered their sacrifices and presented their offensive offerings there. They also sent up their pleasing aromas and poured out their drink offerings there. ²⁹ So I asked them, "What is this high place you are going to?" And it is still called Bamah^A today.' Ezk 6:13; Rm 2:24

³⁰ "Therefore say to the house of Israel, 'This is what the Lord God says: Are you defiling yourselves the way your fathers did, and prostituting yourselves with their abhorrent things? ³¹ When you offer your gifts, sacrificing your children in the fire,^B you still continue to defile yourselves with all your idols today. So should I let you inquire of me, house of Israel? As I live — this is the declaration of the Lord God — I will not let you inquire of me!

Israel's Restoration

³² " 'When you say, "Let us be like the nations, like the clans of other countries, serving wood and stone," what you have in mind will never happen. ³³ As I live — the declaration of the Lord God — I will reign over you with a strong hand, an outstretched arm, and outpoured wrath. ³⁴ I will bring you from the peoples and gather you from the countries where you were scattered, with a strong hand, an outstretched arm, and outpoured wrath. ³⁵ I will lead you into the wilderness of the peoples and enter into judgment with you there face to face. ³⁶ Just as I entered into judgment with your fathers in the wilderness of the land of Egypt, so I will enter into judgment with you. This is the declaration of the Lord God. ³⁷ I will make you pass under the rod and will bring you into the bond of the covenant. ³⁸ I will purge you of those who rebel and transgress against me. I will bring them out of the land where they live as foreign residents, but they will not enter the land of Israel. Then you will know that I am the Lord. Dt 4:28; 2Kg 19:18; Ezk 11:5; Rv 9:20

³⁹ " 'As for you, house of Israel, this is what the Lord God says: Go and serve your idols, each of you. But afterward you will surely listen to me, and you will no longer defile my holy name with your gifts and idols. ⁴⁰ For on my holy mountain, Israel's high mountain — the declaration of the Lord God — there the entire house of Israel, all of them, will serve me in the land. There I will accept them and will require your contributions and choicest gifts, all your holy offerings. ⁴¹ When I bring you from the peoples and gather you from the countries where you have been scattered, I will accept you as a pleasing aroma. And I will demonstrate my holiness through you in the sight of the nations. ⁴² When I lead you into the land of Israel, the land I swore to give your fathers, you will know that I am the Lord. ⁴³ There you will remember your ways and all your deeds by which you have defiled yourself, and you will loathe yourselves for all the evil things you have done. ⁴⁴ You will know that I am the Lord, house of Israel, when I have dealt with you for the sake of my name rather than according to your evil ways

^A20:29 = High Place   ^B20:31 Lit *gifts, making your children pass through the fire*

and corrupt acts. This is the declaration of the Lord GOD.'"   Is 5:16

Fire in the South

⁴⁵ The word of the LORD came to me: ⁴⁶ "Son of man, face the south and preach against it. Prophesy against the forest land in the Negev, ⁴⁷ and say to the forest there, 'Hear the word of the LORD! This is what the Lord GOD says: I am about to ignite a fire in you, and it will devour every green tree and every dry tree in you. The blazing flame will not be extinguished, and every face from the south to the north will be scorched by it. ⁴⁸ Then all people will see that I, the LORD, have kindled it. It will not be extinguished.'"   Ezk 21:2; Jr 21:14

⁴⁹ Then I said, "Oh, Lord GOD, they are saying of me, 'Isn't he just composing parables?'"   Ezk 17:2

God's Sword of Judgment

21 The word of the LORD came to me again: ² "Son of man, face Jerusalem and preach against the sanctuaries. Prophesy against the land of Israel, ³ and say to it, 'This is what the LORD says: I am against you. I will draw my sword from its sheath and cut off from you both the righteous and the wicked. ⁴ Since I will cut offᴬ both the righteous and the wicked, my sword will therefore come out of its sheath against all people from the south to the north. ⁵ So all people will know that I, the LORD, have taken my sword from its sheath — it will not be sheathed again.'

⁶ "But you, son of man, groan! Groan bitterly with a broken heartᴮ right before their eyes. ⁷ And when they ask you, 'Why are you

groaning?' then say, 'Because of the news that is coming. Every heart will melt, and every hand will become weak. Every spirit will be discouraged, and all knees will run with urine.ᶜ Yes, it is coming and it will happen. This is the declaration of the Lord GOD.'"   Ezk 7:26

⁸ The word of the LORD came to me: ⁹ "Son of man, prophesy, 'This is what the Lord says!' You are to proclaim,

'A sword! A sword
     is sharpened   Dt 32:41
     and also polished.   Jr 46:4
¹⁰ It is sharpened
     for slaughter,
     polished to flash
     like lightning!
   Should we rejoice?
   The scepter of my son,
     the sword despises
     every tree.ᴰ
¹¹ The sword is given
     to be polished,
   to be grasped in the hand.
   It is sharpened, and it
     is polished,
   to be put in the hand
     of the slayer.'   Ezk 21:19

¹² "Cry out and wail, son of man, for it is against my people. It is against all the princes of Israel! They are given over to the sword with my people. Therefore strike your thigh in grief. ¹³ Surely it will be a trial! And what if the sword despises even the scepter? The scepter will not continue."ᴰ This is the declaration of the Lord GOD.   Jr 31:19

¹⁴ "So you, son of man, prophesy and clap your hands together:

   Let the sword strike
     two times, even three.
   It is a sword for massacre,

ᴬ**21:4** Lit off from you   ᴮ**21:6** Lit insides, or waist   ᶜ**21:7** Lit knees will go water   ᴰ**21:10,13** Hb obscure

a sword for great massacre —
it surrounds ^A them!

¹⁵ I have appointed a sword
for slaughter^B   Ezk 32:20
at all their gates,
so that their hearts may melt
and many may stumble.
Yes! It is ready to flash
like lightning;   Ezk 21:28
it is drawn^B for slaughter.

¹⁶ Slash to the right;
turn to the left —
wherever your blade
is directed.

¹⁷ I also will clap my hands together,
and I will satisfy my wrath. I, the
LORD, have spoken."   Ezk 5:13

¹⁸ The word of the LORD came to
me: ¹⁹ "Now you, son of man, mark
out two roads that the sword of
Babylon's king can take. Both of
them should originate from the
same land. And make a signpost
at the fork in the road to each city.
²⁰ Mark out a road that the sword
can take to Rabbah of the Am-
monites and to Judah into forti-
fied Jerusalem. ²¹ For the king of
Babylon stands at the split in the
road, at the fork of the two roads,
to practice divination: he shakes
the arrows, consults the idols, and
observes the liver. ²² The answer
marked^C Jerusalem appears in
his right hand, indicating that he
should set up battering rams, give
the order to^D slaughter, raise a battle cry, set battering rams against
the gates, build a ramp, and construct a siege wall. ²³ It will seem
like false divination to those who
have sworn an oath to the Babylonians, ^E but it will draw attention

to their guilt so that they will be
captured.   Jr 49:2; Ezk 4:2; 17:16,18; 26:9

²⁴ "Therefore, this is what the Lord
GOD says: Because you have drawn
attention to your guilt, exposing
your transgressions, so that your
sins are revealed in all your actions
— since you have done this, you
will be captured by them. ²⁵ And
you, profane and wicked prince of
Israel, ^F the day has come for your
punishment. ^G   2Kg 24:20; Ezk 21:29

²⁶ "This is what the Lord GOD says:
Remove the turban,
and take off the crown.
Things will not remain
as they are;^H
exalt the lowly
and bring down the exalted.

²⁷ A ruin, a ruin,
I will make it a ruin!
Yet this will not happen
until he comes;   Jr 23:5-6
I have given the judgment
to him.^I

²⁸ "Now you, son of man, proph-
esy, and say, 'This is what the Lord
GOD says concerning the Ammonites and their contempt.' You are
to proclaim,
'A sword! A sword
is drawn for slaughter,
polished to consume, to flash
like lightning.   Is 31:8; Jr 12:12

²⁹ While they offer false visions
and lying divinations
about you,
the time has come to put you
to the necks of the profane
wicked ones;
the day has come
for final punishment.

---

^A21:14 Or *penetrates*   ^B21:15 Hb obscure   ^C21:22 Lit *The divination for*   ^D21:22 Lit *rams, open the
mouth in*   ^E21:23 Lit *them*   ^F21:25 = King Zedekiah   ^G21:25 Lit *come in the time of the punishment of
the end,* also in v. 29   ^H21:26 Lit *This not this*   ^I21:27 Or *comes to whom it rightfully belongs, and I will
give it to him*

³⁰ " 'Return it to its sheath!

" 'I will judge you ᴬ
in the place
where you were created,
in the land of your origin.
³¹ I will pour out
my indignation on you;
I will blow the fire of my fury
on you.   Ezk 22:20-21
I will hand you over
to brutal men,
skilled at destruction.
³² You will be fuel for the fire.
Your blood will be spilled
within the land.
You will not be remembered,
for I, the LORD, have spoken.' "

Indictment of Sinful Jerusalem

22 The word of the LORD came to me: ² "As for you, son of man, will you pass judgment? Will you pass judgment against the city of blood? Then explain all her detestable practices to her. ³ You are to say, 'This is what the Lord GOD says: A city that sheds blood within her walls so that her time of judgment has come and who makes idols for herself so that she is defiled! ⁴ You are guilty of the blood you have shed, and you are defiled from the idols you have made. You have brought your judgment ᴮ days near and have come to your years of punishment. ᶜ Therefore, I have made you a disgrace to the nations and a mockery to all the lands. ⁵ Those who are near and those far away from you will mock you, you infamous one full of turmoil.   Ezk 16:2; 20:4; 22:6,27

⁶ " 'Look, every prince of Israel within you has used his strength to shed blood. ⁷ Father and mother are treated with contempt, and the resident alien is exploited within you. The fatherless and widow are oppressed in you. ⁸ You despise my holy things and profane my Sabbaths. ⁹ There are men within you who slander in order to shed blood. People who live in you eat at the mountain shrines; ᴰ they commit depraved acts within you. ¹⁰ Men within you have sexual intercourse with their father's wife and violate women during their menstrual impurity. ¹¹ One man within you commits a detestable act with his neighbor's wife; another defiles his daughter-in-law with depravity; and yet another violates his sister, his father's daughter. ¹² People who live in you accept bribes in order to shed blood. You take interest and profit on a loan and brutally extort your neighbors. You have forgotten me. This is the declaration of the Lord GOD.   Ex 20:12; Lv 20:9; 20:17; Is 1:23

¹³ " 'Now look, I clap my hands together against the dishonest profit you have made and against the blood shed among you. ¹⁴ Will your courage endure or your hands be strong in the days when I deal with you? I, the LORD, have spoken, and I will act. ¹⁵ I will disperse you among the nations and scatter you among the countries; I will purge your uncleanness. ¹⁶ You ᴱ will be profaned in the sight of the nations. Then you will know that I am the LORD.' "

Jerusalem as God's Furnace

¹⁷ The word of the LORD came to me: ¹⁸ "Son of man, the house of Israel has become merely dross to me. All of them are copper, tin, iron, and

---

ᴬ**21:30** = the Ammonites   ᴮ**22:4** *judgment* supplied for clarity   ᶜ**22:4** *punishment* supplied for clarity
ᴰ**22:9** Lit *the mountains*   ᴱ**22:16** One Hb ms, LXX, Syr, Vg read *I*

lead inside the furnace; they are just dross from silver. ¹⁹ Therefore, this is what the Lord GOD says: Because all of you have become dross, I am about to gather you into Jerusalem. ²⁰ Just as one gathers silver, copper, iron, lead, and tin into the furnace to blow fire on them and melt them, so I will gather you in my anger and wrath, put you inside, and melt you. ²¹ Yes, I will gather you together and blow on you with the fire of my fury, and you will be melted within the city. ²² As silver is melted inside a furnace, so you will be melted inside the city. Then you will know that I, the LORD, have poured out my wrath on you."

Indictment of a Sinful Land

²³ The word of the LORD came to me: ²⁴ "Son of man, say to her, 'You are a land that has not been cleansed, that has not received rain in the day of indignation.' ²⁵ The conspiracy of her prophets within her is ᴬ like a roaring lion tearing its prey: they devour people, seize wealth and valuables, and multiply the widows within her. ²⁶ Her priests do violence to my instruction and profane my holy things. They make no distinction between the holy and the common, and they do not explain the difference between the clean and the unclean. They close their eyes to my Sabbaths, and I am profaned among them. Jr 11:9; Ezk 24:13

²⁷ "Her officials within her are like wolves tearing their prey, shedding blood, and destroying lives in order to make profit dishonestly. ²⁸ Her prophets plaster for them with whitewash by seeing false visions and lying divinations,

saying, 'This is what the Lord GOD says,' when the LORD has not spoken. ²⁹ The people of the land have practiced extortion and committed robbery. They have oppressed the poor and needy and unlawfully exploited the resident alien. ³⁰ I searched for a man among them who would repair the wall and stand in the gap before me on behalf of the land so that I might not destroy it, but I found no one. ³¹ So I have poured out my indignation on them and consumed them with the fire of my fury. I have brought their conduct down on their own heads." This is the declaration of the Lord GOD. Ezk 9:9; 13:10-15; 22:7

The Two Immoral Sisters

23 The word of the LORD came to me again: ² "Son of man, there were two women, daughters of the same mother, ³ who acted like prostitutes in Egypt, behaving promiscuously in their youth. Their breasts were fondled there, and their virgin nipples caressed. ⁴ The older one was named Oholah, ᴮ and her sister was Oholibah. ᶜ They became mine and gave birth to sons and daughters. As for their names, Oholah represents Samaria and Oholibah represents Jerusalem. Lv 17:7; Jr 3:9; Ezk 16:46

⁵ "Oholah acted like a prostitute even though she was mine. She lusted after her lovers, the Assyrians: warriors ⁶ dressed in blue, governors and prefects, all of them desirable young men, horsemen riding on steeds. ⁷ She offered her sexual favors to them; all of them were the elite of Assyria. She defiled herself with all those she lusted after

ᴬ**22:24-25** LXX reads *indignation,* ²⁵*whose princes within her are*　　ᴮ**23:4** = Her Tent　ᶜ**23:4** = My Tent Is in Her and with all their idols. ⁸ She didn't give up her promiscuity that began in Egypt, when men slept with her in her youth, caressed her virgin nipples, and poured out their lust on her. ⁹ Therefore, I handed her over to her lovers, the Assyrians she lusted for. ¹⁰ They exposed her nakedness, seized her sons and daughters, and killed her with the sword. Since they executed judgment against her, she became notorious among women. 2Kg 15:19; 16:7

¹¹ "Now her sister Oholibah saw this, but she was even more depraved in her lust than Oholah, and made her promiscuous acts worse than those of her sister. ¹² She lusted after the Assyrians: governors and prefects, warriors splendidly dressed, horsemen riding on steeds, all of them desirable young men. ¹³ And I saw that she had defiled herself; both of them had taken the same path. ¹⁴ But she increased her promiscuity when she saw male figures carved on the wall, images of the Chaldeans, engraved in bright red, ¹⁵ wearing belts on their waists and flowing turbans on their heads; all of them looked like officers, a depiction of the Babylonians in Chaldea, their native land. ¹⁶ At the sight of them ᴬ she lusted after them and sent messengers to them in Chaldea. ¹⁷ Then the Babylonians came to her, to the bed of love, and defiled her with their lust. But after she was defiled by them, she turned away from them in disgust. ¹⁸ When she flaunted her promiscuity and exposed her nakedness, I turned away from her in disgust just as I turned away from her sister. ¹⁹ Yet she multiplied her acts of promiscuity, remembering the days of her youth when she acted like a prostitute in the land of Egypt ²⁰ and lusted after their lovers, whose sexual members ᴮ were like those of donkeys and whose emission was like that of stallions. ²¹ So you revisited the depravity of your youth, when the Egyptians caressed your nipples to enjoy your youthful breasts.

²² "Therefore, Oholibah, this is what the Lord GOD says: I am going to incite your lovers against you, those you turned away from in disgust. I will bring them against you from every side: ²³ the Babylonians and all the Chaldeans; Pekod, Shoa, and Koa; and all the Assyrians with them — desirable young men, all of them governors and prefects, officers and administrators, all of them riding on steeds. ²⁴ They will come against you with an assembly of peoples and with weapons, chariots, and ᶜ wagons. They will set themselves against you on every side with large and small shields and helmets. I will delegate judgment to them, and they will judge you by their own standards. ²⁵ When I vent my jealous rage on you, they will deal with you in wrath. They will cut off your nose and ears, and the rest of you ᴰ will fall by the sword. They will seize your sons and daughters, and the rest of you will be consumed by fire. ²⁶ They will strip off your clothes and take your beautiful jewelry. ²⁷ So I will put an end to your depravity and sexual immorality, which began in the land of Egypt, and you will not look longingly at them or remember Egypt anymore.

ᴬ23:16 Lit of her eyes   ᴮ23:20 Lit whose flesh   ᶜ23:24 LXX reads peoples, from the north, chariots and ; Hb obscure   ᴰ23:25 Or and your descendants

²⁸ "For this is what the Lord God says: I am going to hand you over to those you hate, to those you turned away from in disgust. ²⁹ They will treat you with hatred, take all you have worked for, and leave you stark naked, so that the shame of your debauchery will be exposed, both your depravity and promiscuity. ³⁰ These things will be done to you because you acted like a prostitute with the nations, defiling yourself with their idols. ³¹ You have followed the path of your sister, so I will put her cup in your hand." Ezk 16:7,22,39

³² This is what the Lord God says:

"You will drink
    your sister's cup, Ps 75:8; Is 51:17
    which is deep and wide.
You will be an object
    of ^A ridicule and scorn,
for it holds so much. Ezk 22:4-5
³³ You will be filled
    with drunkenness
    and grief,
    with a cup of devastation
    and desolation,
    the cup of your
    sister Samaria.
³⁴ You will drink it and drain it;
    then you will gnaw
    its broken pieces,
    and tear your breasts.
For I have spoken."
    This is the declaration
    of the Lord God.

³⁵ Therefore, this is what the Lord God says: "Because you have forgotten me and cast me behind your back, you must bear the consequences of your indecency and promiscuity." Is 17:10; Jr 3:21; Ezk 22:12

³⁶ Then the Lord said to me: "Son of man, will you pass judgment against Oholah and Oholibah? Then declare their detestable practices to them. ³⁷ For they have committed adultery, and blood is on their hands; they have committed adultery with their idols. And the children they bore to me they have sacrificed in the fire ^B as food for the idols. ³⁸ They also did this to me: they defiled my sanctuary on that same day and profaned my Sabbaths. ³⁹ On the same day they slaughtered their children for their idols, they entered my sanctuary to profane it. Yes, that is what they did inside my house. Jr 1:10; Ezk 20:4; 22:2

⁴⁰ "In addition, they sent for men who came from far away when a messenger was dispatched to them. And look how they came! You bathed, painted your eyes, and adorned yourself with jewelry for them. ⁴¹ You sat on a luxurious couch with a table spread before it, on which you had set my incense and oil. ⁴² The sound of a carefree crowd was there. Drunkards ^C from the desert were brought in, along with common men. They put bracelets on the women's hands and beautiful tiaras on their heads. ⁴³ Then I said concerning this woman worn out by adultery: Will they ^D now have illicit sex with her, even her? ⁴⁴ Yet they had sex with her as one does with a prostitute. This is how they had sex with Oholah and Oholibah, those depraved women. ⁴⁵ But righteous men will judge them the way adulteresses and those who shed blood are judged, for they are adulteresses and blood is on their hands.

⁴⁶ "This is what the Lord God says: Summon ^E an assembly against

---

^A23:32 Or It will bring ^B23:37 Lit have made pass through the fire ^C23:42 Or Sabeans ^D23:43 Or They will ^E23:46 Or I will summon

them and consign them to terror and plunder. **47** The assembly will stone them and cut them down with their swords. They will kill their sons and daughters and burn their houses. **48** So I will put an end to depravity in the land, and all the women will be admonished not to imitate your depraved behavior. **49** They will punish you for your depravity, and you will bear the consequences for your sins of idolatry. Then you will know that I am the Lord GOD." Lv 20:10; Is 59:18; Jr 15:4; 24:9; 29:18

Parable of the Boiling Pot

24 The word of the LORD came to me in the ninth year, in the tenth month, on the tenth day of the month: **2** "Son of man, write down today's date, this very day. The king of Babylon has laid siege to Jerusalem this very day. **3** Now speak a parable to the rebellious house. Tell them, 'This is what the Lord GOD says: 2Kg 25:1; Ezk 17:2; 20:49

Put the pot on the fire —
put it on,
and then pour water into it!
4 Place the pieces of meat in it,
every good piece —
thigh and shoulder.
Fill it with choice bones.
5 Take the choicest of the flock
and also pile up the fuel^A
under it.
Bring it to a boil
and cook the bones in it.

6 " 'Therefore, this is what the Lord GOD says:

Woe to the city of bloodshed,
the pot that has corrosion
inside it,

and its corrosion has not
come out of it!
Empty it piece by piece;
lots should not be cast
for its contents.
7 For the blood she shed^B
is still within her.
She put it out on the bare rock;
she didn't pour it
on the ground
to cover it with dust.   Lv 17:13-14
8 In order to stir up wrath
and take vengeance,   Is 26:21
I have put her blood
on the bare rock,
so that it would not be covered.

9 " 'Therefore, this is what the Lord GOD says:

Woe to the city of bloodshed!
I myself will make the pile
of kindling large.
10 Pile on the logs and kindle
the fire!
Cook the meat well
and mix in the spices!^{C,D}
Let the bones be burned!
11 Set the empty pot on its coals
so that it becomes hot
and its copper glows.
Then its impurity will melt
inside it;
its corrosion will
be consumed.   Ezk 22:15; 23:27
12 It has frustrated every effort;^E
its thick corrosion will not
come off.
Into the fire
with its corrosion!
13 Because of the depravity
of your uncleanness —
since I tried to purify you,
but you would not be purified
from your uncleanness —

---

^A**24:5** Lit bones   ^B**24:7** Lit For her blood   ^C**24:10** Some Hb mss read well; remove the broth ; LXX reads fire so that the meat may be cooked and the broth may be reduced   ^D**24:10** Or and stir the broth   ^E**24:12** Hb obscure

you will not be pure again
until I have satisfied
my wrath on you. Ezk 5:13; 8:18
¹⁴ I, the LORD, have spoken.
It is coming, and I will do it!
I will not refrain, I will not
show pity,
and I will not relent.
I ᴬ will judge you
according to your ways
and deeds. Ezk 18:30; 36:19
This is the declaration
of the Lord GOD.'"

The Death of Ezekiel's Wife: A Sign

¹⁵ Then the word of the LORD came to me: ¹⁶ "Son of man, I am about to take the delight of your eyes away from you with a fatal blow. But you must not lament or weep or let your tears flow. ¹⁷ Groan quietly; do not observe mourning rites for the dead. Put on your turban and strap your sandals on your feet; do not cover your mustache or eat the bread of mourners." ᴮ 1Kg 20:6; Pr 5:18
¹⁸ I spoke to the people in the morning, and my wife died in the evening. The next morning I did just as I was commanded. ¹⁹ Then the people asked me, "Won't you tell us what these things you are doing mean for us?"
²⁰ So I answered them: "The word of the LORD came to me: ²¹ Say to the house of Israel, 'This is what the Lord GOD says: I am about to desecrate my sanctuary, the pride of your power, the delight of your eyes, and the desire of your heart. Also, the sons and daughters you left behind will fall by the sword. ²² Then you will do just as I have done: You will not cover your mustache or eat the bread of mourners.

²³ Your turbans will remain on your heads and your sandals on your feet. You will not lament or weep but will waste away because of your iniquities and will groan to one another. ²⁴ Now Ezekiel will be a sign for you. You will do everything that he has done. When this happens, you will know that I am the Lord GOD.' Jr 6:11; 16:3-4; Ezk 23:25,47
²⁵ "As for you, son of man, know that on that day I will take from them their stronghold — their pride and joy, the delight of their eyes, and the longing of their hearts — as well as their sons and daughters. ²⁶ On that day a fugitive will come to you and report the news. ²⁷ On that day your mouth will be opened to talk with him; you will speak and no longer be mute. So you will be a sign for them, and they will know that I am the LORD." Ezk 3:26-27; 33:21-22

PROPHECIES AGAINST THE NATIONS

Judgment Against Ammon

25 Then the word of the LORD came to me: ² "Son of man, face the Ammonites and prophesy against them. ³ Say to the Ammonites, 'Hear the word of the Lord GOD: This is what the Lord GOD says: Because you said, "Aha!" about my sanctuary when it was desecrated, about the land of Israel when it was laid waste, and about the house of Judah when they went into exile, ⁴ therefore I am about to give you to the people of the east as a possession. They will set up their encampments and pitch their tents among you. They will eat your fruit and drink your milk. ⁵ I will make

ᴬ**24:14** Some Hb mss, LXX, Syr, Tg, Vg; other Hb mss read *They* ᴮ**24:17** Lit *men*, also in v. 22

Rabbah a pasture for camels and Ammon a resting place for sheep. Then you will know that I am the LORD. Jr 49:1-6; Ezk 21:20,28; 26:2

⁶ " 'For this is what the Lord GOD says: Because you clapped your hands, stamped your feet, and rejoiced over the land of Israel with wholehearted contempt, ⁷ therefore I am about to stretch out my hand against you and give you as plunder to the nations. I will cut you off from the peoples and eliminate you from the countries. I will destroy you, and you will know that I am the LORD. Jb 27:23; Nah 3:19; Zph 1:4

Judgment Against Moab

⁸ " 'This is what the Lord GOD says: Because Moab and Seir said, "Look, the house of Judah is like all the other nations." ⁹ Therefore I am about to expose Moab's flank beginning with its^A frontier cities, the splendor of the land: Beth-jeshimoth, Baal-meon, and Kiriathaim. ¹⁰ I will give it along with Ammon to the people of the east as a possession, so that Ammon will not be remembered among the nations. ¹¹ So I will execute judgments against Moab, and they will know that I am the LORD. Is 15:1; Jr 48:1,23; Am 2:1-2

Judgment Against Edom

¹² " 'This is what the Lord GOD says: Because Edom acted vengefully against the house of Judah and incurred grievous guilt by taking revenge on them, ¹³ therefore this is what the Lord GOD says: I will stretch out my hand against Edom and cut off both man and animal from it. I will make it a wasteland; they will fall by the sword from Teman to Dedan. ¹⁴ I will take my vengeance on Edom through my people Israel, and they will deal with Edom according to my anger and wrath. So they will know my vengeance. This is the declaration of the Lord GOD. 2Ch 28:17; Ps 137:7; Is 11:14

Judgment Against Philistia

¹⁵ " 'This is what the Lord GOD says: Because the Philistines acted in vengeance and took revenge with deep contempt, destroying because of their perpetual hatred, ¹⁶ therefore this is what the Lord GOD says: I am about to stretch out my hand against the Philistines, cutting off the Cherethites and wiping out what remains of the coastal peoples. ^B ¹⁷ I will execute severe vengeance against them with furious rebukes. They will know that I am the LORD when I take my vengeance on them.' " Is 14:29-31; Jr 25:20

The Downfall of Tyre

26 In the eleventh year, on the first day of the month, the word of the LORD came to me: ² "Son of man, because Tyre said about Jerusalem, 'Aha! The gateway to the peoples is shattered. She has been turned over to me.^C I will be filled now that she lies in ruins,' ³ therefore this is what the Lord GOD says: See, I am against you, Tyre! I will raise up many nations against you, just as the sea raises its waves. ⁴ They will destroy the walls of Tyre and demolish her towers. I will scrape the soil from her and turn her into a bare rock. ⁵ She will become a place in the sea to spread nets, for I have spoken." This is the declaration of the Lord GOD. "She will become plunder for the nations, ⁶ and her villages on

_{A 25:9 Lit with the cities, with its   B 25:16 Lit the seacoast   C 26:2 Or It has swung open for me}

the mainland will be slaughtered by the sword. Then they will know that I am the LORD." 2Sm 5:11; Is 23:3; Jl 3:4

⁷ For this is what the Lord GOD says: "See, I am about to bring King Nebuchadnezzar ᴬ of Babylon, king of kings, against Tyre from the north with horses, chariots, cavalry, and a huge assembly of troops. ⁸ He will slaughter your villages on the mainland with the sword. He will set up siege works, build a ramp, and raise a wall of shields against you. ⁹ He will direct the blows of his battering rams against your walls and tear down your towers with his iron tools. ¹⁰ His horses will be so numerous that their dust will cover you. When he enters your gates as an army entering a breached city, your walls will shake from the noise of cavalry, wagons, and chariots. ¹¹ He will trample all your streets with the hooves of his horses. He will slaughter your people with the sword, and your mighty pillars will fall to the ground. ¹² They will take your wealth as spoil and plunder your merchandise. They will also demolish your walls and tear down your beautiful homes. Then they will throw your stones, timber, and soil into the water. ¹³ I will put an end to the noise of your songs, and the sound of your lyres will no longer be heard. ¹⁴ I will turn you into a bare rock, and you will be a place to spread nets. You will never be rebuilt, for I, the LORD, have spoken." This is the declaration of the Lord GOD. Jr 52:32; Ezk 21:22; Dn 2:37,47

¹⁵ This is what the Lord GOD says to Tyre: "Won't the coasts and islands quake at the sound of your downfall, when the wounded groan and slaughter occurs within you? ¹⁶ All the princes of the sea will descend from their thrones, remove their robes, and strip off their embroidered garments. They will clothe themselves with trembling; they will sit on the ground, tremble continually, and be appalled at you. ¹⁷ Then they will lament for you and say of you,　　Jr 49:21; Jnh 3:6

'How you have perished,
　　city of renown,
you who were populated
　　from the seas! ᴮ
She who was powerful
　　on the sea,
she and all of her inhabitants
　　inflicted their terror. ᶜ

¹⁸　Now the coastlands tremble
　　on the day of your downfall;
　　the islands in the sea
　　are alarmed
　　　by your demise.' "

¹⁹ For this is what the Lord GOD says: "When I make you a ruined city like other deserted cities, when I raise up the deep against you so that the mighty waters cover you, ²⁰ then I will bring you down to be with those who descend to the Pit, to the people of antiquity. I will make you dwell in the underworld ᴰ like ᴱ the ancient ruins, with those who descend to the Pit, so that you will no longer be inhabited or display your splendor ꜰ in the land of the living. ²¹ I will make you an object of horror, and you will no

---

longer exist. You will be sought but will never be found again." This is the declaration of the Lord God.

The Sinking of Tyre

27 The word of the Lord came to me: ² "Now, son of man, lament for Tyre. ³ Say to Tyre, who is located at the entrance of the sea, merchant of the peoples to many coasts and islands, 'This is what the Lord God says: Is 23:2; Ezk 28:12; 32:2

Tyre, you declared,
"I am perfect in beauty."
⁴ Your realm was in the heart
   of the sea;
your builders perfected
   your beauty.
⁵ They constructed
   all your planking
with pine trees from Senir.
They took a cedar
   from Lebanon
to make a mast for you.
⁶ They made your oars of oaks
   from Bashan.
They made your deck
   of cypress wood
from the coasts of Cyprus,
inlaid with ivory.
⁷ Your sail was made of
   fine embroidered linen
   from Egypt,
and served as your banner.
Your awning was of blue
   and purple fabric
from the coasts of Elishah.
⁸ The inhabitants of Sidon
   and Arvad   Gn 10:18
were your rowers.
Your wise men were
   within you, Tyre;
they were your captains.
⁹ The elders of Gebal and its
   wise men   1Kg 5:18

were within you,
   repairing your leaks.

" 'All the ships of the sea
   and their sailors
came to you to barter
   for your goods.
¹⁰ Men of Persia, Lud, and Put
   were in your army, serving
   as your warriors.
They hung shields
   and helmets in you;
they gave you splendor.
¹¹ Men of Arvad and Helech
   were stationed on your walls
   all around,
and Gammadites were
   in your towers.
They hung their shields ᴬ
   all around your walls;
they perfected your beauty.

¹² " 'Tarshish was your trading partner because of your abundant wealth of every kind. They exchanged silver, iron, tin, and lead for your merchandise. ¹³ Javan, Tubal, and Meshech were your merchants. They exchanged slaves ᴮ and bronze utensils for your goods. ¹⁴ Those from Beth-togarmah exchanged horses, war horses, and mules for your merchandise. ¹⁵ Men of Dedan ᶜ were also your merchants; many coasts and islands were your regular markets. They brought back ivory tusks and ebony as your payment. ¹⁶ Aram ᴰ was your trading partner because of your numerous products. They exchanged turquoise, ᴱ purple and embroidered cloth, fine linen, coral, ᴱ and rubies ᴱ for your merchandise. ¹⁷ Judah and the land of Israel were your merchants. They exchanged wheat from Minnith, meal, ᶠ honey,

---

ᴬ27:11 Or *quivers*; Hb obscure   ᴮ27:13 Lit *souls of men*   ᶜ27:15 LXX reads *Rhodes*   ᴰ27:16 Some Hb mss, Aq, Syr read *Edom*   ᴱ27:16 Hb obscure   ᶠ27:17 Or *resin*; Hb obscure oil, and balm, for your goods. [18] Damascus was also your trading partner because of your numerous products and your abundant wealth of every kind, trading in wine from Helbon and white wool. [A] [19] Vedan [B] and Javan from Uzal [C] dealt in your merchandise; wrought iron, cassia, and aromatic cane were exchanged for your goods. [20] Dedan was your merchant in saddlecloths for riding. [21] Arabia and all the princes of Kedar were your business partners, trading with you in lambs, rams, and goats. [22] The merchants of Sheba and Raamah traded with you. For your merchandise they exchanged the best of all spices and all kinds of precious stones as well as gold. [23] Haran, Canneh, Eden, the merchants of Sheba, Asshur, and Chilmad traded with you. [24] They were your merchants in choice garments, cloaks of blue and embroidered materials, and multicolored carpets, [C] which were bound and secured with cords in your marketplace. [25] Ships of Tarshish were the carriers for your goods.   Gn 10:2,4

" 'So you became full
    and heavily loaded [D]
  in the heart of the sea.
[26] Your rowers have
    brought you
  onto the high seas,   Ezk 26:19
  but the east wind
    has wrecked you
  in the heart of the sea.
[27] Your wealth, merchandise,
    and goods,
  your sailors and captains,
    those who repair your leaks,
    those who barter
      for your goods,
  and all the warriors on board,

with all the other people
    within you,
  sink into the heart of the sea
  on the day of your downfall.
[28] " 'The countryside shakes
    at the sound
    of your sailors' cries.
[29] All the oarsmen
  disembark from their ships.
  The sailors and
    all the captains of the sea
  stand on the shore.
[30] Because of you, they raise
    their voices
  and cry out bitterly.
  They throw dust
    on their heads;   Rv 18:17-19
  they roll in ashes.
[31] They shave their heads
    because of you
  and wrap themselves
    in sackcloth.
  They weep over you
  with deep anguish
    and bitter mourning.
[32] " 'In their wailing they lament
    for you,   Ezk 26:17
  mourning over you:
  "Who was like Tyre,
  silenced [C] in the middle
    of the sea?
[33] When your merchandise
    was unloaded from the seas,
  you satisfied many peoples.
  You enriched the kings
    of the earth
  with your abundant wealth
    and goods.
[34] Now you are wrecked
    by the sea
  in the depths of the waters;
  your goods and the people
    within you

A27:18 Or and wool from Zahar   B27:19 Or Dan   C27:19,24,32 Hb obscure   D27:25 Or and very glorious

have gone down.
³⁵ All the inhabitants
   of the coasts and islands
are appalled at you.   Ezk 26:15-16
Their kings shudder
   with fear;
their faces are contorted.
³⁶ Those who trade
   among the peoples
scoff ᴬ at you;   1Kg 9:8; Jr 19:8; Zph 2:15
you have become an object
   of horror
and will never exist again." ' "

The Fall of Tyre's Ruler

28 The word of the LORD came to me: ² "Son of man, say to the ruler of Tyre, 'This is what the Lord GOD says: Your ᴮ heart is proud, and you have said, "I am a god; I sit in the seat of gods in the heart of the sea." Yet you are a man and not a god, though you have regarded your heart as that of a god. ³ Yes, you are wiser than Daniel; no secret is hidden from you! ⁴ By your wisdom and understanding you have acquired wealth for yourself. You have acquired gold and silver for your treasuries. ⁵ By your great skill in trading you have increased your wealth, but your heart has become proud because of your wealth.   Is 14:14; Dn 1:20; Ac 12:22-23; 2Th 2:4

⁶ " 'Therefore, this is what the Lord GOD says:
Because you regard
   your heart as that of a god,
⁷   I am about to bring strangers
   against you,
ruthless men
   from the nations.
They will draw their swords
against your
   magnificent wisdom

and will pierce
   your splendor.   Ezk 30:11; 31:12
⁸ They will bring you down
   to the Pit,   Ezk 26:20
and you will die
   a violent death
in the heart of the sea.
⁹ Will you still say,
   "I am a god,"
in the presence of those
   who slay ᶜ you?
Yet you will be only a man,
   not a god,
in the hands of those
   who kill you.
¹⁰ You will die the death
   of the uncircumcised
at the hands of strangers.
For I have spoken.
   This is the declaration
   of the Lord GOD.' "

A Lament for Tyre's King

¹¹ The word of the LORD came to me: ¹² "Son of man, lament for the king of Tyre and say to him, 'This is what the Lord GOD says: Ezk 27:2

You were the seal ᴰ
   of perfection, ᴱ
full of wisdom and perfect
   in beauty.   Ezk 27:3
¹³ You were in Eden, the garden
   of God.   Gn 2:8; Ezk 31:9,16,18; 36:35
Every kind of precious stone
   covered you:
carnelian, topaz,
   and diamond, ᴱ
beryl, onyx, and jasper,
lapis lazuli, turquoise ᶠ
   and emerald. ᴳ
Your mountings and settings
   were crafted in gold;
they were prepared
   on the day
   you were created.

ᴬ27:36 Lit *hiss*   ᴮ28:2 Lit *Because your*   ᶜ28:9 Some Hb mss, LXX, Syr, Vg; other Hb mss read *of the one who kills*   ᴰ28:12 Or *sealer*   ᴱ28:12,13 Hb obscure   ᶠ28:13 Or *malachite,* or *garnet*   ᴳ28:13 Or *beryl*

14 You were an anointed
guardian cherub,   Ex 25:18-22
for^A I had appointed you.
You were on
the holy mountain of God;
you walked among
the fiery stones.
15 From the day you
were created
you were blameless
in your ways
until wickedness was found
in you.
16 Through the abundance
of your trade,
you were filled with violence,
and you sinned.
So I expelled you in disgrace
from the mountain of God,
and banished you,
guardian cherub,^B
from among the fiery stones.
17 Your heart became proud
because of your beauty;
For the sake of your splendor
you corrupted your wisdom.
So I threw you down
to the ground;^C
I made you a spectacle
before kings.
18 You profaned
your sanctuaries
by the magnitude
of your iniquities
in your dishonest trade.
So I made fire come
from within you,
and it consumed you.   Ezk 19:14
I reduced you to ashes
on the ground
in the sight of everyone
watching you.
19 All those who know you
among the peoples
are appalled at you.

You have become an object
of horror
and will never exist again.' "

A Prophecy Against Sidon

20 The word of the LORD came to
me: **21** "Son of man, face Sidon and
prophesy against it. **22** You are to
say, 'This is what the Lord GOD says:
Look! I am against you, Sidon,
and I will display my glory
within you.
They will know that I am the
LORD
when I execute judgments
against her   Ezk 30:19
and demonstrate my holiness
through her.
23 I will send a plague
against her   Ezk 38:22
and bloodshed in her streets;
the slain will fall within her,
while the sword is
against her^D on every side.
Then they will know that
I am the LORD.

24 " 'The house of Israel will no
longer be hurt by^E prickly briers
or painful thorns from all their
neighbors who treat them with
contempt. Then they will know
that I am the Lord GOD.   Nm 33:55
25 " 'This is what the Lord GOD
says: When I gather the house of
Israel from the peoples where they
are scattered, I will demonstrate
my holiness through them in the
sight of the nations, and they will
live in their own land, which I gave
to my servant Jacob. **26** They will live
there securely, build houses, and
plant vineyards. They will live securely when I execute judgments
against all their neighbors who

^A **28:14** Or *With an anointed guardian cherub*   ^B **28:16** Or *and the guardian cherub banished you*
^C **28:17** Or *earth*   ^D **28:23** Or *within her by the sword*   ^E **28:24** Lit *longer have*

treat them with contempt. Then they will know that I am the LORD their God.'" Ps 106:47; Jr 23:6; Ezk 20:41; 34:13

A Prophecy of Egypt's Ruin

29 In the tenth year, in the tenth month on the twelfth day of the month, the word of the LORD came to me: ² "Son of man, face Pharaoh king of Egypt and prophesy against him and against all of Egypt. ³ Speak to him and say, 'This is what the Lord GOD says: Is 19:1-17

Look, I am against you,
    Pharaoh king of Egypt,
the great monster[A] lying
    in the middle of his Nile,
who says, "My Nile is
    my own;
I made it for myself."
⁴ I will put hooks in your jaws
    and make the fish
        of your streams
cling to your scales.
I will haul you up
from the middle of your Nile,
    and all the fish
        of your streams
will cling to your scales.
⁵ I will leave you in the desert,
    you and all the fish
        of your streams.
You will fall on
    the open ground
and will not be taken away
    or gathered for burial.   Jr 8:2
I have given you
    to the wild creatures
        of the earth
and the birds of the sky
    as food.   Ezk 39:4

⁶ "Then all the inhabitants
    of Egypt

will know that I am the LORD,
for they[B] have been a staff
    made of reed
to the house of Israel.
⁷ When Israel grasped you
    by the hand,
you splintered, tearing all
    their shoulders;   2Kg 18:21; Is 36:6
when they leaned on you,
you shattered and made all
    their hips unsteady.[C]

⁸ "Therefore, this is what the Lord GOD says: I am going to bring a sword against you and cut off both man and animal from you. ⁹ The land of Egypt will be a desolate ruin. Then they will know that I am the LORD. Because you[D] said, "The Nile is my own; I made it," ¹⁰ therefore, I am against you and your Nile. I will turn the land of Egypt into ruins, a desolate waste from Migdol to Syene, as far as the border of Cush. ¹¹ No human foot will pass through it, and no animal foot will pass through it. It will be uninhabited for forty years. ¹² I will make the land of Egypt a desolation among[E] desolate lands, and its cities will be a desolation among[F] ruined cities for forty years. I will disperse the Egyptians among the nations and scatter them throughout the lands. Ezk 14:17; 30:7-8; 32:13

¹³ "'For this is what the Lord GOD says: At the end of forty years I will gather the Egyptians from the peoples where they were dispersed. ¹⁴ I will restore the fortunes of Egypt and bring them back to the land of Pathros, the land of their origin. There they will be a lowly kingdom. ¹⁵ Egypt will be the lowliest

---

[A]29:3 Or crocodile [B]29:6 LXX, Syr, Vg read you [C]29:7 LXX, Syr, Vg; MT reads and you caused their hips to stand [D]29:9 LXX, Syr, Vg; MT reads he [E]29:12 Or Egypt the most desolate of [F]29:12 Or be the most desolate of of kingdoms and will never again exalt itself over the nations. I will make them so small they cannot rule over the nations. ¹⁶ It will never again be an object of trust for the house of Israel, drawing attention to their iniquity of turning to the Egyptians. Then they will know that I am the Lord GOD.'" Is 19:22-23

Babylon Receives Egypt as Compensation

¹⁷ In the twenty-seventh year, in the first month, on the first day of the month, the word of the LORD came to me: ¹⁸ "Son of man, King Nebuchadnezzar of Babylon made his army labor strenuously against Tyre. Every head was made bald and every shoulder chafed, but he and his army received no compensation from Tyre for the labor he expended against it. ¹⁹ Therefore, this is what the Lord GOD says: I am going to give the land of Egypt to King Nebuchadnezzar of Babylon, and he will carry off its wealth, seizing its spoil and taking its plunder. This will be his army's compensation. ²⁰ I have given him the land of Egypt as the pay he labored for, since they worked for me." This is the declaration of the Lord GOD. ²¹ "In that day I will cause a horn to sprout for the house of Israel, and I will enable you to speak out among them. Then they will know that I am the LORD." Ezk 26:7-12; 30:10,24-25

Egypt's Doom

30 The word of the LORD came to me: ² "Son of man, prophesy and say, 'This is what the Lord GOD says:

Wail, "Woe because of
     that day!" Is 13:6; Ezk 21:12; Jl 1:11,13
³ For a day is near;
  a day belonging to the LORD
     is near. Jl 2:1; Ob 15
It will be a day of clouds,
  a time of doom^A
     for the nations.
⁴ A sword will come
     against Egypt,
and there will be anguish
     in Cush
when the slain fall in Egypt,
and its wealth is taken away,
and its foundations
     are demolished.
⁵ Cush, Put, and Lud, Jr 46:9
  and all the various
     foreign troops,^B
  plus Libya^C and the men
     of the covenant land
  will fall by the sword
     along with them.
⁶ This is what the LORD says:
Those who support Egypt
     will fall,
and its proud strength
     will collapse.
From Migdol to Syene
they will fall within it
     by the sword.
     This is the declaration
     of the Lord GOD.
⁷ They will be desolate
  among^D desolate lands,
and their cities will lie
  among ruined^E cities. Ezk 29:12
⁸ They will know that I am the
     LORD
  when I set fire to Egypt
and all its allies
     are shattered.
⁹ On that day, messengers will go out from me in ships to terrify confident Cush. Anguish will come

---

^A30:3 *of doom* supplied for clarity   ^B30:5 Or *all Arabia*   ^C30:5 Lit *Cub*; Hb obscure   ^D30:7 Or *be the most desolate of*   ^E30:7 Or *will be the most ruined of* over them on the day of Egypt's doom.ᴬ For indeed it is coming.

¹⁰ "This is what the Lord GOD says:
I will put an end
    to the hordesᴮ of Egypt
by the hand of King
    Nebuchadnezzar of Babylon.
¹¹ He along with his people,
    ruthless men from the nations,
will be brought in to destroy
    the land.
They will draw their swords
    against Egypt
and fill the land with the slain.
¹² I will make the streams dry
and sell the land to evil men.
I will bring desolation
on the land and everything
    in it
by the hands of foreigners.
I, the LORD, have spoken.

¹³ "This is what the Lord GOD says:
I will destroy the idols
    and put an end
to the false gods in Memphis.
There will no longer be
a prince from the land
    of Egypt.
And I will instill fear
    in that land.
¹⁴ I will make Pathros desolate,
set fire to Zoan,
and execute judgments
    on Thebes.
¹⁵ I will pour out my wrath
    on Pelusium,
the stronghold of Egypt,
and will wipe out the hordes
    of Thebes.
¹⁶ I will set fire to Egypt;
Pelusium will writhe
    in anguish,

Thebes will be breached,
and Memphis will face foes
    in broad daylight.ᶜ
¹⁷ The young men of Onᴰ
    and Pi-beseth
will fall by the sword,
and those citiesᴱ will go
    into captivity.
¹⁸ The day will be darkᶠ
    in Tehaphnehes,
when I break the yoke
    of Egypt there
and its proud strength
comes to an end in the city.
A cloud will
    cover Tehaphnehes,ᴳ   Ezk 34:12
and its surrounding villages
    will go into captivity.
¹⁹ So I will execute judgments
    against Egypt,
and they will know that
    I am the LORD.'"

Pharaoh's Power Broken

²⁰ In the eleventh year, in the first month, on the seventh day of the month, the word of the LORD came to me: ²¹ "Son of man, I have broken the arm of Pharaoh king of Egypt. Look, it has not been bandaged — no medicine has been applied and no splint put on to bandage it so that it can grow strong enough to handle a sword. ²² Therefore, this is what the Lord GOD says: Look! I am against Pharaoh king of Egypt. I will break his arms, both the strong one and the one already broken, and will make the sword fall from his hand. ²³ I will disperse the Egyptians among the nations and scatter them among the countries. ²⁴ I will strengthen the arms of Babylon's king and place my sword in

---

ᴬ30:9 Lit of Egypt   ᴮ30:10 Or pomp, or wealth, also in v. 15   ᶜ30:16 Or foes daily   ᴰ30:17 LXX, Vg; MT reads iniquity   ᴱ30:17 Or and the women; lit and they   ᶠ30:18 Some Hb mss, LXX, Syr, Tg, Vg; other Hb mss read will withhold   ᴳ30:18 Or Egypt his hand. But I will break the arms of Pharaoh, and he will groan before him as a mortally wounded man. **25** I will strengthen the arms of Babylon's king, but Pharaoh's arms will fall. They will know that I am the LORD when I place my sword in the hand of Babylon's king and he wields it against the land of Egypt. **26** When I disperse the Egyptians among the nations and scatter them among the countries, they will know that I am the LORD."

Downfall of Egypt and Assyria

31 In the eleventh year, in the third month, on the first day of the month, the word of the LORD came to me: **2** "Son of man, say to Pharaoh king of Egypt and to his hordes, Ezk 30:20

'Who are you like
  in your greatness?
3 Think of Assyria, a cedar
  in Lebanon, Is 10:33-34; Ezk 31:16
with beautiful branches
  and shady foliage
  and of lofty height.
Its top was among the clouds. A
4 The waters caused it to grow;
  the underground springs
    made it tall,
directing their rivers
    all around
the place where the tree
    was planted
and sending their channels
  to all the trees of the field.
5 Therefore the cedar
  became greater in height
  than all the trees of the field.
Its branches multiplied,
  and its boughs grew long
  as it spread them out
because of the
    abundant water. Ezk 17:5

6 All the birds of the sky
  nested in its branches, Ezk 17:23
and all the animals
    of the field
gave birth beneath its boughs;
all the great nations lived
    in its shade.
7 It was beautiful in its size,
  in the length of its limbs,
for its roots extended
  to abundant water.
8 The cedars in God's garden
  could not eclipse it; Gn 2:8
the pine trees couldn't
  compare with its branches,
nor could the plane trees
  match its boughs.
No tree in the garden of God
could compare with it
  in beauty.
9 I made it beautiful with its
    many limbs,
and all the trees of Eden,
which were in God's garden,
    envied it.

10 " 'Therefore, this is what the Lord GOD says: Since it B towered high in stature and set its top among the clouds, and it C grew proud on account of its height, **11** I determined to hand it over to a ruler of nations; he would surely deal with it. I banished it because of its wickedness. **12** Foreigners, ruthless men from the nations, cut it down and left it lying. Its limbs fell on the mountains and in every valley; its boughs lay broken in all the earth's ravines. All the peoples of the earth left its shade and abandoned it. **13** All the birds of the sky nested on its fallen trunk, and all the animals of the field were among its boughs. **14** This happened so that no trees planted beside water would

A31:3 Or *thick foliage*, also in vv. 10,14 B31:10 Syr, Vg; MT, LXX read *you* C31:10 Lit *its heart* become great in height and set their tops among the clouds, and so that no other well-watered trees would reach them in height. For they have all been consigned to death, to the underworld, among the people [A] who descend to the Pit.

15 " 'This is what the Lord GOD says: I caused grieving on the day the cedar went down to Sheol. I closed off the underground deep because of it: [B] I held back the rivers of the deep, and its abundant water was restrained. I made Lebanon mourn on account of it, and all the trees of the field fainted because of it. 16 I made the nations quake at the sound of its downfall, when I threw it down to Sheol to be with those who descend to the Pit. Then all the trees of Eden, the choice and best of Lebanon, all the well-watered trees, were comforted in the underworld. 17 They too descended with it to Sheol, to those slain by the sword. As its allies [C,D] they had lived in its shade among the nations. Ezk 26:15

18 " 'Who then are you like in glory and greatness among Eden's trees? You also will be brought down to the underworld to be with the trees of Eden. You will lie among the uncircumcised with those slain by the sword. This is Pharaoh and all his hordes. This is the declaration of the Lord GOD.' " Ezk 28:10; 32:19,21

A Lament for Pharaoh

32 In the twelfth year, in the twelfth month, on the first day of the month, the word of the LORD came to me: 2 "Son of man, lament for Pharaoh king of Egypt and say to him, Ezk 19:1; 27:2; 28:12

'You compare yourself
to a lion of the nations,
but [E] you are like a monster [F]
in the seas. Is 27:1
You thrash about
in your rivers,
churn up the waters
with your feet,
and muddy the [G] rivers.

3 " 'This is what the Lord GOD says:
I will spread my net
over you Ezk 12:13
with an assembly
of many peoples,
and they [H] will haul you up
in my net.
4 I will abandon you
on the land
and throw you
onto the open field.
I will cause all the birds
of the sky
to settle on you
and let the wild creatures
of the entire earth
eat their fill of you. Ezk 29:3-5
5 I will put your flesh
on the mountains Ezk 31:12
and fill the valleys
with your carcass.
6 I will drench the land
with the flow of your blood,
even to the mountains;
the ravines will be filled
with your gore.

7 " 'When I snuff you out,
I will cover the heavens
and darken their stars.
I will cover the sun
with a cloud, Jl 2:2,31; 3:15; Am 8:9
and the moon will not give
its light.

[A] **31:14** Or *the descendants of Adam*   [B] **31:15** Or *I covered it with the underground deep*   [C] **31:17** LXX, Syr read *offspring*   [D] **31:17** Lit *arm*   [E] **32:2** Or *'Lion of the nations, you are destroyed;*   [F] **32:2** Or *crocodile* [G] **32:2** Lit *their*   [H] **32:3** LXX, Vg read *I*

8 I will darken all
      the shining lights
   in the heavens over you,
   and will bring darkness
      on your land.
      This is the declaration
      of the Lord GOD.

9 " 'I will trouble the hearts
      of many peoples,
   when I bring about
      your destruction
   among the nations,
   in countries
      you have not known.
10 I will cause many peoples
      to be appalled at you,
   and their kings will shudder
      with fear because of you
   when I brandish my sword
      in front of them.
   On the day of your downfall
   each of them will tremble
   every moment for his life.

11 " 'For this is what the Lord GOD
   says:
      The sword of Babylon's king
      will come against you!
12 I will make your hordes fall
   by the swords of warriors,
   all of them ruthless men
      from the nations. Ezk 28:7; 31:12
   They will ravage
      Egypt's pride,
   and all its hordes
      will be destroyed.
13 I will slaughter all its cattle
   that are beside many waters.
   No human foot
      will churn them again,
   and no cattle hooves
      will disturb them. Ezk 29:11
14 Then I will let their
      waters settle

and will make their rivers
      flow like oil.
      This is the declaration
      of the Lord GOD.
15 When I make the land
      of Egypt a desolation,
   so that it is emptied of
      everything in it,
   when I strike down all
      who live there,
   then they will know that
      I am the LORD.   Ex 7:5

16 " 'The daughters of the nations
will chant that lament. They will
chant it over Egypt and all its
hordes. This is the declaration of
the Lord GOD.' " 2Sm 1:17; 2Ch 35:25; Jr 9:17

Egypt in Sheol

17 In the twelfth year, A on the fifteenth day of the month, the word
of the LORD came to me: 18 "Son of
man, wail over the hordes of Egypt
and bring Egypt and the daughters
of mighty nations down to the underworld, B to be with those who
descend to the Pit: Ezk 26:20
19   Who do you surpass
         in loveliness?
   Go down and be laid to rest
      with the uncircumcised!
20 They will fall
      among those slain
      by the sword.
   A sword is appointed! Ezk 21:15
   They drag her and all
      her hordes away.
21 Warrior leaders
      will speak
   from the middle of Sheol
   about him C and his allies:
   'They have come down;
   the uncircumcised lie
      slain by the sword.' Is 14:9-11

A32:17 LXX reads year, in the first month,   B32:18 Lit the lower parts of the earth, also in v. 24
C32:21 Either Pharaoh or Egypt

22 "Assyria is there with
    her whole assembly;
  her graves are all around her.
  All of them are slain, fallen
    by the sword.
23 Her graves are set
    in the deepest regions
    of the Pit,
  and her assembly is
    all around her burial place.
  All of them are slain, fallen
    by the sword —
  those who once
    spread terror
  in the land of the living.

24 "Elam is there   Gn 10:22
  with all her hordes
    around her grave.
  All of them are slain, fallen
    by the sword —
  those who went down
    to the underworld
    uncircumcised,
  who once spread their terror
  in the land of the living.
  They bear their disgrace
  with those who descend
    to the Pit.
25 Among the slain
  they prepare a bed for Elam
    with all her hordes.
  Her graves are all
    around her.
  All of them are
    uncircumcised,
  slain by the sword,
  although their terror
    was once spread
  in the land of the living.
  They bear their disgrace
  with those who descend
    to the Pit.
  They are placed
    among the slain.

26 "Meshech and Tubal[A]
    are there,   Gn 10:2; Ezk 27:13; 38:2-3
  with all their hordes.
  Their graves are all
    around them.
  All of them are
    uncircumcised,
    slain by the sword,
  although their terror was
    once spread
  in the land of the living.
27 They do not lie down
  with the fallen warriors
    of the uncircumcised,[B]
  who went down to Sheol
  with their weapons of war,
  whose swords were placed
    under their heads[C]
  and their shields[D]
  rested on their bones,
  although the terror
    of these warriors
  was once in the land
    of the living.
28 But you will be shattered
  and will lie down
    among the uncircumcised,
  with those slain
    by the sword.   Is 14:18

29 "Edom is there, her kings
    and all her princes,   Ezk 25:12-14
  who, despite their strength,
    have been placed
  among those slain
    by the sword.
  They lie down
    with the uncircumcised,
  with those who descend
    to the Pit.
30 All the leaders of the north
  and all the Sidonians
    are there.   Ezk 28:21-23
  They went down in shame
    with the slain,

[A]32:26 Lit *Meshech-tubal*   [B]32:27 LXX reads *of antiquity*   [C]32:27 Or *Do they not . . . heads?*
[D]32:27 Emended; MT reads *iniquities*

despite the terror
their strength inspired.
They lie down uncircumcised
with those slain
by the sword.
They bear their disgrace
with those who descend
to the Pit.

³¹ "Pharaoh will see them
and be comforted over all
his hordes —　　　Ezk 31:16-18
Pharaoh and his whole army,
slain by the sword."
This is the declaration
of the Lord GOD.

³² "For I will spread my ᴬ terror
in the land of the living,
so Pharaoh and all his hordes
will be laid to rest
among the uncircumcised,
with those slain
by the sword."
This is the declaration
of the Lord GOD.

Ezekiel as Israel's Watchman

33 The word of the LORD came
to me: ² "Son of man, speak
to your people and tell them, 'Suppose I bring the sword against a
land, and the people of that land
select a man from among them, appointing him as their watchman.
³ And suppose he sees the sword
coming against the land and blows
his trumpet to warn the people.
⁴ Then, if anyone hears the sound of
the trumpet but ignores the warning, and the sword comes and takes
him away, his death will be his own
fault. ᴮ ⁵ Since he heard the sound of
the trumpet but ignored the warning, his death is his own fault. ᶜ If he
had taken warning, he would have

saved his life. ⁶ However, suppose
the watchman sees the sword coming but doesn't blow the trumpet,
so that the people aren't warned,
and the sword comes and takes
away their lives. Then they have
been taken away because of their
iniquity, but I will hold the watchman accountable for their blood.'

⁷ "As for you, son of man, I have
made you a watchman for the
house of Israel. When you hear a
word from my mouth, give them a
warning from me. ⁸ If I say to the
wicked, 'Wicked one, you will surely die,' but you do not speak out to
warn him about his way, that wicked person will die for his iniquity,
yet I will hold you responsible for
his blood. ⁹ But if you warn a wicked person to turn from his way and
he doesn't turn from it, he will die
for his iniquity, but you will have
rescued yourself.　　Ezk 3:17-19; 18:4

¹⁰ "Now as for you, son of man,
say to the house of Israel, 'You have
said this: "Our transgressions and
our sins are heavy on us, and we
are wasting away because of them!
How then can we survive?"' ¹¹ Tell
them, 'As I live — this is the declaration of the Lord GOD — I take no
pleasure in the death of the wicked, but rather that the wicked person should turn from his way and
live. Repent, repent of your evil
ways! Why will you die, house of
Israel?'　　Lv 26:39; Ezk 4:17; 24:23; 37:11

¹² "Now, son of man, say to your
people, 'The righteousness of the
righteous person will not save
him on the day of his transgression; neither will the wickedness
of the wicked person cause him to
stumble on the day he turns from

ᴬ**32:32** Alt Hb tradition, LXX, Syr read *his*　ᴮ**33:4** Lit *his blood will be on his head*　ᶜ**33:5** Lit *his blood will be on him* his wickedness. The righteous person won't be able to survive by his righteousness on the day he sins. ¹³ When I tell the righteous person that he will surely live, but he trusts in his righteousness and acts unjustly, then none of his righteousness will be remembered, and he will die because of the injustice he has committed. Ezk 3:20; 18:24,26

¹⁴ " 'So when I tell the wicked person, "You will surely die," but he repents of his sin and does what is just and right — ¹⁵ he returns collateral, makes restitution for what he has stolen, and walks in the statutes of life without committing injustice — he will certainly live; he will not die. ¹⁶ None of the sins he committed will be held^A against him. He has done what is just and right; he will certainly live. Lv 18:5

¹⁷ " 'But your people say, "The Lord's way isn't fair," even though it is their own way that isn't fair. ¹⁸ When a righteous person turns from his righteousness and commits injustice, he will die for it. ¹⁹ But if a wicked person turns from his wickedness and does what is just and right, he will live because of it. ²⁰ Yet you say, "The Lord's way isn't fair." I will judge each of you according to his ways, house of Israel.' " Ezk 18:25-30

The News of Jerusalem's Fall

²¹ In the twelfth year of our exile, in the tenth month, on the fifth day of the month, a fugitive from Jerusalem came to me and reported, "The city has been taken!" ²² Now the hand of the LORD had been on me the evening before the fugitive arrived, and he opened my mouth before the man came to me in the morning. So my mouth was opened and I was no longer mute. Ezk 3:26-27

Israel's Continued Rebellion

²³ Then the word of the LORD came to me: ²⁴ "Son of man, those who live in the^B ruins in the land of Israel are saying, 'Abraham was only one person, yet he received possession of the land. But we are many; surely the land has been given to us as a possession.' ²⁵ Therefore say to them, 'This is what the Lord GOD says: You eat meat with blood in it, look to your idols, and shed blood. Should you then receive possession of the land? ²⁶ You have relied on your swords, you have committed detestable acts, and each of you has defiled his neighbor's wife. Should you then receive possession of the land?' Gn 15:7; 28:4; Lv 19:26; Is 51:2; Ezk 36:2

²⁷ "Tell them this: 'This is what the Lord GOD says: As surely as I live, those who are in the ruins will fall by the sword, those in the open field I have given to wild animals to be devoured, and those in the strongholds and caves will die by plague. ²⁸ I will make the land a desolate waste, and its proud strength will come to an end. The mountains of Israel will become desolate, with no one passing through. ²⁹ They will know that I am the LORD when I make the land a desolate waste because of all the detestable acts they have committed.' Ezk 5:12

³⁰ "As for you, son of man, your people are talking about you near the city walls and in the doorways of their houses. One person speaks to another, each saying to his brother, 'Come and hear what the message is that comes from the LORD!' ³¹ So my people come

to you in crowds,[A] sit in front of you, and hear your words, but they don't obey them. Their mouths go on passionately, but their hearts pursue dishonest profit. [32] Yes, to them you are like a singer of passionate songs who has a beautiful voice and plays skillfully on an instrument. They hear your words, but they don't obey them. [33] Yet when all this comes true — and it definitely will — then they will know that a prophet has been among them." Jr 28:9; Ezk 33:29

The Shepherds and God's Flock

34 The word of the Lord came to me: [2] "Son of man, prophesy against the shepherds of Israel. Prophesy, and say to them, 'This is what the Lord God says to the shepherds: Woe to the shepherds of Israel, who have been feeding themselves! Shouldn't the shepherds feed their flock? [3] You eat the fat, wear the wool, and butcher the fattened animals, but you do not tend the flock. [4] You have not strengthened the weak, healed the sick, bandaged the injured, brought back the strays, or sought the lost. Instead, you have ruled them with violence and cruelty. [5] They were scattered for lack of a shepherd; they became food for all the wild animals when they were scattered. [6] My flock went astray on all the mountains and every high hill. My flock was scattered over the whole face of the earth, and there was no one searching or seeking for them.

[7] " 'Therefore, you shepherds, hear the word of the Lord. [8] As I live — this is the declaration of the Lord God — because my flock, lacking a shepherd, has become prey and food for every wild animal, and because my shepherds do not search for my flock, and because the shepherds feed themselves rather than my flock, [9] therefore, you shepherds, hear the word of the Lord!

[10] "'This is what the Lord God says: Look, I am against the shepherds. I will demand my flock from them[B] and prevent them from shepherding the flock. The shepherds will no longer feed themselves, for I will rescue my flock from their mouths so that they will not be food for them. Jr 21:13; Ezk 5:8; 13:8

[11] " 'For this is what the Lord God says: See, I myself will search for my flock and look for them. [12] As a shepherd looks for his sheep on the day he is among his scattered flock, so I will look for my flock. I will rescue them from all the places where they have been scattered on a day of clouds and total darkness. [13] I will bring them out from the peoples, gather them from the countries, and bring them to their own soil. I will shepherd them on the mountains of Israel, in the ravines, and in all the inhabited places of the land. [14] I will tend them in good pasture, and their grazing place will be on Israel's lofty mountains. There they will lie down in a good grazing place; they will feed in rich pasture on the mountains of Israel. [15] I will tend my flock and let them lie down. This is the declaration of the Lord God. [16] I will seek the lost, bring back the strays, bandage the injured, and strengthen the weak, but I will destroy[C] the fat and the strong. I will shepherd them with justice. Ps 23:1-2; Jr 23:3; Hs 6:1

[A]**33:31** Lit *you like the coming of a people*   [B]**34:10** Lit *their hand*   [C]**34:16** Some Hb mss, LXX, Syr, Vg read *watch over*

17 " 'As for you, my flock, the Lord GOD says this: Look, I am going to judge between one sheep and another, between the rams and goats. 18 Isn't it enough for you to feed on the good pasture? Must you also trample the rest of the pasture with your feet? Or isn't it enough that you drink the clear water? Must you also muddy the rest with your feet? 19 Yet my flock has to feed on what your feet have trampled, and drink what your feet have muddied.   Mt 25:31-33

20 " 'Therefore, this is what the Lord GOD says to them: See, I myself will judge between the fat sheep and the lean sheep. 21 Since you have pushed with flank and shoulder and butted all the weak ones with your horns until you scattered them all over, 22 I will save my flock. They will no longer be prey, and I will judge between one sheep and another. 23 I will establish over them one shepherd, my servant David, and he will shepherd them. He will tend them himself and will be their shepherd. 24 I, the LORD, will be their God, and my servant David will be a prince among them. I, the LORD, have spoken.

25 " 'I will make a covenant of peace with them and eliminate dangerous creatures from the land, so that they may live securely in the wilderness and sleep in the forest. 26 I will make them and the area around my hill a blessing: I will send down showers in their season; they will be showers of blessing. 27 The trees of the field will yield their fruit, and the land will yield its produce; my flock will be secure in their land. They will know that I am the LORD when I

break the bars of their yoke and rescue them from the power of those who enslave them. 28 They will no longer be prey for the nations, and the wild creatures of the earth will not consume them. They will live securely, and no one will frighten them. 29 I will establish for them a place renowned for its agriculture, A and they will no longer be victims of famine in the land. They will no longer endure the insults of the nations. 30 Then they will know that I, the LORD their God, am with them, and that they, the house of Israel, are my people. This is the declaration of the Lord GOD. 31 You are my flock, the human flock of my pasture, and I am your God. This is the declaration of the Lord GOD.' "   Is 11:6-9; Ezk 28:26; 37:26

A Prophecy Against Edom

35 The word of the LORD came to me: 2 "Son of man, face Mount Seir and prophesy against it. 3 Say to it, 'This is what the Lord GOD says: Ezk 25:12-14

Look! I am against you,
    Mount Seir.
I will stretch out my hand
    against you
and make you
    a desolate waste.   Ezk 6:14
4 I will turn your cities
    into ruins,
and you will become
    a desolation.
Then you will know that
    I am the LORD.

5 " 'Because you maintained a perpetual hatred and gave the Israelites over to the power of the sword in the time of their disaster, the time of final punishment,

A 34:29 LXX, Syr read a plant of peace

⁶ therefore, as I live — this is the declaration of the Lord GOD — I will destine you for bloodshed, and it will pursue you. Since you did not hate bloodshed, it will pursue you. ⁷ I will make Mount Seir a desolate waste and will cut off from it those who come and go. ⁸ I will fill its mountains with the slain; those slain by the sword will fall on your hills, in your valleys, and in all your ravines. ⁹ I will make you a perpetual desolation; your cities will not be inhabited. Then you will know that I am the LORD. Ps 137:7

¹⁰ " 'Because you said, "These two nations and two lands will be mine, and we will possess them" — though the LORD was there — ¹¹ therefore, as I live — this is the declaration of the Lord GOD — I will treat you according to the anger and jealousy you showed in your hatred of them. I will make myself known among them[A] when I judge you. ¹² Then you will know that I, the LORD, have heard all the blasphemies you uttered against the mountains of Israel, saying, "They are desolate. They have been given to us to devour!" ¹³ You boasted against me with your mouth, and spoke many words against me. I heard it myself! Ps 48:1-3; Ezk 48:35; Ob 12

¹⁴ " 'This is what the Lord GOD says: While the whole world rejoices, I will make you a desolation. ¹⁵ Just as you rejoiced over the inheritance of the house of Israel because it became a desolation, I will deal the same way with you: you will become a desolation, Mount Seir, and so will all Edom in its entirety. Then they will know that I am the LORD.'

Restoration of Israel's Mountains

36 "Son of man, prophesy to the mountains of Israel and say, 'Mountains of Israel, hear the word of the LORD. ² This is what the Lord GOD says: Because the enemy has said about you, "Aha! The ancient heights have become our possession," ' ³ therefore, prophesy and say: 'This is what the Lord GOD says: Because they have made you desolate and have trampled you from every side, so that you became a possession for the rest of the nations and an object of people's gossip and slander, ⁴ therefore, mountains of Israel, hear the word of the Lord GOD. This is what the Lord GOD says to the mountains and hills, to the ravines and valleys, to the desolate ruins and abandoned cities, which have become plunder and a mockery to the rest of the nations all around. Ezk 6:2; 26:2

⁵ " 'This is what the Lord GOD says: Certainly in my burning zeal I speak against the rest of the nations and all of Edom, who took[B] my land as their own possession with wholehearted rejoicing and utter contempt so that its pastureland became[C] plunder. ⁶ Therefore, prophesy concerning the land of Israel and say to the mountains and hills, to the ravines and valleys: This is what the Lord GOD says: Look, I speak in my burning zeal because you have endured the insults of the nations. ⁷ Therefore, this is what the Lord GOD says: I swear[D] that the nations all around you will endure their own insults. Dt 4:24; Ps 74:10

⁸ " 'You, mountains of Israel, will produce your branches and bear your fruit for my people Israel,

A **35:11** LXX reads *you* B **36:5** Lit *gave* C **36:5** Or *contempt, to empty it of*; Hb obscure D **36:7** Lit *lift up my hand* since their arrival is near. ⁹ Look! I am on your side; I will turn toward you, and you will be tilled and sown. ¹⁰ I will fill you with people, with the whole house of Israel in its entirety. The cities will be inhabited and the ruins rebuilt. ¹¹ I will fill you with people and animals, and they will increase and be fruitful. I will make you inhabited as you once were and make you better off than you were before. Then you will know that I am the Lord. ¹² I will cause people, my people Israel, to walk on you; they will possess you, and you will be their inheritance. You will no longer deprive them of their children.

¹³ " 'This is what the Lord God says: Because some are saying to you, "You devour people and deprive your nation of children," ¹⁴ therefore, you will no longer devour people and deprive your nation of children.ᴬ This is the declaration of the Lord God. ¹⁵ I will no longer allow the insults of the nations to be heard against you, and you will not have to endure the reproach of the peoples anymore; you will no longer cause your nation to stumble.ᴮ This is the declaration of the Lord God.' " Nm 13:32; Ezk 34:29

Restoration of Israel's People

¹⁶ The word of the Lord came to me: ¹⁷ "Son of man, while the house of Israel lived in their land, they defiled it with their conduct and actions. Their behavior before me was like menstrual impurity. ¹⁸ So I poured out my wrath on them because of the blood they had shed on the land, and because they had defiled it with their idols. ¹⁹ I

dispersed them among the nations, and they were scattered among the countries. I judged them according to their conduct and actions. ²⁰ When they came to the nations where they went, they profaned my holy name, because it was said about them, 'These are the people of the Lord, yet they had to leave his land in exile.' ²¹ Then I had concern for my holy name, which the house of Israel profaned among the nations where they went. Jr 2:7

²² "Therefore, say to the house of Israel, 'This is what the Lord God says: It is not for your sake that I will act, house of Israel, but for my holy name, which you profaned among the nations where you went. ²³ I will honor the holiness of my great name, which has been profaned among the nations — the name you have profaned among them. The nations will know that I am the Lord — this is the declaration of the Lord God — when I demonstrate my holiness through you in their sight. Dt 9:5; Ps 115:1; Is 43:25

²⁴ " 'For I will take you from the nations and gather you from all the countries, and will bring you into your own land. ²⁵ I will also sprinkle clean water on you, and you will be clean. I will cleanse you from all your impurities and all your idols. ²⁶ I will give you a new heart and put a new spirit within you; I will remove your heart of stoneᶜ and give you a heart of flesh. ²⁷ I will place my Spirit within you and cause you to follow my statutes and carefully observe my ordinances. ²⁸ You will live in the land that I gave your fathers; you will be my people, and I will be your God. ²⁹ I will save

---

ᴬ 36:14 Alt Hb tradition reads and cause your nation to stumble　ᴮ 36:15 Some Hb mss, Tg read no longer bereave your nation of children　ᶜ 36:26 Lit stone from your flesh you from all your uncleanness. I will summon the grain and make it plentiful, and I will not bring famine on you. ³⁰ I will also make the fruit of the trees and the produce of the field plentiful, so that you will no longer experience reproach among the nations on account of famine. Ps 51:7; Ezk 34:13; 37:21; Heb 9:13,19

³¹ " 'You will remember your evil ways and your deeds that were not good, and you will loathe yourselves for your iniquities and detestable practices. ³² It is not for your sake that I will act — this is the declaration of the Lord GOD — let this be known to you. Be ashamed and humiliated because of your ways, house of Israel!

³³ " 'This is what the Lord GOD says: On the day I cleanse you from all your iniquities, I will cause the cities to be inhabited, and the ruins will be rebuilt. ³⁴ The desolate land will be cultivated instead of lying desolate in the sight of everyone who passes by. ³⁵ They will say, "This land that was desolate has become like the garden of Eden. The cities that were once ruined, desolate, and demolished are now fortified and inhabited." ³⁶ Then the nations that remain around you will know that I, the LORD, have rebuilt what was demolished and have replanted what was desolate. I, the LORD, have spoken and I will do it. Is 51:3

³⁷ " 'This is what the Lord GOD says: I will respond to the house of Israel and do this for them: I will multiply them in number like a flock.ᴬ ³⁸ So the ruined cities will be filled with a flock of people, just as Jerusalem is filled with a flock of sheep for sacrificeᴮ during its appointed festivals. Then they will know that I am the LORD.' " Ezk 14:3

The Valley of Dry Bones

37 The hand of the LORD was on me, and he brought me out by his Spirit and set me down in the middle of the valley; it was full of bones. ² He led me all around them. There were a great many of them on the surface of the valley, and they were very dry. ³ Then he said to me, "Son of man, can these bones live?" Ezk 1:3; 8:3; 11:24

I replied, "Lord GOD, only you know." Dt 32:39; 1Sm 2:6

⁴ He said to me, "Prophesy concerning these bones and say to them: Dry bones, hear the word of the LORD! ⁵ This is what the Lord GOD says to these bones: I will cause breath to enter you, and you will live. ⁶ I will put tendons on you, make flesh grow on you, and cover you with skin. I will put breath in you so that you come to life. Then you will know that I am the LORD."

⁷ So I prophesied as I had been commanded. While I was prophesying, there was a noise, a rattling sound, and the bones came together, bone to bone. ⁸ As I looked, tendons appeared on them, flesh grew, and skin covered them, but there was no breath in them. ⁹ He said to me, "Prophesy to the breath,ᶜ prophesy, son of man. Say to it: This is what the Lord GOD says: Breath, come from the four winds and breathe into these slain so that they may live!" ¹⁰ So I prophesied as he commanded me; the breath entered them, and they came to life and stood on their feet, a vast army. Ps 104:30; Rv 11:11

ᴬ36:37 Lit flock of people　ᴮ36:38 Lit as the consecrated flock, as the flock of Jerusalem　ᶜ37:9 Or wind, or spirit, also in v. 10

¹¹ Then he said to me, "Son of man, these bones are the whole house of Israel. Look how they say, 'Our bones are dried up, and our hope has perished; we are cut off.' ¹² Therefore, prophesy and say to them: 'This is what the Lord GOD says: I am going to open your graves and bring you up from them, my people, and lead you into the land of Israel. ¹³ You will know that I am the LORD, my people, when I open your graves and bring you up from them. ¹⁴ I will put my Spirit in you, and you will live, and I will settle you in your own land. Then you will know that I am the LORD. I have spoken, and I will do it. This is the declaration of the LORD.'" Ps 141:7; Ezk 36:10

The Reunification of Israel

¹⁵ The word of the LORD came to me: ¹⁶ "Son of man, take a single stick and write on it: Belonging to Judah and the Israelites associated with him. Then take another stick and write on it: Belonging to Joseph — the stick of Ephraim — and all the house of Israel associated with him. ¹⁷ Then join them together into a single stick so that they become one in your hand. ¹⁸ When your people ask you, 'Won't you explain to us what you mean by these things?' — ¹⁹ tell them, 'This is what the Lord GOD says: I am going to take the stick of Joseph, which is in the hand of Ephraim, and the tribes of Israel associated with him, and put them together with the stick of Judah. I will make them into a single stick so that they become one in my hand.' Nm 17:2-3; 2Ch 11:11-17; Is 11:13

²⁰ "When the sticks you have written on are in your hand and in full view of the people, ²¹ tell them, 'This is what the Lord GOD says: I am going to take the Israelites out of the nations where they have gone. I will gather them from all around and bring them into their own land. ²² I will make them one nation in the land, on the mountains of Israel, and one king will rule over all of them. They will no longer be two nations and will no longer be divided into two kingdoms. ²³ They will not defile themselves anymore with their idols, their abhorrent things, and all their transgressions. I will save them from all their apostasies by which ᴬ they sinned, and I will cleanse them. Then they will be my people, and I will be their God. ²⁴ My servant David will be king over them, and there will be one shepherd for all of them. They will follow my ordinances, and keep my statutes and obey them. Ezk 12:3

²⁵ "They will live in the land that I gave to my servant Jacob, where your fathers lived. They will live in it forever with their children and grandchildren, and my servant David will be their prince forever. ²⁶ I will make a covenant of peace with them; it will be a permanent covenant with them. I will establish and multiply them and will set my sanctuary among them forever. ²⁷ My dwelling place will be with them; I will be their God, and they will be my people. ²⁸ When my sanctuary is among them forever, the nations will know that I, the LORD, sanctify Israel.'" Is 54:10; 60:21; Jn 12:34

The Defeat of Gog

38 The word of the LORD came to me: ² "Son of man, face Gog, of the land of Magog, the chief prince of ᴮ Meshech and Tubal.

ᴬ**37:23** Some Hb mss, LXX, Sym; other Hb mss read *their settlements where*   ᴮ**38:2** Or *the prince of Rosh,*

Prophesy against him [3] and say, 'This is what the Lord God says: Look, I am against you, Gog, chief prince of Meshech and Tubal. [4] I will turn you around, put hooks in your jaws, and bring you out with all your army, including horses and riders, who are all splendidly dressed, a huge assembly armed with large and small shields, all of them brandishing swords. [5] Persia, Cush, and Put are with them, all of them with shields and helmets; [6] Gomer with all its troops; and Beth-togarmah from the remotest parts of the north along with all its troops — many peoples are with you. Gn 10:2; Ezk 39:1; Rv 20:8

[7] "'Be prepared and get yourself ready, you and your whole assembly that has been mobilized around you; you will be their guard. [8] After a long time you will be summoned. In the last years you will enter a land that has been restored from war[A] and regathered from many peoples to the mountains of Israel, which had long been a ruin. They were brought out from the peoples, and all of them now live securely. [9] You, all of your troops, and many peoples with you will advance, coming like a thunderstorm; you will be like a cloud covering the land. Ezk 36:8-11

[10] "'This is what the Lord God says: On that day, thoughts will arise in your mind, and you will devise an evil plan. [11] You will say, "I will advance against a land of open villages; I will come against a tranquil people who are living securely, all of them living without walls and without bars or gates" — [12] in order to seize spoil and carry off plunder, to turn your hand against ruins now inhabited and against a people gathered from the nations, who have been acquiring cattle and possessions and who live at the center of the world. [13] Sheba and Dedan and the merchants of Tarshish with all its rulers[B] will ask you, "Have you come to seize spoil? Have you mobilized your assembly to carry off plunder, to make off with silver and gold, to take cattle and possessions, to seize plenty of spoil?"' Jdg 18:7; Is 10:6; Jr 49:31; Ezk 29:19

[14] "Therefore prophesy, son of man, and say to Gog, 'This is what the Lord God says: On that day when my people Israel are dwelling securely, will you not know this [15] and come from your place in the remotest parts of the north — you and many peoples with you, who are all riding horses — a huge assembly, a powerful army? [16] You will advance against my people Israel like a cloud covering the land. It will happen in the last days, Gog, that I will bring you against my land so that the nations may know me, when I show myself holy through you in their sight. Jr 23:6; Ezk 39:2

[17] "'This is what the Lord God says: Are you the one I spoke about in former times through my servants, the prophets of Israel, who for years prophesied in those times that I would bring you against them? [18] Now on that day, the day when Gog comes against the land of Israel — this is the declaration of the Lord God — my wrath will flare up.[C] [19] I swear in my zeal and fiery rage: On that day there will be a great earthquake in the land of Israel. [20] The fish of the sea, the birds of the sky, the animals of the field, every creature that crawls

---

A 38:8 Lit *from the sword*   B 38:13 Lit *young lions*, or *villages*   C 38:18 Lit *up in my anger* on the ground, and every human being on the face of the earth will tremble before me. The mountains will be demolished, the cliffs will collapse, and every wall will fall to the ground. ²¹ I will call for a sword against him on all my mountains — this is the declaration of the Lord God — and every man's sword will be against his brother. ²² I will execute judgment on him with plague and bloodshed. I will pour out torrential rain, hailstones, fire, and burning sulfur on him, as well as his troops and the many peoples who are with him. ²³ I will display my greatness and holiness, and will reveal myself in the sight of many nations. Then they will know that I am the Lord.'   Ezk 36:6

The Disposal of Gog

39 "As for you, son of man, prophesy against Gog and say, 'This is what the Lord God says: Look, I am against you, Gog, chief prince of ᴬ Meshech and Tubal. ² I will turn you around, drive you on, and lead you up from the remotest parts of the north. I will bring you against the mountains of Israel. ³ Then I will knock your bow from your left hand and make your arrows drop from your right hand. ⁴ You, all your troops, and the peoples who are with you will fall on the mountains of Israel. I will give you as food to every kind of predatory bird and to the wild animals. ⁵ You will fall on the open field, for I have spoken. This is the declaration of the Lord God.   Ezk 38:2-4

⁶ " 'I will send fire against Magog and those who live securely on the coasts and islands. Then they will know that I am the Lord. ⁷ So I will make my holy name known among my people Israel and will no longer allow it to be profaned. Then the nations will know that I am the Lord, the Holy One in Israel. ⁸ Yes, it is coming, and it will happen. This is the declaration of the Lord God. This is the day I have spoken about.

⁹ " 'Then the inhabitants of Israel's cities will go out, kindle fires, and burn the weapons — the small and large shields, the bows and arrows, the clubs and spears. For seven years they will use them to make fires. ¹⁰ They will not gather wood from the countryside or cut it down from the forests, for they will use the weapons to make fires. They will take the loot from those who looted them and plunder those who plundered them. This is the declaration of the Lord God.   Is 14:2; 33:1

¹¹ " 'Now on that day I will give Gog a burial place there in Israel — the Travelers' Valley ᴮ east of the Sea. It will block those who travel through, for Gog and all his hordes will be buried there. So it will be called Hordes of Gog ᶜ Valley. ¹² The house of Israel will spend seven months burying them in order to cleanse the land. ¹³ All the people of the land will bury them and their fame will spread on the day I display my glory. This is the declaration of the Lord God.   Dt 21:23; Jr 33:9

¹⁴ " 'They will appoint men on a full-time basis to pass through the land and bury the invaders ᴰ who remain on the surface of the ground, in order to cleanse it. They will make their search at the end of the seven months. ¹⁵ When they pass through the land and one of

---

ᴬ39:1 Or Gog, prince of Rosh,   ᴮ39:11 Hb obscure   ᶜ39:11 = Hamon-gog, also in v. 15   ᴰ39:14 Or basis, some to pass through the land, and with them some to bury those them sees a human bone, he will set up a marker next to it until the buriers have buried it in Hordes of Gog Valley. ¹⁶ There will even be a city named Hamonah[A] there. So they will cleanse the land.'

¹⁷ "Son of man, this is what the Lord God says: Tell every kind of bird and all the wild animals, 'Assemble and come! Gather from all around to my sacrificial feast that I am slaughtering for you, a great feast on the mountains of Israel; you will eat flesh and drink blood. ¹⁸ You will eat the flesh of mighty men and drink the blood of the earth's princes: rams, lambs, male goats, and all the fattened bulls of Bashan. ¹⁹ You will eat fat until you are satisfied and drink blood until you are drunk, at my sacrificial feast that I have prepared for you. ²⁰ At my table you will eat your fill of horses and riders, of mighty men and all the warriors. This is the declaration of the Lord God.' Rv 19:17-18

Israel's Restoration to God

²¹ "I will display my glory among the nations, and all the nations will see the judgment I have executed and the hand I have laid on them. ²² From that day forward the house of Israel will know that I am the Lord their God. ²³ And the nations will know that the house of Israel went into exile on account of their iniquity, because they dealt unfaithfully with me. Therefore, I hid my face from them and handed them over to their enemies, so that they all fell by the sword. ²⁴ I dealt with them according to their uncleanness and transgressions, and I hid my face from them.

²⁵ "So this is what the Lord God says: Now I will restore the fortunes of Jacob and have compassion on the whole house of Israel, and I will be jealous for my holy name. ²⁶ They will feel remorse for[B,C] their disgrace and all the unfaithfulness they committed against me, when they live securely in their land with no one to frighten them. ²⁷ When I bring them back from the peoples and gather them from the countries of their enemies, I will demonstrate my holiness through them in the sight of many nations. ²⁸ They will know that I am the Lord their God when I regather them to their own land after having exiled them among the nations. I will leave none of them behind.[D] ²⁹ I will no longer hide my face from them, for I will pour out my Spirit on the house of Israel." This is the declaration of the Lord God. Is 27:12-13; Jr 33:7; Ezk 34:13

The New Temple

40 In the twenty-fifth year of our exile, at the beginning of the year, on the tenth day of the month in the fourteenth year after Jerusalem had been captured, on that very day the Lord's hand was on me, and he brought me there. ² In visions of God he took me to the land of Israel and set me down on a very high mountain. On its southern slope was a structure resembling a city. ³ He brought me there, and I saw a man whose appearance was like bronze, with a linen cord and a measuring rod in his hand. He was standing by the city gate. ⁴ He spoke to me: "Son of man, look with your eyes, listen with your ears, and pay attention to

---

[A]**39:16** In Hb, *Hamonah* is related to the word "horde." [B]**39:26** Some emend to *will forget* [C]**39:26** Lit *will bear* [D]**39:28** Lit *behind there any longer* everything I am going to show you, for you have been brought here so that I might show it to you. Report everything you see to the house of Israel." 2Kg 25:1-7; Jr 39:1-9; 52:4-11; Ezk 33:21

The Wall and Outer Gates

5 Now there was a wall surrounding the outside of the temple. The measuring rod in the man's hand was six units of twenty-one inches; A each unit was the standard length plus three inches. B He measured the thickness of the wall structure; it was 10 ½ feet, C and its height was the same. 6 Then he came to the gate that faced east and climbed its steps. He measured the threshold of the gate; it was 10 ½ feet deep — one threshold was 10 ½ feet deep. 7 Each recess was 10 ½ feet long and 10 ½ feet deep, and there was a space of 8 ¾ feet D between the recesses. The inner threshold of the gate on the temple side next to the gate's portico was 10 ½ feet. 8 Next he measured the gate's portico; 9 it E was 14 feet, F and its jambs were 3 ½ feet. G The gate's portico was on the temple side. Is 26:1; Ezk 43:1

10 There were three recesses on each side of the east gate, each with the same measurements, and the jambs on either side also had the same measurements. 11 Then he measured the width of the gate's entrance; it was 17 ½ feet, H while the width I of the gate was 22 ¾ feet. J 12 There was a barrier of 21 inches K in front of the recesses on both sides, and the recesses on

each side were 10 ½ feet L square. 13 Then he measured the gate from the roof of one recess to the roof of the opposite one; the distance was 43 ¾ feet. M The openings of the recesses faced each other. 14 Next, he measured the porch — 105 feet. N,O 15 The distance from the front of the gate at the entrance to the front of the gate's portico on the inside was 87 ½ feet. P 16 The recesses and their jambs had beveled windows all around the inside of the gate. The porticoes also had windows all around on the inside. Each jamb was decorated with palm trees.

17 Then he brought me into the outer court, and there were chambers and a paved surface laid out all around the court. Thirty chambers faced the pavement, 18 which flanked the courtyard's gates and corresponded to the length of the gates; this was the lower pavement. 19 Then he measured the distance from the front of the lower gate to the exterior front of the inner court; it was 175 feet. Q This was the east; next the north is described.

20 He measured the gate of the outer court facing north, both its length and width. 21 Its three recesses on each side, its jambs, and its portico had the same measurements as the first gate: 87 ½ feet long and 43 ¾ feet wide. 22 Its windows, portico, and palm trees had the same measurements as those of the gate that faced east. Seven steps led up to the gate, and its portico was ahead of them. 23 The inner

A 40:5 = a long cubit　B 40:5 Lit six cubits by the cubit and a handbreadth　C 40:5 Lit was one rod, also in v. 7　D 40:7 Lit five cubits, also in v. 30　E 40:8-9 Some Hb mss, Syr, Vg; other Hb mss read gate facing the temple side; it was one rod. 9 Then he measured the gate's portico; it　F 40:9 Lit eight cubits　G 40:9 Lit two cubits　H 40:11 Lit 10 cubits　I 40:11 Lit length　J 40:11 Lit 13 cubits　K 40:12 Lit one cubit, also in v. 42　L 40:12 Lit six cubits　M 40:13 Lit 25 cubits, also in vv. 21,25,29,33,36　N 40:14 MT adds To the jamb of the court, the gate was all around; Hb obscure　O 40:14 Lit 60 cubits　P 40:15 Lit 50 cubits, also in vv. 21,25,29,33,36　Q 40:19 Lit 100 cubits, also in vv. 23,27,47 court had a gate facing the north gate, like the one on the east. He measured the distance from gate to gate; it was 175 feet.

²⁴ He brought me to the south side, and there was also a gate on the south. He measured its jambs and portico; they had the same measurements as the others. ²⁵ Both the gate and its portico had windows all around, like the other windows. It was 87½ feet long and 43¾ feet wide. ²⁶ Its stairway had seven steps, and its portico was ahead of them. It had palm trees on its jambs, one on each side. ²⁷ The inner court had a gate on the south. He measured from gate to gate on the south; it was 175 feet.

The Inner Gates

²⁸ Then he brought me to the inner court through the south gate. When he measured the south gate, it had the same measurements as the others. ²⁹ Its recesses, jambs, and portico had the same measurements as the others. Both it and its portico had windows all around. It was 87½ feet long and 43¾ feet wide. ³⁰ (There were porticoes all around, 43¾ feet long and 8¾ feet wide. ᴬ) ³¹ Its portico faced the outer court, and its jambs were decorated with palm trees. Its stairway had eight steps.

³² Then he brought me to the inner court on the east side. When he measured the gate, it had the same measurements as the others. ³³ Its recesses, jambs, and portico had the same measurements as the others. Both it and its portico had windows all around. It was 87½ feet long and 43¾ feet wide. ³⁴ Its portico faced the outer court, and its jambs were decorated with palm trees on each side. Its stairway had eight steps.

³⁵ Then he brought me to the north gate. When he measured it, it had the same measurements as the others, ³⁶ as did its recesses, jambs, and portico. It also had windows all around. It was 87½ feet long and 43¾ feet wide. ³⁷ Its portico ᴮ faced the outer court, and its jambs were decorated with palm trees on each side. Its stairway had eight steps.   Ezk 47:2

Rooms for Preparing Sacrifices

³⁸ There was a chamber whose door opened into the gate's portico. ᶜ The burnt offering was to be washed there. ³⁹ Inside the gate's portico there were two tables on each side, on which to slaughter the burnt offering, sin offering, and guilt offering. ⁴⁰ Outside, as one approaches the entrance of the north gate, there were two tables on one side and two more tables on the other side of the gate's portico. ⁴¹ So there were four tables inside the gate and four outside, eight tables in all on which the slaughtering was to be done. ⁴² There were also four tables of cut stone for the burnt offering, each 31½ inches ᴰ long, 31½ inches wide, and 21 inches high. The utensils used to slaughter the burnt offerings and other sacrifices were placed on them. ⁴³ There were three-inch ᴱ hooks ᶠ fastened all around the inside of the room, and the flesh of the offering was to be laid on the tables.   Lv 1:3-4; 2Ch 4:6

ᴬ40:30 Some Hb mss, LXX omit v. 30   ᴮ40:37 LXX; MT reads *jambs*   ᶜ40:38 Text emended; MT reads *door was by the jambs, at the gates*   ᴰ40:42 Lit *one and a half cubits*   ᴱ40:43 Lit *one handbreadth*   ᶠ40:43 Or *ledges*

Rooms for Singers and Priests

⁴⁴ Outside the inner gate, within the inner court, there were chambers for the singers: ᴬ one ᴮ beside the north gate, facing south, and another beside the south ᶜ gate, facing north. ⁴⁵ Then the man said to me: "This chamber that faces south is for the priests who keep charge of the temple. ⁴⁶ The chamber that faces north is for the priests who keep charge of the altar. These are the sons of Zadok, the ones from the sons of Levi who may approach the LORD to serve him." ⁴⁷ Next he measured the court. It was square, 175 feet long and 175 feet wide. The altar was in front of the temple.

⁴⁸ Then he brought me to the portico of the temple and measured the jambs of the portico; they were 8 ¾ feet thick on each side. The width of the gate was 24 ½ feet, ᴰ and the side walls of the gate were ᴱ 5 ¼ feet ᶠ wide on each side. ⁴⁹ The portico was 35 feet ᴳ across and 21 ᴴ feet ᴵ deep, and 10 steps led ᴶ up to it. There were pillars by the jambs, one on each side.   1Kg 6:3; 7:15-22

Inside the Temple

41 Next he brought me into the great hall and measured the jambs; on each side the width of the jamb was 10 ½ feet. ᴷ,ᴸ ² The width of the entrance was 17 ½ feet, ᴹ and the side walls of the entrance were 8 ¾ feet ᴺ wide on each side. He also measured the length of the great hall, 70 feet, ᴼ and the width, 35 feet. ᴾ ³ He went inside the next room and measured the jambs at the entrance; they were 3 ½ feet ᵠ wide. The entrance was 10 ½ feet wide, and the width of the entrance's side walls on each side ᴿ was 12 ¼ feet. ˢ ⁴ He then measured the length of the room adjacent to the great hall, 35 feet, and the width, 35 feet. And he said to me, "This is the most holy place." Ezk 40:2-3,17

Outside the Temple

⁵ Then he measured the wall of the temple; it was 10 ½ feet thick. The width of the side rooms all around the temple was 7 feet. ᵀ ⁶ The side rooms were arranged one above another in three stories of thirty rooms each. ᵁ There were ledges on the wall of the temple all around to serve as supports for the side rooms, so that the supports would not be in the temple wall itself. ⁷ The side rooms surrounding the temple widened at each successive story, for the structure surrounding the temple went up by stages. This was the reason for the temple's broadness as it rose. And so, one would go up from the lowest story to the highest by means of the middle one. ⱽ   1Kg 6:5-10

⁸ I saw that the temple had a raised platform surrounding it; this foundation for the side rooms was 10 ½ feet high. ᵂ ⁹ The thickness of the outer wall of the side rooms

---

ᴬ40:44 LXX reads *were two chambers*   ᴮ40:44 LXX; MT reads *singers, which was*   ᶜ40:44 LXX; MT reads *east*   ᴰ40:48 Lit *14 cubits*   ᴱ40:48 LXX; MT omits *24½ feet, and the side walls of the gate were*   ᶠ40:48 Lit *three cubits*   ᴳ40:49 Lit *20 cubits*   ᴴ40:49 LXX; MT reads *19¼*   ᴵ40:49 Lit *12 cubits*   ᴶ40:49 MT reads *and it was on steps that they would go*   ᴷ41:1 LXX; MT reads *jambs; they were 10½ feet wide on each side — the width of the tabernacle*   ᴸ41:1 Lit *six cubits*, also in vv. 3,5   ᴹ41:2 Lit *10 cubits*   ᴺ41:2 Lit *five cubits*, also in vv. 9,11,12   ᴼ41:2 Lit *40 cubits*   ᴾ41:2 Lit *20 cubits*, also in vv. 4,10   ᵠ41:3 Lit *two cubits*, also in v. 22   ᴿ41:3 LXX; MT reads *width of the entrance*   ˢ41:3 Lit *seven cubits*   ᵀ41:5 Lit *four cubits*   ᵁ41:6 Lit *another three and thirty times*   ⱽ41:7 Hb obscure   ᵂ41:8 Lit *a full rod of six cubits of a joint*; Hb obscure was 8¾ feet. The free space between the side rooms of the temple[10] and the outer chambers was 35 feet wide all around the temple. [11] The side rooms opened into the free space, one entrance toward the north and another to the south. The area of free space was 8¾ feet wide all around. Ezk 40:5,17

[12] Now the building that faced the temple yard toward the west was 122½ feet[A] wide. The wall of the building was 8¾ feet thick on all sides, and the building's length was 157½ feet.[B]

[13] Then the man measured the temple; it was 175 feet[C] long. In addition, the temple yard and the building, including its walls, were 175 feet long. [14] The width of the front of the temple along with the temple yard to the east was 175 feet. [15] Next he measured the length of the building facing the temple yard to the west, with its galleries[D] on each side; it was 175 feet.

Interior Wooden Structures

The interior of the great hall and the porticoes of the court — [16] the thresholds, the beveled windows, and the balconies all around with their three levels opposite the threshold — were overlaid with wood on all sides. They were paneled from the ground to the windows (but the windows were covered), [17] reaching to the top of the entrance, and as far as the inner temple and on the outside. On every wall all around, on the inside and outside, was a pattern [18] carved with cherubim and palm trees. There was a palm tree between each pair of cherubim. Each cherub had two faces: [19] a human face turned toward the palm tree on one side, and a lion's face turned toward it on the other. They were carved throughout the temple on all sides. [20] Cherubim and palm trees were carved from the ground to the top of the entrance and on the wall of the great hall. 1Kg 6:4,15; Ezk 40:16,25

[21] The doorposts of the great hall were square, and the front of the sanctuary had the same appearance. [22] The altar was[E] made of wood, 5¼ feet[F] high and 3½ feet long.[G] It had corners, and its length[H] and sides were of wood. The man told me, "This is the table that stands before the LORD."

[23] The great hall and the sanctuary each had a double door, [24] and each of the doors had two swinging panels. There were two panels for one door and two for the other. [25] Cherubim and palm trees were carved on the doors of the great hall like those carved on the walls. There was a wooden canopy[I] outside, in front of the portico. [26] There were beveled windows and palm trees on both sides, on the side walls of the portico, the side rooms of the temple, and the canopies.[I] 1Kg 6:31-35; 7:6

The Priests' Chambers

42 Then the man led me out by way of the north gate into the outer court. He brought me to the group of chambers opposite the temple yard and opposite the building to the north. [2] Along the length of the chambers, which was

---

A 41:12 Lit 70 cubits   B 41:12 Lit 90 cubits   C 41:13 Lit 100 cubits   D 41:15 Or ledges   E 41:21-22 Or and in front of the sanctuary was something that looked like [22] an altar   F 41:22 Lit three cubits   G 41:22 LXX reads long and 3 1/2 feet wide   H 41:22 LXX reads base   I 41:25,26 Hb obscure

175 feet,[A] there was an entrance on the north; the width was 87 1/2 feet.[B] 3 Opposite the 35 foot space[C] belonging to the inner court and opposite the paved surface belonging to the outer court, the structure rose gallery by gallery in three tiers. 4 In front of the chambers was a walkway toward the inside, 17 1/2 feet[D] wide and 175 feet long,[E] and their entrances were on the north. 5 The upper chambers were narrower because the galleries took away more space from them than from the lower and middle stories of the building. 6 For they were arranged in three stories and had no pillars like the pillars of the courts; therefore the upper chambers were set back from the ground more than the lower and middle stories. 7 A wall on the outside ran in front of the chambers, parallel to them, toward the outer court; it was 87 1/2 feet long. 8 For the chambers on the outer court were 87 1/2 feet long, while those facing the great hall were 175 feet long. 9 At the base of these chambers there was an entryway on the east side as one enters them from the outer court. Ezk 40:17,28,48; 41:1,12; 42:10,13

10 In the thickness of the wall of the court toward the south,[F] there were chambers facing the temple yard and the western building, 11 with a passageway in front of them, just like the chambers that faced north. Their length and width, as well as all their exits, measurements, and entrances, were identical. 12 The entrance at the beginning of the passageway, the way in front of the corresponding[G] wall as one enters on the east side, was similar to the entrances of the chambers that were on the south side. Ezk 42:1,4

13 Then the man said to me, "The northern and southern chambers that face the courtyard are the holy chambers where the priests who approach the LORD will eat the most holy offerings. There they will deposit the most holy offerings — the grain offerings, sin offerings, and guilt offerings — for the place is holy. 14 Once the priests have entered, they are not to go out from the holy area to the outer court until they have removed the clothes they minister in, for these are holy. They are to put on other clothes before they approach the public area." Lv 7:6; 10:3; Dt 21:5; Ezk 40:46

Outside Dimensions of the Temple Complex

15 When he finished measuring inside the temple complex, he led me out by way of the gate that faced east and measured all around the complex. Ezk 40:6; 43:1

16 He measured the east side with a measuring rod; it was 875 feet[H] by the measuring rod.[I] 17 He[J] measured the north side; it was 875 feet by the measuring rod. 18 He[K] measured the south side; it was 875 feet by the measuring rod. 19 Then he turned to the west side and measured 875 feet by the measuring rod.

A42:2 Lit 100 cubits, also in vv. 4,8 B42:2 Lit 50 cubits, also in v. 7 C42:3 Lit 20 cubits D42:4 Lit 10 cubits E42:4 LXX, Syr; MT reads wide, a way of one cubit F42:10 LXX; MT reads east G42:12 Or protective; Hb obscure H42:16 Lit 500 in rods, also in vv. 17,18,19 I42:16 Lit rod all around, also in vv. 17,18,19 J42:17 LXX reads Then he turned to the north and K42:18 LXX reads Then he turned to the south and

20 He measured the temple complex on all four sides. It had a wall all around it, 875 feet long and 875 feet wide, to separate the holy from the common. Is 60:18; Ezk 40:5; Zch 2:5

Return of the LORD's Glory

43 He led me to the gate, the one that faces east, 2 and I saw the glory of the God of Israel coming from the east. His voice sounded like the roar of a huge torrent, and the earth shone with his glory. 3 The vision I saw was like the one I had seen when he A came to destroy the city, and like the ones I had seen by the Chebar Canal. I fell facedown. 4 The glory of the LORD entered the temple by way of the gate that faced east. 5 Then the Spirit lifted me up and brought me to the inner court, and the glory of the LORD filled the temple. Ezk 10:19

6 While the man was standing beside me, I heard someone speaking to me from the temple. 7 He said to me: "Son of man, this is the place of my throne and the place for the soles of my feet, where I will dwell among the Israelites forever. The house of Israel and their kings will no longer defile my holy name by their religious prostitution and by the corpses B of their kings at their high places. C 8 Whenever they placed their threshold next to my threshold and their doorposts beside my doorposts, with only a wall between me and them, they were defiling my holy name by the detestable acts they committed. So I destroyed them in my anger. 9 Now let them remove their prostitution and the corpses of their kings far from me, and I will dwell among them forever. Ps 47:8; Ezk 1:26; 37:26-28

10 "As for you, son of man, describe the temple to the house of Israel, so that they may be ashamed of their iniquities. Let them measure its pattern, 11 and they will be ashamed of all that they have done. Reveal D the design of the temple to them — its layout with its exits and entrances — its complete design along with all its statutes, design specifications, and laws. Write it down in their sight so that they may observe its complete design and all its statutes and may carry them out. 12 This is the law of the temple: All its surrounding territory on top of the mountain will be especially holy. Yes, this is the law of the temple. Ezk 40:4

The Altar

13 "These are the measurements of the altar in units of length (each unit being the standard length plus three inches): E The gutter is 21 inches F deep and 21 inches wide, with a rim of nine inches G around its edge. This is the base H of the altar. 14 The distance from the gutter on the ground to the lower ledge is 3 ½ feet, I and the width of the ledge is 21 inches. There are 7 feet J from the small ledge to the large ledge, whose width is also 21 inches. 15 The altar hearth K is 7 feet high, and four horns project upward from the hearth. 16 The hearth is square, 21 feet L long by 21 feet wide. 17 The

---

A 43:3 Some Hb mss, Theod, Vg; other Hb mss, LXX, Syr read I   B 43:7 Or monuments, also in v. 9
C 43:7 Some Hb mss, Theod, Tg read their death   D 43:10-11 LXX, Vg; MT reads pattern. 11 And if they are ashamed . . . done, reveal   E 43:13 Lit in cubits (a cubit being a cubit plus a handbreadth)
F 43:13 Lit one cubit, also in vv. 14,17   G 43:13 Lit one span   H 43:15 LXX reads height   I 43:14 Lit two cubits   J 43:14 Lit four cubits, also in v. 15   K 43:15 Hb obscure   L 43:16 Lit 12 cubits

ledge is 24½ feet^A long by 24½ feet wide, with four equal sides. The rim all around it is 10½ inches,^B and its gutter is 21 inches all around it. The altar's steps face east." Ex 27:1-8; 2Ch 4:1

¹⁸ Then he said to me: "Son of man, this is what the Lord God says: These are the statutes for the altar on the day it is constructed, so that burnt offerings may be sacrificed on it and blood may be splattered on it: ¹⁹ You are to give a bull from the herd as a sin offering to the Levitical priests who are from the offspring of Zadok, who approach me in order to serve me." This is the declaration of the Lord God. ²⁰ "You are to take some of its blood and apply it to the four horns of the altar, the four corners of the ledge, and all around the rim. In this way you will purify the altar and make atonement for it. ²¹ Then you are to take away the bull for the sin offering, and it must be burned outside the sanctuary in the place appointed for the temple. Ezk 2:1

²² "On the second day you are to present an unblemished male goat as a sin offering. They will purify the altar just as they did with the bull. ²³ When you have finished the purification, you are to present a young, unblemished bull and an unblemished ram from the flock. ²⁴ You are to present them before the Lord; the priests will throw salt on them and sacrifice them as a burnt offering to the Lord. ²⁵ You will offer a goat for a sin offering each day for seven days. A young bull and a ram from the flock, both unblemished, are also to be offered. ²⁶ For seven days the priests are to make atonement for the altar and cleanse it. In this way

they will consecrate it^{C 27} and complete the days of purification. Then on the eighth day and afterward, the priests will offer your burnt offerings and fellowship offerings on the altar, and I will accept you." This is the declaration of the Lord God.

The Prince's Privilege

44 The man then brought me back toward the sanctuary's outer gate that faced east, and it was closed. ² The Lord said to me: "This gate will remain closed. It will not be opened, and no one will enter through it, because the Lord, the God of Israel, has entered through it. Therefore it will remain closed. ³ The prince himself will sit in the gate to eat a meal before the Lord. He is to enter by way of the portico of the gate and go out the same way." Gn 31:54; Ex 24:9-11; 43:2-4; 46:2,8-10

⁴ Then the man brought me by way of the north gate to the front of the temple. I looked, and the glory of the Lord filled his temple. And I fell facedown. ⁵ The Lord said to me: "Son of man, pay attention; look with your eyes and listen with your ears to everything I tell you about all the statutes and laws of the Lord's temple. Take careful note of the entrance of the temple along with all the exits of the sanctuary. Dt 32:46; Is 6:3; Ezk 1:28; 3:23; 43:3,5

The Levites' Duties and Privileges

⁶ "Say to the rebellious people, the house of Israel, 'This is what the Lord God says: I have had enough of all your detestable practices, house of Israel. ⁷ When you brought in foreigners, uncircumcised in both heart and flesh, to occupy

^A**43:17** Lit *14 cubits*   ^B**43:17** Lit *one-half cubit*   ^C**43:26** Lit *will fill its hands*

my sanctuary, you defiled my temple while you offered my food — the fat and the blood. You^A broke my covenant by all your detestable practices. ⁸ You have not kept charge of my holy things but have appointed others to keep charge of my sanctuary for you.' Ezk 2:5-7; 3:9

⁹ "This is what the Lord God says: No foreigner, uncircumcised in heart and flesh, may enter my sanctuary, not even a foreigner who is among the Israelites. ¹⁰ Surely the Levites who wandered away from me when Israel went astray, and who strayed from me after their idols, will bear the consequences of their iniquity. ¹¹ Yet they will occupy my sanctuary, serving as guards at the temple gates and ministering at the temple. They will slaughter the burnt offerings and other sacrifices for the people and will stand before them to serve them. ¹² Because they ministered to the house of Israel before their idols and became a sinful stumbling block to them, therefore I swore an oath^B against them" — this is the declaration of the Lord God — "that they would bear the consequences of their iniquity. ¹³ They must not approach me to serve me as priests or come near any of my holy things or the most holy things. They will bear their disgrace and the consequences of the detestable acts they committed. ¹⁴ Yet I will make them responsible for the duties of the temple — for all its work and everything done in it. 2Kg 23:8-9

The Priests' Duties and Privileges

¹⁵ "But the Levitical priests descended from Zadok, who kept charge of my sanctuary when the Israelites went astray from me, will approach me to serve me. They will stand before me to offer me fat and blood." This is the declaration of the Lord God. ¹⁶ "They are the ones who may enter my sanctuary and approach my table to serve me. They will keep my mandate. ¹⁷ When they enter the gates of the inner court they are to wear linen garments; they must not have on them anything made of wool when they minister at the gates of the inner court and within it. ¹⁸ They are to wear linen turbans on their heads and linen undergarments around their waists. They are not to put on anything that makes them sweat. ¹⁹ Before they go out to the outer court,^C to the people, they must take off the clothes they have been ministering in, leave them in the holy chambers, and dress in other clothes so that they do not transmit holiness to the people through their clothes. Lv 6:27; Ezk 40:46

²⁰ "They may not shave their heads or let their hair grow long, but are to carefully trim their hair. ²¹ No priest may drink wine before he enters the inner court. ²² He is not to marry a widow or a divorced woman, but may marry only a virgin from the offspring of the house of Israel, or a widow who is the widow of a priest. ²³ They are to teach my people the difference between the holy and the common, and explain to them the difference between the clean and the unclean. Lv 10:9; 21:5; Nm 6:5

²⁴ "In a dispute, they will officiate as judges and decide the case according to my ordinances. They

---

^A 44:7 LXX, Syr, Vg; MT reads *They*   ^B 44:12 Lit *I lifted my hand*   ^C 44:19 Some Hb mss, LXX, Syr, Vg; other Hb mss read *court, to the outer court* are to observe my laws and statutes regarding all my appointed festivals, and keep my Sabbaths holy. [25] A priest may not come near a dead person so that he becomes defiled. However, he may defile himself for a father, a mother, a son, a daughter, a brother, or an unmarried sister. [26] After he is cleansed, he is to count off seven days for himself. [27] On the day he goes into the sanctuary, into the inner court to minister in the sanctuary, he is to present his sin offering." This is the declaration of the Lord God.

[28] "This will be their inheritance: I am their inheritance. You are to give them no possession in Israel: I am their possession. [29] They will eat the grain offering, the sin offering, and the guilt offering. Everything in Israel that is permanently dedicated to the Lord will belong to them. [30] The best of all the firstfruits of every kind and contribution of every kind from all your gifts will belong to the priests. You are to give your first batch of dough to the priest so that a blessing may rest on your homes. [31] The priests may not eat any bird or animal that died naturally or was mauled by wild beasts.   Nm 18:20; Dt 18:2; Jos 13:33

The Sacred Portion of the Land

45 "When you divide the land by lot as an inheritance, set aside a donation to the Lord, a holy portion of the land, 8 1/3 miles [A] long and 6 2/3 miles [B] wide. This entire region will be holy. [2] In this area there will be a square section [C] for the sanctuary, 875 by 875 feet, [D] with 87 1/2 feet [E] of open space all around it. [3] From this holy portion, [F] you will measure off an area 8 1/3 miles long and 3 1/3 miles [G] wide, in which the sanctuary, the most holy place, will stand. [H] [4] It will be a holy area of the land to be used by the priests who minister in the sanctuary, who approach to serve the Lord. It will be a place for their houses, as well as a holy area for the sanctuary. [5] There will be another area 8 1/3 miles long and 3 1/3 miles wide for the Levites who minister in the temple; it will be their possession for towns to live in. [I]

[6] "As the property of the city, set aside an area 1 2/3 miles [J] wide and 8 1/3 miles long, adjacent to the holy donation of land. It will be for the whole house of Israel. [7] And the prince will have the area on each side of the holy donation of land and the city's property, adjacent to the holy donation and the city's property, stretching to the west on the west side and to the east on the east side. Its length will correspond to one of the tribal portions from the western boundary to the eastern boundary. [8] This will be his land as a possession in Israel. My princes will no longer oppress my people but give the rest of the land to the house of Israel according to their tribes.   Ezk 19:7; 22:27; 48:15-18,21

[9] "This is what the Lord God says: You have gone too far, [K] princes of Israel! Put away violence and oppression and do what is just and right. Put an end to your evictions of my people." This is the declaration of the Lord God. [10] "You are to have

honest scales, an honest dry measure, [A] and an honest liquid measure. [B] 11 The dry measure [C] and the liquid measure [D] will be uniform, with the liquid measure containing 5 ½ gallons [E] and the dry measure holding half a bushel. [E] Their measurement will be a tenth of the standard larger capacity measure. [F] 12 The shekel [G] will weigh twenty gerahs. Your mina will equal sixty shekels. Lv 19:36; Dt 25:15; Jr 22:3; Ezk 44:6

The People's Contribution to the Sacrifices

13 "This is the contribution you are to offer: Three quarts [H] from five bushels [I] of wheat and [J] three quarts from five bushels of barley. 14 The quota of oil in liquid measures [K] will be one percent of every [L] cor. The cor equals ten liquid measures or one standard larger capacity measure, [M] since ten liquid measures equal one standard larger capacity measure. 15 And the quota from the flock is one animal out of every two hundred from the well-watered pastures of Israel. These are for the grain offerings, burnt offerings, and fellowship offerings, to make atonement for the people." This is the declaration of the Lord God. 16 "All the people of the land must take part in this contribution for the prince in Israel. 17 Then the burnt offerings, grain offerings, and drink offerings for the festivals, New Moons, and Sabbaths — for all the appointed times of the house of Israel — will be the prince's responsibility.

He will provide the sin offerings, grain offerings, burnt offerings, and fellowship offerings to make atonement on behalf of the house of Israel. Lv 1:4; 6:30

18 "This is what the Lord God says: In the first month, on the first day of the month, you are to take a young, unblemished bull and purify the sanctuary. 19 The priest is to take some of the blood from the sin offering and apply it to the temple doorposts, the four corners of the altar's ledge, and the doorposts of the gate of the inner court. 20 You are to do the same thing on the seventh day of the month for everyone who sins unintentionally or through ignorance. In this way you will make atonement for the temple. Ezk 43:20

21 "In the first month, on the fourteenth day of the month, you are to celebrate the Passover, a festival of seven days during which unleavened bread will be eaten. 22 On that day the prince will provide a bull as a sin offering on behalf of himself and all the people of the land. 23 During the seven days of the festival, he will provide seven bulls and seven rams without blemish as a burnt offering to the Lord on each of the seven days, along with a male goat each day for a sin offering. 24 He will also provide a grain offering of half a bushel [N] per bull and half a bushel per ram, along with a gallon [O] of oil for every half bushel. 25 At the festival that begins on the fifteenth day of the seventh month, [P] he will provide the same things for seven days — the same

A 45:10 Lit an honest ephah　B 45:10 Lit and an honest bath　C 45:11 Lit The ephah　D 45:11 Lit the bath　E 45:11, 45:11 Lit one-tenth of a homer　F 45:11 Lit be based on the homer　G 45:12 A shekel is about two-fifths of an ounce of silver　H 45:13 Lit One-sixth of an ephah　I 45:13 Lit a homer　J 45:13 LXX, Vg; MT reads and you are to give　K 45:14 Lit oil, the bath, the oil　L 45:14 Lit be a tenth of the bath from the　M 45:14 Lit 10 baths, a homer　N 45:24 Lit an ephah　O 45:24 Lit a hin　P 45:25 = the Festival of Shelters sin offerings, burnt offerings, grain offerings, and oil. Ex 12:18; Lv 23:4-8; Dt 16:1

Sacrifices at Appointed Times

46 "This is what the Lord GOD says: The gate of the inner court that faces east is to be closed during the six days of work, but it will be opened on the Sabbath day and opened on the day of the New Moon. ² The prince should enter from the outside by way of the gate's portico and stand at the gate's doorpost while the priests sacrifice his burnt offerings and fellowship offerings. He will bow in worship at the gate's threshold and then depart, but the gate is not to be closed until evening. ³ The people of the land will also bow in worship before the LORD at the entrance of that gate on the Sabbaths and New Moons. Ex 20:9-10

⁴ "The burnt offering that the prince presents to the LORD on the Sabbath day is to be six unblemished lambs and an unblemished ram. ⁵ The grain offering will be half a bushel ᴬ with the ram, and the grain offering with the lambs will be whatever he wants to give, as well as a gallon ᴮ of oil for every half bushel. ⁶ On the day of the New Moon, the burnt offering is to be a young, unblemished bull, as well as six lambs and a ram without blemish. ⁷ He will provide a grain offering of half a bushel with the bull, half a bushel with the ram, and whatever he can afford with the lambs, together with a gallon of oil for every half bushel. ⁸ When the prince enters, he is to go in by way of the gate's portico and go out the same way. Nm 28:9; Ezk 45:17

⁹ "When the people of the land come before the LORD at the appointed times, ᶜ whoever enters by way of the north gate to worship is to go out by way of the south gate, and whoever enters by way of the south gate is to go out by way of the north gate. No one may return through the gate by which he entered, but is to go out by the opposite gate. ¹⁰ When the people enter, the prince will enter with them, and when they leave, he will leave. ¹¹ At the festivals and appointed times, the grain offering will be half a bushel with the bull, half a bushel with the ram, and whatever he wants to give with the lambs, along with a gallon of oil for every half bushel. Ex 23:14-17

¹² "When the prince makes a freewill offering, whether a burnt offering or a fellowship offering as a freewill offering to the LORD, the gate that faces east is to be opened for him. He is to offer his burnt offering or fellowship offering just as he does on the Sabbath day. Then he will go out, and the gate is to be closed after he leaves. Lv 23:38

¹³ "You are to offer an unblemished year-old male lamb as a daily burnt offering to the LORD; you will offer it every morning. ¹⁴ You are also to prepare a grain offering every morning along with it: three quarts, ᴰ with one-third of a gallon ᴱ of oil to moisten the fine flour — a grain offering to the LORD. This is a permanent statute to be observed regularly. ¹⁵ They will offer the lamb, the grain offering, and the oil every morning as a regular burnt offering. Ex 29:38

ᴬ**46:5** Lit *an ephah*, also in vv. 7,11   ᴮ**46:5** Lit *a hin*, also in vv. 7,11   ᶜ**46:9** Or *the festivals*   ᴰ**46:14** Lit *one-sixth of an ephah*   ᴱ**46:14** Lit *one-third of a hin*

Transfer of Royal Lands

[16] "This is what the Lord God says: If the prince gives a gift to each of his sons as their inheritance, it will belong to his sons. It will become their property by inheritance. [17] But if he gives a gift from his inheritance to one of his servants, it will belong to that servant until the year of freedom, when it will revert to the prince. His inheritance belongs only to his sons; it is theirs. [18] The prince must not take any of the people's inheritance, evicting them from their property. He is to provide an inheritance for his sons from his own property, so that none of my people will be displaced from his own property."   Lv 25:10; Ezk 45:8-9

The Temple Kitchens

[19] Then he brought me through the entrance that was at the side of the gate, into the priests' holy chambers, which faced north. I saw a place there at the far western end. [20] He said to me, "This is the place where the priests will boil the guilt offering and the sin offering, and where they will bake the grain offering, so that they do not bring them into the outer court and transmit holiness to the people." [21] Next he brought me into the outer court and led me past its four corners. There was a separate court in each of its corners. [22] In the four corners of the outer court there were enclosed[A] courts, 70 feet[B] long by 52½ feet[C] wide. All four corner areas had the same dimensions. [23] There was a stone wall[D] around the inside of them, around the four of them, with ovens built at the base of the walls on all sides. [24] He said to me: "These are the kitchens where those who minister at the temple will cook the people's sacrifices."

The Life-Giving River

47 Then he brought me back to the entrance of the temple and there was water flowing from under the threshold of the temple toward the east, for the temple faced east. The water was coming down from under the south side of the threshold of the temple, south of the altar. [2] Next he brought me out by way of the north gate and led me around the outside to the outer gate that faced east; there the water was trickling from the south side. [3] As the man went out east with a measuring line in his hand, he measured off a third of a mile[E] and led me through the water. It came up to my ankles. [4] Then he measured off a third of a mile and led me through the water. It came up to my knees. He measured off another third of a mile and led me through the water. It came up to my waist. [5] Again he measured off a third of a mile, and it was a river that I could not cross on foot. For the water had risen; it was deep enough to swim in, a river that could not be crossed on foot.

[6] He asked me, "Do you see this, son of man?" Then he led me back to the bank of the river. [7] When I had returned, I saw a very large number of trees along both sides of the riverbank. [8] He said to me, "This water flows out to the eastern region and goes down to the Arabah. When it enters the sea, the sea of foul water,[F,G] the water

---

[A]**46:22** Hb obscure   [B]**46:22** Lit *40 cubits*   [C]**46:22** Lit *30 cubits*   [D]**46:23** Or *a row*   [E]**47:3** Lit *1,000 cubits*, also in vv. 4,5   [F]**47:8** Or *enters the sea, being brought out to the sea* ; Hb obscure   [G]**47:8** = the Dead Sea of the sea becomes fresh. [9] Every kind of living creature that swarms will live wherever the river flows, [A] and there will be a huge number of fish because this water goes there. Since the water will become fresh, there will be life everywhere the river goes. [10] Fishermen will stand beside it from En-gedi to En-eglaim. [B] These will become places where nets are spread out to dry. Their fish will consist of many different kinds, like the fish of the Mediterranean Sea. [11] Yet its swamps and marshes will not be healed; they will be left for salt. [12] All kinds of trees providing food will grow along both banks of the river. Their leaves will not wither, and their fruit will not fail. Each month they will bear fresh fruit because the water comes from the sanctuary. Their fruit will be used for food and their leaves for medicine."

The Borders of the Land

[13] This is what the Lord God says: "This is [C] the border you will use to divide the land as an inheritance for the twelve tribes of Israel. Joseph will receive two shares. [14] You will inherit it in equal portions, since I swore [D] to give it to your ancestors. So this land will fall to you as an inheritance. Dt 1:8

[15] This is to be the border of the land:

On the north side it will extend from the Mediterranean Sea by way of Hethlon and Lebo-hamath to Zedad, [E] [16] Berothah, and Sibraim (which is between the border of Damascus and the border of Hamath), as far as Hazer-hatticon, which is on the border of Hauran. [17] So the border will run from the sea to Hazar-enon at the border of Damascus, with the territory of Hamath to the north. This will be the northern side. Nm 34:7-9

[18] On the east side it will run between Hauran and Damascus, along the Jordan between Gilead and the land of Israel; you will measure from the northern border to the eastern sea. [F] This will be the eastern side.

[19] On the south side it will run from Tamar to the Waters of Meribath-kadesh, [G] and on to the Brook of Egypt as far as the Mediterranean Sea. This will be the southern side. Nm 34:5

[20] On the west side the Mediterranean Sea will be the border, from the southern border up to a point opposite Lebo-hamath. This will be the western side.

[21] "You are to divide this land among yourselves according to the tribes of Israel. [22] You will allot it as an inheritance for yourselves and for the aliens residing among you, who have fathered children among you. You will treat them [H] like native-born Israelites; along with you, they will be allotted an inheritance among the tribes of Israel. [23] In whatever tribe the alien resides, you will assign his inheritance there." This is the declaration of the Lord God. Ezk 45:1; Ac 11:18

[A] 47:9 LXX, Vg; MT reads the two rivers flow   [B] 47:10 Two springs near the Dead Sea   [C] 47:13 Tg, Vg; Syr reads The valley of   [D] 47:14 Lit lifted my hand   [E] 47:15 LXX; MT reads and Lebo to Zedad, Hamath; Ezk 48:1   [F] 47:18 = the Dead Sea   [G] 47:19 = Kadesh-barnea   [H] 47:22 Lit They will be to you

The Tribal Allotments

48 "Now these are the names of the tribes:
From the northern end, along the road of Hethlon, to Lebo-hamath as far as Hazar-enon, at the northern border of Damascus, alongside Hamath and extending from the eastern side to the sea, will be Dan — one portion. ² Next to the territory of Dan, from the east side to the west, will be Asher — one portion. ³ Next to the territory of Asher, from the east side to the west, will be Naphtali — one portion. ⁴ Next to the territory of Naphtali, from the east side to the west, will be Manasseh — one portion. ⁵ Next to the territory of Manasseh, from the east side to the west, will be Ephraim — one portion. ⁶ Next to the territory of Ephraim, from the east side to the west, will be Reuben — one portion. ⁷ Next to the territory of Reuben, from the east side to the west, will be Judah — one portion.

⁸ "Next to the territory of Judah, from the east side to the west, will be the portion you donate to the LORD, 8⅓ miles ᴬ wide, and as long as one of the tribal portions from the east side to the west. The sanctuary will be in the middle of it. ⁹ "The special portion you donate to the LORD will be 8⅓ miles long and 3⅓ miles ᴮ wide. ¹⁰ This holy donation will be set apart for the priests alone. It will be 8⅓ miles long on the northern side, 3⅓ miles wide on the western side, 3⅓ miles wide on the eastern side, and 8⅓ miles long on the southern side. The LORD's sanctuary will be in the middle of it. ¹¹ It is for the consecrated priests, the sons of Zadok, who kept my charge and did not go astray as the Levites did when the Israelites went astray. ¹² It will be a special donation for them out of the holy donation of the land, a most holy place adjacent to the territory of the Levites. Ezk 44:10,15

¹³ "Next to the territory of the priests, the Levites will have an area 8⅓ miles long and 3⅓ miles wide. The total length will be 8⅓ miles and the width 3⅓ miles. ¹⁴ They must not sell or exchange any of it, and they must not transfer this choice part of the land, for it is holy to the LORD. Lv 25:34; Ezk 45:1

¹⁵ "The remaining area, 1⅔ miles ᶜ wide and 8⅓ miles long, will be for common use by the city, for both residential and open space. The city will be in the middle of it. ¹⁶ These are the city's measurements: Ezk 45:6
1½ miles ᴰ on the north side;
1½ miles on the south side;
1½ miles on the east side;
and 1½ miles on the west side.
¹⁷ The city's open space will extend:
425 feet ᴱ to the north,
425 feet to the south,
425 feet to the east,
and 425 feet to the west.

¹⁸ "The remainder of the length alongside the holy donation will be 3⅓ miles to the east and 3⅓

ᴬ 48:8 Lit *25,000 cubits*, also in vv. 9,10,13,15,20,21   ᴮ 48:9 Lit *10,000 cubits*, also in vv. 10,13,18
ᶜ 48:15 Lit *5,000 cubits*   ᴰ 48:16 Lit *4,500 cubits*, also in vv. 30,32,33,34   ᴱ 48:17 Lit *250 cubits*

miles to the west. It will run alongside the holy donation. Its produce will be food for the workers of the city. ¹⁹ The city's workers from all the tribes of Israel will cultivate it. ²⁰ The entire donation will be 8 ⅓ miles by 8 ⅓ miles; you are to set apart the holy donation along with the city property as a square area.   Ezk 45:6

²¹ "The remaining area on both sides of the holy donation and the city property will belong to the prince. He will own the land adjacent to the tribal portions, next to the 8 ⅓ miles of the donation as far as the eastern border and ᴬ next to the 8 ⅓ miles of the donation as far as the western border. The holy donation and the sanctuary of the temple will be in the middle of it. ²² Except for the Levitical property and the city property in the middle of the area belonging to the prince, the area between the territory of Judah and that of Benjamin will belong to the prince.   Jos 18:21-28; Ezk 34:24; 45:7

²³ "As for the rest of the tribes: From the east side to the west, will be Benjamin — one portion.

²⁴ Next to the territory of Benjamin, from the east side to the west, will be Simeon — one portion.

²⁵ Next to the territory of Simeon, from the east side to the west, will be Issachar — one portion.

²⁶ Next to the territory of Issachar, from the east side to the west, will be Zebulun — one portion.

²⁷ Next to the territory of Zebulun, from the east side to the west, will be Gad — one portion.

²⁸ Next to the territory of Gad toward the south side, the border will run from Tamar to the Waters of Meribath-kadesh, to the Brook of Egypt, and out to the Mediterranean Sea. ²⁹ This is the land you are to allot as an inheritance to Israel's tribes, and these will be their portions." This is the declaration of the Lord GOD.   2Ch 20:2; Ezk 47:13-20

The New City

³⁰ "These are the exits of the city: On the north side, which measures 1 ½ miles, ³¹ there will be three gates facing north, the gates of the city being named for the tribes of Israel: one, the gate of Reuben; one, the gate of Judah; and one, the gate of Levi. ³² On the east side, which is 1 ½ miles, there will be three gates: one, the gate of Joseph; one, the gate of Benjamin; and one, the gate of Dan. ³³ On the south side, which measures 1 ½ miles, there will be three gates: one, the gate of Simeon; one, the gate of Issachar; and one, the gate of Zebulun. ³⁴ On the west side, which is 1 ½ miles, there will be three gates: one, the gate of Gad; one, the gate of Asher; and one, the gate of Naphtali. ³⁵ The perimeter of the city will be six miles, ᴮ and the name of the city from that day on will be, The LORD Is There."   Is 12:6; 14:32; 24:23; Jr 3:17; 8:19; 14:9

ᴬ48:21 Lit border, and to the west,   ᴮ48:35 Lit 18,000 cubits

DANIEL

Daniel's Captivity in Babylon

1 In the third year of the reign of King Jehoiakim of Judah, King Nebuchadnezzar[A] of Babylon came to Jerusalem and laid siege to it. [2] The Lord handed King Jehoiakim of Judah over to him, along with some of the vessels from the house of God. Nebuchadnezzar carried them to the land of Babylon,[B] to the house of his god,[C] and put the vessels in the treasury of his god. 2Kg 24:1-2; 2Ch 36:5-6; Ezr 5:14; Jr 25:1

[3] The king ordered Ashpenaz, his chief eunuch,[D] to bring some of the Israelites from the royal family and from the nobility — [4] young men without any physical defect, good-looking, suitable for instruction in all wisdom, knowledgeable, perceptive, and capable of serving in the king's palace. He was to teach them the Chaldean language and literature. [5] The king assigned them daily provisions from the royal food and from the wine that he drank. They were to be trained for three years, and at the end of that time they were to attend the king.[E] [6] Among them, from the Judahites, were Daniel, Hananiah, Mishael, and Azariah. [7] The chief eunuch gave them names; he gave the name Belteshazzar to Daniel, Shadrach to Hananiah, Meshach to Mishael, and Abednego to Azariah.

Faithfulness in Babylon

[8] Daniel determined that he would not defile himself with the king's food or with the wine he drank. So he asked permission from the chief eunuch not to defile himself. [9] God had granted Daniel kindness and compassion from the chief eunuch, [10] yet he said to Daniel, "I fear my lord the king, who assigned your food and drink. What if he sees your faces looking thinner than the other young men your age? You would endanger my life[F] with the king." Lv 3:17; 11:47; Ps 141:4; Pr 23:1-2; Ezk 4:13

[11] So Daniel said to the guard whom the chief eunuch had assigned to Daniel, Hananiah, Mishael, and Azariah, [12] "Please test your servants for ten days. Let us be given vegetables to eat and water to drink. [13] Then examine our appearance and the appearance of the young men who are eating the king's food, and deal with your servants based on what you see." [14] He agreed with them about this and tested them for ten days. [15] At the end of ten days they looked better and healthier[G] than all the young men who were eating the king's food. [16] So the guard continued to remove their food and the wine they were to drink and gave them vegetables. Ex 23:25

Faithfulness Rewarded

[17] God gave these four young men knowledge and understanding in every kind of literature and wisdom. Daniel also understood visions and dreams of every kind. [18] At the end of the time that the

A1:1 Or *Nebuchadrezzar* B1:2 Lit *Shinar* C1:2 Or *gods* D1:3 Or *his eunuchs* E1:5 Lit *to stand before the king* F1:10 Lit *would make my head guilty* G1:15 Lit *fatter of flesh* king had said to present them, the chief eunuch presented them to Nebuchadnezzar. ¹⁹ The king interviewed them, and among all of them, no one was found equal to Daniel, Hananiah, Mishael, and Azariah. So they began to attend the king. ²⁰ In every matter of wisdom and understanding that the king consulted them about, he found them ten times ^A better than all the magicians and mediums in his entire kingdom. ²¹ Daniel remained there until the first year of King Cyrus.   1Kg 3:10-12; Jb 32:8; Ac 7:22; Jms 1:5

Nebuchadnezzar's Dream

2 In the second year of his reign, Nebuchadnezzar had dreams that troubled him, and sleep deserted him. ² So the king gave orders to summon the magicians, mediums, sorcerers, and Chaldeans ^B to tell the king his dreams. When they came and stood before the king, ³ he said to them, "I have had a dream and am anxious to understand it."

⁴ The Chaldeans spoke to the king (Aramaic ^C begins here): "May the king live forever. Tell your servants the dream, and we will give the interpretation." 1Kg 1:31; Ezr 4:7; Is 36:11; Dn 3:9

⁵ The king replied to the Chaldeans, "My word is final: If you don't tell me the dream and its interpretation, you will be torn limb from limb, ^D and your houses will be made a garbage dump. ⁶ But if you make the dream and its interpretation known to me, you'll receive gifts, a reward, and great honor from me. So make the dream and its interpretation known to me."

⁷ They answered a second time, "May the king tell the dream to his servants, and we will make known the interpretation."

⁸ The king replied, "I know for certain you are trying to gain some time, because you see that my word is final. ⁹ If you don't tell me the dream, there is one decree for you. You have conspired to tell me something false or fraudulent until the situation changes. So tell me the dream and I will know you can give me its interpretation."

¹⁰ The Chaldeans answered the king, "No one on earth can make known what the king requests. Consequently, no king, however great and powerful, has ever asked anything like this of any magician, medium, or Chaldean. ¹¹ What the king is asking is so difficult that no one can make it known to him except the gods, whose dwelling is not with mortals." ¹² Because of this, the king became violently angry and gave orders to destroy all the wise men of Babylon. ¹³ The decree was issued that the wise men were to be executed, and they searched for Daniel and his friends, to execute them.   Ex 29:45; Is 57:15; Dn 5:11-16

¹⁴ Then Daniel responded with tact and discretion to Arioch, the captain of the king's guard, ^E who had gone out to execute the wise men of Babylon. ¹⁵ He asked Arioch, the king's officer, "Why is the decree from the king so harsh?" ^F Then Arioch explained the situation to Daniel. ¹⁶ So Daniel went and asked the king to give him some time, so that he could give the king the interpretation.   Gn 37:36; Dn 3:22

¹⁷ Then Daniel went to his house and told his friends Hananiah, Mishael, and Azariah about the

---

^A 1:20 Lit hands   ^B 2:2 In this chap. Chaldeans are influential Babylonian wise men.   ^C 2:4 Dn 2:4–7:28 is written in Aramaic.   ^D 2:5 Lit be made into limbs   ^E 2:14 Or executioners   ^F 2:15 Or urgent matter, ¹⁸ urging them to ask the God of the heavens for mercy concerning this mystery, so Daniel and his friends would not be destroyed with the rest of Babylon's wise men. ¹⁹ The mystery was then revealed to Daniel in a vision at night, and Daniel praised the God of the heavens ²⁰ and declared:

May the name of God
be praised forever and ever,
for wisdom and power
belong to him.   Jb 12:13; Is 28:29
²¹ He changes the times
and seasons;
he removes kings
and establishes kings.   Dn 4:17
He gives wisdom to the wise
and knowledge to those
who have understanding.
²² He reveals the deep
and hidden things;
he knows what is
in the darkness,   Jb 12:22; Jr 23:24
and light dwells with him.
²³ I offer thanks and praise
to you,
God of my fathers,   Gn 31:42; Ex 3:15
because you have given me
wisdom and power.
And now you have
let me know
what we asked of you,
for you have let us know
the king's mystery.ᴬ

²⁴ Therefore Daniel went to Arioch, whom the king had assigned to destroy the wise men of Babylon. He came and said to him, "Don't destroy the wise men of Babylon! Bring me before the king, and I will give him the interpretation."

²⁵ Then Arioch quickly brought Daniel before the king and said to him, "I have found a man among the Judean exiles who can let the king know the interpretation."

²⁶ The king said in reply to Daniel, whose name was Belteshazzar, "Are you able to tell me the dream I had and its interpretation?"

²⁷ Daniel answered the king: "No wise man, medium, magician, or diviner is able to make known to the king the mystery he asked about. ²⁸ But there is a God in heaven who reveals mysteries, and he has let King Nebuchadnezzar know what will happen in the last days. Your dream and the visions that came into your mind as you lay in bed were these: ²⁹ Your Majesty, while you were in your bed, thoughts came to your mind about what will happen in the future.ᴮ The revealer of mysteries has let you know what will happen. ³⁰ As for me, this mystery has been revealed to me, not because I have more wisdom than anyone living, but in order that the interpretation might be made known to the king, and that you may understand the thoughts of your mind.   Is 2:2; Dn 1:20; 4:7; 5:7, 11; Hs 3:5

The Dream's Interpretation

³¹ "Your Majesty, as you were watching, suddenly a colossal statue appeared. That statue, tall and dazzling, was standing in front of you, and its appearance was terrifying. ³² The head of the statue was pure gold, its chest and arms were silver, its stomach and thighs were bronze, ³³ its legs were iron, and its feet were partly iron and partly fired clay. ³⁴ As you were watching, a stone broke off without a hand touching it,ᶜ struck the statue on its feet of iron and fired clay, and crushed them. ³⁵ Then the iron, the

fired clay, the bronze, the silver, and the gold were shattered and became like chaff from the summer threshing floors. The wind carried them away, and not a trace of them could be found. But the stone that struck the statue became a great mountain and filled the whole earth. Jb 34:20; Lm 4:6; Dn 8:25; Mt 21:44; 2Co 5:1

[36] "This was the dream; now we will tell the king its interpretation. [37] Your Majesty, you are king of kings. The God of the heavens has given you sovereignty, power, strength, and glory. [38] Wherever people live — or wild animals, or birds of the sky — he has handed them over to you and made you ruler over them all. You are the head of gold. Pr 8:15; Is 47:5; Jr 27:6-7; Ezk 26:7

[39] "After you, there will arise another kingdom, inferior to yours, and then another, a third kingdom, of bronze, which will rule the whole earth. [40] A fourth kingdom will be as strong as iron; for iron crushes and shatters everything, and like iron that smashes, it will crush and smash all the others.[A] [41] You saw the feet and toes, partly of a potter's fired clay and partly of iron — it will be a divided kingdom, though some of the strength of iron will be in it. You saw the iron mixed with clay, [42] and that the toes of the feet were partly iron and partly fired clay — part of the kingdom will be strong, and part will be brittle. [43] You saw the iron mixed with clay — the peoples will mix with one another[B] but will not hold together, just as iron does not mix with fired clay. Dn 5:28,31; 7:6-7,23

[44] "In the days of those kings, the God of the heavens will set up a kingdom that will never be destroyed, and this kingdom will not be left to another people. It will crush all these kingdoms and bring them to an end, but will itself endure forever. [45] You saw a stone break off from the mountain without a hand touching it,[C] and it crushed the iron, bronze, fired clay, silver, and gold. The great God has told the king what will happen in the future. The dream is certain, and its interpretation reliable." Ps 145:13; Ezk 37:25

Nebuchadnezzar's Response

[46] Then King Nebuchadnezzar fell facedown, worshiped Daniel, and gave orders to present an offering and incense to him. [47] The king said to Daniel, "Your God is indeed God of gods, Lord of kings, and a revealer of mysteries, since you were able to reveal this mystery." [48] Then the king promoted Daniel and gave him many generous gifts. He made him ruler over the entire province of Babylon and chief governor over all the wise men of Babylon. [49] At Daniel's request, the king appointed Shadrach, Meshach, and Abednego to manage the province of Babylon. But Daniel remained at the king's court. Mt 8:2; Ac 10:25; 14:13

Nebuchadnezzar's Gold Statue

3 King Nebuchadnezzar made a gold statue, ninety feet high and nine feet wide.[D] He set it up on the plain of Dura in the province of Babylon. [2] King Nebuchadnezzar sent word to assemble the satraps, prefects, governors, advisers, treasurers, judges, magistrates, and all the rulers of the provinces to attend the dedication of the statue

---

[A]2:40 Lit all these   [B]2:43 Lit another in the seed of men   [C]2:45 Lit mountain, not by hands   [D]3:1 Lit statue, its height sixty cubits, its width six cubits

King Nebuchadnezzar had set up. ³ So the satraps, prefects, governors, advisers, treasurers, judges, magistrates, and all the rulers of the provinces assembled for the dedication of the statue the king had set up. Then they stood before the statue Nebuchadnezzar had set up. 1Kg 12:28; Is 46:6; Jr 16:20; Hs 2:8; 8:4; Hab 2:19

⁴ A herald loudly proclaimed, "People of every nation and language, you are commanded: ⁵ When you hear the sound of the horn, flute, zither, ᴬ lyre, ᴮ harp, drum, ᶜ and every kind of music, you are to fall facedown and worship the gold statue that King Nebuchadnezzar has set up. ⁶ But whoever does not fall down and worship will immediately be thrown into a furnace of blazing fire." Gn 4:21

⁷ Therefore, when all the people heard the sound of the horn, flute, zither, lyre, harp, and every kind of music, people of every nation and language fell down and worshiped the gold statue that King Nebuchadnezzar had set up.

The Furnace of Blazing Fire

⁸ Some Chaldeans took this occasion to come forward and maliciously accuse ᴰ the Jews. ⁹ They said to King Nebuchadnezzar, "May the king live forever. ¹⁰ You as king have issued a decree that everyone who hears the sound of the horn, flute, zither, lyre, harp, drum, and every kind of music must fall down and worship the gold statue. ¹¹ Whoever does not fall down and worship will be thrown into a furnace of blazing fire. ¹² There are some Jews you have appointed to manage the province of Babylon:

Shadrach, Meshach, and Abednego. These men have ignored you, the king; they do not serve your gods or worship the gold statue you have set up." Ezr 4:12-16; Dn 2:2,4-5,10

¹³ Then in a furious rage Nebuchadnezzar gave orders to bring in Shadrach, Meshach, and Abednego. So these men were brought before the king. ¹⁴ Nebuchadnezzar asked them, "Shadrach, Meshach, and Abednego, is it true that you don't serve my gods or worship the gold statue I have set up? ¹⁵ Now if you're ready, when you hear the sound of the horn, flute, zither, lyre, harp, drum, and every kind of music, fall down and worship the statue I made. But if you don't worship it, you will immediately be thrown into a furnace of blazing fire — and who is the god who can rescue you from my power?" Ex 5:20; Jr 50:2; Dn 2:12

¹⁶ Shadrach, Meshach, and Abednego replied to the king, "Nebuchadnezzar, we don't need to give you an answer to this question. ¹⁷ If the God we serve exists, then he can rescue us from the furnace of blazing fire, and he can ᴱ rescue us from the power of you, the king. ¹⁸ But even if he does not rescue us, ᶠ we want you as king to know that we will not serve your gods or worship the gold statue you set up."

¹⁹ Then Nebuchadnezzar was filled with rage, and the expression on his face changed toward Shadrach, Meshach, and Abednego. He gave orders to heat the furnace seven times more than was customary, ²⁰ and he commanded some of the best soldiers in his army to tie up Shadrach, Meshach, and Abednego and throw them into the furnace

---

ᴬ3:5 Or lyre   ᴮ3:5 Or sambuke   ᶜ3:5 Or pipe   ᴰ3:8 Lit and eat the pieces of   ᴱ3:17 Or If the God whom we serve is willing to save us from the furnace of blazing fire, then he will   ᶠ3:18 Lit But if not of blazing fire. ²¹ So these men, in their trousers, robes, head coverings, ᴬ and other clothes, were tied up and thrown into the furnace of blazing fire. ²² Since the king's command was so urgent ᴮ and the furnace extremely hot, the raging flames ᶜ killed those men who carried Shadrach, Meshach, and Abednego up. ²³ And these three men, Shadrach, Meshach, and Abednego fell, bound, into the furnace of blazing fire.   Est 7:7; Dn 2:15

Delivered from the Fire

²⁴ Then King Nebuchadnezzar jumped up in alarm. He said to his advisers, "Didn't we throw three men, bound, into the fire?"   Dn 4:19

"Yes, of course, Your Majesty," they replied to the king.

²⁵ He exclaimed, "Look! I see four men, not tied, walking around in the fire unharmed; and the fourth looks like a son of the gods." ᴰ

²⁶ Nebuchadnezzar then approached the door of the furnace of blazing fire and called: "Shadrach, Meshach, and Abednego, you servants of the Most High God — come out!" So Shadrach, Meshach, and Abednego came out of the fire. ²⁷ When the satraps, prefects, governors, and the king's advisers gathered around, they saw that the fire had no effect on ᴱ the bodies of these men: not a hair of their heads was singed, their robes were unaffected, and there was no smell of fire on them. ²⁸ Nebuchadnezzar exclaimed, "Praise to the God of Shadrach, Meshach, and Abednego! He sent his angel ᶠ and rescued his servants who trusted in him. They violated the king's command and risked their lives rather than serve or worship any god except their own God. ²⁹ Therefore I issue a decree that anyone of any people, nation, or language who says anything offensive against the God of Shadrach, Meshach, and Abednego will be torn limb from limb and his house made a garbage dump. For there is no other god who is able to deliver like this." ³⁰ Then the king rewarded Shadrach, Meshach, and Abednego in the province of Babylon.   Dt 29:5; Ps 34:7; Dn 4:2; Heb 1:14; 11:34

Nebuchadnezzar's Proclamation

4 King Nebuchadnezzar,

To those of every people, nation, and language, who live on the whole earth: Dn 6:25

May your prosperity increase. ² I am pleased to tell you about the miracles and wonders the Most High God has done for me.   Dn 6:27; Jn 4:48; Ac 2:22; 2Co 12:12; 2Pt 1:2

³   How great are his miracles,
      and how mighty his wonders!
      His kingdom is
         an eternal kingdom,   Ps 145:13
      and his dominion is
         from generation
         to generation.   Is 9:7; Dn 6:26

The Dream

⁴ I, Nebuchadnezzar, was at ease in my house and flourishing in my palace. ⁵ I had a dream, and it frightened me; while in my bed, the images and visions in my mind alarmed me. ⁶ So I issued a decree to bring all the wise men of Babylon to me in order that they might make

---

ᴬ3:21 The identity of these articles of clothing is uncertain.   ᴮ3:22 Or harsh   ᶜ3:22 Lit the flame of the fire   ᴰ3:25 Or of a divine being   ᴱ3:27 Lit fire had not overcome   ᶠ3:28 Or messenger the dream's interpretation known to me. **7** When the magicians, mediums, Chaldeans, and diviners came in, I told them the dream, but they could not make its interpretation known to me. Ps 30:6; Is 47:7-8; Dn 2:28; 7:15

8 Finally Daniel, named Belteshazzar after the name of my god — and a spirit of the holy gods is in him — came before me. I told him the dream: **9** "Belteshazzar, head of the magicians, because I know that you have the spirit of the holy gods and that no mystery puzzles you, explain to me the visions of my dream that I saw, and its interpretation. **10** In the visions of my mind as I was lying in bed, I saw this: Gn 41:38; Dn 1:7; 2:11; 5:11

There was a tree
in the middle of the earth,
and it was very tall.
11 The tree grew large
and strong;
its top reached to the sky,
and it was visible to the ends
of the^A earth.
12 Its leaves were beautiful,
its fruit was abundant,
and on it was food for all.
Wild animals found shelter
under it,
the birds of the sky lived
in its branches, Ezk 17:23; Mt 13:32
and every creature was fed
from it. Ezk 31:3-6

13 "As I was lying in my bed, I also saw in the visions of my mind a watcher, a holy one,^B coming down from heaven. **14** He called out loudly:

Cut down the tree
and chop off its branches;
strip off its leaves and scatter
its fruit.

Let the animals flee
from under it,
and the birds
from its branches. Ezk 31:10-14
15 But leave the stump
with its roots in the ground
and with a band of iron
and bronze around it
in the tender grass
of the field.
Let him be drenched
with dew from the sky
and share the plants
of the earth Gn 3:18
with the animals.
16 Let his mind be changed
from that of a human,
and let him be given the mind
of an animal
for seven periods of time.^C,D
17 This word is by decree
of the watchers,
and the decision
is by command
from the holy ones.
This is so that the living
will know
that the Most High is ruler
over human kingdoms.
He gives them to anyone
he wants
and sets the lowliest of people
over them. 1Sm 2:8; Ps 9:16

18 This is the dream that I, King Nebuchadnezzar, had. Now, Belteshazzar, tell me the interpretation, because none of the wise men of my kingdom can make the interpretation known to me. But you can, because you have a spirit of the holy gods."

The Dream Interpreted

19 Then Daniel, whose name is Belteshazzar, was stunned for a moment, and his thoughts alarmed

^A**4:11** Lit *of all the*   ^B**4:13** = an angel   ^C**4:16** Lit *animal as seven times pass over him*   ^D**4:16** Perhaps seven years him. The king said, "Belteshazzar, don't let the dream or its interpretation alarm you."

Belteshazzar answered, "My lord, may the dream apply to those who hate you, and its interpretation to your enemies! ²⁰ The tree you saw, which grew large and strong, whose top reached to the sky and was visible to the whole earth, ²¹ and whose leaves were beautiful and its fruit abundant — and on it was food for all, under it the wild animals lived, and in its branches the birds of the sky lived — ²² that tree is you, Your Majesty. For you have become great and strong: your greatness has grown and even reaches the sky, and your dominion extends to the ends of the earth. 2Sm 18:32; Jr 27:6-8

²³ "The king saw a watcher, a holy one, coming down from heaven and saying, 'Cut down the tree and destroy it, but leave the stump with its roots in the ground and with a band of iron and bronze around it in the tender grass of the field. Let him be drenched with dew from the sky and share food with the wild animals for seven periods of time.' ²⁴ This is the interpretation, Your Majesty, and this is the decree of the Most High that has been issued against my lord the king: ²⁵ You will be driven away from people to live with the wild animals. You will feed on grass like cattle and be drenched with dew from the sky for seven periods of time, until you acknowledge that the Most High is ruler over human kingdoms, and he gives them to anyone he wants. ²⁶ As for the command to leave the tree's stump with its roots, your kingdom will be restored^A to you as soon as you acknowledge that Heaven^B rules. ²⁷ Therefore,

may my advice seem good to you my king. Separate yourself from your sins by doing what is right, and from your injustices by showing mercy to the needy. Perhaps there will be an extension of your prosperity."

The Sentence Executed

²⁸ All this happened to King Nebuchadnezzar. ²⁹ At the end of twelve months, as he was walking on the roof of the royal palace in Babylon, ³⁰ the king exclaimed, "Is this not Babylon the Great that I have built to be a royal residence by my vast power and for my majestic glory?"

³¹ While the words were still in the king's mouth, a voice came from heaven: "King Nebuchadnezzar, to you it is declared that the kingdom has departed from you. ³² You will be driven away from people to live with the wild animals, and you will feed on grass like cattle for seven periods of time, until you acknowledge that the Most High is ruler over human kingdoms, and he gives them to anyone he wants."

³³ At that moment the message against Nebuchadnezzar was fulfilled. He was driven away from people. He ate grass like cattle, and his body was drenched with dew from the sky, until his hair grew like eagles' feathers and his nails like birds' claws. Dn 5:21

Nebuchadnezzar's Praise

³⁴ But at the end of those days, I, Nebuchadnezzar, looked up to heaven, and my sanity returned to me. Then I praised the Most High and honored and glorified him who lives forever: Dn 6:26; 12:7; Rv 4:10

For his dominion is
    an everlasting dominion,

^A 4:26 Lit enduring   ^B 4:26 = God

and his kingdom is
　　from generation
　　to generation.　Ps 145:13; Jr 10:10
35 All the inhabitants
　　of the earth are counted
　　as nothing,　Is 40:15-17
and he does what he wants
　　with the army of heaven
　　and the inhabitants
　　of the earth.
There is no one
　　who can block his hand
　　or say to him,
　　"What have you done?"

36 At that time my sanity returned to me, and my majesty and splendor returned to me for the glory of my kingdom. My advisers and my nobles sought me out, I was reestablished over my kingdom, and even more greatness came to me. **37** Now I, Nebuchadnezzar, praise, exalt, and glorify the King of the heavens, because all his works are true and his ways are just. He is able to humble those who walk in pride. Dt 32:4; 2Ch 33:12-13; Ps 33:4; Pr 22:4

Belshazzar's Feast

5 King Belshazzar held a great feast for a thousand of his nobles and drank wine in their presence. **2** Under the influence of[A] the wine, Belshazzar gave orders to bring in the gold and silver vessels that his predecessor[B] Nebuchadnezzar had taken from the temple in Jerusalem, so that the king and his nobles, wives, and concubines could drink from them. **3** So they brought in the gold[C] vessels that had been taken from the temple, the house of God in Jerusalem, and the king and

his nobles, wives, and concubines drank from them. **4** They drank the wine and praised their gods made of gold and silver, bronze, iron, wood, and stone. 1Kg 7:51; 2Kg 24:13; Ezr 5:14; Dn 7:1; 8:1

The Handwriting on the Wall

5 At that moment the fingers of a man's hand appeared and began writing on the plaster of the king's palace wall next to the lampstand. As the king watched the hand[D] that was writing, **6** his face turned pale,[E] and his thoughts so terrified him that he soiled himself[F] and his knees knocked together. **7** The king shouted to bring in the mediums, Chaldeans, and diviners. He said to these wise men of Babylon, "Whoever reads this inscription and gives me its interpretation will be clothed in purple, have a gold chain around his neck, and have the third highest position in the kingdom." **8** So all the king's wise men came in, but none could read the inscription or make its interpretation known to him. **9** Then King Belshazzar became even more terrified, his face turned pale,[G] and his nobles were bewildered. Gn 41:42; Dn 2:1; 5:6; 7:28

10 Because of the outcry of the king and his nobles, the queen[H] came to the banquet hall. "May the king live forever," she said. "Don't let your thoughts terrify you or your face be pale.[I] **11** There is a man in your kingdom who has a spirit of the holy gods in him. In the days of your predecessor he was found to have insight, intelligence, and wisdom like the wisdom of the gods. Your predecessor, King Nebuchadnezzar,

---

A**5:2** Or When he tasted　B**5:2** Or father, or grandfather　C**5:3** Theod, Vg add and silver　D**5:5** Lit part of the hand　E**5:5-6** Lit writing, 6the king's brightness changed　F**5:6** Lit that the knots of his loins were loosed　G**5:9** Lit his brightness changed on him　H**5:10** Perhaps the queen mother　I**5:10** Lit your brightness change appointed him chief of the magicians, mediums, Chaldeans, and diviners. Your own predecessor, the king, [12] did this because Daniel, the one the king named Belteshazzar, was found to have an extraordinary spirit, knowledge and intelligence, and the ability to interpret dreams, explain riddles, and solve problems. Therefore, summon Daniel, and he will give the interpretation."

Daniel Before the King

[13] Then Daniel was brought before the king. The king said to him, "Are you Daniel, one of the Judean exiles that my predecessor the king brought from Judah? [14] I've heard that you have a spirit of the gods in you, and that insight, intelligence, and extraordinary wisdom are found in you. [15] Now the wise men and mediums were brought before me to read this inscription and make its interpretation known to me, but they could not give its interpretation. [16] However, I have heard about you that you can give interpretations and solve problems. Therefore, if you can read this inscription and give me its interpretation, you will be clothed in purple, have a gold chain around your neck, and have the third highest position in the kingdom." Gn 40:8; Dn 1:3-4; 2:25

[17] Then Daniel answered the king, "You may keep your gifts and give your rewards to someone else; however, I will read the inscription for the king and make the interpretation known to him. [18] Your Majesty, the Most High God gave sovereignty, greatness, glory, and majesty to your predecessor Nebuchadnezzar. [19] Because of the greatness he gave him, all peoples, nations, and languages were terrified and fearful of him. He killed anyone he wanted and kept alive anyone he wanted; he exalted anyone he wanted and humbled anyone he wanted. [20] But when his heart was exalted and his spirit became arrogant, he was deposed from his royal throne and his glory was taken from him. [21] He was driven away from people, his mind was like an animal's, he lived with the wild donkeys, he was fed grass like cattle, and his body was drenched with dew from the sky until he acknowledged that the Most High God is ruler over human kingdoms and sets anyone he wants over them. 2Kg 5:15-16; Dn 3:6; 4:2

[22] "But you his successor, Belshazzar, have not humbled your heart, even though you knew all this. [23] Instead, you have exalted yourself against the Lord of the heavens. The vessels from his house were brought to you, and as you and your nobles, wives, and concubines drank wine from them, you praised the gods made of silver and gold, bronze, iron, wood, and stone, which do not see or hear or understand. But you have not glorified the God who holds your life-breath in his hand and who controls the whole course of your life. [A] [24] Therefore, he sent the hand, and this writing was inscribed. Ex 10:3; 2Ch 33:23; 36:12

The Inscription's Interpretation

[25] "This is the writing that was inscribed: MENE, MENE, TEKEL, and PARSIN. [26] This is the interpretation of the message:

'Mene'[B] means that God has numbered[C] the days of your

---

kingdom and brought it to an end.   Is 13:17-19; Dn 2:44; 6:26; Hs 1:4

²⁷ 'Tekel'ᴬ means that you have been weighedᴮ on the balance and found deficient.

²⁸ 'Peres'ᶜ,ᴰ means that your kingdom has been divided and given to the Medes and Persians."ᴱ

²⁹ Then Belshazzar gave an order, and they clothed Daniel in purple, placed a gold chain around his neck, and issued a proclamation concerning him that he should be the third ruler in the kingdom.   Dn 5:7,16

³⁰ That very night Belshazzar the king of the Chaldeans was killed, ³¹ and Darius the Mede received the kingdom at the age of sixty-two.

The Plot Against Daniel

6 Darius decidedᶠ to appoint 120 satraps over the kingdom, stationed throughout the realm, ² and over them three administrators, including Daniel. These satraps would be accountable to them so that the king would not be defrauded. ³ Danielᴳ distinguished himself above the administrators and satraps because he had an extraordinary spirit, so the king planned to set him over the whole realm. ⁴ The administrators and satraps, therefore, kept trying to find a charge against Daniel regarding the kingdom. But they could find no charge or corruption, for he was trustworthy, and no negligence or corruption was found in him. ⁵ Then these men said, "We will

never find any charge against this Daniel unless we find something against him concerning the law of his God."   Ezr 4:22; Est 7:4; Dn 2:48-49; 5:16,29

⁶ So the administrators and satraps went together to the king and said to him, "May King Darius live forever. ⁷ All the administrators of the kingdom, the prefects, satraps, advisers, and governors have agreed that the king should establish an ordinance and enforce an edict that for thirty days, anyone who petitions any god or man except you, the king, will be thrown into the lions' den. ⁸ Therefore, Your Majesty, establish the edict and sign the document so that, as a law of the Medes and Persians, it is irrevocable and cannot be changed." ⁹ So King Darius signed the written edict.   Neh 2:3; Dn 2:4; 5:10; 6:21

Daniel in the Lions' Den

¹⁰ When Daniel learned that the document had been signed, he went into his house. The windows in its upstairs room opened toward Jerusalem, and three times a day he got down on his knees, prayed, and gave thanks to his God, just as he had done before. ¹¹ Then these men went as a group and found Daniel petitioning and imploring his God. ¹² So they approached the king and asked about his edict: "Didn't you sign an edict that for thirty days any person who petitions any god or man except you, the king, will be thrown into the lions' den?"

The king answered, "As a law of the Medes and Persians, the order standsᴴ and is irrevocable."   Est 1:19

ᴬ5:27 Or a shekel   ᴮ5:27 The Aramaic word for weighed sounds like tekel.   ᶜ5:28 Or half a shekel
ᴰ5:28 In Aramaic, the word peres is the sg form of "parsin" in v. 25.   ᴱ5:28 The Aramaic word for divided
and Persians sounds like peres.   ᶠ6:1 Lit It was pleasing before Darius   ᴳ6:3 Lit Now this Daniel
ᴴ6:12 Lit the word is certain

¹³ Then they replied to the king, "Daniel, one of the Judean exiles, has ignored you, the king, and the edict you signed, for he prays three times a day." ¹⁴ As soon as the king heard this, he was very displeased; he set his mind on rescuing Daniel and made every effort until sundown to deliver him.   Est 3:8; Dn 3:12

¹⁵ Then these men went together to the king and said to him, "You know, Your Majesty, that it is a law of the Medes and Persians that no edict or ordinance the king establishes can be changed."   Est 8:8

¹⁶ So the king gave the order, and they brought Daniel and threw him into the lions' den. The king said to Daniel, "May your God, whom you continually serve, rescue you!" ¹⁷ A stone was brought and placed over the mouth of the den. The king sealed it with his own signet ring and with the signet rings of his nobles, so that nothing in regard to Daniel could be changed. ¹⁸ Then the king went to his palace and spent the night fasting. No diversions ^A were brought to him, and he could not sleep.   2Sm 3:39; Jr 38:5

Daniel Released

¹⁹ At the first light of dawn the king got up and hurried to the lions' den. ²⁰ When he reached the den, he cried out in anguish to Daniel. "Daniel, servant of the living God," the king said, ^B "has your God, whom you continually serve, been able to rescue you from the lions?"   Gn 18:14; Nm 11:23; Jr 32:17; Dn 3:17

²¹ Then Daniel spoke with the king: "May the king live forever. ²² My God sent his angel and shut the lions' mouths; and they haven't

harmed me, for I was found innocent before him. And also before you, Your Majesty, I have not done harm."   Nm 20:16; Is 63:9; Dn 3:28; Ac 12:11

²³ The king was overjoyed and gave orders to take Daniel out of the den. When Daniel was brought up from the den, he was found to be unharmed, for he trusted in his God. ²⁴ The king then gave the command, and those men who had maliciously accused Daniel ^C were brought and thrown into the lions' den — they, their children, and their wives. They had not reached the bottom of the den before the lions overpowered them and crushed all their bones.   1Ch 5:20; 2Ch 20:20; Ps 118:8-9; Is 26:3

Darius Honors God

²⁵ Then King Darius wrote to those of every people, nation, and language who live on the whole earth: "May your prosperity abound. ²⁶ I issue a decree that in all my royal dominion, people must tremble in fear before the God of Daniel: Ezr 4:17; 6:8-12; 1Pt 1:2

For he is the living God,
and he endures forever;
his kingdom will never
   be destroyed,   Ps 93:1-2; Dn 2:44
and his dominion
   has no end.
²⁷ He rescues and delivers;
he performs signs
   and wonders
in the heavens
   and on the earth,   Dn 4:2-3
for he has rescued Daniel
from the power of the lions."

²⁸ So Daniel prospered during the reign of Darius and ^D the reign of Cyrus the Persian.   2Ch 36:22-23; Dn 1:21

^A **6:18** Aramaic obscure   ^B **6:20** Lit *said to Daniel*   ^C **6:24** Lit *had eaten his pieces*   ^D **6:28** Or *Darius, even*

Daniel's Vision of the Four Beasts

7 In the first year of King Bel-shazzar of Babylon, Daniel had a dream with visions in his mind as he was lying in his bed. He wrote down the dream, and here is the summary[A] of his account. [2] Daniel said, "In my vision at night I was watching, and suddenly the four winds of heaven stirred up the great sea. [3] Four huge beasts came up from the sea, each different from the other. Jb 33:14-16

[4] "The first was like a lion but had eagle's wings. I continued watching until its wings were torn off. It was lifted up from the ground, set on its feet like a man, and given a human mind. Jr 4:7; 25:9; Rv 13:2

[5] "Suddenly, another beast appeared, a second one, that looked like a bear. It was raised up on one side, with three ribs in its mouth between its teeth. It was told, 'Get up! Gorge yourself on flesh.' Rv 13:2

[6] "After this, while I was watching, suddenly another beast appeared. It was like a leopard with four wings of a bird on its back. It had four heads, and it was given dominion. Dn 8:22; Hab 1:8; Rv 13:2

[7] "After this, while I was watching in the night visions, suddenly a fourth beast appeared, frightening and dreadful, and incredibly strong, with large iron teeth. It devoured and crushed, and it trampled with its feet whatever was left. It was different from all the beasts before it, and it had ten horns. Dn 7:19,23; Rv 12:3

[8] "While I was considering the horns, suddenly another horn, a little one, came up among them, and three of the first horns were uprooted before it. And suddenly in this horn there were eyes like

the eyes of a human and a mouth that was speaking arrogantly.

The Ancient of Days and the Son of Man

[9] "As I kept watching,
thrones were set in place,
and the Ancient of Days
took his seat.
His clothing was white
like snow, Mk 9:3
and the hair of his head
like whitest wool. Is 1:18; Rv 1:14
His throne was flaming fire;
its wheels were blazing fire.
[10] A river of fire was flowing,
coming out
from his presence.
Thousands upon thousands
served him; Dt 33:2; 1Kg 22:19
ten thousand times
ten thousand
stood before him. Ps 96:11-13
The court was convened,
and the books were opened.

[11] "I watched, then, because of the sound of the arrogant words the horn was speaking. As I continued watching, the beast was killed and its body destroyed and given over to the burning fire. [12] As for the rest of the beasts, their dominion was removed, but an extension of life was granted to them for a certain period of time. [13] I continued watching in the night visions, Dn 7:26
and suddenly one like a son
of man Mt 16:27-28; 24:30; Lk 21:27
was coming with the clouds
of heaven. Mt 26:64; Mk 13:26; 14:62
He approached the Ancient
of Days
and was escorted before him.
[14] He was given dominion, Jn 3:35
and glory, and a kingdom;

A **7:1** Lit *beginning*

so that those of every people, nation, and language Ps 72:11 should serve him. Dn 3:14,17-18,28 His dominion is

an everlasting dominion
that will not pass away,
and his kingdom is one
that will not be destroyed.

Interpretation of the Vision

¹⁵ "As for me, Daniel, my spirit was deeply distressed within me, ᴬ and the visions in my mind terrified me. ¹⁶ I approached one of those who were standing by and asked him to clarify all this. So he let me know the interpretation of these things: ¹⁷ 'These huge beasts, four in number, are four kings who will rise from the earth. ¹⁸ But the holy ones of the Most High will receive the kingdom and possess it forever, yes, forever and ever.' Dn 4:19; 7:1

¹⁹ "Then I wanted to be clear about the fourth beast, the one different from all the others, extremely terrifying, with iron teeth and bronze claws, devouring, crushing, and trampling with its feet whatever was left. ²⁰ I also wanted to know about the ten horns on its head and about the other horn that came up, before which three fell — the horn that had eyes, and a mouth that spoke arrogantly, and that looked bigger than the others. ²¹ As I was watching, this horn waged war against the holy ones and was prevailing over them ²² until the Ancient of Days arrived and a judgment was given in favor of the holy ones of the Most High, for the time had come, and the holy ones took possession of the kingdom.

²³ "This is what he said: 'The fourth beast will be a fourth kingdom on the earth, different from all the other kingdoms. It will devour the whole earth, trample it down, and crush it. ²⁴ The ten horns are ten kings who will rise from this kingdom. Another king, different from the previous ones, will rise after them and subdue three kings. ²⁵ He will speak words against the Most High and oppress ᴮ the holy ones of the Most High. He will intend to change religious festivals ᶜ and laws, and the holy ones will be handed over to him for a time, times, and half a time. ᴰ ²⁶ But the court will convene, and his dominion will be taken away, to be completely destroyed forever. ²⁷ The kingdom, dominion, and greatness of the kingdoms under all of heaven will be given to the people, the holy ones of the Most High. His kingdom will be an everlasting kingdom, and all rulers will serve and obey him.' Dn 7:7; 11:36; 12:14; Rv 17:12

²⁸ "This is the end of the account. As for me, Daniel, my thoughts terrified me greatly, and my face turned pale, ᴱ but I kept the matter to myself." Dn 4:19; Lk 2:19,51

The Vision of a Ram and a Goat

8 In the third year of King Belshazzar's reign, a vision appeared to me, Daniel, after the one that had appeared to me earlier. ² I saw the vision, and as I watched, I was in the fortress city of Susa, in the province of Elam. I saw in the vision that I was beside the Ulai Canal. ³ I looked up, ᶠ and there was a ram standing beside the canal. He

---

ᴬ **7:15** Lit *was distressed in the middle of its sheath* ᴮ **7:25** Lit *wear out* ᶜ **7:25** Lit *change times*
ᴰ **7:25** Or *for three and a half years* ᴱ **7:28** Lit *my brightness changed on me* ᶠ **8:3** Lit *I lifted my eyes and looked*

had two horns. The two horns were long, but one was longer than the other, and the longer one came up last. [4] I saw the ram charging to the west, the north, and the south. No animal could stand against him, and there was no rescue from his power. He did whatever he wanted and became great. Dn 5:1; 7:1

[5] As I was observing, a male goat appeared, coming from the west across the surface of the entire earth without touching the ground. The goat had a conspicuous horn[A] between his eyes. [6] He came toward the two-horned ram I had seen standing beside the canal and rushed at him with savage fury. [7] I saw him approaching the ram, and infuriated with him, he struck the ram, breaking his two horns, and the ram was not strong enough to stand against him. The goat threw him to the ground and trampled him, and there was no one to rescue the ram from his power. [8] Then the male goat acted even more arrogantly, but when he became powerful, the large horn was broken. Four conspicuous horns came up in its place, pointing toward the four winds of heaven. Dn 5:20; 8:21

The Little Horn

[9] From one of them a little horn emerged and grew extensively toward the south and the east and toward the beautiful land. [B] [10] It grew as high as the heavenly army, made some of the army and some of the stars[C] fall to the earth, and trampled them. [11] It acted arrogantly even against the Prince of the heavenly army; it revoked his regular sacrifice and overthrew the place of his sanctuary. [12] In the rebellion, the army was given up, together with the regular sacrifice. The horn threw truth to the ground and was successful in what it did. Ps 48:2; Dn 7:8; 8:23; 11:16,41

[13] Then I heard a holy one speaking, and another holy one said to the speaker, "How long will the events of this vision last — the regular sacrifice, the rebellion that makes desolate, and the giving over of the sanctuary and of the army to be trampled?" Dn 4:13,23; 1Pt 1:12

[14] He said to me,[D] "For 2,300 evenings and mornings; then the sanctuary will be restored."

Interpretation of the Vision

[15] While I, Daniel, was watching the vision and trying to understand it, there stood before me someone who appeared to be a man. [16] I heard a human voice calling from the middle of the Ulai: "Gabriel, explain the vision to this man."

[17] So he approached where I was standing; when he came near, I was terrified and fell facedown. "Son of man," he said to me, "understand that the vision refers to the time of the end." [18] While he was speaking to me, I fell into a deep sleep, with my face to the ground. Then he touched me, made me stand up, [19] and said, "I am here to tell you what will happen at the conclusion of the time of wrath, because it refers to the appointed time of the end. [20] The two-horned ram that you saw represents the kings of Media and Persia. [21] The shaggy goat represents the king of Greece, and the large horn between his eyes represents the first

---

[A]8:5 Lit a horn of a vision　　[B]8:9 = Israel　　[C]8:10 Or some of the army, that is, some of the stars
[D]8:14 LXX, Theod, Syr, Vg read him

king.^A 22 The four horns that took the place of the broken horn represent four kingdoms. They will rise from that nation, but without its power. Ezk 1:28; 44:4; Dn 2:46; 10:9; Rv 1:17

23 Near the end
     of their kingdoms,
when the rebels have reached
the full measure of their sin,^B
a ruthless^C king, skilled
     in intrigue,^D
will come to the throne.

24 His power will be great,
but it will not be his own.
He will cause
     outrageous destruction
and succeed in whatever
     he does.
He will destroy the powerful
along with the holy people.

25 He will cause deceit
     to prosper
through his cunning
     and by his influence,
and in his own mind he will
     exalt himself.
He will destroy many in a
     time of peace;
he will even stand
     against the Prince of princes.
Yet he will be broken —
     not by human hands. Jb 34:20

26 The vision of the evenings
     and the mornings
that has been told is true.
Now you are to seal up
     the vision   Ezk 12:27; Dn 12:4,9
because it refers
     to many days in the future."

27 I, Daniel, was overcome and lay sick for days. Then I got up and went about the king's business. I was greatly disturbed by the vision and could not understand it. Dn 7:28

Daniel's Prayer

9 In the first year of Darius, the son of Ahasuerus, a Mede by birth, who was made king over the Chaldean kingdom — 2 in the first year of his reign, I, Daniel, understood from the books according to the word of the LORD to the prophet Jeremiah that the number of years for the desolation of Jerusalem would be seventy. 3 So I turned my attention to the Lord God to seek him by prayer and petitions, with fasting, sackcloth, and ashes. 2 Ch 36:21; Ezr 1:1; Dn 5:31; 6:1; 11:1

4 I prayed to the LORD my God and confessed:

Ah, Lord — the great and awe-inspiring God who keeps his gracious covenant with those who love him and keep his commands — 5 we have sinned, done wrong, acted wickedly, rebelled, and turned away from your commands and ordinances. 6 We have not listened to your servants the prophets, who spoke in your name to our kings, leaders, fathers, and all the people of the land. Dt 7:21

7 Lord, righteousness belongs to you, but this day public shame belongs to us: the men of Judah, the residents of Jerusalem, and all Israel — those who are near and those who are far, in all the countries where you have banished them because of the disloyalty they have shown toward you. 8 LORD, public shame belongs to us, our kings, our leaders, and our fathers, because we have sinned against you. 9 Compassion and

---

^A 8:21 = Alexander the Great   ^B 8:23 Lit *have become complete*   ^C 8:23 Lit *strong of face*   ^D 8:23 Lit *king, and understanding riddles* forgiveness belong to the Lord our God, though we have rebelled against him [10] and have not obeyed the LORD our God by following his instructions that he set before us through his servants the prophets. Jr 23:6

[11] All Israel has broken your law and turned away, refusing to obey you. The promised curse[A] written in the law of Moses, the servant of God, has been poured out on us because we have sinned against him. [12] He has carried out his words that he spoke against us and against our rulers[B] by bringing on us a disaster that is so great that nothing like what has been done to Jerusalem has ever been done under all of heaven. [13] Just as it is written in the law of Moses, all this disaster has come on us, yet we have not sought the favor of the LORD our God by turning from our iniquities and paying attention to your truth. [14] So the LORD kept the disaster in mind and brought it on us, for the LORD our God is righteous in all he has done. But we have not obeyed him. Is 1:3-4; Jr 8:5-10

[15] Now, Lord our God, who brought your people out of the land of Egypt with a strong hand and made your name renowned as it is this day, we have sinned, we have acted wickedly. [16] Lord, in keeping with all your righteous acts, may your anger and wrath turn away from your city

Jerusalem, your holy mountain; for because of our sins and the iniquities of our fathers, Jerusalem and your people have become an object of ridicule to all those around us.

[17] Therefore, our God, hear the prayer and the petitions of your servant. Make your face shine on your desolate sanctuary for the Lord's sake. [18] Listen closely,[C] my God, and hear. Open your eyes and see our desolations and the city that bears your name. For we are not presenting our petitions before you based on our righteous acts, but based on your abundant compassion. [19] Lord, hear! Lord, forgive! Lord, listen and act! My God, for your own sake, do not delay, because your city and your people bear your name. Nm 6:25; Ps 31:17; 67:2; Lm 5:18

The Seventy Weeks of Years

[20] While I was speaking, praying, confessing my sin and the sin of my people Israel, and presenting my petition before the LORD my God concerning the holy mountain of my God — [21] while I was praying, Gabriel, the man I had seen in the first vision, reached me in my extreme weariness, about the time of the evening offering. [22] He gave me this explanation: "Daniel, I've come now to give you understanding. [23] At the beginning of your petitions an answer went out, and I have come to give it, for you are treasured by God.[D] So consider the message and understand the vision: Ezr 9:4; Ps 145:18; Is 58:9; Dn 8:16; 9:3; 10:12

A 9:11 Lit The curse and the oath   B 9:12 Lit against rulers who ruled us   C 9:18 Lit Stretch out your ear
D 9:23 by God added for clarity

²⁴ Seventy weeks are decreed
about your people
and your holy city —
to bring the rebellion
to an end,
to put a stop to sin,
to atone for iniquity,
to bring in
everlasting righteousness,
to seal up vision
and prophecy,
and to anoint
the most holy place.
²⁵ Know and understand this:
From the issuing
of the decree
to restore
and rebuild Jerusalem
until an Anointed One,
the ruler,ᴬ   Mt 1:17; Jn 1:41; 4:25
will be seven weeks
and sixty-two weeks.
It will be rebuilt with a plaza
and a moat,
but in difficult times.
²⁶ After those sixty-two weeks
the Anointed One will be
cut off   Is 53:8; Mk 9:12; Lk 24:26
and will have nothing.
The people
of the coming ruler
will destroy the city
and the sanctuary.ᴮ   Mt 24:2
Theᶜ end will come
with a flood,   Nah 1:8
and until the end
there will beᴰ war;
desolations are decreed.
²⁷ He will make
a firm covenantᴱ
with many for one week,
but in the middle of the week

he will put a stop to sacrifice
and offering.
And the abomination
of desolation   Dn 11:31; Mt 24:15
will be on a wing
of the templeᶠ·ᴳ   Is 7:7-8; Mt 4:5
until the decreed destruction
is poured out
on the desolator."

Vision of a Glorious One

10 In the third year of King Cyrus of Persia, a message was
revealed to Daniel, who was named
Belteshazzar. The message was true
and was about a great conflict. He
understood the message and had
understanding of the vision.

² In those days I, Daniel, was
mourning for three full weeks. ³ I
didn't eat any rich food, no meat
or wine entered my mouth, and I
didn't put any oil on my body until the three weeks were over. ⁴ On
the twenty-fourth day of the first
month,ᴴ as I was standing on the
bank of the great river, the Tigris,
⁵ I looked up, and there was a man
dressed in linen, with a belt of gold
from Uphazᴵ around his waist.
⁶ His body was like beryl,ᴶ his face
like the brilliance of lightning, his
eyes like flaming torches, his arms
and feet like the gleam of polished
bronze, and the sound of his words
like the sound of a multitude.

⁷ Only I, Daniel, saw the vision.
The men who were with me did
not see it, but a great terror fell on
them, and they ran and hid. ⁸ I was
left alone, looking at this great vision. No strength was left in me; my

---

ᴬ**9:25** Or *until an anointed one, a prince*   ᴮ**9:26** MT; Theod, some mss read *The city and the sanctuary*
will be destroyed when the ruler comes.   ᶜ**9:26** Lit *Its,* or *His*   ᴰ**9:26** Or *end of a*   ᴱ**9:27** Or *will enforce*
a covenant   ᶠ**9:27** LXX; MT reads *of abominations*   ᴳ**9:27** Or *And the desolator will be on the wing of*
abominations, or *And the desolator will come on the wings of monsters* (or *of horror*); Hb obscure
ᴴ**10:4** = Nisan (March–April)   ᴵ**10:5** Some Hb mss read *Ophir*   ᴶ**10:6** The identity of this stone is uncertain.

face grew deathly pale,[A] and I was powerless. [9] I heard the words he said, and when I heard them I fell into a deep sleep,[B] with my face to the ground.   2Kg 6:17-20; Ezk 12:18; Ac 9:7

Angelic Conflict

[10] Suddenly, a hand touched me and set me shaking on my hands and knees. [11] He said to me, "Daniel, you are a man treasured by God.[C] Understand the words that I'm saying to you. Stand on your feet, for I have now been sent to you." After he said this to me, I stood trembling.

[12] "Don't be afraid, Daniel," he said to me, "for from the first day that you purposed to understand and to humble yourself before your God, your prayers were heard. I have come because of your prayers. [13] But the prince of the kingdom of Persia opposed me for twenty-one days. Then Michael, one of the chief princes, came to help me after I had been left there with the kings of Persia. [14] Now I have come to help you understand what will happen to your people in the last days, for the vision refers to those days."

[15] While he was saying these words to me, I turned my face toward the ground and was speechless. [16] Suddenly one with human likeness touched my lips. I opened my mouth and said to the one standing in front of me, "My lord, because of the vision, anguish overwhelms me and I am powerless. [17] How can someone like me, your servant,[D] speak with someone like you, my lord? Now I have no strength, and there is no breath in me."   Ezk 3:26

[18] Then the one with a human appearance touched me again and strengthened me. [19] He said, "Don't be afraid, you who are[E] treasured by God. Peace to you; be very strong!"   Jdg 6:23; Is 35:3-4; 43:1; Dn 10:11-12

As he spoke to me, I was strengthened and said, "Let my lord speak, for you have strengthened me."

[20] He said, "Do you know why I've come to you? I must return at once to fight against the prince of Persia, and when I leave, the prince of Greece will come. [21] However, I will tell you what is recorded in the book of truth. (No one has the courage to support me against those princes except Michael, your prince. [1] In the first year of Darius the Mede, I stood up to strengthen and protect him.) [2] Now I will tell you the truth.   Dn 5:31; 9:1

11

Prophecies About Persia and Greece

"Three more kings will arise in Persia, and the fourth will be far richer than the others. By the power he gains through his riches, he will stir up everyone against the kingdom of Greece. [3] Then a warrior king will arise; he will rule a vast realm and do whatever he wants. [4] But as soon as he is established, his kingdom will be broken up and divided to the four winds of heaven, but not to his descendants; it will not be the same kingdom that he ruled, because his kingdom will be uprooted and will go to others besides them.   Dn 5:19; 8:4,8,21; 10:20

Kings of the South and the North

[5] "The king of the South will grow powerful, but one of his commanders will grow more powerful and will rule a kingdom greater than

---

[A]**10:8** Lit *my splendor was turned on me to ruin*   [B]**10:9** Lit *a sleep on my face*   [C]**10:11** *by God* added for clarity, also in v. 19   [D]**10:17** Lit *Can I, a servant of my lord*   [E]**10:19** Lit *afraid, man* his. ⁶ After some years they will form an alliance, and the daughter of the king of the South will go to the king of the North to seal the agreement. She will not retain power, and his strength will not endure. She will be given up, together with her entourage, her father, ᴬ and the one who supported her during those times. ⁷ In the place of the king of the South, one from her family ᴮ will rise up, come against the army, and enter the fortress of the king of the North. He will take action against them and triumph. ⁸ He will take even their gods captive to Egypt, with their metal images and their precious articles of silver and gold. For some years he will stay away from the king of the North, ⁹ who will enter the kingdom of the king of the South and then return to his own land. Is 37:19; Dn 11:9,11,14,25,40

¹⁰ "His sons will mobilize for war and assemble a large number of armed forces. They will advance, sweeping through like a flood, ᶜ and will again wage war as far as his fortress. ¹¹ Infuriated, the king of the South will march out to fight with the king of the North, who will raise a large army, but they will be handed over to his enemy. ¹² When the army is carried off, he will become arrogant and cause tens of thousands to fall, but he will not triumph. ¹³ The king of the North will again raise a multitude larger than the first. After some years ᴰ he will advance with a great army and many supplies. Is 8:8; Jr 46:7-8; 51:42

¹⁴ "In those times many will rise up against the king of the South.

Violent ones among your own people will assert themselves to fulfill a vision, but they will fail. ¹⁵ Then the king of the North will come, build up a siege ramp, and capture a well-fortified city. The forces of the South will not stand; even their select troops will not be able to resist. ¹⁶ The king of the North who comes against him will do whatever he wants, and no one can oppose him. He will establish himself in the beautiful land ᴱ with total destruction in his hand. ¹⁷ He will resolve to come with the force of his whole kingdom and will reach an agreement with him. ᶠ He will give him a daughter in marriage ᴳ to destroy it, ᴴ but she will not stand with him or support him. ¹⁸ Then he will turn his attention to the coasts and islands ᴵ and capture many. But a commander will put an end to his taunting; instead, he will turn his taunts against him. ¹⁹ He will turn his attention back to the fortresses of his own land, but he will stumble, fall, and be no more. Jr 6:6; Ezk 4:2

²⁰ "In his place one will arise who will send out a tax collector for the glory of the kingdom; but within a few days he will be broken, though not in anger ᴶ or in battle. 2Kg 23:35

²¹ "In his place a despised person will arise; royal honors will not be given to him, but he will come during a time of peace ᴷ and seize the kingdom by intrigue. ²² A flood of forces will be swept away before him; they will be broken, as well as the covenant prince. ²³ After an alliance is made with him, he will act deceitfully. He will rise to power

---

ᴬ11:6 Some Hb mss, Theod read *the child*; Syr, Vg read *her children*   ᴮ11:7 Lit *from the shoot of her roots*
ᶜ11:10 Lit *advance and overflow and pass through*   ᴰ11:13 Lit *At the end of the times*   ᴱ11:16 = Israel
ᶠ11:17 = the king of the South   ᴳ11:17 Lit *him the daughter of women*   ᴴ11:17 Perhaps the kingdom
ᴵ11:18 of the Mediterranean   ᴶ11:20 Or *not openly*   ᴷ11:21 Or *come without warning*

with a small nation.^A ²⁴ During a time of peace,^B he will come into the richest parts of the province and do what his fathers and predecessors never did. He will lavish plunder, loot, and wealth on his followers, and he will make plans against fortified cities, but only for a time. _{Nm 13:20; Neh 9:25; Is 53:3; Dn 8:25; 11:24}

²⁵ "With a large army he will stir up his power and his courage against the king of the South. The king of the South will prepare for battle with an extremely large and powerful army, but he will not succeed, because plots will be made against him. ²⁶ Those who eat his provisions will destroy him; his army will be swept away, and many will fall slain. ²⁷ The two kings, whose hearts are bent on evil, will speak lies at the same table but to no avail, for still the end will come at the appointed time. ²⁸ The king of the North will return to his land with great wealth, but his heart will be set against the holy covenant;^C he will take action, then return to his own land. _{Ps 12:2; Jr 9:3-5; Dn 1:5,8,13,15}

²⁹ "At the appointed time he will come again to the South, but this time^D will not be like the first. ³⁰ Ships of Kittim^E will come against him, and being intimidated, he will withdraw. Then he will rage against the holy covenant and take action. On his return, he will favor those who abandon the holy covenant. ³¹ His forces will rise up and desecrate the temple fortress. They will abolish the regular sacrifice and set up the abomination of desolation. ³² With flattery he will corrupt those who act wickedly toward the covenant, but the people who

know their God will be strong and take action. ³³ Those who have insight among the people will give understanding to many, yet they will fall by the sword and flame, and be captured and plundered for a time. ³⁴ When they fall, they will be helped by some, but many others will join them insincerely. ³⁵ Some of those who have insight will fall so that they may be refined, purified, and cleansed until the time of the end, for it will still come at the appointed time. _{Gn 10:4; Nm 24:24; 1Ch 1:7}

³⁶ "Then the king will do whatever he wants. He will exalt and magnify himself above every god, and he will say outrageous things against the God of gods. He will be successful until the time of wrath is completed, because what has been decreed will be accomplished. ³⁷ He will not show regard for the gods^F of his fathers, the god desired by women, or for any other god, because he will magnify himself above all. ³⁸ Instead, he will honor a god of fortresses — a god his fathers did not know — with gold, silver, precious stones, and riches. ³⁹ He will deal with the strongest fortresses with the help of a foreign god. He will greatly honor those who acknowledge him,^G making them rulers over many and distributing land as a reward.

⁴⁰ "At the time of the end, the king of the South will engage him in battle, but the king of the North will storm against him with chariots, horsemen, and many ships. He will invade countries and sweep through them like a flood. ⁴¹ He will also invade the beautiful land, and many will fall. But these will escape

from his power: Edom, Moab, and the prominent people[A] of the Ammonites. [42] He will extend his power against the countries, and not even the land of Egypt will escape. [43] He will get control over the hidden treasures of gold and silver and over all the riches of Egypt. The Libyans and Cushites will also be in submission.[B] [44] But reports from the east and the north will terrify him, and he will go out with great fury to annihilate and completely destroy many. [45] He will pitch his royal tents between the sea and[C] the beautiful holy mountain, but he will meet his end with no one to help him.   Is 5:28; 11:14; Jr 4:13; Dn 11:10,26

12 At that time
Michael, the great prince
who stands watch
over your people,
will rise up.
There will be a time of distress
such as never has occurred
since nations came into being
until that time.   Rv 16:18
But at that time all your people
who are found written
in the book will escape.
[2] Many who sleep in the dust
of the earth will awake,
some to eternal life,   Mt 25:46
and some to disgrace
and eternal contempt.
[3] Those who have insight
will shine
like the bright expanse
of the heavens,   Gn 1:6; Ps 19:1
and those who lead many
to righteousness,   Is 53:11
like the stars
forever and ever.

[4] "But you, Daniel, keep these words secret and seal the book until the time of the end. Many will roam about, and knowledge will increase."[D]   Is 8:16; Dn 8:26; 12:9; Rv 10:4

[5] Then I, Daniel, looked, and two others were standing there, one on this bank of the river and one on the other. [6] One of them said to the man dressed in linen, who was above the water of the river, "How long until the end of these wondrous things?" [7] Then I heard the man dressed in linen, who was above the water of the river. He raised both his hands[E] toward heaven and swore by him who lives eternally that it would be for a time, times, and half a time. When the power of the holy people is shattered, all these things will be completed.   Ezk 9:2; Dn 10:5; 8:13,16; Mt 24:3

[8] I heard but did not understand. So I asked, "My lord, what will be the outcome of these things?"

[9] He said, "Go on your way, Daniel, for the words are secret and sealed until the time of the end. [10] Many will be purified, cleansed, and refined, but the wicked will act wickedly; none of the wicked will understand, but those who have insight will understand. [11] From the time the daily sacrifice is abolished and the abomination of desolation is set up, there will be 1,290 days. [12] Happy is the one who waits for and reaches 1,335 days. [13] But as for you, go on your way to the end;[F] you will rest, and then you will stand to receive your allotted inheritance at the end of the days."   Dn 12:4; Zch 13:9; Ac 1:6-7; Rv 10:4

[A]11:41 Lit *the first*   [B]11:43 Lit *Cushites at his steps*   [C]11:45 Or *the seas at*   [D]12:4 LXX reads *and the earth will be filled with unrighteousness*   [E]12:7 Lit *raised his right and his left*   [F]12:13 LXX omits *to the end*

HOSEA

1

The word of the LORD that came to Hosea son of Beeri during the reigns of Uzziah, Jotham, Ahaz, and Hezekiah, kings of Judah, and of Jeroboam son of Jehoash, king of Israel. 2Kg 15:5; 2Ch 26:1-23; Is 1:1; Am 1:1

Hosea's Marriage and Children

² When the LORD first spoke to Hosea, he said this to him:

Go and marry a woman of
promiscuity, Hs 3:1
and have children
of promiscuity,
for the land is committing
blatant acts of promiscuity
by abandoning the LORD.

³ So he went and married Gomer daughter of Diblaim, and she conceived and bore him a son. ⁴ Then the LORD said to him: Ezk 23:4

Name him Jezreel, A
for in a little while Hs 2:22
I will bring the bloodshed
of Jezreel 2Kg 9:24–10:11
on the house of Jehu 2Kg 9:7
and put an end to the kingdom
of the house of Israel.
⁵ On that day I will break
the bow of Israel Gn 49:24
in the Valley of Jezreel. Jos 17:16

⁶ She conceived again and gave birth to a daughter, and the LORD said to him:

Name her Lo-ruhamah, B
for I will no longer
have compassion
on the house of Israel.

I will certainly take them away.
⁷ But I will have compassion
on the house of Judah,
and I will deliver them by
the LORD their God. Jr 25:5-6
I will not deliver them
by bow, sword, or war,
or by horses and cavalry.

⁸ After Gomer had weaned Lo-ruhamah, she conceived and gave birth to a son. ⁹ Then the LORD said:

Name him Lo-ammi, C
for you are not my people,
and I will not be your God. D
¹⁰ Yet the number
of the Israelites
will be like the sand of the sea,
which cannot be measured
or counted.
And in the place where
they were told:
You are not my people,
they will be called:
Sons of the living God.
¹¹ And the Judeans
and the Israelites
will be gathered together.
They will appoint
for themselves a single ruler
and go up from E the land.
For the day of Jezreel
will be great. Ezk 36:9-11

2

Call F your brothers:
My People
and your sisters: Compassion.

Israel's Adultery Rebuked

² Rebuke your mother;
rebuke her. Ezk 23:45

A 1:4 = God Sows   B 1:6 = No Compassion   C 1:9 = Not My People   D 1:9 Lit *not be yours*   E 1:11 Or *and flourish in* ; Hb obscure   F 2:1 Lit *Say to*

For she is not my wife
and I am not her husband.
Let her remove
the promiscuous look
from her face   Jr 3:1,9,13
and her adultery
from between her breasts.
3 Otherwise, I will strip
her naked   Ezk 16:7,22,39
and expose her as she was
on the day of her birth.
I will make her like a desert
and like a parched land,
and I will let her die of thirst.
4 I will have no compassion
on her children   Jr 13:14
because they are the children
of promiscuity.
5 Yes, their mother
is promiscuous;
she conceived them
and acted shamefully.   Is 1:21
For she thought, "I will follow
my lovers,   Jr 2:25
the men who give me
my food and water,
my wool and flax, my oil
and drink."   Jr 44:17-18
6 Therefore, this is what I will do:
I will block her^A way
with thorns;   Jb 19:8; Hs 9:6; 10:8
I will enclose her with a wall,
so that she cannot find
her paths.   Jr 18:15
7 She will pursue her lovers
but not catch them;   Hs 5:13
she will look for them
but not find them.
Then she will think,
"I will go back
to my former husband,   Jr 2:2
for then it was better for me
than now."   Jr 14:22; Hs 13:6
8 She does not recognize   Is 1:3
that it is I who gave her
the grain,   Ezk 16:19

the new wine,
and the fresh oil.
I lavished silver and gold
on her,
which they used for Baal.
9 Therefore, I will take back
my grain in its time   Hs 8:7; 9:2
and my new wine
in its season;
I will take away my wool
and linen,
which were to cover
her nakedness.
10 Now I will expose her shame
in the sight of her lovers,
and no one will rescue her
from my power.
11 I will put an end to all
her celebrations: Jr 7:34; 16:9
her feasts, New Moons,
and Sabbaths —   Hs 3:4; Am 5:21
all her festivals.
12 I will devastate her vines
and fig trees.   Jr 5:17; 8:13
She thinks that these are
her wages
that her lovers have given her.
I will turn them
into a thicket,   Ps 80:12; Is 5:5; 7:23
and the wild animals
will eat them.   Is 32:13-15
13 And I will punish her
for the days of the Baals,
to which she burned incense.
She put on her rings and her
jewelry   Ezk 16:12,17; 23:40
and followed her lovers,
but she forgot me.   Hs 4:6; 8:14; 13:6
This is
the LORD's declaration.

Israel's Adultery Forgiven

14 Therefore, I am going
to persuade her,
lead her to the wilderness,
and speak tenderly to her.^B

^A 2:6 LXX, Syr; MT reads *your*   ^B 2:14 Lit *speak to her heart*

¹⁵ There I will give
　　her vineyards back to her
　　and make the Valley
　　　of Achor ^A   Jos 7:26
　　into a gateway of hope.
　　There she will respond
　　　as she did
　　in the days of her youth,   Jr 2:1-3
　　as in the day she came out
　　　of the land of Egypt.
¹⁶ In that day —
　　this is
　　the LORD's declaration —
　　you will call me,
　　　"My husband,"   Is 54:5
　　and no longer call me,
　　　"My Baal." ^B
¹⁷ For I will remove the names
　　　of the Baals
　　from her mouth;
　　they will no longer
　　　be remembered
　　by their names.
¹⁸ On that day I will make
　　　a covenant for them
　　with the wild animals,
　　　the birds of the sky,
　　and the creatures that crawl
　　　on the ground.   Jb 5:23; Is 11:6-9
　　I will shatter bow, sword,
　　and weapons of war
　　　in the land ^C
　　　　　　　　　　　 Ezk 39:1-10
　　and will enable the people
　　　to rest securely.   Ezk 34:25
¹⁹ I will take you to be
　　　my wife forever.   Is 62:4-5
　　I will take you to be my wife
　　　in righteousness,
　　justice, love,
　　　and compassion.   Is 1:27; 54:6-8
²⁰ I will take you to be my wife
　　　in faithfulness,
　　and you will know the LORD.
²¹ On that day
　　　I will respond —   Is 55:10

this is
　　the LORD's declaration.
I will respond to the sky,
　　and it will respond
　　　to the earth.
²² The earth will respond
　　　to the grain,   Jr 31:12; Jl 2:19
　　the new wine,
　　　and the fresh oil,
　　and they will respond
　　　to Jezreel.
²³ I will sow her ^D in the land
　　　for myself,   Jr 31:37
　　and I will have compassion
　　　on Lo-ruhamah;
　　I will say to Lo-ammi: Hs 1:9
　　You are my people,   Hs 2:1; Rm 9:25
　　and he will say, "You are
　　　my God."

Waiting for Restoration

3 Then the LORD said to me, "Go
　　again; show love to a woman
who is loved by another man and
is an adulteress, just as the LORD
loves the Israelites though they
turn to other gods and love raisin
cakes."   2Sm 6:19; 1Ch 16:3; Sg 2:5; Hs 1:2
² So I bought her for fifteen shek-
els of silver and five bushels of barley. ^E,F ³ I said to her, "You are to live
with me many days. You must not
be promiscuous or belong to any
man, and I will act the same way
toward you."   Ru 4:10
⁴ For the Israelites must live
many days without king or prince,
without sacrifice or sacred pillar,
and without ephod or household
idols. ⁵ Afterward, the people of
Israel will return and seek the
LORD their God and David their
king. They will come with awe to
the LORD and to his goodness in
the last days.   Dn 9:27; 11:31; 12:11; Hs 13:10-11

^A **2:15** = Trouble   ^B **2:16** Or *My Master*   ^C **2:18** Or *war on the earth*   ^D **2:23** = Israel   ^E **3:2** LXX reads
barley and a measure of wine   ^F **3:2** Lit *silver, a homer of barley, and a lethek of barley*

God's Case Against Israel

4 Hear the word of the LORD,
    people of Israel,   Hs 5:1
for the LORD has a case   Hs 12:2
against the inhabitants
    of the land:
There is no truth,
    no faithful love,   Is 59:4; Jr 7:28
and no knowledge of God
    in the land!   Hs 5:4
2 Cursing, lying,
    murder, stealing,   Hs 7:3; 10:4
and adultery are rampant;
one act of bloodshed
    follows another.   Hs 6:8; 12:14
3 For this reason
    the land mourns,   Is 24:4; 33:9
and everyone who lives
    in it languishes,
along with the wild animals
    and the birds of the sky;
even the fish
    of the sea disappear.
4 But let no one dispute;
    let no one argue,   Ezk 3:26
for my case is
    against you priests. A,B
5 You will stumble by day;   Hs 5:5
the prophet
    will also stumble with you
    by night.
And I will destroy
    your mother.   Hs 2:2,5
6 My people are destroyed
    for lack of knowledge.   Is 5:13
Because you have
    rejected knowledge,   Mal 2:7-8
I will reject you from serving
    as my priest.   Zch 11:8-9,15-17
Since you have forgotten
    the law of your God,   Hs 2:13
I will also forget your sons.
7 The more they multiplied,

the more they sinned
    against me.
I C will change their D honor
    into disgrace.   Hab 2:16
8 They feed on the sin E
    of my people;   Hs 10:13
they have an appetite
    for their iniquity.   Is 56:11; Mc 3:11
9 The same judgment
    will happen
to both people and priests.
I will punish them
    for their ways   Hs 8:13; 9:9
and repay them
    for their deeds.
10 They will eat
    but not be satisfied;   Lv 26:26
they will be promiscuous
    but not multiply.   Hs 7:4
For they have abandoned
    their devotion to the LORD.
11 Promiscuity, wine,
    and new wine   Hs 5:4
take away
    one's understanding.   Is 5:12

12 My people consult
    their wooden idols,   Is 44:19
and their divining rods
    inform them.
For a spirit of promiscuity
    leads them astray;   Hs 5:4
they act promiscuously   Hs 9:1
in disobedience to F their God.
13 They sacrifice
    on the mountaintops,   Jr 3:6
and they burn offerings
    on the hills,   Hs 2:13; 11:2
and under oaks, poplars,
    and terebinths,   Jr 2:20
because their shade
    is pleasant.
And so your daughters
    act promiscuously

A 4:4 Text emended; MT reads *argue, and your people are like those contending with a priest*   B 4:4 Hb
obscure   C 4:7 Alt Hb tradition, Syr, Tg read *They*   D 4:7 Alt Hb tradition reads *my*   E 4:8 Or *sin offerings*
F 4:12 Lit *promiscuously from under*

and your daughters-in-law
   commit adultery.
14 I will not punish
   your daughters
when they act promiscuously
or your daughters-in-law
when they commit adultery,
for the men themselves
   go off with prostitutes   Hs 7:4
and make sacrifices
   with cult prostitutes.   Dt 23:17
People without discernment
   are doomed.   Hs 5:4

Warnings for Israel and Judah

15 Israel, if you
   act promiscuously,
don't let Judah become guilty!
Do not go to Gilgal   Hs 9:15; 12:1
or make a pilgrimage
   to Beth-aven, ^A   1Kg 12:28-29; Hs 5:8
and do not swear an oath:
   As the LORD lives!   Jr 5:2; 44:26
16 For Israel is as obstinate
   as a stubborn cow.   Ps 78:8
Can the LORD now
   shepherd them
like a lamb
   in an open meadow?   Is 5:17
17 Ephraim is attached to idols;
   leave him alone!   Ps 81:12; Hs 4:4
18 When their drinking is over,
they turn to promiscuity.
Israel's leaders ^B fervently
   love disgrace. ^C
19 A wind with its wings will
   carry them off, ^D   Hs 12:1; 13:5
and they will be ashamed
   of their sacrifices.

5 Hear this, priests!   Hs 4:1
Pay attention, house of Israel!
Listen, royal house!
For the judgment applies
   to you

because you have been
   a snare at Mizpah   Hs 9:8
and a net spread out
   on Tabor.
2 Rebels are deeply involved
   in slaughter;   Hs 4:2; 6:9; 9:15
I will be a punishment
   for all of them. ^C
3 I know Ephraim,   Hs 6:4; 7:1; Am 3:2
and Israel is not hidden
   from me.
For now, Ephraim,   Hs 6:10
you have acted promiscuously;
Israel is defiled.
4 Their actions do not
   allow them
to return to their God,   Hs 4:11
for a spirit of promiscuity
   is among them,   Hs 4:12
and they do not know
   the LORD.   Hs 4:6,11,14
5 Israel's arrogance testifies
   against them. ^E   Hs 7:10
Both Israel
   and Ephraim stumble
because of their iniquity;
even Judah will stumble
   with them.   Ezk 23:31-35
6 They go with their flocks
   and herds
to seek the LORD   Hs 8:13; Mc 6:6-7
but do not find him;   Is 1:15; Jr 14:12
he has withdrawn from them.
7 They betrayed the LORD;   Is 48:8
indeed, they gave birth
   to illegitimate children.
Now the New Moon
   will devour them   Hs 2:11
along with their fields.   Is 1:14
8 Blow the horn in Gibeah,
the trumpet in Ramah;   Is 10:29
raise the war cry
   in Beth-aven: Hs 4:15
Look behind you, ^F Benjamin!

---

^A 4:15 = House of Wickedness   ^B 4:18 Lit *Her shields* ; Ps 47:9; 89:18   ^C 4:18; 5:2 Hb obscure   ^D 4:19 Lit
wind will bind it in its wings   ^E 5:5 Lit *against his face*   ^F 5:8 Or *We will follow you*

⁹ Ephraim will become
  a desolation   Is 28:1-4; Hs 9:11-17
on the day of punishment;
I announce what is certain
  among the tribes of Israel.
¹⁰ The princes of Judah are
  like those
who move boundary markers;
I will pour out my fury
  on them like water.   Ezk 7:8
¹¹ Ephraim is oppressed,
  crushed in judgment,   Hs 9:16
for he is determined to follow
  what is worthless. ᴬ
¹² So I am like rot to Ephraim
and like decay to the house
  of Judah.
¹³ When Ephraim saw
  his sickness
and Judah his wound,
Ephraim went to Assyria
and sent a delegation
  to the great king. ᴮ   Hs 10:6
But he cannot cure you
  or heal your wound.   Hs 14:3
¹⁴ For I am like a lion
  to Ephraim   Ps 7:2; Hs 13:7; Am 3:4
and like a young lion
  to the house of Judah.
Yes, I will tear them to pieces
  and depart.   Ps 50:22
I will carry them off,
and no one can rescue them.
¹⁵ I will depart and return
  to my place
until they recognize
  their guilt and seek my face;
they will search for me
  in their distress.   Ps 50:15; 78:34

A Call to Repentance

6 Come, let us return
  to the LORD.   Jr 50:4-5
For he has torn us,   Hs 5:14
and he will heal us;   Hs 14:4

he has wounded us,
and he will bind up
  our wounds.   Is 30:26
² He will revive us
  after two days,   Ps 30:5
and on the third day
  he will raise us up
so we can live
  in his presence.   Dt 32:39
³ Let us strive to know the LORD.
His appearance is as sure as
  the dawn.   Ps 19:6; Mc 5:2
He will come to us
  like the rain,   Jl 2:23
like the spring showers
  that water the land.

The LORD's First Lament

⁴ What am I going to do
  with you, Ephraim?   Hs 7:1; 11:8
What am I going to do
  with you, Judah?
Your love is like
  the morning mist   Ps 78:34-37
and like the early dew
  that vanishes.
⁵ This is why I have used
  the prophets
to cut them down; ᶜ   1Sm 15:32-33
I have killed them
  with the words
  from my mouth.
My judgment strikes
  like lightning. ᴰ
⁶ For I desire faithful love
  and not sacrifice,
the knowledge of God
  rather than burnt offerings.

⁷ But they, like Adam, ᴱ
  have violated the covenant;
there they have betrayed me.
⁸ Gilead is a city of evildoers,
  tracked
  with bloody footprints.

ᴬ**5:11** Or *follow a command*; Hb obscure   ᴮ**5:13** Or *to King Yareb*   ᶜ**6:5** Or *have cut down the prophets*
ᴰ**6:5** LXX, Syr, Tg; MT reads *Your judgments go out as light*   ᴱ**6:7** Or *they, as at Adam*, or *they, like men,*

⁹ Like raiders who wait
　　in ambush for someone,
a band of priests murders
　　on the road to Shechem.
They commit atrocities.
¹⁰ I have seen something
　　horrible in the house
　　of Israel:　　　　　　Jr 5:30-31; 23:14
Ephraim's promiscuity
　　is there; Israel is defiled.
¹¹ A harvest is also appointed
　　for you, Judah.　　Jr 51:33; Jl 3:13

When I ᴬ return my people
　　from captivity,　　Zph 2:7

7 ¹ when I heal Israel,　　Ezk 24:13
the iniquity of Ephraim
　　and the crimes of Samaria
will be exposed.
For they practice fraud;　Hs 4:2
a thief breaks in;
a raiding party
　　pillages outside.　　Hs 6:9
² But they never consider
　　that I remember
　　all their evil.　　Ps 25:7; Jr 14:10; 17:1
Now their actions are
　　all around them;　　Jr 2:19; 4:18
they are right in front
　　of my face.

Israel's Corruption

³ They please the king
　　with their evil,　　Jr 28:1-4; Mc 7:3
the princes with their lies.
⁴ All of them commit adultery;
they are like an oven heated
　　by a baker
who stops stirring the fire
　　from the kneading
　　of the dough
　　until it is leavened.
⁵ On the day of our king,
the princes are sick
　　with the heat of wine —

there is a conspiracy
　　with traitors. ᴮ
⁶ For they — their hearts
　　like an oven —
draw him into their oven.
Their anger smolders
　　all night;
in the morning it blazes
　　like a flaming fire.
⁷ All of them are as hot
　　as an oven,　　Ps 21:9
and they consume
　　their rulers.　　Hs 13:10
All their kings fall;
not one of them calls on me. ᶜ

⁸ Ephraim has allowed
　　himself to get mixed up
　　with the nations.
Ephraim is unturned bread
　　baked on a griddle.
⁹ Foreigners consume
　　his strength,　　Is 1:7
but he does not notice.　Hs 4:6
Even his hair is streaked
　　with gray,
but he does not notice.
¹⁰ Israel's arrogance testifies
　　against them, ᴰ　　Hs 5:5
yet they do not return to the
　　Lᴏʀᴅ their God,　　Hs 5:4
and for all this, they do not
　　seek him.

¹¹ So Ephraim has become
　　like a silly, senseless dove;
they call to Egypt,
　　and they go to Assyria.
¹² As they are going,
　　I will spread my net
　　over them;　　Ezk 12:13
I will bring them down
　　like birds of the sky.
I will discipline them
　　in accordance

ᴬ**6:11** Or *you, Judah, when I*　ᴮ**7:5** Lit *wine — he stretches out his hand to scorners*; Hb obscure
ᶜ**7:3-7** These vv. may refer to a king's assassination; Hb obscure.　ᴰ**7:10** Lit *against his face*

with the news that reaches^A
their assembly.

The Lord's Second Lament

13 Woe to them, for they fled
from me;   Jr 14:10; Hs 9:12,17
destruction to them,
for they rebelled
against me!
Though I want
to redeem them,   Jr 51:9; Hs 7:1
they speak lies against me.
14 They do not cry to me
from their hearts;
rather, they wail
on their beds.
They slash themselves^B
for grain and new wine;
they turn away from me.
15 I trained and strengthened
their arms,   Hs 11:3
but they plot evil against me.
16 They turn, but not to what
is above;^C
they are like a faulty bow.
Their leaders will fall
by the sword
because of their
insolent tongue.   Ps 12:3-4; 17:10
They will be ridiculed for this
in the land of Egypt.   Ezk 23:32

Israel's False Hopes

8 Put the horn to your mouth!
One like an eagle comes
against the house
of the Lord,   Dt 28:49
because they transgress
my covenant   Hs 6:7
and rebel against my law.
2 Israel cries out to me,   Hs 7:14
"My God, we know you!"
3 Israel has rejected
what is good;   Hs 3:5
an enemy will pursue him.

4 They have installed kings,
but not through me.
They have appointed leaders,
but without my approval.
They make their silver
and gold   Hs 2:8; 13:1-2
into idols for themselves
for their own destruction.^D
5 Your calf-idol^E
is rejected, Samaria.   Hs 10:5
My anger burns
against them.
How long will they be
incapable of innocence?
6 For this thing is
from Israel —
a craftsman made it,
and it is not God.   Hs 13:2
The calf of Samaria
will be smashed to bits!
7 Indeed, they sow the wind
and reap the whirlwind.
There is no standing grain;
what sprouts fails
to yield flour.   Hs 2:9
Even if they did,
foreigners would
swallow it up.
8 Israel is swallowed up!   Jr 51:34
Now they are
among the nations
like discarded pottery.   Jr 25:34
9 For they have gone up
to Assyria   Hs 7:11
like a wild donkey going off
on its own.
Ephraim has paid for love.
10 Even though they hire lovers
among the nations,
I will now round them up,
and they will begin
to decrease in number   Jr 42:2
under the burden of the king
and leaders.   Is 10:8

^A7:12 Lit news to   ^B7:14 Some Hb mss, LXX; other Hb mss read They stay   ^C7:16 Some emend to turn to
what is useless   ^D8:4 Lit themselves that it might be cut off   ^E8:5 Lit calf

11 When Ephraim multiplied
  his altars for sin,   Hs 10:1; 12:11
they became his altars
  for sinning.
12 Though I were to write out
  for him
ten thousand points
  of my instruction,   Hs 4:6
they would be^A regarded
  as something strange.
13 Though they offer
  sacrificial gifts^B   Hs 5:6; 9:4
and eat the flesh,   Jr 6:20; 7:21
the LORD does not accept them.
Now he will remember
  their guilt   Hs 7:2; Lk 12:2; 1Co 4:5
and punish their sins;   Hs 4:9; 9:7
they will return to Egypt.
14 Israel has forgotten
  his Maker
  and built palaces;   Hs 2:13; 4:6
Judah has also multiplied
  fortified cities.
I will send fire on their cities,
and it will consume
  their citadels.

The Coming Exile

9 Israel, do not
  rejoice jubilantly
  as the nations do,   Is 22:12-13
for you have acted
  promiscuously,
  leaving your God.   Hs 4:12
You love the wages
  of a prostitute
on every
  grain-threshing floor.   Hs 7:14
2 Threshing floor and wine vat
  will not sustain them,   Hs 2:9
and the new wine
  will fail them.
3 They will not stay in the land
  of the LORD.
Instead, Ephraim will return
  to Egypt,   Hs 7:16; 8:13

and they will eat
  unclean food in Assyria.
4 They will not pour out
  their wine offerings
  to the LORD,   Nm 15:5,7,10
and their sacrifices
  will not please him.
Their food will be
  like the bread of mourners;
all who eat it become defiled.
For their bread will be
  for their appetites alone;
it will not enter the house
  of the LORD.
5 What will you do
  on a festival day,   Is 10:3; Jr 5:31
on the day of the LORD's feast?
6 For even if they flee
  from devastation,
Egypt will gather
  them, and Memphis
  will bury them.   Is 19:13; Jr 2:16
Thistles will take possession
  of their precious silver;
thorns will invade their tents.

7 The days of punishment
  have come;   Is 10:3; Jr 10:15; Mc 7:4
the days of retribution
  have come.   Is 34:8; Jr 16:18; 25:14
Let Israel recognize it!
The prophet is a fool,   Lm 2:14
and the inspired man
  is insane,   Is 44:25
because of the magnitude
of your iniquity and hostility.
8 Ephraim's watchman is
  with my God.
Yet the prophet encounters
  a bird trap
on all his pathways.   Pr 29:5-6
Hostility is in the house
  of his God!
9 They have deeply
  corrupted themselves   Is 31:6

^A 8:12 Or *Though I wrote out . . . instruction, they are*   ^B 8:13 Hb obscure

as in the days of Gibeah. Hs 5:8
He will remember
　　their iniquity;
he will punish their sins. Hs 7:2

Ephraim Bereaved of Offspring

10 I discovered Israel
　　like grapes in the wilderness.
I saw your fathers
　　like the first fruit
　　　of the fig tree
　　　in its first season. Jr 24:2
But they went to Baal-peor,
consecrated themselves
　　to Shame,^A Jr 11:13; Hs 4:18
and became abhorrent, Ezk 20:8
like the thing they loved.

11 Ephraim's glory will fly away
　　like a bird: Hs 4:7; 10:4
no birth, no pregnancy,
　　no conception. Hs 4:10

12 Even if they raise children,
　　I will bereave them
　　　of each one.
Yes, woe to them
　　when I depart from them!

13 I have seen Ephraim
　　like Tyre, Ezk 27:3-4
planted in a meadow,
so Ephraim will bring out
　　his children
　　to the executioner.

14 Give them, LORD —
What should you give?
Give them a womb
　　that miscarries
and breasts that are dry!

15 All their evil appears
　　at Gilgal, Hs 4:15; 12:11
for there I began
　　to hate them.
I will drive them
　　from my house
because of their evil,
　　wicked actions. Hs 4:9; 7:2; 12:2

I will no longer love them;
all their leaders
　　are rebellious. Hs 5:2

16 Ephraim is struck down;
their roots are withered;
they cannot bear fruit. Hs 8:7
Even if they bear children,
I will kill the precious
　　offspring of their wombs.

17 My God will reject them
because they have not
　　listened to him; Hs 4:10
they will become wanderers
　　among the nations. Hs 7:13

The Vine and the Calf

10 Israel is a lush^B vine; Is 5:1-7
　　it yields fruit for itself.
The more his fruit increased,
the more he increased
　　the altars. Hs 8:11; 12:11
The better his land produced,
the better they made
　　the sacred pillars. 1Kg 14:23

2 Their hearts are devious;^C
now they must bear their guilt.
The LORD will break down
　　their altars Mc 5:13
and demolish
　　their sacred pillars.

3 In fact, they are now saying,
"We have no king!
For we do not fear the LORD.
What can a king do for us?"

4 They speak mere words,
taking false oaths
　　while making covenants.
So lawsuits break out
like poisonous weeds
　　in the furrows of a field.

5 The residents of Samaria
　　will have anxiety Hs 7:1
over the calf of Beth-aven.
Indeed, its idolatrous priests
　　rejoiced over it;

^A 9:10 = Baal   ^B 10:1 Or ravaged   ^C 10:2 Or divided

the people will mourn over it,
over its glory. Hs 9:11
It will certainly go into exile.
6 The calf itself will be taken
to Assyria Hs 11:5
as an offering
to the great king.^A Hs 5:13
Ephraim will
experience shame; Hs 4:7
Israel will be ashamed
of its counsel. Is 30:3; Jr 7:24
7 Samaria's king
will disappear^B Hs 13:11
like foam^C on the surface
of the water.
8 The high places of Aven,
the sin of Israel, Dt 12:2; Hs 4:13
will be destroyed;
thorns and thistles will grow
over their altars. Is 32:13; Hs 9:6
They will say
to the mountains,
"Cover us!" Lk 23:30; Rv 6:16
and to the hills, "Fall on us!"

Israel's Defeat Because of Sin

9 Israel, you have sinned
since the days of Gibeah; Hs 5:8
they have taken
their stand there.
Will not war against
the unjust
overtake them in Gibeah?
10 I will discipline them
at my discretion; Ezk 5:13; Hs 4:9
nations will be gathered
against them
to put them in bondage^D
for their double iniquity.

11 Ephraim is a well-trained
calf Jr 5:11; Hs 4:16
that loves to thresh,
but I will place a yoke on^E her
fine neck. Jr 28:14

I will harness Ephraim; Ps 66:12
Judah will plow;
Jacob will do the
final plowing.
12 Sow righteousness
for yourselves Pr 11:18
and reap faithful love;
break up
your unplowed ground.
It is time to seek the Lord
until he comes
and sends righteousness
on you like the rain. Is 44:3; 45:8

13 You have plowed wickedness
and reaped injustice; Jb 4:8
you have eaten the fruit
of lies. Hs 4:2; 7:3; 11:12
Because you have trusted
in your own way^F
and in your large number
of soldiers, Ps 33:16
14 the roar of battle will rise
against your people,
and all your fortifications
will be demolished Is 17:3
in a day of war,
like Shalman's destruction
of Beth-arbel.
Mothers will be dashed
to pieces
along with their children.
15 So it will be done
to you, Bethel, Hs 4:15; 10:5
because of
your extreme evil.
At dawn the king of Israel
will be totally destroyed.

The Lord's Love for Israel

11 When Israel was a child,
I loved him, Dt 4:37; 7:6-8; Is 41:8
and out of Egypt I called
my son. Ex 4:22-23; Dt 32:5-6, 18-20
2 Israel called to the Egyptians

^A10:6 Or to King Yareb ^B10:7 Or will be cut off ^C10:7 Or a stick ^D10:10 LXX, Syr, Vg read against
them when they are disciplined ^E10:11 Lit will pass over ^F10:13 LXX reads your chariots

even as Israel was leaving
  them. ᴬ
They kept sacrificing
  to the Baals   Hs 2:13; 4:13
and burning offerings
  to idols.   Is 65:7; Jr 18:15
³ It was I who taught Ephraim
  to walk,   Hs 7:15
taking them ᴮ by the hand, ᶜ
but they never knew
  that I healed them.   Ex 15:26
⁴ I led them with human cords,
with ropes of love.   Jr 31:2-3
To them I was like one
who eases the yoke
  from their jaws;   Hs 10:11
I bent down
  to give them food.   Ex 16:32
⁵ Israel will not return
  to the land of Egypt
and Assyria will be his king,
because they refused
  to repent.   Hs 7:16
⁶ A sword will whirl
  through his cities;   Hs 13:16
it will destroy and devour
  the bars of his gates, ᴰ   Lm 2:9
because of their schemes.
⁷ My people are bent
  on turning from me.   Jr 8:5
Though they call to him
  on high,
he will not exalt them at all.

⁸ How can I give you
  up, Ephraim?   Hs 6:4; 7:1
How can I surrender
  you, Israel?
How can I make you
  like Admah?   Gn 14:8; Dt 29:23
How can I treat you
  like Zeboiim?   Gn 14:2; 19:1-29
I have had a change of heart;
my compassion is stirred!

⁹ I will not vent the full fury
  of my anger;   Dt 13:17
I will not turn back
  to destroy Ephraim.   Jr 26:3
For I am God and not man,
the Holy One among you;
I will not come in rage. ᴱ
¹⁰ They will follow the LORD;
he will roar like a lion.   Is 31:4
When he roars,
his children
  will come trembling
  from the west.   Is 66:2-5
¹¹ They will be roused like birds
  from Egypt
and like doves from the land
  of Assyria.   Is 11:11; 60:8; Hs 7:11
Then I will settle them
  in their homes.   Ezk 34:27-28
This is
the LORD's declaration.
¹² Ephraim surrounds me
  with lies,   Hs 4:2; 7:3
the house of Israel,
  with deceit.
Judah still wanders with God
and is faithful
  to the holy ones. ᶠ

God's Case Against Jacob's Heirs

12 Ephraim chases ᴳ the wind
and pursues
the east wind.   Gn 41:6; Ezk 17:10
He continually multiplies lies
  and violence.
He makes a covenant
  with Assyria,   Hs 5:13; 7:11; 8:9
and olive oil is carried
  to Egypt.   2Kg 17:4

² The LORD also has a dispute
  with Judah.
He is about to punish Jacob
  according to his conduct;

ᴬ**11:2** Lit *They called to them; thus they went from before them*   ᴮ**11:3** LXX, Syr, Vg; MT reads *him*
ᶜ**11:3** Lit *them on his arms*   ᴰ**11:6** Or *devour his empty talkers*, or *devour his limbs*; Hb obscure
ᴱ**11:9** Or *come into any city*; Hb obscure   ᶠ**11:12** Hb obscure   ᴳ**12:1** Or *grazes on*, or *tends*

he will repay him based on
　　his actions.
3 In the womb he grasped
　　his brother's heel, Gn 25:26
and as an adult he wrestled
　　with God. Gn 32:24-28
4 Jacob struggled with
　　the angel and prevailed;
he wept and sought his favor.
He found him at Bethel,
and there he spoke with him. A
5 The Lord is
　　the God of Armies;
the Lord is his name. Ex 3:15
6 But you must return
　　to your God. Hs 6:1-3;10:12
Maintain love and justice,
and always put your hope
　　in God. Mc 7:7

7 A merchant loves to extort
with dishonest scales
　　in his hands. Pr 11:1; Am 8:5; Mc 6:11
8 But Ephraim thinks,
"How rich I have become;
I made it all myself.
In all my earnings,
no one can find any iniquity
　　in me Hs 4:8;14:1; Am 3:15; 6:4-6
that I can be punished for!" B

Judgment on Apostate Israel

9 I have been the Lord your God
ever since C the land of Egypt.
I will make you live
　　in tents again, Lv 23:42
as in the festival days.
10 I will speak
　　through the prophets Jr 7:25
and grant many visions;
I will give parables
　　through the prophets.
11 Since Gilead is full of evil,
they will certainly come
　　to nothing.

They sacrifice bulls
　　in Gilgal; Hs 4:15; 9:15
even their altars will be
　　like piles of rocks Hs 8:11;10:1-2
on the furrows of a field.

Further Indictment of Jacob's Heirs

12 Jacob fled to the territory
　　of Aram. Gn 28:5
Israel worked to earn
　　a wife; Gn 29:20
he tended flocks for a wife.
13 The Lord brought Israel
　　from Egypt by a prophet,
and Israel was tended
　　by a prophet.
14 Ephraim has provoked
　　bitter anger, 2Kg 17:7-18
so his Lord will leave
　　his bloodguilt on him
and repay him
　　for his contempt. Dn 11:18

13 When Ephraim spoke,
　　there was trembling;
he was exalted in Israel. Jdg 8:1
But he incurred guilt
　　through Baal and died.

2 Now they continue to sin
and make themselves
　　a cast image, Is 46:6; Jr 10:4; Hs 2:8
idols skillfully made
　　from their silver, Is 44:17-20
all of them the work
　　of craftsmen. Hs 8:6
People say about them,
"Let the men who sacrifice D
　　kiss the calves." Hs 8:5-6;10:5
3 Therefore, they will be
　　like the morning mist, Hs 6:4
like the early dew
　　that vanishes,

A 12:4 LXX, Syr; MT reads us　B 12:8 Lit iniquity which is sin　C 12:9 LXX reads God who brought you out of　D 13:2 Or "Those who make human sacrifices

like chaff blown
    from a threshing floor,   Ps 1:4
or like smoke from a window.

Death and Resurrection

4 I have been the LORD your God
ever since [A] the land of Egypt;
you know no God but me,
and no Savior exists
    besides me.   Is 43:11; 45:21-22

5 I knew [B] you in the wilderness,
in the land of drought.

6 When they had pasture,
they became satisfied;   Dt 8:12,14
they were satisfied,
and their hearts
    became proud.   Hs 7:14
Therefore they forgot me.

7 So I will be like a lion
    to them;   Hs 5:14
I will lurk like a leopard
    on the path.   Jr 5:6

8 I will attack them
like a bear robbed of her cubs
and tear open the rib cage
    over their hearts.
I will devour them there
    like a lioness,   Ps 50:22
like a wild beast that
    would rip them open.

9 I will destroy you, Israel;
you have no help but me. [C]

10 Where now is your king, [D]
that he may save you in all
    your cities,
and the [E] rulers [F] you
    demanded, saying,   Hs 7:7
"Give me a king and leaders"?

11 I give you a king in my anger
and take away a king
    in my wrath.   1Kg 14:7-10; Hs 10:7

12 Ephraim's guilt is preserved;
his sin is stored up.   Dt 32:34-35

13 Labor pains come on him.
He is not a wise son;   Dt 32:6
when the time comes,
he will not be born. [G]   Is 37:3; 66:9

14 I will ransom them
    from the power of Sheol.
I will redeem [H] them
    from death.   Hs 6:1-2
Death, where are your barbs?
Sheol, where is your sting?
Compassion is hidden
    from my eyes.   Jr 20:16; 31:35-37

The Coming Judgment

15 Although he flourishes
    among his brothers, [I]   Gn 49:22
an east wind will come,   Gn 41:6
a wind from the LORD
    rising up from the desert.
His water source will fail,
and his spring will run dry.
The wind [J] will plunder
    the treasury   Jr 20:5
of every precious item.

16 Samaria will bear her guilt
because she has rebelled
    against her God.   Hs 7:14
They will fall by the sword;
their children will be dashed
    to pieces,   Hs 10:14
and their pregnant women
    ripped open.   2Kg 15:16

A Plea to Repent

14 Israel, return to the LORD
    your God,   Hs 6:1; 10:12; 12:6
for you have stumbled
    in your iniquity.   Hs 4:8; 5:5; 9:7

[A]**13:4** DSS, LXX read *God who brought you out of destruction, Israel, who will help you?*   [B]**13:5** LXX, Syr read *fed*   [C]**13:9** LXX reads *At your*   [D]**13:10** LXX, Syr, Vg; MT reads *I will be your king*   [E]**13:10** Lit *your*   [F]**13:10** Or *judges*   [G]**13:13** Lit *he will not present himself at the opening of the womb for sons*   [H]**13:14** Or *Should I ransom . . . ? Should I redeem . . . ?*   [I]**13:15** Or *among reeds*   [J]**13:15** Probably the Assyrian king

2 Take words of repentance
with you   Mc 7:18-19
and return to the LORD.
Say to him: "Forgive all
our iniquity
and accept what is good,
so that we may repay you
with praise[A] from our[B] lips.
3 Assyria will not save us,   Hs 5:13
we will not ride on horses,
and we will no longer
proclaim, 'Our gods!'   Hs 4:12
to the work of our hands.
For the fatherless
receives compassion in you."

A Promise of Restoration

4 I will heal their apostasy;
I will freely love them,   Zph 3:17
for my anger will have turned
from him.   Is 12:1
5 I will be like the dew to Israel;
he will blossom like the lily
and take root like
the cedars of Lebanon.   Is 35:2
6 His new branches will spread,
and his splendor will be
like the olive tree,   Jr 11:16

his fragrance, like
the forest of Lebanon.   Sg 4:11
7 The people will return
and live beneath his shade.
They will grow grain   Hs 2:21-22
and blossom like the vine.
His renown will be
like the wine of Lebanon.

8 Ephraim, why should I[C] have
anything more
to do with idols?   Jb 34:32
It is I who answer and watch
over him.
I am like
a flourishing pine tree;
your fruit comes from me.

9 Let whoever is wise
understand these things,
and whoever is insightful
recognize them.
For the ways of the LORD
are right,   Ps 111:7-8; Zph 3:5
and the righteous walk
in them,   Is 26:7
but the rebellious stumble
in them.   Is 1:28

[A]14:2 LXX reads with the fruit   [B]14:2 Lit repay the bulls of our   [C]14:8 LXX reads he

JOEL

1 The word of the Lord that came to Joel son of Pethuel: Hs 1:1; Mc 1:1

A Plague of Locusts

2 Hear this, you elders;   Hs 4:1; 5:1
listen, all you inhabitants
of the land.
Has anything like this
ever happened in your days
or in the days
of your ancestors?
3 Tell your children about it,
and let your children
tell their children,
and their children
the next generation.
4 What the devouring locust
has left,   Ex 10:4; Jl 2:25; Am 4:9
the swarming locust
has eaten;
what the swarming locust
has left,
the young locust has eaten;
and what the young locust
has left,
the destroying locust
has eaten.   Ps 78:46; Is 33:4

5 Wake up, you drunkards,
and weep;   Jl 3:3
wail, all you wine drinkers,
because of the sweet wine,
for it has been taken
from your mouth.
6 For a nation has invaded
my land,   Jl 2:2,11,25
powerful
and without number;
its teeth are the teeth of a lion,
and it has the fangs
of a lioness.   Rv 9:7-8

7 It has devastated
my grapevine
and splintered my fig tree.
It has stripped off its bark
and thrown it away;
its branches
have turned white.
8 Grieve like a young woman
dressed in sackcloth,   Is 22:12
mourning for the husband
of her youth.
9 Grain and drink offerings
have been cut off   Hs 9:4; Jl 2:14
from the house of the Lord;
the priests, who
are ministers
of the Lord, mourn.   Hs 10:5
10 The fields are destroyed;   Is 24:4
the land grieves;
indeed, the grain
is destroyed;
the new wine is dried up;
and the fresh oil fails.   Dt 28:51
11 Be ashamed, you farmers,
wail, you vinedressers,^A
over the wheat
and the barley,
because the harvest
of the field has perished.
12 The grapevine is dried up,
and the fig tree is withered;
the pomegranate,
the date palm,
and the apple —   Sg 7:8; Hg 2:19
all the trees of the orchard —
have withered.
Indeed, human joy
has dried up.   Is 16:10; 24:11

13 Dress in sackcloth
and lament, you priests;

A 1:11 Or *The farmers are dismayed, the vinedressers wail*

wail, you ministers
of the altar.   Jr 9:10
Come and spend the night
in sackcloth,   1Kg 21:27
you ministers of my God,
because grain
and drink offerings
are withheld from the house
of your God.

14 Announce a sacred fast;
proclaim an assembly!
Gather the elders   Jl 1:2
and all the residents
of the land
at the house of the LORD
your God,   2Ch 20:3; Neh 9:1; Jr 36:6,9
and cry out to the LORD.   Jnh 3:8

The Day of the LORD

15 Woe because of that day!
For the day of the LORD is near
and will come as devastation
from the Almighty.   Is 13:6,9
16 Hasn't the food been cut off
before our eyes,   Is 3:7
joy and gladness   Is 16:10; Jr 48:33
from the house of our God?
17 The seeds lie shriveled
in their casings. A   Is 17:10-11
The storehouses are in ruin,
and the granaries are
broken down,
because the grain has
withered away.
18 How the animals groan!   Jr 12:4
The herds of cattle wander
in confusion
since they have no pasture.
Even the flocks of sheep and
goats suffer punishment.
19 I call to you, LORD,   Ps 50:15; Mc 7:7
for fire has consumed
the pastures
of the wilderness,   Jr 9:10; Am 7:4
and flames have devoured
all the trees of the orchard.

20 Even the wild animals
cry out to B you,   Ps 104:21; 147:9
for the river beds
are dried up,   1Kg 17:7; 18:5
and fire has consumed
the pastures
of the wilderness.

2 Blow the horn in Zion;   Jr 4:5
sound the alarm
on my holy mountain!
Let all the residents
of the land tremble,
for the day of the LORD
is coming;   Jl 1:15; 2:11,31; 3:14
in fact, it is near —
2 a day of darkness and gloom,
a day of clouds
and total darkness,   Is 60:2
like the dawn spreading
over the mountains;
a great
and strong people appears,
such as never existed
in ages past   Lm 1:12; Dn 9:12; 12:1
and never will again
in all the generations to come.

3 A fire devours in front of them,
and behind them
a flame blazes.
The land in front of them
is like the garden of Eden,
but behind them,
it is like a desert wasteland;
there is no escape from them.
4 Their appearance is like that
of horses,   Rv 9:7
and they gallop
like war horses.
5 They bound on the tops
of the mountains.
Their sound is like the sound
of chariots,   Rv 9:9
like the sound of fiery flames
consuming stubble,   Is 5:24

A 1:17 Or clods; Hb obscure   B 1:20 Or animals pant for; Hb obscure

like a mighty army deployed
  for war.

6 Nations writhe in horror
    before them;   Is 13:8; Nah 2:10
  all faces turn pale.
7 They attack
    as warriors attack;
  they scale walls as men
    of war do.
  Each goes on his own path,
  and they do not change
    their course.
8 They do not push each other;
  each proceeds
    on his own path.
  They dodge the arrows,
    never stopping.
9 They storm the city;
  they run on the wall;
  they climb into the houses;
  they enter
    through the windows
    like thieves.   Jr 9:21

10 The earth quakes
    before them;   Ps 18:7; Nah 1:5
  the sky shakes.
  The sun and moon
    grow dark,   Is 13:10; 34:4; Jr 4:23
  and the stars cease
    their shining.   Jl 3:15
11 The LORD makes his voice
    heard   Ps 46:6; Is 13:4
  in the presence of his army.
  His camp is very large;
  those who carry out
    his command are powerful.
  Indeed, the day of the LORD
    is terrible and dreadful —
    who can endure it?   Ezk 22:14

God's Call for Repentance

12 Even now —
    this is
    the LORD's declaration —

A 2:16 Or *elders*

turn to me with all
    your heart,   1Kg 8:35-40; 2Ch 7:14
  with fasting, weeping,
    and mourning.   Est 4:3
13 Tear your hearts,   Ps 51:17; Is 57:15
  not just your clothes,   Jr 41:5
  and return to the LORD
    your God.
  For he is gracious
    and compassionate,
  slow to anger,
    abounding in faithful love,
  and he relents
    from sending disaster.
14 Who knows? He may turn
    and relent   Jnh 3:9
  and leave a blessing
    behind him,   Hg 2:19
  so you can offer grain
    and wine
  to the LORD your God.   Jl 1:9,13

15 Blow the horn in Zion!   Jl 2:1
  Announce a sacred fast;
  proclaim an assembly.
16 Gather the people;
  sanctify the congregation;
  assemble the aged;A   2Ch 20:3
  gather the infants,
  even babies nursing
    at the breast.
  Let the groom
    leave his bedroom,   Ps 19:5
  and the bride
    her honeymoon chamber.
17 Let the priests,
    the LORD's ministers,   Jl 1:9
  weep between the portico
    and the altar.   Hs 10:5; Jl 1:13
  Let them say:
  "Have pity
    on your people, LORD,   Is 37:20
  and do not make
    your inheritance a disgrace,
  an object of scorn
    among the nations.

Why should it be said
    among the peoples,
    'Where is their God?'" Ps 42:3,10

God's Response to His People

¹⁸ Then the LORD became jealous
for his land and spared his people.
¹⁹ The LORD answered his people:
Look, I am about to send you
    grain, new wine,
        and fresh oil.   Jr 31:12; Hs 2:21-22
You will be satiated with them,
and I will no longer make you
    a disgrace
        among the nations.   Ezk 34:29

²⁰ I will drive the northerner
        far from you   Jr 1:14-15
    and banish him to a dry
        and desolate land,
    his front ranks
        into the Dead Sea,   Zch 14:8
    and his rear guard into
        the Mediterranean Sea.
    His stench will rise;
    yes, his rotten smell will rise,
    for he has done
        astonishing things.

²¹ Don't be afraid, land;   Jl 1:10
    rejoice and be glad,
    for the LORD has done
        astonishing things.   Ps 126:2-3
²² Don't be afraid, wild animals,
    for the wilderness pastures
        have turned green,   Ps 65:12
    the trees bear their fruit,
    and the fig tree
        and grapevine yield
        their riches.
²³ Children of Zion, rejoice
        and be glad   Ps 149:2
    in the LORD your God,   Is 12:2-6
    because he gives you
        the autumn rain
    for your vindication.ᴬ Dt 11:13-15

ᴬ 2:23 Or righteousness

He sends showers for you,
    both autumn and spring rain
        as before.   Hs 6:3; Zch 10:1
²⁴ The threshing floors
        will be full of grain,   Lv 26:10
    and the vats will overflow
    with new wine and fresh oil.

²⁵ I will repay you for the years
    that the swarming locust ate,
    the young locust,
        the destroying locust,
    and the devouring locust —
    my great army that I sent
        against you.
²⁶ You will have plenty to eat
    and be satisfied.   Dt 11:15; Is 62:9
    You will praise the name
        of the LORD your God,   Ps 113:1
    who has dealt wondrously
        with you.   Ps 126:2; Is 25:1
    My people will never again
        be put to shame.   Is 45:17
²⁷ You will know
    that I am present in Israel
    and that I am the LORD
        your God,
    and there is no other.   Dt 4:35,39
    My people will never again
        be put to shame.   Is 49:23

God's Promise of His Spirit

²⁸ After this   Ac 2:17-21
    I will pour out my Spirit
        on all humanity;   Is 32:15; 44:3
    then your sons
        and your daughters
        will prophesy,
    your old men
        will have dreams,
    and your young men
        will see visions.
²⁹ I will even pour out my Spirit
    on the male and female slaves
        in those days.   1Co 12:13
³⁰ I will display wonders

in the heavens and on
the earth: Lk 21:11,25-26
blood, fire, and columns
of smoke.

31 The sun will be turned
to darkness
and the moon to blood   Is 13:9-10
before the great and terrible
day of the LORD comes.

32 Then everyone who calls
on the name of the LORD
will be saved,   Rm 10:13
for there will be an escape
for those on Mount Zion
and in Jerusalem,
as the LORD promised,   Ob 17
among the survivors
the LORD calls.

Judgment of the Nations

3 Yes, in those days
and at that time,
when I restore the fortunes
of Judah and Jerusalem,

2 I will gather all the nations
and take them to the Valley
of Jehoshaphat. A   Jl 3:12,14
I will enter into judgment
with them there   Is 66:16; Jr 25:31
because of my people,
my inheritance Israel.
The nations have scattered
the Israelites
in foreign countries   Jr 50:17
and divided up my land.

3 They cast lots for my people;
they bartered a boy
for a prostitute
and sold a girl for wine
to drink.   Am 2:6

4 And also: Tyre, Sidon, and all
the territories of Philistia — what
are you to me? Are you paying me
back or trying to get even with me?

I will quickly bring retribution on
your heads. 5 For you took my silver and gold and carried my finest
treasures to your temples. 6 You
sold the people of Judah and Jerusalem to the Greeks to remove
them far from their own territory.
7 Look, I am about to rouse them
up from the place where you sold
them; I will bring retribution on
your heads. 8 I will sell your sons
and daughters to the people of Judah, and they will sell them to the
Sabeans, B to a distant nation, for
the LORD has spoken.   Am 1:9; Zch 9:2-4

9 Proclaim this
among the nations: Jr 51:27-28
Prepare for holy war;   Jr 6:4
rouse the warriors;   Is 8:9-10
let all the men of war
advance and attack!

10 Beat your plows into swords
and your pruning knives
into spears.   Is 2:4; Mc 4:3
Let even the weakling say,
"I am a warrior."

11 Come quickly, C all
you surrounding nations;
gather yourselves.   Ezk 38:15-16
Bring down
your warriors there, LORD.

12 Let the nations be roused
and come to the Valley
of Jehoshaphat,
for there I will sit down
to judge all
the surrounding nations.

13 Swing the sickle
because the harvest is ripe.
Come and trample the grapes
because the winepress is full;
the wine vats overflow
because the wickedness
of the nations is extreme.

A 3:2 = The LORD Will Judge   B 3:8 Probably the south Arabian kingdom of Sheba (modern Yemen)
C 3:11 LXX, Syr, Tg read Gather yourselves and come; Hb obscure

14 Multitudes, multitudes Is 34:2-8
  in the valley of decision!
  For the day of the Lord is near
  in the valley of decision.
15 The sun and moon
    will grow dark,
  and the stars will cease
    their shining. Jl 2:10,31
16 The Lord will roar from Zion
  and make his voice heard
    from Jerusalem; Jr 25:30; Am 1:2
  heaven and earth will shake.
  But the Lord will be a refuge
    for his people, Ps 46:1; 62:8
  a stronghold for the Israelites.

Israel Blessed

17 Then you will know
  that I am the Lord your God,
  who dwells in Zion,
    my holy mountain. Is 11:9; 56:7
  Jerusalem will be holy, Is 4:3
  and foreigners will never
    overrun it again. Is 52:1; Nah 1:15
18 In that day

the mountains will drip
    with sweet wine, Am 9:13
  and the hills will flow
    with milk. Ex 3:8
  All the streams of Judah
    will flow with water, Is 30:25
  and a spring will issue
    from the Lord's house,
  watering the Valley
    of Acacias. A Nm 25:1; Ezk 47:8
19 Egypt will become desolate,
  and Edom
    a desert wasteland,
  because of the violence done
    to the people of Judah Ob 10
  in whose land they shed
    innocent blood.
20 But Judah will be
    inhabited forever, Ezk 37:25
  and Jerusalem
    from generation
    to generation.
21 I will pardon their bloodguilt, B
  which I have not pardoned,
  for the Lord dwells in Zion.

A 3:18 Or *Shittim* B 3:21 LXX, Syr read *I will avenge their blood*

AMOS

1 The words of Amos, who was one of the sheep breeders[A] from Tekoa — what he saw regarding Israel in the days of King Uzziah of Judah and Jeroboam son of Jehoash, king of Israel, two years before the earthquake. 2Kg 3:4; Am 7:14-15

² He said:

The LORD roars from Zion
and makes his voice heard
from Jerusalem;
the pastures
of the shepherds mourn, [B]
and the summit
of Carmel withers. Am 9:3

Judgment on Israel's Neighbors

³ The LORD says:
I will not relent
from punishing Damascus
for three crimes, even four,
because they threshed Gilead
with iron sledges.
⁴ Therefore, I will send fire
against Hazael's palace,
and it will consume
Ben-hadad's citadels.
⁵ I will break down the gates [C]
of Damascus. Gn 22:17; Neh 1:3
I will cut off the ruler
from the Valley of Aven,
and the one who
wields the scepter
from Beth-eden.
The people of Aram
will be exiled to Kir. 2Kg 16:9
The LORD has spoken.

⁶ The LORD says:
I will not relent
from punishing Gaza

for three crimes, even four,
because they exiled
a whole community,
handing them over
to Edom.
⁷ Therefore, I will send fire
against the walls of Gaza,
and it will consume
its citadels.
⁸ I will cut off the ruler
from Ashdod, 2Ch 26:6; Am 3:9
and the one who wields
the scepter from Ashkelon.
I will also turn my hand
against Ekron,
and the remainder
of the Philistines
will perish. Is 14:29-31; Ezk 25:16
The Lord GOD has spoken.

⁹ The LORD says:
I will not relent
from punishing Tyre Is 23
for three crimes, even four,
because they handed over
a whole community of exiles
to Edom
and broke [D] a treaty
of brotherhood. 1Kg 5:1,12
¹⁰ Therefore, I will send fire
against the walls of Tyre,
and it will consume
its citadels.

¹¹ The LORD says:
I will not relent
from punishing Edom
for three crimes, even four,
because he pursued
his brother with the sword.
He stifled his compassion,

A 1:1 Or the shepherds   B 1:2 Or dry up   C 1:5 Lit gate bars   D 1:9 Lit and did not remember

his anger tore
    at him continually,   Gn 37:33
and he harbored
    his rage incessantly.

¹² Therefore, I will send fire
    against Teman,   Jr 49:7,20
and it will consume
    the citadels of Bozrah.

¹³ The Lord says:
I will not relent
    from punishing
    the Ammonites   Jr 49:1-6
for three crimes, even four,
because they ripped open
the pregnant women
    of Gilead   2Kg 8:12; 15:16; Hs 13:16
in order to enlarge
    their territory.   Is 5:8; Ezk 35:10

¹⁴ Therefore, I will set fire
    to the walls of Rabbah,   Jr 49:2
and it will consume
    its citadels.
There will be shouting
    on the day of battle   Ezk 21:22
and a violent wind on the day
    of the storm.   Is 29:6; 30:30

¹⁵ Their king and his princes
will go into exile together.
The Lord has spoken.

2 The Lord says:
I will not relent
    from punishing Moab   Jr 48
for three crimes, even four,
because he burned
    the bones
of the king of Edom to lime.

² Therefore, I will send fire
    against Moab,
and it will consume
    the citadels of Kerioth.
Moab will die with a tumult,
with shouting and the sound
    of the ram's horn.

³ I will cut off the judge
    from the land   Ps 2:10; 141:6

and kill all its officials
    with him.   Jb 12:21; Is 40:23
The Lord has spoken.

Judgment on Judah

⁴ The Lord says:
I will not relent
    from punishing Judah   Hs 2:12
for three crimes, even four,
because they have rejected
    the instruction of the Lord
and have not kept
    his statutes.   Jr 44:10; Ezk 5:7
The lies that
    their ancestors followed
have led them astray.

⁵ Therefore, I will send fire
    against Judah,   Jr 17:27; 21:10
and it will consume
    the citadels of Jerusalem.

Judgment on Israel

⁶ The Lord says:
I will not relent
    from punishing Israel
for three crimes, even four,
because they sell
    a righteous person
    for silver
and a needy person for a pair
    of sandals.   Dt 16:18-20; Am 5:12; 8:6

⁷ They trample the heads
    of the poor   Am 5:11; 8:4; Mc 2:2,9
on the dust of the ground
and obstruct the path
    of the needy.   Jb 24:4
A man and his father
    have sexual relations
with the same girl,   Hs 4:14
profaning my holy name.

⁸ They stretch out beside
    every altar   Am 3:14
on garments taken
    as collateral,   Ex 22:26
and in the house of their God
they drink wine obtained
    through fines.   Am 4:1; 6:6

9 Yet I destroyed the Amorite
   as Israel advanced;   Jos 10:12
his height was
   like the cedars,   Nm 13:28-33
and he was as sturdy
   as the oaks;
I destroyed his fruit above
   and his roots beneath.   Mal 4:1
10 And I brought you
   from the land of Egypt   Am 3:1
and led you forty years
   in the wilderness   Dt 2:7
in order to possess the land
   of the Amorite.   Nm 21:25
11 I raised up some of your sons
   as prophets   Dt 18:18-19; Jr 1:4-5
and some of your young men
   as Nazirites.   Nm 6:1-21; Jdg 13:2-5
Is this not the case, Israelites?
This is
   the LORD's declaration.
12 But you made the Nazirites
   drink wine
and commanded
   the prophets,
"Do not prophesy."   Jr 11:21
13 Look, I am about
   to crush^A you in your place
as a wagon crushes when full
   of grain.
14 Escape will fail the swift,
the strong one will not
   maintain his strength,   Jr 9:23
and the warrior will not save
   his life.
15 The archer will not stand
   his ground,   Jr 51:56; Ezk 39:3
the one who is swift of foot
   will not save himself,
and the one riding a horse
   will not save his life.   Is 31:3
16 Even the most courageous
   of the warriors
will flee naked on that day —
this is
   the LORD's declaration.

^A 2:13 Or *hinder*; Hb obscure

God's Reasons for Punishing Israel

3 Listen to this message that the
LORD has spoken against you,
Israelites, against the entire clan
that I brought from the land of
Egypt: Am 2:10
2 I have known only you   Ex 19:5-6
out of all the clans of the earth;
therefore, I will punish you
   for all your iniquities.   Jr 14:10
3 Can two walk together
   without agreeing to meet?
4 Does a lion roar in the forest
   when it has no prey?
Does a young lion growl
   from its lair
unless it has
   captured something?
5 Does a bird land in a trap
   on the ground
if there is no bait for it?
Does a trap spring
   from the ground
when it has caught nothing?
6 If a ram's horn is blown
   in a city,   Jr 4:5,19,21; 6:1; Hs 5:8
aren't people afraid?   Nm 10:9
If a disaster occurs in a city,
   hasn't the LORD done it?
7 Indeed, the Lord GOD
   does nothing
without revealing
   his counsel
to his servants the prophets.
8 A lion has roared;   Am 1:2
   who will not fear?
The Lord GOD has spoken;
   who will not prophesy?

9 Proclaim on the citadels
   in Ashdod   1Sm 5:1; Am 1:8
and on the citadels in
   the land of Egypt:
Assemble on the mountains
   of Samaria,   Am 4:1; 6:1

and see the great turmoil
　　in the city
and the acts of oppression
　　within it.　　　　　Am 5:11; 6:8
10　The people are incapable
　　of doing right —　　Ps 14:4; Jr 4:22
　　this is
　　the LORD's declaration —
　　those who store up violence
　　and destruction　　　Hab 2:8-10
　　in their citadels.
11 Therefore, the Lord GOD says:
　　An enemy will surround
　　　the land;
　　he will destroy　　　　Am 6:14
　　your strongholds　　　Am 2:14
　　and plunder your citadels.

12　The LORD says:
　　As the shepherd snatches
　　　two legs
　　or a piece of an ear
　　from the lion's mouth,
　　so the Israelites who live
　　　in Samaria
　　will be rescued
　　with only the corner of a bed
　　or the A cushion B of a couch. C

13　Listen and testify
　　against the house
　　of Jacob —　　　　　Ezk 2:7
　　this is the declaration
　　of the Lord GOD,
　　the God of Armies.
14　I will punish the altars
　　of Bethel　　Hs 10:5-8,14-15; Am 4:4
　　on the day I punish Israel
　　　for its crimes;
　　the horns of the altar will be
　　　cut off　　Lv 8:15; 16:18-19; 1Kg 1:50-51
　　and fall to the ground.　　Hs 10:1-2
15　I will demolish
　　the winter house　　　Jr 36:22
　　and the summer house;

the houses inlaid with ivory
　　will be destroyed,　　1Kg 22:39
and the great houses
　　will come to an end.　　Am 2:5
This is
　　the LORD's declaration.

Social and Spiritual Corruption

4 Listen to this message,
　　you cows of Bashan　　Ps 22:12
who are on the hill
　　of Samaria,
women who oppress the poor
and crush the needy,　　Ex 23:3,6
who say to their husbands,
"Bring us something to drink."

2 The Lord GOD has sworn by his
holiness:　　　　Ps 89:35; Am 6:8; 8:7
　　Look, the days are coming D
　　when you will be taken away
　　　with hooks,　　Is 37:29; Ezk 38:4
　　every last one of you
　　　with fishhooks.　　　2Kg 19:28
3　You will go through breaches
　　　in the wall,　　　　Jr 52:7
　　each woman straight ahead,
　　and you will be driven along
　　　toward Harmon.
　　This is
　　the LORD's declaration.

4　Come to Bethel and rebel;
　　rebel even more at Gilgal!
　　Bring your sacrifices
　　　every morning,　　Am 5:21-22
　　your tenths every three days.
5　Offer leavened bread as
　　　a thank offering,　　Lv 7:12
　　and loudly proclaim
　　　your freewill offerings,
　　for that is what you Israelites
　　　love to do!　　Jr 7:9-10; Hs 9:1,10
　　This is declaration of the
　　Lord GOD.

A 3:12 Or *Israelites will be rescued, those who sit in Samaria on a corner of a bed or a*　　B 3:12 Hb obscure
C 3:12 LXX, Aq, Sym, Theod, Syr, Tg, Vg read *or in Damascus*　　D 4:2 Lit *coming on you*

God's Discipline and Israel's Apostasy

6 I gave you absolutely nothing
       to eat^A   Is 3:1; Jr 14:18
in all your cities,
a shortage of food in all
       your communities,
yet you did not return to me.
       This is
       the LORD's declaration.

7 I also withheld the rain
       from you   Jr 3:1-3; 5:23-25
while there were still
       three months until harvest.
I sent rain on one city
but no rain on another.
One field received rain
while a field
       with no rain withered.

8 Two or three cities staggered
to another city to drink water
but were not satisfied,   Ezk 4:16
yet you did not return to me.
       This is
       the LORD's declaration.

9 I struck you with blight
       and mildew;   Dt 28:22; Hg 2:17
the locust devoured   Jl 1:4
your many gardens
       and vineyards,
your fig trees and olive trees,
yet you did not return to me.
       This is
       the LORD's declaration.

10 I sent plagues like those
       of Egypt;   Ex 11:4-5; Dt 28:27,60
I killed your young men
       with the sword,   Jr 11:22; 18:21
along with
       your captured horses.
I caused the stench
       of your camp
to fill your nostrils,   Is 34:3

yet you did not return to me.
       This is
       the LORD's declaration.

11 I overthrew some of you
       as I^B overthrew Sodom
       and Gomorrah,   Gn 19:24-25
and you were
       like a burning stick
snatched from a fire,   Zch 3:1-2
yet you did not return
       to me —   Is 9:13
       This is
       the LORD's declaration.

12 Therefore, Israel, that is what
       I will do to you,
and since I will do that to you,
Israel, prepare to meet
       your God!   Is 32:11; 64:2; Jr 5:22

13 He is here:
the one who forms
       the mountains,   Jb 38:4-7; Ps 65:6
creates the wind,   Ps 135:7
and reveals his thoughts
       to man,   Ps 139:2; Dn 2:30
the one who makes the dawn
       out of darkness
and strides on the heights
       of the earth.   Mc 1:3
The LORD, the God of Armies,
       is his name.   Am 5:8-9,27; 9:5-6

Lamentation for Israel

5 Listen to this message that I
   am singing for you, a lament,
house of Israel: Jr 7:29; 9:10,17; Ezk 19:1

2 She has fallen;
Virgin Israel will never
       rise again.   Jr 14:17; 31:4,21; Am 8:14
She lies abandoned
       on her land
with no one to raise her up.

3 For the Lord GOD says:
The city that marches out
       a thousand strong

---

^A 4:6 Lit you cleanness of teeth   ^B 4:11 Lit God

will have only
   a hundred left,   Is 6:13
and the one that marches out
   a hundred strong
will have only ten left
   in the house of Israel.   Am 6:9

Seek God and Live

⁴ For the LORD says to the house of
Israel:
   Seek me and live!   Dt 4:29; 32:46-47
⁵ Do not seek Bethel   1Kg 12:28-29
   or go to Gilgal   1Sm 7:16; 11:14
   or journey to Beer-sheba,
   for Gilgal will certainly go
      into exile,
   and Bethel will come
      to nothing.
⁶ Seek the LORD and live,
   or he will spread like fire
   throughout the house
      of Joseph;
   it will consume everything
   with no one at Bethel
      to extinguish it.   Is 33:14; 66:24
⁷ Those who turn justice
      into wormwood   Am 6:12
   also throw righteousness
      to the ground.

⁸ The one who made
      the Pleiades and Orion,   Jb 9:9
   who turns darkness ᴬ
      into dawn   Gn 1:2-3; Jb 38:12
   and darkens day into night,
   who summons the water
      of the sea   Ps 104:6-9; Jr 10:13
   and pours it out
      over the surface
      of the earth —   Jb 36:27-30
   the LORD is his name.   Am 4:13
⁹ He brings destruction ᴮ
      on the strong, ᶜ   Is 29:5
   and it falls
      on the fortress.   Mc 5:11

¹⁰ They hate the one
   who convicts the guilty
at the city gate,
and they despise the one
   who speaks with integrity.
¹¹ Therefore, because you
      trample on the poor   Am 3:9
and exact a grain tax
   from him,
you will never live
   in the houses of cut stone
you have built;
you will never drink the wine
from the lush vineyards
you have planted.   Dt 28:30; Mc 6:15
¹² For I know your crimes
      are many
and your sins innumerable.
They oppress the righteous,
   take a bribe,   Is 1:23; 5:23
and deprive the poor
   of justice at the city gates.
¹³ Therefore, those who have
      insight will keep silent ᴰ
at such a time,
for the days are evil.

¹⁴ Pursue good and not evil
so that you may live,
and the LORD, the God
   of Armies,
will be with you
as you have claimed.   Is 48:1-2
¹⁵ Hate evil and love good;
   establish justice in the city
      gate.   Is 1:17
Perhaps the LORD, the God
   of Armies,
   will be gracious   Jl 2:14
to the remnant of Joseph.

¹⁶ Therefore the LORD, the God of
Armies, the Lord, says:
There will be wailing in all
   the public squares;   Jr 9:10,18-20

ᴬ5:8 Or *turns the shadow of death*   ᴮ5:9 Hb obscure   ᶜ5:9 Or *stronghold*   ᴰ5:13 Or *who are prudent
will perish*

they will cry out in anguish[A]
   in all the streets.
The farmer will be called on
   to mourn,   Jl 1:11
and professional mourners[B]
   to wail.   Jr 9:17

17 There will be wailing in all
   the vineyards,   Is 16:10; Jr 48:33
for I will pass among you.
The LORD has spoken.

The Day of the LORD

18 Woe to you who long for
   the day of the LORD!   Is 5:19
What will the day of the LORD
   be for you?
It will be darkness
   and not light.   Is 5:30

19 It will be like a man who flees
   from a lion   Jb 20:24; Is 24:17
only to have a bear
   confront him.
He goes home and
   rests his hand
   against the wall
only to have a snake bite him.

20 Won't the day of the LORD
be darkness rather than light,
even gloom
   without any brightness
   in it?   Jl 2:2; Zph 1:15

21 I hate, I despise, your feasts!
I can't stand the stench
of your solemn assemblies.

22 Even if you offer me
your burnt offerings
   and grain offerings,   Mc 6:6-7
I will not accept them;   Jr 14:12
I will have no regard
for your fellowship offerings
   of fattened cattle.   Lv 7:11-15

23 Take away from me the noise
   of your songs!
I will not listen to the music
   of your harps.   Is 5:12

24 But let justice flow like water,
   and righteousness,
   like an unfailing stream.

25 "House of Israel, was it sacrifices and grain offerings that you presented to me during the forty years in the wilderness? 26 But you have taken up[C] Sakkuth your king and Kaiwan your star god,[D] images you have made for yourselves. 27 So I will send you into exile beyond Damascus." The LORD, the God of Armies, is his name. He has spoken.   Dt 32:17; Jos 24:14; Neh 9:18-21; Ac 7:42-43

Woe to the Complacent

6 Woe to those who are at ease
   in Zion   Is 32:9-11; Zph 1:12
and to those who feel secure
   on the hill of Samaria —
the notable people in this
   first of the nations,
those the house of Israel
   comes to.

2 Cross over to Calneh and see;
go from there
   to great Hamath;   1Kg 8:65; Is 10:9
then go down to Gath
   of the Philistines.   1Sm 5:8
Are you better than
   these kingdoms?
Is their territory larger
   than yours?

3 You dismiss any thought
   of the evil day   Am 9:10
and bring in a reign
   of violence.   Am 3:10

4 They lie on beds
   inlaid with ivory,   Am 3:15
sprawled out
   on their couches,   Am 3:12
and dine on lambs
   from the flock   Ezk 34:2-3

[A]5:16 Lit will say, "Alas! Alas!"   [B]5:16 Lit and those skilled in lamentation   [C]5:26 Or you will lift up
[D]5:26 LXX reads taken up the tent of Molech and the star of your god Rephan; Ac 7:43

and calves from the stall.
5 They improvise songs[A]
   to the sound of the harp
   and invent[B] their own
   musical instruments
   like David.   1Ch 15:16
6 They drink wine
   by the bowlful   Am 2:8; 4:1
   and anoint themselves
   with the finest oils
   but do not grieve
   over the ruin of Joseph.
7 Therefore, they will now go
   into exile
   as the first of the captives,
   and the feasting of those
   who sprawl out   1Kg 20:16-21
   will come to an end.

Israel's Pride Judged

8 The Lord God has sworn by himself — this is the declaration of the
Lord, the God of Armies: Gn 22:16
   I loathe Jacob's pride   Lv 26:30
   and hate his citadels,   Am 3:10-11
   so I will hand over the city
   and everything in it.   Hs 11:6

9 And if there are ten men left in
one house, they will die. 10 A close
relative[C] and burner[D] will remove
his corpse[E] from the house. He will
call to someone in the inner recesses of the house, "Any more with
you?"   1Sm 31:12; 2Ch 16:14; Jr 34:5; Am 5:3
   That person will reply, "None."
   Then he will say, "Silence, because
the Lord's name must not be in-
voked."   Is 48:1; Jr 44:26; Hs 4:15
11 For the Lord commands:
   The large house
      will be smashed to pieces,
   and the small house
      to rubble.   Am 1:1; 9:9

12 Do horses gallop
      on the cliffs?
   Does anyone plow there
      with oxen?[F]
   Yet you have turned justice
      into poison   1Kg 21:7-13; Is 59:13-14
   and the fruit of righteousness
      into wormwood —   Is 5:20
13 you who rejoice over Lo-debar
   and say, "Didn't we
      capture Karnaim
   for ourselves by our
      own strength?"   Ps 75:4
14 But look, I am raising up
      a nation
   against you, house of Israel —
      this is the declaration
      of the Lord,
      the God of Armies —
   and they will oppress you
   from the entrance of Hamath[G]
   to the Brook of the Arabah.[H]

First Vision: Locusts

7 The Lord God showed me this:
   He was forming a swarm of locusts at the time the spring crop
first began to sprout — after the
cutting of the king's hay. 2 When the
locusts finished eating the vegetation of the land, I said, "Lord God,
please forgive! How will Jacob survive since he is so small?"   Ex 10:12-15
3 The Lord relented concerning
this. "It will not happen," he said.

Second Vision: Fire

4 The Lord God showed me this: The
Lord God was calling for a judgment by fire. It consumed the great
deep and devoured the land. 5 Then
I said, "Lord God, please stop! How
will Jacob survive since he is so
small?"   Ps 85:4; Am 1:3–2:5; Jl 2:17

[A]6:5 Hb obscure   [B]6:5 Or *compose on*   [C]6:10 Lit *His uncle*   [D]6:10 A burner of incense, a memorial fire,
or a body; Hb obscure   [E]6:10 Lit *remove bones*   [F]6:12 Some emend to *plow the sea*   [G]6:14 Or *from
Lebo-hamath*   [H]6:14 Probably the Valley of Zared at the southeast end of the Dead Sea

⁶ The LORD relented concerning this. "This will not happen either," said the Lord GOD.   Ps 106:45; Jnh 3:10

Third Vision: A Plumb Line

⁷ He showed me this: The Lord was standing there by a vertical wall with a plumb line in his hand. ⁸ The LORD asked me, "What do you see, Amos?"   Jr 1:11; Am 8:2

I replied, "A plumb line."

Then the Lord said, "I am setting a plumb line among my people Israel; I will no longer spare them:

⁹   Isaac's high places
        will be deserted,   2Kg 17:9-13
    and Israel's sanctuaries
        will be in ruins;   Lv 26:31; Is 63:18
    I will rise up against
        the house of Jeroboam
        with a sword."

Amaziah's Opposition

¹⁰ Amaziah the priest of Bethel sent word to King Jeroboam of Israel, saying, "Amos has conspired against you right here in the house of Israel. The land cannot endure all his words, ¹¹ for Amos has said this: 'Jeroboam will die by the sword, and Israel will certainly go into exile from its homeland.'"   1Kg 12:31-32

¹² Then Amaziah said to Amos, "Go away, you seer! Flee to the land of Judah. Earn your living^A and give your prophecies there, ¹³ but don't ever prophesy at Bethel again, for it is the king's sanctuary and a royal temple."   1Kg 12:29; Am 2:12; Mt 8:34; Ac 4:18

¹⁴ So Amos answered Amaziah, "I was ^B not a prophet or the son of a prophet;^C rather, I was ^B a herdsman, and I took care of sycamore figs. ¹⁵ But the LORD took me from following the flock and said to me,

'Go, prophesy to my people Israel.'"   2Sm 7:8; 2Kg 2:3; 4:38; 2Ch 19:2; Jr 1:7; Am 1:1

¹⁶ Now hear the word of the LORD. You say:

    Do not prophesy
        against Israel;   Am 2:12
    do not preach
        against the house of Isaac.

¹⁷ Therefore, this is what the LORD says:

    Your wife will be a prostitute
        in the city,   Hs 4:13-14
    your sons and daughters
        will fall by the sword,   Jr 14:16
    and your land will be
        divided up
    with a measuring line.
    You yourself will die
        on pagan^D soil,   2Kg 17:6; Ezk 4:13
    and Israel will certainly go
        into exile   Jr 36:29-31
    from its homeland.

Fourth Vision: A Basket of Summer Fruit

8 The Lord GOD showed me this: a basket of summer fruit. ² He asked me, "What do you see, Amos?"

I replied, "A basket of summer fruit."^E   Jr 24:3

The LORD said to me, "The end has come for my people Israel; I will no longer spare them. ³ In that day the temple^F songs will become wailing" — this is the Lord GOD's declaration. "Many dead bodies, thrown everywhere! Silence!"

⁴   Hear this, you who trample
        on the needy   Am 2:7; 5:11-12
    and do away with the poor
        of the land,   Is 10:2
⁵   asking, "When will
        the New Moon be over
        so we may sell grain,   Nm 28:11

and the Sabbath,
so we may market wheat?
We can reduce the measure
while increasing the price [A]
and cheat
with dishonest scales.   Hs 12:7

6 We can buy the poor
with silver
and the needy for a pair
of sandals   Am 2:6
and even sell the chaff! "

7 The LORD has sworn by the Pride
of Jacob: [B]   Dt 33:26,29; Ps 47:4; Am 4:2; 6:8
I will never forget
all their deeds.   Ps 10:11; Hs 7:2

8 Because of this,
won't the land quake   Ps 18:7
and all who dwell in it mourn?
All of it will rise like the Nile;
it will surge and then subside
like the Nile in Egypt.   Am 9:5

9 And in that day —
this is the declaration
of the Lord GOD —
I will make the sun go down
at noon;   Is 13:10; Ezk 32:7; Jl 2:10,31
I will darken the land
in the daytime.   Is 59:9-10; Am 4:13

10 I will turn your feasts
into mourning   Jb 20:23; Am 5:21
and all your songs
into lamentation;   Lm 5:15
I will cause everyone [C]
to wear sackcloth   Ezk 7:18
and every head to be shaved.
I will make that grief
like mourning for an only son
and its outcome
like a bitter day.

11 Look, the days are coming —
this is the declaration
of the Lord GOD —

when I will send a famine
through the land:
not a famine of bread
or a thirst for water,
but of hearing the words
of the LORD.   Mc 3:6-7

12 People will stagger from sea
to sea
and roam from north to east
seeking the word
of the LORD,   Ezk 20:3,31
but they will not find it.

13 In that day the beautiful
young women,   Lm 1:18; 2:21
the young men also, will faint
from thirst.   Is 41:17; Hs 2:3

14 Those who swear by the guilt
of Samaria   Hs 8:5
and say,
"As your god lives, Dan,"
or, "As the way [D,E]
of Beer-sheba lives" —
they will fall,
never to rise again.   Am 5:2

Fifth Vision: The Lord Beside the Altar

9 I saw the Lord standing beside
the altar, and he said: Am 3:14
Strike the capitals
of the pillars   Zph 2:14
so that the thresholds shake;
knock them down
on the heads of all
the people.
Then I will kill the rest
of them with the sword.
None of those who flee
will get away;   Jr 11:11
none of the fugitives
will escape.

2 If they dig down to Sheol,
from there my hand
will take them;
if they climb up to heaven,

[A] 8:5 Lit reduce the ephah and make the shekel great every waist   [D] 8:14 LXX reads god   [E] 8:14 Or power   [B] 8:7 = the LORD or the promised land   [C] 8:10 Lit

from there I will
  bring them down.
3 If they hide
on the top of Carmel,
from there I will track
  them down   Jb 34:22; Ps 139:9-10
and seize them;
if they conceal themselves
from my sight
  on the sea floor,   Jnh 2:2-6
from there I will command
the sea serpent to bite them.
4 And if they are driven
by their enemies
  into captivity,   Lv 26:33
from there I will command
the sword to kill them.   Jr 23:24
I will keep my eye on them
for harm and not for good.

5 The Lord, the GOD
  of Armies —
he touches the earth;   Ps 104:32
it melts, and all who dwell
  in it mourn;
all of it rises like the Nile
and subsides like the Nile
  of Egypt.   Am 8:8
6 He builds
  his upper chambers
in the heavens   Ps 104:3,13
and lays the foundation
  of his vault
on the earth.   Ps 102:25; Is 48:13; 51:13
He summons the water
  of the sea
and pours it out
  over the surface of the earth.
The LORD is his name.   Am 4:13

Announcement of Judgment

7 Israelites, are you not
like the Cushites to me?
This is
the LORD's declaration.

Didn't I bring Israel
  from the land of Egypt,
the Philistines
  from Caphtor, ^A   Dt 2:23; Jr 47:4
and the Arameans
  from Kir?   2Kg 16:9; Is 22:6
8 Look, the eyes of the Lord
  GOD
are on the sinful kingdom,
and I will obliterate it
from the face of the earth.
However, I will not
  totally destroy
the house of Jacob —   Jr 5:10
  this is
  the LORD's declaration —
9 for I am about to give
  the command,
and I will shake the house
  of Israel   Is 30:28; Lk 22:31
among all the nations,
as one shakes a sieve,
but not a pebble will fall
  to the ground.
10 All the sinners
  among my people   Is 33:14
who say: "Disaster will never
  overtake ^B
or confront us,"   Jr 5:12; 23:17; Am 6:3
will die by the sword.

Announcement of Restoration

11 In that day
I will restore
  the fallen shelter of David:
I will repair its gaps,
restore its ruins,   Is 44:26
and rebuild it as in the days
  of old,   Is 63:11; Jr 46:26
12 so that they may possess
  the remnant of Edom   Ezk 36:5
and all the nations
  that bear my name^c —   Is 43:6-7
  this is the declaration
  of the LORD; he will do this.

¹³ Look, the days are coming —
   this is
   the Lord's declaration —
when the plowman
   will overtake the reaper
and the one
   who treads grapes,
the sower of seed.
The mountains will drip
   with sweet wine,
and all the hills will flow
   with it.   Jl 2:24; 3:18

¹⁴ I will restore the fortunes
   of my people Israel.^A   Dt 30:3

They will rebuild and occupy
   ruined cities,   Jr 30:18; 33:10-11
plant vineyards and drink
   their wine,
make gardens and eat
   their produce.   Is 65:21; Jr 31:5

¹⁵ I will plant them
   on their land,
and they will never again
   be uprooted
from the land I have
   given them.   2Sm 7:10; Jr 24:6
The Lord your God
   has spoken.

OBADIAH

The vision of Obadiah.

Edom's Certain Judgment

This is what the Lord God has said about Edom: Gn 25:30; Ps 137:7; Is 21:11-12

> We have heard a message
>   from the Lord; Jr 49:14-16
> an envoy has been sent
>   among the nations: Is 18:2; 30:4
> "Rise up, and let us go to war
>   against her."ᴬ Jr 6:4-5

² Look, I will make
    you insignificant Nm 24:18
among the nations;
you will be deeply despised.

³ Your arrogant heart
    has deceived you, Is 16:6
you who live in clefts
    of the rockᴮ,ᶜ 2Kg 14:7; 2Ch 25:12
in your home on the heights,
who say to yourself,
"Who can bring me down
    to the ground?" Is 14:13-15

⁴ Though you seem to soarᴰ
    like an eagle Jb 20:6-7; Hab 2:9
and make your nest
    among the stars, Is 14:12-15
even from there I will
    bring you down.
    This is
    the Lord's declaration.

⁵ If thieves came to you, Jr 49:9
if marauders by night —
how ravaged
    you would be! —
wouldn't they steal only
    what they wanted?
If grape pickers came to you,
wouldn't they leave
    some grapes? Lv 19:10; 25:5,11

⁶ How Esau will be pillaged,
his hidden treasures
    searched out! Mal 1:2-3

⁷ Everyone who has a treaty
    with you Ps 55:20; Jr 30:14; Am 1:9
will drive you to the border;
everyone at peace with you
will deceive and conquer you.
Those who eat your bread
will setᴱ a trap for you.
He will be unaware of it. Jr 49:7

⁸ In that day —
    this is
    the Lord's declaration —
will I not eliminate
    the wise ones of Edom Jb 4:1
and those who understand
from the hill country of Esau?

⁹ Teman,ᶠ your warriors
    will be terrified Gn 36:11; 1Ch 1:45
so that everyone
    from the hill country of Esau
will be destroyed
    by slaughter. Is 34:5-8; 63:1-3; Ob 5

Edom's Sins Against Judah

¹⁰ You will be covered
    with shame
and destroyed forever
because of violence done
    to your brother Jacob. Jl 3:19

¹¹ On the day you stood aloof,
on the day strangers
    captured his wealth,ᴳ
while foreigners entered
    his city gate
and cast lots for Jerusalem,
you were just like one of them.

ᴬ**1** = Edom ᴮ**3** Or *in Sela* ; probably = Petra ᶜ**3** Probably Petra ᴰ**4** Or *to build high* ᴱ**7** Some LXX mss, Sym, Tg, Vg; MT reads *They will set your bread as* ᶠ**9** = a region or city in Edom ᴳ**11** Or *forces*

¹² Do not^A gloat over
   your brother   Mc 4:11; 7:10
in the day of his calamity;
do not rejoice
   over the people of Judah
in the day of their destruction;
do not boastfully mock^B
in the day of distress.   Gn 35:3
¹³ Do not enter my
   people's city gate
in the day of their disaster.
Yes, you — do not gloat
   over their misery
in the day of their disaster,
and do not appropriate
   their possessions   Ezk 35:10
in the day of their disaster.
¹⁴ Do not stand
   at the crossroads^C   Is 16:3-4
to cut off their fugitives,
and do not hand over
   their survivors
in the day of distress.

Judgment of the Nations

¹⁵ For the day of the LORD
   is near,   Jl 1:15; 2:1,11,31; Am 5:18,20
against all the nations.   Is 13:6
As you have done, it will be
   done to you;   Jr 50:29; 51:56
what you deserve will return
   on your own head.   Jr 50:15
¹⁶ As you have drunk
   on my holy mountain, Jr 49:12
so all the nations will
   drink continually.   Is 51:22-23
They will drink and gulp down
and be as though they had
   never been.
¹⁷ But there will be a deliverance
   on Mount Zion,   Is 4:2-3
and it will be holy; Is 66:20; Jl 2:32
the house of Jacob
   will dispossess   Is 14:1-2

those who
   dispossessed them.^D
¹⁸ Then the house of Jacob
   will be a blazing fire, Is 5:24
and the house of Joseph,
   a burning flame,
but the house of Esau
   will be stubble;
Jacob^E will set them on fire
   and consume Edom.^F
Therefore no survivor
   will remain   Jr 11:23
of the house of Esau,
for the LORD has spoken.

Future Blessing for Israel

¹⁹ People from the Negev
   will possess   Is 11:14
the hill country of Esau;
those from the Judean
   foothills will possess
the land of
   the Philistines.   Is 11:14
They^G will possess
the territories of Ephraim
   and Samaria,   Jr 31:5; 32:44
while Benjamin
   will possess Gilead.
²⁰ The exiles of the Israelites
   who are in Halah^H
and who are among
   the Canaanites
as far as Zarephath 1Kg 17:9-10
as well as the exiles
   of Jerusalem who are
   in Sepharad
will possess the cities
   of the Negev.   Jr 32:44; 33:13
²¹ Saviors^I will ascend
   Mount Zion   Neh 9:27; Is 4:5; 18:7
to rule over the hill country
   of Esau,
but the kingdom will be
   the LORD's.   Ps 22:28; 47:7-9; 67:4

^A**12-14** Or *You should not* throughout vv. 12-14 ^B**12** Lit *not make your mouth big* ^C**14** Hb obscure ^D**17** DSS, LXX, Syr, Vg, Tg; MT reads *Jacob will possess its inheritance* ^E**18** Lit *they* ^F**18** Lit *them* ^G**19** = The house of Jacob ^H**20** Or *of this host of the Israelites*; Hb obscure ^I**21** Or *Those who have been delivered*

JONAH

Jonah's Flight

1 The word of the LORD came to Jonah son of Amittai: ² "Get up! Go to the great city of Nineveh and preach against it because their evil has come up before me." ³ Jonah got up to flee to Tarshish from the LORD's presence. He went down to Joppa and found a ship going to Tarshish. He paid the fare and went down into it to go with them to Tarshish from the LORD's presence.

⁴ But the LORD threw a great wind onto the sea, and such a great storm arose on the sea that the ship threatened to break apart. ⁵ The sailors were afraid, and each cried out to his god. They threw the ship's cargo into the sea to lighten the load. Meanwhile, Jonah had gone down to the lowest part of the vessel and had stretched out and fallen into a deep sleep. **1Sm 18:11**

⁶ The captain approached him and said, "What are you doing sound asleep? Get up! Call to your god.ᴬ Maybe this god will consider us, and we won't perish." **Ps 107:28**

⁷ "Come on!" the sailors said to each other. "Let's cast lots. Then we'll know who is to blame for this trouble we're in." So they cast lots, and the lot singled out Jonah. ⁸ Then they said to him, "Tell us who is to blame for this trouble we're in. What is your business, and where are you from? What is your country, and what people are you from?" **Jos 7:14-18; 1Sm 10:20-21; 14:41-42**

⁹ He answered them, "I'm a Hebrew. I worshipᴮ the LORD, the God of the heavens, who made the sea and the dry land." **Gn 14:13; 39:14; Ex 1:15**

¹⁰ Then the men were seized by a great fear and said to him, "What is this you've done?" The men knew he was fleeing from the LORD's presence because he had told them. ¹¹ So they said to him, "What should we do to you so that the sea will calm down for us?" For the sea was getting worse and worse. **Jnh 1:3**

¹² He answered them, "Pick me up and throw me into the sea so that it will calm down for you, for I know that I'm to blame for this great storm that is against you." ¹³ Nevertheless, the men rowed hard to get back to dry land, but they couldn't because the sea was raging against them more and more.

¹⁴ So they called out to the LORD: "Please, LORD, don't let us perish because of this man's life, and don't charge us with innocent blood! For you, LORD, have done just as you pleased." ¹⁵ Then they picked up Jonah and threw him into the sea, and the sea stopped its raging. ¹⁶ The men were seized by great fear of the LORD, and they offered a sacrifice to the LORD and made vows.

¹⁷ The LORD appointed a great fish to swallow Jonah, and Jonah was in the belly of the fish three days and three nights. **Gn 9:2; Nm 11:22; Ps 8:8**

Jonah's Prayer

2 Jonah prayed to the LORD his God from the belly of the fish:
² I called to the LORD
in my distress, **1Sm 30:6; Ps 18:4-6**

ᴬ**1:6** Or *God* ᴮ**1:9** Or *fear*

and he answered me.
I cried out for help
    from deep inside^A Sheol;
you heard my voice.   Ps 34:7
³ You threw me into the depths,
    into the heart of the seas,
and the current^B overcame me.
All your breakers
    and your billows
    swept over me.   Ps 42:7
⁴ But I said,
    "I have been banished   Lv 21:7
    from your sight,   Ps 31:22-23; Jr 7:15
    yet I will look once more^C
    toward your holy temple.
⁵ The water engulfed me up
    to the neck;^D   Ps 69:1-2; 105:18
the watery depths
    overcame me;
seaweed was wrapped
    around my head.   Ps 18:4-5
⁶ I sank to the foundations
    of the mountains,   Ps 116:3
the earth's gates shut
    behind me forever!   Jb 38:10
Then you raised my life
    from the Pit, LORD my God!
⁷ As my life was fading away,
I remembered the LORD,
and my prayer came to you,
to your holy temple.   Ps 11:4; 65:4
⁸ Those who
    cherish worthless idols
abandon their faithful love,
⁹ but as for me, I will sacrifice
    to you   Ps 50:14,23; Jr 33:11; Hs 14:2
with a voice of thanksgiving.
I will fulfill
    what I have vowed.   Jb 22:27
Salvation^E belongs
    to the LORD."   Ps 3:8; Is 12:2; 45:17

¹⁰ Then the LORD commanded the
fish, and it vomited Jonah onto dry
land.   Jnh 1:17

Jonah's Preaching

3 The word of the LORD came
to Jonah a second time: ² "Get
up! Go to the great city of Nineveh
and preach the message that I tell
you." ³ Jonah got up and went to
Nineveh according to the LORD's
command.   Jr 1:17; Ezk 2:7; Jnh 1:1; Zph 2:13-15

Now Nineveh was an extremely
great city,^F a three-day walk. ⁴ Jonah set out on the first day of his
walk in the city and proclaimed,
"In forty days Nineveh will be demolished!" ⁵ Then the people of
Nineveh believed God. They proclaimed a fast and dressed in sackcloth — from the greatest of them
to the least.

⁶ When word reached the king
of Nineveh, he got up from his
throne, took off his royal robe,
put on sackcloth, and sat in ashes.
⁷ Then he issued a decree in Nin-
eveh: 1Kg 21:27; Est 4:1-4; Jr 6:26; Ezk 27:30-31
By order of the king and his
    nobles: No person or animal,
    herd or flock, is to taste any-
    thing at all. They must not eat
    or drink water. ⁸ Furthermore,
    both people and animals must
    be covered with sackcloth,
    and everyone must call out
    earnestly to God. Each must
    turn from his evil ways and
    from his wrongdoing.^G ⁹ Who
    knows? God may turn and
    relent; he may turn from his
    burning anger so that we will
    not perish.   Ps 130:1; Is 1:16-19; Jnh 1:6,14

¹⁰ God saw their actions — that
they had turned from their evil
ways — so God relented from the
disaster he had threatened them
with. And he did not do it.   2Kg 17:13

---

^A**2:2** Lit *from the stomach of*   ^B**2:3** Lit *river*   ^C**2:4** LXX reads *said, "Indeed, will I look . . . ?*   ^D**2:5** Or *me,
threatening my life*   ^E**2:9** Or *Deliverance*   ^F**3:3** Or *was a great city to God*   ^G**3:8** Or *injustice,* or *violence*

Jonah's Anger

4 Jonah was greatly displeased and became furious. [2] He prayed to the LORD: "Please, LORD, isn't this what I thought while I was still in my own country? That's why I fled toward Tarshish in the first place. I knew that you are a gracious and compassionate God, slow to anger, abounding in faithful love, and one who relents from sending disaster. [3] And now, LORD, take my life from me, for it is better for me to die than to live." Jr 20:7; Jnh 1:3; 4:9; Mt 20:15; Lk 15:28

[4] The LORD asked, "Is it right for you to be angry?"

[5] Jonah left the city and found a place east of it. He made himself a shelter there and sat in its shade to see what would happen to the city. [6] Then the LORD God appointed a plant, and it grew over Jonah to provide shade for his head to rescue him from his trouble.[A] Jonah was greatly pleased with the plant. [7] When dawn came the next day, God appointed a worm that attacked the plant, and it withered.

[8] As the sun was rising, God appointed a scorching east wind. The sun beat down on Jonah's head so much that he almost fainted, and he wanted to die. He said, "It's better for me to die than to live."

[9] Then God asked Jonah, "Is it right for you to be angry about the plant?"

"Yes, it's right!" he replied. "I'm angry enough to die!"

[10] So the LORD said, "You cared about the plant, which you did not labor over and did not grow. It appeared in a night and perished in a night. [11] But may I not care about the great city of Nineveh, which has more than a hundred and twenty thousand people who cannot distinguish between their right and their left, as well as many animals?" Dt 1:39; Is 7:16; Ps 36:6; Jnh 3:10

A 4:6 Or *disaster,* or *evil*

MICAH

1 The word of the LORD that came to Micah the Moreshite — what he saw regarding Samaria and Jerusalem in the days of Jotham, Ahaz, and Hezekiah, kings of Judah. ^{2Ch 29:5-11; 32:24-26; Is 1:1; Hs 1:1; Jl 1:1}

Coming Judgment on Israel

² Listen, all you peoples; ^{Jr 6:19}
    pay attention, earth ^A
    and everyone in it! ^{Ps 24:1}
The Lord GOD will be
    a witness against you, ^{Ps 50:7}
the Lord,
    from his holy temple. ^{Ps 11:4}
³ Look, the LORD is leaving
    his place ^{Is 26:21}
and coming down to trample
    the heights ^B of the earth.
⁴ The mountains will melt
    beneath him,
and the valleys will split apart,
like wax near a fire, ^{Ps 97:5}
like water cascading down
    a mountainside.
⁵ All this will happen
    because of Jacob's rebellion
and the sins of the house
    of Israel.
What is the rebellion of Jacob?
    Isn't it Samaria? ^{Is 7:9; Am 8:14}
And what is the high place
    of Judah? ^{2Ch 34:3-4}
Isn't it Jerusalem?
⁶ Therefore, I will make Samaria
    a heap of ruins
    in the countryside, ^{Mc 3:12}
a planting area for a vineyard.
I will roll her stones
    into the valley ^{Lm 4:1}

and expose her foundations.
⁷ All her carved images
    will be smashed to pieces;
all her wages will be burned
    in the fire, ^{Dt 23:18}
and I will destroy all her idols.
Since she collected the wages
    of a prostitute, ^{Dt 23:18}
they will be used again
    for a prostitute.

Micah's Lament

⁸ Because of this I will lament
    and wail;
I will walk barefoot
    and naked. ^{Is 20:2-4; 32:11}
I will howl like the jackals
and mourn like ostriches. ^C
⁹ For her wound is incurable
and has reached even Judah;
it has approached my
    people's city gate, ^{Mc 1:12}
as far as Jerusalem.
¹⁰ Don't announce it in Gath,
    don't weep at all.
Roll in the dust
    in Beth-leaphrah.
¹¹ Depart in
    shameful nakedness,
you residents of Shaphir;
the residents of Zaanan
    will not come out. ^{Jos 15:37}
Beth-ezel is lamenting;
its support ^D is taken
    from you.
¹² Though the residents
    of Maroth
anxiously wait for
    something good, ^{Is 59:9-11}

---

^A**1:2** Or *land*   ^B**1:3** Or *high places*   ^C**1:8** Or *eagle owls* ; lit *daughters of the desert*   ^D**1:11** Lit *its standing place* ; Hb obscure

disaster has come
  from the LORD   Jdg 2:15; 2Kg 17:7
to the gate of Jerusalem.
¹³ Harness the horses
  to the chariot,
you residents of Lachish.
This was the beginning of sin
  for Daughter Zion
because Israel's acts of
  rebellion can be traced
  to you.   Mc 1:5
¹⁴ Therefore, send farewell gifts
  to Moresheth-gath;   2Kg 16:8
the houses of Achzib are
  a deception   Jos 15:44; Jr 15:18
to the kings of Israel.
¹⁵ I will again bring a conqueror
against you who live
  in Mareshah.   Jos 15:44
The nobility[A] of Israel
  will come to Adullam.
¹⁶ Shave yourselves bald
  and cut off your hair   Jb 1:20
in sorrow for your
  precious children;
make yourselves as bald
  as an eagle,
for they have been taken
  from you into exile.   2Kg 17:6

Oppressors Judged

2 Woe to those who dream
  up wickedness
and prepare evil plans
  on their beds!   Ps 36:4; Is 32:7
At morning light they
  accomplish it   Hs 7:6-7
because the power is
  in their hands.   Gn 31:29; Dt 28:32
² They covet fields
  and seize them;   Jr 22:17; Am 8:4
they also take houses.
They deprive a man
  of his home,   1Kg 21:1-15
a person of his inheritance.

³ Therefore, the LORD says:
I am now planning a disaster
  against this nation;   Jr 8:3; Am 3:1-2
you cannot free your necks
  from it.   Lm 1:14; 5:5
Then you will not walk
  so proudly   Is 2:11-12
because it will be
  an evil time.   Am 5:13
⁴ In that day one will take up
  a taunt against you   Hab 2:6
and lament
  mournfully, saying,   Mc 1:8
"We are totally ruined!" Is 6:11
He measures out
  the allotted land
  of my people.
How he removes it from me!
He allots our fields
  to traitors."   Jr 6:12; 8:10
⁵ Therefore, there will be
  no one
in the assembly of the LORD
  to divide the land
  by casting lots.[B]   Nm 34:13,16-29

God's Word Rejected

⁶ "Quit your preaching,"
  they[C] preach.   Is 30:10; Am 2:12; 7:16
"They should not preach
  these things;   Is 29:10; Mc 3:6
shame will not overtake us."[D]
⁷ House of Jacob, should it
  be asked,
"Is the Spirit
  of the LORD impatient? Is 50:2
Are these the things
  he does?"
Don't my words bring good
  to the one who
  walks uprightly?   Ps 15:2; 84:11
⁸ But recently my people
  have risen up
like an enemy: Jr 12:8
You strip off the splendid robe

[A]**1:15** Lit *glory*   [B]**2:5** Lit LORD *stretching the measuring line by lot*   [C]**2:6** = the prophets   [D]**2:6** Text emended; MT reads *things. Shame will not depart*

from those who are
passing through confidently,
like those returning from war.

9 You force the women
of my people   Jr 10:20
out of their
comfortable homes,
and you take my blessing ᴬ
from their children forever.

10 Get up and leave,
for this is not your place
of rest   Dt 3:19-20; 12:8-10
because defilement
brings destruction —
a grievous destruction!

11 If a man comes
and utters empty lies —
"I will preach to you
about wine and beer" —
he would be just the preacher
for this people!   Is 30:10-11

The Remnant Regathered

12 I will indeed gather all
of you, Jacob;   Mc 4:6-7
I will collect the remnant
of Israel.   2Kg 19:31; Mc 5:7-8; 7:18
I will bring them together
like sheep in a pen,
like a flock in the middle
of its pasture.
It will be noisy with people.

13 One who breaks open the way
will advance before them;
they will break out, pass
through the city gate,
and leave by it.
Their King will pass through
before them,
the LORD as their leader.

Unjust Leaders Judged

3 Then I said, "Now listen,
leaders of Jacob,   Is 1:10; Mc 3:9
you rulers of the house
of Israel.

Aren't you supposed to know
what is just?   Ps 82:1-5; Jr 5:5
2 You hate good and love evil.
You tear off people's skin
and strip their flesh
from their bones.
3 You eat the flesh of my people
after you strip their skin
from them
and break their bones.
You chop them up   Ezk 11:3,6-7
like flesh for the cooking pot,
like meat in a cauldron."
4 Then they will cry out
to the LORD,   Ps 18:41; Pr 1:28; Is 1:15
but he will not answer them.
He will hide his face
from them at that time
because of the crimes
they have committed.

False Prophets Judged

5 This is what the LORD says
concerning the prophets
who lead my people astray,
who proclaim peace   Jr 6:14
when they have food to sink
their teeth into
but declare war
against the one
who puts nothing
in their mouths.
6 Therefore, it will be night
for you —   Is 8:20-22; 29:10-12
without visions;
it will grow dark for you —
without divination.   Dt 18:10
The sun will set on
these prophets,   Is 59:10
and the daylight
will turn black over them.
7 Then the seers will
be ashamed   Zch 13:4
and the diviners disappointed.
They will all cover
their mouths ᴮ   Lv 13:45; Lm 4:13-15

ᴬ2:9 Perhaps the land   ᴮ3:7 Lit *mustache*

because there will be
no answer from God. 1Sm 28:6

8 As for me, however, I am
filled with power Is 61:1-2; Jr 1:18
by the Spirit of the LORD,
with justice and courage,
to proclaim to Jacob
his rebellion
and to Israel his sin. Is 58:1

Zion's Destruction

9 Listen to this, leaders
of the house of Jacob, Mc 3:1
you rulers of the house
of Israel,
who abhor justice Ps 58:1-2; Is 1:23
and pervert everything
that is right,
10 who build Zion
with bloodshed Jr 22:13,17
and Jerusalem with injustice.
11 Her leaders issue rulings
for a bribe, Is 1:23; Mc 7:3
her priests teach
for payment, Jr 6:13
and her prophets
practice divination
for silver.
Yet they lean
on the LORD, saying,
"Isn't the LORD among us?
No disaster will overtake us."
12 Therefore, because of you,
Zion will be plowed
like a field,
Jerusalem will become ruins,
and the temple's mountain
will be a high thicket. Jr 26:18

The LORD's Rule from Restored Zion

4 In the last days Is 2:2-4; Dn 2:28; 10:14
the mountain
of the LORD's house Ezk 43:12
will be established
at the top of the mountains

and will be raised
above the hills.
Peoples will stream to it,
2 and many nations will come
and say, Zch 2:11; 14:16
"Come, let us go up
to the mountain
of the LORD, Is 56:6-7; Jr 31:6
to the house of the God
of Jacob.
He will teach us
about his ways Ps 25:8-9,12
so we may walk in his paths."
For instruction will go out
of Zion Is 42:1-4; Zch 14:8-9
and the word of the LORD
from Jerusalem.
3 He will settle disputes
among many peoples Is 11:3-5
and provide arbitration
for strong nations
that are far away.
They will beat their swords
into plows
and their spears
into pruning knives.
Nation will not take up
the sword against nation,
and they will never
again train for war.
4 But each person will sit
under his grapevine 1Kg 4:25
and under his fig tree
with no one to frighten him.
For the mouth of the LORD
of Armies Is 1:20; 40:5
has spoken.
5 Though all the peoples
each walk
in the name of their gods,
we will walk in the name
of the LORD our God Zch 10:12
forever and ever. Jos 24:15

6 On that day —
this is
the LORD's declaration —

I will assemble the lame
and gather the scattered,
those I have injured.
7 I will make the lame
    into a remnant,   Mc 5:7-8; 7:18
those far removed
    into a strong nation.
Then the LORD will reign
    over them in Mount Zion
from this time on and forever.
8 And you, watchtower
    for the flock,   Ps 48:3,12; 61:3
fortified hill[A]
of Daughter Zion,
the former rule will come
    to you;   Is 1:26; Zch 9:10
sovereignty will come
    to Daughter Jerusalem.

From Exile to Victory

9 Now, why are you
    shouting loudly?   Jr 8:19
Is there no king with you?
Has your counselor perished
so that anguish grips you
    like a woman in labor?
10 Writhe and cry out,[B]
    Daughter Zion,   Mc 5:3
like a woman in labor,
for now you will leave the city
and camp in the open fields.
You will go to Babylon;
there you will be rescued;
there the LORD
    will redeem you   Is 48:20; 52:9-12
from the grasp
    of your enemies!
11 Many nations have
    now assembled against you;
they say, "Let her be defiled,
and let us feast our eyes
    on Zion."
12 But they do not know
    the LORD's intentions
or understand his plan,
that he has gathered them

like sheaves
    to the threshing floor.
13 Rise and thresh,
    Daughter Zion,   Is 41:15
for I will make
    your horns iron
and your hooves bronze
so you can crush
    many peoples.   Jr 51:20-23
Then you[C] will set apart
    their plunder   Is 60:9
for the LORD,
their wealth for the Lord
    of the whole earth.

From Defeated Ruler to Conquering King

5 Now, daughter who is
    under attack,
you slash yourself in grief;
a siege is set against us!
They are striking the judge
    of Israel   1Kg 22:24; Jb 16:10; Lm 3:30
on the cheek with a rod.
2 Bethlehem Ephrathah,   Gn 35:19
you are small
    among the clans of Judah;
one will come from you   Is 11:1
to be ruler over Israel for me.
His origin[D] is from antiquity,
from ancient times.
3 Therefore, Israel will be
    abandoned until the time
when she who is in labor
    has given birth;   Mc 4:9-10
then the rest of the ruler's
    brothers will return   Mc 5:7-8
to the people of Israel.   Mc 4:6-7
4 He will stand
    and shepherd them   Is 40:11
in the strength of the LORD,
in the majestic name of the
    LORD his God.
They will live securely,
for then his greatness
    will extend

A4:8 Or flock, Ophel   B4:10 Hb obscure   C4:13 LXX, Syr, Tg; MT reads I   D5:2 Lit His going out to the ends of the earth. Is 45:22

5 He will be their peace. Is 9:6
When Assyria invades
    our land, Is 8:7-8; 10:24-27
when it marches
    against our fortresses,
we will raise against it
    seven shepherds,
even eight leaders of men.

6 They will shepherd the land
    of Assyria with the sword,
the land of Nimrod
    with a drawn blade. A
So he will rescue us
    from Assyria Is 14:25; 37:36-37
when it invades our land,
when it marches
    against our territory.

The Glorious and Purified Remnant

7 Then the remnant of Jacob
will be among many peoples
like dew from the LORD, Dt 32:2
like showers on the grass,
which do not wait for anyone
or linger for mankind.

8 Then the remnant of Jacob
will be among the nations,
    among many peoples,
like a lion among animals
    of the forest, Gn 49:9; Nm 24:9
like a young lion
    among flocks of sheep,
which tramples and tears
    as it passes through, Ps 44:5
and there is no one
    to rescue them. Ps 50:22

9 Your hand will be lifted up
    against your adversaries,
and all your enemies
    will be destroyed.

10 In that day —
    this is
    the LORD's declaration —
I will remove your horses
    from you Dt 17:16; Is 2:7; Hs 14:3
and wreck your chariots.

11 I will remove the cities
    of your land Is 1:7; 6:11
and tear down all
    your fortresses. Is 2:12-17; Am 5:9

12 I will remove sorceries
    from your hands, Dt 18:10-12
and you will not have
    any more fortune-tellers.

13 I will remove
    your carved images Is 2:18,20
and sacred pillars from you
so that you will no
    longer worship
the work of your hands.

14 I will pull up the Asherah
    poles from among you
and demolish your cities. B

15 I will take vengeance
    in anger and wrath Is 1:24
against the nations that
    have not obeyed me.

God's Lawsuit Against Judah

6 Now listen to what the LORD
is saying:
Rise, plead your case
    before the mountains,
and let the hills hear
    your complaint. C

2 Listen to the LORD's lawsuit,
you mountains
    and enduring foundations
    of the earth, 2Sm 22:16; Ps 104:5
because the LORD has a case
    against his people, Is 1:18; Hs 4:1
and he will argue it
    against Israel.

3 My people, what have I done
    to you, Ps 50:7; Jr 2:5
or how have I wearied you?
Testify against me!

4 Indeed, I brought you up
    from the land of Egypt Ex 20:2

A 5:6 Aq, Vg; MT, Sym read *Nimrod at its gateways*   B 5:14 Or *shrines*   C 6:1 Lit *voice*

and redeemed you
   from that place of slavery.
I sent Moses, Aaron,
   and Miriam ahead of you.
⁵ My people,
   remember what King
   Balak of Moab proposed,
what Balaam son of Beor
   answered him,   Nm 22–24
and what happened from
   the Acacia Grove^A to Gilgal
so that you may acknowledge
   the Lord's righteous acts.

⁶ What should I bring
   before the Lord   Ps 40:6-8
when I come to bow
   before God on high?
Should I come before him
   with burnt offerings,
with year-old calves?
⁷ Would the Lord be pleased
   with thousands of rams
or with ten thousand
   streams of oil?
Should I give my firstborn
   for my transgression,   Lv 18:21
the offspring of my body
   for my own sin?

⁸ Mankind, he has told each of
   you what is good   Dt 30:15
and what it is the Lord
   requires of you: Dt 10:12
to act justly,   Is 56:1; Jr 22:3; Mt 23:23
to love faithfulness,   Hs 6:6
and to walk humbly
   with your God.   Is 57:15; 66:2

Verdict of Judgment

⁹ The voice of the Lord
   calls out to the city^B
(and it is wise to fear
   your name):

"Pay attention to the rod
and the one
   who ordained it.^C
¹⁰ Are there still^D the treasures
   of wickedness   Jr 5:26-27; Am 3:10
and the accursed
   short measure   Ezk 45:9-10; Am 8:5
in the house of the wicked?
¹¹ Can I excuse wicked scales
or bags of deceptive weights?
¹² For the wealthy of the city
   are full of violence,   Is 1:23; 5:7
and its residents speak lies;
the tongues in their mouths
   are deceitful.   Is 3:8

¹³ "As a result, I have begun
   to strike you severely,^E   Mc 1:9
bringing desolation
   because of your sins.   Is 1:7
¹⁴ You will eat but not
   be satisfied,   Is 9:20
for there will be hunger
   within you.
What you acquire,
   you cannot save,   Is 30:6
and what you do save,
I will give to the sword.^D
¹⁵ You will sow but not reap;
you will press olives
but not anoint yourself
   with oil;
and you will tread grapes
but not drink the wine.   Am 5:11
¹⁶ The statutes of Omri
and all the practices
   of Ahab's house
have been observed;
you have followed
   their policies.   1Kg 16:25-34; Jr 7:24
Therefore, I will make you
   a desolate place   Jr 18:16
and the city's^F residents
   an object of contempt;^G

---

^A 6:5 Or *from Shittim* ^B 6:9 = Jerusalem ^C 6:9 Or *attention, you tribe. Who has ordained it?*; Hb obscure
^D 6:10,14 Hb obscure ^E 6:13 LXX, Aq, Theod, Syr, Vg; MT reads *I have made you sick by striking you down*
^F 6:16 Lit *and its* ^G 6:16 Lit *residents a hissing*

you will bear the scorn
  of my people."[A]   Ps 44:13; Jr 51:51

Israel's Moral Decline

7 How sad for me!
For I am like one who —
when the summer fruit
  has been gathered
after the gleaning
  of the grape harvest —
finds no grape cluster
  to eat,
no early fig, which I crave.

2 Faithful people have
  vanished from the land;
there is no one upright
  among the people.   1Kg 19:10
All of them wait in ambush
  to shed blood;   Is 59:7; Mc 3:10
they hunt each other
  with a net.   Jr 5:26; Hs 5:1

3 Both hands are good
  at accomplishing evil:
the official and the judge
  demand a bribe;   Am 5:12; Mc 3:11
when the powerful
  man communicates
  his evil desire,
they plot it together.

4 The best of them is
  like a brier;   Ezk 2:6; 28:24
the most upright is worse
  than a hedge of thorns.
The day of your watchmen,
the day of your punishment,
  is coming;   Is 10:3; Hs 9:7
at this time their panic
  is here.   Is 22:5

5 Do not rely on a friend;   Jr 9:4
don't trust
  in a close companion.
Seal your mouth
from the woman who lies
  in your arms.

6 Surely a son considers
  his father a fool,   Mt 10:21,35-36

a daughter opposes
  her mother,
and a daughter-in-law is
  against her mother-in-law;
a man's enemies are the men
  of his own household.

7 But I will look to the LORD;
I will wait for the God
  of my salvation.   Ps 130:5; Is 25:9
My God will hear me.   Ps 4:3

Zion's Vindication

8 Do not rejoice over me,
  my enemy!   Ob 12
Though I have fallen,
  I will stand up;   Am 9:11
though I sit in darkness,
  the LORD will be my light.   Is 9:2

9 Because I have sinned
  against him,
I must endure
  the LORD's rage
until he champions my cause
and establishes justice
  for me.   Jb 23:3-7; Lm 3:58
He will bring me
  into the light;   Ps 37:6; Is 42:7,16
I will see his salvation.[B]   Is 46:13

10 Then my enemy will see,
and she will be covered
  with shame,
the one who said to me,
"Where is the LORD
  your God?"   Ps 42:3,10; 79:10; 115:2
My eyes will look at her
  in triumph;
at that time she
  will be trampled
like mud in the streets.   Ps 18:42

11 A day will come
  for rebuilding your walls;
on that day your boundary
  will be extended.   Zph 2:2

12 On that day people will come
  to you   Is 19:23-25; 60:4,9

[A]**6:16** LXX reads *of the peoples*   [B]**7:9** Or *righteousness*

from Assyria and the cities
of Egypt,
even from Egypt
to the Euphrates River
and from sea to sea
and mountain to mountain.
¹³ Then the earth will become
a wasteland   Jr 25:11; Mc 6:13
because of its inhabitants
and as a result of
their actions.   Is 3:10-11; Mc 3:4

Micah's Prayer Answered

¹⁴ Shepherd your people
with your staff,   Ps 95:7; Is 40:11
the flock that is
your possession.
They live alone
in a woodland   Nm 23:9; Dt 33:28
surrounded by pastures.
Let them graze in Bashan
and Gilead   Jr 50:19
as in ancient times.   Am 9:11

¹⁵ I will perform miracles
for them[A]
as in the days of your exodus
from the land of Egypt.   Ex 3:20
¹⁶ Nations will see
and be ashamed
of[B] all their power.
They will put their hands
over their mouths,   Mc 3:7

and their ears will
become deaf.
¹⁷ They will lick the dust
like a snake;   Ps 72:9; Is 49:23
they will come trembling
out of their hiding places
like reptiles slithering
on the ground.   Dt 32:24
They will tremble
in the presence of the LORD
our God;   Is 25:3; 59:19
they will stand in awe of you.

¹⁸ Who is a God like you,   Ex 15:11
forgiving iniquity
and passing over rebellion
for the remnant
of his inheritance?   Mc 2:12; 4:7
He does not hold on
to his anger forever
because he delights
in faithful love.   Jr 32:41
¹⁹ He will again
have compassion on us;
he will vanquish
our iniquities.   Jr 50:20
You will cast all our[C] sins
into the depths of the sea.
²⁰ You will show loyalty
to Jacob   Gn 24:27; 32:10
and faithful love to Abraham,
as you swore to our fathers
from days long ago.

NAHUM

1 The pronouncement concerning Nineveh. The book of the vision of Nahum the Elkoshite. Is 13:1; 30:6

God's Vengeance

² The LORD is a jealous
  and avenging God;
the LORD takes vengeance
  and is fierce in^A wrath.
The LORD takes vengeance
  against his foes; Dt 32:35, 41,43
he is furious
  with his enemies. Dt 6:15; Ps 94:1
³ The LORD is slow to anger
  but great in power;
the LORD will never leave
  the guilty unpunished.
His path is in the whirlwind
  and storm, Pr 1:27; 10:25; Is 66:15
and clouds are the dust
  beneath his feet. Dt 33:26; Ps 68:4
⁴ He rebukes the sea
  and dries it up,
and he makes all the rivers
  run dry. 2Sm 22:16; Ps 106:9; Is 50:2
Bashan and Carmel wither;
even the flower
  of Lebanon withers.
⁵ The mountains quake
  before him,
and the hills melt;
the earth trembles^B,C
  at his presence —
the world and all who live
  in it. Jdg 5:5; Ps 18:7; 46:2-3; 97:5; Is 5:25
⁶ Who can withstand
  his indignation?
Who can endure
  his burning anger? Ps 7:11

His wrath is poured out
  like fire; Ps 21:9; Is 9:19; 30:30; Jr 4:4
even rocks are shattered
  before him.

Destruction of Nineveh

⁷ The LORD is good,
  a stronghold in a day
  of distress;
he cares for those
  who take refuge in him.
⁸ But he will completely
  destroy Nineveh^D
with an overwhelming flood,
and he will chase his enemies
  into darkness.

⁹ Whatever you^E plot
  against the LORD,
he will bring it
  to complete destruction;
oppression will not rise up
  a second time.
¹⁰ For they will be consumed
  like entangled thorns, Mal 4:1
like the drink of a drunkard
and like straw that is
  fully dry.^F
¹¹ One has gone out from you,^G
  who plots evil against
  the LORD,
and is a wicked counselor.

Promise of Judah's Deliverance

¹² This is what the LORD says:
  Though they are strong^H
  and numerous,
  they will still be mowed down,
  and he^I will pass away.

^A1:2 Lit *is a master of*   ^B1:5 Some emend to *earth is laid waste*   ^C1:5 Lit *lifts*   ^D1:8 Lit *her place*
^E1:9 = Nineveh   ^F1:10 Hb obscure   ^G1:11 Possibly Nineveh   ^H1:12 Lit *intact*   ^I1:12 Either the king of
Assyria or his army

Though I have
punished you,^A Is 10:5-34
I will punish you no longer.
13 For I will now break off
his yoke from you
and tear off your shackles.

The Assyrian King's Demise

14 The LORD has issued an order
concerning you:
There will be no offspring
to carry on your name.^B Lv 20:3
I will eliminate the carved idol
and cast image
from the house of your gods;
I will prepare your grave,
for you are contemptible.

15 Look to the mountains —
the feet of the herald, Is 52:7; 61:1
who proclaims peace.
Celebrate
your festivals, Judah;
fulfill your vows.
For the wicked one
will never again
march through you;
he will be entirely wiped out.

Attack Against Nineveh

2 One who scatters
is coming up against you.
Man the fortifications!
Watch the road!
Brace^C yourself!
Summon all your strength!

2 For the LORD will restore
the majesty of Jacob, Ps 47:4
yes,^D the majesty of Israel,
though ravagers
have ravaged them Is 24:1,3
and ruined
their vine branches. Jr 12:10

3 The shields of his^E warriors
are dyed red;
the valiant men are dressed
in scarlet. Ezk 23:14
The fittings
of the chariot flash like fire
on the day
of its battle preparations,
and the spears
are brandished.
4 The chariots dash madly
through the streets;
they rush around
in the plazas.
They look like torches;
they dart back and forth
like lightning.
5 He gives orders
to his officers;
they stumble
as they advance.
They race to its wall;
the protective shield is set
in place.
6 The river gates are opened,
and the palace erodes away.
7 Beauty^F is stripped;^G
she is carried away;
her ladies-in-waiting moan
like the sound of doves Is 38:14
and beat their breasts. Is 32:12
8 Nineveh has been like a pool
of water
from her first days,^G
but they are fleeing.
"Stop! Stop!" they cry,
but no one turns back.
9 "Plunder the silver!
Plunder the gold!" Ezk 38:13
There is no end
to the treasure,
an abundance
of every precious thing.

¹⁰ Desolation, decimation,
    devastation!
  Hearts melt,   Dt 20:8; Jos 7:5; Is 13:7
  knees tremble,   Is 35:3
  insides churn,   Ps 69:23
  every face grows pale!   Is 21:3

¹¹ Where is the lions' lair,   Is 2:15
    or the feeding ground
    of the young lions,
  where the lion
    and lioness prowled,
  and the lion's cub,
  with nothing to frighten
    them away?   Lv 26:6; Dt 28:26
¹² The lion mauled whatever
    its cubs needed
  and strangled prey
    for its lionesses.
  It filled up its dens
    with the kill,
  and its lairs
    with mauled prey.   Jb 38:39-40
¹³ Beware, I am against you.
  This is the declaration
    of the LORD of Armies.
  I will make your chariots
    go up in smoke,ᴬ
  and the sword will devour
    your young lions.   Is 31:8; Jr 46:10
  I will cut off your prey
    from the earth,
  and the sound
    of your messengers
  will never be heard again.

Nineveh's Downfall

3 Woe to the city of blood,   Ezk 9:9
    totally deceitful,
  full of plunder,
    never without prey.   Nah 2:9
² The crack of the whip
    and rumble of the wheel,
  galloping horse
    and jolting chariot!   Jdg 5:22

³ Charging horseman,
  flashing sword,
  shining spear;
  heaps of slain,
  mounds of corpses,   Lv 26:30
  dead bodies without end —
  they stumble
    over their dead.
⁴ Because of the
    continual prostitution
    of the prostitute,
  the attractive mistress
    of sorcery,
  who treats nations
    and clans like merchandise
  by her prostitution
    and sorcery,   2Kg 9:22; Pr 7:10-23
⁵ I am against you.   Nah 2:13
  This is the declaration
    of the LORD of Armies.
  I will lift your skirts
    over your face
  and display your nakedness
    to nations,
  your shame to kingdoms.
⁶ I will throw filth on you
  and treat you with contempt;
  I will make a spectacle
    of you.
⁷ Then all who see you
    will recoil from you, saying,
  "Nineveh is devastated;
  who will show sympathy
    to her?"
  Where can I find anyone
    to comfort you?

⁸ Are you better than Thebesᴮ
  that sat along the Nile
  with water surrounding her,
  whose rampart was the sea,
  the riverᶜ,ᴰ her wall?
⁹ Cush and Egypt were
    her endless source
    of strength;

ᴬ**2:13** Lit *will burn her chariots in smoke*   ᴮ**3:8** Hb *No-amon*   ᶜ**3:8** LXX, Syr, Vg read *water*   ᴰ**3:8** Lit *sea from sea*

Put and Libya were
  among her[A] allies.
10 Yet she became an exile;
she went into captivity.
Her children were also
  dashed to pieces   2Kg 8:12
at the head of every street.
They cast lots
  for her dignitaries,   Ob 11
and all her nobles
were bound in chains.
11 You[B] also
  will become drunk;
you will hide.[C]
You also will seek refuge
  from the enemy.

12 All your fortresses are
  fig trees
with figs that ripened first;
when shaken, they fall —
right into the mouth
  of the eater!

13 Look, your troops
  are like women among you;
your land's city gates
are wide open
  to your enemies.
Fire will devour the bars
  of your gates.

14 Draw water for the siege;
strengthen your fortresses.
Step into the clay and tread
  the mortar;
take hold of the brick-mold!
15 The fire will devour
  you there;
the sword will cut you down.

It will devour you
  like the young locust.   Jl 1:4
Multiply yourselves
  like the young locust;
multiply like
  the swarming locust!
16 You have made
  your merchants   Ezk 16:29; 17:4
more numerous than
  the stars of the sky.
The young locust strips[D]
  the land
and flies away.
17 Your court officials are
  like the swarming locust,
and your scribes like clouds
  of locusts,
which settle on the walls
  on a cold day;
when the sun rises,
  they take off,
and no one knows
  where they are.

18 King of Assyria,
  your shepherds slumber;
your officers sleep.
Your people are scattered
  across the mountains
with no one to gather
  them together.   1Kg 22:17
19 There is no remedy
  for your injury;
your wound is severe.   Jr 10:19
All who hear the news
  about you
will clap their hands
  because of you,   Ps 47:1; 98:8
for who has not experienced
  your constant cruelty?

A 3:9 Lit *your*   B 3:11 = Nineveh   C 3:11 Or *will be overcome*   D 3:16 Or *sheds its skin*

HABAKKUK

1

The pronouncement that the prophet Habakkuk saw. Is 13:1

Habakkuk's First Prayer

2 How long, LORD, must I call
for help Jb 19:7; Ps 4:2; 5:2; 6:3; 13:1
and you do not listen
or cry out to you
about violence Jr 6:7; Ezk 7:11,23
and you do not save?
3 Why do you force me to look
at injustice? Jb 4:8; Ps 5:5; Is 5:7
Why do you
tolerate^A wrongdoing?
Oppression and violence
are right in front of me.
Strife is ongoing,
and conflict escalates.
4 This is why the law
is ineffective
and justice never emerges.
For the wicked restrict
the righteous; Jdg 20:43; Ps 22:12
therefore, justice
comes out perverted. Ex 23:6

God's First Answer

5 Look at the nations^B
and observe — Gn 15:5; Ps 2:1
be utterly astounded! Gn 43:33
For I am doing something
in your days
that you will not believe
when you hear about it.
6 Look! I am raising up
the Chaldeans,^C Ru 4:5
that bitter, impetuous nation
that marches across
the earth's open spaces

to seize territories
not its own.
7 They are fierce
and terrifying; Sg 6:4,10
their views of justice
and sovereignty
stem from themselves.
8 Their horses are swifter
than leopards 2Sm 1:23; Is 11:6
and more fierce^D than wolves
of the night.
Their horsemen
charge ahead;
their horsemen come
from distant lands.
They fly like eagles,
swooping to devour. Dt 28:49
9 All of them come
to do violence;
their faces are set
in determination.^E Gn 48:11
They gather prisoners
like sand. Dt 11:14; Jos 11:4
10 They mock kings, 2Kg 2:23
and rulers are a joke to them.
They laugh at every fortress
and build siege ramps
to capture it. Nm 21:32
11 Then they sweep by
like the wind Is 8:8
and pass through.
They are guilty;^F
their strength is their god.

Habakkuk's Second Prayer

12 Are you not from eternity,
LORD my God? 1Ch 29:10; Ps 90:2
My Holy One,
you^G will not die. Is 1:4

---

^A 1:3 Lit observe, also in v. 13 ^B 1:5 DSS, LXX, Syr read Look, you treacherous people ^C 1:6 = the Babylonians ^D 1:8 Or and quicker ^E 1:9 Hb obscure ^F 1:11 Or wind, and transgress and incur guilt ^G 1:12 Alt Hb tradition reads we

LORD, you appointed them
  to execute judgment;
my Rock, you destined them
  to punish us.   Dt 32:4; Ps 18:2
13 Your eyes are too pure
  to look on evil,   2Ch 6:20; 16:9
and you cannot
  tolerate wrongdoing.
So why do you tolerate those
  who are treacherous?
Why are you silent
while one[A] who is wicked
  swallows up
one[B] who is more righteous
  than himself?
14 You have made mankind
like the fish of the sea,   Ec 9:12
like marine creatures
  that have no ruler.
15 The Chaldeans pull them all
  up with a hook,
catch them in their dragnet,
and gather them
  in their fishing net;
that is why they are glad
  and rejoice.
16 That is why they sacrifice
  to their dragnet
and burn incense
  to their fishing net,
for by these things
  their portion is rich
and their food plentiful.   Dt 8:17
17 Will they therefore empty
  their net
and continually slaughter
  nations without mercy?

Habakkuk Waits for God's Response

2 I will stand at my guard post
  and station myself
    on the lookout tower.   1Ch 9:27
  I will watch to see what
    he will say to me   Ps 85:8

and what I should[C] reply
  about my complaint.

God's Second Answer

2 The LORD answered me:
  Write down this vision;   1Sm 3:1
  clearly inscribe it on tablets
  so one may easily read it.[D]
3 For the vision is yet
  for the appointed time;
it testifies about the end
  and will not lie.
Though it delays, wait for it,
since it will certainly come
  and not be late.   Dn 10:1,14; 11:35
4 Look, his ego is inflated;[E]
he is without integrity.
But the righteous one
  will live by his faith.[F]   Rm 1:17
5 Moreover, wine[G] betrays;
an arrogant man is never
  at rest.[H]
He enlarges his appetite
  like Sheol,
and like Death he is
  never satisfied.   Pr 27:20; 30:15-16
He gathers all the nations
  to himself;   Is 13:4; 43:9; 66:18; Jr 3:17
he collects all the peoples
  for himself.

The Five Woe Oracles

6 Won't all of these take up
  a taunt against him,   Is 14:4
with mockery and riddles
  about him?
They will say:

Woe to him who amasses
  what is not his —
how much longer? —   1Kg 18:21
and loads himself with goods
  taken in pledge.   Dt 24:10-13
7 Won't your creditors
  suddenly arise,

[A]1:13 = Babylon   [B]1:13 = Judah   [C]2:1 Syr reads *what he will*   [D]2:2 Lit *one who reads in it may run*
[E]2:4 Hb obscure   [F]2:4 Or *faithfulness*   [G]2:5 DSS read *wealth*   [H]2:5 Or *man does not endure*; Hb obscure

and those who disturb you
    wake up?
Then you will become spoil
    for them. 2Kg 21:14; Is 42:22,24

8 Since you have plundered
    many nations, Is 10:13; Ezk 36:4
all the peoples who remain
    will plunder you — Zph 3:8
because of human bloodshed
and violence
    against lands, cities, Jr 6:7
and all who live in them. Is 33:1

9 Woe to him
    who dishonestly makes
wealth for his house[A] Pr 1:9; 15:27
to place his nest on high,
to escape the grasp
    of disaster! Pr 11:28; Jr 22:13; 49:16
10 You have planned shame
    for your house
by wiping out many peoples
and sinning against
    your own self.
11 For the stones will cry out
    from the wall, Lk 19:40
and the rafters
    will answer them
from the woodwork.

12 Woe to him who builds a city
    with bloodshed
and founds a town
    with injustice! Ezk 22:2-3; Mc 3:10
13 Is it not from the LORD
    of Armies
that the peoples labor
    only to fuel the fire
and countries
    exhaust themselves
    for nothing? Jr 51:58
14 For the earth will be filled
    with the knowledge
    of the LORD's glory,
as the water covers the sea.

15 Woe to him who gives
    his neighbors drink,
pouring out your wrath[B]
and even making
    them drunk,
in order to look
    at their nakedness!
16 You will be filled
    with disgrace
    instead of glory.
You also — drink,
and expose
    your uncircumcision![C]
The cup in the LORD's
    right hand
will come around to you,
and utter disgrace will cover
    your glory. Rv 14:8-10
17 For your violence
    against Lebanon
will overwhelm you;
    the destruction of animals
    will terrify you[D]
because of your human
    bloodshed and violence
against lands, cities, and all
    who live in them.

18 What use is a carved idol
    after its craftsman carves it?
It is only a cast image,
    a teacher of lies.
For the one who crafts
    its shape trusts in it
and makes idols
    that cannot speak.
19 Woe to him who says
    to wood: Wake up!
or to mute stone:
    Come alive!
Can it teach?
Look! It may be plated
    with gold and silver,
yet there is no breath in it
    at all. Ex 32:4; Dt 27:15; Jdg 17:4; Is 30:22

[A]2:9 Or dynasty [B]2:15 Or venom [C]2:16 DSS, LXX, Aq, Syr, Vg read and stagger [D]2:17 DSS, LXX, Aq, Syr, Tg, Vg; MT reads them

²⁰ But the LORD is
in his holy temple;   Ps 11:4
let the whole earth
be silent in his presence.

Habakkuk's Third Prayer

3 A prayer of the prophet Habakkuk. According to *Shigionoth.* ^A
² LORD, I have heard the report
about you;
LORD, I stand in awe
of your deeds.   Ps 44:1; 64:9; 77:12
Revive your work
in these years;
make it known
in these years.
In your wrath
remember mercy!   Is 60:10

³ God comes from Teman,
the Holy One
from Mount Paran.   *Selah*
His splendor covers
the heavens,
and the earth is full
of his praise.   1Ch 29:11; Jb 37:22
⁴ His brilliance is like light;
rays are flashing
from his hand.
This is where his power
is hidden.
⁵ Plague goes before him,
and pestilence follows
in his steps.
⁶ He stands and shakes ^B
the earth;   Jb 9:6; Is 13:13; 24:19; Jl 2:10
he looks and startles
the nations.
The age-old mountains
break apart;
the ancient hills sink down.
His pathways are ancient.
⁷ I see the tents of Cushan ^C
in distress;

the tent curtains of the land
of Midian tremble.
⁸ Are you angry
at the rivers, LORD?
Is your wrath
against the rivers?
Or is your rage against the sea
when you ride
on your horses,
your victorious chariot?
⁹ You took the sheath
from your bow;
the arrows are ready ^D
to be used
with an oath. ^E   *Selah*
You split the earth
with rivers.
¹⁰ The mountains see you
and shudder;   Ps 77:16
a downpour of water
sweeps by.
The deep roars with its voice
and lifts its waves ^F high.
¹¹ Sun and moon stand still
in their lofty residence,
at the flash
of your flying arrows,
at the brightness
of your shining spear.
¹² You march across the earth
with indignation;
you trample
down the nations in wrath.
¹³ You come out to save
your people,   Dt 33:29; Jdg 2:18
to save your anointed. ^G
You crush the leader
of the house of the wicked
and strip him from foot ^H
to neck.   *Selah*
¹⁴ You pierce his head
with his own spears;
his warriors storm out
to scatter us,

---

^A**3:1** Perhaps a passionate song with rapid changes of rhythm, or a dirge   ^B**3:6** Or *surveys*   ^C**3:7** = Midian
^D**3:9** Or *set*   ^E**3:9** Hb obscure   ^F**3:10** Lit *hands*   ^G**3:13** The Davidic king or the nation of Israel   ^H**3:13** Lit
foundation

gloating as if ready to
  secretly devour the weak.
15 You tread the sea
  with your horses,
stirring up the vast water.

Habakkuk's Confidence in God Expressed

16 I heard,
  and I trembled within; Rv 1:17
my lips quivered
  at the sound.
Rottenness entered
  my bones;
I trembled where I stood.
Now I must quietly wait
  for the day of distress Is 37:3
to come against the people
  invading us.
17 Though the fig tree
  does not bud

and there is no fruit
  on the vines,
though the olive crop fails
and the fields produce
  no food,
though the flocks disappear
  from the pen
and there are no herds
  in the stalls,
18 yet I will celebrate in
  the LORD;
I will rejoice in the God
  of my salvation! 1Sm 2:1; Ps 9:14
19 The LORD my Lord
  is my strength; 1Sm 30:6; 1Ch 16:11
he makes my feet like those
  of a deer Ps 18:33
and enables me to walk
  on mountain heights! Ps 18:33
For the choir director: on A stringed
instruments.

A 3:19 Lit on my

ZEPHANIAH

1 The word of the LORD that came to Zephaniah son of Cushi, son of Gedaliah, son of Amariah, son of Hezekiah, in the days of Josiah son of Amon, king of Judah. Jr 1:2

The Great Day of the LORD

2 I will completely
sweep away everything
from the face of the earth —
this is
the LORD's declaration.
3 I will sweep away people
and animals; 1Kg 14:10; Ezk 14:17
I will sweep away the birds
of the sky
and the fish of the sea,
and the ruins[A] along with
the wicked. Is 13:9-12; Mt 13:41
I will cut off mankind
from the face of the earth.
This is
the LORD's declaration.

4 I will stretch out my hand
against Judah Ex 3:20; Ps 138:7
and against all the residents
of Jerusalem.
I will cut off every vestige
of Baal 1Kg 16:30-32
from this place,
the names
of the pagan priests 2Kg 23:5
along with the priests;
5 those who bow in worship
on the rooftops Jr 19:13; 32:29
to the stars in the sky;
those who bow
and pledge loyalty
to the LORD Dt 6:13; Is 48:1
but also pledge loyalty
to Milcom;[B] 1Kg 11:5; 2Kg 23:13
6 and those who turn back
from following the LORD,
who do not seek the LORD
or inquire of him.
7 Be silent in the presence
of the Lord GOD, Nm 13:30
for the day of the LORD
is near. Zph 1:14,18; 2:2-3
Indeed, the LORD
has prepared a sacrifice;
he has consecrated
his guests. Lv 7:11-21; 1Sm 16:5

8 On the day
of the LORD's sacrifice
I will punish the officials,
the king's sons,
and all who are dressed
in foreign clothing.
9 On that day I will punish
all who skip over
the threshold,[C] 1Sm 5:5
who fill their master's house
with violence and deceit.

10 On that day —
this is
the LORD's declaration —
there will be an outcry
from the Fish Gate, 2Ch 33:14
a wailing
from the Second District,
and a loud crashing
from the hills.
11 Wail, you residents
of the Hollow,[D]
for all the merchants[E]
will be silenced;

A 1:3 Perhaps objects connected with idolatry B 1:5 Some LXX mss, Syr, Vg; MT, other LXX mss read *their king* C 1:9 Hb obscure D 1:11 Or *the market district* E 1:11 Or *Canaanites*

all those loaded with silver
   will be cut off.

¹² And at that time I will
   search Jerusalem
   with lamps
and punish
   those who settle down
   comfortably,ᴬ   Ex 15:8; Is 25:6
who say to themselves:
The Lᴏʀᴅ will not do good
   or evil.   Mal 2:17
¹³ Their wealth will
   become plunder
and their houses a ruin.
They will build houses
   but never live in them,
plant vineyards
   but never drink their wine.

¹⁴ The great day of the Lᴏʀᴅ
   is near,   Is 13:6,9; Jl 1:15; 2:1,11,31; 3:14
near and
   rapidly approaching.
Listen, the day of the Lᴏʀᴅ —
then the warrior's cry is bitter.
¹⁵ That day is a day of wrath,
   a day of trouble and distress,
a day of destruction
   and desolation,
a day of darkness and gloom,
a day of clouds and total
   darkness,   Ps 97:2; Ezk 34:12; Jl 2:2
¹⁶ a day of trumpet blast
   and battle cry
against the fortified cities,
and against
   the high corner towers.
¹⁷ I will bring distress
   on mankind,
and they will walk
   like the blind   Lm 4:14
because they have sinned
   against the Lᴏʀᴅ.
Their blood will be
   poured out like dust

and their flesh like dung.
¹⁸ Their silver and their gold
will be unable to rescue them
   on the day
   of the Lᴏʀᴅ's wrath.   Ezk 7:19
The whole earth
   will be consumed
by the fire of his jealousy,
for he will make a complete,
yes, a horrifying end
of all the inhabitants
   of the earth.

A Call to Repentance

2 Gather yourselves together;
   gather together,
   undesirableᴮ nation,
²   before the decree
   takes effect   Jb 23:14; Ps 2:7; 148:6
and the day passes like chaff,
before the burning
   of the Lᴏʀᴅ's anger
   overtakes you,   Nm 25:4; 32:14
before the day
   of the Lᴏʀᴅ's anger
   overtakes you.   Lm 2:22
³ Seek the Lᴏʀᴅ,
   all you humble of the earth,
who carry out
   what he commands.
Seek righteousness,
   seek humility;
perhaps you will
   be concealed   Gn 4:14; Ex 3:6
on the day
   of the Lᴏʀᴅ's anger.

Judgment Against the Nations

⁴ For Gaza will be abandoned,
and Ashkelon will become
   a ruin.
Ashdod will be driven out
   at noon,
and Ekron will be uprooted.
⁵ Woe, inhabitants
   of the seacoast,

ᴬ**1:12** Lit *who thicken on their dregs*   ᴮ**2:1** Or *shameless*

nation of the Cherethites!^A
The word of the LORD is
  against you,   Is 37:22; Jr 16:10; 42:19
Canaan, land
  of the Philistines:
I will destroy you until
  there is no one left.   Is 5:9; 6:11

⁶ The seacoast will
  become pasturelands
with caves for shepherds
  and pens for sheep.
⁷ The coastland will belong
to the remnant of the house
  of Judah;
they will find pasture there.
They will lie down
  in the evening
among the houses
  of Ashkelon,
for the LORD their God
  will return to them
and restore their fortunes.

⁸ I have heard the taunting
  of Moab   Ps 42:10; 102:8; 119:42
and the insults
  of the Ammonites,   Am 1:13
who have taunted my people
and threatened
  their territory.
⁹ Therefore, as I live —
  this is the declaration
  of the LORD of Armies,
  the God of Israel —
Moab will be like Sodom   Is 1:9
and the Ammonites
  like Gomorrah: Gn 19:24-25
a place overgrown
  with weeds,
a salt pit, and
  a perpetual wasteland.
The remnant of my people
  will plunder them;
the remainder of my nation
  will dispossess them.

¹⁰ This is what they get
  for their pride,
because they have taunted
  and acted arrogantly   Jr 48:42
against the people
  of the LORD of Armies.
¹¹ The LORD will be terrifying
  to them
when he starves all the gods
  of the earth.
Then all the distant coasts
  and islands of the nations
will bow in worship to him,
  each in its own place.

¹² You Cushites will also
  be slain by my sword.   Is 18:1-7

¹³ He will also stretch out
  his hand against the north
and destroy Assyria;
he will make Nineveh
  a desolate ruin,   Nah 2:8; 3:7
dry as the desert.
¹⁴ Herds will lie down
  in the middle of it,
every kind of wild animal.^B
Both eagle owls^C and herons^D
will roost in the capitals
  of its pillars.
Their calls will sound^E
  from the window,
but devastation^F will be
  on the threshold,
for he will expose
  the cedar work.^G
¹⁵ This is the jubilant city   Is 13:3
that lives in security,
that thinks to herself:
I exist, and there is
  no one else.
What a desolation
  she has become,
a place for wild animals
  to lie down!

^A**2:5** = Sea Peoples   ^B**2:14** Lit *every wild animal of a nation*   ^C**2:14** Or *the pelicans*   ^D**2:14** Or *the hedgehogs*   ^E**2:14** Lit *sing*   ^F**2:14** LXX, Vg read *ravens*   ^G**2:14** Hb obscure

Everyone who passes by her
scoffs[A] and shakes his fist.

Woe to Oppressive Jerusalem

3 Woe to the city
that is rebellious[B]
and defiled, Ex 23:21; Dt 9:24; Is 59:3
the oppressive city!
[2] She has not obeyed; 1Sm 15:22
she has not
accepted discipline. Jb 5:17
She has not trusted in the
LORD;
she has not drawn near
to her God. Pr 3:5
[3] The[C] princes within her are
roaring lions; Ezk 22:25
her judges are wolves
of the night, Hab 1:8; Mt 7:15
which leave nothing
for[D] the morning.
[4] Her prophets are reckless —
treacherous men.
Her priests profane
the sanctuary;
they do violence
to instruction. Ezk 22:26
[5] The righteous LORD is in her;
he does no wrong. Ps 92:15
He applies his justice
morning by morning;
he does not fail at dawn,
yet the one who does wrong
knows no shame. Jr 8:12

[6] I have cut off nations;
their corner towers
are destroyed. Zph 1:16
I have laid waste
their streets,
with no one to pass through.
Their cities lie devastated,
without a person,
without an inhabitant. Jr 44:2

[7] I thought: You
will certainly fear me
and accept correction.
Then her dwelling place[E]
would not be cut off
based on
all that I had allocated
to her.
However, they became
more corrupt
in all their actions.
[8] Therefore, wait for me —
this is
the LORD's declaration —
until the day I rise up
for plunder.[F]
For my decision is
to gather nations,
to assemble kingdoms,
in order to pour out
my indignation on them,
all my burning anger;
for the whole earth
will be consumed
by the fire of my jealousy.

Final Restoration Promised

[9] For I will then restore
pure speech to the peoples
so that all of them may call
on the name of the LORD
and serve him
with a single purpose.[G]
[10] From beyond the rivers
of Cush Is 18:1-3
my supplicants,
my dispersed people,
will bring an offering to me.
[11] On that day you[H] will not
be put to shame Gn 2:25; Ps 25:3
because of everything
you have done
in rebelling against me. Is 1:2
For then I will remove

[A]2:15 Or hisses   [B]3:1 Or filthy   [C]3:3 Lit Her   [D]3:3 Or that had nothing to gnaw in   [E]3:7 LXX, Syr read her eyes   [F]3:8 LXX, Syr read for a witness; Vg reads up forever   [G]3:9 Lit with one shoulder   [H]3:11 = Israel

from among you your
jubilant, arrogant people,
and you will never again
be haughty
on my holy mountain.   Is 11:9
¹² I will leave
a meek and humble people
among you,   Is 66:2
and they will take refuge
in the name of the LORD.
¹³ The remnant of Israel will
no longer   Gn 45:7; 2Kg 19:31; Jr 23:3
do wrong or tell lies;
a deceitful tongue will not
be found
in their mouths.
They will pasture
and lie down,
with nothing to make
them afraid.   Gn 42:28; Jr 50:19

¹⁴ Sing for joy, Daughter Zion;
shout loudly, Israel!
Be glad and celebrate with all
your heart,
Daughter Jerusalem!
¹⁵ The LORD has removed
your punishment;
he has turned back
your enemy.
The King of Israel, the LORD,
is among you;
you need no longer
fear harm.
¹⁶ On that day it will be said
to Jerusalem:
"Do not fear;

Zion, do not let your hands
grow weak.   Jr 6:24; 50:43
¹⁷ The LORD your God
is among you,
a warrior who saves.   Jos 1:14
He will rejoice over you
with gladness.   Dt 28:63; 30:9
He will be quiet ᴬ in his love.
He will delight in you
with singing."   Ps 30:5
¹⁸ I will gather those
who have been driven   Lm 3:33
from the appointed festivals;
they will be a tribute
from you ᴮ
and a reproach on her. ᶜ
¹⁹ Yes, at that time
I will deal with all
who oppress you.
I will save the lame
and gather the outcasts;
I will make those
who were disgraced
throughout the earth
receive praise and fame.
²⁰ At that time I will bring
you ᴰ back,
yes, at the time
I will gather you.
I will give you
fame and praise
among all the peoples
of the earth,
when I restore your fortunes
before your eyes.   Jb 42:10; Hs 6:11
The LORD has spoken.

HAGGAI

Command to Rebuild the Temple

1 In the second year of King Darius,[A] on the first day of the sixth month, the word of the LORD came through the prophet Haggai to Zerubbabel son of Shealtiel, the governor of Judah, and to Joshua son of Jehozadak, the high priest: ² "The LORD of Armies says this: These people say: The time has not come for the house of the LORD to be rebuilt." **Ezr 1:3** ³ The word of the LORD came through the prophet Haggai: ⁴ "Is it a time for you yourselves to live in your paneled houses, while this house[B] lies in ruins?" ⁵ Now, the LORD of Armies says this: "Think carefully about[C] your ways: **1Kg 7:7**

⁶ You have planted much
but harvested little.
You eat
but never have enough
to be satisfied.
You drink
but never have enough
to be happy.
You put on clothes
but never have enough
to get warm.
The wage earner
puts his wages
into a bag with a hole in it."

⁷ The LORD of Armies says this: "Think carefully about your ways. ⁸ Go up into the hills, bring down lumber, and build the house; and I will be pleased with it and be glorified," says the LORD.

⁹ "You expected much, but then it amounted to little. When you brought the harvest to your house, I ruined[D] it. Why?" This is the declaration of the LORD of Armies. "Because my house still lies in ruins, while each of you is busy with his own house.

¹⁰ So on your account,[E]
the skies have withheld
the dew
and the land its crops. **Lv 26:20**
¹¹ I have summoned a drought
on the fields and the hills,
on the grain, new wine,
fresh oil,
and whatever
the ground yields,
on man and animal,
and on all that
your hands produce."

The People's Response

¹² Then Zerubbabel son of Shealtiel, the high priest Joshua son of Jehozadak, and the entire remnant of the people obeyed the LORD their God and the words of the prophet Haggai, because the LORD their God had sent him. So the people feared the LORD. **1Ch 13:9; Ezr 3:8; Neh 12:1; Hg 2:2**

¹³ Then Haggai, the LORD's messenger, delivered the LORD's message to the people: "I am with you — this is the LORD's declaration."

¹⁴ The LORD roused the spirit of Zerubbabel son of Shealtiel, governor of Judah, the spirit of the high priest Joshua son of Jehozadak, and the spirit of all the remnant of the

people. They began work on the house of the LORD of Armies, their God, [15] on the twenty-fourth day of the sixth month, in the second year of King Darius.   1Ch 5:26; Ezr 1:1,5; Is 13:17

Encouragement and Promise

2 On the twenty-first day of the seventh month, the word of the LORD came through the prophet Haggai: [2] "Speak to Zerubbabel son of Shealtiel, governor of Judah, to the high priest Joshua son of Jehozadak, and to the remnant of the people: [3] 'Who is left among you who saw this house in its former glory? How does it look to you now? Doesn't it seem to you like nothing by comparison? [4] Even so, be strong, Zerubbabel — this is the LORD's declaration. Be strong, Joshua son of Jehozadak, high priest. Be strong, all you people of the land — this is the LORD's declaration. Work! For I am with you — the declaration of the LORD of Armies. [5] This is the promise I made to you when you came out of Egypt, and my Spirit is present among you; don't be afraid.'"   Lv 23:33-43; 2Ch 7:8-10

[6] For the LORD of Armies says this: "Once more, in a little while, I am going to shake the heavens and the earth, the sea and the dry land. [7] I will shake all the nations so that the treasures of all the nations will come, and I will fill this house with glory," says the LORD of Armies. [8] "The silver and gold belong to me" — this is the declaration of the LORD of Armies. [9] "The final glory of this house [A] will be greater than the first," says the LORD of Armies. "I will provide peace in this place" — this is the declaration of the LORD of Armies.   Is 64:2; Hg 2:21

From Deprivation to Blessing

[10] On the twenty-fourth day of the ninth month, in the second year of Darius, the word of the LORD came to the prophet Haggai: [11] "This is what the LORD of Armies says: Ask the priests for a ruling. [12] If a man is carrying consecrated meat in the fold of his garment, and it touches bread, stew, wine, oil, or any other food, does it become holy?"   Jr 11:15; Mal 2:7

The priests answered, "No."

[13] Then Haggai asked, "If someone defiled by contact with a corpse touches any of these, does it become defiled?"   Lv 11:39; 22:4-6

The priests answered, "It becomes defiled."

[14] Then Haggai replied, "So is this people, and so is this nation before me — this is the LORD's declaration. And so is every work of their hands; even what they offer there is defiled.

[15] "Now from this day on, think carefully: Before one stone was placed on another in the LORD's temple, [16] what state were you in? [B] When someone came to a grain heap of twenty measures, it only amounted to ten; when one came to the winepress to dip fifty measures from the vat, it only amounted to twenty. [17] I struck you — all the work of your hands — with blight, mildew, and hail, but you didn't turn to me — this is the LORD's declaration. [18] "From this day on, think carefully; from the twenty-fourth day of the ninth month, from the day the foundation of the LORD's temple was laid; think carefully. [19] Is there still seed left in the granary? The vine, the fig, the pomegranate, and the olive tree have not

^A 2:9 Or *The glory of this latter house*   ^B 2:16 Hb obscure yet produced. But from this day on I will bless you." Dt 28:22; 1Kg 8:37; Am 4:9

Promise to Zerubbabel

20 The word of the LORD came to Haggai a second time on the twenty-fourth day of the month: 21 "Speak to Zerubbabel, governor of Judah: I am going to shake the heavens and the earth. 22 I will overturn royal thrones and destroy the power of the Gentile kingdoms. I will overturn chariots and their riders. Horses and their riders will fall, each by his brother's sword. 23 On that day" — this is the declaration of the LORD of Armies — "I will take you, Zerubbabel son of Shealtiel, my servant" — this is the LORD's declaration — "and make you like my signet ring, for I have chosen you." This is the declaration of the LORD of Armies. Gn 19:25; Est 8:8; Ezk 38:19-20; Hg 2:6-7

ZECHARIAH

A Plea for Repentance

1 In the eighth month, in the second year of Darius, the word of the LORD came to the prophet Zechariah son of Berechiah, son of Iddo: ² "The LORD was extremely angry with your ancestors. ³ So tell the people, 'This is what the LORD of Armies says: Return to me — this is the declaration of the LORD of Armies — and I will return to you, says the LORD of Armies. ⁴ Do not be like your ancestors; the earlier prophets proclaimed to them: This is what the LORD of Armies says: Turn from your evil ways and your evil deeds. But they did not listen or pay attention to me — this is the LORD's declaration. ⁵ Where are your ancestors now? And do the prophets live forever? ⁶ But didn't my words and my statutes that I commanded my servants the prophets overtake your ancestors?'" Ezr 4:5,24; 5:5-7; Hg 1:1,15

So the people repented and said, "As the LORD of Armies decided to deal with us for our ways and our deeds, so he has dealt with us."

THE NIGHT VISIONS

⁷ On the twenty-fourth day of the eleventh month, which is the month of Shebat, in the second year of Darius, the word of the LORD came to the prophet Zechariah son of Berechiah, son of Iddo:

First Vision: Horsemen

⁸ I looked out in the night and saw a man riding on a chestnut ^A^ horse. He was standing among the myrtle trees in the valley. ^B^ Behind him were chestnut, brown, and white horses. ⁹ I asked, "What are these, my lord?" Rv 6:4

The angel who was talking to me replied, "I will show you what they are."

¹⁰ Then the man standing among the myrtle trees explained, "They are the ones the LORD has sent to patrol the earth."

¹¹ They reported to the angel of the LORD standing among the myrtle trees, "We have patrolled the earth, and right now the whole earth is calm and quiet." Jos 11:23; Jdg 5:31; Is 14:7

¹² Then the angel of the LORD responded, "How long, LORD of Armies, will you withhold mercy from Jerusalem and the cities of Judah that you have been angry with these seventy years?" ¹³ The LORD replied with kind and comforting words to the angel who was speaking with me. Ps 13:1; 79:5; 89:46

¹⁴ So the angel who was speaking with me said, "Proclaim: The LORD of Armies says: I am extremely jealous for Jerusalem and Zion. ¹⁵ I am fiercely angry with the nations that are at ease, for I was a little angry, but they made the destruction worse. ^C^ ¹⁶ Therefore, this is what the LORD says: In mercy, I have returned to Jerusalem; my house will be rebuilt within it — this is the declaration of the LORD of Armies — and a measuring line will be stretched out over Jerusalem. Ex 20:5; 34:14; Dt 4:24; 5:9; 6:15; Jos 24:19

^A^1:8 Lit *red*   ^B^1:8 Lit *depths*   ^C^1:15 Lit *they helped for evil*

¹⁷ "Proclaim further: This is what the LORD of Armies says: My cities will again overflow with prosperity; the LORD will once more comfort Zion and again choose Jerusalem."

Second Vision: Four Horns and Craftsmen

¹⁸ Then I looked up and saw four horns. ¹⁹ So I asked the angel who was speaking with me, "What are these?"   Ezk 43:15,20

And he said to me, "These are the horns that scattered Judah, Israel, and Jerusalem."

²⁰ Then the LORD showed me four craftsmen. ²¹ I asked, "What are they coming to do?"

He replied, "These are the horns that scattered Judah so no one could raise his head. These craftsmen have come to terrify them, to cut off^A the horns of the nations that raised a horn against the land of Judah to scatter it."

Third Vision: Surveyor

2 I looked up and saw a man with a measuring line in his hand. ² I asked, "Where are you going?"

He answered me, "To measure Jerusalem to determine its width and length."

³ Then the angel who was speaking with me went out, and another angel went out to meet him. ⁴ He said to him, "Run and tell this young man: Jerusalem will be inhabited without walls because of the number of people and livestock in it." ⁵ The declaration of the LORD: "I myself will be a wall of fire around it, and I will be the glory within it."   Is 49:19

⁶ "Listen! Listen! Flee from the land of the north" — this is the LORD's declaration — "for I have scattered you like the four winds of heaven" — this is the LORD's declaration. ⁷ "Listen, Zion! Escape, you who are living with Daughter Babylon." ⁸ For the LORD of Armies says this: "In pursuit of his glory, he sent me against the nations plundering you, for whoever touches you touches the pupil^B of my^C eye. ⁹ For look, I am raising my hand against them, and they will become plunder for their own servants. Then you will know that the LORD of Armies has sent me.   Is 11:15; 19:16; Jr 6:22; 10:22

¹⁰ "Daughter Zion, shout for joy and be glad, for I am coming to dwell among you" — this is the LORD's declaration. ¹¹ "Many nations will join themselves to the LORD on that day and become my^D people. I will dwell among you, and you will know that the LORD of Armies has sent me to you. ¹² The LORD will take possession of Judah as his portion in the Holy Land, and he will once again choose Jerusalem. ¹³ Let all people be silent before the LORD, for from his holy dwelling he has roused himself."   Ps 47:9; Is 42:6; Mc 4:2

Fourth Vision: High Priest and Branch

3 Then he showed me the high priest Joshua standing before the angel of the LORD, with Satan^E standing at his right side to accuse him. ² The LORD^F said to Satan: "The LORD rebuke you, Satan! May the LORD who has chosen Jerusalem rebuke you! Isn't this man a burning stick snatched from the fire?"   Dt 4:20; Am 4:11

³ Now Joshua was dressed with filthy^G clothes as he stood before

---

^A1:21 Lit throw down   ^B2:8 Or apple   ^C2:8 Alt Hb tradition; MT reads his   ^D2:11 LXX, Syr read his
^E3:1 Or the accuser   ^F3:2 Syr reads The Angel of the LORD   ^G3:3 Probably stained with human excrement

the angel. ⁴ So the angel of the LORDᴬ spoke to thoseᴮ standing before him, "Take off his filthy clothes!" Then he said to him, "See, I have removed your iniquity from you, and I will clothe you with festive robes." Lv 22:3; Dt 23:13; 2Sm 24:10; Is 4:4

⁵ Then I said, "Let them put a clean turban on his head." So a clean turban was placed on his head, and they clothed him in garments while the angel of the LORD was standing nearby. Ex 28:36-38

⁶ Then the angel of the LORD charged Joshua: ⁷ "This is what the LORD of Armies says: If you walk in my ways and keep my mandates, you will both rule my house and take care of my courts; I will also grant you access among these who are standing here.

⁸ "Listen, High Priest Joshua, you and your colleagues sitting before you; indeed, these men are a sign that I am about to bring my servant, the Branch. ⁹ Notice the stone I have set before Joshua; on that one stone are seven eyes. I will engrave an inscription on it" — this is the declaration of the LORD of Armies — "and I will take away the iniquity of this land in a single day. ¹⁰ On that day, each of you will invite his neighbor to sit under his vine and fig tree." This is the declaration of the LORD of Armies. Is 4:2; 11:1; Jr 23:5; 33:15; Ezk 17:22-24

Fifth Vision: Gold Lampstand

4 The angel who was speaking with me then returned and roused me as one awakened out of sleep. ² He asked me, "What do you see?"

I replied, "I see a solid gold lampstand with a bowl at the top. The lampstand also has seven lamps at the top with seven spouts for each ofᶜ the lamps. ³ There are also two olive trees beside it, one on the right of the bowl and the other on its left."

⁴ Then I asked the angel who was speaking with me, "What are these, my lord?"

⁵ "Don't you know what they are?" replied the angel who was speaking with me.

I said, "No, my lord."

⁶ So he answered me, "This is the word of the LORD to Zerubbabel: 'Not by strength or by might, but by my Spirit,' says the LORD of Armies. ⁷ 'What are you, great mountain? Before Zerubbabel you will become a plain. And he will bring out the capstone accompanied by shouts of: Grace, grace to it!'" Is 40:4; Hs 1:7; Hg 2:4-5; Mt 17:20; 21:21

⁸ Then the word of the LORD came to me: ⁹ "Zerubbabel's hands have laid the foundation of this house, and his hands will complete it. Then you will know that the LORD of Armies has sent me to you. ¹⁰ For who despises the day of small things? These seven eyes of the LORD, which scan throughout the whole earth, will rejoice when they see the ceremonial stoneᴰ in Zerubbabel's hand." Ezr 3:8-11; 5:16; Pr 15:3; Zch 6:9

¹¹ I asked him, "What are the two olive trees on the right and left of the lampstand?" ¹² And I questioned him further, "What are the two streamsᴱ of the olive trees, from which the golden oil is pouring through the two golden conduits?"

¹³ Then he inquired of me, "Don't you know what these are?"

"No, my lord," I replied.

ᴬ3:4 Lit *he*   ᴮ3:4 = the angels   ᶜ4:2 Or *seven lips to*   ᴰ4:10 Lit *the tin stone*   ᴱ4:12 Or *branches*

[14] "These are the two anointed ones,"[A] he said, "who stand by the Lord of the whole earth." Jr 33:17-22

Sixth Vision: Flying Scroll

5 I looked up again and saw a flying scroll. [2] "What do you see?" he asked me. Ezk 2:9-10; Rv 5:1; 10:2

"I see a flying scroll," I replied, "thirty feet[B] long and fifteen feet[C] wide." Ex 26:15-25; 1Kg 6:3; 1Pt 4:17

[3] Then he said to me, "This is the curse that is going out over the whole land, for everyone who is a thief, contrary to what is written on one side, has gone unpunished,[D] and everyone who swears falsely, contrary to what is written on the other side, has gone unpunished. [4] I will send it out," — this is the declaration of the LORD of Armies — "and it will enter the house of the thief and the house of the one who swears falsely by my name. It will stay inside his house and destroy it along with its timbers and stones."

Seventh Vision: Woman in the Basket

[5] Then the angel who was speaking with me came forward and told me, "Look up and see what this is that is approaching."

[6] So I asked, "What is it?"

He responded, "It's a measuring basket[E] that is approaching." And he continued, "This is their iniquity[F] in all the land." [7] Then a lead cover was lifted, and there was a woman sitting inside the basket. [8] "This is Wickedness," he said. He shoved her down into the basket and pushed the lead weight over its opening. [9] Then I looked up and saw two women approaching with the wind in their wings. Their wings were like those of a stork, and they lifted up the basket between earth and sky. Lv 19:36; Dt 25:14; Hs 9:15; Rv 17:1

[10] So I asked the angel who was speaking with me, "Where are they taking the basket?"

[11] "To build a shrine for it in the land of Shinar," he told me. "When that is ready, the basket will be placed there on its pedestal." Gn 11:9

Eighth Vision: Four Chariots

6 Then I looked up again and saw four chariots coming from between two mountains. The mountains were made of bronze. [2] The first chariot had chestnut[G] horses, the second chariot black horses, [3] the third chariot white horses, and the fourth chariot dappled horses — all strong horses. [4] So I inquired of the angel who was speaking with me, "What are these, my lord?" Rv 6:2, 4-6; 19:11

[5] The angel told me, "These are the four spirits[H] of heaven going out after presenting themselves to the Lord of the whole earth. [6] The one with the black horses is going to the land of the north, the white horses are going after them, but the dappled horses are going to the land of the south." [7] As the strong horses went out, they wanted to go patrol the earth, and the LORD said, "Go, patrol the earth." So they patrolled the earth. [8] Then he summoned me saying, "See, those going to the land of the north have pacified my Spirit in the northern land."

Crowning of the Branch

[9] The word of the LORD came to me: [10] "Take an offering from the exiles,

from Heldai, Tobijah, and Jedaiah, who have arrived from Babylon, and go that same day to the house of Josiah son of Zephaniah. [11] Take silver and gold, make a crown, [A] and place it on the head of Joshua son of Jehozadak, the high priest. [12] You are to tell him: This is what the LORD of Armies says: Here is a man whose name is Branch; he will branch out from his place and build the LORD's temple. [13] Yes, he will build the LORD's temple; he will be clothed in splendor and will sit on his throne and rule. There will also be a priest on his throne, and there will be peaceful counsel between the two of them. [14] The crown will reside in the LORD's temple as a memorial to Heldai, Tobijah, Jedaiah, and Hen [B] son of Zephaniah. [15] People who are far off will come and build the LORD's temple, and you will know that the LORD of Armies has sent me to you. This will happen when you fully obey the LORD your God."   1Ch 16:27; Zch 3:8; 4:8

Disobedience and Fasting

7 In the fourth year of King Darius, the word of the LORD came to Zechariah on the fourth day of the ninth month, which is Chislev. [2] Now the people of Bethel had sent Sharezer, Regem-melech, and their men to plead for the LORD's favor [3] by asking the priests who were at the house of the LORD of Armies as well as the prophets, "Should we mourn and fast in the fifth month as we have done these many years?"   Zch 1:1; 8:21-22

[4] Then the word of the LORD of Armies came to me: [5] "Ask all the people of the land and the priests: When you fasted and lamented

in the fifth and in the seventh months for these seventy years, did you really fast for me? [6] When you eat and drink, don't you eat and drink simply for yourselves? [7] Aren't these the words that the LORD proclaimed through the earlier prophets when Jerusalem was inhabited and secure, [C] along with its surrounding cities, and when the southern region and the Judean foothills were inhabited? "

[8] The word of the LORD came to Zechariah: [9] "The LORD of Armies says this: 'Make fair decisions. Show faithful love and compassion to one another. [10] Do not oppress the widow or the fatherless, the resident alien or the poor, and do not plot evil in your hearts against one another.' [11] But they refused to pay attention and turned a stubborn shoulder; they closed their ears so they could not hear. [12] They made their hearts like a rock so as not to obey the law or the words that the LORD of Armies had sent by his Spirit through the earlier prophets. Therefore intense anger came from the LORD of Armies. [13] Just as he had called, and they would not listen, so when they called, I would not listen, says the LORD of Armies. [14] I scattered them with a windstorm over all the nations that had not known them, and the land was left desolate behind them, with no one coming or going. They turned a pleasant land into a desolation."   Ex 18:19-23; Zch 8:16

Obedience and Feasting

8 The word of the LORD of Armies came: [2] The LORD of Armies says this: "I am extremely jealous for Zion; I am jealous for her with great wrath." [3] The LORD says this: "I will return to Zion and live in Jerusalem. Then Jerusalem will be called the Faithful City; the mountain of the LORD of Armies will be called the Holy Mountain." [4] The LORD of Armies says this: "Old men and women will again sit along the streets of Jerusalem, each with a staff in hand because of advanced age. [5] The streets of the city will be filled with boys and girls playing in them." [6] The LORD of Armies says this: "Though it may seem impossible to the remnant of this people in those days, should it also seem impossible to me?" — this is the declaration of the LORD of Armies. [7] The LORD of Armies says this: "I will save my people from the land of the east and the land of the west.[A] [8] I will bring them back to live in Jerusalem. They will be my people, and I will be their faithful and righteous God."   Is 1:26; Zch 1:14

[9] The LORD of Armies says this: "Let your hands be strong, you who now hear these words that the prophets spoke when the foundations were laid for the rebuilding of the temple, the house of the LORD of Armies. [10] For prior to those days neither man nor animal had wages. There was no safety from the enemy for anyone who came or went, for I turned everyone against his neighbor. [11] But now, I will not treat the remnant of this people as in the former days" — this is the declaration of the LORD of Armies. [12] "For they will sow in peace: the vine will yield its fruit, the land will yield its produce, and the skies will yield their dew. I will give the remnant of this people all these things as an inheritance. [13] As you have been a

curse among the nations, house of Judah and house of Israel, so I will save you, and you will be a blessing. Don't be afraid; let your hands be strong." [14] For the LORD of Armies says this: "As I resolved to treat you badly when your fathers provoked me to anger, and I did not relent," says the LORD of Armies, [15] "so I have resolved again in these days to do what is good to Jerusalem and the house of Judah. Don't be afraid. [16] These are the things you must do: Speak truth to one another; make true and sound decisions within your city gates. [17] Do not plot evil in your hearts against your neighbor, and do not love perjury, for I hate all this" — this is the LORD's declaration.   Dt 31:7; Jos 1:6; Is 49:8

[18] Then the word of the LORD of Armies came to me: [19] The LORD of Armies says this: "The fast of the fourth month, the fast of the fifth, the fast of the seventh, and the fast of the tenth will become times of joy, gladness, and cheerful festivals for the house of Judah. Therefore, love truth and peace." [20] The LORD of Armies says this: "Peoples will yet come, the residents of many cities; [21] the residents of one city will go to another, saying: Let's go at once to plead for the LORD's favor and to seek the LORD of Armies. I am also going. [22] Many peoples and strong nations will come to seek the LORD of Armies in Jerusalem and to plead for the LORD's favor." [23] The LORD of Armies says this: "In those days, ten men from nations of every language will grab the robe of a Jewish man tightly, urging: Let us go with you, for we have heard that God is with you."   2Kg 25:3-4; Is 4:1; Jr 39:2

<hr>

[A] 8:7 Lit *sunset*

Judgment of Zion's Enemies

9 A pronouncement:
The word of the LORD
is against the land
of Hadrach,
and Damascus is
its resting place — Gn 15:2
for the eyes of humanity
and all the tribes of Israel
are on the LORD[A] —
2 and also against Hamath,
which borders it, 2Kg 14:25
as well as Tyre and Sidon,
though they are very shrewd.
3 Tyre has built herself
a fortress;
she has heaped up silver
like dust
and gold like the dirt
of the streets.
4 Listen! The Lord will
impoverish her
and cast her wealth
into the sea;
she herself will be consumed
by fire. Ezk 26:4-6; 27:27
5 Ashkelon will see it
and be afraid;
Gaza too, and will writhe
in great pain,
as will Ekron, for her hope
will fail.
There will cease to be a king
in Gaza,
and Ashkelon will
become uninhabited.
6 A mongrel people will live
in Ashdod,
and I will destroy the pride
of the Philistines. Am 1:6-8
7 I will remove the blood
from their mouths
and the abhorrent things
from between their teeth.
Then they too will become
a remnant for our God;

they will become like a clan
in Judah
and Ekron like the Jebusites.
8 I will encamp at my house
as a guard,
against those who march
back and forth,
and no oppressor will march
against them again,
for now I have seen
with my own eyes.

The Coming of Zion's King

9 Rejoice greatly,
Daughter Zion!
Shout in triumph,
Daughter Jerusalem!
Look, your King is coming
to you;
he is righteous
and victorious,[B]
humble and riding
on a donkey,
on a colt, the foal of a donkey.
10 I will cut off the chariot
from Ephraim
and the horse
from Jerusalem.
The bow of war
will be removed,
and he will proclaim peace
to the nations.
His dominion will extend
from sea to sea,
from the Euphrates River
to the ends of the earth. Ps 72:8
11 As for you,
because of the blood
of your covenant, Heb 10:29
I will release your prisoners
from the waterless cistern.
12 Return to a stronghold,
you prisoners
who have hope;
today I declare that
I will restore double to you.

[A]9:1 Or *eyes of the LORD are on mankind* — [B]9:9 Or *and has salvation*

¹³ For I will bend Judah
        as my bow;
I will fill that bow
        with Ephraim.
I will rouse your
        sons, Zion,
against your sons, Greece. ᴬ
I will make you
        like a warrior's sword.
¹⁴ Then the LORD will appear
        over them,
and his arrow will fly
        like lightning.
The Lord GOD will sound
        the trumpet
and advance
        with the southern storms.
¹⁵ The LORD of Armies will
        defend them.
They will consume
        and conquer
        with slingstones;
they will drink and be rowdy
        as if with wine.   Nm 23:24
They will be as full as
        the sprinkling basin,   Ex 27:3
like those at the corners
        of the altar.   Lv 1:5,11; 3:2
¹⁶ The LORD their God will
        save them on that day
as the flock of his people;
for they are like jewels
        in a crown,   Lv 8:9
sparkling over his land.
¹⁷ How lovely and beautiful!
Grain will make
        the young men flourish,
and new wine,
        the young women.

The LORD Restores His People

10 Ask the LORD for rain
        in the season of spring rain.
The LORD makes
        the rain clouds,
and he will give them
        showers of rain
and crops in the field
        for everyone.   Dt 28:12; Is 30:23
² For the idols speak falsehood,
and the diviners see illusions;
they relate empty dreams
and offer empty comfort.
Therefore the people wander
        like sheep;
they suffer affliction because
        there is no shepherd.
³ My anger burns
        against the shepherds,
so I will punish the leaders. ᴮ
For the LORD of Armies
        has tended his flock,
the house of Judah;
he will make them
        like his majestic steed
        in battle.
⁴ The cornerstone will come
        from Judah. ᶜ   Jdg 20:2; 1Sm 14:38
The tent peg will come
        from them   Jdg 4:21
and also the battle bow and
        every ᴰ ruler.   2Kg 13:15-17; Rv 6:2
Together ⁵ they will be
        like warriors in battle
trampling down the mud
        of the streets.
They will fight because
        the LORD is with them,
and they will put horsemen
        to shame.
⁶ I will strengthen the house
        of Judah
and deliver the house
        of Joseph. ᴱ
I will restore ᶠ them
because I have compassion
        on them,
and they will be
as though I had never
        rejected them.   Ps 103:12

ᴬ9:13 Lit *Javan*   ᴮ10:3 Lit *male goats*   ᶜ10:4 Lit *him*   ᴰ10:4 Lit *also from him the . . . , from him every*
ᴱ10:6 = the northern kingdom   ᶠ10:6 Other Hb mss, LXX read *settle*

For I am the LORD their God,
and I will answer them.
7 Ephraim will be like a warrior,
and their hearts will be glad
as if with wine.
Their children will see it
and be glad;   Ex 4:14; Ps 16:9
their hearts will rejoice
in the LORD.

8 I will whistle and gather them
because I have
redeemed them;   Ex 13:13; 21:8
they will be as numerous as
they once were.
9 Though I sow them
among the nations,   Gn 26:12
they will remember me
in the distant lands;   Gn 40:23
they and their children
will live and return.
10 I will bring them back
from the land of Egypt
and gather them
from Assyria.
I will bring them to the land
of Gilead   Gn 31:21; Dt 34:1; Ps 60:7
and to Lebanon,
but it will not be enough
for them.
11 The LORD^A will pass through
the sea of distress
and strike the waves of the sea;
all the depths of the Nile
will dry up.   Gn 8:7; Jos 2:10; 4:23
The pride of Assyria will be
brought down,
and the scepter of Egypt
will come to an end.
12 I will strengthen them
in the LORD,   Zch 10:6
and they will march
in his name —   Jos 6:3; Ps 68:7
this is
the LORD's declaration.

Israel's Shepherds: Good and Bad

11 Open your gates, Lebanon,
and fire will consume
your cedars.   Jdg 9:15; 2Kg 19:23
2 Wail, cypress, for the cedar
has fallen;   Is 14:8
the glorious trees
are destroyed!
Wail, oaks of Bashan,   Is 2:13
for the stately forest has fallen!
3 Listen to the wail
of the shepherds,   Is 15:8; Zph 1:10
for their glory is destroyed.
Listen to the roar
of young lions,   Jb 4:10; Ps 34:10
for the thickets of the Jordan
are^B destroyed.   Jr 49:19

4 The LORD my God says this: "Shepherd the flock intended for slaughter. 5 Those who buy them slaughter them but are not punished. Those who sell them say: Blessed be the LORD because I have become rich! Even their own shepherds have no compassion for them. 6 Indeed, I will no longer have compassion on the inhabitants of the land" — this is the LORD's declaration. "Instead, I will turn everyone over to his neighbor and his king. They will devastate the land, and I will not rescue it from their hand."   Lm 2:2,17,21; Ps 34:22; Jr 13:14

7 So I shepherded the flock intended for slaughter, the oppressed of the flock.^C I took two staffs, calling one Favor and the other Union, and I shepherded the flock. 8 In one month I got rid of three shepherds. I became impatient with them, and they also detested me. 9 Then I said, "I will no longer shepherd you. Let what is dying die, and let what is perishing perish; let the rest devour

---

^A10:11 Lit *He*   ^B11:3 Lit *for the majesty of the Jordan is*   ^C11:7 LXX reads *slaughter that belonged to the sheep merchants* each other's flesh." ¹⁰ Next I took my staff called Favor and cut it in two, annulling the covenant I had made with all the peoples. ¹¹ It was annulled on that day, and so the oppressed of the flock ᴬ who were watching me knew that it was the word of the LORD. ¹² Then I said to them, "If it seems right to you, give me my wages; but if not, keep them." So they weighed my wages, thirty pieces of silver. Ps 90:17; Zch 11:10

¹³ "Throw it to the potter," ᴮ the LORD said to me — this magnificent price I was valued by them. So I took the thirty pieces of silver and threw it into the house of the LORD, to the potter. ᶜ ¹⁴ Then I cut in two my second staff, Union, annulling the brotherhood between Judah and Israel. Mt 26:15; 27:3-10

¹⁵ The LORD also said to me: "Take the equipment of a foolish shepherd. ¹⁶ I am about to raise up a shepherd in the land who will not care for those who are perishing, and he will not seek the lost ᴰ or heal the broken. He will not sustain the healthy, ᴱ but he will devour the flesh of the fat sheep and tear off their hooves. Ezk 34:3-4

¹⁷   Woe to
        the worthless shepherd
        who deserts the flock!   Jr 23:2
    May a sword strike ᶠ his arm
        and his right eye!
    May his arm wither away
        and his right eye go
        completely blind! "

Judah's Security

12 A pronouncement:
The word of the LORD
concerning Israel.

A declaration of the LORD,

who stretched out
    the heavens,   Is 45:12; 51:13; Jr 10:12
laid the foundation
    of the earth,   Jb 38:4; Heb 1:10
and formed the spirit of man
    within him.

² "Look, I will make Jerusalem a cup that causes staggering for the peoples who surround the city. The siege against Jerusalem will also involve Judah. ³ On that day I will make Jerusalem a heavy stone for all the peoples; all who try to lift it will injure themselves severely when all the nations of the earth gather against her. ⁴ On that day" — this is the LORD's declaration — "I will strike every horse with panic and its rider with madness. I will keep a watchful eye on the house of Judah but strike all the horses of the nations with blindness. ⁵ Then each of the leaders of Judah will think to himself: The residents of Jerusalem are my strength through the LORD of Armies, their God. ⁶ On that day I will make the leaders of Judah like a firepot in a woodpile, like a flaming torch among sheaves; they will consume all the peoples around them on the right and the left, while Jerusalem continues to be inhabited on its site, in Jerusalem. ⁷ The LORD will save the tents of Judah first, so that the glory of David's house and the glory of Jerusalem's residents may not be greater than that of Judah. ⁸ On that day the LORD will defend the inhabitants of Jerusalem, so that on that day the one who is weakest among them will be like David on that day, and the house of David will be like God,

---

ᴬ**11:11** LXX reads *and the sheep merchants*   ᴮ**11:13** Syr reads *treasury*   ᶜ**11:13** One Hb ms, Syr read *treasury*   ᴰ**11:16** Or *young*   ᴱ**11:16** Or *exhausted*   ᶠ**11:17** Lit *be against* like the angel of the LORD, before them. ⁹ On that day I will set out to destroy all the nations that come against Jerusalem. Is 51:22-23; Jr 25:15-16

Mourning for the Pierced One

¹⁰ "Then I will pour out a spirit ᴬ of grace and prayer on the house of David and the residents of Jerusalem, and they will look at ᴮ me whom they pierced. They will mourn for him as one mourns for an only child and weep bitterly for him as one weeps for a firstborn. ¹¹ On that day the mourning in Jerusalem will be as great as the mourning of Hadad-rimmon in the plain of Megiddo. ¹² The land will mourn, every family by itself: the family of David's house by itself and their women by themselves; the family of Nathan's ᶜ house by itself and their women by themselves; ¹³ the family of Levi's house by itself and their women by themselves; the family of Shimei ᴰ by itself and their women by themselves; ¹⁴ all the remaining families, every family by itself, and their women by themselves. Is 44:3; Ezk 36:27; 39:29; Jl 2:28-29; Zch 4:6

God's People Cleansed

13 "On that day a fountain will be opened for the house of David and for the residents of Jerusalem, to wash away sin and impurity. ² On that day" — this is the declaration of the LORD of Armies — "I will remove the names of the idols from the land, and they will no longer be remembered. I will banish the prophets ᴱ and the unclean spirit from the land. ³ If a man still prophesies, his father and his mother who bore him will

say to him: You cannot remain alive because you have spoken a lie in the name of the LORD. When he prophesies, his father and his mother who bore him will pierce him through. ⁴ On that day every prophet will be ashamed of his vision when he prophesies; they will not put on a hairy cloak in order to deceive. ⁵ He will say: I am not a prophet; I work the land, for a man purchased ᶠ me as a servant since my youth. ⁶ If someone asks him: What are these wounds on your chest? ᴳ — then he will answer: I received the wounds in the house of my friends. Ps 36:9; 68:26; Pr 14:27; Jr 2:13

⁷ Sword, awake
     against my shepherd,
   against the man who is
     my associate —
     this is the declaration
     of the LORD of Armies.
   Strike the shepherd,
     and the sheep
     will be scattered;   Mt 26:31
   I will turn my hand
     against the little ones.
⁸ In the whole land —
     this is
     the LORD's declaration —
   two-thirds ᴴ will be cut off
     and die,
   but a third will be left in it.
⁹ I will put this third
     through the fire;
   I will refine them as silver
     is refined
   and test them as gold
     is tested.   Ps 66:10; Pr 17:3; Is 48:10
   They will call on my name,
   and I will answer them.   Ps 20:9
   I will say: They are my people,
   and they will say: The LORD is
     our God."   Ex 6:7; Lv 26:12; Jr 7:23; 11:4

ᴬ **12:10** Or *out the Spirit*   ᴮ **12:10** Or *to*   ᶜ **12:12** = a son of David   ᴰ **12:13** = a descendant of Levi
ᴱ **13:2** = false prophets   ᶠ **13:5** Or *sold*   ᴳ **13:6** Lit *wounds between your hands*   ᴴ **13:8** Lit *two-thirds in it*

The Lord's Triumph and Reign

14 Look, a day belonging to the Lord is coming when the plunder taken from you will be divided in your presence. ² I will gather all the nations against Jerusalem for battle. The city will be captured, the houses looted, and the women raped. Half the city will go into exile, but the rest of the people will not be removed from the city. Jl 3:2

³ Then the Lord will go out to fight against those nations as he fights on a day of battle. ⁴ On that day his feet will stand on the Mount of Olives, which faces Jerusalem on the east. The Mount of Olives will be split in half from east to west, forming a huge valley, so that half the mountain will move to the north and half to the south. ⁵ You will flee by my mountain valley, ᴬ for the valley of the mountains will extend to Azal. You will flee as you fled ᴮ from the earthquake in the days of King Uzziah of Judah. Then the Lord my God will come and all the holy ones with him. ꟲ Mt 24:3; Rv 19:11-21

⁶ On that day there will be no light; the sunlight and moonlight will diminish. ᴰ,ᴱ ⁷ It will be a unique day known only to the Lord, without day or night, but there will be light at evening. Is 13:10; Jl 2:10; 3:15; Mt 24:36

⁸ On that day living water will flow out from Jerusalem, half of it toward the eastern sea ꟳ and the other half toward the western sea, ꟾ in summer and winter alike. ⁹ On that day the Lord will become King over the whole earth — the Lord alone, and his name

alone. ¹⁰ All the land from Geba to Rimmon south of Jerusalem will be changed into a plain. But Jerusalem will be raised up and will remain ᴴ on its site from the Benjamin Gate to the place of the First Gate, ꟷ to the Corner Gate, and from the Tower of Hananel to the royal winepresses. ¹¹ People will live there, and never again will there be a curse of complete destruction. So Jerusalem will dwell in security. Ezk 41:7; 47:1-12; Jl 3:18; Rv 8:8-9; 16:3

¹² This will be the plague with which the Lord strikes all the people who have warred against Jerusalem: their flesh will rot while they stand on their feet, their eyes will rot in their sockets, and their tongues will rot in their mouths. ¹³ On that day a great panic from the Lord will be among them, so that each will seize the hand of another, and the hand of one will rise against the other. ¹⁴ Judah will also fight at Jerusalem, and the wealth of all the surrounding nations will be collected: gold, silver, and clothing in great abundance. ¹⁵ The same plague as the previous one will strike Ꞵ the horses, mules, camels, donkeys, and all the animals that are in those camps. Mc 4:13; Hg 2:7

¹⁶ Then all the survivors from the nations that came against Jerusalem will go up year after year to worship the King, the Lord of Armies, and to celebrate the Festival of Shelters. ¹⁷ Should any of the families of the earth not go up to Jerusalem to worship the King,

---

ᴬ**14:5** Some Hb mss, LXX, Sym, Tg read *The valley of my mountains will be blocked*   ᴮ**14:5** LXX reads *It will be blocked as it was blocked*   ꟲ**14:5** Some Hb mss, LXX, Vg, Tg, Syr; other Hb mss read *you*
ᴰ**14:6** LXX, Sym, Syr, Tg, Vg read *no light or cold or ice*   ᴱ**14:6** Lit *no light; the precious ones will congeal*
ꟳ**14:8** = the Dead Sea   ꟲ**14:8** = the Mediterranean Sea   ᴴ**14:10** Or *will be inhabited*   ꟾ**14:10** Or *the former gate*   Ꞵ**14:15** Lit *be on*

the LORD of Armies, rain will not fall on them. ¹⁸ And if the people ᴬ of Egypt will not go up and enter, then rain will not fall on them; this will be the plague the LORD inflicts on the nations who do not go up to celebrate the Festival of Shelters. ¹⁹ This will be the punishment of Egypt and all the nations that do not go up to celebrate the Festival of Shelters.   Lv 23:33-36

²⁰ On that day, the words HOLY TO THE LORD will be on the bells of the horses. The pots in the house of the LORD will be like the sprinkling basins before the altar. ²¹ Every pot in Jerusalem and in Judah will be holy to the LORD of Armies. All who sacrifice will come and use the pots to cook in. And on that day there will no longer be a Canaanite ᴮ in the house of the LORD of Armies.

MALACHI

The LORD's Love for Israel

1 A pronouncement: Is 13:1; Zch 9:1
The word of the LORD to Israel
through Malachi.^A   Hs 1:1; Jl 1:1; Mc 1:1

² "I have loved you," says the
LORD.   Dt 4:37; 7:6-8; 10:14-15; Neh 13:26; Ps 78:68
Yet you ask, "How have you loved
us?"

"Wasn't Esau Jacob's brother?"
This is the LORD's declaration. "Even
so, I loved Jacob, ³ but I hated Esau. I
turned his mountains into a wasteland, and gave his inheritance to
the desert jackals."   Gn 36:19

⁴ Though Edom says: "We have
been devastated, but we will re-
build^B the ruins," the LORD of Armies says this: "They may build,
but I will demolish. They will be
called a wicked country and the
people the LORD has cursed^C forever. ⁵ Your own eyes will see this, and
you yourselves will say, 'The LORD
is great, even beyond^D the borders
of Israel.'   Is 34:5-17; Jr 49:17-18; Mal 3:12,15

Disobedience of the Priests

⁶ "A son honors his father, and a
servant his master. But if I am a
father, where is my honor? And if
I am a master, where is your fear
of me? says the LORD of Armies to
you priests, who despise my name."

Yet you ask: "How have we despised your name?"

⁷ "By presenting defiled food on
my altar."

"How have we defiled you?" you
ask.   Ezk 22:26

When you say: "The LORD's table
is contemptible."   Ezk 41:22; 44:16

⁸ "When you present a blind animal for sacrifice, is it not wrong?
And when you present a lame or
sick animal, is it not wrong? Bring
it to your governor! Would he be
pleased with you or show you favor?" asks the LORD of Armies.
⁹ "And now plead for God's favor.
Will he be gracious to us? Since this
has come from your hands, will he
show any of you favor?" asks the
LORD of Armies. ¹⁰ "I wish one of
you would shut the temple doors,
so that you would no longer kindle
a useless fire on my altar! I am not
pleased with you," says the LORD of
Armies, "and I will accept no offering from your hands.   Lv 22:18-25
¹¹ "My name will be great among
the nations, from the rising of the
sun to its setting. Incense^E and pure
offerings will be presented in my
name in every place because my
name will be great among the nations,"^F says the LORD of Armies.
¹² "But you are profaning it when
you say: 'The Lord's table is defiled,
and its product, its food, is contemptible.' ¹³ You also say: 'Look,
what a nuisance!' And you scorn^G
it,"^H says the LORD of Armies. "You
bring stolen,^I lame, or sick animals.
You bring this as an offering! Am I
to accept that from your hands?"
asks the LORD.   Lv 22:2; Ezk 13:19; 22:26
¹⁴ "The deceiver is cursed who has
an acceptable male in his flock and

---

^A 1:1 = My Messenger   ^B 1:4 Or *will return and build*   ^C 1:4 Or *LORD is angry with*   ^D 1:5 Or *great over*
^E 1:11 Or *Burnt offerings*   ^F 1:11 Or *is great . . . are presented . . . is great*   ^G 1:13 Lit *blow at*   ^H 1:13 Alt
Hb tradition reads *me*   ^I 1:13 Or *injured*

makes a vow but sacrifices a defective animal to the Lord. For I am a great King," says the LORD of Armies, "and my name will be feared among the nations. Lv 22:18-25; 27:9-10

Warning to the Priests

2 "Therefore, this decree is for you priests: [2] If you don't listen, and if you don't take it to heart to honor my name," says the LORD of Armies, "I will send a curse among you, and I will curse your blessings. In fact, I have already begun to curse them because you are not taking it to heart. Is 42:25; 57:1; Nah 1:14

[3] "Look, I am going to rebuke your descendants, and I will spread animal waste[A] over your faces, the waste from your festival sacrifices, and you will be taken away with it. [4] Then you will know that I sent you this decree, so that my covenant with Levi may continue," says the LORD of Armies. [5] "My covenant with him was one of life and peace, and I gave these to him; it called for reverence, and he revered me and stood in awe of my name. [6] True instruction was in his mouth, and nothing wrong was found on his lips. He walked with me in peace and integrity and turned many from iniquity. [7] For the lips of a priest should guard knowledge, and people should desire instruction from his mouth, because he is the messenger of the LORD of Armies. Ex 29:14; Lv 16:27; Hs 4:6-8

[8] "You, on the other hand, have turned from the way. You have caused many to stumble by your instruction. You have violated[B] the covenant of Levi," says the LORD of

Armies. [9] "So I in turn have made you despised and humiliated before all the people because you are not keeping my ways but are showing partiality in your instruction."

Judah's Marital Unfaithfulness

[10] Don't all of us have one Father? Didn't one God create us? Why then do we act treacherously against one another, profaning the covenant of our fathers? [11] Judah has acted treacherously, and a detestable act has been done in Israel and in Jerusalem. For Judah has profaned the LORD's sanctuary,[C] which he loves, and has married the daughter of a foreign god.[D] [12] May the LORD cut off from the tents of Jacob the man who does this, whoever he may be,[E] even if he presents an offering to the LORD of Armies. Ex 4:22-23; Is 63:16; Hs 11:1; Mal 1:6

[13] This is another thing you do. You are covering the LORD's altar with tears, with weeping and groaning, because he no longer respects your offerings or receives them gladly from your hands. [14] And you ask, "Why?" Because even though the LORD has been a witness between you and the wife of your youth, you have acted treacherously against her. She was your marriage partner and your wife by covenant. [15] Didn't God make them one and give them a portion of spirit? What is the one seeking?[E] Godly offspring. So watch yourselves carefully,[F] so that no one acts treacherously against the wife of his[G] youth. Gn 31:50-53

[16] "If he hates and divorces his wife," says the LORD God of Israel,

---

[A]2:3 Dung or entrails　[B]2:8 Lit corrupted　[C]2:11 Or profaned what is holy to the LORD　[D]2:11 = a woman who worshiped a foreign god　[E]2:12,15 Hb obscure　[F]2:15 Lit So guard yourselves in your spirit　[G]2:15 Lit your "he^A covers his garment with injustice," says the LORD of Armies. Therefore, watch yourselves carefully,^B and do not act treacherously.

Judgment at the LORD's Coming

^17 You have wearied the LORD with your words.   Is 43:22-24

Yet you ask, "How have we wearied him?"

When you say, "Everyone who does what is evil is good in the LORD's sight, and he is delighted with them, or else where is the God of justice?"   Dt 25:16; Neh 9:33; Mal 3:15

3 "See, I am going to send my messenger, and he will clear the way before me. Then the Lord you seek will suddenly come to his temple, the Messenger of the covenant you delight in — see, he is coming," says the LORD of Armies. ^2 But who can endure the day of his coming? And who will be able to stand when he appears? For he will be like a refiner's fire and like launderer's bleach.^C ^3 He will be like a refiner and purifier of silver; he will purify the sons of Levi and refine them like gold and silver. Then they will present offerings to the LORD in righteousness. ^4 And the offerings of Judah and Jerusalem will please the LORD as in days of old and years gone by.   Ex 23:20; 33:2; Is 40:3

^5 "I will come to you in judgment, and I will be ready to witness against sorcerers and adulterers; against those who swear falsely; against those who oppress the hired worker, the widow, and the fatherless; and against those who deny justice to the resident alien. They do not fear me," says the LORD of Armies.

^6 "Because I, the LORD, have not changed, you descendants of Jacob have not been destroyed.^D

Robbing God

^7 "Since the days of your fathers, you have turned from my statutes; you have not kept them. Return to me, and I will return to you," says the LORD of Armies.   Jos 1:7; 23:6; 1Kg 8:58

Yet you ask, "How can we return?"
^8 "Will a man rob God? Yet you are robbing me!"   Pr 22:22-23

"How do we rob you?" you ask.

"By not making the payments of the tenth and the contributions. ^9 You are suffering under a curse, yet^E you — the whole nation — are still robbing me. ^10 Bring the full tenth into the storehouse so that there may be food in my house. Test me in this way," says the LORD of Armies. "See if I will not open the floodgates of heaven and pour out a blessing for you without measure. ^11 I will rebuke the devourer^F for you, so that it will not ruin the produce of your land and your vine in your field will not fail to produce fruit," says the LORD of Armies. ^12 "Then all the nations will consider you fortunate, for you will be a delightful land," says the LORD of Armies.   Lv 7:14,32-33

The Righteous and the Wicked

^13 "Your words against me are harsh," says the LORD.   Ezk 35:13

Yet you ask, "What have we spoken against you?"

^14 You have said: "It is useless to serve God. What have we gained by keeping his requirements and walking mournfully before the

---

^A 2:16 Or The LORD God of Israel says that he hates divorce and the one who   ^B 2:16 Lit Therefore, guard yourselves in your spirit   ^C 3:2 Lit cleansing agent   ^D 3:6 Or Because I, the LORD, do not change, you descendants of Jacob are not destroyed   ^E 3:9 Or because   ^F 3:11 Perhaps locusts

LORD of Armies? [15] So now we consider the arrogant to be fortunate. Not only do those who commit wickedness prosper, they even test God and escape." Lv 8:35; Dt 11:1

[16] At that time those who feared the LORD spoke to one another. The LORD took notice and listened. So a book of remembrance was written before him for those who feared the LORD and had high regard for his name. [17] "They will be mine," says the LORD of Armies, "my own possession on the day I am preparing. I will have compassion on them as a man has compassion on his son who serves him. [18] So you will again see the difference between the righteous and the wicked, between one who serves God and one who does not serve him. Ex 14:2; 32:32

The Day of the LORD

4 "For look, the day is coming, burning like a furnace, when all the arrogant and everyone who commits wickedness will become stubble. The coming day will consume them," says the LORD of Armies, "not leaving them root or branches. [2] But for you who fear my name, the sun of righteousness will rise with healing in its wings, and you will go out and playfully jump like calves from the stall. [A] [3] You will trample the wicked, for they will be ashes under the soles of your feet on the day I am preparing," says the LORD of Armies. Ps 37:6; Is 58:8

A Final Warning

[4] "Remember the instruction of Moses my servant, the statutes and ordinances I commanded him at Horeb for all Israel. [5] Look, I am going to send you the prophet Elijah before the great and terrible day of the LORD comes. [6] And he will turn the hearts of fathers to their children and the hearts of children to their fathers. Otherwise, I will come and strike the land [B] with a curse." Dt 4:10,15; 5:2; Jl 2:31; Mt 11:13-14; Ac 2:20

[A] 4:2 Or like stall-fed calves   [B] 4:6 Or earth

THE NEW TESTAMENT

MATTHEW

The Genealogy of Jesus Christ

1 An account of the genealogy of Jesus Christ, the Son of David, the Son of Abraham: Ru 4:18-22; Mk 12:26

From Abraham to David

2 Abraham fathered^A Isaac,
Isaac fathered Jacob,
Jacob fathered Judah
and his brothers, Gn 29:35
3 Judah fathered
Perez and Zerah by Tamar,
Perez fathered Hezron,
Hezron fathered Aram, Gn 46:12
4 Aram fathered Amminadab,
Amminadab fathered
Nahshon,
Nahshon fathered Salmon,
5 Salmon fathered Boaz
by Rahab,
Boaz fathered Obed by Ruth,
Obed fathered Jesse, Ru 1:4; 2:1
6 and Jesse fathered
King David.

From David to the Babylonian Exile

David fathered Solomon^B
by Uriah's wife, 1Sm 16:1; 17:12
7 Solomon fathered
Rehoboam,
Rehoboam fathered Abijah,
Abijah fathered Asa,^C
8 Asa^C fathered Jehoshaphat,
Jehoshaphat fathered
Joram,^D
Joram fathered Uzziah, 1Kg 14:31
9 Uzziah fathered Jotham,
Jotham fathered Ahaz,
Ahaz fathered Hezekiah,

10 Hezekiah fathered Manasseh,
Manasseh fathered Amon,^E
Amon fathered Josiah, 2Kg 16:20
11 and Josiah fathered Jeconiah
and his brothers
at the time of the exile
to Babylon. 2Kg 24:6,14; Is 5:13

From the Exile to the Christ

12 After the exile to Babylon
Jeconiah fathered Shealtiel,
Shealtiel fathered
Zerubbabel,
13 Zerubbabel fathered Abiud,
Abiud fathered Eliakim,
Eliakim fathered Azor, Gn 10:10
14 Azor fathered Zadok,
Zadok fathered Achim,
Achim fathered Eliud,
15 Eliud fathered Eleazar,
Eleazar fathered Matthan,
Matthan fathered Jacob,
16 and Jacob fathered Joseph
the husband of Mary,
who gave birth to Jesus
who is called the Christ.

17 So all the generations from Abraham to David were fourteen generations; and from David until the exile to Babylon, fourteen generations; and from the exile to Babylon until the Christ, fourteen generations. 2Kg 24:14; Jr 27:20; Dn 9:25-26

The Nativity of the Christ

18 The birth of Jesus Christ came about this way: After his mother Mary had been engaged^F to Joseph, it was discovered before they

---

^A 1:2 In vv. 2-16 either a son, as here, or a later descendant, as in v. 8 ^B 1:6 Other mss add *King*
^C 1:7,8 Other mss read *Asaph* ^D 1:8 = Jehoram ^E 1:10 Other mss read *Amos* ^F 1:18 Or *betrothed*

came together that she was pregnant from the Holy Spirit. ¹⁹ So her husband Joseph, being a righteous man, and not wanting to disgrace her publicly, decided to divorce her secretly.   Mt 12:46; 13:17; Mk 10:12; Lk 1:27, 35

²⁰ But after he had considered these things, an angel of the Lord appeared to him in a dream, saying, "Joseph, son of David, don't be afraid to take Mary as your wife, because what has been conceived in her is from the Holy Spirit. ²¹ She will give birth to a son, and you are to name him Jesus, because he will save his people from their sins."   Mt 27:19; Jn 6:20

²² Now all this took place to fulfill what was spoken by the Lord through the prophet:

²³ **See, the virgin will**
   become pregnant
   and give birth to a son,
   and they will
   name him Immanuel, ᴬ

which is translated "God is with us."

²⁴ When Joseph woke up, he did as the Lord's angel had commanded him. He married her ²⁵ but did not have sexual relations with her until she gave birth to a son. ᴮ And he named him Jesus.   Mt 1:6; 13:49; Lk 1:1

Wise Men Visit the King

2 After Jesus was born in Bethlehem of Judea in the days of King Herod, wise men from the east arrived in Jerusalem, ² saying, "Where is he who has been born king of the Jews? For we saw his star at its rising and have come to worship him." ᶜ   Gn 25:6; 1Kg 4:30; Lk 1:5; 2:4-7

³ When King Herod heard this, he was deeply disturbed, and all Jerusalem with him. ⁴ So he assembled all the chief priests and scribes of the people and asked them where the Christ would be born.   Mt 16:21

⁵ "In Bethlehem of Judea," they told him, "because this is what was written by the prophet:

⁶ **And you, Bethlehem,**
   in the land of Judah,
   are by no means least
   among the rulers
   of Judah:
   Because out of you
   will come a ruler
   who will shepherd
   my people Israel." ᴰ   2Sm 5:2

⁷ Then Herod secretly summoned the wise men and asked them the exact time the star appeared. ⁸ He sent them to Bethlehem and said, "Go and search carefully for the child. When you find him, report back to me so that I too can go and worship him." ᴱ   Mk 5:6; Lk 1:7; Ac 13:6; Rv 1:16

⁹ After hearing the king, they went on their way. And there it was — the star they had seen at its rising. It led them until it came and stopped above the place where the child was. ¹⁰ When they saw the star, they were overwhelmed with joy. ¹¹ Entering the house, they saw the child with Mary his mother, and falling to their knees, they worshiped him. ᶠ Then they opened their treasures and presented him with gifts: gold, frankincense, and myrrh. ¹² And being warned in a dream not to go back to Herod, they returned to their own country by another route.   Ps 72:10; Is 60:6; Mt 1:18; 12:46

The Flight into Egypt

¹³ After they were gone, an angel of the Lord appeared to Joseph in a dream, saying, "Get up! Take

---

ᴬ**1:23** Is 7:14   ᴮ**1:25** Other mss read *to her firstborn son*   ᶜ**2:2** Or *to pay him homage*   ᴰ**2:6** Mc 5:2
ᴱ**2:8** Or *and pay him homage*   ᶠ**2:11** Or *they paid him homage*

the child and his mother, flee to Egypt, and stay there until I tell you. For Herod is about to search for the child to kill him." ¹⁴ So he got up, took the child and his mother during the night, and escaped to Egypt. ¹⁵ He stayed there until Herod's death, so that what was spoken by the Lord through the prophet might be fulfilled: **Out of Egypt I called my Son.** ^A Mt1:20; 13:49

The Massacre of the Innocents

¹⁶ Then Herod, when he realized that he had been outwitted by the wise men, flew into a rage. He gave orders to massacre all the boys in and around Bethlehem who were two years old and under, in keeping with the time he had learned from the wise men. ¹⁷ Then what was spoken through Jeremiah the prophet was fulfilled: Is 59:7; Mk 10:34

¹⁸ **A voice was heard**
   in Ramah,
weeping, ^B **and**
   great mourning,
Rachel weeping
   for her children;
and she refused
   to be consoled,
because they are no more. ^C

The Return to Nazareth

¹⁹ After Herod died, an angel of the Lord appeared in a dream to Joseph in Egypt, ²⁰ saying, "Get up, take the child and his mother, and go to the land of Israel, because those who intended to kill the child are dead." ²¹ So he got up, took the child and his mother, and entered the land of Israel. ²² But when he heard that Archelaus was ruling over Judea in place of his father Herod, he was afraid to go there. And being warned in a dream, he withdrew to the region of Galilee. ²³ Then he went and settled in a town called Nazareth to fulfill what was spoken through the prophets, that he would be called a Nazarene.   Mt 1:20; 13:49; Lk 1:5,11; Jd 5

The Herald of the Christ

3 In those days John the Baptist came, preaching in the wilderness of Judea ² and saying, "Repent, because the kingdom of heaven has come near!" ³ For he is the one spoken of through the prophet Isaiah, who said: Mk 1:3-8; Lk 3:2-17; Jn 1:6-8,19-28

   A voice of one crying out
      in the wilderness:
   Prepare the way
      for the Lord;
   make his paths straight! ^D

⁴ Now John had a camel-hair garment with a leather belt around his waist, and his food was locusts and wild honey. ⁵ Then people from Jerusalem, all Judea, and all the vicinity of the Jordan were going out to him, ⁶ and they were baptized by him in the Jordan River, confessing their sins.   Mt 23:37; Mk 1:5; Lk 3:3; Jn 15:22

⁷ When he saw many of the Pharisees and Sadducees coming to his baptism, he said to them, "Brood of vipers! Who warned you to flee from the coming wrath? ⁸ Therefore produce fruit consistent with ^E repentance. ⁹ And don't presume to say to yourselves, 'We have Abraham as our father.' For I tell you that God is able to raise up children for Abraham from these stones. ¹⁰ The ax is already at the root of the trees. Therefore,

---

^A **2:15** Hs 11:1   ^B **2:18** Other mss read *Ramah, lamentation, and weeping,*   ^C **2:18** Jr 31:15   ^D **3:3** Is 40:3
^E **3:8** Lit *fruit worthy of*

every tree that doesn't produce good fruit will be cut down and thrown into the fire.   Mt 16:1; 22:23

¹¹ "I baptize you with^A water for repentance, but the one who is coming after me is more powerful than I. I am not worthy to remove^B his sandals. He himself will baptize you with the Holy Spirit and fire. ¹² His winnowing shovel is in his hand, and he will clear his threshing floor and gather his wheat into the barn. But the chaff he will burn with fire that never goes out."   Is 4:4; Mk 1:4,8; Jn 1:26,33; Ac 1:5

The Baptism of Jesus

¹³ Then Jesus came from Galilee to John at the Jordan, to be baptized by him. ¹⁴ But John tried to stop him, saying, "I need to be baptized by you, and yet you come to me?"

¹⁵ Jesus answered him, "Allow it for now, because this is the way for us to fulfill all righteousness." Then John allowed him to be baptized.

¹⁶ When Jesus was baptized, he went up immediately from the water. The heavens suddenly opened for him,^C and he saw the Spirit of God descending like a dove and coming down on him. ¹⁷ And a voice from heaven said: "This is my beloved Son, with whom I am well-pleased."   Mt 24:35; Lk 12:33; Ac 17:24; Eph 6:9

The Temptation of Jesus

4 Then Jesus was led up by the Spirit into the wilderness to be tempted by the devil. ² After he had fasted forty days and forty nights, he was hungry. ³ Then the tempter approached him and said, "If you are the Son of God, tell these stones to become bread."   Mk 1:12-13; Lk 4:1-13

⁴ He answered, "It is written: Man must not live on bread alone but on every word that comes from the mouth of God."^D   Dt 8:3

⁵ Then the devil took him to the holy city, had him stand on the pinnacle of the temple, ⁶ and said to him, "If you are the Son of God, throw yourself down. For it is written:

He will give his angels
   orders concerning you,
and they will support you
   with their hands
so that you will not strike
   your foot against a stone."^E

⁷ Jesus told him, "It is also written: Do not test the Lord your God."^F

⁸ Again, the devil took him to a very high mountain and showed him all the kingdoms of the world and their splendor. ⁹ And he said to him, "I will give you all these things if you will fall down and worship me."^G

¹⁰ Then Jesus told him, "Go away,^H Satan! For it is written: Worship the Lord your God, and serve only him."^I   Dt 6:13; 1Ch 21:1

¹¹ Then the devil left him, and angels came and began to serve him.

Ministry in Galilee

¹² When he heard that John had been arrested, he withdrew into Galilee. ¹³ He left Nazareth and went to live in Capernaum by the sea, in the region of Zebulun and Naphtali. ¹⁴ This was to fulfill what was spoken through the prophet Isaiah:

¹⁵   Land of Zebulun and land
     of Naphtali,
   along the road by the sea,
   beyond the Jordan,
   Galilee of the Gentiles.

---

^A3:11 Or *in*   ^B3:11 Or *to carry*   ^C3:16 Other mss omit *for him*   ^D4:4 Dt 8:3   ^E4:6 Ps 91:11-12
^F4:7 Dt 6:16   ^G4:9 Or *and pay me homage*   ^H4:10 Other mss read *"Get behind me*   ^I4:10 Dt 6:13

¹⁶ The people who live
    in darkness
    have seen a great light,
    and for those living
    in the land of the shadow
    of death,
    a light has dawned. ^{A,B}   Is 9:1-2
¹⁷ From then on Jesus began to preach, "Repent, because the kingdom of heaven has come near."

The First Disciples

¹⁸ As he was walking along the Sea of Galilee, he saw two brothers, Simon (who is called Peter), and his brother Andrew. They were casting a net into the sea — for they were fishermen. ¹⁹ "Follow me," he told them, "and I will make you fish for^C people." ²⁰ Immediately they left their nets and followed him.   Mk 7:31

²¹ Going on from there, he saw two other brothers, James the son of Zebedee, and his brother John. They were in a boat with Zebedee their father, preparing their nets, and he called them. ²² Immediately they left the boat and their father and followed him.

Teaching, Preaching, and Healing

²³ Now Jesus began to go all over Galilee, teaching in their synagogues, preaching the good news of the kingdom, and healing every^D disease and sickness^E among the people. ²⁴ Then the news about him spread throughout Syria. So they brought to him all those who were afflicted, those suffering from various diseases and intense pains, the demon-possessed, the epileptics, and the paralytics. And he healed them. ²⁵ Large crowds followed him from Galilee, the Decapolis,

Jerusalem, Judea, and beyond the Jordan.   Mk 1:35-39; 13:54; 24:14; Lk 4:42-44

THE SERMON ON THE MOUNT

5 When he saw the crowds, he went up on the mountain, and after he sat down, his disciples came to him. ² Then^F he began to teach them, saying: Mk 3:13; Lk 9:28; 18:14

The Beatitudes

³ "Blessed are the poor in
    spirit,   Is 57:15; 66:2
    for the kingdom of heaven
    is theirs.   Mt 19:14; 25:34; Mk 10:14
⁴ Blessed are those who
    mourn,   Is 61:2; Mt 11:29; 21:5; Jn 16:20
    for they will be comforted.
⁵ Blessed are the humble,   Ps 37:11
    for they will inherit
    the earth.
⁶ Blessed are those who
    hunger and thirst
    for righteousness,   Is 55:1-2
    for they will be filled.
⁷ Blessed are the merciful,
    for they will be shown mercy.
⁸ Blessed are the pure in heart,
    for they will see God.   Ps 24:4
⁹ Blessed are the peacemakers,
    for they will be called
    sons of God.   Mt 5:45; Lk 6:35; 1Jn 3:1
¹⁰ Blessed are those who
    are persecuted because
    of righteousness,
    for the kingdom of heaven
    is theirs.   Mt 19:14; 25:34; Mk 10:14

¹¹ "You are blessed when they insult you and persecute you and falsely say every kind of evil against you because of me. ¹² Be glad and rejoice, because your reward is great in heaven. For that is how

^A4:16 Lit *dawned on them*   ^B4:15-16 Is 9:1-2   ^C4:19 Or *you fishers of*   ^D4:23 Or *every kind of*
^E4:23 Or *physical ailment*   ^F5:2 Lit *Then opening his mouth*

they persecuted the prophets who were before you. Mt 2:23; Ac 7:52; 2Tm 3:12

Believers Are Salt and Light

[13] "You are the salt of the earth. But if the salt should lose its taste, how can it be made salty?[A] It's no longer good for anything but to be thrown out and trampled under people's feet. Mk 9:50; Lk 14:34

[14] "You are the light of the world. A city situated on a hill cannot be hidden. [15] No one lights a lamp and puts it under a basket, but rather on a lampstand, and it gives light for all who are in the house. [16] In the same way, let your light shine before others, so that they may see your good works and give glory to your Father in heaven. Pr 4:18; Jn 8:12

Christ Fulfills the Law

[17] "Don't think that I came to abolish the Law or the Prophets. I did not come to abolish but to fulfill. [18] For truly I tell you, until heaven and earth pass away, not the smallest letter[B] or one stroke of a letter will pass away from the law until all things are accomplished. [19] Therefore, whoever breaks one of the least of these commands and teaches others to do the same will be called least in the kingdom of heaven. But whoever does and teaches these commands will be called great in the kingdom of heaven. [20] For I tell you, unless your righteousness surpasses that of the scribes and Pharisees, you will never get into the kingdom of heaven. Mt 7:12; Rm 3:31; 10:4; 13:8; Gl 3:24

Murder Begins in the Heart

[21] "You have heard that it was said to our ancestors, **Do not murder,**[C] and whoever murders will be subject to judgment. [22] But I tell you, everyone who is angry with his brother or sister[D] will be subject to judgment. Whoever insults[E] his brother or sister, will be subject to the court.[F] Whoever says, 'You fool!' will be subject to hellfire.[G] [23] So if you are offering your gift on the altar, and there you remember that your brother or sister has something against you, [24] leave your gift there in front of the altar. First go and be reconciled with your brother or sister, and then come and offer your gift. [25] Reach a settlement quickly with your adversary while you're on the way with him to the court, or your adversary will hand you over to the judge, and the judge to[H] the officer, and you will be thrown into prison. [26] Truly I tell you, you will never get out of there until you have paid the last penny.[I] Ex 20:13; Dt 5:17

Adultery Begins in the Heart

[27] "You have heard that it was said, **Do not commit adultery.**[J] [28] But I tell you, everyone who looks at a woman lustfully has already committed adultery with her in his heart. [29] If your right eye causes you to sin, gouge it out and throw it away. For it is better that you lose one of the parts of your body than for your whole body to be thrown into hell. [30] And if your right hand causes you to sin, cut it off and

---

[A] 5:13 Or *how can the earth be salted?* [B] 5:18 Or *not one iota*; *iota* is the smallest letter of the Gk alphabet. [C] 5:21 Ex 20:13; Dt 5:17 [D] 5:22 Other mss add *without a cause* [E] 5:22 Lit *Whoever says 'Raca'*; an Aramaic term of abuse that puts someone down, insulting one's intelligence [F] 5:22 Lit *Sanhedrin* [G] 5:22 Lit *the gehenna of fire* [H] 5:25 Other mss read *judge will hand you over to* [I] 5:26 Lit *quadrans*, the smallest and least valuable Roman coin, worth 1/64 of a daily wage [J] 5:27 Ex 20:14; Dt 5:18

throw it away. For it is better that you lose one of the parts of your body than for your whole body to go into hell. Ex 20:14; Dt 5:18; 2Sm 11:2; Jb 31:1

Divorce Practices Censured

31 "It was also said, **Whoever divorces his wife must give her a written notice of divorce.** [A] 32 But I tell you, everyone who divorces his wife, except in a case of sexual immorality, causes her to commit adultery. And whoever marries a divorced woman commits adultery. Dt 24:1; Jr 3:1; Mt 19:7,9; Mk 10:4

Tell the Truth

33 "Again, you have heard that it was said to our ancestors, **You must not break your oath, but you must keep your oaths to the Lord.** [B] 34 But I tell you, don't take an oath at all: either by heaven, because it is God's throne; 35 or by the earth, because it is his footstool; or by Jerusalem, because it is the city of the great King. 36 Do not swear by your head, because you cannot make a single hair white or black. 37 But let your 'yes' mean 'yes,' and your 'no' mean 'no.' Anything more than this is from the evil one. Lv 19:12; Nm 30:2

Go the Second Mile

38 "You have heard that it was said, **An eye for an eye** and **a tooth for a tooth.** [C] 39 But I tell you, don't resist [D] an evildoer. On the contrary, if anyone slaps you on your right cheek, turn the other to him also. 40 As for the one who wants to sue you and take away your shirt, let him have your coat as well. 41 And if anyone forces you to go one mile, go with him two. 42 Give to the one who asks you, and don't turn away from the one who wants to borrow from you. Ex 21:24; Lv 24:20; Dt 19:21; Lk 6:29-30

Love Your Enemies

43 "You have heard that it was said, **Love your neighbor** [E] and hate your enemy. 44 But I tell you, love your enemies [F] and pray for those who [G] persecute you, 45 so that you may be [H] children of your Father in heaven. For he causes his sun to rise on the evil and the good, and sends rain on the righteous and the unrighteous. 46 For if you love those who love you, what reward will you have? Don't even the tax collectors do the same? 47 And if you greet only your brothers and sisters, what are you doing out of the ordinary? [I] Don't even the Gentiles [J] do the same? 48 Be perfect, therefore, as your heavenly Father is perfect. Lv 19:18; Dt 23:6; Lk 6:27; 10:29

How to Give

6 "Be careful not to practice your righteousness [K] in front of others to be seen by them. Otherwise, you have no reward with your Father in heaven. 2 So whenever you give to the poor, don't sound a trumpet before you, as the hypocrites do in the synagogues and on the streets, to be applauded by people. Truly I tell you, they have their reward. 3 But when you give to the poor, don't let your left hand know what your right hand is doing, 4 so

---

[A] 5:31 Dt 24:1　[B] 5:33 Lv 19:12; Nm 30:2; Dt 23:21　[C] 5:38 Ex 21:24; Lv 24:20; Dt 19:21　[D] 5:39 Or *don't set yourself against*, or *don't retaliate against*　[E] 5:43 Lv 19:18　[F] 5:44 Other mss add *bless those who curse you, do good to those who hate you*,　[G] 5:44 Other mss add *mistreat you and*　[H] 5:45 Or *may become*, or *may show yourselves to be*　[I] 5:47 Or *doing that is superior*; lit *doing more*　[J] 5:47 Other mss read *tax collectors*　[K] 6:1 Other mss read *charitable giving* that your giving may be in secret. And your Father who sees in secret will reward you.^A Mt 23:5; Lk 6:24

How to Pray

5 "Whenever you pray, you must not be like the hypocrites, because they love to pray standing in the synagogues and on the street corners to be seen by people. Truly I tell you, they have their reward. 6 But when you pray, go into your private room, shut your door, and pray to your Father who is in secret. And your Father who sees in secret will reward you.^B 7 When you pray, don't babble like the Gentiles, since they imagine they'll be heard for their many words. 8 Don't be like them, because your Father knows the things you need before you ask him. Mt 6:16; Mk 11:25; Lk 6:24; 18:11

The Lord's Prayer

9 "Therefore, you should pray like this: Lk 11:1-13

Our Father in heaven,
your name be honored as holy.
10 Your kingdom come.
Your will be done
on earth as it is in heaven.
11 Give us today
our daily bread.^C
12 And forgive us our debts,
as we also have forgiven
our debtors.   Pr 30:8; Rm 4:4; Gl 5:3
13 And do not bring us
into^D temptation,   Mt 26:41
but deliver us
from the evil one.^E   Mt 5:37

14 "For if you forgive others their offenses, your heavenly Father will forgive you as well. 15 But if you don't forgive others,^F your Father will not forgive your offenses.   Mk 11:25; Eph 4:32; Col 3:13

How to Fast

16 "Whenever you fast, don't be gloomy like the hypocrites. For they make their faces unattractive^G so that their fasting is obvious to people. Truly I tell you, they have their reward. 17 But when you fast, put oil on your head and wash your face, 18 so that your fasting isn't obvious to others but to your Father who is in secret. And your Father who sees in secret will reward you.^B   Is 58:5; Mt 18:35; Jms 2:13

God and Possessions

19 "Don't store up for yourselves treasures^H on earth, where moth and rust destroy and where thieves break in and steal. 20 But store up for yourselves treasures in heaven, where neither moth nor rust destroys, and where thieves don't break in and steal. 21 For where your treasure is, there your heart will be also.   Pr 23:4; Mt 19:21; Lk 12:33; 18:22; Heb 13:5

22 "The eye is the lamp of the body. If your eye is healthy, your whole body will be full of light. 23 But if your eye is bad, your whole body will be full of darkness. So if the light within you is darkness, how deep is that darkness!   Mt 4:16; 8:12

24 "No one can serve two masters, since either he will hate one and love the other, or he will be devoted to one and despise the other. You cannot serve both God and money.   Lk 16:13; Gl 1:10; Jms 4:4

---

^A6:4 Other mss read will himself reward you openly   ^B6:6,18 Other mss add openly   ^C6:11 Or our necessary bread, or our bread for tomorrow   ^D6:13 Or do not cause us to come into   ^E6:13 Or from evil ; some later mss add For yours is the kingdom and the power and the glory forever. Amen.   ^F6:15 Other mss add their wrongdoing   ^G6:16 Or unrecognizable, or disfigured   ^H6:19 Or valuables

The Cure for Anxiety

25 "Therefore I tell you: Don't worry about your life, what you will eat or what you will drink; or about your body, what you will wear. Isn't life more than food and the body more than clothing? 26 Consider the birds of the sky: They don't sow or reap or gather into barns, yet your heavenly Father feeds them. Aren't you worth more than they? 27 Can any of you add one moment to his life span[A] by worrying? 28 And why do you worry about clothes? Observe how the wildflowers of the field grow: They don't labor or spin thread. 29 Yet I tell you that not even Solomon in all his splendor was adorned like one of these. 30 If that's how God clothes the grass of the field, which is here today and thrown into the furnace tomorrow, won't he do much more for you — you of little faith? 31 So don't worry, saying, 'What will we eat?' or 'What will we drink?' or 'What will we wear?' 32 For the Gentiles eagerly seek all these things, and your heavenly Father knows that you need them. 33 But seek first the kingdom of God[B] and his righteousness, and all these things will be provided for you. 34 Therefore don't worry about tomorrow, because tomorrow will worry about itself. Each day has enough trouble of its own.   Lk 10:41; 12:22-31; Php 4:6; 1Pt 5:7

Do Not Judge

7 "Do not judge, so that you won't be judged. 2 For you will be judged by the same standard with which you judge others, and you will be measured by the same measure you use. 3 Why do you look at the splinter in your brother's eye but don't notice the beam of wood in your own eye? 4 Or how can you say to your brother, 'Let me take the splinter out of your eye,' and look, there's a beam of wood in your own eye? 5 Hypocrite! First take the beam of wood out of your eye, and then you will see clearly to take the splinter out of your brother's eye. 6 Don't give what is holy to dogs or toss your pearls before pigs, or they will trample them under their feet, turn, and tear you to pieces.   Mk 4:24-25; Lk 6:37-42

Ask, Search, Knock

7 "Ask, and it will be given to you. Seek, and you will find. Knock, and the door[C] will be opened to you. 8 For everyone who asks receives, and the one who seeks finds, and to the one who knocks, the door will be opened. 9 Who among you, if his son asks him for bread, will give him a stone? 10 Or if he asks for a fish, will give him a snake? 11 If you then, who are evil, know how to give good gifts to your children, how much more will your Father in heaven give good things to those who ask him. 12 Therefore, whatever you want others to do for you, do also the same for them, for this is the Law and the Prophets.

Entering the Kingdom

13 "Enter through the narrow gate. For the gate is wide and the road broad that leads to destruction, and there are many who go through it. 14 How narrow is the gate and difficult the road that leads to life, and few find it.   Mt 26:8; Mk 14:4; Lk 13:23-24

15 "Be on your guard against false prophets who come to you in sheep's clothing but inwardly

A 6:27 Or add a single cubit to his height   B 6:33 Other mss omit of God   C 7:7 Lit and it are ravaging wolves. ¹⁶ You'll recognize them by their fruit. Are grapes gathered from thornbushes or figs from thistles? ¹⁷ In the same way, every good tree produces good fruit, but a bad tree produces bad fruit. ¹⁸ A good tree can't produce bad fruit; neither can a bad tree produce good fruit. ¹⁹ Every tree that doesn't produce good fruit is cut down and thrown into the fire. ²⁰ So you'll recognize them by their fruit.

²¹ "Not everyone who says to me, 'Lord, Lord,' will enter the kingdom of heaven, but only the one who does the will of my Father in heaven. ²² On that day many will say to me, 'Lord, Lord, didn't we prophesy in your name, drive out demons in your name, and do many miracles in your name?' ²³ Then I will announce to them, 'I never knew you. **Depart from me, you lawbreakers!**' ᴬ·ᴮ Ps 143:10; Mt 3:2; 18:3; Mk 9:43

The Two Foundations

²⁴ "Therefore, everyone who hears these words of mine and acts on them will be like a wise man who built his house on the rock. ²⁵ The rain fell, the rivers rose, and the winds blew and pounded that house. Yet it didn't collapse, because its foundation was on the rock. ²⁶ But everyone who hears these words of mine and doesn't act on them will be like a foolish man who built his house on the sand. ²⁷ The rain fell, the rivers rose, the winds blew and pounded that house, and it collapsed. It collapsed with a great crash." Mt 12:36; Lk 6:47-49

²⁸ When Jesus had finished saying these things, the crowds were astonished at his teaching, ²⁹ because he was teaching them like one who had authority, and not like their scribes. Mt 11:1; 13:53-54; 19:1; 22:23; 26:1

A Man Cleansed

8 When he came down from the mountain, large crowds followed him. ² Right away a man with leprosyᶜ came up and knelt before him, saying, "Lord, if you are willing, you can make me clean."

³ Reaching out his hand, Jesus touched him, saying, "I am willing; be made clean." Immediately his leprosy was cleansed. ⁴ Then Jesus told him, "See that you don't tell anyone; but go, show yourself to the priest, and offer the gift that Moses commanded, as a testimony to them." Mt 9:30; 17:9; Mk 5:43; 7:36; 8:30

A Centurion's Faith

⁵ When he entered Capernaum, a centurion came to him, pleading with him, ⁶ "Lord, my servant is lying at home paralyzed, in terrible agony." Lk 7:1-10; Jn 4:46-54

⁷ He said to him, "Am I to come and heal him?"ᴰ

⁸ "Lord," the centurion replied, "I am not worthy to have you come under my roof. But just say the word, and my servant will be healed. ⁹ For I too am a man under authority, having soldiers under my command.ᴱ I say to this one, 'Go,' and he goes; and to another, 'Come,' and he comes; and to my servant, 'Do this!' and he does it."

¹⁰ Hearing this, Jesus was amazed and said to those following him, "Truly I tell you, I have not found anyone in Israel with so great a faith. ¹¹ I tell you that many will come from east and west to share

---

ᴬ**7:23** Lit *you who work lawlessness*　ᴮ**7:23** Ps 6:8　ᶜ**8:2** Gk *lepros*; a term for various skin diseases, also in v. 3; see Lv 13–14　ᴰ**8:7** Or *"I will come and heal him."*　ᴱ**8:9** Lit *under me* the banquet[A] with Abraham, Isaac, and Jacob in the kingdom of heaven. [12] But the sons of the kingdom will be thrown into the outer darkness where there will be weeping and gnashing of teeth." [13] Then Jesus told the centurion, "Go. As you have believed, let it be done for you." And his servant was healed that very moment.[B]   Is 49:12; 59:19; Mk 1:11

Healings at Capernaum

[14] Jesus went into Peter's house and saw his mother-in-law lying in bed with a fever. [15] So he touched her hand, and the fever left her. Then she got up and began to serve him. [16] When evening came, they brought to him many who were demon-possessed. He drove out the spirits with a word and healed all who were sick, [17] so that what was spoken through the prophet Isaiah might be fulfilled: Mk 1:29-34

He himself took
    our weaknesses
    and carried our diseases.[C]

The Cost of Following Jesus

[18] When Jesus saw a large crowd[D] around him, he gave the order to go to the other side of the sea. [19] A scribe approached him and said, "Teacher, I will follow you wherever you go."   Mt 14:22; Mk 4:35; Lk 8:22

[20] Jesus told him, "Foxes have dens, and birds of the sky have nests, but the Son of Man has no place to lay his head."   Dn 7:14; Mt 9:6

[21] "Lord," another of his disciples said, "first let me go bury my father."

[22] But Jesus told him, "Follow me, and let the dead bury their own dead."

Wind and Waves Obey Jesus

[23] As he got into the boat, his disciples followed him. [24] Suddenly, a violent storm arose on the sea, so that the boat was being swamped by the waves — but Jesus kept sleeping. [25] So the disciples came and woke him up, saying, "Lord, save us! We're going to die!"   Mt 10:1; Mk 4:36-41; Lk 8:22-25

[26] He said to them, "Why are you afraid, you of little faith?" Then he got up and rebuked the winds and the sea, and there was a great calm. [27] The men were amazed and asked, "What kind of man is this? Even the winds and the sea obey him!"   Mk 1:27; Lk 5:9

Demons Driven Out by Jesus

[28] When he had come to the other side, to the region of the Gadarenes,[E] two demon-possessed men met him as they came out of the tombs. They were so violent that no one could pass that way. [29] Suddenly they shouted, "What do you have to do with us,[F] Son of God? Have you come here to torment us before the time?"   Mk 5:1-17; Lk 8:26-37

[30] A long way off from them, a large herd of pigs was feeding. [31] "If you drive us out," the demons begged him, "send us into the herd of pigs."

[32] "Go!" he told them. So when they had come out, they entered the pigs, and the whole herd rushed down the steep bank into the sea and perished in the water. [33] Then the men who tended them fled. They went into the city and reported everything, especially what had happened to those who were demon-possessed. [34] At that, the whole town went out to meet Jesus. When

[A]8:11 Lit recline at the table   [B]8:13 Or that hour; lit very hour   [C]8:17 Is 53:4   [D]8:18 Other mss read saw large crowds   [E]8:28 Other mss read Gergesenes   [F]8:29 Other mss add Jesus they saw him, they begged him to leave their region. 1Kg 17:18; Lk 5:8

The Son of Man Forgives and Heals

9 So he got into a boat, crossed over, and came to his own town. ² Just then some men[A] brought to him a paralytic lying on a stretcher. Seeing their faith, Jesus told the paralytic, "Have courage, son, your sins are forgiven." Mt 4:13; Mk 5:21

³ At this, some of the scribes said to themselves, "He's blaspheming!"

⁴ Perceiving their thoughts, Jesus said, "Why are you thinking evil things in your hearts?[B] ⁵ For which is easier: to say, 'Your sins are forgiven,' or to say, 'Get up and walk'? ⁶ But so that you may know that the Son of Man has authority on earth to forgive sins" — then he told the paralytic, "Get up, take your stretcher, and go home." ⁷ So he got up and went home. ⁸ When the crowds saw this, they were awestruck[C,D] and gave glory to God, who had given such authority to men. Mt 12:25; Lk 6:8

The Call of Matthew

⁹ As Jesus went on from there, he saw a man named Matthew sitting at the toll booth, and he said to him, "Follow me," and he got up and followed him. Mt 10:3; Mk 2:14-22; Lk 5:27-38

¹⁰ While he was reclining at the table in the house, many tax collectors and sinners came to eat with Jesus and his disciples. ¹¹ When the Pharisees saw this, they asked his disciples, "Why does your teacher eat with tax collectors and sinners?"

¹² Now when he heard this, he said, "It is not those who are well

who need a doctor, but those who are sick. ¹³ Go and learn what this means: **I desire mercy and not sacrifice.**[E] For I didn't come to call the righteous, but sinners."[F] Mk 2:17; Lk 5:31

A Question About Fasting

¹⁴ Then John's disciples came to him, saying, "Why do we and the Pharisees fast often, but your disciples do not fast?" Mt 11:2; 14:12; 15:2

¹⁵ Jesus said to them, "Can the wedding guests[G] be sad while the groom is with them? The time[H] will come when the groom will be taken away from them, and then they will fast. ¹⁶ No one patches an old garment with unshrunk cloth, because the patch pulls away from the garment and makes the tear worse. ¹⁷ And no one puts[I] new wine into old wineskins. Otherwise, the skins burst, the wine spills out, and the skins are ruined. No, they put new wine into fresh wineskins, and both are preserved."

A Girl Restored and a Woman Healed

¹⁸ As he was telling them these things, suddenly one of the leaders came and knelt down before him, saying, "My daughter just died,[J] but come and lay your hand on her, and she will live." ¹⁹ So Jesus and his disciples got up and followed him. Mt 8:2-3; Mk 5:22-43; Lk 8:41-56

²⁰ Just then, a woman who had suffered from bleeding for twelve years approached from behind and touched the end of his robe, ²¹ for she said to herself, "If I can just touch his robe, I'll be made well."[K] Lv 15:25; Nm 15:38; Dt 22:12; Mt 14:36; 23:5

[A]9:2 Lit then they   [B]9:4 Or minds   [C]9:8 Other mss read amazed   [D]9:8 Lit afraid   [E]9:13 Hs 6:6
[F]9:13 Other mss add to repentance   [G]9:15 Lit the sons of the bridal chamber   [H]9:15 Lit days   [I]9:17 Lit And they do not put   [J]9:18 Lit daughter has now come to the end   [K]9:21 Or be saved

²² Jesus turned and saw her. "Have courage, daughter," he said. "Your faith has saved you."ᴬ And the woman was made well from that moment.ᴮ   Mt 15:28; Mk 10:52; Lk 7:50; 17:19

²³ When Jesus came to the leader's house, he saw the flute players and a crowd lamenting loudly. ²⁴ "Leave," he said, "because the girl is not dead but asleep." And they laughed at him. ²⁵ After the crowd had been put outside, he went in and took her by the hand, and the girl got up. ²⁶ Then news of this spread throughout that whole area.   Jr 9:17

Healing the Blind

²⁷ As Jesus went on from there, two blind men followed him, calling out, "Have mercy on us, Son of David!"   Mt 1:1; 12:23; 15:22; 20:30-31; Mk 10:47

²⁸ When he entered the house, the blind men approached him, and Jesus said to them, "Do you believe that I can do this?"   Mk 11:24; Jn 3:16

They said to him, "Yes, Lord."

²⁹ Then he touched their eyes, saying, "Let it be done for you according to your faith." ³⁰ And their eyes were opened. Then Jesus warned them sternly, "Be sure that no one finds out." ³¹ But they went out and spread the news about him throughout that whole area.

Driving Out a Demon

³² Just as they were going out, a demon-possessed man who was unable to speak was brought to him. ³³ When the demon had been driven out, the man who had been mute spoke, and the crowds were amazed, saying, "Nothing like this has ever been seen in Israel!"

³⁴ But the Pharisees said, "He drives out demons by the ruler of the demons."   Mk 3:22; Jn 7:20

The Lord of the Harvest

³⁵ Jesus continued going around to all the towns and villages, teaching in their synagogues, preaching the good news of the kingdom, and healing everyᶜ disease and every sickness.ᴰ,ᴱ ³⁶ When he saw the crowds, he felt compassion for them, because they were distressed and dejected, like sheep without a shepherd. ³⁷ Then he said to his disciples, "The harvest is abundant, but the workers are few. ³⁸ Therefore, pray to the Lord of the harvest to send out workers into his harvest."   Mt 4:23; 14:14; 15:32; Mk 8:2

Commissioning the Twelve

10 Summoning his twelve disciples, he gave them authority over unclean spirits, to drive them out and to heal everyᶜ disease and sickness.ᴱ ² These are the names of the twelve apostles: First, Simon, who is called Peter, and Andrew his brother; James the son of Zebedee, and John his brother; ³ Philip and Bartholomew; Thomas and Matthew the tax collector; James the son of Alphaeus, and Thaddaeus;ᶠ ⁴ Simon the Zealot,ᴳ and Judas Iscariot, who also betrayed him.   Mt 9:35; Mk 3:13-19; 6:13-16

⁵ Jesus sent out these twelve after giving them instructions: "Don't take the road that leads to the Gentiles, and don't enter any Samaritan town. ⁶ Instead, go to the lost sheep of the house of Israel. ⁷ As you go, proclaim: 'The kingdom of

---

ᴬ**9:22** Or *has made you well*   ᴮ**9:22** Lit *hour*   ᶜ**9:35; 10:1** Or *every kind of*   ᴰ**9:35** Other mss add *among the people*   ᴱ**9:35; 10:1** Or *physical ailment*   ᶠ**10:3** Other mss read *and Lebbaeus, whose surname was Thaddaeus*   ᴳ**10:4** Lit *the Cananaean* heaven has come near.' ⁸ Heal the sick, raise the dead, cleanse those with leprosy,ᴬ drive out demons. Freely you received, freely give. ⁹ Don't acquire gold, silver, or copper for your money-belts. ¹⁰ Don't take a traveling bag for the road, or an extra shirt, sandals, or a staff, for the worker is worthy of his food. ¹¹ When you enter any town or village, find out who is worthy, and stay there until you leave. ¹² Greet a household when you enter it, ¹³ and if the household is worthy, let your peace be on it; but if it is unworthy, let your peace return to you. ¹⁴ If anyone does not welcome you or listen to your words, shake the dust off your feet when you leave that house or town. ¹⁵ Truly I tell you, it will be more tolerable on the day of judgment for the land of Sodom and Gomorrah than for that town. 2Kg 17:24; Lk 9:52; 17:16; Jn 4:9

Persecutions Predicted

¹⁶ "Look, I'm sending you out like sheep among wolves. Therefore be as shrewd as serpents and as innocent as doves. ¹⁷ Beware of them, because they will hand you over to local courtsᴮ and flog you in their synagogues. ¹⁸ You will even be brought before governors and kings because of me, to bear witness to them and to the Gentiles. ¹⁹ But when they hand you over, don't worry about how or what you are to speak. For you will be given what to say at that hour, ²⁰ because it isn't you speaking, but the Spirit of your Father is speaking through you. Gn 3:1; Lk 10:3; Rm 16:19; Php 2:15

²¹ "Brother will betray brother to death, and a father his child. Children will rise up against parents and have them put to death. ²² You will be hated by everyone because of my name. But the one who endures to the end will be saved. ²³ When they persecute you in one town, flee to another. For truly I tell you, you will not have gone through the towns of Israel before the Son of Man comes. ²⁴ A discipleᶜ is not above his teacher, or a slave above his master. ²⁵ It is enough for a disciple to become like his teacher and a slave like his master. If they called the head of the house 'Beelzebul,' how much more the members of his household! Mc 7:6; Mt 10:35-36; Mk 13:12; Ac 8:1

Fear God

²⁶ "Therefore, don't be afraid of them, since there is nothing covered that won't be uncovered and nothing hidden that won't be made known. ²⁷ What I tell you in the dark, speak in the light. What you hear in a whisper,ᴰ proclaim on the housetops. ²⁸ Don't fear those who kill the body but are not able to kill the soul; rather, fear him who is able to destroy both soul and body in hell. ²⁹ Aren't two sparrows sold for a penny?ᴱ Yet not one of them falls to the ground without your Father's consent.ᶠ ³⁰ But even the hairs of your head have all been counted. ³¹ So don't be afraid; you are worth more than many sparrows. Mt 24:17; Mk 4:22; Lk 8:17; 12:2-9

Acknowledging Christ

³² "Therefore, everyone who will acknowledge me before others, I will also acknowledge him before

---

ᴬ**10:8** Gk *lepros*; a term for various skin diseases; see Lv 13–14   ᴮ**10:17** Or *sanhedrins*   ᶜ**10:24** Or *student*
ᴰ**10:27** Lit *in the ear*   ᴱ**10:29** Gk *assarion*, a small copper coin   ᶠ**10:29** Lit *ground apart from your Father*

my Father in heaven. ³³ But whoever denies me before others, I will also deny him before my Father in heaven. ³⁴ Don't assume that I came to bring peace on the earth. I did not come to bring peace, but a sword. ³⁵ For I came to turn   Mk 8:38 ; Lk 12:8; Rm 10:9-10; Rv 3:5

> a man against his father,
> a daughter against
>   her mother,
> a daughter-in-law against
>   her mother-in-law;
> ³⁶   and a man's enemies
>   will be
>   the members
>   of his household. ^A   Ps 41:9

³⁷ The one who loves a father or mother more than me is not worthy of me; the one who loves a son or daughter more than me is not worthy of me. ³⁸ And whoever doesn't take up his cross and follow me is not worthy of me. ³⁹ Anyone who finds his life will lose it, and anyone who loses his life because of me will find it.   Mt 16:25; Lk 9:24 ; 14:25-27

A Cup of Cold Water

⁴⁰ "The one who welcomes you welcomes me, and the one who welcomes me welcomes him who sent me. ⁴¹ Anyone who welcomes a prophet because he is a prophet ^B will receive a prophet's reward. And anyone who welcomes a righteous person because he's righteous ^C will receive a righteous person's reward. ⁴² And whoever gives even a cup of cold water to one of these little ones because he is a disciple, ^D truly I tell you, he will never lose his reward."   Mt 18:5; Lk 10:16; Jn 13:20; Gl 4:14

John the Baptist Doubts

11 When Jesus had finished giving instructions to his twelve disciples, he moved on from there to teach and preach in their towns. ² Now when John heard in prison what the Christ was doing, he sent a message through his disciples ³ and asked him, "Are you the one who is to come, or should we expect someone else? "   Mt 7:28; 9:35; 11:27

⁴ Jesus replied to them, "Go and report to John what you hear and see: ⁵ The blind receive their sight, the lame walk, those with leprosy ^E are cleansed, the deaf hear, the dead are raised, and the poor are told the good news, ⁶ and blessed is the one who isn't offended by me."   Is 8:14-15; 35:5; 61:1; Lk 4:18; Jms 2:5

⁷ As these men were leaving, Jesus began to speak to the crowds about John: "What did you go out into the wilderness to see? A reed swaying in the wind? ⁸ What then did you go out to see? A man dressed in soft clothes? See, those who wear soft clothes are in royal palaces. ⁹ What then did you go out to see? A prophet? Yes, I tell you, and more than a prophet. ¹⁰ This is the one about whom it is written: Mt 3:1; Eph 4:14

> See, I am sending
>   my messenger
>   ahead of you;
> he will prepare your way
>   before you. ^F   Mal 3:1; Mk 1:2

¹¹ "Truly I tell you, among those born of women no one greater than John the Baptist has appeared, ^G but the least in the kingdom of heaven is greater than he. ¹² From the days of John the Baptist until now, the kingdom of heaven has been suffering

^A**10:35-36** Mc 7:6   ^B**10:41** Lit *prophet in the name of a prophet*   ^C**10:41** Lit *person in the name of a righteous person*   ^D**10:42** Lit *little ones in the name of a disciple*   ^E**11:5** Gk *lepros* ; a term for various skin diseases; see Lv 13–14   ^F**11:10** Mal 3:1   ^G**11:11** Lit *arisen* violence,[A] and the violent have been seizing it by force. [13] For all the prophets and the law prophesied until John. [14] And if you're willing to accept it, he is the Elijah who is to come. [15] Let anyone who has ears[B] listen.   Mal 4:5; Mt 17:10-13; Mk 9:11-13

An Unresponsive Generation

[16] "To what should I compare this generation? It's like children sitting in the marketplaces who call out to other children:

[17] We played the flute for you,
    but you didn't dance;
    we sang a lament,
    but you didn't mourn![C]

[18] For John came neither eating nor drinking, and they say, 'He has a demon!' [19] The Son of Man came eating and drinking, and they say, 'Look, a glutton and a drunkard, a friend of tax collectors and sinners!' Yet wisdom is vindicated[D] by her deeds."[E]   Mt 3:4; 9:10; Lk 1:15; 7:36

[20] Then he proceeded to denounce the towns where most of his miracles were done, because they did not repent: [21] "Woe to you, Chorazin! Woe to you, Bethsaida! For if the miracles that were done in you had been done in Tyre and Sidon, they would have repented in sackcloth and ashes long ago. [22] But I tell you, it will be more tolerable for Tyre and Sidon on the day of judgment than for you. [23] And you, Capernaum, will you be exalted to heaven? No, you will go down to Hades. For if the miracles that were done in you had been done in Sodom, it would have remained until today. [24] But I tell you, it will be more tolerable for the land of Sodom on the day of judgment than for you."   Mk 6:45; Lk 9:10; 10:12-15; Jn 12:21

The Son Gives Knowledge and Rest

[25] At that time Jesus said, "I praise you, Father, Lord of heaven and earth, because you have hidden these things from the wise and intelligent and revealed them to infants. [26] Yes, Father, because this was your good pleasure.[F] [27] All things have been entrusted to me by my Father. No one knows the Son except the Father, and no one knows the Father except the Son and anyone to whom the Son desires[G] to reveal him.   Ps 8:2; Lk 10:21-22

[28] "Come to me, all of you who are weary and burdened, and I will give you rest. [29] Take up my yoke and learn from me, because I am lowly and humble in heart, and you will find rest for your souls. [30] For my yoke is easy and my burden is light."   Jr 31:25; Jn 7:37; 13:15; Eph 4:20; Php 2:5

Lord of the Sabbath

12 At that time Jesus passed through the grainfields on the Sabbath. His disciples were hungry and began to pick and eat some heads of grain. [2] When the Pharisees saw this, they said to him, "See, your disciples are doing what is not lawful to do on the Sabbath."   Mt 10:1; 26:56; Mk 2:23-28; Lk 6:1-5

[3] He said to them, "Haven't you read what David did when he and those who were with him were hungry: [4] how he entered the house of God, and they ate[H] the bread of the Presence — which is not lawful for him or for those with him

---

to eat, but only for the priests? ⁵ Or haven't you read in the law that on Sabbath days the priests in the temple violate the Sabbath and are innocent? ⁶ I tell you that something greater than the temple is here. ⁷ If you had known what this means, I **desire mercy and not sacrifice,** ᴬ you would not have condemned the innocent. ⁸ For the Son of Man is Lord of the Sabbath." Ex 25:30; Mal 3:1

The Man with the Shriveled Hand

⁹ Moving on from there, he entered their synagogue. ¹⁰ There he saw a man who had a shriveled hand, and in order to accuse him they asked him, "Is it lawful to heal on the Sabbath?" Mk 3:1-6; Lk 6:6-11

¹¹ He replied to them, "Who among you, if he had a sheep that fell into a pit on the Sabbath, wouldn't take hold of it and lift it out? ¹² A person is worth far more than a sheep; so it is lawful to do what is good on the Sabbath." Ex 23:4-5; Dt 22:4; Lk 14:5

¹³ Then he told the man, "Stretch out your hand." So he stretched it out, and it was restored, as good as the other. ¹⁴ But the Pharisees went out and plotted against him, how they might kill him. 1Kg 13:4; Mt 8:3; 27:1

The Servant of the Lord

¹⁵ Jesus was aware of this and withdrew. Large crowds ᴮ followed him, and he healed them all. ¹⁶ He warned them not to make him known, ¹⁷ so that what was spoken through the prophet Isaiah might be fulfilled: Mt 4:23; 10:23; 19:2; Mk 3:7

¹⁸   **Here is my servant**
        whom I have chosen,
      my beloved in whom
        I delight;

      I will put my Spirit on him,
      and he will proclaim
        justice to the nations.
¹⁹   **He will not argue or shout,**
      and no one will hear
        his voice in the streets.
²⁰   **He will not break**
        a bruised reed,
      and he will not put out
        a smoldering wick,
      until he has led justice
        to victory. ᶜ
²¹   **The nations will put**
        their hope in his name. ᴰ

A House Divided

²² Then a demon-possessed man who was blind and unable to speak was brought to him. He healed him, so that the man ᴱ could both speak and see. ²³ All the crowds were astounded and said, "Could this be the Son of David?" Mt 4:24; Lk 11:14-15

²⁴ When the Pharisees heard this, they said, "This man drives out demons only by Beelzebul, the ruler of the demons." Mt 9:34; 10:25; Mk 3:22

²⁵ Knowing their thoughts, he told them: "Every kingdom divided against itself is headed for destruction, and no city or house divided against itself will stand. ²⁶ If Satan drives out Satan, he is divided against himself. How then will his kingdom stand? ²⁷ And if I drive out demons by Beelzebul, by whom do your sons drive them out? For this reason they will be your judges. ²⁸ If I drive out demons by the Spirit of God, then the kingdom of God has come upon you. ²⁹ How can someone enter a strong man's house and steal his possessions unless he first ties up the strong man? Then he can plunder his house. ³⁰ Anyone who

ᴬ**12:7** Hs 6:6   ᴮ**12:15** Other mss read *Many*   ᶜ**12:20** Or *until he has successfully put forth justice*
ᴰ**12:18-21** Is 42:1-4   ᴱ**12:22** Lit *mute*

is not with me is against me, and anyone who does not gather with me scatters. ³¹ Therefore, I tell you, people will be forgiven every sin and blasphemy, but the blasphemy against ^A the Spirit will not be forgiven. ^B ³² Whoever speaks a word against the Son of Man, it will be forgiven him; but whoever speaks against the Holy Spirit, it will not be forgiven him, either in this age or in the one to come. Mk 3:23-27

A Tree and Its Fruit

³³ "Either make the tree good and its fruit will be good, or make the tree bad ^C and its fruit will be bad; for a tree is known by its fruit. ³⁴ Brood of vipers! How can you speak good things when you are evil? For the mouth speaks from the overflow of the heart. ³⁵ A good person produces good things from his storeroom of good, and an evil person produces evil things from his storeroom of evil. ³⁶ I tell you that on the day of judgment people will have to account for every careless ^D word they speak. ^E ³⁷ For by your words you will be acquitted, and by your words you will be condemned."

The Sign of Jonah

³⁸ Then some of the scribes and Pharisees said to him, "Teacher, we want to see a sign from you."

³⁹ He answered them, "An evil and adulterous generation demands a sign, but no sign will be given to it except the sign of the prophet Jonah. ⁴⁰ For as Jonah was in the belly of the huge fish ^F three days and three nights, so the Son of Man will be in the heart of the earth three days and three nights. ⁴¹ The men of Nineveh will stand up at the judgment with this generation and condemn it, because they repented at Jonah's preaching; and look — something greater than Jonah is here. ⁴² The queen of the south will rise up at the judgment with this generation and condemn it, because she came from the ends of the earth to hear the wisdom of Solomon; and look — something greater than Solomon is here. Is 57:3

An Unclean Spirit's Return

⁴³ "When an unclean spirit comes out of a person, it roams through waterless places looking for rest but doesn't find any. ⁴⁴ Then it says, 'I'll go back to my house that I came from.' Returning, it finds the house vacant, swept, and put in order. ⁴⁵ Then it goes and brings with it seven other spirits more evil than itself, and they enter and settle down there. As a result, that person's last condition is worse than the first. That's how it will also be with this evil generation." Lk 11:24-26

True Relationships

⁴⁶ While he was still speaking with the crowds, his mother and brothers were standing outside wanting to speak to him. ⁴⁷ Someone told him, "Look, your mother and your brothers are standing outside, wanting to speak to you." ^G Mk 3:31-35

⁴⁸ He replied to the one who was speaking to him, "Who is my mother and who are my brothers?" ⁴⁹ Stretching out his hand toward his disciples, he said, "Here are my mother and my brothers! ⁵⁰ For whoever does the will of my

---

^A 12:31 Or of   ^B 12:31 Other mss add people   ^C 12:33 Or decayed; lit rotten   ^D 12:36 Lit worthless
^E 12:36 Lit will speak   ^F 12:40 Or sea creature; Jnh 1:17   ^G 12:47 Other mss omit this v.

Father in heaven is my brother and sister and mother." Mt 10:42; 28:19; Jn 8:31

The Parable of the Sower

13 On that day Jesus went out of the house and was sitting by the sea. ² Such large crowds gathered around him that he got into a boat and sat down, while the whole crowd stood on the shore. Mk 4:1-12

³ Then he told them many things in parables, saying: "Consider the sower who went out to sow. ⁴ As he sowed, some seed fell along the path, and the birds came and devoured them. ⁵ Other seed fell on rocky ground where it didn't have much soil, and it grew up quickly since the soil wasn't deep. ⁶ But when the sun came up, it was scorched, and since it had no root, it withered away. ⁷ Other seed fell among thorns, and the thorns came up and choked it. ⁸ Still other seed fell on good ground and produced fruit: some a hundred, some sixty, and some thirty times what was sown. ⁹ Let anyone who has ears^A listen." Mt 13:10, 34-36; 15:15; 21:33, 45; 22:1

Why Jesus Used Parables

¹⁰ Then the disciples came up and asked him, "Why are you speaking to them in parables?" Mt 9:10; Mk 10:10

¹¹ He answered, "Because the secrets of the kingdom of heaven have been given for you to know, but it has not been given to them. ¹² For whoever has, more will be given to him, and he will have more than enough; but whoever does not have, even what he has will be taken away from him. ¹³ That is why I speak to them in parables, because looking they do not see, and hearing they do not listen or understand.

¹⁴ Isaiah's prophecy is fulfilled in them, which says:

You will listen and listen,
but never understand;
you will look and look,
but never perceive. Is 6:9; Lk 8:10
¹⁵ For this people's heart
has grown callous;
their ears are hard
of hearing,
and they have shut
their eyes;
otherwise they might see
with their eyes,
and hear with their ears,
and
understand
with their hearts,
and turn back —
and I would heal them.^B

¹⁶ "Blessed are your eyes because they do see, and your ears because they do hear. ¹⁷ For truly I tell you, many prophets and righteous people longed to see the things you see but didn't see them, to hear the things you hear but didn't hear them. Mt 16:17; Lk 10:23-24; Jn 8:56; 20:29

The Parable of the Sower Explained

¹⁸ "So listen to the parable of the sower: ¹⁹ When anyone hears the word about the kingdom and doesn't understand it, the evil one comes and snatches away what was sown in his heart. This is the one sown along the path. ²⁰ And the one sown on rocky ground — this is one who hears the word and immediately receives it with joy. ²¹ But he has no root and is short-lived. When distress or persecution comes because of the word, immediately he falls away. ²² Now the one sown among the thorns — this is

^A **13:9** Other mss add *to hear*   ^B **13:14-15** Is 6:9-10 one who hears the word, but the worries of this age and the deceitfulness[A] of wealth choke the word, and it becomes unfruitful. [23] But the one sown on the good ground — this is one who hears and understands the word, who does produce fruit and yields: some a hundred, some sixty, some thirty times what was sown." Mt 4:23; 5:37; Mk 4:13-20; Lk 8:11-15

The Parable of the Wheat and the Weeds

[24] He presented another parable to them: "The kingdom of heaven may be compared to a man who sowed good seed in his field. [25] But while people were sleeping, his enemy came, sowed weeds among the wheat, and left. [26] When the plants sprouted and produced grain, then the weeds also appeared. [27] The landowner's servants came to him and said, 'Master, didn't you sow good seed in your field? Then where did the weeds come from?' Mt 18:23; 20:1 [28] " 'An enemy did this,' he told them.

" 'So, do you want us to go and pull them up?' the servants asked him. [29] " 'No,' he said. 'When you pull up the weeds, you might also uproot the wheat with them. [30] Let both grow together until the harvest. At harvest time I'll tell the reapers: Gather the weeds first and tie them in bundles to burn them, but collect the wheat in my barn.' "

The Parables of the Mustard Seed and of the Leaven

[31] He presented another parable to them: "The kingdom of heaven is like a mustard seed that a man took and sowed in his field. [32] It's the smallest of all the seeds, but when grown, it's taller than the garden plants and becomes a tree, so that the birds of the sky come and nest in its branches." Mk 4:30-32

[33] He told them another parable: "The kingdom of heaven is like leaven[B] that a woman took and mixed into fifty pounds[C] of flour until all of it was leavened." Gn 18:6; Lk 13:21; Gl 5:9

Using Parables Fulfills Prophecy

[34] Jesus told the crowds all these things in parables, and he did not tell them anything without a parable, [35] so that what was spoken through the prophet might be fulfilled: Mk 4:34; Jn 10:6; 16:25

> I will open my mouth
>   in parables;
> I will declare things
>   kept secret
> from the foundation
>   of the world.[D,E] Ps 78:2; 1Co 2:7

Jesus Interprets the Parable of the Wheat and the Weeds

[36] Then he left the crowds and went into the house. His disciples approached him and said, "Explain to us the parable of the weeds in the field." Mt 13:3; 15:15; 21:33,45; 22:1; 24:32 [37] He replied: "The one who sows the good seed is the Son of Man; [38] the field is the world; and the good seed — these are the children of the kingdom. The weeds are the children of the evil one, [39] and the enemy who sowed them is the devil. The harvest is the end of the age, and the harvesters are angels. [40] Therefore, just as the weeds are gathered and burned in the fire, so it will be at the end of the age. [41] The Son of Man will send out his angels,

A**13:22** Or *pleasure*   B**13:33** Or *yeast*   C**13:33** Lit *three sata* ; about 40 liters   D**13:35** Some mss omit *of the world*   E**13:35** Ps 78:2

and they will gather from his kingdom all who cause sin[A] and those guilty of lawlessness.[B] [42] They will throw them into the blazing furnace where there will be weeping and gnashing of teeth. [43] Then the righteous will shine like the sun in their Father's kingdom. Let anyone who has ears[C] listen. Mt 8:12; Jn 8:44

The Parables of the Hidden Treasure and of the Priceless Pearl

[44] "The kingdom of heaven is like treasure, buried in a field, that a man found and reburied. Then in his joy he goes and sells everything he has and buys that field. Is 55:1

[45] "Again, the kingdom of heaven is like a merchant in search of fine pearls. [46] When he found one priceless[D] pearl, he went and sold everything he had and bought it.

The Parable of the Net

[47] "Again, the kingdom of heaven is like a large net thrown into the sea. It collected every kind of fish, [48] and when it was full, they dragged it ashore, sat down, and gathered the good fish into containers, but threw out the worthless ones. [49] So it will be at the end of the age. The angels will go out, separate the evil people from the righteous, [50] and throw them into the blazing furnace, where there will be weeping and gnashing of teeth. Mt 3:2; 13:39-40,44; 22:10; 25:32

The Storehouse of Truth

[51] "Have you understood all these things?"[E]

They answered him, "Yes."

[52] "Therefore," he said to them, "every teacher of the law[F] who has become a disciple in the kingdom of heaven is like the owner of a house who brings out of his storeroom treasures new and old." Mt 12:35; 28:19

Rejection at Nazareth

[53] When Jesus had finished these parables, he left there. [54] He went to his hometown and began to teach them in their synagogue, so that they were astonished and said, "Where did this man get this wisdom and these miraculous powers? [55] Isn't this the carpenter's son? Isn't his mother called Mary, and his brothers James, Joseph,[G] Simon, and Judas? [56] And his sisters, aren't they all with us? So where does he get all these things?" [57] And they were offended by him. Mk 6:1-6

Jesus said to them, "A prophet is not without honor except in his hometown and in his household." [58] And he did not do many miracles there because of their unbelief. Jr 11:21; 12:6; Lk 4:24; Jn 4:44

John the Baptist Beheaded

14 At that time Herod the tetrarch heard the report about Jesus. [2] "This is John the Baptist," he told his servants. "He has been raised from the dead, and that's why miraculous powers are at work in him." Mk 6:14-29; Lk 3:19; 9:7-9

[3] For Herod had arrested John, chained[H] him, and put him in prison on account of Herodias, his brother Philip's wife, [4] since John had been telling him, "It's not lawful for you to have her." [5] Though Herod

---

A 13:41 Or stumbling   B 13:41 Or those who do lawlessness   C 13:43 Other mss add to hear   D 13:46 Or very precious   E 13:51 Other mss add Jesus asked them   F 13:52 Or every scribe   G 13:55 Other mss read Joses; Mk 6:3   H 14:3 Or bound wanted to kill John, he feared the crowd since they regarded John as a prophet. Lv 18:16; 20:21; Mt 4:12; 11:2; Jn 3:24

⁶ When Herod's birthday celebration came, Herodias's daughter danced before them ^A and pleased Herod. ⁷ So he promised with an oath to give her whatever she asked. ⁸ Prompted by her mother, she answered, "Give me John the Baptist's head here on a platter." ⁹ Although the king regretted it, he commanded that it be granted because of his oaths and his guests. ¹⁰ So he sent orders and had John beheaded in the prison. ¹¹ His head was brought on a platter and given to the girl, who carried it to her mother. ¹² Then his disciples came, removed the corpse, ^B buried it, and went and reported to Jesus.

Feeding of the Five Thousand

¹³ When Jesus heard about it, he withdrew from there by boat to a remote place to be alone. When the crowds heard this, they followed him on foot from the towns. ¹⁴ When he went ashore, ^C he saw a large crowd, had compassion on them, and healed their sick. Jn 6:1-13

¹⁵ When evening came, the disciples approached him and said, "This place is deserted, and it is already late. ^D Send the crowds away so that they can go into the villages and buy food for themselves." Mt 10:1; 26:56; Mk 3:7; 16:20; Lk 6:13

¹⁶ "They don't need to go away," Jesus told them. "You give them something to eat."

¹⁷ "But we only have five loaves and two fish here," they said to him.

¹⁸ "Bring them here to me," he said. ¹⁹ Then he commanded the crowds to sit down on the grass. He took the five loaves and the two fish, and looking up to heaven, he blessed them. He broke the loaves and gave them to the disciples, and the disciples gave them to the crowds. ²⁰ Everyone ate and was satisfied. They picked up twelve baskets full of leftover pieces. ²¹ Now those who ate were about five thousand men, besides women and children. 1Sm 9:13

Walking on the Water

²² Immediately he ^E made the disciples get into the boat and go ahead of him to the other side, while he dismissed the crowds. ²³ After dismissing the crowds, he went up on the mountain by himself to pray. Well into the night, he was there alone. ²⁴ Meanwhile, the boat was already some distance ^F from land, ^G battered by the waves, because the wind was against them. ²⁵ Jesus came toward them walking on the sea very early in the morning. ^H ²⁶ When the disciples saw him walking on the sea, they were terrified. "It's a ghost!" they said, and they cried out in fear. Mk 6:45-51; Lk 6:12

²⁷ Immediately Jesus spoke to them. "Have courage! It is I. Don't be afraid." Dt 31:6; Is 41:13; 43:1-2; Mt 17:7

²⁸ "Lord, if it's you," Peter answered him, "command me to come to you on the water."

²⁹ He said, "Come."

And climbing out of the boat, Peter started walking on the water and came toward Jesus. ³⁰ But when he saw the strength of the wind, ^I he

---

^A 14:6 Lit *danced in the middle*   ^B 14:12 Other mss read *body*   ^C 14:14 Lit *Coming out* (of the boat)
^D 14:15 Lit *and the time* (for the evening meal) *has already passed*   ^E 14:22 Other mss read *Jesus*
^F 14:24 Lit *already many stadia*; one *stadion* = 600 feet   ^G 14:24 Other mss read *already in the middle of the sea*   ^H 14:25 Lit *fourth watch of the night* = 3 to 6 a.m.   ^I 14:30 Other mss read *saw the wind*

was afraid, and beginning to sink he cried out, "Lord, save me!"

31 Immediately Jesus reached out his hand, caught hold of him, and said to him, "You of little faith, why did you doubt?" Mt 6:30; 8:26; 16:8

32 When they got into the boat, the wind ceased. 33 Then those in the boat worshiped him and said, "Truly you are the Son of God."

Miraculous Healings

34 When they had crossed over, they came to shore at Gennesaret. 35 When the men of that place recognized him, they alerted the whole vicinity and brought to him all who were sick. 36 They begged him that they might only touch the end of his robe, and as many as touched it were healed. Mk 6:53-56; Jn 6:24-25

The Tradition of the Elders

15 Then Jesus was approached by Pharisees and scribes from Jerusalem, who asked, 2 "Why do your disciples break the tradition of the elders? For they don't wash their hands when they eat."A

3 He answered them, "Why do you break God's commandment because of your tradition? 4 For God said:B **Honor your father and your mother;**C and, **Whoever speaks evil of father or mother must be put to death.**D 5 But you say, 'Whoever tells his father or mother, "Whatever benefit you might have received from me is a gift committed to the temple,"6 he does not have to honor his father.'E In this way, you have nullified the

word of GodF because of your tradition. 7 Hypocrites! Isaiah prophesied correctly about you when he said: Ex 20:12; 21:17; Lv 20:9; Dt 5:16; Eph 6:2

8 **This people**G **honors me
     with their lips,
     but their heart is far
     from me.**
9 **They worship me in vain,
     teaching as doctrines
     human commands."**H Is 29:13

Defilement Is from Within

10 Summoning the crowd, he told them, "Listen and understand: 11 It's not what goes into the mouth that defiles a person, but what comes out of the mouth — this defiles a person." Mt 15:18; Mk 7:15; Ac 21:28; Heb 9:13

12 Then the disciples came up and told him, "Do you know that the Pharisees took offense when they heard what you said?"

13 He replied, "Every plant that my heavenly Father didn't plant will be uprooted. 14 Leave them alone! They are blind guides.I And if the blind guide the blind, both will fall into a pit." Is 60:21; 61:3; Jn 15:2; 1Co 3:9

15 Then Peter said, "Explain this parable to us." Mt 13:36; Mk 7:17

16 "Do you still lack understanding?" heJ asked. 17 "Don't you realizeK that whatever goes into the mouth passes into the stomach and is eliminated?L 18 But what comes out of the mouth comes from the heart, and this defiles a person. 19 For from the heart come evil thoughts, murders, adulteries, sexual immoralities, thefts, false testimonies, slander. 20 These are

---

A15:2 Lit eat bread = eat a meal   B15:4 Other mss read commanded, saying   C15:4 Ex 20:12; Dt 5:16
D15:4 Ex 21:17; Lv 20:9   E15:6 Other mss read then he does not have to honor his father or mother
F15:6 Other mss read commandment   G15:8 Other mss add draw near to me with their mouths, and
H15:8-9 Is 29:13 LXX   I15:14 Other mss add for the blind   J15:16 Other mss read Jesus   K15:17 Other
mss add yet   L15:17 Lit and goes out into the toilet

the things that defile a person; but eating with unwashed hands does not defile a person." Mt 12:34; Jms 3:6

A Gentile Mother's Faith

²¹ When Jesus left there, he withdrew to the area of Tyre and Sidon. ²² Just then a Canaanite woman from that region came and kept crying out,ᴬ "Have mercy on me, Lord, Son of David! My daughter is severely tormented by a demon." Mt 11:21; Mk 7:24-30

²³ Jesus did not say a word to her. His disciples approached him and urged him, "Send her away because she's crying out after us." Mt 16:20

²⁴ He replied, "I was sent only to the lost sheep of the house of Israel." Mt 10:6,23; Jn 4:22; Rm 15:8

²⁵ But she came, knelt before him, and said, "Lord, help me!"

²⁶ He answered, "It isn't right to take the children's bread and throw it to the dogs." Ex 22:31; 2Kg 9:10; Mt 8:2

²⁷ "Yes, Lord," she said, "yet even the dogs eat the crumbs that fall from their masters' table."

²⁸ Then Jesus replied to her, "Woman, your faith is great. Let it be done for you as you want." And from that momentᴮ her daughter was healed. Mt 9:22; 17:18; Jn 4:52-53

Healing Many People

²⁹ Moving on from there, Jesus passed along the Sea of Galilee. He went up on a mountain and sat there, ³⁰ and large crowds came to him, including the lame, the blind, the crippled, those unable to speak, and many others. They put them at his feet, and he healed them. ³¹ So the crowd was amazed when they saw those unable to speak talking, the crippled restored, the lame walking, and the blind seeing, and they gave glory to the God of Israel. Is 29:23; Mt 9:8; 18:8; Mk 7:31-37; 9:43

Feeding of the Four Thousand

³² Jesus called his disciples and said, "I have compassion on the crowd, because they've already stayed with me three days and have nothing to eat. I don't want to send them away hungry, otherwise they might collapse on the way." Mt 14:14-21

³³ The disciples said to him, "Where could we get enough bread in this desolate place to feed such a crowd?" Mk 8:4; 2Co 11:26; Heb 11:38

³⁴ "How many loaves do you have?" Jesus asked them.

"Seven," they said, "and a few small fish."

³⁵ After commanding the crowd to sit down on the ground, ³⁶ he took the seven loaves and the fish, gave thanks, broke them, and gave them to the disciples, and the disciples gave them to the crowds. ³⁷ They all ate and were satisfied. They collected the leftover pieces — seven large baskets full. ³⁸ Now there were four thousand men who had eaten, besides women and children. ³⁹ After dismissing the crowds, he got into the boat and went to the region of Magadan.ᶜ Mt 26:27; Lk 22:17; Jn 6:11,23; Ac 27:35

The Leaven of the Pharisees and the Saducees

16 The Pharisees and Sadducees approached, and tested him, asking him to show them a sign from heaven. ² He replied, "When evening comes you say, 'It will be good weather because the sky is red.' ³ And in the morning, 'Today will be stormy because the sky is

ᴬ15:22 Other mss read and cried out to him   ᴮ15:28 Lit hour   ᶜ15:39 Other mss read Magdala red and threatening.' You^A know how to read the appearance of the sky, but you can't read the signs of the times.^B ⁴ An evil and adulterous generation demands a sign, but no sign will be given to it except the sign of^C Jonah." Then he left them and went away.   Mt 12:38-39; Mk 8:11-21

⁵ The disciples reached the other shore,^D and they had forgotten to take bread. ⁶ Then Jesus told them, "Watch out and beware of the leaven^E of the Pharisees and Sadducees."   Mt 3:7; 8:15; Lk 12:1; 1Co 5:6-8; Gl 5:9

⁷ They were discussing among themselves, "We didn't bring any bread."

⁸ Aware of this, Jesus said, "You of little faith, why are you discussing among yourselves that you do not have bread? ⁹ Don't you understand yet? Don't you remember the five loaves for the five thousand and how many baskets you collected? ¹⁰ Or the seven loaves for the four thousand and how many large baskets you collected? ¹¹ Why is it you don't understand that when I told you, 'Beware of the leaven of the Pharisees and Sadducees,' it wasn't about bread?" ¹² Then they understood that he had not told them to beware of the leaven in bread, but of the teaching of the Pharisees and Sadducees.   Mt 6:30; 8:26

Peter's Confession of the Messiah

¹³ When Jesus came to the region of Caesarea Philippi,^F he asked his disciples, "Who do people say that the Son of Man is?"^G   Mk 8:27-29

¹⁴ They replied, "Some say John the Baptist; others, Elijah; still others, Jeremiah or one of the prophets."   Mt 14:2; 17:10; Mk 6:15; Lk 9:8; Jn 1:21

¹⁵ "But you," he asked them, "who do you say that I am?"

¹⁶ Simon Peter answered, "You are the Messiah, the Son of the living God."   Mt 1:16; Jn 11:27

¹⁷ Jesus responded, "Blessed are you, Simon son of Jonah,^H because flesh and blood did not reveal this to you, but my Father in heaven. ¹⁸ And I also say to you that you are Peter, and on this rock I will build my church, and the gates of Hades will not overpower it. ¹⁹ I will give you the keys of the kingdom of heaven, and whatever you bind on earth will have been bound^I in heaven, and whatever you loose on earth will have been loosed^J in heaven." ²⁰ Then he gave the disciples orders to tell no one that he was^K the Messiah.   Jn 1:42; 21:15-17; Gl 1:16

His Death and Resurrection Predicted

²¹ From then on Jesus began to point out to his disciples that it was necessary for him to go to Jerusalem and suffer many things from the elders, chief priests, and scribes, be killed, and be raised the third day. ²² Peter took him aside and began to rebuke him, "Oh no,^L Lord! This will never happen to you!"

²³ Jesus turned and told Peter, "Get behind me, Satan! You are a hindrance to me because you're not thinking about God's concerns^M but human concerns."   2Sm 19:22

---

^A**16:3** Other mss read *Hypocrites! You*   ^B**16:2-3** Other mss omit *When* (v. 2) through end of v. 3   ^C**16:4** Other mss add *the prophet*   ^D**16:5** Lit *disciples went to the other side*   ^E**16:6** Or *yeast*, also in vv. 11,12   ^F**16:13** A town north of Galilee at the base of Mount Hermon   ^G**16:13** Other mss read *that I, the Son of Man, am*   ^H**16:17** Or *son of John*   ^I**16:19** Or *earth will be bound*   ^J**16:19** Or *earth will be loosed*   ^K**16:20** Other mss add *Jesus*   ^L**16:22** Lit *"Mercy to you = "May God have mercy on you*   ^M**16:23** Lit *about the things of God*

Take Up Your Cross

²⁴ Then Jesus said to his disciples, "If anyone wants to follow after me, let him deny himself, take up his cross, and follow me. ²⁵ For whoever wants to save his life will lose it, but whoever loses his life because of me will find it. ²⁶ For what will it benefit someone if he gains the whole world yet loses his life? Or what will anyone give in exchange for his life? ²⁷ For the Son of Man is going to come with his angels in the glory of his Father, and then he will reward each according to what he has done. ²⁸ Truly I tell you, there are some standing here who will not taste death until they see the Son of Man coming in his kingdom."   Mt 10:38-39; Lk 14:27; Jn 12:25; Ac 1:11

The Transfiguration

17 After six days Jesus took Peter, James, and his brother John and led them up on a high mountain by themselves. ² He was transfigured in front of them, and his face shone like the sun; his clothes became as white as the light. ³ Suddenly, Moses and Elijah appeared to them, talking with him. ⁴ Then Peter said to Jesus, "Lord, it's good for us to be here. I will set up ᴬ three shelters here: one for you, one for Moses, and one for Elijah."   Mk 9:2-8

⁵ While he was still speaking, suddenly a bright cloud covered ᴮ them, and a voice from the cloud said: "This is my beloved Son, with whom I am well-pleased. Listen to him!" ⁶ When the disciples heard this, they fell facedown and were terrified.   Is 42:1; Mt 3:17; 10:1; Mk 1:11; Lk 3:22

⁷ Jesus came up, touched them, and said, "Get up; don't be afraid." ⁸ When they looked up they saw no one except Jesus alone.   Dn 8:18; 9:21

⁹ As they were coming down the mountain, Jesus commanded them, "Don't tell anyone about the vision until the Son of Man is raised ᶜ from the dead."   Mk 9:9-13

¹⁰ So the disciples asked him, "Why then do the scribes say that Elijah must come first?"   Mal 4:5

¹¹ "Elijah is coming ᴰ and will restore everything," he replied. ᴱ ¹² "But I tell you: Elijah has already come, and they didn't recognize him. On the contrary, they did whatever they pleased to him. In the same way the Son of Man is going to suffer at their hands." ¹³ Then the disciples understood that he had spoken to them about John the Baptist.   Mal 4:6; Mt 14:3,10; 16:21; Lk 1:16-17

The Power of Jesus over a Demon

¹⁴ When they reached the crowd, a man approached and knelt down before him. ¹⁵ "Lord," he said, "have mercy on my son, because he has seizures ᶠ and suffers terribly. He often falls into the fire and often into the water. ¹⁶ I brought him to your disciples, but they couldn't heal him."   Mk 9:14-29; Lk 9:37-43

¹⁷ Jesus replied, "You unbelieving and perverse generation, how long will I be with you? How long must I put up with you? Bring him here to me." ¹⁸ Then Jesus rebuked the demon, ᴳ and it ᴴ came out of him, and from that moment ᴵ the boy was healed.   Zch 3:2; Mt 8:26; Jn 14:9; 20:27; Php 2:15

ᴬ**17:4** Other mss read *Let's make*   ᴮ**17:5** Or *enveloped*; Ex 40:34-35   ᶜ**17:9** Other mss read *Man has risen*   ᴰ**17:11** Other mss add *first*   ᴱ**17:11** Other mss read *Jesus said to them*   ᶠ**17:15** Lit *he is moonstruck*; thought to be a form of epilepsy   ᴳ**17:18** Lit *rebuked him*, or *it*   ᴴ**17:18** Lit *the demon* ᴵ**17:18** Lit *hour*

¹⁹ Then the disciples approached Jesus privately and said, "Why couldn't we drive it out?"

²⁰ "Because of your little faith," heᴬ told them. "For truly I tell you, if you have faith the size ofᴮ a mustard seed, you will tell this mountain, 'Move from here to there,' and it will move. Nothing will be impossible for you."ᶜ Mt 21:21-22; Mk 11:23

The Second Prediction of His Death

²² As they were gathering togetherᴰ in Galilee, Jesus told them, "The Son of Man is about to be betrayed into the hands of men. ²³ They will kill him, and on the third day he will be raised up." And they were deeply distressed. Mt 16:21; 20:17; Mk 8:31

Paying the Temple Tax

²⁴ When they came to Capernaum, those who collected the temple tax approached Peter and said, "Doesn't your teacher pay the temple tax?" Ex 30:13; 38:26; Mk 9:33

²⁵ "Yes," he said.

When he went into the house, Jesus spoke to him first,ᴱ "What do you think, Simon? From whom do earthly kings collect tariffs or taxes? From their sons or from strangers?"ᶠ Mt 22:17,19; Mk 12:14; Rm 13:7

²⁶ "From strangers," he said. ᴳ

"Then the sons are free," Jesus told him. ²⁷ "But, so we won't offend them, go to the sea, cast in a fishhook, and take the first fish that you catch. When you open its mouth you'll find a coin.ᴴ Take it and give it to them for me and you."

Who Is the Greatest?

18 At that time¹ the disciples came to Jesus and asked, "So who is greatest in the kingdom of heaven?" ² He called a child and had him stand among them. ³ "Truly I tell you," he said, "unless you turn and become like children, you will never enter the kingdom of heaven. ⁴ Therefore, whoever humbles himself like this child — this one is the greatest in the kingdom of heaven. ⁵ And whoever welcomes ᴶ one child like this in my name welcomes me. Mt 7:21; 9:10; Mk 9:33-37; Lk 9:46-48

⁶ "But whoever causes one of these little ones who believe in me to fall away — it would be better for him if a heavy millstone were hung around his neck and he were drowned in the depths of the sea. ⁷ Woe to the world because of offenses. For offenses will inevitably come, but woe to that person by whom the offense comes. ⁸ If your hand or your foot causes you to fall away, cut it off and throw it away. It is better for you to enter life maimed or lame than to have two hands or two feet and be thrown into the eternal fire. ⁹ And if your eye causes you to fall away, gouge it out and throw it away. It is better for you to enter life with one eye than to have two eyes and be thrown into hellfire.ᴷ Mk 9:42; Lk 17:2

The Parable of the Lost Sheep

¹⁰ "See to it that you don't despise one of these little ones, because I tell you that in heaven their angels continually view the face of my Father in heaven.ᴸ ¹² What do you

---

ᴬ17:20 Other mss read *your unbelief, Jesus* ᴮ17:20 Lit *faith like* ᶜ17:20 Some mss include v. 21: *"However, this kind does not come out except by prayer and fasting."* ᴰ17:22 Other mss read *were staying* ᴱ17:25 Lit *Jesus anticipated him by saying* ᶠ17:25 Or *foreigners* ᴳ17:26 Other mss read *Peter said to him* ᴴ17:27 Gk *stater*, worth 2 double-drachmas ¹18:1 Lit *hour* ᴶ18:5 Or *receives* ᴷ18:9 Lit *gehenna of fire.* ᴸ18:10 Some mss include v. 11: *For the Son of Man has come to save the lost.*

think? If someone has a hundred sheep, and one of them goes astray, won't he leave the ninety-nine on the hillside and go and search for the stray? [13] And if he finds it, truly I tell you, he rejoices over that sheep[A] more than over the ninety-nine that did not go astray. [14] In the same way, it is not the will of your Father in heaven that one of these little ones perish. Est 1:14; Lk 1:19

Restoring a Brother

[15] "If your brother sins against you,[B] go and rebuke him in private.[C] If he listens to you, you have won your brother. [16] But if he won't listen, take one or two others with you, so that **by the testimony[D] of two or three witnesses every fact may be established.**[E] [17] If he doesn't pay attention to them, tell the church.[F] If he doesn't pay attention even to the church, let him be like a Gentile and a tax collector to you. [18] Truly I tell you, whatever you bind on earth will have been bound[G] in heaven, and whatever you loose on earth will have been loosed[H] in heaven. [19] Again, truly I tell you, if two of you on earth agree about any matter that you[I] pray for, it will be done for you[J] by my Father in heaven. [20] For where two or three are gathered together in my name, I am there among them." Lv 19:17; Lk 17:3; Gl 6:1; 2Th 3:15

The Parable of the Unforgiving Servant

[21] Then Peter approached him and asked, "Lord, how many times shall I forgive my brother or sister who sins against me? As many as seven times?" Lk 17:3-4; Col 3:13

[22] "I tell you, not as many as seven," Jesus replied, "but seventy times seven.[K]

[23] "For this reason, the kingdom of heaven can be compared to a king who wanted to settle accounts with his servants. [24] When he began to settle accounts, one who owed ten thousand talents[L] was brought before him. [25] Since he did not have the money to pay it back, his master commanded that he, his wife, his children, and everything he had be sold to pay the debt. Ex 21:2; Lv 25:39

[26] "At this, the servant fell facedown before him and said, 'Be patient with me, and I will pay you everything.' [27] Then the master of that servant had compassion, released him, and forgave him the loan.

[28] "That servant went out and found one of his fellow servants who owed him a hundred denarii.[M] He grabbed him, started choking him, and said, 'Pay what you owe!' Mt 20:2; 22:19; Mk 6:37; 14:5; Lk 7:41; 10:35

[29] "At this, his fellow servant fell down[N] and began begging him, 'Be patient with me, and I will pay you back.' [30] But he wasn't willing. Instead, he went and threw him into prison until he could pay what was owed. [31] When the other servants saw what had taken place, they were deeply distressed and went and reported to their master everything that had happened. [32] Then, after he had summoned him, his master said to him, 'You

---

A18:13 Lit *over it*   B18:15 Other mss omit *against you*   C18:15 Lit *him between you and him alone*
D18:16 Lit *mouth*   E18:16 Dt 19:15   F18:17 Or *congregation*   G18:18 Or *earth will be bound*   H18:18 Or *earth will be loosed*   I18:19 Lit *they*   J18:19 Lit *for them*   K18:22 Or *but seventy-seven times*
L18:24 A talent is worth about 6,000 denarii, or twenty years' wages for a laborer   M18:28 A denarius = one day's wage   N18:29 Other mss add *at his feet*

wicked servant! I forgave you all that debt because you begged me. [33] Shouldn't you also have had mercy on your fellow servant, as I had mercy on you?' [34] And because he was angry, his master handed him over to the jailers to be tortured until he could pay everything that was owed. [35] So also my heavenly Father will do to you unless every one of you forgives his brother or sister[A] from your[B] heart."   Mt 6:12

The Question of Divorce

19 When Jesus had finished saying these things, he departed from Galilee and went to the region of Judea across the Jordan. [2] Large crowds followed him, and he healed them there. [3] Some Pharisees approached him to test him. They asked, "Is it lawful for a man to divorce his wife on any grounds?"

[4] "Haven't you read," he replied, "that he who created[C] them in the beginning **made them male and female,**[D] [5] and he also said, 'For this reason a man will leave his father and mother and be joined to his wife, and the two will become one flesh'?[E] [6] So they are no longer two, but one flesh. Therefore, what God has joined together, let no one separate."   Gn 2:18,24

[7] "Why then," they asked him, "did Moses command us to give divorce papers and to send her away?"

[8] He told them, "Moses permitted you to divorce your wives because of the hardness of your hearts, but it was not like that from the beginning. [9] I tell you, whoever divorces his wife, except for sexual immorality, and marries another commits adultery."[F]   Mt 5:32; Lk 16:18

[10] His disciples said to him, "If the relationship of a man with his wife is like this, it's better not to marry."

[11] He responded, "Not everyone can accept this saying, but only those to whom it has been given. [12] For there are eunuchs who were born that way from their mother's womb, there are eunuchs who were made by men, and there are eunuchs who have made themselves that way because of the kingdom of heaven. The one who is able to accept it should accept it."   Mt 13:11

Blessing the Children

[13] Then children were brought to Jesus for him to place his hands on them and pray, but the disciples rebuked them. [14] Jesus said, "Leave the children alone, and don't try to keep them from coming to me, because the kingdom of heaven belongs to such as these."[G] [15] After placing his hands on them, he went on from there.   Mt 18:3; Mk 10:13-16

The Rich Young Ruler

[16] Just then someone came up and asked him, "Teacher, what good must I do to have eternal life?"

[17] "Why do you ask me about what is good?"[H] he said to him. "There is only one who is good.[I] If you want to enter into life, keep the commandments."   Lv 18:5; Neh 9:29; Ezk 20:21

[18] "Which ones?" he asked him.

Jesus answered: **Do not murder; do not commit adultery; do not steal; do not bear false witness;** [19] **honor your father and your**

[A]**18:35** Other mss add *their trespasses*   [B]**18:35** Lit *his*   [C]**19:4** Other mss read *made*   [D]**19:4** Gn 1:27; 5:2 [E]**19:5** Gn 2:24   [F]**19:9** Other mss add *Also whoever marries a divorced woman commits adultery*; Mt 5:32 [G]**19:14** Lit *heaven is of such ones*   [H]**19:17** Other mss read *"Why do you call me good?"*   [I]**19:17** Other mss read *"No one is good but one — God* mother; and love your neighbor as yourself.[A]   Ex 20:12-16; Dt 5:17-20

²⁰ "I have kept all these,"[B] the young man told him. "What do I still lack?"

²¹ "If you want to be perfect,"[C] Jesus said to him, "go, sell your belongings and give to the poor, and you will have treasure in heaven. Then come, follow me."   Lk 12:33; 16:9

²² When the young man heard that, he went away grieving, because he had many possessions.

Possessions and the Kingdom

²³ Jesus said to his disciples, "Truly I tell you, it will be hard for a rich person to enter the kingdom of heaven. ²⁴ Again I tell you, it is easier for a camel to go through the eye of a needle than for a rich person to enter the kingdom of God."   Mt 13:22

²⁵ When the disciples heard this, they were utterly astonished and asked, "Then who can be saved?"

²⁶ Jesus looked at them and said, "With man this is impossible, but with God all things are possible."

²⁷ Then Peter responded to him, "See, we have left everything and followed you. So what will there be for us?"

²⁸ Jesus said to them, "Truly I tell you, in the renewal of all things, when the Son of Man sits on his glorious throne, you who have followed me will also sit on twelve thrones, judging the twelve tribes of Israel. ²⁹ And everyone who has left houses or brothers or sisters or father or mother[D] or children or fields because of my name will receive a hundred times more and will inherit eternal life. ³⁰ But many who are first will be last, and the last first.   Is 65:17; 66:22; 2Pt 3:13; Rv 21:1

The Parable of the Vineyard Workers

20 "For the kingdom of heaven is like a landowner who went out early in the morning to hire workers for his vineyard. ² After agreeing with the workers on one denarius,[E] he sent them into his vineyard for the day. ³ When he went out about nine in the morning,[F] he saw others standing in the marketplace doing nothing. ⁴ He said to them, 'You also go into my vineyard, and I'll give you whatever is right.' So off they went. ⁵ About noon and about three,[G] he went out again and did the same thing. ⁶ Then about five[H] he went and found others standing around[I] and said to them, 'Why have you been standing here all day doing nothing?'   Mt 13:24; 21:28,33

⁷ "'Because no one hired us,' they said to him.

"'You also go into my vineyard,' he told them.[J] ⁸ When evening came, the owner of the vineyard told his foreman, 'Call the workers and give them their pay, starting with the last and ending with the first.'   Lv 19:13

⁹ "When those who were hired about five came, they each received one denarius. ¹⁰ So when the first ones came, they assumed they would get more, but they also received a denarius each. ¹¹ When they received it, they began to complain to the landowner: ¹² 'These last men put in one hour, and you

---

[A]**19:18-19** Ex 20:12-16; Lv 19:18; Dt 5:16-20   [B]**19:20** Other mss add *from my youth*   [C]**19:21** Or *complete*
[D]**19:29** Other mss add *or wife*   [E]**20:2** A denarius = one day's wage, also in vv. 9,10,13   [F]**20:3** Lit *about the third hour*   [G]**20:5** Lit *about the sixth hour and the ninth hour*   [H]**20:6** Lit *about the eleventh hour*, also in v. 9   [I]**20:6** Other mss add *doing nothing*   [J]**20:7** Other mss add *'and you'll get whatever is right.'*

made them equal to us who bore the burden of the day's work and the burning heat.' Jnh 4:8; Lk 12:55 [13] "He replied to one of them, 'Friend, I'm doing you no wrong. Didn't you agree with me on a denarius? [14] Take what's yours and go. I want to give this last man the same as I gave you. [15] Don't I have the right to do what I want with what is mine? Are you jealous[A] because I'm generous?'"[B] Mt 22:12; 26:50 [16] "So the last will be first, and the first last."[C]   Mt 19:30; Mk 10:31; Lk 13:30

The Third Prediction of His Death

[17] While going up to Jerusalem, Jesus took the twelve disciples aside privately and said to them on the way, [18] "See, we are going up to Jerusalem. The Son of Man will be handed over to the chief priests and scribes, and they will condemn him to death. [19] They will hand him over to the Gentiles to be mocked, flogged,[D] and crucified, and on the third day he will be raised."[E] Mt 16:21; Mk 10:32-34; Lk 18:31-33

Suffering and Service

[20] Then the mother of Zebedee's sons approached him with her sons. She knelt down to ask him for something. [21] "What do you want?" he asked her.   Mt 4:21; Mk 10:35-45 "Promise,"[F] she said to him, "that these two sons of mine may sit, one on your right and the other on your left, in your kingdom." Mt 16:28; 19:28 [22] Jesus answered, "You don't know what you're asking. Are you able to drink the cup that I am about to drink?"[G]   Is 51:22; Jr 49:12; Mk 14:36

"We are able," they said to him. [23] He told them, "You will indeed drink my cup,[H] but to sit at my right and left is not mine to give; instead, it is for those for whom it has been prepared by my Father." Ac 12:2; Rv 1:9 [24] When the ten disciples heard this, they became indignant with the two brothers. [25] Jesus called them over and said, "You know that the rulers of the Gentiles lord it over them, and those in high positions act as tyrants over them. [26] It must not be like that among you. On the contrary, whoever wants to become great among you must be your servant, [27] and whoever wants to be first among you must be your slave; [28] just as the Son of Man did not come to be served, but to serve, and to give his life as a ransom for many." Mt 23:11; Mk 9:35; Lk 22:27; Jn 13:13-15

Two Blind Men Healed

[29] As they were leaving Jericho, a large crowd followed him. [30] There were two blind men sitting by the road. When they heard that Jesus was passing by, they cried out, "Lord, have mercy on us, Son of David!" [31] The crowd demanded that they keep quiet, but they cried out all the more, "Lord, have mercy on us, Son of David!" Mt 9:27; Mk 10:46-52; Lk 18:35-43 [32] Jesus stopped, called them, and said, "What do you want me to do for you?" [33] "Lord," they said to him, "open our eyes." [34] Moved with compassion, Jesus touched their eyes. Immediately they could see, and they followed him.

[A]**20:15** Lit *Is your eye evil*; an idiom for jealousy or stinginess   [B]**20:15** Lit *good*   [C]**20:16** Other mss add *"For many are called, but few are chosen."*   [D]**20:19** Or *scourged*   [E]**20:19** Other mss read *will rise again*   [F]**20:21** Lit *Say*   [G]**20:22** Other mss add *and (or) to be baptized with the baptism which I am baptized?"*   [H]**20:23** Other mss add *and be baptized with the baptism with which I am baptized.*

The Triumphal Entry

21 When they approached Jerusalem and came to Bethphage at the Mount of Olives, Jesus then sent two disciples, ² telling them, "Go into the village ahead of you. At once you will find a donkey tied there with her foal. Untie them and bring them to me. ³ If anyone says anything to you, say that the Lord needs them, and he will send them at once." Mk 11:1-10; Jn 12:12-19

⁴ This took place so that what was spoken through the prophet might be fulfilled:

⁵ **Tell Daughter Zion,**
"See, your King is coming
to you,
gentle, and mounted
on a donkey,
and on a colt,
the foal of a donkey." ᴬ Is 62:11

⁶ The disciples went and did just as Jesus directed them. ⁷ They brought the donkey and its foal; then they laid their clothes on them, and he sat on them. ⁸ A very large crowd spread their clothes on the road; others were cutting branches from the trees and spreading them on the road. ⁹ Then the crowds who went ahead of him and those who followed shouted:

Hosanna to the Son of David!
Blessed is he who comes
in the name
of the Lord! ᴮ
Hosanna
in the highest heaven!

¹⁰ When he entered Jerusalem, the whole city was in an uproar, saying, "Who is this?" ¹¹ The crowds were saying, "This is the prophet Jesus from Nazareth in Galilee." Mk 6:15

Cleansing the Temple

¹² Jesus went into the temple ᶜ and threw out all those buying and selling. He overturned the tables of the money changers and the chairs of those selling doves. ¹³ He said to them, "It is written, **my house will be called a house of prayer,** ᴰ but you are making it **a den of thieves!"** ᴱ Mk 11:15-18; Lk 19:45-47

Children Praise Jesus

¹⁴ The blind and the lame came to him in the temple, and he healed them. ¹⁵ When the chief priests and the scribes saw the wonders that he did and the children shouting in the temple, "*Hosanna* to the Son of David!" they were indignant ¹⁶ and said to him, "Do you hear what these children are saying?"

Jesus replied, "Yes, have you never read:

You have prepared ᶠ **praise**
from the mouths of infants
and nursing babies?" ᴳ

¹⁷ Then he left them, went out of the city to Bethany, and spent the night there. Mt 26:6; Mk 11:1; Lk 19:29; 24:50; Jn 11:18

The Barren Fig Tree

¹⁸ Early in the morning, as he was returning to the city, he was hungry. ¹⁹ Seeing a lone fig tree by the road, he went up to it and found nothing on it except leaves. And he said to it, "May no fruit ever come from you again!" At once the fig tree withered. Mk 11:12-14, 20-24

²⁰ When the disciples saw it, they were amazed and said, "How did the fig tree wither so quickly?"

²¹ Jesus answered them, "Truly I tell you, if you have faith and do not doubt, you will not only do what

ᴬ21:5 Is 62:11; Zch 9:9   ᴮ21:9 Ps 118:25-26   ᶜ21:12 Other mss add *of God*   ᴰ21:13 Is 56:7   ᴱ21:13 Jr 7:11
ᶠ21:16 Or *restored*   ᴳ21:16 Ps 8:2

was done to the fig tree, but even if you tell this mountain, 'Be lifted up and thrown into the sea,' it will be done. ²² And if you believe, you will receive whatever you ask for in prayer." Mt 17:20; Lk 17:6; 1Co 13:2; Jms 1:6

The Authority of Jesus Challenged

²³ When he entered the temple, the chief priests and the elders of the people came to him as he was teaching and said, "By what authority are you doing these things? Who gave you this authority?" Mk 11:27-33

²⁴ Jesus answered them, "I will also ask you one question, and if you answer it for me, then I will tell you by what authority I do these things. ²⁵ Did John's baptism come from heaven, or was it of human origin?"

They discussed it among themselves, "If we say, 'From heaven,' he will say to us, 'Then why didn't you believe him?' ²⁶ But if we say, 'Of human origin,' we're afraid of the crowd, because everyone considers John to be a prophet." ²⁷ So they answered Jesus, "We don't know."

And he said to them, "Neither will I tell you by what authority I do these things.

The Parable of the Two Sons

²⁸ "What do you think? A man had two sons. He went to the first and said, 'My son, go work in the vineyard today.' Mt 20:1

²⁹ "He answered, 'I don't want to,' but later he changed his mind and went. ³⁰ Then the man went to the other and said the same thing. 'I will, sir,' he answered, but he didn't go. ³¹ Which of the two did his father's will?"

They said, "The first."

Jesus said to them, "Truly I tell you, tax collectors and prostitutes are entering the kingdom of God before you. ³² For John came to you in the way of righteousness, and you didn't believe him. Tax collectors and prostitutes did believe him; but you, when you saw it, didn't even change your minds then and believe him. Pr 8:20; Mt 3:8-12

The Parable of the Vineyard Owner

³³ "Listen to another parable: There was a landowner, who planted a vineyard, put a fence around it, dug a winepress in it, and built a watchtower. He leased it to tenant farmers and went away. ³⁴ When the time came to harvest fruit, he sent his servants to the farmers to collect his fruit. ³⁵ The farmers took his servants, beat one, killed another, and stoned a third. ³⁶ Again, he sent other servants, more than the first group, and they did the same to them. ³⁷ Finally, he sent his son to them. 'They will respect my son,' he said. Mt 13:3,34-36; 22:1; Mk 12:1-12; Lk 20:9-19

³⁸ "But when the tenant farmers saw the son, they said to each other, 'This is the heir. Come, let's kill him and take his inheritance.' ³⁹ So they seized him, threw him out of the vineyard, and killed him. ⁴⁰ Therefore, when the owner of the vineyard comes, what will he do to those farmers?" Ps 2:8; Heb 1:2

⁴¹ "He will completely destroy those terrible men," they told him, "and lease his vineyard to other farmers who will give him his fruit at the harvest." Mt 8:11; Ac 13:46; 18:6; 28:28

⁴² Jesus said to them, "Have you never read in the Scriptures:

The stone that
the builders rejected

has become
the cornerstone.^A
This is what the Lord has
done
and it is wonderful
in our eyes?^B   Ps 118:22-23; Ac 4:11
⁴³ Therefore I tell you, the kingdom of God will be taken away from you and given to a people producing its fruit. ⁴⁴ Whoever falls on this stone will be broken to pieces; but on whomever it falls, it will shatter him."^C   Is 8:14-15; Rm 9:32-33; 1Pt 2:8

⁴⁵ When the chief priests and the Pharisees heard his parables, they knew he was speaking about them. ⁴⁶ Although they were looking for a way to arrest him, they feared the crowds, because the people regarded him as a prophet.   Mt 13:3,35; 15:15

The Parable of the Wedding Banquet

22 Once more Jesus spoke to them in parables: ² "The kingdom of heaven is like a king who gave a wedding banquet for his son. ³ He sent his servants to summon those invited to the banquet, but they didn't want to come. ⁴ Again, he sent out other servants and said, 'Tell those who are invited: See, I've prepared my dinner; my oxen and fattened cattle have been slaughtered, and everything is ready. Come to the wedding banquet.'   Mt 13:24; Lk 12:36; 14:16-24; Jn 2:2; Rv 19:7

⁵ "But they paid no attention and went away, one to his own farm, another to his business, ⁶ while the rest seized his servants, mistreated them, and killed them. ⁷ The king^D was enraged, and he sent out his

troops, killed those murderers, and burned down their city.

⁸ "Then he told his servants, 'The banquet is ready, but those who were invited were not worthy. ⁹ Go then to where the roads exit the city and invite everyone you find to the banquet.' ¹⁰ So those servants went out on the roads and gathered everyone they found, both evil and good. The wedding banquet^E was filled with guests.^F ¹¹ When the king came in to see the guests, he saw a man there who was not dressed for a wedding. ¹² So he said to him, 'Friend, how did you get in here without wedding clothes?' The man was speechless.   Ezk 21:21; Ob 14; Mt 10:11; Ac 13:46

¹³ "Then the king told the attendants, 'Tie him up hand and foot,^G and throw him into the outer darkness, where there will be weeping and gnashing of teeth.'

¹⁴ "For many are invited, but few are chosen."   Mt 20:16; Rv 17:14

God and Caesar

¹⁵ Then the Pharisees went and plotted how to trap him by what he said.^H ¹⁶ So they sent their disciples to him, along with the Herodians. "Teacher," they said, "we know that you are truthful and teach truthfully the way of God. You don't care what anyone thinks nor do you show partiality.^I ¹⁷ Tell us, then, what you think. Is it lawful to pay taxes to Caesar or not?"   Mk 2:8; 3:6; 12:13-17; Lk 20:20-26

¹⁸ Perceiving their malicious intent, Jesus said, "Why are you testing me, hypocrites? ¹⁹ Show me the

---

^A21:42 Lit *the head of the corner*   ^B21:42 Ps 118:22-23   ^C21:44 Some mss omit this verse   ^D22:7 Other mss read *But when the (that) king heard about it he*   ^E22:10 Other mss read *wedding hall*   ^F22:10 Lit *those reclining* (to eat)   ^G22:13 Other mss add *take him away*   ^H22:15 Lit *trap him in a word*   ^I22:16 Lit *don't look on the face of men*

coin used for the tax." They brought him a denarius.[A] 20 "Whose image and inscription is this?" he asked them.

21 "Caesar's," they said to him.

Then he said to them, "Give, then, to Caesar the things that are Caesar's, and to God the things that are God's." 22 When they heard this, they were amazed. So they left him and went away. Mt 17:25; Rm 13:7

The Sadducees and the Resurrection

23 That same day some Sadducees, who say there is no resurrection, came up to him and questioned him: 24 "Teacher, Moses said, **if a man dies, having no children, his brother is to marry his wife and raise up offspring for his brother.**[B] 25 Now there were seven brothers among us. The first got married and died. Having no offspring, he left his wife to his brother. 26 The same thing happened to the second also, and the third, and so on to all seven. 27 Last of all, the woman died. 28 In the resurrection, then, whose wife will she be of the seven? For they all had married her."[C] Mt 3:7; Mk 12:18-27; Lk 20:27-38; Ac 4:1

29 Jesus answered them, "You are mistaken, because you don't know the Scriptures or the power of God. 30 For in the resurrection they neither marry nor are given in marriage but are like[D] angels in heaven. 31 Now concerning the resurrection of the dead, haven't you read what was spoken to you by God: 32 **I am the God of Abraham and the God of Isaac and the God of** Jacob?[E] He[F] is not the God of the dead, but of the living." Ex 3:6; Mt 24:38

33 And when the crowds heard this, they were astonished at his teaching.

The Primary Commands

34 When the Pharisees heard that he had silenced the Sadducees, they came together. 35 And one of them, an expert in the law, asked a question to test him: 36 "Teacher, which command in the law is the greatest?" Mk 12:28-33; Lk 7:30; 10:25-28; 11:45

37 He said to him, "**Love the Lord your God with all your heart, with all your soul, and with all your mind.**[G] 38 This is the greatest and most important[H] command. 39 The second is like it: **Love your neighbor as yourself.**[I] 40 All the Law and the Prophets depend[J] on these two commands." Dt 6:5; Lk 10:27

The Question About the Christ

41 While the Pharisees were together, Jesus questioned them, 42 "What do you think about the Messiah? Whose son is he?" Mk 12:35-37

They replied, "David's."

43 He asked them, "How is it then that David, inspired by the Spirit,[K] calls him 'Lord': 2Sm 23:2; Rv 1:10; 4:2

44 　**The Lord declared
　　　　to my Lord,
　'Sit at my right hand
　　until I put your enemies
　　　　under your feet'?**[L,M] Ps 110:1

45 "If David calls him 'Lord,' how then can he be his son?" 46 No one was able to answer him at all,[N] and from that day no one dared to question him anymore. Mk 12:34; Lk 14:6; 20:40

Religious Hypocrites Denounced

23 Then Jesus spoke to the crowds and to his disciples: [2] "The scribes and the Pharisees are seated in the chair of Moses. [3] Therefore do whatever they tell you, and observe it. But don't do what they do, because they don't practice what they teach. [4] They tie up heavy loads that are hard to carry[A] and put them on people's shoulders, but they themselves aren't willing to lift a finger to move them. [5] They do everything[B] to be seen by others: They enlarge their phylacteries and lengthen their tassels.[C] [6] They love the place of honor at banquets, the front seats in the synagogues, [7] greetings in the marketplaces, and to be called 'Rabbi' by people. Mt 10:42; Mk 12:38-39

[8] "But you are not to be called 'Rabbi,' because you have one Teacher,[D] and you are all brothers and sisters. [9] Do not call anyone on earth your father, because you have one Father, who is in heaven. [10] You are not to be called instructors either, because you have one Instructor, the Messiah. [11] The greatest among you will be your servant. [12] Whoever exalts himself will be humbled, and whoever humbles himself will be exalted. Mk 9:5; 10:51; Jn 1:38,49; 11:8; Jms 3:1

[13] "Woe to you, scribes and Pharisees, hypocrites! You shut the door of the kingdom of heaven in people's faces. For you don't go in, and you don't allow those entering to go in.[E] Mt 23:15,23,25; Lk 11:52

[15] "Woe to you, scribes and Pharisees, hypocrites! You travel over land and sea to make one convert, and when he becomes one, you make him twice as fit for hell[F] as you are! Ac 2:11; 6:5; 13:43

[16] "Woe to you, blind guides, who say, 'Whoever takes an oath by the temple, it means nothing. But whoever takes an oath by the gold of the temple is bound by his oath.'[G] [17] Blind fools! For which is greater, the gold or the temple that sanctified the gold? [18] Also, 'Whoever takes an oath by the altar, it means nothing; but whoever takes an oath by the gift that is on it is bound by his oath.' [19] Blind people![H] For which is greater, the gift or the altar that sanctifies the gift? [20] Therefore, the one who takes an oath by the altar takes an oath by it and by everything on it. [21] The one who takes an oath by the temple takes an oath by it and by him who dwells in it. [22] And the one who takes an oath by heaven takes an oath by God's throne and by him who sits on it. Lv 19:12; Mt 15:14; 23:24; Ac 1:16; Rm 2:19

[23] "Woe to you, scribes and Pharisees, hypocrites! You pay a tenth of[I] mint, dill, and cumin, and yet you have neglected the more important matters of the law — justice, mercy, and faithfulness.[J] These things should have been done without neglecting the others. [24] Blind guides! You strain out a gnat, but gulp down a camel! 1Sm 15:22; Ps 33:5; Jr 5:1; Mc 6:8; Zch 7:9

[25] "Woe to you, scribes and Pharisees, hypocrites! You clean the outside of the cup and dish, but inside

---

[A]**23:4** Other mss omit *that are hard to carry*   [B]**23:5** Lit *do all their works*   [C]**23:5** Other mss add *on their robes*   [D]**23:8** Other mss add *the Christ*   [E]**23:13** Some mss include v. 14: *"Woe to you, scribes and Pharisees, hypocrites! You devour widows' houses and make long prayers just for show. This is why you will receive a harsher punishment.*   [F]**23:15** Lit *twice the son of gehenna*   [G]**23:16** Lit *is obligated*, also in v. 18   [H]**23:19** Other mss read *Fools and blind*   [I]**23:23** Or *You tithe*   [J]**23:23** Or *faith* they are full of greed[A] and self-indulgence. [26] Blind Pharisee! First clean the inside of the cup,[B] so that the outside of it[C] may also become clean. Mk 7:4; Lk 11:39

[27] "Woe to you, scribes and Pharisees, hypocrites! You are like whitewashed tombs, which appear beautiful on the outside, but inside are full of the bones of the dead and every kind of impurity. [28] In the same way, on the outside you seem righteous to people, but inside you are full of hypocrisy and lawlessness. Lk 11:44; Ac 23:3

[29] "Woe to you, scribes and Pharisees, hypocrites! You build the tombs of the prophets and decorate the graves of the righteous, [30] and you say, 'If we had lived in the days of our ancestors, we wouldn't have taken part with them in shedding the prophets' blood.' [31] So you testify against yourselves that you are descendants of those who murdered the prophets. [32] Fill up, then, the measure of your ancestors' sins! Gn 15:16; Ac 7:51; 1Th 2:15-16

[33] "Snakes! Brood of vipers! How can you escape being condemned to hell?[D] [34] This is why I am sending you prophets, sages, and scribes. Some of them you will kill and crucify, and some of them you will flog in your synagogues and pursue from town to town. [35] So all the righteous blood shed on the earth will be charged to you,[E] from the blood of righteous Abel to the blood of Zechariah, son of Berechiah, whom you murdered between the sanctuary and the altar. [36] Truly I tell you, all these things will come on this generation. Mt 3:7; 5:22; 12:34

Jesus's Lamenting over Jerusalem

[37] "Jerusalem, Jerusalem, who kills the prophets and stones those who are sent to her. How often I wanted to gather your children together, as a hen gathers her chicks[F] under her wings, but you were not willing! [38] See, your house is left to you desolate. [39] For I tell you, you will not see me again until you say, 'Blessed is he who comes in the name of the Lord'!"[G] Jr 12:7; Lk 13:34-35

Destruction of the Temple Predicted

24 As Jesus left and was going out of the temple, his disciples came up and called his attention to its buildings. [2] He replied to them, "Do you see all these things? Truly I tell you, not one stone will be left here on another that will not be thrown down." Mk 13:1-37

Signs of the End of the Age

[3] While he was sitting on the Mount of Olives, the disciples approached him privately and said, "Tell us, when will these things happen? And what is the sign of your coming and of the end of the age?"

[4] Jesus replied to them: "Watch out that no one deceives you. [5] For many will come in my name, saying, 'I am the Messiah,' and they will deceive many. [6] You are going to hear of wars and rumors of wars. See that you are not alarmed, because these things must take place, but the end is not yet. [7] For nation will rise up against nation, and kingdom against kingdom. There will be

---

[A]23:25 Or *full of violence*　[B]23:26 Other mss add *and dish*　[C]23:26 Other mss read *of them*　[D]23:33 Lit *escape from the judgment of gehenna*　[E]23:35 Lit *will come on you*　[F]23:37 Or *as a mother bird gathers her young*　[G]23:39 Ps 118:26

famines [A] and earthquakes in various places. [8] All these events are the beginning of labor pains.

Persecutions Predicted

[9] "Then they will hand you over to be persecuted, and they will kill you. You will be hated by all nations because of my name. [10] Then many will fall away, betray one another, and hate one another. [11] Many false prophets will rise up and deceive many. [12] Because lawlessness will multiply, the love of many will grow cold. [13] But the one who endures to the end will be saved. [14] This good news of the kingdom will be proclaimed in all the world [B] as a testimony to all nations, and then the end will come. Is 44:25; Mt 10:17,22; Jn 16:2

The Great Tribulation

[15] "So when you see the abomination of desolation, [C] spoken of by the prophet Daniel, standing in the holy place" (let the reader understand), [16] "then those in Judea must flee to the mountains. [17] A man on the housetop [D] must not come down to get things out of his house, [18] and a man in the field must not go back to get his coat. [19] Woe to pregnant women and nursing mothers in those days! [20] Pray that your escape may not be in winter or on a Sabbath. [21] For at that time there will be great distress, [E] the kind that hasn't taken place from the beginning of the world until now and never will again. [22] Unless those days were cut short, no one would [F] be saved. But those days will be cut short because of the elect. Dn 9:27; 11:31; 12:11; Mk 13:14

[23] "If anyone tells you then, 'See, here is the Messiah!' or, 'Over here!' do not believe it. [24] For false messiahs and false prophets will arise and perform great signs and wonders to lead astray, if possible, even the elect. [25] Take note: I have told you in advance. [26] So if they tell you, 'See, he's in the wilderness!' don't go out; or, 'See, he's in the storerooms!' do not believe it. [27] For as the lightning comes from the east and flashes as far as the west, so will be the coming of the Son of Man. [28] Wherever the carcass is, there the vultures [G] will gather. Dt 13:1-3; Mk 11:24; Lk 17:3; 21:28; Jn 6:64

The Coming of the Son of Man

[29] "Immediately after the distress of those days, the sun will be darkened, and the moon will not shed its light; the stars will fall from the sky, and the powers of the heavens will be shaken. [30] Then the sign of the Son of Man will appear in the sky, and then all the peoples of the earth [H] will mourn; [I] and they will see the Son of Man coming on the clouds of heaven with power and great glory. [31] He will send out his angels with a loud trumpet, and they will gather his elect from the four winds, from one end of the sky to the other. Is 13:10; 24:23; Ezk 32:7

The Parable of the Fig Tree

[32] "Learn this lesson from the fig tree: As soon as its branch becomes tender and sprouts leaves, you know that summer is near. [33] In the same way, when you see all these things, recognize [J] that he [K]

[A] **24:7** Other mss add *epidemics* [B] **24:14** Or *in all the inhabited earth* [C] **24:15** Dn 9:27 [D] **24:17** Or *roof*
[E] **24:21** Or *tribulation*, also in v. 29 [F] **24:22** Lit *short, all flesh would not* [G] **24:28** Or *eagles* [H] **24:30** Or
all the tribes of the land [I] **24:30** Lit *will beat*; that is, beat their chests [J] **24:33** Or *things, you know*
[K] **24:33** Or *it*; that is, summer

is near — at the door. [34] Truly I tell you, this generation will certainly not pass away until all these things take place. [35] Heaven and earth will pass away, but my words will never pass away.   Mt 13:3,34-36; 15:15; 21:33,45

No One Knows the Day or Hour

[36] "Now concerning that day and hour no one knows — neither the angels of heaven nor the Son[A] — except the Father alone. [37] As the days of Noah were, so the coming of the Son of Man will be. [38] For in those days before the flood they were eating and drinking, marrying and giving in marriage, until the day Noah boarded the ark. [39] They didn't know until the flood came and swept them all away. This is the way the coming of the Son of Man will be. [40] Then two men will be in the field; one will be taken and one left. [41] Two women will be grinding grain with a hand mill; one will be taken and one left. [42] Therefore be alert, since you don't know what day[B] your Lord is coming. [43] But know this: If the homeowner had known what time[C] the thief was coming, he would have stayed alert and not let his house be broken into. [44] This is why you are also to be ready, because the Son of Man is coming at an hour you do not expect.   Gn 6:5; Zch 14:7; Mt 25:13; Mk 13:32; Ac 1:7

Faithful Service to Christ

[45] "Who then is a faithful and wise servant, whom his master has put in charge of his household, to give them food at the proper time? [46] Blessed is that servant whom the master finds doing his job when he comes. [47] Truly I tell you, he will put him in charge of all his possessions. [48] But if that wicked servant says in his heart, 'My master is delayed,' [49] and starts to beat his fellow servants, and eats and drinks with drunkards, [50] that servant's master will come on a day he does not expect him and at an hour he does not know. [51] He will cut him to pieces and assign him a place with the hypocrites, where there will be weeping and gnashing of teeth.   Mt 7:24; 10:16; 25:2,21; Lk 12:42-46; Jn 13:17

The Parable of the Ten Virgins

25 "At that time the kingdom of heaven will be like ten virgins[D] who took their lamps[E] and went out to meet the groom. [2] Five of them were foolish and five were wise. [3] When the foolish took their lamps, they didn't take oil with them; [4] but the wise ones took oil in their flasks with their lamps. [5] When the groom was delayed, they all became drowsy and fell asleep.   Mt 13:24; Ac 20:8; Rv 4:5; 19:7; 21:2,9

[6] "In the middle of the night there was a shout: 'Here's the groom! Come out to meet him.'

[7] "Then all the virgins got up and trimmed their lamps. [8] The foolish ones said to the wise ones, 'Give us some of your oil, because our lamps are going out.'

[9] "The wise ones answered, 'No, there won't be enough for us and for you. Go instead to those who sell oil, and buy some for yourselves.'

[10] "When they had gone to buy some, the groom arrived, and those who were ready went in with him to the wedding banquet, and the door was shut. [11] Later the rest of

---

[A]24:36 Other mss omit *nor the Son*   [B]24:42 Other mss read *hour*; = time   [C]24:43 Lit *watch*; a division of the night in ancient times   [D]25:1 Or *bridesmaids*   [E]25:1 Or *torches*, also in vv. 3,4,7,8 the virgins also came and said, 'Master, master, open up for us!'

¹² "He replied, 'Truly I tell you, I don't know you!'

¹³ "Therefore be alert, because you don't know either the day or the hour.ᴬ

The Parable of the Talents

¹⁴ "For it is just like a man about to go on a journey. He called his own servants and entrusted his possessions to them. ¹⁵ To one he gave five talents,ᴮ to another two talents, and to another one talent, depending on each one's ability. Then he went on a journey. Immediately ¹⁶ the man who had received five talents went, put them to work, and earned five more. ¹⁷ In the same way the man with two earned two more. ¹⁸ But the man who had received one talent went off, dug a hole in the ground, and hid his master's money.   Lk 19:12-27

¹⁹ "After a long time the master of those servants came and settled accounts with them. ²⁰ The man who had received five talents approached, presented five more talents, and said, 'Master, you gave me five talents. See, I've earned five more talents.'

²¹ "His master said to him, 'Well done, good and faithful servant! You were faithful over a few things; I will put you in charge of many things. Share your master's joy.'

²² "The man with two talents also approached. He said, 'Master, you gave me two talents. See, I've earned two more talents.'

²³ "His master said to him, 'Well done, good and faithful servant!

You were faithful over a few things; I will put you in charge of many things. Share your master's joy.'

²⁴ "The man who had received one talent also approached and said, 'Master, I know you. You're a harsh man, reaping where you haven't sown and gathering where you haven't scattered seed. ²⁵ So I was afraid and went off and hid your talent in the ground. See, you have what is yours.'   1Sm 25:3; 2Co 8:12

²⁶ "His master replied to him, 'You evil, lazy servant! If you knew that I reap where I haven't sown and gather where I haven't scattered, ²⁷ thenᶜ you should have deposited my money with the bankers, and I would have received my moneyᴰ back with interest when I returned.

²⁸ "'So take the talent from him and give it to the one who has ten talents. ²⁹ For to everyone who has, more will be given, and he will have more than enough. But from the one who does not have, even what he has will be taken away from him. ³⁰ And throw this good-for-nothing servant into the outer darkness, where there will be weeping and gnashing of teeth.'   Mt 13:12; Mk 4:25

The Sheep and the Goats

³¹ "When the Son of Man comes in his glory, and all the angelsᴱ with him, then he will sit on his glorious throne. ³² All the nationsᶠ will be gathered before him, and he will separate them one from another, just as a shepherd separates the sheep from the goats. ³³ He will put the sheep on his right and the goats on the left. ³⁴ Then the King will say to those on his right, 'Come, you who

---

ᴬ**25:13** Other mss add *in which the Son of Man is coming.*   ᴮ**25:15** A talent is worth about 6,000 denarii, or twenty years' wages for a laborer   ᶜ**25:26-27** Or *So you knew . . . scattered? Then* (as a question)   ᴰ**25:27** Lit *received what is mine*   ᴱ**25:31** Other mss read *holy angels*   ᶠ**25:32** Or *the Gentiles* are blessed by my Father; inherit the kingdom prepared for you from the foundation of the world. Gn 16:7 ³⁵ " 'For I was hungry and you gave me something to eat; I was thirsty and you gave me something to drink; I was a stranger and you took me in; ³⁶ I was naked and you clothed me; I was sick and you took care of me; I was in prison and you visited me.' Jb 31:32; Is 58:7; Ezk 18:7; 2Tm 1:16

³⁷ "Then the righteous will answer him, 'Lord, when did we see you hungry and feed you, or thirsty and give you something to drink? ³⁸ When did we see you a stranger and take you in, or without clothes and clothe you? ³⁹ When did we see you sick, or in prison, and visit you?'

⁴⁰ "And the King will answer them, 'Truly I tell you, whatever you did for one of the least of these brothers and sisters of mine, you did for me.' Pr 19:17; Mt 10:42; 25:34; Heb 6:10

⁴¹ "Then he will also say to those on the left, 'Depart from me, you who are cursed, into the eternal fire prepared for the devil and his angels! ⁴² For I was hungry and you gave me nothing to eat; I was thirsty and you gave me nothing to drink; ⁴³ I was a stranger and you didn't take me in; I was naked and you didn't clothe me, sick and in prison and you didn't take care of me.'

⁴⁴ "Then they too will answer, 'Lord, when did we see you hungry, or thirsty, or a stranger, or without clothes, or sick, or in prison, and not help you?'

⁴⁵ "Then he will answer them, 'Truly I tell you, whatever you did not do for one of the least of these, you did not do for me.' Pr 14:31; 17:5; Ac 9:5

⁴⁶ "And they will go away into eternal punishment, but the righteous into eternal life." Dn 12:2; Jn 5:21

The Plot to Kill Jesus

26 When Jesus had finished saying all these things, he told his disciples, ² "You know^A that the Passover takes place after two days, and the Son of Man will be handed over to be crucified." Mk 14:1-2; Lk 22:1-2

³ Then the chief priests^B and the elders of the people assembled in the courtyard of the high priest, who was named Caiaphas, ⁴ and they conspired to arrest Jesus in a treacherous way and kill him. ⁵ "Not during the festival," they said, "so there won't be rioting among the people." Ps 2:2; Mt 26:57; Lk 3:2; Jn 11:47

The Anointing at Bethany

⁶ While Jesus was in Bethany at the house of Simon the leper,^C ⁷ a woman approached him with an alabaster jar of very expensive perfume. She poured it on his head as he was reclining at the table. ⁸ When the disciples saw it, they were indignant. "Why this waste?" they asked. ⁹ "This might have been sold for a great deal and given to the poor." Mt 10:1; 26:56; Mk 14:3-9; Jn 12:1-8

¹⁰ Aware of this, Jesus said to them, "Why are you bothering this woman? She has done a noble thing for me. ¹¹ You always have the poor with you, but you do not always have me. ¹² By pouring this perfume on my body, she has prepared me for burial. ¹³ Truly I tell you, wherever this gospel is proclaimed in the whole world, what she has done will also be told in memory of her." Dt 15:11; Mt 24:14; Jn 12:8

---

^A 26:2 Or "Know (as a command)   ^B 26:3 Other mss add and the scribes   ^C 26:6 Gk lepros; a term for various skin diseases; see Lv 13–14

¹⁴ Then one of the Twelve, the man called Judas Iscariot, went to the chief priests ¹⁵ and said, "What are you willing to give me if I hand him over to you?" So they weighed out thirty pieces of silver for him. ¹⁶ And from that time he started looking for a good opportunity to betray him. Mt 10:4; Mk 14:10-11; Lk 22:3-6

Betrayal at the Passover

¹⁷ On the first day of Unleavened Bread the disciples came to Jesus and asked, "Where do you want us to make preparations for you to eat the Passover?" Mk 14:12-16; Lk 22:7-13

¹⁸ "Go into the city to a certain man," he said, "and tell him, 'The Teacher says: My time is near; I am celebrating the Passover at your place^A with my disciples.'" ¹⁹ So the disciples did as Jesus had directed them and prepared the Passover. ²⁰ When evening came, he was reclining at the table with the Twelve. ²¹ While they were eating, he said, "Truly I tell you, one of you will betray me." Jn 7:6,8; 8:20; 13:1

²² Deeply distressed, each one began to say to him, "Surely not I, Lord?"

²³ He replied, "The one who dipped his hand with me in the bowl — he will betray me. ²⁴ The Son of Man will go just as it is written about him, but woe to that man by whom the Son of Man is betrayed! It would have been better for him if he had not been born." Dn 9:26; Mk 9:12; Ac 17:2-3

²⁵ Judas, his betrayer, replied, "Surely not I, Rabbi?" Lk 22:70; Jn 1:38

"You have said it," he told him.

The First Lord's Supper

²⁶ As they were eating, Jesus took bread, blessed and broke it, gave it to the disciples, and said, "Take and eat it; this is my body." ²⁷ Then he took a cup, and after giving thanks, he gave it to them and said, "Drink from it, all of you. ²⁸ For this is my blood of the covenant,^B which is poured out for many for the forgiveness of sins. ²⁹ But I tell you, I will not drink from this fruit of the vine from now on until that day when I drink it new with you in my Father's kingdom." ³⁰ After singing a hymn, they went out to the Mount of Olives. Mt 10:1; Mk 14:22-25

Peter's Denial Predicted

³¹ Then Jesus said to them, "Tonight all of you will fall away because of me, for it is written:

> **I will strike the shepherd,**
> **and the sheep of the flock**
> **will be scattered.**^C   Zch 13:7

³² But after I have risen, I will go ahead of you to Galilee." Mt 28:7,10,16

³³ Peter told him, "Even if everyone falls away because of you, I will never fall away."

³⁴ "Truly I tell you," Jesus said to him, "tonight, before the rooster crows, you will deny me three times." Mt 26:75; Lk 22:34; Jn 13:38

³⁵ "Even if I have to die with you," Peter told him, "I will never deny you," and all the disciples said the same thing.

The Prayer in the Garden

³⁶ Then Jesus came with them to a place called Gethsemane, and he told the disciples, "Sit here while I go over there and pray." ³⁷ Taking along Peter and the two sons of Zebedee, he began to be sorrowful and troubled. ³⁸ He said to them, "I am deeply grieved^D to the point of

^A 26:18 Lit Passover with you   ^B 26:28 Other mss read new covenant   ^C 26:31 Zch 13:7   ^D 26:38 Lit "My soul is swallowed up in sorrow death. Remain here and stay awake with me." **39** Going a little farther,[A] he fell facedown and prayed, "My Father, if it is possible, let this cup pass from me. Yet not as I will, but as you will." Mt 4:21; Mk 14:32-42; Lk 22:40-46 **40** Then he came to the disciples and found them sleeping. He asked Peter, "So, couldn't you stay awake with me one hour? **41** Stay awake and pray, so that you won't enter into temptation. The spirit is willing, but the flesh is weak."

42 Again, a second time, he went away and prayed, "My Father, if this[B] cannot pass[C] unless I drink it, your will be done." **43** And he came again and found them sleeping, because they could not keep their eyes open. Mt 26:39; Mk 14:36; Jn 6:38

44 After leaving them, he went away again and prayed a third time, saying the same thing once more. **45** Then he came to the disciples and said to them, "Are you still sleeping and resting? See, the time is near. The Son of Man is betrayed into the hands of sinners. **46** Get up; let's go. See, my betrayer is near." Jn 12:27; 13:1

Judas's Betrayal of Jesus

47 While he was still speaking, Judas, one of the Twelve, suddenly arrived. A large mob with swords and clubs was with him from the chief priests and elders of the people. **48** His betrayer had given them a sign: "The one I kiss, he's the one; arrest him." **49** So immediately he went up to Jesus and said, "Greetings, Rabbi!" and kissed him.

50 "Friend," Jesus asked him, "why have you come?"[D] Mt 20:13; 22:12

Then they came up, took hold of Jesus, and arrested him. **51** At that moment one of those with Jesus reached out his hand and drew his sword. He struck the high priest's servant and cut off his ear. Lk 22:38

52 Then Jesus told him, "Put your sword back in its place because all who take up the sword will perish by the sword. **53** Or do you think that I cannot call on my Father, and he will provide me here and now with more than twelve legions of angels? **54** How, then, would the Scriptures be fulfilled that say it must happen this way?" Gn 9:6; 2Kg 6:17; Dn 7:10; Rv 13:10

55 At that time Jesus said to the crowds, "Have you come out with swords and clubs, as if I were a criminal,[E] to capture me? Every day I used to sit, teaching in the temple, and you didn't arrest me. **56** But all this has happened so that the writings of the prophets would be fulfilled." Then all the disciples deserted him and ran away. Mk 12:35

Jesus Faces the Sanhedrin

57 Those who had arrested Jesus led him away to Caiaphas the high priest, where the scribes and the elders had convened. **58** Peter was following him at a distance right to the high priest's courtyard. He went in and was sitting with the servants to see the outcome. Jn 7:32

59 The chief priests and the whole Sanhedrin were looking for false testimony against Jesus so that they could put him to death, **60** but they could not find any, even though many false witnesses came forward.[F] Finally, two[G] who came forward[61] stated, "This man said, 'I

[A]**26:39** Other mss read *Drawing nearer* [B]**26:42** Other mss add *cup* [C]**26:42** Other mss add *from me* [D]**26:50** Or *Jesus told him, "do what you have come for."* [E]**26:55** Lit *as against a criminal* [F]**26:60** Other mss add *they found none* [G]**26:60** Other mss add *false witnesses* can destroy the temple of God and rebuild it in three days.'" Mt 5:22

⁶² The high priest stood up and said to him, "Don't you have an answer to what these men are testifying against you?" ⁶³ But Jesus kept silent. The high priest said to him, "I charge you under oath by the living God: Tell us if you are the Messiah, the Son of God." Lk 22:67-71

⁶⁴ "You have said it," Jesus told him. "But I tell you, in the future^A you will see **the Son of Man seated at the right hand** of Power and **coming on the clouds of heaven.**"^B

⁶⁵ Then the high priest tore his robes and said, "He has blasphemed! Why do we still need witnesses? See, now you've heard the blasphemy. ⁶⁶ What is your decision?" Nm 14:6; Mk 3:29; 14:63; Jn 10:33

They answered, "He deserves death!" ⁶⁷ Then they spat in his face and beat him; others slapped him ⁶⁸ and said, "Prophesy to us, Messiah! Who was it that hit you?"

Peter Denies His Lord

⁶⁹ Now Peter was sitting outside in the courtyard. A servant girl approached him and said, "You were with Jesus the Galilean too."

⁷⁰ But he denied it in front of everyone: "I don't know what you're talking about."

⁷¹ When he had gone out to the gateway, another woman saw him and told those who were there, "This man was with Jesus the Nazarene!" Mk 14:67; Ac 6:14

⁷² And again he denied it with an oath: "I don't know the man!"

⁷³ After a little while those standing there approached and said to Peter, "You really are one of them, since even your accent^C gives you away."

⁷⁴ Then he started to curse and to swear with an oath, "I don't know the man!" Immediately a rooster crowed, ⁷⁵ and Peter remembered the words Jesus had spoken, "Before the rooster crows, you will deny me three times." And he went outside and wept bitterly. Mt 26:34

Jesus Handed Over to Pilate

27 When daybreak came, all the chief priests and the elders of the people plotted against Jesus to put him to death. ² After tying him up, they led him away and handed him over to Pilate,^D the governor. Mt 20:19; Mk 15:1; Lk 22:66; Jn 18:28

Judas Hangs Himself

³ Then Judas, his betrayer, seeing that Jesus had been condemned, was full of remorse and returned the thirty pieces of silver to the chief priests and elders. ⁴ "I have sinned by betraying innocent blood," he said. Mt 21:29; 26:14-15

"What's that to us?" they said. "See to it yourself!" ⁵ So he threw the silver into the temple and departed. Then he went and hanged himself. 2Sm 17:23; Lk 1:19,21; Ac 1:18

⁶ The chief priests took the silver and said, "It's not permitted to put it into the temple treasury, since it is blood money." ⁷ They conferred together and bought the potter's field with it as a burial place for foreigners. ⁸ Therefore that field has been called "Blood Field" to this day. ⁹ Then what was spoken through the prophet Jeremiah was fulfilled: **They took^E the thirty pieces of silver, the price of him whose**

^A**26:64** Lit *you, from now*   ^B**26:64** Ps 110:1; Dn 7:13   ^C**26:73** Or *speech*   ^D**27:2** Other mss read *Pontius Pilate*   ^E**27:9** Or *I took* price was set by the Israelites, ¹⁰ and they gave ᴬ them for the potter's field, as the Lord directed me. ᴮ Jr 32:6-9; Zch 11:12-13; Mk 2:24; Jn 18:31

Jesus Faces the Governor

¹¹ Now Jesus stood before the governor. "Are you the King of the Jews?" the governor asked him. Mk 15:2-5

Jesus answered, "You say so." ¹² While he was being accused by the chief priests and elders, he didn't answer. Mt 2:2; 26:63; 1Tm 6:13

¹³ Then Pilate said to him, "Don't you hear how much they are testifying against you?" ¹⁴ But he didn't answer him on even one charge, so that the governor was quite amazed. Mk 15:5; Lk 23:9

Jesus or Barabbas

¹⁵ At the festival the governor's custom was to release to the crowd a prisoner they wanted. ¹⁶ At that time they had a notorious prisoner called Barabbas. ᶜ ¹⁷ So when they had gathered together, Pilate said to them, "Who is it you want me to release for you — Barabbas, or Jesus who is called Christ?" ¹⁸ For he knew it was because of envy that they had handed him over.

¹⁹ While he was sitting on the judge's bench, his wife sent word to him, "Have nothing to do with that righteous man, for today I've suffered terribly in a dream because of him." Gn 20:6; Nm 12:6; Jb 33:14-16

²⁰ The chief priests and the elders, however, persuaded the crowds to ask for Barabbas and to execute Jesus. ²¹ The governor asked them, "Which of the two do you want me to release for you?"

"Barabbas!" they answered.

²² Pilate asked them, "What should I do then with Jesus, who is called Christ?"

They all answered, "Crucify him!"

²³ Then he said, "Why? What has he done wrong?"

But they kept shouting all the more, "Crucify him!" Lk 23:41; Jn 8:46

²⁴ When Pilate saw that he was getting nowhere, but that a riot was starting instead, he took some water, washed his hands in front of the crowd, and said, "I am innocent of this man's blood. ᴰ See to it yourselves!" Dt 21:6-8; Ps 26:6; Mt 26:5

²⁵ All the people answered, "His blood be on us and on our children!" ²⁶ Then he released Barabbas to them and, after having Jesus flogged, handed him over to be crucified. Jos 2:19; Is 53:5; Mk 15:15; Lk 23:16; Ac 5:28

Mocked by the Military

²⁷ Then the governor's soldiers took Jesus into the governor's residence and gathered the whole company ᴱ around him. ²⁸ They stripped him and dressed him in a scarlet robe. ²⁹ They twisted together a crown of thorns, put it on his head, and placed a staff in his right hand. And they knelt down before him and mocked him: "Hail, King of the Jews!" ³⁰ Then they spat on him, took the staff, and kept hitting him on the head. ³¹ After they had mocked him, they stripped him of the robe, put his own clothes on him, and led him away to crucify him. Mk 15:16-20; Jn 18:28,33; 19:2-3,9

Crucified Between Two Criminals

³² As they were going out, they found a Cyrenian man named Simon. They forced him to carry

ᴬ27:10 Some mss read I gave ᴮ27:9-10 Jr 32:6-9; Zch 11:12-13 ᶜ27:16 Other mss read Jesus Barabbas, also in v. 17 ᴰ27:24 Other mss read this righteous man's blood ᴱ27:27 Lit cohort his cross. [33] When they came to a place called *Golgotha* (which means Place of the Skull), [34] they gave him wine[A] mixed with gall to drink. But when he tasted it, he refused to drink it. [35] After crucifying him, they divided his clothes by casting lots. [B] [36] Then they sat down and were guarding him there. [37] Above his head they put up the charge against him in writing: THIS IS JESUS, THE KING OF THE JEWS. Nm 15:35; Mk 15:21; Lk 23:26; Heb 13:12

[38] Then two criminals[C] were crucified with him, one on the right and one on the left. [39] Those who passed by were yelling insults at[D] him, shaking their heads [40] and saying, "You who would destroy the temple and rebuild it in three days, save yourself! If you are the Son of God, come down from the cross!" [41] In the same way the chief priests, with the scribes and elders,[E] mocked him and said, [42] "He saved others, but he cannot save himself! He is the King of Israel! Let him[F] come down now from the cross, and we will believe in him. [43] He trusts in God; let God rescue him now — if he takes pleasure in him![G] For he said, 'I am the Son of God.'" [44] In the same way even the criminals who were crucified with him taunted him. Is 53:12; Mt 20:21

The Death of Jesus

[45] From noon until three in the afternoon[H] darkness came over the whole land.[I] [46] About three in the afternoon Jesus cried out with a loud voice, "*Elí, Elí, lemá j sabachtháni?*"

that is, "My God, my God, why have you abandoned me?"[K] Mk 15:33-41

[47] When some of those standing there heard this, they said, "He's calling for Elijah."

[48] Immediately one of them ran and got a sponge, filled it with sour wine, put it on a stick, and offered him a drink. [49] But the rest said, "Let's see if Elijah comes to save him." Ps 69:21; Mk 15:36; Lk 23:36; Jn 19:29

[50] But Jesus cried out again with a loud voice and gave up his spirit. [51] Suddenly, the curtain of the sanctuary was torn in two from top to bottom, the earth quaked, and the rocks were split. [52] The tombs were also opened and many bodies of the saints who had fallen asleep were raised. [53] And they came out of the tombs after his resurrection, entered the holy city, and appeared to many. Mk 15:37; Lk 23:46; Jn 10:18; 19:30

[54] When the centurion and those with him, who were keeping watch over Jesus, saw the earthquake and the things that had happened, they were terrified and said, "Truly this man was the Son of God!" Jn 5:19

[55] Many women who had followed Jesus from Galilee and looked after him were there, watching from a distance. [56] Among them were Mary Magdalene, Mary the mother of James and Joseph, and the mother of Zebedee's sons.

The Burial of Jesus

[57] When it was evening, a rich man from Arimathea named Joseph came, who himself had also

---

[A] 27:34 Other mss read *sour wine* [B] 27:35 Other mss add *that what was spoken by the prophet might be fulfilled: "They divided my clothes among them, and for my clothing they cast lots."* [C] 27:38 Or *revolutionaries* [D] 27:39 Lit *passed by blasphemed*, or *were blaspheming* [E] 27:41 Other mss add *and Pharisees* [F] 27:42 Other mss read *If he . . . Israel, let him* [G] 27:43 Or *if he wants him* [H] 27:45 Lit *From the sixth hour to the ninth hour* [I] 27:45 Or *whole earth* [J] 27:46 Some mss read *lama*; other mss read *lima* [K] 27:46 Ps 22:1

become a disciple of Jesus. [58] He approached Pilate and asked for Jesus's body. Then Pilate ordered that it [A] be released. [59] So Joseph took the body, wrapped it in clean, fine linen, [60] and placed it in his new tomb, which he had cut into the rock. He left after rolling a great stone against the entrance of the tomb. [61] Mary Magdalene and the other Mary were seated there, facing the tomb. Mk 15:42-47; Lk 23:50-56

The Closely Guarded Tomb

[62] The next day, which followed the preparation day, the chief priests and the Pharisees gathered before Pilate [63] and said, "Sir, we remember that while this deceiver was still alive he said, 'After three days I will rise again.' [64] So give orders that the tomb be made secure until the third day. Otherwise, his disciples may come, steal him, and tell the people, 'He has been raised from the dead,' and the last deception will be worse than the first." Mk 15:42; Lk 23:54; Jn 19:14,31,42

[65] "You have [B] a guard of soldiers," Pilate told them. "Go and make it as secure as you know how." [66] They went and secured the tomb by setting a seal on the stone and placing the guard. Dn 6:17; Mt 28:2,11

Resurrection Morning

28 After the Sabbath, as the first day of the week was dawning, Mary Magdalene and the other Mary went to view the tomb. [2] There was a violent earthquake, because an angel of the Lord descended from heaven and approached the tomb. He rolled back the stone and was sitting on it. [3] His appearance was like lightning, and his clothing was as white as snow. [4] The guards were so shaken by fear of him that they became like dead men. Dn 7:9; Mk 16:1-8; Lk 24:1-10; Jn 20:1-8

[5] The angel told the women, "Don't be afraid, because I know you are looking for Jesus who was crucified. [6] He is not here. For he has risen, just as he said. Come and see the place where he lay. [7] Then go quickly and tell his disciples, 'He has risen from the dead and indeed he is going ahead of you to Galilee; you will see him there.' Listen, I have told you." Mt 14:27; 28:10

[8] So, departing quickly from the tomb with fear and great joy, they ran to tell his disciples the news. [9] Just then [C] Jesus met them and said, "Greetings!" They came up, took hold of his feet, and worshiped him. [10] Then Jesus told them, "Do not be afraid. Go and tell my brothers to leave for Galilee, and they will see me there." Mk 16:9; Jn 20:14

The Soldiers Bribed to Lie

[11] As they were on their way, some of the guards came into the city and reported to the chief priests everything that had happened. [12] After the priests [D] had assembled with the elders and agreed on a plan, they gave the soldiers a large sum of money [13] and told them, "Say this, 'His disciples came during the night and stole him while we were sleeping.' [14] If this reaches the governor's ears, we will deal with [E] him and keep you out of trouble." [15] They took the money and did as they were instructed, and this story has been spread among Jewish people to this day. Mt 27:2,8; Ac 12:20

[A] **27:58** Other mss read *that the body*　[B] **27:65** Or *"Take to tell the news to his disciples*　[C] **28:9** Other mss add *as they were on their way*　[D] **28:12** Lit *After they*　[E] **28:14** Lit *will persuade*

The Great Commission

¹⁶ The eleven disciples traveled to Galilee, to the mountain where Jesus had directed them. ¹⁷ When they saw him, they worshiped, ᴬ but some doubted. ¹⁸ Jesus came near and said to them, "All authority has been given to me in heaven and on earth. ¹⁹ Go, therefore, and make disciples of ᴮ all nations, baptizing them in the name of the Father and of the Son and of the Holy Spirit, ²⁰ teaching them to observe everything I have commanded you. And remember, ᶜ I am with you always, ᴰ to the end of the age."

MARK

The Messiah's Herald

1 The beginning of the gospel of Jesus Christ, the Son of God. [A] [2] As it is written in Isaiah the prophet: [B] Mt 3:1-12; Lk 3:1-18; Jn 1:1; Php 4:15

> See, I am sending
>   my messenger ahead
>   of you; Mt 13:49
> he will prepare your way. [C,D]
> [3] A voice of one crying out
>   in the wilderness: Jn 1:23
> Prepare the way
>   for the Lord; Lk 10:1; 17:5
> make his paths straight! [E]

[4] John came baptizing [F] in the wilderness and proclaiming a baptism of repentance for the forgiveness of sins. [5] The whole Judean countryside and all the people of Jerusalem were going out to him, and they were baptized by him in the Jordan River, confessing their sins. [6] John wore a camel-hair garment with a leather belt around his waist and ate locusts and wild honey. Lk 7:29; Ac 22:16; Rv 12:6

[7] He proclaimed, "One who is more powerful than I am is coming after me. I am not worthy to stoop down and untie the strap of his sandals. [8] I baptize you with [G] water, but he will baptize you with the Holy Spirit." Mt 3:11; Jn 1:15; Rv 18:8

The Baptism of Jesus

[9] In those days Jesus came from Nazareth in Galilee and was baptized in the Jordan by John. [10] As soon as he came up out of the water, he saw the heavens being torn open and the Spirit descending on him like a dove. [11] And a voice came from heaven: "You are my beloved Son; with you I am well-pleased." Mt 2:23; 3:13-17; 4:13; Lk 3:21-23

The Temptation of Jesus

[12] Immediately the Spirit drove him into the wilderness. [13] He was in the wilderness forty days, being tempted by Satan. He was with the wild animals, and the angels were serving him. Mt 4:1-11; Lk 4:1-13; Jn 1:33

Ministry in Galilee

[14] After John was arrested, Jesus went to Galilee, proclaiming the good news [H,I] of God: [15] "The time is fulfilled, and the kingdom of God has come near. Repent and believe the good news!" Mt 3:12; 4:17; 9:1; Jn 4:45

The First Disciples

[16] As he passed alongside the Sea of Galilee, he saw Simon and Andrew, Simon's brother, casting a net into the sea — for they were fishermen. [17] "Follow me," Jesus told them, "and I will make you fish for [J] people." [18] Immediately they left their nets and followed him. [19] Going on a little farther, he saw James the son of Zebedee and his brother John in a boat putting their nets in order. [20] Immediately he called them, and they left their father Zebedee in the boat with the hired men and followed him. Mt 4:18-22; Lk 5:1-11

[A] **1:1** Some mss omit *the Son of God* [B] **1:2** Other mss read *in the prophets* [C] **1:2** Other mss add *before you* [D] **1:2** Mal 3:1 [E] **1:3** Is 40:3 [F] **1:4** Or *John the Baptist came* [G] **1:8** Or *in* [H] **1:14** Other mss add *of the kingdom* [I] **1:14** Or *gospel* [J] **1:17** Or *you to become fishers of*

Driving Out an Unclean Spirit

²¹ They went into Capernaum, and right away he entered the synagogue on the Sabbath and began to teach. ²² They were astonished at his teaching because he was teaching them as one who had authority, and not like the scribes. Lk 4:31-35

²³ Just then a man with an unclean spirit was in their synagogue. He cried out, ²⁴ "What do you have to do with us, Jesus of Nazareth? Have you come to destroy us? I know who you are — the Holy One of God!" Lk 11:24; 2Co 6:17 ²⁵ Jesus rebuked him saying, "Be silent, and come out of him!" ²⁶ And the unclean spirit threw him into convulsions, shouted with a loud voice, and came out of him. 2Tm 4:2

²⁷ They were all amazed, and so they began to ask each other: "What is this? A new teaching with authority!ᴬ He commands even the unclean spirits, and they obey him." ²⁸ At once the news about him spread throughout the entire vicinity of Galilee. Mk 10:24,32

Healings at Capernaum

²⁹ As soon as they left the synagogue, they went into Simon and Andrew's house with James and John. ³⁰ Simon's mother-in-law was lying in bed with a fever, and they told him about her at once. ³¹ So he went to her, took her by the hand, and raised her up. The fever left her,ᴮ and she began to serve them.

³² When evening came, after the sun had set, they brought to him all those who were sick and demon-possessed. ³³ The whole town was assembled at the door, ³⁴ and he healed many who were sick with various diseases and drove out many demons. And he would not permit the demons to speak, because they knew him. Mt 8:16-17

Preaching in Galilee

³⁵ Very early in the morning, while it was still dark, he got up, went out, and made his way to a deserted place; and there he was praying. ³⁶ Simon and his companions searched for him, ³⁷ and when they found him they said, "Everyone is looking for you." Mt 4:23-25; Lk 4:42-44 ³⁸ And he said to them, "Let's go on to the neighboring villages so that I may preach there too. This is why I have come." Mk 1:4

A Man Cleansed

³⁹ He went into all of Galilee, preaching in their synagogues and driving out demons. ⁴⁰ Then a man with leprosyᶜ came to him and, on his knees,ᴰ begged him: "If you are willing, you can make me clean." ⁴¹ Moved with compassion,ᴱ Jesus reached out his hand and touched him. "I am willing," he told him. "Be made clean." ⁴² Immediately the leprosy left him, and he was made clean. ⁴³ Then he sternly warned him and sent him away at once, ⁴⁴ telling him, "See that you say nothing to anyone; but go and show yourself to the priest, and offer what Moses commanded for your cleansing, as a testimony to them."ᶠ ⁴⁵ Yet he went out and began to proclaim it widely and to spread the news, with the result that Jesus could no longer enter a town openly. But he was out in

---

ᴬ**1:27** Other mss read *"What is this? What is this new teaching? For with authority* ᴮ**1:31** Other mss add *at once* ᶜ**1:40** Gk *lepros* ; a term for various skin diseases, also in v. 42; see Lv 13–14 ᴰ**1:40** Other mss omit *on his knees* ᴱ**1:41** Other mss *Moved with indignation* ᶠ**1:44** Or *against them*

THE BOOKS OF THE
GOSPELS
AND NEW TESTAMENT
HISTORY

Like the Old Testament, the New Testament is separated into five divisions. The first division consists of four books called the Gospels. The second division, History, has only one book, Acts. The Gospels contain Christ's birth, ministry, death, and resurrection. Acts shares how the church was shaped because of those events.

MATTHEW was originally written for the Jews and shows Jesus as the Messiah and King, in whom the Old Testament prophecies were fulfilled.

MARK was written for the Gentiles, especially the Romans. This Gospel presents Jesus as the Son of Man.

LUKE was written for the Greeks. Luke, who seems to have been a physician of Gentile birth and a friend to Paul, wrote this book. He wrote about Jesus' humanity and His death on the cross.

JOHN emphasizes that Jesus is the Son of God and that by believing in Him people can have eternal life.

ACTS, the only New Testament book of History, tells what the apostles did during the time after Jesus' crucifixion, resurrection, and return to heaven. Luke wrote this book and reported the coming of the Holy Spirit and the spread of the church under Peter's and Paul's leadership.

THE LIFE OF
JESUS

**WORSHIPED BY
THE WISE MEN**

Greeted by
Simeon and Anna
in the temple

**BORN IN
BETHLEHEM**

Preached
the Sermon
on the Mount

**CALMED
THE STORM**

FED THE 5,000

Visited Mary
and Martha

Raised Lazarus
from the dead

Had the Last
Supper with
the disciples

Prayed in
Gethsemane

**CRUCIFIED
ON THE CROSS**

Arrested
and tried

**RESURRECTED—
JESUS IS ALIVE!**

Buried in
the tomb

LEARNED AT THE TEMPLE

BAPTIZED BY JOHN

Met the Samaritan woman at the well

CALLED PETER, ANDREW, JAMES, AND JOHN

BLESSED THE CHILDREN

Healed blind Bartimaeus

Visited Zacchaeus

COOKED BREAKFAST FOR DISCIPLES

ENTERED JERUSALEM TRIUMPHANTLY

Met two disciples on the Emmaus road

Appeared to disciples in the upper room

Ascended to heaven

KIDS
IN THE BIBLE

The Bible has many stories about children. Find some of these kids in your Bible to discover facts about their lives and their families. Who were their parents? What did these kids do? Why do you think their stories are in the Bible?

CAIN AND ABEL
Genesis 4:1–16

ISHMAEL
Genesis 1–3, 15–16; 21:8–20

ISAAC
Genesis 21:1–7; 22:1–19

JACOB AND ESAU
Genesis 25:19–26

JOSEPH
Genesis 37:2–11

MOSES
Exodus 2:1–10

SAMSON
Judges 13:1–14, 24

OBED
Ruth 4:13–17

SAMUEL
1 Samuel 1; 2:18–21; 3:1–19

DAVID
1 Samuel 16:1–13

THE WIDOW'S SONS
2 Kings 4:1–7

NAAMAN'S WIFE'S SERVANT
2 Kings 5:1–6

JOSIAH
2 Kings 22:1–2

DANIEL
Daniel 1

SHOUTING CHILDREN
Matthew 21:14–16

BLESSED CHILDREN
Mark 10:13–16

JOHN
Luke 1:5–20, 57–66, 80

JESUS
Luke 2

RHODA
Acts 12:5–16

TIMOTHY
2 Timothy 1:5; 3:14–15

deserted places, and they came to him from everywhere. Mt 17:22; Mk 3:1

The Son of Man Forgives and Heals

2 When he entered Capernaum again after some days, it was reported that he was at home. ² So many people gathered together that there was no more room, not even in the doorway, and he was speaking the word to them. ³ They came to him bringing a paralytic, carried by four of them. ⁴ Since they were not able to bring him to ᴬ Jesus because of the crowd, they removed the roof above him, and after digging through it, they lowered the mat on which the paralytic was lying. ⁵ Seeing their faith, Jesus told the paralytic, "Son, your sins are forgiven."   Mt 9:1-8; Lk 5:17-26; 10:15

⁶ But some of the scribes were sitting there, questioning in their hearts: ⁷ "Why does he speak like this? He's blaspheming! Who can forgive sins but God alone?"

⁸ Right away Jesus perceived in his spirit that they were thinking like this within themselves and said to them, "Why are you thinking these things in your hearts? ⁹ Which is easier: to say to the paralytic, 'Your sins are forgiven,' or to say, 'Get up, take your mat, and walk'? ¹⁰ But so that you may know that the Son of Man has authority on earth to forgive sins" — he told the paralytic — ¹¹ "I tell you: get up, take your mat, and go home." Lk 5:22
¹² Immediately he got up, took the mat, and went out in front of everyone. As a result, they were all astounded and gave glory to God,

saying, "We have never seen anything like this!" Jn 11:4; 17:1; Ac 10:45

The Call of Levi

¹³ Jesus went out again beside the sea. The whole crowd was coming to him, and he was teaching them. ¹⁴ Then, passing by, he saw Levi the son of Alphaeus sitting at the toll booth, and he said to him, "Follow me," and he got up and followed him.   Mt 9:9-13; 28:20; Lk 5:27-32; Ac 4:2

¹⁵ While he was reclining at the table in Levi's house, many tax collectors and sinners were eating ᴮ with Jesus and his disciples, for there were many who were following him. ¹⁶ When the scribes who were Pharisees ᶜ saw that he was eating with sinners and tax collectors, they asked his disciples, "Why does he eat ᴰ with tax collectors and sinners?"   Mt 9:10; Lk 3:12; 18:13

¹⁷ When Jesus heard this, he told them, "It is not those who are well who need a doctor, but those who are sick. I didn't come to call the righteous, but sinners." Mt 6:8; Col 4:14

A Question About Fasting

¹⁸ Now John's disciples and the Pharisees ᴱ were fasting. People came and asked him, "Why do John's disciples and the Pharisees' disciples fast, but your disciples do not fast?" Mt 9:14-17; Mk 1:4; Lk 5:33-39; Jn 3:25

¹⁹ Jesus said to them, "The wedding guests cannot fast while the groom is with them, can they? As long as they have the groom with them, they cannot fast. ²⁰ But the time ᶠ will come when the groom will be taken away from them, and then they will fast on that day. ²¹ No

---

ᴬ**2:4** Other mss read *able to get near*   ᴮ**2:15** Lit *reclining together*   ᶜ**2:16** Other mss read *scribes and Pharisees*   ᴰ**2:16** Other mss add *and drink*   ᴱ**2:18** Other mss read *The disciples of John and of the Pharisees*   ᶠ**2:20** Or *the days* one sews a patch of unshrunk cloth on an old garment. Otherwise, the new patch pulls away from the old cloth, and a worse tear is made. ²² And no one puts new wine into old wineskins. Otherwise, the wine will burst the skins, and the wine is lost as well as the skins. No, new wine is put into fresh wineskins."

Lord of the Sabbath

²³ On the Sabbath he was going through the grainfields, and his disciples began to make their way, picking some heads of grain. ²⁴ The Pharisees said to him, "Look, why are they doing what is not lawful on the Sabbath?" Mt12:1-8; Mk7:3; Lk6:1-5

²⁵ He said to them, "Have you never read what David and those who were with him did when he was in need and hungry — ²⁶ how he entered the house of God in the time of Abiathar the high priest and ate the bread of the Presence — which is not lawful for anyone to eat except the priests — and also gave some to his companions?" ²⁷ Then he told them, "The Sabbath was made for^A man and not man for the Sabbath. ²⁸ So then, the Son of Man is Lord even of the Sabbath."

3 Jesus entered the synagogue again, and a man was there who had a shriveled hand. ² In order to accuse him, they were watching him closely to see whether he would heal him on the Sabbath. ³ He told the man with the shriveled hand, "Stand before us." ⁴ Then he said to them, "Is it lawful to do good on the Sabbath or to do evil, to save life or to kill?" But they were silent. ⁵ After looking around at them with anger, he was grieved at the hardness of their hearts and told the man, "Stretch out your hand." So he stretched it out, and his hand was restored. ⁶ Immediately the Pharisees went out and started plotting with the Herodians against him, how they might kill him. Mt12:9-14; Mk1:21,39; Lk6:6-11; Jms2:2

Ministering to the Multitude

⁷ Jesus departed with his disciples to the sea, and a large crowd followed from Galilee, and a large crowd followed from Judea, ⁸ Jerusalem, Idumea, beyond the Jordan, and around Tyre and Sidon. The large crowd came to him because they heard about everything he was doing. ⁹ Then he told his disciples to have a small boat ready for him, so that the crowd wouldn't crush him. ¹⁰ Since he had healed many, all who had diseases were pressing toward him to touch him. ¹¹ Whenever the unclean spirits saw him, they fell down before him and cried out, "You are the Son of God!" ¹² And he would strongly warn them not to make him known. Mt4:24-25; 12:15-16; Lk6:17-19

The Twelve Apostles

¹³ Jesus went up the mountain and summoned those he wanted, and they came to him. ¹⁴ He appointed twelve, whom he also named apostles,^B to be with him, to send them out to preach, ¹⁵ and to have authority to^C drive out demons. ¹⁶ He appointed the Twelve:^D To Simon, he gave the name Peter; ¹⁷ and to James the son of Zebedee, and to his brother John, he gave the name "Boanerges" (that is, "Sons of Thunder"); ¹⁸ Andrew; Philip and

---

^A**2:27** Or *because of*   ^B**3:14** Other mss omit *he also named them apostles*   ^C**3:15** Other mss add *heal diseases, and to*   ^D**3:16** Other mss omit *He appointed the Twelve*

Bartholomew; Matthew and Thomas; James the son of Alphaeus, and Thaddaeus; Simon the Zealot,[19] and Judas Iscariot, who also betrayed him.   Mt 4:8; 10:2-4; Lk 6:12-16

A House Divided

[20] Jesus entered a house, and the crowd gathered again so that they were not even able to eat.[A] [21] When his family heard this, they set out to restrain him, because they said, "He's out of his mind."   Lk 2:48; Jn 7:3

[22] The scribes who had come down from Jerusalem said, "He is possessed by Beelzebul," and, "He drives out demons by the ruler of the demons."   Mt 2:4; 10:25; 12:24,27; 3Jn 10

[23] So he summoned them and spoke to them in parables: "How can Satan drive out Satan? [24] If a kingdom is divided against itself, that kingdom cannot stand. [25] If a house is divided against itself, that house cannot stand. [26] And if Satan opposes himself and is divided, he cannot stand but is finished. [27] But no one can enter a strong man's house and plunder his possessions unless he first ties up the strong man. Then he can plunder his house.   Mk 1:13; 4:15; 8:33; 12:1; Lk 18:16

[28] "Truly I tell you, people will be forgiven for all sins and whatever blasphemies they utter. [29] But whoever blasphemes against the Holy Spirit never has forgiveness, but is guilty of an eternal sin"[B] — [30] because they were saying, "He has an unclean spirit."   Mt 12:31-32; Lk 12:10; Ac 7:51

True Relationships

[31] His mother and his brothers came, and standing outside, they sent word to him and called him.

[32] A crowd was sitting around him and told him, "Look, your mother, your brothers, and your sisters[C] are outside asking for you."   Mt 1:16

[33] He replied to them, "Who are my mother and my brothers?" [34] Looking at those sitting in a circle around him, he said, "Here are my mother and my brothers! [35] Whoever does the will of God is my brother and sister and mother."   Ac 9:30

The Parable of the Sower

4 Again he began to teach by the sea, and a very large crowd gathered around him. So he got into a boat on the sea and sat down, while the whole crowd was by the sea on the shore. [2] He taught them many things in parables, and in his teaching he said to them: [3] "Listen! Consider the sower who went out to sow. [4] As he sowed, some seed fell along the path, and the birds came and devoured it. [5] Other seed fell on rocky ground where it didn't have much soil, and it grew up quickly, since the soil wasn't deep. [6] When the sun came up, it was scorched, and since it had no root, it withered away. [7] Other seed fell among thorns, and the thorns came up and choked it, and it didn't produce fruit. [8] Still other seed fell on good ground and it grew up, producing fruit that increased thirty, sixty, and a hundred times." [9] Then he said, "Let anyone who has ears to hear listen."   Mt 13:1-15; Lk 8:4-10; Ac 4:2

Why Jesus Used Parables

[10] When he was alone, those around him with the Twelve, asked him about the parables. [11] He answered them, "The secret of the kingdom

---

[A]**3:20** Or *eat a meal*; lit *eat bread*   [B]**3:29** Other mss read *is subject to eternal judgment*   [C]**3:32** Other mss omit *and your sisters* of God has been given to you, but to those outside, everything comes in parables [12] so that

Mk 11:11; 12:1

> they may indeed look,
> and yet not perceive;
> they may indeed listen,
> and yet not understand;
> otherwise, they might
>   turn back
> and be forgiven."[A,B]   Is 6:9-10

The Parable of the Sower Explained

[13] Then he said to them: "Don't you understand this parable? How then will you understand all of the parables? [14] The sower sows the word. [15] Some are like the word sown on the path. When they hear, immediately Satan comes and takes away the word sown in them.[C] [16] And others are like seed sown on rocky ground. When they hear the word, immediately they receive it with joy. [17] But they have no root; they are short-lived. When distress or persecution comes because of the word, they immediately fall away. [18] Others are like seed sown among thorns; these are the ones who hear the word, [19] but the worries of this age, the deceitfulness[D] of wealth, and the desires for other things enter in and choke the word, and it becomes unfruitful. [20] And those like seed sown on good ground hear the word, welcome it, and produce fruit thirty, sixty, and a hundred times what was sown."

Using Your Light

[21] He also said to them, "Is a lamp brought in to be put under a basket or under a bed? Isn't it to be put on a lampstand? [22] For there is nothing hidden that will not be revealed, and nothing concealed that will not be brought to light. [23] If anyone has ears to hear, let him listen." [24] And he said to them, "Pay attention to what you hear. By the measure you use, it will be measured to you — and more will be added to you. [25] For whoever has, more will be given to him, and whoever does not have, even what he has will be taken away from him."

The Parable of the Growing Seed

[26] "The kingdom of God is like this," he said. "A man scatters seed on the ground. [27] He sleeps and rises night and day; the seed sprouts and grows, although he doesn't know how. [28] The soil produces a crop by itself — first the blade, then the head, and then the full grain on the head. [29] As soon as the crop is ready, he sends for the sickle, because the harvest has come."   Jn 9:4

The Parable of the Mustard Seed

[30] And he said, "With what can we compare the kingdom of God, or what parable can we use to describe it? [31] It's like a mustard seed that, when sown upon the soil, is the smallest of all the seeds on the ground. [32] And when sown, it comes up and grows taller than all the garden plants, and produces large branches, so that the birds of the sky can nest in its shade."

Using Parables

[33] He was speaking the word to them with many parables like these, as they were able to understand. [34] He did not speak to them without a parable. Privately,

---

[A]4:12 Other mss read *and their sins be forgiven them hearts*   [D]4:19 Or *seduction*   [B]4:12 Is 6:9-10   [C]4:15 Other mss read *in their* however, he explained everything to his own disciples.   Lk 6:47; Jn 18:32

Wind and Wave Obey Jesus

35 On that day, when evening had come, he told them, "Let's cross over to the other side of the sea." 36 So they left the crowd and took him along since he was in the boat. And other boats were with him. 37 A great windstorm arose, and the waves were breaking over the boat, so that the boat was already being swamped. 38 He was in the stern, sleeping on the cushion. So they woke him up and said to him, "Teacher! Don't you care that we're going to die?"   Mt 8:23-27; Lk 8:22-25

39 He got up, rebuked the wind, and said to the sea, "Silence! Be still!" The wind ceased, and there was a great calm. 40 Then he said to them, "Why are you afraid? Do you still have no faith?"   2Tm 4:2

41 And they were terrified A and asked one another, "Who then is this? Even the wind and the sea obey him!"   Jnh 1:10,16; Mk 1:27

Demons Driven Out by Jesus

5 They came to the other side of the sea, to the region of the Gerasenes. B 2 As soon as he got out of the boat, a man with an unclean spirit came out of the tombs and met him. 3 He lived in the tombs, and no one was able to restrain him anymore — not even with a chain — 4 because he often had been bound with shackles and chains, but had torn the chains apart and smashed the shackles. No one was strong enough to subdue him. 5 Night and day among the tombs and on the mountains, he was always crying out and cutting himself with stones.   Mt 8:28-34

6 When he saw Jesus from a distance, he ran and knelt down before him. 7 And he cried out with a loud voice, "What do you have to do with me, Jesus, Son of the Most High God? I beg you before God, don't torment me!" 8 For he had told him, "Come out of the man, you unclean spirit!"   Jn 5:19; Heb 1:2

9 "What is your name?" he asked him.

"My name is Legion," he answered him, "because we are many." 10 And he begged him earnestly not to send them out of the region.   Mt 26:53; Lk 8:30

11 A large herd of pigs was there, feeding on the hillside. 12 The demons C begged him, "Send us to the pigs, so that we may enter them." 13 So he gave them permission, and the unclean spirits came out and entered the pigs. The herd of about two thousand rushed down the steep bank into the sea and drowned there.   Mt 7:6; 8:30-32; Lk 8:32-33

14 The men who tended them D ran off and reported it in the town and the countryside, and people went to see what had happened. 15 They came to Jesus and saw the man who had been demon-possessed, sitting there, dressed and in his right mind; and they were afraid. 16 Those who had seen it described to them what had happened to the demon-possessed man and told about the pigs. 17 Then they began to beg him to leave their region.

18 As he was getting into the boat, the man who had been demon-possessed begged him earnestly that

---

A 4:41 Or were filled with awe   B 5:1 Some mss read Gadarenes; other mss read Gergesenes
C 5:12 Other mss read All the demons   D 5:14 Other mss read tended the pigs

he might remain with him. ¹⁹ Jesus did not let him but told him, "Go home to your own people, and report to them how much the Lord has done for you and how he has had mercy on you." ²⁰ So he went out and began to proclaim in the Decapolis how much Jesus had done for him, and they were all amazed. Mk 1:4; Lk 1:25; 8:39; Ac 15:17; Col 4:1; Jd 5

A Girl Restored and a Woman Healed

²¹ When Jesus had crossed over again by boat ᴬ to the other side, a large crowd gathered around him while he was by the sea. ²² One of the synagogue leaders, named Jairus, came, and when he saw Jesus, he fell at his feet ²³ and begged him earnestly, "My little daughter is dying. Come and lay your hands on her so that she can get well ᴮ and live." ²⁴ So Jesus went with him, and a large crowd was following and pressing against him. Mt 9:18-26; Mk 2:4

²⁵ Now a woman suffering from bleeding for twelve years ²⁶ had endured much under many doctors. She had spent everything she had and was not helped at all. On the contrary, she became worse. ²⁷ Having heard about Jesus, she came up behind him in the crowd and touched his clothing. ²⁸ For she said, "If I just touch his clothes, I'll be made well." ²⁹ Instantly her flow of blood ceased, and she sensed in her body that she was healed of her affliction. Lk 8:43; Jn 20:17; Php 1:29; Col 4:14

³⁰ At once Jesus realized in himself that power had gone out from him. He turned around in the crowd and said, "Who touched my clothes?" Mk 2:13; Lk 5:17; 6:19; 8:46

³¹ His disciples said to him, "You see the crowd pressing against you, and yet you say, 'Who touched me?'" ³² But he was looking around to see who had done this. ³³ The woman, with fear and trembling, knowing what had happened to her, came and fell down before him, and told him the whole truth. ³⁴ "Daughter," he said to her, "your faith has saved you. Go in peace and be healed from your affliction." Mt 8:10; 9:22; Mk 6:56; Lk 8:47; Jn 14:6

³⁵ While he was still speaking, people came from the synagogue leader's house and said, "Your daughter is dead. Why bother the teacher anymore?" Mk 4:38; Eph 4:11

³⁶ When Jesus overheard ᶜ what was said, he told the synagogue leader, "Don't be afraid. Only believe." ³⁷ He did not let anyone accompany him except Peter, James, and John, James's brother. ³⁸ They came to the leader's house, and he saw a commotion — people weeping and wailing loudly. ³⁹ He went in and said to them, "Why are you making a commotion and weeping? The child is not dead but asleep." ⁴⁰ They laughed at him, but he put them all outside. He took the child's father, mother, and those who were with him, and entered the place where the child was. ⁴¹ Then he took the child by the hand and said to her, "Talitha koum" ᴰ (which is translated, "Little girl, I say to you, get up"). ⁴² Immediately the girl got up and began to walk. (She was twelve years old.) At this they were utterly astounded. ⁴³ Then he gave them strict orders that no one should know about this

ᴬ5:21 Other mss omit by boat   ᴮ5:23 Or she might be saved   ᶜ5:36 Or ignored   ᴰ5:41 An Aramaic expression and told them to give her something to eat. Lk 6:14; Jn 6:20; 21:7; Ac 12:2

Rejection at Nazareth

6 He left there and came to his hometown, and his disciples followed him. ² When the Sabbath came, he began to teach in the synagogue, and many who heard him were astonished. "Where did this man get these things?" they said. "What is this wisdom that has been given to him, and how are these miracles performed by his hands? ³ Isn't this the carpenter, the son of Mary, and the brother of James, Joses, Judas, and Simon? And aren't his sisters here with us?" So they were offended by him. Mt 13:53-58; Jd 1

⁴ Jesus said to them, "A prophet is not without honor except in his hometown, among his relatives, and in his household." ⁵ He was not able to do a miracle there, except that he laid his hands on a few sick people and healed them. ⁶ And he was amazed at their unbelief. He was going around the villages teaching. Mt 2:23; 13:57; 1Co 4:10; 12:23

Commissioning the Twelve

⁷ He summoned the Twelve and began to send them out in pairs and gave them authority over unclean spirits. ⁸ He instructed them to take nothing for the road except a staff — no bread, no traveling bag, no money in their belts, ⁹ but to wear sandals and not put on an extra shirt. ¹⁰ He said to them, "Whenever you enter a house, stay there until you leave that place. ¹¹ If any place does not welcome you or listen to you, when you leave there, shake the dust off your feet as a testimony against them." A ¹² So they went out and preached that people should repent. ¹³ They drove out many demons, anointed many sick people with oil and healed them. Mt 10:5-42; Mk 11:11; Lk 9:1-6; 18:16

John the Baptist Beheaded

¹⁴ King Herod heard about it, because Jesus's name had become well known. Some B said, "John the Baptist has been raised from the dead, and that's why miraculous powers are at work in him." ¹⁵ But others said, "He's Elijah." Still others said, "He's a prophet, like one of the prophets from long ago."

¹⁶ When Herod heard of it, he said, "John, the one I beheaded, has been raised!" Mt 14:1; 26:32; Mk 1:4

¹⁷ For Herod himself had given orders to arrest John and to chain him in prison on account of Herodias, his brother Philip's wife, because he had married her. ¹⁸ John had been telling Herod, "It is not lawful for you to have your brother's wife." ¹⁹ So Herodias held a grudge against him and wanted to kill him. But she could not, ²⁰ because Herod feared John and protected him, knowing he was a righteous and holy man. When Herod heard him he would be very perplexed, C and yet he liked to listen to him. Mt 14:3,6-12; 20:21; Mk 15:1

²¹ An opportune time came on his birthday, when Herod gave a banquet for his nobles, military commanders, and the leading men of Galilee. ²² When Herodias's own daughter D came in and danced, she pleased Herod and his guests.

A 6:11 Other mss add *Truly I tell you, it will be more tolerable for Sodom or Gomorrah on judgment day than for that town.*   B 6:14 Other mss read *He*   C 6:20 Other mss read *When he heard him, he did many things*   D 6:22 Other mss read *When his daughter Herodias*

The king said to the girl, "Ask me whatever you want, and I'll give it to you." ²³ He promised her with an oath: "Whatever you ask me I will give you, up to half my kingdom."

²⁴ She went out and said to her mother, "What should I ask for?"

"John the Baptist's head," she said.   Mk 1:4

²⁵ At once she hurried to the king and said, "I want you to give me John the Baptist's head on a platter immediately." ²⁶ Although the king was deeply distressed, because of his oaths and the guests^A he did not want to refuse her. ²⁷ The king immediately sent for an executioner and commanded him to bring John's head. So he went and beheaded him in prison, ²⁸ brought his head on a platter, and gave it to the girl. Then the girl gave it to her mother. ²⁹ When John's disciples heard about it, they came and removed his corpse and placed it in a tomb.   Mt 14:8; 26:38; Mk 14:34; Lk 7:20

Feeding of the Five Thousand

³⁰ The apostles gathered around Jesus and reported to him all that they had done and taught. ³¹ He said to them, "Come away by yourselves to a remote place and rest for a while." For many people were coming and going, and they did not even have time to eat. Mt 14:13-21; Ac 1:2

³² So they went away in the boat by themselves to a remote place, ³³ but many saw them leaving and recognized them, and they ran on foot from all the towns and arrived ahead of them.^B

³⁴ When he went ashore, he saw a large crowd and had compassion on them, because they were like sheep without a shepherd. Then he began to teach them many things.

³⁵ When it grew late, his disciples approached him and said, "This place is deserted, and it is already late. ³⁶ Send them away so that they can go into the surrounding countryside and villages to buy themselves something to eat."   Mk 10:10

³⁷ "You give them something to eat," he responded.

They said to him, "Should we go and buy two hundred denarii^C worth of bread and give them something to eat?"

³⁸ He asked them, "How many loaves do you have? Go and see."

When they found out they said, "Five, and two fish." ³⁹ Then he instructed them to have all the people sit down in groups on the green grass. ⁴⁰ So they sat down in groups of hundreds and fifties. ⁴¹ He took the five loaves and the two fish, and looking up to heaven, he blessed and broke the loaves. He kept giving them to his disciples to set before the people. He also divided the two fish among them all. ⁴² Everyone ate and was satisfied. ⁴³ They picked up twelve baskets full of pieces of bread and fish. ⁴⁴ Now those who had eaten the loaves were five thousand men.   Mt 5:6

Walking on the Water

⁴⁵ Immediately he made his disciples get into the boat and go ahead of him to the other side, to Bethsaida, while he dismissed the crowd. ⁴⁶ After he said good-bye to them, he went away to the mountain to pray. ⁴⁷ Well into the night, the boat was in the middle of the sea, and he was alone on the land. ⁴⁸ He

---

^A **6:26** Lit *and those reclining at the table*   ^B **6:33** Other mss add *and gathered around him*
^C **6:37** A denarius = one day's wage

saw them straining at the oars, [A] because the wind was against them. Very early in the morning [B] he came toward them walking on the sea and wanted to pass by them. ⁴⁹ When they saw him walking on the sea, they thought it was a ghost and cried out, ⁵⁰ because they all saw him and were terrified. Immediately he spoke with them and said, "Have courage! It is I. Don't be afraid." ⁵¹ Then he got into the boat with them, and the wind ceased. They were completely astounded, ⁵² because they had not understood about the loaves. Instead, their hearts were hardened.   Mt 4:8; 14:22-36; Jn 6:16-21; 12:21

Miraculous Healings

⁵³ When they had crossed over, they came to shore at Gennesaret and anchored there.   Mt 14:34; Lk 5:1

⁵⁴ As they got out of the boat, people immediately recognized him. ⁵⁵ They hurried throughout that region and began to carry the sick on mats to wherever they heard he was. ⁵⁶ Wherever he went, into villages, towns, or the country, they laid the sick in the marketplaces and begged him that they might touch just the end of his robe. And everyone who touched it was healed.   Mt 9:20; 14:36; 23:5; Lk 5:31

The Traditions of the Elders

7 The Pharisees and some of the scribes who had come from Jerusalem gathered around him. ² They observed that some of his disciples were eating bread with unclean — that is, unwashed — hands. ³ (For the Pharisees and all the Jews do not eat unless they give their hands a ceremonial washing, keeping the tradition of the elders. ⁴ When they come from the marketplace, they do not eat unless they have washed. And there are many other customs they have received and keep, like the washing of cups, pitchers, kettles, and dining couches. [C]) ⁵ So the Pharisees and the scribes asked him, "Why don't your disciples live according to the tradition of the elders, instead of eating bread with ceremonially unclean [D] hands?"   Mt 2:4; 15:1-20; Mk 7:3

⁶ He answered them, "Isaiah prophesied correctly about you hypocrites, as it is written: Mt 3:3

> This people honors me
>   with their lips,   1Tm 5:3
> but their heart is far
>   from me.
> ⁷ They worship me in vain,
>   teaching as doctrines
>   human commands. [E]   Mt 28:20

⁸ Abandoning the command of God, you hold on to human tradition." [F] ⁹ He also said to them, "You have a fine way of invalidating God's command in order to set up [G] your tradition! ¹⁰ For Moses said: **Honor your father and your mother;** [H] and **Whoever speaks evil of father or mother must be put to death.** [I] ¹¹ But you say, 'If anyone tells his father or mother: Whatever benefit you might have received from me is *corban*'" (that is, an offering devoted to God), ¹² "you no longer let him do anything for his father or mother. ¹³ You nullify the word of God by your tradition

---

[A] **6:48** Or *them being battered as they rowed*   [B] **6:48** Lit *Around the fourth watch of the night* = 3 to 6 a.m.   [C] **7:4** Other mss omit *and dining couches*   [D] **7:5** Other mss read *with unwashed*   [E] **7:6-7** Is 29:13   [F] **7:8** Other mss add *The washing of jugs, and cups, and many other similar things you practice.*   [G] **7:9** Or *to maintain*   [H] **7:10** Ex 20:12; Dt 5:16   [I] **7:10** Ex 21:17; Lv 20:9

that you have handed down. And you do many other similar things."

¹⁴ Summoning the crowd again, he told them, "Listen to me, all of you, and understand: ¹⁵ Nothing that goes into a person from outside can defile him but the things that come out of a person are what defile him." ᴬ   Mt 13:13; Lk 18:16

¹⁷ When he went into the house away from the crowd, his disciples asked him about the parable. ¹⁸ He said to them, "Are you also as lacking in understanding? Don't you realize that nothing going into a person from the outside can defile him? ¹⁹ For it doesn't go into his heart but into the stomach and is eliminated" (thus he declared all foods clean ᴮ). ²⁰ And he said, "What comes out of a person is what defiles him. ²¹ For from within, out of people's hearts, come evil thoughts, sexual immoralities, thefts, murders, ²² adulteries, greed, evil actions, deceit, self-indulgence, envy, ᶜ slander, pride, and foolishness. ²³ All these evil things come from within and defile a person."   Php 3:19; 1Th 4:3; 1Jn 1:7

A Gentile Mother's Faith

²⁴ He got up and departed from there to the region of Tyre. ᴰ He entered a house and did not want anyone to know it, but he could not escape notice. ²⁵ Instead, immediately after hearing about him, a woman whose little daughter had an unclean spirit came and fell at his feet. ²⁶ The woman was a Gentile, ᴱ a Syrophoenician by birth, and she was asking him to cast the demon out of her daughter. ²⁷ He said to her, "Let the children be fed

first, because it isn't right to take the children's bread and throw it to the dogs."   Mt 15:21-28; Lk 11:24; Ac 21:7

²⁸ But she replied to him, "Lord, even the dogs under the table eat the children's crumbs."   Lk 10:1

²⁹ Then he told her, "Because of this reply, you may go. The demon has left your daughter." ³⁰ When she went back to her home, she found her child lying on the bed, and the demon was gone.

Jesus Does Everything Well

³¹ Again, leaving the region of Tyre, he went by way of Sidon to the Sea of Galilee, through ᶠ the region of the Decapolis. ³² They brought to him a deaf man who had difficulty speaking and begged Jesus to lay his hand on him. ³³ So he took him away from the crowd in private. After putting his fingers in the man's ears and spitting, he touched his tongue. ³⁴ Looking up to heaven, he sighed deeply and said to him, *Ephphatha!* ᴳ (that is, "Be opened!"). ³⁵ Immediately his ears were opened, his tongue was loosened, and he began to speak clearly. ³⁶ He ordered them to tell no one, but the more he ordered them, the more they proclaimed it.   Ac 21:7

³⁷ They were extremely astonished and said, "He has done everything well. He even makes the deaf hear and the mute speak."

Feeding Four Thousand

8 In those days there was again a large crowd, and they had nothing to eat. He called the disciples and said to them, ² "I have compassion on the crowd, because they've

---

ᴬ**7:15** Some mss include v. 16: *"If anyone has ears to hear, let him listen."* ᴮ**7:19** Other mss read *is eliminated, making all foods clean"* ᶜ**7:22** Or *evil eye* ᴰ**7:24** Many early mss add *and Sidon* ᴱ**7:26** Or *a Greek (speaker)* ᶠ**7:31** Or *into* ᴳ**7:34** An Aramaic expression already stayed with me three days and have nothing to eat. ³ If I send them home hungry, they will collapse on the way, and some of them have come a long distance." Lk 18:16

⁴ His disciples answered him, "Where can anyone get enough bread here in this desolate place to feed these people?" Mt 5:6; 15:33

⁵ "How many loaves do you have?" he asked them.

"Seven," they said. ⁶ He commanded the crowd to sit down on the ground. Taking the seven loaves, he gave thanks, broke them, and gave them to his disciples to set before the people. So they served them to the crowd. ⁷ They also had a few small fish, and after he had blessed them, he said these were to be served as well. ⁸ They ate and were satisfied. Then they collected seven large baskets of leftover pieces. ⁹ About four thousand were there. He dismissed them. ¹⁰ And he immediately got into the boat with his disciples and went to the district of Dalmanutha. Mk 14:22

The Leaven of the Pharisees and Herod

¹¹ The Pharisees came and began to argue with him, demanding of him a sign from heaven to test him. ¹² Sighing deeply in his spirit, he said, "Why does this generation demand a sign? Truly I tell you, no sign will be given to this generation." ¹³ Then he left them, got back into the boat, and went to the other side. Mt 16:1-4; Mk 7:3; Jn 2:11

¹⁴ The disciples had forgotten to take bread and had only one loaf with them in the boat. ¹⁵ Then he gave them strict orders: "Watch out! Beware of the leaven^A of the Pharisees and the leaven of Herod." ¹⁶ They were discussing among themselves that they did not have any bread. ¹⁷ Aware of this, he said to them, "Why are you discussing the fact you have no bread? Don't you understand or comprehend? Do you have hardened hearts? ¹⁸ **Do you have eyes and not see; do you have ears and not hear?**^B And do you not remember? ¹⁹ When I broke the five loaves for the five thousand, how many baskets full of leftovers did you collect?" Mt 16:5-12; Lk 13:21; Gl 5:9

"Twelve," they told him.

²⁰ "When I broke the seven loaves for the four thousand, how many baskets full of pieces did you collect?"

"Seven," they said.

²¹ And he said to them, "Don't you understand yet?" Mk 4:40

Healing a Blind Man

²² They came to Bethsaida. They brought a blind man to him and begged him to touch him. ²³ He took the blind man by the hand and brought him out of the village. Spitting on his eyes and laying his hands on him, he asked him, "Do you see anything?" Mt 15:14; Jn 12:21

²⁴ He looked up and said, "I see people — they look like trees walking." Mt 11:5

²⁵ Again Jesus placed his hands on the man's eyes. The man looked intently and his sight was restored and he saw everything clearly. ²⁶ Then he sent him home, saying, "Don't even go into the village."^C

Peter's Confession of the Messiah

²⁷ Jesus went out with his disciples to the villages of Caesarea Philippi.

^A 8:15 Or *yeast*   ^B 8:18 Jr 5:21; Ezk 12:2   ^C 8:26 Other mss add *or tell anyone in the village*

And on the road he asked his disciples, "Who do people say that I am?" ²⁸ They answered him, "John the Baptist; others, Elijah; still others, one of the prophets."   Mk 1:4; Lk 7:20

²⁹ "But you," he asked them, "who do you say that I am?"

Peter answered him, "You are the Messiah." ³⁰ And he strictly warned them to tell no one about him.

His Death and Resurrection Predicted

³¹ Then he began to teach them that it was necessary for the Son of Man to suffer many things and be rejected by the elders, chief priests, and scribes, be killed, and rise after three days. ³² He spoke openly about this. Peter took him aside and began to rebuke him. ³³ But turning around and looking at his disciples, he rebuked Peter and said, "Get behind me, Satan! You are not thinking about God's concerns[A] but human concerns."   Mt 16:21-28; Lk 9:21-27

Take Up Your Cross

³⁴ Calling the crowd along with his disciples, he said to them, "If anyone wants to follow after me, let him deny himself, take up his cross, and follow me. ³⁵ For whoever wants to save his life will lose it, but whoever loses his life because of me and the gospel will save it. ³⁶ For what does it benefit someone to gain the whole world and yet lose his life? ³⁷ What can anyone give in exchange for his life? ³⁸ For whoever is ashamed of me and my words in this adulterous and sinful generation, the Son of Man will also be ashamed of him when he comes in the glory of his Father with the holy angels."   Mk 10:45; Lk 9:23; Jn 8:12; 3Jn 9

[A]8:33 Or about the things of God

9 Then he said to them, "Truly I tell you, there are some standing here who will not taste death until they see the kingdom of God come in power."   Ps 72:19; Rv 22:21

The Transfiguration

² After six days Jesus took Peter, James, and John and led them up a high mountain by themselves to be alone. He was transfigured in front of them, ³ and his clothes became dazzling — extremely white as no launderer on earth could whiten them. ⁴ Elijah appeared to them with Moses, and they were talking with Jesus. ⁵ Peter said to Jesus, "Rabbi, it's good for us to be here. Let us set up three shelters: one for you, one for Moses, and one for Elijah" — ⁶ because he did not know what to say, since they were terrified.   Ex 24:15-18; Hs 6:2; Mt 17:1-8; Lk 9:28-36

⁷ A cloud appeared, overshadowing them, and a voice came from the cloud: "This is my beloved Son; listen to him!"   Ex 24:15; Mt 26:64; Lk 1:35

⁸ Suddenly, looking around, they no longer saw anyone with them except Jesus.

⁹ As they were coming down the mountain, he ordered them to tell no one what they had seen until the Son of Man had risen from the dead. ¹⁰ They kept this word to themselves, questioning what "rising from the dead" meant.

¹¹ Then they asked him, "Why do the scribes say that Elijah must come first?"   Mal 4:5; Mt 2:4

¹² "Elijah does come first and restores all things," he replied. "Why then is it written that the Son of Man must suffer many things and be treated with contempt? ¹³ But I tell you that Elijah has come, and

they did whatever they pleased to him, just as it is written about him."

The Power of Faith over a Demon

¹⁴ When they came to the disciples, they saw a large crowd around them and scribes disputing with them. ¹⁵ When the whole crowd saw him, they were amazed and ran to greet him. ¹⁶ He asked them, "What are you arguing with them about?"   Mk 8:11

¹⁷ Someone from the crowd answered him, "Teacher, I brought my son to you. He has a spirit that makes him unable to speak. ¹⁸ Whenever it seizes him, it throws him down, and he foams at the mouth, grinds his teeth, and becomes rigid. I asked your disciples to drive it out, but they couldn't."

¹⁹ He replied to them, "You unbelieving generation, how long will I be with you? How long must I put up with you? Bring him to me." ²⁰ So they brought the boy to him. When the spirit saw him, it immediately threw the boy into convulsions. He fell to the ground and rolled around, foaming at the mouth. ²¹ "How long has this been happening to him?" Jesus asked his father.   Lk 12:46

"From childhood," he said. ²² "And many times it has thrown him into fire or water to destroy him. But if you can do anything, have compassion on us and help us."   Jn 6:27

²³ Jesus said to him, " 'If you can'?ᴬ Everything is possible for the one who believes."   Mt 17:20; Jn 3:16; 11:40

²⁴ Immediately the father of the boy cried out, "I do believe; help my unbelief!"

²⁵ When Jesus saw that a crowd was quickly gathering, he rebuked the unclean spirit, saying to it, "You mute and deaf spirit, I command you: Come out of him and never enter him again."   Lk 7:22; 2Co 6:17; 2Tm 4:2

²⁶ Then it came out, shrieking and throwing himᴮ into terrible convulsions. The boy became like a corpse, so that many said, "He's dead." ²⁷ But Jesus, taking him by the hand, raised him, and he stood up.   Mk 1:26,31

²⁸ After he had gone into the house, his disciples asked him privately, "Why couldn't we drive it out?"

²⁹ And he told them, "This kind can come out by nothing but prayer."ᶜ   Ac 12:5; 16:13; Phm 22

The Second Prediction of His Death

³⁰ Then they left that place and made their way through Galilee, but he did not want anyone to know it. ³¹ For he was teaching his disciples and telling them, "The Son of Man is going to be betrayedᴰ into the hands of men. They will kill him, and after he is killed, he will rise three days later." ³² But they did not understand this statement, and they were afraid to ask him.   Mt 17:22-23; 28:20; Mk 1:44; Lk 9:43-45

Who Is the Greatest?

³³ They came to Capernaum. When he was in the house, he asked them, "What were you arguing about on the way?" ³⁴ But they were silent, because on the way they had been arguing with one another about who was the greatest. ³⁵ Sitting down, he called the Twelve and said to them, "If anyone wants to be first, he must be last and servant of all."

ᴬ9:23 Other mss add believe   ᴮ9:26 Other mss omit him   ᶜ9:29 Other mss add and fasting   ᴰ9:31 Or handed over

36 He took a child, had him stand among them, and taking him in his arms, he said to them, **37** "Whoever welcomes [A] one little child such as this in my name welcomes me. And whoever welcomes me does not welcome me, but him who sent me." Mt 18:1-11; Mk 1:29; 3:4; Lk 9:46-50; 10:15

In His Name

38 John said to him, "Teacher, we saw someone [B] driving out demons in your name, and we tried to stop him because he wasn't following us." Mk 3:15; 4:38; Jn 10:25; 21:7; Rv 9:20

39 "Don't stop him," said Jesus, "because there is no one who will perform a miracle in my name who can soon afterward speak evil of me. **40** For whoever is not against us is for us. **41** And whoever gives you a cup of water to drink in my name, because you belong to Christ — truly I tell you, he will never lose his reward." Mt 1:17; 12:30; Lk 11:23; Ac 19:11

Warnings from Jesus

42 "But whoever causes one of these little ones who believe in me to fall away — it would be better for him if a heavy millstone were hung around his neck and he were thrown into the sea. Ex 23:33; Jn 6:35

43 "And if your hand causes you to fall away, cut it off. It is better for you to enter life maimed than to have two hands and go to hell, the unquenchable fire. [C] **45** And if your foot causes you to fall away, cut it off. It is better for you to enter life lame than to have two feet and be thrown into hell. [D] **47** And if your eye causes you to fall away, gouge it out. It is better for you to enter the kingdom of God with one eye than to have two eyes and be thrown into hell, **48** where **their worm does not die, and the fire is not quenched.** [E] **49** For everyone will be salted with fire. [F,G] **50** Salt is good, but if the salt should lose its flavor, how can you season it? Have salt among yourselves, and be at peace with one another." Mt 3:12; 5:22,29-30; 15:30-31; 25:41

The Question of Divorce

10 He set out from there and went to the region of Judea and across the Jordan. Then crowds converged on him again, and as was his custom he taught them again. Mt 4:15,25; 19:1-2; Lk 1:5; 3:3

2 Some Pharisees came to test him, asking, "Is it lawful for a man to divorce his wife?" Mk 7:3; Jms 1:13

3 He replied to them, "What did Moses command you?" Ps 77:20

4 They said, "Moses permitted us to write divorce papers and send her away." Dt 24:1,3; Mt 5:31

5 But Jesus told them, "He wrote this command for you because of the hardness of your hearts. **6** But from the beginning of creation God [H] **made them male and female.** [I] **7** For this reason a man will leave his father and mother [J] **8** and the two will become one flesh.** [K] So they are no longer two, but one flesh. **9** Therefore what God has joined together, let no one separate." Mk 16:14; Jn 1:1,3; Ac 26:4; Rv 3:14

10 When they were in the house again, the disciples questioned him

---

[A] **9:37** Or "Whoever receives   [B] **9:38** Other mss add who didn't go along with us   [C] **9:43** Some mss include v. 44: Where their worm does not die, and the fire is not quenched.   [D] **9:45** Some mss include v. 46: Where their worm does not die, and the fire is not quenched.   [E] **9:48** Is 66:24   [F] **9:49** Other mss add and every sacrifice will be salted with salt   [G] **9:49** Lv 2:13; Ezk 43:24   [H] **10:6** Other mss omit God   [I] **10:6** Gn 1:27; 5:2   [J] **10:7** Some mss add and be joined to his wife   [K] **10:7-8** Gn 2:24

about this matter. [11] He said to them, "Whoever divorces his wife and marries another commits adultery against her. [12] Also, if she divorces her husband and marries another, she commits adultery." 1Pt 3:1

Blessing the Children

[13] People were bringing little children to him in order that he might touch them, but the disciples rebuked them. [14] When Jesus saw it, he was indignant and said to them, "Let the little children come to me. Don't stop them, because the kingdom of God belongs to such as these. [15] Truly I tell you, whoever does not receive[A] the kingdom of God like a little child will never enter it." [16] After taking them in his arms, he laid his hands on them and blessed them. Mt 19:13-15; Lk 18:15-17

The Rich Young Ruler

[17] As he was setting out on a journey, a man ran up, knelt down before him, and asked him, "Good teacher, what must I do to inherit eternal life?" Mt 19:16-30; Lk 18:18-30 [18] "Why do you call me good?" Jesus asked him. "No one is good except God alone. [19] You know the commandments: Do not murder; do not commit adultery; do not steal; do not bear false witness; do not defraud; honor your father and mother."[B] Ps 69:16; Mt 5:21

[20] He said to him, "Teacher, I have kept all these from my youth."

[21] Looking at him, Jesus loved him and said to him, "You lack one thing: Go, sell all you have and give to the poor, and you will have treasure in heaven. Then come,[C] follow me." [22] But he was dismayed by this

demand, and he went away grieving, because he had many possessions. Mk 14:7; Lk 6:35; Rm 15:26; 2Th 2:13; Heb 12:6

Possessions and the Kingdom

[23] Jesus looked around and said to his disciples, "How hard it is for those who have wealth to enter the kingdom of God!" Ac 4:37; 8:18,20 [24] The disciples were astonished at his words. Again Jesus said to them, "Children, how hard it is[D] to enter the kingdom of God! [25] It is easier for a camel to go through the eye of a needle than for a rich person to enter the kingdom of God."

[26] They were even more astonished, saying to one another, "Then who can be saved?" Ac 16:30; Eph 2:8 [27] Looking at them, Jesus said, "With man it is impossible, but not with God, because all things are possible with God." Heb 6:4 [28] Peter began to tell him, "Look, we have left everything and followed you." Lk 6:14; Ac 10:32 [29] "Truly I tell you," Jesus said, "there is no one who has left house or brothers or sisters or mother or father[E] or children or fields for my sake and for the sake of the gospel, [30] who will not receive a hundred times more, now at this time — houses, brothers and sisters, mothers and children, and fields, with persecutions — and eternal life in the age to come. [31] But many who are first will be last, and the last first." Mk 1:1; Lk 20:10; 21:8; Php 1:5; Rv 22:21

The Third Prediction of His Death

[32] They were on the road, going up to Jerusalem, and Jesus was walking ahead of them. The disciples were astonished, but those who

A**10:15** Or *not welcome*   B**10:19** Ex 20:12-16; Dt 5:16-20   C**10:21** Other mss add *taking up the cross, and*
D**10:24** Other mss add *for those trusting in wealth*   E**10:29** Other mss add *or wife*

followed him were afraid. Taking the Twelve aside again, he began to tell them the things that would happen to him. ³³ "See, we are going up to Jerusalem. The Son of Man will be handed over to the chief priests and the scribes, and they will condemn him to death. Then they will hand him over to the Gentiles, ³⁴ and they will mock him, spit on him, flog ᴬ him, and kill him, and he will rise after three days."

Suffering and Service

³⁵ James and John, the sons of Zebedee, approached him and said, "Teacher, we want you to do whatever we ask you." Mt 20:20-28; Ac 12:2

³⁶ "What do you want me to do for you?" he asked them.

³⁷ They answered him, "Allow us to sit at your right and at your left in your glory." Mt 19:28; Lk 9:26

³⁸ Jesus said to them, "You don't know what you're asking. Are you able to drink the cup I drink or to be baptized with the baptism I am baptized with?" Ps 75:8; Lk 12:50; Jn 11:22

³⁹ "We are able," they told him.

Jesus said to them, "You will drink the cup I drink, and you will be baptized with the baptism I am baptized with. ⁴⁰ But to sit at my right or left is not mine to give; instead, it is for those for whom it has been prepared." Ac 12:2; Rv 1:9

⁴¹ When the ten disciples heard this, they began to be indignant with James and John. ⁴² Jesus called them over and said to them, "You know that those who are regarded as rulers of the Gentiles lord it over them, and those in high positions act as tyrants over them. ⁴³ But it is not so among you. On the contrary, whoever wants to become

great among you will be your servant, ⁴⁴ and whoever wants to be first among you will be a slave to all. ⁴⁵ For even the Son of Man did not come to be served, but to serve, and to give his life as a ransom for many." ᴮ Mk 9:35; 10:45; Jn 21:7; Ac 19:16; 1Pt 5:3

A Blind Man Healed

⁴⁶ They came to Jericho. And as he was leaving Jericho with his disciples and a large crowd, Bartimaeus (the son of Timaeus), a blind beggar, was sitting by the road. ⁴⁷ When he heard that it was Jesus of Nazareth, he began to cry out, "Jesus, Son of David, have mercy on me!" ⁴⁸ Many warned him to keep quiet, but he was crying out all the more, "Have mercy on me, Son of David!"

⁴⁹ Jesus stopped and said, "Call him."

So they called the blind man and said to him, "Have courage! Get up; he's calling for you." ⁵⁰ He threw off his coat, jumped up, and came to Jesus. Lk 19:36; Jn 16:33

⁵¹ Then Jesus answered him, "What do you want me to do for you?" Mk 1:40

"*Rabboni*," ᶜ the blind man said to him, "I want to see." Jn 20:16

⁵² Jesus said to him, "Go, your faith has saved you." Immediately he could see and began to follow Jesus on the road. Mt 9:22; Mk 6:56; Lk 5:20

The Triumphal Entry

11 When they approached Jerusalem, at Bethphage and Bethany near the Mount of Olives, he sent two of his disciples ² and told them, "Go into the village ahead of you. As soon as you enter it, you will find a colt tied there, on which no one has ever sat. Untie it

ᴬ**10:34** Or *scourge*   ᴮ**10:45** Or *in the place of many*; Is 53:10-12   ᶜ**10:51** Hb word for *my lord* and bring it. ³ If anyone says to you, 'Why are you doing this?' say, 'The Lord needs it and will send it back here right away.'" Mt 21:1-11; Lk 19:28-44

⁴ So they went and found a colt outside in the street, tied by a door. They untied it, ⁵ and some of those standing there said to them, "What are you doing, untying the colt?" ⁶ They answered them just as Jesus had said; so they let them go.

⁷ They brought the donkey to Jesus and threw their clothes on it, and he sat on it. ⁸ Many people spread their clothes on the road, and others spread leafy branches cut from the fields.ᴬ ⁹ Those who went ahead and those who followed shouted:

Hosanna!
Blessed is he who comes in the name of the Lord!ᴮ

10   Blessed is the
         coming kingdom   Mk 1:15; 9:1
    of our father David!   Lk 1:27
Hosanna
         in the highest heaven!   Mk 11:9

¹¹ He went into Jerusalem and into the temple. After looking around at everything, since it was already late, he went out to Bethany with the Twelve.   Mt 23:37; Mk 11:1; Ac 21:26

The Barren Fig Tree Is Cursed

¹² The next day when they went out from Bethany, he was hungry. ¹³ Seeing in the distance a fig tree with leaves, he went to find out if there was anything on it. When he came to it, he found nothing but leaves; for it was not the season for figs. ¹⁴ He said to it, "May no one ever eat fruit from you again!" And his disciples heard it.   Mt 21:12-19; Lk 19:45-48

Cleansing the Temple

¹⁵ They came to Jerusalem, and he went into the temple and began to throw out those buying and selling. He overturned the tables of the money changers and the chairs of those selling doves, ¹⁶ and would not permit anyone to carry goods through the temple. ¹⁷ He was teaching them: "Is it not written, **My house will be called a house of prayer for all nations?**ᶜ But you have made it a **den of thieves!**"ᴰ

¹⁸ The chief priests and the scribes heard it and started looking for a way to kill him. For they were afraid of him, because the whole crowd was astonished by his teaching.

¹⁹ Whenever evening came, they would go out of the city.

The Barren Fig Tree Is Withered

²⁰ Early in the morning, as they were passing by, they saw the fig tree withered from the roots up. ²¹ Then Peter remembered and said to him, "Rabbi, look! The fig tree that you cursed has withered."   Lk 6:14

²² Jesus replied to them, "Have faith in God. ²³ Truly I tell you, if anyone says to this mountain, 'Be lifted up and thrown into the sea,' and does not doubt in his heart, but believes that what he says will happen, it will be done for him. ²⁴ Therefore I tell you, everything you pray and ask for — believe that you have receivedᴱ it and it will be yours. ²⁵ And whenever you stand praying, if you have anything against anyone, forgive him, so that your Father in heaven will also forgive you your wrongdoing."ᶠ   Mt 9:2; 17:20

ᴬ11:8 Other mss read *others were cutting leafy branches from the trees and spreading them on the road* ᴮ11:9 Ps 118:26 ᶜ11:17 Is 56:7 ᴰ11:17 Jr 7:11 ᴱ11:24 Some mss read *you receive* ; other mss read *you will receive* ᶠ11:25 Some mss include v. 26: *"But if you don't forgive, neither will your Father in heaven forgive your wrongdoing."*

The Authority of Jesus Challenged

²⁷ They came again to Jerusalem. As he was walking in the temple, the chief priests, the scribes, and the elders came ²⁸ and asked him, "By what authority are you doing these things? Who gave you this authority to do these things?"

²⁹ Jesus said to them, "I will ask you one question; then answer me, and I will tell you by what authority I do these things. ³⁰ Was John's baptism from heaven or of human origin? Answer me." Mk 4:14; Lk 7:29

³¹ They discussed it among themselves: "If we say, 'From heaven,' he will say, 'Then why didn't you believe him?' ³² But if we say, 'Of human origin'" — they were afraid of the crowd, because everyone thought that John was truly a prophet. ³³ So they answered Jesus, "We don't know." Ac 7:52; 1Jn 5:10

And Jesus said to them, "Neither will I tell you by what authority I do these things."

The Parable of the Vineyard Owner

12 He began to speak to them in parables: "A man planted a vineyard, put a fence around it, dug out a pit for a winepress, and built a watchtower. Then he leased it to tenant farmers and went away. ² At harvest time he sent a servant to the farmers to collect some of the fruit of the vineyard from them. ³ But they took him, beat him, and sent him away empty-handed. ⁴ Again he sent another servant to them, and theyᴬ hit him on the head and treated him shamefully.ᴮ ⁵ Then he sent another, and they killed that one. He also sent many others; some they beat, and others they killed. ⁶ He still had one to send, a beloved son. Finally he sent him to them, saying, 'They will respect my son.' ⁷ But those tenant farmers said to one another, 'This is the heir. Come, let's kill him, and the inheritance will be ours.' ⁸ So they seized him, killed him, and threw him out of the vineyard. ⁹ What then will the ownerᶜ of the vineyard do? He will come and kill the farmers and give the vineyard to others. ¹⁰ Haven't you read this Scripture: Gn 9:20; Mt 21:33-46; Lk 20:9-19

> The stone that
>   the builders rejected
>   has become the cornerstone.
> ¹¹ This came about from
>   the Lord Col 4:1; Jd 5
>   and is wonderful in
>   our eyes?"ᴰ

¹² They were looking for a way to arrest him but feared the crowd because they knew he had spoken this parable against them. So they left him and went away.

God and Caesar

¹³ Then they sent some of the Pharisees and the Herodians to Jesus to trap him in his words. ¹⁴ When they came, they said to him, "Teacher, we know you are truthful and don't care what anyone thinks, nor do you show partiality but teach the way of God truthfully. Is it lawful to pay taxes to Caesar or not? Should we pay or shouldn't we?" Mt 22:15-22

¹⁵ But knowing their hypocrisy, he said to them, "Why are you testing me? Bring me a denariusᴱ to look at." ¹⁶ They brought a coin. "Whose

ᴬ**12:4** Other mss add *threw stones and* ᴮ**12:4** Other mss add *and sent him off* ᶜ**12:9** Or *lord*
ᴰ**12:10-11** Ps 118:22-23 ᴱ**12:15** A denarius = one day's wage

image and inscription is this?" he asked them. Mt 23:28; Lk 12:1; Gl 2:13; 1Tm 4:2

"Caesar's," they replied.

¹⁷ Jesus told them, "Give to Caesar the things that are Caesar's, and to God the things that are God's." And they were utterly amazed at him. Rm 13:7; Rv 17:6

The Sadducees and the Resurrection

¹⁸ Sadducees, who say there is no resurrection, came to him and questioned him: ¹⁹ "Teacher, Moses wrote for us that **if a man's brother dies**, leaving a wife behind but **no child, that man should take the wife and raise up offspring for his brother.** ᴬ ²⁰ There were seven brothers. The first married a woman, and dying, left no offspring. ²¹ The second also took her, and he died, leaving no offspring. And the third likewise. ²² None of the seven ᴮ left offspring. Last of all, the woman died too. ²³ In the resurrection, when they rise, ᶜ whose wife will she be, since the seven had married her?" Mt 22:23-33; Ac 23:6

²⁴ Jesus spoke to them, "Isn't this the reason why you're mistaken: you don't know the Scriptures or the power of God? ²⁵ For when they rise from the dead, they neither marry nor are given in marriage but are like angels in heaven. ²⁶ And as for the dead being raised — haven't you read in the book of Moses, in the passage about the burning bush, how God said to him: **I am the God of Abraham and the God of Isaac and the God of Jacob?** ᴰ ²⁷ He is not the God of the dead but of the living. You are badly mistaken." Mt 26:54; Lk 1:35; 6:19; 2Pt 1:20

The Primary Commands

²⁸ One of the scribes approached. When he heard them debating and saw that Jesus answered them well, he asked him, "Which command is the most important of all?" Mt 2:4

²⁹ Jesus answered, "The most important ᴱ is **Listen, O Israel! The Lord our God, the Lord is one.** ᶠ ³⁰ **Love the Lord your God with all your heart, with all your soul, with all your mind, and with all your strength.** ᴳ,ᴴ ³¹ The second is, **Love your neighbor as yourself.** ᴵ There is no other command greater than these." Dt 6:4; Lk 6:35; Col 4:1; Jd 5

³² Then the scribe said to him, "You are right, teacher. You have correctly said that he is one, and there is no one else except him. ³³ And to love him with all your heart, with all your understanding, ᴶ and with all your strength, and to love your neighbor as yourself, is far more important than all the burnt offerings and sacrifices."

³⁴ When Jesus saw that he answered wisely, he said to him, "You are not far from the kingdom of God." And no one dared to question him any longer. Mk 1:15; Lk 20:40

The Question About the Christ

³⁵ While Jesus was teaching in the temple, he asked, "How can the scribes say that the Messiah is the son of David? ³⁶ David himself says by the Holy Spirit: Ac 21:26

**The Lord declared to
   my Lord,** Lk 17:5

ᴬ12:19 Gn 38:8; Dt 25:5 ᴮ12:22 Other mss add *had taken her and* ᶜ12:23 Other mss omit *when they rise* ᴰ12:26 Ex 3:6,15-16 ᴱ12:29 Other mss add *of all the commands* ᶠ12:29 Or *the Lord our God is Lord alone.* ᴳ12:30 Other mss add *This is the first commandment.* ᴴ12:30 Dt 6:4-5; Jos 22:5 ᴵ12:31 Lv 19:18 ᴶ12:33 Other mss add *with all your soul*

'Sit at my right hand   Mt 20:21
until I put your enemies
under your feet.'[A]   Ps 110:1

[37] David himself calls him 'Lord';
how then can he be his son?" And
the large crowd was listening to
him with delight.

Warning Against the Scribes

[38] He also said in his teaching, "Beware of the scribes, who want to
go around in long robes and who
want greetings in the marketplaces, [39] the best seats in the synagogues, and the places of honor
at banquets. [40] They devour widows' houses and say long prayers
just for show. These will receive
harsher judgment."   Mt 23:1-36; Rv 7:14

The Widow's Gift

[41] Sitting across from the temple treasury, he watched how the
crowd dropped money into the
treasury. Many rich people were
putting in large sums. [42] Then a
poor widow came and dropped
in two tiny coins worth very little. [43] Summoning his disciples, he
said to them, "Truly I tell you, this
poor widow has put more into the
treasury than all the others. [44] For
they all gave out of their surplus,
but she out of her poverty has put
in everything she had — all she
had to live on."   Gn 24:35; Lk 21:1-4; Jn 8:20

Destruction of the
Temple Predicted

13 As he was going out of the
temple, one of his disciples
said to him, "Teacher, look! What
massive stones! What impressive
buildings!"   Mt 24:1-51; Lk 21:5-38; Ac 21:26
[2] Jesus said to him, "Do you see
these great buildings? Not one

stone will be left upon another
— all will be thrown down."

Signs of the End of the Age

[3] While he was sitting on the Mount
of Olives across from the temple,
Peter, James, John, and Andrew
asked him privately, [4] "Tell us,
when will these things happen?
And what will be the sign when
all these things are about to be accomplished?"   Mt 21:1; Lk 6:14; Jn 21:7; Ac 21:26
[5] Jesus told them, "Watch out that
no one deceives you. [6] Many will
come in my name, saying, 'I am
he,' and they will deceive many.
[7] When you hear of wars and rumors of wars, don't be alarmed;
these things must take place, but it
is not yet the end. [8] For nation will
rise up against nation, and kingdom against kingdom. There will
be earthquakes in various places,
and famines.[B] These are the beginning of birth pains.   Ex 3:14; Jn 10:25; 14:13

Persecutions Predicted

[9] "But you, be on your guard! They
will hand you over to local courts,[C]
and you will be flogged in the synagogues. You will stand before governors and kings because of me, as
a witness to them. [10] And it is necessary that the gospel be preached
to all nations. [11] So when they arrest
you and hand you over, don't worry
beforehand what you will say, but
say whatever is given to you at that
time, for it isn't you speaking, but
the Holy Spirit.   Mt 10:17; Lk 22:63; Ac 5:40
[12] "Brother will betray brother
to death, and a father his child.
Children will rise up against parents and have them put to death.
[13] You will be hated by everyone
because of my name, but the one

[A] **12:36** Ps 110:1   [B] **13:8** Other mss add *and disturbances*   [C] **13:9** Or *sanhedrins* who endures to the end will be saved. Is 19:2; Mc 7:6; Mt 10:22; Lk 6:22; Jn 13:21

The Great Tribulation

¹⁴ "When you see **the abomination of desolation** ᴬ standing where it should not be" (let the reader understand), "then those in Judea must flee to the mountains. ¹⁵ A man on the housetop must not come down or go in to get anything out of his house, ¹⁶ and a man in the field must not go back to get his coat. ¹⁷ Woe to pregnant women and nursing mothers in those days! Dn 9:27; 11:31; 12:11; Lk 1:5 ¹⁸ "Pray it ᴮ won't happen in winter. ¹⁹ For those will be days of tribulation, the kind that hasn't been from the beginning of creation until now and never will be again. ²⁰ If the Lord had not cut those days short, no one would be saved. But he cut those days short for the sake of the elect, whom he chose.

²¹ "Then if anyone tells you, 'See, here is the Messiah! See, there!' do not believe it. ²² For false messiahs and false prophets will arise and will perform signs and wonders to lead astray, if possible, the elect. ²³ And you must watch! I have told you everything in advance. Mt 1:17

The Coming of the Son of Man

²⁴ "But in those days, after that tribulation: The sun will be darkened, and the moon will not shed its light; ²⁵ the stars will be falling from the sky, and the powers in the heavens will be shaken. ²⁶ Then they will see the Son of Man coming in clouds with great power and glory. ²⁷ He will send out the angels and gather his elect from the four winds, from the ends of the earth to the ends of heaven. Is 13:10; 2Co 1:4; Rv 1:16

The Parable of the Fig Tree

²⁸ "Learn this lesson from the fig tree: As soon as its branch becomes tender and sprouts leaves, you know that summer is near. ²⁹ In the same way, when you see these things happening, recognize ᶜ that he ᴰ is near — at the door. Jn 7:15; Rv 1:1 ³⁰ "Truly I tell you, this generation will certainly not pass away until all these things take place. ³¹ Heaven and earth will pass away, but my words will never pass away. Ps 72:19

No One Knows the Day or Hour

³² "Now concerning that day or hour no one knows — neither the angels in heaven nor the Son — but only the Father. Mt 13:49; 25:13; Jn 5:19 ³³ "Watch! Be alert! ᴱ For you don't know when the time is coming.

³⁴ "It is like a man on a journey, who left his house, gave authority to his servants, gave each one his work, and commanded the doorkeeper to be alert. ³⁵ Therefore be alert, since you don't know when the master of the house is coming — whether in the evening or at midnight or at the crowing of the rooster or early in the morning. ³⁶ Otherwise, when he comes suddenly he might find you sleeping. ³⁷ And what I say to you, I say to everyone: Be alert!" Lk 12:35-40

The Plot to Kill Jesus

14 It was two days before the Passover and the Festival of Unleavened Bread. The chief priests and the scribes were looking for a cunning way to arrest

---

ᴬ**13:14** Dn 9:27   ᴮ**13:18** Other mss read *"Pray that your escape*   ᶜ**13:29** Or *you know*   ᴰ**13:29** Or *it* ᴱ**13:33** Other mss add *and pray*

Jesus and kill him. ²"Not during the festival," they said, "so that there won't be a riot among the people."

The Anointing at Bethany

³ While he was in Bethany at the house of Simon the leper,ᴬ as he was reclining at the table, a woman came with an alabaster jar of very expensive perfume of pure nard. She broke the jar and poured it on his head. ⁴ But some were expressing indignation to one another: "Why has this perfume been wasted? ⁵ For this perfume might have been sold for more than three hundred denariiᴮ and given to the poor." And they began to scold her.   Mt 26:6-13; Jn 12:2-8

⁶ Jesus replied, "Leave her alone. Why are you bothering her? She has done a noble thing for me. ⁷ You always have the poor with you, and you can do what is good for them whenever you want, but you do not always have me. ⁸ She has done what she could; she has anointed my body in advance for burial. ⁹ Truly I tell you, wherever the gospel is proclaimed in the whole world, what she has done will also be told in memory of her."

¹⁰ Then Judas Iscariot, one of the Twelve, went to the chief priests to betray Jesus to them. ¹¹ And when they heard this, they were glad and promised to give him money. So he started looking for a good opportunity to betray him.   Mt 2:4; 26:14-16

Preparation for Passover

¹² On the first day of Unleavened Bread, when they sacrifice the Passover lamb, his disciples asked him, "Where do you want us to go and prepare the Passover so that you may eat it?"   Mt 26:17-19; Lk 22:7-13

¹³ So he sent two of his disciples and told them, "Go into the city, and a man carrying a jar of water will meet you. Follow him. ¹⁴ Wherever he enters, tell the owner of the house, 'The Teacher says, "Where is my guest room where I may eat the Passover with my disciples?"' ¹⁵ He will show you a large room upstairs, furnished and ready. Make the preparations for us there." ¹⁶ So the disciples went out, entered the city, and found it just as he had told them, and they prepared the Passover.   Mk 4:38; 10:10; Eph 4:11

Betrayal at the Passover

¹⁷ When evening came, he arrived with the Twelve. ¹⁸ While they were reclining and eating, Jesus said, "Truly I tell you, one of you will betray me — one who is eating with me."   Mt 26:20-25; Lk 22:21-23

¹⁹ They began to be distressed and to say to him one by one, "Surely not I?"

²⁰ He said to them, "It is one of the Twelve — the one who is dipping bread in the bowl with me. ²¹ For the Son of Man will go just as it is written about him, but woe to that man by whom the Son of Man is betrayed! It would have been better for him if he had not been born."   Dn 7:21,25; 9:26; Mk 2:10; Rv 9:12

The First Lord's Supper

²² As they were eating, he took bread, blessed and broke it, gave it to them, and said, "Take it; this is my body." ²³ Then he took a cup, and after giving thanks, he gave it to them, and they all drank from it. ²⁴ He said to them, "This is my blood

ᴬ14:3 Gk *lepros*; a term for various skin diseases; see Lv 13–14   ᴮ14:5 A denarius = one day's wage of the covenant,^A which is poured out for many. ^25 Truly I tell you, I will no longer drink of the fruit of the vine until that day when I drink it new^B in the kingdom of God."

^26 After singing a hymn, they went out to the Mount of Olives.

Peter's Denial Predicted

^27 Then Jesus said to them, "All of you will fall away,^C because it is written: Mt 26:31-35; Lk 22:31-38; Jn 13:31-38

> I will strike the shepherd,
>   and the sheep
>   will be scattered.^D   Mt 7:15

^28 But after I have risen, I will go ahead of you to Galilee."   1Co 15:4
^29 Peter told him, "Even if everyone falls away, I will not."   Lk 6:14
^30 "Truly I tell you," Jesus said to him, "today, this very night, before the rooster crows twice, you will deny me three times."   Mk 14:72
^31 But he kept insisting, "If I have to die with you, I will never deny you." And they all said the same thing.

The Prayer in the Garden

^32 Then they came to a place named Gethsemane, and he told his disciples, "Sit here while I pray." ^33 He took Peter, James, and John with him, and he began to be deeply distressed and troubled. ^34 He said to them, "I am deeply grieved^E to the point of death. Remain here and stay awake." ^35 He went a little farther, fell to the ground, and prayed that if it were possible, the hour might pass from him. ^36 And he said, "*Abba*,^F Father! All things are possible for you. Take this cup away from me. Nevertheless, not what I will, but what you will."

^37 Then he came and found them sleeping. He said to Peter, "Simon, are you sleeping? Couldn't you stay awake one hour? ^38 Stay awake and pray so that you won't enter into temptation.^G The spirit is willing, but the flesh is weak."
^39 Once again he went away and prayed, saying the same thing. ^40 And again he came and found them sleeping, because they could not keep their eyes open. They did not know what to say to him. ^41 Then he came a third time and said to them, "Are you still sleeping and resting? Enough! The time has come. See, the Son of Man is betrayed into the hands of sinners. ^42 Get up; let's go. See, my betrayer is near."   Mt 26:36-46; Mk 9:31; 10:10; Lk 22:39-46

Judas's Betrayal of Jesus

^43 While he was still speaking, Judas, one of the Twelve, suddenly arrived. With him was a mob, with swords and clubs, from the chief priests, the scribes, and the elders. ^44 His betrayer had given them a signal. "The one I kiss," he said, "he's the one; arrest him and take him away under guard." ^45 So when he came, immediately he went up to Jesus and said, "Rabbi!" and kissed him. ^46 They took hold of him and arrested him. ^47 One of those who stood by drew his sword, struck the high priest's servant, and cut off his ear.   Mt 26:47-56; Lk 22:47-53; Jn 18:1-2

^48 Jesus said to them, "Have you come out with swords and clubs, as if I were a criminal,^H to capture me? ^49 Every day I was among you, teaching in the temple, and you

---

^A14:24 Other mss read *the new covenant*   ^B14:25 Or *drink new wine*; lit *drink it new*   ^C14:27 Other mss add *because of me this night*   ^D14:27 Zch 13:7   ^E14:34 Or *"My soul is swallowed up in sorrow*   ^F14:36 Aramaic for *father*   ^G14:38 Or *won't be put to the test*   ^H14:48 Or *insurrectionist* didn't arrest me. But the Scriptures must be fulfilled." Ac 21:26; 2Pt 1:20

⁵⁰ Then they all deserted him and ran away. ⁵¹ Now a certain young man, wearing nothing but a linen cloth, was following him. They caught hold of him, ⁵² but he left the linen cloth behind and ran away naked. Am 2:16; Mk 4:40; Jms 4:7

Jesus Faces the Sanhedrin

⁵³ They led Jesus away to the high priest, and all the chief priests, the elders, and the scribes assembled. ⁵⁴ Peter followed him at a distance, right into the high priest's courtyard. He was sitting with the servants,ᴬ warming himself by the fire. Mt 26:3,57-68; Lk 22:54,63-65; Jn 18:24

⁵⁵ The chief priests and the whole Sanhedrin were looking for testimony against Jesus to put him to death, but they could not find any. ⁵⁶ For many were giving false testimony against him, and the testimonies did not agree. ⁵⁷ Some stood up and gave false testimony against him, stating, ⁵⁸ "We heard him say, 'I will destroy this temple made with human hands, and in three days I will build another not made by hands.'" ⁵⁹ Yet their testimony did not agree even on this. Pr 6:19; Mt 10:21; Mk 13:9; Col 2:11; 1Jn 5:10

⁶⁰ Then the high priest stood up before them all and questioned Jesus, "Don't you have an answer to what these men are testifying against you?" ⁶¹ But he kept silent and did not answer. Again the high priest questioned him, "Are you the Messiah, the Son of the Blessed One?" Is 53:7; Mt 27:12,14; Mk 15:5; Lk 23:9; Jn 19:9

⁶² "I am," said Jesus, "and you will see the Son of Man seated at the right hand of Power and coming with the clouds of heaven."ᴮ

⁶³ Then the high priest tore his robes and said, "Why do we still need witnesses? ⁶⁴ You have heard the blasphemy. What is your decision?" They all condemned him as deserving death. Lv 10:6; 21:10; Mt 26:3

⁶⁵ Then some began to spit on him, to blindfold him, and to beat him, saying, "Prophesy!" The temple servants also took him and slapped him. Jn 11:51; 18:18

Peter Denies His Lord

⁶⁶ While Peter was in the courtyard below, one of the high priest's maidservants came. ⁶⁷ When she saw Peter warming himself, she looked at him and said, "You also were with Jesus, the man from Nazareth." Mt 26:69-75; Mk 1:24; Lk 6:14; 22:54-62

⁶⁸ But he denied it: "I don't know or understand what you're talking about." Then he went out to the entryway,ᶜ and a rooster crowed.ᴰ

⁶⁹ When the maidservant saw him again, she began to tell those standing nearby, "This man is one of them."

⁷⁰ But again he denied it. After a little while those standing there said to Peter again, "You certainly are one of them, since you're also a Galilean."ᴱ Jn 4:45

⁷¹ Then he started to curse and swear, "I don't know this man you're talking about!" Mt 5:34

⁷² Immediately a rooster crowed a second time, and Peter remembered when Jesus had spoken the word to him, "Before the rooster crows twice, you will deny me three times." And he broke down and wept. Mk 14:30

ᴬ14:54 Or temple police, or officers, also in v. 65   ᴮ14:62 Ps 110:1; Dn 7:13   ᶜ14:68 Or forecourt
ᴰ14:68 Other mss omit and a rooster crowed   ᴱ14:70 Other mss add and your speech shows it

Jesus Faces Pilate

15 As soon as it was morning, having held a meeting with the elders, scribes, and the whole Sanhedrin, the chief priests tied Jesus up, led him away, and handed him over to Pilate. Mt 27:2,11-14; 3Jn1

² So Pilate asked him, "Are you the King of the Jews?" Lk 19:38; Jn 19:21

He answered him, "You say so."

³ And the chief priests accused him of many things. ⁴ Pilate questioned him again, "Aren't you going to answer? Look how many things they are accusing you of!" ⁵ But Jesus still did not answer, and so Pilate was amazed. 1Tm 6:13

Jesus or Barabbas

⁶ At the festival Pilate used to release for the people a prisoner whom they requested. ⁷ There was one named Barabbas, who was in prison with rebels who had committed murder during the rebellion. ⁸ The crowd came up and began to ask Pilate to do for them as was his custom. ⁹ Pilate answered them, "Do you want me to release the King of the Jews for you?" ¹⁰ For he knew it was because of envy that the chief priests had handed him over. ¹¹ But the chief priests stirred up the crowd so that he would release Barabbas to them instead. ¹² Pilate asked them again, "Then what do you want me to do with the one you call the King of the Jews?" Mt 27:15-26; Mk 14:1; Lk 23:13-25

¹³ Again they shouted, "Crucify him!"

¹⁴ Pilate said to them, "Why? What has he done wrong?"

But they shouted all the more, "Crucify him!"

¹⁵ Wanting to satisfy the crowd, Pilate released Barabbas to them; and after having Jesus flogged, he handed him over to be crucified.

Mocked by the Military

¹⁶ The soldiers led him away into the palace (that is, the governor's residence) and called the whole company together. ¹⁷ They dressed him in a purple robe, twisted together a crown of thorns, and put it on him. ¹⁸ And they began to salute him, "Hail, King of the Jews!" ¹⁹ They were hitting him on the head with a stick and spitting on him. Getting down on their knees, they were paying him homage. ²⁰ After they had mocked him, they stripped him of the purple robe and put his clothes on him. Mt 27:27-31

Crucified Between Two Criminals

They led him out to crucify him. ²¹ They forced a man coming in from the country, who was passing by, to carry Jesus's cross. He was Simon of Cyrene, the father of Alexander and Rufus. Mt 27:32

²² They brought Jesus to the place called *Golgotha* (which means Place of the Skull). ²³ They tried to give him wine mixed with myrrh, but he did not take it. Ps 4:7; Mt 27:33-37

²⁴ Then they crucified him and divided his clothes, casting lots for them to decide what each would get. ²⁵ Now it was nine in the morning[A] when they crucified him. ²⁶ The inscription of the charge written against him was: THE KING OF THE JEWS. ²⁷ They crucified two criminals[B] with him, one on his right and one on his left.[C] Ps 22:18; Lk 19:38

A15:25 Lit *was the third hour*　**B**15:27 Or *revolutionaries*　**C**15:27 Some mss include v. 28: *So the Scripture was fulfilled that says: And he was counted among criminals.*

²⁹ Those who passed by were yelling insults at^A him, shaking their heads, and saying, "Ha! The one who would destroy the temple and rebuild it in three days, ³⁰ save yourself by coming down from the cross!" ³¹ In the same way, the chief priests with the scribes were mocking him among themselves and saying, "He saved others, but he cannot save himself! ³² Let the Messiah, the King of Israel, come down now from the cross, so that we may see and believe." Even those who were crucified with him taunted him. Ex 22:28; Mt 27:39-43; Mk 3:29; Lk 23:35-38

The Death of Jesus

³³ When it was noon,^B darkness came over the whole land until three in the afternoon.^C ³⁴ And at three Jesus cried out with a loud voice, *"Eloi, Eloi, lemá sabachtháni?"* which is translated, "My God, my God, why have you abandoned me?"^D   Mt 27:45-54; Lk 23:44-48

³⁵ When some of those standing there heard this, they said, "See, he's calling for Elijah."

³⁶ Someone ran and filled a sponge with sour wine, fixed it on a stick, offered him a drink, and said, "Let's see if Elijah comes to take him down."   Ps 69:21

³⁷ Jesus let out a loud cry and breathed his last. ³⁸ Then the curtain of the temple was torn in two from top to bottom. ³⁹ When the centurion, who was standing opposite him, saw the way he^E breathed his last, he said, "Truly this man was the Son of God!"^F   Ex 26:31-33; 2Ch 3:14; 9:3

⁴⁰ There were also women watching from a distance. Among them were Mary Magdalene, Mary the mother of James the younger and of Joses, and Salome. ⁴¹ In Galilee these women followed him and took care of him. Many other women had come up with him to Jerusalem.   Mt 27:55-56; 28:1; Lk 23:49; Jn 19:25-27

The Burial of Jesus

⁴² When it was already evening, because it was the day of preparation (that is, the day before the Sabbath), ⁴³ Joseph of Arimathea, a prominent member of the Sanhedrin who was himself looking forward to the kingdom of God, came and boldly went to Pilate and asked for Jesus's body. ⁴⁴ Pilate was surprised that he was already dead. Summoning the centurion, he asked him whether he had already died. ⁴⁵ When he found out from the centurion, he gave the corpse to Joseph. ⁴⁶ After he bought some linen cloth, Joseph took him down and wrapped him in the linen. Then he laid him in a tomb cut out of the rock and rolled a stone against the entrance to the tomb. ⁴⁷ Mary Magdalene and Mary the mother of Joses were watching where he was laid.   Mt 27:57-60; Jd 21

Resurrection Morning

16 When the Sabbath was over, Mary Magdalene, Mary the mother of James, and Salome bought spices, so that they could go and anoint him. ² Very early in the morning, on the first day of the week, they went to the tomb at sunrise. ³ They were saying to one another, "Who will roll away the stone from the entrance to the tomb for us?" ⁴ Looking up, they noticed that the stone — which was very large — had been rolled away.   Mt 28:1

^A15:29 Or passed by blasphemed   ^B15:33 Lit the sixth hour   ^C15:33 Lit the ninth hour, also in v. 34
^D15:34 Ps 22:1   ^E15:39 Other mss read saw that he cried out like this and   ^F15:39 Or a son of God

⁵ When they entered the tomb, they saw a young man dressed in a white robe sitting on the right side; they were alarmed. ⁶ "Don't be alarmed," he told them. "You are looking for Jesus of Nazareth, who was crucified. He has risen! He is not here. See the place where they put him. ⁷ But go, tell his disciples and Peter, 'He is going ahead of you to Galilee; you will see him there just as he told you.' " Mt 28:5-8; Lk 24:3-8

⁸ They went out and ran from the tomb, because trembling and astonishment overwhelmed them. And they said nothing to anyone, since they were afraid. Mk 1:44; Jn 5:28

[Some of the earliest mss conclude with 16:8.]ᴬ

The Longer Ending of Mark: Appearances of the Risen Lord

[⁹ Early on the first day of the week, after he had risen, he appeared first to Mary Magdalene, out of whom he had driven seven demons. ¹⁰ She went and reported to those who had been with him, as they were mourning and weeping. ¹¹ Yet, when they heard that he was alive and had been seen by her, they did not believe it. Lk 8:2; Jn 20:11-18

¹² After this, he appeared in a different form to two of them walking on their way into the country. ¹³ And they went and reported it to the rest, who did not believe them either. Lk 24:13-35; Jn 21:1; 2Co 4:11

The Great Commission

¹⁴ Later he appeared to the Eleven themselves as they were reclining at the table. He rebuked their unbelief and hardness of heart, because they did not believe those who saw him after he had risen. ¹⁵ Then he said to them, "Go into all the world and preach the gospel to all creation. ¹⁶ Whoever believes and is baptized will be saved, but whoever does not believe will be condemned. ¹⁷ And these signs will accompany those who believe: In my name they will drive out demons; they will speak in new tongues;ᴮ ¹⁸ they will pick up snakes;ᶜ if they should drink anything deadly, it will not harm them; they will lay hands on the sick, and they will get well." Lk 24:9,38,41

The Ascension

¹⁹ So the Lord Jesus, after speaking to them, was taken up into heaven and sat down at the right hand of God. ²⁰ And they went out and preached everywhere, while the Lord worked with them and confirmed the word by the accompanying signs. Lk 24:3,51; Ac 1:2,11,22]

ᴬ**16:8** Other mss include vv. 9-20 as a longer ending. The following shorter ending is found in some mss between v. 8 and v. 9 and in one ms after v. 8 (each of which omits vv. 9-20): *And all that had been commanded to them they quickly reported to those around Peter. After these things, Jesus himself sent out through them from east to west, the holy and imperishable proclamation of eternal salvation. Amen.* ᴮ**16:17** = languages ᶜ**16:18** Other mss add *with their hands*

LUKE

The Dedication to Theophilus

1 Many have undertaken to compile a narrative about the events that have been fulfilled[A] among us, [2] just as the original eyewitnesses and servants of the word handed them down to us. [3] It also seemed good to me, since I have carefully investigated everything from the very first, to write to you in an orderly sequence, most honorable Theophilus, [4] so that you may know the certainty of the things about which you have been instructed.[B]

Gabriel Predicts John's Birth

[5] In the days of King Herod of Judea, there was a priest of Abijah's division named Zechariah. His wife was from the daughters of Aaron, and her name was Elizabeth. [6] Both were righteous in God's sight, living without blame according to all the commands and requirements of the Lord. [7] But they had no children because Elizabeth could not conceive, and both of them were well along in years. 1Ch 24:10; Mt 2:1

[8] When his division was on duty and he was serving as priest before God, [9] it happened that he was chosen by lot, according to the custom of the priesthood, to enter the sanctuary of the Lord and burn incense. [10] At the hour of incense the whole assembly of the people was praying outside. [11] An angel of the Lord appeared to him, standing to the right of the altar of incense. [12] When Zechariah saw him, he was terrified and overcome with fear.

[13] But the angel said to him: "Do not be afraid, Zechariah, because your prayer has been heard. Your wife Elizabeth will bear you a son, and you will name him John. [14] There will be joy and delight for you, and many will rejoice at his birth. [15] For he will be great in the sight of the Lord and will never drink wine or beer. He will be filled with the Holy Spirit while still in his mother's womb. [16] He will turn many of the children of Israel to the Lord their God. [17] And he will go before him in the spirit and power of Elijah, to turn the hearts of fathers to their children, and the disobedient to the understanding of the righteous, to make ready for the Lord a prepared people." 1Ch 24:19; 2Ch 8:14

[18] "How can I know this?" Zechariah asked the angel. "For I am an old man, and my wife is well along in years."

[19] The angel answered him, "I am Gabriel, who stands in the presence of God, and I was sent to speak to you and tell you this good news. [20] Now listen. You will become silent and unable to speak until the day these things take place, because you did not believe my words, which will be fulfilled in their proper time." Dn 8:16; 9:21; Lk 1:26

[21] Meanwhile, the people were waiting for Zechariah, amazed that he stayed so long in the sanctuary. [22] When he did come out, he could not speak to them. Then they realized that he had seen a vision in the sanctuary. He was making signs

---

A**1:1** Or *events that have been accomplished,* or *events most surely believed*   B**1:4** Or *informed* to them and remained speechless. ²³ When the days of his ministry were completed, he went back home. Lk 1:62

²⁴ After these days his wife Elizabeth conceived and kept herself in seclusion for five months. She said, ²⁵ "The Lord has done this for me. He has looked with favor in these days to take away my disgrace among the people." Gn 30:23; Is 4:1; 25:8

Gabriel Predicts Jesus's Birth

²⁶ In the sixth month, the angel Gabriel was sent by God to a town in Galilee called Nazareth, ²⁷ to a virgin engaged ᴬ to a man named Joseph, of the house of David. The virgin's name was Mary. ²⁸ And the angel came to her and said, "Greetings, favored woman! The Lord is with you." ᴮ ²⁹ But she was deeply troubled by this statement, wondering what kind of greeting this could be. ³⁰ Then the angel told her: "Do not be afraid, Mary, for you have found favor with God. ³¹ Now listen: You will conceive and give birth to a son, and you will name him Jesus. ³² He will be great and will be called the Son of the Most High, and the Lord God will give him the throne of his father David. ³³ He will reign over the house of Jacob forever, and his kingdom will have no end." Dt 21:23; Mt 2:23; Lk 1:19

³⁴ Mary asked the angel, "How can this be, since I have not had sexual relations with a man?" ᶜ

³⁵ The angel replied to her: "The Holy Spirit will come upon you, and the power of the Most High will overshadow you. Therefore, the holy one to be born will be called the Son of God. ³⁶ And consider your relative Elizabeth — even she has conceived a son in her old age, and this is the sixth month for her who was called childless. ³⁷ For nothing will be impossible with God." Gn 18:14; Mt 1:18; 14:33; Lk 4:3,9,41; 22:70

³⁸ "I am the Lord's servant," said Mary. "May it be done to me according to your word." Then the angel left her.

Mary's Visit to Elizabeth

³⁹ In those days Mary set out and hurried to a town in the hill country of Judah ⁴⁰ where she entered Zechariah's house and greeted Elizabeth. ⁴¹ When Elizabeth heard Mary's greeting, the baby leaped inside her, and Elizabeth was filled with the Holy Spirit. ⁴² Then she exclaimed with a loud cry: "Blessed are you among women, and your child will be blessed! ᴰ ⁴³ How could this happen to me, that the mother of my Lord should come to me? ⁴⁴ For you see, when the sound of your greeting reached my ears, the baby leaped for joy inside me. ⁴⁵ Blessed is she who has believed that the Lord would fulfill what he has spoken to her!" Lk 1:67; Ac 2:4; 4:8

Mary's Praise

⁴⁶ And Mary said:

My soul praises the greatness
of ᴱ the Lord, 1Sm 2:1-10

⁴⁷ and my spirit rejoices in God
my Savior, Ps 35:9; Hab 3:18; 1Tm 1:1

⁴⁸ because he has looked
with favor
on the humble condition
of his servant.
Surely, from now on
all generations
will call me blessed, Lk 11:27

ᴬ1:27 Lit betrothed ᴮ1:28 Other mss add Blessed are you among women. ᶜ1:34 Lit since I do not know a man ᴰ1:42 Lit and the fruit of your abdomen (or womb) is blessed ᴱ1:46 Or soul magnifies

49 because the Mighty One   Ps 89:8
   has done great things for me,
   and his name is holy.   Ps 99:3
50 His mercy is from generation
    to generation   Ps 100:5; 103:11,17
   on those who fear him.
51 He has done a mighty deed
    with his arm;   Ps 89:10; 98:1; 118:15
   he has scattered the proud
   because of the thoughts
    of their hearts;   Lk 2:35; 9:47
52 he has toppled the mighty
    from their thrones
   and exalted the lowly.   1Sm 2:7-8
53 He has satisfied the hungry
    with good things   Ps 34:10; 107:9
   and sent the rich away empty.
54 He has helped
    his servant Israel,
   remembering his mercy
55 to Abraham and his
    descendants[A] forever,   Gn 21:12
   just as he spoke
    to our ancestors.

56 And Mary stayed with her about three months; then she returned to her home.

The Birth and Naming of John

57 Now the time had come for Elizabeth to give birth, and she had a son. 58 Then her neighbors and relatives heard that the Lord had shown her his great mercy, and they rejoiced with her.   Gn 19:19
59 When they came to circumcise the child on the eighth day, they were going to name him Zechariah, after his father. 60 But his mother responded, "No. He will be called John."   Gn 17:12; Lv 12:3; Lk 1:13,63; 2:21; Php 3:5
61 Then they said to her, "None of your relatives has that name." 62 So they motioned to his father to find out what he wanted him

to be called. 63 He asked for a writing tablet and wrote: "His name is John." And they were all amazed. 64 Immediately his mouth was opened and his tongue set free, and he began to speak, praising God. 65 Fear came on all those who lived around them, and all these things were being talked about throughout the hill country of Judea. 66 All who heard about him took it to heart, saying, "What then will this child become?" For, indeed, the Lord's hand was with him.   Lk 1:20,22; Ac 11:21

Zechariah's Prophecy

67 Then his father Zechariah was filled with the Holy Spirit and prophesied: Jl 2:28; Lk 1:41
68 Blessed is the Lord, the God
    of Israel,
   because he has visited   Ps 41:13
   and provided redemption
    for his people.   Lk 1:71; 2:38
69 He has raised up a horn
    of salvation for us   1Sm 2:1,10
   in the house of his servant
    David,   2Sm 7:26; Ps 89:3,20
70 just as he spoke by the mouth
   of his holy prophets
    in ancient times;   2Kg 21:10
71 salvation from our enemies
   and from the hand of those
    who hate us.
72 He has dealt mercifully
    with our fathers   Mc 7:20
   and remembered
    his holy covenant —   Ps 106:45
73 the oath that he swore
    to our father Abraham.
   He has given us the privilege,
74 since we have been rescued
   from the hand of
    our enemies,
   to serve him without fear

A 1:55 Or *offspring*; lit *seed*

75   in holiness
      and righteousness
      in his presence all our days.
76   And you, child, will be called
      a prophet of the Most High,
      for you will go
         before the Lord
      to prepare his ways,   Lk 1:17
77   to give his people knowledge
      of salvation
      through the forgiveness
      of their sins.   Jr 31:34; Mk 1:4
78   Because of our God's
      merciful compassion,
      the dawn from on high
      will visit us   Is 58:8; Jr 23:5; Zch 3:8
79   to shine on those who live
      in darkness
      and the shadow of death,   Is 9:2
      to guide our feet into the way
      of peace.

80 The child grew up and became spiritually strong, and he was in the wilderness until the day of his public appearance to Israel. Lk 2:40

The Birth of Jesus

2 In those days a decree went out from Caesar Augustus that the whole empire ^A should be registered. ² This first registration took place while ^B Quirinius was governing Syria. ³ So everyone went to be registered, each to his own town. ⁴ Joseph also went up from the town of Nazareth in Galilee, to Judea, to the city of David, which is called Bethlehem, because he was of the house and family line of David, ⁵ to be registered along with Mary, who was engaged to him ^C and was pregnant. ⁶ While they

were there, the time came for her to give birth. ⁷ Then she gave birth to her firstborn son, and she wrapped him tightly in cloth and laid him in a manger, ^D because there was no guest room available for them.

The Shepherds and the Angels

⁸ In the same region, shepherds were staying out in the fields and keeping watch at night over their flock. ⁹ Then an angel of the Lord stood before them, and the glory of the Lord shone around them, and they were terrified. ^E ¹⁰ But the angel said to them, "Don't be afraid, for look, I proclaim to you good news of great joy that will be for all the people: ^F ¹¹ Today in the city of David a Savior was born for you, who is the Messiah, the Lord. ¹² This will be the sign for you: You will find a baby wrapped tightly in cloth and lying in a manger." Mt 1:20; 2:13,19; 28:2 ¹³ Suddenly there was a multitude of the heavenly host ^G with the angel, praising God and saying:

14   Glory to God
         in the highest heaven,   Mt 21:9
      and peace on earth to people
      he favors! ^H,I   Lk 3:22; 12:51; Eph 1:9

¹⁵ When the angels had left them and returned to heaven, the shepherds said to one another, "Let's go straight to Bethlehem and see what has happened, which the Lord has made known to us."

¹⁶ They hurried off and found both Mary and Joseph, and the baby who was lying in the manger. ¹⁷ After seeing them, they reported the message they were told about

---

^A 2:1 Or the whole inhabited world   ^B 2:2 Or This registration was the first while, or This registration was before   ^C 2:5 Lit betrothed   ^D 2:7 Or feeding trough, also in vv. 12,16   ^E 2:9 Lit they feared a great fear   ^F 2:10 Or the whole nation   ^G 2:13 Lit heavenly army   ^H 2:14 Other mss read earth good will to people   ^I 2:14 Or earth to men of good will this child, [18] and all who heard it were amazed at what the shepherds said to them. [19] But Mary was treasuring up all these things in her heart and meditating on them. [20] The shepherds returned, glorifying and praising God for all the things they had seen and heard, which were just as they had been told. Lk 1:63; 2:33; 4:22; 8:25; 9:43; 11:14,38; 20:26

The Circumcision and Presentation of Jesus

[21] When the eight days were completed for his circumcision, he was named Jesus — the name given by the angel before he was conceived. [22] And when the days of their purification according to the law of Moses were finished, they brought him up to Jerusalem to present him to the Lord [23] (just as it is written in the law of the Lord, **Every firstborn male will be dedicated**[A] **to the Lord**[B]) [24] and to offer a sacrifice (according to what is stated in the law of the Lord, **a pair of turtledoves or two young pigeons**[C]).

Simeon's Prophetic Praise

[25] There was a man in Jerusalem whose name was Simeon. This man was righteous and devout, looking forward to Israel's consolation, and the Holy Spirit was on him. [26] It had been revealed to him by the Holy Spirit that he would not see death before he saw the Lord's Messiah. [27] Guided by the Spirit, he entered the temple. When the parents brought in the child Jesus to perform for him what was customary under the law, [28] Simeon took him up in his arms, praised God, and said, Ps 135:14; Is 40:1-2,11; 49:10,13; 51:3,12; Lk 1:6

[29] Now, Master,
you can dismiss your servant
in peace,
as you promised.
[30] For my eyes have seen
your salvation. Ps 119:166,174
[31] You have prepared it
in the presence
of all peoples —
[32] a light for revelation
to the Gentiles[D] Is 42:6; 49:6,9
and glory
to your people Israel.

[33] His father and mother[E] were amazed at what was being said about him. [34] Then Simeon blessed them and told his mother Mary: "Indeed, this child is destined to cause the fall and rise of many in Israel and to be a sign that will be opposed[F] — [35] and a sword will pierce your own soul — that the thoughts[G] of many hearts may be revealed." Mt 21:44; 1Co 1:23; 2Co 2:16; 1Pt 2:8

Anna's Testimony

[36] There was also a prophetess, Anna, a daughter of Phanuel, of the tribe of Asher. She was well along in years, having lived with her husband seven years after her marriage, [H] [37] and was a widow for eighty-four years.[I] She did not leave the temple, serving God night and day with fasting and prayers. [38] At that very moment,[J] she came up and began to thank God and to speak about him to all who were looking forward to the redemption of Jerusalem.[K] Jos 19:24; Lk 2:25,38; Ac 21:9

[A]**2:23** Lit *be called holy* [B]**2:23** Ex 13:2,12 [C]**2:24** Lv 5:11; 12:8 [D]**2:32** Or *the nations* [E]**2:33** Other mss read *But Joseph and his mother* [F]**2:34** Or *spoken against* [G]**2:35** Or *schemes* [H]**2:36** Lit *years from her virginity* [I]**2:37** Or *she was a widow until the age of eighty-four* [J]**2:38** Lit *very hour* [K]**2:38** Other mss read *in Jerusalem*

The Family's Return to Nazareth

³⁹ When they had completed everything according to the law of the Lord, they returned to Galilee, to their own town of Nazareth. ⁴⁰ The boy grew up and became strong, filled with wisdom, and God's grace was on him.　Mt 2:23; Lk 1:26,80; 2:51; 4:16

In His Father's House

⁴¹ Every year his parents traveled to Jerusalem for the Passover Festival. ⁴² When he was twelve years old, they went up according to the custom of the festival. ⁴³ After those days were over, as they were returning, the boy Jesus stayed behind in Jerusalem, but his parents[A] did not know it. ⁴⁴ Assuming he was in the traveling party, they went a day's journey. Then they began looking for him among their relatives and friends. ⁴⁵ When they did not find him, they returned to Jerusalem to search for him. ⁴⁶ After three days, they found him in the temple sitting among the teachers, listening to them and asking them questions. ⁴⁷ And all those who heard him were astounded at his understanding and his answers. ⁴⁸ When his parents saw him, they were astonished, and his mother said to him, "Son, why have you treated us like this? Your father and I have been anxiously searching for you."　Ex 12:11; 23:15

⁴⁹ "Why were you searching for me?" he asked them. "Didn't you know that it was necessary for me to be in my Father's house?"[B] ⁵⁰ But they did not understand what he said to them.　Mk 9:32; Lk 9:45; 18:34

In Favor with God and with People

⁵¹ Then he went down with them and came to Nazareth and was obedient to them. His mother kept all these things in her heart. ⁵² And Jesus increased in wisdom and stature, and in favor with God and with people.　Lk 2:19,40

The Messiah's Herald

3 In the fifteenth year of the reign of Tiberius Caesar, while Pontius Pilate was governor of Judea, Herod was tetrarch[C] of Galilee, his brother Philip tetrarch of the region of Iturea and Trachonitis, and Lysanias tetrarch of Abilene, ² during the high priesthood of Annas and Caiaphas, God's word came to John the son of Zechariah in the wilderness. ³ He went into all the vicinity of the Jordan, proclaiming a baptism of repentance for the forgiveness of sins, ⁴ as it is written in the book of the words of the prophet Isaiah:　Mt 27:2; Lk 13:1; 23:1-24,52

> **A voice of one crying out**
> **in the wilderness:**
> **Prepare the way**
> **for the Lord;**
> **make his paths straight!**
> ⁵ **Every valley will be filled,**
> **and every mountain**
> **and hill will be**
> **made low;[D]**
> **the crooked**
> **will become straight,**
> **the rough ways smooth,**
> ⁶ **and everyone will see**
> **the salvation of God.[E]**

⁷ He then said to the crowds who came out to be baptized by him, "Brood of vipers! Who warned you

---

[A]**2:43** Other mss read *but Joseph and his mother*　[B]**2:49** Or *be involved in my Father's interests* (or *things*), or *be among my Father's people*　[C]**3:1** Or *ruler*　[D]**3:5** Lit *be humbled*　[E]**3:4-6** Is 40:3-5 to flee from the coming wrath? [8] Therefore produce fruit consistent with repentance. And don't start saying to yourselves, 'We have Abraham as our father,' for I tell you that God is able to raise up children for Abraham from these stones. [9] The ax is already at the root of the trees. Therefore, every tree that doesn't produce good fruit will be cut down and thrown into the fire." Mt 12:34; 23:33; Lk 3:7; Eph 5:6; Col 3:6

[10] "What then should we do?" the crowds were asking him. Ac 2:37-38

[11] He replied to them, "The one who has two shirts must share with someone who has none, and the one who has food must do the same." Is 58:7

[12] Tax collectors also came to be baptized, and they asked him, "Teacher, what should we do?"

[13] He told them, "Don't collect any more than what you have been authorized."

[14] Some soldiers also questioned him, "What should we do?"

He said to them, "Don't take money from anyone by force or false accusation, and be satisfied with your wages."

[15] Now the people were waiting expectantly, and all of them were questioning in their hearts whether John might be the Messiah. [16] John answered them all, "I baptize you with water, but one who is more powerful than I am is coming. I am not worthy to untie the strap of his sandals. He will baptize you with [A] the Holy Spirit and fire. [17] His winnowing shovel is in his hand to clear his threshing floor and gather the wheat into his barn, but the chaff he will burn with fire that never goes out." [18] Then, along with

many other exhortations, he proclaimed good news to the people. [19] But when John rebuked Herod the tetrarch because of Herodias, his brother's wife, and all the evil things he had done, [20] Herod added this to everything else — he locked up John in prison. Mt 3:11-12; Jn 1:19-20

The Baptism of Jesus

[21] When all the people were baptized, Jesus also was baptized. As he was praying, heaven opened, [22] and the Holy Spirit descended on him in a physical appearance like a dove. And a voice came from heaven: "You are my beloved Son; with you I am well-pleased." Lk 5:16

The Genealogy of Jesus Christ

[23] As he began his ministry, Jesus was about thirty years old and was thought to be the

son of Joseph, son of Heli,
[24] son of Matthat, son of Levi,
son of Melchi, son of Jannai,
son of Joseph,
[25] son of Mattathias,
son of Amos, son of Nahum,
son of Esli, son of Naggai,
[26] son of Maath,
son of Mattathias,
son of Semein, son of Josech,
son of Joda, [27] son of Joanan,
son of Rhesa,
son of Zerubbabel, Hg 1:1,12,14
son of Shealtiel, son of Neri,
[28] son of Melchi, son of Addi,
son of Cosam,
son of Elmadam,
son of Er, [29] son of Joshua,
son of Eliezer, son of Jorim,
son of Matthat, son of Levi,
[30] son of Simeon, son of Judah,
son of Joseph, son of Jonam,
son of Eliakim, [31] son of Melea,

son of Menna, son of Mattatha,
son of Nathan, son of David,
32 son of Jesse, son of Obed,
son of Boaz, son of Salmon, A
son of Nahshon,
33 son of Amminadab,
son of Ram, B son of Hezron,
son of Perez, son of Judah,
34 son of Jacob, son of Isaac,
son of Abraham,
son of Terah,   Gn 11:26-30
son of Nahor, 35 son of Serug,
son of Reu, son of Peleg,
son of Eber, son of Shelah,
36 son of Cainan,
son of Arphaxad,
son of Shem, son of Noah,
son of Lamech,
37 son of Methuselah,
son of Enoch, son of Jared,
son of Mahalalel,
son of Cainan,
38 son of Enos, son of Seth,
son of Adam, son of God.

The Temptation of Jesus

4 Then Jesus left the Jordan, full of the Holy Spirit, and was led by the Spirit in the wilderness ² for forty days to be tempted by the devil. He ate nothing during those days, and when they were over, he was hungry. ³ The devil said to him, "If you are the Son of God, tell this stone to become bread." Mt 4:1-11

⁴ But Jesus answered him, "It is written: **Man must not live on bread alone.**" C,D   Dt 8:3

⁵ So he took him up E and showed him all the kingdoms of the world in a moment of time. ⁶ The devil said to him, "I will give you their splendor and all this authority, because it has been given over to me, and I can give it to anyone I want. ⁷ If you, then, will worship me, F all will be yours." Is 23:17; Jr 25:26; 1Jn 5:19

⁸ And Jesus answered him, G "It is written: **Worship the Lord your God, and serve him only.**" H Dt 6:13

⁹ So he took him to Jerusalem, had him stand on the pinnacle of the temple, and said to him, "If you are the Son of God, throw yourself down from here. ¹⁰ For it is written:

He will give his angels
orders concerning you,
to protect you, I ¹¹ and Ps 91:11
they will support you
with their hands,
so that you will not strike
your foot against a stone." J

¹² And Jesus answered him, "It is said: **Do not test the Lord your God.**" K   Dt 6:16

¹³ After the devil had finished every temptation, he departed from him for a time.

Ministry in Galilee

¹⁴ Then Jesus returned to Galilee in the power of the Spirit, and news about him spread throughout the entire vicinity. ¹⁵ He was teaching in their synagogues, being praised L by everyone. Mt 4:12,24; 9:26,31; Lk 4:37

Rejection at Nazareth

¹⁶ He came to Nazareth, where he had been brought up. As usual, he entered the synagogue on the Sabbath day and stood up to read. ¹⁷ The scroll of the prophet Isaiah

---

A**3:32** Other mss read *Sala*   B**3:33** Other mss read *Amminadab, son of Aram, son of Joram* ; other mss read *Amminadab, son of Admin, son of Arni*   C**4:4** Other mss add *but on every word of God*   D**4:4** Dt 8:3   E**4:5** Other mss read *So the devil took him up on a high mountain*   F**4:7** Lit *will fall down before me*   G**4:8** Other mss add *"Get behind me, Satan!*   H**4:8** Dt 6:13   I**4:10** Ps 91:11   J**4:11** Ps 91:12   K**4:12** Dt 6:16   L**4:15** Or *glorified* was given to him, and unrolling the scroll, he found the place where it was written: Mt 13:54; Mk 6:1-2; Lk 2:39,51

18 The Spirit of the Lord is
　　on me,
　because he has anointed me
　to preach good news
　　to the poor.
　He has sent me[A]
　to proclaim release[B]
　　to the captives
　and recovery of sight
　　to the blind,
　to set free the oppressed,
19 　to proclaim the year
　　of the Lord's favor.[C] Is 61:1-2

20 He then rolled up the scroll, gave it back to the attendant, and sat down. And the eyes of everyone in the synagogue were fixed on him. 21 He began by saying to them, "Today as you listen, this Scripture has been fulfilled." Mt 26:55; Jn 13:18; 15:25; 17:12

22 They were all speaking well of him[D] and were amazed by the gracious words that came from his mouth; yet they said, "Isn't this Joseph's son?" Mt 13:55; Mk 6:3; Jn 6:42

23 Then he said to them, "No doubt you will quote this proverb[E] to me: 'Doctor, heal yourself. What we've heard that took place in Capernaum, do here in your hometown also.'" Mt 11:23; Mk 2:1-12; Jn 4:46-53

24 He also said, "Truly I tell you, no prophet is accepted in his hometown. 25 But I say to you, there were certainly many widows in Israel in Elijah's days, when the sky was shut up for three years and six months while a great famine came over all the land. 26 Yet Elijah was not sent to any of them except a widow at Zarephath in Sidon. 27 And in the prophet Elisha's time, there were many in Israel who had leprosy,[F] and yet not one of them was cleansed except Naaman the Syrian." 1Kg 18:1; Mt 13:57

28 When they heard this, everyone in the synagogue was enraged. 29 They got up, drove him out of town, and brought him to the edge of the hill that their town was built on, intending to hurl him over the cliff. 30 But he passed right through the crowd and went on his way. Nm 15:35

Driving Out an Unclean Spirit

31 Then he went down to Capernaum, a town in Galilee, and was teaching them on the Sabbath. 32 They were astonished at his teaching because his message had authority. 33 In the synagogue there was a man with an unclean demonic spirit who cried out with a loud voice, 34 "Leave us alone! What do you have to do with us, Jesus of Nazareth? Have you come to destroy us? I know who you are — the Holy One of God!" Mt 7:28-29; Mk 1:21-28

35 But Jesus rebuked him and said, "Be silent and come out of him!" And throwing him down before them, the demon came out of him without hurting him at all. Lk 8:24

36 Amazement came over them all, and they were saying to one another, "What is this message? For he commands the unclean spirits with authority and power, and they come out!" 37 And news about him began to go out to every place in the vicinity.

Healings at Capernaum

38 After he left the synagogue, he entered Simon's house. Simon's

---

[A] 4:18 Other mss add to heal the brokenhearted, [B] 4:18 Or freedom, or forgiveness [C] 4:18-19 Is 61:1-2 [D] 4:22 Or They were testifying against him [E] 4:23 Or parable [F] 4:27 Gk lepros; a term for various skin diseases; see Lv 13–14 mother-in-law was suffering from a high fever, and they asked him about her. ³⁹ So he stood over her and rebuked the fever, and it left her. She got up immediately and began to serve them. Mt 8:14-17; 1Co 9:5

⁴⁰ When the sun was setting, all those who had anyone sick with various diseases brought them to him. As he laid his hands on each one of them, he healed them. ⁴¹ Also, demons were coming out of many, shouting and saying, "You are the Son of God!" But he rebuked them and would not allow them to speak, because they knew he was the Christ.

⁴² When it was day, he went out and made his way to a deserted place. But the crowds were searching for him. They came to him and tried to keep him from leaving them. ⁴³ But he said to them, "It is necessary for me to proclaim the good news about the kingdom of God to the other towns also, because I was sent for this purpose." ⁴⁴ And he was preaching in the synagogues of Judea.ᴬ Mt14:13; Mk1:35-38,45

The First Disciples

5 As the crowd was pressing in on Jesus to hear God's word, he was standing by Lake Gennesaret. ² He saw two boats at the edge of the lake; the fishermen had left them and were washing their nets. ³ He got into one of the boats, which belonged to Simon, and asked him to put out a little from the land. Then he sat down and was teaching the crowds from the boat. Dt3:17; Mt4:18-22

⁴ When he had finished speaking, he said to Simon, "Put out into deep water and let down your nets for a catch." Jn 21:3-6

⁵ "Master," Simon replied, "we've worked hard all night long and caught nothing. But if you say so, I'll let down the nets."ᴮ Lk8:24; 9:33,49

⁶ When they did this, they caught a great number of fish, and their netsᴮ began to tear. ⁷ So they signaled to their partners in the other boat to come and help them; they came and filled both boats so full that they began to sink.

⁸ When Simon Peter saw this, he fell at Jesus's knees and said, "Go away from me, because I'm a sinful man, Lord!" ⁹ For he and all those with him were amazed at the catch of fish they had taken, ¹⁰ and so were James and John, Zebedee's sons, who were Simon's partners.

"Don't be afraid," Jesus told Simon. "From now on you will be catching people." ¹¹ Then they brought the boats to land, left everything, and followed him. Mt14:27

A Man Cleansed

¹² While he was in one of the towns, a man was there who had leprosyᶜ all over him. He saw Jesus, fell facedown, and begged him: "Lord, if you are willing, you can make me clean." Mt 8:2-4; Mk 1:40-44

¹³ Reaching out his hand, Jesus touched him, saying, "I am willing; be made clean," and immediately the leprosy left him. ¹⁴ Then he ordered him to tell no one: "But go and show yourself to the priest, and offer what Moses commanded for your cleansing as a testimony to them." Mt8:15; 9:29; 17:7; 20:34; Lk18:15

¹⁵ But the newsᴰ about him spread even more, and large crowds would come together to hear him and to be healed of their sicknesses. ¹⁶ Yet

ᴬ**4:44** Other mss read *Galilee* ᴮ**5:5,6** Other mss read *net* (Gk sg) ᶜ**5:12** Gk *lepros* ; a term for various skin diseases, also in v. 13; see Lv 13–14 ᴰ**5:15** Lit *the word* he often withdrew to deserted places and prayed. Mt 14:23; Mk 1:35; Lk 6:12

The Son of Man Forgives and Heals

¹⁷ On one of those days while he was teaching, Pharisees and teachers of the law were sitting there who had come from every village of Galilee and Judea, and also from Jerusalem. And the Lord's power to heal was in him. ¹⁸ Just then some men came, carrying on a stretcher a man who was paralyzed. They tried to bring him in and set him down before him. ¹⁹ Since they could not find a way to bring him in because of the crowd, they went up on the roof and lowered him on the stretcher through the roof tiles into the middle of the crowd before Jesus. Mk 5:30; Lk 6:19; Ac 5:34; 1Tm 1:7

²⁰ Seeing their faith he said, "Friend, ᴬ your sins are forgiven."

²¹ Then the scribes and the Pharisees began to think to themselves: "Who is this man who speaks blasphemies? Who can forgive sins but God alone?" Is 43:25; Mt 23:2; Lk 11:53; Jn 8:3

²² But perceiving their thoughts, Jesus replied to them, "Why are you thinking this in your hearts? ᴮ ²³ Which is easier: to say, 'Your sins are forgiven you,' or to say, 'Get up and walk'? ²⁴ But so that you may know that the Son of Man has authority on earth to forgive sins"— he told the paralyzed man, "I tell you: Get up, take your stretcher, and go home."

²⁵ Immediately he got up before them, picked up what he had been lying on, and went home glorifying God. ²⁶ Then everyone was astounded, and they were giving glory to God. And they were filled with awe and said, "We have seen incredible things today." Lk 7:16; 13:13

The Call of Levi

²⁷ After this, Jesus went out and saw a tax collector named Levi sitting at the tax office, and he said to him, "Follow me." ²⁸ So, leaving everything behind, he got up and began to follow him. Mt 9:9-17; Mk 2:14-22

²⁹ Then Levi hosted a grand banquet for him at his house. Now there was a large crowd of tax collectors and others who were guests ᶜ with them. ³⁰ But the Pharisees and their scribes were complaining to his disciples, "Why do you eat and drink with tax collectors and sinners?" Mk 2:16; Lk 15:1; Ac 23:9

³¹ Jesus replied to them, "It is not those who are healthy who need a doctor, but those who are sick. ³² I have not come to call the righteous, but sinners to repentance."

A Question about Fasting

³³ Then they said to him, "John's disciples fast often and say prayers, and those of the Pharisees do the same, but yours eat and drink." ᴰ

³⁴ Jesus said to them, "You can't make the wedding guests fast while the groom is with them, can you? ³⁵ But the time ᴱ will come when the groom will be taken away from them — then they will fast in those days." 1Sm 2:31; Ps 37:13; Ec 2:16; 12:1; Lk 17:22

³⁶ He also told them a parable: "No one tears a patch from a new garment and puts it on an old garment. Otherwise, not only will he tear the new, but also the piece from the new garment will not match the old. ³⁷ And no one puts new wine

ᴬ5:20 Lit "Man"   ᴮ5:22 Or minds   ᶜ5:29 Lit were reclining   ᴰ5:33 Other mss read "Why do John's . . . drink?" (as a question)   ᴱ5:35 Lit days into old wineskins. Otherwise, the new wine will burst the skins, it will spill, and the skins will be ruined. ³⁸ No, new wine is put into fresh wineskins.^A ³⁹ And no one, after drinking old wine, wants new, because he says, 'The old is better.'"^B

Lord of the Sabbath

6 On a Sabbath, he passed through the grainfields. His disciples were picking heads of grain, rubbing them in their hands, and eating them. ² But some of the Pharisees said, "Why are you doing what is not lawful on the Sabbath?"

³ Jesus answered them, "Haven't you read what David and those who were with him did when he was hungry — ⁴ how he entered the house of God and took and ate the bread of the Presence, which is not lawful for any but the priests to eat? He even gave some to those who were with him." ⁵ Then he told them, "The Son of Man is Lord of the Sabbath." Ex 25:30; Lv 24:5-9; 1Sm 21:6

⁶ On another Sabbath he entered the synagogue and was teaching. A man was there whose right hand was shriveled. ⁷ The scribes and Pharisees were watching him closely, to see if he would heal on the Sabbath, so that they could find a charge against him. ⁸ But he knew their thoughts and told the man with the shriveled hand, "Get up and stand here."^C So he got up and stood there. ⁹ Then Jesus said to them, "I ask you: Is it lawful to do good on the Sabbath or to do evil, to save life or to destroy it?" ¹⁰ After looking around at them all, he told him, "Stretch out your hand." He did, and his hand was restored.^D

¹¹ They, however, were filled with rage and started discussing with one another what they might do to Jesus. Mt 12:9-14; Mk 3:1-6; Lk 14:1

The Twelve Apostles

¹² During those days he went out to the mountain to pray and spent all night in prayer to God. ¹³ When daylight came, he summoned his disciples, and he chose twelve of them, whom he also named apostles: ¹⁴ Simon, whom he also named Peter, and Andrew his brother; James and John; Philip and Bartholomew; ¹⁵ Matthew and Thomas; James the son of Alphaeus, and Simon called the Zealot; ¹⁶ Judas the son of James, and Judas Iscariot, who became a traitor. Mt 14:23; Lk 5:16

Teaching and Healing

¹⁷ After coming down with them, he stood on a level place with a large crowd of his disciples and a great number of people from all Judea and Jerusalem and from the seacoast of Tyre and Sidon. ¹⁸ They came to hear him and to be healed of their diseases; and those tormented by unclean spirits were made well. ¹⁹ The whole crowd was trying to touch him, because power was coming out from him and healing them all. Mt 9:21; 11:21; 14:36

The Beatitudes

²⁰ Then looking up at his disciples, he said: Mt 5:3-12

　　Blessed are you who are poor,
　　　because the kingdom of God
　　　is yours.
²¹　Blessed are you who are now hungry,
　　　because you will be filled.

---

^A**5:38** Other mss add *And so both are preserved.*　^B**5:39** Other mss read *is good*　^C**6:8** Lit *stand in the middle*　^D**6:10** Other mss add *as sound as the other*

Blessed are you who weep now,
because you will laugh.
²² Blessed are you when people hate you,
when they exclude you,
insult you, _{Jn 9:22; 16:2}
and slander your name as evil
because of the Son of Man.
²³ "Rejoice in that day and leap for joy. Take note — your reward is great in heaven, for this is the way their ancestors used to treat the prophets. Neh 9:26; Ezk 2:1-7; Ac 7:52

Woe to the Self-Satisfied

²⁴ But woe to you who are rich,
for you have received
your comfort.
²⁵ Woe to you who are now full,
for you will be hungry.
Woe to you^A
who are now laughing,
for you will mourn and weep.
²⁶ Woe to you^A
when all people speak well
of you,
for this is the way
their ancestors
used to treat the false prophets.

Love Your Enemies

²⁷ "But I say to you who listen: Love your enemies, do what is good to those who hate you, ²⁸ bless those who curse you, pray for those who mistreat you. ²⁹ If anyone hits you on the cheek, offer the other also. And if anyone takes away your coat, don't hold back your shirt either. ³⁰ Give to everyone who asks you, and from someone who takes your things, don't ask for them back. ³¹ Just as you want others to do for you, do the same for them. ³² If you love those who love you, what credit is that to you? Even sinners love those who love them. ³³ If you do what is good to those who are good to you, what credit is that to you? Even sinners do that. ³⁴ And if you lend to those from whom you expect to receive, what credit is that to you? Even sinners lend to sinners to be repaid in full. ³⁵ But love your enemies, do what is good, and lend, expecting nothing in return. Then your reward will be great, and you will be children of the Most High. For he is gracious to the ungrateful and evil. ³⁶ Be merciful, just as your Father also is merciful.

Do Not Judge

³⁷ "Do not judge, and you will not be judged. Do not condemn, and you will not be condemned. Forgive, and you will be forgiven. ³⁸ Give, and it will be given to you; a good measure — pressed down, shaken together, and running over — will be poured into your lap. For with the measure you use, it will be measured back to you." Mt 7:1-5

³⁹ He also told them a parable: "Can the blind guide the blind? Won't they both fall into a pit? ⁴⁰ A disciple is not above his teacher, but everyone who is fully trained will be like his teacher. Mt 10:24; 15:14

⁴¹ "Why do you look at the splinter in your brother's eye, but don't notice the beam of wood in your own eye? ⁴² Or how can you say to your brother, 'Brother, let me take out the splinter that is in your eye,' when you yourself don't see the beam of wood in your eye? Hypocrite! First take the beam of wood out of your eye, and then you will see clearly to take out the splinter in your brother's eye.

^A6:25,26 Other mss omit *to you*

A Tree and Its Fruit

43 "A good tree doesn't produce bad fruit; on the other hand, a bad tree doesn't produce good fruit. ^A^ 44 For each tree is known by its own fruit. Figs aren't gathered from thornbushes, or grapes picked from a bramble bush. 45 A good person produces good out of the good stored up in his heart. An evil person produces evil out of the evil stored up in his heart, for his mouth speaks from the overflow of the heart. Mt 7:16,18,20; 12:33-35

The Two Foundations

46 "Why do you call me 'Lord, Lord,' and don't do the things I say? 47 I will show you what someone is like who comes to me, hears my words, and acts on them: 48 He is like a man building a house, who dug deep and laid the foundation on the rock. When the flood came, the river crashed against that house and couldn't shake it, because it was well built. 49 But the one who hears and does not act is like a man who built a house on the ground without a foundation. The river crashed against it, and immediately it collapsed. And the destruction of that house was great." Mal 1:6; Mt 7:21

A Centurion's Faith

7 When he had concluded saying all this to the people who were listening, he entered Capernaum. 2 A centurion's servant, who was highly valued by him, was sick and about to die. 3 When the centurion heard about Jesus, he sent some Jewish elders to him, requesting him to come and save the life of his servant. 4 When they reached Jesus, they pleaded with him earnestly, saying, "He is worthy for you to grant this, 5 because he loves our nation and has built us a synagogue." Mt 8:5-13; Ac 10:22

6 Jesus went with them, and when he was not far from the house, the centurion sent friends to tell him, "Lord, don't trouble yourself, since I am not worthy to have you come under my roof. 7 That is why I didn't even consider myself worthy to come to you. But say the word, and my servant will be healed. ^B^ 8 For I too am a man placed under authority, having soldiers under my command. I say to this one, 'Go,' and he goes; and to another, 'Come,' and he comes; and to my servant, 'Do this,' and he does it." Ps 107:20; Mt 8:16

9 Jesus heard this and was amazed at him, and turning to the crowd following him, he said, "I tell you, I have not found so great a faith even in Israel." 10 When those who had been sent returned to the house, they found the servant in good health.

A Widow's Son Raised to Life

11 Afterward he was on his way to a town called Nain. His disciples and a large crowd were traveling with him. 12 Just as he neared the gate of the town, a dead man was being carried out. He was his mother's only son, and she was a widow. A large crowd from the city was also with her. 13 When the Lord saw her, he had compassion on her and said, "Don't weep." 14 Then he came up and touched the open coffin, and the pallbearers stopped. And he said, "Young man, I tell you, get up!" Jdg 11:34; Mt 20:34; Lk 8:42; 9:38; Heb 11:17

^A^6:43 Lit *on the other hand, again, a bad tree doesn't produce good fruit*   ^B^7:7 Other mss read *and let my servant be healed*

¹⁵ The dead man sat up and began to speak, and Jesus gave him to his mother. ¹⁶ Then fear^A came over everyone, and they glorified God, saying, "A great prophet has risen among us," and "God has visited^B his people." ¹⁷ This report about him went throughout Judea and all the vicinity.   1Kg 17:23; 2Kg 4:36; Mt 5:16; Lk 5:26

In Praise of John the Baptist

¹⁸ Then John's disciples told him about all these things. So John summoned two of his disciples ¹⁹ and sent them to the Lord, asking, "Are you the one who is to come, or should we expect someone else?"

²⁰ When the men reached him, they said, "John the Baptist sent us to ask you, 'Are you the one who is to come, or should we expect someone else?'"

²¹ At that time Jesus healed many people of diseases, afflictions, and evil spirits, and he granted sight to many blind people. ²² He replied to them, "Go and report to John what you have seen and heard: The blind receive their sight, the lame walk, those with leprosy^C are cleansed, the deaf hear, the dead are raised, and the poor are told the good news, ²³ and blessed is the one who isn't offended by me."

²⁴ After John's messengers left, he began to speak to the crowds about John: "What did you go out into the wilderness to see? A reed swaying in the wind? ²⁵ What then did you go out to see? A man dressed in soft clothes? See, those who are splendidly dressed and live in luxury are in royal palaces. ²⁶ What then did you go out to see? A prophet? Yes, I tell you, and more than a prophet.

²⁷ This is the one about whom it is written: Mt 14:5; Lk 1:76; 20:6

See, I am sending
    my messenger
    ahead of you;
    he will prepare your way
    before you. ^D   Mal 3:1; Mt 11:10

²⁸ I tell you, among those born of women no one is greater than John,^E but the least in the kingdom of God is greater than he."

²⁹ (And when all the people, including the tax collectors, heard this, they acknowledged God's way of righteousness, because they had been baptized with John's baptism. ³⁰ But since the Pharisees and experts in the law had not been baptized by him, they rejected the plan of God for themselves.)   Mt 21:32; Lk 3:12

An Unresponsive Generation

³¹ "To what then should I compare the people of this generation, and what are they like? ³² They are like children sitting in the marketplace and calling to each other:

We played the flute for you,
    but you didn't dance;
    we sang a lament,
    but you didn't weep!

³³ For John the Baptist did not come eating bread or drinking wine, and you say, 'He has a demon!' ³⁴ The Son of Man has come eating and drinking, and you say, 'Look, a glutton and a drunkard, a friend of tax collectors and sinners!' ³⁵ Yet wisdom is vindicated by all her children."   Mt 9:10-11; Lk 1:15; 15:2; 19:7

Much Forgiveness, Much Love

³⁶ Then one of the Pharisees invited him to eat with him. He entered the Pharisee's house and reclined

---

^A 7:16 Or awe   ^B 7:16 Or come to help   ^C 7:22 Gk lepros ; a term for various skin diseases; see Lv 13–14
^D 7:27 Mal 3:1   ^E 7:28 Other mss read women is not a greater prophet than John the Baptist

at the table. ³⁷ And a woman in the town who was a sinner found out that Jesus was reclining at the table in the Pharisee's house. She brought an alabaster jar of perfume ³⁸ and stood behind him at his feet, weeping, and began to wash his feet with her tears. She wiped his feet with her hair, kissing them and anointing them with the perfume. Mt 26:6-13; Lk 11:37; 14:1; Jn 11:2

³⁹ When the Pharisee who had invited him saw this, he said to himself, "This man, if he were a prophet, would know who and what kind of woman this is who is touching him — she's a sinner!" ⁴⁰ Jesus replied to him, "Simon, I have something to say to you."

He said, "Say it, teacher."

⁴¹ "A creditor had two debtors. One owed five hundred denarii,^A and the other fifty. ⁴² Since they could not pay it back, he graciously forgave them both. So, which of them will love him more?" Mt 18:28

⁴³ Simon answered, "I suppose the one he forgave more."

"You have judged correctly," he told him. ⁴⁴ Turning to the woman, he said to Simon, "Do you see this woman? I entered your house; you gave me no water for my feet, but she, with her tears, has washed my feet and wiped them with her hair. ⁴⁵ You gave me no kiss, but she hasn't stopped kissing my feet since I came in. ⁴⁶ You didn't anoint my head with olive oil, but she has anointed my feet with perfume. ⁴⁷ Therefore I tell you, her many sins have been forgiven; that's why she loved much. But the one who is forgiven little, loves little." ⁴⁸ Then he said to her, "Your sins are forgiven." Gn 18:4; 19:2; 43:24; Jdg 19:21; 1Tm 5:10

^A**7:41** A denarius = one day's wage

⁴⁹ Those who were at the table with him began to say among themselves, "Who is this man who even forgives sins?" Lk 5:21

⁵⁰ And he said to the woman, "Your faith has saved you. Go in peace." 1Sm 1:17; Mt 9:22; Mk 10:52; Lk 17:19; 18:42

Many Women Support Christ's Work

8 Afterward he was traveling from one town and village to another, preaching and telling the good news of the kingdom of God. The Twelve were with him, ² and also some women who had been healed of evil spirits and sicknesses: Mary, called Magdalene (seven demons had come out of her); ³ Joanna the wife of Chuza, Herod's steward; Susanna; and many others who were supporting them from their possessions. Mt 4:23; Mk 6:6; Lk 4:43

The Parable of the Sower

⁴ As a large crowd was gathering, and people were coming to Jesus from every town, he said in a parable: ⁵ "A sower went out to sow his seed. As he sowed, some seed fell along the path; it was trampled on, and the birds of the sky devoured it. ⁶ Other seed fell on the rock; when it grew up, it withered away, since it lacked moisture. ⁷ Other seed fell among thorns; the thorns grew up with it and choked it. ⁸ Still other seed fell on good ground; when it grew up, it produced fruit: a hundred times what was sown." As he said this, he called out, "Let anyone who has ears to hear listen." Gn 26:12

Why Jesus Used Parables

⁹ Then his disciples asked him, "What does this parable mean?"

10 So he said, "The secrets of the kingdom of God have been given for you to know, but to the rest it is in parables, so that   Mt 13:10-11

**Looking they may not see,
and hearing they may
not understand.** ^A   Is 6:9

The Parable of the Sower Explained

11 "This is the meaning of the parable: The seed is the word of God. 12 The seed along the path are those who have heard and then the devil comes and takes away the word from their hearts, so that they may not believe and be saved. 13 And the seed on the rock are those who, when they hear, receive the word with joy. Having no root, these believe for a while and fall away in a time of testing. 14 As for the seed that fell among thorns, these are the ones who, when they have heard, go on their way and are choked with worries, riches, and pleasures of life, and produce no mature fruit. 15 But the seed in the good ground — these are the ones who, having heard the word with an honest and good heart, hold on to it and by enduring, produce fruit. Mt 13:18-23; Mk 4:13-20; Lk 8:21; 11:28; 1Pt 1:23

Using Your Light

16 "No one, after lighting a lamp, covers it with a basket or puts it under a bed, but puts it on a lampstand so that those who come in may see its light. 17 For nothing is concealed that won't be revealed, and nothing hidden that won't be made known and brought to light. 18 Therefore take care how you listen. For whoever has, more will be given to him; and whoever does not have, even what he thinks he has will be taken away from him."

True Relationships

19 Then his mother and brothers came to him, but they could not meet with him because of the crowd. 20 He was told, "Your mother and your brothers are standing outside, wanting to see you." Mt 13:55

21 But he replied to them, "My mother and my brothers are those who hear and do the word of God."

Wind and Wave Obey Jesus

22 One day he and his disciples got into a boat, and he told them, "Let's cross over to the other side of the lake." So they set out, 23 and as they were sailing he fell asleep. Then a fierce windstorm came down on the lake; they were being swamped and were in danger. 24 They came and woke him up, saying, "Master, Master, we're going to die!"

Then he got up and rebuked the wind and the raging waves. So they ceased, and there was a calm. 25 He said to them, "Where is your faith?"

They were fearful and amazed, asking one another, "Who then is this? He commands even the winds and the waves, and they obey him!" Mt 21:10; Lk 1:66; 5:21; 7:49; 9:9

Demons Driven Out by Jesus

26 Then they sailed to the region of the Gerasenes, ^B which is opposite Galilee. 27 When he got out on land, a demon-possessed man from the town met him. For a long time he had worn no clothes and did not stay in a house but in the tombs. 28 When he saw Jesus, he cried out, fell down before him, and said in a loud voice, "What do

^A 8:10 Is 6:9   ^B 8:26 Other mss read *the Gadarenes*

you have to do with me, Jesus, Son of the Most High God? I beg you, don't torment me!" [29] For he had commanded the unclean spirit to come out of the man. Many times it had seized him, and though he was guarded, bound by chains and shackles, he would snap the restraints and be driven by the demon into deserted places.

[30] "What is your name?" Jesus asked him.

"Legion," he said, because many demons had entered him. [31] And they begged him not to banish them to the abyss.   Ps 140:10; Mt 26:53

[32] A large herd of pigs was there, feeding on the hillside. The demons begged him to permit them to enter the pigs, and he gave them permission. [33] The demons came out of the man and entered the pigs, and the herd rushed down the steep bank into the lake and drowned.

[34] When the men who tended them saw what had happened, they ran off and reported it in the town and in the countryside. [35] Then people went out to see what had happened. They came to Jesus and found the man the demons had departed from, sitting at Jesus's feet, dressed and in his right mind. And they were afraid. [36] Meanwhile, the eyewitnesses reported to them how the demon-possessed man was delivered. [37] Then all the people of the Gerasene region[A] asked him to leave them, because they were gripped by great fear. So getting into the boat, he returned.   Lk 5:8; 8:41; 10:39

[38] The man from whom the demons had departed begged him earnestly to be with him. But he sent him away and said, [39] "Go back to your home, and tell all that God has done for you." And off he went, proclaiming throughout the town how much Jesus had done for him.

A Girl Restored and a Woman Healed

[40] When Jesus returned, the crowd welcomed him, for they were all expecting him. [41] Just then, a man named Jairus came. He was a leader of the synagogue. He fell down at Jesus's feet and pleaded with him to come to his house, [42] because he had an only daughter about twelve years old, and she was dying. Lk 9:11

While he was going, the crowds were nearly crushing him. [43] A woman suffering from bleeding for twelve years, who had spent all she had on doctors[B] and yet could not be healed by any, [44] approached from behind and touched the end of his robe. Instantly her bleeding stopped.   Lv 15:25; Mt 9:20-22; Mk 3:9; 5:25-34

[45] "Who touched me?" Jesus asked.

When they all denied it, Peter[C] said, "Master, the crowds are hemming you in and pressing against you."[D]   Lk 5:5

[46] "Someone did touch me," said Jesus. "I know that power has gone out from me." [47] When the woman saw that she was discovered, she came trembling and fell down before him. In the presence of all the people, she declared the reason she had touched him and how she was instantly healed. [48] "Daughter," he said to her, "your faith has saved you.[E] Go in peace." Lk 5:17; 6:19; Ac 10:38

[A]8:37 Other mss read the Gadarenes   [B]8:43 Other mss omit who had spent all she had on doctors
[C]8:45 Other mss add and those with him   [D]8:45 Other mss add and you say, 'Who touched me?'
[E]8:48 Or has made you well

[49] While he was still speaking, someone came from the synagogue leader's house and said, "Your daughter is dead. Don't bother the teacher anymore." Mt 9:23-26

[50] When Jesus heard it, he answered him, "Don't be afraid. Only believe, and she will be saved."[A] [51] After he came to the house, he let no one enter with him except Peter, John, James, and the child's father and mother. [52] Everyone was crying and mourning for her. But he said, "Stop crying, because she is not dead but asleep." Mk 3:17; 14:33

[53] They laughed at him, because they knew she was dead. [54] So he[B] took her by the hand and called out, "Child, get up!" [55] Her spirit returned, and she got up at once. Then he gave orders that she be given something to eat. [56] Her parents were astounded, but he instructed them to tell no one what had happened. Mt 11:5; Mk 1:31; Lk 7:14,22; Jn 11:43

Commissioning the Twelve

9 Summoning the Twelve, he gave them power and authority over all the demons and to heal diseases. [2] Then he sent them to proclaim the kingdom of God and to heal the sick. Mt 10:1,5,7-8; Mk 3:13-15; 6:7; Lk 6:12-16

[3] "Take nothing for the road," he told them, "no staff, no traveling bag, no bread, no money; and don't take an extra shirt. [4] Whatever house you enter, stay there and leave from there. [5] If they do not welcome you, when you leave that town, shake off the dust from your feet as a testimony against them." [6] So they went out and traveled from village to village, proclaiming the good news and healing everywhere. Mt 10:9-15

Herod's Desire to See Jesus

[7] Herod the tetrarch heard about everything that was going on. He was perplexed, because some said that John had been raised from the dead, [8] some that Elijah had appeared, and others that one of the ancient prophets had risen. [9] "I beheaded John," Herod said, "but who is this I hear such things about?" And he wanted to see him. Lk 3:1,19

Feeding of the Five Thousand

[10] When the apostles returned, they reported to Jesus all that they had done. He took them along and withdrew privately to a[C] town called Bethsaida. [11] When the crowds found out, they followed him. He welcomed them, spoke to them about the kingdom of God, and healed those who needed healing.

[12] Late in the day, the Twelve approached and said to him, "Send the crowd away, so that they can go into the surrounding villages and countryside to find food and lodging, because we are in a deserted place here." Mt 15:23; Lk 24:29

[13] "You give them something to eat," he told them.

"We have no more than five loaves and two fish," they said, "unless we go and buy food for all these people." [14] (For about five thousand men were there.) Mt 16:9; Mk 8:19

Then he told his disciples, "Have them sit down[D] in groups of about fifty each." [15] They did what he said, and had them all sit down. [16] Then he took the five loaves and the two fish, and looking up to heaven, he blessed and broke them. He kept giving them to the disciples to set before the crowd.

[A]8:50 Or she will be made well   [B]8:54 Other mss add having put them all outside   [C]9:10 Other mss add deserted place near a   [D]9:14 Lit them recline

[17] Everyone ate and was filled. They picked up twelve baskets of left-over pieces. Mt 26:26; Mk 7:34; Jn 11:41; 17:1

Peter's Confession of the Messiah

[18] While he was praying in private and his disciples were with him, he asked them, "Who do the crowds say that I am?" Mt 16:13-16; Mk 8:27-29 [19] They answered, "John the Baptist; others, Elijah; still others, that one of the ancient prophets has come back."[A] Lk 9:7-8 [20] "But you," he asked them, "who do you say that I am?"

Peter answered, "God's Messiah."

His Death and Resurrection Predicted

[21] But he strictly warned and instructed them to tell this to no one, [22] saying, "It is necessary that the Son of Man suffer many things and be rejected by the elders, chief priests, and scribes, be killed, and be raised the third day." Mt 12:16; 16:20

Take Up Your Cross

[23] Then he said to them all, "If anyone wants to follow after[B] me, let him deny himself, take up his cross daily,[C] and follow me. [24] For whoever wants to save his life will lose it, but whoever loses his life because of me will save it. [25] For what does it benefit someone if he gains the whole world, and yet loses or forfeits himself? [26] For whoever is ashamed of me and my words, the Son of Man will be ashamed of him when he comes in his glory and that of the Father and the holy angels. [27] Truly I tell you, there are some standing here who will not taste death until they see the kingdom of God." Mt 10:38-39; 23:36; Lk 14:27; 2Tm 2:12-13

The Transfiguration

[28] About eight days after this conversation, he took along Peter, John, and James and went up on the mountain to pray. [29] As he was praying, the appearance of his face changed, and his clothes became dazzling white. [30] Suddenly, two men were talking with him — Moses and Elijah. [31] They appeared in glory and were speaking of his departure, which he was about to accomplish in Jerusalem. Mt 17:1-8 [32] Peter and those with him were in a deep sleep,[D] and when they became fully awake, they saw his glory and the two men who were standing with him. [33] As the two men were departing from him, Peter said to Jesus, "Master, it's good for us to be here. Let us set up three shelters: one for you, one for Moses, and one for Elijah" — not knowing what he was saying. [34] While he was saying this, a cloud appeared and overshadowed them. They became afraid as they entered the cloud. [35] Then a voice came from the cloud, saying: "This is my Son, the Chosen One;[E] listen to him!" Ex 24:15-16; Lk 1:35; Ac 5:15; 2Pt 1:16-18 [36] After the voice had spoken, Jesus was found alone. They kept silent, and at that time told no one what they had seen.

The Power of Jesus over a Demon

[37] The next day, when they came down from the mountain, a large crowd met him. [38] Just then a man from the crowd cried out, "Teacher, I beg you to look at my son, because

he's my only child. ³⁹ A spirit seizes him; suddenly he shrieks, and it throws him into convulsions until he foams at the mouth; severely bruising him, it scarcely ever leaves him. ⁴⁰ I begged your disciples to drive it out, but they couldn't."

⁴¹ Jesus replied, "You unbelieving and perverse^A generation, how long will I be with you and put up with you? Bring your son here."

⁴² As the boy was still approaching, the demon knocked him down and threw him into severe convulsions. But Jesus rebuked the unclean spirit, healed the boy, and gave him back to his father. ⁴³ And they were all astonished at the greatness of God. Zch 3:2; Mt 8:26; Mk 1:25

The Second Prediction of His Death

While everyone was amazed at all the things he was doing, he told his disciples, ⁴⁴ "Let these words sink in:^B The Son of Man is about to be betrayed into the hands of men."

⁴⁵ But they did not understand this statement; it was concealed from them so that they could not grasp it, and they were afraid to ask him about it. Mk 6:52; Lk 2:50; 18:34

Who Is the Greatest?

⁴⁶ An argument started among them about who was the greatest of them. ⁴⁷ But Jesus, knowing their inner thoughts,^C took a little child and had him stand next to him. ⁴⁸ He told them, "Whoever welcomes^D this little child in my name welcomes me. And whoever

welcomes me welcomes him who sent me. For whoever is least among you — this one is great."

In His Name

⁴⁹ John responded, "Master, we saw someone driving out demons in your name, and we tried to stop him because he does not follow us."

⁵⁰ "Don't stop him," Jesus told him, "because whoever is not against you is for you."^E Mt 12:30

The Journey to Jerusalem

⁵¹ When the days were coming to a close for him to be taken up, he determined^F to journey to Jerusalem. ⁵² He sent messengers ahead of himself, and on the way they entered a village of the Samaritans to make preparations for him. ⁵³ But they did not welcome him, because he determined to journey to Jerusalem. ⁵⁴ When the disciples James and John saw this, they said, "Lord, do you want us to call down fire from heaven to consume them?"^G

⁵⁵ But he turned and rebuked them,^H ⁵⁶ and they went to another village.

Following Jesus

⁵⁷ As they were traveling on the road someone said to him, "I will follow you wherever you go."

⁵⁸ Jesus told him, "Foxes have dens, and birds of the sky have nests, but the Son of Man has no place to lay his head." ⁵⁹ Then he said to another, "Follow me."

"Lord," he said, "first let me go bury my father."

---

^A 9:41 Or corrupt, or perverted, or twisted; Dt 32:5   ^B 9:44 Lit "Put these words in your ears   ^C 9:47 Lit the thoughts of their hearts   ^D 9:48 Or receives, throughout the verse   ^E 9:50 Other mss read against us is for us   ^F 9:51 Lit he stiffened his face to go; Is 50:7   ^G 9:54 Other mss add as Elijah also did
^H 9:55-56 Other mss add and said, "You don't know what kind of spirit you belong to. ⁵⁶ For the Son of Man did not come to destroy people's lives but to save them,"

⁶⁰ But he told him, "Let the dead bury their own dead, but you go and spread the news of the kingdom of God." Lk 8:1; 9:2; 16:16

⁶¹ Another said, "I will follow you, Lord, but first let me go and say good-bye to those at my house."

⁶² But Jesus said to him, "No one who puts his hand to the plow and looks back is fit for the kingdom of God."

Sending Out the Seventy-Two

10 After this, the Lord appointed seventy-two ᴬ others, and he sent them ahead of him in pairs to every town and place where he himself was about to go. ² He told them, "The harvest is abundant, but the workers are few. Therefore, pray to the Lord of the harvest to send out workers into his harvest. ³ Now go; I'm sending you out like lambs among wolves. ⁴ Don't carry a money-bag, traveling bag, or sandals; don't greet anyone along the road. ⁵ Whatever house you enter, first say, 'Peace to this household.' ⁶ If a person of peace is there, your peace will rest on him; but if not, it will return to you. ⁷ Remain in the same house, eating and drinking what they offer, for the worker is worthy of his wages. Don't move from house to house. ⁸ When you enter any town, and they welcome you, eat the things set before you. ⁹ Heal the sick who are there, and tell them, 'The kingdom of God has come near you.' ¹⁰ When you enter any town, and they don't welcome you, go out into its streets and say, ¹¹ 'We are wiping off even the dust of your town that clings to our feet as a witness against you. Know this

for certain: The kingdom of God has come near.' ¹² I tell you, on that day it will be more tolerable for Sodom than for that town. Mt 9:37-38; Jn 4:35

Unrepentant Towns

¹³ "Woe to you, Chorazin! Woe to you, Bethsaida! For if the miracles that were done in you had been done in Tyre and Sidon, they would have repented long ago, sitting in sackcloth and ashes. ¹⁴ But it will be more tolerable for Tyre and Sidon at the judgment than for you. ¹⁵ And you, Capernaum, will you be exalted to heaven? No, you will go down to Hades. ¹⁶ Whoever listens to you listens to me. Whoever rejects you rejects me. And whoever rejects me rejects the one who sent me." Ezk 16:23; Mt 11:20-24; 23:13-16

The Return of the Seventy-Two

¹⁷ The seventy-two ᴮ returned with joy, saying, "Lord, even the demons submit to us in your name." Ezk 8:11

¹⁸ He said to them, "I watched Satan fall from heaven like lightning. ¹⁹ Look, I have given you the authority to trample on snakes and scorpions and over all the power of the enemy; nothing at all will harm you. ²⁰ However, don't rejoice that ᶜ the spirits submit to you, but rejoice that your names are written in heaven." Mt 4:1,10; Ac 13:10; Rv 12:9

The Son Reveals the Father

²¹ At that time he ᴰ rejoiced in the Holy ᴱ Spirit and said, "I praise ᶠ you, Father, Lord of heaven and earth, because you have hidden these things from the wise and intelligent and revealed them to infants. Yes, Father, because this was

---

ᴬ**10:1** Other mss read *seventy*   ᴮ**10:17** Other mss read *The seventy*   ᶜ**10:20** Lit *don't rejoice in this, that*
ᴰ**10:21** Other mss read *Jesus*   ᴱ**10:21** Other mss omit *Holy*   ᶠ**10:21** Or *thank*, or *confess*

your good pleasure.[A] [22] All things have[B] been entrusted to me by my Father. No one knows who the Son is except the Father, and who the Father is except the Son, and anyone to whom the Son desires[C] to reveal him."   Mt 11:25-27; 13:16-17; Lk 2:27; 4:1

[23] Then turning to his disciples he said privately, "Blessed are the eyes that see the things you see! [24] For I tell you that many prophets and kings wanted to see the things you see but didn't see them; to hear the things you hear but didn't hear them."   Jn 8:56; Heb 11:13; 1Pt 1:10-12

The Parable of the Good Samaritan

[25] Then an expert in the law stood up to test him, saying, "Teacher, what must I do to inherit eternal life?"   Mt 16:1; 22:34-40; Mk 12:28-34; Lk 7:30

[26] "What is written in the law?" he asked him. "How do you read it?"

[27] He answered, "Love the Lord your God with all your heart, with all your soul, with all your strength, and with all your mind;" and "your neighbor as yourself."[D]

[28] "You've answered correctly," he told him. "Do this and you will live."

[29] But wanting to justify himself, he asked Jesus, "And who is my neighbor?"   Ex 20:16-17; Lv 6:2; Lk 16:15

[30] Jesus took up the question and said: "A man was going down from Jerusalem to Jericho and fell into the hands of robbers. They stripped him, beat him up, and fled, leaving him half dead. [31] A priest happened to be going down that road. When he saw him, he passed by on the other side. [32] In the same way, a Levite, when he arrived at the place and saw him, passed by on the other side. [33] But a Samaritan on his journey came up to him, and when he saw the man, he had compassion. [34] He went over to him and bandaged his wounds, pouring on olive oil and wine. Then he put him on his own animal, brought him to an inn, and took care of him. [35] The next day[E] he took out two denarii,[F] gave them to the innkeeper, and said, 'Take care of him. When I come back I'll reimburse you for whatever extra you spend.'   Mt 10:5

[36] "Which of these three do you think proved to be a neighbor to the man who fell into the hands of the robbers?"

[37] "The one who showed mercy to him," he said.   Mt 23:23; Lk 1:72; Jms 2:13

Then Jesus told him, "Go and do the same."

Martha and Mary

[38] While they were traveling, he entered a village, and a woman named Martha welcomed him into her home.[G] [39] She had a sister named Mary, who also sat at the Lord's[H] feet and was listening to what he said.[I] [40] But Martha was distracted by her many tasks, and she came up and asked, "Lord, don't you care that my sister has left me to serve alone? So tell her to give me a hand."[J]   Lk 8:35; Jn 11:1,19-20; 12:2-3

[41] The Lord[K] answered her, "Martha, Martha, you are worried and upset about many things, [42] but one thing is necessary.[L] Mary has made

---

[A]10:21 Lit *was well-pleasing in your sight*   [B]10:22 Other mss read *And turning to the disciples, he said, "Everything has*   [C]10:22 Or *wills*, or *chooses*   [D]10:27 Lv 19:18; Dt 6:5   [E]10:35 Other mss add *as he was leaving*   [F]10:35 A denarius = one day's wage.   [G]10:38 Other mss omit *into her home*   [H]10:39 Other mss read *at Jesus's*   [I]10:39 Lit *to his word*, or *message*   [J]10:40 Or *tell her to help me*   [K]10:41 Other mss read *Jesus*   [L]10:42 Some mss read *few things are necessary*, or *only one* the right choice,[A] and it will not be taken away from her." Lk 12:22; 1Co 7:32

The Lord's Prayer

11 He was praying in a certain place, and when he finished, one of his disciples said to him, "Lord, teach us to pray, just as John also taught his disciples." Lk 3:21

[2] He said to them, "Whenever you pray, say, Mt 6:9-13

Father,[B] Jn 20:17; 1Pt 1:17
your name be honored
as holy. Ps 9:10; Is 29:23; Jn 10:25; 17:6
Your kingdom come.[C] Mk 9:1
[3] Give us each day
our daily bread.[D] Pr 30:8
[4] And forgive us our sins, Lk 6:12
for we ourselves also
forgive everyone
in debt to us.[E] Mt 18:23-35
And do not bring us
into temptation."[F] Mt 26:41

Ask, Search, Knock

[5] He also said to them: "Suppose one of you[G] has a friend and goes to him at midnight and says to him, 'Friend, lend me three loaves of bread, [6] because a friend of mine on a journey has come to me, and I don't have anything to offer him.' [7] Then he will answer from inside and say, 'Don't bother me! The door is already locked, and my children and I have gone to bed. I can't get up to give you anything.' [8] I tell you, even though he won't get up and give him anything because he is his friend, yet because of his friend's shameless boldness,[H] he will get up and give him as much as he needs.

[9] "So I say to you, ask, and it will be given to you. Seek, and you will find. Knock, and the door will be opened to you. [10] For everyone who asks receives, and the one who seeks finds, and to the one who knocks, the door will be opened. [11] What father among you, if his son[I] asks for a fish, will give him a snake instead of a fish? [12] Or if he asks for an egg, will give him a scorpion? [13] If you then, who are evil, know how to give good gifts to your children, how much more will the heavenly Father give the Holy Spirit to those who ask him?" Mt 7:7-11; Jn 14:13-14; 15:7

A House Divided

[14] Now he was driving out a demon that was mute. When the demon came out, the man who had been mute spoke, and the crowds were amazed. [15] But some of them said, "He drives out demons by Beelzebul, the ruler of the demons." [16] And others, as a test, were demanding of him a sign from heaven.

[17] Knowing their thoughts, he told them, "Every kingdom divided against itself is headed for destruction, and a house divided against itself falls. [18] If Satan also is divided against himself, how will his kingdom stand? For you say I drive out demons by Beelzebul. [19] And if I drive out demons by Beelzebul, by whom do your sons drive them out? For this reason they will be your judges. [20] If I drive out demons by the finger of God, then the kingdom of God has come upon you. [21] When a strong man, fully

---

[A]**10:42** Lit *has chosen the good part*, or *has chosen the better portion* ; = the right meal   [B]**11:2** Other mss read *Our Father in heaven*   [C]**11:2** Other mss add *Your will be done on earth as it is in heaven*   [D]**11:3** Or *our bread for tomorrow*   [E]**11:4** Or *everyone who wrongs us*   [F]**11:4** Other mss add *But deliver us from the evil one*   [G]**11:5** Lit *Who of you*   [H]**11:8** Or *persistence*   [I]**11:11** Other mss read *son asks for bread, would give him a stone? Or if he* armed, guards his estate, his possessions are secure. ²² But when one stronger than he attacks and overpowers him, he takes from him all his weapons^A he trusted in, and divides up his plunder. ²³ Anyone who is not with me is against me, and anyone who does not gather with me scatters. Dn 5:28; Lk 5:22

An Unclean Spirit's Return

²⁴ "When an unclean spirit comes out of a person, it roams through waterless places looking for rest, and not finding rest, it then^B says, 'I'll go back to my house that I came from.' ²⁵ Returning, it finds the house swept and put in order. ²⁶ Then it goes and brings seven other spirits more evil than itself, and they enter and settle down there. As a result, that person's last condition is worse than the first."

True Blessedness

²⁷ As he was saying these things, a woman from the crowd raised her voice and said to him, "Blessed is the womb that bore you and the one who nursed you!" Lk 1:48; 12:3

²⁸ He said, "Rather, blessed are those who hear the word of God and keep it." Lk 5:1; 8:21; Ac 13:7; Rv 22:7

The Sign of Jonah

²⁹ As the crowds were increasing, he began saying: "This generation is an evil generation. It demands a sign, but no sign will be given to it except the sign of Jonah.^C ³⁰ For just as Jonah became a sign to the people of Nineveh, so also the Son of Man will be to this generation. ³¹ The queen of the south will rise up at the judgment with the men of this generation and condemn them, because she came from the ends of the earth to hear the wisdom of Solomon, and look — something greater than Solomon is here. ³² The men of Nineveh will stand up at the judgment with this generation and condemn it, because they repented at Jonah's preaching, and look — something greater than Jonah is here. Lk 7:31

The Lamp of the Body

³³ "No one lights a lamp and puts it in the cellar or under a basket,^D but on a lampstand, so that those who come in may see its light. ³⁴ Your eye is the lamp of the body. When your eye is healthy, your whole body is also full of light. But when it is bad, your body is also full of darkness. ³⁵ Take care, then, that the light in you is not darkness. ³⁶ If, therefore, your whole body is full of light, with no part of it in darkness, it will be entirely illuminated, as when a lamp shines its light on you." Jr 24:8; Mt 5:15; 6:22; Mk 4:21; Lk 8:16

Religious Hypocrisy Denounced

³⁷ As he was speaking, a Pharisee asked him to dine with him. So he went in and reclined at the table. ³⁸ When the Pharisee saw this, he was amazed that he did not first perform the ritual washing^E before dinner. ³⁹ But the Lord said to him, "Now you Pharisees clean the outside of the cup and dish, but inside you are full of greed and evil. ⁴⁰ Fools! Didn't he who made the outside make the inside too? ⁴¹ But give from what is within

to the poor,[A] and then everything is clean for you.   Mt 15:2; Lk 7:36; Heb 6:2

[42] "But woe to you Pharisees! You give a tenth[B] of mint, rue, and every kind of herb, and you bypass[C] justice and love for God.[D] These things you should have done without neglecting the others.   Lk 10:13

[43] "Woe to you Pharisees! You love the front seat in the synagogues and greetings in the marketplaces.

[44] "Woe to you![E] You are like unmarked graves; the people who walk over them don't know it."

[45] One of the experts in the law answered him, "Teacher, when you say these things you insult us too."

[46] Then he said: "Woe also to you experts in the law! You load people with burdens that are hard to carry, and yet you yourselves don't touch these burdens with one of your fingers.   Mt 23:4; Ac 15:10; 27:10; Gl 6:5

[47] "Woe to you! You build tombs[F] for the prophets, and your fathers killed them. [48] Therefore, you are witnesses that you approve[G] the deeds of your fathers, for they killed them, and you build their monuments. [H] [49] Because of this, the wisdom of God said, 'I will send them prophets and apostles, and some of them they will kill and persecute,' [50] so that this generation may be held responsible for the blood of all the prophets shed since the foundation of the world[I] — [51] from the blood of Abel to the blood of Zechariah, who perished between the altar and the sanctuary.   Mt 23:35; Ac 7:52

"Yes, I tell you, this generation will be held responsible.[J]

[52] "Woe to you experts in the law! You have taken away the key to knowledge. You didn't go in yourselves, and you hindered those who were trying to go in."   1Co 14:6,39

[53] When he left there,[K] the scribes and the Pharisees began to oppose him fiercely and to cross-examine him about many things; [54] they were lying in wait for him to trap him in something he said.[L]   Mk 6:19

Beware of Religious Hypocrisy

12 Meanwhile, a crowd of many thousands came together, so that they were trampling on one another. He began to say to his disciples first, "Be on your guard against the leaven[M] of the Pharisees, which is hypocrisy. [2] There is nothing covered that won't be uncovered, nothing hidden that won't be made known. [3] Therefore, whatever you have said in the dark will be heard in the light, and what you have whispered in an ear in private rooms will be proclaimed on the housetops.   Jr 9:4; Mt 16:5-6; Mk 8:14-15; Lk 8:5

Fear God

[4] "I say to you, my friends, don't fear those who kill the body, and after that can do nothing more. [5] But I will show you the one to fear: Fear him who has authority to throw people into hell after death. Yes, I say to you, this is the one to fear! [6] Aren't five sparrows sold for two pennies?[N] Yet not one of them is

---

[A] **11:41** Or *But donate from the heart as charity*   [B] **11:42** Or *a tithe*   [C] **11:42** Or *neglect*   [D] **11:42** Lit *the justice and the love of God*   [E] **11:44** Other mss add *scribes and Pharisees, hypocrites!*   [F] **11:47** Or *graves*   [G] **11:48** Lit *witnesses and approve*   [H] **11:48** Other mss omit *their monuments*   [I] **11:50** Lit *so that the blood of all . . . world may be required of this generation,*   [J] **11:51** Lit *you, it will be required of this generation*   [K] **11:53** Other mss read *And as he was saying these things to them*   [L] **11:54** Other mss add *so that they might bring charges against him*   [M] **12:1** Or *yeast*   [N] **12:6** Lit *two assaria*; a small copper coin forgotten in God's sight. [7] Indeed, the hairs of your head are all counted. Don't be afraid; you are worth more than many sparrows.   Ac 27:3

Acknowledging Christ

[8] "And I say to you, anyone who acknowledges me before others, the Son of Man will also acknowledge him before the angels of God, [9] but whoever denies me before others will be denied before the angels of God. [10] Anyone who speaks a word against the Son of Man will be forgiven, but the one who blasphemes against the Holy Spirit will not be forgiven. [11] Whenever they bring you before synagogues and rulers and authorities, don't worry about how you should defend yourselves or what you should say. [12] For the Holy Spirit will teach you at that very hour what must be said."   Mt 7:23; Lk 5:24; 11:30; 15:10; Jn 9:22

The Parable of the Rich Fool

[13] Someone from the crowd said to him, "Teacher, tell my brother to divide the inheritance with me."

[14] "Friend,"[A] he said to him, "who appointed me a judge or arbitrator over you?" [15] He then told them, "Watch out and be on guard against all greed, because one's life is not in the abundance of his possessions."   1Tm 6:20; 2Tm 1:14; 4:15

[16] Then he told them a parable: "A rich man's land was very productive. [17] He thought to himself, 'What should I do, since I don't have anywhere to store my crops? [18] I will do this,' he said. 'I'll tear down my barns and build bigger ones and store all my grain and my goods there. [19] Then I'll say to myself, "You have many goods stored up

for many years. Take it easy; eat, drink, and enjoy yourself."'   Lk 5:36

[20] "But God said to him, 'You fool! This very night your life is demanded of you. And the things you have prepared — whose will they be?'   Ps 39:6; 49:10; Jr 17:11; Lk 11:40

[21] "That's how it is with the one who stores up treasure for himself and is not rich toward God."

The Cure for Anxiety

[22] Then he said to his disciples: "Therefore I tell you, don't worry about your life, what you will eat; or about the body, what you will wear. [23] For life is more than food and the body more than clothing. [24] Consider the ravens: They don't sow or reap; they don't have a storeroom or a barn; yet God feeds them. Aren't you worth much more than the birds? [25] Can any of you add one moment to his life-span[B] by worrying? [26] If then you're not able to do even a little thing, why worry about the rest?   Mt 6:25-34

[27] "Consider how the wildflowers grow: They don't labor or spin thread. Yet I tell you, not even Solomon in all his splendor was adorned like one of these. [28] If that's how God clothes the grass, which is in the field today and is thrown into the furnace tomorrow, how much more will he do for you — you of little faith? [29] Don't strive for what you should eat and what you should drink, and don't be anxious. [30] For the Gentile world eagerly seeks all these things, and your Father knows that you need them.   1Kg 10:4-7; Mt 8:26; 14:31; 16:8; Heb 11:14

[31] "But seek his kingdom, and these things will be provided for you. [32] Don't be afraid, little flock,

[A]12:14 Lit Man   [B]12:25 Or add a cubit to his height

because your Father delights to give you the kingdom. ³³ Sell your possessions and give to the poor. Make money-bags for yourselves that won't grow old, an inexhaustible treasure in heaven, where no thief comes near and no moth destroys. ³⁴ For where your treasure is, there your heart will be also.

Ready for the Master's Return

³⁵ "Be ready for service ᴬ and have your lamps lit. ³⁶ You are to be like people waiting for their master to return from the wedding banquet so that when he comes and knocks, they can open the door for him at once. ³⁷ Blessed will be those servants the master finds alert when he comes. Truly I tell you, he will get ready, ᴮ have them recline at the table, then come and serve them. ³⁸ If he comes in the middle of the night, or even near dawn, ᶜ and finds them alert, blessed are those servants. ³⁹ But know this: If the homeowner had known at what hour the thief was coming, he would not have let his house be broken into. ⁴⁰ You also be ready, because the Son of Man is coming at an hour you do not expect." Mt 24:42-51; 25:1-13; Mk 13:33-37

Rewards and Punishment

⁴¹ "Lord," Peter asked, "are you telling this parable to us or to everyone?"

⁴² The Lord said: "Who then is the faithful and sensible manager his master will put in charge of his household servants to give them their allotted food at the proper time? ⁴³ Blessed is that servant whom the master finds doing his job when he comes. ⁴⁴ Truly I tell you, he will put him in charge of all his possessions. ⁴⁵ But if that servant says in his heart, 'My master is delaying his coming,' and starts to beat the male and female servants, and to eat and drink and get drunk, ⁴⁶ that servant's master will come on a day he does not expect him and at an hour he does not know. He will cut him to pieces ᴰ and assign him a place with the unfaithful. ᴱ ⁴⁷ And that servant who knew his master's will and didn't prepare himself or do it ᶠ will be severely beaten. ⁴⁸ But the one who did not know and did what deserved punishment will receive a light beating. From everyone who has been given much, much will be required; and from the one who has been entrusted with much, even more will be expected. ᴳ Dt 25:2; Lk 16:1; 1 Tm 6:8; 1 Jn 2:28

Not Peace but Division

⁴⁹ "I came to bring fire on the earth, and how I wish it were already set ablaze! ⁵⁰ But I have a baptism to undergo, and how it consumes me until it is finished! ⁵¹ Do you think that I came here to bring peace on the earth? No, I tell you, but rather division. ⁵² From now on, five in one household will be divided: three against two, and two against three.

⁵³ They will be divided, father
  against son,
 son against father,
 mother against daughter,
 daughter against mother,
 mother-in-law against
  her daughter-in-law,
 and daughter-in-law
  against mother-in-law." ᴴ

ᴬ**12:35** Lit *"Let your loins be girded* ; an idiom for tying up loose outer clothing in preparation for action;
Ex 12:11   ᴮ**12:37** Lit *will gird himself*   ᶜ**12:38** Lit *even in the second or third watch*   ᴰ**12:46** Lit *him in two*   ᴱ**12:46** Or *unbelievers*   ᶠ**12:47** Lit *or do toward his will*,   ᴳ**12:48** Or *much*   ᴴ**12:53** Mc 7:6

Interpreting the Time

⁵⁴ He also said to the crowds: "When you see a cloud rising in the west, right away you say, 'A storm is coming,' and so it does. ⁵⁵ And when the south wind is blowing, you say, 'It's going to be hot,' and it is. ⁵⁶ Hypocrites! You know how to interpret the appearance of the earth and the sky, but why don't you know how to interpret this present time?   1Kg 18:43-44; Mt 16:2-3

Settling Accounts

⁵⁷ "Why don't you judge for yourselves what is right? ⁵⁸ As you are going with your adversary to the ruler, make an effort to settle with him on the way. Then he won't drag you before the judge, the judge hand you over to the bailiff, and the bailiff throw you into prison. ⁵⁹ I tell you, you will never get out of there until you have paid the last cent." ᴬ   Pr 25:8; Mt 5:25-26; Lk 21:2; 2Tm 4:8; 1Pt 5:8

Repent or Perish

13 At that time, some people came and reported to him about the Galileans whose blood Pilate had mixed with their sacrifices. ² And he ᴮ responded to them, "Do you think that these Galileans were more sinful than all the other Galileans because they suffered these things? ³ No, I tell you; but unless you repent, you will all perish as well. ⁴ Or those eighteen that the tower in Siloam fell on and killed — do you think they were more sinful than all the other people who live in Jerusalem? ⁵ No, I tell you; but unless you repent, you will all perish as well."   Mt 21:18-19; Mk 11:12-14

The Parable of the Barren Fig Tree

⁶ And he told this parable: "A man had a fig tree that was planted in his vineyard. He came looking for fruit on it and found none. ⁷ He told the vineyard worker, 'Listen, for three years I have come looking for fruit on this fig tree and haven't found any. Cut it down! Why should it even waste the soil?'   Lk 5:35; 12:16

⁸ "But he replied to him, 'Sir, ᶜ leave it this year also, until I dig around it and fertilize it. ⁹ Perhaps it will produce fruit next year, but if not, you can cut it down.' "   Lk 16:3

Healing a Daughter of Abraham

¹⁰ As he was teaching in one of the synagogues on the Sabbath, ¹¹ a woman was there who had been disabled by a spirit ᴰ for over eighteen years. She was bent over and could not straighten up at all. ᴱ ¹² When Jesus saw her, he called out to her, ᶠ "Woman, you are free of your disability." ¹³ Then he laid his hands on her, and instantly she was restored and began to glorify God.   Mt 8:17; Lk 4:31,33; 6:6,18; 7:21; 8:2,29

¹⁴ But the leader of the synagogue, indignant because Jesus had healed on the Sabbath, responded by telling the crowd, "There are six days when work should be done; therefore come on those days and be healed and not on the Sabbath day."   Mt 20:24; 21:15; 26:8; Mk 10:14,41; 14:4

¹⁵ But the Lord answered him and said, "Hypocrites! Doesn't each one of you untie his ox or donkey from the feeding trough on the Sabbath and lead it to water? ¹⁶ Satan has bound this woman, a

---

ᴬ 12:59 Gk *lepton*, the smallest and least valuable copper coin in use   ᴮ 13:2 Other mss read *Jesus*
ᶜ 13:8 Or *Lord*   ᴰ 13:11 Lit *had a spirit of disability*   ᴱ 13:11 Or *straighten up completely*   ᶠ 13:12 Or *he summoned her*

daughter of Abraham, for eighteen years — shouldn't she be untied from this bondage^A on the Sabbath day?" Mt 12:11; Lk 6:42; 14:5,19; 1Co 9:9

^17 When he had said these things, all his adversaries were humiliated, but the whole crowd was rejoicing over all the glorious things he was doing. Lk 21:5; 1Co 16:9; Php 1:28; 1Tm 5:14

The Parables of the Mustard Seed and of the Leaven

^18 He said, therefore, "What is the kingdom of God like, and what can I compare it to? ^19 It's like a mustard seed that a man took and sowed in his garden. It grew and became a tree, and the birds of the sky nested in its branches." Mt 13:31-32

^20 Again he said, "What can I compare the kingdom of God to? ^21 It's like leaven^B that a woman took and mixed into fifty pounds^C of flour until all of it was leavened."

The Narrow Way

^22 He went through one town and village after another, teaching and making his way to Jerusalem. ^23 "Lord," someone asked him, "are only a few people going to be saved?" Mt 22:14; Lk 9:51; 18:26

He said to them, ^24 "Make every effort to enter through the narrow door, because I tell you, many will try to enter and won't be able ^25 once the homeowner gets up and shuts the door. Then you will stand outside and knock on the door, saying, 'Lord, open up for us!' He will answer you, 'I don't know you or where you're from.' ^26 Then you will say, 'We ate and drank in your presence, and you taught in our streets.' ^27 But he will say, 'I tell you, I don't know you or where you're from. Get away from me, all you evildoers!' ^28 There will be weeping and gnashing of teeth in that place, when you see Abraham, Isaac, Jacob, and all the prophets in the kingdom of God, but yourselves thrown out. ^29 They will come from east and west, from north and south, to share the banquet^D in the kingdom of God. ^30 Note this: Some who are last will be first, and some who are first will be last." Mt 7:13-14; 10:33

Jesus and Herod Antipas

^31 At that time some Pharisees came and told him, "Go, get out of here. Herod wants to kill you." Mt 14:1

^32 He said to them, "Go tell that fox, 'Look, I'm driving out demons and performing healings today and tomorrow, and on the third day I will complete my work.'^E ^33 Yet it is necessary that I travel today, tomorrow, and the next day, because it is not possible for a prophet to perish outside of Jerusalem.

Jesus's Lamentation over Jerusalem

^34 "Jerusalem, Jerusalem, who kills the prophets and stones those who are sent to her. How often I wanted to gather your children together, as a hen gathers her chicks under her wings, but you were not willing! ^35 See, your house is abandoned to you. I tell you, you will not see me until the time comes when^F you say, '**Blessed is he who comes in the name of the Lord**'!"^G Mt 23:37-39; Lk 19:41-44; Heb 11:37

---

^A**13:16** Or *isn't it necessary that she be untied from this bondage*   ^B**13:21** Or *yeast*   ^C**13:21** Lit *three sata*; about forty liters   ^D**13:29** Lit *recline at the table*   ^E**13:32** Lit *I will be finished*   ^F**13:35** Other mss omit *the time comes when*   ^G**13:35** Ps 118:26

A Sabbath Controversy

14 One Sabbath, when he went in to eat[A] at the house of one of the leading Pharisees, they were watching him closely. ² There in front of him was a man whose body was swollen with fluid. ³ In response, Jesus asked the law experts and the Pharisees, "Is it lawful to heal on the Sabbath or not?" ⁴ But they kept silent. He took the man, healed him, and sent him away. ⁵ And to them, he said, "Which of you whose son or ox falls into a well, will not immediately pull him out on the Sabbath day?" ⁶ They could find no answer to these things.

Teachings on Humility

⁷ He told a parable to those who were invited, when he noticed how they would choose the best places for themselves: ⁸ "When you are invited by someone to a wedding banquet, don't recline at the best place, because a more distinguished person than you may have been invited by your host. ⁹ The one who invited both of you may come and say to you, 'Give your place to this man,' and then in humiliation, you will proceed to take the lowest place. Lk 5:36; 7:2; 11:43; 13:6; Php 2:29

¹⁰ "But when you are invited, go and recline in the lowest place, so that when the one who invited you comes, he will say to you, 'Friend, move up higher.' You will then be honored in the presence of all the other guests. ¹¹ For everyone who exalts himself will be humbled, and the one who humbles himself will be exalted." Pr 25:6-7; Jn 5:44; 7:18; Rm 2:7

¹² He also said to the one who had invited him, "When you give a lunch or a dinner, don't invite your friends, your brothers or sisters, your relatives, or your rich neighbors, because they might invite you back, and you would be repaid. ¹³ On the contrary, when you host a banquet, invite those who are poor, maimed, lame, or blind. ¹⁴ And you will be blessed, because they cannot repay you; for you will be repaid at the resurrection of the righteous." Lv 22:22; Lk 5:29

The Parable of the Large Banquet

¹⁵ When one of those who reclined at the table with him heard these things, he said to him, "Blessed is the one who will eat bread in the kingdom of God!" Mt 22:1-14; Lk 13:29

¹⁶ Then he told him: "A man was giving a large banquet and invited many. ¹⁷ At the time of the banquet, he sent his servant to tell those who were invited, 'Come, because everything is now ready.'

¹⁸ "But without exception[B] they all began to make excuses. The first one said to him, 'I have bought a field, and I must go out and see it. I ask you to excuse me.'

¹⁹ "Another said, 'I have bought five yoke of oxen, and I'm going to try them out. I ask you to excuse me.'

²⁰ "And another said, 'I just got married, and therefore I'm unable to come.' Dt 24:5

²¹ "So the servant came back and reported these things to his master. Then in anger, the master of the house told his servant, 'Go out quickly into the streets and alleys of the city, and bring in here the poor, maimed, blind, and lame.' Lk 14:13

²² "'Master,' the servant said, 'what you ordered has been done, and there's still room.'

[A] 14:1 Lit *eat bread*   [B] 14:18 Lit *"And from one* (voice)

²³ "Then the master told the servant, 'Go out into the highways and hedges and make them come in, so that my house may be filled. ²⁴ For I tell you, not one of those people who were invited will enjoy my banquet.'"

The Cost of Following Jesus

²⁵ Now great crowds were traveling with him. So he turned and said to them: ²⁶ "If anyone comes to me and does not hate his own father and mother, wife and children, brothers and sisters — yes, and even his own life — he cannot be my disciple. ²⁷ Whoever does not bear his own cross and come after me cannot be my disciple.

²⁸ "For which of you, wanting to build a tower, doesn't first sit down and calculate the cost to see if he has enough to complete it? ²⁹ Otherwise, after he has laid the foundation and cannot finish it, all the onlookers will begin to ridicule him, ³⁰ saying, 'This man started to build and wasn't able to finish.' Pr 24:27

³¹ "Or what king, going to war against another king, will not first sit down and decide if he is able with ten thousand to oppose the one who comes against him with twenty thousand? ³² If not, while the other is still far off, he sends a delegation and asks for terms of peace. ³³ In the same way, therefore, every one of you who does not renounce^A all his possessions cannot be my disciple. Mt 19:21; Php 3:7

³⁴ "Now, salt is good, but if salt should lose its taste, how will it be made salty? ³⁵ It isn't fit for the soil or for the manure pile; they throw it out. Let anyone who has ears to hear listen." Jdg 9:45; Mt 5:13; Mk 9:49-50

The Parable of the Lost Sheep

15 All the tax collectors and sinners were approaching to listen to him. ² And the Pharisees and scribes were complaining, "This man welcomes sinners and eats with them." Mt 11:19; 18:12-14; Lk 5:29; 7:39

³ So he told them this parable: ⁴ "What man among you, who has a hundred sheep and loses one of them, does not leave the ninety-nine in the open field^B and go after the lost one until he finds it? ⁵ When he has found it, he joyfully puts it on his shoulders, ⁶ and coming home, he calls his friends and neighbors together, saying to them, 'Rejoice with me, because I have found my lost sheep!' ⁷ I tell you, in the same way, there will be more joy in heaven over one sinner who repents than over ninety-nine righteous people who don't need repentance. Ps 119:176; Jr 50:6; Mt 10:6; Mk 12:1

The Parable of the Lost Coin

⁸ "Or what woman who has ten silver coins, ^C,D if she loses one coin, does not light a lamp, sweep the house, and search carefully until she finds it? ⁹ When she finds it, she calls her friends and neighbors together, saying, 'Rejoice with me, because I have found the silver coin I lost!' ¹⁰ I tell you, in the same way, there is joy in the presence of God's angels over one sinner who repents." Lk 2:10

The Parable of the Lost Son

¹¹ He also said: "A man had two sons. ¹² The younger of them said to his

---

^A14:33 Or leave   ^B15:4 Or the wilderness   ^C15:8 Gk ten drachmas   ^D15:8 A Gk drachma was equivalent to a Roman denarius = one day's wage father, 'Father, give me the share of the estate I have coming to me.' So he distributed the assets[A] to them. [13] Not many days later, the younger son gathered together all he had and traveled to a distant country, where he squandered his estate in foolish living. [14] After he had spent everything, a severe famine struck that country, and he had nothing.[B] [15] Then he went to work for one of the citizens of that country, who sent him into his fields to feed pigs. [16] He longed to eat his fill from[C] the pods that the pigs were eating, but no one would give him anything. [17] When he came to his senses,[D] he said, 'How many of my father's hired workers have more than enough food, and here I am dying of hunger![E] [18] I'll get up, go to my father, and say to him, "Father, I have sinned against heaven and in your sight. [19] I'm no longer worthy to be called your son. Make me like one of your hired workers."' [20] So he got up and went to his father. But while the son was still a long way off, his father saw him and was filled with compassion. He ran, threw his arms around his neck, and kissed him. [21] The son said to him, 'Father, I have sinned against heaven and in your sight. I'm no longer worthy to be called your son.'   Lk 16:1; Rm 6:2; 8:12; Gl 2:14; Col 3:7

[22] "But the father told his servants, 'Quick! Bring out the best robe and put it on him; put a ring on his finger and sandals on his feet. [23] Then bring the fattened calf and slaughter it, and let's celebrate with a feast, [24] because this son of mine was dead and is alive again;

he was lost and is found!' So they began to celebrate.   Gn 41:42; Zch 3:3-5

[25] "Now his older son was in the field; as he came near the house, he heard music and dancing. [26] So he summoned one of the servants, questioning what these things meant. [27] 'Your brother is here,' he told him, 'and your father has slaughtered the fattened calf because he has him back safe and sound.'[F]

[28] "Then he became angry and didn't want to go in. So his father came out and pleaded with him. [29] But he replied to his father, 'Look, I have been slaving many years for you, and I have never disobeyed your orders, yet you never gave me a goat so that I could celebrate with my friends. [30] But when this son of yours came, who has devoured your assets[G] with prostitutes, you slaughtered the fattened calf for him.'   Pr 29:3

[31] " 'Son,'[H] he said to him, 'you are always with me, and everything I have is yours. [32] But we had to celebrate and rejoice, because this brother of yours was dead and is alive again; he was lost and is found.' "   Jn 8:35

The Parable of the Dishonest Manager

16 Now he said to the disciples: "There was a rich man who received an accusation that his manager was squandering his possessions. [2] So he called the manager in and asked, 'What is this I hear about you? Give an account of your management, because you can no longer be my manager.'   Lk 15:13; 16:19

[A]15:12 Or *life*, or *livelihood*, also in v. 30   [B]15:14 Lit *and he began to be in need*   [C]15:16 Other mss read *to fill his stomach with*   [D]15:17 Lit *to himself*   [E]15:17 Or *dying in the famine*; v. 14   [F]15:27 Lit *him back healthy*   [G]15:30 Or *life*, or *livelihood*   [H]15:31 Lit *Child*

[3] "Then the manager said to himself, 'What will I do since my master is taking the management away from me? I'm not strong enough to dig; I'm ashamed to beg. [4] I know what I'll do so that when I'm removed from management, people will welcome me into their homes.'

[5] "So he summoned each one of his master's debtors. 'How much do you owe my master?' he asked the first one.

[6] " 'A hundred measures of olive oil,' he said.

" 'Take your invoice,' he told him, 'sit down quickly, and write fifty.'

[7] "Next he asked another, 'How much do you owe?'

" 'A hundred measures of wheat,' he said.

" 'Take your invoice,' he told him, 'and write eighty.'

[8] "The master praised the unrighteous manager because he had acted shrewdly. For the children of this age are more shrewd than the children of light in dealing with their own people.[A] [9] And I tell you, make friends for yourselves by means of worldly wealth[B] so that when it fails,[C] they may welcome you into eternal dwellings. [10] Whoever is faithful in very little is also faithful in much, and whoever is unrighteous in very little is also unrighteous in much. [11] So if you have not been faithful with worldly wealth, who will trust you with what is genuine? [12] And if you have not been faithful with what belongs to someone else, who will give you what is your own? [13] No servant can serve two masters, since either he will hate one and love the other, or he will be devoted to one and despise the other. You cannot serve both God and money." Mt 12:32; Lk 18:6

Kingdom Values

[14] The Pharisees, who were lovers of money, were listening to all these things and scoffing at him. [15] And he told them, "You are the ones who justify yourselves in the sight of others, but God knows your hearts. For what is highly admired by people is revolting in God's sight. Lk 18:9

[16] "The Law and the Prophets were until John; since then, the good news of the kingdom of God has been proclaimed, and everyone is urgently invited to enter it.[D] [17] But it is easier for heaven and earth to pass away than for one stroke of a letter in the law to drop out. Mt 5:18

[18] "Everyone who divorces his wife and marries another woman commits adultery, and everyone who marries a woman divorced from her husband commits adultery. Pr 6:32; Mt 1:19; 5:32; 19:9; Mk 10:11-12

The Rich Man and Lazarus

[19] "There was a rich man who would dress in purple and fine linen, feasting lavishly every day. [20] But a poor man named Lazarus, covered with sores, was lying at his gate. [21] He longed to be filled with what fell from the rich man's table, but instead the dogs would come and lick his sores. [22] One day the poor man died and was carried away by the angels to Abraham's side.[E] The rich man also died and was buried. [23] And being in torment in Hades, he looked up and saw Abraham a long way off, with Lazarus at his

---

[A]**16:8** Lit *own generation*   [B]**16:9** Lit *unrighteous money,* also in v. 11   [C]**16:9** Other mss read *when you fail,* or *pass away*   [D]**16:16** Or *everyone is forcing his way into it*   [E]**16:22** Or *to Abraham's bosom* ; lit *to the fold of Abraham's robe* ; Jn 13:23

side. ²⁴ 'Father Abraham!' he called out, 'Have mercy on me and send Lazarus to dip the tip of his finger in water and cool my tongue, because I am in agony in this flame!'

²⁵ "'Son,'ᴬ Abraham said, 'remember that during your life you received your good things, just as Lazarus received bad things, but now he is comforted here, while you are in agony. ²⁶ Besides all this, a great chasm has been fixed between us and you, so that those who want to pass over from here to you cannot; neither can those from there cross over to us.' Lk 6:24

²⁷ "'Father,' he said, 'then I beg you to send him to my father's house — ²⁸ because I have five brothers — to warn them, so they won't also come to this place of torment.'

²⁹ "But Abraham said, 'They have Moses and the prophets; they should listen to them.' Lk 24:27,44

³⁰ "'No, father Abraham,' he said. 'But if someone from the dead goes to them, they will repent.'

³¹ "But he told him, 'If they don't listen to Moses and the prophets, they will not be persuaded if someone rises from the dead.'"

Warnings from Jesus

17 He said to his disciples, "Offenses will certainly come,ᴮ but woe to the one through whom they come! ² It would be better for him if a millstone were hung around his neck and he were thrown into the sea than for him to cause one of these little ones to stumble. ³ Be on your guard. If your brother sins,ᶜ rebuke him, and if he repents, forgive him. ⁴ And if he

sins against you seven times in a day, and comes back to you seven times, saying, 'I repent,' you must forgive him." Mt 18:6-7; Mk 9:42; 1Co 11:19

Faith and Duty

⁵ The apostles said to the Lord, "Increase our faith." Mt 17:19-20; Mk 9:28-29

⁶ "If you have faith the size ofᴰ a mustard seed," the Lord said, "you can say to this mulberry tree, 'Be uprooted and planted in the sea,' and it will obey you. Mt 13:31; Mk 4:31

⁷ "Which one of you having a servant tending sheep or plowing will say to him when he comes in from the field, 'Come at once and sit down to eat'? ⁸ Instead, will he not tell him, 'Prepare something for me to eat, get ready, and serve me while I eat and drink; later you can eat and drink'? ⁹ Does he thank that servant because he did what was commanded?ᴱ ¹⁰ In the same way, when you have done all that you were commanded, you should say, 'We are worthless servants; we've only done our duty.'" Jb 22:2-3

Ten Men Healed

¹¹ While traveling to Jerusalem, he passed betweenᶠ Samaria and Galilee. ¹² As he entered a village, ten men with leprosyᴳ met him. They stood at a distance ¹³ and raised their voices, saying, "Jesus, Master, have mercy on us!" Lk 9:51; Jn 4:3-4

¹⁴ When he saw them, he told them, "Go and show yourselves to the priests." And while they were going, they were cleansed. Mt 8:4

¹⁵ But one of them, seeing that he was healed, returned and, with a loud voice, gave glory to God. ¹⁶ He

ᴬ**16:25** Lit Child   ᴮ**17:1** Lit "It is impossible for offenses not to come   ᶜ**17:3** Other mss add against you
ᴰ**17:6** Lit faith like   ᴱ**17:9** Other mss add I don't think so   ᶠ**17:11** Other mss read through the middle of
ᴳ**17:12** Gk lepros ; a term for various skin diseases; see Lv 13–14

fell facedown at his feet, thanking him. And he was a Samaritan. ¹⁷ Then Jesus said, "Were not ten cleansed? Where are the nine? ¹⁸ Didn't any return to give glory to God except this foreigner?" ¹⁹ And he told him, "Get up and go on your way. Your faith has saved you." ^A

The Coming of the Kingdom

²⁰ Being asked by the Pharisees when the kingdom of God would come, he answered them, "The kingdom of God is not coming with something observable; ²¹ no one will say, ^B 'See here!' or 'There!' For you see, the kingdom of God is in your midst." ^C   Mt 24:23; Mk 13:21; Lk 19:11

²² Then he told the disciples: "The days are coming when you will long to see one of the days of the Son of Man, but you won't see it. ²³ They will say to you, 'See there!' or 'See here!' Don't follow or run after them. ²⁴ For as the lightning flashes from horizon to horizon and lights up the sky, so the Son of Man will be in his day. ²⁵ But first it is necessary that he suffer many things and be rejected by this generation.   Dt 32:35; Is 2:12; Jr 7:32; Am 4:2; Lk 5:35

²⁶ "Just as it was in the days of Noah, so it will be in the days of the Son of Man: ²⁷ People went on eating, drinking, marrying and giving in marriage until the day Noah boarded the ark, and the flood came and destroyed them all. ²⁸ It will be the same as it was in the days of Lot: People went on eating, drinking, buying, selling, planting, building. ²⁹ But on the day Lot left Sodom, fire and sulfur rained from heaven and destroyed them all. ³⁰ It will be like that on the day the Son of Man is revealed. ³¹ On that day, a man on the housetop, whose belongings are in the house, must not come down to get them. Likewise the man who is in the field must not turn back. ³² Remember Lot's wife! ³³ Whoever tries to make his life secure ^{D,E} will lose it, and whoever loses his life will preserve it. ³⁴ I tell you, on that night two will be in one bed; one will be taken and the other will be left. ³⁵ Two women will be grinding grain together; one will be taken and the other left." ^F   Gn 6:14; Mt 24:37-38; Lk 20:34-35

³⁷ "Where, Lord?" they asked him.

He said to them, "Where the corpse is, there also the vultures will be gathered."   Ezk 29:5; 32:4; 39:17-20

The Parable of the Persistent Widow

18 Now he told them a parable on the need for them to pray always and not give up. ² "There was a judge in a certain town who didn't fear God or respect people. ³ And a widow in that town kept coming to him, saying, 'Give me justice against my adversary.'

⁴ "For a while he was unwilling, but later he said to himself, 'Even though I don't fear God or respect people, ⁵ yet because this widow keeps pestering me, ^G I will give her justice, so that she doesn't wear me out ^H by her persistent coming.'"

⁶ Then the Lord said, "Listen to what the unjust judge says. ⁷ Will not God grant justice to his elect who cry out to him day and night?

Will he delay helping them?[A] [8] I tell you that he will swiftly grant them justice. Nevertheless, when the Son of Man comes, will he find faith on earth?" Is 63:4; Mt 24:22; Rm 8:33; Ti 1:1; Rv 6:10

The Parable of the Pharisee and the Tax Collector

[9] He also told this parable to some who trusted in themselves that they were righteous and looked down on everyone else: [10] "Two men went up to the temple to pray, one a Pharisee and the other a tax collector. [11] The Pharisee was standing and praying like this about himself:[B] 'God, I thank you that I'm not like other people — greedy, unrighteous, adulterers, or even like this tax collector. [12] I fast twice a week; I give a tenth[C] of everything I get.' Mt 18:4; 23:12; Lk 14:11

[13] "But the tax collector, standing far off, would not even raise his eyes to heaven but kept striking his chest and saying, 'God, have mercy on me,[D] a sinner!' [14] I tell you, this one went down to his house justified rather than the other; because everyone who exalts himself will be humbled, but the one who humbles himself will be exalted."

Blessing the Children

[15] People were bringing infants to him so he might touch them, but when the disciples saw it, they rebuked them. [16] Jesus, however, invited them: "Let the little children come to me, and don't stop them, because the kingdom of God belongs to such as these. [17] Truly I tell you, whoever does not receive the kingdom of God like a little child will never enter it." Mt 18:3; 19:13-15

The Rich Young Ruler

[18] A ruler asked him, "Good teacher, what must I do to inherit eternal life?" Mt 19:16-30; Mk 10:17-31; Lk 22:28-30

[19] "Why do you call me good?" Jesus asked him. "No one is good except God alone. [20] You know the commandments: **Do not commit adultery; do not murder; do not steal; do not bear false witness; honor your father and mother.**"[E]

[21] "I have kept all these from my youth," he said.

[22] When Jesus heard this, he told him, "You still lack one thing: Sell all you have and distribute it to the poor, and you will have treasure in heaven. Then come, follow me." Lk 5:11; 12:33; 19:8; Ac 2:45; 4:34

[23] After he heard this, he became extremely sad, because he was very rich. Mt 26:38; Mk 6:26; 14:34

Possessions and the Kingdom

[24] Seeing that he became sad,[F] Jesus said, "How hard it is for those who have wealth to enter the kingdom of God! [25] For it is easier for a camel to go through the eye of a needle than for a rich person to enter the kingdom of God."

[26] Those who heard this asked, "Then who can be saved?" Lk 18:42

[27] He replied, "What is impossible with man is possible with God."

[28] Then Peter said, "Look, we have left what we had and followed you."

[29] So he said to them, "Truly I tell you, there is no one who has left a house, wife or brothers or sisters, parents or children because of the kingdom of God, [30] who will not receive many times more at this time, and eternal life in the age to come." Jb 42:10; Mt 6:33; Lk 21:8

[A]**18:7** Or *Will he put up with them?* [B]**18:11** Or *by himself* [C]**18:12** Or *give tithes* [D]**18:13** Or *God, turn your wrath from me* [E]**18:20** Ex 20:12-16; Dt 5:16-20 [F]**18:24** Other mss omit *he became sad*

THE NAMES OF **JESUS**

An angel told Mary that she would give birth to a son and said that His name would be Jesus. That's the first of many names by which Jesus the Son of God is known. The New Testament gives many more names for Jesus. The names tell who He is and what He does.

NAME	REFERENCE	MEANING	ENGLISH NAME
JESUS	Matthew 1:21	Yahweh saves	Jesus
IMMANUEL	Matthew 1:23	God is with us	Immanuel
SON OF DAVID	Matthew 9:27	One who brings in the Kingdom	Son of David
CHRIST	Matthew 16:16	Son of the living God	Messiah
SON OF MAN	Matthew 20:28	A divine title of suffering and exaltation	Son of Man
HOLY ONE	Mark 1:24	Perfect and sinless	Holy One of God
WORD	John 1:1	Eternal God who reveals God	The Word
LAMB OF GOD	John 1:29	Offered His life as a sacrifice for sins	Lamb of God
SAVIOR	John 4:42	One who delivers from sins	Savior of the World
BREAD OF LIFE	John 6:35	Essential to life	Bread of Life
LIGHT OF THE WORLD	John 9:5	One who brings hope and gives guidance	Light of the World
GOOD SHEPHERD	John 10:11	Gives guidance and protection	Good Shepherd
SON OF GOD	John 20:31	Tells of Jesus' unique and special relationship with God	Messiah, the Son of God
LORD	Romans 10:9	Sovereign Creator and Redeemer	Lord
LORD OF GLORY	1 Corinthians 2:8	The power of the Living God	Lord of Glory
CHIEF CORNERSTONE	Ephesians 2:20	A Sure Foundation for life	Cornerstone
HIGH PRIEST	Hebrews 3:1	The Perfect Mediator	Apostle and High Priest
KING OF KINGS, LORD OF LORDS	Revelation 19:16	The Sovereign Almighty	KING of Kings and LORD of Lords
ALPHA AND OMEGA	Revelation 21:6	The Beginning and Ending	The Alpha and the Omega

THE APOSTLES OF
JESUS

Matthew 10:1-4; Mark 3:13-19; Luke 6:12-16

JOHN (SONS OF THUNDER)

John was a fisherman on the Sea of Galilee with his father, Zebedee, and his brother James. Jesus called John to be a disciple while he was mending nets (Matthew 4:21–22). John helped Peter prepare the Passover meal (Luke 22:8), and from the cross, Jesus told John to care for His mother (John 19:26–27).

THADDAEUS
(JUDAS, SON OF JAMES)

Thaddaeus (Judas, not Iscariot) asked Jesus how He was going to reveal Himself to the disciples and not to the world (John 14:22).

JUDAS ISCARIOT

Judas was keeper of the disciples' money bag. Judas betrayed Jesus for thirty pieces of silver (Luke 22:47–48). He was sorry for what he had done and hanged himself (Matthew 27:3–5).

JAMES (SONS OF THUNDER)

James was a fisherman on the Sea of Galilee with his father, Zebedee, and his brother John. Jesus called James to be a disciple while he was mending nets (Matthew 4:21–22). James was the first disciple to be killed for his faith (Acts 12:2).

ANDREW

Andrew was a fisherman with his brother Peter on the Sea of Galilee. Jesus called Andrew to be a disciple while he was fishing (Matthew 4:18–20). Andrew brought his brother Peter to Jesus (John 1:40–42) and told Jesus about the boy with the loaves and fishes (John 6:8–9).

SIMON (PETER OR CEPHAS-ROCK)

Peter was a fisherman with his brother Andrew on the Sea of Galilee. Jesus called Peter to be a disciple while he was fishing (Matthew 4:18–20). Jesus helped Peter to walk on water (Matthew 14:29). Peter denied Jesus before His crucifixion (Luke 22:54–62) and was later forgiven by Jesus (John 21:15–19).

MATTHEW (LEVI)

Jesus called Matthew to be a disciple while he was a tax collector in Capernaum. Matthew invited Jesus to a dinner where his friends could meet Jesus (Matthew 9:9–13).

SIMON THE ZEALOT

The Bible tells nothing about this man except his name.

PHILIP

Jesus called Philip to follow Him as a disciple. Philip found Nathaniel and told him about Jesus (John 1:43–45). Philip went with Andrew to bring some Greeks to Jesus (John 12:20–22).

JAMES, SON OF ALPHAEUS

The Bible tells nothing about this man except his name.

THOMAS (DIDYMUS)

Thomas encouraged the disciples to go with Jesus and die with Him (John 11:16). Thomas wanted evidence that Jesus had risen from the dead (John 20:25). Jesus showed Thomas His hands and side to prove His resurrection (John 20:27).

BARTHOLOMEW (NATHANIEL)

Bartholomew (Nathaniel) was invited to see Jesus by Philip. Jesus called him a "true Israelite" (John 1:45–51).

THE MIRACLES OF
JESUS

Because He is God's Son, Jesus was able to do many things that other people cannot do. These things are called miracles. The Bible tells of many amazing miracles Jesus performed. Some are listed below.

MARK 5:22–43

- Healed a bleeding woman
- Brought Jairus's daughter back to life

MARK 7:24–37

- Healed a Gentile woman's daughter who had a demon
- Healed a man who could not hear or talk clearly

MARK 8:1–10, 22–25

- Healed a blind man
- Fed 4,000 people

LUKE 5:1–26

- Helped Simon Peter catch fish
- Healed a leper
- Healed a man who could not walk

The Third Prediction of His Death

³¹ Then he took the Twelve aside and told them, "See, we are going up to Jerusalem. Everything that is written through the prophets about the Son of Man will be accomplished. ³² For he will be handed over to the Gentiles, and he will be mocked, insulted, spit on; ³³ and after they flog him, they will kill him, and he will rise on the third day." Mt 20:17-19; Lk 9:51

³⁴ They understood none of these things. The meaning of the saying ᴬ was hidden from them, and they did not grasp what was said. Lk 2:50

A Blind Man Receives His Sight

³⁵ As he approached Jericho, a blind man was sitting by the road begging. ³⁶ Hearing a crowd passing by, he inquired what was happening. ³⁷ "Jesus of Nazareth is passing by," they told him. Mt 20:29-34; Mk 10:46-52

³⁸ So he called out, "Jesus, Son of David, have mercy on me!" ³⁹ Then those in front told him to keep quiet, ᴮ but he kept crying out all the more, "Son of David, have mercy on me!" Mt 1:1; 9:27; Lk 1:32; 18:7; Rm 1:3

⁴⁰ Jesus stopped and commanded that he be brought to him. When he came closer, he asked him, ⁴¹ "What do you want me to do for you?"

"Lord," he said, "I want to see."

⁴² "Receive your sight." Jesus told him. "Your faith has saved you." ⁴³ Instantly he could see, and he began to follow him, glorifying God. All the people, when they saw it, gave praise to God. Lk 7:22; Jn 9:11; Ac 9:12

Jesus Visits Zacchaeus

19 He entered Jericho and was passing through. ² There was a man named Zacchaeus who was a chief tax collector, and he was rich. ³ He was trying to see who Jesus was, but he was not able because of the crowd, since he was a short man. ⁴ So running ahead, he climbed up a sycamore tree to see Jesus, since he was about to pass that way. ⁵ When Jesus came to the place, he looked up and said to him, "Zacchaeus, hurry and come down because today it is necessary for me to stay at your house."

⁶ So he quickly came down and welcomed him joyfully. ⁷ All who saw it began to complain, "He's gone to stay with a sinful man."

⁸ But Zacchaeus stood there and said to the Lord, "Look, I'll give half of my possessions to the poor, Lord. And if I have extorted anything from anyone, I'll pay back four times as much." Ex 22:1; Lk 3:14; 18:22

⁹ "Today salvation has come to this house," Jesus told him, "because he too is a son of Abraham. ¹⁰ For the Son of Man has come to seek and to save the lost." Lk 1:77

The Parable of the Ten Minas

¹¹ As they were listening to this, he went on to tell a parable because he was near Jerusalem, and they thought the kingdom of God was going to appear right away.

¹² Therefore he said: "A nobleman traveled to a far country to receive for himself authority to be king ᶜ and then to return. ¹³ He called ten of his servants, gave them ten minas, ᴰ and told them, 'Engage in business until I come back.'

¹⁴ "But his subjects hated him and sent a delegation after him, saying, 'We don't want this man to rule over us.'

ᴬ**18:34** Lit *This saying*   ᴮ**18:39** Or *those in front rebuked him*   ᶜ**19:12** Lit *to receive for himself a kingdom,* or *sovereignty,* also in v. 15   ᴰ**19:13** = Gk coin worth a hundred drachmas or about a hundred days' wages

¹⁵ "At his return, having received the authority to be king, he summoned those servants he had given the money to, so that he could find out how much they had made in business. ¹⁶ The first came forward and said, 'Master, your mina has earned ten more minas.'

¹⁷ " 'Well done, good ᴬ servant!' he told him. 'Because you have been faithful in a very small matter, have authority over ten towns.' Lk 16:10

¹⁸ "The second came and said, 'Master, your mina has made five minas.'

¹⁹ "So he said to him, 'You will be over five towns.'

²⁰ "And another came and said, 'Master, here is your mina. I have kept it safe in a cloth ²¹ because I was afraid of you since you're a harsh man: you collect what you didn't deposit and reap what you didn't sow.' 2Co 8:12

²² "He told him, 'I will condemn you by what you have said, you evil servant! If you knew I was a harsh man, collecting what I didn't deposit and reaping what I didn't sow, ²³ why, then, didn't you put my money in the bank? And when I returned, I would have collected it with interest.' ²⁴ So he said to those standing there, 'Take the mina away from him and give it to the one who has ten minas.'

²⁵ "But they said to him, 'Master, he has ten minas.'

²⁶ " 'I tell you, that to everyone who has, more will be given; and from the one who does not have, even what he does have will be taken away. ²⁷ But bring here these enemies of mine, who did not want me to rule over them, and slaughter ᴮ them in my presence.' " Mt 13:12

The Triumphal Entry

²⁸ When he had said these things, he went on ahead, going up to Jerusalem. ²⁹ As he approached Bethphage and Bethany, at the place called the Mount of Olives, he sent two of the disciples ³⁰ and said, "Go into the village ahead of you. As you enter it, you will find a young donkey tied there, on which no one has ever sat. Untie it and bring it. ³¹ If anyone asks you, 'Why are you untying it?' say this: 'The Lord needs it.' " 2Sm 15:30; 22:39; Mt 21:1-11; Mk 11:1-11; Lk 9:51

³² So those who were sent left and found it just as he had told them. ³³ As they were untying the young donkey, its owners said to them, "Why are you untying the donkey?" Lk 22:13

³⁴ "The Lord needs it," they said. ³⁵ Then they brought it to Jesus, and after throwing their clothes on the donkey, they helped Jesus get on it. ³⁶ As he was going along, they were spreading their clothes on the road. ³⁷ Now he came near the path down the Mount of Olives, and the whole crowd of the disciples began to praise God joyfully with a loud voice for all the miracles they had seen: Zch 9:9; Jn 12:12-15

³⁸ **Blessed is the King who comes** Mt 2:2; 25:34
  in the name of the Lord. ᶜ Ps 118:26; Lk 13:35
  Peace in heaven and glory
    in the highest heaven! Lk 2:14

³⁹ Some of the Pharisees from the crowd told him, "Teacher, rebuke your disciples."

⁴⁰ He answered, "I tell you, if they were to keep silent, the stones would cry out." Hab 2:11

ᴬ**19:17** Or *capable*   ᴮ**19:27** Or *execute*   ᶜ**19:38** Ps 118:26

Jesus's Love for Jerusalem

41 As he approached and saw the city, he wept for it, **42** saying, "If you knew this day what would bring peace — but now it is hidden from your eyes. **43** For the days will come on you when your enemies will build a barricade around you, surround you, and hem you in on every side. **44** They will crush you and your children among you to the ground, and they will not leave one stone on another in your midst, because you did not recognize the time when God visited you."

Cleansing the Temple

45 He went into the temple and began to throw out those who were selling, ^A **46** and he said, "It is written, **my house will be a house of prayer**, but you have made it **a den of thieves!**"^B   Mt 21:12-19; Mk 11:12-19

47 Every day he was teaching in the temple. The chief priests, the scribes, and the leaders of the people were looking for a way to kill him, **48** but they could not find a way to do it, because all the people were captivated by what they heard.   Mt 26:55; Lk 6:11; 11:53-54; 20:1,19

The Authority of Jesus Challenged

20 One day as he was teaching the people in the temple and proclaiming the good news, the chief priests and the scribes, with the elders, came **2** and said to him: "Tell us, by what authority are you doing these things? Who is it who gave you this authority?"   Mt 21:23-27

3 He answered them, "I will also ask you a question. Tell me, **4** was the baptism of John from heaven or of human origin?"

5 They discussed it among themselves: "If we say, 'From heaven,' he will say, 'Why didn't you believe him?' **6** But if we say, 'Of human origin,' all the people will stone us, because they are convinced that John was a prophet." **7** So they answered that they did not know its origin.

8 And Jesus said to them, "Neither will I tell you by what authority I do these things."

The Parable of the Vineyard Owner

9 Now he began to tell the people this parable: "A man planted a vineyard, leased it to tenant farmers, and went away for a long time. **10** At harvest time he sent a servant to the farmers so that they might give him some fruit from the vineyard. But the farmers beat him and sent him away empty-handed. **11** He sent yet another servant, but they beat that one too, treated him shamefully, and sent him away empty-handed. **12** And he sent yet a third, but they wounded this one too and threw him out.   Mt 21:33-46; Mk 12:1-12

13 "Then the owner of the vineyard said, 'What should I do? I will send my beloved son. Perhaps^C they will respect him.'   Mt 17:5; Lk 3:22

14 "But when the tenant farmers saw him, they discussed it among themselves and said, 'This is the heir. Let's kill him, so that the inheritance will be ours.' **15** So they threw him out of the vineyard and killed him.   Lk 16:16

"What then will the owner of the vineyard do to them? **16** He will come and kill those farmers and give the vineyard to others."

But when they heard this they said, "That must never happen!"

17 But he looked at them and said, "Then what is the meaning of this Scripture: A   Lk 4:17; 18:31; 21:22,37; 24:44

The stone that
the builders rejected
has become
the cornerstone? B   Ps 118:22

18 Everyone who falls on that stone will be broken to pieces, but on whomever it falls, it will shatter him."   Is 8:14-15; Dn 2:34-35,44-45; Rm 9:32-33

19 Then the scribes and the chief priests looked for a way to get their hands on him that very hour, because they knew he had told this parable against them, but they feared the people.   Mt 2:4; 20:18; 21:15

God and Caesar

20 They watched closely and sent spies who pretended to be righteous, C so that they could catch him in what he said, to hand him over to the governor's rule and authority. 21 They questioned him, "Teacher, we know that you speak and teach correctly, and you don't show partiality D but teach truthfully the way of God. 22 Is it lawful for us to pay taxes to Caesar or not?"   Mt 20:15-22

23 But detecting their craftiness, he said to them, E 24 "Show me a denarius. F Whose image and inscription does it have?"

"Caesar's," they said.

25 "Well then," he told them, "give to Caesar the things that are Caesar's, and to God the things that are God's."   Mt 22:21

26 They were not able to catch him in what he said in public, and being amazed at his answer, they became silent.   Lk 9:36; 14:4

The Sadducees and the Resurrection

27 Some of the Sadducees, who say there is no resurrection, came up and questioned him: 28 "Teacher, Moses wrote for us that **if a man's brother has a wife, and dies childless, his brother should take the wife and produce offspring for his brother.** G 29 Now there were seven brothers. The first took a wife and died without children. 30 Also the second H 31 and the third took her. In the same way, all seven died and left no children. 32 Finally, the woman died too. 33 In the resurrection, therefore, whose wife will the woman be? For all seven had married her."   Mt 22:23-33,46; Ac 23:6

34 Jesus told them, "The children of this age marry and are given in marriage. 35 But those who are counted worthy to take part in that age and in the resurrection from the dead neither marry nor are given in marriage. 36 For they can no longer die, because they are like angels and are children of God, since they are children of the resurrection. 37 Moses even indicated in the passage about the burning bush that the dead are raised, where he calls the Lord **the God of Abraham and the God of Isaac and the God of Jacob.** I 38 He is not the God of the dead but of the living, because all are living to J him."   Mk 10:30; Lk 16:8; 17:27; Ac 5:41; 2Th 1:5

39 Some of the scribes answered, "Teacher, you have spoken well." 40 And they no longer dared to ask him anything.

A**20:17** Lit "What then is this that is written   B**20:17** Ps 118:22   C**20:20** Or upright   D**20:21** Lit you don't receive a face   E**20:23** Other mss add "Why are you testing me?   F**20:24** A denarius = one day's wage   G**20:28** Dt 25:5   H**20:30** Other mss add took her as wife, and he died without children   I**20:37** Ex 3:6,15   J**20:38** Or with

The Question about the Christ

⁴¹ Then he said to them, "How can they say that the Christ is the son of David? ⁴² For David himself says in the Book of Psalms: Mt 22:41-46

> The Lord declared
> to my Lord,
> 'Sit at my right hand
⁴³ until I make your enemies
> your footstool.'ᴬ Ps 110:1

⁴⁴ David calls him 'Lord'; how then can the Christ be his son?" Rm 1:3-4

Warning against the Scribes

⁴⁵ While all the people were listening, he said to his disciples, ⁴⁶ "Beware of the scribes, who want to go around in long robes and who love greetings in the marketplaces, the best seats in the synagogues, and the places of honor at banquets. ⁴⁷ They devour widows' houses and say long prayers just for show. These will receive harsher judgment."ᴮ Mt 16:6; 23:1-36; Mk 12:37-40; Lk 11:43

The Widow's Gift

21 He looked up and saw the rich dropping their offerings into the temple treasury. ² He also saw a poor widow dropping in two tiny coins.ᶜ ³ "Truly I tell you," he said, "this poor widow has put in more than all of them. ⁴ For all these people have put in gifts out of their surplus, but she out of her poverty has put in all she had to live on." 2Kg 12:9; Mt 27:6; Mk 12:41-44; Jn 8:20

Destruction of the Temple Predicted

⁵ As some were talking about the temple, how it was adorned with beautiful stones and gifts dedicated to God, he said, ⁶ "These things that you see — the days will come when not one stone will be left on another that will not be thrown down." Mt 24:1-51; Mk 13:1-37

Signs of the End of the Age

⁷ "Teacher," they asked him, "so when will these things happen? And what will be the sign when these things are about to take place?" Ac 1:6-7

⁸ Then he said, "Watch out that you are not deceived. For many will come in my name, saying, 'I am he,' and, 'The time is near.' Don't follow them. ⁹ When you hear of wars and rebellions,ᴰ don't be alarmed. Indeed, it is necessary that these things take place first, but the end won't come right away." Jr 29:8; Eph 5:6

¹⁰ Then he told them: "Nation will be raised up against nation, and kingdom against kingdom. ¹¹ There will be violent earthquakes, and famines and plagues in various places, and there will be terrifying sights and great signs from heaven. ¹² But before all these things, they will lay their hands on you and persecute you. They will hand you over to the synagogues and prisons, and you will be brought before kings and governors because of my name. ¹³ This will give you an opportunity to bear witness. ¹⁴ Therefore make up your mindsᴱ not to prepare your defense ahead of time, ¹⁵ for I will give you such words and a wisdom that none of your adversaries will be able to resist or contradict. ¹⁶ You will even be betrayed by parents, brothers, relatives, and friends. They will kill

---

ᴬ20:42-43 Ps 110:1　ᴮ20:47 Or judgment　ᶜ21:2 Lit two lepta; the lepton was the smallest and least valuable Gk coin in use.　ᴰ21:9 Or insurrections, or revolutions, or chaos　ᴱ21:14 Lit Therefore place (determine) in your hearts some of you. ¹⁷ You will be hated by everyone because of my name, ¹⁸ but not a hair of your head will be lost. ¹⁹ By your endurance, gain^A your lives.   2Ch 15:6; Is 19:2; 29:6; Zch 14:5

The Destruction of Jerusalem

²⁰ "When you see Jerusalem surrounded by armies, then recognize that its desolation has come near. ²¹ Then those in Judea must flee to the mountains. Those inside the city must leave it, and those who are in the country must not enter it, ²² because these are days of vengeance to fulfill all the things that are written. ²³ Woe to pregnant women and nursing mothers in those days, for there will be great distress in the land^B and wrath against this people. ²⁴ They will be killed by the sword^C and be led captive into all the nations, and Jerusalem will be trampled by the Gentiles^D until the times of the Gentiles are fulfilled.   Is 34:8; Dn 9:27; Mt 4:8; Lk 17:31; 19:43

The Coming of the Son of Man

²⁵ "Then there will be signs in the sun, moon, and stars; and there will be anguish on the earth among nations bewildered by the roaring of the sea and the waves. ²⁶ People will faint from fear and expectation of the things that are coming on the world, because the powers of the heavens will be shaken. ²⁷ Then they will see the Son of Man coming in a cloud with power and great glory. ²⁸ But when these things begin to take place, stand up and lift up your heads, because your redemption is near."   Is 13:10; 24:23; Ezk 32:7; Jl 2:10

The Parable of the Fig Tree

²⁹ Then he told them a parable: "Look at the fig tree, and all the trees. ³⁰ As soon as they put out leaves you can see for yourselves and recognize that summer is already near. ³¹ In the same way, when you see these things happening, recognize^E that the kingdom of God is near. ³² Truly I tell you, this generation will certainly not pass away until all things take place. ³³ Heaven and earth will pass away, but my words will never pass away.   Lk 9:27

The Need for Watchfulness

³⁴ "Be on your guard, so that your minds are not dulled^F from carousing,^G drunkenness, and worries of life, or that day will come on you unexpectedly ³⁵ like a trap. For it will come on all who live on the face of the whole earth. ³⁶ But be alert at all times, praying that you may have strength^H to escape all these things that are going to take place and to stand before the Son of Man."   Mt 13:22; Mk 4:19; Lk 17:3; Rm 13:13

³⁷ During the day, he was teaching in the temple, but in the evening he would go out and spend the night on what is called the Mount of Olives. ³⁸ Then all the people would come early in the morning to hear him in the temple.   Mt 26:55; Jn 8:1-2

The Plot to Kill Jesus

22 The Festival of Unleavened Bread, which is called Passover, was approaching. ² The chief priests and the scribes were looking for a way to put him to death, because they were afraid of the people.   Ex 12:11; 23:15; Mt 26:1-5; Mk 14:1-2

---

^A**21:19** Other mss read *endurance, you will gain*   ^B**21:23** Or *the earth*   ^C**21:24** Lit *will fall by the edge of the sword*   ^D**21:24** Or *nations*   ^E**21:31** Or *you know*   ^F**21:34** Lit *your hearts are not weighed down*   ^G**21:34** Or *hangovers*   ^H**21:36** Other mss read *you may be counted worthy*

³ Then Satan entered Judas, called Iscariot, who was numbered among the Twelve. ⁴ He went away and discussed with the chief priests and temple police how he could hand him over to them. ⁵ They were glad and agreed to give him silver.ᴬ ⁶ So he accepted the offer and started looking for a good opportunity to betray him to them when the crowd was not present.   Mt 26:14-16

Preparation for Passover

⁷ Then the Day of Unleavened Bread came when the Passover lamb had to be sacrificed. ⁸ Jesus sent Peter and John, saying, "Go and make preparations for us to eat the Passover."   Ex 12:21; Mt 26:17-19; Mk 14:12-16; 1Co 5:7

⁹ "Where do you want us to prepare it?" they asked him.

¹⁰ "Listen," he said to them, "when you've entered the city, a man carrying a water jug will meet you. Follow him into the house he enters. ¹¹ Tell the owner of the house, 'The Teacher asks you, "Where is the guest room where I can eat the Passover with my disciples?"' ¹² Then he will show you a large, furnished room upstairs. Make the preparations there."   Ac 1:13

¹³ So they went and found it just as he had told them, and they prepared the Passover.   Lk 19:32

The First Lord's Supper

¹⁴ When the hour came, he reclined at the table, and the apostles with him. ¹⁵ Then he said to them, "I have fervently desired to eat this Passover with you before I suffer. ¹⁶ For I tell you, I will not eat it againᴮ until it is fulfilled in the kingdom of God." ¹⁷ Then he took a cup, and after giving thanks, he said, "Take this and share it among yourselves. ¹⁸ For I tell you, from now on I will not drink of the fruit of the vine until the kingdom of God comes."

¹⁹ And he took bread, gave thanks, broke it, gave it to them, and said, "This is my body, which is given for you. Do this in remembrance of me."   Jn 6:51-53; Heb 10:3

²⁰ In the same way he also took the cup after supper and said, "This cup is the new covenant in my blood, which is poured out for you.ᶜ ²¹ But look, the hand of the one betraying me is at the table with me. ²² For the Son of Man will go away as it has been determined, but woe to that man by whom he is betrayed!"   Ex 24:8; Jr 31:31; Zch 9:11; 2Co 3:6

²³ So they began to argue among themselves which of them it could be who was going to do it.   Mt 21:25

The Dispute over Greatness

²⁴ Then a dispute also arose among them about who should be considered the greatest. ²⁵ But he said to them, "The kings of the Gentiles lord it over them, and those who have authority over them have themselves calledᴰ 'Benefactors.' ²⁶ It is not to be like that among you. On the contrary, whoever is greatest among you should become like the youngest, and whoever leads, like the one serving. ²⁷ For who is greater, the one at the table or the one serving? Isn't it the one at the table? But I am among you as the one who serves. ²⁸ You are those who stood by me in my trials. ²⁹ I bestow on you a kingdom, just as my Father bestowed one on me, ³⁰ so that you may eat and drink at my table

ᴬ22:5 Or *money*   ᴮ22:16 Other mss omit *again*   ᶜ22:19-20 Other mss omit *which is given for you* (v. 19) through the end of v. 20   ᴰ22:25 Or *them call themselves* in my kingdom. And you will sit on thrones judging the twelve tribes of Israel. Mt 20:25-28; Mk 9:34; 10:42-45; Lk 1:32

Peter's Denial Predicted

[31] "Simon, Simon,[A] look out. Satan has asked to sift you like wheat. [32] But I have prayed for you that your faith may not fail. And you, when you have turned back, strengthen your brothers." Mt 4:10

[33] "Lord," he told him, "I'm ready to go with you both to prison and to death." Mt 26:33-35; Mk 14:29-31; Jn 13:37-38

[34] "I tell you, Peter," he said, "the rooster will not crow today until[B] you deny three times that you know me."

Be Ready for Trouble

[35] He also said to them, "When I sent you out without money-bag, traveling bag, or sandals, did you lack anything?" Mt 10:9-10; Mk 6:8; Lk 9:3; 10:4

"Not a thing," they said.

[36] Then he said to them, "But now, whoever has a money-bag should take it, and also a traveling bag. And whoever doesn't have a sword should sell his robe and buy one. [37] For I tell you, what is written must be fulfilled in me:[C] **And he was counted among the lawless.**[D] Yes, what is written about me is coming to its fulfillment." Is 53:12

[38] "Lord," they said, "look, here are two swords."

"That is enough!" he told them.

The Prayer in the Garden

[39] He went out and made his way as usual to the Mount of Olives, and the disciples followed him. [40] When he reached the place, he told them,

"Pray that you may not fall into temptation." [41] Then he withdrew from them about a stone's throw, knelt down, and began to pray, [42] "Father, if you are willing, take this cup away from me — nevertheless, not my will, but yours, be done." Mt 26:30; Mk 14:26; Lk 4:30; 21:37; Jn 18:1

[43] Then an angel from heaven appeared to him, strengthening him. [44] Being in anguish, he prayed more fervently, and his sweat became like drops of blood falling to the ground.[E] [45] When he got up from prayer and came to the disciples, he found them sleeping, exhausted from their grief. [46] "Why are you sleeping?" he asked them. "Get up and pray, so that you won't fall into temptation." Mt 4:11; Heb 1:14; 5:7

Judas's Betrayal of Jesus

[47] While he was still speaking, suddenly a mob came, and one of the Twelve named Judas was leading them. He came near Jesus to kiss him, [48] but Jesus said to him, "Judas, are you betraying the Son of Man with a kiss?" Mt 26:47-56; Jn 18:3-12

[49] When those around him saw what was going to happen, they asked, "Lord, should we strike with the sword?" [50] Then one of them struck the high priest's servant and cut off his right ear.

[51] But Jesus responded, "No more of this!" And touching his ear, he healed him. [52] Then Jesus said to the chief priests, temple police, and the elders who had come for him, "Have you come out with swords and clubs as if I were a criminal?[F] [53] Every day while I was with you in the temple, you never laid a hand

---

[A] **22:31** Other mss read *Then the Lord said, "Simon, Simon* [B] **22:34** Other mss read *before* [C] **22:37** Or *it is necessary that what is written be fulfilled in me* [D] **22:37** Is 53:12 [E] **22:43-44** Other mss omit vv. 43-44 [F] **22:52** Lit *as against a thief,* or *a bandit* on me. But this is your hour — and the dominion of darkness." Lk 2:46

Peter Denies His Lord

⁵⁴ They seized him, led him away, and brought him into the high priest's house. Meanwhile Peter was following at a distance. ⁵⁵ They lit a fire in the middle of the courtyard and sat down together, and Peter sat among them. ⁵⁶ When a servant saw him sitting in the light, and looked closely at him, she said, "This man was with him too." Mt 26:58,69-75; Mk 14:54; Jn 18:15

⁵⁷ But he denied it: "Woman, I don't know him."

⁵⁸ After a little while, someone else saw him and said, "You're one of them too."

"Man, I am not!" Peter said.

⁵⁹ About an hour later, another kept insisting, "This man was certainly with him, since he's also a Galilean."

⁶⁰ But Peter said, "Man, I don't know what you're talking about!" Immediately, while he was still speaking, a rooster crowed. ⁶¹ Then the Lord turned and looked at Peter. So Peter remembered the word of the Lord, how he had said to him, "Before the rooster crows today, you will deny me three times." ⁶² And he went outside and wept bitterly. Mk 10:21; Lk 22:31-34; Ac 3:13-14

Jesus Mocked and Beaten

⁶³ The men who were holding Jesus started mocking and beating him. ⁶⁴ After blindfolding him, they kept ᴬ asking, "Prophesy! Who was it that hit you?" ⁶⁵ And they were saying many other blasphemous things to him. Mt 26:67-68

Jesus Faces the Sanhedrin

⁶⁶ When daylight came, the elders ᴮ of the people, both the chief priests and the scribes, convened and brought him before their Sanhedrin. ⁶⁷ They said, "If you are the Messiah, tell us." Mt 27:1; Mk 15:1; Jn 18:28

But he said to them, "If I do tell you, you will not believe. ⁶⁸ And if I ask you, you will not answer. ⁶⁹ But from now on, the Son of Man will be seated at the right hand of the power of God." Ps 110:1; Mk 16:19; Ac 7:56

⁷⁰ They all asked, "Are you, then, the Son of God?" Mt 4:3; Lk 1:32,35

And he said to them, "You say that I am." Mt 26:64; 27:11; Lk 23:3

⁷¹ "Why do we need any more testimony," they said, "since we've heard it ourselves from his mouth?"

Jesus Faces Pilate

23 Then their whole assembly rose up and brought him before Pilate. ² They began to accuse him, saying, "We found this man misleading our nation, opposing payment of taxes to Caesar, and saying that he himself is the Messiah, a king." Mt 27:1,11-14; Mk 15:1-5

³ So Pilate asked him, "Are you the king of the Jews?" Mt 27:11; Mk 15:2

He answered him, "You say so." ᶜ

⁴ Pilate then told the chief priests and the crowds, "I find no grounds for charging this man." Mt 27:24

⁵ But they kept insisting, "He stirs up the people, teaching throughout all Judea, from Galilee where he started even to here." Ac 17:5-8,13

Jesus Faces Herod Antipas

⁶ When Pilate heard this, ᴰ he asked if the man was a Galilean. ⁷ Finding that he was under Herod's

---

ᴬ22:64 Other mss add *striking him on the face and*   ᴮ22:66 Or *council of elders*   ᶜ23:3 Or *"That is true."*
ᴰ23:6 Other mss read *heard "Galilee"*

jurisdiction, he sent him to Herod, who was also in Jerusalem during those days. ⁸ Herod was very glad to see Jesus; for a long time he had wanted to see him because he had heard about him and was hoping to see some miracle ᴬ performed by him. ⁹ So he kept asking him questions, but Jesus did not answer him. ¹⁰ The chief priests and the scribes stood by, vehemently accusing him. ¹¹ Then Herod, with his soldiers, treated him with contempt, mocked him, dressed him in bright clothing, and sent him back to Pilate. ¹² That very day Herod and Pilate became friends. ᴮ Previously, they had been enemies. Lk 3:1; 1Tm 6:13

Jesus or Barabbas

¹³ Pilate called together the chief priests, the leaders, and the people, ¹⁴ and said to them, "You have brought me this man as one who misleads the people. But in fact, after examining him in your presence, I have found no grounds to charge this man with those things you accuse him of. ¹⁵ Neither has Herod, because he sent him back to us. Clearly, he has done nothing to deserve death. ¹⁶ Therefore, I will have him whipped ᶜ and then release him." ᴰ Lk 23:35; 24:20; Jn 7:26,48; 12:42

¹⁸ Then they all cried out together, "Take this man away! Release Barabbas to us!" ¹⁹ (He had been thrown into prison for a rebellion that had taken place in the city, and for murder.) Mt 27:15-23; Mk 15:6-14; Jn 18:40; Ac 21:36

²⁰ Wanting to release Jesus, Pilate addressed them again, ²¹ but they kept shouting, "Crucify! Crucify him!" Ac 3:13-14

²² A third time he said to them, "Why? What has this man done wrong? I have found in him no grounds for the death penalty. Therefore, I will have him whipped and then release him." Lk 23:4; Jn 8:46

²³ But they kept up the pressure, demanding with loud voices that he be crucified, and their voices ᴱ won out. ²⁴ So Pilate decided to grant their demand ²⁵ and released the one they were asking for, who had been thrown into prison for rebellion and murder. But he handed Jesus over to their will. Mt 27:24-26

The Way to the Cross

²⁶ As they led him away, they seized Simon, a Cyrenian, who was coming in from the country, and laid the cross on him to carry behind Jesus. ²⁷ A large crowd of people followed him, including women who were mourning and lamenting him. ²⁸ But turning to them, Jesus said, "Daughters of Jerusalem, do not weep for me, but weep for yourselves and your children. ²⁹ Look, the days are coming when they will say, 'Blessed are the women without children, the wombs that never bore, and the breasts that never nursed!' ³⁰ Then they will begin to say to the mountains, 'Fall on us!' and to the hills, 'Cover us!' ᶠ ³¹ For if they do these things when the wood is green, what will happen when it is dry?" Mt 27:31-32; Mk 15:20-21

Crucified Between Two Criminals

³² Two others — criminals — were also led away to be executed with

---

ᴬ 23:8 Or sign   ᴮ 23:12 Lit friends with one another   ᶜ 23:16 Gk paideuo; to discipline or "teach a lesson"
ᴰ 23:16 Some mss include v. 17: For according to the festival he had to release someone to them.
ᴱ 23:23 Other mss add and those of the chief priests   ᶠ 23:30 Hs 10:8

him. [33] When they arrived at the place called The Skull, they crucified him there, along with the criminals, one on the right and one on the left. [34] Then Jesus said, "Father, forgive them, because they do not know what they are doing."[A] And they divided his clothes and cast lots. Is 53:12; Mt 27:38; Mk 15:27; Lk 22:37; Jn 19:18

[35] The people stood watching, and even the leaders were scoffing: "He saved others; let him save himself if this is God's Messiah, the Chosen One!" [36] The soldiers also mocked him. They came offering him sour wine [37] and said, "If you are the King of the Jews, save yourself!" Mt 27:43,48; Mk 15:26,29-32; Jn 19:19,29

[38] An inscription was above him:[B] THIS IS THE KING OF THE JEWS.

[39] Then one of the criminals hanging there began to yell insults at[C] him: "Aren't you the Messiah? Save yourself and us!" Mt 27:44

[40] But the other answered, rebuking him: "Don't you even fear God, since you are undergoing the same punishment? [41] We are punished justly, because we're getting back what we deserve for the things we did, but this man has done nothing wrong." [42] Then he said, "Jesus, remember me[D] when you come into your kingdom." Ps 147:11; Pr 1:7; Ac 10:2

[43] And he said to him, "Truly I tell you, today you will be with me in paradise." 2Co 12:4; Rv 2:7

The Death of Jesus

[44] It was now about noon,[E] and darkness came over the whole land[F] until three,[G] [45] because the sun's light failed.[H] The curtain of the sanctuary was split down the middle. [46] And Jesus called out with a loud voice, "Father, **into your hands I entrust my spirit.**"[I] Saying this, he breathed his last. Ps 31:5

[47] When the centurion saw what happened, he began to glorify God, saying, "This man really was righteous!"[J] [48] All the crowds that had gathered for this spectacle, when they saw what had taken place, went home, striking their chests. [49] But all who knew him, including the women who had followed him from Galilee, stood at a distance, watching these things. Lk 13:13; 18:13

The Burial of Jesus

[50] There was a good and righteous man named Joseph, a member of the Sanhedrin, [51] who had not agreed with their plan and action. He was from Arimathea, a Judean town, and was looking forward to the kingdom of God. [52] He approached Pilate and asked for Jesus's body. [53] Taking it down, he wrapped it in fine linen and placed it in a tomb cut into the rock, where no one had ever been placed.[K] [54] It was the preparation day, and the Sabbath was about to begin.[L] [55] The women who had come with him from Galilee followed along and observed the tomb and how his body was placed. [56] Then they returned and prepared spices and perfumes. And they rested on the Sabbath according to the commandment. Mt 27:57-61; Mk 15:42-47; Ac 2:23

[A]23:34 Other mss omit *Then Jesus said, "Father, forgive them, because they do not know what they are doing."* [B]23:38 Other mss add *written in Greek, Latin, and Hebrew letters* [C]23:39 Or *began to blaspheme* [D]23:42 Other mss add *Lord* [E]23:44 Lit *about the sixth hour* [F]23:44 Or *whole earth* [G]23:44 Lit *the ninth hour* [H]23:45 Other mss read *three, and the sun was darkened* [I]23:46 Ps 31:5 [J]23:47 Or *innocent* [K]23:53 Or *interred*, or *laid* [L]23:54 Lit *was dawning*

Resurrection Morning

24 On the first day of the week, very early in the morning, they[A] came to the tomb, bringing the spices they had prepared. [2] They found the stone rolled away from the tomb. [3] They went in but did not find the body of the Lord Jesus. [4] While they were perplexed about this, suddenly two men stood by them in dazzling clothes. [5] So the women were terrified and bowed down to the ground. Mt 28:1-10; Ac 20:7

"Why are you looking for the living among the dead?" asked the men. [6] "He is not here, but he has risen! Remember how he spoke to you when he was still in Galilee, [7] saying, 'It is necessary that the Son of Man be betrayed into the hands of sinful men, be crucified, and rise on the third day'?" [8] And they remembered his words.

[9] Returning from the tomb, they reported all these things to the Eleven and to all the rest. [10] Mary Magdalene, Joanna, Mary the mother of James, and the other women with them were telling the apostles these things. [11] But these words seemed like nonsense to them, and they did not believe the women. [12] Peter, however, got up and ran to the tomb. When he stooped to look in, he saw only the linen cloths.[B] So he went away, amazed at what had happened. Mk 15:40; 16:1; Ac 1:15-26; 2:14

The Emmaus Disciples

[13] Now that same day two of them were on their way to a village called Emmaus, which was about seven miles[C] from Jerusalem. [14] Together they were discussing everything that had taken place. [15] And while they were discussing and arguing, Jesus himself came near and began to walk along with them. [16] But they[D] were prevented from recognizing him. [17] Then he asked them, "What is this dispute that you're having[E] with each other as you are walking?" And they stopped walking and looked discouraged.

[18] The one named Cleopas answered him, "Are you the only visitor in Jerusalem who doesn't know the things that happened there in these days?" Ac 26:26

[19] "What things?" he asked them.

So they said to him, "The things concerning Jesus of Nazareth, who was a prophet powerful in action and speech before God and all the people, [20] and how our chief priests and leaders handed him over to be sentenced to death, and they crucified him. [21] But we were hoping that he was the one who was about to redeem Israel. Besides all this, it's the third day since these things happened. [22] Moreover, some women from our group astounded us. They arrived early at the tomb, [23] and when they didn't find his body, they came and reported that they had seen a vision of angels who said he was alive. [24] Some of those who were with us went to the tomb and found it just as the women had said, but they didn't see him." Lk 4:34; 18:37; Ac 2:22

[25] He said to them, "How foolish you are, and slow[F] to believe all that the prophets have spoken! [26] Wasn't it necessary for the Messiah to suffer these things and enter into his glory?" [27] Then beginning

---

A**24:1** Other mss add *and other women with them*   B**24:12** Other mss add *lying there*   C**24:13** Lit *about sixty stadia*; one *stadion* = 600 feet   D**24:16** Lit *their eyes*   E**24:17** Lit *"What are these words that you are exchanging*   F**24:25** Lit *slow of heart* with Moses and all the Prophets, he interpreted for them the things concerning himself in all the Scriptures. Lk 16:31; 18:31; 24:44-48; Ac 26:27; 2Pt 1:21

²⁸ They came near the village where they were going, and he gave the impression that he was going farther. ²⁹ But they urged him, "Stay with us, because it's almost evening, and now the day is almost over." So he went in to stay with them. Mk 6:48

³⁰ It was as he reclined at the table with them that he took the bread, blessed and broke it, and gave it to them. ³¹ Then their eyes were opened, and they recognized him, but he disappeared from their sight. ³² They said to each other, "Weren't our hearts burning within us while he was talking with us on the road and explaining the Scriptures to us?" ³³ That very hour they got up and returned to Jerusalem. They found the Eleven and those with them gathered together, ³⁴ who said, "The Lord has truly been raised and has appeared to Simon!" ³⁵ Then they began to describe what had happened on the road and how he was made known to them in the breaking of the bread. 2Kg 6:17; Lk 9:16; 24:16; 22:19

The Reality of the Risen Jesus

³⁶ As they were saying these things, he himself stood in their midst. He said to them, "Peace to you!" ³⁷ But they were startled and terrified and thought they were seeing a ghost. ³⁸ "Why are you troubled?" he asked them. "And why do doubts arise in your hearts? ³⁹ Look at my hands and my feet, that it is I myself! Touch me and see, because a ghost does not have flesh and bones as you can see I have." ⁴⁰ Having said this, he showed them his hands and feet. ⁴¹ But while they still were amazed and in disbelief because of their joy, he asked them, "Do you have anything here to eat?" ⁴² So they gave him a piece of a broiled fish, ^A ⁴³ and he took it and ate in their presence. Lk 2:14; 7:50; 8:48; Jn 20:19-20

⁴⁴ He told them, "These are my words that I spoke to you while I was still with you — that everything written about me in the Law of Moses, the Prophets, and the Psalms must be fulfilled." ⁴⁵ Then he opened their minds to understand the Scriptures. ⁴⁶ He also said to them, "This is what is written:^B The Messiah would suffer and rise from the dead the third day, ⁴⁷ and repentance for^C forgiveness of sins would be proclaimed in his name to all the nations, beginning at Jerusalem. ⁴⁸ You are witnesses of these things. ⁴⁹ And look, I am sending you^D what my Father promised. As for you, stay in the city^E until you are empowered^F from on high." Lk 9:22,44; 17:25; 18:31-33; 22:37

The Ascension of Jesus

⁵⁰ Then he led them out to the vicinity of Bethany, and lifting up his hands he blessed them. ⁵¹ And while he was blessing them, he left them and was carried up into heaven. ⁵² After worshiping him, they returned to Jerusalem with great joy. ⁵³ And they were continually in the temple praising God.^G Ac 1:12

---

^A 24:42 Other mss add *and some honeycomb*   ^B 24:46 Other mss add *and thus it was necessary that*
^C 24:47 Many mss read *repentance and*   ^D 24:49 Lit *upon you*   ^E 24:49 Other mss add *of Jerusalem*
^F 24:49 Lit *clothed with power*   ^G 24:53 Other mss read *praising and blessing God. Amen.*

JOHN

Prologue

1 In the beginning was the Word, and the Word was with God, and the Word was God. ² He was with God in the beginning. ³ All things were created through him, and apart from him not one thing was created that has been created. ⁴ In him was life,^A and that life was the light of men. ⁵ That light shines in the darkness, and yet the darkness did not overcome^B it. Gn 1:1; Col 1:18

⁶ There was a man sent from God whose name was John. ⁷ He came as a witness to testify about the light, so that all might believe through him.^C ⁸ He was not the light, but he came to testify about the light. ⁹ The true light that gives light to everyone, was coming into the world.^D Mk 1:4; Jn 12:46; 15:26; 18:37

¹⁰ He was in the world, and the world was created through him, and yet the world did not recognize him. ¹¹ He came to his own, and his own people did not receive him. ¹² But to all who did receive him, he gave them the right to be^E children of God, to those who believe in his name, ¹³ who were born, not of natural descent,^F or of the will of the flesh, or of the will of man,^G but of God. Mk 1:22; Lk 1:7; Jn 1:3; 5:43; 2Jn 10

¹⁴ The Word became flesh and dwelt^H among us. We observed his glory, the glory as the one and only Son^I from the Father, full of grace and truth. ¹⁵ (John testified concerning him and exclaimed, "This was the one of whom I said, 'The one coming after me ranks ahead of me, because he existed before me.' ") ¹⁶ Indeed, we have all received grace upon^J grace from his fullness, ¹⁷ for the law was given through Moses; grace and truth came through Jesus Christ. ¹⁸ No one has ever seen God. The one and only Son, who is himself God and is at the Father's side^K —he has revealed him. Jn 1:1; 17:24; Php 2:7; 1Jn 4:2; 5:20

John the Baptist's Testimony

¹⁹ This was John's testimony when the Jews from Jerusalem sent priests and Levites to ask him, "Who are you? " Ex 6:19; Mt 23:37; Ac 4:1

²⁰ He didn't deny it but confessed: "I am not the Messiah." Mt 1:17; Eph 5:2

²¹ "What then? " they asked him. "Are you Elijah? " Mal 4:5; Mt 11:14; 17:10-13

"I am not," he said.

"Are you the Prophet? " Dt 18:15

"No," he answered.

²² "Who are you, then? " they asked. "We need to give an answer to those who sent us. What can you tell us about yourself? "

²³ He said, "I am a **voice of one crying out in the wilderness: Make straight the way of the Lord**^L — just as Isaiah the prophet said."

---

^A**1:3-4** Other punctuation is possible: ... *not one thing was created. What was created in him was life* ^B**1:5** Or *grasp*, or *comprehend*, or *overtake* ; Jn 12:35 ^C**1:7** Or *it (the light)* ^D**1:9** Or *The true light who comes into the world gives light to everyone*, or *The true light enlightens everyone coming into the world.* ^E**1:12** Or *become* ^F**1:13** Lit *blood* ^G**1:13** Or *not of human lineage, or of human capacity, or of human volition* ^H**1:14** Or *and dwelt in a tent*; lit *and tabernacled* ^I**1:14** *Son* is implied from the reference to the Father and from Gk usage. ^J**1:16** Or *in place of* ^K**1:18** Other mss read *The one and only Son, who is at the Father's side* ^L**1:23** Is 40:3

²⁴ Now they had been sent from the Pharisees. ²⁵ So they asked him, "Why then do you baptize if you aren't the Messiah, or Elijah, or the Prophet?"   Mk 7:3

²⁶ "I baptize with^A water," John answered them. "Someone stands among you, but you don't know him. ²⁷ He is the one coming after me,^B whose sandal strap I'm not worthy to untie." ²⁸ All this happened in Bethany^C across the Jordan, where John was baptizing.   Mk 1:8; 10:1; Jn 1:15

The Lamb of God

²⁹ The next day John saw Jesus coming toward him and said, "Here is the Lamb of God, who takes away the sin of the world! ³⁰ This is the one I told you about: 'After me comes a man who ranks ahead of me, because he existed before me.' ³¹ I didn't know him, but I came baptizing with water so he might be revealed to Israel." ³² And John testified, "I saw the Spirit descending from heaven like a dove, and he rested on him. ³³ I didn't know him, but he who sent me to baptize with water told me, 'The one you see the Spirit descending and resting on — he is the one who baptizes with the Holy Spirit.' ³⁴ I have seen and testified that this is the Son of God."^D   Is 53:7; Ac 8:32; 1Pt 1:19; Rv 5:6

³⁵ The next day, John was standing with two of his disciples. ³⁶ When he saw Jesus passing by, he said, "Look, the Lamb of God!"

³⁷ The two disciples heard him say this and followed Jesus. ³⁸ When Jesus turned and noticed them following him, he asked them, "What are you looking for?"

They said to him, "Rabbi" (which means "Teacher"), "where are you staying?"   Jn 11:8

³⁹ "Come and you'll see," he replied. So they went and saw where he was staying, and they stayed with him that day. It was about four in the afternoon.^E

⁴⁰ Andrew, Simon Peter's brother, was one of the two who heard John and followed him. ⁴¹ He first found his own brother Simon and told him, "We have found the Messiah"^F (which is translated "the Christ"), ⁴² and he brought Simon to Jesus.   Mt 4:18-22; Mk 1:16-20; Lk 5:2-11

When Jesus saw him, he said, "You are Simon, son of John.^G You will be called Cephas" (which is translated "Peter"^H).   1Co 1:12; 3:22; 9:5

Philip and Nathanael

⁴³ The next day Jesus^I decided to leave for Galilee. He found Philip and told him, "Follow me."   Mk 3:18

⁴⁴ Now Philip was from Bethsaida, the hometown of Andrew and Peter. ⁴⁵ Philip found Nathanael and told him, "We have found the one Moses wrote about in the law (and so did the prophets): Jesus the son of Joseph, from Nazareth."   Mt 2:23; Jn 1:46-49; 12:21; 21:2; Ac 7:52

⁴⁶ "Can anything good come out of Nazareth?" Nathanael asked him.   Gn 1:31

"Come and see," Philip answered.

⁴⁷ Then Jesus saw Nathanael coming toward him and said about him, "Here truly is an Israelite in whom there is no deceit."   2Co 11:22

---

^A 1:26 Or *in*, also in vv. 31,33   ^B 1:27 Other mss add *who came before me*   ^C 1:28 Other mss read *in Bethabara*   ^D 1:34 Other mss read *is the Chosen One of God*   ^E 1:39 Lit *about the tenth hour*   ^F 1:41 Both Hb *Messiah* and Gk *Christos* mean "anointed one"   ^G 1:42 Other mss read *"Simon, son of Jonah*   ^H 1:42 Both Aramaic *Cephas* and Gk *Petros* mean "rock"   ^I 1:43 Lit *he*

⁴⁸ "How do you know me?" Nathanael asked.

"Before Philip called you, when you were under the fig tree, I saw you," Jesus answered.

⁴⁹ "Rabbi," Nathanael replied, "You are the Son of God; you are the King of Israel!" Jn 5:19; 11:8; 12:13

⁵⁰ Jesus responded to him, "Do you believe because I told you I saw you under the fig tree? You will see greater things than this." ⁵¹ Then he said, "Truly I tell you, you will see heaven opened and the angels of God ascending and descending on the Son of Man." Lk 12:8-9; 15:10; Ac 10:3

The First Sign: Turning Water into Wine

2 On the third day a wedding took place in Cana of Galilee. Jesus's mother was there, and ² Jesus and his disciples were invited to the wedding as well. ³ When the wine ran out, Jesus's mother told him, "They don't have any wine." Jn 2:11

⁴ "What does that have to do with you and me,^A woman?" Jesus asked. "My hour has not yet come."

⁵ "Do whatever he tells you," his mother told the servants.

⁶ Now six stone water jars had been set there for Jewish purification. Each contained twenty or thirty gallons.^B Lv 13-14; Heb 1:3

⁷ "Fill the jars with water," Jesus told them. So they filled them to the brim. ⁸ Then he said to them, "Now draw some out and take it to the headwaiter."^C And they did.

⁹ When the headwaiter tasted the water (after it had become wine), he did not know where it came from — though the servants who had drawn the water knew. He called the groom ¹⁰ and told him, "Everyone sets out the fine wine first, then, after people are drunk, the inferior. But you have kept the fine wine until now."

¹¹ Jesus did this, the first of his signs, in Cana of Galilee. He revealed his glory, and his disciples believed in him. Mt 17:22; Jn 2:1; 21:2; 1Jn 1:2

¹² After this, he went down to Capernaum, together with his mother, his brothers, and his disciples, and they stayed there only a few days. Mt 12:46-50; Mk 3:31-35; 6:3; Lk 10:15; Ac 1:14

Cleansing the Temple

¹³ The Jewish Passover was near, and so Jesus went up to Jerusalem. ¹⁴ In the temple he found people selling oxen, sheep, and doves, and he also found the money changers sitting there. ¹⁵ After making a whip out of cords, he drove everyone out of the temple with their sheep and oxen. He also poured out the money changers' coins and overturned the tables. ¹⁶ He told those who were selling doves, "Get these things out of here! Stop turning my Father's house into a marketplace!"^D Ex 12:11

¹⁷ And his disciples remembered that it is written: **Zeal for your house will consume me.**^E Nm 25:13

¹⁸ So the Jews replied to him, "What sign will you show us for doing these things?"

¹⁹ Jesus answered, "Destroy this temple,^F and I will raise it up in three days." Lk 1:21; 9:22

²⁰ Therefore the Jews said, "This temple took forty-six years to build,^G and will you raise it up in three days?" Mk 15:29

---

^A 2:4 Or "You and I see things differently; lit "What to me and to you"; Mt 8:29; Mk 1:24; 5:7; Lk 8:28
^B 2:6 Lit two or three measures   ^C 2:8 Lit ruler of the table   ^D 2:16 Lit a house of business   ^E 2:17 Ps 69:9
^F 2:19 Or sanctuary, also in vv. 20,21   ^G 2:20 Or was built forty-six years ago

²¹ But he was speaking about the temple of his body. ²² So when he was raised from the dead, his disciples remembered that he had said this, and they believed the Scripture and the statement Jesus had made. Mt 26:26; 27:52,58; Mk 14:22; 15:43; Lk 12:4

²³ While he was in Jerusalem during the Passover Festival, many believed in his name when they saw the signs he was doing. ²⁴ Jesus, however, would not entrust himself to them, since he knew them all ²⁵ and because he did not need anyone to testify about man; for he himself knew what was in man.

Jesus and Nicodemus

3 There was a man from the Pharisees named Nicodemus, a ruler of the Jews. ² This man came to him at night and said, "Rabbi, we know that you are a teacher who has come from God, for no one could perform these signs you do unless God were with him." Mk 7:3

³ Jesus replied, "Truly I tell you, unless someone is born again,ᴬ he cannot see the kingdom of God."

⁴ "How can anyone be born when he is old?" Nicodemus asked him. "Can he enter his mother's womb a second time and be born?"

⁵ Jesus answered, "Truly I tell you, unless someone is born of water and the Spirit, he cannot enter the kingdom of God. ⁶ Whatever is born of the flesh is flesh, and whatever is born of the Spirit is spirit. ⁷ Do not be amazed that I told you that you must be born again. ⁸ The wind blows where it pleases, and you hear its sound, but you don't know where it comes from or where it is going. So it is with everyone born of the Spirit." Ezk 36:25-27; Mk 9:43; Ac 22:16

⁹ "How can these things be?" asked Nicodemus.

¹⁰ "Are you a teacherᴮ of Israel and don't know these things?" Jesus replied. ¹¹ "Truly I tell you, we speak what we know and we testify to what we have seen, but you do not accept our testimony. ¹² If I have told you about earthly things and you don't believe, how will you believe if I tell you about heavenly things? ¹³ No one has ascended into heaven except the one who descended from heaven — the Son of Man.ᶜ ¹⁴ "Just as Moses lifted up the snake in the wilderness, so the Son of Man must be lifted up, ¹⁵ so that everyone who believes in him mayᴰ have eternal life. ¹⁶ For God loved the world in this way:ᴱ He gaveᶠ his one and only Son, so that everyone who believes in him will not perish but have eternal life. ¹⁷ For God did not send his Son into the world to condemn the world, but to save the world through him. ¹⁸ Anyone who believes in him is not condemned, but anyone who does not believe is already condemned, because he has not believed in the name of the one and only Son of God. ¹⁹ This is the judgment: The light has come into the world, and people loved darkness rather than the light because their deeds were evil. ²⁰ For everyone who does evil hates the light and avoids it,ᴳ so that his deeds may not be exposed. ²¹ But anyone who lives byᴴ the truth comes to the light, so

---

ᴬ3:3 Or from above, also in v. 7 ᴮ3:10 Or the teacher ᶜ3:13 Other mss add who is in heaven
ᴰ3:15 Other mss add not perish, but ᴱ3:16 Or this much ᶠ3:16 Or For in this way God loved the world, and so he gave, or For God so loved the world that he gave ᴳ3:20 Lit and does not come to the light
ᴴ3:21 Lit who does

that his works may be shown to be accomplished by God." Ps 77:20; Mt 8:4

Jesus and John the Baptist

²² After this, Jesus and his disciples went to the Judean countryside, where he spent time with them and baptized.

²³ John also was baptizing in Aenon near Salim, because there was plenty of water there. People were coming and being baptized, ²⁴ since John had not yet been thrown into prison. Mk 1:4,14

²⁵ Then a dispute arose between John's disciples and a Jew ᴬ about purification. ²⁶ So they came to John and told him, "Rabbi, the one you testified about, and who was with you across the Jordan, is baptizing — and everyone is going to him." Mt 9:14; 11:2; 14:12; Mk 2:18; 6:29; Lk 5:33; 11:1

²⁷ John responded, "No one can receive anything unless it has been given to him from heaven. ²⁸ You yourselves can testify that I said, 'I am not the Messiah, but I've been sent ahead of him.' ²⁹ He who has the bride is the groom. But the groom's friend, who stands by and listens for him, rejoices greatly ᴮ at the groom's voice. So this joy of mine is complete. ³⁰ He must increase, but I must decrease." Mt 1:17

The One from Heaven

³¹ The one who comes from above is above all. The one who is from the earth is earthly and speaks in earthly terms. ᶜ The one who comes from heaven is above all. ³² He testifies to what he has seen and heard, and yet no one accepts his testimony. ³³ The one who has accepted his testimony has affirmed that God is true. ³⁴ For the one whom God sent speaks God's words, since he ᴰ gives the Spirit without measure. ³⁵ The Father loves the Son and has given all things into his hands. ³⁶ The one who believes in the Son has eternal life, but the one who rejects the Son ᴱ will not see life; instead, the wrath of God remains on him. Jn 8:23

Jesus and the Samaritan Woman

4 When Jesus ᶠ learned that the Pharisees had heard he was making and baptizing more disciples than John ² (though Jesus himself was not baptizing, but his disciples were), ³ he left Judea and went again to Galilee. ⁴ He had to travel through Samaria; ⁵ so he came to a town of Samaria called Sychar near the property ᴳ that Jacob had given his son Joseph. ⁶ Jacob's well was there, and Jesus, worn out from his journey, sat down at the well. It was about noon. ᴴ   Mt 28:19-20; Mk 1:4; 7:3; Lk 1:5; Ac 1:8

⁷ A woman of Samaria came to draw water. Gn 24:11-17; 29:2-12

"Give me a drink," Jesus said to her, ⁸ because his disciples had gone into town to buy food.

⁹ "How is it that you, a Jew, ask for a drink from me, a Samaritan woman?" she asked him. For Jews do not associate with ᴵ Samaritans. ᴶ

¹⁰ Jesus answered, "If you knew the gift of God, and who is saying to you, 'Give me a drink,' you would ask him, and he would give you living water." Gn 26:19; Ps 36:7-9; Is 49:10; Ac 8:20

ᴬ3:25 Other mss read *and the Jews*   ᴮ3:29 Lit *with joy rejoices*   ᶜ3:31 Or *of earthly things*
ᴰ3:34 Other mss read *since God*   ᴱ3:36 Or *refuses to believe in the Son*, or *disobeys the Son*
ᶠ4:1 Other mss read *the Lord*   ᴳ4:5 Lit *piece of land*   ᴴ4:6 Lit *about the sixth hour*   ᴵ4:9 Or *do not share vessels with*   ᴶ4:9 Other mss omit *For Jews do not associate with Samaritans.*

¹¹ "Sir," said the woman, "you don't even have a bucket, and the well is deep. So where do you get this 'living water'? ¹² You aren't greater than our father Jacob, are you? He gave us the well and drank from it himself, as did his sons and livestock." Mt 1:2; Lk 1:33; 10:1

¹³ Jesus said, "Everyone who drinks from this water will get thirsty again. ¹⁴ But whoever drinks from the water that I will give him will never get thirsty again. In fact, the water I will give him will become a well^A of water springing up in him for eternal life." Jn 6:35

¹⁵ "Sir," the woman said to him, "give me this water so that I won't get thirsty and come here to draw water."

¹⁶ "Go call your husband," he told her, "and come back here."

¹⁷ "I don't have a husband," she answered.

"You have correctly said, 'I don't have a husband,' " Jesus said. ¹⁸ "For you've had five husbands, and the man you now have is not your husband. What you have said is true."

¹⁹ "Sir," the woman replied, "I see that you are a prophet. ²⁰ Our fathers worshiped on this mountain, but you Jews say that the place to worship is in Jerusalem." Dt 27:3

²¹ Jesus told her, "Believe me, woman, an hour is coming when you will worship the Father neither on this mountain nor in Jerusalem. ²² You Samaritans worship what you do not know. We worship what we do know, because salvation is from the Jews. ²³ But an hour is coming, and is now here, when the true worshipers will worship the Father in Spirit and in truth.^B Yes, the Father wants such people

to worship him. ²⁴ God is spirit, and those who worship him must worship in Spirit and in truth." Gn 12:1-7

²⁵ The woman said to him, "I know that the Messiah is coming" (who is called Christ). "When he comes, he will explain everything to us."

²⁶ Jesus told her, "I, the one speaking to you, am he." Ex 3:14; Ps 45:8; Jn 8:24

The Ripened Harvest

²⁷ Just then his disciples arrived, and they were amazed that he was talking with a woman. Yet no one said, "What do you want? " or "Why are you talking with her? "

²⁸ Then the woman left her water jar, went into town, and told the people, ²⁹ "Come, see a man who told me everything I ever did. Could this be the Messiah? " ³⁰ They left the town and made their way to him. Mt 1:17; Mk 1:45

³¹ In the meantime the disciples kept urging him, "Rabbi, eat something." Jn 11:8

³² But he said, "I have food to eat that you don't know about."

³³ The disciples said to one another, "Could someone have brought him something to eat? "

³⁴ "My food is to do the will of him who sent me and to finish his work," Jesus told them. ³⁵ "Don't you say, 'There are still four more months, and then comes the harvest'? Listen to what I'm telling you: Open^C your eyes and look at the fields, because they are ready^D for harvest. ³⁶ The reaper is already receiving pay and gathering fruit for eternal life, so that the sower and reaper can rejoice together. ³⁷ For in this case the saying is true: 'One sows and another reaps.' ³⁸ I sent you to reap what you didn't

---

^A 4:14 Or spring   ^B 4:23 Or in spirit and truth, also in v. 24   ^C 4:35 Lit Raise   ^D 4:35 Lit white labor for; others have labored, and you have benefited from [A] their labor." Mk 10:17; Jn 5:30,36; Eph 1:9; 1Jn 2:17

The Savior of the World

[39] Now many Samaritans from that town believed in him because of what the woman said [B] when she testified, "He told me everything I ever did." [40] So when the Samaritans came to him, they asked him to stay with them, and he stayed there two days. [41] Many more believed because of what he said. [C] [42] And they told the woman, "We no longer believe because of what you said, since we have heard for ourselves and know that this really is the Savior of the world." [D] Lk 9:52; Jn 15:26; Ac 1:8; 26:5

A Galilean Welcome

[43] After two days he left there for Galilee. [44] (Jesus himself had testified that a prophet has no honor in his own country.) [45] When they entered Galilee, the Galileans welcomed him because they had seen everything he did in Jerusalem during the festival. For they also had gone to the festival. Is 9:1-2; Mk 6:4

The Second Sign: Healing an Official's Son

[46] He went again to Cana of Galilee, where he had turned the water into wine. There was a certain royal official whose son was ill at Capernaum. [47] When this man heard that Jesus had come from Judea into Galilee, he went to him and pleaded with him to come down and heal his son, since he was about to die. Lk 1:5; 10:15; Jn 2:1,11; 21:2

[48] Jesus told him, "Unless you people see signs and wonders, you will not believe." Ex 7:3-4; Mk 13:22

[49] "Sir," the official said to him, "come down before my boy dies."

[50] "Go," Jesus told him, "your son will live." The man believed what [E] Jesus said to him and departed.

[51] While he was still going down, his servants met him saying that his boy was alive. [52] He asked them at what time he got better. "Yesterday at one in the afternoon [F] the fever left him," they answered. [53] The father realized this was the very hour at which Jesus had told him, "Your son will live." So he himself believed, along with his whole household. Lk 11:11; Col 3:21

[54] Now this was also the second sign Jesus performed after he came from Judea to Galilee. Mt 17:22; Jn 2:11

The Third Sign: Healing the Sick

5 After this, a Jewish festival took place, and Jesus went up to Jerusalem. [2] By the Sheep Gate in Jerusalem there is a pool, called Bethesda [G] in Aramaic, which has five colonnades. [3] Within these lay a large number of the disabled — blind, lame, and paralyzed. [H] Mt 23:37

[5] One man was there who had been disabled for thirty-eight years. [6] When Jesus saw him lying there and realized he had already been there a long time, he said to him, "Do you want to get well?" Jn 6:6

[7] "Sir," the disabled man answered, "I have no one to put me

---

[A] 4:38 Lit *you have entered into*　[B] 4:39 Lit *because of the woman's word*　[C] 4:41 Lit *because of his word*　[D] 4:42 Other mss add , *the Messiah*　[E] 4:50 Lit *the word*　[F] 4:52 Lit *at the seventh hour*　[G] 5:2 Some mss read *Bethzatha*; other mss read *Bethsaida*　[H] 5:3 Some mss include vv. 3b-4: *— waiting for the moving of the water,* [4]*because an angel would go down into the pool from time to time and stir up the water. Then the first one who got in after the water was stirred up recovered from whatever ailment he had.*

into the pool when the water is stirred up, but while I'm coming, someone goes down ahead of me."

⁸ "Get up," Jesus told him, "pick up your mat and walk." ⁹ Instantly the man got well, picked up his mat, and started to walk.

Now that day was the Sabbath, ¹⁰ and so the Jews said to the man who had been healed, "This is the Sabbath. The law prohibits you from picking up your mat." Mk 2:23

¹¹ He replied, "The man who made me well told me, 'Pick up your mat and walk.'" Ti 2:8

¹² "Who is this man who told you, 'Pick up your mat and walk'?" they asked. ¹³ But the man who was healed did not know who it was, because Jesus had slipped away into the crowd that was there.ᴬ

¹⁴ After this, Jesus found him in the temple and said to him, "See, you are well. Do not sin anymore, so that something worse doesn't happen to you." ¹⁵ The man went and reported to the Jews that it was Jesus who had made him well. ¹⁶ Therefore, the Jews began persecuting Jesusᴮ because he was doing these things on the Sabbath. Ac 21:26; Ti 2:8

Honoring the Father and the Son

¹⁷ Jesus responded to them, "My Father is still working, and I am working also." ¹⁸ This is why the Jews began trying all the more to kill him: Not only was he breaking the Sabbath, but he was even calling God his own Father, making himself equal to God. Mt 5:16; 11:27; 27:1

¹⁹ Jesus replied, "Truly I tell you, the Son is not able to do anything on his own, but only what he sees the Father doing. For whatever the Fatherᶜ does, the Son likewise does these things. ²⁰ For the Father loves the Son and shows him everything he is doing, and he will show him greater works than these so that you will be amazed. ²¹ And just as the Father raises the dead and gives them life, so the Son also gives life to whom he wants. ²² The Father, in fact, judges no one but has given all judgment to the Son, ²³ so that all people may honor the Son just as they honor the Father. Anyone who does not honor the Son does not honor the Father who sent him. Jn 3:35; 6:38; 7:16,28; 8:26-42

Life and Judgment

²⁴ "Truly I tell you, anyone who hears my word and believes him who sent me has eternal life and will not come under judgment but has passed from death to life.

²⁵ "Truly I tell you, an hour is coming, and is now here, when the dead will hear the voice of the Son of God, and those who hear will live. ²⁶ For just as the Father has life in himself, so also he has granted to the Son to have life in himself. ²⁷ And he has granted him the right to pass judgment, because he is the Son of Man. ²⁸ Do not be amazed at this, because a time is coming when all who are in the graves will hear his voice ²⁹ and come out — those who have done good things, to the resurrection of life, but those who have done wicked things, to the resurrection of condemnation. Jn 4:23

³⁰ "I can do nothing on my own. I judge only as I hear, and my judgment is just, because I do not seek my own will, but the will of him who sent me. Mt 6:33; 6:38; 12:41; 2Th 1:5

ᴬ 5:13 Lit slipped away, there being a crowd in that place   ᴮ 5:16 Other mss add and trying to kill him   ᶜ 5:19 Lit whatever that one

Witnesses to Jesus

³¹ "If I testify about myself, my testimony is not true. ³² There is another who testifies about me, and I know that the testimony he gives about me is true. ³³ You sent messengers to John, and he testified to the truth. ³⁴ I don't receive human testimony, but I say these things so that you may be saved. ³⁵ John ᴬ was a burning and shining lamp, and you were willing to rejoice for a while in his light.   Ps 119:142; 1Jn 5:20

³⁶ "But I have a greater testimony than John's because of the works that the Father has given me to accomplish. These very works I am doing testify about me that the Father has sent me. ³⁷ The Father who sent me has himself testified about me. You have not heard his voice at any time, and you haven't seen his form. ³⁸ You don't have his word residing in you, because you don't believe the one he sent. ³⁹ You pore over the Scriptures because you think you have eternal life in them, and yet they testify about me. ⁴⁰ But you are not willing to come to me so that you may have life.   Jn 15:24

⁴¹ "I do not accept glory from people, ⁴² but I know you — that you have no love for God within you. ⁴³ I have come in my Father's name, and yet you don't accept me. If someone else comes in his own name, you will accept him. ⁴⁴ How can you believe, since you accept glory from one another but don't seek the glory that comes from the only God? ⁴⁵ Do not think that I will accuse you to the Father. Your accuser is Moses, on whom you have set your hope. ⁴⁶ For if you believed Moses, you would believe me, because he wrote about me.

⁴⁷ But if you don't believe what he wrote, how will you believe my words?"   Lk 10:27; Jn 17:24; Php 3:19; 1Pt 5:4

The Fourth Sign: Feeding of the Five Thousand

6 After this, Jesus crossed the Sea of Galilee (or Tiberias). ² A huge crowd was following him because they saw the signs that he was performing by healing the sick. ³ Jesus went up a mountain and sat down there with his disciples.   Mt 14:13-21

⁴ Now the Passover, a Jewish festival, was near. ⁵ So when Jesus looked up and noticed a huge crowd coming toward him, he asked Philip, "Where will we buy bread so that these people can eat?" ⁶ He asked this to test him, for he himself knew what he was going to do.   Ex 15:25; Mk 1:45; 3:18

⁷ Philip answered him, "Two hundred denarii ᴮ worth of bread wouldn't be enough for each of them to have a little."   Mt 18:28

⁸ One of his disciples, Andrew, Simon Peter's brother, said to him, ⁹ "There's a boy here who has five barley loaves and two fish — but what are they for so many?"   Mt 4:18

¹⁰ Jesus said, "Have the people sit down."

There was plenty of grass in that place; so they sat down. The men numbered about five thousand. ¹¹ Then Jesus took the loaves, and after giving thanks he distributed them to those who were seated — so also with the fish, as much as they wanted.   2Kg 4:42-44; Mt 14:21

¹² When they were full, he told his disciples, "Collect the leftovers so that nothing is wasted." ¹³ So they collected them and filled twelve baskets with the pieces from the

---

ᴬ**5:35** Lit *That man*   ᴮ**6:7** A denarius = one day's wage five barley loaves that were left over by those who had eaten.

[14] When the people saw the sign[A] he had done, they said, "This truly is the Prophet who is to come into the world." Dt 18:15; Mt 11:3; Lk 7:19-20; Rm 5:14

[15] Therefore, when Jesus realized that they were about to come and take him by force to make him king, he withdrew again to the mountain by himself. Jn 19:21

The Fifth Sign: Walking on Water

[16] When evening came, his disciples went down to the sea, [17] got into a boat, and started across the sea to Capernaum. Darkness had already set in, but Jesus had not yet come to them. [18] A high wind arose, and the sea began to churn. [19] After they had rowed about three or four miles,[B] they saw Jesus walking on the sea. He was coming near the boat, and they were afraid. [20] But he said to them, "It is I.[C] Don't be afraid." [21] Then they were willing to take him on board, and at once the boat was at the shore where they were heading. Mt 14:22-36; Lk 10:15

The Bread of Life

[22] The next day, the crowd that had stayed on the other side of the sea saw there had been only one boat.[D] They also saw that Jesus had not boarded the boat with his disciples, but that his disciples had gone off alone. [23] Some boats from Tiberias came near the place where they had eaten the bread after the Lord had given thanks. [24] When the crowd saw that neither Jesus nor his disciples were there, they got into the boats and went

to Capernaum looking for Jesus. [25] When they found him on the other side of the sea, they said to him, "Rabbi, when did you get here?"

[26] Jesus answered, "Truly I tell you, you are looking for me, not because you saw[E] the signs, but because you ate the loaves and were filled. [27] Don't work for the food that perishes but for the food that lasts for eternal life, which the Son of Man will give you, because God the Father has set his seal of approval on him." Is 55:2; Jn 12:25; Ac 13:48

[28] "What can we do to perform the works of God?" they asked.

[29] Jesus replied, "This is the work of God — that you believe in the one he has sent." Mk 9:37; Jn 1:6; 5:36

[30] "What sign, then, are you going to do so we may see and believe you?" they asked. "What are you going to perform? [31] Our ancestors ate the manna in the wilderness, just as it is written: **He gave them bread from heaven to eat."**[F]

[32] Jesus said to them, "Truly I tell you, Moses didn't give you the bread from heaven, but my Father gives you the true bread from heaven. [33] For the bread of God is the one who comes down from heaven and gives life to the world."

[34] Then they said, "Sir, give us this bread always."

[35] "I am the bread of life," Jesus told them. "No one who comes to me will ever be hungry, and no one who believes in me will ever be thirsty again. [36] But as I told you, you've seen me,[G] and yet you do not believe. [37] Everyone the Father gives me will come to me, and the one who comes to me I will never

---

[A] 6:14 Other mss read signs   [B] 6:19 Lit twenty-five or thirty stadia; one stadion = 600 feet   [C] 6:20 Lit "I am
[D] 6:22 Other mss add into which his disciples had entered   [E] 6:26 Or perceived   [F] 6:31 Ex 16:4; Ps 78:24
[G] 6:36 Other mss omit me

cast out. ³⁸ For I have come down from heaven, not to do my own will, but the will of him who sent me. ³⁹ This is the will of him who sent me: that I should lose none of those he has given me but should raise them up on the last day. ⁴⁰ For this is the will of my Father: that everyone who sees the Son and believes in him will have eternal life, and I will raise him up on the last day." _{Lk 14:26; Jn 4:14; 8:24; Rv 7:16,38}

⁴¹ **Therefore the Jews started complaining about him because he said,** "I am the bread that came down from heaven." ⁴² **They were saying,** "Isn't this Jesus the son of Joseph, whose father and mother we know? How can he now say, 'I have come down from heaven'?"

⁴³ **Jesus answered them,** "Stop complaining among yourselves. ⁴⁴ No one can come to me unless the Father who sent me draws ᴬ him, and I will raise him up on the last day. ⁴⁵ It is written in the Prophets: **And they will all be taught by God.** ᴮ Everyone who has listened to and learned from the Father comes to me — ⁴⁶ not that anyone has seen the Father except the one who is from God. He has seen the Father. _{Is 54:13; Mt 2:23; Ac 7:52; 1Co 2:13; 1Th 4:9}

⁴⁷ "Truly I tell you, anyone who believes ᶜ has eternal life. ⁴⁸ I am the bread of life. ⁴⁹ Your ancestors ate the manna in the wilderness, and they died. ⁵⁰ This is the bread that comes down from heaven so that anyone may eat of it and not die. ⁵¹ I am the living bread that came down from heaven. If anyone eats of this bread he will live forever. The bread that I will give for the life of the world is my flesh." _{Ex 16:12-36}

⁵² At that, the Jews argued among themselves, "How can this man give us his flesh to eat?" _{2Tm 2:24}

⁵³ So Jesus said to them, "Truly I tell you, unless you eat the flesh of the Son of Man and drink his blood, you do not have life in yourselves. ⁵⁴ The one who eats my flesh and drinks my blood has eternal life, and I will raise him up on the last day, ⁵⁵ because my flesh is true food and my blood is true drink. ⁵⁶ The one who eats my flesh and drinks my blood remains in me, and I in him. ⁵⁷ Just as the living Father sent me and I live because of the Father, so the one who feeds on me will live because of me. ⁵⁸ This is the bread that came down from heaven; it is not like the manna ᴰ your ancestors ate — and they died. The one who eats this bread will live forever."

⁵⁹ He said these things while teaching in the synagogue in Capernaum. _{Lk 10:15; Jms 2:2}

Many Disciples Desert Jesus

⁶⁰ Therefore, when many of his disciples heard this, they said, "This teaching is hard. Who can accept ᴱ it?"

⁶¹ Jesus, knowing in himself that his disciples were complaining about this, asked them, "Does this offend you? ⁶² Then what if you were to observe the Son of Man ascending to where he was before? ⁶³ The Spirit is the one who gives life. The flesh doesn't help at all. The words that I have spoken to you are spirit and are life. ⁶⁴ But there are some among you who don't believe." (For Jesus knew from the beginning those who did not ꟳ believe and the one who would

---

ᴬ**6:44** Or *brings,* or *leads*　ᴮ**6:45** Is 54:13　ᶜ**6:47** Other mss add *in me*　ᴰ**6:58** Other mss omit *the manna*
ᴱ**6:60** Lit *hear*　ꟳ**6:64** Other mss omit *not*

betray him.) ⁶⁵ He said, "This is why I told you that no one can come to me unless it is granted to him by the Father." Mk 10:32; Jn 1:47-48

⁶⁶ From that moment^A many of his disciples turned back and no longer accompanied him. ⁶⁷ So Jesus said to the Twelve, "You don't want to go away too, do you?"

⁶⁸ Simon Peter answered, "Lord, to whom will we go? You have the words of eternal life. ⁶⁹ We have come to believe and know that you are the Holy One of God."^B Lk 6:14

⁷⁰ Jesus replied to them, "Didn't I choose you, the Twelve? Yet one of you is a devil." ⁷¹ He was referring to Judas, Simon Iscariot's son,^C one of the Twelve, because he was going to betray him. Mt 4:1,10; Jn 13:18

The Unbelief of Jesus's Brothers

7 After this, Jesus traveled in Galilee, since he did not want to travel in Judea because the Jews were trying to kill him. ² The Jewish Festival of Shelters^D was near. ³ So his brothers said to him, "Leave here and go to Judea so your disciples can see your works that you are doing. ⁴ For no one does anything in secret while he's seeking public recognition. If you do these things, show yourself to the world." ⁵ (For not even his brothers believed in him.) Mt 17:22; Lk 1:5; Jn 11:36

⁶ Jesus told them, "My time has not yet arrived, but your time is always at hand. ⁷ The world cannot hate you, but it does hate me because I testify about it — that its works are evil. ⁸ Go up to the festival yourselves. I'm not going up to this festival,^E because my time has not yet fully come." ⁹ After he

had said these things, he stayed in Galilee. Ps 37:39; Lk 6:27; 19:14; 20:10; Jn 7:8

Jesus at the Festival of Shelters

¹⁰ After his brothers had gone up to the festival, then he also went up, not openly but secretly. ¹¹ The Jews were looking for him at the festival and saying, "Where is he?" ¹² And there was a lot of murmuring about him among the crowds. Some were saying, "He's a good man." Others were saying, "No, on the contrary, he's deceiving the people." ¹³ Still, nobody was talking publicly about him for fear of the Jews. Gn 1:31

¹⁴ When the festival was already half over, Jesus went up into the temple and began to teach. ¹⁵ Then the Jews were amazed and said, "How is this man so learned, since he hasn't been trained?" Ac 21:26

¹⁶ Jesus answered them, "My teaching isn't mine but is from the one who sent me. ¹⁷ If anyone wants to do his will, he will know whether the teaching is from God or whether I am speaking on my own. ¹⁸ The one who speaks on his own seeks his own glory; but he who seeks the glory of the one who sent him is true, and there is no unrighteousness in him. ¹⁹ Didn't Moses give you the law? Yet none of you keeps the law. Why are you trying to kill me?" Jn 5:19,30; Rm 8:27

²⁰ "You have a demon!" the crowd responded. "Who is trying to kill you?"

²¹ "I performed one work, and you are all amazed," Jesus answered. ²² "This is why Moses has given you circumcision — not that it comes from Moses but from the fathers — and you circumcise a man on

---

^A 6:66 Or Because of this   ^B 6:69 Other mss read you are the Messiah, the Son of the Living God
^C 6:71 Or Judas Iscariot, Simon's son   ^D 7:2 Or Tabernacles, or Booths   ^E 7:8 Other mss add yet

the Sabbath. ²³ If a man receives circumcision on the Sabbath so that the law of Moses won't be broken, are you angry at me because I made a man entirely well on the Sabbath? ²⁴ Stop judging according to outward appearances; rather judge according to righteous judgment." Jn 5:36; Heb 3:9

The Identity of the Messiah

²⁵ Some of the people of Jerusalem were saying, "Isn't this the man they are trying to kill? ²⁶ Yet, look, he's speaking publicly and they're saying nothing to him. Can it be true that the authorities know he is the Messiah? ²⁷ But we know where this man is from. When the Messiah comes, nobody will know where he is from." Mt 23:37; Lk 8:41; 12:58

²⁸ As he was teaching in the temple, Jesus cried out, "You know me and you know where I am from. Yet I have not come on my own, but the one who sent me is true. You don't know him; ²⁹ I know him because I am from him, and he sent me."

³⁰ Then they tried to seize him. Yet no one laid a hand on him because his hour had not yet come. ³¹ However, many from the crowd believed in him and said, "When the Messiah comes, he won't perform more signs than this man has done, will he?" ³² The Pharisees heard the crowd murmuring these things about him, and so the chief priests and the Pharisees sent servants^A to arrest him. Mt 2:4; Mk 7:3; Jn 15:24

³³ Then Jesus said, "I am only with you for a short time. Then I'm going to the one who sent me. ³⁴ You will look for me, but you will not find me; and where I am, you cannot come." Jn 12:35; 14:12,19; 16:5,16

³⁵ Then the Jews said to one another, "Where does he intend to go so we won't find him? He doesn't intend to go to the Jewish people dispersed^B among the Greeks and teach the Greeks, does he? ³⁶ What is this remark he made: 'You will look for me, and you will not find me; and where I am, you cannot come'?" Jn 8:21; 11:36; Gl 2:3; Jms 1:1; 1Pt 1:1

The Promise of the Spirit

³⁷ On the last and most important day of the festival, Jesus stood up and cried out, "If anyone is thirsty, let him come to me^C and drink. ³⁸ The one who believes in me, as the Scripture has said, will have streams of living water flow from deep within him." ³⁹ He said this about the Spirit. Those who believed in Jesus were going to receive the Spirit, for the Spirit^D had not yet been given^E because Jesus had not yet been glorified. Nm 29:35

The People Are Divided over Jesus

⁴⁰ When some from the crowd heard these words, they said, "This truly is the Prophet." ⁴¹ Others said, "This is the Messiah." But some said, "Surely the Messiah doesn't come from Galilee, does he? ⁴² Doesn't the Scripture say that the Messiah comes from David's offspring^F and from the town of Bethlehem, where David lived?" ⁴³ So the crowd was divided because of him. ⁴⁴ Some of them wanted to seize him, but no one laid hands on him. Lk 1:27; Jn 6:14; 2Pt 1:20

---

^A7:32 Or temple police, or officers, also in vv. 45,46   ^B7:35 Gk diaspora ; Jewish people scattered throughout Gentile lands   ^C7:37 Other mss omit to me   ^D7:39 Other mss read Holy Spirit   ^E7:39 Lit the Spirit was not yet   ^F7:42 Lit seed

Debate over Jesus's Claims

⁴⁵ Then the servants came to the chief priests and Pharisees, who asked them, "Why didn't you bring him?" Mt 2:4; Jn 18:18

⁴⁶ The servants answered, "No man ever spoke like this!"ᴬ

⁴⁷ Then the Pharisees responded to them: "Are you fooled too? ⁴⁸ Have any of the rulers or Pharisees believed in him? ⁴⁹ But this crowd, which doesn't know the law, is accursed." Lk 8:41; Rv 20:10

⁵⁰ Nicodemus — the one who came to him previously and who was one of them — said to them, ⁵¹ "Our law doesn't judge a man before it hears from him and knows what he's doing, does it?" Jn 3:1; 19:39

⁵² "You aren't from Galilee too, are you?" they replied. "Investigate and you will see that no prophet arises from Galilee." 2Kg 14:25; Mt 17:22

[The earliest mss do not include 7:53–8:11.]ᴮ

8 [⁵³ Then each one went to his house. ¹ But Jesus went to the Mount of Olives. Mt 21:1

An Adulteress Forgiven

² At dawn he went to the temple again, and all the people were coming to him. He sat down and began to teach them. Mk 1:45; 9:35; Ac 21:26

³ Then the scribes and the Pharisees brought a woman caught in adultery, making her stand in the center. ⁴ "Teacher," they said to him, "this woman was caught in the act of committing adultery. ⁵ In the law Moses commanded us to stone such women. So what do you say?" ⁶ They asked this to trap him, in order that they might have evidence to accuse him. Mk 7:3

Jesus stooped down and started writing on the ground with his finger. ⁷ When they persisted in questioning him, he stood up and said to them, "The one without sin among you should be the first to throw a stone at her." ⁸ Then he stooped down again and continued writing on the ground. ⁹ When they heard this, they left one by one, starting with the older men. Only he was left, with the woman in the center. ¹⁰ When Jesus stood up, he said to her, "Woman, where are they? Has no one condemned you?" Rm 3:23

¹¹ "No one, Lord,"ᶜ she answered.

"Neither do I condemn you," said Jesus. "Go, and from now on do not sin anymore."] Jn 3:17

The Light of the World

¹² Jesus spoke to them again: "I am the light of the world. Anyone who follows me will never walk in the darkness but will have the light of life." Ex 3:14; Ps 36:9; Jn 8:24,58; 12:46; 1Jn 2:8

¹³ So the Pharisees said to him, "You are testifying about yourself. Your testimony is not valid."

¹⁴ "Even if I testify about myself," Jesus replied, "My testimony is true, because I know where I came from and where I'm going. But you don't know where I come from or where I'm going. ¹⁵ You judge by human standards.ᴰ I judge no one. ¹⁶ And if I do judge, my judgment is true, because it is not I alone who judge, but I and the Father who sent me.

ᴬ**7:46** Other mss read *like this man*   ᴮ**7:53–8:11** Other mss include all or some of the passage after Jn 7:36,44,52; 21:25; or Lk 21:38.   ᶜ**8:11** Or *Sir*; Jn 4:15,49; 5:7; 6:34; 9:36   ᴰ**8:15** Lit *You judge according to the flesh*

¹⁷ Even in your law it is written that the testimony of two witnesses is true. ¹⁸ I am the one who testifies about myself, and the Father who sent me testifies about me."   Jn 3:8

¹⁹ Then they asked him, "Where is your Father?"

"You know neither me nor my Father," Jesus answered. "If you knew me, you would also know my Father." ²⁰ He spoke these words by the treasury, while teaching in the temple. But no one seized him, because his hour had not yet come.

Jesus Predicts His Departure

²¹ Then he said to them again, "I'm going away; you will look for me, and you will die in your sin. Where I'm going, you cannot come."

²² So the Jews said again, "He won't kill himself, will he, since he says, 'Where I'm going, you cannot come'?"   Jn 8:21

²³ "You are from below," he told them, "I am from above. You are of this world; I am not of this world. ²⁴ Therefore I told you that you will die in your sins. For if you do not believe that I am he, you will die in your sins."   Jn 3:13,31; 18:36; Col 3:1-2; 1Jn 4:5

²⁵ "Who are you?" they questioned.

"Exactly what I've been telling you from the very beginning," Jesus told them. ²⁶ "I have many things to say and to judge about you, but the one who sent me is true, and what I have heard from him — these things I tell the world."

²⁷ They did not know he was speaking to them about the Father. ²⁸ So Jesus said to them, "When you lift up the Son of Man, then you will know that I am he, and that I do nothing on my own. But just as the Father taught me, I say these things. ²⁹ The one who sent me is with me. He has not left me alone, because I always do what pleases him."   Mk 2:10; 6:5; Jn 8:24; 9:33; 15:5

Truth and Freedom

³⁰ As he was saying these things, many believed in him.

³¹ Then Jesus said to the Jews who had believed him, "If you continue in my word, ^A you really are my disciples. ³² You will know the truth, and the truth will set you free."

³³ "We are descendants ^B of Abraham," they answered him, "and we have never been enslaved to anyone. How can you say, 'You will become free'?"   Gn 16:15; Jn 8:37; Heb 2:16

³⁴ Jesus responded, "Truly I tell you, everyone who commits sin is a slave of sin. ³⁵ A slave does not remain in the household forever, but a son does remain forever. ³⁶ So if the Son sets you free, you really will be free. ³⁷ I know you are descendants of Abraham, but you are trying to kill me because my word has no place among you. ³⁸ I speak what I have seen in the presence of the Father; ^C so then, you do what you have heard from your father."

³⁹ "Our father is Abraham," they replied.

"If you were Abraham's children," Jesus told them, "you would do what Abraham did. ⁴⁰ But now you are trying to kill me, a man who has told you the truth that I heard from God. Abraham did not do this. ⁴¹ You're doing what your father does."   Ps 119:142; Jn 14:6; Gl 3:7,9; 2Jn 9

"We weren't born of sexual immorality," they said. "We have one Father — God."   Hs 2:4; 1Th 4:3; 1Jn 2:29

^A 8:31 Or *my teaching*, or *my message*, also in v. 37   ^B 8:33 Or *offspring*; lit *seed*, also in v. 37; Jn 7:42
^C 8:38 Other mss read *of my Father*

⁴² Jesus said to them, "If God were your Father, you would love me, because I came from God and I am here. For I didn't come on my own, but he sent me. ⁴³ Why don't you understand what I say? Because you cannot listen toᴬ my word. ⁴⁴ You are of your father the devil, and you want to carry out your father's desires. He was a murderer from the beginning and does not stand in the truth, because there is no truth in him. When he tells a lie, he speaks from his own nature,ᴮ because he is a liar and the father of lies. ⁴⁵ Yet because I tell the truth, you do not believe me. ⁴⁶ Who among you can convict me of sin? If I am telling the truth, why don't you believe me? ⁴⁷ The one who is from God listens to God's words. This is why you don't listen, because you are not from God."   Dt 6:5; Lk 10:27; 1Jn 5:1

Jesus and Abraham

⁴⁸ The Jews responded to him, "Aren't we right in saying that you're a Samaritan and have a demon?"

⁴⁹ "I do not have a demon," Jesus answered. "On the contrary, I honor my Father and you dishonor me. ⁵⁰ I do not seek my own glory; there is one who seeks it and judges. ⁵¹ Truly I tell you, if anyone keeps my word, he will never see death."   Jn 15:20; 17:24

⁵² Then the Jews said, "Now we know you have a demon. Abraham died and so did the prophets. You say, 'If anyone keeps my word, he will never taste death.' ⁵³ Are you greater than our father Abraham who died? And the prophets died. Who do you claim to be?"

⁵⁴ "If I glorify myself," Jesus answered, "my glory is nothing. My Father — about whom you say, 'He is our God' — he is the one who glorifies me. ⁵⁵ You do not know him, but I know him. If I were to say I don't know him, I would be a liar like you. But I do know him, and I keep his word. ⁵⁶ Your father Abraham rejoiced to see my day; he saw it and was glad."   Mt 11:27; Lk 10:24; Jn 7:28; Heb 11:13-19

⁵⁷ The Jews replied, "You aren't fifty years old yet, and you've seen Abraham?"ᶜ

⁵⁸ Jesus said to them, "Truly I tell you, before Abraham was, I am."

⁵⁹ So they picked up stones to throw at him. But Jesus was hiddenᴰ and went out of the temple.ᴱ

The Sixth Sign: Healing a Man Born Blind

9 As he was passing by, he saw a man blind from birth. ² His disciples asked him: "Rabbi, who sinned, this man or his parents, that he was born blind?"   Jn 11:8

³ "Neither this man nor his parents sinned," Jesus answered. "This came about so that God's works might be displayed in him. ⁴ Weᶠ must do the works of him who sent meᴳ while it is day. Night is coming when no one can work. ⁵ As long as I am in the world, I am the light of the world."   Jn 5:36; 6:28-29; Rm 14:20

⁶ After he said these things he spit on the ground, made some mud from the saliva, and spread the mud on his eyes. ⁷ "Go," he told him, "wash in the pool of Siloam" (which means "Sent"). So he left, washed, and came back seeing.   Gn 2:7; Is 35:5; Lk 13:4; Jn 9:11

ᴬ**8:43** Or *cannot hear*   ᴮ**8:44** Lit *from his own things*   ᶜ**8:57** Other mss read *and Abraham has seen you?*   ᴰ**8:59** Or *Jesus hid himself*   ᴱ**8:59** Other mss add *and having gone through their midst, he passed by*   ᶠ**9:4** Other mss read *I*   ᴳ**9:4** Other mss read *us*

⁸ His neighbors and those who had seen him before as a beggar said, "Isn't this the one who used to sit begging?" ⁹ Some said, "He's the one." Others were saying, "No, but he looks like him."

He kept saying, "I'm the one."

¹⁰ So they asked him, "Then how were your eyes opened?"

¹¹ He answered, "The man called Jesus made mud, spread it on my eyes, and told me, 'Go to Siloam and wash.' So when I went and washed I received my sight."   Jn 9:7; Ac 9:12

¹² "Where is he?" they asked.

"I don't know," he said.

The Healed Man's Testimony

¹³ They brought the man who used to be blind to the Pharisees. ¹⁴ The day that Jesus made the mud and opened his eyes was a Sabbath. ¹⁵ Then the Pharisees asked him again how he received his sight.   Mk 2:23; 7:3

"He put mud on my eyes," he told them. "I washed and I can see."

¹⁶ Some of the Pharisees said, "This man is not from God, because he doesn't keep the Sabbath." But others were saying, "How can a sinful man perform such signs?" And there was a division among them.

¹⁷ Again they asked the blind man, "What do you say about him, since he opened your eyes?"

"He's a prophet," he said.   Jn 6:14

¹⁸ The Jews did not believe this about him — that he was blind and received sight — until they summoned the parents of the one who had received his sight.

¹⁹ They asked them, "Is this your son, the one you say was born blind? How then does he now see?"

²⁰ "We know this is our son and that he was born blind," his parents answered. ²¹ "But we don't know how he now sees, and we don't know who opened his eyes. Ask him; he's of age. He will speak for himself." ²² His parents said these things because they were afraid of the Jews, since the Jews had already agreed that if anyone confessed him as the Messiah, he would be banned from the synagogue. ²³ This is why his parents said, "He's of age; ask him."   Mt 1:17; Eph 5:2

²⁴ So a second time they summoned the man who had been blind and told him, "Give glory to God. We know that this man is a sinner."

²⁵ He answered, "Whether or not he's a sinner, I don't know. One thing I do know: I was blind, and now I can see!"

²⁶ Then they asked him, "What did he do to you? How did he open your eyes?"

²⁷ "I already told you," he said, "and you didn't listen. Why do you want to hear it again? You don't want to become his disciples too, do you?"

²⁸ They ridiculed him: "You're that man's disciple, but we're Moses's disciples. ²⁹ We know that God has spoken to Moses. But this man — we don't know where he's from."   Ps 77:20; Mt 8:4; Jn 7:27-28; 8:14; Heb 3:2

³⁰ "This is an amazing thing!" the man told them. "You don't know where he is from, and yet he opened my eyes. ³¹ We know God doesn't listen to sinners, but if anyone is God-fearing and does his will, he listens to him. ³² Throughout history^A no one has ever heard of someone opening the eyes of a person born blind. ³³ If this man were not from God, he wouldn't be able to do anything."   Jb 27:9; Pr 28:9

^A 9:32 Lit From the age

³⁴ "You were born entirely in sin," they replied, "and are you trying to teach us?" Then they threw him out. *Ps 51:5; Is 66:5*

Spiritual Blindness

³⁵ Jesus heard that they had thrown the man out, and when he found him, he asked, "Do you believe in the Son of Man?"ᴬ *Mk 2:10*
³⁶ "Who is he, Sir, that I may believe in him?" he asked. *Lk 10:1*
³⁷ Jesus answered, "You have seen him; in fact, he is the one speaking with you."
³⁸ "I believe, Lord!" he said, and he worshiped him.
³⁹ Jesus said, "I came into this world for judgment, in order that those who do not see will see and those who do see will become blind." *Mk 12:40; Lk 4:18; Jn 5:22-30; 18:37*
⁴⁰ Some of the Pharisees who were with him heard these things and asked him, "We aren't blind too, are we?"
⁴¹ "If you were blind," Jesus told them, "you wouldn't have sin. But now that you say, 'We see,' your sin remains." *Jn 15:22,24; 1Jn 1:8; 3:5*

The Good Shepherd

10 "Truly I tell you, anyone who doesn't enter the sheep pen by the gate but climbs in some other way is a thief and a robber. ² The one who enters by the gate is the shepherd of the sheep. ³ The gatekeeper opens it for him, and the sheep hear his voice. He calls his own sheep by name and leads them out. ⁴ When he has brought all his own outside, he goes ahead of them. The sheep follow him because they know his voice. ⁵ They will never follow a stranger; instead they will run away from him, because they don't know the voice of strangers." ⁶ Jesus gave them this figure of speech, but they did not understand what he was telling them. *Jr 7:11; Hs 6:9; 1Th 5:2,4*

⁷ Jesus said again, "Truly I tell you, I am the gate for the sheep. ⁸ All who came before meᴮ are thieves and robbers, but the sheep didn't listen to them. ⁹ I am the gate. If anyone enters by me, he will be saved and will come in and go out and find pasture. ¹⁰ A thief comes only to steal and kill and destroy. I have come so that they may have life and have it in abundance. *Ex 3:14; Ps 45:8*

¹¹ "I am the good shepherd. The good shepherd lays down his life for the sheep. ¹² The hired hand, since he is not the shepherd and doesn't own the sheep, leaves themᶜ and runs away when he sees a wolf coming. The wolf then snatches and scatters them. ¹³ This happens because he is a hired hand and doesn't care about the sheep. *Ps 23; Is 40:11*

¹⁴ "I am the good shepherd. I know my own, and my own know me, ¹⁵ just as the Father knows me, and I know the Father. I lay down my life for the sheep. ¹⁶ But I have other sheep that are not from this sheep pen; I must bring them also, and they will listen to my voice. Then there will be one flock, one shepherd. ¹⁷ This is why the Father loves me, because I lay down my life so that I may take it up again. ¹⁸ No one takes it from me, but I lay it down on my own. I have the right to lay it down, and I have the right to take it up again. I have received this command from my Father." *Is 56:8; Mt 11:27*

¹⁹ Again the Jews were divided because of these words. ²⁰ Many of them were saying, "He has a demon

ᴬ**9:35** Other mss read *the Son of God*   ᴮ**10:8** Other mss omit *before me*   ᶜ**10:12** Lit *leaves the sheep* and he's crazy. Why do you listen to him?" [21] Others were saying, "These aren't the words of someone who is demon-possessed. Can a demon open the eyes of the blind?" Jn 7:43

Jesus at the Festival of Dedication

[22] Then the Festival of Dedication took place in Jerusalem, and it was winter. [23] Jesus was walking in the temple in Solomon's Colonnade. [24] The Jews surrounded him and asked, "How long are you going to keep us in suspense? [A] If you are the Messiah, tell us plainly." [B] Ac 3:11; 5:12

[25] "I did tell you and you don't believe," Jesus answered them. "The works that I do in my Father's name testify about me. [26] But you don't believe because you are not of my sheep. [C] [27] My sheep hear my voice, I know them, and they follow me. [28] I give them eternal life, and they will never perish. No one will snatch them out of my hand. [29] My Father, who has given them to me, is greater than all. No one is able to snatch them out of the Father's hand. [30] I and the Father are one." Jn 5:36; 6:28-29; Rm 14:20; Heb 3:9

Renewed Efforts to Stone Jesus

[31] Again the Jews picked up rocks to stone him. Jn 11:8

[32] Jesus replied, "I have shown you many good works from the Father. For which of these works are you stoning me?" Jn 5:36; 15:24

[33] "We aren't stoning you for a good work," the Jews answered, "but for blasphemy, because you — being a man — make yourself God." Lv 24:16; Mt 9:3; 26:62-66; Jn 5:18; 8:59

[34] Jesus answered them, "Isn't it written in your law, [D] I said, you are gods? [E] [35] If he called those whom the word of God came to 'gods' — and the Scripture cannot be broken — [36] do you say, 'You are blaspheming' to the one the Father set apart and sent into the world, because I said: I am the Son of God? [37] If I am not doing my Father's works, don't believe me. [38] But if I am doing them and you don't believe me, believe the works. This way you will know and understand [F] that the Father is in me and I in the Father." [39] Then they were trying again to seize him, but he eluded their grasp. Ps 82:6; Lk 8:21

Many Beyond the Jordan Believe in Jesus

[40] So he departed again across the Jordan to the place where John had been baptizing earlier, and he remained there. [41] Many came to him and said, "John never did a sign, but everything John said about this man was true." [42] And many believed in him there. Mk 10:1; Lk 3:3

Lazarus Dies at Bethany

11 Now a man was sick, Lazarus from Bethany, the village of Mary and her sister Martha. [2] Mary was the one who anointed the Lord with perfume and wiped his feet with her hair, and it was her brother Lazarus who was sick. [3] So the sisters sent a message to him: "Lord, the one you love is sick." Mk 11:1; Lk 7:38; 10:38-42; Jn 12:3

[4] When Jesus heard it, he said, "This sickness will not end in death but is for the glory of God, so that

the Son of God may be glorified through it." ⁵ Now Jesus loved Martha, her sister, and Lazarus. ⁶ So when he heard that he was sick, he stayed two more days in the place where he was. ⁷ Then after that, he said to the disciples, "Let's go to Judea again." Lk 9:32; Jn 9:3; 10:38; 11:40; 17:24

⁸ "Rabbi," the disciples told him, "just now the Jews tried to stone you, and you're going there again?"

⁹ "Aren't there twelve hours in a day?" Jesus answered. "If anyone walks during the day, he doesn't stumble, because he sees the light of this world. ¹⁰ But if anyone walks during the night, he does stumble, because the light is not in him." Mt 5:14; Jn 8:12; 9:4

¹¹ He said this, and then he told them, "Our friend Lazarus has fallen asleep, but I'm on my way to wake him up." Ac 13:36; 1Co 11:30

¹² Then the disciples said to him, "Lord, if he has fallen asleep, he will get well."

¹³ Jesus, however, was speaking about his death, but they thought he was speaking about natural sleep. ¹⁴ So Jesus then told them plainly, "Lazarus has died. ¹⁵ I'm glad for you that I wasn't there so that you may believe. But let's go to him."

¹⁶ Then Thomas (called "Twin"ᴬ) said to his fellow disciples, "Let's go too so that we may die with him."

The Resurrection and the Life

¹⁷ When Jesus arrived, he found that Lazarus had already been in the tomb four days. ¹⁸ Bethany was near Jerusalem (less than two milesᴮ away). ¹⁹ Many of the Jews had come to Martha and Mary to comfort them about their brother. Jn 5:28

²⁰ As soon as Martha heard that Jesus was coming, she went to meet him, but Mary remained seated in the house. ²¹ Then Martha said to Jesus, "Lord, if you had been here, my brother wouldn't have died. ²² Yet even now I know that whatever you ask from God, God will give you."

²³ "Your brother will rise again," Jesus told her. Mk 9:27

²⁴ Martha said to him, "I know that he will rise again in the resurrection at the last day." Jn 2:4; 6:39

²⁵ Jesus said to her, "I am the resurrection and the life. The one who believes in me, even if he dies, will live. ²⁶ Everyone who lives and believes in me will never die. Do you believe this?" Ex 3:14; Jn 6:35; 8:24,51,58

²⁷ "Yes, Lord," she told him, "I believe you are the Messiah, the Son of God, who comes into the world."

Jesus Shares the Sorrow of Death

²⁸ Having said this, she went back and called her sister Mary, saying in private, "The Teacher is here and is calling for you."

²⁹ As soon as Mary heard this, she got up quickly and went to him. ³⁰ Jesus had not yet come into the village but was still in the place where Martha had met him. ³¹ The Jews who were with her in the house consoling her saw that Mary got up quickly and went out. They followed her, supposing that she was going to the tomb to cry there. Mk 1:45; Jn 5:28

³² As soon as Mary came to where Jesus was and saw him, she fell at his feet and told him, "Lord, if you had been here, my brother would not have died!" Rv 19:10

ᴬ11:16 Gk *Didymus*   ᴮ11:18 Lit *fifteen stadia*; one *stadion* = 600 feet

³³ When Jesus saw her crying, and the Jews who had come with her crying, he was deeply moved^A in his spirit and troubled. ³⁴ "Where have you put him?" he asked.

"Lord," they told him, "come and see."

³⁵ Jesus wept.   Lk 19:41

³⁶ So the Jews said, "See how he loved him!" ³⁷ But some of them said, "Couldn't he who opened the blind man's eyes also have kept this man from dying?"   Mk 14:44; Jn 5:20

The Seventh Sign: Raising Lazarus from the Dead

³⁸ Then Jesus, deeply moved again, came to the tomb. It was a cave, and a stone was lying against it. ³⁹ "Remove the stone," Jesus said.

Martha, the dead man's sister, told him, "Lord, there is already a stench because he has been dead four days."

⁴⁰ Jesus said to her, "Didn't I tell you that if you believed you would see the glory of God?"   Mk 9:23; Jn 17:24

⁴¹ So they removed the stone. Then Jesus raised his eyes and said, "Father, I thank you that you heard me. ⁴² I know that you always hear me, but because of the crowd standing here I said this, so that they may believe you sent me." ⁴³ After he said this, he shouted with a loud voice, "Lazarus, come out!" ⁴⁴ The dead man came out bound hand and foot with linen strips and with his face wrapped in a cloth. Jesus said to them, "Unwrap him and let him go."   Mk 8:6; 9:37; Jn 1:6; 9:31; Rm 1:8

The Plot to Kill Jesus

⁴⁵ Therefore, many of the Jews who came to Mary and saw what he did believed in him. ⁴⁶ But some of them went to the Pharisees and told them what Jesus had done.   Mk 7:3; Jn 2:23; 12:11

⁴⁷ So the chief priests and the Pharisees convened the Sanhedrin and were saying, "What are we going to do since this man is doing many signs? ⁴⁸ If we let him go on like this, everyone will believe in him, and the Romans will come and take away both our place and our nation."   Mk 13:9; Ac 16:21

⁴⁹ One of them, Caiaphas, who was high priest that year, said to them, "You know nothing at all! ⁵⁰ You're not considering that it is to your^B advantage that one man should die for the people rather than the whole nation perish." ⁵¹ He did not say this on his own, but being high priest that year he prophesied that Jesus was going to die for the nation, ⁵² and not for the nation only, but also to unite the scattered children of God. ⁵³ So from that day on they plotted to kill him.   Mt 26:3,57; Lk 3:2; Jn 18:13-14,24,28

⁵⁴ Jesus therefore no longer walked openly among the Jews but departed from there to the countryside near the wilderness, to a town called Ephraim, and he stayed there with the disciples.

⁵⁵ Now the Jewish Passover was near, and many went up to Jerusalem from the country to purify themselves before the Passover. ⁵⁶ They were looking for Jesus and asking one another as they stood in the temple: "What do you think? He won't come to the festival, will he?" ⁵⁷ The chief priests and the Pharisees had given orders that if anyone knew where he was, he should report it so that they could arrest him.   Ex 12:11; Mt 23:37; Jn 2:23; Ac 21:26

^A 11:33 Or *angry*, also in v. 38   ^B 11:50 Other mss read *to our*

The Anointing at Bethany

12 Six days before the Passover, Jesus came to Bethany where Lazarus[A] was, the one Jesus had raised from the dead. [2] So they gave a dinner for him there; Martha was serving them, and Lazarus was one of those reclining at the table with him. [3] Then Mary took a pound of perfume, pure and expensive nard, anointed Jesus's feet, and wiped his feet with her hair. So the house was filled with the fragrance of the perfume. Mt 26:6-13; Mk 11:1; Jn 11:1,43-44

[4] Then one of his disciples, Judas Iscariot (who was about to betray him), said, [5] "Why wasn't this perfume sold for three hundred denarii[B] and given to the poor?" [6] He didn't say this because he cared about the poor but because he was a thief. He was in charge of the money-bag and would steal part of what was put in it. Mt 26:14

[7] Jesus answered, "Leave her alone; she has kept it for the day of my burial. [8] For you always have the poor with you, but you do not always have me." Dt 15:11; Jn 19:40

The Decision to Kill Lazarus

[9] Then a large crowd of the Jews learned he was there. They came not only because of Jesus but also to see Lazarus, the one he had raised from the dead. [10] But the chief priests had decided to kill Lazarus also, [11] because he was the reason many of the Jews were deserting them[C] and believing in Jesus.

The Triumphal Entry

[12] The next day, when the large crowd that had come to the festival heard that Jesus was coming to Jerusalem, [13] they took palm branches and went out to meet him. They kept shouting: Lv 23:40; Mt 21:1-11; Mk 11:1-11

"*Hosanna!* Lk 1:42

Blessed is he who comes in the name of the Lord[D] —
the King of Israel!" Ps 118:25-26

[14] Jesus found a young donkey and sat on it, just as it is written: Lk 13:15

[15] **Do not be afraid,** Jn 6:20
**Daughter Zion. Look, your King is coming,
sitting on a donkey's colt.**[E]

[16] His disciples did not understand these things at first. However, when Jesus was glorified, then they remembered that these things had been written about him and that they had done these things to him. [17] Meanwhile, the crowd, which had been with him when he called Lazarus out of the tomb and raised him from the dead, continued to testify.[F] [18] This is also why the crowd met him, because they heard he had done this sign. [19] Then the Pharisees said to one another, "You see? You've accomplished nothing. Look, the world has gone after him!" Mk 15:6-15; Lk 19:39-44; Jn 5:28; 19:15

Jesus Predicts His Crucifixion

[20] Now some Greeks were among those who went up to worship at the festival. [21] So they came to Philip, who was from Bethsaida in Galilee, and requested of him, "Sir, we want to see Jesus." [22] Philip went and told Andrew; then Andrew and Philip went and told Jesus. Mt 11:21; Mk 3:18; 6:45; 8:22; Lk 9:10

[23] Jesus replied to them, "The hour has come for the Son of Man to be

---

glorified. [24] Truly I tell you, unless a grain of wheat falls to the ground and dies, it remains by itself. But if it dies, it produces much fruit. [25] The one who loves his life will lose it, and the one who hates his life in this world will keep it for eternal life. [26] If anyone serves me, he must follow me. Where I am, there my servant also will be. If anyone serves me, the Father will honor him.   Mk 2:10; Lk 6:27; 16:7; Jn 10:28; 1Co 15:36

[27] "Now my soul is troubled. What should I say — Father, save me from this hour? But that is why I came to this hour. [28] Father, glorify your name." [A]   Ps 3:7; Jn 10:25; Ac 15:14

Then a voice came from heaven: "I have glorified it, and I will glorify it again."   Jn 5:37; 11:4; 17:1; Rv 14:13

[29] The crowd standing there heard it and said it was thunder. Others said, "An angel has spoken to him."

[30] Jesus responded, "This voice came, not for me, but for you. [31] Now is the judgment of this world. Now the ruler of this world will be cast out. [32] As for me, if I am lifted up [B] from the earth I will draw all people to myself." [33] He said this to indicate what kind of death he was about to die.   Lk 4:6; Jn 3:16; 11:42; 14:30

[34] Then the crowd replied to him, "We have heard from the law that the Messiah will remain forever. So how can you say, 'The Son of Man must be lifted up'? Who is this Son of Man?"   Ps 89:36; Mk 2:10; Jn 15:4; 1Jn 2:17

[35] Jesus answered, "The light will be with you only a little longer. Walk while you have the light so that darkness doesn't overtake you. The one who walks in darkness doesn't know where he's going. [36] While you have the light, believe in the light so that you may become children of light." Jesus said this, then went away and hid from them.   Ps 36:9; 118:27; Jn 7:33; 8:14; 9:4

Isaiah's Prophecies Fulfilled

[37] Even though he had performed so many signs in their presence, they did not believe in him. [38] This was to fulfill the word of Isaiah the prophet, who said: [C]   Mt 1:22; 3:3; 4:14

Lord, who has believed
our message?
And to whom has the arm
of the Lord
been revealed? [D]   Ex 15:16; Is 53:1

[39] This is why they were unable to believe, because Isaiah also said:
[40] He has blinded their eyes
and hardened their hearts,
so that they would not see
with their eyes
or understand
with their hearts,
and turn,   Is 56:3,6; Mt 18:3; 23:15
and I would heal them. [E]

[41] Isaiah said these things because [F] he saw his glory and spoke about him.   Mk 10:37; Jn 17:24

[42] Nevertheless, many did believe in him even among the rulers, but because of the Pharisees they did not confess him, so that they would not be banned from the synagogue. [43] For they loved human praise more than praise from God.   Lk 8:41; 9:32; 2Co 3:18; Php 3:19

A Summary of Jesus's Mission

[44] Jesus cried out, "The one who believes in me believes not in me, but in him who sent me. [45] And the one who sees me sees him who sent

---

[A] 12:28 Other mss read your Son   [B] 12:32 Or exalted, also in v. 34   [C] 12:38 Lit which he said
[D] 12:38 Is 53:1   [E] 12:40 Is 6:10   [F] 12:41 Other mss read when

me. ⁴⁶ I have come as light into the world, so that everyone who believes in me would not remain in darkness. ⁴⁷ If anyone hears my words and doesn't keep them, I do not judge him; for I did not come to judge the world but to save the world. ⁴⁸ The one who rejects me and doesn't receive my sayings has this as his judge: ᴬ The word I have spoken will judge him on the last day. ⁴⁹ For I have not spoken on my own, but the Father himself who sent me has given me a command to say everything I have said. ⁵⁰ I know that his command is eternal life. So the things that I speak, I speak just as the Father has told me." Lk 11:28; Jn 6:35; 14:9; 2Tm 1:14; 2Pt 3:17

Jesus Washes His Disciples' Feet

13 Before the Passover Festival, Jesus knew that his hour had come to depart from this world to the Father. Having loved his own who were in the world, he loved them to the end. Jn 6:37; 10:18; 12:23; 16:28 ² Now when it was time for supper, the devil had already put it into the heart of Judas, Simon Iscariot's son, ᴮ to betray him. ³ Jesus knew that the Father had given everything into his hands, that he had come from God, and that he was going back to God. ⁴ So he got up from supper, laid aside his outer clothing, took a towel, and tied it around himself. ⁵ Next, he poured water into a basin and began to wash his disciples' feet and to dry them with the towel tied around him. Mt 4:1,10; 10:4; Mk 3:19; Jn 8:44; Ac 13:10 ⁶ He came to Simon Peter, who asked him, "Lord, are you going to wash my feet?" Mt 16:17

⁷ Jesus answered him, "What I'm doing you don't realize now, but afterward you will understand."

⁸ "You will never wash my feet," Peter said.

Jesus replied, "If I don't wash you, you have no part with me."

⁹ Simon Peter said to him, "Lord, not only my feet, but also my hands and my head."

¹⁰ "One who has bathed," Jesus told him, "doesn't need to wash anything except his feet, but he is completely clean. You are clean, but not all of you." ¹¹ For he knew who would betray him. This is why he said, "Not all of you are clean."

The Meaning of Foot Washing

¹² When Jesus had washed their feet and put on his outer clothing, he reclined again and said to them, "Do you know what I have done for you? ¹³ You call me Teacher and Lord — and you are speaking rightly, since that is what I am. ¹⁴ So if I, your Lord and Teacher, have washed your feet, you also ought to wash one another's feet. ¹⁵ For I have given you an example, that you also should do just as I have done for you. 1Tm 5:10; 1Pt 2:21; 5:5 ¹⁶ "Truly I tell you, a servant is not greater than his master, ᶜ and a messenger is not greater than the one who sent him. ¹⁷ If you know these things, you are blessed if you do them. Mt 7:24-25; Lk 6:47; 11:28; Jn 15:20 ¹⁸ "I'm not speaking about all of you; I know those I have chosen. But the Scripture must be fulfilled: **The one who eats my bread** ᴰ **has raised his heel against me.** ᴱ ¹⁹ I am telling you now before it happens, so that when it does happen you

---

ᴬ12:48 Lit *has the one judging him*   ᴮ13:2 Or *Judas Iscariot, Simon's son*   ᶜ13:16 Or *lord*
ᴰ13:18 Other mss read *eats bread with me*   ᴱ13:18 Ps 41:9

will believe that I am he. ²⁰ Truly I tell you, whoever receives anyone I send receives me, and the one who receives me receives him who sent me."   Ps 41:9; Mt 1:22; 26:54; Jn 6:70; Eph 1:4

Judas's Betrayal Predicted

²¹ When Jesus had said this, he was troubled in his spirit and testified, "Truly I tell you, one of you will betray me."   Mt 26:20-25; Mk 14:17-21; Lk 22:21-23

²² The disciples started looking at one another — uncertain which one he was speaking about. ²³ One of his disciples, the one Jesus loved, was reclining close beside Jesus.ᴬ ²⁴ Simon Peter motioned to him to find out who it was he was talking about. ²⁵ So he leaned back against Jesus and asked him, "Lord, who is it?"   Jn 19:26; 20:2; 21:7,20

²⁶ Jesus replied, "He's the one I give the piece of bread to after I have dipped it." When he had dipped the bread, he gave it to Judas, Simon Iscariot's son.ᴮ ²⁷ After Judas ate the piece of bread, Satan entered him. So Jesus told him, "What you're doing, do quickly."

²⁸ None of those reclining at the table knew why he said this to him. ²⁹ Since Judas kept the money-bag, some thought that Jesus was telling him, "Buy what we need for the festival," or that he should give something to the poor. ³⁰ After receiving the piece of bread, he immediately left. And it was night.   Mk 3:19; Jn 2:23

The New Command

³¹ When he had left, Jesus said, "Now the Son of Man is glorified, and God is glorified in him. ³² If God is glorified in him,ᶜ God will also

glorify him in himself and will glorify him at once. ³³ Children, I am with you a little while longer. You will look for me, and just as I told the Jews, so now I tell you: 'Where I am going, you cannot come.'

³⁴ "I give you a new command: Love one another. Just as I have loved you, you are also to love one another. ³⁵ By this everyone will know that you are my disciples, if you love one another."

Peter's Denials Predicted

³⁶ "Lord," Simon Peter said to him, "where are you going?"

Jesus answered, "Where I am going you cannot follow me now, but you will follow later."   Jn 14:2; 16:5

³⁷ "Lord," Peter asked, "why can't I follow you now? I will lay down my life for you."   Mk 14:31; 1Jn 3:16

³⁸ Jesus replied, "Will you lay down your life for me? Truly I tell you, a rooster will not crow until you have denied me three times.

The Way to the Father

14 "Don't let your heart be troubled. Believeᴰ in God; believe also in me. ² In my Father's house are many rooms; if not, I would have told you. I am going away to prepare a place for you. ³ If I go away and prepare a place for you, I will come again and take you to myself, so that where I am you may be also. ⁴ You know the way to where I am going."ᴱ   Jn 14:27; Ac 16:34

⁵ "Lord," Thomas said, "we don't know where you're going. How can we know the way?"   Mk 3:18

⁶ Jesus told him, "I am the way, the truth, and the life. No one comes

---

ᴬ**13:23** Lit *reclining at Jesus's breast*; that is, on his right; Jn 1:18   ᴮ**13:26** Or *Judas Iscariot, Simon's son*
ᶜ**13:32** Other mss omit *If God is glorified in him*   ᴰ**14:1** Or *You believe*   ᴱ**14:4** Other mss read this verse: *And you know where I am going, and you know the way*

to the Father except through me. [7] If you know me, you will also know[A] my Father. From now on you do know him and have seen him."

Jesus Reveals the Father

[8] "Lord," said Philip, "show us the Father, and that's enough for us."

[9] Jesus said to him, "Have I been among you all this time and you do not know me, Philip? The one who has seen me has seen the Father. How can you say, 'Show us the Father'? [10] Don't you believe that I am in the Father and the Father is in me? The words I speak to you I do not speak on my own. The Father who lives in me does his works. [11] Believe me that I am in the Father and the Father is in me. Otherwise, believe[B] because of the works themselves.　Jn 5:19,37

Praying in Jesus's Name

[12] "Truly I tell you, the one who believes in me will also do the works that I do. And he will do even greater works than these, because I am going to the Father. [13] Whatever you ask in my name, I will do it so that the Father may be glorified in the Son. [14] If you ask me[C] anything in my name, I will do it.[D]　Jn 5:20; 6:35

Another Counselor Promised

[15] "If you love me, you will keep[E] my commands. [16] And I will ask the Father, and he will give you another Counselor[F] to be with you forever. [17] He is the Spirit of truth. The world is unable to receive him because it doesn't see him or know him. But you do know him, because he remains with you and will be[G] in you.

The Father, the Son, and the Holy Spirit

[18] "I will not leave you as orphans; I am coming to you. [19] In a little while the world will no longer see me, but you will see me. Because I live, you will live too. [20] On that day you will know that I am in my Father, you are in me, and I am in you. [21] The one who has my commands and keeps them is the one who loves me. And the one who loves me will be loved by my Father. I also will love him and will reveal myself to him."

[22] Judas (not Iscariot) said to him, "Lord, how is it you're going to reveal yourself to us and not to the world?"　Lk 6:16; Ac 1:13; 10:40-41

[23] Jesus answered, "If anyone loves me, he will keep my word. My Father will love him, and we will come to him and make our home with him. [24] The one who doesn't love me will not keep my words. The word that you hear is not mine but is from the Father who sent me.

[25] "I have spoken these things to you while I remain with you. [26] But the Counselor, the Holy Spirit, whom the Father will send in my name, will teach you all things and remind you of everything I have told you.　Ps 51:11; Jn 1:33; Ac 2:4; Rm 8:9; Gl 5:25

Jesus's Gift of Peace

[27] "Peace I leave with you. My peace I give to you. I do not give to you as the world gives. Don't let your heart be troubled or fearful. [28] You have heard me tell you, 'I am going away and I am coming to you.' If you loved me, you would rejoice that I am going to the Father, because the Father is greater than I.

[A] **14:7** Other mss read *If you had known me, you would have known*　　[B] **14:11** Other mss read *believe me*　　[C] **14:14** Other mss omit *me*　　[D] **14:14** Other mss omit all of v. 14　　[E] **14:15** Other mss read *"If you love me, keep* (as a command)　　[F] **14:16** Or *advocate,* or *comforter,* also in v. 26　　[G] **14:17** Other mss read *and is*

²⁹ I have told you now before it happens so that when it does happen you may believe. ³⁰ I will not talk with you much longer, because the ruler of the world is coming. He has no power over me.ᴬ ³¹ On the contrary, so that the world may know that I love the Father, I do as the Father commanded me.   Jn 16:5; 2Tm 1:7

"Get up; let's leave this place.

The Vine and the Branches

15 "I am the true vine, and my Father is the gardener. ² Every branch in me that does not produce fruit he removes, and he prunes every branch that produces fruit so that it will produce more fruit. ³ You are already clean because of the word I have spoken to you. ⁴ Remain in me, and I in you. Just as a branch is unable to produce fruit by itself unless it remains on the vine, neither can you unless you remain in me. ⁵ I am the vine; you are the branches. The one who remains in me and I in him produces much fruit, because you can do nothing without me. ⁶ If anyone does not remain in me, he is thrown aside like a branch and he withers. They gather them, throw them into the fire, and they are burned. ⁷ If you remain in me and my words remain in you, ask whatever you want and it will be done for you. ⁸ My Father is glorified by this: that you produce much fruit and prove to beᴮ my disciples.

Christlike Love

⁹ "As the Father has loved me, I have also loved you. Remain in my love. ¹⁰ If you keep my commands you will remain in my love, just as I have kept my Father's commands and remain in his love.   Col 1:13; 1Jn 5:20; Jd 21

¹¹ "I have told you these things so that my joy may be in you and your joy may be complete.   1Jn 1:4; 2Jn 12

¹² "This is my command: Love one another as I have loved you. ¹³ No one has greater love than this: to lay down his life for his friends. ¹⁴ You are my friends if you do what I command you. ¹⁵ I do not call you servants anymore, because a servant doesn't know what his masterᶜ is doing. I have called you friends, because I have made known to you everything I have heard from my Father. ¹⁶ You did not choose me, but I chose you. I appointed you to go and produce fruit and that your fruit should remain, so that whatever you ask the Father in my name, he will give you.   Jn 3:16; Rm 5:8

¹⁷ "This is what I command you: Love one another.

Persecutions Predicted

¹⁸ "If the world hates you, understand that it hated me before it hated you. ¹⁹ If you were of the world, the world would love you as its own. However, because you are not of the world, but I have chosen you out of it, the world hates you. ²⁰ Remember the word I spoke to you: 'A servant is not greater than his master.' If they persecuted me, they will also persecute you. If they kept my word, they will also keep yours. ²¹ But they will do all these things to you on account of my name, because they don't know the one who sent me. ²² If I had not come and spoken to them, they would not be guilty of sin. Now they have no excuse for their sin. ²³ The one who hates me also hates my Father. ²⁴ If I had not done the works among them that no one else has done,

ᴬ**14:30** Lit *He has nothing in me*   ᴮ**15:8** Or *and become*   ᶜ**15:15** Or *lord* they would not have sin. Now they have seen and hated both me and my Father. [25] But this happened so that the statement written in their law might be fulfilled: **They hated me for no reason.** [A] Lk 6:27; 19:14; Eph 1:4

The Counselor's Ministry

[26] "When the Counselor comes, the one I will send to you from the Father — the Spirit of truth who proceeds from the Father — he will testify about me. [27] You also will testify, because you have been with me from the beginning. Jn 1:33; 14:16

16 "I have told you these things to keep you from stumbling. [2] They will ban you from the synagogues. In fact, a time is coming when anyone who kills you will think he is offering service to God. [3] They will do these things because they haven't known the Father or me. [4] But I have told you these things so that when their time [B] comes you will remember I told them to you. I didn't tell you these things from the beginning, because I was with you. [5] But now I am going away to him who sent me, and not one of you asks me, 'Where are you going?' [6] Yet, because I have spoken these things to you, sorrow has filled your heart. [7] Nevertheless, I am telling you the truth. It is for your benefit that I go away, because if I don't go away the Counselor will not come to you. If I go, I will send him to you. [8] When he comes, he will convict the world about sin, righteousness, and judgment: [9] About sin, because they do not believe in me; [10] about righteousness, because I am going to the Father and you will no longer

see me; [11] and about judgment, because the ruler of this world has been judged. Ex 12:25; Jn 7:28; 9:22; 12:42

[12] "I still have many things to tell you, but you can't bear them now. [13] When the Spirit of truth comes, he will guide you into all the truth. For he will not speak on his own, but he will speak whatever he hears. He will also declare to you what is to come. [14] He will glorify me, because he will take from what is mine and declare it to you. [15] Everything the Father has is mine. This is why I told you that he takes from what is mine and will declare it to you. Mk 4:33; Jn 1:17; 14:6; Rm 3:7; 1Jn 4:6

Sorrow Turned to Joy

[16] "A little while and you will no longer see me; again a little while and you will see me." [C] Mk 2:20; 14:19; Jn 7:33

[17] Then some of his disciples said to one another, "What is this he's telling us: 'A little while and you will not see me; again a little while and you will see me,' and, 'Because I am going to the Father'?" [18] They said, "What is this he is saying, [D] 'A little while'? We don't know what he's talking about." Jn 14:12; 16:10

[19] Jesus knew they wanted to ask him, and so he said to them, "Are you asking one another about what I said, 'A little while and you will not see me; again a little while and you will see me'? [20] Truly I tell you, you will weep and mourn, but the world will rejoice. You will become sorrowful, but your sorrow will turn to joy. [21] When a woman is in labor, she has pain because her time has come. But when she has given birth to a child, she no longer remembers the suffering

---

[A]**15:25** Ps 69:4　[B]**16:4** Other mss read *when the time Father*　[C]**16:16** Other mss add *because I am going to the Father*　[D]**16:18** Other mss omit *he is saying* because of the joy that a person has been born into the world. ²² So you also have sorrow^A now. But I will see you again. Your hearts will rejoice, and no one will take away your joy from you. Mt 11:17; Lk 7:32; 23:27

²³ "In that day you will not ask me anything. Truly I tell you, anything you ask the Father in my name, he will give you. ²⁴ Until now you have asked for nothing in my name. Ask and you will receive, so that your joy may be complete. Jn 11:22; 14:13-14

Jesus the Victor

²⁵ "I have spoken these things to you in figures of speech. A time is coming when I will no longer speak to you in figures, but I will tell you plainly about the Father. ²⁶ On that day you will ask in my name, and I am not telling you that I will ask the Father on your behalf. ²⁷ For the Father himself loves you, because you have loved me and have believed that I came from God.^B ²⁸ I came from the Father and have come into the world. Again, I am leaving the world and going to the Father." Jn 6:46; 8:42; 10:25; 14:16,21

²⁹ His disciples said, "Look, now you're speaking plainly and not using any figurative language. ³⁰ Now we know that you know everything and don't need anyone to question you. By this we believe that you came from God." Mk 2:8; Jn 1:48; 2:24-25

³¹ Jesus responded to them, "Do you now believe? ³² Indeed, an hour is coming, and has come, when each of you will be scattered to his own home, and you will leave me alone. Yet I am not alone, because the Father is with me. ³³ I have told you these things so that in me you

may have peace. You will have suffering in this world. Be courageous! I have conquered the world."

Jesus Prays for Himself

17 Jesus spoke these things, looked up to heaven, and said: "Father, the hour has come. Glorify your Son so that the Son may glorify you, ² since you gave him authority over all flesh,^C so that he may give eternal life to everyone you have given him. ³ This is eternal life: that they may know you, the only true God, and the one you have sent — Jesus Christ. ⁴ I have glorified you on the earth by completing the work you gave me to do. ⁵ Now, Father, glorify me in your presence with that glory I had with you before the world existed. Jn 5:19; 12:25,28; Php 3:3; Heb 1:2

Jesus Prays for His Disciples

⁶ "I have revealed your name to the people you gave me from the world. They were yours, you gave them to me, and they have kept your word. ⁷ Now they know that everything you have given me is from you, ⁸ because I have given them the words you gave me. They have received them and have known for certain that I came from you. They have believed that you sent me. Jn 13:1

⁹ "I pray^D for them. I am not praying for the world but for those you have given me, because they are yours. ¹⁰ Everything I have is yours, and everything you have is mine, and I am glorified in them. ¹¹ I am no longer in the world, but they are in the world, and I am coming to you. Holy Father, protect^E them by your name that you have given

---

^A**16:22** Other mss read *will have sorrow*   ^B**16:27** Other mss read *from the Father*   ^C**17:2** Or *people*
^D**17:9** Lit *ask* (throughout this passage)   ^E**17:11** Lit *keep* (throughout this passage)

me, so that they may be one as we are one. ¹² While I was with them, I was protecting them by your name that you have given me. I guarded them and not one of them is lost, except the son of destruction, ^A so that the Scripture may be fulfilled. ¹³ Now I am coming to you, and I speak these things in the world so that they may have my joy completed in them. ¹⁴ I have given them your word. The world hated them because they are not of the world, just as I am not of the world. ¹⁵ I am not praying that you take them out of the world but that you protect them from the evil one. ¹⁶ They are not of the world, just as I am not of the world. ¹⁷ Sanctify them by the truth; your word is truth. ¹⁸ As you sent me into the world, I also have sent them into the world. ¹⁹ I sanctify myself for them, so that they also may be sanctified by the truth.　　Ps 20:6; Jn 13:3; 14:12; 16:15; Rm 9:11

Jesus Prays for All Believers

²⁰ "I pray not only for these, but also for those who believe in me through their word. ²¹ May they all be one, as you, Father, are in me and I am in you. May they also be ^B in us, so that the world may believe you sent me. ²² I have given them the glory you have given me, so that they may be one as we are one. ²³ I am in them and you are in me, so that they may be made completely one, that the world may know you have sent me and have loved them as you have loved me.　　Jn 11:52; 17:11

²⁴ "Father, I want those you have given me to be with me where I am, so that they will see my glory, which you have given me because

you loved me before the world's foundation. ²⁵ Righteous Father, the world has not known you. However, I have known you, and they have known that you sent me. ²⁶ I made your name known to them and will continue to make it known, so that the love you have loved me with may be in them and I may be in them."　　Mt 11:27; Lk 10:22; Jn 10:25; 12:26

Jesus Betrayed

18 After Jesus had said these things, he went out with his disciples across the Kidron Valley, where there was a garden, and he and his disciples went into it. ² Judas, who betrayed him, also knew the place, because Jesus often met there with his disciples. ³ So Judas took a company of soldiers and some officials ^C from the chief priests and the Pharisees and came there with lanterns, torches, and weapons.　　Mt 26:47-56; Mk 14:43-52

⁴ Then Jesus, knowing everything that was about to happen to him, went out and said to them, "Who is it that you're seeking?"　　Jn 16:30

⁵ "Jesus of Nazareth," they answered.

"I am he," Jesus told them.

Judas, who betrayed him, was also standing with them. ⁶ When Jesus told them, "I am he," they stepped back and fell to the ground. ⁷ Then he asked them again, "Who is it that you're seeking?"

"Jesus of Nazareth," they said.

⁸ "I told you I am he," Jesus replied. "So if you're looking for me, let these men go." ⁹ This was to fulfill the words he had said: "I have not lost one of those you have given me."　　Mt 1:22; Jn 17:6,12

---

^A **17:12** The one destined for destruction, loss, or perdition　^B **17:21** Other mss add *one*　^C **18:3** Or *temple police*, or *officers*, also in vv. 12,18,22

¹⁰ Then Simon Peter, who had a sword, drew it, struck the high priest's servant, and cut off his right ear. (The servant's name was Malchus.) Mt 16:17; Mk 14:47; Lk 6:14; Ac 10:32

¹¹ At that, Jesus said to Peter, "Put your sword away! Am I not to drink the cup the Father has given me?"

Jesus Arrested and Taken to Annas

¹² Then the company of soldiers, the commander, and the Jewish officials arrested Jesus and tied him up. ¹³ First they led him to Annas, since he was the father-in-law of Caiaphas, who was high priest that year. ¹⁴ Caiaphas was the one who had advised the Jews that it would be better for one man to die for the people. Mt 26:3; Lk 3:2; Jn 11:49; 18:24; Ac 4:6

Peter Denies Jesus

¹⁵ Simon Peter was following Jesus, as was another disciple. That disciple was an acquaintance of the high priest; so he went with Jesus into the high priest's courtyard. ¹⁶ But Peter remained standing outside by the door. So the other disciple, the one known to the high priest, went out and spoke to the girl who was the doorkeeper and brought Peter in. Lk 6:14

¹⁷ Then the servant girl who was the doorkeeper said to Peter, "You aren't one of this man's disciples too, are you?"

"I am not." he said. ¹⁸ Now the servants and the officials had made a charcoal fire, because it was cold. They were standing there warming themselves, and Peter was standing with them, warming himself.

ᴬ18:23 Or him, "testify

Jesus Before Annas

¹⁹ The high priest questioned Jesus about his disciples and about his teaching. Mt 26:3

²⁰ "I have spoken openly to the world," Jesus answered him. "I have always taught in the synagogue and in the temple, where all the Jews congregate, and I haven't spoken anything in secret. ²¹ Why do you question me? Question those who heard what I told them. Look, they know what I said." Jms 2:2

²² When he had said these things, one of the officials standing by slapped Jesus, saying, "Is this the way you answer the high priest?"

²³ "If I have spoken wrongly," Jesus answered him, "give evidenceᴬ about the wrong; but if rightly, why do you hit me?" ²⁴ Then Annas sent him bound to Caiaphas the high priest. Gn 1:31; Mt 26:57-75; Jn 18:13

Peter Denies Jesus Twice More

²⁵ Now Simon Peter was standing and warming himself. They said to him, "You aren't one of his disciples too, are you?"

He denied it and said, "I am not."

²⁶ One of the high priest's servants, a relative of the man whose ear Peter had cut off, said, "Didn't I see you with him in the garden?" ²⁷ Peter denied it again. Immediately a rooster crowed. Jn 13:38

Jesus Before Pilate

²⁸ Then they led Jesus from Caiaphas to the governor's headquarters. It was early morning. They did not enter the headquarters themselves; otherwise they would be defiled and unable to eat the Passover. Mt 27:2,11-14; Mk 15:1-5,16; Lk 23:25

²⁹ So Pilate came out to them and said, "What charge do you bring against this man?" 1Tm 5:19; 6:13

³⁰ They answered him, "If this man weren't a criminal,ᴬ we wouldn't have handed him over to you."

³¹ Pilate told them, "You take him and judge him according to your law."

"It's not legal for us to put anyone to death," the Jews declared. ³² They said this so that Jesus's words might be fulfilled indicating what kind of death he was going to die. Jn 12:32-33

³³ Then Pilate went back into the headquarters, summoned Jesus, and said to him, "Are you the King of the Jews?" Jn 19:21

³⁴ Jesus answered, "Are you asking this on your own, or have others told you about me?"

³⁵ "I'm not a Jew, am I?" Pilate replied. "Your own nation and the chief priests handed you over to me. What have you done?"

³⁶ "My kingdom is not of this world," said Jesus. "If my kingdom were of this world, my servants would fight, so that I wouldn't be handed over to the Jews. But as it is,ᴮ my kingdom is not from here."

³⁷ "You are a king then?" Pilate asked.

"You say that I'm a king," Jesus replied. "I was born for this, and I have come into the world for this: to testify to the truth. Everyone who is of the truth listens to my voice." Jn 1:9; 3:19; 6:14; 9:39; 11:27; 12:46; 16:28

³⁸ "What is truth?" said Pilate.

Jesus or Barabbas

After he had said this, he went out to the Jews again and told them, "I find no grounds for charging him. ³⁹ You have a custom that I release one prisoner to you at the Passover. So, do you want me to release to you the King of the Jews?" Mt 27:37

⁴⁰ They shouted back, "Not this man, but Barabbas!" Now Barabbas was a revolutionary.ᶜ Mk 15:7

Jesus Flogged and Mocked

19 Then Pilate took Jesus and had him flogged. ² The soldiers also twisted together a crown of thorns, put it on his head, and clothed him in a purple robe. ³ And they kept coming up to him and saying, "Hail, King of the Jews!" and were slapping his face. Mk 15:17

⁴ Pilate went outside again and said to them, "Look, I'm bringing him out to you to let you know I find no grounds for charging him." ⁵ Then Jesus came out wearing the crown of thorns and the purple robe. Pilate said to them, "Here is the man!" Zch 6:12; Lk 19:36; Jn 18:38

Pilate Sentences Jesus to Death

⁶ When the chief priests and the temple servantsᴰ saw him, they shouted, "Crucify! Crucify!"

Pilate responded, "Take him and crucify him yourselves, since I find no grounds for charging him."

⁷ "We have a law," the Jews replied to him, "and according to that law he ought to die, because he made himself the Son of God." Lv 24:16

⁸ When Pilate heard this statement, he was more afraid than ever. ⁹ He went back into the headquarters and asked Jesus, "Where are you from?" But Jesus did not give him an answer. ¹⁰ So Pilate said to him, "Do you refuse to speak to me?

ᴬ18:30 Lit an evil doer ᴮ18:36 Or But now ᶜ18:40 Or robber; see Jn 10:1,8 for the same Gk word used here ᴰ19:6 Or temple police, or officers

Don't you know that I have the authority to release you and the authority to crucify you?" Mk 15:16

¹¹ "You would have no authority over me at all," Jesus answered him, "if it hadn't been given you from above. This is why the one who handed me over to you has the greater sin." Jn 15:22; 18:13-14,19-24,28

¹² From that moment Pilate kept trying^A to release him. But the Jews shouted, "If you release this man, you are not Caesar's friend. Anyone who makes himself a king opposes Caesar!"

¹³ When Pilate heard these words, he brought Jesus outside. He sat down on the judge's seat in a place called the Stone Pavement (but in Aramaic,^B *Gabbatha*). ¹⁴ It was the preparation day for the Passover, and it was about noon.^C Then he told the Jews, "Here is your king!"

¹⁵ They shouted, "Take him away! Take him away! Crucify him!"

Pilate said to them, "Should I crucify your king?"

"We have no king but Caesar!" the chief priests answered.

¹⁶ Then he handed him over to be crucified.

The Crucifixion

Then they took Jesus away.^D ¹⁷ Carrying the cross by himself, he went out to what is called Place of the Skull, which in Aramaic is called *Golgotha*. ¹⁸ There they crucified him and two others with him, one on either side, with Jesus in the middle. ¹⁹ Pilate also had a sign made and put on the cross. It said: JESUS OF NAZARETH, THE KING OF THE JEWS. ²⁰ Many of the Jews read this sign, because the place where Jesus was crucified was near the city, and it was written in Aramaic, Latin, and Greek. ²¹ So the chief priests of the Jews said to Pilate, "Don't write, 'The King of the Jews,' but that he said, 'I am the King of the Jews.'" Mt 27:33-37; Mk 15:22-26; Lk 9:23

²² Pilate replied, "What I have written, I have written."

²³ When the soldiers crucified Jesus, they took his clothes and divided them into four parts, a part for each soldier. They also took the tunic, which was seamless, woven in one piece from the top. ²⁴ So they said to one another, "Let's not tear it, but cast lots for it, to see who gets it." This happened that the Scripture might be fulfilled that says:
They divided my clothes among themselves, and they cast lots for my clothing.^E This is what the soldiers did. Ps 22:18; Mt 1:22; 26:54

Jesus's Provision for His Mother

²⁵ Standing by the cross of Jesus were his mother, his mother's sister, Mary the wife of Clopas, and Mary Magdalene. ²⁶ When Jesus saw his mother and the disciple he loved standing there, he said to his mother, "Woman, here is your son." ²⁷ Then he said to the disciple, "Here is your mother." And from that hour the disciple took her into his home. Mt 27:55-56; Mk 15:40-41; Lk 23:49

The Finished Work of Jesus

²⁸ After this, when Jesus knew that everything was now finished that the Scripture might be fulfilled, he said, "I'm thirsty." ²⁹ A jar full of sour wine was sitting there; so they fixed a sponge full of sour wine on

---

^A 19:12 Lit *Pilate was trying*   ^B 19:13 Or *Hebrew*, also in vv. 17,20   ^C 19:14 Lit *about the sixth hour*
^D 19:16 Other mss add *and led him out*   ^E 19:24 Ps 22:18

a hyssop branch and held it up to his mouth. Mt 27:45-54; Mk 15:33-39; Lk 12:50

³⁰ When Jesus had received the sour wine, he said, "It is finished." Then bowing his head, he gave up his spirit. Lk 12:50; Jn 4:34; 17:4; 19:28; 1Jn 5:8

Jesus's Side Pierced

³¹ Since it was the preparation day, the Jews did not want the bodies to remain on the cross on the Sabbath (for that Sabbath was a special^A day). They requested that Pilate have the men's legs broken and that their bodies be taken away. ³² So the soldiers came and broke the legs of the first man and of the other one who had been crucified with him. ³³ When they came to Jesus, they did not break his legs since they saw that he was already dead. ³⁴ But one of the soldiers pierced his side with a spear, and at once blood and water came out. ³⁵ He who saw this has testified so that you also may believe. His testimony is true, and he knows he is telling the truth. ³⁶ For these things happened so that the Scripture would be fulfilled: **Not one of his bones will be broken.**^B ³⁷ Also, another Scripture says: **They will look at the one they pierced.**^C Lk 12:4; Jn 19:14

Jesus's Burial

³⁸ After this, Joseph of Arimathea, who was a disciple of Jesus — but secretly because of his fear of the Jews — asked Pilate that he might remove Jesus's body. Pilate gave him permission; so he came and took his body away. ³⁹ Nicodemus (who had previously come to him at night) also came, bringing a mixture of about seventy-five pounds^D of myrrh and aloes. ⁴⁰ They took Jesus's body and wrapped it in linen cloths with the fragrant spices, according to the burial custom of the Jews. ⁴¹ There was a garden in the place where he was crucified. A new tomb was in the garden; no one had yet been placed in it. ⁴² They placed Jesus there because of the Jewish day of preparation and since the tomb was nearby. Mt 27:57-60; Mk 15:42-46; Lk 23:50-54

The Empty Tomb

20 On the first day of the week Mary Magdalene came to the tomb early, while it was still dark. She saw that the stone had been removed from the tomb. ² So she went running to Simon Peter and to the other disciple, the one Jesus loved, and said to them, "They've taken the Lord out of the tomb, and we don't know where they've put him!" Mt 28:5-8; Mk 16:5-8

³ At that, Peter and the other disciple went out, heading for the tomb. ⁴ The two were running together, but the other disciple outran Peter and got to the tomb first. ⁵ Stooping down, he saw the linen cloths lying there, but he did not go in. ⁶ Then, following him, Simon Peter also came. He entered the tomb and saw the linen cloths lying there. ⁷ The wrapping that had been on his head was not lying with the linen cloths but was folded up in a separate place by itself. ⁸ The other disciple, who had reached the tomb first, then also went in, saw, and believed. ⁹ For they did not yet understand the Scripture that he must rise from the dead. ¹⁰ Then the disciples

---

^A **19:31** Lit *great*   ^B **19:36** Ex 12:46; Nm 9:12; Ps 34:20   ^C **19:37** Zch 12:10   ^D **19:39** Lit *a hundred litrai*; a Roman *litrai* = 12 ounces returned to the place where they were staying. Lk 24:12; Jn 19:40; 20:5-7

Mary Magdalene Sees the Risen Lord

¹¹ But Mary stood outside the tomb, crying. As she was crying, she stooped to look into the tomb. ¹² She saw two angels in white sitting where Jesus's body had been lying, one at the head and the other at the feet. ¹³ They said to her, "Woman, why are you crying?" Mk 16:9-11

"Because they've taken away my Lord," she told them, "and I don't know where they've put him."

¹⁴ Having said this, she turned around and saw Jesus standing there, but she did not know it was Jesus. ¹⁵ "Woman," Jesus said to her, "why are you crying? Who is it that you're seeking?" Jn 21:4

Supposing he was the gardener, she replied, "Sir, if you've carried him away, tell me where you've put him, and I will take him away."

¹⁶ Jesus said to her, "Mary."

Turning around, she said to him in Aramaic,ᴬ "Rabboni!" — which means "Teacher." Mk 4:38; Eph 4:11

¹⁷ "Don't cling to me," Jesus told her, "since I have not yet ascended to the Father. But go to my brothers and tell them that I am ascending to my Father and your Father, to my God and your God." Lk 24:51; Jn 3:13

¹⁸ Mary Magdalene went and announced to the disciples, "I have seen the Lord!" And she told them whatᴮ he had said to her. Mk 16:10

The Disciples Commissioned

¹⁹ When it was evening of that first day of the week, the disciples were gathered together with the doors locked because they feared the Jews. Jesus came, stood among them, and said to them, "Peace be with you." Lk 24:1; Jn 14:27; Ac 20:7; 1Co 16:2

²⁰ Having said this, he showed them his hands and his side. So the disciples rejoiced when they saw the Lord. Lk 24:39-40; Jn 19:34; 20:25-29

²¹ Jesus said to them again, "Peace be with you. As the Father has sent me, I also send you." ²² After saying this, he breathed on them and said,ᶜ "Receive the Holy Spirit. ²³ If you forgive the sins of any, they are forgiven them; if you retain the sins of any, they are retained." Jn 3:17; 16:7

Thomas Sees and Believes

²⁴ But Thomas (called "Twin"ᴰ), one of the Twelve, was not with them when Jesus came. ²⁵ So the other disciples were telling him, "We've seen the Lord!" Mk 3:18; Jn 11:16

But he said to them, "If I don't see the mark of the nails in his hands, put my finger into the mark of the nails, and put my hand into his side, I will never believe." Ps 22:16; Jn 20:20

²⁶ A week later his disciples were indoors again, and Thomas was with them. Even though the doors were locked, Jesus came and stood among them and said, "Peace be with you."

²⁷ Then he said to Thomas, "Put your finger here and look at my hands. Reach out your hand and put it into my side. Don't be faithless, but believe." Nm 12:7

²⁸ Thomas responded to him, "My Lord and my God!"

²⁹ Jesus said, "Because you have seen me, you have believed.ᴱ Blessed are those who have not seen and yet believe." 2Co 5:7; 1Pt 1:8

ᴬ20:16 Or Hebrew ᴮ20:18 Lit these things ᶜ20:22 Lit he breathed and said to them
ᴰ20:24 Gk Didymus ᴱ20:29 Or have you believed?

The Purpose of This Gospel

³⁰ Jesus performed many other signs in the presence of his disciples that are not written in this book. ³¹ But these are written so that you may believe that Jesus is the Messiah, the Son of God, ᴬ and that by believing you may have life in his name. Jn 2:11; 21:25; 1Jn 1:4; 5:1

Jesus's Third Appearance to the Disciples

21 After this, Jesus revealed himself again to his disciples by the Sea of Tiberias. He revealed himself in this way: Mk 16:12

² Simon Peter, Thomas (called "Twin" ᴮ), Nathanael from Cana of Galilee, Zebedee's sons, and two others of his disciples were together. Mt 17:22; Mk 3:18; Lk 6:14; Ac 10:32

³ "I'm going fishing," Simon Peter said to them.

"We're coming with you," they told him. They went out and got into the boat, but that night they caught nothing. Lk 5:5

⁴ When daybreak came, Jesus stood on the shore, but the disciples did not know it was Jesus. ⁵ "Friends," ᶜ Jesus called to them, "you don't have any fish, do you?"

"No," they answered.

⁶ "Cast the net on the right side of the boat," he told them, "and you'll find some." So they did, ᴰ and they were unable to haul it in because of the large number of fish. ⁷ The disciple, the one Jesus loved, said to Peter, "It is the Lord!" Lk 10:1; 1Co 8:6

When Simon Peter heard that it was the Lord, he tied his outer clothing around him (for he had taken it off) and plunged into the sea. ⁸ Since they were not far from land (about a hundred yards ᴱ away), the other disciples came in the boat, dragging the net full of fish. Mk 3:9; Lk 12:25; Jn 6:22-24

⁹ When they got out on land, they saw a charcoal fire there, with fish lying on it, and bread. ¹⁰ "Bring some of the fish you've just caught," Jesus told them. ¹¹ So Simon Peter climbed up and hauled the net ashore, full of large fish — 153 of them. Even though there were so many, the net was not torn. Lk 5:4-10

¹² "Come and have breakfast," Jesus told them. None of the disciples dared ask him, "Who are you?" because they knew it was the Lord. ¹³ Jesus came, took the bread, and gave it to them. He did the same with the fish. ¹⁴ This was now the third time Jesus appeared ᶠ to the disciples after he was raised from the dead. Jn 20:19,26; 21:1; 2Co 4:11; 1Jn 1:2

Jesus's Threefold Restoration of Peter

¹⁵ When they had eaten breakfast, Jesus asked Simon Peter, "Simon, son of John, ᴳ do you love me more than these?"

"Yes, Lord," he said to him, "you know that I love you."

"Feed my lambs," he told him. ¹⁶ A second time he asked him, "Simon, son of John, do you love me?"

"Yes, Lord," he said to him, "you know that I love you."

"Shepherd my sheep," he told him. Mt 7:15; Jn 10:11; 1Pt 5:2

¹⁷ He asked him the third time, "Simon, son of John, do you love me?"

Peter was grieved that he asked him the third time, "Do you love me?" He said, "Lord, you know everything; you know that I love you." Jn 16:30; 2Co 2:2

"Feed my sheep," Jesus said. ¹⁸ "Truly I tell you, when you were younger, you would tie your belt and walk wherever you wanted. But when you grow old, you will stretch out your hands and someone else will tie you and carry you where you don't want to go." ¹⁹ He said this to indicate by what kind of death Peter would glorify God. After saying this, he told him, "Follow me." Jn 1:51; 11:4; 21:15; 2Pt 1:14; Rv 22:21

Correcting a False Report

²⁰ So Peter turned around and saw the disciple Jesus loved following them, the one who had leaned back against Jesus at the supper and asked, "Lord, who is the one that's going to betray you?" ²¹ When Peter saw him, he said to Jesus, "Lord, what about him?" Jn 13:21,23-25; 21:7

²² "If I want him to remain until I come," Jesus answered, "what is that to you? As for you, follow me."

²³ So this rumor[A] spread to the brothers and sisters that this disciple would not die. Yet Jesus did not tell him that he would not die, but, "If I want him to remain until I come, what is that to you?" Ac 9:30

Epilogue

²⁴ This is the disciple who testifies to these things and who wrote them down. We know that his testimony is true.

²⁵ And there are also many other things that Jesus did, which, if every one of them were written down, I suppose not even the world itself could contain the books[B] that would be written. Jn 20:30

ACTS

Prologue

1 I wrote the first narrative, Theophilus, about all that Jesus began to do and teach ² until the day he was taken up, after he had given instructions through the Holy Spirit to the apostles he had chosen. ³ After he had suffered, he also presented himself alive to them by many convincing proofs, appearing to them over a period of forty days and speaking about the kingdom of God. Mt 28:19-20; Lk 1:3; 24:19,47

The Holy Spirit Promised

⁴ While he was ᴬ with them, he commanded them not to leave Jerusalem, but to wait for the Father's promise. "Which," he said, "you have heard me speak about; ⁵ for John baptized with water, but you will be baptized with the Holy Spirit in a few days." Lk 24:49; Jn 14:1; Ac 2:33

⁶ So when they had come together, they asked him, "Lord, are you restoring the kingdom to Israel at this time?"

⁷ He said to them, "It is not for you to know times or periods that the Father has set by his own authority. ⁸ But you will receive power when the Holy Spirit has come on you, and you will be my witnesses in Jerusalem, in all Judea and Samaria, and to the end of the earth." 1Th 5:1

The Ascension

⁹ After he had said this, he was taken up as they were watching, and a cloud took him out of their sight. ¹⁰ While he was going, they were gazing into heaven, and suddenly two men in white clothes stood by them. ¹¹ They said, "Men of Galilee, why do you stand looking up into heaven? This same Jesus, who has been taken from you into heaven, will come in the same way that you have seen him going into heaven." Mt 16:27; 28:13; Mk 16:5; Lk 24:4

United in Prayer

¹² Then they returned to Jerusalem from the Mount of Olives, which is near Jerusalem — a Sabbath day's journey away. ¹³ When they arrived, they went to the room upstairs where they were staying: Peter, John, James, Andrew, Philip, Thomas, Bartholomew, Matthew, James the son of Alphaeus, Simon the Zealot, and Judas the son of James. ¹⁴ They all were continually united in prayer, ᴮ along with the women, including Mary the mother of Jesus, and his brothers.

Matthias Chosen

¹⁵ In those days Peter stood up among the brothers and sisters ᶜ — the number of people who were together was about a hundred and twenty — and said: ¹⁶ "Brothers and sisters, it was necessary that the Scripture be fulfilled that the Holy Spirit through the mouth of David foretold about Judas, who became a guide to those who arrested Jesus. ¹⁷ For he was one of our number and shared in this

ᴬ**1:4** Or *he was eating,* or *he was lodging* ᴮ**1:14** Other mss add *and petition* ᶜ**1:15** Other mss read *disciples* ministry." ¹⁸ Now this man acquired a field with his unrighteous wages. He fell headfirst, his body burst open and his intestines spilled out. ¹⁹ This became known to all the residents of Jerusalem, so that in their own language that field is called *Hakeldama* (that is, Field of Blood). ²⁰ "For it is written in the Book of Psalms: Lk 22:37,47; 24:44

> Let his dwelling become
>   desolate;
> let no one live in it;ᴬ and
> Let someone else take
>   his position.ᴮ   Ps 69:25; 109:8

²¹ "Therefore, from among the men who have accompanied us during the whole time the Lord Jesus went in and out among us — ²² beginning from the baptism of John until the day he was taken up from us — from among these, it is necessary that one become a witness with us of his resurrection."

²³ So they proposed two: Joseph, called Barsabbas, who was also known as Justus, and Matthias. ²⁴ Then they prayed, "You, Lord, know everyone's hearts; show which of these two you have chosen ²⁵ to take the placeᶜ in this apostolic ministry that Judas left to go where he belongs." ²⁶ Then they cast lots for them, and the lot fell to Matthias and he was added to the eleven apostles. Ac 6:6; 15:22; 18:7

Pentecost

2 When the day of Pentecost had arrived, they were all together in one place. ² Suddenly a sound like that of a violent rushing wind came from heaven, and it filled the whole house where they were staying. ³ They saw tongues like flames of fire that separated and rested on each one of them. ⁴ Then they were all filled with the Holy Spirit and began to speak in different tongues,ᴰ as the Spirit enabled them. Lv 23:15; Ac 1:14; 20:16

⁵ Now there were Jews staying in Jerusalem, devout people from every nation under heaven. ⁶ When this sound occurred, a crowd came together and was confused because each one heard them speaking in his own language. ⁷ They were astounded and amazed, saying,ᴱ "Look, aren't all these who are speaking Galileans? ⁸ How is it that each of us can hear them in our own native language? ⁹ Parthians, Medes, Elamites; those who live in Mesopotamia, in Judea and Cappadocia, Pontus and Asia, ¹⁰ Phrygia and Pamphylia, Egypt and the parts of Libya near Cyrene; visitors from Rome (both Jews and converts), ¹¹ Cretans and Arabs — we hear them declaring the magnificent acts of God in our own tongues." ¹² They were all astounded and perplexed, saying to one another, "What does this mean?" ¹³ But some sneered and said, "They're drunk on new wine." Mt 28:19; Rm 1:5

Peter's Sermon

¹⁴ Peter stood up with the Eleven, raised his voice, and proclaimed to them: "Fellow Jews and all you residents of Jerusalem, let me explain this to you and pay attention to my words. ¹⁵ For these people are not drunk, as you suppose, since it's only nine in the morning.ᶠ ¹⁶ On the contrary, this is what was spoken through the prophet Joel:

ᴬ**1:20** Ps 69:25 ᴮ**1:20** Ps 109:8 ᶜ**1:25** Other mss read *to share* ᴰ**2:4** languages, also in v. 11 ᴱ**2:7** Other mss add *to one another* ᶠ**2:15** Lit *it's the third hour of the day*

¹⁷ And it will be
  in the last days, says God,
  that I will pour out
    my Spirit on all people;
  then your sons
    and your daughters
    will prophesy,
  your young men will
    see visions,
  and your old men will
    dream dreams. Is 44:3; Jn 7:38
¹⁸ I will even pour out
    my Spirit
  on my servants
    in those days, both men
    and women
  and they will prophesy. Ac 21:10
¹⁹ I will display wonders
    in the heaven above
  and signs
    on the earth below:
  blood and fire and a cloud
    of smoke.
²⁰ The sun will be turned
    to darkness
  and the moon to blood 1Th 5:2
  before the great and
    glorious day of the
    Lord comes. Is 58:13; Ezk 13:5
²¹ Then everyone who calls
    on the name of the Lord
    will be saved. ^A Jl 2:28-32; Ac 16:31

²² "Fellow Israelites, listen to these words: This Jesus of Nazareth was a man attested to you by God with miracles, wonders, and signs that God did among you through him, just as you yourselves know. ²³ Though he was delivered up according to God's determined plan and foreknowledge, you used ^B lawless people to nail him to a cross and kill him. ²⁴ God raised him up, ending the pains of death, because

it was not possible for him to be held by death. ²⁵ For David says of him: Mt 26:24; Jn 3:2; 4:48; Ac 10:38; Heb 2:4

  I saw the Lord ever
    before me;
  because he is
    at my right hand,
  I will not be shaken.
²⁶ Therefore my heart is glad
  and my tongue rejoices.
  Moreover, my flesh
    will rest in hope,
²⁷ because you will not
    abandon me in Hades
  or allow your holy one
    to see decay. Mt 11:23; Lk 2:26
²⁸ You have revealed
    the paths of life to me;
  you will fill me
    with gladness
  in your presence. ^C Ps 16:8-11

²⁹ "Brothers and sisters, I can confidently speak to you about the patriarch David: He is both dead and buried, and his tomb is with us to this day. ³⁰ Since he was a prophet, he knew that God had sworn an oath to him to seat one of his descendants ^D on his throne. ³¹ Seeing what was to come, he spoke concerning the resurrection of the Messiah: He ^E was not abandoned in Hades, and his flesh did not experience decay. ^F 1Kg 2:10; Neh 3:16

³² "God has raised this Jesus; we are all witnesses of this. ³³ Therefore, since he has been exalted to the right hand of God and has received from the Father the promised Holy Spirit, he has poured out what you both see and hear. ³⁴ For it was not David who ascended into the heavens, but he himself says: Lk 18:33; Ac 2:24; Php 2:9; Heb 10:12

^A2:17-21 Jl 2:28-32 ^B2:23 Other mss read *you have taken* ^C2:25-28 Ps 16:8-11 ^D2:30 Other mss add *according to the flesh to raise up the Messiah* ^E2:31 Other mss read *His soul* ^F2:31 Ps 16:10

**The Lord declared
to my Lord,
'Sit at my right hand
35 until I make your enemies
your footstool.'**^A   Ps 110:1

³⁶ "Therefore let all the house of Israel know with certainty that God has made this Jesus, whom you crucified, both Lord and Messiah."

Call to Repentance

³⁷ When they heard this, they were pierced to the heart and said to Peter and the rest of the apostles: "Brothers, what should we do?"

³⁸ Peter replied, "Repent and be baptized, each of you, in the name of Jesus Christ for the forgiveness of your sins, and you will receive the gift of the Holy Spirit. ³⁹ For the promise is for you and for your children, and for all who are far off, as many as the Lord our God will call." ⁴⁰ With many other words he testified and strongly urged them, saying, "Be saved from this corrupt^B generation!" ⁴¹ So those who accepted his message were baptized, and that day about three thousand people were added to them. Lk 24:47; Ac 3:19; 22:16; 26:20

A Generous and Growing Church

⁴² They devoted themselves to the apostles' teaching, to the fellowship, to the breaking of bread, and to prayer.   Ac 1:14; 5:28; 13:12; 17:19; 1 Co 14:6
⁴³ Everyone was filled with awe, and many wonders and signs were being performed through the apostles. ⁴⁴ Now all the believers were together and held all things in common. ⁴⁵ They sold their possessions and property and distributed the proceeds to all, as any had need. ⁴⁶ Every day they devoted themselves to meeting together in the temple, and broke bread from house to house. They ate their food with joyful and sincere hearts, ⁴⁷ praising God and enjoying the favor of all the people. Every day the Lord added to their number^C those who were being saved.   Mt 19:21; Mk 16:17,20; Ac 4:32; 5:12; 20:7

Healing of a Lame Man

3 Now Peter and John were going up to the temple for the time of prayer at three in the afternoon.^D ² A man who was lame from birth was being carried there. He was placed each day at the temple gate called Beautiful, so that he could beg from those entering the temple. ³ When he saw Peter and John about to enter the temple, he asked for money. ⁴ Peter, along with John, looked straight at him and said, "Look at us." ⁵ So he turned to them, expecting to get something from them. ⁶ But Peter said, "I don't have silver or gold, but what I do have, I give you: In the name of Jesus Christ of Nazareth, get up and walk!" ⁷ Then, taking him by the right hand he raised him up, and at once his feet and ankles became strong. ⁸ So he jumped up and started to walk, and he entered the temple with them — walking, leaping, and praising God. ⁹ All the people saw him walking and praising God, ¹⁰ and they recognized that he was the one who used to sit and beg at the Beautiful Gate of the temple. So they were filled with awe and astonishment at what had happened to him.   Ps 55:17; Mt 27:46; Lk 16:20; Ac 10:3,30

^A**2:34-35** Ps 110:1   ^B**2:40** Or *crooked*, or *twisted*   ^C**2:47** Other mss read *to the church*   ^D**3:1** Lit *at the ninth hour*

Preaching in Solomon's Colonnade

[11] While he[A] was holding on to Peter and John, all the people, utterly astonished, ran toward them in what is called Solomon's Colonnade. [12] When Peter saw this, he addressed the people: "Fellow Israelites, why are you amazed at this? Why do you stare at us, as though we had made him walk by our own power or godliness? [13] The God of Abraham, Isaac, and Jacob, the God of our ancestors, has glorified his servant Jesus, whom you handed over and denied before Pilate, though he had decided to release him. [14] You denied the Holy and Righteous One and asked to have a murderer released to you. [15] You killed the source[B] of life, whom God raised from the dead; we are witnesses of this. [16] By faith in his name, his name has made this man strong, whom you see and know. So the faith that comes through Jesus has given him this perfect health in front of all of you. Lk 22:8; Jn 10:23

[17] "And now, brothers and sisters, I know that you acted in ignorance, just as your leaders also did. [18] In this way God fulfilled what he had predicted through all the prophets — that his Messiah would suffer. [19] Therefore repent and turn back, so that your sins may be wiped out, [20] that seasons of refreshing may come from the presence of the Lord, and that he may send Jesus, who has been appointed for you as the Messiah. [21] Heaven must receive him until the time of the restoration of all things, which God spoke about through his holy prophets from the beginning. [22] Moses said:[C] **The Lord your God will raise up for you a prophet like me from among your brothers and sisters. You must listen to everything he tells you.** [23] **And everyone who does not listen to that prophet will be completely cut off from the people.**[D] Lk 17:3; 23:34; 24:27; Ac 13:27

[24] "In addition, all the prophets who have spoken, from Samuel and those after him, have also foretold these days. [25] You are the sons[E] of the prophets and of the covenant that God made with your ancestors, saying to Abraham, **And all the families of the earth will be blessed through your offspring.**[F] [26] God raised up his servant[G] and sent him first to you to bless you by turning each of you from your evil ways." Ac 2:39

Peter and John Arrested

4 While they were speaking to the people, the priests, the captain of the temple police, and the Sadducees confronted them, [2] because they were annoyed that they were teaching the people and proclaiming in Jesus the resurrection of the dead. [3] So they seized them and took them into custody until the next day since it was already evening. [4] But many of those who heard the message believed, and the number of the men[H] came to about five thousand. Mt 3:7; Lk 22:4

Peter and John Face the Jewish Leadership

[5] The next day, their rulers, elders, and scribes assembled in Jerusalem [6] with Annas the high priest,

---

[A]**3:11** Other mss read *the lame man who was healed* [B]**3:15** Or *the Prince*, or *the Ruler* [C]**3:22** Other mss add *to the fathers* [D]**3:22-23** Dt 18:15-19 [E]**3:25** = heirs [F]**3:25** Gn 12:3; 18:18; 22:18; 26:4 [G]**3:26** Other mss add *Jesus* [H]**4:4** Or *people*

Caiaphas, John, Alexander, and all the members of the high-priestly family. ⁷ After they had Peter and John stand before them, they began to question them: "By what power or in what name have you done this?"   Mt 26:3; Lk 3:2; Jn 18:13

⁸ Then Peter was filled with the Holy Spirit and said to them, "Rulers of the people and elders:ᴬ ⁹ If we are being examined today about a good deed done to a disabled man, by what means he was healed, ¹⁰ let it be known to all of you and to all the people of Israel, that by the name of Jesus Christ of Nazareth, whom you crucified and whom God raised from the dead — by him this man is standing here before you healthy. ¹¹ This Jesus is

the stone rejected by you builders,
which has become the cornerstone.ᴮ   1Pt 2:7

¹² There is salvation in no one else, for there is no other name under heaven given to people by which we must be saved."   Mt 1:21; Ac 10:43

The Boldness of the Disciples

¹³ When they observed the boldness of Peter and John and realized that they were uneducated and untrained men, they were amazed and recognized that they had been with Jesus. ¹⁴ And since they saw the man who had been healed standing with them, they had nothing to say in opposition. ¹⁵ After they ordered them to leave the Sanhedrin, they conferred among themselves, ¹⁶ saying, "What should we do with these men? For an obvious sign has been done through them, clear to everyone living in

Jerusalem, and we cannot deny it. ¹⁷ But so that this does not spread any further among the people, let's threaten them against speaking to anyone in this name again." ¹⁸ So they called for them and ordered them not to speak or teach at all in the name of Jesus.   Mt 11:25; Lk 22:8; Jn 7:15

¹⁹ Peter and John answered them, "Whether it's right in the sight of God for us to listen to you rather than to God, you decide; ²⁰ for we are unable to stop speaking about what we have seen and heard."

²¹ After threatening them further, they released them. They found no way to punish them because the people were all giving glory to God over what had been done. ²² For this sign of healing had been performed on a man over forty years old.   Mt 9:8; 21:26; Lk 20:6,19; 22:2; Ac 5:26

Prayer for Boldness

²³ After they were released, they went to their own people and reported everything the chief priests and the elders had said to them. ²⁴ When they heard this, they raised their voices together to God and said, "Master, you are the one who made the heaven, the earth, and the sea, and everything in them. ²⁵ You said through the Holy Spirit, by the mouth of our father David your servant:ᶜ   Ex 20:11; 2Ch 2:12

Why do the Gentiles rage
and the peoples plot futile things?
²⁶ **The kings of the earth take their stand**
and the rulers assemble together
against the Lord and against his Messiah.ᴰ   Lk 4:18

ᴬ4:8 Other mss add *of Israel*   ᴮ4:11 Ps 118:22   ᶜ4:25 Other mss read *through the mouth of David your servant*   ᴰ4:25-26 Ps 2:1-2

²⁷ "For, in fact, in this city both Herod and Pontius Pilate, with the Gentiles and the people of Israel, assembled together against your holy servant Jesus, whom you anointed, ²⁸ to do whatever your hand and your will had predestined to take place. ²⁹ And now, Lord, consider their threats, and grant that your servants may speak your word with all boldness, ³⁰ while you stretch out your hand for healing, and signs and wonders are performed through the name of your holy servant Jesus." ³¹ When they had prayed, the place where they were assembled was shaken, and they were all filled with the Holy Spirit and began to speak the word of God boldly. Mt 14:1; 27:2; Lk 23:1,12; Ac 9:27; 13:46

All Things in Common

³² Now the entire group of those who believed were of one heart and mind, and no one claimed that any of his possessions was his own, but instead they held everything in common. ³³ With great power the apostles were giving testimony to the resurrection of the Lord Jesus, and great grace was on all of them. ³⁴ For there was not a needy person among them because all those who owned lands or houses sold them, brought the proceeds of what was sold, ³⁵ and laid them at the apostles' feet. This was then distributed to each person as any had need. Lk 24:48; Ac 1:8,22; 2:44; Php 1:27

³⁶ Joseph, a Levite from Cyprus by birth, the one the apostles called Barnabas (which is translated Son of Encouragement), ³⁷ sold a field he owned, brought the money, and laid it at the apostles' feet. Ac 4:35; 5:2; 9:27; 1Co 9:6

Lying to the Holy Spirit

5 But a man named Ananias, with his wife Sapphira, sold a piece of property. ² However, he kept back part of the proceeds with his wife's knowledge, and brought a portion of it and laid it at the apostles' feet.

³ "Ananias," Peter asked, "why has Satan filled your heart to lie to the Holy Spirit and keep back part of the proceeds of the land? ⁴ Wasn't it yours while you possessed it? And after it was sold, wasn't it at your disposal? Why is it that you planned this thing in your heart? You have not lied to people but to God." ⁵ When he heard these words, Ananias dropped dead, and a great fear came on all who heard. ⁶ The young men got up, wrapped his body, carried him out, and buried him. Ezk 11:13; 29:5; Mt 4:10; Lk 22:3; Jn 13:2,27

⁷ About three hours later, his wife came in, not knowing what had happened. ⁸ "Tell me," Peter asked her, "did you sell the land for this price?"

"Yes," she said, "for that price."

⁹ Then Peter said to her, "Why did you agree to test the Spirit of the Lord? Look, the feet of those who have buried your husband are at the door, and they will carry you out." Ac 5:3-4; 15:10; 1Co 10:9

¹⁰ Instantly she dropped dead at his feet. When the young men came in, they found her dead, carried her out, and buried her beside her husband. ¹¹ Then great fear came on the whole church and on all who heard these things.

Apostolic Signs and Wonders

¹² Many signs and wonders were being done among the people through the hands of the apostles. They were all together in Solomon's

Colonnade. [13] No one else dared to join them, but the people spoke well of them. [14] Believers were added to the Lord in increasing numbers — multitudes of both men and women. [15] As a result, they would carry the sick out into the streets and lay them on cots and mats so that when Peter came by, at least his shadow might fall on some of them. [16] In addition, a multitude came together from the towns surrounding Jerusalem, bringing the sick and those who were tormented by unclean spirits, and they were all healed. Ac 2:43; 14:3; 19:11

In and out of Prison

[17] Then the high priest rose up. He and all who were with him, who belonged to the party of the Sadducees, were filled with jealousy. [18] So they arrested the apostles and put them in the public jail. [19] But an angel of the Lord opened the doors of the jail during the night, brought them out, and said, [20] "Go and stand in the temple, and tell the people all about this life." [21] Hearing this, they entered the temple at daybreak and began to teach. Mt 1:20; Lk 1:11; 21:12; Ac 4:1,3; 15:5

The Apostles on Trial Again

When the high priest and those who were with him arrived, they convened the Sanhedrin — the full council of the Israelites — and sent orders to the jail to have them brought. [22] But when the servants[A] got there, they did not find them in the jail, so they returned and reported, [23] "We found the jail securely locked, with the guards standing in front of the doors, but when we opened them, we found no one inside." [24] As[B] the captain of the temple police and the chief priests heard these things, they were baffled about them, wondering what would come of this. Mt 5:22; Ac 4:6

[25] Someone came and reported to them, "Look! The men you put in jail are standing in the temple and teaching the people." [26] Then the commander went with the servants and brought them in without force, because they were afraid the people might stone them. [27] After they brought them in, they had them stand before the Sanhedrin, and the high priest asked, [28] "Didn't we strictly order you not to teach in this name? Look, you have filled Jerusalem with your teaching and are determined to make us guilty of this man's blood." Ac 3:16; 4:21; 5:13

[29] Peter and the apostles replied, "We must obey God rather than people. [30] The God of our ancestors raised up Jesus, whom you had murdered by hanging him on a tree. [31] God exalted this man to his right hand as ruler and Savior, to give repentance to Israel and forgiveness of sins. [32] We are witnesses of these things, and so is the Holy Spirit whom God has given to those who obey him." Ac 2:24; 3:13; 13:29

Gamaliel's Advice

[33] When they heard this, they were enraged and wanted to kill them. [34] But a Pharisee named Gamaliel, a teacher of the law who was respected by all the people, stood up in the Sanhedrin and ordered the men[C] to be taken outside for a little while. [35] He said to them, "Men of Israel, be careful about what you're

---

A5:22 Or temple police, or officers, also in v. 26   B5:24 Other mss add the high priest and   C5:34 Other mss read apostles about to do to these men. [36] Some time ago Theudas rose up, claiming to be somebody, and a group of about four hundred men rallied to him. He was killed, and all his followers were dispersed and came to nothing. [37] After this man, Judas the Galilean rose up in the days of the census and attracted a following. He also perished, and all his followers were scattered. [38] So in the present case, I tell you, stay away from these men and leave them alone. For if this plan or this work is of human origin, it will fail; [39] but if it is of God, you will not be able to overthrow them. You may even be found fighting against God." They were persuaded by him. [40] After they called in the apostles and had them flogged, they ordered them not to speak in the name of Jesus and released them. [41] Then they went out from the presence of the Sanhedrin, rejoicing that they were counted worthy to be treated shamefully on behalf of the Name.[A] [42] Every day in the temple, and in various homes, they continued teaching and proclaiming the good news that Jesus is the Messiah.   Lk 2:46; 5:17; Ac 2:37; 7:54; 8:9; 22:3; Gl 2:6

Seven Chosen to Serve

6 In those days, as the disciples were increasing in number, there arose a complaint by the Hellenistic Jews against the Hebraic Jews that their widows were being overlooked in the daily distribution. [2] The Twelve summoned the whole company of the disciples and said, "It would not be right for us to give up preaching the word of God to wait on tables. [3] Brothers and sisters, select from among you seven men of good reputation, full of the Spirit and wisdom, whom we can appoint to this duty. [4] But we will devote ourselves to prayer and to the ministry of the word." [5] This proposal pleased the whole company. So they chose Stephen, a man full of faith and the Holy Spirit, and Philip, Prochorus, Nicanor, Timon, Parmenas, and Nicolaus, a convert from Antioch. [6] They had them stand before the apostles, who prayed and laid their hands on them.   Mt 9:10; Mk 10:10; Lk 6:1; Jn 6:3

[7] So the word of God spread, the disciples in Jerusalem increased greatly in number, and a large group of priests became obedient to the faith.   Ac 12:24; 19:20; Col 1:6

Stephen Accused of Blasphemy

[8] Now Stephen, full of grace and power, was performing great wonders and signs among the people. [9] Opposition arose, however, from some members of the Freedmen's Synagogue, composed of both Cyrenians and Alexandrians, and some from Cilicia and Asia, and they began to argue with Stephen. [10] But they were unable to stand up against his wisdom and the Spirit by whom he was speaking. [11] Then they secretly persuaded some men to say, "We heard him speaking blasphemous words against Moses and God." [12] They stirred up the people, the elders, and the scribes; so they came, seized him, and took him to the Sanhedrin. [13] They also presented false witnesses who said, "This man never stops speaking against this holy place and the law. [14] For we heard him say that this Jesus of Nazareth will destroy this place and change

[A]**5:41** Other mss add *of Jesus*, or *of Christ*

the customs that Moses handed down to us." [15] And all who were sitting in the Sanhedrin looked intently at him and saw that his face was like the face of an angel.

Stephen's Sermon

7 "Are these things true?" the high priest asked.

[2] "Brothers and fathers," he replied, "listen: The God of glory appeared to our father Abraham when he was in Mesopotamia, before he settled in Haran, [3] and said to him: **Leave your country and relatives, and come to the land that I will show you.** [A]   Gn 11:31; 15:7

[4] "Then he left the land of the Chaldeans and settled in Haran. From there, after his father died, God had him move to this land in which you are now living. [5] He didn't give him an inheritance in it — not even a foot of ground — but he promised to give it to him as a possession, and to his descendants after him, even though he was childless. [6] God spoke in this way: His **descendants** would **be strangers in a foreign country, and they** would **enslave and oppress them for four hundred years.** [7] **I will judge the nation that they will serve as slaves,** God said. **After this, they will come out and worship me in this place.** [B] [8] And so he gave Abraham the covenant of circumcision. After this, he fathered Isaac and circumcised him on the eighth day. Isaac became the father of Jacob, and Jacob became the father of the twelve patriarchs.   Gn 11:31; 12:4-5, 7

The Patriarchs in Egypt

[9] "The patriarchs became jealous of Joseph and sold him into Egypt, but God was with him [10] and rescued him out of all his troubles. He gave him favor and wisdom in the sight of Pharaoh, king of Egypt, who appointed him ruler over Egypt and over his whole household. [11] Now a famine and great suffering came over all of Egypt and Canaan, and our ancestors could find no food. [12] When Jacob heard there was grain in Egypt, he sent our ancestors there the first time. [13] The second time, Joseph revealed himself to his brothers, and Joseph's family became known to Pharaoh. [14] Joseph invited his father Jacob and all his relatives, seventy-five people in all, [15] and Jacob went down to Egypt. He and our ancestors died there, [16] were carried back to Shechem, and were placed in the tomb that Abraham had bought for a sum of silver from the sons of Hamor in Shechem.   Gn 37:11, 28; 39:2, 21; 42:6; 45:4

Moses, a Rejected Savior

[17] "As the time was approaching to fulfill the promise that God had made to Abraham, the people flourished and multiplied in Egypt [18] until a different king who did not know Joseph ruled over Egypt. [C] [19] He dealt deceitfully with our race and oppressed our ancestors by making them abandon their infants outside so that they wouldn't survive. [20] At this time Moses was born, and he was beautiful in God's sight. He was cared for in his father's home for three months. [21] When he was put outside, Pharaoh's daughter adopted and raised him as her own son. [22] So Moses was educated in all the wisdom of the Egyptians and was powerful in his speech and actions.   Gn 15:13; Ex 1:7; Ps 105:24; Is 19:11

[A] **7:3** Gn 12:1   [B] **7:6-7** Gn 15:13-14   [C] **7:18** Other mss omit *over Egypt*

²³ "When he was forty years old, he decided to visit his own people, the Israelites. ²⁴ When he saw one of them being mistreated, he came to his rescue and avenged the oppressed man by striking down the Egyptian. ²⁵ He assumed his people would understand that God would give them deliverance through him, but they did not understand. ²⁶ The next day he showed up while they were fighting and tried to reconcile them peacefully, saying, 'Men, you are brothers. Why are you mistreating each other?' Ex 2:11-14; Heb 11:24-26

²⁷ "But the one who was mistreating his neighbor pushed Moses aside, saying: **Who appointed you a ruler and a judge over us?** ²⁸ **Do you want to kill me, the same way you killed the Egyptian yesterday?** ^A   Ex 2:14; Lk 12:14; Ac 7:35

²⁹ "When he heard this, Moses fled and became an exile in the land of Midian, where he became the father of two sons. ³⁰ After forty years had passed, an angel ^B appeared to him in the wilderness of Mount Sinai, in the flame of a burning bush. ³¹ When Moses saw it, he was amazed at the sight. As he was approaching to look at it, the voice of the Lord came: ³² **I am the God of your ancestors — the God of Abraham, of Isaac, and of Jacob.** ^C Moses began to tremble and did not dare to look.   Ex 2:15,22

³³ "The Lord said to him: **Take off the sandals from your feet, because the place where you are standing is holy ground.** ³⁴ **I have certainly seen the oppression of my people in Egypt; I have heard their groaning and have come down to set them free. And now, come, I will send you to Egypt.** ^D   Ex 3:5, 7-8,10

³⁵ "This Moses, whom they rejected when they said, **Who appointed you a ruler and a judge?** ^A — this one God sent as a ruler and a deliverer through the angel who appeared to him in the bush. ³⁶ This man led them out and performed wonders and signs in the land of Egypt, at the Red Sea, and in the wilderness for forty years.   Ex 14:19

Israel's Rebellion Against God

³⁷ "This is the Moses who said to the Israelites: **God** ^E **will raise up for you a prophet like me from among your brothers and sisters.** ^F ³⁸ He is the one who was in the assembly in the wilderness, with the angel who spoke to him on Mount Sinai, and with our ancestors. He received living oracles to give to us. ³⁹ Our ancestors were unwilling to obey him. Instead, they pushed him aside, and in their hearts turned back to Egypt. ⁴⁰ They told Aaron: **Make us gods who will go before us. As for this Moses who brought us out of the land of Egypt, we don't know what's happened to him.** ^G ⁴¹ They even made a calf in those days, offered sacrifice to the idol, and were celebrating what their hands had made. ⁴² God turned away and gave them up to worship the stars of heaven, as it is written in the book of the prophets: Ex 19:17; Dt 18:15; Is 63:9; Ac 3:22

> House of Israel, did you
>   bring me offerings
>   and sacrifices
> for forty years
>   in the wilderness?

^A7:27-28,35 Ex 2:14   ^B7:30 Other mss add *of the Lord*   ^C7:32 Ex 3:6,15   ^D7:33-34 Ex 3:5,7-8,10
^E7:37 Other mss read *The Lord your God*   ^F7:37 Dt 18:15   ^G7:40 Ex 32:1,23

43 **You took up**
the tent of Moloch
and the star of
your god Rephan,
the images that you made
to worship.
So I will send you into exile
beyond Babylon. A   1Kg 11:7

God's Real Tabernacle

44 "Our ancestors had the tabernacle of the testimony in the wilderness, just as he who spoke to Moses commanded him to make it according to the pattern he had seen. 45 Our ancestors in turn received it and with Joshua brought it in when they dispossessed the nations that God drove out before them, until the days of David. 46 He found favor in God's sight and asked that he might provide a dwelling place for the God B of Jacob. 47 It was Solomon, rather, who built him a house, 48 but the Most High does not dwell in sanctuaries made with hands, as the prophet says:

49 **Heaven is my throne,**
and the earth my footstool.
What sort of house
will you build for me?
says the Lord,
or what will be
my resting place?
50 **Did not my hand make all**
these things? C   Is 66:1-2

Resisting the Holy Spirit

51 "You stiff-necked people with uncircumcised hearts and ears! You are always resisting the Holy Spirit. As your ancestors did, you do also. 52 Which of the prophets did your ancestors not persecute? They even killed those who foretold the coming of the Righteous One, whose betrayers and murderers you have now become. 53 You received the law under the direction of angels and yet have not kept it." Ex 32:9; Lv 26:41; Dt 10:16; Heb 3:13

The First Christian Martyr

54 When they heard these things, they were enraged D and gnashed their teeth at him. 55 Stephen, full of the Holy Spirit, gazed into heaven. He saw the glory of God, and Jesus standing at the right hand of God. 56 He said, "Look, I see the heavens opened and the Son of Man standing at the right hand of God!"

57 They yelled at the top of their voices, covered their ears, and together rushed against him. 58 They dragged him out of the city and began to stone him. And the witnesses laid their garments at the feet of a young man named Saul. 59 While they were stoning Stephen, he called out: "Lord Jesus, receive my spirit!" 60 He knelt down and cried out with a loud voice, "Lord, do not hold this sin against them!" And after saying this, he died. E   Lv 24:14-16

Saul the Persecutor

8 Saul agreed with putting him to death.

On that day a severe persecution broke out against the church in Jerusalem, and all except the apostles were scattered throughout the land of Judea and Samaria. 2 Devout men buried Stephen and mourned deeply over him. 3 Saul, however, was ravaging the church. He would enter house after house, drag off men and women, and put them in prison.   Ac 7:58; 9:31; 11:19; 22:4,19-20

A7:42-43 Am 5:25-27   B7:46 Other mss read house   C7:49-50 Is 66:1-2   D7:54 Or were cut to the quick
E7:60 Lit he fell asleep

Philip in Samaria

⁴ So those who were scattered went on their way preaching the word. ⁵ Philip went down to a ᴬ city in Samaria and proclaimed the Messiah to them. ⁶ The crowds were all paying attention to what Philip said, as they listened and saw the signs he was performing. ⁷ For unclean spirits, crying out with a loud voice, came out of many who were possessed, and many who were paralyzed and lame were healed. ⁸ So there was great joy in that city.

The Response of Simon

⁹ A man named Simon had previously practiced sorcery in that city and amazed the Samaritan people, while claiming to be somebody great. ¹⁰ They all paid attention to him, from the least of them to the greatest, and they said, "This man is called the Great Power of God."ᴮ ¹¹ They were attentive to him because he had amazed them with his sorceries for a long time. ¹² But when they believed Philip, as he proclaimed the good news about the kingdom of God and the name of Jesus Christ, both men and women were baptized. ¹³ Even Simon himself believed. And after he was baptized, he followed Philip everywhere and was amazed as he observed the signs and great miracles that were being performed. Ac 5:36

Simon's Sin

¹⁴ When the apostles who were at Jerusalem heard that Samaria had received the word of God, they sent Peter and John to them. ¹⁵ After they went down there, they prayed for them so the Samaritans might receive the Holy Spirit because he had not yet come down on any of them. ¹⁶ (They had only been baptized in the name of the Lord Jesus.) ¹⁷ Then Peter and John laid their hands on them, and they received the Holy Spirit. Lk 22:8; Ac 8:1

¹⁸ When Simon saw that the Spiritᶜ was given through the laying on of the apostles' hands, he offered them money, ¹⁹ saying, "Give me this power also so that anyone I lay hands on may receive the Holy Spirit."

²⁰ But Peter told him, "May your silver be destroyed with you, because you thought you could obtain the gift of God with money! ²¹ You have no part or share in this matter, because your heart is not right before God. ²² Therefore repent of this wickedness of yours, and pray to the Lord that, if possible, your heart's intent may be forgiven. ²³ For I see you are poisoned by bitterness and bound by wickedness." 2Kg 5:16; Is 55:1; Dn 5:17; Mt 10:8

²⁴ "Pray to the Lord for me," Simon replied, "so that nothing you have said may happen to me." Ex 8:8

²⁵ So, after they had testified and spoken the word of the Lord, they traveled back to Jerusalem, preaching the gospel in many villages of the Samaritans.

The Conversion of the Ethiopian Official

²⁶ An angel of the Lord spoke to Philip: "Get up and go south to the road that goes down from Jerusalem to Gaza." (This is the desert road.ᴰ) ²⁷ So he got up and went. There was an Ethiopian man, a eunuch and high official of Candace, queen of the Ethiopians, who was

ᴬ8:5 Other mss read the   ᴮ8:10 Or "This is the power of God called Great   ᶜ8:18 Other mss add Holy
ᴰ8:26 Or is a desert place

in charge of her entire treasury. He had come to worship in Jerusalem ²⁸ and was sitting in his chariot on his way home, reading the prophet Isaiah aloud. Ps 68:31; 87:4; Ac 5:19; 8:29

²⁹ The Spirit told Philip, "Go and join that chariot." Ac 10:19; 11:12; 13:2; 21:11

³⁰ When Philip ran up to it, he heard him reading the prophet Isaiah, and said, "Do you understand what you're reading?"

³¹ "How can I," he said, "unless someone guides me?" So he invited Philip to come up and sit with him. ³² Now the Scripture passage he was reading was this:

> He was led like a sheep
>   to the slaughter,
> and as a lamb is silent
>   before its shearer,
> so he does not open
>   his mouth.
> ³³ In his humiliation justice
>   was denied him.
> Who will describe
>   his generation?
> For his life is taken
>   from the earth.^A   Is 53:7-8

³⁴ The eunuch said to Philip, "I ask you, who is the prophet saying this about — himself or someone else?" ³⁵ Philip proceeded to tell him the good news about Jesus, beginning with that Scripture.

³⁶ As they were traveling down the road, they came to some water. The eunuch said, "Look, there's water. What would keep me from being baptized?"^B ³⁸ So he ordered the chariot to stop, and both Philip and the eunuch went down into the water, and he baptized him. ³⁹ When they came up out of the water, the Spirit of the Lord carried Philip away, and the eunuch did not see him any longer but went on his way rejoicing. ⁴⁰ Philip appeared in^C Azotus, ^D and he was traveling and preaching the gospel in all the towns until he came to Caesarea.

The Damascus Road

9 Now Saul was still breathing threats and murder against the disciples of the Lord. He went to the high priest ² and requested letters from him to the synagogues in Damascus, so that if he found any men or women who belonged to the Way, he might bring them as prisoners to Jerusalem. ³ As he traveled and was nearing Damascus, a light from heaven suddenly flashed around him. ⁴ Falling to the ground, he heard a voice saying to him, "Saul, Saul, why are you persecuting me?" Mt 9:10; Mk 10:10; Lk 6:1; Jn 6:3

⁵ "Who are you, Lord?" Saul said.

"I am Jesus, the one you are persecuting," he replied. ⁶ "But get up and go into the city, and you will be told what you must do."

⁷ The men who were traveling with him stood speechless, hearing the sound but seeing no one. ⁸ Saul got up from the ground, and though his eyes were open, he could see nothing. So they took him by the hand and led him into Damascus. ⁹ He was unable to see for three days and did not eat or drink. Dn 10:7; Jn 12:29; Ac 22:9

Saul's Baptism

¹⁰ There was a disciple in Damascus named Ananias, and the Lord said to him in a vision, "Ananias."

---

^A**8:32-33** Is 53:7-8   ^B**8:36** Some mss include v. 37: *Philip said, "If you believe with all your heart you may." And he replied, "I believe that Jesus Christ is the Son of God."*   ^C**8:40** Or *Philip was found at,* or *Philip found himself in*   ^D**8:40** Or *Ashdod*

"Here I am, Lord," he replied. ¹¹ "Get up and go to the street called Straight," the Lord said to him, "to the house of Judas, and ask for a man from Tarsus named Saul, since he is praying there. ¹² In a vision ^A he has seen a man named Ananias coming in and placing his hands on him so that he may regain his sight." Mk 5:23; Ac 9:30; 11:25; 21:39; 22:3

¹³ "Lord," Ananias answered, "I have heard from many people about this man, how much harm he has done to your saints in Jerusalem. ¹⁴ And he has authority here from the chief priests to arrest all who call on your name." Ac 8:3; 9:32

¹⁵ But the Lord said to him, "Go, for this man is my chosen instrument to take my name to Gentiles, kings, and Israelites. ¹⁶ I will show him how much he must suffer for my name." Mt 28:19; Ac 13:2; Rm 1:1; Gl 1:15

¹⁷ Ananias went and entered the house. He placed his hands on him and said, "Brother Saul, the Lord Jesus, who appeared to you on the road you were traveling, has sent me so that you may regain your sight and be filled with the Holy Spirit." Ac 6:6; 22:13

¹⁸ At once something like scales fell from his eyes, and he regained his sight. Then he got up and was baptized. ¹⁹ And after taking some food, he regained his strength.

Saul Proclaiming the Messiah

Saul was with the disciples in Damascus for some time. ²⁰ Immediately he began proclaiming Jesus in the synagogues: "He is the Son of God." Mt 4:3; Ac 13:5,14

²¹ All who heard him were astounded and said, "Isn't this the man in Jerusalem who was causing havoc for those who called on this name and came here for the purpose of taking them as prisoners to the chief priests?" Ac 8:3; 9:13-14

²² But Saul grew stronger and kept confounding the Jews who lived in Damascus by proving that Jesus is the Messiah.

²³ After many days had passed, the Jews conspired to kill him, ²⁴ but Saul learned of their plot. So they were watching the gates day and night intending to kill him, ²⁵ but his disciples took him by night and lowered him in a large basket through an opening in the wall. Jos 2:15; Ac 20:3,19; 23:12,30; 25:3; 2Co 11:26

Saul in Jerusalem

²⁶ When he arrived in Jerusalem, he tried to join the disciples, but they were all afraid of him, since they did not believe he was a disciple. ²⁷ Barnabas, however, took him and brought him to the apostles and explained to them how Saul had seen the Lord on the road and that the Lord had talked to him, and how in Damascus he had spoken boldly in the name of Jesus. ²⁸ Saul was coming and going with them in Jerusalem, speaking boldly in the name of the Lord. ²⁹ He conversed and debated with the Hellenistic Jews, but they tried to kill him. ³⁰ When the brothers found out, they took him down to Caesarea and sent him off to Tarsus. Ac 13:46; 14:3; 22:17; 26:20; Gl 1:17

The Church's Growth

³¹ So the church throughout all Judea, Galilee, and Samaria had peace and was strengthened. Living in the fear of the Lord and encouraged by the Holy Spirit, it increased in numbers. Mt 16:18; 1Co 14:4; Rv 1:4

^A9:12 Other mss omit *In a vision*

The Healing of Aeneas

[32] As Peter was traveling from place to place, he also came down to the saints who lived in Lydda. [33] There he found a man named Aeneas, who was paralyzed and had been bedridden for eight years. [34] Peter said to him, "Aeneas, Jesus Christ heals you. Get up and make your bed," [A] and immediately he got up. [35] So all who lived in Lydda and Sharon saw him and turned to the Lord.   1Ch 8:12; Ezr 2:23; Rm 1:7; Eph 5:3; 6:18

Dorcas Restored to Life

[36] In Joppa there was a disciple named Tabitha (which is translated Dorcas). She was always doing good works and acts of charity. [37] About that time she became sick and died. After washing her, they placed her in a room upstairs. [38] Since Lydda was near Joppa, the disciples heard that Peter was there and sent two men to him who urged him, "Don't delay in coming with us." [39] Peter got up and went with them. When he arrived, they led him to the room upstairs. And all the widows approached him, weeping and showing him the robes and clothes that Dorcas had made while she was with them. [40] Peter sent them all out of the room. He knelt down, prayed, and turning toward the body said, "Tabitha, get up." She opened her eyes, saw Peter, and sat up. [41] He gave her his hand and helped her stand up. He called the saints and widows and presented her alive. [42] This became known throughout Joppa, and many believed in the Lord. [43] Peter stayed for some time in Joppa with Simon, a leather tanner.   Jos 19:46; 2Ch 2:16; Ezr 3:7; Jnh 1:3

Cornelius's Vision

10 There was a man in Caesarea named Cornelius, a centurion of what was called the Italian Regiment. [2] He was a devout man and feared God along with his whole household. He did many charitable deeds for the Jewish people and always prayed to God. [3] About three in the afternoon [B] he distinctly saw in a vision an angel of God who came in and said to him, "Cornelius."   Mt 27:27; Mk 15:16; Ac 3:1

[4] Staring at him in awe, he said, "What is it, Lord?"

The angel told him, "Your prayers and your acts of charity have ascended as a memorial offering before God. [5] Now send men to Joppa and call for Simon, who is also named Peter. [6] He is lodging with Simon, a tanner, whose house is by the sea."   Lk 16:13; Ac 9:43; 11:14; Rm 14:4

[7] When the angel who spoke to him had gone, he called two of his household servants and a devout soldier, who was one of those who attended him. [8] After explaining everything to them, he sent them to Joppa.

Peter's Vision

[9] The next day, as they were traveling and nearing the city, Peter went up to pray on the roof about noon. [C] [10] He became hungry and wanted to eat, but while they were preparing something, he fell into a trance. [11] He saw heaven opened and an object that resembled a large sheet coming down, being lowered by its four corners to the earth. [12] In it were all the four-footed animals and reptiles of the earth, and the birds of the sky. [13] A voice said to him, "Get up, Peter; kill and eat."   Ac 11:5-14

A **9:34** Or and get ready to eat   B **10:3** Lit About the ninth hour   C **10:9** Lit about the sixth hour

¹⁴ "No, Lord!" Peter said. "For I have never eaten anything impure and ritually unclean." Lv 11:4; 20:25

¹⁵ Again, a second time, the voice said to him, "What God has made clean, do not call impure." ¹⁶ This happened three times, and suddenly the object was taken up into heaven. Mt 15:11; Mk 7:19; Rm 14:14; 1Co 10:25

Peter Visits Cornelius

¹⁷ While Peter was deeply perplexed about what the vision he had seen might mean, right away the men who had been sent by Cornelius, having asked directions to Simon's house, stood at the gate. ¹⁸ They called out, asking if Simon, who was also named Peter, was lodging there.

¹⁹ While Peter was thinking about the vision, the Spirit told him, "Three men are here looking for you. ²⁰ Get up, go downstairs, and go with them with no doubts at all, because I have sent them." Ac 8:29

²¹ Then Peter went down to the men and said, "Here I am, the one you're looking for. What is the reason you're here?"

²² They said, "Cornelius, a centurion, an upright and God-fearing man, who has a good reputation with the whole Jewish nation, was divinely directed by a holy angel to call you to his house and to hear a message from you." ²³ Peter then invited them in and gave them lodging. Mk 8:38; Ac 10:2; 11:14

The next day he got up and set out with them, and some of the brothers from Joppa went with him. ²⁴ The following day he entered Caesarea. Now Cornelius was expecting them and had called together his relatives and close friends. ²⁵ When Peter entered, Cornelius met him, fell at his feet, and worshiped him. Ac 10:45

²⁶ But Peter lifted him up and said, "Stand up. I myself am also a man." ²⁷ While talking with him, he went in and found a large gathering of people. ²⁸ Peter said to them, "You know it's forbidden for a Jewish man to associate with or visit a foreigner, but God has shown me that I must not call any person impure or unclean. ²⁹ That's why I came without any objection when I was sent for. So may I ask why you sent for me?" Jn 4:9; 18:28; Ac 14:15; Rv 19:10; 22:8

³⁰ Cornelius replied, "Four days ago at this hour, at three in the afternoon, ᴬ I was ᴮ praying in my house. Just then a man in dazzling clothing stood before me ³¹ and said, 'Cornelius, your prayer has been heard, and your acts of charity have been remembered in God's sight. ³² Therefore send someone to Joppa and invite Simon here, who is also named Peter. He is lodging in Simon the tanner's house by the sea.' ᶜ ³³ So I immediately sent for you, and it was good of you to come. So now we are all in the presence of God to hear everything you have been commanded by the Lord." Ac 1:10; 3:1

Good News for Gentiles

³⁴ Peter began to speak: "Now I truly understand that God doesn't show favoritism, ³⁵ but in every nation the person who fears him and does what is right is acceptable to him. ³⁶ He sent the message to the Israelites, proclaiming the good news of peace through Jesus Christ — he is Lord of all. ³⁷ You

ᴬ**10:30** Lit *at the ninth hour*   ᴮ**10:30** Other mss add *fasting and*   ᶜ**10:32** Other mss add *When he arrives, he will speak to you.*

know the events that took place throughout all Judea, beginning from Galilee after the baptism that John preached: [38] how God anointed Jesus of Nazareth with the Holy Spirit and with power, and how he went about doing good and healing all who were under the tyranny of the devil, because God was with him. [39] We ourselves are witnesses of everything he did in both the Judean country and in Jerusalem, and yet they killed him by hanging him on a tree. [40] God raised up this man on the third day and caused him to be seen, [41] not by all the people, but by us whom God appointed as witnesses, who ate and drank with him after he rose from the dead. [42] He commanded us to preach to the people and to testify that he is the one appointed by God to be the judge of the living and the dead. [43] All the prophets testify about him that through his name everyone who believes in him receives forgiveness of sins." Dt 10:17; 2Ch 19:7

Gentile Conversion and Baptism

[44] While Peter was still speaking these words, the Holy Spirit came down on all those who heard the message. [45] The circumcised believers who had come with Peter were amazed because the gift of the Holy Spirit had been poured out even on the Gentiles. [46] For they heard them speaking in other tongues[A] and declaring the greatness of God.

Then Peter responded, [47] "Can anyone withhold water and prevent these people from being baptized, who have received the Holy Spirit just as we have?" [48] He commanded them to be baptized in the name of

Jesus Christ. Then they asked him to stay for a few days. Ac 2:4; 8:36; 11:17

Gentile Salvation Defended

11 The apostles and the brothers and sisters who were throughout Judea heard that the Gentiles had also received the word of God. [2] When Peter went up to Jerusalem, the circumcision party criticized him, [3] saying, "You went to uncircumcised men and ate with them." Ac 10:28,45; Gl 2:12; Col 4:11; 1Tm 1:10

[4] Peter began to explain to them step by step: [5] "I was in the town of Joppa praying, and I saw, in a trance, an object that resembled a large sheet coming down, being lowered by its four corners from heaven, and it came to me. [6] When I looked closely and considered it, I saw the four-footed animals of the earth, the wild beasts, the reptiles, and the birds of the sky. [7] I also heard a voice telling me, 'Get up, Peter; kill and eat.' Ac 10:9-32

[8] "'No, Lord!' I said. 'For nothing impure or ritually unclean has ever entered my mouth.' [9] But a voice answered from heaven a second time, 'What God has made clean, you must not call impure.'

[10] "Now this happened three times, and everything was drawn up again into heaven. [11] At that very moment, three men who had been sent to me from Caesarea arrived at the house where we were. [12] The Spirit told me to accompany them with no doubts at all. These six brothers also accompanied me, and we went into the man's house. [13] He reported to us how he had seen the angel standing in his house and saying, 'Send[B] to Joppa, and call for Simon, who is also named Peter.

A 10:46 languages   B 11:13 Other mss add *men*

¹⁴ He will speak a message to you by which you and all your household will be saved.' Ac 8:29; 10:23; 15:9

¹⁵ "As I began to speak, the Holy Spirit came down on them, just as on us at the beginning. ¹⁶ I remembered the word of the Lord, how he said, 'John baptized with water, but you will be baptized with the Holy Spirit.' ¹⁷ If, then, God gave them the same gift that he also gave to us when we believed in the Lord Jesus Christ, how could I possibly hinder God?" Mt 3:11; Mk 1:8; Ac 2:4; 10:44

¹⁸ When they heard this they became silent. And they glorified God, saying, "So then, God has given repentance resulting in life even to the Gentiles." Rm 10:12-13; 2Co 7:10

The Church in Antioch

¹⁹ Now those who had been scattered as a result of the persecution that started because of Stephen made their way as far as Phoenicia, Cyprus, and Antioch, speaking the word to no one except Jews. ²⁰ But there were some of them, men from Cyprus and Cyrene, who came to Antioch and began speaking to the Greeks^A also, proclaiming the good news about the Lord Jesus. ²¹ The Lord's hand was with them, and a large number who believed turned to the Lord. ²² News about them reached^B the church in Jerusalem, and they sent out Barnabas to travel^C as far as Antioch. ²³ When he arrived and saw the grace of God, he was glad and encouraged all of them to remain true to the Lord with devoted hearts, ²⁴ for he was a good man, full of the Holy Spirit and of faith. And large numbers of people were added to the Lord.

²⁵ Then he^D went to Tarsus to search for Saul, ²⁶ and when he found him he brought him to Antioch. For a whole year they met with the church and taught large numbers. The disciples were first called Christians at Antioch. Ac 6:1

Famine Relief

²⁷ In those days some prophets came down from Jerusalem to Antioch. ²⁸ One of them, named Agabus, stood up and predicted by the Spirit that there would be a severe famine throughout the Roman world.^E This took place during the reign of Claudius. ²⁹ Each of the disciples, according to his ability, determined to send relief to the brothers and sisters who lived in Judea. ³⁰ They did this, sending it to the elders by means of Barnabas and Saul. Ac 13:1; 15:32; 18:2; 1Co 12:28

James Martyred and Peter Jailed

12 About that time King Herod violently attacked some who belonged to the church, ² and he executed James, John's brother, with the sword. ³ When he saw that it pleased the Jews, he proceeded to arrest Peter too, during the Festival of Unleavened Bread. ⁴ After the arrest, he put him in prison and assigned four squads of four soldiers each to guard him, intending to bring him out to the people after the Passover. ⁵ So Peter was kept in prison, but the church was praying fervently to God for him. Mt 4:21; 20:23

Peter Rescued

⁶ When Herod was about to bring him out for trial, that very night Peter, bound with two chains, was

---

^A **11:20** Lit *Hellenists* ^B **11:22** Lit *reached the ears of* ^C **11:22** Other mss omit *to travel* ^D **11:25** Other mss read *Barnabas* ^E **11:28** Or *the whole world* sleeping between two soldiers, while the sentries in front of the door guarded the prison. [7] Suddenly an angel of the Lord appeared, and a light shone in the cell. Striking Peter on the side, he woke him up and said, "Quick, get up!" And the chains fell off his wrists. [8] "Get dressed," the angel told him, "and put on your sandals." And he did. "Wrap your cloak around you," he told him, "and follow me." [9] So he went out and followed, and he did not know that what the angel did was really happening, but he thought he was seeing a vision. [10] After they passed the first and second guards, they came to the iron gate that leads into the city, which opened to them by itself. They went outside and passed one street, and suddenly the angel left him.   Lk 1:11; 2:9; 5:19; 16:26; Col 4:1; Jd 5

[11] When Peter came to himself, he said, "Now I know for certain that the Lord has sent his angel and rescued me from Herod's grasp and from all that the Jewish people expected." [12] As soon as he realized this, he went to the house of Mary, the mother of John Mark,[A] where many had assembled and were praying. [13] He knocked at the door of the outer gate, and a servant named Rhoda came to answer. [14] She recognized Peter's voice, and because of her joy, she did not open the gate but ran in and announced that Peter was standing at the outer gate.   Ps 33:18-19; 34:7; Dn 3:28; 6:22; Lk 15:17

[15] "You're out of your mind!" they told her. But she kept insisting that it was true, and they said, "It's his angel." [16] Peter, however, kept on knocking, and when they opened the door and saw him, they were amazed.   Mt 18:10; Lk 24:21

[17] Motioning to them with his hand to be silent, he described to them how the Lord had brought him out of the prison. "Tell these things to James and the brothers," he said, and he left and went to another place.   Ac 13:16; 15:13; 19:33; 21:40

[18] At daylight, there was a great commotion among the soldiers as to what had become of Peter. [19] After Herod had searched and did not find him, he interrogated the guards and ordered their execution. Then Herod went down from Judea to Caesarea and stayed there.

Herod's Death

[20] Herod had been very angry with the people of Tyre and Sidon. Together they presented themselves before him. After winning over Blastus, who was in charge of the king's bedroom, they asked for peace, because their country was supplied with food from the king's country. [21] On an appointed day, dressed in royal robes and seated on the throne, Herod delivered a speech to them. [22] The assembled people began to shout, "It's the voice of a god and not of a man!" [23] At once an angel of the Lord struck him because he did not give the glory to God, and he was eaten by worms and died.   1Kg 5:11

[24] But the word of God flourished and multiplied. [25] After they had completed their relief mission, Barnabas and Saul returned to[B] Jerusalem, taking along John who was called Mark.   Ac 4:36; 6:7; 11:30; 12:12; 19:20

Preparing for the Mission Field

13 Now in the church at Antioch there were prophets and teachers: Barnabas, Simeon who

---

[A]**12:12** Lit *John who was called Mark*   [B]**12:25** Other mss read *from* was called Niger, Lucius of Cyrene, Manaen, a close friend of Herod the tetrarch, and Saul. Mt 14:1

² As they were worshiping^A the Lord and fasting, the Holy Spirit said, "Set apart for me Barnabas and Saul for the work to which I have called them." ³ Then after they had fasted, prayed, and laid hands on them, they sent them off. Ac 8:29

The Mission to Cyprus

⁴ So being sent out by the Holy Spirit, they went down to Seleucia, and from there they sailed to Cyprus. ⁵ Arriving in Salamis, they proclaimed the word of God in the Jewish synagogues. They also had John as their assistant. ⁶ When they had traveled the whole island as far as Paphos, they came across a sorcerer, a Jewish false prophet named Bar-Jesus. ⁷ He was with the proconsul, Sergius Paulus, an intelligent man. This man summoned Barnabas and Saul and wanted to hear the word of God. ⁸ But Elymas the sorcerer (that is the meaning of his name) opposed them and tried to turn the proconsul away from the faith. Mt 7:15; Ac 8:9; 9:20; 12:12; 18:12

⁹ But Saul — also called Paul — filled with the Holy Spirit, stared straight at Elymas ¹⁰ and said, "You are full of all kinds of deceit and trickery, you son of the devil and enemy of all that is right. Won't you ever stop perverting the straight paths of the Lord? ¹¹ Now, look, the Lord's hand is against you. You are going to be blind, and will not see the sun for a time." Immediately a mist and darkness fell on him, and he went around seeking someone to lead him by the hand. Mt 13:38

¹² Then, when he saw what happened, the proconsul believed, because he was astonished at the teaching of the Lord. Ac 13:49; 15:35-36

Paul's Sermon in Antioch of Pisidia

¹³ Paul and his companions set sail from Paphos and came to Perga in Pamphylia, but John left them and went back to Jerusalem. ¹⁴ They continued their journey from Perga and reached Pisidian Antioch. On the Sabbath day they went into the synagogue and sat down. ¹⁵ After the reading of the Law and the Prophets, the leaders of the synagogue sent word to them, saying, "Brothers, if you have any word of encouragement for the people, you can speak." Ac 9:20; 12:12; 13:6; 15:38; 16:3

¹⁶ Paul stood up and motioned with his hand and said: "Fellow Israelites, and you who fear God, listen! ¹⁷ The God of this people Israel chose our ancestors, made the people prosper during their stay in the land of Egypt, and led them out of it with a mighty^B arm. ¹⁸ And for about forty years he put up with them^C in the wilderness; ¹⁹ and after destroying seven nations in the land of Canaan, he gave them their land as an inheritance. ²⁰ This all took about 450 years. After this, he gave them judges until Samuel the prophet. ²¹ Then they asked for a king, and God gave them Saul the son of Kish, a man of the tribe of Benjamin, for forty years. ²² After removing him, he raised up David as their king and testified about him: '**I have found David** the son of Jesse to be **a man after my own heart**,^D who will carry out all my will.' Ex 1:6; 6:6; Ac 10:2; 12:17

---

^A **13:2** Or *were ministering to*   ^B **13:17** Lit *with an uplifted*   ^C **13:18** Other mss read *he cared for them*
^D **13:22** 1Sm 13:14; Ps 89:20

23 "From this man's descendants, as he promised, God brought to Israel the Savior, Jesus.[A] 24 Before his coming to public attention, John had previously proclaimed a baptism of repentance to all the people of Israel. 25 Now as John was completing his mission, he said, 'Who do you think I am? I am not the one. But one is coming after me, and I am not worthy to untie the sandals on his feet.' Ps 132:1; Mt 1:1

26 "Brothers and sisters, children of Abraham's race, and those among you who fear God, it is to us that the word of this salvation has been sent. 27 Since the residents of Jerusalem and their rulers did not recognize him or the sayings of the prophets that are read every Sabbath, they have fulfilled their words by condemning him. 28 Though they found no grounds for the death sentence, they asked Pilate to have him killed. 29 When they had carried out all that had been written about him, they took him down from the tree and put him in a tomb. 30 But God raised him from the dead, 31 and he appeared for many days to those who came up with him from Galilee to Jerusalem, who are now his witnesses to the people. 32 And we ourselves proclaim to you the good news of the promise that was made to our ancestors. 33 God has fulfilled this for us, their children, by raising up Jesus, as it is written in the second Psalm: Lk 24:27; Ac 3:17; 4:12; 5:20

You are my Son;
today I have become
your Father.[B,C]   Ps 2:7; Heb 1:5; 5:5

34 As to his raising him from the dead, never to return to decay, he has spoken in this way, **I will give you the holy and sure promises of David.**[D] 35 Therefore he also says in another passage, **You will not let your Holy One see decay.**[E] 36 For David, after serving God's purpose in his own generation, fell asleep, was buried with his fathers, and decayed, 37 but the one God raised up did not decay. 38 Therefore, let it be known to you, brothers and sisters, that through this man forgiveness of sins is being proclaimed to you. 39 Everyone who believes is justified[F] through him from everything that you could not be justified from through the law of Moses. 40 So beware that what is said in the prophets does not happen to you: Is 55:3

41 **Look, you scoffers,**
    marvel and vanish away,
    because I am doing a work
    in your days,
    a work that you will
    never believe,
    even if someone were
    to explain it to you."[G] Is 29:14

Paul and Barnabas in Antioch

42 As they were leaving, the people[H] urged them to speak about these matters the following Sabbath. 43 After the synagogue had been dismissed, many of the Jews and devout converts to Judaism followed Paul and Barnabas, who were speaking with them and urging them to continue in the grace of God. Ac 11:23; 14:22

44 The following Sabbath almost the whole town assembled to hear the word of the Lord.[I] 45 But when the Jews saw the crowds, they were filled with jealousy and began to

contradict what Paul was saying, insulting him. Ac 18:6; 1Th 2:16; 1Pt 4:4; Jd 10

46 Paul and Barnabas boldly replied, "It was necessary that the word of God be spoken to you first. Since you reject it and judge yourselves unworthy of eternal life, we are turning to the Gentiles. **47** For this is what the Lord has commanded us: Mt 21:43; Ac 3:26; 18:6; 22:21; 28:28

**I have made you
a light for the Gentiles
to bring salvation
to the end of the earth."** A

48 When the Gentiles heard this, they rejoiced and honored the word of the Lord, and all who had been appointed to eternal life believed. **49** The word of the Lord spread through the whole region. **50** But the Jews incited the prominent God-fearing women and the leading men of the city. They stirred up persecution against Paul and Barnabas and expelled them from their district. **51** But Paul and Barnabas shook the dust off their feet against them and went to Iconium. **52** And the disciples were filled with joy and the Holy Spirit. Lk 9:5; Ac 14:2,19

Growth and Persecution in Iconium

14 In Iconium they entered the Jewish synagogue, as usual, and spoke in such a way that a great number of both Jews and Greeks believed. **2** But the unbelieving Jews stirred up the Gentiles and poisoned their minds against the brothers. **3** So they stayed there a long time and spoke boldly for the Lord, who testified to the message of his grace by enabling them to do signs and wonders. **4** But the people of the city were divided, some

siding with the Jews and others with the apostles. **5** When an attempt was made by both the Gentiles and Jews, with their rulers, to mistreat and stone them, **6** they found out about it and fled to the Lycaonian towns of Lystra and Derbe and to the surrounding countryside. **7** There they continued preaching the gospel. Ac 13:5,51; 14:19

Mistaken for Gods in Lystra

8 In Lystra a man was sitting who was without strength in his feet, had never walked, and had been lame from birth. **9** He listened as Paul spoke. After looking directly at him and seeing that he had faith to be healed, **10** Paul said in a loud voice, "Stand up on your feet!" And he jumped up and began to walk around. Mk 6:56; Php 2:12

11 When the crowds saw what Paul had done, they shouted, saying in the Lycaonian language, "The gods have come down to us in human form!" **12** Barnabas they called Zeus, and Paul, Hermes, because he was the chief speaker. **13** The priest of Zeus, whose temple was just outside the town, brought bulls and wreaths to the gates because he intended, with the crowds, to offer sacrifice. Ac 8:10; 28:6

14 The apostles Barnabas and Paul tore their robes when they heard this and rushed into the crowd, shouting: **15** "People! Why are you doing these things? We are people also, just like you, and we are proclaiming good news to you, that you turn from these worthless things to the living God, **who made the heaven, the earth, the sea, and everything in them.** B **16** In past generations he allowed all the

A **13:47** Is 49:6   B **14:15** Ex 20:11; Ps 146:6

nations to go their own way, ¹⁷ although he did not leave himself without a witness, since he did what is good by giving you rain from heaven and fruitful seasons and filling you with food and your^A hearts with joy." ¹⁸ Even though they said these things, they barely stopped the crowds from sacrificing to them.   1Sm 12:21; Mt 26:65; Mk 14:63

¹⁹ Some Jews came from Antioch and Iconium, and when they won over the crowds, they stoned Paul and dragged him out of the city, thinking he was dead. ²⁰ After the disciples gathered around him, he got up and went into the town. The next day he left with Barnabas for Derbe.   Ac 11:26; 13:45,51; 2Co 11:25; 2Tm 3:11

Church Planting

²¹ After they had preached the gospel in that town and made many disciples, they returned to Lystra, to Iconium, and to Antioch, ²² strengthening the^B disciples by encouraging them to continue in the faith and by telling them, "It is necessary to go through many hardships to enter the kingdom of God." ²³ When they had appointed elders for them in every church and prayed with fasting, they committed them to the Lord in whom they had believed.   Mt 28:19; Ac 13:43,51

²⁴ They passed through Pisidia and came to Pamphylia. ²⁵ After they had spoken the word in Perga, they went down to Attalia. ²⁶ From there they sailed back to Antioch where they had been commended to the grace of God for the work they had now completed. ²⁷ After they arrived and gathered the church together, they reported everything God had done

with them and that he had opened the door of faith to the Gentiles. ²⁸ And they spent a considerable time with the disciples.   Ac 11:19; 13:3

Dispute in Antioch

15 Some men came down from Judea and began to teach the brothers: "Unless you are circumcised according to the custom prescribed by Moses, you cannot be saved." ² After Paul and Barnabas had engaged them in serious argument and debate, Paul and Barnabas and some others were appointed to go up to the apostles and elders in Jerusalem about this issue. ³ When they had been sent on their way by the church, they passed through both Phoenicia and Samaria, describing in detail the conversion of the Gentiles, and they brought great joy to all the brothers and sisters.   Ac 15:24; Gl 2:12

⁴ When they arrived at Jerusalem, they were welcomed by the church, the apostles, and the elders, and they reported all that God had done with them. ⁵ But some of the believers who belonged to the party of the Pharisees stood up and said, "It is necessary to circumcise them and to command them to keep the law of Moses."   Ac 14:27

The Jerusalem Council

⁶ The apostles and the elders gathered to consider this matter. ⁷ After there had been much debate, Peter stood up and said to them: "Brothers and sisters, you are aware that in the early days God made a choice among you,^C that by my mouth the Gentiles would hear the gospel message and believe. ⁸ And God, who knows the heart, bore witness

to them by giving them the Holy Spirit, just as he also did to us. ⁹ He made no distinction between us and them, cleansing their hearts by faith. ¹⁰ Now then, why are you testing God by putting a yoke on the disciples' necks that neither our ancestors nor we have been able to bear? ¹¹ On the contrary, we believe that we are saved through the grace of the Lord Jesus in the same way they are." Ac 1:24; 10:44,47

¹² The whole assembly became silent and listened to Barnabas and Paul describe all the signs and wonders God had done through them among the Gentiles. ¹³ After they stopped speaking, James responded: "Brothers and sisters, listen to me. ¹⁴ Simeon^A has reported how God first intervened to take from the Gentiles a people for his name. ¹⁵ And the words of the prophets agree with this, as it is written:

¹⁶ **After these things**
   I will return
   and rebuild
      David's fallen tent.
   I will rebuild its ruins
   and set it up again,
¹⁷ **so the rest of humanity**
   may seek the Lord —
   even all the Gentiles
   who are called
   by my name —
   declares the Lord
   who makes these things
      ¹⁸ **known from long ago.** ^B,C

¹⁹ Therefore, in my judgment, we should not cause difficulties for those among the Gentiles who turn to God, ²⁰ but instead we should write to them to abstain from things polluted by idols, from

sexual immorality, from eating anything that has been strangled, and from blood. ²¹ For since ancient times, Moses has had those who proclaim him in every city, and every Sabbath day he is read aloud in the synagogues." 1Co 8:7,13; 10:7-8,14-28

The Letter to the Gentile Believers

²² Then the apostles and the elders, with the whole church, decided to select men who were among them and to send them to Antioch with Paul and Barnabas: Judas, called Barsabbas, and Silas, both leading men among the brothers. ²³ They wrote: Ac 1:23; 15:2; 1Pt 5:12

"From the apostles and the elders, your brothers,
To the brothers and sisters among the Gentiles in Antioch, Syria, and Cilicia: Ac 15:1; 23:26; Jms 1:1
Greetings.
²⁴ Since we have heard that some without our authorization went out from us and troubled you with their words and unsettled your hearts, ^D ²⁵ we have unanimously decided to select men and send them to you along with our dearly loved Barnabas and Paul, ²⁶ who have risked their lives for the name of our Lord Jesus Christ. ²⁷ Therefore we have sent Judas and Silas, who will personally report the same things by word of mouth. ²⁸ For it was the Holy Spirit's decision — and ours — not to place further burdens on you beyond these requirements: ²⁹ that you abstain from food offered to

---

^A **15:14** Simon (Peter) ^B **15:17-18** Other mss read *says the Lord who does all these things. Known to God from long ago are all his works.* ^C **15:16-18** Am 9:11-12; Is 45:21 ^D **15:24** Other mss add *by saying, 'Be circumcised and keep the law,'* idols, from blood, from eating anything that has been strangled, and from sexual immorality. You will do well if you keep yourselves from these things. Farewell."

The Outcome of the Jerusalem Letter

³⁰ So they were sent off and went down to Antioch, and after gathering the assembly, they delivered the letter. ³¹ When they read it, they rejoiced because of its encouragement. ³² Both Judas and Silas, who were also prophets themselves, encouraged the brothers and sisters and strengthened them with a long message. ³³ After spending some time there, they were sent back in peace by the brothers and sisters to those who had sent them. ^A,B ³⁵ But Paul and Barnabas, along with many others, remained in Antioch, teaching and proclaiming the word of the Lord. Ac 14:22; 15:1

Paul and Barnabas Part Company

³⁶ After some time had passed, Paul said to Barnabas, "Let's go back and visit the brothers and sisters in every town where we have preached the word of the Lord and see how they're doing." ³⁷ Barnabas wanted to take along John Mark. ^C ³⁸ But Paul insisted that they should not take along this man who had deserted them in Pamphylia and had not gone on with them to the work. ³⁹ They had such a sharp disagreement that they parted company, and Barnabas took Mark with him and sailed off to Cyprus. ⁴⁰ But Paul chose Silas and departed, after

being commended by the brothers and sisters to the grace of the Lord. ⁴¹ He traveled through Syria and Cilicia, strengthening the churches. Ac 12:1; 13:4,13-14,51; 14:6,24

Paul Selects Timothy

16 Paul went on to Derbe and Lystra, where there was a disciple named Timothy, the son of a believing Jewish woman, but his father was a Greek. ² The brothers and sisters at Lystra and Iconium spoke highly of him. ³ Paul wanted Timothy to go with him; so he took him and circumcised him because of the Jews who were in those places, since they all knew that his father was a Greek. ⁴ As they traveled through the towns, they delivered the decisions reached by the apostles and elders at Jerusalem for the people to observe. ⁵ So the churches were strengthened in the faith and grew daily in numbers. Ac 17:14-15; 18:5; 19:22; 20:4

Evangelization of Europe

⁶ They went through the region of Phrygia and Galatia; they had been forbidden by the Holy Spirit to speak the word in Asia. ⁷ When they came to Mysia, they tried to go into Bithynia, but the Spirit of Jesus did not allow them. ⁸ Passing by Mysia they went down to Troas. ⁹ During the night Paul had a vision in which a Macedonian man was standing and pleading with him, "Cross over to Macedonia and help us!" ¹⁰ After he had seen the vision, we immediately made efforts to set out for Macedonia, concluding that God had called us to preach the gospel to them.

^A 15:33 Other mss read *the brothers to the apostles stay there.* ^B 15:33 Other mss add v. 34: *But Silas decided to* ^C 15:37 Lit *John who was called Mark*

Lydia's Conversion

¹¹ From Troas we put out to sea and sailed straight for Samothrace, the next day to Neapolis, ¹² and from there to Philippi, a Roman colony and a leading city of the district of Macedonia. We stayed in that city for several days. ¹³ On the Sabbath day we went outside the city gate by the river, where we expected to find a place of prayer. We sat down and spoke to the women gathered there. ¹⁴ A God-fearing woman named Lydia, a dealer in purple cloth from the city of Thyatira, was listening. The Lord opened her heart to respond to what Paul was saying. ¹⁵ After she and her household were baptized, she urged us, "If you consider me a believer in the Lord, come and stay at my house." And she persuaded us.

Paul and Silas in Prison

¹⁶ Once, as we were on our way to prayer, a slave girl met us who had a spirit by which she predicted the future. She made a large profit for her owners by fortune-telling. ¹⁷ As she followed Paul and us she cried out, "These men, who are proclaiming to you ^A the way of salvation, are the servants of the Most High God." ¹⁸ She did this for many days. Paul was greatly annoyed. Turning to the spirit, he said, "I command you in the name of Jesus Christ to come out of her!" And it came out right away. Mk 5:7; 16:17

¹⁹ When her owners realized that their hope of profit was gone, they seized Paul and Silas and dragged them into the marketplace to the authorities. ²⁰ Bringing them before the chief magistrates, they said, "These men are seriously disturbing our city. They are Jews ²¹ and are promoting customs that are not legal for us as Romans to adopt or practice." ²² The crowd joined in the attack against them, and the chief magistrates stripped off their clothes and ordered them to be beaten with rods. ²³ After they had severely flogged them, they threw them in jail, ordering the jailer to guard them carefully. ²⁴ Receiving such an order, he put them into the inner prison and secured their feet in the stocks. Mt 10:18; Ac 8:3

A Midnight Deliverance

²⁵ About midnight Paul and Silas were praying and singing hymns to God, and the prisoners were listening to them. ²⁶ Suddenly there was such a violent earthquake that the foundations of the jail were shaken, and immediately all the doors were opened, and everyone's chains came loose. ²⁷ When the jailer woke up and saw the doors of the prison standing open, he drew his sword and was going to kill himself, since he thought the prisoners had escaped. Ac 4:31; 5:19; 12:7,10

²⁸ But Paul called out in a loud voice, "Don't harm yourself, because we're all here!"

²⁹ The jailer called for lights, rushed in, and fell down trembling before Paul and Silas. ³⁰ He escorted them out and said, "Sirs, what must I do to be saved?" Ac 2:37; 22:10

³¹ They said, "Believe in the Lord Jesus, and you will be saved — you and your household." ³² And they spoke the word of the Lord to him along with everyone in his house. ³³ He took them the same hour of the night and washed their wounds. Right away he and all his

^A16:17 Other mss read us

family were baptized. ³⁴ He brought them into his house, set a meal before them, and rejoiced because he had come to believe in God with his entire household. Mk 16:16; Ac 11:14; 16:15

An Official Apology

³⁵ When daylight came, the chief magistrates sent the police to say, "Release those men."

³⁶ The jailer reported these words to Paul: "The magistrates have sent orders for you to be released. So come out now and go in peace."

³⁷ But Paul said to them, "They beat us in public without a trial, although we are Roman citizens, and threw us in jail. And now are they going to send us away secretly? Certainly not! On the contrary, let them come themselves and escort us out." Ac 22:25-29

³⁸ The police reported these words to the magistrates. They were afraid when they heard that Paul and Silas were Roman citizens. ³⁹ So they came to appease them, and escorting them from prison, they urged them to leave town. ⁴⁰ After leaving the jail, they came to Lydia's house, where they saw and encouraged the brothers and sisters, and departed. Mt 8:34; Ac 16:14

A Short Ministry in Thessalonica

17 After they passed through Amphipolis and Apollonia, they came to Thessalonica, where there was a Jewish synagogue. ² As usual, Paul went into the synagogue, and on three Sabbath days reasoned with them from the Scriptures, ³ explaining and proving that it was necessary for the Messiah to suffer and rise from the dead: "This Jesus I am proclaiming to you is the Messiah." ⁴ Some of them were persuaded and joined Paul and Silas, including a large number of God-fearing Greeks, as well as a number of the leading women.

Riot in the City

⁵ But the Jews became jealous, and they brought together some wicked men from the marketplace, formed a mob, and started a riot in the city. Attacking Jason's house, they searched for them to bring them out to the public assembly. ⁶ When they did not find them, they dragged Jason and some of the brothers before the city officials, shouting, "These men who have turned the world upside down have come here too, ⁷ and Jason has welcomed them. They are all acting contrary to Caesar's decrees, saying that there is another king — Jesus." ⁸ The crowd and city officials who heard these things were upset. ⁹ After taking a security bond from Jason and the others, they released them. Ac 17:13; Rm 16:21; 1Th 2:14-16

The Bereans Search the Scriptures

¹⁰ As soon as it was night, the brothers and sisters sent Paul and Silas away to Berea. Upon arrival, they went into the synagogue of the Jews. ¹¹ The people here were of more noble character than those in Thessalonica, since they received the word with eagerness and examined the Scriptures daily to see if these things were so. ¹² Consequently, many of them believed, including a number of the prominent Greek women as well as men. ¹³ But when the Jews from Thessalonica found out that the word of God had been proclaimed by Paul at Berea, they came there

too, agitating and upsetting[A] the crowds. ¹⁴ Then the brothers and sisters immediately sent Paul away to go to the coast, but Silas and Timothy stayed on there. ¹⁵ Those who escorted Paul brought him as far as Athens, and after receiving instructions for Silas and Timothy to come to him as quickly as possible, they departed.   Ac 17:13-14; 20:4

Paul in Athens

¹⁶ While Paul was waiting for them in Athens, he was deeply distressed when he saw that the city was full of idols. ¹⁷ So he reasoned in the synagogue with the Jews and with those who worshiped God, as well as in the marketplace every day with those who happened to be there. ¹⁸ Some of the Epicurean and Stoic philosophers also debated with him. Some said, "What is this ignorant show-off[B] trying to say?"

Others replied, "He seems to be a preacher of foreign deities" — because he was telling the good news about Jesus and the resurrection. ¹⁹ They took him and brought him to the Areopagus,[C] and said, "May we learn about this new teaching you are presenting? ²⁰ Because what you say sounds strange to us, and we want to know what these things mean." ²¹ Now all the Athenians and the foreigners residing there spent their time on nothing else but telling or hearing something new.   Mk 1:27; Ac 17:22

The Areopagus Address

²² Paul stood in the middle of the Areopagus and said: "People of Athens! I see that you are extremely religious in every respect. ²³ For as I was passing through and observing the objects of your worship, I even found an altar on which was inscribed: 'To an Unknown God.' Therefore, what you worship in ignorance, this I proclaim to you. ²⁴ The God who made the world and everything in it — he is Lord of heaven and earth — does not live in shrines made by hands. ²⁵ Neither is he served by human hands, as though he needed anything, since he himself gives everyone life and breath and all things. ²⁶ From one man[D] he has made every nationality to live over the whole earth and has determined their appointed times and the boundaries of where they live. ²⁷ He did this so that they might seek God, and perhaps they might reach out and find him, though he is not far from each one of us. ²⁸ For in him we live and move and have our being, as even some of your own poets have said, 'For we are also his offspring.' ²⁹ Since we are God's offspring then, we shouldn't think that the divine nature is like gold or silver or stone, an image fashioned by human art and imagination.   Dt 10:14; Jb 33:4; Ps 115:16; Is 42:5

³⁰ "Therefore, having overlooked the times of ignorance, God now commands all people everywhere to repent, ³¹ because he has set a day when he is going to judge the world in righteousness by the man he has appointed. He has provided proof of this to everyone by raising him from the dead."   Lk 24:47

³² When they heard about the resurrection of the dead, some began to ridicule him, but others said, "We'd like to hear from you

---

[A]**17:13** Other mss omit *and upsetting*   [B]**17:18** Lit *this seed picker*   [C]**17:19** Or *Mars Hill*   [D]**17:26** Other mss read *blood* again about this." ³³ So Paul left their presence. ³⁴ However, some people joined him and believed, including Dionysius the Areopagite, a woman named Damaris, and others with them.

Founding the Corinthian Church

18 After this, heᴬ left Athens and went to Corinth, ² where he found a Jew named Aquila, a native of Pontus, who had recently come from Italy with his wife Priscilla because Claudius had ordered all the Jews to leave Rome. Paul came to them, ³ and since they were of the same occupation, tentmakers by trade, he stayed with them and worked. ⁴ He reasoned in the synagogue every Sabbath and tried to persuade both Jews and Greeks.

⁵ When Silas and Timothy arrived from Macedonia, Paul devoted himself to preaching the wordᴮ and testified to the Jews that Jesus is the Messiah. ⁶ When they resisted and blasphemed, he shook out his clothes and told them, "Your blood is on your own heads! I am innocent.ᶜ From now on I will go to the Gentiles." ⁷ So he left there and went to the house of a man named Titius Justus, a worshiper of God, whose house was next door to the synagogue. ⁸ Crispus, the leader of the synagogue, believed in the Lord, along with his whole household. Many of the Corinthians, when they heard, believed and were baptized. Jb 32:18; Ac 15:22; 16:1,9; 18:28

⁹ The Lord said to Paul in a night vision, "Don't be afraid, but keep on speaking and don't be silent. ¹⁰ For I am with you, and no one will lay a hand on you to hurt you, because I have many people in this city." ¹¹ He stayed there a year and a half, teaching the word of God among them. Mt 28:20; Ac 23:11

¹² While Gallio was proconsul of Achaia, the Jews made a united attack against Paul and brought him to the tribunal. ¹³ "This man," they said, "is persuading people to worship God in ways contrary to the law." Ac 13:7; 18:27

¹⁴ As Paul was about to open his mouth, Gallio said to the Jews, "If it were a matter of wrongdoing or of a serious crime, it would be reasonable for me to put up with you Jews. ¹⁵ But if these are questions about words, names, and your own law, see to it yourselves. I refuse to be a judge of such things." ¹⁶ So he drove them from the tribunal. ¹⁷ And they allᴰ seized Sosthenes, the leader of the synagogue, and beat him in front of the tribunal, but none of these things mattered to Gallio. Ac 23:29; 25:11,19; 1Co 1:1

The Return Trip to Antioch

¹⁸ After staying for some time, Paul said farewell to the brothers and sisters and sailed away to Syria, accompanied by Priscilla and Aquila. He shaved his head at Cenchreae because of a vow he had taken. ¹⁹ When they reached Ephesus he left them there, but he himself entered the synagogue and debated with the Jews. ²⁰ When they asked him to stay for a longer time, he declined, ²¹ but he said farewell and added,ᴱ "I'll come back to you again, if God wills." Then he set sail from Ephesus. Nm 6:2,5,9,18; Ac 21:24; Rm 16:1

ᴬ**18:1** Other mss read *Paul* ᴮ**18:5** Other mss read *was urged by the Spirit* ᶜ**18:6** Lit *clean* ᴰ**18:17** Other mss read *Then all the Greeks* ᴱ**18:21** Other mss add *"By all means it is necessary to keep the coming festival in Jerusalem. But*

²² On landing at Caesarea, he went up to Jerusalem and greeted the church, then went down to Antioch.   Ac 8:40; 11:19

²³ After spending some time there, he set out, traveling through one place after another in the region of Galatia and Phrygia, strengthening all the disciples.   Ac 14:22; 16:6

The Eloquent Apollos

²⁴ Now a Jew named Apollos, a native Alexandrian, an eloquent man who was competent in the use of the Scriptures, arrived in Ephesus. ²⁵ He had been instructed in the way of the Lord; and being fervent in spirit, ᴬ he was speaking and teaching accurately about Jesus, although he knew only John's baptism. ²⁶ He began to speak boldly in the synagogue. After Priscilla and Aquila heard him, they took him aside ᴮ and explained the way of God to him more accurately. ²⁷ When he wanted to cross over to Achaia, the brothers and sisters wrote to the disciples to welcome him. After he arrived, he was a great help to those who by grace had believed. ²⁸ For he vigorously refuted the Jews in public, demonstrating through the Scriptures that Jesus is the Messiah.   Ac 19:1

Twelve Disciples of John the Baptist

19 While Apollos was in Corinth, Paul traveled through the interior regions and came to Ephesus. He found some disciples ² and asked them, "Did you receive the Holy Spirit when you believed?"

"No," they told him, "we haven't even heard that there is a Holy Spirit."   Jn 7:39; Ac 8:16; 11:16

³ "Into what then were you baptized?" he asked them.

"Into John's baptism," they replied.   Ac 18:25

⁴ Paul said, "John baptized with a baptism of repentance, telling the people that they should believe in the one who would come after him, that is, in Jesus."   Mt 3:11; Lk 3:3; Ac 13:24

⁵ When they heard this, they were baptized into the name of the Lord Jesus. ⁶ And when Paul had laid his hands on them, the Holy Spirit came on them, and they began to speak in other tongues ᶜ and to prophesy. ⁷ Now there were about twelve men in all.   Mk 16:17; Ac 6:6; 8:17

In the Lecture Hall of Tyrannus

⁸ Paul entered the synagogue and spoke boldly over a period of three months, arguing and persuading them about the kingdom of God. ⁹ But when some became hardened and would not believe, slandering the Way in front of the crowd, he withdrew from them, taking the disciples, and conducted discussions every day in the lecture hall of Tyrannus. ¹⁰ This went on for two years, so that all the residents of Asia, both Jews and Greeks, heard the word of the Lord.   Ac 1:3; 9:20; 28:23

Demonism Defeated at Ephesus

¹¹ God was performing extraordinary miracles by Paul's hands, ¹² so that even facecloths or aprons ᴰ that had touched his skin were brought to the sick, and the diseases left them, and the evil spirits came out of them.   Ac 5:15; 8:13

¹³ Now some of the itinerant Jewish exorcists also attempted to pronounce the name of the Lord Jesus over those who had evil spirits,

ᴬ**18:25** Or *in the Spirit*   ᴮ**18:26** Lit *they received him*   ᶜ**19:6** languages   ᴰ**19:12** Or *sweat cloths* saying, "I command you by the Jesus that Paul preaches!" [14] Seven sons of Sceva, a Jewish high priest, were doing this. [15] The evil spirit answered them, "I know Jesus, and I recognize Paul — but who are you?" [16] Then the man who had the evil spirit jumped on them, overpowered them all, and prevailed against them, so that they ran out of that house naked and wounded. [17] When this became known to everyone who lived in Ephesus, both Jews and Greeks, they became afraid, and the name of the Lord Jesus was held in high esteem. Mt 12:27; Mk 9:38; Lk 11:19; Ac 8:16; 21:13

[18] And many who had become believers came confessing and disclosing their practices, [19] while many of those who had practiced magic collected their books and burned them in front of everyone. So they calculated their value and found it to be fifty thousand pieces of silver. [20] In this way the word of the Lord flourished and prevailed.

The Riot in Ephesus

[21] After these events, Paul resolved by the Spirit[A] to pass through Macedonia and Achaia and go to Jerusalem. "After I've been there," he said, "It is necessary for me to see Rome as well." [22] After sending to Macedonia two of those who assisted him, Timothy and Erastus, he himself stayed in Asia for a while. Ac 16:9; 18:12; 20:16,22; Rm 15:24-25,28

[23] About that time there was a major disturbance about the Way. [24] For a person named Demetrius, a silversmith who made silver shrines of Artemis, provided a great deal of business for the craftsmen. [25] When he had assembled them, as well as the workers engaged in this type of business, he said: "Men, you know that our prosperity is derived from this business. [26] You see and hear that not only in Ephesus, but in almost all of Asia, this man Paul has persuaded and misled a considerable number of people by saying that gods made by hand are not gods. [27] Not only do we run a risk that our business may be discredited, but also that the temple of the great goddess Artemis may be despised and her magnificence come to the verge of ruin — the very one all of Asia and the world worship." Dt 4:28; Ps 115:4; Ac 9:2; 2Co 1:8

[28] When they had heard this, they were filled with rage and began to cry out, "Great is Artemis of the Ephesians!" [29] So the city was filled with confusion, and they rushed all together into the amphitheater, dragging along Gaius and Aristarchus, Macedonians who were Paul's traveling companions. [30] Although Paul wanted to go in before the people, the disciples did not let him. [31] Even some of the provincial officials of Asia, who were his friends, sent word to him, pleading with him not to venture[B] into the amphitheater. [32] Some were shouting one thing and some another, because the assembly was in confusion, and most of them did not know why they had come together. [33] Some Jews in the crowd gave instructions to Alexander[C] after they pushed him to the front. Motioning with his hand, Alexander wanted to make his defense to the people. [34] But when they recognized that he was a Jew, they all shouted in unison for about two hours: "Great is Artemis of the Ephesians!" Rm 16:23

A 19:21 Or in his spirit   B 19:31 Lit not to give himself   C 19:33 Or thought it was about Alexander

³⁵ When the city clerk had calmed the crowd down, he said, "People of Ephesus! What person is there who doesn't know that the city of the Ephesians is the temple guardian of the great ᴬ Artemis, and of the image that fell from heaven? ³⁶ Therefore, since these things are undeniable, you must keep calm and not do anything rash. ³⁷ For you have brought these men here who are not temple robbers or blasphemers of our ᴮ goddess. ³⁸ So if Demetrius and the craftsmen who are with him have a case against anyone, the courts are in session, and there are proconsuls. Let them bring charges against one another. ³⁹ But if you seek anything further, it must be decided in a legal assembly. ⁴⁰ In fact, we run a risk of being charged with rioting for what happened today, since there is no justification that we can give as a reason for this disturbance." ⁴¹ After saying this, he dismissed the assembly. Mt 26:5; 27:24; Ac 13:7; Rm 2:22

Paul in Macedonia

20 After the uproar was over, Paul sent for the disciples, encouraged them, and after saying farewell, departed to go to Macedonia. ² And when he had passed through those areas and offered them many words of encouragement, he came to Greece ³ and stayed three months. The Jews plotted against him when he was about to set sail for Syria, and so he decided to go back through Macedonia. ⁴ He was accompanied ᶜ by Sopater son of Pyrrhus ᴰ from Berea, Aristarchus and Secundus from Thessalonica, Gaius

from Derbe, Timothy, and Tychicus and Trophimus from the province of Asia. ⁵ These men went on ahead and waited for us in Troas, ⁶ but we sailed away from Philippi after the Festival of Unleavened Bread. In five days we reached them at Troas, where we spent seven days.

Eutychus Revived at Troas

⁷ On the first day of the week, we ᴱ assembled to break bread. Paul spoke to them, and since he was about to depart the next day, he kept on talking until midnight. ⁸ There were many lamps in the room upstairs where we were assembled, ⁹ and a young man named Eutychus was sitting on a window sill and sank into a deep sleep as Paul kept on talking. When he was overcome by sleep, he fell down from the third story and was picked up dead. ¹⁰ But Paul went down, bent over him, embraced him, and said, "Don't be alarmed, because he's alive." ¹¹ After going upstairs, breaking the bread, and eating, Paul talked a long time until dawn. Then he left. ¹² They brought the boy home alive and were greatly comforted. Ac 2:42

From Troas to Miletus

¹³ We went on ahead to the ship and sailed for Assos, where we were going to take Paul on board, because these were his instructions, since he himself was going by land. ¹⁴ When he met us at Assos, we took him on board and went on to Mitylene. ¹⁵ Sailing from there, the next day we arrived off Chios. The following day we crossed over to Samos, and ᶠ the day after, we came to Miletus. ¹⁶ For Paul had decided to

---

ᴬ**19:35** Other mss add *goddess*   ᴮ**19:37** Other mss read *your*   ᶜ**20:4** Other mss add *to Asia*   ᴰ**20:4** Other mss omit *son of Pyrrhus*   ᴱ**20:7** Other mss read *the disciples*   ᶠ**20:15** Other mss add *after staying at Trogyllium* sail past Ephesus to avoid spending time in the province of Asia, because he was hurrying to be in Jerusalem, if possible, for the day of Pentecost. _{Ac 2:1; 18:19; 20:17; 2Tm 4:20}

Farewell Address to the Ephesian Elders

¹⁷ Now from Miletus, he sent to Ephesus and summoned the elders of the church. ¹⁸ When they came to him, he said to them: "You know, from the first day I set foot in Asia, how I was with you the whole time, ¹⁹ serving the Lord with all humility, with tears, and during the trials that came to me through the plots of the Jews. ²⁰ You know that I did not avoid proclaiming to you anything that was profitable or from teaching you publicly and from house to house. ²¹ I testified to both Jews and Greeks about repentance toward God and faith in our Lord Jesus. _{Mk 1:15; 18:5; Ac 18:19; 19:1,10; 20:3,27}

²² "And now I am on my way to Jerusalem, compelled by the Spirit,ᴬ not knowing what I will encounter there, ²³ except that in every town the Holy Spirit warns me that chains and afflictions are waiting for me. ²⁴ But I consider my life of no value to myself; my purpose is to finish my courseᴮ and the ministry I received from the Lord Jesus, to testify to the gospel of God's grace. ²⁵ "And now I know that none of you, among whom I went about preaching the kingdom, will ever see me again. ²⁶ Therefore I declare to you this day that I am innocentᶜ of the blood of all of you, ²⁷ because I did not avoid declaring to you the whole plan of God. ²⁸ Be on guard for yourselves and for all the flock of which the Holy Spirit has appointed you as overseers, to shepherd the church of God,ᴰ which he purchased with his own blood. ²⁹ I know that after my departure savage wolves will come in among you, not sparing the flock. ³⁰ Men will rise up even from your own number and distort the truth to lure the disciples into following them. ³¹ Therefore be on the alert, remembering that night and day for three years I never stopped warning each one of you with tears. _{Ac 18:6; 20:38; 28:31}

³² "And nowᴱ I commit you to God and to the word of his grace, which is able to build you up and to give you an inheritance among all who are sanctified. ³³ I have not coveted anyone's silver or gold or clothing. ³⁴ You yourselves know that I worked with my own hands to support myself and those who are with me. ³⁵ In every way I've shown you that it is necessary to help the weak by laboring like this and to remember the words of the Lord Jesus, because he said, 'It is more blessed to give than to receive.' "

³⁶ After he said this, he knelt down and prayed with all of them. ³⁷ There were many tears shed by everyone. They embraced Paul and kissed him, ³⁸ grieving most of all over his statement that they would never see his face again. And they accompanied him to the ship.

Warnings on the Journey to Jerusalem

21 After we tore ourselves away from them, we set sail straight for Cos, the next day to Rhodes, and from there to Patara.

ᴬ20:22 Or *in my spirit* ᴮ20:24 Other mss add *with joy of the Lord*; other mss read *church of the Lord and God* ᶜ20:26 Lit *clean* ᴰ20:28 Some mss read *church* ᴱ20:32 Other mss add *brothers and sisters*

[2] Finding a ship crossing over to Phoenicia, we boarded and set sail. [3] After we sighted Cyprus, passing to the south of it, [A] we sailed on to Syria and arrived at Tyre, since the ship was to unload its cargo there. [4] We sought out the disciples and stayed there seven days. Through the Spirit they told Paul not to go to Jerusalem. [5] When our time had come to an end, we left to continue our journey, while all of them, with their wives and children, accompanied us out of the city. After kneeling down on the beach to pray, [6] we said farewell to one another and boarded the ship, and they returned home.   Ac 11:26; 16:10-11

[7] When we completed our voyage [B] from Tyre, we reached Ptolemais, where we greeted the brothers and sisters and stayed with them for a day. [8] The next day we left and came to Caesarea, where we entered the house of Philip the evangelist, who was one of the Seven, and stayed with him. [9] This man had four virgin daughters who prophesied.   Jn 21:23

[10] After we had been there for several days, a prophet named Agabus came down from Judea. [11] He came to us, took Paul's belt, tied his own feet and hands, and said, "This is what the Holy Spirit says: 'In this way the Jews in Jerusalem will bind the man who owns this belt and deliver him over to the Gentiles.'" [12] When we heard this, both we and the local people pleaded with him not to go up to Jerusalem.   1Kg 22:11

[13] Then Paul replied, "What are you doing, weeping and breaking my heart? For I am ready not only to be bound but also to die in Jerusalem for the name of the Lord Jesus."   Ac 5:41; 9:16; 20:24

[14] Since he would not be persuaded, we said no more except, "The Lord's will be done."   Mt 6:10; Lk 22:42

Conflict over the Gentile Mission

[15] After this we got ready and went up to Jerusalem. [16] Some of the disciples from Caesarea also went with us and brought us to Mnason of Cyprus, an early disciple, with whom we were to stay.   Ac 8:40

[17] When we reached Jerusalem, the brothers and sisters welcomed us warmly. [18] The following day Paul went in with us to James, and all the elders were present. [19] After greeting them, he reported in detail what God had done among the Gentiles through his ministry.   Ac 12:17; 15:4; 21:7

[20] When they heard it, they glorified God and said, "You see, brother, how many thousands of Jews there are who have believed, and they are all zealous for the law. [21] But they have been informed about you — that you are teaching all the Jews who are among the Gentiles to abandon Moses, telling them not to circumcise their children or to live according to our customs. [22] So what is to be done? [C] They will certainly hear that you've come. [23] Therefore do what we tell you: We have four men who have made a vow. [24] Take these men, purify yourself along with them, and pay for them to get their heads shaved. Then everyone will know that what they were told about you amounts to nothing, but that you yourself are also careful about observing the law. [25] With regard to the Gentiles who have believed, we have written a letter

containing our decision that[A] they should keep themselves from food sacrificed to idols, from blood, from what is strangled, and from sexual immorality." Ac 6:14; 22:3; Rm 10:12; Gl 1:14

The Riot in the Temple

[26] So the next day, Paul took the men, having purified himself along with them, and entered the temple, announcing the completion of the purification days when the offering would be made for each of them. [27] When the seven days were nearly over, some Jews from the province of Asia saw him in the temple, stirred up the whole crowd, and seized him, [28] shouting, "Fellow Israelites, help! This is the man who teaches everyone everywhere against our people, our law, and this place. What's more, he also brought Greeks into the temple and has defiled this holy place." [29] For they had previously seen Trophimus the Ephesian in the city with him, and they supposed that Paul had brought him into the temple. Nm 6:13; Ac 24:18

[30] The whole city was stirred up, and the people rushed together. They seized Paul, dragged him out of the temple, and at once the gates were shut. 2Kg 11:15; Ac 16:19; 26:21

[31] As they were trying to kill him, word went up to the commander of the regiment that all Jerusalem was in chaos. [32] Taking along soldiers and centurions, he immediately ran down to them. Seeing the commander and the soldiers, they stopped beating Paul. [33] Then the commander approached, took him into custody, and ordered him to be bound with two chains. He asked who he was and what he had

done. [34] Some in the crowd were shouting one thing and some another. Since he was not able to get reliable information because of the uproar, he ordered him to be taken into the barracks. [35] When Paul got to the steps, he had to be carried by the soldiers because of the violence of the crowd, [36] for the mass of people followed, yelling, "Get rid of him!" Ac 2:9; 12:6; 20:23; 21:11

Paul's Defense Before the Jerusalem Mob

[37] As he was about to be brought into the barracks, Paul said to the commander, "Am I allowed to say something to you?"

He replied, "You know how to speak Greek? [38] Aren't you the Egyptian who started a revolt some time ago and led four thousand men of the Assassins into the wilderness?"

[39] Paul said, "I am a Jewish man from Tarsus of Cilicia, a citizen of an important city. Now I ask you, let me speak to the people." Ac 9:11

[40] After he had given permission, Paul stood on the steps and motioned with his hand to the people. When there was a great hush, he addressed them in Aramaic:[B]

22 [1] "Brothers and fathers, listen now to my defense before you." [2] When they heard that he was addressing them in Aramaic,[B] they became even quieter. [3] He continued, "I am a Jew, born in Tarsus of Cilicia but brought up in this city, educated at the feet of Gamaliel according to the law of our ancestors. I was zealous for God, just as all of you are today. [4] I persecuted this Way to the death, arresting and putting both men and women in jail, [5] as both the high priest and

[A]**21:25** Other mss add *they should observe no such thing, except that*   [B]**21:40; 22:2** Or *Hebrew* the whole council of elders can testify about me. After I received letters from them to the brothers, I traveled to Damascus to arrest those who were there and bring them to Jerusalem to be punished.

Paul's Testimony

⁶ "As I was traveling and approaching Damascus, about noon an intense light from heaven suddenly flashed around me. ⁷ I fell to the ground and heard a voice saying to me, 'Saul, Saul, why are you persecuting me?' Ac 9:3-8; 26:12-18

⁸ "I answered, 'Who are you, Lord?'

"He said to me, 'I am Jesus of Nazareth, the one you are persecuting.' ⁹ Now those who were with me saw the light,ᴬ but they did not hear the voice of the one who was speaking to me. Dn 10:7; Ac 9:7; 26:13

¹⁰ "I said, 'What should I do, Lord?'

"The Lord told me, 'Get up and go into Damascus, and there you will be told everything that you have been assigned to do.'

¹¹ "Since I couldn't see because of the brightness of the light,ᴮ I was led by the hand by those who were with me, and went into Damascus. ¹² Someone named Ananias, a devout man according to the law, who had a good reputation with all the Jews living there, ¹³ came and stood by me and said, 'Brother Saul, regain your sight.' And in that very hour I looked up and saw him. ¹⁴ And he said, 'The God of our ancestors has appointed you to know his will, to see the Righteous One, and to hear the words from his mouth, ¹⁵ since you will be a witness for him to all people of what you have seen and heard. ¹⁶ And now, why are you delaying? Get up and be baptized, and wash away your sins, calling on his name.' Ac 3:13; 9:8,10,15,17; 10:22; 16:30

¹⁷ "After I returned to Jerusalem and was praying in the temple, I fell into a trance ¹⁸ and saw him telling me, 'Hurry and get out of Jerusalem quickly, because they will not accept your testimony about me.'

¹⁹ "But I said, 'Lord, they know that in synagogue after synagogue I had those who believed in you imprisoned and beaten. ²⁰ And when the blood of your witness Stephen was being shed, I stood there giving approvalᶜ and guarding the clothes of those who killed him.' Mt 10:17

²¹ "He said to me, 'Go, because I will send you far away to the Gentiles.' " Ac 9:15; 13:46

Paul's Roman Protection

²² They listened to him up to this point. Then they raised their voices, shouting, "Wipe this man off the face of the earth! He should not be allowed to live!" Ac 21:36; 25:24

²³ As they were yelling and flinging aside their garments and throwing dust into the air, ²⁴ the commander ordered him to be brought into the barracks, directing that he be interrogated with the scourge to discover the reason they were shouting against him like this. ²⁵ As they stretched him out for the lash, Paul said to the centurion standing by, "Is it legal for you to scourge a man who is a Roman citizen and is uncondemned?" 2Sm 16:13; Ac 7:58; Ac 16:37; 21:34

²⁶ When the centurion heard this, he went and reported to the commander, saying, "What are you

---

ᴬ**22:9** Other mss add *and were afraid*   ᴮ**22:11** Lit *the glory of that light*   ᶜ**22:20** Other mss add *of his murder* going to do? For this man is a Roman citizen."

²⁷ The commander came and said to him, "Tell me, are you a Roman citizen?"

"Yes," he said.

²⁸ The commander replied, "I bought this citizenship for a large amount of money."

"But I was born a citizen," Paul said.

²⁹ So those who were about to examine him withdrew from him immediately. The commander too was alarmed when he realized Paul was a Roman citizen and he had bound him.   Ac 16:38; 21:33

Paul Before the Sanhedrin

³⁰ The next day, since he wanted to find out exactly why Paul was being accused by the Jews, he released him ᴬ and instructed the chief priests and all the Sanhedrin to convene. He brought Paul down and placed him before them.

23 ¹ Paul looked straight at the Sanhedrin and said, "Brothers, I have lived my life before God in all good conscience to this day." ² The high priest Ananias ordered those who were standing next to him to strike him on the mouth. ³ Then Paul said to him, "God is going to strike you, you whitewashed wall! You are sitting there judging me according to the law, and yet in violation of the law are you ordering me to be struck?"   Ac 24:16; 1Co 4:4

⁴ Those standing nearby said, "Do you dare revile God's high priest?"

⁵ "I did not know, brothers, that he was the high priest," replied Paul. "For it is written, **You must not speak evil of a ruler of your people.**" ᴮ ⁶ When Paul realized that

one part of them were Sadducees and the other part were Pharisees, he cried out in the Sanhedrin, "Brothers, I am a Pharisee, a son of Pharisees. I am being judged because of the hope of the resurrection of the dead!" ⁷ When he said this, a dispute broke out between the Pharisees and the Sadducees, and the assembly was divided. ⁸ For the Sadducees say there is no resurrection, and neither angel nor spirit, but the Pharisees affirm them all.   Ex 22:28; Ac 24:17; 26:5; Php 3:5

⁹ The shouting grew loud, and some of the scribes of the Pharisees' party got up and argued vehemently: "We find nothing evil in this man. What if a spirit or an angel has spoken to him?" ᶜ

¹⁰ When the dispute became violent, the commander feared that Paul might be torn apart by them and ordered the troops to go down, take him away from them, and bring him into the barracks. ¹¹ The following night, the Lord stood by him and said, "Have courage! For as you have testified about me in Jerusalem, so it is necessary for you to testify in Rome."   Ac 19:21; 21:34

The Plot Against Paul

¹² When it was morning, the Jews formed a conspiracy and bound themselves under a curse not to eat or drink until they had killed Paul. ¹³ There were more than forty who had formed this plot. ¹⁴ These men went to the chief priests and elders and said, "We have bound ourselves under a solemn curse that we won't eat anything until we have killed Paul. ¹⁵ So now you, along with the Sanhedrin, make a request to the commander that he

ᴬ**22:30** Other mss add *from his chains*   ᴮ**23:5** Ex 22:28   ᶜ**23:9** Other mss add *Let us not fight God.*

bring him down to you^A as if you were going to investigate his case more thoroughly. But, before he gets near, we are ready to kill him."

¹⁶ But the son of Paul's sister, hearing about their ambush, came and entered the barracks and reported it to Paul. ¹⁷ Paul called one of the centurions and said, "Take this young man to the commander, because he has something to report to him."

¹⁸ So he took him, brought him to the commander, and said, "The prisoner Paul called me and asked me to bring this young man to you, because he has something to tell you."

¹⁹ The commander took him by the hand, led him aside, and inquired privately, "What is it you have to report to me?"

²⁰ "The Jews," he said, "have agreed to ask you to bring Paul down to the Sanhedrin tomorrow, as though they are going to hold a somewhat more careful inquiry about him. ²¹ Don't let them persuade you, because there are more than forty of them lying in ambush — men who have bound themselves under a curse not to eat or drink until they have killed him. Now they are ready, waiting for your consent." Lk 11:54; Ac 23:12,14

²² So the commander dismissed the young man and instructed him, "Don't tell anyone that you have informed me about this."

To Caesarea by Night

²³ He summoned two of his centurions and said, "Get two hundred soldiers ready with seventy cavalry and two hundred spearmen to go to Caesarea at nine tonight.^B ²⁴ Also provide mounts for Paul to ride and bring him safely to Felix the governor." Ac 8:40; 23:33

²⁵ He wrote the following letter:^C ²⁶ Claudius Lysias,

To the most excellent governor Felix:

Greetings. Lk 1:3; Ac 15:23; 24:3; 26:25

²⁷ When this man had been seized by the Jews and was about to be killed by them, I arrived with my troops and rescued him because I learned that he is a Roman citizen. ²⁸ Wanting to know the charge they were accusing him of, I brought him down before their Sanhedrin. ²⁹ I found out that the accusations were concerning questions of their law, and that there was no charge that merited death or imprisonment. ³⁰ When I was informed that there was a plot against the man,^D I sent him to you right away. I also ordered his accusers to state their case against him in your presence.^E

³¹ So the soldiers took Paul during the night and brought him to Antipatris as they were ordered. ³² The next day, they returned to the barracks, allowing the cavalry to go on with him. ³³ When these men entered Caesarea and delivered the letter to the governor, they also presented Paul to him. ³⁴ After he^F read it, he asked what province he was from. When he learned he was from Cilicia, ³⁵ he said, "I will give you a hearing whenever your

---

^A23:15 Other mss add *tomorrow*   ^B23:23 Lit *at the third hour tonight*   ^C23:25 Or *He wrote a letter to this effect:*   ^D23:30 Other mss add *by the Jews*   ^E23:30 Other mss add *Farewell*   ^F23:34 Other mss read *the governor* accusers also get here." He ordered that he be kept under guard in Herod's palace. [A] Ac 6:9; 8:40; 23:23-24,26; 25:1

The Accusation Against Paul

24 Five days later Ananias the high priest came down with some elders and a lawyer named Tertullus. These men presented their case against Paul to the governor. [2] When Paul was called in, Tertullus began to accuse him and said: "We enjoy great peace because of you, and reforms are taking place for the benefit of this nation because of your foresight. [3] We acknowledge this in every way and everywhere, most excellent Felix, with utmost gratitude. [4] But, so that I will not burden you any further, I request that you would be kind enough to give us a brief hearing. [5] For we have found this man to be a plague, an agitator among all the Jews throughout the Roman world, and a ringleader of the sect of the Nazarenes. [6] He even tried to desecrate the temple, and so we apprehended him. [B] By examining him yourself you will be able to discern the truth about these charges we are bringing against him." [9] The Jews also joined in the attack, alleging that these things were true. Lk 1:3; Ac 21:27; 23:2,24,30

Paul's Defense Before Felix

[10] When the governor motioned for him to speak, Paul replied: "Because I know you have been a judge of this nation for many years, I am glad to offer my defense in what concerns me. [11] You can verify for yourself that it is no more than twelve days since I went up to worship in Jerusalem. [12] They didn't find me arguing with anyone or causing a disturbance among the crowd, either in the temple or in the synagogues or anywhere in the city. [13] Neither can they prove the charges they are now making against me. [14] But I admit this to you: I worship the God of my ancestors according to the Way, which they call a sect, believing everything that is in accordance with the law and written in the prophets. [15] I have a hope in God, which these men themselves also accept, that there will be a resurrection, [C] both of the righteous and the unrighteous. [16] I always strive to have a clear conscience toward God and men. [17] After many years, I came to bring charitable gifts and offerings to my people. [18] While I was doing this, some Jews from Asia found me ritually purified in the temple, without a crowd and without any uproar. [19] It is they who ought to be here before you to bring charges, if they have anything against me. [20] Or let these men here state what wrongdoing they found in me when I stood before the Sanhedrin, [21] other than this one statement I shouted while standing among them, 'Today I am on trial before you concerning the resurrection of the dead.'" Ac 23:24; 1Th 2:16

The Verdict Postponed

[22] Since Felix was well informed about the Way, he adjourned the hearing, saying, "When Lysias the commander comes down, I will decide your case." [23] He ordered that the centurion keep Paul

---

[A] **23:35** Or *headquarters*   [B] **24:6** Some mss include vv. 6b-8a: *and wanted to judge him according to our law. [7] But Lysias the commander came and took him from our hands with great force, [8] commanding his accusers to come to you.*   [C] **24:15** Other mss add *of the dead* under guard, though he could have some freedom, and that he should not prevent any of his friends from meeting[A] his needs. Ac 9:2; 22:4; 24:14

24 Several days later, when Felix came with his wife Drusilla, who was Jewish, he sent for Paul and listened to him on the subject of faith in Christ Jesus. 25 Now as he spoke about righteousness, self-control, and the judgment to come, Felix became afraid and replied, "Leave for now, but when I have an opportunity I'll call for you." 26 At the same time he was also hoping that Paul would offer him money.[B] So he sent for him quite often and conversed with him. Gl 5:23; Ti 2:12

27 After two years had passed, Porcius Festus succeeded Felix, and because Felix wanted to do the Jews a favor, he left Paul in prison.

Appeal to Caesar

25 Three days after Festus arrived in the province, he went up to Jerusalem from Caesarea. 2 The chief priests and the leaders of the Jews presented their case against Paul to him; and they appealed, 3 asking for a favor against Paul, that Festus summon him to Jerusalem. They were, in fact, preparing an ambush along the road to kill him. 4 Festus, however, answered that Paul should be kept at Caesarea, and that he himself was about to go there shortly. 5 "Therefore," he said, "let those of you who have authority go down with me and accuse him, if he has done anything wrong." Ac 8:40; 23:34; 24:1; 25:15

6 When he had spent not more than eight or ten days among them, he went down to Caesarea. The next day, seated at the tribunal, he commanded Paul to be brought in. 7 When he arrived, the Jews who had come down from Jerusalem stood around him and brought many serious charges that they were not able to prove. 8 Then Paul made his defense: "Neither against the Jewish law, nor against the temple, nor against Caesar have I sinned in any way." Mt 27:19; Mk 15:3; Lk 23:2,10; Ac 25:10,17

9 But Festus, wanting to do the Jews a favor, replied to Paul, "Are you willing to go up to Jerusalem to be tried before me there on these charges?" Ac 24:27; 25:20

10 Paul replied: "I am standing at Caesar's tribunal, where I ought to be tried. I have done no wrong to the Jews, as even you yourself know very well. 11 If then I did anything wrong and am deserving of death, I am not trying to escape death; but if there is nothing to what these men accuse me of, no one can give me up to them. I appeal to Caesar!" Ac 25:21,25; 26:32; 28:19

12 Then after Festus conferred with his council, he replied, "You have appealed to Caesar; to Caesar you will go."

King Agrippa and Bernice Visit Festus

13 Several days later, King Agrippa and Bernice arrived in Caesarea and paid a courtesy call on Festus. 14 Since they were staying there several days, Festus presented Paul's case to the king, saying, "There's a man who was left as a prisoner by Felix. 15 When I was in Jerusalem, the chief priests and the elders of the Jews presented their case and asked that he be condemned. 16 I answered them that it is not the Roman custom to give

A**24:23** Other mss add *or visiting*   B**24:26** Other mss add *so that he might release him* someone up^A before the accused faces the accusers and has an opportunity for a defense against the charges. ¹⁷ So when they had assembled here, I did not delay. The next day I took my seat at the tribunal and ordered the man to be brought in. ¹⁸ The accusers stood up but brought no charge against him of the evils I was expecting. ¹⁹ Instead they had some disagreements with him about their own religion and about a certain Jesus, a dead man Paul claimed to be alive. ²⁰ Since I was at a loss in a dispute over such things, I asked him if he wanted to go to Jerusalem and be tried there regarding these matters. ²¹ But when Paul appealed to be held for trial by the Emperor,^B I ordered him to be kept in custody until I could send him to Caesar."

²² Agrippa said to Festus, "I would like to hear the man myself."

"Tomorrow you will hear him," he replied. Ac 9:15; 25:9,11

Paul Before Agrippa

²³ So the next day, Agrippa and Bernice came with great pomp and entered the auditorium with the military commanders and prominent men of the city. When Festus gave the command, Paul was brought in. ²⁴ Then Festus said: "King Agrippa and all men present with us, you see this man. The whole Jewish community has appealed to me concerning him, both in Jerusalem and here, shouting that he should not live any longer. ²⁵ I found that he had not done anything deserving of death, but when he himself appealed to the Emperor, I decided to send him. ²⁶ I have nothing definite to write to my lord about him. Therefore, I have brought him before all of you, and especially before you, King Agrippa, so that after this examination is over, I may have something to write. ²⁷ For it seems unreasonable to me to send a prisoner without indicating the charges against him." Ac 22:22; 23:29; 25:2,7,13; 26:30

Paul's Defense Before Agrippa

26 Agrippa said to Paul, "You have permission to speak for yourself."

Then Paul stretched out his hand and began his defense: ² "I consider myself fortunate, that it is before you, King Agrippa, I am to make my defense today against all the accusations of the Jews, ³ especially since you are very knowledgeable about all the Jewish customs and controversies. Therefore I beg you to listen to me patiently.

⁴ "All the Jews know my way of life from my youth, which was spent from the beginning among my own people and in Jerusalem. ⁵ They have known me for a long time, if they are willing to testify, that according to the strictest sect of our religion I lived as a Pharisee. ⁶ And now I stand on trial because of the hope in what God promised to our ancestors, ⁷ the promise our twelve tribes hope to reach as they earnestly serve him night and day. King Agrippa, I am being accused by the Jews because of this hope. ⁸ Why do any of you consider it incredible that God raises the dead? ⁹ In fact, I myself was convinced that it was necessary to do many things in opposition to the name of Jesus of Nazareth. ¹⁰ I actually did this in Jerusalem, and I locked

^A **25:16** Other mss add *to destruction*　^B **25:21** Lit *his majesty*, also in v. 25

up many of the saints in prison, since I had received authority for that from the chief priests. When they were put to death, I was in agreement against them. [11] In all the synagogues I often punished them and tried to make them blaspheme. Since I was terribly enraged at them, I pursued them even to foreign cities. Ac 6:14; 22:3; 25:19; Gl 1:13

Paul's Account of His Conversion and Commission

[12] "I was traveling to Damascus under these circumstances with authority and a commission from the chief priests. [13] King Agrippa, while on the road at midday, I saw a light from heaven brighter than the sun, shining around me and those traveling with me. [14] We all fell to the ground, and I heard a voice speaking to me in Aramaic,[A] 'Saul, Saul, why are you persecuting me? It is hard for you to kick against the goads.' Ac 9:3-8; 21:40; 22:6-11

[15] "I asked, 'Who are you, Lord?'

"And the Lord replied: 'I am Jesus, the one you are persecuting. [16] But get up and stand on your feet. For I have appeared to you for this purpose, to appoint you as a servant and a witness of what you have seen and will see of me. [17] I will rescue you from your people and from the Gentiles. I am sending you to them [18] to open their eyes so that they may turn[B] from darkness to light and from the power of Satan to God, that they may receive forgiveness of sins and a share among those who are sanctified by faith in me.'

[19] "So then, King Agrippa, I was not disobedient to the heavenly vision. [20] Instead, I preached to those in Damascus first, and to those in Jerusalem and in all the region of Judea, and to the Gentiles, that they should repent and turn to God, and do works worthy of repentance. [21] For this reason the Jews seized me in the temple and were trying to kill me. [22] To this very day, I have had help from God, and I stand and testify to both small and great, saying nothing other than what the prophets and Moses said would take place — [23] that the Messiah must suffer, and that, as the first to rise from the dead, he would proclaim light to our people and to the Gentiles." Mt 3:8; Lk 3:8; Ac 9:19-20,22,26-29

Agrippa Not Quite Persuaded

[24] As he was saying these things in his defense, Festus exclaimed in a loud voice, "You're out of your mind, Paul! Too much study is driving you mad." 2Kg 9:11; Jn 10:20; 1Co 1:23; 2:14

[25] But Paul replied, "I'm not out of my mind, most excellent Festus. On the contrary, I'm speaking words of truth and good judgment. [26] For the king knows about these matters, and I can speak boldly to him. For I am convinced that none of these things has escaped his notice, since this was not done in a corner. [27] King Agrippa, do you believe the prophets? I know you believe."

[28] Agrippa said to Paul, "Are you going to persuade me to become a Christian so easily?"[C]

[29] "I wish before God," replied Paul, "that whether easily or with difficulty,[D] not only you but all who listen to me today might become as I am — except for these chains."

[30] The king, the governor, Bernice, and those sitting with them got

A26:14 Or Hebrew   B26:18 Or to turn them   C26:28 Or so quickly   D26:29 Or whether a short time or long up, [31] and when they had left they talked with each other and said, "This man is not doing anything to deserve death or imprisonment."

[32] Agrippa said to Festus, "This man could have been released if he had not appealed to Caesar."

Sailing for Rome

27 When it was decided that we were to sail to Italy, they handed over Paul and some other prisoners to a centurion named Julius, of the Imperial Regiment. [A] [2] When we had boarded a ship of Adramyttium, we put to sea, intending to sail to ports along the coast of Asia. Aristarchus, a Macedonian of Thessalonica, was with us. [3] The next day we put in at Sidon, and Julius treated Paul kindly and allowed him to go to his friends to receive their care. [4] When we had put out to sea from there, we sailed along the northern coast [B] of Cyprus because the winds were against us. [5] After sailing through the open sea off Cilicia and Pamphylia, we reached Myra in Lycia. [6] There the centurion found an Alexandrian ship sailing for Italy and put us on board. [7] Sailing slowly for many days, with difficulty we arrived off Cnidus. Since the wind did not allow us to approach it, we sailed along the south side of Crete off Salmone. [8] With still more difficulty we sailed along the coast and came to a place called Fair Havens near the city of Lasea. Ac 10:1; 16:10; 20:4

Paul's Advice Ignored

[9] By now much time had passed, and the voyage was already dangerous. Since the Day of Atonement [C] was already over, Paul gave his advice [10] and told them, "Men, I can see that this voyage is headed toward disaster and heavy loss, not only of the cargo and the ship but also of our lives." [11] But the centurion paid attention to the captain and the owner of the ship rather than to what Paul said. [12] Since the harbor was unsuitable to winter in, the majority decided to set sail from there, hoping somehow to reach Phoenix, a harbor on Crete facing the southwest and northwest, and to winter there. Lv 16:29-31; 23:27-29; Ac 2:11

Storm-Tossed Ship

[13] When a gentle south wind sprang up, they thought they had achieved their purpose. They weighed anchor and sailed along the shore of Crete. [14] But before long, a fierce wind called the "northeaster" rushed down from the island. [15] Since the ship was caught and unable to head into the wind, we gave way to it and were driven along. [16] After running under the shelter of a little island called Cauda, [D] we were barely able to get control of the skiff. [17] After hoisting it up, they used ropes and tackle and girded the ship. Fearing they would run aground on the Syrtis, they lowered the drift-anchor, and in this way they were driven along. [18] Because we were being severely battered by the storm, they began to jettison the cargo the next day. [19] On the third day, they threw the ship's tackle overboard with their own hands. [20] For many days neither sun nor stars appeared, and the severe storm kept raging. Finally all hope was fading that we would be saved. Jnh 1:5; Ac 27:38

A 27:1 Or *Augustan Cohort*   B 27:4 Lit *sailed under the lee*, also in v. 7   C 27:9 Lit *the Fast*   D 27:16 Or *Clauda*

²¹ Since they had been without food for a long time, Paul then stood up among them and said, "You men should have followed my advice not to sail from Crete and sustain this damage and loss. ²² Now I urge you to take courage, because there will be no loss of any of your lives, but only of the ship. ²³ For last night an angel of the God I belong to and serve stood by me ²⁴ and said, 'Don't be afraid, Paul. It is necessary for you to appear before Caesar. And indeed, God has graciously given you all those who are sailing with you.' ²⁵ So take courage, men, because I believe God that it will be just the way it was told to me. ²⁶ But we have to run aground on some island." Dn 6:16; Ac 18:9; 23:11; Rm 1:9; 2Tm 4:17

²⁷ When the fourteenth night came, we were drifting in the Adriatic Sea, and about midnight the sailors thought they were approaching land. ²⁸ They took soundings and found it to be a hundred and twenty feet[A] deep; when they had sailed a little farther and sounded again, they found it to be ninety feet[B] deep. ²⁹ Then, fearing we might run aground on the rocks, they dropped four anchors from the stern and prayed for daylight to come. ³⁰ Some sailors tried to escape from the ship; they had let down the skiff into the sea, pretending that they were going to put out anchors from the bow. ³¹ Paul said to the centurion and the soldiers, "Unless these men stay in the ship, you cannot be saved." ³² Then the soldiers cut the ropes holding the skiff and let it drop away.

³³ When it was about daylight, Paul urged them all to take food, saying, "Today is the fourteenth day that you have been waiting and going without food, having eaten nothing. ³⁴ So I urge you to take some food. For this is for your survival, since none of you will lose a hair from your head." ³⁵ After he said these things and had taken some bread, he gave thanks to God in the presence of all of them, and after he broke it, he began to eat. ³⁶ They all were encouraged and took food themselves. ³⁷ In all there were 276 of us on the ship. ³⁸ When they had eaten enough, they began to lighten the ship by throwing the grain overboard into the sea. 1Kg 1:52; Mt 10:30; Lk 21:18; Mt 14:19; 7:14

Shipwreck

³⁹ When daylight came, they did not recognize the land but sighted a bay with a beach. They planned to run the ship ashore if they could. ⁴⁰ After cutting loose the anchors, they left them in the sea, at the same time loosening the ropes that held the rudders. Then they hoisted the foresail to the wind and headed for the beach. ⁴¹ But they struck a sandbar and ran the ship aground. The bow jammed fast and remained immovable, while the stern began to break up by the pounding of the waves. ⁴² The soldiers' plan was to kill the prisoners so that no one could swim away and escape. ⁴³ But the centurion kept them from carrying out their plan because he wanted to save Paul, and so he ordered those who could swim to jump overboard first and get to land. ⁴⁴ The rest were to follow, some on planks and some on debris from the ship. In this way, everyone safely reached the shore. Ac 27:18; 28:1

A 27:28 Lit twenty fathoms   B 27:28 Lit fifteen fathoms

Malta's Hospitality

28 Once safely ashore, we then learned that the island was called Malta. [2] The local people showed us extraordinary kindness. They lit a fire and took us all in, since it was raining and cold. [3] As Paul gathered a bundle of brushwood and put it on the fire, a viper came out because of the heat and fastened itself on his hand. [4] When the local people saw the snake hanging from his hand, they said to one another, "This man, no doubt, is a murderer. Even though he has escaped the sea, Justice has not allowed him to live." [5] But he shook the snake off into the fire and suffered no harm. [6] They expected that he would begin to swell up or suddenly drop dead. After they waited a long time and saw nothing unusual happen to him, they changed their minds and said he was a god.   Ac 16:10; 27:1

Ministry in Malta

[7] Now in the area around that place was an estate belonging to the leading man of the island, named Publius, who welcomed us and entertained us hospitably for three days. [8] Publius's father was in bed suffering from fever and dysentery. Paul went to him, and praying and laying his hands on him, he healed him. [9] After this, the rest of those on the island who had diseases also came and were healed. [10] So they heaped many honors on us, and when we sailed, they gave us what we needed.   Ac 9:40; Jms 5:14-15

Rome at Last

[11] After three months we set sail in an Alexandrian ship that had wintered at the island, with the Twin Gods[A] as its figurehead. [12] Putting in at Syracuse, we stayed three days. [13] From there, after making a circuit along the coast,[B] we reached Rhegium. After one day a south wind sprang up, and the second day we came to Puteoli. [14] There we found brothers and sisters and were invited to stay a week with them. And so we came to Rome. [15] Now the brothers and sisters from there had heard the news about us and had come to meet us as far as the Forum of Appius and the Three Taverns. When Paul saw them, he thanked God and took courage. [16] When we entered Rome,[C] Paul was allowed to live by himself with the soldier who guarded him.   Jn 21:23; Ac 1:16; 24:23; 27:3

Paul's First Interview with Roman Jews

[17] After three days he called together the leaders of the Jews. When they had gathered he said to them: "Brothers, although I have done nothing against our people or the customs of our ancestors, I was delivered as a prisoner from Jerusalem into the hands of the Romans. [18] After they examined me, they wanted to release me, since there was no reason for the death penalty in my case. [19] Because the Jews objected, I was compelled to appeal to Caesar; even though I had no charge to bring against my people. [20] For this reason I've asked to see you and speak to you. In fact, it is for the hope of Israel that I'm wearing this chain."   Ac 6:14; 23:29; 25:8

[21] Then they said to him, "We haven't received any letters about you from Judea. None of the brothers

---

[A] 28:11 Gk *Dioscuri*, twin sons of Zeus, Castor and Pollux   [B] 28:13 Other mss read *From there, casting off,*
[C] 28:16 Other mss add *the centurion turned the prisoners over to the military commander; but*

has come and reported or spoken anything evil about you. **22** But we want to hear what your views are, since we know that people everywhere are speaking against this sect."　　Lk 2:34; Ac 24:5; 1Pt 2:12; 4:14

The Response to Paul's Message

23 After arranging a day with him, many came to him at his lodging. From dawn to dusk he expounded and testified about the kingdom of God. He tried to persuade them about Jesus from both the Law of Moses and the Prophets. **24** Some were persuaded by what he said, but others did not believe.　　Ac 8:35

25 Disagreeing among themselves, they began to leave after Paul made one statement:[A] "The Holy Spirit was right in saying to your[B] ancestors through the prophet Isaiah **26** when he said,

> Go to these people and say:
> You will always be listening,
> but never understanding;
> and you will always be
> looking,
> but never perceiving.
> **27** For the hearts
> of these people
> have grown callous,
> their ears are hard
> of hearing,
> and they have shut
> their eyes;
> otherwise they might see
> with their eyes
> and hear with their ears,
> understand
> with their heart
> and turn,
> and I would heal them.[C]

28 Therefore, let it be known to you that this salvation of God has been sent to the Gentiles; they will listen."[D]

Paul's Ministry Unhindered

30 Paul stayed two whole years in his own rented house. And he welcomed all who visited him, **31** proclaiming the kingdom of God and teaching about the Lord Jesus Christ with all boldness and without hindrance.　　Mt 4:23; Ac 20:25; 28:23

A **28:25** Or *after they began to leave, Paul made one statement*　　B **28:25** Other mss read *our*
C **28:26-27** Is 6:9-10　　D **28:28** Some mss include v. 29: *After he said these things, the Jews departed, while engaging in a vigorous debate among themselves.*

ROMANS

The Gospel of God for Rome

1 Paul, a servant of Christ Jesus, called as an apostle^A and set apart for the gospel of God — ² which he promised beforehand through his prophets in the Holy Scriptures — ³ concerning his Son, Jesus Christ our Lord, who was a descendant of David^B according to the flesh ⁴ and was appointed to be the powerful Son of God according to the Spirit of holiness^C by the resurrection of the dead. ⁵ Through him we have received grace and apostleship to bring about^D the obedience of faith for the sake of his name among all the Gentiles, ^E ⁶ including you who are also called by Jesus Christ. Ac 9:15; 1Co 1:1; 9:1; 2Co 1:1

⁷ To all who are in Rome, loved by God, called as saints. Rm 5:5; 8:39

Grace to you and peace from God our Father and the Lord Jesus Christ.

Paul's Desire to Visit Rome

⁸ First, I thank my God through Jesus Christ for all of you because the news of your faith^F is being reported in all the world. ⁹ God is my witness, whom I serve with my spirit in telling the good news about his Son — that I constantly mention you, ¹⁰ always asking in my prayers that if it is somehow in God's will, I may now at last succeed in coming to you. ¹¹ For I want very much to see you, so that I may impart to you some spiritual gift to strengthen you, ¹² that is, to be mutually encouraged by each other's faith, both yours and mine. Rm 16:19

¹³ Now I don't want you to be unaware, brothers and sisters, that I often planned to come to you (but was prevented until now) in order that I might have a fruitful ministry^G among you, just as I have had among the rest of the Gentiles. ¹⁴ I am obligated both to Greeks and barbarians, ^H both to the wise and the foolish. ¹⁵ So I am eager to preach the gospel to you also who are in Rome. Jn 4:36; Ac 19:21; 1Co 10:1; 11:3

The Righteous Will Live by Faith

¹⁶ For I am not ashamed of the gospel,^I because it is the power of God for salvation to everyone who believes, first to the Jew, and also to the Greek. ¹⁷ For in it the righteousness of God is revealed from faith to faith,^J just as it is written: **The righteous will live by faith.**^{K,L}

The Guilt of the Gentile World

¹⁸ For God's wrath is revealed from heaven against all godlessness and unrighteousness of people who by their unrighteousness suppress the truth, ¹⁹ since what can be known^M about God is evident among them, because God has shown it to them. ²⁰ For his invisible attributes, that is, his eternal power and divine nature, have been clearly seen since the

---

^A**1:1** Or *Jesus, a called apostle*   ^B**1:3** Lit *was of the seed of David*   ^C**1:4** Or *the spirit of holiness,* or *the Holy Spirit*   ^D**1:5** Or *him for;* lit *him into*   ^E**1:5** Or *nations,* also in v. 13   ^F**1:8** Or *because your faith*   ^G**1:13** Lit *have some fruit*   ^H**1:14** Or *non-Greeks*   ^I**1:16** Other mss add *of Christ*   ^J**1:17** Or *revealed out of faith into faith*   ^K**1:17** Or *The one who is righteous by faith will live*   ^L**1:17** Hab 2:4   ^M**1:19** Or *what is known*

creation of the world, being understood through what he has made. As a result, people are without excuse. [21] For though they knew God, they did not glorify him as God or show gratitude. Instead, their thinking became worthless, and their senseless hearts were darkened. [22] Claiming to be wise, they became fools [23] and exchanged the glory of the immortal God for images resembling mortal man, birds, four-footed animals, and reptiles. Rm 5:9; Eph 5:6; Col 3:6; 2Th 2:6-10

[24] Therefore God delivered them over in the desires of their hearts to sexual impurity, so that their bodies were degraded among themselves. [25] They exchanged the truth of God for a lie, and worshiped and served what has been created instead of the Creator, who is praised forever. Amen. Is 44:20; Jr 10:14; 13:25; Eph 2:3; 4:19

From Idolatry to Depravity

[26] For this reason God delivered them over to disgraceful passions. Their women[A] exchanged natural sexual relations[B] for unnatural ones. [27] The men[C] in the same way also left natural relations with women and were inflamed in their lust for one another. Men committed shameless acts with men and received in their own persons[D] the appropriate penalty of their error. Lv 18:22; 20:13; 1Th 4:5

[28] And because they did not think it worthwhile to acknowledge God, God delivered them over to a corrupt mind so that they do what is not right. [29] They are filled with all unrighteousness,[E] evil, greed, and wickedness. They are full of envy, murder, quarrels, deceit, and malice. They are gossips, [30] slanderers, God-haters, arrogant, proud, boastful, inventors of evil, disobedient to parents, [31] senseless, untrustworthy, unloving,[F] and unmerciful. [32] Although they know God's just sentence — that those who practice such things deserve to die[G] — they not only do them, but even applaud[H] others who practice them. Ps 5:5; 2Co 12:20; 2Tm 3:2

God's Righteous Judgment

2 Therefore, every one of you[I] who judges is without excuse. For when you judge another, you condemn yourself, since you, the judge, do the same things. [2] We know that God's judgment on those who do such things is based on the truth. [3] Do you really think — anyone of you who judges those who do such things yet do the same — that you will escape God's judgment? [4] Or do you despise the riches of his kindness, restraint, and patience, not recognizing[J] that God's kindness is intended to lead you to repentance? [5] Because of your hardened and unrepentant heart you are storing up wrath for yourself in the day of wrath, when God's righteous judgment is revealed. [6] **He will repay each one according to his works:**[K] [7] eternal life to those who by persistence in doing good seek glory, honor, and immortality; [8] but wrath and anger to those who are self-seeking and disobey the truth while obeying unrighteousness. [9] There will be affliction and distress for every human

---

[A]1:26 Lit *females*, also in v. 27   [B]1:26 Lit *natural use*, also in v. 27   [C]1:27 Lit *males*, also later in v.
[D]1:27 Or *in themselves*   [E]1:29 Other mss add *sexual immorality*   [F]1:31 Other mss add *unforgiving*
[G]1:32 Lit *things are worthy of death*   [H]1:32 Lit *even take pleasure in*   [I]2:1 Lit *Therefore, O man, every one*   [J]2:4 Or *patience, because you do not recognize*   [K]2:6 Ps 62:12; Pr 24:12

being who does evil, first to the Jew, and also to the Greek; ¹⁰ but glory, honor, and peace for everyone who does what is good, first to the Jew, and also to the Greek. ¹¹ For there is no favoritism with God.

¹² All who sin without the law will also perish without the law, and all who sin under ᴬ the law will be judged by the law. ¹³ For the hearers of the law are not righteous before God, but the doers of the law will be justified. ᴮ ¹⁴ So, when Gentiles, who do not by nature have the law, do ᶜ what the law demands, they are a law to themselves even though they do not have the law. ¹⁵ They show that the work of the law ᴰ is written on their hearts. Their consciences confirm this. Their competing thoughts either accuse or even excuse them ᴱ ¹⁶ on the day when God judges what people have kept secret, according to my gospel through Christ Jesus.   1Co 9:21

Jewish Violation of the Law

¹⁷ Now if ᶠ you call yourself a Jew, and rely on the law, and boast in God, ¹⁸ and know his will, and approve the things that are superior, being instructed from the law, ¹⁹ and if you are convinced that you are a guide for the blind, a light to those in darkness, ²⁰ an instructor of the ignorant, a teacher of the immature, having the embodiment of knowledge and truth in the law — ²¹ you then, who teach another, don't you teach yourself? You who preach, "You must not steal" — do you steal? ²² You who say, "You must not commit adultery" — do you commit adultery?

You who detest idols, do you rob their temples? ²³ You who boast in the law, do you dishonor God by breaking the law? ²⁴ For, as it is written: **The name of God is blasphemed among the Gentiles because of you.** ᴳ   Mc 3:11; Jn 5:45; Rm 9:4

Circumcision of the Heart

²⁵ Circumcision benefits you if you observe the law, but if you are a lawbreaker, your circumcision has become uncircumcision. ²⁶ So if an uncircumcised man keeps the law's requirements, will not his uncircumcision be counted as circumcision? ²⁷ A man who is physically uncircumcised, but who keeps the law, will judge you who are a lawbreaker in spite of having the letter of the law and circumcision. ²⁸ For a person is not a Jew who is one outwardly, and true circumcision is not something visible in the flesh. ²⁹ On the contrary, a person is a Jew who is one inwardly, and circumcision is of the heart — by the Spirit, not the letter. ᴴ That person's praise is not from people but from God.   Jr 4:4; 9:25; Rm 3:30; 8:4; 1Co 7:19

Paul Answers an Objection

3 So what advantage does the Jew have? Or what is the benefit of circumcision? ² Considerable in every way. First, they were entrusted with the very words of God. ³ What then? If some were unfaithful, will their unfaithfulness nullify God's faithfulness? ⁴ Absolutely not! Let God be true, even though everyone is a liar, as it is written: Dt 4:8; Ps 147:19

**That you may be justified
in your words**

ᴬ**2:12** Lit *in*   ᴮ**2:13** Or *acquitted*   ᶜ**2:14** Or *who do not have the law, instinctively do*   ᴰ**2:15** The code of conduct required by the law   ᴱ**2:15** Internal debate, either in a person or among the pagan moralists
ᶠ**2:17** Other mss read *Look* —   ᴳ**2:24** Is 52:5   ᴴ**2:29** Or *heart — spiritually, not literally*

and triumph
  when you judge.[A]   Ps 51:4

[5] But if our unrighteousness highlights[B] God's righteousness, what are we to say? I am using a human argument:[C] Is God unrighteous to inflict wrath? [6] Absolutely not! Otherwise, how will God judge the world? [7] But if by my lie God's truth abounds to his glory, why am I also still being judged as a sinner? [8] And why not say, just as some people slanderously claim we say, "Let us do what is evil so that good may come"? Their condemnation is deserved!   Rm 4:1; 5:8; 7:7; 8:31; 2Co 6:4; Gl 2:18

The Whole World Guilty Before God

[9] What then? Are we any better off?[D] Not at all! For we have already charged that both Jews and Gentiles[E] are all under sin,[F] [10] as it is written: Rm 1:18-32; 2:1-29; 3:19,23; 11:32

  There is no one righteous,
    not even one.
[11] There is no one
    who understands;
  there is no one
    who seeks God.
[12] All have turned away;
  all alike have become
    worthless.
  There is no one who does
    what is good,
  not even one.[G]   Ps 14:1-3; 53:1-3
[13] Their throat is
    an open grave;
  they deceive
    with their tongues.[H]   Ps 5:9
  Vipers' venom is
    under their lips.[I]   Ps 140:3
[14] Their mouth is
    full of cursing
    and bitterness.[J]   Ps 10:7
[15] Their feet are swift
    to shed blood;
[16] ruin and wretchedness are
    in their paths,
[17] and the path of peace
    they have not known.[K]
[18] There is no fear of God
    before their eyes.[L]   Ps 36:1

[19] Now we know that whatever the law says, it speaks to those who are subject to the law,[M] so that every mouth may be shut and the whole world may become subject to God's judgment.[N] [20] For no one will be justified[O] in his sight by the works of the law, because the knowledge of sin comes through the law.   Ps 143:2; Jn 10:34; Rm 2:12; 7:7

The Righteousness of God Through Faith

[21] But now, apart from the law, the righteousness of God has been revealed, attested by the Law and the Prophets.[P] [22] The righteousness of God is through faith in Jesus Christ[Q] to all who believe, since there is no distinction. [23] For all have sinned and fall short of the[R] glory of God. [24] They are justified freely by his grace through the redemption that is in Christ Jesus. [25] God presented him as an atoning sacrifice[S] in his blood, received

---

[A]3:4 Ps 51:4   [B]3:5 Or *shows*, or *demonstrates*   [C]3:5 Lit *I speak as a man*   [D]3:9 Are we Jews any better than the Gentiles?   [E]3:9 Lit *Greeks*   [F]3:9 Under sin's power or dominion   [G]3:10-12 Ps 14:1-3; 53:1-3; Ec 7:20   [H]3:13 Ps 5:9   [I]3:13 Ps 140:3   [J]3:14 Ps 10:7   [K]3:15-17 Is 59:7-8   [L]3:18 Ps 36:1   [M]3:19 Lit *those in the law*   [N]3:19 Or *become guilty before God*, or *may be accountable to God*   [O]3:20 Or *will be declared righteous*, or *will be acquitted*   [P]3:21 When capitalized, *the Law and the Prophets* = OT   [Q]3:22 Or *through the faithfulness of Jesus Christ*   [R]3:23 Or *and lack the*   [S]3:25 Or *a propitiation*, or *a place of atonement* through faith, to demonstrate his righteousness, because in his restraint God passed over the sins previously committed. [26] God presented him to demonstrate his righteousness at the present time, so that he would be righteous and declare righteous[A] the one who has faith in Jesus. Ac 10:43; Rm 1:2,17; 9:30

Boasting Excluded

[27] Where, then, is boasting? It is excluded. By what kind of law?[B] By one of works? No, on the contrary, by a law[C] of faith. [28] For we conclude that a person is justified by faith apart from the works of the law. [29] Or is God the God of Jews only? Is he not the God of Gentiles too? Yes, of Gentiles too, [30] since there is one God who will justify the circumcised by faith and the uncircumcised through faith. [31] Do we then nullify the law through faith? Absolutely not! On the contrary, we uphold the law. Rm 2:17,23

Abraham Justified by Faith

4 What then will we say that Abraham, our forefather according to the flesh, has found?[D] [2] If Abraham was justified[E] by works, he has something to boast about — but not before God. [3] For what does the Scripture say? **Abraham believed God, and it was credited to him for righteousness.**[F] [4] Now to the one who works, pay is not credited as a gift, but as something owed. [5] But to the one who does not work, but believes on him who declares the ungodly to be righteous, his faith is credited for righteousness. Rm 1:3

David Celebrating the Same Truth

[6] Just as David also speaks of the blessing of the person to whom God credits righteousness apart from works:

[7]   **Blessed are those whose
      lawless acts are forgiven
      and whose sins
      are covered.**
[8]   **Blessed is the person
      the Lord will never charge
      with sin.**[G]   Ps 32:1-2; 2Co 5:19

Abraham Justified Before Circumcision

[9] Is this blessing only for the circumcised, then? Or is it also for the uncircumcised? For we say, **Faith was credited to Abraham for righteousness.**[F] [10] In what way then was it credited — while he was circumcised, or uncircumcised? It was not while he was circumcised, but uncircumcised. [11] And he received the sign of circumcision as a seal of the righteousness that he had by faith[H] while still uncircumcised. This was to make him the father of all who believe but are not circumcised, so that righteousness may be credited to them also. [12] And he became the father of the circumcised, who are not only circumcised but who also follow in the footsteps of the faith our father Abraham had while he was still uncircumcised. Rm 3:30

The Promise Granted Through Faith

[13] For the promise to Abraham or to his descendants that he would

---

[A]3:26 Or and justify, or and acquit   [B]3:27 Or what principle?   [C]3:27 Or a principle   [D]4:1 Or What then shall we say? Have we found Abraham to be our forefather according to the flesh? or What, then, shall we say that Abraham our forefather found according to the flesh?   [E]4:2 Or was declared righteous, or was acquitted   [F]4:3,9 Gn 15:6   [G]4:7-8 Ps 32:1-2   [H]4:11 Lit righteousness of faith, also in v. 13

inherit the world was not through the law, but through the righteousness that comes by faith. [14] If those who are of the law are heirs, faith is made empty and the promise nullified, [15] because the law produces wrath. And where there is no law, there is no transgression.   Rm 9:8

[16] This is why the promise is by faith, so that it may be according to grace, to guarantee it to all the descendants — not only to those who are of the law[A] but also to those who are of Abraham's faith. He is the father of us all. [17] As it is written: **I have made you the father of many nations.**[B] He is our father in God's sight, in whom Abraham believed — the God who gives life to the dead and calls things into existence that do not exist. [18] He believed, hoping against hope, so that he became **the father of many nations**[B] according to what had been spoken: **So will your descendants be.**[C] [19] He did not weaken in faith when he considered[D] his own body to be already dead (since he was about a hundred years old) and also the deadness of Sarah's womb. [20] He did not waver in unbelief at God's promise but was strengthened in his faith and gave glory to God, [21] because he was fully convinced that what God had promised, he was also able to do. [22] Therefore, **it was credited to him for righteousness.**[E] [23] Now **it was credited to him**[E] was not written for Abraham alone, [24] but also for us. It will be credited to us who believe in him who raised Jesus our Lord from the dead. [25] He was delivered up for[F] our trespasses and raised for our justification.   Rm 3:24; 9:8

Faith Triumphs

5 Therefore, since we have been declared righteous by faith, we have peace[G] with God through our Lord Jesus Christ. [2] We have also obtained access through him by faith[H] into this grace in which we stand, and we rejoice[I] in the hope of the glory of God. [3] And not only that, but we also rejoice in our afflictions, because we know that affliction produces endurance, [4] endurance produces proven character, and proven character produces hope. [5] This hope will not disappoint us, because God's love has been poured out in our hearts through the Holy Spirit who was given to us.   Rm 3:28; 5:11; Eph 2:18; 3:12

Those Declared Righteous Are Reconciled

[6] For while we were still helpless, at the right time, Christ died for the ungodly. [7] For rarely will someone die for a just person — though for a good person perhaps someone might even dare to die. [8] But God proves his own love for us in that while we were still sinners, Christ died for us. [9] How much more then, since we have now been declared righteous by his blood, will we be saved through him from wrath. [10] For if, while we were enemies, we were reconciled to God through the death of his Son, then how much more, having been reconciled, will we be saved by his life. [11] And not only that, but we also rejoice in

---

[A]4:16 Or *not to those who are of the law only*   [B]4:17,18 Gn 17:5   [C]4:18 Gn 15:5   [D]4:19 Other mss read *He did not consider*   [E]4:22,23 Gn 15:6   [F]4:25 Or *because of*   [G]5:1 Other mss read *faith, let us have peace*, which can also be translated *faith, let us grasp the fact that we have peace*   [H]5:2 Other mss omit *by faith*   [I]5:2 Lit *boast*, also in vv. 3,11

God through our Lord Jesus Christ, through whom we have now received this reconciliation.   Gl 4:4

Death Through Adam and Life Through Christ

[12] Therefore, just as sin entered the world through one man, and death through sin, in this way death spread to all people, because all sinned.[A] [13] In fact, sin was in the world before the law, but sin is not charged to a person's account when there is no law. [14] Nevertheless, death reigned from Adam to Moses, even over those who did not sin in the likeness of Adam's transgression. He is a type of the Coming One.   Gn 2:17; 3:6,19; Hs 6:7; 1Co 15:21

[15] But the gift is not like the trespass. For if by the one man's trespass the many died, how much more have the grace of God and the gift which comes through the grace of the one man Jesus Christ overflowed to the many. [16] And the gift is not like the one man's sin, because from one sin came the judgment, resulting in condemnation, but from many trespasses came the gift, resulting in justification.[B] [17] Since by the one man's trespass, death reigned through that one man, how much more will those who receive the overflow of grace and the gift of righteousness reign in life through the one man, Jesus Christ.   Ac 15:11; 1Co 11:32; 2Tm 2:12; Rv 22:5

[18] So then, as through one trespass there is condemnation for everyone, so also through one righteous act there is justification leading to life for everyone. [19] For just as through one man's disobedience the many were made sinners, so also through the one man's obedience the many will be made righteous. [20] The law came along to multiply the trespass. But where sin multiplied, grace multiplied even more [21] so that, just as sin reigned in death, so also grace will reign through righteousness, resulting in eternal life through Jesus Christ our Lord.   Rm 4:25; 11:32

The New Life in Christ

6 What should we say then? Should we continue in sin so that grace may multiply? [2] Absolutely not! How can we who died to sin still live in it? [3] Or are you unaware that all of us who were baptized into Christ Jesus were baptized into his death? [4] Therefore we were buried with him by baptism into death, in order that, just as Christ was raised from the dead by the glory of the Father, so we too may walk in newness[C] of life. [5] For if we have been united with him in the likeness of his death, we will certainly also be[D] in the likeness of his resurrection. [6] For we know that our old self[E] was crucified with him so that the body ruled by sin[F] might be rendered powerless so that we may no longer be enslaved to sin, [7] since a person who has died is freed[G] from sin. [8] Now if we died with Christ, we believe that we will also live with him, [9] because we know that Christ, having been raised from the dead, will not die again. Death no longer rules over him. [10] For the death he died, he died to sin once for all time; but the life he lives, he lives to God. [11] So, you too consider yourselves dead

---

[A]**5:12** Or *have sinned*   [B]**5:16** Or *acquittal*   [C]**6:4** Or *a new way*   [D]**6:5** Be joined with him   [E]**6:6** Lit *man*
[F]**6:6** Lit *that the body of sin*   [G]**6:7** Or *justified*; lit *acquitted*

to sin and alive to God in Christ Jesus. ^A   Lk 20:16; Rm 3:5,88; 6:15; 7:4,6

¹² Therefore do not let sin reign in your mortal body, so that you obey ^B its desires. ¹³ And do not offer any parts ^C of it to sin as weapons for unrighteousness. But as those who are alive from the dead, offer yourselves to God, and all the parts of yourselves to God as weapons for righteousness. ¹⁴ For sin will not rule over you, because you are not under the law but under grace.   Rm 7:5; 12:1; 2Co 5:14; Col 3:5

From Slaves of Sin to Slaves of God

¹⁵ What then? Should we sin because we are not under the law but under grace? Absolutely not! ¹⁶ Don't you know that if you offer yourselves to someone ^D as obedient slaves, you are slaves of that one you obey — either of sin leading to death or of obedience leading to righteousness? ¹⁷ But thank God that, although you used to be slaves of sin, you obeyed from the heart that pattern of teaching to which you were handed ^E over, ¹⁸ and having been set free from sin, you became enslaved to righteousness. ¹⁹ I am using a human analogy because of the weakness of your flesh. ^F For just as you offered the parts of yourselves as slaves to impurity, and to greater and greater lawlessness, so now offer them as slaves to righteousness, which results in sanctification. ²⁰ For when you were slaves of sin, you were free with regard to righteousness. ^G ²¹ So what fruit was produced ^H then from the things

you are now ashamed of? The outcome of those things is death. ²² But now, since you have been set free from sin and have become enslaved to God, you have your fruit, which results in sanctification — and the outcome is eternal life! ²³ For the wages of sin is death, but the gift of God is eternal life in Christ Jesus our Lord.   Lk 20:16; Rm 6:1; 11:2; 1Co 3:16; 5:6

An Illustration from Marriage

7 Since I am speaking to those who know the law, brothers and sisters, don't you know that the law rules over someone as long as he lives? ² For example, a married woman is legally bound to her husband while he lives. But if her husband dies, she is released from the law regarding the husband. ³ So then, if she is married to another man while her husband is living, she will be called an adulteress. But if her husband dies, she is free from that law. Then, if she is married to another man, she is not an adulteress.   Rm 1:13; 1Co 7:39

⁴ Therefore, my brothers and sisters, you also were put to death in relation to the law through the body of Christ so that you may belong to another. You belong to him who was raised from the dead in order that we may bear fruit for God. ⁵ For when we were in the flesh, the sinful passions aroused through the law were working in us ^I to bear fruit for death. ⁶ But now we have been released from the law, since we have died to what held us, so that we may serve in the newness of the Spirit and not in the old letter of the law.   Rm 6:2; 8:2; Gl 2:19; 5:18

^A **6:11** Other mss add *our Lord*   ^B **6:12** Other mss add *sin* (lit *it*) *in*   ^C **6:13** Or *members*, also in v. 19
^D **6:16** Lit *that to whom you offer yourselves*   ^E **6:17** Or *entrusted*   ^F **6:19** Or *your human nature*
^G **6:20** Lit *free to righteousness*   ^H **6:21** Lit *what fruit do you have*   ^I **7:5** Lit *in our members*

Sin's Use of the Law

⁷ What should we say then? Is the law sin? Absolutely not! On the contrary, I would not have known sin if it were not for the law. For example, I would not have known what it is to covet if the law had not said, **Do not covet.** ^A ⁸ And sin, seizing an opportunity through the commandment, produced in me coveting of every kind. For apart from the law sin is dead. ⁹ Once I was alive apart from the law, but when the commandment came, sin sprang to life again ¹⁰ and I died. The commandment that was meant for life resulted in death for me. ¹¹ For sin, seizing an opportunity through the commandment, deceived me, and through it killed me. ¹² So then, the law is holy, and the commandment is holy and just and good. ¹³ Therefore, did what is good become death to me? Absolutely not! On the contrary, sin, in order to be recognized as sin, was producing death in me through what is good, so that through the commandment, sin might become sinful beyond measure. Lk 20:16; Rm 3:5

The Problem of Sin in Us

¹⁴ For we know that the law is spiritual, but I am of the flesh, ^B sold as a slave to sin. ^C ¹⁵ For I do not understand what I am doing, because I do not practice what I want to do, but I do what I hate. ¹⁶ Now if I do what I do not want to do, I agree with the law that it is good. ¹⁷ So now I am no longer the one doing it, but it is sin living in me. ¹⁸ For I know that nothing good lives in me, that

is, in my flesh. For the desire to do what is good is with me, but there is no ability to do it. ¹⁹ For I do not do the good that I want to do, but I practice the evil that I do not want to do. ²⁰ Now if I do what I do not want, I am no longer the one that does it, but it is the sin that lives in me. ²¹ So I discover this law: ^D When I want to do what is good, ^E evil is present with me. ²² For in my inner self ^F I delight in God's law, ²³ but I see a different law in the parts of my body, ^G waging war against the law of my mind and taking me prisoner to the law of sin in the parts of my body. ²⁴ What a wretched man I am! Who will rescue me from this body of death? ²⁵ Thanks be to God through Jesus Christ our Lord! So then, with my mind I myself am serving the law of God, but with my flesh, the law of sin. Rm 6:6; 1Co 3:1

The Life-Giving Spirit

8 Therefore, there is now no condemnation for those in Christ Jesus, ^H ² because the law of the Spirit of life in Christ Jesus has set you ^I free from the law of sin and death. ³ What the law could not do since it was weakened by the flesh, God did. He condemned sin in the flesh by sending his own Son in the likeness of sinful flesh as a sin offering, ^J ⁴ in order that the law's requirement would be fulfilled in us who do not walk according to the flesh but according to the Spirit. ⁵ For those who live according to the flesh have their minds set on the things of the flesh, but those who live according to

^A 7:7 Ex 20:17   ^B 7:14 Or *unspiritual*   ^C 7:14 Lit *under sin*   ^D 7:21 Or *principle*   ^E 7:21 Or *I find with respect to the law that when I want to do good*   ^F 7:22 Lit *inner man*   ^G 7:23 Lit *my members*   ^H 8:1 Other mss add *who do not walk according to the flesh but according to the Spirit*   ^I 8:2 Other mss read *me*   ^J 8:3 Or *for sin* the Spirit have their minds set on the things of the Spirit. [6] Now the mind-set of the flesh is death, but the mind-set of the Spirit is life and peace. [7] The mind-set of the flesh is hostile to God because it does not submit to God's law. Indeed, it is unable to do so. [8] Those who are in the flesh cannot please God. [9] You, however, are not in the flesh, but in the Spirit, if indeed the Spirit of God lives in you. If anyone does not have the Spirit of Christ, he does not belong to him. [10] Now if Christ is in you, the body is dead because of sin, but the Spirit[A] gives life[B] because of righteousness. [11] And if the Spirit of him who raised Jesus from the dead lives in you, then he who raised Christ from the dead will also bring your mortal bodies to life through[C] his Spirit who lives in you.   Rm 5:16; 8:9-11,34,39; 16:3

The Holy Spirit's Ministries

[12] So then, brothers and sisters, we are not obligated to the flesh to live according to the flesh, [13] because if you live according to the flesh, you are going to die. But if by the Spirit you put to death the deeds of the body, you will live. [14] For all those led by God's Spirit are God's sons. [15] For you did not receive a spirit of slavery to fall back into fear. Instead, you received the Spirit of adoption, by whom we cry out, "Abba,[D] Father!" [16] The Spirit himself testifies together with our spirit that we are God's children, [17] and if children, also heirs — heirs of God and coheirs with Christ — if indeed we suffer with him so that we may also be glorified with him.   Col 3:5; Gl 5:18; 4:7

From Groans to Glory

[18] For I consider that the sufferings of this present time are not worth comparing with the glory that is going to be revealed to us. [19] For the creation eagerly waits with anticipation for God's sons to be revealed. [20] For the creation was subjected to futility — not willingly, but because of him who subjected it — in the hope [21] that the creation itself will also be set free from the bondage to decay into the glorious freedom of God's children. [22] For we know that the whole creation has been groaning together with labor pains until now. [23] Not only that, but we ourselves who have the Spirit as the firstfruits — we also groan within ourselves, eagerly waiting for adoption, the redemption of our bodies. [24] Now in this hope we were saved, but hope that is seen is not hope, because who hopes for what he sees? [25] Now if we hope for what we do not see, we eagerly wait for it with patience.   Rm 1:5; 2Co 4:17; Col 3:4; Ti 2:13; 1Pt 4:13

[26] In the same way the Spirit also helps us in our weakness, because we do not know what to pray for as we should, but the Spirit himself intercedes for us[E] with unspoken groanings. [27] And he who searches our hearts knows the mind of the Spirit, because he intercedes for the saints according to the will of God.   Mt 20:22; Jn 14:16; Rm 8:15-16; 2Co 12:8

[28] We know that all things work together[F] for the good[G] of those who love God, who are called according to his purpose. [29] For those he foreknew he also predestined to be conformed to the image of

---

[A] 8:10 Or spirit   [B] 8:10 Or your spirit is alive   [C] 8:11 Other mss read because of   [D] 8:15 Aramaic for father   [E] 8:26 Some mss omit for us   [F] 8:28 Other mss read that God works together in all things   [G] 8:28 The ultimate good his Son, so that he would be the firstborn among many brothers and sisters. ³⁰ And those he predestined, he also called; and those he called, he also justified; and those he justified, he also glorified. Rm 9:24; 11:29; 1Co 1:9; Gl 1:6,15; 5:8; Eph 1:11

The Believer's Triumph

³¹ What then are we to say about these things? If God is for us, who is against us? ³² He did not even spare his own Son but offered him up for us all. How will he not also with him grant us everything? ³³ Who can bring an accusation against God's elect? God is the one who justifies. ³⁴ Who is the one who condemns? Christ Jesus is the one who died, but even more, has been raised; he also is at the right hand of God and intercedes for us. ³⁵ Who can separate us from the love of Christ? Can affliction or distress or persecution or famine or nakedness or danger or sword? ³⁶ As it is written: Ps 118:6; Rm 3:5; 4:1

**Because of you
we are being put to death
all day long;**   Ac 20:24; 1Co 4:9
**we are counted as sheep
to be slaughtered.**ᴬ   Is 53:7

³⁷ No, in all these things we are more than conquerors through him who loved us. ³⁸ For I am persuaded that neither death nor life, nor angels nor rulers, nor things present nor things to come, nor powers, ³⁹ nor height nor depth, nor any other created thing will be able to separate us from the love of God that is in Christ Jesus our Lord.   Jn 16:33; 1Co 15:57; Gl 2:20; Eph 5:2; Rv 1:5

Israel's Rejection of Christ

9 I speak the truth in Christ — I am not lying; my conscience testifies to me through the Holy Spiritᴮ — ² that I have great sorrow and unceasing anguish in my heart. ³ For I could wish that I myself were cursed and cut offᶜ from Christ for the benefit of my brothers and sisters, my own flesh and blood. ⁴ They are Israelites, and to them belong the adoption, the glory, the covenants, the giving of the law, the temple service, and the promises. ⁵ The ancestors are theirs, and from them, by physical descent,ᴰ came the Christ, who is God over all, praised forever.ᴱ Amen.   Rm 1:9

God's Gracious Election of Israel

⁶ Now it is not as though the word of God has failed, because not all who are descended from Israel are Israel. ⁷ Neither are all of Abraham's children his descendants.ᶠ On the contrary, **your offspring will be traced**ᴳ **through Isaac.**ᴴ ⁸ That is, it is not the children by physical descentᴵ who are God's children, but the children of the promise are considered to be the offspring. ⁹ For this is the statement of the promise: **At this time I will come, and Sarah will have a son.**ᴶ ¹⁰ And not only that, but Rebekah conceived children through one man, our father Isaac. ¹¹ For though her sons had not been born yet or done anything good or bad, so that God's purpose according to election might stand — ¹² not from works but from the one who calls — she was told, **The older will serve**

ᴬ**8:36** Ps 44:22   ᴮ**9:1** Or *testifying with me by the Holy Spirit*   ᶜ**9:3** Lit *to be anathema*   ᴰ**9:5** Lit *them, according to the flesh*   ᴱ**9:5** Or *the Messiah, the one who is over all, the God who is blessed forever,* or *Messiah. God, who is over all, be blessed forever*   ᶠ**9:7** Lit *seed*   ᴳ**9:7** Lit *called*   ᴴ**9:7** Gn 21:12   ᴵ**9:8** Lit *children of the flesh*   ᴶ**9:9** Gn 18:10,14 the younger.[A] [13] As it is written: I have loved Jacob, but I have hated Esau.[B]   Nm 23:19; Jn 1:47; Rm 2:28-29; Gl 6:16

God's Selection Is Just

[14] What should we say then? Is there injustice with God? Absolutely not! [15] For he tells Moses, I will show mercy to whom I will show mercy, and I will have compassion on whom I will have compassion.[C] [16] So then, it does not depend on human will or effort but on God who shows mercy. [17] For the Scripture tells Pharaoh, I raised you up for this reason so that I may display my power in you and that my name may be proclaimed in the whole earth.[D] [18] So then, he has mercy on whom he wants to have mercy and he hardens whom he wants to harden.   2Ch 19:7; Lk 20:16; Rm 2:11; 3:5; Gl 2:2

[19] You will say to me, therefore, "Why then does he still find fault? For who can resist his will?" [20] But who are you, a mere man, to talk back to God? Will what is formed say to the one who formed it, "Why did you make me like this?" [21] Or has the potter no right over the clay, to make from the same lump one piece of pottery for honor and another for dishonor? [22] And what if God, wanting to display his wrath and to make his power known, endured with much patience objects of wrath prepared for destruction? [23] And what if he did this to make known the riches of his glory on objects of mercy that he prepared beforehand for glory — [24] on us, the ones he also called, not only from the Jews but also from the Gentiles? [25] As it[E] also says in Hosea,   Rm 11:19; Jms 2:18

I will call Not My People,
My People,
and she who is Unloved,
Beloved.[F]   Hs 2:23; 1Pt 2:10

[26] And it will be in the place
where they were told,
you are not my people,
there they will be called
sons of the living God.[G]

[27] But Isaiah cries out concerning Israel,

Though the number
of Israelites
is like the sand of the sea,
only the remnant
will be saved;   Rm 11:5
[28] since the Lord will execute
his sentence
completely and decisively
on the earth.[H,I]   Is 10:22-23; 28:22

[29] And just as Isaiah predicted:

If the Lord of Hosts[J]
had not left us offspring,
we would have become
like Sodom,
and we would
have been made
like Gomorrah.[K]   Dt 29:23; Is 1:9

Israel's Present State

[30] What should we say then? Gentiles, who did not pursue righteousness, have obtained righteousness — namely the righteousness that comes from faith. [31] But Israel, pursuing the law of righteousness, has not achieved the righteousness of the law.[L] [32] Why is that? Because they did not pursue it by faith, but as if it were by works.[M] They stumbled over the stumbling stone. [33] As it is written,   Rm 1:17; 3:21; 9:14; 10:6; Gl 2:16

[A]9:12 Gn 25:23   [B]9:13 Mal 1:2-3   [C]9:15 Ex 33:19   [D]9:17 Ex 9:16   [E]9:25 Or he   [F]9:25 Hs 2:23   [G]9:26 Hs 1:10   [H]9:28 Or land   [I]9:27-28 Is 10:22-23; 28:22; Hs 1:10   [J]9:29 Gk Sabaoth; or the Lord of Armies   [K]9:29 Is 1:9   [L]9:31 Other mss read the law for righteousness   [M]9:32 Other mss add of the law

Look, I am putting a stone
  in Zion to stumble over
and a rock to trip over,
and the one who believes
  on him   Rm 10:11
will not be put to shame. ^A

Righteousness by Faith Alone

10 Brothers and sisters, my
heart's desire and prayer to
God concerning them ^B is for their
salvation. ² I can testify about them
that they have zeal for God, but not
according to knowledge. ³ Since
they are ignorant of the righteousness of God and attempted to establish their own righteousness,
they have not submitted to God's
righteousness. ⁴ For Christ is the
end ^C of the law for righteousness
to everyone who believes, ⁵ since
Moses writes about the righteousness that is from the law: **The one
who does these things will live
by them.** ^D ⁶ But the righteousness
that comes from faith speaks like
this: **Do not say in your heart,
"Who will go up to heaven?"** ^E
that is, to bring Christ down ⁷ or,
**"Who will go down into the
abyss?"** ^F that is, to bring Christ up
from the dead. ⁸ On the contrary,
what does it say? **The message is
near you, in your mouth and in
your heart.** ^G This is the message
of faith that we proclaim: ⁹ If you
confess with your mouth, "Jesus
is Lord," and believe in your heart
that God raised him from the dead,
you will be saved. ¹⁰ One believes
with the heart, resulting in righteousness, and one confesses with
the mouth, resulting in salvation.
¹¹ For the Scripture says, **Everyone**

who believes on him will not
be put to shame, ^H ¹² since there
is no distinction between Jew and
Greek, because the same Lord of
all richly blesses all who call on
him. ¹³ For **everyone who calls
on the name of the Lord will be
saved.** ^I   Ac 21:20; Rm 1:17; 7:1-4

Israel's Rejection of the Message

¹⁴ How, then, can they call on him
they have not believed in? And how
can they believe without hearing
about him? And how can they hear
without a preacher? ¹⁵ And how
can they preach unless they are
sent? As it is written: **How beautiful ^J are the feet of those who
bring good news.** ^K ¹⁶ But not all
obeyed the gospel. For Isaiah
says, **Lord, who has believed our
message?** ^L ¹⁷ So faith comes from
what is heard, and what is heard
comes through the message about
Christ. ^M ¹⁸ But I ask, "Did they not
hear?" Yes, they did: Eph 2:17; 4:21; Ti 1:3

Their voice has gone out to
  the whole earth,
and their words to the ends
  of the world. ^N   Ps 19:4; Rm 1:8
¹⁹ But I ask, "Did Israel not understand?" First, Moses said,

I will make you jealous
  of those who are not
  a nation;   Rm 11:11,14
I will make you angry
  by a nation
  that lacks understanding. ^O
²⁰ And Isaiah says boldly,

I was found
  by those who were not
  looking for me;
I revealed myself

^A 9:33 Is 8:14; 28:16   ^B 10:1 Other mss read *God for Israel*   ^C 10:4 Or *goal*   ^D 10:5 Lv 18:5   ^E 10:6 Dt 9:4; 30:12   ^F 10:7 Dt 30:13   ^G 10:8 Dt 30:14   ^H 10:11 Is 28:16   ^I 10:13 Jl 2:32   ^J 10:15 Or *welcome*, or *timely*   ^K 10:15 Is 52:7; Nah 1:15   ^L 10:16 Is 53:1   ^M 10:17 Other mss read *God*   ^N 10:18 Ps 19:4   ^O 10:19 Dt 32:21

to those who were not
asking for me.[A]   Is 65:1; Rm 9:30
²¹ But to Israel he says, **All day long
I have held out my hands to a disobedient and defiant people.**[B]

Israel's Rejection Not Total

11 I ask, then, has God rejected
his people? Absolutely not!
For I too am an Israelite, a descendant of Abraham, from the tribe
of Benjamin. ² God has not rejected
his people whom he foreknew. Or
don't you know what the Scripture
says in the passage about Elijah —
how he pleads with God against Israel? ³ **Lord, they have killed your
prophets and torn down your altars. I am the only one left, and
they are trying to take my life!**[C]
⁴ But what was God's answer to him?
**I have left seven thousand for my-
self who have not bowed down to
Baal.**[D] ⁵ In the same way, then, there
is also at the present time a remnant
chosen by grace. ⁶ Now if by grace,
then it is not by works; otherwise
grace ceases to be grace.[E]   1Sm 12:22
⁷ What then? Israel did not find
what it was looking for, but the
elect did find it. The rest were hardened, ⁸ as it is written,   Mk 6:52; Rm 9:31

**God gave them a spirit
of stupor,
eyes that cannot see
and ears that cannot hear,
to this day.**[F]   Dt 29:4; Is 29:10
⁹ And David says,
**Let their table become
a snare and a trap,
a pitfall and a retribution
to them.**
¹⁰ **Let their eyes be darkened
so that they cannot see,**

and their backs be bent
continually.[G]   Ps 69:22-23

Israel's Rejection Not Final

¹¹ I ask, then, have they stumbled
so as to fall? Absolutely not! On the
contrary, by their transgression,
salvation has come to the Gentiles to make Israel jealous. ¹² Now
if their transgression brings riches for the world, and their failure
riches for the Gentiles, how much
more will their fullness bring!

¹³ Now I am speaking to you Gentiles. Insofar as I am an apostle to
the Gentiles, I magnify my ministry, ¹⁴ if I might somehow make
my own people[H] jealous and save
some of them. ¹⁵ For if their rejec-
tion brings reconciliation to the
world, what will their acceptance
mean but life from the dead? ¹⁶ Now
if the firstfruits are holy, so is the
whole batch. And if the root is holy,
so are the branches.   Gn 29:14; Ac 9:15

¹⁷ Now if some of the branches
were broken off, and you, though
a wild olive branch, were grafted
in among them and have come to
share in the rich root[I] of the cultivated olive tree, ¹⁸ do not boast
that you are better than those
branches. But if you do boast —
you do not sustain the root, but
the root sustains you. ¹⁹ Then you
will say, "Branches were broken
off so that I might be grafted in."
²⁰ True enough; they were broken
off because of unbelief, but you
stand by faith. Do not be arrogant,
but beware,[J] ²¹ because if God did
not spare the natural branches, he
will not spare you either. ²² Therefore, consider God's kindness and

[A]**10:20** Is 65:1 [B]**10:21** Is 65:2 [C]**11:3** 1Kg 19:10,14 [D]**11:4** 1Kg 19:18 [E]**11:6** Other mss add *But if of works
it is no longer grace; otherwise work is no longer work.* [F]**11:8** Dt 29:4; Is 29:10 [G]**11:9-10** Ps 69:22-23
[H]**11:14** Lit *flesh* [I]**11:17** Other mss read *the root and the richness* [J]**11:20** Lit *fear*

severity: severity toward those who have fallen but God's kindness toward you — if you remain in his kindness. Otherwise you too will be cut off. ²³ And even they, if they do not remain in unbelief, will be grafted in, because God has the power to graft them in again. ²⁴ For if you were cut off from your native wild olive tree and against nature were grafted into a cultivated olive tree, how much more will these — the natural branches — be grafted into their own olive tree? Jr 11:16; Jn 4:22; 15:2; Rm 9:19; Eph 2:12-13

²⁵ I don't want you to be ignorant of this mystery, brothers and sisters, so that you will not be conceited: A partial hardening has come upon Israel until the fullness of the Gentiles has come in. ²⁶ And in this way all ᴬ Israel will be saved, as it is written, Mt 13:11; Rm 1:13; 12:16; 16:25

**The Deliverer will come
    from Zion;
  he will turn godlessness
    away from Jacob.**
²⁷ **And this will be
    my covenant with them ᴮ
  when I take away
    their sins.** ᶜ Jr 31:31-34; Heb 8:10,12

²⁸ Regarding the gospel, they are enemies for your advantage, but regarding election, they are loved because of the patriarchs, ²⁹ since God's gracious gifts and calling are irrevocable. ᴰ ³⁰ As you once disobeyed God but now have received mercy through their disobedience, ³¹ so they too have now disobeyed, resulting in mercy to you, so that they also may now ᴱ receive mercy. ³² For God has imprisoned all in disobedience so that he may have mercy on all.   Dt 7:8; 10:15; Rm 5:10; 9:5

A Hymn of Praise

³³ Oh, the depth of the riches
    both of the wisdom
    and of the knowledge
    of God!   Eph 3:10; Col 2:3
  How unsearchable
    his judgments   Jb 5:9; 11:7; 15:8
  and untraceable his ways!
³⁴ **For who has known
    the mind of the Lord?
  Or who has been
    his counselor?**
³⁵ **And who has ever given
    to God,
  that he should be repaid?** ᶠ
³⁶ For from him and through him
    and to him are all things.
  To him be the glory
    forever. Amen.

A Living Sacrifice

12 Therefore, brothers and sisters, in view of the mercies of God, I urge you to present your bodies as a living sacrifice, holy and pleasing to God; this is your true worship. ᴳ ² Do not be conformed to this age, but be transformed by the renewing of your mind, so that you may discern what is the good, pleasing, and perfect will of God.

Many Gifts but One Body

³ For by the grace given to me, I tell everyone among you not to think of himself more highly than he should think. Instead, think sensibly, as God has distributed a measure of faith to each one. ⁴ Now as we have many parts in one body, and all the parts do not have the same function, ⁵ in the same way we who are many are one body in Christ and individually members of one another. ⁶ According

---

ᴬ**11:26** Or *And then all*   ᴮ**11:26-27** Is 59:20-21   ᶜ**11:27** Jr 31:31-34   ᴰ**11:29** Or *are not taken back*   ᴱ**11:31** Other mss omit *now*   ᶠ**11:34-35** Jb 41:11; Is 40:13; Jr 23:18   ᴳ**12:1** Or *your reasonable service* to the grace given to us, we have different gifts: If prophecy, use it according to the proportion of one's [A] faith; [7] if service, use it in service; if teaching, in teaching; [8] if exhorting, in exhortation; giving, with generosity; leading, with diligence; showing mercy, with cheerfulness. Rm 1:5; 15:15; 1Co 3:10; 15:10

Christian Ethics

[9] Let love be without hypocrisy. Detest evil; cling to what is good. [10] Love one another deeply as brothers and sisters. Outdo one another in showing honor. [11] Do not lack diligence in zeal; be fervent in the Spirit; [B] serve the Lord. [12] Rejoice in hope; be patient in affliction; be persistent in prayer. [13] Share with the saints in their needs; pursue hospitality. [14] Bless those who persecute you; bless and do not curse. [15] Rejoice with those who rejoice; weep with those who weep. [16] Live in harmony with one another. Do not be proud; instead, associate with the humble. Do not be wise in your own estimation. [17] Do not repay anyone evil for evil. Give careful thought to do what is honorable in everyone's eyes. [18] If possible, as far as it depends on you, live at peace with everyone. [19] Friends, do not avenge yourselves; instead, leave room for God's wrath, because it is written, **Vengeance belongs to me; I will repay,** [C] says the Lord. [20] But 2Co 6:6

**If your enemy is hungry,
   feed him.** Mt 5:44; Lk 6:27
**If he is thirsty, give him
   something to drink.
For in so doing
   you will be heaping
   fiery coals on his head.** [D]

[21] Do not be conquered by evil, but conquer evil with good.

A Christian's Duties to the State

13 Let everyone submit to the governing authorities, since there is no authority except from God, and the authorities that exist are instituted by God. [2] So then, the one who resists the authority is opposing God's command, and those who oppose it will bring judgment on themselves. [3] For rulers are not a terror to good conduct, but to bad. Do you want to be unafraid of the authority? Do what is good, and you will have its approval. [4] For it is God's servant for your good. But if you do wrong, be afraid, because it does not carry the sword for no reason. For it is God's servant, an avenger that brings wrath on the one who does wrong. [5] Therefore, you must submit, not only because of wrath but also because of your conscience. [6] And for this reason you pay taxes, since the authorities are God's servants, continually attending to these tasks. [E] [7] Pay your obligations to everyone: taxes to those you owe taxes, tolls to those you owe tolls, respect to those you owe respect, and honor to those you owe honor. Dn 2:21; 4:17; Jn 19:1; Ti 3:1

Love, Our Primary Duty

[8] Do not owe anyone anything, except to love one another, for the one who loves another has fulfilled the law. [9] The commandments, **Do not commit adultery; do not murder; do not steal;** [F] **do not covet;** [G] and any other commandment, are summed up by this commandment: **Love your neighbor as yourself.** [H]

[A] **12:6** Or *the*, also in v. 19   [B] **12:11** Or *in spirit*   [C] **12:19** Dt 32:35   [D] **12:20** Pr 25:21-22   [E] **13:6** Lit *to this very thing*   [F] **13:9** Other mss add *do not bear false witness*   [G] **13:9** Ex 20:13-17; Dt 5:17-21   [H] **13:9** Lv 19:18

[10] Love does no wrong to a neighbor. Love, therefore, is the fulfillment of the law.   Mt 7:12; 22:39; Jn 13:34

Put On Christ

[11] Besides this, since you know the time, it is already the hour for you[B] to wake up from sleep, because now our salvation is nearer than when we first believed. [12] The night is nearly over, and the day is near; so let us discard the deeds of darkness and put on the armor of light. [13] Let us walk with decency, as in the daytime: not in carousing and drunkenness; not in sexual impurity and promiscuity; not in quarreling and jealousy. [14] But put on the Lord Jesus Christ, and don't make plans to gratify the desires of the flesh.   1Co 7:29

The Law of Liberty

14 Accept anyone who is weak in faith, but don't argue about disputed matters. [2] One person believes he may eat anything, while one who is weak eats only vegetables. [3] One who eats must not look down on one who does not eat, and one who does not eat must not judge one who does, because God has accepted him. [4] Who are you to judge another's household servant? Before his own Lord he stands or falls. And he will stand, because the Lord is able[C] to make him stand.   Ac 28:2; Rm 11:15; 12:3; 15:1,7

[5] One person judges one day to be more important than another day. Someone else judges every day to be the same. Let each one be fully convinced in his own mind. [6] Whoever observes the day, observes it for the honor of the Lord.[D] Whoever

eats, eats for the Lord, since he gives thanks to God; and whoever does not eat, it is for the Lord that he does not eat it, and he gives thanks to God. [7] For none of us lives for himself, and no one dies for himself. [8] If we live, we live for the Lord; and if we die, we die for the Lord. Therefore, whether we live or die, we belong to the Lord. [9] Christ died and returned to life for this: that he might be Lord over both the dead and the living. [10] But you, why do you judge your brother or sister? Or you, why do you despise your brother or sister? For we will all stand before the judgment seat of God.[E] [11] For it is written,   Lk 1:1; Gl 4:10

**As I live, says the Lord,
every knee will bow to me,
and every tongue will give
praise to God.**[F]   Is 45:23; 49:18

[12] So then, each of us will give an account of himself to God.   Mt 12:36

The Law of Love

[13] Therefore, let us no longer judge one another. Instead decide never to put a stumbling block or pitfall in the way of your brother or sister. [14] I know and am persuaded in the Lord Jesus that nothing is unclean in itself. Still, to someone who considers a thing to be unclean, to that one it is unclean. [15] For if your brother or sister is hurt by what you eat, you are no longer walking according to love. Do not destroy, by what you eat, someone for whom Christ died. [16] Therefore, do not let your good be slandered, [17] for the kingdom of God is not eating and drinking, but righteousness, peace, and

B13:11 Other mss read *for us*   **C**14:4 Other mss read *For God has the power*   **D**14:6 Other mss add *but whoever does not observe the day, it is to the Lord that he does not observe it*   **E**14:10 Other mss read *of Christ*   **F**14:11 Is 45:23; 49:18

joy in the Holy Spirit. [18] Whoever serves Christ in this way is acceptable to God and receives human approval.

[19] So then, let us pursue what promotes peace and what builds up one another. [20] Do not tear down God's work because of food. Everything is clean, but it is wrong to make someone fall by what he eats. [21] It is a good thing not to eat meat, or drink wine, or do anything that makes your brother or sister stumble. [A] [22] Whatever you believe about these things, keep between yourself and God. Blessed is the one who does not condemn himself by what he approves. [23] But whoever doubts stands condemned if he eats, because his eating is not from faith, [B] and everything that is not from faith is sin. Ps 34:14; Rm 12:18

Pleasing Others, Not Ourselves

15 Now we who are strong have an obligation to bear the weaknesses of those without strength, and not to please ourselves. [2] Each one of us is to please his neighbor for his good, to build him up. [3] For even Christ did not please himself. On the contrary, as it is written, **The insults of those who insult you have fallen on me.** [C] [4] For whatever was written in the past was written for our instruction, so that we may have hope through endurance and through the encouragement from the Scriptures. [5] Now may the God who gives [D] endurance and encouragement grant you to live in harmony with one another, according to Christ Jesus, [6] so that you may glorify the God and Father

of our Lord Jesus Christ with one mind and one voice. Rm 14:1; Rv 1:6

Glorifying God Together

[7] Therefore accept one another, just as Christ also accepted you, to the glory of God. [8] For I say that Christ became a servant of the circumcised [E] on behalf of God's truth, to confirm the promises to the fathers, [9] and so that Gentiles may glorify God for his mercy. As it is written,

Therefore I will praise you among the Gentiles, and I will sing praise to your name. [F] 2Sm 22:50

[10] Again it says, **Rejoice, you Gentiles, with his people!** [G] [11] And again,

Praise the Lord, all you Gentiles; let all the peoples praise him! [H] Ps 117:1

[12] And again, Isaiah says,

The root of Jesse will appear, the one who rises to rule the Gentiles; the Gentiles will hope in him. [I] Is 11:10; Mt 12:21

[13] Now may the God of hope fill you with all joy and peace as you believe so that you may overflow with hope by the power of the Holy Spirit.

From Jerusalem to Illyricum

[14] My brothers and sisters, I myself am convinced about you that you also are full of goodness, filled with all knowledge, and able to instruct one another. [15] Nevertheless, I have written to remind you more boldly on some points [J] because of the grace given me by God [16] to be a minister of Christ Jesus to the Gentiles, serving as a priest of the gospel of

---

[A] **14:21** Other mss add *or offended or weakened* [B] **14:23** Or *conviction* [C] **15:3** Ps 69:9 [D] **15:5** Lit *God of*
[E] **15:8** The Jews [F] **15:9** 2Sm 22:50; Ps 18:49 [G] **15:10** Dt 32:43 [H] **15:11** Ps 117:1 [I] **15:12** Is 11:10
[J] **15:15** Other mss add *brothers*

God. My purpose is that the Gentiles may be an acceptable offering, sanctified by the Holy Spirit. [17] Therefore I have reason to boast in Christ Jesus regarding what pertains to God. [18] For I would not dare say anything except what Christ has accomplished through me by word and deed for the obedience of the Gentiles, [19] by the power of miraculous signs and wonders, and by the power of God's Spirit. As a result, I have fully proclaimed the gospel of Christ from Jerusalem all the way around to Illyricum.[A] [20] My aim is to preach the gospel where Christ has not been named, so that I will not build on someone else's foundation, [21] but, as it is written, Eph 5:9

> Those who were not told
> about him will see,
> and those who have not
> heard will understand.[B]

Paul's Travel Plans

[22] That is why I have been prevented many times from coming to you. [23] But now I no longer have any work to do in these regions,[C] and I have strongly desired for many years to come to you [24] whenever I travel to Spain.[D] For I hope to see you when I pass through and to be assisted by you for my journey there, once I have first enjoyed your company for a while. [25] Right now I am traveling to Jerusalem to serve the saints, [26] because Macedonia and Achaia were pleased to make a contribution for the poor among the saints in Jerusalem. [27] Yes, they were pleased, and indeed are indebted to them. For if the Gentiles have shared in their spiritual benefits, then they are obligated to minister to them in material needs. [28] So when I have finished this and safely delivered the funds[E] to them,[F] I will visit you on the way to Spain. [29] I know that when I come to you, I will come in the fullness of the blessing[G] of Christ. Rm 1:13; 1Th 2:18; 2:13

[30] Now I appeal to you, brothers and sisters, through our Lord Jesus Christ and through the love of the Spirit, to strive together with me in fervent prayers to God on my behalf. [31] Pray that I may be rescued from the unbelievers in Judea, that my ministry to[H] Jerusalem may be acceptable to the saints, [32] and that, by God's will, I may come to you with joy and be refreshed together with you. 2Co 1:11; Gl 5:22; Col 1:8; 4:12

[33] May the God of peace be with all of you. Amen. Rm 16:20; 2Co 13:11

Paul's Commendation of Phoebe

16 I commend to you our sister Phoebe, who is a servant[I] of the church in Cenchreae. [2] So you should welcome her in the Lord in a manner worthy of the saints and assist her in whatever matter she may require your help. For indeed she has been a benefactor of many — and of me also. Ac 18:18; 2Co 3:1

Greeting to Roman Christians

[3] Give my greetings to Prisca[J] and Aquila, my coworkers in Christ Jesus, [4] who risked their own necks

---

[A]15:19 A Roman province northwest of Greece on the eastern shore of the Adriatic Sea　[B]15:21 Is 52:15
[C]15:23 Lit *now, having no longer a place in these parts*　[D]15:24 Other mss add *I will come to you.*
[E]15:28 Lit *delivered this fruit*　[F]15:28 Or *and placed my seal of approval on this fruit for them*
[G]15:29 Other mss add *of the gospel*　[H]15:31 Lit *that my service for*　[I]16:1 Others interpret this term in a technical sense: *deacon*, or *deaconess*, or *minister*, or *courier*　[J]16:3 Traditionally, *Priscilla*, as in Ac 18:2,18,26

for my life. Not only do I thank them, but so do all the Gentile churches. ⁵ Greet also the church that meets in their home. Greet my dear friend Epaenetus, who is the first convert^A to Christ from Asia. ^{B 6} Greet Mary,^C who has worked very hard for you.^D ⁷ Greet Andronicus and Junia, my fellow Jews^E and fellow prisoners. They are noteworthy in the eyes of the apostles,^F and they were also in Christ before me. ⁸ Greet Ampliatus, my dear friend in the Lord. ⁹ Greet Urbanus, our coworker in Christ, and my dear friend Stachys. ¹⁰ Greet Apelles, who is approved in Christ. Greet those who belong to the household of Aristobulus. ¹¹ Greet Herodion, my fellow Jew.^G Greet those who belong to the household of Narcissus who are in the Lord. ¹² Greet Tryphaena and Tryphosa, who have worked hard in the Lord. Greet my dear friend Persis, who has worked very hard in the Lord. ¹³ Greet Rufus, chosen in the Lord; also his mother — and mine. ¹⁴ Greet Asyncritus, Phlegon, Hermes, Patrobas, Hermas, and the brothers and sisters who are with them. ¹⁵ Greet Philologus and Julia, Nereus and his sister, and Olympas, and all the saints who are with them. ¹⁶ Greet one another with a holy kiss. All the churches of Christ send you greetings.   Ac 18:2; Rm 8:11

Warning Against Divisive People

¹⁷ Now I urge you, brothers and sisters, to watch out for those who create divisions and obstacles contrary to the teaching that you learned. Avoid them, ¹⁸ because such people do not serve our Lord Christ but their own appetites.^H They deceive the hearts of the unsuspecting with smooth talk and flattering words.   Mt 7:15; 1Tm 1:3; 6:3

Paul's Gracious Conclusion

¹⁹ The report of your obedience has reached everyone. Therefore I rejoice over you, but I want you to be wise about what is good, and yet innocent about what is evil. ²⁰ The God of peace will soon crush Satan under your feet. The grace of our Lord Jesus be with you.   Rm 1:8

²¹ Timothy, my coworker, and Lucius, Jason, and Sosipater, my fellow countrymen, greet you.   Ac 16:1

²² I Tertius, who wrote this letter, greet you in the Lord.^I   1Co 16:21; Gl 6:11

²³ Gaius, who is host to me and to the whole church, greets you. Erastus, the city treasurer, and our brother Quartus greet you.^J   Ac 20:4

Glory to God

²⁵ Now to him who is able to strengthen you according to my gospel and the proclamation about Jesus Christ, according to the revelation of the mystery kept silent for long ages ²⁶ but now revealed and made known through the prophetic Scriptures, according to the command of the eternal God to advance the obedience of faith among all the Gentiles — ²⁷ to the only wise God, through Jesus Christ — to him be the glory forever!^K Amen.   Eph 3:20

---

^A**16:5** Lit *the firstfruits*   ^B**16:5** Other mss read *Achaia*   ^C**16:6** Or *Maria*   ^D**16:6** Other mss read *us*
^E**16:7** Or *family members*   ^F**16:7** Or *They are noteworthy among the apostles*   ^G**16:11** Or *family member*
^H**16:18** Lit *belly*   ^I**16:22** Or *letter in the Lord, greet you*   ^J**16:23** Some mss include v. 24: *The grace of our Lord Jesus Christ be with you all.*   ^K**16:25-27** Other mss have these vv. at the end of chap. 14 or 15.

1 CORINTHIANS

Greeting

1 Paul, called as an apostle of Christ Jesus by God's will, and Sosthenes our brother: Ac 13:9; Rm 1:1 ² To the church of God at Corinth, to those sanctified in Christ Jesus, called as saints, with all those in every place who call on the name of Jesus Christ our Lord — both their Lord and ours. Ac 18:1; 19:1; 2Tm 4:20 ³ Grace to you and peace from God our Father and the Lord Jesus Christ. Rm 1:7; 2Co 1:2; Gl 1:3; Eph 1:2; Php 1:2; Ti 1:4

Thanksgiving

⁴ I always thank my God for you because of the grace of God given to you in Christ Jesus, ⁵ that you were enriched in him in every way, in all speech and all knowledge. ⁶ In this way, the testimony about Christ was confirmed among you, ⁷ so that you do not lack any spiritual gift as you eagerly wait for the revelation of our Lord Jesus Christ. ⁸ He will also strengthen you to the end, so that you will be blameless in the day of our Lord Jesus Christ. ⁹ God is faithful; you were called by him into fellowship with his Son, Jesus Christ our Lord. Rm 1:8; Php 1:3

Divisions at Corinth

¹⁰ Now I urge you, brothers and sisters, in the name of our Lord Jesus Christ, that all of you agree in what you say, that there be no divisions among you, and that you be united with the same understanding and the same conviction. ¹¹ For it has been reported to me about you, my brothers and sisters, by members of Chloe's people, that there is rivalry among you. ¹² What I am saying is this: One of you says, "I belong to Paul," or "I belong to Apollos," or "I belong to Cephas," or "I belong to Christ." ¹³ Is Christ divided? Was Paul crucified for you? Or were you baptized in Paul's name? ¹⁴ I thank God^(A,B) that I baptized none of you except Crispus and Gaius, ¹⁵ so that no one can say you were baptized in my name. ¹⁶ I did, in fact, baptize the household of Stephanas; beyond that, I don't recall if I baptized anyone else. ¹⁷ For Christ did not send me to baptize, but to preach the gospel — not with eloquent wisdom, so that the cross of Christ will not be emptied of its effect. Mt 23:9-10; Jn 1:42; 1Co 12:5; Ti 3:9,13

Christ the Power and Wisdom of God

¹⁸ For the word of the cross is foolishness to those who are perishing, but it is the power of God to us who are being saved. ¹⁹ For it is written,

> **I will destroy the wisdom of the wise,**
> **and I will set aside the intelligence of the intelligent.**^(C) Is 29:14

²⁰ Where is the one who is wise? Where is the teacher of the law?^(D) Where is the debater of this age? Hasn't God made the world's wisdom foolish? ²¹ For since, in God's wisdom, the world did not know God through wisdom, God was pleased to save those who believe

^A1:14 Other mss omit *God*   ^B1:14 Or *I am thankful*   ^C1:19 Is 29:14   ^D1:20 Or *scholar* through the foolishness of what is preached. ²² For the Jews ask for signs and the Greeks seek wisdom, ²³ but we preach Christ crucified, a stumbling block to the Jews and foolishness to the Gentiles. ^A ²⁴ Yet to those who are called, both Jews and Greeks, Christ is the power of God and the wisdom of God, ²⁵ because God's foolishness is wiser than human wisdom, and God's weakness is stronger than human strength.   Mt 12:38; Lk 16:8; 23:26; 1 Co 2:2

Boasting Only in the Lord

²⁶ Brothers and sisters, consider your calling: Not many were wise from a human perspective, ^B not many powerful, not many of noble birth. ²⁷ Instead, God has chosen what is foolish in the world to shame the wise, and God has chosen what is weak in the world to shame the strong. ²⁸ God has chosen what is insignificant and despised in the world — what is viewed as nothing — to bring to nothing what is viewed as something, ²⁹ so that no one ^C may boast in his presence. ³⁰ It is from him that you are in Christ Jesus, who became wisdom from God for us — our righteousness, sanctification, and redemption, ³¹ in order that, as it is written: **Let the one who boasts, boast in the Lord.** ^D

Paul's Proclamation

2 When I came to you, brothers and sisters, announcing the mystery ^E of God to you, I did not come with brilliance of speech or wisdom. ² I decided to know nothing among you except Jesus Christ

and him crucified. ³ I came to you in weakness, in fear, and in much trembling. ⁴ My speech and my preaching were not with persuasive words of wisdom ^F but with a demonstration of the Spirit's power, ⁵ so that your faith might not be based on human wisdom but on God's power.   1 Co 1:23-24; Col 4:6; 1 Tm 2:2

Spiritual Wisdom

⁶ We do, however, speak a wisdom among the mature, but not a wisdom of this age, or of the rulers of this age, who are coming to nothing. ⁷ On the contrary, we speak God's hidden wisdom in a mystery, a wisdom God predestined before the ages for our glory. ⁸ None of the rulers of this age knew this wisdom, because if they had known it, they would not have crucified the Lord of glory. ⁹ But as it is written,

**What no eye has seen, no
  ear has heard,
  and no human heart
    has conceived —
  God has prepared
    these things for those
    who love him.** ^G   Is 52:15; 64:4

¹⁰ Now God has revealed these things to us by the Spirit, since the Spirit searches everything, even the depths of God. ¹¹ For who knows a person's thoughts ^H except his spirit within him? In the same way, no one knows the thoughts of God except the Spirit of God. ¹² Now we have not received the spirit of the world, but the Spirit who comes from God, so that we may understand what has been freely given to us by God. ¹³ We also speak these things, not in words taught by

---

^A 1:23 Other mss read *Greeks*   ^B 1:26 Lit *wise according to the flesh*   ^C 1:29 Lit *that not all flesh*
^D 1:31 Jr 9:24   ^E 2:1 Other mss read *testimony*   ^F 2:4 Other mss read *human wisdom*   ^G 2:9 Is 52:15; 64:4
^H 2:11 Or *things*

human wisdom, but in those taught by the Spirit, explaining spiritual things to spiritual people. [A] [14] But the person without the Spirit [B] does not receive what comes from God's Spirit, because it is foolishness to him; he is not able to understand it since it is evaluated [C] spiritually. [15] The spiritual person, however, can evaluate [D] everything, and yet he himself cannot be evaluated by anyone. [16] For Ps 17:3; Jn 14:26; Rm 8:39; 11:33

> who has known
> the Lord's mind,
> that he may instruct him? [E]

But we have the mind of Christ.

The Problem of Immaturity

3 For my part, brothers and sisters, I was not able to speak to you as spiritual people but as people of the flesh, as babies in Christ. [2] I gave you milk to drink, not solid food, since you were not yet ready for it. In fact, you are still not ready, [3] because you are still worldly. For since there is envy and strife [F] among you, are you not worldly and behaving like mere humans? [4] For whenever someone says, "I belong to Paul," and another, "I belong to Apollos," are you not acting like mere humans? 1Co 14:20; Ti 3:9

The Role of God's Servants

[5] What then is Apollos? What is Paul? They are servants through whom you believed, and each has the role the Lord has given. [6] I planted, Apollos watered, but God gave the growth. [7] So then neither the one who plants nor the one who waters is anything, but only God who gives the growth. [8] Now he who plants and he who waters are one, [G] and each will receive his own reward according to his own labor. [9] For we are God's coworkers. [H] You are God's field, God's building.

[10] According to God's grace that was given to me, I have laid a foundation as a skilled master builder, [I] and another builds on it. But each one is to be careful how he builds on it. [11] For no one can lay any other foundation than what has been laid down. That foundation is Jesus Christ. [12] If anyone builds on the foundation with gold, silver, costly stones, wood, hay, or straw, [13] each one's work will become obvious. For the day will disclose it, because it will be revealed by fire; the fire will test the quality of each one's work. [14] If anyone's work that he has built survives, he will receive a reward. [15] If anyone's work is burned up, he will experience [J] loss, but he himself will be saved — but only as through fire.

[16] Don't you yourselves know that you are God's temple and that the Spirit of God lives in you? [17] If anyone destroys God's temple, God will destroy him; for God's temple is holy, and that is what you are.

The Folly of Human Wisdom

[18] Let no one deceive himself. If anyone among you thinks he is wise in this age, let him become a fool so that he can become wise. [19] For the wisdom of this world is foolishness with God, since it is written, **He catches the wise in their craftiness;** [K] [20] and again, **The Lord knows**

[A] **2:13** Or *things with spiritual words*   [B] **2:14** Lit *natural person*   [C] **2:14** Or *judged,* or *discerned,* also in v. 15   [D] **2:15** Or *judge,* or *discern*   [E] **2:16** Is 40:13   [F] **3:3** Other mss add *and divisions*   [G] **3:8** Or *of equal status,* or *united in purpose*   [H] **3:9** Or *are coworkers belonging to God*   [I] **3:10** Or *wise master builder*   [J] **3:15** Or *suffer*   [K] **3:19** Jb 5:13

that the reasonings of the wise are futile.[A] [21] So let no one boast in human leaders, for everything is yours — [22] whether Paul or Apollos or Cephas or the world or life or death or things present or things to come — everything is yours, [23] and you belong to Christ, and Christ belongs to God. Is 5:21; Mt 5:22; Lk 16:8; 2Co 11:3

The Faithful Manager

4 A person should think of us in this way: as servants of Christ and managers of the mysteries of God. [2] In this regard, it is required that managers be found faithful. [3] It is of little importance to me that I should be judged by you or by any human court.[B] In fact, I don't even judge myself. [4] For I am not conscious of anything against myself, but I am not justified by this. It is the Lord who judges me. [5] So don't judge anything prematurely, before the Lord comes, who will both bring to light what is hidden in darkness and reveal the intentions of the hearts. And then praise will come to each one from God. 1Co 2:7

The Apostles' Example of Humility

[6] Now, brothers and sisters, I have applied these things to myself and Apollos for your benefit, so that you may learn from us the meaning of the saying: "Nothing beyond what is written." The purpose is that none of you will be arrogant, favoring one person over another. [7] For who makes you so superior? What do you have that you didn't receive? If, in fact, you did receive it, why do you boast as if you hadn't received it? [8] You are already full! You are already rich!

You have begun to reign as kings without us — and I wish you did reign, so that we could also reign with you! [9] For I think God has displayed us, the apostles, in last place, like men condemned to die: We have become a spectacle to the world, both to angels and to people. [10] We are fools for Christ, but you are wise in Christ! We are weak, but you are strong! You are distinguished, but we are dishonored! [11] Up to the present hour we are both hungry and thirsty; we are poorly clothed, roughly treated, homeless; [12] we labor, working with our own hands. When we are reviled, we bless; when we are persecuted, we endure it; [13] when we are slandered, we respond graciously. Even now, we are like the scum of the earth, like everyone's garbage. Ac 9:30; 18:3; Ti 3:13; 1Pt 5:14; 2Jn 8

Paul's Fatherly Care

[14] I'm not writing this to shame you, but to warn you as my dear children. [15] For you may have countless instructors in Christ, but you don't have many fathers. For I became your father in Christ Jesus through the gospel. [16] Therefore I urge you to imitate me. [17] This is why I have sent Timothy to you. He is my dearly loved and faithful child in the Lord. He will remind you about my ways in Christ Jesus, just as I teach everywhere in every church. Phm 1; 2Co 9:3; Gl 4:19; 1Th 2:11; Phm 10

[18] Now some are arrogant, as though I were not coming to you. [19] But I will come to you soon, if the Lord wills, and I will find out not the talk, but the power of those who are arrogant. [20] For the kingdom of God is not a matter of talk but of

A**3:20** Ps 94:11   B**4:3** Lit *a human day*

power. [21] What do you want? Should I come to you with a rod, or in love and a spirit of gentleness? Ac 19:21

Immoral Church Members

5 It is actually reported that there is sexual immorality among you, and the kind of sexual immorality that is not even tolerated[A] among the Gentiles — a man is sleeping with his father's wife. [2] And you are arrogant! Shouldn't you be filled with grief and remove from your congregation the one who did this? [3] Even though I am absent in the body, I am present in spirit. As one who is present with you in this way, I have already pronounced judgment on the one who has been doing such a thing. [4] When you are assembled in the name of our Lord Jesus, and I am with you in spirit, with the power of our Lord Jesus, [5] hand that one over to Satan for the destruction of the flesh, so that his spirit may be saved in the day of the Lord. Lv 18:8; 1Th 4:3; Gl 1:16

[6] Your boasting is not good. Don't you know that a little leaven[B] leavens the whole batch of dough? [7] Clean out the old leaven so that you may be a new unleavened batch, as indeed you are. For Christ our Passover lamb has been sacrificed.[C] [8] Therefore, let us observe the feast, not with old leaven or with the leaven of malice and evil, but with the unleavened bread of sincerity and truth. Lk 13:21; Gl 5:9

Church Discipline

[9] I wrote to you in a letter not to associate with sexually immoral people. [10] I did not mean the immoral people of this world or the greedy and swindlers or idolaters; otherwise you would have to leave the world. [11] But actually, I wrote[D] you not to associate with anyone who claims to be a brother or sister and is sexually immoral or greedy, an idolater or verbally abusive, a drunkard or a swindler. Do not even eat with such a person. [12] For what business is it of mine to judge outsiders? Don't you judge those who are inside? [13] God judges outsiders. **Remove the evil person from among you.**[E]   2Th 3:14

Lawsuits Among Believers

6 If any of you has a dispute against another, how dare you take it to court before the unrighteous,[F] and not before the saints? [2] Or don't you know that the saints will judge the world? And if the world is judged by you, are you unworthy to judge the trivial cases? [3] Don't you know that we will judge angels — how much more matters of this life? [4] So if you have such matters, do you appoint as your judges those who have no standing in the church? [5] I say this to your shame! Can it be that there is not one wise person among you who is able to arbitrate between fellow believers? [6] Instead, brother goes to court against brother, and that before unbelievers! Mt 18:15-17; Lk 18:9

[7] As it is, to have legal disputes against one another is already a defeat for you. Why not rather be wronged? Why not rather be cheated? [8] Instead, you yourselves do wrong and cheat — and you do this to brothers and sisters! [9] Don't you know that the unrighteous will not inherit God's kingdom?

[A]5:1 Other mss read named   [B]5:6 Or yeast, also in vv. 7, 8   [C]5:7 Other mss add for us   [D]5:11 Or But now I am writing   [E]5:13 Dt 17:7   [F]6:1 Unbelievers; v. 6

Do not be deceived: No sexually immoral people, idolaters, adulterers, or males who have sex with males,[A] [10] no thieves, greedy people, drunkards, verbally abusive people, or swindlers will inherit God's kingdom. [11] And some of you used to be like this. But you were washed, you were sanctified, you were justified in the name of the Lord Jesus Christ and by the Spirit of our God. Mk 10:19; Lk 16:10; Rm 11:12; Rv 2:11

Glorifying God in Body and Spirit

[12] "Everything is permissible for me," but not everything is beneficial. "Everything is permissible for me," but I will not be mastered by anything. [13] "Food is for the stomach and the stomach for food," and God will do away with both of them. However, the body is not for sexual immorality but for the Lord, and the Lord for the body. [14] God raised up the Lord and will also raise us up by his power. [15] Don't you know that your bodies are a part of Christ's body? So should I take a part of Christ's body and make it part of a prostitute? Absolutely not! [16] Don't you know that anyone joined to a prostitute is one body with her? For Scripture says, **The two will become one flesh.**[B] [17] But anyone joined to the Lord is one spirit with him. Mk 5:30; Jn 18:31; 1Th 4:3; 1Tm 6:8

[18] Flee sexual immorality! Every other sin[C] a person commits is outside the body, but the person who is sexually immoral sins against his own body. [19] Don't you know that your body is a temple of the Holy Spirit who is in you, whom you have from God? You are not your own, [20] for you were bought at a price. So glorify God with your body.[D] Lk 1:21; Rm 8:9,23; 1Co 10:8; Jms 4:7; Jd 19

Principles of Marriage

7 Now in response to the matters you wrote[E] about: "It is good for a man not to use[F] a woman for sex." [2] But because sexual immorality is so common,[G] each man should have sexual relations with his own wife, and each woman should have sexual relations with her own husband. [3] A husband should fulfill his marital duty to his wife, and likewise a wife to her husband. [4] A wife does not have the right over her own body, but her husband does. In the same way, a husband does not have the right over his own body, but his wife does. [5] Do not deprive one another — except when you agree for a time, to devote yourselves to[H] prayer. Then come together again; otherwise, Satan may tempt you because of your lack of self-control. [6] I say this as a concession, not as a command. [7] I wish that all people were as I am. But each has his own gift from God, one person has this gift, another has that. Mt 1:6; Rm 13:7; 1Th 4:3; 1Pt 3:1

A Word to the Unmarried

[8] I say to the unmarried[I] and to widows: It is good for them if they remain as I am. [9] But if they do not have self-control, they should marry, since it is better to marry than to burn with desire. 1Co 9:25; Jms 1:27

[A]6:9 Both passive and active participants in homosexual acts　[B]6:16 Gn 2:24　[C]6:18 Lit *Every sin*　[D]6:20 Other mss add *and in your spirit, which belong to God.*　[E]7:1 Other mss add *to me*　[F]7:1 Lit *"It is good for a man not to touch a woman*　[G]7:2 Lit *because of immoralities*　[H]7:5 Other mss add *fasting and to*　[I]7:8 Or *widowers*

About Married People

¹⁰ To the married I give this command — not I, but the Lord — a wife is not to leaveᴬ her husband. ¹¹ But if she does leave, she must remain unmarried or be reconciled to her husband — and a husband is not to divorce his wife. ¹² But I (not the Lord) say to the rest: If any brother has an unbelieving wife and she is willing to live with him, he must not divorce her. ¹³ Also, if any woman has an unbelieving husband and he is willing to live with her, she must not divorce her husband. ¹⁴ For the unbelieving husband is made holy by the wife, and the unbelieving wife is made holy by the husband.ᴮ Otherwise your children would be unclean, but as it is they are holy. ¹⁵ But if the unbeliever leaves, let him leave. A brother or a sister is not bound in such cases. God has called youᶜ to live in peace. ¹⁶ Wife, for all you know, you might save your husband. Husband, for all you know, you might save your wife.ᴰ Dt 22:19; Ac 9:30; 1Tm 5:14

Various Situations of Life

¹⁷ Let each one live his life in the situation the Lord assigned when God called him.ᴱ This is what I command in all the churches. ¹⁸ Was anyone already circumcised when he was called? He should not undo his circumcision. Was anyone called while uncircumcised? He should not get circumcised. ¹⁹ Circumcision does not matter and uncircumcision does not matter. Keeping God's commands is what matters. ²⁰ Let each of you remain in the situationᶠ in which he was called. ²¹ Were you called while a slave? Don't let it concern you. But if you can become free, by all means take the opportunity.ᴳ ²² For he who is called by the Lord as a slave is the Lord's freedman. Likewise he who is called as a free man is Christ's slave. ²³ You were bought at a price; do not become slaves of people. ²⁴ Brothers and sisters, each person is to remain with God in the situation in which he was called. Rm 1:1; Col 3:15

About the Unmarried and Widows

²⁵ Now about virgins:ᴴ I have no command from the Lord, but I do give an opinion as one who by the Lord's mercy is faithful. ²⁶ Because of the present distress, I think that it is good for a man to remain as he is. ²⁷ Are you bound to a wife? Do not seek to be released. Are you released from a wife? Do not seek a wife. ²⁸ However, if you do get married, you have not sinned, and if a virginᴵ marries, she has not sinned. But such people will have trouble in this life,ᴶ and I am trying to spare you. Nm 12:7; Mt 5:7; Mk 5:19; Lk 1:50; 1Tm 5:14

²⁹ This is what I mean, brothers and sisters: The time is limited, so from now on those who have wives should be as though they had none, ³⁰ those who weep as though they did not weep, those who rejoice as though they did not rejoice, those who buy as though they didn't own anything, ³¹ and those who use the

---

ᴬ**7:10** Or *separate from*, or *divorce*   ᴮ**7:14** Lit *the brother*   ᶜ**7:15** Other mss read *us*   ᴰ**7:16** Or *Wife, how do you know that you will save your husband? Husband, how do you know that you will save your wife?*   ᴱ**7:17** Lit *called each*   ᶠ**7:20** Lit *in the calling*   ᴳ**7:21** Or *But even though you can become free, make the most of your position as a slave*   ᴴ**7:25** Or *betrothed*, or *those not yet married*   ᴵ**7:28** Or *betrothed woman*   ᴶ**7:28** Lit *in the flesh* world as though they did not make full use of it. For this world in its current form is passing away.

³² I want you to be without concerns. The unmarried man is concerned about the things of the Lord — how he may please the Lord. ³³ But the married man is concerned about the things of the world — how he may please his wife — ³⁴ and his interests are divided. The unmarried woman or virgin is concerned about the things of the Lord, so that she may be holy both in body and in spirit. But the married woman is concerned about the things of the world — how she may please her husband. ³⁵ I am saying this for your own benefit, not to put a restraint on you, but to promote what is proper and so that you may be devoted to the Lord without distraction. 1Th 4:1; 1Tm 5:5

³⁶ If any man thinks he is acting improperly toward the virgin he is engaged to,ᴬ if she is getting beyond the usual age for marriage, and he feels he should marry — he can do what he wants. He is not sinning; they can get married. ³⁷ But he who stands firm in his heart (who is under no compulsion, but has control over his own will) and has decided in his heart to keep her as his fiancée, will do well. ³⁸ So then he who marriesᴮ his fiancée does well, but he who does not marryᶜ will do better. Jn 1:13

³⁹ A wife is boundᴰ as long as her husband is living. But if her husband dies, she is free to be married to anyone she wants — only in the Lord. ⁴⁰ But she is happier if she remains as she is, in my opinion. And I think that I also have the Spirit of God.

Food Offered to Idols

8 Now about food sacrificed to idols: We know that "we all have knowledge." Knowledge puffs up, but love builds up. ² If anyone thinks he knows anything, he does not yet know it as he ought to know it. ³ But if anyone loves God, he is known by him. Ac 15:29; 21:25; 1Co 10:19

⁴ About eating food sacrificed to idols, then, we know that "an idol is nothing in the world,"ᴱ and that "there is no God but one." ⁵ For even if there are so-called gods, whether in heaven or on earth — as there are many "gods" and many "lords" — ⁶ yet for us there is one God, the Father. All things are from him, and we exist for him. And there is one Lord, Jesus Christ. All things are through him, and we exist through him. Dt 6:4; Mt 5:16; 2Th 2:4

⁷ However, not everyone has this knowledge. Some have been so used to idolatry up until now that when they eat food sacrificed to an idol, their conscience, being weak, is defiled. ⁸ Food will not bring us close to God.ᶠ We are not worse off if we don't eat, and we are not better if we do eat. ⁹ But be careful that this right of yours in no way becomes a stumbling block to the weak. ¹⁰ For if someone sees you, the one who has knowledge, dining in an idol's temple, won't his weak conscience be encouragedᴳ to eat food offered to idols? ¹¹ So the weak person, the brother or sister for whom Christ died, is ruinedᴴ by your knowledge. ¹² Now when

---

ᴬ**7:36** Or *toward his virgin daughter*   ᴮ**7:38** Or *marries off*   ᶜ**7:38** Or *marry her off*   ᴰ**7:39** Other mss add *by law*   ᴱ**8:4** Or *an idol has no real existence*   ᶠ**8:8** Or *bring us before* (the judgment seat of) *God*   ᴳ**8:10** Or *built up*   ᴴ**8:11** Or *destroyed* you sin like this against brothers and sisters and wound their weak conscience, you are sinning against Christ. [13] Therefore, if food causes my brother or sister to fall, I will never again eat meat, so that I won't cause my brother or sister to fall.   Ex 23:33; Jn 11:51; Rm 8:34; 14:17,20

Paul's Example as an Apostle

9 Am I not free? Am I not an apostle? Have I not seen Jesus our Lord? Are you not my work in the Lord? [2] If I am not an apostle to others, at least I am to you, because you are the seal of my apostleship in the Lord.   Rv 5:1

[3] My defense to those who examine me is this: [4] Don't we have the right to eat and drink? [5] Don't we have the right to be accompanied by a believing wife[A] like the other apostles, the Lord's brothers, and Cephas? [6] Or do only Barnabas and I have no right to refrain from working? [7] Who serves as a soldier at his own expense? Who plants a vineyard and does not eat its fruit? Or who shepherds a flock and does not drink the milk from the flock?   Jn 1:42; Ac 4:36; 2Th 3:8-9; Jd 17

[8] Am I saying this from a human perspective? Doesn't the law also say the same thing? [9] For it is written in the law of Moses, **Do not muzzle an ox while it treads out grain.**[B] Is God really concerned about oxen? [10] Isn't he really saying it for our sake? Yes, this is written for our sake, because he who plows ought to plow in hope, and he who threshes should thresh in hope of sharing the crop. [11] If we have sown spiritual things for you, is it too much if we reap material benefits from you? [12] If others have this right to receive benefits from you, don't we even more? Nevertheless, we have not made use of this right; instead, we endure everything so that we will not hinder the gospel of Christ.   Dt 25:4; Lk 13:15

[13] Don't you know that those who perform the temple services eat the food from the temple, and those who serve at the altar share in the offerings of the altar? [14] In the same way, the Lord has commanded that those who preach the gospel should earn their living by the gospel.   Lv 6:16,26; 7:6,31-32; Nm 5:9-10; Dt 18:1

[15] For my part I have used none of these rights, nor have I written these things that they may be applied in my case. For it would be better for me to die than for anyone to deprive me of my boast! [16] For if I preach the gospel, I have no reason to boast, because I am compelled to preach[C] — and woe to me if I do not preach the gospel! [17] For if I do this willingly, I have a reward, but if unwillingly, I am entrusted with a commission. [18] What then is my reward? To preach the gospel and offer it free of charge and not make full use of my rights in the gospel.   Lk 16:11; 2Co 11:7; 12:13

[19] Although I am free from all and not anyone's slave, I have made myself a slave to everyone, in order to win more people. [20] To the Jews I became like a Jew, to win Jews; to those under the law, like one under the law — though I myself am not under the law[D] — to win those under the law. [21] To those who are without the law, like one without the law — though I am not without God's law but under the law of

---

A**9:5** Lit *a sister as a wife*   B**9:9** Dt 25:4   C**9:16** Lit *because necessity is laid upon me*   D**9:20** Other mss omit *though I myself am not under the law*

Christ — to win those without the law. ²² To the weak I became weak, in order to win the weak. I have become all things to all people, so that I may by every possible means save some. ²³ Now I do all this because of the gospel, so that I may share in the blessings. Ac 16:3; 1Pt 3:1

²⁴ Don't you know that the runners in a stadium all race, but only one receives the prize? Run in such a way to win the prize. ²⁵ Now everyone who competes exercises self-control in everything. They do it to receive a perishable crown, but we an imperishable crown. ²⁶ So I do not run like one who runs aimlessly or box like one beating the air. ²⁷ Instead, I discipline my body and bring it under strict control, so that after preaching to others, I myself will not be disqualified. Col 2:18; Jd 3

Warnings from Israel's Past

10 Now I do not want you to be unaware, brothers and sisters, that our ancestors were all under the cloud, all passed through the sea, ² and all were baptized into Moses in the cloud and in the sea. ³ They all ate the same spiritual food, ⁴ and all drank the same spiritual drink. For they drank from the spiritual rock that followed them, and that rock was Christ. ⁵ Nevertheless God was not pleased with most of them, since they were struck down in the wilderness. Ex 13:21; Ps 44:1; Ac 7:11

⁶ Now these things took place as examples for us, so that we will not desire evil things as they did. ᴬ ⁷ Don't become idolaters as some of them were; as it is written,

The people sat down to eat and drink, and got up to party. ᴮ,ᶜ ⁸ Let us not commit sexual immorality as some of them did, ᴰ and in a single day twenty-three thousand people died. ⁹ Let us not test Christ as some of them did ᴱ and were destroyed by snakes. ¹⁰ And don't complain as some of them did, ᶠ and were killed by the destroyer. ᴳ ¹¹ These things happened to them as examples, and they were written for our instruction, on whom the ends of the ages ᴴ have come. ¹² So, whoever thinks he stands must be careful not to fall. ¹³ No temptation has come upon you except what is common to humanity. But God is faithful; he will not allow you to be tempted beyond what you are able, but with the temptation he will also provide a way out so that you may be able to bear it. Mt 27:23

Warning Against Idolatry

¹⁴ So then, my dear friends, flee from idolatry. ¹⁵ I am speaking as to sensible people. Judge for yourselves what I am saying. ¹⁶ The cup of blessing that we bless, is it not a sharing in the blood of Christ? The bread that we break, is it not a sharing in the body of Christ? ¹⁷ Because there is one bread, we who are many are one body, since all of us share the one bread. ¹⁸ Consider the people of Israel. ᴵ Do not those who eat the sacrifices participate in the altar? ¹⁹ What am I saying then? That food sacrificed to idols is anything, or that an idol is anything? ²⁰ No, but I do say that what they ᴶ sacrifice, they sacrifice to demons

ᴬ10:6 Lit *they desired*　　ᴮ10:7 Or *to dance*　　ᶜ10:7 Ex 32:6　　ᴰ10:8 Lit *them committed sexual immorality*　　ᴱ10:9 Lit *them tested*　　ᶠ10:10 Lit *them complained*　　ᴳ10:10 Or *the destroying angel*　　ᴴ10:11 Or *goals of the ages,* or *culmination of the ages*　　ᴵ10:18 Lit *Look at Israel according to the flesh*　　ᴶ10:20 Other mss read *Gentiles* and not to God. I do not want you to be participants with demons! ²¹ You cannot drink the cup of the Lord and the cup of demons. You cannot share in the Lord's table and the table of demons. ²² Or are we provoking the Lord to jealousy? Are we stronger than he?   Mt 26:27

Christian Liberty

²³ "Everything is permissible,"ᴬ but not everything is beneficial. "Everything is permissible,"ᴬ but not everything builds up. ²⁴ No one is to seek his own good, but the good of the other person.   Mk 10:45; Php 2:4

²⁵ Eat everything that is sold in the meat market, without raising questions for the sake of conscience, ²⁶ since **the earth is the Lord's, and all that is in it.**ᴮ ²⁷ If any of the unbelievers invites you over and you want to go, eat everything that is set before you, without raising questions for the sake of conscience. ²⁸ But if someone says to you, "This is food from a sacrifice," do not eat it, out of consideration for the one who told you, and for the sake of conscience.ᶜ ²⁹ I do not mean your own conscience, but the other person's. For why is my freedom judged by another person's conscience? ³⁰ If I partake with thanksgiving, why am I criticized because of something for which I give thanks?   Ps 24:1; Mk 13:19

³¹ So, whether you eat or drink, or whatever you do, do everything for the glory of God. ³² Give no offense to Jews or Greeks or the church of God, ³³ just as I also try to please everyone in everything, not seeking my own benefit, but the benefit of many, so that they may be saved.

11 ¹ Imitate me, as I also imitate Christ.   Php 2:5; 1Pt 2:21

Instructions About Head Coverings

² Now I praise youᴰ because you remember me in everything and hold fast to the traditions just as I delivered them to you. ³ But I want you to know that Christ is the head of every man, and the man is the head of the woman,ᴱ and God is the head of Christ. ⁴ Every man who prays or prophesies with something on his head dishonors his head. ⁵ Every woman who prays or prophesies with her head uncovered dishonors her head, since that is one and the same as having her head shaved. ⁶ For if a woman doesn't cover her head, she should have her hair cut off. But if it is disgraceful for a woman to have her hair cut off or her head shaved, let her head be covered.   2Th 2:15; 3:6; Jd 3

⁷ A man should not cover his head, because he is the image and glory of God. So too, woman is the glory of man. ⁸ For man did not come from woman, but woman came from man. ⁹ Neither was man created for the sake of woman, but woman for the sake of man. ¹⁰ This is why a woman should have a symbol of authority on her head, because of the angels. ¹¹ In the Lord, however, woman is not independent of man, and man is not independent of woman. ¹² For just as woman came from man, so man comes through woman, and all things come from God.

¹³ Judge for yourselves: Is it proper for a woman to pray to God with her head uncovered? ¹⁴ Does not even nature itself teach you that if

---

ᴬ**10:23** Other mss add *for me*   ᴮ**10:26** Ps 24:1   ᶜ**10:28** Other mss add *"For the earth is the Lord's and all that is in it."*   ᴰ**11:2** Other mss add *brothers,*   ᴱ**11:3** Or *the husband is the head of the wife*

THE BOOKS OF
PAUL'S LETTERS

The books of Paul's Letters make up one of the ten divisions of the Bible. Paul wrote thirteen letters to churches and individuals to help them know what God wanted them to do and how He wanted them to live like Christ.

ROMANS was written to Christians in Rome and is about living in ways that please God because of faith in Him. Romans also recognizes the power of Christ's life, death, and resurrection to bring us back to God.

FIRST & SECOND CORINTHIANS were written to the Christians at Corinth in Greece. In the first letter, Paul wrote about sin in the church at Corinth and stressed church unity. In the second letter, Paul defended his own authority and spoke against the false teachers in Corinth. Paul stresses the importance of the church and its members to live by the example of Christ.

GALATIANS was written to the Christians in the province of Galatia, in Asia Minor. The primary theme is the freedom of the gospel through Christ rather than being bound by the law.

EPHESIANS was written to teach Christians that they have been saved by grace and should live how God wants them to live so that they can stand against the ways of Satan. This way of living is best represented in Jesus Christ.

PHILIPPIANS, written to the church in Philippi, thanked the believers for their kindnesses toward Paul and explained true joy in Christ.

COLOSSIANS encouraged the church in Colossae to obey Jesus' teachings and warned the people to stay away from teachings that are not true.

FIRST & SECOND THESSALONIANS addressed the church in Thessalonica in Macedonia. In the first letter, Paul praised the church's faithfulness and helped the church understand more about Christ's return. The second letter told about events that will happen before Jesus' return and stressed patience.

FIRST & SECOND TIMOTHY are letters of encouragement and wisdom that Paul wrote to his young helper Timothy. The first letter is about church leadership. The second letter gave final instructions and encouragement to Timothy. These letters highlight Christ's reason for coming to earth, salvation through grace.

TITUS is a letter to a young church leader on the island of Crete. In this letter, Paul instructed and encouraged Titus to live right and do good things because of what Christ has done for us.

PHILEMON was written to a person of that name in Colossae. Paul encouraged Philemon to forgive his runaway slave Onesimus and treat him as a brother in Christ. Paul also reminds us that Christ is available to all.

PAUL'S MISSIONARY JOURNEYS

City

Paul's first missionary journey

Paul's second missionary journey

Paul's third missionary journey

Paul's voyage to Rome

Paul resumes his missionary travels

Paul and Barnabas mistaken for gods

Proconsul Sergius Paulus converted

Porcius Festus sends Paul to Rome to appeal to Caesar

Jerusalem Conference A.D. 49

Paul restores life to young Eutychus

Luke joins Paul

Paul speaks to the Areopagus

Ship lost in storm

Paul spends two years preaching the gospel as he awaits his appeal to Nero a man has long hair it is a disgrace to him, [15] but that if a woman has long hair, it is her glory? For her hair is given to her[A] as a covering. [16] If anyone wants to argue about this, we have no other[B] custom, nor do the churches of God.　Jn 5:22-30

The Lord's Supper

[17] Now in giving this instruction I do not praise you, since you come together not for the better but for the worse. [18] For to begin with, I hear that when you come together as a church there are divisions among you, and in part I believe it. [19] Indeed, it is necessary that there be factions among you, so that those who are approved may be recognized among you. [20] When you come together, then, it is not to eat the Lord's Supper. [21] For at the meal, each one eats his own supper.[C] So one person is hungry while another gets drunk! [22] Don't you have homes in which to eat and drink? Or do you despise the church of God and humiliate those who have nothing? What should I say to you? Should I praise you? I do not praise you in this matter!

[23] For I received from the Lord what I also passed on to you: On the night when he was betrayed, the Lord Jesus took bread, [24] and when he had given thanks, broke it, and said,[D] "This is my body, which is[E] for you. Do this in remembrance of me."　Lk 22:19; Jd 3

[25] In the same way also he took the cup, after supper, and said, "This cup is the new covenant in my blood. Do this, as often as you drink it, in remembrance of me."[26] For as often as you eat this bread and drink the cup, you proclaim the Lord's death until he comes.　Lk 22:20; Jn 6:54; Php 2:8; 3:10

Self-Examination

[27] So then, whoever eats the bread or drinks the cup of the Lord in an unworthy manner will be guilty of sin against the body[F] and blood of the Lord. [28] Let a person examine himself; in this way let him eat the bread and drink from the cup. [29] For whoever eats and drinks without recognizing the body,[G] eats and drinks judgment on himself. [30] This is why many are sick and ill among you, and many have fallen asleep. [31] If we were properly judging ourselves, we would not be judged, [32] but when we are judged by the Lord, we are disciplined, so that we may not be condemned with the world.　Mk 12:40; Jn 11:11; Ac 7:60; 1Jn 5:16

[33] Therefore, my brothers and sisters, when you come together to eat, welcome one another.[H] [34] If anyone is hungry, he should eat at home, so that when you gather together you will not come under judgment. I will give instructions about the other matters whenever I come.　1Co 4:19

Diversity of Spiritual Gifts

12 Now concerning spiritual gifts:[I] brothers and sisters, I do not want you to be unaware. [2] You know that when you were pagans, you used to be enticed and led astray by mute idols. [3] Therefore I want you to know that no one speaking by the Spirit of God

---

[A]**11:15** Other mss omit *to her*　[B]**11:16** Or *no such*　[C]**11:21** Or *eats his own supper ahead of others*
[D]**11:24** Other mss add *"Take, eat.*　[E]**11:24** Other mss add *broken*　[F]**11:27** Lit *be guilty of the body*
[G]**11:29** Other mss read *drinks unworthily, not discerning the Lord's body*　[H]**11:33** Or *wait for one another*
[I]**12:1** Or *spiritual things*, or *spiritual people*

says, "Jesus is cursed," and no one can say, "Jesus is Lord," except by the Holy Spirit. Ac 8:32; 1Co 14:10; 2Pt 2:16 ⁴ Now there are different gifts, but the same Spirit. ⁵ There are different ministries, but the same Lord. ⁶ And there are different activities, but the same God produces each gift in each person. ⁷ A manifestation of the Spirit is given to each person for the common good: ⁸ to one is given a message of wisdom through the Spirit, to another, a message of knowledge by the same Spirit, ⁹ to another, faith by the same Spirit, to another, gifts of healing by the one Spirit, ¹⁰ to another, the performing of miracles, to another, prophecy, to another, distinguishing between spirits, to another, different kinds of tongues, ᴬ to another, interpretation of tongues. ¹¹ One and the same Spirit is active in all these, distributing to each person as he wills.

Unity Yet Diversity in the Body

¹² For just as the body is one and has many parts, and all the parts of that body, though many, are one body — so also is Christ. ¹³ For we were all baptized by ᴮ one Spirit into one body — whether Jews or Greeks, whether slaves or free — and we were all given one Spirit to drink. ¹⁴ Indeed, the body is not one part but many. ¹⁵ If the foot should say, "Because I'm not a hand, I don't belong to the body," it is not for that reason any less a part of the body. ¹⁶ And if the ear should say, "Because I'm not an eye, I don't belong to the body," it is not for that reason any less a part of the body. ¹⁷ If the whole body were an eye, where would the hearing be? If the whole body were an ear, where would the sense of smell be? ¹⁸ But as it is, God has arranged each one of the parts in the body just as he wanted. ¹⁹ And if they were all the same part, where would the body be? ²⁰ As it is, there are many parts, but one body. ²¹ The eye cannot say to the hand, "I don't need you!" Or again, the head can't say to the feet, "I don't need you!" ²² On the contrary, those parts of the body that are weaker are indispensable. ²³ And those parts of the body that we consider less honorable, we clothe these with greater honor, and our unrespectable parts are treated with greater respect, ²⁴ which our respectable parts do not need.

Instead, God has put the body together, giving greater honor to the less honorable, ²⁵ so that there would be no division in the body, but that the members would have the same concern for each other. ²⁶ So if one member suffers, all the members suffer with it; if one member is honored, all the members rejoice with it. 1Co 1:10

²⁷ Now you are the body of Christ, and individual members of it. ²⁸ And God has appointed these in the church: first apostles, second prophets, third teachers, next miracles, then gifts of healing, helping, administrating, various kinds of tongues. ᶜ ²⁹ Are all apostles? Are all prophets? Are all teachers? Do all do miracles? ³⁰ Do all have gifts of healing? Do all speak in other tongues? Do all interpret? ³¹ But desire the greater gifts. And I will show you an even better way. Mt 16:18; 1Co 14:4; Eph 1:23; Col 1:18; Jms 3:1

Love: The Superior Way

13 If I speak human or angelic tongues ᴰ but do not have love, I am a noisy gong or a clanging cymbal. ² If I have the gift of

---

ᴬ 12:10 languages   ᴮ 12:13 Or *with*, or *in*   ᶜ 12:28 languages, also in v. 30   ᴰ 13:1 languages, also in v. 8

prophecy and understand all mysteries and all knowledge, and if I have all faith so that I can move mountains but do not have love, I am nothing. ³ And if I give away all my possessions, and if I give over my body in order to boast ᴬ but do not have love, I gain nothing.

⁴ Love is patient, love is kind. Love does not envy, is not boastful, is not arrogant, ⁵ is not rude, is not self-seeking, is not irritable, and does not keep a record of wrongs. ⁶ Love finds no joy in unrighteousness but rejoices in the truth. ⁷ It bears all things, believes all things, hopes all things, endures all things.

⁸ Love never ends. But as for prophecies, they will come to an end; as for tongues, they will cease; as for knowledge, it will come to an end. ⁹ For we know in part, and we prophesy in part, ¹⁰ but when the perfect comes, the partial will come to an end. ¹¹ When I was a child, I spoke like a child, I thought like a child, I reasoned like a child. When I became a man, I put aside childish things. ¹² For now we see only a reflection ᴮ as in a mirror, but then face to face. Now I know in part, but then I will know fully, as I am fully known. ¹³ Now these three remain: faith, hope, and love — but the greatest of these is love.

Prophecy: A Superior Gift

14 Pursue love and desire spiritual gifts, and especially that you may prophesy. ² For the person who speaks in another tongue ᶜ is not speaking to people but to God, since no one understands him; he speaks mysteries in the Spirit. ᴰ ³ On the other hand, the person who prophesies speaks to people for their strengthening, ᴱ encouragement, and consolation. ⁴ The person who speaks in another tongue builds himself up, but the one who prophesies builds up the church. ⁵ I wish all of you spoke in other tongues, ᶠ but even more that you prophesied. The person who prophesies is greater than the person who speaks in tongues, unless he interprets so that the church may be built up. 1Co 12:10

⁶ So now, brothers and sisters, if I come to you speaking in other tongues, how will I benefit you unless I speak to you with a revelation or knowledge or prophecy or teaching? ⁷ Even lifeless instruments that produce sounds — whether flute or harp — if they don't make a distinction in the notes, how will what is played on the flute or harp be recognized? ⁸ In fact, if the bugle makes an unclear sound, who will prepare for battle? ⁹ In the same way, unless you use your tongue for intelligible speech, how will what is spoken be known? For you will be speaking into the air. ¹⁰ There are doubtless many different kinds of languages in the world, none is without meaning. ¹¹ Therefore, if I do not know the meaning of the language, I will be a foreigner ᴳ to the speaker, and the speaker will be a foreigner to me. ¹² So also you — since you are zealous for spiritual gifts, ᴴ seek to excel in building up the church. 1Pt 4:13; Rv 5:8; 14:2

¹³ Therefore the person who speaks in another tongue should

pray that he can interpret. ¹⁴ For if I pray in another tongue, my spirit prays, but my understanding is unfruitful. ¹⁵ What then? I will pray with the spirit, and I will also pray with my understanding. I will sing praise with the spirit, and I will also sing praise with my understanding. ¹⁶ Otherwise, if you praise with the spirit, ᴬ how will the outsider ᴮ say "Amen" at your giving of thanks, since he does not know what you are saying? ¹⁷ For you may very well be giving thanks, but the other person is not being built up. ¹⁸ I thank God that I speak in other tongues more than all of you; ¹⁹ yet in the church I would rather speak five words with my understanding, in order to teach others also, than ten thousand words in another tongue. Ps 51:12; Gl 5:22; Ti 3:14

²⁰ Brothers and sisters, don't be childish in your thinking, but be infants in regard to evil and adult in your thinking. ²¹ It is written in the law, Ps 131:2; Is 28:9; Mt 18:3; Rm 16:19

I will speak to this people by people of other tongues and by the lips of foreigners, and even then, they will not listen to me, ᶜ Is 28:11-12

says the Lord. ²² Speaking in other tongues, then, is intended as a sign, not for believers but for unbelievers, while prophecy is not for unbelievers but for believers. ²³ If, therefore, the whole church assembles together and all are speaking in other tongues and people who are outsiders or unbelievers come in, will they not say that you are out of your minds? ²⁴ But if all are prophesying and some unbeliever

or outsider comes in, he is convicted by all and is called to account by all. ²⁵ The secrets of his heart will be revealed, and as a result he will fall facedown and worship God, proclaiming, "God is really among you." Is 45:14; Zch 8:23

Order in Church Meetings

²⁶ What then, brothers and sisters? Whenever you come together, each one ᴰ has a hymn, a teaching, a revelation, another tongue, or an interpretation. Everything is to be done for building up. ²⁷ If anyone speaks in another tongue, there are to be only two, or at the most three, each in turn, and let someone interpret. ²⁸ But if there is no interpreter, that person is to keep silent in the church and speak to himself and God. ²⁹ Two or three prophets should speak, and the others should evaluate. ³⁰ But if something has been revealed to another person sitting there, the first prophet should be silent. ³¹ For you can all prophesy one by one, so that everyone may learn and everyone may be encouraged. ³² And the prophets' spirits are subject to the prophets, ³³ since God is not a God of disorder but of peace. Lk 16:25; 1Co 12:10; 1Jn 4:1

As in all the churches of the saints, ³⁴ the women ᴱ should be silent in the churches, for they are not permitted to speak, but are to submit themselves, as the law also says. ³⁵ If they want to learn something, let them ask their own husbands at home, since it is disgraceful for a woman to speak in the church. ³⁶ Or did the word of God originate from you, or did it come to you only? Eph 6:18; 1Tm 2:11-12

ᴬ**14:16** Or praise by the Spirit   ᴮ**14:16** Lit the one filling the place of the uninformed   ᶜ**14:21** Is 28:11-12
ᴰ**14:26** Other mss add of you   ᴱ**14:34** Other mss read your women

[37] If anyone thinks he is a prophet or spiritual, he should recognize that what I write to you is the Lord's command. [38] If anyone ignores this, he will be ignored. [A] [39] So then, my brothers and sisters, be eager to prophesy, and do not forbid speaking in other tongues. [40] But everything is to be done decently and in order. Nm 25:13; Rm 13:13; Gl 4:17

Resurrection Essential to the Gospel

15 Now I want to make clear for you, brothers and sisters, the gospel I preached to you, which you received, on which you have taken your stand [2] and by which you are being saved, if you hold to the message I preached to you — unless you believed in vain. [3] For I passed on to you as most important what I also received: that Christ died for our sins according to the Scriptures, [4] that he was buried, that he was raised on the third day according to the Scriptures, [5] and that he appeared to Cephas, then to the Twelve. [6] Then he appeared to over five hundred brothers and sisters at one time; most of them are still alive, but some have fallen asleep. [7] Then he appeared to James, then to all the apostles. [8] Last of all, as to one born at the wrong time, [B] he also appeared to me. Pr 24:16; Gl 4:11

[9] For I am the least of the apostles, not worthy to be called an apostle, because I persecuted the church of God. [10] But by the grace of God I am what I am, and his grace toward me was not in vain. On the contrary, I worked harder than any of them, yet not I, but the grace of God that

was with me. [11] Whether, then, it is I or they, so we proclaim and so you have believed. Eph 3:8; 1Tm 1:16-17

Resurrection Essential to the Faith

[12] Now if Christ is proclaimed as raised from the dead, how can some of you say, "There is no resurrection of the dead"? [13] If there is no resurrection of the dead, then not even Christ has been raised; [14] and if Christ has not been raised, then our proclamation is in vain, and so is your faith. [C] [15] Moreover, we are found to be false witnesses about God, because we have testified wrongly about God that he raised up Christ — whom he did not raise up, if in fact the dead are not raised. [16] For if the dead are not raised, not even Christ has been raised. [17] And if Christ has not been raised, your faith is worthless; you are still in your sins. [18] Those, then, who have fallen asleep in Christ have also perished. [19] If we have put our hope in Christ for this life only, we should be pitied more than anyone. Mt 17:9; 22:23; Mk 12:18; Lk 20:27; Ac 23:8

Christ's Resurrection Guarantees Ours

[20] But as it is, Christ has been raised from the dead, the firstfruits of those who have fallen asleep. [21] For since death came through a man, the resurrection of the dead also comes through a man. [22] For just as in Adam all die, so also in Christ all will be made alive. Ex 23:19; Lv 2:12

[23] But each in his own order: Christ, the firstfruits; afterward, at his coming, those who belong

[A] **14:38** Other mss read *he should be ignored* [B] **15:8** Or *one whose birth was unusual* [C] **15:14** Or *proclamation is useless, and your faith also is useless*, or *proclamation is empty, and your faith also is empty* to Christ. ²⁴ Then comes the end, when he hands over the kingdom to God the Father, when he abolishes all rule and all authority and power. ²⁵ For he must reign until he puts all his enemies under his feet. ²⁶ The last enemy to be abolished is death. ²⁷ For **God has put everything under his feet.** ᴬ Now when it says "everything" is put under him, it is obvious that he who puts everything under him is the exception. ²⁸ When everything is subject to Christ, then the Son himself will also be subject to the one who subjected everything to him, so that God may be all in all. 1Th 4:17

Resurrection Supported by Christian Experience

²⁹ Otherwise what will they do who are being baptized for the dead? ᴮ If the dead are not raised at all, then why are people baptized for them? ᶜ ³⁰ Why are we in danger every hour? ³¹ I face death every day, as surely as I may boast about you, brothers and sisters, in Christ Jesus our Lord. ³² If I fought wild beasts in Ephesus as a mere man, what good did that do me? If the dead are not raised, **Let us eat and drink, for tomorrow we die.** ᴰ ³³ Do not be deceived: "Bad company corrupts good morals." ³⁴ Come to your senses ᴱ and stop sinning; for some people are ignorant about God. I say this to your shame. Rm 8:36; Eph 1:1

The Nature of the Resurrection Body

³⁵ But someone will ask, "How are the dead raised? What kind of body will they have when they come?" ³⁶ You fool! What you sow does not come to life unless it dies. ³⁷ And as for what you sow — you are not sowing the body that will be, but only a seed, perhaps of wheat or another grain. ³⁸ But God gives it a body as he wants, and to each of the seeds its own body. ³⁹ Not all flesh is the same flesh; there is one flesh for humans, another for animals, another for birds, and another for fish. ⁴⁰ There are heavenly bodies and earthly bodies, but the splendor of the heavenly bodies is different from that of the earthly ones. ⁴¹ There is a splendor of the sun, another of the moon, and another of the stars; in fact, one star differs from another star in splendor. ⁴² So it is with the resurrection of the dead: Sown in corruption, raised in incorruption; ⁴³ sown in dishonor, raised in glory; sown in weakness, raised in power; ⁴⁴ sown a natural body, raised a spiritual body. If there is a natural body, there is also a spiritual body. ⁴⁵ So it is written, **The first man Adam became a living being;** ᶠ the last Adam became a life-giving spirit. ⁴⁶ However, the spiritual is not first, but the natural, then the spiritual. Pr 16:9; Jn 12:24

⁴⁷ The first man was from the earth, a man of dust; the second man is ᴳ from heaven. ⁴⁸ Like the man of dust, so are those who are of the dust; like the man of heaven, so are those who are of heaven. ⁴⁹ And just as we have borne the image of the man of dust, we will also bear the image of the man of heaven. Gn 2:7; 3:19; Ps 90:3; Php 3:20-21; 1Jn 3:2

Victorious Resurrection

⁵⁰ What I am saying, brothers and sisters, is this: Flesh and blood

---

ᴬ**15:27** Ps 8:6   ᴮ**15:29** Or *baptized on account of the dead*   ᶜ**15:29** Other mss read *for the dead*
ᴰ**15:32** Is 22:13   ᴱ**15:34** Lit *Sober up*   ᶠ**15:45** Gn 2:7   ᴳ**15:47** Other mss add *the Lord*

cannot inherit the kingdom of God, nor can corruption inherit incorruption. ⁵¹ Listen, I am telling you a mystery: We will not all fall asleep, but we will all be changed, ⁵² in a moment, in the twinkling of an eye, at the last trumpet. For the trumpet will sound, and the dead will be raised incorruptible, and we will be changed. ⁵³ For this corruptible body must be clothed with incorruptibility, and this mortal body must be clothed with immortality. ⁵⁴ When this corruptible body is clothed with incorruptibility, and this mortal body is clothed with immortality, then the saying that is written will take place: Php 3:3

> **Death has been swallowed up in victory.**ᴬ   Is 25:8; Mt 23:24
> ⁵⁵ **Where, death, is your victory?**
> **Where, death, is your sting?**ᴮ   Hs 13:14

⁵⁶ The sting of death is sin, and the power of sin is the law. ⁵⁷ But thanks be to God, who gives us the victory through our Lord Jesus Christ!

⁵⁸ Therefore, my dear brothers and sisters, be steadfast, immovable, always excelling in the Lord's work, because you know that your labor in the Lord is not in vain. Mk 14:6

Collection for the Jerusalem Church

16 Now about the collection for the saints: Do the same as I instructed the Galatian churches. ² On the first day of the week, each of you is to set something aside and save in keeping with how he is prospering, so that no collections will need to be made when I come. ³ When I arrive, I will send with letters those you recommend to carry your gift to Jerusalem. ⁴ If it is suitable for me to go as well, they will travel with me. Ac 11:30; Gl 1:2

Paul's Travel Plans

⁵ I will come to you after I pass through Macedonia — for I will be traveling through Macedonia — ⁶ and perhaps I will remain with you or even spend the winter, so that you may send me on my way wherever I go. ⁷ I don't want to see you now just in passing, since I hope to spend some time with you, if the Lord allows. ⁸ But I will stay in Ephesus until Pentecost, ⁹ because a wide door for effective ministry has opened for meᶜ — yet many oppose me. ¹⁰ If Timothy comes, see that he has nothing to fear while with you, because he is doing the Lord's work, just as I am. ¹¹ So let no one look down on him. Send him on his way in peace so that he can come to me, because I am expecting him with the brothers. Ac 16:9

¹² Now about our brother Apollos: I strongly urged him to come to you with the brothers, but he was not at all willing to come now. However, he will come when he has an opportunity. Ti 3:13

Final Exhortation

¹³ Be alert, stand firm in the faith, be courageous,ᴰ be strong. ¹⁴ Do everything in love. 1Co 13:1; Jd 3

¹⁵ Brothers and sisters, you know the household of Stephanas: They are the firstfruits of Achaia and have devoted themselves to serving the saints. I urge you ¹⁶ also to submit to such people, and to everyone who works and labors

---

ᴬ**15:54** Is 25:8   ᴮ**15:55** Hs 13:14   ᶜ**16:9** Lit *door has opened to me, great and effective*   ᴰ**16:13** Lit *act like men* with them. [17] I am delighted to have Stephanas, Fortunatus, and Achaicus present, because these men have made up for your absence. [18] For they have refreshed my spirit and yours. Therefore recognize such people.   Lv 2:12; Ps 51:12; Ac 18:12

Conclusion

[19] The churches of Asia send you greetings. Aquila and Priscilla send you greetings warmly in the Lord, along with the church that meets in their home. [20] All the brothers and sisters send you greetings. Greet one another with a holy kiss.   Ac 6:9

[21] This greeting is in my own hand — Paul. [22] If anyone does not love the Lord, a curse be on him. Our Lord, come! [A] [23] The grace of the Lord Jesus be with you. [24] My love be with all of you in Christ Jesus.

[A] **16:22** Aramaic *Marana tha*

2 CORINTHIANS

Greeting

1 Paul, an apostle of Christ Jesus by God's will, and Timothy our[A] brother: 1Co 1:1; Eph 1:1; Col 1:1; 1Th 3:2; 2Tm 1:1

To the church of God at Corinth, with all the saints who are throughout Achaia. Ac 18:12; 1Co 1:2; Php 1:1

² Grace to you and peace from God our Father and the Lord Jesus Christ. Mt 5:16; Lk 12:51; Rm 1:7; 2Tm 1:2; 3Jn 14

The God of Comfort

³ Blessed be the God and Father of our Lord Jesus Christ, the Father of mercies and the God of all comfort. ⁴ He comforts us in all our affliction,[B] so that we may be able to comfort those who are in any kind of affliction, through the comfort we ourselves receive from God. ⁵ For just as the sufferings of Christ overflow to us, so also through Christ our comfort overflows. ⁶ If we are afflicted, it is for your comfort and salvation. If we are comforted, it is for your comfort, which produces in you patient endurance of the same sufferings that we suffer. ⁷ And our hope for you is firm, because we know that as you share in the sufferings, so you will also share in the comfort. Mk 14:61; Lk 2:25; Gl 5:24; Php 3:10; Heb 10:28

⁸ We don't want you to be unaware, brothers and sisters, of our affliction that took place in Asia. We were completely overwhelmed — beyond our strength — so that we even despaired of life itself. ⁹ Indeed, we felt that we had received the sentence of death, so that we would not trust in ourselves but in God who raises the dead. ¹⁰ He has delivered us from such a terrible death, and he will deliver us. We have put our hope in him that he will deliver us again ¹¹ while you join in helping us by your prayers. Then many will give thanks on our[C] behalf for the gift that came to us through the prayers of many.

A Clear Conscience

¹² Indeed, this is our boast: The testimony of our conscience is that we have conducted ourselves in the world, and especially toward you, with godly sincerity and purity, not by human wisdom but by God's grace. ¹³ For we are writing nothing to you other than what you can read and also understand. I hope you will understand completely — ¹⁴ just as you have partially understood us — that we are your reason for pride, just as you also are ours in the day of our[D] Lord Jesus.

A Visit Postponed

¹⁵ Because of this confidence, I planned to come to you first, so that you could have a second benefit,[E] ¹⁶ and to visit you on my way to Macedonia, and then come to you again from Macedonia and be helped by you on my journey to Judea. ¹⁷ Now when I planned this, was I of two minds? Or what I plan, do I plan in a purely human[F] way so that I say "Yes, yes" and "No,

---

[A] **1:1** Lit *the* [B] **1:4** Or *trouble*, or *tribulation*, or *trials*, or *oppression* [C] **1:11** Other mss read *your* [D] **1:14** Other mss omit *our* [E] **1:15** Other mss read *a second joy* [F] **1:17** Or *a worldly*, or *a fleshly*, or *a selfish* no" at the same time? [18] As God is faithful, our message to you is not "Yes and no." [19] For the Son of God, Jesus Christ, whom we proclaimed among you — Silvanus, [A] Timothy, and I — did not become "Yes and no." On the contrary, in him it is always "Yes." [20] For every one of God's promises is "Yes" in him. Therefore, through him we also say "Amen" to the glory of God. [21] Now it is God who strengthens us together with you in Christ, and who has anointed us. [22] He has also put his seal on us and given us the Spirit in our hearts as a down payment.   Lk 1:5; Ac 16:9; 18:1-18; 20:38; 1Co 4:19

[23] I call on God as a witness, on my life, that it was to spare you that I did not come to Corinth. [24] I do not mean that we lord it over your faith, but we are workers with you for your joy, because you stand firm in your faith. **2** [1] In fact, I made up my mind about this: I would not come to you on another painful visit. [B] [2] For if I cause you pain, then who will cheer me other than the one being hurt by me? [C] [3] I wrote this very thing so that when I came I wouldn't have pain from those who ought to give me joy, because I am confident about all of you that my joy will also be yours. [4] For I wrote to you with many tears out of an extremely troubled and anguished heart — not to cause you pain, but that you should know the abundant love I have for you.   Pr 24:16; Php 1:25

A Sinner Forgiven

[5] If anyone has caused pain, he has caused pain not so much to me but to some degree — not to exaggerate — to all of you. [6] This punishment by the majority is sufficient for that person. [7] As a result, you should instead forgive and comfort him. Otherwise, he may be overwhelmed by excessive grief. [8] Therefore I urge you to reaffirm your love to him. [9] I wrote for this purpose: to test your character to see if you are obedient in everything. [10] Anyone you forgive, I do too. For what I have forgiven — if I have forgiven anything — it is for your benefit in the presence of Christ, [11] so that we may not be taken advantage of by Satan. For we are not ignorant of his schemes.   Mt 6:12; Rm 5:4; Php 2:8; 2Th 3:8

A Trip to Macedonia

[12] When I came to Troas to preach the gospel of Christ, even though the Lord opened a door for me, [13] I had no rest in my spirit because I did not find my brother Titus. Instead, I said good-bye to them and left for Macedonia.   Ac 16:8; Col 4:3; 2Th 1:7

A Ministry of Life or Death

[14] But thanks be to God, who always leads us in Christ's triumphal procession and through us spreads the aroma of the knowledge of him in every place. [15] For to God we are the fragrance of Christ among those who are being saved and among those who are perishing. [16] To some we are an aroma of death leading to death, but to others, an aroma of life leading to life. Who is adequate for these things? [17] For we do not market the word of God for profit like so many. [D] On the contrary, we speak with sincerity in Christ, as from God and before God.   Jn 17:3; 1Co 15:57; Eph 5:2; 1Jn 4:8

[A] **1:19** Or *Silas* ; Ac 15:22-32; 16:19-40; 17:1-16   [B] **2:1** Lit *not again in sorrow to come to you*   [C] **2:2** Lit *the one pained*   [D] **2:17** Other mss read *like the rest*

Living Letters

3 Are we beginning to commend ourselves again? Or do we need, like some, letters of recommendation to you or from you? ² You yourselves are our letter, written on our hearts, known and read by everyone. ³ You show that you are Christ's letter, delivered^A by us, not written with ink but with the Spirit of the living God — not on tablets of stone but on tablets of human hearts. ^B Ex 24:12; Dt 5:26; Pr 3:3; 1Co 9:2; Phm 13

Paul's Competence

⁴ Such is the confidence we have through Christ before God. ⁵ It is not that we are competent in ^C ourselves to claim anything as coming from ourselves, but our adequacy is from God. ⁶ He has made us competent to be ministers of a new covenant, not of the letter, but of the Spirit. For the letter kills, but the Spirit gives life. Lk 22:20; 1Co 15:10; Heb 7:22

New Covenant Ministry

⁷ Now if the ministry that brought death, chiseled in letters on stones, came with glory, so that the Israelites were not able to gaze steadily at Moses's face because of its glory, which was set aside, ⁸ how will the ministry of the Spirit not be more glorious? ⁹ For if the ministry that brought condemnation had glory, the ministry that brings righteousness overflows with even more glory. ¹⁰ In fact, what had been glorious is not glorious now by comparison because of the glory that surpasses it. ¹¹ For if what was set aside was glorious, what endures will be even more glorious. Ex 34:29-35; Mk 10:37; Lk 9:32

¹² Since, then, we have such a hope, we act with great boldness. ¹³ We are not like Moses, who used to put a veil over his face to prevent the Israelites from gazing steadily until the end^D of the glory of what was being set aside, ¹⁴ but their minds were hardened. For to this day, at the reading of the old covenant, the same veil remains; it is not lifted, because it is set aside only in Christ. ¹⁵ Yet still today, whenever Moses is read, a veil lies over their hearts, ¹⁶ but whenever a person turns to the Lord, the veil is removed. ¹⁷ Now the Lord is the Spirit, and where the Spirit of the Lord is, there is freedom. ¹⁸ We all, with unveiled faces, are looking as in a mirror at^E the glory of the Lord and are being transformed into the same image from glory to glory; this is from the Lord who is the Spirit. ^F Ex 34:33; Mk 8:17; 1Th 1:3; Heb 3:13

The Light of the Gospel

4 Therefore, since we have this ministry because we were shown mercy, we do not give up. ² Instead, we have renounced secret and shameful things, not acting deceitfully or distorting the word of God, but commending ourselves before God to everyone's conscience by an open display of the truth. ³ But if our gospel is veiled, it is veiled to those who are perishing. ⁴ In their case, the god of this age has blinded the minds of the unbelievers to keep them from seeing the light of the gospel of the glory of Christ, ^G who is the image of God. ⁵ For we are not proclaiming ourselves but Jesus Christ as Lord,

^A**3:3** Lit *ministered to*   ^B**3:3** Lit *fleshly hearts*   ^C**3:5** Lit *from*   ^D**3:13** Or *at the outcome*   ^E**3:18** Or *are reflecting*   ^F**3:18** Or *from the Spirit of the Lord*, or *from the Lord, the Spirit*   ^G**4:4** Or *the gospel of the glorious Christ*, or *the glorious gospel of Christ* and ourselves as your servants for Jesus's sake. [6] For God who said, "Let light shine out of darkness," has shone in our hearts to give the light of the knowledge of God's glory in the face of Jesus Christ. Mt 5:7

Treasure in Clay Jars

[7] Now we have this treasure in clay jars, so that this extraordinary power may be from God and not from us. [8] We are afflicted in every way but not crushed; we are perplexed but not in despair; [9] we are persecuted but not abandoned; we are struck down but not destroyed. [10] We always carry the death of Jesus in our body, so that the life of Jesus may also be displayed in our body. [11] For we who live are always being given over to death for Jesus's sake, so that Jesus's life may also be displayed in our mortal flesh. [12] So then, death is at work in us, but life in you. [13] And since we have the same spirit of faith in keeping with what is written, **I believed, therefore I spoke,** [A] we also believe, and therefore speak. [14] For we know that the one who raised the Lord Jesus will also raise us with Jesus and present us with you. [15] Indeed, everything is for your benefit so that, as grace extends through more and more people, it may cause thanksgiving to increase to the glory of God.

[16] Therefore we do not give up. Even though our outer person is being destroyed, our inner person is being renewed day by day. [17] For our momentary light affliction is producing for us an absolutely incomparable eternal weight of glory. [18] So we do not focus on what is seen, but on what is unseen. For

what is seen is temporary, but what is unseen is eternal. Rm 7:22; 2Th 3:13

Our Future After Death

5 For we know that if our earthly tent we live in is destroyed, we have a building from God, an eternal dwelling in the heavens, not made with hands. [2] Indeed, we groan in this tent, desiring to put on our heavenly dwelling, [3] since, when we have taken it off, [B] we will not be found naked. [4] Indeed, we groan while we are in this tent, burdened as we are, because we do not want to be unclothed but clothed, so that mortality may be swallowed up by life. [5] Now the one who prepared us for this very purpose is God, who gave us the Spirit as a down payment. 2Pt 1:13; Eph 6:9; 8:23

[6] So we are always confident and know that while we are at home in the body we are away from the Lord. [7] For we walk by faith, not by sight. [8] In fact, we are confident, and we would prefer to be away from the body and at home with the Lord. [9] Therefore, whether we are at home or away, we make it our aim to be pleasing to him. [10] For we must all appear before the judgment seat of Christ, so that each may be repaid for what he has done in the body, whether good or evil. Mt 8:10; Ac 3:16

[11] Therefore, since we know the fear of the Lord, we try to persuade people. What we are is plain to God, and I hope it is also plain to your consciences. [12] We are not commending ourselves to you again, but giving you an opportunity to be proud of us, so that you may have a reply for those who take pride in outward appearance rather than in the heart. [13] For if we are out of

[A]**4:13** Ps 116:10 LXX   [B]**5:3** Other mss read *when we have put on* our mind, it is for God; if we are in our right mind, it is for you. [14] For the love of Christ compels us, since we have reached this conclusion: If one died for all, then all died. [15] And he died for all so that those who live should no longer live for themselves, but for the one who died for them and was raised.

The Ministry of Reconciliation

[16] From now on, then, we do not know anyone from a worldly perspective. [A] Even if we have known Christ from a worldly perspective, [B] yet now we no longer know him in this way. [17] Therefore, if anyone is in Christ, he is a new creation; the old has passed away, and see, the new has [C] come! [18] Everything is from God, who has reconciled us to himself through Christ and has given us the ministry of reconciliation. [19] That is, in Christ, God was reconciling the world to himself, not counting their trespasses against them, and he has committed the message of reconciliation to us. Is 43:19; 65:17; Jn 1:3; Rm 8:24; Ti 2:11; Rv 3:14

[20] Therefore, we are ambassadors for Christ, since God is making his appeal through us. We plead on Christ's behalf: "Be reconciled to God." [21] He made the one who did not know sin to be sin [D] for us, so that in him we might become the righteousness of God. Eph 6:20; Php 1:29

6 Working together with him, we also appeal to you, "Don't receive the grace of God in vain." [2] For he says:

> At an acceptable time I
> listened to you,
> and in the day of salvation I
> helped you. [E]   Is 49:8

See, now is the acceptable time; now is the day of salvation! Is 49:8

The Character of Paul's Ministry

[3] We are not giving anyone an occasion for offense, so that the ministry will not be blamed. [4] Instead, as God's ministers, we commend ourselves in everything: by great endurance, by afflictions, by hardships, by difficulties, [5] by beatings, by imprisonments, by riots, by labors, by sleepless nights, by times of hunger, [6] by purity, by knowledge, by patience, by kindness, by the Holy Spirit, by sincere love, [7] by the word of truth, [F] by the power of God; through weapons of righteousness for the right hand and the left, [8] through glory and dishonor, through slander and good report; regarded as deceivers, yet true; [9] as unknown, yet recognized; as dying, yet see — we live; as being disciplined, yet not killed; [10] as grieving, yet always rejoicing; as poor, yet enriching many; as having nothing, yet possessing everything. [11] We have spoken openly to you, Corinthians; our heart has been opened wide. [12] We are not withholding our affection from you, but you are withholding yours from us. [13] I speak as to my children; as a proper response, open your heart to us. Ex 34:6; Jdg 16:21; 2Co 11:3; Php 3:8; 1Jn 4:8

Separation to God

[14] Don't become partners with those who do not believe. For what partnership is there between righteousness and lawlessness? Or what fellowship does light have with darkness? [15] What agreement

---

[A]5:16 Lit *anyone according to the flesh*   [B]5:16 Lit *Christ according to the flesh*   [C]5:17 Other mss read *look, all new things have*   [D]5:21 Or *be a sin offering*   [E]6:2 Is 49:8   [F]6:7 Or *by truthful speech* does Christ have with Belial?[A] Or what does a believer have in common with an unbeliever? [16] And what agreement does the temple of God have with idols? For we[B] are the temple of the living God, as God said: Mt 6:23; 13:41; Jn 12:46; 1Co 8:4

I will dwell   Jms 4:5
and walk among them,
and I will be their God,
and they will be my people.[C]

[17] Therefore, **come out**
       from among them
     and **be separate,**
       says the Lord;
     do not touch
       any unclean thing,
     and I will welcome you.[D]

[18] And **I will be a Father** to you,
     and you will be **sons**
       and daughters **to me,**   Mt 5:9
     says the Lord Almighty.[E]

7 So then, dear friends, since we have these promises, let us cleanse ourselves from every impurity of the flesh and spirit, bringing holiness to completion[F] in the fear of God.   Gn 12:7; Ps 51:12; 147:11; Pr 1:7

Joy and Repentance

[2] Make room for us in your hearts. We have wronged no one, corrupted no one, taken advantage of no one. [3] I don't say this to condemn you, since I have already said that you are in our hearts, to die together and to live together. [4] I am very frank with you; I have great pride in you. I am filled with encouragement; I am overflowing with joy in all our afflictions.   1Co 3:17; 15:33; 2Co 11:3

[5] In fact, when we came into Macedonia, we[G] had no rest. Instead, we were troubled in every way: conflicts on the outside, fears within. [6] But God, who comforts the downcast, comforted us by the arrival of Titus, [7] and not only by his arrival but also by the comfort he received from you. He told us about your deep longing, your sorrow, and your zeal for me, so that I rejoiced even more. [8] For even if I grieved you with my letter, I don't regret it. And if I regretted it — since I saw that the letter grieved you, yet only for a while — [9] I now rejoice, not because you were grieved, but because your grief led to repentance. For you were grieved as God willed, so that you didn't experience any loss from us. [10] For godly grief produces a repentance that leads to salvation without regret, but worldly grief produces death. [11] For consider how much diligence this very thing — this grieving as God wills — has produced in you: what a desire to clear yourselves, what indignation, what fear, what deep longing, what zeal, what justice! In every way you showed yourselves to be pure in this matter. [12] So even though I wrote to you, it was not because of the one who did wrong, or because of the one who was wronged, but in order that your devotion to us might be made plain to you in the sight of God. [13] For this reason we have been comforted.   Jn 7:13; 8:51; Ac 16:9; Jms 4:1; Ti 3:9

In addition to our own comfort, we rejoiced even more over the joy Titus had, because his spirit was refreshed by all of you. [14] For if I have made any boast to him about you, I have not been disappointed; but as I have spoken everything to you in truth, so our boasting to Titus

---

has also turned out to be the truth. [15] And his affection toward you is even greater as he remembers the obedience of all of you, and how you received him with fear and trembling. [16] I rejoice that I have complete confidence in you.   Ti 1:4

Appeal to Complete the Collection

8 We want you to know, brothers and sisters, about the grace of God that was given to the churches of Macedonia: [2] During a severe trial brought about by affliction, their abundant joy and their extreme poverty overflowed in a wealth of generosity on their part. [3] I can testify that, according to their ability and even beyond their ability, of their own accord, [4] they begged us earnestly for the privilege of sharing in the ministry to the saints, [5] and not just as we had hoped. Instead, they gave themselves first to the Lord and then to us by God's will. [6] So we urged Titus that just as he had begun, so he should also complete among you this act of grace.   Mt 16:18; Ac 16:9; 1Co 14:4; Php 4:10; Rv 1:4

[7] Now as you excel in everything — in faith, speech, knowledge, and in all diligence, and in your love for us[A] — excel also in this act of grace. [8] I am not saying this as a command. Rather, by means of the diligence of others, I am testing the genuineness of your love. [9] For you know the grace of our Lord Jesus Christ: Though he was rich, for your sake he became poor, so that by his poverty you might become rich. [10] And in this matter I am giving advice because it is profitable for you, who began last year

not only to do something but also to want to do it. [11] Now also finish the task, so that just as there was an eager desire, there may also be a completion, according to what you have. [12] For if the eagerness is there, the gift is acceptable according to what a person has, not according to what he does not have. [13] It is not that there should be relief for others and hardship for you, but it is a question of equality.[B] [14] At the present time your surplus is available for their need, so that their abundance may in turn meet your need, in order that there may be equality. [15] As it is written: **The person who had much did not have too much, and the person who had little did not have too little.**[C]

Administration of the Collection

[16] Thanks be to God, who put the same concern for you into the heart of Titus. [17] For he welcomed our appeal and, being very diligent, went out to you by his own choice. [18] We have sent with him the brother who is praised among all the churches for his gospel ministry.[D] [19] And not only that, but he was also appointed by the churches to accompany us with this gracious gift that we are administering for the glory of the Lord himself and to show our eagerness to help. [20] We are taking this precaution so that no one will criticize us about this large sum that we are administering. [21] Indeed, we are giving careful thought to do what is right, not only before the Lord but also before people. [22] We have also sent with them our brother. We have often tested him in many circumstances

[A] 8:7 Other mss read in our love for you   [B] 8:13 Lit but from equality   [C] 8:15 Ex 16:18   [D] 8:18 Lit churches, in the gospel and found him to be diligent — and now even more diligent because of his great confidence in you. ²³ As for Titus, he is my partner and co-worker for you; as for our brothers, they are the messengers of the churches, the glory of Christ. ²⁴ Therefore, show them proof before the churches of your love and of our boasting about you. 2Co 12:18

Motivations for Giving

9 Now concerning the ministry to the saints, it is unnecessary for me to write to you. ² For I know your eagerness, and I boast about you to the Macedonians: "Achaia has been ready since last year," and your zeal has stirred up most of them. ³ But I am sending the brothers so that our boasting about you in this matter would not prove empty, and so that you would be ready just as I said. ⁴ Otherwise, if any Macedonians come with me and find you unprepared, we, not to mention you, would be put to shame in that situation.ᴬ ⁵ Therefore I considered it necessary to urge the brothers to go on ahead to you and arrange in advance the generous gift you promised, so that it will be ready as a gift and not as an extortion. Ac 16:9; 18:12

⁶ The point is this:ᴮ The person who sows sparingly will also reap sparingly, and the person who sows generously will also reap generously. ⁷ Each person should do as he has decided in his heart — not reluctantly or out of compulsion, since God loves a cheerful giver. ⁸ And God is able to make every grace overflow to you, so that in every way, always having everything you need, you may excel in every good work. ⁹ As it is written:

He distributed freely; Jn 16:32
he gave to the poor;
his righteousness
endures forever.ᶜ Ps 112:9

¹⁰ Now the one who provides seed for the sower and bread for food will also provide and multiply your seed and increase the harvest of your righteousness. ¹¹ You will be enriched in every way for all generosity, which produces thanksgiving to God through us. ¹² For the ministry of this service is not only supplying the needs of the saints but is also overflowing in many expressions of thanks to God. ¹³ Because of the proof provided by this ministry, they will glorify God for your obedient confession of the gospel of Christ, and for your generosity in sharing with them and with everyone. ¹⁴ And as they pray on your behalf, they will have deep affection for you because of the surpassing grace of God in you. ¹⁵ Thanks be to God for his indescribable gift! Is 55:10-11; Hs 10:12; 1Co 1:5

Paul's Apostolic Authority

10 Now I Paul, myself, appeal to you by the meekness and gentleness of Christ — I who am humble among you in person but bold toward you when absent. ² I beg you that when I am present I will not need to be bold with the confidence by which I plan to challenge certain people who think we are behaving according to the flesh. ³ For although we live in the flesh, we do not wage war according to the flesh, ⁴ since the weapons of our warfare are not of the flesh, but are powerful through God for the demolition of strongholds. We demolish arguments ⁵ and every proud

ᴬ9:4 Or in this confidence   ᴮ9:6 Lit And this   ᶜ9:9 Ps 112:9

thing that is raised up against the knowledge of God, and we take every thought captive to obey Christ. [6] And we are ready to punish any disobedience, once your obedience is complete. Jn 17:3; Ac 25:5; Php 3:3; 1Tm 1:18

[7] Look at what is obvious. [A] If anyone is confident that he belongs to Christ, let him remind himself of this: Just as he belongs to Christ, so do we. [8] For if I boast a little too much about our authority, which the Lord gave for building you up and not for tearing you down, I will not be put to shame. [9] I don't want to seem as though I am trying to terrify you with my letters. [10] For it is said, "His letters are weighty and powerful, but his physical presence is weak and his public speaking amounts to nothing." [11] Let such a person consider this: What we are in our letters, when we are absent, we will also be in our actions when we are present. 1Co 3:23; 14:3; Gl 5:24

[12] For we don't dare classify or compare ourselves with some who commend themselves. But in measuring themselves by themselves and comparing themselves to themselves, they lack understanding. [13] We, however, will not boast beyond measure but according to the measure of the area of ministry that God has assigned to us, which reaches even to you. [14] For we are not overextending ourselves, as if we had not reached you, since we have come to you with the gospel of Christ. [15] We are not boasting beyond measure about other people's labors. On the contrary, we have the hope that as your faith increases, our area of ministry will be greatly enlarged, [16] so that we

may preach the gospel to the regions beyond you without boasting about what has already been done in someone else's area of ministry. [17] So **let the one who boasts, boast in the Lord.** [B] [18] For it is not the one commending himself who is approved, but the one the Lord commends.   Pr 26:12; 27:2; Mt 13:13; Gl 2:18

Paul and the False Apostles

11 I wish you would put up with a little foolishness from me. Yes, do put up with me! [C] [2] For I am jealous for you with a godly jealousy, because I have promised you in marriage to one husband — to present a pure virgin to Christ. [3] But I fear that, as the serpent deceived Eve by his cunning, your minds may be seduced from a sincere and pure [D] devotion to Christ. [4] For if a person comes and preaches another Jesus, whom we did not preach, or you receive a different spirit, which you had not received, or a different gospel, which you had not accepted, you put up with it splendidly! Mk 7:22; 2Co 11:17,21; Jms 3:16

[5] Now I consider myself in no way inferior to those "super-apostles." [6] Even if I am untrained in public speaking, I am certainly not untrained in knowledge. Indeed, we have in every way made that clear to you in everything. [7] Or did I commit a sin by humbling myself so that you might be exalted, because I preached the gospel of God to you free of charge? [8] I robbed other churches by taking pay from them to minister to you. [9] When I was present with you and in need, I did not burden anyone, since the brothers who came from

---

[A]**10:7** Or *You are looking at things outwardly*   [B]**10:17** Jr 9:24   [C]**11:1** Or *Yes, you are putting up with me*
[D]**11:3** Other mss omit *and pure*

Macedonia supplied my needs. I have kept myself, and will keep myself, from burdening you in any way. ¹⁰ As the truth of Christ is in me, this boasting of mine will not be stopped ᴬ in the regions of Achaia. ¹¹ Why? Because I don't love you? God knows I do!   1Co 1:17; 1Jn 4:8; Jd 17

¹² But I will continue to do what I am doing, in order to deny ᴮ an opportunity to those who want to be regarded as our equals in what they boast about. ¹³ For such people are false apostles, deceitful workers, disguising themselves as apostles of Christ. ¹⁴ And no wonder! For Satan disguises himself as an angel of light. ¹⁵ So it is no great surprise if his servants also disguise themselves as servants of righteousness. Their end will be according to their works.   Gl 3:10; Rv 2:2

Paul's Sufferings for Christ

¹⁶ I repeat: Let no one consider me a fool. But if you do, at least accept me as a fool so that I can also boast a little. ¹⁷ What I am saying in this matter ᶜ of boasting, I don't speak as the Lord would, but as it were, foolishly. ¹⁸ Since many boast according to the flesh, I will also boast. ¹⁹ For you, being so wise, gladly put up with fools! ²⁰ In fact, you put up with it if someone enslaves you, if someone exploits you, if someone takes advantage of you, if someone is arrogant toward you, if someone slaps you in the face. ²¹ I say this to our shame: We have been too weak for that!   Pr 3:7; Mt 5:39; Gl 5:15

But in whatever anyone dares to boast — I am talking foolishly — I also dare: ²² Are they Hebrews? So am I. Are they Israelites? So am I.

Are they the descendants of Abraham? So am I. ²³ Are they servants of Christ? I'm talking like a madman — I'm a better one: with far more labors, many more imprisonments, far worse beatings, many times near death.   Gn 16:15; Gl 3:29; Php 3:5

²⁴ Five times I received the forty lashes minus one from the Jews. ²⁵ Three times I was beaten with rods. Once I received a stoning. Three times I was shipwrecked. I have spent a night and a day in the open sea. ²⁶ On frequent journeys, I faced dangers from rivers, dangers from robbers, dangers from my own people, dangers from Gentiles, dangers in the city, dangers in the wilderness, dangers at sea, and dangers among false brothers; ²⁷ toil and hardship, many sleepless nights, hunger and thirst, often without food, cold, and without clothing. ²⁸ Not to mention ᴰ other things, there is the daily pressure on me: my concern for all the churches. ²⁹ Who is weak, and I am not weak? Who is made to stumble, and I do not burn with indignation?   Dt 25:3

³⁰ If boasting is necessary, I will boast about my weaknesses. ³¹ The God and Father of the Lord Jesus, who is blessed forever, knows I am not lying. ³² In Damascus, a ruler ᴱ under King Aretas guarded the city of Damascus in order to arrest me. ³³ So I was let down in a basket through a window in the wall and escaped from his hands.   Mt 5:16; 11:27

Sufficient Grace

12 Boasting is necessary. It is not profitable, but I will move on to visions and revelations of the Lord. ² I know a man in Christ who

---

ᴬ**11:10** Or *silenced*   ᴮ**11:12** Lit *cut off*   ᶜ**11:17** Or *business*, or *confidence*   ᴰ**11:28** Lit *Apart from*
ᴱ**11:32** Gk *ethnarches* ; a leader of an ethnic community

was caught up to the third heaven fourteen years ago. Whether he was in the body or out of the body, I don't know; God knows. [3] I know that this man — whether in the body or out of the body I don't know; God knows — [4] was caught up into paradise and heard inexpressible words, which a human being is not allowed to speak. [5] I will boast about this person, but not about myself, except of my weaknesses. Lk 1:22; 23:43; 1Th 4:17; 1Pt 4:13

[6] For if I want to boast, I wouldn't be a fool, because I would be telling the truth. But I will spare you, so that no one can credit me with something beyond what he sees in me or hears from me, [7] especially because of the extraordinary revelations. Therefore, so that I would not exalt myself, a thorn in the flesh was given to me, a messenger of Satan to torment me so that I would not exalt myself. [8] Concerning this, I pleaded with the Lord three times that it would leave me. [9] But he said to me, "My grace is sufficient for you, for my power is perfected in weakness." Ps 119:142; Jn 8:14; 14:6; 2Co 11:10

Therefore, I will most gladly boast all the more about my weaknesses, so that Christ's power may reside in me. [10] So I take pleasure in weaknesses, insults, hardships, persecutions, and in difficulties, for the sake of Christ. For when I am weak, then I am strong.

Signs of an Apostle

[11] I have been a fool; you forced it on me. You ought to have commended me, since I am not in any way inferior to those "super-apostles," even though I am nothing. [12] The signs of an apostle were performed with unfailing endurance among you, including signs and wonders and miracles. [13] So in what way are you worse off than the other churches, except that I personally did not burden you? Forgive me for this wrong! Mk 13:22; Ac 1:2; Gl 6:3; Heb 2:4; Jd 17

Paul's Concern for the Corinthians

[14] Look, I am ready to come to you this third time. I will not burden you, since I am not seeking what is yours, but you. For children ought not save up for their parents, but parents for their children. [15] I will most gladly spend and be spent for you. [A] If I love you more, am I to be loved less? [16] Now granted, I did not burden you; yet sly as I am, I took you in by deceit! [17] Did I take advantage of you by any of those I sent you? [18] I urged Titus to go, and I sent the brother with him. Titus didn't take advantage of you, did he? Didn't we walk in the same spirit and in the same footsteps? Ac 18; 2Co 1:6; 2:1; 13:1; Php 2:17; Ti 1:4

[19] Have you been thinking all along that we were defending ourselves to you? No, in the sight of God we are speaking in Christ, and everything, dear friends, is for building you up. [20] For I fear that perhaps when I come I will not find you to be what I want, and you may not find me to be what you want. Perhaps there will be quarreling, jealousy, angry outbursts, selfish ambitions, slander, gossip, arrogance, and disorder. [21] I fear that when I come my God will again [B] humiliate me in your presence, and I will grieve for many who sinned before and have not repented of the moral impurity,

sexual immorality, and sensuality they practiced.

Final Warnings and Exhortations

13 This is the third time I am coming to you. **Every matter must be established by the testimony of two or three witnesses.**[A] [2] I gave a warning when I was present the second time, and now I give a warning while I am absent to those who sinned before and to all the rest: If I come again, I will not be lenient, [3] since you seek proof of Christ speaking in me. He is not weak in dealing with you, but powerful among you. [4] For he was crucified in weakness, but he lives by the power of God. For we also are weak in him, but in dealing with you we will live with him by God's power. Dt 17:6; 19:15; 2Co 12:14

[5] Test yourselves to see if you are in the faith. Examine yourselves. Or do you yourselves not recognize that Jesus Christ is in you? — unless you fail the test.[B] [6] And I hope you will recognize that we ourselves do not fail the test. [7] But we pray to God that you do nothing wrong — not that we may appear to pass the test, but that you may do what is right, even though we may appear to fail. [8] For we can't do anything against the truth, but only for the truth. [9] We rejoice when we are weak and you are strong. We also pray that you become fully mature.[C] [10] This is why I am writing these things while absent, so that when I am there I may not have to deal harshly with you, in keeping with the authority the Lord gave me for building up and not for tearing down. Ac 25:5; 1Co 14:3; 2Th 2:10; Jms 1:13; 1Pt 2:1

[11] Finally, brothers and sisters, rejoice.[D] Become mature, be encouraged,[E] be of the same mind, be at peace, and the God of love and peace will be with you. [12] Greet one another with a holy kiss. All the saints send you greetings.

[13] The grace of the Lord Jesus Christ, and the love of God, and the fellowship of the Holy Spirit be with you all.[F] 1Co 13:1; 2Th 3:16; 1Jn 4:16

[A] **13:1** Dt 17:6; 19:15 [B] **13:5** Or *you are disqualified*, or *you are counterfeit* [C] **13:9** Or *become complete*, or *be restored* [D] **13:11** Or *farewell* [E] **13:11** Or *listen to my appeal* [F] **13:12-13** Some translations divide these two vv. into three vv. so that v. 13 begins with *All the saints . . .* and v. 14 begins with *The grace of . . .*

GALATIANS

Greeting

1 Paul, an apostle — not from men or by man, but by Jesus Christ and God the Father who raised him from the dead — [2] and all the brothers who are with me: Mt 5:16; 6:1; Ac 13:9

To the churches of Galatia. Ac 16:6

[3] Grace to you and peace from God the Father and our Lord[A] Jesus Christ, [4] who gave himself for our sins to rescue us from this present evil age, according to the will of our God and Father. [5] To him be the glory forever and ever. Amen. Mt 20:28; Rm 4:25; 6:23; Gl 2:20; Ti 2:14

No Other Gospel

[6] I am amazed that you are so quickly turning away from him who called you by the grace of Christ and are turning to a different gospel — [7] not that there is another gospel, but there are some who are troubling you and want to distort the gospel of Christ. [8] But even if we or an angel from heaven should preach to you a gospel contrary to what we have preached to you, a curse be on him![B] [9] As we have said before, I now say again: If anyone is preaching to you a gospel contrary to what you received, a curse be on him! Ac 4:12; 1Co 3:11; Col 3:15; 1Pt 1:15

[10] For am I now trying to persuade people,[C] or God? Or am I striving to please people? If I were still trying to please people, I would not be a servant of Christ. 1Th 2:4

Paul Defends His Apostleship

[11] For I want you to know, brothers and sisters, that the gospel preached by me is not of human origin. [12] For I did not receive it from a human source and I was not taught it, but it came by a revelation of Jesus Christ. 1Pt 4:13

[13] For you have heard about my former way of life in Judaism: I intensely persecuted God's church and tried to destroy it. [14] I advanced in Judaism beyond many contemporaries among my people, because I was extremely zealous for the traditions of my ancestors. [15] But when God, who from my mother's womb set me apart and called me by his grace, was pleased [16] to reveal his Son in me, so that I could preach him among the Gentiles, I did not immediately consult with anyone.[D] [17] I did not go up to Jerusalem to those who had become apostles before me; instead I went to Arabia and came back to Damascus. Ac 8:1–9:2; 26:4; Php 3:5-6; 2Pt 3:11

[18] Then after three years I did go up to Jerusalem to get to know Cephas,[E] and I stayed with him fifteen days. [19] But I didn't see any of the other apostles except James, the Lord's brother. [20] I declare in the sight of God: I am not lying in what I write to you. Jn 1:42; Ac 9:26; Jd 1

[21] Afterward, I went to the regions of Syria and Cilicia. [22] I remained personally unknown to the Judean churches that are in Christ. [23] They

---

[A]1:3 Other mss read *God our Father and the Lord*   [B]1:8 Or *you, let him be condemned*, or *you, let him be condemned to hell*; Gk *anathema*   [C]1:10 Or *win the approval of people*   [D]1:16 Lit *flesh and blood*   [E]1:18 Other mss read *Peter* simply kept hearing: "He who formerly persecuted us now preaches the faith he once tried to destroy." [24] And they glorified God because of me. [A]   Nm 23:7; Lk 2:2; Ac 8:1-3; 9:30; 11:25-26

Paul Defends His Gospel at Jerusalem

2 Then after fourteen years I went up again to Jerusalem with Barnabas, taking Titus along also. [2] I went up according to a revelation and presented to them the gospel I preach among the Gentiles, but privately to those recognized as leaders. I wanted to be sure I was not running, and had not been running, in vain. [3] But not even Titus, who was with me, was compelled to be circumcised, even though he was a Greek. [4] This matter arose because some false brothers had infiltrated our ranks to spy on the freedom we have in Christ Jesus in order to enslave us. [5] But we did not give up and submit to these people for even a moment, so that the truth of the gospel would be preserved for you.   Ac 4:36; 15:2-30; Ti 1:4; 1Pt 4:13; 2Pt 2:1

[6] Now from those recognized as important (what they [B] once were makes no difference to me; God does not show favoritism [C]) — they added nothing to me. [7] On the contrary, they saw that I had been entrusted with the gospel for the uncircumcised, just as Peter was for the circumcised, [8] since the one at work in Peter for an apostleship to the circumcised was also at work in me for the Gentiles. [9] When James, Cephas, [D] and John — those recognized as pillars — acknowledged the grace that had been given to me, they gave the right hand of fellowship to me and Barnabas, agreeing that we should go to the Gentiles and they to the circumcised. [10] They asked only that we would remember the poor, which I had made every effort to do.

Freedom from the Law

[11] But when Cephas [D] came to Antioch, I opposed him to his face because he stood condemned. [E] [12] For he regularly ate with the Gentiles before certain men came from James. However, when they came, he withdrew and separated himself, because he feared those from the circumcision party. [13] Then the rest of the Jews joined his hypocrisy, so that even Barnabas was led astray by their hypocrisy. [14] But when I saw that they were deviating from the truth of the gospel, I told Cephas [D] in front of everyone, "If you, who are a Jew, live like a Gentile and not like a Jew, how can you compel Gentiles to live like Jews?" [F]   Mk 12:15; Rm 1:13; 2:28-29; 14:2

[15] We are Jews by birth and not "Gentile sinners," [16] and yet because we know that a person is not justified by the works of the law but by faith in Jesus Christ, [G] even we ourselves have believed in Christ Jesus. This was so that we might be justified by faith in Christ [H] and not by the works of the law, because by the works of the law no human being will [I] be justified. [17] But if we ourselves are also found to be "sinners" while seeking to be justified by Christ,

---

[A] **1:24** Or in me   [B] **2:6** Lit the recognized ones   [C] **2:6** Or God is not a respecter of persons; lit God does not receive the face of man   [D] **2:9,11,14** Other mss read Peter   [E] **2:11** Or he was in the wrong   [F] **2:14** Some translations continue the quotation through v. 16 or v. 21.   [G] **2:16** Or by the faithfulness of Jesus Christ   [H] **2:16** Or by the faithfulness of Christ   [I] **2:16** Lit law all flesh will not is Christ then a promoter[A] of sin? Absolutely not! [18] If I rebuild those things that I tore down, I show myself to be a lawbreaker. [19] For through the law I died to the law, so that I might live for God. [20] I have been crucified with Christ, and I no longer live, but Christ lives in me. The life I now live in the body,[B] I live by faith in the Son of God, who loved me and gave himself for me. [21] I do not set aside the grace of God, for if righteousness comes through the law, then Christ died for nothing. Rm 3:20; 7:4

Justification Through Faith

3 You foolish Galatians! Who has cast a spell on you,[C] before whose eyes Jesus Christ was publicly portrayed[D] as crucified? [2] I only want to learn this from you: Did you receive the Spirit by the works of the law or by believing what you heard?[E] [3] Are you so foolish? After beginning by the Spirit, are you now finishing by the flesh? [4] Did you experience[F] so much for nothing — if in fact it was for nothing? [5] So then, does God give you the Spirit and work miracles among you by your doing the works of the law? Or is it by believing what you heard — [6] just like Abraham who **believed God, and it was credited to him for righteousness?**[G] Mt 27:22; Jn 14:1 [7] You know, then, that those who have faith, these are Abraham's sons. [8] Now the Scripture saw in advance that God would justify the Gentiles by faith and proclaimed

the gospel ahead of time to Abraham, saying, **All the nations[H] will be blessed through you.**[19] Consequently those who have faith are blessed with Abraham, who had faith.[J] Gn 12:3; 16:15; Jn 8:37,39; Heb 2:16

Law and Promise

[10] For all who rely on the works of the law are under a curse, because it is written, **Everyone who does not do everything written in the book of the law is cursed.**[K] [11] Now it is clear that no one is justified before God by the law, because **the righteous will live by faith.**[L] [12] But the law is not based on faith; instead, **the one who does these things will live by them.**[M] [13] Christ redeemed us from the curse of the law by becoming a curse for us, because it is written, **Cursed is everyone who is hung on a tree.**[N] [14] The purpose was that the blessing of Abraham would come to the Gentiles by Christ Jesus, so that we could receive the promised Spirit through faith. Dt 27:26; Ac 15:15; Jms 3:10

[15] Brothers and sisters, I'm using a human illustration. No one sets aside or makes additions to a validated human will.[O] [16] Now the promises were spoken to Abraham and to his seed. He does not say "and to seeds," as though referring to many, but referring to one, **and to your seed,**[P] who is Christ. [17] My point is this: The law, which came 430 years later, does not invalidate a covenant previously established by God[Q] and thus cancel the promise. [18] For if the inheritance is based

on the law, it is no longer based on the promise; but God has graciously given it to Abraham through the promise. Gn 12:7; 13:15; 15:13; 17:8; 24:7

The Purpose of the Law

[19] Why then was the law given? It was added for the sake of transgressions[A] until the Seed to whom the promise was made would come. The law was put into effect through angels by means of a mediator. [20] Now a mediator is not just for one person alone, but God is one. [21] Is the law therefore contrary to God's promises? Absolutely not! For if the law had been granted with the ability to give life, then righteousness would certainly be on the basis of the law. [22] But the Scripture imprisoned everything under sin's power,[B] so that the promise might be given on the basis of faith in Jesus Christ to those who believe. [23] Before this faith came, we were confined under the law, imprisoned until the coming faith was revealed. [24] The law, then, was our guardian until Christ, so that we could be justified by faith. [25] But since that faith has come, we are no longer under a guardian, [26] for through faith you are all sons of God in Christ Jesus. Gn 16:7; Mt 13:49; Rm 4:15; 5:20

Sons and Heirs

[27] For those of you who were baptized into Christ have been clothed with Christ. [28] There is no Jew or Greek, slave or free, male and female; since you are all one in Christ Jesus. [29] And if you belong to Christ, then you are Abraham's seed, heirs

according to the promise. [1] Now I say that as long as the heir is a child, he differs in no way from a slave, though he is the owner of everything. [2] Instead, he is under guardians and trustees until the time set by his father. [3] In the same way we also, when we were children, were in slavery under the elements[C] of the world. [4] When the time came to completion, God sent his Son, born of a woman, born under the law, [5] to redeem those under the law, so that we might receive adoption as sons. [6] And because you are sons, God sent the Spirit of his Son into our[D] hearts, crying, "Abba,[E] Father!" [7] So you are no longer a slave but a son, and if a son, then God has made you an heir. Nm 26:52-62; Lk 2:7; Rm 4:13; 7:6; Col 3:22

Paul's Concern for the Galatians

[8] But in the past, since you didn't know God, you were enslaved to things[F] that by nature are not gods. [9] But now, since you know God, or rather have become known by God, how can you turn back again to the weak and worthless elements? Do you want to be enslaved to them all over again? [10] You are observing special days, months, seasons, and years. [11] I am fearful for you, that perhaps my labor for you has been wasted. Pr 2:6; Jn 7:28; Php 3:8

[12] I beg you, brothers and sisters: Become like me, for I also became like you. You have not wronged me; [13] you know[G] that previously I preached the gospel to you because of a weakness of the flesh. [14] You did not despise or reject me

A[3:19] Or because of transgressions   B[3:22] Lit under sin   C[4:3] Or spirits, or principles   D[4:6] Other mss read your   E[4:6] Aramaic for father   F[4:8] Or beings   G[4:12-13] Or [12] Become like I am, because I—inasmuch as you are brothers and sisters—am not requesting anything of you. You wronged me. [13] You know though my physical condition was a trial for you.[A] On the contrary, you received me as an angel of God, as Christ Jesus himself.

¹⁵ Where, then, is your blessing? For I testify to you that, if possible, you would have torn out your eyes and given them to me. ¹⁶ So then, have I become your enemy because I told you the truth? ¹⁷ They court you eagerly, but not for good. They want to exclude you from me, so that you would pursue them. ¹⁸ But it is always good to be pursued[B] in a good manner — and not just when I am with you. ¹⁹ My children, I am again suffering labor pains for you until Christ is formed in you. ²⁰ I would like to be with you right now and change my tone of voice, because I don't know what to do about you. 1Co 4:15; Eph 4:15; 1Th 2:11

Sarah and Hagar: Two Covenants

²¹ Tell me, you who want to be under the law, don't you hear the law? ²² For it is written that Abraham had two sons, one by a slave and the other by a free woman. ²³ But the one by the slave was born as a result of the flesh, while the one by the free woman was born through promise. ²⁴ These things are being taken figuratively, for the women represent two covenants. One is from Mount Sinai and bears children into slavery — this is Hagar. ²⁵ Now Hagar represents Mount Sinai in Arabia and corresponds to the present Jerusalem, for she is in slavery with her children. ²⁶ But the Jerusalem above is free, and she is our mother. ²⁷ For it is written, Gn 16:15; Jn 8:37

**Rejoice, childless woman,
unable to give birth.**

**Burst into song and shout,
you who are not in labor,
for the children
of the desolate woman
will be many,
more numerous than those
of the woman who has
a husband.**[C]   Is 54:1

²⁸ Now you too, brothers and sisters, like Isaac, are children of promise. ²⁹ But just as then the child born as a result of the flesh persecuted the one born as a result of the Spirit, so also now. ³⁰ But what does the Scripture say? **"Drive out the slave and her son, for the son of the slave will never be a coheir with the son of the free woman."**[D] ³¹ Therefore, brothers and sisters, we are not children of a slave but of the free woman. Ps 105:9; Jms 2:21

Freedom of the Christian

5 For freedom, Christ set us free. Stand firm then and don't submit again to a yoke of slavery. ² Take note! I, Paul, am telling you that if you get yourselves circumcised, Christ will not benefit you at all. ³ Again I testify to every man who gets himself circumcised that he is obligated to do the entire law. ⁴ You who are trying to be justified by the law are alienated from Christ; you have fallen from grace. ⁵ For we eagerly await through the Spirit, by faith, the hope of righteousness. ⁶ For in Christ Jesus neither circumcision nor uncircumcision accomplishes anything; what matters is faith working through love. Rm 14:4; Gl 4:22

⁷ You were running well. Who prevented you from being persuaded regarding the truth?[E] ⁸ This

A 4:14 Other mss read me   B 4:18 Lit zealously courted   C 4:27 Is 54:1   D 4:30 Gn 21:10   E 5:7 Or obeying the truth persuasion does not come from the one who calls you. ⁹ A little leaven[A] leavens the whole batch of dough. ¹⁰ I myself am persuaded in the Lord you will not accept any other view. But whoever it is that is confusing you will pay the penalty. ¹¹ Now brothers and sisters, if I still preach circumcision, why am I still persecuted? In that case the offense of the cross has been abolished. ¹² I wish those who are disturbing you might also let themselves be mutilated!   Jn 8:14

¹³ For you were called to be free, brothers and sisters; only don't use this freedom as an opportunity[B] for the flesh, but serve one another through love. ¹⁴ For the whole law is fulfilled in one statement: **Love your neighbor as yourself.**[C] ¹⁵ But if you bite and devour one another, watch out, or you will be consumed by one another.   Mt 1:22; Col 3:15

The Spirit Versus the Flesh

¹⁶ I say then, walk by the Spirit and you will certainly not carry out the desire of the flesh. ¹⁷ For the flesh desires what is against the Spirit, and the Spirit desires what is against the flesh; these are opposed to each other, so that you don't do what you want. ¹⁸ But if you are led by the Spirit, you are not under the law.   Rm 8:4; 1Tm 3:16; 1Pt 2:11; 2Pt 1:4; 2:10

¹⁹ Now the works of the flesh are obvious:[D] sexual immorality, moral impurity, promiscuity, ²⁰ idolatry, sorcery, hatreds, strife, jealousy, outbursts of anger, selfish ambitions, dissensions, factions, ²¹ envy,[E] drunkenness, carousing, and anything similar. I am warning you about these things — as I warned you before — that those who practice such things will not inherit the kingdom of God.   Mk 7:21; 1Th 4:3

²² But the fruit of the Spirit is love, joy, peace, patience, kindness, goodness, faithfulness, ²³ gentleness, and self-control. The law is not against such things.[F] ²⁴ Now those who belong to Christ Jesus have crucified the flesh with its passions and desires. ²⁵ If we live by the Spirit, let us also keep in step with the Spirit. ²⁶ Let us not become conceited, provoking one another, envying one another.   Rm 6:21

Carry One Another's Burdens

6 Brothers and sisters, if someone is overtaken in any wrongdoing, you who are spiritual, restore such a person with a gentle spirit,[G] watching out for yourselves so that you also won't be tempted. ² Carry one another's burdens; in this way you will fulfill the law of Christ. ³ For if anyone considers himself to be something when he is nothing, he deceives himself. ⁴ Let each person examine his own work, and then he can take pride in himself alone, and not compare himself with someone else. ⁵ For each person will have to carry his own load.   Ps 51:12; 1Co 9:21; Jms 1:13; 3:13

⁶ Let the one who is taught the word share all his good things with the teacher. ⁷ Don't be deceived: God is not mocked. For whatever a person sows he will also reap, ⁸ because the one who sows to his flesh will reap destruction from the flesh, but the one who sows to the Spirit will reap eternal life

---

[A]5:9 Or yeast   [B]5:13 Lit a pretext; a military term for abuse of position   [C]5:14 Lv 19:18   [D]5:19 Other mss add adultery,   [E]5:21 Other mss add murders,   [F]5:23 Or Against such things there is no law   [G]6:1 Or with the Spirit of gentleness from the Spirit. [9] Let us not get tired of doing good, for we will reap at the proper time if we don't give up. [10] Therefore, as we have opportunity, let us work for the good of all, especially for those who belong to the household of faith. Ps 51:11; Ac 2:4

Concluding Exhortation

[11] Look at what large letters I use as I write to you in my own handwriting. [12] Those who want to make a good impression in the flesh are the ones who would compel you to be circumcised — but only to avoid being persecuted for the cross of Christ. [13] For even the circumcised don't keep the law themselves, and yet they want you to be circumcised in order to boast about your flesh. [14] But as for me, I will never boast about anything except the cross of our Lord Jesus Christ. The world has been crucified to me through the cross, and I to the world. [15] For [A] both circumcision and uncircumcision mean nothing; what matters instead is a new creation. [16] May peace come to all those who follow this standard, and mercy even to the Israel of God! [B]   Ac 15:1; Php 3:3,18; 2Tm 3:12

[17] From now on, let no one cause me trouble, because I bear on my body the marks of Jesus. [18] Brothers and sisters, the grace of our Lord Jesus Christ be with your spirit. Amen.   Ps 51:12; Php 3:10

[A]6:15 Other mss add *in Christ Jesus*   [B]6:16 Or *And for those who follow this standard, may peace and mercy be upon them, even upon the Israel of God,* or *And as many who will follow this standard, peace be upon them and mercy even upon the Israel of God.*

EPHESIANS

Greeting

1 Paul, an apostle of Christ Jesus by God's will: Ac 13:9; Eph 1:9

To the faithful saints in Christ Jesus[A] at Ephesus.[B] Ac 18:19-21; Eph 5:2

² Grace to you and peace from God our Father and the Lord Jesus Christ.

God's Rich Blessings

³ Blessed is the God and Father of our Lord Jesus Christ, who has blessed us with every spiritual blessing in the heavens in Christ. ⁴ For he chose us in him, before the foundation of the world, to be holy and blameless in love before him.[C] ⁵ He predestined us to be adopted as sons through Jesus Christ for himself, according to the good pleasure of his will, ⁶ to the praise of his glorious grace that he lavished on us in the Beloved One. Eph 1:20; 2:6; 3:10; 6:12

⁷ In him we have redemption through his blood, the forgiveness of our trespasses, according to the riches of his grace ⁸ that he richly poured out on us with all wisdom and understanding.[D] ⁹ He made known to us the mystery of his will, according to his good pleasure that he purposed in Christ ¹⁰ as a plan for the right time[E] — to bring everything together in Christ, both things in heaven and things on earth in him. Ps 25:11; Mt 9:2; Heb 9:12

¹¹ In him we have also received an inheritance,[F] because we were predestined according to the plan of the one who works out everything in agreement with the purpose of his will, ¹² so that we who had already put our hope in Christ might bring praise to his glory.

¹³ In him you also were sealed with the promised Holy Spirit when you heard the word of truth, the gospel of your salvation, and when you believed. ¹⁴ The Holy Spirit is the down payment of our inheritance, until the redemption of the possession, to the praise of his glory. Ps 51:11; Jn 1:33; Ac 2:4; Rm 8:9; Col 1:5; 2 Th 2:10

Prayer for Spiritual Insight

¹⁵ This is why, since I heard about your faith in the Lord Jesus and your love for all the saints, ¹⁶ I never stop giving thanks for you as I remember you in my prayers. ¹⁷ I pray that the God of our Lord Jesus Christ, the glorious Father,[G] would give you the Spirit[H] of wisdom and revelation in the knowledge of him. ¹⁸ I pray that the eyes of your heart may be enlightened so that you may know what is the hope of his calling, what is the wealth of his glorious inheritance in the saints, ¹⁹ and what is the immeasurable greatness of his power toward us who believe, according to the mighty working of his strength. Ps 51:12

God's Power in Christ

²⁰ He exercised this power in Christ by raising him from the dead and seating him at his right

---

A 1:1 Or *to the saints, the believers in Christ Jesus*   **B** 1:1 Other mss omit *at Ephesus*   **C** 1:4 Or *in his sight. In love*   **D** 1:8 Or *on us. With all wisdom and understanding*   **E** 1:10 Or *the fulfillment of times*   **F** 1:11 Or *In him we are also an inheritance*,   **G** 1:17 Or *the Father of glory*   **H** 1:17 Or *a spirit* hand in the heavens — ²¹ far above every ruler and authority, power and dominion, and every title given, ^A not only in this age but also in the one to come. ²² And **he subjected everything under his feet** ^B and appointed him ^C as head over everything for the church, ²³ which is his body, the fullness of the one who fills all things in every way.   Php 2:6,9

From Death to Life

2 And you were dead in your trespasses and sins ² in which you previously lived according to the ways of this world, according to the ruler of the power of the air, the spirit now working in the disobedient. ^D ³ We too all previously lived among them in our fleshly desires, carrying out the inclinations of our flesh and thoughts, and we were by nature children under wrath as the others were also. ⁴ But God, who is rich in mercy, because of his great love that he had for us, ^E ⁵ made us alive with Christ even though we were dead in trespasses. You are saved by grace! ⁶ He also raised us up with him and seated us with him in the heavens in Christ Jesus, ⁷ so that in the coming ages he might display the immeasurable riches of his grace through his kindness to us in Christ Jesus. ⁸ For you are saved by grace through faith, and this is not from yourselves; it is God's gift — ⁹ not from works, so that no one can boast. ¹⁰ For we are his workmanship, created in Christ Jesus for good works, which God prepared ahead of time for us to do.   Jn 5:25; 1Co 2:12; Php 3:3; 2Pt 2:10,20; Jd 8

Unity in Christ

¹¹ So then, remember that at one time you were Gentiles in the flesh — called "the uncircumcised" by those called "the circumcised," which is done in the flesh by human hands. ¹² At that time you were without Christ, excluded from the citizenship of Israel, and foreigners to the covenants of promise, without hope and without God in the world. ¹³ But now in Christ Jesus, you who were far away have been brought near by the blood of Christ. ¹⁴ For he is our peace, who made both groups one and tore down the dividing wall of hostility. In his flesh, ¹⁵ he made of no effect the law consisting of commands and expressed in regulations, so that he might create in himself one new man from the two, resulting in peace. ¹⁶ He did this so that he might reconcile both to God in one body through the cross by which he put the hostility to death. ^F ¹⁷ He came and proclaimed the good news of peace to you who were far away and peace to those who were near. ¹⁸ For through him we both have access in one spirit to the Father. ¹⁹ So then you are no longer foreigners and strangers, but fellow citizens with the saints, and members of God's household, ²⁰ built on the foundation of the apostles and prophets, with Christ Jesus himself as the cornerstone. ²¹ In him the whole building, being put together, grows into a holy temple in the Lord. ²² In him you are also being built together for God's dwelling in the Spirit.   Gn 12:7; Gl 6:15; Php 3:3; 1Th 1:3

---

^A 1:21 Lit *every name named*   ^B 1:22 Ps 8:6   ^C 1:22 Lit *gave him*   ^D 2:2 Lit *sons of disobedience*   ^E 2:4 Lit *love with which he loved us*   ^F 2:16 Or *death in himself*

Paul's Ministry to the Gentiles

3 For this reason, I, Paul, the prisoner of Christ Jesus on behalf of you Gentiles — [2] you have heard, haven't you, about the administration of God's grace that he gave to me for you? [3] The mystery was made known to me by revelation, as I have briefly written above. [4] By reading this you are able to understand my insight into the mystery of Christ. [5] This was not made known to people[A] in other generations as it is now revealed to his holy apostles and prophets by the Spirit: [6] The Gentiles are coheirs, members of the same body, and partners in the promise in Christ Jesus through the gospel. [7] I was made a servant of this gospel by the gift of God's grace that was given to me by the working of his power.   2Tm 1:8; 1Pt 4:13

[8] This grace was given to me — the least of all the saints — to proclaim to the Gentiles the incalculable riches of Christ, [9] and to shed light for all about the administration of the mystery hidden for ages in God who created all things. [10] This is so that God's multi-faceted wisdom may now be made known through the church to the rulers and authorities in the heavens. [11] This is according to his eternal purpose accomplished in Christ Jesus our Lord. [12] In him we have boldness and confident access through faith in him.[B] [13] So then I ask you not to be discouraged over my afflictions on your behalf, for they are your glory.   Rm 1:15; 10:12; 11:12

Prayer for Spiritual Power

[14] For this reason I kneel before the Father[C] [15] from whom every family in heaven and on earth is named. [16] I pray that he may grant you, according to the riches of his glory, to be strengthened with power in your inner being through his Spirit, [17] and that Christ may dwell in your hearts through faith. I pray that you, being rooted and firmly established in love, [18] may be able to comprehend with all the saints what is the length and width, height and depth of God's love, [19] and to know Christ's love that surpasses knowledge, so that you may be filled with all the fullness of God.   Lk 8:14; Php 2:10

[20] Now to him who is able to do above and beyond all that we ask or think according to the power that works in us — [21] to him be glory in the church and in Christ Jesus to all generations, forever and ever. Amen.   Mk 14:36; 16:25; Rm 16:25; 2Co 9:8; Jd 24

Unity and Diversity in the Body of Christ

4 Therefore I, the prisoner in the Lord, urge you to live worthy of the calling you have received, [2] with all humility and gentleness, with patience, bearing with one another in love, [3] making every effort to keep the unity of the Spirit through the bond of peace. [4] There is one body and one Spirit — just as you were called to one hope[D] at your calling — [5] one Lord, one faith, one baptism, [6] one God and Father of all, who is above all and through all and in all.   Col 3:12; 2Tm 1:8

[7] Now grace was given to each one of us according to the measure of Christ's gift. [8] For it says: 1Co 12:7-11

When he ascended on high,
  he took the captives captive;
  he gave gifts to people.[E]

A **3:5** Lit *to the sons of men*   B **3:12** Or *through his faithfulness*   C **3:14** Other mss add *of our Lord Jesus Christ*   D **4:4** Lit *called in one hope*   E **4:8** Ps 68:18

⁹ But what does "he ascended" mean except that he ^A also descended to the lower parts of the earth? ^B ¹⁰ The one who descended is also the one who ascended far above all the heavens, to fill all things. ¹¹ And he himself gave some to be apostles, some prophets, some evangelists, some pastors and teachers, ¹² equipping the saints for the work of ministry, to build up the body of Christ, ¹³ until we all reach unity in the faith and in the knowledge of God's Son, growing into maturity with a stature measured by Christ's fullness. ¹⁴ Then we will no longer be little children, tossed by the waves and blown around by every wind of teaching, by human cunning with cleverness in the techniques of deceit. ¹⁵ But speaking the truth in love, let us grow in every way into him who is the head — Christ. ¹⁶ From him the whole body, fitted and knit together by every supporting ligament, promotes the growth of the body for building up itself in love by the proper working of each individual part.   Jn 3:13; 6:62; Rm 10:6-7

Living the New Life

¹⁷ Therefore, I say this and testify in the Lord: You should no longer live as the Gentiles live, in the futility of their thoughts. ¹⁸ They are darkened in their understanding, excluded from the life of God, because of the ignorance that is in them and because ^C of the hardness of their hearts. ¹⁹ They became callous and gave themselves over to promiscuity for the practice of every kind of impurity with a desire for more and more. ^D   1Th 4:17

²⁰ But that is not how you came to know Christ, ²¹ assuming you heard about him and were taught by him, as the truth is in Jesus, ²² to take off ^E your former way of life, the old self that is corrupted by deceitful desires, ²³ to be renewed ^F in the spirit of your minds, ²⁴ and to put on ^G the new self, the one created according to God's likeness in righteousness and purity of the truth.

²⁵ Therefore, putting away lying, **speak the truth, each one to his neighbor,** ^H because we are members of one another. ²⁶ **Be angry and do not sin.** ^I Don't let the sun go down on your anger, ²⁷ and don't give the devil an opportunity. ²⁸ Let the thief no longer steal. Instead, he is to do honest work with his own hands, so that he has something to share with anyone in need. ²⁹ No foul language should come from your mouth, but only what is good for building up someone in need, ^J so that it gives grace to those who hear. ³⁰ And don't grieve God's Holy Spirit. You were sealed by him ^K for the day of redemption. ³¹ Let all bitterness, anger and wrath, shouting and slander be removed from you, along with all malice. ³² And be kind and compassionate to one another, forgiving one another, just as God also forgave you ^L in Christ.   Ps 4:4; 37:8; Pr 31:25; Zch 8:16; Mt 18:21

5 Therefore, be imitators of God, as dearly loved children, ² and walk in love, as Christ also loved us and gave himself for us, a sacrificial and fragrant offering to

---

^A **4:9** Other mss add *first*   ^B **4:9** Or *the lower parts, namely, the earth*   ^C **4:18** Or *in them because*   ^D **4:19** Lit *with greediness*   ^E **4:21-22** Or *Jesus. This means: take off* (as a command)   ^F **4:22-23** Or *desires; renew* (as a command)   ^G **4:23-24** Or *minds; and put on* (as a command)   ^H **4:25** Zch 8:16   ^I **4:26** Ps 4:4   ^J **4:29** Lit *for the building up of the need*   ^K **4:30** Or *Spirit, by whom you were sealed*   ^L **4:32** Other mss read *us*

God. [3] But sexual immorality and any impurity or greed should not even be heard of [A] among you, as is proper for saints. [4] Obscene and foolish talking or crude joking are not suitable, but rather giving thanks. [5] For know and recognize this: Every sexually immoral or impure or greedy person, who is an idolater, does not have an inheritance in the kingdom of Christ and of God.   1Th 4:3,7; 2Th 2:13; Ti 2:14

Light Versus Darkness

[6] Let no one deceive you with empty arguments, for God's wrath is coming on the disobedient [B] because of these things. [7] Therefore, do not become their partners. [8] For you were once darkness, but now you are light in the Lord. Live as children of light — [9] for the fruit of the light [C] consists of all goodness, righteousness, and truth — [10] testing what is pleasing to the Lord. [11] Don't participate in the fruitless works of darkness, but instead expose them. [12] For it is shameful even to mention what is done by them in secret. [13] Everything exposed by the light is made visible, [14] for what makes everything visible is light. Therefore it is said: Is 2:5; Rm 2:5; Rv 6:16

> Get up, sleeper, and rise up
>   from the dead,   Pr 6:4; Jn 5:25
> and Christ will shine on you.

Consistency in the Christian Life

[15] Pay careful attention, then, to how you live — not as unwise people but as wise — [16] making the most of the time, [D] because the days are evil. [17] So don't be foolish, but understand what the Lord's will is.

[18] And don't get drunk with wine, which leads to reckless living, but be filled by the Spirit: [19] speaking to one another in psalms, hymns, and spiritual songs, singing and making music with your heart to the Lord, [20] giving thanks always for everything to God the Father in the name of our Lord Jesus Christ, [21] submitting to one another in the fear of Christ.   Jr 31:31-34; Rm 12:2; Col 4:5

Wives and Husbands

[22] Wives, submit [E] to your husbands as to the Lord, [23] because the husband is the head of the wife as Christ is the head of the church. He is the Savior of the body. [24] Now as the church submits to Christ, so also wives are to submit to their husbands in everything. [25] Husbands, love your wives, just as Christ loved the church and gave himself for her [26] to make her holy, cleansing [F] her with the washing of water by the word. [27] He did this to present the church to himself in splendor, without spot or wrinkle or anything like that, but holy and blameless. [28] In the same way, husbands are to love their wives as their own bodies. He who loves his wife loves himself. [29] For no one ever hates his own flesh but provides and cares for it, just as Christ does for the church, [30] since we are members of his body. [G] [31] **For this reason a man will leave his father and mother and be joined to his wife, and the two will become one flesh.** [H] [32] This mystery is profound, but I am talking about Christ and the church. [33] To sum up, each one of

---

[A]**5:3** Or *be named*   [B]**5:6** Lit *sons of disobedience*   [C]**5:9** Other mss read *fruit of the Spirit*   [D]**5:16** Lit *buying back the time*   [E]**5:22** Other mss omit *submit*   [F]**5:26** Or *having cleansed*   [G]**5:30** Other mss add *and of his flesh and of his bones*   [H]**5:31** Gn 2:24

you is to love his wife as himself, and the wife is to respect her husband. Gn 3:16; 1Co 11:3,7-9,11-12; Col 3:18; 1Pt 3:1

Children and Parents

6 Children, obey your parents in the Lord, because this is right. [2] **Honor your father and mother**, which is the first commandment with a promise, [3] **so that it may go well with you and that you may have a long life in the land.**[A,B] [4] Fathers, don't stir up anger in your children, but bring them up in the training and instruction of the Lord. Ex 20:12; Pr 1:8; 6:20; 23:22; Rm 10:19; Col 3:20

Slaves and Masters

[5] Slaves, obey your human[C] masters with fear and trembling, in the sincerity of your heart, as you would Christ. [6] Don't work only while being watched, as people-pleasers, but as slaves of Christ, do God's will from your heart. [7] Serve with a good attitude, as to the Lord and not to people, [8] knowing that whatever good each one does, slave or free, he will receive this back from the Lord. [9] And masters, treat your slaves the same way, without threatening them, because you know that both their Master and yours is in heaven, and there is no favoritism with him. Col 3:22; 1Pt 2:18

Christian Warfare

[10] Finally, be strengthened by the Lord and by his vast strength. [11] Put on the full armor of God so that you can stand against the schemes of the devil. [12] For our struggle is not against flesh and blood, but against the rulers, against the authorities, against the cosmic powers of this darkness, against evil, spiritual forces in the heavens. [13] For this reason take up the full armor of God, so that you may be able to resist in the evil day, and having prepared everything, to take your stand. [14] Stand, therefore, with truth like a belt around your waist, righteousness like armor on your chest, [15] and your feet sandaled with readiness for the gospel of peace. [16] In every situation take up the shield of faith with which you can extinguish all the flaming arrows of the evil one. [17] Take the helmet of salvation and the sword of the Spirit — which is the word of God. [18] Pray at all times in the Spirit with every prayer and request, and stay alert with all perseverance and intercession for all the saints. [19] Pray also for me, that the message may be given to me when I open my mouth to make known with boldness the mystery of the gospel. [20] For this I am an ambassador in chains. Pray that I might be bold enough to speak about it as I should. Pr 31:25; Ac 4:33; Eph 2:6; 6:11-17

Paul's Farewell

[21] Tychicus, our dearly loved brother and faithful servant[D] in the Lord, will tell you all the news about me so that you may be informed. [22] I am sending him to you for this very reason, to let you know how we are and to encourage your hearts. Lk 16:25; Col 4:8; Ti 3:12

[23] Peace to the brothers and sisters, and love with faith, from God the Father and the Lord Jesus Christ. [24] Grace be with all who have undying love for our Lord Jesus Christ.[E,F] Mt 5:16; 11:27; Lk 11:13; Jn 8:42

A **6:3** Or *life on the earth*   B **6:2-3** Ex 20:12   C **6:5** Lit *according to the flesh*   D **6:21** Or *deacon*
E **6:24** Other mss add *Amen.*   F **6:24** Lit *all who love our Lord Jesus Christ in incorruption*

PHILIPPIANS

Greeting

1 Paul and Timothy, servants of Christ Jesus: Ac 13:9; 16:1; 1Tm 1:2 To all the saints in Christ Jesus who are in Philippi, including the overseers and deacons. Ac 16:12-40 ² Grace to you and peace from God our Father and the Lord Jesus Christ.

Thanksgiving and Prayer

³ I give thanks to my God for every remembrance of you, ᴬ ⁴ always praying with joy for all of you in my every prayer, ⁵ because of your partnership in the gospel from the first day until now. ⁶ I am sure of this, that he who started a good work in you ᴮ will carry it on to completion until the day of Christ Jesus. ⁷ Indeed, it is right for me to think this way about all of you, because I have you in my heart, ᶜ and you are all partners with me in grace, both in my imprisonment and in the defense and confirmation of the gospel. ⁸ For God is my witness, how deeply I miss all of you with the affection of Christ Jesus. ⁹ And I pray this: that your love will keep on growing in knowledge and every kind of discernment, ¹⁰ so that you may approve the things that are superior and may be pure and blameless in the day of Christ, ¹¹ filled with the fruit of righteousness that comes through Jesus Christ to the glory and praise of God. Ac 16:12-40; 2Co 11:7-9

Advance of the Gospel

¹² Now I want you to know, brothers and sisters, that what has happened to me has actually advanced the gospel, ¹³ so that it has become known throughout the whole imperial guard, and to everyone else, that my imprisonment is because I am in Christ. ¹⁴ Most of the brothers have gained confidence in the Lord from my imprisonment and dare even more to speak the word ᴰ fearlessly. ¹⁵ To be sure, some preach Christ out of envy and rivalry, but others out of good will. ¹⁶ These preach out of love, knowing that I am appointed for the defense of the gospel; ¹⁷ the others proclaim Christ out of selfish ambition, not sincerely, thinking that they will cause me trouble in my imprisonment. ¹⁸ What does it matter? Only that in every way, whether from false motives or true, Christ is proclaimed, and in this I rejoice. Yes, and I will continue to rejoice ¹⁹ because I know this will lead to my salvation ᴱ through your prayers and help from the Spirit of Jesus Christ. ²⁰ My eager expectation and hope is that I will not be ashamed about anything, but that now as always, with all courage, Christ will be highly honored in my body, whether by life or by death. Mk 13:9

Living Is Christ

²¹ For me, to live is Christ and to die is gain. ²² Now if I live on in the flesh, this means fruitful work for

---

ᴬ1:3 Or *for your every remembrance of me*   ᴮ1:6 Or *work among you*   ᶜ1:7 Or *because you have me in your heart*   ᴰ1:14 Other mss add *of God*   ᴱ1:19 Or *vindication* me; and I don't know which one I should choose. ²³ I am torn between the two. I long to depart and be with Christ — which is far better — ²⁴ but to remain in the flesh is more necessary for your sake. ²⁵ Since I am persuaded of this, I know that I will remain and continue with all of you for your progress and joy in the faith, ²⁶ so that, because of my coming to you again, your boasting in Christ Jesus may abound. Rm 14:7-9; Gl 2:19-20; Php 1:11,15; 3:7

²⁷ Just one thing: As citizens of heaven, live your life worthy of the gospel of Christ. Then, whether I come and see you or am absent, I will hear about you that you are standing firm in one spirit, in one accord, ^A contending together for the faith of the gospel, ²⁸ not being frightened in any way by your opponents. This is a sign of destruction for them, but of your salvation — and this is from God. ²⁹ For it has been granted to you on Christ's behalf not only to believe in him, but also to suffer for him, ³⁰ since you are engaged in the same struggle that you saw I had and now hear that I have. Ac 23:1; 1Co 16:13; Gl 5:1; Eph 6:13-17

Christian Humility

2 If then there is any encouragement in Christ, if any consolation of love, if any fellowship with the Spirit, if any affection and mercy, ² make my joy complete by thinking the same way, having the same love, united in spirit, intent on one purpose. ³ Do nothing out of selfish ambition or conceit, but in humility consider others as more important than yourselves. ⁴ Everyone should look out not only for his own interests, but also for the interests of others. Rm 5:8; 15:30; 2Th 2:16

Christ's Humility and Exaltation

⁵ Adopt the same attitude as that of Christ Jesus,

⁶ who, existing in the form of God,
did not consider equality with God   Is 9:6; Jn 1:1,14; 20:28
as something to be exploited. ^B
⁷ Instead he emptied himself by assuming the form of a servant,   Is 42:1; 53:12; Mt 20:28
taking on the likeness of humanity.   Jn 1:14; Rm 8:3; Gl 4:4
And when he had come as a man,
⁸ he humbled himself by becoming obedient to the point of death — even to death on a cross.
⁹ For this reason God highly exalted him   Is 52:13
and gave him the name that is above every name,
¹⁰ so that at the name of Jesus every knee will bow —   Is 45:23
in heaven and on earth   2Co 5:1
and under the earth —   Mt 28:18
¹¹ and every tongue will confess   Is 45:23; Rm 10:9; 14:11
that Jesus Christ is Lord, to the glory of God the Father.   Lk 9:32; Jn 17:24; 2Co 3:18

Lights in the World

¹² Therefore, my dear friends, just as you have always obeyed, so now, not only in my presence but even more in my absence, work out your own salvation with fear and trembling. ¹³ For it is God who is working in you both to will and to work according to his good purpose. ¹⁴ Do everything without grumbling and

^A 1:27 Lit *soul*   ^B 2:6 Or *to be grasped*, or *to be held on to* arguing, [15] so that you may be blameless and pure, children of God who are faultless in a crooked and perverted generation, among whom you shine like stars in the world, [16] by holding firm to the word of life. Then I can boast in the day of Christ that I didn't run or labor for nothing. [17] But even if I am poured out as a drink offering on the sacrificial service of your faith, I am glad and rejoice with all of you. [18] In the same way you should also be glad and rejoice with me. Mk 1:27; Ac 6:1; Phm 1

Timothy and Epaphroditus

[19] Now I hope in the Lord Jesus to send Timothy to you soon so that I too may be encouraged by news about you. [20] For I have no one else like-minded who will genuinely care about your interests; [21] all seek their own interests, not those of Jesus Christ. [22] But you know his proven character, because he has served with me in the gospel ministry like a son with a father. [23] Therefore, I hope to send him as soon as I see how things go with me. [24] I am confident in the Lord that I myself will also come soon. Lk 24:3; Ac 16:1

[25] But I considered it necessary to send you Epaphroditus — my brother, coworker, and fellow soldier, as well as your messenger and minister to my need — [26] since he has been longing for all of you and was distressed because you heard that he was sick. [27] Indeed, he was so sick that he nearly died. However, God had mercy on him, and not only on him but also on me, so that I would not have sorrow upon sorrow. [28] For this reason, I am very eager to send him so that you may rejoice again when you see him and

I may be less anxious. [29] Therefore, welcome him in the Lord with great joy and hold people like him in honor, [30] because he came close to death for the work of Christ, risking his life to make up what was lacking in your ministry to me. Mt 6:8; Mk 14:6

Knowing Christ

3 In addition, my brothers and sisters, rejoice in the Lord. To write to you again about this is no trouble for me and is a safeguard for you. Rm 12:12; 2Co 6:10; Php 1:18

[2] Watch out for the dogs, watch out for the evil workers, watch out for those who mutilate the flesh. [3] For we are the circumcision, the ones who worship by the Spirit of God, boast in Christ Jesus, and do not put confidence in the flesh — [4] although I have reasons for confidence in the flesh. If anyone else thinks he has grounds for confidence in the flesh, I have more: [5] circumcised the eighth day; of the nation of Israel, of the tribe of Benjamin, a Hebrew born of Hebrews; regarding the law, a Pharisee; [6] regarding zeal, persecuting the church; regarding the righteousness that is in the law, blameless. Rm 8:4; 2Co 3:7; Gl 5:4,25; 6:15

[7] But everything that was a gain to me, I have considered to be a loss because of Christ. [8] More than that, I also consider everything to be a loss in view of the surpassing value of knowing Christ Jesus my Lord. Because of him I have suffered the loss of all things and consider them as dung, so that I may gain Christ [9] and be found in him, not having a righteousness of my own from the law, but one that is through faith in Christ[A] — the righteousness from

[A]**3:9** Or through the faithfulness of Christ

God based on faith. [10] My goal is to know him and the power of his resurrection and the fellowship of his sufferings, being conformed to his death, [11] assuming that I will somehow reach the resurrection from among the dead.   Jn 17:3; 2Co 4:6; Php 2:3

Reaching Forward to God's Goal

[12] Not that I have already reached the goal or am already perfect, but I make every effort to take hold of it because I also have been taken hold of by Christ Jesus. [13] Brothers and sisters, I do not [A] consider myself to have taken hold of it. But one thing I do: Forgetting what is behind and reaching forward to what is ahead, [14] I pursue as my goal the prize promised by God's heavenly [B] call in Christ Jesus. [15] Therefore, let all of us who are mature think this way. And if you think differently about anything, God will reveal this also to you. [16] In any case, we should live up to whatever truth we have attained. [17] Join in imitating me, brothers and sisters, and pay careful attention to those who live according to the example you have in us. [18] For I have often told you, and now say again with tears, that many live as enemies of the cross of Christ. [19] Their end is destruction; their god is their stomach; their glory is in their shame. They are focused on earthly things, [20] but our citizenship is in heaven, and we eagerly wait for a Savior from there, the Lord Jesus Christ. [21] He will transform the body of our humble condition into the likeness of his glorious body, by the power that enables him to subject everything to himself.   Jn 1:5; 12:35; Rm 9:30

[4] So then, my dearly loved and longed for brothers and sisters, my joy and crown, in this manner stand firm in the Lord, dear friends.

Practical Counsel

[2] I urge Euodia and I urge Syntyche to agree in the Lord. [3] Yes, I also ask you, true partner, [C] to help these women who have contended for the gospel at my side, along with Clement and the rest of my coworkers whose names are in the book of life. [4] Rejoice in the Lord always. I will say it again: Rejoice! [5] Let your graciousness [D] be known to everyone. The Lord is near. [6] Don't worry about anything, but in everything, through prayer and petition with thanksgiving, present your requests to God. [7] And the peace of God, which surpasses all understanding, will guard your hearts and minds in Christ Jesus.   1Co 16:22

[8] Finally [E] brothers and sisters, whatever is true, whatever is honorable, whatever is just, whatever is pure, whatever is lovely, whatever is commendable — if there is any moral excellence and if there is anything praiseworthy — dwell on these things. [9] Do what you have learned and received and heard from me, and seen in me, and the God of peace will be with you.   Ti 2:2

Appreciation of Support

[10] I rejoiced in the Lord greatly because once again you renewed your care for me. You were, in fact, concerned about me but lacked the opportunity to show it. [11] I don't say this out of need, for I have learned to be content in whatever circumstances I find myself. [12] I know both

---

[A] 3:13 Other mss read not yet   [B] 3:14 Or upward   [C] 4:3 Or true Syzygus, possibly a person's name   [D] 4:5 Or gentleness   [E] 4:8 Or In addition how to make do with little, and I know how to make do with a lot. In any and all circumstances I have learned the secret of being content — whether well fed or hungry, whether in abundance or in need. [13] I am able to do all things through him[A] who strengthens me. [14] Still, you did well by partnering with me in my hardship.   2Co 8:1-2; 11:9; Php 1:5

[15] And you Philippians know that in the early days of the gospel, when I left Macedonia, no church shared with me in the matter of giving and receiving except you alone. [16] For even in Thessalonica you sent gifts for my need several times. [17] Not that I seek the gift, but I seek the profit[B] that is increasing to your account. [18] But I have received everything in full, and I have an abundance. I am fully supplied,[C] having received from Epaphroditus what you provided — a fragrant offering, an acceptable sacrifice, pleasing to God. [19] And my God will supply all your needs according to his riches in glory in Christ Jesus. [20] Now to our God and Father be glory forever and ever. Amen.   Ac 16:6-40; 17:1; Php 1:1,5

Final Greetings

[21] Greet every saint in Christ Jesus. The brothers who are with me send you greetings. [22] All the saints send you greetings, especially those who belong to Caesar's household. [23] The grace of the Lord Jesus Christ be with your spirit. [D]   Mt 22:17

[A]**4:13** Other mss read *Christ*   [B]**4:17** Lit *fruit*   [C]**4:18** Or *Here, then, is my receipt for everything, I have an abundance, for I am fully supplied*   [D]**4:23** Other mss add *Amen.*

COLOSSIANS

Greeting

1 Paul, an apostle of Christ Jesus by God's will, and Timothy our brother: Ac 16:1; 1Co 1:1; 2Co 1:1; Eph 1:1; 2Tm 1:1 ² To the saints in Christ at Colossae, who are faithful brothers and sisters.

Grace to you and peace from God our Father.ᴬ

Thanksgiving

³ We always thank God, the Father of our Lord Jesus Christ, when we pray for you, ⁴ for we have heard of your faith in Christ Jesus and of the love you have for all the saints ⁵ because of the hope reserved for you in heaven. You have already heard about this hope in the word of truth, the gospel ⁶ that has come to you. It is bearing fruit and growing all over the world, just as it has among you since the day you heard it and came to truly appreciate God's grace.ᴮ ⁷ You learned this from Epaphras, our dearly loved fellow servant. He is a faithful minister of Christ on yourᶜ behalf, ⁸ and he has told us about your love in the Spirit. Ps 119:142; Jn 14:6; 2Co 11:10; Eph 1:13

Prayer for Spiritual Growth

⁹ For this reason also, since the day we heard this, we haven't stopped praying for you. We are asking that you may be filled with the knowledge of his will in all wisdom and spiritual understanding,ᴰ ¹⁰ so that you may walk worthy of the Lord, fully pleasing to him: bearing fruit in every good work and growing in the knowledge of God, ¹¹ being strengthened with all power, according to his glorious might, so that you may have great endurance and patience, joyfully ¹² giving thanks to the Father, who has enabled youᴱ to share in the saints' inheritance in the light. ¹³ He has rescued us from the domain of darkness and transferred us into the kingdom of the Son he loves. ¹⁴ In him we have redemption,ᶠ the forgiveness of sins. Pr 2:6; Jn 14:13; Jms 1:5

The Centrality of Christ

¹⁵ He is the image
  of the invisible God, Php 2:6
  the firstborn over all creation.
¹⁶ For everything was created
  by him, Gn 1:1; Mk 13:19
in heaven and on earth,
  the visible and the invisible,
  whether thrones
  or dominions
  or rulers or authorities —
all things have been created
  through him and for him.
¹⁷ He is before all things, Jn 1:1-2
and by him all things
  hold together. Ps 104:24
¹⁸ He is also the head
  of the body, the church;
he is the beginning, Gn 1:1; Mk 1:1
  the firstborn from the dead,
so that he might come to have
  first place in everything.
¹⁹ For God was pleased to have

all his fullness dwell in him,
20 and through him to reconcile
everything to himself,
whether things on earth
or things in heaven,
by making peace   Ac 7:26; Eph 2:14
through his blood, shed
on the cross. [A]   Lk 9:23; Heb 9:12

21 Once you were alienated and hostile in your minds expressed in your evil actions. 22 But now he has reconciled you by his physical body through his death, to present you holy, faultless, and blameless before him — 23 if indeed you remain grounded and steadfast in the faith and are not shifted away from the hope of the gospel that you heard. This gospel has been proclaimed in all creation under heaven, and I, Paul, have become a servant of it.   2Co 4:14; Gl 2:16; Php 2:8; Jd 24

Paul's Ministry

24 Now I rejoice in my sufferings for you, and I am completing in my flesh what is lacking in Christ's afflictions for his body, that is, the church. 25 I have become its servant, according to God's commission that was given to me for you, to make the word of God fully known, 26 the mystery hidden for ages and generations but now revealed to his saints. 27 God wanted to make known among the Gentiles the glorious wealth of this mystery, which is Christ in you, the hope of glory. 28 We proclaim him, warning and teaching everyone with all wisdom, so that we may present everyone mature in Christ. 29 I labor for this, striving with his strength that works powerfully in me.   2Co 1:4

2 For I want you to know how greatly I am struggling for you, for those in Laodicea, and for all who have not seen me in person. 2 I want their hearts to be encouraged and joined together in love, so that they may have all the riches of complete understanding and have the knowledge of God's mystery — Christ. [B] 3 In him are hidden all the treasures of wisdom and knowledge.   Col 4:13-16; 2Tm 4:7; Rv 1:11; 3:14

Christ Versus the Colossian Heresy

4 I am saying this so that no one will deceive you with arguments that sound reasonable. 5 For I may be absent in body, but I am with you in spirit, rejoicing to see how well ordered you are and the strength of your faith in Christ.   Ps 51:12; 1Th 2:17

6 So then, just as you have received Christ Jesus as Lord, continue to live in him, 7 being rooted and built up in him and established in the faith, just as you were taught, and overflowing with gratitude.   Eph 2:20; 3:11; 4:21; Heb 13:9; Jd 3

8 Be careful that no one takes you captive through philosophy and empty deceit based on human tradition, based on the elements of the world, rather than Christ. 9 For the entire fullness of God's nature dwells bodily [c] in Christ, 10 and you have been filled by him, who is the head over every ruler and authority. 11 You were also circumcised in him with a circumcision not done with hands, by putting off the body of flesh, in the circumcision of Christ, 12 when you were buried with him in baptism, in which you were also raised with him through

[A] 1:20 Other mss add through him   [B] 2:2 Other mss read mystery of God, both of the Father and of Christ; other ms variations exist on this v.   [C] 2:9 Or nature lives in a human body faith in the working of God, who raised him from the dead. [13] And when you were dead in trespasses and in the uncircumcision of your flesh, he made you alive with him and forgave us all our trespasses. [14] He erased the certificate of debt, with its obligations, that was against us and opposed to us, and has taken it away by nailing it to the cross. [15] He disarmed the rulers and authorities and disgraced them publicly; he triumphed over them in him.[A]   Mk 7:3; Eph 4:15; 1Tm 6:20

[16] Therefore, don't let anyone judge you in regard to food and drink or in the matter of a festival or a new moon or a Sabbath day.[B] [17] These are a shadow of what was to come; the substance is[C] Christ. [18] Let no one condemn[D] you by delighting in ascetic practices and the worship of angels, claiming access to a visionary realm. Such people are inflated by empty notions of their unspiritual[E] mind. [19] He doesn't hold on to the head, from whom the whole body, nourished and held together by its ligaments and tendons, grows with growth from God.   Lk 6:37; Jn 6:55; 1Co 8:4

[20] If you died with Christ to the elements of this world, why do you live as if you still belonged to the world? Why do you submit to regulations: [21] "Don't handle, don't taste, don't touch"? [22] All these regulations refer to what is destined to perish by being used up; they are human commands and doctrines. [23] Although these have a reputation for wisdom by promoting self-made religion, false humility, and severe treatment of the body, they are not of any value in curbing self-indulgence.[F]   Rm 6:8; Ac 7:22; 1Tm 4:8; 1Pt 2:24

The Life of the New Man

3 So if you have been raised with Christ, seek the things above, where Christ is, seated at the right hand of God. [2] Set your minds on things above, not on earthly things. [3] For you died, and your life is hidden with Christ in God. [4] When Christ, who is your[G] life, appears, then you also will appear with him in glory.   Rm 6:8; 2Co 4:11; Php 3:19; Heb 10:12

[5] Therefore, put to death what belongs to your earthly nature: sexual immorality, impurity, lust, evil desire, and greed, which is idolatry. [6] Because of these, God's wrath is coming upon the disobedient,[H] [7] and you once walked in these things when you were living in them. [8] But now, put away all the following: anger, wrath, malice, slander, and filthy language from your mouth. [9] Do not lie to one another, since you have put off the old self with its practices [10] and have put on the new self. You are being renewed in knowledge according to the image of your[I] Creator. [11] In Christ there is not Greek and Jew, circumcision and uncircumcision, barbarian, Scythian, slave and free; but Christ is all and in all.   1Th 4:3,7

The Christian Life

[12] Therefore, as God's chosen ones, holy and dearly loved, put on compassion, kindness, humility, gentleness, and patience, [13] bearing with one another and forgiving one another if anyone has a grievance against another. Just as the

---

[A]2:15 Or *them through it* [B]2:16 Or *or sabbaths* [C]2:17 Or *substance belongs to* [D]2:18 Or *disqualify* [E]2:18 Lit *fleshly* [F]2:23 Lit *value against indulgence of the flesh* [G]3:4 Other mss read *our* [H]3:6 Other mss omit *upon the disobedient* [I]3:10 Lit *his*

Lord has forgiven you, so you are also to forgive. [14] Above all, put on love, which is the perfect bond of unity. [15] And let the peace of Christ, to which you were also called in one body, rule your hearts. And be thankful. [16] Let the word of Christ dwell richly among you, in all wisdom teaching and admonishing one another through psalms, hymns, and spiritual songs,[A] singing to God with gratitude in your hearts. [17] And whatever you do, in word or in deed, do everything in the name of the Lord Jesus, giving thanks to God the Father through him.   Jn 3:16; Ac 20:19; 2Co 6:6; 2Th 2:13; Rv 12:11

Christ in Your Home

[18] Wives, submit yourselves to your husbands, as is fitting in the Lord. [19] Husbands, love your wives and don't be bitter toward them. [20] Children, obey your parents in everything, for this pleases the Lord. [21] Fathers, do not exasperate your children, so that they won't become discouraged. [22] Slaves, obey your human masters in everything. Don't work only while being watched, as people-pleasers, but work wholeheartedly, fearing the Lord. [23] Whatever you do, do it from the heart, as something done for the Lord and not for people, [24] knowing that you will receive the reward of an inheritance from the Lord. You serve the Lord Christ. [25] For the wrongdoer will be paid back for whatever wrong he has done, and there is no favoritism.

4 Masters, deal with your slaves justly and fairly, since you know that you too have a Master in heaven.   Col 3:22

Speaking to God and Others

[2] Devote yourselves to prayer; stay alert in it with thanksgiving. [3] At the same time, pray also for us that God may open a door to us for the word, to speak the mystery of Christ, for which I am in chains, [4] so that I may make it known as I should. [5] Act wisely toward outsiders, making the most of the time. [6] Let your speech always be gracious, seasoned with salt, so that you may know how you should answer each person.   Ac 14:27; Rm 12:12

Final Greetings

[7] Tychicus, our dearly loved brother, faithful minister, and fellow servant in the Lord, will tell you all the news about me. [8] I have sent him to you for this very purpose, so that you may know how we are[B] and so that he may encourage your hearts. [9] He is coming with Onesimus, a faithful and dearly loved brother, who is one of you. They will tell you about everything here.   Nm 23:19; Lk 16:25; Ac 20:4; Col 2:2; Ti 3:12

[10] Aristarchus, my fellow prisoner, sends you greetings, as does Mark, Barnabas's cousin (concerning whom you have received instructions: if he comes to you, welcome him), [11] and so does Jesus who is called Justus. These alone of the circumcised are my coworkers for the kingdom of God, and they have been a comfort to me. [12] Epaphras, who is one of you, a servant of Christ Jesus, sends you greetings. He is always wrestling for you in his prayers, so that you can stand mature and fully assured[C] in everything God wills. [13] For I testify about him that he works hard[D] for you, for

---

[A] 3:16 Or and songs prompted by the Spirit   [B] 4:8 Other mss read that he may know how you are   [C] 4:12 Other mss read and complete   [D] 4:13 Other mss read he has a great zeal those in Laodicea, and for those in Hierapolis. [14] Luke, the dearly loved physician, and Demas send you greetings. [15] Give my greetings to the brothers and sisters in Laodicea, and to Nympha and the church in her home. [16] After this letter has been read at your gathering, have it read also in the church of the Laodiceans; and see that you also read the letter from Laodicea. [17] And tell Archippus, "Pay attention to the ministry you have received in the Lord, so that you can accomplish it." Ac 4:36; Gl 1:4; Col 1:7; Phm 23-24; Jd 3

[18] I, Paul, am writing this greeting with my own hand. Remember my chains. Grace be with you. [A] Php 1:7

1 THESSALONIANS

Greeting

1 Paul, Silvanus,[A] and Timothy:
To the church of the Thessalonians in God the Father and the Lord Jesus Christ.   Ac 17:1
Grace to you and peace.[B]

Thanksgiving

[2] We always thank God for all of you, making mention of you constantly in our prayers. [3] We recall, in the presence of our God and Father, your work produced by faith, your labor motivated by love, and your endurance inspired by hope in our Lord Jesus Christ. [4] For we know, brothers and sisters loved by God, that he has chosen you, [5] because our gospel did not come to you in word only, but also in power, in the Holy Spirit, and with full assurance. You know how we lived among you for your benefit, [6] and you yourselves became imitators of us and of the Lord when, in spite of severe persecution, you welcomed the message with joy from the Holy Spirit. [7] As a result, you became an example to all the believers in Macedonia and Achaia. [8] For the word of the Lord rang out from you, not only in Macedonia and Achaia, but in every place that your faith[C] in God has gone out. Therefore, we don't need to say anything, [9] for they themselves report[D] what kind of reception we had from you: how you turned to God from idols to serve the living and true God[10] and to wait for his Son from heaven, whom he raised from the dead — Jesus, who rescues us from the coming wrath.   Gl 5:6

Paul's Conduct

2 For you yourselves know, brothers and sisters, that our visit with you was not without result. [2] On the contrary, after we had previously suffered and were treated outrageously in Philippi, as you know, we were emboldened by our God to speak the gospel of God to you in spite of great opposition. [3] For our exhortation didn't come from error or impurity or an intent to deceive. [4] Instead, just as we have been approved by God to be entrusted with the gospel, so we speak, not to please people, but rather God, who examines our hearts. [5] For we never used flattering speech, as you know, or had greedy motives — God is our witness — [6] and we didn't seek glory from people, either from you or from others. [7] Although we could have been a burden as Christ's apostles, instead we were gentle[E] among you, as a nurse[F] nurtures her own children. [8] We cared so much for you that we were pleased to share with you not only the gospel of God but also our own lives, because you had become dear to us. [9] For you remember our labor and hardship, brothers and sisters. Working night and day so that we

---

[A]**1:1** Or *Silas*; Ac 15:22-32; 16:19-40; 17:1-16   [B]**1:1** Other mss add *from God our Father and the Lord Jesus Christ*   [C]**1:8** Or *in every place news of your faith*   [D]**1:9** Lit *report about us*   [E]**2:7** Many mss read *infants*   [F]**2:7** Or *nursing mother* would not burden any of you, we preached God's gospel to you. [10] You are witnesses, and so is God, of how devoutly, righteously, and blamelessly we conducted ourselves with you believers. [11] As you know, like a father with his own children, [12] we encouraged, comforted, and implored each one of you to live worthy of God, who calls you into his own kingdom and glory. Ac 17:1-9

Reception and Opposition to the Message

[13] This is why we constantly thank God, because when you received the word of God that you heard from us, you welcomed it not as a human message, but as it truly is, the word of God, which also works effectively in you who believe. [14] For you, brothers and sisters, became imitators of God's churches in Christ Jesus that are in Judea, since you have also suffered the same things from people of your own country, just as they did from the Jews [15] who killed the Lord Jesus and the prophets and persecuted us. They displease God and are hostile to everyone, [16] by keeping us from speaking to the Gentiles so that they may be saved. As a result, they are constantly filling up their sins to the limit, and wrath has overtaken them at last. [A] Lk 1:5; 8:21; Php 1:29; 2Th 3:1

Paul's Desire to See Them

[17] But as for us, brothers and sisters, after we were forced to leave you [B] for a short time (in person, not in heart), we greatly desired and made every effort to return and see you face to face. [18] So we wanted to come to you — even I, Paul, time and again — but Satan hindered us. [19] For who is our hope or joy or crown of boasting in the presence of our Lord Jesus at his coming? Is it not you? [20] Indeed you are our glory and joy! Col 2:5; 1Th 3:10

Anxiety in Athens

3 Therefore, when we could no longer stand it, we thought it was better to be left alone in Athens. [2] And we sent Timothy, our brother and God's coworker [C] in the gospel of Christ, to strengthen and encourage you concerning your faith, [3] so that no one will be shaken by these afflictions. For you yourselves know that we are appointed to this. [4] In fact, when we were with you, we told you in advance that we were going to experience affliction, and as you know, it happened. [5] For this reason, when I could no longer stand it, I also sent him to find out about your faith, fearing that the tempter had tempted you and that our labor might be for nothing. Ac 16:1; 17:15; 1Tm 1:2; Php 1:27

Encouraged by Timothy

[6] But now Timothy has come to us from you and brought us good news about your faith and love. He reported that you always have good memories of us and that you long to see us, as we also long to see you. [7] Therefore, brothers and sisters, in all our distress and affliction, we were encouraged about you through your faith. [8] For now we live, if you stand firm in the Lord. [9] How can we thank God for you in return for all the joy we experience before our God because of you, [10] as we pray very earnestly night and day to see you face to face and to

[A] **2:16** Or to the end   [B] **2:17** Lit orphaned from you   [C] **3:2** Other mss read servant complete what is lacking in your faith? Ac 18:5; Rm 14:4; 1Co 11:2; 16:13; Php 1:8

Prayer for the Church

[11] Now may our God and Father himself, and our Lord Jesus, direct our way to you. [12] And may the Lord cause you to increase and overflow with love for one another and for everyone, just as we do for you. [13] May he make your hearts blameless in holiness before our God and Father at the coming of our Lord Jesus with all his saints. Amen. [A]   Jn 8:42; Php 4:20

The Call to Sanctification

4 Additionally then, brothers and sisters, we ask and encourage you in the Lord Jesus, that as you have received instruction from us on how you should live and please God — as you are doing [B] — do this even more. [2] For you know what commands we gave you through the Lord Jesus.

[3] For this is God's will, your sanctification: that you keep away from sexual immorality, [4] that each of you knows how to control his own body [C] in holiness and honor, [5] not with lustful passions, like the Gentiles, who don't know God. [6] This means one must not transgress against and take advantage of a brother or sister in this manner, because the Lord is an avenger of all these offenses, as we also previously told and warned you. [7] For God has not called us to impurity but to live in holiness. [8] Consequently, anyone who rejects this does not reject man, but God, who gives you his Holy Spirit. Rm 6:19,22; 1Th 5:18; 1Pt 1:2

Loving and Working

[9] About brotherly love: You don't need me to write you because you yourselves are taught by God to love one another. [10] In fact, you are doing this toward all the brothers and sisters in the entire region of Macedonia. But we encourage you, brothers and sisters, to do this even more, [11] to seek to lead a quiet life, to mind your own business, [D] and to work with your own hands, as we commanded you, [12] so that you may behave properly in the presence of outsiders and not be dependent on anyone. [E]   Lk 14:4; Jn 6:45; Ac 16:9; 1Jn 3:11

The Comfort of Christ's Coming

[13] We do not want you to be uninformed, brothers and sisters, concerning those who are asleep, so that you will not grieve like the rest, who have no hope. [14] For if we believe that Jesus died and rose again, in the same way, through Jesus, God will bring with him those who have fallen asleep. [15] For we say this to you by a word from the Lord: We who are still alive at the Lord's coming will certainly not precede those who have fallen asleep. [16] For the Lord himself will descend from heaven with a shout, [F] with the archangel's voice, and with the trumpet of God, and the dead in Christ will rise first. [17] Then we who are still alive, who are left, will be caught up together with them in the clouds to meet the Lord in the air, and so we will always be with the Lord. [18] Therefore encourage [G] one another with these words. Jr 14:19; Lk 18:33; Eph 2:12; 1Th 1:3

[A] 3:13 Other mss omit *Amen.*   [B] 4:1 Lit *walking*   [C] 4:4 Or *to acquire his own wife*; lit *to possess his own vessel*   [D] 4:11 Lit *to practice one's own things*   [E] 4:12 Or *not need anything,* or *not be in need*   [F] 4:16 Or *command*   [G] 4:18 Or *comfort*

The Day of the Lord

5 About the times and the seasons: Brothers and sisters, you do not need anything to be written to you. [2] For you yourselves know very well that the day of the Lord will come just like a thief in the night. [3] When they say, "Peace and security," then sudden destruction will come upon them, like labor pains on a pregnant woman, and they will not escape. [4] But you, brothers and sisters, are not in the dark, for this day to surprise you like a thief. [5] For you are all children of light and children of the day. We do not belong to the night or the darkness. [6] So then, let us not sleep, like the rest, but let us stay awake and be self-controlled. [7] For those who sleep, sleep at night, and those who get drunk, get drunk at night. [8] But since we belong to the day, let us be self-controlled and put on the armor of faith and love, and a helmet of the hope of salvation. [9] For God did not appoint us to wrath, but to obtain salvation through our Lord Jesus Christ, [10] who died for us, so that whether we are awake or asleep, we may live together with him. [11] Therefore encourage one another and build each other up as you are already doing. Dn 2:21; Jl 2:1; Mt 25:13; Ac 1:7; 2:20

Exhortations and Blessings

[12] Now we ask you, brothers and sisters, to give recognition to those who labor among you and lead you[A] in the Lord and admonish you, [13] and to regard them very highly in love because of their work. Be at peace among yourselves. [14] And we exhort you, brothers and sisters: warn those who are idle,[B] comfort the discouraged, help the weak, be patient with everyone. [15] See to it that no one repays evil for evil to anyone, but always pursue what is good for one another and for all. [16] Rejoice always, [17] pray constantly, [18] give thanks in everything; for this is God's will for you in Christ Jesus. [19] Don't stifle the Spirit. [20] Don't despise prophecies, [21] but test all things. Hold on to what is good. [22] Stay away from every kind of evil. Mk 9:50; Lk 18:7; 1Co 16:18; Php 2:29; 2Th 3:15

[23] Now may the God of peace himself sanctify you completely. And may your whole spirit, soul, and body be kept sound and blameless at the coming of our Lord Jesus Christ. [24] He who calls you is faithful; he will do it. [25] Brothers and sisters, pray for us also. [26] Greet all the brothers and sisters with a holy kiss. [27] I charge you by the Lord that this letter be read to all the brothers and sisters. [28] The grace of our Lord Jesus Christ be with you.

A5:12 Or care for you B5:14 Or who are disorderly, or who are undisciplined

2 THESSALONIANS

Greeting

1 Paul, Silvanus, [A] and Timothy:
To the church of the Thessalonians in God our Father and the Lord Jesus Christ. Ac 17:1

² Grace to you and peace from God our Father and the Lord Jesus Christ.

God's Judgment and Glory

³ We ought to thank God always for you, brothers and sisters, and rightly so, since your faith is flourishing and the love each one of you has for one another is increasing. ⁴ Therefore, we ourselves boast about you among God's churches — about your perseverance and faith in all the persecutions and afflictions that you are enduring. ⁵ It is clear evidence of God's righteous judgment that you will be counted worthy of God's kingdom, for which you also are suffering, ⁶ since it is just for God to repay with affliction those who afflict you ⁷ and to give relief to you who are afflicted, along with us. This will take place at the revelation of the Lord Jesus from heaven with his powerful angels, ⁸ when he takes vengeance with flaming fire on those who don't know God and on those who don't obey the gospel of our Lord Jesus. ⁹ They will pay the penalty of eternal destruction from the Lord's presence and from his glorious strength ¹⁰ on that day when he comes to be glorified by his saints and to be marveled at by all those who have believed, because our testimony among you was believed. ¹¹ In view of this, we always pray for you that our God will make you worthy of his calling, and by his power fulfill your every desire to do good [B] and your work produced by faith, ¹² so that the name of our Lord Jesus will be glorified by you, and you by him, according to the grace of our God and the Lord Jesus Christ. 1Co 13:1

The Man of Lawlessness

2 Now concerning the coming of our Lord Jesus Christ and our being gathered to him: We ask you, brothers and sisters, ² not to be easily upset or troubled, either by a prophecy [C] or by a message or by a letter supposedly from us, alleging that the day of the Lord [D] has come. ³ Don't let anyone deceive you in any way. For that day will not come unless the apostasy [E] comes first and the man of lawlessness [F] is revealed, the man doomed to destruction. ⁴ He opposes and exalts himself above every so-called god or object of worship, so that he sits [G] in God's temple, proclaiming that he himself is God. 1Th 1:10; 1Jn 2:28; Rv 11:8

⁵ Don't you remember that when I was still with you I used to tell you about this? ⁶ And you know what currently restrains him, so that he will be revealed in his time. ⁷ For

---

[A] **1:1** Or *Silas*; Ac 15:22-32; 16:19-40; 17:1-16   [B] **1:11** Or *power bring to fruition your desire to do good*
[C] **2:2** Or *spiritual utterance*   [D] **2:2** Other mss read *Christ*   [E] **2:3** Or *rebellion*   [F] **2:3** Other mss read *man of sin*   [G] **2:4** Other mss add *as God*

the mystery of lawlessness is already at work, but the one now restraining will do so until he is out of the way, [8] and then the lawless one will be revealed. The Lord Jesus will destroy him with the breath of his mouth and will bring him to nothing at the appearance of his coming. [9] The coming of the lawless one is based on Satan's working, with all kinds of false miracles, signs, and wonders, [10] and with every wicked deception among those who are perishing. They perish because they did not accept the love of the truth and so be saved. [11] For this reason God sends them a strong delusion so that they will believe the lie, [12] so that all will be condemned — those who did not believe the truth but delighted in unrighteousness.   Is 11:4; Mt 13:41; Lk 21:8

Stand Firm

[13] But we ought to thank God always for you, brothers and sisters loved by the Lord, because from the beginning[A] God has chosen you for salvation through sanctification by the Spirit and through belief in the truth. [14] He called you to this through our gospel, so that you might obtain the glory of our Lord Jesus Christ. [15] So then, brothers and sisters, stand firm and hold to the traditions you were taught, whether by what we said or what we wrote.   Rm 6:19; 9:11; 11:5; Eph 1:4; 1Th 1:4

[16] May our Lord Jesus Christ himself and God our Father, who has loved us and given us eternal encouragement and good hope by grace, [17] encourage your hearts and strengthen you in every good work and word.   Jn 3:16; Rv 12:11

Pray for Us

3 In addition, brothers and sisters, pray for us that the word of the Lord may spread rapidly and be honored, just as it was with you, [2] and that we may be delivered from wicked and evil people, for not all have faith. [B] [3] But the Lord is faithful; he will strengthen and guard you from the evil one. [4] We have confidence in the Lord about you, that you are doing and will continue to do what we command. [5] May the Lord direct your hearts to God's love and Christ's endurance.   Mt 27:43; Rm 15:31; 1Th 2:13

Warning Against Irresponsible Behavior

[6] Now we command you, brothers and sisters, in the name of our Lord Jesus Christ, to keep away from every brother or sister who is idle and does not live according to the tradition received from us. [7] For you yourselves know how you should imitate us: We were not idle among you; [8] we did not eat anyone's food free of charge; instead, we labored and toiled, working night and day, so that we would not be a burden to any of you. [9] It is not that we don't have the right to support, but we did it to make ourselves an example to you so that you would imitate us. [10] In fact, when we were with you, this is what we commanded you: "If anyone isn't willing to work, he should not eat." [11] For we hear that there are some among you who are idle. They are not busy but busybodies. [12] Now we command and exhort such people by the Lord Jesus Christ to work quietly and provide for themselves. [C] [13] But as for you,

---

[A] **2:13** Other mss read *because as a firstfruit*   [B] **3:2** Or *for the faith is not in everyone*   [C] **3:12** Lit *they may eat their own bread* brothers and sisters, do not grow weary in doing good. Jn 14:13 ¹⁴ If anyone does not obey our instruction in this letter, take note of that person; don't associate with him, so that he may be ashamed. ¹⁵ Yet don't consider him as an enemy, but warn him as a brother.

Final Greetings

¹⁶ May the Lord of peace himself give you peace always in every way. The Lord be with all of you. ¹⁷ I, Paul, am writing this greeting with my own hand, which is an authenticating mark in every letter; this is how I write. ¹⁸ The grace of our Lord Jesus Christ be with you all. 1Th 5:23

1 TIMOTHY

Greeting

1 Paul, an apostle of Christ Jesus by the command of God our Savior and of Christ Jesus our hope: ² To Timothy, my true son in the faith. _{Ac 16:1; 20:4; 1Co 4:17; 16:10}

Grace, mercy, and peace from God the^A Father and Christ Jesus our Lord.

False Doctrine and Misuse of the Law

³ As I urged you when I went to Macedonia, remain in Ephesus so that you may instruct certain people not to teach false doctrine ⁴ or to pay attention to myths and endless genealogies. These promote empty speculations rather than God's plan, which operates by faith. ⁵ Now the goal of our instruction is love that comes from a pure heart, a good conscience, and a sincere faith. ⁶ Some have departed from these and turned aside to fruitless discussion. ⁷ They want to be teachers of the law, although they don't understand what they are saying or what they are insisting on. ⁸ But we know that the law is good, provided one uses it legitimately. ⁹ We know that the law is not meant for a righteous person, but for the lawless and rebellious, for the ungodly and sinful, for the unholy and irreverent, for those who kill their fathers and mothers, for murderers, ¹⁰ for the sexually immoral and homosexuals, for slave traders, liars, perjurers, and for whatever else is contrary to the sound teaching ¹¹ that conforms to the gospel concerning the glory of the blessed God, which was entrusted to me. _{Ac 16:9; Eph 1:1; Ti 1:14; Jd 4}

Paul's Testimony

¹² I give thanks to Christ Jesus our Lord who has strengthened me, because he considered me faithful, appointing me to the ministry — ¹³ even though I was formerly a blasphemer, a persecutor, and an arrogant man. But I received mercy because I acted out of ignorance in unbelief, ¹⁴ and the grace of our Lord overflowed, along with the faith and love that are in Christ Jesus. ¹⁵ This saying is trustworthy and deserving of full acceptance: "Christ Jesus came into the world to save sinners" — and I am the worst of them. ¹⁶ But I received mercy for this reason, so that in me, the worst of them, Christ Jesus might demonstrate his extraordinary patience as an example to those who would believe in him for eternal life. ¹⁷ Now to the King eternal, immortal, invisible, the only^B God, be honor and glory forever and ever. Amen. _{Ac 6:11; 9:22; Php 4:13; 2Tm 3:2; 2Pt 2:11}

Engage in Battle

¹⁸ Timothy, my son, I am giving you this instruction in keeping with the prophecies previously made about you, so that by recalling them you may fight the good fight, ¹⁹ having faith and a good conscience. Some have rejected these and have shipwrecked their faith. ²⁰ Among

^A**1:2** Other mss read *our*   ^B**1:17** Other mss add *wise* them are Hymenaeus and Alexander, whom I have delivered to Satan, so that they may be taught not to blaspheme. 1Co 13:2; 1Tm 4:14; 2Tm 1:6

Instructions on Prayer

2 First of all, then, I urge that petitions, prayers, intercessions, and thanksgivings be made for everyone, [2] for kings and all those who are in authority, so that we may lead a tranquil and quiet life in all godliness and dignity. [3] This is good, and it pleases God our Savior, [4] who wants everyone to be saved and to come to the knowledge of the truth. Ezr 6:10; Rm 13:1; 1Co 2:1; 2Pt 1:3; Ti 2:7

[5] For there is one God and one mediator between God and humanity, the man Christ Jesus, [6] who gave himself as a ransom for all, a testimony at the proper time. Dt 6:4

[7] For this I was appointed a herald, an apostle (I am telling the truth;[A] I am not lying), and a teacher of the Gentiles in faith and truth. Ac 9:15

Instructions to Men and Women

[8] Therefore, I want the men in every place to pray, lifting up holy hands without anger or argument. [9] Also, the women are to dress themselves in modest clothing, with decency and good sense, not with elaborate hairstyles, gold, pearls, or expensive apparel, [10] but with good works, as is proper for women who profess to worship God. [11] A woman is to learn quietly with full submission. [12] I do not allow a woman to teach or to have authority over a man; instead, she is to remain quiet. [13] For Adam was formed first, then Eve. [14] And Adam was not deceived, but the woman was deceived and transgressed.

[15] But she will be saved through childbearing, if they continue in faith, love, and holiness, with good sense. Mk 7:21; Lk 9:46-47; 24:38; Rm 14:1; Php 2:14

Qualifications for Overseers and Deacons

3 This saying is trustworthy: "If anyone aspires to be an overseer,[B] he desires a noble work." [2] An overseer, therefore, must be above reproach, the husband of one wife, self-controlled, sensible, respectable, hospitable, able to teach, [3] not an excessive drinker, not a bully but gentle, not quarrelsome, not greedy. [4] He must manage his own household competently and have his children under control with all dignity. [5] (If anyone does not know how to manage his own household, how will he take care of God's church?) [6] He must not be a new convert, or he might become conceited and incur the same condemnation as the devil. [7] Furthermore, he must have a good reputation among outsiders, so that he does not fall into disgrace and the devil's trap. Ac 20:28; Php 1:1; 1Tm 1:15; 4:9; Ti 1:7

[8] Deacons, likewise, should be worthy of respect, not hypocritical, not drinking a lot of wine, not greedy for money, [9] holding the mystery of the faith with a clear conscience. [10] They must also be tested first; if they prove blameless, then they can serve as deacons. [11] Wives,[C] too, must be worthy of respect, not slanderers, self-controlled, faithful in everything. [12] Deacons are to be husbands of one wife, managing their children and their own households competently. [13] For those who have served well as deacons acquire a good standing for themselves and

[A]2:7 Other mss add in Christ   [B]3:1 Or bishop, pastor   [C]3:11 Or The women great boldness in the faith that is in Christ Jesus. Php 1:1,27; 1Tm 1:2,19

The Mystery of Godliness

[14] I write these things to you, hoping to come to you soon. [15] But if I should be delayed, I have written so that you will know how people ought to conduct themselves in God's household, which is the church of the living God, the pillar and foundation of the truth. [16] And most certainly, the mystery of godliness is great: 1Co 3:16; 2Co 6:16; 1Tm 4:13

He[A] was manifested
   in the flesh, Jn 1:14; Php 2:7; 1Jn 4:2
vindicated in the Spirit,
seen by angels,
preached among the nations,
believed on in the world,
taken up in glory. Mk 16:19; Jn 20:17

Demonic Influence

4 Now the Spirit explicitly says that in later times some will depart from the faith, paying attention to deceitful spirits and the teachings of demons, [2] through the hypocrisy of liars whose consciences are seared. [3] They forbid marriage and demand abstinence from foods that God created to be received with gratitude by those who believe and know the truth. [4] For everything created by God is good, and nothing is to be rejected if it is received with thanksgiving, [5] since it is sanctified by the word of God and by prayer. Jn 14:17; 16:13; Jd 3

A Good Servant of Jesus Christ

[6] If you point these things out to the brothers and sisters, you will be a good servant of Christ Jesus, nourished by the words of the faith and the good teaching that you have followed. [7] But have nothing to do with pointless and silly myths. Rather, train yourself in godliness. [8] For the training of the body has limited benefit, but godliness is beneficial in every way, since it holds promise for the present life and also for the life to come. [9] This saying is trustworthy and deserves full acceptance. [10] For this reason we labor and strive, [B] because we have put our hope in the living God, who is the Savior of all people, especially of those who believe. Php 1:27

Instructions for Ministry

[11] Command and teach these things. [12] Don't let anyone despise your youth, but set an example for the believers in speech, in conduct, in love, [C] in faith, and in purity. [13] Until I come, give your attention to public reading, exhortation, and teaching. [14] Don't neglect the gift that is in you; it was given to you through prophecy, with the laying on of hands by the council of elders. [15] Practice these things; be committed to them, so that your progress may be evident to all. [16] Pay close attention to your life and your teaching; persevere in these things, for in doing this you will save both yourself and your hearers. Pr 12:6; 1Co 13:1; 1Tm 5:2; 2Pt 3:11; Jd 23

5 Don't rebuke an older man, but exhort him as a father, younger men as brothers, [2] older women as mothers, and the younger women as sisters with all purity.

The Support of Widows

[3] Support[D] widows who are genuinely in need. [4] But if any widow

---

has children or grandchildren, let them learn to practice godliness toward their own family first and to repay their parents, for this pleases God. [5] The widow who is truly in need and left all alone has put her hope in God and continues night and day in her petitions and prayers; [6] however, she who is self-indulgent is dead even while she lives. [7] Command this also, so that they will be above reproach. [8] But if anyone does not provide for his own family, especially for his own household, he has denied the faith and is worse than an unbeliever. Ex 22:22; Lk 15:24; 1Co 7:34; Jms 1:27

[9] No widow is to be enrolled on the list for support unless she is at least sixty years old, has been the wife of one husband, [10] and is well known for good works — that is, if she has brought up children, shown hospitality, washed the saints' feet, helped the afflicted, and devoted herself to every good work. [11] But refuse to enroll younger widows, for when they are drawn away from Christ by desire, they want to marry [12] and will therefore receive condemnation because they have renounced their original pledge. [13] At the same time, they also learn to be idle, going from house to house; they are not only idle, but are also gossips and busybodies, saying things they shouldn't say. [14] Therefore, I want younger women to marry, have children, manage their households, and give the adversary no opportunity to accuse us. [15] For some have already turned away to follow Satan. [16] If any [A] believing woman has widows in her family, let her help

them. Let the church not be burdened, so that it can help widows in genuine need. Mk 14:6; 2Co 9:8; Gl 3:10

Honoring the Elders

[17] The elders who are good leaders are to be considered worthy of double honor, [B] especially those who work hard at preaching and teaching. [18] For the Scripture says: **Do not muzzle an ox while it is treading out the grain,** [C] and, "The worker is worthy of his wages." Dt 25:4; 1Th 5:12

[19] Don't accept an accusation against an elder unless it is supported by two or three witnesses. [20] Publicly rebuke those who sin, so that the rest will be afraid. [21] I solemnly charge you before God and Christ Jesus and the elect angels to observe these things without prejudice, doing nothing out of favoritism. [22] Don't be too quick to appoint [D] anyone as an elder, and don't share in the sins of others. Keep yourself pure. [23] Don't continue drinking only water, but use a little wine because of your stomach and your frequent illnesses. [24] Some people's sins are obvious, preceding them to judgment, but the sins of others surface [E] later. [25] Likewise, good works are obvious, and those that are not obvious cannot remain hidden. Dt 19:15; Lk 11:28

Honoring Masters

6 All who are under the yoke as slaves should regard their own masters [F] as worthy of all respect, so that God's name and his teaching will not be blasphemed. [2] Let those who have believing masters not be disrespectful to them because they are brothers, but serve them even better, since those who benefit from their service are believers and dearly loved.[A] Jn 10:25; Ac 15:14

False Doctrine and Human Greed

Teach and encourage these things. [3] If anyone teaches false doctrine and does not agree with the sound teaching of our Lord Jesus Christ and with the teaching that promotes godliness, [4] he is conceited and understands nothing, but has an unhealthy interest in disputes and arguments over words. From these come envy, quarreling, slander, evil suspicions, [5] and constant disagreement among people whose minds are depraved and deprived of the truth, who imagine that godliness is a way to material gain.[B] [6] But godliness with contentment is great gain. [7] For we brought nothing into the world, and[C] we can take nothing out. [8] If we have food and clothing,[D] we will be content with these. [9] But those who want to be rich fall into temptation, a trap, and many foolish and harmful desires, which plunge people into ruin and destruction. [10] For the love of money is a root[E] of all kinds of evil, and by craving it, some have wandered away from the faith and pierced themselves with many griefs. Ps 37:1; 2Tm 2:14,23; Ti 3:9; 2Pt 1:3; Rv 11:8

Fight the Good Fight

[11] But you, man of God, flee from these things, and pursue righteousness, godliness, faith, love, endurance, and gentleness. [12] Fight the good fight of the faith. Take hold of eternal life to which you were called and about which you have made a good confession in the presence of many witnesses. [13] In the presence of God, who gives life to all, and of Christ Jesus, who gave a good confession before Pontius Pilate, I charge you [14] to keep this command without fault or failure until the appearing of our Lord Jesus Christ. [15] God will bring this about in his own time. He is the blessed and only Sovereign, the King of kings, and the Lord of lords, [16] who alone is immortal and who lives in unapproachable light, whom no one has seen or can see, to him be honor and eternal power. Amen. 1Co 13:1; 2Tm 4:7; Ti 2:13; Jd 3; Rv 13:10

Instructions to the Rich

[17] Instruct those who are rich in the present age not to be arrogant or to set their hope on the uncertainty of wealth, but on God,[F] who richly provides us with all things to enjoy. [18] Instruct them to do what is good, to be rich in good works, to be generous and willing to share, [19] storing up treasure for themselves as a good foundation for the coming age, so that they may take hold of what is truly life. 1Sm 2:3; Ec 7:8; Rm 11:20

Guard the Heritage

[20] Timothy, guard what has been entrusted to you, avoiding irreverent and empty speech and contradictions from what is falsely called knowledge. [21] By professing it, some people have departed from the faith. 1Tm 1:11; 2Tm 1:12,14; 4:4

Grace be with you all.

[A]6:2 Or because, as believers who are dearly loved, they are devoted to others' welfare   [B]6:5 Other mss add From such people withdraw yourself.   [C]6:7 Other mss add it is clear that   [D]6:8 Or food and shelter   [E]6:10 Or is the root   [F]6:17 Other mss read on the living God

2 TIMOTHY

Greeting

1 Paul, an apostle of Christ Jesus by God's will, for the sake of the promise of life in Christ Jesus: Col 1 ² To Timothy, my dearly loved son.

Grace, mercy, and peace from God the Father and Christ Jesus our Lord. 1Tm 1:2; 2Jn 3

Thanksgiving

³ I thank God, whom I serve with a clear conscience as my ancestors did, when I constantly remember you in my prayers night and day. ⁴ Remembering your tears, I long to see you so that I may be filled with joy. ⁵ I recall your sincere faith that first lived in your grandmother Lois and in your mother Eunice and now, I am convinced, is in you also. Ac 23:1; 24:16; Rm 9:1; 2Co 1:12; 1Tm 1:19; 3:9

⁶ Therefore, I remind you to rekindle the gift of God that is in you through the laying on of my hands. ⁷ For God has not given us a spirit of fear, but one of power, A love, and sound judgment. 1Tm 4:14; 5:22

Not Ashamed of the Gospel

⁸ So don't be ashamed of the testimony about our Lord, or of me his prisoner. Instead, share in suffering for the gospel, relying on the power of God. ⁹ He has saved us and called us with a holy calling, not according to our works, but according to his own purpose and grace, which was given to us in Christ Jesus before time began. ¹⁰ This has now been made evident through the appearing of our Savior Christ Jesus, who has abolished death and has brought life and immortality to light through the gospel. ¹¹ For this gospel I was appointed a herald, apostle, and teacher, B ¹² and that is why I suffer these things. But I am not ashamed, because I know whom I have believed and am persuaded that he is able to guard what has been entrusted to me C until that day. Mk 8:38; Ac 4:33; Rm 1:16; 1Co 1:6; 2Tm 1:12,16

Be Loyal to the Faith

¹³ Hold on to the pattern of sound teaching that you have heard from me, in the faith and love that are in Christ Jesus. ¹⁴ Guard the good deposit through the Holy Spirit who lives in us. ¹⁵ You know that all those in the province of Asia have deserted me, including Phygelus and Hermogenes. ¹⁶ May the Lord grant mercy to the household of Onesiphorus, because he often refreshed me and was not ashamed of my chains. ¹⁷ On the contrary, when he was in Rome, he diligently searched for me and found me. ¹⁸ May the Lord grant that he obtain mercy from him on that day. You know very well how much he ministered at Ephesus. 1Tm 1:10; 2:1

Be Strong in Grace

2 You, therefore, my son, be strong in the grace that is in Christ Jesus. ² What you have heard from me in the presence of many

---

A 1:7 Or For the Spirit God gave us does not make us fearful, but gives us power   B 1:11 Other mss add of the Gentiles   C 1:12 Or guard what I have entrusted to him, or guard my deposit witnesses, commit to faithful men[A] who will be able to teach others also. Nm 12:7; Gl 1:6; 2Tm 1:13; 2Pt 3:18

[3] Share in suffering as a good soldier of Christ Jesus. [4] No one serving as a soldier gets entangled in the concerns of civilian life; he seeks to please the commanding officer. [5] Also, if anyone competes as an athlete, he is not crowned unless he competes according to the rules. [6] The hardworking farmer ought to be the first to get a share of the crops. [7] Consider what I say, for the Lord will give you understanding in everything. 1Tm 1:18

[8] Remember Jesus Christ, risen from the dead and descended from David, according to my gospel, [9] for which I suffer to the point of being bound like a criminal. But the word of God is not bound. [10] This is why I endure all things for the elect: so that they also may obtain salvation, which is in Christ Jesus, with eternal glory. [11] This saying is trustworthy: Mt 17:9; Lk 9:32; Jn 21:14; Jms 1:12

For if we died with him, Jn 8:51
we will also live with him;
[12] if we endure,
we will also reign with him;
if we deny him, he will also deny us;
[13] if we are faithless,
he remains faithful,
for he cannot deny himself.

An Approved Worker

[14] Remind them of these things, and charge them before God[B] not to fight about words. This is useless and leads to the ruin of those who listen. [15] Be diligent to present yourself to God as one approved, a worker who doesn't need to be ashamed, correctly teaching the word of truth. [16] Avoid irreverent and empty speech, since those who engage in it will produce even more godlessness, [17] and their teaching will spread like gangrene. Hymenaeus and Philetus are among them. [18] They have departed from the truth, saying that the resurrection has already taken place, and are ruining the faith of some. [19] Nevertheless, God's solid foundation stands firm, bearing this inscription: **The Lord knows those who are his,**[C] and let everyone who calls on the name of[D] the Lord turn away from wickedness. Eph 1:13; Col 1:5; 1Tm 6:4

[20] Now in a large house there are not only gold and silver vessels, but also those of wood and clay; some for honorable[E] use and some for dishonorable.[F] [21] So if anyone purifies himself from anything dishonorable,[G] he will be a special[H] instrument, set apart, useful to the Master, prepared for every good work. Rm 9:21; 2Co 9:8; Gl 3:10; 1Tm 5:10

[22] Flee from youthful passions, and pursue righteousness, faith, love, and peace, along with those who call on the Lord from a pure heart. [23] But reject foolish and ignorant disputes, because you know that they breed quarrels. [24] The Lord's servant must not quarrel, but must be gentle to everyone, able to teach,[I] and patient, [25] instructing his opponents with gentleness. Perhaps God will grant them repentance leading them to the knowledge of the truth. [26] Then they may come to their senses and escape the trap of the devil, who

[A]2:2 Or faithful people [B]2:14 Other mss read before the Lord [C]2:19 Nm 16:5 [D]2:19 Lit everyone who names the name of [E]2:20 Or special [F]2:20 Or ordinary [G]2:21 Lit from these [H]2:21 Or an honorable [I]2:24 Or everyone, skillful in teaching has taken them captive to do his will. Lk 12:51; 1Tm 4:12; 6:11; 2Tm 1:2

Difficult Times Ahead

3 But know this: Hard times will come in the last days. [2] For people will be lovers of self, lovers of money, boastful, proud, demeaning, disobedient to parents, ungrateful, unholy, [3] unloving, irreconcilable, slanderers, without self-control, brutal, without love for what is good, [4] traitors, reckless, conceited, lovers of pleasure rather than lovers of God, [5] holding to the form of godliness but denying its power. Avoid these people. Jn 6:39; Php 1:6; 1Pt 1:5; 2Pt 3:3; Jd 18

[6] For among them are those who worm their way into households and deceive gullible women overwhelmed by sins and led astray by a variety of passions, [7] always learning and never able to come to a knowledge of the truth. [8] Just as Jannes and Jambres resisted Moses, so these also resist the truth. They are men who are corrupt in mind and worthless in regard to the faith. [9] But they will not make further progress, for their foolishness will be clear to all, as was the foolishness of Jannes and Jambres. 2Co 11:10; 1Tm 2:4; 2Tm 2:25; 2Pt 1:4; 2:10

Struggles in the Christian Life

[10] But you have followed my teaching, conduct, purpose, faith, patience, love, and endurance, [11] along with the persecutions and sufferings that came to me in Antioch, Iconium, and Lystra. What persecutions I endured — and yet the Lord rescued me from them all. [12] In fact, all who want to live a godly life in Christ Jesus will be persecuted. [13] Evil people and impostors will become worse, deceiving and being deceived. [14] But as for you, continue in what you have learned and firmly believed. You know those who taught you, [15] and you know that from infancy you have known the sacred Scriptures, which are able to give you wisdom for salvation through faith in Christ Jesus. [16] All Scripture is inspired by God[A] and is profitable for teaching, for rebuking, for correcting, for training in righteousness, [17] so that the man of God may be complete, equipped for every good work. Pr 19:21; Ac 11:23; 1Co 13:1; 1Jn 4:16

Fulfill Your Ministry

4 I solemnly charge you before God and Christ Jesus, who is going to judge the living and the dead, and because of his appearing and his kingdom: [2] Preach the word; be ready in season and out of season; rebuke, correct, and encourage with great patience and teaching. [3] For the time will come when people will not tolerate sound doctrine, but according to their own desires, will multiply teachers for themselves because they have an itch to hear what they want to hear. [4] They will turn away from hearing the truth and will turn aside to myths. [5] But as for you, exercise self-control in everything, endure hardship, do the work of an evangelist, fulfill your ministry. Jn 5:22-30; Rm 5:18; 1Pt 4:5

[6] For I am already being poured out as a drink offering, and the time for my departure is close. [7] I have fought the good fight, I have finished the race, I have kept the faith. [8] There is reserved for me the

A3:16 Lit *breathed out by God*

crown of righteousness, which the Lord, the righteous Judge, will give me on that day, and not only to me, but to all those who have loved his appearing.[A] Gn 35:14; Jn 15:17; Php 2:17; Rv 12:1

Final Instructions

[9] Make every effort to come to me soon, [10] because Demas has deserted me, since he loved this present world, and has gone to Thessalonica. Crescens has gone to Galatia, Titus to Dalmatia. [11] Only Luke is with me. Bring Mark with you, for he is useful to me in the ministry. [12] I have sent Tychicus to Ephesus. [13] When you come, bring the cloak I left in Troas with Carpus, as well as the scrolls, especially the parchments. [14] Alexander the coppersmith did great harm to me. The Lord will repay him according to his works. [15] Watch out for him yourself because he strongly opposed our words. Col 4:14; Ti 3:12; Phm 24

[16] At my first defense, no one stood by me, but everyone deserted me. May it not be counted against them. [17] But the Lord stood with me and strengthened me, so that I might fully preach the word and all the Gentiles might hear it. So I was rescued from the lion's mouth. [18] The Lord will rescue me from every evil work and will bring me safely into his heavenly kingdom. To him be the glory forever and ever! Amen. Mk 1:15; Ac 20:25; 2Tm 1:15

Benediction

[19] Greet Prisca and Aquila, and the household of Onesiphorus. [20] Erastus has remained at Corinth; I left Trophimus sick at Miletus. [21] Make every effort to come before winter. Eubulus greets you, as do Pudens, Linus, Claudia, and all the brothers and sisters. Ac 18:2; 19:22; 20:4; 2Tm 1:16

[22] The Lord be with your spirit. Grace be with you all.

[A]4:8 Or *have longed for his appearing*

TITUS

Greeting

1 Paul, a servant of God and an apostle of Jesus Christ, for[A] the faith of God's elect and their knowledge of the truth that leads[B] to godliness, ² in the hope of eternal life that God, who cannot lie, promised before time began. ³ In his own time he has revealed his word in the preaching with which I was entrusted by the command of God our Savior: Ac 13:9; 16:17; Rm 1:1

⁴ To Titus, my true son in our common faith. 2Co 2:13; 7:6,13-14; 8:6,16,23

Grace and peace from God the Father and Christ Jesus our Savior.

Titus's Ministry in Crete

⁵ The reason I left you in Crete was to set right what was left undone and, as I directed you, to appoint elders in every town. ⁶ An elder must be blameless: the husband of one wife, with faithful[C] children who are not accused of wildness or rebellion. ⁷ As an overseer of God's household, he must be blameless: not arrogant, not hot-tempered, not an excessive drinker, not a bully, not greedy for money, ⁸ but hospitable, loving what is good, sensible, righteous, holy, self-controlled, ⁹ holding to the faithful message as taught, so that he will be able both to encourage with sound teaching and to refute those who contradict it. Ac 27:7,12-13; 1Tm 3:1-7; 5:17

¹⁰ For there are many rebellious people, full of empty talk and deception, especially those from the circumcision party. ¹¹ It is necessary to silence them; they are ruining entire households by teaching what they shouldn't in order to get money dishonestly. ¹² One of their very own prophets said, "Cretans are always liars, evil beasts, lazy gluttons." ¹³ This testimony is true. For this reason, rebuke them sharply, so that they may be sound in the faith ¹⁴ and may not pay attention to Jewish myths and the commands of people who reject the truth. Jn 8:14; 1Tm 1:4

¹⁵ To the pure, everything is pure, but to those who are defiled and unbelieving nothing is pure; in fact, both their mind and conscience are defiled. ¹⁶ They claim to know God, but they deny him by their works. They are detestable, disobedient, and unfit for any good work. Jn 7:28

Sound Teaching and Christian Living

2 But you are to proclaim things consistent with sound teaching. ² Older men are to be self-controlled, worthy of respect, sensible, and sound in faith, love, and endurance. ³ In the same way, older women are to be reverent in behavior, not slanderers, not slaves to excessive drinking. They are to teach what is good, ⁴ so that they may encourage the young women to love their husbands and to love their children, ⁵ to be self-controlled, pure, workers at home, kind, and in submission to their husbands, so that God's word will not be slandered. 1Co 13:1; 1Tm 5:1-2; Ti 1:9; 1Jn 4:16

A **1:1** Or *according to*   B **1:1** Or *corresponds*   C **1:6** Or *believing*

⁶ In the same way, encourage the young men to be self-controlled ⁷ in everything. Make yourself an example of good works with integrity and dignity ^A in your teaching. ⁸ Your message is to be sound beyond reproach, so that any opponent will be ashamed, because he doesn't have anything bad to say about us.   1Tm 2:2; 5:1; 1Pt 5:5; 1Jn 2:13-14

⁹ Slaves are to submit to their masters in everything, and to be well-pleasing, not talking back ¹⁰ or stealing, but demonstrating utter faithfulness, so that they may adorn the teaching of God our Savior in everything.   Eph 6:5-9; Col 3:22; Jd 4

¹¹ For the grace of God has appeared, bringing salvation ^B for all people, ¹² instructing us to deny godlessness and worldly lusts and to live in a sensible, righteous, and godly way in the present age, ¹³ while we wait for the blessed hope, the appearing of the glory of our great God and Savior, Jesus Christ. ¹⁴ He gave himself for us to redeem us from all lawlessness and to cleanse for himself a people for his own possession, eager to do good works.   Ac 1:8; Rm 10:14; 2Co 5:18-21

¹⁵ Proclaim these things; encourage and rebuke with all authority. Let no one disregard ^C you.

Christian Living Among Outsiders

3 Remind them to submit to rulers and authorities, to obey, to be ready for every good work, ² to slander no one, to avoid fighting, and to be kind, always showing gentleness to all people. ³ For we too were once foolish, disobedient, deceived, enslaved by various passions and pleasures, living in malice and envy, hateful, detesting one another.   Rm 13:1-7; Jms 3:13; 1Pt 2:13-14

⁴ But when the kindness of God our Savior and his love for mankind appeared, ⁵ he saved us — not by works of righteousness that we had done, but according to his mercy — through the washing of regeneration and renewal by the Holy Spirit. ⁶ He poured out his Spirit on us abundantly through Jesus Christ our Savior ⁷ so that, having been justified by his grace, we may become heirs with the hope of eternal life. ⁸ This saying is trustworthy. I want you to insist on these things, so that those who have believed God might be careful to devote themselves to good works. These are good and profitable for everyone. ⁹ But avoid foolish debates, genealogies, quarrels, and disputes about the law, because they are unprofitable and worthless. ¹⁰ Reject a divisive person after a first and second warning. ¹¹ For you know that such a person has gone astray and is sinning; he is self-condemned.   1Tm 1:1; 2:3; Ti 1:3; 2:10

Final Instructions and Closing

¹² When I send Artemas or Tychicus to you, make every effort to come to me in Nicopolis, because I have decided to spend the winter there. ¹³ Diligently help Zenas the lawyer and Apollos on their journey, so that they will lack nothing.   Ac 20:4; Eph 6:21; Col 4:7; 2Tm 4:12

¹⁴ Let our people learn to devote themselves to good works for pressing needs, so that they will not be unfruitful. ¹⁵ All those who are with me send you greetings. Greet those who love us in the faith. Grace be with all of you.   Mt 13:22; Jd 12

^A 2:7 Other mss add *and incorruptibility*   ^B 2:11 Or *appeared with saving power*   ^C 2:15 Or *despise*

PHILEMON

Greeting

¹ Paul, a prisoner of Christ Jesus, and Timothy our brother: Ac 13:9

To Philemon our dear friend and coworker, ² to Apphia our sister,[A] to Archippus our fellow soldier, and to the church that meets in your home. Ac 12:12; Rm 16:5; Col 4:17; Php 2:25

³ Grace to you and peace from God our Father and the Lord Jesus Christ.

Philemon's Love and Faith

⁴ I always thank my God when I mention you in my prayers, ⁵ because I hear of your love for all the saints and the faith that you have in the Lord Jesus. ⁶ I pray that your participation in the faith may become effective through knowing every good thing that is in us[B] for the glory of Christ. ⁷ For I have great joy and encouragement from your love, because the hearts of the saints have been refreshed through you, brother. Dt 6:5; Mt 22:37; Gl 5:6,22; Eph 6:23

An Appeal for Onesimus

⁸ For this reason, although I have great boldness in Christ to command you to do what is right, ⁹ I appeal to you, instead, on the basis of love. I, Paul, as an elderly man[C] and now also as a prisoner of Christ Jesus, ¹⁰ appeal to you for my son, Onesimus.[D] I became his father while I was in chains.

¹¹ Once he was useless to you, but now he is useful both to you and to me. ¹² I am sending him back to you — I am sending my very own heart.[E,F] ¹³ I wanted to keep him with me, so that in my imprisonment for the gospel he might serve me in your place. ¹⁴ But I didn't want to do anything without your consent, so that your good deed might not be out of obligation, but of your own free will. ¹⁵ For perhaps this is why he was separated from you for a brief time, so that you might get him back permanently, ¹⁶ no longer as a slave, but more than a slave — as a dearly loved brother. He is especially so to me, but how much more to you, both in the flesh and in the Lord. 1Th 2:11; 2Tm 1:8; Heb 13:3

¹⁷ So if you consider me a partner, welcome him as you would me. ¹⁸ And if he has wronged you in any way, or owes you anything, charge that to my account. ¹⁹ I, Paul, write this with my own hand: I will repay it — not to mention to you that you owe me even your very self. ²⁰ Yes, brother, may I benefit from you in the Lord; refresh my heart in Christ. ²¹ Since I am confident of your obedience, I am writing to you, knowing that you will do even more than I say. ²² Meanwhile, also prepare a guest room for me, since I hope that through your prayers I will be restored to you. Rm 5:13; 14:1; 1Co 16:21
[A] 2 Other mss read our beloved   [B] 6 Other mss read in you   [C] 9 Or an ambassador   [D] 10 In Gk, Onesimus means "useful"   [E] 12 Other mss read him back. Receive him, my own heart.   [F] 12 Lit you — that is, my own heart

Final Greetings

²³ Epaphras, my fellow prisoner in Christ Jesus, sends you greetings, and so do ²⁴ Mark, Aristarchus, Demas, and Luke, my coworkers. ²⁵ The grace of the Lord[A] Jesus Christ be with your spirit.   2Th 3:18

HEBREWS

The Nature of the Son

1 Long ago God spoke to the fathers by the prophets at different times and in different ways. ² In these last days, he has spoken to us by his Son. God has appointed him heir of all things and made the universe[A] through him. ³ The Son is the radiance[B] of God's glory and the exact expression[C] of his nature, sustaining all things by his powerful word. After making purification for sins,[D] he sat down at the right hand of the Majesty on high.[E] ⁴ So he became superior to the angels, just as the name he inherited is more excellent than theirs.   2Kg 17:13; 21:10; 24:2; Jn 9:29; Heb 2:2-3

The Son Superior to Angels

⁵ For to which of the angels did he ever say,

> You are my Son;
> today I have become your
>   Father,[F,G]

or again,

> I will be his Father,
> and he will be my Son?[H]

⁶ Again, when he[I] brings his firstborn into the world, he says,   Rv 1:5

> And let all God's angels
>   worship him.[J]   Dt 32:43; Ps 97:7

⁷ And about the angels he says:

> He makes his angels
>   winds,[K]
> and his servants[L]
>   a fiery flame,[M]   Ps 104:4

⁸ but to[N] the Son:

> Your throne, O God,
> is forever and ever,
> and the scepter
>   of your kingdom
> is a scepter of justice.   Ps 45:6-7

⁹ You have loved
>   righteousness
> and hated lawlessness;
> this is why God, your God,
> has anointed you
> with the oil of joy   Is 61:1,3
> beyond your companions.[O,P]

¹⁰ And:

> In the beginning, Lord,
> you established the earth,
> and the heavens are
>   the works of your hands;
¹¹ they will perish,
>   but you remain.
> They will all wear out
>   like clothing;   Is 50:9; 51:6
¹² you will roll them up
>   like a cloak,[Q]
> and they will be changed
>   like clothing.
> But you are the same,
> and your years
>   will never end.[R]   Ps 102:26-27

¹³ Now to which of the angels has he ever said:

> Sit at my right hand
> until I make your enemies
>   your footstool?[S]   Jos 10:24

¹⁴ Are they not all ministering spirits sent out to serve those who are going to inherit salvation?   Ps 103:20

[A]**1:2** Lit ages   [B]**1:3** Or reflection   [C]**1:3** Or representation, or copy, or reproduction   [D]**1:3** Other mss read for our sins by himself   [E]**1:3** Or he sat down on high at the right hand of the Majesty   [F]**1:5** Or have begotten you   [G]**1:5** Ps 2:7   [H]**1:5** 2Sm 7:14; 1Ch 17:13   [I]**1:6** Or When he again   [J]**1:6** Dt 32:43 LXX; Ps 97:7   [K]**1:7** Or spirits   [L]**1:7** Or ministers   [M]**1:7** Ps 104:4   [N]**1:8** Or about   [O]**1:9** Or associates   [P]**1:8-9** Ps 45:6-7   [Q]**1:12** Other mss omit like a cloak   [R]**1:10-12** Ps 102:25-27   [S]**1:13** Ps 110:1

Warning Against Neglect

2 For this reason, we must pay attention all the more to what we have heard, so that we will not drift away. ² For if the message spoken through angels was legally binding^A and every transgression and disobedience received a just punishment, ³ how will we escape if we neglect such a great salvation? This salvation had its beginning when it was spoken of by the Lord, and it was confirmed to us by those who heard him. ⁴ At the same time, God also testified by signs and wonders, various miracles, and distributions of gifts from the Holy Spirit according to his will.   Jos 24:27; Mc 5:13; 1Co 9:27

Jesus and Humanity

⁵ For he has not subjected to angels the world to come that we are talking about. ⁶ But someone somewhere has testified:

**What is man
     that you remember him,
     or the son of man
     that you care for him?**
⁷ **You made him lower
     than the angels
     for a short time;
     you crowned him
     with glory and honor**^B
⁸   **and subjected everything
     under his feet.**^C

For in **subjecting everything** to him, he left nothing that is not subject to him. As it is, we do not yet see **everything subjected** to him. ⁹ But we do see Jesus — **made lower than the angels for a short time** so that by God's grace he might taste death for everyone — **crowned with glory**

and honor because he suffered death.   Jb 7:17; Ps 8:4-6; Mt 22:44; Ac 2:35; 3:13

¹⁰ For in bringing many sons and daughters to glory, it was entirely appropriate that God — for whom and through whom all things exist — should make the source^D of their salvation perfect through sufferings. ¹¹ For the one who sanctifies and those who are sanctified all have one Father.^E That is why Jesus is not ashamed to call them brothers and sisters, ¹² saying:

**I will proclaim your name
     to my brothers and sisters;
I will sing hymns to you
     in the congregation.**^F
¹³ Again, **I will trust in him.**^G And again, **Here I am with the children God gave me.**^H   Ps 18:2; Is 8:17-18

¹⁴ Now since the children have flesh and blood in common, Jesus also shared in these, so that through his death he might destroy the one holding the power of death — that is, the devil — ¹⁵ and free those who were held in slavery all their lives by the fear of death. ¹⁶ For it is clear that he does not reach out to help angels, but to help Abraham's offspring. ¹⁷ Therefore, he had to be like his brothers and sisters in every way, so that he could become a merciful and faithful high priest in matters^I pertaining to God, to make atonement^J for the sins of the people. ¹⁸ For since he himself has suffered when he was tempted, he is able to help those who are tempted.

Our Apostle and High Priest

3 Therefore, holy brothers and sisters, who share in a heavenly calling, consider Jesus, the apostle

---

^A**2:2** Or *valid,* or *reliable*   ^B**2:7** Other mss add *and set him over the works of your hands*   ^C**2:6-8** Ps 8:5-7 LXX   ^D**2:10** Or *pioneer,* or *leader*   ^E**2:11** Or *father,* or *origin;* lit *all are of one*   ^F**2:12** Ps 22:22   ^G**2:13** 2Sm 22:3 LXX; Is 8:17 LXX; 12:2 LXX   ^H**2:13** Is 8:18 LXX   ^I**2:17** Lit *things*   ^J**2:17** Or *propitiation* and high priest of our confession. [2] He was faithful to the one who appointed him, just as Moses was in all God's household. [3] For Jesus is considered worthy of more glory than Moses, just as the builder has more honor than the house. [4] Now every house is built by someone, but the one who built everything is God. [5] Moses was faithful as a servant in all God's household, as a testimony to what would be said in the future. [6] But Christ was faithful as a Son over his household. And we are that household if we hold on to our confidence and the hope in which we boast. [A] Rm 15:8; Php 3:14

Warning Against Unbelief

[7] Therefore, as the Holy Spirit says:

Today, if you hear his voice,
[8] **do not harden your hearts**
as in the rebellion,
on the day of testing
in the wilderness,
[9] **where your fathers**
tested me, tried me,
and saw my works
[10] **for forty years.**
Therefore I was
provoked to anger
with that generation
and said, "They always
go astray in their hearts,
and they have not known
my ways."
[11] **So I swore in my anger,**
"They will not enter
my rest." [B] Ps 95:7-11; Ac 7:36

[12] Watch out, brothers and sisters, so that there won't be in any of you an evil, unbelieving heart that turns away from the living God. [13] But encourage each other daily, while it is still called **today**, so that none of you is hardened by sin's deception. [14] For we have become participants in Christ if we hold firmly until the end the reality [C] that we had at the start. [15] As it is said:

Today, if you hear his voice,
do not harden your hearts
as in the rebellion. [D] Ps 95:7-8

[16] For who heard and rebelled? Wasn't it all who came out of Egypt under Moses? [17] With whom was God angry for forty years? Wasn't it with those who sinned, whose bodies fell in the wilderness? [18] And to whom did he swear that they would not enter his rest, if not to those who disobeyed? [19] So we see that they were unable to enter because of unbelief. Nm 14:2; Dt 1:35-38

The Promised Rest

4 Therefore, since the promise to enter his rest remains, let us beware [E] that none of you be found to have fallen short. [F] [2] For we also have received the good news just as they did. But the message they heard did not benefit them, since they were not united with those who heard it in faith. [G] [3] For we who have believed enter the rest, in keeping with what [H] he has said,

So I swore in my anger,
"They will not enter
my rest," [I] Ps 95:11; Heb 3:11

even though his works have been finished since the foundation of the world. [4] For somewhere he has spoken about the seventh day in this way: **And on the seventh day God rested from all his works.** [J] [5] Again, in that passage he says, **They will never enter my rest.** [K]

[6] Therefore, since it remains for some to enter it, and those who formerly received the good news did not enter because of disobedience, [7] he again specifies a certain day — **today**. He specified this speaking through David after such a long time: Gn 2:2; Ex 20:11; Ps 95:11; Heb 3:19

Today, if you hear his voice, do not harden your hearts. [A]

[8] For if Joshua had given them rest, God would not have spoken later about another day. [9] Therefore, a Sabbath rest remains for God's people. [10] For the person who has entered his rest has rested from his own works, just as God did from his. [11] Let us then make every effort to enter that rest, so that no one will fall into the same pattern of disobedience. Jos 22:4; Heb 4:4; Rv 14:13

[12] For the word of God is living and effective and sharper than any double-edged sword, penetrating as far as the separation of soul and spirit, joints and marrow. It is able to judge the thoughts and intentions of the heart. [13] No creature is hidden from him, but all things are naked and exposed to the eyes of him to whom we must give an account. Is 49:2; Jr 23:29; Eph 6:17; 1Pt 1:23

Our Great High Priest

[14] Therefore, since we have a great high priest who has passed through the heavens — Jesus the Son of God — let us hold fast to our confession. [15] For we do not have a high priest who is unable to sympathize with our weaknesses, but one who has been tempted in every way as we are, yet without sin. [16] Therefore, let us approach the throne of grace with boldness, so that we may receive mercy and find grace to help us in time of need. Heb 3:1; 6:20; 10:23

Christ, a High Priest

5 For every high priest taken from among men is appointed in matters pertaining to God for the people, to offer both gifts and sacrifices for sins. [2] He is able to deal gently with those who are ignorant and are going astray, since he is also clothed with weakness. [3] Because of this, he must make an offering for his own sins as well as for the people. [4] No one takes this honor on himself; instead, a person is called by God, just as Aaron was. [5] In the same way, Christ did not exalt himself to become a high priest, but God who said to him, Lv 4:3; Heb 2:18; 4:15; 7:28

You are my Son; today I have become your Father, [B,C] Ps 2:7; Jn 8:54

[6] also says in another place,

You are a priest forever according to the order of Melchizedek. [D] Ps 110:4

[7] During his earthly life, [E] he offered prayers and appeals with loud cries and tears to the one who was able to save him from death, and he was heard because of his reverence. [8] Although he was the Son, he learned obedience from what he suffered. [9] After he was perfected, he became the source of eternal salvation for all who obey him, [10] and he was declared by God a high priest according to the order of Melchizedek. Mt 26:39; Mk 14:36

The Problem of Immaturity

[11] We have a great deal to say about this, and it is difficult to explain,

---

[A] 4:7 Ps 95:7-8   [B] 5:5 Lit *I have begotten you*   [C] 5:5 Ps 2:7   [D] 5:6 Gn 14:18-20; Ps 110:4   [E] 5:7 Lit *In the days of his flesh* since you have become too lazy to understand. [12] Although by this time you ought to be teachers, you need someone to teach you the basic principles of God's revelation again. You need milk, not solid food. [13] Now everyone who lives on milk is inexperienced with the message about righteousness, because he is an infant. [14] But solid food is for the mature — for those whose senses have been trained to distinguish between good and evil.   Is 7:15; 1Co 2:6; 3:2; Heb 6:1; 1Pt 2:21

Warning Against Falling Away

6 Therefore, let us leave the elementary teaching about Christ and go on to maturity, not laying again a foundation of repentance from dead works, faith in God, [2] teaching about ritual washings, [A] laying on of hands, the resurrection of the dead, and eternal judgment. [3] And we will do this if God permits.   Jn 3:25; Ac 6:6; Php 3:13; Heb 5:12; 9:14

[4] For it is impossible to renew to repentance those who were once enlightened, who tasted the heavenly gift, who shared in the Holy Spirit, [5] who tasted God's good word and the powers of the coming age, [6] and who have fallen away. This is because, [B] to their own harm, they are recrucifying the Son of God and holding him up to contempt. [7] For the ground that drinks the rain that often falls on it and that produces vegetation useful to those for whom it is cultivated receives a blessing from God. [8] But if it produces thorns and thistles, it is worthless and about to be cursed, and at the end will be burned.   Gl 3:3; Eph 2:8; Heb 10:29,32

[9] Even though we are speaking this way, dearly loved friends, in your case we are confident of things that are better and that pertain to salvation. [10] For God is not unjust; he will not forget your work and the love [C] you demonstrated for his name by serving the saints — and by continuing to serve them. [11] Now we desire each of you to demonstrate the same diligence for the full assurance of your hope until the end, [12] so that you won't become lazy but will be imitators of those who inherit the promises through faith and perseverance.   Pr 19:17; Mt 10:42; 25:40; 2Co 8:4

Inheriting the Promise

[13] For when God made a promise to Abraham, since he had no one greater to swear by, he swore by himself: [14] **I will indeed bless you, and I will greatly multiply you.** [D] [15] And so, after waiting patiently, Abraham obtained the promise. [16] For people swear by something greater than themselves, and for them a confirming oath ends every dispute. [17] Because God wanted to show his unchangeable purpose even more clearly to the heirs of the promise, he guaranteed it with an oath, [18] so that through two unchangeable things, in which it is impossible for God to lie, we who have fled for refuge might have strong encouragement to seize the hope set before us. [19] We have this hope as an anchor for the soul, firm and secure. It enters the inner sanctuary behind the curtain. [20] Jesus has entered there on our behalf as a forerunner, because he has become a high priest forever according to the order of Melchizedek.   Gn 21:5; 22:16-17; Ex 22:11; Lk 1:73

The Greatness of Melchizedek

7 For this Melchizedek, king of Salem, priest of God Most High, met Abraham and blessed him as he returned from defeating the kings, [2] and Abraham gave him a tenth of everything. First, his name means king of righteousness, then also, king of Salem, meaning king of peace. [3] Without father, mother, or genealogy, having neither beginning of days nor end of life, but resembling the Son of God, he remains a priest forever. Gn 14:18-20; Mt 4:3; Mk 5:7

[4] Now consider how great this man was: even Abraham the patriarch gave a tenth of the plunder to him. [5] The sons of Levi who receive the priestly office have a command according to the law to collect a tenth from the people — that is, from their brothers and sisters — though they have also descended from Abraham. [6] But one without this[A] lineage collected a tenth from Abraham and blessed the one who had the promises. [7] Without a doubt, the inferior is blessed by the superior. [8] In the one case, men who will die receive a tenth, but in the other case, Scripture testifies that he lives. [9] And in a sense Levi himself, who receives a tenth, has paid a tenth through Abraham, [10] for he was still within his ancestor[B] when Melchizedek met him. Gn 14:20; Nm 18:21,26; Ac 2:29; 7:8-9

A Superior Priesthood

[11] Now if perfection came through the Levitical priesthood (for on the basis of it the people received the law), what further need was there for another priest to appear, said to be according to the order of Melchizedek and not according to the order of Aaron? [12] For when there is a change of the priesthood, there must be a change of law as well. [13] For the one these things are spoken about belonged to a different tribe. No one from it has served at the altar. [14] Now it is evident that our Lord came from Judah, and Moses said nothing about that tribe concerning priests. Gl 2:21; Heb 7:18-19; 8:7; 10:1

[15] And this becomes clearer if another priest like Melchizedek appears, [16] who did not become a priest based on a legal regulation about physical[C] descent but based on the power of an indestructible life. [17] For it has been testified:

> **You are a priest forever**
> **according to the order**
> **of Melchizedek.**[D]　Ps 110:4

[18] So the previous command is annulled because it was weak and unprofitable [19] (for the law perfected nothing), but a better hope is introduced, through which we draw near to God. Ac 13:39; Rm 3:20; 8:3; Gl 4:9

[20] None of this happened without an oath. For others became priests without an oath, [21] but he became a priest with an oath made by the one who said to him:

> **The Lord has sworn**
> **and will not change**
> **his mind,**
> **"You are a priest forever."**[D]

[22] Because of this oath, Jesus has also become the guarantee of a better covenant. Heb 8:6-10; 9:15; 12:24; 13:20

[23] Now many have become Levitical priests, since they are prevented by death from remaining in office. [24] But because he remains forever, he holds his priesthood permanently. [25] Therefore, he is able to save completely those who come to God through him, since

---

[A]**7:6** Lit *their*　[B]**7:10** Lit *still in his father's loins*　[C]**7:16** Or *fleshly*　[D]**7:17,21** Ps 110:4

he always lives to intercede for them. Rm 8:34; Heb 9:24

26 For this is the kind of high priest we need: holy, innocent, undefiled, separated from sinners, and exalted above the heavens. 27 He doesn't need to offer sacrifices every day, as high priests do — first for their own sins, then for those of the people. He did this once for all time when he offered himself. 28 For the law appoints as high priests men who are weak, but the promise of the oath, which came after the law, appoints a Son, who has been perfected forever. 2Co 5:21; Eph 5:2; Heb 4:15; 5:1,3; 9:12,28

A Heavenly Priesthood

8 Now the main point of what is being said is this: We have this kind of high priest, who sat down at the right hand of the throne of the Majesty in the heavens, 2 a minister of the sanctuary and the true tabernacle that was set up by the Lord and not man. 3 For every high priest is appointed to offer gifts and sacrifices; therefore, it was necessary for this priest also to have something to offer. 4 Now if he were on earth, he wouldn't be a priest, since there are those[A] offering the gifts prescribed by the law. 5 These serve as a copy and shadow of the heavenly things, as Moses was warned when he was about to complete the tabernacle. For God said, **Be careful that you make everything according to the pattern that was shown to you on the mountain.**[B] 6 But Jesus has now obtained a superior ministry, and to that degree he is the mediator of a better covenant, which has been established on better promises. Col 3:1; Heb 2:17; 9:14

A Superior Covenant

7 For if that first covenant had been faultless, there would have been no occasion for a second one. 8 But finding fault with his people,[C] he says:[D]

See, the days are coming,
  says the Lord,
when I will make
  a new covenant
with the house of Israel
and with the house
  of Judah —
9 not like the covenant
  that I made
  with their ancestors
  on the day I took them
  by the hand
  to lead them out of the land
  of Egypt.
I showed no concern for
  them, says the Lord,
because they
  did not continue
  in my covenant.
10 For this is the covenant
  that I will make
  with the house of Israel
  after those days,
  says the Lord:
I will put my laws
  into their minds
and write them
  on their hearts.
I will be their God,
and they will be
  my people. Zch 8:8; 2Co 3:3
11 And each person
  will not teach
  his fellow citizen,[E]
and each his brother
  or sister, saying,
  "Know the Lord,"
because they will all
  know me,

A 8:4 Other mss read *priests*   B 8:5 Ex 25:40   C 8:8 Lit *with them*   D 8:8 Other mss read *finding fault, he says to them*   E 8:11 Other mss read *neighbor*

from the least
   to the greatest of them.
12 For I will forgive
    their wrongdoing,
    and I will never again
    remember their sins. A,B

13 By saying **a new covenant**, he has declared that the first is obsolete. And what is obsolete and growing old is about to pass away.   2Co 5:17

Old Covenant Ministry

9 Now the first covenant also had regulations for ministry and an earthly sanctuary. ² For a tabernacle was set up, and in the first room, which is called the holy place, were the lampstand, the table, and the presentation loaves. ³ Behind the second curtain was a tent called the most holy place. ⁴ It had the gold altar of incense and the ark of the covenant, covered with gold on all sides, in which was a gold jar containing the manna, Aaron's staff that budded, and the tablets of the covenant. ⁵ The cherubim of glory were above the ark overshadowing the mercy seat. It is not possible to speak about these things in detail right now.   Ex 25:8-9,23-39; 26:1; Lv 24:5-8

⁶ With these things prepared like this, the priests enter the first room repeatedly, performing their ministry. ⁷ But the high priest alone enters the second room, and he does that only once a year, and never without blood, which he offers for himself and for the sins the people had committed in ignorance. ⁸ The Holy Spirit was making it clear that the way into the most holy place had not yet been disclosed while the first tabernacle was still standing.

⁹ This is a symbol for the present time, during which gifts and sacrifices are offered that cannot perfect the worshiper's conscience. ¹⁰ They are physical regulations and only deal with food, drink, and various washings imposed until the time of the new order.   Ex 30:10; Lv 16:15,34; Nm 28:3

New Covenant Ministry

¹¹ But Christ has appeared as a high priest of the good things that have come. C In the greater and more perfect tabernacle not made with hands (that is, not of this creation), ¹² he entered the most holy place once for all time, not by the blood of goats and calves, but by his own blood, having obtained eternal redemption. ¹³ For if the blood of goats and bulls and the ashes of a young cow, sprinkling those who are defiled, sanctify for the purification of the flesh, ¹⁴ how much more will the blood of Christ, who through the eternal Spirit offered himself without blemish to God, cleanse our D consciences from dead works so that we can serve the living God?   Dn 9:24; Heb 2:17; 8:2; 10:1

¹⁵ Therefore, he is the mediator of a new covenant, E so that those who are called might receive the promise of the eternal inheritance, because a death has taken place for redemption from the transgressions committed under the first covenant. ¹⁶ Where a will exists, the death of the one who made it must be established. ¹⁷ For a will is valid only when people die, since it is never in effect while the one who made it is living. ¹⁸ That is why even the first covenant was inaugurated

---

A **8:12** Other mss add *and their lawless deeds*   B **8:8-12** Jr 31:31-34   C **9:11** Other mss read *that are to come*   D **9:14** Other mss read *your*   E **9:15** The Gk word used here can be translated covenant, will, or testament, also in vv. 16,17,18.

with blood. ¹⁹ For when every command had been proclaimed by Moses to all the people according to the law, he took the blood of calves and goats, ^A^ along with water, scarlet wool, and hyssop, and sprinkled the scroll itself and all the people, ²⁰ saying, **This is the blood of the covenant that God has ordained for you.** ^B^ ²¹ In the same way, he sprinkled the tabernacle and all the articles of worship with blood. ²² According to the law almost everything is purified with blood, and without the shedding of blood there is no forgiveness.   Jr 31:31-34; 1Tm 2:5; Heb 8:6; 12:24

²³ Therefore, it was necessary for the copies of the things in the heavens to be purified with these sacrifices, but the heavenly things themselves to be purified with better sacrifices than these. ²⁴ For Christ did not enter a sanctuary made with hands (only a model ^C^ of the true one) but into heaven itself, so that he might now appear in the presence of God for us. ²⁵ He did not do this to offer himself many times, as the high priest enters the sanctuary yearly with the blood of another. ²⁶ Otherwise, he would have had to suffer many times since the foundation of the world. But now he has appeared one time, at the end of the ages, for the removal of sin by the sacrifice of himself. ²⁷ And just as it is appointed for people to die once — and after this, judgment — ²⁸ so also Christ, having been offered once to bear the sins of many, will appear a second time, not to bear sin, but ^D^ to bring salvation to those who are waiting for him.   Rm 8:34; Heb 7:25; 8:2,5; 9:7; 10:19

The Perfect Sacrifice

10 Since the law has only a shadow of the good things to come, and not the reality itself of those things, it can never perfect the worshipers by the same sacrifices they continually offer year after year. ² Otherwise, wouldn't they have stopped being offered, since the worshipers, purified once and for all, would no longer have any consciousness of sins? ³ But in the sacrifices there is a reminder of sins year after year. ⁴ For it is impossible for the blood of bulls and goats to take away sins.   Col 2:17; Heb 8:5

⁵ Therefore, as he was coming into the world, he said:

> You did not desire sacrifice
>   and offering,
> but you prepared a body
>   for me.
⁶ You did not delight
>   in whole burnt offerings
>   and sin offerings.
⁷ Then I said, "See —
>   it is written about me
>   in the scroll —
> I have come to do your will,
>   O God." ^E^   Ps 40:6-8; Jr 36:2; Heb 1:6

⁸ After he says above, **You did not desire or delight in sacrifices and offerings, whole burnt offerings and sin offerings** (which are offered according to the law), ⁹ he then says, **See, I have come to do your will.** ^F^ He takes away the first to establish the second. ¹⁰ By this will, we have been sanctified through the offering of the body of Jesus Christ once for all time.   Mk 12:33; Heb 9:12; 10:5-6

¹¹ Every priest stands day after day ministering and offering the same sacrifices time after time,

---

^A^ **9:19** Some mss omit *and goats*   ^B^ **9:20** Ex 24:8   ^C^ **9:24** Or *antitype,* or *figure*   ^D^ **9:28** Lit *time, apart from sin,*   ^E^ **10:5-7** Ps 40:6-8   ^F^ **10:9** Other mss add *God* which can never take away sins. [12] But this man, after offering one sacrifice for sins forever, sat down at the right hand of God.[A] [13] He is now waiting until his enemies are made his footstool. [14] For by one offering he has perfected forever those who are sanctified. [15] The Holy Spirit also testifies to us about this. For after he says: Nm 28:3; Heb 5:1

[16]   **This is the covenant
      I will make with them
      after those days,
the Lord says,
      I will put my laws
      on their hearts
      and write them
      on their minds**,

[17]   and **I will never again
      remember
      their sins** and
      their lawless acts.[B]

[18] Now where there is forgiveness of these, there is no longer an offering for sin.

Exhortations to Godliness

[19] Therefore, brothers and sisters, since we have boldness to enter the sanctuary through the blood of Jesus — [20] he has inaugurated[C] for us a new and living way through the curtain (that is, through his flesh) — [21] and since we have a great high priest over the house of God, [22] let us draw near with a true heart in full assurance of faith, with our hearts sprinkled clean from an evil conscience and our bodies washed in pure water. [23] Let us hold on to the confession of our hope without wavering, since he who promised is faithful. [24] And let us watch out for one another

to provoke love and good works, [25] not neglecting to gather together, as some are in the habit of doing, but encouraging each other, and all the more as you see the day approaching. Jn 10:9; Eph 2:18; Heb 9:3,8,25

Warning Against Deliberate Sin

[26] For if we deliberately go on sinning after receiving the knowledge of the truth, there no longer remains a sacrifice for sins, [27] but a terrifying expectation of judgment and the fury of a fire about to consume the adversaries. [28] Anyone who disregarded the law of Moses died without mercy, based on the testimony of two or three witnesses. [29] How much worse punishment do you think one will deserve who has trampled on the Son of God, who has regarded as profane[D] the blood of the covenant by which he was sanctified, and who has insulted the Spirit of grace? [30] For we know the one who has said, Nm 15:30; Dt 17:12

      **Vengeance belongs to me;
      I will repay**,[E,F]
and again,
      **The Lord will judge
      his people**.[G] Dt 32:35-36; Ps 135:14

[31] It is a terrifying thing to fall into the hands of the living God. Mt 16:16

[32] Remember the earlier days when, after you had been enlightened, you endured a hard struggle with sufferings. [33] Sometimes you were publicly exposed to taunts and afflictions, and at other times you were companions of those who were treated that way. [34] For you sympathized with the prisoners[H] and accepted with joy the confiscation of your possessions,

---

[A]**10:12** Or *offering one sacrifice for sins, sat down forever at the right hand of God*   [B]**10:16-17** Jr 31:33-34
[C]**10:20** Or *opened*   [D]**10:29** Or *ordinary*   [E]**10:30** Other mss add *says the Lord*   [F]**10:30** Dt 32:35
[G]**10:30** Dt 32:36   [H]**10:34** Other mss read *sympathized with my imprisonment*

because you know that you yourselves have a better and enduring possession.^A ^35 So don't throw away your confidence, which has a great reward. ^36 For you need endurance, so that after you have done God's will, you may receive what was promised. 1Co 4:9; Php 1:29-30; 4:14; Heb 6:4

^37   For yet in **a very little while,**
     the Coming One will come
     and not delay.

^38   **But my righteous one**^B
     will live by faith;
     and if he draws back,
     I have no pleasure^C **in him.**^D

^39 But we are not those who draw back and are destroyed, but those who have faith and are saved.

Living by Faith

11 Now faith is the reality^E of what is hoped for, the proof^F of what is not seen. ^2 For by it our ancestors won God's approval.

^3 By faith we understand that the universe was^G created by the word of God, so that what is seen was made from things that are not visible.^H   Gn 1:1; Jn 1:3; 2Pt 3:5

^4 By faith Abel offered to God a better sacrifice than Cain did. By faith he was approved as a righteous man, because God approved his gifts, and even though he is dead, he still speaks through his faith.   Gn 4:4; 1Jn 3:12

^5 By faith Enoch was taken away, and so he did not experience death. **He was not to be found because God took him away.**^I For before he was taken away, he was approved as one who pleased God.

^6 Now without faith it is impossible to please God, since the one who draws near to him must believe that he exists and that he rewards those who seek him.   Gn 5:21-24; 2Kg 2:11

^7 By faith Noah, after he was warned about what was not yet seen and motivated by godly fear, built an ark to deliver his family. By faith he condemned the world and became an heir of the righteousness that comes by faith.   Gn 6:13-22

^8 By faith Abraham, when he was called, obeyed and set out for a place that he was going to receive as an inheritance. He went out, even though he did not know where he was going. ^9 By faith he stayed as a foreigner in the land of promise, living in tents as did Isaac and Jacob, coheirs of the same promise. ^10 For he was looking forward to the city that has foundations, whose architect and builder is God.   Gn 12:1-4, 7-8; 18:1; Ac 7:2,5; Heb 6:17; 13:14

^11 By faith even Sarah herself, when she was unable to have children, received power to conceive offspring, even though she was past the age, since she^J considered that the one who had promised was faithful. ^12 Therefore, from one man — in fact, from one as good as dead — came offspring as numerous as the stars of the sky and as innumerable as the grains of sand along the seashore.   Gn 17:19; 18:11-14; 21:2

^13 These all died in faith, although they had not received the things that were promised. But they saw them from a distance, greeted them, and confessed that

^A10:34 Other mss add *in heaven*   ^B10:38 Other mss read *the righteous one*   ^C10:38 Lit *my soul has no pleasure*   ^D10:37-38 Is 26:20 LXX; Hab 2:3-4   ^E11:1 Or *assurance*   ^F11:1 Or *conviction*   ^G11:3 Or *the worlds were,* or *the ages were*   ^H11:3 Or *so that what is seen was made out of what was not visible*   ^I11:5 Gn 5:21-24   ^J11:11 Or *By faith Abraham, even though he was past age — and Sarah herself was barren — received the ability to procreate since he* they were foreigners and temporary residents on the earth. [14] Now those who say such things make it clear that they are seeking a homeland. [15] If they were thinking about where they came from, they would have had an opportunity to return. [16] But they now desire a better place — a heavenly one. Therefore, God is not ashamed to be called their God, for he has prepared a city for them. Gn 23:4; Ps 39:12; Mt 13:17; Jn 8:56; Heb 11:39

[17] By faith Abraham, when he was tested, offered up Isaac. He received the promises and yet he was offering his one and only son, [18] the one to whom it had been said, **Your offspring**[A] **will be traced through Isaac.**[B] [19] He considered God to be able even to raise someone from the dead; therefore, he received him back, figuratively speaking.[C]

[20] By faith Isaac blessed Jacob and Esau concerning things to come. [21] By faith Jacob, when he was dying, blessed each of the sons of Joseph, and **he worshiped, leaning on the top of his staff.**[D] [22] By faith Joseph, as he was nearing the end of his life, mentioned[E] the exodus of the Israelites and gave instructions concerning his bones.

[23] By faith Moses, after he was born, was hidden by his parents for three months, because they saw that the child was beautiful, and they didn't fear the king's edict. [24] By faith Moses, when he had grown up, refused to be called the son of Pharaoh's daughter [25] and chose to suffer with the people of God rather than to enjoy the fleeting pleasure of sin. [26] For he considered reproach for the sake of Christ to be greater wealth than the treasures of Egypt,

since he was looking ahead to the reward. Ex 1:16,22; 2:2,10-11; Ps 84:10

[27] By faith he left Egypt behind, not being afraid of the king's anger, for Moses persevered as one who sees him who is invisible. [28] By faith he instituted the Passover and the sprinkling of the blood, so that the destroyer of the firstborn might not touch the Israelites. [29] By faith they crossed the Red Sea as though they were on dry land. When the Egyptians attempted to do this, they were drowned. Rm 1:20; Col 1:15-16

[30] By faith the walls of Jericho fell down after being marched around by the Israelites for seven days. [31] By faith Rahab the prostitute welcomed the spies in peace and didn't perish with those who disobeyed. Jos 2:1; 6:23

[32] And what more can I say? Time is too short for me to tell about Gideon, Barak, Samson, Jephthah, David, Samuel, and the prophets, [33] who by faith conquered kingdoms, administered justice, obtained promises, shut the mouths of lions, [34] quenched the raging of fire, escaped the edge of the sword, gained strength in weakness, became mighty in battle, and put foreign armies to flight. [35] Women received their dead, raised to life again. Other people were tortured, not accepting release, so that they might gain a better resurrection. [36] Others experienced mockings and scourgings, as well as bonds and imprisonment. [37] They were stoned,[F] they were sawed in two, they died by the sword, they wandered about in sheepskins, in goatskins, destitute, afflicted, and mistreated. [38] The world was not worthy of them. They

[A]**11:18** Lit *seed* [B]**11:18** Gn 21:12 [C]**11:19** Or *back, as a foreshadowing,* or *as a type* [D]**11:21** Gn 47:31 [E]**11:22** Or *remembered* [F]**11:37** Other mss add *they were tempted,* wandered in deserts and on mountains, hiding in caves and holes in the ground. Jdg 4:6; 11:1; 13:24; 1Sm 1:20; 16:1, 13 **39** All these were approved through their faith, but they did not receive what was promised, **40** since God had provided something better for us, so that they would not be made perfect without us.

The Call to Endurance

12 Therefore, since we also have such a large cloud of witnesses surrounding us, let us lay aside every hindrance and the sin that so easily ensnares us. Let us run with endurance the race that lies before us, **2** keeping our eyes on Jesus, ^A the source and perfecter ^B of our faith. For the joy that lay before him, ^C he endured the cross, despising the shame, and sat down at the right hand of the throne of God.   1Co 9:24; Heb 11:2, 4-5, 39

Fatherly Discipline

3 For consider him who endured such hostility from sinners against himself, so that you won't grow weary and give up. **4** In struggling against sin, you have not yet resisted to the point of shedding your blood. **5** And you have forgotten the exhortation that addresses you as sons: Mt 10:24; Gl 6:9

My son, do not take
   the Lord's
   discipline lightly
   or lose heart when you are
   reproved by him,
6 **for the Lord disciplines**
   the one he loves
   and punishes every son
   he receives. ^D   Jb 5:17; Ps 94:12

7 Endure suffering as discipline: God is dealing with you as sons. For what son is there that a father does not discipline? **8** But if you are without discipline — which all receive ^E — then you are illegitimate children and not sons. **9** Furthermore, we had human fathers discipline us, and we respected them. Shouldn't we submit even more to the Father of spirits and live? **10** For they disciplined us for a short time based on what seemed good to them, but he does it for our benefit, so that we can share his holiness. **11** No discipline seems enjoyable at the time, but painful. Later on, however, it yields the peaceful fruit of righteousness to those who have been trained by it.   Nm 16:22; Dt 8:5; 1Pt 5:9

12 Therefore, strengthen your tired hands and weakened knees, **13** and make straight paths for your feet, so that what is lame may not be dislocated ^F but healed instead.   Jb 4:3-4

Warning Against Rejecting God's Grace

14 Pursue peace with everyone, and holiness — without it no one will see the Lord. **15** Make sure that no one falls short of the grace of God and that no root of bitterness springs up, causing trouble and defiling many. **16** And make sure that there isn't any immoral ^G or irreverent person like Esau, who sold his birthright in exchange for a single meal. **17** For you know that later, when he wanted to inherit the blessing, he was rejected, even though he sought it with tears, because he didn't find any opportunity for repentance.   Rm 6:22; 14:19; Gl 5:4

^A **12:2** Or us, looking to Jesus   ^B **12:2** Or the founder and completer, or pioneer and perfecter   ^C **12:2** Or who instead of the joy lying before him   ^D **12:6** Pr 3:11-12   ^E **12:8** Lit discipline, of which all have become participants   ^F **12:13** Or so that the lame will not be turned aside   ^G **12:16** Or sexually immoral

¹⁸ For you have not come to what could be touched, to a blazing fire, to darkness, gloom, and storm, ¹⁹ to the blast of a trumpet, and the sound of words. Those who heard it begged that not another word be spoken to them, ²⁰ for they could not bear what was commanded: **If even an animal touches the mountain, it must be stoned.** ᴬ ²¹ The appearance was so terrifying that Moses said, **I am trembling with fear.** ᴮ ²² Instead, you have come to Mount Zion, to the city of the living God (the heavenly Jerusalem), to myriads of angels, a festive gathering, ²³ to the assembly of the firstborn whose names have been written ᶜ in heaven, to a Judge, who is God of all, to the spirits of righteous people made perfect, ²⁴ and to Jesus, the mediator of a new covenant, and to the sprinkled blood, which says better things than the blood of Abel.   Ex 19:12-13,18; 20:18-21; Dt 4:11; 5:5,25

²⁵ See to it that you do not reject the one who speaks. For if they did not escape when they rejected him who warned them on earth, even less will we if we turn away from him who warns us from heaven. ²⁶ His voice shook the earth at that time, but now he has promised, **Yet once more I will shake not only the earth but also the heavens.** ᴰ ²⁷ This expression, "Yet once more," indicates the removal of what can be shaken — that is, created things — so that what is not shaken might remain. ²⁸ Therefore, since we are receiving a kingdom that cannot be shaken, let us be thankful. By it, we may serve God acceptably, with reverence and awe, ²⁹ for our God is a consuming fire.

Heb 2:2-4; 8:5; 11:7

Final Exhortations

13 Let brotherly love continue. ² Don't neglect to show hospitality, for by doing this some have welcomed angels as guests without knowing it. ³ Remember those in prison, as though you were in prison with them, and the mistreated, ᴱ as though you yourselves were suffering bodily. ᶠ ⁴ Marriage is to be honored by all and the marriage bed kept undefiled, because God will judge the sexually immoral and adulterers. ⁵ Keep your life free from the love of money. Be satisfied with what you have, for he himself has said, **I will never leave you or abandon you.** ᴳ ⁶ Therefore, we may boldly say,

Gn 18:3; Mt 25:35; Rm 12:10; 1Pt 1:22

The Lord is my helper;
I will not be afraid.
What can man do to me? ᴴ

⁷ Remember your leaders who have spoken God's word to you. As you carefully observe the outcome of their lives, imitate their faith. ⁸ Jesus Christ is the same yesterday, today, and forever. ⁹ Don't be led astray by various kinds of strange teachings; for it is good for the heart to be established by grace and not by food regulations, since those who observe them have not benefited. ¹⁰ We have an altar from which those who worship at the tabernacle do not have a right to eat. ¹¹ For the bodies of those animals whose blood is brought into the most holy place by the high priest as a sin offering are burned

---

ᴬ**12:20** Ex 19:12   ᴮ**12:21** Dt 9:19   ᶜ**12:23** Or *registered*   ᴰ**12:26** Hg 2:6   ᴱ**13:3** Or *tortured*
ᶠ**13:3** Or *mistreated, since you are also in a body*   ᴳ**13:5** Dt 31:6   ᴴ**13:6** Ps 118:6

outside the camp. [12] Therefore, Jesus also suffered outside the gate, so that he might sanctify[A] the people by his own blood. [13] Let us then go to him outside the camp, bearing his disgrace. [14] For we do not have an enduring city here; instead, we seek the one to come. [15] Therefore, through him let us continually offer up to God a sacrifice of praise, that is, the fruit of lips that confess his name. [16] Don't neglect to do what is good and to share, for God is pleased with such sacrifices. [17] Obey your leaders[B] and submit to them, since they keep watch over your souls as those who will give an account, so that they can do this with joy and not with grief, for that would be unprofitable for you. [18] Pray for us, for we are convinced that we have a clear conscience, wanting to conduct ourselves honorably in everything. [19] And I urge you all the more to pray[C] that I may be restored to you very soon. Jn 8:58; Heb 6:12; 13:17,24

Benediction and Farewell

[20] Now may the God of peace, who brought up from the dead our Lord Jesus — the great Shepherd of the sheep — through the blood of the everlasting covenant, [21] equip[D] you with everything good to do his will, working in us what is pleasing in his sight, through Jesus Christ, to whom be glory forever and ever.[E] Amen. Zch 9:11; Jn 10:11; Ac 2:24; Rm 15:33

[22] Brothers and sisters, I urge you to receive this message of exhortation, for I have written to you briefly. [23] Be aware that our brother Timothy has been released. If he comes soon enough, he will be with me when I see you. [24] Greet all your leaders and all the saints. Those who are from Italy send you greetings. [25] Grace be with you all.

A **13:12** Or set apart, or consecrate   B **13:17** Or rulers   C **13:19** Lit to do this   D **13:21** Or perfect
E **13:21** Other mss omit and ever

JAMES

Greeting

1 James, a servant of God and of the Lord Jesus Christ: Mt 13:55; Jd 1
To the twelve tribes dispersed abroad.^A Gn 49:28; Ex 24:4; Ezk 47:13; Mt 19:28
Greetings. Ti 1:1

Trials and Maturity

² Consider it a great joy, my brothers and sisters, whenever you experience various trials, ³ because you know that the testing of your faith produces endurance. ⁴ And let endurance have its full effect, so that you may be mature and complete, lacking nothing. Mt 5:12; 1Pt 1:6

⁵ Now if any of you lacks wisdom, he should ask God — who gives to all generously and ungrudgingly — and it will be given to him. ⁶ But let him ask in faith without doubting.^B For the doubter is like the surging sea, driven and tossed by the wind. ⁷ That person should not expect to receive anything from the Lord, ⁸ being double-minded and unstable in all his ways.^C 1Kg 3:9; Pr 2:3-6; Mt 7:7

⁹ Let the brother of humble circumstances boast in his exaltation, ¹⁰ but let the rich boast in his humiliation because he will pass away like a flower of the field. ¹¹ For the sun rises and, together with the scorching wind, dries up the grass; its flower falls off, and its beautiful appearance perishes. In the same way, the rich person will wither away while pursuing his activities.

¹² Blessed is the one who endures trials, because when he has stood the test he will receive the crown of life that God^D has promised to those who love him. 1Co 9:25; 2Tm 4:8

¹³ No one undergoing a trial should say, "I am being tempted by God," since God is not tempted by evil, and he himself doesn't tempt anyone. ¹⁴ But each person is tempted when he is drawn away and enticed by his own evil desire. ¹⁵ Then after desire has conceived, it gives birth to sin, and when sin is fully grown, it gives birth to death. Jb 15:35; Ps 7:14; Pr 7:6-23

¹⁶ Don't be deceived, my dear brothers and sisters. ¹⁷ Every good and perfect gift is from above, coming down from the Father of lights, who does not change like shifting shadows. ¹⁸ By his own choice, he gave us birth by the word of truth so that we would be a kind of firstfruits of his creatures. 1Co 6:9; Jms 1:19

Hearing and Doing the Word

¹⁹ My dear brothers and sisters, understand this: Everyone should be quick to listen, slow to speak, and slow to anger, ²⁰ for human anger does not accomplish God's righteousness. ²¹ Therefore, ridding yourselves of all moral filth and the evil that is so prevalent,^E humbly receive the implanted word, which is able to save your souls. Pr 10:19

²² But be doers of the word and not hearers only, deceiving yourselves. ²³ Because if anyone is a hearer of the word and not a doer, he is like someone looking at his

---

^A1:1 Gk *diaspora* ; Jewish people scattered throughout Gentile lands   ^B1:6 Or *without divided loyalties*
^C1:8 Or *in all his conduct*   ^D1:12 Other mss read *that the Lord*   ^E1:21 Or *the abundance of evil*

own face^A in a mirror. ²⁴ For he looks at himself, goes away, and immediately forgets what kind of person he was. ²⁵ But the one who looks intently into the perfect law of freedom and perseveres in it, and is not a forgetful hearer but a doer who works — this person will be blessed in what he does. Jms 2:12

²⁶ If anyone^B thinks he is religious without controlling his tongue, his religion is useless and he deceives himself. ²⁷ Pure and undefiled religion before God the Father is this: to look after orphans and widows in their distress and to keep oneself unstained from the world. Ps 34:13; 39:1; 141:3; Jms 3:2-3; 1Pt 3:10

The Sin of Favoritism

2 My brothers and sisters, do not show favoritism as you hold on to the faith in our glorious Lord Jesus Christ. ² For if someone comes into your meeting wearing a gold ring and dressed in fine clothes, and a poor person dressed in filthy clothes also comes in, ³ if you look with favor on the one wearing the fine clothes and say, "Sit here in a good place," and yet you say to the poor person, "Stand over there," or "Sit here on the floor by my footstool," ⁴ haven't you made distinctions among yourselves and become judges with evil thoughts? Lv 19:15; Dt 1:17; Ac 10:34; Rm 2:11

⁵ Listen, my dear brothers and sisters: Didn't God choose the poor in this world to be rich in faith and heirs of the kingdom that he has promised to those who love him? ⁶ Yet you have dishonored the poor. Don't the rich oppress you and drag you into court? ⁷ Don't they blaspheme the good name that was invoked over you? Jb 34:19; 1Co 1:27; Rv 2:9

⁸ Indeed, if you fulfill the royal law prescribed in the Scripture, **Love your neighbor as yourself**,^C you are doing well. ⁹ If, however, you show favoritism, you commit sin and are convicted by the law as transgressors. ¹⁰ For whoever keeps the entire law, and yet stumbles at one point, is guilty of breaking it all. ¹¹ For he who said, **Do not commit adultery**,^D also said, **Do not murder**.^E So if you do not commit adultery, but you murder, you are a lawbreaker. Lv 19:18

¹² Speak and act as those who are to be judged by the law of freedom. ¹³ For judgment is without mercy to the one who has not shown mercy. Mercy triumphs over judgment. Mt 7:12,24-29; 19:17-21; 22:36-40; 28:20

Faith and Works

¹⁴ What good is it, my brothers and sisters, if someone claims to have faith but does not have works? Can such faith save him?

¹⁵ If a brother or sister is without clothes and lacks daily food ¹⁶ and one of you says to them, "Go in peace, stay warm, and be well fed," but you don't give them what the body needs, what good is it? ¹⁷ In the same way faith, if it doesn't have works, is dead by itself.

¹⁸ But someone will say, "You have faith, and I have works."^F Show me your faith without works, and I will show you faith by my works. ¹⁹ You believe that God is one. Good! Even the demons believe — and they shudder. Dt 6:4; Rm 3:28; Heb 11:33; Jms 3:13

²⁰ Senseless person! Are you willing to learn that faith without works is useless? ²¹ Wasn't Abraham our

THE BOOKS OF THE
GENERAL LETTERS
AND NEW TESTAMENT
PROPHECY

The Bible has sixty-six books and ten divisions. The General Letters is the next to the last division of the Bible and consists of eight books. The last division is New Testament Prophecy and has one book, Revelation. These last divisions help Christians know how to stand true to faith in Christ even in difficult times while preparing for His second coming.

HEBREWS explains why Jesus came to earth to be the Savior of the world and encouraged Jewish Christians by helping them understand how Jesus fulfilled their law.

JAMES was written by Jesus' brother and tells that true faith is shown in right behavior. Christ is the ultimate example of doing right through faith.

FIRST & SECOND PETER were written by the Apostle Peter. In the first letter, he encouraged Christians to be patient during persecution. In the second letter, he encouraged them to be holy and to be careful about false teachers. Peter promised Christians that their suffering and faithfulness would bring joy when Christ returns.

FIRST, SECOND, & THIRD JOHN were written by the same man who wrote the Gospel of John. In the first letter, he reminded Christians of God's love, encouraged them to love one another, and warns them about false teaching. The second letter has messages about love and truth and also warned about false teaching. In the third letter, John thanked a man named Gaius for his kindness toward missionaries. These books illustrate how Christ came to earth as God and man to allow us to once again have fellowship with God the Father.

JUDE, written by Jesus' and James's brother, encouraged all Christians to stand firm in the faith. Jude prepares us for the promise that awaits us when Christ returns.

REVELATION is the only New Testament book of Prophecy and was written by the apostle John. In beautiful, symbolic language, John encouraged and warned Christians about events leading up to the end of time and the coming of "a new heaven and a new earth." Ultimately, this book brings us to the conclusion of Christ's return and His victory over sin.

PRAYERS IN THE **BIBLE**

Prayer is a way to talk with God. The Bible tells about prayer and about how to pray. When you pray, start by praising and thanking God. Then ask for His forgiveness, pray for others, and ask for His help for your own problems. Close by telling God you will do what He wants you to do and asking for His blessing.

TYPE OF PRAYER	DEFINITION	OLD TESTAMENT EXAMPLE	NEW TESTAMENT EXAMPLE	JESUS' TEACHING
PRAISE	Honoring God for who He is	In 1 Chronicles 29:10–13, David honored God for His greatness.	In Luke 1:46–55, Mary honored God in a praise song.	In Matthew 6:9, Jesus taught the disciples to begin their prayers by honoring God.
THANKSGIVING	Thanking God for what He has done for you	In Psalm 100:4–5, the psalmist thanked God for His goodness.	In 1 Thessalonians 5:16–18, Paul told the church to give thanks in all things.	In Luke 17:11–19, Jesus met a man with leprosy who was thankful for healing.
CONFESSION	Telling God about your sin and asking for His forgiveness	In Psalm 51, David told God about his sin and asked for forgiveness.	In Luke 18:13, Jesus told about a tax collector who asked God for forgiveness.	In Luke 18:9–14, Jesus taught about the importance of asking for forgiveness.
INTERCESSION	Praying for other people	In Exodus 32:11–13, 31–32, Moses prayed for the Hebrew people.	In Philippians 1:9–11, Paul prayed for the church at Philippi.	In John 17:9, 20–23, Jesus prayed for His disciples and for believers today.
PETITION	Asking God for help for yourself	In Genesis 24:12–14, Abraham's servant asked God to help him find a wife for Isaac.	In John 17:1–5, Jesus prayed for Himself.	In Matthew 7:7–12, Jesus taught about asking God for help.
COMMITMENT	Telling God that you will do what He wants you to do	In 1 Kings 8:56–61, Solomon told God the people would obey His commands.	In Acts 4:24–30, the believers prayed for God to help them tell others about Jesus.	In Matthew 6:10, Jesus taught His disciples to ask for God's will to be done.
BENEDICTION	Asking for God's blessing	In Numbers 6:24–26, God taught Moses and Aaron a blessing for the Hebrew people.	In Ephesians 6:23–24, Paul prays for God's peace and grace on all who love the Lord.	In Luke 11:28, Jesus said those who obeyed God's Word would be blessed.

father justified by works in offering Isaac his son on the altar? ²² You see that faith was active together with his works, and by works, faith was made complete, ²³ and the Scripture was fulfilled that says, **Abraham believed God, and it was credited to him as righteousness,** ^A and he was called God's friend. ²⁴ You see that a person is justified by works and not by faith alone. ²⁵ In the same way, wasn't Rahab the prostitute also justified by works in receiving the messengers and sending them out by a different route? ²⁶ For just as the body without the spirit is dead, so also faith without works is dead.   Gn 15:6; 22:9; Rm 4:3; 1Th 1:3; Heb 11:17

Controlling the Tongue

3 Not many should become teachers, my brothers, ^B because you know that we will receive a stricter judgment. ² For we all stumble in many ways. If anyone does not stumble in what he says, he is mature, able also to control the whole body. ³ Now if we put bits into the mouths of horses so that they obey us, we direct their whole bodies. ⁴ And consider ships: Though very large and driven by fierce winds, they are guided by a very small rudder wherever the will of the pilot directs. ⁵ So too, though the tongue is a small part of the body, it boasts great things. Consider how a small fire sets ablaze a large forest. ⁶ And the tongue is a fire. The tongue, a world of unrighteousness, is placed^C among our members. It stains the whole body, sets the course of life on fire, and is itself set on fire by hell. ⁷ Every kind of animal, bird, reptile, and fish is tamed and has

been tamed by humankind, ⁸ but no one can tame the tongue. It is a restless evil, full of deadly poison. ⁹ With the tongue we bless our Lord and Father, and with it we curse people who are made in God's likeness. ¹⁰ Blessing and cursing come out of the same mouth. My brothers and sisters, these things should not be this way. ¹¹ Does a spring pour out sweet and bitter water from the same opening? ¹² Can a fig tree produce olives, my brothers and sisters, or a grapevine produce figs? Neither can a saltwater spring yield fresh water.   1Kg 8:46; Mt 23:8; Rm 2:20-21

The Wisdom from Above

¹³ Who among you is wise and understanding? By his good conduct he should show that his works are done in the gentleness that comes from wisdom. ¹⁴ But if you have bitter envy and selfish ambition in your heart, don't boast and deny the truth. ¹⁵ Such wisdom does not come down from above but is earthly, unspiritual, demonic. ¹⁶ For where there is envy and selfish ambition, there is disorder and every evil practice. ¹⁷ But the wisdom from above is first pure, then peace-loving, gentle, compliant, full of mercy and good fruits, unwavering, without pretense. ¹⁸ And the fruit of righteousness is sown in peace by those who cultivate peace.   Rm 2:8; 13:13; 2Co 12:20; Gl 6:8; Jms 1:21; 2:18

Proud or Humble

4 What is the source of wars and fights among you? Don't th[ey] come from your passion[s that] wage war within you[r...] sire and do not ha[ve...]

^A**2:23** Gn 15:6   ^B**3:1** Or brothers and sisters   ^C**3:6** Or places itself, or appe[...] members and covet and cannot obtain. You fight and wage war.^A You do not have because you do not ask. ³ You ask and don't receive because you ask with wrong motives, so that you may spend it on your pleasures. Ps 18:41; Rm 7:23; Ti 3:9; 1Jn 3:22; 5:14

⁴ You adulterous people!^B Don't you know that friendship with the world is hostility toward God? So whoever wants to be the friend of the world becomes the enemy of God. ⁵ Or do you think it's without reason that the Scripture says: The spirit he made to dwell in us envies intensely?^C Jn 15:19; 1Co 6:19; Jms 1:27; 1Jn 2:15

⁶ But he gives greater grace. Therefore he says:

> **God resists the proud,**
> **but gives grace**
> **to the humble.**^D Ps 138:6; Pr 3:34

⁷ Therefore, submit to God. Resist the devil, and he will flee from you. ⁸ Draw near to God, and he will draw near to you. Cleanse your hands, sinners, and purify your hearts, you double-minded. ⁹ Be miserable and mourn and weep. Let your laughter be turned to mourning and your joy to gloom. ¹⁰ Humble yourselves before the Lord, and he will exalt you. Eph 4:27; 6:11; 1Pt 5:8-9

¹¹ Don't criticize one another, brothers and sisters. Anyone who defames or judges a fellow believer^E defames and judges the law. If you judge the law, you are ... of the law but a judge. ... lawgiver and judge^F ... e and to destroy. ... judge your ... 4; Jms 1:22; 1Pt 2:1

Our Will and God's Will

¹³ Come now, you who say, "Today or tomorrow we will travel to such and such a city and spend a year there and do business and make a profit." ¹⁴ Yet you do not know what tomorrow will bring — what your life will be! For you are like vapor that appears for a little while, then vanishes. Jb 7:7; Ps 102:3; Pr 27:1; Lk 12:18-20

¹⁵ Instead, you should say, "If the Lord wills, we will live and do this or that." ¹⁶ But as it is, you boast in your arrogance. All such boasting is evil. ¹⁷ So it is sin to know the good and yet not do it. Jn 9:41; Ac 18:21; 1Co 5:6

Warning to the Rich

5 Come now, you rich people, weep and wail over the miseries that are coming on you. ² Your wealth has rotted and your clothes are moth-eaten. ³ Your gold and silver are corroded, and their corrosion will be a witness against you and will eat your flesh like fire. You have stored up treasure in the last days. ⁴ Look! The pay that you withheld from the workers who mowed your fields cries out, and the outcry of the harvesters has reached the ears of the Lord of Hosts.^G ⁵ You have lived luxuriously on the earth and have indulged yourselves. You have fattened your hearts in a day of slaughter. ⁶ You have condemned, you have murdered the righteous, who does not resist you. Jb 13:28; Pr 11:28; Is 50:9; Lk 6:24

Waiting for the Lord

⁷ Therefore, brothers and sisters, be patient until the Lord's coming.

... u murder. You covet and cannot obtain, so you fight and wage ... ure says: He jealously yearns for the spirit he made to live ... dwell in us longs jealously?   ^D4:6 Pr 3:34   ^E4:11 Or his ... e   ^G5:4 Gk Sabaoth; or the Lord of Armies

See how the farmer waits for the precious fruit of the earth and is patient with it until it receives the early and the late rains. **8** You also must be patient. Strengthen your hearts, because the Lord's coming is near. Dt 11:14; Jr 5:24; Hs 6:3; Rm 13:11; Php 4:5

9 Brothers and sisters, do not complain about one another, so that you will not be judged. Look, the judge stands at the door!

10 Brothers and sisters, take the prophets who spoke in the Lord's name as an example of suffering and patience. **11** See, we count as blessed those who have endured.^A You have heard of Job's endurance and have seen the outcome that the Lord brought about — the Lord is compassionate and merciful. Ex 34:6; Nm 14:18; Jb 1:21-22; 2:10; 42:10-12

Truthful Speech

12 Above all, my brothers and sisters, do not swear, either by heaven or by earth or with any other oath. But let your "yes" mean "yes," and your "no" mean "no," so that you won't fall under judgment.^B Mt 5:33-37; 23:16-22; Mk 7:9-13

Effective Prayer

13 Is anyone among you suffering? He should pray. Is anyone cheerful? He should sing praises. **14** Is anyone among you sick? He should call for the elders of the church, and they are to pray over him, anointing him with oil in the name of the Lord. **15** The prayer of faith will save the sick person, and the Lord will raise him up; if he has committed sins, he will be forgiven. **16** Therefore, confess your sins to one another and pray for one another, so that you may be healed. The prayer of a righteous person is very powerful in its effect. **17** Elijah was a human being as we are, and he prayed earnestly that it would not rain, and for three years and six months it did not rain on the land. **18** Then he prayed again, and the sky gave rain and the land produced its fruit. Ps 50:15; Col 3:16

19 My brothers and sisters, if any among you strays from the truth, and someone turns him back, **20** let that person know that whoever turns a sinner from the error of his way will save his soul from death and cover a multitude of sins. Gl 6:1

---

^A**5:11** Or *persevered*　^B**5:12** Other mss read *fall into hypocrisy*

1 PETER

Greeting

1 Peter, an apostle of Jesus Christ: To those chosen, living as exiles dispersed abroad [A] in Pontus, Galatia, Cappadocia, Asia, and Bithynia, chosen [2] according to the foreknowledge of God the Father, through the sanctifying work of the Spirit, to be obedient and to be sprinkled with the blood of Jesus Christ. Gn 23:4; Ps 39:12; Heb 11:9,13; 1Pt 2:11

May grace and peace be multiplied to you.

A Living Hope

[3] Blessed be the God and Father of our Lord Jesus Christ. Because of his great mercy he has given us new birth into a living hope through the resurrection of Jesus Christ from the dead [4] and into an inheritance that is imperishable, undefiled, and unfading, kept in heaven for you. [5] You are being guarded by God's power through faith for a salvation that is ready to be revealed in the last time. [6] You rejoice in this, [B] even though now for a short time, if necessary, you suffer grief in various trials [7] so that the proven character of your faith — more valuable than gold which, though perishable, is refined by fire — may result in praise, glory, and honor at the revelation of Jesus Christ. [8] Though you have not seen him, you love him; though not seeing him now, you believe in him, and you rejoice with inexpressible and glorious joy, [9] because you are receiving the goal of your faith, the salvation of your souls. Jn 1:13; 2Co 1:3; Gl 6:16; Eph 1:3; Ti 3:5

[10] Concerning this salvation, the prophets, who prophesied about the grace that would come to you, searched and carefully investigated. [11] They inquired into what time or what circumstances the Spirit of Christ within them was indicating when he testified in advance to the sufferings of Christ and the glories that would follow. [C] [12] It was revealed to them that they were not serving themselves but you. These things have now been announced to you through those who preached the gospel to you by the Holy Spirit sent from heaven — angels long to catch a glimpse of these things. Lk 1:70; 10:24; 16:16,29; 18:31

A Call to Holy Living

[13] Therefore, with your minds ready for action, be sober-minded and set your hope completely on the grace to be brought to you at the revelation of Jesus Christ. [14] As obedient children, do not be conformed to the desires of your former ignorance. [15] But as the one who called you is holy, you also are to be holy in all your conduct; [16] for it is written, **Be holy, because I am holy.** [D] [17] If you appeal to the Father who judges impartially according to each one's work, you are to conduct yourselves in reverence during your time living as strangers. [18] For you know that you

were redeemed from your empty way of life inherited from your fathers, not with perishable things like silver or gold, [19] but with the precious blood of Christ, like that of an unblemished and spotless lamb. [20] He was foreknown before the foundation of the world but was revealed in these last times for you. [21] Through him you believe in God, who raised him from the dead and gave him glory, so that your faith and hope are in God.   Ex 12:11; Mt 12:21; Rm 8:24; 1Th 1:3; 1Pt 5:8

[22] Since you have purified yourselves by your obedience to the truth,[A] so that you show sincere brotherly love for each other, from a pure[B] heart love one another constantly,[C] [23] because you have been born again — not of perishable seed but of imperishable — through the living and enduring word of God. [24] For   Zch 7:9; Jn 13:34

All flesh is like grass,
and all its glory
    like a flower of the grass.
The grass withers,
    and the flower falls,
[25]   **but the word of the Lord**
    endures forever.[D]   Is 40:6-8

And this word is the gospel that was proclaimed to you.

The Living Stone and a Holy People

2 Therefore, rid yourselves of all malice, all deceit, hypocrisy, envy, and all slander. [2] Like newborn infants, desire the pure milk of the word,[E] so that you may

grow up into your salvation,[F] [3] if **you have tasted that the Lord is good.**[G] [4] As you come to him, a living stone — rejected by people but chosen and honored by[H] God — [5] you yourselves, as living stones, a spiritual house, are being built to be a holy priesthood[I] to offer spiritual sacrifices acceptable to God through Jesus Christ. [6] For it stands in Scripture: Rm 13:12; 2Co 12:20

See, I lay a stone in Zion,
a chosen and honored[J]
    cornerstone,   Eph 2:20
and the one who believes
    in him
will never be put
    to shame.[K]   Is 28:16; Rm 9:33; 10:11

[7] So honor will come to you who believe; but for the unbelieving,

The stone that the builders
    rejected —
this one has become
    the cornerstone,[L]   Ps 118:22

[8] and

A stone to stumble over,
    and a rock to trip over.[M]

They stumble because they disobey the word; they were destined for this.   Ac 2:23; 4:27-28; Rm 9:22; 11:7; Jd 4

[9] But you are **a chosen race,**[N,O] **a royal priesthood,**[P] **a holy nation,**[Q] **a people for his possession,**[R] **so that you may proclaim the praises**[S,T] of the one who called you out of darkness into his marvelous light. [10] Once you were not a people, but now you are God's people; you had not received mercy, but now you have received mercy.   Dt 7:6; 10:15; Is 43:20

[A]**1:22** Other mss add *through the Spirit*   [B]**1:22** Other mss omit *pure*   [C]**1:22** Or *fervently*   [D]**1:24-25** Is 40:6-8   [E]**2:2** Or *desire pure spiritual milk*   [F]**2:2** Other mss omit *for your salvation*   [G]**2:3** Ps 34:8   [H]**2:4** Or *precious to*   [I]**2:5** Or *you yourselves, as living stones, are being built into a spiritual house for a holy priesthood*   [J]**2:6** Or *precious*   [K]**2:6** Is 28:16 LXX   [L]**2:7** Ps 118:22   [M]**2:8** Is 8:14   [N]**2:9** Or *generation*, or *nation*   [O]**2:9** Dt 7:6; 10:15; Is 43:20 LXX   [P]**2:9** Ex 19:6; 23:22 LXX; Is 61:6   [Q]**2:9** Ex 19:6; 23:22 LXX   [R]**2:9** Ex 19:5; 23:22 LXX; Dt 4:20; 7:6; Is 43:21 LXX   [S]**2:9** Or *the mighty deeds*   [T]**2:9** Is 42:12; 43:21

A Call to Good Works

[11] Dear friends, I urge you as strangers and exiles to abstain from sinful desires that wage war against the soul. [12] Conduct yourselves honorably among the Gentiles,[A] so that when they slander you as evildoers, they will observe your good works and will glorify God on the day he visits.   1Tm 4:3; 1Pt 1:1

[13] Submit to every human authority because of the Lord, whether to the emperor[B] as the supreme authority [14] or to governors as those sent out by him to punish those who do what is evil and to praise those who do what is good. [15] For it is God's will that you silence the ignorance of foolish people by doing good. [16] Submit as free people, not using your freedom as a cover-up for evil, but as God's slaves. [17] Honor everyone. Love the brothers and sisters. Fear God. Honor the emperor.   Rm 13:1-7; Gl 1:4; Ti 3:1

Submission of Slaves to Masters

[18] Household slaves, submit to your masters with all reverence not only to the good and gentle ones but also to the cruel. [19] For it brings favor if, because of a consciousness of God, someone endures grief from suffering unjustly. [20] For what credit is it there if when you do wrong and are beaten, you endure it? But when you do what is good and suffer, if you endure it, this brings favor with God.   Eph 6:5; Col 3:22; Ti 2:9; Jd 4

[21] For you were called to this, because Christ also suffered for you, leaving you an example, that you should follow in his steps. [22] He did not commit sin, **and no deceit was found in his mouth;**[C] [23] when he was insulted, he did not insult in return; when he suffered, he did not threaten but entrusted himself to the one who judges justly. [24] He himself bore our sins in his body on the tree; so that, having died to sins, we might live for righteousness. **By his wounds**[D] **you have been healed.** [25] For you **were like sheep going astray,**[E] but you have now returned to the Shepherd and Overseer[F] of your souls.   Mk 8:31; Jn 8:12; 13:15; 1Pt 3:18; 1Jn 3:16

Wives and Husbands

3 In the same way, wives, submit yourselves to your own husbands so that, even if some disobey the word, they may be won over without a word by the way their wives live [2] when they observe your pure, reverent lives. [3] Don't let your beauty consist of outward things like elaborate hairstyles and wearing gold jewelry or fine clothes, [4] but rather what is inside the heart[G] — the imperishable quality of a gentle and quiet spirit, which is of great worth in God's sight. [5] For in the past, the holy women who put their hope in God also adorned themselves in this way, submitting to their own husbands, [6] just as Sarah obeyed Abraham, calling him lord. You have become her children when you do what is good and do not fear any intimidation.   Eph 5:22-33; Col 3:18-19; 1Tm 3:11; Ti 2:5

[7] Husbands, in the same way, live with your wives in an understanding way, as with a weaker partner, showing them honor as coheirs of the grace of life, so that your prayers will not be hindered.   Mt 1:19; 1Co 14:35

[A] **2:12** Or *among the nations,* or *among the pagans*   [B] **2:13** Or *king*   [C] **2:22** Is 53:9   [D] **2:24** Is 53:5
[E] **2:25** Is 53:6   [F] **2:25** Or *Guardian*   [G] **3:4** Or *rather, the hidden person of the heart*

Do No Evil

[8] Finally, all of you be like-minded and sympathetic, love one another, and be compassionate and humble,[A] [9] not paying back evil for evil or insult for insult but, on the contrary, giving a blessing, since you were called for this, so that you may inherit a blessing. Eph 4:32; Heb 13:1

[10] For the one who wants
    to love life Ps 34:12-16
    and to see good days,
    let him keep his tongue
        from evil Jms 1:26
    and his lips
        from speaking deceit,
[11] and let him turn away
        from evil Ps 37:27
    and do what is good.
    Let him seek peace
        and pursue it, Lk 12:51; 2Tm 1:2
[12] because the eyes
        of the Lord are
        on the righteous
    and his ears are open
        to their prayer.
    But the face of the Lord
        is against
    those who do what is evil.[B]

Undeserved Suffering

[13] Who then will harm you if you are devoted to what is good? [14] But even if you should suffer for righteousness, you are blessed. Do not fear what they fear[C] or be intimidated,[D] [15] but in your hearts regard[E] Christ[F] the Lord as holy, ready at any time to give a defense to anyone who asks you for a reason for the hope that is in you. [16] Yet do this with gentleness and respect, keeping a clear conscience, so that when you are accused, [6] those who disparage your good conduct in Christ will be put to shame. [17] For it is better to suffer for doing good, if that should be God's will, than for doing evil. Mt 6:33; Jn 6:20; Rm 1:17; 2Pt 1:1

[18] For Christ also suffered for sins once for all, the righteous for the unrighteous, that he might bring you to God. He was put to death in the flesh[H] but made alive by the Spirit,[I] [19] in which[J] he also went and made proclamation to the spirits in prison [20] who in the past were disobedient, when God patiently waited in the days of Noah while the ark was being prepared. In it a few — that is, eight people[K] — were saved through water. [21] Baptism, which corresponds to this, now saves you (not as the removal of dirt from the body, but the pledge[L] of a good conscience toward God) through the resurrection of Jesus Christ, [22] who has gone into heaven and is at the right hand of God with angels, authorities, and powers subject to him. Mk 8:31; Rm 5:8; 6:10

Following Christ

4 Therefore, since Christ suffered[M] in the flesh, arm yourselves also with the same understanding[N] — because the one who suffers in the flesh is finished with sin[O] — [2] in order to live the remaining time in the flesh no longer for human desires, but for God's will. [3] For there has already been enough

A3:8 Other mss read courteous   B3:10-12 Ps 34:12-16   C3:14 Or Do not fear them   D3:14 Is 8:12
E3:15 Or sanctify, or set apart   F3:15 Other mss read set God   G3:16 Other mss read when they speak
against you as evildoers   H3:18 Or by the flesh, or in the fleshly realm   I3:18 Or in the spirit, or in the
Spirit, or in the spiritual realm   J3:19 Or by whom, or in whom, or at that time   K3:20 Or souls   L3:21 Or
the appeal   M4:1 Other mss read suffered for us   N4:1 Or perspective, or attitude   O4:1 Or the one who
suffered in the flesh has finished with sin

time spent in doing what the Gentiles choose to do: carrying on in unrestrained behavior, evil desires, drunkenness, orgies, carousing, and lawless idolatry. ⁴ They are surprised that you don't join them in the same flood of wild living — and they slander^A you. ⁵ They will give an account to the one who stands ready to judge the living and the dead. ⁶ For this reason the gospel was also preached to those who are now dead,^B so that, although they might be judged in the flesh according to human standards, they might live in the spirit according to God's standards. Rm 6:10

End-Time Ethics

⁷ The end of all things is near; therefore, be alert and sober-minded for prayer. ⁸ Above all, maintain constant love for one another, since **love covers a multitude of sins.**^C ⁹ Be hospitable to one another without complaining. ¹⁰ Just as each one has received a gift, use it to serve others, as good stewards of the varied grace of God. ¹¹ If anyone speaks, let it be as one who speaks God's words; if anyone serves, let it be from the strength God provides, so that God may be glorified through Jesus Christ in everything. To him be the glory and the power forever and ever. Amen. Rm 13:11-12

Christian Suffering

¹² Dear friends, don't be surprised when the fiery ordeal comes among you to test you as if something unusual were happening to you. ¹³ Instead, rejoice as you share in the sufferings of Christ, so that you may also rejoice with great joy when his glory is revealed. ¹⁴ If you are ridiculed for the name of Christ, you are blessed, because the Spirit of glory and of God^D rests on you. ¹⁵ Let none of you suffer as a murderer, a thief, an evildoer, or a meddler.^E ¹⁶ But if anyone suffers as a Christian, let him not be ashamed but let him glorify God in having that name.^F ¹⁷ For the time has come for judgment to begin with God's household, and if it begins with us, what will the outcome be for those who disobey the gospel of God?

¹⁸ And **if a righteous person
is saved with difficulty,
what will become
of the ungodly
and the sinner?**^G   Pr 11:31

¹⁹ So then, let those who suffer according to God's will entrust themselves to a faithful Creator while doing what is good.   Ps 10:14; 2Co 1:9

About the Elders

5 I exhort the elders among you as a fellow elder and witness to the sufferings of Christ, as well as one who shares in the glory about to be revealed: ² Shepherd God's flock among you, not overseeing^H out of compulsion but willingly, as God would have you;^I not out of greed for money but eagerly; ³ not lording it over those entrusted to you, but being examples to the flock. ⁴ And when the chief Shepherd appears, you will receive the unfading crown of glory. ⁵ In the same way, you who are younger, be subject to the elders. All of you clothe yourselves with^J humility toward one another, because Col 3:4

^A4:4 Or *blaspheme*   ^B4:6 Or *those who are dead*   ^C4:8 Pr 10:12   ^D4:14 Or *God's glorious Spirit*   ^E4:15 Or *as one who defrauds others*   ^F4:16 Other mss read *in that case*   ^G4:18 Pr 11:31 LXX   ^H5:2 Other mss omit *overseeing*   ^I5:2 Other mss omit *as God would have you*   ^J5:5 Or *you tie around yourselves*

**God resists the proud
but gives grace
to the humble.**[A]   Pr 3:34; Jms 4:6

Conclusion

[6] Humble yourselves, therefore, under the mighty hand of God, so that he may exalt you at the proper time, [7] casting all your cares on him, because he cares about you. [8] Be sober-minded, be alert. Your adversary the devil is prowling around like a roaring lion, looking for anyone he can devour. [9] Resist him, firm in the faith, knowing that the same kind of sufferings are being experienced by your fellow believers throughout the world.   1Kg 8:42; 2Ch 6:32; Lk 14:11

[10] The God of all grace, who called you to his eternal glory in Christ,[B] will himself restore, establish, strengthen, and support you after you have suffered a little while.[C] [11] To him be dominion[D] forever.[E] Amen.   1Pt 5:1,4; 2Pt 3:18

[12] Through Silvanus,[F] a faithful brother (as I consider him), I have written to you briefly in order to encourage you and to testify that this is the true grace of God. Stand firm in it! [13] She who is in Babylon, chosen together with you, sends you greetings, as does Mark, my son. [14] Greet one another with a kiss of love. Peace to all of you who are in Christ.[G]   Ac 15:22; 1Th 1:1; 2Th 1:1; Rv 14:8; 16:19

[A] **5:5** Pr 3:34 LXX   [B] **5:10** Other mss read *in Christ Jesus*   [C] **5:10** Or *to a small extent*   [D] **5:11** Some mss read *dominion and glory*; other mss read *glory and dominion*   [E] **5:11** Other mss read *forever and ever*   [F] **5:12** Or *Silas*; Ac 15:22-32; 16:19-40; 17:1-16   [G] **5:14** Other mss read *Christ Jesus. Amen.*

2 PETER

Greeting

1 Simeon[A] Peter, a servant and an apostle of Jesus Christ: Mt 16:17 To those who have received a faith equal to ours through the righteousness of our God and Savior Jesus Christ. Rm 5:17,21; Php 1:11; Ti 2:13 ² May grace and peace be multiplied to you through the knowledge of God and of Jesus our Lord.

Growth in the Faith

³ His[B] divine power has given us everything required for life and godliness through the knowledge of him who called us by[C] his own glory and goodness. ⁴ By these he has given us very great and precious promises, so that through them you may share in the divine nature, escaping the corruption that is in the world because of evil desire. ⁵ For this very reason, make every effort to supplement your faith with goodness, goodness with knowledge, ⁶ knowledge with self-control, self-control with endurance, endurance with godliness, ⁷ godliness with brotherly affection, and brotherly affection with love. ⁸ For if you possess these qualities in increasing measure, they will keep you from being useless or unfruitful in the knowledge of our Lord Jesus Christ. ⁹ The person who lacks these things is blind and shortsighted and has forgotten the cleansing from his past sins. ¹⁰ Therefore, brothers and sisters, make every effort to confirm your calling and election, because if you do these things you will never stumble. ¹¹ For in this way, entry into the eternal kingdom of our Lord and Savior Jesus Christ will be richly provided for you. Jn 17:3; Php 3:8; 1Pt 1:5

¹² Therefore I will always remind you about these things, even though you know them and are established in the truth you now have. ¹³ I think it is right, as long as I am in this bodily tent, to wake you up with a reminder, ¹⁴ since I know that I will soon lay aside my tent, as our Lord Jesus Christ has indeed made clear to me. ¹⁵ And I will also make every effort so that you are able to recall these things at any time after my departure.[D] 2Co 11:10; Col 1:5-6

The Trustworthy Prophetic Word

¹⁶ For we did not follow cleverly contrived myths when we made known to you the power and coming of our Lord Jesus Christ; instead, we were eyewitnesses of his majesty. ¹⁷ For he received honor and glory from God the Father when the voice came to him from the Majestic Glory, saying "This is my beloved Son,[E] with whom I am well-pleased!" ¹⁸ We ourselves heard this voice when it came from heaven while we were with him on the holy mountain. ¹⁹ We also have the prophetic word strongly confirmed, and you will do well to pay attention to it, as to a lamp shining in a dark place, until the day dawns and the morning star

---

[A]1:1 Other mss read *Simon* [B]1:3 Lit *As his* [C]1:3 Or *to* [D]1:15 Or *death* [E]1:17 Other mss read *my Son, my beloved* rises in your hearts. ²⁰ Above all, you know this: No prophecy of Scripture comes from the prophet's own interpretation, ²¹ because no prophecy ever came by the will of man; instead, men spoke from God as they were carried along by the Holy Spirit.   Mk 13:26; 14:62; 1Th 2:19

The Judgment of False Teachers

2 There were indeed false prophets among the people, just as there will be false teachers among you. They will bring in destructive heresies, even denying the Master who bought them, and will bring swift destruction on themselves. ² Many will follow their depraved ways, and the way of truth will be maligned because of them. ³ They will exploit you in their greed with made-up stories. Their condemnation, pronounced long ago, is not idle, and their destruction does not sleep.   Dt 13:1-5; Mt 7:15; Ac 20:29; 2Co 11:13-15

⁴ For if God didn't spare the angels who sinned but cast them into hell^A and delivered them in chains^B of utter darkness to be kept for judgment; ⁵ and if he didn't spare the ancient world, but protected Noah, a preacher of righteousness, and seven others,^C when he brought the flood on the world of the ungodly; ⁶ and if he reduced the cities of Sodom and Gomorrah to ashes and condemned them to extinction,^D making them an example of what is coming to the ungodly;^{E 7} and if he rescued righteous Lot, distressed by the depraved behavior of the immoral ⁸ (for as that righteous man lived among them

day by day, his righteous soul was tormented by the lawless deeds he saw and heard) — ⁹ then the Lord knows how to rescue the godly from trials and to keep the unrighteous under punishment for the day of judgment, ¹⁰ especially those who follow the polluting desires of the flesh and despise authority.   Mt 25:41; Rm 8:32; Jd 6-7; Rv 20:2-3,10

Bold, arrogant people! They are not afraid to slander the glorious ones; ¹¹ however, angels, who are greater in might and power, do not bring a slanderous charge against them before the Lord.^{F 12} But these people, like irrational animals — creatures of instinct born to be caught and destroyed — slander what they do not understand, and in their destruction they too will be destroyed. ¹³ They will be paid back with harm for the harm they have done. They consider it a pleasure to carouse in broad daylight. They are spots and blemishes, delighting in their deceptions^G while they feast with you. ¹⁴ They have eyes full of adultery that never stop looking for sin. They seduce unstable people and have hearts trained in greed. Children under a curse! ¹⁵ They have gone astray by abandoning the straight path and have followed the path of Balaam, the son of Bosor,^H who loved the wages of wickedness ¹⁶ but received a rebuke for his lawlessness: A speechless donkey spoke with a human voice and restrained the prophet's madness.   Jr 23:14; Hs 4:2; Mt 5:27-28; Eph 2:3

¹⁷ These people are springs without water, mists driven by a storm.

---

^A**2:4** Gk *Tartarus*   ^B**2:4** Other mss read *in pits*   ^C**2:5** Lit *Noah, the eighth, a preacher of righteousness*   ^D**2:6** Other mss omit *to extinction*   ^E**2:6** Other mss read *an example of what is going to happen to the ungodly*   ^F**2:11** Other mss read *them from the Lord*   ^G**2:13** Other mss read *delighting in the love feasts* ^H**2:15** Other mss read *Beor*

The gloom of darkness has been reserved for them. [18] For by uttering boastful, empty words, they seduce, with fleshly desires and debauchery, people who have barely escaped[A] from those who live in error. [19] They promise them freedom, but they themselves are slaves of corruption, since people are enslaved to whatever defeats them. [20] For if, having escaped the world's impurity through the knowledge of the Lord[B] and Savior Jesus Christ, they are again entangled in these things and defeated, the last state is worse for them than the first. [21] For it would have been better for them not to have known the way of righteousness than, after knowing it, to turn back from the holy command delivered to them. [22] It has happened to them according to the true proverb: **A dog returns to its own vomit**,[C] and, "A washed sow returns to wallowing in the mud." Jn 8:34; Jd 13,16

The Day of the Lord

3 Dear friends, this is now the second letter I have written to you; in both letters, I want to stir up your sincere understanding by way of reminder, [2] so that you recall the words previously spoken by the holy prophets and the command of our Lord and Savior given through your apostles. [3] Above all, be aware of this: Scoffers will come in the last days scoffing and following their own evil desires, [4] saying, "Where is his 'coming' that he promised? Ever since our ancestors fell asleep, all things continue as they have

been since the beginning of creation." [5] They deliberately overlook this: By the word of God the heavens came into being long ago and the earth was brought about from water and through water. [6] Through these the world of that time perished when it was flooded. [7] By the same word, the present heavens and earth are stored up for fire, being kept for the day of judgment and destruction of the ungodly. Php 1:10; 2Tm 3:1; 1Pt 1:1

[8] Dear friends, don't overlook this one fact: With the Lord one day is like a thousand years, and a thousand years like one day. [9] The Lord does not delay his promise, as some understand delay, but is patient with you, not wanting any to perish but all to come to repentance. Ps 90:4; Ezk 18:23,32; Hab 2:3; Ti 2:11

[10] But the day of the Lord will come like a thief;[D] on that day the heavens will pass away with a loud noise, the elements will burn and be dissolved, and the earth and the works on it will be disclosed.[E,F] [11] Since all these things are to be dissolved in this way, it is clear what sort of people you should be in holy conduct and godliness [12] as you wait for the day of God and hasten its coming.[G] Because of that day, the heavens will be dissolved with fire and the elements will melt with heat. [13] But based on his promise, we wait for new heavens and a new earth, where righteousness dwells. Mt 24:43; Php 1:6; 1Th 5:2

Conclusion

[14] Therefore, dear friends, while you wait for these things, make

---

A2:18 Or *people who are actually escaping*   B2:20 Other mss read *our Lord*   C2:22 Pr 26:11
D3:10 Other mss add *in the night*   E3:10 Other mss read *will be burned up*   F3:10 Some Syriac and Coptic mss read *will not be found*   G3:12 Or *and speed the coming*

every effort to be found without spot or blemish in his sight, at peace. ¹⁵ Also, regard the patience of our Lord as salvation, just as our dear brother Paul has written to you according to the wisdom given to him. ¹⁶ He speaks about these things in all his letters. There are some matters that are hard to understand. The untaught and unstable will twist them to their own destruction, as they also do with the rest of the Scriptures. Php 2:15; 1Th 5:23; 1Tm 6:14

¹⁷ Therefore, dear friends, since you know this in advance, be on your guard, so that you are not led away by the error of lawless people and fall from your own stable position. ¹⁸ But grow in the grace and knowledge of our Lord and Savior Jesus Christ. To him be the glory both now and to the day of eternity.ᴬ Lk 12:15; 2Tm 1:14; 4:15; 2Pt 1:2; Rv 1:6

1 JOHN

Prologue: Our Declaration

1 What was from the beginning, what we have heard, what we have seen with our eyes, what we have observed and have touched with our hands, concerning the word of life — ² that life was revealed, and we have seen it and we testify and declare to you the eternal life that was with the Father and was revealed to us — ³ what we have seen and heard we also declare to you, so that you may also have fellowship with us; and indeed our fellowship is with the Father and with his Son Jesus Christ. ⁴ We are writing these things ᴬ so that our ᴮ joy may be complete. Ps 119:25; Jn 1:1; 1Jn 2:13-14

Fellowship with God

⁵ This is the message we have heard from him and declare to you: God is light, and there is absolutely no darkness in him. ⁶ If we say, "We have fellowship with him," and yet we walk in darkness, we are lying and are not practicing the truth. ⁷ If we walk in the light as he himself is in the light, we have fellowship with one another, and the blood of Jesus his Son cleanses us from all sin. ⁸ If we say, "We have no sin," we are deceiving ourselves, and the truth is not in us. ⁹ If we confess our sins, he is faithful and righteous to forgive us our sins and to cleanse us from all unrighteousness. ¹⁰ If we say, "We have not sinned," we make him a liar, and his word is not in us. Ps 27:1; 36:9; Jn 12:46; 1Tm 6:16; 1Jn 2:5

2 My little children, I am writing you these things so that you may not sin. But if anyone does sin, we have an advocate with the Father — Jesus Christ the righteous one. ² He himself is the atoning sacrifice ᶜ for our sins, and not only for ours, but also for those of the whole world. Jn 14:26; Rm 3:25; 2Co 5:21

God's Commands

³ This is how we know that we know him: if we keep his commands. ⁴ The one who says, "I have come to know him," and yet doesn't keep his commands, is a liar, and the truth is not in him. ⁵ But whoever keeps his word, truly in him the love of God is made complete. This is how we know we are in him: ⁶ The one who says he remains in him should walk just as he walked. Jn 13:35; 1Jn 2:5; 3:19,24

⁷ Dear friends, I am not writing you a new command but an old command that you have had from the beginning. The old command is the word you have heard. ⁸ Yet I am writing you a new command, which is true in him and in you, because the darkness is passing away and the true light is already shining. ⁹ The one who says he is in the light but hates his brother or sister is in the darkness until now. ¹⁰ The one who loves his brother or sister remains in the light, and there is no cause for stumbling in him. ᴰ ¹¹ But the one who hates his brother or sister is in the darkness, walks in the darkness, and doesn't know where he's going,

ᴬ**1:4** Other mss add *to you* ᴮ**1:4** Other mss read *your* ᶜ**2:2** Or *the propitiation* ᴰ**2:10** Or *it* because the darkness has blinded his eyes. Mk 7:8; Lk 6:47; Jn 8:12; 13:34; 2Jn 5

Reasons for Writing

¹² I am writing to you,
    little children,
since your sins have
    been forgiven
on account of his name. Ac 2:38
¹³ I am writing to you, fathers,
because you have come
    to know
the one who is
    from the beginning. 1Jn 1:1
I am writing to you,
    young men,
because you have conquered
    the evil one. Jn 16:33; 17:15; Eph 6:10
¹⁴ I have written to you,
    children,
because you have come
    to know the Father.
I have written to you, fathers,
because you have come
    to know
the one who is
    from the beginning.
I have written to you,
    young men,
because you are strong,
God's word remains in you,
and you have
    conquered the evil one.

A Warning About the World

¹⁵ Do not love the world or the things in the world. If anyone loves the world, the love of the Father is not in him. ¹⁶ For everything in the world — the lust of the flesh, the lust of the eyes, and the pride in one's possessions — is not from the Father, but is from the world. ¹⁷ And the world with its lust is passing away, but the one who does the will of God remains forever.

The Last Hour

¹⁸ Children, it is the last hour. And as you have heard that antichrist is coming, even now many antichrists have come. By this we know that it is the last hour. ¹⁹ They went out from us, but they did not belong to us; for if they had belonged to us, they would have remained with us. However, they went out so that it might be made clear that none of them belongs to us. Jn 2:4; 1Pt 4:7; 1Jn 2:22

²⁰ But you have an anointing from the Holy One, and all of you know the truth. ^A ²¹ I have not written to you because you don't know the truth, but because you do know it, and because no lie comes from the truth. ²² Who is the liar, if not the one who denies that Jesus is the Christ? This one is the antichrist: the one who denies the Father and the Son. ²³ No one who denies the Son has the Father; he who confesses the Son has the Father as well. Ps 89:18; Mk 1:24; Jn 20:31; Ac 10:38; 2Co 1:21

Remaining with God

²⁴ What you have heard from the beginning is to remain in you. If what you have heard from the beginning remains in you, then you will remain in the Son and in the Father. ²⁵ And this is the promise that he himself made to us: eternal life. Jn 15:4-7; 1Jn 2:6, 27-28; 3:6, 24; 4:13, 15-16

²⁶ I have written these things to you concerning those who are trying to deceive you. ²⁷ As for you, the anointing you received from him remains in you, and you don't need anyone to teach you. Instead, his anointing teaches you about all things and is true and is not a lie; just as it has taught you, ^B remain in him. Jn 14:26; 15:4-7; 1Jn 2:6; 3:6, 24

^A2:20 Other mss read *and you know all things* ^B2:27 Or *as he has taught you*

God's Children

[28] So now, little children, remain in him so that when he appears we may have confidence and not be ashamed before him at his coming. [29] If you know that he is righteous, you know this as well: Everyone who does what is right has been

3 born of him. [1] See what great love[A] the Father has given us that we should be called God's children — and we are! The reason the world does not know us is that it didn't know him. [2] Dear friends, we are God's children now, and what we will be has not yet been revealed. We know that when he appears,[B] we will be like him because we will see him as he is. [3] And everyone who has this hope in him purifies himself just as he is pure.   Jn 1:12-13; 3:3-7; 8:41; 1Jn 3:9

[4] Everyone who commits sin practices lawlessness; and sin is lawlessness. [5] You know that he was revealed so that he might take away sins,[C] and there is no sin in him. [6] Everyone who remains in him does not sin;[D] everyone who sins[E] has not seen him or known him.   Jn 1:29; 1Co 15:3; 2Co 5:21; Heb 10:4; 1Pt 2:24

[7] Children, let no one deceive you. The one who does what is right is righteous, just as he is righteous. [8] The one who commits[F] sin is of the devil, for the devil has sinned from the beginning. The Son of God was revealed for this purpose: to destroy the devil's works. [9] Everyone who has been born of God does not sin,[G] because his seed remains in him; he is not able to sin,[H] because he has been born of God. [10] This is how God's children and the devil's

children become obvious. Whoever does not do what is right is not of God, especially the one who does not love his brother or sister.   Mk 1:11

Love in Action

[11] For this is the message you have heard from the beginning: We should love one another, [12] unlike Cain, who was of the evil one and murdered his brother. And why did he murder him? Because his deeds were evil, and his brother's were righteous.   Gn 4:1; 2Th 3:3; Jd 11

[13] Do not be surprised, brothers and sisters, if the world hates you. [14] We know that we have passed from death to life because we love our brothers and sisters. The one who does not love remains in death. [15] Everyone who hates his brother or sister is a murderer, and you know that no murderer has eternal life residing in him. [16] This is how we have come to know love: He laid down his life for us. We should also lay down our lives for our brothers and sisters. [17] If anyone has this world's goods and sees a fellow believer[I] in need but withholds compassion from him — how does God's love reside in him? [18] Little children, let us not love in word or speech, but in action and in truth.   Jn 8:51; 17:14

[19] This is how we will know that we belong to the truth and will reassure our hearts before him [20] whenever our hearts condemn us; for God is greater than our hearts, and he knows all things.   Jn 14:6; 2Co 11:10

[21] Dear friends, if our hearts don't condemn us, we have confidence before God [22] and receive whatever we ask from him because we keep

---

[A]**3:1** Or *what sort of love*   [B]**3:2** Or *when it appears*   [C]**3:5** Other mss read *our sins*   [D]**3:6** Or *not keep on sinning*   [E]**3:6** Or *who keeps on sinning*   [F]**3:8** Or *practices*   [G]**3:9** Or *not practice sin*   [H]**3:9** Or *to keep on sinning*   [I]**3:17** Lit *sees his brother or sister* his commands and do what is pleasing in his sight. ²³ Now this is his command: that we believe in the name of his Son Jesus Christ, and love one another as he commanded us. ²⁴ The one who keeps his commands remains in him, and he in him. And the way we know that he remains in us is from the Spirit he has given us.   Mk 7:8; Jn 1:12; 14:15; 1Jn 2:3; 5:2

The Spirit of Truth and the Spirit of Error

4 Dear friends, do not believe every spirit, but test the spirits to see if they are from God, because many false prophets have gone out into the world.   1Th 5:21

² This is how you know the Spirit of God: Every spirit that confesses that Jesus Christ has come in the flesh is from God, ³ but every spirit that does not confess Jesus ᴬ is not from God. This is the spirit of the antichrist, which you have heard is coming; even now it is already in the world.   Jn 1:14; 1Co 12:3; Php 2:7; 3:3

⁴ You are from God, little children, and you have conquered them, because the one who is in you is greater than the one who is in the world. ⁵ They are from the world. Therefore what they say is from the world, and the world listens to them. ⁶ We are from God. Anyone who knows God listens to us; anyone who is not from God does not listen to us. This is how we know the Spirit of truth and the spirit of deception.   Rm 8:31; Col 1:27; 1Jn 3:20

Knowing God Through Love

⁷ Dear friends, let us love one another, because love is from God, and everyone who loves has been born of God and knows God. ⁸ The one who does not love does not know God, because God is love. ⁹ God's love was revealed among us ᴮ in this way: God sent his one and only Son into the world so that we might live through him. ¹⁰ Love consists in this: not that we loved God, but that he loved us and sent his Son to be the atoning sacrifice ᶜ for our sins. ¹¹ Dear friends, if God loved us in this way, we also must love one another. ¹² No one has ever seen God. If we love one another, God remains in ᴰ us and his love is made complete in us. ¹³ This is how we know that we remain in him and he in us: He has given us of his Spirit. ¹⁴ And we have seen and we testify that the Father has sent his Son as the world's Savior. ¹⁵ Whoever confesses that Jesus is the Son of God — God remains in him and he in God. ¹⁶ And we have come to know and to believe the love that God has for us.   Mk 9:37; Jn 1:14,18; 1Jn 2:29

God is love, and the one who remains in love remains in God, and God remains in him. ¹⁷ In this, love is made complete with us so that we may have confidence in the day of judgment, because as he is, so also are we in this world. ¹⁸ There is no fear in love; instead, perfect love drives out fear, because fear involves punishment. ᴱ So the one who fears is not complete in love. ¹⁹ We love ᶠ because he first loved us. ²⁰ If anyone says, "I love God," and yet hates his brother or sister, he is a liar. For the person who does not love his brother or sister whom he has seen cannot love God whom he has not seen. ᴳ ²¹ And we

---

ᴬ4:3 Other mss read *confess that Jesus has come in the flesh*   ᴮ4:9 Or *in us*   ᶜ4:10 Or *the propitiation*
ᴰ4:12 Or *remains among*   ᴱ4:18 Or *fear has its own punishment* or *torment*   ᶠ4:19 Other mss add *him*
ᴳ4:20 Other mss read *has seen, how is he able to love . . . seen?* (as a question)

have this command from him: The one who loves God must also love his brother and sister. Mt10:15;11:22,24

5 Everyone who believes that Jesus is the Christ has been born of God, and everyone who loves the Father[A] also loves the one born of him. [2] This is how we know that we love God's children: when we love God and obey[B] his commands. [3] For this is what love for God is: to keep his commands. And his commands are not a burden, [4] because everyone who has been born of God conquers the world. This is the victory that has conquered the world: our faith. Dt 30:11; Mt 11:30; 23:4,23; 1Jn 2:29

The Certainty of God's Testimony

[5] Who is the one who conquers the world but the one who believes that Jesus is the Son of God? [6] Jesus Christ — he is the one who came by water and blood, not by water only, but by water and by blood. And the Spirit is the one who testifies, because the Spirit is the truth. [7] For there are three that testify:[C] [8] the Spirit, the water, and the blood — and these three are in agreement. [9] If we accept human testimony, God's testimony is greater, because it is God's testimony that he has given about his Son. [10] The one who believes in the Son of God has this testimony within himself. The one who does not believe God has made him a liar, because he has not believed in the testimony God has given about his Son. [11] And this is the testimony: God has given us eternal life, and this life is in his Son. [12] The one

who has the Son has life. The one who does not have the Son of God does not have life. [13] I have written these things to you who believe in the name of the Son of God so that you may know that you have eternal life. Jn 5:19; 14:1; 1Co 15:57; 2Pt 2:20

Effective Prayer

[14] This is the confidence we have before him: If we ask anything according to his will, he hears us. [15] And if we know that he hears whatever we ask, we know that we have what we have asked of him. Mt 7:7-8; Jn 9:31; 14:13; 1Jn 3:22

[16] If anyone sees a fellow believer[D] committing a sin that doesn't lead to death, he should ask, and God will give life to him — to those who commit sin that doesn't lead to death. There is sin[E] that leads to death. I am not saying he should pray about that. [17] All unrighteousness is sin, and there is sin that doesn't lead to death.

Conclusion

[18] We know that everyone who has been born of God does not sin, but the one who is born of God keeps him,[F] and the evil one does not touch him. [19] We know that we are of God, and the whole world is under the sway of the evil one. [20] And we know that the Son of God has come and has given us understanding so that we may know the true one.[G] We are in the true one — that is, in his Son Jesus Christ. He is the true God and eternal life. Jn 1:14; 17:12; 1Pt 1:5; Jd 24; Rv 3:10

[21] Little children, guard yourselves from idols.

[A]**5:1** Or *loves the one who has given birth*   [B]**5:2** Other mss read *keep*   [C]**5:7-8** A few late Gk mss and some late Vg mss add *testify in heaven: the Father, the Word, and the Holy Spirit, and these three are one.* ⁸*And there are three who bear witness on earth:*   [D]**5:16** Lit *sees his brother or sister*   [E]**5:16** Or *is a sin*   [F]**5:18** Other mss read *himself*   [G]**5:20** Other mss read *the true God*

2 JOHN

Greeting

[1] The elder:

To the elect lady and her children, whom I love in the truth — and not only I, but also all who know the truth — [2] because of the truth that remains in us and will be with us forever.   Jn 8:32; 14:6; Rm 16:13; 1Pt 5:13; 2Jn 13

[3] Grace, mercy, and peace will be with us from God the Father and from Jesus Christ, the Son of the Father, in truth and love.   1Tm 1:2

Truth and Deception

[4] I was very glad to find some of your children walking in truth, in keeping with a command we have received from the Father. [5] So now I ask you, dear lady — not as if I were writing you a new command, but one we have had from the beginning — that we love one another. [6] This is love: that we walk according to his commands. This is the command as you have heard it from the beginning: that you walk in love. [A]   Ps 103:18; 1Jn 2:5; 3:11; 5:3; 3Jn 3-4

[7] Many deceivers have gone out into the world; they do not confess the coming of Jesus Christ in the flesh. This is the deceiver and the antichrist. [8] Watch yourselves so you don't lose what we [B] have worked for, but that you may receive a full reward. [9] Anyone who does not remain in Christ's teaching but goes beyond it does not have God. The one who remains in that teaching, this one has both the Father and the Son. [10] If anyone comes to you and does not bring this teaching, do not receive him into your home, and don't greet him; [11] for the one who greets him shares in his evil works.   Php 3:3; 1Jn 2:18,22; 4:3; 2Pt 2:13

Farewell

[12] Though I have many things to write to you, I don't want to use paper and ink. Instead, I hope to come to you and talk face to face so that our joy may be complete.

[13] The children of your elect sister send you greetings.

[A] 6 Or in it   [B] 8 Other mss read you

3 JOHN

Greeting

¹ The elder: 2Jn 1

To my dear friend Gaius, whom I love in the truth. Jn 14:6; 1Jn 5:20

² Dear friend, I pray that you are prospering in every way and are in good health, just as your whole life is going well.[A] ³ For I was very glad when fellow believers came and testified to your fidelity to the truth — how you are walking in truth. ⁴ I have no greater joy than this: to hear that my children are walking in truth. Jn 15:26; Ac 26:5; 1Tm 1:10

Gaius Commended

⁵ Dear friend, you are acting faithfully in whatever you do for the brothers and sisters, especially when they are strangers. ⁶ They have testified to your love before the church. You will do well to send them on their journey in a manner worthy of God, ⁷ since they set out for the sake of the Name, accepting nothing from pagans.[B] ⁸ Therefore, we ought to support such people so that we can be coworkers with the truth. Mt 16:18; 21:5

Diotrephes and Demetrius

⁹ I wrote something to the church, but Diotrephes, who loves to have first place among them, does not receive our authority. ¹⁰ This is why, if I come, I will remind him of the works he is doing, slandering us with malicious words. And he is not satisfied with that! He not only refuses to welcome fellow believers, but he even stops those who want to do so and expels them from the church. Mt 20:25-28; 23:5-12; Col 1:18; 2Jn 9

¹¹ Dear friend, do not imitate what is evil, but what is good. The one who does good is of God; the one who does evil has not seen God. ¹² Everyone speaks well of Demetrius — even the truth itself. And we also speak well of him, and you know that our testimony is true. Ex 33:20; 1Pt 3:17; 1Jn 2:20-21; 4:4

Farewell

¹³ I have many things to write you, but I don't want to write to you with pen and ink. ¹⁴ I hope to see you soon, and we will talk face to face.

¹⁵ Peace to you. The friends send you greetings. Greet the friends by name.

[A]2 Or as your soul prospers   [B]7 Or Gentiles

JUDE

Greeting

¹ Jude, a servant of Jesus Christ and a brother of James: Mt 13:55; Mk 6:3

To those who are the called, loved ᴬ by God the Father and kept for Jesus Christ. Rm 1:7; 1Co 1:24; 1Th 1:4

² May mercy, peace, and love be multiplied to you. 1Pt 1:2; 2Pt 1:2

Jude's Purpose in Writing

³ Dear friends, although I was eager to write you about the salvation we share, I found it necessary to write, appealing to you to contend for the faith that was delivered to the saints once for all. ⁴ For some people, who were designated for this judgment long ago, ᴮ have come in by stealth; they are ungodly, turning the grace of our God into sensuality and denying Jesus Christ, our only Master and Lord. 1Tm 6:12; 2Tm 4:7; Ti 1:4; 1Pt 2:8; 2Pt 2:21

Apostates: Past and Present

⁵ Now I want to remind you, although you came to know all these things once and for all, that Jesus ᶜ saved a people out of Egypt and later destroyed those who did not believe; ⁶ and the angels who did not keep their own position but abandoned their proper dwelling, he has kept in eternal chains in deep darkness for the judgment on the great day. ⁷ Likewise, Sodom and Gomorrah and the surrounding towns committed sexual immorality and perversions, ᴰ and serve as an example by undergoing the punishment of eternal fire. Gn 6:1-4; 1Co 10:1-11; 2Pt 2:4

⁸ In the same way these people — relying on their dreams — defile their flesh, reject authority, and slander glorious ones. ⁹ Yet when Michael the archangel was disputing with the devil in an argument about Moses's body, he did not dare utter a slanderous condemnation against him but said, "The Lord rebuke you!" ¹⁰ But these people blaspheme anything they do not understand. And what they do understand by instinct — like irrational animals — by these things they are destroyed. ¹¹ Woe to them! For they have gone the way of Cain, have plunged into Balaam's error for profit, and have perished in Korah's rebellion. Dn 10:13,21; 12:1; 2Pt 2:10

The Apostates' Doom

¹² These people are dangerous reefs ᴱ at your love feasts as they eat with you without reverence. They are shepherds who only look after themselves. They are waterless clouds carried along by winds; trees in late autumn — fruitless, twice dead and uprooted. ¹³ They are wild waves of the sea, foaming up their shameful deeds; wandering stars for whom the blackness of darkness is reserved forever. 1Co 11:17-22; 2Pt 2:13

¹⁴ It was about these that Enoch, in the seventh generation from Adam, prophesied: "Look! The Lord comes with tens of thousands of his

ᴬ1 Other mss read *sanctified*   ᴮ4 Or *whose judgment was written about long ago*   ᶜ5 Other mss read *the Lord,* or *God*   ᴰ7 Or *and went after other flesh*   ᴱ12 Other mss read *are like blemishes* holy ones [15] to execute judgment on all and to convict all the ungodly concerning all the ungodly acts that they have done in an ungodly way, and concerning all the harsh things ungodly sinners have said against him." [16] These people are discontented grumblers, living according to their desires; their mouths utter arrogant words, flattering people for their own advantage. Gn 5:18; Dt 33:2; Dn 7:10; Mk 8:38; 1Th 3:13

[17] But you, dear friends, remember what was predicted by the apostles of our Lord Jesus Christ. [18] They told you, "In the end time there will be scoffers living according to their own ungodly desires." [19] These people create divisions and are worldly, not having the Spirit. 1Tm 4:1; 2Tm 3:1; 1Pt 1:5,20

Exhortation and Benediction

[20] But you, dear friends, as you build yourselves up in your most holy faith, praying in the Holy Spirit, [21] keep yourselves in the love of God, waiting expectantly for the mercy of our Lord Jesus Christ for eternal life. [22] Have mercy on those who waver; [23] save others by snatching them from the fire; have mercy on others but with fear, hating even the garment defiled by the flesh. Eph 6:18

[24] Now to him who is able to protect you from stumbling and to make you stand in the presence of his glory, without blemish and with great joy, [25] to the only God our Savior, through Jesus Christ our Lord, A be glory, majesty, power, and authority before all time, B now and forever. Amen. Rm 16:25; 5:27

A **25** Other mss omit *through Jesus Christ our Lord*   B **25** Other mss omit *before all time*

REVELATION

Prologue

1 The revelation of[A] Jesus Christ that God gave him to show his servants what must soon take place. He made it known by sending his angel to his servant John, [2] who testified to the word of God and to the testimony[B] of Jesus Christ, whatever he saw.[C] [3] Blessed is the one who reads aloud the words of this prophecy, and blessed are those who hear the words of this prophecy and keep[D] what is written in it, because the time is near. Ac 2:18; Rm 6:19

[4] John: To the seven churches in Asia. Grace and peace to you from[E] the one who is, who was, and who is to come, and from the seven spirits[F] before his throne, [5] and from Jesus Christ, the faithful witness, the firstborn from the dead and the ruler of the kings of the earth. Ti 1:4; Rv 1:8,17; 3:1; 4:5,8; 16:5

To him who loves us and has set us free[G] from our sins by his blood, [6] and made us a kingdom,[H] priests[I] to his God and Father — to him be glory and dominion forever and ever. Amen. Ex 19:6; Dt 7:8; Rm 8:2; 1Pt 2:9; 20:6

[7] Look, he is coming
with the clouds, Is 19:1
and every eye will see him,
even those who pierced him.
And all the tribes[J]
of the earth[K] Gn 12:3; 28:14
will mourn over him.[L,M]
So it is to be. Amen.

[8] "I am the Alpha and the Omega," says the Lord God, "the one who is, who was, and who is to come, the Almighty." Is 44:6; Rv 21:6; 22:13

John's Vision of the Risen Lord

[9] I, John, your brother and partner in the affliction, kingdom, and endurance that are in Jesus, was on the island called Patmos because of the word of God and the testimony of Jesus. [10] I was in the Spirit[N] on the Lord's day, and I heard a loud voice behind me like a trumpet [11] saying, "Write on a scroll[O] what you see and send it to the seven churches: Ephesus, Smyrna, Pergamum, Thyatira, Sardis, Philadelphia, and Laodicea." Jn 16:33; Ac 14:22; Rm 5:3; 2Tm 2:12

[12] Then I turned to see whose voice it was that spoke to me. When I turned I saw seven golden lampstands, [13] and among the lampstands was one like the Son of Man,[P] dressed in a robe and with a golden sash wrapped around his chest. [14] The hair of his head was white as wool — white as snow — and his eyes like a fiery flame. [15] His feet were like fine bronze as it is fired in a furnace, and his voice like the sound of cascading[Q] waters. [16] He had seven stars in his right hand; a sharp double-edged sword came from his mouth, and his face was shining like the sun at full strength. Ex 20:18; 25:37; 37:23; Zch 4:2

A1:1 Or *Revelation of*, or *A revelation of*   B1:2 Or *witness*   C1:2 Or *as many as he saw*   D1:3 Or *follow*, or *obey*   E1:4 Other mss add *God*   F1:4 Or *the sevenfold Spirit*   G1:5 Other mss read *has washed us*   H1:6 Other mss read *kings and*   I1:6 Or *made us into* (or *to be*) *a kingdom of priests*; Ex 19:6   J1:7 Or *peoples*   K1:7 Gn 12:3; 28:14; Zch 14:17   L1:7 Or *will wail because of him*   M1:7 Dn 7:13; Zch 12:10   N1:10 Or *in spirit*; lit *I became in the Spirit*   O1:11 Or *book*   P1:13 Or *like a son of man*   Q1:15 Lit *many*

¹⁷ When I saw him, I fell at his feet like a dead man. He laid his right hand on me and said, "Don't be afraid. I am the First and the Last, ¹⁸ and the Living One. I was dead, but look — I am alive forever and ever, and I hold the keys of death and Hades. ¹⁹ Therefore write what you have seen, what is, and what will take place after this. ²⁰ The mystery of the seven stars you saw in my right hand and of the seven golden lampstands is this: The seven stars are the angels^A of the seven churches, and the seven lampstands^B are the seven churches.　Gn 17:3; Jdg 6:22-23

THE LETTERS TO THE SEVEN CHURCHES

The Letter to Ephesus

2 "Write to the angel^C of the church in Ephesus: Thus says the one who holds the seven stars in his right hand and who walks among the seven golden lampstands: ² I know your works, your labor, and your endurance, and that you cannot tolerate evil people. You have tested those who call themselves apostles and are not, and you have found them to be liars. ³ I know that you have persevered and endured hardships for the sake of my name, and have not grown weary. ⁴ But I have this against you: You have abandoned the love you had at first. ⁵ Remember then how far you have fallen; repent, and do the works you did at first. Otherwise, I will come to you^D and remove your lampstand from its place, unless you repent. ⁶ Yet you do have this: You hate the practices of the Nicolaitans, which I also hate.　Ac 21:11; Rv 1:16,20; 2:19; 3:1,8,15

⁷ "Let anyone who has ears to hear listen to what the Spirit says to the churches. To the one who conquers, I will give the right to eat from the tree of life, which is in^E the paradise of God.　Gn 2:8-9; Lk 23:43; 1Jn 5:4-5

The Letter to Smyrna

⁸ "Write to the angel of the church in Smyrna: Thus says the First and the Last, the one who was dead and came to life: ⁹ I know your^F affliction and poverty, but you are rich. I know the slander of those who say they are Jews and are not, but are a synagogue of Satan. ¹⁰ Don't be afraid of what you are about to suffer. Look, the devil is about to throw some of you into prison to test you, and you will experience affliction for ten days. Be faithful to the point of death, and I will give you the crown^G of life.　Mt 4:1; Rv 1:17; 3:9-10

¹¹ "Let anyone who has ears to hear listen to what the Spirit says to the churches. The one who conquers will never be harmed by the second death.　Rv 20:6,14; 21:8

The Letter to Pergamum

¹² "Write to the angel of the church in Pergamum: Thus says the one who has the sharp, double-edged sword: ¹³ I know^H where you live — where Satan's throne is. Yet you are holding on to my name and did not deny your faith in me,^I even in the days of Antipas, my faithful witness who was put to death among you, where Satan lives. ¹⁴ But I have a few things against you. You have some there who hold to the teaching of

---

^A**1:20** Or *messengers*　^B**1:20** Other mss add *that you saw*　^C**2:1** Or *messenger*, also in vv. 8,12,18
^D**2:5** Other mss add *quickly*　^E**2:7** Other mss read *in the midst of*　^F**2:9** Other mss add *works and*
^G**2:10** Or *wreath*　^H**2:13** Other mss add *your works and*　^I**2:13** Or *deny my faith*

Balaam, who taught Balak to place a stumbling block[A] in front of the Israelites: to eat meat sacrificed to idols and to commit sexual immorality. [15] In the same way, you also have those who hold to the teaching of the Nicolaitans.[B] [16] So repent! Otherwise, I will come to you quickly and fight against them with the sword of my mouth.   Is 49:2; Heb 4:12

[17] "Let anyone who has ears to hear listen to what the Spirit says to the churches. To the one who conquers, I will give some of the hidden manna.[C] I will also give him a white stone, and on the stone a new name is inscribed that no one knows except the one who receives it.

The Letter to Thyatira

[18] "Write to the angel of the church in Thyatira: Thus says the Son of God, the one whose eyes are like a fiery flame and whose feet are like fine bronze: [19] I know your works — your love, faithfulness,[D] service, and endurance. I know that your last works are greater than the first. [20] But I have this against you: You tolerate the woman Jezebel, who calls herself a prophetess and teaches and deceives my servants to commit sexual immorality and to eat meat sacrificed to idols. [21] I gave her time to repent, but she does not want to repent of her sexual immorality. [22] Look, I will throw her into a sickbed and those who commit adultery with her into great affliction. Unless they repent of her[E] works, [23] I will strike her children dead.[F] Then all the churches will know that I am the one who examines minds and hearts, and I will give to each of you according to your works. [24] I say to the rest of you in Thyatira, who do not hold this teaching, who haven't known "the so-called secrets[G] of Satan" — as they say — I am not putting any other burden on you. [25] Only hold on to what you have until I come. [26] The one who conquers and who keeps my works to the end: I will give him authority over the nations —   Ps 2:7-9; Rv 1:14-15

[27] **and he will rule[H] them
with an iron scepter;
he will shatter them
like pottery[I] —**   Ps 2:9

[28] just as I have received this from my Father. I will also give him the morning star.   Is 14:12; 2Pt 1:19; Rv 22:1

[29] "Let anyone who has ears to hear listen to what the Spirit says to the churches.

The Letter to Sardis

3 "Write to the angel[J] of the church in Sardis: Thus says the one who has the seven spirits of God and the seven stars: I know your works; you have a reputation[K] for being alive, but you are dead. [2] Be alert and strengthen[L] what remains, which is about to die,[M] for I have not found your works complete before my God. [3] Remember, then, what you have received and heard; keep it, and repent. If you are not alert, I will come[N] like a thief, and you have no idea at what hour I will come upon you. [4] But you have a few people[O] in Sardis who have

---

[A]**2:14** Or *to place a trap*   [B]**2:15** Other mss add *which I hate*   [C]**2:17** Other mss add *to eat*   [D]**2:19** Or *faith*
[E]**2:22** Other mss read *their*   [F]**2:23** Or *with a plague*   [G]**2:24** Or *the secret things*   [H]**2:27** Or *shepherd*
[I]**2:27** Ps 2:9   [J]**3:1** Or *messenger,* also in vv. 7,14   [K]**3:1** Or *have a name*   [L]**3:2** Other mss read *guard*
[M]**3:2** Or *strengthen who remain, who are about to die*   [N]**3:3** Other mss add *upon you*   [O]**3:4** Lit *few
names*

not defiled[A] their clothes, and they will walk with me in white, because they are worthy.   Rv 1:4,16,20; 4:5; 5:6

⁵ "In the same way, the one who conquers will be dressed in white clothes, and I will never erase his name from the book of life but will acknowledge his name before my Father and before his angels.

⁶ "Let anyone who has ears to hear listen to what the Spirit says to the churches.   Mt 11:15; 13:9,43; Lk 8:8

The Letter to Philadelphia

⁷ "Write to the angel of the church in Philadelphia: Thus says the Holy One, the true one, the one who has the key of David, who opens and no one will close, and who closes and no one opens: ⁸ I know your works. Look, I have placed before you an open door that no one can close because you have but little power; yet you have kept my word and have not denied my name. ⁹ Note this: I will make those from the synagogue of Satan, who claim to be Jews and are not, but are lying — I will make them come and bow down at your feet, and they will know that I have loved you. ¹⁰ Because you have kept my command to endure, I will also keep you from the hour of testing that is going to come on the whole world to test those who live on the earth. ¹¹ I am coming soon. Hold on to what you have, so that no one takes your crown.   Is 22:22; Mt 16:19; 1Jn 5:20; Rv 6:10; 19:11

¹² "The one who conquers I will make a pillar in the temple of my God, and he will never go out again. I will write on him the name of my God and the name of the city of my God — the new Jerusalem, which comes down out of heaven from my God — and my new name.   2Ch 3:17

¹³ "Let anyone who has ears to hear listen to what the Spirit says to the churches.

The Letter to Laodicea

¹⁴ "Write to the angel of the church in Laodicea: Thus says the Amen, the faithful and true witness, the originator[B] of God's creation: ¹⁵ I know your works, that you are neither cold nor hot. I wish that you were cold or hot. ¹⁶ So, because you are lukewarm, and neither hot nor cold, I am going to vomit[C] you out of my mouth. ¹⁷ For you say, 'I'm rich; I have become wealthy and need nothing,' and you don't realize that you are wretched, pitiful, poor, blind, and naked. ¹⁸ I advise you to buy from me gold refined in the fire so that you may be rich, white clothes so that you may be dressed and your shameful nakedness not be exposed, and ointment to spread on your eyes so that you may see. ¹⁹ As many as I love, I rebuke and discipline. So be zealous and repent. ²⁰ See! I stand at the door and knock. If anyone hears my voice and opens the door, I will come in to him and eat with him, and he with me.   Mk 10:6; 13:19; 2Co 1:20

²¹ "To the one who conquers I will give the right to sit with me on my throne, just as I also conquered and sat down with my Father on his throne.   Mt 19:28; 2Tm 2:12

²² "Let anyone who has ears to hear listen to what the Spirit says to the churches."

The Throne Room of Heaven

4 After this I looked, and there in heaven was an open door. The first voice that I had heard speaking to me like a trumpet said, "Come up here, and I will

[A] **3:4** Or *soiled*   [B] **3:14** Or *beginning of God's creation,* or *ruler of God's creation*   [C] **3:16** Or *spit* show you what must take place after this." Ex 19:19; 20:18; Ps 47:5; Zch 9:14

² Immediately I was in the Spirit, and there was a throne in heaven and someone was seated on it. ³ The one seated ᴬ there had the appearance of jasper and carnelian stone. A rainbow that had the appearance of an emerald surrounded the throne. Ac 19:21; Rm 8:9; 14:17

⁴ Around the throne were twenty-four thrones, and on the thrones sat twenty-four elders dressed in white clothes, with golden crowns on their heads. Mt 19:28; Rv 5:8; 11:16; 19:4

⁵ Flashes of lightning and rumblings and peals of thunder came from the throne. Seven fiery torches were burning before the throne, which are the seven spirits of God. ⁶ Something like a sea of glass, similar to crystal, was also before the throne. Ex 19:16; 20:18; Ps 77:18; Rv 8:5; 11:19

Four living creatures covered with eyes in front and in back were around the throne on each side. ⁷ The first living creature was like a lion; the second living creature was like an ox; the third living creature had a face like a man; and the fourth living creature was like a flying eagle. ⁸ Each of the four living creatures had six wings; they were covered with eyes around and inside. Day and night they never stop, ᴮ saying, Is 6:2; Ezk 1:5-28; 10:9-14; Rv 7:15

Holy, holy, holy,
Lord God, the Almighty,
who was, who is,
   and who is to come. Is 6:3

⁹ Whenever the living creatures give glory, honor, and thanks to the one seated on the throne, the one who lives forever and ever, ¹⁰ the twenty-four elders fall down before the one seated on the throne and worship the one who lives forever and ever. They cast their crowns before the throne and say, 2Ch 20:18; Rv 10:6; 15:7

¹¹ Our Lord and God, ᶜ
   you are worthy to receive
   glory and honor and power,
   because you have created
      all things, Gn 1:1; Ac 14:15; Rv 10:6
   and by your will
   they exist and were created.

The Lamb Takes the Scroll

5 Then I saw in the right hand of the one seated on the throne a scroll with writing on both sides, sealed with seven seals. ² I also saw a mighty angel proclaiming with a loud voice, "Who is worthy to open the scroll and break its seals?" ³ But no one in heaven or on earth or under the earth was able to open the scroll or even to look in it. ⁴ I wept and wept because no one was found worthy to open ᴰ the scroll or even to look in it. ⁵ Then one of the elders said to me, "Do not weep. Look, the Lion from the tribe of Judah, the Root of David, has conquered so that he is able to open the scroll and ᴱ its seven seals." Is 29:11; Ezk 2:9-10

⁶ Then I saw one like a slaughtered lamb standing in the midst of the throne and the four living creatures and among the elders. He had seven horns and seven eyes, which are the seven spirits of God sent into all the earth. ⁷ He went and took the scroll out of the right hand of the one seated on the throne. Rv 1:4; 5:12; 13:8

The Lamb Is Worthy

⁸ When he took the scroll, the four living creatures and the twenty-four

---

ᴬ4:3 Other mss omit *The one seated* ᴮ4:8 Or *rest* ᶜ4:11 Some mss add *the Holy One*; other mss read *Lord* ᴰ5:4 Other mss add *and read* ᴱ5:5 Other mss add *loose* elders fell down before the Lamb. Each one had a harp and golden bowls filled with incense, which are the prayers of the saints. ⁹ And they sang a new song: Ps 33:2; 71:22; 96:1

> You are worthy to take
>   the scroll
> and to open its seals,
> because you
>   were slaughtered,
> and you purchased[A] people[B]
> for God by your blood
> from every tribe and language
> and people and nation.   Ex 19:5
> ¹⁰ You made them a kingdom[C]
> and priests to our God,   Ex 19:6
> and they will reign
>   on the earth.

¹¹ Then I looked and heard the voice of many angels around the throne, and also of the living creatures and of the elders. Their number was countless thousands, plus thousands of thousands. ¹² They said with a loud voice,   Dn 7:10

> Worthy is the Lamb who was
>   slaughtered
> to receive power and riches
> and wisdom and strength
> and honor and glory
> and blessing!

¹³ I heard every creature in heaven, on earth, under the earth, on the sea, and everything in them say,

> Blessing and honor and glory
>   and power
> be to the one seated
>   on the throne,
> and to the Lamb, forever
>   and ever!

¹⁴ The four living creatures said, "Amen," and the elders fell down and worshiped.

The First Seal on the Scroll

6 Then I saw the Lamb open one of the seven[D] seals, and I heard one of the four living creatures say with a voice like thunder, "Come!" ² I looked, and there was a white horse. Its rider held a bow; a crown was given to him, and he went out as a conqueror in order to conquer.[E]   Zch 6:1-3; Rv 14:2; 19:6,11

The Second Seal

³ When he opened the second seal, I heard the second living creature say, "Come!" ⁴ Then another horse went out, a fiery red one, and its rider was allowed to take peace from the earth, so that people would slaughter one another. And a large sword was given to him.   Zch 1:8; 6:2; Mt 10:34

The Third Seal

⁵ When he opened the third seal, I heard the third living creature say, "Come!" And I looked, and there was a black horse. Its rider held a set of scales in his hand. ⁶ Then I heard something like a voice among the four living creatures say, "A quart of wheat for a denarius,[F] and three quarts of barley for a denarius, but do not harm the oil and the wine."   1Sm 2:3; Jb 6:2; 31:6; Zch 6:2,6

The Fourth Seal

⁷ When he opened the fourth seal, I heard the voice of the fourth living creature say, "Come!" ⁸ And I looked, and there was a pale green[G] horse. Its rider was named Death, and Hades was following after him. They were[H] given authority over a fourth of the earth, to kill by the sword, by famine, by

---

^A**5:9** Or *redeemed*   ^B**5:9** Other mss read *us*   ^C**5:10** Other mss read *them kings*   ^D**6:1** Other mss omit *seven*   ^E**6:2** Or *went out conquering and in order to conquer*   ^F**6:6** A denarius = one day's wage   ^G**6:8** Or *a greenish gray*   ^H**6:8** Other mss read *He was* plague, and by the wild animals of the earth. Hs 13:14; Mt 10:1; 28:18; Rv 1:18; 20:13

The Fifth Seal

⁹ When he opened the fifth seal, I saw under the altar the souls of those who had been slaughtered because of the word of God and the testimony they had given.ᴬ ¹⁰ They cried out with a loud voice: "Lord,ᴮ the one who is holy and true, how long until you judge those who live on the earth and avenge our blood? " ¹¹ So they were each given a white robe, and they were told to rest a little while longer until the number would be completed of their fellow servants and their brothers and sisters, who were going to be killed just as they had been. Rv 1:2,9; 12:17; 19:10

The Sixth Seal

¹² Then I saw him openᶜ the sixth seal. A violent earthquake occurred; the sun turned black like sackcloth made of hair; the entire moonᴰ became like blood; ¹³ the starsᴱ of heaven fell to the earth as a fig tree drops its unripe figs when shaken by a high wind; ¹⁴ the sky was split apart like a scroll being rolled up; and every mountain and island was moved from its place. Is 13:10; 50:3; Jl 2:10; Rv 11:13; 16:18
¹⁵ Then the kings of the earth, the nobles, the generals, the rich, the powerful, and every slave and free person hid in the caves and among the rocks of the mountains. ¹⁶ And they said to the mountains and to the rocks, "Fall on us and hide us from the face of the one seated on the throne and from the wrath of the Lamb, ¹⁷ because the great day

of theirᶠ wrath has come! And who is able to stand? " Jdg 6:2; 1Sm 13:6; Hs 10:8

The Sealed of Israel

7 After this I saw four angels standing at the four corners of the earth, restraining the four winds of the earth so that no wind could blow on the earth or on the sea or on any tree. ² Then I saw another angel rising up from the east, who had the seal of the living God. He cried out in a loud voice to the four angels who were allowed to harm the earth and the sea: ³ "Don't harm the earth or the sea or the trees until we seal the servants of our God on their foreheads." ⁴ And I heard the number of the sealed: Is 11:12; Jr 49:36; Ezk 7:2; Rv 9:14

144,000 sealed from every tribe of the Israelites:
⁵ 12,000 sealed from the tribe of Judah,
12,000ᴳ from the tribe of Reuben,
12,000 from the tribe of Gad,
⁶ 12,000 from the tribe of Asher,
12,000 from the tribe of Naphtali,
12,000 from the tribe of Manasseh,
⁷ 12,000 from the tribe of Simeon,
12,000 from the tribe of Levi,
12,000 from the tribe of Issachar,
⁸ 12,000 from the tribe of Zebulun,
12,000 from the tribe of Joseph,
12,000 sealed from the tribe of Benjamin.

ᴬ6:9 Other mss add about the Lamb ᴮ6:10 Or "Master" ᶜ6:12 Or I saw when he opened ᴰ6:12 Or the full moon ᴱ6:13 Perhaps meteors ᶠ6:17 Other mss read his ᴳ7:5-8 Other mss add sealed after each number

A Multitude from the Great Tribulation

⁹ After this I looked, and there was a vast multitude from every nation, tribe, people, and language, which no one could number, standing before the throne and before the Lamb. They were clothed in white robes with palm branches in their hands. ¹⁰ And they cried out in a loud voice: Gn 15:5; 32:12; Rv 5:9; 11:9; 13:7; 14:6

Salvation belongs to our God,
who is seated on the throne,
and to the Lamb!

¹¹ All the angels stood around the throne, and along with the elders and the four living creatures they fell facedown before the throne and worshiped God, ¹² saying,

Amen! Blessing and glory
and wisdom
and thanksgiving and honor
and power and strength
be to our God forever
and ever. Amen.   Rv 4:11

¹³ Then one of the elders asked me, "Who are these people in white robes, and where did they come from?"

¹⁴ I said to him, "Sir,[A] you know." Then he told me: These are the ones coming out of the great tribulation. They washed their robes and made them white in the blood of the Lamb. Dn 12:1; Mk 13:19; Rv 3:10; 6:11

¹⁵ For this reason they are
before the throne of God,
and they serve him
day and night in his temple.
The one seated on the throne
will shelter[B] them: Ps 27:5; 61:4

¹⁶ They will no longer hunger;
they will no longer thirst;
the sun will no longer
strike them,

nor will any scorching heat.
¹⁷ For the Lamb who is
at the center of the throne
will shepherd them;   Ps 23:1
he will guide them to springs
of the waters of life,   Ps 23:2
and God will wipe away
every tear
from their eyes. Is 25:8; Rv 21:4

The Seventh Seal

8 When he opened the seventh seal, there was silence in heaven for about half an hour. ² Then I saw the seven angels who stand in the presence of God; seven trumpets were given to them. ³ Another angel, with a golden incense burner, came and stood at the altar. He was given a large amount of incense to offer with the prayers of all the saints on the golden altar in front of the throne. ⁴ The smoke of the incense, with the prayers of the saints, went up in the presence of God from the angel's hand. ⁵ The angel took the incense burner, filled it with fire from the altar, and hurled it to the earth; there were peals of thunder, rumblings, flashes of lightning, and an earthquake. Hab 2:20; Zph 1:7; Zch 2:13; Lk 1:19; 16:1

The Seven Trumpets

⁶ And the seven angels who had the seven trumpets prepared to blow them.

The First Trumpet

⁷ The first angel blew his trumpet, and hail and fire, mixed with blood, were hurled to the earth. So a third of the earth was burned up, a third of the trees were burned up, and all the green grass was burned up. Ex 9:13-35; Ezk 5:12; 38:22; Jl 2:30-31; Zch 13:8-9

[A]7:14 Or "My lord   [B]7:15 Or will spread his tent over

The Second Trumpet

[8] The second angel blew his trumpet, and something like a great mountain ablaze with fire was hurled into the sea. So a third of the sea became blood, [9] a third of the living creatures in the sea died, and a third of the ships were destroyed.   Ex 7:20-21; Jr 51:25; Mk 11:23

The Third Trumpet

[10] The third angel blew his trumpet, and a great star, blazing like a torch, fell from heaven. It fell on a third of the rivers and springs of water. [11] The name of the star is Wormwood, and a third of the waters became wormwood. So, many of the people died from the waters, because they had been made bitter.   Pr 5:3-4; Is 14:12; Jr 9:15; Lm 3:19; Rv 9:1

The Fourth Trumpet

[12] The fourth angel blew his trumpet, and a third of the sun was struck, a third of the moon, and a third of the stars, so that a third of them were darkened. A third of the day was without light and also a third of the night.   Ex 10:21-23; Is 13:10

[13] I looked and heard an eagle[A] flying high overhead, crying out in a loud voice, "Woe! Woe! Woe to those who live on the earth, because of the remaining trumpet blasts that the three angels are about to sound!"   Rv 9:12; 11:14; 12:12

The Fifth Trumpet

9 The fifth angel blew his trumpet, and I saw a star that had fallen from heaven to earth. The key for the shaft to the abyss was given to him. [2] He opened the shaft to the abyss, and smoke came up out of the shaft like smoke from a great[B] furnace so that the sun and the air were darkened by the smoke from the shaft. [3] Then locusts came out of the smoke on to the earth, and power[C] was given to them like the power that scorpions have on the earth. [4] They were told not to harm the grass of the earth, or any green plant, or any tree, but only those people who do not have God's seal on their foreheads. [5] They were not permitted to kill them but were to torment them for five months; their torment is like the torment caused by a scorpion when it stings someone. [6] In those days people will seek death and will not find it; they will long to die, but death will flee from them.   Is 14:12; Lk 8:31; 10:18; Rv 8:10

[7] The appearance of the locusts was like horses prepared for battle. Something like golden crowns was on their heads; their faces were like human faces; [8] they had hair like women's hair; their teeth were like lions' teeth; [9] they had chests like iron breastplates; the sound of their wings was like the sound of many chariots with horses rushing into battle; [10] and they had tails with stingers like scorpions, so that with their tails they had the power to harm people for five months. [11] They had as their king[D] the angel of the abyss; his name in Hebrew is Abaddon,[E] and in Greek he has the name Apollyon.[F]   Jl 2:4-5

[12] The first woe has passed. There are still two more woes to come after this.   Rv 8:13; 11:14

The Sixth Trumpet

[13] The sixth angel blew his trumpet. From the four[G] horns of the golden

---

altar that is before God, I heard a voice [14] say to the sixth angel who had the trumpet, "Release the four angels bound at the great river Euphrates." [15] So the four angels who were prepared for the hour, day, month, and year were released to kill a third of the human race. [16] The number of mounted troops was two hundred million; [A] I heard their number. [17] This is how I saw the horses and their riders in the vision: They had breastplates that were fiery red, hyacinth blue, and sulfur yellow. The heads of the horses were like the heads of lions, and from their mouths came fire, smoke, and sulfur. [18] A third of the human race was killed by these three plagues — by the fire, the smoke, and the sulfur that came from their mouths. [19] For the power of the horses is in their mouths and in their tails, because their tails, which resemble snakes, have heads that inflict injury. Ex 39:38; 40:5; Rv 7:1-2

[20] The rest of the people, who were not killed by these plagues, did not repent of the works of their hands to stop worshiping demons and idols of gold, silver, bronze, stone, and wood, which cannot see, hear, or walk. [21] And they did not repent of their murders, their sorceries, their sexual immorality, or their thefts. 1Kg 13:33; 2Ch 34:25; Ps 7:12

The Mighty Angel and the Small Scroll

10 Then I saw another mighty angel coming down from heaven, wrapped in a cloud, with a rainbow over his head. [B] His face was like the sun, his legs [C] were like pillars of fire, [2] and he held a little scroll opened in his hand. He put his right foot on the sea, his left on the land, [3] and he called out with a loud voice like a roaring lion. When he cried out, the seven thunders raised their voices. [4] And when the seven thunders spoke, I was about to write, but I heard a voice from heaven, saying, "Seal up what the seven thunders said, and do not write it down!" Dn 8:26; Rv 3:12; 4:3; 5:2; 18:21

[5] Then the angel that I had seen standing on the sea and on the land raised his right hand to heaven. [6] He swore by the one who lives forever and ever, who created heaven and what is in it, the earth and what is in it, and the sea and what is in it: "There will no longer be a delay, [7] but in the days when the seventh angel will blow his trumpet, then the mystery of God will be completed, as he announced to his servants the prophets." Dn 12:7; Rv 11:15

[8] Then the voice that I heard from heaven spoke to me again and said, "Go, take the scroll that lies open in the hand of the angel who is standing on the sea and on the land."

[9] So I went to the angel and asked him to give me the little scroll. He said to me, "Take and eat it; it will be bitter in your stomach, but it will be as sweet as honey in your mouth." Ps 119:103; Jr 15:16; Ezk 2:8–3:3

[10] Then I took the little scroll from the angel's hand and ate it. It was as sweet as honey in my mouth, but when I ate it, my stomach became bitter. [11] And they said to me, "You must prophesy again about [D] many peoples, nations, languages, and kings." Nm 5:24; Ezk 3:1-3; Dn 3:4,7; 4:1; 7:9

[A]**9:16** Other mss read *a hundred million*   [B]**10:1** Or *a halo on his head*   [C]**10:1** Or *feet*   [D]**10:11** Or *prophesy again against*

The Two Witnesses

11 Then I was given a measuring reed like a rod,[A] with these words: "Go[B] and measure the temple of God and the altar, and count those who worship there. [2] But exclude the courtyard outside the temple. Don't measure it, because it is given to the nations,[C] and they will trample the holy city for forty-two months. [3] I will grant[D] my two witnesses authority to prophesy for 1,260 days, dressed in sackcloth." [4] These are the two olive trees and the two lampstands that stand before the Lord[E] of the earth. [5] If anyone wants to harm them, fire comes from their mouths and consumes their enemies; if anyone wants to harm them, he must be killed in this way. [6] They have authority to close up the sky so that it does not rain during the days of their prophecy. They also have power over the waters to turn them into blood and to strike the earth with every plague whenever they want.   Ezk 40:3,5; 42:14-19; Rv 21:15

The Witnesses Martyred

[7] When they finish their testimony, the beast that comes up out of the abyss will make war on them, conquer them, and kill them. [8] Their dead bodies[F] will lie in the main street[G] of the great city, which figuratively[H] is called Sodom and Egypt, where also their Lord was crucified. [9] And some of[I] the peoples, tribes, languages, and nations will view their bodies for three and a half days and not permit their bodies to be put into a tomb. [10] Those who live on the earth will gloat over them and celebrate and send gifts to one another because these two prophets had tormented those who live on the earth.   Ps 140:10; Dn 7:11; Rv 13:1-18; 17:8

The Witnesses Resurrected

[11] But after three and a half days, the breath[J] of life from God entered them, and they stood on their feet. Great fear fell on those who saw them. [12] Then they heard[K] a loud voice from heaven saying to them, "Come up here." They went up to heaven in a cloud, while their enemies watched them. [13] At that moment a violent earthquake took place, a tenth of the city fell, and seven thousand people were killed in the earthquake. The survivors were terrified and gave glory to the God of heaven.   Gn 2:7; 6:17; 7:15,22

[14] The second woe has passed. Take note: The third woe is coming soon!   Rv 8:13; 9:12

The Seventh Trumpet

[15] The seventh angel blew his trumpet, and there were loud voices in heaven saying,   Is 27:13

The kingdom of the world
has become the kingdom
of our Lord and of his Christ,
and he will reign forever
and ever.   2Sm 7:16; Is 37:16; Dn 7:14,18

[16] The twenty-four elders, who were seated before God on their thrones, fell facedown and worshiped God, [17] saying,

We give you thanks,
Lord God, the Almighty,
who is and who was,[L]   Rv 1:4,8

[A]11:1 Other mss add *and the angel stood up*   [B]11:1 Lit *"Arise*   [C]11:2 Or *Gentiles*   [D]11:3 Or *I will give to*
[E]11:4 Other mss read *God*   [F]11:8 Or *Their corpse*   [G]11:8 Or *lie on the broad street*   [H]11:8 Or *spiritually*
[I]11:9 Lit *And from*   [J]11:11 Or *spirit*   [K]11:12 Other mss read *Then I heard*   [L]11:17 Other mss add *and who is to come*

because you have taken
your great power
and have begun to reign.
¹⁸ The nations were angry,   Ps 2:1
but your wrath has come.
The time has come
for the dead to be judged
and to give the reward
to your servants the prophets,
to the saints, and to those
who fear your name,
both small and great,   2Kg 23:2
and the time has come
to destroy
those who destroy the earth.

¹⁹ Then the temple of God in heaven was opened, and the ark of his covenant ᴬ appeared in his temple. There were flashes of lightning, rumblings and peals of thunder, an earthquake, ᴮ and severe hail.   Rv 4:5; 8:5

The Woman, the Child, and the Dragon

12 A great sign ᶜ appeared in heaven: a woman clothed with the sun, with the moon under her feet and a crown of twelve stars on her head. ² She was pregnant and cried out in labor and agony as she was about to give birth. ³ Then another sign ᴰ appeared in heaven: There was a great fiery red dragon having seven heads and ten horns, and on its heads were seven crowns. ᴱ ⁴ Its tail swept away a third of the stars in heaven and hurled them to the earth. And the dragon stood in front of the woman who was about to give birth, so that when she did give birth it might devour her child. ⁵ She gave birth to a

Son, a male who is going to rule ᶠ all nations with an iron rod. Her child was caught up to God and to his throne. ⁶ The woman fled into the wilderness, where she had a place prepared by God, to be nourished there ᴳ for 1,260 days.   Gn 37:9-10; Mt 24:30

The Dragon Thrown Out of Heaven

⁷ Then war broke out in heaven: Michael and his angels fought against the dragon. The dragon and his angels also fought, ⁸ but he could not prevail, and there was no place for them in heaven any longer. ⁹ So the great dragon was thrown out — the ancient serpent, who is called the devil and Satan, the one who deceives the whole world. He was thrown to earth, and his angels with him. ¹⁰ Then I heard a loud voice in heaven say,   1Sm 2:9; Jb 2:1; Dn 10:13, 21; 12:1; Jd 9

The salvation and the power
and the kingdom of our God
and the authority
of his Christ
have now come,   Rv 11:17; 19:1
because the accuser
of our brothers and sisters,
who accuses them
before our God
day and night,
has been thrown down.
¹¹ They conquered him
by the blood of the Lamb   Rv 5:9
and by the word
of their testimony;   Rv 6:9
for they did not love
their lives
to the point of death.   Lk 14:26
¹² Therefore rejoice,
you heavens,
and you who dwell in them!

ᴬ**11:19** Other mss read *ark of the covenant of the Lord*   ᴮ**11:19** Other mss omit *an earthquake*   ᶜ**12:1** Or *great symbolic display*; see Rv 12:3   ᴰ**12:3** Or *another symbolic display*   ᴱ**12:3** Or *diadems*   ᶠ**12:5** Or *shepherd*   ᴳ**12:6** Or *God, that they might feed her there*

Woe to the earth and the sea,
because the devil
has come down to you
with great fury,
because he knows his time
is short.

The Woman Persecuted

¹³ When the dragon saw that he had been thrown down to the earth, he persecuted ᴬ the woman who had given birth to the male child. ¹⁴ The woman was given two wings of a great eagle, so that she could fly from the serpent's presence to her place in the wilderness, where she was nourished for a time, times, and half a time. ¹⁵ From his mouth the serpent spewed water like a river flowing after the woman, to sweep her away with a flood. ¹⁶ But the earth helped the woman. The earth opened its mouth and swallowed up the river that the dragon had spewed from his mouth. ¹⁷ So the dragon was furious with the woman and went off to wage war against the rest of her offspring ᴮ — those who keep the commands of God and hold firmly to the testimony about Jesus.   Ex 19:4; Dt 32:10-11

The Beast from the Sea

¹⁸ The dragon ᶜ stood on the sand of the sea. ᴰ

13 And I saw a beast coming up out of the sea. It had ten horns and seven heads. On its horns were ten crowns, ᴱ and on its heads were blasphemous names. ᶠ ² The beast I saw was like a leopard, its feet were like a bear's, and its mouth was like a lion's mouth. The dragon gave the beast his power, his throne, and great authority. ³ One of its heads appeared to be fatally wounded, but its fatal wound was healed.   Dn 7:3-6; Rv 12:3; 17:3

The whole earth was amazed and followed the beast. ⁴ They worshiped the dragon because he gave authority to the beast. And they worshiped the beast, saying, "Who is like the beast? Who is able to wage war against it?"   Ex 15:11; Rv 12:3; 17:8

⁵ The beast was given a mouth to utter boasts and blasphemies. It was allowed to exercise authority ᴳ,ᴴ for forty-two months. ⁶ It began to speak ' blasphemies against God: to blaspheme his name and his dwelling — those who dwell in heaven. ⁷ And it was permitted to wage war against the saints and to conquer them. It was also given authority over every tribe, people, language, and nation. ⁸ All those who live on the earth will worship it, everyone whose name was not written from the foundation of the world in the book ᴶ of life of the Lamb who was slaughtered. ᴷ   Dn 7:8,11,20; Rv 11:2; 12:17

⁹ If anyone has ears to hear, let him listen.   Mt 11:15; Rv 2:7,11,17,19; 3:6,13,22
¹⁰   If anyone is to be
taken captive,
into captivity he goes.
If anyone is to be killed ᴸ
with a sword,
with a sword
he will be killed.   Jr 15:2; 43:11
This calls for endurance ᴹ and faithfulness from the saints.   Rv 14:12

ᴬ**12:13** Or pursued   ᴮ**12:17** Or seed   ᶜ**12:18** Or he; other mss read I   ᴰ**12:18** Some translations put Rv 12:18 either in Rv 12:17 or Rv 13:1.   ᴱ**13:1** Or diadems   ᶠ**13:1** Other mss read heads was a blasphemous name   ᴳ**13:5** Other mss read to wage war   ᴴ**13:5** Or to rule   ' **13:6** Or He opened his mouth in   ᴶ**13:8** Or scroll   ᴷ**13:8** Or written in the book of life of the Lamb who was slaughtered from the foundation of the world   ᴸ**13:10** Other mss read anyone kills   ᴹ**13:10** Or Here is the perseverance

The Beast from the Earth

[11] Then I saw another beast coming up out of the earth; it had two horns like a lamb,[A] but it spoke like a dragon. [12] It exercises all the authority of the first beast on its behalf and compels the earth and those who live on it to worship the first beast, whose fatal wound was healed. [13] It also performs great signs, even causing fire to come down from heaven to earth in front of people. [14] It deceives those who live on the earth because of the signs that it is permitted to perform in the presence of the beast, telling those who live on the earth to make an image[B] of the beast who was wounded by the sword and yet lived. [15] It was permitted to give breath[C] to the image of the beast, so that the image of the beast could both speak and cause whoever would not worship the image of the beast to be killed. [16] And it makes everyone — small and great, rich and poor, free and slave — to receive a mark on his right hand or on his forehead, [17] so that no one can buy or sell unless he has the mark: the beast's name or the number of its name.   Dt 13:1-3; Dn 8:3; Mk 13:22; 2Th 2:9-11

[18] This calls for wisdom:[D] Let the one who has understanding calculate[E] the number of the beast, because it is the number of a person. Its number is 666.[F]   Rv 17:9

The Lamb and the 144,000

14 Then I looked, and there was the Lamb, standing on Mount Zion, and with him were 144,000 who had his name and his Father's name written on their foreheads.

[2] I heard a sound[G] from heaven like the sound of cascading waters and like the rumbling of loud thunder. The sound I heard was like harpists playing on their harps. [3] They sang[H] a new song before the throne and before the four living creatures and the elders, but no one could learn the song except the 144,000 who had been redeemed from the earth. [4] These are the ones who have not defiled themselves with women, since they remained virgins. These are the ones who follow the Lamb wherever he goes. They were redeemed[I] from humanity as the firstfruits for God and the Lamb. [5] No lie was found in their mouths; they are blameless.   Is 18:7; 24:23; Mc 4:7

The Proclamation of Three Angels

[6] Then I saw another angel flying high overhead, with the eternal gospel to announce to the inhabitants of the earth — to every nation, tribe, language, and people. [7] He spoke with a loud voice: "Fear God and give him glory, because the hour of his judgment has come. Worship the one who made heaven and earth, the sea and the springs of water."   Rv 7:2; 8:3,13; 14:15,17-18; 18:1

[8] And another, a second angel, followed, saying, "It has fallen, Babylon the Great has fallen.[J] She made all the nations drink the wine of her sexual immorality,[K] which brings wrath."   Is 21:9; Dn 4:30; Rv 16:19; 17:5; 18:2

[9] And another, a third angel, followed them and spoke with a loud voice: "If anyone worships the beast and its image and receives

---

[A]13:11 Or ram   [B]13:14 Or a statue, or a likeness   [C]13:15 Or a spirit, or life   [D]13:18 Or Here is wisdom   [E]13:18 Or count, or figure out   [F]13:18 Other Gk mss read 616   [G]14:2 Or voice   [H]14:3 Other mss add as it were   [I]14:4 Other mss add by Jesus   [J]14:8 Other mss omit the second has fallen   [K]14:8 Or wine of her passionate immorality a mark on his forehead or on his hand, [10] he will also drink the wine of God's wrath, which is poured full strength into the cup of his anger. He will be tormented with fire and sulfur in the sight of the holy angels and in the sight of the Lamb, [11] and the smoke of their torment will go up forever and ever. There is no rest[A] day or night for those who worship the beast and its image, or anyone who receives the mark of its name. [12] This calls for endurance from the saints, who keep God's commands and their faith in Jesus."[B]   Ps 75:8; Is 51:17; Jr 25:15-17

[13] Then I heard a voice from heaven saying, "Write: Blessed are the dead who die in the Lord from now on."   Rv 1:3; 16:15; 19:9; 20:6; 22:7,14

"Yes," says the Spirit, "so they will rest from their labors, since their works follow them."

Reaping the Earth's Harvest

[14] Then I looked, and there was a white cloud, and one like the Son of Man[C] was seated on the cloud, with a golden crown on his head and a sharp sickle in his hand. [15] Another angel came out of the temple, crying out in a loud voice to the one who was seated on the cloud, "Use your sickle and reap, for the time to reap has come, since the harvest of the earth is ripe." [16] So the one seated on the cloud swung his sickle over the earth, and the earth was harvested.   Dn 7:13; Lk 21:27; Rv 1:13

[17] Then another angel who also had a sharp sickle came out of the temple in heaven. [18] Yet another angel, who had authority over fire, came from the altar, and he called with a loud voice to the one who had the sharp sickle, "Use your sharp sickle and gather the clusters of grapes from the vineyard of the earth, because its grapes have ripened." [19] So the angel swung his sickle at the earth and gathered the grapes from the vineyard of the earth, and he threw them into the great winepress of God's wrath. [20] Then the press was trampled outside the city, and blood flowed out of the press up to the horses' bridles for about 180 miles.[D]   Is 63:1-6; Rv 16:19; 19:15

Preparation for the Bowl Judgments

15 Then I saw another great and awe-inspiring sign[E] in heaven: seven angels with the seven last plagues; for with them God's wrath will be completed. [2] I also saw something like a sea of glass mixed with fire, and those who had won the victory over the beast, its image,[F] and the number of its name, were standing on the sea of glass with harps from God. [3] They sang the song of God's servant Moses and the song of the Lamb: Mt 16:1; 24:30; Lk 21:11; Ac 2:19; Rv 12:1,3

Great and awe-inspiring are
  your works,
Lord God, the Almighty;
just and true are your ways,
King of the nations.[G]   Dn 2:37
[4] Lord, who will not fear
and glorify your name?
For you alone are holy.   Is 8:13
All the nations will come
and worship before you   Ps 86:9
because your righteous acts
have been revealed.

---

⁵ After this I looked, and the heavenly temple — the tabernacle of testimony — was opened. ⁶ Out of the temple came the seven angels with the seven plagues, dressed in pure, bright linen, with golden sashes wrapped around their chests. ⁷ One of the four living creatures gave the seven angels seven golden bowls filled with the wrath of God who lives forever and ever. ⁸ Then the temple was filled with smoke from the glory of God and from his power, and no one could enter the temple until the seven plagues of the seven angels were completed.   Ex 38:21; Nm 17:7; 18:2; Rv 11:19

The First Bowl

16 Then I heard a loud voice from the temple saying to the seven angels, "Go and pour out the seven^A bowls of God's wrath on the earth." ² The first went and poured out his bowl on the earth, and severely painful sores broke out on the people who had the mark of the beast and who worshiped its image.   Ex 9:9-11; Rv 8:2,6; 15:1,6-8; 17:1; 21:9

The Second Bowl

³ The second^B poured out his bowl into the sea. It turned to blood like that of a dead person, and all life in the sea died.   Rv 8:8-9

The Third Bowl

⁴ The third^B poured out his bowl into the rivers and the springs of water, and they became blood. ⁵ I heard the angel of the waters say,   Ex 7:17-21

You are just,
the Holy One, who is
and who was,   Is 5:19; 41:20; 45:11

because you have passed
judgment on these things.
⁶ Because they poured out
the blood of the saints
and the prophets,   2Kg 9:7
you have given them blood
to drink;
they deserve it!   Is 49:26
⁷ I heard the altar say,
Yes, Lord God, the Almighty,
true and just are
your judgments.   Rv 19:2,9

The Fourth Bowl

⁸ The fourth^B poured out his bowl on the sun. It was allowed to scorch people with fire, ⁹ and people were scorched by the intense heat. So they blasphemed the name of God, who has the power^C over these plagues, and they did not repent and give him glory.   Lv 24:11; Is 52:5; Rv 13:6

The Fifth Bowl

¹⁰ The fifth^B poured out his bowl on the throne of the beast, and its kingdom was plunged into darkness. People^D gnawed their tongues because of their pain ¹¹ and blasphemed the God of heaven because of their pains and their sores, but they did not repent of their works.   Ex 10:21; Rv 2:13; 13:2,6

The Sixth Bowl

¹² The sixth^B poured out his bowl on the great river Euphrates, and its water was dried up to prepare the way for the kings from the east. ¹³ Then I saw three unclean spirits like frogs coming from the dragon's mouth, from the beast's mouth, and from the mouth of the false prophet. ¹⁴ For they are demonic spirits performing signs, who travel to the kings of the whole

^A **16:1** Other mss omit *seven*   ^B **16:3,4,8,10,12** Other mss add *angel*   ^C **16:9** Or *authority*   ^D **16:10** Lit *They* world to assemble them for the battle on the great day of God, the Almighty. [15] "Look, I am coming like a thief. Blessed is the one who is alert and remains clothed [A] so that he may not go around naked and people see his shame." [16] So they assembled the kings at the place called in Hebrew, Armageddon. [B]   Gn 2:14; 15:18; Dt 11:24; 1Kg 4:21; Rv 9:14

The Seventh Bowl

[17] Then the seventh [C] poured out his bowl into the air, [D] and a loud voice came out of the temple [E] from the throne, saying, "It is done!" [18] There were flashes of lightning, rumblings, and peals of thunder. And a severe earthquake occurred like no other since people have been on the earth, so great was the quake. [19] The great city split into three parts, and the cities of the nations [F] fell. Babylon the Great was remembered in God's presence; he gave her the cup filled with the wine of his fierce anger. [20] Every island fled, and the mountains disappeared. [21] Enormous hailstones, each weighing about a hundred pounds, [G] fell from the sky on people, and they blasphemed God for the plague of hail because that plague was extremely severe.   Ex 19:16-19; Is 66:6; Rv 4:5; 8:5; 11:19; 19:15

The Woman and the Scarlet Beast

17 Then one of the seven angels who had the seven bowls came and spoke with me: "Come, I will show you the judgment of the notorious prostitute [H] who is seated on many [I] waters. [2] The kings of the earth committed sexual immorality with her, and those who live on the earth became drunk on the wine of her sexual immorality." [3] Then he carried me away in the Spirit [J] to a wilderness.

I saw a woman sitting on a scarlet beast that was covered [K] with blasphemous names and had seven heads and ten horns. [4] The woman was dressed in purple and scarlet, adorned with gold, jewels, and pearls. She had a golden cup in her hand filled with everything detestable and with the impurities of her [L] prostitution. [5] On her forehead was written a name, a mystery: BABYLON THE GREAT, THE MOTHER OF PROSTITUTES AND OF THE DETESTABLE THINGS OF THE EARTH. [6] Then I saw that the woman was drunk with the blood of the saints and with the blood of the witnesses to Jesus. When I saw her, I was greatly astonished.   Rv 12:3, 6; 13:1; 14:1

The Meaning of the Woman and of the Beast

[7] Then the angel said to me, "Why are you astonished? I will explain to you the mystery of the woman and of the beast, with the seven heads and the ten horns, that carries her. [8] The beast that you saw was, and is not, and is about to come up from the abyss and go to destruction. Those who live on the earth whose names have not been written in the book of life from the foundation of the world

---

[A]16:15 Or and guards his clothes   [B]16:16 Some mss read Armageddon; other mss read Harmegedon; other mss read Mageddon; other mss read Magedon   [C]16:17 Other mss add angel   [D]16:17 Or bowl on the air   [E]16:17 Other mss add of heaven   [F]16:19 Or the Gentile cities   [G]16:21 Lit about a talent; talents varied in weight upwards from 75 pounds   [H]17:1 Traditionally translated the great whore   [I]17:1 Or by many   [J]17:3 Or in spirit   [K]17:3 Or was filled   [L]17:4 Other mss read earth's they see the beast that was, and is not, and is to come. ⁹ This calls for a mind that has wisdom. ᴬ

"The seven heads are seven mountains on which the woman is seated. They are also seven kings: ¹⁰ Five have fallen, one is, the other has not yet come, and when he comes, he must remain for only a little while. ¹¹ The beast that was and is not, is itself an eighth king, but it belongs to the seven and is going to destruction. ¹² The ten horns you saw are ten kings who have not yet received a kingdom, but they will receive authority as kings with the beast for one hour. ¹³ These have one purpose, and they give their power and authority to the beast. ¹⁴ These will make war against the Lamb, but the Lamb will conquer them because he is Lord of lords and King of kings. Those with him are called, chosen, and faithful." ᴾ

140:10; Lk 8:31; 11:7

¹⁵ He also said to me, "The waters you saw, where the prostitute was seated, are peoples, multitudes, nations, and languages. ¹⁶ The ten horns you saw, and the beast, will hate the prostitute. They will make her desolate and naked, devour her flesh, and burn her up with fire. ¹⁷ For God has put it into their hearts to carry out his plan by having one purpose and to give their kingdom ᴮ to the beast until the words of God are fulfilled. ¹⁸ And the woman you saw is the great city that has royal power over the kings of the earth." Is 17:12; Jr 51:13

The Fall of Babylon the Great

18 After this I saw another angel with great authority coming down from heaven, and the earth was illuminated by his splendor. ² He called out in a mighty voice: Dn 4:13,23; Rv 10:1; 20:1

It has fallen, ᶜ
Babylon the Great has fallen!
She has become a home
for demons,
a haunt for
every unclean spirit,
a haunt for
every unclean bird,
and a haunt ᴰ for
every unclean
and despicable beast. ᴱ Mal 1:3
³ For all the nations
have drunk ᶠ
the wine of her
sexual immorality,
which brings wrath. Rv 14:8; 17:2
The kings of the earth
have committed
sexual immorality with her,
and the merchants
of the earth
have grown wealthy
from her sensuality
and excess. Ezk 16:29
⁴ Then I heard another voice from heaven:
Come out of her, my people,
so that you will not share
in her sins Is 52:11; Jr 50:8; 51:6,9,45
or receive any of her plagues.
⁵ For her sins are piled up ᴳ
to heaven, Jr 51:9
and God has remembered
her crimes. 2Sm 19:19; Neh 6:14
⁶ Pay her back the way
she also paid, Jr 50:29

and double it
    according to her works.
In the cup in which she mixed,
    mix a double portion for her.
7 As much as she
    glorified herself
    and indulged her sensual
    and excessive ways,
give her that much torment
    and grief.
For she says in her heart,
"I sit as a queen;
I am not a widow,
    and I will never see grief."
8 For this reason her plagues
    will come in just one day —
    death and grief and famine.
She will be burned up
    with fire,   Ps 21:9; 97:3; Is 33:12; 47:14
because the Lord God
    who judges her is mighty.

The World Mourns Babylon's Fall

9 The kings of the earth who have committed sexual immorality and shared her sensual and excessive ways will weep and mourn over her when they see the smoke from her burning. 10 They will stand far off in fear of her torment, saying,   Ezk 26:16-18

Woe, woe, the great city,   Rv 11:8
Babylon, the mighty city!
For in a single hour
    your judgment has come.

11 The merchants of the earth will weep and mourn over her, because no one buys their cargo any longer — 12 cargo of gold, silver, jewels, and pearls; fine linen, purple, silk, and scarlet; all kinds of fragrant wood products; objects of ivory; objects of expensive wood, brass, A iron, and marble; 13 cinnamon, spice, B incense, myrrh, C and

frankincense; wine, olive oil, fine flour, and grain; cattle and sheep; horses and carriages; and slaves — human lives.   Gn 36:6; Nm 31:32-35
14 The fruit you craved
    has left you.
All your splendid
    and glamorous things
    are gone;
they will never
    find them again.

15 The merchants of these things, who became rich from her, will stand far off in fear of her torment, weeping and mourning, 16 saying,

Woe, woe, the great city,
    dressed in fine linen, purple,
    and scarlet,
    adorned with gold, jewels,
    and pearls;   Rv 17:4
17 for in a single hour
    such fabulous wealth
    was destroyed!

And every shipmaster, seafarer, the sailors, and all who do business by sea, stood far off 18 as they watched the smoke from her burning and kept crying out: "Who was like the great city?" 19 They threw dust on their heads and kept crying out, weeping, and mourning,   Ex 15:11; Dt 33:29; 2Sm 7:23; Ezk 27:32; Rv 13:4

Woe, woe, the great city,
    where all those
    who have ships on the sea
    became rich from her wealth;
for in a single hour
    she was destroyed.
20 Rejoice over her, heaven,
    and you saints, apostles,
    and prophets,   Rv 12:12
because God has pronounced
    on her the judgment she
    passed on you!   Ps 48:11; 97:8

A18:12 Or *bronze*, or *copper*   B18:13 Other mss omit *spice*   C18:13 Or *perfume*

The Finality of Babylon's Fall

²¹ Then a mighty angel picked up a stone like a large millstone and threw it into the sea, saying, Rv 5:2

In this way, Babylon
the great city
will be thrown down violently
and never be found again.

²² The sound of harpists,
musicians,
flutists, and trumpeters
will never be heard
in you again; Is 24:8
no craftsman of any trade
will ever be found
in you again;
the sound of a mill
will never be heard
in you again;

²³ the light of a lamp
will never shine in you again;
and the voice of a groom
and bride
will never be heard
in you again. Jr 25:10
All this will happen
because your merchants
were the nobility
of the earth,
because all the nations
were deceived
by your sorcery.

²⁴ In her was found the blood
of prophets and saints,
and of all those slaughtered
on the earth. Rv 6:10; 16:6

Celebration in Heaven

19 After this I heard something like the loud voice of a vast multitude in heaven, saying, Rv 7:9

Hallelujah! Ps 104:35; 106:1,48; 146:10
Salvation, glory, and power
belong to our God, Jb 12:13

² because his judgments
are true[A] and righteous,

because he has judged
the notorious prostitute
who corrupted the earth
with her sexual immorality;
and he has avenged the blood
of his servants
that was on her hands. Dt 32:43

³ A second time they said,
Hallelujah!
Her smoke ascends forever
and ever! Is 34:8-10; Rv 14:11

⁴ Then the twenty-four elders and the four living creatures fell down and worshiped God, who is seated on the throne, saying, Rv 4:8-10; 5:6-14

Amen! Hallelujah! Ps 106:48

⁵ A voice came from the throne, saying,

Praise our God,
all his servants, and the ones
who fear him,
both small and great! Dt 1:17

⁶ Then I heard something like the voice of a vast multitude, like the sound of cascading waters, and like the rumbling of loud thunder, saying, Ezk 1:24; 43:2; Rv 1:15; 14:2

Hallelujah, because
our Lord God, the Almighty,
reigns! Ex 15:18; Ps 93:1; 96:10; 97:1; 99:1

⁷ Let us be glad, rejoice,
and give him glory, Mt 5:12
because the marriage
of the Lamb has come,
and his bride
has prepared herself. Is 54:5-7

⁸ She was given fine linen to
wear, bright and pure. Rv 15:6
For the fine linen represents the righteous acts of the saints. Eph 2:10

⁹ Then he[B] said to me, "Write: Blessed are those invited to the marriage feast of the Lamb!" He also said to me, "These words of God are true." ¹⁰ Then I fell at his feet to worship him, but he said to me, "Don't

---

A **19:2** Valid; Jn 8:16; 19:35   B **19:9** Probably an angel; Rv 17:1; 22:8-9 do that! I am a fellow servant with you and your brothers and sisters who hold firmly to the testimony of Jesus. Worship God, because the testimony of Jesus is the spirit[A] of prophecy." Is 25:6-8; Lk 13:29; Rv 17:1; 22:8-9

The Rider on a White Horse

[11] Then I saw heaven opened, and there was a white horse. Its rider is called Faithful and True, and he judges and makes war with justice. [12] His eyes were like a fiery flame, and many crowns[B] were on his head. He had a name written that no one knows except himself. [13] He wore a robe dipped in blood, and his name is called the Word of God. [14] The armies that were in heaven followed him on white horses, wearing pure white linen. [15] A sharp[C] sword came from his mouth, so that he might strike the nations with it. He will rule[D] them with an iron rod. He will also trample the winepress of the fierce anger of God, the Almighty. [16] And he has a name written on his robe and on his thigh: KING OF KINGS AND LORD OF LORDS. Jn 1:51; Rv 4:1; 11:19; 13:1

The Beast and Its Armies Defeated

[17] Then I saw an angel standing in the sun, and he called out in a loud voice, saying to all the birds flying high overhead, "Come, gather together for the great supper of God, [18] so that you may eat the flesh of kings, the flesh of military commanders, the flesh of the mighty, the flesh of horses and of their riders, and the flesh of everyone, both free and slave, small and great." [19] Then I saw the beast, the kings of the earth, and their armies

gathered together to wage war against the rider on the horse and against his army. [20] But the beast was taken prisoner, and along with it the false prophet, who had performed the signs in its presence. He deceived those who accepted the mark of the beast and those who worshiped its image with these signs. Both of them were thrown alive into the lake of fire that burns with sulfur. [21] The rest were killed with the sword that came from the mouth of the rider on the horse, and all the birds ate their fill of their flesh. Nm 27:3; Jdg 6:33; Rv 16:13-14; 17:2; 18:3,9

Satan Bound

20 Then I saw an angel coming down from heaven holding the key to the abyss and a great chain in his hand. [2] He seized the dragon, that ancient serpent who is the devil and Satan,[E] and bound him for a thousand years. [3] He threw him into the abyss, closed it, and put a seal on it so that he would no longer deceive the nations until the thousand years were completed. After that, he must be released for a short time. Ps 140:10

The Saints Reign with Christ

[4] Then I saw thrones, and people seated on them who were given authority to judge. I also saw the souls of those who had been beheaded because of their testimony about Jesus and because of the word of God, who had not worshiped the beast or his image, and who had not accepted the mark on their foreheads or their hands. They came to life and reigned with Christ for a thousand years. [5] The

A**19:10** Or *the Spirit*   B**19:12** Or *diadems*   C**19:15** Other mss add *double-edged*   D**19:15** Or *shepherd*
E**20:2** Other mss add *who deceives the whole world*

rest of the dead did not come to life until the thousand years were completed. Dn 7:22; Mt 19:28; 1Co 6:2-3; Rv 3:21

This is the first resurrection. ⁶ Blessed and holy is the one who shares in the first resurrection! The second death has no power^A over them, but they will be priests of God and of Christ, and they will reign with him for a thousand years.

Satanic Rebellion Crushed

⁷ When the thousand years are completed, Satan will be released from his prison ⁸ and will go out to deceive the nations at the four corners of the earth, Gog and Magog, to gather them for battle. Their number is like the sand of the sea. ⁹ They came up across the breadth of the earth and surrounded the encampment of the saints, the beloved city. Then fire came down from heaven^B and consumed them. ¹⁰ The devil who deceived them was thrown into the lake of fire and sulfur where the beast and the false prophet are, and they will be tormented day and night forever and ever. Gn 3:13; 2Co 11:3; 1Tm 2:14; 2Jn 7; Rv 12:9

The Great White Throne Judgment

¹¹ Then I saw a great white throne and one seated on it. Earth and heaven fled from his presence, and no place was found for them. ¹² I also saw the dead, the great and the small, standing before the throne, and books were opened. Another book was opened, which is the book of life, and the dead were judged according to their works by what was written in the books.

¹³ Then the sea gave up the dead that were in it, and death and Hades gave up the dead that were in them; each one was judged according to their works. ¹⁴ Death and Hades were thrown into the lake of fire. This is the second death, the lake of fire. ^C ¹⁵ And anyone whose name was not found written in the book of life was thrown into the lake of fire. Is 51:6; Mt 24:35; 2Pt 3:10; Rv 18:21

The New Creation

21 Then I saw a new heaven and a new earth; for the first heaven and the first earth had passed away, and the sea was no more. ² I also saw the holy city, the new Jerusalem, coming down out of heaven from God, prepared like a bride adorned for her husband. Is 52:1; 65:17

³ Then I heard a loud voice from the throne:^D Look, God's dwelling^E is with humanity, and he will live with them. They will be his peoples,^F and God himself will be with them and will be their God.^G ⁴ He will wipe away every tear from their eyes. Death will be no more; grief, crying, and pain will be no more, because the previous things^H have passed away. Dt 5:22; Ezk 9:1; Jn 11:43

⁵ Then the one seated on the throne said, "Look, I am making everything new." He also said, "Write, because these words¹ are faithful and true." ⁶ Then he said to me, "It is done! I am the Alpha and the Omega, the beginning and the end. I will freely give to the thirsty from the spring of the water of life. ⁷ The one who conquers will inherit these things, and I will be his God, and he will be my son. ⁸ But the cowards,

---

^A 20:6 Or *authority*   ^B 20:9 Other mss add *from God*   ^C 20:14 Other mss omit *the lake of fire*
^D 21:3 Other mss read *from heaven*   ^E 21:3 Or *tent,* or *tabernacle*   ^F 21:3 Other mss read *people*
^G 21:3 Other mss omit *and will be their God*   ^H 21:4 Or *the first things*   ^I 21:5 Other mss add *of God*

faithless, [A] detestable, murderers, sexually immoral, sorcerers, idolaters, and all liars — their share will be in the lake that burns with fire and sulfur, which is the second death." Rv 1:8; 3:14; 16:17; 19:11; 22:6,13

The New Jerusalem

[9] Then one of the seven angels, who had held the seven bowls filled with the seven last plagues, came and spoke with me: "Come, I will show you the bride, the wife of the Lamb." [10] He then carried me away in the Spirit [B] to a great, high mountain and showed me the holy city, Jerusalem, coming down out of heaven from God, [11] arrayed with God's glory. Her radiance was like a precious jewel, like a jasper stone, clear as crystal. [12] The city had a massive high wall, with twelve gates. Twelve angels were at the gates; the names of the twelve tribes of Israel's sons were inscribed on the gates. [13] There were three gates on the east, three gates on the north, three gates on the south, and three gates on the west. [14] The city wall had twelve foundations, and the twelve names of the twelve apostles of the Lamb were on the foundations. Ezk 40:2; Rv 1:10; 4:2; 16:1; 17:3

[15] The one who spoke with me had a golden measuring rod to measure the city, its gates, and its wall. [16] The city is laid out in a square; its length and width are the same. He measured the city with the rod at 12,000 *stadia*. [C] Its length, width, and height are equal. [17] Then he measured its wall, 144 cubits according to human measurement,

which the angel used. [18] The building material of its wall was jasper, and the city was pure gold clear as glass. [19] The foundations of the city wall were adorned with every kind of jewel: the first foundation is jasper, the second sapphire, the third chalcedony, the fourth emerald, [20] the fifth sardonyx, the sixth carnelian, the seventh chrysolite, the eighth beryl, the ninth topaz, the tenth chrysoprase, the eleventh jacinth, the twelfth amethyst. [21] The twelve gates are twelve pearls; each individual gate was made of a single pearl. The main street [D] of the city was pure gold, transparent as glass. Ex 28:15-21; Is 54:11; Ezk 40:3; Rv 11:1

[22] I did not see a temple in it, because the Lord God the Almighty and the Lamb are its temple. [23] The city does not need the sun or the moon to shine on it, because the glory of God illuminates it, and its lamp is the Lamb. [24] The nations [E] will walk by its light, and the kings of the earth will bring their glory into it. [F] [25] Its gates will never close by day because it will never be night there. [26] They will bring the glory and honor of the nations into it. [G] [27] Nothing unclean will ever enter it, nor anyone who does what is detestable or false, but only those written in the Lamb's book of life. Is 24:23; 30:26; 60:19-20; Rv 22:5

The Source of Life

22 Then he showed me the river [H] of the water of life, clear as crystal, flowing from the throne of God and of the Lamb [2] down the middle of the city's main street.

[A] **21:8** Other mss add *the sinful,*   [B] **21:10** Or *in spirit*   [C] **21:16** A *stadion* (sg) = about 600 feet; 12,000 *stadia* = 1,400 miles.   [D] **21:21** Or *The public square*   [E] **21:24** Other mss add *of those who are saved*   [F] **21:24** Other mss read *will bring to him the nations' glory and honor*   [G] **21:26** Other mss add *in order that they might go in*   [H] **22:1** Other mss read *pure river*

The tree of life was on each side of the river, bearing twelve kinds of fruit, producing its fruit every month. The leaves of the tree are for healing the nations, ³ and there will no longer be any curse. The throne of God and of the Lamb will be in the city, and his servants will worship him. ⁴ They will see his face, and his name will be on their foreheads. ⁵ Night will be no more; people will not need the light of a lamp or the light of the sun, because the Lord God will give them light, and they will reign forever and ever.   Ps 46:4; Jr 2:13; 17:13; Jn 4:10; Rv 4:6

The Time Is Near

⁶ Then he said to me, "These words are faithful ᴬ and true. The Lord, the God of the spirits of the prophets, ᴮ has sent his angel to show his servants what must soon take place."   Dn 2:28-29, 45; Rv 1:1; 3:14; 19:11; 21:5

⁷ "Look, I am coming soon! Blessed is the one who keeps the words of the prophecy of this book."   Rv 3:11

⁸ I, John, am the one who heard and saw these things. When I heard and saw them, I fell down to worship at the feet of the angel who had shown them to me. ⁹ But he said to me, "Don't do that! I am a fellow servant with you, your brothers the prophets, and those who keep the words of this book. Worship God!"   Rv 19:10

¹⁰ Then he said to me, "Don't seal up the words of the prophecy of this book, because the time is near. ¹¹ Let the unrighteous go on in unrighteousness; let the filthy still be filthy; let the righteous go on in righteousness; let the holy still be holy."   Is 8:16; 9:24

¹² "Look, I am coming soon, and my reward is with me to repay each person according to his work. ¹³ I am the Alpha and the Omega, the first and the last, the beginning and the end.   Ps 62:12; Is 40:10; 59:18; 62:11; Jr 17:10

¹⁴ "Blessed are those who wash their robes, ᶜ so that they may have the right to the tree of life and may enter the city by the gates. ¹⁵ Outside are the dogs, the sorcerers, the sexually immoral, the murderers, the idolaters, and everyone who loves and practices falsehood.

¹⁶ "I, Jesus, have sent my angel to attest these things to you for the churches. I am the root and descendant of David, the bright morning star."   Nm 24:17; Is 11:1, 10; Rm 1:3; Rv 2:28; 5:5;

¹⁷ Both the Spirit and the bride say, "Come!" Let anyone who hears, say, "Come!" Let the one who is thirsty come. Let the one who desires take the water of life freely.   Is 55:1; Jn 4:10

¹⁸ I testify to everyone who hears the words of the prophecy of this book: If anyone adds to them, God will add to him the plagues that are written in this book. ¹⁹ And if anyone takes away from the words of the book of this prophecy, God will take away his share of the tree of life and the holy city, which are written about in this book.   Dt 4:2

²⁰ He who testifies about these things says, "Yes, I am coming soon."

Amen! Come, Lord Jesus!   1Co 16:22

²¹ The grace of the Lord Jesus ᴰ be with everyone. ᴱ Amen. ᶠ

ᴬ22:6 Or *trustworthy*   ᴮ22:6 Other mss read *God of the holy prophets*   ᶜ22:14 Other mss read *who keep his commands*   ᴰ22:21 Other mss add *Christ*   ᴱ22:21 Other mss read *with all the saints*
ᶠ22:21 Other mss omit *Amen.*

Where to Turn

Table of Weights and Measures

Weights

Biblical Unit	Language	Biblical Measure	U.S. Equivalent	Metric Equivalent	Various Translations
Gerah	Hebrew	½0 shekel	½0 ounce	.6 gram	gerah; oboli
Bekah	Hebrew	½ shekel or 10 gerahs	⅕ ounce	5.7 grams	bekah; half a shekel; quarter ounce; fifty cents
Pim	Hebrew	⅔ shekel	⅓ ounce	7.6 grams	⅔ of a shekel; quarter
Shekel	Hebrew	2 bekahs	⅖ ounce	11.5 grams	shekel; piece; dollar; fifty dollars
Litra (pound)	Greco-Roman	30 shekels	12 ounces	.4 kilogram	pound; pounds
Mina	Hebrew/Greek	50 shekels	1¼ pounds	.6 kilogram	mina; pound
Talent	Hebrew/Greek	3,000 shekels or 60 minas	75 pounds/ 88 pounds	34 kilograms/ 40 kilograms	talent/talents; 100 pounds

Length

Handbreadth	Hebrew	⅙ cubit or ⅓ span	3 inches	8 centimeters	handbreadth; three inches; four inches
Span	Hebrew	½ cubit or 3 handbreadths	9 inches	23 centimeters	span
Cubit/ Pechys	Hebrew/Greek	2 spans	18 inches	.5 meter	cubit/cubits; yard; half a yard; foot
Fathom	Greco-Roman	4 cubits	2 yards	2 meters	fathom; six feet
Kalamos	Greco-Roman	6 cubits	3 yards	3 meters	rod; reed; measuring rod
Stadion	Greco-Roman	⅛ milion or 400 cubits	⅛ mile	185 meters	miles; furlongs; race
Milion	Greco-Roman	8 stadia	1,620 yards	1.5 kilometers	mile

Dry Measure

Biblical Unit	Language	Biblical Measure	U.S. Equivalent	Metric Equivalent	Various Translations
Xestes	Greco-Roman	½ cab	1⅙ pints	.5 liter	pots; pitchers; kettles; copper pots; copper bowls; vessels of bronze
Cab	Hebrew	⅟₁₈ ephah	1 quart	1 liter	cab; kab
Choinix	Greco-Roman	⅟₁₈ ephah	1 quart	1 liter	measure; quart
Omer	Hebrew	⅟₁₀ ephah	2 quarts	2 liters	omer; tenth of a deal; tenth of an ephah; six pints
Seah/Saton	Hebrew/Greek	⅓ ephah	7 quarts	7.3 liters	measures; pecks; large amounts
Modios	Greco-Roman	4 omers	1 peck or ¼ bushel	9 liters	bushel; bowl; peck
Ephah [Bath]	Hebrew	10 omers	⅗ bushel	22 liters	bushel; peck; deal; part; measure; six pints; seven pints
Lethek	Hebrew	5 ephahs	3 bushels	110 liters	half homer; half sack
Kor [Homer]/Koros	Hebrew/Greek	10 ephahs	6 bushels or 200 quarts	220 liters/525 liters	cor; homer; sack; measures; bushels

Liquid Measure

Log	Hebrew	⅟₇₂ bath	⅓ quart	.3 liter	log; pint; cotulus
Xestes	Greco-Roman	⅛ hin	1⅙ pints	.5 liter	pots; pitchers; kettles; copper bowls; vessels of bronze
Hin	Hebrew	⅙ bath	1 gallon or 4 quarts	4 liters	hin; pints
Bath/Batos	Hebrew/Greek	1 ephah	6 gallons	22 liters	gallon(s); barrels; liquid measures
Metretes	Greco-Roman	10 hins	10 gallons	39 liters	firkins; gallons

Topical Concordance

Ability

From God. 1Pt 4:11.

Giving according to. Ezr 2:69; Ac 11:29.

Greater, promised. Jn 14:12.

Limited only by faith. Mk 9:23.

Measured by one's readiness. 2Co 8:12.

Spiritual, assigned by God. Rm 12:3-8.

Spiritual, inspired by the Spirit. 1Co 12:4-11.

Talents given according to. Mt 25:15.

Abstinence

From sexual immorality. 1Co 6:18-20; Gl 5:19-21; Eph 5:3-5; 1Th 4:3-5; Rv 22:14-15.

Acceptance

By the grace of God. Rm 5:17; Eph 1:6.

Of prayers. Gn 19:21.

Of sacrifices. Ps 119:108.

Of sinners. Ezk 20:40-41; 36:23-29.

Affections

Of believers, supremely set on God. Ps 42:1; 73:25; 119:10.

Blessedness of making God the object of. Ps 91:14.

Christ claims the first place in. Mt 10:37; Lk 14:26.

False teachers seek to captivate. Gl 1:10; 4:17; 2Tm 3:6; 2Pt 2:3,18; Rv 2:14,20.

Kindled by communion with Christ and Scripture. Lk 24:32.

Should be set:

    Upon the commandments of God. Ps 19:8-10; 119:20,97,103,167.

    Upon God supremely. Dt 6:5; 12:30.

    Upon heavenly things. Col 3:1-2.

    Upon the people of God. Ps 16:3; Rm 12:10; 2Co 7:13-15; 1Th 2:8.

Should be zealously engaged for God. Ps 69:9; 119:139; Gl 4:18.

Should not grow cold. Ps 106:12-13; Mt 24:12; Gl 4:15; Rv 2:4.

Of the wicked, not sincerely set on God. Is 58:1-2; Ezk 33:31-32; Lk 8:13.

Worldly, crucified in believers. Rm 6:6; Gl 5:24.

Worldly, should be put to death. Rm 8:13; 13:14; 1Co 9:27; Col 3:5; 1Th 4:5.

Afflictions

Always less than we deserve. Ezr 9:13; Ps 103:10.

Are consequences of the fall. Gn 3:16-19.

Believers appointed to. 1Th 3:3.

Believers are to expect. Jn 16:33; Ac 14:22.

Of believers, but temporary. Ps 30:5; 103:9; Is 54:7-8; Jn 16:20; 1Pt 1:6; 5:10.

Of believers, comparatively light. Ac 20:23-24; Rm 8:18; 2Co 4:17.

Of believers, end in joy and blessedness. Ps 126:5-6; Is 61:2-3; Mt 5:4; 1Pt 4:13-14.

Believers have joy under. Jb 5:17; Jms 5:11.

Frequently result in good. Gn 50:20; Ex 1:11-12; Dt 8:15-16; Jr 24:5-6; Ezk 20:37.

God appoints. 2Kg 6:33; Jb 5:6,17; Ps 66:11; Am 3:6; Mc 6:9.

God determines the continuance of. Gn 15:13-14; Nm 14:33; Is 10:25; Jr 29:10.

God dispenses, as he will. Jb 11:10; Is 10:15; 45:7.

God regulates the measure of. Ps 80:5; Is 9:1; Jr 46:28.

Man is born to. Jb 5:6-7; 14:1.

Often arise from being the followers of Jesus Christ. Mt 24:9; Jn 15:21; 2Tm 3:11-12.

Sin produces. Jb 4:8; 20:11; Pr 1:31.

Sin visited with. 2Sm 12:14; Ps 89:30-32; Is 57:17; Ac 13:10-11.

Tempered with mercy. Ps 78:38-39; 106:43-46; Is 30:18-21; Lm 3:32; Mc 7:7-9; Nah 1:12.

Afflictions, Made beneficial

In convincing us of sin. Jb 36:8-9; Ps 119:67; Lk 15:16-18.

In exercising our patience. Ps 40:1; Rm 5:3; Jms 1:3; 1Pt 2:20.

In exhibiting the power and faithfulness of God. Ps 34:19-20; 2Co 4:8-11.

In furthering the gospel. Ac 8:3-4; 11:19-21; Php 1:12; 2Tm 2:9-10; 4:16-17.

In humbling us. Dt 8:3,16; 2Ch 7:13-14; Lm 3:19-20; 2Co 12:7.

In keeping us from again departing from God.
Jb 34:31-32; Is 10:20; Ezk 14:10-11.

In leading us to confession of sin. Nm 21:7;
Ps 32:5; 51:35.

In leading us to seek God in prayer. Jdg 4:3;
Jr 31:18; Lm 2:17-19;
Hs 5:14-15; Jnh 2:1.

In promoting the glory of God. Jn 9:1-3; 11:3-4;
21:18-19.

In purifying us. Ec 7:2-3; Is 1:25-26; 48:10;
Jr 9:6-7; Zch 13:9; Mal 3:2-3.

In testing and exhibiting our sincerity.
Jb 23:10; Ps 66:10; Pr 17:3.

In trying our faith and obedience. Gn 22:1-2;
Ex 15:23-25; Dt 8:2,16;
Heb 11:17; 1Pt 1:7; Rv 2:10.

In turning us to God. Dt 4:30-31;
Neh 1:8-9; Ps 78:34; Is 10:20-21; Hs 2:6-7.

Afflictions, Ministry to those experiencing

Bear them in mind. Heb 13:3.

Comfort them. Jb 16:5; 29:25; 2Cor 1:4;
1Th 4:18.

Have compassion on them. Jb 6:14.

Pray for them. Ac 12:5; Php 1:16,19;
Jms 5:14-16.

Protect them. Ps 82:3; Pr 22:22; 31:5.

Relieve them. Jb 31:19-20; Is 58:10; Php 4:14.

Sympathize with them. Rm 12:15; Gl 6:2.

Visit them. Jms 1:27.

Afflictions, Prayer in the midst of

For deliverance. Ps 25:17,22; 39:10;
Is 64:9-12; Jr 17:14.

For divine comfort. Ps 4:6; 119:76.

For divine teaching and direction. Jb 34:32;
Ps 27:11; 143:10.

Encouragement to. Jms 5:13-16.

For increase of faith. Mk 9:24.

For mercy. Ps 6:2; Hab 3:2.

For pardon and deliverance from sin. Ps 39:8;
51:1; 79:8.

For the presence and support of God.
Ps 10:1; 102:2.

For protection and preservation from enemies.
2Kg 19:19; 2Ch 20:12; Ps 17:8-9.

For restoration to joy. Ps 51:8,12; 69:29;
90:14-15.

That we may be taught the uncertainty of life.
Ps 39:4.

That we may be turned to God. Ps 80:7;
85:4-6; Jr 31:18.

That we may know the causes of our trouble.
Jb 6:24; 10:2; 13:23-24.

Angels

Announced the ascension and second coming
of Christ. Ac 1:11.

Birth of Christ. Lk 2:10-12.

Conception of Christ. Mt 1:20-21; Lk 1:31.

Conception of John the Baptist. Lk 1:13,36.

Resurrection of Christ. Mt 28:5-7; Lk 24:23.

Are ministering spirits. 1Kg 19:5; Ps 68:17;
104:4; Lk 16:22; Ac 12:7-11; 27:23;
Heb 1:7,14.

Not to be worshiped. Col 2:18; Rv 19:10; 22:9.

Subject to Christ. Eph 1:21; Col 1:16; 2:10;
1Pt 3:22.

Wise. 2Sm 14:20.

Celebrate the praises of God. Jb 38:7; Ps 148:2;
Is 6:3; Lk 2:13-14; Rv 5:11-12; 7:11-12.

Execute the judgments of God. 2Sm 24:16;
2Kg 19:35; Ps 35:6; Ac 12:23; Rv 16:1.

Execute the purposes of God. Nm 22:22;
Ps 103:21; Mt 13:39-42; 28:2; Jn 5:4; Rv 5:2.

Have charge over the children of God. Ps 34:7;
91:11-12.

Know and delight in the gospel of Christ.
Eph 3:9-10.

The law given by. Ps 68:17; Ac 7:53; Heb 2:2.

Rejoice over every repentant sinner.
Luke 15:7,10.

Will attend Christ at his second coming.
Mt 16:27; 25:31; Mk 8:38; 2Th 1:7.

Anger

Be slow to. Pr 15:18; 16:32; 19:11; Ti 1:7;
Jms 1:19.

Characteristic of fools. Pr 12:16; 14:29; 27:3.

Children should not be stirred up to. Eph 6:4;
Col 3:21.

Pray without. 1Tm 2:8.

A work of sinful nature. Gl 5:20.

Anxiety

The cure for. Mt 6:25-34; Php 2:28; 1Pt 5:7.

Prevented. Ps 121:4; 1Pt 5:7.

Appearance

Can be deceiving. Mt 23:27-28.

Do not judge by. Jms 2:2-4.

Inner versus outward. 1Sm 16:7; 1Pt 3:1-6.

Assurance

Abundant in the understanding of the gospel. Col 2:2; 1Th 1:5.

Confirmed by love. 1Jn 3:14,19; 4:18.

Eternal life. Rm 8:28-39; 1Th 1:5; 1Jn 5:13.

Give diligence to attain. 2Pt 1:10-11.

In Christ. Jn 6:39; 17:12; 18:9.

Made full by hope. Heb 6:19.

Produced by faith. Eph 3:12; 2Tm 1:12; Heb 10:22.

Baptism

Jesus was baptized. Mt 3:13-16.

Believers were baptized at Pentecost. Ac 2:41.

The Ethiopian eunuch. Ac 8:36.

Paul was baptized. Ac 9:18.

A sign of repentance and sins forgiven. Mk 1:4; Ac 2:38.

Shows identification with Jesus Christ. Rm 6:3-8.

A command for all believers. Mt 28:18-20.

Belief

In Christ. Jn 3:16; 14:1; 20:31; Ac 8:37.

In God required. 2Ch 20:20.

Making all things possible. Mk 9:23.

In devils. Jms 2:19.

Producing healing. Mt 9:22.

Bible

Inspired by God. Jr 36:1-2; 2Tm 3:14-17.

Inspired by the Holy Spirit. Ac 1:16; 2Pt 1:21.

Points to Christ. Jn 5:39; Ac 18:28.

Learn about salvation from. 2Tm 3:15.

An unerring guide. 2Pt 1:19.

Sharp as a sword. Eph 6:17; Heb 4:12.

Hearing is not enough. Jms 1:22.

Received message, not from men, but from God. 1Th 2:13.

Everything should be tested against. Is 8:20; Ac 17:11.

Warning against those who add to or take from. Dt 4:2; Rv 22:18-19.

Body

Is the temple of Holy Spirit. 1Co 6:19.

Will be resurrected. 1Co 15:12-58.

Capital Punishment

For adultery. Lv 20:10; Jn 8:3-11.

For murder. Gn 9:5-6; Ex 21:12; Nm 35:33.

For violating the Sabbath. Ex 31:14.

Warning against putting innocent to death. Ex 23:7.

Celibacy

Jesus's teaching concerning. Mt 19:10-12.

Paul's teaching concerning. 1Co 7:1-9, 25-26,32-39.

Wrongly insisted on. 1Tm 4:1-3.

Children

Christ taught. Mk 10:13-16.

Gifts from God. Gn 33:5; Ps 127:3.

Should honor the aged. Lv 19:32; 1Pt 5:5.

Should obey parents. Ex 20:12; Pr 6:20; Eph 6:1.

Should take care of parents. 1Tm 5:4.

Should be treated with respect. Eph 6:2.

Christ

Preexistence. Jn 1:1-18.

Genealogy traced through Joseph. Mt 1:1-17.

Genealogy traced through Mary. Lk 3:23-38.

Birth of. Mt 1:18-25; Lk 2:1-20.

Circumcision and naming of. Lk 2:21.

Childhood. Lk 2:41-52.

Baptism. Mt 3:13-17.

Tempted by Satan. Mt 4:1-11; Mk 1:12-13; Lk 4:1-13.

Calls his first disciples. Jn 1:35-51.

Mission. Lk 4:16-21.

Manner of relating to people. Mt 12:18-21.

Sinless. Jn 8:46; 2Co 5:21; Heb 4:14-16.

Forgives sins. Col 3:13; Mk 2:7,10-11.

One with the Father. Jn 10:30,38; 12:45; 14:7-10; 17:10.

Fully God. Col 2:9; Heb 1:3.

Eternally the same. Heb 1:12; 13:8.

Fully human. Jn 1:14; Heb 2:14.

The only mediator between God and man. 1Tm 2:5.

Church

Christ will build. Mt 16:18.

Commission of. Mt 28:18-20.

Is the bride of Christ. Rv 19:7-8.

Christ is the head. Col 1:18.

Is like a body. 1Co 12:12-13.

Circumcision

Abolished by the gospel. Gl 2:3-5; Eph 2:11,15; Php 3:3; Col 2:11; 3:11.

Described. Gn 17:9-11; Ex 4:25.

Civil rights
Exercised by Paul. Ac 16:35-40; 22:24-29.

Contentment
With wages and possessions. Lk 3:14;
   Heb 13:5.
With food and clothing. 1Tm 6:8.
With godliness is great gain. Ps 37:16;
   1Tm 6:6.

Counselor
Necessary for victory. Pr 11:14; 24:6.
A title of Christ. Is 9:6.
A role of the Spirit. Jn 14:16,26; 15:26; 16:7.

Courage
Commanded. Dt 31:6; Jos 1:7; Is 41:10.

Covenant
Abraham's. Gn 12:1-3; 15:7-18; 17:2-14;
   1Ch 16:16-17; Lk 1:72-75; Ac 3:25; Gl 3:16.
David's. 2Sm 23:5; Ps 89:3-4.
Isaac's. Gn 17:19,21; 26:3-4.
Jacob's. Gn 28:13-14.
Israel's. Ex 6:4; Ac 3:25.
New. Jr 31:31-33; Rm 11:27; Heb 8:8-10,13.

Creation
By Christ. Jn 1:3,10; Col 1:16.
By God. Gn 1:1; 2:4-5; Pr 26:10.
For God's pleasure. Pr 16:4; Rv 4:11.
Glorifies God. Neh 9:6; Ps 19:1; 136:3-9;
   145:10; 148:5.

Crown
A reward. 1Co 9:25; 2Tm 2:5; 4:8; Jms 1:12;
   1Pt 5:4; Rv 3:11.
Symbolic. Rv 4:4,10; 6:2; 9:7; 12:1,3; 13:1;
   14:14; 19:12.
Of thorns. Mt 27:29; Jn 19:5.

Crucifixion
Of Christ. Mt 27:32-56.
Symbolic. Rm 6:6; Gl 2:20.

Dancing
Praising God with. Ex 15:20; 2Sm 6:14;
   Ps 150:4.
Example of sinful. Ex 32:19,25; Mt 14:6.

Death
A consequence of sin. Gn 2:17;
   Rm 5:12-14; 6:23.
Christ delivers from the fear of. Heb 2:15.
Conquered by Christ. Rm 6:9; Rv 1:18.

Described as sleep. Dt 31:16; Jn 11:11-14;
   Ac 7:59-60; 13:36; 1Co 15:6.
Everyone will experience. Jb 30:23; 1Co 15:22;
   1Tm 6:7; Heb 9:27.
For believers, a passage to God. 2Co 5:1-8;
   Php 1:21-24.
For believers, a place of rest. Jb 3:17;
   Lk 16:22,25; Php 1:23; Rv 14:13.
Precious in God's sight. Ps 116:15.

Debt
Borrower is slave of lender. Pr 22:7.
Owe no one anything. Rm 13:8.

Demons
Jesus casts out. Mt 17:14-21; Lk 4:31-36.
Disciples cast out. Mk 16:17; Lk 10:17-20;
   Ac 5:16.
Paul casts out. Ac 16:16-18; 19:12.

Devil
Assumes the form of an angel of light.
   2Co 11:14.
Believers should resist. Jms 4:7; 1Pt 5:9.
Ultimately defeated. Gn 3:15; 2Pt 2:4; Jd 6;
   Rv 20:10.
Is our adversary. Jb 1:6-12; Zch 3:1; 1Th 2:18.
Cunning in deception. 2Co 11:3.

Discipleship
Cost of. Mt 16:24-28.
Tests of. Mt 10:32-39; Lk 14:26-27,33;
   Jn 21:15-19.

Discipling
Commanded. Dt 6:6-7; Mt 28:18-20; 2Tm 2:2.

Disease (see also Healing)
Relationship to sin. Ps 107:17; Mt 9:1-8;
   Mk 2:1-12; Ac 12:20-25; Rm 1:26-27;
   1Co 11:27-34; Jms 5:14-16.

Divorce
Jesus's teaching concerning. Mt 19:1-10;
   Mk 10:2-12.

Doubt (see also Assurance)
God's help in. Ps 73:13-17; Is 40:27-28.
Jesus's response to. Mt 11:1-19; Mk 9:14-29;
   Jn 20:24-29.

Drugs
Honor God with body. Rm 12:1; 1Co 6:19-20.
Mind should stay alert. Eph 5:18; 1Pt 1:13;
   1Th 5:6.

Drunkenness
Avoid those given to. Pr 23:20; 1Co 5:11.
To be avoided. Pr 23:29-35; Lk 21:34;
   Rm 13:13; Eph 5:18.
Results in punishment. Is 28:1-3; Mt 24:49-51;
   1Co 6:10; Gl 5:21.

Earth
Believers will inherit. Ps 25:13; Mt 5:5.
Is the Lord's. 1Co 10:26.
Not to be flooded again. 2Pt 3:6-7.
To be renewed. 2Pt 3:13.
Eagerly longs for redemption. Rm 8:19-22.

Edification
All to be done for. 2Co 12:19; Eph 4:29.
Described. Eph 4:12-16.
Exhortation to. Jd 20-21.
Gospel as the instrument of. Ac 20:32.
Love leads to. 1Co 8:1.

Education
Of children in God's Word. Dt 6:7; Eph 6:4;
   2Tm 3:15-16.
From nature. Pr 6:6.
In the pastoral ministry. 1Tm 4:11.
From personal experience. Ps 78:1-8.

Election
Of Israel. Dt 7:6; Is 45:4.
Of believers. Ps 65:4; Is 65:9; Jn 6:44; 13:18;
   Ac 13:48; 22:14; Rm 8:28-30; 9:11-16;
   Eph 1:4-6,11; 2:10; 1Th 1:4; 2Th 2:13;
   1Pt 1:2.
Should be evidenced by diligence. 2Pt 1:10.
Should lead to godliness. Col 3:12.

Encouragement
Exhorted. 1Th 4:18; 5:11; Ti 2:15; Heb 3:13;
   10:25.
Through fellow believers. Ac 14:22; 15:31-32;
   Rm 1:12.
Through God's Word. Rm 15:4.
Through the Spirit. Ac 9:31.

Endurance
God gives. Rm 15:5.

Enemies
Should be loved. Mt 5:44.
Should be prayed for. Ac 7:60.
Christ forgave. Lk 23:34.
God delivers from. Dt 32:35;
   Ps 18:48; 61:3.

Equality
Among believers. Gn 13:8; Mt 23:8.
In Christ. Gl 3:28.
Under God. Pr 22:2.
In justice. Pr 24:23.
In salvation. Jn 3:16; Rm 5:18-21.
In sin and guilt. Rm 3:10-19; 5:12-21.

Eternal life
May have assurance of. 1Jn 5:13.
To know God and Christ is. Jn 17:3.
To those who believe in Christ. Jn 3:15-16;
   6:40,47.

Euthanasia
May lead to devaluing of life. Gn 1:27.
Violates God's command. Ex 20:13.

Evangelism
Commanded by Christ. Mt 28:18-20.

Evolution
Contrary to the consistent teaching of
   Scripture. Gn 1–2; Jb 38–39; Jn 1:1-3;
   Col 1:16-17; Heb 11:3.

Excuses
Adam and Eve to the Lord. Gn 3:12-13.
A disciple to Jesus. Mt 8:21.
Elisha to Elijah. 1Kg 19:19-21.
Felix to Paul. Ac 24:25.
Humanity to God. Rm 1:20.
Moses to the Lord. Ex 4:1-14.
Saul to the Lord. 1Sm 15:13-15.

Fairness
God's. 2Ch 19:7; Ps 98:9; 99:4; Ezk 18:29;
   Rm 3:3-6.
In business. Lv 19:36; Dt 25:15; Pr 11:1;
   1Tm 5:18.
In legal judgment. Ex 23:3; Dt 1:17; 16:19;
   Pr 29:14.
In treatment of slaves. Col 4:1.
Through wisdom. Pr 8:15.
Lacking. Ps 82:2-4; Is 59:9-11; Mc 3:9;
   Hab 1:4.

Faith
Demonstrated by a pagan soldier. Lk 7:1-10.
All things should be done in. Rm 14:22;
   Heb 11:6.
Have full assurance of. 2Tm 1:12; Heb 10:22.
The gift of God. Rm 12:3; Eph 2:8; 6:23;
   Php 1:29.

Christ the source and perfecter of. Heb 12:2.
Proof of things not seen. Heb 11:1.
Examine whether you are in. 2Co 13:5.
A gift of the Holy Spirit. 1Co 12:9.
Right with God by. Gn 15:6; Rm 4:16.
Necessary in prayer. Mt 21:22; Jms 1:6.
Produces confidence. 1Pt 2:6.
Scripture designed to produce. Jn 20:31;
    2Tm 3:14-16.
The wicked often profess. Ac 8:9-24.

Family
Believers' families blessed. Ps 128:3-6.
Honoring God in. Dt 6:6-7; Jos 24:15;
    Eph 5:22—6:9.
Jesus's family. Mk 3:31-35.
Paul's family. Ac 23:16.
Timothy's family. 2Tm 1:5.
Church leaders' families. 1Tm 3:1-13.

Fasting
Expected of Christians. Mt 6:16; 9:15.
Along with prayer, when seeking God's grace.
    1Sm 7:5-6; Neh 1:4; Dn 9:3; Ac 13:3; 14:23.
Wrong way and right way compared.
    Is 58:3-12; Zch 7:5-10; Mt 6:16-18.

Father
God in heaven. Mt 6:9; 23:9.
Duties of godly. Dt 6:6-7; Eph 6:4.
To be honored. Ex 20:12; Pr 23:22; Eph 6:2;
    Col 3:17.

Fear
Of God, advantages of. Pr 9:10; 15:16; 19:23;
    2Co 7:1.
Godly delivered from. Ps 27:1; Pr 1:33;
    1Jn 4:16-18.

Fellowship
Blessings of. 1Jn 1:7.
In Christ. Mt 18:20; 1Co 1:9; Rv 3:20.
In the Holy Spirit. 2Co 13:14.

Flattery
Beware of. Ps 5:9; 12:3; Pr 29:5; Rm 16:18;
    Jd 16.

Flood
Noah's. Gn 6—8.
Came suddenly and unexpectedly.
    Mt 24:38-39.
Whole earth affected by. Gn 7:23;
    2Pt 3:5-6.

Noah warned of. Gn 6:13; Heb 11:7.
Wicked warned of. 1Pt 3:19-20; 2Pt 2:5.

Forgiveness
Of sins, from God. Ex 34:6-7; Ps 103:1-4;
    Dn 9:9.
Of sins, through Christ. Ac 4:11-12; 1Jn 2:12.
Of each other. Mt 6:14-15; 18:21-35;
    Mk 11:25; Eph 4:32; Jms 2:13.

Freedom
Of God. Ac 4:24-28.
Result of truth. Jn 8:32.
From condemnation. Rm 8:1,33-39.
From sin's power. Rm 8:2-4; Rv 1:5.

Friends
Constancy of. Pr 17:17; 18:24.
David and Jonathan. 1Sm 18:1-4; 20:1-29.
Jesus called his disciples. Jn 15:13-15.

Gambling
Can result in destructive lifestyle. 1Tm 6:9.
Harms the poor and families. Pr 14:23; 1Tm 5:8.
Poor example for those who may become
    addicted. 1Co 8:13; Rm 14:21.
Practiced by those who crucified Jesus.
    Mk 12:30.
Stems from covetousness. Lk 12:15; 1Tm 6:10.

Genders, Relationship between (see also Women in Roles of Responsibility)
Be subject to one another. Eph 5:21.
Male and female in image of God. Gn 1:26-27;
    5:1-2.
Men and women equal as regards salvation.
    Ac 10:34; Rm 2:9-11; Gl 3:28.
One flesh in marriage. Gn 2:24.
Partnership in child-rearing. Pr 1:8; Eph 6:1-4;
    Col 3:20.
Woman a suitable helper of man. Gn 2:18.

Genealogies
Of patriarchs. Gn 4:16-22; 5; 10; 11:10-32;
    22:20-24; 25:1-4,12-16; 35:23-26; 36;
    Ru 4:18-20; 1Ch 1—9.
Of Christ. Mt 1:1-17; Lk 3:23-38.
No spiritual value. Mt 3:9; 1Tm 1:4; Ti 3:9.

Giving
Blessings connected with. Ps 41:1; Pr 22:9;
    28:27; Ec 11:1-2; Is 58:10; Ac 20:35.
Encouraged. Lk 6:38; 2Co 8:1-12.
Toward enemies. Pr 25:21.

God

Is all knowing. Is 55:9; Dn 2:20; Rm 11:33.

Is all powerful. Jr 32:27; Lk 1:37; Rv 1:8.

Is faithful. Ps 89:24,33; Is 49:7; Lm 3:23;
1Co 1:9; 1Th 5:24; 2Th 3:3; 2Tm 2:13.

Is good. Ps 25:8; 119:68.

Is holy. 1Sm 2:2; Is 57:15; 1Pt 1:15-16.

Is judge. Ps 9:7; Jms 4:12.

Is just. Dt 32:4; Ezk 18:25; Rm 3:26; 9:14.

Is kind. Rm 2:4.

Is knowable. Jr 31:34; Eph 1:17.

Is love. Dt 7:8; Jr 31:3; Hs 11:4; 1Jn 4:16.

Is our Father. Hs 1:10; Mt 6:9; Rm 8:15.

Is sovereign. Ex 18:11; Dt 10:14; 2Kg 19:15;
Ps 24:1; 115:3; 135:6; 146:10; Is 40:23;
45:23; Lm 3:37; Dn 4:35; Rm 9:16; Col 2:13.

Is spirit. Jn 4:24.

Is to be glorified. 1Ch 16:28-29; Is 42:12;
Dn 5:23; Rm 1:21; 1Co 6:20.

Is unchanging. Ps 102:26-27; Jms 1:17.

Gospel

Predicted. Is 41:27; 52:7; 61:1-3.

Described. 1Co 15:1-4.

Brings peace. Lk 2:10-14.

Veiled to the lost. 2Co 4:3.

There is only one. Gl 1:8.

Must be believed. Mk 1:15; Heb 4:2.

The power of God for salvation. Rm 1:16;
1Co 1:18; 1Th 1:5.

Produces hope. 1Co 1:23.

Grace

Came by Christ. Jn 1:17; Rm 5:15.

Believers should grow in. 2Pt 3:18.

God's work completed in believers by.
2Th 1:11-12.

Justifies sinners. Ps 51:1-12; Rm 5:1-21.

Not to be abused. Rm 3:8; 6:1,15; 2Co 6:1; Jd 4.

Salvation by. Ac 15:11; Eph 2:1-10; Ti 2:11.

Guidance

Of believers. Ps 32:8; Jn 10:3.

Hate

Embitters life. Pr 15:17.

Of neighbors, prohibited. Lv 19:17; 1Jn 3:15.

Of evil, condoned. Ps 97:10; 119:104; 139:21;
Pr 8:13.

Believers should expect. Mt 10:22;
Jn 15:18-19.

Return good for. Mt 5:44.

Healing

Comes from God. Ex 15:26; Ps 103:3.

Proof that Jesus is the Messiah. Mt 11:5.

Son of a royal official. Jn 4:46-54.

Heaven

Believers rewarded in. Is 65:17-25; Mt 5:12;
1Pt 1:4; Rv 21:1-7.

Jesus entered. Ac 3:21; Heb 6:20.

God's dwelling place. Ps 11:4; 115:3; Is 66:1;
Mt 6:9.

Believers names are written in. Lk 10:20;
Heb 12:23.

Wicked are excluded from. Gl 5:21; Eph 5:5;
Rv 22:15.

Hell

The beast, false prophet, and the devil thrown
into. Rv 19:20; 20:10.

Body suffers in. Mt 5:29; 10:28.

Described as everlasting fire. Is 1:28-31; 66:24;
Mt 3:12; 25:41,46.

Destruction, away from God's presence.
2Th 1:9.

Strive to keep others from. Mt 18:14; Jd 23.

Holiness

God's, as standard. Lv 19:2; Eph 5:1.

Believers called to. Lv 11:45; 20:7; Lk 1:74-75;
Rm 6:13,19; 8:29; 12:1; Eph 1:4; 5:8;
1Th 4:7; Heb 12:14; 1Pt 1:14-16.

Holy Spirit

Believers receive. 1Jn 2:20.

Guides into all truth. Is 30:21; Ezk 36:27;
Jn 16:13; 1Jn 2:27.

Baptism of, through Christ. Ti 3:6.

Communicates joy. Rm 14:17; Gl 5:22;
1Th 1:6.

Given by the Father. Neh 9:20; Ezk 36:27;
Jl 2:28; Jn 14:15-18.

Gives new birth. Jn 3:5-6.

Called God. Ac 5:3-4.

Convinces of sin. Neh 9:30; Mc 3:8;
Jn 16:8-11.

Lives in believers. Is 59:21; Hg 2:5;
Jn 14:16-17; 1Co 3:16; 6:19; Eph 5:18;
1Pt 4:14.

Blasphemy against is unpardonable.
Zch 7:12-13; Mt 12:31-32; 1Jn 5:16.

Can be grieved. Is 63:10; Eph 4:30; 1Th 5:19.

Believers sealed by. 2Co 1:22; Eph 1:13; 4:30.

Homosexuality

Prohibited. Lv 18:22; 20:13.

Condemned. Gn 18:20-21; 19:4-7;
Rm 1:26-27; 1Co 6:9; 1Tm 1:8-10.

Honesty

Commanded. Dt 25:13; Lv 19:35; Pr 11:1;
12:22; Am 8:4-7; Zch 8:16; 2Co 4:2.

Necessary in speaking. Ps 101:7; Pr 12:19;
17:20; Mt 5:33-37; Eph 4:25; Rv 22:15.

Hope

In God. Ps 39:7; Ti 1:2; 1Pt 1:21.

Be ready to give a reason for your.
1Pt 3:15.

Believers enjoy. Rm 5:2; 12:12; Ti 2:13.

Leads to patience. Rm 8:25; 1Th 1:3.

Hospitality

Commanded. Rm 12:13; 1Tm 3:2; 5:10; Ti 1:8;
1Pt 4:9.

To enemies. 2Kg 6:22-23; Rm 12:20.

To the poor. Is 58:7; Lk 14:13-14.

To strangers. Heb 13:2.

Humility

Afflictions intended to produce. Lv 26:41;
Dt 8:3.

Averts punishment. 2Ch 7:14; 12:6-7.

Before honor. Pr 15:33.

Brings wisdom. Pr 11:2; Mt 11:25.

Christ's example. Mt 11:29; Jn 13:14-15;
Php 2:5-8.

In believers. Mc 6:8; Rm 12:16; Eph 4:1-2;
Php 2:3; Col 3:12; 1Pt 5:5.

Husband

To love wife. Gn 2:23-24; Eph 5:25-30;
Col 3:19.

To respect wife. 1Pt 3:7.

Should have only one wife. Mt 19:3-9;
Mk 10:6-8; 1Co 7:2-4; 1Tm 3:12.

Idolatry, Idols

Forbidden by the law. Ex 20:4-5;
Dt 4:15-19.

Provokes God. Dt 31:20; Is 65:3; Jr 25:6.

Ridiculed. Is 44:10-20; 45:20; Jr 10:3-5;
Hab 2:18-19; 1Co 12:2.

Not gods. Jr 5:7; Gl 4:8.

Nothing. Is 41:24; 1Co 8:4.

Believers should avoid. Ex 34:16;
Dt 7:3-5,26; Ac 14:15; 1Co 10:14,19-21.

Image of God

Man created in. Gn 1:26-27; 5:1; 9:5; Jms 3:9.

Christ as. Col 1:15; Heb 1:3.

Immortality

David's hope. 2Sm 12:23.

Jesus's promise of. Jn 6:39-58.

Incest

Forbidden. Lv 18:6-18; 1Co 5:1.

Amnon and Tamar. 2Sm 13:14.

Herod. Mt 14:3-4.

Judah and Tamar. Gn 38:16-18.

Lot's daughters. Gn 19:31-36.

Integrity

Required. Dt 6:5.

Characterizes righteous men. Nm 16:15;
Jb 27:5; Ps 25:21; 26:11; Pr 11:3.

Intercession

Should be made for everyone. 1Tm 2:1;
Eph 6:18.

Christ's example. Jn 17:1-26; Rm 8:34;
Heb 7:25; 1Jn 2:1.

Holy Spirit's example. Rm 8:26.

Job's example. Jb 42:8-10.

Moses's example. Nm 14:19.

Stephen's example. Ac 7:60.

Intolerance, Religious

Proper. Ex 22:20; Dt 13; 17:1-7; 1Kg 18:40;
2Kg 10:18-30; 2Ch 15:12-13.

Improper. Nm 11:24-30; Mk 9:38-39;
Ac 4:1-3; 13:50; 17:5; 18:13; 21:28-31;
22:22.

Jealousy

God's righteous. Ex 20:5; 1Kg 14:22; Ps 78:58;
1Co 10:22.

Consequences of man's. Gn 4:4-8; 37:4-8, 18,28;
Mt 2:16-18.

Jesus the Christ

Preexistence. Jn 1:1-18; Col 1:16; Heb 1:2.

Genealogy traced through Joseph.
Mt 1:1-17.

Genealogy traced through Mary. Lk 3:23-38.

Birth of. Mt 1:18-25; Lk 2:1-20.

Circumcision and naming of. Lk 2:21.

Childhood. Lk 2:41-52.

Baptism. Mt 3:13-17.

Tempted by Satan. Mt 4:1-11; Mk 1:12-13;
Lk 4:1-13.

Calls his first disciples. Jn 1:35-51.

Mission. Lk 4:16-21.

Manner of relating to people. Mt 12:18-21.

Sinless. Jn 8:46; 2Co 5:21; Heb 4:14-16.

Forgives sins. Col 3:13; Mk 2:7,10-11.

One with the Father. Jn 10:30,38; 12:45;
14:7-10; 17:10.

Fully God. Col 2:9; Heb 1:3.

Eternally the same. Heb 1:12; 13:8.

Fully human. Jn 1:14; Heb 2:14.

Humility of attitude rewarded. Php 2:5-11.

The only mediator between God and man.
1Tm 2:5.

Joy

Commanded of believers. Ps 32:11; Zch 9:9;
Php 3:1.

Despite difficulties. Hab 3:17-18;
Mt 5:11-12; Jms 1:2; 1Pt 1:6.

Over sinners who repent. Lk 15:1-32.

In answer to prayer. Jn 16:24.

In fellowship. 2Tm 1:4; 1Jn 1:3-4; 2Jn 12.

A fruit of the Spirit. Gl 5:22.

Judgment

By God for words spoken. Nm 14:29;
Mt 12:36.

Of Christians. Rm 14:10; 2Co 5:10;
Jms 2:12-13.

After death. Heb 9:27.

Not by outward appearances. Jn 7:24.

Will be in righteousness. Neh 9:33; Ps 98:9;
Dn 9:14; Ac 17:31.

Justice

Rewarded. Dt 16:20; Ps 119:121; Pr 21:15;
Is 33:15-16; 56:1; Jr 7:5,7; Ezk 18:8-9.

Kindness

An attribute of God. Ru 2:20; Hs 11:4;
Eph 2:7; Ti 3:4-7.

A quality of believers. Col 3:12; 2Pt 1:7;
1Co 13:4.

Knowledge

Fear of the Lord is the beginning of. Pr 1:7.

Of God among all human beings. Rm 1:20.

Jesus's disciples have. Lk 8:10; Col 2:2-3.

Every disciple's goal. Php 3:10; Col 1:9;
2Pt 3:18.

Of salvation. Lk 1:77; 1Jn 5:13.

Needed to guide zeal. Rm 10:2-3.

Law

1. Ceremonial: Israel's worship. Lv 7:37-38;
Heb 9:1-7.

2. Civil: Israel's justice. Ex 21:1.

3. Moral: universal, timeless. Ex 20:1-17;
Dt 6:5; Mt 22:37-39.

Jesus fulfills. Mt 5:17-20; Gl 3:24-25.

Jesus's interpretation of. Mt 12:9-14;
Mk 2:23-28.

Man's sinful nature and the law.
Rm 7:7-25.

Lawsuits

Symbolic, of God. Pr 23:11; Is 3:14;
Jr 2:9; 25:31; Hs 4:1; Mc 6:2.

To be avoided. Pr 25:8-10; Mt 5:25-26;
1Co 6:1-8.

Laziness

Characteristics of. Pr 18:9; 26:13-16.

Consequences of. Pr 6:6-9; 10:26; 12:24;
15:19; 19:15; 20:4; 21:25; 24:30-34;
Ec 10:18.

Contrasted with diligence. Pr 13:4.

Love

Covers sin. Pr 10:12.

For God. Dt 6:5; Mt 22:36-40.

Described. 1Co 13:4-7.

Fulfills the law. Rm 13:8; Gl 5:6.

God is. 1Jn 4:7-8,16.

Marks the child of God. Jn 13:35;
1Jn 2:15; 4:7.

Lust

Condemned. Pr 5:15-20; Php 4:8.

Must be controlled by God. Rm 13:14;
Gl 5:17.

Same as committing adultery. Jb 31:1;
Mt 5:27-28.

Leads to trouble. 2Sm 11:2-5; Pr 5:3-5;
6:25-35; Jms 1:14-15.

Results in perverted sexual behavior.
2Sm 13:1-18; Rm 1:26-27.

Lying

A characteristic of unbelief and apostasy.
2Th 2:9; 1Tm 4:2; 1Jn 2:4.

The devil is the father of. Jn 8:44.

Forbidden. Lv 19:11; Pr 12:22; Zch 1:16;
Col 3:9.

Punished. Ps 5:6; 120:3-4; Pr 19:5; Rv 21:8.

Male and Female
Equally saved in Christ. Gl 3:28.
Mutual love. 1Co 7:3-4; Col 3:19; Ti 2:4.
Different roles. Gn 3:16-19; 1Co 14:34-35;
Eph 5:22-33; Col 3:18-19; 1Tm 2:11;
Ti 2:2-5; 1Pt 3:1-7.

Mankind
Made in God's image. Gn 1:26-27; Jms 3:9.
More valuable than animals. Gn 1:28;
9:3-6; Ps 8:4-8; Mt 10:31; 12:11-12.
Object of God's love. Jn 3:16.

Marriage
Jesus blesses. Jn 2:1-11.
Honorable for all. 1Tm 4:3; Heb 13:4.
Not believer with unbeliever. Dt 7:3-4;
1Co 7:39; 2Co 6:14.
Should be permanent. Pr 5:15-19; Mal 2:14;
Mt 19:6; 1Co 7:39.
Illustrates Christ and the church.
Eph 5:22-32.

Materialism
More to life than. Lk 12:15.
Root of all evil. 1Tm 6:10.
Makes entry into God's kingdom difficult.
Mk 10:23-25.
Can't provide what humans need most.
1Pt 1:18-19.

Meditation
Characterizes the godly person. Ps 1:1-2.
On the Lord. Ps 63:6-7; 119:148; 143:5.
On what is good. Php 4:8.

Mercy
Blessedness of showing. Pr 14:21; Mt 5:7.
Denunciations against those lacking.
Mt 18:23-35; Jms 2:13.
Encouraged. 2Kg 6:21-23; Lk 6:36;
Rm 12:20-21.

Mind
Love God with. Mt 22:36-40.
Renewed, key to spirituality. Rm 12:2;
Eph 4:23.
To be prepared before taking action.
1Pt 1:13.
God puts law in believer's. Heb 8:10.
Have a sound. 2Tm 1:7.
Use while praying or singing.
1Co 14:15-16.

Miracles
Purpose is to encourage belief. Ex 4:1-5;
Mk 16:20; Jn 20:30-31.
Insufficient to produce conversion. Ps 106:7;
Lk 16:31.
Jesus proved to be the Messiah by. Mt 11:4-6;
Lk 7:20-22; Jn 5:36.
Performed by false prophets. Ex 7:12;
Dt 13:1-3; Mt 24:24; 2Th 2:9; Rv 19:20.

Missions
All believers are called to. Mt 28:18-20;
Mk 16:15.
Principle of. 2Co 5:14-15.
Obligations to engage in. Lk 10:2;
Ac 4:19-20; Rm 1:13-15; 10:14-15;
1Co 9:16.

Money
Must choose between God or money. Mt 6:24.
Cannot rescue one. Pr 11:4; Ezk 7:19; Zph 1:18.
Use your money to benefit others. Lk 16:9.
Test of repentance. Lk 3:10-14.
Love of is root of all evil. 1Tm 6:9-10.

Monotheism
There is only one God. Dt 4:39; 6:4; 1Co 8:4,6;
Eph 4:5-6.
Christ and his Father are one. Jn 10:30.
The Holy Spirit is the Spirit of God and of
Christ. Rm 8:9,14; 1Co 3:16.

Morality
Exalts a nation. Pr 14:34.
Sermon on the Mount. Mt 5–7.
Ten Commandments. Ex 20:1-17.
The heart of religion. Am 5:21,24;
Mc 6:6-8; Ti 2:7; 1Jn 2:29.

Mother
To be honored and cared for. Pr 23:22;
Jn 19:27; Eph 6:2.

Motives
Key to sin. Mt 5:21-30.
Right, required. Mt 6:1-18; 2Co 9:7;
Eph 6:5-6; Heb 11:6.

Murder
Hatred is. Mt 5:21-22; 1Jn 3:15.
God despises. Gn 4:11; 9:6; Ex 20:13;
Pr 6:16-17.
Punished by death. Gn 9:5-6; Ex 21:12;
Nm 35:16,30.

Music
Used in the temple. 1Ch 16:4-6; 23:5-6; 25:1;
2Ch 29:25.
Used by Christians. Eph 5:19.

Name
God's, not taken in vain. Ex 20:7.
God's, restored. Ezk 20:9,14,22,44.
Importance of good. Pr 22:1; Ec 7:1.

Neighbor
Care for. Pr 3:28-29; Mt 25:34-46.
Love as you love yourself. Lv 19:18;
Lk 10:25-37; Rm 13:8-10; Gl 5:13-15;
Jms 2:8.

New Birth
Prophesied. Ezk 11:19; 36:26.
All believers partake of. Jn 3:3-9; 1Pt 1:23;
1Jn 2:29; 3:9; 4:7; 5:1,4,18.

New Creation
Christ brings about. Rm 6:4; 2Co 5:14-17;
Gl 6:14-15.
Will transform the entire universe.
Rm 8:18-21; 2Pt 3:7-13; Rv 21:1-8.

Oaths
Permitted. Is 65:16; Jr 12:16; Heb 6:16.
False, condemned. Lv 6:3; Zch 5:4; Mal 3:5.
Forbidden in the name of idol or created thing.
Jos 23:7; Mt 5:34-36; Jms 5:12.

Occult
Denounced by God. Lv 19:26,31;
Dt 18:9-14.
Severe punishment for. Ex 22:18; Lv 20:27;
Dt 13:5; Gl 5:20-21.
Saul and the medium. 1Sm 28:7-25.

Pain
None in heaven. Rv 21:4.
Presence in hell. Lk 16:24; Rv 16:10.

Parables
Why Jesus spoke in. Mt 13:10-17.

Paradise
The place of the glorified spirits. Lk 23:43;
2Co 12:4; Rv 2:7.

Patience
Waiting for God. Ps 37:7; 40:1.
Believers receive from God. Col 1:11.
Exercise, toward all. 1Th 5:14.
Running the race with. Heb 12:1.

Peace
Takes the place of worry. Php 4:6-7.
Believers have. Ps 85:8; Is 26:3; 53:5; Rm 5:1;
Jn 14:27; Col 1:19-20.
Believers will have forever. Is 57:2;
Ezk 34:25.
Wicked do not know. Is 48:22; 59:8; Jr 6:14;
Rm 3:17.

Persecution
Christ's followers will have. Mt 16:21-26;
2Tm 3:12.
God will deliver from. Dn 3:25,28; 2Co 1:10;
4:9; 2Tm 3:11.

Poor
Jesus preached to. Lk 4:18.
God cares for. 1Sm 2:8; Ps 35:10; 68:10;
Is 41:17.
Do not despise. Dt 15:7; Pr 14:21,31;
Jms 2:2-17.

Praise (see also Worship)
Offered continually. Ps 35:28; 71:6.
Christ is worthy of. Rv 5:1-14.

Prayer
Jesus's way. Mt 6:5-13.
Acceptable through Christ. Jn 14:13-14.
Husband and wife relationship important for.
1Pt 3:7.
At all times. Ps 88:1; 1Th 5:17; 1Tm 5:5.
Regarding everything. Php 4:6.
For others. 1Tm 2:1; Jms 5:13-18; 1Jn 5:16.

Preaching
Purpose of. 2Tm 4:1-4.

Predestination
Of the crucifixion. Acts 4:28.
Of salvation. Rm 8:28-33; 9:11-29; 11:5-8;
1Co 2:7; Eph 1:5,11.

Pride
Warnings against. 1Sm 2:3; Pr 21:4;
1Co 8:1-2; 10:12.
God sees and judges. Is 2:12; Zph 2:10-11;
Lk 1:51.

Prophecy
Blessing for those who listen. 1Th 5:20;
Rv 1:3; 22:7.
Does not come by human will. Jr 1:5;
Am 7:14-15; 2Pt 1:20-21.

Purity
Demanded. Rm 13:13; Eph 5:5-6; Php 4:8;
   Col 3:5; Heb 13:4.

Quiet
Achievement of. Is 32:17.
Power of. Is 30:15.
Value of. Ec 4:6.

Racism
Rejected since all are from one man.
   Gn 9:18-19; Ac 17:26.
No racial distinction in the law. Lv 24:22;
   Dt 24:17.
No racial distinction in Christ. Gl 3:28-29;
   Eph 2:19; Rv 5:9-10.

Rape
Forbidden. Dt 22:25-28.

Redemption
Is by the blood of Christ. Heb 9:12;
   1Pt 1:18-19; Rv 5:9.

Repentance
Given by God. Ac 11:18; 2Tm 2:25.
Godly grief produces. Ezr 9:6-9; Jr 31:19;
   Zch 12:10; 2Co 7:10.
Commanded. Ezk 18:30-32; Mk 1:15; Ac 17:30.
Results are changed attitudes and behavior.
   2Ch 6:26; Lk 3:7-14; 2Co 7:11.

Resurrection
OT doctrine of. Jb 19:26; Ps 16:10; 49:15;
   Is 26:19; Dn 12:2; Hs 13:14.
Of Jesus, the historical event. Mt 28:5-10.
Preached by the apostles. Ac 4:2.
Of the body. Is 26:19; 1Co 15:42-45.
First principle of the gospel. 1Co 15:1-19.

Revenge
Law of. Ex 21:23-25.
Prohibited. Lv 19:18; Rm 12:17-19;
   1Th 5:15; 1Pt 3:9.
Alternatives to. Pr 20:22; Mt 5:38-42;
   Rm 12:14.

Righteousness
Our own does not save. Ti 3:5.
God gives. Ps 24:5; Is 61:10.
Given through Christ. Rm 3:21-26; Php 3:4-11.

Sabbath
Grounds of its institution. Gn 2:2-3; Ex 20:11.
Made for man. Mk 2:27.

Observance of, perpetual. Ex 31:16-17;
   Mt 5:17-18.
Works of mercy lawful on. Mt 12:12; Lk 13:16;
   Jn 9:14.

Salvation
From God. Ps 3:8; Is 45:21-22; Jr 3:23.
In Jesus alone. Ac 4:11-12; Rm 10:9.
Gospel is power of God to. Rm 1:16; 1Co 1:21.

Sanctification
Through Christ. Rm 8:29-30; 1Co 1:2,30;
   Heb 10:10; 13:12.
Through the Word of God. Jn 17:17,19;
   Eph 5:26.

Second Coming of Christ
Jesus predicted. Mt 25:31; Jn 14:3.
In same way as he ascended into heaven.
   Dn 7:13; Ac 1:9-11.
Will complete salvation of believers. Heb 9:28.
Time of, unknown and sudden. Mt 24:36,44;
   Mk 13:32-37; Lk 12:40; 1Th 5:1-11;
   2Th 1:3-12; 2Pt 3:10-13.

Self-esteem
Cautions regarding. Rm 12:3; 2Co 10:7-13;
   Gl 6:1-3; Php 2:3.
Self-confidence in Christ. Rm 8:1; 2Co 3:5;
   Php 3:4-7; 4:13.

Sex (see also Abstinence; Homosexuality; Lust; Marriage; Rape)
Prohibited outside marriage. Sg 2:7;
   1Co 6:15-20; Heb 13:4.
Blessed within marriage. Sg 4:1–5:1.
Not to be withheld in marriage. 1Co 7:3-5.

Sin
Begins in the mind. Mt 5:27-28;
   Jms 1:14-15.
All have committed. Rm 3:23.
Confession of followed by forgiveness.
   2Sm 12:13; Ps 32:5; 1Jn 1:9.
God helps believers resist. Ps 119:11;
   1Co 10:13.
Christ's blood removes. Mt 26:28; Eph 1:7;
   1Jn 1:7.

Singing (see also Worship)
Commanded. 1Ch 16:9; Ps 100:2; Eph 5:19;
   Col 3:16; Jms 5:13.
From God. Ps 40:3.

Stealing
Prohibited. Ex 20:15.
From the poor, especially forbidden. Pr 22:22.
Do honest work instead. Eph 4:28.

Talent (Ability)
Differs in different individuals. Mt 25:15.
Given by God. 1Co 12:4.
To be used. 1Tm 4:14; Rm 12:6.

Tax
Jesus paid. Mt 17:24-27.

Thankfulness
Commanded. Ps 50:14; Php 4:6.
Accompanies prayer. Php 4:6; Col 4:2.
In all things. Eph 5:20; 1Th 5:18; 1Tm 4:4-5.

Tithe
Preceded law. Gn 14:20; Heb 7:6.
Given to the Levites for their services.
    Nm 18:21,24; Neh 10:37.
Punishment for withholding. Mal 3:8.

Trinity
Reference to. Rm 8:9; 1Co 12:3-6; Eph 4:4-6;
    2Th 2:13-14; Ti 3:4-6; 1Pt 1:2; Jd 20-21.
Evident at Jesus's baptism. Mt 3:16-17.
To be baptized in the name of.
    Mt 28:18-20.
The apostolic benediction. 2Co 13:13.

Truth
Leaders should be men of. Ex 18:21; Pr 20:28.
The Holy Spirit guides believers into. Jn 14:17;
    16:13.
The Word of God is. Dn 10:21; Jn 17:17.

Unbelief
Is sin. Jn 16:8-11.
Questions truthfulness of God. 2Kg 17:13-15;
    Ps 106:24; 1Jn 5:10.

Unity
The early church a picture of. Ac 4:32.
Paul's urging believers toward. Rm 12:16;
    14:19; 15:5; Php 2:2; 3:16-17.

Vegetarianism
In creation. Gn 2:16; Is 11:7; 65:25.
Tolerance for. Rm 14:1-3.

Voyeurism
Abstain from. Jb 31:1.
David and Bathsheba. 2Sm 11:2.
Same as adultery. Mt 5:28.

Widows
Cared for. Dt 10:18; Ps 68:5; Ac 6:1.
Allowed to marry again. Rm 7:3; 1Co 7:39.
Paul's commandments concerning.
    1Co 7:8-9; 1Tm 5:3-16.

Wife
A helper to complement man. Gn 2:18-23.
A capable. Pr 31:10-31.
A blessing to her husband. Pr 12:4; 31:10,12.
Submissive to her husband. 1Co 11:3-12;
    Eph 5:22-33.
Win unbelieving husband by her life.
    1Pt 3:1-2.

Women in Roles of Responsibility
Deborah. Jdg 4–5.
Huldah. 2Kg 22:12-20.
Virtuous woman. Pr 31:10-31.
Mary. Mt 28:1-10.
Miriam. Ex 15:20; Mc 6:4.
Phoebe. Rm 16:1.
Priscilla. Rm 16:3-4.

Work
Believers should. Pr 10:4; 13:4,11; Eph 6:5-8;
    2Th 3:10-12.

Works
Do not save. Rm 3:20; Gl 2:16; Eph 2:8-9;
    2Tm 1:9; Ti 3:5.
Are the fruit of true faith. Mt 3:8; Eph 2:10;
    Jms 2:14-26.

Worship
With fear and reverence. Ps 5:7; 96:9;
    Is 6:1-7.
With music. Ps 57:7-8; 150.
With a new song. Ps 33:3; 96:1; 98:1; 149:1;
    Is 42:10; Rv 5:9; 14:3.
With dance. 2Sm 6:14-16; Ps 149:3.
Bowing down. 1Ch 29:20; Ps 95:6; Mt 2:11.
Authentic. Jn 4:19-26.

Youth
Examples of. 1Sm 2:11; 17:1-54.
Should be an example. 1Tm 4:12.

Zeal
Sometimes not according to knowledge.
    Ac 21:20; Rm 10:2; Gl 1:14.
Sometimes wrongly directed. 2Sm 21:2;
    Ac 22:3-4; Php 3:6.
Stimulates others to do good. 2Co 9:2.

THE ROUTE OF THE
EXODUS

THE ROUTE OF THE EXODUS

EXOD 13:17–19:3;
NUM 10:11–12:16; 33:1–36

Northern route
Central route
Alternate central route
Southern route
Alternate route from Jebel
Musa to Kadesh-barnea

○ City
○ City (uncertain location)
▲ Mountain peak
▲ Possible locations for Mt. Sinai
Major roads

THE TRAVELS OF
JACOB & JOSEPH

Carchemish · Haran
PADDAN-ARAM

Jacob produces large family

36 N

· Aleppo

Ugarit · · Ebla
Qatna · · Hamath

Euphrates R.

Byblos · · Tadmor

34 N

Sidon
Tyre · · Damascus

MEDITERRANEAN SEA

Shechem · · Ramoth-gilead

32 N

Jacob and his sons reunite and journey to Egypt

Bethel (Luz)
Jerusalem
Hebron
Beersheba

Syro-Arabian Desert

Succoth ·

Goshen
On (Heliopolis) ·
· Noph (Memphis)

Beer-lahai-roi ·

Area enlarged below

Mt. Seir

(EDOM)
Ezion-geber

EGYPT

W. Tumilat

Sinai Desert

0   50 Miles
0   50 Kilometers

TRAVELS OF JACOB
GEN. 28–33; 35

● City
○ City (uncertain location)
← Jacob's journey
← Jacob's sons seek pasturage
← Esau's journey

35 E   36 E

Sea of Galilee

Dor ·   · Megiddo

Laban overtakes Jacob

Taanach ·   Ramoth-gilead ·

GILEAD

Dothan ·

Jacob named "Israel"

· Mizpah
Penuel ·

Jacob builds an altar upon his return from Paddan-Aram (Gen. 35:1–15)

Shechem ·   Succoth

Jacob and Esau reunited (Gen. 33)

MEDITERRANEAN SEA

Aphek ·

Joppa ·

Bethel (Luz) ·   Mahanaim
· Rabbah

32 N

God reaffirms to Jacob the covenant made with Abraham (Gen. 28:10–22)

· Ai   Jericho ·

· Gezer

Jerusalem ·

Traditional site of Rachel's burial

Ashkelon ·   Beth-zur ·   · Bethlehem

Mamre ·   Kiriathaim ·

CANAAN   · Hebron

Jacob tricks brother of birthright

DEAD SEA

Gerar ·

· Arad

Beersheba ·

Negeb

31 N

0 10 20 30 40 50 Miles
0 10 20 30 40 50 Kilometers

(EDOM)   Mt. Seir   36 E

THE JOURNEYS OF JOSEPH
GEN. 37; 39–46

City
City (uncertain location)
Migration of Jacob and his sons
Migration of Jacob's sons
Joseph's journey into slavery
Joseph's brothers' and Jacob's journeys from Canaan
Ancient canal

MEDITERRANEAN SEA

Sea of Galilee
Beth-shan
Megiddo
Dor
Dothan
Joseph sold into slavery
Succoth
Rabbah
Dibon
Jordan
Jericho
Shechem
Bethel (Luz)
Jerusalem
Joppa
Hebron
Lachish
Gerar
Sharuhen
Gaza
Beersheba
Arad
Burial of Jacob at Cave of Machpelah
DEAD SEA
Punon
Arabah
Negeb

W. el-'Arish

Way to Shur
Wilderness of Shur

Sinai Desert

Lake Sirbonis
Lake Menzaleh
Delta
Nile R.
Avaris (T. ed-Dab'a)
The Hyksos capital of Egypt
Goshen
Succoth
W. Tumilat
Pithom
Lake Timsah
Great Bitter Lake
Little Bitter Lake
Gulf of Suez

Tell el-Yahudiya
On (Heliopolis)
Joseph's father-in-law (Potiphera) was a priest at On
Noph (Memphis)
Itjowy
XII Dynasty capital of Egypt
EGYPT

30 N
32 N
30 N
32 E
34 E

0   10   20   30   40 Miles
0 10 20 30 40 Kilometers

THE KINGDOMS OF
ISRAEL & JUDAH

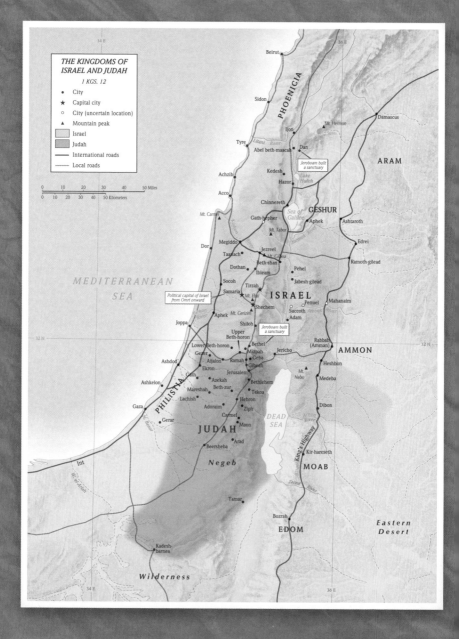

THE KINGDOMS OF ISRAEL AND JUDAH
1 KGS. 12

- • City
- ★ Capital city
- ○ City (uncertain location)
- ▲ Mountain peak
- ▢ Israel
- ▢ Judah
- — International roads
- — Local roads

0 10 20 30 40 50 Miles
0 10 20 30 40 50 Kilometers

PHOENICIA
ARAM
GESHUR
ISRAEL
JUDAH
AMMON
MOAB
EDOM
PHILISTIA

MEDITERRANEAN SEA
DEAD SEA
Sea of Galilee
Lake Huleh

Beirut
Sidon
Tyre
Ijon
Abel beth-maacah
Dan
Mt. Hermon
Damascus
Kedesh
Hazor
Achzib
Acco
Chinnereth
Gath-hepher
Aphek
Ashtaroth
Mt. Carmel
Mt. Tabor
Edrei
Dor
Megiddo
Jezreel
Taanach
Mt. Gilboa
Beth-shan
Ramoth-gilead
Dothan
Ibleam
Pehel
Jabesh-gilead
Socoh
Tirzah
Samaria
Mt. Ebal
ISRAEL
Penuel
Mahanaim
Joppa
Aphek
Mt. Gerizim
Shechem
Succoth
Adam
Shiloh
Upper Beth-horon
Bethel
Lower Beth-horon
Mizpah
Jericho
Rabbah (Amman)
Gezer
Geba
Heshbon
Ajalon
Ramah
Gibeon
Ekron
Jerusalem
Ashdod
Gath
Azekah
Bethlehem
Mt. Nebo
Medeba
Ashkelon
Mareshah
Beth-zur
Tekoa
Lachish
Hebron
Zipth
Dibon
Gaza
Adoraim
Carmel
Maon
Gerar
JUDAH
Arad
Beersheba
Kir-hareseth
Negeb
MOAB
Int.
Tamar
Bozrah
Eastern Desert
Kadesh-barnea
EDOM
Wilderness

Jeroboam built a sanctuary
Political capital of Israel from Omri onward
Jeroboam built a sanctuary

JESUS' BIRTH
AND EARLY CHILDHOOD

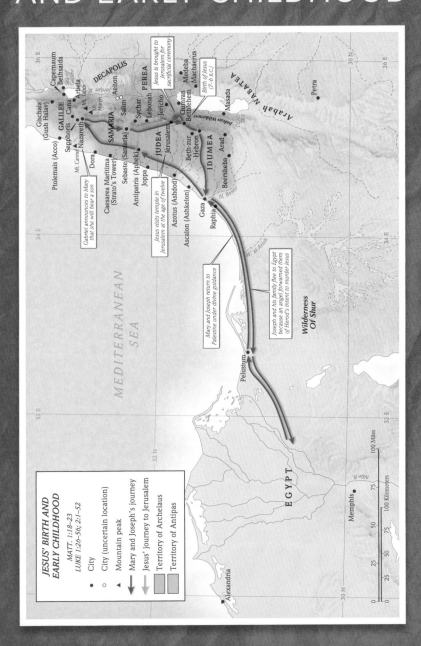

JESUS' BIRTH AND EARLY CHILDHOOD

MATT. 1:18–23
LUKE 1:26–56; 2:1–52

- City
- ○ City (uncertain location)
- ▲ Mountain peak
- ↓ Mary and Joseph's journey
- ↓ Jesus' journey to Jerusalem
- Territory of Archelaus
- Territory of Antipas

Gabriel announces to Mary that she will bear a son

Jesus visits temple in Jerusalem at the age of twelve

Jesus is brought to Jerusalem for sacrificial ceremony

Birth of Jesus (7–6 B.C.)

Joseph and his family flee to Egypt because an angel forewarned them of Herod's intent to murder Jesus

Mary and Joseph return to Palestine under divine guidance

MEDITERRANEAN SEA

EGYPT

Wilderness Of Shur

100 Miles
100 Kilometers

ISRAEL IN THE TIME OF
JESUS

ISRAEL IN THE TIME OF JESUS

- • City
- ◦ City (uncertain location)
- ⬡ Decapolis city
- ⬡ Decapolis city (uncertain location)
- ★ Administrative capital
- ▲ Mountain peak
- —— Major roads
- — Other roads
- First Procuratorship
- Territory of Antipas
- Territory of Phillip
- Syrian territory

Coponius was named the first prefect and established the Administrative capital at Caesarea Maritima

35°E · 33°N · 32°N · 31°N · 36°E

ABILENE

Sidon

ITUREA

Mt. Hermon ▲

Damascus · Abana R.

Caesarea-Philippi (Paneas)

Pharpar R.

PHOENICIA (TYRE)

Tyre

GAULANITIS

King's Highway

Raphana

Cadasa (Kedesh)
Gischala (Gush Halav)

Ptolemais (Acco)

GALILEE

Capernaum
Bethsaida

Sea of Galilee
Gergesa (Kursi)
Gamala

BATANEA

TRACHONITIS

Canatha

Mt. Hauran ▲

Sepphoris
Jotapata
Geba
Nazareth
Xaloth (Chesulloth)
Legio (Megiddo)

Mt. Tabor ▲
Tiberias
Hippos
Gadara
Abila

Adraa (Edrei)

AURANITIS

Bostra

Dora

Esdraelon Valley

Mt. Gilboa ▲

Caesarea Maritima (Strato's Tower) ★

MEDITERRANEAN SEA

SAMARIA

Ginae (Jenin)
Aenon
Salim

Scythopolis (Beth-shan)

Pella

Dion

Gerasa (Jerash)

DECAPOLIS

Sebaste (Samaria)
Mt. Ebal
Neapolis (Shechem)
Mt. Gerizim
Coreae

Amathus

Apollonia

Antipatris (Aphek)

Joppa

Jordan R.

Ephraim (Ophrah)

Alexandrium

Gedor (Gadara)

PEREA

Lydda

JUDEA

Archelais

Philadelphia (Amman)

Jamnia

Emmaus (Nicopolis)

Jericho

Cyprus

Mt. Nebo

Esbus (Heshbon)

Azotus (Ashdod)

Jerusalem

Bethany

Hyrcania

Medeba

Ascalon (Ashkelon)

Mesad Hasidim (Qumran)

Betogabris (Beth-guvrin)

Hebron

Machaerus

Gaza

En-gedi

Callirrhoe (Zereth-shahar)

DEAD SEA

IDUMEA

Masada

King's Highway

Arnon R.

Eastern Desert

Raphia

Beersheba

Malatha

Arad

N. Besor

NABATEA

Arabah

Khirbet Tannur

Zered R.

0 · 10 · 20 · 30 · 40 · 50 Miles
0 · 10 · 20 · 30 · 40 · 50 Kilometers

THE PASSION WEEK IN
JERUSALEM

THE PASSION WEEK IN JERUSALEM

-][Gate
- ⌐ Tower
- ⋯⋯ Wall
- ● Possible locations of the Chamber of Hewn Stone

MOVEMENTS OF JESUS

- ← Sunday
- ← Monday
- ← Thursday/Friday
- ◄--- Jesus before the Sanhedrin

Begun by Herod Agrippa I (A.D. 41–44) and completed later

Josephus' Third North Wall

Josephus' Second North Wall

Tyropoeon Valley

Kidron Valley

Sunday
Jesus descends from Bethany and enters the temple precincts

Sunday night
Jesus returns to Bethany to lodge with His friends

Mt. of Olives

To Bethany (see inset below)

Tuesday
Jesus teaches His disciples about end times on the Mount of Olives

Tower of Psephinus

Bezetha

Golgotha (Gordon's Calvary)

Antonia Fortress

Monday
Cleansing of the temple

Via Dolorosa

Fish Gate

Sheep Gate

Gethsemane

Thursday night
3. Jesus is arrested

Friday morning
9. Jesus is crucified

Golgotha (traditional location)

Wilson's Arch (bridge)

Temple Mount

Solomon's Portico

Shushan Gate

Beautiful Gate

Friday daybreak
5. Jesus before the Sanhedrin

Tower of Hippicus

Friday morning
8. Jesus again before Pilate

Gennath Gate

Josephus

Tower of Phasael

First N. Wall

Xystus Gate

Warren's Gate

Barclay's Gate

Royal Portico

Altar

Temple

Huldah Gates

Friday daybreak
6. Jesus before Pilate

Tower of Mariamne

Praetorium

Upper City

Antipas' Palace

Robinson's Arch (stairs)

Valley Gate

Pinnacle of Temple (traditional location)

Herod's Family Tomb(s)

Thursday/Friday
4. Jesus is taken to the house of Caiaphas for a preliminary hearing

Herod's Palace

Theater

House of Caiaphas, the High Priest

Serpent's

Ophel

Citadel

Gihon Spring

Thursday evening
2. Jesus retires to Gethsemane with His disciples

Friday morning
7. Jesus before Herod Antipas

Lower City

Hezekiah's Tunnel

Essene Quarter

City of David

Thursday
1. Jesus shares the Passover meal with His disciples

Upper Room (traditional location)

Essene Gate

Water Gate

| 0 | 1/8 | 1/4 Mile |

| 0 | 150 | 300 Meters |

Hinnom Valley

30 E   40 E   40 N

MEDITERRANEAN SEA

PRESENT-DAY ISRAEL

Area enlarged below

30 N   30 N

33 N

MEDITERRANEAN SEA

Jordan R.

Emmaus   Jerusalem
Bethany

Area enlarged at left

32 N

DEAD SEA

31 N

30 N

CHURCHES OF THE
REVELATION

CHURCHES OF THE REVELATION

- City
- Cities of the Seven Churches
- Major road

John writes Revelation encouraging Christians to remain faithful.